Philip J Gerson pgerson_8@msn.com
9057 East Shorewood Dr
Apt 2311
Mercer Island,Wa 98040
425-890-8685

MW061934

THE SCHOTTENSTEIN EDITION

סליחות שמחת יהושע
לימים נוראים

SELICHOS

THE COMPLETE SELICHOS
WITH AN INTERLINEAR TRANSLATION

The ArtScroll Series®

Rabbi Nosson Scherman / Rabbi Meir Zlotowitz

General Editors

A PROJECT OF THE

Mesorah Heritage Foundation

סליחות

שמחת יהושע

Published by

Mesorah Publications, ltd

THE SCHOTTENSTEIN EDITION

selichos

THE COMPLETE SELICHOS
WITH AN INTERLINEAR TRANSLATION

SEFARD — מנהג פולין

Edited by
Rabbi Menachem Davis

Contributing Editors:
Rabbi Yaakov Lavon
Rabbi Avie Gold
Rabbi Nosson Scherman   *Designed by*
Rabbi Meir Zlotowitz   Rabbi Sheah Brander

FIRST EDITION
First Impression ... August 2011

Published and Distributed by
MESORAH PUBLICATIONS, Ltd.
4401 Second Avenue
Brooklyn, New York 11232

Distributed in Europe by
LEHMANNS
Unit E, Viking Business Park
Rolling Mill Road
Jarrow, Tyne & Wear NE32 3DP
England

Distributed in Australia & New Zealand by
GOLDS WORLD OF JUDAICA
3-13 William Street
Balaclava, Melbourne 3183
Victoria Australia

Distributed in Israel by
SIFRIATI / A. GITLER — BOOKS
6 Hayarkon Street
Bnei Brak 51127

Distributed in South Africa by
KOLLEL BOOKSHOP
Ivy Common 105 William Road
Norwood 2192, Johannesburg, South Africa

THE ARTSCROLL SERIES® / SCHOTTENSTEIN EDITION
"SELICHOS SIMCHAS YESHOSHUA / THE ARTSCROLL INTERLINEAR SELICHOS"
Sefard (Minhag Polin)

© *Copyright 2011, by* MESORAH PUBLICATIONS, Ltd.
4401 Second Avenue / Brooklyn, N.Y. 11232 / (718) 921-9000 / www.artscroll.com

---

Hard cover — ISBN 10: 1-4226-1120-5 / ISBN 13: 978-1-4226-1120-3

Typography by CompuScribe at ArtScroll Studios, Ltd., Brooklyn, NY
Bound by **Sefercraft, Inc.,** Brooklyn, NY

This volume is dedicated to the memory of a very dear friend of everyone who ever met him. He exuded genuine love and brought joy and dignity to thousands and thousands of lives

Rabbi Yossie Raichik ז"ל

His broad smile, exuberant personality, deep understanding, and selfless concern for others had an electric effect when he entered a room. He could not be passive when others were hurting. No one will ever know how many burdens he lifted from how many people by the sheer force of his kindness and concern.

His wife and children knew him as a loving, caring partner and father. The world knew him as the charismatic, innovative, dynamic leader who created **Children of Chernobyl** and brought children from the Ukrainian valley of tears to a new life of hope, health and happiness in Israel.

When the nuclear power plant in Chernobyl melted down, people shook their heads and worried about the fallout. **Yossie Raichik** worried about the children. He fashioned a magic carpet that brought **2,547** children to Israel on **81** flights He gave them love, medical care, education, housing, and a new future. And he gave Israel a generation of productive, successful citizens.

And then, tragedy struck. Yossie was taken from this world much too soon. He was only 55.

Such a short life, but such a fruitful life.

The world lost a great leader. We and countless others lost a treasured friend who enriched our lives with his warm embrace, contagious joy, and sincere idealism.

He will never be forgotten.

Jay and Jeanie Schottenstein

Joseph Aaron and Lindsay Brooke,
Jacob Meir, Jonah Philip, and Emma Blake

Jonathan Richard, and Jeffrey Adam

⊰ TABLE OF CONTENTS ⊱

Selichos listed in alphabetical order

ﮊ The Interlinear Translation — How to Read it

There is a difficulty inherent in any interlinear translation of Hebrew to English: the fact that English and Hebrew are read in opposite directions. ArtScroll has developed a patented system of notations that helps the reader navigate the two languages simultaneously, without confusion.

These notations consist of the following:

1) single arrow notations 〈 between English phrases direct the reader's eye toward the next English phrase, reading right to left, for example:

אַשְׁרֵי   יוֹשְׁבֵי   בֵיתֶךָ,

《 in Your house, 〈 are those who dwell 〈 Praiseworthy,

2) Double arrow notations 《 indicate a logical break between phrases, equivalent to a period, semicolon, dash and many commas.

3) Bold double arrow notations **《** indicate the completion of a sentence at the end of a verse.

With these double arrows, the reader need not search for commas, semicolons, and periods. This was done to make the translation as user-friendly as possible; it allows the reader to continue following the Hebrew moving to the left, without the distraction of looking for English punctuation marks on the *right* side of the English words.

The arrows also identify the specific Hebrew word or words that are translated by the English phrase. This is especially useful where two or more Hebrew words are translated as a unit.

For quotations, one further convention was used: Wherever text would normally be set off by quotation marks, the quotation has been set in italics.

✎§ Publisher's Preface

T he approach of the Days of Awe is a time when the Jew's mind turns to self-examination and improvement. Where have I fallen short? How can I achieve the goals I set for myself a year ago? How can I accomplish more in the coming year than in the last one? How can I better fulfill the will of my Maker and make myself the person He wants me to be?

Such questions flood the mind and heart of the Jew as the season of judgment and repentance draws near. *Selichos* — the special supplications of this period — are the prayers that express these longings and contemplations. But these moving prayers are so poetic and complex, both in language and construction, that all but scholars of unusual breadth find them extremely difficult. They are so important, yet so distant.

That is why the publication of the classic ArtScroll *Selichos* in 1992 was greeted so enthusiastically. It made the *Selichos* accessible in an unprecedented way. It quickly became the standard *Selichos* for countless people, and with good reason. Its authors presented the language of the prayers and their underlying meaning accurately, gracefully, and movingly. It became the prayer companion of serious, thoughtful people throughout the *Selichos* season, bringing them understanding and inspiration.

Since then, the SCHOTTENSTEIN INTERLINEAR SERIES, born in 2001, has inaugurated a new era in study and prayer. It began with the publication of the Interlinear Tehillim / Psalms. The response was electrifying. Immediately it became obvious that more such works must be produced. Our hope was that the Interlinear Series would inaugurate a new and greater degree of learning and prayer, as people began to understand it word by word and phrase by phrase. That hope has been realized many times over. The SCHOTTENSTEIN INTERLINEAR SERIES includes such classics as the Siddur, Machzor, Chumash and others. Now, the publication of this brilliant treatment of *Selichos,* in addition to the previously published Rosh Hashanah and Yom Kippur Machzorim, completes the prayers of the Days of Awe season.

This series has been made possible by JAY AND JEANIE SCHOTTENSTEIN and their children, JOSEPH AND LINDSAY, JONATHAN, AND JEFFREY. It is another milestone in their long list of achievements for the benefit of the Jewish people and for the enhancement of Torah study and prayer.

The Schottenstein family has dedicated this volume in memory of their dear friend RABBI YOSSI RAICHIK z"l. Multitudes were touched by his warmth and devotion to anyone in need. Thanks to him, thousands of children were saved from the nuclear peril of Chernobyl.

◆§ Contents This volume contains the full text of the *Selichos* according to *Minhag Polin [Sefard]*. For the convenience of the user, every passage is presented in its entirety every time it appears, so that the reader will not have to turn pages constantly. The Overview presents a *hashkafah* / philosophical introduction to the concept and historical background of the *Selichos*.

◆§ How is the Interlinear Format Unique? A look at a page of this Selichos provides the answer. Even someone fluent in Hebrew will often come across an unfamiliar word or phrase. To search in an adjoining column or facing page for the translation will solve the problem, but often at the price of a loss of concentration. Once the mind focuses away from the Hebrew text to the English translation, one may find it difficult to return to the exact Hebrew phrase of the prayer. Next time, the worshiper may well decide to forgo the translation in favor of continuing the prayer without a lapse. The result is a frequent, if not constant, tug of war between the desire for understanding and the need not to interrupt the recitation, especially if one is praying with the congregation.

This new format provides the best solution yet to this problem. It is called "interlinear," a word that may sound cryptic, but whose meaning is immediately obvious when one looks at the page. The translation is directly beneath each word or phrase — not opposite the line, but intermingled with it. Instantly, the worshiper sees the meaning and continues his recitation.

This basic concept was first used in an English Siddur in 1874. Why has it not become a common feature of Torah works in English? Because the sentence structure of Hebrew is very different from that of English, and this complicates the task of translation. For example, take the very familiar phrase תְּהִלַּת ה' יְדַבֶּר פִּי, which our *Tehillim* and Siddur translate quite accurately and understandably as *May my mouth declare the praise of* HASHEM. But a literal, word-by-word translation is *The praise of* HASHEM *will declare my mouth* — accurate, perhaps, but hardly comprehensible. Undoubtedly, the difficulty of making an interlinear translation both accurate and readable led to its disuse. Thus, the editor of this interlinear translation had to be a master of both syntax and meaning, often adding a word here and there in order to do justice both to translation and comprehensibility.

But there is another, more basic, problem — the discrepancy between the Hebrew that reads right to left, and the English that reads left to right. The eye is confused, as it were, like an American stepping off a curb in England, and instinctively looking to his left, while traffic speeds toward him from the right. Consequently, in order to make this interlinear treatment convenient and practical, a way had to be found to solve the right-left problem. Another glance at a page in this edition will show the solution. After each English word or phrase, there is a barely obtrusive arrow, which directs the eye in the direction of the Hebrew. We have tested this device, and found that it solves the problem to an amazing degree. These arrows keep the reader's eye moving in the direction of the Hebrew without interfering with his reading of the English. To indicate a comma or pause, there is a double arrow, and to indicate a period at the end of a verse, the double arrow is bold. This revolutionary new graphics icon is patented. It was developed in conjunction with RABBI BENYAMIN GOHARI, whose efforts we gratefully acknowledge.

⋙Translation The interlinear translation strives to maintain the literary flavor of the original ArtScroll translation that sought to balance the lofty beauty of the heavily nuanced text with a readily understood English rendering. Obviously, the word-by-word nature of this work constrains the fluidity of the language, but nevertheless it flows. Where a choice had to be made, we generally preferred fidelity to the text over inaccurate simplicity, but occasionally, we had to stray from the literal translation in order to capture the essence of a phrase in an accessible English idiom. Due to the poetic nature of the *Selichos*, we had to go beyond a strictly literal translation, and sometimes rely on the commentary to clarify the meaning of the text.

Out of respect for the sanctity and skill of the paytanim, the translator has endeavored to maintain the poetic style and construction of the Hebrew, even though this may occasionally detract from the smooth flow of the English.

⋙Layout and Typography Though this Siddur's interlinear system sets it apart dramatically from others, it fundamentally maintains the pattern of the ArtScroll Siddur, which has been greatly praised for its ease of use and clarity of layout. This *Selichos*, with its clear instructions, and precise page headings, was designed to make the service easy for everyone to follow. Paragraphs begin with bold-type words to facilitate finding the individual tefillos; portions said aloud by the chazzan are indicated by either the symbol ∴ or the word chazzan. An asterisk (*) after a word indicates that the word or phrase is treated in the commentary. Numbered footnotes give the Scriptural sources of countless verses that have been melded into the prayers, as well as variant readings. A footnote beginning "Cf." indicates that the Scriptural source is paraphrased.

◈§**Hebrew Grammar**   As a general rule in the Hebrew language, the accent is on the last syllable. Where the accent is on an earlier syllable, it is indicated with a *messeg*, a vertical line below the accented letter: שִׁירוּ. A שְׁוָא נָע [*sh'va na*] is indicated by a hyphen mark above the letter: בָּֽרְכוּ; except for a *sh'va* on the first letter of a word, which is always a *sh'va na*. In identifying a *sh'va na*, we have followed the rules of the Vilna Gaon and Rabbi Yaakov Emden.

◈§ *Acknowledgments*

We are grateful to the great Roshei Hayeshivah זצוק"ל of the previous two generations for their encouragement and guidance. Thanks to them, the ArtScroll Series became a reality and gained acceptance. להבחל"ח, the great Torah leaders of our time, in Israel and America, continue that tradition. Words are inadequate to express our gratitude.

Only thanks to the MESORAH HERITAGE FOUNDATION is it possible to produce scholarly works of this nature and quality. We are grateful to the Trustees of the Foundation who volunteer their time, prestige, and expertise. The members of the Board of Governors honor us with their friendship and support. The names of the Trustees and Governors are listed earlier in this volume.

Many hundreds of titles have been published by ArtScroll/Mesorah thanks to generous and visionary friends and supporters who have dedicated entire series and individual volumes. They are named and acknowledged in other volumes. Thanks to such people, Torah and tefillah are flourishing throughout the world. There is a thirst for learning, and they are slaking it.

The original ArtScroll *Selichos* was dedicated by MR. AND MRS. ELLIOT GLASER and their children, in memory of Mr. Glaser's mother, after whom it is named, and Mrs. Glaser's father. The Glasers are people of uncommon kindness and concern for worthy causes and the needy.

RABBI MENACHEM DAVIS has edited the entire Interlinear project since its inception. He brings uncommon skills to this very difficult task and accomplishes it brilliantly. He has a rare sensitivity to the subtleties and nuances of Hebrew and English, and the ability to convert even complex syntactical constructions into the interlinear format, in a literate, graceful manner.

The design of the interlinear page remains a challenge even for our cherished friend and colleague REB SHEAH BRANDER, the acknowledged genius in this demanding field — and he has again produced a masterpiece. Reb Sheah was ably assisted in every facet of the production and layout by MRS. SURY ENGLARD and by SHLOIME BRANDER.

In this volume, we have utilized the services of ZEV TEICH, a brilliant technological consultant who designed systems to maximize the efficient functioning of the entire process.

REB ELI KROEN designed the cover with his customary good taste and imagination.

AVROHOM BIDERMAN and MENDY HERZBERG always contribute expertise and efficiency in shepherding the production from beginning to end, whatever the need.

MRS. LEA BRAFMAN is our dedicated and outstanding comptroller. She is ably assisted by MRS. SARALEA HOBERMAN and MRS. LEYA RABINOWITZ.

SHMUEL BLITZ directs our Jerusalem office with extraordinary efficiency, and his prowess helps in all our work.

We are grateful to them all.

With Hashem's help, ArtScroll / Mesorah has over 1,400 titles in print, and the SCHOTTENSTEIN INTERLINEAR SERIES is one of our crown jewels. We are grateful for the *z'chus* of serving His people by bringing them closer to His Torah. We close with the prayer that this year's *Selichos* and the prayers of the Days of Awe will be answered for all of Klal Yisrael, with good health, peace, the coming of Mashiach and the building of the Third Bais HaMikdash.

Rabbi Meir Zlotowitz   Rabbi Nosson Scherman

Menachem Av 5771 / August 2011

◦§ Editor's Preface

T he source for our reciting *Selichos* is the Gemara (*Rosh Hashanah* 17b) that describes how Hashem first taught Moses the Thirteen Attributes of Mercy by "wrapping Himself in a *tallis* like a prayer leader and demonstrating the order of prayer."

R' Yochanan and Rav Yehudah in that Gemara make remarkable statements about the Thirteen Attributes that Moses was taught. R' Yochanan declares, "Were the verse not written [*And* HASHEM *passed before him (Moses) and proclaimed*] it would not be possible to say it." Thus, in order for us to be able to recite the Thirteen Attributes, Hashem had to demonstrate their recitation to Moses. Why was this demonstration of a "prayer" that seems to be nothing but a string of descriptions of God, without a request for forgiveness imbedded in it, necessary? Furthermore, Rav Yehudah states, "A covenant had been made regarding the Thirteen Attributes that they never return without having an effect." Why are the Thirteen Attributes described as having guaranteed effectiveness — unlike other prayers? My Rebbi, Rav Yosef Dov Soloveitchik זצ"ל, suggested that while it is true that these are but descriptions of God's nature, they are activated in the world only when Israel invokes them. When we declare that God is Merciful, He acts in a merciful way. This is the extraordinary power of the Thirteen Attributes. It therefore stands to reason that Hashem Himself had to appear to Moses wrapped in a *tallis* in order to model the effect of the Attributes.

The *halachah* is that the *chazzan* for *Selichos* must cover his head and wrap his body with a *tallis* even in the middle of the night, a time when the *tallis* is not usually worn. Rav Soloveitchik suggested further that just as then, at Sinai, Hashem was under the *tallis,* so in every generation, Hashem is there under the *tallis,* assisting the *chazzan* in his request for forgiveness for the congregation. Just as the *Kohanim* cover their heads and hands with the *tallis* during the Priestly Blessing because Hashem is present between their fingers, blessing His people as well, so must the *chazzan* for *Selichos* be covered by the *tallis* out of respect for Hashem's Presence. Under every *chazzan's tallis,* in every generation, Hashem is there to activate this power of the Thirteen Attributes.

May our recitation of *Selichos* bring the blessing and forgiveness that we desperately need and that only Hashem's Presence in our midst can provide.

❦ ❦ ❦

With the completion of the *Selichos* for the יָמִים נוֹרָאִים, the Days of Awe, another significant milestone in the SCHOTTENSTEIN INTERLINEAR SERIES has been reached. Together with the publication of the Interlinear Kinnos, now the two most difficult standard prayer texts have been made available in the easy to understand Interlinear format. I was surprised when after this *Tishah B'Av,* friends and colleagues somewhat sheepishly thanked me for making the recitation of *Kinnos* "enjoyable." Obviously one does not enjoy reading about the tragedies and horrors of the destruction of the Temples and further catastrophes through the millennia. But the inability of even rabbis and scholars to understand what one is saying in *Kinnos* or *Selichos* creates an intense frustration that the Interlinear system mitigates.

This week, ArtScroll received a letter of appreciation from someone in Israel whose first introduction to the Interlinear series was the SCHOTTENSTEIN EDITION INTERLINEAR KINNOS. She wrote: "For the first time in my life I was able to finally understand what I was saying! … What was especially nice was [that] each word was translated and the extra words which one needed to really understand the **one** written word were written under the word …. I really said [the *Kinnos*] and got something out of it instead of just mumbling meaningless words." The SCHOTTENSTEIN EDITION INTERLINEAR SELICHOS should enable the same satisfying comprehension of our special prayers for forgiveness at this holiest time of the year.

❦ ❦ ❦

I wish to acknowledge the support and encouragement of many of the scholars who are part of the ArtScroll family. First and foremost, RABBI MEIR ZLOTOWITZ, the source of the vision and energy behind the unique ArtScroll dynamic. May he succeed in envisioning and incubating many more projects — to enlighten and to inspire. RABBI SHEAH BRANDER is one of the wonders of the publishing world. The interlinear format is one of the most challenging of layouts, even if there were unlimited time within which to produce each volume. In addition, the diversity of poetic styles of the *Selichos* presents a truly daunting task.

R' Sheah magically creates his masterpieces. But R' Sheah is much more than the supreme artisan of the printed word; he is also an editor par excellence and a *talmid chacham* of deep insight. His sage advice has improved the Interlinear Series in myriad ways. And perhaps more important, Reb Sheah is a friend.

Other scholars contributed to the interlinear project in those subtle ways that inspire and spur one's efforts to unanticipated heights. They include: RABBI NOSSON SCHERMAN, who is renowned for his eloquence and depth in expressing so many concepts of the ArtScroll oeuvre, and who is always available for consultation and for discovering the ideal way to express an elusive concept; RABBI MENACHEM SILBER, whose encyclopedic knowledge was readily proferred, and who provided access to critical volumes from his personal library; RABBI MOSHE ROSENBLUM, a consummate scholar of Hebrew, *Mikra*, and *piyut*; and RABBI AVROHOM SHERESHEVSKY, an expert in Hebrew grammar and *Mikra*.

MRS. SURY ENGLARD prepared all of the various files for editing, and she and SHLOIME BRANDER assisted in the production and layout. MRS. ESTI DICKER and MRS. ESTHER FEIERSTEIN typed the many files that were not available in electronic format.

AVROHOM YITZCHOK DEUTSCH proofread the Hebrew text to assure the greatest degree of accuracy. MOSHE DEUTSCH prepared the book for print. RABBI YECHEZKEL SOCHACZEWSKI, ensured the accuracy of this volume, as he has for so many others, with skill and dedication. RABBI YEHUDA LICHT provided assistance to ensure that the text of the *Selichos* is grammatically correct.

MRS. FRIMY EISNER reviewed everything for language, consistency, and accuracy. MRS. FAYGIE WEINBAUM and MRS. MINDY STERN proofread with their customary diligence.

Even more than in previous volumes, my wife EDNA served as an editor extraordinaire, assisting with numerous translations and helping me meet the rigorous schedule that producing the two volumes of *Selichos — Ashkenaz /* מנהג ליטא and *Sefard /* מנהג פולין — in one year entailed. All this, in addition to her inspiration and enthusiasm that continually encourage me to greater achievement. May Hashem grant that we be *zocheh* to enjoy further growth in Torah and *yiras Shamayim*, together with our children and all of *Klal Yisrael*.

Menachem Davis

Menachem Av 5771 / August 2011
Brooklyn, N.Y.

⋅§ An Overview
Selichos — The Almighty's Own Prayer

אַף עַל פִּי שֶׁהַתְּשׁוּבָה וְהַצְּעָקָה יָפָה לְעוֹלָם, בַּעֲשֶׂרֶת הַיָּמִים שֶׁבֵּין
רֹאשׁ הַשָּׁנָה לְיוֹם הַכִּפּוּרִים הִיא יָפָה בְּיוֹתֵר, וּמִתְקַבֶּלֶת הִיא מִיָּד,
שֶׁנֶּאֱמַר דִּרְשׁוּ ה' בְּהִמָּצְאוֹ

Although repentance and outcry are always appropriate,
during the ten days between Rosh Hashanah and Yom
Kippur they are especially appropriate and are answered
immediately, as it is written (Isaiah 55:6): Seek HASHEM
when He is found [call to Him when He is near] ...
(Rambam, Hil. Teshuvah 2:6).

I. The Father's Hope

THE DAYS OF AWE AND JUDGMENT, of reflection and repentance, are a
time when Jews use their prayers to seek the Father Who hovers nearby
awaiting their call. The Talmud explains that, of course, God can always
be found and He is always near, but during the ten days from Rosh
Hashanah through Yom Kippur, He is especially available, especially
close, especially hopeful that His children will have the good sense to
seek Him out.

Rabbi Bunam of P'shischa used the parable of a king who banished his
son because he failed to live up to his royal responsibilities. The recal-
citrant young man acclimated himself to the rough life of a rural village,
and before long was more a villager than a prince. His father, meanwhile,
kept watch over his beloved, though wayward, son. He accomplished
this through agents who reported back to the palace and unobtrusively
shepherded the young man through frequent difficulties.

Finally, unable to bear the degradation and poverty that his son was
suffering, the king gave him a chance to redeem himself. The king sent
an official with a message: "Your father loves you and is ready to grant
you anything you want. Make a wish."

The prince did not have to think very long. "Tell my father how grateful
I am for his concern. And tell him that it is cold here and my coat is worn.
Please ask him to send me a new, warm, fur-lined coat!"

Can one imagine the heartbreak of the father who wanted his son back in the palace? The boy could have asked for a chance to visit his family. He could have asked for a reconciliation. He could have asked for the kingdom. But he had forgotten where he belonged. He had traded the palace for the corral; traded his destiny for a coat.

So, too, R' Bunam said, "We come to the Days of Awe when God longs for us to say, 'Father, we want to come home to You!' And all we think to ask for in our prayers is a bit more money, a nicer home, a warmer coat. Can we even begin to imagine the extent of our foolishness and the anguish we cause God?"

The Ten Days of Repentance, that begin on Rosh Hashanah and reach their climax with the sunset of Yom Kippur, is our Father's invitation to us to become princes again. One thing should be clear: The call of the season is to return to our roots, to return to the destiny that was mapped out for us in past millennia and is spelled out in our tradition and Torah literature. What should be our goal? Where will we find it? How are we to achieve it? What has the genius of our past told us about the way to remake the future?

II. Origins of Selichos

ORIGINALLY, THE CUSTOM WAS to recite *Selichos* only during the Ten Days of Repentance, from Rosh Hashanah to Yom Kippur (see *Hil. Teshuvah* **Early Start** 3:4). But the spiritual genius of the Jewish people decreed that ten days was not enough, that we had to enter the judgment of Rosh Hashanah with the process of prayer and repentance already under way.

Sephardic communities have adopted the practice of reciting *Selichos* from the first day of Elul to Yom Kippur, to commemorate the forty days that Moses spent on Mount Sinai to receive the Second Tablets of the Law. Those forty days were a time of hope and trepidation, because the first time Moses had been away, the people had built the Golden Calf. The people had repented, but what guarantee was there that they would not fall again while Moses was absent? So his forty days on the Mount was a time of intense spiritual striving, when the people had to remember that human aspirations are fragile and require constant encouragement and strengthening.

The climax of the forty days was the tenth of Tishrei, when Moses came back to the camp to find the nation even more elevated than when he had left it, a nation deserving of the Tablets of the Law, which would remain their eternal testimony that God had accepted their repentance and con-secrated them once again as His Chosen People [see *Exodus* Chs. 32-34].

Just as our ancestors devoted those forty days to self-improvement, so too that period has become a time of striving in all communities — and Sephardic Jews arise every night before dawn to recite *Selichos* as part of the process.

ASHKENAZIC COMMUNITIES began reciting *Selichos* before Rosh Hashanah, and in deciding when to begin the recitation, they based the **Two Symbols** decision on two criteria: the twenty-fifth of Elul, and *Motzaei Shabbos* [the night after the Sabbath]. If we can understand the significance of these two considerations, we will go a long way toward understanding the significance of the *Selichos*.

According to Rabbi Eliezer *(Rosh Hashanah* 8a), Adam and Eve were created on Rosh Hashanah, a Friday, which was the sixth day of Creation. This means that Creation began on Sunday, the twenty-fifth of Elul. Therefore, the Jews of Barcelona and its environs adopted the custom of beginning the recitation of *Selichos* on that day *(Ran* to *Rosh Hashanah* 16a). According to this comment, it would seem that the purpose of *Selichos* is nothing less than to remind us that within our minds and hearts we must re-create the pristine state of the beginning of Creation. What is the message of that day?

When God created the world, it was clear that there was only One power in the universe and that everything from the mightiest galaxy to the tiniest gnat owed its existence to Him alone. The Song of the Day of Sunday, which was sung in the Temple by the Levites and which we recite in our Sunday morning prayer, is *Hashem's is the world and its fullness (Psalms* 24), because, as the Talmud explains, on that day God created heaven and earth and manifested His sole sovereignty over the universe *(Rosh Hashanah* 31a). When one recognizes that reality, there is no place for sin. Sin is caused by self-deception. As the Talmud puts it, no one sins unless a spirit of foolishness enters him. If someone recognized without a doubt that there is no power or master but the One God, that only He gives the breath of life and the strength to exist, and that no deed goes unrecorded or unrequited by Him, it would be impossible for him to sin — unless he were struck by an attack of lunacy. On the first day of Creation, when God's omnipotence was indisputable, sin was inconceivable. And by beginning to recite *Selichos* on that date, the Jew attempts to re-adopt that primeval conviction.

THE RABBIS ALSO WANTED there to be at least four days of *Selichos* before Rosh Hashanah — to symbolize the four days that an animal must

Motzaei Shabbos

be checked for flaws before it is used as an offering. This concept brings home to man that he should analyze himself carefully before he "presents" himself to God on Rosh Hashanah. Consequently, when Rosh Hashanah falls on Monday or Tuesday, *Selichos* must begin sooner — and it is moved up a week, to the previous *Motzaei Shabbos*. Obviously, therefore, the Sabbath, too, is closely related to the beginning of *Selichos*.

The author of *Terumas HaDeshen* explains that the Torah is associated with the Sabbath, the day on which God gave the Ten Commandments. Because the Sabbath is a day when people are free from their weekday activities, they can spend more time studying the Torah, and

> Therefore it is good to begin [reciting *Selichos*] at the beginning of the first day, when people are joyous because of the *mitzvah* of the Torah that they study on the Sabbath, and also because of the pleasure [engendered by] the Sabbath. And as the Talmud teaches (*Shabbos* 30b), the *Shechinah* does not rest amid sadness or laziness, only amid the joy of [the performance of] the commandments. Therefore it is good to begin to pray amid joy of the commandments (*Lekket Yosher*).

As the Torah and the Sages stress, the Sabbath — the culmination of the six days of Creation — bears witness that God is the Creator. So the Sabbath, like the twenty-fifth of Elul, focuses our attention on the beginning of time and it reinforces our responsibility — and, it is to be hoped, our resolve — to do our share in making the world what it was intended to be. For the Jew is called upon to make the world a better place, and the primary way for him to begin is by making himself a better person. After one breaks his mirrors so he will not see his own flaws, it would be vainglorious and futile to think that he can then concentrate on the flaws of everyone else.

JUDAISM TEACHES THAT AN individual human being is a microcosm of the universe. One's primary duty is to perfect *that* universe, his per-

Individuals Matter

sonal one, before moving on to change the rest of society. If enough people rise toward perfection, the world will change, not only through the accumulation of many good people, but also because spirituality is indivisible. The very fact that people study the Torah and perform its commandments with sincerity elevates everyone else in the world. Abraham and Sarah were a minority of two in a world awash with idolatry and immorality, yet they saved the entire world from destruction.

Everyone makes a difference. The Sages said that one should imagine that the entire world is balanced between virtue and sin, and that if he performs *one mitzvah*, he will tip the scales of all humanity to the side of merit; but if he commits *one sin*, he will cause the whole world to be condemned. The responsibility is awesome, but so is the privilege. Especially in today's crowded societies, it is easy to think that one lonely individual cannot make a difference and one vote can never matter. That may be true in economics and politics. But Jews are grandchildren of the Patriarchs, the people who proved that majorities are meaningless in determining spiritual accomplishment.

The confluence of the Sabbath and the first day of Creation shed light on what the *Selichos* are meant to, and *can*, accomplish. They are to create a new world, to provide a new resting place for God's Presence, to prepare us for the year that we pray will bring the fulfillment of the prophecies for the coming of Messiah and the End of Days.

III. The Leader of Prayer*

וַיַּעֲבֹר ה' עַל פָּנָיו וַיִּקְרָא. אָמַר ר' יוֹחָנָן אִלְמָלֵא מִקְרָא כָּתוּב אִי אֶפְשָׁר לְאָמְרוֹ. מְלַמֵּד שֶׁנִּתְעַטֵּף הַקָּדוֹשׁ בָּרוּךְ הוּא כִּשְׁלִיחַ צִבּוּר וְאָמַר לְמֹשֶׁה, כָּל זְמַן שֶׁיִּשְׂרָאֵל חוֹטְאִים לְפָנַי יַעֲשׂוּ לְפָנַי כְּסֵדֶר הַזֶּה וַאֲנִי מוֹחֵל לָהֶם.

HASHEM passed before him [Moses] *and proclaimed* (*Exodus 34:6*). *R' Yochanan said, "If the Scriptural verse had not been written, it would be impossible to say it! This teaches that the Holy One, Blessed is He, wrapped Himself* [in a tallis] *like a leader of prayer, and said to Moses: 'Whenever the Jews sin before Me, let them perform this procedure and I shall forgive them'"* (*Rosh Hashanah* 17b).

---

* This section of the Overview is based on *Maharal* in *Be'er HaGolah* and *Chiddushei Aggados, Rosh Hashanah* 17b.

AFTER THE TRAGIC EPISODE of the Golden Calf, God wrathfully told Moses that Israel was worthy of extermination, and that he, Moses, would be-

Moses' Request

come the forerunner of a new and better nation. But Moses could not bear to see his beloved brethren wiped out, even though they had sinned grievously. He pleaded for them and risked his own survival for their sake, being so bold as to declare that if they were doomed, then he wanted to share their fate (*Exodus* 32:32). God granted his wish and spared the people.

Moses wanted to understand God's ways, to comprehend His justice, and to learn the role of prayer. In response, God told him that no human being, not even Moses, the "master of all prophets," could presume to understand the totality of God's ways, but God showed Moses as much of the Divine glory as he could absorb (ibid. 33:18-23). After that, God conveyed to Moses the teaching that was not only for him, but for all generations of Jews, the teaching that became the pattern of our order of *Selichos*.

AS CITED ABOVE, GOD APPEARED to Moses in the form of a cantor wrapped in a *tallis*, leading his congregation in prayer. As Moses watched and lis-

God's Tallis

tened, God taught him the prayer that, He assured, would always bring forth God's mercy. Whenever Jews are in distress, let them recite these words, God told Moses, and they will be forgiven. Those words were the Thirteen Attributes of Mercy:

ה', ה', אֵל, רַחוּם, וְחַנּוּן, אֶרֶךְ אַפַּיִם, וְרַב חֶסֶד, וֶאֱמֶת, נֹצֵר חֶסֶד לָאֲלָפִים, נֹשֵׂא עָוֹן, וָפֶשַׁע, וְחַטָאָה, וְנַקֵּה.

HASHEM, HASHEM, God, Compassionate and Gracious, Slow to anger, and Abundant in Kindness and Truth, Preserver of kindness for thousands of generations, Forgiver of iniquity, willful sin, and error, and Who cleanses.

R' Yochanan says, quite understandably, that if the Torah did not allude to this scenario, we would not dare suggest that God gave Moses a personal demonstration, as it were, of how Jews should pray. How did R' Yochanan know that God did so?

Maharal explains that the verses themselves indicate it. The Torah says:

HASHEM descended in a cloud and stood with him [i.e., Moses] *there, and He called out with the Name HASHEM. HASHEM passed before him and proclaimed, HASHEM, HASHEM . . . (Exodus* 34:5-6).

The plain meaning of the verses is that God spoke to Moses and recited the Thirteen Attributes to him, teaching him this new and potent order of prayer. Because of this, R' Yochanan infers that if God came to teach Moses how to pray, He must have shown him everything he and future generations would need to know — not only the text, but how it should be recited, meaning that God, as it were, "wrapped Himself in a *tallis*." But this merely begs the question, *Maharal* asserts. Why was it so important for God to *demonstrate* the procedure of the prayer?

Moses had begged of God, "*Show me now Your glory*" (ibid. 33:18). He wanted to know how man can attain maximum closeness to God. It was an honest, legitimate request. Moses had seen how even the spiritual height of prophecy can be ephemeral, how the nation that heard God's voice proclaiming, "*I am Hashem your God*" (ibid. 20:2), had danced around a Golden Calf only forty days later singing, "*This is your god, O Israel*" (ibid. 32:8). If that could happen once, then Moses realized that there had to be a more enduring way to elevate the nation. By appearing in a manner symbolizing someone leading his fellows in prayer, God taught Moses the way to achieve the closeness for which he longed, not only for himself, but for us.

GOD APPEARED AS A LEADER of prayer wrapped in his *tallis*, reciting the Thirteen Attributes of Mercy. The *tallis*, drawn over His head and shielding His eyes from outside influences and stimuli, **Total** was to show how a Jew must react to, and interact **Concentration** with, his prayers. The point is not that all one need do is drape a woolen garment around the shoulders and head of the people's leader; in isolation, such an act is superficial, and superficiality does not lead to spiritual growth. To the contrary, superficiality is harmful, for if a person deceives himself into thinking that he can come closer to God through external deeds, he will only drift further away than he was when he started. God responds to those who seek Him, but only to the extent that they do so sincerely.

In the words of *Maharal*:

> God is just as accessible to a person as the person is accessible to God. If a person concentrates on the content of his prayer and does not turn away from Hashem, God will be accessible to him completely.

This was the message of the *tallis*. When praying, one must insulate oneself from everything but closeness to God. In the physical sense, the *tallis* shields one's eyes and ears from distraction. But that, too, is not enough — isolation from a corrosive environment enables one to concentrate on the prayers, but it is the *import* of the prayers that matters. What was the prayer to teach?

BY TEACHING MOSES the Attributes of Mercy, God was teaching the Jewish people that in order for their prayers to be efficacious, they must

Emulating God   emulate the merciful traits of the One to Whom they pray. As R' Yochanan put it, God told Moses, "Let them *perform* this procedure"; God did not teach Moses words alone; He told him that the message of the words must be carried out. The "procedure" to be performed was the content of the Attributes of Mercy.

God thus showed Moses that in order to merit *God's* mercy, Jews must be merciful to one another — single-mindedly so, for just as the *tallis* draped around them shuts out physical distractions, so it must shut out the thousand reasons why one person does not deserve mercy, another is unworthy of patience, and a third has forfeited his right to forgiveness. By coupling the attitude of prayer with the text that proclaimed the infinite nature of Divine mercy, God was signifying that closeness to God implies emulation of His merciful traits.

How often have Jews wondered why their countless tearful recitations of the Thirteen Attributes have gone unanswered! Did not R' Yochanan teach that they would always be accepted?

Alshich explains that R' Yochanan made it very clear that words are not enough, even if they are recited with feeling. *Perform* this procedure, God pleaded. Do not merely *speak* about *God's* mercy. Show *human* mercy. Only then does God guarantee that He will respond to us in kind (quoted by *Eitz Yosef* to *Ein Yaakov, Rosh Hashanah* 17b).

In the famous homily of *Kedushas Levi*, King David says צִלְּךָ 'ה, *HASHEM is your protector (Psalms* 121:4). The phrase can also be rendered *HASHEM is your shadow,* for just as a shadow follows and imitates the actions of a person, so God is in a sense, the shadow of a person's deeds. If we are kind, He is kind to us. If we are forgiving, He is forgiving to us. And, unfortunately, vice versa. This is the sort of behavior that God called for, not words but emulation of God's mercy.

IV. Before and After

ה' ה', אֲנִי הוּא קוֹדֶם שֶׁיֶּחֱטָא אָדָם, אֲנִי הוּא לְאַחַר שֶׁיֶּחֱטָא אָדָם
וְיַעֲשֶׂה תְשׁוּבָה

*[The Talmud explains why the first two Attributes are a
repetition of God's Four-letter Name.] Hashem, Hashem
… [This means] I am He before a person sins, and I am
He after a person sins and repents (Rosh Hashanah 17b).*

GOD'S FOUR-LETTER NAME SYMBOLIZES His mercy. The repetition of the
Name in the Thirteen Attributes, the Talmud teaches, means that He

**Conditioned
to Act**

treats people mercifully both before they sin and after
they sin. *Rabbeinu Asher [Rosh]* asks why it is necessary for God to show mercy *before* the sin; someone
who is uncontaminated should not require mercy. He explains that God
is merciful even though He knows that someone *will* sin.

It is axiomatic in spiritual matters that nothing happens in a vacuum.
When someone sins it is because he has begun to condition himself,
emotionally and intellectually, to the idea that it is possible, permissible,
even desirable to defy God's will. Even before he has acted, he has prepared the way for the act. It would be quite logical, therefore, for God to
remove His mercy from such a person. But He does not. As long as the
potential sinner has not become an *actual* sinner, the first Attribute —
HASHEM — remains in place, and He continues to shower His mercy upon
the person who has within himself seeds of defiance that are soon to
break through to the surface.

The second Attribute indicated by the Name *HASHEM* is that God is
merciful even after one has sinned and repented. Even after repentance, mercy cannot be taken for granted, for it is not at all reasonable
to expect that a person should be able to repent from his sins and have
them wiped away. By sinning, one has changed himself for the worse.
Just as a criminal cannot expect regret to absolve him from all punishment, and a compulsive gambler who has lost a fortune cannot expect
his bank account to be replenished because he regrets his foolishness,
so too a transgressor cannot logically expect to be made whole again
merely because he has repented. But the Attribute of *HASHEM* comes
into play in defiance of all logic; even after the sin, God accepts repentance and is merciful to the erstwhile sinner as if the misdeed had never
occurred.

IN EXPLAINING WHY MERCY IS NEEDED both before and after a sin, *Maharal* disagrees with the basic premise of the *Rosh*. Far from having no need of

Constant Mercy

mercy before he sins, man always requires it; to think otherwise is to ignore his constant needs and deficiencies. Air, water, food, sun, the very breath of life — all these and more are the basic necessities of man's existence. What has he done to earn them, even if he has not sinned? Yet God brings man into a finished world and supplies him with the essentials of life and the ability to enjoy it and find fulfillment. Is this not a display of boundless mercy, even if a sin has never been committed? So it is that man always needs mercy and God always gives it, before the sin and surely after the repentance.

> לֹא הָיוּ יִשְׂרָאֵל רְאוּיִים לְאוֹתוֹ מַעֲשֶׂה אֶלָּא כְדֵי לְהוֹרוֹת תְּשׁוּבָה לָרַבִּים
> *Israel would not have been susceptible to that sin* [of the Golden Calf] *except to teach repentance to the multitude (Avodah Zarah* 4a).

THAT GOD CHOSE TO BEGIN the Attributes of Mercy with the double use of the Four-letter Name provides an insight into man's mission on earth,

Lesson for the Future*

especially during the *Selichos* days that call out for our repentance. God uses the same Name for His mercy after the sin as before to show that a sinner can return to the state of purity he enjoyed before he stumbled. The Name is repeated because man has the challenge of coming back after he sins. Thanks to one of God's greatest demonstrations of mercy, repentance can erase sins and bring man back to his pristine state of prior perfection. It can restore him to what he was before he lapsed, so he can once again enjoy the mercy that God extends to those who have not yet fallen short, cognizant though He is that imperfect man is never more than a breath away from stumbling. Sin is cause for chagrin, but never for despair — and certainly not for surrender. Hashem is always there, before and after, with His support and open arms, awaiting the return of His fallen children.

The lesson of national repentance came in the earliest days of Israel's national history, in the Wilderness, only a few months after the Exodus. As the Sages taught, under normal circumstances, the sin of the Golden Calf would not have happened. The nation that had heard Hashem announce Himself to them as their God should have been able to withstand the fear and temptation that led them to ask for the Golden Calf. The only reason the sin took place was to demonstrate the power of

---

* This section of the Overview is based on *Ohr Gedalyahu*, to *Elul*.

repentance, and its efficacy in achieving atonement even for a multitude that has sinned *(Avodah Zarah* 4b).

When the Sages tell us that Israel sinned only in order to show the way of repentance, they do not mean to say that God *forced* them to sin. That would have been unjust, and God is never unjust.

What happened in the Wilderness was that God withdrew the mercy that He normally gives before there is a sin. He knew that that august generation could overcome temptation to do evil, because of the combination of their own greatness and God's merciful protection. But He also knew that His people still had flaws that could result in the failure of future generations, which would be neither so lofty nor so worthy of mercy. For such generations, there had to be a well-trodden way back up from the depths of a spiritual fall. If there was any generation that had the capacity to set the example for its offspring, it was the generation that had received the Torah. So God withdrew His mercy, His spiritual shelter, from them so that they could show how Jews can redeem themselves after falling.

They were being tested to see if they could withstand a very powerful temptation, and they would have to do it without Divine assistance. Their downfall was surely not inevitable — for "Israel would not have been susceptible to that sin" *(Avodah Zarah* 4b) — and if God had been giving them the degree of mercy that would normally have been theirs, they would not have sinned. But the mercy was not there and the temptation was — so they danced around the Golden Calf.

That was not the end of it, however. Because of their initial failure, Moses prayed and God appeared to him in the form of a leader of prayer, and taught him the Thirteen Attributes. Only a generation as great as that one could have been worthy of such an exalted teaching, a teaching that has been the mainstay of their offspring for over thirty-three centuries. They taught repentance. They taught that Jews can fall and rise again. They taught that *we* can rise. They became the teachers and the examples of repentance for all generations.

IT IS ILLUSTRATIVE TO SEE what that repentance brought. Prior to the sin of the Golden Calf, Moses had received the Tablets of the Law from

Legacy of the Downfall Sinai. When he saw the painful spectacle of the nation of God prancing around a false god, he smashed the Tablets — something he had to do because the people no longer deserved them. Then came a long period of prayer, highlighted by the vision of God showing Moses how to pray and what to say, and the promise that if Israel would *perform* this prayer — by making themselves agents of mercy to others — then they could rely on His help in the worst situations. The result was that Moses came back from Mount Sinai on Yom Kippur with the Second Tablets.

This was a lesson for all time. Jews can lose the Torah and get it back. They can lose God's mercy and win it back. God loves us and wants us so much that He shows us how to pray and promises that His ear is always cocked, as it were, waiting for us to call Him, to repent, to evoke His mercy, and to come back to where we were before we fell.

This is the secret of *Selichos*. It is as if God had told Moses and the Children of Israel that He had given them a special service for repentance when they needed it most, when they had lost the greatest gift God had ever given man — the Torah — and longed to get it back. Repentance and Torah went hand in hand, then and now, for the Sages teach that Yom Kippur is a *festival*, because it was the day that God gave the Torah to Israel for a second time (*Taanis* 30b).

Let us take the lesson of *Selichos* to heart. By falling and rising, our ancestors in the Wilderness taught us that hope is never lost, even when the protection of God's mercy is absent. God is merciful when we fall short of His expectations, but only if we emulate Him by being merciful to those who fall short of our expectations of them.

Let us begin, and may this year's *Selichos* be climaxed by a Yom Kippur as climactic as the one when Moses brought back the Second Tablets.

Rabbi Nosson Scherman

Menachem Av 5761
August 2011

⋙ *Introduction*

Within the *Siddur* and synagogue service, the mood of repentance is expressed in the סְלִיחוֹת [*Selichos*], *prayers of supplication*. They are of ancient origin; some of them are even mentioned in the Mishnah (*Taanis* Ch. 2) where special prayers for rain are discussed, but almost all of them were composed between the 8th and 16th centuries. The composers of these *Selichos* include some of the outstanding figures of ancient times, among them *Geonim* (7th-10th century Torah authorities) and *Rishonim* (11th-15th century authorities). Consequently, it should be clear that their compositions are not merely inspired poetry.

The central theme of all *Selichos,* as well as of the Yom Kippur *Maariv* and *Neilah* services, is שְׁלֹשׁ עֶשְׂרֵה מִדּוֹת הָרַחֲמִים, *the Thirteen Attributes of Mercy.* This passage appears in the Torah (*Exodus* 34:6-7) at the time when God proclaimed His readiness to do away with the Jewish people after the sin of the Golden Calf. According to R' Yochanan's interpretation (*Rosh Hashanah* 17b), Moses felt that Israel's sin was so grievous that there was no possibility of his intercession on their behalf. Thereupon, God appeared to him in the form of a *chazzan* wrapped in a *tallis* and taught him the Thirteen Attributes, saying, "Whenever Israel sins, let them recite this in its proper order and I will forgive them." Thus, this appeal to God's mercy reassures us both that repentance is always possible and that God always awaits our return to Him. The implication is also plain that if we emulate God's merciful ways, He will treat us mercifully in return.

When it appears in the *Selichos* service, the Thirteen Attributes is introduced by one of two prayers: The first time during each *Selichos* service, it is introduced by אֵל אֶרֶךְ אַפַּיִם, *O God — [You are] slow to anger* .... All other times, the introduction is אֵל מֶלֶךְ יוֹשֵׁב, *O God, King Who sits* .... Brief explanations of these introductions, as well as of the Thirteen Attributes, appear in the commentary.* After the Thirteen Attributes there is always a direct prayer for forgiveness, following the example of Moses, who, after being taught the Thirteen Attributes, pleaded that God forgive Israel (*Exodus* 34:8-9).

---

* Among the *Rishonim,* the *Acharonim,* and the different schools of philosophical and Kabbalistic thought, the Thirteen Attributes have been numbered and explained in many ways. In this volume we have adopted the view of Rabbeinu Tam (*Rosh Hashanah* 17b). The Hebrew reader interested in a deeper understanding and a survey of the various interpretations would do well to study שַׁעֲרֵי רַחֲמִים, by Rabbi Yaakov Y. Hamburger.

Types of *Selichos*

Each of the *piyutim* (liturgical poems) recited during the *Selichos* service is properly called a סְלִיחָה, *selichah*, literally, *forgiveness*. Certain *selichos* are further identified by category, according to their poetic form, subject matter, or location in the service. Some of these classifications are:

פְּתִיחָה, *pesichah* (opening): a *selichah* recited near the beginning of some *Selichos* services, even before the first recitation of the Thirteen Attributes.

שְׁנִיָּה, *sheniyah* (twofold): a *piyut* composed exclusively of couplets, or two-lined stanzas.

שְׁלִישִׁיָּה, *shelishiyah* (threefold): a *piyut* composed exclusively of triplets, or three-lined stanzas.

שַׁלְמוֹנִית, *shalmonis* (whole): a *piyut* composed exclusively of quatrains, or four-lined stanzas. According to some commentaries, the word *shalmonis* means *of Shlomo*, an allusion to R' Shlomo HaBavli, who wrote most of his *piyutim* in this genre.

פִּזְמוֹן, *pizmon* (response; calling out): a *piyut* having a refrain, and usually recited responsively between *chazzan* and congregation. At least one *pizmon* is recited at each *Selichos* service.

שִׁירְשׁוּר, *shirshur* (chain): a *piyut* in which the last word of one stanza (or verse) is repeated as the first word of the next stanza (or verse).

עֲקֵדָה, *akeidah* (binding): a *selichah* that recounts the time Abraham was tested by being asked to sacrifice his son Isaac on the altar. An *akeidah* pleads that the merit of that act should shield the offspring of Abraham and Isaac from harsh judgment when they come before the Heavenly Tribunal.

תּוֹכָחָה, *tochachah* (rebuke): a *piyut* that, unlike the *selichah* that calls upon God to forgive His people, calls on the people to repent and return to God.

חָטָאנוּ, *chatanu* (We have sinned!) a *selichah* with the refrain חָטָאנוּ צוּרֵנוּ, סְלַח לָנוּ יוֹצְרֵנוּ, *We have sinned, our Rock! Forgive us, our Molder!*

שְׁמַע יִשְׂרָאֵל, *Shema Yisrael* (Hear, O Israel): A *selichah* with the first verse of the *Shema* as its refrain.

תְּחִנָּה, *techinah* (supplication): a *selichah* juxtaposed with the recital of *Tachanun* just before the close of the *Selichos* service.

The Daily *Selichos* Service

In the various Ashkenazic *Selichos* rites [the best known of which are *Minhag Lita* (Lithuania), *Minhag Polin* (Poland), *Minhag Ungarin* (Hungary), and *Minhag Ashkenaz* (Germany)], different prayers are recited each day of the *Selichos* period. Nevertheless, the basic format is the same every day. The *selichos* compositions are inserted into "windows" in a "framework" of Scriptural verses and supplications. In most rites, the framework begins with *Ashrei* (*Psalm* 145 with added verses) and Half-*Kaddish*, followed by some fifty verses, mostly from *Psalms*. It closes with another series of verses, the threefold recitation of the *Viduy*/Confession (some, however, recite *Viduy* only once), more verses, supplications, and, finally, *Tachanun* and the Full *Kaddish*.

In *Minhag Lita*, the rite used in this volume, the first day's service includes a *pesichah*, two *selichos*, and a *pizmon*. On the remaining days before Erev Rosh Hashanah, two *selichos* and a *pizmon* are recited.

The ceremony is much longer on Erev Rosh Hashanah, when the recitation includes: a *pesichah*, six *sheniyos*, two *shelishiyos*, two *shalmoniyos*, two *pizmonim*, an *akeidah*, a *techinah*, and four other *selichos*. A multipartite supplication is also interpolated at various points during the regular threefold *Viduy* recitation.

In deference to the preparations for Yom Kippur, the *Selichos* service for Erev Yom Kippur comprises only a *sheniyah*, a *shelishiyah*, a *pizmon*, and a greatly abridged framework.

Mention of Intermediaries

The propriety and permissibility of channeling prayer through angelic intercessors, rather than directly to God, is a point of halachic contention.* The debate revolves around supplications such as, מַכְנִיסֵי רַחֲמִים, *O you who usher in [pleas for] mercy* (p. 66), מַלְאֲכֵי רַחֲמִים, *O angels of mercy* (p. 149), and תְּפִלָּה תִּקַּח, *Accept prayer* (p. 608), which request ministering angels to bring our supplications and tears before God, and to beseech Him to accept them favorably.

---

* It is not within the scope of this article to even attempt to reconcile the two sides in this centuries-old debate. We have only tried to show that each view is firmly entrenched and based on the tradition of millennia. Those wishing to study the issue further are advised to see the *Mavo* to *Siddur Otzer HaTefillos*, section 3, לְמִי מִתְפַּלְלִין.

Some *selichos* do not go quite so far as to request angelic intervention, but nevertheless are not addressed directly to God. Some of these
are: שְׁלֹשׁ עֶשְׂרֵה מִדּוֹת, *Thirteen Attributes* (p. 537), which entreats not God
but His Attributes; תּוֹרָה הַקְּדוֹשָׁה, *Holy Torah* (p. 733), which pleads with
the Torah to act as an advocate on Israel's behalf; and שְׁבֶת הַכִּסֵּא, *May
the Throne of Glory* (p. 829), which invokes God's celestial Throne to
intercede and pray for us.

Those opposed to the recitation of such prayers cite a passage in the
Jerusalem Talmud to support their view:

> When a man supported by a patron finds himself in dif-
> ficult straits, he does not suddenly enter [his patron's
> chambers to demand assistance or succor]. Rather, he
> stands at the door and asks a servant or a family mem-
> ber to announce his presence. [Even then his success is
> not assured.] Perhaps he will be admitted, perhaps he
> will not. But with the Holy one, Blessed is He, such is
> not the case, [for He says,] "If one is in difficult straits,
> he should not call to [the angel] Michael or to [the
> angel] Gabriel. Rather, he should call to Me and I will
> answer him immediately" (*Yerushalmi, Berachos* 9:1).

The *Rishonim* expound on and expand this prohibition. In the fifth
of his Thirteen Principles of Faith, Maimonides writes:

> It is the Blessed One Whom it is proper to worship,
> to exalt, to propagate His greatness, and to fulfill His
> commandments. But one must not do so for anything
> of lower existence [than God Himself], such as the
> angels, the stars, the spheres, the elements, and what-
> ever is composed of them .... It is likewise improper
> to pray that they act as intercessors to present [our
> prayers] to Him. Only to Him shall one's thoughts be
> directed; and all besides Him should be ignored ...
> (*Rambam, Pirush HaMishnayos, Sanhedrin* 10).

Nachmanides writes similarly: "The third form of idolatry is consider-
ing the angels capable of serving as intermediaries between God and
His worshipers .... Realize that even to pray to them for this purpose is
forbidden to us ..." (*Ramban, Toras Hashem Temimah*).

In later generations, the Maharal of Prague wrote strongly against
supplications addressed to angelic advocates. In the course of his

argument, the Maharal distinguishes between celestial beings on the one hand, and the Patriarchs, Matriarchs, and righteous *tzaddikim* of every generation. Why may one seek the intercession of human intermediaries, yet be prohibited from beseeching the angels to advocate his cause? Man is commanded to perform acts of kindness with his fellow man. Thus, by requesting another person to pray for his welfare, one presents his fellow with an opportunity to perform an act of kindness. Angels, on the other hand, are neither commanded nor given the free will to perform such acts. They may do only the specific deed or deeds for which they were created and regarding which they were commanded by God. A request to an angel must therefore be considered not just asking for friendly help, but a prayer; and Heaven forbid that any Jew should utter such a prayer (*Nesivos Olam, Nesiv HaAvodah* 12).

R' Yosef Albo, in a lengthy dissertation, explains that even if there were no halachic problem regarding such prayers, they nevertheless would remain useless for pragmatic reasons. For one to be able to grant the needs of another on an on-going basis, (a) the provider must be eternal and unchanging; then the beneficence will remain unchangingly appropriate and good for the recipient — only God fits this requirement; (b) the provider must be independent and not need the assistance of another party — only God fits this requirement; (c) the provider must be able to supply items of opposite natures, for example, heat and cold, fire and water, because sometimes man needs one, at other times the other — only God fits this requirement; and (d) there must be nothing in the world that can prevent the provider from fulfilling his desire — only God fits this requirement. Thus, in order for prayer to be effective, it must be received favorably by God, even if it is directed elsewhere. So from a practical sense, prayer should be addressed only to God (*Ikkarim* 4:17).

Elsewhere R' Albo explains that although worshiping an angel is forbidden, showing reverence or honor to the angel as an emissary of God is permitted. For this reason Joshua was able to bow to the angel that appeared to him in Jericho (see *Joshua* 5:13-15). But one who bows to an angel as an act of worship is guilty of idolatry (*Ikkarim* 2:28).

❧ ❧ ❧

Those who permit the recitation of supplications addressed to angelic intercessors cite a passage from *Midrash Shir HaShirim* (not found in extant editions):

> The Congregation of Israel says to the angels standing at the [heavenly] Gates of Prayer and Gates of Tears, "Usher in my prayer and my tears before the Holy One, Blessed is He; and act as advocates before Him, that He pardon me for both intentional and inadvertent sins." And so it is stated (*Job* 33:23): *If there be for him but one advocate angel from among a thousand* ... (*Shibbolei HaLeket* 282; *Tanya Rabbasi*, Cremona edition, p. 102a).

Another source for this viewpoint is in the Talmud. "R' Yochanan says: A person should always seek mercy that all should invigorate and encourage him, and that he not have enemies on high" (*Sanhedrin* 44b). According to *Rashi* this means that one should seek to have the ministering angels plead for mercy for him and not become his accusers in heaven.

Another Talmudic passage is cited. "Rav Yehudah said: A person should never request his needs in the Aramaic tongue. And R' Yochanan said: If anyone requests his needs in the Aramaic tongue, the ministering angels ignore him, for the angels do not understand Aramaic" (*Shabbos* 12b). According to R' Sherira Gaon, Rav Yehudah and R' Yochanan are speaking of a person who directs his request to an angel. One who speaks directly to God, however, may use any language. R' Sherira explains although angels have no independent power to grant bounty or withhold it, some angels are given parameters within which they may function at their own discretion. For example, an angel may be assigned to accompany a traveler and protect him from harm along the road. Nevertheless, the guardian is permitted to remove its protection if the wayfarer acts sinfully. Thus, when God informed Moses that He would send an angel to lead and protect the nation on the way to *Eretz Yisrael*, He warned: *"Be careful before him; follow his words; do not rebel against him, for he will not forgive your rebelliousness, because My Name is within him"* (*Exodus* 23:21).

Of course, it is needless to add that the *paytanim* who composed the controversial *selichos* were certainly of the opinion that such prayer is permitted. And their number includes some of the greatest scholars and halachic authorities of all generations.

◈ The Names of God

The Four-Letter Name of HASHEM [יְ־ה־ו־ה] indicates that God is timeless and infinite, since the letters of this Name are those of the words הָיָה הֹוֶה וְיִהְיֶה, *He was, He is, and He will be*. This Name appears in some editions with vowel points [יְ־הֹ־וָ־ה] and in others, such as the present edition, without vowels. In either case, this Name is *never* pronounced as it is spelled.

During prayer, or when a blessing is recited, or when Torah verses are read, the Four-Letter Name should be pronounced as if it were spelled אֲדֹנָי, *Adōnoy,* the Name that identifies God as the Master of All. At other times, it should be pronounced הַשֵּׁם, *Hashem,* literally, "the Name."

According to the *Shulchan Aruch,* one should have both meanings — the Master of All and the Timeless, Infinite One — in mind when reciting the Four-Letter Name during prayer (*Orach Chaim* Ch. 5). According to the *Vilna Gaon,* however, one need have in mind only the meaning of the Name as it is pronounced — the Master of All (ibid.).

When the Name is spelled אֲדֹנָי in the prayer or verse, all agree that one should have in mind that God is the Master of All.

The Name אֱלֹהִים, *Elōhim, God,* refers to Him as the One Who is all-powerful and Who is in direct overlordship of the universe (ibid.). This is also used as a generic name for the angels, a court, rulers, and even idols. However, when the term אֱלֹהִים is used for the God of Israel, it means the One Omniscient God, Who is uniquely identified with His Chosen People.

In this work, the Four-Letter Name of God is translated "HASHEM," the pronunciation traditionally used for the Name to avoid pronouncing it unnecessarily. This pronunciation should be used when studying the meanings of the prayers. However, if one prays in English, he should say "God" or "Lord" or he should pronounce the Name in the proper Hebrew way — *Adōnoy* — in accord with the ruling of most halachic authorities.

◈ Pronouncing the Names of God

The following table gives the pronunciations of the Name when it appears with a prefix. In all these cases, the accent is on the last syllable (*noy*). The phrase "מֹשֶׁה" מֹוצִיא "וְכָלֵב" מַכְנִיס is used as a mnemonic. The prefixes מ, ש, and ה do not absorb or assimilate the vowel from the first letter of God's Name, while the prefixes ו, כ, ל, and ב do absorb the vowel that follows.

בַּ־יְ־ה־ו־ה	*Ba-dōnoy*
דַּ־יְ־ה־ו־ה	*Da-dōnoy*
הַ־יְ־ה־ו־ה	*Ha-adōnoy*
וַ־יְ־ה־ו־ה	*Va-dōnoy*
כַּ־יְ־ה־ו־ה	*Ka-dōnoy*
לַ־יְ־ה־ו־ה	*La-dōnoy*
מֵ־יְ־ה־ו־ה	*May-adōnoy*
שֶׁ־יְ־ה־ו־ה	*She-adōnoy*

Sometimes the Name appears with the vowelization יֱ־הֹ־וִ־ה. This version of the Name is pronounced as if it were spelled אֱלֹהִים, *Elōhim,* the Name that refers to God as the One Who is all-powerful. When it appears with a prefix לֵ־יהֹ־וִ־ה, it is pronounced *Lay-lōhim.* We have translated this Name as HASHEM / ELOHIM to indicate that it refers to the aspects inherent in each of those Names.

סְלִיחוֹת / Selichos

Within the framework of the *Siddur* and synagogue service, the mood of repentance is expressed in the סְלִיחוֹת [*selichos*], *prayers of supplication*. They are of ancient origin; some of them are even mentioned in the Mishnah (*Taanis* ch. 2) where special prayers for rain are discussed, but almost all of them were composed between the eighth and sixteenth centuries. The composers of these *selichos* include some of the outstanding figures of ancient times, among them *Geonim* (7th-10th century Torah authorities) and *Rishonim* (11th-15th century authorities). Consequently, it should be clear that their compositions are not merely inspired poetry.

The central theme of all *selichos,* as well as of the Yom Kippur *Maariv* and *Neilah* services, is שְׁלֹשׁ עֶשְׂרֵה מִדּוֹת הָרַחֲמִים, *the Thirteen Attributes of Mercy*. This passage appears in the Torah (*Exodus* 34:6-7) at the time when God proclaimed His readiness to do away with the Jewish people after the sin of the Golden Calf. According to R' Yochanan's interpretation (*Rosh Hashanah* 17b), Moses felt that Israel's sin was so grievous that there was no possibility of his intercession on their behalf. Thereupon, God appeared to him in the form of a *chazzan* wrapped in a *tallis* and taught him the Thirteen Attributes, saying, 'Whenever Israel sins, let them recite this in its proper order and I will forgive them.' Thus, this appeal to God's mercy reassures us both that repentance is always possible and that God always awaits our return to Him. The implication is also plain that if we emulate God's merciful ways, He will treat us mercifully in return.

When it appears in the *Selichos* service, the Thirteen Attributes is introduced by one of two prayers: The first time during each *Selichos* service, it is introduced by אֵל אֶרֶךְ אַפַּיִם, *God Who is slow to anger* . . . All other times, the introduction is אֵל מֶלֶךְ יוֹשֵׁב, *O God, King Who sits* . . . Brief explanations of these introductions, as well as of the Thirteen Attributes, appear in the commentary. After the Thirteen Attributes there is always a direct prayer for forgiveness, following the example of Moses, who, after being taught the Thirteen Attributes, pleaded that God forgive Israel (*Exodus* 34:8-9).

❧ יום ראשון / FIRST DAY ❧

אַ֫שְׁרֵי יוֹשְׁבֵי בֵיתֶךָ, עוֹד יְהַלְלוּךָ סֶּלָה.¹ אַשְׁרֵי

⟨ Praise-worthy ⟨ Selah. ⟨ they will praise You, ⟨ con-tinually ⟨ in Your house, ⟨ are those who dwell ⟨ Praiseworthy

הָעָם שֶׁכָּכָה לּוֹ, אַשְׁרֵי הָעָם שֶׁיהוה אֱלֹהָיו.²

⟨ is their God. ⟨ that ⟨ is the people ⟨ praise-worthy ⟨ is their lot; ⟨ that such ⟨ is the people

——— תהלים קמה / Psalm 145 ———

תְּהִלָּה* לְדָוִד, אֲרוֹמִמְךָ* אֱלוֹהַי הַמֶּלֶךְ, וַאֲבָרְכָה

⟨ and I will bless ⟨ the King, ⟨ my God ⟨ I will exalt You,* ⟨ by David: ⟨ A psalm of praise*

שִׁמְךָ לְעוֹלָם וָעֶד. בְּכָל יוֹם אֲבָרְכֶךָּ,* וַאֲהַלְלָה

⟨ and I will laud ⟨ I will bless You,* ⟨ day ⟨ Every ⟨ and ever. ⟨ for ever ⟨ Your Name

שִׁמְךָ לְעוֹלָם וָעֶד. גָּדוֹל יהוה וּמְהֻלָּל מְאֹד,

⟨ exceedingly, ⟨ and lauded ⟨ is HASHEM ⟨ Great ⟨ and ever. ⟨ for ever ⟨ Your Name

(1) *Psalms* 84:5. (2) 144:15.

אַשְׁרֵי❧ / **Ashrei**

The *Selichos* service is best begun with the recital of the exalted praises of *Kaddish*. However, since *Kaddish* cannot be recited except after Scriptural verses, it is customary to recite Psalm 145 [אַשְׁרֵי, *Ashrei*] first (*Levush*). The selection of *Ashrei* is based on the similarity between *Selichos* and the daily *Shacharis* service. Each day's morning prayers begin with *Pesukei D'Zimrah*, of which *Ashrei* is a major component. The *selichah* passages and the Thirteen Attributes recited with them are similar to the *Shemoneh Esrei*. And as with *Shacharis*, the *Selichos* service ends with וִדּוּי, *Confession*, and תַּחֲנוּן, *the Tachanun supplication*. It is noteworthy that the Full *Kaddish*, usually recited after *Shemoneh Esrei*, is also recited after *Selichos*, further adding to the similarity between the regular morning prayers and *Selichos* (*Likkutei Maharich*).

Psalm 145 begins with the verse תְּהִלָּה לְדָוִד; the two preliminary verses, each beginning with the word אַשְׁרֵי, are affixed to תְּהִלָּה לְדָוִד for two reasons: (a) By expressing the idea that those who dwell in God's house of prayer and service are praiseworthy, these verses set the stage for the succeeding psalm of praise, for we, the praiseworthy ones, are about to laud the God in Whose house we dwell; and (b) the word אַשְׁרֵי is found three times in these verses. This alludes to the Talmudic dictum that one who recites Psalm 145 three times a day is assured of a share in the World to Come (*Berachos* 4b); thus, those who do so are indeed אַשְׁרֵי, *praiseworthy*.

תְּהִלָּה ... אֲרוֹמִמְךָ — *A psalm of praise ... I will exalt You*. Beginning with the word אֲרוֹמִמְךָ, the initials of the respective verses follow the order of the *aleph-beis*. According to *Abudraham*, the *aleph-beis* structure symbolizes that we praise God with every sound available to the organs of speech. *Midrash Tadshei* records that the Psalmists and Sages used the *aleph-beis* formula in chapters that they wanted people to follow more easily or to memorize.

בְּכָל יוֹם אֲבָרְכֶךָּ — *Every day I will bless You*. True, no mortal can pretend to know God's essence, but each of us is equipped to appreciate life, health, sustenance,

וְלִגְדֻלָּתוֹ אֵין חֵקֶר.* **דּוֹר** לְדוֹר יְשַׁבַּח מַעֲשֶׂיךָ,

‹ Your actions, ‹ will praise ‹ to generation ‹ Generation » is beyond investigation.* ‹ and His greatness

וּגְבוּרֹתֶיךָ יַגִּידוּ. **הֲדַר** כְּבוֹד הוֹדֶךָ, וְדִבְרֵי

‹ and Your deeds ‹ of Your majesty ‹ glory ‹ The splendrous » they will recount. » and Your mighty deeds

נִפְלְאֹתֶיךָ אָשִׂיחָה. וֶעֱזוּז נוֹרְאֹתֶיךָ יֹאמֵרוּ,

» they will speak, ‹ of Your awesome deeds ‹ And of the might » I shall discuss. ‹ that are wondrous

וּגְדוּלָּתְךָ אֲסַפְּרֶנָּה. זֵכֶר רַב טוּבְךָ יַבִּיעוּ, וְצִדְקָתְךָ

‹ and of Your righteousness » they will utter, ‹ of Your abundant goodness ‹ A recollection » I shall relate. ‹ and Your greatness

יְרַנֵּנוּ. חַנּוּן וְרַחוּם* יהוה, אֶרֶךְ אַפַּיִם וּגְדָל חָסֶד.

» in [bestowing] kindness. ‹ and great ‹ to anger, ‹ slow » is ‹ HASHEM, ‹ and merciful* ‹ Gracious » they will sing joyfully.

טוֹב יהוה לַכֹּל, וְרַחֲמָיו עַל כָּל מַעֲשָׂיו. יוֹדוּךָ יהוה

» HASHEM ‹ They will » His ‹ all ‹ are on ‹ His » to all; ‹ HASHEM is good
thank You, creations. mercies

כָּל מַעֲשֶׂיךָ, וַחֲסִידֶיךָ יְבָרְכוּכָה. **כְּבוֹד** מַלְכוּתְךָ

‹ of Your kingdom ‹ Of the glory » will bless You. » and Your devout ones » Your creations — ‹ — all

יֹאמֵרוּ, וּגְבוּרָתְךָ יְדַבֵּרוּ. **לְהוֹדִיעַ** לִבְנֵי הָאָדָם

‹ mankind ‹ To inform » they will declare. ‹ and of Your power » they will speak, » they will speak,

גְּבוּרֹתָיו, וּכְבוֹד הֲדַר מַלְכוּתוֹ. **מַלְכוּתְךָ** מַלְכוּת

‹ is a kingdom ‹ Your kingdom » of His kingdom. ‹ splendor ‹ and of the glorious » of His mighty deeds,

כָּל עֹלָמִים, וּמֶמְשַׁלְתְּךָ בְּכָל דּוֹר וָדֹר. **סוֹמֵךְ** יהוה*

‹ HASHEM supports* » after generation. ‹ generation ‹ is throughout ‹ and Your dominion » eternities, ‹ [spanning] all

---

sunshine, rainfall, and so on. For these and their daily renewal, we give daily blessings (*Siach Yitzchak*).

וְלִגְדֻלָּתוֹ אֵין חֵקֶר — *And His greatness is beyond investigation.* Much though we may try, we can understand neither God's essence nor His ways through human analysis, for He is infinite. We *must* rely on the traditions that have come to us from earlier generations, as the next verse

suggests (*Rama*).

חַנּוּן וְרַחוּם — *Gracious and merciful.* Because God is *merciful*, He is אֶרֶךְ אַפַּיִם, *slow to anger,* so that punishment, although deserved, is delayed as long as possible to allow time for repentance. And because He is *gracious*, He is גְּדָל חָסֶד, *great in [bestowing] kindness* (*Siach Yitzchak*).

סוֹמֵךְ ה׳ — *HASHEM supports.* No verse in *Ashrei* begins with a נ, because in the

לְכָל הַנֹּפְלִים, וְזוֹקֵף לְכָל הַכְּפוּפִים. עֵינֵי כֹל אֵלֶיךָ

‹ to You ‹ of all ‹ The eyes ≪ those who are bent. ‹ all ‹ and ≪ those who straightens are fallen, ‹ all

יְשַׂבֵּרוּ,* וְאַתָּה נוֹתֵן לָהֶם אֶת אָכְלָם בְּעִתּוֹ.

≪ in its proper time. ‹ their food ‹ them ‹ give ‹ and You ≪ do look with hope,*

CONCENTRATE INTENTLY WHILE RECITING THE VERSE פּוֹתֵחַ, YOU OPEN.

פּוֹתֵחַ* אֶת יָדֶךָ, וּמַשְׂבִּיעַ לְכָל חַי רָצוֹן. ❖ צַדִּיק*

‹ Righteous* ≪ [with its] desire. ‹ living thing ‹ every ‹ and satisfy ≪ Your hand, ‹ You open*

יהוה בְּכָל דְּרָכָיו, וְחָסִיד* בְּכָל מַעֲשָׂיו. קָרוֹב

‹ Close ≪ His deeds. ‹ in all ‹ and magnanimous* ≪ His ways, ‹ in all ‹ is HASHEM

יהוה לְכָל קֹרְאָיו, לְכֹל אֲשֶׁר יִקְרָאֻהוּ בֶאֱמֶת.

≪ sincerely. ‹ call upon Him ‹ who ‹ to all ≪ who call upon Him, ‹ to all ‹ is HASHEM

רְצוֹן יְרֵאָיו יַעֲשֶׂה, וְאֶת שַׁוְעָתָם יִשְׁמַע וְיוֹשִׁיעֵם.

≪ and He will save them. ‹ He will hear, ‹ and their cry ≪ He will do; ‹ of those who fear Him ‹ The will

שׁוֹמֵר יהוה אֶת כָּל אֹהֲבָיו, וְאֵת כָּל הָרְשָׁעִים

‹ the wicked ‹ but all ≪ who love Him; ‹ all ‹ HASHEM protects

יַשְׁמִיד. תְּהִלַּת יהוה יְדַבֶּר פִּי, וִיבָרֵךְ כָּל בָּשָׂר

‹ flesh ‹ may all ‹ and bless ≪ may my mouth declare, ‹ of HASHEM ‹ The praise ≪ He will destroy.

context of this verse that speaks of God supporting the fallen, the letter נ can be taken as an allusion to נְפִילָה, Israel's future *downfall*, ח"ו and the Psalmist refused to use a letter that could suggest such tragedy. Nevertheless, knowing that downfalls would take place, the Psalmist comforted Israel by saying, *God supports all those who are fallen*. Even when a dreaded downfall happens, the people can look forward to His support (*Berachos* 4b). *Maharsha* comments that by omitting a direct mention of downfall, the Psalmist implies that even when Israel *does* suffer reverses, those reverses will never be final. Rather, as the next verse declares, God will support the fallen.

עֵינֵי כֹל אֵלֶיךָ יְשַׂבֵּרוּ — *The eyes of all to You do look with hope.* Even animals instinct-

ively rely upon God for their sustenance [how much more so should man recognize the beneficence of his Maker!] (*Radak*).

פּוֹתֵחַ — *You open.* When reciting this verse, one should have in mind the meaning of the words because this declaration of God's universal goodness is one of the two reasons the Sages required the thrice-daily recitation of this psalm. This verse should be recited with great joy at the knowledge that God cares for every creature (*Yesod V'Shoresh HaAvodah*).

צַדִּיק ... וְחָסִיד — *Righteous ... and magnanimous.* God's ways are just and *right-eous*, meaning that He judges people only according to their deeds. Nevertheless, even when justice calls for harsh punishment, He is *magnanimous* in softening the

שֵׁם קָדְשׁוֹ לְעוֹלָם וָעֶד. וַאֲנַחְנוּ נְבָרֵךְ* יָהּ מֵעַתָּה

⟨ from this time ⟨ God ⟨ will bless* ⟨ But we « and ever. ⟨ for ever ⟨ of His Holiness ⟨ the Name

וְעַד עוֹלָם; הַלְלוּיָהּ.*¹

« Halleluyah!* « eternity. ⟨ until

THE CHAZZAN RECITES חֲצִי קַדִּישׁ, HALF-KADDISH:

יִתְגַּדַּל וְיִתְקַדַּשׁ שְׁמֵהּ רַבָּא.* (.אָמֵן — Cong.) בְּעָלְמָא

⟨ — in the world « (Amen.)* « that is great!—* ⟨ may His Name ⟨ and be sanctified ⟨ Grow exalted

דִּי בְרָא כִרְעוּתֵהּ.* וְיַמְלִיךְ מַלְכוּתֵהּ, וְיַצְמַח פֻּרְקָנֵהּ

⟨ His salvation, ⟨ and cause to sprout « to His kingship, ⟨ and may He give reign « according to His will,* ⟨ He created ⟨ that

וִיקָרֵב מְשִׁיחֵהּ. (.אָמֵן — Cong.) בְּחַיֵּיכוֹן* וּבְיוֹמֵיכוֹן וּבְחַיֵּי

⟨ and in the lifetimes ⟨ and in your days, ⟨ in your lifetimes* « (Amen.) « His Messiah, ⟨ and bring near

דְּכָל בֵּית יִשְׂרָאֵל, בַּעֲגָלָא וּבִזְמַן קָרִיב.* וְאִמְרוּ: אָמֵן.

« Amen. ⟨ Now respond: « that comes soon.* ⟨ and at a time ⟨ swiftly « of Israel, ⟨ Family ⟨ of the entire

---

(1) *Psalms* 115:18.

blow, for He is merciful (*Vilna Gaon*).

וַאֲנַחְנוּ נְבָרֵךְ — *But we will bless.* This verse is appended to *Ashrei*, for having recited *Ashrei*, which holds an assurance of the World to Come, we express the hope that we will bless God *forever* — that is, in both worlds (*Levush*).

הַלְלוּיָהּ — *Halleluyah.* This word is composed of two words: הַלְלוּ, *praise, and* יָהּ, *God.* הַלְלוּ denotes crying out in exultation, while the unique meaning implied by the Name יָהּ is *the One Who is forever.* The Psalmist addresses everyone: Use your energy to be *excited* over God — and only God — and nothing else (*R' Avigdor Miller*).

קַדִּישׁ / Kaddish ≈§

יִתְגַּדַּל וְיִתְקַדַּשׁ שְׁמֵהּ רַבָּא — *Grow exalted and be sanctified may His Name that is great.* The ultimate sanctification of God's Name will come when Israel is redeemed; in this sense *Kaddish* is a plea for the Final Redemption. It is also an expression of Israel's mission to bring recognition of His sovereignty primarily upon the community as a whole, and *Kaddish* is therefore recited

only in the presence of a *minyan* [a quorum of ten males over *bar mitzvah*] (*R' Munk*).

אָמֵן — *Amen.* The word אָמֵן, *Amen*, is the listener's acknowledgment that he believes in what the reader has just said. It is derived from the same root as אֱמוּנָה, *faithfulness* (*Tur, Orach Chaim* 124). Additionally, it stands for אֵל מֶלֶךְ נֶאֱמָן, *God, King Who is trustworthy* (*Shabbos* 119b).

בְּעָלְמָא דִּי בְרָא כִרְעוּתֵהּ — *In the world that He created according to His will.* God had His concept of a perfect world before He began creation. Then He began to create in accordance with His prior will (*Ran*). Or it refers to the *future.* Only then will mankind function in accordance with God's original intention (*R' Yehudah ben Yakar*).

בְּחַיֵּיכוֹן — *In your lifetimes.* The one reciting the *Kaddish* expresses the hope that his fellow congregants may all live to witness the Redemption of Israel and the sanctification of God's Name (*Abudraham*).

בַּעֲגָלָא וּבִזְמַן קָרִיב — *Swiftly and at a time that comes soon.* May the travail preceding the Messianic epoch be over *swiftly*

CONGREGATION RESPONDS:

אָמֵן. יְהֵא שְׁמֵהּ רַבָּא* מְבָרַךְ לְעָלַם וּלְעָלְמֵי עָלְמַיָּא.

》 and for all eternity. 〈 forever 〈 be blessed 〈 that is great* 〈 His Name 〈 May 》 Amen.

CHAZZAN CONTINUES:

יְהֵא שְׁמֵהּ רַבָּא מְבָרַךְ לְעָלַם וּלְעָלְמֵי עָלְמַיָּא. יִתְבָּרַךְ*

〈 Blessed,* 》 and for all eternity. 〈 forever 〈 be blessed 〈 that is great 〈 His Name 〈 May

וְיִשְׁתַּבַּח וְיִתְפָּאַר וְיִתְרוֹמַם וְיִתְנַשֵּׂא וְיִתְהַדָּר וְיִתְעַלֶּה

〈 elevated, 〈 honored, 〈 upraised, 〈 exalted, 〈 glorified, 〈 praised,

וְיִתְהַלָּל שְׁמֵהּ דְּקֻדְשָׁא בְּרִיךְ הוּא (.Cong — בְּרִיךְ הוּא)

》(is He) 〈(Blessed 》 is He 〈 Blessed 〈 of the Holy One, 〈 be the Name 〈 and lauded

— לְעֵלָּא מִן כָּל בִּרְכָתָא* וְשִׁירָתָא תֻּשְׁבְּחָתָא וְנֶחֱמָתָא

〈 and consolation 〈 praise 》 and song, 〈 blessing* 》 any 〈 beyond

דַּאֲמִירָן בְּעָלְמָא. וְאִמְרוּ: אָמֵן. (.Cong — אָמֵן.)

》 (Amen.) 》 Amen. 〈 Now respond: 》 in the world. 〈 that are uttered

ALL:

לְךָ יהוה הַצְּדָקָה, וְלָנוּ בּֽשֶׁת הַפָּנִים.¹ מַה

》What 》 is shamefacedness. 〈 and ours 》 is the right-eousness, 〈 O Lord, 〈 Yours,

נִּתְאוֹנֵן,² מַה נֹּאמַר, מַה נְּדַבֵּר, וּמַה נִּצְטַדָּק.³

》 justification can we offer? 〈 What 》 can we declare? 〈 What 》can we say? 〈 What 》 complaint can we make?

---

(1) *Daniel* 9:7. (2) Cf. *Lamentations* 3:39. (3) Cf. *Genesis* 44:16.

and not be drawn out; and may it begin very soon (*Aruch HaShulchan*).

יְהֵא שְׁמֵהּ רַבָּא — *May His Name that is great.* The Talmud stresses in several places that the response, יְהֵא שְׁמֵהּ רַבָּא, *May His Name that is great* …, has an enormous cosmic effect. Indeed, the halachah states that an opportunity to respond to *Kaddish* takes precedence over an opportunity to respond to any other prayer, even *Kedushah* and *Borchu*. Consequently, if *Kaddish* is about to be recited in one room and *Kedushah* in another, one should go to hear *Kaddish* (*Mishnah Berurah* 56:6).

The Talmud (*Shabbos* 19b) teaches that one must respond יְהֵא שְׁמֵהּ רַבָּא *with all his power*, meaning his total concentration (*Rashi, Tosafos*). Though it is preferable to raise one's voice when saying it, one should not say it so loudly that he will invite ridicule (*R' Yonah*). And it must be enunciated clearly (*Maharal*).

יִתְבָּרַךְ — *Blessed.* This begins a series of praises that continue the central theme of *Kaddish:* In time to come, God's greatness will be acknowledged by all of mankind (*Emek Berachah*).

לְעֵלָּא מִן כָּל בִּרְכָתָא — *Beyond any blessing.* No words or ideas adequately praise God.

נַחְפְּשָׂה דְרָכֵינוּ וְנַחְקְרָה, וְנָשׁוּבָה אֵלֶיךָ, כִּי יְמִינְךָ [1]

⟨ Your ⟨ for ⟪ to You, ⟨ and return ⟨ and investigate ⟨ our ways ⟨ Let us
right hand   them,   examine

פְּשׁוּטָה לְקַבֵּל שָׁבִים. לֹא בְחֶסֶד וְלֹא בְמַעֲשִׂים

⟨ with [merit for ⟨ nor ⟨ with [merit] ⟨ Nei- ⟪ those who ⟨ to accept ⟨ is extended
good] deeds   for kindness   ther   return.

בָּאנוּ לְפָנֶיךָ, כְּדַלִּים וּכְרָשִׁים דָּפַקְנוּ דְלָתֶיךָ.

⟪ on Your ⟨ before You; ⟪ and as destitute ⟨ but as ⟪ before You; ⟨ do we
doors.   we have   people   paupers   come
knocked

דְלָתֶיךָ דָּפַקְנוּ רַחוּם וְחַנּוּן, נָא אַל תְּשִׁיבֵנוּ

⟨ turn us ⟨ do ⟨ Please ⟪ and Gra- ⟨ O Compas- ⟨ we have ⟨ On Your
away   not   cious One.   sionate One   knocked,   doors

רֵיקָם מִלְּפָנֶיךָ. מִלְּפָנֶיךָ מַלְכֵּנוּ רֵיקָם אַל תְּשִׁיבֵנוּ,

⟪ turn us ⟨ do ⟨ empty- ⟨ Our King, ⟨ From before ⟪ from before ⟨ empty-
away,   not   handed   You,   You.   handed

כִּי אַתָּה שׁוֹמֵעַ תְּפִלָּה.

⟪ prayer. ⟨ Who hears ⟨ You are ⟨ for
the One

שׁוֹמֵעַ תְּפִלָּה,* עָדֶיךָ כָּל בָּשָׂר יָבְאוּ. [2] יָבוֹא

⟨ Come ⟪ will come. ⟨ flesh ⟨ all ⟨ unto You ⟪ prayer,* ⟨ You Who hears

כָּל בָּשָׂר לְהִשְׁתַּחֲוֹת לְפָנֶיךָ יהוה. [3] יָבְאוּ וְיִשְׁתַּחֲווּ

⟨ and bow ⟨ They will ⟪ O ⟨ before ⟨ to bow down ⟨ will all flesh
down   come   HASHEM.   You,

לְפָנֶיךָ אֲדֹנָי, וִיכַבְּדוּ לִשְׁמֶךָ. [4] בֹּאוּ נִשְׁתַּחֲוֶה וְנִכְרָעָה,

⟪ and bow, ⟨ Let us prostrate ⟨ Come! ⟪ to Your ⟨ and they will ⟪ O Lord, ⟨ before
ourselves   Name.   show honor   You,

נִבְרְכָה לִפְנֵי יהוה עֹשֵׂנוּ. [5] נָבוֹאָה לְמִשְׁכְּנוֹתָיו,*

⟪ to His Tabernacles,* ⟨ Let us come ⟪ our Maker. ⟨ HASHEM, ⟨ before ⟨ let us kneel

נִשְׁתַּחֲוֶה לַהֲדֹם רַגְלָיו.* [6] בֹּאוּ שְׁעָרָיו בְּתוֹדָה,

⟪ with ⟨ His ⟨ Enter ⟪ for His feet.* ⟨ at the ⟨ let us prostrate
thanksgiving,   gates   stool   ourselves

---

(1) Cf. *Lamentations* 3:40. (2) *Psalms* 65:3. (3) Cf. *Isaiah* 66:23. (4) *Psalms* 86:9. (5) 95:6. (6) 132:7.

---

§ שׁוֹמֵעַ תְּפִלָּה — *You Who hears prayer.* This collection of verses introduces the daily *Selichos*. It speaks simultaneously to God and to Israel. To God, it declares that we acknowledge His complete mastery over everything and His uncontested ability to bring us salvation. To Israel, it urges everyone to join us in worshiping Him and begging forgiveness.

לְמִשְׁכְּנוֹתָיו ... לַהֲדֹם רַגְלָיו — *... to His Tabernacles ... at the stool for His feet.* In

חֲצֵרֹתָיו בִּתְהִלָּה, הוֹדוּ לוֹ בָּרְכוּ שְׁמוֹ.¹ וַאֲנַחְנוּ

⟨ But we, ⟪ His Name. ⟨ bless ⟪ to Him, ⟨ give thanks ⟪ with praise; ⟨ His courtyards

בְּרֹב חַסְדְּךָ נָבוֹא בֵיתֶךָ, נִשְׁתַּחֲוֶה אֶל הֵיכַל קָדְשְׁךָ

⟨ Your Holy Sanctuary ⟨ toward ⟨ we will prostrate ourselves ⟪ Your House; ⟨ will we enter ⟨ of Your kindness ⟨ through the abundance

בְּיִרְאָתֶךָ.² הִנֵּה בָּרְכוּ אֶת יהוה כָּל עַבְדֵי יהוה,

⟨ of HASHEM, ⟨ you ⟨ all ⟨ servants ⟨ HASHEM, ⟨ bless ⟪ Indeed, ⟪ in awe of You.

הָעֹמְדִים* בְּבֵית יהוה בַּלֵּילוֹת.*³ שְׂאוּ יְדֵכֶם קֹדֶשׁ

⟨ in the Sanctuary ⟨ your hands ⟨ Lift ⟪ in the nights.* ⟨ of HASHEM ⟨ in the House ⟨ who stand*

וּבָרְכוּ אֶת יהוה.⁴ רוֹמְמוּ יהוה אֱלֹהֵינוּ, וְהִשְׁתַּחֲווּ

⟨ and bow down ⟨ our God, ⟨ HASHEM, ⟨ Exalt ⟪ HASHEM. ⟨ and bless

לַהֲדֹם רַגְלָיו, קָדוֹשׁ הוּא.⁵ רוֹמְמוּ יהוה אֱלֹהֵינוּ,

⟨ our God, ⟨ HASHEM, ⟨ Exalt ⟪ is He! ⟨ holy ⟪ at His footstool;

וְהִשְׁתַּחֲווּ לְהַר קָדְשׁוֹ, כִּי קָדוֹשׁ יהוה אֱלֹהֵינוּ.⁶

⟪ our God. ⟨ is HASHEM, ⟨ holy ⟨ for ⟪ of His Holiness; ⟨ at the Mount ⟨ and bow

הִשְׁתַּחֲווּ לַיהוה בְּהַדְרַת קֹדֶשׁ,* חִילוּ מִפָּנָיו כָּל

⟨ everyone ⟨ before Him, ⟨ tremble ⟪ of holiness;* ⟨ in the splendor ⟨ before HASHEM ⟨ Bow down

הָאָרֶץ.⁷ נִשְׁתַּחֲוֶה אֶל הֵיכַל קָדְשְׁךָ וְנוֹדֶה אֶת שְׁמֶךָ,

⟨ Your Name ⟨ and we will thank ⟪ Your Holy Sanctuary, ⟨ toward ⟨ We will prostrate ourselves ⟪ on earth.

---

(1) *Psalms* 100:4. (2) Cf. 5:8. (3) 134:1. (4) 134:2. (5) 99:5. (6) 99:9. (7) 96:9.

its Scriptural sense this verse from *Psalms* refers to the Temple. In the context of the *Selichos* service, it refers to our synagogues and study halls, because our places of prayer and Torah study take the place of the Temple, until it is rebuilt (see *Ezekiel* 11:16). The plural form, *Tabernacles*, alludes to the fact that the Sanctuary on earth corresponds to the spiritual Sanctuary in heaven. Thus, the earthly Sanctuary is like a *footstool* for God, Who hovers above it (*Alshich*).

הָעֹמְדִים ... בַּלֵּילוֹת — *Who stand ... in the nights.* The loyal servants of God bless

Him constantly, even at night. *Night* in this verse can be understood literally: during the nighttime hours, an interpretation that is especially apt regarding the *Selichos*, which are ideally recited during the last third of the night. Or it can have a figurative meaning: They *stand* in the reverent attitude that is proper during praise or prayer, and remain loyal even during the *night* of suffering and exile.

בְּהַדְרַת קֹדֶשׁ — *In the splendor of holiness,* the Temple. Once again, this alludes, by extension, to our synagogues.

עַל חַסְדְּךָ וְעַל אֲמִתֶּךָ, כִּי הִגְדַּלְתָּ עַל כָּל שִׁמְךָ*

《 Your 〈 — even 《 You have 〈 for 《 Your 〈 and 〈 Your 〈 for
Name* — beyond exalted faithfulness; for kindness

אִמְרָתֶךָ.[1] יהוה אֱלֹהֵי צְבָאוֹת, מִי כָמוֹךָ חֲסִין

〈 O Strong 《 is like 〈 — who 《 of 〈 God 〈 HASHEM, 《 Your promise.
One, You, Legions

יָהּ, וֶאֱמוּנָתְךָ סְבִיבוֹתֶיךָ.[2]* כִּי מִי בַשַּׁחַק יַעֲרֹךְ

〈 can be 〈 in the sky 〈 who 〈 For 《 surrounds You.* 〈 and Your 《 God? —
compared faithfulness

לַיהוה, יִדְמֶה לַיהוה בִּבְנֵי אֵלִים.[3] כִּי גָדוֹל אַתָּה

〈 are You 〈 great 〈 For 《 among the angels? 〈 to HASHEM 〈 be likened 《 to HASHEM;

וְעוֹשֵׂה נִפְלָאוֹת, אַתָּה אֱלֹהִים לְבַדֶּךָ.[4] כִּי גָדוֹל

〈 great 〈 For 《 alone. 〈 O God, 〈 You, 《 of wonders; 〈 and a worker

מֵעַל שָׁמַיִם חַסְדֶּךָ, וְעַד שְׁחָקִים אֲמִתֶּךָ.[5] גָּדוֹל

〈 Great 《 is Your 〈 the upper 〈 and 《 is Your 〈 the very 〈 above
truth. heights until kindness, heavens

יהוה וּמְהֻלָּל מְאֹד, וְלִגְדֻלָּתוֹ אֵין חֵקֶר. (כִּי)[6] גָדוֹל

〈 great 〈 (For) 《 investiga- 〈 is 〈 and His 《 exceed- 〈 and 〈 is
tion. beyond greatness ingly, lauded HASHEM

יהוה וּמְהֻלָּל מְאֹד, נוֹרָא הוּא עַל כָּל אֱלֹהִים.[7] כִּי

〈 For 《 heavenly 〈 all 〈 above 〈 is He 〈 awesome 《 exceed- 〈 and 〈 is
powers. ingly; lauded HASHEM

אֵל גָּדוֹל יהוה, וּמֶלֶךְ גָּדוֹל עַל כָּל אֱלֹהִים.[8] אֲשֶׁר

〈 For 《 heavenly 〈 all 〈 above 〈 and a great King 《 is 〈 a great God
powers. HASHEM,

מִי אֵל בַּשָּׁמַיִם וּבָאָרֶץ, אֲשֶׁר יַעֲשֶׂה כְמַעֲשֶׂיךָ

〈 like unto 〈 can do 〈 that 〈 or in the 〈 is there in 〈 power 〈 what
Your deeds earth the heaven

וְכִגְבוּרֹתֶיךָ.[9] מִי לֹא יִרָאֲךָ מֶלֶךְ הַגּוֹיִם, כִּי לְךָ

〈 to 〈 For 《 of nations? 〈 O King 《 fear You, 〈 would 〈 Who 《 and like unto Your
You not mighty acts?

(1) Cf. *Psalms* 138:2. (2) 89:9. (3) 89:7. (4) 86:10. (5) 108:5.
(6) 145:3. (7) 96:4. (8) 95:3. (9) *Deuteronomy* 3:24.

עַל כָּל שִׁמְךָ — *Even beyond Your Name.*
Though He is known by Names that suggest strict judgment, His promise of mercy
overpowers His Attribute of justice (*Rashi*).

וֶאֱמוּנָתְךָ סְבִיבוֹתֶיךָ — *And Your faithfulness
surrounds You.* God is surrounded by His
angels, who testify to His absolute faithfulness. No word of God goes unfulfilled.

יָאֵתָה, כִּי בְכָל חַכְמֵי הַגּוֹיִם וּבְכָל מַלְכוּתָם מֵאֵין
‹ there is ‹ their ‹ and in all ‹ of the ‹ the wise ‹ among ‹ for « [kingship]
none   kingdoms   nations   men   all   befits;

כָּמוֹךָ.[1] מֵאֵין כָּמוֹךָ יהוה, גָּדוֹל אַתָּה וְגָדוֹל שְׁמֶךָ
‹ is Your ‹ and great ‹ are You ‹ Great « O ‹ like You, ‹ There is « like You.
Name   HASHEM!   none

בִּגְבוּרָה.[2] לְךָ זְרוֹעַ עִם גְּבוּרָה, תָּעֹז יָדְךָ* תָּרוּם
‹ uplifted « is Your ‹ strength- « power; ‹ with ‹ is the ‹ Yours « in might.
hand,* ened   arm

יְמִינֶךָ.*[3] לְךָ יוֹם,* אַף לְךָ לָיְלָה,* אַתָּה הֲכִינוֹתָ מָאוֹר
‹ the ‹ prepared ‹ You « is the ‹ Yours ‹ also « is the ‹ Yours « is Your
luminary   night;*   day,*   right hand.*

וָשָׁמֶשׁ.[4] אֲשֶׁר בְּיָדוֹ מֶחְקְרֵי אָרֶץ,* וְתוֹעֲפוֹת הָרִים
‹ of the ‹ and the « of the ‹ are the hidden ‹ in His ‹ For « and the
mountains   summits   earth,*   mysteries   power   sun.

לוֹ.[6] מִי יְמַלֵּל גְּבוּרוֹת יהוה, יַשְׁמִיעַ כָּל תְּהִלָּתוֹ.
« of His ‹ all ‹ [who] can « of ‹ the mighty ‹ can ‹ Who « are
praise?   make heard HASHEM; acts   express   His.

לְךָ יהוה הַגְּדֻלָּה* וְהַגְּבוּרָה, וְהַתִּפְאֶרֶת וְהַנֵּצַח
‹ the ‹ the glory, ‹ the strength, ‹ is the ‹ HASHEM, ‹ Yours,
triumph,   greatness,*

וְהַהוֹד, כִּי כֹל בַּשָּׁמַיִם וּבָאָרֶץ; לְךָ יהוה הַמַּמְלָכָה,
‹ is the ‹ HASHEM, ‹ Yours, « and on ‹ in heaven ‹ every- ‹ for « and the
kingdom   earth   thing   majesty;
[is Yours];

---

(1) *Jeremiah* 10:7. (2) 10:6. (3) *Psalms* 89:14. (4) 74:16. (5) 95:4. (6) 106:2.

יָדְךָ ... יְמִינֶךָ — *Your hand ... Your right hand.* The verse refers to two hands, as it were. The first is God's *[left] hand*, meaning His judgment against the wicked; the second is His *right hand*, meaning His goodness to the righteous or downtrodden. Whichever mode of conduct God chooses to exercise, no one can resist Him.

יוֹם ... לָיְלָה — *The day ... the night.* Whether in the *day* of good times or the *night* of exile, the Jewish people maintain their faith in You. To serve as our guide in all seasons, You gave us the Torah, which is our luminary in darkness and our sun in times of joy.

מֶחְקְרֵי אָרֶץ — *The hidden mysteries of the earth.* God's power is expressed allegorically in earthly terms. He knows the solution to all the earth's mysteries and He reigns over the mightiest peaks.

לְךָ ה' הַגְּדֻלָּה — *Yours, HASHEM, is the greatness.* David uttered this verse in the presence of the entire congregation at one of the supreme moments of his life, when he had assembled the necessary contributions and materials for his heir, Solomon, to build the Temple. In this moment of public glory, David proclaimed that his every achievement was possible only because God made it so.

וְהַמִּתְנַשֵּׂא לְכֹל לְרֹאשׁ.¹ לְךָ שָׁמַיִם, אַף לְךָ אֶָרֶץ,

《 is the 〈 Yours 〈 also 《 are the 〈 Yours 《 leader. 〈 over 〈 and the
earth; heavens, every sovereignty

תֵּבֵל וּמְלֹאָהּ אַתָּה יְסַדְתָּם.² אַתָּה הִצַּבְתָּ כָּל גְּבוּלוֹת

〈 the 〈 all 〈 established 〈 You 《 founded 〈 You 〈 and its 〈 the
boundaries them. fullness, world

אֶרֶץ, קַיִץ וָחֹרֶף אַתָּה יְצַרְתָּם.³ אַתָּה רִצַּצְתָּ רָאשֵׁי

〈 the 〈 crushed 〈 You 《 fashioned 〈 You 〈 and 〈 summer 《 of
heads them. winter, earth;

לִוְיָתָן,* תִּתְּנֶנּוּ מַאֲכָל לְעַם לְצִיִּים. אַתָּה בָקַעְתָּ מַעְיָן

〈 fountain 〈 split 〈 You 《 [destined] for 〈 to the 〈 as food 〈 You will 《 of
open the desolate people serve it Leviathan;*
wilderness.

וָנָחַל, אַתָּה הוֹבַשְׁתָּ נַהֲרוֹת אֵיתָן.⁴ אַתָּה פוֹרַרְתָּ

〈 shattered 〈 You 《 that are mighty. 〈 rivers 〈 dried 〈 You 《 and stream;

בְּעָזְּךָ יָם, שִׁבַּרְתָּ רָאשֵׁי תַנִּינִים עַל הַמָּיִם.⁵ אַתָּה

〈 You 《 the water. 〈 upon 〈 of sea 〈 the heads 〈 You 《 the 〈 with Your
serpents smashed sea; might

מוֹשֵׁל בְּגֵאוּת הַיָּם, בְּשׂוֹא גַלָּיו אַתָּה תְשַׁבְּחֵם.⁶

《 calm them. 〈 You 〈 its waves, 〈 when it raises 《 of the sea; 〈 the grandeur 〈 rule

גָּדוֹל יהוה וּמְהֻלָּל מְאֹד, בְּעִיר אֱלֹהֵינוּ הַר קָדְשׁוֹ.⁷

《 of His 〈 Mount 〈 of our God, 〈 in the 〈 and much praised, 〈 is 〈 Great
Holiness. City HASHEM

יהוה צְבָאוֹת, אֱלֹהֵי יִשְׂרָאֵל, יוֹשֵׁב הַכְּרֻבִים,* אַתָּה

〈 it is 《 upon the 〈 en- 〈 of Israel, 〈 God 〈 Master of 〈 HASHEM,
You Cherubim,* throned Legions,

הוּא הָאֱלֹהִים לְבַדֶּךָ.⁸ אֵל נַעֲרָץ בְּסוֹד קְדוֹשִׁים רַבָּה,

《 in the great assemblage 〈 is 〈 God 《 alone. 〈 God 〈 Who
of the holy [angels], revered are

---

(1) I Chronicles 29:11. (2) Psalms 89:12. (3) 74:17. (4) 74:14-15. (5) 74:13. (6) 89:10. (7) 48:2. (8) Isaiah 37:16.

רָאשֵׁי לִוְיָתָן — *The heads of Leviathan.* The Psalmist describes Israel's Exodus from Egypt and God's mercy in the Wilderness. The Egyptian army, which pursued the Jews into the Sea of Reeds, is likened to a sea monster; while Pharaoh and his generals are alluded to as Leviathan heads. God smashed the Egyptians and their leaders and distributed their spoils to Israel, the nation of twelve tribal legions. In the Wilderness, He provided water for Israel and dried the mighty Jordan River so that the people could cross into the Land of Canaan.

יוֹשֵׁב הַכְּרֻבִים — *Enthroned upon the Cherubim.* God's Presence rested upon the Cherubim in the Holiest of the Holies. The Cherubim were in the form of angels with the faces of children, carved from the solid gold cover

וְנוֹרָא עַל כָּל סְבִיבָיו.¹ וְיוֹדוּ שָׁמַיִם פִּלְאֲךָ יהוה, אַף

and is / over / all / who surround Him. / Acknowledge / will the / heavens / Your wonders, / HASHEM, / also
awesome

אֱמוּנָתְךָ בִּקְהַל קְדֹשִׁים.² לְכוּ נְרַנְּנָה לַיהוה, נָרִיעָה

Your faithfulness, / in the assembly / of holy ones. / Come! / Let us sing joyfully / to HASHEM, / let us call out

לְצוּר יִשְׁעֵנוּ.* נְקַדְּמָה פָנָיו בְּתוֹדָה, בִּזְמִרוֹת נָרִיעַ

to the Rock / of our salvation.* / Let us greet / Him / with thanksgiving, / with praiseful songs / let us call out

לוֹ.³ צֶדֶק וּמִשְׁפָּט מְכוֹן כִּסְאֶךָ, חֶסֶד וֶאֱמֶת יְקַדְּמוּ

to Him. / Righteousness / and justice / are the foundation / of Your throne; / kindness / and truth / precede

פָנֶיךָ.⁴ אֲשֶׁר יַחְדָּו נַמְתִּיק סוֹד,* בְּבֵית אֱלֹהִים נְהַלֵּךְ

Your countenance. / For / together / let us take sweet / counsel;* / in the House / of God / let us walk

בְּרָגֶשׁ.⁵ אֲשֶׁר לוֹ הַיָּם וְהוּא עָשָׂהוּ, וְיַבֶּשֶׁת יָדָיו

in company. / For / His / is the sea / and He / perfected it, / and the dry land, / His hands

יָצָרוּ.⁶ אֲשֶׁר בְּיָדוֹ נֶפֶשׁ כָּל חָי, וְרוּחַ כָּל בְּשַׂר אִישׁ.⁷

fashioned. / For / in His hand / is the soul / of all / living / the / and the spirit / of all / mankind.

❖ הַנְּשָׁמָה לָךְ וְהַגּוּף פָּעֳלָךְ, חוּסָה עַל עֲמָלָךְ.

The soul / is Yours / and the body / is Your handiwork; / take pity / on / Your labor.

הַנְּשָׁמָה לָךְ וְהַגּוּף שֶׁלָּךְ, יהוה עֲשֵׂה לְמַעַן שְׁמֶךָ.*

The soul / is Yours / and the body / is Yours; / HASHEM, / O / act / for the sake / of Your Name.*

אָתָאנוּ עַל שְׁמֶךָ, יהוה, עֲשֵׂה לְמַעַן שְׁמֶךָ. בַּעֲבוּר

We have come / [relying] on / Your Name; / HASHEM; / O / act / for the sake / of Your Name; / because of / [act]

---

(1) Psalms 89:8. (2) 89:6. (3) 95:1-2. (4) 89:15. (5) 55:15. (6) 95:5. (7) Job 12:10.

of the Holy Ark in the *Beis HaMikdash.*

לְצוּר יִשְׁעֵנוּ — *To the Rock of our salvation.* No matter how imminent Israel's destruction has often seemed, the Rock of our salvation has always prevented the "inevitable" from happening (*Avnei Eliyahu*).

נַמְתִּיק סוֹד — *Let us take sweet counsel.* Let us all gather in the study hall [*the House of God*], to discuss the pleasant secrets of Torah (*Rashi*).

לְמַעַן שְׁמֶךָ — *For the sake of Your Name.* Since we are Yours, body and soul, we implore You to spare us for Your sake, though we know we are undeserving.

לְמַעַן *.שְׁמֶךָ וְרַחוּם חַנּוּן אֵל כִּי שְׁמֶךָ, כְּבוֹד

‹ For the sake «‹ is Your Name.* ‹ and Merciful ‹ Who is Gracious ‹ God ‹ for «‹ of Your Name, ‹ the glory

שְׁמֶךָ יהוה, וְסָלַחְתָּ לַעֲוֹנֵנוּ כִּי רַב הוּא.[1]

‹ it is great. ‹ though ‹ our iniquity, ‹ forgive «‹ HASHEM, ‹ of Your Name,

CONGREGATION, THEN *CHAZZAN:*

סְלַח לָנוּ אָבִינוּ, כִּי בְרוֹב אִוַּלְתֵּנוּ שָׁגִינוּ,

«‹ we have erred; ‹ of our folly ‹ in the abundance ‹ for ‹ our Father, ‹ us, ‹ Forgive

מְחַל לָנוּ מַלְכֵּנוּ, כִּי רַבּוּ עֲוֹנֵינוּ.

«‹ our iniquities. ‹ many are ‹ for ‹ our King, ‹ us, ‹ pardon

---

סליחה א / SELICHAH 1
(פתיחה)

ALL:

(אֱלֹהֵינוּ וֵאלֹהֵי אֲבוֹתֵינוּ:)

«‹ of our forefathers): ‹ and God ‹ (Our God

אֵיךְ נִפְתַּח פֶּה* לְפָנֶיךָ, דָּר מְתוּחִים,

«‹ in the [heavens] spread out? ‹ Who dwells «‹ before You, ‹ [our] mouth* ‹ can we open ‹ How

בְּאֵלוּ פָנִים נִשְׁפֹּךְ שִׂיחִים,[2]

«‹ [our] supplications? ‹ may we pour forth ‹ manner ‹ In what

גָּעַלְנוּ נְתִיבוֹתֶיךָ הַיְשָׁרִים וְהַנִּכֹחִים,

«‹and straightforward; ‹ that are honest ‹ Your paths ‹ We despised

דָּבַקְנוּ בְּתוֹעֵבוֹת וּבְמַעֲשִׂים זְנוּחִים.

«‹ that are despicable. ‹ and deeds ‹ to [idolatrous] abominations ‹we adhered

הָלַכְנוּ אַחֲרֵי מַשְׂאוֹת שָׁוְא וּמַדּוּחִים,[3]

«‹ and deception; ‹ of uselessness ‹ visions ‹ after ‹ We went

---

(1) Cf. *Psalms* 25:11. (2) Cf. 102:1. (3) *Lamentations* 2:14.

שְׁמֶךָ — *Is Your Name.* Graciousness and mercy are so intrinsic to You that Your very Name is *God Who is Gracious and Merciful.*

אֵיךְ נִפְתַּח פֶּה — *How can we open [our] mouth.* This פְּתִיחָה *[pesichah],* introductory *selichah,* contains an *aleph-beis* acrostic. The

וְהִקְשִׁינוּ עֹרֶף וְהֵעַזְנוּ מְצָחִים,
‏《 our faces.   〈 made brazen   《 our necks,   〈 we obstinately made stiff

זַעַמְתָּ בְּשֶׁלָנוּ, בֵּית מִשְׁכְּנוֹת מִבְטָחִים,*1
〈 in security*   〈 of Dwelling Place   《 [and] the Place   《 on account of us;   〈 You raged

חָרַב* וּפַס רֵיחַ נִיחֹחִים.
‏《 that was satisfying.   〈 was the aroma [of the offerings]   〈 and vanished   《 was destroyed;*

טֹרְדוּ וְטֻלְטְלוּ כֹּהֲנִים מְשׁוּחִים,
‏《 who were anointed,   〈 were the Kohanim   〈 and forced to wander   〈 Driven out

יוֹדְעֵי עֲרֶךְ* עוֹלוֹת וּזְבָחִים,
‏《 and [all other] sacrifices.   〈 burnt-offerings   〈 how to arrange [on the Altar pyre]*   〈 who knew

כַּמֶּה יִסַּרְתָּנוּ עַל יְדֵי צִירִים וּשְׁלוּחִים,
‏《 and messengers!   〈 of [the prophets, Your] emissaries   〈 the hands   〈 at   〈 You   〈 How chastised us

לֹא הִקְשַׁבְנוּ לִשְׁמֹעַ לְמוֹכִיחִים.
‏《 to those who rebuked [us].   〈 to listen   〈 [But] we were not attentive

---

(1) Cf. *Isaiah* 32:18.

paytan hid his name — בִּנְיָמִין — *Binyamin* — in the first two words of the next-to-last stich: בִּנְוֹרָאוֹת יְמִינְךָ. It is uncertain whether he was R' Binyamin ben Zerach [see below] or another *paytan* with the same first name.

According to *Emek HaBacha* (by R' Yosef HaKohen of 16th-century France and Italy), R' Binyamin ben Zerach flourished in late 7th-century Germany and was the first *dayan* (judge of Torah law) in that country. Others find allusions to the First Crusade (1096) in his works and place him in that era. In either case, he was a prolific *paytan*; seven of his *selichos* appear in *Selichos* of *Nusach Lita*, many more in *Nusach Ashkenaz*. The commentary *Arugas HaBosem* refers to him as *R' Binyamin HaGadol* (the Great).

בֵּית מִשְׁכְּנוֹת מִבְטָחִים — *The Place of Dwelling in security*. The juxtaposition of this verse with the cessation of the Temple offerings (in the next line) indicates that it refers to the *Beis HaMikdash*. Alternatively, it may refer to the Land of Israel in general or to Jerusalem in particular, for that is how the phrase is used in *Isaiah* (32:18).

זַעַמְתָּ בְּשֶׁלָנוּ בֵּית מִשְׁכְּנוֹת מִבְטָחִים חָרַב — *You raged on account of us; [and] the Place of Dwelling in security was destroyed.* This translation includes the word חָרַב, *was destroyed*, from the next stich, as part of this one. An alternative rendering that maintains the alphabetical acrostic and the rhyme scheme within the stich is: *You raged at what was ours, the Place of Dwelling in security — the Place of Dwelling in security* describing what was ours.

יוֹדְעֵי עֲרֶךְ — *Who knew how to arrange [on the Altar pyre].* Alternatively, *who knew the worth of.*

מֵאָז* וְעַד עַתָּה אֲנַחְנוּ נִדָּחִים,

《   have been 〈 we 〈 now 〈 until 〈 From
driven into exile,   then*

נֶהֱרָגִים וְנִשְׁחָטִים וְנִטְבָּחִים,

《 and butchered. 〈 slaughtered, 〈 slain,

שָׂרַדְנוּ מְתֵי מְעַט¹ בֵּין קוֹצִים כְּסוּחִים,*

《   that are cut, 〈 thorns 〈 [scattered] 〈 who were 〈 as a 〈 We have
[dry, and sharp,]*   among   but few   people   survived

עֵינֵינוּ כָלוֹת בְּלִי מְצֹא רְוָחִים.

《   relief. 〈 finding 〈 without 〈 yearn [for 〈 while our
Your salvation]   eyes

פּוֹרְכֵי עַמְּךָ אֲשֶׁר לַבַּל* שׁוֹחֲחִים,

《   bow down, 〈 to idols* 〈 who 《 Your 〈 Those who
people,   crushingly
enslave

צָפַר וָעֶרֶב לָמָה מַצְלִיחִים,

《 do they succeed? 〈 why 《 [to] 〈 [from]
evening,   morning

קָמִים לְמוּלָךְ נְאָצוֹת שׁוֹחֲחִים,

《 do they speak: 〈 and 〈 against 〈 They
blasphemy   You,   rise up

רְצוּצִים, בַּמֶּה אַתֶּם בּוֹטְחִים.

《   trust? 〈 do you 〈 In 《 You who are
what   crushed [in exile]!

---

(1) Cf. *Deuteronomy* 26:5.

מֵאָז — *From then.* The verses from מ to ר present the conquering nations in a less-than-favorable light. Thus, they have been the targets of censorship. In some editions, these verses have been completely eliminated. In others, they have been replaced with stanzas that continue the theme of the כ and ל verses; namely, that Israel did not heed the reproach of the prophets. The text presented here is probably the least-altered version and is the version that appears in virtually all editions of *Selichos* printed during the last century.

בֵּין קוֹצִים כְּסוּחִים — *[Scattered] among thorns that are cut, [dry, and sharp].* The phrase קוֹצִים כְּסוּחִים as used in *Isaiah* (33:12) means *cut thorns.* It refers to the Assyrian hordes

who would eventually be destroyed like thorns that have been cut down and have become dry, easily burned tinder. Perhaps the *paytan* intends both meanings: *Our oppressors presently are like thorns that are dry and sharp, but, when the proper time arrives, they will become like cut-down thorns that are readily consumed by the fire.*

לַבַּל — *To idols* [lit., *to the Bel*]. The *Bel* or *Baal* was a genre of idolatry common in the days of the prophets. Its use here obviously refers to idolatry in general, since the nations of which this verse speaks did not worship the *Baal* idols. Some early editions of *Selichos* read לַמֵּת, *to the dead,* and that is probably the original uncensored version.

❖ שׁוֹכֵן עַד וְקָדוֹשׁ, צָפָה בְּעֶלְבּוֹן אֲנוּחִים,

‹ of those who ‹ the shame ‹ behold ‹ and Who ‹ forever ‹ O He
[can but] sigh,   is holy,   Who dwells

תְּמוּכִים עָלֶיךָ וּבְךָ מִתְאָחִים,

‹ are joined like ‹ and who ‹ on You, ‹ [those] who
brothers.   to You   depend

בְּנוֹרָאוֹת יְמִינְךָ נִוָּשַׁע לִנְצָחִים,

‹ for ever, ‹ may we be ‹ of Your ‹ By the awesome
redeemed   right hand   deeds

כִּי עַל רַחֲמֶיךָ הָרַבִּים[1] אָנוּ בְטוּחִים.

‹ do we trust. ‹ that is abundant ‹ Your mercy ‹ upon ‹ for

ALL:

כִּי עַל רַחֲמֶיךָ הָרַבִּים[1] אָנוּ בְטוּחִים, וְעַל צִדְקוֹתֶיךָ

‹ Your ‹ and ‹ trust, ‹ we ‹ that is ‹ Your ‹ upon ‹ For
righteousness   upon   abundant   mercy

אָנוּ נִשְׁעָנִים, וְלִסְלִיחוֹתֶיךָ אָנוּ מְקַוִּים, וְלִישׁוּעָתְךָ

‹ and for Your ‹ hope, ‹ we ‹ and for Your ‹ rely, ‹ we
salvation   forgiveness

אָנוּ מְצַפִּים. אַתָּה הוּא מֶלֶךְ, אוֹהֵב צְדָקוֹת מִקֶּדֶם,

‹ since the ‹ righteous- ‹ Who ‹ the King ‹ are ‹ You ‹ await eagerly. ‹ we
beginning   ness   loves
of time,

מַעֲבִיר עֲוֹנוֹת עַמּוֹ, וּמֵסִיר חַטֹּאת יְרֵאָיו. כּוֹרֵת

‹ He es- ‹ of those who ‹ the sins ‹ and ‹ of His ‹ the ‹ Who
tablished   revere Him.   removes   people   iniquities   overlooks

בְּרִית לָרִאשׁוֹנִים, וּמְקַיֵּם שְׁבוּעָה לָאַחֲרוֹנִים. אַתָּה

‹ You ‹ to the descendants. ‹ [His] oath ‹ and fulfills ‹ with the ancestors ‹ a covenant

הוּא, שֶׁיָּרַדְתָּ בַּעֲנַן כְּבוֹדְךָ עַל הַר סִינַי,[2] וְהֶרְאֵיתָ

‹ and You ‹ Sinai, ‹ Mount ‹ upon ‹ of Your ‹ in the ‹ Who ‹ are the
showed   glory   cloud   descended   One

דַּרְכֵי טוּבְךָ לְמֹשֶׁה עַבְדֶּךָ.[3] וְאָרְחוֹת חֲסָדֶיךָ גִּלִּיתָ

‹ You ‹ of Your ‹ The paths ‹ Your ‹ to Moses ‹ of Your ‹ the
revealed   kindness   servant.   goodness   ways

לוֹ, וְהוֹדַעְתּוֹ כִּי אַתָּה אֵל רַחוּם וְחַנּוּן, אֶרֶךְ אַפַּיִם

‹ to ‹ Slow ‹ and ‹ Compas- ‹ God, ‹ You are ‹ that ‹ and You ‹ to
anger   Gracious,   sionate   let him know   him,

---

(1) *Daniel* 9:18. (2) Cf. *Exodus* 34:5. (3) Cf. 33:13.

וְרַב חֶֽסֶד[1] וּמַרְבֶּה לְהֵטִיב, וּמַנְהִיג אֶת כָּל הָעוֹלָם

⟨ world ⟨ the whole ⟨ and Who ⟪ beneficent, ⟨ Who is ⟨ in ⟨ and
guides   abundantly Kindness, Abundant

כֻּלּוֹ בְּמִדַּת הָרַחֲמִים. ❖וְכֵן כָּתוּב, וַיֹּאמֶר אֲנִי אַעֲבִיר

⟨ shall cause ⟨ "I ⟪ And He ⟪ it is ⟨ And ⟪ of Mercy. ⟨ with the ⟨ in its
to pass   said,   written: so   Attribute entirety

כָּל טוּבִי עַל פָּנֶֽיךָ, וְקָרֵֽאתִי בְשֵׁם יהוה לְפָנֶֽיךָ, וְחַנֹּֽתִי

⟨ I shall ⟪ before ⟨ HASHEM ⟨ with the ⟨ and I shall ⟪ your ⟨ before ⟨ My ⟨ all
show favor   you;   Name   call out   face,   goodness

אֶת אֲשֶׁר אָחֹן, וְרִחַמְתִּי אֶת אֲשֶׁר אֲרַחֵם.[2]

⟪ I choose to ⟨ whom- ⟨ to ⟨ and I shall ⟪ I choose to ⟨ whom- ⟨ to
show mercy."   ever   show mercy   show favor,   ever

ALL, WHILE STANDING

אֵל אֶֽרֶךְ אַפַּֽיִם אַתָּה,

⟪ You are, ⟨ to anger, ⟨ Who is slow ⟨ God

וּבַֽעַל הָרַחֲמִים נִקְרֵֽאתָ, וְדֶֽרֶךְ תְּשׁוּבָה הוֹרֵֽיתָ.

⟪ You have ⟨ of ⟨ and the ⟪ You are ⟨ of Mercy ⟨ and
taught. repentance way   called;   Master

גְּדֻלַּת רַחֲמֶֽיךָ וַחֲסָדֶֽיךָ,

⟨ and Your ⟨ of Your ⟨ The
kindness   mercy   greatness

תִּזְכּוֹר הַיּוֹם וּבְכָל יוֹם לְזֶֽרַע יְדִידֶֽיךָ.

⟪ of Your ⟨ for the ⟪ day, ⟨ and ⟨ this day ⟨ may You
beloved ones. offspring   every   remember,

תֵּֽפֶן אֵלֵֽינוּ בְּרַחֲמִים, כִּי אַתָּה הוּא בַּֽעַל הָרַחֲמִים.

⟪ of Mercy. ⟨ the Master ⟨ are ⟨ You ⟨ for ⟪ in mercy, ⟨ to us ⟨ Turn

בְּתַחֲנוּן וּבִתְפִלָּה פָּנֶֽיךָ נְקַדֵּם, כְּהוֹדַעְתָּ לֶעָנָיו מִקֶּֽדֶם.

⟪ in ⟨ to the ⟨ in the manner ⟪ we ⟨ Your ⟨ and prayer ⟨ With
ancient humble one that You made approach, Presence   supplication
times. [Moses] known

---

(1) *Exodus* 34:6. (2) 33:19.

❧ אֵל אֶֽרֶךְ אַפַּֽיִם ⧉
God Who Is Slow to Anger

After declaring that God's patience with sinful people and His boundless mercy are our primary hope, we beg Him to be as merciful to us now as He was on the day He taught the Thirteen Attributes to Moses on Mount Sinai. On that day, God assured Moses that He would continue to protect Israel despite the nation's grievous sin. So may He heed and protect us, and be merciful to us now.

מֵחֲרוֹן אַפְּךָ שׁוּב,¹ כְּמוֹ בְתוֹרָתְךָ כָּתוּב.²

《 it is ⟨ in Your Torah ⟨ as 《 turn ⟨ of Your ⟨ From the
written. back, anger fierceness

וּבְצֵל כְּנָפֶיךָ נֶחֱסֶה³ וְנִתְלוֹנָן, כְּיוֹם וַיֵּרֶד יהוה בֶּעָנָן.

《 in a ⟨ when HASHEM ⟨ as on 《 and may ⟨ may we ⟨ of Your ⟨ In the
cloud. descended the day we dwell find shelter wings shadow

❖ תַּעֲבוֹר עַל פֶּשַׁע וְתִמְחֶה אָשָׁם,

《 guilt, ⟨ and erase ⟨ sin ⟨ Overlook

כְּיוֹם וַיִּתְיַצֵּב עִמּוֹ שָׁם.

《 there. ⟨ with him ⟨ when He ⟨ as on
[Moses] [God] stood the day

תַּאֲזִין שַׁוְעָתֵנוּ וְתַקְשִׁיב מֶנּוּ מַאֲמַר,

《 [our] declaration, ⟨ from us ⟨ and hear ⟨ to our cry ⟨ Give heed

כְּיוֹם וַיִּקְרָא בְשֵׁם יהוה,*⁴ וְשָׁם נֶאֱמַר:

《 it was said: ⟨ and ⟨ of 《 with the ⟨ when He ⟨ as on
there HASHEM,* Name called out the day

CONGREGATION, THEN CHAZZAN:

וַיַּעֲבֹר יהוה עַל פָּנָיו וַיִּקְרָא:

《 and 《 [Moses'] ⟨ before ⟨ And HASHEM passed
proclaimed: face,

(1) Cf. *Exodus* 32:12. (2) See 32:14. (3) Cf. *Psalms* 36:8. (4) *Exodus* 34:5.

וַיִּקְרָא בְשֵׁם ה' — *He called out with the Name of HASHEM.* According to *Mizrachi's* understanding of *Rashi* (*Exodus* 34:5), Moses called out God's Name. However, *Gur Aryeh's* interpretation of *Rashi, Ibn Ezra,* and *Sforno* comment that God called out His Own Name, teaching Moses the order of the Thirteen Attributes.

י"ג מִדּוֹת / The Thirteen Attributes

The central theme of all the *Selichos* is the שְׁלֹשׁ עֶשְׂרֵה מִדּוֹת הָרַחֲמִים, *Thirteen Attributes of Divine Mercy,* beginning 'ה ה', *HASHEM, HASHEM.* This passage appears in the Torah (*Exodus* 34:6-7) at the time when God acceded to Moses' pleading not to destroy Israel after the sin of the Golden Calf. Moses then requested that God make known to him His ways, so that he could comprehend His justice and learn the role of prayer. While God responded that no human being could presume to understand the totality of God's ways, He taught Moses what was not only for him but for all generations of Jews — the pattern for our order of *Selichos.* According to R' Yochanan (*Rosh Hashanah* 17b), God appeared to him in the guise of a *chazzan* wrapped in a *tallis* and taught him the Thirteen Attributes. God said, "Whenever Israel sins, let them perform this procedure and I will forgive them." Thus, this appeal for God's mercy reassures us both that repentance is always possible and that God always awaits our return to Him. The implication is also plain that if we emulate God's merciful ways, He will treat us mercifully in return.

Whenever the Thirteen Attributes appears in the *Selichos,* it is introduced the first time by the paragraph אֵל אֶרֶךְ אַפַּיִם, *God Who is slow to anger,* and then by the paragraph אֵל מֶלֶךְ יוֹשֵׁב, *O God, King Who sits ....* After the Thirteen Attributes there is always a direct prayer for forgiveness, following the example of Moses who, after being taught the Thirteen Attributes, pleaded that God forgive Israel (*Exodus* 34:8-9).

CONGREGATION AND *CHAZZAN* RECITE LOUDLY AND IN UNISON:

יהוה, יהוה,* אֵל, רַחוּם, וְחַנּוּן, אֶרֶךְ אַפַּיִם,

⟨ to anger, ⟨ Slow ⟪and Gracious,⟨ Compassionate⟨ God, ⟨ HASHEM,* ⟨ HASHEM,

וְרַב חֶסֶד, וֶאֱמֶת, נֹצֵר חֶסֶד לָאֲלָפִים, נֹשֵׂא עָוֹן,

⟨ of ⟨ Forgiver ⟪ for thousands ⟨ of ⟨ Preserver ⟪ and ⟨ in ⟨ and
iniquity,   [of generations], kindness   Truth,   Kindness Abundant

וָפֶשַׁע, וְחַטָּאָה, וְנַקֵּה.¹ וְסָלַחְתָּ לַעֲוֹנֵנוּ וּלְחַטָּאתֵנוּ

⟪ and our sins, ⟨ our ⟨ May You ⟪ and Who ⟨ and inadvertent⟨ willful sin,
iniquities   forgive   absolves.   sin,

(1) *Exodus* 34:6-7.

ה' ה' — *HASHEM, HASHEM.* There are various opinions regarding how to enumerate the Thirteen Attributes. We follow the generally accepted view of *Rabbeinu Tam* (*Rosh Hashanah* 17b):

(1) ה' — *HASHEM.* This Name [containing the letters of הָיָה, הֹוֶה, יִהְיֶה, *He was, He is, He will be*] designates God as the מְהַוֶּה, *Prime Cause,* of everything. It is only natural that He wishes to assure the survival of all that He brought into being. Consequently, this Name represents the Attribute of Mercy. In addition, the Name's spelling implies God's timelessness. Though man may sin, he can repent and call upon the timeless God to restore him to his original innocent state. As the Talmud states: אֲנִי הוּא קֹדֶם שֶׁיֶּחֱטָא הָאָדָם, *I am He* [the God of Mercy] *before a person sins,* וַאֲנִי הוּא לְאַחַר שֶׁיֶּחֱטָא הָאָדָם וְיַעֲשֶׂה תְּשׁוּבָה, *and I am He after a person sins and repents* (*Rosh Hashanah* 17b). Based on this dictum, *Rabbeinu Tam* counts the twin use of the Name *HASHEM* as two attributes. The first is that God is merciful before a person sins, even though He knows that the sin will be committed. And ...

(2) ה' — *HASHEM.* God is merciful after the sin has been committed, by granting the sinner time to repent, and by accepting his repentance, though it may be imperfect.

(3) אֵל — *God.* This Name denotes the power of God's mercy, which sometimes surpasses even the compassion indicated by the name *HASHEM.* He displays this higher degree of mercy to genuinely righteous people who sin, but repent. In return for their previous behavior, God exerts Himself, as it were, to ensure their survival.

(4) רַחוּם — *Compassionate.* In response to

pleas for mercy, God eases the suffering of those being punished for their sins. Another manifestation of compassion is that God does not confront deserving people with overpowering temptation.

(5) וְחַנּוּן — *And Gracious.* God is gracious even to those unworthy of His kindness. Also, if someone finds himself lacking in the willpower to avoid sin and he seeks God's help, he will be given it.

(6) אֶרֶךְ אַפַּיִם — *Slow to anger,* so that the sinner will have time to repent.

(7) וְרַב חֶסֶד — *And Abundant in Kindness.* God shows great kindness to those who lack personal merits. The Talmud teaches, as described below, that God exercises this attribute by removing sins from the scale of justice, thus tilting the scales in favor of merit.

(8) וֶאֱמֶת — *And Truth.* God never reneges; His promise to reward the deserving will be carried out unequivocally.

(9) נֹצֵר חֶסֶד לָאֲלָפִים — *Preserver of kindness for thousands* [*of generations*]. The deeds of the righteous — especially those who serve Him out of intense love — bring benefits to their offspring far into the future.

(10) נֹשֵׂא עָוֹן — *Forgiver of iniquity.* God forgives the intentional sinner, if he repents.

(11) וָפֶשַׁע — [*Forgiver of*] *willful sin.* Even the one who rebels against God and purposely seeks to anger Him is given an opportunity to repent.

(12) וְחַטָּאָה — *And* [*Forgiver of*] *inadvertent sin.* God forgives the person who repents of sins committed out of carelessness or apathy. Having already praised God as the Forgiver of intentional sin and rebelliousness, why do we revert to praising Him for this seemingly lesser level of mercy?

וּנְחַלְתָּנוּ. סְלַח לָנוּ אָבִינוּ כִּי חָטָאנוּ, מְחַל לָנוּ[1]

‏« and make us ‹ us, ‹ pardon « we have ‹ for « our Father, ‹ us, ‹ Forgive
Your heritage.   sinned;

מַלְכֵּנוּ כִּי פָשָׁעְנוּ. כִּי אַתָּה אֲדֹנָי טוֹב וְסַלָּח,*

‏« and ‹ are ‹ O Lord, ‹ You, ‹ For « we have ‹ for « our King,
forgiving,* good   willfully sinned.

וְרַב חֶסֶד לְכָל קֹרְאֶיךָ.[2]

‏« who call ‹ to all ‹ kind ‹ and
upon You.   abundantly

PREFATORY VERSES TO SELICHAH 2 / פסוקי הקדמה לסליחה ב

יהוה בְּקֶר תִּשְׁמַע קוֹלֵנוּ, בְּקֶר נַעֲרָךְ לְךָ וַאֲצַפֶּה.[3]

‏« and we ‹ to ‹ as we ‹ at « our ‹ hear ‹ at ‹ HASHEM,
await You arrange dawn voice; dawn
expectantly. [our prayer]

שְׁמַע קוֹל תַּחֲנוּנֵינוּ בְּשַׁוְּעֵנוּ אֵלֶיךָ, בְּנָשְׂאֵנוּ יָדֵינוּ

‹ our ‹ when ‹ to You; ‹ when we ‹ of our ‹ the ‹ Hear
hands we lift cry out supplications sound

אֶל דְּבִיר קָדְשֶׁךָ.[4] שְׁמַע יהוה קוֹלֵנוּ נִקְרָא, וְחָנֵּנוּ

‹ show us « when we ‹ our voice ‹ HASHEM, ‹ Hear, « Your Holy Sanctuary. ‹ toward
favor call,

וַעֲנֵנוּ.[5] שׁוּבֵנוּ אֱלֹהֵי יִשְׁעֵנוּ, וְהָפֵר כַּעַסְךָ עִמָּנוּ.[6]

‏« with us. ‹ Your ‹ and « of our ‹ O God ‹ Return us, « and
anger annul salvation, answer us.

וְאֵין קוֹרֵא בְשִׁמְךָ מִתְעוֹרֵר לְהַחֲזִיק בָּךְ.[7] שִׁמְעָה

‹ Hear « to ‹ to hold fast ‹ who arouses ‹ in Your ‹ who ‹ And there
You. himself Name, calls out is no one

---

(1) Exodus 34:9. (2) Psalms 86:5. (3) Cf. 5:4. (4) Cf. 28:2. (5) Cf. 27:7. (6) 85:5. (7) Isaiah 64:6.

Because if someone repents out of fear rather than love, his intentional sins are reduced in severity and are treated by God as if they had been done inadvertently. Thus, even after having partially forgiven the intentional sins by reducing their severity, God further forgives those who continue to repent for these lesser sins.

(13) וְנַקֵּה — And Who absolves. God wipes away the sins of those who repent sincerely, as if they had never existed.

In the Torah, the verse continues לֹא יְנַקֶּה, He does not absolve. The simple interpreta-

tion of the verse is that God does not completely erase the sin, but He exacts retribution in minute stages. The Talmud (Yoma 86a), however, explains that He absolves the sins of those who truly repent; but He does not absolve the sins of those who do not repent.

טוֹב וְסַלָּח — Are good and forgiving. God is good to the righteous; even though they may have had hard lives on earth, their reward will be generous in the World to Come. He is forgiving to sinners who make an effort to repent.

תְּפִלָּתֵנוּ, יהוה, וְשַׁוְעָתֵנוּ הַאֲזִינָה, אֶל דִּמְעָתֵנוּ
⟨ our tears ⟨ to ⟪ listen; ⟨ and to our cry ⟪ HASHEM; ⟨ our prayer,

אַל תֶּחֱרַשׁ.[1]
⟪ mute. ⟨ be not

כְּרַחֵם אָב עַל בָּנִים, כֵּן תְּרַחֵם יהוה עָלֵינוּ.[2]
⟪ on us. ⟨ HASHEM, ⟨ have ⟨ so ⟪ his ⟨ toward ⟨ a ⟨ As merciful as
mercy, children, father is

לַיהוה הַיְשׁוּעָה, עַל עַמְּךָ בִרְכָתֶךָ סֶּלָה.[3] יהוה
⟨ HASHEM, ⟪ Selah. ⟪ is Your ⟨ Your ⟨ upon ⟪ is salvation, ⟨ To HASHEM
blessing, people

צְבָאוֹת עִמָּנוּ, מִשְׂגָּב לָנוּ אֱלֹהֵי יַעֲקֹב סֶלָה.[4]
⟪ Selah. ⟪ of Jacob, ⟨ is the God ⟨ for us ⟨ a ⟪ is with us, ⟨ Master of
stronghold Legions,

יהוה צְבָאוֹת, אַשְׁרֵי אָדָם בֹּטֵחַ בָּךְ.[5] יהוה הוֹשִׁיעָה,
⟪ save! ⟨ HASHEM, ⟪ in You. ⟨ who ⟨ is the ⟨ — praise- ⟪ Master of ⟨ HASHEM,
trusts man worthy Legions

הַמֶּלֶךְ יַעֲנֵנוּ בְיוֹם קָרְאֵנוּ.[6]
⟪ we call. ⟨ on the ⟨ answer ⟨ May the
day us King

**IN MOST CONGREGATIONS THE FOLLOWING VERSES ARE RECITED ALOUD RESPONSIVELY,
AS INDICATED; IN OTHERS THEY ARE RECITED SILENTLY.**

CONGREGATION, ALOUD, FOLLOWED BY *CHAZZAN,* **ALOUD:**

סְלַח נָא* לַעֲוֹן הָעָם הַזֶּה כְּגֹדֶל חַסְדֶּךָ, וְכַאֲשֶׁר
⟨ just as ⟪ of Your ⟨ according to ⟨ of this people ⟨ the ⟨ please,* ⟨ Forgive,
kindness, the greatness iniquity

נָשָׂאתָה לָעָם הַזֶּה מִמִּצְרַיִם וְעַד הֵנָּה,[7] וְשָׁם נֶאֱמַר:
⟪ it was ⟨ And ⟪ now. ⟨ until ⟨ from Egypt ⟨ this people ⟨ You have
said: there forgiven

ALL, ALOUD AND IN UNISON:

וַיֹּאמֶר יהוה סָלַחְתִּי כִּדְבָרֶךָ.[8]
⟪ according to ⟨ I have forgiven ⟪ And HASHEM said:
your word!

---

(1) Cf. *Psalms* 39:13. (2) Cf. 103:13. (3) 3:9. (4) 46:8. (5) 84:13. (6) 20:10. (7) *Numbers* 14:19. (8) 14:20.

§ סְלַח נָא — *Forgive, please.* This verse was Moses' plea to God that He forgive Israel after the sin of the spies, when the entire nation loudly expressed its lack of faith that God could bring them safely into *Eretz Yisrael.* In response, God answered סָלַחְתִּי, *I have forgiven.* In our prayers today, we beg for a similar response.

ALL CONTINUE:

הַטֵּה אֱלֹהַי אָזְנְךָ* וּשְׁמָע, פְּקַח עֵינֶיךָ וּרְאֵה

⟨ and see ⟨ Your eyes ⟨ open ⟪ and listen; ⟨ Your ear,* ⟨ my God, ⟨ Incline,

שֹׁמְמֹתֵינוּ, וְהָעִיר אֲשֶׁר נִקְרָא שִׁמְךָ עָלֶיהָ, כִּי לֹא

⟨ not ⟨ for ⟪ upon; ⟨ Your Name is ⟨ which ⟨ and that ⟨ our desolation
proclaimed [of] the city

עַל צִדְקֹתֵינוּ אֲנַחְנוּ מַפִּילִים תַּחֲנוּנֵינוּ לְפָנֶיךָ, כִּי

⟨ but ⟪ before ⟨ our ⟨ cast ⟨ do we ⟨ of our ⟨ be-
You; supplications righteousness cause

עַל רַחֲמֶיךָ הָרַבִּים. אֲדֹנָי שְׁמָעָה, אֲדֹנָי סְלָחָה,

⟪ forgive; ⟨ O Lord, ⟪ heed; ⟨ O Lord, ⟪ which is ⟨ of Your ⟨ be-
abundant. compassion, cause

אֲדֹנָי הַקְשִׁיבָה, וַעֲשֵׂה אַל תְּאַחַר, לְמַעַנְךָ אֱלֹהַי,

⟪ my God, ⟨ for Your sake, ⟪ delay; ⟨ do not ⟪ and act, ⟨ be attentive, ⟨ O Lord,

כִּי שִׁמְךָ נִקְרָא* עַל עִירְךָ וְעַל עַמֶּךָ.[1]

⟪ Your ⟨ and ⟨ Your City ⟨ upon ⟨ is ⟨ Your ⟨ for
people. upon proclaimed* Name

סליחה ב / SELICHAH 2

ALL:

אֱלֹהֵינוּ וֵאלֹהֵי אֲבוֹתֵינוּ:

⟪ of our forefathers: ⟨ and God ⟨ Our God

אֵין מִי יִקְרָא בְצֶדֶק,*[2]

⟪ with right- ⟨ who calls ⟨ one ⟨ There
eousness;* [to You] is no

---

(1) *Daniel* 9:18-19. (2) *Isaiah* 59:2.

הַטֵּה אֱלֹהַי אָזְנְךָ — *Incline, my God, Your ear.* Even if we are not deserving, at least let God help for the sake of His Name that is desecrated by the destruction of His City and the persecution of His people.

כִּי שִׁמְךָ נִקְרָא — *For Your Name is proclaimed.* Each nation has an angel that is appointed to oversee its fortunes, but God Himself maintains personal dominion over Israel and Jerusalem (*Tikkunei Zohar*).

אֵין מִי יִקְרָא בְצֶדֶק — *There is no one who calls [to You] with righteousness.* This *selichah* follows a double alphabetical scheme.

The acrostic of the final quatrain forms the name of the *paytan*, שְׁלֹמֹה, *Shlomo*. Most *selichos* bearing the signature *Shlomo* are ascribed to R' Shlomo bar Yehudah, who was known as R' Shlomo HaBavli. He flourished more than one thousand years ago and passed away about 990. (According to some, he lived a century earlier than that; see commentary to *Selichah* 61, s.v. זֶה פַּעֲמַיִם קָצִיר.) R' Shlomo was a contemporary of R' Sherira Gaon and his son R' Hai Gaon. One of Rashi's mentors, R' Yitzchak ben Yehudah, ranks R' Shlomo [together with

אִישׁ טוֹב נִמְשַׁל כְּחֶדֶק,*1

《 to a thorn.* 〈 is 〈 who is 〈 [today]
compared good the man

בַּקֵּשׁ רַחֲמִים בְּעַד שְׁחוּקֵי הָדָק,

《 to dust, 〈 those pounded 〈 for 〈 mercy 〈 To ask

בְּשׁוּם פָּנִים אֵין בְּדָק.

《 to be 〈 is there 〈 way 〈 in no
found. anyone

גֶּבֶר תָּמִים וְנִבָר אָפֵס, גָּמַר חָסִיד² וְצַדִּיק נִרְפַּס,

《 are 〈 the 《 are the 〈 gone 《 have 〈 and the 〈 who are 〈 Men
trampled righteous devout, disappeared; pure- sincere,
upon. hearted

דּוֹר עָנִי בַּעֲוֹנוֹ נִתְפַּס, דְּרָכָיו לְהַגִּיד* מִי יֵחָפֵשׂ.

《 can be 〈 who 《 is able 〈 [for, some- 《 is caught: 〈 in its 《 A generation that
found? to teach,* one who] iniquity is poor [without
His ways righteous people],

הוֹסַפְנוּ בַחֲטָאֵינוּ חֵמָה לְהַבְעִיר,

《 to inflame, 〈 [God's] 〈 with our sins 〈 We have
rage continued

הַמִּתְנַדְּבִים כִּבְנֵי בַיִת* לְהַפְעִיר,

《 must open their 《 of [His] 〈 — who 《 [therefore the
mouths [to pray house- are like righteous] who
for us]. hold —* members volunteered

---

(1) Cf. *Micah* 7:4. (2) Cf. *II Samuel* 22:26-27, *Psalms* 18:26-27; cf. *Psalms* 12:2.

R' Elazar HaKalir] among the קְדוֹשֵׁי עֶלְיוֹן, *exalted, holy ones.* His *piyutim* are cited by various *Rishonim.*

אִישׁ טוֹב נִמְשַׁל כְּחֶדֶק — *[Today] the man who is good is compared to a thorn.* The Talmud relates that a non-believer once called the Talmudic sage R' Yehoshua bar Chananiah, "חִדְקָאָה, *Thorny one!* For about people like you the prophet [*Micah* 7:4] states: טוֹבָם כְּחֵדֶק, *The good one among them is like a thorn.*"

"Fool," replied the sage, "continue the verse: יָשָׁר מִמְּסוּכָה, *the upright is better than a shelter.* Clearly the verse is complimentary, not derogatory! It means that just as thorns guard the breach in a fence, so too, the best of us protects the others" (*Eruvin* 101a).

The *paytan* here, according to most commentaries, follows the derogatory connotation of the phrase: even the best of men today

is merely a vexing thorn. And this interpretation has been used in the translation. An alternative opinion understands the phrase in its Scriptural context. Thus: *There are no longer any of those good people who are compared to protective thorns who can call to You with righteousness.* Both views are cited in the medieval commentary *Arugas HaBosem.*

דְּרָכָיו לְהַגִּיד — *[For, someone who] His ways is able to teach* [lit., *to tell*]. Who is capable of teaching God's ways to the iniquitous generation? Or, דְּרָכָיו may be rendered *its ways;* who can teach this generation the proper way for it to follow? Some early editions read דְּבָרָיו לְהַגִּיד, which means *to relate its* [the generation's] *concerns* [before God]; in other words, to plead its case.

הַמִּתְנַדְּבִים כִּבְנֵי בַיִת — *[Therefore the righteous] who volunteered — who are like mem-*

וּמַה יַּעֲצוֹר כֹּחַ¹ רַב וְצָעִיר,

⟨ or young ⟨ by ⟨ [enough] ⟨can there be⟨ How
old strength gathered then

וְדוּי וּפֶלֶל לְקָדִישׁ וָעִיר.²

《 the Ever- 《 to the ⟨ and pray ⟨ to
Awake? Holy One, confess

זָחַלְתִּי וָאִירָא בְּעַד מַחַן,

《 of the Camp ⟨ on 《 and am ⟨ I tremble,
[of Israel], behalf afraid,

זַעַק לְחַוּוֹת³ לְחוֹקֵר וּבוֹחֵן,⁴

《 and evaluates ⟨ to the One ⟨ to express ⟨ my cry
[hearts]. Who investigates

חֲסַר חֶסֶד וְיִתּוּר צָחַן, חֵן אֵיךְ אֶמְצָא בְּתַחַן.

《 through ⟨ will I find ⟨ how ⟨ — favor 《 of [sin's] ⟨ and having ⟨ deeds of ⟨ Lacking
supplication? then stench an excess kindness,

טוֹב לְקוֹרְאֶיךָ בְּנֶפֶשׁ רְחַב,

《 embold- ⟨ with a soul ⟨ to those who ⟨ [You Who
ened, call upon You are] Good

טָרְחָם נְשֹׂא וּלְכַלְכֵּל יַהַב,

《 You give ⟨ and ⟨ You ⟨ their
[them]; sustenance bear trouble

יְקַר חַסְדְּךָ עָלַי יִרְהַב, יַעַן קוֹלִי לְהַאֲזִין בְּאַהַב.

《 with ⟨ You listen ⟨ to my ⟨ in order 《 let flow ⟨ upon ⟨ kindness ⟨ Your
love! voice that plentifully, me precious

כְּהָגוּן מִדּוֹת* וּבִתְפִלָּה שָׁלֵם,

《 proficient, ⟨ and in prayer ⟨ character,* ⟨ Like one
of good

כְּזָקֵן וְרָגִיל* וְלֹא כְגֹלֶם,

《 like an ⟨ and 《 who is ex- ⟨ like an
ignoramus not perienced* elder

לְהֵחָשֵׁב נֶגְדְּךָ דְּבָאִי מִלְּהִכָּלֵם,

《 and not ⟨ my ⟨ before ⟨ — so that
be shamed broken You should be con-
[in my prayer]. [heart], sidered worthy

(1) Cf. *II Chronicles* 2:5. (2) Cf. *Daniel* 4:10 with *Rashi*. (3) Cf. *Job* 32:6. (4) Some editions read לְחוֹקֵר בְּבוֹחֵן, *to Him Who probes with an examination.*

bers *[of His]* household. Alternatively, *[even against the righteous]* who volunteered, who are like members *[of His]* household ....

כְּהָגוּן מִדּוֹת ... כְּזָקֵן וְרָגִיל — *Like one of good character ... like an elder who is experienced* — some of the qualifications of a

לְרַוְחָתִי זָכְרָה רַחֲמֶיךָ מֵהִתְעַלֵּם.[1]

《 not to disregard [my prayer]. 〈 Your mercy 〈 remember 〈 To [bring] my relief,

מֵרַבִּים צְרָכֵינוּ וְאֵין לְהֵאָמֵר,

《 be expressed, 〈 that they cannot 〈 are our needs, 〈 [So] many

מִקֹּצֶר דֵּעָה[2] וּמֵרֹב מֶמֶר,

《 of bitterness. 〈 and [our] excess 〈 of [our] knowledge 〈 because of the paucity

נֶגְדְּךָ הַכֹּל יוֹצֵר חֹמֶר, נוֹהֵג וְרוֹעֶה צֵל וְשׁוֹמֵר.[3]

《 and Guard. 〈 Pro-tector 《 and Shepherd, 〈 [our] Leader 《 [as of] 〈 Clay, O Molder 〈 is it all, 〈 Before You

שָׂרַדְנוּ כְתֹרֶן הַר בְּדוֹדֵנוּ,

《 in our isolation, 〈 atop a mountain 〈 like a signal pole 〈 We have survived

סְחִי וּמָאוֹס הוּשַׂם כְּבוֹדֵנוּ,

《 our glory; 〈 was transformed 〈 and repugnance 〈 into filth

עֲנֵנוּ וּתְנֵנוּ מִחְיָה בְּשִׁעְבּוּדֵנוּ,

《 in our bondage, 〈 sustenance 〈 grant us 〈 answer us,

עוֹד לִמְנְיָנְךָ בַּקֵּשׁ אֲבוּדֵינוּ.[4]

《 our lost ones. 〈 seek out 〈 to complete the census of your [nation] 〈 yet again

פְּקֻדַת נִגְעֵי תוֹכְחוֹתֶיךָ שְׁבוּטִים,[5]

〈 and beaten with rods 〈 of Your rebukes 〈 with the blows 〈 Those punished

פְּזוּרִים פְּרוּדִים וּבַגּוֹיִם עֲבוּטִים,

《 held hostage; 〈 among the nations 〈 divided, 〈 are scattered,

צָפְנֵם בְּסֻכָּךְ מֵרִיב[6] וּשְׁפָטִים,

《 and [harsh] judgment [of the gentiles] 〈 from the strife 〈 in Your shelter 〈 hide them

---

(1) Cf. *Psalms* 25:6; *Lamentations* 3:56. (2) See *Berachos* 29b. (3) Cf. *Psalms* 80:2; 121:5.
(4) Cf. *Ezekiel* 34:16. (5) Cf. *Psalms* 89:33, *II Samuel* 7:14. (6) Cf. *Psalms* 31:21.

chazzan listed in the Talmud (*Taanis* 16a).

צָפִיתָ תִּפְאַרְתְּךָ לָמוֹ מַבָּטִים.[1]

« their ‹ is for ‹ on Your glory ‹ — for to
yearning.   them   gaze

קוֹל כֹּחֲךָ לַהַב חוֹצֵב,[2] קֶצֶב טוֹב וְחִלּוּפוֹ קוֹצֵב,

« You ‹ or its ‹ of a good ‹ the « it cuts ‹ the ‹ of Your ‹ The
allocate; opposite portion allotment through, flames might, sound

רֵעֶיךָ דוֹפְקִים בְּקוֹל עָצֵב,

« that is ‹ with a ‹ are ‹ Your loved
sad — voice knocking ones

רְצוֹת נִדְבָתָם וּבְקִרְבָּם הִתְיַצֵּב.

« rest Your ‹ and in their « their offered ‹ accept
Presence. midst prayer favorably

שׁוֹקְדִים בְּצוֹם לִבָּם לְהַכְנִיעַ,

« to subdue; ‹ so as their « in ‹ They are
heart fasting, conscientious

שְׁאוֹנָם מִזַּעַם בַּחֲדָרֶיךָ[3] תַּצְנִיעַ,

« hide. ‹ in Your chambers ‹ from wrath ‹ their multitude

תּוֹבְעִים בְּלַחַשׁ שָׂפָה לְהָנִיעַ,*

« are they ‹ [just] ‹ in whispered ‹ They beseech
moving;* their lips [prayer],

תַּאֲוָתָם אַל נָא תַמְנִיעַ.

« withhold from them. ‹ please, ‹ do not, ‹ their desire

❖ שִׁמְךָ אֱלֹהִים חַיִּים מִתְפָּאֵר,

« is glorified; ‹ of life ‹ God ‹ Your Name

לְחַיִּים טוֹבִים מִמְּךָ נִשְׁאָר,

« let us ‹ that comes ‹ that is ‹ with a life
continue from You good

מְקוֹר חַיִּים עִמְּךָ[4] מִתְבָּאֵר,

« becomes clear. ‹ is with ‹ of life ‹ — that the
You source

הַבִּיטָה וַעֲנֵנוּ וְעֵינֵינוּ הָאֵר.[5]

« enlighten! ‹ and our « and ‹ Look [at our
eyes answer us; situation]

---

(1) Cf. *Isaiah* 20.5. (2) Cf. *Psalms* 29:4,7. (3) Cf. *Isaiah* 26:20. (4) Cf. *Psalms* 36:10. (5) Cf. 13:4.

תּוֹבְעִים בְּלַחַשׁ שָׂפָה לְהָנִיעַ — *They beseech in whispered [prayer], [just] their lips are they moving*, translating שָׂפָה in its literal meaning *lip*, as Hannah's prayer is described (*I Samuel* 1:13). *Matteh Levi* understands שָׂפָה as *speech* or *language*, rendering *that*

ALL, WHILE STANDING:

אֵל מֶלֶךְ* יוֹשֵׁב עַל כִּסֵּא רַחֲמִים, מִתְנַהֵג

⟨ O God, ⟩ ⟨ King* ⟩ ⟨ Who sits ⟩ ⟨ on ⟩ ⟨ the throne ⟩ ⟨ of mercy, ⟩ ⟨ Who acts ⟩

בַּחֲסִידוּת,* מוֹחֵל עֲוֹנוֹת עַמּוֹ,* מַעֲבִיר רִאשׁוֹן

⟨ with kindness,* ⟩ ⟨ Who pardons ⟩ ⟨ the sins ⟩ ⟨ of His people,* ⟩ ⟨ Who removes ⟩ ⟨ [sins,] one ⟩

רִאשׁוֹן,*¹ מַרְבֶּה מְחִילָה* לַחַטָּאִים וּסְלִיחָה

⟨ by one,* ⟩ ⟨ Who abundantly grants ⟩ ⟨ pardon* ⟩ ⟨ to unintentional sinners ⟩ ⟨ and forgiveness ⟩

לְפוֹשְׁעִים, עֹשֶׂה צְדָקוֹת* עִם כָּל בָּשָׂר וָרוּחַ,

⟨ to willful sinners, ⟩ ⟨ Who performs ⟩ ⟨ acts of generosity* ⟩ ⟨ with ⟩ ⟨ all ⟩ ⟨ [beings of] flesh ⟩ ⟨ and spirit ⟩

לֹא כְרָעָתָם תִּגְמוֹל. ❖ אֵל הוֹרֵיתָ לָּנוּ לוֹמַר*

⟨ — not ⟩ ⟨ in accord with their wickedness ⟩ ⟨ do You repay them! ⟩ ⟨ O God, ⟩ ⟨ You taught ⟩ ⟨ us ⟩ ⟨ to recite ⟩

(1) *Rosh Hashanah* 17a.

---

the [Accuser's] speech be set aside.

אֵל מֶלֶךְ **—** *O God, King* .... [The commentary to the introductory paragraph is based on *Sh'lah*.] אֵל connotes God as dominating and all-powerful. Despite this awesome strength, He sits on the *throne of mercy,* always anxious to show compassion.

בַּחֲסִידוּת **—** *With kindness.* A genuinely kind person tends not to avenge himself against those who wrong him. So too, God finds ways to avoid meting out punishment to sinners.

מוֹחֵל עֲוֹנוֹת עַמּוֹ **—** *Who pardons the sins of His people.* This expresses God's kindness in forgiving even those who antagonize Him with their deeds. However, the Talmud (*Rosh Hashanah* 17a-b) notes, this applies to those who subjugate themselves to Him even though they are too weak to avoid sin. [This may be alluded to by the word עַמּוֹ, *His people;* God pardons those who desire to remain *His,* despite their shortcomings.]

מַעֲבִיר רִאשׁוֹן רִאשׁוֹן **—** *Who removes [sins,] one by one.* According to the teachings of Beis Hillel [the Academy of Hillel], God, Who is רַב חֶסֶד, *Abundant in Kindness,* מַטֶּה כְּלַפֵּי חֶסֶד, *tips* [*the scales of justice*] *toward kindness.* The Academy of R' Yishmael explains that God accomplishes

this by removing sins one by one, meaning that if one's good deeds are equivalent to his sins, God removes a sin from the balance so that the side of virtue outweighs the side of sin (*Rashi*). *Rif* interprets that if someone has committed a particular sin for the first time, God holds it in abeyance and does not include it in the calculation, as long as it has not yet become habitual. *Rambam,* based on *Yoma* 86b, writes that the first *two* sins are removed (*Hil. Teshuvah* 3:5).

מַרְבֶּה מְחִילָה **—** *Who abundantly grants pardon.* Not only does God forgive those who sin out of carelessness, He even forgives rebels who sin out of defiance against Him. Furthermore, He pardons abundantly, meaning that God transforms even sins into virtues, provided the sinner's repentance was motivated by love of God (*Yoma* 86b). [See Overview.]

עֹשֶׂה צְדָקוֹת **—** *Who performs acts of generosity.* Even though someone may have sinned grievously, God does not withhold reward for any good he may have done. God does not repay them in accord with their evil; God does not say that they are so evil that even their *mitzvos* deserve to be ignored.

הוֹרֵיתָ לָּנוּ לוֹמַר **—** *You taught us to recite.* God taught Moses that whenever Israel

שְׁלֹשׁ עֶשְׂרֵה, וּזְכוֹר לָנוּ הַיּוֹם בְּרִית שְׁלֹשׁ עֶשְׂרֵה,*

《 of [these] Thirteen,* 〈 the 〈 today 〈 for us 〈 remem- 《 the Thirteen
                  covenant   ber   [Attributes of Mercy];

כְּמוֹ שֶׁהוֹדַעְתָּ לֶעָנָיו* מִקֶּדֶם, כְּמוֹ שֶׁכָּתוּב,

《 it is written: 〈 as 《 in ancient 〈 to the humble 〈 You made 〈 as
                    times,   one [Moses]*   known

וַיֵּרֶד יהוה* בֶּעָנָן וַיִּתְיַצֵּב עִמּוֹ שָׁם, וַיִּקְרָא

〈 and He 《 there, 〈 with 〈 and stood 〈 in a 〈 And HASHEM
called out   him   cloud   descended*

בְשֵׁם יהוה.*[1]

《 of 〈 with the
HASHEM.*   Name

CONGREGATION, THEN *CHAZZAN*:

וַיַּעֲבֹר יהוה עַל פָּנָיו וַיִּקְרָא:

《 and 《 [Moses'] 〈 before 〈 And HASHEM passed
proclaimed: face,

CONGREGATION AND *CHAZZAN* RECITE LOUDLY AND IN UNISON:

יהוה, יהוה, אֵל, רַחוּם, וְחַנּוּן, אֶרֶךְ אַפַּיִם,

〈 to anger, 〈 Slow 《 and Gracious, 〈 Compassionate 〈 God, 〈 HASHEM, 〈 HASHEM,

וְרַב חֶסֶד, וֶאֱמֶת, נֹצֵר חֶסֶד לָאֲלָפִים, נֹשֵׂא עָוֹן,

〈 of 〈 Forgiver 《 for thousands 〈 of 〈 Preserver 《 and 〈 in 〈 and
iniquity,   [of generations], kindness   Truth,   Kindness Abundant

וָפֶשַׁע, וְחַטָּאָה, וְנַקֵּה.[2] וְסָלַחְתָּ לַעֲוֹנֵנוּ וּלְחַטָּאתֵנוּ

《 and our sins, 〈 our 〈 May You 《 and Who 〈 and inadvertent 〈 willful sin,
            iniquities   forgive   absolves.   sin,

וּנְחַלְתָּנוּ.[3] סְלַח לָנוּ אָבִינוּ כִּי חָטָאנוּ, מְחַל לָנוּ

〈 us, 〈 pardon 《 we have 〈 for 《 our Father, 〈 us, 〈 Forgive 《 and make us
           sinned;   Your heritage.

---

(1) *Exodus* 34:5. (2) 34:6-7. (3) 34:9.

---

would be in a time of crisis, they should
pray for mercy by reciting the Thirteen Attributes (see below).

בְּרִית שְׁלֹשׁ עֶשְׂרֵה — *The covenant of [these]
Thirteen.* R' Yehudah taught that God sealed
a covenant with Moses and Israel that the
recitation of the Thirteen Attributes would
never be in vain (*Rosh Hashanah* 17b).

לֶעָנָיו — *To the humble one [Moses].*

Moses was the humblest of men (*Numbers*
12:3).

וַיֵּרֶד ה' — *And HASHEM descended.* God
descended, as if to stand with Moses.

וַיִּקְרָא בְּשֵׁם ה' — *And He called out with
the Name of HASHEM.* There, God called
out the Name HASHEM, as He taught Moses
the Thirteen Attributes that begin with
that Name.

מַלְכֵּנוּ כִּי פָשָֽׁעְנוּ. כִּי אַתָּה אֲדֹנָי טוֹב וְסַלָּח,

‹ our King, ‹ for ‹‹ we have ‹ For ‹‹ You, ‹ O Lord, ‹ good ‹ are ‹‹ and
forgiving, ‹ willfully sinned.

וְרַב חֶֽסֶד לְכָל קֹרְאֶֽיךָ.¹

‹‹ abundantly ‹ and ‹ kind ‹ to all ‹ who call
upon You.

פסוקי הקדמה לסליחה ג / PREFATORY VERSES TO SELICHAH 3

תָּבֹא לְפָנֶֽיךָ תְּפִלָּתֵֽנוּ,² וְאַל תִּתְעַלַּם מִתְּחִנָּתֵֽנוּ.³

‹ Let come ‹ before You ‹‹ our prayer; ‹ do not ‹ disregard ‹‹ our pleas.

תָּבֹא אֵלֶֽיךָ תְּפִלָּתֵֽנוּ, אֶל הֵיכַל קָדְשֶֽׁךָ.⁴ תָּבוֹא לְפָנֶֽיךָ

‹ Let
come ‹ to You ‹‹ our prayer; ‹ to ‹ Your Holy Temple ‹ Let come ‹ before
You

אֶנְקַת אָסִיר; כְּגֹֽדֶל זְרוֹעֲךָ הוֹתֵר בְּנֵי תְמוּתָה.⁵

‹ the groan ‹ of the
prisoner; ‹‹ as [befits] ‹ the greatness ‹ of Your ‹ spare ‹ those ‹‹ to die.
might, ‹ condemned

אֱלֹהֵֽינוּ בֹּֽשְׁנוּ בְמַעֲשֵֽׂינוּ וְנִכְלַֽמְנוּ בַּעֲוֹנֵֽינוּ.⁶

‹ Our God ‹ we are ‹ of our actions ‹ and we are ‹‹ by our
ashamed ‹ humiliated ‹ iniquities.

כְּרַחֵם אָב עַל בָּנִים, כֵּן תְּרַחֵם יהוה עָלֵֽינוּ.⁷

‹ As merciful as ‹ a ‹ toward ‹ his ‹ so ‹‹ have ‹ HASHEM, ‹‹ on us.
father is ‹ children, ‹ mercy,

לַיהוה הַיְשׁוּעָה, עַל עַמְּךָ בִרְכָתֶֽךָ סֶּֽלָה.⁸ יהוה

‹ To HASHEM ‹ is salvation, ‹‹ upon ‹ Your ‹ is Your ‹‹ Selah. ‹‹ HASHEM,
people ‹ blessing,

צְבָאוֹת עִמָּֽנוּ, מִשְׂגָּב לָֽנוּ אֱלֹהֵי יַעֲקֹב סֶֽלָה.⁹

‹ Master of ‹ is with us, ‹‹ a ‹ for us ‹ is the God ‹ of Jacob, ‹‹ Selah.
Legions, ‹ stronghold

יהוה צְבָאוֹת, אַשְׁרֵי אָדָם בֹּטֵֽחַ בָּךְ.¹⁰ יהוה הוֹשִֽׁיעָה,

‹‹ HASHEM, ‹ Master of ‹‹ — praise- ‹ is the ‹ who ‹ in You. ‹ HASHEM, ‹ save!
Legions ‹ worthy ‹ man ‹ trusts

הַמֶּֽלֶךְ יַעֲנֵֽנוּ בְיוֹם קָרְאֵֽנוּ.¹¹

‹ May the ‹ answer ‹ on the ‹ we call.
King ‹ us ‹ day ‹‹

---

(1) *Psalms* 86:5. (2) Cf. 88:3. (3) Cf. 55:2. (4) Cf. *Jonah* 2:8. (5) *Psalms* 79:11.
(6) This is not a Scriptural verse. (7) Cf. *Psalms* 103:13. (8) 3:9. (9) 46:8. (10) 84:13. (11) 20:10.

SELICHAH 3 / סליחה ג

ALL:

אֱלֹהֵינוּ וֵאלֹהֵי אֲבוֹתֵינוּ:

《 of our forefathers: 〈 and God 〈 Our God

תָּבֹא לְפָנֶיךָ שַׁוְעַת חִנּוּן,*

《 of our supplication,* 〈 the cry 〈 before You 〈 Let come

תְּהִי נָא אָזְנְךָ קַשֶּׁבֶת תַּחֲנוּן,[1]

《 to [our] supplication; 〈 be attentive 〈 Your ear 〈 please, 〈 let,

שִׁמְעָה יהוה צֶדֶק, הַקְשִׁיבָה רִנּוּן,[2]

《 to [our] entreaty, 〈 be attentive 《 [our] righteous [plea], 〈 HASHEM, 〈 hear,

שָׁר מֵישָׁרִים וּמַעֲלִים מֵרֶנּוּן.

《 defamation. 〈 and ignore 〈 at uprightness 〈 You Who look

רֹאשׁ לְהָרִים נִכְלַמְנוּ בְּשֵׁנוּ,[3]

《 ashamed, 〈 we are embarrassed 〈 to lift up 〈 Our head

רֵיחַ נִרְדֵּנוּ כִּי הִבְאַשְׁנוּ,

《 we have made the foul-smelling; 〈 indeed 〈 of our fragrant spice 〈 the scent

קִלְקַלְנוּ יְשָׁרִים, וְתוֹרוֹת שִׁבַּשְׁנוּ,*

《 we have perverted,* 〈 and the Torahs 〈 the straight [paths] 〈 we have spoiled

קַרְקַע פָּנֵינוּ בְּכֵן כָּבַשְׁנוּ.

《 we averted. 〈 therefore, 〈 our faces, 〈 and to the ground,

---

(1) *Nehemiah* 1:6. (2) Cf. *Psalms* 17:1. (3) Cf. *Ezra* 9:6.

⊷§ תָּבֹא לְפָנֶיךָ שַׁוְעַת חִנּוּן — *Let come before You the cry of our supplication.* This *selichah* contains a double תַּשְׁרַ"ק (reversed aleph-beis) acrostic. The author signed his name — שְׁלֹמֹה הַקָּטָן וְהַצָּעִיר יְחִי, *Shlomo, the lesser and the younger, may he live* [see prefatory comment to *Selichah* 2], as indicated by the bold type. Others read

the signature שְׁלֹמֹה הַלֵוִי, *Shlomo HaLevi*, the letters of הַלֵוִי, being the initials of the words הַקָּטָן ... לְאֶלֶף ... וְהַצָּעִיר ... יְחַד.

וְתוֹרוֹת שִׁבַּשְׁנוּ — *And the Torahs we have perverted.* The plural form alludes to תּוֹרָה שֶׁבִּכְתָב, *the Written Torah*, Scripture, and תּוֹרָה שֶׁבְּעַל פֶּה, *the Oral Torah*, the traditional interpretation of the Written

צַר וּמָצוֹק מִכָּל צַד, צֹאן נִדְחָה מֵאֵין מִצַּד,

《 a protecting 〈 without 〈 that are 〈 [we are] 《 side, 〈 on 〈 and 〈 Distress
shelter. going astray sheep every anguish

פָּנָה לִימִין וַיִּגְזֹר מַעֲצָד, פַּחַד מִשְּׂמֹאל וְצַיָּד הַצָּד.

《 who 〈 and the 〈 is to the left 〈 fear 《 by the axe; 〈 we are 〈 to the 〈 [If we]
stalks. hunter hacked right, turn

עֵינֶיךָ רֹאוֹת תִּהְיֶינָה פְּקוּחוֹת,[1]

〈 let them be vigilant 《 that are 〈 Your eyes
all-seeing,

עָנְיִ וְעָנוּי מִצָּרוֹת הַמָּתוּחוֹת,

《 that are 〈 from 〈 and 〈 [to observe
prolonged. troubles torment our] poverty

סֶפֶד לְרִנָּה וּלְרִצּוּי תּוֹכָחוֹת,

《 from rebukes 〈 and to 〈 to 〈 [From]
reconciliation song, lamentation

סַבּוֹת וַהֲפֹךְ בִּדְרָכֶיךָ הַנְּכֹחוֹת.

《 that are 〈 with 〈 and trans- 〈 —turn them
straightforward. Your ways form them around

נִתַּנּוּ בַּעֲוֹנֵינוּ לְשֶׁבִי וּלְבִזָּה,

《 and pillage; 〈 to 〈 due to our 〈 We have
captivity iniquities been delivered

נַחְנוּ מְלָכֵינוּ כֹּהֲנֵינוּ לְבוּזָה,[2]

《 have been 〈 and our 〈 our kings, 〈 we,
put to shame. Kohanim

מֵרוֹם נִכְבָּדוֹת וְאַהֲבָה עַזָּה,

《 so 〈 and love 〈 so glorious 〈 From the
intense, heights

מִגַּרְתָּ לָאָרֶץ לְשַׁמָּה וּלְעִזָּה.

《 and ridicule. 〈 to [suffer] 〈 to earth 〈 You have
desolation thrown [us] down

לֹא חִלִּינוּ פָנֶיךָ לְהַפִּיל תְּחִנָּה,

《 [our] 〈 pouring 《 before 〈 We did not
supplication, out You, beseech

(1) Cf. *Nehemiah* 1:6; *Jeremiah* 32:19. (2) Cf. *Ezra* 9:7; some editions of *Selichos* read לְבִזָּה, *for pillage*.

Torah as taught by Moses and transmitted orally through the generations until it was formally recorded in the Mishnah and Talmud.

לְהַשְׂכִּיל בַּאֲמִתֶּךְ מַעֲלוֹת צַחֲנָה,*

≪ of the stench   ⟨ to prevent   ⟨ in Your truth   ⟨ [nor did we]
[of sin].*   the rise   seek wisdom

בָּלִינוּ כִּסְדוֹם בְּשֵׁפַל קוֹל הַטַּחֲנָה,*[1]

≪ of the mill   ⟨ is the   ⟨ — when   ⟨ like Sodom   ⟨ We would
[the voice of   sound   grown   have been
Torah study]* —   fainter   destroyed

בִּמְעַט רֶגַע לוּלֵי תְחִנָּה.[2]

≪ Your bestowed favor. ⟨ if not for ≪ moment, ⟨ in a fleeting

יֶתֶר הַפְּלֵטָה* לְהַשְׁאִיר[3] חָסְתָּ,

≪ You took   ⟨ to leave over   ⟨ of the [First Tem- ⟨ A
pity;   ple] survivors*   remnant

יָתֵד וְגָדֵר תַּתָּה וְכִנַּסְתָּ,

≪ and gathered ⟨ You   ⟨ and a   ⟨ a stake
them in.   provided   fence

טִלְטַלְתָּנוּ כְּנֶגֶד שָׁלֹשׁ* מָאַסְתָּ,

≪ that You   ⟨ to the   ⟨ [because of ⟨ Then You sent
loathe,   three*   the one sin]   us into exile
               equal   [again],

טִירַת כֶּסֶף* בִּגְלָלֵנוּ רָמַסְתָּ.

≪ You   ⟨ because   ⟨ longed   ⟨ and the
trampled.   of us   for*   Tower

---

(1) *Ecclesiastes* 12:4. (2) Cf. *Ezra* 9:8. (3) Cf. 9:14-15.

לְהַשְׂכִּיל בַּאֲמִתֶּךְ מַעֲלוֹת צַחֲנָה — *[Nor did we]
seek wisdom in Your truth to prevent the
rise of the stench [of sin].* Had we but considered the truth of Your ways, we would
have cleansed ourselves of sin. Alternatively,
the stich means: *[Nor did we] seek wisdom
in Your truth, because we reeked of sin.*

קוֹל הַטַּחֲנָה — *The sound of the mill [the
voice of Torah study]*, the sound of Torah
scholars debating and clarifying their subject matter. The Midrash (*Koheles Rabbah*
12:7) explains that Torah study is compared
to a flour mill. Just as a mill runs day and
night and never ceases to turn, so are we
bidden to study Torah day and night, as it
is written: וְהָגִיתָ בּוֹ יוֹמָם וָלַיְלָה, *And you shall
ponder it day and night* (*Joshua* 1:8).

יֶתֶר הַפְּלֵטָה — *A remnant of the [First
Temple] survivors.* God allowed a remnant of the nation to survive the destruction

of the First Temple, and He established them
firmly — a stake and a fence — in the Second Temple.

כְּנֶגֶד שָׁלֹשׁ — *[Because of the one sin] equal
to the three.* The Talmud compares the underlying causes of the destruction of the two
Temples:

Why was the First *Beis HaMikdash*
destroyed? Because of three [evil] things:
idolatry, adultery, and murder .... Why then
was the Second *Beis HaMikdash* destroyed?
Hadn't the nation involved itself in the
study of Torah, the performance of *mitzvos*,
and acts of kindness? Because of unwarranted hatred [that was prevalent among
the people]. This teaches that unwarranted
hatred is equal to the three cardinal sins:
idolatry, adultery, and murder (*Yoma* 9b).

טִירַת כֶּסֶף — *The Tower longed for.* This
is a play on words, for Scripture alludes to

חֶבֹל חָבַלְנוּ¹ מֵעַל לְמַעַל,² חִבַּלְנוּ מֵעַל אֶל עַל,

《 another 〈 to 〈 from one 〈 now we are 《 to commit; 〈 treachery 〈 We have acted
yoke.　　yoke [of exile]　wounded,　　　　　　　　corruptly,

זְכֹר צִוִּיתָ בְּלִי לִגְעַל,³ זְרוּיִם לְקַבֵּץ וּבָם לִבְעַל.

《　to rule. 〈 and over 〈　to　〈　the　《 to abhor 〈 not 〈 You 〈 Remem-
　　　　them　gather,　dispersed　　　[us],　　　　promised　ber

וְאַתָּה אַחֲרֵי כָּל הַבָּא,⁴ וַדַּאי וְצַדִּיק, וְלָנוּ הַדִּבָּה,

《　is the　〈 and in 〈 that You are 《 we are 《 that has 〈 all 〈 after 〈 And You,
　　fault.　　us　righteous,　certain　happened
　　　　　　　　　　　　　　[to us],

הַיּוֹם כְּמֵאָז בְּלִי סִבָה, הִנְנוּ לְפָנֶיךָ בְּאַשְׁמָה רַבָּה.

《 that is 〈　with guilt 〈 before 〈 we are 《 change 〈 without 〈 as of 〈 Today,
vast.　　　　　You,　here　[of heart],　　old,

דַּלַּת עַם לְקֶלֶס וְחֵרוּף,

《　　　and　〈 [are subject] 〈 of the 〈 The
　　derision,　　to scorn　people　poorest

דְּחוּפִים סְחוּפִים נְתוּנִים לְטֵרוּף,

《 to be ripped apart 〈 given over 〈 swept away, 〈 pushed away,

גָּלוּת וְשִׁעְבּוּד בְּנִסָּיוֹן⁵ וְצֵרוּף,

《　　and　〈 provided 〈　and　〈 —[their]
purification;　testing　enslavement　exile

גַּלְגֵּל בְּחֶסֶד לִסְלִיחָה וְתֵרוּף.

《 and healing. 〈　to pardon　〈 in kindness 〈 turn now

בְּרַחֲמֶיךָ עוֹד בִּרְבוֹת עִתִּים,*

《　times,* 〈 as [You have 〈 yet, 〈 In Your mercy,
　　　　done] so many

בְּךָ נִוָּשֵׁעָה קַיֵּם וְהוֹשַׁעְתִּים,⁶

《　I will save 《 Fulfill [Your 《 we will 〈 by
them!　promise],　be saved.　You

אֵלֶּה מֵרָחוֹק יָבֹאוּ⁷ כֻּתִּים,

《 in groups, 〈 will come 〈 from afar 〈 These

---

(1) *Nehemiah* 1:7. (2) Cf. 1:8. (3) Cf. *Leviticus* 26:44. (4) Cf. *Ezra* 9:13.
(5) Some editions read וְנִסָּיוֹן, but the meaning is the same. (6) *Hosea* 1:7. (7) *Isaiah* 49:12.

the *Beis HaMikdash* as כֶּסֶף טִירַת, *a Tower*　　בִּרְבוֹת עִתִּים — As [You have done] so many
of silver (*Song of Songs* 8:9). Indeed, many　　times. The grammatical sense of this verse
early editions of *Selichos* read כֶּסֶף instead　　is ambiguous, and the word רְבוֹת can mean
of כֹּסֶף.　　　　　　　　　　　　　　　　　　　　*much* or *many*. Thus, this phrase can have

וְאֵלֶּה מִצָּפוֹן וְצִיִּים וְכִתִּים.*¹

《 from Kittim 〈 on large 《 from the 〈 those
[Rome].*   ships   north,

שֶׁלְּךָ הֵם עֲבָדֶיךָ וְעַמֶּךָ,

《 and Your 〈 Your 《 they 〈 Yours
people.   servants   are:

לַבֵּב* כִּימֵי קֶדֶם מַנְעִימֶיךָ,*

《 Your pleasant 〈 of old 〈 as in 〈 Hearten*
ones.*   days

מָשְׁכֵנוּ אַחֲרֶיךָ שִׂימֵנוּ בִּרְשׁוּמֶיךָ,

《 among Your ones 〈 place us 《 after You, 〈 Draw us
inscribed [for life],

הַכֹּל חֲפֵצִים לְיִרְאָה אֶת שְׁמֶךָ.²

《 Your Name. 〈 to revere 〈 who desire 〈 all

❖ הַקָּטֹן לָאֶלֶף גַּדֵּל רַחוּמֵנוּ,

《 O our 〈 increase, 〈 a thou- 〈 The smallest
Beloved One!   sandfold   [people]

וְהַצָּעִיר לְגוֹי לְהָעֲצִים³ בִּתְחוּמֵנוּ,

《 in all Your 《 that grows 〈 into a 〈 And [make]
righteousness,   mightily   nation   the younger
within our border,   [son of Isaac]

יַחַד בְּכָל צִדְקוֹתֶיךָ לְרַחֲמֵנוּ.

《 have compassion 〈 Your 〈 with 《 [when we
upon us;   righteousness,   all   are] united,

יָשָׁב נָא אַפְּךָ וּתְנַחֲמֵנוּ.⁴

《 and console us. 〈 Your 〈 please, 〈 turn
anger,   back,

---

(1) Cf. *Numbers* 24:24; *Daniel* 11:30. (2) Cf. *Nehemiah* 1:11. (3) Cf. *Isaiah* 60:22.
(4) Cf. 12:1; *Daniel* 9:16; in keeping with the Scriptural verse,
some editions of *Selichos* read בְּכָל, *in accordance with all*, instead of בְּכָל, *in all*.

any of three meanings: *As [You have done]
so many times; In the fullness of time*
(when much time has elapsed); or, *For such
a long time.*

וְצִיִּים וְכִתִּים — *On large ships from Kittim
[Rome].* The translation is based on *Rashi's*
interpretation of the phrase וְצִים מִיַד כִּתִּים
(*Numbers* 24:24 and *Sanhedrin* 106a).
Elsewhere, *Rashi* renders צִיִּים כִּתִּים as *Ro-
man legions* (*Daniel* 11:30). *R' Saadiah*

Gaon (ibid.) interprets צִיִּים as *Lombardians*
[from Northern Italy], and כִּתִּים as *Romans*
[from Central Italy]. Accordingly, our text
would read (as it does in some editions)
וּמֵצִיִּים וְכִתִּים, *and from Lombardy and from
Rome.*

לַבֵּב ... מַנְעִימֶיךָ — *Hearten ... Your pleasant
ones.* The word לַבֵּב may also be translated
take to heart or *cherish.* And מַנְעִימֶיךָ can
mean *those who sing Your sweet praises.*

ALL, WHILE STANDING:

אֵל מֶלֶךְ יוֹשֵׁב עַל כִּסֵּא רַחֲמִים, מִתְנַהֵג
⟨ Who acts ⟩ ⟪ of mercy, ⟩ ⟨ the throne ⟨ on ⟩ ⟨ Who sits ⟩ ⟨ King ⟩ ⟨ O God,

בַּחֲסִידוּת, מוֹחֵל עֲוֹנוֹת עַמּוֹ, מַעֲבִיר רִאשׁוֹן רִאשׁוֹן,[1]
⟪ by one, ⟩ ⟨ [sins] one ⟩ ⟨ Who ⟩ ⟪ of His ⟩ ⟨ the sins ⟩ ⟨ Who ⟩ ⟪ with kindness,
                 removes   people,   pardons

מַרְבֶּה מְחִילָה לְחַטָּאִים וּסְלִיחָה לַפּוֹשְׁעִים, עֹשֶׂה
⟨ Who ⟩ ⟪ to willful ⟩ ⟨ and ⟩ ⟨ to unintentional ⟨ pardon ⟩ ⟨ Who abun-
performs   sinners,   forgiveness   sinners   dantly grants

צְדָקוֹת עִם כָּל בָּשָׂר וָרוּחַ, לֹא כְרָעָתָם תִּגְמוֹל.
⟪ do You ⟩ ⟨ in accord with ⟨ — not ⟪ and spirit ⟨ [beings ⟨ all ⟩ ⟨ with ⟩ ⟨ acts of
repay them! their wickedness   of] flesh   generosity

❖ אֵל הוֹרֵיתָ לָּנוּ לוֹמַר שְׁלֹשׁ עֶשְׂרֵה, וּזְכוֹר לָנוּ
⟨ for ⟨ remember ⟪ the Thirteen ⟩ ⟨ to recite ⟨ us ⟩ ⟨ You taught ⟨ O God,
us   [Attributes of Mercy];

הַיּוֹם בְּרִית שְׁלֹשׁ עֶשְׂרֵה, כְּמוֹ שֶׁהוֹדַעְתָּ לֶעָנָיו
⟨ to the humble ⟨ You made ⟩ ⟨ as ⟩ ⟪ of [these] Thirteen, ⟩ ⟨ the ⟩ ⟨ today
one [Moses]   known   covenant

מִקֶּדֶם, כְּמוֹ שֶׁכָּתוּב, וַיֵּרֶד יהוה בֶּעָנָן וַיִּתְיַצֵּב עִמּוֹ
⟨ with ⟩ ⟨ and stood ⟩ ⟨ in a ⟩ ⟨ And HASHEM ⟪ it is written: ⟩ ⟨ as ⟪ in ancient
him   cloud   descended   times,

שָׁם, וַיִּקְרָא בְשֵׁם יהוה.[2]
⟪ of ⟩ ⟨ with the ⟨ and He ⟪ there,
HASHEM.   Name   called out

CONGREGATION, THEN *CHAZZAN*:

וַיַּעֲבֹר יהוה עַל פָּנָיו וַיִּקְרָא:
⟪ and ⟩ ⟪ [Moses'] ⟨ before ⟩ ⟨ And HASHEM passed
proclaimed: face,

CONGREGATION AND *CHAZZAN* RECITE LOUDLY AND IN UNISON:

יהוה, יהוה, אֵל, רַחוּם, וְחַנּוּן, אֶרֶךְ אַפַּיִם,
⟨ to anger, ⟩ ⟨ Slow ⟪ and ⟩ ⟨ Compassionate ⟨ God, ⟩ ⟨ HASHEM, ⟩ ⟨ HASHEM,
Gracious,

וְרַב חֶסֶד, וֶאֱמֶת, נֹצֵר חֶסֶד לָאֲלָפִים, נֹשֵׂא עָוֹן,
⟨ of ⟨ Forgiver ⟪ for thousands ⟩ ⟨ of ⟨ Preserver ⟪ and ⟩ ⟨ in ⟨ and
iniquity,   [of generations], kindness   Truth,   Kindness Abundant

---

(1) *Rosh Hashanah* 17a. (2) *Exodus* 34:5.

וָפֶשַׁע, וְחַטָּאָה, וְנַקֵּה.¹ וְסָלַחְתָּ לַעֲוֹנֵנוּ וּלְחַטָּאתֵנוּ
《 and our sins, 〈 our iniquities 〈 May You forgive 《 and Who absolves. 〈 and inadvertent sin, 〈 willful sin,

וּנְחַלְתָּנוּ.² סְלַח לָנוּ אָבִינוּ כִּי חָטָאנוּ, מְחַל לָנוּ
〈 us, 〈 pardon 《 we have sinned; 〈 for 《 our Father, 〈 us, 〈 Forgive 《 and make us Your heritage.

מַלְכֵּנוּ כִּי פָשָׁעְנוּ. כִּי אַתָּה אֲדֹנָי טוֹב וְסַלָּח,
《 and forgiving, 〈 are 〈 good 〈 O Lord, 〈 You, 〈 For 《 we have willfully sinned. 〈 for 《 our King,

וְרַב חֶסֶד לְכָל קֹרְאֶיךָ.³
《 who call upon You. 〈 to all 〈 kind 〈 and abundantly

סליחה ד / SELICHAH 4
(פזמון)

CHAZZAN, THEN CONGREGATION:

בְּמוֹצָאֵי מְנוּחָה,* קַדַּמְנוּךְ תְּחִלָּה,
《 first of all; 〈 we approach You 《 [of the day] of rest,* 〈 At the departure

הַט אָזְנְךָ מִמָּרוֹם, יוֹשֵׁב תְּהִלָּה,⁴
《 upon the praises [of Israel] — 〈 [O You] Who are enthroned 《 from On High, 〈 Your 〈 incline ear

לִשְׁמֹעַ אֶל הָרִנָּה וְאֶל הַתְּפִלָּה.⁵
《 [our] prayer. 〈 and to 〈 [our] song of praise 〈 to 〈 O [that You] listen

CONGREGATION, THEN CHAZZAN:

אֶת יְמִין עֹז עוֹרְרָה, לַעֲשׂוֹת חָיִל,⁶
《 of valor [against our accusers], 〈 to do deeds 〈 arouse 〈 that is mighty 〈 Your right hand

בְּצֶדֶק נֶעֱקַד, וְנִשְׁחַט תְּמוּרוֹ אָיִל,
《 was a ram; 〈 in his stead 〈 but 《 of [Isaac] who was bound [on the altar], 〈 by the merit

---

(1) *Exodus* 34:6-7. (2) 34:9. (3) *Psalms* 86:5. (4) Cf. 22:4. (5) *I Kings* 8:28. (6) Cf. *Psalms* 118:15.

§**בְּמוֹצָאֵי מְנוּחָה** — *At the departure [of the day] of rest.* This *selichah* is called a *pizmon*, which indicates that it has a refrain. It begins by stating the time of its recital, at the departure of the Sabbath. Anonymously written, it follows an *aleph-beis* acrostic (after the first stanza). It is usually recited in responsive fashion: The *chazzan* recites the first stanza, which is then repeated by the congregation; each succeeding stanza

גְּנוֹן נָא גִזְעוֹ, בְּזַעֲקָם בְּעוֹד לָיִל,

《 night — 〈 while it is 〈 when they 〈 his de- 〈 please, 〈 protect,
still cry [to You] scendants

לִשְׁמֹעַ אֶל הָרִנָּה וְאֶל הַתְּפִלָּה.

《 [our] prayer. 〈 and to 〈 [our] song 〈 to 〈 O [that You]
of praise listen

CONGREGATION, THEN *CHAZZAN:*

דְּרוֹשׁ נָא דּוֹרְשֶׁיךָ, בְּדָרְשָׁם פָּנֶיךָ,

《 Your 〈 as they seek 〈 those who 〈 please, 〈 Seek,
Presence; seek You

הִדָּרֵשׁ לָמוֹ מִשְּׁמֵי מְעוֹנֶךָ,

《 abode, 〈 from Your 〈 to 〈 make Your-
Heavenly them self available

וּלְשַׁוְעַת חִנּוּנָם אַל תַּעְלֵם אָזְנֶךָ,[1]

《 Your ear — 〈 shut 〈 do 〈 of their 〈 and to the cry
not supplication

לִשְׁמֹעַ אֶל הָרִנָּה וְאֶל הַתְּפִלָּה.

《 [our] prayer. 〈 and to 〈 [our] song 〈 to 〈 O [that You]
of praise listen

CONGREGATION, THEN *CHAZZAN:*

זוֹחֲלִים וְרוֹעֲדִים מִיּוֹם בּוֹאֶךָ,

《 of Your 〈 aware of 〈 and tremble, 〈 They are
coming, the day fearful

חָלִים כְּמַבְכִּירָה מֵעֶבְרַת מַשָּׂאֶךָ,

《 when You are 〈 before 〈 like a woman first 〈 frightened
elevated [in judgment], Your wrath giving birth

טְנוּפָם מְחֵה נָא וְיוֹדוּ פְלָאֶיךָ,[2]

《 Your 〈 and they will 〈 please, 〈 wipe 〈 their filth
wonders — acknowledge away [of sin]

לִשְׁמֹעַ אֶל הָרִנָּה וְאֶל הַתְּפִלָּה.

《 [our] prayer. 〈 and to 〈 [our] song 〈 to 〈 O [that You]
of praise listen

CONGREGATION, THEN *CHAZZAN:*

יוֹצֵר אַתָּה לְכָל יְצִיר נוֹצָר,

《 that is created; 〈 creature 〈 of every 〈 You are 〈 The Creator

---

(1) Cf. *Lamentations* 3:56. (2) Cf. *Psalms* 89:6.

---

is recited first by the congregation, then repeated by the *chazzan*. This mode is fol- lowed with most of the *selichos* recited re- sponsively (one or two per day of *Selichos*).

כּוֹנַנְתָּ מֵאָז תֶּרֶף* לְחַלְּצָם מִמֵּצָר,[1]

《 from [sin's] 〈 to release 〈 a 〈 long 〈 You
trouble,   them   remedy*   ago   prepared

לְחוֹנְנָם חִנָּם מֵאוֹצָר הַמְּנֻצָּר,*

《 that are reserved 〈 from the 〈 gratis 〈 by granting
[for those without   repository   them
merits]* —   [for rewards]

לִשְׁמֹעַ אֶל הָרִנָּה וְאֶל הַתְּפִלָּה.

《 [our] prayer. 〈 and to 〈 [our] song 〈 to 〈 O [that You]
   of praise   listen

CONGREGATION, THEN *CHAZZAN:*

מָרוֹם, אִם עָצְמוּ פִּשְׁעֵי קְהָלֶךָ,

《 of Your 〈 have the 〈 become more 〈 if 《 O Exalted
congregation,   willful sins   numerous   One,

נָא שַׂגְּבֵם מֵאוֹצָר הַמּוּכָן בִּזְבוּלֶךָ,

《 in Your 〈 that is 〈 from the 〈 sustain 〈 please,
heavens.   prepared   repository   them

עָדֶיךָ לָחֹן חִנָּם, בָּאִים אֵלֶיךָ,[2]

《 to You — 〈 they come 〈 gratis 〈 to be grant- 〈 Unto
     ed [reward]   You

לִשְׁמֹעַ אֶל הָרִנָּה וְאֶל הַתְּפִלָּה.

《 [our] prayer. 〈 and to 〈 [our] song 〈 to 〈 O [that You]
   of praise   listen

CONGREGATION, THEN *CHAZZAN:*

פְּנֵה נָא אֶל הַתְּלָאוֹת וְאַל לַחֲטָאוֹת,

《 toward [their] 〈 and 〈 [their] 〈 toward 〈 please, 〈 Turn,
sins;   not   suffering,

צַדֵּק צוֹעֲקֶיךָ מַפְלִיא פְּלָאוֹת,

《 wondrous 〈 Who 〈 those who cry 〈 justify
deeds!   performs   to You,

---

(1) Some editions read מִמַּעְצָר, *from the [punishing]
constraints [imposed by their sins].* (2) Cf. *Psalms* 65:3.

כּוֹנַנְתָּ מֵאָז תֶּרֶף — *You prepared long ago
a remedy.* The Talmud states that seven
things were created before the world itself:
Torah, the concept of *teshuvah* (repentance), *Gan Eden, Gehinnom,* the Throne
of Glory, the *Beis HaMikdash,* and the
name of the Messiah (*Nedarim* 39b). Here
the *paytan* refers to *teshuvah,* the remedy
prepared long ago to remedy the ills of sin.

מֵאוֹצָר הַמְּנֻצָּר — *From the repository [for
rewards] that are reserved [for those without merits].* When God permitted Moses a
glimpse of His glory (see *Exodus* 33:17-23),
He displayed before Moses all of the celestial
storehouses in which are kept the rewards
to be meted out to the righteous. At each,
Moses asked its purpose. At one, God said,
"This treasure is for the Torah scholars";

קְשׁוֹב נָא חִנּוּנָם, אֱלֹהִים יהוה צְבָאוֹת,

《 Master of 〈 HASHEM, 〈 God, 《 to their 〈 please, 〈 Be
Legions —　　　　　　　　　　supplication,　　　　attentive,

לִשְׁמֹעַ אֶל הָרִנָּה וְאֶל הַתְּפִלָּה.

《 [our] prayer. 〈 and to 〈 [our] song 〈 to 〈 O [that You]
　　　　　　　　of praise　　　　　listen

CONGREGATION, THEN *CHAZZAN:*

רְצֵה עֲתִירָתָם בְּעָמְדָם בַּלֵּילוֹת,

《 in the night, 〈 as they stand 〈 toward their 〈 Show
　　　　　　　　　　　　entreaty　　favor

שְׁעֵה נָא בְרָצוֹן כְּקָרְבַּן כָּלִיל וְעוֹלוֹת,*1

《 and burnt- 〈 in its entirety 〈 as [if it were] a 〈 [to it] 〈 please, 〈 attend,
offerings.*　consumed　[meal-] offering　with favor

תַּרְאֵם נִסֶּיךָ עוֹשֵׂה עוֹשֶׂה גְדוֹלוֹת,²

《 of great 〈 O Doer 《 Your 〈 Show
deeds —　　　　　miracles,　them

לִשְׁמֹעַ אֶל הָרִנָּה וְאֶל הַתְּפִלָּה.

《 [our] prayer. 〈 and to 〈 [our] song 〈 to 〈 O [that You]
　　　　　　　　of praise　　　　　listen

ALL, WHILE STANDING:

אֵל מֶלֶךְ יוֹשֵׁב עַל כִּסֵּא רַחֲמִים, מִתְנַהֵג

〈 Who acts 《 of mercy, 〈 the throne 〈 on 〈 Who sits 〈 King 〈 O God,

---

(1) Cf. *Psalms* 51:21. (2) *Job* 5:9, 9:10.

at another, "This is for those who honor Torah scholars"; and at a third, "Here waits the reward for those who raise orphans as their own children." Finally, they reached the largest repository of all. God told Moses, "Those who perform *mitzvos* receive their just compensation from the appropriate repository. But for those who have not earned their own merits, I provide, by My grace, from this treasury" (*Tanchuma, Ki Sisa* 27; *Shemos Rabbah* 45:6).

כְּקָרְבַּן כָּלִיל וְעוֹלוֹת — *As [if it were] a [meal-] offering in its entirety consumed and burnt-offerings* [lit., *as a completely consumed offering and olah-offerings*]. Unlike other personal offerings, the flesh of which is eaten by the owner and/or the *Kohanim*, the *olah*-offering, often referred to as the burnt-offering, is totally

consumed by the Altar fire; no part of its flesh is eaten by either the *Kohanim* or the owner. This is usually referred to as כֻּלוֹ כָּלִיל, *consumed in its entirety*. The word כָּלִיל, then, refers to another Altar offering completely consumed by the fire, the flour-offering of a *Kohen*. Although a portion of the *minchah*, or flour-offering, of a non-*Kohen* was eaten by the *Kohanim*, the *minchah* of a *Kohen* was completely burnt (*Leviticus* 6:16). Alternatively, the stich "repeats the same idea in different words" (*Radak* to *Psalms* 51:21). Additionally, כָּלִיל can mean *completion*. It would then allude to the *tamid*, or continual-offering, which was the final Altar offering each day, and thus "completed" the day's service. In fact, the reading in some editions is תָּמִיד וְעוֹלוֹת, *the tamid-offering and olah-offerings.*

בַּחֲסִידוּת, מוֹחֵל עֲוֹנוֹת עַמּוֹ, מַעֲבִיר רִאשׁוֹן
‹ [sins] one ‹ Who removes ‹‹ of His people, ‹ the sins ‹ Who pardons ‹‹ with kindness,

רִאשׁוֹן,[1] מַרְבֶּה מְחִילָה לַחַטָּאִים וּסְלִיחָה לַפּוֹשְׁעִים,
‹‹ to willful sinners, ‹ and forgiveness ‹ to unintentional sinners ‹ pardon ‹ Who abun-dantly grants ‹‹ by one,

עֹשֶׂה צְדָקוֹת עִם כָּל בָּשָׂר וָרוּחַ, לֹא כְרָעָתָם
‹ in accord with their wickedness ‹ — not ‹‹ and spirit ‹ [beings of] flesh ‹ all ‹ with ‹ acts of generosity ‹ Who performs

תִּגְמוֹל. ❖ אֵל הוֹרֵיתָ לָּנוּ לוֹמַר שְׁלֹשׁ עֶשְׂרֵה,
‹‹ the Thirteen [Attributes of Mercy]; ‹ to recite ‹ us ‹ You taught ‹ O God, ‹‹ do You repay them!

וּזְכֹר לָנוּ הַיּוֹם בְּרִית שְׁלֹשׁ עֶשְׂרֵה, כְּמוֹ שֶׁהוֹדַעְתָּ
‹ You made known ‹ as ‹‹ of [these] Thirteen, ‹ the covenant ‹ today ‹ for us ‹ remember

לֶעָנָיו מִקֶּדֶם, כְּמוֹ שֶׁכָּתוּב, וַיֵּרֶד יהוה בֶּעָנָן
‹ in a cloud ‹ And HASHEM descended ‹‹ it is written: ‹ as ‹‹ in ancient times, ‹ to the humble one [Moses]

וַיִּתְיַצֵּב עִמּוֹ שָׁם, וַיִּקְרָא בְשֵׁם יהוה.[2]
‹‹ of HASHEM. ‹ with the Name ‹ and He called out ‹‹ there, ‹ with him ‹ and stood

CONGREGATION, THEN CHAZZAN:

וַיַּעֲבֹר יהוה עַל פָּנָיו וַיִּקְרָא:
‹‹ and proclaimed: ‹‹ [Moses'] ‹ before ‹ And HASHEM passed face,

CONGREGATION AND CHAZZAN RECITE LOUDLY AND IN UNISON:

יהוה, יהוה, אֵל, רַחוּם, וְחַנּוּן, אֶרֶךְ אַפַּיִם,
‹ to anger, ‹ Slow ‹‹ and Gracious, ‹ Compassionate ‹ God, ‹ HASHEM, ‹ HASHEM,

וְרַב חֶסֶד, וֶאֱמֶת, נֹצֵר חֶסֶד לָאֲלָפִים, נֹשֵׂא עָוֹן,
‹ of iniquity, ‹ Forgiver ‹‹ for thousands [of generations], ‹ of ‹ Preserver ‹‹ and kindness ‹‹ in Truth, ‹ and Kindness Abundant

וָפֶשַׁע, וְחַטָּאָה, וְנַקֵּה.[3] וְסָלַחְתָּ לַעֲוֹנֵנוּ וּלְחַטָּאתֵנוּ
‹‹ and our sins, ‹ our iniquities ‹ May You forgive ‹‹ and Who absolves. ‹ and inadvertent sin, ‹ willful sin,

וּנְחַלְתָּנוּ.[4] סְלַח לָנוּ אָבִינוּ כִּי חָטָאנוּ, מְחַל לָנוּ
‹ us, ‹ pardon ‹‹ we have sinned; ‹ for ‹‹ our Father, ‹ us, ‹ Forgive ‹‹ and make us Your heritage.

---

(1) *Rosh Hashanah* 17a. (2) *Exodus* 34:5. (3) 34:6-7. (4) 34:9.

מַלְכֵּנוּ כִּי פָשָׁעְנוּ. כִּי אַתָּה אֲדֹנָי טוֹב וְסַלָּח,
《 and 〈 are 〈 O Lord, 〈 You, 〈 For 《 we have 〈 for 《 our King,
forgiving, good willfully sinned.

וְרַב חֶסֶד לְכָל קֹרְאֶיךָ.[1]
《 who call 〈 to all 〈 kind 〈 and
upon You. abundantly

ALL:

זְכֹר רַחֲמֶיךָ* יהוה וַחֲסָדֶיךָ, כִּי מֵעוֹלָם הֵמָה.[2]
《 are 〈 eternal 〈 for 《 and Your 〈 HASHEM, 〈 Your 〈 Remember
they. kindnesses, mercies,*

זָכְרֵנוּ יהוה בִּרְצוֹן עַמֶּךָ, פָּקְדֵנוּ בִּישׁוּעָתֶךָ. זְכֹר*[3]
〈 Re- 《 with Your 〈 recall us 《 to Your 〈 when You 〈 HASHEM, 〈 Remem-
member* salvation. people; show favor ber us,

עֲדָתְךָ קָנִיתָ קֶּדֶם, גָּאַלְתָּ שֵׁבֶט נַחֲלָתֶךָ, הַר צִיּוֹן זֶה
〈 the one 〈 of 〈 the 《 of Your 〈 the 〈 You 《 long 〈 which You 〈 Your con-
[where] Zion, mountain heritage; tribe redeemed ago, acquired gregation,

שָׁכַנְתָּ בּוֹ.[4] זְכֹר יהוה חִבַּת יְרוּשָׁלַיִם, אַהֲבַת
〈 the love 《 of Jerusalem; 〈 the 〈 HASHEM, 〈 Remem- 《 there. 〈 You rested
affection ber, Your Presence

צִיּוֹן אַל תִּשְׁכַּח לָנֶצַח.[5] אַתָּה תָקוּם תְּרַחֵם צִיּוֹן כִּי
〈 for 《 to 〈 and show 〈 will arise 〈 You 《 forever. 〈 forget 〈 do not 〈 of
Zion, mercy Zion

עֵת לְחֶנְנָהּ, כִּי בָא מוֹעֵד.[6] זְכֹר יהוה לִבְנֵי אֱדוֹם
〈 of 〈 [to repay] 〈 HASHEM, 〈 Re- 《 the appointed time 〈 for 《 [there will come]
Edom the offspring, member, will have come. the time to favor her,

אֵת יוֹם יְרוּשָׁלָיִם,* הָאֹמְרִים עָרוּ עָרוּ עַד הַיְסוֹד
〈 the very 〈 to 〈 Destroy 《 Destroy! 《 [to repay] 《 of Jerusalem;* 〈 for the day
foundation those who say,

---

(1) *Psalms* 86:5. (2) 25:6. (3) Cf. 106:4. (4) 74:2. (5) This is not a Scriptural verse. (6) *Psalms* 102:14.

זְכֹר רַחֲמֶיךָ •§ — *Remember Your mer-cies.* This collection of verses, in slightly different orders and with some omissions or additions, begins the conclusion of the *Selichos* prayers on all fast days and on Yom Kippur. It has three themes: (a) a plea that God remember His ancient prom-ises to the Patriarchs and His covenant to have mercy on their offspring; (b) a plea that He end our exile and return us to a

rebuilt Temple; and (c) a plea for forgive-ness.

זְכֹר — *Remember.* The Psalmist asks God to remember three facts that show Israel to be His Chosen People, and thereby to be deserving of His redemption (*Malbim*).

אֵת יוֹם יְרוּשָׁלָיִם — *For the day of Jerusalem.* Remember when Rome, the offspring of Edom, destroyed Jerusalem.

בֵּהּ. זְכֹר לְאַבְרָהָם לְיִצְחָק וּלְיִשְׂרָאֵל עֲבָדֶיךָ,
《 Your servants, 〈 and for Israel, 〈 for Isaac, 〈 for Abraham, 〈 Remember 《 of it!

אֲשֶׁר נִשְׁבַּעְתָּ לָהֶם בָּךְ וַתְּדַבֵּר אֲלֵהֶם, אַרְבֶּה
〈 I shall increase 《 to them, 〈 and You said 《 by Your Being, 〈 to them 〈 You swore 〈 that

אֶת זַרְעֲכֶם כְּכוֹכְבֵי הַשָּׁמָיִם, וְכָל הָאָרֶץ הַזֹּאת אֲשֶׁר
〈 of which 〈 of this land 〈 and all 《 of the heavens; 〈 like the stars 〈 Your offspring

אָמַרְתִּי, אֶתֵּן לְזַרְעֲכֶם, וְנָחֲלוּ לְעֹלָם. זְכֹר לַעֲבָדֶיךָ
〈 of Your servants, 〈 Remember 《 [the merits] forever. 〈 and they will inherit it 〈 to your offspring, 〈 I will give 〈 I spoke

לְאַבְרָהָם לְיִצְחָק וּלְיַעֲקֹב, אַל תֵּפֶן אֶל קְשִׁי
〈 the stubbornness 〈 to 〈 pay attention 〈 do not 《 and of Jacob; 〈 of Isaac, 〈 of Abraham,

הָעָם הַזֶּה וְאֶל רִשְׁעוֹ וְאֶל חַטָּאתוֹ. זְכוֹר לָנוּ
〈 for us 〈 Remember 《 its sinfulness. 〈 and to 《 its wickedness, 〈 to 《 of this people,

בְּרִית אָבוֹת, כַּאֲשֶׁר אָמַרְתָּ: וְזָכַרְתִּי אֶת בְּרִיתִי
〈 My covenant 〈 And I will remember 《 You said: 〈 as 《 of the Patriarchs, 〈 the covenant

יַעֲקֹוב, וְאַף אֶת בְּרִיתִי יִצְחָק, וְאַף אֶת בְּרִיתִי
〈 My covenant 〈 and also 《 [with] Isaac, 〈 My covenant 〈 and also 《 [with] Jacob,

אַבְרָהָם אֶזְכֹּר, וְהָאָרֶץ אֶזְכֹּר.
《 I will remember. 〈 and the Land 《 I will remember; 〈 [with] Abraham

זְכוֹר לָנוּ* בְּרִית רִאשׁוֹנִים, כַּאֲשֶׁר אָמַרְתָּ: וְזָכַרְתִּי
〈 And I will remember 《 You said: 〈 as 《 of the ancient ones, 〈 the covenant 〈 for us* 〈 Remember

לָהֶם בְּרִית רִאשׁוֹנִים, אֲשֶׁר הוֹצֵאתִי אֹתָם מֵאֶרֶץ
〈 from the land 〈 I took them out 〈 that 《 of the ancient ones, 〈 the covenant 〈 for them

מִצְרַיִם לְעֵינֵי הַגּוֹיִם, לִהְיוֹת לָהֶם לֵאלֹהִים, אֲנִי
〈 I am 《 a God; 〈 to them 〈 to be 《 of the nations, 〈 in the very sight 〈 of Egypt

---

(1) *Psalms* 137:7. (2) *Exodus* 32:13. (3) *Deuteronomy* 9:27. (4) *Leviticus* 26:42.

§⇐ **זְכוֹר לָנוּ** — *Remember for us.* In some editions of *Selichos*, the verses of this sup- plication appear in a different order.

יהוה.‎1 עֲשֵׂה עִמָּנוּ כְּמָה שֶׁהִבְטַחְתָּנוּ: וְאַף גַּם

⟨ all ⟨ And ⟪ You promised us: ⟨ as ⟨ with us ⟨ Do ⟪ HASHEM.
despite

זֹאת* בִּהְיוֹתָם בְּאֶרֶץ אֹיְבֵיהֶם, לֹא מְאַסְתִּים וְלֹא

⟨ nor ⟨ despise them ⟨ I will ⟪ of their ⟨ in the land ⟨ when they ⟪ this,*
not enemies, will be

גְעַלְתִּים לְכַלֹּתָם לְהָפֵר בְּרִיתִי אִתָּם, כִּי אֲנִי יהוה

⟨ HASHEM, ⟨ I am ⟨ for ⟪ with ⟨ My ⟨ to annul ⟪ to destroy ⟨ abhor them
them, covenant them,

אֱלֹהֵיהֶם.‎2 הָשֵׁב שְׁבוּתֵנוּ וְרַחֲמֵנוּ, כְּמָה שֶׁכָּתוּב:

⟪ it is ⟨ as ⟪ and have ⟨ our captivity ⟨ Bring ⟪ their God.
written: mercy on us, back

וְשָׁב יהוה אֱלֹהֶיךָ אֶת שְׁבוּתְךָ וְרַחֲמֶךָ, וְשָׁב וְקִבֶּצְךָ

⟨ gather ⟨ and He ⟪ and He will ⟨ your captivity, ⟨ your ⟨ will ⟨ Then bring
you in will once have mercy God, HASHEM, back
again upon you,

מִכָּל הָעַמִּים אֲשֶׁר הֱפִיצְךָ יהוה אֱלֹהֶיךָ שָׁמָּה.‎3

⟪ thereto. ⟨ your God ⟨ has ⟨ scattered ⟨ that ⟨ the ⟨ from
HASHEM you peoples all

קַבֵּץ נִדָּחֵינוּ, כְּמָה שֶׁכָּתוּב: אִם יִהְיֶה נִדַּחֲךָ בִּקְצֵה

⟨ at the ⟨ your dispersed ⟨ If ⟨ it is written: ⟨ as ⟨ our ⟨ Gather
ends will be dispersed ones,

הַשָּׁמָיִם, מִשָּׁם יְקַבֶּצְךָ יהוה אֱלֹהֶיךָ, וּמִשָּׁם יִקָּחֶךָ.‎4

⟪ He will ⟨ and from ⟪ your God, ⟨ will ⟨ gather ⟨ from ⟪ of heaven,
take you. there HASHEM, you in there

מְחֵה פְשָׁעֵינוּ כָעָב וְכֶעָנָן, כְּמָה שֶׁכָּתוּב: מָחִיתִי

⟨ I have ⟪ it is written: ⟨ as ⟪ and like a ⟨ like a ⟨ our sins ⟨ Wipe
wiped away cloud, mist away

כָעָב פְּשָׁעֶיךָ וְכֶעָנָן חַטֹּאתֶיךָ, שׁוּבָה אֵלַי כִּי

⟨ for ⟨ to ⟨ return ⟪ your ⟨ and like ⟨ your willful ⟨ like a
Me, transgressions; a cloud sins, mist

גְאַלְתִּיךָ.*5 מְחֵה פְשָׁעֵינוּ לְמַעַנְךָ, כַּאֲשֶׁר אָמַרְתָּ:

⟪ You have ⟨ as ⟪ for Your ⟨ our sins ⟨ Wipe ⟪ I have
said: sake, away redeemed you.

(1) *Leviticus* 26:45. (2) 26:44. (3) 30:3. (4) 30:4. (5) *Isaiah* 44:22.

וְאַף גַּם זֹאת — *And despite all this.* Even though
Israel may have sinned so gravely that God
will destroy the Temple and exile the people,
He will not permit Israel to be destroyed.

כִּי גְאַלְתִּיךָ — *For I have redeemed you.*
Because God has redeemed Israel from past
exiles, we should repent, for we can be sure
He will redeem us again (*Radak*).

אָנֹכִי אָנֹכִי הוּא מֹחֶה פְשָׁעֶיךָ לְמַעֲנִי, וְחַטֹּאתֶיךָ לֹא

⟨ I shall ⟨ and your ⟪ for ⟨ your ⟨ Who wipes ⟨ am the ⟨ [only] I, ⟨ I,
not transgressions My sake, willful sins away One

אֶזְכֹּר.[1] הַלְבֵּן חֲטָאֵינוּ כַּשֶּׁלֶג וְכַצֶּמֶר, כְּמָה שֶׁכָּתוּב:

⟪ it is written: ⟨ as ⟪ and like wool, ⟨ like snow ⟨ our sins ⟨ Whiten ⟪ recall.

לְכוּ נָא וְנִוָּכְחָה, יֹאמַר יהוה, אִם יִהְיוּ חֲטָאֵיכֶם

⟨ your sins may be ⟨ Though ⟪ HASHEM. ⟨ says ⟪ let us reason ⟨ now, ⟨ Come,
together,

כַשָּׁנִים כַּשֶּׁלֶג יַלְבִּינוּ, אִם יַאְדִּימוּ כַתּוֹלָע, כַּצֶּמֶר

⟨ like [white] ⟪ as crimson, ⟨ they may ⟨ though ⟪ they will be ⟨ like ⟪ like
wool be red whitened; snow scarlet,

יִהְיוּ.[2] זְרֹק עָלֵינוּ מַיִם טְהוֹרִים וְטַהֲרֵנוּ, כְּמָה שֶׁכָּתוּב:

⟪ it is written: ⟨ as ⟪ and purify us, ⟨ pure water ⟨ upon us ⟨ Pour ⟪ they will
become.

וְזָרַקְתִּי עֲלֵיכֶם מַיִם טְהוֹרִים וּטְהַרְתֶּם, מִכֹּל

⟨ from ⟪ and you will ⟨ pure water ⟨ upon you ⟨ I shall pour
all become pure;

טֻמְאוֹתֵיכֶם וּמִכָּל גִּלּוּלֵיכֶם אֲטַהֵר אֶתְכֶם.[3] רַחֵם

⟨ Have ⟪ you. ⟨ I will ⟨ your ⟨ and ⟨ your
mercy purify abominations from all contaminations

עָלֵינוּ וְאַל תַּשְׁחִיתֵנוּ, כְּמָה שֶׁכָּתוּב: כִּי אֵל רַחוּם

⟨ a merciful God ⟨ For ⟪ it is written: ⟨ as ⟪ destroy us, ⟨ and do not ⟨ on us

יהוה אֱלֹהֶיךָ, לֹא יַרְפְּךָ וְלֹא יַשְׁחִיתֶךָ, וְלֹא יִשְׁכַּח

⟨ will He ⟨ nor ⟪ will He ⟨ nor ⟨ relinquish ⟨ He will ⟪ your God; ⟨ is
forget destroy you, you not HASHEM,

אֶת בְּרִית אֲבֹתֶיךָ אֲשֶׁר נִשְׁבַּע לָהֶם.[4] מוֹל

⟨ Circumcise ⟪ to them. ⟨ He swore ⟨ which ⟨ with your forefathers, ⟨ the covenant

אֶת לְבָבֵנוּ* לְאַהֲבָה וּלְיִרְאָה אֶת שְׁמֶךָ, כְּמָה שֶׁכָּתוּב:

⟪ it is written: ⟨ as ⟪ Your Name, ⟨ and to fear ⟨ to love ⟨ our hearts*

וּמָל יהוה אֱלֹהֶיךָ אֶת לְבָבְךָ וְאֶת לְבַב זַרְעֶךָ,

⟪ of your ⟨ and the heart ⟨ your heart ⟨ HASHEM, your God,
offspring, will circumcise

(1) Isaiah 43:25. (2) 1:18. (3) Ezekiel 36:25. (4) Deuteronomy 4:31.

מוֹל אֶת לְבָבֵנוּ — *Circumcise our hearts.* A person's accumulation of sins builds a barrier of habits, self-justification, and materialism over his heart, making it very hard for him to experience love of God and Torah. When we try to repent, God helps by cutting away this barrier, thereby exposing the true inner yearning of our heart.

לְאַהֲבָה אֶת יהוה אֱלֹהֶיךָ, בְּכָל לְבָבְךָ וּבְכָל
⟨ and ⟨ your ⟨ with all ⟨ your God, ⟨ HASHEM, ⟨ to love
with all heart

נַפְשֶׁךָ, לְמַעַן חַיֶּיךָ.¹ הַמָּצֵא לָנוּ בְּבַקָּשָׁתֵנוּ, כְּמָה
⟨ as ≪ in our quest, ⟨ to us ⟨ Be ≪ you may ⟨ so that ≪ your soul,
accessible live.

שֶׁכָּתוּב: וּבִקַּשְׁתֶּם מִשָּׁם אֶת יהוה אֱלֹהֶיךָ וּמָצָאתָ,
≪ and you will ⟨ your God, ⟨ HASHEM, ⟨ from ⟨ And you ≪ it is written:
find [Him], there will seek

כִּי תִדְרְשֶׁנּוּ בְּכָל לְבָבְךָ וּבְכָל נַפְשֶׁךָ.²·• תְּבִיאֵנוּ אֶל
⟨ to ⟨ Bring us ≪ your soul. ⟨ and with ⟨ your ⟨ with ⟨ you search ⟨ when
all heart all Him out

הַר קָדְשֶׁךָ, וְשַׂמְּחֵנוּ בְּבֵית תְּפִלָּתֶךָ, כְּמָה שֶׁכָּתוּב:
≪ it is ⟨ as ≪ of Prayer, ⟨ in Your ⟨ and gladden ⟨ Your holy
written: House us mountain

וַהֲבִיאוֹתִים אֶל הַר קָדְשִׁי, וְשִׂמַּחְתִּים בְּבֵית תְּפִלָּתִי,
≪ of Prayer; ⟨ in My ⟨ and I will ≪ My holy ⟨ to ⟨ And I will bring
House gladden them mountain, them

עוֹלֹתֵיהֶם וְזִבְחֵיהֶם לְרָצוֹן עַל מִזְבְּחִי, כִּי בֵיתִי
⟨ My ⟨ for ≪ My Altar, ⟨ on ⟨ will find ⟨ and their feast- ⟨ their burnt-
House favor offerings offerings

בֵּית תְּפִלָּה יִקָּרֵא לְכָל הָעַמִּים.³
≪ nations. ⟨ for all ⟨ will be ⟨ of Prayer" ⟨ "a
called House

THE ARK IS OPENED.

CHAZZAN, THEN CONGREGATION:

שְׁמַע קוֹלֵנוּ* יהוה אֱלֹהֵינוּ, חוּס וְרַחֵם עָלֵינוּ,
≪ on us, ⟨ and have ⟨ have ≪ our God; ⟨ HASHEM, ⟨ our voice,* ⟨ Hear
compassion pity

וְקַבֵּל בְּרַחֲמִים וּבְרָצוֹן אֶת תְּפִלָּתֵנוּ.⁴
≪ our prayer. ⟨ and favor ⟨ with compassion ⟨ and accept

---

(1) *Deuteronomy* 30:6. (2) 4:29. (3) *Isaiah* 56:7. (4) From the weekday *Shemoneh Esrei*.

שְׁמַע קוֹלֵנוּ ❧ — *Hear our voice.* With the Ark opened and the congregation standing, these verses are recited aloud and passionately. Their recitation calls forth strong fervor and emotion in virtually all congregations. The theme expressed by this collection of verses is that we must rely upon God to desire our survival and, therefore, to help us come closer to Him through repentance. We acknowledge that we are unworthy, but we also declare that we wish to improve and will do so if God eases the

CHAZZAN, THEN CONGREGATION:

הֲשִׁיבֵנוּ יהוה אֵלֶיךָ וְנָשׁוּבָה, חַדֵּשׁ יָמֵינוּ כְּקֶדֶם.¹

《 as of old. 〈 our days 〈 renew 《 and we shall return, 〈 to You, 〈 HASHEM, 〈 Bring us back,

CHAZZAN, THEN CONGREGATION:

אֲמָרֵינוּ הַאֲזִינָה יהוה, בִּינָה הֲגִיגֵנוּ.²

《 our thoughts. 〈 perceive 《 HASHEM; 〈 hear, 〈 Our words

THE FOLLOWING VERSE IS RECITED QUIETLY:

יִהְיוּ לְרָצוֹן אִמְרֵי פִינוּ וְהֶגְיוֹן לִבֵּנוּ לְפָנֶיךָ,

《 before You, 《 of our heart — 〈 and the thoughts 〈 of our mouth 〈 — the expressions 《 find favor 〈 May they

יהוה צוּרֵנוּ וְגֹאֲלֵנוּ.³

《 and our Redeemer. 〈 our Rock 〈 HASHEM,

CHAZZAN, THEN CONGREGATION:

אַל תַּשְׁלִיכֵנוּ מִלְּפָנֶיךָ, וְרוּחַ קָדְשְׁךָ אַל תִּקַּח מִמֶּנּוּ.⁴

《 from us. 〈 take 〈 do not 〈 of Your Holiness 〈 and the Spirit 《 from Your Presence, 〈 cast us away 〈 Do not

CHAZZAN, THEN CONGREGATION:

אַל תַּשְׁלִיכֵנוּ לְעֵת זִקְנָה, כִּכְלוֹת כֹּחֵנוּ אַל תַּעַזְבֵנוּ.⁵

《 forsake us not. 〈 does our strength, 〈 when fail 《 of old 〈 in time 〈 age; 〈 cast us away 〈 Do not

ALL CONTINUE (SOME CONGREGATIONS RECITE THE NEXT VERSE RESPONSIVELY):

אַל תַּעַזְבֵנוּ יהוה, אֱלֹהֵינוּ אַל תִּרְחַק מִמֶּנּוּ.⁶

《 from us. 〈 be not distant 〈 our God, 《 O HASHEM; 〈 Forsake us not,

עֲשֵׂה עִמָּנוּ אוֹת לְטוֹבָה, וְיִרְאוּ שׂוֹנְאֵינוּ וְיֵבֹשׁוּ,

《 and be ashamed, 〈 may our enemies 〈 so that see it 《 for good; 〈 a sign 〈 for us 〈 Display

כִּי אַתָּה יהוה עֲזַרְתָּנוּ וְנִחַמְתָּנוּ.⁷ כִּי לְךָ יהוה

〈 HASHEM, 〈 for 〈 Because 《 and consoled us. 〈 will have helped us 〈 HASHEM, 〈 You, 〈 for

הוֹחָלְנוּ, אַתָּה תַעֲנֶה אֲדֹנָי אֱלֹהֵינוּ.⁸

《 our God. 〈 O Lord, 〈 will answer, 〈 You 《 do we wait;

THE ARK IS CLOSED.

---

(1) *Lamentations* 5:21. (2) Cf. *Psalms* 5:2. (3) Cf. 19:15.
(4) 51:13. (5) Cf. 71:9. (6) Cf. 38:22. (7) Cf. 86:17. (8) Cf. 38:16.

---

way for us to come back to Him. Therefore, though we are old and "worn out" in terms of our spiritual freshness, we implore God not to cast us off.

EACH INDIVIDUAL CONTINUES UNTIL THE END OF *SELICHOS*.

CONFESSION / וִדּוּי

**DURING THE RECITATION OF THE וִדּוּי, *CONFESSION*, STAND WITH
HEAD AND BODY SLIGHTLY BOWED, IN SUBMISSIVE CONTRITION.**

אֱלֹהֵֽינוּ וֵאלֹהֵי אֲבוֹתֵֽינוּ, תָּבֹא לְפָנֶֽיךָ תְּפִלָּתֵֽנוּ,¹

《 may our prayer, 〈 before You 〈 come 《 of our forefathers, 〈 and the God 〈 Our God

וְאַל תִּתְעַלַּם מִתְּחִנָּתֵֽנוּ,² שֶׁאֵין אָֽנוּ עַזֵּי פָנִים

〈 faced 〈 so brazen- 〈 For we are not 《 our supplication. 〈 ignore 〈 and do not

וּקְשֵׁי עֹֽרֶף, לוֹמַר לְפָנֶֽיךָ יהוה אֱלֹהֵֽינוּ וֵאלֹהֵי

〈 and the God 〈 our God, 〈 HASHEM, 《 before You, 〈 as to say 〈 necked 〈 and stiff-

אֲבוֹתֵֽינוּ, צַדִּיקִים אֲנַֽחְנוּ וְלֹא חָטָֽאנוּ, אֲבָל אֲנַֽחְנוּ

〈 we 《 —for 《 sinned 〈 and 〈 we are, 〈 that 《 of our
　　　indeed,　　　　　have not　　　　righteous　forefathers,

וַאֲבוֹתֵֽינוּ חָטָֽאנוּ.³

《 have sinned. 〈 and our forefathers

**STRIKE THE LEFT SIDE OF THE CHEST WITH THE RIGHT FIST WHILE RECITING
EACH OF THE SINS OF THE FOLLOWING CONFESSIONAL LITANY:**

אָשַֽׁמְנוּ, בָּגַֽדְנוּ, גָּזַֽלְנוּ, דִּבַּֽרְנוּ דֹֽפִי. הֶעֱוִֽינוּ,

《 We have com- 《 slander. 〈 we have 《 we have 《 we have 《 We have been
　mitted iniquity;　　　　spoken　robbed;　betrayed;　　guilty;

וְהִרְשַֽׁעְנוּ, זַֽדְנוּ, חָמַֽסְנוּ, טָפַֽלְנוּ שֶֽׁקֶר. יָעַֽצְנוּ

〈 We have 《 false 〈 we have 《 we have 《 we have sinned 《 we have commit-
given advice　accusations.　made　extorted;　willfully;　ted wickedness;

רָע, כִּזַּֽבְנוּ, לַֽצְנוּ, מָרַֽדְנוּ, נִאַֽצְנוּ, סָרַֽרְנוּ,

《 we have 《 we have provoked 《 we have 《 we have 《 we have been 《 that is
　strayed;　[God's anger];　rebelled;　scorned;　deceitful;　bad;

עָוִֽינוּ, פָּשַֽׁעְנוּ, צָרַֽרְנוּ, קִשִּֽׁינוּ עֹֽרֶף. רָשַֽׁעְנוּ,

《 We have 《 our 〈 we have 《 we have caused 《 we have sinned 《 we have been
been wicked;　necks.　stiffened　distress;　rebelliously;　iniquitous;

שִׁחַֽתְנוּ, תִּעַֽבְנוּ, תָּעִֽינוּ, תִּעְתָּֽעְנוּ.

《 we have 《 we have 《 we have 《 we have
　scoffed.　gone astray;　committed　been corrupt;
　　　　　　　　　　abominations;

סַֽרְנוּ מִמִּצְוֹתֶֽיךָ וּמִמִּשְׁפָּטֶֽיךָ הַטּוֹבִים, וְלֹא שָֽׁוָה

〈 worth- 〈 and it 《 that are 〈 and from 〈 from Your 〈 We have
　while　was not　good,　Your laws　commandments　turned away

---

(1) Cf. *Psalms* 88:3. (2) Cf. 55:2. (3) Cf. 106:6, *Jeremiah* 3:25.

1. לָנוּ. וְאַתָּה צַדִּיק עַל כָּל הַבָּא עָלֵינוּ, כִּי אֱמֶת

⟨ truth- ⟨ for ⟨ upon us, ⟨ that has ⟨ all ⟨ in ⟨ are ⟨ And You ⟪ for us.
fully   come   righteous

2. עָשִׂיתָ וַאֲנַחְנוּ הִרְשָׁעְנוּ.

⟪ have acted ⟨ while we ⟪ have You
wickedly.   acted,

אָשַׁמְנוּ מִכָּל עָם, בּֽשְׁנוּ מִכָּל דּוֹר, גָּלָה מִמֶּנּוּ

⟨ from ⟨ Departed ⟪ genera- ⟨ more ⟨ We have ⟪ people. ⟨ more than ⟨ We have
us   tion.   than any   been   any other   been guilty
     other   ashamed

מָשׂוֹשׂ, דָּוָה לִבֵּנוּ בַּחֲטָאֵינוּ, הֻחְבַּל אַוֵּינוּ, וְנִפְרַע

⟨ uncov- ⟪ was our de- ⟨ Seized ⟪ because of ⟨ is our ⟨ Sickened ⟪ has joy.
ered   sired [Temple],   our sins.   heart

פְּאֵרֵנוּ, זְבוּל בֵּית מִקְדָּשֵׁנוּ חָרַב בַּעֲוֹנֵינוּ, טִירָתֵנוּ

⟨ Our Palace ⟪ because of ⟨ has been ⟨ our Holy Temple ⟨ for [His] ⟪ was our
   our iniquities. destroyed   abode,   splendor;

הָיְתָה לְשַׁמָּה, יְפִי אַדְמָתֵנוּ לְזָרִים, כֹּחֵנוּ לְנָכְרִים.

⟪ [was given] ⟨ our ⟪ is controlled ⟨ of our ⟨ [Jerusalem,] ⟪ desolate. ⟨ has
to foreigners. wealth   by strangers,   Land   the beauty   become

וַעֲדַיִן לֹא שַׁבְנוּ מִטָּעוּתֵנוּ וְהֵיךְ נָעִיז פָּנֵינוּ וְנַקְשֶׁה

⟨ and ⟨ faced ⟨ can we be ⟨ So ⟪ from our ⟨ we have not ⟨ But still
stiffen   so brazen- how   willful errors. repented

עָרְפֵּנוּ, לוֹמַר לְפָנֶיךָ יהוה אֱלֹהֵינוּ וֵאלֹהֵי אֲבוֹתֵינוּ,

⟪ of our ⟨ and the ⟨ our God ⟨ HASHEM, ⟨ before ⟨ so as to ⟨ our neck
forefathers, God   You,   say

צַדִּיקִים אֲנַחְנוּ וְלֹא חָטָאנוּ, אֲבָל אֲנַחְנוּ וַאֲבוֹתֵינוּ

⟨ and our ⟨ both we ⟨ for in ⟪ and we have ⟪ we are ⟨ that
fathers   truth,   not sinned,   righteous

3. חָטָאנוּ.

⟪ have sinned.

**STRIKE THE LEFT SIDE OF THE CHEST WITH THE RIGHT FIST WHILE RECITING
EACH OF THE SINS OF THE FOLLOWING CONFESSIONAL LITANY:**

אָשַׁמְנוּ, בָּגַדְנוּ, גָּזַלְנוּ, דִּבַּרְנוּ דְפִי. הֶעֱוִינוּ,

⟪ We have com- ⟪ slander. ⟨ we have ⟪ we have ⟪ we have ⟪ We have been
mitted iniquity;   spoken   robbed;   betrayed;   guilty;

---

(1) Cf. *Job* 33:27. (2) *Nehemiah* 9:33. (3) Cf. *Psalms* 106:6; *Jeremiah* 3:25.

וְהִרְשַׁעְנוּ, זַדְנוּ, חָמַסְנוּ, טָפַלְנוּ שֶׁקֶר. יָעַצְנוּ

< We have « false < we have « we have «we have sinned «we have commit-
given advice accusations. made extorted; willfully; ted wickedness;

רָע, כִּזַּבְנוּ, לַצְנוּ, מָרַדְנוּ, נִאַצְנוּ, סָרַרְנוּ,

« we have « we have provoked « we have « we have « we have been « that is
strayed; [God's anger]; rebelled; scorned; deceitful; bad;

עָוִינוּ, פָּשַׁעְנוּ, צָרַרְנוּ, קִשִּׁינוּ עֹרֶף. רָשַׁעְנוּ,

« We have « our < we have « we have « we have « we have
been wicked; necks. stiffened caused sinned been
distress; rebelliously; iniquitous;

שִׁחַתְנוּ, תִּעַבְנוּ, תָּעִינוּ, תִּעְתָּעְנוּ.

« we have « we have « we have « we have
scoffed. gone astray; committed been corrupt;
abominations;

סַרְנוּ מִמִּצְוֹתֶיךָ וּמִמִּשְׁפָּטֶיךָ הַטּוֹבִים, וְלֹא שָׁוָה

< worth- < and it « that are < and from < from Your < We have
while was not good, Your laws commandments turned away

לָנוּ.[1] וְאַתָּה צַדִּיק עַל כָּל הַבָּא עָלֵינוּ, כִּי אֶמֶת

< truth- < for « upon us, < that has < all < in < are < And You « for us.
fully come righteous

עָשִׂיתָ וַאֲנַחְנוּ הִרְשָׁעְנוּ.[2]

« have acted wickedly. < while we « have You acted,

לְעֵינֵנוּ עָשְׁקוּ עֲמָלֵנוּ, מְמֻשָּׁךְ וּמְמוֹרָט מִמֶּנּוּ,

« from < and cut off < [it was] « the product < have they < Before our
us. pulled away of our labor; stolen eyes

נָתְנוּ עֹלָם עָלֵינוּ, סָבַלְנוּ עַל שִׁכְמֵנוּ, עֲבָדִים

< Slaves « our < upon < we bore it « upon us, < their < They have
shoulders. yoke placed

מָשְׁלוּ בָנוּ, פֹּרֵק אֵין מִיָּדָם, צָרוֹת רַבּוֹת

< that are < Troubles « from their there < a « over < have
manifold hand. was not redeemer us; ruled

סְבָבוּנוּ, קְרָאֲנוּךָ יהוה אֱלֹהֵינוּ, רָחַקְתָּ מִמֶּנּוּ

< from < but You have dis- « our God, < HASHEM, < we called « have
us tanced Yourself upon You, surrounded us,

בַּעֲוֹנֵינוּ, שַׁבְנוּ מֵאַחֲרֶיךָ, תָּעִינוּ וְאָבַדְנוּ.

« we have « we have « from following < We have « because of
become lost. gone astray; after You; turned away our iniquities.

(1) Cf. *Job* 33:27. (2) *Nehemiah* 9:33.

וַעֲדַיִן לֹא שַׁבְנוּ מִטָּעוּתֵנוּ וְהֵיךְ נָעִיז פָּנֵינוּ וְנַקְשֶׁה

‹ and ‹ faced ‹ can we be ‹ So ≪ from our ‹ we have not ‹ But still
stiffen   so brazen-   how   willful errors.   repented

עָרְפֵּנוּ, לוֹמַר לְפָנֶיךָ יהוה אֱלֹהֵינוּ וֵאלֹהֵי אֲבוֹתֵינוּ,

≪ of our ‹ and the ‹ our God ‹ HASHEM, ‹ before ‹ so as to ‹ our neck
forefathers,   God   You,   say

צַדִּיקִים אֲנַחְנוּ וְלֹא חָטָאנוּ, אֲבָל אֲנַחְנוּ וַאֲבוֹתֵינוּ

‹ and our ‹ both we ‹ for in ≪ and we have ≪ we are ‹ that
fathers   truth,   not sinned,   righteous

חָטָאנוּ.[1]

≪ have sinned.

**STRIKE THE LEFT SIDE OF THE CHEST WITH THE RIGHT FIST WHILE RECITING
EACH OF THE SINS OF THE FOLLOWING CONFESSIONAL LITANY:**

אָשַׁמְנוּ, בָּגַדְנוּ, גָּזַלְנוּ, דִּבַּרְנוּ דֹפִי. הֶעֱוִינוּ,

≪ We have com- ≪ slander. ‹ we have ≪ we have ≪ we have ≪ We have been
mitted iniquity;   spoken   robbed;   betrayed;   guilty;

וְהִרְשַׁעְנוּ, זַדְנוּ, חָמַסְנוּ, טָפַלְנוּ שֶׁקֶר. יָעַצְנוּ

‹ We have ≪ false ‹ we have ≪ we have ≪ we have sinned ≪ we have commit-
given advice   accusations.   made   extorted;   willfully;   ted wickedness;

רָע, כִּזַּבְנוּ, לַצְנוּ, מָרַדְנוּ, נִאַצְנוּ, סָרַרְנוּ,

≪ we have ≪ we have provoked ≪ we have ≪ we have ≪ we have been ≪ that is
strayed;   [God's anger];   rebelled;   scorned;   deceitful;   bad;

עָוִינוּ, פָּשַׁעְנוּ, צָרַרְנוּ, קִשִּׁינוּ עֹרֶף. רָשַׁעְנוּ,

≪ We have ≪ our ‹ we have ≪ we have caused ≪ we have sinned ≪ we have been
been wicked;   necks.   stiffened   distress;   rebelliously;   iniquitous;

שִׁחַתְנוּ, תִּעַבְנוּ, תָּעִינוּ, תִּעְתָּעְנוּ.

≪ we have ≪ we have ≪ we have commit- ≪ we have
scoffed.   gone astray;   ted abominations;   been corrupt;

סַרְנוּ מִמִּצְוֹתֶיךָ וּמִמִּשְׁפָּטֶיךָ הַטּוֹבִים, וְלֹא שָׁוָה

‹ worth- ‹ and it ≪ that are ‹ and from ‹ from Your ‹ We have
while   was not   good,   Your laws   commandments   turned away

לָנוּ.[2] וְאַתָּה צַדִּיק עַל כָּל הַבָּא עָלֵינוּ, כִּי אֱמֶת

‹ truth- ‹ for ≪ upon us, ‹ that has ‹ all ‹ in ‹ are ‹ And You ≪ for us.
fully   come   righteous

עָשִׂיתָ וַאֲנַחְנוּ הִרְשָׁעְנוּ.[3]

≪ have acted wickedly. ‹ while we ≪ have You acted,

___

(1) Cf. *Psalms* 106:6; *Jeremiah* 3:25. (2) Cf. *Job* 33:27. (3) *Nehemiah* 9:33.

הִרְשַׁעְנוּ* וּפָשַׁעְנוּ, לָכֵן לֹא נוֹשָׁעְנוּ. וְתֵן בְּלִבֵּנוּ

⟨ in our ⟨ Place ⟪ been ⟨ we have ⟨ there- ⟪ and we have ⟨ We have acted
hearts   saved.   not   fore sinned rebelliously;   wickedly*

לַעֲזוֹב דֶּרֶךְ רֶשַׁע, וְחִישׁ לָנוּ יֶשַׁע, כַּכָּתוּב עַל יַד

⟨ the ⟨ by ⟨ as it is ⟪ salvation; ⟨ to us ⟨ and ⟪ of ⟨ the ⟨ [the will]
hand   written   hasten wickedness, path to abandon

נְבִיאֶךָ: יַעֲזֹב רָשָׁע דַּרְכּוֹ, וְאִישׁ אָוֶן מַחְשְׁבֹתָיו,

⟪ [abandon] ⟨ of ⟨ and ⟪ his way, ⟨ the wicked ⟨ Let ⟪ of Your
his thoughts; iniquity the man   one   abandon   prophet:

וְיָשֹׁב אֶל יהוה וִירַחֲמֵהוּ, וְאֶל אֱלֹהֵינוּ כִּי

⟨ for ⟨ our God, ⟨ and to ⟪ and He will have ⟨ HASHEM, ⟨ to ⟨ and let
                          compassion on him,   him return

יַרְבֶּה לִסְלוֹחַ.¹

⟪ forgiving. ⟨ He is abundantly

מְשִׁיחַ צִדְקֶךָ* אָמַר לְפָנֶיךָ, שְׁגִיאוֹת מִי יָבִין,

⟪ can ⟨ who ⟨ Mistakes ⟪ before You: ⟨ said ⟨ who is righteous ⟨ Your
discern?   [David]*   anointed one

מִנִּסְתָּרוֹת נַקֵּנִי.² נַקֵּנוּ יהוה אֱלֹהֵינוּ מִכָּל פְּשָׁעֵינוּ,

⟨ our sins ⟨ of all ⟨ our God, ⟨ HASHEM, ⟨ Cleanse ⟪ cleanse ⟨ From
                                              us,   me. unperceived faults

וְטַהֲרֵנוּ מִכָּל טֻמְאוֹתֵינוּ, וּזְרוֹק עָלֵינוּ מַיִם טְהוֹרִים

⟨ pure water ⟨ upon us ⟨ Pour ⟪ our contaminations. ⟨ of all ⟨ and purify us

וְטַהֲרֵנוּ, כַּכָּתוּב עַל יַד נְבִיאֶךָ: וְזָרַקְתִּי עֲלֵיכֶם

⟨ upon you ⟨ I shall pour ⟪ of Your ⟨ the ⟨ by ⟨ as it is ⟪ and purify us,
                          prophet: hand   written

מַיִם טְהוֹרִים וּטְהַרְתֶּם, מִכֹּל טֻמְאוֹתֵיכֶם וּמִכָּל

⟨ and ⟨ your ⟨ from ⟪ and you will ⟨ pure water
from all   contaminations all   become pure;

גִּלּוּלֵיכֶם אֲטַהֵר אֶתְכֶם.*³ עַמְּךָ וְנַחֲלָתְךָ, רְעֵבֵי

⟨ who ⟪ and Your ⟨ Your ⟪ you.* ⟨ I will purify ⟨ your
hunger   heritage, people   abominations

---

(1) Isaiah 55:7. (2) Psalms 19:13. (3) Ezekiel 36:25.

הִרְשַׁעְנוּ §— We have acted wickedly.
Though our deeds have been wicked, God
assures us that He does not desire the death
of the wicked, but their repentance.

מְשִׁיחַ צִדְקֶךָ §— Your anointed one who is
righteous [David]. These verses deal with

the theme of purity — becoming purified
from the spiritual contamination of sin, and
saying that God will remove from us the
contamination that our sins brought upon
us.

אֲטַהֵר אֶתְכֶם—I will purify you. God Himself,

טוּבְךָ, צְמֵאֵי חַסְדֶּךָ, תְּאֵבֵי יִשְׁעֶךָ, יַכִּירוּ וְיֵדְעוּ

❮ and ❮ — may they ❰ for Your ❮ and ❰ for Your ❮ who ❰ for Your
know recognize salvation who long kindness, thirst goodness,

כִּי לַיהוה אֱלֹהֵינוּ הָרַחֲמִים וְהַסְּלִיחוֹת.

❰ and forgiveness. ❮ belong mercy ❮ our God, ❮ to HASHEM, ❮ that

אֵל רַחוּם* שְׁמֶךָ, אֵל חַנּוּן שְׁמֶךָ,¹ בָּנוּ נִקְרָא שְׁמֶךָ.²

❰ is Your Name ❮ upon ❰ is Your ❮ Gracious God ❰ is Your ❮ Merciful God*
proclaimed, us Name, Name,

יהוה עֲשֵׂה לְמַעַן שְׁמֶךָ, עֲשֵׂה לְמַעַן אֲמִתָּךְ,* עֲשֵׂה³

❮ act ❰ Your truth;* ❮ for the ❰ Act ❮ Your ❮ for the ❮ act ❰ HASHEM,
sake of Name. sake of

לְמַעַן בְּרִיתָךְ, עֲשֵׂה לְמַעַן גָּדְלָךְ וְתִפְאַרְתָּךְ,*

❮ and Your ❮ Your ❮ for the ❮ act ❮ Your ❮ for the
splendor;* greatness sake of covenant; sake of

---

(1) Cf. *Exodus* 34:6. (2) Cf. *Deuteronomy* 28:10. (3) *Jeremiah* 14:7.

as it were, promises to cleanse Israel of its sins. This inspiring pledge makes clear to us that even when we have strayed far from Him, God continues to love us so much that He personally will remove the filth of our sins.

אֵל רַחוּם ❧— *Merciful God.* The first twenty-two of the verses that begin with עֲשֵׂה לְמַעַן, *act for the sake of,* list attributes of God following the order of the *aleph-beis.* The same list appears in the *Hoshana* service for the first day of Succos. These terms are based on Scriptural verses in most cases, and occasionally, on sayings of the Talmudic sages [see ArtScroll *Hoshanos* pp. 38-45 for a full commentary on each of these terms].

Although many editions of *Selichos* follow the vowelization that appears above, some vowelize the word endings differently; thus אֲמִתָּךְ becomes אֲמִתֶּךָ; and בְּרִיתָךְ becomes בְּרִיתֶךָ, etc. The meaning is unchanged.

אֲמִתָּךְ — *Your truth.* During the long and difficult period of exile, we have seen the fulfillment of the prophecy: וְתַשְׁלֵךְ אֱמֶת אַרְצָה, *It will throw truth to the earth* (*Daniel* 8:12). Truth has become ridiculed and despised, therefore we pray: *for the sake of Your truth.*

גָּדְלָךְ וְתִפְאַרְתָּךְ — *Your greatness and Your splendor.* This phrase is based on King David's last public declaration of God's praise: *To You,* HASHEM, *is the greatness* [גְּדֻלָה] *and the power* [גְּבוּרָה] *and the splendor* [תִּפְאֶרֶת] (*I Chronicles* 29:11).

The present stich deviates from the rest of this stanza by combining two attributes, instead of listing only one. This anomaly is compounded by the exclusion of גְּבוּרָה, *power,* which (a) fits the alphabetical scheme whereas תִּפְאֶרֶת, *splendor,* does not; and (b) follows immediately after *greatness* in King David's formula.

Bnei Yisas'char explains: Kabbalistically, the attributes of גְּדוּלָה גְּבוּרָה תִּפְאֶרֶת, *greatness, power,* and *splendor,* are equivalent to חֶסֶד דִּין אֱמֶת, *kindness, justice,* and *mercy,* respectively. The latter three are symbolic of the judges on the Heavenly Tribunal through which God passes judgment on His world, each one representing a different response to man's deeds. While Justice tends to strictness, Kindness and Mercy lean toward leniency. Hence, we beseech God, *"Act for the sake of Your Greatness/Kindness and Your Splendor/Mercy"* — the attributes of compassion which outweigh the severity of Power/Justice.

עֲשֵׂה לְמַעַן דָּתָךְ,* עֲשֵׂה לְמַעַן הוֹדֶךָ,* עֲשֵׂה
‹ act ‹‹ Your for the ‹ act ‹‹ Your for the ‹ act
glory;* sake of Law;* sake of

לְמַעַן וְעוּדָךְ,* עֲשֵׂה לְמַעַן זִכְרָךְ,*[1] עֲשֵׂה לְמַעַן
‹ for the ‹ act ‹‹ Your for the ‹ act ‹‹ Your Meeting ‹ for the
sake of remembrance;* sake of House;* sake of

חַסְדָּךְ,[2] עֲשֵׂה לְמַעַן טוּבָךְ, עֲשֵׂה לְמַעַן יִחוּדָךְ,
‹‹ Your for the ‹ act ‹‹ Your for the ‹ act ‹‹ Your
Oneness; sake of goodness; sake of kindness;

עֲשֵׂה לְמַעַן כְּבוֹדָךְ, עֲשֵׂה לְמַעַן לִמּוּדָךְ,*[3] עֲשֵׂה
‹ act ‹‹ Your for the ‹ act ‹‹ Your honor; for the ‹ act
students;* sake of sake of

לְמַעַן מַלְכוּתָךְ,* עֲשֵׂה לְמַעַן נִצְחָךְ,* עֲשֵׂה לְמַעַן
‹ for the ‹ act ‹‹ Your eternal ‹ for the ‹ act ‹‹ Your kingship;* ‹ for the
sake of [Name];* sake of sake of

---

(1) Cf. *Exodus* 3:15. (2) *Psalms* 6:5. (3) Cf. *Isaiah* 54:13.

דָּתָךְ ... הוֹדֶךָ — *Your Law ... Your glory.* Law refers to the Torah; *glory* to the *Beis HaMikdash.* The *Zohar* relates the destruction of the Holy Temple to the defilement of God's הוֹד, *glory.* Both blows, the destruction and the defilement, can be remedied through the same medium. Only through study of Torah can God's glory be restored; and only through study of Torah can the Holy Temple be rebuilt. Thus the juxtaposition of דָּתָךְ, *Your Law,* the Torah, with הוֹדֶךָ, *Your glory,* the Temple.

וְעוּדָךְ — *Your Meeting House.* This is another allusion to the Holy Temple where the *Shechinah* and Israel came together.

זִכְרָךְ — *Your remembrance.* Moses asked of God: *When I come to the Children of Israel and say to them, "The God of your ancestors has sent me to you," and they will respond, "What is His Name?" — what shall I say to them?*

God replied: "HASHEM, God of your ancestors ... זֶה שְּׁמִי, *This is My Name eternally, ...* וְזֶה זִכְרִי, *and this is My remembrance in every generation"* (*Exodus* 3:13,15).

לִמּוּדָךְ — *Your students.* In the World to Come, Israel shall be taught Torah directly by God, as the prophets declare: *All your children shall be* לִמּוּדֵי ה', *students of HASHEM* (*Isaiah* 54:13). Just as God is eternal so is His [direct] teaching eternal. Torah taught in this way can never be forgotten (*Yalkut Shimoni II* 479).

מַלְכוּתָךְ — *Your kingship.* On Rosh Hashanah, just before reciting the *Kaddish* before *Mussaf,* R' Levi Yitzchak of Berditchev would cry out: The czar of Russia claims that the world is his; so it is that every monarch claims possession of the world. But we, Your Jewish nation, say, יִתְגַּדֵּל וְיִתְקַדֵּשׁ ..., *Grow exalted and be sanctified may His Name that is great, in the world ...* וְיַמְלִיךְ מַלְכוּתֵה, *and may He give reign to His Kingship.*

Likewise we pray for salvation which will lead to the day when HASHEM shall be King over the entire earth (*Zechariah* 14:9).

נִצְחָךְ — *Your eternal [Name].* The word also has many other meanings, several of which are accurate in the sense of this *piyut: strength, supervision, victory, triumph.*

סֽוֹדָךְ, עֲשֵׂה לְמַעַן **עֻזָּךְ,** עֲשֵׂה לְמַעַן **פְּאֵרָךְ,**
《 Your secret [revealed to those who fear You]; 〈 act 〈 for the sake of 《 Your power; 〈 act 〈 for the sake of 《 Your glory;

עֲשֵׂה לְמַעַן **צִדְקָתָךְ,** עֲשֵׂה לְמַעַן **קְדֻשָּׁתָךְ,** עֲשֵׂה
〈 act 《 Your righteousness; 〈 for the sake of 〈 act 《 Your sanctity; 〈 for the sake of 〈 act

לְמַעַן **רַחֲמֶיךָ** הָרַבִּים, עֲשֵׂה לְמַעַן **שְׁכִינָתָךְ,** עֲשֵׂה
〈 for the sake of 《 Your mercy 〈 that is abundant; 〈 act 〈 for the sake of 《 Your Divine Presence; 〈 act

לְמַעַן **תְּהִלָּתָךְ,** עֲשֵׂה לְמַעַן אוֹהֲבֶיךָ שׁוֹכְנֵי עָפָר,²
〈 for the sake of 《 Your praise; 〈 act 〈 for the sake of 〈 those who loved You 〈 who rest 《 in the dust;

עֲשֵׂה לְמַעַן **אַבְרָהָם** יִצְחָק וְיַעֲקֹב, עֲשֵׂה לְמַעַן
〈 for the sake of 〈 act 《 Abraham, 〈 Isaac, 〈 and Jacob; 《 for the sake of 〈 act

מֹשֶׁה וְאַהֲרֹן, עֲשֵׂה לְמַעַן **דָּוִד** וּשְׁלֹמֹה, עֲשֵׂה
〈 Moses 《 and Aaron; 〈 act 〈 for the sake of 〈 David 《 and Solomon; 〈 act

לְמַעַן **יְרוּשָׁלַיִם** עִיר **קָדְשֶׁךָ,³** עֲשֵׂה לְמַעַן **צִיּוֹן**
〈 for the sake of 〈 Jerusalem, 〈 the City 《 of Your Holiness; 〈 act 〈 for the sake of 〈 Zion,

מִשְׁכַּן **כְּבוֹדֶךָ,⁴** עֲשֵׂה לְמַעַן **שִׁמְמוֹת הֵיכָלֶךָ,⁵** עֲשֵׂה
〈 the abode 《 of Your glory; 〈 act 〈 for the sake of 《 the desolation 〈 of Your Temple; 〈 act

לְמַעַן **הֲרִיסוּת** מִזְבְּחֶךָ, עֲשֵׂה לְמַעַן **הֲרוּגִים** עַל
〈 for the sake of 〈 the devastation 《 of Your Altar; 〈 act 〈 for the sake of 〈 those killed 〈 for

שֵׁם **קָדְשֶׁךָ,** עֲשֵׂה לְמַעַן **טְבוּחִים** עַל **יִחוּדֶךָ,** עֲשֵׂה
〈 act 《 Your holy Name; 〈 for the sake of 〈 those slaughtered 〈 for 《 Your Oneness; 〈 act

לְמַעַן **בָּאֵי** בָאֵשׁ וּבַמַּיִם עַל **קִדּוּשׁ שְׁמֶךָ,** עֲשֵׂה לְמַעַן
〈 for the sake of 〈 those who entered 〈 fire 〈 and water 〈 for 《 of Your Name; sanctification 〈 act 〈 for the sake of

יוֹנְקֵי שָׁדַיִם⁷ שֶׁלֹּא **חָטָאוּ,** עֲשֵׂה לְמַעַן **גְּמוּלֵי חָלָב⁸**
〈 the [infants] sucking 〈 at the breast 《 who did not sin; 〈 act 〈 for the sake of 〈 the [babies] weaned 〈 from milk

---

(1) Cf. *Psalms* 25:14. (2) *Isaiah* 26:19. (3) Cf. *Daniel* 9:16,24. (4) *Psalms* 26:8.
(5) Cf. *Jeremiah* 51:26. (6) Cf. *Isaiah* 49:19. (7) *Joel* 2:16. (8) *Isaiah* 28:9.

שֶׁלֹא פָּשָׁעוּ, עֲשֵׂה לְמַעַן תִּינוֹקוֹת שֶׁל בֵּית רַבָּן,¹

‹ who ‹‹ transgress; ‹ act ‹ for the ‹ the children ‹ of ‹‹ their teachers'
did not　　　　　　　　　　sake of　　　　　　　　　　　　school;

עֲשֵׂה לְמַעַנְךָ אִם לֹא לְמַעֲנֵנוּ, עֲשֵׂה לְמַעַנְךָ וְהוֹשִׁיעֵנוּ.

act ‹ for Your sake ‹ not ‹ if ‹ for our sake; ‹‹ for our sake, ‹ act ‹ for Your sake ‹‹ and save us.

עֲנֵנוּ* יהוה עֲנֵנוּ, עֲנֵנוּ אֱלֹהֵינוּ עֲנֵנוּ, עֲנֵנוּ **אָבִינוּ**²

Answer ‹ HASHEM, ‹‹ answer ‹ answer ‹ our God, ‹ answer ‹‹ answer ‹ our
us;*　　　　　　us;　　us;　　　　　　　us;　　us;　　Father,

עֲנֵנוּ, עֲנֵנוּ **בּוֹרְאֵנוּ**³ עֲנֵנוּ, עֲנֵנוּ **גּוֹאֲלֵנוּ**⁴ עֲנֵנוּ עֲנֵנוּ

‹‹ answer ‹ answer ‹ our Creator, ‹ answer ‹‹ answer ‹ our ‹ answer ‹‹ answer
us;　　us;　　　　　　　　us;　　us;　　Redeemer,　us;　　us;

דּוֹרְשֵׁנוּ⁵ עֲנֵנוּ, עֲנֵנוּ **הָאֵל** הַנֶּאֱמָן⁶ עֲנֵנוּ, עֲנֵנוּ **וָתִיק**

‹ You Who ‹‹ answer ‹ answer ‹ God ‹ Who is ‹‹ answer ‹ answer ‹ stead-
searches us out, us;　　us;　　　　faithful,　　　us;　　us;　　fast

וְחָסִיד עֲנֵנוּ, עֲנֵנוּ **זַךְ** וְיָשָׁר⁷ עֲנֵנוּ, עֲנֵנוּ **חַי** וְקַיָּם⁸

‹ and kind ‹‹ answer ‹ answer ‹ pure ‹ and ‹ answer ‹‹ answer ‹ living ‹ and endur-
One,　　us;　　us;　　upright One　us;　　us;　　　　ing One,

עֲנֵנוּ, עֲנֵנוּ **טוֹב** וּמֵטִיב⁹ עֲנֵנוּ, עֲנֵנוּ **יוֹדֵעַ** יֵצֶר¹⁰ עֲנֵנוּ,

‹‹ answer ‹ answer ‹ good ‹ and bene- ‹ answer ‹‹ answer ‹ Knower ‹ of incli- ‹‹ answer
us;　　us;　　　ficent One,　　us;　　us;　　　nations,　　us;

עֲנֵנוּ **כּוֹבֵשׁ** כְּעָסִים עֲנֵנוּ, עֲנֵנוּ **לוֹבֵשׁ** צְדָקוֹת¹¹ עֲנֵנוּ,

‹ answer ‹ Suppressor ‹ of wrath, ‹‹ answer ‹‹ answer ‹ Donner ‹ of ‹ answer
us;　　　　　　　　　　us;　　us;　　　　righteousness,　us;

עֲנֵנוּ **מֶלֶךְ** מַלְכֵי הַמְּלָכִים¹² עֲנֵנוּ, עֲנֵנוּ **נוֹרָא** וְנִשְׂגָּב¹³

‹ answer ‹ King ‹ over ‹ of kings, ‹‹ answer ‹ answer ‹ awesome ‹ and power-
us,　　　　kings　　　　　　us;　　us;　　　　　　ful One,

עֲנֵנוּ, עֲנֵנוּ **סוֹלֵחַ** וּמוֹחֵל עֲנֵנוּ, עֲנֵנוּ **עוֹנֶה** בְּעֵת

‹‹ answer ‹ answer ‹ You Who ‹ and ‹‹ answer ‹ answer ‹ You Who ‹ in time
us;　　us;　　forgives ‹ pardons,　us;　　us;　　answers

צָרָה¹⁴ עֲנֵנוּ, עֲנֵנוּ **פּוֹדֶה** וּמַצִּיל¹⁵ עֲנֵנוּ, עֲנֵנוּ **צַדִּיק**

‹ of ‹‹ answer ‹ answer ‹ Redeemer ‹ and ‹‹ answer ‹ answer ‹ righteous
distress,　us;　　us;　　　　Rescuer,　　us;　　us;

---

(1) *Shabbos* 119b. (2) *Isaiah* 64:7. (3) Cf. 43:1. (4) 47:4. (5) Cf. *Ezekiel* 34:11. (6) *Deuteronomy* 7:9.
(7) *Job* 8:6; cf. *Proverbs* 20:11. (8) Cf. *Daniel* 6:27. (9) Cf. *Psalms* 119:68. (10) Cf. 103:14.
(11) Cf. *Isaiah* 59:17. (12) *Ethics of the Fathers* 3:1. (13) *Psalms* 47:3; 148:13.
(14) Cf. *Isaiah* 49:8; *Psalms* 37:39. Alternate text: בְּעֵת רָצוֹן, *in time of favor*. (15) Cf. 34:23,18.

◆§ עֲנֵנוּ — *Answer us.* This *piyut* refers to 　　　and attributes based mostly on Scriptural
God in an alphabetical listing of Names 　　　verses and, in some instances, on Talmudic

וְיָשָׁר[1] עֲנֵנוּ, עֲנֵנוּ קָרוֹב לְקוֹרְאָיו[2] עֲנֵנוּ, עֲנֵנוּ קָשֶׁה

⟨ You Who ⟨answer ⟪answer⟨ to those who ⟨ He Who ⟨ answer ⟪ answer ⟨ and up-
with difficulty us, us; call upon Him, is close us, us; right One,

לִכְעוֹס[3] עֲנֵנוּ, עֲנֵנוּ רַךְ לִרְצוֹת[4] עֲנֵנוּ, עֲנֵנוּ רַחוּם

⟨ merciful ⟨ answer ⟪ answer ⟨ appeased, ⟨ You Who ⟨answer ⟪ answer ⟨ becomes
us, us; are easily us, us; angry,

וְחַנּוּן[5] עֲנֵנוּ, עֲנֵנוּ שׁוֹמֵעַ אֶל אֶבְיוֹנִים[6] עֲנֵנוּ, עֲנֵנוּ

⟨answer ⟪answer⟨ the destitute, ⟨ to ⟨ You Who ⟨ answer ⟨answer ⟨ and gra-
us, us; listens us, us; cious One,

תּוֹמֵךְ תְּמִימִים עֲנֵנוּ, עֲנֵנוּ אֱלֹהֵי אֲבוֹתֵינוּ עֲנֵנוּ,

⟪answer ⟨ of our ⟨ God ⟨ answer ⟪ answer ⟨ the ⟨ You Who
us; forefathers, us, us; wholesome, supports

עֲנֵנוּ אֱלֹהֵי אַבְרָהָם[7] עֲנֵנוּ, עֲנֵנוּ פַּחַד יִצְחָק עֲנֵנוּ,

⟪ answer ⟨ of Isaac, ⟨ Awesome ⟨answer ⟪ answer ⟨ of Abraham, ⟨ God ⟨ answer
us; One us, us; us,

עֲנֵנוּ אֲבִיר יַעֲקֹב[8] עֲנֵנוּ, עֲנֵנוּ עֶזְרַת הַשְּׁבָטִים עֲנֵנוּ,

⟪answer ⟨ of the tribes, ⟨ Helper ⟨ answer ⟪ answer ⟨ of Jacob,⟨ Mighty ⟨ answer
us; us, us; One us,

עֲנֵנוּ מִשְׂגָּב אִמָּהוֹת עֲנֵנוּ, עֲנֵנוּ עוֹנֶה בְּעֵת רָצוֹן[9] עֲנֵנוּ,

⟪answer ⟨ of favor, ⟨ in a ⟨ You Who ⟨ answer ⟪ answer ⟨ of the ⟨ Stronghold ⟨ answer
us; time answers us, us; Matriarchs, us,

עֲנֵנוּ אֲבִי יְתוֹמִים[10] עֲנֵנוּ, עֲנֵנוּ דַּיַּן אַלְמָנוֹת[10] עֲנֵנוּ.

⟪ answer ⟨ of widows, ⟨ Judge ⟨ answer ⟪answer ⟨ of orphans, ⟨ Father ⟨ answer
us. us, us; us,

מִי שֶׁעָנָה* לְאַבְרָהָם* אָבִינוּ בְּהַר הַמּוֹרִיָּה[11]

⟪ Moriah ⟨ on Mount ⟨ our father ⟨ Abraham* ⟨ Who answered* ⟨ He

הוּא יַעֲנֵנוּ.

⟪ answer ⟨ — may He
us. He

(1) *Deuteronomy* 32:4. (2) Cf. *Psalms* 145:18. (3) *Ethics of the Fathers* 5:14.
(4) Cf. 5:14. (5) *Exodus* 34:6. (6) *Psalms* 69:34. (7) *Genesis* 31:42. (8) *Isaiah* 49:26.
(9) Cf. 49:8; *Psalms* 69:14. Alternate text: בְּעֵת צָרָה, *in time of distress.* (10) 68:6. (11) *Genesis* 22:12.

and Midrashic statements.

❧ **מִי שֶׁעָנָה** — *He Who answered.* Whenever *Eretz Yisrael* is afflicted with a drought, the *beis din* declares a series of public fast days devoted to prayer and repentance. The special supplications of the day include seven blessings, each of which contains the plea, "He Who answered … may He answer us" (*Taanis* 15a). This litany, in a greatly ex-

panded version, has been appended to the *Selichos* prayers. In this commentary, we will give a very brief description of the particular event to which the verse refers (except for those that are very well known) and a Scriptural reference for each of them.

אַבְרָהָם — *Abraham* was the first Jew to be saved by God's intervention, when he was rescued from Nimrod's attempt to burn him

מִי שֶׁעָנָה לְיִצְחָק בְּנוֹ כְּשֶׁנֶּעֱקַד עַל גַּבֵּי הַמִּזְבֵּחַ[1]
《 of the altar 〈 top 〈 on 〈 when he was bound 〈 his son 〈 Isaac 〈 Who answered 〈 He

הוּא יַעֲנֵנוּ.
《 answer 〈 — may
us.　　　He

מִי שֶׁעָנָה לְיַעֲקֹב* בְּבֵית אֵל[2]
《　　 in Beth-el 〈 Jacob* 〈 Who 〈 He
answered

הוּא יַעֲנֵנוּ.
《 answer 〈 — may
us.　　　He

מִי שֶׁעָנָה לְיוֹסֵף בְּבֵית הָאֲסוּרִים[3]
《　 in the prison 〈 Joseph 〈 Who 〈 He
answered

הוּא יַעֲנֵנוּ.
《 answer 〈 — may
us.　　　He

מִי שֶׁעָנָה לַאֲבוֹתֵינוּ עַל יַם סוּף[4]
《 of 〈 the 〈 at 〈 our forefathers 〈 Who 〈 He
Reeds　Sea　　　　　　 answered

הוּא יַעֲנֵנוּ.
《 answer 〈 — may
us.　　　He

מִי שֶׁעָנָה לְמֹשֶׁה* בְּחוֹרֵב[5]
《 in Horeb 〈 Moses* 〈 Who 〈 He
answered

הוּא יַעֲנֵנוּ.
《 answer 〈 — may
us.　　　He

מִי שֶׁעָנָה לְאַהֲרֹן* בַּמַּחְתָּה[6]
《 with the fire-pan 〈 Aaron* 〈 Who 〈 He
answered

הוּא יַעֲנֵנוּ.
《 answer 〈 — may
us.　　　He

מִי שֶׁעָנָה לְפִינְחָס* בְּקוּמוֹ מִתּוֹךְ הָעֵדָה[7]
《the congregation 〈 from 〈 when he 〈 Phinehas* 〈 Who 〈 He
amid　　arose　　　　　　 answered

הוּא יַעֲנֵנוּ.
《 answer 〈 — may
us.　　　He

מִי שֶׁעָנָה לִיהוֹשֻׁעַ* בַּגִּלְגָּל[8]
《 in Gilgal 〈 Joshua* 〈 Who 〈 He
answered

הוּא יַעֲנֵנוּ.
《 answer 〈 — may
us.　　　He

---

(1) *Genesis* 22:12. (2) 35:3. (3) 39:21. (4) *Exodus* Ch. 14. (5) 17:6,11; *Deuteronomy* 9:19.
(6) *Numbers* 17:11-13. (7) 25:7-13. (8) *Joshua* 6:1-20; 7:6-15; 10:12-14.

to death. At a later date, on Mount Moriah, when Abraham bound Isaac on the altar, he prayed that God would always come to the defense of the Jewish people in times of future danger (*Yerushalmi, Taanis* 2:4).

יַעֲקֹב — *Jacob's* vision of the angels on a ladder, and God's promise to protect him, took place at Beth-el (*Genesis* 28:13-19).

מֹשֶׁה — *Moses* prayed in Horeb that Israel not be destroyed for worshiping the Golden

Calf (*Deuteronomy* 9:19,26).

אַהֲרֹן — *Aaron.* When Israel was struck by a plague, Moses commanded Aaron to take a fire-pan of incense and use it to bring atonement for the people (*Numbers* 17:11-13).

פִּינְחָס — *Phinehas* arose from among the people and single-handedly dealt with the wrongdoers whose lewd acts brought a plague upon Israel (*Numbers* 25:7).

יְהוֹשֻׁעַ — *Joshua* was encamped in Gilgal

מִי שֶׁעָנָה לִשְׁמוּאֵל* בַּמִּצְפָּה[1] הוּא יַעֲנֵנוּ.

‹ He › Who answered › Samuel* › in Mizpah ≪ — may He › answer us. ≫

מִי שֶׁעָנָה לְדָוִד וּשְׁלֹמֹה בְנוֹ בִּירוּשָׁלָיִם[2] הוּא יַעֲנֵנוּ.

‹ He › Who answered › David › and Solomon › his son ≪ in Jerusalem ≪ — may He › answer us. ≫

מִי שֶׁעָנָה לְאֵלִיָּהוּ בְּהַר הַכַּרְמֶל[3] הוּא יַעֲנֵנוּ.

‹ He › Who › Elijah › on Mount › Carmel ≪ — may He › answer us. ≫

מִי שֶׁעָנָה לֶאֱלִישָׁע* בִּירִיחוֹ[4] הוּא יַעֲנֵנוּ.

‹ He › Who › Elisha* › in Jericho ≪ — may He › answer us. ≫

מִי שֶׁעָנָה לְיוֹנָה בִּמְעֵי הַדָּגָה[5] הוּא יַעֲנֵנוּ.

‹ He › Who › Jonah › in the innards › of the fish ≪ — may He › answer us. ≫

מִי שֶׁעָנָה לְחִזְקִיָּהוּ* מֶלֶךְ יְהוּדָה בְּחָלְיוֹ[6]

‹ He › Who answered › Hezekiah,* › king › of Judah, › in his illness ≫

הוּא יַעֲנֵנוּ.

‹ — may He › answer us. ≫

מִי שֶׁעָנָה לַחֲנַנְיָה* מִישָׁאֵל וַעֲזַרְיָה

‹ He › Who answered › Hananiah,* › Mishael, › and Azariah ›

בְּתוֹךְ כִּבְשַׁן הָאֵשׁ[7] הוּא יַעֲנֵנוּ.

‹ inside › the furnace › of fire ≪ — may He › answer us. ≫

מִי שֶׁעָנָה לְדָנִיֵּאל בְּגוֹב הָאֲרָיוֹת[8] הוּא יַעֲנֵנוּ.

‹ He › Who answered › Daniel › in the den › of lions ≪ — may He › answer us. ≫

(1) *I Samuel* 7:9. (2) *II Samuel* 7:5-16; 21:1,14; 24:25; *I Kings* 9:3. (3) 18:36-38. (4) *II Kings* 2:21. (5) *Jonah* 2:2-11. (6) *II Kings* 20:1-6; *Isaiah* 38:2-8. (7) *Daniel* 3:21-26. (8) 6:17-23.

when the miraculous conquest of Jericho took place (*Joshua* 6:20).

שְׁמוּאֵל — *Samuel* prayed at Mizpah for God's help against the Philistines (*I Samuel* 7:9).

אֱלִישָׁע — *Elisha*. At Jericho, Elijah's spirit of prophetic greatness descended upon his disciple Elisha (*II Kings* Ch. 2).

חִזְקִיָּהוּ — *Hezekiah* was told by the prophet Isaiah that he would die. Hezekiah prayed to God, Who responded with a promise that he would live another fifteen years (*II Kings* 20:1-6).

חֲנַנְיָה — *Hananiah* .... Nebuchadnezzar ordered that these three Jews (known in Babylonian as Shadrach, Mesach, and Abad Nego) be thrown into a furnace, but God saved them from the flames (*Daniel* 3:21-26).

מִי שֶׁעָנָה לְמָרְדְּכַי וְאֶסְתֵּר בְּשׁוּשַׁן הַבִּירָה¹
He ⟩ Who answered ⟩ Mordechai ⟩ and Esther ⟩ in Shushan ⟨ the capital ⟩

הוּא יַעֲנֵנוּ.
— may ⟩ answer ⟪
He   us.

מִי שֶׁעָנָה לְעֶזְרָא בַּגּוֹלָה*²
He ⟩ Who ⟩ Ezra ⟩ in the exile* ⟪
answered

הוּא יַעֲנֵנוּ.
— may ⟩ answer ⟪
He   us.

מִי שֶׁעָנָה לְכָל הַצַּדִּיקִים וְהַחֲסִידִים וְהַתְּמִימִים
He ⟩ Who answered ⟩ all ⟩ the righteous, ⟩ the devout, ⟩ the wholesome,

וְהַיְשָׁרִים
and the ⟪
upright

הוּא יַעֲנֵנוּ.
— may ⟩ answer ⟪
He   us.

רַחֲמָנָא דְּעָנֵי לַעֲנִיֵּי, עֲנֵינַן. רַחֲמָנָא דְּעָנֵי לִתְבִירֵי
Merciful One ⟩ Who ⟩ the poor, ⟪ answer ⟪ Who ⟩ Merciful One ⟩ those of
answers   us!   answers   broken

לִבָּא, עֲנֵינַן. רַחֲמָנָא דְּעָנֵי לְמַכִּיכֵי רוּחָא, עֲנֵינַן.
hearts, ⟪ answer ⟪ Merciful ⟩ Who ⟩ those of ⟩ spirit, ⟪ answer⟪
us!   One   answers   crushed   us!

רַחֲמָנָא עֲנֵינַן. רַחֲמָנָא חוּס. רַחֲמָנָא פְּרוֹק. רַחֲמָנָא
Merciful ⟩ answer ⟪ Merciful ⟩ have ⟪ Merciful ⟩ redeem! ⟪ Merciful ⟩
One,   us!   One,   pity!   One,   One,

שְׁזִיב. רַחֲמָנָא רְחַם עֲלָן, הַשְׁתָּא בַּעֲגָלָא וּבִזְמַן קָרִיב.
save! ⟪ Merciful ⟩ have ⟩ on us ⟪ — now, ⟩ swiftly, ⟩ and at ⟩ that comes⟪
One,   mercy   a time   soon.

---

(1) *Esther* Ch. 8. (2) *Ezra* 8:21-23.

עֶזְרָא בַּגּוֹלָה — *Ezra in the exile* decided to
ascend from Babylonia to *Eretz Yisrael*, and
God influenced King Darius to grant all of
Ezra's requests (*Ezra* 7:6).

נְפִילַת אַפַּיִם / Putting Down the Head

The act of נְפִילַת אַפַּיִם, *putting down
the head,* "burying" one's face in submissive supplication, is based on the actions of
Moses, Aaron, and Joshua, who fell on their
faces before God in times of stress and tragedy (*Numbers* 16:22; *Joshua* 7:6).
This passage is called *Tachanun* and is recited with the head down, resting on the left

arm, and preferably in a sitting position. The
head should not rest on the bare arm; rather,
the arm should be covered with a sleeve, *tallis*, or even a cloth. This posture is an indication of the feelings of despair and guilt that
combine with the undying hope that God's
mercy will rescue the supplicant no matter
how hopeless his plight. Since Joshua fell
on his face before the Holy Ark, the act of
falling on the face is done only in the presence of a Torah Scroll, i.e., an Ark containing a Torah Scroll. If a Torah is not present,
Tachanun is recited with the head held erect.

PUTTING DOWN THE HEAD / נפילת אפים

RECITE UNTIL יבשו רגע WITH THE HEAD RESTING ON THE LEFT ARM, PREFERABLY WHILE SEATED.

(וַיֹּאמֶר דָּוִד* אֶל גָּד, צַר לִי מְאֹד, נִפְּלָה נָּא בְיַד יהוה,

‹‹ of ‹ into the ‹ now ‹ Let us ‹‹ exceed- ‹ am I ‹ Dis- ‹‹(Gad, ‹ to ‹ (And David said*
HASHEM, hand fall ingly. tressed

כִּי רַבִּים רַחֲמָיו, וּבְיַד אָדָם אַל אֶפֹּלָה.[1]

‹‹ let me not fall.) ‹ but into human ‹‹ are His ‹ abundant ‹ for
hands mercies,

רַחוּם וְחַנּוּן* חָטָאתִי לְפָנֶיךָ. יהוה מָלֵא

‹ Who is full ‹ HASHEM, ‹‹ before You. ‹ I have sinned ‹ and gracious One,* ‹ O merciful

רַחֲמִים, רַחֵם עָלַי וְקַבֵּל תַּחֲנוּנָי.

‹‹ my supplications. ‹ and accept ‹ on me ‹ have mercy ‹‹ of mercy,

———— תהלים ו:ב-יא / Psalms 6:2-11 ————

יהוה, אַל בְּאַפְּךָ* תוֹכִיחֵנִי, וְאַל בַּחֲמָתְךָ תְיַסְּרֵנִי.

‹‹ chastise me. ‹ in Your wrath ‹ nor ‹ rebuke me, ‹ in Your anger* ‹ do not ‹ HASHEM,

חָנֵּנִי יהוה כִּי אֻמְלַל אָנִי, רְפָאֵנִי יהוה כִּי נִבְהֲלוּ

‹ shudder ‹ for ‹ HASHEM, ‹ heal me, ‹‹ am I; ‹ feeble ‹ for ‹ HASHEM, ‹ Favor
with terror, me,

עֲצָמָי. וְנַפְשִׁי נִבְהֲלָה מְאֹד, וְאַתָּה יהוה עַד מָתָי.*

‹‹ when?* ‹ until ‹ HASHEM, ‹ and You, ‹‹ utterly, ‹ is terrified ‹ My soul ‹‹ do my bones.

שׁוּבָה יהוה חַלְּצָה נַפְשִׁי, הוֹשִׁיעֵנִי לְמַעַן חַסְדֶּךָ.

‹‹ Your kindness. ‹ as befits ‹ save me ‹‹ my soul; ‹ release ‹ HASHEM, ‹ Desist,

(1) II Samuel 24:14.

וַיֹּאמֶר דָּוִד — *And David said.* King David had sinned by taking a census of the Jews in a manner contrary to that prescribed in the Torah (see *Exodus* 30:12). God, through the agency of the prophet Gad, gave King David a choice of three calamities, one of which he and his people would have to suffer in atonement for his sin: seven years of hunger; three months of defeat in battle; or a three-day death plague. David chose the last because that one would be inflicted directly by God, Whose mercy is ever-present even when His wrath is aroused. His choice proved wise when God mercifully halted the plague after a duration of only half a day. Similarly, in *Tachanun*, we cast ourselves upon God's compassion.

רַחוּם וְחַנּוּן — *O merciful and gracious One.* This verse is not of Scriptural origin. It is based on the dictum that God tempers the judgment of someone who confesses that he has sinned (*Eitz Yosef*).

ה' אַל בְּאַפְּךָ — *HASHEM, do not in Your anger.* David composed this psalm when he was sick and in pain. He intended this prayer to apply to every person in distress, and particularly to Israel when it suffered oppression and deprivation.

Even if he must be punished for his deeds, David pleaded, let God do so gradually, but not in anger, for then it would be beyond human endurance (*Radak*).

עַד מָתָי — *Until when?* How long will You watch my suffering and not cure me?

כִּי אֵין בַּמָּוֶת זִכְרֶךָ, בִּשְׁאוֹל מִי יוֹדֶה לָךְ. יָגַעְתִּי

‹ I am ‹ You? ‹ will ‹ who ‹ in the ‹ is there men- ‹ in ‹ not ‹ For
wearied　　　praise　　　grave　　tion of You;　death

בְּאַנְחָתִי, אַשְׂחֶה בְכָל לַיְלָה מִטָּתִי, בְּדִמְעָתִי

‹ with my tears ‹ my bed; ‹ night ‹ every ‹ I drench ‹ with my sigh;

עַרְשִׂי אַמְסֶה. עָשְׁשָׁה מִכַּעַס עֵינִי, עָתְקָה בְּכָל

‹ by all ‹ aged ‹ is my ‹ because of ‹ Dimmed ‹ I soak. ‹ my couch
　　　　　　　　eye,　　anger

צוֹרְרָי. סוּרוּ מִמֶּנִּי כָּל פֹּעֲלֵי אָוֶן, כִּי שָׁמַע יהוה

‹ Hashem has heard ‹ for ‹ of evil, ‹ doers ‹ all ‹ from me, ‹ Depart ‹ my tormentors.

קוֹל בִּכְיִי. שָׁמַע יהוה תְּחִנָּתִי, יהוה תְּפִלָּתִי יִקָּח.

‹ will ‹ my prayer ‹ Hashem ‹ my plea, ‹ Hashem ‹ of my ‹ the
accept.　　　　　　　　　　　has heard　　weeping.　sound

יֵבֹשׁוּ וְיִבָּהֲלוּ מְאֹד כָּל אֹיְבָי, יָשֻׁבוּ יֵבֹשׁוּ רָגַע.

‹ in an ‹ and be ‹ may they ‹ my ‹ all ‹ utterly, ‹ and con- ‹ Let them
instant.　shamed　regret　enemies;　　　　　founded　be shamed

מָחֵי וּמַסֵּי מֵמִית וּמְחַיֶּה, מַסִּיק מִן שְׁאוֹל

‹ the ‹ from ‹ Who raises ‹ and Who ‹ Who causes ‹ and Who ‹ [O God,]
grave　　　[the dead]　restores life,　death　　heals,　Who wounds

לְחַיֵּי עָלְמָא, בְּרָא כַּד חָטֵי אֲבוּהִי לָקְיֵהּ, אֲבוּהִי

‹ but a ‹ would ‹ his father ‹ sin, ‹ should ‹ A son ‹ eternal: ‹ to life
father　strike him,　　　　　　　he

דְּחַיֵּס אַסֵּי לִכְאֵבֵהּ. עַבְדָּא דְּמָרִיד נָפִיק בְּקוֹלָר,

‹ in chains, ‹ he is ‹ who rebels, ‹ A slave ‹ his [son's] ‹ will ‹ who is com-
led out　　　　　　　　　　pain.　　heal　passionate

מָרֵהּ תָּאִיב וְתַבִּיר קוֹלָרֵהּ.

‹ his chains. ‹ he breaks ‹ desires, ‹ but [if]
his master

בְּרָךְ בְּכְרָךְ אֲנַן וְחָטֵינַן קַמָּךְ, הָא רָוֵי נַפְשִׁין

‹ has our ‹ satiated ‹ indeed ‹ before ‹ and we have ‹ we ‹ Your ‹ Your
soul been　　　　　　　You;　sinned　are,　firstborn,　son,

בְּגִידִין מְרָרִין וּמְרוֹדִינַן אֲנַן עַבְדָּךְ, קַמָּךְ,

‹ before ‹ and we have ‹ we ‹ Your ‹ that is bitter. ‹ with
You;　rebelled　are　servants　　　　wormwood

הָא בְּבִזְתָא, הָא בְּשִׁבְיָא, הָא בְּמַלְקְיוּתָא.

‹ by the lash. ‹ and ‹ in captivity, ‹ some ‹ from ‹ [indeed we have
some　　　　　　　looting,　suffered,] some

בְּמָטוּ מִנָּךְ בְּרַחֲמָךְ דִּנְפִישִׁין, אַסֵּי לִכְאֵבִין
⟨ the pains ⟨ heal ⟨ that is abundant,⟨ in Your compassion ⟨ of You, ⟨ We beg

דְּתִקּוֹף עֲלָן, עַד דְּלָא נֶהֱוֵי גְמִירָא בְּשִׁבְיָא.
≪ in captivity. ⟨ completely ⟨ we are not ⟨ while ⟨ us, ⟨ that have
      annihilated   yet   overwhelmed

מַכְנִיסֵי רַחֲמִים, הַכְנִיסוּ רַחֲמֵינוּ, לִפְנֵי בַּעַל
⟨ the ⟨ before ⟨ our [plea for] ⟨ may you ⟨ [pleas for] mercy,* ⟨ O you who
Master   mercy*   usher in   usher in

הָרַחֲמִים. מַשְׁמִיעֵי תְפִלָּה, הַשְׁמִיעוּ תְפִלָּתֵנוּ, לִפְנֵי
⟨ before ⟨ of our ⟨ may you aid ≪ of prayer, ⟨ O you who aid ≪ of mercy.
     prayer   the hearing   the hearing

שׁוֹמֵעַ תְּפִלָּה. מַשְׁמִיעֵי צְעָקָה, הַשְׁמִיעוּ צַעֲקָתֵנוּ,
⟨ of our outcries* ⟨ may you aid ≪ of outcries,⟨ O you who aid ≪ of ⟨ the Hearer
      the hearing   the hearing   prayer.

לִפְנֵי שׁוֹמֵעַ צְעָקָה. מַכְנִיסֵי דִמְעָה, הַכְנִיסוּ
⟨ may you usher in ≪ tears, ⟨ O you who usher in ≪ of outcries. ⟨ the Hearer ⟨ before

דִמְעוֹתֵינוּ, לִפְנֵי מֶלֶךְ מִתְרַצֶּה בִּדְמָעוֹת.
≪ through tears. ⟨Who is appeased ⟨ the King ⟨ before ⟨ our tears*

הִשְׁתַּדְּלוּ וְהַרְבּוּ תְּחִנָּה וּבַקָּשָׁה, לִפְנֵי מֶלֶךְ אֵל
⟨ God, ⟨ the King, ⟨ before ⟨ and pleas ⟨ supplications ⟨ and intensify ⟨ Exert yourselves

רָם וְנִשָּׂא. הַזְכִּירוּ לְפָנָיו, הַשְׁמִיעוּ לְפָנָיו
⟨ before Him, ⟨ aid to be heard ≪ before Him, ⟨ Mention ≪ and uplifted. ⟨ exalted

תּוֹרָה וּמַעֲשִׂים טוֹבִים שֶׁל שׁוֹכְנֵי עָפָר.
≪ in the ⟨ [the Patriarchs and ⟨ of ⟨ that are ⟨ and the deeds ⟨ the
dust.   Matriarchs] who dwell   good   Torah

⊱ **מַכְנִיסֵי רַחֲמִים** — *O you who usher in [pleas for] mercy.* The propriety and permissibility of channeling a prayer through intermediaries — rather than directly to God — is a point of halachic contention. The debate revolves around supplications, such as the one before us, that request ministering angels to bring our supplications and tears before God, and to beseech Him to accept them favorably.

Shibbolei HaLeket (282) and *Tanya Rabbasi* (Cremona, end of Ch. 72, p. 102a) cite a proem from *Midrash Shir HaShirim* (not found in extant editions of the Midrash) upon which this supplication obviously was based:

The Congregation of Israel says to the angels standing at the [heavenly] Gates of Prayer and Gates of Tears, "Usher in my prayer and my tears before the Holy One, Blessed is He; and act as advocates before Him, that He pardon me for both intentional and inadvertent sins." And so it is stated: *If there be for him but one advocate angel from among a thousand ... (Job 33:23).*

— רַחֲמֵינוּ ... תְּפִלָּתֵנוּ ... צַעֲקָתֵנוּ ... דִּמְעוֹתֵינוּ *Our [plea for] mercy ... our prayer ... our outcries ... our tears. Machzor Kol Bo* suggests that these four modes of supplication to God invoke the merit of Abraham, Isaac, Jacob, and David, respectively.

יִזְכֹּר אַהֲבָתָם וִיחַיֶּה זַרְעָם, שֶׁלֹּא תֹאבַד שְׁאֵרִית

⟨ shall the remnant ⟨ lost ⟨ so that not ⟨ to their offspring, ⟨ and grant life ⟨ their love ⟨ May He remember

יַעֲקֹב. כִּי צֹאן רוֹעֶה נֶאֱמָן הָיָה לְחֶרְפָּה,

《 a disgrace; ⟨ has become ⟨ who is faith-ful [Moses] ⟨ of the shepherd ⟨ the flock ⟨ For 《 of Jacob be.

יִשְׂרָאֵל גּוֹי אֶחָד לְמָשָׁל וְלִשְׁנִינָה.

《 and a simile. ⟨ a parable 《 that is unique, ⟨ the nation 《 Israel,

מַהֵר עֲנֵנוּ אֱלֹהֵי יִשְׁעֵנוּ, וּפְדֵנוּ מִכָּל גְּזֵרוֹת קָשׁוֹת

《 that are harsh; ⟨ decrees ⟨ from all ⟨ and re-deem us ⟨ of our salvation, ⟨ O God ⟨ answer us, 《 Swiftly

וְהוֹשִׁיעָה בְּרַחֲמֶיךָ הָרַבִּים, מְשִׁיחַ צִדְקֶךָ וְעַמֶּךָ.

《 and Your people. ⟨ Your righteous anointed one ⟨ that is abundant, ⟨ in Your mercy ⟨ and may You save,

מָרָן דִּבִשְׁמַיָּא לָךְ מִתְחַנְּנַן, כְּבַר שִׁבְיָא דְמִתְחַנֵּן

⟨ who supplicates ⟨ in captivity ⟨ as one 《 do we supplicate, ⟨ to You 《 Who is in heaven, ⟨ Our Master

לִשְׁבוּיֵהּ. כֻּלְּהוֹן בְּנֵי שִׁבְיָא בְּכַסְפָּא מִתְפָּרְקִין,

《 are redeemed, ⟨ through money ⟨ in captivity, ⟨ those ⟨ [for] all 《 before his captors;

וְעַמָּךְ יִשְׂרָאֵל בְּרַחֲמֵי וּבְתַחֲנוּנֵי, הַב לָן שְׁאִילְתִין

⟨ our requests ⟨ us ⟨ O 《 and grant ⟨ supplication. ⟨ through compassion ⟨ Israel ⟨ but Your people

וּבָעוּתִין, דְּלָא נֶהְדַּר רֵיקָם מִן קָדָמָךְ.

《 before You. ⟨ from ⟨ empty-handed ⟨ that we not be turned away ⟨ and our prayers

מָרָן דִּבִשְׁמַיָּא לָךְ מִתְחַנְּנַן, כְּעַבְדָּא דְמִתְחַנֵּן

⟨ who supplicates ⟨ as a slave 《 do we supplicate, ⟨ to You 《 Who is in heaven, ⟨ Our Master

לְמָרֵיהּ, עֲשִׁיקֵי אֲנָן וּבַחֲשׁוֹכָא שָׁרִינָן, מְרִירָן

⟨ embittered 《 do we abide, ⟨ and in darkness ⟨ are we ⟨ Oppressed 《 to his master:

נַפְשִׁין מֵעַקְתִין דִּנְפִישִׁין, חֵילָא לֵית בָּן לְרַצּוּיָךְ.

《 to appease You. ⟨ within us ⟨ is lacking ⟨ Strength 《 that is excessive. ⟨ from distress ⟨ are [our] souls

מָרָן, עֲבִיד בְּדִיל קַיָּמָא דִּגְזַרְתָּ עִם אֲבָהָתָנָא.

《 our Patriarchs. ⟨ with ⟨ that You established ⟨ of the covenant ⟨ for the sake ⟨ act ⟨ Our Master,

שׁוֹמֵר יִשְׂרָאֵל,* שְׁמוֹר שְׁאֵרִית יִשְׂרָאֵל, וְאַל

‹ O Guardian ‹ of Israel,* ‹ safeguard ‹ the remnant ‹ of Israel; ‹ let not »

יֹאבַד יִשְׂרָאֵל, הָאֹמְרִים שְׁמַע יִשְׂרָאֵל.[1]

« Israel be destroyed — ‹ those who proclaim: ‹ Hear, ‹ O Israel. »

שׁוֹמֵר גּוֹי אֶחָד, שְׁמוֹר שְׁאֵרִית עַם אֶחָד, וְאַל

‹ O Guardian ‹ of the ‹ nation that is unique, « safeguard ‹ the remnant ‹ of the people that is unique; « let not »

יֹאבַד גּוֹי אֶחָד, הַמְיַחֲדִים שִׁמְךָ, יהוה אֱלֹהֵינוּ

« be the nation ‹ that is unique, « those who proclaim the Oneness ‹ of Your Name: « HASHEM, ‹ is our God,

יהוה אֶחָד.

« HASHEM is « the One [and Only]! ‹

שׁוֹמֵר גּוֹי קָדוֹשׁ, שְׁמוֹר שְׁאֵרִית עַם קָדוֹשׁ, וְאַל

‹ O Guardian ‹ of the ‹ nation that is holy, « safeguard ‹ the remnant ‹ of the people that is holy; « let not »

יֹאבַד גּוֹי קָדוֹשׁ, הַמְשַׁלְּשִׁים בְּשָׁלֹשׁ קְדֻשּׁוֹת לְקָדוֹשׁ.

« be the nation ‹ that is holy, « those who proclaim three times ‹ the threefold ‹ sanctifications ‹ to the Holy One. »

מִתְרַצֶּה* בְּרַחֲמִים וּמִתְפַּיֵּס בְּתַחֲנוּנִים, הִתְרַצֵּה

‹ You Who becomes favorable* ‹ through compassion ‹ and Who becomes conciliatory ‹ through supplications, « be favorable »

וְהִתְפַּיֵּס לְדוֹר עָנִי, כִּי אֵין עוֹזֵר. אָבִינוּ מַלְכֵּנוּ,

« and be conciliatory ‹ to the ‹ generation ‹ that is poor, ‹ for ‹ there is no « helper. ‹ Our Father, « our King,

חָנֵּנוּ וַעֲנֵנוּ, כִּי אֵין בָּנוּ מַעֲשִׂים, עֲשֵׂה עִמָּנוּ

‹ be gracious with us ‹ and answer us, ‹ though ‹ we have no « worthy deeds; « treat ‹ us »

צְדָקָה וָחֶסֶד וְהוֹשִׁיעֵנוּ.

« with charity ‹ and kindness, ‹ and save us. »

---

(1) *Deuteronomy* 6:4.

שׁוֹמֵר יִשְׂרָאֵל — *O Guardian of Israel.* Although this plea stresses that we are helpless and totally dependent on God's mercy, we do not come to God empty-handed. Each paragraph beginning שׁוֹמֵר, *O Guardian,* expresses an aspect of Israel's importance to God. Israel deserves God's mercy because: (a) Israel proclaims its allegiance to God by reciting the *Shema* twice daily; (b) Israel is unique in that it demonstrates to the world that God is One and Unique; and (c) like the angels, Israel praises and exalts God with the trebled proclamation of His holiness, *Kedushah.*

מִתְרַצֶּה — *You Who becomes favorable.*

STAND AFTER THE WORDS וַאֲנַחְנוּ לֹא נֵדַע, UNTIL CONCLUSION OF THE PARAGRAPH.

וַאֲנַחְנוּ לֹא נֵדַע מַה נַּעֲשֶׂה,* כִּי עָלֶיךָ עֵינֵינוּ.¹

⟨ are our ⟨ upon ⟨ rather, ⟨⟨ we should ⟨ what ⟨ know not ⟨ We
eyes. You do,*

זְכֹר רַחֲמֶיךָ יהוה וַחֲסָדֶיךָ, כִּי מֵעוֹלָם הֵמָּה. יְהִי²

⟨ May ⟨⟨ are they. ⟨ eternal ⟨ for ⟨ and Your ⟨ HASHEM, ⟨ Your ⟨Remem-
kindnesses, mercies, ber

חַסְדְּךָ יהוה עָלֵינוּ, כַּאֲשֶׁר יִחַלְנוּ לָךְ.³* אַל תִּזְכָּר

⟨ recall ⟨ Do not ⟨⟨ You.* ⟨ we awaited ⟨ just as ⟨⟨ be upon us, ⟨ HASHEM, ⟨Your kindness,

לָנוּ עֲוֹנוֹת רִאשׁוֹנִים, מַהֵר יְקַדְּמוּנוּ רַחֲמֶיךָ, כִּי

⟨for ⟨⟨ may Your ⟨ advance to ⟨ swiftly ⟨⟨ of the ancients; ⟨ the sins ⟨against
mercies, meet us us

דַלּוֹנוּ מְאֹד.⁴* עֶזְרֵנוּ בְּשֵׁם יהוה, עֹשֵׂה שָׁמַיִם

⟨ of ⟨ Maker ⟨⟨ of HASHEM, ⟨ is through ⟨ Our help ⟨⟨ exceed- ⟨⟨ we have become
heaven the Name ingly.* impoverished

וָאָרֶץ.⁵ חָנֵּנוּ יהוה חָנֵּנוּ, כִּי רַב שָׂבַעְנוּ בוּז.⁶ בְּרֹגֶז

⟨⟨ Amid ⟨⟨ with ⟨ sated ⟨ we are ⟨ for ⟨⟨ favor us, ⟨ HASHEM, ⟨ Favor us, ⟨⟨ and earth.
wrath, contempt. fully

רַחֵם תִּזְכּוֹר.⁷ בְּרֹגֶז עֲקֵדָה תִּזְכּוֹר. בְּרֹגֶז תְּמִימוֹת

⟨ the perfect ⟨⟨ Amid ⟨⟨ You should ⟨the binding ⟨⟨ Amid ⟨ You should ⟨ to be
ones wrath, remember! [of Isaac] wrath, remember! merciful

תִּזְכּוֹר. יהוה הוֹשִׁיעָה, הַמֶּלֶךְ יַעֲנֵנוּ בְיוֹם קָרְאֵנוּ.⁸

⟨⟨ we call. ⟨ on the ⟨ answer ⟨ May the ⟨⟨ save! ⟨ HASHEM, ⟨⟨ You should
day us King remember!

כִּי הוּא יָדַע יִצְרֵנוּ, זָכוּר כִּי עָפָר אֲנָחְנוּ.⁹

⟨⟨ are we. ⟨ dust ⟨ that ⟨ He is mindful ⟨⟨ our nature, ⟨ knew ⟨ He ⟨ For

---

(1) *II Chronicles* 20:12. (2) *Psalms* 25:6. (3) 33:22. (4) 79:8. (5) 121:2.
(6) 123:3. (7) *Habakkuk* 3:2. (8) *Psalms* 20:10. (9) 103:14.

May we have succeeded through our supplications in arousing God's mercy.

§**וַאֲנַחְנוּ לֹא נֵדַע מַה נַּעֲשֶׂה** — *We know not
what we should do.* We have prayed in
every possible manner: sitting, standing,
and casting ourselves down in supplication.
Moses, too, prayed in these three postures.
Now, we beg of God to help, for "we know
not what else we should do." To allude to this
concept it is customary to sit while reciting
the first three words of this prayer and then
to stand (*Abudraham*).

We are like orphaned children who depend
totally on their guardian. Similarly, we look
to God for His help and mercy, recognizing
that only He can rescue us from our plight
(*Eitz Yosef*). Appropriately, this verse is from
the prayer of King Jehoshaphat, who prayed
for help against an overwhelming invasion.

כַּאֲשֶׁר יִחַלְנוּ לָךְ — *Just as we awaited You.*
If we are undeserving, O God, then help
us because You will thereby sanctify Your
Name (*Alshich*).

כִּי דַלּוֹנוּ מְאֹד — *For we have become impov-*

❖ עָזְרֵנוּ אֱלֹהֵי יִשְׁעֵנוּ עַל דְּבַר כְּבוֹד שְׁמֶךָ, וְהַצִּילֵנוּ

⟨ rescue us ⟪ of Your ⟨ of the ⟨ the ⟨ for ⟨ of our ⟨ O God ⟨ Assist us,
Name; glory sake salvation

וְכַפֵּר עַל חַטֹּאתֵינוּ לְמַעַן שְׁמֶךָ.¹

⟪ of Your ⟨ for the ⟨ our sins ⟨ for ⟨ and grant
Name. sake atonement

FULL KADDISH / קדיש שלם

THE *CHAZZAN* RECITES קַדִּישׁ שָׁלֵם, FULL *KADDISH.*

יִתְגַּדַּל וְיִתְקַדַּשׁ שְׁמֵהּ רַבָּא. (אָמֵן. — Cong.) בְּעָלְמָא

⟨ — in the ⟪ (Amen.) ⟪ that is ⟨ may His ⟨ and be ⟨ Grow
world great! — Name sanctified exalted

דִּי בְרָא כִרְעוּתֵהּ, וְיַמְלִיךְ מַלְכוּתֵהּ, וְיַצְמַח פֻּרְקָנֵהּ

⟨ His ⟨ and cause ⟪ to His ⟨ and may He ⟪ according ⟨ He ⟨ that
salvation, to sprout kingship, give reign to His will, created

וִיקָרֵב מְשִׁיחֵהּ. (אָמֵן. — Cong.) בְּחַיֵּיכוֹן וּבְיוֹמֵיכוֹן וּבְחַיֵּי

⟨ and in the ⟨ and in ⟨ in your ⟪ (Amen.) ⟪ His Messiah, ⟨ and bring
lifetimes your days, lifetimes near

דְכָל בֵּית יִשְׂרָאֵל, בַּעֲגָלָא וּבִזְמַן קָרִיב. וְאִמְרוּ: אָמֵן.

⟪ Amen. ⟨ Now ⟪ that comes ⟨ and at a ⟨ swiftly ⟪ of Israel, ⟨ Family ⟨ of the
respond: soon. time entire

CONGREGATION RESPONDS:

אָמֵן. יְהֵא שְׁמֵהּ רַבָּא מְבָרַךְ לְעָלַם וּלְעָלְמֵי עָלְמַיָּא.

⟪ and for all eternity. ⟨ forever ⟨ be ⟨ that is ⟨ His ⟨ May ⟪ Amen.
blessed great Name

CHAZZAN CONTINUES:

יְהֵא שְׁמֵהּ רַבָּא מְבָרַךְ לְעָלַם וּלְעָלְמֵי עָלְמַיָּא. יִתְבָּרַךְ

⟨ Blessed, ⟪ and for all eternity. ⟨ forever ⟨ be ⟨ that is ⟨ His ⟨ May
blessed great Name

וְיִשְׁתַּבַּח וְיִתְפָּאַר וְיִתְרוֹמַם וְיִתְנַשֵּׂא וְיִתְהַדָּר וְיִתְעַלֶּה

⟨ elevated, ⟨ honored, ⟨ upraised, ⟨ exalted, ⟨ glorified, ⟨ praised,

וְיִתְהַלָּל שְׁמֵהּ דְּקֻדְשָׁא בְּרִיךְ הוּא (— Cong.) בְּרִיךְ הוּא)

⟪ is He) ⟨ (Blessed ⟪ is He ⟨ Blessed ⟨ of the Holy ⟨ be the ⟨ and lauded
One, Name

— לְעֵלָּא מִן כָּל בִּרְכָתָא וְשִׁירָתָא תֻּשְׁבְּחָתָא וְנֶחֱמָתָא

⟨ and ⟨ praise ⟪ and song, ⟨ blessing ⟨ any ⟨ beyond
consolation

---

(1) *Psalms* 79:9.

---

erished exceedingly. The prayer concludes   mightily and that God in His mercy knows
with the plea that we have already suffered   that we are helpless without Him.

דַּאֲמִירָן בְּעָלְמָא. וְאִמְרוּ: אָמֵן. (Cong.) — אָמֵן.)

(Amen.)   Amen. Now respond: in the world.   that are uttered

CONGREGATION:

(קַבֵּל בְּרַחֲמִים וּבְרָצוֹן אֶת תְּפִלָּתֵנוּ.)

our prayers.) and with favor   with mercy   (Accept

CHAZZAN CONTINUES:

תִּתְקַבֵּל צְלוֹתְהוֹן וּבָעוּתְהוֹן דְּכָל בֵּית יִשְׂרָאֵל קֳדָם

before   Israel   Family of   of the entire   and supplications   the prayers   May accepted be

אֲבוּהוֹן דִּי בִשְׁמַיָּא. וְאִמְרוּ: אָמֵן. (Cong.) — אָמֵן.)

(Amen.)   Amen. Now respond: is in Heaven.   Who   their Father

CONGREGATION:

(יְהִי שֵׁם יהוה מְבֹרָךְ, מֵעַתָּה וְעַד עוֹלָם.[1])

eternity.) until from this time   be blessed,   HASHEM   the Name   (Let

CHAZZAN CONTINUES:

יְהֵא שְׁלָמָא רַבָּא מִן שְׁמַיָּא וְחַיִּים טוֹבִים עָלֵינוּ וְעַל כָּל

all   and upon   upon us   that is good,   and life   Heaven   from   that is abundant   peace   May there be

יִשְׂרָאֵל. וְאִמְרוּ: אָמֵן. (Cong.) — אָמֵן.)

(Amen.)   Amen. Now respond: Israel.

CONGREGATION:

(עֶזְרִי מֵעִם יהוה, עֹשֵׂה שָׁמַיִם וָאָרֶץ.[2])

and earth.) of heaven   Maker   HASHEM,   is from   (My help

CHAZZAN BOWS; TAKES THREE STEPS BACK. BOWS LEFT AND SAYS "... עֹשֶׂה שָׁלוֹם, HE WHO MAKES PEACE . . ."; BOWS RIGHT AND SAYS "... הוּא, MAY HE . . ."; BOWS FORWARD AND SAYS "... וְעַל כָּל יִשְׂרָאֵל, AND UPON ALL ISRAEL . . ."; REMAINS IN PLACE FOR A FEW MOMENTS, THEN TAKES THREE STEPS FORWARD.

עֹשֶׂה שָׁלוֹם בִּמְרוֹמָיו, הוּא יַעֲשֶׂה שָׁלוֹם עָלֵינוּ, וְעַל כָּל

all   and upon   upon us,   peace   make   may He   in His heights,   peace   He Who makes

יִשְׂרָאֵל. וְאִמְרוּ: אָמֵן. (Cong.) — אָמֵן.)

(Amen.)   Amen. Now respond: Israel.

(1) *Psalms* 113:2. (2) 121:2.

﷽ SECOND DAY / יום שני ﷽

אַשְׁרֵי יוֹשְׁבֵי בֵיתֶךָ, עוֹד יְהַלְלוּךָ סֶּלָה.[1] אַשְׁרֵי

⟨ Praise-
worthy ⟩ ⟨ Selah. ⟩ ⟨ they will
praise You, ⟩ ⟨ con-
tinually ⟩ ⟨ in Your
house, ⟩ ⟨ are those
who dwell ⟩ ⟨ Praiseworthy

הָעָם שֶׁכָּכָה לּוֹ, אַשְׁרֵי הָעָם שֶׁיהוה אֱלֹהָיו.[2]

⟨ is their
God. ⟩ ⟨ that ⟩ ⟨ is the
people ⟩ ⟨ praise-
worthy ⟩ ⟨ is ⟩ ⟨ that such ⟩ ⟨ is the
people ⟩ their lot;

——— תהלים קמה / Psalm 145 ———

תְּהִלָּה לְדָוִד, אֲרוֹמִמְךָ אֱלוֹהַי הַמֶּלֶךְ, וַאֲבָרְכָה

⟨ and I
will bless ⟩ ⟨ the King, ⟩ ⟨ my God ⟩ ⟨ I will exalt You, ⟩ ⟨ by David: ⟩ ⟨ A psalm of
praise

שִׁמְךָ לְעוֹלָם וָעֶד. בְּכָל יוֹם אֲבָרְכֶךָ, וַאֲהַלְלָה שִׁמְךָ

⟨ Your
Name ⟩ ⟨ and I
will laud ⟩ ⟨ I will
bless You, ⟩ ⟨ day ⟩ ⟨ Every ⟩ ⟨ and
ever. ⟩ ⟨ for ever ⟩ ⟨ Your
Name

לְעוֹלָם וָעֶד. גָּדוֹל יהוה וּמְהֻלָּל מְאֹד, וְלִגְדֻלָּתוֹ

⟨ and His
greatness ⟩ ⟨ exceedingly, ⟩ ⟨ and
lauded ⟩ ⟨ is ⟩ ⟨ Great ⟩ ⟨ HASHEM ⟩ ⟨ and
ever. ⟩ ⟨ for ever

אֵין חֵקֶר. דּוֹר לְדוֹר יְשַׁבַּח מַעֲשֶׂיךָ, וּגְבוּרֹתֶיךָ יַגִּידוּ.

⟨ they will
recount. ⟩ ⟨ and Your
mighty deeds ⟩ ⟨ Your
actions, ⟩ ⟨ will
praise ⟩ ⟨ to ⟩ ⟨ Gen-
generation ⟩ ⟨ eration ⟩ ⟨ is beyond
investigation.

הֲדַר כְּבוֹד הוֹדֶךָ, וְדִבְרֵי נִפְלְאֹתֶיךָ אָשִׂיחָה. וֶעֱזוּז

⟨ And of
the might ⟩ ⟨ I shall
discuss. ⟩ ⟨ that are
wondrous ⟩ ⟨ and Your
deeds ⟩ ⟨ of Your
majesty ⟩ ⟨ glory ⟩ ⟨ The
splendrous

נוֹרְאֹתֶיךָ יֹאמֵרוּ, וּגְדוּלָּתְךָ אֲסַפְּרֶנָּה. זֵכֶר רַב טוּבְךָ

⟨ of Your abun-
dant goodness ⟩ ⟨ A recol-
lection ⟩ ⟨ I shall
relate. ⟩ ⟨ and Your
greatness ⟩ ⟨ they will
speak, ⟩ ⟨ of Your
awesome deeds

יַבִּיעוּ, וְצִדְקָתְךָ יְרַנֵּנוּ. חַנּוּן וְרַחוּם יהוה, אֶרֶךְ אַפַּיִם

⟨ to
anger, ⟩ ⟨ slow ⟩ ⟨ is ⟩ ⟨ and ⟩ ⟨ Gracious ⟩ ⟨ they will ⟩ ⟨ and of Your ⟩ ⟨ they
HASHEM, ⟩ merciful ⟩ sing joyfully. ⟩ righteousness ⟩ will utter,

וּגְדָל חָסֶד. טוֹב יהוה לַכֹּל, וְרַחֲמָיו עַל כָּל מַעֲשָׂיו.

⟨ His
creations. ⟩ ⟨ all
on ⟩ ⟨ are ⟩ ⟨ His
mercies ⟩ ⟨ to all; ⟩ ⟨ HASHEM
is good ⟩ ⟨ in [bestowing]
kindness. ⟩ ⟨ and
great

יוֹדוּךָ יהוה כָּל מַעֲשֶׂיךָ, וַחֲסִידֶיךָ יְבָרְכוּכָה. כְּבוֹד

⟨ Of the
glory ⟩ ⟨ will
bless You. ⟩ ⟨ and Your
devout ones ⟩ ⟨ Your
creations — ⟩ ⟨ — all ⟩ ⟨ HASHEM ⟩ ⟨ They will
thank You,

———

(1) *Psalms* 84:5. (2) 144:15.

מַלְכוּתְךָ יֹאמֵרוּ, וּגְבוּרָתְךָ יְדַבֵּרוּ. לְהוֹדִיעַ לִבְנֵי הָאָדָם

> of Your kingdom ‹ they will speak, « and of Your power ‹ they will declare. » To inform ‹ mankind ‹

גְּבוּרֹתָיו, וּכְבוֹד הֲדַר מַלְכוּתוֹ. מַלְכוּתְךָ מַלְכוּת כָּל

» of His mighty deeds, ‹ and of the « splendor ‹ of His kingdom. » Your kingdom ‹ is a ‹ [span-ning] all kingdom

עֹלָמִים, וּמֶמְשַׁלְתְּךָ בְּכָל דּוֹר וָדֹר. סוֹמֵךְ יהוה

« eternities, ‹ and Your dominion » is ‹ throughout ‹ gen-eration ‹ after generation. « HASHEM ‹ supports

לְכָל הַנֹּפְלִים, וְזוֹקֵף לְכָל הַכְּפוּפִים. עֵינֵי כֹל

‹ all « those who are fallen, ‹ and » straightens ‹ all « those who are bent. ‹ The eyes ‹ of all

אֵלֶיךָ יְשַׂבֵּרוּ, וְאַתָּה נוֹתֵן לָהֶם אֶת אָכְלָם בְּעִתּוֹ.

‹ to You « do look with hope, ‹ and You » give ‹ them ‹ their food ‹ « in its proper time.

CONCENTRATE INTENTLY WHILE RECITING THE VERSE פּוֹתֵחַ, YOU OPEN.

פּוֹתֵחַ אֶת יָדֶךָ, וּמַשְׂבִּיעַ לְכָל חַי רָצוֹן. ✧ צַדִּיק

‹ You open ‹ Your hand, « and satisfy ‹ every ‹ living thing « [with its] desire. ✧ Righteous ‹

יהוה בְּכָל דְּרָכָיו, וְחָסִיד בְּכָל מַעֲשָׂיו. קָרוֹב יהוה

HASHEM ‹ in all ‹ His ways, « and magnanimous ‹ in all ‹ His deeds. « Close ‹ is HASHEM

לְכָל קֹרְאָיו, לְכֹל אֲשֶׁר יִקְרָאֻהוּ בֶאֱמֶת. רְצוֹן יְרֵאָיו

‹ to all ‹ who call upon Him, ‹ to all ‹ who « call upon Him ‹ sincerely. « The will ‹ of those who fear Him

יַעֲשֶׂה, וְאֶת שַׁוְעָתָם יִשְׁמַע וְיוֹשִׁיעֵם. שׁוֹמֵר יהוה

‹ He will do; « He ‹ and their cry ‹ He will hear, « and He will save them. « HASHEM protects ‹

אֶת כָּל אֹהֲבָיו, וְאֶת כָּל הָרְשָׁעִים יַשְׁמִיד. תְּהִלַּת

‹ all « who love Him; ‹ but all ‹ the wicked « He will destroy. ‹ The praise ‹

יהוה יְדַבֶּר פִּי, וִיבָרֵךְ כָּל בָּשָׂר שֵׁם קָדְשׁוֹ לְעוֹלָם

‹ of HASHEM ‹ may my mouth declare, « and bless ‹ may ‹ all ‹ flesh ‹ the Name ‹ Holiness ‹ of His ‹ for ever

וָעֶד. וַאֲנַחְנוּ נְבָרֵךְ יָהּ מֵעַתָּה וְעַד עוֹלָם; הַלְלוּיָהּ.[1]

« and ever. ‹ But we ‹ will bless ‹ God ‹ from this time ‹ until ‹ eternity. « Halleluyah! «

(1) *Psalms* 115:18.

THE CHAZZAN RECITES חֲצִי קַדִּישׁ, HALF-KADDISH:

יִתְגַּדַּל וְיִתְקַדַּשׁ שְׁמֵהּ רַבָּא. (Cong. — אָמֵן.) בְּעָלְמָא
‹ — in the world   « (Amen.)   « that is great! — ‹ may His Name ‹ and be sanctified ‹ Grow exalted

דִּי בְרָא כִרְעוּתֵהּ, וְיַמְלִיךְ מַלְכוּתֵהּ, וְיַצְמַח פֻּרְקָנֵהּ
‹ His salvation, ‹ and cause to sprout « to His kingship, ‹ and may He give reign « according to His will, ‹ He created ‹ that

וִיקָרֵב מְשִׁיחֵהּ. (Cong. — אָמֵן.) בְּחַיֵּיכוֹן וּבְיוֹמֵיכוֹן וּבְחַיֵּי
‹ and in the lifetimes ‹ and in your days, ‹ in your lifetimes « (Amen.) « His Messiah, ‹ and bring near

דְכָל בֵּית יִשְׂרָאֵל, בַּעֲגָלָא וּבִזְמַן קָרִיב. וְאִמְרוּ: אָמֵן.
« Amen. ‹ Now respond: « that comes soon. ‹ and at a time ‹ swiftly « of Israel, ‹ Family ‹ of the entire

CONGREGATION RESPONDS:

אָמֵן. יְהֵא שְׁמֵהּ רַבָּא מְבָרַךְ לְעָלַם וּלְעָלְמֵי עָלְמַיָּא.
« and for all eternity. ‹ forever ‹ be blessed ‹ that is great ‹ His Name ‹ May « Amen.

CHAZZAN CONTINUES:

יְהֵא שְׁמֵהּ רַבָּא מְבָרַךְ לְעָלַם וּלְעָלְמֵי עָלְמַיָּא. יִתְבָּרַךְ
‹ Blessed, « and for all eternity. ‹ forever ‹ be blessed ‹ that is great ‹ His Name ‹ May

וְיִשְׁתַּבַּח וְיִתְפָּאַר וְיִתְרוֹמַם וְיִתְנַשֵּׂא וְיִתְהַדָּר וְיִתְעַלֶּה
‹ elevated, ‹ honored, ‹ upraised, ‹ exalted, ‹ glorified, ‹ praised,

וְיִתְהַלָּל שְׁמֵהּ דְּקֻדְשָׁא בְּרִיךְ הוּא (Cong. — בְּרִיךְ הוּא)
« is He) ‹ (Blessed « is He ‹ Blessed ‹ of the Holy One, ‹ be the Name ‹ and lauded

— לְעֵלָּא מִן כָּל בִּרְכָתָא וְשִׁירָתָא תֻּשְׁבְּחָתָא וְנֶחֱמָתָא
‹ and consolation ‹ praise « and song, ‹ blessing ‹ any ‹ beyond

דַּאֲמִירָן בְּעָלְמָא. וְאִמְרוּ: אָמֵן. (Cong. — אָמֵן.)
« (Amen.) « Amen. ‹ Now respond: « in the world. ‹ that are uttered

ALL:

לְךָ יהוה הַצְּדָקָה, וְלָנוּ בֹּשֶׁת הַפָּנִים.[1] מַה
« What « is shamefacedness. ‹ and ours « is the righteousness, ‹ O Lord, ‹ Yours,

נִתְאוֹנֵן,[2] מַה נֹּאמַר, מַה נְּדַבֵּר, וּמַה נִּצְטַדָּק.[3]
« justification can we offer? ‹ What « can we declare? ‹ What « can we say? ‹ What « complaint can we make?

(1) *Daniel* 9:7. (2) Cf. *Lamentations* 3:39. (3) Cf. *Genesis* 44:16.

נַחְפְּשָׂה דְרָכֵינוּ וְנַחְקְרָה, וְנָשׁוּבָה אֵלֶיךָ,¹ כִּי יְמִינְךָ

⟨ Your right hand ⟨ for ⟪ to You, ⟨ and return ⟨ and investigate them, ⟨ our ways ⟨ Let us examine

פְּשׁוּטָה לְקַבֵּל שָׁבִים. לֹא בְחֶסֶד וְלֹא בְמַעֲשִׂים

⟨ with [merit for good] deeds ⟨ nor ⟨ with [merit] for kindness ⟨ Nei-ther ⟪ those who return. ⟨ to accept ⟨ is extended

בָּאנוּ לְפָנֶיךָ, כְּדַלִּים וּכְרָשִׁים דָּפַקְנוּ דְלָתֶיךָ.

⟪ on Your doors. ⟨ we have knocked ⟨ and as destitute people ⟨ but as paupers ⟪ before You; ⟨ do we come

דְלָתֶיךָ דָּפַקְנוּ רַחוּם וְחַנּוּן, נָא אַל תְּשִׁיבֵנוּ

⟨ turn us away ⟨ do not ⟨ Please ⟪ and Gra-cious One. ⟨ O Compas-sionate One ⟨ we have knocked, ⟨ On Your doors

רֵיקָם מִלְּפָנֶיךָ. מִלְּפָנֶיךָ מַלְכֵּנוּ רֵיקָם אַל תְּשִׁיבֵנוּ,

⟪ turn us away, ⟨ do not ⟨ empty-handed ⟨ Our King, ⟨ From before You, ⟪ from before You. ⟨ empty-handed

כִּי אַתָּה שׁוֹמֵעַ תְּפִלָּה.

⟪ prayer. ⟨ Who hears ⟨ You are ⟨ for the One

שֹׁמֵעַ תְּפִלָּה, עָדֶיךָ כָּל בָּשָׂר יָבֹאוּ.² יָבוֹא

⟨ Come ⟪ will come. ⟨ flesh ⟨ all ⟨ unto You ⟪ prayer, ⟨ You Who hears

כָל בָּשָׂר לְהִשְׁתַּחֲוֹת לְפָנֶיךָ יהוה.³ יָבֹאוּ וְיִשְׁתַּחֲווּ

⟨ and bow down ⟨ They will come ⟪ O HASHEM. ⟨ before You, ⟨ to bow down ⟨ will all flesh

לְפָנֶיךָ אֲדֹנָי, וִיכַבְּדוּ לִשְׁמֶךָ.⁴ בֹּאוּ נִשְׁתַּחֲוֶה וְנִכְרָעָה,

⟪ and bow, ⟨ Let us prostrate ourselves ⟨ Come! ⟪ to Your Name. ⟨ and they will show honor ⟪ O Lord, ⟨ before You,

נִבְרְכָה לִפְנֵי יהוה עֹשֵׂנוּ.⁵ נָבוֹאָה לְמִשְׁכְּנוֹתָיו,

⟪ to His Tabernacles, ⟨ Let us come ⟪ our Maker. ⟨ HASHEM, ⟨ before ⟨ let us kneel

נִשְׁתַּחֲוֶה לַהֲדֹם רַגְלָיו.⁶ בֹּאוּ שְׁעָרָיו בְּתוֹדָה,

⟪ with thanksgiving, ⟨ His gates ⟨ Enter ⟪ for His feet. ⟨ at the stool ⟨ let us prostrate ourselves

חֲצֵרֹתָיו בִּתְהִלָּה, הוֹדוּ לוֹ בָּרְכוּ שְׁמוֹ.⁷ וַאֲנַחְנוּ

⟨ But we, ⟪ His Name. ⟨ bless ⟪ to Him, ⟨ give thanks ⟪ with praise; ⟨ His courtyards

---

(1) Cf. *Lamentations* 3:40. (2) *Psalms* 65:3. (3) Cf. *Isaiah* 66:23.
(4) *Psalms* 86:9. (5) 95:6. (6) 132:7. (7) 100:4.

בְּרֹב חַסְדְּךָ נָבוֹא בֵיתֶךָ, נִשְׁתַּחֲוֶה אֶל הֵיכַל קָדְשְׁךָ

בְּיִרְאָתֶךָ.[1] הִנֵּה בָּרְכוּ אֶת יהוה כָּל עַבְדֵי יהוה,

הָעֹמְדִים בְּבֵית יהוה בַּלֵּילוֹת.[2] שְׂאוּ יְדֵיכֶם קֹדֶשׁ

וּבָרְכוּ אֶת יהוה.[3] רוֹמְמוּ יהוה אֱלֹהֵינוּ, וְהִשְׁתַּחֲווּ

לַהֲדֹם רַגְלָיו, קָדוֹשׁ הוּא.[4] רוֹמְמוּ יהוה אֱלֹהֵינוּ,

וְהִשְׁתַּחֲווּ לְהַר קָדְשׁוֹ, כִּי קָדוֹשׁ יהוה אֱלֹהֵינוּ.[5]

הִשְׁתַּחֲווּ לַיהוה בְּהַדְרַת קֹדֶשׁ, חִילוּ מִפָּנָיו כָּל

הָאָרֶץ.[6] נִשְׁתַּחֲוֶה אֶל הֵיכַל קָדְשְׁךָ וְנוֹדֶה אֶת שְׁמֶךָ,

עַל חַסְדְּךָ וְעַל אֲמִתֶּךָ, כִּי הִגְדַּלְתָּ עַל כָּל שִׁמְךָ

אִמְרָתֶךָ.[7] יהוה אֱלֹהֵי צְבָאוֹת, מִי כָמוֹךָ חֲסִין

יָהּ, וֶאֱמוּנָתְךָ סְבִיבוֹתֶיךָ.[8] כִּי מִי בַשַּׁחַק יַעֲרֹךְ

לַיהוה, יִדְמֶה לַיהוה בִּבְנֵי אֵלִים.[9] כִּי גָדוֹל אַתָּה

וְעֹשֵׂה נִפְלָאוֹת, אַתָּה אֱלֹהִים לְבַדֶּךָ.[10] כִּי גָדוֹל

(1) Cf. *Psalms* 5:8. (2) 134:1. (3) 134:2. (4) 99:5. (5) 99:9. (6) 96:9. (7) Cf. 138:2. (8) 89:9. (9) 89:7. (10) 86:10.

מֵעַל שָׁמַיִם חַסְדֶּךָ, וְעַד שְׁחָקִים אֲמִתֶּךָ.¹ גָּדוֹל

⟨ Great ⟫ is Your truth. ⟨ the upper heights ⟨ and until ⟫ is Your kindness, ⟨ the very heavens ⟨ above

יהוה וּמְהֻלָּל מְאֹד, וְלִגְדֻלָּתוֹ אֵין חֵקֶר. (כִּי)² גָּדוֹל

⟨ great ⟨ (For) ⟫ investiga- tion. ⟨ is beyond ⟨ and His greatness ⟫ exceed- ingly, ⟨ and lauded ⟨ is HASHEM

יהוה וּמְהֻלָּל מְאֹד, נוֹרָא הוּא עַל כָּל אֱלֹהִים.³ כִּי

⟨ For ⟫ heavenly powers. ⟨ all ⟨ above ⟨ is He ⟨ awesome ⟫ exceed- ingly; ⟨ and lauded ⟨ is HASHEM

אֵל גָּדוֹל יהוה, וּמֶלֶךְ גָּדוֹל עַל כָּל אֱלֹהִים.⁴ אֲשֶׁר

⟨ For ⟫ heavenly powers. ⟨ all ⟨ above ⟨ and a great King ⟫ is HASHEM, ⟨ a great God

מִי אֵל בַּשָּׁמַיִם וּבָאָרֶץ, אֲשֶׁר יַעֲשֶׂה כְמַעֲשֶׂיךָ

⟨ like unto Your deeds ⟨ can do ⟨ that ⟨ or in the earth ⟨ is there in the heaven ⟨ power ⟨ what

וְכִגְבוּרֹתֶיךָ.⁵ מִי לֹא יִרָאֲךָ מֶלֶךְ הַגּוֹיִם, כִּי לְךָ

⟨ to You ⟨ For ⟫ of nations? ⟨ O King ⟫ fear You, ⟨ would not ⟨ Who ⟫ and like unto Your mighty acts?

יָאָתָה, כִּי בְכָל חַכְמֵי הַגּוֹיִם וּבְכָל מַלְכוּתָם מֵאֵין

⟨ there is none ⟨ their kingdoms ⟨ and in all ⟨ of the nations ⟨ the wise men ⟨ among all ⟨ for ⟫ [kingship] befits;

כָּמוֹךָ.⁶ מֵאֵין כָּמוֹךָ יהוה, גָּדוֹל אַתָּה וְגָדוֹל שִׁמְךָ

⟨ is Your Name ⟨ and great ⟨ are You ⟨ Great ⟫ O HASHEM! ⟨ like You, ⟨ There is none ⟫ like You.

בִּגְבוּרָה.⁷ לְךָ זְרוֹעַ עִם גְּבוּרָה, תָּעֹז יָדְךָ תָּרוּם

⟨ uplifted ⟫ is Your hand, ⟨ strength- ened ⟫ power; ⟨ with ⟨ is the arm ⟨ Yours ⟫ in might.

יְמִינֶךָ.⁸ לְךָ יוֹם, אַף לְךָ לָיְלָה, אַתָּה הֲכִינוֹתָ מָאוֹר

⟨ the luminary ⟨ prepared ⟨ You ⟫ is the night; ⟨ Yours ⟨ also ⟫ is the day, ⟨ Yours ⟫ is Your right hand.

וָשָׁמֶשׁ.⁹ אֲשֶׁר בְּיָדוֹ מֶחְקְרֵי אָרֶץ, וְתוֹעֲפוֹת הָרִים

⟨ of the mountains ⟨ and the summits ⟫ of the earth, ⟨ are the hidden mysteries ⟨ in His power ⟨ For ⟫ and the sun.

לוֹ.¹⁰ מִי יְמַלֵּל גְּבוּרוֹת יהוה, יַשְׁמִיעַ כָּל תְּהִלָּתוֹ.¹¹

⟫ of His praise? ⟨ all ⟨ [who] can ⟫ of make heard ⟨ of HASHEM; ⟨ the mighty acts ⟨ can express ⟨ Who ⟫ are His.

---

(1) *Psalms* 108:5. (2) 145:3. (3) 96:4. (4) 95:3. (5) *Deuteronomy* 3:24.
(6) *Jeremiah* 10:7. (7) 10:6. (8) *Psalms* 89:14. (9) 74:16. (10) 95:4. (11) 106:2.

לְךָ יהוה הַגְּדֻלָּה וְהַגְּבוּרָה, וְהַתִּפְאֶרֶת וְהַנֵּצַח

‹ the ‹ the glory, ‹ the strength, ‹ is the ‹ HASHEM, ‹ Yours,
triumph,   greatness,

וְהַהוֹד, כִּי כֹל בַּשָּׁמַיִם וּבָאָרֶץ; לְךָ יהוה הַמַּמְלָכָה,

‹ is the ‹ HASHEM, ‹ Yours, « and on ‹ in heaven ‹ every- ‹ for « and the
kingdom   earth;   thing   majesty;
[is Yours];

וְהַמִּתְנַשֵּׂא לְכֹל לְרֹאשׁ.¹ לְךָ שָׁמַיִם, אַף לְךָ אָרֶץ,

« is the ‹ Yours ‹ also « are the ‹ Yours « leader. ‹ over ‹ and the
earth;   heavens,   every   sovereignty

תֵּבֵל וּמְלֹאָהּ אַתָּה יְסַדְתָּם.² אַתָּה הִצַּבְתָּ כָּל גְּבוּלוֹת

‹ the ‹ all ‹ established ‹ You « founded ‹ You ‹ and its ‹ the
boundaries   them.   fullness,   world

אָרֶץ, קַיִץ וָחֹרֶף אַתָּה יְצַרְתָּם.³ אַתָּה רִצַּצְתָּ רָאשֵׁי

‹ the ‹ crushed ‹ You « fashioned ‹ You ‹ and ‹ summer « of
heads   them.   winter,   earth;

לִוְיָתָן, תִּתְּנֶנּוּ מַאֲכָל לְעָם לְצִיִּים. אַתָּה בָקַעְתָּ מַעְיָן

‹ fountain ‹ split ‹ You « [destined] for ‹ to the ‹ as food ‹ You will « of
open   the desolate   people   serve it   Leviathan;
wilderness.

וָנָחַל, אַתָּה הוֹבַשְׁתָּ נַהֲרוֹת אֵיתָן.⁴ אַתָּה פוֹרַרְתָּ

‹ shattered ‹ You « that are mighty. ‹ rivers ‹ dried ‹ You « and stream;

בְעָזְּךָ יָם, שִׁבַּרְתָּ רָאשֵׁי תַנִּינִים עַל הַמָּיִם.⁵ אַתָּה

‹ You « the water. ‹ upon ‹ of sea ‹ the heads ‹ You « the ‹ with Your
serpents   smashed   sea;   might

מוֹשֵׁל בְּגֵאוּת הַיָּם, בְּשׂוֹא גַלָּיו אַתָּה תְשַׁבְּחֵם.⁶

« calm them. ‹ You ‹ its ‹ when it « of the ‹ the ‹ rule
waves,   raises   sea;   grandeur

גָּדוֹל יהוה וּמְהֻלָּל מְאֹד, בְּעִיר אֱלֹהֵינוּ הַר קָדְשׁוֹ.⁷

« of His ‹ Mount ‹ of our God, ‹ in the ‹ and much praised, ‹ is ‹ Great
Holiness.   City   HASHEM

יהוה צְבָאוֹת, אֱלֹהֵי יִשְׂרָאֵל, יוֹשֵׁב הַכְּרֻבִים, אַתָּה

‹ it is « upon the ‹ en- ‹ of Israel, ‹ God ‹ Master of ‹ HASHEM,
You   Cherubim,   throned   Legions,

הוּא הָאֱלֹהִים לְבַדֶּךָ.⁸ אֵל נַעֲרָץ בְּסוֹד קְדוֹשִׁים רַבָּה,

« in the great assemblage ‹ is ‹ God « alone. ‹ God ‹ Who
of the holy [angels],   revered   are

---

(1) *I Chronicles* 29:11. (2) *Psalms* 89:12. (3) 74:17. (4) 74:14-15. (5) 74:13. (6) 89:10. (7) 48:2. (8) *Isaiah* 37:16.

וְנוֹרָא עַל כָּל סְבִיבָיו.¹ וְיוֹדוּ שָׁמַיִם פִּלְאֲךָ יהוה, אַף

⟨ also ⟩ HASHEM, ⟨ Your ⟩ will the ⟨ Acknowl- ⟨ who sur- ⟨ all ⟨ over ⟨ and is
wonders, heavens edge round Him. awesome

אֱמוּנָתְךָ בִּקְהַל קְדֹשִׁים. לְכוּ נְרַנְּנָה לַיהוה, נָרִיעָה

⟨ let us ⟨⟨ to ⟨ Let us sing ⟨ Come! ⟨⟨ of holy ⟨ in the ⟨ Your
call out HASHEM, joyfully ones. assembly faithfulness,

לְצוּר יִשְׁעֵנוּ. נְקַדְּמָה פָנָיו בְּתוֹדָה, בִּזְמִרוֹת נָרִיעַ

⟨ let us ⟨ with praiseful ⟨⟨ with ⟨ Him ⟨ Let us greet ⟨⟨ of our ⟨ to the
call out songs thanksgiving, salvation. Rock

לוֹ.³ צֶדֶק וּמִשְׁפָּט מְכוֹן כִּסְאֶךָ, חֶסֶד וֶאֱמֶת יְקַדְּמוּ

⟨ precede ⟨ and ⟨ kindness ⟨ of Your ⟨ are the ⟨ and ⟨ Righteous- ⟨⟨ to
truth throne; foundation justice ness Him.

פָנֶיךָ.⁴ אֲשֶׁר יַחְדָּו נַמְתִּיק סוֹד, בְּבֵית אֱלֹהִים נְהַלֵּךְ

⟨ let us ⟨ of God ⟨ in the ⟨⟨ counsel; ⟨ let us ⟨ together ⟨ For ⟨⟨ Your coun-
walk House take sweet tenance.

בְּרָגֶשׁ.⁵ אֲשֶׁר לוֹ הַיָּם וְהוּא עָשָׂהוּ, וְיַבֶּשֶׁת יָדָיו

⟨ His ⟨⟨ and the ⟨⟨ perfected ⟨ and He ⟨ is the ⟨ His ⟨ For ⟨⟨ in company.
hands dry land, it, sea

יָצָרוּ.⁶ אֲשֶׁר בְּיָדוֹ נֶפֶשׁ כָּל חָי, וְרוּחַ כָּל בְּשַׂר אִישׁ.⁷

⟨⟨ mankind. ⟨ of all ⟨ and the ⟨⟨ the ⟨ of ⟨ is the ⟨ in His ⟨ For ⟨⟨ fashioned.
spirit living all soul hand

✿ הַנְּשָׁמָה לָךְ וְהַגּוּף פָּעֳלָךְ, חוּסָה עַל עֲמָלָךְ.

⟨⟨ Your ⟨ on ⟨ take pity ⟨⟨ is Your ⟨ and the ⟨ is ⟨ The soul
labor. handiwork; body Yours

הַנְּשָׁמָה לָךְ וְהַגּוּף שֶׁלָּךְ, יהוה עֲשֵׂה לְמַעַן שְׁמֶךָ.

⟨⟨ of Your ⟨ for the ⟨ act ⟨ O ⟨⟨ is Yours; ⟨ and the ⟨ is ⟨ The soul
Name. sake HASHEM, body Yours

אָתָאנוּ עַל שִׁמְךָ, יהוה, עֲשֵׂה לְמַעַן שְׁמֶךָ. בַּעֲבוּר

⟨ [act] ⟨⟨ of Your ⟨ for the ⟨ act ⟨⟨ O ⟨⟨ Your ⟨ [relying] ⟨ We have
because of Name; sake HASHEM; Name, on come

כְּבוֹד שְׁמֶךָ, כִּי אֵל חַנּוּן וְרַחוּם שְׁמֶךָ. לְמַעַן

⟨ For the ⟨⟨ is Your ⟨ and ⟨ Who is ⟨ God ⟨ for ⟨⟨ of Your ⟨ the glory
sake Name. Merciful Gracious Name,

שִׁמְךָ יהוה, וְסָלַחְתָּ לַעֲוֹנֵנוּ כִּי רַב הוּא.⁸

⟨ it is great. ⟨ though ⟨ our ⟨ forgive ⟨⟨ HASHEM, ⟨ of Your
iniquity, Name,

---

(1) *Psalms* 89:8. (2) 89:6. (3) 95:1-2. (4) 89:15. (5) 55:15. (6) 95:5. (7) *Job* 12:10. (8) Cf. *Psalms* 25:11.

CONGREGATION, THEN *CHAZZAN*:

סְלַח לָנוּ אָבִינוּ, כִּי בְרוֹב אִוַּלְתֵּנוּ שָׁגִינוּ,

《 we have 〈 of our folly 〈 in the 〈 for 〈 our Father, 〈 us, 〈 Forgive
erred; abundance

מְחַל לָנוּ מַלְכֵּנוּ, כִּי רַבּוּ עֲוֹנֵינוּ.

《 our 〈 many 〈 for 〈 our King, 〈 us, 〈 pardon
iniquities. are

ALL, WHILE STANDING

אֵל אֶרֶךְ אַפַּיִם אַתָּה,

《 You are, 〈 to anger, 〈 Who is slow 〈 God

וּבַעַל הָרַחֲמִים נִקְרֵאתָ, וְדֶרֶךְ תְּשׁוּבָה הוֹרֵיתָ.

《 You have 〈 of 〈 and the 《 You are 〈 of Mercy 〈 and
taught. repentance way called; Master

גְּדֻלַּת רַחֲמֶיךָ וַחֲסָדֶיךָ,

〈 and Your 〈 of Your 〈 The
kindness mercy greatness

תִּזְכּוֹר הַיּוֹם וּבְכָל יוֹם לְזֶרַע יְדִידֶיךָ.

《 of Your 〈 for the 《 day, 〈 and 〈 this day 〈 may You
beloved ones. offspring every remember,

תֵּפֶן אֵלֵינוּ בְּרַחֲמִים,

《 in mercy, 〈 to us 〈 Turn

כִּי אַתָּה הוּא בַּעַל הָרַחֲמִים.

《 of Mercy. 〈 the Master 〈 are 〈 You 〈 for

בְּתַחֲנוּן וּבִתְפִלָּה פָּנֶיךָ נְקַדֵּם, כְּהוֹדַעְתָּ לֶעָנָיו מִקֶּדֶם.

《 in ancient 〈 to the 〈 in the manner 《 we 〈 Your 〈 and prayer 〈 With
times. humble one that You made approach, Presence supplication
[Moses] known

מֵחֲרוֹן אַפְּךָ שׁוּב,[1] כְּמוֹ בְּתוֹרָתְךָ כָּתוּב.[2]

《 it is 〈 in Your Torah 〈 as 《 turn 〈 of Your 〈 From the
written. back, anger fierceness

וּבְצֵל כְּנָפֶיךָ נֶחֱסֶה וְנִתְלוֹנָן,[3] כְּיוֹם וַיֵּרֶד יהוה בֶּעָנָן.

《 in a 〈 when HASHEM 〈 as on 《 and may 〈 may we find 〈 of Your 〈 In the
cloud. descended the day we dwell, shelter wings shadow

❖ תַּעֲבוֹר עַל פֶּשַׁע וְתִמְחֶה אָשָׁם,

《 guilt, 〈 and erase 〈 sin 〈 Overlook

---

(1) Cf. *Exodus* 32:12. (2) See 32:14. (3) Cf. *Psalms* 36:8.

כְּיוֹם וַיִּתְיַצֵּב עִמּוֹ שָׁם.

《 there. 〈 with him 〈 when *He* 〈 as on the
            [Moses]   [God] stood   day

תַּאֲזִין שַׁוְעָתֵנוּ וְתַקְשִׁיב מֶנּוּ מַאֲמָר,

《 [our] 〈 from 〈 and hear 〈 to our cry 〈 Give heed
  declaration, us

כְּיוֹם וַיִּקְרָא בְשֵׁם יהוה,[1] וְשָׁם נֶאֱמַר:

《 it was said: 〈 and 《 of *Hashem*, 〈 with the 〈 when *He* 〈 as on
              there   Name   called out   the day

CONGREGATION, THEN *CHAZZAN*:

וַיַּעֲבֹר יהוה עַל פָּנָיו וַיִּקְרָא:

《   and   《 [Moses'] 〈 before 〈 *And Hashem passed*
  proclaimed: face,

CONGREGATION AND *CHAZZAN* RECITE LOUDLY AND IN UNISON:

יהוה, יהוה, אֵל, רַחוּם, וְחַנּוּן, אֶרֶךְ אַפַּיִם,

〈 to anger, 〈 Slow 《 and Gracious, 〈 Compassionate 〈 God, 〈 *Hashem*, 〈 *Hashem*,

וְרַב חֶסֶד, וֶאֱמֶת, נֹצֵר חֶסֶד לָאֲלָפִים, נֹשֵׂא עָוֹן,

〈 of 〈 Forgiver 《 for thousands 〈 of 〈 Preserver 《 and 〈 in 〈 and
iniquity,   [of generations], kindness   Truth,   Kindness Abundant

וָפֶשַׁע, וְחַטָּאָה, וְנַקֵּה.[2] וְסָלַחְתָּ לַעֲוֹנֵנוּ וּלְחַטָּאתֵנוּ

《 and our sins, 〈 our 〈 May You 《 and Who 〈 and inadvertent 〈 willful sin,
              iniquities forgive   absolves.   sin,

וּנְחַלְתָּנוּ.[3] סְלַח לָנוּ אָבִינוּ כִּי חָטָאנוּ, מְחַל לָנוּ

〈 us, 〈 pardon 《 we have 〈 for 《 our Father, 〈 us, 〈 Forgive 《 and make us
              sinned;   Your heritage.

מַלְכֵּנוּ כִּי פָשָׁעְנוּ. כִּי אַתָּה אֲדֹנָי טוֹב וְסַלָּח, וְרַב

〈 and 《 and 〈 are 〈 O Lord, 〈 You, 〈 For 《 we have 〈 for 《 our King,
abundantly forgiving, good   willfully sinned.

חֶסֶד לְכָל קֹרְאֶיךָ.[4]

《 who call upon You. 〈 to all 〈 kind

פסוקי הקדמה לסליחה ה / PREFATORY VERSES TO SELICHAH 5

מִקְוֵה יִשְׂרָאֵל מוֹשִׁיעוֹ בְּעֵת צָרָה. לָמָּה תִהְיֶה

〈 should 〈 why 《 of 〈 in time 〈 its 《 of Israel, 〈 O Hope
  You be   trouble,   Redeemer

(1) *Exodus* 34:5. (2) 34:6-7. (3) 34:9. (4) *Psalms* 86:5.

כְּגֵר בָּאָרֶץ וּכְאֹרֵחַ נָטָה לָלוּן. לָמָּה תִהְיֶה כְּאִישׁ

⟨ like a ⟨ should ⟨ Why ⟪ to sleep ⟨ who ⟨ like a ⟨ in the land, ⟨ like a
man You be overnight? turns off traveler stranger
[the road]

נִדְהָם, כְּגִבּוֹר לֹא יוּכַל לְהוֹשִׁיעַ.¹ קוּמָה עֶזְרָתָה

⟨ Assist ⟪ Arise! ⟪ to save. ⟨ able ⟨ is not ⟨like a hero who ⟪ in shock,

לָּנוּ, וּפְדֵנוּ לְמַעַן חַסְדֶּךָ.²

⟪ of Your ⟨ for the ⟨ And ⟪ us!
kindness! sake redeem us

כְּרַחֵם אָב עַל בָּנִים, כֵּן תְּרַחֵם יהוה עָלֵינוּ.³

⟪ on us. ⟨ HASHEM, ⟨ have ⟨ so ⟪ his ⟨ toward ⟨ a ⟨ As merciful as
mercy, children, father is

לַיהוה הַיְשׁוּעָה, עַל עַמְּךָ בִרְכָתֶךָ סֶּלָה.⁴ יהוה

⟨ HASHEM, ⟪ Selah. ⟪ is Your ⟨ Your ⟨ upon ⟪ is salvation, ⟨ To HASHEM
blessing, people

צְבָאוֹת עִמָּנוּ, מִשְׂגָּב לָנוּ אֱלֹהֵי יַעֲקֹב סֶלָה.⁵

⟪ Selah. ⟪ of Jacob, ⟨ is the God ⟨ for us ⟨ a stronghold ⟪ is with us, ⟨ Master of Legions,

יהוה צְבָאוֹת, אַשְׁרֵי אָדָם בֹּטֵחַ בָּךְ.⁶ יהוה הוֹשִׁיעָה,

⟪ save! ⟨ HASHEM, ⟪ in ⟨ who ⟨ is the ⟨ — praise- ⟪ Master of ⟨ HASHEM,
You. trusts man worthy Legions

הַמֶּלֶךְ יַעֲנֵנוּ בְיוֹם קָרְאֵנוּ.⁷

⟪ we call. ⟨ on the day ⟨ answer us ⟨ May the King

IN MOST CONGREGATIONS THE FOLLOWING VERSES ARE RECITED ALOUD RESPONSIVELY,
AS INDICATED; IN OTHERS THEY ARE RECITED SILENTLY.

CONGREGATION ALOUD, FOLLOWED BY *CHAZZAN*, ALOUD:

סְלַח נָא לַעֲוֹן הָעָם הַזֶּה כְּגֹדֶל חַסְדֶּךָ, וְכַאֲשֶׁר

⟨ just as ⟪ of Your ⟨ according to ⟨ of this people ⟨ the ⟨ please, ⟨ Forgive,
kindness, the greatness iniquity

נָשָׂאתָה לָעָם הַזֶּה מִמִּצְרַיִם וְעַד הֵנָּה,⁸ וְשָׁם נֶאֱמַר:

⟪ it was said: ⟨ And there ⟪ now. ⟨ until ⟨ from Egypt ⟨ this people ⟨ You have forgiven

ALL, ALOUD AND IN UNISON:

וַיֹּאמֶר יהוה סָלַחְתִּי כִּדְבָרֶךָ.⁹

⟪ according ⟨ I have forgiven ⟪ And HASHEM said:
to your word!

(1) *Jeremiah* 14:8-9. (2) *Psalms* 44:27. (3) Cf. 103:13. (4) 3:9.
(5) 46:8. (6) 84:13. (7) 20:10. (8) *Numbers* 14:19. (9) 14:20.

ALL CONTINUE:

הַטֵּה אֱלֹהַי אָזְנְךָ וּשֲׁמָע, פְּקַח עֵינֶיךָ וּרְאֵה
⟨ and see ⟨ Your eyes ⟨ open ⟪ and listen; ⟨ Your ear, ⟨ my God, ⟨ Incline,

שֹׁמְמֹתֵינוּ, וְהָעִיר אֲשֶׁר נִקְרָא שִׁמְךָ עָלֶיהָ, כִּי לֹא
⟨ not ⟨ for ⟪ upon; ⟨　Your Name is　⟨ which ⟨ and that ⟨ our desolation
　　　　　　　　　　proclaimed　　　　　　　　　　　[of] the city

עַל צִדְקֹתֵינוּ אֲנַחְנוּ מַפִּילִים תַּחֲנוּנֵינוּ לְפָנֶיךָ,
⟪ before ⟨　our　⟨ cast ⟨ do we ⟨　of our　⟨ because
　You;　supplications　　　　　　　righteousness

כִּי עַל רַחֲמֶיךָ הָרַבִּים. אֲדֹנָי שְׁמָעָה, אֲדֹנָי סְלָחָה,
⟪ forgive; ⟨ O Lord, ⟪ heed; ⟨ O Lord, ⟪ which is ⟨ of Your ⟨ be- ⟨ but
　　　　　　　　　　　　　　　abundant.　compassion, cause

אֲדֹנָי הַקְשִׁיבָה, וַעֲשֵׂה אַל תְּאַחַר, לְמַעַנְךָ אֱלֹהַי,
⟪ my God, ⟨ for Your sake, ⟪ delay; ⟨ do not ⟪ and act, ⟨ be attentive, ⟨ O Lord,

כִּי שִׁמְךָ נִקְרָא עַל עִירְךָ וְעַל עַמֶּךָ.¹
⟪　Your　⟨ and ⟨　Your　⟨ upon ⟨　is　⟨　Your　⟨ for
　people.　upon　City　proclaimed　Name

SELICHAH 5 / סליחה ה

ALL:

אֱלֹהֵינוּ וֵאלֹהֵי אֲבוֹתֵינוּ:
⟪ of our forefathers: ⟨ and God ⟨ Our God

אִם עֲוֹנֵינוּ* רַבּוּ לְהַגְדִּיל,² בָּנוּ עָנוּ³ עֲבוֹת כִּגְדִיל,*
⟪ that are ⟨ and [drag us] as ⟨ they ⟨ against ⟪ until they are ⟨ have ⟨　our　⟨ If
twisted,* with thick ropes testify　us　enormous, multiplied iniquities*

גָּרְמוּ לָנוּ בֵּינָתַיִם לְהַבְדִּיל,⁴
⟪　a rift be　⟨ that between ⟨ for ⟨ [if our sins]
　created,　[God and] us　us　have caused

דַּרְכֵי רַחֲמֶיךָ לֹא תַחְדִּיל.
⟪ You will not withhold. ⟨ of Your mercy ⟨ the ways

---

(1) *Daniel* 9:18-19. (2) Cf. *Ezra* 9:6. (3) Cf. *Jeremiah* 14:7. (4) Cf. *Isaiah* 59:2.

◆§ **אִם עֲוֹנֵינוּ —** *If our iniquities.* The acrostic of this *selichah* forms the *aleph-beis*, followed by the *paytan's* signature — שְׁלֹמֹה הַקָּטָן יְחִי, *Shlomo the lesser, may he live* [see prefatory comment to *Selichah* 2].

עֲבוֹת כִּגְדִיל — *And [drag us] as with thick ropes that are twisted.* The Evil Inclination, or *Yetzer Hara*, at first is as delicate as a spider's strand, but eventually becomes as thick and strong as the rope used to harness

הִתְנַהֵג בְּמִדַּת חֶסֶד הַתְּנִיתָ,

《 You have 〈 of 〈 with the 〈 To act
promised, Kindness Attribute

וְאַתָּה הוּא שֶׁמִּקֶּדֶם הָיִיתָ,*

《 [always] 〈 Who from 〈 it is 〈 and You
was.* the beginning

זְכֹר עֲדָתְךָ אֲשֶׁר קָנִיתָ,*[1] חֹן שִׁירֵי בְּכוֹר[2] כֻּנִיתָ.

《 You 〈 of those 〈 to the 〈 and be 《 You have 〈 that 〈 Your con- 〈 Re-
designated. whom as remnants gracious acquired,* gregation member
[My] firstborn

טַעֲנְתָּנוּ גַּפֵּי קֶרֶת[3] נְתוּנִים,

《 we were 〈 of the 〈 and upon 〈 You
placed, [Holy] City the height bore us

יְשַׁבְתָּנוּ שֵׁן סֶלַע אֵיתָנִים,*

《 of the mighty 〈 of the rocky 〈 upon the 〈 You
[Patriarchs].* mountain summit settled us

בְּאֶחָד דְּכִיתָנוּ בִּמְקוֹם תַּנִּים,[4]

《 of 〈 in the place 〈 You 〈 In a
serpents. crushed us moment

---

(1) Cf. *Psalms* 74:2; some editions read זְכֹר עֲדָתְךָ קֶדֶם קָנִיתָ, *Remember Your flock that You long ago acquired.* (2) See *Exodus* 4:22. (3) Cf. *Proverbs* 9:3. (4) Cf. *Psalms* 44:20.

---

a draft animal to its wagon (*Succah* 52a). The *Yetzer Hara* seduces a person to sin in this world, then testifies against him in the future (ibid. 52b).

שֶׁמִּקֶּדֶם הָיִיתָ — *Who from the beginning [always] was.* That is, You have never changed since the beginning of Creation. [Indeed, some editions of *Selichos* read: וְאַתָּה הוּא לֹא שֵׁנִיתָ, *It is You Who has never changed* (cf. *Malachi* 3:6).] When You created the world, You established it on three pillars: Torah, Divine Worship, and Kindness. Thus it is written: כִּי אָמַרְתִּי עוֹלָם חֶסֶד יִבָּנֶה, *For I have said, ''The world shall be built upon kindness''* (*Psalms* 89:3; *Avos* 1:2 with *Rashi*). So we pray that God fulfill His ancient promise to conduct His affairs with mankind in accordance with His Attribute of Kindness.

אֲשֶׁר קָנִיתָ — *That You have acquired.* In the Song at the Sea, Israel is called עַם זוּ קָנִיתָ, *this people that You have acquired* (*Exodus* 15:16). The root קנה usually refers to acquisition through a business transaction. In other words, the verse implies that God acquired

Israel from someone else! But since everything belongs to God in the first place, how can He ''acquire'' anything from someone else? *Rashi* explains that God did not actually acquire Israel from someone else. Rather, God's love for Israel is so strong that it may be compared to a person's love for a precious possession that he bought for a vast sum and treasures dearly (ad loc. and *Pesachim* 87b).

שֵׁן סֶלַע אֵיתָנִים — *Upon the summit of the rocky mountain of the mighty [Patriarchs].* The word אֵיתָנִים is a noun and means *mighty ones*, a term often used to describe the Patriarchs Abraham, Isaac, and Jacob (see *Rosh Hashanah* 11a; see also commentary below, s.v. תָּם וְצָבוּר וּבַנַּאי אֵיתָנַי). Since it was in the merit of the Patriarchs that Israel inherited *Eretz Yisrael*, a land that is mountainous and rocky in many places, the *paytan* refers to the Land as *the summit of the rocky mountain of the mighty [Patriarchs].*

[Although many commentaries treat אֵיתָנִים as an adjective and render this phrase *on the mighty summit of the rocky moun-*

לִרְוָיָה צֵאת כַּמָּה מְתוּנִים.

《 must we have 〈 how 〈 we go 〈 Until to
patience?   long   forth,   liberty

מֶרֹב פְּקֻדּוֹת וּבֶהָלָה מְחַלְחֶלֶת,

《 that causes 〈 and the 〈 [evil] 〈 Due to
trembling,   panic   occurrences, the many

נָקְטָה נַפְשִׁי,*[1] לֶעָפָר בּוֹחֶלֶת,

《 it found 〈 [it is bent] 〈 is my 〈 in turmoil
repulsive. to the dust   soul,*

סָמְכָה בֶטֶן לָאָרֶץ[2] נִשְׁחֶלֶת,

《 is pulled! 〈 to the 〈 the one 〈 Support
ground whose belly

עוּרָה לָמָּה תִישַׁן[3] תּוֹחֶלֶת.

《 [our] Hope? 《 do You seem 〈 Why 《 Awaken!
to sleep,

פְּקַח קוֹחַ קְרֹא אֲסִירֶיךָ[4] חָפוֹץ,

《 by Your 〈 to Your 〈 cry out 〈 the 〈 Open
will,   prisoners   prisons!

צוּק הָעִתִּים[5] חֶשְׁבּוֹנָם קָפֵץ.

《 jump 〈 in its 《 designated for a 〈 and the
ahead. reckoning   fixed duration, suffering

קַבֵּץ פְּזוּרֶיךָ עֵדֶר הַנָּפֵץ, רְאוֹת עַוְלָתָה פִּיהָ תִּקְפֹּץ.[6]

《 to shut. 〈 its 〈 [will cause] 〈 seeing 《 that is 〈 the 《 Your dis- 〈 Gather
mouth wickedness [this] scattered; flock persed ones, up

שְׁמֹר שְׁבוּעַת חֶסֶד וּתְנַאי, תָּם וְצָבוּר וּבַנַּאי אֵיתָנַי,*

《 — my 《 and the 〈 the 〈 with the 〈 and the 〈 of 〈 the vow 〈 Keep
mighty builder heaped whole- pact kindness
[Patriarchs].* one, some one,

---

(1) Some editions of *Selichos* read, נָקְטָה שָׁחָה נַפְשִׁי, *My soul is bent, it is in turmoil*; some read,
נָקְטָה נַפְשִׁי שָׁחָה, *My soul is in turmoil, it is bent*; but most editions omit the word שָׁחָה.
(2) Cf. *Psalms* 44:26. (3) 44:24. (4) Cf. *Isaiah* 61:1. (5) *Daniel* 9:25. (6) Cf. *Psalms* 107:42; *Job* 5:16.

---

tains, the plural form אֵיתָנִים is grammatically inconsistent with the singular noun שֵׁן סֶלַע, *summit of the rocky mountain*.]

נָקְטָה נַפְשִׁי — *In turmoil is my soul*. The translation follows *Rashi* (to *Job* 10:1). According to *Targum* and *Ralbag*, the meaning is *doomed is my soul*.

תָּם וְצָבוּר וּבַנַּאי אֵיתָנַי — *With the wholesome one, the heaped one, and the builder — my*

mighty [*Patriarchs*]. The word אֵיתָנַי alludes to the Patriarchs [see above, s.v. שֵׁן סֶלַע אֵיתָנִים]. Jacob is described as אִישׁ תָּם, *a man who is wholesome* (*Genesis* 25:27); Isaac is considered as the ashes of an offering צָבוּר, *heaped*, upon the Altar (*Midrash Tanchuma, Vayeira* 23); and Abraham is called *the builder* because וַיִּבֶן ... אֶת הַמִּזְבֵּחַ, *he built ... the altar*, on which to offer Isaac (*Genesis* 22:9).

שְׁלוֹמוֹ יְצַוֶּה לִבְלִי גְנַאי, הֲפֹךְ וְשַׁנּוֹת לְטוֹבָה הַפְּנַאי.[1]

» Your atten- ‹ to good ‹ and ‹ trans- » [be] ‹ so that ‹ may He ‹ His peace
tion [to us]. changing forming disdained, we not command, [to us]

❖ קָטֹן כִּי יַעֲקֹב[2] וָדָל, יָדְוּעַ חֳלִי נִבְזֶה וַחֲדָל,[3]

» and ‹ scorned, » to ‹ accus- » and ‹ Jacob is, ‹ though ‹ Small
isolated, sickness, tomed poor,

חַיִּים וָחֶסֶד מָעֹז וּמִגְדָּל, כַּאֲשֶׁר עַתָּה כֹּחֲךָ יִגְדָּל.[4]

» is [revealed ‹ Your ‹ [even] ‹ as » and a tower ‹ a » and ‹ [yet we
in its] strength now [from God], fortress kindness, ask that he
greatness. have] life

ALL, WHILE STANDING:

אֵל מֶלֶךְ יוֹשֵׁב עַל כִּסֵּא רַחֲמִים, מִתְנַהֵג

‹ Who acts » of mercy, ‹ the throne ‹ on ‹ Who sits ‹ King ‹ O God,

בַּחֲסִידוּת, מוֹחֵל עֲוֹנוֹת עַמּוֹ, מַעֲבִיר רִאשׁוֹן

‹ [sins,] one ‹ Who » of His ‹ the sins ‹ Who » with kindness,
removes people, pardons

רִאשׁוֹן,[5] מַרְבֶּה מְחִילָה לְחַטָּאִים וּסְלִיחָה לַפּוֹשְׁעִים,

» to willful ‹ and ‹ to unintentional ‹ pardon ‹ Who abun- » by one,
sinners, forgiveness sinners dantly grants

עֹשֶׂה צְדָקוֹת עִם כָּל בָּשָׂר וָרוּחַ, לֹא כְּרָעָתָם

‹ in accord with ‹ — not » and ‹ [beings ‹ all ‹ with ‹ acts of ‹ Who
their wickedness spirit of] flesh generosity performs

תִּגְמוֹל. ❖ אֵל הוֹרֵיתָ לָנוּ לוֹמַר שְׁלֹשׁ עֶשְׂרֵה, וּזְכוֹר

‹ remem- » the Thirteen ‹ to ‹ us ‹ You ‹ O God, » do You
ber [Attributes of Mercy]; recite taught repay them!

לָנוּ הַיּוֹם בְּרִית שְׁלֹשׁ עֶשְׂרֵה, כְּמוֹ שֶׁהוֹדַעְתָּ לֶעָנָיו

‹ to the ‹ You made ‹ as » of [these] Thirteen, ‹ the ‹ today ‹ for us
humble one known covenant
[Moses]

מִקֶּדֶם, כְּמוֹ שֶׁכָּתוּב, וַיֵּרֶד יהוה בֶּעָנָן וַיִּתְיַצֵּב עִמּוֹ

‹ with ‹ and stood ‹ in a ‹ And Hashem » it is written: ‹ as » in ancient
him cloud descended times,

שָׁם, וַיִּקְרָא בְשֵׁם יהוה.[6]

» of ‹ with the ‹ and He » there,
Hashem. Name called out

---

(1) Cf. *Leviticus* 26:9,17. (2) Cf. *Amos* 7:2. (3) Cf. *Isaiah* 53:3.
(4) Cf. *Numbers* 14:17. (5) *Rosh Hashanah* 17a. (6) *Exodus* 34:5.

CONGREGATION, THEN *CHAZZAN:*

וַיַּעֲבֹר יהוה עַל פָּנָיו וַיִּקְרָא:

《 and 　《 [Moses'] 〈 before 〈 And Hashem passed
proclaimed: 　face,

CONGREGATION AND *CHAZZAN* **RECITE LOUDLY AND IN UNISON:**

יהוה, יהוה, אֵל, רַחוּם, וְחַנּוּן, אֶרֶךְ אַפַּיִם,

〈 to anger, 〈 Slow 《 and Gracious, 〈 Compassionate 〈 God, 〈 Hashem, 〈 Hashem,

וְרַב חֶסֶד, וֶאֱמֶת, נֹצֵר חֶסֶד לָאֲלָפִים, נֹשֵׂא עָוֹן,

〈 of 〈 Forgiver 《 for thousands 〈 of 〈 Preserver 《 and 〈 in 〈 and
iniquity, 　　[of generations], kindness 　Truth, Kindness Abundant

וָפֶשַׁע, וְחַטָּאָה, וְנַקֵּה.¹ וְסָלַחְתָּ לַעֲוֹנֵנוּ וּלְחַטָּאתֵנוּ

《 and our sins, 〈 our 〈 May You 《 and Who 〈 and inadvertent 〈 willful sin,
iniquities forgive absolves. sin,

וּנְחַלְתָּנוּ.² סְלַח לָנוּ אָבִינוּ כִּי חָטָאנוּ, מְחַל לָנוּ

〈 us, 〈 pardon 《 we have 〈 for 《 our 〈 us, 〈 Forgive 《 and make us
sinned; Father, Your heritage.

מַלְכֵּנוּ כִּי פָשָׁעְנוּ. כִּי אַתָּה אֲדֹנָי טוֹב וְסַלָּח,

《 and 〈 are 〈 O Lord, 〈 You, 〈 For 《 we have 〈 for 《 our King,
forgiving, good willfully sinned.

וְרַב חֶסֶד לְכָל קֹרְאֶיךָ.³

《 who call 〈 to all 〈 kind 〈 and
upon You. abundantly

PREFATORY VERSES TO SELICHAH 6 / פסוקי הקדמה לסליחה ו

לֹא כַחֲטָאֵינוּ תַּעֲשֶׂה לָנוּ, וְלֹא כַעֲוֹנֹתֵינוּ תִּגְמֹל

〈 shall You 〈 according to 〈 and 《 us, 〈 shall You 〈 according to 〈 Not
repay our iniquities not treat our sins

עָלֵינוּ.⁴ אִם עֲוֹנֵינוּ עָנוּ בָנוּ, יהוה, עֲשֵׂה לְמַעַן שְׁמֶךָ.⁵

《 of Your 〈 for the 〈 act 〈 Hashem, 《 against 〈 testify 〈 our 〈 Even 《 us.
Name. sake us, iniquities if

אִם עֲוֹנוֹת תִּשְׁמָר יָהּ, אֲדֹנָי, מִי יַעֲמֹד.⁶ אִם בָּנֶיךָ

〈 Your 〈 If 《 could 〈 who 〈 O 《 O 〈 You 〈 iniquities 〈 If
sons survive? Lord, God, preserve,

חָטְאוּ לָךְ, אַל תְּשַׁלְּחֵם בְּיַד פִּשְׁעָם.⁷ נַפְשֵׁנוּ חִבְּתָה

〈 longed 〈 Our soul 《 of their 〈 into the 〈 send them 〈 do 《 against 〈 sinned
own sin. hand not You

---

(1) *Exodus* 34:6-7. (2) 34:9. (3) *Psalms* 86:5. (4) Cf. 103:10. (5) *Jeremiah* 14:7. (6) *Psalms* 130:3. (7) Cf. *Job* 8:4.

לַיהוה, עֶזְרֵנוּ וּמָגִנֵּנוּ הוּא.[1]
《 is He. ⟨ and our shield ⟨ our help 《 for HASHEM;

כְּרַחֵם אָב עַל בָּנִים, כֵּן תְּרַחֵם יהוה עָלֵינוּ.[2]
《 on us. ⟨ HASHEM, ⟨ have mercy, ⟨ so 《 his children, ⟨ toward ⟨ a father is ⟨ As merciful as

לַיהוה הַיְשׁוּעָה, עַל עַמְּךָ בִרְכָתֶךָ סֶּלָה.[3] יהוה
⟨ HASHEM, 《 Selah. 《 is Your blessing, ⟨ Your people ⟨ upon 《 is salvation, ⟨ To HASHEM

צְבָאוֹת עִמָּנוּ, מִשְׂגָּב לָנוּ אֱלֹהֵי יַעֲקֹב סֶלָה.[4]
《 Selah. 《 of Jacob, ⟨ is the God ⟨ for us ⟨ a stronghold 《 is with us, ⟨ Master of Legions,

יהוה צְבָאוֹת, אַשְׁרֵי אָדָם בֹּטֵחַ בָּךְ.[5] יהוה הוֹשִׁיעָה,
《 save! ⟨ HASHEM, 《 in You. ⟨ who trusts ⟨ is the man ⟨ — praise-worthy 《 Master of Legions ⟨ HASHEM,

הַמֶּלֶךְ יַעֲנֵנוּ בְיוֹם קָרְאֵנוּ.[6]
《 we call. ⟨ on the day ⟨ answer us ⟨ May the King

SELICHAH 6 / ו סליחה

ALL:

אֱלֹהֵינוּ וֵאלֹהֵי אֲבוֹתֵינוּ:
《 of our forefathers: ⟨ and God ⟨ Our God

אֵין כְּמִדַּת בָּשָׂר* מִדָּתֶךָ.*
《 is Your nature;* ⟨ of flesh [and blood]* ⟨ like the nature ⟨ Not

אַיֵּה קִנְאָתְךָ[7] וַעֲצַת עֲמִידָתֶךָ,[8]
《 that is enduring? ⟨ and Your counsel ⟨ is Your jealousy [on our behalf], ⟨ where, [then,]

---

(1) *Psalms* 33:20. (2) Cf. 103:13. (3) 3:9 (4) 46:8. (5) 84:13. (6) 20:10. (7) *Isaiah* 63:15. (8) Cf. *Psalms* 33:11.

§⊷ **אֵין כְּמִדַּת בָּשָׂר** — *Not like the nature of flesh [and blood].* Ascribed to R' Shlomo HaBavli (whose signature uncharacteristically does not appear in the composition; see prefatory note to *Selichah* 2), this *selichah* contains a double *aleph-beis* acrostic.

אֵין כְּמִדַּת בָּשָׂר מִדָּתֶךָ — *Not like the nature of flesh [and blood] is Your nature.* As Scripture states: *Do You have eyes of*

flesh? *Do You see as man sees?* (*Job* 10:4). Unlike man whose vision is limited, You are able to see everything; nothing is hidden from Your sight (*Arugas HaBosem*).

Alternatively: Unlike man who cannot always fulfill his wishes, You גּוֹזֵר וּמְקַיֵּם, *decree and fulfill.* None can prevent You from doing whatever You desire (*Matteh Levi*).

בַּת בָּחַרְתָּ לְבֵית חֶמְדָּתֶךָ,*

⟨ that is Your ⟨ for the ⟨ You ⟨ The
desire*   House   chose   daughter

בְּעָלוּהָ אֲדוֹנִים¹ וְאֵין לִצְמִידָתֶךָ.*

《 to hold tightly ⟨ and [she] ⟨ by [strange] ⟨ is ruled
to You.*   is not able   lords,   over

גּוֹעָה, לְדוֹדִי אֲנִי מְאֹרֶסֶת,

《 betrothed! ⟨ I am ⟨ To my ⟨ She
Beloved   moans,

גּוֹעַל רוֹדִי אֵיךְ נִדְרֶסֶת,

《 allow me to ⟨ how ⟨ by [the tyrant] ⟨ Loathed
be trampled?   [does my   who rules
Beloved]   over me,

דִּין הֶרֶג לְעַצְמָהּ מַקְנֶסֶת,*

《 she ⟨ upon ⟨ of death ⟨ A sen-
pronounces,*   herself   [as a martyr]   tence

דְּחוּיָה וְגַם כִּי נֶאֱנֶסֶת.

《 coerced. ⟨ when ⟨ and ⟨ [even when]
also   pushed out
[into exile]

הַאֵם בְּלִי סֵפֶר שִׁלּוּחַ,²

《 was sent ⟨ a document ⟨ without ⟨ The
out;   [of divorce],   mother,

הַבֵּן כִּיָתוֹם אוֹבֵד שָׁלוּחַ,

《was sent off. 《 wander- ⟨ — like an ⟨ the
ing —   orphan,   son

---

(1) Cf. *Isaiah* 26:13. (2) Cf. 50:1.

בַּת בָּחַרְתָּ לְבֵית חֶמְדָּתֶךָ — *The daughter You chose for the House that is Your desire.* The words בַּת, *daughter*, and בֵּית, *house*, are often used as euphemisms for *wife*. Thus, when Scripture states that *Mordechai took Esther as a daughter (Esther 2:7),* the Sages explain that he married her (*Megillah* 13a). Similarly here, the *paytan* refers to God's chosen mate, Israel (*Arugas HaBosem*).

Others interpret: *The nation You chose to serve in Your Holy Temple.*

וְאֵין לִצְמִידָתֶךָ — *And [she] is not able to hold tightly to You. Matteh Levi* reverses the persons: *And You do not hold tightly to her.*

According to *Arugas HaBosem,* the phrase modifies אֲדוֹנִים, *[strange] lords,* and means *who cannot be compared to You.*

דִּין הֶרֶג לְעַצְמָהּ מַקְנֶסֶת — *A sentence of death [as a martyr] upon herself she pronounces.* In every generation, the Jew has proudly surrendered his life to sanctify God's Name. *Meshech Chochmah (Genesis 22:14)* explains that martyrdom became ingrained in the Jewish character when the Patriarch Isaac readily encouraged his father, Abraham, to sacrifice him in accordance with God's command.

וְגַן נָעוּל¹ הֶפְקֵר כְּמַלּוּחַ,*

《 like an ined- ⟨ is made ⟨ that is ⟨ And the
ible weed,* ownerless locked [Israel] garden

וּמַעְיָן חָתוּם¹ נִרְפָּס דָּלוּחַ.²

《 and ⟨ is ⟨ that is sealed ⟨ the
muddied. trampled [Israel] spring

זַעַם כְּרֶגַע³ וְעַתָּה לְהִפּוּךְ, זֵרֵי קֹדֶשׁ* עַתָּה לִשְׁפּוּךְ,⁴

《 poured out ⟨ are now ⟨ of ⟨ The 《 it has ⟨ but now 《 for a ⟨ Your
[like trash]. holiness* crowns changed [to [mere] anger
longlasting]. moment, [was once]

חַבַּת רֵעַ כְּקֶרֶן הַפּוּךְ,*⁵

《 gem,* ⟨ [once as beautiful 《 of the ⟨ The
as Job's daughters,] Friend, beloved
as a brilliant

חֲשׁוּבָה וַעֲזוּבָה כְּקוֹרַעַת בַּפּוּךְ.⁶

《 [her eyes] ⟨ like [a harlot] ⟨ and is ⟨ is [now] con-
with mascara. elongating abandoned sidered to be

טוֹב הַתֹּאַר קְדוֹרַנִּית מִפֶּרֶךְ,

《 from hard ⟨ she is [now] ⟨ appear- ⟨ [Formerly]
labor, blackened ance, of beautiful

טְרִיָּה מַכָּה מִבְּלִי אֶרֶךְ,⁷

《 a cure. ⟨ without ⟨ are her ⟨ raw
wounds,

---

(1) Cf. *Song of Songs* 4:12. (2) Cf. *Ezekiel* 32:2. (3) Cf. *Isaiah* 26:20.
(4) Cf. *Lamentations* 4:1. (5) *Job* 42:14. (6) Cf. *Jeremiah* 4:30. (7) Cf. *Isaiah* 1:6.

כְּמַלּוּחַ — *Like an inedible weed.* According to *Rashi* (to *Job* 30:4) and *Arugas HaBosem*, this is the name of a very bitter herb. *Matteh Levi* understands it as an adjective describing herbs grown in אֶרֶץ מְלֵחָה, *salty earth,* and thus lacking in nutritional value.

זֵרֵי קֹדֶשׁ — *The crowns of holiness.* In describing the appointments of the *Mishkan* (Tabernacle), the Torah uses the expression זֵר זָהָב סָבִיב, *a crown of gold all around,* three times: for the Ark of the Covenant (*Exodus* 25:11); for the Table of the *Panim* Loaves (ibid. v. 24); and for the Incense Altar (ibid. 30:3). According to the Talmud, the crown of the Ark represents the Crown of Torah scholarship; the crown of the Table alludes to the Crown of Kingship; and the crown of the Altar stands for the Crown of Priesthood (*Yoma* 72b with *Rashi*; see also *Avos* 4:17). These Crowns — once borne so proudly by the Sages, the House of David, and the *Kohanim* — have been dashed by our conquerors and discarded like trash.

כְּקֶרֶן הַפּוּךְ — *[Once as beautiful as Job's daughters,] as a brilliant gem.* The reference here is to Job's third daughter, Keren Happuch, who, with her two older sisters, Jemimah and Keziah, was the fairest in the land (see *Job* 42:14-15). According to the *Targum* and *Metzudos*, קֶרֶן means *shine* and פּוּךְ is the name of a precious stone (see *Isaiah* 54:11). Hence Keren Happuch means *a brilliant gem.* According to *Rashi*, קֶרֶן means *horn* and refers to a horn-shaped case used to carry פּוּךְ, *mascara* (see *Jeremiah* 4:30).

יוֹם נָקָם¹ נִסְתַּם דֶּרֶךְ, יוֹם שָׁלוּם¹ נֶחְתַּם חֶרֶף.

《 is the 〈 — sealed 《 of 〈 to [view] 《 is the 〈 — closed 《 of ven- 〈 To [arrive
lattice. up reckoning the day path; off geance at] the day

כֹּחַ הַסַּבָּל הִכְשִׁיל² נֶטַל,

《 from the bur- 〈 failed 〈 of the one who 〈 The
den [of exile]; bears [Israel] strength

כָּסוּל וְשָׂחוּל הַנִּשְׁאָר מְקֻטָּל,

《 from the slaughter. 〈 are those left 〈 and lame 〈 limping

לֹא לְמַרְגּוֹעַ נָד וּמְטַלְטָל, לְעָמֵל וְיָגֵעַ וְאַחֵר נוֹטֵל.

《 take [their 〈 — only to 《 unto 〈 then toil 《 and roam, 〈 they 〈 rest 〈 Without
fruits]. have others weariness wander

מַטַּע קֶרֶן* שָׁמֵן הַמִּדְרָשָׁן,³

《 and 〈 that is 〈 in a 〈 [Israel, the
fruitful; fertile corner vine] planted

מִרְמָס מַדּוּעַ כַּחֲרֻלֵּי כְבָשָׁן,

《 [destined] for 〈 like thorns 《 — why — 《 to be
the furnace? trampled

נוֹצֵר לְמַעְלָה* לֹא יִישָׁן, נִטְעוֹ לְמִשְׁלוֹחַ פָּרוֹת הַבָּשָׁן.*

《 of the 〈 for the 〈 is turned into 〈 His 《 let Him 〈 on High* 〈 The
Bashan.* [fat] cows pastureland planting not sleep! Watchman

שׁוֹרֵקָה מַה בֶּצַע וְנִקְטֶפֶת,

《 if [its fruit] has 〈 profit is 〈 what 《 [From] the
been plucked? there vine-branch,

סוֹרֵחַת מַה יִּתְרוֹן וְנֶחֱטֶפֶת,

《 if it has been 〈 benefit 〈 what 《 [From] the
plundered? is there spreading vine,

---

(1) Cf. *Isaiah* 34:8; some editions of *Selichos* read יוֹם גְּאֻלָּה, *a day of redemption*,
instead of יוֹם שָׁלוּם. (2) Cf. *Nehemiah* 4:4. (3) Cf. *Isaiah* 5:1.

קֶרֶן — *In a corner*. The translation follows *Rashi* (to *Isaiah* 5:1). *Targum*, however, renders *peak*. According to *Ibn Ezra*, this alludes to a particularly fertile area near Jerusalem. *Radak* understands it as a reference to the Holy Land in general.

נוֹצֵר לְמַעְלָה — *The Watchman on High*. The Midrash lists sixteen ways in which Israel is compared to a grapevine. One of these is that just as the vine's watchman stands above it to protect it, so does Israel's Guardian stand over the nation to pro-

tect it (*Vayikra Rabbah* 36:2).

פָּרוֹת הַבָּשָׁן — *For the [fat] cows of the Bashan*. The land of Bashan had extremely rich pasturage, and the herds of cattle that grazed there were world renowned for the quality of their meat. The prophet (*Amos* 4:1) uses *cows of Bashan* as an epithet for the wives of wealthy aristocrats who need not work for a living, but fatten themselves on the labor of others (see commentaries to *Amos* 4:1; *Shabbos* 32b). Here, it is a reference to the oppressor nations that plunder

עַל יַד חֲקוּקָה וְטוֹטָפֶת,* עַל מָה אַהֲבָתָה נִשְׁטֶפֶת.¹

» washed away?   ‹ is [His] love for her   ‹ what for   ‹ reason   » and [on His] crown —*   ‹ is engraved   ‹ [She who] on [God's] arm

פְּעֻלַּת הָרוֹבִים מְעוּט מְלֶאכֶת,*

« work,*   ‹ are but little   ‹ of the youths [the nations]   ‹ The [good] deeds

פְּרִיעַת שָׂכָר רַבָּה וְהוֹלֶכֶת,

« and ever-increasing.   ‹ is excessive   ‹ of their wages   ‹ [yet] the payment

צוֹפֶה הַפָּנוֹת וְעִתָּה נִמְשֶׁכֶת,

« drags on,   ‹ but its time [of coming]   » You turning Your attention [to us],   ‹ [We] anticipate

צָרָה פְּקוּדָה וְאַחֶרֶת נִסְמֶכֶת.

« follows right after.   ‹ another   ‹ strikes,   ‹ [while] one trouble

קֹדֶשׁ רֵאשִׁית* עֲרֵמַת שְׂעָרִים,

« of the highest price,   ‹ heaps of [grain]   » of the first-fruits,*   ‹ The holiness

קַצְוֵי אֶרֶץ זְרוּיִים כִּשְׂעוֹרִים,

«   ‹ as barley is [winnowed].   ‹ is scattered   ‹ of the earth   ‹ [to] the ends

---

(1) Cf. *Song of Songs* 8:7.

the fruits of Israel's labor.

עַל יַד ... וְטוֹטָפֶת — *[She who] on [God's] arm ... and [on His] crown.* The Talmud adduces various verses to show that God wears *tefillin*. Moreover, just as Israel's *tefillin* contain Torah passages that declare God's praises, so do God's *tefillin* contain passages that praise Israel (*Berachos* 6a). Thus, Israel is engraved in the *tefillin* that God wears on His arm and on His head.

פְּעֻלַּת הָרוֹבִים מִיעוּט מְלֶאכֶת — *The [good] deeds of the youths [the nations] are but little work.* The Midrash uses a parable to compare Israel's service with that of the other nations: A king once hired many פּוֹעֲלִים, *laborers*, one of whom toiled long days [thus accomplishing much more than any of the others]. When the workers came to receive their wages, the king took this worker and

said, "To you, my son, will I turn my attention! הָרוֹבִים הַלָּלוּ, *These youths*, who did for me מְלָאכָה מוּעֶטֶת, *little work*, I shall give but small wages. But you I shall recompense with great reward in the future!"

So does God say unto Israel, "To you, My son, will I turn My attention! These nations who did little work on My behalf [— they had only seven *mitzvos* to keep —] I shall give but small wages in this world. But you [who fulfilled six hundred and thirteen *mitzvos*] I shall recompense with great reward in the World to Come" (*Sifra, Bechukosai* 2:5:5).

קֹדֶשׁ רֵאשִׁית — *The holiness of the first-fruits.* A reference to Israel, as the prophet proclaims: קֹדֶשׁ יִשְׂרָאֵל לַה׳, *Israel is holy unto HASHEM*, רֵאשִׁית תְּבוּאָתוֹ, *the first of His grain crop (Jeremiah* 2:3).

רוּחַ מְנַשֶּׁבֶת בַּעֲלֵי יְעָרִים,

《 of the 〈 among 〈 blowing 〈 Like a
forests, the leaves wind

רָדוּף נִשְׁמֶטֶת נָסִים וְנִסְעָרִים.

《 in terror. 〈 they flee 〈 with drawn 〈 as if
swords pursued

❖ שְׁמֹנֶה וְתִשְׁעִים הָאָלוֹת הָאֵלֶּה.[1]

《 those that [the 《 are the 〈 and ninety 〈 Eight
Torah decreed]; curses,

שָׁלְמוּ אֵלֶּה מֵאֵלֶּה וְכָאֵלֶּה.*

《 and a similar 〈 — all 《 have been 〈 fulfilled
amount besides.* these these [upon us]

תְּרַחֵם תְּקַבְּצֵנוּ מִקַּרְנוֹת אֵלֶּה.

《 from these corners 〈 gather us in 〈 Have mercy,
[of the world];

אָז יֹאמְרוּ בַגּוֹיִם, הִגְדִּיל יהוה לַעֲשׂוֹת עִם אֵלֶּה.[2]

《 these 〈 with 〈 done 〈 has 〈 Greatly 《 among the 〈 will they 〈 then
[people]! HASHEM nations, declare

ALL, WHILE STANDING:

אֵל מֶלֶךְ יוֹשֵׁב עַל כִּסֵּא רַחֲמִים, מִתְנַהֵג

〈 Who acts 《 of mercy, 〈 the throne 〈 on 〈 Who sits 〈 King 〈 O God,

---

(1) See *Deuteronomy* 28:15-68. (2) *Psalms* 126:2.

שְׁמֹנָה וְתִשְׁעִים הָאָלוֹת הָאֵלֶּה. שָׁלְמוּ אֵלֶּה מֵאֵלֶּה וְכָאֵלֶּה — *Eight and ninety are the curses, those that [the Torah decreed]; fulfilled [upon us] have these — all these and a similar amount besides.* The *Tochachah* (passage of rebuke) in *Deuteronomy* (28:15-68) contains ninety-eight curses or threats of retribution that will come upon Israel if it will not follow the *mitzvos* of the Torah. The *paytan* here bemoans the fact that many more than ninety-eight punishments, pogroms, exiles, oppressions, and other forms of Divine retribution have come upon us. "Therefore," he pleads, "have mercy and gather us from the four corners of our dispersion."

Alternatively, the words אֵלֶּה מֵאֵלֶּה וְכָאֵלֶּה, literally, *these, from these, and like these,* allude to the Altar offerings. *Rashi* (to *Numbers* 29:18) teaches that the fourteen lambs brought as part of the *mussaf*-offering on each of the seven days

of Succos served to protect Israel against the ninety-eight (fourteen times seven) curses of *Deuteronomy*. Similarly, the *paytan* here assumes, other Altar offerings must have served the same purpose. Thus, he states: שָׁלְמוּ, *They have been fulfilled* — the offerings alluded to by the words אֵלֶּה מֵאֵלֶּה and כָאֵלֶּה. For the last, summarizing verse in the chapter describing the Festival *mussaf*-offerings begins, אֵלֶּה תַּעֲשׂוּ, *These [offerings] shall you make* (*Numbers* 29:39). The laws of the *minchah*-offering state: *You shall bring the minchah-offering that has been made* מֵאֵלֶּה, *from these [aforementioned ingredients]* (*Leviticus* 2:8). And the *mussaf*-offerings of Pesach are summarized, כָּאֵלֶּה תַּעֲשׂוּ, *like these shall you make* (*Numbers* 28:24). Thus, since we are no longer able to bring the offerings described as אֵלֶּה מֵאֵלֶּה and כָאֵלֶּה, we are afflicted with the ninety-eight curses of the *Tochachah*.

בַּחֲסִידוּת, מוֹחֵל עֲוֹנוֹת עַמּוֹ, מַעֲבִיר רִאשׁוֹן

‹ [sins,] one ‹ Who removes ‹‹ of His people, ‹ the sins ‹ Who pardons ‹‹ with kindness,

רִאשׁוֹן,[1] מַרְבֶּה מְחִילָה לַחַטָּאִים וּסְלִיחָה לַפּוֹשְׁעִים,

‹‹ to willful sinners, ‹ and forgiveness ‹ to unintentional sinners ‹ pardon ‹ Who abundantly grants ‹‹ by one,

עֹשֶׂה צְדָקוֹת עִם כָּל בָּשָׂר וָרוּחַ, לֹא כְרָעָתָם

‹ in accord with their wickedness ‹ — not ‹‹ and spirit ‹ [beings of] flesh ‹ all ‹ with ‹ acts of generosity ‹ Who performs

תִּגְמוֹל. ❖ אֵל הוֹרֵיתָ לָּנוּ לוֹמַר שְׁלֹשׁ עֶשְׂרֵה, וּזְכוֹר

‹ remember ‹‹ the Thirteen [Attributes of Mercy]; ‹ to recite ‹ us ‹ You taught ‹ O God, ‹‹ do You repay them!

לָּנוּ הַיּוֹם בְּרִית שְׁלֹשׁ עֶשְׂרֵה, כְּמוֹ שֶׁהוֹדַעְתָּ לֶעָנָיו

‹ to the humble one [Moses] ‹ You made ‹ as ‹‹ of [these] Thirteen, ‹ the covenant ‹ today ‹ for us

מִקֶּדֶם, כְּמוֹ שֶׁכָּתוּב, וַיֵּרֶד יהוה בֶּעָנָן וַיִּתְיַצֵּב עִמּוֹ

‹ with him ‹ and stood ‹ in a cloud ‹ And HASHEM descended ‹‹ it is written: ‹ as ‹‹ in ancient times,

שָׁם, וַיִּקְרָא בְשֵׁם יהוה.[2]

‹‹ of HASHEM. ‹ with the Name ‹ and He called out ‹‹ there,

CONGREGATION, THEN *CHAZZAN:*

וַיַּעֲבֹר יהוה עַל פָּנָיו וַיִּקְרָא:

‹‹ and proclaimed: ‹‹ [Moses'] ‹ before ‹ And HASHEM passed face,

CONGREGATION AND *CHAZZAN* **RECITE LOUDLY AND IN UNISON:**

יהוה, יהוה, אֵל, רַחוּם, וְחַנּוּן, אֶרֶךְ אַפַּיִם,

‹ to anger, ‹ Slow ‹‹ and Gracious, ‹ Compassionate ‹ God, ‹ HASHEM, ‹ HASHEM,

וְרַב חֶסֶד, וֶאֱמֶת, נֹצֵר חֶסֶד לָאֲלָפִים, נֹשֵׂא עָוֹן,

‹ of iniquity, ‹ Forgiver ‹‹ for thousands [of generations], ‹ of kindness ‹ Preserver ‹‹ and Truth, ‹ in ‹ and Kindness Abundant

וָפֶשַׁע, וְחַטָּאָה, וְנַקֵּה.[3] וְסָלַחְתָּ לַעֲוֹנֵנוּ וּלְחַטָּאתֵנוּ

‹‹ and our sins, ‹ our iniquities ‹ May You forgive ‹‹ and Who absolves. ‹ and inadvertent sin, ‹ willful sin,

---

(1) *Rosh Hashanah* 17a. (2) *Exodus* 34:5. (3) 34:6-7.

וּנְחַלְתָּנוּ.[1] סְלַח לָנוּ אָבִינוּ כִּי חָטָאנוּ, מְחַל לָנוּ

《 us, 〈 pardon 《 we have 〈 for 《 our 〈 us, 〈 Forgive 《 and make us
                sinned;   Father,   Your heritage.

מַלְכֵּנוּ כִּי פָשָׁעְנוּ. כִּי אַתָּה אֲדֹנָי טוֹב וְסַלָּח,

《 and 〈 are 〈 O Lord, 〈 You, 〈 For 《 we have 〈 for 《 our King,
forgiving, good   willfully sinned.

וְרַב חֶסֶד לְכָל קֹרְאֶיךָ.[2]

《 who call 〈 to all 〈 kind 〈 and
upon You.   abundantly

סְלִיחָה ז / SELICHAH 7

(פזמון)

CHAZZAN, THEN CONGREGATION:

מַלְאֲכֵי רַחֲמִים* מְשָׁרְתֵי עֶלְיוֹן,

《 of the Supreme One, 〈 servants 〈 of mercy,* 〈 O angels

חַלּוּ נָא פְּנֵי אֵל[3] בְּמֵיטַב הִגָּיוֹן,

《 expression: 〈 with eloquent 〈 God 〈 before 〈 please, 〈 entreat,

אוּלַי יָחוֹס עַם עָנִי[4] וְאֶבְיוֹן, אוּלַי יְרַחֵם.

《 He will 〈 perhaps 《 and 〈 who 〈 on [His] 〈 He will 〈 Perhaps
have mercy.   destitute; are poor people have pity

CONGREGATION, THEN CHAZZAN:

אוּלַי יְרַחֵם שְׁאֵרִית יוֹסֵף,[5]

《 of 〈 on the 〈 He will 〈 Perhaps
Joseph,   remnant   have mercy

שְׁפָלִים וְנִבְזִים[6] פְּשׁוּחֵי[7] שֶׁסֶף,[8]

〈 and hewed 〈 split open 〈 and 〈 degraded,
down,   disgraced,

שְׁבוּיֵי חִנָּם מְכוּרֵי בְּלֹא כֶסֶף.[9]

《 money. 〈 for no 〈 sold 〈 without 〈 taken
                              reason, captive

---

(1) *Exodus* 34:9. (2) *Psalms* 86:5. (3) *Malachi* 1:9. (4) Cf. *Zephaniah* 3:12. (5) Cf. *Amos* 5:15;
see commentary to *Selichah* 67, s.v. בְּכוֹר שׁוֹר. (6) Cf. *Malachi* 2:9. (7) Cf. *Lamentations* 3:11.
(8) Cf. *I Samuel* 15:33. (9) Cf. *Isaiah* 52:3; see commentary to *Selichah* 11, s.v. לִמְכוּרֵי חִנָּם.

ﬦﬤ מַלְאֲכֵי רַחֲמִים — *O angels of mercy*. The
propriety and permissibility of requesting angelic intervention in bringing our
prayers before God is a very controversial
halachic issue in the area of prayers. See

the introduction for a full discussion.

The *paytan* signed his name — שְׁמוּאֵל
כֹּהֵן יְחִי, *Shmuel the Kohen, may he live*
— in the acrostic of the verses, as indicated
by the bold type. Some speculate that he

שׁוֹאֲגִים בִּתְפִלָּה וּמְבַקְשִׁים רִשָׁיוֹן,

⟪ for permission: ⟩ and plead ⟨ in prayer ⟨ They cry out

אוּלַי יָחוֹס עַם עָנִי וְאֶבְיוֹן, אוּלַי יְרַחֵם.

⟪ He will ⟨ perhaps ⟪ and ⟨ who ⟨ on [His] ⟨ He will ⟨ Perhaps
have mercy.   destitute; are poor people have pity

CONGREGATION, THEN *CHAZZAN:*

אוּלַי יְרַחֵם מְעֻנֵּי כֶבֶל,[1]

⟪ by ⟨ on those ⟨ He will ⟨ Perhaps
chains, tortured have mercy

מְלֻמְּדֵי מַכּוֹת בְּעִנּוּי סֵבֶל,

⟪ of [their] ⟨ in the ⟨ to blows ⟨ accustomed
suffering, oppression

מְנוֹד רֹאשׁ[2] נְתוּנִים בְּיוֹשְׁבֵי תֵבֵל.

⟪ of the ⟨ by the ⟨ they are ⟨ of ⟨ [to ridicule]
world, inhabitants subjected heads by a shaking

מָשָׁל בָּעַמִּים[3] בְּקֶצֶף וּבִזָּיוֹן,[4]

⟪ and ⟨ with wrath ⟨ among the ⟨ a byword
contempt: peoples [for contempt]

אוּלַי יָחוֹס עַם עָנִי וְאֶבְיוֹן, אוּלַי יְרַחֵם.

⟪ He will ⟨ perhaps ⟪ and ⟨ who ⟨ on [His] ⟨ He will ⟨ Perhaps
have mercy.   destitute; are poor people have pity

CONGREGATION, THEN *CHAZZAN:*

אוּלַי יְרַחֵם וְיֵרֶא בָּעֳנִי עַמּוֹ,[5]

⟪ of His ⟨ the ⟨ and see ⟨ He will ⟨ Perhaps
people, suffering have mercy

וְיַקְשֵׁב וְיִשְׁמַע[6] הַצָּגִים לְעֻמּוֹ,

⟪ before ⟨ those ⟨ and hear ⟨ and listen
Him, standing to

וְעוֹדִים בְּלַחַשׁ מוּסָר לָמוֹ.[7]

⟪ them, ⟨ [when He] ⟨ in silent ⟨ gathered
chastises prayer

וְעֵינֵיהֶם תּוֹלִים לִמְצֹא רִצָּיוֹן,

⟪ favor: ⟨ to find ⟨ they raise ⟨ as their eyes

---

(1) Cf. *Psalms* 105:18. (2) 44:15, cf. 22:8. (3) Cf. 44:15. (4) Cf. *Esther* 1:18. (5) Cf. *Exodus* 3:7. (6) *Malachi* 3:16. (7) Cf. *Isaiah* 26:16.

---

is R' Shmuel ben R' Yehudah HaKohen of Mainz, Germany, who, along with his wife and children, was martyred during the First Crusade in 1096.

אוּלַי יָחוֹס עַם עָנִי וְאֶבְיוֹן, אוּלַי יְרַחֵם.

《 He will 〈 perhaps 《 and 〈 who 〈 on [His] 〈 He will 〈 Perhaps
have mercy.   destitute;   are poor people   have pity

CONGREGATION, THEN *CHAZZAN:*

אוּלַי יְרַחֵם אוֹמְרֵי סְלַח נָא,[1]

《 Forgive please! 〈 on those 〈 He will 〈 Perhaps
who say,   have mercy

אוֹמְצֵי שְׁבָחוֹ בְּכָל עֵת וְעוֹנָה,

《 and season, 〈 time 〈 at every 〈 His praise 〈 who intensify

אֲגוּדִים בַּצָּרָה לִשְׁפּוֹךְ תְּחִנָּה.

《 supplication; 〈 to pour out 〈 in distress 〈 united

אֶת פְּנֵי אֱלֹהֵיהֶם שׁוֹפְכִים לֵב דִּוָּיוֹן,

《 full of 〈 a 〈 they pour 〈 their God 〈 before
anguish: heart   out

אוּלַי יָחוֹס עַם עָנִי וְאֶבְיוֹן, אוּלַי יְרַחֵם.

《 He will 〈 perhaps 《 and 〈 who 〈 on [His] 〈 He will 〈 Perhaps
have mercy.   destitute;   are poor people   have pity

CONGREGATION, THEN *CHAZZAN:*

אוּלַי יְרַחֵם לָקְתָה בְּכִפְלַיִם,[2]

《 doubly, 〈 on [the 〈 He will 〈 Perhaps
nation that] have mercy
was punished

לְעוּטָה אֲרָיוֹת כְּמוֹ בְּפִי שַׁחֲלַיִם,[*3]

《 of lions 〈 by the 〈 as well 〈 by lions 〈 devoured
[Rome],*   mouth   as   [Babylon],

לֻקָּה וּמִשְׁתַּלֶּמֶת[4] בַּעֲוֹן שׁוּלַיִם,[5]

《 [visible] on the 〈 for its 〈 and is repaid 〈 received
bottom of its   sins   beatings
garments,

לֹא שָׁכְחָה בְּכָל זֹאת מִכְתָּב עֹז חֶבְיוֹן,[6]

《 that was 〈 of [God's] 〈 the 《 this, 〈 despite 《 forgotten, 〈 yet has
hidden   might,   Scripture   all   not
[until Sinai]:

---

(1) *Numbers* 14:19. (2) Some editions of *Selichos* read לָקְחָה כִּפְלַיִם,
she has received [lit., *taken*] *double* [*punishment*]; cf. *Isaiah* 40:2.
(3) *Hosea* 13:7. (4) *Makkos* 4b. (5) Cf. *Jeremiah* 13:22. (6) Cf. *Habakkuk* 3:4.

שַׁחֲלִים ... אֲרָיוֹת — *Lions ... lions.* The Talmud records six Scriptural names for the

lion: אֲרִי, כְּפִיר, לָבִיא, לַיִשׁ, שַׁחַל, שַׁחַץ (*San-*
hedrin 95a).

אוּלַי יָחוֹס עַם עָנִי וְאֶבְיוֹן, אוּלַי יְרַחֵם.

» He will 〈 perhaps » and 〈 who 〈 on [His] 〈 He will 〈 Perhaps
have mercy.   destitute; are poor people have pity

CONGREGATION, THEN *CHAZZAN*:

אוּלַי יְרַחֵם כְּבוּשֵׁי פָנִים,

» their faces 〈 on those 〈 He will 〈 Perhaps
[in shame], who hide have mercy

הַשּׁוֹמְעִים חֶרְפָּתָם וְלֹא מְשִׁיבִים[1] וְעוֹנִים,

» or answer. 〈 respond 〈 but do 〈 insults directed 〈 who hear
not at them

נִצְחוֹ מְקַוִּים וּלְיִשְׁעוֹ נִשְׁעָנִים.

» they rely, 〈 and on His 〈 they 〈 For [God's]
salvation hope, triumph

כִּי לֹא כָלוּ רַחֲמָיו[2] בְּכִלָּיוֹן,

» totally: 〈 are His 〈 finished 〈 not 〈 for
mercies

אוּלַי יָחוֹס עַם עָנִי וְאֶבְיוֹן, אוּלַי יְרַחֵם.

» He will 〈 perhaps » and 〈 who 〈 on [His] 〈 He will 〈 Perhaps
have mercy.   destitute; are poor people have pity

CONGREGATION, THEN *CHAZZAN*:

אוּלַי יְרַחֵם יְחַלֵּץ עָנִי בְעָנְיוֹ,[3]

» from its 〈 the 〈 and 〈 He will 〈 Perhaps
affliction, afflicted set free have mercy
[nation]

חֲבוּשׁוֹ יַתִּיר מֵאֶרֶץ שְׁבִיו,

» of its 〈 from the 〈 he shall 〈 His
captivity, land release imprisoned
[nation]

יִגְהֶה מְזוֹרוֹ[4] וְיַחְבּוֹשׁ חָלָיו.

» its disease, 〈 and curing 〈 its wound 〈 healing

צַעֲקָתוֹ יִשְׁמַע וְיָחִישׁ עֵת פִּדְיוֹן,

» of 〈 the 〈 and He will 〈 He will 〈 its outcry
redemption: time hasten hear

אוּלַי יָחוֹס עַם עָנִי וְאֶבְיוֹן, אוּלַי יְרַחֵם.

» He will 〈 perhaps » and 〈 who 〈 on [His] 〈 He will 〈 Perhaps
have mercy.   destitute; are poor people have pity

---

(1) Cf. *Shabbos* 88b. (2) *Lamentations* 3:22. (3) *Job* 36:15. (4) Cf. *Hosea* 5:13.

ALL, WHILE STANDING:

אֵל מֶלֶךְ יוֹשֵׁב עַל כִּסֵּא רַחֲמִים, מִתְנַהֵג

⟨ Who acts ⟪ of mercy, ⟨ the throne ⟨ on ⟨ Who sits ⟨ King ⟨ O God,

בַּחֲסִידוּת, מוֹחֵל עֲוֹנוֹת עַמּוֹ, מַעֲבִיר רִאשׁוֹן

⟨ [sins] one ⟨ Who removes ⟪of His people, ⟨ the sins ⟨ Who pardons ⟪ with kindness,

רִאשׁוֹן,¹ מַרְבֶּה מְחִילָה לַחַטָּאִים וּסְלִיחָה לַפּוֹשְׁעִים,

⟪ to willful ⟨ and ⟨ to unintentional ⟨ pardon ⟨ Who abun- ⟪ by one,
sinners,   forgiveness   sinners   dantly grants

עֹשֶׂה צְדָקוֹת עִם כָּל בָּשָׂר וָרוּחַ, לֹא כְרָעָתָם

⟨ in accord with ⟨ — not ⟪ and spirit ⟨ [beings ⟨ all ⟨ with ⟨ acts of ⟨ Who
their wickedness   of] flesh   generosity   performs

תִגְמוֹל. ❖ אֵל הוֹרֵיתָ לָּנוּ לוֹמַר שְׁלֹשׁ עֶשְׂרֵה,

⟪ the Thirteen ⟨ to recite ⟨ us ⟨ You taught ⟨ O God, ⟪ do You
[Attributes of Mercy];   repay them!

וּזְכוֹר לָנוּ הַיּוֹם בְּרִית שְׁלֹשׁ עֶשְׂרֵה, כְּמוֹ שֶׁהוֹדַעְתָּ

⟨ You made ⟨ as ⟪ of [these] Thirteen, ⟨ the ⟨ today ⟨ for ⟨ remember
known   covenant   us

לֶעָנָיו מִקֶּדֶם, כְּמוֹ שֶׁכָּתוּב, וַיֵּרֶד יהוה בֶּעָנָן

⟨ in a ⟨ And HASHEM ⟪ it is written: ⟨ as ⟪ in ancient ⟨ to the humble
cloud   descended   times,   one [Moses]

וַיִּתְיַצֵּב עִמּוֹ שָׁם, וַיִּקְרָא בְשֵׁם יהוה.²

⟪ of ⟨ with the ⟨ and He ⟪ there, ⟨ with ⟨ and stood
HASHEM.   Name   called out   him

CONGREGATION, THEN *CHAZZAN:*

וַיַּעֲבֹר יהוה עַל פָּנָיו וַיִּקְרָא:

⟪ and ⟪ [Moses'] ⟨ before ⟨ And HASHEM passed
proclaimed: face,

CONGREGATION AND *CHAZZAN* **RECITE LOUDLY AND IN UNISON:**

יהוה, יהוה, אֵל, רַחוּם, וְחַנּוּן, אֶרֶךְ אַפַּיִם,

⟨ to anger, ⟨ Slow ⟪ and Gracious, ⟨ Compassionate ⟨ God, ⟨ HASHEM, ⟨ HASHEM,

וְרַב חֶסֶד, וֶאֱמֶת, נֹצֵר חֶסֶד לָאֲלָפִים, נֹשֵׂא עָוֹן,

⟨ of ⟨ Forgiver ⟪ for thousands ⟨ of ⟨ Preserver ⟪ and ⟨ in ⟨ and
iniquity,   [of generations], kindness   Truth,   Kindness Abundant

וָפֶשַׁע, וְחַטָּאָה, וְנַקֵּה.³ וְסָלַחְתָּ לַעֲוֹנֵנוּ וּלְחַטָּאתֵנוּ

⟪ and our sins, ⟨ our ⟨ May You ⟪ and Who ⟨ and inadvertent ⟨ willful sin,
iniquities   forgive   absolves.   sin,

(1) *Rosh Hashanah* 17a. (2) *Exodus* 34:5. (3) 34:6-7.

1. וּנְחַלְתָּנוּ. סְלַח לָנוּ אָבִינוּ כִּי חָטָאנוּ, מְחַל לָנוּ

  ⟨ us, ⟨ pardon ⟪ we have ⟨ for ⟪ our ⟨ us, ⟨ Forgive ⟪ and make us
            sinned;   Father,   Your heritage.

מַלְכֵּנוּ כִּי פָשָׁעְנוּ. כִּי אַתָּה אֲדֹנָי טוֹב וְסַלָּח,

  ⟪ and ⟨ are ⟨ O Lord, ⟨ You, ⟨ For ⟪ we have ⟨ for ⟪ our King,
   forgiving,   good   willfully sinned.

2. וְרַב חֶסֶד לְכָל קֹרְאֶיךָ.

  ⟪ who call ⟨ to all ⟨ kind ⟨ and
   upon You.   abundantly

ALL:

3. זְכֹר רַחֲמֶיךָ יהוה וַחֲסָדֶיךָ, כִּי מֵעוֹלָם הֵמָּה.

  ⟪ are ⟨ eternal ⟨ for ⟪ and Your ⟨ HASHEM, ⟨ Your ⟨ Remember
   they.   kindnesses,   mercies,

4. זָכְרֵנוּ יהוה בִּרְצוֹן עַמֶּךָ, פָּקְדֵנוּ בִּישׁוּעָתֶךָ. זְכֹר

  ⟨ Re- ⟪ with Your ⟨ recall us ⟪ to Your ⟨ when You ⟨ HASHEM, ⟨ Remem-
   member   salvation.   people;   show favor   ber us,

עֲדָתְךָ קָנִיתָ קֶּדֶם, גָּאַלְתָּ שֵׁבֶט נַחֲלָתֶךָ, הַר צִיּוֹן זֶה

  ⟨ the one ⟨ of ⟨ the ⟪ of Your ⟨ the ⟨ You ⟪ long ⟨ which You ⟨ Your con-
   [where] Zion, mountain heritage;   tribe redeemed   ago, acquired gregation,

5. שָׁכַנְתָּ בּוֹ. זְכֹר יהוה חִבַּת יְרוּשָׁלַיִם, אַהֲבַת

  ⟨ the love ⟪ of Jerusalem; ⟨ the ⟨ HASHEM, ⟨ Remem- ⟪ there. ⟨ You rested
               affection   ber,   Your Presence

6. צִיּוֹן אַל תִּשְׁכַּח לָנֶצַח. אַתָּה תָקוּם תְּרַחֵם צִיּוֹן כִּי

  ⟨ for ⟪ to ⟨ and show ⟨ will arise ⟨ You ⟪ forever. ⟨ forget ⟨ do not ⟨ of
   Zion,   mercy   Zion

עֵת לְחֶנְנָהּ, כִּי בָא מוֹעֵד. זְכֹר יהוה לִבְנֵי אֱדוֹם

  ⟨ of ⟨ [to repay] ⟨ HASHEM, ⟨ Re- ⟪ the appointed time ⟨ for ⟪ [there will come]
   Edom the offspring,   member, will have come.   the time to favor her,

אֵת יוֹם יְרוּשָׁלָיִם, הָאֹמְרִים עָרוּ עָרוּ עַד הַיְסוֹד

  ⟨ the very ⟨ to ⟨ Destroy ⟪ Destroy! ⟪ [to repay] ⟪ of Jerusalem; ⟨ for the day
   foundation   those who say,

8. בָּהּ. זְכֹר לְאַבְרָהָם לְיִצְחָק וּלְיִשְׂרָאֵל עֲבָדֶיךָ,

  ⟪ Your servants, ⟨ and for Israel, ⟨ for Isaac, ⟨ for Abraham, ⟨ Remember ⟪ of it!

אֲשֶׁר נִשְׁבַּעְתָּ לָהֶם בָּךְ, וַתְּדַבֵּר אֲלֵהֶם, אַרְבֶּה

  ⟨ I shall ⟪ to them, ⟨ and ⟪ by Your ⟨ to them ⟨ You swore ⟨ that
   increase   You said   Being,

---

(1) *Exodus* 34:9. (2) *Psalms* 86:5. (3) 25:6. (4) Cf. 106:4. (5) 74:2.
(6) This is not a Scriptural verse. (7) *Psalms* 102:14. (8) 137:7.

אֶת זַרְעֲכֶם כְּכוֹכְבֵי הַשָּׁמַיִם, וְכָל הָאָרֶץ הַזֹּאת אֲשֶׁר
⟨ of ⟨ of this land ⟨ and all ⟪ of the ⟨ like the stars ⟨ Your offspring
which heavens;

אָמַרְתִּי, אֶתֵּן לְזַרְעֲכֶם, וְנָחֲלוּ לְעֹלָם.¹ זְכֹר לַעֲבָדֶיךָ
⟨ of Your ⟨ Remember ⟪ forever. ⟨ and they ⟨ to your ⟨ I will ⟨ I spoke
servants, [the merits] will inherit it offspring, give

לְאַבְרָהָם לְיִצְחָק וּלְיַעֲקֹב, אַל תֵּפֶן אֶל קְשִׁי
⟨ the stub- ⟨ to ⟨ pay ⟨ do ⟪ and of Jacob; ⟨ of Isaac, ⟨ of Abraham,
bornness attention not

הָעָם הַזֶּה וְאֶל רִשְׁעוֹ וְאֶל חַטָּאתוֹ.² זְכוֹר לָנוּ בְּרִית
⟨ the ⟨ for ⟨ Remember ⟪ its ⟨ and ⟪ its ⟨ to ⟪ of this people,
covenant us sinfulness. to wickedness,

אָבוֹת, כַּאֲשֶׁר אָמַרְתָּ: וְזָכַרְתִּי אֶת בְּרִיתִי יַעֲקוֹב,
⟪ [with] ⟨ My covenant ⟨ And I will ⟪ You said: ⟨ as ⟪ of the
Jacob, remember Patriarchs,

וְאַף אֶת בְּרִיתִי יִצְחָק, וְאַף אֶת בְּרִיתִי אַבְרָהָם
⟨ [with] ⟨ My covenant ⟨ and ⟪ [with] Isaac, ⟨ My covenant ⟨ and also
Abraham also

אֶזְכֹּר, וְהָאָרֶץ אֶזְכֹּר.³
⟪ I will ⟨ and the ⟪ I will
remember. Land remember;

זְכוֹר לָנוּ בְּרִית רִאשׁוֹנִים, כַּאֲשֶׁר אָמַרְתָּ: וְזָכַרְתִּי
⟨ And I will ⟪ You said: ⟨ as ⟪ of the ⟨ the ⟨ for us ⟨ Remember
remember ancient ones, covenant

לָהֶם בְּרִית רִאשׁוֹנִים, אֲשֶׁר הוֹצֵאתִי אֹתָם מֵאֶרֶץ
⟨ from ⟨ I took them out ⟨ that ⟪ of the ⟨ the ⟨ for
the land ancient ones, covenant them

מִצְרַיִם לְעֵינֵי הַגּוֹיִם, לִהְיוֹת לָהֶם לֵאלֹהִים, אֲנִי
⟨ I am ⟪ a God; ⟨ to them ⟨ to be ⟪ of the ⟨ in the ⟨ of Egypt
nations, very sight

יהוה.⁴ עָשָׂה עִמָּנוּ כְּמָה שֶׁהִבְטַחְתָּנוּ: וְאַף גַּם
⟨ all ⟨ And ⟪ You promised us: ⟨ as ⟨ with us ⟨ Do ⟪ HASHEM.
despite

זֹאת בִּהְיוֹתָם בְּאֶרֶץ אֹיְבֵיהֶם, לֹא מְאַסְתִּים וְלֹא
⟨ nor ⟨ despise them ⟨ I will ⟪ of their ⟨ in the land ⟨ when they ⟪ this,
not enemies, will be

(1) *Exodus* 32:13. (2) *Deuteronomy* 9:27. (3) *Leviticus* 26:42. (4) 26:45.

גְּעַלְתִּים לְכַלֹּתָם לְהָפֵר בְּרִיתִי אִתָּם, כִּי אֲנִי יהוה

⟨HASHEM, ⟨I am ⟨for ⟪with ⟨My ⟨to annul ⟪to destroy ⟨abhor them
them, covenant them,

אֱלֹהֵיהֶם.¹ הָשֵׁב שְׁבוּתֵנוּ וְרַחֲמֵנוּ, כְּמָה שֶׁכָּתוּב:

⟪it is ⟨as ⟪and have ⟨our captivity ⟨Bring ⟪their God.
written: mercy on us, back

וְשָׁב יהוה אֱלֹהֶיךָ אֶת שְׁבוּתְךָ וְרִחֲמֶךָ, וְשָׁב וְקִבֶּצְךָ

⟨gather ⟨and He ⟪and He will ⟨your captivity, ⟨your ⟨will ⟨Then bring
you in will once have mercy God, HASHEM, back
again upon you,

מִכָּל הָעַמִּים אֲשֶׁר הֱפִיצְךָ יהוה אֱלֹהֶיךָ שָׁמָּה.²

⟪thereto. ⟨your God ⟨has ⟨scattered ⟨that ⟨the ⟨from
HASHEM you peoples all

קַבֵּץ נִדָּחֵינוּ, כְּמָה שֶׁכָּתוּב: אִם יִהְיֶה נִדַּחֲךָ בִּקְצֵה

⟨at the ⟨your dispersed ⟨If ⟨it is written: ⟨as ⟨our ⟨Gather
ends will be dispersed ones,

הַשָּׁמָיִם, מִשָּׁם יְקַבֶּצְךָ יהוה אֱלֹהֶיךָ, וּמִשָּׁם יִקָּחֶךָ.³

⟪He will ⟨and from ⟪your God, ⟨will ⟨gather ⟨from ⟪of heaven,
take you. there HASHEM, you in there

מְחֵה פְשָׁעֵינוּ כָעָב וְכֶעָנָן, כְּמָה שֶׁכָּתוּב: מָחִיתִי

⟨I have ⟪it is written: ⟨as ⟪and like a ⟨like a ⟨our sins ⟨Wipe
wiped away cloud, mist away

כָעָב פְּשָׁעֶיךָ וְכֶעָנָן חַטֹּאתֶיךָ, שׁוּבָה אֵלַי כִּי

⟨for ⟨to ⟨return ⟪your ⟨and like ⟨your willful ⟨like a
Me, transgressions; a cloud sins, mist

גְאַלְתִּיךָ.⁴ מְחֵה פְשָׁעֵינוּ לְמַעֲנָךְ, כַּאֲשֶׁר אָמָרְתָּ:

⟪You have ⟨as ⟪for Your ⟨our sins ⟨Wipe ⟪I have
said: sake, away redeemed you.

אָנֹכִי אָנֹכִי הוּא מֹחֶה פְשָׁעֶיךָ לְמַעֲנִי, וְחַטֹּאתֶיךָ לֹא

⟨I shall ⟨and your ⟪for ⟨your ⟨Who wipes ⟨am the ⟨[only] I, ⟨I,
not transgressions My sake, willful sins away One

אֶזְכֹּר.⁵ הַלְבֵּן חֲטָאֵינוּ כַּשֶּׁלֶג וְכַצֶּמֶר, כְּמָה שֶׁכָּתוּב:

⟪it is written: ⟨as ⟪and like wool, ⟨like snow ⟨our sins ⟨Whiten ⟪recall.

לְכוּ נָא וְנִוָּכְחָה, יֹאמַר יהוה, אִם יִהְיוּ חֲטָאֵיכֶם

⟨your sins may be ⟨Though ⟪HASHEM. ⟨says ⟪let us reason ⟨now, ⟨Come,
together,

---

(1) *Leviticus* 26:44. (2) 30:3. (3) 30:4. (4) *Isaiah* 44:22. (5) 43:25.

כַּשָּׁנִים כַּשֶּׁלֶג יַלְבִּינוּ, אִם יַאְדִּימוּ כַתּוֹלָע, כַּצֶּמֶר
‹ like [white] ‹‹ as crimson, ‹ they may ‹ though ‹‹ they will be ‹ like ‹‹ like
wool   be red   whitened;   snow   scarlet,

יִהְיוּ.[1] זְרוֹק עָלֵינוּ מַיִם טְהוֹרִים וְטַהֲרֵנוּ, כְּמָה שֶׁכָּתוּב:
‹‹ it is written: ‹ as ‹‹ and purify us, ‹ pure water ‹ upon us ‹ Pour ‹‹ they will
become.

וְזָרַקְתִּי עֲלֵיכֶם מַיִם טְהוֹרִים וּטְהַרְתֶּם, מִכֹּל
‹ from ‹‹ and you will ‹ pure water ‹ upon you ‹ I shall pour
all   become pure;

טֻמְאוֹתֵיכֶם וּמִכָּל גִּלּוּלֵיכֶם אֲטַהֵר אֶתְכֶם.[2] רַחֵם
‹ Have ‹‹ you. ‹ I will ‹ your ‹ and ‹ your
mercy   purify   abominations   from all   contaminations

עָלֵינוּ וְאַל תַּשְׁחִיתֵנוּ, כְּמָה שֶׁכָּתוּב: כִּי אֵל רַחוּם
‹ a merciful God ‹ For ‹‹ it is written: ‹ as ‹‹ destroy us, ‹ and do not ‹ on us

יהוה אֱלֹהֶיךָ, לֹא יַרְפְּךָ וְלֹא יַשְׁחִיתֶךָ, וְלֹא יִשְׁכַּח
‹ will He ‹ nor ‹‹ will He ‹ nor ‹ relinquish ‹ He will ‹‹ your God; ‹ is
forget   destroy you,   you   not   HASHEM,

אֶת בְּרִית אֲבֹתֶיךָ אֲשֶׁר נִשְׁבַּע לָהֶם.[3] מוֹל
‹ Circumcise ‹‹ to them. ‹ He swore ‹ which ‹ with your forefathers, ‹ the covenant

אֶת לְבָבֵנוּ לְאַהֲבָה וּלְיִרְאָה אֶת שְׁמֶךָ, כְּמָה שֶׁכָּתוּב:
‹‹ it is written: ‹ as ‹‹ Your Name, ‹ and to fear ‹ to love ‹ our hearts

וּמָל יהוה אֱלֹהֶיךָ אֶת לְבָבְךָ וְאֶת לְבַב זַרְעֶךָ,
‹‹ of your ‹ and the heart ‹ your heart ‹ HASHEM, your God,
offspring,   will circumcise

לְאַהֲבָה אֶת יהוה אֱלֹהֶיךָ, בְּכָל לְבָבְךָ וּבְכָל
‹ and with all ‹ your heart ‹ with all ‹ your God, ‹ HASHEM, ‹ to love

נַפְשֶׁךָ, לְמַעַן חַיֶּיךָ.[4] הִמָּצֵא לָנוּ בְּבַקְשָׁתֵנוּ, כְּמָה
‹ as ‹‹ in our quest, ‹ to us ‹ Be ‹‹ you may ‹ so that ‹‹ your soul,
accessible   live.

שֶׁכָּתוּב: וּבִקַּשְׁתֶּם מִשָּׁם אֶת יהוה אֱלֹהֶיךָ וּמָצָאתָ,
‹‹ and you will ‹ your God, ‹ HASHEM, ‹ from ‹ And you ‹‹ it is written:
find [Him],   there   will seek

כִּי תִדְרְשֶׁנּוּ בְּכָל לְבָבְךָ וּבְכָל נַפְשֶׁךָ.[5] ✧ תְּבִיאֵנוּ אֶל
‹ to ‹ Bring us ‹‹ your soul. ‹ and with ‹ your ‹ with ‹ you search ‹ when
all   heart   all   Him out

---

(1) *Isaiah* 1:18. (2) *Ezekiel* 36:25. (3) *Deuteronomy* 4:31. (4) 30:6. (5) 4:29.

הַר קָדְשֶׁךָ, וְשַׂמַּחְתֵּנוּ בְּבֵית תְּפִלָּתֶךָ, כְּמָה שֶׁכָּתוּב:

‹‹ it is ‹ as ‹‹ of Prayer, ‹ in Your ‹ and gladden ‹ Your holy
written: House   us   mountain

וַהֲבִיאוֹתִים אֶל הַר קָדְשִׁי, וְשִׂמַּחְתִּים בְּבֵית תְּפִלָּתִי,

‹‹ of Prayer; ‹ in My ‹ and I will ‹‹ My holy ‹ to ‹ And I will bring
   House   gladden them   mountain,   them

עוֹלֹתֵיהֶם וְזִבְחֵיהֶם לְרָצוֹן עַל מִזְבְּחִי, כִּי בֵיתִי

‹ My ‹ for ‹‹ My Altar, ‹ on ‹ will find ‹ and their feast- ‹ their burnt-
House   favor   offerings   offerings

בֵית תְּפִלָּה יִקָּרֵא לְכָל הָעַמִּים.¹

‹‹ nations. ‹ for all ‹ will be ‹ of Prayer" ‹ "a
      called   House

THE ARK IS OPENED.

CHAZZAN, THEN CONGREGATION:

שְׁמַע קוֹלֵנוּ יהוה אֱלֹהֵינוּ, חוּס וְרַחֵם עָלֵינוּ,

‹‹ on us, ‹ and have ‹ have ‹‹ our God; ‹ HASHEM, ‹ our voice, ‹ Hear
     compassion   pity

וְקַבֵּל בְּרַחֲמִים וּבְרָצוֹן אֶת תְּפִלָּתֵנוּ.²

‹‹ our prayer. ‹ and favor ‹ with ‹ and accept
       compassion

CHAZZAN, THEN CONGREGATION:

הֲשִׁיבֵנוּ יהוה אֵלֶיךָ וְנָשׁוּבָה, חַדֵּשׁ יָמֵינוּ כְּקֶדֶם.³

‹‹ as of old. ‹ our ‹ renew ‹‹ and we shall ‹ to You, ‹ HASHEM, ‹ Bring us back,
    days   return,

CHAZZAN, THEN CONGREGATION:

אֲמָרֵינוּ הַאֲזִינָה יהוה, בִּינָה הֲגִיגֵנוּ.⁴

‹‹ our thoughts. ‹ perceive ‹‹ HASHEM; ‹ hear, ‹ Our words

THE FOLLOWING VERSE IS RECITED QUIETLY:

יִהְיוּ לְרָצוֹן אִמְרֵי פִינוּ וְהֶגְיוֹן לִבֵּנוּ לְפָנֶיךָ,

‹‹ before ‹‹ of our ‹ and the ‹ of our ‹ — the ex- ‹‹ find ‹ May
You,   heart —   thoughts   mouth   pressions   favor   they

יהוה צוּרֵנוּ וְגוֹאֲלֵנוּ.⁵

‹‹ and our ‹ our Rock ‹ HASHEM,
Redeemer.

---

(1) *Isaiah* 56:7. (2) From the weekday *Shemoneh Esrei*.
(3) *Lamentations* 5:21. (4) Cf. *Psalms* 5:2. (5) Cf. 19:15.

CHAZZAN, THEN CONGREGATION:

אַל תַּשְׁלִיכֵנוּ מִלְּפָנֶיךָ, וְרוּחַ קָדְשְׁךָ אַל תִּקַּח מִמֶּנּוּ.¹

《 from us. 〈 take 〈 do 〈 of Your 〈 and the 《 from Your 〈 cast us away 〈 Do
                           not Holiness   Spirit   Presence,   not

CHAZZAN, THEN CONGREGATION:

אַל תַּשְׁלִיכֵנוּ לְעֵת זִקְנָה, כִּכְלוֹת כֹּחֵנוּ אַל תַּעַזְבֵנוּ.²

《 forsake us not. 〈 does our 〈 when fail 《 of old 〈 in time 〈 cast us away 〈 Do
                         strength,   age;   not

ALL CONTINUE (SOME CONGREGATIONS RECITE THE NEXT VERSE RESPONSIVELY):

אַל תַּעַזְבֵנוּ יהוה, אֱלֹהֵינוּ אַל תִּרְחַק מִמֶּנּוּ.³

《 from us. 〈 be not distant 〈 our God, 《 O HASHEM; 〈 Forsake us not,

עֲשֵׂה עִמָּנוּ אוֹת לְטוֹבָה, וְיִרְאוּ שׂוֹנְאֵינוּ וְיֵבֹשׁוּ,

《 and be 〈 may our 〈 so that 《 for good; 〈 a sign 〈 for us 〈 Display
ashamed,   enemies   see it

כִּי אַתָּה יהוה עֲזַרְתָּנוּ וְנִחַמְתָּנוּ.⁴ כִּי לְךָ יהוה

〈 HASHEM, 〈 for 〈 Because 《 and 〈 will have 〈 HASHEM, 〈 You, 〈 for
You,   consoled us. helped us

הוֹחָלְנוּ, אַתָּה תַעֲנֶה אֲדֹנָי אֱלֹהֵינוּ.⁵

《 our God. 〈 O Lord, 〈 will answer, 〈 You 《 do we wait;

THE ARK IS CLOSED.

EACH INDIVIDUAL CONTINUES UNTIL THE END OF *SELICHOS.*

CONFESSION / וִדּוּי

DURING THE RECITATION OF THE וִדּוּי, *CONFESSION*, STAND WITH
HEAD AND BODY SLIGHTLY BOWED, IN SUBMISSIVE CONTRITION.

אֱלֹהֵינוּ וֵאלֹהֵי אֲבוֹתֵינוּ, תָּבֹא לְפָנֶיךָ תְּפִלָּתֵנוּ,⁶

《 may our 〈 before 〈 come 《 of our 〈 and the 〈 Our God
prayer,   You   forefathers,   God

וְאַל תִּתְעַלַּם מִתְּחִנָּתֵנוּ,⁷ שֶׁאֵין אָנוּ עַזֵּי פָנִים

〈 faced 〈 so brazen- 〈 For we are not 《 our supplication. 〈 ignore 〈 and do not

וּקְשֵׁי עֹרֶף, לוֹמַר לְפָנֶיךָ יהוה אֱלֹהֵינוּ וֵאלֹהֵי

〈 and the God 〈 our God, 〈 HASHEM, 《 before You, 〈 as to say 〈 necked 〈 and stiff-

אֲבוֹתֵינוּ, צַדִּיקִים אֲנַחְנוּ וְלֹא חָטָאנוּ, אֲבָל אֲנַחְנוּ

〈 we 《 —for 《 sinned 〈 and 〈 we are, 〈 that 《 of our
indeed,   have not   righteous   forefathers,

---

(1) *Psalms* 51:13. (2) Cf. 71:9. (3) Cf. 38:22. (4) Cf. 86:17. (5) Cf. 38:16. (6) Cf. 88:3. (7) Cf. 55:2.

וַאֲבוֹתֵינוּ חָטָאנוּ.[1]

‹ have sinned. ‹ and our forefathers

STRIKE THE LEFT SIDE OF THE CHEST WITH THE RIGHT FIST WHILE RECITING EACH OF THE SINS OF THE FOLLOWING CONFESSIONAL LITANY:

אָשַׁמְנוּ, בָּגַדְנוּ, גָּזַלְנוּ, דִּבַּרְנוּ דְפִי. הֶעֱוִינוּ,

‹ We have committed iniquity; ‹ slander. ‹ we have spoken ‹ we have robbed; ‹ we have betrayed; ‹ We have been guilty;

וְהִרְשַׁעְנוּ, זַדְנוּ, חָמַסְנוּ, טָפַלְנוּ שֶׁקֶר. יָעַצְנוּ

‹ We have given advice ‹ false accusations. ‹ we have made ‹ we have extorted; ‹ we have sinned willfully; ‹ we have committed wickedness;

רָע, כִּזַּבְנוּ, לַצְנוּ, מָרַדְנוּ, נִאַצְנוּ, סָרַרְנוּ,

‹ we have strayed; ‹ we have provoked [God's anger]; ‹ we have rebelled; ‹ we have scorned; ‹ we have been deceitful; ‹ that is bad;

עָוִינוּ, פָּשַׁעְנוּ, צָרַרְנוּ, קִשִּׁינוּ עֹרֶף. רָשַׁעְנוּ,

‹ We have been wicked; ‹ our necks. ‹ we have stiffened ‹ we have caused distress; ‹ we have sinned rebelliously; ‹ we have been iniquitous;

שִׁחַתְנוּ, תִּעַבְנוּ, תָּעִינוּ, תִּעְתָּעְנוּ.

‹ we have scoffed. ‹ we have gone astray; ‹ we have committed abominations; ‹ we have been corrupt;

סַרְנוּ מִמִּצְוֹתֶיךָ וּמִמִּשְׁפָּטֶיךָ הַטּוֹבִים, וְלֹא שָׁוָה

‹ worthwhile ‹ and it was not ‹ that are good, ‹ and from Your laws ‹ from Your commandments ‹ We have turned away

לָנוּ.[2] וְאַתָּה צַדִּיק עַל כָּל הַבָּא עָלֵינוּ, כִּי אֱמֶת

‹ truthfully ‹ for ‹ upon us, ‹ that has come ‹ all ‹ in ‹ are righteous ‹ And You ‹ for us.

עָשִׂיתָ וַאֲנַחְנוּ הִרְשָׁעְנוּ.[3]

‹ have acted wickedly. ‹ while we ‹ have You acted,

אָשַׁמְנוּ מִכָּל עָם, בֹּשְׁנוּ מִכָּל דּוֹר, גָּלָה מִמֶּנּוּ

‹ from us ‹ Departed ‹ generation. ‹ more than any other ‹ We have been ashamed ‹ people. ‹ more than any other ‹ We have been guilty

מָשׂוֹשׂ, דָּוָה לִבֵּנוּ בַּחֲטָאֵינוּ, הֻחְבַּל אֲוּוּיֵנוּ, וְנִפְרַע

‹ uncovered ‹ was our desired [Temple], ‹ Seized ‹ because of our sins. ‹ is our heart ‹ Sickened ‹ has joy.

(1) Cf. *Psalms* 106:6, *Jeremiah* 3:25. (2) Cf. *Job* 33:27. (3) *Nehemiah* 9:33.

פְּאֵרֵנוּ, זְבוּל בֵּית מִקְדָּשֵׁנוּ חָרַב בַּעֲוֹנֵינוּ, טִירָתֵנוּ

⟨ Our Palace ⟩ ❮ because of ⟨ has been ⟨ our Holy Temple ⟨ for [His] ❮ was our
our iniquities. destroyed   abode,   splendor;

הָיְתָה לְשַׁמָּה, יְפִי אַדְמָתֵנוּ לְזָרִים, בֹּחֵנוּ לְנָכְרִים.

❮ [was given] ⟨ our ❮ is controlled ⟨ of our ⟨ [Jerusalem,] ❮desolate. ⟨ has
to foreigners. wealth by strangers,   Land   the beauty   become

וַעֲדַיִן לֹא שַׁבְנוּ מִטָּעוּתֵנוּ וְהֵיךְ נָעִיז פָּנֵינוּ וְנַקְשֶׁה

⟨ and ⟨ faced ⟨ can we be ⟨ So ❮ from our ⟨ we have not ⟨ But still
stiffen   so brazen-   how   willful errors.   repented

עָרְפֵּנוּ, לוֹמַר לְפָנֶיךָ יהוה אֱלֹהֵינוּ וֵאלֹהֵי אֲבוֹתֵינוּ,

❮ of our ⟨ and the ⟨ our God ⟨ HASHEM, ⟨ before ⟨ so as to ⟨ our neck
forefathers, God   You,   say

צַדִּיקִים אֲנַחְנוּ וְלֹא חָטָאנוּ, אֲבָל אֲנַחְנוּ וַאֲבוֹתֵינוּ

⟨ and our ⟨ both we ⟨ for in ❮ and we have ❮ we are ⟨ that
fathers   truth,   not sinned,   righteous

חָטָאנוּ.[1]

❮ have sinned.

**STRIKE THE LEFT SIDE OF THE CHEST WITH THE RIGHT FIST WHILE RECITING
EACH OF THE SINS OF THE FOLLOWING CONFESSIONAL LITANY:**

אָשַׁמְנוּ, בָּגַדְנוּ, גָּזַלְנוּ, דִּבַּרְנוּ דֹפִי. הֶעֱוִינוּ,

❮ We have com- ❮ slander. ⟨ we have ❮ we have ❮ we have ❮ We have been
mitted iniquity;   spoken   robbed;   betrayed;   guilty;

וְהִרְשַׁעְנוּ, זַדְנוּ, חָמַסְנוּ, טָפַלְנוּ שֶׁקֶר. יָעַצְנוּ

⟨ We have ❮ false ⟨ we have ❮ we have ❮we have sinned ❮we have commit-
given advice accusations. made   extorted;   willfully;   ted wickedness;

רָע, כִּזַּבְנוּ, לַצְנוּ, מָרַדְנוּ, נִאַצְנוּ, סָרַרְנוּ,

❮ we have ❮ we have provoked ❮ we have ❮ we have ❮ we have been ❮ that is
strayed;   [God's anger];   rebelled;   scorned;   deceitful;   bad;

עָוִינוּ, פָּשַׁעְנוּ, צָרַרְנוּ, קִשִּׁינוּ עֹרֶף. רָשַׁעְנוּ,

❮ We have ❮ our ⟨ we have ❮ we have ❮ we have ❮ we have
been wicked;   necks.   stiffened   caused   sinned   been
                                      distress;   rebelliously; iniquitous;

שִׁחַתְנוּ, תִּעַבְנוּ, תָּעִינוּ, תִּעְתָּעְנוּ.

❮ we have ❮ we have ❮ we have ❮ we have
scoffed.   gone astray; committed   been corrupt;
                          abominations;

---

(1) Cf. *Psalms* 106:6; *Jeremiah* 3:25.

סַרְנוּ מִמִּצְוֹתֶיךָ וּמִמִּשְׁפָּטֶיךָ הַטּוֹבִים, וְלֹא שָׁוָה

⟨ worth- ⟨ and it ⟪ that are ⟨ and from ⟨ from Your ⟨ We have
while was not good, Your laws commandments turned away

לָנוּ.[1] וְאַתָּה צַדִּיק עַל כָּל הַבָּא עָלֵינוּ, כִּי אֱמֶת

⟨ truth- ⟨ for ⟪ upon us, ⟨ that has ⟨ all ⟨ in ⟨ are ⟨ And You ⟪ for us.
fully come righteous

עָשִׂיתָ וַאֲנַחְנוּ הִרְשָׁעְנוּ.[2]

⟪ have acted ⟨ while we ⟪ have You
wickedly. acted,

לְעֵינֵנוּ עָשְׁקוּ עֲמָלֵנוּ, **מְמֻשָּׁךְ** וּמְמוֹרָט מִמֶּנּוּ,

⟪ from ⟨ and cut off ⟪ [it was] ⟪ the product ⟨ have they ⟨ Before our
us. pulled away of our labor; stolen eyes

נָתְנוּ עָלָם עָלֵינוּ, **סָבַלְנוּ** עַל שִׁכְמֵנוּ, עֲבָדִים

⟨ Slaves ⟪ our ⟨ upon ⟨ we bore it ⟪ upon us, ⟨ their ⟨ They have
shoulders. yoke placed

מָשְׁלוּ בָנוּ, **פֹּרֵק** אֵין מִיָּדָם, **צָרוֹת** רַבּוֹת

⟨ that are ⟨ Troubles ⟪ from their there ⟨ a ⟪ over ⟨ have
manifold hand. was not redeemer us; ruled

סְבָבוּנוּ, **קְרָאנוּךָ** יהוה אֱלֹהֵינוּ, רָחַקְתָּ מִמֶּנּוּ

⟨ from ⟨ but You have dis- ⟪ our God, ⟨ HASHEM, ⟨ we called ⟪ have
us tanced Yourself upon You, surrounded us,

בַּעֲוֹנֵינוּ, שַׁבְנוּ מֵאַחֲרֶיךָ, תָּעִינוּ וְאָבָדְנוּ.

⟪ we have ⟪ we have ⟪ from following ⟨ We have ⟪ ⟪ because of
become lost. gone astray; after You; turned away our iniquities.

וַעֲדַיִן לֹא שַׁבְנוּ מִטָּעוּתֵנוּ וְהֵיךְ נָעִיז פָּנֵינוּ וְנַקְשֶׁה

⟨ and ⟨ faced ⟨ can we be ⟨ So ⟪ from our ⟨ we have not ⟨ But still
stiffen so brazen- how willful errors. repented

עׇרְפֵּנוּ, לוֹמַר לְפָנֶיךָ יהוה אֱלֹהֵינוּ וֵאלֹהֵי אֲבוֹתֵינוּ,

⟪ of our ⟨ and the ⟨ our God ⟨ HASHEM, ⟨ before ⟨ so as to ⟨ our neck
forefathers, God You, say

צַדִּיקִים אֲנַחְנוּ וְלֹא חָטָאנוּ, אֲבָל אֲנַחְנוּ וַאֲבוֹתֵינוּ

⟨ and our ⟨ both we ⟨ for in ⟪ and we have ⟪ we are ⟨ that
fathers truth, not sinned, righteous

חָטָאנוּ.[3]

⟪ have sinned.

---

(1) Cf. *Job* 33:27. (2) *Nehemiah* 9:33. (3) Cf. *Psalms* 106:6; *Jeremiah* 3:25.

**STRIKE THE LEFT SIDE OF THE CHEST WITH THE RIGHT FIST WHILE RECITING
EACH OF THE SINS OF THE FOLLOWING CONFESSIONAL LITANY:**

אָשַׁמְנוּ, בָּגַדְנוּ, גָּזַלְנוּ, דִּבַּרְנוּ דְפִי. הֶעֱוִינוּ,

《 We have com-　《 slander.　〈 we have　　《 we have　　《 we have　　《 We have been
mitted iniquity;　　　　　　spoken　　　 robbed;　　　 betrayed;　　　guilty;

וְהִרְשַׁעְנוּ, זַדְנוּ, חָמַסְנוּ, טָפַלְנוּ שֶׁקֶר. יָעַצְנוּ

〈 We have　　《 false　　〈 we have　　《 we have 《we have sinned 《we have commit-
given advice　accusations.　made　　　 extorted;　　willfully;　　ted wickedness;

רָע, כִּזַּבְנוּ, לַצְנוּ, מָרַדְנוּ, נִאַצְנוּ, סָרַרְנוּ,

《 we have　《 we have provoked 《 we have　　《 we have　〈 we have been 《 that is
strayed;　　[God's anger];　　rebelled;　　scorned;　　deceitful;　　bad;

עָוִינוּ, פָּשַׁעְנוּ, צָרַרְנוּ, קִשִּׁינוּ עֹרֶף. רָשַׁעְנוּ,

《 We have　　《 our　　〈 we have 《we have caused 《we have sinned 《we have been
been wicked;　necks.　stiffened　　distress;　　rebelliously;　　iniquitous;

שִׁחַתְנוּ, תִּעַבְנוּ, תָּעִינוּ, תִּעְתָּעְנוּ.

　　　　　　　《　　we have　　《 we have 《we have commit-《 we have
　　　　　　　scoffed.　gone astray;　ted abominations;　been corrupt;

סַרְנוּ מִמִּצְוֹתֶיךָ וּמִמִּשְׁפָּטֶיךָ הַטּוֹבִים, וְלֹא שָׁוָה

〈 worth-　〈 and it　《 that are　〈 and from　〈 from Your　〈 We have
while　was not　good,　Your laws　commandments　turned away

לָנוּ.[1] וְאַתָּה צַדִּיק עַל כָּל הַבָּא עָלֵינוּ, כִּי אֱמֶת

〈 truth-　〈 for　《 upon us, 〈 that has　〈 all　〈 in 〈　are　〈 And You 《 for us.
fully　　　　　　　　come　　　　　　　　righteous

עָשִׂיתָ וַאֲנַחְנוּ הִרְשָׁעְנוּ.[2]

　　　　　《　　have acted　　〈 while we　　《 have You
　　　　　wickedly.　　　　　　　　　　acted,

הִרְשַׁעְנוּ וּפָשַׁעְנוּ, לָכֵן לֹא נוֹשָׁעְנוּ. וְתֵן בְּלִבֵּנוּ

〈 in our　〈 Place　《 been　〈 we have 〈 there-　《　and we　　〈 We have acted
hearts　　　saved.　　not　　fore　　have sinned　　wickedly
　　　　　　　　　　　　　　　　rebelliously;

לַעֲזוֹב דֶּרֶךְ רֶשַׁע, וְחִישׁ לָנוּ יֶשַׁע, כַּכָּתוּב עַל יַד

〈 the 〈　by　〈 as it is 《 salvation; 〈 to us 〈 and 《　of　　〈 the 〈 [the will]
hand　　written　　　　　　　　　　hasten　wickedness,　path　to abandon

נְבִיאֶךָ: יַעֲזֹב רָשָׁע דַּרְכּוֹ, וְאִישׁ אָוֶן מַחְשְׁבֹתָיו,

《 [abandon]　〈 of　〈 and　　《 his way, 〈 the wicked 〈　Let　　《 of Your
his thoughts;　iniquity　the man　　　　　one　　abandon　prophet:

_____

(1) Cf. *Job* 33:27. (2) *Nehemiah* 9:33.

וְיָשֹׁב אֶל יהוה וִירַחֲמֵהוּ, וְאֶל אֱלֹהֵינוּ כִּי
⟨ for ⟨ our God, ⟨ and to ⟨⟨ and He will have ⟨ HASHEM, ⟨ to ⟨ and let
compassion on him, him return

יַרְבֶּה לִסְלוֹחַ.[1]
⟨⟨ forgiving. ⟨ He is
abundantly

מְשִׁיחַ צִדְקֶךָ אָמַר לְפָנֶיךָ, שְׁגִיאוֹת מִי יָבִין,
⟨⟨ can ⟨ who ⟨ Mistakes ⟨⟨ before You: ⟨ said ⟨ who is righteous ⟨ Your
discern? [David] anointed one

מִנִּסְתָּרוֹת נַקֵּנִי.[2] נַקֵּנוּ יהוה אֱלֹהֵינוּ מִכָּל פְּשָׁעֵינוּ,
⟨ our sins ⟨ of all ⟨ our God, ⟨ HASHEM, ⟨ Cleanse ⟨⟨ cleanse ⟨ From
us, me. unperceived faults

וְטַהֲרֵנוּ מִכָּל טֻמְאוֹתֵינוּ, וּזְרוֹק עָלֵינוּ מַיִם טְהוֹרִים
⟨ pure water ⟨ upon us ⟨ Pour ⟨⟨ our contaminations. ⟨ of all ⟨ and purify us

וְטַהֲרֵנוּ, כַּכָּתוּב עַל יַד נְבִיאֶךָ: וְזָרַקְתִּי עֲלֵיכֶם
⟨ upon you ⟨ I shall pour ⟨⟨ of Your ⟨ the ⟨ by ⟨ as it is ⟨⟨ and purify us,
prophet: hand written

מַיִם טְהוֹרִים וּטְהַרְתֶּם, מִכֹּל טֻמְאוֹתֵיכֶם וּמִכָּל
⟨ and ⟨ your ⟨ from ⟨⟨ and you will ⟨ pure water
from all contaminations all become pure;

גִּלּוּלֵיכֶם אֲטַהֵר אֶתְכֶם.[3] עַמְּךָ וְנַחֲלָתֶךָ, רְעֵבֵי
⟨ who ⟨⟨ and Your ⟨ Your ⟨⟨ you. ⟨ I will purify ⟨ your
hunger heritage, people abominations

טוּבְךָ, צְמֵאֵי חַסְדֶּךָ, תְּאֵבֵי יִשְׁעֶךָ, יַכִּירוּ וְיֵדְעוּ
⟨ and ⟨ — may they ⟨⟨ for Your ⟨ and ⟨⟨ for Your ⟨ who ⟨⟨ for Your
know recognize salvation who long kindness, thirst goodness,

כִּי לַיהוה אֱלֹהֵינוּ הָרַחֲמִים וְהַסְּלִיחוֹת.
⟨⟨ and forgiveness. ⟨ belong mercy ⟨ our God, ⟨ to HASHEM, ⟨ that

אֵל רַחוּם שְׁמֶךָ, אֵל חַנּוּן שְׁמֶךָ, בָּנוּ נִקְרָא שְׁמֶךָ.[5]
⟨⟨ is Your Name ⟨ upon ⟨⟨ is Your ⟨ Gracious God ⟨⟨ is Your ⟨ Merciful God
proclaimed, us Name, Name,

יהוה עֲשֵׂה לְמַעַן שְׁמֶךָ,[6] עֲשֵׂה לְמַעַן אֲמִתָּךָ, עֲשֵׂה
⟨ act ⟨⟨ Your truth; ⟨ for the ⟨ Act ⟨⟨ Your ⟨ for the ⟨ act ⟨ HASHEM,
sake of Name. sake of

(1) *Isaiah* 55:7. (2) *Psalms* 19:13. (3) *Ezekiel* 36:25.
(4) Cf. *Exodus* 34:6. (5) Cf. *Deuteronomy* 28:10. (6) *Jeremiah* 14:7.

לְמַעַן **בְּרִיתֶךָ**, עֲשֵׂה לְמַעַן **גָּדְלֶךָ** וְתִפְאַרְתֶּךָ, עֲשֵׂה

‹ act › ‹‹ and Your splendor; › ‹ Your greatness › ‹ for the sake of › ‹ act › ‹‹ Your covenant; › ‹ for the sake of ›

לְמַעַן **דָתֶךָ**, עֲשֵׂה לְמַעַן **הוֹדֶךָ**, עֲשֵׂה לְמַעַן **וְעוּדֶךָ**,

‹‹ Your Meeting House; › ‹ for the sake of › ‹ act › ‹‹ Your glory; › ‹ for the sake of › ‹ act › ‹‹ Your Law; › ‹ for the sake of ›

עֲשֵׂה לְמַעַן **זִכְרְךָ**,[1] עֲשֵׂה לְמַעַן **חַסְדֶּךָ**,[2] עֲשֵׂה לְמַעַן

‹ for the sake of › ‹ act › ‹‹ Your kindness; › ‹ for the sake of › ‹ act › ‹‹ Your remembrance; › ‹ for the sake of › ‹ act ›

טוּבֶךָ, עֲשֵׂה לְמַעַן **יִחוּדֶךָ**, עֲשֵׂה לְמַעַן **כְּבוֹדֶךָ**, עֲשֵׂה

‹ act › ‹‹ Your honor; › ‹ for the sake of › ‹ act › ‹‹ Your Oneness; › ‹ for the sake of › ‹ act › ‹‹ Your goodness; ›

לְמַעַן **לִמּוּדֶךָ**,[3] עֲשֵׂה לְמַעַן **מַלְכוּתֶךָ**, עֲשֵׂה לְמַעַן

‹ for the sake of › ‹ act › ‹‹ Your kingship; › ‹ for the sake of › ‹ act › ‹‹ Your students; › ‹ for the sake of ›

נִצְחָךָ, עֲשֵׂה לְמַעַן **סוֹדֶךָ**,[4] עֲשֵׂה לְמַעַן **עֻזֶּךָ**, עֲשֵׂה

‹ act › ‹‹ Your power; › ‹ for the sake of › ‹ act › ‹‹ Your secret [revealed to those who fear You]; › ‹ for the sake of › ‹ act › ‹‹ Your eternal [Name]; ›

לְמַעַן **פְּאֵרֶךָ**, עֲשֵׂה לְמַעַן **צִדְקָתֶךָ**, עֲשֵׂה לְמַעַן

‹ for the sake of › ‹ act › ‹‹ Your righteousness; › ‹ for the sake of › ‹ act › ‹‹ Your glory; › ‹ for the sake of ›

קְדֻשָּׁתֶךָ, עֲשֵׂה לְמַעַן **רַחֲמֶיךָ** הָרַבִּים, עֲשֵׂה לְמַעַן

‹ for the sake of › ‹ act › ‹‹ that is abundant; › ‹ Your mercy › ‹ for the sake of › ‹ act › ‹‹ Your sanctity; ›

שְׁכִינָתֶךָ, עֲשֵׂה לְמַעַן **תְּהִלָּתֶךָ**, עֲשֵׂה לְמַעַן **אוֹהֲבֶיךָ**

‹ those who loved You › ‹ for the sake of › ‹ act › ‹‹ Your praise; › ‹ for the sake of › ‹ act › ‹‹ Your Divine Presence; ›

שׁוֹכְנֵי עָפָר,[5] עֲשֵׂה לְמַעַן אַבְרָהָם יִצְחָק וְיַעֲקֹב,

‹‹ and Jacob; › ‹ Isaac, › ‹ Abraham, › ‹ for the sake of › ‹ act › ‹‹ in the dust; › ‹ who rest ›

עֲשֵׂה לְמַעַן מֹשֶׁה וְאַהֲרֹן, עֲשֵׂה לְמַעַן דָוִד וּשְׁלֹמֹה,

‹‹ and Solomon; › ‹ David › ‹ for the sake of › ‹ act › ‹‹ and Aaron; › ‹ Moses › ‹ for the sake of › ‹ act ›

עֲשֵׂה לְמַעַן יְרוּשָׁלַיִם עִיר קָדְשֶׁךָ,[6] עֲשֵׂה לְמַעַן צִיּוֹן

‹ Zion, › ‹ for the sake of › ‹ act › ‹‹ of Your Holiness; › ‹ the City › ‹ Jerusalem, › ‹ for the sake of › ‹ act ›

---

(1) Cf. *Exodus* 3:15. (2) *Psalms* 6:5. (3) Cf. *Isaiah* 54:13.
(4) Cf. *Psalms* 25:14. (5) *Isaiah* 26:19. (6) Cf. *Daniel* 9:16,24.

מִשְׁכַּן כְּבוֹדֶךָ, ¹עֲשֵׂה לְמַעַן שְׁמָמוֹת ²הֵיכָלֶךָ, עֲשֵׂה

⟨ act ⟪ of Your ⟨ the ⟨ for the ⟨ act ⟪ of Your ⟨ the
Temple;   desolation   sake of   glory;   abode

לְמַעַן הֲרִיסוּת ³מִזְבְּחֶךָ, עֲשֵׂה לְמַעַן הֲרוּגִים עַל

⟨ for ⟨ those killed ⟨ for the ⟨ act ⟪ of Your ⟨ the ⟨ for the
    sake of   Altar;   devastation   sake of

שֵׁם קָדְשֶׁךָ, עֲשֵׂה לְמַעַן טְבוּחִים עַל יִחוּדֶךָ, עֲשֵׂה

⟨ act ⟪ Your ⟨ for ⟨ those ⟨ for the ⟨ act ⟪ Your holy Name;
  Oneness;   slaughtered   sake of

לְמַעַן בָּאֵי בָאֵשׁ וּבַמַּיִם עַל קִדּוּשׁ שְׁמֶךָ, עֲשֵׂה לְמַעַן

⟨ for the ⟨ act ⟪ of Your ⟨ the ⟨ for ⟨ and water ⟨ fire ⟨ those who ⟨ for the
sake of   Name; sanctification   entered   sake of

⁵יוֹנְקֵי שָׁדַיִם שֶׁלֹּא חָטְאוּ, עֲשֵׂה לְמַעַן גְּמוּלֵי חָלָב

⟨ from ⟨ the [babies] ⟨ for the ⟨ act ⟪ sin; ⟨ who did ⟨ at the ⟨ the [infants]
milk   weaned   sake of   not   breast   sucking

⁶שֶׁלֹּא פָשָׁעוּ, עֲשֵׂה לְמַעַן תִּינוֹקוֹת שֶׁל בֵּית רַבָּן,

⟪ their teachers' ⟨ of ⟨ the children ⟨ for the ⟨ act ⟪ transgress; ⟨ who
school;   sake of   did not

עֲשֵׂה לְמַעַנְךָ אִם לֹא לְמַעֲנֵנוּ, עֲשֵׂה לְמַעַנְךָ וְהוֹשִׁיעֵנוּ.

⟪ and save us. ⟨ for Your sake ⟨ act ⟪ for our sake; ⟨ not ⟨ if ⟨ for Your sake ⟨ act

⁷עֲנֵנוּ יהוה עֲנֵנוּ, עֲנֵנוּ אֱלֹהֵינוּ עֲנֵנוּ, עֲנֵנוּ **אָבִינוּ**

⟨ our ⟨ answer ⟪ answer ⟨ our God, ⟨ answer ⟪ answer ⟨ Hashem, ⟨ Answer
Father,   us;   us;   us;   us;

עֲנֵנוּ, עֲנֵנוּ **בּוֹרְאֵנוּ** עֲנֵנוּ, עֲנֵנוּ ⁹**גּוֹאֲלֵנוּ** עֲנֵנוּ, עֲנֵנוּ

⟨ answer ⟪ answer ⟨ our ⟨ answer ⟪ answer ⟨ our Creator, ⟨ answer ⟪ answer
us;   us;   Redeemer,   us;   us;   us;   us;

¹⁰**דּוֹרְשֵׁנוּ** עֲנֵנוּ, עֲנֵנוּ **הָאֵל** הַנֶּאֱמָן ¹¹עֲנֵנוּ, עֲנֵנוּ וָתִיק

⟨ stead- ⟨ answer ⟪ answer ⟨ Who is ⟨ God ⟨ answer ⟪ answer ⟨ You Who
fast   us;   us;   faithful,   us;   us;   searches us out,

וְחָסִיד עֲנֵנוּ, עֲנֵנוּ ¹²זַךְ וְיָשָׁר עֲנֵנוּ, עֲנֵנוּ **חַי** וְקַיָּם ¹³

⟨ and endur- ⟨ living ⟨ answer ⟪ answer ⟨ and ⟨ pure ⟨ answer ⟪ answer ⟨ and kind
ing One,   us;   us;   upright One   us;   us;   One,

עֲנֵנוּ, עֲנֵנוּ **טוֹב** וּמֵטִיב ¹⁴עֲנֵנוּ, עֲנֵנוּ **יוֹדֵעַ** יֵצֶר עֲנֵנוּ,

⟪ answer ⟨ of incli- ⟨ Knower ⟨ answer ⟪ answer ⟨ and bene- ⟨ good ⟨ answer ⟪ answer
us;   nations,   us;   us;   ficent One,   us;   us;

---

(1) *Psalms* 26:8. (2) Cf. *Jeremiah* 51:26. (3) Cf. *Isaiah* 49:19. (4) *Joel* 2:16. (5) *Isaiah* 28:9.
(6) *Shabbos* 119b. (7) *Isaiah* 64:7. (8) Cf. 43:1. (9) 47:4. (10) Cf. *Ezekiel* 34:11. (11) *Deuteronomy* 7:9.
(12) *Job* 8:6; cf. *Proverbs* 20:11. (13) Cf. *Daniel* 6:27. (14) Cf. *Psalms* 119:68. (15) Cf. 103:14.

עֲנֵנוּ **כּוֹבֵשׁ** כְּעָסִים עֲנֵנוּ, עֲנֵנוּ לוֹבֵשׁ צְדָקוֹת[1] עֲנֵנוּ,

‹ answer ‹ of ‹ Donner ‹ answer ‹‹ answer ‹ of wrath, ‹ Suppressor ‹ answer
us;   righteousness,   us,   us;   us;

עֲנֵנוּ **מֶלֶךְ** מַלְכֵי הַמְּלָכִים[2] עֲנֵנוּ, עֲנֵנוּ **נוֹרָא** וְנִשְׂגָּב[3]

‹ and power- ‹ awesome ‹ answer ‹‹ answer ‹ of kings, ‹ over ‹ King ‹ answer
ful One,   us,   us;   kings   us;

עֲנֵנוּ, עֲנֵנוּ **סוֹלֵחַ** וּמוֹחֵל עֲנֵנוּ, עֲנֵנוּ עוֹנֶה בְּעֵת

‹ in time ‹ You Who ‹ answer ‹‹ answer ‹ and ‹ You Who ‹ answer ‹ answer
  answers   us,   us;   pardons,   forgives   us,   us;

צָרָה[4] עֲנֵנוּ, עֲנֵנוּ **פּוֹדֶה** וּמַצִּיל[5] עֲנֵנוּ, עֲנֵנוּ **צַדִּיק**

‹ righteous ‹ answer ‹‹ answer ‹ and ‹ Redeemer ‹ answer ‹‹ answer ‹ of
  us,   us;   Rescuer,   us,   us;   distress,

וְיָשָׁר[6] עֲנֵנוּ, עֲנֵנוּ **קָרוֹב** לְקוֹרְאָיו[7] עֲנֵנוּ, עֲנֵנוּ **קָשֶׁה**

‹ You Who ‹ answer ‹‹ answer ‹ to those who ‹ He Who ‹ answer ‹‹ answer ‹ and up-
with difficulty   us,   us;   call upon Him,   is close   us,   us;   right One,

לִכְעוֹס[8] עֲנֵנוּ, עֲנֵנוּ **רַךְ** לִרְצוֹת[9] עֲנֵנוּ, עֲנֵנוּ **רַחוּם**

‹ merciful ‹ answer ‹‹ answer ‹ appeased, ‹ You Who ‹ answer ‹‹ answer ‹ becomes
  us,   us;   are easily   us,   us;   angry,

וְחַנּוּן[10] עֲנֵנוּ, עֲנֵנוּ **שׁוֹמֵעַ** אֶל אֶבְיוֹנִים[11] עֲנֵנוּ, עֲנֵנוּ

‹ answer ‹‹ answer ‹ the destitute, ‹ to ‹ You Who ‹ answer ‹‹ answer ‹ and gra-
us;   us;   listens   us,   us;   cious One,

תּוֹמֵךְ תְּמִימִים עֲנֵנוּ, עֲנֵנוּ אֱלֹהֵי אֲבוֹתֵינוּ עֲנֵנוּ,

‹‹ answer ‹ of our ‹ God ‹ answer ‹‹ answer ‹ the ‹ You Who
us;   forefathers,   us,   us;   wholesome,   supports

עֲנֵנוּ אֱלֹהֵי אַבְרָהָם[12] עֲנֵנוּ, עֲנֵנוּ פַּחַד יִצְחָק[13] עֲנֵנוּ,

‹‹ answer ‹ of Isaac, ‹ Awesome ‹ answer ‹‹ answer ‹ of Abraham, ‹ God ‹ answer
us;   One   us,   us;   us,

עֲנֵנוּ אֲבִיר יַעֲקֹב[13] עֲנֵנוּ, עֲנֵנוּ עֶזְרַת הַשְּׁבָטִים עֲנֵנוּ,

‹‹ answer ‹ of the tribes, ‹ Helper ‹ answer ‹‹ answer ‹ of Jacob, ‹ Mighty ‹ answer
us;   us,   us;   One

עֲנֵנוּ מִשְׂגָּב אִמָּהוֹת עֲנֵנוּ, עֲנֵנוּ עוֹנֶה בְּעֵת רָצוֹן[14] עֲנֵנוּ,

‹‹ answer ‹ of favor, ‹ in a ‹ You Who ‹ answer ‹‹ answer ‹ of the ‹ Stronghold ‹ answer
us;   time   answers   us,   us;   Matriarchs,   us;

עֲנֵנוּ אֲבִי יְתוֹמִים[15] עֲנֵנוּ, עֲנֵנוּ דַּיַּן אַלְמָנוֹת[15] עֲנֵנוּ.

‹‹ answer ‹ of widows, ‹ Judge ‹ answer ‹‹ answer ‹ of orphans, ‹ Father ‹ answer
us.   us,   us;   us,

---

(1) Cf. *Isaiah* 59:17. (2) *Ethics of the Fathers* 3:1. (3) *Psalms* 47:3; 148:13. (4) Cf. *Isaiah* 49:8; *Psalms* 37:39.
Alternate text: בְּעֵת רָצוֹן, *in time of favor*. (5) Cf. 34:23,18. (6) *Deuteronomy* 32:4. (7) Cf. *Psalms* 145:18.
(8) *Ethics of the Fathers* 5:14. (9) Cf. 5:14. (10) *Exodus* 34:6. (11) *Psalms* 69:34. (12) *Genesis* 31:42.
(13) *Isaiah* 49:26. (14) Cf. 49:8; *Psalms* 69:14. Alternate text: בְּעֵת צָרָה, *in time of distress*. (15) 68:6.

מִי שֶׁעָנָה לְאַבְרָהָם אָבִינוּ בְּהַר הַמּוֹרִיָּה[1]

He ⟨ Who answered ⟨ Abraham ⟨ our father ⟨ on Mount ⟨ Moriah ≪

הוּא יַעֲנֵנוּ.

may — ⟨ answer ≪
He us.

מִי שֶׁעָנָה לְיִצְחָק בְּנוֹ כְּשֶׁנֶּעֱקַד עַל גַּבֵּי הַמִּזְבֵּחַ[1]

He ⟨ Who answered ⟨ Isaac ⟨ his son ⟨ when he was bound ⟨ on ⟨ top ⟨ of the altar ≪

הוּא יַעֲנֵנוּ.

may — ⟨ answer ≪
He us.

מִי שֶׁעָנָה לְיַעֲקֹב בְּבֵית אֵל[2]

He ⟨ Who answered ⟨ Jacob* ⟨ in Beth-el ≪

הוּא יַעֲנֵנוּ.

may — ⟨ answer ≪
He us.

מִי שֶׁעָנָה לְיוֹסֵף בְּבֵית הָאֲסוּרִים[3]

He ⟨ Who answered ⟨ Joseph ⟨ in the prison ≪

הוּא יַעֲנֵנוּ.

may — ⟨ answer ≪
He us.

מִי שֶׁעָנָה לַאֲבוֹתֵינוּ עַל יַם סוּף[4]

He ⟨ Who answered ⟨ our forefathers ⟨ at ⟨ the ⟨ of Reeds Sea ≪

הוּא יַעֲנֵנוּ.

may — ⟨ answer ≪
He us.

מִי שֶׁעָנָה לְמֹשֶׁה בְּחוֹרֵב[5]

He ⟨ Who answered ⟨ Moses ⟨ in Horeb ≪

הוּא יַעֲנֵנוּ.

may — ⟨ answer ≪
He us.

מִי שֶׁעָנָה לְאַהֲרֹן בַּמַּחְתָּה[6]

He ⟨ Who answered ⟨ Aaron ⟨ with the fire-pan ≪

מִי שֶׁעָנָה לְפִינְחָס בְּקוּמוֹ מִתּוֹךְ הָעֵדָה[7]

He ⟨ Who answered ⟨ Phinehas ⟨ when he arose ⟨ from amid ⟨ the congregation ≪

הוּא יַעֲנֵנוּ.

may — ⟨ answer ≪
He us.

מִי שֶׁעָנָה לִיהוֹשֻׁעַ בַּגִּלְגָּל[8]

He ⟨ Who answered ⟨ Joshua ⟨ in Gilgal ≪

הוּא יַעֲנֵנוּ.

may — ⟨ answer ≪
He us.

---

(1) *Genesis* 22:12. (2) 35:3. (3) 39:21. (4) *Exodus* Ch. 14. (5) 17:6,11; *Deuteronomy* 9:19.
(6) *Numbers* 17:11-13. (7) 25:7-13. (8) *Joshua* 6:1-20; 7:6-15; 10:12-14.

מִי שֶׁעָנָה לִשְׁמוּאֵל בַּמִּצְפָּה¹ הוּא יַעֲנֵנוּ.

He › Who › Samuel › in Mizpah « — may › He answer « us.
answered

מִי שֶׁעָנָה לְדָוִד וּשְׁלֹמֹה בְנוֹ בִּירוּשָׁלַיִם² הוּא יַעֲנֵנוּ.

He › Who › David › and › his « in Jerusalem « — may › He answer « us.
answered Solomon son

מִי שֶׁעָנָה לְאֵלִיָּהוּ בְּהַר הַכַּרְמֶל³ הוּא יַעֲנֵנוּ.

He › Who › Elijah › on › Carmel « — may › He answer « us.
answered Mount

מִי שֶׁעָנָה לֶאֱלִישָׁע בִּירִיחוֹ⁴ הוּא יַעֲנֵנוּ.

He › Who › Elisha › in Jericho « — may › He answer « us.
answered

מִי שֶׁעָנָה לְיוֹנָה בִּמְעֵי הַדָּגָה⁵ הוּא יַעֲנֵנוּ.

He › Who › Jonah › in the › of the « — may › He answer « us.
answered innards fish

מִי שֶׁעָנָה לְחִזְקִיָּהוּ מֶלֶךְ יְהוּדָה בְּחָלְיוֹ⁶ הוּא יַעֲנֵנוּ.

He › Who › Hezekiah, › king › of Judah, › in his « — may › He answer « us.
answered illness

מִי שֶׁעָנָה לַחֲנַנְיָה מִישָׁאֵל וַעֲזַרְיָה

He › Who › Hananiah, › Mishael, › and Azariah ›
answered

בְּתוֹךְ כִּבְשַׁן הָאֵשׁ⁷ הוּא יַעֲנֵנוּ.

inside › the furnace › of fire « He › Who — may › He answer « us.

מִי שֶׁעָנָה לְדָנִיֵּאל בְּגוֹב הָאֲרָיוֹת⁸ הוּא יַעֲנֵנוּ.

He › Who › Daniel › in the › of lions « — may › He answer « us.
answered den

מִי שֶׁעָנָה לְמָרְדְּכַי וְאֶסְתֵּר בְּשׁוּשַׁן הַבִּירָה⁹

He › Who › Mordechai › and Esther › in Shushan « the capital «
answered

הוּא יַעֲנֵנוּ.

He › Who — may › He answer « us.

מִי שֶׁעָנָה לְעֶזְרָא בַּגּוֹלָה¹⁰ הוּא יַעֲנֵנוּ.

He › Who › Ezra › in the exile « — may › He answer « us.
answered

(1) I Samuel 7:9. (2) II Samuel 7:5-16; 21:1,14; 24:25; I Kings 9:3. (3) 18:36-38.
(4) II Kings 2:21. (5) Jonah 2:2-11. (6) II Kings 20:1-6; Isaiah 38:2-8.
(7) Daniel 3:21-26. (8) 6:17-23. (9) Esther Ch. 8. (10) Ezra 8:21-23.

מִי שֶׁעָנָה לְכָל הַצַּדִּיקִים וְהַחֲסִידִים וְהַתְּמִימִים

⟨ the wholesome, ⟨ the devout, ⟨ the righteous, ⟨ all ⟨ Who ⟨ He
answered

וְהַיְשָׁרִים הוּא יַעֲנֵנוּ.

《 answer ⟨ — may 《 and the
us. He upright

רַחֲמָנָא דְּעָנֵי לַעֲנִיֵּי, עֲנֵינָן. רַחֲמָנָא דְּעָנֵי לִתְבִירֵי

⟨ those of ⟨ Who ⟨ Merciful 《 answer 《 the poor, ⟨ Who ⟨ Merciful One
broken answers One us! answers

לִבָּא, עֲנֵינָן. רַחֲמָנָא דְּעָנֵי לִמְכִיכֵי רוּחָא, עֲנֵינָן.

《 answer 《 spirit, ⟨ those of ⟨ Who ⟨ Merciful 《 answer 《 hearts,
us! crushed answers One us!

רַחֲמָנָא עֲנֵינָן. רַחֲמָנָא חוּס. רַחֲמָנָא פְּרוֹק. רַחֲמָנָא

⟨ Merciful 《 redeem! ⟨ Merciful 《 have ⟨ Merciful 《 answer ⟨ Merciful
One, One, pity! One, us! One,

שְׁזִיב. רַחֲמָנָא רְחַם עֲלָן, הַשְׁתָּא בַּעֲגָלָא וּבִזְמַן קָרִיב.

《that comes⟨ and at ⟨ swiftly, ⟨ — now, 《 on us ⟨ have ⟨ Merciful 《 save!
soon. a time mercy One,

PUTTING DOWN THE HEAD / נפילת אפים

RECITE UNTIL יָבֵשׁ רָגַע WITH THE HEAD RESTING ON THE LEFT ARM,
PREFERABLY WHILE SEATED.

(וַיֹּאמֶר דָּוִד אֶל גָּד, צַר לִי מְאֹד, נִפְּלָה נָּא בְיַד יהוה,

《 of ⟨ into the⟨ now ⟨ Let us 《 exceed- ⟨ am ⟨ Dis- 《Gad, ⟨ to ⟨ (And David said
HASHEM, hand fall ingly. I tressed

כִּי רַבִּים רַחֲמָיו, וּבְיַד אָדָם אַל אֶפְּלָה.(1)

《 let me not fall.) ⟨ but into human 《 are His ⟨ abundant ⟨ for
hands mercies,

רַחוּם וְחַנּוּן חָטָאתִי לְפָנֶיךָ. יהוה מָלֵא רַחֲמִים,

《 of mercy, ⟨ Who ⟨ HASHEM, 《 before ⟨ I have ⟨ and gracious ⟨ O merciful
is full You. sinned One,

רַחֵם עָלַי וְקַבֵּל תַּחֲנוּנָי.

《 my ⟨ and ⟨ on me ⟨ have
supplications. accept mercy

———— תהלים ו:ב-יא / Psalms 6:2-11 ————

יהוה, אַל בְּאַפְּךָ תוֹכִיחֵנִי, וְאַל בַּחֲמָתְךָ תְיַסְּרֵנִי.

《chastise me. ⟨ in Your wrath ⟨ nor ⟨ rebuke me, ⟨ in Your anger ⟨ do not ⟨ HASHEM,

(1) II Samuel 24:14.

חָנֵּנִי יהוה כִּי אֻמְלַל אָנִי, רְפָאֵנִי יהוה כִּי נִבְהֲלוּ

⟨ shudder ⟨ for ⟨ Hashem, ⟨ heal me, ⟪ am I; ⟨ feeble ⟨ for ⟨ Hashem, ⟨ Favor
with terror,   me,

עֲצָמָי. וְנַפְשִׁי נִבְהֲלָה מְאֹד, וְאַתָּה יהוה עַד מָתָי.

⟪ when? ⟨ until ⟨ Hashem, ⟨ and You, ⟪ utterly, ⟨ is terrified ⟨ My soul ⟪ do my bones.

שׁוּבָה יהוה חַלְּצָה נַפְשִׁי, הוֹשִׁיעֵנִי לְמַעַן חַסְדֶּךָ.

⟪ Your kindness. ⟨ as befits ⟨ save me ⟪ my soul; ⟨ release ⟨ Hashem, ⟨ Desist,

כִּי אֵין בַּמָּוֶת זִכְרֶךָ, בִּשְׁאוֹל מִי יוֹדֶה לָּךְ. יָגַעְתִּי

⟨ I am ⟪ You? ⟨ will ⟨ who ⟨ in the ⟪ is there men- ⟨ in ⟨ not ⟨ For
wearied   praise   grave   tion of You;   death

בְאַנְחָתִי, אַשְׂחֶה בְכָל לַיְלָה מִטָּתִי, בְּדִמְעָתִי

⟨ with my tears ⟪ my bed; ⟨ night ⟪ every ⟨ I drench ⟪ with my sigh;

עַרְשִׂי אַמְסֶה. עָשְׁשָׁה מִכַּעַס עֵינִי, עָתְקָה בְּכָל

⟨ by all ⟨ aged ⟨ is my ⟨ because of ⟨ Dimmed ⟪ I soak. ⟨ my couch
     eye,   anger

צוֹרְרָי. סוּרוּ מִמֶּנִּי כָּל פֹּעֲלֵי אָוֶן, כִּי שָׁמַע יהוה

⟨ Hashem has heard ⟨ for ⟪ of evil, ⟨ doers ⟨ all ⟨ from me, ⟨ Depart ⟪ my
tormentors.

קוֹל בִּכְיִי. שָׁמַע יהוה תְּחִנָּתִי, יהוה תְּפִלָּתִי יִקָּח.

⟪ will ⟨ my prayer ⟨ Hashem ⟪ my plea, ⟨ Hashem ⟪ of my ⟨ the
accept.   has heard   weeping. sound

יֵבֹשׁוּ וְיִבָּהֲלוּ מְאֹד כָּל אֹיְבָי, יָשֻׁבוּ יֵבֹשׁוּ רָגַע.

⟪ in an ⟨ and be ⟨ may they ⟪ my ⟨ all ⟨ utterly, ⟨ and con- ⟨ Let them
instant. shamed regret enemies;   founded be shamed

מָחֵי וּמַסֵּי מֵמִית וּמְחַיֶּה, מַסִּיק מִן שְׁאוֹל

⟨ the ⟨ from ⟨ Who raises ⟪ and Who ⟨ Who causes ⟪ and Who ⟨ [O God,]
grave [the dead] restores life, death heals, Who wounds

לְחַיֵּי עָלְמָא, בְּרָא כַּד חָטֵי אֲבוּהִי לַקְיֵהּ, אֲבוּהִי

⟨ but a ⟪ would ⟨ his father ⟨ sin, ⟨ should ⟨ A son ⟨ eternal: ⟨ to life
father strike him, he

דְחָיֵס אַסֵּי לִכְאֵבֵהּ. עַבְדָּא דְמָרִיד נָפִיק בְּקוֹלָר,

⟪ in chains, ⟨ he is ⟪ who rebels, ⟨ A slave ⟨ his [son's] ⟨ will ⟨ who is com-
led out pain. heal passionate

מָרֵהּ תָּאִיב וְתַבִּיר קוֹלָרֵהּ.

⟪ his chains. ⟨ he breaks ⟨ desires, ⟨ but [if]
his master

בְּרָךְ בְּכִרְךָ אֲנָן וְחָטִינָן קַמָּךְ, הָא רָוֵי נַפְשִׁין

⟨ Your son, ⟨ Your firstborn, ⟨ we are, ⟨ and we have sinned ⟨ before You; ⟨ indeed ⟨ satiated ⟨ has our soul been

בִּגְגִידִין מְרָרִין, עַבְדָּךְ אֲנָן וּמְרוֹדִינָן קַמָּךְ,

⟨ with wormwood ⟨ that is bitter. ⟨ Your servants ⟨ we are ⟨ and we have rebelled ⟨ before You;

הָא בִּבְזְתָא, הָא בִּשְׁבִיָא, הָא בְּמַלְקְיוּתָא.

⟨ [indeed we have suffered,] some ⟨ from looting, ⟨ some ⟨ in captivity, ⟨ and some ⟨ by the lash.

בְּמָטוּ מִנָּךְ בְּרַחֲמָךְ דִּנְפִישִׁין, אַסֵּי לִכְאָבִין

⟨ We beg ⟨ of You, ⟨ in Your compassion ⟨ that is abundant, ⟨ heal ⟨ the pains

דִּתְקוֹף עֲלָן, עַד דְּלָא נֶהֱוֵי גְמִירָא בְּשִׁבְיָא.

⟨ that have overwhelmed ⟨ us, ⟨ while yet ⟨ we are not ⟨ completely annihilated ⟨ in captivity.

מַכְנִיסֵי רַחֲמִים, הַכְנִיסוּ רַחֲמֵינוּ, לִפְנֵי בַּעַל

⟨ O you who usher in ⟨ [pleas for] mercy, ⟨ may you usher in ⟨ our [plea for] mercy, ⟨ before ⟨ the Master

הָרַחֲמִים. מַשְׁמִיעֵי תְפִלָּה, הַשְׁמִיעוּ תְפִלָּתֵנוּ, לִפְנֵי

⟨ of mercy. ⟨ O you who aid the hearing ⟨ of prayer, ⟨ may you aid the hearing ⟨ of our prayer ⟨ before

שׁוֹמֵעַ תְּפִלָּה. מַשְׁמִיעֵי צְעָקָה, הַשְׁמִיעוּ צַעֲקָתֵנוּ,

⟨ the Hearer ⟨ of prayer. ⟨ O you who aid the hearing ⟨ of outcries, ⟨ may you aid the hearing ⟨ of our outcries

לִפְנֵי שׁוֹמֵעַ צְעָקָה. מַכְנִיסֵי דִמְעָה, הַכְנִיסוּ

⟨ before ⟨ the Hearer ⟨ of outcries. ⟨ O you who usher in ⟨ tears, ⟨ may you usher in

דִמְעוֹתֵינוּ, לִפְנֵי מֶלֶךְ מִתְרַצֶּה בִדְמָעוֹת.

⟨ our tears ⟨ before ⟨ the King ⟨ Who is appeased ⟨ through tears.

הִשְׁתַּדְּלוּ וְהַרְבּוּ תְּחִנָּה וּבַקָּשָׁה, לִפְנֵי מֶלֶךְ אֵל

⟨ Exert yourselves ⟨ and intensify ⟨ supplications ⟨ and pleas ⟨ before ⟨ the King, ⟨ God,

רָם וְנִשָּׂא. הַזְכִּירוּ לְפָנָיו, הַשְׁמִיעוּ לְפָנָיו תּוֹרָה

⟨ exalted ⟨ and uplifted. ⟨ Mention ⟨ before Him, ⟨ aid to be heard ⟨ before Him, ⟨ the Torah

וּמַעֲשִׂים טוֹבִים שֶׁל שׁוֹכְנֵי עָפָר.

⟨ and the deeds ⟨ that are good ⟨ of ⟨ [the Patriarchs and Matriarchs] who dwell ⟨ in the dust.

יִזְכֹּר אַהֲבָתָם וִיחַיֶּה זַרְעָם, שֶׁלֹּא תֹאבַד שְׁאֵרִית

⟨ May He remember ⟨ their love ⟩ and grant ⟨ life ⟨ to their offspring, ⟨ so that not ⟨ lost ⟨ shall the remnant

יַעֲקֹב. כִּי צֹאן רוֹעֶה נֶאֱמָן הָיָה לְחֶרְפָּה,

《 of Jacob be. ⟨ For ⟨ the flock ⟨ of the shepherd ⟨ who is faithful [Moses] ⟨ has become 《 a disgrace;

יִשְׂרָאֵל גּוֹי אֶחָד לְמָשָׁל וְלִשְׁנִינָה.

《 and a simile. ⟨ a parable 《 that is ⟨ the unique, ⟨ the nation ⟨ Israel,

מַהֵר עֲנֵנוּ אֱלֹהֵי יִשְׁעֵנוּ, וּפְדֵנוּ מִכָּל גְּזֵרוֹת קָשׁוֹת

《 that are harsh; ⟨ decrees ⟨ from all ⟨ and redeem us ⟨ of our salvation, ⟨ O God ⟨ answer us, ⟨ Swiftly

וְהוֹשִׁיעָה בְּרַחֲמֶיךָ הָרַבִּים, מְשִׁיחַ צִדְקָךְ וְעַמָּךְ.

《 and Your people. ⟨ Your righteous anointed one ⟨ that is abundant, ⟨ in Your mercy ⟨ and may You save,

מָרָן דְּבִשְׁמַיָּא לָךְ מִתְחַנְּנָן, כְּבַר שְׁבִיָּא דְּמִתְחַנֵּן

⟨ who supplicates ⟨ in captivity ⟨ as one 《 do we ⟨ to You 《 Who is in heaven, ⟨ Our Master

לְשָׁבוּיֵהּ. כֻּלְּהוֹן בְּנֵי שְׁבִיָּא בְּכַסְפָּא מִתְפָּרְקִין,

《 are redeemed, ⟨ through money ⟨ in captivity, ⟨ those ⟨ [for] all 《 before his captors;

וְעַמָּךְ יִשְׂרָאֵל בְּרַחֲמֵי וּבְתַחֲנוּנֵי, הַב לָן שְׁאֵילְתִּין

⟨ our requests ⟨ us ⟨ O 《 grant ⟨ and supplication. ⟨ through compassion ⟨ Israel ⟨ but Your people

וּבָעוּתִין, דְּלָא נְהַדַּר רֵיקָם מִן קֳדָמָךְ.

《 before You. ⟨ from ⟨ emptyhanded ⟨ that we not be turned away ⟨ and our prayers

מָרָן דְּבִשְׁמַיָּא לָךְ מִתְחַנְּנָן, כְּעַבְדָּא דְּמִתְחַנֵּן

⟨ who supplicates ⟨ as a slave 《 do we ⟨ to You 《 Who is in heaven, ⟨ Our Master

לְמָרֵיהּ, עֲשִׁיקֵי אֲנָן וּבַחֲשׁוֹכָא שָׁרִינָן, מְרִירָן נַפְשִׁין

⟨ are [our] souls ⟨ embittered 《 do we ⟨ and in darkness ⟨ are we ⟨ Oppressed 《 to his master:

מֵעַקְתִין דְּנַפִישִׁין, חֵילָא לֵית בָּן לְרַצּוּיָךְ. מָרָן,

⟨ Our Master, 《 to appease ⟨ within us ⟨ is lacking ⟨ Strength 《 that is excessive. ⟨ from distress

עֲבִיד בְּדִיל קַיָּמָא דִּגְזַרְתָּ עִם אֲבָהָתָנָא.

« our Patriarchs. ‹ with ‹ that You ‹ of the ‹ for the ‹ act
established covenant sake

שׁוֹמֵר יִשְׂרָאֵל, שְׁמוֹר שְׁאֵרִית יִשְׂרָאֵל, וְאַל

‹ let not « of Israel; ‹ the remnant ‹ safeguard « of Israel, ‹ O Guardian

יֹאבַד יִשְׂרָאֵל, הָאוֹמְרִים שְׁמַע יִשְׂרָאֵל.[1]

« O Israel. ‹ Hear, ‹ those who « Israel be destroyed —
proclaim:

שׁוֹמֵר גּוֹי אֶחָד, שְׁמוֹר שְׁאֵרִית עַם אֶחָד, וְאַל

‹ let not « that is ‹ of the ‹ the remnant ‹ safeguard « that is ‹ of the ‹ O Guardian
unique; people unique, nation

יֹאבַד גּוֹי אֶחָד, הַמְיַחֲדִים שִׁמְךָ, יהוה אֱלֹהֵינוּ

‹ is our God, ‹ HASHEM « of Your ‹ those who proclaim « that is ‹ the ‹ be
Name: the Oneness unique, nation destroyed

יהוה אֶחָד.

« the One ‹ HASHEM
[and Only]! is

שׁוֹמֵר גּוֹי קָדוֹשׁ, שְׁמוֹר שְׁאֵרִית עַם קָדוֹשׁ, וְאַל

‹ let not « that is ‹ of the ‹ the remnant ‹ safeguard « that is ‹ of the ‹ O Guardian
holy; people holy, nation

יֹאבַד גּוֹי קָדוֹשׁ, הַמְשַׁלְּשִׁים בְּשָׁלֹשׁ קְדֻשּׁוֹת לְקָדוֹשׁ.

« to the ‹ sancti- ‹ the ‹ those who proclaim « that is ‹ the ‹ be
Holy One. fications threefold three times holy, nation destroyed

מִתְרַצֶּה בְּרַחֲמִים וּמִתְפַּיֵּס בְּתַחֲנוּנִים, הִתְרַצֵּה

‹ be « through ‹ and Who becomes ‹ through ‹ You Who becomes
favorable supplications, conciliatory compassion favorable

וְהִתְפַּיֵּס לְדוֹר עָנִי, כִּי אֵין עוֹזֵר. אָבִינוּ מַלְכֵּנוּ,

« our King, ‹ Our « helper. ‹ there ‹ for « that is ‹ to the ‹ and be
Father, is no poor, generation conciliatory

חָנֵּנוּ וַעֲנֵנוּ, כִּי אֵין בָּנוּ מַעֲשִׂים, עֲשֵׂה עִמָּנוּ

‹ us ‹ treat « worthy deeds; ‹ we have no ‹ though ‹ and ‹ be gracious
answer us, with us

צְדָקָה וָחֶסֶד וְהוֹשִׁיעֵנוּ.

« and save us. ‹ and kindness, ‹ with charity

---

(1) *Deuteronomy* 6:4.

STAND AFTER THE WORDS וַאֲנַחְנוּ לֹא נֵדַע, UNTIL CONCLUSION OF THE PARAGRAPH.

וַאֲנַ֫חְנוּ לֹא נֵדַע מַה נַּעֲשֶׂה, כִּי עָלֶיךָ עֵינֵינוּ.[1]

《 are our 〈 upon 〈 rather, 《 we should 〈 what 〈 know not 〈   We
eyes.   You   do,

זְכֹר רַחֲמֶיךָ יהוה וַחֲסָדֶיךָ, כִּי מֵעוֹלָם הֵמָּה.[2] יְהִי

〈 May 《 are they. 〈 eternal 〈 for 〈 and Your 〈 HASHEM, 〈 Your 〈 Remem-
                                  kindnesses,   mercies,   ber

חַסְדְּךָ יהוה עָלֵינוּ, כַּאֲשֶׁר יִחַלְנוּ לָךְ.[3] אַל תִּזְכָּר

〈 recall 〈 Do not 《 You. 〈 we awaited 〈 just as 《 be upon us, 〈 HASHEM, 〈 Your kindness,

לָנוּ עֲוֹנוֹת רִאשׁוֹנִים, מַהֵר יְקַדְּמוּנוּ רַחֲמֶיךָ, כִּי

〈 for 《 may Your 〈 advance to 〈 swiftly 《 of the ancients; 〈 the sins 〈 against
        mercies,   meet us   us

דַלּוֹנוּ מְאֹד.[4] עָזְרֵנוּ בְּשֵׁם יהוה, עֹשֵׂה שָׁמַיִם

〈 of 〈 Maker 〈 of HASHEM, 〈 is through 《 Our help 《 exceed- 〈 we have
heaven   the Name   ingly.   become
                                                                impoverished

וָאָרֶץ.[5] חָנֵּנוּ יהוה חָנֵּנוּ, כִּי רַב שָׂבַעְנוּ בוּז.[6] בְּרֹגֶז

《 Amid 《 with 〈 sated 〈 we are 〈 for 《 favor us, 〈 HASHEM, 〈 Favor us, 《 and earth.
wrath, contempt.   fully

רַחֵם תִּזְכּוֹר.[7] בְּרֹגֶז עֲקֵדָה תִּזְכּוֹר. בְּרֹגֶז תְּמִימוֹת

〈 the perfect 《 Amid 《 You should 〈 the binding 《 Amid 《 You should 〈 to be
ones   wrath, remember!   [of Isaac]   wrath, remember!   merciful

תִּזְכּוֹר. יהוה הוֹשִׁיעָה, הַמֶּלֶךְ יַעֲנֵנוּ בְיוֹם קָרְאֵנוּ.[8]

《 we call. 〈 on the 〈 answer 〈 May the 《 save! 〈 HASHEM, 《 You should
           day   us   King   remember!

כִּי הוּא יָדַע יִצְרֵנוּ, זָכוּר כִּי עָפָר אֲנָחְנוּ.[9]

《 are we. 〈 dust 〈 that 〈 He is 《 our nature, 〈 knew 〈 He 〈 For
                         mindful

❖ עָזְרֵנוּ אֱלֹהֵי יִשְׁעֵנוּ עַל דְּבַר כְּבוֹד שְׁמֶךָ, וְהַצִּילֵנוּ

〈 rescue us 《 of Your 〈 of the 〈 the 〈 for 〈 of our 〈 O God 〈 Assist us,
            Name;   glory   sake   salvation

וְכַפֵּר עַל חַטֹּאתֵינוּ לְמַעַן שְׁמֶךָ.[10]

《 of Your 〈 for the 〈 our sins 〈 for 〈 and grant
Name.   sake   atonement

(1) *II Chronicles* 20:12. (2) *Psalms* 25:6. (3) *ibid.* 33:22. (4) 79:8. (5) 121:2.
(6) 123:3. (7) *Habakkuk* 3:2. (8) *Psalms* 20:10. (9) 103:14. (10) 79:9.

FULL KADDISH / קדיש שלם

THE *CHAZZAN* RECITES קַדִּישׁ שָׁלֵם, FULL *KADDISH*.

יִתְגַּדַּל וְיִתְקַדַּשׁ שְׁמֵהּ רַבָּא. (Cong. — אָמֵן.) בְּעָלְמָא
‹ Grow exalted ‹ and be sanctified ‹ may His Name ‹ that is great! — 《 (Amen.) 《 — in the world

דִּי בְרָא כִרְעוּתֵהּ, וְיַמְלִיךְ מַלְכוּתֵהּ, וְיַצְמַח פֻּרְקָנֵהּ
‹ that ‹ He created ‹ according to His will, 《 and may He give reign ‹ to His kingship, ‹ and cause to sprout ‹ His salvation,

וִיקָרֵב מְשִׁיחֵהּ. (Cong. — אָמֵן.) בְּחַיֵּיכוֹן וּבְיוֹמֵיכוֹן וּבְחַיֵּי
‹ and bring near 《 His Messiah, 《 (Amen.) 《 in your lifetimes ‹ and in your days, ‹ and in the lifetimes

דְכָל בֵּית יִשְׂרָאֵל, בַּעֲגָלָא וּבִזְמַן קָרִיב. וְאִמְרוּ: אָמֵן.
‹ of the entire ‹ Family ‹ of Israel, 《 swiftly ‹ and at a time 《 that comes soon. ‹ Now respond: 《Amen.

CONGREGATION RESPONDS:

אָמֵן. יְהֵא שְׁמֵהּ רַבָּא מְבָרַךְ לְעָלַם וּלְעָלְמֵי עָלְמַיָּא.
《 Amen. ‹ May 《 His Name ‹ that is great ‹ be blessed ‹ forever ‹ and for all eternity. 《

CHAZZAN CONTINUES:

יְהֵא שְׁמֵהּ רַבָּא מְבָרַךְ לְעָלַם וּלְעָלְמֵי עָלְמַיָּא. יִתְבָּרַךְ
‹ May ‹ His Name ‹ that is great ‹ be blessed ‹ forever ‹ and for all eternity. 《 Blessed,

וְיִשְׁתַּבַּח וְיִתְפָּאַר וְיִתְרוֹמַם וְיִתְנַשֵּׂא וְיִתְהַדָּר וְיִתְעַלֶּה
‹ praised, ‹ glorified, ‹ exalted, ‹ upraised, ‹ honored, ‹ elevated,

וְיִתְהַלָּל שְׁמֵהּ דְּקֻדְשָׁא בְּרִיךְ הוּא (Cong. — בְּרִיךְ הוּא)
‹ and lauded ‹ be the Name ‹ of the Holy One, ‹ Blessed 《 is He 《 (Blessed ‹ is He)

— לְעֵלָּא מִן כָּל בִּרְכָתָא וְשִׁירָתָא תֻּשְׁבְּחָתָא וְנֶחֱמָתָא
‹ beyond ‹ any ‹ blessing ‹ and song, 《 and praise ‹ and consolation

דַּאֲמִירָן בְּעָלְמָא. וְאִמְרוּ: אָמֵן. (Cong. — אָמֵן.)
‹ that are uttered ‹ in the world. 《 Now respond: ‹ Amen. 《 (Amen.)

CONGREGATION:

(קַבֵּל בְּרַחֲמִים וּבְרָצוֹן אֶת תְּפִלָּתֵנוּ.)
《 our prayers.) ‹ and with favor ‹ with mercy ‹ (Accept

CHAZZAN CONTINUES:

תִּתְקַבֵּל צְלוֹתְהוֹן וּבָעוּתְהוֹן דְּכָל בֵּית יִשְׂרָאֵל קֳדָם
‹ before ›   Israel   ‹ Family ›   ‹ of the ›   ‹ and ›   ‹ the prayers ›   ‹ May
                           of   entire   supplications   accepted be

אֲבוּהוֹן דִּי בִשְׁמַיָּא. וְאִמְרוּ: אָמֵן. (Cong. — אָמֵן.)
《 (Amen.)   《 Amen. ‹ Now ›   《 is in ‹ Who › their
                                    respond: Heaven.   Father

CONGREGATION:

(יְהִי שֵׁם יהוה מְבֹרָךְ, מֵעַתָּה וְעַד עוֹלָם.[1])
《 eternity.) ‹ until › ‹ from ›   《 be   ‹ of › ‹ the › 《 (Let
                        this time   blessed,   HASHEM   Name

CHAZZAN CONTINUES:

יְהֵא שְׁלָמָא רַבָּא מִן שְׁמַיָּא וְחַיִּים טוֹבִים עָלֵינוּ וְעַל כָּל
‹ all › ‹ and › ‹ upon us › ‹ that is ‹ and life › ‹ Heaven › ‹ from › ‹ that is › ‹ peace › ‹ May
        upon   good,   abundant   there be

יִשְׂרָאֵל. וְאִמְרוּ: אָמֵן. (Cong. — אָמֵן.)
《 (Amen.)   《 Amen. ‹ Now ›   《 Israel.
                        respond:

CONGREGATION:

(עֶזְרִי מֵעִם יהוה, עֹשֵׂה שָׁמַיִם וָאָרֶץ.[2])
《   and   ‹   of   › ‹ Maker 《HASHEM, ‹   is   › 《 (My
    earth.)   heaven   from   help

CHAZZAN BOWS; TAKES THREE STEPS BACK. BOWS LEFT AND SAYS "... עֹשֶׂה שָׁלוֹם, *HE WHO MAKES
PEACE ...";* BOWS RIGHT AND SAYS "... הוּא, *MAY HE ...";* BOWS FORWARD AND SAYS "... וְעַל כָּל יִשְׂרָאֵל,
AND UPON ALL ISRAEL ..."; REMAINS IN PLACE FOR A FEW MOMENTS, THEN TAKES THREE STEPS FORWARD.

עֹשֶׂה שָׁלוֹם בִּמְרוֹמָיו, הוּא יַעֲשֶׂה שָׁלוֹם עָלֵינוּ, וְעַל כָּל
‹ all › ‹ and › ‹ upon us, › ‹ peace › ‹ make › ‹ may 《 in His   ‹ peace › ‹ He Who
        upon   He   heights,   makes

יִשְׂרָאֵל. וְאִמְרוּ: אָמֵן. (Cong. — אָמֵן.)
《 (Amen.)   《 Amen. ‹ Now ›   《 Israel.
                        respond:

---

(1) *Psalms* 113:2. (2) 121:2.

﷽ יום שלישי / THIRD DAY ﴾

אַשְׁרֵי יוֹשְׁבֵי בֵיתֶךָ, עוֹד יְהַלְלוּךָ סֶּלָה.[1] אַשְׁרֵי

⟨ Praise-worthy ⟩ are those who dwell ⟨ in Your house, ⟩ continually ⟨ they will praise You, ⟩ Selah. ⟨ Praiseworthy

הָעָם שֶׁכָּכָה לּוֹ, אַשְׁרֵי הָעָם שֶׁיהוה אֱלֹהָיו.[2]

is the people ⟨ that such ⟨ is their lot; ⟨ praiseworthy ⟩ is the people ⟨ that HASHEM ⟨ is their God.

——— תהלים קמה / Psalm 145 ———

תְּהִלָּה לְדָוִד, אֲרוֹמִמְךָ אֱלוֹהַי הַמֶּלֶךְ, וַאֲבָרְכָה

⟨ A psalm of praise ⟨ by David: ⟩ I will exalt You, ⟨ my God ⟨ the King, ⟩ and I will bless

שִׁמְךָ לְעוֹלָם וָעֶד. **בְּכָל** יוֹם אֲבָרְכֶךָּ, וַאֲהַלְלָה שִׁמְךָ

⟨ Your Name ⟩ for ever and ever. ⟨ Every ⟨ day ⟩ I will bless You, ⟩ and I will laud ⟨ Your Name

לְעוֹלָם וָעֶד. **גָּדוֹל** יהוה וּמְהֻלָּל מְאֹד, וְלִגְדֻלָּתוֹ

⟨ for ever and ever. ⟨ Great ⟩ is HASHEM ⟨ and ⟨ lauded ⟩ exceedingly, ⟨ and His greatness

אֵין חֵקֶר. **דּוֹר** לְדוֹר יְשַׁבַּח מַעֲשֶׂיךָ, וּגְבוּרֹתֶיךָ יַגִּידוּ.

is beyond investigation. ⟨ Gen-eration ⟨ to ⟨ generation ⟨ will praise ⟨ Your actions, ⟩ and Your mighty deeds ⟨ they will recount.

הֲדַר כְּבוֹד הוֹדֶךָ, וְדִבְרֵי נִפְלְאֹתֶיךָ אָשִׂיחָה. וֶעֱזוּז

⟨ The splendrous ⟨ glory ⟨ of Your majesty ⟨ and Your deeds ⟨ that are wondrous ⟨ I shall discuss. ⟨ And of the might

נוֹרְאֹתֶיךָ יֹאמֵרוּ, וּגְדוּלָּתְךָ אֲסַפְּרֶנָּה. **זֵכֶר** רַב טוּבְךָ

⟨ of Your awesome deeds ⟩ they will speak, ⟨ and Your greatness ⟨ I shall relate. ⟨ A recol-lection ⟨ of Your abun-dant goodness

יַבִּיעוּ, וְצִדְקָתְךָ יְרַנֵּנוּ. **חַנּוּן** וְרַחוּם יהוה, אֶרֶךְ אַפַּיִם

⟨ they will utter, ⟨ and of Your righteousness ⟩ they will sing joyfully. ⟨ Gracious ⟨ and ⟨ merciful ⟩ is HASHEM, ⟨ slow ⟨ to anger,

וּגְדָל חָסֶד. **טוֹב** יהוה לַכֹּל, וְרַחֲמָיו עַל כָּל מַעֲשָׂיו.

⟨ and ⟨ great ⟩ in [bestowing] ⟨ kindness. ⟨ HASHEM ⟨ is good ⟨ to all; ⟩ His ⟨ mercies ⟨ are ⟨ on ⟨ all ⟩ His creations.

יוֹדוּךָ יהוה כָּל מַעֲשֶׂיךָ, וַחֲסִידֶיךָ יְבָרְכוּכָה. **כְּבוֹד**

⟨ They will thank You, ⟨ HASHEM ⟨ — all ⟨ Your creations — ⟨ Your ⟨ devout ones ⟩ will bless You. ⟨ Of the glory

———

(1) *Psalms* 84:5. (2) 144:15.

מַלְכוּתְךָ יֹאמֵרוּ, וּגְבוּרָתְךָ יְדַבֵּרוּ. **לְהוֹדִיעַ** לִבְנֵי הָאָדָם
⟨ mankind ⟨ To inform ⟫ they will ⟨ and of Your ⟫ they will ⟨ of Your
declare. power speak, kingdom

גְּבוּרֹתָיו, וּכְבוֹד הֲדַר מַלְכוּתוֹ. **מַלְכוּתְךָ** מַלְכוּת כָּל
⟨ [span- ⟨ is a ⟨ Your kingdom ⟫ of His ⟨ splendor ⟨ and of the ⟫ of His mighty
ning] all kingdom kingdom. glorious deeds,

עֹלָמִים, וּמֶמְשַׁלְתְּךָ בְּכָל דּוֹר וָדֹר. **סוֹמֵךְ** יהוה
⟨ HASHEM ⟫ after ⟨ gen- ⟨ is ⟨ and Your ⟫ eternities,
supports generation. eration throughout dominion

לְכָל הַנֹּפְלִים, וְזוֹקֵף לְכָל הַכְּפוּפִים. **עֵינֵי** כֹל
⟨ of all ⟨ The ⟫ those who ⟨ all ⟨ and ⟫ those who ⟨ all
eyes are bent. straightens are fallen.

אֵלֶיךָ יְשַׂבֵּרוּ, וְאַתָּה נוֹתֵן לָהֶם אֶת אָכְלָם בְּעִתּוֹ.
⟫ in its ⟨ their food ⟨ them ⟨ give ⟨ and You ⟫ do look ⟨ to You
proper time. with hope,

CONCENTRATE INTENTLY WHILE RECITING THE VERSE **פּוֹתֵחַ**, YOU OPEN.

פּוֹתֵחַ אֶת יָדֶךָ, וּמַשְׂבִּיעַ לְכָל חַי רָצוֹן. ✧ **צַדִּיק**
⟨ Righteous ⟫ [with its] ⟨ living ⟨ every ⟨ and satisfy ⟫ Your hand, ⟨ You open
desire. thing

יהוה בְּכָל דְּרָכָיו, וְחָסִיד בְּכָל מַעֲשָׂיו. **קָרוֹב** יהוה
⟨ is ⟨ Close ⟫ His deeds. ⟨ in all ⟨ and ⟫ His ways, ⟨ in all ⟨ is
HASHEM magnanimous HASHEM

לְכָל קֹרְאָיו, לְכֹל אֲשֶׁר יִקְרָאֻהוּ בֶאֱמֶת. **רְצוֹן** יְרֵאָיו
⟨ of those ⟨ The ⟫ sincerely. ⟨ call upon ⟨ who ⟨ to all ⟫ who call ⟨ to all
who fear Him will Him upon Him,

יַעֲשֶׂה, וְאֶת שַׁוְעָתָם יִשְׁמַע וְיוֹשִׁיעֵם. **שׁוֹמֵר** יהוה
⟨ HASHEM protects ⟫ and He will ⟨ He will ⟨ and their cry ⟫ He
save them. hear, will do;

אֶת כָּל אֹהֲבָיו, וְאֵת כָּל הָרְשָׁעִים יַשְׁמִיד. **תְּהִלַּת**
⟨ The praise ⟫ He will destroy. ⟨ the wicked ⟨ but all ⟫ who love Him; ⟨ all

יהוה יְדַבֶּר פִּי, וִיבָרֵךְ כָּל בָּשָׂר שֵׁם קָדְשׁוֹ לְעוֹלָם
⟨ for ever ⟨ of His ⟨ the ⟨ flesh ⟨ may ⟨ and bless ⟫ may my ⟨ of
Holiness Name all mouth declare, HASHEM

וָעֶד. וַאֲנַחְנוּ נְבָרֵךְ יָהּ מֵעַתָּה וְעַד עוֹלָם; הַלְלוּיָהּ.[1]
⟫ Halleluyah! ⟫ eternity. ⟨ until ⟨ from ⟨ God ⟨ will ⟨ But we ⟫ and
this time bless ever.

(1) *Psalms* 115:18.

THE CHAZZAN RECITES חֲצִי קַדִּישׁ, HALF-KADDISH:

בְּעָלְמָא (אָמֵן. — Cong.) רַבָּא. שְׁמֵהּ וְיִתְקַדַּשׁ **יִתְגַּדַּל**

⟨ — in the world   ⟨⟨ (Amen.)   ⟨⟨ that is great! —   ⟨ may His Name   ⟨ and be sanctified   ⟨ Grow exalted

פֻּרְקָנֵהּ וְיַצְמַח מַלְכוּתֵהּ, וְיַמְלִיךְ כִרְעוּתֵהּ, בְרָא דִּי

⟨ His salvation,   ⟨ and cause to sprout   ⟨⟨ to His kingship,   ⟨ and may He give reign   ⟨⟨ according to His will,   ⟨ He created   ⟨ that

וּבְחַיֵּי וּבְיוֹמֵיכוֹן בְּחַיֵּיכוֹן (אָמֵן. — Cong.) מְשִׁיחֵהּ. וִיקָרֵב

⟨ and in the lifetimes   ⟨ and in your days,   ⟨ in your lifetimes   ⟨⟨ (Amen.)   ⟨⟨ His Messiah,   ⟨ and bring near

אָמֵן. וְאִמְרוּ: קָרִיב. וּבִזְמַן בַּעֲגָלָא יִשְׂרָאֵל, בֵּית דְכָל

⟨⟨ Amen.   ⟨ Now respond: ⟨⟨ that comes soon.   ⟨ and at a time   ⟨ swiftly   ⟨⟨ of Israel,   ⟨ Family   ⟨ of the entire

CONGREGATION RESPONDS:

עָלְמַיָּא. וּלְעָלְמֵי לְעָלַם מְבָרַךְ רַבָּא שְׁמֵהּ יְהֵא אָמֵן.

⟨⟨ and for all eternity.   ⟨ forever   ⟨ be blessed   ⟨ that is great   ⟨ His Name   ⟨ May   ⟨⟨ Amen.

CHAZZAN CONTINUES:

יִתְבָּרַךְ עָלְמַיָּא. וּלְעָלְמֵי לְעָלַם מְבָרַךְ רַבָּא שְׁמֵהּ יְהֵא

⟨ Blessed,   ⟨⟨ and for all eternity.   ⟨ forever   ⟨ be blessed   ⟨ that is great   ⟨ His Name   ⟨ May

וְיִתְעַלֶּה וְיִתְהַדָּר וְיִתְנַשֵּׂא וְיִתְרוֹמַם וְיִתְפָּאַר וְיִשְׁתַּבַּח

⟨ elevated,   ⟨ honored,   ⟨ upraised,   ⟨ exalted,   ⟨ glorified,   ⟨ praised,

(הוּא בְּרִיךְ — Cong.) הוּא בְּרִיךְ דְּקֻדְשָׁא שְׁמֵהּ וְיִתְהַלָּל

⟨⟨ is He)   ⟨ (Blessed   ⟨⟨ is He   ⟨ Blessed   ⟨ of the Holy One,   ⟨ be the Name   ⟨ and lauded

וְנֶחֱמָתָא תֻּשְׁבְּחָתָא וְשִׁירָתָא בִּרְכָתָא כָּל מִן לְעֵלָּא —

⟨ and consolation   ⟨ praise   ⟨⟨ and song,   ⟨ blessing   ⟨ any   ⟨ beyond

(אָמֵן. — Cong.) וְאִמְרוּ: אָמֵן. בְּעָלְמָא. דַּאֲמִירָן

⟨⟨ (Amen.)   ⟨⟨ Amen.   ⟨ Now respond: ⟨⟨ in the world.   ⟨ that are uttered

ALL:

מַה הַפָּנִים.[1] בֹּשֶׁת וְלָנוּ הַצְּדָקָה, **יהוה לְךָ**

⟨⟨ What   ⟨⟨ is shamefacedness.   ⟨ and ours   ⟨⟨ is the righteousness,   ⟨ O Lord,   ⟨ Yours,

נִצְטַדָּק.[3] וּמַה נְּדַבֵּר, מַה נֹּאמַר, מַה נִּתְאוֹנֵן,[2]

⟨⟨ justification can we offer?   ⟨ What   ⟨ can we declare?   ⟨⟨ can we say?   ⟨ What   ⟨⟨ complaint can we make?

(1) Daniel 9:7. (2) Cf. Lamentations 3:39. (3) Cf. Genesis 44:16.

נַחְפְּשָׂה דְרָכֵינוּ וְנַחְקֹרָה, וְנָשׁוּבָה אֵלֶיךָ,¹ כִּי יְמִינְךָ

⟨ Your right hand ⟨ for ⟪ to You, ⟨ and return ⟨ and investigate ⟨ our ways ⟨ Let us examine
them,

פְּשׁוּטָה לְקַבֵּל שָׁבִים. לֹא בְחֶסֶד וְלֹא בְמַעֲשִׂים

⟨ with [merit for good] deeds ⟨ nor ⟨ with [merit] for kindness ⟨ Neither ⟪ those who return. ⟨ to accept ⟨ is extended

בָּאנוּ לְפָנֶיךָ, כְּדַלִּים וּכְרָשִׁים דָּפַקְנוּ דְלָתֶיךָ.

⟪ on Your doors. ⟨ we have knocked ⟨ and as destitute people ⟨ but as paupers ⟪ before You; ⟨ do we come

דְלָתֶיךָ דָּפַקְנוּ רַחוּם וְחַנּוּן, נָא אַל תְּשִׁיבֵנוּ

⟨ turn us away ⟨ do not ⟨ Please ⟪ and Gracious One. ⟨ O Compassionate One ⟨ we have knocked, ⟨ On Your doors

רֵיקָם מִלְּפָנֶיךָ. מִלְּפָנֶיךָ מַלְכֵּנוּ רֵיקָם אַל תְּשִׁיבֵנוּ,

⟪ turn us away, ⟨ do not ⟨ empty-handed ⟨ Our King, ⟨ From before You, ⟪ from before You. ⟨ empty-handed

כִּי אַתָּה שׁוֹמֵעַ תְּפִלָּה.

⟪ prayer. ⟨ Who hears ⟨ You are ⟨ for the One

שֹׁמֵעַ תְּפִלָּה, עָדֶיךָ כָּל בָּשָׂר יָבֹאוּ.² יָבוֹא

⟨ Come ⟪ will come. ⟨ flesh ⟨ all ⟨ unto You ⟪ prayer, ⟨ You Who hears

כָל בָּשָׂר לְהִשְׁתַּחֲוֹת לְפָנֶיךָ יהוה.³ יָבֹאוּ וְיִשְׁתַּחֲווּ

⟨ and bow down ⟨ They will come ⟪ O HASHEM. ⟨ before You, ⟨ to bow down ⟨ will all flesh

לְפָנֶיךָ אֲדֹנָי, וִיכַבְּדוּ לִשְׁמֶךָ.⁴ בֹּאוּ נִשְׁתַּחֲוֶה וְנִכְרָעָה,

⟪ and bow, ⟨ Let us prostrate ourselves ⟨ Come! ⟪ to Your Name. ⟨ and they will show honor ⟪ O Lord, ⟨ before You,

נִבְרְכָה לִפְנֵי יהוה עֹשֵׂנוּ.⁵ נָבוֹאָה לְמִשְׁכְּנוֹתָיו,

⟪ to His Tabernacles, ⟨ Let us come ⟪ our Maker. ⟨ HASHEM, ⟨ before ⟨ let us kneel

נִשְׁתַּחֲוֶה לַהֲדֹם רַגְלָיו.⁶ בֹּאוּ שְׁעָרָיו בְּתוֹדָה,

⟪ with thanksgiving, ⟨ His gates ⟨ Enter ⟪ for His feet. ⟨ at the stool ⟨ let us prostrate ourselves

חֲצֵרֹתָיו בִּתְהִלָּה, הוֹדוּ לוֹ בָּרְכוּ שְׁמוֹ.⁷ וַאֲנַחְנוּ

⟨ But we, ⟪ His Name. ⟨ bless ⟪ to Him, ⟨ give thanks ⟪ with praise; ⟨ His courtyards

---

(1) Cf. *Lamentations* 3:40. (2) *Psalms* 65:3. (3) Cf. *Isaiah* 66:23.
(4) *Psalms* 86:9. (5) 95:6. (6) 132:7. (7) 100:4.

בְּרֹב חַסְדְּךָ נָבוֹא בֵיתֶךָ, נִשְׁתַּחֲוֶה אֶל הֵיכַל קָדְשְׁךָ

Your Holy ‹ toward ‹ we will pros- ‹‹ Your ‹ will we ‹ of Your ‹ through the
Sanctuary   trate ourselves   House;   enter   kindness   abundance

בְּיִרְאָתֶךָ.¹ הִנֵּה בָּרְכוּ אֶת יהוה כָּל עַבְדֵי יהוה,

of ‹ you ‹ all ‹ HASHEM, ‹ bless ‹‹ Indeed, ‹‹ in awe
HASHEM,   servants   of You.

הָעֹמְדִים בְּבֵית יהוה בַּלֵּילוֹת.² שְׂאוּ יְדֵיכֶם קֹדֶשׁ

‹ in the ‹ your ‹ Lift ‹‹ in the nights. ‹ of ‹ in the ‹ who stand
Sanctuary hands   HASHEM   House

וּבָרְכוּ אֶת יהוה.³ רוֹמְמוּ יהוה אֱלֹהֵינוּ, וְהִשְׁתַּחֲווּ

‹ and bow down ‹ our God, ‹ HASHEM, ‹ Exalt ‹‹ HASHEM. ‹ and bless

לַהֲדֹם רַגְלָיו, קָדוֹשׁ הוּא.⁴ רוֹמְמוּ יהוה אֱלֹהֵינוּ,

‹ our God, ‹ HASHEM, ‹ Exalt ‹‹ is He! ‹ holy ‹‹ at His footstool;

וְהִשְׁתַּחֲווּ לְהַר קָדְשׁוֹ, כִּי קָדוֹשׁ יהוה אֱלֹהֵינוּ.⁵

‹‹ our God. ‹ is ‹ holy ‹ for ‹‹ of His ‹ at the ‹ and bow
          HASHEM,   Holiness;   Mount

הִשְׁתַּחֲווּ לַיהוה בְּהַדְרַת קֹדֶשׁ, חִילוּ מִפָּנָיו כָּל

‹ every- ‹ before ‹ tremble ‹‹ of ‹ in the ‹ before ‹ Bow down
one   Him,   holiness; splendor   HASHEM

הָאָרֶץ.⁶ נִשְׁתַּחֲוֶה אֶל הֵיכַל קָדְשְׁךָ וְנוֹדֶה אֶת שְׁמֶךָ,

‹ Your Name ‹ and we ‹‹ Your Holy ‹ toward ‹ We will pros- ‹‹ on earth.
            will thank   Sanctuary,   trate ourselves

עַל חַסְדְּךָ וְעַל אֲמִתֶּךָ, כִּי הִגְדַּלְתָּ עַל כָּל שִׁמְךָ

‹‹ Your ‹ — even ‹‹ You have ‹ for ‹‹ faithfulness; ‹ and ‹ Your ‹ for
Name —   beyond   exalted   for   kindness

אִמְרָתֶךָ.⁷ יהוה אֱלֹהֵי צְבָאוֹת, מִי כָמוֹךָ חֲסִין

‹ O Strong ‹‹ is like ‹ — who ‹‹ of ‹ God ‹ HASHEM, ‹‹ Your promise.
One   You,   Legions

יָהּ, וֶאֱמוּנָתְךָ סְבִיבוֹתֶיךָ.⁸ כִּי מִי בַשַּׁחַק יַעֲרֹךְ

‹ can be ‹ in the sky ‹ who ‹ For ‹‹ surrounds You. ‹ and Your ‹‹ God? —
compared   faithfulness

לַיהוה, יִדְמֶה לַיהוה בִּבְנֵי אֵלִים.⁹ כִּי גָדוֹל אַתָּה

‹ are You ‹ great ‹ For ‹‹ among the angels? ‹ to HASHEM ‹ be likened ‹‹ to HASHEM;

וְעוֹשֵׂה נִפְלָאוֹת, אַתָּה אֱלֹהִים לְבַדֶּךָ.¹⁰ כִּי גָדוֹל

‹ great ‹ For ‹‹ alone. ‹ O God, ‹ You, ‹‹ of wonders; ‹ and a worker

(1) Cf. *Psalms* 5:8. (2) 134:1. (3) 134:2. (4) 99:5. (5) 99:9. (6) 96:9. (7) Cf. 138:2. (8) 89:9. (9) 89:7. (10) 86:10.

גָּדוֹל ‎.1מֵעַל שָׁמַיִם חַסְדֶּךָ, וְעַד שְׁחָקִים אֲמִתֶּךָ.
⟨ Great ⟩ 《 is Your truth. ⟨ the upper heights ⟨ and until 《 is Your kindness, ⟨ the very heavens ⟨ above

גָּדוֹל ‎(כִּי) .2יהוה וּמְהֻלָּל מְאֹד, וְלִגְדֻלָּתוֹ אֵין חֵקֶר.
⟨ great ⟨ (For) 《 investigation. ⟨ is beyond ⟨ and His greatness 《 exceedingly, ⟨ and lauded ⟨ is HASHEM

כִּי ‎.3יהוה וּמְהֻלָּל מְאֹד, נוֹרָא הוּא עַל כָּל אֱלֹהִים.
⟨ For 《 heavenly powers. ⟨ all ⟨ above ⟨ is He ⟨ awesome 《 exceedingly; ⟨ and lauded ⟨ is HASHEM

אֲשֶׁר ‎.4אֵל גָּדוֹל יהוה, וּמֶלֶךְ גָּדוֹל עַל כָּל אֱלֹהִים.
⟨ For 《 heavenly powers. ⟨ all ⟨ above ⟨ and a great King 《 is ⟨ a great God HASHEM,

כְמַעֲשֶׂיךָ מִי אֵל בַּשָּׁמַיִם וּבָאָרֶץ, אֲשֶׁר יַעֲשֶׂה
⟨ like unto Your deeds ⟨ can do ⟨ that ⟨ or in the earth ⟨ is there in the heaven ⟨ power ⟨ what

וְכִגְבוּרֹתֶיךָ.‎5 מִי לֹא יִרָאֲךָ מֶלֶךְ הַגּוֹיִם, כִּי לְךָ
⟨ to You ⟨ For 《 of nations? ⟨ O King 《 fear You, ⟨ would not ⟨ Who 《 and like unto Your mighty acts?

יָאָתָה, כִּי בְכָל חַכְמֵי הַגּוֹיִם וּבְכָל מַלְכוּתָם מֵאֵין
⟨ there is none ⟨ their kingdoms ⟨ and in all ⟨ of the nations ⟨ the wise men ⟨ among ⟨ for 《 [kingship] befits;

כָּמוֹךָ.‎6 מֵאֵין כָּמוֹךָ יהוה, גָּדוֹל אַתָּה וְגָדוֹל שְׁמֶךָ
⟨ is Your Name ⟨ and great ⟨ are You ⟨ Great 《 O HASHEM! ⟨ like You, ⟨ There is none 《 like You.

בִּגְבוּרָה.‎7 לְךָ זְרוֹעַ עִם גְּבוּרָה, תָּעֹז יָדְךָ תָּרוּם
⟨ uplifted 《 is Your hand, ⟨ strengthened 《 power; ⟨ with ⟨ is the arm ⟨ Yours 《 in might.

יְמִינֶךָ.‎8 לְךָ יוֹם, אַף לְךָ לָיְלָה, אַתָּה הֲכִינוֹתָ מָאוֹר
⟨ the luminary ⟨ prepared ⟨ You 《 is the night; ⟨ Yours ⟨ also 《 is the day, ⟨ Yours 《 is Your right hand.

וָשָׁמֶשׁ.‎9 אֲשֶׁר בְּיָדוֹ מֶחְקְרֵי אָרֶץ, וְתוֹעֲפוֹת הָרִים
⟨ of the mountains ⟨ and the summits 《 of the earth, ⟨ are the hidden mysteries ⟨ in His power ⟨ For 《 and the sun.

לוֹ.‎10 מִי יְמַלֵּל גְּבוּרוֹת יהוה, יַשְׁמִיעַ כָּל תְּהִלָּתוֹ.‎11
《 of His praise? ⟨ all ⟨ [who] can 《 of ⟨ the mighty ⟨ can ⟨ Who 《 are His. make heard HASHEM; acts express

---

(1) *Psalms* 108:5. (2) 145:3. (3) 96:4. (4) 95:3. (5) *Deuteronomy* 3:24.
(6) *Jeremiah* 10:7. (7) 10:6. (8) *Psalms* 89:14. (9) 74:16. (10) 95:4. (11) 106:2.

לְךָ יהוה הַגְּדֻלָּה וְהַגְּבוּרָה, וְהַתִּפְאֶרֶת וְהַנֵּצַח
⟨ the ⟨ the glory, ⟨ the strength, ⟨ is the ⟨ HASHEM, ⟨ Yours,
triumph, greatness,

וְהַהוֹד, כִּי כֹל בַּשָּׁמַיִם וּבָאָרֶץ; לְךָ יהוה הַמַּמְלָכָה,
⟨ is the ⟨ HASHEM, ⟨ Yours, « and on ⟨ in heaven ⟨ every- ⟨ for « and the
kingdom earth thing majesty;
[is Yours];

וְהַמִּתְנַשֵּׂא לְכֹל לְרֹאשׁ.[1] לְךָ שָׁמַיִם, אַף לְךָ אָרֶץ,
« is the ⟨ Yours ⟨ also « are the ⟨ Yours « leader. ⟨ over ⟨ and the
earth; heavens, every sovereignty

תֵּבֵל וּמְלֹאָהּ אַתָּה יְסַדְתָּם.[2] אַתָּה הִצַּבְתָּ כָּל גְּבוּלוֹת
⟨ the ⟨ all ⟨ established ⟨ You « founded ⟨ You ⟨ and its ⟨ the
boundaries them. fullness, world

אֶרֶץ, קַיִץ וָחֹרֶף אַתָּה יְצַרְתָּם.[3] אַתָּה רִצַּצְתָּ רָאשֵׁי
⟨ the ⟨ crushed ⟨ You « fashioned ⟨ You ⟨ and ⟨ summer « of
heads them. winter, earth;

לִוְיָתָן, תִּתְּנֶנּוּ מַאֲכָל לְעָם לְצִיִּים. אַתָּה בָקַעְתָּ מַעְיָן
⟨ fountain ⟨ split ⟨ You «[destined] for ⟨ to the ⟨ as food ⟨ You will « of
open the desolate people serve it Leviathan;
wilderness.

וָנָחַל, אַתָּה הוֹבַשְׁתָּ נַהֲרוֹת אֵיתָן.[4] אַתָּה פוֹרַרְתָּ
⟨ shattered ⟨ You « that are mighty. ⟨ rivers ⟨ dried ⟨ You « and stream;

בְעָזְךָ יָם, שִׁבַּרְתָּ רָאשֵׁי תַנִּינִים עַל הַמָּיִם.[5] אַתָּה
⟨ You « the water. ⟨ upon ⟨ of sea ⟨ the heads ⟨ You « the ⟨ with Your
serpents smashed sea; might

מוֹשֵׁל בְּגֵאוּת הַיָּם, בְּשׂוֹא גַלָּיו אַתָּה תְשַׁבְּחֵם.[6]
« calm them. ⟨ You ⟨ its ⟨ when it « of the ⟨ the ⟨ rule
waves, raises sea; grandeur

גָּדוֹל יהוה וּמְהֻלָּל מְאֹד, בְּעִיר אֱלֹהֵינוּ הַר קָדְשׁוֹ.[7]
« of His ⟨ Mount ⟨ of our God, ⟨ in the ⟨ and much praised, ⟨ is ⟨ Great
Holiness. City HASHEM

יהוה צְבָאוֹת, אֱלֹהֵי יִשְׂרָאֵל, יוֹשֵׁב הַכְּרֻבִים, אַתָּה
⟨ it is « upon the ⟨ en- ⟨ of Israel, ⟨ God ⟨ Master of ⟨ HASHEM,
You Cherubim, throned Legions,

הוּא הָאֱלֹהִים לְבַדֶּךָ.[8] אֵל נַעֲרָץ בְּסוֹד קְדוֹשִׁים רַבָּה,
« in the great assemblage ⟨ is ⟨ God « alone. ⟨ God ⟨ Who
of the holy [angels], revered are

---

(1) *I Chronicles* 29:11. (2) *Psalms* 89:12. (3) 74:17. (4) 74:14-15. (5) 74:13. (6) 89:10. (7) 48:2. (8) *Isaiah* 37:16.

וְנוֹרָא עַל כָּל סְבִיבָיו.[1] וְיוֹדוּ שָׁמַיִם פִּלְאֲךָ יהוה, אַף
‹ also ‹‹ Hashem, ‹ Your ‹ will the ‹ Acknowl- ‹‹ who sur- ‹ all ‹ over ‹ and is
wonders, heavens edge round Him. awesome

אֱמוּנָתְךָ בִּקְהַל קְדֹשִׁים.[2] לְכוּ נְרַנְּנָה לַיהוה, נָרִיעָה
‹ let us ‹‹ to ‹ Let us sing ‹ Come! ‹‹ of holy ‹ in the ‹ Your
call out Hashem, joyfully ones. assembly faithfulness,

לְצוּר יִשְׁעֵנוּ. נְקַדְּמָה פָנָיו בְּתוֹדָה, בִּזְמִירוֹת נָרִיעַ
‹ let us ‹ with praiseful ‹‹ with ‹ Him ‹ Let us greet ‹‹ of our ‹ to the
call out songs thanksgiving, salvation. Rock

לוֹ.[3] צֶדֶק וּמִשְׁפָּט מְכוֹן כִּסְאֶךָ, חֶסֶד וֶאֱמֶת יְקַדְּמוּ
‹ precede ‹ and ‹ kindness ‹‹ of Your ‹ are the ‹ and ‹ Righteous- ‹‹ to
truth throne; foundation justice ness Him.

פָנֶיךָ.[4] אֲשֶׁר יַחְדָּו נַמְתִּיק סוֹד, בְּבֵית אֱלֹהִים נְהַלֵּךְ
‹ let us ‹ of God ‹ in the ‹‹ counsel; ‹ let us ‹ together ‹ For ‹‹ Your coun-
walk House take sweet tenance.

בְּרָגֶשׁ.[5] אֲשֶׁר לוֹ הַיָּם וְהוּא עָשָׂהוּ, וְיַבֶּשֶׁת יָדָיו
‹ His ‹‹ and the ‹‹ perfected ‹ and He ‹ is the ‹ His ‹ For ‹‹ in company.
hands dry land, it, sea

יָצָרוּ.[6] אֲשֶׁר בְּיָדוֹ נֶפֶשׁ כָּל חָי, וְרוּחַ כָּל בְּשַׂר אִישׁ.[7]
‹‹ mankind. ‹ of all ‹ and the ‹‹ the ‹ of ‹ is the ‹ in His ‹ For ‹‹ fashioned.
spirit living all soul hand

❖ הַנְּשָׁמָה לָךְ וְהַגוּף פָּעֳלָךְ, חוּסָה עַל עֲמָלָךְ.
‹‹ Your ‹ on ‹ take pity ‹‹ is Your ‹ and the ‹ is ‹ The soul
labor. handiwork; body Yours

הַנְּשָׁמָה לָךְ וְהַגוּף שֶׁלָּךְ, יהוה עֲשֵׂה לְמַעַן שְׁמֶךָ.
‹‹ of Your ‹ for the ‹ act ‹ O ‹‹ is Yours; ‹ and the ‹ is ‹ The soul
Name. sake Hashem, body Yours

אָתָאנוּ עַל שִׁמְךָ, יהוה, עֲשֵׂה לְמַעַן שְׁמֶךָ. בַּעֲבוּר
‹ [act] ‹‹ of Your ‹ for the ‹ act ‹‹ O ‹‹ Your ‹ [relying] ‹ We have
because of Name; sake Hashem; Name, on come

כְּבוֹד שְׁמֶךָ, כִּי אֵל חַנּוּן וְרַחוּם שְׁמֶךָ. לְמַעַן
‹ For the ‹‹ is Your ‹ and ‹ Who is ‹ God ‹ for ‹‹ of Your ‹ the glory
sake Name. Merciful Gracious Name,

שְׁמֶךָ יהוה, וְסָלַחְתָּ לַעֲוֹנֵנוּ כִּי רַב הוּא.[8]
‹ it is great. ‹ though ‹ our ‹ forgive ‹‹ Hashem, ‹ of Your
iniquity, Name,

---

(1) *Psalms* 89:8. (2) 89:6. (3) 95:1-2. (4) 89:15. (5) 55:15. (6) 95:5. (7) *Job* 12:10. (8) Cf. *Psalms* 25:11.

CONGREGATION, THEN *CHAZZAN*:

סְלַח לָנוּ אָבִינוּ, כִּי בְרוֹב אִוַּלְתֵּנוּ שָׁגִינוּ,

《 we have 〈 of our folly 〈 in the 〈 for 〈 our Father, 〈 us, 〈 Forgive
erred;   abundance

מְחַל לָנוּ מַלְכֵּנוּ, כִּי רַבּוּ עֲוֹנֵינוּ.

《 our 〈 many 〈 for 〈 our King, 〈 us, 〈 pardon
iniquities.   are

ALL, WHILE STANDING

אֵל אֶרֶךְ אַפַּיִם אַתָּה,

《 You are, 〈 to anger, 〈 Who is slow 〈 God

וּבַעַל הָרַחֲמִים נִקְרֵאתָ, וְדֶרֶךְ תְּשׁוּבָה הוֹרֵיתָ.

《 You have 〈 of 〈 and the 《 You are 〈 of Mercy 〈 and
taught.   repentance way   called;   Master

גְּדֻלַּת רַחֲמֶיךָ וַחֲסָדֶיךָ,

〈 and Your 〈 of Your 〈 The
kindness   mercy   greatness

תִּזְכּוֹר הַיּוֹם וּבְכָל יוֹם לְזֶרַע יְדִידֶיךָ.

《 of Your 〈 for the 《 day, 〈 and 〈 this day 〈 may You
beloved ones. offspring   every   remember,

תֵּפֶן אֵלֵינוּ בְּרַחֲמִים,

《 in mercy, 〈 to us 〈 Turn

כִּי אַתָּה הוּא בַּעַל הָרַחֲמִים.

《 of Mercy. 〈 the Master 〈 are 〈 You 〈 for

בְּתַחֲנוּן וּבִתְפִלָּה פָּנֶיךָ נְקַדֵּם, כְּהוֹדַעְתָּ לֶעָנָיו מִקֶּדֶם.

《in ancient 〈 to the 〈 in the manner 《 we 〈 Your 〈 and prayer 〈 With
times.   humble one that You made approach, Presence   supplication
         [Moses]   known

מֵחֲרוֹן אַפְּךָ שׁוּב,[1] כְּמוֹ בְתוֹרָתְךָ כָּתוּב.[2]

《 it is 〈 in Your Torah 〈 as 《 turn 〈 of Your 〈 From the
written.   back,   anger   fierceness

וּבְצֵל כְּנָפֶיךָ נֶחֱסֶה[3] וְנִתְלוֹנָן, כְּיוֹם וַיֵּרֶד יהוה בֶּעָנָן.

《 in a 〈 when HASHEM 〈 as on 《 and may 〈 may we find 〈 of Your 〈 In the
cloud. descended the day we dwell, shelter   wings   shadow

❖ תַּעֲבוֹר עַל פֶּשַׁע וְתִמְחֶה אָשָׁם,

《 guilt, 〈 and erase 〈 sin 〈 Overlook

---

(1) Cf. *Exodus* 32:12. (2) See 32:14. (3) Cf. *Psalms* 36:8.

כְּיוֹם וַיִּתְיַצֵּב עִמּוֹ שָׁם.

《 there. 〈 with him 〈 when He 〈 as on the
　　　　　　　[Moses] [God] stood　　day

תַּאֲזִין שַׁוְעָתֵנוּ וְתַקְשִׁיב מֶנּוּ מַאֲמַר,

《 [our] 〈 from 〈 and hear 〈 to our cry 〈 Give heed
declaration,　us

כְּיוֹם וַיִּקְרָא בְשֵׁם יהוה,[1] וְשָׁם נֶאֱמַר:

《 it was said:〈 and 《 of HASHEM,〈 with the 〈 when He 〈 as on
　　　　there　　　　　　Name　called out　the day

CONGREGATION, THEN *CHAZZAN:*

וַיַּעֲבֹר יהוה עַל פָּנָיו וַיִּקְרָא:

《 and 《 [Moses'] 〈 before 〈 And HASHEM passed
proclaimed:　face,

CONGREGATION AND *CHAZZAN* RECITE LOUDLY AND IN UNISON:

יהוה, יהוה, אֵל, רַחוּם, וְחַנּוּן, אֶרֶךְ אַפַּיִם,

〈 to anger, 〈 Slow 《and Gracious,〈Compassionate〈 God, 〈 HASHEM, 〈 HASHEM,

וְרַב חֶסֶד, וֶאֱמֶת, נֹצֵר חֶסֶד לָאֲלָפִים, נֹשֵׂא עָוֹן,

〈 of 〈 Forgiver 《 for thousands 〈 of 〈 Preserver 《 and 〈 in 〈 and
iniquity,　[of generations], kindness　　　Truth,　Kindness Abundant

וָפֶשַׁע, וְחַטָּאָה, וְנַקֵּה.[2] וְסָלַחְתָּ לַעֲוֹנֵנוּ וּלְחַטָּאתֵנוּ

《 and our sins, 〈 our 〈 May You 《 and Who 〈 and inadvertent 〈 willful sin,
　　　　　iniquities　forgive　absolves.　sin,

וּנְחַלְתָּנוּ.[3] סְלַח לָנוּ אָבִינוּ כִּי חָטָאנוּ, מְחַל לָנוּ

〈 us, 〈 pardon 《 we have 〈 for 《our Father, 〈 us, 〈 Forgive 《 and make us
　　　　　sinned;　　　　　　　　　　　　　Your heritage.

מַלְכֵּנוּ כִּי פָשָׁעְנוּ. כִּי אַתָּה אֲדֹנָי טוֹב וְסַלָּח, וְרַב

〈 and 《 and 〈 are 〈 O Lord, 〈 You, 〈 For 《 we have 〈 for 《 our King,
abundantly forgiving, good　　　　　　　willfully sinned.

חֶסֶד לְכָל קֹרְאֶיךָ.[4]

《 who call upon You. 〈 to all 〈 kind

הוֹשִׁיעָה יהוה כִּי גָמַר חָסִיד, כִּי פַסּוּ אֱמוּנִים

〈 have truthful 〈 van- 〈 for 《 is the 〈 gone 〈 for 〈 HASHEM, 〈 Save [us],
people　ished　　　devout one,

(1) *Exodus* 34:5. (2) 34:6-7. (3) 34:9. (4) *Psalms* 86:5.

מִבְּנֵי אָדָם.¹ לוּלֵי יהוה שֶׁהָיָה לָנוּ, בְּקוּם עָלֵינוּ
from mankind. « Had not ‹ Hashem › been ‹ with us » when ‹ against us » rise up

אָדָם. אֲזַי חַיִּים בְּלָעוּנוּ, בַּחֲרוֹת אַפָּם בָּנוּ.²
did men, » then ‹ alive ‹ they would have » swallowed us, when ‹ flare up › their anger » against us.

כְּרַחֵם אָב עַל בָּנִים, כֵּן תְּרַחֵם יהוה עָלֵינוּ.³
As merciful as ‹ a ‹ father is ‹ toward ‹ his children, » so ‹ have mercy, ‹ Hashem, » on us.

לַיהוה הַיְשׁוּעָה, עַל עַמְּךָ בִרְכָתֶךָ סֶּלָה.⁴ יהוה
To Hashem ‹ is salvation, » upon ‹ Your people ‹ Your blessing, is Your » Selah. « Hashem,

צְבָאוֹת עִמָּנוּ, מִשְׂגָּב לָנוּ אֱלֹהֵי יַעֲקֹב סֶלָה.⁵
Master of Legions, «is with us, » a stronghold ‹ for us ‹ is the God ‹ of Jacob, » Selah. «

יהוה צְבָאוֹת, אַשְׁרֵי אָדָם בֹּטֵחַ בָּךְ.⁶ יהוה הוֹשִׁיעָה,
Hashem, ‹ Master of » Legions, — praise- ‹ worthy ‹ is the ‹ who ‹ man trusts You. in » Hashem, ‹ save! «

הַמֶּלֶךְ יַעֲנֵנוּ בְיוֹם קָרְאֵנוּ.⁷
May the King ‹ answer us ‹ on the day » we call. «

**IN MOST CONGREGATIONS THE FOLLOWING VERSES ARE RECITED ALOUD RESPONSIVELY,
AS INDICATED; IN OTHERS THEY ARE RECITED SILENTLY.**

CONGREGATION, ALOUD, FOLLOWED BY *CHAZZAN,* **ALOUD:**

סְלַח נָא לַעֲוֹן הָעָם הַזֶּה כְּגֹדֶל חַסְדֶּךָ, וְכַאֲשֶׁר
Forgive, ‹ please, ‹ the ‹ iniquity ‹ of this people ‹ according to ‹ of Your » just as ‹ the greatness kindness,

נָשָׂאתָה לָעָם הַזֶּה מִמִּצְרַיִם וְעַד הֵנָּה,⁸ וְשָׁם נֶאֱמַר:
You have forgiven ‹ this people ‹ from Egypt ‹ until ‹ now. » And there » it was said:

ALL, ALOUD AND IN UNISON:

וַיֹּאמֶר יהוה סָלַחְתִּי כִּדְבָרֶךָ.⁹
And Hashem said: » ‹ I have forgiven » according to your word!

---

(1) *Psalms* 12:2. (2) 124:2-3. (3) Cf. 103:13. (4) 3:9. (5) 46:8.
(6) 84:13. (7) 20:10. (8) *Numbers* 14:19. (9) 14:20.

ALL CONTINUE:

הַטֵּה אֱלֹהַי אָזְנְךָ וּשְׁמָע, פְּקַח עֵינֶיךָ וּרְאֵה
⟨ and see ⟨ Your eyes ⟨ open ⟪ and listen; ⟨ Your ear, ⟨ my God, ⟨ Incline,

שֹׁמְמֹתֵינוּ, וְהָעִיר אֲשֶׁר נִקְרָא שִׁמְךָ עָלֶיהָ, כִּי לֹא
⟨ not ⟨ for ⟪ upon; ⟨ Your Name is ⟨ which ⟨ and that ⟨ our desolation
　　　　　　　　　　　proclaimed　　　　　　　　[of] the city

עַל צִדְקֹתֵינוּ אֲנַחְנוּ מַפִּילִים תַּחֲנוּנֵינוּ לְפָנֶיךָ,
⟪ before ⟨ our ⟨ cast ⟨ do we ⟨ of our ⟨ because
　 You;　　supplications　　　　　　　　　righteousness

כִּי עַל רַחֲמֶיךָ הָרַבִּים. אֲדֹנָי שְׁמָעָה, אֲדֹנָי סְלָחָה,
⟪ forgive; ⟨ O Lord, ⟪ heed; ⟨ O Lord, ⟪ which is ⟨ of Your ⟨ be- ⟨ but
　　　　　　　　　　　　　　　　abundant.　compassion, cause

אֲדֹנָי הַקְשִׁיבָה, וַעֲשֵׂה אַל תְּאַחַר, לְמַעַנְךָ אֱלֹהַי,
⟪ my God, ⟨ for Your sake, ⟪ delay; ⟨ do not ⟪ and act, ⟨ be attentive, ⟨ O Lord,

כִּי שִׁמְךָ נִקְרָא עַל עִירְךָ וְעַל עַמֶּךָ.[1]
⟪ Your ⟨ and ⟨ Your ⟨ upon ⟨ is ⟨ Your ⟨ for
　 people.　upon　　City　　　　proclaimed　Name

SELICHAH 8 / ח סליחה

ALL:

אֱלֹהֵינוּ וֵאלֹהֵי אֲבוֹתֵינוּ:
⟪ of our forefathers: ⟨ and God ⟨ Our God

יִשְׂרָאֵל עַמְּךָ* תְּחִנָּה עוֹרְכִים,
⟪ they arrange, ⟨ [their] ⟨ Your ⟨ Israel,
　　　　　　supplication　people,*

שֶׁהֵם מְצֵרִים וּלְהִוָּשַׁע צְרִיכִים,
⟪ they have need. ⟨ and to be saved ⟨ are distressed ⟨ for they

צָרֵיהֶם עֲלֵיהֶם עֹל מַאֲרִיכִים,
⟪ prolong. ⟨ their yoke ⟨ upon them ⟨ Their foes

---

(1) *Daniel* 9:18-19.

◆§ יִשְׂרָאֵל עַמְּךָ — *Israel, Your people.* This
selichah bewails the tribulations caused by
the First Crusade (1096). It is the work of
יִצְחָק הַקָּטָן בְּרַבִּי מֵאִיר, *Yitzchak the lesser,*
son of R' Meir, as attested to by the acrostic.
Best known as רִיבַם, *Rivam,* R' Yitzchak was

a noted Tosafist, a grandson to Rashi, and a
brother of Rashbam and Rabbeinu Tam. He
lived in Ramerupt, France (c. 1090-c. 1130),
and died at a relatively young age, leaving
seven orphans.

כָּל זֹאת הַגִּעַתָּם וְשִׁמְךָ מְבָרְכִים.

《   they bless. 〈 yet Your 《 has befallen 〈 this 〈 All
name   them,

חֲלִי וּמַכְאוֹב לְהִכָּתֵב לֹא נִמְסָר,

《   be 〈 can- 〈 to writing 《 and pain, 〈 The
committed;   not   sickness

עֲלוּבִים מִנַּעַר וּמֵהֶם לֹא הוּסָר,

《 been 〈 [the degradation]〈 and from 〈 from [their]〈 they are
removed.   has never   them   youth,   degraded

קָדוֹשׁ בְּיָדְךָ לְפַתֵּחַ מוּסָר,[1]

《 [their] 〈 to break 〈 it is in Your〈 O Holy
bonds,   open   power   One,

כְּאֱמָנוּתְךָ הַנְּקִיָּה וְלֹא כְּאֱמָנוּת בָּשָׂר.

《 of 〈 the practice 〈 and 《 which is 〈 as is Your
humans.   unlike   pure,   practice

הַלּוֹבֵשׁ צְדָקָה וְלוֹ כַּמְּעִיל עֲטוּיָה,[2]

《 it is draped, 〈 like a coat 〈 and for 《 righteous- 〈 The One
Whom   ness,   Who dons

וּמִמַּכָּה עַצְמָהּ מְתַקֵּן רְטִיָּה,*[3]

《 its healing 〈 fashions 〈 itself 〈 and Who from
bandage,*   the wound

---

(1) Cf. *Job* 12:18. (2) Cf. *Isaiah* 59:17; 61:10. (3) Cf. *Jeremiah* 30:17.

וּמִמַּכָּה עַצְמָהּ מְתַקֵּן רְטִיָּה — *And Who from the wound itself fashions its healing bandage.* God is the Doctor par excellence, as the Torah states: כִּי אֲנִי ה' רֹפְאֶךָ, *for I am HASHEM your Healer* (Exodus 15:26). The prophets declared: *Let us go and return to HASHEM, for He has torn and He shall heal us; He has smitten and He shall bandage us* (Hosea 6:1); *Heal me, O HASHEM, and I shall be healed; save me, and I shall be saved* (Jeremiah 17:14); and, *For I shall bring a cure for you, from your very wound itself shall I heal you* — *the word of HASHEM* (ibid. 30:17).

The Midrash expounds on the differences between the craft of human physicians and that of Hashem: The way of the human doctor is that when a person is wounded with a knife, the doctor prepares a bandage for the wound. But that is not My way of healing; rather, *"from your very wound itself shall I heal you."* God smote Job with a storm wind

— *He pushed me with a storm wind, and caused me multiple wounds* (Job 9:17). And He cured him with a storm wind — *And HASHEM replied to Job from the storm wind ...* (ibid. 38:1). He caused Israel to be exiled with clouds — *Alas, how He has beclouded in His anger ...* (Lamentations 2:1). And He will return Israel from exile with clouds — *Who are these that fly like a cloud?* (Isaiah 60:8). He dispersed Israel like doves — *And their fugitives will flee and be upon the mountain like doves of the valleys, all of them moaning, each in his sin* (Ezekiel 7:16). And He will gather them and return them to their land like doves — *[Who are these that fly] as doves to their cotes?* (Isaiah 60:8). Thus, in God's medical practice, the cure and healing are always derived from the sickness or wound itself (Mechilta to Shemos 14:24, see also Pesikta Rabbasi 34:13 for thirty other examples).

קוֹמֵם עֲדָתְךָ מִנְּפִילָתָהּ הַמְּטוּיָה,
《 into the depths,《 from its 〈 Your 〈 raise up
downfall congregation

בְּכֹחֲךָ הַגָּדוֹל וּבִזְרֹעֲךָ הַנְּטוּיָה.[1]
《 that is 〈 and with 〈 that is great 〈 with Your
outstretched. Your arm strength

טְמֵאִים[2] הָאוֹמְרִים נַחֲלָתְךָ לְחַבֵּל,
《 to destroy, 〈 Your 《 who declare 〈 The unclean
heritage [their intention]: ones

כְּבוֹדְךָ לְהָמִיר וּבַהֶבֶל לְהִתְהַבֵּל,[3]
《 and become 〈 for 〈 to 〈 and Your
worthless themselves; worthlessness exchange glory

נֵצֶר נִתְעָב לֶאֱלוֹהַּ לְקַבֵּל,[4]
《 to accept, 〈 as a god 〈 that is vile 〈 The
offshoot

וְיִרְאָתְךָ הַקְּדוֹשָׁה לִנְטֹשׁ וּלְנַבֵּל.
《 and to 〈 to 〈 that is holy 〈 and Your
revile. abandon reverence

בְּאַהֲבָתְךָ וּבְחֶמְלָתְךָ מְנַשֵּׂא וּמְנַטֵּל,[5]
《 and bears 〈 O You 〈 and with Your 〈 With Your love
[us], Who uplifts compassion,

עֲצָתָם תְּסַכֵּל[6] וּמַחְשְׁבוֹתָם תְּבַטֵּל,
《 nullify. 〈 and their intentions 《 confound, 〈 their plans

רַבָּה מְהוּמָה[7] בֵּינֵיהֶם הַטֵּל,
〈 cast 〈 among them 〈 confusion 〈 Great

וּמַלְאָךְ אַכְזָרִי*[8] דּוֹחֶה[9] וּמְטַלְטֵל.
《 and moving 〈 repulsing 〈 who is cruel,*〈 with an
them about. emissary

---

(1) *Deuteronomy* 9:29. (2) This verse and the next have come under the heavy hand of the censors; some editions read, טוֹעִים, *misguided ones*, for טְמֵאִים, *unclean ones*; others omit these two verses altogether. (3) Cf. *Jeremiah* 2:11,5; some editions of *Selichos* read, וּבַהֶבֶל לְהִתְבַּלְבֵּל, *and to become confused with emptiness*. (4) Cf. *Isaiah* 14:19; see commentary to *Selichah* 12, s.v. בָּאֱמֶנַת נוֹצֵר; some editions read, נוֹצֵר אָדָם, *the creation of man*; others read, נְטוֹת מִדְּרָכֶיךָ וְתֹהוּ לְקַבֵּל, *to veer from Your ways and nonsensical beliefs to accept*. (5) Cf. 63:9. (6) Some editions read, עֲצַת צוֹרְרֶיךָ תְּסַכֵּל, *confound Your enemies' counsel*; others read עֲצַת הָרָעִים תְּמַחֶה, *eradicate the counsel of the evil ones*. (7) Cf. *Zechariah* 14:13. (8) *Proverbs* 17:11. (9) Cf. *Psalms* 35:5.

וּמַלְאָךְ אַכְזָרִי — *With an emissary who is cruel*. Repulse and remove from Your presence the cruel angel who accuses us before You. Alternatively, send a cruel angel to repulse and scatter our oppressors (*Arugas HaBosem*).

בַּעֲבוּר כְּבוֹד עַצְמְךָ¹ וְשֵׁם קָדְשְׁךָ הַמְהֻלָּל,

《 which is   〈 of Your   〈 and that of 〈 of Your own honor   〈 For the sake
lauded,   holiness   the Name

נוֹרָאוֹת הַפְלֵא לְבַל בַּגּוֹיִם יִתְחַלָּל,²

《 be   〈 among the 〈 so that 《 perform 〈 awesome
desecrated.   nations   It not   wondrously,   deeds

יוֹעֲצֵיהֶם וְאֵיתָנֵיהֶם תּוֹלִיךְ שׁוֹלָל,³

《 to folly, 〈 lead   〈 and strong men 〈 Their advisors

וּבָהֶם תְּעוֹלֵל כַּאֲשֶׁר בִּי הִתְעוֹלָל.⁴

《 they inflicted. 〈 upon 〈 what   〈 inflict   〈 and upon
me   them

מֵקִים מֵעָפָר דָּל וְאֶבְיוֹן מֵאַשְׁפָּה,⁵

《 from the   〈 and the 《 the 〈 from the 〈 The One
trash heap,   destitute   needy,   dust   Who raises

כְּנֶסָתְךָ אַל תִּתֵּן לְכָלָה וּלְחֶרְפָּה,

《 and disgrace. 〈 to   〈 deliver 〈 do 〈 Your
destruction   not   congregation

אִם בְּפִקּוּדֶיךָ מִתְעַצֶּלֶת וּמַרְפָּה,

《 and indolent, 〈 it is lazy   〈 in [fulfilling] 〈 If
Your commands

עַל כָּל פְּשָׁעֶיהָ אַהֲבָתְךָ תְּהֵא מְחַפָּה.⁶

《 cover up. 〈 should 〈 Your love 〈 their sins 〈 all 〈 over

יְתֵרָה חִבָּתָם⁷ לְפָנֶיךָ אֲדוֹנֵי הָאֲדוֹנִים,

《 of lords;   〈 O Lord 《 before 〈 is the love 〈 Intense
You,   of them

בֵּין כָּךְ וּבֵין כָּךְ קְרוּאִים לְךָ בָּנִים,*

《 children.* 〈 Your 〈 they are 〈 that   〈 or   〈 this 〈wheth-
called   way   whether   way   er
[sinful],   [virtuous]

---

(1) Some editions read, כְּבוֹד שְׁמֶךָ, *Your Name's honor.* (2) Cf. *Ezekiel* 36:23. (3) Cf. *Job* 12:17,19.
(4) Cf. *Lamentations* 1:22. (5) Cf. *I Samuel* 2:8; *Psalms* 113:7. (6) Cf. *Proverbs* 10:12. (7) See *Avos* 3:18.

בֵּין כָּךְ וּבֵין כָּךְ קְרוּאִים לְךָ בָּנִים — *Whether this way [virtuous] or whether that way [sinful], they are called Your children.* The *paytan* follows the view of R' Meir in his explanation of the verse, בָּנִים אַתֶּם לַה׳ אֱלֹהֵיכֶם, *You are children to* HASHEM, *your God* (Deuteronomy 14:1). According to R' Yehudah, this verse applies only when Israel acts like

obedient children. But when they do not act like obedient children, they are not considered God's children. R' Meir, however, adduces four verses (*Jeremiah* 4:22, *Deuteronomy* 32:20, *Isaiah* 1:4, *Hosea* 2:1) to prove that בֵּין כָּךְ וּבֵין כָּךְ, *whether like this or like that,* whether or not they are obedient, they are called [God's] children (*Kiddushin* 36a).

רַחֲמֶיךָ יְקַדְּמוּנוּ אֱלֹהֵי עֶלְיוֹנִים וְתַחְתּוֹנִים,

⟨ May Your ⟨ O God ⟪ advance ⟨ of the upper ⟨ and lower realms,
mercy toward us,

טֶרֶם יִשְׁטְפוּנוּ הַמַּיִם הַזֵּידוֹנִים.[1]

⟨ before ⟪ they inundate ⟨ — the ⟨ that are ⟪
us waters treacherous.

❖ חֲפֵצֵי קִרְבָתֶךָ[2] עַל כָּל הַבָּאוֹת,[3]

⟨ To those who ⟨ of Your ⟨ whatever ⟨ befalls ⟪
are desirous nearness, [them] —

הָחִישָׁה לָמוֹ יְשׁוּעוֹת הַנְּבָאוֹת,

⟨ hasten ⟨ for ⟨ the salvations ⟨ that were ⟪
them prophesied.

קָדוֹשׁ עֲשֵׂה עִמָּם לְטוֹבָה אוֹת,[4]

⟨ O Holy One, ⟨ perform ⟨ for them ⟨ a good ⟨ sign, ⟪

חָזָק וְאַמִּיץ גּוֹאֲלָם יהוה צְבָאוֹת.[5]

⟨ [for] ⟨ and ⟨ is their ⟪ HASHEM, ⟨ Master of ⟪
strong powerful Redeemer, Legions.

ALL, WHILE STANDING:

אֵל מֶלֶךְ יוֹשֵׁב עַל כִּסֵּא רַחֲמִים, מִתְנַהֵג

⟨ O God, ⟨ King ⟨ Who sits ⟨ on ⟨ the throne ⟪ of mercy, ⟪ Who acts ⟨

בַּחֲסִידוּת, מוֹחֵל עֲוֹנוֹת עַמּוֹ, מַעֲבִיר רִאשׁוֹן

⟪ with kindness, ⟨ Who ⟨ the sins ⟪ of His ⟨ Who ⟨ [sins,] one ⟨
pardons people, removes

רִאשׁוֹן,[6] מַרְבֶּה מְחִילָה לַחַטָּאִים וּסְלִיחָה לַפּוֹשְׁעִים,

⟪ by one, ⟨ Who abun- ⟨ pardon ⟨ to unintentional ⟨ and ⟨ to willful ⟪
dantly grants sinners forgiveness sinners,

עֹשֶׂה צְדָקוֹת עִם כָּל בָּשָׂר וָרוּחַ, לֹא כְרָעָתָם

⟨ Who ⟨ acts of ⟨ with ⟨ all ⟨ [beings ⟪ and ⟨ — not ⟨ in accord with
performs generosity of] flesh spirit their wickedness

תִּגְמוֹל. ❖ אֵל הוֹרֵיתָ לָּנוּ לוֹמַר שְׁלֹשׁ עֶשְׂרֵה, וּזְכוֹר

⟨ do You ⟪ O God, ⟨ You ⟨ us ⟨ to ⟨ the Thirteen ⟪ remem-
repay them! taught recite [Attributes of Mercy]; ber

לָּנוּ הַיּוֹם בְּרִית שְׁלֹשׁ עֶשְׂרֵה, כְּמוֹ שֶׁהוֹדַעְתָּ לֶעָנָיו

⟨ for us ⟨ today ⟨ the ⟪ of [these] Thirteen, ⟨ as ⟨ You made ⟨ to the humble
covenant known one [Moses]

---

(1) Cf. *Psalms* 124:4-5. (2) Cf. *Isaiah* 58:2. (3) Cf. *Nehemiah* 9:33. (4) Cf. *Psalms* 86:17.
(5) Cf. *Isaiah* 47:4; *Jeremiah* 50:34. (6) *Rosh Hashanah* 17a.

מִקֶּדֶם, כְּמוֹ שֶׁכָּתוּב, וַיֵּרֶד יהוה בֶּעָנָן וַיִּתְיַצֵּב עִמּוֹ
《 in ancient   as 《 it is written: 《 And HASHEM 〈 in a 〈 and stood 〈 with
times,   descended   cloud   him

שָׁם, וַיִּקְרָא בְשֵׁם יהוה.[1]
《 of 〈 with the 〈 and He 《 there,
HASHEM.   Name   called out

CONGREGATION, THEN CHAZZAN:

וַיַּעֲבֹר יהוה עַל פָּנָיו וַיִּקְרָא:
《 and 《 [Moses'] 〈 before 〈 And HASHEM passed
proclaimed: face,

CONGREGATION AND CHAZZAN RECITE LOUDLY AND IN UNISON:

יהוה, יהוה, אֵל, רַחוּם, וְחַנּוּן, אֶרֶךְ אַפַּיִם,
〈 to anger, 〈 Slow 《 and Gracious, 〈 Compassionate 〈 God, 〈 HASHEM, 〈 HASHEM,

וְרַב חֶסֶד, וֶאֱמֶת, נֹצֵר חֶסֶד לָאֲלָפִים, נֹשֵׂא עָוֹן,
〈 of 〈 Forgiver 《 for thousands 〈 of 〈 Preserver 《 and 〈 in 〈 and
iniquity,   [of generations],   kindness   Truth,   Kindness Abundant

וָפֶשַׁע, וְחַטָּאָה, וְנַקֵּה.[2] וְסָלַחְתָּ לַעֲוֹנֵנוּ וּלְחַטָּאתֵנוּ
《 and our sins, 〈 our 〈 May You 《 and Who 〈 and inadvertent 〈 willful sin,
     iniquities   forgive   absolves.   sin,

וּנְחַלְתָּנוּ.[3] סְלַח לָנוּ אָבִינוּ כִּי חָטָאנוּ, מְחַל לָנוּ
〈 us, 〈 pardon 《 we have 〈 for 《 our 〈 us, 〈 Forgive 《 and make us
     sinned;   Father,   Your heritage.

מַלְכֵּנוּ כִּי פָשָׁעְנוּ. כִּי אַתָּה אֲדֹנָי טוֹב וְסַלָּח,
《 and 〈 are 〈 O Lord, 〈 You, 〈 For 《 we have 〈 for 《 our King,
forgiving,   good   willfully sinned.

וְרַב חֶסֶד לְכָל קֹרְאֶיךָ.[4]
《 who call 〈 to all 〈 kind 〈 and
upon You.   abundantly

PREFATORY VERSES TO SELICHAH 9 / פסוקי הקדמה לסליחה ט

נְשָׂא לְבָבֵנוּ אֶל כַּפָּיִם, אֶל אֵל בַּשָּׁמָיִם.[5] תָּבוֹא
〈 Let there 《 in Heaven. 〈 God 〈 to 〈 our 〈 together 〈 our hearts 〈 Let us lift
come   hands   with   [in prayer]

לְפָנֶיךָ אֶנְקַת אָסִיר; כְּגֹדֶל זְרוֹעֲךָ הוֹתֵר בְּנֵי תְמוּתָה.[6]
《 to die. 〈 those 〈 spare 《 of Your 〈 as [befits] 《 of the 〈 the 〈 before
condemned   might,   the greatness   prisoner;   groan   You

---

(1) Exodus 34:5. (2) 34:6-7. (3) 34:9. (4) Psalms 86:5. (5) Lamentations 3:41. (6) Psalms 79:11.

לַאדֹנָי אֱלֹהֵינוּ הָרַחֲמִים וְהַסְּלִיחוֹת, כִּי מָרַדְנוּ בּוֹ.[1]

《 against 《 we have 《 for 《 and forgiveness, 〈 belong mercy 〈 our God 〈 To the
Him. rebelled Lord,

כְּרַחֵם אָב עַל בָּנִים, כֵּן תְּרַחֵם יהוה עָלֵינוּ.[2]

《 on us. 〈 HASHEM, 〈 have 〈 so 《 his 〈 toward 〈 a 〈 As merciful as
mercy, children, father is

לַיהוה הַיְשׁוּעָה, עַל עַמְּךָ בִרְכָתֶךָ סֶּלָה.[3] יהוה

〈 HASHEM, 《 Selah. 《 is Your 〈 Your 〈 upon 《 is salvation, 〈 To HASHEM
blessing, people

צְבָאוֹת עִמָּנוּ, מִשְׂגָּב לָנוּ אֱלֹהֵי יַעֲקֹב סֶלָה.[4]

《 Selah. 〈 of Jacob, 〈 is the God 〈 for us 〈 a 《 is with us, 〈 Master of
stronghold Legions,

יהוה צְבָאוֹת, אַשְׁרֵי אָדָם בֹּטֵחַ בָּךְ.[5] יהוה הוֹשִׁיעָה,

《 save! 〈 HASHEM, 《 in You. 〈 who 〈 is the 〈 — praise- 《 Master of 〈 HASHEM,
trusts man worthy Legions

הַמֶּלֶךְ יַעֲנֵנוּ בְיוֹם קָרְאֵנוּ.[6]

《 we call. 〈 on the 〈 answer 〈 May the
day us King

סליחה ט / SELICHAH 9

ALL:

אֱלֹהֵינוּ וֵאלֹהֵי אֲבוֹתֵינוּ:

《 of our forefathers: 〈 and God 〈 Our God

אֵלֶיךָ נְשׂוּאוֹת עֵינֵינוּ,[7]*

《 our eyes,* 〈 are raised 〈 To You

בְּכָל פִּנָּה וּפִנָּה אֲשֶׁר זֵרִיתָנוּ.

《 You have 〈 where 〈 single corner 〈 in every
scattered us.

גַּעֲיַת קוֹלֵנוּ בְּרָמָה נִשְׁמַע,

《 is heard, 〈 on high 〈 of our voice 〈 The cry

---

(1) *Daniel* 9:9. (2) Cf. *Psalms* 103:13. (3) 3:9 (4) 46:8. (5) 84:13. (6) 20:10.
(7) Cf. *Psalms* 123:1; according to *Arugas HaBosem*, this line reads
אֵלֶיךָ נְשׂוּאוֹת עֵינֵינוּ לְהוֹשִׁיעֵנוּ, *To You are raised our eyes, that You should save us.*

◆§ **אֵלֶיךָ נְשׂוּאוֹת עֵינֵינוּ** — *To You are raised*   lows an alphabetical acrostic.
our eyes. This anonymous *selichah* fol-

הֲלֹף בְּכִי תַמְרוּרִים נִדְמָע.[1]

《 do we cry 〈 in bitterness, 〈 from our 〈 dripping
our tears.   weeping

הֲצִיקָתָנוּ בְּטָנֵנוּ בְּרֹב[2] תַּחֲלוּאוֹת,

《   ills; 〈 with 〈 do our 〈 Trouble us
manifold   innards

וּמִתְּלָאוֹת הַבָּאוֹת אַחֲרֵי תְלָאוֹת.

《 hardships. 〈 after 〈 that follow 〈 and from hardships

זוּלָתֶךְ בְּעָלוּנוּ אֲדוֹנִים,[3]

《 [other] lords, 〈 there have 《 Other
ruled over us   than You,

חוֹרְשִׁים זֶה אַחַר זֶה כַּמָּה שָׁנִים.

《 years. 〈 for so 〈 another, 〈 after 〈 one 《 plowing
many   [our backs],

טְרוּפָה פָרָתְךָ* בְּפִצְעֵי חַבּוּרִים,*

《 and bruises,* 〈 with wounds 〈 is Your herd* 〈 Torn apart

יְגוּעָה וּכְבָר אֵין לָךְ בָּהֶן צֹרֶךְ וְלֹא לַאֲחֵרִים.

《 do others 〈 nor 《 any need 〈 for 〈 You do not 〈 — already 《 worn out
[because they   [because of   them   have
are worn out].   their sins],

כָּל הַיּוֹם עָלֶיךָ הֲרוּגִים,[4]

《 we are killed, 〈 for Your sake 〈 day long 〈 All

לְכַפָּרָה אֵין אָנוּ מַשִּׂיגִים.

《   we do not achieve. 〈 yet atonement

מַה נְּתַנֶּה וּמַה נְּקַדֵּם,

〈 can we 〈 How 《 can we 〈 What
approach,   relate?

נֶגְדְּךָ מִלְּבוֹשׁ וּמִלְּהִתְאַדֵּם.*

《 and without 〈 without 〈 before
blushing?*   being ashamed   You

---

(1) Cf. *Jeremiah* 31:14. (2) Some editions read מֵרֹב, *from manifold* . . . .
(3) Cf. *Isaiah* 26:13. (4) Cf. *Psalms* 44:23.

פָרָתְךָ — *Your herd* [lit., *cow*]. The prophet refers to the wayward nation as פָּרָה סֹרֵרָה, *a rebellious cow* (*Hosea* 4:16).

בְּפִצְעֵי חַבּוּרִים — *With wounds and bruises.* The parallel phrase in the singular פֶּצַע וְחַבּוּרָה, *wound and bruise* (*Isaiah* 1:6), is

rendered *defiant and rebellious* by *Targum Yonasan*. Thus the whole stich implies: "Your nation is suffering from its own sinfulness" (*Masbir*).

וּמִלְּהִתְאַדֵּם — *Without blushing* [lit., *without reddening ourselves*]. The translation

שִׂיחַ שִׂפְתוֹתֵינוּ אִם נְבָרֵר כְּשׁוֹשָׁן,

《 like a rose, 〈 we would 〈— even 《 of our lips 〈 The
purify it though   prayer

עֲוֺנֵנוּ נֶגְדֵּנוּ יָשָׁן נוֹשָׁן.

《 of the 〈 the 〈 are 〈 our
old.   oldest before us, iniquities

פִּגְרֵינוּ אִם תַּצְמִית וְדָמֵנוּ אִם תִּשְׁפֹּךְ,

《 You choose 〈 though 〈 our 《 You choose to cut 〈 though 〈 Our
to spill,   blood, down [for our sins],   corpses,

צְדָקָה אֶרֶץ* וּמִבְּלִי רֹגֶז תַּהֲפֹךְ.

《 have You chosen 〈 cause for 〈 but why 《 is the Land 〈 still,
to overturn it? anger without   [Israel]*; righteous

קוּמוּ רְבוּצֵי מַכְפֵּל סְעָדוּנוּ בִּשׁוּעָה,

《 with prayer! 〈 bolster us 《 in the Mach- 〈 O sleepers 〈 Arise,
pelah Cave,

רְאוּ כִלָּיוֹן אַיֵּה שְׁבוּעָה.

《 the oath 〈 Where 《 the 〈 See
[sworn to you]? is destruction!

❖ שׁוֹמְרֵי הַצֹּאן* הָקִיצוּ וְהִשְׁתּוֹמֵמוּ,

《 and be appalled! 〈 awaken 《 of the flock,* 〈 Guardians

שֶׁקָּדַמְתֶּם טְרַחְתֶּם וּבַבֶּהָלוֹת הִתַּמּוּ.

《 they waste 〈 but in waves 《 and labored 〈 You were
away. of terror [to protect them], diligent

תִּפְאֶרֶת עֻזָּמוֹ עוּרָה לָמָּה תִישָׁן,

《 do You sleep? 〈 Why 《 awake! 《 of their 〈 O Splendor
power,

תְּהִלּוֹת יִשְׂרָאֵל¹ יוֹשֵׁב הִנֵּה לֹא יָנוּם וְלֹא יִישָׁן.²

《 sleeps. 〈 nor 〈 slumbers 〈 [He] 《 indeed,《 is en- 〈 of Israel 〈 He Who upon
neither throned, the praises

_____

(1) Some editions read תּוֹחֶלֶת יִשְׂרָאֵל, *O Hope of Israel*;
either way, the allusion is to God. (2) *Psalms* 121:4.

follows *Arugas HaBosem.* According to *Masbir*, this word alludes to the verse, *Though your sins are like scarlet, they shall become white as snow; though they are red like crimson, they shall become as wool* (Isaiah 1:18). If so, our stich reads: *How can we approach before You without being ashamed at having reddened ourselves with sin.*

אֶרֶץ — *The Land [Israel].* The translation

follows *Masbir* who interprets this stich as a lament over the deplorable condition of *Eretz Yisrael* during these millennia of our exile. If *we* are guilty, why must the *Land* suffer? Was it not spared the ravages of the Flood in the time of Noah (see *Zevachim* 113a), despite the sinfulness of its inhabitants?

שׁוֹמְרֵי הַצֹּאן — *Guardians of the flock.* A reference to Moses, Aaron, Joshua, and all

ALL, WHILE STANDING:

אֵל מֶלֶךְ יוֹשֵׁב עַל כִּסֵּא רַחֲמִים, מִתְנַהֵג

⟨ O God, ⟩ King ⟨ Who sits ⟩ on ⟨ the throne ⟩ of mercy, ⟩ the ⟨ Who acts ⟩

בַּחֲסִידוּת, מוֹחֵל עֲוֹנוֹת עַמּוֹ, מַעֲבִיר רִאשׁוֹן

⟨ with kindness, ⟩ Who pardons ⟨ the sins ⟩ of His people, ⟩ Who removes ⟨ [sins,] one ⟩

רִאשׁוֹן,¹ מַרְבֶּה מְחִילָה לַחַטָּאִים וּסְלִיחָה לַפּוֹשְׁעִים,

⟨ by one, ⟩ Who abundantly grants ⟩ pardon ⟨ to unintentional sinners ⟩ and forgiveness ⟨ to willful sinners, ⟩

עֹשֶׂה צְדָקוֹת עִם כָּל בָּשָׂר וָרוּחַ, לֹא כְרָעָתָם

⟨ Who performs ⟩ acts of generosity ⟨ with ⟩ all ⟨ [beings of] flesh ⟩ and spirit ⟨ — not ⟩ in accord with their wickedness ⟩

תִּגְמוֹל. ❖ אֵל הוֹרֵיתָ לָּנוּ לוֹמַר שְׁלֹשׁ עֶשְׂרֵה, וּזְכוֹר

⟨ do You repay them! ⟩ O God, ⟨ You taught ⟩ us ⟨ to recite ⟩ the Thirteen [Attributes of Mercy]; ⟩ remember ⟨

לָנוּ הַיּוֹם בְּרִית שְׁלֹשׁ עֶשְׂרֵה, כְּמוֹ שֶׁהוֹדַעְתָּ לֶעָנָיו

⟨ for us ⟩ today ⟨ the covenant ⟩ of [these] Thirteen, ⟨ as ⟩ You made known ⟨ to the humble one [Moses] ⟩

מִקֶּדֶם, כְּמוֹ שֶׁכָּתוּב, וַיֵּרֶד יהוה בֶּעָנָן וַיִּתְיַצֵּב עִמּוֹ

⟨ in ancient times, ⟩ as ⟨ it is written: ⟩ And HASHEM descended ⟨ in a cloud ⟩ and stood ⟨ with him ⟩

שָׁם, וַיִּקְרָא בְשֵׁם יהוה.²

⟨ there, ⟩ and He called out ⟨ with the Name ⟩ of HASHEM. ⟩

CONGREGATION, THEN CHAZZAN:

וַיַּעֲבֹר יהוה עַל פָּנָיו וַיִּקְרָא:

⟨ And HASHEM passed ⟩ before ⟨ [Moses'] face, ⟩ and proclaimed: ⟩

CONGREGATION AND CHAZZAN RECITE LOUDLY AND IN UNISON:

יהוה, יהוה, אֵל, רַחוּם, וְחַנּוּן, אֶרֶךְ אַפַּיִם,

⟨ HASHEM, ⟩ HASHEM, ⟨ God, ⟩ Compassionate ⟨ and Gracious, ⟩ Slow ⟨ to anger, ⟩

וְרַב חֶסֶד, וֶאֱמֶת, נֹצֵר חֶסֶד לָאֲלָפִים, נֹשֵׂא עָוֹן,

⟨ and Abundant ⟩ in Kindness ⟨ and ⟩ Truth, ⟨ Preserver ⟩ of kindness ⟨ for thousands [of generations], ⟩ Forgiver ⟨ of iniquity, ⟩

---

(1) *Rosh Hashanah* 17a. (2) *Exodus* 34:5.

---

the prophets who succeeded them (*Arugas HaBosem; Masbir*).

וָפֶשַׁע, וְחַטָּאָה, וְנַקֵּה.¹ וְסָלַחְתָּ לַעֲוֹנֵנוּ וּלְחַטָּאתֵנוּ

《 and our sins, 〈 our 〈 May You 《 *and Who* 〈 *and inadvertent* 〈 *willful sin,*
iniquities   forgive   *absolves.*   *sin,*

וּנְחַלְתָּנוּ.² סְלַח לָנוּ אָבִינוּ כִּי חָטָאנוּ, מְחַל לָנוּ

〈 us, 〈 pardon 《 we have   〈 for 《 our 〈 us, 〈 Forgive 《 and make us
sinned;   Father,   Your heritage.

מַלְכֵּנוּ כִּי פָשָׁעְנוּ. כִּי אַתָּה אֲדֹנָי טוֹב וְסַלָּח,

《 and   〈 are   〈 O Lord, 〈 You,   〈 For 《 we have 〈 for 《 our King,
forgiving,   good   willfully sinned.

וְרַב חֶסֶד לְכָל קֹרְאֶיךָ.³

《 who call 〈 to all 〈 kind 〈 and
upon You.   abundantly

סְלִיחָה י / SELICHAH 10
(פִּזְמוֹן)

CHAZZAN, THEN CONGREGATION:

יִשְׂרָאֵל* נוֹשַׁע בַּיהוה תְּשׁוּעַת עוֹלָמִים,⁴

《 that is eternal; 〈 [with] a 〈 through 〈 is saved 〈 Israel*
salvation   HASHEM

גַּם הַיּוֹם יִוָּשְׁעוּ מִפִּיךָ, שׁוֹכֵן מְרוֹמִים,

《 in the 〈 O 《 by Your 〈 may they 〈 today 〈 Also
Heights —   Dweller   word,   be saved

כִּי אַתָּה רַב סְלִיחוֹת וּבַעַל הָרַחֲמִים.

《 of mercies. 〈 and are 〈 forgiving 〈 abun- 〈 You are 〈 for
the Master   dantly

CONGREGATION, THEN CHAZZAN:

שַׁעֲרֶיךָ הֵם דּוֹפְקִים כַּעֲנִיִּים וְדַלִּים,

《 and destitute 〈 like poor 〈 knock 〈 they 〈 At Your gates
[people];

---

(1) *Exodus* 34:6-7. (2) 34:9. (3) *Psalms* 86:5. (4) *Isaiah* 45:17.

יִשְׂרָאֵל — *Israel.* The acrostic (of the stanzas after the first) spells the author's name — שְׁפַטְיָה, *Shephatiah.* He was a well-known Kabbalist and lived in Oria, Italy. When the Byzantine emperor Basil I issued anti-Jewish decrees (about 873 C.E.), R' Shephatiah traveled to Constantinople in an attempt to convince the emperor to annul his decrees. Although unsuccessful in his overall mission, while he was in Basil's court, R' Shephatiah cured a daughter of the emperor who had been "possessed." As a reward, Basil released the Jews of Oria, as well as four other Jewish communities, from his decrees. Both R' Shephatiah and his son and successor, R' Amittai [see *Selichah* 82], often allude to the persecutions and forced conversions that Basil inflicted upon the Jews.

צְקוֹן לַחֲשָׁם¹ קְשֹׁב יָהּ שׁוֹכֵן מְעָלִים,

‹ to the ‹ of their ‹ be ‹ O ‹ Who ‹ aloft —
outpouring silent prayer attentive, God dwells

כִּי אַתָּה רַב סְלִיחוֹת וּבַעַל הָרַחֲמִים.

‹ for ‹ You are ‹ abun-‹ forgiving ‹ and are ‹ of mercies.
dantly the Master

CONGREGATION, THEN *CHAZZAN:*

פְּחוּדִים הֵם מִכָּל צָרוֹת מִמְּחָרְפֵּיהֶם וּמִלּוֹחֲצֵיהֶם,²

‹ Frightened ‹ they ‹ by all ‹ the troubles ‹ from those who ‹ and from those
are [they endure], curse them who oppress them;

נָא אַל תַּעַזְבֵם, יהוה אֱלֹהֵי אֲבוֹתֵיהֶם,

‹ please ‹ do ‹ forsake ‹ HASHEM, ‹ God ‹ of their
not them forefathers —

כִּי אַתָּה רַב סְלִיחוֹת וּבַעַל הָרַחֲמִים.

‹ for ‹ You are ‹ abun-‹ forgiving ‹ and are ‹ of mercies.
dantly the Master

CONGREGATION, THEN *CHAZZAN:*

טוֹבוֹתֶיךָ יְקַדְּמוּ לָהֶם בְּיוֹם תּוֹכֵחָה,

‹ May Your ‹ precede ‹ them ‹ on the ‹ of
goodness day admonishment,

וּמִתּוֹךְ צָרָה הַמְצִיאֵם פְּדוּת וּרְוָחָה,

‹ and from ‹ [their] ‹ [may You] pro-‹ redemp-‹ and relief —
amid troubles vide for them tion

כִּי אַתָּה רַב סְלִיחוֹת וּבַעַל הָרַחֲמִים.

‹ for ‹ You are ‹ abun-‹ forgiving ‹ and are ‹ of mercies.
dantly the Master

CONGREGATION, THEN *CHAZZAN:*

יִוָּשְׁעוּ לְעֵין כֹּל, וְאַל יִמְשְׁלוּ בָם רְשָׁעִים,

‹ May they ‹ in view ‹ of ‹ everyone, ‹ and ‹ dominate ‹ them ‹ the wicked
be saved let not [any more].

כַּלֵּה שֵׂעִיר וְחוֹתְנוֹ,* וְיַעֲלוּ לְצִיּוֹן מוֹשִׁיעִים,³

‹ Destroy ‹ Seir ‹ and his ‹ and let there ‹ to Zion ‹ saviors —
father-in-law,* ascend

(1) *Isaiah* 26:16. (2) Some editions read וּמִמְּנַגְּדֵיהֶם,
and from those who curse them. (3) Cf. *Obadiah* 1:21.

שֵׂעִיר וְחוֹתְנוֹ — *Seir and his father-in-law.*
Seir refers to Esau [Edom] because he settled
on and then took over Mount Seir (see

Genesis 32:4 and 36:8). His father-in-law
was Ishmael (see ibid. 28:9).
Rashi (to *Zechariah* 5:11) cites a Midrash

כִּי אַתָּה רַב סְלִיחוֹת וּבַעַל הָרַחֲמִים.

《 of mercies. 〈 and are 〈 forgiving 〈 abun- 〈 You are 〈 for
the Master   dantly

CONGREGATION, THEN CHAZZAN:

הַקְשִׁיבָה אָדוֹן לְקוֹל שַׁוְעָתָם,

《 of their 〈 to the 〈 O 〈 Be attentive,
outcry;   sound   Master,

וְלִמְכוֹן שִׁבְתְּךָ הַשָּׁמַיִם תַּעֲלֶה תְפִלָּתָם,

《 their prayer — 〈 may there 〈 in heaven 〈 of Your dwell- 〈 and to the
ascend   ing place   foundation

כִּי אַתָּה רַב סְלִיחוֹת וּבַעַל הָרַחֲמִים.

《 of mercies. 〈 and are 〈 forgiving 〈 abun- 〈 You are 〈 for
the Master   dantly

ALL, WHILE STANDING:

אֵל מֶלֶךְ יוֹשֵׁב עַל כִּסֵּא רַחֲמִים, מִתְנַהֵג

〈 Who acts 《 of mercy, 〈 the throne 〈 on 〈 Who sits 〈 King 〈 O God,

בַּחֲסִידוּת, מוֹחֵל עֲוֹנוֹת עַמּוֹ, מַעֲבִיר רִאשׁוֹן

〈 [sins] one 〈 Who 《 of His 〈 the sins 〈 Who 《 with kindness,
removes   people,   pardons

רִאשׁוֹן,[1] מַרְבֶּה מְחִילָה לְחַטָּאִים וּסְלִיחָה לַפּוֹשְׁעִים,

《 to willful 〈 and 〈 to unintentional 〈 pardon 〈 Who abun- 《 by one,
sinners,   forgiveness   sinners   dantly grants

עֹשֶׂה צְדָקוֹת עִם כָּל בָּשָׂר וָרוּחַ, לֹא כְרָעָתָם

〈 in accord with 〈 — not 《 and spirit 〈 [beings 〈 all 〈 with 〈 acts of 〈 Who
their wickedness   of] flesh   generosity   performs

תִגְמוֹל. ❖ אֵל הוֹרֵיתָ לָנוּ לוֹמַר שְׁלֹשׁ עֶשְׂרֵה,

《 the Thirteen 〈 to recite 〈 us 〈 You taught 〈 O God, 《 do You
[Attributes of Mercy];   repay them!

וּזְכוֹר לָנוּ הַיּוֹם בְּרִית שְׁלֹשׁ עֶשְׂרֵה, כְּמוֹ שֶׁהוֹדַעְתָּ

〈 You made 〈 as 《 of [these] Thirteen, 〈 the 〈 today 〈 for 〈 remember
known   covenant   us

---

(1) *Rosh Hashanah* 17a.

(*Shocher Tov* 6:1) that states that the four kingdoms that rule over Israel during its four periods of exile were actually eight, for each consisted of two empires: (a) Babylon and Chaldea; (b) Medea and Persia; (c) Greece and Macedonia; and (d) Edom and Ishmael.

Thus, when the fourth kingdom — Seir and his father-in-law — will have ended, then *ascend will the saviors up Mount Zion to judge the mountain of Esau, and to HASHEM will be the kingship* (*Obadiah* 1:21).

לְעָנָיו מִקֶּדֶם, כְּמוֹ שֶׁכָּתוּב, וַיֵּרֶד יהוה בֶּעָנָן

‹ in a cloud ‹ And HASHEM descended ‹‹ it is written: ‹ as ‹‹ in ancient times, ‹ to the humble one [Moses]

וַיִּתְיַצֵּב עִמּוֹ שָׁם, וַיִּקְרָא בְשֵׁם יהוה.[1]

‹‹ of HASHEM. ‹ with the Name ‹ and He called out ‹‹ there, ‹ with him ‹ and stood

CONGREGATION, THEN *CHAZZAN*:

וַיַּעֲבֹר יהוה עַל פָּנָיו וַיִּקְרָא:

‹‹ and proclaimed: ‹‹ [Moses'] face, ‹ before ‹ And HASHEM passed

CONGREGATION AND *CHAZZAN* RECITE LOUDLY AND IN UNISON:

יהוה, יהוה, אֵל, רַחוּם, וְחַנּוּן, אֶרֶךְ אַפַּיִם,

‹ to anger, ‹ Slow ‹‹ and Gracious, ‹ Compassionate ‹ God, ‹ HASHEM, ‹ HASHEM,

וְרַב חֶסֶד, וֶאֱמֶת, נֹצֵר חֶסֶד לָאֲלָפִים, נֹשֵׂא עָוֹן,

‹ of iniquity, ‹ Forgiver ‹‹ for thousands [of generations], ‹ of kindness ‹ Preserver ‹‹ and Truth, ‹ in Kindness ‹ and Abundant

וָפֶשַׁע, וְחַטָּאָה, וְנַקֵּה.[2] וְסָלַחְתָּ לַעֲוֹנֵנוּ וּלְחַטָּאתֵנוּ

‹‹ and our sins, ‹ our iniquities ‹ May You forgive ‹‹ and Who absolves. ‹ and inadvertent sin, ‹ willful sin,

וּנְחַלְתָּנוּ.[3] סְלַח לָנוּ אָבִינוּ כִּי חָטָאנוּ, מְחַל לָנוּ

‹ us, ‹ pardon ‹‹ we have sinned; ‹ for ‹‹ our Father, ‹ us, ‹ Forgive ‹‹ and make us Your heritage.

מַלְכֵּנוּ כִּי פָשָׁעְנוּ. כִּי אַתָּה אֲדֹנָי טוֹב וְסַלָּח,

‹‹ and forgiving, ‹ are good ‹ O Lord, ‹ You, ‹ For ‹‹ we have willfully sinned. ‹ for ‹‹ our King,

וְרַב חֶסֶד לְכָל קֹרְאֶיךָ.[4]

‹‹ who call upon You. ‹ to all ‹ kind ‹ and abundantly

ALL:

זְכֹר רַחֲמֶיךָ יהוה וַחֲסָדֶיךָ, כִּי מֵעוֹלָם הֵמָּה.[5]

‹‹ are they. ‹ eternal ‹ for ‹‹ and Your kindnesses, ‹ HASHEM, ‹ Your mercies, ‹ Remember

זָכְרֵנוּ יהוה בִּרְצוֹן עַמֶּךָ, פָּקְדֵנוּ בִּישׁוּעָתֶךָ.[6] זְכֹר

‹ Re-member ‹‹ with Your salvation. ‹ recall us ‹‹ to Your people; ‹ when You show favor ‹ HASHEM, ‹ Remem-ber us,

---

(1) *Exodus* 35:4. (2) 34:6-7. (3) 34:9. (4) *Psalms* 86:5. (5) 25:6. (6) Cf. 106:4.

עֲדָתְךָ קָנִיתָ קֶּדֶם, גָּאַלְתָּ שֵׁבֶט נַחֲלָתֶךָ, הַר צִיּוֹן זֶה

⟨the one ⟨ of ⟨ the ⟪ of Your ⟨ the ⟨ You ⟪ long ⟨ which You ⟨ Your con-
[where] Zion, mountain heritage; tribe redeemed ago, acquired gregation,

שָׁכַנְתָּ בּוֹ.¹ זְכֹר יהוה חִבַּת יְרוּשָׁלַיִם, אַהֲבַת

⟨ the love ⟪ of Jerusalem; ⟨ the ⟨ HASHEM, ⟨ Remem- ⟪there. ⟨ You rested
affection ber, Your Presence

צִיּוֹן אַל תִּשְׁכַּח לָנֶצַח.² אַתָּה תָקוּם תְּרַחֵם צִיּוֹן כִּי

⟨ for ⟪ to ⟨ and show ⟨ will arise ⟨ You ⟪ forever. ⟨ forget ⟨ do not ⟨ of
Zion, mercy Zion

עֵת לְחֶנְנָהּ, כִּי בָא מוֹעֵד.³ זְכֹר יהוה לִבְנֵי אֱדוֹם

⟨ of ⟨ [to repay] ⟨ HASHEM, ⟨ Re- ⟪ the appointed time ⟨ for ⟪ [there will come]
Edom the offspring, member, will have come. the time to favor her,

אֵת יוֹם יְרוּשָׁלָיִם, הָאֹמְרִים עָרוּ עָרוּ עַד הַיְסוֹד

⟨ the very ⟨ to ⟨ Destroy ⟪ Destroy! ⟪ [to repay] ⟪ of Jerusalem; ⟨ for the day
foundation those who say,

בָּהּ.⁴ זְכֹר לְאַבְרָהָם לְיִצְחָק וּלְיִשְׂרָאֵל עֲבָדֶיךָ,

⟪ Your servants, ⟨ and for Israel, ⟨ for Isaac, ⟨ for Abraham, ⟨ Remember ⟪ of it!

אֲשֶׁר נִשְׁבַּעְתָּ לָהֶם בָּךְ, וַתְּדַבֵּר אֲלֵהֶם, אַרְבֶּה

⟨ I shall ⟪ to them, ⟨ and ⟪ by Your ⟨ to them ⟨ You swore ⟨ that
increase You said Being,

אֶת זַרְעֲכֶם כְּכוֹכְבֵי הַשָּׁמָיִם, וְכָל הָאָרֶץ הַזֹּאת אֲשֶׁר

⟨ of ⟨ of this land ⟨ and all ⟪ of the ⟨ like the stars ⟨ Your offspring
which heavens;

אָמַרְתִּי, אֶתֵּן לְזַרְעֲכֶם, וְנָחֲלוּ לְעֹלָם.⁵ זְכֹר לַעֲבָדֶיךָ

⟨ of Your ⟨ Remember ⟪ forever. ⟨ and they ⟨ to your ⟨ I will ⟨ I spoke
servants, [the merits] will inherit it offspring, give

לְאַבְרָהָם לְיִצְחָק וּלְיַעֲקֹב, אַל תֵּפֶן אֶל קְשִׁי

⟨ the stub- ⟨ to ⟨ pay ⟨ do ⟪ and of Jacob; ⟨ of Isaac, ⟨ of Abraham,
bornness attention not

הָעָם הַזֶּה וְאֶל רִשְׁעוֹ וְאֶל חַטָּאתוֹ.⁶ זְכוֹר לָנוּ בְּרִית

⟨ the ⟨ for ⟨ Remember ⟪ its ⟨ and ⟪ its ⟨ to ⟪ of this people,
covenant us sinfulness. to wickedness,

אָבוֹת, כַּאֲשֶׁר אָמַרְתָּ: וְזָכַרְתִּי אֶת בְּרִיתִי יַעֲקוֹב,

⟪ [with] ⟨ My covenant ⟨ And I will ⟪ You said: ⟨ as ⟪ of the
Jacob, remember Patriarchs,

---

(1) *Psalms* 74:2. (2) This is not a Scriptural verse. (3) *Psalms* 102:14.
(4) 137:7. (5) *Exodus* 32:13. (6) *Deuteronomy* 9:27.

וְאַף אֶת בְּרִיתִי יִצְחָק, וְאַף אֶת בְּרִיתִי אַבְרָהָם

⟨ [with] ⟨ My covenant ⟨ and ⟪ [with] Isaac, ⟨ My covenant ⟨ and also
Abraham also

אֶזְכֹּר, וְהָאָרֶץ אֶזְכֹּר.¹

⟪ I will ⟨ and the ⟪ I will
remember. Land remember;

זְכוֹר לָנוּ בְּרִית רִאשׁוֹנִים, כַּאֲשֶׁר אָמָרְתָּ: וְזָכַרְתִּי

⟨ And I will ⟪ You said: ⟨ as ⟪ of the ⟨ the ⟨ for us ⟨ Remember
remember ancient ones, covenant

לָהֶם בְּרִית רִאשׁוֹנִים, אֲשֶׁר הוֹצֵאתִי אֹתָם מֵאֶרֶץ

⟨ from ⟨ I took them out ⟨ that ⟪ of the ⟨ the ⟨ for
the land ancient ones, covenant them

מִצְרַיִם לְעֵינֵי הַגּוֹיִם, לִהְיוֹת לָהֶם לֵאלֹהִים, אֲנִי

⟨ I am ⟪ a God; ⟨ to them ⟨ to be ⟪ of the ⟨ in the ⟨ of Egypt
nations, very sight

יהוה.² עֲשֵׂה עִמָּנוּ כְּמָה שֶׁהִבְטַחְתָּנוּ: וְאַף גַּם

⟨ all ⟨ And despite ⟪ You promised us: ⟨ as ⟨ with us ⟨ Do ⟪ HASHEM.

זֹאת בִּהְיוֹתָם בְּאֶרֶץ אֹיְבֵיהֶם, לֹא מְאַסְתִּים וְלֹא

⟨ nor ⟨ despise them ⟨ I will ⟪ of their ⟨ in the land ⟨ when they ⟪ this,
not enemies, will be

גְעַלְתִּים לְכַלֹּתָם לְהָפֵר בְּרִיתִי אִתָּם, כִּי אֲנִי יהוה

⟨ HASHEM, ⟨ I am ⟨ for ⟪ with ⟨ My ⟨ to annul ⟪ to destroy ⟨ abhor them
them, covenant them,

אֱלֹהֵיהֶם.³ הָשֵׁב שְׁבוּתֵנוּ וְרַחֲמֵנוּ, כְּמָה שֶׁכָּתוּב:

⟪ it is ⟨ as ⟪ and have ⟨ our captivity ⟨ Bring ⟪ their God.
written: mercy on us, back

וְשָׁב יהוה אֱלֹהֶיךָ אֶת שְׁבוּתְךָ וְרִחֲמֶךָ, וְשָׁב וְקִבֶּצְךָ

⟨ gather ⟨ and He ⟪ and He will ⟨ your captivity, ⟨ your ⟨ will ⟨ Then bring
you in will once have mercy God, HASHEM, back
again upon you,

מִכָּל הָעַמִּים אֲשֶׁר הֱפִיצְךָ יהוה אֱלֹהֶיךָ שָׁמָּה.⁴

⟪ thereto. ⟨ your God ⟨ has ⟨ scattered ⟨ that ⟨ the ⟨ from
HASHEM you peoples all

קַבֵּץ נִדָּחֵינוּ, כְּמָה שֶׁכָּתוּב: אִם יִהְיֶה נִדַּחֲךָ בִּקְצֵה

⟨ at the ⟨ your dispersed ⟨ If ⟨ it is written: ⟨ as ⟨ our ⟨ Gather
ends will be dispersed ones,

---

(1) Leviticus 26:42. (2) 26:45. (3) 26:44. (4) 30:3.

הַשָּׁמַיִם, מִשָּׁם יְקַבֶּצְךָ יהוה אֱלֹהֶיךָ, וּמִשָּׁם יִקָּחֶךָ.[1]

« He will take you. ‹ and from there « your God, ‹ will HASHEM, ‹ gather you in ‹ from there « of heaven,

מָחָה פְשָׁעֵינוּ כָּעָב וְכֶעָנָן, כְּמָה שֶׁכָּתוּב: מָחִיתִי

‹ I have wiped away « it is written: ‹ as « and like a cloud, ‹ like a mist ‹ our sins ‹ Wipe away

כָעָב פְּשָׁעֶיךָ וְכֶעָנָן חַטֹּאתֶיךָ, שׁוּבָה אֵלַי כִּי

‹ for ‹ to Me, ‹ return « your transgressions; ‹ and like a cloud ‹ your willful sins, ‹ like a mist

גְאַלְתִּיךָ.[2]   מָחֵה פְשָׁעֵינוּ לְמַעַנְךָ, כַּאֲשֶׁר אָמַרְתָּ:

«You have said: ‹ as « for Your sake, ‹ our sins ‹ Wipe away «I have redeemed you.

אָנֹכִי אָנֹכִי הוּא מֹחֶה פְשָׁעֶיךָ לְמַעֲנִי, וְחַטֹּאתֶיךָ לֹא

‹ I shall not ‹ and your transgressions « for My sake, ‹ your willful sins « Who wipes away ‹ am the One ‹ [only] I, ‹ I,

אֶזְכֹּר.[3] הַלְבֵּן חֲטָאֵינוּ כַּשֶּׁלֶג וְכַצֶּמֶר, כְּמָה שֶׁכָּתוּב:

« it is written: ‹ as « and like wool, ‹ like snow ‹ our sins ‹ Whiten « recall.

לְכוּ נָא וְנִוָּכְחָה, יֹאמַר יהוה, אִם יִהְיוּ חֲטָאֵיכֶם

‹ your sins may be ‹ Though «HASHEM. ‹ says « let us reason ‹ now, ‹ Come, together,

כַּשָּׁנִים כַּשֶּׁלֶג יַלְבִּינוּ, אִם יַאְדִּימוּ כַתּוֹלָע, כַּצֶּמֶר

‹ like [white] wool « as crimson, ‹ they may be red ‹ though « they will be whitened; ‹ like snow « like scarlet,

יִהְיוּ.[4] זָרוֹק עָלֵינוּ מַיִם טְהוֹרִים וְטַהֲרֵנוּ, כְּמָה שֶׁכָּתוּב:

« it is written: ‹ as « and purify us, ‹ pure water ‹ upon us ‹ Pour « they will become.

וְזָרַקְתִּי עֲלֵיכֶם מַיִם טְהוֹרִים וּטְהַרְתֶּם, מִכֹּל

‹ from all « and you will become pure; ‹ pure water ‹ upon you ‹ I shall pour

טֻמְאוֹתֵיכֶם וּמִכָּל גִּלּוּלֵיכֶם אֲטַהֵר אֶתְכֶם.[5] רַחֵם

‹ Have mercy ‹ you. ‹ I will purify ‹ your abominations ‹ and from all ‹ your contaminations

עָלֵינוּ וְאַל תַּשְׁחִיתֵנוּ, כְּמָה שֶׁכָּתוּב: כִּי אֵל רַחוּם

‹ a merciful God ‹ For « it is written: ‹ as « destroy us, ‹ and do not ‹ on us

יהוה אֱלֹהֶיךָ, לֹא יַרְפְּךָ וְלֹא יַשְׁחִיתֶךָ, וְלֹא יִשְׁכַּח

‹ will He forget ‹ nor « will He destroy you, ‹ nor ‹ relinquish ‹ He will not « your God; ‹ is HASHEM,

(1) *Leviticus* 30:4. (2) *Isaiah* 44:22. (3) 43:25. (4) 1:18. (5) *Ezekiel* 36:25.

מוֹל   אֶת בְּרִית אֲבֹתֶיךָ אֲשֶׁר נִשְׁבַּע לָהֶם.[1]

‹ Circumcise ‹‹ to them. ‹ He swore ‹ which ‹ with your forefathers, ‹ the covenant

אֶת לְבָבֵנוּ לְאַהֲבָה וּלְיִרְאָה אֶת שְׁמֶךָ, כְּמָה שֶׁכָּתוּב:

‹‹ it is written: ‹ as ‹‹ Your Name, ‹ and to fear ‹ to love ‹ our hearts

וּמָל יהוה אֱלֹהֶיךָ אֶת לְבָבְךָ וְאֶת לְבַב זַרְעֶךָ, לְאַהֲבָה

‹ to love ‹‹ of your offspring, ‹ and the heart ‹ your heart ‹ HASHEM, your God, will circumcise

אֶת יהוה אֱלֹהֶיךָ, בְּכָל לְבָבְךָ וּבְכָל נַפְשְׁךָ, לְמַעַן

‹ so that ‹‹ your soul, ‹ and with all ‹ your heart ‹ with all ‹ your God, ‹ HASHEM,

חַיֶּיךָ.[2] הַמָּצֵא לָנוּ בְּבַקָּשָׁתֵנוּ, כְּמָה שֶׁכָּתוּב: וּבִקַּשְׁתֶּם

‹ And you will seek ‹‹ it is written: ‹ as ‹‹ in our quest, ‹ to us ‹ Be accessible ‹‹ you may live.

מִשָּׁם אֶת יהוה אֱלֹהֶיךָ וּמָצָאתָ, כִּי תִדְרְשֶׁנּוּ בְּכָל

‹ with all ‹ you search Him out ‹ when ‹‹ and you will find [Him], ‹ your God, ‹ HASHEM, ‹ from there

לְבָבְךָ וּבְכָל נַפְשֶׁךָ.[3] ✧ תְּבִיאֵנוּ אֶל הַר קָדְשֶׁךָ,

‹ Your holy mountain ‹ to ‹ Bring us ‹‹ your soul. ‹ and with all ‹ your heart

וְשַׂמְּחֵנוּ בְּבֵית תְּפִלָּתֶךָ, כְּמָה שֶׁכָּתוּב: וַהֲבִיאוֹתִים

‹ And I will bring them ‹‹ it is written: ‹ as ‹‹ of Prayer, ‹ in Your House ‹ and gladden us

אֶל הַר קָדְשִׁי, וְשִׂמַּחְתִּים בְּבֵית תְּפִלָּתִי, עוֹלֹתֵיהֶם

‹ their burnt-offerings ‹‹ of Prayer; ‹ in My House ‹ and I will gladden them ‹‹ My holy mountain, ‹ to

וְזִבְחֵיהֶם לְרָצוֹן עַל מִזְבְּחִי, כִּי בֵיתִי בֵּית תְּפִלָּה

‹ of Prayer" ‹ "a House ‹ My House ‹ for ‹‹ My Altar, ‹ on ‹ will find favor ‹ and their feast-offerings

יִקָּרֵא לְכָל הָעַמִּים.[4]

‹‹ nations. ‹ for all ‹ will be called

THE ARK IS OPENED.

CHAZZAN, THEN CONGREGATION:

שְׁמַע קוֹלֵנוּ יהוה אֱלֹהֵינוּ, חוּס וְרַחֵם עָלֵינוּ,

‹‹ on us, ‹ and have compassion ‹ have pity ‹‹ our God; ‹ HASHEM, ‹ our voice, ‹ Hear

וְקַבֵּל בְּרַחֲמִים וּבְרָצוֹן אֶת תְּפִלָּתֵנוּ.[5]

‹‹ our prayer. ‹ and favor ‹ with compassion ‹ and accept

(1) *Deuteronomy* 4:31. (2) 30:6. (3) 4:29. (4) *Isaiah* 56:7. (5) From the weekday *Shemoneh Esrei*.

CHAZZAN, THEN CONGREGATION:

הֲשִׁיבֵנוּ יהוה אֵלֶיךָ וְנָשׁוּבָה, חַדֵּשׁ יָמֵינוּ כְּקֶדֶם.¹

《 as of old.   〈 our   〈 renew 《 and we shall 〈 to You, 〈 HASHEM, 〈Bring us back,
                 days   return,

CHAZZAN, THEN CONGREGATION:

אֲמָרֵינוּ הַאֲזִינָה יהוה, בִּינָה הֲגִיגֵנוּ.²

《 our thoughts. 〈 perceive 《 HASHEM; 〈   hear,   〈 Our words

THE FOLLOWING VERSE IS RECITED QUIETLY:

יִהְיוּ לְרָצוֹן אִמְרֵי פִינוּ וְהֶגְיוֹן לִבֵּנוּ לְפָנֶיךָ,

《 before 《 of our   〈 and the 〈 of our 〈 — the ex- 《 find   〈 May
   You,   heart —   thoughts mouth   pressions   favor   they

יהוה צוּרֵנוּ וְגוֹאֲלֵנוּ.³

《   and our   〈 our Rock 〈 HASHEM,
           Redeemer.

CHAZZAN, THEN CONGREGATION:

אַל תַּשְׁלִיכֵנוּ מִלְּפָנֶיךָ, וְרוּחַ קָדְשְׁךָ אַל תִּקַּח מִמֶּנּוּ.⁴

《 from us. 〈 take   〈 do 〈 of Your 〈 and the 《 from Your 〈 cast us away 〈 Do
             not   Holiness   Spirit   Presence,   not

CHAZZAN, THEN CONGREGATION:

אַל תַּשְׁלִיכֵנוּ לְעֵת זִקְנָה, כִּכְלוֹת כֹּחֵנוּ אַל תַּעַזְבֵנוּ.⁵

《 forsake us not. 〈 does our 〈 when fail 《 of old 〈 in time 〈 cast us away 〈 Do
                    strength,   age;   not

ALL CONTINUE (SOME CONGREGATIONS RECITE THE NEXT VERSE RESPONSIVELY):

אַל תַּעַזְבֵנוּ יהוה, אֱלֹהֵינוּ אַל תִּרְחַק מִמֶּנּוּ.⁶

《 from us.   be not distant 〈 our God, 《 O HASHEM; 〈 Forsake us not,

עֲשֵׂה עִמָּנוּ אוֹת לְטוֹבָה, וְיִרְאוּ שׂוֹנְאֵינוּ וְיֵבְשׁוּ,

《 and be   〈 may our   〈 so that 《 for good; 〈 a sign 〈 for us 〈 Display
   ashamed,   enemies   see it

כִּי אַתָּה יהוה עֲזַרְתָּנוּ וְנִחַמְתָּנוּ.⁷ כִּי לְךָ יהוה

〈 HASHEM, 〈 for 〈 Because 《   and   〈 will have 〈 HASHEM, 〈 You, 〈 for
            You,   consoled us. helped us

הוֹחָלְנוּ, אַתָּה תַעֲנֶה אֲדֹנָי אֱלֹהֵינוּ.⁸

《   our God. 〈 O Lord, 〈 will answer, 〈 You   《 do we wait;

THE ARK IS CLOSED.

---

(1) *Lamentations* 5:21. (2) Cf. *Psalms* 5:2. (3) Cf. 19:15.
(4) 51:13. (5) Cf. 71:9. (6) Cf. 38:22. (7) Cf. 86:17. (8) Cf. 38:16.

EACH INDIVIDUAL CONTINUES UNTIL THE END OF *SELICHOS*.

CONFESSION / וִדּוּי

**DURING THE RECITATION OF THE וִדּוּי, *CONFESSION*, STAND WITH
HEAD AND BODY SLIGHTLY BOWED, IN SUBMISSIVE CONTRITION.**

אֱלֹהֵינוּ ¹ וֵאלֹהֵי אֲבוֹתֵינוּ, תָּבֹא לְפָנֶיךָ תְּפִלָּתֵנוּ,

Our God ‹ and the ‹ of our ‹ come ‹ before ‹ may our
       God   forefathers,   You   prayer,

וְאַל תִּתְעַלַּם מִתְּחִנָּתֵנוּ, ² שֶׁאֵין אָנוּ עַזֵּי פָנִים

faced ‹ so brazen- ‹ For we are not ‹ our supplication. ‹ ignore ‹ and do not

וּקְשֵׁי עֹרֶף, לוֹמַר לְפָנֶיךָ יהוה אֱלֹהֵינוּ וֵאלֹהֵי

and the God ‹ our God, ‹ Hashem, ‹ before You, ‹ as to say ‹ necked ‹ and stiff-

אֲבוֹתֵינוּ, צַדִּיקִים אֲנַחְנוּ וְלֹא חָטָאנוּ, אֲבָל

—for indeed, ‹ sinned ‹ and have not ‹ we are, ‹ that righteous ‹ of our forefathers,

אֲנַחְנוּ וַאֲבוֹתֵינוּ חָטָאנוּ. ³

have sinned. ‹ and our forefathers ‹ we

**STRIKE THE LEFT SIDE OF THE CHEST WITH THE RIGHT FIST WHILE RECITING
EACH OF THE SINS OF THE FOLLOWING CONFESSIONAL LITANY:**

אָשַׁמְנוּ, בָּגַדְנוּ, גָּזַלְנוּ, דִּבַּרְנוּ דֹפִי. הֶעֱוִינוּ,

We have com- ‹ slander. ‹ we have ‹ we have ‹ we have ‹ We have been
mitted iniquity;   spoken   robbed;   betrayed;   guilty;

וְהִרְשַׁעְנוּ, זַדְנוּ, חָמַסְנוּ, טָפַלְנוּ שֶׁקֶר. יָעַצְנוּ

We have ‹ false ‹ we have ‹ we have ‹ we have sinned ‹ we have commit-
given advice   accusations.   made   extorted;   willfully;   ted wickedness;

רָע, כִּזַּבְנוּ, לַצְנוּ, מָרַדְנוּ, נִאַצְנוּ, סָרַרְנוּ,

we have ‹ we have provoked ‹ we have ‹ we have ‹ we have been ‹ that is
strayed;   [God's anger];   rebelled;   scorned;   deceitful;   bad;

עָוִינוּ, פָּשַׁעְנוּ, צָרַרְנוּ, קִשִּׁינוּ עֹרֶף. רָשַׁעְנוּ,

We have ‹ our ‹ we have ‹ we have caused ‹ we have sinned ‹ we have been
been wicked;   necks.   stiffened   distress;   rebelliously;   iniquitous;

שִׁחַתְנוּ, תִּעַבְנוּ, תָּעִינוּ, תִּעְתָּעְנוּ.

we have ‹ we have ‹ we have ‹ we have
scoffed.   gone astray;   committed   been corrupt;
                  abominations;

סַרְנוּ מִמִּצְוֹתֶיךָ וּמִמִּשְׁפָּטֶיךָ הַטּוֹבִים, וְלֹא שָׁוָה

worth- ‹ and it ‹ that are ‹ and from ‹ from Your ‹ We have
while   was not   good,   Your laws   commandments   turned away

---

(1) Cf. *Psalms* 88:3. (2) Cf. 55:2. (3) Cf. 106:6, *Jeremiah* 3:25.

לָנוּ.¹ וְאַתָּה צַדִּיק עַל כָּל הַבָּא עָלֵינוּ, כִּי
⟨ for ⟩ ⟨ upon us, ⟩ ⟨ that has come ⟩ ⟨ all ⟩ ⟨ in ⟩ ⟨ are righteous ⟩ ⟨ And You ⟩ ⟪ for us.

אֱמֶת עָשִׂיתָ וַאֲנַחְנוּ הִרְשָׁעְנוּ.²
⟪ have acted wickedly. ⟩ while we ⟪ have You acted, ⟩ truthfully

אָשַׁמְנוּ מִכָּל עָם, בֹּשְׁנוּ מִכָּל דּוֹר, גָּלָה מִמֶּנּוּ
⟨ from ⟩ ⟨ Departed ⟪ genera- ⟨ more ⟩ ⟨ We have ⟪ people. ⟩ more than ⟩ We have
us   tion.   than any   been ashamed   any other   been guilty
                              other

מָשׂוֹשׂ, דָּוָה לִבֵּנוּ בַּחֲטָאֵינוּ, הֻחְבַּל אִוּוּיֵנוּ, וְנִפְרַע
⟨ uncov- ⟪ was our de- ⟨ Seized ⟪ because of ⟨ is our ⟨ Sickened ⟪ has joy.
ered   sired [Temple],   our sins.   heart

פְּאֵרֵנוּ, זְבוּל בֵּית מִקְדָּשֵׁנוּ חָרַב בַּעֲוֹנֵינוּ, טִירָתֵנוּ
⟨ Our Palace ⟪ because of ⟨ has been ⟨ our Holy Temple ⟨ for [His] ⟪ was our
                our iniquities. destroyed   abode,   splendor;

הָיְתָה לְשַׁמָּה, יְפִי אַדְמָתֵנוּ לְזָרִים, בֹּחֵנוּ לְנָכְרִים.
⟪ [was given] ⟨ our ⟪ is controlled ⟨ of our ⟨ [Jerusalem,] ⟪ desolate. ⟨ has
to foreigners.   wealth by strangers,   Land   the beauty   become

וַעֲדַיִן לֹא שַׁבְנוּ מִטָּעוּתֵנוּ וְהֵיךְ נָעִיז פָּנֵינוּ וְנַקְשֶׁה
⟨ and ⟩ ⟨ faced ⟨ can we be ⟨ So ⟪ from our ⟨ we have not ⟨ But still
stiffen   so brazen- how   willful errors. repented

עָרְפֵּנוּ, לוֹמַר לְפָנֶיךָ יהוה אֱלֹהֵינוּ וֵאלֹהֵי אֲבוֹתֵינוּ,
⟪ of our ⟨ and the ⟨ our God ⟨ HASHEM, ⟨ before ⟨ so as to ⟨ our neck
forefathers, God   You,   say

צַדִּיקִים אֲנַחְנוּ וְלֹא חָטָאנוּ, אֲבָל אֲנַחְנוּ וַאֲבוֹתֵינוּ
⟨ and our ⟨ both we ⟨ for in ⟪ and we have ⟪ we are ⟨ that
fathers   truth,   not sinned,   righteous

חָטָאנוּ.³
⟪ have sinned.

**STRIKE THE LEFT SIDE OF THE CHEST WITH THE RIGHT FIST WHILE RECITING
EACH OF THE SINS OF THE FOLLOWING CONFESSIONAL LITANY:**

אָשַׁמְנוּ, בָּגַדְנוּ, גָּזַלְנוּ, דִּבַּרְנוּ דֹּפִי. הֶעֱוִינוּ,
⟪ We have com- ⟪ slander. ⟨ we have ⟪ we have ⟪ we have ⟪ We have been
mitted iniquity;   spoken   robbed;   betrayed;   guilty;

וְהִרְשַׁעְנוּ, זַדְנוּ, חָמַסְנוּ, טָפַלְנוּ שֶׁקֶר. יָעַצְנוּ
⟨ We have ⟪ false ⟨ we have ⟪ we have ⟪ we have sinned ⟪ we have commit-
given advice accusations. made   extorted;   willfully;   ted wickedness;

―――――――――
(1) Cf. *Job* 33:27. (2) *Nehemiah* 9:33. (3) Cf. *Psalms* 106:6; *Jeremiah* 3:25.

רָע, כִּזַּבְנוּ, לַצְנוּ, מָרַדְנוּ, נִאַצְנוּ, סָרַרְנוּ,

《 that is bad; 《 we have been deceitful; 《 we have scorned; 《 we have rebelled; 《 we have provoked [God's anger]; 《 we have strayed;

עָוִינוּ, פָּשַׁעְנוּ, צָרַרְנוּ, קִשִּׁינוּ עֹרֶף. רָשַׁעְנוּ,

《 we have been iniquitous; 《 we have sinned rebelliously; 《 we have caused distress; 〈 we have stiffened 《 our necks. 《 We have been wicked;

שִׁחַתְנוּ, תִּעַבְנוּ, תָּעִינוּ, תִּעְתָּעְנוּ.

《 we have been corrupt; 《 we have committed abominations; 《 we have gone astray; 《 we have scoffed.

סַרְנוּ מִמִּצְוֹתֶיךָ וּמִמִּשְׁפָּטֶיךָ הַטּוֹבִים, וְלֹא שָׁוָה

〈 worth- while 〈 and it was not 《 that are good, 〈 and from Your laws 〈 from Your commandments 〈 We have turned away

לָנוּ.[1] וְאַתָּה צַדִּיק עַל כָּל הַבָּא עָלֵינוּ, כִּי אֱמֶת

〈 truth- fully 〈 for 《 upon us, 〈 that has come 〈 all 〈 in 〈 are righteous 〈 And You 《 for us.

עָשִׂיתָ וַאֲנַחְנוּ הִרְשָׁעְנוּ.[2]

《 have acted wickedly. 〈 while we 《 have You acted,

לְעֵינֵינוּ עָשְׁקוּ עֲמָלֵנוּ, מִמְּשָׁךְ, [it was] וּמְמוֹרָט מִמֶּנּוּ,

《 from us. 〈 and cut off 〈 [it was] pulled away 《 the product of our labor; 〈 have they stolen 〈 Before our eyes

נָתְנוּ עֹלָם עָלֵינוּ, סָבַלְנוּ עַל שִׁכְמֶנוּ, עֲבָדִים

〈 Slaves 《 our shoulders. 〈 upon 〈 we bore it 《 upon us, 〈 their yoke 〈 They have placed

מָשְׁלוּ בָנוּ, פֹּרֵק אֵין מִיָּדָם, צָרוֹת רַבּוֹת

〈 that are manifold 〈 Troubles 《 from their hand. there was not 〈 a redeemer 《 over us; 〈 have ruled

סְבָבוּנוּ, קְרָאנוּךָ יהוה אֱלֹהֵינוּ, רָחַקְתָּ מִמֶּנּוּ

〈 from us 〈 but You have dis- tanced Yourself 《 our God, 〈 HASHEM, 〈 we called upon You, 《 have surrounded us,

בַּעֲוֹנֵינוּ, שַׁבְנוּ מֵאַחֲרֶיךָ, תָּעִינוּ וְאָבָדְנוּ.

《 we have become lost. 《 we have gone astray; 《 from following after You; 〈 We have turned away 《 because of our iniquities.

---

(1) Cf. *Job* 33:27. (2) *Nehemiah* 9:33.

וַעֲדַיִן לֹא שַׁבְנוּ מִטָּעוּתֵנוּ וְהֵיךְ נָעִיז פָּנֵינוּ וְנַקְשֶׁה

⟨ and ⟨ faced ⟨ can we be ⟨ So 《 from our ⟨ we have not ⟨ But still
stiffen   so brazen- how willful errors. repented

עָרְפֵּנוּ, לוֹמַר לְפָנֶיךָ יהוה אֱלֹהֵינוּ וֵאלֹהֵי אֲבוֹתֵינוּ,

《 of our ⟨ and the ⟨ our God ⟨ HASHEM, ⟨ before ⟨ so as to ⟨ our neck
forefathers, God   You, say

צַדִּיקִים אֲנַחְנוּ וְלֹא חָטָאנוּ, אֲבָל אֲנַחְנוּ וַאֲבוֹתֵינוּ

⟨ and our ⟨ both we ⟨ for in 《 and we have 《 we are ⟨ that
fathers   truth, not sinned,   righteous

חָטָאנוּ.[1]

《 have sinned.

**STRIKE THE LEFT SIDE OF THE CHEST WITH THE RIGHT FIST WHILE RECITING
EACH OF THE SINS OF THE FOLLOWING CONFESSIONAL LITANY:**

אָשַׁמְנוּ, בָּגַדְנוּ, גָּזַלְנוּ, דִּבַּרְנוּ דֹפִי. הֶעֱוִינוּ,

《 We have com- 《 slander. ⟨ we have 《 we have 《 we have 《 We have been
mitted iniquity;   spoken robbed; betrayed; guilty;

וְהִרְשַׁעְנוּ, זַדְנוּ, חָמַסְנוּ, טָפַלְנוּ שֶׁקֶר. יָעַצְנוּ

⟨ We have 《 false ⟨ we have 《 we have 《we have sinned 《we have commit-
given advice accusations. made extorted; willfully; ted wickedness;

רָע, כִּזַּבְנוּ, לַצְנוּ, מָרַדְנוּ, נִאַצְנוּ, סָרַרְנוּ,

《 we have 《 we have provoked 《 we have 《 we have 《 we have been 《 that is
strayed; [God's anger]; rebelled; scorned; deceitful; bad;

עָוִינוּ, פָּשַׁעְנוּ, צָרַרְנוּ, קִשִּׁינוּ עֹרֶף. רָשַׁעְנוּ,

《 We have 《 our ⟨ we have 《we have caused 《we have sinned 《we have been
been wicked; necks. stiffened distress; rebelliously; iniquitous;

שִׁחַתְנוּ, תִּעַבְנוּ, תָּעִינוּ, תִּעְתָּעְנוּ.

《 we have 《 we have 《we have commit- 《 we have
scoffed. gone astray; ted abominations; been corrupt;

סַרְנוּ מִמִּצְוֹתֶיךָ וּמִמִּשְׁפָּטֶיךָ הַטּוֹבִים, וְלֹא שָׁוָה

⟨ worth- ⟨ and it 《 that are ⟨ and from ⟨ from Your ⟨ We have
while was not good, Your laws commandments turned away

לָנוּ.[2] וְאַתָּה צַדִּיק עַל כָּל הַבָּא עָלֵינוּ, כִּי אֱמֶת

⟨ truth- ⟨ for 《 upon us, ⟨ that has ⟨ all ⟨ in ⟨ are ⟨ And You 《 for us.
fully   come   righteous

עָשִׂיתָ וַאֲנַחְנוּ הִרְשָׁעְנוּ.[3]

《 have acted wickedly. ⟨ while we 《 have You acted,

---

(1) Cf. *Psalms* 106:6; *Jeremiah* 3:25. (2) Cf. *Job* 33:27. (3) *Nehemiah* 9:33.

הִרְשַׁעְנוּ וּפָשַׁעְנוּ, לָכֵן לֹא נוֹשָׁעְנוּ. וְתֵן בְּלִבֵּנוּ

⟨ in our ⟨ Place ⟨ been ⟨ we have ⟨ there- ⟨ and we ⟨ We have acted
hearts　　　　　saved.　　　not　　fore　　have sinned　　wickedly
　　　　　　　　　　　　　　　　　　　　　　rebelliously;

לַעֲזוֹב דֶּרֶךְ רֶשַׁע, וְחִישׁ לָנוּ יֶשַׁע, כַּכָּתוּב עַל יַד

⟨ the ⟨ by ⟨ as it is ⟨ salvation; ⟨ to us ⟨ and ⟨ of ⟨ the ⟨ [the will]
hand　　　written　　　　　　　　hasten　wickedness,　path　to abandon

נְבִיאֶךָ: יַעֲזֹב רָשָׁע דַּרְכּוֹ, וְאִישׁ אָוֶן מַחְשְׁבֹתָיו,

⟨ [abandon] ⟨ of ⟨ and ⟨ his way, ⟨ the wicked ⟨ Let ⟨ of Your
his thoughts;　iniquity　the man　　　　　one　abandon　prophet:

וְיָשֹׁב אֶל יהוה וִירַחֲמֵהוּ, וְאֶל אֱלֹהֵינוּ כִּי

⟨ for ⟨ our God, ⟨ and to ⟨ and He will have ⟨ HASHEM, ⟨ to ⟨ and let
　　　　　　　　　　compassion on him,　　　　　　　　　him return

יַרְבֶּה לִסְלוֹחַ.[1]

⟨ forgiving. ⟨ He is
　　　　　　abundantly

מָשִׁיחַ צִדְקֶךָ אָמַר לְפָנֶיךָ, שְׁגִיאוֹת מִי יָבִין,

⟨ can ⟨ who ⟨ Mistakes ⟨ before You: ⟨ said ⟨ who is righteous ⟨ Your
discern?　　　　　　　　　　　　　　　　　[David]　anointed one

מִנִּסְתָּרוֹת נַקֵּנִי.[2] נַקֵּנוּ יהוה אֱלֹהֵינוּ מִכָּל פְּשָׁעֵינוּ,

⟨ our sins ⟨ of all ⟨ our God, ⟨ HASHEM, ⟨ Cleanse ⟨ cleanse ⟨ From
　　　　　　　　　　　　　　　us,　　me.　　unperceived faults

וְטַהֲרֵנוּ מִכָּל טֻמְאוֹתֵינוּ, וּזְרוֹק עָלֵינוּ מַיִם טְהוֹרִים

⟨ pure water ⟨ upon us ⟨ Pour ⟨ our contaminations. ⟨ of all ⟨ and purify us

וְטַהֲרֵנוּ, כַּכָּתוּב עַל יַד נְבִיאֶךָ: וְזָרַקְתִּי עֲלֵיכֶם

⟨ upon you ⟨ I shall pour ⟨ of Your ⟨ the ⟨ by ⟨ as it is ⟨ and purify us,
　　　　　　　　　　prophet:　hand　　　written

מַיִם טְהוֹרִים וּטְהַרְתֶּם, מִכֹּל טֻמְאוֹתֵיכֶם וּמִכָּל

⟨ and ⟨ your ⟨ from ⟨ and you will ⟨ pure water
from all　contaminations　all　become pure;

גִּלּוּלֵיכֶם אֲטַהֵר אֶתְכֶם.[3] עַמְּךָ וְנַחֲלָתֶךָ, רְעֵבֵי

⟨ who ⟨ and Your ⟨ Your ⟨ you. ⟨ I will purify ⟨ your
hunger　heritage,　people　　　　　　　abominations

טוּבְךָ, צְמֵאֵי חַסְדֶּךָ, תְּאֵבֵי יִשְׁעֶךָ, יַכִּירוּ וְיֵדְעוּ

⟨ and ⟨ — may they ⟨ for Your ⟨ and ⟨ for Your ⟨ who ⟨ for Your
know　recognize　salvation　who long　kindness,　thirst　goodness,

(1) *Isaiah* 55:7. (2) *Psalms* 19:13. (3) *Ezekiel* 36:25.

כִּי לַיהוה אֱלֹהֵינוּ הָרַחֲמִים וְהַסְּלִיחוֹת.

《 and forgiveness. 〈 belong mercy 〈 our God, 〈 to HASHEM, 〈 that

אֵל רַחוּם שְׁמֶךָ, אֵל חַנּוּן שְׁמֶךָ,[1] בָּנוּ נִקְרָא שְׁמֶךָ.[2]

《 is Your Name 〈 upon 《 is Your 〈 *Gracious God* 《 is Your 〈 *Merciful God*
proclaimed, us Name, Name,

יהוה עֲשֵׂה לְמַעַן שְׁמֶךָ,[3] עֲשֵׂה לְמַעַן אֲמִתָּךְ, עֲשֵׂה

〈 act 《 Your truth; 〈 for the 〈 Act 《 Your 〈 for the 〈 act 〈 HASHEM,
sake of Name. sake of

לְמַעַן בְּרִיתָךְ, עֲשֵׂה לְמַעַן גָּדְלָךְ וְתִפְאַרְתָּךְ, עֲשֵׂה

〈 act 《 and Your 〈 Your 〈 for the 〈 act 《 Your 〈 for the
splendor; greatness sake of covenant; sake of

לְמַעַן דָּתָךְ, עֲשֵׂה לְמַעַן הוֹדָךְ, עֲשֵׂה לְמַעַן וְעוּדָךְ,

《 Your Meet- 〈 for the 〈 act 《 Your 〈 for the 〈 act 《 Your 〈 for the
ing House; sake of glory; sake of Law; sake of

עֲשֵׂה לְמַעַן זִכְרָךְ,[4] עֲשֵׂה לְמַעַן חַסְדָּךְ, עֲשֵׂה לְמַעַן

〈 for the 〈 act 《 Your 〈 for the 〈 act 《 Your 〈 for the 〈 act
sake of kindness; sake of remembrance; sake of

טוּבָךְ, עֲשֵׂה לְמַעַן יִחוּדָךְ, עֲשֵׂה לְמַעַן כְּבוֹדָךְ, עֲשֵׂה

〈 act 《 Your 〈 for the 〈 act 《 Your 〈 for the 〈 act 《 Your
honor; sake of Oneness; sake of goodness;

לְמַעַן לִמּוּדָךְ,[6] עֲשֵׂה לְמַעַן מַלְכוּתָךְ, עֲשֵׂה לְמַעַן

〈 for the 〈 act 《 Your kingship; 〈 for the 〈 act 《 Your 〈 for the
sake of sake of students; sake of

נִצְחָךְ, עֲשֵׂה לְמַעַן סוֹדָךְ,[7] עֲשֵׂה לְמַעַן עֻזָּךְ, עֲשֵׂה

〈 act 《 Your 〈 for the 〈 act 《 Your secret [re- 〈 for the 〈 act 《 Your eternal
power; sake of vealed to those sake of [Name];
who fear You];

לְמַעַן פְּאֵרָךְ, עֲשֵׂה לְמַעַן צִדְקָתָךְ, עֲשֵׂה לְמַעַן

〈 for the 〈 act 《 Your 〈 for the 〈 act 《 Your 〈 for the
sake of righteousness; sake of glory; sake of

קְדֻשָּׁתָךְ, עֲשֵׂה לְמַעַן רַחֲמֶיךָ הָרַבִּים, עֲשֵׂה לְמַעַן

〈 for the 〈 act 《 that is 〈 Your mercy 〈 for the 〈 act 《 Your sanctity;
sake of abundant; sake of

שְׁכִינָתָךְ, עֲשֵׂה לְמַעַן תְּהִלָּתָךְ, עֲשֵׂה לְמַעַן אוֹהֲבֶיךָ

〈 those who 〈 for the 〈 act 《 Your praise; 〈 for the 〈 act 《 Your Divine
loved You sake of sake of Presence;

(1) Cf. *Exodus* 34:6. (2) Cf. *Deuteronomy* 28:10. (3) *Jeremiah* 14:7.
(4) Cf. *Exodus* 3:15. (5) *Psalms* 6:5. (6) Cf. *Isaiah* 54:13. (7) Cf. *Psalms* 25:14.

שׁוֹכְנֵי עָפָר, ¹עֲשֵׂה לְמַעַן אַבְרָהָם יִצְחָק וְיַעֲקֹב,

‹ and Jacob; ‹ Isaac, ‹ Abraham, ‹ for the sake of ‹ act ‹‹ in the dust; ‹ who rest

עֲשֵׂה לְמַעַן מֹשֶׁה וְאַהֲרֹן, עֲשֵׂה לְמַעַן דָּוִד וּשְׁלֹמֹה,

‹ and Solomon; ‹ David ‹ for the sake of ‹ act ‹‹ and Aaron; ‹ Moses ‹ for the sake of ‹ act

²עֲשֵׂה לְמַעַן יְרוּשָׁלַיִם עִיר קָדְשֶׁךָ, עֲשֵׂה לְמַעַן צִיּוֹן

‹ Zion, ‹ for the sake of ‹ act ‹‹ of Your Holiness; ‹ the City ‹‹ Jerusalem, ‹ for the sake of ‹ act

מִשְׁכַּן כְּבוֹדֶךָ, ³עֲשֵׂה לְמַעַן שִׁמְמוֹת⁴ הֵיכָלֶךָ, עֲשֵׂה

‹ act ‹‹ of Your Temple; ‹ the desolation ‹ for the sake of ‹ act ‹‹ of Your glory; ‹ the abode

לְמַעַן הֲרִיסוּת⁵ מִזְבְּחֶךָ, עֲשֵׂה לְמַעַן הֲרוּגִים עַל

‹ for ‹ those killed ‹ for the sake of ‹ act ‹‹ of Your Altar; ‹ the devastation ‹ for the sake of

שֵׁם קָדְשֶׁךָ, עֲשֵׂה לְמַעַן טְבוּחִים עַל יִחוּדֶךָ, עֲשֵׂה

‹ act ‹‹ Your Oneness; ‹ for ‹ those slaughtered ‹ for the sake of ‹ act ‹‹ Your holy Name;

לְמַעַן בָּאֵי בָאֵשׁ וּבַמַּיִם עַל קִדּוּשׁ שְׁמֶךָ, עֲשֵׂה לְמַעַן

‹ for the sake of ‹ act ‹‹ of Your Name; ‹ the sanctification ‹ for ‹ and water ‹ fire ‹ those who entered ‹ for the sake of

⁷יוֹנְקֵי שָׁדַיִם שֶׁלֹּא חָטָאוּ, עֲשֵׂה לְמַעַן גְּמוּלֵי חָלָב,

‹ from milk ‹ the [babies] weaned ‹ for the sake of ‹ act ‹‹ sin; ‹ who did not ‹ at the breast ‹ the [infants] sucking

⁸שֶׁלֹּא פָשָׁעוּ, עֲשֵׂה לְמַעַן תִּינוֹקוֹת שֶׁל בֵּית רַבָּן,

‹‹ their teachers' school; ‹ of ‹ the children ‹ for the sake of ‹ act ‹‹ transgress; ‹ who did not

עֲשֵׂה לְמַעַנְךָ אִם לֹא לְמַעֲנֵנוּ, עֲשֵׂה לְמַעַנְךָ וְהוֹשִׁיעֵנוּ.

‹‹ and save us. ‹ for Your sake ‹ act ‹‹ for our sake; ‹ not ‹ if ‹ for Your sake ‹ act

עֲנֵנוּ יהוה עֲנֵנוּ, עֲנֵנוּ אֱלֹהֵינוּ עֲנֵנוּ, עֲנֵנוּ **אָבִינוּ**⁹

‹ our Father, ‹ answer us, ‹‹ answer us; ‹ our God, ‹ answer us, ‹‹ answer us; ‹ HASHEM, ‹ Answer us;

עֲנֵנוּ, עֲנֵנוּ **בוֹרְאֵנוּ**¹⁰ עֲנֵנוּ, עֲנֵנוּ **גוֹאֲלֵנוּ**¹¹ עֲנֵנוּ, עֲנֵנוּ

‹ answer us; ‹‹ answer us; ‹ our Redeemer, ‹ answer us, ‹‹ answer us; ‹ our Creator, ‹ answer us ‹‹ answer us;

(1) *Isaiah* 26:19. (2) Cf. *Daniel* 9:16,24. (3) *Psalms* 26:8. (4) Cf. *Jeremiah* 51:26. (5) Cf. *Isaiah* 49:19. (6) *Joel* 2:16. (7) *Isaiah* 28:9. (8) *Shabbos* 119b. (9) *Isaiah* 64:7. (10) Cf. 43:1. (11) 47:4.

דּוֹרְשֵׁנוּ[1] עֲנֵנוּ, עֲנֵנוּ הָאֵל הַנֶּאֱמָן[2] עֲנֵנוּ, עֲנֵנוּ וָתִיק

⟨stead- ⟨answer ⟨⟨answer ⟨ Who is ⟨ God ⟨answer ⟨⟨answer ⟨ You Who
fast us, us; faithful, us, us; searches us out,

וְחָסִיד עֲנֵנוּ, עֲנֵנוּ זַךְ וְיָשָׁר[3] עֲנֵנוּ, עֲנֵנוּ חַי וְקַיָּם[4]

⟨and endur-⟨living ⟨answer ⟨⟨answer ⟨ and ⟨ pure ⟨answer ⟨⟨answer ⟨ and kind
ing One, us, us; upright One us, us; One,

עֲנֵנוּ, עֲנֵנוּ **טוֹב** וּמֵטִיב[5] עֲנֵנוּ, עֲנֵנוּ יוֹדֵעַ יֵצֶר[6] עֲנֵנוּ,

⟨⟨answer ⟨ of incli- ⟨ Knower ⟨ answer ⟨⟨ answer ⟨ and bene- ⟨ good ⟨answer ⟨⟨ answer
us; nations, us, us; ficent One, us, us;

עֲנֵנוּ **כּוֹבֵשׁ** כְּעָסִים עֲנֵנוּ, עֲנֵנוּ **לוֹבֵשׁ** צְדָקוֹת[7] עֲנֵנוּ,

⟨⟨answer ⟨ of ⟨ Donner ⟨ answer ⟨⟨answer ⟨ of wrath, ⟨ Suppressor ⟨answer
us; righteousness, us, us;

עֲנֵנוּ **מֶלֶךְ** מַלְכֵי הַמְּלָכִים[8] עֲנֵנוּ, עֲנֵנוּ **נוֹרָא** וְנִשְׂגָּב[9]

⟨ and power-⟨awesome ⟨answer ⟨⟨answer ⟨ of kings, ⟨ over ⟨ King ⟨ answer
ful One, us, us; kings us,

עֲנֵנוּ, עֲנֵנוּ **סוֹלֵחַ** וּמוֹחֵל עֲנֵנוּ, עֲנֵנוּ עוֹנֶה בְּעֵת

⟨ in time ⟨ You Who ⟨ answer ⟨⟨ answer ⟨ and ⟨ You Who ⟨ answer ⟨⟨ answer
answers us, us; pardons forgives us, us;

צָרָה[10] עֲנֵנוּ, עֲנֵנוּ **פּוֹדֶה** וּמַצִּיל[11] עֲנֵנוּ, עֲנֵנוּ צַדִּיק

⟨righteous ⟨answer ⟨⟨ answer ⟨ and ⟨ Redeemer ⟨ answer ⟨⟨answer ⟨ of
us, us; Rescuer, us, us; distress,

וְיָשָׁר[12] עֲנֵנוּ, עֲנֵנוּ **קָרוֹב** לְקוֹרְאָיו[13] עֲנֵנוּ, עֲנֵנוּ קָשֶׁה

⟨ You Who ⟨answer ⟨⟨answer ⟨ to those who ⟨ He Who ⟨ answer ⟨⟨ answer ⟨ and up-
with difficulty us, us; call upon Him, is close us, us; right One,

לִכְעוֹס[14] עֲנֵנוּ, עֲנֵנוּ **רַךְ** לִרְצוֹת[15] עֲנֵנוּ, עֲנֵנוּ רַחוּם

⟨ merciful ⟨ answer ⟨⟨ answer ⟨ appeased, ⟨ You Who ⟨answer ⟨⟨ answer ⟨ becomes
us, us; are easily us, us; angry,

וְחַנּוּן[16] עֲנֵנוּ, עֲנֵנוּ **שׁוֹמֵעַ** אֶל אֶבְיוֹנִים[17] עֲנֵנוּ, עֲנֵנוּ

⟨answer ⟨⟨answer ⟨ the destitute, ⟨ to ⟨ You Who ⟨ answer ⟨⟨answer ⟨ and gra-
us, us; listens us, us; cious One,

תּוֹמֵךְ תְּמִימִים עֲנֵנוּ, עֲנֵנוּ אֱלֹהֵי אֲבוֹתֵינוּ עֲנֵנוּ,

⟨⟨answer ⟨ of our ⟨ God ⟨ answer ⟨⟨ answer ⟨ the ⟨ You Who
us; forefathers, us, us; wholesome, supports

עֲנֵנוּ אֱלֹהֵי אַבְרָהָם[18] עֲנֵנוּ, עֲנֵנוּ פַּחַד יִצְחָק עֲנֵנוּ,

⟨⟨ answer ⟨ of Isaac, ⟨ Awesome ⟨answer ⟨⟨ answer ⟨ of Abraham, ⟨ God ⟨ answer
us; One us, us; us,

---

(1) Cf. *Ezekiel* 34:11. (2) *Deuteronomy* 7:9. (3) *Job* 8:6; cf. *Proverbs* 20:11. (4) Cf. *Daniel* 6:27.
(5) Cf. *Psalms* 119:68. (6) Cf. 103:14. (7) Cf. *Isaiah* 59:17. (8) *Ethics of the Fathers* 3:1.
(9) *Psalms* 47:3; 148:13. (10) Cf. *Isaiah* 49:8; *Psalms* 37:39. Alternate text: בְּעֵת רָצוֹן, *in time of favor.*
(11) Cf. 34:23,18. (12) *Deuteronomy* 32:4. (13) Cf. *Psalms* 145:18. (14) *Ethics of the Fathers* 5:14.
(15) Cf. 5:14. (16) *Exodus* 34:6. (17) *Psalms* 69:34. (18) *Genesis* 31:42.

עֲנֵנוּ אֲבִיר יַעֲקֹב¹ עֲנֵנוּ, עֲנֵנוּ עֶזְרַת הַשְּׁבָטִים עֲנֵנוּ,

《answer us; 〉 of the tribes, 〉 Helper 〉 answer 《answer us; 〉 of Jacob, 〉 Mighty One 〉 answer us,

עֲנֵנוּ מִשְׂגָּב אִמָּהוֹת עֲנֵנוּ, עֲנֵנוּ עוֹנֶה בְּעֵת רָצוֹן² עֲנֵנוּ,

《answer us; 〉 of favor, 〉 in a time 〉 You Who answers 〉 answer us, 《answer us; 〉 of the Matriarchs, 〉 Stronghold 〉 answer us,

עֲנֵנוּ אֲבִי יְתוֹמִים³ עֲנֵנוּ, עֲנֵנוּ דַּיַּן אַלְמָנוֹת³ עֲנֵנוּ.

《 answer us. 〉 of widows, 〉 Judge 〉 answer us; 《 answer us; 〉 of orphans, 〉 Father 〉 answer us,

מִי שֶׁעָנָה לְאַבְרָהָם אָבִינוּ בְּהַר הַמּוֹרִיָּה⁴

《 Moriah 〉 on Mount 〉 our father 〉 Abraham 〉 Who answered 〉 He

הוּא יַעֲנֵנוּ.

《 answer us. 〉 — may He

מִי שֶׁעָנָה לְיִצְחָק בְּנוֹ כְּשֶׁנֶּעֱקַד עַל גַּבֵּי הַמִּזְבֵּחַ⁴

《 of the altar 〉 top 〉 on 〉 when he was bound 〉 his son 〉 Isaac 〉 Who answered 〉 He

הוּא יַעֲנֵנוּ.

《 answer us. 〉 — may He

מִי שֶׁעָנָה לְיַעֲקֹב בְּבֵית אֵל⁵   הוּא יַעֲנֵנוּ.

《 in Beth-el 〉 Jacob 〉 Who answered 〉 He   《 answer us. 〉 — may He

מִי שֶׁעָנָה לְיוֹסֵף בְּבֵית הָאֲסוּרִים⁶   הוּא יַעֲנֵנוּ.

《 in the prison 〉 Joseph 〉 Who answered 〉 He   《 answer us. 〉 — may He

מִי שֶׁעָנָה לַאֲבוֹתֵינוּ עַל יַם סוּף⁷   הוּא יַעֲנֵנוּ.

《 of Reeds 〉 the Sea 〉 at 〉 our forefathers 〉 Who answered 〉 He   《 answer us. 〉 — may He

מִי שֶׁעָנָה לְמֹשֶׁה בְּחוֹרֵב⁸   הוּא יַעֲנֵנוּ.

《 in Horeb 〉 Moses 〉 Who answered 〉 He   《 answer us. 〉 — may He

מִי שֶׁעָנָה לְאַהֲרֹן בַּמַּחְתָּה⁹   הוּא יַעֲנֵנוּ.

《 with the fire-pan 〉 Aaron 〉 Who answered 〉 He   《 answer us. 〉 — may He

---

(1) *Isaiah* 49:26. (2) Cf. 49:8; *Psalms* 69:14. Alternate text: בְּעֵת צָרָה, *in time of distress.*
(3) 68:6. (4) *Genesis* 22:12. (5) 35:3. (6) 39:21. (7) *Exodus* Ch. 14.
(8) *Exodus* 17:6,11; *Deuteronomy* 9:19. (9) *Numbers* 17:11-13.

מִי שֶׁעָנָה לְפִינְחָס בְּקוּמוֹ מִתּוֹךְ הָעֵדָה¹

He ⟩ Who ⟩ Phinehas ⟨ when he ⟩ from ⟨ the
answered   arose   amid   congregation ⟪

הוּא יַעֲנֵנוּ.

may ⟩ He — ⟨ answer ⟪
He   us.

מִי שֶׁעָנָה לִיהוֹשֻׁעַ בַּגִּלְגָּל²

He ⟩ Who ⟩ Joshua ⟨ in Gilgal ⟪
answered

הוּא יַעֲנֵנוּ.

may ⟩ He — ⟨ answer ⟪
He   us.

מִי שֶׁעָנָה לִשְׁמוּאֵל בַּמִּצְפָּה³

He ⟩ Who ⟩ Samuel ⟨ in Mizpah ⟪
answered

הוּא יַעֲנֵנוּ.

may ⟩ He — ⟨ answer ⟪
He   us.

מִי שֶׁעָנָה לְדָוִד וּשְׁלֹמֹה בְנוֹ בִּירוּשָׁלָיִם⁴

He ⟩ Who ⟩ David ⟨ and ⟨ his ⟩ in Jerusalem ⟪
answered   Solomon   son

הוּא יַעֲנֵנוּ.

may ⟩ He — ⟨ answer ⟪
He   us.

מִי שֶׁעָנָה לְאֵלִיָּהוּ בְּהַר הַכַּרְמֶל⁵

He ⟩ Who ⟩ Elijah ⟨ on ⟨ Carmel ⟪
answered   Mount

הוּא יַעֲנֵנוּ.

may ⟩ He — ⟨ answer ⟪
He   us.

מִי שֶׁעָנָה לֶאֱלִישָׁע בִּירִיחוֹ⁶

He ⟩ Who ⟩ Elisha ⟨ in Jericho ⟪
answered

הוּא יַעֲנֵנוּ.

may ⟩ He — ⟨ answer ⟪
He   us.

מִי שֶׁעָנָה לְיוֹנָה בִּמְעֵי הַדָּגָה⁷

He ⟩ Who ⟩ Jonah ⟨ in the ⟨ of the ⟪
answered   innards   fish

הוּא יַעֲנֵנוּ.

may ⟩ He — ⟨ answer ⟪
He   us.

מִי שֶׁעָנָה לְחִזְקִיָּהוּ מֶלֶךְ יְהוּדָה בְּחָלְיוֹ⁸

He ⟩ Who ⟩ Hezekiah, ⟨ king ⟨ of Judah, ⟨ in his ⟪
answered   illness

הוּא יַעֲנֵנוּ.

may ⟩ He — ⟨ answer ⟪
He   us.

מִי שֶׁעָנָה לַחֲנַנְיָה מִישָׁאֵל וַעֲזַרְיָה

He ⟩ Who ⟩ Hananiah, ⟨ Mishael, ⟨ and Azariah ⟨
answered

בְּתוֹךְ כִּבְשַׁן הָאֵשׁ⁹

inside ⟩ the furnace ⟨ of fire ⟪

הוּא יַעֲנֵנוּ.

may ⟩ He — ⟨ answer ⟪
He   us.

מִי שֶׁעָנָה לְדָנִיֵּאל בְּגוֹב הָאֲרָיוֹת¹⁰

He ⟩ Who ⟩ Daniel ⟨ in the ⟨ of lions ⟪
answered   den

הוּא יַעֲנֵנוּ.

may ⟩ He — ⟨ answer ⟪
He   us.

---

(1) *Numbers* 25:7-13. (2) *Joshua* 6:1-20; 7:6-15; 10:12-14. (3) *I Samuel* 7:9.
(4) *II Samuel* 7:5-16; 21:1,14; 24:25; *I Kings* 9:3. (5) 18:36-38. (6) *II Kings* 2:21.
(7) *Jonah* 2:2-11. (8) *II Kings* 20:1-6; *Isaiah* 38:2-8. (9) *Daniel* 3:21-26. (10) 6:17-23.

מִי שֶׁעָנָה לְמָרְדְּכַי וְאֶסְתֵּר בְּשׁוּשַׁן הַבִּירָה[1]

‹ He › Who answered › Mordechai › and Esther › in Shushan › the capital ⟪

הוּא יַעֲנֵנוּ.

⟪ answer us. ‹ — may He

מִי שֶׁעָנָה לְעֶזְרָא בַּגּוֹלָה[2]

‹ He › Who answered › Ezra › in the exile ⟪

הוּא יַעֲנֵנוּ.

⟪ answer us. ‹ — may He

מִי שֶׁעָנָה לְכָל הַצַּדִּיקִים וְהַחֲסִידִים וְהַתְּמִימִים

‹ He › Who answered › all › the righteous, › the devout, › the wholesome,

וְהַיְשָׁרִים

⟪ and the upright

הוּא יַעֲנֵנוּ.

⟪ answer us. ‹ — may He

רַחֲמָנָא דְּעָנֵי לַעֲנִיֵּי, עֲנֵינָן. רַחֲמָנָא דְּעָנֵי לִתְבִירֵי

‹ those of broken › Who answers › Merciful One ⟪ answer us! ⟪ the poor, ‹ Who answers ‹ Merciful One

לִבָּא, עֲנֵינָן. רַחֲמָנָא דְּעָנֵי לִמְכִיכֵי רוּחָא, עֲנֵינָן.

⟪ answer us! ⟪ spirit, ‹ those of crushed › Who answers ‹ Merciful One ⟪ answer us! ⟪ hearts,

רַחֲמָנָא עֲנֵינָן. רַחֲמָנָא חוּס. רַחֲמָנָא פְּרוֹק. רַחֲמָנָא

‹ Merciful One, ⟪ redeem! ‹ Merciful One, ⟪ have pity! ‹ Merciful One, ⟪ answer us! ‹ Merciful One,

שֵׁזִיב. רַחֲמָנָא רְחַם עֲלָן, הַשְׁתָּא בַּעֲגָלָא וּבִזְמַן קָרִיב.

⟪ that comes soon. ‹ and at a time ‹ swiftly, ‹ — now, ⟪ on us ‹ have mercy ‹ Merciful One, ⟪ save!

נפילת אפים / PUTTING DOWN THE HEAD

RECITE UNTIL יַבֵּשׁ רֶגַע WITH THE HEAD RESTING ON THE LEFT ARM,
PREFERABLY WHILE SEATED.

(וַיֹּאמֶר דָּוִד אֶל גָּד, צַר לִי מְאֹד, נִפְּלָה נָּא בְיַד יהוה,

⟪ of HASHEM, ‹ into the hand ‹ now ‹ Let us fall ⟪ exceedingly. ‹ am I ‹ Dis- tressed ⟪ Gad, ‹ to ‹ (And David said

כִּי רַבִּים רַחֲמָיו, וּבְיַד אָדָם אַל אֶפֹּלָה.[3]

⟪ let me not fall.) ‹ but into human hands ⟪ are His mercies, ‹ abundant ‹ for

---

(1) Esther Ch. 8. (2) Ezra 8:21-23. (3) II Samuel 24:14.

רַחוּם וְחַנּוּן חָטָאתִי לְפָנֶיךָ. יהוה מָלֵא רַחֲמִים,

《 of mercy, 〈 Who 〈 HASHEM, 《 before 〈 I have 〈 and gracious 〈 O merciful
　　　　　　is full　　　　　You.　　sinned　　　　One,

רַחֵם עָלַי וְקַבֵּל תַּחֲנוּנָי.

　　　　《　　my　　　〈 and 〈 on me 〈 have
　　　supplications.　accept　　　　　mercy

——— *Psalms 6:2-11* / תהלים ו:ב-יא ———

יהוה, אַל בְּאַפְּךָ תוֹכִיחֵנִי, וְאַל בַּחֲמָתְךָ תְיַסְּרֵנִי.

《chastise me. 〈 in Your wrath 〈 nor 〈 rebuke me, 〈in Your anger 〈 do not 〈 HASHEM,

חָנֵּנִי יהוה כִּי אֻמְלַל אָנִי, רְפָאֵנִי יהוה כִּי נִבְהֲלוּ

〈 shudder 〈 for 〈 HASHEM, 〈 heal me, 《 am I; 〈 feeble 〈 for 〈 HASHEM, 〈 Favor
with terror,　　　　　　　　　　　　　　　　　　　　　　　　　me,

עֲצָמָי. וְנַפְשִׁי נִבְהֲלָה מְאֹד, וְאַתָּה יהוה עַד מָתָי.

《when? 〈 until 〈 HASHEM, 〈 and You, 《 utterly, 〈 is terrified 〈 My soul 《do my bones.

שׁוּבָה יהוה חַלְּצָה נַפְשִׁי, הוֹשִׁיעֵנִי לְמַעַן חַסְדֶּךָ.

《Your kindness. 〈 as befits 〈 save me 《 my soul; 〈 release 〈 HASHEM, 〈 Desist,

כִּי אֵין בַּמָּוֶת זִכְרֶךָ, בִּשְׁאוֹל מִי יוֹדֶה לָּךְ. יָגַעְתִּי

〈 I am 《 You? 〈 will 〈 who 〈 in the 《 is there men- 〈 in 〈 not 〈 For
wearied　　　praise　　　　grave　tion of You;　death

בְּאַנְחָתִי, אַשְׂחֶה בְכָל לַיְלָה מִטָּתִי, בְּדִמְעָתִי

〈 with my tears 《 my bed; 〈 night 〈 every 〈 I drench 《 with my sigh;

עַרְשִׂי אַמְסֶה. עָשְׁשָׁה מִכַּעַס עֵינִי, עָתְקָה בְּכָל

〈 by all 〈 aged 〈 is my 〈 because of 〈 Dimmed 《 I soak. 〈 my couch
　　　　　　eye,　　anger

צוֹרְרָי. סוֹרוּ מִמֶּנִּי כָּל פֹּעֲלֵי אָוֶן, כִּי שָׁמַע יהוה

〈 HASHEM has heard 〈 for 《 of evil, 〈 doers 〈 all 〈 from me, 〈 Depart 《 my
　　　　　　　　　　　　　　　　　　　　　　　　　　　tormentors.

קוֹל בִּכְיִי. שָׁמַע יהוה תְּחִנָּתִי, יהוה תְּפִלָּתִי יִקָּח.

《 will 〈 my prayer 〈 HASHEM 《 my plea, 〈 HASHEM 《 of my 〈 the
accept.　　　　　　　　　　　　　　　　has heard　weeping. sound

יֵבֹשׁוּ וְיִבָּהֲלוּ מְאֹד כָּל אֹיְבָי, יָשֻׁבוּ יֵבֹשׁוּ רָגַע.

《 in an 〈 and be 〈 may they 《 my 〈 all 〈 utterly, 〈 and con- 〈 Let them
instant. shamed　regret　enemies;　　　　　　founded　be shamed

מַחֵי וּמַסֵּי מֵמִית וּמְחַיֶּה, מַסִּיק מִן שְׁאוֹל

〈 the 〈 from 〈 Who raises 《 and Who 〈 Who causes 《 and Who 〈 [O God,]
grave　　[the dead]　restores life,　death　　heals,　Who wounds

לְחַיֵּי עָלְמָא, בְּרָא כַּד חָטֵי אֲבוּהִי לַקְיֵהּ, אֲבוּהִי

⟨ but a father ⟨ would strike him, ⟨ his father ⟨ sin, ⟨ should he ⟨ A son ⟨ eternal: ⟨ to life

דְּחָיֵס אַסֵּי לִכְאֵבֵהּ. עַבְדָּא דְּמָרִיד נָפִיק בְּקוֹלָר,

⟨ in chains, ⟨ he is led out ⟨ who rebels, ⟨ A slave ⟨ his [son's] pain. ⟨ will heal ⟨ who is compassionate

מָרֵהּ תָּאִיב וְתַבִּיר קוֹלָרֵהּ.

⟨ his chains. ⟨ he breaks ⟨ desires, ⟨ but [if] his master

בְּרָךְ בְּכְרָךְ אֲנָן וְחָטֵינָן קַמָּךְ, הָא רָוֵי נַפְשִׁין

⟨ has our soul been ⟨ satiated ⟨ indeed ⟨ before You; ⟨ and we have sinned ⟨ we are, ⟨ Your firstborn, ⟨ Your son,

בְּגִידִין מְרָרִין, אֲנָן עַבְדָּךְ, וּמְרוֹדִינָן קַמָּךְ,

⟨ before You; ⟨ and we have rebelled ⟨ we are ⟨ Your servants ⟨ that is bitter. ⟨ with wormwood

הָא בְּבִזְּתָא, הָא בְּשִׁבְיָא, הָא בְּמַלְקִיּוּתָא.

⟨ by the lash. ⟨ and some ⟨ in captivity, ⟨ some ⟨ from looting, ⟨ [indeed we have suffered,] some

בְּמָטוּ מִנָּךְ בְּרַחֲמָךְ דִּנְפִישִׁין, אַסֵּי לִכְאֵבִין

⟨ the pains ⟨ heal ⟨ that is abundant, ⟨ in Your compassion ⟨ of You, ⟨ We beg

דִּתְקוֹף עֲלָן, עַד דְּלָא נֶהֱוֵי גְּמִירָא בְּשִׁבְיָא.

⟨ in captivity. ⟨ completely annihilated ⟨ we are not ⟨ while yet ⟨ us, ⟨ that have overwhelmed

מַכְנִיסֵי רַחֲמִים, הַכְנִיסוּ רַחֲמֵינוּ, לִפְנֵי בַּעַל

⟨ the Master ⟨ before ⟨ our [plea for] mercy, ⟨ may you usher in ⟨ [pleas for] mercy, ⟨ O you who usher in

הָרַחֲמִים. מַשְׁמִיעֵי תְפִלָּה, הַשְׁמִיעוּ תְפִלָּתֵנוּ, לִפְנֵי

⟨ before ⟨ of our prayer ⟨ may you aid the hearing ⟨ of prayer, ⟨ O you who aid the hearing ⟨ of mercy.

שׁוֹמֵעַ תְּפִלָּה. מַשְׁמִיעֵי צְעָקָה, הַשְׁמִיעוּ צַעֲקָתֵנוּ,

⟨ of our outcries ⟨ may you aid the hearing ⟨ of outcries, ⟨ O you who aid the hearing ⟨ of prayer. ⟨ the Hearer

לִפְנֵי שׁוֹמֵעַ צְעָקָה. מַכְנִיסֵי דִמְעָה, הַכְנִיסוּ

⟨ may you usher in ⟨ tears, ⟨ O you who usher in ⟨ of outcries. ⟨ the Hearer ⟨ before

דִמְעוֹתֵינוּ, לִפְנֵי מֶלֶךְ מִתְרַצֶּה בִּדְמָעוֹת.

⟨ through tears. ⟨ Who is appeased ⟨ the King ⟨ before ⟨ our tears

הִשְׁתַּדְּלוּ וְהַרְבּוּ תְּחִנָּה וּבַקָּשָׁה, לִפְנֵי מֶלֶךְ אֵל
‹ God, ‹ the King, ‹ before ‹ and pleas ‹ supplications ‹ and intensify ‹ Exert yourselves

רָם וְנִשָּׂא. הַזְכִּירוּ לְפָנָיו, הַשְׁמִיעוּ לְפָנָיו תּוֹרָה
‹ the Torah ‹ before Him, ‹ aid to be heard « before Him, ‹ Mention « and uplifted. ‹ exalted

וּמַעֲשִׂים טוֹבִים שֶׁל שׁוֹכְנֵי עָפָר.
« in the dust. ‹ [the Patriarchs and Matriarchs] who dwell ‹ of ‹ that are good ‹ and the deeds

יִזְכֹּר אַהֲבָתָם וִיחַיֶּה זַרְעָם, שֶׁלֹּא תֹאבַד שְׁאֵרִית
‹ shall the remnant ‹ lost ‹ so that not ‹ to their offspring, ‹ and grant life ‹ their love ‹ May He remember

יַעֲקֹב. כִּי צֹאן רוֹעֶה נֶאֱמָן הָיָה לְחֶרְפָּה,
« a disgrace; ‹ has become ‹ who is faithful [Moses] ‹ of the shepherd ‹ the flock ‹ For « of Jacob be.

יִשְׂרָאֵל גּוֹי אֶחָד לִמְשָׁל וְלִשְׁנִינָה.
« and a simile. ‹ a parable « that is unique, ‹ the nation « Israel,

מַהֵר עֲנֵנוּ אֱלֹהֵי יִשְׁעֵנוּ, וּפְדֵנוּ מִכָּל גְּזֵרוֹת קָשׁוֹת
« that are harsh; ‹ decrees ‹ from all ‹ and redeem us ‹ of our salvation, ‹ O God ‹ answer us, ‹ Swiftly

וְהוֹשִׁיעָה בְּרַחֲמֶיךָ הָרַבִּים, מְשִׁיחַ צִדְקֶךָ וְעַמֶּךָ.
« and Your people. ‹ Your righteous anointed one ‹ that is abundant, ‹ in Your mercy ‹ and may You save,

מָרַן דְּבִשְׁמַיָּא לָךְ מִתְחַנְּנָן, כְּבַר שְׁבִיָּא דְמִתְחַנַּן
‹ who supplicates ‹ in captivity ‹ as one « do we ‹ to You « Who is in heaven, ‹ Our Master

לִשְׁבוּיֵהּ. כֻּלְּהוֹן בְּנֵי שְׁבִיָּא בְּכַסְפָּא מִתְפָּרְקִין,
« are redeemed, ‹ through money ‹ in captivity, ‹ those ‹ [for] all « before his captors;

וְעַמָּךְ יִשְׂרָאֵל בְּרַחֲמֵי וּבְתַחֲנוּנֵי, הַב לָן שְׁאִילְתִּין
‹ our requests ‹ us ‹ O « grant supplication. ‹ and ‹ through compassion ‹ Israel ‹ but Your people

וּבָעוּתִין, דְּלָא נֶהְדַּר רֵיקָם מִן קֳדָמָךְ.
« before You. ‹ from ‹ empty-handed ‹ that we not be turned away ‹ and our prayers

מָרָן דִּבִשְׁמַיָּא לָךְ מִתְחַנְּנָן, כְּעַבְדָּא דְּמִתְחַנֵּן

⟨ who supplicates ⟨ as a slave ⟨⟨ do we supplicate, ⟨ to You ⟨⟨ Who is in heaven, ⟨ Our Master

לְמָרֵיהּ, עֲשִׁיקֵי אֲנָן וּבַחֲשׁוֹכָא שָׁרִינָן, מְרִירָן נַפְשִׁין

⟨ are [our] souls ⟨ embittered ⟨⟨ do we abide, ⟨ and in darkness ⟨ are we ⟨ Oppressed ⟨⟨ to his master:

מֵעַקְתִּין דִּנְפִישִׁין, חֵילָא לֵית בֵּן לְרַצּוּיָךְ. מָרָן,

⟨ Our Master, ⟨⟨ to appease You. ⟨ within us ⟨ is lacking ⟨ Strength ⟨⟨ that is excessive. ⟨ from distress

עֲבִיד בְּדִיל קַיָּמָא דִּגְזַרְתָּ עִם אֲבָהָתָנָא.

⟨⟨ our Patriarchs. ⟨ with ⟨ that You established ⟨ of the covenant ⟨ for the sake ⟨ act

שׁוֹמֵר יִשְׂרָאֵל, שְׁמוֹר שְׁאֵרִית יִשְׂרָאֵל, וְאַל

⟨ let not ⟨⟨ of Israel; ⟨ the remnant ⟨ safeguard ⟨⟨ of Israel, ⟨ O Guardian

יֹאבַד יִשְׂרָאֵל, הָאוֹמְרִים שְׁמַע יִשְׂרָאֵל.[1]

⟨⟨ O Israel. ⟨ Hear, ⟨ those who proclaim ⟨⟨ Israel be destroyed —

שׁוֹמֵר גּוֹי אֶחָד, שְׁמוֹר שְׁאֵרִית עַם אֶחָד, וְאַל

⟨ let not ⟨⟨ that is unique; ⟨ of the people ⟨ the remnant ⟨ safeguard ⟨ that is unique, ⟨ of the nation ⟨ O Guardian

יֹאבַד גּוֹי אֶחָד, הַמְיַחֲדִים שִׁמְךָ, יהוה אֱלֹהֵינוּ

⟨ is our God, ⟨ HASHEM ⟨ of Your Name: ⟨ those who proclaim the Oneness ⟨⟨ that is unique, ⟨ the nation ⟨ be destroyed

יהוה אֶחָד.

⟨⟨ the One [and Only]! ⟨ HASHEM is

שׁוֹמֵר גּוֹי קָדוֹשׁ, שְׁמוֹר שְׁאֵרִית עַם קָדוֹשׁ, וְאַל

⟨ let not ⟨⟨ that is holy; ⟨ of the people ⟨ the remnant ⟨ safeguard ⟨ that is holy, ⟨ of the nation ⟨ O Guardian

יֹאבַד גּוֹי קָדוֹשׁ, הַמְשַׁלְּשִׁים בְּשָׁלֹשׁ קְדֻשּׁוֹת לְקָדוֹשׁ.

⟨⟨ to the Holy One. ⟨ the sanctifications ⟨ the threefold ⟨ those who proclaim three times ⟨⟨ that is holy, ⟨ the nation ⟨ be destroyed

מִתְרַצֶּה בְּרַחֲמִים וּמִתְפַּיֵּס בְּתַחֲנוּנִים, הִתְרַצֵּה

⟨ be favorable ⟨⟨ through supplications, ⟨ and Who becomes conciliatory ⟨ through compassion ⟨ You Who becomes favorable

(1) *Deuteronomy* 6:4.

וְהִתְפַּיֵּס לְדוֹר עָנִי, כִּי אֵין עוֹזֵר. אָבִינוּ מַלְכֵּנוּ,

《 our King,　〈 Our Father,　《 helper.　〈 there is no　〈 for　《 that is　〈 to the generation　〈 and be conciliatory　〈 poor,

חָנֵּנוּ וַעֲנֵנוּ, כִּי אֵין בָּנוּ מַעֲשִׂים, עֲשֵׂה עִמָּנוּ

〈 us　〈 treat　《 worthy deeds;　〈 we have no　〈 though　〈 and answer us,　〈 be gracious with us

צְדָקָה וָחֶסֶד וְהוֹשִׁיעֵנוּ.

《 and save us.　〈 and kindness,　〈 with charity

STAND AFTER THE WORDS וַאֲנַחְנוּ לֹא נֵדַע UNTIL CONCLUSION OF THE PARAGRAPH.

וַאֲנַחְנוּ לֹא נֵדַע מַה נַּעֲשֶׂה, כִּי עָלֶיךָ עֵינֵינוּ.[1]

《 are our eyes.　〈 upon　〈 rather,　《 we should do,　〈 what　〈 know not　〈 You　〈 We

זְכֹר רַחֲמֶיךָ יהוה וַחֲסָדֶיךָ, כִּי מֵעוֹלָם הֵמָּה.[2] יְהִי

〈 May　《 are they.　〈 eternal　〈 for　〈 and Your kindnesses,　〈 HASHEM,　〈 Your mercies,　〈 Remember

חַסְדְּךָ יהוה עָלֵינוּ, כַּאֲשֶׁר יִחַלְנוּ לָךְ.[3] אַל תִּזְכָּר

〈 recall　〈 Do not　《 You.　〈 we awaited　〈 just as　《 be upon us,　〈 HASHEM,　〈 Your kindness,

לָנוּ עֲוֹנוֹת רִאשׁוֹנִים, מַהֵר יְקַדְּמוּנוּ רַחֲמֶיךָ, כִּי

〈 for　《 may Your mercies,　〈 advance to meet us　〈 swiftly　《 of the ancients;　〈 the sins　〈 against us

דַלּוֹנוּ מְאֹד.[4] עֶזְרֵנוּ בְּשֵׁם יהוה, עֹשֵׂה שָׁמַיִם

〈 of heaven　〈 Maker　《 of HASHEM,　〈 is through the Name　〈 Our help　《 exceedingly.　〈 we have become impoverished

וָאָרֶץ.[5] חָנֵּנוּ יהוה חָנֵּנוּ, כִּי רַב שָׂבַעְנוּ בוּז.[6] בִּרְגֹּז

《 Amid wrath,　《 with contempt.　〈 sated　〈 we are fully　〈 for　《 favor us,　〈 HASHEM,　〈 Favor us,　《 and earth.

רַחֵם תִּזְכּוֹר.[7] בִּרְגֹּז עֲקֵדָה תִּזְכּוֹר. בִּרְגֹּז תְּמִימוֹת

〈 the perfect ones　《 Amid wrath,　《 You should remember!　〈 the binding [of Isaac]　《 Amid wrath,　《 You should remember!　〈 to be merciful

תִּזְכּוֹר. יהוה הוֹשִׁיעָה, הַמֶּלֶךְ יַעֲנֵנוּ בְיוֹם קָרְאֵנוּ.[8]

《 we call.　〈 on the day　〈 answer us　〈 May the King　《 save!　〈 HASHEM,　《 You should remember!

כִּי הוּא יָדַע יִצְרֵנוּ, זָכוּר כִּי עָפָר אֲנָחְנוּ.[9]

《 are we.　〈 dust　〈 that　〈 He is mindful　《 our nature,　〈 knew　〈 He　〈 For

(1) *II Chronicles* 20:12. (2) *Psalms* 25:6. (3) 33:22. (4) 79:8. (5) 121:2.
(6) 123:3. (7) *Habakkuk* 3:2. (8) *Psalms* 20:10. (9) 103:14.

❖ עָזְרֵנוּ אֱלֹהֵי יִשְׁעֵנוּ עַל דְּבַר כְּבוֹד שְׁמֶךָ, וְהַצִּילֵנוּ

⟨ rescue us ⟨ of Your ⟨ of the ⟨ the ⟨ for ⟨ of our ⟨ O God ⟨ Assist us,
Name; glory sake salvation

וְכַפֵּר עַל חַטֹּאתֵינוּ לְמַעַן שְׁמֶךָ.[1]

⟪ of Your ⟨ for the ⟨ our sins ⟨ for ⟨ and grant
Name. sake atonement

FULL KADDISH / קדיש שלם

THE CHAZZAN RECITES קדיש שָׁלֵם, FULL KADDISH.

יִתְגַּדַּל וְיִתְקַדַּשׁ שְׁמֵהּ רַבָּא. (אָמֵן. — Cong.) בְּעָלְמָא

⟨ — in the ⟪ (Amen.) ⟪ that is ⟨ may His ⟨ and be ⟨ Grow
world great! — Name sanctified exalted

דִּי בְרָא כִרְעוּתֵהּ. וְיַמְלִיךְ מַלְכוּתֵהּ, וְיַצְמַח פֻּרְקָנֵהּ

⟨ His ⟨ and cause ⟪ to His ⟨ and may He ⟪ according ⟨ He ⟨ that
salvation, to sprout kingship, give reign to His will, created

וִיקָרֵב מְשִׁיחֵהּ. (אָמֵן. — Cong.) בְּחַיֵּיכוֹן וּבְיוֹמֵיכוֹן וּבְחַיֵּי

⟨ and in the ⟨ and in ⟨ in your ⟪ (Amen.) ⟪ His Messiah, ⟨ and bring
lifetimes your days, lifetimes near

דְכָל בֵּית יִשְׂרָאֵל, בַּעֲגָלָא וּבִזְמַן קָרִיב. וְאִמְרוּ: אָמֵן.

⟪Amen. ⟨ Now ⟪ that comes ⟨ and at a ⟨ swiftly ⟪ of Israel, ⟨ Family ⟨ of the
respond: soon. time entire

CONGREGATION RESPONDS:

אָמֵן. יְהֵא שְׁמֵהּ רַבָּא מְבָרַךְ לְעָלַם וּלְעָלְמֵי עָלְמַיָּא.

⟪ and for all eternity. ⟨ forever ⟨ be ⟨ that is ⟨ His ⟨ May ⟪ Amen.
blessed great Name

CHAZZAN CONTINUES:

יְהֵא שְׁמֵהּ רַבָּא מְבָרַךְ לְעָלַם וּלְעָלְמֵי עָלְמַיָּא. יִתְבָּרַךְ

⟨ Blessed, ⟪ and for all eternity. ⟨ forever ⟨ be ⟨ that is ⟨ His ⟨ May
blessed great Name

וְיִשְׁתַּבַּח וְיִתְפָּאַר וְיִתְרוֹמַם וְיִתְנַשֵּׂא וְיִתְהַדָּר וְיִתְעַלֶּה

⟨ elevated, ⟨ honored, ⟨ upraised, ⟨ exalted, ⟨ glorified, ⟨ praised,

וְיִתְהַלָּל שְׁמֵהּ דְּקֻדְשָׁא בְּרִיךְ הוּא (אָמֵן. — Cong.) — בְּרִיךְ הוּא

⟪ is He) ⟨ (Blessed ⟪ is He ⟨ Blessed ⟨ of the Holy ⟨ be the ⟨ and lauded
One, Name

— לְעֵלָּא מִן כָּל בִּרְכָתָא וְשִׁירָתָא תֻּשְׁבְּחָתָא וְנֶחֱמָתָא

⟨ and ⟨ praise ⟪ and song, ⟨ blessing ⟪ any ⟨ beyond
consolation

---

(1) *Psalms* 79:9.

דַּאֲמִירָן בְּעָלְמָא. וְאִמְרוּ: אָמֵן. (.Cong —) אָמֵן.

《 (Amen.)   《 Amen. 〈 Now   《 in the   〈 that are
                             respond: world.   uttered

CONGREGATION:

(קַבֵּל בְּרַחֲמִים וּבְרָצוֹן אֶת תְּפִלָּתֵנוּ.)

《 our prayers.) 〈 and   〈 with mercy 〈 (Accept
              with favor

CHAZZAN **CONTINUES:**

תִּתְקַבֵּל צְלוֹתְהוֹן וּבָעוּתְהוֹן דְּכָל בֵּית יִשְׂרָאֵל קֳדָם

〈 before 〈 Israel 〈 Family 〈 of the 〈 and   〈 the prayers 〈 May
                       of   entire supplications   accepted be

אֲבוּהוֹן דִּי בִשְׁמַיָּא. וְאִמְרוּ: אָמֵן. (.Cong —) אָמֵן.

《 (Amen.)   《 Amen. 〈 Now   《 is in   〈 Who 〈 their
                             respond: Heaven.   Father

CONGREGATION:

(יְהִי שֵׁם יהוה מְבֹרָךְ, מֵעַתָּה וְעַד עוֹלָם.[1])

《 eternity.) 〈 until 〈 from   《 be   〈 of 〈 the 〈 (Let
                   this time blessed, HASHEM Name

CHAZZAN **CONTINUES:**

יְהֵא שְׁלָמָא רַבָּא מִן שְׁמַיָּא וְחַיִּים טוֹבִים עָלֵינוּ וְעַל כָּל

〈 all 〈 and 〈 upon us 〈 that is 〈 and life 〈 Heaven 〈 from 〈 that is 〈 peace 〈 May
       upon   good,   abundant   there be

יִשְׂרָאֵל. וְאִמְרוּ: אָמֵן. (.Cong —) אָמֵן.

《 (Amen.)   《 Amen. 〈 Now   《 Israel.
                             respond:

CONGREGATION:

(עֶזְרִי מֵעִם יהוה, עֹשֵׂה שָׁמַיִם וָאָרֶץ.[2])

《 and   〈 of   〈 Maker 《 HASHEM, 〈 is   〈 (My
  earth.) heaven   from   help

CHAZZAN BOWS; TAKES THREE STEPS BACK. BOWS LEFT AND SAYS "... עֹשֶׂה שָׁלוֹם, *HE WHO MAKES PEACE* ...", BOWS RIGHT AND SAYS "... הוּא, *MAY HE* ...", BOWS FORWARD AND SAYS "... וְעַל כָּל יִשְׂרָאֵל, *AND UPON ALL ISRAEL* ..."; REMAINS IN PLACE FOR A FEW MOMENTS, THEN TAKES THREE STEPS FORWARD.

עֹשֶׂה שָׁלוֹם בִּמְרוֹמָיו, הוּא יַעֲשֶׂה שָׁלוֹם עָלֵינוּ, וְעַל כָּל

〈 all 〈 and 〈 upon us, 〈 peace 〈 make 〈 may 《 in His   〈 peace 〈 He Who
       upon   He   heights,   makes

יִשְׂרָאֵל. וְאִמְרוּ: אָמֵן. (.Cong —) אָמֵן.

《 (Amen.)   《 Amen. 〈 Now   《 Israel.
                             respond:

---

(1) *Psalms* 113:2. (2) 121:2.

❧ יום רביעי / FOURTH DAY ❧

אַשְׁרֵי יוֹשְׁבֵי בֵיתֶךָ, עוֹד יְהַלְלוּךָ סֶּלָה.[1] אַשְׁרֵי

‹ Praise- ‹‹ Selah. ‹‹ they will ‹ con- ‹‹ in Your ‹ are those ‹ Praiseworthy
worthy   praise You,   tinually   house,   who dwell

הָעָם שֶׁכָּכָה לּוֹ, אַשְׁרֵי הָעָם שֶׁיהוה אֱלֹהָיו.[2]

‹‹ is their ‹ that ‹ is the ‹ praise- ‹‹ is ‹ that such ‹ is the
God.   HASHEM   people   worthy   their lot;   people

—— תהלים קמה / Psalm 145 ——

תְּהִלָּה לְדָוִד, אֲרוֹמִמְךָ אֱלוֹהַי הַמֶּלֶךְ, וַאֲבָרְכָה

‹ and I ‹‹ the King, ‹ my God ‹ I will exalt You, ‹‹ by David: ‹ A psalm of
will bless   praise

שִׁמְךָ לְעוֹלָם וָעֶד. בְּכָל יוֹם אֲבָרְכֶךָ, וַאֲהַלְלָה שִׁמְךָ

‹ Your ‹ and I ‹‹ I will ‹ day ‹ Every ‹‹ and ‹ for ever ‹ Your
Name   will laud   bless You,   ever.   Name

לְעוֹלָם וָעֶד. גָּדוֹל יהוה וּמְהֻלָּל מְאֹד, וְלִגְדֻלָּתוֹ

‹ and His ‹‹ exceedingly, ‹ and ‹ is ‹ Great ‹‹ and ‹ for ever
greatness   lauded   HASHEM   ever.

אֵין חֵקֶר. דּוֹר לְדוֹר יְשַׁבַּח מַעֲשֶׂיךָ, וּגְבוּרֹתֶיךָ יַגִּידוּ.

‹‹ they will ‹ and Your ‹‹ Your ‹ will ‹ to ‹ Gen- ‹‹ is beyond
recount.   mighty deeds   actions,   praise   generation   eration   investigation.

הֲדַר כְּבוֹד הוֹדֶךָ, וְדִבְרֵי נִפְלְאֹתֶיךָ אָשִׂיחָה. וֶעֱזוּז

‹ And of ‹‹ I shall ‹ that are ‹ and Your ‹ of Your ‹ glory ‹ The
the might   discuss.   wondrous   deeds   majesty   splendrous

נוֹרְאֹתֶיךָ יֹאמֵרוּ, וּגְדוּלָּתְךָ אֲסַפְּרֶנָּה. זֵכֶר רַב טוּבְךָ

‹ of Your abun- ‹ A recol- ‹‹ I shall ‹ and Your ‹‹ they will ‹ of Your
dant goodness   lection   relate.   greatness   speak,   awesome deeds

יַבִּיעוּ, וְצִדְקָתְךָ יְרַנֵּנוּ. חַנּוּן וְרַחוּם יהוה, אֶרֶךְ אַפַּיִם

‹ to ‹ slow ‹‹ is ‹ and ‹ Gracious ‹‹ they will ‹ and of Your ‹‹ they
anger,   HASHEM,   merciful   sing joyfully.   righteousness   will utter,

וּגְדָל חָסֶד. טוֹב יהוה לַכֹּל, וְרַחֲמָיו עַל כָּל מַעֲשָׂיו.

‹‹ His ‹ all ‹ are ‹ His ‹‹ to all; ‹ HASHEM ‹‹ in [bestowing] ‹ and
creations.   on   mercies   is good   kindness.   great

יוֹדוּךָ יהוה כָּל מַעֲשֶׂיךָ, וַחֲסִידֶיךָ יְבָרְכוּכָה. כְּבוֹד

‹ Of the ‹‹ will ‹ and Your ‹‹ Your ‹ — all ‹‹ HASHEM ‹ They will
glory   bless You.   devout ones   creations —   thank You,

---

(1) *Psalms* 84:5. (2) 144:15.

מַלְכוּתְךָ יֹאמֵרוּ, וּגְבוּרָתְךָ יְדַבֵּרוּ. **לְהוֹדִיעַ** לִבְנֵי הָאָדָם

mankind ⟨ To inform ⟨ they will declare. ⟨ and of Your power ⟨ they will speak, ⟨ of Your kingdom

גְּבוּרֹתָיו, וּכְבוֹד הֲדַר מַלְכוּתוֹ. **מַלְכוּתְךָ** מַלְכוּת כָּל

⟨[span-ning] all ⟨ is a kingdom ⟨ Your kingdom ⟨ of His kingdom. ⟨ splendor ⟨ and of the glorious ⟨ of His mighty deeds,

עֹלָמִים, וּמֶמְשַׁלְתְּךָ בְּכָל דּוֹר וָדֹר. **סוֹמֵךְ** יְהוה

⟨ HASHEM supports ⟨ after ⟨ generation. gen-eration ⟨ is throughout ⟨ and Your dominion ⟨ eternities,

לְכָל הַנֹּפְלִים, וְזוֹקֵף לְכָל הַכְּפוּפִים. **עֵינֵי** כֹל

⟨ of all ⟨ The eyes ⟨ those who are bent. ⟨ all ⟨ and straightens ⟨ those who are fallen, ⟨ all

אֵלֶיךָ יְשַׂבֵּרוּ, וְאַתָּה נוֹתֵן לָהֶם אֶת אָכְלָם בְּעִתּוֹ.

⟨ in its proper time. ⟨ their food ⟨ them ⟨ give ⟨ and You ⟨ do look with hope, ⟨ to You

CONCENTRATE INTENTLY WHILE RECITING THE VERSE **פּוֹתֵחַ**, YOU OPEN.

פּוֹתֵחַ אֶת יָדֶךָ, וּמַשְׂבִּיעַ לְכָל חַי רָצוֹן. ✣**צַדִּיק**

⟨ Righteous ⟨ [with its] desire. ⟨ living thing ⟨ every ⟨ and satisfy ⟨ Your hand, ⟨ You open

יְהוה בְּכָל דְּרָכָיו, וְחָסִיד בְּכָל מַעֲשָׂיו. **קָרוֹב** יְהוה

⟨ is HASHEM ⟨ Close ⟨ His deeds. ⟨ in all ⟨ and magnanimous ⟨ His ways, ⟨ in all ⟨ is HASHEM

לְכָל קֹרְאָיו, לְכֹל אֲשֶׁר יִקְרָאֻהוּ בֶאֱמֶת. **רְצוֹן** יְרֵאָיו

⟨ of those who fear Him ⟨ The will ⟨ sincerely. ⟨ call upon Him ⟨ who ⟨ to all ⟨ who call upon Him, ⟨ to all

יַעֲשֶׂה, וְאֶת שַׁוְעָתָם יִשְׁמַע וְיוֹשִׁיעֵם. **שׁוֹמֵר** יְהוה

⟨ HASHEM protects ⟨ and He will save them. ⟨ He will hear, ⟨ and their cry ⟨ He will do;

אֶת כָּל אֹהֲבָיו, וְאֶת כָּל הָרְשָׁעִים יַשְׁמִיד. **תְּהִלַּת**

⟨ The praise ⟨ He will destroy. ⟨ the wicked ⟨ but all ⟨ who love Him; ⟨ all

יְהוה יְדַבֶּר פִּי, וִיבָרֵךְ כָּל בָּשָׂר שֵׁם קָדְשׁוֹ לְעוֹלָם

⟨ for ever ⟨ of His Holiness ⟨ the Name ⟨ flesh ⟨ may all ⟨ and bless ⟨ may my mouth declare, ⟨ of HASHEM

וָעֶד. וַאֲנַחְנוּ נְבָרֵךְ יָהּ מֵעַתָּה וְעַד עוֹלָם; הַלְלוּיָהּ.[1]

⟨ Halleluyah! ⟨ eternity. ⟨ until ⟨ from this time ⟨ God ⟨ will bless ⟨ But we ⟨ and ever.

---

(1) *Psalms* 115:18.

THE *CHAZZAN* RECITES חֲצִי קַדִּישׁ, HALF-*KADDISH*:

יִתְגַּדַּל וְיִתְקַדַּשׁ שְׁמֵהּ רַבָּא. (.Cong — אָמֵן.) בְּעָלְמָא

⟨ Grow exalted ⟨ and be sanctified ⟨ may His Name ⟨ that is great! — ⟪ (Amen.) ⟪ — in the world

דִּי בְרָא כִרְעוּתֵהּ. וְיַמְלִיךְ מַלְכוּתֵהּ, וְיַצְמַח פֻּרְקָנֵהּ

⟨ that ⟨ He created ⟪ according to His will, ⟨ and may He give reign ⟪ to His kingship, ⟪ and cause to sprout ⟨ His salvation,

וִיקָרֵב מְשִׁיחֵהּ. (.Cong — אָמֵן.) בְּחַיֵּיכוֹן וּבְיוֹמֵיכוֹן וּבְחַיֵּי

⟨ and bring near ⟨ His Messiah, ⟪ His ⟪ (Amen.) ⟨ in your lifetimes ⟨ and in your days, ⟨ and in the lifetimes

דְכָל בֵּית יִשְׂרָאֵל, בַּעֲגָלָא וּבִזְמַן קָרִיב. וְאִמְרוּ: אָמֵן.

⟨ of the entire ⟨ Family ⟨ of Israel, ⟪ swiftly ⟨ and at a time ⟨ that comes ⟨ soon. ⟪ Now respond: ⟪Amen.

CONGREGATION RESPONDS:

אָמֵן. יְהֵא שְׁמֵהּ רַבָּא מְבָרַךְ לְעָלַם וּלְעָלְמֵי עָלְמַיָּא.

⟪ Amen. ⟨ May ⟨ His Name ⟨ that is great ⟨ be blessed ⟨ forever ⟪ and for all eternity.

CHAZZAN CONTINUES:

יְהֵא שְׁמֵהּ רַבָּא מְבָרַךְ לְעָלַם וּלְעָלְמֵי עָלְמַיָּא. יִתְבָּרַךְ

⟨ May ⟨ His Name ⟨ that is great ⟨ be blessed ⟨ forever ⟪ and for all eternity. ⟪ Blessed, ⟩

וְיִשְׁתַּבַּח וְיִתְפָּאַר וְיִתְרוֹמַם וְיִתְנַשֵּׂא וְיִתְהַדָּר וְיִתְעַלֶּה

⟨ praised, ⟨ glorified, ⟨ exalted, ⟨ upraised, ⟨ honored, ⟨ elevated,

וְיִתְהַלָּל שְׁמֵהּ דְּקֻדְשָׁא בְּרִיךְ הוּא (.Cong — בְּרִיךְ הוּא)

⟨ and lauded ⟨ be the Name ⟨ of the Holy One, ⟨ Blessed ⟪ is He ⟨ (Blessed ⟪ is He)

— לְעֵלָּא מִן כָּל בִּרְכָתָא וְשִׁירָתָא תֻּשְׁבְּחָתָא וְנֶחֱמָתָא

⟨ beyond ⟨ any ⟨ blessing ⟨ and song, ⟪ and song, ⟨ praise ⟨ and consolation ⟩

דַּאֲמִירָן בְּעָלְמָא. וְאִמְרוּ: אָמֵן. (.Cong — אָמֵן.)

⟨ that are uttered ⟨ in the world. ⟪ Now respond: ⟨ Amen. ⟪ (Amen.)

ALL:

לְךָ יהוה הַצְּדָקָה, וְלָנוּ בֹּשֶׁת הַפָּנִים.[1] מַה

⟨ Yours, ⟨ O Lord, ⟨ is the righteousness, ⟪ and ours ⟪ is shamefacedness. ⟪What

נִּתְאוֹנֵן,[2] מַה נֹּאמַר, מַה נְּדַבֵּר, וּמַה נִּצְטַדָּק.[3]

⟪ complaint can we make? ⟨ What ⟪can we say? ⟨ What ⟨ can we declare? ⟪ What ⟨ justification can we offer?

---

(1) *Daniel* 9:7. (2) Cf. *Lamentations* 3:39. (3) Cf. *Genesis* 44:16.

נַחְפְּשָׂה דְרָכֵינוּ וְנַחְקֹרָה, וְנָשׁוּבָה אֵלֶיךָ,¹ כִּי יְמִינְךָ
‹ Your right hand ‹ for ‹‹ to You, ‹ and return ‹ and investigate them, ‹ our ways ‹ Let us examine

פְּשׁוּטָה לְקַבֵּל שָׁבִים. לֹא בְחֶסֶד וְלֹא בְמַעֲשִׂים
‹ with [merit for good] deeds ‹ nor ‹ with [merit] for kindness ‹ Neither ‹‹ those who return. ‹ to accept ‹ is extended

בָּאנוּ לְפָנֶיךָ, כְּדַלִּים וּכְרָשִׁים דָּפַקְנוּ דְלָתֶיךָ.
‹‹ on Your doors. ‹ we have knocked ‹ and as destitute people ‹ but as paupers ‹‹ before You; ‹ do we come

דְלָתֶיךָ דָּפַקְנוּ רַחוּם וְחַנּוּן, נָא אַל תְּשִׁיבֵנוּ
‹ turn us away ‹ do not ‹ Please ‹‹ and Gracious One. ‹ O Compassionate One ‹ we have knocked, ‹ On Your doors

רֵיקָם מִלְּפָנֶיךָ. מִלְּפָנֶיךָ מַלְכֵּנוּ רֵיקָם אַל תְּשִׁיבֵנוּ,
‹‹ turn us away, ‹ do not ‹ empty-handed ‹ Our King, ‹ From before You, ‹‹ from before You. ‹ empty-handed

כִּי אַתָּה שׁוֹמֵעַ תְּפִלָּה.
‹‹ prayer. ‹ Who hears ‹ You are ‹ for the One

שֹׁמֵעַ תְּפִלָּה, עָדֶיךָ כָּל בָּשָׂר יָבֹאוּ.² יָבוֹא
‹ Come ‹‹ will come. ‹ flesh ‹ all ‹ unto You ‹‹ prayer, ‹ You Who hears

כָּל בָּשָׂר לְהִשְׁתַּחֲוֹת לְפָנֶיךָ יהוה.³ יָבֹאוּ וְיִשְׁתַּחֲווּ
‹ and bow down ‹ They will come ‹‹ O HASHEM. ‹ before You, ‹ to bow down ‹ will all flesh

לְפָנֶיךָ אֲדֹנָי, וִיכַבְּדוּ לִשְׁמֶךָ.⁴ בֹּאוּ נִשְׁתַּחֲוֶה וְנִכְרָעָה,
‹‹ and bow, ‹ Let us prostrate ourselves ‹ Come! ‹‹ to Your Name. ‹ and they will show honor ‹‹ O Lord, ‹ before You,

נִבְרְכָה לִפְנֵי יהוה עֹשֵׂנוּ.⁵ נָבוֹאָה לְמִשְׁכְּנוֹתָיו,
‹‹ to His Tabernacles, ‹ Let us come ‹‹ our Maker. ‹ HASHEM, ‹ before ‹ let us kneel

נִשְׁתַּחֲוֶה לַהֲדֹם רַגְלָיו.⁶ בֹּאוּ שְׁעָרָיו בְּתוֹדָה,
‹‹ with thanksgiving, ‹ His gates ‹ Enter ‹‹ for His feet. ‹ at the stool ‹ let us prostrate ourselves

חֲצֵרֹתָיו בִּתְהִלָּה, הוֹדוּ לוֹ בָּרְכוּ שְׁמוֹ.⁷ וַאֲנַחְנוּ
‹ But we, ‹‹ His Name. ‹ bless ‹‹ to Him, ‹ give thanks ‹‹ with praise; ‹ His courtyards

(1) Cf. *Lamentations* 3:40. (2) *Psalms* 65:3. (3) Cf. *Isaiah* 66:23.
(4) *Psalms* 86:9. (5) 95:6. (6) 132:7. (7) 100:4.

בְּרֹב חַסְדְּךָ נָבוֹא בֵיתֶךָ, נִשְׁתַּחֲוֶה אֶל הֵיכַל קָדְשְׁךָ

Your Holy Sanctuary ‹ toward ‹ we will prostrate ourselves ‹‹ Your House; ‹ will we ‹ enter ‹ of Your kindness ‹ through the abundance

בְּיִרְאָתֶךָ. [1] הִנֵּה בָּרְכוּ אֶת יהוה כָּל עַבְדֵי יהוה,

of HASHEM, ‹ you ‹ all ‹ servants ‹ HASHEM, ‹ bless ‹‹ Indeed, ‹‹ in awe of You.

הָעֹמְדִים בְּבֵית יהוה בַּלֵּילוֹת. [2] שְׂאוּ יְדֵיכֶם קֹדֶשׁ

in the Sanctuary ‹ your hands ‹ Lift ‹‹ in the nights. ‹ of HASHEM ‹ in the House ‹ who stand

וּבָרְכוּ אֶת יהוה. [3] רוֹמְמוּ יהוה אֱלֹהֵינוּ, וְהִשְׁתַּחֲווּ

and bow down ‹ our God, ‹ HASHEM, ‹ Exalt ‹‹ HASHEM. ‹ and bless

לַהֲדֹם רַגְלָיו, קָדוֹשׁ הוּא. [4] רוֹמְמוּ יהוה אֱלֹהֵינוּ,

our God, ‹ HASHEM, ‹ Exalt ‹‹ is He! ‹ holy ‹‹ at His footstool;

וְהִשְׁתַּחֲווּ לְהַר קָדְשׁוֹ, כִּי קָדוֹשׁ יהוה אֱלֹהֵינוּ. [5]

our God. ‹ is ‹ holy ‹ for ‹‹ of His Holiness; ‹ at the Mount ‹ and bow HASHEM,

הִשְׁתַּחֲווּ לַיהוה בְּהַדְרַת קֹדֶשׁ, חִילוּ מִפָּנָיו כָּל

every- one ‹ before Him, ‹ tremble ‹‹ of holiness; ‹ in the splendor ‹ before HASHEM ‹ Bow down

הָאָרֶץ. [6] נִשְׁתַּחֲוֶה אֶל הֵיכַל קָדְשְׁךָ וְנוֹדֶה אֶת שְׁמֶךָ,

Your Name ‹ and we will thank ‹‹ Your Holy Sanctuary, ‹ toward ‹ We will prostrate ourselves ‹‹ on earth.

עַל חַסְדְּךָ וְעַל אֲמִתֶּךָ, כִּי הִגְדַּלְתָּ עַל כָּל שְׁמֶךָ

Your Name — ‹ — even beyond ‹‹ You have exalted ‹ for ‹‹ Your faithfulness; ‹ and for ‹ Your kindness ‹ for

אִמְרָתֶךָ. [7] יהוה אֱלֹהֵי צְבָאוֹת, מִי כָמוֹךָ חֲסִין

O Strong One, ‹ is like ‹ You, ‹ — who ‹‹ of Legions ‹ God ‹ HASHEM, ‹‹ Your promise.

יָהּ, וֶאֱמוּנָתְךָ סְבִיבוֹתֶיךָ. [8] כִּי מִי בַשַּׁחַק יַעֲרֹךְ

can be compared ‹ in the sky ‹ who ‹ For ‹‹ surrounds You. ‹ and Your faithfulness ‹‹ God? —

לַיהוה, יִדְמֶה לַיהוה בִּבְנֵי אֵלִים. [9] כִּי גָדוֹל אַתָּה

are You ‹ great ‹ For ‹‹ among the angels? ‹ to HASHEM ‹ be likened ‹‹ to HASHEM;

וְעוֹשֶׂה נִפְלָאוֹת, אַתָּה אֱלֹהִים לְבַדֶּךָ. [10] כִּי גָדוֹל

great ‹ For ‹‹ alone. ‹ O God, ‹ You, ‹‹ of wonders; ‹ and a worker

(1) Cf. *Psalms* 5:8. (2) 134:1. (3) 134:2. (4) 99:5. (5) 99:9. (6) 96:9. (7) Cf. 138:2. (8) 89:9. (9) 89:7. (10) 86:10.

מֵעַל שָׁמַיִם חַסְדֶּךָ, וְעַד שְׁחָקִים אֲמִתֶּךָ.[1] גָּדוֹל

⟨ Great   « is Your   ⟨ the upper   ⟨ and   « is Your   ⟨ the very   ⟨ above
truth.   heights   until   kindness,   heavens

יהוה וּמְהֻלָּל מְאֹד, וְלִגְדֻלָּתוֹ אֵין חֵקֶר.[2] (כִּי) גָּדוֹל

⟨ great   ⟨ (For) «investiga- ⟨ is   ⟨   and His   « exceed- ⟨ and   ⟨ is
tion.   beyond   greatness   ingly,   lauded   HASHEM

יהוה וּמְהֻלָּל מְאֹד, נוֹרָא הוּא עַל כָּל אֱלֹהִים.[3] כִּי

⟨For « heavenly   ⟨ all ⟨ above ⟨ is He ⟨ awesome «exceed- ⟨ and   ⟨ is
powers.   ingly;   lauded HASHEM

אֵל גָּדוֹל יהוה, וּמֶלֶךְ גָּדוֹל עַל כָּל אֱלֹהִים.[4] אֲשֶׁר

⟨ For   « heavenly   ⟨ all ⟨ above ⟨ and a great King « is ⟨ a great God
powers.   HASHEM,

מִי אֵל בַּשָּׁמַיִם וּבָאָרֶץ, אֲשֶׁר יַעֲשֶׂה כְמַעֲשֶׂיךָ

⟨ like unto   ⟨ can do   ⟨ that ⟨ or in the   ⟨ is there in ⟨ power ⟨what
Your deeds   earth   the heaven

וְכִגְבוּרֹתֶיךָ.[5] מִי לֹא יִרָאֲךָ מֶלֶךְ הַגּוֹיִם, כִּי לְךָ

⟨ to ⟨ For « of nations? ⟨ O King « fear You, ⟨ would ⟨ Who « and like unto Your
You   not   mighty acts?

יָאָתָה, כִּי בְּכָל חַכְמֵי הַגּוֹיִם וּבְכָל מַלְכוּתָם מֵאֵין

⟨ there is ⟨   their   ⟨ and in all ⟨ of the ⟨ the wise ⟨ among ⟨ for « [kingship]
none   kingdoms   nations   men   all   befits;

כָּמוֹךָ.[6] מֵאֵין כָּמוֹךָ יהוה, גָּדוֹל אַתָּה וְגָדוֹל שְׁמֶךָ

⟨ is Your ⟨ and great ⟨ are You ⟨ Great «   O   ⟨ like You, ⟨ There is « like You.
Name   HASHEM!   none

בִּגְבוּרָה.[7] לְךָ זְרוֹעַ עִם גְּבוּרָה, תָּעֹז יָדְךָ תָּרוּם

⟨ uplifted « is Your ⟨ strength- « power; ⟨ with ⟨ is the ⟨ Yours « in might.
hand,   ened   arm

יְמִינֶךָ.[8] לְךָ יוֹם, אַף לְךָ לָיְלָה, אַתָּה הֲכִינוֹתָ מָאוֹר

⟨ the   ⟨ prepared ⟨ You « is the ⟨ Yours ⟨ also «is the ⟨ Yours « is Your
luminary   night;   day,   right hand.

וָשָׁמֶשׁ.[9] אֲשֶׁר בְּיָדוֹ מֶחְקְרֵי אָרֶץ, וְתוֹעֲפוֹת הָרִים

⟨ of the ⟨   and the « of the ⟨ are the hidden ⟨ in His ⟨ For « and the
mountains   summits   earth,   mysteries   power   sun.

לוֹ.[10] מִי יְמַלֵּל גְּבוּרוֹת יהוה, יַשְׁמִיעַ כָּל תְּהִלָּתוֹ.[11]

« of His ⟨ all ⟨ [who] can « of ⟨ the mighty ⟨ can ⟨ Who « are
praise?   make heard HASHEM;   acts   express   His.

(1) *Psalms* 108:5. (2) 145:3. (3) 96:4. (4) 95:3. (5) *Deuteronomy* 3:24.
(6) *Jeremiah* 10:7. (7) 10:6. (8) *Psalms* 89:14. (9) 74:16. (10) 95:4. (11) 106:2.

לְךָ יהוה הַגְּדֻלָּה וְהַגְּבוּרָה, וְהַתִּפְאֶרֶת וְהַנֵּצַח
Yours, ‹ HASHEM, ‹ is the ‹ the strength, ‹ the glory, ‹ the triumph,
greatness,

וְהַהוֹד, כִּי כֹל בַּשָּׁמַיִם וּבָאָרֶץ; לְךָ יהוה הַמַּמְלָכָה,
and the ‹ and the ‹ for ‹ every- ‹ in heaven ‹ Yours, ‹ HASHEM, ‹ is the
majesty; thing and on kingdom
earth
[is Yours];

וְהַמִּתְנַשֵּׂא לְכֹל לְרֹאשׁ. לְךָ שָׁמַיִם, אַף לְךָ אָרֶץ,
and the ‹ over ‹ leader. ‹ are the ‹ Yours ‹ also ‹ is the
sovereignty every heavens, earth;

תֵּבֵל וּמְלֹאָהּ אַתָּה יְסַדְתָּם. אַתָּה הִצַּבְתָּ כָּל גְּבוּלוֹת
the ‹ and its ‹ You ‹ founded ‹ You ‹ established ‹ all ‹ the
world fullness, them. boundaries

אָרֶץ, קַיִץ וָחֹרֶף אַתָּה יְצַרְתָּם. אַתָּה רִצַּצְתָּ רָאשֵׁי
of ‹ summer ‹ and ‹ You ‹ fashioned ‹ You ‹ crushed ‹ the
earth; winter, them. heads

לִוְיָתָן, תִּתְּנֶנּוּ מַאֲכָל לְעַם לְצִיִּים. אַתָּה בָקַעְתָּ מַעְיָן
of ‹ You will ‹ as food ‹ to the ‹ [destined] for ‹ split ‹ fountain
Leviathan; serve it the desolate people open
wilderness.

וָנָחַל, אַתָּה הוֹבַשְׁתָּ נַהֲרוֹת אֵיתָן. אַתָּה פוֹרַרְתָּ
and stream; ‹ that are mighty. ‹ rivers ‹ dried ‹ You ‹ shattered ‹ You

בְּעָזְּךָ יָם, שִׁבַּרְתָּ רָאשֵׁי תַנִּינִים עַל הַמָּיִם. אַתָּה
with Your ‹ the ‹ You ‹ the heads ‹ of sea ‹ upon ‹ the water. ‹ You
might sea; smashed serpents

מוֹשֵׁל בְּגֵאוּת הַיָּם, בְּשׂוֹא גַלָּיו אַתָּה תְשַׁבְּחֵם.
rule ‹ the ‹ of the ‹ when it ‹ its ‹ You ‹ calm them.
grandeur sea; raises waves,

גָּדוֹל יהוה וּמְהֻלָּל מְאֹד, בְּעִיר אֱלֹהֵינוּ הַר קָדְשׁוֹ.
Great ‹ is ‹ and much praised, ‹ in the ‹ of our God, ‹ Mount ‹ of His
HASHEM City Holiness.

יהוה צְבָאוֹת, אֱלֹהֵי יִשְׂרָאֵל, יוֹשֵׁב הַכְּרֻבִים, אַתָּה
HASHEM, ‹ Master of ‹ God ‹ of Israel, ‹ en- ‹ upon the ‹ it is
Legions, throned Cherubim, You

הוּא הָאֱלֹהִים לְבַדֶּךָ. אֵל נַעֲרָץ בְּסוֹד קְדֹשִׁים רַבָּה,
in the great assemblage ‹ is ‹ God ‹ alone. ‹ God ‹ Who
of the holy [angels], revered are

(1) I Chronicles 29:11. (2) Psalms 89:12. (3) 74:17. (4) 74:14-15. (5) 74:13. (6) 89:10. (7) 48:2. (8) Isaiah 37:16.

וְנוֹרָא עַל כָּל סְבִיבָיו. וְיוֹדוּ שָׁמַיִם פִּלְאֲךָ יהוה, אַף[1]

‹ also › HASHEM, ‹ Your ‹ will the ‹ Acknowl- › who sur- ‹ all ‹ over ‹ and is
wonders, heavens edge round Him. awesome

אֱמוּנָתְךָ בִּקְהַל קְדֹשִׁים. לְכוּ נְרַנְּנָה לַיהוה, נָרִיעָה[2]

‹ let us › to ‹ Let us sing ‹ Come! › of holy ‹ in the ‹ Your
call out HASHEM, joyfully ones. assembly faithfulness,

לְצוּר יִשְׁעֵנוּ. נְקַדְּמָה פָנָיו בְּתוֹדָה, בִּזְמִירוֹת נָרִיעַ

‹ let us ‹ with praiseful › with ‹ Him ‹ Let us greet › of our ‹ to the
call out songs thanksgiving, salvation. Rock

לוֹ.[3] צֶדֶק וּמִשְׁפָּט מְכוֹן כִּסְאֶךָ, חֶסֶד וֶאֱמֶת יְקַדְּמוּ

‹ precede › and ‹ of Your ‹ are the ‹ and ‹ Righteous- › to
truth throne; foundation justice ness Him.

פָנֶיךָ.[4] אֲשֶׁר יַחְדָּו נַמְתִּיק סוֹד, בְּבֵית אֱלֹהִים נְהַלֵּךְ

‹ let us ‹ of God ‹ in the › counsel; ‹ let us ‹ together ‹ For › Your coun-
walk House take sweet tenance.

בְּרָגֶשׁ.[5] אֲשֶׁר לוֹ הַיָּם וְהוּא עָשָׂהוּ, וְיַבֶּשֶׁת יָדָיו

‹ His › and the › perfected ‹ and He ‹ is the ‹ His ‹ For › in company.
hands dry land, it, sea

יָצָרוּ.[6] אֲשֶׁר בְּיָדוֹ נֶפֶשׁ כָּל חָי, וְרוּחַ כָּל בְּשַׂר אִישׁ.[7]

› mankind. ‹ of all ‹ and the › the ‹ of ‹ is the ‹ in His ‹ For › fashioned.
spirit living all soul hand

❖ הַנְּשָׁמָה לָךְ וְהַגּוּף פָּעֳלָךְ, חוּסָה עַל עֲמָלָךְ.

› Your ‹ on ‹ take pity › is Your ‹ and the ‹ is ‹ The soul
labor. handiwork; body Yours

הַנְּשָׁמָה לָךְ וְהַגּוּף שֶׁלָּךְ, יהוה עֲשֵׂה לְמַעַן שְׁמֶךָ.

› of Your ‹ for the ‹ act ‹ O › is Yours; ‹ and the ‹ is ‹ The soul
Name. sake HASHEM, body Yours

אָתָאנוּ עַל שְׁמָךְ, יהוה, עֲשֵׂה לְמַעַן שְׁמָךְ. בַּעֲבוּר

‹ [act] › of Your ‹ for the ‹ act › O › Your ‹ [relying] ‹ We have
because of Name; sake HASHEM; Name, on come

כְּבוֹד שְׁמָךְ, כִּי אֵל חַנּוּן וְרַחוּם שְׁמֶךָ. לְמַעַן

‹ For the › is Your ‹ and ‹ Who is ‹ God ‹ for › of Your ‹ the glory
sake Name. Merciful Gracious Name,

שְׁמָךְ יהוה, וְסָלַחְתָּ לַעֲוֹנֵנוּ כִּי רַב הוּא.[8]

‹ it is great. ‹ though ‹ our ‹ forgive › HASHEM, ‹ of Your
iniquity, Name,

---

(1) *Psalms* 89:8. (2) 89:6. (3) 95:1-2. (4) 89:15. (5) 55:15. (6) 95:5. (7) *Job* 12:10. (8) Cf. *Psalms* 25:11.

CONGREGATION, THEN *CHAZZAN*:

סְלַח לָנוּ אָבִינוּ, כִּי בְרוֹב אִוַּלְתֵּנוּ שָׁגִינוּ,

Forgive ‹ us, ‹ our Father, ‹ for ‹ in the ‹ of our folly ‹ we have erred; »
abundance

מְחַל לָנוּ מַלְכֵּנוּ, כִּי רַבּוּ עֲוֹנֵינוּ.

pardon ‹ us, ‹ our King, ‹ for ‹ many ‹ our iniquities. »
are

ALL, WHILE STANDING

אֵל אֶרֶךְ אַפַּיִם אַתָּה,

God ‹ Who is slow ‹ to anger, ‹ You are, »

וּבַעַל הָרַחֲמִים נִקְרֵאתָ, וְדֶרֶךְ תְּשׁוּבָה הוֹרֵיתָ.

and ‹ of Mercy ‹ You are ‹ and the » way ‹ of ‹ You have »
Master called; repentance taught.

גְּדֻלַּת רַחֲמֶיךָ וַחֲסָדֶיךָ,

The ‹ of Your ‹ and Your
greatness mercy kindness

תִּזְכּוֹר הַיּוֹם וּבְכָל יוֹם לְזֶרַע יְדִידֶיךָ.

may You ‹ this day ‹ and » day, ‹ every ‹ for the ‹ of Your »
remember, every offspring beloved ones.

תֵּפֶן אֵלֵינוּ בְּרַחֲמִים,

Turn ‹ to us ‹ in mercy, »

כִּי אַתָּה הוּא בַּעַל הָרַחֲמִים.

for ‹ You ‹ are ‹ the Master ‹ of Mercy. »

בְּתַחֲנוּן וּבִתְפִלָּה פָּנֶיךָ נְקַדֵּם, כְּהוֹדַעְתָּ לֶעָנָיו מִקֶּדֶם.

With ‹ and prayer ‹ Your ‹ we ‹ in the manner ‹ to the ‹ in ancient »
supplication Presence approach, that You made humble one times.
known [Moses]

מֵחֲרוֹן אַפְּךָ שׁוּב,[1] כְּמוֹ בְּתוֹרָתְךָ כָּתוּב.[2]

From the ‹ anger ‹ turn ‹ as ‹ in Your Torah ‹ it is »
fierceness of Your back, written.

וּבְצֵל כְּנָפֶיךָ נֶחֱסֶה וְנִתְלוֹנָן, כְּיוֹם וַיֵּרֶד יהוה בֶּעָנָן.[3]

In the ‹ of Your ‹ may we find ‹ and may ‹ as on ‹ when HASHEM ‹ in a »
shadow wings shelter we dwell the day descended cloud.

❖ תַּעֲבוֹר עַל פֶּשַׁע וְתִמְחֶה אָשָׁם,

Overlook ‹ sin ‹ and erase ‹ guilt, »

---

(1) Cf. *Exodus* 32:12. (2) See 32:14. (3) Cf. *Psalms* 36:8.

כְּיוֹם וַיִּתְיַצֵּב עִמּוֹ שָׁם.
《 there. 〈 with him 〈 when He 〈 as on the
[Moses] [God] stood day

תַּאֲזִין שַׁוְעָתֵנוּ וְתַקְשִׁיב מֶנּוּ מַאֲמַר,
《 [our] 〈 from 〈 and hear 〈 to our cry 〈 Give heed
declaration, us

כְּיוֹם וַיִּקְרָא בְּשֵׁם יהוה,¹ וְשָׁם נֶאֱמַר:
《 it was said:〈 and 《 of HASHEM,〈 with the 〈 when He 〈 as on
there Name called out the day

CONGREGATION, THEN *CHAZZAN:*

וַיַּעֲבֹר יהוה עַל פָּנָיו וַיִּקְרָא:
《 and 《 [Moses'] 〈 before 〈 And HASHEM passed
proclaimed: face,

CONGREGATION AND *CHAZZAN* RECITE LOUDLY AND IN UNISON:

יהוה, יהוה, אֵל, רַחוּם, וְחַנּוּן, אֶרֶךְ אַפַּיִם,
〈 to anger, 〈 Slow 《 and Gracious,〈 Compassionate 〈 God, 〈 HASHEM, 〈 HASHEM,

וְרַב חֶסֶד, וֶאֱמֶת, נֹצֵר חֶסֶד לָאֲלָפִים, נֹשֵׂא עָוֹן,
〈 of 〈 Forgiver 《 for thousands 〈 of 〈 Preserver 《 and 〈 in 〈 and
iniquity, [of generations], kindness Truth, Kindness Abundant

וָפֶשַׁע, וְחַטָּאָה, וְנַקֵּה.² וְסָלַחְתָּ לַעֲוֹנֵנוּ וּלְחַטָּאתֵנוּ
《 and our sins, 〈 our 〈 May You 《 and Who 〈 and inadvertent 〈 willful sin,
iniquities forgive absolves. sin,

וּנְחַלְתָּנוּ.³ סְלַח לָנוּ אָבִינוּ כִּי חָטָאנוּ, מְחַל לָנוּ
〈 us, 〈 pardon 《 we have 〈 for 《 our Father, 〈 us, 〈 Forgive 《 and make us
sinned; Your heritage

מַלְכֵּנוּ כִּי פָשָׁעְנוּ. כִּי אַתָּה אֲדֹנָי טוֹב וְסַלָּח, וְרַב
〈 and 《 and 〈 are 〈 O Lord, 〈 You, 〈 For 《 we have 〈 for 《 our King,
abundantly forgiving, good willfully sinned.

חֶסֶד לְכָל קֹרְאֶיךָ.⁴
《 who call upon You. 〈 to all 〈 kind

לָמָה יהוה תַּעֲמֹד בְּרָחוֹק, תַּעְלִים לְעִתּוֹת בַּצָּרָה.⁵
《 of 〈 in times 〈 do You con- 《 at a 〈 do You 〈 HASHEM, 〈 Why,
trouble? ceal Yourself distance, stand

---

(1) *Exodus* 34:5. (2) 34:6-7. (3) 34:9. (4) *Psalms* 86:5. (5) 10:1.

לָמָּה פָנֶיךָ תַסְתִּיר, תִּשְׁכַּח עָנְיֵנוּ וְלַחֲצֵנוּ.[1] וְאַל

‹ Why ‹ Your ‹‹ do You ‹ [why] do ‹ our ‹‹ and our ‹ Do
   face   conceal;   You forget   affliction   oppression?   not

תַּסְתֵּר פָּנֶיךָ מֵעַבְדֶּךָ; כִּי צַר לִי, מַהֵר עֲנֵנִי.[2] עֲנֵנוּ

‹ hide ‹ Your ‹‹ from Your ‹ because ‹‹ I am ‹‹ quickly ‹‹ answer ‹Answer
       face   servant,   distressed,   me.   me

יהוה כִּי טוֹב חַסְדֶּךָ, כְּרֹב רַחֲמֶיךָ פְּנֵה אֵלֵינוּ.[3]

‹ HASHEM, ‹ for ‹ good‹ is Your ‹‹ according to ‹ of Your ‹ turn ‹‹ toward
               kindness; the abundance mercy   us.

אַל יָשֹׁב דַּךְ נִכְלָם, עָנִי וְאֶבְיוֹן יְהַלְלוּ שְׁמֶךָ.[4]

‹ Let ‹ be turned ‹‹ the oppressed ‹ in ‹‹ let the ‹ and the ‹ destitute ‹‹ Your
  not   back   shame,   poor   praise   Name.

כְּרַחֵם אָב עַל בָּנִים, כֵּן תְּרַחֵם יהוה עָלֵינוּ.[5]

‹ As merciful as ‹ a ‹ toward ‹ his ‹‹ so ‹ have ‹ HASHEM, ‹‹ on us.
           father is   children,   mercy,

לַיהוה הַיְשׁוּעָה, עַל עַמְּךָ בִרְכָתֶךָ סֶּלָה.[6] יהוה

‹ To HASHEM ‹ is salvation, ‹‹ upon ‹ Your ‹ is Your ‹‹ Selah. ‹‹ HASHEM,
                 people   blessing,

צְבָאוֹת עִמָּנוּ, מִשְׂגָּב לָנוּ אֱלֹהֵי יַעֲקֹב סֶלָה.[7]

‹ Master of ‹‹ is with us, ‹ a ‹ for us ‹ is the God ‹ of Jacob, ‹‹ Selah.
  Legions,   stronghold

יהוה צְבָאוֹת, אַשְׁרֵי אָדָם בֹּטֵחַ בָּךְ.[8] יהוה הוֹשִׁיעָה,

‹ HASHEM ‹ Master of ‹‹ praise- ‹ man ‹ is the ‹ who ‹‹ in ‹ HASHEM, ‹‹ save!
      Legions   worthy   trusts   You.

הַמֶּלֶךְ יַעֲנֵנוּ בְיוֹם קָרְאֵנוּ.[9]

‹ May the ‹ answer us ‹ on the ‹‹ we call.
  King   day

IN MOST CONGREGATIONS THE FOLLOWING VERSES ARE RECITED ALOUD RESPONSIVELY,
AS INDICATED; IN OTHERS THEY ARE RECITED SILENTLY.

CONGREGATION, ALOUD, FOLLOWED BY *CHAZZAN*, ALOUD:

סְלַח נָא לַעֲוֹן הָעָם הַזֶּה כְּגֹדֶל חַסְדֶּךָ, וְכַאֲשֶׁר

‹ just as ‹‹ of Your ‹ according to ‹ of this people ‹ the ‹ please, ‹ Forgive,
          kindness,   the greatness   iniquity

נָשָׂאתָה לָעָם הַזֶּה מִמִּצְרַיִם וְעַד הֵנָּה,[10] וְשָׁם נֶאֱמַר:

‹‹ it was ‹ And ‹‹ now. ‹ until ‹ from Egypt ‹ this people ‹ You have
   said: there   forgiven

(1) *Psalms* 44:25. (2) 69:18. (3) Cf. 69:17. (4) 74:21. (5) Cf. 103:13.
(6) 3:9. (7) 46:8. (8) 84:13. (9) 20:10. (10) *Numbers* 14:19.

ALL, ALOUD AND IN UNISON:

וַיֹּאמֶר יהוה סָלַחְתִּי כִּדְבָרֶךָ.[1]

《 according 〈 I have forgiven 《 And HASHEM said:
to your word!

ALL CONTINUE:

הַטֵּה אֱלֹהַי אָזְנְךָ וּשְׁמָע, פְּקַח עֵינֶיךָ וּרְאֵה
〈 and see 〈 Your eyes 〈 open 《 and listen; 〈 Your ear, 〈 my God, 〈 Incline,

שֹׁמְמֹתֵינוּ, וְהָעִיר אֲשֶׁר נִקְרָא שִׁמְךָ עָלֶיהָ, כִּי לֹא
〈 not 〈 for 《 upon; 〈 Your Name is 〈 which 〈 and that 〈 our desolation
proclaimed [of] the city

עַל צִדְקֹתֵינוּ אֲנַחְנוּ מַפִּילִים תַּחֲנוּנֵינוּ לְפָנֶיךָ,
《 before 〈 our 〈 cast 〈 do we 〈 of our 〈 because
You; supplications righteousness

כִּי עַל רַחֲמֶיךָ הָרַבִּים. אֲדֹנָי שְׁמָעָה, אֲדֹנָי סְלָחָה,
《 forgive; 〈 O Lord, 《 heed; 〈 O Lord, 《 which is 〈 of Your 〈 be- 〈 but
abundant. compassion, cause

אֲדֹנָי הַקְשִׁיבָה, וַעֲשֵׂה אַל תְּאַחַר, לְמַעַנְךָ אֱלֹהַי,
《 my God, 〈 for Your sake, 《 delay; 〈 do not 《 and act, 〈 be attentive, 〈 O Lord,

כִּי שִׁמְךָ נִקְרָא עַל עִירְךָ וְעַל עַמֶּךָ.[2]
《 Your 〈 and 〈 Your 〈 upon 〈 is 〈 Your 〈 for
people. upon City proclaimed Name

סליחה יא / SELICHAH 11

ALL:

אֱלֹהֵינוּ וֵאלֹהֵי אֲבוֹתֵינוּ:
《 of our forefathers: 〈 and God 〈 Our God

אֲנִי יוֹם אִירָא* אֵלֶיךָ[3] אֶקְרָא,
《 I call, 〈 to You 〈 I am 〈 on 〈 I,
afraid,* the day

בַּל יַעַשְׁקוּנִי זֵדִים[4] עוֹזְבֵי יְקָרָה,
《 forsakers of the 〈 should the 〈 exploit me 〈 that
precious [Torah]. willful sinners, not

---

(1) *Numbers* 14:20. (2) *Daniel* 9:18-19. (3) Cf. *Psalms* 56:4. (4) Cf. 119:122.

אֲנִי יוֹם אִירָא § — *I, on the day I am afraid.*
This *selichah* was written by R' Shlomo Ha-
Bavli [see prefatory comment to *Selichah* 2],

whose name appears in the acrostic, after the
aleph-beis — שְׁלֹמֹה הַקָּטָן יִגְדַּל בְּתוֹרָה, *Shlomo
the lesser, may he become great in Torah.*

גְּמוּל לְהָשִׁיב לָהֶם, שֵׁב לְבַקְּרָה,[1]

‹ to examine ‹ [when] ‹‹ to them, ‹ pay back ‹ What they
[in judgment] you] sit   deserve

דִּין רָשָׁע וְעַוָּל, מְלוֹאָם[2] יְקְרָא.*

‹‹ they ‹ that in their ‹ and wicked ‹ of the ‹ the
proclaim.*   councils   ones   evil   decrees

הַחוֹשְׁבִים לְהַשְׁכִּיחַ שֵׁם[3] קֹדֶשׁ הַנִּכְבָּד,

‹‹ that is ‹ of ‹ the ‹ to make ‹ They plot
revered,   holiness   Name   [us] forget

וּלְהַרְגִּיל שֵׁם טֻמְאָה נְקֵלָה וְנֶעֱבָד,*[4]

‹‹ idolatry.* ‹ of vile ‹ of ‹ to a ‹ and to
        defilement, name   accustom [us]

זֶה דַרְכָּם, טוֹבֵי עַם אָבָד,

‹‹ has been ‹ of our ‹ the ‹ method ‹ Through
lost;   people   best   of theirs,   this

חֲשֹׂךְ הַשְׁאָר מִכַּתְּשָׁם בְּבֵית הַבָּד.

‹‹ in the olive press. ‹ from being crushed ‹ the remnant ‹ save

טְרֹף טֶרֶף אָדָם, לִמְּדוּ[5] כִּמְדֻבָּר,[6]

‹‹ as stated [by ‹ they have ‹ of men ‹ their ‹ To tear
the prophet].   learned,   prey   apart

יַדּוּ גוֹרָל* כְּעַל הֶפְקֵר בַּמִּדְבָּר,

‹‹ in the ‹ a thing left ‹ as if ‹ lots,* ‹ [And]
desert.   ownerless   for   they cast

---

(1) Cf. *Lamentations* 3:64. (2) Cf. *Job* 36:17. (3) Cf. *Jeremiah* 23:27. (4) Cf. *Proverbs* 12:9.
(5) Some editions read לְמְדוּ, *they have been taught.* (6) Cf. *Ezekiel* 19:3.

דִּין רָשָׁע וְעַוָּל מְלוֹאָם יְקְרָא — *The decrees of the evil and wicked ones that in their councils they proclaim.* The translation follows *Arugas HaBosem* and alludes to the anti-Semitic decrees to which the composer was a witness. Others translate this stich as a supplication: *Let the sentence of the wicked and the evildoers be proclaimed in full.* A third opinion repunctuates the verse and synthesizes the first two interpretations: דִּין רָשָׁע, *Let the wicked decree,* וְעַוָּל מְלוֹאָם, *and the evil of their councils,* יְקְרָא, *be proclaimed [against them].*

וּלְהַרְגִּיל שֵׁם טֻמְאָה נְקֵלָה וְנֶעֱבָד — *And to accustom [us] to a name of defilement, of vile idolatry.* One of the most heavily censored stiches in all of the *selichos,* this line is omitted entirely in some editions, and altered in many others. One edition went so far as to rewrite the entire verse: וַאֲנַחְנוּ שֵׁם אֱלֹהֵינוּ נַזְכִּיר לְבָד, *But we mention only the Name of our God.* In most emended versions, however, the words שֵׁם טֻמְאָה, *an unclean name,* are replaced by either שֵׁם אַחֵר, *another's name,* or שֵׁם אֱלִיל, *an idol's name.*

The literal meaning of נְקֵלָה is *despised,* while the word וְנֶעֱבָד has been translated as *worshiped* or *manufactured by man.* In some editions the word is spelled וְנָאֱבָד and means *and ruined;* still other versions read וְנֶעֱכָר, *and murky.*

יַדּוּ גוֹרָל — *[And] they cast lots.* To decide who would get Jerusalem (*Obadiah* 1:11), who would enslave its honored citizens

בִּמְעַט כִּלּוּ, וְלֹא יַעַדְּרוּ דָבָר,[1]

« any ‹ and indeed « destroyed‹ They
means, they did not lack [us], almost

לוּלֵי רַחֲמֶיךָ, אָדוֹן בְּחֶסֶד דַּבֵּר.

« leads. ‹ Who with ‹ Lord ‹ for Your ‹ were it
kindness mercy, not

מִי יְהַרְהֵר אַחַר מִדּוֹתֶיךָ לְדַיְּנָה,

« or judge them? ‹ Your ways ‹ with ‹ can find fault ‹ Who

נִכְחֲךָ לְהָשִׁיב מֵחֲלָצָיו לְזַיְּנָה,

« gird with ‹ [who] would ‹ to argue ‹ Or against
strength? himself You

סַרְנוּ וְסֹעַרְנוּ,* וְנִשְׁמְטָה חֶרֶב הַיּוֹנָה.*[2]

« that is blood- ‹ was the ‹ and drawn « and we have ‹ We have turned
intoxicated as [enemy's] been storm away [from the
from wine.* sword tossed,* Torah],

עִמְּךָ הַדִּין, וְיָדְךָ עַל הָעֶלְיוֹנָה.

« is ascendant. ‹ and Your « is ‹With You
hand justice,

פֶּן יֹאמַר יָכֹלְתִּי,[3] בַּעַל הַמּוֹט,

« of the club; ‹ shall the « I overcame! ‹ proclaim ‹ Lest
master

צָרֵי יְהוּדָה יָגִילוּ כִּי אֶמּוֹט,[4]

« I falter. ‹ when‹ rejoice ‹ of ‹ [lest] the
Judah tormenters

קְרָא לִמְכוּרֵי חִנָּם,* שְׁנַת שְׁמוֹט,

« of ‹ the ‹ for ‹ for those who ‹ Proclaim
remission, year nothing* were sold

---

(1) I Kings 5:7. (2) Jeremiah 46:16. (3) Cf. Ezekiel 19:3. (4) Cf. Psalms 13:5.

(Nahum 3:10), and who would rule over Israel in general (Joel 4:3).

וְסֹעַרְנוּ — And we have been storm tossed. The translation follows Arugas HaBosem. According to Rashi (to Isaiah 54:11), the word may be rendered, [our hearts] have become turbulent.

חֶרֶב הַיּוֹנָה — Was the [enemy's] sword that is blood-intoxicated as from wine. The translation follows Targum and Rashi's primary interpretation (to Jeremiah 46:16), who derive יוֹנָה from יַיִן, wine, and paraphrase, the enemy's sword that is blood-

intoxicated as from wine. According to Radak and Rashi's secondary interpretation, the word is related to אוֹנָאָה and means oppressive.

לִמְכוּרֵי חִנָּם — For those who were sold for nothing; they gained nothing from the sinfulness that caused God to give them over into the hands of their captors (Rashi to Isaiah 52:3). Alternatively, He gave them over to their captors, not for money but as punishment for their sins. Thus, as the verse there continues, they cannot be redeemed with money, but only with repentance (Radak).

רָשָׁע הַפּוֹשֵׁט יָד, יִסֹּג אָחוֹר וְיִקְמֹט.

《 and shrivels. 〈 falls back 〈 a hand [to hit] 〈 who extends 〈 while the evil one

שְׁטָרְךָ קוֹדֵם וְלוֹ נוֹשִׁים מְבַקְשִׁים,

《 who demand [payment of their debt]; 〈 creditors 〈 they have 《 predates [all others], 〈 Although Your contract of indebtedness

שֶׁעֲבוּדָךְ לְהַרְחִיק, רַבּוּ צוֹרְרִים קָשִׁים,

《 who are harsh! 〈 are the bitter enemies 〈 so many 《 [they attempt] to push away, 〈 Your [prior] lien [against us]

תְּחוּמֵי סְמָנֵי מִצְרֶיךָ, לַעֲקֹר מְבַקְשִׁים,

《 they seek, 〈 to uproot 《 of Your domain [the Torah], 〈 markers [the mitzvos] 〈 The boundary-

תְּבוּאָה קִדַּשְׁתָּ,¹ בְּלוֹעָהּ מְלִילוֹת וְקָשִׁים.*

《 as well as straw.* 〈 kernels of grain 〈 [they seek] to swallow up, 《 that You sanctified, 〈 and the wheat [Israel]

שְׁפֶט רָעָה, תָּבֹא עֲלֵיהֶם וְהַאֲשִׁימֵם,¹

《 and find them guilty. 〈 upon them 〈 come 〈 for their evil 〈 [With] justice

לָמוֹ עוֹלֵל, וְהִתְעוֹלֵל בְּכֹבֶד יְשִׁימֵם,²

《 You devastate them. 〈 as heavily 〈 and taunt them 〈 do [as they did to us,] 〈 To them

מְנָת כּוֹסָם,* פַּחֲיֵי מִפַּח הַגְּשִׁימֵם,³

《 rain down on them; 〈 of despair 〈 coals 〈 of their cup [of retribution],* 〈 The measure

הֲשִׁיבֵם שִׁבְעָתָיִם,*⁴ נְקַם בְּרִית⁵ וְהַשְׁמֵם.

《 and devastate them. 〈 of the covenant, 〈 the vengeance 《 sevenfold* 〈 repay

---

(1) Cf. *Jeremiah* 2:3. (2) Cf. *I Samuel* 5:6. (3) Cf. *Psalms* 11:6. (4) Cf. 79:12. (5) *Leviticus* 26:25.

מְלִילוֹת וְקָשִׁים — *Kernels of grain as well as straw.* The word מְלִילוֹת refers to the kernels that have been completely separated from the shells and other forms of chaff. Thus, it alludes to the righteous *tzaddikim* who have succeeded in winning their freedom from the *klippos* (spiritual shells) and the *Yetzer Hara* (Evil Inclination) that prevent man from fulfilling his soul's potential. קָשִׁים, *straw,* has been emptied of its grain and represents those who are devoid of *mitzvos.* The *paytan* intimates that the anti-Semite is not selective in choosing which Jews to oppress; he will persecute the good along with the bad, the observant along with the irreligious.

מְנָת כּוֹסָם ... שִׁבְעָתָיִם — *The measure of their cup [of retribution] ... sevenfold.* The stiches seem to contradict each other. First we pray that they be punished according to *the measure of their cup,* i.e., in equal measure to their acts against us. But then we ask that they be paid back *sevenfold!* Moreover, since it is axiomatic

❖ הָעִיר קִרְיַת טִירַת נָוֶךְ, נַהֲלֵנוּ,

《 lead us, 〈 of Your 〈 of the 〈 metropolis 〈 To the city
            abode,   tower   [Jerusalem],

יַם גְּאוּלִים דֶּרֶךְ לַעֲבֹר קְהָלֵנוּ,

《 may our 〈 so that 〈 a way, 〈 for the 〈 [make
gathered people. pass through   redeemed the] sea

בְּךָ תוֹחַלְתֵּנוּ, וְאַתָּה רַב (הָאֵל) מְחוֹלְלֵנוּ,

《 Who 〈 (O God), 〈 [our] 〈 for 《 is our longing, 〈 In You
fashioned us;   Master, You are

נַחֲמֵנוּ נָא, יְהִי חַסְדְּךָ עָלֵינוּ.[1]

《 be upon 〈 Your 〈 may 《 please; 〈 comfort
   us.   kindness   us,

ALL, WHILE STANDING:

אֵל מֶלֶךְ יוֹשֵׁב עַל כִּסֵּא רַחֲמִים, מִתְנַהֵג

〈 Who acts 《 of mercy, 〈 the throne 〈 on 〈 Who sits 〈 King 〈 O God,

בַּחֲסִידוּת, מוֹחֵל עֲוֹנוֹת עַמּוֹ, מַעֲבִיר רִאשׁוֹן

〈 [sins,] one 〈 Who 《 of His 〈 the sins 〈 Who 《 with kindness,
              removes   people,   pardons

רִאשׁוֹן,[2] מַרְבֶּה מְחִילָה לְחַטָּאִים וּסְלִיחָה לַפּוֹשְׁעִים,

《 to willful 〈 and 〈 to unintentional 〈 pardon 〈 Who abun- 《 by one,
sinners,   forgiveness   sinners   dantly grants

עֹשֶׂה צְדָקוֹת עִם כָּל בָּשָׂר וָרוּחַ, לֹא כְרָעָתָם

〈 in accord 〈 — not 《 and 〈 [beings 〈 all 〈 with 〈 acts of 〈 Who
with their   spirit   of] flesh   generosity   performs
wickedness

---

(1) Cf. *Psalms* 33:22. (2) *Rosh Hashanah* 17a.

that God always punishes מִדָּה כְּנֶגֶד מִדָּה,
measure for measure, why do we pray
that He *pay them back sevenfold?* Is that
not unjust? This very contradiction also
appears in Scripture: Jeremiah prayed,
"*Pay them back their due,* HASHEM,
as they have done" (*Lamentations* 3:64),
in equal measure to their sins. But David
prayed, "*Pay back our neighbors sevenfold*" (*Psalms* 79:12). The Midrash
(*Yalkut Shimoni* to *Psalms* 79:12 citing
Midrash Eichah) explains: There is no
contradiction. Jeremiah was referring to
the oppressive nations' acts against Israel,

"*Pay them back their due, as they have
done [to us],*" while David spoke of their
sins against the Torah, which is described
as מְזֻקָּק שִׁבְעָתָיִם, *refined sevenfold* (ibid.
12:7).

שִׁבְעָתָיִם — *Sevenfold.* Although *Rashi*
usually tries to find a reason for the number seven whenever it appears in Scripture (see, e.g., *Leviticus* 26:18; *I Samuel* 2:5),
other commentaries understand the num-
ber seven as a synonym for *many* (see *Ibn
Ezra* and *Radak* ibid.); or as "a mystical
number whose secret is known to very few
people" (*Ibn Ezra* to *Numbers* 23:1).

תִּגְמוֹל. ❖ אֵל הוֹרֵיתָ לָנוּ לוֹמַר שְׁלֹשׁ עֶשְׂרֵה, וּזְכוֹר

⟨ remember ⟨ the Thirteen ⟨ to ⟨ us ⟨ You ⟨ O God, ⟨ do You
ber [Attributes of Mercy]; recite taught repay them!

לָנוּ הַיּוֹם בְּרִית שְׁלֹשׁ עֶשְׂרֵה, כְּמוֹ שֶׁהוֹדַעְתָּ לֶעָנָיו

⟨ to the humble ⟨ You made ⟨ as ⟨ of [these] Thirteen, ⟨ the ⟨ today ⟨ for us
one [Moses] known covenant

מִקֶּדֶם, כְּמוֹ שֶׁכָּתוּב, וַיֵּרֶד יהוה בֶּעָנָן וַיִּתְיַצֵּב עִמּוֹ

⟨ with ⟨ and stood ⟨ in a ⟨ And HASHEM ⟨ it is written: ⟨ as ⟨ in ancient
him cloud descended times,

שָׁם, וַיִּקְרָא בְשֵׁם יהוה.[1]

⟨ of ⟨ with the ⟨ and He ⟨ there,
HASHEM. Name called out

CONGREGATION, THEN CHAZZAN:

וַיַּעֲבֹר יהוה עַל פָּנָיו וַיִּקְרָא:

⟨ and ⟨ [Moses'] ⟨ before ⟨ And HASHEM passed
proclaimed: face,

CONGREGATION AND CHAZZAN RECITE LOUDLY AND IN UNISON:

יהוה, יהוה, אֵל, רַחוּם, וְחַנּוּן, אֶרֶךְ אַפַּיִם,

⟨ to anger, ⟨ Slow ⟨ and ⟨ Compassionate ⟨ God, ⟨ HASHEM, ⟨ HASHEM,
Gracious,

וְרַב חֶסֶד, וֶאֱמֶת, נֹצֵר חֶסֶד לָאֲלָפִים, נֹשֵׂא עָוֹן,

⟨ of ⟨ Forgiver ⟨ for thousands ⟨ of ⟨ Preserver ⟨ and ⟨ in ⟨ and
iniquity, [of generations], kindness Truth, Kindness Abundant

וָפֶשַׁע, וְחַטָּאָה, וְנַקֵּה.[2] וְסָלַחְתָּ לַעֲוֹנֵנוּ וּלְחַטָּאתֵנוּ

⟨ and our sins, ⟨ our ⟨ May You ⟨ and Who ⟨ and inadvertent ⟨ willful sin,
iniquities forgive absolves. sin,

וּנְחַלְתָּנוּ.[3] סְלַח לָנוּ אָבִינוּ כִּי חָטָאנוּ, מְחַל לָנוּ

⟨ us, ⟨ pardon ⟨ we have ⟨ for ⟨ our ⟨ us, ⟨ Forgive ⟨ and make us
sinned; Father, Your heritage.

מַלְכֵּנוּ כִּי פָשָׁעְנוּ. כִּי אַתָּה אֲדֹנָי טוֹב וְסַלָּח,

⟨ and ⟨ are ⟨ O Lord, ⟨ You, ⟨ For ⟨ we have ⟨ for ⟨ our King,
forgiving, good willfully sinned.

וְרַב חֶסֶד לְכָל קֹרְאֶיךָ.[4]

⟨ who call ⟨ to all ⟨ kind ⟨ and
upon You. abundantly

(1) *Exodus* 34:5. (2) 34:6-7. (3) 34:9. (4) *Psalms* 86:5.

פסוקי הקדמה לסליחה יב / PREFATORY VERSES TO SELICHAH 12

הַבֵּט מִשָּׁמַיִם וּרְאֵה מִזְּבֻל קָדְשְׁךָ וְתִפְאַרְתֶּךָ,

‹ and splendor; › ‹ of holiness › ‹ from Your abode › ‹ and see › ‹ from Heaven › ‹ Look down

אַיֵּה קִנְאָתְךָ וּגְבוּרֹתֶיךָ, הֲמוֹן מֵעֶיךָ וְרַחֲמֶיךָ

‹ and Your mercy › ‹ of Your inner [feelings] › ‹ The yearnings › « and Your might? › ‹ Your zealousness › ‹ where is

אֵלֵינוּ הִתְאַפָּקוּ.¹ אַתָּה פוֹרַרְתָּ בְעָזְּךָ יָם, שִׁבַּרְתָּ

‹ You smashed › « the sea; › ‹ with Your might › ‹ shattered › ‹ You « ‹ withheld. › ‹ are from us

רָאשֵׁי תַנִּינִים עַל הַמָּיִם.² אִם עֲוֹנֵינוּ עָנוּ

‹ testify › ‹ our iniquities › ‹ Even if › « the water. › ‹ upon › ‹ of sea serpents [Egyptians] › ‹ the heads

בָּנוּ, יהוה עֲשֵׂה לְמַעַן שְׁמֶךָ.³

« of Your Name. › ‹ for the sake › ‹ act › ‹ HASHEM, « ‹ against us,

כְּרַחֵם אָב עַל בָּנִים, כֵּן תְּרַחֵם יהוה עָלֵינוּ.⁴

« on us. › ‹ HASHEM, › ‹ have mercy, › ‹ so « ‹ his children, › ‹ toward › ‹ a father is › ‹ As merciful as

לַיהוה הַיְשׁוּעָה, עַל עַמְּךָ בִרְכָתֶךָ סֶּלָה.⁵ יהוה

‹ HASHEM, « ‹ Selah. « ‹ is Your blessing, › ‹ Your people › ‹ upon « ‹ is salvation, › ‹ To HASHEM

צְבָאוֹת עִמָּנוּ, מִשְׂגָּב לָנוּ אֱלֹהֵי יַעֲקֹב סֶלָה.⁶

« Selah. « ‹ of Jacob, › ‹ is the God › ‹ for us › ‹ a stronghold « ‹ is with us, › ‹ Master of Legions,

יהוה צְבָאוֹת, אַשְׁרֵי אָדָם בֹּטֵחַ בָּךְ.⁷ יהוה הוֹשִׁיעָה,

« save! › ‹ HASHEM, « in You. › ‹ who trusts › ‹ is the man › ‹ — praise-worthy « ‹ Master of Legions › ‹ HASHEM,

הַמֶּלֶךְ יַעֲנֵנוּ בְיוֹם קָרְאֵנוּ.⁸

« we call. › ‹ on the day › ‹ answer us › ‹ May the King

---

(1) Cf. *Isaiah* 63:15. (2) *Psalms* 74:13. (3) *Jeremiah* 14:7.
(4) Cf. *Psalms* 103:13. (5) 3:9 (6) 46:8. (7) 84:13. (8) 20:10.

סליחה יב / SELICHAH 12

ALL:

אֱלֹהֵינוּ וֵאלֹהֵי אֲבוֹתֵינוּ:

《 of our forefathers: 〈 and God 〈 Our God

אַיֵּה כָל נִפְלְאוֹתֶיךָ* הַגְּדוֹלוֹת וְהַנּוֹרָאוֹת,

〈 and that are 〈 that are great 〈 Your wonders* 〈 all 〈 Where
awesome, are

אֲשֶׁר סִפְּרוּ לָנוּ אֲבוֹתֵינוּ,[1] יהוה צְבָאוֹת,

《 Master of 〈 O 《 did our fathers, 〈 to us 〈 tell 〈 that
Legions? HASHEM,

בְּרֶדֶת יִשְׂרָאֵל מִצְרַיְמָה בְּשִׁעְבּוּד וּתְלָאוֹת,

《 and 〈 into slavery 〈 to Egypt 〈 did Israel 〈 When
tribulations, descend

בְּחַבְלֵי אָדָם מְשַׁכְתָּם[2] וְלֹא בְשַׁלְשְׁלָאוֹת.*

《 with chains.* 〈 and 〈 You drew them 〈 that were 〈 with ropes
not [to Egypt], humane

---

(1) Cf. *Judges* 6:13. (2) Cf. *Hosea* 11:4.

אַיֵּה כָּל נִפְלְאוֹתֶיךָ — *Where are all Your wonders?* This *selichah* contains an alphabetical acrostic, followed by the *paytan*'s signature — גֵּרְשׁם בַּר יְהוּדָה, *Gershom bar Yehudah*. Better known as Rabbeinu Gershom Meor HaGolah [Light of the Diaspora], he lived in Mainz, Germany, in the early part of the 11th century and maintained a yeshivah there. He was also a member of that city's *beis din* together with R' Shimon HaGadol [see prefatory comment to *Selichah* 53].

R' Gershom's best-known contributions are the enactments adopted by rabbinic synods at his behest, and accepted as law throughout Ashkenazic Jewry, and in some instances by the entire Diaspora. Two of these enactments have had a profound effect upon Jewish family life. They are his bans against polygamy and against divorce without the wife's consent. He also prohibited the shaming of those who renounced Judaism under duress, once they had returned to the Jewish fold.

This last enactment was necessitated by the common Christian tactic of forcibly converting Jews by threatening them with death or expulsion. Halachah requires Jews to submit to death rather than renounce their faith. Indeed, entire Jewish communities in Germany and France gave up their lives to sanctify God's Name. But some individuals were unable to withstand the test. R' Gershom's only son was compelled to convert to Christianity, and when he died soon after without having had the chance to return to his faith, R' Gershom observed a two-week period of mourning: one week for the loss of his life, and another for the loss of his soul.

The terrible suffering of his people in those times is depicted in R' Gershom's *selichos*.

בְּחַבְלֵי אָדָם מְשַׁכְתָּם וְלֹא בְשַׁלְשְׁלָאוֹת — *With ropes that were humane* [lit., *cords of man*] *You drew them [to Egypt], and not with chains.* Rabban Yochanan taught that the Patriarch Jacob actually should have descended to Egypt in iron chains [since his descent was the fulfillment of the decree of exile, foretold to Abraham at the Covenant Between the Parts (*Genesis* 15:13)]. However, his personal merits rescued him

גַּם מַעֲבִידֵיהֶם בְּקָשֶׁה עֲבוֹדָה,

⟨ labor, ⟨ at hard ⟨ those who ⟨ Also
enslaved them

גָּזְרוּ בַּיְאוֹר זְכוּרֵיהֶם לְאַבְּדָה,

《 should be ⟨ their sons ⟨ that in ⟨ [and] who
destroyed — the Nile commanded

דַּנְתָּם בְּסָאסְאָה,*1 מִדָּה בְמִדָּה,

《 for ⟨ measure 《 bushel ⟨ You judged
measure, for bushel,* them,

דְּגָלִים הוֹצֵאתָ, בִּרְכוּשׁ כָּל חֲמְדָה.

《 that [to the ⟨ — all 《 [laden] ⟨ You brought ⟨ [and] the
Egyptians] was with wealth out bannered
precious. [tribes]

הַיָּם וְגַלָּיו בְּעָזְּךָ פּוֹרֲרוּ,2

《 were ⟨ by Your ⟨ and its ⟨ The sea
shattered; might waves

הַיַּרְדֵּן הוֹבַשְׁתָּ, וּבְרֶגֶל עָבֳרוּ,3

《 [the tribes] ⟨ and on ⟨ You dried up, ⟨ The Jordan
crossed it. foot

וּבַמִּדְבָּר כִּלְכַּלְתָּם, וְדָבָר לֹא חָסֵרוּ,4

《 were they ⟨ and nothing ⟨ You sustained ⟨ In the desert
lacking, them

וּמַמְלָכוֹת וַעֲמָמִים בְּיָדָם נִמְסָרוּ.5

《 were ⟨ into their ⟨ and peoples ⟨ and kingdoms
delivered. hand

---

(1) Cf. *Isaiah* 27:8; some editions of *Selichos* read סְאָה בְּסָאָה (see commentary).
(2) Cf. *Psalms* 74:13. (3) Cf. *Joshua* 5:1. (4) Cf. *Nehemiah* 9:21. (5) Cf. 9:22.

---

from that ignominious fate. Thus, the prophet (*Hosea* 11:4) states, *"I drew them with cords of man, with bands of love ..."* (*Shabbos* 89b).

The Midrash explains Jacob's honorable descent to Egypt with a parable. A cow stubbornly refused to follow its owner to the slaughterhouse. So he led her calf there instead. When the cow saw her calf being led away, she quickly went after it. Thus her owner was able to bring her to the slaughterhouse without having to drag her against her will. Similarly, when God wanted Jacob to leave the Holy Land

and go into the Egyptian exile, He first sent Joseph, Jacob's favorite son, down to Egypt. Then Jacob offered no resistance and did not have to go down in chains (*Bereishis Rabbah* 86:2).

בְּסָאסְאָה — *Bushel for bushel.* The Talmud adduces a Scriptural verse (*Isaiah* 27:8) as proof that God recompenses man's deeds in the same measure as they are performed: בְּסָאסְאָה בְּשַׁלְחָהּ תְּרִיבֶנָּה, *When You banish her, You demand her measure from her* (*Sotah* 8b). The word בְּסָאסְאָה is thus to be understood as if it were written סְאָה בְּסָאָה, *bushel for bushel,* i.e., measure for measure.

זָנְחוּ הַטּוֹב,* וּרְדָפוּם¹ מַכְנִיעִים,

《 did subjugating 〈 and pursue 〈 the Good 〈 They
nations;   them   One,*   spurned

זְעָקוּךְ וְשָׁמַעְתָּ, וְהֶעֱמַדְתָּ לָהֶם מוֹשִׁיעִים,

《   rescuers. 〈 for 〈 and 《 and 〈 they called
   them   established   You heard,   to You,

חָנוּ בְאַרְצָם כָּל טוּב שְׂבֵעִים,

《 they were 〈 that is 〈 with 《 in their 〈 They
  sated;   good   everything   land;   settled

חָטְאוּ וְגָלוּ וּפְקַדְתָּם לְשִׁבְעִים.

《 after seventy 〈 until You 〈 and 〈 [then]
  years.   remembered   were   they
    them   exiled   sinned,

טָפְלוּ שֶׁקֶר² וְנִתְּנוּ לְמִרְמָס,

《 to be 〈 and were 〈 with false 〈 They as-
  trampled;   consigned   [ideologies]   sociated

טֹרְדוּם לְמַדְחֵפוֹת אַנְשֵׁי חָמָס,³

《 who were 〈 by men 〈 pushed out 〈 they were
  violent.   [into exile]   chased away,

יָצְאוּ מֵאַרְצָם וְקֵץ חֲזָרָתָם נִכְמָס,

《 remains hidden 〈 of their 〈 but the 〈 from their 〈 They
  [from them],   return   date   land,   went out

יָשְׁבוּ בַגּוֹיִם וְהָיוּ לָמַס.⁴

《 payers of 〈 and 〈 among the 〈 they
  tribute.   became   nations   dwelt

כֹּחַ אַמֵּץ פְּלֵיטָה הַנִּשְׁאֶרֶת,

《 that survives, 〈 of the 〈 fortify 〈 The
    remnant   strength

בָּשַׁל כֹּחָהּ, מִכֹּבֶד רָעָה מַמְאֶרֶת,

《 that is 〈 of evil 〈 by the 〈 is its 〈 for
  malignant.   burden   strength   exhausted

---

(1) Cf. *Hosea* 8:3. (2) Cf. *Psalms* 119:69. (3) Cf. *140:12.* (4) Cf. *Lamentations* 1:3,1.

הַטּוֹב — *The Good One.* The translation follows *Ibn Ezra* and *Radak* (to *Hosea* 8:3) and is based upon Hezekiah's prayer (*II Chronicles* 30:18), *May* HASHEM, *the Good One, forgive ....* According to *Targum Yonasan* (*Hosea* 8:3), the word הַטּוֹב, *the good,* alludes to the Divine service that

is rewarded with God's beneficence and bounty. By rejecting the service, they cut themselves off from the flow of heavenly *goodness* that had sustained them. *Matteh Levi* understands הַטּוֹב as a reference to the Torah, which is described as לֶקַח טוֹב, *a good teaching* (*Proverbs* 4:2).

לְעֵת רִאשׁוֹנָה פְּקוּדָה מְשֻׁאֶרֶת,¹

《 still remains, 〈 calamity 〈 that [the pain of]〈 At the
the first   time

לָבֹא שְׁנִיָּה אָצָה וּמְמַהֶרֶת.²

《 and hurries. 〈 rushes 〈 of the 〈 the
second   advent

מֵעֵת לְעֵת צָרָתִי מִרְבָּה,

《 increases; 〈 my pain 〈 to 〈 From
moment   moment

מִיּוֹם שֶׁעָבַר קָשֶׁה הַבָּא,

《 of the one 〈 is the 《 that 〈 for more than
to come. harshness passed, of the day

נִלְאֵיתִי נִשֹׂא עַל מַדְהֵבָה,

《 the gold- 〈 the yoke 〈 with 〈 I am worn out
extorting nation, [of Babylon,] bearing

נוֹאֶמֶת מִדֹּד וְהָבֵא הֲבָאָה רַבָּה.*

《 that is 〈 an offering 〈 and 〈 Measure 《 [as] the
large!*   bring [your gold] [conquerors]
declaim,

סְגֻלָּתְךָ דוֹחֵק צוֹרֵר הַצָּר,

《 who 〈 by the 〈 is being 〈 Your most
oppresses, oppressor coerced beloved treasure [Israel]

סִבְרָהּ, לְהָמִיר בַּאֲמָנַת נוֹצָר,³*

《 in a created 〈 for belief 〈 to exchange 〈 her Hope,
being.*   [God,]

---

(1) Some editions read מְשֻׁמֶּרֶת, *guarded*. (2) Cf. *Sanhedrin* 97a. (3) The two stiches beginning
with the letter ס have been the targets of heavy censorship (see commentary); some editions
omit one or both of these lines (yet, strangely, include them in the Yiddish translation); some
read, סִבְרָהּ ,סְגֻלָּתְךָ דּוֹחֶקֶת קְדָּשֶׁתְךָ מִלִּנְצוֹר, *Your precious one is pushed to stop guarding Your laws,*
לְהָמִיר כְּבוֹדְךָ בְּעֵת צָר [*The enemy*] *hoped* [*Israel*] *would exchange Your glory in* (*times of*) *stress;*
others read, סְגֻלָּתְךָ קוֹרְאִים בַּצָּר, *Your precious ones call out from the straits,* סִבְרָם לָאֵל בּוֹרֵא וְיוֹצֵר,
Their hope is to God, Creator and Maker.

עַל מַדְהֵבָה — *The yoke*
of [Babylon,] *...* מִדֹּד וְהָבֵא הֲבָאָה רַבָּה
of [Babylon,] *the gold-extorting nation ...*
"*Measure* [*your gold*] *and bring an offer-*
ing that is large!" The prophet (*Isaiah* 14:4)
refers to Babylon as מַדְהֵבָה, a word most
commentaries understand as *abundant with*
gold, from the Aramaic דַּהֲבָה, *gold*. The Talmud interprets it as a play on words: מַדְהֵבָה
is the nation that exclaims, "מְדוֹד וְהָבֵא,
Weigh out and bring!" Alternatively, "מְאֹד

מְאֹד הָבִיא בְּלֹא מִדָּה, *Bring very very much,*
without measure!" (*Shabbos* 149b).

סִבְרָהּ לְהָמִיר בַּאֲמָנַת נוֹצָר — *Her Hope,* [*God,*]
to exchange for belief in a created being.
See footnote for various censored versions
of this stich. According to *Arugas Ha-*
Bosem, the word נוֹצָר means *the Nazarene*
(his text reads בְּתָלוּי נוֹצָר), and the stich
refers to forced baptism and conversions
perpetrated throughout the centuries by

עַד אָנָה יהוה אֶקְרָא מִמֵּצָר,

《 from my 〈 must I 〈 O 〈 when, 〈 Until
straits? call out HASHEM,

עֲנֵנִי בַמֶּרְחָב יָהּ¹ כִּי יָדְךָ לֹא תִקְצָר.²

《 limited. 〈 is not 〈 Your 〈 for 《 O 〈 with 〈 Answer
hand God, expansiveness, me

פְּשָׁעִים אִם עָצְמוּ בֵּינִי וּבֵינְךָ לְהַבְדִּילָה,³

《 they create a divide, 〈 and 〈 that 〈 they are so 〈 — if 《 [My] sins
between between numerous
You me

פַּרְגּוֹד אִם נִנְעַל בִּפְנֵי הַתְּפִלָּה,⁴

《 [my] prayer, 〈 before 〈 it is 〈 — if 《 the Heavenly
closed Curtain

צוּר, בְּכִסֵּא כְבוֹדְךָ חֲתֹר מְחִלָּה,⁵

〈 a tunnel 〈 dig 〈 of Glory 〈 in Your Throne 《 O Rock!

צַעֲקָתֵנוּ לְפָנֶיךָ תָבֹא, פְּנֵי כְבוֹדְךָ לְהִתְקַבְּלָה.

《 be accepted. 〈 Your glory 〈 and 《 may 〈 before 〈 [so that]
before You our cry
come,

קְרָא שְׁנַת רָצוֹן,⁶ מֵעֹצֶב לְהַנְפִּישִׁי,

《 to provide 〈 [so as] 〈 of favor, 〈 a year 〈 Proclaim
me rest; from misery

קַבֵּץ נְפוּצוֹתַי וַעֲבֹר בְּרֹאשִׁי,⁷

《 [to lead] 〈 and pass 〈 my dispersed 〈 gather
at my head. ahead ones,

רִיבָה יהוה רִיבֵי נַפְשִׁי,⁸

《 of my 〈 the 〈 O 〈 Fight,
soul; battles HASHEM,

רְצֵה לְהַצִּילֵנִי,⁹ אֱלֹהֵי קָדְשִׁי.

《 my Holy 〈 O my 《 to rescue me, 〈 May it be
One. God, Your will

שִׁנֵּי רְשָׁעִים בְּחָצָץ תִּגְרֹס,¹⁰

《 shatter; 〈 with gravel 〈 of the 〈 The
wicked teeth

---

(1) Cf. *Psalms* 118:5. (2) Cf. *Numbers* 11:23; *Isaiah* 59:1. (3) Cf. 59:2.
(4) Cf. *Bava Metzia* 59a. (5) Cf. *Sanhedrin* 103a. (6) Cf. *Isaiah* 61:2. (7) Cf. *Micah* 2:12-13.
(8) Cf. *Lamentations* 3:58. (9) Cf. *Psalms* 40:14; some editions of *Selichos* read
רְצֵה לְהַחֲלִיצֵנִי, *May it be Your will to give me rest.* (10) Cf. *Lamentations* 3:16.

---

zealous missionaries. See prefatory comment to this *selichah*.

שְׁכוֹל וְאַלְמוֹן*[1] אוֹתָם תַּהֲרֹס,

《 You shall 〈 and 〈 [by] be-
destroy them.   widowhood*   reavement

תִּשְׁפֹּךְ דָּמָם אַרְצָה לָרוֹס,

《 to mix 〈 onto the 〈 their 〈 May You
[with it],   earth   blood   pour

תְּמוּתָה* הוֹתֵר[2] וּבֶאֱמוּנָה לְאֵרוֹס.[3]

《 betroth them. 〈   and with 《 spare, 〈 [those] con-
fidelity   demned to die
[for Your sake]*

גְּדוֹר פִּרְצַת סֻכַּת דָּוִד הַנֹּפֶלֶת,*[4]

《 that is fallen,* 〈 of 〈 of the 〈 the breach 〈 Repair
David   succah

רוֹמֵם קִרְיָה, עַד עָפָר מַשְׁפִּלֶת,[5]

《 has been 〈 the 〈 that 〈 the City 〈 raise up
lowered.   dust   unto   [of
Jerusalem]

שְׁבוּיָה נַחֵם, נֶחָמָה מְכֻפֶּלֶת,*[6]

《 that is 〈 with a 〈 comfort 〈 The captive
doubled:*   consolation   [nation]

מְאוֹרָהּ הָאֵר, וְתָאִיר מְאַפֶּלֶת.

《 the one in the 〈 and shine 〈 shine 〈 Her [special]
darkness [of exile].   light upon   upon them   light

---

(1) *Isaiah* 47:8. (2) Cf. *Psalms* 79:11. (3) Cf. *Hosea* 2:22. (4) *Amos* 9:11. (5) Cf. *Isaiah* 26:5. (6) Cf. 40:1.

שְׁכוֹל וְאַלְמוֹן — *[By] bereavement and wid-owhood.* The translation follows the ma-jority of the commentaries to the *Selichos*. According to *Rashi* (*Isaiah* 47:9), the phrase alludes to a land whose citizens have been exiled and whose king has been taken, for the citizens are considered the land's chil-dren and the king its husband.

תְּמוּתָה — *[Those] condemned to die [for Your sake].* The translation follows most commentaries to *Psalms* 79:11, who derive the word from מוּת, *to die.* According to *Arugas HaBosem,* the word is from תמם, *wholeness* and *perfection,* and means *the wholesome nation.*

סֻכַּת דָּוִד הַנֹּפֶלֶת — *Of the succah of David that is fallen.* This refers to the Davidic dynasty (*Targum, Rashi,* et al., to *Amos* 9:11), the *Beis HaMikdash* (*Mahari Kara,*

ibid.), or Jerusalem (*Maglei Tzedek*). This last interpretation is borne out by the stich below, בְּנֵה עִירְךָ כִּימֵי עוֹלָם, *Build Your City as in days of old,* which, without the word עִירְךָ, *Your city,* appears in the same verse in *Amos* as the phrase *the succah of David that is fallen.*

נֶחָמָה מְכֻפֶּלֶת — *With a consolation that is doubled.* The Midrash (*Pesikta*) expounds on certain double expressions found in Scrip-tures: חֵטְא חָטְאָה יְרוּשָׁלַיִם, *Jerusalem sinned doubly* (*Lamentations* 1:8), and so she was punished, כִּפְלַיִם בְּכָל חַטֹּאתֶיהָ, *double for all her sins* (*Isaiah* 40:2). בָּכוֹ תִבְכֶּה, *She cried doubly* (*Lamentations* 1:2), and so she will be doubly consoled, as it is written נַחֲמוּ נַחֲמוּ עַמִּי, *Console, console My people* (*Isaiah* 40:1).

Other expressions of double consolation appear in *Isaiah* 51: עוּרִי עוּרִי, *Awaken!*

❖ בְּנֵה עִירְךָ כִּימֵי עוֹלָם,[1]

《 of old, 〈 as in days 〈 Your City 〈 Build

רַפֵּא מִזְבַּחֲךָ[2] הֵיכָל וְאוּלָם,[3]

《 and Antechamber. 〈 Sanctuary, 〈 Your Altar, 〈 repair

יְהוּדָה וְיִשְׂרָאֵל, שָׁם יַעַבְדוּךָ כֻּלָּם,

《 — all of them, 《 shall serve You 〈 there 〈 and Israel 〈 Judah

יִגְדַּל שִׁמְךָ מֵעוֹלָם וְעַד עוֹלָם.[4]

《 eternity. 〈 until 〈 for ever 〈 Your Name 〈 [and] great will be

ALL, WHILE STANDING:

אֵל מֶלֶךְ יוֹשֵׁב עַל כִּסֵּא רַחֲמִים, מִתְנַהֵג

〈 Who acts 《 of mercy, 〈 the throne 〈 on 〈 Who sits 〈 King 〈 O God,

בַּחֲסִידוּת, מוֹחֵל עֲווֹנוֹת עַמּוֹ, מַעֲבִיר רִאשׁוֹן

〈 [sins,] one 〈 Who removes 《 Who of His 〈 the sins 〈 Who pardons 《 with kindness, people,

רִאשׁוֹן,[5] מַרְבֶּה מְחִילָה לַחַטָּאִים וּסְלִיחָה לַפּוֹשְׁעִים,

《 to willful sinners, 〈 and forgiveness 〈 to unintentional sinners 〈 pardon 〈 Who abundantly grants 《 by one,

עֹשֶׂה צְדָקוֹת עִם כָּל בָּשָׂר וָרוּחַ, לֹא כְרָעָתָם

〈 in accord with their wickedness 〈 — not 《 and spirit 〈 [beings of] flesh 〈 all 〈 with 〈 acts of generosity 〈 Who performs

תִּגְמוֹל. ❖ אֵל הוֹרֵיתָ לָּנוּ לוֹמַר שְׁלֹשׁ עֶשְׂרֵה, וּזְכוֹר

〈 remember 《 the Thirteen [Attributes of Mercy]; 〈 to recite 〈 us 〈 You taught 〈 O God, 《 do You repay them!

לָנוּ הַיּוֹם בְּרִית שְׁלֹשׁ עֶשְׂרֵה, כְּמוֹ שֶׁהוֹדַעְתָּ לֶעָנָיו

〈 to the humble one [Moses] 〈 You made 〈 as 《 of [these] Thirteen, 〈 the covenant 〈 today 〈 for us

מִקֶּדֶם, כְּמוֹ שֶׁכָּתוּב, וַיֵּרֶד יהוה בֶּעָנָן וַיִּתְיַצֵּב עִמּוֹ

〈 with him 〈 and stood 〈 in a cloud 〈 And HASHEM descended 《 it is written: 〈 as 《 in ancient times,

שָׁם, וַיִּקְרָא בְשֵׁם יהוה.[6]

《 of HASHEM. 〈 with the Name 〈 and He called out 《 there,

---

(1) Cf. *Amos* 9:11. (2) Cf. *I Kings* 18:30. (3) See 6:3.
(4) Cf. *II Samuel* 7:26. (5) *Rosh Hashanah* 17a. (6) *Exodus* 34:5.

Awaken! (v. 9); אָנֹכִי אָנֹכִי הוּא מְנַחֶמְכֶם, *I, I am*   הִתְעוֹרְרִי, *Awaken yourself! Awaken your-*
He that consoles you (v. 12); and הִתְעוֹרְרִי   *self!* (v. 17).

CONGREGATION, THEN *CHAZZAN:*

וַיַּעֲבֹר יהוה עַל פָּנָיו וַיִּקְרָא:

《 and 《 [Moses'] 〈 before 〈 And HASHEM passed
proclaimed: face,

CONGREGATION AND *CHAZZAN* RECITE LOUDLY AND IN UNISON:

יהוה, יהוה, אֵל, רַחוּם, וְחַנּוּן, אֶרֶךְ אַפַּיִם,

〈 to anger, 〈 Slow 《 and Gracious, 〈 Compassionate 〈 God, 〈 HASHEM, 〈 HASHEM,

וְרַב חֶסֶד, וֶאֱמֶת, נֹצֵר חֶסֶד לָאֲלָפִים, נֹשֵׂא עָוֹן,

〈 of 〈 Forgiver 《 for thousands 〈 of 〈 Preserver 《 and 〈 in 〈 and
iniquity,   [of generations], kindness   Truth,   Kindness Abundant

וָפֶשַׁע, וְחַטָּאָה, וְנַקֵּה.¹ וְסָלַחְתָּ לַעֲוֹנֵנוּ וּלְחַטָּאתֵנוּ

《 and our sins, 〈 our 〈 May You 《 and Who 〈 and inadvertent 〈 willful sin,
iniquities forgive absolves.   sin,

וּנְחַלְתָּנוּ.² סְלַח לָנוּ אָבִינוּ כִּי חָטָאנוּ, מְחַל לָנוּ

〈 us, 〈 pardon 《 we have 〈 for 《 our 〈 us, 〈 Forgive 《 and make us
sinned; Father, Your heritage.

מַלְכֵּנוּ כִּי פָשָׁעְנוּ. כִּי אַתָּה אֲדֹנָי טוֹב וְסַלָּח,

《 and 〈 are 〈 O Lord, 〈 You, 〈 For 《 we have 〈 for 《 our King,
forgiving, good willfully sinned.

וְרַב חֶסֶד לְכָל קֹרְאֶיךָ.³

《 who call 〈 to all 〈 kind 〈 and
upon You.   abundantly

סליחה יג / SELICHAH 13
(פזמון)

CHAZZAN, THEN CONGREGATION:

בְּאַשְׁמֹרֶת הַבֹּקֶר* קְרָאתִיךָ אֵל מְהֻלָּל,⁴

《 Who is praised; 〈 O God 〈 I call You, 《 of the morning,* 〈 At the watch

יֶעֱרַב לְךָ חִין עֶרְכִּי, יוֹם לִבִּי לְךָ סוֹלֵל,

《 extols, 〈 to 〈 that my 〈 on the 《 that is 〈 — my 《 to 〈 may it
You heart day structured — prayer You be sweet

---

(1) *Exodus* 34:6-7. (2) 34:9. (3) *Psalms* 86:5. (4) Cf. 18:4.

בְּאַשְׁמֹרֶת הַבֹּקֶר — *At the watch of the morning.* The night is divided into three (or four) periods, called מִשְׁמָרוֹת, *watches,* during which different legions of angels sing praises before the Throne of Glory (see *Berachos* 3a). The last of these periods is called

אַשְׁמֹרֶת הַבֹּקֶר (see *Exodus* 14:24 with *Rashi*), and is the ideal time for the *Selichos* prayers.

The *paytan* signed his name — יִצְחָק, *Yitzchak* — starting with the initial letters of the second line of the first stanza and the first words of the others. All we know of R'

וְתַגִּיהַּ אֶת חָשְׁכִּי[1] וּכְאוֹר בְּקֶר יְהֻלָּל,

《 it shines, 〈 of 〈 until like 〈 my darkness 〈 and
morning   light   brighten

מַלְכִּי וֵאלֹהַי כִּי אֵלֶיךָ אֶתְפַּלָּל.[2]

《 do I pray. 〈 to You 〈 for 〈 and my 〈 O my
          God,   King

CONGREGATION, THEN *CHAZZAN:*

צָרַי מַזְעִימֶיךָ בְּאַף חֵרְפוּ עַמֶּךָ,

《 Your 〈 vilify 〈 with 《 who infuriate 〈 My tor-
people,   anger   You,   mentors,

וְנָשָׂאתִי אֵימֶךָ[3] בְּרֶגֶשׁ שְׁאוֹן קָמֶיךָ,[4]

《 of Your 〈 tumult 〈 despite the 〈 [my] awe 〈 but I have
opponents.   thronging   of You   borne

שְׁפוֹךְ עֲלֵיהֶם זַעְמֶךָ וַחֲרוֹן אַף[5] מִמְּרוֹמֶיךָ,

《 from Your 〈 anger 〈 and the 《 Your fury, 〈 upon them 〈 Pour out
heights,   fierce

וְקַנֵּא אֵל לְשִׁמְךָ[6] אֲשֶׁר בַּגּוֹיִם מְחֻלָּל,[7]

《 is 〈 among the 〈 that 〈 for Your 〈 O 〈 and take
desecrated,   nations   Name   God,   vengeance,

מַלְכִּי וֵאלֹהַי כִּי אֵלֶיךָ אֶתְפַּלָּל.

《 do I pray. 〈 to You 〈 for 〈 and my 〈 O my
          God,   King

CONGREGATION, THEN *CHAZZAN:*

חַי רוֹכֵב עַל עָב קַל,[8] אִם תַּעֲלֵנִי בְּמִשְׁקָל,

《 onto a scale, 〈 You should 《 that is 〈 a 〈 upon 〈 Who 〈 O Living
lift me   swift,   cloud   rides   One,

צִדְקִי כְּחוֹל יָם יִתְקַל,[9] וְרִשְׁעִי כְּנוֹצָה יֵקַל,

《 be 〈 like a 〈 and my 〈 weigh 〈 of the 〈 [as heavy] 〈 let my right-
light;   feather   wickedness   sea   as the sand   eousness

וְאִם נְתִיב אָרְחִי מְעֻקָּל וְדִינִי כְּשׁוֹר הַנִּסְקָל, *

《 that is to 〈 is like 〈 and my 《 is crooked, 〈 of my 〈 the 〈 and if
be stoned,*   the ox   sentence   path   route

---

(1) Cf. *Psalms* 18:29. (2) 5:3. (3) Cf. 88:16. (4) 74:23. (5) Cf. 69:25.
(6) Cf. *Ezekiel* 39:25. (7) Cf. 36:23. (8) *Isaiah* 19:1. (9) Cf. *Job* 6:2-3.

Yitzchak is that he flourished some time before 1234, because his *selichah* is commented
upon in *Arugas HaBosem*, which was written in that year. Although some identify the

composer as R' Yitzchak ben Yehudah ibn
Gias of 11th-century Lucena, Spain, there is
no solid basis for this assertion.

כְּשׁוֹר הַנִּסְקָל — *Like the ox that is to be*

שְׁקְלָה בְּפֶלֶס מְהֻלָּל, אִישׁ מִפְּשָׁעִים מְחוֹלָל,*1

《 is desecrated,* 〈 who by 〈 [for I am] 《 that is 〈 on a scale 〈 then weigh
wanton sins   a man   praised,   [me]

מַלְכִּי וֵאלֹהַי כִּי אֵלֶיךָ אֶתְפַּלָּל.

《 do I pray. 〈 to You 〈 for 〈 and my 〈 O my
God,   King

CONGREGATION, THEN *CHAZZAN:*

קוֹמֵם אָרוֹן וּבַדָּיו, וְהַלְבֵּשׁ אַהֲרֹן מַדָּיו,

《 in his [priestly] 〈 Aaron 〈 and dress 《 and its 〈 the Ark 〈 Restore
garments;   poles,

וְרוֹבֶה וְצוֹדֶה* בְּצֵידָיו יֹאכַל פְּרִי מַעֲבָדָיו,

《 of his actions. 〈 the 〈 shall 〈 with his 〈 and the 〈 and the
fruit   [each]   traps,   trapper   archer
eat   [Esau]*   [Ishmael]

וְאִישׁ נוֹחֵם עַל מִרְדָּיו2 לְשׁוֹן אֵשׁ תֹּאכַל בַּדָּיו,3

《 his branches 〈 consume 〈 of fire 〈 — let a 《 his 〈 about 〈 who 〈 And the
[descendants];   tongue rebellion   roars man [Esau]

וּבָעֲרוּ שְׁנֵיהֶם יַחְדָּו4 כַּאֲשֶׁר יְבַעֵר הַגָּלָל,5

《 dung, 〈 one 〈 as 〈 together, 〈 both of 〈 let them
disposes of   them   burn,

מַלְכִּי וֵאלֹהַי כִּי אֵלֶיךָ אֶתְפַּלָּל.

《 do I pray. 〈 to You 〈 for 〈 and my 〈 O my
God,   King

CONGREGATION, THEN *CHAZZAN:*

קָדוֹשׁ עַל כָּל אָדוֹן, עִם כָּל יְצוּרָיו נָדוֹן,

《 He passes 〈 His 〈 all 〈 upon 《 lord, 〈 every 〈 Who is 〈 O Holy
judgment, creatures   above   One,

חֲזֵה יְרִיבִי אִישׁ מָדוֹן מְדַבֵּר עָלַי בְּזָדוֹן,

《 maliciously, 〈 about 〈 how he 《 of 〈 who is 〈 my 〈 see
me   speaks contention, a man Adversary

---

(1) Cf. *Isaiah* 53:5. (2) Cf. 5:29. (3) Cf. 5:24; *Job* 18:13. (4) *Isaiah* 1:31. (5) *I Kings* 14:10.

---

stoned. The Torah decrees death by stoning as the punishment of an ox that kills a person (see *Exodus* 21:28).

אִישׁ מִפְּשָׁעִים מְחוֹלָל — *[For I am] a man who by wanton sins is desecrated.* The translation is based on the commentaries to *Isaiah* 53:5. Other renderings are: *man who is created sinful* (*Arugas HaBosem*, based on

Genesis 8:21 and *Deuteronomy* 32:18); *man who is conceived in sin* (*Masbir*; see *Rashi* to *Psalms* 51:7).

וְרוֹבֶה וְצוֹדֶה — *The archer [Ishmael] and the trapper [Esau].* Ishmael is described as an archer (*Genesis* 21:20), Esau as a hunter (ibid. 25:27; 27:3).

Thus, the phrase refers to their descen-

וְנוֹכְחִי יְעוֹרֵר כִּידוֹן וְתוֹתָח בִּי יָדוֹן,

he ⟨ at ⟨ and [his] ⟨ his spear ⟨ he wields ⟨ toward me
directs. me catapult

תְּנָה אֶת נַפְשִׁי לִשְׁלָל,¹ מוֹלִיךְ יוֹעֲצִים שׁוֹלָל,²

《 into folly, ⟨ counselors ⟨ [O God] 《 its freedom, ⟨ my soul ⟨ Grant
[of evil] Who leads

מַלְכִּי וֵאלֹהָי כִּי אֵלֶיךָ אֶתְפַּלָּל.

《 do I pray. ⟨ to You ⟨ for ⟨ and my ⟨ O my
God, King

ALL, WHILE STANDING:

אֵל מֶלֶךְ יוֹשֵׁב עַל כִּסֵּא רַחֲמִים, מִתְנַהֵג

⟨ Who acts 《 of mercy, ⟨ the throne ⟨ on ⟨ Who sits ⟨ King ⟨ O God,

בַּחֲסִידוּת, מוֹחֵל עֲוֹנוֹת עַמּוֹ, מַעֲבִיר רִאשׁוֹן

⟨ [sins] one ⟨ Who ⟨ of His 《 the sins ⟨ Who 《 with kindness,
removes people, pardons

רִאשׁוֹן,³ מַרְבֶּה מְחִילָה לְחַטָּאִים וּסְלִיחָה לַפּוֹשְׁעִים,

《 to willful ⟨ and ⟨ to unintentional⟨ pardon ⟨ Who abun- 《 by one,
sinners, forgiveness sinners dantly grants

עֹשֶׂה צְדָקוֹת עִם כָּל בָּשָׂר וָרוּחַ, לֹא כְּרָעָתָם

⟨ in accord with ⟨ — not 《 and spirit ⟨ [beings ⟨ all ⟨ with ⟨ acts of ⟨ Who
their wickedness of] flesh generosity performs

תִּגְמוֹל. ❖ אֵל הוֹרֵיתָ לָּנוּ לוֹמַר שְׁלֹשׁ עֶשְׂרֵה,

《 the Thirteen ⟨ to recite ⟨ us ⟨ You taught ⟨ O God, 《 do You
[Attributes of Mercy]; repay them!

וּזְכוֹר לָנוּ הַיּוֹם בְּרִית שְׁלֹשׁ עֶשְׂרֵה, כְּמוֹ שֶׁהוֹדַעְתָּ

⟨ You made ⟨ as 《 of [these] Thirteen, ⟨ the ⟨ today ⟨ for ⟨ remember
known covenant us

לֶעָנָיו מִקֶּדֶם, כְּמוֹ שֶׁכָּתוּב, וַיֵּרֶד יהוה בֶּעָנָן

⟨ in a ⟨ And HASHEM 《 it is written: ⟨ as 《 in ancient ⟨ to the humble
cloud descended times, one [Moses]

וַיִּתְיַצֵּב עִמּוֹ שָׁם, וַיִּקְרָא בְשֵׁם יהוה.⁴

《 of ⟨ with the ⟨ and He 《 there, ⟨ with ⟨ and stood
HASHEM. Name called out him

---

(1) Cf. *Jeremiah* 21:9. (2) *Job* 12:17. (3) *Rosh Hashanah* 17a. (4) *Exodus* 35:4.

dants who have oppressed Israel throughout
the centuries (*Masbir*). Alternatively: Both
terms refer to Ishmael, while the stich about

the one who roars about his rebellion alludes to Esau (*Arugas HaBosem*) or Assyria
(*Pardes*, based on *Isaiah* 5:29).

CONGREGATION, THEN *CHAZZAN*:

וַיַּעֲבֹר יהוה עַל פָּנָיו וַיִּקְרָא:

《 and 《 [Moses'] 〈 before 〈 And HASHEM passed
proclaimed: face,

CONGREGATION AND *CHAZZAN* RECITE LOUDLY AND IN UNISON:

יהוה, יהוה, אֵל, רַחוּם, וְחַנּוּן, אֶרֶךְ אַפַּיִם,

〈 to anger, 〈 Slow 《 and 〈 Compassionate 〈 God, 〈 HASHEM, 〈 HASHEM,
                        Gracious,

וְרַב חֶסֶד, וֶאֱמֶת, נֹצֵר חֶסֶד לָאֲלָפִים, נֹשֵׂא עָוֹן,

〈 of 〈 Forgiver 《 for 〈 of 〈 Preserver 《 and 〈 in 〈 and
iniquity,   thousands [of   kindness   Truth,   Kindness Abundant
                 generations],

וָפֶשַׁע, וְחַטָּאָה, וְנַקֵּה.[1] וְסָלַחְתָּ לַעֲוֹנֵנוּ וּלְחַטָּאתֵנוּ

《 and our sins, 〈 our 〈 May You 《 and Who 〈 and inadvertent 〈 willful sin,
                 iniquities forgive absolves. sin,

וּנְחַלְתָּנוּ.[2] סְלַח לָנוּ אָבִינוּ כִּי חָטָאנוּ, מְחַל לָנוּ

〈 us, 〈 pardon 《 we have 〈 for 《 our 〈 us, 〈 Forgive 《 and make us
                sinned;   Father,   Your heritage.

מַלְכֵּנוּ כִּי פָשָׁעְנוּ. כִּי אַתָּה אֲדֹנָי טוֹב וְסַלָּח,

《 and 〈 are 〈 O Lord, 〈 You, 〈 For 《 we have 〈 for 《 our King,
forgiving, good   willfully sinned.

וְרַב חֶסֶד לְכָל קֹרְאֶיךָ.[3]

《 who call 〈 to all 〈 kind 〈 and
upon You.   abundantly

ALL:

זְכֹר רַחֲמֶיךָ יהוה וַחֲסָדֶיךָ, כִּי מֵעוֹלָם הֵמָּה.[4]

《 are 〈 eternal 〈 for 《 and Your 〈 HASHEM, 〈 Your 〈 Remember
they.   kindnesses,   mercies,

זָכְרֵנוּ יהוה בִּרְצוֹן עַמֶּךָ, פָּקְדֵנוּ בִּישׁוּעָתֶךָ.[5] זְכֹר

〈 Re- 《 with Your 〈 recall us 《 to Your 〈 when You 〈 HASHEM, 〈 Remem-
member salvation.   people;   show favor   ber us,

עֲדָתְךָ קָנִיתָ קֶּדֶם, גָּאַלְתָּ שֵׁבֶט נַחֲלָתֶךָ, הַר צִיּוֹן זֶה

〈 the 〈 of 〈 the 《 of Your 〈 the 〈 You 《 long 〈 which 〈 Your con-
one Zion, mountain heritage; tribe redeemed ago, You gregation,
[where]   acquired

(1) *Exodus* 34:6-7. (2) 34:9. (3) *Psalms* 86:5. (4) 25:6. (5) Cf. 106:4.

שָׁכַנְתָּ בּוֹ.¹ זְכֹר יהוה חִבַּת יְרוּשָׁלַיִם, אַהֲבַת

⟨ the love ⟫ of Jerusalem; ⟨ the ⟨ HASHEM, ⟨ Remem- ⟫there. ⟨ You rested
affection ber, Your Presence

צִיּוֹן אַל תִּשְׁכַּח לָנֶצַח.² אַתָּה תָקוּם תְּרַחֵם צִיּוֹן כִּי

⟨ for ⟫ to ⟨ and show ⟨ will arise ⟨ You ⟫ forever. ⟨ forget ⟨ do not ⟨ of
Zion, mercy Zion

עֵת לְחֶנְנָהּ, כִּי בָא מוֹעֵד.³ זְכֹר יהוה לִבְנֵי אֱדוֹם

⟨ of ⟨ [to repay] ⟨ HASHEM, ⟨ Re- ⟫ the appointed time ⟨ for ⟫ [there will come]
Edom the offspring, member, will have come. the time to favor her,

אֵת יוֹם יְרוּשָׁלָיִם, הָאֹמְרִים עָרוּ עָרוּ עַד הַיְסוֹד

⟨ the very ⟨ to ⟨ Destroy ⟫ Destroy! ⟫ [to repay] ⟫ of Jerusalem; ⟨ for the day
foundation those who say,

בָּהּ.⁴ זְכֹר לְאַבְרָהָם לְיִצְחָק וּלְיִשְׂרָאֵל עֲבָדֶיךָ,

⟫Your servants, ⟨ and for Israel, ⟨ for Isaac, ⟨ for Abraham, ⟨ Remember ⟫ of it!

אֲשֶׁר נִשְׁבַּעְתָּ לָהֶם בָּךְ, וַתְּדַבֵּר אֲלֵהֶם, אַרְבֶּה

⟨ I shall ⟫ to them, ⟨ and ⟫ by Your ⟨ to them ⟨ You swore ⟨ that
increase You said Being,

אֶת זַרְעֲכֶם כְּכוֹכְבֵי הַשָּׁמָיִם, וְכָל הָאָרֶץ הַזֹּאת אֲשֶׁר

⟨ of ⟨ of this land ⟨ and all ⟫ of the ⟨ like the stars ⟨ Your offspring
which heavens;

אָמַרְתִּי, אֶתֵּן לְזַרְעֲכֶם, וְנָחֲלוּ לְעֹלָם.⁵ זְכֹר לַעֲבָדֶיךָ

⟨ of Your ⟨ Remember ⟫ forever. ⟨ and they ⟨ to your ⟨ I will ⟨ I spoke
servants, [the merits] will inherit it offspring, give

לְאַבְרָהָם לְיִצְחָק וּלְיַעֲקֹב, אַל תֵּפֶן אֶל קְשִׁי

⟨ the stub- ⟨ to ⟨ pay ⟨ do ⟫ and of Jacob; ⟨ of Isaac, ⟨ of Abraham,
bornness attention not

הָעָם הַזֶּה וְאֶל רִשְׁעוֹ וְאֶל חַטָּאתוֹ.⁶ זְכֹר לָנוּ בְּרִית

⟨ the ⟨ for ⟨ Remember ⟫ its ⟨ and ⟫ its ⟨ to ⟫ of this people,
covenant us sinfulness. to wickedness,

אָבוֹת, כַּאֲשֶׁר אָמַרְתָּ: וְזָכַרְתִּי אֶת בְּרִיתִי יַעֲקוֹב,

⟫ [with] ⟨ My covenant ⟨ And I will ⟫ You said: ⟨ as ⟫ of the
Jacob, remember Patriarchs,

וְאַף אֶת בְּרִיתִי יִצְחָק, וְאַף אֶת בְּרִיתִי אַבְרָהָם

⟨ [with] ⟨ My covenant ⟨ and ⟫ [with] Isaac, ⟨ My covenant ⟨ and also
Abraham also

---

(1) *Psalms* 74:2. (2) This is not a Scriptural verse. (3) *Psalms* 102:14.
(4) 137:7. (5) *Exodus* 32:13. (6) *Deuteronomy* 9:27.

אֶזְכֹּר, וְהָאָרֶץ אֶזְכֹּר.¹

《 I will remember. 〈 and the Land 《 I will remember;

זְכוֹר לָנוּ בְּרִית רִאשׁוֹנִים, כַּאֲשֶׁר אָמַרְתָּ: וְזָכַרְתִּי

〈 And I will remember 《 You said: 〈 as 《 of the ancient ones, 〈 the covenant 〈 for us 〈 Remember

לָהֶם בְּרִית רִאשׁוֹנִים, אֲשֶׁר הוֹצֵאתִי אֹתָם מֵאֶרֶץ

〈 from the land 〈 I took them out 〈 that 《 of the ancient ones, 〈 the covenant 〈 for them

מִצְרַיִם לְעֵינֵי הַגּוֹיִם, לִהְיוֹת לָהֶם לֵאלֹהִים, אֲנִי

〈 I am 《 a God; 〈 to them 〈 to be 《 of the nations, 〈 in the very sight 〈 of Egypt

יהוה.² עָשֵׂה עִמָּנוּ כְּמָה שֶׁהִבְטַחְתָּנוּ: וְאַף גַּם

〈 all 〈 And despite 《 You promised us: 〈 as 〈 with us 〈 Do 《 HASHEM.

זֹאת בִּהְיוֹתָם בְּאֶרֶץ אֹיְבֵיהֶם, לֹא מְאַסְתִּים וְלֹא

〈 nor 〈 despise them 〈 I will not 《 of their enemies, 〈 in the land 〈 when they will be 《 this,

גְעַלְתִּים לְכַלֹּתָם לְהָפֵר בְּרִיתִי אִתָּם, כִּי אֲנִי יהוה

〈 HASHEM, 〈 I am 〈 for 《 with them, 〈 My covenant 〈 to annul 《 to destroy them, 〈 abhor them

אֱלֹהֵיהֶם.³ הָשֵׁב שְׁבוּתֵנוּ וְרַחֲמֵנוּ, כְּמָה שֶׁכָּתוּב:

《 it is written: 〈 as 《 and have mercy on us, 〈 our captivity 〈 Bring back 《 their God.

וְשָׁב יהוה אֱלֹהֶיךָ אֶת שְׁבוּתְךָ וְרִחֲמֶךָ, וְשָׁב וְקִבֶּצְךָ

〈 gather you in 〈 and He will once again 《 and He will have mercy upon you, 〈 your captivity, 〈 your God, 〈 will HASHEM, 〈 Then bring back

מִכָּל הָעַמִּים אֲשֶׁר הֱפִיצְךָ יהוה אֱלֹהֶיךָ שָׁמָּה.⁴

《 thereto. 〈 your God 〈 has HASHEM 〈 scattered you 〈 that 〈 the peoples 〈 from all

קַבֵּץ נִדָּחֵינוּ, כְּמָה שֶׁכָּתוּב: אִם יִהְיֶה נִדַּחֲךָ בִּקְצֵה

〈 at the ends 〈 your dispersed will be 〈 If 〈 it is written: 〈 as 〈 our dispersed ones, 〈 Gather

---

(1) *Leviticus* 26:42. (2) 26:45. (3) 26:44. (4) 30:3.

הַשָּׁמַיִם, מִשָּׁם יְקַבֶּצְךָ יהוה אֱלֹהֶיךָ, וּמִשָּׁם יִקָּחֶךָ.[1]

> of heaven, ‹ from ‹« gather ‹ will ‹ your God, «› and from « He will take you. ‹ there ‹ you in HASHEM, there

מָחָה פְשָׁעֵינוּ כָּעָב וְכֶעָנָן, כְּמָה שֶׁכָּתוּב: מָחִיתִי

> Wipe ‹ our sins ‹ like a ‹ like a ‹« and like a « as ‹ it is written: «› I have away mist cloud, wiped away

כָעָב פְּשָׁעֶיךָ וְכֶעָנָן חַטֹּאתֶיךָ, שׁוּבָה אֵלַי כִּי

> like a ‹ your willful ‹ and like ‹« your ‹ return «› to ‹ for mist sins, a cloud transgressions; Me,

גְאַלְתִּיךָ.[2] מָחָה פְשָׁעֵינוּ לְמַעַנָךְ, כַּאֲשֶׁר אָמָרְתָּ:

> «› I have redeemed you. « Wipe away ‹ our sins «› for Your sake, ‹ as «› You have said:

אָנֹכִי אָנֹכִי הוּא מֹחֶה פְשָׁעֶיךָ לְמַעֲנִי, וְחַטֹּאתֶיךָ לֹא

> I, ‹ [only] I, ‹ am the ‹« Who wipes ‹ your ‹ for ‹« and your ‹ I shall One away willful sins My sake, transgressions not

אֶזְכֹּר.[3] הַלְבֵּן חֲטָאֵינוּ כַּשֶּׁלֶג וְכַצֶּמֶר, כְּמָה שֶׁכָּתוּב:

> recall. «› Whiten ‹ our sins ‹ like snow ‹« and like wool, «› as « it is written:

לְכוּ נָא וְנִוָּכְחָה, יֹאמַר יהוה, אִם יִהְיוּ חֲטָאֵיכֶם

> Come, ‹ now, ‹« let us reason ‹ says «› HASHEM. ‹« Though ‹ your sins may be together,

כַּשֶּׁלֶג יַלְבִּינוּ, אִם יַאְדִּימוּ כַתּוֹלָע, כַּצֶּמֶר

> like ‹« like ‹ they will be ‹« though ‹ they may ‹ as crimson, «› like [white] ‹ scarlet snow whitened; be red wool

יִהְיוּ.[4] זְרוֹק עָלֵינוּ מַיִם טְהוֹרִים וְטַהֲרֵנוּ, כְּמָה שֶׁכָּתוּב:

> they will «› Pour ‹ upon us ‹ pure water ‹ and purify us, «› as ‹ it is written: «› become.

וְזָרַקְתִּי עֲלֵיכֶם מַיִם טְהוֹרִים וּטְהַרְתֶּם, מִכֹּל

> I shall pour ‹ upon you ‹ pure water ‹ and you will «› from become pure; all

טֻמְאוֹתֵיכֶם וּמִכָּל גִּלּוּלֵיכֶם אֲטַהֵר אֶתְכֶם.[5] רַחֵם

> your ‹ and ‹ your ‹« I will ‹ you. «› Have contaminations from all abominations purify mercy

עָלֵינוּ וְאַל תַּשְׁחִיתֵנוּ, כְּמָה שֶׁכָּתוּב: כִּי אֵל רַחוּם

> on us ‹ and do not ‹ destroy us, «› as ‹ it is written: «› For ‹ a merciful God

יהוה אֱלֹהֶיךָ, לֹא יַרְפְּךָ וְלֹא יַשְׁחִיתֶךָ, וְלֹא יִשְׁכַּח

> is ‹ your God; «› He will ‹ nor ‹ relinquish ‹ He will ‹ nor ‹« will He HASHEM, not you destroy you, forget

---

(1) *Leviticus* 30:4. (2) *Isaiah* 44:22. (3) 43:25. (4) 1:18. (5) *Ezekiel* 36:25.

מוֹל　¹.אֶת בְּרִית אֲבֹתֶיךָ אֲשֶׁר נִשְׁבַּע לָהֶם.

‹ Circumcise 《 to them.　‹ He swore　‹ which ‹ with your forefathers, ‹　the covenant

אֶת לְבָבֵנוּ לְאַהֲבָה וּלְיִרְאָה אֶת שְׁמֶךָ, כְּמָה שֶׁכָּתוּב:

《 it is written: ‹　as　《　Your Name,　‹ and to fear　‹　to love　‹　our hearts

וּמָל יהוה אֱלֹהֶיךָ אֶת לְבָבְךָ וְאֶת לְבַב זַרְעֶךָ, לְאַהֲבָה

‹　to love　《 of your　‹　and the　‹　your heart　‹　HASHEM, your God,
　　　　　　　offspring,　　　heart　　　　　　　　　　　will circumcise

אֶת יהוה אֱלֹהֶיךָ, בְּכָל לְבָבְךָ וּבְכָל נַפְשְׁךָ, לְמַעַן

‹ so that 《 your soul, ‹ and with all ‹ your heart ‹ with all　‹　your God,　‹　HASHEM,

חַיֶּיךָ.². הַמָּצֵא לָנוּ בְּבַקָּשָׁתֵנוּ, כְּמָה שֶׁכָּתוּב: וּבִקַּשְׁתֶּם

‹　And you　《 it is written: ‹　as　《 in our quest, ‹ to us ‹　Be 《　you may
　will seek　　　　　　　　　　　　　　　　　　　accessible　　　live.

מִשָּׁם אֶת יהוה אֱלֹהֶיךָ וּמָצָאתָ, כִּי תִדְרְשֶׁנּוּ בְּכָל

‹ with　‹　you search ‹ when 《 and you will ‹ your God,　‹　HASHEM,　‹　from
　all　　　Him out　　　　find [Him],　　　　　　　　　　　　　　　there

לְבָבְךָ וּבְכָל נַפְשֶׁךָ.³. ❖ תְּבִיאֵנוּ אֶל הַר קָדְשֶׁךָ,

‹ Your holy mountain ‹　to　‹　Bring us　《　your soul. ‹ and with all ‹ your heart

וְשִׂמַּחְנוּ בְּבֵית תְּפִלָּתֶךָ, כְּמָה שֶׁכָּתוּב: וַהֲבִיאוֹתִים

‹ And I will bring them 《 it is written: ‹　as　《 of Prayer, ‹ in Your House ‹ and gladden us

אֶל הַר קָדְשִׁי, וְשִׂמַּחְתִּים בְּבֵית תְּפִלָּתִי, עוֹלֹתֵיהֶם

‹　their burnt-　《 of Prayer; ‹　in My　‹　and I will　《　My holy　‹　to
　offerings　　　　　　　　House　　　gladden them　　　mountain,

וְזִבְחֵיהֶם לְרָצוֹן עַל מִזְבְּחִי, כִּי בֵיתִי בֵּית תְּפִלָּה

‹　of　‹　"a　‹　My　‹ for 《 My Altar,　‹　on　‹ will find ‹ and their feast-
　Prayer"　House　House　　　　　　　　　　　favor　　　offerings

יִקָּרֵא לְכָל הָעַמִּים.⁴.

《　nations.　‹ for all ‹ will be called

THE ARK IS OPENED.

CHAZZAN, THEN CONGREGATION:

שְׁמַע קוֹלֵנוּ יהוה אֱלֹהֵינוּ, חוּס וְרַחֵם עָלֵינוּ,

《 on us, ‹ and have ‹ have 《 our God; ‹ HASHEM, ‹ our voice, ‹　Hear
　　　　compassion　pity

וְקַבֵּל בְּרַחֲמִים וּבְרָצוֹן אֶת תְּפִלָּתֵנוּ.⁵.

《　　our prayer.　‹ and favor ‹ with compassion ‹ and accept

---

(1) *Deuteronomy* 4:31. (2) 30:6. (3) 4:29. (4) *Isaiah* 56:7. (5) From the weekday *Shemoneh Esrei*.

CHAZZAN, THEN CONGREGATION:

הֲשִׁיבֵנוּ יהוה אֵלֶיךָ וְנָשׁוּבָה, חַדֵּשׁ יָמֵינוּ כְּקֶדֶם.[1]

« as of old. ⟨ our days ⟨ renew « and we shall return, ⟨ to You, ⟨ HASHEM, ⟨ Bring us back,

CHAZZAN, THEN CONGREGATION:

אֲמָרֵינוּ הַאֲזִינָה יהוה, בִּינָה הֲגִיגֵנוּ.[2]

« our thoughts. ⟨ perceive « HASHEM; ⟨ hear, ⟨ Our words

THE FOLLOWING VERSE IS RECITED QUIETLY:

יִהְיוּ לְרָצוֹן אִמְרֵי פִינוּ וְהֶגְיוֹן לִבֵּנוּ לְפָנֶיךָ,

« before You, « of our heart — ⟨ and the thoughts ⟨ of our mouth « the expressions « find favor ⟨ May they

יהוה צוּרֵנוּ וְגֹאֲלֵנוּ.[3]

« and our Redeemer. ⟨ our Rock ⟨ HASHEM,

CHAZZAN, THEN CONGREGATION:

אַל תַּשְׁלִיכֵנוּ מִלְּפָנֶיךָ, וְרוּחַ קָדְשְׁךָ אַל תִּקַּח מִמֶּנּוּ.[4]

« from us. ⟨ take ⟨ do not ⟨ of Your Holiness ⟨ and the Spirit « from Your Presence, ⟨ cast us away ⟨ Do not

CHAZZAN, THEN CONGREGATION:

אַל תַּשְׁלִיכֵנוּ לְעֵת זִקְנָה, כִּכְלוֹת כֹּחֵנוּ אַל תַּעַזְבֵנוּ.[5]

« forsake us not. ⟨ does our strength, ⟨ when fail « of old age; ⟨ in time ⟨ cast us away ⟨ Do not

ALL CONTINUE (SOME CONGREGATIONS RECITE THE NEXT VERSE RESPONSIVELY):

אַל תַּעַזְבֵנוּ יהוה, אֱלֹהֵינוּ אַל תִּרְחַק מִמֶּנּוּ.[6]

« from us. ⟨ be not distant ⟨ our God, « O HASHEM; ⟨ Forsake us not,

עֲשֵׂה עִמָּנוּ אוֹת לְטוֹבָה, וְיִרְאוּ שׂוֹנְאֵינוּ וְיֵבֹשׁוּ,

« and be ashamed, ⟨ may our enemies ⟨ so that see it « for good; ⟨ a sign ⟨ for us ⟨ Display

כִּי אַתָּה יהוה עֲזַרְתָּנוּ וְנִחַמְתָּנוּ.[7] כִּי לְךָ יהוה

⟨ HASHEM, ⟨ for You, ⟨ Because « and consoled us. ⟨ will have helped us ⟨ HASHEM, ⟨ You, ⟨ for

הוֹחָלְנוּ, אַתָּה תַעֲנֶה אֲדֹנָי אֱלֹהֵינוּ.[8]

« our God. ⟨ O Lord, ⟨ will answer, ⟨ You « do we wait;

THE ARK IS CLOSED.

---

(1) *Lamentations* 5:21. (2) Cf. *Psalms* 5:2. (3) Cf. 19:15.
(4) 51:13. (5) Cf. 71:9. (6) Cf. 38:22. (7) Cf. 86:17. (8) Cf. 38:16.

EACH INDIVIDUAL CONTINUES UNTIL THE END OF *SELICHOS*.

CONFESSION / וִדּוּי

**DURING THE RECITATION OF THE וִדּוּי, *CONFESSION*, STAND WITH
HEAD AND BODY SLIGHTLY BOWED, IN SUBMISSIVE CONTRITION.**

אֱלֹהֵינוּ וֵאלֹהֵי אֲבוֹתֵינוּ, תָּבֹא לְפָנֶיךָ תְּפִלָּתֵנוּ,[1]

《 may our   〈 before   〈 come   《   of our   〈 and the   〈 Our God
   prayer,   You   forefathers,   God

וְאַל תִּתְעַלַּם מִתְּחִנָּתֵנוּ,[2] שֶׁאֵין אָנוּ עַזֵּי פָנִים

〈 faced 〈 so brazen- 〈 For we are not 《 our supplication. 〈 ignore 〈 and do not

וּקְשֵׁי עֹרֶף, לוֹמַר לְפָנֶיךָ יהוה אֱלֹהֵינוּ וֵאלֹהֵי

〈 and the God 〈 our God,   〈 HASHEM, 《 before You, 〈 as to say 〈 necked 〈 and stiff-

אֲבוֹתֵינוּ, צַדִּיקִים אֲנַחְנוּ וְלֹא חָטָאנוּ, אֲבָל

《—for indeed, 《 sinned 〈 and have not 〈 we are, 〈 that righteous 《 of our forefathers,

אֲנַחְנוּ וַאֲבוֹתֵינוּ חָטָאנוּ.[3]

《 have sinned. 〈 and our forefathers 〈 we

**STRIKE THE LEFT SIDE OF THE CHEST WITH THE RIGHT FIST WHILE RECITING
EACH OF THE SINS OF THE FOLLOWING CONFESSIONAL LITANY:**

אָשַׁמְנוּ, בָּגַדְנוּ, גָּזַלְנוּ, דִּבַּרְנוּ דֹּפִי. הֶעֱוִינוּ,

《 We have com- 《 slander. 〈 we have 《 we have 《 we have 《 We have been
   mitted iniquity;   spoken   robbed;   betrayed;   guilty;

וְהִרְשַׁעְנוּ, זַדְנוּ, חָמַסְנוּ, טָפַלְנוּ שֶׁקֶר. יָעַצְנוּ

〈 We have 《 false 〈 we have 《 we have 《we have sinned 《we have commit-
given advice accusations. made   extorted;   willfully;   ted wickedness;

רָע, כִּזַּבְנוּ, לַצְנוּ, מָרַדְנוּ, נִאַצְנוּ, סָרַרְנוּ,

《 we have 《 we have provoked 《 we have 《 we have 《 we have been 《 that is
   strayed;   [God's anger];   rebelled;   scorned;   deceitful;   bad;

עָוִינוּ, פָּשַׁעְנוּ, צָרַרְנוּ, קִשִּׁינוּ עֹרֶף. רָשַׁעְנוּ,

《 We have 《 our 〈 we have 《we have caused 《 we have sinned 《we have been
been wicked; necks. stiffened   distress;   rebelliously;   iniquitous;

שִׁחַתְנוּ, תִּעַבְנוּ, תָּעִינוּ, תִּעְתָּעְנוּ.

《   we have 《 we have 《 we have 《 we have
      scoffed.   gone astray; committed   been corrupt;
                          abominations;

סַרְנוּ מִמִּצְוֹתֶיךָ וּמִמִּשְׁפָּטֶיךָ הַטּוֹבִים, וְלֹא שָׁוָה

〈 worth- 〈 and it 《 that are 〈 and from 〈 from Your 〈 We have
   while   was not good,   Your laws   commandments turned away

---

(1) Cf. *Psalms* 88:3. (2) Cf. 55:2. (3) Cf. 106:6, *Jeremiah* 3:25.

לָנוּ.[1] וְאַתָּה צַדִּיק עַל כָּל הַבָּא עָלֵינוּ, כִּי

《 for 《 upon us, 〈 that has come 〈 all 〈 in 〈 are righteous 〈 And You 《 for us.

אֱמֶת עָשִׂיתָ וַאֲנַחְנוּ הִרְשָׁעְנוּ.[2]

《 have acted wickedly. 〈 while we 《 have You acted, 〈 truthfully

אָשַׁמְנוּ מִכָּל עָם, בּֽשְׁנוּ מִכָּל דּוֹר, גָּלָה מִמֶּנּוּ

〈 from 〈 Departed 《 genera- 〈 more 〈 We have 《 people. 〈 more than 〈 We have
us tion. than any been been guilty
other ashamed

מָשׂוֹשׂ, דָּוָה לִבֵּנוּ בַּחֲטָאֵינוּ, הֻחֲבַּל אֲוּוּיֵנוּ, וְנִפְרַע

〈 uncov- 《 was our de- 〈 Seized 《 because of 〈 is our 〈 Sickened 〈 has joy.
ered sired [Temple], our sins. heart

פְּאָרֵנוּ, זְבוּל בֵּית מִקְדָּשֵׁנוּ חָרַב בַּעֲוֹנֵינוּ, טִירָתֵנוּ

〈 Our Palace 《 because of 〈 has been 〈 our Holy Temple, 〈 for [His] 《 was our
our iniquities. destroyed abode, splendor;

הָיְתָה לְשַׁמָּה, יְפִי אַדְמָתֵנוּ לְזָרִים, כֹּחֵנוּ לְנָכְרִים.

《 [was given] 〈 our 《 is controlled 〈 of our 〈 [Jerusalem,] 《 desolate. 〈 has
to foreigners. wealth by strangers, Land the beauty become

וַעֲדַיִן לֹא שַׁבְנוּ מִטָּעוּתֵנוּ וְהֵיךְ נָעִיז פָּנֵינוּ וְנַקְשֶׁה

〈 and 〈 faced 〈 can we be 〈 So 《 from our 〈 we have not 〈 But still
stiffen so brazen- how willful errors. repented

עָרְפֵּנוּ, לוֹמַר לְפָנֶיךָ יְהוָה אֱלֹהֵינוּ וֵאלֹהֵי אֲבוֹתֵינוּ,

《 of our 〈 and the 〈 our God 〈 HASHEM, 〈 before 〈 so as to 〈 our neck
forefathers, God You, say

צַדִּיקִים אֲנַחְנוּ וְלֹא חָטָאנוּ, אֲבָל אֲנַחְנוּ וַאֲבוֹתֵינוּ

〈 and our 〈 both we 〈 for in 《 and we have 《 we are 〈 that
fathers truth, not sinned, righteous

חָטָאנוּ.[3]

《 have sinned.

**STRIKE THE LEFT SIDE OF THE CHEST WITH THE RIGHT FIST WHILE RECITING
EACH OF THE SINS OF THE FOLLOWING CONFESSIONAL LITANY:**

אָשַׁמְנוּ, בָּגַדְנוּ, גָּזַלְנוּ, דִּבַּרְנוּ דֹפִי. הֶעֱוִינוּ,

《 We have com- 《 slander. 〈 we have 《 we have 《 we have 《 We have been
mitted iniquity; spoken robbed; betrayed; guilty;

וְהִרְשַׁעְנוּ, זַדְנוּ, חָמַסְנוּ, טָפַלְנוּ שֶׁקֶר. יָעַצְנוּ

〈 We have 《 false 〈 we have 《 we have 《 we have sinned 《 we have commit-
given advice accusations. made extorted; willfully; ted wickedness;

(1) Cf. *Job* 33:27. (2) *Nehemiah* 9:33. (3) Cf. *Psalms* 106:6; *Jeremiah* 3:25.

רָע, בְּזַבְנוּ, לַצְנוּ, מָרַדְנוּ, נִאַצְנוּ, סָרַרְנוּ,
《 that is 《 we have been 《 we have 《 we have 《 we have provoked 《 we have
bad; deceitful; scorned; rebelled; [God's anger]; strayed;

עָוִינוּ, פָּשַׁעְנוּ, צָרַרְנוּ, קִשִּׁינוּ עֹרֶף. רָשַׁעְנוּ.
《 we have 《 we have 《 we have 〈 we have 〈 our 《 We have
been sinned caused stiffened necks. been wicked;
iniquitous; rebelliously; distress;

שִׁחַתְנוּ, תִּעַבְנוּ, תָּעִינוּ, תִּעְתָּעְנוּ.
《 we have 《 we have 《 we have 《 we have
been corrupt; committed gone astray; scoffed.
abominations;

סַרְנוּ מִמִּצְוֹתֶיךָ וּמִמִּשְׁפָּטֶיךָ הַטּוֹבִים, וְלֹא שָׁוָה
〈 worth- 〈 and it 《 that are 〈 and from 〈 from Your 〈 We have
while was not good, Your laws commandments turned away

לָנוּ.[1] וְאַתָּה צַדִּיק עַל כָּל הַבָּא עָלֵינוּ, כִּי אֱמֶת
〈 truth- 〈 for 《 upon us, 〈 that has 〈 all 〈 in 〈 are 〈 And You 《 for us.
fully come righteous

עָשִׂיתָ וַאֲנַחְנוּ הִרְשָׁעְנוּ.[2]
《 have acted 〈 while we 《 have You
wickedly. acted,

לְעֵינֵינוּ עָשְׁקוּ עֲמָלֵנוּ, מִמְשָׁךְ וּמְמוֹרָט מִמֶּנּוּ,
《 from 〈 and cut off 〈 [it was] 《 the product 〈 have they 〈 Before our
us. pulled away of our labor; stolen eyes

נָתְנוּ עָלֵם עָלֵינוּ, סָבַלְנוּ עַל שִׁכְמֵנוּ, עֲבָדִים
〈 Slaves 《 our 〈 upon 〈 we bore it 《 upon us, 〈 their 〈 They have
shoulders. yoke placed

מָשְׁלוּ בָנוּ, פֹּרֵק אֵין מִיָּדָם, צָרוֹת רַבּוֹת
〈 that are 〈 Troubles 《 from their there 〈 a 《 over 〈 have
manifold hand. was not redeemer us; ruled

סְבָבוּנוּ, קְרָאנוּךָ יהוה אֱלֹהֵינוּ, רָחַקְתָּ מִמֶּנּוּ
〈 from 〈 but You have dis- 《 our God, 〈 HASHEM, 〈 we called 《 have
us tanced Yourself upon You, surrounded us,

בַּעֲוֹנֵינוּ, שַׁבְנוּ מֵאַחֲרֶיךָ, תָּעִינוּ וְאָבַדְנוּ.
《 we have 《 we have 《 from following 〈 We have 《 because of
become lost. gone astray; after You; turned away our iniquities.

___

(1) Cf. *Job* 33:27. (2) *Nehemiah* 9:33.

וַעֲדַיִן לֹא שַׁבְנוּ מִטָּעוּתֵנוּ וְהֵיךְ נָעֵיז פָּנֵינוּ וְנַקְשֶׁה

‹ and stiffen ‹ can we be ‹ faced ‹ can we be so brazen- « from our willful errors. ‹ we have not repented ‹ But still

עָרְפֵּנוּ, לוֹמַר לְפָנֶיךָ יהוה אֱלֹהֵינוּ וֵאלֹהֵי אֲבוֹתֵינוּ,

« of our forefathers, ‹ and the God ‹ our God ‹ Hashem, ‹ before You, ‹ so as to say ‹ our neck

צַדִּיקִים אֲנַחְנוּ וְלֹא חָטָאנוּ, אֲבָל אֲנַחְנוּ וַאֲבוֹתֵינוּ

‹ and our fathers ‹ both we ‹ for in truth, « and we have not sinned, « we are ‹ that righteous

חָטָאנוּ.[1]

« have sinned.

STRIKE THE LEFT SIDE OF THE CHEST WITH THE RIGHT FIST WHILE RECITING EACH OF THE SINS OF THE FOLLOWING CONFESSIONAL LITANY:

אָשַׁמְנוּ, בָּגַדְנוּ, גָּזַלְנוּ, דִּבַּרְנוּ דֹפִי. הֶעֱוִינוּ,

« We have committed iniquity; « slander. ‹ we have spoken « we have robbed; « we have betrayed; « We have been guilty;

וְהִרְשַׁעְנוּ, זַדְנוּ, חָמַסְנוּ, טָפַלְנוּ שֶׁקֶר. יָעַצְנוּ

‹ We have given advice « false accusations. ‹ we have made « we have extorted; « we have sinned willfully; « we have committed wickedness;

רָע, כִּזַּבְנוּ, לַצְנוּ, מָרַדְנוּ, נִאַצְנוּ, סָרַרְנוּ,

« we have strayed; « we have provoked [God's anger]; « we have rebelled; « we have scorned; « we have been deceitful; « that is bad;

עָוִינוּ, פָּשַׁעְנוּ, צָרַרְנוּ, קִשִּׁינוּ עֹרֶף. רָשַׁעְנוּ,

« We have been wicked; « our necks. ‹ we have stiffened « we have caused distress; « we have sinned rebelliously; « we have been iniquitous;

שִׁחַתְנוּ, תִּעַבְנוּ, תָּעִינוּ, תִּעְתָּעְנוּ.

« we have scoffed. « we have gone astray; « we have committed abominations; « we have been corrupt;

סַרְנוּ מִמִּצְוֹתֶיךָ וּמִמִּשְׁפָּטֶיךָ הַטּוֹבִים, וְלֹא שָׁוָה

‹ worthwhile ‹ and it was not « that are good, ‹ and from Your laws ‹ from Your commandments ‹ We have turned away

לָנוּ.[2] וְאַתָּה צַדִּיק עַל כָּל הַבָּא עָלֵינוּ, כִּי אֱמֶת

‹ truthfully ‹ for « upon us, ‹ that has come ‹ all ‹ in ‹ are ‹ And You « for us. are righteous

עָשִׂיתָ וַאֲנַחְנוּ הִרְשָׁעְנוּ.[3]

« have acted wickedly. ‹ while we « have You acted,

---

(1) Cf. *Psalms* 106:6; *Jeremiah* 3:25. (2) Cf. *Job* 33:27. (3) *Nehemiah* 9:33.

הִרְשַׁעְנוּ וּפָשַׁעְנוּ, לָכֵן לֹא נוֹשָׁעְנוּ. וְתֵן בְּלִבֵּנוּ

⟨ in our ⟨ Place ⟫ been ⟨ we have ⟨ there- ⟫ and we ⟨ We have acted
hearts saved. not fore have sinned wickedly
rebelliously;

לַעֲזוֹב דֶּרֶךְ רֶשַׁע, וְחִישׁ לָנוּ יֶשַׁע, כַּכָּתוּב עַל יַד

⟨ the ⟨ by ⟨ as it is ⟫ salvation; ⟨ to us ⟨ and ⟫ of ⟨ the ⟨ [the will]
hand written hasten wickedness, path to abandon

נְבִיאֶךָ: יַעֲזֹב רָשָׁע דַּרְכּוֹ, וְאִישׁ אָוֶן מַחְשְׁבֹתָיו,

⟫ [abandon] ⟨ of ⟨ and ⟫ his way, ⟨ the wicked ⟨ Let ⟫ of Your
his thoughts; iniquity the man one abandon prophet:

וְיָשֹׁב אֶל יהוה וִירַחֲמֵהוּ, וְאֶל אֱלֹהֵינוּ כִּי

⟨ for ⟨ our God, ⟨ and to ⟫ and He will have ⟨ HASHEM, ⟨ to ⟨ and let
compassion on him, him return

יַרְבֶּה לִסְלוֹחַ.[1]

⟫ forgiving. ⟨ He is
abundantly

מְשִׁיחַ צִדְקֶךָ אָמַר לְפָנֶיךָ, שְׁגִיאוֹת מִי יָבִין,

⟫ can ⟨ who ⟨ Mistakes ⟫ before You: ⟨ said ⟨ who is righteous ⟨ Your
discern? [David] anointed one

מִנִּסְתָּרוֹת נַקֵּנִי.[2] נַקֵּנוּ יהוה אֱלֹהֵינוּ מִכָּל פְּשָׁעֵינוּ,

⟨ our sins ⟨ of all ⟨ our God, ⟨ HASHEM, ⟨ Cleanse ⟫ cleanse ⟨ From
us, me. unperceived faults

וְטַהֲרֵנוּ מִכָּל טֻמְאוֹתֵינוּ, וּזְרוֹק עָלֵינוּ מַיִם טְהוֹרִים

⟨ pure water ⟨ upon us ⟨ Pour ⟫ our contaminations. ⟨ of all ⟨ and purify us

וְטַהֲרֵנוּ, כַּכָּתוּב עַל יַד נְבִיאֶךָ: וְזָרַקְתִּי עֲלֵיכֶם

⟨ upon you ⟨ I shall pour ⟫ of Your ⟨ the ⟨ by ⟨ as it is ⟫ and purify us,
prophet: hand written

מַיִם טְהוֹרִים וּטְהַרְתֶּם, מִכֹּל טֻמְאוֹתֵיכֶם וּמִכָּל

⟨ and ⟨ your ⟨ from ⟫ and you will ⟨ pure water
from all contaminations all become pure;

גִּלּוּלֵיכֶם אֲטַהֵר אֶתְכֶם.[3] עַמְּךָ וְנַחֲלָתְךָ, רְעֵבֵי

⟨ who ⟫ and Your ⟨ Your ⟫ you. ⟨ I will purify ⟨ your
hunger heritage, people abominations

טוּבְךָ, צְמֵאֵי חַסְדֶּךָ, תְּאֵבֵי יִשְׁעֶךָ, יַכִּירוּ וְיֵדְעוּ

⟨ and ⟨ — may they ⟫ for Your ⟨ and ⟫ for Your ⟨ who ⟫ for Your
know recognize salvation who long kindness, thirst goodness,

---

(1) *Isaiah* 55:7. (2) *Psalms* 19:13. (3) *Ezekiel* 36:25.

כִּי לַיהוה אֱלֹהֵינוּ הָרַחֲמִים וְהַסְּלִיחוֹת.

that ⟨ to HASHEM, ⟨ our God, ⟨ belong mercy ⟨ and forgiveness. ⟩

אֵל רַחוּם שְׁמֶךָ, אֵל חַנּוּן שְׁמֶךָ, בָּנוּ נִקְרָא שְׁמֶךָ.

Merciful God ⟨ is Your Name, ⟨ Gracious God ⟨ is Your Name, ⟨ upon us ⟨ is Your Name proclaimed,

יהוה עֲשֵׂה לְמַעַן שְׁמֶךָ, עֲשֵׂה לְמַעַן אֲמִתָּךְ, עֲשֵׂה

HASHEM, ⟨ act ⟨ for the sake of ⟨ Your Name. ⟨ Act ⟨ for the sake of ⟨ Your truth; ⟩ act ⟩

לְמַעַן בְּרִיתָךְ, עֲשֵׂה לְמַעַן גָּדְלָךְ וְתִפְאַרְתָּךְ, עֲשֵׂה

for the sake of ⟨ Your covenant ⟩ act ⟨ for the sake of ⟨ Your greatness ⟨ and Your splendor; ⟩ act ⟩

לְמַעַן דָּתָךְ, עֲשֵׂה לְמַעַן הוֹדָךְ, עֲשֵׂה לְמַעַן וְעוּדָךְ,

for the sake of ⟨ Your Law; ⟨ act ⟨ for the sake of ⟨ Your glory; ⟨ act ⟨ for the sake of ⟨ Your Meeting House; ⟩

עֲשֵׂה לְמַעַן זִכְרָךְ, עֲשֵׂה לְמַעַן חַסְדָּךְ, עֲשֵׂה לְמַעַן

act ⟨ for the sake of ⟨ Your remembrance; ⟨ act ⟨ for the sake of ⟨ Your kindness; ⟨ act ⟨ for the sake of ⟩

טוּבָךְ, עֲשֵׂה לְמַעַן יִחוּדָךְ, עֲשֵׂה לְמַעַן כְּבוֹדָךְ, עֲשֵׂה

Your goodness; ⟨ act ⟨ for the sake of ⟨ Your Oneness; ⟨ act ⟨ for the sake of ⟨ Your honor; ⟩ act ⟩

לְמַעַן לִמּוּדָךְ, עֲשֵׂה לְמַעַן מַלְכוּתָךְ, עֲשֵׂה לְמַעַן

for the sake of ⟨ Your students; ⟨ act ⟨ for the sake of ⟨ Your kingship; ⟨ act ⟨ for the sake of ⟩

נִצְחָךְ, עֲשֵׂה לְמַעַן סוֹדָךְ, עֲשֵׂה לְמַעַן עֻזָּךְ, עֲשֵׂה

Your eternal [Name]; ⟨ act ⟨ for the sake of ⟨ Your secret [revealed to those who fear You]; ⟨ act ⟨ for the sake of ⟨ Your power; ⟩ act ⟩

לְמַעַן פְּאֵרָךְ, עֲשֵׂה לְמַעַן צִדְקָתָךְ, עֲשֵׂה לְמַעַן

for the sake of ⟨ Your glory; ⟨ act ⟨ for the sake of ⟨ Your righteousness; ⟨ act ⟨ for the sake of ⟩

קְדֻשָּׁתָךְ, עֲשֵׂה לְמַעַן רַחֲמֶיךָ הָרַבִּים, עֲשֵׂה לְמַעַן

Your sanctity; ⟨ act ⟨ for the sake of ⟨ Your mercy ⟨ that is abundant; ⟨ act ⟨ for the sake of ⟩

שְׁכִינָתָךְ, עֲשֵׂה לְמַעַן תְּהִלָּתָךְ, עֲשֵׂה לְמַעַן אוֹהֲבֶיךָ

Your Divine Presence; ⟨ act ⟨ for the sake of ⟨ Your praise; ⟨ act ⟨ for the sake of ⟨ those who loved You;

(1) Cf. *Exodus* 34:6. (2) Cf. *Deuteronomy* 28:10. (3) *Jeremiah* 14:7.
(4) Cf. *Exodus* 3:15. (5) *Psalms* 6:5. (6) Cf. *Isaiah* 54:13. (7) Cf. *Psalms* 25:14.

שׁוֹכְנֵי עָפָר, עֲשֵׂה לְמַעַן אַבְרָהָם יִצְחָק וְיַעֲקֹב,

and Jacob; ‹ Isaac, ‹ Abraham, ‹ for the sake of ‹ act ‹ in the dust; ‹ who rest

עֲשֵׂה לְמַעַן מֹשֶׁה וְאַהֲרֹן, עֲשֵׂה לְמַעַן דָּוִד וּשְׁלֹמֹה,

and Solomon; ‹ David ‹ for the sake of ‹ act ‹ and Aaron; ‹ Moses ‹ for the sake of ‹ act

עֲשֵׂה לְמַעַן יְרוּשָׁלַיִם עִיר קָדְשֶׁךָ, עֲשֵׂה לְמַעַן צִיּוֹן

Zion, ‹ for the sake of ‹ act ‹ of Your Holiness; ‹ the City ‹ Jerusalem, ‹ for the sake of ‹ act

מִשְׁכַּן כְּבוֹדֶךָ, עֲשֵׂה לְמַעַן שִׁמְמוֹת הֵיכָלֶךָ, עֲשֵׂה

act ‹ of Your Temple; ‹ the desolation ‹ for the sake of ‹ act ‹ of Your glory; ‹ the abode

לְמַעַן הֲרִיסוּת מִזְבְּחֶךָ, עֲשֵׂה לְמַעַן הֲרוּגִים עַל

for ‹ those killed ‹ for the sake of ‹ act ‹ of Your Altar; ‹ the devastation ‹ for the sake of

שֵׁם קָדְשֶׁךָ, עֲשֵׂה לְמַעַן טְבוּחִים עַל יִחוּדֶךָ, עֲשֵׂה

act ‹ Your Oneness; ‹ for ‹ those slaughtered ‹ for the sake of ‹ act ‹ Your holy Name;

לְמַעַן בָּאֵי בָאֵשׁ וּבַמַּיִם עַל קִדּוּשׁ שְׁמֶךָ, עֲשֵׂה לְמַעַן

for the sake of ‹ act ‹ of Your Name; sanctification ‹ the ‹ for ‹ and water ‹ fire ‹ those who entered ‹ for the sake of

יוֹנְקֵי שָׁדַיִם שֶׁלֹא חָטְאוּ, עֲשֵׂה לְמַעַן גְּמוּלֵי חָלָב

from milk ‹ the [babies] weaned ‹ for the sake of ‹ act ‹ sin; ‹ who did not ‹ at the breast ‹ the [infants] sucking

שֶׁלֹא פָשְׁעוּ, עֲשֵׂה לְמַעַן תִּינוֹקוֹת שֶׁל בֵּית רַבָּן,

their teachers' school; ‹ of ‹ the children ‹ for the sake of ‹ act ‹ transgress; ‹ who did not

עֲשֵׂה לְמַעַנְךָ אִם לֹא לְמַעֲנֵנוּ, עֲשֵׂה לְמַעַנְךָ וְהוֹשִׁיעֵנוּ.

and save us. ‹ for Your sake ‹ act ‹ for our sake; ‹ not ‹ if ‹ for Your sake ‹ act

עֲנֵנוּ יהוה עֲנֵנוּ, עֲנֵנוּ אֱלֹהֵינוּ עֲנֵנוּ, עֲנֵנוּ אָבִינוּ

our Father, ‹ answer us; ‹ answer us; ‹ our God, ‹ answer us; ‹ answer us; ‹ HASHEM, ‹ Answer us;

עֲנֵנוּ, עֲנֵנוּ בּוֹרְאֵנוּ עֲנֵנוּ, עֲנֵנוּ גוֹאֲלֵנוּ עֲנֵנוּ, עֲנֵנוּ

answer us; ‹ answer us; ‹ our Redeemer, ‹ answer us; ‹ answer us; ‹ our Creator, ‹ answer us; ‹ answer us;

---

(1) *Isaiah* 26:19. (2) Cf. *Daniel* 9:16,24. (3) *Psalms* 26:8. (4) Cf. *Jeremiah* 51:26. (5) Cf. *Isaiah* 49:19.
(6) *Joel* 2:16. (7) *Isaiah* 28:9. (8) *Shabbos* 119b. (9) *Isaiah* 64:7. (10) Cf. 43:1. (11) 47:4.

דּוֹרְשֵׁנוּ¹ עֲנֵנוּ, עֲנֵנוּ הָאֵל הַנֶּאֱמָן² עֲנֵנוּ, עֲנֵנוּ וָתִיק

וְחָסִיד עֲנֵנוּ, עֲנֵנוּ זַךְ וְיָשָׁר³ עֲנֵנוּ, עֲנֵנוּ חַי וְקַיָּם⁴

עֲנֵנוּ, עֲנֵנוּ טוֹב וּמֵטִיב⁵ עֲנֵנוּ, עֲנֵנוּ יוֹדֵעַ יֵצֶר⁶ עֲנֵנוּ,

עֲנֵנוּ כּוֹבֵשׁ כְּעָסִים עֲנֵנוּ, עֲנֵנוּ לוֹבֵשׁ צְדָקוֹת⁷ עֲנֵנוּ,

עֲנֵנוּ מֶלֶךְ מַלְכֵי הַמְּלָכִים⁸ עֲנֵנוּ, עֲנֵנוּ נוֹרָא וְנִשְׂגָּב⁹

עֲנֵנוּ, עֲנֵנוּ סוֹלֵחַ וּמוֹחֵל עֲנֵנוּ, עֲנֵנוּ עוֹנֶה בְּעֵת

צָרָה¹⁰ עֲנֵנוּ, עֲנֵנוּ פּוֹדֶה וּמַצִּיל¹¹ עֲנֵנוּ, עֲנֵנוּ צַדִּיק

וְיָשָׁר¹² עֲנֵנוּ, עֲנֵנוּ קָרוֹב לְקוֹרְאָיו¹³ עֲנֵנוּ, עֲנֵנוּ קָשֶׁה

לִכְעוֹס¹⁴ עֲנֵנוּ, עֲנֵנוּ רַךְ לִרְצוֹת¹⁵ עֲנֵנוּ, עֲנֵנוּ רַחוּם

וְחַנּוּן¹⁶ עֲנֵנוּ, עֲנֵנוּ שׁוֹמֵעַ אֶל אֶבְיוֹנִים¹⁷ עֲנֵנוּ, עֲנֵנוּ

תּוֹמֵךְ תְּמִימִים עֲנֵנוּ, עֲנֵנוּ אֱלֹהֵי אֲבוֹתֵינוּ עֲנֵנוּ,

עֲנֵנוּ אֱלֹהֵי אַבְרָהָם¹⁸ עֲנֵנוּ, עֲנֵנוּ פַּחַד יִצְחָק עֲנֵנוּ,

Interlinear translation:
You Who searches us out, « answer us, « answer us; God, Who is faithful, answer us; « answer us; steadfast and enduring One, living One, « answer us, « answer us; and pure and upright One, answer us; « answer us; and kind One, « answer us, « answer us; good and beneficent One, answer us; « answer us; Knower of inclinations, answer us, « answer us; Suppressor of wrath, answer us; « answer us; Donner of righteousness, « answer us; answer us, King over kings King of kings, answer us; « answer us; awesome and powerful One, answer us, « answer us; You Who forgives and pardons, answer us; « answer us; You Who answers in time of distress, answer us, « answer us; Redeemer and Rescuer, answer us; « answer us; righteous and upright One, answer us, « answer us; He Who is close to those who call upon Him, answer us; « answer us; Who is hard to anger, answer us, « answer us; You Who are easily appeased, answer us; « answer us; merciful and gracious One, answer us, « answer us; You Who listens to the destitute, answer us; « answer us; You Who supports the wholesome, answer us, « answer us; the God of our forefathers, answer us; « answer us; God of Abraham, answer us, « answer us; Awesome One of Isaac, answer us;

---

(1) Cf. *Ezekiel* 34:11. (2) *Deuteronomy* 7:9. (3) *Job* 8:6; cf. *Proverbs* 20:11. (4) Cf. *Daniel* 6:27.
(5) Cf. *Psalms* 119:68. (6) Cf. 103:14. (7) Cf. *Isaiah* 59:17. (8) *Ethics of the Fathers* 3:1.
(9) *Psalms* 47:3; 148:13. (10) Cf. *Isaiah* 49:8; *Psalms* 37:39. Alternate text: בְּעֵת רָצוֹן, *in time of favor.*
(11) Cf. 34:23,18. (12) *Deuteronomy* 32:4. (13) Cf. *Psalms* 145:18. (14) *Ethics of the Fathers* 5:14.
(15) Cf. 5:14. (16) *Exodus* 34:6. (17) *Psalms* 69:34. (18) *Genesis* 31:42.

עֲנֵנוּ אֲבִיר יַעֲקֹב¹ עֲנֵנוּ, עֲנֵנוּ עֶזְרַת הַשְּׁבָטִים עֲנֵנוּ,

עֲנֵנוּ מִשְׂגַּב אִמָּהוֹת עֲנֵנוּ, עֲנֵנוּ עוֹנֶה בְּעֵת רָצוֹן² עֲנֵנוּ,

עֲנֵנוּ אֲבִי יְתוֹמִים³ עֲנֵנוּ, עֲנֵנוּ דַּיַּן אַלְמָנוֹת³ עֲנֵנוּ.

מִי שֶׁעָנָה לְאַבְרָהָם אָבִינוּ בְּהַר הַמּוֹרִיָּה⁴ הוּא יַעֲנֵנוּ.

מִי שֶׁעָנָה לְיִצְחָק בְּנוֹ כְּשֶׁנֶּעֱקַד עַל גַּבֵּי הַמִּזְבֵּחַ⁴ הוּא יַעֲנֵנוּ.

מִי שֶׁעָנָה לְיַעֲקֹב בְּבֵית אֵל⁵ הוּא יַעֲנֵנוּ.

מִי שֶׁעָנָה לְיוֹסֵף בְּבֵית הָאֲסוּרִים⁶ הוּא יַעֲנֵנוּ.

מִי שֶׁעָנָה לַאֲבוֹתֵינוּ עַל יַם סוּף⁷ הוּא יַעֲנֵנוּ.

מִי שֶׁעָנָה לְמֹשֶׁה בְּחוֹרֵב⁸ הוּא יַעֲנֵנוּ.

מִי שֶׁעָנָה לְאַהֲרֹן בַּמַּחְתָּה⁹ הוּא יַעֲנֵנוּ.

---

(1) *Isaiah* 49:26. (2) Cf. 49:8; *Psalms* 69:14. Alternate text: בְּעֵת צָרָה, *in time of distress.*
(3) 68:6. (4) *Genesis* 22:12. (5) 35:3. (6) 39:21. (7) *Exodus* Ch. 14.
(8) 17:6,11; *Deuteronomy* 9:19. (9) *Numbers* 17:11-13.

מִי שֶׁעָנָה לְפִינְחָס בְּקוּמוֹ מִתּוֹךְ הָעֵדָה[1]

He ⟩ Who ⟨ Phinehas ⟨ when he ⟨ from ⟨ the
answered   arose   amid   congregation «

הוּא יַעֲנֵנוּ.

He ⟩ may — ⟨ answer «
   us.

מִי שֶׁעָנָה לִיהוֹשֻׁעַ בַּגִּלְגָּל[2]

He ⟩ Who ⟨ Joshua ⟨ in Gilgal «
answered

הוּא יַעֲנֵנוּ.

He ⟩ may — ⟨ answer «
   us.

מִי שֶׁעָנָה לִשְׁמוּאֵל בַּמִּצְפֶּה[3]

He ⟩ Who ⟨ Samuel ⟨ in Mizpah «
answered

הוּא יַעֲנֵנוּ.

He ⟩ may — ⟨ answer «
   us.

מִי שֶׁעָנָה לְדָוִד וּשְׁלֹמֹה בְנוֹ בִּירוּשָׁלַיִם[4]

He ⟩ Who ⟨ David ⟨ and ⟨ his ⟨ in Jerusalem «
answered   Solomon   son

הוּא יַעֲנֵנוּ.

He ⟩ may — ⟨ answer «
   us.

מִי שֶׁעָנָה לְאֵלִיָּהוּ בְּהַר הַכַּרְמֶל[5]

He ⟩ Who ⟨ Elijah ⟨ on ⟨ Carmel «
answered   Mount

הוּא יַעֲנֵנוּ.

He ⟩ may — ⟨ answer «
   us.

מִי שֶׁעָנָה לֶאֱלִישָׁע בִּירִיחוֹ[6]

He ⟩ Who ⟨ Elisha ⟨ in Jericho «
answered

הוּא יַעֲנֵנוּ.

He ⟩ may — ⟨ answer «
   us.

מִי שֶׁעָנָה לְיוֹנָה בִּמְעֵי הַדָּגָה[7]

He ⟩ Who ⟨ Jonah ⟨ in the ⟨ of the «
answered   innards   fish

הוּא יַעֲנֵנוּ.

He ⟩ may — ⟨ answer «
   us.

מִי שֶׁעָנָה לְחִזְקִיָּהוּ מֶלֶךְ יְהוּדָה בְּחָלְיוֹ[8]

He ⟩ Who ⟨ Hezekiah, ⟨ king ⟨ of Judah, ⟨ in his «
answered   illness

הוּא יַעֲנֵנוּ.

He ⟩ may — ⟨ answer «
   us.

מִי שֶׁעָנָה לַחֲנַנְיָה מִישָׁאֵל וַעֲזַרְיָה

He ⟩ Who ⟨ Hananiah, ⟨ Mishael, ⟨ and Azariah ⟩
answered

בְּתוֹךְ כִּבְשַׁן הָאֵשׁ[9]

inside ⟨ the furnace ⟨ of fire «

הוּא יַעֲנֵנוּ.

He ⟩ may — ⟨ answer «
   us.

מִי שֶׁעָנָה לְדָנִיֵּאל בְּגוֹב הָאֲרָיוֹת[10]

He ⟩ Who ⟨ Daniel ⟨ in the ⟨ of lions «
answered   den

הוּא יַעֲנֵנוּ.

He ⟩ may — ⟨ answer «
   us.

(1) *Numbers* 25:7-13. (2) *Joshua* 6:1-20; 7:6-15; 10:12-14. (3) *I Samuel* 7:9.
(4) *II Samuel* 7:5-16; 21:1,14; 24:25; *I Kings* 9:3. (5) 18:36-38. (6) *II Kings* 2:21.
(7) *Jonah* 2:2-11. (8) *II Kings* 20:2-6; *Isaiah* 38:2-8. (9) *Daniel* 3:21-27. (10) 6:17-23.

מִי שֶׁעָנָה לְמָרְדְּכַי וְאֶסְתֵּר בְּשׁוּשַׁן הַבִּירָה¹

《 the capital 〈 in Shushan 〈 and Esther 〈 Mordechai 〈 Who 〈 He
answered

הוּא יַעֲנֵנוּ.

《 answer 〈 — may
us. He

מִי שֶׁעָנָה לְעֶזְרָא בַּגּוֹלָה²

《 in the exile 〈 Ezra 〈 Who 〈 He
answered

הוּא יַעֲנֵנוּ.

《 answer 〈 — may
us. He

מִי שֶׁעָנָה לְכָל הַצַּדִּיקִים וְהַחֲסִידִים וְהַתְּמִימִים

〈 the wholesome, 〈 the devout, 〈 the righteous, 〈 all 〈 Who 〈 He
answered

וְהַיְשָׁרִים

《 and the
upright

הוּא יַעֲנֵנוּ.

《 answer 〈 — may
us. He

רַחֲמָנָא דְּעָנֵי לַעֲנִיֵּי, עֲנֵינָן. רַחֲמָנָא דְּעָנֵי לִתְבִירֵי

〈 those of 〈 Who 〈 Merciful 《 answer 《 the poor, 〈 Who 〈 Merciful One
broken answers One us! answers

לִבָּא, עֲנֵינָן. רַחֲמָנָא דְּעָנֵי לִמְכִיכֵי רוּחָא, עֲנֵינָן.

《 answer 《 spirit, 〈 those of 〈 Who 〈 Merciful 《 answer 《 hearts,
us! crushed answers One us!

רַחֲמָנָא עֲנֵינָן. רַחֲמָנָא חוּס. רַחֲמָנָא פְּרוֹק. רַחֲמָנָא

〈 Merciful 《 redeem! 〈 Merciful 《 have 〈 Merciful 《 answer 〈 Merciful
One, One, pity! One, us! One,

שֵׁזִיב. רַחֲמָנָא רְחַם עֲלָן, הַשְׁתָּא בַּעֲגָלָא וּבִזְמַן קָרִיב.

《 that comes 〈 and at 〈 swiftly, 〈 — now, 《 on us 〈 have 〈 Merciful 《 save!
soon. a time mercy One,

PUTTING DOWN THE HEAD / נפילת אפים

RECITE UNTIL יְבֹשׁוּ רָגַע WITH THE HEAD RESTING ON THE LEFT ARM,
PREFERABLY WHILE SEATED.

(וַיֹּאמֶר דָּוִד אֶל גָּד, צַר לִי מְאֹד, נִפְּלָה נָּא בְיַד יהוה,

《 of 〈 into the 〈 now 〈 Let us 《 exceed- 〈 am 〈 Dis- 《 Gad, 〈 to 〈 (And David said
HASHEM, hand fall ingly. I tressed

כִּי רַבִּים רַחֲמָיו, וּבְיַד אָדָם אַל אֶפֹּלָה.³)

《 let me not fall.) 〈 but into human 《 are His 〈 abundant 〈 for
hands mercies,

---

(1) *Esther* Ch. 8. (2) *Ezra* 8:21-23. (3) *II Samuel* 24:14.

רַחוּם וְחַנּוּן חָטָאתִי לְפָנֶיךָ. יהוה מָלֵא רַחֲמִים,

‹‹ of mercy, ‹ Who ‹ HASHEM, ‹‹ before ‹ I have ‹ and gracious ‹ O merciful
is full   You.   sinned   One,

רַחֵם עָלַי וְקַבֵּל תַּחֲנוּנָי.

‹‹ my ‹ and ‹ on me ‹ have
supplications. accept   mercy

——— תהלים ו:ב-יא / Psalms 6:2-11 ———

יהוה, אַל בְּאַפְּךָ תוֹכִיחֵנִי, וְאַל בַּחֲמָתְךָ תְיַסְּרֵנִי.

‹‹chastise me. ‹ in Your wrath ‹ nor ‹ rebuke me, ‹in Your anger ‹ do not ‹ HASHEM,

חָנֵּנִי יהוה כִּי אֻמְלַל אָנִי, רְפָאֵנִי יהוה כִּי נִבְהֲלוּ

‹ shudder ‹ for ‹ HASHEM, ‹ heal me, ‹‹ am I; ‹ feeble ‹ for ‹ HASHEM, ‹ Favor
with terror   me,

עֲצָמָי. וְנַפְשִׁי נִבְהֲלָה מְאֹד, וְאַתָּה יהוה עַד מָתָי.

‹‹when? ‹ until ‹ HASHEM, ‹ and You, ‹‹ utterly, ‹ is terrified ‹ My soul ‹‹do my bones.

שׁוּבָה יהוה חַלְּצָה נַפְשִׁי, הוֹשִׁיעֵנִי לְמַעַן חַסְדֶּךָ.

‹‹Your kindness. ‹ as befits ‹ save me ‹‹ my soul; ‹ release ‹ HASHEM, ‹ Desist,

כִּי אֵין בַּמָּוֶת זִכְרֶךָ, בִּשְׁאוֹל מִי יוֹדֶה לָךְ. יָגַעְתִּי

‹ I am ‹‹ You? ‹ will ‹ who ‹ in the ‹‹ is there men- ‹ in ‹ not ‹ For
wearied   praise   grave   tion of You; death

בְּאַנְחָתִי, אַשְׂחֶה בְכָל לַיְלָה מִטָּתִי, בְּדִמְעָתִי

‹ with my tears ‹‹ my bed; ‹ night ‹ every ‹ I drench ‹‹ with my sigh;

עַרְשִׂי אַמְסֶה. עָשְׁשָׁה מִכַּעַס עֵינִי, עָתְקָה בְּכָל

‹ by all ‹ aged ‹ is my ‹ because of ‹ Dimmed ‹‹ I soak. ‹ my couch
eye,   anger

צוֹרְרָי. סוּרוּ מִמֶּנִּי כָּל פֹּעֲלֵי אָוֶן, כִּי שָׁמַע יהוה

‹ HASHEM has heard ‹ for ‹‹ of evil, ‹ doers ‹ all ‹ from me, ‹ Depart ‹‹ my
tormentors.

קוֹל בִּכְיִי. שָׁמַע יהוה תְּחִנָּתִי, יהוה תְּפִלָּתִי יִקָּח.

‹‹ will ‹ my prayer ‹ HASHEM ‹‹ my plea, ‹ HASHEM ‹‹ of my ‹ the
accept.   has heard   weeping. sound

יֵבֹשׁוּ וְיִבָּהֲלוּ מְאֹד כָּל אֹיְבָי, יָשֻׁבוּ יֵבֹשׁוּ רָגַע.

‹‹ in an ‹ and be ‹ may they ‹‹ my ‹ all ‹ utterly, ‹ and con- ‹ Let them
instant. shamed regret enemies;   founded be shamed

מַחִי וּמַסִּי מֵמִית וּמְחַיֶּה, מַסִּיק מִן שְׁאוֹל

‹ the ‹ from ‹ Who raises ‹‹ and Who ‹ Who causes ‹‹ and Who ‹ [O God,]
grave   [the dead]   restores life,   death   heals, Who wounds

לְחַיֵּי עָלְמָא, בְּרָא כַּד חָטֵי אֲבוּהִי לַקְיֵהּ, אֲבוּהִי

‹ but a ‹‹ would ‹ his father ‹ sin, ‹ should ‹ A son ‹ eternal: ‹ to life
father　strike him,　　　　　　he

דְּחָיֵס אַסֵּי לִכְאֵבֵהּ. עַבְדָּא דְּמָרִיד נָפִיק בְּקוֹלָר,

‹‹ in chains, ‹ he is ‹‹ who rebels, ‹ A slave ‹‹ his [son's] ‹ will ‹ who is com-
led out　　　　　　pain.　　heal　passionate

מָרֵהּ תָּאִיב וְתַבִּיר קוֹלָרֵהּ.

‹‹ his chains. ‹ he breaks ‹ desires, ‹ but [if]
his master

בְּרָךְ בְּכְרָךְ אֲנַן וְחָטֵינָן קַמָּךְ, הָא רָוֵי נַפְשִׁין

‹ has our ‹ satiated ‹ indeed ‹‹ before ‹ and we have ‹ we ‹ Your ‹ Your
soul been　　　　　　You;　　sinned　are, firstborn,　son,

בְּגִידִין מְרָרִין אֲנַן עַבְדָּךְ, וּמְרוֹדִינָן קַמָּךְ,

‹‹ before ‹ and we have ‹ we ‹ Your ‹‹ that is bitter. ‹ with
You;　rebelled　are　servants　　　wormwood

הָא בִּבְזְתָא, הָא בְּשִׁבְיָא, הָא בְּמַלְקְיוּתָא.

‹‹ by the lash. ‹ and ‹ in captivity, ‹ some ‹ from ‹ [indeed we have
some　　　　　　looting, suffered,] some

בְּמָטוּ מִנָּךְ בְּרַחֲמָךְ דִּנְפִישִׁין, אַסֵּי לִכְאֵבִין

‹ the pains ‹ heal ‹ that is ‹ in Your ‹ of You, ‹ We beg
abundant,　compassion

דִּתְקוֹף עֲלָן, עַד דְּלָא נֶהֱוֵי גְּמִירָא בְּשִׁבְיָא.

‹‹ in captivity. ‹ completely ‹ we are not ‹ while ‹ us, ‹ that have
annihilated　　　yet　　overwhelmed

מַכְנִיסֵי רַחֲמִים, הַכְנִיסוּ רַחֲמֵינוּ, לִפְנֵי בַּעַל

‹ the ‹ before ‹ our [plea for] ‹ may you ‹ [pleas for] mercy, ‹ O you who
Master　　mercy　usher in　　usher in

הָרַחֲמִים. מַשְׁמִיעֵי תְפִלָּה, הַשְׁמִיעוּ תְפִלָּתֵנוּ, לִפְנֵי

‹ before ‹ of our prayer ‹ may you aid ‹‹ of prayer, ‹ O you who aid ‹‹ of mercy.
the hearing　　　　the hearing

שׁוֹמֵעַ תְּפִלָּה. מַשְׁמִיעֵי צְעָקָה, הַשְׁמִיעוּ צַעֲקָתֵנוּ,

‹ of our ‹ may you aid ‹‹ of outcries, ‹ O you who aid ‹‹ of ‹ the Hearer
outcries　the hearing　　　the hearing　prayer.

לִפְנֵי שׁוֹמֵעַ צְעָקָה. מַכְנִיסֵי דִמְעָה, הַכְנִיסוּ

‹ may you usher in ‹‹ tears, ‹ O you who usher in ‹‹ of outcries. ‹ the Hearer ‹ before

דִּמְעוֹתֵינוּ, לִפְנֵי מֶלֶךְ מִתְרַצֶּה בִּדְמָעוֹת.

‹‹ through tears. ‹ Who is appeased ‹ the King ‹ before ‹ our tears

הִשְׁתַּדְּלוּ וְהַרְבּוּ תְּחִנָּה וּבַקָּשָׁה, לִפְנֵי מֶלֶךְ אֵל

‹ God, ‹ the King, ‹ before ‹ and pleas ‹ supplications ‹ and ‹ Exert
intensify   yourselves

רָם וְנִשָּׂא. הַזְכִּירוּ לְפָנָיו, הַשְׁמִיעוּ לְפָנָיו תּוֹרָה

‹ the ‹ before ‹ aid to ‹‹ before ‹ Mention ‹‹ and ‹ exalted
Torah   Him,   be heard   Him,   uplifted.

וּמַעֲשִׂים טוֹבִים שֶׁל שׁוֹכְנֵי עָפָר.

‹‹ in the ‹ [the Patriarchs ‹ of ‹ that are ‹ and the deeds
dust.   and Matriarchs]   good
who dwell

יִזְכֹּר אַהֲבָתָם וִיחַיֶּה זַרְעָם, שֶׁלֹּא תֹאבַד שְׁאֵרִית

‹ shall the ‹ lost ‹ so that ‹ to their ‹ and grant ‹ their love ‹ May He
remnant   not   offspring,   life   remember

יַעֲקֹב. כִּי צֹאן רוֹעֶה נֶאֱמָן הָיָה לְחֶרְפָּה,

‹‹ a disgrace; ‹ has ‹ who is faith- ‹ of the ‹ the ‹ For ‹‹ of Jacob
become   ful [Moses]   shepherd   flock   be.

יִשְׂרָאֵל גּוֹי אֶחָד לְמָשָׁל וְלִשְׁנִינָה.

‹‹ and a simile. ‹ a parable ‹‹ that is ‹ the ‹‹ Israel,
unique,   nation

מַהֵר עֲנֵנוּ אֱלֹהֵי יִשְׁעֵנוּ, וּפְדֵנוּ מִכָּל גְּזֵרוֹת קָשׁוֹת

‹‹ that are ‹ decrees ‹ from all ‹ and re- ‹ of our ‹ O God ‹ answer ‹ Swiftly
harsh;   deem us   salvation,   us,

וְהוֹשִׁיעָה בְּרַחֲמֶיךָ הָרַבִּים, מְשִׁיחַ צִדְקֶךָ וְעַמֶּךָ.

‹‹ and Your ‹ Your righteous ‹ that is ‹ in Your mercy ‹ and may You
people.   anointed one   abundant,   save,

מָרָן דְּבִשְׁמַיָּא לָךְ מִתְחַנְּנַן, כְּבָר שְׁבִיָּא דְמִתְחַנַּן

‹ who ‹ in ‹ as one ‹ do we ‹ to You ‹‹ Who is in ‹ Our
supplicates   captivity   supplicate,   heaven,   Master

לִשְׁבוּיֵהּ. כֻּלְּהוֹן בְּנֵי שְׁבִיָּא בְּכַסְפָּא מִתְפָּרְקִין,

‹‹ are redeemed, ‹ through ‹ in ‹ those ‹ [for] all ‹‹ before his
money   captivity,   captors;

וְעַמָּךְ יִשְׂרָאֵל בְּרַחֲמֵי וּבְתַחֲנוּנֵי, הַב לָן שְׁאִילְתִּין

‹ our requests ‹ us ‹ O ‹‹ and ‹ through ‹ Israel ‹ but Your
grant   supplication.   compassion   people

וּבָעוּתִין, דְּלָא נֶהְדַּר רֵיקָם מִן קֳדָמָךְ.

‹‹ before ‹ from ‹ empty- ‹ that we not be ‹ and our prayers
You.   handed   turned away

מָרָן דִּבִשְׁמַיָּא לָךְ מִתְחַנְּנָן, כְּעַבְדָּא דְּמִתְחַנֵּן
‹ Our › ‹ Who is in › ‹ to You » do we « ‹ as a slave › who
Master heaven, supplicate, supplicates

לְמָרֵיהּ, עֲשִׁיקֵי אֲנָן וּבַחֲשׁוֹכָא שָׁרִינָן, מְרִירָן נַפְשִׁין
‹ to his » are ‹ Oppressed › are ‹ and in darkness » do we ‹ embittered › are [our] ‹
master: we abide, souls

מֵעַקְתִין דִּנְפִישִׁין, חֵילָא לֵית בָּן לְרַצּוּיָךְ. מָרָן,
‹ from distress › that is « ‹ Strength › is ‹ within › to appease » ‹ Our
excessive. lacking us You. Master,

עָבִיד בְּדִיל קַיָּמָא דִּגְזַרְתָּ עִם אֲבָהָתָנָא.
act ‹ for the › of the › that You › with ‹ our Patriarchs. »
sake covenant established

שׁוֹמֵר יִשְׂרָאֵל, שְׁמוֹר שְׁאֵרִית יִשְׂרָאֵל, וְאַל
O Guardian › of Israel, » safeguard ‹ the remnant › of Israel; « let not ‹

יֹאבַד יִשְׂרָאֵל, הָאוֹמְרִים שְׁמַע יִשְׂרָאֵל.¹
Israel be destroyed — » those who › Hear, ‹ O Israel. › »
proclaim:

שׁוֹמֵר גּוֹי אֶחָד, שְׁמוֹר שְׁאֵרִית עַם אֶחָד, וְאַל
O Guardian › of the › that is › safeguard « the remnant › of the › that is › let not ‹
nation unique, people unique; »

יֹאבַד גּוֹי אֶחָד, הַמְיַחֲדִים שִׁמְךָ, יהוה אֱלֹהֵינוּ
be ‹ the ‹ that is » those who proclaim › of Your › HASHEM « ‹ is our God, ›
destroyed nation unique, the Oneness Name:

יהוה אֶחָד.
is ‹ HASHEM › the One «
[and Only]!

שׁוֹמֵר גּוֹי קָדוֹשׁ, שְׁמוֹר שְׁאֵרִית עַם קָדוֹשׁ, וְאַל
O Guardian › of the › that is › safeguard « the remnant › of the › that is « let not ‹
nation holy, people holy;

יֹאבַד גּוֹי קָדוֹשׁ, הַמְשַׁלְּשִׁים בְּשָׁלֹשׁ קְדֻשּׁוֹת לְקָדוֹשׁ.
be ‹ the ‹ that is » those who proclaim ‹ the ‹ sancti- ‹ to the »
destroyed nation holy, three times threefold fications Holy One.

מִתְרַצֶּה בְּרַחֲמִים וּמִתְפַּיֵּס בְּתַחֲנוּנִים, הִתְרַצֵּה
be ‹ through » and Who becomes ‹ through ‹ You Who becomes ‹
favorable supplications, conciliatory compassion favorable

---
(1) *Deuteronomy* 6:4.

וְהִתְפַּיֵּס לְדוֹר עָנִי, כִּי אֵין עוֹזֵר. אָבִינוּ מַלְכֵּנוּ,

《 our King, 〈 Our Father, 《 helper. 〈 there is no 〈 for 〈 that is poor, 〈 to the generation 〈 and be conciliatory

חָנֵּנוּ וַעֲנֵנוּ, כִּי אֵין בָּנוּ מַעֲשִׂים, עֲשֵׂה עִמָּנוּ

〈 us 〈 treat 《 worthy deeds; 〈 we have no 〈 though 〈 and answer us, 〈 be gracious with us

צְדָקָה וָחֶסֶד וְהוֹשִׁיעֵנוּ.

《 and save us. 〈 and kindness, 〈 with charity

STAND AFTER THE WORDS וַאֲנַחְנוּ לֹא נֵדַע, UNTIL CONCLUSION OF THE PARAGRAPH.

וַאֲנַחְנוּ לֹא נֵדַע מַה נַּעֲשֶׂה, כִּי עָלֶיךָ עֵינֵינוּ.[1]

《 are our eyes. 〈 upon You 〈 rather, 《 we should do, 〈 what 〈 know not 〈 We

זְכֹר רַחֲמֶיךָ יהוה וַחֲסָדֶיךָ, כִּי מֵעוֹלָם הֵמָּה.[2] יְהִי

〈 May 《 are they. 〈 eternal 〈 for 〈 and Your kindnesses, 《 Hashem, 〈 Your mercies, 〈 Remember

חַסְדְּךָ יהוה עָלֵינוּ, כַּאֲשֶׁר יִחַלְנוּ לָךְ.[3] אַל תִּזְכָּר

〈 recall 〈 Do not 《 You. 〈 we awaited 〈 just as 《 be upon us, 〈 Hashem, 〈 Your kindness,

לָנוּ עֲוֹנוֹת רִאשׁוֹנִים, מַהֵר יְקַדְּמוּנוּ רַחֲמֶיךָ, כִּי

〈 for 《 may Your mercies, 〈 advance to meet us 〈 swiftly 〈 of the ancients; 〈 the sins 〈 against us

דַלּוֹנוּ מְאֹד.[4] עֶזְרֵנוּ בְּשֵׁם יהוה, עֹשֵׂה שָׁמַיִם

〈 of heaven 〈 Maker 《 of Hashem, 〈 is through the Name 〈 Our help 《 exceedingly 〈 we have become impoverished

וָאָרֶץ.[5] חָנֵּנוּ יהוה חָנֵּנוּ, כִּי רַב שָׂבַעְנוּ בוּז.[6] בְּרֹגֶז

《 Amid wrath, 《 with contempt. 〈 sated fully 〈 we are 〈 for 《 favor us, 〈 Hashem, 〈 Favor us, 《 and earth.

רַחֵם תִּזְכּוֹר.[7] בְּרֹגֶז עֲקֵדָה תִּזְכּוֹר. בְּרֹגֶז תְּמִימוֹת

〈 the perfect ones 《 Amid wrath, 《 You should remember! 〈 the binding [of Isaac] 《 Amid wrath, 《 You should remember! 〈 to be merciful

תִּזְכּוֹר. יהוה הוֹשִׁיעָה, הַמֶּלֶךְ יַעֲנֵנוּ בְיוֹם קָרְאֵנוּ.[8]

《 we call. 〈 on the day 〈 answer us 〈 May the King 《 save! 〈 Hashem, 《 You should remember!

כִּי הוּא יָדַע יִצְרֵנוּ, זָכוּר כִּי עָפָר אֲנָחְנוּ.[9]

《 are we. 〈 dust 〈 that 〈 He is mindful 《 our nature, 〈 knew 〈 He 〈 For

---

(1) *II Chronicles* 20:12. (2) *Psalms* 25:6. (3) 33:22. (4) 79:8. (5) 121:2. (6) 123:3. (7) *Habakkuk* 3:2. (8) *Psalms* 20:10. (9) 103:14.

עֲזְרֵנוּ אֱלֹהֵי יִשְׁעֵנוּ עַל דְּבַר כְּבוֹד שְׁמֶךָ, וְהַצִּילֵנוּ ❖

⟨ rescue us ⟨⟨ of Your ⟨ of the ⟨ the ⟨ for ⟨ of our ⟨ O God ⟨ Assist us,
Name; glory sake salvation

וְכַפֵּר עַל חַטֹּאתֵינוּ לְמַעַן שְׁמֶךָ.¹

⟨⟨ of Your ⟨ for the ⟨ our sins ⟨ for ⟨ and grant
Name. sake atonement

FULL KADDISH / קדיש שלם

THE *CHAZZAN* RECITES קַדִּישׁ שָׁלֵם, FULL *KADDISH*.

יִתְגַּדַּל וְיִתְקַדַּשׁ שְׁמֵהּ רַבָּא. (אָמֵן. — Cong.) בְּעָלְמָא

⟨ — in the ⟨⟨ (Amen.) ⟨⟨ that is ⟨ may His ⟨ and be ⟨ Grow
world great! — Name sanctified exalted

דִּי בְרָא כִרְעוּתֵהּ. וְיַמְלִיךְ מַלְכוּתֵהּ, וְיַצְמַח פֻּרְקָנֵהּ

⟨ His ⟨ and cause ⟨⟨ to His ⟨ and may He ⟨⟨ according ⟨ He ⟨ that
salvation, to sprout kingship, give reign to His will, created

וִיקָרֵב מְשִׁיחֵהּ. (אָמֵן. — Cong.) בְּחַיֵּיכוֹן וּבְיוֹמֵיכוֹן וּבְחַיֵּי

⟨ and in the ⟨ and in ⟨ in your ⟨⟨ (Amen.) ⟨⟨ His Messiah, ⟨ and bring
lifetimes your days, lifetimes near

דְכָל בֵּית יִשְׂרָאֵל, בַּעֲגָלָא וּבִזְמַן קָרִיב. וְאִמְרוּ: אָמֵן.

⟨⟨Amen. ⟨ Now ⟨⟨ that comes ⟨ and at a ⟨ swiftly ⟨⟨ of Israel, ⟨ Family ⟨ of the
respond: soon. time entire

CONGREGATION RESPONDS:

אָמֵן. יְהֵא שְׁמֵהּ רַבָּא מְבָרַךְ לְעָלַם וּלְעָלְמֵי עָלְמַיָּא.

⟨⟨ and for all eternity. ⟨ forever ⟨ be ⟨ that is ⟨ His ⟨ May ⟨⟨ Amen.
blessed great Name

CHAZZAN CONTINUES:

יְהֵא שְׁמֵהּ רַבָּא מְבָרַךְ לְעָלַם וּלְעָלְמֵי עָלְמַיָּא. יִתְבָּרַךְ

⟨ Blessed, ⟨⟨ and for all eternity. ⟨ forever ⟨ be ⟨ that is ⟨ His ⟨ May
blessed great Name

וְיִשְׁתַּבַּח וְיִתְפָּאַר וְיִתְרוֹמַם וְיִתְנַשֵּׂא וְיִתְהַדָּר וְיִתְעַלֶּה

⟨ elevated, ⟨ honored, ⟨ upraised, ⟨ exalted, ⟨ glorified, ⟨ praised,

וְיִתְהַלָּל שְׁמֵהּ דְּקֻדְשָׁא בְּרִיךְ הוּא (בְּרִיךְ הוּא — Cong.)

⟨⟨ is He) ⟨ (Blessed ⟨⟨ is He ⟨ Blessed ⟨ of the Holy ⟨ be the ⟨ and lauded
One, Name

לְעֵלָּא מִן כָּל בִּרְכָתָא וְשִׁירָתָא תֻּשְׁבְּחָתָא וְנֶחֱמָתָא —

⟨ and ⟨ praise ⟨⟨ and song, ⟨ blessing ⟨ any ⟨ beyond
consolation

---

(1) *Psalms* 79:9.

דַּאֲמִירָן בְּעָלְמָא. וְאִמְרוּ: אָמֵן. (Cong.) — אָמֵן.)

《 (Amen.)   《 Amen. 〈 Now respond: 《 in the world. 〈 that are uttered

CONGREGATION:

(קַבֵּל בְּרַחֲמִים וּבְרָצוֹן אֶת תְּפִלָּתֵנוּ.)

《 our prayers.) 〈 and with favor 〈 with mercy 〈 (Accept

CHAZZAN CONTINUES:

תִּתְקַבֵּל צְלוֹתְהוֹן וּבָעוּתְהוֹן דְּכָל בֵּית יִשְׂרָאֵל קֳדָם

〈 before 〈 Israel 〈 Family of 〈 of the entire 〈 and supplications 〈 the prayers 〈 May accepted be

אֲבוּהוֹן דִּי בִשְׁמַיָּא. וְאִמְרוּ: אָמֵן. (Cong.) — אָמֵן.)

《 (Amen.)   《 Amen. 〈 Now respond: 《 is in Heaven. 〈 Who 〈 their Father

CONGREGATION:

(יְהִי שֵׁם יהוה מְבֹרָךְ, מֵעַתָּה וְעַד עוֹלָם.[1])

《 eternity.) 〈 until 〈 from this time 《 be blessed, 〈 of HASHEM 〈 the Name 〈 (Let

CHAZZAN CONTINUES:

יְהֵא שְׁלָמָא רַבָּא מִן שְׁמַיָּא וְחַיִּים טוֹבִים עָלֵינוּ וְעַל כָּל

〈 all 〈 and upon 〈 upon us 〈 that is good, 〈 and life 〈 Heaven 〈 from 〈 that is abundant 〈 peace 〈 May there be

יִשְׂרָאֵל. וְאִמְרוּ: אָמֵן. (Cong.) — אָמֵן.)

《 (Amen.)   《 Amen. 〈 Now respond: 《 Israel.

CONGREGATION:

(עֶזְרִי מֵעִם יהוה, עֹשֵׂה שָׁמַיִם וָאָרֶץ.[2])

《 and earth.) 〈 of heaven 〈 Maker 《 HASHEM, 〈 is from 〈 (My help

CHAZZAN BOWS; TAKES THREE STEPS BACK. BOWS LEFT AND SAYS "… עֹשֶׂה שָׁלוֹם, *HE WHO MAKES PEACE* …"; BOWS RIGHT AND SAYS "… הוּא, *MAY HE* …"; BOWS FORWARD AND SAYS "… וְעַל כָּל יִשְׂרָאֵל, *AND UPON ALL ISRAEL* …"; REMAINS IN PLACE FOR A FEW MOMENTS, THEN TAKES THREE STEPS FORWARD.

עֹשֶׂה שָׁלוֹם בִּמְרוֹמָיו, הוּא יַעֲשֶׂה שָׁלוֹם עָלֵינוּ, וְעַל כָּל

〈 all 〈 and upon 〈 upon us, 〈 peace 〈 make 《 may He 《 in His heights, 〈 peace 〈 He Who makes

יִשְׂרָאֵל. וְאִמְרוּ: אָמֵן. (Cong.) — אָמֵן.)

《 (Amen.)   《 Amen. 〈 Now respond: 《 Israel.

---

(1) *Psalms* 113:2. (2) 121:2.

﷽ FIFTH DAY / יום חמישי ﷽

אַשְׁרֵי יוֹשְׁבֵי בֵיתֶךָ, עוֹד יְהַלְלוּךָ סֶּלָה.¹ אַשְׁרֵי

⟨ Praise-worthy ⟩ « Selah. « they will praise You, « con-tinually « in Your house, ⟨ are those who dwell ⟨ Praiseworthy

הָעָם שֶׁכָּכָה לּוֹ, אַשְׁרֵי הָעָם שֶׁיהוה אֱלֹהָיו.²

« is their God. ⟨ that ⟨ HASHEM ⟨ is the people ⟨ praise-worthy « is their lot; ⟨ that such ⟨ is the people

——————— תהלים קמה / Psalm 145 ———————

תְּהִלָּה לְדָוִד, אֲרוֹמִמְךָ אֱלוֹהַי הַמֶּלֶךְ, וַאֲבָרְכָה

⟨ and I will bless « the King, ⟨ my God ⟨ I will exalt You, « by David: ⟨ A psalm of praise

שִׁמְךָ לְעוֹלָם וָעֶד. בְּכָל יוֹם אֲבָרְכֶךָ, וַאֲהַלְלָה שִׁמְךָ

⟨ Your Name ⟨ and I will laud « I will bless You, ⟨ day ⟨ Every « and ever. ⟨ for ever ⟨ Your Name

לְעוֹלָם וָעֶד. גָּדוֹל יהוה וּמְהֻלָּל מְאֹד, וְלִגְדֻלָּתוֹ

⟨ and His greatness «exceedingly, ⟨ and lauded ⟨ is ⟨ HASHEM ⟨ Great « and ever. ⟨ for ever

אֵין חֵקֶר. דּוֹר לְדוֹר יְשַׁבַּח מַעֲשֶׂיךָ, וּגְבוּרֹתֶיךָ יַגִּידוּ.

« they will recount. ⟨ and Your mighty deeds « Your actions, ⟨ will ⟨ to praise ⟨ Gen-eration « is beyond investigation.

הֲדַר כְּבוֹד הוֹדֶךָ, וְדִבְרֵי נִפְלְאֹתֶיךָ אָשִׂיחָה. וֶעֱזוּז

⟨ And of the might « I shall discuss. ⟨ that are wondrous ⟨ and Your deeds ⟨ of Your majesty ⟨ glory ⟨ The splendrous

נוֹרְאֹתֶיךָ יֹאמֵרוּ, וּגְדוּלָּתְךָ אֲסַפְּרֶנָּה. זֵכֶר רַב טוּבְךָ

⟨ of Your abun-dant goodness ⟨ A recol-lection « I shall relate. ⟨ and Your greatness « they will speak. ⟨ of Your awesome deeds

יַבִּיעוּ, וְצִדְקָתְךָ יְרַנֵּנוּ. חַנּוּן וְרַחוּם יהוה, אֶרֶךְ אַפַּיִם

⟨ to anger, ⟨ slow « is ⟨ and ⟨ Gracious « they will ⟨ and of Your « they will utter, sing joyfully. HASHEM, merciful righteousness

וּגְדָל חָסֶד. טוֹב יהוה לַכֹּל, וְרַחֲמָיו עַל כָּל מַעֲשָׂיו.

« His creations. ⟨ all ⟨ are ⟨ His ⟨ on mercies « to all; ⟨ HASHEM is good « in [bestowing] ⟨ and kindness. great

יוֹדוּךָ יהוה כָּל מַעֲשֶׂיךָ, וַחֲסִידֶיךָ יְבָרְכוּכָה. כְּבוֹד

⟨ Of the glory « will bless You. ⟨ and Your devout ones « Your creations — ⟨ — all «HASHEM ⟨ They will thank You,

───────────────
(1) Psalms 84:5. (2) 144:15.

מַלְכוּתְךָ יֹאמֵרוּ, וּגְבוּרָתְךָ יְדַבֵּרוּ. לְהוֹדִיעַ לִבְנֵי הָאָדָם

< mankind < To inform « they will < and of Your « they will < of Your
declare. power speak, kingdom

גְּבוּרֹתָיו, וּכְבוֹד הֲדַר מַלְכוּתוֹ. מַלְכוּתְךָ מַלְכוּת כָּל

<[span- < is a < Your kingdom « of His < splendor < and of the « of His mighty
ning] all kingdom kingdom. glorious deeds,

עֹלָמִים, וּמֶמְשַׁלְתְּךָ בְּכָל דּוֹר וָדֹר. סוֹמֵךְ יהוה

< HASHEM « after < gen- < is < and Your « eternities,
supports generation. eration throughout dominion

לְכָל הַנֹּפְלִים, וְזוֹקֵף לְכָל הַכְּפוּפִים. עֵינֵי כֹל

< of all < The « those who < all < and « those who < all
eyes are bent. straightens are fallen,

אֵלֶיךָ יְשַׂבֵּרוּ, וְאַתָּה נוֹתֵן לָהֶם אֶת אָכְלָם בְּעִתּוֹ.

« in its < their food < them < give < and You « do look < to You
proper time. with hope,

CONCENTRATE INTENTLY WHILE RECITING THE VERSE פּוֹתֵחַ, *YOU OPEN.*

פּוֹתֵחַ אֶת יָדֶךָ, וּמַשְׂבִּיעַ לְכָל חַי רָצוֹן. ❖ צַדִּיק

< Righteous « [with its] < living < every < and satisfy « Your hand, < You open
desire. thing

יהוה בְּכָל דְּרָכָיו, וְחָסִיד בְּכָל מַעֲשָׂיו. קָרוֹב יהוה

< is < Close « His deeds. < in all < and « His ways, < in all < is
HASHEM magnanimous HASHEM

לְכָל קֹרְאָיו, לְכֹל אֲשֶׁר יִקְרָאֻהוּ בֶאֱמֶת. רְצוֹן יְרֵאָיו

< of those < The « sincerely. < call upon < who < to all « who call < to all
who fear Him will Him upon Him,

יַעֲשֶׂה, וְאֶת שַׁוְעָתָם יִשְׁמַע וְיוֹשִׁיעֵם. שׁוֹמֵר יהוה

< HASHEM protects « and He will < He will < and their cry « He
save them. hear, will do;

אֶת כָּל אֹהֲבָיו, וְאֵת כָּל הָרְשָׁעִים יַשְׁמִיד. תְּהִלַּת

< The praise « He will destroy. < the wicked < but all « who love Him; < all

יהוה יְדַבֶּר פִּי, וִיבָרֵךְ כָּל בָּשָׂר שֵׁם קָדְשׁוֹ לְעוֹלָם

< for ever < of His < the < flesh < may < and bless « may my < of
Holiness Name all mouth declare, HASHEM

וָעֶד. וַאֲנַחְנוּ נְבָרֵךְ יָהּ מֵעַתָּה וְעַד עוֹלָם; הַלְלוּיָהּ.[1]

« Halleluyah! « eternity. < until < from < God < will < But we « and
this time bless ever.

(1) *Psalms* 115:18.

THE *CHAZZAN* RECITES חֲצִי קַדִּישׁ, HALF-*KADDISH*:

יִתְגַּדַּל וְיִתְקַדַּשׁ שְׁמֵהּ רַבָּא. (Cong. — אָמֵן.) בְּעָלְמָא

‹ Grow exalted › ‹ and be sanctified › ‹ may His Name › ‹ that is great! — › « (Amen.) ‹ — in the world

דִּי בְרָא כִרְעוּתֵהּ. וְיַמְלִיךְ מַלְכוּתֵהּ, וְיַצְמַח פֻּרְקָנֵהּ

‹ that › ‹ He created › « according to His will, › ‹ and may He give reign › « to His kingship, › ‹ and cause to sprout › ‹ His salvation,

וִיקָרֵב מְשִׁיחֵהּ. (Cong. — אָמֵן.) בְּחַיֵּיכוֹן וּבְיוֹמֵיכוֹן וּבְחַיֵּי

‹ and bring near › « His Messiah, › « (Amen.) › ‹ in your lifetimes › ‹ and in your days, › ‹ and in the lifetimes

דְכָל בֵּית יִשְׂרָאֵל, בַּעֲגָלָא וּבִזְמַן קָרִיב. וְאִמְרוּ: אָמֵן.

‹ of the entire › ‹ Family › ‹ of Israel, › « swiftly › ‹ and at a time › « that comes soon. › ‹ Now respond: › « Amen.

CONGREGATION RESPONDS:

אָמֵן. יְהֵא שְׁמֵהּ רַבָּא מְבָרַךְ לְעָלַם וּלְעָלְמֵי עָלְמַיָּא.

« and for all eternity. ‹ forever › ‹ be blessed › ‹ that is great › ‹ His Name › ‹ May › « Amen.

CHAZZAN CONTINUES:

יְהֵא שְׁמֵהּ רַבָּא מְבָרַךְ לְעָלַם וּלְעָלְמֵי עָלְמַיָּא. יִתְבָּרַךְ

‹ Blessed, › « and for all eternity. ‹ forever › ‹ be blessed › ‹ that is great › ‹ His Name › ‹ May

וְיִשְׁתַּבַּח וְיִתְפָּאַר וְיִתְרוֹמַם וְיִתְנַשֵּׂא וְיִתְהַדָּר וְיִתְעַלֶּה

‹ elevated, › ‹ honored, › ‹ upraised, › ‹ exalted, › ‹ glorified, › ‹ praised,

וְיִתְהַלָּל שְׁמֵהּ דְּקֻדְשָׁא בְּרִיךְ הוּא (Cong. — בְּרִיךְ הוּא)

« is He) ‹ (Blessed « is He ‹ Blessed ‹ of the Holy One, › ‹ be the Name › ‹ and lauded

— לְעֵלָּא מִן כָּל בִּרְכָתָא וְשִׁירָתָא תֻּשְׁבְּחָתָא וְנֶחֱמָתָא

‹ and consolation ‹ praise « and song, ‹ blessing ‹ any ‹ beyond

דַּאֲמִירָן בְּעָלְמָא. וְאִמְרוּ: אָמֵן. (Cong. — אָמֵן.)

« (Amen.) « Amen. ‹ Now respond: ‹ in the world. ‹ that are uttered

ALL:

לְךָ יהוה הַצְּדָקָה, וְלָנוּ בֹּשֶׁת הַפָּנִים.[1] מַה

« What « is shamefacedness. ‹ and ours « is the righteousness, ‹ O Lord, ‹ Yours,

נִּתְאוֹנֵן,[2] מַה נֹּאמַר, מַה נְּדַבֵּר, וּמַה נִּצְטַדָּק.[3]

« justification ‹ What « can we offer? ‹ What « can we declare? ‹ What « can we say? ‹ What « complaint can we make?

---

(1) *Daniel* 9:7. (2) Cf. *Lamentations* 3:39. (3) Cf. *Genesis* 44:16.

נַחְפְּשָׂה דְרָכֵינוּ וְנַחְקְרָה, וְנָשׁוּבָה אֵלֶיךָ, כִּי יְמִינְךָ¹
‹ Your   ‹ for ‹ « to You, ‹ and return ‹ and investigate ‹ our ways ‹ Let us
right hand   them,   examine

פְּשׁוּטָה לְקַבֵּל שָׁבִים. לֹא בְחֶסֶד וְלֹא בְמַעֲשִׂים
‹ with [merit for ‹ nor ‹ with [merit] ‹ Nei- « those who ‹ to accept ‹ is extended
good] deeds   for kindness   ther   return.

בָּאנוּ לְפָנֶיךָ, כְּדַלִּים וּכְרָשִׁים דָּפַקְנוּ דְלָתֶיךָ.
« on Your ‹ we have ‹ and as destitute ‹ but as « before You; ‹ do we
doors.   knocked   people   paupers   come

דְּלָתֶיךָ דָּפַקְנוּ רַחוּם וְחַנּוּן, נָא אַל תְּשִׁיבֵנוּ
‹ turn us ‹ do ‹ Please « and Gra- ‹ O Compas- ‹ we have ‹ On Your
away   not   cious One.   sionate One   knocked,   doors

רֵיקָם מִלְּפָנֶיךָ. מִלְּפָנֶיךָ מַלְכֵּנוּ רֵיקָם אַל תְּשִׁיבֵנוּ,
« turn us ‹ do ‹ empty- ‹ Our King, ‹ From before « from before ‹ empty-
away,   not   handed   You,   You.   handed

כִּי אַתָּה שׁוֹמֵעַ תְּפִלָּה.
« prayer. ‹ Who hears ‹ You are ‹ for
the One

שׁוֹמֵעַ תְּפִלָּה, עָדֶיךָ כָּל בָּשָׂר יָבֹאוּ.² יָבוֹא
‹ Come « will come. ‹ flesh ‹ all ‹ unto You « prayer, ‹ You Who
hears

כָּל בָּשָׂר לְהִשְׁתַּחֲוֹת לְפָנֶיךָ יהוה. יָבֹאוּ וְיִשְׁתַּחֲווּ³
‹ and bow ‹ They will « O ‹ before ‹ to bow down ‹ will all flesh
down   come   HASHEM.   You,

לְפָנֶיךָ אֲדֹנָי, וִיכַבְּדוּ לִשְׁמֶךָ.⁴ בֹּאוּ נִשְׁתַּחֲוֶה וְנִכְרָעָה,
« and bow, ‹ Let us prostrate ‹ Come! « to Your ‹ and they will « O Lord, ‹ before
ourselves   Name.   show honor   You,

נִבְרְכָה לִפְנֵי יהוה עֹשֵׂנוּ.⁵ נָבוֹאָה לְמִשְׁכְּנוֹתָיו,
« to His Tabernacles, ‹ Let us come « our Maker. ‹ HASHEM, ‹ before ‹ let us kneel

נִשְׁתַּחֲוֶה לַהֲדֹם רַגְלָיו.⁶ בֹּאוּ שְׁעָרָיו בְּתוֹדָה,
« with ‹ His ‹ Enter « for His feet. ‹ at the ‹ let us prostrate
thanksgiving,   gates   stool   ourselves

חֲצֵרֹתָיו בִּתְהִלָּה, הוֹדוּ לוֹ בָּרְכוּ שְׁמוֹ.⁷ וַאֲנַחְנוּ
‹ But we, « His ‹ bless « to ‹ give « with praise; ‹ His courtyards
Name.   Him,   thanks

(1) Cf. *Lamentations* 3:40. (2) *Psalms* 65:3. (3) Cf. *Isaiah* 66:23.
(4) *Psalms* 86:9. (5) 95:6. (6) 132:7. (7) 100:4.

בְּרֹב חַסְדְּךָ נָבוֹא בֵיתֶךָ, נִשְׁתַּחֲוֶה אֶל הֵיכַל קָדְשְׁךָ

‹ Your Holy Sanctuary ‹ toward ‹ we will prostrate ourselves ≪ Your House; ‹ will we enter ‹ of Your kindness ‹ through the abundance

בְּיִרְאָתֶךָ.¹ הִנֵּה בָּרְכוּ אֶת יהוה כָּל עַבְדֵי יהוה,

‹ of HASHEM, ‹ you servants ‹ all ‹ HASHEM, ‹ bless ≪ Indeed, ≪ in awe of You.

הָעֹמְדִים בְּבֵית יהוה בַּלֵּילוֹת.² שְׂאוּ יְדֵיכֶם קֹדֶשׁ

‹ in the Sanctuary ‹ your hands ‹ Lift ≪ in the nights. ‹ of HASHEM ‹ in the House ‹ who stand

וּבָרְכוּ אֶת יהוה.³ רוֹמְמוּ יהוה אֱלֹהֵינוּ, וְהִשְׁתַּחֲווּ

‹ and bow down ‹ our God, ‹ HASHEM, ‹ Exalt ≪ HASHEM. ‹ and bless

לַהֲדֹם רַגְלָיו, קָדוֹשׁ הוּא.⁴ רוֹמְמוּ יהוה אֱלֹהֵינוּ,

‹ our God, ‹ HASHEM, ‹ Exalt ≪ is He! ‹ holy ≪ at His footstool;

וְהִשְׁתַּחֲווּ לְהַר קָדְשׁוֹ, כִּי קָדוֹשׁ יהוה אֱלֹהֵינוּ.⁵

≪ our God. ‹ is HASHEM, ‹ holy ‹ for ≪ of His Holiness; ‹ at the Mount ‹ and bow

הִשְׁתַּחֲווּ לַיהוה בְּהַדְרַת קֹדֶשׁ, חִילוּ מִפָּנָיו כָּל

‹ everyone ‹ before Him, ‹ tremble ≪ of holiness; ‹ in the splendor ‹ before HASHEM ‹ Bow down

הָאָרֶץ.⁶ נִשְׁתַּחֲוֶה אֶל הֵיכַל קָדְשְׁךָ וְנוֹדֶה אֶת שְׁמֶךָ,

‹ Your Name ‹ and we will thank ≪ Your Holy Sanctuary, ‹ toward ‹ We will prostrate ourselves ≪ on earth.

עַל חַסְדְּךָ וְעַל אֲמִתֶּךָ, כִּי הִגְדַּלְתָּ עַל כָּל שְׁמֶךָ

≪ Your Name — ‹ — even beyond ≪ You have exalted ‹ for ≪ Your faithfulness; ‹ and for ‹ Your kindness ‹ for

אִמְרָתֶךָ.⁷ יהוה אֱלֹהֵי צְבָאוֹת, מִי כָמוֹךָ חֲסִין

‹ O Strong One, ≪ is like You, ‹ — who ≪ of Legions ‹ God ‹ HASHEM, ≪ Your promise.

יָהּ, וֶאֱמוּנָתְךָ סְבִיבוֹתֶיךָ.⁸ כִּי מִי בַשַּׁחַק יַעֲרֹךְ

‹ can be compared ‹ in the sky ‹ who ‹ For ≪ surrounds You. ‹ and Your faithfulness ≪ God? —

לַיהוה, יִדְמֶה לַיהוה בִּבְנֵי אֵלִים.⁹ כִּי גָדוֹל אַתָּה

‹ are You ‹ great ‹ For ≪ among the angels? ‹ to HASHEM ‹ be likened ≪ to HASHEM;

וְעוֹשֵׂה נִפְלָאוֹת, אַתָּה אֱלֹהִים לְבַדֶּךָ.¹⁰ כִּי גָדוֹל

‹ great ‹ For ≪ alone. ‹ O God, ‹ You, ≪ of wonders; ‹ and a worker

(1) Cf. *Psalms* 5:8. (2) 134:1. (3) 134:2. (4) 99:5. (5) 99:9. (6) 96:9. (7) Cf. 138:2. (8) 89:9. (9) 89:7. (10) 86:10.

גָּדוֹל ^{1.}אֲמִתֶּךָ. שְׁחָקִים וְעַד חַסְדֶּךָ, שָׁמַיִם מֵעַל

‹ Great « is Your ‹ the upper ‹ and « is Your ‹ the very ‹ above
truth. heights until kindness, heavens

גָּדוֹל (כִּי) ^{2.}חֵקֶר. אֵין וְלִגְדֻלָּתוֹ מְאֹד, וּמְהֻלָּל יהוה

‹ great ‹ (For) « investiga- ‹ is ‹ and His « exceed- ‹ and ‹ is
tion. beyond greatness ingly, lauded HASHEM

כִּי ^{3.}אֱלֹהִים. כָּל עַל הוּא נוֹרָא מְאֹד, וּמְהֻלָּל יהוה

‹ For « heavenly ‹ all ‹ above ‹ is He ‹ awesome « exceed- ‹ and ‹ is
powers. ingly; lauded HASHEM

אֲשֶׁר ^{4.}אֱלֹהִים. כָּל עַל גָּדוֹל וּמֶלֶךְ יהוה, גָּדוֹל אֵל

‹ For « heavenly ‹ all ‹ above ‹ and a great King « is ‹ a great God
powers. HASHEM,

כְמַעֲשֶׂיךָ יַעֲשֶׂה אֲשֶׁר וּבָאָרֶץ, בַּשָּׁמַיִם אֵל מִי

‹ like unto ‹ can do ‹ that ‹ or in the ‹ is there in ‹ power ‹ what
Your deeds earth the heaven

לָּךְ כִּי הַגּוֹיִם, מֶלֶךְ יִרָאֲךָ לֹא מִי ^{5.}וְכִגְבוּרֹתֶיךָ.

‹ to ‹ For « of nations? ‹ O King « fear You, ‹ would ‹ Who « and like unto Your
You not mighty acts?

מֵאֵין מַלְכוּתָם וּבְכָל הַגּוֹיִם חַכְמֵי בְּכָל כִּי יָאָתָה,

‹ there is ‹ their ‹ and in all ‹ of the ‹ the wise ‹ among ‹ for « [kingship]
none kingdoms nations men all befits;

שְׁמֶךָ וְגָדוֹל אַתָּה גָּדוֹל יהוה, כָמוֹךָ מֵאֵין ^{6.}כָּמוֹךָ.

‹ is Your ‹ and great ‹ are You ‹ Great « O ‹ like You, ‹ There is « like You.
Name HASHEM! none

תָּרוּם יָדְךָ תָּעֹז גְּבוּרָה, עִם זְרוֹעַ לְךָ ^{7.}בִּגְבוּרָה.

‹ uplifted « is Your ‹ strength- « power; ‹ with ‹ is the ‹ Yours « in might.
hand, ened arm

מָאוֹר הֲכִינוֹתָ אַתָּה לָיְלָה, לְךָ אַף יוֹם, לְךָ ^{8.}יְמִינֶךָ.

‹ the ‹ prepared ‹ You « is the ‹ Yours ‹ also « is the ‹ Yours « is Your
luminary night; day, right hand.

הָרִים וְתוֹעֲפוֹת אָרֶץ, מְחְקְרֵי בְּיָדוֹ אֲשֶׁר ^{9.}וָשָׁמֶשׁ.

‹ of the ‹ and the « of the ‹ are the hidden ‹ in His ‹ For « and the
mountains summits earth, mysteries power sun.

תְּהִלָּתוֹ. כָּל יַשְׁמִיעַ יהוה, גְּבוּרוֹת יְמַלֵּל מִי ^{10.}לוֹ. ^{11.}

« of His ‹ all « [who] can « of ‹ the mighty ‹ can ‹ Who « are
praise? make heard HASHEM; acts express His.

---

(1) *Psalms* 108:5. (2) 145:3. (3) 96:4. (4) 95:3. (5) *Deuteronomy* 3:24.
(6) *Jeremiah* 10:7. (7) 10:6. (8) *Psalms* 89:14. (9) 74:16. (10) 95:4. (11) 106:2.

לְךָ יהוה הַגְּדֻלָּה וְהַגְּבוּרָה, וְהַתִּפְאֶרֶת וְהַנֵּצַח

‹ the ‹ the glory, ‹ the strength, ‹ is the ‹ HASHEM, ‹ Yours,
triumph,   greatness,

וְהַהוֹד, כִּי כֹל בַּשָּׁמַיִם וּבָאָרֶץ; לְךָ יהוה הַמַּמְלָכָה,

‹ is the ‹ HASHEM, ‹ Yours, « and on ‹ in heaven ‹ every- ‹ for « and the
kingdom   earth   thing   majesty;
[is Yours];

וְהַמִּתְנַשֵּׂא לְכֹל לְרֹאשׁ. לְךָ שָׁמַיִם, אַף לְךָ אָרֶץ,

« is the ‹ Yours ‹ also « are the ‹ Yours « leader. ‹ over ‹ and the
earth;   heavens,   every   sovereignty

תֵּבֵל וּמְלֹאָהּ אַתָּה יְסַדְתָּם. אַתָּה הִצַּבְתָּ כָּל גְּבוּלוֹת

‹ the ‹ all ‹ established ‹ You « founded ‹ You ‹ and its ‹ the
boundaries   them.   fullness,   world

אָרֶץ, קַיִץ וָחֹרֶף אַתָּה יְצַרְתָּם. אַתָּה רִצַּצְתָּ רָאשֵׁי

‹ the ‹ crushed ‹ You « fashioned ‹ You ‹ and ‹ summer « of
heads   them.   winter,   earth;

לִוְיָתָן, תִּתְּנֶנּוּ מַאֲכָל לְעָם לְצִיִּים. אַתָּה בָקַעְתָּ מַעְיָן

‹ fountain ‹ split ‹ You « [destined] for ‹ to the ‹ as food ‹ You will « of
open   the desolate   people   serve it   Leviathan;
wilderness.

וָנָחַל, אַתָּה הוֹבַשְׁתָּ נַהֲרוֹת אֵיתָן. אַתָּה פוֹרַרְתָּ

‹ shattered ‹ You « that are mighty. ‹ rivers ‹ dried ‹ You « and stream;

בְעָזְּךָ יָם, שִׁבַּרְתָּ רָאשֵׁי תַנִּינִים עַל הַמָּיִם. אַתָּה

‹ You « the water. ‹ upon ‹ of sea ‹ the heads ‹ You « the ‹ with Your
serpents   smashed   sea;   might

מוֹשֵׁל בְּגֵאוּת הַיָּם, בְּשׂוֹא גַלָּיו אַתָּה תְשַׁבְּחֵם.

« calm them. ‹ You ‹ its ‹ when it « of the ‹ the ‹ rule
waves,   raises   sea;   grandeur

גָּדוֹל יהוה וּמְהֻלָּל מְאֹד, בְּעִיר אֱלֹהֵינוּ הַר קָדְשׁוֹ.

« of His ‹ Mount ‹ of our God, ‹ in the ‹ and much praised, ‹ is ‹ Great
Holiness.   City   HASHEM

יהוה צְבָאוֹת, אֱלֹהֵי יִשְׂרָאֵל, יוֹשֵׁב הַכְּרֻבִים, אַתָּה

‹ it is « upon the ‹ en- ‹ of Israel, ‹ God ‹ Master of ‹ HASHEM,
You   Cherubim,   throned   Legions,

הוּא הָאֱלֹהִים לְבַדְּךָ. אֵל נַעֲרָץ בְּסוֹד קְדוֹשִׁים רַבָּה,

« in the great assemblage ‹ is ‹ God « alone. ‹ God ‹ Who
of the holy [angels],   revered   are

---

(1) *I Chronicles* 29:11. (2) *Psalms* 89:12. (3) 74:17. (4) 74:14-15. (5) 74:13. (6) 89:10. (7) 48:2. (8) *Isaiah* 37:16.

וְנוֹרָא עַל כָּל סְבִיבָיו.[1] וְיוֹדוּ שָׁמַיִם פִּלְאֲךָ יהוה, אַף

‹ and is ‹ over ‹ all ‹ who sur- « ‹ Acknowl- › will the › ‹ Your « HASHEM, « also ›
awesome round Him. edge heavens wonders,

אֱמוּנָתְךָ בִּקְהַל קְדֹשִׁים.[2] לְכוּ נְרַנְּנָה לַיהוה, נָרִיעָה

‹ Your ‹ in the ‹ of holy « ‹ Come! ‹ Let us sing » to « let us ›
faithfulness, assembly ones. joyfully HASHEM, call out

לְצוּר יִשְׁעֵנוּ. נְקַדְּמָה פָנָיו בְּתוֹדָה, בִּזְמִרוֹת נָרִיעַ

‹ to the ‹ of our « Let us greet › ‹ Him › with ‹ with praiseful › let us ›
Rock salvation. thanksgiving, songs call out

לוֹ.[3] צֶדֶק וּמִשְׁפָּט מְכוֹן כִּסְאֶךָ, חֶסֶד וֶאֱמֶת יְקַדְּמוּ

‹ to « ‹ Righteous- ‹ and » of Your › ‹ are the › ‹ and ‹ kindness › ‹ precede ›
Him. ness justice foundation throne; truth

פָנֶיךָ.[4] אֲשֶׁר יַחְדָּו נַמְתִּיק סוֹד, בְּבֵית אֱלֹהִים נְהַלֵּךְ

‹ Your coun- « For › together › let us « counsel; › in the › of God › let us ›
tenance. take sweet House walk

בְּרָגֶשׁ.[5] אֲשֶׁר לוֹ הַיָּם וְהוּא עָשָׂהוּ, וְיַבֶּשֶׁת יָדָיו

« in company. » For › His › is the › and He › perfected « and the « His ›
sea it, dry land, hands

יְצָרוּ.[6] אֲשֶׁר בְּיָדוֹ נֶפֶשׁ כָּל חָי, וְרוּחַ כָּל בְּשַׂר אִישׁ.[7]

« fashioned. For › in His › the › of › is the › the «and the‹ of all › mankind. «
hand soul all living spirit

❖ הַנְּשָׁמָה לָךְ וְהַגּוּף פָּעֳלֶךָ, חוּסָה עַל עֲמָלֶךָ.

« Your › on › take pity « is Your › and the › is › The soul «
labor. handiwork; body Yours

הַנְּשָׁמָה לָךְ וְהַגּוּף שֶׁלָּךְ, יהוה עֲשֵׂה לְמַעַן שְׁמֶךָ.

«of Your › for the › act › O « is Yours; ‹ and the › is › The soul «
Name. sake HASHEM, body Yours

אָתָאנוּ עַל שִׁמְךָ, יהוה, עֲשֵׂה לְמַעַן שְׁמֶךָ. בַּעֲבוּר

‹ [act] « of Your › for the › act › O « Your › [relying] ‹ We have ›
because of Name; sake HASHEM; Name, on come

כְּבוֹד שְׁמֶךָ, כִּי אֵל חַנּוּן וְרַחוּם שְׁמֶךָ. לְמַעַן

‹ For the « is Your › and › Who is › God › for « of Your › the glory ›
sake Name. Merciful Gracious Name,

שִׁמְךָ יהוה, וְסָלַחְתָּ לַעֲוֹנֵנוּ כִּי רַב הוּא.[8]

‹ it is great. ‹ though ‹ our ‹ forgive « HASHEM, ‹ of Your
iniquity, Name,

---

(1) *Psalms* 89:8. (2) 89:6. (3) 95:1-2. (4) 89:15. (5) 55:15. (6) 95:5. (7) *Job* 12:10. (8) Cf. *Psalms* 25:11.

CONGREGATION, THEN *CHAZZAN*:

סְלַח לָנוּ אָבִינוּ, כִּי בְרוֹב אִוַּלְתֵּנוּ שָׁגִינוּ,

《 we have 〈 of our folly 〈 in the 〈 for 〈 our Father, 〈 us, 〈 Forgive
erred;　　　　　　　　abundance

מְחַל לָנוּ מַלְכֵּנוּ, כִּי רַבּוּ עֲוֹנֵינוּ.

《 our 〈 many 〈 for 〈 our King, 〈 us, 〈 pardon
iniquities.　are

ALL, WHILE STANDING

אֵל אֶֽרֶךְ אַפַּֽיִם אַתָּה,

《 You are, 〈 to anger, 〈 Who is slow 〈 God

וּבַֽעַל הָרַחֲמִים נִקְרֵֽאתָ, וְדֶֽרֶךְ תְּשׁוּבָה הוֹרֵֽיתָ.

《 You have 〈 of 〈 and the 《 You are 〈 of Mercy 〈 and
taught.　repentance　way　called;　Master

גְּדֻלַּת רַחֲמֶֽיךָ וַחֲסָדֶֽיךָ,

〈 and Your 〈 of Your 〈 The
kindness　mercy　greatness

תִּזְכּוֹר הַיּוֹם וּבְכָל יוֹם לְזֶֽרַע יְדִידֶֽיךָ.

《 of Your 〈 for the 《 day, 〈 and 〈 this day 〈 may You
beloved ones.　offspring　every　remember,

תֵּֽפֶן אֵלֵֽינוּ בְּרַחֲמִים,

《 in mercy, 〈 to us 〈 Turn

כִּי אַתָּה הוּא בַּֽעַל הָרַחֲמִים.

《 of Mercy. 〈 the Master 〈 are 〈 You 〈 for

בְּתַחֲנוּן וּבִתְפִלָּה פָּנֶֽיךָ נְקַדֵּם, כְּהוֹדַֽעְתָּ לֶעָנָיו מִקֶּֽדֶם.

《in ancient 〈 to the 〈 in the manner 《 we 〈 Your 〈 and prayer 〈 With
times.　humble one　that You made　approach,　Presence　supplication
[Moses]　known

מֵחֲרוֹן אַפְּךָ שׁוּב,[1] כְּמוֹ בְתוֹרָתְךָ כָּתוּב.[2]

《 it is 〈 in Your Torah 〈 as 《 turn 〈 of Your 〈 From the
written.　back,　anger　fierceness

וּבְצֵל כְּנָפֶֽיךָ נֶחֱסֶה[3] וְנִתְלוֹנָן, כְּיוֹם וַיֵּֽרֶד יהוה בֶּעָנָן.

《 in a 〈 when HASHEM 〈 as on 《 and may 〈 may we find 〈 of Your 〈 In the
cloud.　descended　the day　we dwell,　shelter　wings　shadow

❖ תַּעֲבוֹר עַל פֶּֽשַׁע וְתִמְחֶה אָשָׁם,

《 guilt, 〈 and erase 〈 sin 〈 Overlook

---

(1) Cf. *Exodus* 32:12. (2) See 32:14. (3) Cf. *Psalms* 36:8.

כְּיוֹם וַיִּתְיַצֵּב עִמּוֹ שָׁם.

《 there. 〈 with him 〈 when He 〈 as on the
         [Moses]   [God] stood   day

תַּאֲזִין שַׁוְעָתֵנוּ וְתַקְשִׁיב מֶנּוּ מַאֲמַר,

《 [our] 〈 from 〈 and hear 〈 to our cry 〈 Give heed
declaration,   us

כְּיוֹם וַיִּקְרָא בְשֵׁם יהוה,¹ וְשָׁם נֶאֱמַר:

《 it was said: 〈 and 《 of HASHEM, 〈 with the 〈 when He 〈 as on
    there   Name   called out   the day

CONGREGATION, THEN CHAZZAN:

וַיַּעֲבֹר יהוה עַל פָּנָיו וַיִּקְרָא:

《 and 《 [Moses'] 〈 before 〈 And HASHEM passed
proclaimed: face,

CONGREGATION AND CHAZZAN RECITE LOUDLY AND IN UNISON:

יהוה, יהוה, אֵל, רַחוּם, וְחַנּוּן, אֶרֶךְ אַפַּיִם,

〈 to anger, 〈 Slow 《 and Gracious, 〈 Compassionate 〈 God, 〈 HASHEM, 〈 HASHEM,

וְרַב חֶסֶד, וֶאֱמֶת, נֹצֵר חֶסֶד לָאֲלָפִים, נֹשֵׂא עָוֹן,

〈 of 〈 Forgiver 《 for thousands 〈 of 〈 Preserver 《 and 〈 in 〈 and
iniquity,   [of generations],   kindness   Truth,   Kindness Abundant

וָפֶשַׁע, וְחַטָּאָה, וְנַקֵּה.² וְסָלַחְתָּ לַעֲוֹנֵנוּ וּלְחַטָּאתֵנוּ

《 and our sins, 〈 our 〈 May You 《 and Who 〈 and inadvertent 〈 willful sin,
    iniquities   forgive   absolves.   sin,

וּנְחַלְתָּנוּ.³ סְלַח לָנוּ אָבִינוּ כִּי חָטָאנוּ, מְחַל לָנוּ

〈 us, 〈 pardon 《 we have 〈 for 《 our Father, 〈 us, 〈 Forgive 《 and make us
       sinned;   Your heritage.

מַלְכֵּנוּ כִּי פָשָׁעְנוּ. כִּי אַתָּה אֲדֹנָי טוֹב וְסַלָּח, וְרַב

〈 and 《 and 〈 are 〈 O Lord, 〈 You, 〈 For 《 we have 〈 for 《 our King,
abundantly forgiving, good   willfully sinned.

חֶסֶד לְכָל קֹרְאֶיךָ.⁴

《 who call upon You. 〈 to all 〈 kind

פְּסוּקֵי הַקְדָּמָה לִסְלִיחָה יד / PREFATORY VERSES TO SELICHAH 14

וְאֵין קוֹרֵא בְשִׁמְךָ מִתְעוֹרֵר לְהַחֲזִיק בָּךְ.⁵ הוֹשִׁיעָה

《 Save, 《 to 〈 to hold fast 〈 who arouses 〈 in Your 〈 who calls 〈 There is
      You.   himself   Name   out   no one

---

(1) *Exodus* 34:5. (2) 34:6-7. (3) 34:9. (4) *Psalms* 86:5. (5) *Isaiah* 64:7.

יהוה כִּי גָמַר חָסִיד, כִּי פַסּוּ אֱמוּנִים מִבְּנֵי אָדָם.¹

« from mankind. ‹ have truthful ‹ vanished ‹ for « is the ‹ gone ‹ for « O
                    people   devout one,   HASHEM,

הוֹשַׁע יהוה אֶת עַמְּךָ אֶת שְׁאֵרִית יִשְׂרָאֵל.²

« of Israel. ‹   the remnant   « Your people, « HASHEM « Save,

כְּרַחֵם אָב עַל בָּנִים, כֵּן תְּרַחֵם יהוה עָלֵינוּ.³

« on us. ‹ HASHEM, ‹   have   ‹ so « his ‹ toward ‹ a ‹ As merciful as
                          mercy,   children,   father is

לַיהוה הַיְשׁוּעָה, עַל עַמְּךָ בִרְכָתֶךָ סֶּלָה.⁴ יהוה

‹ HASHEM, « Selah. « is Your ‹ Your ‹ upon « is salvation, ‹ To HASHEM
                        blessing,   people

צְבָאוֹת עִמָּנוּ, מִשְׂגָּב לָנוּ אֱלֹהֵי יַעֲקֹב סֶלָה.⁵

« Selah. ‹ of Jacob, ‹ is the God ‹ for us ‹ a « is with us, ‹ Master of
                                      stronghold   Legions,

יהוה צְבָאוֹת, אַשְׁרֵי אָדָם בֹּטֵחַ בָּךְ.⁶ יהוה הוֹשִׁיעָה,

« save! ‹ HASHEM, « in ‹ who ‹ is the ‹ — praise- « Master of ‹ HASHEM,
            You. trusts man   worthy   Legions

הַמֶּלֶךְ יַעֲנֵנוּ בְיוֹם קָרְאֵנוּ.⁷

« we call. ‹ on the ‹ answer us ‹ May the
              day   King

IN MOST CONGREGATIONS THE FOLLOWING VERSES ARE RECITED ALOUD RESPONSIVELY,
AS INDICATED; IN OTHERS THEY ARE RECITED SILENTLY.

CONGREGATION, ALOUD, FOLLOWED BY *CHAZZAN*, ALOUD:

סְלַח נָא לַעֲוֹן הָעָם הַזֶּה כְּגֹדֶל חַסְדֶּךָ, וְכַאֲשֶׁר

‹ just as « of Your ‹ according to ‹ of this people ‹ the ‹ please, ‹ Forgive,
              kindness,   the greatness   iniquity

נָשָׂאתָה לָעָם הַזֶּה מִמִּצְרַיִם וְעַד הֵנָּה,⁸ וְשָׁם נֶאֱמַר:

« it was ‹ And « now. ‹ until ‹ from Egypt ‹ this people ‹ You have
  said: there   forgiven

ALL, ALOUD AND IN UNISON:

וַיֹּאמֶר יהוה סָלַחְתִּי כִּדְבָרֶךָ.⁹

«   according   ‹ I have forgiven « And HASHEM said:
  to your word!

(1) *Psalms* 12:2. (2) *Jeremiah* 31:6. (3) Cf. *Psalms* 103:13. (4) 3:9.
(5) 46:8. (6) 84:13. (7) 20:10. (8) *Numbers* 14:19. (9) 14:20.

ALL CONTINUE:

הַטֵּה אֱלֹהַי אָזְנְךָ וּשְׁמָע, פְּקַח עֵינֶיךָ וּרְאֵה
‹ and see ‹ Your eyes ‹ open ‹‹ and listen; ‹ Your ear, ‹ my God, ‹ Incline,

שֹׁמְמֹתֵינוּ, וְהָעִיר אֲשֶׁר נִקְרָא שִׁמְךָ עָלֶיהָ, כִּי לֹא
‹ not ‹ for ‹‹ upon; ‹ Your Name is proclaimed ‹ which ‹ and that ‹ our desolation [of] the city

עַל צִדְקֹתֵינוּ אֲנַחְנוּ מַפִּילִים תַּחֲנוּנֵינוּ לְפָנֶיךָ,
‹‹ before You; ‹ our supplications ‹ cast ‹ do we ‹ of our righteousness ‹ because

כִּי עַל רַחֲמֶיךָ הָרַבִּים. אֲדֹנָי שְׁמָעָה, אֲדֹנָי סְלָחָה,
‹‹ forgive; ‹ O Lord, ‹‹ heed; ‹ O Lord, ‹‹ which is abundant. ‹ of Your compassion, ‹ be-cause ‹ but

אֲדֹנָי הַקְשִׁיבָה, וַעֲשֵׂה אַל תְּאַחַר, לְמַעַנְךָ אֱלֹהַי,
‹‹ my God, ‹ for Your sake, ‹‹ delay; ‹ do not ‹‹ and act, ‹ be attentive, ‹ O Lord,

כִּי שִׁמְךָ נִקְרָא עַל עִירְךָ וְעַל עַמֶּךָ.¹
‹‹ Your people. ‹ and upon ‹ Your City ‹ upon ‹ is proclaimed ‹ Your Name ‹ for

---

סליחה יד / SELICHAH 14

ALL:

אֱלֹהֵינוּ וֵאלֹהֵי אֲבוֹתֵינוּ:
‹‹ of our forefathers: ‹ and God ‹ Our God

אִוִּיתִיךָ קִוִּיתִיךָ* מֵאֶרֶץ מֶרְחַקִּים.
‹‹ far away, ‹ in a land ‹ I place my hope in You* ‹ I yearn for You,

בְּקִרְבִּי שִׁחַרְתִּיךָ קְרָאתִיךָ מִמַּעֲמַקִּים.²
‹‹ from the depths. ‹ I call to You ‹‹ I seek You; ‹ from within me

גָּרַסְתִּי לְתַאֲוָתְךָ כְּאַיָּל עַל אֲפִיקִים.³
‹‹ brooks of water. ‹ for ‹ as a deer [yearns] ‹ by my yearning for You ‹ I am broken

---

(1) *Daniel* 9:18-19. (3) Cf. *Psalms* 130:1. (3) Cf. 42:2.

אִוִּיתִיךָ קִוִּיתִיךָ — *I yearn for You, I place my hope in You.* The verses follow an alphabetical scheme, followed by the composer's signature — אֵלִיָּה בַּר שְׁמַעְיָהוּ, *Eliyah bar Shemayahu* — as indicated by the bold type. R' Eliyah lived in Bari, Italy, during the late-10th and early-11th centuries. About forty of his *selichos* are extant. Characteristically, they describe the plight of Israel in exile and the nation's hope for a speedy redemption.

דְּרַשְׁתִּיךְ וּבִקַּשְׁתִּיךְ בָּרְחוֹבוֹת וּבַשְּׁוָקִים.¹

《 and in the 〈 in the streets 〈 and searched 〈 I have
marketplaces. for You sought You

הִנֵּה הָעֵת תַּרְוִיחַ לִדְחוּקִים.

《 to the 〈 for You to 〈 it is the 〈 Indeed,
oppressed, bring relief time

וְתַעֲשֶׂה דִין וּמִשְׁפָּט לַעֲשׁוּקִים.²

《 in the cause of the victimized. 〈 and restitution 〈 justice 〈 and achieve

זְמוֹרֵיהֶם* שֻׁחָתוּ וּבְקָקוּם בּוֹקְקִים.³

《 by pillagers, 〈 stripped 《 were 〈 Their vine
[of their fruit] destroyed; branches*

חֲמוּסִים נְגוּשִׂים בְּיַד מְדִיקִים.

《 of the 〈 by the 〈 and bullied 〈 and they are
oppressor. hand robbed

טְפוּלֶיךָ⁴ שֶׁעֲשַׁעְתָּ כִּילָדִים רַכִּים.⁵

《 who are 〈 like 〈 [with whom] You 〈 Those who
tender, children [once] delighted cling to You,

יָמִים רַבִּים לְחוּצִים וּדְפוּקִים.⁵

《 and driven hard, 〈 they have 〈 for many days
been oppressed

כֹּל חָסְרוּ מִטּוּב רֵקִים.

《 they are 〈 of [any- 《 they are 〈 of every-
empty, thing] good deprived; thing

לְבָאִים שְׁנֵּיהֶם עָלֵימוֹ חוֹרְקִים.⁶

《 gnash. 〈 at them 〈 their teeth 〈 [while] lions

מָאַסְתָּ וְזָנַחְתָּ וְנָטַשְׁתָּ דְּבֵקִים.

《 those who 〈 You 〈 You 〈 You
cling [to You]; abandoned rejected, despised,

נֵאַרְתָּ בְּרִית שְׁלֹשֶׁת הַחֲשׁוּקִים.

《 beloved 〈 of the 〈 the 〈 You shook
[Patriarchs]. three covenant off

סְחִי שַׂמְתָּנוּ מֻכִּים וְלוֹקִים.

《 and beaten, 〈 we are 《You have made us 〈 Loath-
battered [to the nations]; some

---

(1) Cf. *Song of Songs* 3:2. (2) Cf. *Psalms* 140:13, 146:7. (3) Cf. *Nahum* 2:3.
(4) Some editions read טְלָאֶיךָ, *Your flock*. (5) Cf. *Genesis* 33:13. (6) Cf. *Psalms* 35:16.

זְמוֹרֵיהֶם — *Their vine branches.* Oppressed been plundered, its fruits stripped from its
Israel is compared to a vineyard that has vines (see *Hosea* 10:1).

עֲצוּמֵי גָזָם וַאֲכוּלֵי יָלֶק.*

over- ‹ by the › and ‹ by the › overwhelmed ‹ gazam › devoured ‹ yelek.*

פְּצוּעֵי חַבּוּרוֹת[1] וְאֵבָרִים מִתְפָּרְקִים.

Wounded ‹ with bruises ‹ and with ‹ dislocated; [our] limbs

צָרֵי חָדַלְנוּ וְדַלְנוּ מִתַּמְרוּקִים.

balm ‹ we have ‹ and we ‹ healing salves. no more, lack

קוּמָה עֶזְרָתָה[2] לְנֶאֱנָחִים וְנֶאֱנָקִים.

Arise! » Assist ‹ those who sigh ‹ and those who groan!

רוֹמֵם מֵאַשְׁפּוֹת וּמֵעָפָר תָּקִים.[3]

Lift [us] ‹ from the ‹ from the dirt ‹ raise [us] up trash heaps, up.

שִׁלְטוֹן בְּיָדְךָ יְרוּדֶיךָ לְהָקִים.

The power ‹ is in Your ‹ Your downtrod- ‹ to raise up: hand den [people]

תָּקְפְּךָ בַּשַּׁחַק וּמֶמְשַׁלְתְּךָ בָּאֲרָקִים.

Your ‹ is in ‹ and Your ‹ is in [all] might the sky dominion the earth.

אַךְ לְשִׁמְךָ יוֹדוּ הַצַּדִּיקִים.[4]

They ‹ to Your ‹ give ‹ will the alone Name thanks righteous;

בִּנְשָׂאֲךָ רֹאשׁ[5] שִׁבְעָתַיִם מְזֻקָּקִים.

when You ‹ [Israel's] ‹ — sevenfold, ‹ they are raise head purified.

❖ עַתָּה יֹאמְרוּ הַקְּרוֹבִים וְהָרְחוֹקִים.

Now ‹ they will say ‹ — those near ‹ and those far away,

כְּהוֹשִׁיעֲךָ חוֹכֶיךָ בְּמִצְוֹתֶיךָ מִתְחַזְּקִים.[6]

when You ‹ those who ‹ who in Your ‹ are ever-strengthening redeem yearn for You, commandments themselves —

---

(1) Cf. *Isaiah* 1:6. (2) *Psalms* 44:27. (3) Cf. *I Samuel* 2:8; *Psalms* 113:7. (4) Cf. 140:14.
(5) Cf. *Genesis* 40:13. (6) Some editions omit this line and read the next two lines
חָזָק וְאַמִּיץ דְּבָרוֹ הֵקִים, *The Strong One, the Mighty One has fulfilled His word,*
קִיֵּם מַאֲמָרוֹ שׁוֹכֵן שְׁחָקִים, *fulfilled His promise has He Who dwells in the highest heavens.*

יָלֶק ... גָזָם — *The gazam ... the yelek.* The prophet Joel (Ch. 1) describes a devastating visitation of four species of locust coming in four waves. The species are *gazam, arbeh,* *yelek,* and *chasil.* According to *Arugas Ha-Bosem,* these represent the four kingdoms that would eventually subjugate Israel: Babylon, Persia, Greece, and Rome.

חָזָק וְאַמִּיץ דְּבָרוֹ הֵקִים.

⟨ He has ⟨ His ⟨ the Mighty ⟨ The Strong
fulfilled word One, One,

לַחֲבַצֶּלֶת הַשָּׁרוֹן שׁוֹשַׁנַּת הָעֲמָקִים.[1]

《 of the valleys! ⟨ to the ever- 《 of Sharon, ⟨ to the rose
fresh rose

ALL, WHILE STANDING:

אֵל מֶלֶךְ יוֹשֵׁב עַל כִּסֵּא רַחֲמִים, מִתְנַהֵג

⟨ Who acts 《 of mercy, ⟨ the throne ⟨ on ⟨ Who sits ⟨ King ⟨ O God,

בַּחֲסִידוּת, מוֹחֵל עֲוֹנוֹת עַמּוֹ, מַעֲבִיר רִאשׁוֹן

⟨ [sins,] one ⟨ Who 《 of His ⟨ the sins ⟨ Who 《 with kindness,
removes people, pardons

רִאשׁוֹן,[2] מַרְבֶּה מְחִילָה לַחַטָּאִים וּסְלִיחָה לַפּוֹשְׁעִים,

《 to willful ⟨ and ⟨ to unintentional ⟨ pardon ⟨ Who abun- 《 by one,
sinners, forgiveness sinners dantly grants

עֹשֶׂה צְדָקוֹת עִם כָּל בָּשָׂר וָרוּחַ, לֹא כְרָעָתָם

⟨ in accord ⟨ — not 《 and ⟨ [beings ⟨ all ⟨ with ⟨ acts of ⟨ Who
with their spirit of] flesh generosity performs
wickedness

תִּגְמוֹל. ❖ אֵל הוֹרֵיתָ לָּנוּ לוֹמַר שְׁלֹשׁ עֶשְׂרֵה, וּזְכוֹר

⟨ remem- 《 the Thirteen ⟨ to ⟨ us ⟨ You ⟨ O God, 《 do You
ber [Attributes of Mercy]; recite taught repay them!

לָּנוּ הַיּוֹם בְּרִית שְׁלֹשׁ עֶשְׂרֵה, כְּמוֹ שֶׁהוֹדַעְתָּ לֶעָנָיו

⟨ to the humble ⟨ You made ⟨ as 《 of [these] Thirteen, ⟨ the ⟨ today ⟨ for us
one [Moses] known covenant

מִקֶּדֶם, כְּמוֹ שֶׁכָּתוּב, וַיֵּרֶד יהוה בֶּעָנָן וַיִּתְיַצֵּב עִמּוֹ

⟨ with ⟨ and stood ⟨ in a ⟨ And HASHEM 《 it is written: ⟨ as 《 in ancient
him cloud descended times,

שָׁם, וַיִּקְרָא בְשֵׁם יהוה.[3]

《 of ⟨ with the ⟨ and He 《 there,
HASHEM. Name called out

CONGREGATION, THEN *CHAZZAN:*

וַיַּעֲבֹר יהוה עַל פָּנָיו וַיִּקְרָא:

《 and 《 [Moses'] ⟨ before ⟨ And HASHEM passed
proclaimed: face,

---

(1) Cf. *Song of Songs* 2:1. (2) *Rosh Hashanah* 17a. (3) *Exodus* 34:5.

CONGREGATION AND *CHAZZAN* RECITE LOUDLY AND IN UNISON:

יְהוה, יְהוה, אֵל, רַחוּם, וְחַנּוּן, אֶרֶךְ אַפַּיִם,
⟨ to anger, ⟨ Slow ⟪ and Gracious, ⟨ Compassionate ⟨ God, ⟨ HASHEM, ⟨ HASHEM,

וְרַב חֶסֶד, וֶאֱמֶת, נֹצֵר חֶסֶד לָאֲלָפִים, נֹשֵׂא עָוֹן,
⟨ of ⟨ Forgiver ⟪ for thousands ⟨ of ⟨ Preserver ⟪ and ⟨ in ⟨ and
iniquity, [of generations], kindness Truth, Kindness Abundant

וָפֶשַׁע, וְחַטָּאָה, וְנַקֵּה.[1] וְסָלַחְתָּ לַעֲוֹנֵנוּ וּלְחַטָּאתֵנוּ
⟪ and our sins, ⟨ our ⟨ May You ⟪ and Who ⟨ and inadvertent ⟨ willful sin,
iniquities forgive absolves. sin,

וּנְחַלְתָּנוּ.[2] סְלַח לָנוּ אָבִינוּ כִּי חָטָאנוּ, מְחַל לָנוּ
⟨ us, ⟨ pardon ⟪ we have ⟨ for ⟪ our ⟨ us, ⟨ Forgive ⟪ and make us
sinned; Father, Your heritage.

מַלְכֵּנוּ כִּי פָשָׁעְנוּ. כִּי אַתָּה אֲדֹנָי טוֹב וְסַלָּח,
⟪ and ⟨ are ⟨ O Lord, ⟨ You, ⟨ For ⟪ we have ⟨ for ⟪ our King,
forgiving, good willfully sinned.

וְרַב חֶסֶד לְכָל קֹרְאֶיךָ.[3]
⟪ who call ⟨ to all ⟨ kind ⟨ and
upon You. abundantly

פסוקי הקדמה לסליחה טו / PREFATORY VERSES TO SELICHAH 15

אַל תִּזְכָּר לָנוּ עֲוֹנֹת רִאשֹׁנִים; מַהֵר יְקַדְּמוּנוּ
⟨ advance to ⟨ swiftly ⟪ of the ancients; ⟨ the sins ⟨ against ⟨ recall ⟨ Do not
meet us us

רַחֲמֶיךָ, כִּי דַלּוֹנוּ מְאֹד.[4] יְהוה אֱלֹהֵינוּ, בְּעָלוּנוּ
⟨ ruled ⟨ Our God, ⟨ HASHEM, ⟪ exceed- ⟨ we have become ⟨ for ⟪ may Your
over us ingly. impoverished mercies,

אֲדֹנִים זוּלָתֶךָ, לְבַד בְּךָ נַזְכִּיר שְׁמֶךָ.[5] כִּי עָלֶיךָ
⟨ for ⟨ Because ⟪ Your ⟨ that we ⟨ about ⟨ but it ⟪ other ⟨ have
Your sake Name. mention You is only than You; masters

הֹרַגְנוּ כָל הַיּוֹם, נֶחְשַׁבְנוּ כְּצֹאן טִבְחָה.[6]
⟪ for ⟨ as sheep ⟨ we are ⟪ day long, ⟨ all ⟨ we are
slaughter. considered killed

כְּרַחֵם אָב עַל בָּנִים, כֵּן תְּרַחֵם יְהוה עָלֵינוּ.[7]
⟪ on us. ⟨ HASHEM, ⟨ have ⟨ so ⟪ his ⟨ toward ⟨ a ⟨ As merciful as
mercy, children, father is

---

(1) *Exodus* 34:6-7. (2) 34:9. (3) *Psalms* 86:5. (4) 79:8. (5) *Isaiah* 26:13. (6) *Psalms* 44:23. (7) Cf. 103:13.

לַיהוה הַיְשׁוּעָה, עַל עַמְּךָ בִרְכָתֶךָ סֶּלָה.[1] יהוה

⟨ HASHEM, ⟪ Selah. ⟪ is Your ⟨ Your ⟨ upon ⟪ is salvation, ⟨ To HASHEM
blessing, people

צְבָאוֹת עִמָּנוּ, מִשְׂגָּב לָנוּ אֱלֹהֵי יַעֲקֹב סֶּלָה.[2]

⟪ Selah. ⟪ of Jacob, ⟨ is the God ⟨ for us ⟨ a ⟪ is with us, ⟨ Master of
stronghold Legions,

יהוה צְבָאוֹת, אַשְׁרֵי אָדָם בֹּטֵחַ בָּךְ.[3] יהוה הוֹשִׁיעָה,

⟪ save! ⟨ HASHEM, ⟪ in You. ⟨ who ⟨ is the ⟨ — praise- ⟪ Master of ⟨ HASHEM,
trusts man worthy Legions

הַמֶּלֶךְ יַעֲנֵנוּ בְיוֹם קָרְאֵנוּ.[4]

⟪ we call. ⟨ on the ⟨ answer ⟨ May the
day us King

SELICHAH 15 / סליחה טו

ALL:

אֱלֹהֵינוּ וֵאלֹהֵי אֲבוֹתֵינוּ:

⟪ of our forefathers: ⟨ and God ⟨ Our God

אַיֵּה קִנְאָתְךָ* וּגְבוּרֹתֶיךָ,[5]

⟪ and Your mighty ⟨ Your ⟨ Where
deeds [on our behalf], zealousness* are

בַּעֲשׂוֹתְךָ נוֹרָאוֹת[6] לְזֶרַע כֹּרְתֵי בְרִיתֶךָ,[7]

⟪ Your ⟨ with ⟨ for the ⟨ awesome ⟨ when You
covenant? whom You descendants [of deeds performed
established the Patriarchs]

גֵּרוּשִׁים נְטוּשִׁים אֲנַחְנוּ מִנַּחֲלָתֶךָ,[8]

⟪ from Your ⟨ are we ⟨ and ⟨ Chased out
heritage; abandoned

יהוה אֱלֹהֵינוּ בְּעָלוּנוּ אֲדֹנִים זוּלָתֶךָ.[9]

⟪other than ⟨ have lords ⟨ ruled over us ⟨ our God, ⟨ HASHEM,
You.

דַּאֲגַת עֲנִיֶּיךָ גָּדְלָה עַד לִמְאֹד.[10]

⟪ an extreme, ⟨ to ⟨ have grown ⟨ of Your ⟨ The
great poor ones worries

---

(1) *Psalms* 3:9 (2) 46:8. (3) 84:13. (4) 20:10. (5) *Isaiah* 63:15. (6) 64:2. (7) Cf. *Psalms* 50:5.
(8) Cf. *Jeremiah* 12:7. (9) *Isaiah* 26:13; some editions of *Selichos* read אֱלֹהִים, *God,* instead of
אֱלֹהֵינוּ, *our God,* but that reading needlessly alters the Scriptural verse. (10) Cf. *Genesis* 27:33.

⊷§ **אַיֵּה קִנְאָתְךָ** — *Where are Your zealous*
ness .... The author of this *selichah* signed
his name בִּנְיָמִן, *Binyamin,* after the alphabetic acrostic. He is probably Binyamin bar
Zerach [see prefatory comment to *Selichah*
1].

הַסּוֹבְלִים עַל מוֹרָאֲךָ בְּלֵב וָנֶפֶשׁ וּמְאֹד,[1]

» and ⟨ and soul ⟨ with ⟨ of reverence ⟨ the ⟨ they bear
resources,   heart   for You   yoke

וְהֵם שָׁחִים וּמֻשְׁפָּלִים[2] עַד מְאֹד,

» an ⟨ to ⟨ and humiliated ⟨ are bowed ⟨ while
extreme.   they

מַהֵר יְקַדְּמוּנוּ רַחֲמֶיךָ, כִּי דַלּוֹנוּ מְאֹד.[3]

» exceed- ⟨ we have ⟨ for ⟨ may Your ⟨ advance ⟨ Swiftly
ingly.   become   mercies,   to meet us
impoverished

זִיוֵנוּ שׁוֹנָה,[4] מִפְּנֵי מְחָרְפִים יוֹם יוֹם,[5]

» after ⟨ day ⟨ those who ⟨ because ⟨ is ⟨ Our facial
day,   revile us   of   changed appearance

חוֹרְקִים שֵׁן וְשׁוֹחֲחִים, אַךְ זֶה הַיּוֹם,[6]

» is the day! ⟨ this ⟨ Indeed, » and declare, ⟨ their ⟨ [who] gnash
teeth

טֶכֶס מֶמְשַׁלְתְּךָ גַּלֵּה, אָיוֹם,

» O Awesome One, ⟨ reveal, ⟨ of Your rule ⟨ The plan

כִּי עָלֶיךָ הֹרַגְנוּ כָל הַיּוֹם.[7]

» day ⟨ all ⟨ we are ⟨ for Your ⟨ Because
long.   killed   sake

יִחַלְנוּ קֵץ גְּאֻלָּה וְנֶחָמָה,

» and ⟨ of ⟨ for the ⟨ We long
consolation,   Redemption   time

כִּי כִּסָּתְנוּ בוּשָׁה וְעֲטַתְנוּ כְלִמָּה,[8]

» has ⟨ and ⟨ has shame ⟨ covered us ⟨ for
humiliation.   enwrapped us

לְחוּצִים וַעֲבוּדִים תַּחַת יַד כָּל אֻמָּה,[9]

» of every nation, ⟨ the ⟨ under ⟨ and enslaved ⟨ [We are]
hand   oppressed

וְאֵין אִתָּנוּ יוֹדֵעַ עַד מָה.[10]

» when. ⟨ until ⟨ who ⟨ among ⟨ and there
knows   us   is none

---

(1) Cf. *Deuteronomy* 6:5. (2) Cf. *Isaiah* 2:9. (3) *Psalms* 79:8. (4) Cf. *Daniel* 5:9. (5) Cf. *Psalms* 102:9.
(6) Cf. *Lamentations* 2:16. (7) *Psalms* 44:23. (8) Cf. 71:13. (9) This stich has been a target of the
censors and appears in many variant forms; some editions read תַּחַת יַד רְשָׁעִים [זָרִים] הָעֲצוּמָה,
under the powerful hand of the wicked [or, *the strangers*]; others read יַד קְצָת אֻמָּה,
the hand of some nation; some omit the stich altogether; while still others substitute
לֹא עַתָּה קַרְנֵנוּ רָמָה, *Our pride is not raised at present.* (10) Cf. *Psalms* 74:9.

מֶלֶךְ מַלְכִים, זְכֹר רַחֲמֶיךָ הַיְּשָׁנִים,
‮《 from of old! 〈 Your mercies 〈 remember 《 of kings, 〈 King‬

נוֹצְרֵי יִחוּדֶךָ מַלֵּט מֵאוּדִים הָעֲשֵׁנִים,*[1]
‮《 that are 〈 from the 〈 rescue 《 Your 〈 Those who‬
‮smoking.* firebrands Oneness, guard‬

סָאַב צַחֲנָתָם לַבֵּן, הַמִּתְלָע כַּשָּׁנִים,[2]
‮《 or like 〈 [though it be] 《 whiten, 〈 of their 〈 The filth‬
‮scarlet; crimson [sins'] stench‬

אַל תִּזְכָּר לָנוּ עֲוֹנוֹת רִאשׁוֹנִים.[3]
‮《 of the ancients. 〈 the sins 〈 against 〈 recall 〈 Do‬
‮us not‬

עַל הַר צִיּוֹן שֶׁשָּׁמֵם,[4]
‮〈 that became 〈 Zion 〈 Mount 〈 For‬
‮desolate‬

פָּנַי כְּבוּשִׁים וְלִבִּי יִשְׁתּוֹמֵם,[5]
‮《 is appalled. 〈 and my 〈 is downcast 〈 my‬
‮heart face‬

צָרִים אֲשֶׁר שִׁמְּמוּהוּ הַאֲשִׁימֵם,
‮《 condemn them, 《 destroyed 〈 who 〈 The‬
‮[the Temple], oppressors‬

וְהָאֵר פָּנֶיךָ עַל מִקְדָּשְׁךָ הַשָּׁמֵם.[6]
‮《 which is 〈 Your 〈 upon 〈 Your 〈 and‬
‮desolate. Sanctuary countenance shine‬

קִנְיָן* הַנִּקְנֶה מֵאָז[7] לְשֵׁם תִּפְאַרְתֶּךָ,
‮《 of Your splendor, 〈 in the 〈 long 〈 that You 〈 [Israel,] the‬
‮Name ago acquired possession,*‬

---

(1) Cf. *Isaiah* 7:4. (2) Cf. 1:18. (3) *Psalms* 79:8. (4) *Lamentations* 5:18.
(5) Cf. *Psalms* 143:4. (6) *Daniel* 9:17. (7) Cf. *Exodus* 15:16.

מֵאוּדִים הָעֲשֵׁנִים — *From the firebrands that are smoking.* These are the dying embers that no longer have the power to burn, yet raise an irritating smoke; they allude to those nations that rage and threaten but do not really have the power to wreak destruction (see *Ibn Ezra* and *Radak* to *Isaiah* 7:4). Thus, we pray that God save us, not only from those capable of destroying us, but even from those whose bark is worse than their bite.

קִנְיָן — *[Israel,] the possession.* This refers to Israel the nation. According to the Mishnah (*Avos* 6:10), God singled out five things from the entire universe that uniquely advance the goals of Creation. One of these is Israel, as it is written: *Until Your people pass through, HASHEM, until this people You have acquired pass through* (*Exodus* 15:16). The other four are: Torah; heaven and earth; the Patriarch Abraham; and the Holy Temple.

רַחֵם וְאַל תַּשְׁחֵת וְהִיא תְהִלָּתֶךָ,*

《 Your praise.* **〈** for that **《** destroy [it], **〈** and **〈** have mercy
    is   do not   [on it]

שֹׁכֵן הִבְטִיחָנוּ נֶאֱמַן בֵּיתֶךָ,[1]

《 of Your **〈** the **《** [Moses] **〈** For so
house: trusted one promised us,

כִּי אֵל רַחוּם יהוה אֱלֹהֶיךָ,

《 your, **〈** is **〈** Who is **〈** a **〈** For
God; HASHEM, merciful God

לֹא יַרְפְּךָ וְלֹא יַשְׁחִיתֶךָ.[2]

《 and He will not **〈** He will not
destroy you. let go of you

❖ תִּזְכֹּר תַּבְנִית תָּם בְּכִסְאֲךָ מְחֻקָּה,*

《 is engraved,* **〈** [who] on **〈** of the **〈** the image **〈** You should
Your throne wholesome   remember
[Jacob]

נָאוֹר,* יְלָדָיו מִנַּחַל עֲדָנֶיךָ תַשְׁקֶה,[3]

《 give to drink. **〈** of Your **〈** from the **〈** his **《** O Illuminat-
delight stream children ed One,*

יֵשַׁע הַמְצִיאֵם אוֹתָם נַקֵּה,[4]

《 cleanse them **《** bring forth **〈** Salvation
[of sin], for them,

נֹשֵׂא עָוֹן וְעֹבֵר עַל פֶּשַׁע וְנַקֵּה.[5]

《 and Who **〈** willful **〈** and **〈** iniquity, **〈** O You Who
absolves. sin overlooks forgives

ALL, WHILE STANDING:

אֵל מֶלֶךְ יוֹשֵׁב עַל כִּסֵּא רַחֲמִים, מִתְנַהֵג

〈 Who acts **《** of mercy, **〈** the throne **〈** on **〈** Who sits **〈** King **〈** O God,

---

(1) Cf. *Numbers* 12:7. (2) *Deuteronomy* 4:31. (3) Cf. *Psalms* 36:9. (4) Cf. 19:14.
(5) Cf. *Exodus* 34:7; some editions of *Selichos* read נֹשֵׂא עָוֹן וָפֶשַׁע וְחַטָּאָה וְנַקֵּה, *Who forgives iniquity, willful sin, and error, and Who cleanses*, as in the Scriptural verse.

וְהִיא תְהִלָּתֶךָ — *For that is Your praise.* God Himself declares that His merciful restraint in meting out punishment to sinners is the source of His praise (see *Isaiah* 48:9). Some translate: *For she [Israel] is [the one that recites] Your praise.* If this is correct, the feminine word הִיא, *she*, does not refer to קִנְיָן, *the possession*, a masculine noun, but to the אֻמָּה, *nation*, which is grammatically feminine.

תַּבְנִית תָּם בְּכִסְאֲךָ מְחֻקָּה — *The image of the wholesome [Jacob, who] on Your throne is engraved.* God engraved the image of Jacob [who is called תָּם, *the wholesome* or *perfect one* (*Genesis* 25:27)] on His Throne of Glory (*Bereishis Rabbah* 68:12).

נָאוֹר — *O Illuminated One.* The translation follows *Targum, Ibn Ezra,* and *Radak* (to *Psalms* 76:5). *Rashi* renders, *the One Who destroys those who oppose Him.*

בַּחֲסִידוּת, מוֹחֵל עֲוֹנוֹת עַמּוֹ, מַעֲבִיר רִאשׁוֹן רִאשׁוֹן,[1]

《 by one, 〈 [sins,] one 〈 Who 《 of His 〈 the sins 〈 Who 《 with kindness,
removes people, pardons

מַרְבֶּה מְחִילָה לַחֲטָאִים וּסְלִיחָה לַפּוֹשְׁעִים, עֹשֶׂה

〈 Who 《 to willful 〈 and 〈 to unintentional 〈 pardon 〈 Who abun-
performs sinners, forgiveness sinners dantly grants

צְדָקוֹת עִם כָּל בָּשָׂר וָרוּחַ, לֹא כְרָעָתָם תִּגְמוֹל.

《 do You 〈 in accord with 〈 — not 《 and 〈 [beings 〈 all 〈 with 〈 acts of
repay them! their wickedness spirit of] flesh generosity

∴ אֵל הוֹרֵיתָ לָּנוּ לוֹמַר שְׁלֹשׁ עֶשְׂרֵה, וּזְכוֹר

〈 remem- 《 the Thirteen 〈 to 〈 us 〈 You 〈 O God,
ber [Attributes of Mercy]; recite taught

לָנוּ הַיּוֹם בְּרִית שְׁלֹשׁ עֶשְׂרֵה, כְּמוֹ שֶׁהוֹדַעְתָּ לֶעָנָיו

〈 to the humble 〈 You made 〈 as 《 of [these] Thirteen, 〈 the 〈 today 〈 for us
one [Moses] known covenant

מִקֶּדֶם, כְּמוֹ שֶׁכָּתוּב, וַיֵּרֶד יהוה בֶּעָנָן וַיִּתְיַצֵּב עִמּוֹ

〈 with 〈 and stood 〈 in a 〈 And HASHEM 《 it is written: 〈 as 《 in ancient
him cloud descended times,

שָׁם, וַיִּקְרָא בְשֵׁם יהוה.[2]

《 of 〈 with the 〈 and He 《 there,
HASHEM. Name called out

CONGREGATION, THEN *CHAZZAN*:

וַיַּעֲבֹר יהוה עַל פָּנָיו וַיִּקְרָא:

《 and 《 [Moses'] 〈 before 〈 And HASHEM passed
proclaimed: face,

CONGREGATION AND *CHAZZAN* RECITE LOUDLY AND IN UNISON:

יהוה, יהוה, אֵל, רַחוּם, וְחַנּוּן, אֶרֶךְ אַפַּיִם,

〈 to anger, 〈 Slow 《 and 〈 Compassionate 〈 God, 〈 HASHEM, 〈 HASHEM,
Gracious,

וְרַב חֶסֶד, וֶאֱמֶת, נֹצֵר חֶסֶד לָאֲלָפִים, נֹשֵׂא עָוֹן,

〈 of 〈 Forgiver 《 for thousands 〈 of 〈 Preserver 《 and 〈 in 〈 and
iniquity, [of generations], kindness Truth, Kindness Abundant

וָפֶשַׁע, וְחַטָּאָה, וְנַקֵּה.[3] וְסָלַחְתָּ לַעֲוֹנֵנוּ וּלְחַטָּאתֵנוּ

《 and our sins, 〈 our 〈 May You 《 and Who 〈 and inadvertent 〈 willful sin,
iniquities forgive absolves. sin,

---

(1) *Rosh Hashanah* 17a. (2) *Exodus* 34:5. (3) 34:6-7.

וּנְחַלְתָּנוּ.[1] סְלַח לָנוּ אָבִינוּ כִּי חָטָאנוּ, מְחַל לָנוּ

‹ us, ‹ pardon   « we have ‹ for « our ‹ us, ‹ Forgive « and make us
      sinned;   Father,   Your heritage.

מַלְכֵּנוּ כִּי פָשָׁעְנוּ. כִּי אַתָּה אֲדֹנָי טוֹב וְסַלָּח,

« and ‹ are ‹ O Lord, ‹ You, ‹ For « we have ‹ for « our King,
forgiving,   good   willfully sinned.

וְרַב חֶסֶד לְכָל קֹרְאֶיךָ.[2]

« who call ‹ to all ‹ kind ‹ and
upon You.   abundantly

SELICHAH 16 / סליחה טז

(פזמון)

CHAZZAN, THEN CONGREGATION:

שַׁחַר קַמְתִּי* לְהוֹדוֹת לְךָ[3] אֱלֹהֵי תְהִלָּתִי,[3]

« of my praise; ‹ O God « to You, ‹ to offer thanks ‹ I rose* ‹ At dawn

וַאֲרַנֵּן לְךָ בְּקֶר[4] וְאוֹדִיעֲךָ חַטָּאתִי,[5]

« my sin. ‹ and let You ‹ in the ‹ to ‹ I will sing
know   morning   You

תִּנָּתֶן לִי[6] בָזֶה שָׂכָר לִפְעֻלָּתִי,[7]

« for my action: ‹ a reward ‹ for this ‹ to ‹ Let there
me be granted

נַפְשִׁי בִּשְׁאֵלָתִי, וְעַמִּי בְּבַקָּשָׁתִי.[8]

« at my petition. ‹ and my ‹ at my request, ‹ [Grant me]
people   my life

CONGREGATION, THEN CHAZZAN:

לְפָנִים זֹאת בְּיִשְׂרָאֵל[9] מַקְרִיבֵי הַקָּרְבָּן,

« a sacrifice, ‹ those who « [the practice] ‹ this ‹ Of old
offered   in Israel,   was

---

(1) *Exodus* 34:9. (2) *Psalms* 86:5. (3) Cf. 119:62. (4) 109:1. (5) Cf. 59:17.
(6) Cf. 32:5. (7) Cf. *Jeremiah* 31:15. (8) *Esther* 7:3. (9) Cf. *Ruth* 4:7.

⧼8 שַׁחַר קַמְתִּי — *At dawn I rose.* Although most of the *selichos* bearing the signature שְׁלֹמֹה הַקָּטָן חֲזַק, *Shlomo the lesser, may he be strong,* are attributed to R' Shlomo HaBavli [see prefatory comment to *Selichah* 2], this one is ascribed to R' Shlomo Ibn Gabirol [see prefatory comment to *Selichah* 71]. Like *Selichah* 22, this *selichah* uses the words of Queen Esther, נַפְשִׁי בִּשְׁאֵלָתִי, *[Grant me] my life at my*

request, וְעַמִּי בְּבַקָּשָׁתִי, *and my people at my petition* (*Esther* 7:3), as its refrain. But the similarity does not end there, for the meters and rhyme schemes of the two *selichos* are also very close to each other. If indeed this one is the work of Ibn Gabirol and *Selichah* 22 is by Ibn Gias, the similarity may be more than coincidence. The two *paytanim* lived in Southern Spain at the same time, and were about the same age. Moreover,

אִם חַטָאתִי כַּשָׁנִי כֻּלּוֹ הָפַךְ לָבָן,[1]

《 white. 〈 turn 〈 it would 《 [will be] 〈 my sin 〈 if
completely like scarlet,

וַאֲדַדֶּה כָּל שְׁנוֹתַי*[2] וַאֲאַנִין עַל הַחָרְבָּן,

《 the [Temple's] 〈 over 〈 and mourn 〈 my years* 〈 all 〈 [Therefore]
destruction, I will shake
[my head]

וְאֵין לִי לְבַד מִלָּתִי, וְעוֹלָתִי תְפִלָּתִי,

《 is my prayer: 〈 my burnt- 《 my word; 〈 besides 〈 for 〈 [as now]
offering me there is
naught

נַפְשִׁי בִּשְׁאֵלָתִי, וְעַמִּי בְּבַקָּשָׁתִי.

《at my petition. 〈 and my 《 at my request, 〈[Grant me]
people my life

CONGREGATION, THEN *CHAZZAN:*

מִזְבֵּחַ בִּהְיוֹתוֹ וְקָדָשִׁים לִזְבִיחָה,

《 for slaughter, 〈 with sanctified 《 while it 〈 The Altar,
offerings still existed

וְהֵבִיא אִישׁ אֶת זִבְחוֹ וְחַטָּאתוֹ נִמְחָה,[3]

《 was wiped away. 〈 and his sin 〈 his sacrifice 〈 a man would bring

אָפֵס מֶנִּי מְכַהֵן, וְאֵין זֶבַח וְאֵין מִנְחָה,

《 meal- 〈 nor 〈 animal 〈and there 《 is the 〈 from 〈 But
offering. offering is neither Kohen, me gone

תּוֹדָתִי זְבִיחָתִי, שִׂיחָתִי מִנְחָתִי,

《 is my meal- 〈 my prayer 《 is my animal 〈 My
offering. offering, confession

נַפְשִׁי בִּשְׁאֵלָתִי, וְעַמִּי בְּבַקָּשָׁתִי.

《at my petition. 〈 and my 《 at my request, 〈[Grant me]
people my life

CONGREGATION, THEN *CHAZZAN:*

הֵן בִּהְיוֹת הָעֲבוֹדָה וְכֹהֲנִים עַל מִשְׁמֶרֶת,

《 their watches, 〈[serving]〈 with the 〈 the Temple 〈 while there 〈 In-
at priests service, still was deed,

---

(1) Cf. *Isaiah* 1:18; *Leviticus* 13:13. (2) Cf. *Isaiah* 38:15.
(3) Some editions read וְנִתְכַּפֵּר בִּסְלִיחָה, *and he was atoned with forgiveness.*

---

for a time, they were both supported by
(and may have been students of) R' Shmuel
HaNaggid.

וַאֲדַדֶּה כָּל שְׁנוֹתַי — *[Therefore] I will shake
[my head] all my years.* The translation follows *Targum* (to *Isaiah* 38:15) who considers

הֲלֹא חַטָּאת מְכַפֶּרֶת וְהָעוֹלָה מַכְשֶׁרֶת,

« authorized. ‹ and a burnt- ‹ atone, ‹ a sin- ‹ would
offering offering not

וְאֵין חַטָּאת וְאֵין עוֹלָה וְלֹא חֵלֶב וְיוֹתֶרֶת,

« and internal ‹ fats ‹ and no « burnt- ‹ nor ‹ sin- ‹ [But today]
organs offering, offering there is
[on the Altar], neither

וְאֶשְׁפֹּךְ אֶת רִנָּתִי וְאַפִּיל תְּחִנָּתִי,

« my supplication: ‹ and present ‹ my song ‹ so I pour out

נַפְשִׁי בִּשְׁאֵלָתִי, וְעַמִּי בְּבַקָּשָׁתִי.

« at my petition. ‹ and my « at my request, ‹ [Grant me]
people my life

CONGREGATION, THEN *CHAZZAN:*

הֵן קֶדֶם בַּמִּקְדָּשׁ בְּקוּם זְרִיזִים בְּאַשְׁמֹרֶת,

« before dawn, ‹ would the ‹ when ‹ in the Holy ‹ of old « In-
alacritous rise Temple, deed,
[Kohanim]

טְהוֹרִים נִצְּבוּ לְהָפִיס, חֲדָשִׁים לִקְטֹרֶת,*

« [would offer] ‹ [only] new « to cast lots: ‹ would ‹ the purified
the incense.* ones stand ones

וְאֵין לְבוֹנָה וְאֵין קְטֹרֶת, וְנִשְׁאַרְתִּי שְׁחַרְחֹרֶת,

« blackened [by sin]; ‹ so I remain « incense, ‹ nor ‹ frankin- ‹ [But today]
cense there is neither

בְּהִתְוַדּוֹת חַטָּאתִי תְּהִי כְקָרְבָּן תּוֹדָתִי,

« my ‹ as an ‹ let be « my sins, ‹ [thus]
confession. offering [considered] as I confess

נַפְשִׁי בִּשְׁאֵלָתִי, וְעַמִּי בְּבַקָּשָׁתִי.

« at my petition. ‹ and my « at my request, ‹ [Grant me]
people my life

CONGREGATION, THEN *CHAZZAN:*

חֵזֶה קָדוֹשׁ כִּי יָדִי כָּבְדָה עַל אַנְחָתִי,[1]

« my groaning ‹ than ‹ are ‹ the ‹ that ‹ O Holy ‹ See,
[about them], heavier blows I One,
received

(1) *Job* 23:2; see *Targum* and *Rashi* there.

שְׁנוֹתַי a derivative of שָׁנָה, *year*. According to *Rashi*, the word is derived from שֵׁנָה, *sleep*, and the phrase means, *[Therefore] I will wander [instead of] all my sleep.*

חֲדָשִׁים לִקְטֹרֶת — *[Only] new ones [would offer] the incense.* Whenever possible, the Incense service was limited to *Kohanim* who had never yet burned the incense.

וְאֵין מִי יַעֲמֹד בַּעֲדִי, וְאֵין לִי בֵּית מְנוּחָתִי,[1]

《 of Rest. 〈 [my Temple,]〈 do I 〈 nor 《 for me; 〈 to stand 〈 any- 〈and there
          my House   have   up   one   is not

לְבַד בְּךָ אַזְכִּיר שְׁמֶךָ,[2] מָעוֹז צוּר יְשׁוּעָתִי,[3]

《 of my 〈 the 〈 [for You 《 Your 〈 do I 〈 upon 〈 Only
Salvation; Rock are] the   Name, [rely and] You,
            Stronghold,   mention

הַעֲבֵר אֶת אַשְׁמָתִי, וְעָנְתָה בִּי צִדְקָתִי,[4]

《 my right- 〈 for 〈 and let 〈 my guilt, 〈 clear away
eousness: me   answer

נַפְשִׁי בִּשְׁאֵלָתִי, וְעַמִּי בְּבַקָּשָׁתִי.

《at my petition. 〈 and my 《 at my request, 〈[Grant me]
                 people   my life

ALL, WHILE STANDING:

אֵל מֶלֶךְ יוֹשֵׁב עַל כִּסֵּא רַחֲמִים, מִתְנַהֵג

〈 Who acts 《 of mercy, 〈 the throne 〈 on 〈 Who sits 〈 King 〈 O God,

בַּחֲסִידוּת, מוֹחֵל עֲוֹנוֹת עַמּוֹ, מַעֲבִיר רִאשׁוֹן

〈 [sins] one 〈 Who 《 of His 〈 the sins 〈 Who 《 with kindness,
           removes people,   pardons

רִאשׁוֹן,[5] מַרְבֶּה מְחִילָה לַחֲטָאִים וּסְלִיחָה לַפּוֹשְׁעִים,

《 to willful 〈 and 〈 to unintentional 〈 pardon 〈 Who abun- 《 by one,
   sinners, forgiveness sinners   dantly grants

עֹשֶׂה צְדָקוֹת עִם כָּל בָּשָׂר וָרוּחַ, לֹא כְרָעָתָם

〈 in accord 〈 — not 《 and spirit 〈 [beings 〈 all 〈 with 〈 acts of 〈 Who
with their   of] flesh   generosity performs
wickedness

תִּגְמוֹל. ❖ אֵל הוֹרֵיתָ לָנוּ לוֹמַר שָׁלֹשׁ עֶשְׂרֵה,

《 the Thirteen 〈 to recite 〈 us 〈 You taught 〈 O God, 《 do You
[Attributes of Mercy];   repay them!

וּזְכוֹר לָנוּ הַיּוֹם בְּרִית שָׁלֹשׁ עֶשְׂרֵה, כְּמוֹ שֶׁהוֹדַעְתָּ

〈 You made 〈 as 《 of [these] Thirteen, 〈 the 〈 today 〈 for 〈remember
  known   covenant   us

---

(1) Cf. *I Chronicles* 28:2. (2) Cf. *Isaiah* 26:13. (3) Cf. *Psalms* 31:3; 28:8.
(4) *Genesis* 30:33. (5) *Rosh Hashanah* 17a.

Tradition, based on *Deuteronomy* 33:10-11, teaches that this service increased the wealth of the *Kohen* who performed it. Therefore, care was taken to give every *Kohen* at least one opportunity to burn the incense (*Yoma* 26a).

לְעָנָיו מִקֶּדֶם, כְּמוֹ שֶׁכָּתוּב, וַיֵּרֶד יהוה בֶּעָנָן
‹ in a ‹ And HASHEM ‹‹ it is written: ‹ as ‹‹ in ancient ‹ to the humble
cloud descended times, one [Moses]

וַיִּתְיַצֵּב עִמּוֹ שָׁם, וַיִּקְרָא בְשֵׁם יהוה.[1]
‹‹ of ‹ with the ‹ and He ‹‹ there, ‹ with ‹ and stood
HASHEM. Name called out him

CONGREGATION, THEN *CHAZZAN:*

וַיַּעֲבֹר יהוה עַל פָּנָיו וַיִּקְרָא:
‹‹ and ‹‹ [Moses'] ‹ before ‹ And HASHEM passed
proclaimed: face,

CONGREGATION AND *CHAZZAN* **RECITE LOUDLY AND IN UNISON:**

יהוה, יהוה, אֵל, רַחוּם, וְחַנּוּן, אֶרֶךְ אַפַּיִם,
‹ to anger, ‹ Slow ‹‹ and ‹ Compassionate ‹ God, ‹ HASHEM, ‹ HASHEM,
Gracious,

וְרַב חֶסֶד, וֶאֱמֶת, נֹצֵר חֶסֶד לָאֲלָפִים, נֹשֵׂא עָוֹן,
‹ of ‹ Forgiver ‹‹ for thousands ‹ of ‹ Preserver ‹‹ and ‹ in ‹ and
iniquity, [of generations], kindness Truth, Kindness Abundant

וָפֶשַׁע, וְחַטָּאָה, וְנַקֵּה.[2] וְסָלַחְתָּ לַעֲוֹנֵנוּ וּלְחַטָּאתֵנוּ
‹‹ and our sins, ‹ our ‹ May You ‹‹ and Who ‹ and inadvertent ‹ willful sin,
iniquities forgive absolves. sin,

וּנְחַלְתָּנוּ.[3] סְלַח לָנוּ אָבִינוּ כִּי חָטָאנוּ, מְחַל לָנוּ
‹ us, ‹ pardon ‹‹ we have ‹ for ‹‹ our ‹ us, ‹ Forgive ‹‹ and make us
sinned; Father, Your heritage.

מַלְכֵּנוּ כִּי פָשָׁעְנוּ. כִּי אַתָּה אֲדֹנָי טוֹב וְסַלָּח,
‹‹ and ‹ are ‹ O Lord, ‹ You, ‹ For ‹‹ we have ‹ for ‹‹ our King,
forgiving, good willfully sinned.

וְרַב חֶסֶד לְכָל קֹרְאֶיךָ.[4]
‹‹ who call ‹ to all ‹ kind ‹ and
upon You. abundantly

ALL:

זְכֹר רַחֲמֶיךָ יהוה וַחֲסָדֶיךָ, כִּי מֵעוֹלָם הֵמָּה.[5]
‹‹ are ‹ eternal ‹ for ‹‹ and Your ‹ HASHEM, ‹ Your ‹ Remember
they. kindnesses, mercies,

זָכְרֵנוּ יהוה בִּרְצוֹן עַמֶּךָ, פָּקְדֵנוּ בִּישׁוּעָתֶךָ.[6] זְכֹר
‹ Re- ‹‹ with Your ‹ recall us ‹ to Your ‹ when You ‹ HASHEM, ‹ Remem-
member salvation. people; show favor ber us,

---

(1) *Exodus* 35:4. (2) 34:6-7. (3) 34:9. (4) *Psalms* 86:5. (5) 25:6. (6) Cf. 106:4.

עֲדָתְךָ קָנִיתָ קֶּדֶם, גָּאַלְתָּ שֵׁבֶט נַחֲלָתֶךָ, הַר צִיּוֹן זֶה

Your congregation, which You acquired long ago, You redeemed the tribe of Your heritage; the mountain, Zion [where]

שָׁכַנְתָּ בּוֹ.¹ זְכֹר יהוה חִבַּת יְרוּשָׁלַיִם, אַהֲבַת

You rested Your Presence there. Remember, HASHEM, the affection of Jerusalem; the love

צִיּוֹן אַל תִּשְׁכַּח לָנֶצַח.² אַתָּה תָקוּם תְּרַחֵם צִיּוֹן כִּי

of Zion do not forget forever. You will arise and show mercy to Zion, for

עֵת לְחֶנְנָהּ, כִּי בָא מוֹעֵד.³ זְכֹר יהוה לִבְנֵי אֱדוֹם

[there will come] the time to favor her, for the appointed time will have come. Remember, HASHEM, [to repay] for the offspring of Edom

אֵת יוֹם יְרוּשָׁלַיִם, הָאֹמְרִים עָרוּ עָרוּ עַד הַיְסוֹד

the day of Jerusalem; those who say, Destroy! Destroy! [to repay] to the very foundation

בָּהּ.⁴ זְכֹר לְאַבְרָהָם לְיִצְחָק וּלְיִשְׂרָאֵל עֲבָדֶיךָ,

of it! Remember for Abraham, for Isaac, and for Israel, Your servants,

אֲשֶׁר נִשְׁבַּעְתָּ לָהֶם בָּךְ, וַתְּדַבֵּר אֲלֵהֶם, אַרְבֶּה

that You swore to them by Your Being, and You said to them, I shall increase

אֶת זַרְעֲכֶם כְּכוֹכְבֵי הַשָּׁמָיִם, וְכָל הָאָרֶץ הַזֹּאת אֲשֶׁר

Your offspring like the stars of the heavens; and all of this land of which

אָמַרְתִּי, אֶתֵּן לְזַרְעֲכֶם, וְנָחֲלוּ לְעֹלָם.⁵ זְכֹר לַעֲבָדֶיךָ

I spoke I will give to your offspring, and they will inherit it forever. Remember [the merits] of Your servants,

לְאַבְרָהָם לְיִצְחָק וּלְיַעֲקֹב, אַל תֵּפֶן אֶל קְשִׁי

of Abraham, of Isaac, and of Jacob; do not pay attention to the stubbornness

הָעָם הַזֶּה וְאֶל רִשְׁעוֹ וְאֶל חַטָּאתוֹ.⁶ זְכוֹר לָנוּ בְּרִית

of this people, to its wickedness, and to its sinfulness. Remember for us the covenant

אָבוֹת, כַּאֲשֶׁר אָמַרְתָּ: וְזָכַרְתִּי אֶת בְּרִיתִי יַעֲקוֹב,

of the Patriarchs, as You said: And I will remember My covenant [with] Jacob,

---

(1) *Psalms* 74:2. (2) This is not a Scriptural verse. (3) *Psalms* 102:14.
(4) 137:7. (5) *Exodus* 32:13. (6) *Deuteronomy* 9:27.

וְאַף אֶת בְּרִיתִי יִצְחָק, וְאַף אֶת בְּרִיתִי אַבְרָהָם

‹ [with] Abraham ‹ My covenant ‹ and « [with] Isaac, ‹ My covenant ‹ and also

אֶזְכֹּר, וְהָאָרֶץ אֶזְכֹּר.¹

« I will remember. ‹ and the Land « I will remember;

זְכוֹר לָנוּ בְּרִית רִאשׁוֹנִים, כַּאֲשֶׁר אָמַרְתָּ: וְזָכַרְתִּי

‹ And I will remember « You said: ‹ as « of the ancient ones, ‹ the covenant ‹ for us ‹ Remember

לָהֶם בְּרִית רִאשׁוֹנִים, אֲשֶׁר הוֹצֵאתִי אֹתָם מֵאֶרֶץ

‹ from the land ‹ I took them out ‹ that « of the ancient ones, ‹ the covenant ‹ for them

מִצְרַיִם לְעֵינֵי הַגּוֹיִם, לִהְיוֹת לָהֶם לֵאלֹהִים, אֲנִי

‹ I am « a God; ‹ to them ‹ to be « of the nations, ‹ in the very sight ‹ of Egypt

יהוה.² עֲשֵׂה עִמָּנוּ כְּמָה שֶׁהִבְטַחְתָּנוּ: וְאַף גַּם

‹ all ‹ And despite « You promised us: ‹ as ‹ with us ‹ Do « HASHEM.

זֹאת בִּהְיוֹתָם בְּאֶרֶץ אֹיְבֵיהֶם, לֹא מְאַסְתִּים וְלֹא

‹ nor ‹ despise them ‹ I will not « of their enemies, ‹ in the land ‹ when they will be ‹ this,

גְעַלְתִּים לְכַלֹּתָם לְהָפֵר בְּרִיתִי אִתָּם, כִּי אֲנִי יהוה

‹ HASHEM, ‹ I am ‹ for « with them, ‹ My covenant ‹ to annul « to destroy them, ‹ abhor them

אֱלֹהֵיהֶם.³ הָשֵׁב שְׁבוּתֵנוּ וְרַחֲמֵנוּ, כְּמָה שֶׁכָּתוּב:

« it is written: ‹ as « and have mercy on us, ‹ our captivity ‹ Bring back « their God.

וְשָׁב יהוה אֱלֹהֶיךָ אֶת שְׁבוּתְךָ וְרִחֲמֶךָ, וְשָׁב וְקִבֶּצְךָ

‹ gather you in ‹ and He will once again « and He will have mercy upon you, ‹ your captivity, ‹ your God, ‹ will HASHEM, ‹ Then bring back

מִכָּל הָעַמִּים אֲשֶׁר הֱפִיצְךָ יהוה אֱלֹהֶיךָ שָׁמָּה.⁴

« thereto. ‹ your God ‹ has HASHEM ‹ scattered you ‹ that ‹ the peoples ‹ from all

קַבֵּץ נִדְחֵינוּ, כְּמָה שֶׁכָּתוּב: אִם יִהְיֶה נִדַּחֲךָ בִּקְצֵה

‹ at the ends ‹ your dispersed will be ‹ If ‹ it is written: ‹ as ‹ our dispersed ones, ‹ Gather

(1) Leviticus 26:42. (2) 26:45. (3) 26:44. (4) 30:3.

הַשָּׁמַיִם, מִשָּׁם יְקַבֶּצְךָ יהוה אֱלֹהֶיךָ, וּמִשָּׁם יִקָּחֶךָ.[1]

⟨ He will ⟨ and from ⟨⟨ your God, ⟨ will ⟨ gather ⟨ from ⟨⟨ of heaven,
take you. there HASHEM, you in there

מְחֵה פְשָׁעֵינוּ כָּעָב וְכֶעָנָן, כְּמָה שֶׁכָּתוּב: מָחִיתִי

⟨ I have ⟨⟨ it is written: ⟨ as ⟨⟨ and like a ⟨ like a ⟨ our sins ⟨ Wipe
wiped away cloud, mist away

כָעָב פְּשָׁעֶיךָ וְכֶעָנָן חַטֹּאתֶיךָ, שׁוּבָה אֵלַי כִּי

⟨ for ⟨ to ⟨ return ⟨⟨ your ⟨ and like ⟨ your willful ⟨ like a
Me, transgressions; a cloud sins, mist

גְאַלְתִּיךָ.[2] מְחֵה פְשָׁעֵינוּ לְמַעַנְךָ, כַּאֲשֶׁר אָמַרְתָּ:

⟨⟨ You have said: ⟨ as ⟨⟨ for Your sake, ⟨ our sins ⟨ Wipe away ⟨⟨ I have redeemed you.

אָנֹכִי אָנֹכִי הוּא מֹחֶה פְשָׁעֶיךָ לְמַעֲנִי, וְחַטֹּאתֶיךָ לֹא

⟨ I shall ⟨ and your ⟨⟨ for ⟨ your ⟨⟨ Who wipes ⟨ am the ⟨ [only] I, ⟨ I,
not transgressions My sake, willful sins away One

אֶזְכֹּר.[3] הַלְבֵּן חֲטָאֵינוּ כַּשֶּׁלֶג וְכַצֶּמֶר, כְּמָה שֶׁכָּתוּב:

⟨⟨ it is written: ⟨ as ⟨⟨ and like wool, ⟨ like snow ⟨ our sins ⟨ Whiten ⟨⟨ recall.

לְכוּ נָא וְנִוָּכְחָה, יֹאמַר יהוה, אִם יִהְיוּ חֲטָאֵיכֶם

⟨ your sins may be ⟨ Though ⟨⟨ HASHEM. ⟨ says ⟨⟨ let us reason ⟨ now, ⟨ Come,
together,

כַּשָּׁנִים כַּשֶּׁלֶג יַלְבִּינוּ, אִם יַאְדִּימוּ כַתּוֹלָע, כַּצֶּמֶר

⟨ like [white] ⟨⟨ as crimson, ⟨ they may ⟨ though ⟨⟨ they will be ⟨ like ⟨⟨ like
wool be red whitened; snow scarlet,

יִהְיוּ.[4] זְרוֹק עָלֵינוּ מַיִם טְהוֹרִים וְטַהֲרֵנוּ, כְּמָה שֶׁכָּתוּב:

⟨⟨ it is written: ⟨ as ⟨⟨ and purify us, ⟨ pure water ⟨ upon us ⟨ Pour ⟨⟨ they will
become.

וְזָרַקְתִּי עֲלֵיכֶם מַיִם טְהוֹרִים וּטְהַרְתֶּם, מִכֹּל

⟨ from ⟨⟨ and you will ⟨ pure water ⟨ upon you ⟨ I shall pour
all become pure;

טֻמְאוֹתֵיכֶם וּמִכָּל גִּלּוּלֵיכֶם אֲטַהֵר אֶתְכֶם.[5] רַחֵם

⟨ Have ⟨⟨ you. ⟨ I will ⟨ your ⟨ and ⟨ your
mercy purify abominations from all contaminations

עָלֵינוּ וְאַל תַּשְׁחִיתֵנוּ, כְּמָה שֶׁכָּתוּב: כִּי אֵל רַחוּם

⟨ a merciful God ⟨ For ⟨⟨ it is written: ⟨ as ⟨⟨ destroy us, ⟨ and do not ⟨ on us

יהוה אֱלֹהֶיךָ, לֹא יַרְפְּךָ וְלֹא יַשְׁחִיתֶךָ, וְלֹא יִשְׁכַּח

⟨ will He ⟨ nor ⟨⟨ will He ⟨ nor ⟨ relinquish ⟨ He will ⟨⟨ your God; ⟨ is
forget destroy you, you not HASHEM,

---

(1) *Leviticus* 30:4. (2) *Isaiah* 44:22. (3) 43:25. (4) 1:18. (5) *Ezekiel* 36:25.

אֶת בְּרִית אֲבֹתֶיךָ אֲשֶׁר נִשְׁבַּע לָהֶם.[1] מוּל
⟨ Circumcise ⟪ to them. ⟨ He swore ⟨ which ⟨ with your forefathers, ⟨ the covenant

אֶת לְבָבֵנוּ לְאַהֲבָה וּלְיִרְאָה אֶת שְׁמֶךָ, כְּמָה שֶׁכָּתוּב:
⟪ it is written: ⟨ as ⟪ Your Name, ⟨ and to fear ⟨ to love ⟨ our hearts

וּמָל יהוה אֱלֹהֶיךָ אֶת לְבָבְךָ וְאֶת לְבַב זַרְעֶךָ, לְאַהֲבָה
⟨ to love ⟪ of your ⟨ and the ⟨ your heart ⟨ HASHEM, your God, offspring, heart will circumcise

אֶת יהוה אֱלֹהֶיךָ, בְּכָל לְבָבְךָ וּבְכָל נַפְשְׁךָ, לְמַעַן
⟨ so that ⟪ your soul, ⟨ and with all ⟨ your heart ⟨ with all ⟨ your God, ⟨ HASHEM,

חַיֶּיךָ.[2] הַמָּצֵא לָנוּ בְּבַקָּשָׁתֵנוּ, כְּמָה שֶׁכָּתוּב: וּבִקַּשְׁתֶּם
⟨ And you ⟪ it is written: ⟨ as ⟪ in our quest, ⟨ to us ⟨ Be ⟪ you may will seek accessible live.

מִשָּׁם אֶת יהוה אֱלֹהֶיךָ וּמָצָאתָ, כִּי תִדְרְשֶׁנּוּ בְּכָל
⟨ with ⟨ you search ⟨ when ⟪ and you will ⟨ your God, ⟨ HASHEM, ⟨ from all Him out find [Him], there

לְבָבְךָ וּבְכָל נַפְשֶׁךָ.[3] ✧ תְּבִיאֵנוּ אֶל הַר קָדְשֶׁךָ,
⟨ Your holy mountain ⟨ to ⟨ Bring us ⟪ your soul. ⟨ and with all ⟨ your heart

וְשַׂמְּחֵנוּ בְּבֵית תְּפִלָּתֶךָ, כְּמָה שֶׁכָּתוּב: וַהֲבִיאוֹתִים
⟨ And I will bring them ⟪ it is written: ⟨ as ⟪ of Prayer, ⟨ in Your House ⟨ and gladden us

אֶל הַר קָדְשִׁי, וְשִׂמַּחְתִּים בְּבֵית תְּפִלָּתִי, עוֹלֹתֵיהֶם
⟨ their burnt- ⟪ of Prayer; ⟨ in My ⟨ and I will ⟪ My holy ⟨ to offerings House gladden them mountain,

וְזִבְחֵיהֶם לְרָצוֹן עַל מִזְבְּחִי, כִּי בֵיתִי בֵּית תְּפִלָּה
⟨ of ⟨ "a ⟨ My ⟨ for ⟪ My Altar, ⟨ on ⟨ will find ⟨ and their feast-
Prayer" House House favor offerings

יִקָּרֵא לְכָל הָעַמִּים.[4]
⟪ nations. ⟨ for all ⟨ will be called

THE ARK IS OPENED.

CHAZZAN, THEN CONGREGATION:

שְׁמַע קוֹלֵנוּ יהוה אֱלֹהֵינוּ, חוּס וְרַחֵם עָלֵינוּ,
⟪ on us, ⟨ and have ⟨ have ⟪ our God; ⟨ HASHEM, ⟨ our voice, ⟨ Hear
compassion pity

וְקַבֵּל בְּרַחֲמִים וּבְרָצוֹן אֶת תְּפִלָּתֵנוּ.[5]
⟪ our prayer. ⟨ and favor ⟨ with compassion ⟨ and accept

---

(1) *Deuteronomy* 4:31. (2) 30:6. (3) 4:29. (4) *Isaiah* 56:7. (5) From the weekday *Shemoneh Esrei*.

CHAZZAN, THEN CONGREGATION:

הֲשִׁיבֵנוּ יהוה אֵלֶיךָ וְנָשׁוּבָה, חַדֵּשׁ יָמֵינוּ כְּקֶדֶם.[1]

《 as of old. 〈 our days 〈 renew 《 and we shall return, 〈 to You, 〈 HASHEM, 〈 Bring us back,

CHAZZAN, THEN CONGREGATION:

אֲמָרֵינוּ הַאֲזִינָה יהוה, בִּינָה הֲגִיגֵנוּ.[2]

《 our thoughts. 〈 perceive 《 HASHEM; 〈 hear, 〈 Our words

THE FOLLOWING VERSE IS RECITED QUIETLY:

יִהְיוּ לְרָצוֹן אִמְרֵי פִינוּ וְהֶגְיוֹן לִבֵּנוּ לְפָנֶיךָ,

《 before You, 《 of our heart — 〈 and the thoughts 〈 of our mouth 〈 — the ex- pressions 《 find favor 〈 May they

יהוה צוּרֵנוּ וְגוֹאֲלֵנוּ.[3]

《 and our Redeemer. 〈 our Rock 〈 HASHEM,

CHAZZAN, THEN CONGREGATION:

אַל תַּשְׁלִיכֵנוּ מִלְּפָנֶיךָ, וְרוּחַ קָדְשְׁךָ אַל תִּקַּח מִמֶּנּוּ.[4]

《 from us. 〈 take not 〈 do not 〈 of Your Holiness 〈 and the Spirit 《 from Your Presence, 〈 cast us away 〈 Do not

CHAZZAN, THEN CONGREGATION:

אַל תַּשְׁלִיכֵנוּ לְעֵת זִקְנָה, כִּכְלוֹת כֹּחֵנוּ אַל תַּעַזְבֵנוּ.[5]

《 forsake us not. 〈 does our strength, 〈 when fail 《 of old 〈 in time 〈 cast us away 〈 Do not

ALL CONTINUE (SOME CONGREGATIONS RECITE THE NEXT VERSE RESPONSIVELY):

אַל תַּעַזְבֵנוּ יהוה, אֱלֹהֵינוּ אַל תִּרְחַק מִמֶּנּוּ.[6]

《 from us. 〈 be not distant 〈 our God, 《 O HASHEM; 〈 Forsake us not,

עֲשֵׂה עִמָּנוּ אוֹת לְטוֹבָה, וְיִרְאוּ שׂוֹנְאֵינוּ וְיֵבֹשׁוּ,

《 and be ashamed, 〈 may our enemies 〈 so that see it 《 for good; 〈 a sign 〈 for us 〈 Display

כִּי אַתָּה יהוה עֲזַרְתָּנוּ וְנִחַמְתָּנוּ.[7] כִּי לְךָ יהוה

〈 HASHEM, 〈 for You, 〈 Because 《 and consoled us. 〈 will have helped us 〈 HASHEM, 〈 You, 〈 for

הוֹחָלְנוּ, אַתָּה תַעֲנֶה אֲדֹנָי אֱלֹהֵינוּ.[8]

《 our God. 〈 O Lord, 〈 will answer, 〈 You 《 do we wait;

THE ARK IS CLOSED.

---

(1) *Lamentations* 5:21. (2) Cf. *Psalms* 5:2. (3) Cf. 19:15.
(4) 51:13. (5) Cf. 71:9. (6) Cf. 38:22. (7) Cf. 86:17. (8) Cf. 38:16.

EACH INDIVIDUAL CONTINUES UNTIL THE END OF *SELICHOS*.

CONFESSION / וִדּוּי

**DURING THE RECITATION OF THE וִדּוּי, *CONFESSION*, STAND WITH
HEAD AND BODY SLIGHTLY BOWED, IN SUBMISSIVE CONTRITION.**

אֱלֹהֵינוּ וֵאלֹהֵי אֲבוֹתֵינוּ, תָּבֹא לְפָנֶיךָ תְּפִלָּתֵנוּ,[1]

| may our prayer, | before You | come | of our forefathers, | and the God | Our God |

וְאַל תִּתְעַלַּם מִתְּחִנָּתֵנוּ,[2] שֶׁאֵין אָנוּ עַזֵּי פָנִים

| faced | so brazen- | For we are not | our supplication. | ignore | and do not |

וּקְשֵׁי עֹרֶף, לוֹמַר לְפָנֶיךָ יהוה אֱלֹהֵינוּ וֵאלֹהֵי

| and the God | our God, | HASHEM, | before You, | as to say | necked | and stiff- |

אֲבוֹתֵינוּ, צַדִּיקִים אֲנַחְנוּ וְלֹא חָטָאנוּ, אֲבָל

| —for indeed, | sinned | and have not | we are, | that righteous | of our forefathers, |

אֲנַחְנוּ וַאֲבוֹתֵינוּ חָטָאנוּ.[3]

| have sinned. | and our forefathers | we |

**STRIKE THE LEFT SIDE OF THE CHEST WITH THE RIGHT FIST WHILE RECITING
EACH OF THE SINS OF THE FOLLOWING CONFESSIONAL LITANY:**

אָשַׁמְנוּ, בָּגַדְנוּ, גָּזַלְנוּ, דִּבַּרְנוּ דֹּפִי. הֶעֱוִינוּ,

| We have com-mitted iniquity; | slander. | we have spoken | we have robbed; | we have betrayed; | We have been guilty; |

וְהִרְשַׁעְנוּ, זַדְנוּ, חָמַסְנוּ, טָפַלְנוּ שֶׁקֶר. יָעַצְנוּ

| We have given advice | false accusations. | we have made | we have extorted; | we have sinned willfully; | we have committed wickedness; |

רָע, כִּזַּבְנוּ, לַצְנוּ, מָרַדְנוּ, נִאַצְנוּ, סָרַרְנוּ,

| we have strayed; | we have provoked [God's anger]; | we have rebelled; | we have scorned; | we have been deceitful; | that is bad; |

עָוִינוּ, פָּשַׁעְנוּ, צָרַרְנוּ, קִשִּׁינוּ עֹרֶף. רָשַׁעְנוּ,

| We have been wicked; | our necks. | we have stiffened | we have caused distress; | we have sinned rebelliously; | we have been iniquitous; |

שִׁחַתְנוּ, תִּעַבְנוּ, תָּעִינוּ, תִּעְתָּעְנוּ.

| we have scoffed. | we have gone astray; | we have committed abominations; | we have been corrupt; |

סַרְנוּ מִמִּצְוֹתֶיךָ וּמִמִּשְׁפָּטֶיךָ הַטּוֹבִים, וְלֹא שָׁוָה

| worth-while | and it was not | that are good, | and from Your laws | from Your commandments | We have turned away |

---

(1) Cf. *Psalms* 88:3. (2) Cf. 55:2. (3) Cf. 106:6, *Jeremiah* 3:25.

1. לָנוּ. וְאַתָּה צַדִּיק עַל כָּל הַבָּא עָלֵינוּ, כִּי
⟨ for ⟩ ⟪ upon us, ⟨ that has come ⟨ all ⟨ in ⟨ are righteous ⟨ And You ⟪ for us.

2. אֱמֶת עָשִׂיתָ וַאֲנַחְנוּ הִרְשָׁעְנוּ.
⟪ have acted wickedly. ⟨ while we ⟪ have You acted, ⟨ truthfully

אָשַׁמְנוּ מִכָּל עָם, בִּשְׁנוּ מִכָּל דּוֹר, גָּלָה מִמֶּנּוּ
⟨ from ⟨ Departed ⟪ genera- ⟨ more ⟨ We have ⟪ people. ⟨ more than ⟨ We have
us tion. than any been any other been guilty
other ashamed

מָשׂוֹשׂ, דָּוָה לִבֵּנוּ בַּחֲטָאֵינוּ, הֶחְבַּל אַוִּינוּ, וְנִפְרַע
⟨ uncov- ⟪ was our de- ⟨ Seized ⟪ because of ⟨ is our ⟨ Sickened ⟪ has joy.
ered sired [Temple], our sins. heart

פְּאֵרֵנוּ, זְבוּל בֵּית מִקְדָּשֵׁנוּ חָרַב בַּעֲוֹנֵינוּ, טִירָתֵנוּ
⟨ Our Palace ⟪ because of ⟨ has been ⟨ our Holy Temple, ⟨ for [His] ⟪ was our
our iniquities. destroyed abode, splendor;

הָיְתָה לְשַׁמָּה, יְפִי אַדְמָתֵנוּ לְזָרִים, בֹּחֵנוּ לְנָכְרִים.
⟪ [was given] ⟨ our ⟪ is controlled ⟨ of our ⟨ [Jerusalem,] ⟪ desolate. ⟨ has
to foreigners. wealth by strangers, Land the beauty become

וַעֲדַיִן לֹא שַׁבְנוּ מִטְּעוּתֵנוּ וְהֵיךְ נָעִיז פָּנֵינוּ וְנַקְשֶׁה
⟨ and ⟨ faced ⟨ can we be ⟨ So ⟪ from our ⟨ we have not ⟨ But still
stiffen so brazen- how willful errors. repented

עָרְפֵּנוּ, לוֹמַר לְפָנֶיךָ יהוה אֱלֹהֵינוּ וֵאלֹהֵי אֲבוֹתֵינוּ,
⟪ of our ⟨ and the ⟨ our God ⟨ HASHEM, ⟨ before ⟨ so as to ⟨ our neck
forefathers, God You, say

צַדִּיקִים אֲנַחְנוּ וְלֹא חָטָאנוּ, אֲבָל אֲנַחְנוּ וַאֲבוֹתֵינוּ
⟨ and our ⟨ both we ⟨ for in ⟪ and we have ⟪ we are ⟨ that
fathers truth, not sinned, righteous

3. חָטָאנוּ.
⟪ have sinned.

**STRIKE THE LEFT SIDE OF THE CHEST WITH THE RIGHT FIST WHILE RECITING
EACH OF THE SINS OF THE FOLLOWING CONFESSIONAL LITANY:**

אָשַׁמְנוּ, בָּגַדְנוּ, גָּזַלְנוּ, דִּבַּרְנוּ דֹפִי. הֶעֱוִינוּ,
⟪ We have com- ⟪ slander. ⟨ we have ⟪ we have ⟪ we have ⟨ We have been
mitted iniquity; spoken robbed; betrayed; guilty;

וְהִרְשַׁעְנוּ, זַדְנוּ, חָמַסְנוּ, טָפַלְנוּ שֶׁקֶר. יָעַצְנוּ
⟨ We have ⟪ false ⟨ we have ⟪ we have ⟪ we have sinned ⟪ we have commit-
given advice accusations. made extorted; willfully; ted wickedness;

(1) Cf. *Job* 33:27. (2) *Nehemiah* 9:33. (3) Cf. *Psalms* 106:6; *Jeremiah* 3:25.

רָע, בְּזַבְנוּ, לַצְנוּ, מָרַדְנוּ, נִאַצְנוּ, סָרַרְנוּ,
《 we have 《 we have provoked 《 we have 《 we have 《 we have been 《 that is
strayed; [God's anger]; rebelled; scorned; deceitful; bad;

עָוִינוּ, פָּשַׁעְנוּ, צָרַרְנוּ, קִשִּׁינוּ עֹרֶף. רָשַׁעְנוּ,
《 We have 《 our 〈 we have 《 we have 《 we have 《 we have
been wicked; necks. stiffened caused sinned been
distress; rebelliously; iniquitous;

שִׁחַתְנוּ, תִּעַבְנוּ, תָּעִינוּ, תִּעְתָּעְנוּ.
《 we have 《 we have 《 we have 《 we have
scoffed. gone astray; committed been corrupt;
abominations;

סַרְנוּ מִמִּצְוֹתֶיךָ וּמִמִּשְׁפָּטֶיךָ הַטּוֹבִים, וְלֹא שָׁוָה
〈 worth- 〈 and it 《 that are 〈 and from 〈 from Your 〈 We have
while was not good, Your laws commandments turned away

לָנוּ.[1] וְאַתָּה צַדִּיק עַל כָּל הַבָּא עָלֵינוּ, כִּי אֱמֶת
〈 truth- 〈 for 《 upon us, 〈 that has 〈 all 〈 in 〈 are 〈 And You 《 for us.
fully come righteous

עָשִׂיתָ וַאֲנַחְנוּ הִרְשָׁעְנוּ.[2]
《 have acted 〈 while we 《 have You
wickedly. acted,

לְעֵינוּ עָשְׁקוּ עֲמָלֵנוּ, מְמַשָּׁךְ וּמְמוֹרָט מִמֶּנּוּ.
《 from 〈 and cut off 〈 [it was] 《 the product 〈 have they 〈 Before our
us. pulled away of our labor; stolen eyes

נָתְנוּ עֹל עָלֵינוּ, סָבַלְנוּ עַל שִׁכְמֵנוּ, עֲבָדִים
〈 Slaves 《 our 〈 upon 〈 we bore it 《 upon us, 〈 their 〈 They have
shoulders. yoke placed

מָשְׁלוּ בָנוּ, **פֹּרֵק** אֵין מִיָּדָם, צָרוֹת רַבּוֹת
〈 that are 〈 Troubles 《 from their there 〈 a 《 over 〈 have
manifold hand. was not redeemer us; ruled

סְבָבוּנוּ, **קְרָאנוּךָ** יהוה אֱלֹהֵינוּ, רָחַקְתָּ מִמֶּנּוּ
〈 from 〈 but You have dis- 《 our God, 〈 HASHEM, 〈 we called 《 have
us tanced Yourself upon You, surrounded us,

בַּעֲוֹנֵינוּ, שַׁבְנוּ מֵאַחֲרֶיךָ, תָּעִינוּ וְאָבָדְנוּ.
《 we have 《 we have 《 from following 〈 We have 《 because of
become lost. gone astray; after You; turned away our iniquities.

---

(1) Cf. *Job* 33:27. (2) *Nehemiah* 9:33.

וַעֲדַיִן לֹא שַׁבְנוּ מִטָּעוּתֵנוּ וְהֵיךְ נָעִיז פָּנֵינוּ וְנַקְשֶׁה

‹ and   ‹ faced ‹ can we be ‹ So   « from our   ‹ we have not   ‹ But still
stiffen   so brazen-   how   willful errors.   repented

עָרְפֵּנוּ, לוֹמַר לְפָנֶיךָ יהוה אֱלֹהֵינוּ וֵאלֹהֵי אֲבוֹתֵינוּ,

« of our   ‹ and the ‹ our God ‹ HASHEM, ‹ before ‹ so as to ‹ our neck
forefathers,   God   You,   say

צַדִּיקִים אֲנַחְנוּ וְלֹא חָטָאנוּ, אֲבָל אֲנַחְנוּ וַאֲבוֹתֵינוּ

‹ and our   ‹ both we ‹ for in «   and we have «   we are ‹   that
fathers   truth,   not sinned,   righteous

חָטָאנוּ.[1]

« have sinned.

**STRIKE THE LEFT SIDE OF THE CHEST WITH THE RIGHT FIST WHILE RECITING
EACH OF THE SINS OF THE FOLLOWING CONFESSIONAL LITANY:**

אָשַׁמְנוּ, בָּגַדְנוּ, גָּזַלְנוּ, דִּבַּרְנוּ דְפִי. הֶעֱוִינוּ,

« We have com- « slander. ‹ we have   « we have   « we have   « We have been
mitted iniquity;   spoken   robbed;   betrayed;   guilty;

וְהִרְשַׁעְנוּ, זַדְנוּ, חָמַסְנוּ, טָפַלְנוּ שֶׁקֶר. יָעַצְנוּ

‹ We have   «   false   ‹ we have « we have «we have sinned «we have commit-
given advice accusations.   made   extorted;   willfully;   ted wickedness;

רָע, כִּזַּבְנוּ, לַצְנוּ, מָרַדְנוּ, נִאַצְנוּ, סָרַרְנוּ,

« we have   « we have provoked « we have   « we have « we have been « that is
strayed;   [God's anger];   rebelled;   scorned;   deceitful;   bad;

עָוִינוּ, פָּשַׁעְנוּ, צָרַרְנוּ, קִשִּׁינוּ עֹרֶף. רָשַׁעְנוּ,

« We have   «   our   ‹ we have «we have caused «we have sinned «we have been
been wicked;   necks.   stiffened   distress;   rebelliously;   iniquitous;

שִׁחַתְנוּ, תִּעַבְנוּ, תָּעִינוּ, תִּעְתָּעְנוּ.

«   we have   « we have «we have commit- « we have
scoffed.   gone astray; ted abominations; been corrupt;

סַרְנוּ מִמִּצְוֹתֶיךָ וּמִמִּשְׁפָּטֶיךָ הַטּוֹבִים, וְלֹא שָׁוָה

‹ worth- ‹ and it   « that are ‹   and from   ‹ from Your   ‹ We have
while   was not   good,   Your laws   commandments   turned away

לָנוּ.[2] וְאַתָּה צַדִּיק עַל כָּל הַבָּא עָלֵינוּ, כִּי אֱמֶת

‹ truth-   ‹ for « upon us, ‹ that has ‹ all ‹ in ‹   are   ‹ And You « for us.
fully   come   righteous

עָשִׂיתָ וַאֲנַחְנוּ הִרְשָׁעְנוּ.[3]

« have acted wickedly. ‹ while we « have You acted,

(1) Cf. *Psalms* 106:6; *Jeremiah* 3:25. (2) Cf. *Job* 33:27. (3) *Nehemiah* 9:33.

הִרְשַׁעְנוּ וּפָשַׁעְנוּ, לָכֵן לֹא נוֹשָׁעְנוּ. וְתֵן בְּלִבֵּנוּ
We have acted ‹ and we ‹› there- ‹ we have ‹ been ‹› Place ‹ in our
wickedly ‹ have sinned ‹ fore ‹ not ‹ saved. ‹› ‹ hearts
‹ rebelliously;

לַעֲזוֹב דֶּרֶךְ רֶשַׁע, וְחִישׁ לָנוּ יֶשַׁע, כַּכָּתוּב עַל יַד
[the will] ‹ the ‹› to abandon ‹ of ‹› wickedness, ‹ and ‹ to us ‹ salvation; ‹ as it is ‹ by ‹ the
to abandon ‹ path ‹ hasten ‹ ‹ written ‹ hand

נְבִיאֶךָ: יַעֲזֹב רָשָׁע דַּרְכּוֹ, וְאִישׁ אָוֶן מַחְשְׁבֹתָיו,
of Your ‹› Let ‹ the wicked ‹ his way, ‹ and ‹ of ‹ [abandon]
prophet: ‹ abandon ‹ one ‹ the man ‹ iniquity ‹ his thoughts;

וְיָשֹׁב אֶל יהוה וִירַחֲמֵהוּ, וְאֶל אֱלֹהֵינוּ כִּי
and let ‹ to ‹ HASHEM, ‹ and He will have ‹› and to ‹ our God, ‹ for
him return ‹ ‹ compassion on him,

יַרְבֶּה לִסְלוֹחַ.¹
He is ‹ forgiving. ‹›
abundantly

מְשִׁיחַ צִדְקֶךָ אָמַר לְפָנֶיךָ, שְׁגִיאוֹת מִי יָבִין,
Your ‹ who is righteous ‹ said ‹ who ‹ before You: ‹› Mistakes ‹ who ‹ can
anointed one ‹ [David] ‹ ‹ discern?

מִנִּסְתָּרוֹת נַקֵּנִי.² נַקֵּנוּ יהוה אֱלֹהֵינוּ מִכָּל פְּשָׁעֵינוּ,
From ‹ cleanse ‹› Cleanse ‹ HASHEM, ‹ our God, ‹ of all ‹ our sins
unperceived faults ‹ me. ‹ us,

וְטַהֲרֵנוּ מִכָּל טֻמְאוֹתֵינוּ, וּזְרוֹק עָלֵינוּ מַיִם טְהוֹרִים
and purify us ‹ of all ‹ our contaminations. ‹› Pour ‹ upon us ‹ pure water

וְטַהֲרֵנוּ, כַּכָּתוּב עַל יַד נְבִיאֶךָ: וְזָרַקְתִּי עֲלֵיכֶם
and purify us, ‹ as it is ‹ by ‹ the ‹ of Your ‹ I shall pour ‹› upon you
‹ written ‹ hand ‹ prophet:

מַיִם טְהוֹרִים וּטְהַרְתֶּם, מִכֹּל טֻמְאוֹתֵיכֶם וּמִכָּל
pure water ‹ and you will ‹ from ‹ your ‹ and
‹ become pure; ‹ all ‹ contaminations ‹ from all

גִּלּוּלֵיכֶם אֲטַהֵר אֶתְכֶם.³ עַמְּךָ וְנַחֲלָתְךָ, רְעֵבֵי
your ‹ I will purify ‹ you. ‹› Your ‹› and Your ‹› who
abominations ‹ ‹ people ‹ heritage, ‹ hunger

טוּבְךָ, צְמֵאֵי חַסְדֶּךָ, תְּאֵבֵי יִשְׁעֶךָ, יַכִּירוּ וְיֵדְעוּ
for Your ‹› who ‹ for Your ‹› and ‹ for Your ‹› — may they ‹ and
goodness, ‹ thirst ‹ kindness, ‹ who long ‹ salvation ‹ recognize ‹ know

---

(1) *Isaiah* 55:7. (2) *Psalms* 19:13. (3) *Ezekiel* 36:25.

כִּי לַיהוה אֱלֹהֵינוּ הָרַחֲמִים וְהַסְּלִיחוֹת.

《 and forgiveness. 〈 belong mercy 〈 our God, 〈 to HASHEM, 〈 that

אֵל רַחוּם שְׁמֶךָ, אֵל חַנּוּן שְׁמֶךָ,[1] בָּנוּ נִקְרָא שְׁמֶךָ.[2]

《 is Your Name 〈 upon 《 is Your 〈 Gracious God 《 is Your 〈 Merciful God
proclaimed, us Name,

יהוה עֲשֵׂה לְמַעַן שְׁמֶךָ,[3] עֲשֵׂה לְמַעַן אֲמִתָּךְ, עֲשֵׂה

〈 act 《 Your truth; 〈 for the 〈 Act 《 Your 〈 for the 〈 act 〈 HASHEM,
sake of Name. sake of

לְמַעַן בְּרִיתָךְ, עֲשֵׂה לְמַעַן גָּדְלָךְ וְתִפְאַרְתָּךְ, עֲשֵׂה

〈 act 《 and Your 〈 Your 〈 for the 〈 act 《 Your 〈 for the
splendor; greatness sake of covenant; sake of

לְמַעַן דָּתָךְ, עֲשֵׂה לְמַעַן הוֹדָךְ, עֲשֵׂה לְמַעַן וְעוּדָךְ,

《 Your Meet- 〈 for the 〈 act 《 Your 〈 for the 〈 act 《 Your 〈 for the
ing House; sake of glory; sake of Law; sake of

עֲשֵׂה לְמַעַן זִכְרָךְ,[4] עֲשֵׂה לְמַעַן חַסְדָּךְ, עֲשֵׂה לְמַעַן

〈 for the 〈 act 《 Your 〈 for the 〈 act 《 Your 〈 for the 〈 act
sake of kindness; sake of remembrance; sake of

טוּבָךְ, עֲשֵׂה לְמַעַן יִחוּדָךְ, עֲשֵׂה לְמַעַן כְּבוֹדָךְ, עֲשֵׂה

〈 act 《 Your 〈 for the 〈 act 《 Your 〈 for the 〈 act 《 Your
honor; sake of Oneness; sake of goodness;

לְמַעַן לִמּוּדָךְ,[6] עֲשֵׂה לְמַעַן מַלְכוּתָךְ, עֲשֵׂה לְמַעַן

〈 for the 〈 act 《 Your kingship; 〈 for the 〈 act 《 Your 〈 for the
sake of sake of students; sake of

נִצְחָךְ, עֲשֵׂה לְמַעַן סוֹדָךְ,[7] עֲשֵׂה לְמַעַן עֻזָּךְ, עֲשֵׂה

〈 act 《 Your 〈 for the 〈 act 《 Your secret [re- 〈 for the 〈 act 《 Your eternal
power; sake of vealed to those sake of [Name];
who fear You];

לְמַעַן פְּאֵרָךְ, עֲשֵׂה לְמַעַן צִדְקָתָךְ, עֲשֵׂה לְמַעַן

〈 for the 〈 act 《 Your 〈 for the 〈 act 《 Your 〈 for the
sake of righteousness; sake of glory; sake of

קְדֻשָּׁתָךְ, עֲשֵׂה לְמַעַן רַחֲמֶיךָ הָרַבִּים, עֲשֵׂה לְמַעַן

〈 for the 〈 act 《 that is 〈 Your mercy 〈 for the 〈 act 《 Your sanctity;
sake of abundant; sake of

שְׁכִינָתָךְ, עֲשֵׂה לְמַעַן תְּהִלָּתָךְ, עֲשֵׂה לְמַעַן אוֹהֲבֶיךָ

〈 those who 〈 for the 〈 act 《 Your praise; 〈 for the 〈 act 《 Your Divine
loved You sake of sake of Presence;

(1) Cf. *Exodus* 34:6. (2) Cf. *Deuteronomy* 28:10. (3) *Jeremiah* 14:7.
(4) Cf. *Exodus* 3:15. (5) *Psalms* 6:5. (6) Cf. *Isaiah* 54:13. (7) Cf. *Psalms* 25:14.

שׁוֹכְנֵי עָפָר, עֲשֵׂה לְמַעַן אַבְרָהָם יִצְחָק וְיַעֲקֹב,
‹ who rest ‹ in the dust; ›› ‹ act ‹ for the sake of ›› Abraham, ‹ Isaac, ‹ and Jacob; ››

עֲשֵׂה לְמַעַן מֹשֶׁה וְאַהֲרֹן, עֲשֵׂה לְמַעַן דָּוִד וּשְׁלֹמֹה,
‹ act ‹ for the sake of ‹ Moses ›› and Aaron; ‹ act ‹ for the sake of ‹ David ‹ and Solomon;

עֲשֵׂה לְמַעַן יְרוּשָׁלַיִם עִיר קָדְשֶׁךָ, עֲשֵׂה לְמַעַן צִיּוֹן
‹ act ‹ for the sake of ‹ Jerusalem, ‹ the City ‹ of Your Holiness; ›› ‹ act ‹ for the sake of ‹ Zion,

מִשְׁכַּן כְּבוֹדֶךָ, עֲשֵׂה לְמַעַן שִׁמְמוֹת הֵיכָלֶךָ, עֲשֵׂה
‹ the abode ‹ of Your glory; ›› ‹ act ‹ for the sake of ‹ the desolation ‹ of Your Temple; ›› ‹ act

לְמַעַן הֲרִיסוּת מִזְבְּחֶךָ, עֲשֵׂה לְמַעַן הַהֲרוּגִים עַל
‹ for the sake of ‹ the devastation ‹ of Your Altar; ›› ‹ act ‹ for the sake of ‹ those killed ‹ for

שֵׁם קָדְשֶׁךָ, עֲשֵׂה לְמַעַן טְבוּחִים עַל יִחוּדֶךָ, עֲשֵׂה
‹ Your holy Name; ›› ‹ act ‹ for the sake of ‹ those slaughtered ‹ for ‹ Your Oneness; ›› ‹ act

לְמַעַן בָּאֵי בָאֵשׁ וּבַמַּיִם עַל קִדּוּשׁ שְׁמֶךָ, עֲשֵׂה לְמַעַן
‹ for the sake of ‹ those who entered ‹ fire ‹ and water ‹ for ‹ the sanctification ‹ of Your Name; ›› ‹ act ‹ for the sake of

יוֹנְקֵי שָׁדַיִם שֶׁלֹּא חָטְאוּ, עֲשֵׂה לְמַעַן גְּמוּלֵי חָלָב
‹ the [infants] sucking ‹ at the breast ‹ who did not ‹ sin; ›› ‹ act ‹ for the sake of ‹ the [babies] weaned ‹ from milk

שֶׁלֹּא פָשָׁעוּ, עֲשֵׂה לְמַעַן תִּינוֹקוֹת שֶׁל בֵּית רַבָּן,
‹ who did not ‹ transgress; ›› ‹ act ‹ for the sake of ‹ the children ‹ of ‹ their teachers' school; ››

עֲשֵׂה לְמַעַנְךָ אִם לֹא לְמַעֲנֵנוּ, עֲשֵׂה לְמַעַנְךָ וְהוֹשִׁיעֵנוּ.
‹ act ‹ for Your sake ‹ if ‹ not ‹ for our sake; ›› ‹ act ‹ for Your sake ›› and save us.

עֲנֵנוּ יהוה עֲנֵנוּ, עֲנֵנוּ אֱלֹהֵינוּ עֲנֵנוּ, עֲנֵנוּ אָבִינוּ
‹ Answer us; ‹ HASHEM, ›› ‹ answer us; ‹ answer ‹ our God, ›› ‹ answer us; ‹ answer ‹ our Father,

עֲנֵנוּ, עֲנֵנוּ בוֹרְאֵנוּ עֲנֵנוּ, עֲנֵנוּ גוֹאֲלֵנוּ עֲנֵנוּ, עֲנֵנוּ
‹ answer us; ›› ‹ answer ‹ our Creator, ›› ‹ answer us; ‹ answer ‹ our Redeemer, ›› ‹ answer us; ›› ‹ answer us;

---

(1) *Isaiah* 26:19. (2) Cf. *Daniel* 9:16,24. (3) *Psalms* 26:8. (4) Cf. *Jeremiah* 51:26. (5) Cf. *Isaiah* 49:19. (6) *Joel* 2:16. (7) *Isaiah* 28:9. (8) *Shabbos* 119b. (9) *Isaiah* 64:7. (10) Cf. 43:1. (11) 47:4.

דּוֹרְשֵׁנוּ¹ עֲנֵנוּ, עֲנֵנוּ הָאֵל הַנֶּאֱמָן² עֲנֵנוּ, עֲנֵנוּ וָתִיק

⟨ You Who searches us out, answer us; « answer us, ⟨ God Who is faithful, ⟨ answer us, « answer us, ⟨ stead-fast

וְחָסִיד עֲנֵנוּ, עֲנֵנוּ זַךְ וְיָשָׁר³ עֲנֵנוּ, עֲנֵנוּ חַי וְקַיָּם⁴

⟨ and kind One, ⟨ answer us, « answer us; ⟨ pure ⟨ and upright One ⟨ answer us, « answer us; ⟨ living ⟨ and enduring One,

עֲנֵנוּ, עֲנֵנוּ טוֹב וּמֵטִיב עֲנֵנוּ, עֲנֵנוּ יוֹדֵעַ יֵצֶר⁶ עֲנֵנוּ,

« answer us; ⟨ answer us, ⟨ good ⟨ and beneficent One, ⟨ answer us « answer us; ⟨ Knower ⟨ of inclinations, « answer us;

עֲנֵנוּ כּוֹבֵשׁ כְּעָסִים עֲנֵנוּ, עֲנֵנוּ לוֹבֵשׁ צְדָקוֹת⁷ עֲנֵנוּ,

⟨ answer us ⟨ Suppressor ⟨ of wrath, « answer us, ⟨ answer us; ⟨ Donner ⟨ of righteousness, « answer us;

עֲנֵנוּ מֶלֶךְ מַלְכֵי הַמְּלָכִים⁸ עֲנֵנוּ, עֲנֵנוּ נוֹרָא וְנִשְׂגָּב⁹

⟨ answer us, ⟨ King ⟨ over kings ⟨ of kings, « answer us; ⟨ answer us, ⟨ awesome ⟨ and powerful One,

עֲנֵנוּ, עֲנֵנוּ סוֹלֵחַ וּמוֹחֵל עֲנֵנוּ, עֲנֵנוּ עוֹנֶה בְּעֵת

« answer us ⟨ answer us, ⟨ You Who forgives ⟨ and pardons, « answer us; ⟨ answer us, ⟨ You Who answers ⟨ in time

צָרָה¹⁰ עֲנֵנוּ, עֲנֵנוּ פּוֹדֶה וּמַצִּיל¹¹ עֲנֵנוּ, עֲנֵנוּ צַדִּיק

⟨ of distress, « answer us ⟨ answer us, ⟨ Redeemer ⟨ and Rescuer, « answer us; ⟨ answer us, ⟨ righteous

וְיָשָׁר¹² עֲנֵנוּ, עֲנֵנוּ קָרוֹב לְקוֹרְאָיו¹³ עֲנֵנוּ, עֲנֵנוּ קָשֶׁה

⟨ and upright One, « answer us ⟨ answer us; ⟨ He Who is close ⟨ to those who call upon Him, « answer us ⟨ answer us, ⟨ You Who with difficulty

לִכְעוֹס¹⁴ עֲנֵנוּ, עֲנֵנוּ רַךְ לִרְצוֹת¹⁵ עֲנֵנוּ, עֲנֵנוּ רַחוּם

⟨ becomes angry, « answer us ⟨ answer us, ⟨ You Who are easily appeased, « answer us ⟨ answer us; ⟨ merciful

וְחַנּוּן¹⁶ עֲנֵנוּ, עֲנֵנוּ שׁוֹמֵעַ אֶל אֶבְיוֹנִים¹⁷ עֲנֵנוּ, עֲנֵנוּ

⟨ and gracious One, « answer us ⟨ answer us, ⟨ You Who listens ⟨ to ⟨ the destitute, « answer us ⟨ answer us,

תּוֹמֵךְ תְּמִימִים עֲנֵנוּ, עֲנֵנוּ אֱלֹהֵי אֲבוֹתֵינוּ עֲנֵנוּ,

⟨ You Who supports ⟨ the wholesome, « answer us; ⟨ answer us, ⟨ God ⟨ of our forefathers, « answer us;

עֲנֵנוּ אֱלֹהֵי אַבְרָהָם¹⁸ עֲנֵנוּ, עֲנֵנוּ פַּחַד יִצְחָק עֲנֵנוּ,

⟨ answer us ⟨ God ⟨ of Abraham, « answer us, ⟨ answer us ⟨ Awesome One ⟨ of Isaac, « answer us;

---

(1) Cf. Ezekiel 34:11. (2) Deuteronomy 7:9. (3) Job 8:6; cf. Proverbs 20:11. (4) Cf. Daniel 6:27.
(5) Cf. Psalms 119:68. (6) Cf. 103:14. (7) Cf. Isaiah 59:17. (8) Ethics of the Fathers 3:1.
(9) Psalms 47:3; 148:13. (10) Cf. Isaiah 49:8; Psalms 37:39. Alternate text: בְּעֵת רָצוֹן, in time of favor.
(11) Cf. 34:23,18. (12) Deuteronomy 32:4. (13) Cf. Psalms 145:18. (14) Ethics of the Fathers 5:14.
(15) Cf. 5:14. (16) Exodus 34:6. (17) Psalms 69:34. (18) Genesis 31:42.

עֲנֵנוּ אֲבִיר יַעֲקֹב¹ עֲנֵנוּ, עֲנֵנוּ עֶזְרַת הַשְּׁבָטִים עֲנֵנוּ,

answer us; of the tribes, Helper answer us, answer us; of Jacob, Mighty One answer us;

עֲנֵנוּ מִשְׂגַּב אִמָּהוֹת עֲנֵנוּ, עֲנֵנוּ עוֹנֶה בְּעֵת רָצוֹן² עֲנֵנוּ,

answer us; of favor, in a time You Who answers answer us; answer us; of the Matriarchs, Stronghold answer us,

עֲנֵנוּ אֲבִי יְתוֹמִים³ עֲנֵנוּ, עֲנֵנוּ דַּיַּן אַלְמָנוֹת³ עֲנֵנוּ.

answer us. of widows, Judge answer us; answer us; of orphans, Father answer us,

מִי שֶׁעָנָה לְאַבְרָהָם אָבִינוּ בְּהַר הַמּוֹרִיָּה⁴

Moriah on Mount our father Abraham Who answered He

הוּא יַעֲנֵנוּ.

answer us. — may He

מִי שֶׁעָנָה לְיִצְחָק בְּנוֹ כְּשֶׁנֶּעֱקַד עַל גַּבֵּי הַמִּזְבֵּחַ⁴

of the altar top on when he was bound his son Isaac Who answered He

הוּא יַעֲנֵנוּ.

answer us. — may He

הוּא יַעֲנֵנוּ.

answer us. — may He

מִי שֶׁעָנָה לְיַעֲקֹב בְּבֵית אֵל⁵

in Beth-el Jacob Who answered He

מִי שֶׁעָנָה לְיוֹסֵף בְּבֵית הָאֲסוּרִים⁶

in the prison Joseph Who answered He

הוּא יַעֲנֵנוּ.

answer us. — may He

מִי שֶׁעָנָה לַאֲבוֹתֵינוּ עַל יַם סוּף⁷

of Reeds the Sea at our forefathers Who answered He

הוּא יַעֲנֵנוּ.

answer us. — may He

מִי שֶׁעָנָה לְמֹשֶׁה בְּחוֹרֵב⁸

in Horeb Moses Who answered He

הוּא יַעֲנֵנוּ.

answer us. — may He

מִי שֶׁעָנָה לְאַהֲרֹן בַּמַּחְתָּה⁹

with the fire-pan Aaron Who answered He

הוּא יַעֲנֵנוּ.

answer us. — may He

---

(1) *Isaiah* 49:26. (2) Cf. 49:8; *Psalms* 69:14. Alternate text: בְּעֵת צָרָה, *in time of distress.*
(3) 68:6. (4) *Genesis* 22:12. (5) 35:3. (6) 39:21. (7) *Exodus* Ch. 14.
(8) 17:6,11; *Deuteronomy* 9:19. (9) *Numbers* 17:11-13.

מִי שֶׁעָנָה לְפִינְחָס בְּקוּמוֹ מִתּוֹךְ הָעֵדָה¹

He ⟩ Who ⟩ Phinehas ⟩ when he ⟩ from ⟩ the ⟩⟩
answered   arose   amid   congregation

הוּא יַעֲנֵנוּ.

may ⟩ — He ⟩ answer ⟩⟩
He   us.

מִי שֶׁעָנָה לִיהוֹשֻׁעַ בַּגִּלְגָּל²

He ⟩ Who ⟩ Joshua ⟩ in Gilgal ⟩⟩
answered

הוּא יַעֲנֵנוּ.

may ⟩ — He ⟩ answer ⟩⟩
He   us.

מִי שֶׁעָנָה לִשְׁמוּאֵל בַּמִּצְפָּה³

He ⟩ Who ⟩ Samuel ⟩ in Mizpah ⟩⟩
answered

הוּא יַעֲנֵנוּ.

may ⟩ — He ⟩ answer ⟩⟩
He   us.

מִי שֶׁעָנָה לְדָוִד וּשְׁלֹמֹה בְנוֹ בִּירוּשָׁלַיִם⁴

He ⟩ Who ⟩ David ⟩ and ⟩ his ⟩ in Jerusalem ⟩⟩
answered   Solomon   son

הוּא יַעֲנֵנוּ.

may ⟩ — He ⟩ answer ⟩⟩
He   us.

מִי שֶׁעָנָה לְאֵלִיָּהוּ בְּהַר הַכַּרְמֶל⁵

He ⟩ Who ⟩ Elijah ⟩ on ⟩ Carmel ⟩⟩
answered   Mount

הוּא יַעֲנֵנוּ.

may ⟩ — He ⟩ answer ⟩⟩
He   us.

מִי שֶׁעָנָה לֶאֱלִישָׁע בִּירִיחוֹ⁶

He ⟩ Who ⟩ Elisha ⟩ in Jericho ⟩⟩
answered

הוּא יַעֲנֵנוּ.

may ⟩ — He ⟩ answer ⟩⟩
He   us.

מִי שֶׁעָנָה לְיוֹנָה בִּמְעֵי הַדָּגָה⁷

He ⟩ Who ⟩ Jonah ⟩ in the ⟩ of the ⟩⟩
answered   innards   fish

הוּא יַעֲנֵנוּ.

may ⟩ — He ⟩ answer ⟩⟩
He   us.

מִי שֶׁעָנָה לְחִזְקִיָּהוּ מֶלֶךְ יְהוּדָה בְּחָלְיוֹ⁸

He ⟩ Who ⟩ Hezekiah, ⟩ king ⟩ of Judah, ⟩ in his ⟩⟩
answered   illness

הוּא יַעֲנֵנוּ.

may ⟩ — He ⟩ answer ⟩⟩
He   us.

מִי שֶׁעָנָה לַחֲנַנְיָה מִישָׁאֵל וַעֲזַרְיָה

He ⟩ Who ⟩ Hananiah, ⟩ Mishael, ⟩ and Azariah ⟩
answered

בְּתוֹךְ כִּבְשַׁן הָאֵשׁ⁹

inside ⟩ the furnace ⟩ of fire ⟩⟩

הוּא יַעֲנֵנוּ.

may ⟩ — He ⟩ answer ⟩⟩
He   us.

מִי שֶׁעָנָה לְדָנִיֵּאל בְּגוֹב הָאֲרָיוֹת¹⁰

He ⟩ Who ⟩ Daniel ⟩ in the ⟩ of lions ⟩⟩
answered   den

הוּא יַעֲנֵנוּ.

may ⟩ — He ⟩ answer ⟩⟩
He   us.

(1) *Numbers* 25:7-13. (2) *Joshua* 6:1-20; 7:6-15; 10:12-14. (3) *I Samuel* 7:9.
(4) *II Samuel* 7:5-16; 21:1,14; 24:25; *I Kings* 9:3. (5) 18:36-38. (6) *II Kings* 2:21.
(7) *Jonah* 2:2-11. (8) *II Kings* 20:2-6; *Isaiah* 38:2-8. (9) *Daniel* 3:21-27. (10) 6:17-23.

מִי שֶׁעָנָה לְמָרְדְּכַי וְאֶסְתֵּר בְּשׁוּשַׁן הַבִּירָה¹

‹ He › Who ‹ Mordechai › and Esther ‹ in Shushan › the capital 》
     answered

הוּא יַעֲנֵנוּ.

‹ — may › answer 》
He   us.

מִי שֶׁעָנָה לְעֶזְרָא בַגּוֹלָה²

‹ He › Who ‹ Ezra › in the exile 》
answered

הוּא יַעֲנֵנוּ.

‹ — may › answer 》
He   us.

מִי שֶׁעָנָה לְכָל הַצַּדִּיקִים וְהַחֲסִידִים וְהַתְּמִימִים

‹ He › Who ‹ all › the righteous, ‹ the devout, ‹ the wholesome, ›
answered

וְהַיְשָׁרִים

and the 》
upright

הוּא יַעֲנֵנוּ.

‹ — may › answer 》
He   us.

רַחֲמָנָא דְעָנֵי לַעֲנִיֵּי, עֲנֵינָן. רַחֲמָנָא דְעָנֵי לִתְבִירֵי

‹ those of ‹ Who ‹ Merciful 》 answer 》 the poor, ‹ Who ‹ Merciful One
broken   answers   One   us!   answers

לִבָּא, עֲנֵינָן. רַחֲמָנָא דְעָנֵי לִמְכִיכֵי רוּחָא, עֲנֵינָן.

》answer 》 spirit, ‹ those of ‹ Who ‹ Merciful 》 answer 》 hearts,
us!   crushed   answers   One   us!

רַחֲמָנָא עֲנֵינָן. רַחֲמָנָא חוּס. רַחֲמָנָא פְּרוֹק. רַחֲמָנָא

‹ Merciful 》redeem! ‹ Merciful 》 have ‹ Merciful 》 answer ‹ Merciful
One,   One,   pity!   One,   us!   One,

שְׁזִיב. רַחֲמָנָא רְחַם עֲלָן, הַשְׁתָּא בַּעֲגָלָא וּבִזְמַן קָרִיב.

》that comes‹ and at ‹ swiftly, ‹ — now, 》 on us ‹ have ‹ Merciful 》 save!
soon.   a time   mercy   One,

PUTTING DOWN THE HEAD / נפילת אפים

RECITE UNTIL יֵבֹשׁוּ רָגַע WITH THE HEAD RESTING ON THE LEFT ARM,
PREFERABLY WHILE SEATED.

(וַיֹּאמֶר דָּוִד אֶל גָּד, צַר לִי מְאֹד, נִפְּלָה נָּא בְיַד יהוה,

》 of ‹ into the ‹ now ‹ Let us 》 exceed- ‹ am ‹ Dis- 》Gad, ‹ to ‹ (And David said
HASHEM, hand   fall   ingly.   I   tressed

כִּי רַבִּים רַחֲמָיו, וּבְיַד אָדָם אַל אֶפֹּלָה.³)

》 let me not fall.) ‹ but into human 》 are His ‹ abundant ‹ for
hands   mercies,

---

(1) *Esther* Ch. 8. (2) *Ezra* 8:21-23. (3) *II Samuel* 24:14.

רַחוּם וְחַנּוּן חָטָאתִי לְפָנֶיךָ. יהוה מָלֵא רַחֲמִים,

O merciful One, and gracious, I have sinned before You. HASHEM, Who is full of mercy,

רַחֵם עָלַי וְקַבֵּל תַּחֲנוּנָי.

have mercy on me and accept my supplications.

—— תהלים ו:ב-יא / Psalms 6:2-11 ——

יהוה, אַל בְּאַפְּךָ תוֹכִיחֵנִי, וְאַל בַּחֲמָתְךָ תְיַסְּרֵנִי.

HASHEM, do not in Your anger rebuke me, nor in Your wrath chastise me.

חָנֵּנִי יהוה כִּי אֻמְלַל אָנִי, רְפָאֵנִי יהוה כִּי נִבְהֲלוּ

Favor me, HASHEM, for feeble am I; heal me, HASHEM, for shudder with terror

עֲצָמָי. וְנַפְשִׁי נִבְהֲלָה מְאֹד, וְאַתָּה יהוה עַד מָתָי.

do my bones. My soul is terrified utterly, and You, HASHEM, until when?

שׁוּבָה יהוה חַלְּצָה נַפְשִׁי, הוֹשִׁיעֵנִי לְמַעַן חַסְדֶּךָ.

Desist, HASHEM, release my soul; save me as befits Your kindness.

כִּי אֵין בַּמָּוֶת זִכְרֶךָ, בִּשְׁאוֹל מִי יוֹדֶה לָּךְ. יָגַעְתִּי

For not in death is there mention of You; in the grave who will praise You? I am wearied

בְּאַנְחָתִי, אַשְׂחֶה בְכָל לַיְלָה מִטָּתִי, בְּדִמְעָתִי

with my sigh; I drench every night my bed; with my tears

עַרְשִׂי אַמְסֶה. עָשְׁשָׁה מִכַּעַס עֵינִי, עָתְקָה בְּכָל

my couch I soak. Dimmed because of anger is my eye, aged by all

צוֹרְרָי. סוּרוּ מִמֶּנִּי כָּל פֹּעֲלֵי אָוֶן, כִּי שָׁמַע יהוה

my tormentors. Depart from me, all doers of evil, for HASHEM has heard

קוֹל בִּכְיִי. שָׁמַע יהוה תְּחִנָּתִי, יהוה תְּפִלָּתִי יִקָּח.

the sound of my weeping. HASHEM has heard my plea, HASHEM my prayer will accept.

יֵבֹשׁוּ וְיִבָּהֲלוּ מְאֹד כָּל אֹיְבָי, יָשֻׁבוּ יֵבֹשׁוּ רָגַע.

Let them be shamed and confounded utterly, all my enemies; may they regret and be shamed in an instant.

מַחֲי וּמַסִּי מֵמִית וּמְחַיֶּה, מַסִּיק מִן שְׁאוֹל

[O God,] Who wounds and Who heals, Who causes death and Who restores life, Who raises [the dead] from the grave

לְחַיֵּי עָלְמָא, בְּרָא כַּד חָטֵי אֲבוּהִי לַקְיֵהּ, אֲבוּהִי

to life › eternal: › A son › should he › sin, › his father › would strike him, › but a father

דְּחָיֵס אַסֵּי לִכְאֵבֵהּ. עַבְדָּא דְּמָרִיד נָפִיק בְּקוֹלָר,

who is compassionate › will heal › his [son's] pain. › A slave › who rebels, › he is led out › in chains,

מָרֵהּ תָּאִיב וְתַבִּיר קוֹלָרֵהּ.

but [if] his master › desires, › he breaks › his chains.

בְּרָךְ בְּכְרָךְ אֲנַן וְחָטִינָן קַמָּךְ, הָא רָוֵי נַפְשִׁין

Your son, › Your firstborn, › we are, › and we have sinned › before You; › indeed › satiated › has our soul been

בְּגִידִין מְרָרִין, עַבְדָּךְ אֲנַן וּמְרוֹדִינָן קַמָּךְ,

with wormwood › that is bitter. › Your servants › we are › and we have rebelled › before You;

הָא בְּבִזְּתָא, הָא בְּשִׁבְיָא, הָא בְּמַלְקִיּוּתָא.

[indeed we have suffered,] some › from looting, › some › in captivity, › and some › by the lash.

בְּמָטוּ מִנָּךְ בְּרַחֲמָךְ דִּנְפִישִׁין, אַסֵּי לִכְאֵבִין

We beg › of You, › in Your compassion › that is abundant, › heal › the pains

דִּתְקוֹף עֲלָן, עַד דְּלָא נֶהֱוֵי גְּמִירָא בְּשִׁבְיָא.

that have overwhelmed › us, › while yet › we are not › completely annihilated › in captivity.

מַכְנִיסֵי רַחֲמִים, הַכְנִיסוּ רַחֲמֵינוּ, לִפְנֵי בַּעַל

O you who usher in › [pleas for] mercy, › may you usher in › our [plea for] mercy, › before › the Master

הָרַחֲמִים. מַשְׁמִיעֵי תְפִלָּה, הַשְׁמִיעוּ תְפִלָּתֵנוּ, לִפְנֵי

of mercy. › O you who aid the hearing › of prayer, › may you aid the hearing › of our prayer, › before

שׁוֹמֵעַ תְּפִלָּה. מַשְׁמִיעֵי צְעָקָה, הַשְׁמִיעוּ צַעֲקָתֵנוּ,

the Hearer › of prayer. › O you who aid the hearing › of outcries, › may you aid the hearing › of our outcries

לִפְנֵי שׁוֹמֵעַ צְעָקָה. מַכְנִיסֵי דִמְעָה, הַכְנִיסוּ

before › the Hearer › of outcries. › O you who usher in › tears, › may you usher in

דִּמְעוֹתֵינוּ, לִפְנֵי מֶלֶךְ מִתְרַצֶּה בִּדְמָעוֹת.

our tears › before › the King › Who is appeased › through tears.

הִשְׁתַּדְּלוּ וְהַרְבּוּ תְּחִנָּה וּבַקָּשָׁה, לִפְנֵי מֶלֶךְ אֵל

‹ God, ‹ the King, ‹ before ‹ and pleas ‹ supplications ‹ and intensify ‹ Exert yourselves

רָם וְנִשָּׂא. הַזְכִּירוּ לְפָנָיו, הַשְׁמִיעוּ לְפָנָיו תּוֹרָה

‹ the Torah ‹ before Him, ‹ aid to be heard « before Him, ‹ Mention « and uplifted. ‹ exalted

וּמַעֲשִׂים טוֹבִים שֶׁל שׁוֹכְנֵי עָפָר.

« in the dust. ‹ [the Patriarchs and Matriarchs] who dwell ‹ of ‹ that are good ‹ and the deeds

יִזְכֹּר אַהֲבָתָם וִיחַיֶּה זַרְעָם, שֶׁלֹּא תֹאבַד שְׁאֵרִית

‹ shall the remnant ‹ lost ‹ so that not ‹ to their offspring, ‹ and grant life ‹ their love ‹ May He remember

יַעֲקֹב. כִּי צֹאן רוֹעֵה נֶאֱמָן הָיָה לְחֶרְפָּה,

« a disgrace; ‹ has become ‹ who is faithful [Moses] ‹ of the shepherd ‹ the flock ‹ For « of Jacob be.

יִשְׂרָאֵל גּוֹי אֶחָד לִמְשָׁל וְלִשְׁנִינָה.

« and a simile. ‹ a parable « that is the unique, ‹ the nation « Israel,

מַהֵר עֲנֵנוּ אֱלֹהֵי יִשְׁעֵנוּ, וּפְדֵנוּ מִכָּל גְּזֵרוֹת קָשׁוֹת

« that are harsh; ‹ decrees ‹ from all ‹ and redeem us ‹ of our salvation, ‹ O God ‹ answer us, ‹ Swiftly

וְהוֹשִׁיעָה בְּרַחֲמֶיךָ הָרַבִּים, מְשִׁיחַ צִדְקֶךָ וְעַמֶּךָ.

« and Your people. ‹ Your righteous anointed one ‹ that is abundant, ‹ in Your mercy ‹ and may You save,

מָרָן דִּבִשְׁמַיָּא לָךְ מִתְחַנְּנָן, כְּבַר שְׁבִיָּא דְּמִתְחַנָּן

‹ who supplicates ‹ in captivity ‹ as one « do we supplicate, ‹ to You « Who is in heaven, ‹ Our Master

לִשְׁבוּיֵהּ. כֻּלְּהוֹן בְּנֵי שְׁבִיָּא בְּכַסְפָּא מִתְפָּרְקִין,

« are redeemed, ‹ through money ‹ in captivity, ‹ those ‹ [for] all « before his captors;

וְעַמָּךְ יִשְׂרָאֵל בְּרַחֲמֵי וּבְתַחֲנוּנֵי, הַב לָן שְׁאֵילְתִּין

‹ our requests ‹ us ‹ O « and grant supplication. ‹ through compassion ‹ Israel ‹ but Your people

וּבָעוּתִין, דְּלָא נֶהְדַר רֵיקָם מִן קֳדָמָךְ.

« before You. ‹ from ‹ empty-handed ‹ that we not be turned away ‹ and our prayers

מָרַן דְּבִשְׁמַיָּא לָךְ מִתְחַנְּנַן, כְּעַבְדָּא דְּמִתְחַנֵּן
‹ who supplicates ‹ as a slave « do we ‹ to You « Who is in « Our
supplicates, heaven, Master

לְמָרֵיהּ, עֲשִׁיקֵי אֲנַן וּבַחֲשׁוֹכָא שָׁרֵינַן, מְרִירָן נַפְשִׁין
‹ are [our] ‹ embittered « do we ‹ and in darkness ‹ are « Oppressed « to his
souls abide, we master:

מֵעָקָתִין דְּנַפִּישִׁין, חֵילָא לֵית בָּן לְרַצּוּיָךְ. מָרַן,
‹ Our « to appease ‹ within ‹ is ‹ Strength « that is ‹ from distress
Master, You. us lacking excessive.

עֲבִיד בְּדִיל קַיָּמָא דִּגְזַרְתָּ עִם אֲבָהָתָנָא.
« our Patriarchs. ‹ with ‹ that You ‹ of the ‹ for the ‹ act
established covenant sake

שׁוֹמֵר יִשְׂרָאֵל, שְׁמוֹר שְׁאֵרִית יִשְׂרָאֵל, וְאַל
‹ let not « of Israel; ‹ the remnant ‹ safeguard « of Israel, ‹ O Guardian

יֹאבַד יִשְׂרָאֵל, הָאוֹמְרִים שְׁמַע יִשְׂרָאֵל.[1]
« O Israel. ‹ Hear, ‹ those who « Israel be destroyed —
proclaim:

שׁוֹמֵר גּוֹי אֶחָד, שְׁמוֹר שְׁאֵרִית עַם אֶחָד, וְאַל
‹ let not « that is ‹ of the ‹ the remnant ‹ safeguard « that is ‹ of the ‹ O Guardian
unique; people unique, nation

יֹאבַד גּוֹי אֶחָד, הַמְּיַחֲדִים שְׁמֶךָ, יהוה אֱלֹהֵינוּ
‹ is our God, ‹ HASHEM « of Your ‹ those who proclaim « that is ‹ the ‹ be
Name: the Oneness unique, nation destroyed

יהוה אֶחָד.
« the One ‹ HASHEM
[and Only]! is

שׁוֹמֵר גּוֹי קָדוֹשׁ, שְׁמוֹר שְׁאֵרִית עַם קָדוֹשׁ, וְאַל
‹ let not « that is ‹ of the ‹ the remnant ‹ safeguard « that is ‹ of the ‹ O Guardian
holy; people holy, nation

יֹאבַד גּוֹי קָדוֹשׁ, הַמְּשַׁלְּשִׁים בְּשָׁלֹשׁ קְדֻשּׁוֹת לְקָדוֹשׁ.
« to the ‹ sancti- ‹ the ‹ those who proclaim « that is ‹ the ‹ be
Holy One. fications threefold three times holy, nation destroyed

מִתְרַצֶּה בְּרַחֲמִים וּמִתְפַּיֵּס בְּתַחֲנוּנִים, הִתְרַצֵּה
‹ be « through ‹ and Who becomes ‹ through ‹ You Who becomes
favorable supplications, conciliatory compassion favorable

(1) Deuteronomy 6:4.

וְהִתְפַּיֵס לְדוֹר עָנִי, כִּי אֵין עוֹזֵר. אָבִינוּ מַלְכֵּנוּ,

《 our King,　〈 Our Father,　《 helper.　〈 there is no　〈 for　《 that is　〈 to the　〈 and be conciliatory poor,　generation

חָנֵּנוּ וַעֲנֵנוּ, כִּי אֵין בָּנוּ מַעֲשִׂים, עֲשֵׂה עִמָּנוּ

〈 us　〈 treat　《 worthy deeds;　〈 we have no　〈 though　〈 and　〈 be gracious answer us,　with us

צְדָקָה וָחֶסֶד וְהוֹשִׁיעֵנוּ.

《 and save us. 〈 and kindness, 〈 with charity

STAND AFTER THE WORDS וַאֲנַחְנוּ לֹא נֵדַע UNTIL CONCLUSION OF THE PARAGRAPH.

וַאֲנַחְנוּ לֹא נֵדַע מַה נַּעֲשֶׂה, כִּי עָלֶיךָ עֵינֵינוּ.[1]

《 are our eyes.　〈 upon You　〈 rather,　《 we should do,　〈 what　〈 know not　〈 We

זְכֹר רַחֲמֶיךָ יהוה וַחֲסָדֶיךָ, כִּי מֵעוֹלָם הֵמָּה.[2] יְהִי

〈 May 《 are they.　〈 eternal　〈 for　〈 and Your kindnesses,　〈 HASHEM,　〈 Your mercies,　〈 Remember

חַסְדְּךָ יהוה עָלֵינוּ, כַּאֲשֶׁר יִחַלְנוּ לָךְ.[3] אַל תִּזְכָּר

〈 recall　〈 Do not　《 You.　〈 we awaited　〈 just as　《 be upon us, 〈 HASHEM, 〈 Your kindness,

לָנוּ עֲוֹנוֹת רִאשׁוֹנִים, מַהֵר יְקַדְּמוּנוּ רַחֲמֶיךָ, כִּי

〈 for 《 may Your mercies,　〈 advance to meet us　〈 swiftly　《 of the ancients;　〈 the sins　〈 against us

דַלּוֹנוּ מְאֹד.[4] עֶזְרֵנוּ בְּשֵׁם יהוה, עֹשֵׂה שָׁמַיִם

〈 of heaven　〈 Maker　《 of HASHEM,　〈 is through the Name　〈 Our help　《 exceedingly.　〈 we have become impoverished

וָאָרֶץ.[5] חָנֵּנוּ יהוה חָנֵּנוּ, כִּי רַב שָׂבַעְנוּ בוּז.[6] בְּרֹגֶז

《 Amid wrath,　《 with contempt.　〈 sated fully　〈 we are　〈 for 《 favor us,　〈 HASHEM, 〈 Favor us,　《 and earth.

רַחֵם תִּזְכּוֹר.[7] בְּרֹגֶז עֲקֵדָה תִּזְכּוֹר. בְּרֹגֶז תְּמִימוֹת

〈 the perfect ones　《 Amid wrath,　《 You should remember!　〈 the binding [of Isaac]　《 Amid wrath,　《 You should remember!　〈 to be merciful

תִּזְכּוֹר.[8] יהוה הוֹשִׁיעָה, הַמֶּלֶךְ יַעֲנֵנוּ בְיוֹם קָרְאֵנוּ.[9]

《 we call.　〈 on the day　〈 answer us　〈 May the King　《 save!　〈 HASHEM, 《 You should remember!

כִּי הוּא יָדַע יִצְרֵנוּ, זָכוּר כִּי עָפָר אֲנָחְנוּ.[9]

《 are we.　〈 dust　〈 that　〈 He is mindful　《 our nature,　〈 knew　〈 He　〈 For

---

(1) *II Chronicles* 20:12. (2) *Psalms* 25:6. (3) 33:22. (4) 79:8. (5) 121:2.
(6) 123:3. (7) *Habakkuk* 3:2. (8) *Psalms* 20:10. (9) 103:14.

❖ עָזְרֵנוּ אֱלֹהֵי יִשְׁעֵנוּ עַל דְּבַר כְּבוֹד שְׁמֶךָ, וְהַצִּילֵנוּ

‹ rescue us › « of Your ‹ of the ‹ the ‹ for ‹ of our ‹ O God ‹ Assist us,
Name; glory sake salvation

וְכַפֵּר עַל חַטֹּאתֵינוּ לְמַעַן שְׁמֶךָ.[1]

« of Your ‹ for the ‹ our sins ‹ for ‹ and grant
Name. sake atonement

FULL KADDISH / קדיש שלם

THE *CHAZZAN* RECITES קדיש שלם, FULL *KADDISH*.

יִתְגַּדַּל וְיִתְקַדַּשׁ שְׁמֵהּ רַבָּא. (אָמֵן. — Cong.) בְּעָלְמָא

‹ — in the « (Amen.) « that is ‹ may His ‹ and be ‹ Grow
world great! — Name sanctified exalted

דִּי בְרָא כִרְעוּתֵהּ. וְיַמְלִיךְ מַלְכוּתֵהּ, וְיַצְמַח פֻּרְקָנֵהּ

‹ His ‹ and cause « to His ‹ and may He « according ‹ He ‹ that
salvation, to sprout kingship, give reign to His will, created

וִיקָרֵב מְשִׁיחֵהּ. (אָמֵן. — Cong.) בְּחַיֵּיכוֹן וּבְיוֹמֵיכוֹן וּבְחַיֵּי

‹ and in the ‹ and in ‹ in your « (Amen.) « His Messiah, ‹ and bring
lifetimes your days, lifetimes near

דְכָל בֵּית יִשְׂרָאֵל, בַּעֲגָלָא וּבִזְמַן קָרִיב. וְאִמְרוּ: אָמֵן.

« Amen. ‹ Now « that comes ‹ and at a ‹ swiftly « of Israel, ‹ Family ‹ of the
respond: soon. time entire

CONGREGATION RESPONDS:

אָמֵן. יְהֵא שְׁמֵהּ רַבָּא מְבָרַךְ לְעָלַם וּלְעָלְמֵי עָלְמַיָּא.

« and for all eternity. ‹ forever ‹ be ‹ that is ‹ His ‹ May « Amen.
blessed great Name

CHAZZAN CONTINUES:

יְהֵא שְׁמֵהּ רַבָּא מְבָרַךְ לְעָלַם וּלְעָלְמֵי עָלְמַיָּא. יִתְבָּרַךְ

‹ Blessed, « and for all eternity. ‹ forever ‹ be ‹ that is ‹ His ‹ May
blessed great Name

וְיִשְׁתַּבַּח וְיִתְפָּאַר וְיִתְרוֹמַם וְיִתְנַשֵּׂא וְיִתְהַדָּר וְיִתְעַלֶּה

‹ elevated, ‹ honored, ‹ upraised, ‹ exalted, ‹ glorified, ‹ praised,

וְיִתְהַלָּל שְׁמֵהּ דְּקֻדְשָׁא בְּרִיךְ הוּא (בְּרִיךְ הוּא — Cong.)

« is He) ‹ (Blessed « is He ‹ Blessed ‹ of the Holy ‹ be the ‹ and lauded
One, Name

— לְעֵלָּא מִן כָּל בִּרְכָתָא וְשִׁירָתָא תֻּשְׁבְּחָתָא וְנֶחָמָתָא

‹ and ‹ praise « and song, ‹ blessing ‹ any ‹ beyond
consolation

(1) *Psalms* 79:9.

דַּאֲמִירָן בְּעָלְמָא. וְאִמְרוּ: אָמֵן. (Cong. — אָמֵן.)

《 (Amen.) 《 Amen. 〈 Now respond: 《 in the world. 〈 that are uttered

CONGREGATION:

(קַבֵּל בְּרַחֲמִים וּבְרָצוֹן אֶת תְּפִלָּתֵנוּ.)

《 our prayers.) 〈 and with favor 〈 with mercy 〈 (Accept

CHAZZAN CONTINUES:

תִּתְקַבֵּל צְלוֹתְהוֹן וּבָעוּתְהוֹן דְּכָל בֵּית יִשְׂרָאֵל קֳדָם

〈 before 〈 Israel 〈 Family of 〈 of the entire 〈 and supplications 〈 the prayers 〈 May accepted be

אֲבוּהוֹן דִּי בִשְׁמַיָּא. וְאִמְרוּ: אָמֵן. (Cong. — אָמֵן.)

《 (Amen.) 《 Amen. 〈 Now respond: 《 is in Heaven. 〈 Who 〈 their Father

CONGREGATION:

(יְהִי שֵׁם יהוה מְבֹרָךְ, מֵעַתָּה וְעַד עוֹלָם.[1])

《 eternity.) 〈 until 〈 from this time 《 be blessed, 〈 of 〈 the HASHEM Name 〈 (Let

CHAZZAN CONTINUES:

יְהֵא שְׁלָמָא רַבָּא מִן שְׁמַיָּא וְחַיִּים טוֹבִים עָלֵינוּ וְעַל כָּל

〈 all upon 〈 and upon us 〈 that is good, 〈 and life 〈 Heaven 〈 from 〈 that is abundant 〈 peace 〈 May there be

יִשְׂרָאֵל. וְאִמְרוּ: אָמֵן. (Cong. — אָמֵן.)

《 (Amen.) 《 Amen. 〈 Now respond: 《 Israel.

CONGREGATION:

(עֶזְרִי מֵעִם יהוה, עֹשֵׂה שָׁמַיִם וָאָרֶץ.[2])

《 and earth.) 〈 of heaven 〈 Maker 《 HASHEM, 〈 is from 〈 (My help

CHAZZAN BOWS; TAKES THREE STEPS BACK. BOWS LEFT AND SAYS "... עֹשֶׂה שָׁלוֹם, *HE WHO MAKES PEACE ...";* BOWS RIGHT AND SAYS "... הוּא, *MAY HE ...";* BOWS FORWARD AND SAYS "... וְעַל כָּל יִשְׂרָאֵל, *AND UPON ALL ISRAEL ...";* REMAINS IN PLACE FOR A FEW MOMENTS, THEN TAKES THREE STEPS FORWARD.

עֹשֶׂה שָׁלוֹם בִּמְרוֹמָיו, הוּא יַעֲשֶׂה שָׁלוֹם עָלֵינוּ, וְעַל כָּל

〈 all upon 〈 and 〈 upon us, 〈 peace 〈 make 〈 may He 《 in His heights, 〈 peace 〈 He Who makes

יִשְׂרָאֵל. וְאִמְרוּ: אָמֵן. (Cong. — אָמֵן.)

《 (Amen.) 《 Amen. 〈 Now respond: 《 Israel.

(1) *Psalms* 113:2. (2) 121:2.

⚜ SIXTH DAY / יום ששי ⚜

אַשְׁרֵי יוֹשְׁבֵי בֵיתֶךָ, עוֹד יְהַלְלוּךָ סֶּלָה.[1] אַשְׁרֵי

< Praise-   « Selah.   « they will   < con-   « in Your   < are those   < Praiseworthy
worthy   praise You,   tinually   house,   who dwell

הָעָם שֶׁכָּכָה לּוֹ, אַשְׁרֵי הָעָם שֶׁיהוה אֱלֹהָיו.[2]

« is their   < that   < is the   < praise-   « is   < that such   < is the
God.   HASHEM   people   worthy   their lot;   people

———— תהלים קמה / Psalm 145 ————

תְּהִלָּה לְדָוִד, אֲרוֹמִמְךָ אֱלוֹהַי הַמֶּלֶךְ, וַאֲבָרְכָה

< and I   « the King,   < my God   < I will exalt You,   « by David: < A psalm of
will bless   praise

שִׁמְךָ לְעוֹלָם וָעֶד. בְּכָל יוֹם אֲבָרְכֶךָ, וַאֲהַלְלָה שִׁמְךָ

< Your   < and I   « I will   < day   < Every   « and   < for ever   < Your
Name   will laud   bless You,   ever.   Name

לְעוֹלָם וָעֶד. גָּדוֹל יהוה וּמְהֻלָּל מְאֹד, וְלִגְדֻלָּתוֹ

< and His   « exceedingly,   < and   < is   < Great   « and   < for ever
greatness   lauded   HASHEM   ever.

אֵין חֵקֶר. דּוֹר לְדוֹר יְשַׁבַּח מַעֲשֶׂיךָ, וּגְבוּרֹתֶיךָ יַגִּידוּ.

« they will   < and Your   « Your   < will   < to   < Gen-   « is beyond
recount.   mighty deeds   actions,   praise   generation   eration   investigation.

הֲדַר כְּבוֹד הוֹדֶךָ, וְדִבְרֵי נִפְלְאֹתֶיךָ אָשִׂיחָה. וֶעֱזוּז

< And of   « I shall   < that are   < and Your   < of Your   < glory   < The
the might   discuss.   wondrous   deeds   majesty   splendrous

נוֹרְאֹתֶיךָ יֹאמֵרוּ, וּגְדוּלָּתְךָ אֲסַפְּרֶנָּה. זֵכֶר רַב טוּבְךָ

< of Your abun-   < A recol-   < I shall   < and Your   « they will   < of Your
dant goodness   lection   relate.   greatness   speak,   awesome deeds

יַבִּיעוּ, וְצִדְקָתְךָ יְרַנֵּנוּ. חַנּוּן וְרַחוּם יהוה, אֶרֶךְ אַפַּיִם

< to   < slow   « is   < and   < Gracious   « they will   < and of Your   « they
anger,   HASHEM,   merciful   sing joyfully.   righteousness   will utter,

וּגְדָל חָסֶד. טוֹב יהוה לַכֹּל, וְרַחֲמָיו עַל כָּל מַעֲשָׂיו.

« His   < all   < are   < His   « to all;   < HASHEM   « in [bestowing]   < and
creations.   on   mercies   is good   kindness.   great

יוֹדוּךָ יהוה כָּל מַעֲשֶׂיךָ, וַחֲסִידֶיךָ יְבָרְכוּכָה. כְּבוֹד

< Of the   « will   < and Your   « Your   < — all   « HASHEM   < They will
glory   bless You.   devout ones   creations —   thank You,

———

(1) *Psalms* 84:5. (2) 144:15.

מַלְכוּתְךָ יֹאמֵרוּ, וּגְבוּרָתְךָ יְדַבֵּרוּ. לְהוֹדִיעַ לִבְנֵי הָאָדָם
‹ mankind ‹ To inform » they will ‹ and of Your » they will ‹ of Your
declare. power speak, kingdom

גְּבוּרֹתָיו, וּכְבוֹד הֲדַר מַלְכוּתוֹ. מַלְכוּתְךָ מַלְכוּת כָּל
‹[span- ‹ is a ‹ Your kingdom » of His ‹ splendor ‹ and of the » of His mighty
ning] all kingdom kingdom. glorious deeds,

עֹלָמִים, וּמֶמְשַׁלְתְּךָ בְּכָל דּוֹר וָדֹר. סוֹמֵךְ יהוה
‹ Hashem » after ‹ gen- ‹ is ‹ and Your » eternities,
supports generation. eration throughout dominion

לְכָל הַנֹּפְלִים, וְזוֹקֵף לְכָל הַכְּפוּפִים. עֵינֵי כֹל
‹ of all ‹ The » those who ‹ all ‹ and » those who ‹ all
eyes are bent. straightens are fallen,

אֵלֶיךָ יְשַׂבֵּרוּ, וְאַתָּה נוֹתֵן לָהֶם אֶת אָכְלָם בְּעִתּוֹ.
» in its ‹ their food ‹ them ‹ give ‹ and You » do look ‹ to You
proper time. with hope,

CONCENTRATE INTENTLY WHILE RECITING THE VERSE פּוֹתֵחַ, *YOU OPEN.*

פּוֹתֵחַ אֶת יָדֶךָ, וּמַשְׂבִּיעַ לְכָל חַי רָצוֹן. ❖ צַדִּיק
‹ Righteous » [with its] ‹ living ‹ every ‹ and satisfy » Your hand, ‹ You open
desire. thing

יהוה בְּכָל דְּרָכָיו, וְחָסִיד בְּכָל מַעֲשָׂיו. קָרוֹב יהוה
‹ is ‹ Close » His deeds. ‹ in all ‹ and » His ways, ‹ in all ‹ is
Hashem magnanimous Hashem

לְכָל קֹרְאָיו, לְכֹל אֲשֶׁר יִקְרָאֻהוּ בֶאֱמֶת. רְצוֹן יְרֵאָיו
‹ of those ‹ The » sincerely. ‹ call upon ‹ who ‹ to all » who call ‹ to all
who fear Him will Him upon Him,

יַעֲשֶׂה, וְאֶת שַׁוְעָתָם יִשְׁמַע וְיוֹשִׁיעֵם. שׁוֹמֵר יהוה
‹ Hashem protects » and He will ‹ He will ‹ and their cry » He
save them. hear, will do;

אֶת כָּל אֹהֲבָיו, וְאֵת כָּל הָרְשָׁעִים יַשְׁמִיד. תְּהִלַּת
‹ The praise » He will destroy. ‹ the wicked ‹ but all » who love Him; ‹ all

יהוה יְדַבֶּר פִּי, וִיבָרֵךְ כָּל בָּשָׂר שֵׁם קָדְשׁוֹ לְעוֹלָם
‹ for ever ‹ of His ‹ the ‹ flesh ‹ may ‹ and bless » may my ‹ of
Holiness Name all mouth declare, Hashem

וָעֶד. וַאֲנַחְנוּ נְבָרֵךְ יָהּ מֵעַתָּה וְעַד עוֹלָם; הַלְלוּיָהּ.[1]
» Halleluyah! » eternity. ‹ until ‹ from ‹ God ‹ will ‹ But we » and
this time bless ever.

---

(1) *Psalms* 115:18.

THE *CHAZZAN* RECITES חֲצִי קַדִּישׁ, HALF-*KADDISH*:

יִתְגַּדַּל וְיִתְקַדַּשׁ שְׁמֵהּ רַבָּא. (—Cong. אָמֵן.) בְּעָלְמָא
⟨ Grow exalted ⟩ and be sanctified ⟨ may His Name ⟩ that is great! — ⟫ (Amen.) ⟫ — in the world

דִּי בְרָא כִרְעוּתֵהּ, וְיַמְלִיךְ מַלְכוּתֵהּ, וְיַצְמַח פֻּרְקָנֵהּ
⟨ that ⟨ He created ⟨ according to His will, ⟫ and may He give reign ⟨ to His kingship, ⟫ and cause to sprout ⟨ His salvation,

וִיקָרֵב מְשִׁיחֵהּ. (—Cong. אָמֵן.) בְּחַיֵּיכוֹן וּבְיוֹמֵיכוֹן וּבְחַיֵּי
⟨ and bring near ⟨ His Messiah, ⟫ (Amen.) ⟨ in your lifetimes ⟨ and in your days, ⟨ and in the lifetimes

דְּכָל בֵּית יִשְׂרָאֵל, בַּעֲגָלָא וּבִזְמַן קָרִיב. וְאִמְרוּ: אָמֵן.
⟨ of the entire ⟨ Family ⟨ of Israel, ⟫ swiftly ⟨ and at a time ⟫ that comes soon. ⟨ Now respond: ⟫Amen.

CONGREGATION RESPONDS:

אָמֵן. יְהֵא שְׁמֵהּ רַבָּא מְבָרַךְ לְעָלַם וּלְעָלְמֵי עָלְמַיָּא.
⟫ Amen. ⟨ May ⟨ His Name ⟨ that is great ⟨ be blessed ⟨ forever ⟨ and for all eternity. ⟫

CHAZZAN CONTINUES:

יְהֵא שְׁמֵהּ רַבָּא מְבָרַךְ לְעָלַם וּלְעָלְמֵי עָלְמַיָּא. יִתְבָּרַךְ
⟨ May ⟨ His Name ⟨ that is great ⟨ be blessed ⟨ forever ⟫ and for all eternity. ⟨ Blessed,

וְיִשְׁתַּבַּח וְיִתְפָּאַר וְיִתְרוֹמַם וְיִתְנַשֵּׂא וְיִתְהַדָּר וְיִתְעַלֶּה
⟨ praised, ⟨ glorified, ⟨ exalted, ⟨ upraised, ⟨ honored, ⟨ elevated,

וְיִתְהַלָּל שְׁמֵהּ דְּקֻדְשָׁא בְּרִיךְ הוּא (—Cong. בְּרִיךְ הוּא)
⟨ and lauded ⟨ be the Name ⟨ of the Holy One, ⟨ Blessed ⟨ is He ⟫ (Blessed ⟨ is He)

— לְעֵלָּא מִן כָּל בִּרְכָתָא וְשִׁירָתָא תֻּשְׁבְּחָתָא וְנֶחֱמָתָא
⟨ beyond ⟨ any ⟨ blessing ⟨ and song, ⟫ praise ⟨ and consolation ⟩

דַּאֲמִירָן בְּעָלְמָא. וְאִמְרוּ: אָמֵן. (—Cong. אָמֵן.)
⟨ that are uttered ⟫ in the world. ⟫ Now respond: ⟨ Amen. ⟫ (Amen.)

ALL:

לְךָ יהוה הַצְּדָקָה, וְלָנוּ בֹּשֶׁת הַפָּנִים.[1] מַה
⟨ Yours, ⟨ O Lord, ⟨ is the righteousness, ⟫ and ours ⟫ is shamefacedness. ⟫What

נִּתְאוֹנֵן,[2] מַה נֹּאמַר, מַה נְּדַבֵּר, וּמַה נִּצְטַדָּק.[3]
⟫ complaint can we make? ⟫can we say? ⟨ What ⟨ What can we declare? ⟫ justification can we offer?

---

(1) *Daniel* 9:7. (2) Cf. *Lamentations* 3:39. (3) Cf. *Genesis* 44:16.

נַחְפְּשָׂה דְרָכֵינוּ וְנַחְקְרָה, וְנָשׁוּבָה אֵלֶיךָ, כִּי יְמִינְךָ[1]

‹ Let us examine ‹ our ways ‹ and investigate them, « and return ‹ to You, ‹ for » Your right hand

פְּשׁוּטָה לְקַבֵּל שָׁבִים. לֹא בְחֶסֶד וְלֹא בְמַעֲשִׂים

‹ is extended ‹ to accept » those who return. « Nei-ther ‹ with [merit] for kindness ‹ nor ‹ with [merit for good] deeds

בָּאנוּ לְפָנֶיךָ, כְּדַלִּים וּכְרָשִׁים דָּפַקְנוּ דְלָתֶיךָ.

‹ do we come » before You; ‹ but as paupers ‹ and as destitute people ‹ we have knocked » on Your doors.

דְלָתֶיךָ דָּפַקְנוּ רַחוּם וְחַנּוּן, נָא אַל תְּשִׁיבֵנוּ

‹ On Your doors ‹ we have knocked, ‹ O Compassionate One » and Gracious One. « Please ‹ do not ‹ turn us away

רֵיקָם מִלְּפָנֶיךָ. מִלְּפָנֶיךָ מַלְכֵּנוּ רֵיקָם אַל תְּשִׁיבֵנוּ,

‹ empty-handed » from before You. ‹ From before You, ‹ Our King, ‹ empty-handed ‹ do not « turn us away,

כִּי אַתָּה שׁוֹמֵעַ תְּפִלָּה.

‹ for ‹ You are ‹ Who hears « prayer.

שְׁמַע תְּפִלָּה, עָדֶיךָ כָּל בָּשָׂר יָבֹאוּ.[2] יָבוֹא

‹ You Who hears » prayer, ‹ unto You ‹ all ‹ flesh « will come. ‹ Come

כָּל בָּשָׂר לְהִשְׁתַּחֲוֹת לְפָנֶיךָ יהוה.[3] יָבֹאוּ וְיִשְׁתַּחֲווּ

will all flesh ‹ to bow down ‹ before You, « O HASHEM. ‹ They will come « and bow down

לְפָנֶיךָ אֲדֹנָי, וִיכַבְּדוּ לִשְׁמֶךָ.[4] בֹּאוּ נִשְׁתַּחֲוֶה וְנִכְרָעָה,

‹ before You, ‹ O Lord, « and they will show honor ‹ to Your Name. « Come! ‹ Let us prostrate ourselves « and bow,

נִבְרְכָה לִפְנֵי יהוה עֹשֵׂנוּ.[5] נָבוֹאָה לְמִשְׁכְּנוֹתָיו,

‹ let us kneel ‹ before ‹ HASHEM, « our Maker. ‹ Let us come « to His Tabernacles,

נִשְׁתַּחֲוֶה לַהֲדֹם רַגְלָיו.[6] בֹּאוּ שְׁעָרָיו בְּתוֹדָה,

‹ let us prostrate ourselves ‹ at the stool « for His feet. « Enter ‹ His gates « with thanksgiving,

חֲצֵרֹתָיו בִּתְהִלָּה, הוֹדוּ לוֹ בָּרְכוּ שְׁמוֹ.[7] וַאֲנַחְנוּ

‹ His courtyards « with praise; ‹ give thanks ‹ to Him, « bless ‹ His Name. ‹ But we,

---

(1) Cf. *Lamentations* 3:40. (2) *Psalms* 65:3. (3) Cf. *Isaiah* 66:23.
(4) *Psalms* 86:9. (5) 95:6. (6) 132:7. (7) 100:4.

בְּרֹב חַסְדְּךָ נָבוֹא בֵיתֶךָ, נִשְׁתַּחֲוֶה אֶל הֵיכַל קָדְשְׁךָ

‹ Your Holy Sanctuary ‹ toward ‹ we will prostrate ourselves ‹‹ Your House; ‹ will we ‹ of Your ‹ through the kindness abundance

בְּיִרְאָתֶךָ.[1] הִנֵּה בָּרְכוּ אֶת יהוה כָּל עַבְדֵי יהוה,

‹ of HASHEM, ‹ you ‹ all ‹ HASHEM, ‹ bless ‹‹ Indeed, ‹‹ in awe of You. servants

הָעֹמְדִים בְּבֵית יהוה בַּלֵּילוֹת.[2] שְׂאוּ יְדֵיכֶם קֹדֶשׁ

‹ in the ‹ your ‹ Lift ‹‹ in the nights. ‹ of ‹ in the ‹ who stand Sanctuary hands HASHEM House

וּבָרְכוּ אֶת יהוה.[3] רוֹמְמוּ יהוה אֱלֹהֵינוּ, וְהִשְׁתַּחֲווּ

‹ and bow down ‹ our God, ‹ HASHEM, ‹ Exalt ‹‹ HASHEM. ‹ and bless

לַהֲדֹם רַגְלָיו, קָדוֹשׁ הוּא.[4] רוֹמְמוּ יהוה אֱלֹהֵינוּ,

‹ our God, ‹ HASHEM, ‹ Exalt ‹‹ is He! ‹ holy ‹‹ at His footstool;

וְהִשְׁתַּחֲווּ לְהַר קָדְשׁוֹ, כִּי קָדוֹשׁ יהוה אֱלֹהֵינוּ.[5]

‹‹ our God. ‹ is ‹ holy ‹ for ‹‹ of His ‹ at the ‹ and bow HASHEM, Holiness; Mount

הִשְׁתַּחֲווּ לַיהוה בְּהַדְרַת קֹדֶשׁ, חִילוּ מִפָּנָיו כָּל

‹ every- ‹ before ‹ tremble ‹‹ of ‹ in the ‹ before ‹ Bow down one Him, holiness; splendor HASHEM

הָאָרֶץ.[6] נִשְׁתַּחֲוֶה אֶל הֵיכַל קָדְשְׁךָ וְנוֹדֶה אֶת שְׁמֶךָ,

‹ Your Name ‹ and we ‹‹ Your Holy ‹ toward ‹ We will pros- ‹‹ on earth. will thank Sanctuary, trate ourselves

עַל חַסְדְּךָ וְעַל אֲמִתֶּךָ, כִּי הִגְדַּלְתָּ עַל כָּל שִׁמְךָ

‹‹ Your ‹ — even ‹‹ You have ‹ for ‹‹ Your ‹ and ‹ Your ‹ for Name — beyond exalted faithfulness; for kindness

אִמְרָתֶךָ.[7] יהוה אֱלֹהֵי צְבָאוֹת, מִי כָמוֹךָ חֲסִין

‹ O Strong ‹‹ is like ‹ — who ‹‹ of ‹ God ‹ HASHEM, ‹‹ Your promise. One, You, Legions

יָהּ, וֶאֱמוּנָתְךָ סְבִיבוֹתֶיךָ.[8] כִּי מִי בַשַּׁחַק יַעֲרֹךְ

‹ can be ‹ in the sky ‹ who ‹ For ‹‹ surrounds You. ‹ and Your ‹‹ God? — compared faithfulness

לַיהוה, יִדְמֶה לַיהוה בִּבְנֵי אֵלִים.[9] כִּי גָדוֹל אַתָּה

‹ are You ‹ great ‹ For ‹‹ among the angels? ‹ to HASHEM ‹ be likened ‹‹ to HASHEM;

וְעוֹשֵׂה נִפְלָאוֹת, אַתָּה אֱלֹהִים לְבַדֶּךָ.[10] כִּי גָדוֹל

‹ great ‹ For ‹‹ alone. ‹ O God, ‹ You, ‹‹ of wonders; ‹ and a worker

---

(1) Cf. *Psalms* 5:8. (2) 134:1. (3) 134:2. (4) 99:5. (5) 99:9. (6) 96:9. (7) Cf. 138:2. (8) 89:9. (9) 89:7. (10) 86:10.

מֵעַל שָׁמַיִם חַסְדֶּךָ, וְעַד שְׁחָקִים אֲמִתֶּךָ.¹ גָּדוֹל

‹ Great » is Your ‹ the upper ‹ and » is Your ‹ the very ‹ above
truth. heights until kindness, heavens

יהוה וּמְהֻלָּל מְאֹד, וְלִגְדֻלָּתוֹ אֵין חֵקֶר.² (כִּי) גָּדוֹל

‹ great ‹ (For) » investiga- ‹ is ‹ and His » exceed- ‹ and ‹ is
tion. beyond greatness ingly, lauded HASHEM

יהוה וּמְהֻלָּל מְאֹד, נוֹרָא הוּא עַל כָּל אֱלֹהִים.³ כִּי

‹ For » heavenly ‹ all ‹ above ‹ is He ‹ awesome » exceed- ‹ and ‹ is
powers. ingly; lauded HASHEM

אֵל גָּדוֹל יהוה, וּמֶלֶךְ גָּדוֹל עַל כָּל אֱלֹהִים.⁴ אֲשֶׁר

‹ For » heavenly ‹ all ‹ above ‹ and a great King » is ‹ a great God
powers. HASHEM,

מִי אֵל בַּשָּׁמַיִם וּבָאָרֶץ, אֲשֶׁר יַעֲשֶׂה כְמַעֲשֶׂיךָ

‹ like unto ‹ can do ‹ that ‹ or in the ‹ is there in ‹ power ‹ what
Your deeds earth the heaven

וְכִגְבוּרֹתֶיךָ.⁵ מִי לֹא יִרָאֲךָ מֶלֶךְ הַגּוֹיִם, כִּי לְךָ

‹ to ‹ For » of nations? ‹ O King » fear You, ‹ would ‹ Who » and like unto Your
You not mighty acts?

יָאָתָה, כִּי בְכָל חַכְמֵי הַגּוֹיִם וּבְכָל מַלְכוּתָם מֵאֵין

‹ there is ‹ their ‹ and in all ‹ of the ‹ the wise ‹ among ‹ for » [kingship]
none kingdoms nations men all befits;

כָּמוֹךָ.⁶ מֵאֵין כָּמוֹךָ יהוה, גָּדוֹל אַתָּה וְגָדוֹל שְׁמֶךָ

‹ is Your ‹ and great ‹ are You ‹ Great » O ‹ like You, ‹ There is » like You.
Name HASHEM! none

בִּגְבוּרָה.⁷ לְךָ זְרוֹעַ עִם גְּבוּרָה, תָּעֹז יָדְךָ תָּרוּם

‹ uplifted » is Your ‹ strength- » power; ‹ with ‹ is the ‹ Yours » in might.
hand, ened arm

יְמִינֶךָ.⁸ לְךָ יוֹם, אַף לְךָ לָיְלָה, אַתָּה הֲכִינוֹתָ מָאוֹר

‹ the ‹ prepared ‹ You » is the ‹ Yours ‹ also » is the ‹ Yours » is Your
luminary night; day, right hand.

וָשָׁמֶשׁ.⁹ אֲשֶׁר בְּיָדוֹ מֶחְקְרֵי אָרֶץ, וְתוֹעֲפוֹת הָרִים

‹ of the ‹ and the » of the ‹ are the hidden ‹ in His ‹ For » and the
mountains summits earth, mysteries power sun.

לוֹ.¹⁰ מִי יְמַלֵּל גְּבוּרוֹת יהוה, יַשְׁמִיעַ כָּל תְּהִלָּתוֹ.¹¹

» of His ‹ all ‹ [who] can » of ‹ the mighty ‹ can ‹ Who » are
praise? make heard HASHEM; acts express His.

---

(1) Psalms 108:5. (2) 145:3. (3) 96:4. (4) 95:3. (5) Deuteronomy 3:24.
(6) Jeremiah 10:7. (7) 10:6. (8) Psalms 89:14. (9) 74:16. (10) 95:4. (11) 106:2.

לְךָ יהוה הַגְּדֻלָּה וְהַגְּבוּרָה, וְהַתִּפְאֶרֶת וְהַנֵּצַח

Yours, ‹ HASHEM, ‹ is the / greatness, › the strength, ‹ the glory, ‹ the / triumph,

וְהַהוֹד, כִּי כֹל בַּשָּׁמַיִם וּבָאָרֶץ; לְךָ יהוה הַמַּמְלָכָה,

and the / majesty; » and on / earth / [is Yours]; ‹ in heaven ‹ every- / thing › Yours, ‹ HASHEM, » is the / kingdom

וְהַמִּתְנַשֵּׂא לְכֹל לְרֹאשׁ.¹ לְךָ שָׁמַיִם, אַף לְךָ אֶרֶץ,

and the / sovereignty ‹ over / every » leader. ‹ Yours › are the / heavens, » Yours also ‹ is the / earth;

תֵּבֵל וּמְלֹאָהּ אַתָּה יְסַדְתָּם.² אַתָּה הִצַּבְתָּ כָּל גְּבוּלוֹת

the / world ‹ and its / fullness, ‹ You ‹ founded / them. » You ‹ established ‹ all ‹ the / boundaries

אֶרֶץ, קַיִץ וָחֹרֶף אַתָּה יְצַרְתָּם.³ אַתָּה רִצַּצְתָּ רָאשֵׁי

of / earth; » summer ‹ and / winter, ‹ You ‹ fashioned / them. » You ‹ crushed ‹ the / heads

לִוְיָתָן, תִּתְּנֶנּוּ מַאֲכָל לְעָם לְצִיִּים. אַתָּה בָקַעְתָּ מַעְיָן

of / Leviathan; ‹ You will / serve it » as food ‹ to the / desolate / wilderness. ‹ [destined] for / the people » You ‹ split / open ‹ fountain

וָנַחַל, אַתָּה הוֹבַשְׁתָּ נַהֲרוֹת אֵיתָן.⁴ אַתָּה פוֹרַרְתָּ

and stream; » You ‹ dried ‹ rivers ‹ that are mighty. » You ‹ shattered

בְּעָזְּךָ יָם, שִׁבַּרְתָּ רָאשֵׁי תַנִּינִים עַל הַמָּיִם.⁵ אַתָּה

with Your / might » the / sea; ‹ You / smashed ‹ the heads ‹ of sea / serpents ‹ upon ‹ the / water. » You

מוֹשֵׁל בְּגֵאוּת הַיָּם, בְּשׂוֹא גַלָּיו אַתָּה תְשַׁבְּחֵם.⁶

rule ‹ the / grandeur ‹ of the / sea; ‹ when it / raises ‹ its / waves, ‹ You » calm them.

גָּדוֹל יהוה וּמְהֻלָּל מְאֹד, בְּעִיר אֱלֹהֵינוּ הַר קָדְשׁוֹ.⁷

Great ‹ is / HASHEM ‹ and much praised, ‹ in the / City ‹ of our God, ‹ Mount › of His / Holiness. »

יהוה צְבָאוֹת, אֱלֹהֵי יִשְׂרָאֵל, יוֹשֵׁב הַכְּרֻבִים, אַתָּה

HASHEM ‹ Master of / Legions, ‹ God ‹ of Israel, ‹ en- / throned ‹ upon the / Cherubim, » it is / You

הוּא הָאֱלֹהִים לְבַדְּךָ.⁸ אֵל נַעֲרָץ בְּסוֹד קְדוֹשִׁים רַבָּה,

Who / are ‹ God ‹ God » alone. ‹ is / revered ‹ God » in the great assemblage / of the holy [angels],

(1) I Chronicles 29:11. (2) Psalms 89:12. (3) 74:17. (4) 74:14-15. (5) 74:13. (6) 89:10. (7) 48:2. (8) Isaiah 37:16.

וְנוֹרָא עַל כָּל סְבִיבָיו.¹ וְיוֹדוּ שָׁמַיִם פִּלְאֲךָ יהוה, אַף
⟨ also ⟩⟪ HASHEM, ⟩ Your ⟨ will the ⟨ Acknowl- ⟨ who sur- ⟨ all ⟨ over ⟨ and is
　　　　　　　wonders, heavens edge round Him.　　　　　awesome

אֱמוּנָתְךָ בִּקְהַל קְדֹשִׁים.² לְכוּ נְרַנְּנָה לַיהוה, נָרִיעָה
⟨ let us ⟪ to ⟨ Let us sing ⟨ Come! ⟪ of holy ⟨ in the ⟨ Your
call out HASHEM, joyfully　　　ones. assembly faithfulness,

לְצוּר יִשְׁעֵנוּ. נְקַדְּמָה פָנָיו בְּתוֹדָה, בִּזְמִירוֹת נָרִיעַ
⟨ let us ⟨ with praiseful ⟪ with ⟨ Him ⟨ Let us greet ⟪ of our ⟨ to the
call out songs thanksgiving, salvation. Rock

לוֹ.³ צֶדֶק וּמִשְׁפָּט מְכוֹן כִּסְאֶךָ, חֶסֶד וֶאֱמֶת יְקַדְּמוּ
⟨ precede ⟨ and ⟨ kindness ⟪ of Your ⟨ are the ⟨ and ⟨ Righteous- ⟪ to
truth throne; foundation justice ness Him.

פָנֶיךָ.⁴ אֲשֶׁר יַחְדָּו נַמְתִּיק סוֹד, בְּבֵית אֱלֹהִים נְהַלֵּךְ
⟨ let us ⟨ of God ⟨ in the ⟪ counsel; ⟨ let us ⟨ together ⟨ For ⟪ Your coun-
walk House take sweet tenance.

בְּרָגֶשׁ.⁵ אֲשֶׁר לוֹ הַיָּם וְהוּא עָשָׂהוּ, וְיַבֶּשֶׁת יָדָיו
⟨ His ⟪ and the ⟪ perfected ⟨ and He ⟨ is the ⟨ His ⟨ For ⟪ in company.
hands dry land, it, sea

יְצָרוּ.⁶ אֲשֶׁר בְּיָדוֹ נֶפֶשׁ כָּל חָי, וְרוּחַ כָּל בְּשַׂר אִישׁ.⁷
⟪ mankind. ⟨ of all ⟨ and the ⟪ the ⟨ of ⟨ is the ⟨ in His ⟨ For ⟪ fashioned.
spirit living all soul hand

❖ הַנְּשָׁמָה לָךְ וְהַגּוּף פָּעֳלָךְ, חוּסָה עַל עֲמָלָךְ.
⟪ Your ⟨ on ⟨ take pity ⟪ is Your ⟨ and the ⟨ is ⟨ The soul
labor. handiwork; body Yours

הַנְּשָׁמָה לָךְ וְהַגּוּף שֶׁלָּךְ, יהוה עֲשֵׂה לְמַעַן שְׁמֶךָ.
⟪ of Your ⟨ for the ⟨ act ⟨ O ⟪ is Yours; ⟨ and the ⟨ is ⟨ The soul
Name. sake HASHEM, body Yours

אָתָאנוּ עַל שִׁמְךָ, יהוה, עֲשֵׂה לְמַעַן שְׁמֶךָ. בַּעֲבוּר
⟨ [act] ⟪ of Your ⟨ for the ⟨ act ⟪ O ⟪ Your ⟨ [relying] ⟨ We have
because of Name; sake HASHEM; Name, on come

כְּבוֹד שְׁמֶךָ, כִּי אֵל חַנּוּן וְרַחוּם שְׁמֶךָ. לְמַעַן
⟨ For the ⟪ is Your ⟨ and ⟨ Who is ⟨ God ⟨ for ⟪ of Your ⟨ the glory
sake Name. Merciful Gracious Name,

שִׁמְךָ יהוה, וְסָלַחְתָּ לַעֲוֺנֵנוּ כִּי רַב הוּא.⁸
⟨ it is great. ⟨ though ⟨ our ⟨ forgive ⟪ HASHEM, ⟨ of Your
iniquity, Name,

---

(1) *Psalms* 89:8. (2) 89:6. (3) 95:1-2. (4) 89:15. (5) 55:15. (6) 95:5. (7) *Job* 12:10. (8) Cf. *Psalms* 25:11.

CONGREGATION, THEN *CHAZZAN:*

סְלַח לָנוּ אָבִינוּ, כִּי בְרוֹב אִוַּלְתֵּנוּ שָׁגִינוּ,

《 we have erred; 〈 of our folly 〈 in the abundance 〈 for 〈 our Father, 〈 us, 〈 Forgive

מְחַל לָנוּ מַלְכֵּנוּ, כִּי רַבּוּ עֲוֹנֵינוּ.

《 our iniquities. 〈 many are 〈 for 〈 our King, 〈 us, 〈 pardon

ALL, WHILE STANDING

אֵל אֶרֶךְ אַפַּיִם אַתָּה,

《 You are, 〈 to anger, 〈 Who is slow 〈 God

וּבַעַל הָרַחֲמִים נִקְרֵאתָ, וְדֶרֶךְ תְּשׁוּבָה הוֹרֵיתָ.

《 You have taught. 〈 of repentance 〈 and the way 《 You are called; 〈 of Mercy 〈 and Master

גְּדֻלַּת רַחֲמֶיךָ וַחֲסָדֶיךָ,

〈 and Your kindness 〈 of Your mercy 〈 The greatness

תִּזְכּוֹר הַיּוֹם וּבְכָל יוֹם לְזֶרַע יְדִידֶיךָ.

《 of Your beloved ones. 〈 for the offspring 《 day, 〈 and every 〈 this day 〈 may You remember,

תֵּפֶן אֵלֵינוּ בְּרַחֲמִים,

《 in mercy, 〈 to us 〈 Turn

כִּי אַתָּה הוּא בַּעַל הָרַחֲמִים.

《 of Mercy. 〈 the Master 〈 are 〈 You 〈 for

בְּתַחֲנוּן וּבִתְפִלָּה פָּנֶיךָ נְקַדֵּם, כְּהוֹדַעְתָּ לֶעָנָיו מִקֶּדֶם.

《in ancient 〈 to the 〈 in the manner 《 we 〈 Your 〈 and prayer 〈 With times. humble one [Moses] that You made known approach, Presence supplication

מֵחֲרוֹן אַפְּךָ שׁוּב,[1] כְּמוֹ בְתוֹרָתְךָ כָּתוּב.[2]

《 it is written. 〈 in Your Torah 〈 as 《 turn back, 〈 of Your anger 〈 From the fierceness

וּבְצֵל כְּנָפֶיךָ נֶחֱסֶה[3] וְנִתְלוֹנָן, כְּיוֹם וַיֵּרֶד יהוה בֶּעָנָן.

《 in a cloud. 〈 when HASHEM descended 〈 as on the day 《 and may we dwell, 〈 may we find shelter 〈 of Your wings 〈 In the shadow

❖ תַּעֲבוֹר עַל פֶּשַׁע וְתִמְחֶה אָשָׁם,

《 guilt, 〈 and erase 〈 sin 〈 Overlook

---

(1) Cf. *Exodus* 32:12. (2) See 32:14. (3) Cf. *Psalms* 36:8.

כִּיוֹם וַיִּתְיַצֵּב עִמּוֹ שָׁם.

《 there. 〈 with him 〈 when He 〈 as on the
　　　　　　[Moses] [God] stood　　day

תַּאֲזִין שַׁוְעָתֵנוּ וְתַקְשִׁיב מֶנּוּ מַאֲמַר,

《 [our] 〈 from 〈 and hear 〈 to our cry 〈 Give heed
declaration, us

כְּיוֹם וַיִּקְרָא בְשֵׁם יהוה,¹ וְשָׁם נֶאֱמַר:

《 it was said: 〈 and 《 of HASHEM, 〈 with the 〈 when He 〈 as on
　　　　　there　　　　　　　Name　called out　the day

CONGREGATION, THEN *CHAZZAN***:**

וַיַּעֲבֹר יהוה עַל פָּנָיו וַיִּקְרָא:

《 and 《 [Moses'] 〈 before 〈 And HASHEM passed
proclaimed: face,

CONGREGATION AND *CHAZZAN* **RECITE LOUDLY AND IN UNISON:**

יהוה, יהוה, אֵל, רַחוּם, וְחַנּוּן, אֶרֶךְ אַפַּיִם,

〈 to anger, 〈 Slow 《and Gracious, 〈 Compassionate 〈 God, 〈 HASHEM, 〈 HASHEM,

וְרַב חֶסֶד, וֶאֱמֶת, נֹצֵר חֶסֶד לָאֲלָפִים, נֹשֵׂא עָוֹן,

〈 of 〈 Forgiver 《 for thousands 〈 of 〈 Preserver 《 and 〈 in 〈 and
iniquity, [of generations], kindness Truth, Kindness Abundant

וָפֶשַׁע, וְחַטָּאָה, וְנַקֵּה.² וְסָלַחְתָּ לַעֲוֹנֵנוּ וּלְחַטָּאתֵנוּ

《 and our sins, 〈 our 〈 May You 《 and Who 〈 and inadvertent 〈 willful sin,
　　　　　iniquities forgive absolves.　sin,

וּנְחַלְתָּנוּ.³ סְלַח לָנוּ אָבִינוּ כִּי חָטָאנוּ, מְחַל לָנוּ

〈 us, 〈 pardon 《 we have 〈 for 《 our Father, 〈 us, 〈 Forgive 《 and make us
　　　　　　sinned;　　　　　　　　　　　　　Your heritage.

מַלְכֵּנוּ כִּי פָשָׁעְנוּ. כִּי אַתָּה אֲדֹנָי טוֹב וְסַלָּח, וְרַב

〈 and 《 and 〈 are 〈 O Lord, 〈 You, 〈 For 《 we have 〈 for 《 our King,
abundantly forgiving, good　　　　　　　　willfully sinned.

חֶסֶד לְכָל קֹרְאֶיךָ.⁴

《 who call 〈 to all 〈 kind
upon You.

פסוקי הקדמה לסליחה יז / PREFATORY VERSES TO SELICHAH 17

כְּאַיָּל תַּעֲרֹג עַל אֲפִיקֵי מָיִם, כֵּן נַפְשִׁי תַעֲרֹג

〈 long 〈 our souls 〈 so 《 of water, 〈 brooks 〈 for 〈 longs 〈 As the deer

---

(1) *Exodus* 34:5. (2) 34:6-7. (3) 34:9. (4) *Psalms* 86:5.

אֵלֶיךָ אֱלֹהִים.¹ כִּי שָׁחָה לֶעָפָר נַפְשֵׁנוּ, דָּבְקָה

‹ stuck « is our soul, ‹ to the dust ‹ prostrated ‹ For « O God. ‹ for You,

לָאָרֶץ בִּטְנֵנוּ.² שְׁפֹךְ חֲמָתְךָ אֶל הַגּוֹיִם אֲשֶׁר לֹא

‹ do not ‹ that ‹ the nations ‹ upon ‹ Your wrath ‹ Pour « is our belly. ‹ to the earth

יְדָעוּךָ, וְעַל מַמְלָכוֹת אֲשֶׁר בְּשִׁמְךָ לֹא קָרָאוּ. כִּי

‹ For « call. ‹ do not ‹ upon Your Name ‹ that ‹ the kingdoms ‹ and upon « recognize You,

אָכַל אֶת יַעֲקֹב וְאֶת נָוֵהוּ הֵשַׁמּוּ.³ קוּמָה עֶזְרָתָה

‹ Assist « Arise! « they have destroyed. ‹ and His habitation ‹ Jacob ‹ they have devoured

לָּנוּ, וּפְדֵנוּ לְמַעַן חַסְדֶּךָ.⁴

« of Your kindness! ‹ for the sake ‹ And redeem us « us!

כְּרַחֵם אָב עַל בָּנִים, כֵּן תְּרַחֵם יהוה עָלֵינוּ.⁵

« on us. ‹ HASHEM, ‹ have mercy, ‹ so « his ‹ toward ‹ a father is ‹ As merciful as children,

לַיהוה הַיְשׁוּעָה, עַל עַמְּךָ בִרְכָתֶךָ סֶּלָה.⁶ יהוה

‹ HASHEM, « Selah. « is Your blessing, ‹ Your people ‹ upon « is salvation, ‹ To HASHEM

צְבָאוֹת עִמָּנוּ, מִשְׂגָּב לָנוּ אֱלֹהֵי יַעֲקֹב סֶלָה.⁷

« Selah. « of Jacob, ‹ is the God ‹ for us ‹ a stronghold « is with us, ‹ Master of Legions,

יהוה צְבָאוֹת, אַשְׁרֵי אָדָם בֹּטֵחַ בָּךְ.⁸ יהוה הוֹשִׁיעָה,

« save! ‹ HASHEM, « in You. ‹ who trusts ‹ is the man ‹ — praise-worthy « Master of Legions ‹ HASHEM,

הַמֶּלֶךְ יַעֲנֵנוּ בְיוֹם קָרְאֵנוּ.⁹

« we call. ‹ on the day ‹ answer us ‹ May the King

IN MOST CONGREGATIONS THE FOLLOWING VERSES ARE RECITED ALOUD RESPONSIVELY, AS INDICATED; IN OTHERS THEY ARE RECITED SILENTLY.

CONGREGATION, ALOUD, FOLLOWED BY *CHAZZAN*, ALOUD:

סְלַח נָא לַעֲוֹן הָעָם הַזֶּה כְּגֹדֶל חַסְדֶּךָ, וְכַאֲשֶׁר

‹ just as « of Your kindness, ‹ according to the greatness ‹ of this people ‹ the iniquity ‹ please, ‹ Forgive,

---

(1) Cf. *Psalms* 42:2. (2) 44:26. (3) 79:6-7. (4) 44:27. (5) *Jeremiah* 31:6.
(6) Cf. *Psalms* 103:13. (7) 3:9. (8) 46:8. (9) 84:13.

נְשָׂאתָה לָעָם הַזֶּה מִמִּצְרַיִם וְעַד הֵנָּה,¹ וְשָׁם נֶאֱמַר:

‹ it was said: ‹ And there ‹ now. ‹ until ‹ from Egypt ‹ this people ‹ You have forgiven

ALL, ALOUD AND IN UNISON:

וַיֹּאמֶר יהוה סָלַחְתִּי כִּדְבָרֶךָ.²

‹ according to your word! ‹ I have forgiven ‹ And HASHEM said:

ALL CONTINUE:

הַטֵּה אֱלֹהַי אָזְנְךָ וּשְׁמָע, פְּקַח עֵינֶיךָ וּרְאֵה

‹ and see ‹ Your eyes ‹ open ‹ and listen; ‹ Your ear, ‹ my God, ‹ Incline,

שֹׁמְמֹתֵינוּ, וְהָעִיר אֲשֶׁר נִקְרָא שִׁמְךָ עָלֶיהָ, כִּי לֹא

‹ not ‹ for ‹ upon; ‹ Your Name is proclaimed ‹ which ‹ and that [of the city] ‹ our desolation

עַל צִדְקֹתֵינוּ אֲנַחְנוּ מַפִּילִים תַּחֲנוּנֵינוּ לְפָנֶיךָ,

‹ before You; ‹ our supplications ‹ cast ‹ do we ‹ of our righteousness ‹ because

כִּי עַל רַחֲמֶיךָ הָרַבִּים. אֲדֹנָי שְׁמָעָה, אֲדֹנָי סְלָחָה,

‹ forgive; ‹ O Lord, ‹ heed; ‹ O Lord, ‹ which is abundant. ‹ of Your compassion, ‹ be- cause ‹ but

אֲדֹנָי הַקְשִׁיבָה, וַעֲשֵׂה אַל תְּאַחַר, לְמַעַנְךָ אֱלֹהַי,

‹ my God, ‹ for Your sake, ‹ delay; ‹ do not ‹ and act, ‹ be attentive, ‹ O Lord,

כִּי שִׁמְךָ נִקְרָא עַל עִירְךָ וְעַל עַמֶּךָ.³

‹ Your people. ‹ and upon ‹ Your City ‹ upon ‹ is proclaimed ‹ Your Name ‹ for

---

SELICHAH 17 / סליחה יז

ALL:

אֱלֹהֵינוּ וֵאלֹהֵי אֲבוֹתֵינוּ:

‹ of our forefathers: ‹ and the God ‹ Our God

תַּעֲרֹג אֵלֶיךָ* כְּאַיָּל עַל אֲפִיקִים,⁴

‹ brooks [of water], ‹ for ‹ like a deer ‹ for You* ‹ She [Israel] longs

---

(1) *Numbers* 14:19. (2) 14:20. (3) *Daniel* 9:18-19. (4) Cf. *Psalms* 42:2.

§⇥ תַּעֲרֹג אֵלֶיךָ — *She [Israel] longs for You.* This *selichah* bears a reverse alphabetical scheme, followed by the *paytan's* signature — שְׁלֹמֹה הַקָּטָן, *Shlomo the lesser* [see prefa-

שָׁחָה* לְקֵץ רְוָיָה וְאֵין מְפִיקִים,

《 achieving it; 〈 but 《 for 〈 for the 〈 bent over,
    not freedom and   end,   yearning*
    abundance,

רָחוֹק וְעָמֹק וְלִדְלוֹת לֹא מַסְפִּיקִים,

《 they are unable. 〈 and to 《 and 〈 it is far
         draw it up   deep,   away

קֹוִים וְחוֹכִים, וַאֲמָנָה לֹא מַפְסִיקִים.

《 they do not pause. 〈 in [their] 〈 they wait, 〈 They
          faith   hope,

צְמֵאֶיךָ צוֹק לָהֶם יָחוּל לְבָבָם,

《 of their 〈 the 〈 for 〈 pour 〈 [For] those who
   heart,   hope   them   forth   thirst for You

פָּנֶיךָ לֵרָאוֹת בֵּית מְעוֹן חֲבִיבָם,*

《 that is their 〈 Dwelling 〈 in the 〈 to appear 〈 before
   beloved,*   Temple   You

עֲבֹר בַּסָּךְ¹ וְעַמּוּד אֵשׁ* סְבִיבָם,

《 around 〈 of fire* 〈 with a 〈 with the 〈 to pass
   them,   pillar   throng

סוּר עָרֵל וְטָמֵא*² בַּעֲלֵי דְבָבָם.

《 their enemies. 《 and the 〈 the uncir- 〈 remove
         unclean,*   cumcised

נִכְחִידֵם נִירָשָׁה³ לָמוֹ נָמוּ חָרָשׁוּ,

《 they 〈 they 《 for our- 〈 Let us 《 Let us
  plotted.   said,   selves!   conquer   obliterate them!

---

(1) Cf. *Psalms* 42:5. (2) *Isaiah* 52:1. (3) Cf. *Psalms* 83:5,13.

tory comment to *Selichah* 2].

שָׁחָה . . . תָּעְרֹג — *She [Israel] longs . . . bent over, yearning.* The translation follows *Masbir* and *Matteh Levi*, who understand the feminine verb forms as an allusion to כְּנֶסֶת יִשְׂרָאֵל, *the Assembly of Israel.* According to *Arugas HaBosem*, the reference is to the speaker's soul, which has been bent to the ground in unfulfilled anticipation (see *Psalms* 44:26).

מְעוֹן חֲבִיבָם — *Dwelling that is their beloved.* The translation follows *Arugas HaBosem* and *Matteh Levi.* Alternatively: *the Dwelling of [You,] their Beloved,* or, *the Dwelling that is [in the portion of Benjamin who is*

called God's] beloved (*Pardes*).

וְעַמּוּד אֵשׁ — *With a pillar of fire.* The angels are called pillars of fire (*Arugas HaBosem*). Just as we merited to be led through the Wilderness by a pillar of fire when we left Egypt, so may we merit to be led out of our present exile by a pillar of fire (*Pardes*).

סוּר עָרֵל וְטָמֵא — *Remove the uncircumcised and the unclean.* This term includes all the nations that are hostile to Israel (see *Jeremiah* 9:25). Alternatively: עָרֵל, *Uncircumcised,* and טָמֵא, *Unclean,* are two of the seven names of the Evil Inclination (*Succos* 52a; see commentary to *Selichah* 24, s.v. מִכְשׁוֹל).

מִירֻשָּׁתְךָ אֲשֶׁר הוֹרַשְׁתָּ עַמְּךָ גֵּרְשׁוּ,[1]

《 they have 《 to Your 〈 You 〈 that 〈 [Your people]
expelled. people, bequeathed from Your
inheritance

לְהַשְׁמִיד יוֹם יוֹם עוֹד יִדְרֹשׁוּ,[2]

《 they still seek, 〈 by day 〈 day 〈 To destroy [Israel],

בֹּנֵס מַס וְחָמָס וַעֲנִיֶּיךָ יְרוֹשֵׁשׁוּ.

《 making yet 〈 Your poor 《 and 〈 taxes 〈 gather-
more destitute. people booty, ing

יְבַזּוּ יְבַזּוּ יְדִידֶיךָ יְכַנּוּם כְּלָבִים,

《 dogs. 〈 they call 《 Your beloved 〈 they 〈 They
them people, revile despoil,

טִפֵּשׁ וְנָבָל כְּמֹר תַּעַר הַגַּלָּבִים.*[3]

《 of the 〈 [shorn with] 〈 the 〈 the 〈 [Who are
barbers.* the razor priest scoundrel, they?]
The fool,

חֶרְפָּתָם שׁוֹמְעִים עֲלוּבִים וְלֹא עוֹלְבִים,[4]

《 insult; 〈 but do 〈 and remain 〈 they [Your 〈 Their abuse
not insulted people] hear,

זָר לֹא נִשְׁלָבִים וְעָלֶיךָ נִצְלָבִים.

《 they are 〈 and for 《 they do not 〈 a strange
crucified. Your sake embrace, [god]

וַאֲנַחְנוּ נֶגְדְּךָ זֶה עִנּוּיֵינוּ,

《 torment 〈 let 〈 — considered 《 As for us
of ours. be this before You

הַעַל אֵלֶּה תִתְאַפַּק תֶּחֱשֶׁה וּתְעַנֵּנוּ,[5]

《 and [allow us] 〈 Will You 《 will You restrain 〈 all these 〈 In the
to be tormented? be silent Yourself? face of

דִּכִּיתָנוּ בִּמְקוֹם תַּנִּים[6] וְאֵלֶיךָ עֵינֵינוּ,[7]

《 are our 〈 yet to You 《 of 〈 in the place 〈 You have
eyes, serpents, crushed us

---

(1) Cf. *II Chronicles* 20:11. (2) Cf. *Isaiah* 58:2. (3) Cf. *Ezekiel* 5:1; in some editions of *Selichos*
this stich has been censored to read טִפְּשִׁים יִשְׁמָעֵאל, *the Ishmaelite fools* [or טִפֵּשׁ גּוֹי, *the foolish
nation*], נָבָל תַּעַר הַגַּלָּבִים, *the scoundrel, shorn with the razor of the barbers*; in others it has been
changed to טָהוֹרֵי לֵב עָלֶיךָ מַשְׁלִיכִים יְהָבִים, *[while] the pure of heart cast their burden upon You*
(based on *Psalms* 55:23). (4) Cf. *Shabbos* 88b. (5) Cf. *Isaiah* 64:11. (6) Cf. *Psalms* 44:20; 23:4.
(7) Cf. *II Chronicles* 20:12; *Psalms* 123:2.

כְּמֹר תַּעַר הַגַּלָּבִים — *The priest [shorn with]
the razor of the barbers.* The priests, fri-
ars, and other church functionaries of

medieval times were [as are certain of their
present-day counterparts] virulent anti-
Semites.

גַּם גֵּיא צַלְמָוֶת,¹ שָׁמוּ מְעוֹנֵנוּ.

《 our 〈 they have 〈 overshadowed 〈 into the 〈 even
dwellings. turned by death valley though

בְּנוּ נִקְרָא שִׁמְךָ אַל יִתְחַלָּל,

《 be 〈— let 《 Your Name 〈 is read 〈 Within
desecrated! it not [Isra-El] us

בְּךָ כָּל זֶרַע יִשְׂרָאֵל יִתְהַלָּל,

《 are praised. 〈 of Israel 〈 the 〈 all 〈 Through
seed You

אִם עֲוֹנֵינוּ רַבּוּ וּמָלְאוּ חָלָל,

《 the world's 〈 enough 《 are 〈 our sins 〈 Though
expanse, to fill many,

אָנֹכִי מוֹחֶה פְשָׁעֶיךָ,² פִּיךָ מִלָּל.

《 has said. 〈 Your mouth 《 your sins, 〈 wipe away 〈 I

שְׁגִיאוֹת שִׂים זֵדִים וְלֹא קוֹנֵס,

《 punish; 〈 and 《 deliber- 〈 convert 〈 Into inad-
do not ate sin, vertent sins

לִפְנִים מִשּׁוּרַת הַדִּין לָנוּ הִכָּנֵס,

《 may You 〈 for us 《 of Your 〈 the strict line 〈 beyond
step. law,

מִפְּנֵי קֹשֶׁט סֶלָה, יֵבוֹשׁ הָאוֹנֵס,

《 the 〈 let be 《 eternal, 〈 of truth 〈 For the
oppressor; shamed sake

הַנֵּס יִתְנוֹסֵס³ וְנִדְחֵי יִשְׂרָאֵל יְכַנֵּס.⁴

《 let HASHEM 〈 of Israel 〈 and the 《 be raised 〈 let the
gather in. dispersed high, [Messiah's]
banner

❖ הָרֵץ בַּת פּוּצִי וְקָרְבָּן תֵּשַׁע,

《 turn; 〈 and to [her 〈 of my 〈 with the 〈 Find
prayer in place scattered daughter favor
of an] offering nation,

קַבֵּץ יַחַד עֲשִׂירִית עִם תֵּשַׁע,*

《 the nine 〈 with 《 the Tenth 〈 together 〈 gather
[preceding it].* [Exile], in

---

(1) Cf. *Psalms* 44:20; 23:4. (2) Cf. *Isaiah* 43:25. (3) Cf. *Psalms* 60:6. (4) Cf. 147:2.

עֲשִׂירִית עִם תֵּשַׁע — *The Tenth [Exile], with
the nine [preceding it].* The commentary
Arugas HaBosem cites various Midrashim

that discuss the stages by which Israel was
exiled from the Land, during and after the
First Destruction and after the Second. He

טַבַּע חֵטְא וְלֹא יִזָּכֵר רֶשַׁע,
《 wickedness, 〈 be re- 〈 and let 〈 sin, 〈 Drown
membered not

נֹשֵׂא עָוֹן וְעֹבֵר עַל פֶּשַׁע.¹
《 sin. 〈 over 〈 and 〈 iniquity 〈 [O God]
passes Who bears

ALL, WHILE STANDING:

אֵל מֶלֶךְ יוֹשֵׁב עַל כִּסֵּא רַחֲמִים, מִתְנַהֵג
〈 Who acts 《 of mercy, 〈 the throne 〈 on 〈 Who sits 〈 King 〈 O God,

בַּחֲסִידוּת, מוֹחֵל עֲוֹנוֹת עַמּוֹ, מַעֲבִיר רִאשׁוֹן
〈 [sins,] one 〈 Who 《 of His 〈 the sins 〈 Who 《 with kindness,
removes people, pardons

רִאשׁוֹן,² מַרְבֶּה מְחִילָה לַחַטָּאִים וּסְלִיחָה לַפּוֹשְׁעִים,
《 to willful 〈 and 〈 to unintentional 〈 pardon 〈 Who abun- 《 by one,
sinners, forgiveness sinners dantly grants

עֹשֶׂה צְדָקוֹת עִם כָּל בָּשָׂר וָרוּחַ, לֹא כְרָעָתָם
〈 in accord 〈 — not 《 and 〈 [beings 〈 all 〈 with 〈 acts of 〈 Who
with their spirit of] flesh generosity performs
wickedness

תִּגְמוֹל. ❖ אֵל הוֹרֵיתָ לָּנוּ לוֹמַר שְׁלֹשׁ עֶשְׂרֵה, וּזְכוֹר
〈 remem- 《 the Thirteen 〈 to 〈 us 〈 You 〈 O God, 《 do You
ber [Attributes of Mercy]; recite taught repay them!

לָּנוּ הַיּוֹם בְּרִית שְׁלֹשׁ עֶשְׂרֵה, כְּמוֹ שֶׁהוֹדַעְתָּ לֶעָנָיו
〈 to the 〈 You made 〈 as 《 of [these] Thirteen, 〈 the 〈 today 〈 for us
humble one known covenant
[Moses]

מִקֶּדֶם, כְּמוֹ שֶׁכָּתוּב, וַיֵּרֶד יהוה בֶּעָנָן וַיִּתְיַצֵּב עִמּוֹ
〈 with 〈 and stood 〈 in a 〈 And Hashem 《 it is written: 〈 as 《 in ancient
him cloud descended times,

שָׁם, וַיִּקְרָא בְשֵׁם יהוה.³
《 of 〈 with the 〈 and He 《 there,
Hashem. Name called out

---

(1) *Micah* 7:18. (2) *Rosh Hashanah* 17a. (3) *Exodus* 34:5.

---

counts six for the First Temple — three by
Sennacherib and three by Nebuchadnezzar (*Tanchuma, Masei* 13), and four for

the Second (*Seder Olam*), culminating in
the almost two-thousand-year *galus* of
today.

CONGREGATION, THEN *CHAZZAN*:

וַיַּעֲבֹר יהוה עַל פָּנָיו וַיִּקְרָא:

⟪ and ⟪ [Moses'] ⟨ before ⟨ And HASHEM passed
proclaimed: face,

CONGREGATION AND *CHAZZAN* RECITE LOUDLY AND IN UNISON:

יהוה, יהוה, אֵל, רַחוּם, וְחַנּוּן, אֶרֶךְ אַפַּיִם,

⟨ to anger, ⟨ Slow ⟪and Gracious,⟨ Compassionate ⟨ God, ⟨ HASHEM, ⟨ HASHEM,

וְרַב חֶסֶד, וֶאֱמֶת, נֹצֵר חֶסֶד לָאֲלָפִים, נֹשֵׂא עָוֹן,

⟨ of ⟨ Forgiver ⟪ for thousands ⟨ of ⟨ Preserver ⟪ and ⟨ in ⟨ and
iniquity, [of generations], kindness Truth, Kindness Abundant

וָפֶשַׁע, וְחַטָּאָה, וְנַקֵּה.[1] וְסָלַחְתָּ לַעֲוֹנֵנוּ וּלְחַטָּאתֵנוּ

⟪ and our sins, ⟨ our ⟨ May You ⟪ and Who ⟨ and inadvertent ⟨ willful sin,
iniquities forgive absolves. sin,

וּנְחַלְתָּנוּ.[2] סְלַח לָנוּ אָבִינוּ כִּי חָטָאנוּ, מְחַל לָנוּ

⟨ us, ⟨ pardon ⟪ we have ⟨ for ⟪ our ⟨ us, ⟨ Forgive ⟪ and make us
sinned; Father, Your heritage.

מַלְכֵּנוּ כִּי פָשָׁעְנוּ. כִּי אַתָּה אֲדֹנָי טוֹב וְסַלָּח,

⟪ and ⟨ are ⟨ O Lord, ⟨ You, ⟨ For ⟪ we have ⟨ for ⟪ our King,
forgiving, good willfully sinned.

וְרַב חֶסֶד לְכָל קֹרְאֶיךָ.[3]

⟪ who call ⟨ to all ⟨ kind ⟨ and
upon You. abundantly

SELICHAH 18 / סליחה יח

ALL:

אֱלֹהֵינוּ וֵאלֹהֵי אֲבוֹתֵינוּ:

⟪ of our forefathers: ⟨ and God ⟨ Our God

אָרְכוּ הַיָּמִים* וּדְבַר חָזוֹן,*[4]

⟪ of the [prophetic]⟨ and the ⟨ have the days ⟨ Grown
vision;* words [until Redemption]* long

---

(1) *Exodus* 34:6-7. (2) 34:9. (3) *Psalms* 86:5. (4) Cf. *Ezekiel* 12:22-23.

⟰§ **אָרְכוּ הַיָּמִים** — *Grown long have the days [until Redemption].* The acrostic of this *selichah* comprises the *aleph-beis*, followed by the author's name — שִׁמְעוֹן בַּר יִצְחָק חֲזַק, *Shimon bar Yitzchak, may he be strong* — each respective letter appearing twice. Known as R' Shimon *HaGadol* (the

Great), this prolific *paytan* lived in Mainz, Germany, about 950-1020, where he served on the *beis din* together with R' Gershom Meor HaGolah [see prefatory comment to *Selichah* 12].

Because of his great wisdom and impressive appearance, R' Shimon was often sent

אַרְמוֹן נָטַשׁ וְחָדַל פְּרָזוֹן,*[1]

《 are unwalled 〈 and aban- 〈 is 〈 our Temple-
villages.* doned deserted, palace

בִּקּוּוִי מַרְפֵּא בְּעָתָה[2] וְרָזוֹן,

《 and 〈 there were 《 for 〈 Where we
emaciation; terror healing, hoped

בִּטְחָה וְהַשְׁקֵט לִמְנוּסָה וְחִפָּזוֹן.

《 and panic. 〈 turned to flight 〈 and quiet 〈 security

גְּאֻלָּה נֶאֱחֶרֶת וְתוֹחֶלֶת מְמֻשָּׁכָה,

《 is stretched 〈 hope 《 is delayed, 〈 Redemption
out so long.

גּוֹלָה וְסוּרָה[3] קְדוֹרַנִּית חֲשׁוּכָה,

《 in darkness, 〈 despondent, 《 and wandering, 〈 Exiled

דִּמְעָתָהּ מְצוּיָה בִּלְחָיֶיהָ[4] לְמָשְׁכָה,

《 [seemingly] forever. 〈 on her cheek 〈 is found 〈 her tear

---

(1) Cf. *Judges* 5:7. (2) Cf. *Jeremiah* 8:15. (3) *Isaiah* 49:21. (4) Cf. *Lamentations* 1:2.

by the community to persuade monarchs and clergymen to abolish harsh decrees proposed against the Jews, and in many cases he succeeded. In a responsum, Rabbeinu Tam describes him as, "R' Shimon ben Yitzchak *HaGadol*, with whom miracles were common."

According to a popular story, R' Shimon had two sons, Yitzchak and Elchanan. Elchanan was kidnaped by the family's trusted gentile maid, who handed him over to a monastery where he was raised in the Christian faith. His keen mind absorbed so much knowledge that he was continually raised in rank, until he eventually became pope. Some time after his son's election, R' Shimon journeyed to Rome in order to gain an audience with the new pope and plead with him to nullify a cruel edict against the Jews. During this visit the pope invited his guest to play a game of chess. R' Shimon, a master at chess who had never before been defeated, was stunned when the pope checkmated him. R' Shimon, who had taught chess to his sons, suspected that the pope might have acquired his chess training from him. When he questioned the pope concerning his skills, the truth surfaced, and father and son embraced.

After issuing many decrees in favor of the Jews. Elchanan disappeared with his father, and became an outstanding Talmudic scholar.

R' Shimon often wrote very sharply against those who persecuted the Jews for refusing to believe in a god of flesh and blood. Thus, many of his compositions have suffered the heavy hand of Christian censorship. The numbered footnotes of the *selichah* point out many instances of such tampering.

אָרְכוּ הַיָּמִים וּדְבַר חָזוֹן — *Grown long have the days [until Redemption] and the words of the [prophetic] vision.* In this paraphrase of the prophet's words, the *paytan* bemoans the length of the present exile and the lack of fulfillment of the prophetic visions that foretold of its end.

וְחָדַל פְּרָזוֹן — *And abandoned are unwalled villages.* Unwalled cities are no longer viable dwelling places, for they provide no protection from the ever-present enemy (*Masbir* based on *Judges* 5:7). Alternatively, the *paytan* refers to the loss of prophecy, a homiletical interpretation of the verse in *Judges* (see *Pesachim* 66b). If so, this stich repeats the theme of the opening stich, which also speaks of the absence of prophecy.

דְּרוּסָה בְּעוּטָה נְגוּחָה נְשׁוּכָה.*

《 and bitten.* 〈 gored, 〈 kicked, 〈 She is clawed,

הוּבָאָה בַּחֹשֶׁךְ וְיוֹשֶׁבֶת דּוּמָם,[1]

《 silent, 〈 she sits 〈 into darkness, 〈 Brought

הוֹמֶה לִבָּהּ וּבְתוֹכָהּ יִשְׁתּוֹמָם,

《 is desolation; 〈 and within her 〈 is her heart, 〈 in turmoil

וְעֵינֶיהָ מְיַחֲלוֹת לַיְלָה וְיוֹמָם,

《 and by day, 〈 by night 〈 are pining, 〈 and her eyes

וְעָצוּר בְּעַצְמוֹתֶיהָ כְּגַחֶלֶת לַחֲמָם.[2]

《 that is burning. 〈 is a coal 〈 within her bones 〈 caged

(1) Cf. *Isaiah* 47:5. (2) Cf. *Jeremiah* 20:9.

דְּרוּסָה בְּעוּטָה נְגוּחָה נְשׁוּכָה — *She is clawed, kicked, gored, and bitten.* Throughout the Talmud and Midrash, and based on the Vision of the Four Beasts in the Book of *Daniel* (Chs. 7-8), Israel's long series of exiles and persecutions are always treated as four main periods of subjugation to foreign oppressors — either in *Eretz Yisrael* or in the Diaspora. These periods are known collectively as אַרְבַּע מַלְכִיּוֹת, *the Four Kingdoms* (*Daniel* 8:22), and each is called by the name of the empire dominant in the world at that particular time.

The first, called גָּלוּת בָּבֶל, *the Babylonian Exile*, began when King Nebuchadnezzar of Babylon conquered the Land of Israel and destroyed the First Temple. The second, called גָּלוּת מָדַי וּפָרַס, *the Median-Persian Exile* (ibid. 8:20), began when that empire captured the Babylonians and became the leading world power. Although the Medes permitted the Jewish return to *Eretz Yisrael* and the building of the Second Temple, the early years of that *Beis HaMikdash* were still considered a part of the exile, because Israel was not sovereign in its Land. During the entire third period, גָּלוּת יָוָן, *the Greek Exile* (ibid. 8:21), paradoxically, Israel lived on its Land and the Temple stood. Nevertheless, it was a very turbulent era marked with civil strife, foreign domination, vicious anti-religious

campaigns, and the rejection of Torah values by a large number of Jews who adopted Greek culture with all its abominations. The downfall of the Greek Empire and the rise of Rome marked the beginning of גָּלוּת אֱדוֹם, *the Edomite* or *Roman Exile.* It is this millennia-long exile that we are still in today.

According to *Arugas HaBosem,* the *selichah* refers to the Four Kingdoms as they are variously described in Scripture: In his vision, Daniel was shown allegorically the four nations in whose domains Israel would be exiled. The first exile, the Babylonian, was represented by a lion with eagle's wings (7:4). In our *selichah,* Israel, subjugated by that beast, is alluded to as דְּרוּסָה, *clawed.* The Median-Persians are depicted in the Vision as a bear (v. 5); and our *paytan* describes Israel as בְּעוּטָה, *kicked,* by them. Although, in his Vision, Daniel saw Greece as a four-headed, four-winged leopard (v. 6), he later identifies the Greek king as a goat (8:21); our stich states that during this exile, Israel was נְגוּחָה, *gored.* Finally, the Romans are seen by Daniel as an unnamed ten-horned iron-toothed monster (7:7). However, another prophet describes the period of the Roman exile as וּנְשָׁכוֹ הַנָּחָשׁ, *and a snake bit him* (*Amos* 5:19); thus, the *selichah* refers to Israel during this exile as נְשׁוּכָה, *bitten.*

זְמַנֵּי קְצֶיהָ מְאֹד חֲתָמוּ,[1]

《 sealed. 〈 are very 〈 when Her 〈 The times
well redemption should arrive

זוֹהֲרוֹת נֵרוֹתֶיהָ בְּעֶבְרָה נֶעְתָּמוּ,

《 is darkened. 〈 by [God's] fury 〈 of her radiance 〈 The gleam

חֶבְאוּ נִדָּחֶיהָ וּבְמַסְגֵּר נִסְתָּמוּ,

《 shut away — 〈 in prison 《 are her dis- 〈 Hidden
persed people,

חֲטָאֶיהָ הִשִּׂיגוּהָ כִּי נִכְתָּמוּ.

《 they are stub- 〈 for 《 have caught 〈 Her sins
bornly stained. up with her,

טוֹפְלֵי שֶׁקֶר יִשְׁלָיוּ בְּשֶׁקֶט,

《 in 〈 are serene 〈 to false- 〈 Those
tranquility, hood connected

טִירוֹתָם בְּטוּחוֹת כְּעַל שְׁמָרֵי שָׁקֶט,

《 that are quiet 〈 lees 〈 like 〈 are secure 〈 their towers
[without [wine] on
agitation].

יַעֲצִיבוּ רַעְיָתְךָ בְּרֹגֶז לְמַקֵּט,

《 they 〈 as in 《 do Your be- 《 They grieve,
torment her, anger loved people,

יְגוֹזְזוּהָ כְּרָחֵל גִּזּוֹתֶיהָ לְלַקֵּט.

《 to gather. 〈 her wool 《 like a ewe, 〈 shearing her

כָּשַׁל כֹּחָהּ מִכֹּבֶד סֵבֶל,

《 of her 〈 under the 〈 has her 〈 Failed
burden; weight strength

כִּנּוֹרָהּ לִבְכִי וְעוּגָבָהּ לְאֵבֶל,[2]

《 to 〈 her flute 《 turned to 〈 her harp
mourning. weeping,

לְנֶגְדָּהּ כְּלִמָּתָהּ מִצָּרֶיהָ לְהִתְנַבֵּל,

〈 she is degraded 〈 by her 《 is her 〈 Before her
oppressors humiliation;

לֵאמֹר נוֹאַשְׁתֶּם לָצֵאת מִכֶּבֶל.

《 the chains! 〈 to escape 〈 You have no 《 when they
hope say,

---

(1) Cf. *Daniel* 12:9. (2) Cf. *Job* 30:31.

מָאס נִמְאַסְתֶּם¹ בְּגָלוּת לְנִדָּח,

You are utterly despised, ⟩ in exile ⟩ banished. ⟪

מְנוּסְכֶם אָבַד וְכִיקוּד מְקָדָח,

Your refuge ⟩ is lost, ⟪ and is like a blazing ⟩ inferno. ⟪

נוֹתַרְתֶּם כַּנֵּס וְכִצְבִי מֻדָּח,²

You are left ⟩ like a [forsaken] flagpole; ⟪ like a deer ⟩ chased away. ⟪

נִהְיָה יְקַרְכֶם כְּאֹפֶל מְנֻדָּח.³

Transformed ⟩ is your glory ⟩ as if to darkness ⟩ it has been banished. ⟪

סַלְעֵינוּ וּמְצוּדָתֵנוּ בְּשִׁמְךָ נָרוּץ,⁴

Our Rock, ⟩ our Fortress, ⟩ to [the protection of] Your Name ⟩ we run, ⟪

סְבוּל עָלֶיךָ כִּלָּיוֹן וְחָרוּץ,⁵

suffering ⟩ for Your sake ⟩ destruction ⟩ that was intense. ⟪

עֲנוּשִׁים וּמֻכִּים בְּפֶרֶץ פָּרוּץ,

Punished, ⟩ beaten ⟩ [through] the breaches ⟩ that breach [our wall] ⟩

עֲבוּר מַהֲמִירֶךָ בְּחֹמֶר קָרוּץ.⁶

to force us ⟩ to exchange You ⟩ for [a man who] out of clay ⟩ was formed. ⟪

פְּנֵה לְהָחִישׁ לְעֶזְרָתִי אֱיָלוּתִי,⁷

Turn ⟩ and rush ⟩ to my aid, ⟪ O my strength, ⟪

פֶּן יֹאמַר הָאוֹיֵב יְכָלְתִּי,

lest ⟩ the enemy boast, ⟪ I have overcome [him]. ⟪

צָרַי יָגִילוּ⁸ כִּי שָׁכֹלְתִּי, צוּר הֲקִימֵנִי כִּי נָפָלְתִּי.

My tormentors ⟩ would rejoice ⟩ that ⟩ I have been bereaved — ⟪ O Rock! ⟪ Raise me up, ⟩ for ⟩ I have fallen. ⟪

(1) Cf. *Lamentations* 5:22. (2) Cf. *Isaiah* 13:14. (3) Cf. 8:22. (4) Cf. *Psalms* 18:3. (5) Cf. *Isaiah* 10:22, 28:22. (6) This reference to flesh-and-blood deities has been censored out of many editions of *Selichos*; in some it is omitted altogether; in most it is replaced with עַמְּךָ כָּלִים בְּכִלָּיוֹן חָרוּץ, *Your people are decimated with ruthless destruction*. (7) Cf. *Psalms* 22:20. (8) Cf. 13:5; in some editions of *Selichos* the word הָאוֹיֵב, *the enemy*, has been changed to יִשְׁמָעֵאל, *Ishmael*, a ploy obviously intended to appease Christian censors.

קוּמָה וְהִנָּשֵׂא בְּעַבְרוֹת צוֹרְרִים,[1]

《 over the tormentors. 〈 in fury 〈 be raised up 《 Arise,

קָרֵב יוֹם יִקְרְאוּ נוֹצְרִים,[2]

《 will the 〈 when called 〈 the 〈 Bring
watchmen be, [out of exile] day near

רֵעֵי גוֹיִם[3] לִהְיוֹת מִצְרִים, רְאוֹת דְּרִיכַת בּוֹצְרִים.[4]

《 [as if] in the 〈 trampled 〈 as they see 〈 suffering 〈 will be 〈 of the 〈 and the
wine press. [themselves] nations cohorts

שׁוּר בְּעַמֶּךְ לְהוֹסִיף אָמְצוֹ,

《 its 〈 and increase 〈 to Your 〈 Look
strength; people

שְׁקֹד לְטַהֲרוֹ וּלְנַקּוֹתוֹ מִשְּׁמְצוֹ,

《 of its blemish. 〈 and cleanse it 〈 purify it 〈 diligently

תִּשְׁמֹר עֶדְרְךָ כְּרוֹעֶה לְרִבְצוֹ,

《 and see 《 like a 〈 Your flock 〈 Guard
that it rests. shepherd,

תַּשְׁמִיעַ מִזְרֵה יִשְׂרָאֵל יְקַבְּצוֹ.[5]

《 shall gather 〈 Israel 〈 He that 《 Proclaim,
them in! scattered

שַׁנֵּן בְּרַק חֶרֶב בְּזַעְמֶךְ, שַׁכֵּר חִצֶּיךָ מִגּוֹי מַזְעִימֶךְ,[7]

《 that angers 〈 with [the 〈 Your 〈 intoxicate 《 in Your fury; 〈 of the 〈 the 〈 Sharpen
You, blood of] arrows sword edge
the nation

מֵרֹאשׁ פַּרְעוֹת אוֹיֵב בְּהִתְנַקֶּמֶךְ,

〈 when You avenge 《 of the 〈 depredations 〈 because of
enemy, the earliest

מִמַּה שֶּׁעָשׂוּ בְּחַלְלֵי עַמֶּךְ.[8]

《 of Your 〈 to the slain 〈 they did 〈 what
people. bodies

עֲבוּר נִקְמָתְךָ גוֹיִם הַרְנִינוּ,[9]

《 will sing; 〈 the 〈 Your 〈 Because
nations vengeance of

---

(1) Cf. *Psalms* 7:7. (2) Cf. *Jeremiah* 31:5. (3) Once again, the censor's hand has tampered with our
selichah; many editions read רֵעֵי יִשְׁמָעֵאל, *Ishmael's cohorts*. An alternate text, רָעֵי גוֹיִם,
the most wicked nations, matches *Ezekiel* 7:24. (4) Cf. *Isaiah* 63:1-3. (5) Cf. *Jeremiah* 31:9.
(6) Cf. *Deuteronomy* 32:41; some editions omit the sixteen lines beginning שַׁנֵּן בְּרַק חֶרֶב,
Sharpen the edge of the sword. (7) Here too, some editions read מִישְׁמָעֵאל מַזְעִימֶךְ,
from Ishmael who angers You. (8) Cf. *Deuteronomy* 32:41-42. (9) Cf. 32:43.

עֲלִיּוֹת תַּחְתִּיּוֹת הָרִיעוּ רָנּוּ,
《with song; 〈 will shout 〈 and earth below 〈 heaven above

וְהַר וָגֶבַע וְאִילָנוֹת יְרַנֵּנוּ,[1] וְגַם יוֹשְׁבֵי סֶלַע יָרֹנּוּ.[2]
《 will 〈 in Mach- 〈those who〈 Also 《 will joy- 〈 and trees 〈 and 〈 and
sing. pelah Cave dwell ously sing. hill mountain

נְקַם הַדָּם וּנְקַם הֶחָמָס,
〈 for robbery 〈 and 〈 for 〈 Ven-
vengeance blood geance

נִמְסָךְ לְצָרִים[3] לְהַגִּירָם נִכְמָס,
〈 [the poison] 〈 pouring 《 for the 〈 will be
hidden out for them tormentors, mixed

בְּכוֹס[4] עָמֹק וְרָחָב לְהֶחָמֵס,[5]
《 to ravage them. 〈 and wide, 〈 deep 〈 in a cup,

בִּשְׂחוֹק וּבְלַעַג כֹּחָם יִמָּס.[6]
《 will melt 〈 their 〈 and 〈 Amid [Heav-
away. power scorn enly] laughter

רִאשׁוֹנָה תְשַׁלֵּם מִשְׁנֵה עֲוֹנוֹתֵיהֶם,
《 iniquities — 〈 for their 〈 You will 〈 First
repeated pay them

רְאֵה חַלְּלָם[7] אַרְצְךָ בְּשַׁחִיתוֹתֵיהֶם,
《 with their abominations! 〈 of Your land 〈their desecration 〈 see

יֵבוֹשׁוּ צָרִים[8] בְּשֶׁקֶר עַוְּתוֹתֵיהֶם,[9]
《 of their 〈 by the 〈 let the 〈 Be
crookedness, falsehood tormentors, shamed

יוּפְקְדוּ מֵרֹב יָמִים בְּחַטֹּאתֵיהֶם.[10]
《 of their sinfulness. 〈 period 〈 for the 〈 recalled to
prolonged be punished

צְרַפְנוּ כַּכֶּסֶף בְּמוּעָקָה[11] לְגוֹלְלָה,
《 that keep us 〈 placed in 《 like [refined] 〈 We have
spinning; constraints silver, been smelted
[in exile]

---

(1) Cf. *Isaiah* 44:23. (2) Cf. 42:11; the four lines beginning, עֲבוּר נִקְמָתְךָ גּוֹיִם הַרְנִינוּ, *Because of Your vengeance the nations will sing,* are based upon *Sifrei* to *Deuteronomy* 32:43. (3) Cf. *Deuteronomy* 32:43; the word לְצָרִים, *for the tormentors,* has been changed in some editions of *Selichos* to לַיִּשְׁמְעֵאלִים, *to the Ishmaelites.* (4) Cf. *Psalms* 75:9. (5) Many editions read לְהַעֲמֵס, which can mean either *to weigh down upon them,* or *to be filled to the brim.* (6) Cf. *Ezekiel* 23:32; the four lines beginning נְקַם הַדָּם, *Vengeance for blood,* are based on *Sifrei* to *Deuteronomy* 32:34. (7) Cf. *Jeremiah* 16:18; some editions of *Selichos* read חַלְּלֵי, *those who desecrate,* for חַלְּלָם, *their desecration.* (8) Some editions read זֵדִים, *the wanton.* (9) Some editions read עֲוֹנוֹתֵיהֶם, *their iniquities.* (10) Cf. *Isaiah* 24:22. (11) Cf. *Psalms* 66:10-11.

צָמַתְנוּ וְנוֹאַשְׁנוּ* לִכְלוֹת בַּגּוֹלָה,¹

《 in the exile. 〈 [certain] 《 we despair,* 《we have been
of perishing closed off,

חֻלְּלָה לְנַפֵּץ יָד עַם סְגֻלָּה,

《 that is 〈 of the 〈 the 〈shattering 〈 Profaned,
Treasured; People power

חֵפֶץ פְּרוּטָה מִכִּיס אָזְלָה.

《 is gone. 〈 from our 〈 even a 〈any object
pockets penny [of value],

קַנֵּא לִשְׁמְךָ וְלִקְדֻשָּׁתְךָ חַס,

《 have 〈 on Your holiness 〈 for Your 〈 Be
pity; Name's sake, zealous

קָרְבֵנוּ אֵלֶיךָ וּבְצִלְּךָ נֶחַס,

《 shall we be〈 and in Your 〈 to You, 〈 bring us
sheltered. shadow near

חֲזֵה כִּי אֵין מַפְגִּיעַ עָלֵינוּ לְהָחֵס,

《 and arouse 〈 for us 〈 to pray 〈there is〈 that 〈 See
mercy, no one

חַלּוֹתְךָ כְּמֹשֶׁה וְאַהֲרֹן וּפִינְחָס.*

《 or Phinehas.* 〈 or Aaron 〈 like Moses 〈beseeching You

❖ זְכוֹר בְּרִית חֶסֶד קְדוּמִים,

《 [with the Patriarchs]〈 of 〈 the 〈 Remem-
in earliest times. kindness covenant ber

וַעֲקָתֵנוּ שְׁעֵה מִשְּׁמֵי מְרוֹמִים,

《 of heavens. 〈 from the 〈 pay heed 〈 To our
highest outcry

קַיֵּם לְעַמְּךָ בְּרִית שְׁלוֹמִים,

《 of peace, 〈 the 〈 for Your 〈 Fulfill
covenant people

אֵל מֶלֶךְ יוֹשֵׁב עַל כִּסֵּא רַחֲמִים.

《 of mercy! 〈 the throne 〈 on 〈 Who sits 〈 King 〈 God,

---

(1) Some editions read וְנוֹאַשְׁנוּ מִן הַגְאֻלָּה, we despair of the Redemption.

וְנוֹאַשְׁנוּ — *We despair.* The Midrash (*Sifrei* to *Deuteronomy* 32:36) and Talmud (*Sanhedrin* 97a) enumerate various signs that will indicate the imminent arrival of the Messiah. Among them are: despair of the *galus* ever ending; despair of the Redemption ever coming; and the last penny will be gone. The *paytan* incorporates all of these signs into his prayer for the end of this longest of all our exiles.

חַלּוֹתְךָ כְּמֹשֶׁה וְאַהֲרֹן וּפִינְחָס — *Beseeching You like Moses or Aaron or Phinehas.* Another

ALL, WHILE STANDING:

אֵל מֶלֶךְ יוֹשֵׁב עַל כִּסֵּא רַחֲמִים, מִתְנַהֵג
⟨ Who acts   ⟪ of mercy,   ⟨ the throne   ⟨ on   ⟨ Who sits   ⟨ King   ⟨ O God,

בַּחֲסִידוּת, מוֹחֵל עֲוֹנוֹת עַמּוֹ, מַעֲבִיר רִאשׁוֹן רִאשׁוֹן,[1]
⟪ by one,   ⟨ [sins,] one   ⟨ Who   ⟪ of His   ⟨ the sins   ⟨ Who   ⟪ with kindness,
                           removes   people,   pardons

מַרְבֶּה מְחִילָה לַחֲטָאִים וּסְלִיחָה לַפּוֹשְׁעִים, עֹשֶׂה
⟨ Who   ⟪ to willful   ⟨ and   ⟨ to unintentional   ⟨ pardon   ⟨ Who abun-
performs   sinners,   forgiveness   sinners   dantly grants

צְדָקוֹת עִם כָּל בָּשָׂר וָרוּחַ, לֹא כְרָעָתָם תִּגְמוֹל.
⟪ do You   ⟨ in accord with   ⟨ — not   ⟪ and   ⟨ [beings   ⟨ all   ⟨ with   ⟨ acts of
repay them!   their wickedness   spirit   of] flesh   generosity

❖ אֵל הוֹרֵיתָ לָּנוּ לוֹמַר שְׁלֹשׁ עֶשְׂרֵה, וּזְכוֹר לָנוּ
⟨ for   ⟨ remember   ⟪ the Thirteen   ⟨ to   ⟨ us   ⟨ You   ⟨ O God,
us   [Attributes of Mercy];   recite   taught

הַיּוֹם בְּרִית שְׁלֹשׁ עֶשְׂרֵה, כְּמוֹ שֶׁהוֹדַעְתָּ לֶעָנָיו
⟨ to the humble   ⟨ You made   ⟨ as   ⟪ of [these] Thirteen,   ⟨ the   ⟨ today
one [Moses]   known   covenant

מִקֶּדֶם, כְּמוֹ שֶׁכָּתוּב, וַיֵּרֶד יהוה בֶּעָנָן וַיִּתְיַצֵּב עִמּוֹ
⟨ with   ⟨ and stood   ⟨ in a   ⟨ And HASHEM   ⟪ it is written: ⟨ as   ⟪ in ancient
him   cloud   descended   times,

שָׁם, וַיִּקְרָא בְשֵׁם יהוה.[2]
⟪ of   ⟨ with the   ⟨ and He   ⟪ there,
HASHEM.   Name   called out

CONGREGATION, THEN *CHAZZAN:*

וַיַּעֲבֹר יהוה עַל פָּנָיו וַיִּקְרָא:
⟪ and   ⟪ [Moses']   ⟨ before   ⟨ And HASHEM passed
proclaimed: face,

CONGREGATION AND *CHAZZAN* **RECITE LOUDLY AND IN UNISON:**

יהוה, יהוה, אֵל, רַחוּם, וְחַנּוּן, אֶרֶךְ אַפַּיִם,
⟨ to anger,   ⟨ Slow   ⟪ and   ⟨ Compassionate   ⟨ God,   ⟨ HASHEM,   ⟨ HASHEM,
Gracious,

---

(1) *Rosh Hashanah* 17a. (2) *Exodus* 34:5.

sign of the Messiah's coming will be the
lack of proper advocates on Israel's behalf
before the Heavenly Tribunal. There will
be none to pray as did Moses (see *Psalms*
106:23), Aaron (see *Numbers* 17:12-13), and

Phinehas (see *Psalms* 106:30), who were able
to appease God's anger at Israel's sins (*Sifrei*
to *Deuteronomy* 32:36). This too has come to
pass in our time.

וְרַב חֶֽסֶד, וֶאֱמֶת, נֹצֵר חֶֽסֶד לָאֲלָפִים, נֹשֵׂא עָוֹן,

‹ of ‹ Forgiver « for thousands ‹ of ‹ Preserver « and ‹ in ‹ and
iniquity, [of generations], kindness Truth, Kindness Abundant

וָפֶֽשַׁע, וְחַטָּאָה, וְנַקֵּה.[1] וְסָלַֽחְתָּ לַעֲוֹנֵֽנוּ וּלְחַטָּאתֵֽנוּ

« and our sins, ‹ our ‹ May You « and Who ‹ and inadvertent ‹ willful sin,
iniquities forgive absolves. sin,

וּנְחַלְתָּֽנוּ.[2] סְלַח לָֽנוּ אָבִֽינוּ כִּי חָטָֽאנוּ, מְחַל לָֽנוּ

‹ us, ‹ pardon « we have ‹ for « our ‹ us, ‹ Forgive « and make us
sinned; Father, Your heritage.

מַלְכֵּֽנוּ כִּי פָשָֽׁעְנוּ. כִּי אַתָּה אֲדֹנָי טוֹב וְסַלָּח,

« and ‹ are ‹ O Lord, ‹ You, ‹ For « we have ‹ for « our King,
forgiving, good willfully sinned.

וְרַב חֶֽסֶד לְכָל קֹרְאֶֽיךָ.[3]

« who call ‹ to all ‹ kind ‹ and
upon You. abundantly

סליחה יט / SELICHAH 19
(פזמון)

CHAZZAN, THEN CONGREGATION:

חָנֵּֽנוּ יהוה חָנֵּֽנוּ,[4]* עֲנֵֽנוּ יהוה עֲנֵֽנוּ,[5]

« answer ‹ HASHEM, ‹ Answer « be gracious ‹ HASHEM, ‹ Be gracious
us! us, with us!* with us,

עָזְרֵֽנוּ אֱלֹהֵי יִשְׁעֵֽנוּ,[6] כִּי עָלֶֽיךָ נִשְׁעָֽנוּ.[7]

« we rely. ‹ upon ‹ for « of our ‹ O God ‹ Help us,
You salvation,

CONGREGATION, THEN CHAZZAN:

אֵֽלֶּה בִּשְׁלִישֵׁימוֹ, וְאֵֽלֶּה בְּפָרָשֵׁימוֹ בְּקֶֽרֶב,

« in battle; ‹ in their cavalrymen ‹ and those « in their officers, ‹ These [trust]

---

(1) *Exodus* 34:6-7. (2) 34:9. (3) *Psalms* 86:5. (4) *Psalms* 123:3. (5) Cf. *I Kings* 18:37.
(6) *Psalms* 79:9. (7) Cf. *II Chronicles* 14:10; some editions of *Selichos* read נִשְׁעֵנוּ
as in the Scriptural verse; the meaning is the same.

חָנֵּֽנוּ ה' חָנֵּֽנוּ ⊷ — *Be gracious with us,*
HASHEM, *be gracious with us.* In declaring Israel's reliance upon God, the Psalmist
states, אֵֽלֶּה בָרֶֽכֶב וְאֵֽלֶּה בַסּוּסִים, *These [trust] in*
the chariot, and those in the horses, וַאֲנַֽחְנוּ,
but we, בְּשֵׁם ה' אֱלֹהֵֽינוּ נַזְכִּיר, *we mention the*
Name of HASHEM, *our God (Psalms 20:8).*
This *pizmon* paraphrases that verse, begin-

ning the first line of each quatrain with אֵֽלֶּה
בְּ-, *These [trust] in…;* the second line with
וְאֵֽלֶּה בְּ-, *and those in…;* and the third line
with וַאֲנַֽחְנוּ בְּ-, *but we….*

The *paytan* signed his name — שְׁלֹמֹה
הַקָּטָן, *Shlomo the lesser* — in the second letter of the second word of the respective stanzas [see prefatory comment to *Selichah* 2].

וַאֲנַחְנוּ בְּשֵׁם קָדְשְׁךָ לְהִתְעָרֵב,
but we [trust] ⟩ in the Name ⟩ of Your holiness ⟩ to be secure — 《

שׁוֹכֵן שַׁחַק לְיִשְׁעֵנוּ תִקְרָב.
O Dweller ⟩ in the heavens, ⟩ to our salvation ⟩ draw near! 《

עָזְרֵנוּ אֱלֹהֵי יִשְׁעֵנוּ, כִּי עָלֶיךָ נִשְׁעָנּוּ.
Help us, ⟩ O God ⟩ of our salvation, ⟩ for ⟩ upon You ⟩ we rely. 《

CONGREGATION, THEN *CHAZZAN*:

אֵלֶּה בְּלִגְיוֹנָם, **וְאֵלֶּה** בְּגָאוֹנָם מִתְפָּאֲרִים,
These [trust] ⟩ in their legions, 《 and those 《 in their power ⟩ take pride; 《

וַאֲנַחְנוּ בְּרַב לְהוֹשִׁיעַ מִתְגַּבְּרִים,
but we ⟩ in Him Who is abundantly ⟩ able to save ⟩ find strength, 《

לַעֲזֹר לְאֵין כֹּחַ מַכְבִּירִים.[1]
that He help ⟩ those without ⟩ power, 《 we pray fervently. 《

עָזְרֵנוּ אֱלֹהֵי יִשְׁעֵנוּ, כִּי עָלֶיךָ נִשְׁעָנּוּ.
Help us, ⟩ O God ⟩ of our salvation, 《 for ⟩ upon You ⟩ we rely. 《

CONGREGATION, THEN *CHAZZAN*:

אֵלֶּה בְּמָגִנָּתָם, **וְאֵלֶּה** בְּצִנָּתָם מִסְתַּחֲרִים,
These [trust] ⟩ in their shield, 《 and those ⟩ behind their armor ⟩ they fortify themselves; 《

וַאֲנַחְנוּ בְּאִמְרָתְךָ מַחֲס תָּרִים,
but we ⟩ in Your word ⟩ our shelter ⟩ do we see, 《

מֵרוּחַ עָרִיצִים הֱיוֹת נִסְתָּרִים.[2]
from the anger ⟩ of tyrants ⟩ we are hidden. 《

עָזְרֵנוּ אֱלֹהֵי יִשְׁעֵנוּ, כִּי עָלֶיךָ נִשְׁעָנּוּ.
Help us, ⟩ O God ⟩ of our salvation, ⟩ for 《 upon You ⟩ we rely. 《

CONGREGATION, THEN *CHAZZAN*:

אֵלֶּה בְּהַצְהָלָה* וְשֶׁעַט, **וְאֵלֶּה** בְּצַחְצוּחַ וּמַעַט,
These [trust] ⟩ in neighing [horses]* ⟩ and ⟩ and those 《 in flashing [of swords] ⟩ and [in] armor; 《 hoof-beats,

---

(1) Some editions read לַעֲזֹר לְאֵין כֹּחַ מִכַּבִּירִים, *to help those without power against the mighty [foe]*. (2) See *Radak* to *Isaiah* 25:4.

אֵלֶּה בְּהַצְהָלָה — *These [trust] in neighing [horses]*. From this point the *paytan* para- | phrases the words of a *mishnah* (*Sotah* 8:1). The Torah dictates (*Deuteronomy* 20:1-9)

וַאֲנַחְנוּ בְּאוֹר כַּשַּׂלְמָה עֹט,[1] מֵרוֹם שָׂרָם דְּכוּי בָּעַט.

and ⟨crushed⟨ their ⟨Who from ⟨⟨ dons, ⟨ like a ⟨[look] to Him⟨ but we
kicked out.   angel,   on high   garment   Who light

עֶזְרֵנוּ אֱלֹהֵי יִשְׁעֵנוּ, כִּי עָלֶיךָ נִשְׁעָנּוּ.

⟨⟨ we rely. ⟨ upon You ⟨ for ⟨⟨of our salvation, ⟨O God ⟨ Help us,

CONGREGATION, THEN *CHAZZAN:*

אֵלֶּה בְּהַגָּפַת תְּרֵסִים, וְאֵלֶּה בְּשִׁפְעַת קַלְגַּסִּים,

⟨⟨ of soldiers; ⟨ in multitudes ⟨ **and those** ⟨⟨ of shields, ⟨ in clanging ⟨**These [trust]**

וַאֲנַחְנוּ בְּמָגֵן[2] חוֹסִים בְּמָגֵן מִתְגַּיְּסִים,

⟨⟨ to those who ⟨ in the ⟨⟨ take refuge, ⟨ in the ⟨ but we
gather round Him, Shield   Shield

שׁוֹבֵר מַטֵּה גְאוֹן גַּסִּים.

⟨⟨ of the ⟨ of pride ⟨ the staff ⟨ Who
haughty.   breaks

עֶזְרֵנוּ אֱלֹהֵי יִשְׁעֵנוּ, כִּי עָלֶיךָ נִשְׁעָנּוּ.

⟨⟨ we rely. ⟨ upon You ⟨ for ⟨⟨of our salvation, ⟨O God ⟨ Help us,

CONGREGATION, THEN *CHAZZAN:*

אֵלֶּה בְּקַרְנֵי נְבָחִים, וְאֵלֶּה בְּקוֹל צֹרְחִים,

⟨⟨ of shouting; ⟨ in the ⟨ **and those** ⟨⟨ blaring, ⟨ in trumpets ⟨ **These
sound   [trust]**

וַאֲנַחְנוּ בְּקוֹלוֹ בְּמֵי שְׁבָחִים,[3]

⟨⟨ that are ⟨ is over the ⟨ in Him ⟨ but we
mighty, waters Whose voice [trust]

מְפָרֵק וּמְפוֹצֵץ סַלְעֵי צְחִיחִים.

⟨⟨ that are ⟨ boulders ⟨ and shatters ⟨Who breaks
[sun-]baked.   apart

עֶזְרֵנוּ אֱלֹהֵי יִשְׁעֵנוּ, כִּי עָלֶיךָ נִשְׁעָנּוּ.

⟨⟨ we rely. ⟨ upon You ⟨ for ⟨⟨of our salvation, ⟨O God ⟨ Help us,

(1) Cf. *Psalms* 104:2. (2) Cf. 18:31, *Proverbs* 30:5.
(3) See *Targum Yonasan / Yerushalmi* to *Exodus* 15:10.

that in the event of a war, whether defensive or offensive, the Jewish troops conscripted for service must be addressed by a *Kohen* designated for that purpose, before they enter the battle. According to the *mishnah*, that *Kohen's* charge to the troops included the statement: "Let not your heart become faint from the neighing of the horses or the flashing of the swords. Do not fear the clanging of the shields or the multitude of soldiers. Do not become terrified at the sound of trumpets nor broken from the sound of shouting. For it is Hashem, your God, Who goes with you. They come [trusting] in the triumph of flesh and blood, but you come [trusting] in the triumph of the Omnipresent ...."

CONGREGATION, THEN *CHAZZAN*:

אֵלֶּה בִטְכּוּס עֶרְכָּן, וְאֵלֶּה בְּטַכְסִיס צָרְכָן,

‹ These [trust] › in the battle-plan › array [of forces], › **and those** » in strategies ‹ » for logistics;

וַאֲנַחְנוּ בְּאֵין כְּעֶרְכּוֹ, אַרְכוֹן¹ וְאַרְכָן,

‹ but we [trust] › in the One that there is no › comparison to Him, » Ruler ‹ and Patient One,

מֵקִים מֻרְכָּן לְבָמוֹת דִּרְכָן.

‹ Who raises up › the bent over › [until on the en- emy's] high places › they tread. »

עָזְרֵנוּ אֱלֹהֵי יִשְׁעֵנוּ, כִּי עָלֶיךָ נִשְׁעָנּוּ.

‹ Help us, › O God › of our salvation, » for ‹ upon You ‹ we rely. »

CONGREGATION, THEN *CHAZZAN*:

אֵלֶּה בְּנַצְחָנֵימוֹ, וְאֵלֶּה בְּרַצְחָנֵימוֹ הַבְטַחוֹת,

‹ These [trust] › in their victories, » **and those** ‹ in their murderers › feel secure; »

וַאֲנַחְנוּ בְּשֵׁם נֵצַח יִשְׂרָאֵל כַּפֵּינוּ שְׁטוּחוֹת,

‹ but we › in the Name › of the Trium- phant One ‹ of Israel › our hands › stretch out [in prayer], »

מֵלַּעֲרֹץ וּמִלִּירָא וּמִלֵּרַךְ טוּחוֹת.²

‹ that we not let [our spirit] be broken › nor be fearful › nor be faint ‹ of heart. »

עָזְרֵנוּ אֱלֹהֵי יִשְׁעֵנוּ, כִּי עָלֶיךָ נִשְׁעָנּוּ.

‹ Help us, › O God › of our salvation, » for ‹ upon You ‹ we rely. »

ALL, WHILE STANDING:

אֵל מֶלֶךְ יוֹשֵׁב עַל כִּסֵּא רַחֲמִים, מִתְנַהֵג

‹ O God, › King ‹ Who sits › on ‹ the throne ‹ of mercy, » ‹ Who acts

בַּחֲסִידוּת, מוֹחֵל עֲוֹנוֹת עַמּוֹ, מַעֲבִיר רִאשׁוֹן רִאשׁוֹן,³

» with kindness, › Who pardons › the sins › of His people, › Who removes ‹ [sins] one › by one, »

מַרְבֶּה מְחִילָה לַחַטָּאִים וּסְלִיחָה לַפּוֹשְׁעִים, עֹשֶׂה

‹ Who abun- dantly grants › pardon › to unintentional sinners › and forgiveness ‹ to willful sinners, » ‹ Who performs

צְדָקוֹת עִם כָּל בָּשָׂר וָרוּחַ, לֹא כְּרָעָתָם תִּגְמוֹל.

‹ acts of generosity › with ‹ all ‹ [beings of] flesh › and spirit » — not ‹ in accord with their wickedness ‹ do You repay them! »

---

(1) Some editions read עֶרְכָן, but the meaning is the same; the two readings are based on two readings of *Bava Basra* 164b. (2) Cf. *Deuteronomy* 20:3. (3) *Rosh Hashanah* 17a.

❖ אֵל הוֹרֵיתָ לָּנוּ לוֹמַר שְׁלֹשׁ עֶשְׂרֵה, וּזְכוֹר לָנוּ הַיּוֹם

⟨ today ⟨ for us ⟨ remem-⟨⟨   the Thirteen   ⟨   to   ⟨ us ⟨ You ⟨ O God,
             ber   [Attributes of Mercy];   recite   taught

בְּרִית שְׁלֹשׁ עֶשְׂרֵה, כְּמוֹ שֶׁהוֹדַעְתָּ לֶעָנָיו מִקֶּדֶם,

⟨⟨ in ancient ⟨ to the humble ⟨ You made ⟨ as ⟨⟨ of [these] Thirteen, ⟨ the
   times,   one [Moses]   known   covenant

כְּמוֹ שֶׁכָּתוּב, וַיֵּרֶד יהוה בֶּעָנָן וַיִּתְיַצֵּב עִמּוֹ שָׁם,

⟨⟨ there, ⟨ with ⟨ and stood ⟨ in a ⟨ And HASHEM ⟨⟨ it is written: ⟨ as
          him   cloud   descended

וַיִּקְרָא בְשֵׁם יהוה.[1]

⟨⟨   of   ⟨ with the ⟨ and He
     HASHEM.   Name   called out

CONGREGATION, THEN *CHAZZAN*:

וַיַּעֲבֹר יהוה עַל פָּנָיו וַיִּקְרָא:

⟨⟨ and proclaimed: ⟨⟨ [Moses'] face, ⟨ before ⟨ And HASHEM passed

CONGREGATION AND *CHAZZAN* RECITE LOUDLY AND IN UNISON:

יהוה, יהוה, אֵל, רַחוּם, וְחַנּוּן, אֶרֶךְ אַפַּיִם,

⟨ to anger, ⟨ Slow ⟨⟨ and Gracious, ⟨ Compassionate ⟨ God, ⟨ HASHEM, ⟨ HASHEM,

וְרַב חֶסֶד, וֶאֱמֶת, נֹצֵר חֶסֶד לָאֲלָפִים, נֹשֵׂא עָוֹן,

⟨ of ⟨ Forgiver ⟨⟨ for thousands ⟨ of ⟨ Preserver ⟨⟨ and ⟨ in ⟨ and
iniquity,   [of generations], kindness   Truth, Kindness Abundant

וָפֶשַׁע, וְחַטָּאָה, וְנַקֵּה.[2] וְסָלַחְתָּ לַעֲוֹנֵנוּ וּלְחַטָּאתֵנוּ

⟨⟨ and our sins, ⟨ our ⟨ May You ⟨⟨ and Who ⟨ and inadvertent ⟨ willful sin,
                iniquities forgive   absolves.   sin,

וּנְחַלְתָּנוּ.[3] סְלַח לָנוּ אָבִינוּ כִּי חָטָאנוּ, מְחַל לָנוּ

⟨ us, ⟨ pardon ⟨⟨ we have ⟨ for ⟨⟨ our ⟨ us, ⟨ Forgive ⟨⟨ and make us
               sinned;   Father,   Your heritage.

מַלְכֵּנוּ כִּי פָשָׁעְנוּ. כִּי אַתָּה אֲדֹנָי טוֹב וְסַלָּח, וְרַב

⟨ and ⟨⟨ and ⟨ are ⟨ O Lord, ⟨ You, ⟨ For ⟨⟨ we have ⟨ for ⟨⟨ our King,
abundantly forgiving, good   willfully sinned.

חֶסֶד לְכָל קֹרְאֶיךָ.[4]

⟨⟨ who call upon You. ⟨ to all ⟨ kind

ALL:

זְכֹר רַחֲמֶיךָ יהוה וַחֲסָדֶיךָ, כִּי מֵעוֹלָם הֵמָּה.[5]

⟨⟨ are they. ⟨ eternal ⟨ for ⟨⟨ and Your ⟨ HASHEM, ⟨ Your mercies, ⟨ Remember
                               kindnesses,

_____
(1) *Exodus* 35:4. (2) 34:6-7. (3) 34:9. (4) *Psalms* 86:5. (5) 25:6.

זָכְרֵנוּ יהוה בִּרְצוֹן עַמֶּךָ, פָּקְדֵנוּ בִּישׁוּעָתֶךָ. ¹ זְכֹר

⟨ Re- ⟪ with Your ⟨ recall us ⟪ to Your ⟨ when You ⟨ HASHEM, ⟨ Remem-
member salvation. people; show favor ber us,

עֲדָתְךָ קָנִיתָ קֶּדֶם, גָּאַלְתָּ שֵׁבֶט נַחֲלָתֶךָ, הַר צִיּוֹן זֶה

⟨the one⟨ of ⟨ the ⟪ of Your ⟨ the ⟨ You ⟪ long ⟨ which You ⟨ Your con-
[where] Zion, mountain heritage; tribe redeemed ago, acquired gregation,

שָׁכַנְתָּ בּוֹ. ² זְכֹר יהוה חִבַּת יְרוּשָׁלַיִם, אַהֲבַת

⟨ the love ⟪ of Jerusalem; ⟨ the ⟨ HASHEM, ⟨ Remem- ⟪there. ⟨ You rested
affection ber, Your Presence

צִיּוֹן אַל תִּשְׁכַּח לָנֶצַח. ³ אַתָּה תָקוּם תְּרַחֵם צִיּוֹן כִּי

⟨for ⟪ to ⟨ and show ⟨ will arise ⟨ You ⟪ forever. ⟨ forget ⟨ do not ⟨ of
Zion, mercy Zion

עֵת לְחֶנְנָהּ, כִּי בָא מוֹעֵד. ⁴ זְכֹר יהוה לִבְנֵי אֱדוֹם

⟨ of ⟨ [to repay] ⟨ HASHEM, ⟨ Re- ⟪ the appointed time ⟨ for ⟪ [there will come]
Edom the offspring, member, will have come. the time to favor her,

אֵת יוֹם יְרוּשָׁלַיִם, הָאֹמְרִים עָרוּ עָרוּ עַד הַיְסוֹד בָּהּ. ⁵

⟪of it! ⟨ the very ⟨ to⟨ Destroy!⟪Destroy!⟪ [to repay] ⟪ of Jerusalem; ⟨ for the day
foundation those who say,

זְכֹר לְאַבְרָהָם לְיִצְחָק וּלְיִשְׂרָאֵל עֲבָדֶיךָ, אֲשֶׁר נִשְׁבַּעְתָּ

⟨ You ⟨ that ⟪ Your ⟨ and for Israel, ⟨ for Isaac, ⟨ for ⟨ Remem-
swore servants, Abraham, ber

לָהֶם בָּךְ, וַתְּדַבֵּר אֲלֵהֶם, אַרְבֶּה אֶת זַרְעֲכֶם כְּכוֹכְבֵי

⟨ like the ⟨ Your offspring ⟪ I shall ⟨ to them, ⟨ and ⟪ by Your⟨ to
stars increase You said Being, them

הַשָּׁמַיִם, וְכָל הָאָרֶץ הַזֹּאת אֲשֶׁר אָמַרְתִּי, אֶתֵּן

⟨ I will give ⟨ I spoke ⟨ of which ⟨ of this land ⟨ and all ⟪ of the heavens;

לְזַרְעֲכֶם, וְנָחֲלוּ לְעֹלָם. ⁶ זְכֹר לַעֲבָדֶיךָ לְאַבְרָהָם

⟨ of Abraham, ⟨ of Your ⟨ Remember ⟪ forever. ⟨ and they ⟨ to your
servants, [the merits] will inherit it offspring,

לְיִצְחָק וּלְיַעֲקֹב, אַל תֵּפֶן אֶל קְשִׁי הָעָם הַזֶּה וְאֶל

⟨ to ⟪ of this people, ⟨ the stub- ⟨ to ⟨ pay ⟨ do ⟪ and of Jacob; ⟨ of Isaac,
bornness attention not

רִשְׁעוֹ וְאֶל חַטָּאתוֹ. ⁷ זְכוֹר לָנוּ בְּרִית אָבוֹת, כַּאֲשֶׁר

⟨ as ⟪ of the ⟨ the ⟨ for⟨ Remember ⟪ its ⟨ and ⟪ its
Patriarchs, covenant us sinfulness. to wickedness,

---

(1) Cf. *Psalms* 106:4. (2) 74:2. (3) This is not a Scriptural verse.
(4) *Psalms* 102:14. (5) 137:7. (6) *Exodus* 32:13. (7) *Deuteronomy* 9:27.

אָמַרְתָּ: וְזָכַרְתִּי אֶת בְּרִיתִי יַעֲקוֹב, וְאַף אֶת בְּרִיתִי
‹ My covenant ‹ and also ‹‹ [with] ‹ My covenant ‹ And I will ‹‹ You said:
Jacob,   remember

יִצְחָק, וְאַף אֶת בְּרִיתִי אַבְרָהָם אֶזְכּוֹר, וְהָאָרֶץ אֶזְכּוֹר.[1]
‹‹ I will ‹ and the ‹‹ I will ‹ [with] ‹ My covenant ‹ and ‹‹ [with]
remember. Land   remember; Abraham   also   Isaac,

זְכוֹר לָנוּ בְּרִית רִאשׁוֹנִים, כַּאֲשֶׁר אָמַרְתָּ: וְזָכַרְתִּי
‹ And I will ‹‹ You said: ‹ as ‹‹ of the ‹ the ‹ for us ‹ Remember
remember   ancient ones, covenant

לָהֶם בְּרִית רִאשׁוֹנִים, אֲשֶׁר הוֹצֵאתִי אֹתָם מֵאֶרֶץ
‹ from ‹ I took them out ‹ that ‹‹ of the ‹ the ‹ for
the land   ancient ones, covenant them

מִצְרַיִם לְעֵינֵי הַגּוֹיִם, לִהְיוֹת לָהֶם לֵאלֹהִים, אֲנִי
‹ I am ‹‹ a God; ‹ to them ‹ to be ‹‹ of the ‹ in the ‹ of Egypt
nations, very sight

יהוה.[2] עֲשֵׂה עִמָּנוּ כְּמָה שֶׁהִבְטַחְתָּנוּ: וְאַף גַּם
‹ all ‹ And despite ‹‹ You promised us: ‹ as ‹ with us ‹ Do ‹‹ HASHEM.

זֹאת בִּהְיוֹתָם בְּאֶרֶץ אֹיְבֵיהֶם, לֹא מְאַסְתִּים וְלֹא
‹ nor ‹ despise them ‹ I will ‹‹ of their ‹ in the land ‹ when they ‹‹ this,
not   enemies,   will be

גְעַלְתִּים לְכַלֹּתָם לְהָפֵר בְּרִיתִי אִתָּם, כִּי אֲנִי יהוה
‹ HASHEM, ‹ I am ‹ for ‹‹ with ‹ My ‹ to annul ‹‹ to destroy ‹ abhor them
them, covenant   them,

אֱלֹהֵיהֶם.[3] הָשֵׁב שְׁבוּתֵנוּ וְרַחֲמֵנוּ, כְּמָה שֶׁכָּתוּב:
‹‹ it is ‹ as ‹‹ and have ‹ our captivity ‹ Bring ‹‹ their God.
written: mercy on us,   back

וְשָׁב יהוה אֱלֹהֶיךָ אֶת שְׁבוּתְךָ וְרִחֲמֶךָ, וְשָׁב וְקִבֶּצְךָ
‹ gather ‹ and He ‹‹ and He will ‹ your captivity, ‹ your ‹ will ‹ Then bring
you in will once have mercy   God, HASHEM, back
again   upon you,

מִכָּל הָעַמִּים אֲשֶׁר הֱפִיצְךָ יהוה אֱלֹהֶיךָ שָׁמָּה.[4]
‹‹ thereto. ‹ your God ‹ has ‹ scattered ‹ that ‹ the ‹ from
HASHEM   you   peoples   all

קַבֵּץ נִדָּחֵינוּ, כְּמָה שֶׁכָּתוּב: אִם יִהְיֶה נִדַּחֲךָ בִּקְצֵה
‹ at the ‹ your dispersed ‹ If ‹ it is written: ‹ as ‹ our ‹ Gather
ends   will be   dispersed ones,

(1) *Leviticus* 26:42. (2) 26:45. (3) 26:44. (4) 30:3.

הַשָּׁמַיִם, מִשָּׁם יְקַבֶּצְךָ יהוה אֱלֹהֶיךָ, וּמִשָּׁם יִקָּחֶךָ.[1]

‹ He will take you. ‹ and from there ‹ your God, ‹ will gather you in ‹ from there ‹ of heaven,

מְחֵה פְשָׁעֵינוּ כָעָב וְכֶעָנָן, כְּמָה שֶׁכָּתוּב: מָחִיתִי

‹ I have wiped away ‹ it is written: ‹ as ‹ and like a cloud, ‹ like a mist ‹ our sins ‹ Wipe away

כָעָב פְּשָׁעֶיךָ וְכֶעָנָן חַטֹּאתֶיךָ, שׁוּבָה אֵלַי כִּי

‹ for ‹ to Me, ‹ return ‹ your transgressions; ‹ and like a cloud ‹ your willful sins, ‹ like a mist

גְאַלְתִּיךָ.[2] מְחֵה פְשָׁעֵינוּ לְמַעֲנָךְ, כַּאֲשֶׁר אָמָרְתָּ:

‹ You have said: ‹ as ‹ for Your sake, ‹ our sins ‹ Wipe away ‹ I have redeemed you.

אָנֹכִי אָנֹכִי הוּא מֹחֶה פְשָׁעֶיךָ לְמַעֲנִי, וְחַטֹּאתֶיךָ לֹא

‹ I shall not ‹ and your transgressions ‹ for My sake, ‹ your willful sins ‹ Who wipes away ‹ am the One ‹ [only] I, ‹ I,

אֶזְכֹּר.[3] הַלְבֵּן חֲטָאֵינוּ כַּשֶּׁלֶג וְכַצֶּמֶר, כְּמָה שֶׁכָּתוּב:

‹ it is written: ‹ as ‹ and like wool, ‹ like snow ‹ our sins ‹ Whiten ‹ recall.

לְכוּ נָא וְנִוָּכְחָה, יֹאמַר יהוה, אִם יִהְיוּ חֲטָאֵיכֶם

‹ your sins may be ‹ Though ‹ HASHEM. ‹ says ‹ let us reason together, ‹ now, ‹ Come,

כַּשָּׁנִים כַּשֶּׁלֶג יַלְבִּינוּ, אִם יַאְדִּימוּ כַתּוֹלָע, כַּצֶּמֶר

‹ like [white] wool ‹ as crimson, ‹ they may be red ‹ though ‹ they will be whitened; ‹ like snow ‹ like scarlet,

יִהְיוּ.[4] זְרוֹק עָלֵינוּ מַיִם טְהוֹרִים וְטַהֲרֵנוּ, כְּמָה שֶׁכָּתוּב:

‹ it is written: ‹ as ‹ and purify us, ‹ pure water ‹ upon us ‹ Pour ‹ they will become.

וְזָרַקְתִּי עֲלֵיכֶם מַיִם טְהוֹרִים וּטְהַרְתֶּם, מִכֹּל

‹ from all ‹ and you will become pure; ‹ pure water ‹ upon you ‹ I shall pour

טֻמְאוֹתֵיכֶם וּמִכָּל גִּלּוּלֵיכֶם אֲטַהֵר אֶתְכֶם.[5] רַחֵם

‹ Have mercy ‹ you. ‹ I will purify ‹ your abominations ‹ and from all ‹ your contaminations

עָלֵינוּ וְאַל תַּשְׁחִיתֵנוּ, כְּמָה שֶׁכָּתוּב: כִּי אֵל רַחוּם

‹ a merciful God ‹ For ‹ it is written: ‹ as ‹ destroy us, ‹ and do not ‹ on us

יהוה אֱלֹהֶיךָ, לֹא יַרְפְּךָ וְלֹא יַשְׁחִיתֶךָ, וְלֹא יִשְׁכַּח

‹ will He forget ‹ nor ‹ will He destroy you, ‹ nor ‹ relinquish you ‹ He will not ‹ your God; ‹ is HASHEM,

(1) *Leviticus* 30:4. (2) *Isaiah* 44:22. (3) 43:25. (4) 1:18. (5) *Ezekiel* 36:25.

מוֹל   ¹.לָהֶם נִשְׁבַּע אֲשֶׁר אֲבֹתֶיךָ בְּרִית אֶת
⟨ Circumcise ⟪ to them. ⟨ He swore ⟨ which ⟨ with your forefathers, ⟨ the covenant

שֶׁכָּתוּב: כְּמָה שְׁמֶךָ, אֶת וּלְיִרְאָה לְאַהֲבָה לְבָבֵנוּ אֶת
⟪ it is written: ⟨ as ⟪ Your Name, ⟨ and to fear ⟨ to love ⟨ our hearts

לְאַהֲבָה זַרְעֶךָ, לְבַב וְאֶת לְבָבְךָ אֶת אֱלֹהֶיךָ יהוה וּמָל
⟨ to love ⟪ of your ⟨ and the ⟨ your heart ⟨ HASHEM, your God,
    offspring, heart   will circumcise

לְמַעַן נַפְשֶׁךָ, וּבְכָל לְבָבְךָ בְּכָל אֱלֹהֶיךָ, יהוה אֶת
⟨ so that ⟪ your soul, ⟨ and with all ⟨ your heart ⟨ with all ⟨ your God, ⟨ HASHEM,

וּבִקַּשְׁתֶּם שֶׁכָּתוּב: כְּמָה בְּבַקָּשָׁתֵנוּ, לָּנוּ הַמָּצֵא ².חַיֶּיךָ
⟨ And you ⟪ it is written: ⟨ as ⟪ in our quest, ⟨ to us ⟨ Be ⟪ you may
 will seek   accessible live.

בְּכָל תִדְרְשֶׁנּוּ כִּי וּמָצָאתָ, אֱלֹהֶיךָ יהוה אֶת מִשָּׁם
⟨ with ⟨ you search ⟨ when ⟪ and you will ⟨ your God, ⟨ HASHEM, ⟨ from
 all Him out   find [Him],   there

קָדְשֶׁךָ, הַר אֶל תְּבִיאֵנוּ ∻³.נַפְשֶׁךָ וּבְכָל לְבָבְךָ
⟨ Your holy mountain ⟨ to ⟨ Bring us ⟪ your soul. ⟨ and with all ⟨ your heart

וַהֲבִיאוֹתִים שֶׁכָּתוּב: כְּמָה תְּפִלָּתֶךָ, בְּבֵית וְשַׂמְּחֵנוּ
⟨ And I will bring them ⟪ it is written: ⟨ as ⟪ of Prayer, ⟨ in Your House ⟨ and gladden us

עוֹלֹתֵיהֶם תְּפִלָּתִי, בְּבֵית וְשִׂמַּחְתִּים קָדְשִׁי, הַר אֶל
⟨ their burnt- ⟪ of Prayer; ⟨ in My ⟨ and I will ⟪ My holy ⟨ to
 offerings   House gladden them mountain,

תְּפִלָּה בֵית בֵיתִי כִּי מִזְבְּחִי, עַל לְרָצוֹן וְזִבְחֵיהֶם
⟨ of ⟨ "a ⟨ My ⟨ for ⟪ My Altar, ⟨ on ⟨ will find ⟨ and their feast-
 Prayer" House House   favor offerings

⁴.הָעַמִּים לְכָל יִקָּרֵא
⟪ nations. ⟨ for all ⟨ will be called

THE ARK IS OPENED.

CHAZZAN, THEN CONGREGATION:

עָלֵינוּ, וְרַחֵם חוּס אֱלֹהֵינוּ, יהוה **קוֹלֵנוּ** **שְׁמַע**
⟪ on us, ⟨ and have ⟨ have ⟪ our God; ⟨ HASHEM, ⟨ our voice, ⟨ Hear
   compassion pity

⁵.תְּפִלָּתֵנוּ אֶת וּבְרָצוֹן בְּרַחֲמִים וְקַבֵּל
⟪ our prayer. ⟨ and favor ⟨ with compassion ⟨ and accept

(1) *Deuteronomy* 4:31. (2) 30:6. (3) 4:29. (4) *Isaiah* 56:7. (5) From the weekday *Shemoneh Esrei*.

CHAZZAN, THEN CONGREGATION:

הֲשִׁיבֵנוּ יהוה אֵלֶיךָ וְנָשׁוּבָה, חַדֵּשׁ יָמֵינוּ כְּקֶדֶם.[1]

《 as of old. ‹ our ‹ renew 《 and we shall ‹ to You, ‹ HASHEM, ‹Bring us back,
days return,

CHAZZAN, THEN CONGREGATION:

אֲמָרֵינוּ הַאֲזִינָה יהוה, בִּינָה הֲגִיגֵנוּ.[2]

《 our thoughts. ‹ perceive 《 HASHEM; ‹ hear, ‹ Our words

THE FOLLOWING VERSE IS RECITED QUIETLY:

יִהְיוּ לְרָצוֹן אִמְרֵי פִינוּ וְהֶגְיוֹן לִבֵּנוּ לְפָנֶיךָ,

《 before 《 of our ‹ and the ‹ of our ‹ — the ex- 《 find ‹ May
You, heart — thoughts mouth pressions favor they

יהוה צוּרֵנוּ וְגֹאֲלֵנוּ.[3]

《 and our ‹ our Rock ‹ HASHEM,
Redeemer.

CHAZZAN, THEN CONGREGATION:

אַל תַּשְׁלִיכֵנוּ מִלְּפָנֶיךָ, וְרוּחַ קָדְשְׁךָ אַל תִּקַּח מִמֶּנּוּ.[4]

《 from us. ‹ take ‹ do ‹ of Your ‹ and the 《 from Your ‹ cast us away ‹ Do
not Holiness Spirit Presence, not

CHAZZAN, THEN CONGREGATION:

אַל תַּשְׁלִיכֵנוּ לְעֵת זִקְנָה, כִּכְלוֹת כֹּחֵנוּ אַל תַּעַזְבֵנוּ.[5]

《 forsake us not. ‹ does our ‹ when fail 《 of old ‹ in time ‹ cast us away ‹ Do
strength, age; not

ALL CONTINUE (SOME CONGREGATIONS RECITE THE NEXT VERSE RESPONSIVELY):

אַל תַּעַזְבֵנוּ יהוה, אֱלֹהֵינוּ אַל תִּרְחַק מִמֶּנּוּ.[6]

《 from us. ‹ be not distant ‹ our God, 《 O HASHEM; ‹ Forsake us not,

עֲשֵׂה עִמָּנוּ אוֹת לְטוֹבָה, וְיִרְאוּ שׂוֹנְאֵינוּ וְיֵבֹשׁוּ,

《 and be ‹ may our ‹ so that 《 for good; ‹ a sign ‹ for us ‹ Display
ashamed, enemies see it

כִּי אַתָּה יהוה עֲזַרְתָּנוּ וְנִחַמְתָּנוּ.[7] כִּי לְךָ יהוה

‹ HASHEM, ‹ for ‹ Because 《 and ‹ will have ‹ HASHEM, ‹ You, ‹ for
You, consoled us. helped us

הוֹחָלְנוּ, אַתָּה תַעֲנֶה אֲדֹנָי אֱלֹהֵינוּ.[8]

《 our God. ‹ O Lord, ‹ will answer, ‹ You 《 do we wait;

THE ARK IS CLOSED.

(1) *Lamentations* 5:21. (2) Cf. *Psalms* 5:2. (3) Cf. 19:15.
(4) 51:13. (5) Cf. 71:9. (6) Cf. 38:22. (7) Cf. 86:17. (8) Cf. 38:16.

EACH INDIVIDUAL CONTINUES UNTIL THE END OF SELICHOS.

CONFESSION / וִדּוּי

**DURING THE RECITATION OF THE וִדּוּי, CONFESSION, STAND WITH
HEAD AND BODY SLIGHTLY BOWED, IN SUBMISSIVE CONTRITION.**

אֱלֹהֵינוּ וֵאלֹהֵי אֲבוֹתֵינוּ, תָּבֹא לְפָנֶיךָ תְּפִלָּתֵנוּ,¹

⟪ may our ⟨ before ⟨ come ⟪ of our ⟨ and the ⟨ Our God
prayer, You forefathers, God

וְאַל תִּתְעַלַּם מִתְּחִנָּתֵנוּ,² שֶׁאֵין אָנוּ עַזֵּי פָנִים

⟨ faced ⟨ so brazen- ⟨ For we are not ⟪ our supplication. ⟨ ignore ⟨ and do not

וּקְשֵׁי עֹרֶף, לוֹמַר לְפָנֶיךָ יהוה אֱלֹהֵינוּ וֵאלֹהֵי

⟨ and the God ⟨ our God, ⟨ Hashem, ⟪ before You, ⟨ as to say ⟨ necked ⟨ and stiff-

אֲבוֹתֵינוּ, צַדִּיקִים אֲנַחְנוּ וְלֹא חָטָאנוּ, אֲבָל

⟪—for indeed, ⟪ sinned ⟨ and have not ⟨ we are, ⟨ that righteous ⟪of our forefathers,

אֲנַחְנוּ וַאֲבוֹתֵינוּ חָטָאנוּ.³

⟪ have sinned. ⟨ and our forefathers ⟨ we

**STRIKE THE LEFT SIDE OF THE CHEST WITH THE RIGHT FIST WHILE RECITING
EACH OF THE SINS OF THE FOLLOWING CONFESSIONAL LITANY:**

אָשַׁמְנוּ, בָּגַדְנוּ, גָּזַלְנוּ, דִּבַּרְנוּ דֹּפִי. הֶעֱוִינוּ,

⟪ We have com- ⟪ slander. ⟨ we have ⟪ we have ⟪ we have ⟪ We have been
mitted iniquity; spoken robbed; betrayed; guilty;

וְהִרְשַׁעְנוּ, זַדְנוּ, חָמַסְנוּ, טָפַלְנוּ שֶׁקֶר. יָעַצְנוּ

⟨ We have ⟪ false ⟨ we have ⟪ we have ⟪we have sinned ⟪we have commit-
given advice accusations. made extorted; willfully; ted wickedness;

רָע, כִּזַּבְנוּ, לַצְנוּ, מָרַדְנוּ, נִאַצְנוּ, סָרַרְנוּ,

⟪ we have ⟪ we have provoked ⟪ we have ⟪ we have ⟪ we have been ⟨ that is
strayed; [God's anger]; rebelled; scorned; deceitful; bad;

עָוִינוּ, פָּשַׁעְנוּ, צָרַרְנוּ, קִשִּׁינוּ עֹרֶף. רָשַׁעְנוּ,

⟪ We have ⟪ our ⟨ we have ⟪ we have caused ⟪ we have sinned ⟪we have been
been wicked; necks. stiffened distress; rebelliously; iniquitous;

שִׁחַתְנוּ, תִּעַבְנוּ, תָּעִינוּ, תִּעְתָּעְנוּ.

⟪ we have ⟪ we have ⟪ we have ⟪ we have
scoffed. gone astray; committed been corrupt;
abominations;

סַרְנוּ מִמִּצְוֹתֶיךָ וּמִמִּשְׁפָּטֶיךָ הַטּוֹבִים, וְלֹא שָׁוָה

⟨ worth- ⟨ and it ⟪ that are ⟨ and from ⟨ from Your ⟨ We have
while was not good, Your laws commandments turned away

---

(1) Cf. *Psalms* 88:3. (2) Cf. 55:2. (3) Cf. 106:6, *Jeremiah* 3:25.

כִּי עָלֵינוּ, כָּל הַבָּא עַל צַדִּיק וְאַתָּה לָנוּ.[1]

‹ for ‹‹ upon us, ‹ that has come ‹ all ‹ in ‹are righteous ‹ And You ‹‹ for us.

אֱמֶת עָשִׂיתָ וַאֲנַחְנוּ הִרְשָׁעְנוּ.[2]

‹‹ have acted wickedly. ‹ while we ‹‹ have You acted, ‹ truthfully

מִמֶּנּוּ גָּלָה דּוֹר, מִכָּל בְּשְׁנוּ עָם, מִכָּל אָשַׁמְנוּ

‹ from us ‹ Departed ‹‹ genera- tion. ‹ more than any other ‹ We have been ashamed ‹‹ people. ‹ more than any other ‹ We have been guilty

וְנִפְרַע אֲוִיֵּנוּ הֶחֱבַּל בַּחֲטָאֵינוּ לִבֵּנוּ דָּוָה מָשׂוֹשׂ,

‹ uncov- ered ‹‹ was our de- sired [Temple], ‹ Seized ‹‹ because of our sins. ‹ is our heart ‹ Sickened ‹ has joy.

טִירָתֵנוּ בַּעֲוֹנֵינוּ חָרַב מִקְדָּשֵׁנוּ בֵּית זְבוּל פְּאֵרֵנוּ,

‹ Our Palace ‹‹ because of our iniquities. ‹ has been destroyed ‹ our Holy Temple ‹ for [His] abode, ‹‹ was our splendor;

לְנָכְרִים. כֹּחֵנוּ לְזָרִים, אַדְמָתֵנוּ יְפִי לְשַׁמָּה, הָיְתָה

‹‹ [was given] to foreigners. ‹ our wealth ‹‹ is controlled by strangers, ‹ of our Land ‹ [Jerusalem,] ‹‹ desolate. ‹ the beauty ‹ has become

וְנִקְשֶׁה פָּנֵינוּ נָעִיז וְהֵיךְ מִטָּעוּתֵנוּ שַׁבְנוּ לֹא וַעֲדַיִן

‹ and stiffen ‹ faced ‹ can we be so brazen- ‹ So how ‹‹ from our willful errors. ‹ we have not repented ‹ But still

אֲבוֹתֵינוּ, וֵאלֹהֵי אֱלֹהֵינוּ יהוה לְפָנֶיךָ לוֹמַר עׇרְפֵּנוּ,

‹‹ of our forefathers, ‹ and the God ‹ our God ‹ HASHEM, ‹ before You, ‹ so as to say ‹ our neck

וַאֲבוֹתֵינוּ אֲנַחְנוּ אֲבָל חָטָאנוּ, וְלֹא אֲנַחְנוּ צַדִּיקִים

‹ and our fathers ‹ both we ‹ for in truth, ‹‹ and we have not sinned, ‹‹ we are ‹ that righteous

חָטָאנוּ.[3]

‹‹ have sinned.

STRIKE THE LEFT SIDE OF THE CHEST WITH THE RIGHT FIST WHILE RECITING EACH OF THE SINS OF THE FOLLOWING CONFESSIONAL LITANY:

הֶעֱוִינוּ. דֹּפִי. דִּבַּרְנוּ גָּזַלְנוּ, בָּגַדְנוּ, אָשַׁמְנוּ,

‹‹ We have com- mitted iniquity; ‹‹ slander. ‹ we have spoken ‹‹ we have robbed; ‹‹ we have betrayed; ‹‹ We have been guilty;

יָעַצְנוּ שֶׁקֶר. טָפַלְנוּ חָמַסְנוּ, זַדְנוּ, וְהִרְשָׁעְנוּ,

‹ We have given advice ‹‹ false accusations. ‹ we have made ‹‹ we have extorted; ‹‹ we have sinned willfully; ‹‹ we have commit- ted wickedness;

(1) Cf. Job 33:27. (2) Nehemiah 9:33. (3) Cf. Psalms 106:6; Jeremiah 3:25.

רָע, כִּזַּבְנוּ, לַצְנוּ, מָרַדְנוּ, נִאַצְנוּ, סָרַרְנוּ,

《 we have strayed; 《 we have provoked [God's anger]; 《 we have rebelled; 《 we have scorned; 《 we have been deceitful; 《 that is bad;

עָוִינוּ, פָּשַׁעְנוּ, צָרַרְנוּ, קִשִּׁינוּ עֹרֶף. רָשַׁעְנוּ,

《 We have been wicked; 《 our necks. ‹ we have stiffened 《 we have caused distress; 《 we have sinned rebelliously; 《 we have been iniquitous;

שִׁחַתְנוּ, תִּעַבְנוּ, תָּעִינוּ, תִּעְתָּעְנוּ.

《 we have scoffed. 《 we have gone astray; 《 we have committed abominations; 《 we have been corrupt;

סַרְנוּ מִמִּצְוֹתֶיךָ וּמִמִּשְׁפָּטֶיךָ הַטּוֹבִים, וְלֹא שָׁוָה

‹ worth-while ‹ and it was not 《 that are good, ‹ and from Your laws ‹ from Your commandments ‹ We have turned away

לָנוּ.[1] וְאַתָּה צַדִּיק עַל כָּל הַבָּא עָלֵינוּ, כִּי אֱמֶת

‹ truth-fully ‹ for 《 upon us, ‹ that has come ‹ all ‹ in ‹ are righteous ‹ And You 《 for us.

עָשִׂיתָ וַאֲנַחְנוּ הִרְשָׁעְנוּ.[2]

《 have acted wickedly. ‹ while we 《 have You acted,

לְעֵינֵינוּ עָשְׁקוּ עֲמָלֵנוּ, מִמְּשָׁךְ וּמְמוֹרָט מִמֶּנּוּ,

《 from us. ‹ and cut off ‹ [it was] pulled away 《 the product of our labor; ‹ have they stolen ‹ Before our eyes

נָתְנוּ עֹלָם עָלֵינוּ, סָבַלְנוּ עַל שִׁכְמֵנוּ, עֲבָדִים

‹ Slaves 《 our shoulders. ‹ upon ‹ we bore it ‹ upon us, ‹ their yoke ‹ They have placed

מָשְׁלוּ בָנוּ, פֹּרֵק אֵין מִיָּדָם, צָרוֹת רַבּוֹת

‹ that are manifold ‹ Troubles 《 from their hand. there was not ‹ a redeemer 《 over us; ‹ have ruled

סְבָבוּנוּ, קְרָאנוּךָ יהוה אֱלֹהֵינוּ, רָחַקְתָּ מִמֶּנּוּ

‹ from us ‹ but You have dis-tanced Yourself 《 our God, ‹ HASHEM, ‹ we called upon You, 《 have surrounded us,

בַּעֲוֺנֵינוּ, שַׁבְנוּ מֵאַחֲרֶיךָ, תָּעִינוּ וְאָבָדְנוּ.

《 we have become lost. 《 we have gone astray; 《 from following after You; ‹ We have turned away 《 because of our iniquities.

---

(1) Cf. Job 33:27. (2) Nehemiah 9:33.

וַעֲדַיִן לֹא שַׁבְנוּ מִטָּעוּתֵנוּ וְהֵיךְ נָעִיז פָּנֵינוּ וְנַקְשֶׁה

‹ and ‹ faced ‹ can we be ‹ So ≪ from our ‹ we have not ‹ But still
stiffen so brazen- how willful errors. repented

עָרְפֵּנוּ, לוֹמַר לְפָנֶיךָ יהוה אֱלֹהֵינוּ וֵאלֹהֵי אֲבוֹתֵינוּ,

≪ of our ‹ and the ‹ our God ‹ HASHEM, ‹ before ‹ so as to ‹ our neck
forefathers, God You, say

צַדִּיקִים אֲנַחְנוּ וְלֹא חָטָאנוּ, אֲבָל אֲנַחְנוּ וַאֲבוֹתֵינוּ

‹ and our ‹ both we ‹ for in ≪ and we have ≪ we are ‹ that
fathers truth, not sinned, righteous

חָטָאנוּ.[1]

≪ have sinned.

**STRIKE THE LEFT SIDE OF THE CHEST WITH THE RIGHT FIST WHILE RECITING
EACH OF THE SINS OF THE FOLLOWING CONFESSIONAL LITANY:**

אָשַׁמְנוּ, בָּגַדְנוּ, גָּזַלְנוּ, דִּבַּרְנוּ דְפִי. הֶעֱוִינוּ,

≪ We have com- ≪ slander. ‹ we have ≪ we have ≪ we have ≪ We have been
mitted iniquity; spoken robbed; betrayed; guilty;

וְהִרְשַׁעְנוּ, זַדְנוּ, חָמַסְנוּ, טָפַלְנוּ שֶׁקֶר. יָעַצְנוּ

‹ We have ≪ false ‹ we have ≪ we have ≪ we have sinned ≪ we have commit-
given advice accusations. made extorted; willfully; ted wickedness;

רָע, כִּזַּבְנוּ, לַצְנוּ, מָרַדְנוּ, נִאַצְנוּ, סָרַרְנוּ,

≪ we have ≪ we have provoked ≪ we have ≪ we have ≪ we have been ‹ that is
strayed; [God's anger]; rebelled; scorned; deceitful; bad;

עָוִינוּ, פָּשַׁעְנוּ, צָרַרְנוּ, קִשִּׁינוּ עֹרֶף. רָשַׁעְנוּ,

≪ We have ≪ our ‹ we have ≪ we have caused ≪ we have sinned ≪ we have been
been wicked; necks. stiffened distress; rebelliously; iniquitous;

שִׁחַתְנוּ, תִּעַבְנוּ, תָּעִינוּ, תִּעְתָּעְנוּ.

≪ we have ≪ we have ≪ we have commit- ≪ we have
scoffed. gone astray; ted abominations; been corrupt;

סַרְנוּ מִמִּצְוֹתֶיךָ וּמִמִּשְׁפָּטֶיךָ הַטּוֹבִים, וְלֹא שָׁוָה

‹ worth- ‹ and it ≪ that are ‹ and from ‹ from Your ‹ We have
while was not good, Your laws commandments turned away

לָנוּ.[2] וְאַתָּה צַדִּיק עַל כָּל הַבָּא עָלֵינוּ, כִּי אֱמֶת

‹ truth- ‹ for ≪ upon us, ‹ that has ‹ all ‹ in ‹ are ‹ And You ≪ for us.
fully come righteous

עָשִׂיתָ וַאֲנַחְנוּ הִרְשָׁעְנוּ.[3]

≪ have acted wickedly. ‹ while we ≪ have You acted,

---

(1) Cf. *Psalms* 106:6; *Jeremiah* 3:25. (2) Cf. *Job* 33:27. (3) *Nehemiah* 9:33.

הִרְשַׁעְנוּ וּפָשַׁעְנוּ, לָכֵן לֹא נוֹשָׁעְנוּ. וְתֵן בְּלִבֵּנוּ

‹ in our ‹ Place ‹‹ been ‹ we have ‹ there- ‹‹ and we ‹ We have acted
hearts saved. not fore have sinned wickedly
rebelliously;

לַעֲזוֹב דֶּרֶךְ רֶשַׁע, וְחִישׁ לָנוּ יֶשַׁע, כַּכָּתוּב עַל יַד

‹ the ‹ by ‹ as it is ‹‹ salvation; ‹ to us ‹ and ‹‹ of ‹ the ‹ [the will]
hand written hasten wickedness, path to abandon

נְבִיאֶךָ: יַעֲזֹב רָשָׁע דַּרְכּוֹ, וְאִישׁ אָוֶן מַחְשְׁבֹתָיו,

‹‹ [abandon] ‹ of ‹ and ‹‹ his way, ‹ the wicked ‹ Let ‹‹ of Your
his thoughts; iniquity the man one abandon prophet:

וְיָשֹׁב אֶל יהוה וִירַחֲמֵהוּ, וְאֶל אֱלֹהֵינוּ כִּי

‹ for ‹ our God, ‹ and to ‹‹ and He will have ‹ HASHEM, ‹ to ‹ and let
compassion on him, him return

יַרְבֶּה לִסְלוֹחַ.[1]

‹‹ forgiving. ‹ He is
abundantly

מְשִׁיחַ צִדְקֶךָ אָמַר לְפָנֶיךָ, שְׁגִיאוֹת מִי יָבִין,

‹‹ can ‹ who ‹ Mistakes ‹‹ before You: ‹ said ‹ who is righteous ‹ Your
discern? [David] anointed one

מִנִּסְתָּרוֹת נַקֵּנִי.[2] נַקֵּנוּ יהוה אֱלֹהֵינוּ מִכָּל פְּשָׁעֵינוּ,

‹ our sins ‹ of all ‹ our God, ‹ HASHEM, ‹ Cleanse ‹‹ cleanse ‹ From
us, me. unperceived faults

וְטַהֲרֵנוּ מִכָּל טֻמְאוֹתֵינוּ, וּזְרוֹק עָלֵינוּ מַיִם טְהוֹרִים

‹ pure water ‹ upon us ‹ Pour ‹‹ our contaminations. ‹ of all ‹ and purify us

וְטַהֲרֵנוּ, כַּכָּתוּב עַל יַד נְבִיאֶךָ: וְזָרַקְתִּי עֲלֵיכֶם

‹ upon you ‹ I shall pour ‹‹ of Your ‹ the ‹ by ‹ as it is ‹‹ and purify us,
prophet: hand written

מַיִם טְהוֹרִים וּטְהַרְתֶּם, מִכֹּל טֻמְאוֹתֵיכֶם וּמִכָּל

‹ and ‹ your ‹ from ‹‹ and you will ‹ pure water
from all contaminations all become pure;

גִּלּוּלֵיכֶם אֲטַהֵר אֶתְכֶם.[3] עַמְּךָ וְנַחֲלָתֶךָ, רְעֵבֵי

‹ who ‹‹ and Your ‹ Your ‹‹ you. ‹ I will purify ‹ your
hunger heritage, people abominations

טוּבְךָ, צְמֵאֵי חַסְדֶּךָ, תְּאֵבֵי יִשְׁעֶךָ, יַכִּירוּ וְיֵדְעוּ

‹ and ‹ — may they ‹‹ for Your ‹ and ‹‹ for Your ‹ who ‹‹ for Your
know recognize salvation who long kindness, thirst goodness,

(1) *Isaiah* 55:7. (2) *Psalms* 19:13. (3) *Ezekiel* 36:25.

כִּי לַיהוה אֱלֹהֵינוּ הָרַחֲמִים וְהַסְּלִיחוֹת.

《 and forgiveness. 〈 belong mercy 〈 our God, 〈 to Hashem, 〈 that

אֵל רַחוּם שְׁמֶךָ, אֵל חַנּוּן שְׁמֶךָ, בָּנוּ נִקְרָא שְׁמֶךָ.[2]

《 is Your Name 〈 upon 《 is Your 〈 *Gracious God* 《 is Your 〈 *Merciful God*
proclaimed, us Name, Name.

יהוה עֲשֵׂה לְמַעַן שְׁמֶךָ,[3] עֲשֵׂה לְמַעַן אֲמִתֶּךָ, עֲשֵׂה

〈 act 《 Your truth; 〈 for the 〈 Act 〈 Your 〈 for the 〈 act 〈 Hashem,
sake of Name. sake of

לְמַעַן בְּרִיתֶךָ, עֲשֵׂה לְמַעַן גָּדְלְךָ וְתִפְאַרְתֶּךָ, עֲשֵׂה

〈 act 《 and Your 〈 Your 〈 for the 〈 act 《 Your 〈 for the
splendor; greatness sake of covenant; sake of

לְמַעַן דָּתֶךָ, עֲשֵׂה לְמַעַן הוֹדֶךָ, עֲשֵׂה לְמַעַן וְעוּדֶךָ,

《Your Meet- 〈 act 〈 Your 〈 for the 〈 act 《 Your 〈 for the
ing House; sake of glory; sake of Law; sake of

עֲשֵׂה לְמַעַן זִכְרְךָ,[4] עֲשֵׂה לְמַעַן חַסְדֶּךָ, עֲשֵׂה לְמַעַן

〈 for the 〈 act 《 Your 〈 for the 〈 act 《 Your 〈 for the 〈 act
sake of kindness; sake of remembrance; sake of

טוּבֶךָ, עֲשֵׂה לְמַעַן יִחוּדֶךָ, עֲשֵׂה לְמַעַן כְּבוֹדֶךָ, עֲשֵׂה

〈 act 《 Your 〈 for the 〈 act 《 Your 〈 for the 〈 act 《 Your
honor; sake of Oneness; sake of goodness;

לְמַעַן **לִמּוּדֶךָ**,[6] עֲשֵׂה לְמַעַן **מַלְכוּתֶךָ**, עֲשֵׂה לְמַעַן

〈 for the 〈 act 《 Your kingship; 〈 for the 〈 act 《 Your 〈 for the
sake of sake of students; sake of

נִצְחֶךָ, עֲשֵׂה לְמַעַן **סוֹדֶךָ**,[7] עֲשֵׂה לְמַעַן **עֶזָּךְ**, עֲשֵׂה

〈 act 《 Your 〈 for the 〈 act 《Your secret [re- 〈 for the 〈 act 《 Your eternal
power; sake of vealed to those sake of [Name];
who fear You];

לְמַעַן **פְּאֵרְךָ**, עֲשֵׂה לְמַעַן **צִדְקָתֶךָ**, עֲשֵׂה לְמַעַן

〈 for the 〈 act 《 Your 〈 for the 〈 act 《 Your 〈 for the
sake of righteousness; sake of glory; sake of

קְדֻשָּׁתֶךָ, עֲשֵׂה לְמַעַן **רַחֲמֶיךָ הָרַבִּים**, עֲשֵׂה לְמַעַן

〈 for the 〈 act 《 that is 〈 Your mercy 〈 for the 〈 act 《 Your sanctity;
sake of abundant; sake of

שְׁכִינָתֶךָ, עֲשֵׂה לְמַעַן **תְּהִלָּתֶךָ**, עֲשֵׂה לְמַעַן **אוֹהֲבֶיךָ**

〈 those who 〈 for the 〈 act 《 Your praise; 〈 for the 〈 act 《 Your Divine
loved You sake of sake of Presence;

---

(1) Cf. *Exodus* 34:6. (2) Cf. *Deuteronomy* 28:10. (3) *Jeremiah* 14:7.
(4) Cf. *Exodus* 3:15. (5) *Psalms* 6:5. (6) Cf. *Isaiah* 54:13. (7) Cf. *Psalms* 25:14.

שׁוֹכְנֵי עָפָר,¹ עֲשֵׂה לְמַעַן אַבְרָהָם יִצְחָק וְיַעֲקֹב,
‹‹ and Jacob; ‹ Isaac, ‹ Abraham, ‹ for the sake of ‹ act ‹‹ in the dust; ‹ who rest

עֲשֵׂה לְמַעַן מֹשֶׁה וְאַהֲרֹן, עֲשֵׂה לְמַעַן דָּוִד וּשְׁלֹמֹה,
‹‹ and Solomon; ‹ David ‹ for the sake of ‹ act ‹‹ and Aaron; ‹ Moses ‹ for the sake of ‹ act

עֲשֵׂה לְמַעַן יְרוּשָׁלַיִם עִיר קָדְשֶׁךָ,² עֲשֵׂה לְמַעַן צִיּוֹן
‹ Zion, ‹ for the sake of ‹ act ‹‹ of Your Holiness; ‹ the City ‹ Jerusalem, ‹ for the sake of ‹ act

מִשְׁכַּן כְּבוֹדֶךָ,³ עֲשֵׂה לְמַעַן שִׁמְמוֹת הֵיכָלֶךָ⁴ עֲשֵׂה
‹ act ‹‹ of Your Temple; ‹ the desolation ‹ for the sake of ‹ act ‹‹ of Your glory; ‹ the abode

לְמַעַן הֲרִיסוּת⁵ מִזְבְּחֶךָ, עֲשֵׂה לְמַעַן הַהֲרוּגִים עַל
‹ for ‹ those killed ‹ for the sake of ‹ act ‹‹ of Your Altar; ‹ the devastation ‹ for the sake of

שֵׁם קָדְשֶׁךָ, עֲשֵׂה לְמַעַן טְבוּחִים עַל יִחוּדֶךָ, עֲשֵׂה
‹ act ‹‹ Your Oneness; ‹ for ‹ those slaughtered ‹ for the sake of ‹ act ‹‹ Your holy Name;

לְמַעַן בָּאֵי בָאֵשׁ וּבַמַּיִם עַל קִדּוּשׁ שְׁמֶךָ, עֲשֵׂה לְמַעַן
‹ for the sake of ‹ act ‹‹ of Your Name; sanctification ‹ the ‹ for ‹ and water ‹ fire ‹ those who entered ‹ for the sake of

יוֹנְקֵי שָׁדַיִם⁶ שֶׁלֹּא חָטָאוּ, עֲשֵׂה לְמַעַן גְּמוּלֵי חָלָב,⁷
‹ from ‹ the [babies] ‹ for the sake of ‹ act ‹‹ sin; ‹ who did not ‹ at the breast ‹ the [infants] sucking
milk weaned

שֶׁלֹּא פָשָׁעוּ, עֲשֵׂה לְמַעַן תִּינוֹקוֹת שֶׁל בֵּית רַבָּן,⁸
‹‹ their teachers' school; ‹ of ‹ the children ‹ for the sake of ‹ act ‹‹ transgress; ‹ who did not

עֲשֵׂה לְמַעַנְךָ אִם לֹא לְמַעֲנֵנוּ, עֲשֵׂה לְמַעַנְךָ וְהוֹשִׁיעֵנוּ.
‹‹ and save us. ‹ for Your sake ‹ act ‹‹ for our sake; ‹ not ‹ if ‹ for Your sake ‹ act

עֲנֵנוּ יהוה עֲנֵנוּ, עֲנֵנוּ אֱלֹהֵינוּ עֲנֵנוּ, עֲנֵנוּ אָבִינוּ⁹
‹ our Father, ‹ answer us, ‹‹ answer us; ‹ our God, ‹ answer us, ‹‹ answer us; ‹ HASHEM, ‹ Answer us;

עֲנֵנוּ, עֲנֵנוּ **בּוֹרְאֵנוּ**¹⁰ עֲנֵנוּ, עֲנֵנוּ **גּוֹאֲלֵנוּ**¹¹ עֲנֵנוּ, עֲנֵנוּ
‹ answer us, ‹‹ answer us; ‹ our Redeemer, ‹ answer us, ‹‹ answer us; ‹ our Creator, ‹ answer us, ‹‹ answer us;

(1) *Isaiah* 26:19. (2) Cf. *Daniel* 9:16,24. (3) *Psalms* 26:8. (4) Cf. *Jeremiah* 51:26. (5) Cf. *Isaiah* 49:19.
(6) *Joel* 2:16. (7) *Isaiah* 28:9. (8) *Shabbos* 119b. (9) *Isaiah* 64:7. (10) Cf. 43:1. (11) 47:4.

דּוֹרְשֵׁנוּ¹ עֲנֵנוּ, עֲנֵנוּ הָאֵל הַנֶּאֱמָן² עֲנֵנוּ, עֲנֵנוּ וָתִיק

⟨ stead-fast ⟨ answer us, ⟪ answer us; ⟨ Who is faithful, ⟨ God ⟨ answer us, ⟪ answer us; ⟨ You Who searches us out,

וְחָסִיד עֲנֵנוּ, עֲנֵנוּ זַךְ³ וְיָשָׁר עֲנֵנוּ, עֲנֵנוּ חַי וְקַיָּם⁴

⟨ and endur-ing One, ⟨ living One ⟨ answer us, ⟪ answer us; ⟨ and upright One ⟨ pure ⟨ answer us, ⟪ answer us; ⟨ and kind One,

עֲנֵנוּ, עֲנֵנוּ טוֹב וּמֵטִיב⁵ עֲנֵנוּ, עֲנֵנוּ יוֹדֵעַ יֵצֶר⁶ עֲנֵנוּ,

⟪ answer us; ⟨ of incli-nations, ⟨ Knower ⟨ answer us, ⟪ answer us; ⟨ and bene-ficent One, ⟨ good ⟨ answer us, ⟪ answer us;

עֲנֵנוּ כּוֹבֵשׁ כְּעָסִים עֲנֵנוּ, עֲנֵנוּ לוֹבֵשׁ צְדָקוֹת⁷ עֲנֵנוּ,

⟪ answer us; ⟨ of righteousness, ⟨ Donner ⟨ answer us, ⟪ answer us; ⟨ of wrath, ⟨ Suppressor ⟨ answer us,

עֲנֵנוּ מֶלֶךְ מַלְכֵי הַמְּלָכִים⁸ עֲנֵנוּ, עֲנֵנוּ נוֹרָא וְנִשְׂגָּב⁹

⟨ and power-ful One, ⟨ awesome ⟨ answer us, ⟪ answer us; ⟨ of kings, ⟨ over kings ⟨ King ⟨ answer us,

עֲנֵנוּ, עֲנֵנוּ סוֹלֵחַ וּמוֹחֵל עֲנֵנוּ, עֲנֵנוּ עוֹנֶה בְּעֵת

⟨ in time ⟨ You Who answers ⟨ answer us, ⟪ answer us; ⟨ and pardons, ⟨ You Who forgives ⟨ answer us, ⟪ answer us;

צָרָה¹⁰ עֲנֵנוּ, עֲנֵנוּ פּוֹדֶה וּמַצִּיל¹¹ עֲנֵנוּ, עֲנֵנוּ צַדִּיק

⟨ righteous ⟨ answer us, ⟪ answer us; ⟨ and Rescuer, ⟨ Redeemer ⟨ answer us, ⟪ answer us; ⟨ of distress,

וְיָשָׁר¹² עֲנֵנוּ, עֲנֵנוּ קָרוֹב לְקוֹרְאָיו¹³ עֲנֵנוּ, עֲנֵנוּ קָשֶׁה

⟨ You Who with difficulty ⟨ answer us, ⟪ answer us; ⟨ to those who call upon Him, ⟨ He Who is close ⟨ answer us, ⟪ answer us; ⟨ and up-right One,

לִכְעוֹס¹⁴ עֲנֵנוּ, עֲנֵנוּ רַךְ לִרְצוֹת¹⁵ עֲנֵנוּ, עֲנֵנוּ רַחוּם

⟨ merciful ⟨ answer us, ⟪ answer us; ⟨ appeased, ⟨ You Who are easily ⟨ answer us, ⟪ answer us; ⟨ becomes angry,

וְחַנּוּן¹⁶ עֲנֵנוּ, עֲנֵנוּ שׁוֹמֵעַ אֶל אֶבְיוֹנִים¹⁷ עֲנֵנוּ, עֲנֵנוּ

⟨ answer us, ⟪ answer us; ⟨ the destitute, ⟨ to ⟨ You Who listens ⟨ answer us, ⟪ answer us; ⟨ and gra-cious One,

תּוֹמֵךְ תְּמִימִים עֲנֵנוּ, עֲנֵנוּ אֱלֹהֵי אֲבוֹתֵינוּ עֲנֵנוּ,

⟪ answer us; ⟨ of our forefathers, ⟨ God ⟨ answer us, ⟪ answer us; ⟨ the wholesome, ⟨ You Who supports

עֲנֵנוּ אֱלֹהֵי אַבְרָהָם¹⁸ עֲנֵנוּ, עֲנֵנוּ פַּחַד יִצְחָק¹⁸ עֲנֵנוּ,

⟪ answer us; ⟨ of Isaac, ⟨ Awesome One ⟨ answer us, ⟪ answer us; ⟨ of Abraham, ⟨ God ⟨ answer us,

(1) Cf. *Ezekiel* 34:11. (2) *Deuteronomy* 7:9. (3) *Job* 8:6; cf. *Proverbs* 20:11. (4) Cf. *Daniel* 6:27.
(5) Cf. *Psalms* 119:68. (6) Cf. 103:14. (7) Cf. *Isaiah* 59:17. (8) *Ethics of the Fathers* 3:1.
(9) *Psalms* 47:3; 148:13. (10) Cf. *Isaiah* 49:8; *Psalms* 37:39. Alternate text: בְּעֵת רָצוֹן, *in time of favor.*
(11) Cf. 34:23,18. (12) *Deuteronomy* 32:4. (13) Cf. *Psalms* 145:18. (14) *Ethics of the Fathers* 5:14.
(15) Cf. 5:14. (16) *Exodus* 34:6. (17) *Psalms* 69:34. (18) *Genesis* 31:42.

עֲנֵנוּ אָבִיר יַעֲקֹב¹ עֲנֵנוּ, עֲנֵנוּ עֶזְרַת הַשְּׁבָטִים עֲנֵנוּ,

answer us, Mighty One ⟩ of Jacob, ⟩ answer us, ⟩ Helper ⟩ answer us; ⟩ of the tribes, ⟩ answer us;

עֲנֵנוּ מִשְׂגַּב אִמָּהוֹת עֲנֵנוּ, עֲנֵנוּ עוֹנֶה בְּעֵת רָצוֹן² עֲנֵנוּ,

answer us, Stronghold ⟩ of the Matriarchs, ⟩ answer us; ⟩ answer us, ⟩ You Who answers ⟩ in a time ⟩ of favor, ⟩ answer us;

עֲנֵנוּ אֲבִי יְתוֹמִים³ עֲנֵנוּ, עֲנֵנוּ דַּיַּן אַלְמָנוֹת עֲנֵנוּ.

answer us, Father ⟩ of orphans, ⟩ answer us; ⟩ answer us, ⟩ Judge ⟩ of widows, ⟩ answer us.

מִי שֶׁעָנָה לְאַבְרָהָם אָבִינוּ בְּהַר הַמּוֹרִיָּה⁴

He ⟩ Who answered ⟩ Abraham ⟩ our father ⟩ on Mount ⟩ Moriah

הוּא יַעֲנֵנוּ.

He ⟩ — may ⟩ answer us.

מִי שֶׁעָנָה לְיִצְחָק בְּנוֹ כְּשֶׁנֶּעֱקַד עַל גַּבֵּי הַמִּזְבֵּחַ⁴

He ⟩ Who answered ⟩ Isaac ⟩ his son ⟩ when he was bound ⟩ on ⟩ top ⟩ of the altar

הוּא יַעֲנֵנוּ.

He ⟩ — may ⟩ answer us.

מִי שֶׁעָנָה לְיַעֲקֹב בְּבֵית אֵל⁵

He ⟩ Who answered ⟩ Jacob ⟩ in Beth-el

הוּא יַעֲנֵנוּ.

He ⟩ — may ⟩ answer us.

מִי שֶׁעָנָה לְיוֹסֵף בְּבֵית הָאֲסוּרִים⁶

He ⟩ Who answered ⟩ Joseph ⟩ in the prison

הוּא יַעֲנֵנוּ.

He ⟩ — may ⟩ answer us.

מִי שֶׁעָנָה לַאֲבוֹתֵינוּ עַל יַם סוּף⁷

He ⟩ Who answered ⟩ our forefathers ⟩ at ⟩ the ⟩ Sea of Reeds

הוּא יַעֲנֵנוּ.

He ⟩ — may ⟩ answer us.

מִי שֶׁעָנָה לְמֹשֶׁה בְּחוֹרֵב⁸

He ⟩ Who answered ⟩ Moses ⟩ in Horeb

הוּא יַעֲנֵנוּ.

He ⟩ — may ⟩ answer us.

מִי שֶׁעָנָה לְאַהֲרֹן בַּמַּחְתָּה⁹

He ⟩ Who answered ⟩ Aaron ⟩ with the fire-pan

הוּא יַעֲנֵנוּ.

He ⟩ — may ⟩ answer us.

---

(1) *Isaiah* 49:26. (2) Cf. 49:8; *Psalms* 69:14. Alternate text: בְּעֵת צָרָה, *in time of distress.*
(3) 68:6. (4) *Genesis* 22:12. (5) 35:3. (6) 39:21. (7) *Exodus* Ch. 14.
(8) 17:6,11; *Deuteronomy* 9:19. (9) *Numbers* 17:11-13.

מִי שֶׁעָנָה לְפִינְחָס בְּקוּמוֹ מִתּוֹךְ הָעֵדָה[1]

‹ He › Who ‹ Phinehas ‹ when he › from ‹ the
answered   arose amid congregation

הוּא יַעֲנֵנוּ.

‹ may › — ‹ answer ≪
He   us.

מִי שֶׁעָנָה לִיהוֹשֻׁעַ בַּגִּלְגָּל[2]

‹ He › Who ‹ Joshua ‹ in Gilgal ≪
answered

הוּא יַעֲנֵנוּ.

‹ may › — ‹ answer ≪
He   us.

מִי שֶׁעָנָה לִשְׁמוּאֵל בַּמִּצְפָּה[3]

‹ He › Who ‹ Samuel ‹ in Mizpah ≪
answered

הוּא יַעֲנֵנוּ.

‹ may › — ‹ answer ≪
He   us.

מִי שֶׁעָנָה לְדָוִד וּשְׁלֹמֹה בְנוֹ בִּירוּשָׁלָיִם[4] הוּא יַעֲנֵנוּ.

‹ He › Who ‹ David ‹ and ‹ his ‹ in Jerusalem ≪ ‹ answer ≪ — ‹ may
answered   Solomon son   us. He

מִי שֶׁעָנָה לְאֵלִיָּהוּ בְּהַר הַכַּרְמֶל[5]

‹ He › Who ‹ Elijah ‹ on ‹ Carmel ≪
answered   Mount

הוּא יַעֲנֵנוּ.

‹ may › — ‹ answer ≪
He   us.

מִי שֶׁעָנָה לֶאֱלִישָׁע בִּירִיחוֹ[6]

‹ He › Who ‹ Elisha ‹ in Jericho ≪
answered

הוּא יַעֲנֵנוּ.

‹ may › — ‹ answer ≪
He   us.

מִי שֶׁעָנָה לְיוֹנָה בִּמְעֵי הַדָּגָה[7]

‹ He › Who ‹ Jonah ‹ in the ‹ of the ≪
answered   innards fish

הוּא יַעֲנֵנוּ.

‹ may › — ‹ answer ≪
He   us.

מִי שֶׁעָנָה לְחִזְקִיָּהוּ מֶלֶךְ יְהוּדָה בְּחָלְיוֹ[8] הוּא יַעֲנֵנוּ.

‹ He › Who ‹ Hezekiah, ‹ king ‹ of Judah, ‹ in his ≪ ‹ answer ≪ — ‹ may
answered   illness   us. He

מִי שֶׁעָנָה לַחֲנַנְיָה מִישָׁאֵל וַעֲזַרְיָה

‹ He › Who ‹ Hananiah, ‹ Mishael, ‹ and Azariah ‹
answered

בְּתוֹךְ כִּבְשַׁן הָאֵשׁ[9]

‹ inside › the furnace ‹ of fire ≪

הוּא יַעֲנֵנוּ.

‹ may › — ‹ answer ≪
He   us.

מִי שֶׁעָנָה לְדָנִיֵּאל בְּגוֹב הָאֲרָיוֹת[10]

‹ He › Who ‹ Daniel ‹ in the ‹ of lions ≪
answered   den

הוּא יַעֲנֵנוּ.

‹ may › — ‹ answer ≪
He   us.

---

(1) *Numbers* 25:7-13. (2) *Joshua* 6:1-20; 7:6-15; 10:12-14. (3) *I Samuel* 7:9.
(4) *II Samuel* 7:5-16; 21:1,14; 24:25; *I Kings* 9:3. (5) 18:36-38. (6) *II Kings* 2:21.
(7) *Jonah* 2:2-11. (8) *II Kings* 20:2-6; *Isaiah* 38:2-8. (9) *Daniel* 3:21-27. (10) 6:17-23.

מִי שֶׁעָנָה לְמָרְדְּכַי וְאֶסְתֵּר בְּשׁוּשַׁן הַבִּירָה¹

⟪ the capital ⟨ in Shushan ⟨ and Esther ⟨ Mordechai ⟨ Who answered ⟨ He

הוּא יַעֲנֵנוּ.

⟪ answer ⟨ — may He us.

מִי שֶׁעָנָה לְעֶזְרָא בַגּוֹלָה²

⟪ in the exile ⟨ Ezra ⟨ Who answered ⟨ He

הוּא יַעֲנֵנוּ.

⟪ answer ⟨ — may He us.

מִי שֶׁעָנָה לְכָל הַצַּדִּיקִים וְהַחֲסִידִים וְהַתְּמִימִים

⟨ the wholesome, ⟨ the devout, ⟨ the righteous, ⟨ all ⟨ Who answered ⟨ He

וְהַיְשָׁרִים

⟪ and the upright

הוּא יַעֲנֵנוּ.

⟪ answer ⟨ — may He us.

רַחֲמָנָא דְּעָנֵי לַעֲנִיֵּי, עֲנֵינָן. רַחֲמָנָא דְּעָנֵי לִתְבִירֵי

⟨ those of ⟨ Who ⟨ Merciful ⟪ answer ⟪ the poor, ⟨ Who ⟨ Merciful One
broken answers One us! answers

לִבָּא, עֲנֵינָן. רַחֲמָנָא דְּעָנֵי לְמַכִּיכֵי רוּחָא, עֲנֵינָן.

⟪ answer ⟪ spirit, ⟨ those of ⟨ Who ⟨ Merciful ⟪ answer ⟪ hearts,
us! crushed answers One us!

רַחֲמָנָא עֲנֵינָן. רַחֲמָנָא חוּס. רַחֲמָנָא פְּרוֹק. רַחֲמָנָא

⟨ Merciful ⟪ redeem! ⟨ Merciful ⟪ have ⟨ Merciful ⟪ answer ⟨ Merciful
One, One, pity! One, us! One,

שְׁזִיב. רַחֲמָנָא רְחַם עֲלָן, הַשְׁתָּא בַּעֲגָלָא וּבִזְמַן קָרִיב.

⟪ that comes ⟨ and at ⟨ swiftly, ⟨ — now, ⟪ on us ⟨ have ⟨ Merciful ⟪ save!
soon. a time mercy One,

PUTTING DOWN THE HEAD / נפילת אפים

RECITE UNTIL יֵבֹשׁוּ רָגַע WITH THE HEAD RESTING ON THE LEFT ARM,
PREFERABLY WHILE SEATED.

(וַיֹּאמֶר דָּוִד אֶל גָּד, צַר לִי מְאֹד, נִפְּלָה נָּא בְיַד יהוה,

⟪ of ⟨ into the ⟨ now ⟨ Let us ⟪ exceed- ⟨ am ⟨ Dis- ⟪ Gad, ⟨ to ⟨ (And David said
HASHEM, hand fall ingly. I tressed

כִּי רַבִּים רַחֲמָיו, וּבְיַד אָדָם אַל אֶפְּלָה.³)

⟪ let me not fall.) ⟨ but into human ⟪ are His ⟨ abundant ⟨ for
hands mercies,

---

(1) Esther Ch. 8. (2) Ezra 8:21-23. (3) II Samuel 24:14.

רַחוּם וְחַנּוּן חָטָאתִי לְפָנֶיךָ. יהוה מָלֵא רַחֲמִים,

‹ of mercy, ‹ Who ‹ HASHEM, ‹ before ‹ I have ‹ and gracious ‹ O merciful
is full   You.   sinned   One,

רַחֵם עָלַי וְקַבֵּל תַּחֲנוּנָי.

‹ my ‹ and ‹ on me ‹ have
supplications.   accept   mercy

———— *Psalms 6:2-11* / תהלים ו:ב-יא ————

יהוה, אַל בְּאַפְּךָ תוֹכִיחֵנִי, וְאַל בַּחֲמָתְךָ תְיַסְּרֵנִי.

‹ chastise me. ‹ in Your wrath ‹ nor ‹ rebuke me, ‹ in Your anger ‹ do not ‹ HASHEM,

חָנֵּנִי יהוה כִּי אֻמְלַל אָנִי, רְפָאֵנִי יהוה כִּי נִבְהֲלוּ

‹ shudder ‹ for ‹ HASHEM, ‹ heal me, ‹ am I; ‹ feeble ‹ for ‹ HASHEM, ‹ Favor
with terror   me,

עֲצָמָי. וְנַפְשִׁי נִבְהֲלָה מְאֹד, וְאַתָּה יהוה עַד מָתָי.

‹ when? ‹ until ‹ HASHEM, ‹ and You, ‹ utterly, ‹ is terrified ‹ My soul ‹ do my bones.

שׁוּבָה יהוה חַלְּצָה נַפְשִׁי, הוֹשִׁיעֵנִי לְמַעַן חַסְדֶּךָ.

‹ Your kindness. ‹ as befits ‹ save me ‹ my soul; ‹ release ‹ HASHEM, ‹ Desist,

כִּי אֵין בַּמָּוֶת זִכְרֶךָ, בִּשְׁאוֹל מִי יוֹדֶה לָּךְ. יָגַעְתִּי

‹ I am ‹ You? ‹ will ‹ who ‹ in the ‹ is there men- ‹ in ‹ not ‹ For
wearied   praise   grave   tion of You;   death

בְּאַנְחָתִי, אַשְׂחֶה בְכָל לַיְלָה מִטָּתִי, בְּדִמְעָתִי

‹ with my tears ‹ my bed; ‹ night ‹ every ‹ I drench ‹ with my sigh;

עַרְשִׂי אַמְסֶה. עָשְׁשָׁה מִכַּעַס עֵינִי, עָתְקָה בְּכָל

‹ by all ‹ aged ‹ is my ‹ because of ‹ Dimmed ‹ I soak. ‹ my couch
   eye,   anger

צוֹרְרָי. סוּרוּ מִמֶּנִּי כָּל פֹּעֲלֵי אָוֶן, כִּי שָׁמַע יהוה

‹ HASHEM has heard ‹ for ‹ of evil, ‹ doers ‹ all ‹ from me, ‹ Depart ‹ my
tormentors.

קוֹל בִּכְיִי. שָׁמַע יהוה תְּחִנָּתִי, יהוה תְּפִלָּתִי יִקָּח.

‹ will ‹ my prayer ‹ HASHEM ‹ my plea, ‹ HASHEM ‹ of my ‹ the
accept.   has heard   weeping.   sound

יֵבֹשׁוּ וְיִבָּהֲלוּ מְאֹד כָּל אֹיְבָי, יָשֻׁבוּ יֵבֹשׁוּ רָגַע.

‹ in an ‹ and be ‹ may they ‹ my ‹ all ‹ utterly, ‹ and con- ‹ Let them
instant. shamed   regret   enemies;   founded   be shamed

מָחִי וּמַסִּי מֵמִית וּמְחַיֶּה, מַסִּיק מִן שְׁאוֹל

‹ the ‹ from ‹ Who raises ‹ and Who ‹ Who causes ‹ and Who ‹ [O God,]
grave   [the dead]   restores life,   death   heals,   Who wounds

לְחַיֵּי עָלְמָא, בְּרָא כַּד חָטֵי אֲבוּהִי לַקְיֵהּ, אֲבוּהִי

〈 but a 《 would 〈 his father 〈 sin, 〈 should 〈 A son 〈 eternal: 〈 to life
father · strike him, · · he

דְחַיֵּס אַסֵי לִכְאֵבֵהּ. עַבְדָּא דְמָרִיד נָפִיק בְּקוֹלָר,

《 in chains, 〈 he is 《 who rebels, 〈 A slave 《 his [son's] 〈 will 〈 who is com-
· led out · · pain. · heal · passionate

מָרֵהּ תָּאִיב וְתַבִּיר קוֹלָרֵהּ.

《 his chains. 〈 he breaks 〈 desires, 〈 but [if]
· · his master

בְּרָךְ בִּכְרָךְ אֲנָן וְחָטֵינָן קַמָּךְ, הָא רָוֵי נַפְשִׁין

〈 has our 〈 satiated 〈 indeed 《 before 〈 and we have 〈 we 〈 Your 〈 Your
soul been · · · You; · sinned · are, · firstborn, · son,

בִּגְדִין מְרָרִין אֲנָן עַבְדָּךְ וּמְרוֹדִינָן קַמָּךְ,

《 before 〈 and we have 〈 we 〈 Your 《 that is bitter. 〈 with
You; · rebelled · are · servants · · wormwood

הָא בְּבִזְתָּא, הָא בְּשִׁבְיָא, הָא בְּמַלְקִיוּתָא.

《 by the lash. 〈 and 〈 in captivity, 〈 some 〈 from 〈 [indeed we have
· some · · · looting, · suffered,] some

בְּמָטוּ מִנָּךְ בְּרַחֲמָךְ דִּנְפִישִׁין, אַסֵי לִכְאֵבִין

〈 the pains 〈 heal 〈 that is 〈 in Your 〈 of You, 〈 We beg
· · abundant, · compassion

דִּתְקוֹף עֲלָן, עַד דְּלָא נֶהֱוֵי גְמִירָא בְּשִׁבְיָא.

《 in captivity. 〈 completely 〈 we are not 〈 while 〈 us, 〈 that have
· annihilated · · yet · overwhelmed

מַכְנִיסֵי רַחֲמִים, הַכְנִיסוּ רַחֲמֵינוּ, לִפְנֵי בַּעַל

〈 the 〈 before 〈 our [plea for] 〈 may you 〈 [pleas for] mercy, 〈 O you who
Master · · mercy · usher in · · usher in

הָרַחֲמִים. מַשְׁמִיעֵי תְפִלָּה, הַשְׁמִיעוּ תְפִלָּתֵנוּ, לִפְנֵי

〈 before 〈 of our prayer 〈 may you aid 《 of prayer, 〈 O you who aid 《 of mercy.
· · the hearing · · the hearing

שׁוֹמֵעַ תְּפִלָּה. מַשְׁמִיעֵי צְעָקָה, הַשְׁמִיעוּ צַעֲקָתֵנוּ,

〈 of our 〈 may you aid 《 of outcries, 〈 O you who aid 《 of 〈 the Hearer
outcries · the hearing · · the hearing · prayer.

לִפְנֵי שׁוֹמֵעַ צְעָקָה. מַכְנִיסֵי דִמְעָה, הַכְנִיסוּ

〈 may you usher in 《 tears, 〈 O you who usher in 《 of outcries. 〈 the Hearer 〈 before

דִמְעוֹתֵינוּ, לִפְנֵי מֶלֶךְ מִתְרַצֶּה בִּדְמָעוֹת.

《 through tears. 〈 Who is appeased 〈 the King 〈 before 〈 our tears

הִשְׁתַּדְּלוּ וְהַרְבּוּ תְּחִנָּה וּבַקָּשָׁה, לִפְנֵי מֶלֶךְ אֵל

⟨ God, ⟨ the King, ⟨ before ⟨ and pleas ⟨ supplications ⟨ and intensify ⟨ Exert yourselves

רָם וְנִשָּׂא. הַזְכִּירוּ לְפָנָיו, הַשְׁמִיעוּ לְפָנָיו תּוֹרָה

⟨ the Torah ⟨ before Him, ⟨ aid to be heard ≪ before Him, ⟨ Mention ≪ and ⟨ exalted uplifted.

וּמַעֲשִׂים טוֹבִים שֶׁל שׁוֹכְנֵי עָפָר.

≪ in the dust. ⟨ [the Patriarchs and Matriarchs] who dwell ⟨ of ⟨ that are good ⟨ and the deeds

יִזְכֹּר אַהֲבָתָם וִיחַיֶּה זַרְעָם, שֶׁלֹּא תֹאבַד שְׁאֵרִית

⟨ shall the remnant ⟨ lost ⟨ so that not ⟨ to their offspring, ⟨ and grant life ⟨ their love ⟨ May He remember

יַעֲקֹב. כִּי צֹאן רוֹעֶה נֶאֱמָן הָיָה לְחֶרְפָּה,

≪ a disgrace; ⟨ has become ⟨ who is faithful [Moses] ⟨ of the shepherd ⟨ the flock ⟨ For ≪ of Jacob be.

יִשְׂרָאֵל גּוֹי אֶחָד לְמָשָׁל וְלִשְׁנִינָה.

≪ and a simile. ⟨ a parable ≪ that is the unique, ⟨ the nation ≪ Israel,

מַהֵר עֲנֵנוּ אֱלֹהֵי יִשְׁעֵנוּ, וּפְדֵנוּ מִכָּל גְּזֵרוֹת קָשׁוֹת

≪ that are harsh; ⟨ decrees ⟨ from all ⟨ and redeem us ⟨ of our salvation, ⟨ O God ⟨ answer us, ≪ Swiftly

וְהוֹשִׁיעָה בְּרַחֲמֶיךָ הָרַבִּים, מְשִׁיחַ צִדְקֶךָ וְעַמֶּךָ.

≪ and Your people. ⟨ Your righteous anointed one ⟨ that is abundant, ⟨ in Your mercy ⟨ and may You save,

מָרָן דְּבִשְׁמַיָּא לָךְ מִתְחַנְּנַן, כְּבַר שְׁבִיָּא דְמִתְחַנַּן

⟨ who supplicates ⟨ in captivity ⟨ as one ⟨ do we supplicate, ⟨ to You ≪ Who is in heaven, ⟨ Our Master

לִשְׁבוּיֵהּ. כֻּלְּהוֹן בְּנֵי שְׁבִיָּא בְּכַסְפָּא מִתְפָּרְקִין,

≪ are redeemed, ⟨ through money ⟨ in captivity, ⟨ those ⟨ [for] all ≪ before his captors; ⟨ are redeemed,

וְעַמָּךְ יִשְׂרָאֵל בְּרַחֲמֵי וּבְתַחֲנוּנֵי, הַב לָן שְׁאֵלָתִין

⟨ our requests ⟨ us ⟨ O ≪ grant ⟨ and supplication. ⟨ through compassion ⟨ Israel ⟨ but Your people

וּבָעוּתִין, דְּלָא נֶהֱדַר רֵיקָם מִן קֳדָמָךְ.

≪ before You. ⟨ from ⟨ empty-handed ⟨ that we not be turned away ⟨ and our prayers

מָרַן דְּבִשְׁמַיָּא לָךְ מִתְחַנְּנַן, כְּעַבְדָּא דְּמִתְחַנֵּן
‹ who supplicates ‹ as a slave « do we supplicate, ‹ to You « Who is in heaven, ‹ Our Master

לְמָרֵיהּ, עֲשִׁיקֵי אֲנָן וּבַחֲשׁוֹכָא שָׁרִינַן, מְרִירָן נַפְשִׁין
‹ are [our] souls ‹ embittered « do we abide, ‹ and in darkness ‹ are we ‹ Oppressed « to his master:

מֵעָקְתִין דִּנְפִישִׁין, חֵילָא לֵית בָּן לְרַצּוּיָךְ. מָרַן,
‹ Our Master, « to appease ‹ within us ‹ is lacking ‹ Strength « that is excessive. ‹ from distress

עֲבִיד בְּדִיל קַיָּמָא דִּגְזַרְתָּ עִם אֲבָהָתָנָא.
« our Patriarchs. ‹ with ‹ that You established ‹ of the covenant ‹ for the sake ‹ act

שׁוֹמֵר יִשְׂרָאֵל, שְׁמוֹר שְׁאֵרִית יִשְׂרָאֵל, וְאַל
‹ let not « of Israel; ‹ the remnant ‹ safeguard « of Israel, ‹ O Guardian

יֹאבַד יִשְׂרָאֵל, הָאֹמְרִים שְׁמַע יִשְׂרָאֵל.[1]
« O Israel. ‹ Hear, ‹ those who proclaim « Israel be destroyed —

שׁוֹמֵר גּוֹי אֶחָד, שְׁמוֹר שְׁאֵרִית עַם אֶחָד, וְאַל
‹ let not « that is unique; ‹ of the people ‹ the remnant ‹ safeguard « that is unique, ‹ of the nation ‹ O Guardian

יֹאבַד גּוֹי אֶחָד, הַמְּיַחֲדִים שִׁמְךָ, יהוה אֱלֹהֵינוּ
‹ is our God, ‹ HASHEM « of Your Name: ‹ those who proclaim the Oneness « that is unique, ‹ the nation ‹ be destroyed

יהוה אֶחָד.
« the One [and Only]! ‹ HASHEM is

שׁוֹמֵר גּוֹי קָדוֹשׁ, שְׁמוֹר שְׁאֵרִית עַם קָדוֹשׁ, וְאַל
‹ let not « that is holy; ‹ of the people ‹ the remnant ‹ safeguard « that is holy, ‹ of the nation ‹ O Guardian

יֹאבַד גּוֹי קָדוֹשׁ, הַמְשַׁלְּשִׁים בְּשָׁלֹשׁ קְדֻשּׁוֹת לְקָדוֹשׁ.
« to the Holy One. ‹ sanctifications ‹ the threefold ‹ those who proclaim three times « that is holy, ‹ the nation ‹ be destroyed

מִתְרַצֶּה בְּרַחֲמִים וּמִתְפַּיֵּס בְּתַחֲנוּנִים, הִתְרַצֵּה
‹ be favorable « through supplications, ‹ and Who becomes conciliatory ‹ through compassion ‹ You Who becomes favorable

---

(1) *Deuteronomy* 6:4.

וְהִתְפַּיֵּס לְדוֹר עָנִי, כִּי אֵין עוֹזֵר. אָבִינוּ מַלְכֵּנוּ,

《 our King, 〈 Our Father, 《 helper. 〈 there is no 〈 for 《 that is poor, 〈 to the generation 〈 and be conciliatory

חָנֵּנוּ וַעֲנֵנוּ, כִּי אֵין בָּנוּ מַעֲשִׂים, עֲשֵׂה עִמָּנוּ

〈 us 〈 treat 《 worthy deeds; 〈 we have no 〈 though 〈 and answer us, 〈 be gracious with us

צְדָקָה וָחֶסֶד וְהוֹשִׁיעֵנוּ.

《 and save us. 〈 and kindness, 〈 with charity

STAND AFTER THE WORDS וַאֲנַחְנוּ לֹא נֵדַע UNTIL CONCLUSION OF THE PARAGRAPH.

וַאֲנַחְנוּ לֹא נֵדַע מַה נַּעֲשֶׂה, כִּי עָלֶיךָ עֵינֵינוּ.[1]

《 are our eyes. 〈 upon You 〈 rather, 《 we should do, 〈 what 〈 know not 〈 We

זְכֹר רַחֲמֶיךָ יהוה וַחֲסָדֶיךָ, כִּי מֵעוֹלָם הֵמָּה.[2] יְהִי

〈 May 《 are they. 〈 eternal 〈 for 〈 and Your kindnesses, 〈 HASHEM, 〈 Your mercies, 〈 Remember

חַסְדְּךָ יהוה עָלֵינוּ, כַּאֲשֶׁר יִחַלְנוּ לָךְ.[3] אַל תִּזְכָּר

〈 recall 〈 Do not 《 You. 〈 we awaited 〈 just as 《 be upon us, 〈 HASHEM, 〈 Your kindness,

לָנוּ עֲוֺנוֹת רִאשֹׁנִים, מַהֵר יְקַדְּמוּנוּ רַחֲמֶיךָ, כִּי

〈 for 《 may Your mercies, 〈 advance to meet us 〈 swiftly 《 of the ancients; 〈 the sins 〈 against us

דַלּוֹנוּ מְאֹד.[4] עֶזְרֵנוּ בְּשֵׁם יהוה, עֹשֵׂה שָׁמַיִם

〈 of heaven 〈 Maker 《 of HASHEM, 〈 is through the Name 〈 Our help 《 exceedingly. 〈 we have become impoverished

וָאָרֶץ.[5] חָנֵּנוּ יהוה חָנֵּנוּ, כִּי רַב שָׂבַעְנוּ בוּז.[6] בְּרֹגֶז

《 Amid wrath, 《 with contempt. 〈 sated 〈 we are fully 〈 for 《 favor us, 〈 HASHEM, 〈 Favor us, 《 and earth.

רַחֵם תִּזְכּוֹר.[7] בְּרֹגֶז עֲקֵדָה תִּזְכּוֹר. בְּרֹגֶז תְּמִימוֹת

〈 the perfect ones 《 Amid wrath, 《 You should remember! 〈 the binding [of Isaac] 《 Amid wrath, 《 You should remember! 〈 to be merciful

תִּזְכּוֹר. יהוה הוֹשִׁיעָה, הַמֶּלֶךְ יַעֲנֵנוּ בְיוֹם קָרְאֵנוּ.[8]

《 we call. 〈 on the day 〈 answer us 〈 May the King 《 save! 〈 HASHEM, 《 You should remember!

כִּי הוּא יָדַע יִצְרֵנוּ, זָכוּר כִּי עָפָר אֲנָחְנוּ.[9]

《 are we. 〈 dust 〈 that 〈 He is mindful 《 our nature, 〈 knew 〈 He 〈 For

---

(1) *II Chronicles* 20:12. (2) *Psalms* 25:6. (3) 33:22. (4) 79:8. (5) 121:2.
(6) 123:3. (7) *Habakkuk* 3:2. (8) *Psalms* 20:10. (9) 103:14.

❖ עָזְרֵנוּ אֱלֹהֵי יִשְׁעֵנוּ עַל דְּבַר כְּבוֹד שְׁמֶךָ, וְהַצִּילֵנוּ

⟨ rescue us ⟪ of Your ⟨ of the ⟨ the ⟨ for ⟨ of our ⟨ O God ⟨ Assist us,
Name; glory sake salvation

וְכַפֵּר עַל חַטֹּאתֵינוּ לְמַעַן שְׁמֶךָ.¹

⟪ of Your ⟨ for the ⟨ our sins ⟨ for ⟨ and grant
Name. sake atonement

FULL KADDISH / קדיש שלם

THE CHAZZAN RECITES קַדִּישׁ שָׁלֵם, FULL *KADDISH*.

יִתְגַּדַּל וְיִתְקַדַּשׁ שְׁמֵהּ רַבָּא. (אָמֵן. — Cong.) בְּעָלְמָא

⟨ — in the ⟪ (Amen.) ⟪ that is ⟨ may His ⟨ and be ⟨ Grow
world great! — Name sanctified exalted

דִּי בְרָא כִרְעוּתֵהּ. וְיַמְלִיךְ מַלְכוּתֵהּ, וְיַצְמַח פֻּרְקָנֵהּ

⟨ His ⟨ and cause ⟪ to His ⟨ and may He ⟪ according ⟨ He ⟨ that
salvation, to sprout kingship, give reign to His will, created

וִיקָרֵב מְשִׁיחֵהּ. (אָמֵן. — Cong.) בְּחַיֵּיכוֹן וּבְיוֹמֵיכוֹן וּבְחַיֵּי

⟨ and in the ⟨ and in ⟨ in your ⟪ (Amen.) ⟪ His Messiah, ⟨ and bring
lifetimes your days, lifetimes near

דְכָל בֵּית יִשְׂרָאֵל, בַּעֲגָלָא וּבִזְמַן קָרִיב. וְאִמְרוּ: אָמֵן.

⟪ Amen. ⟨ Now ⟪ that comes ⟨ and at a ⟨ swiftly ⟪ of Israel, ⟨ Family ⟨ of the
respond: soon. time entire

CONGREGATION RESPONDS:

אָמֵן. יְהֵא שְׁמֵהּ רַבָּא מְבָרַךְ לְעָלַם וּלְעָלְמֵי עָלְמַיָּא.

⟪ and for all eternity. ⟨ forever ⟨ be ⟨ that is ⟨ His ⟨ May ⟪ Amen.
blessed great Name

CHAZZAN CONTINUES:

יְהֵא שְׁמֵהּ רַבָּא מְבָרַךְ לְעָלַם וּלְעָלְמֵי עָלְמַיָּא. יִתְבָּרַךְ

⟨ Blessed, ⟪ and for all eternity. ⟨ forever ⟨ be ⟨ that is ⟨ His ⟨ May
blessed great Name

וְיִשְׁתַּבַּח וְיִתְפָּאַר וְיִתְרוֹמַם וְיִתְנַשֵּׂא וְיִתְהַדָּר וְיִתְעַלֶּה

⟨ elevated, ⟨ honored, ⟨ upraised, ⟨ exalted, ⟨ glorified, ⟨ praised,

וְיִתְהַלָּל שְׁמֵהּ דְּקֻדְשָׁא בְּרִיךְ הוּא (בְּרִיךְ הוּא — Cong.)

⟪ is He) ⟨ (Blessed ⟪ is He ⟨ Blessed ⟨ of the Holy ⟨ be the ⟨ and lauded
One, Name

— לְעֵלָּא מִן כָּל בִּרְכָתָא וְשִׁירָתָא תֻּשְׁבְּחָתָא וְנֶחֱמָתָא

⟨ and ⟨ praise ⟪ and song, ⟨ blessing ⟨ any ⟨ beyond
consolation

---

(1) *Psalms* 79:9.

דַּאֲמִירָן בְּעָלְמָא. וְאִמְרוּ: אָמֵן. (.Cong — אָמֵן.)
‹‹ (Amen.) ‹‹ Amen. ‹ Now respond: ‹‹ in the world. ‹ that are uttered

CONGREGATION:

(קַבֵּל בְּרַחֲמִים וּבְרָצוֹן אֶת תְּפִלָּתֵנוּ.)
‹‹ our prayers.) ‹ and with favor ‹ with mercy ‹ (Accept

CHAZZAN CONTINUES:

תִּתְקַבֵּל צְלוֹתְהוֹן וּבָעוּתְהוֹן דְּכָל בֵּית יִשְׂרָאֵל קֳדָם
‹ before ‹ Israel ‹ Family of ‹ of the entire ‹ and supplications ‹ the prayers ‹ May accepted be

אֲבוּהוֹן דִּי בִשְׁמַיָּא. וְאִמְרוּ: אָמֵן. (.Cong — אָמֵן.)
‹‹ (Amen.) ‹‹ Amen. ‹ Now respond: ‹‹ is in Heaven. ‹ Who ‹ their Father

CONGREGATION:

(יְהִי שֵׁם יהוה מְבֹרָךְ, מֵעַתָּה וְעַד עוֹלָם.[1])
‹‹ eternity.) ‹ until ‹ from this time ‹‹ be blessed, ‹ of ‹ the HASHEM Name ‹ (Let

CHAZZAN CONTINUES:

יְהֵא שְׁלָמָא רַבָּא מִן שְׁמַיָּא וְחַיִּים טוֹבִים עָלֵינוּ וְעַל כָּל
‹ all ‹ and upon ‹ upon us ‹ that is good, ‹ and life ‹ Heaven ‹ from ‹ that is abundant ‹ peace ‹ May there be

יִשְׂרָאֵל. וְאִמְרוּ: אָמֵן. (.Cong — אָמֵן.)
‹‹ (Amen.) ‹‹ Amen. ‹ Now respond: ‹‹ Israel.

CONGREGATION:

(עֶזְרִי מֵעִם יהוה, עֹשֵׂה שָׁמַיִם וָאָרֶץ.[2])
‹‹ and earth.) ‹ of heaven ‹ Maker ‹‹ HASHEM, ‹ is from ‹ (My help

CHAZZAN BOWS; TAKES THREE STEPS BACK. BOWS LEFT AND SAYS "... עֹשֶׂה שָׁלוֹם, *HE WHO MAKES PEACE* ..."; BOWS RIGHT AND SAYS "... הוּא, *MAY HE* ..."; BOWS FORWARD AND SAYS "... וְעַל כָּל יִשְׂרָאֵל, *AND UPON ALL ISRAEL* ..."; REMAINS IN PLACE FOR A FEW MOMENTS, THEN TAKES THREE STEPS FORWARD.

עֹשֶׂה שָׁלוֹם בִּמְרוֹמָיו, הוּא יַעֲשֶׂה שָׁלוֹם עָלֵינוּ, וְעַל כָּל
‹ all ‹ and upon ‹ upon us, ‹ peace ‹ make ‹‹ may He ‹‹ in His heights, ‹ peace ‹ He Who makes

יִשְׂרָאֵל. וְאִמְרוּ: אָמֵן. (.Cong — אָמֵן.)
‹‹ (Amen.) ‹‹ Amen. ‹ Now respond: ‹‹ Israel.

(1) *Psalms* 113:2. (2) 121:2.

❧ SEVENTH DAY / יוֹם שְׁבִיעִי ❧

אַשְׁרֵי יוֹשְׁבֵי בֵיתֶךָ, עוֹד יְהַלְלוּךָ סֶּלָה.¹ אַשְׁרֵי

⟨ Praise-
worthy ⟩ ≪ Selah. ≪ they will
praise You, ⟨ con-
tinually ≪ in Your
house, ⟨ are those
who dwell ⟨ Praiseworthy

הָעָם שֶׁכָּכָה לוֹ, אַשְׁרֵי הָעָם שֶׁיהוה אֱלֹהָיו.²

≪ is their
God. ⟨ that
HASHEM ⟨ is the
people ⟨ praise-
worthy ≪ is
their lot; ⟨ that such ⟨ is the
people

———— תהלים קמה / Psalm 145 ————

תְּהִלָּה לְדָוִד, אֲרוֹמִמְךָ אֱלוֹהַי הַמֶּלֶךְ, וַאֲבָרְכָה

⟨ and I
will bless ≪ the King, ⟨ my God ⟨ I will exalt You, ≪ by David: ⟨ A psalm of
praise

שִׁמְךָ לְעוֹלָם וָעֶד. בְּכָל יוֹם אֲבָרְכֶךָּ, וַאֲהַלְלָה שִׁמְךָ

⟨ Your
Name ⟨ and I
will laud ≪ I will
bless You, ⟨ day ⟨ Every ≪ and
ever. ⟨ for ever ⟨ Your
Name

לְעוֹלָם וָעֶד. גָּדוֹל יהוה וּמְהֻלָּל מְאֹד, וְלִגְדֻלָּתוֹ

⟨ and His
greatness ≪ exceedingly, ⟨ and
lauded ⟨ is
HASHEM ⟨ Great ≪ and
ever. ⟨ for ever

אֵין חֵקֶר. דּוֹר לְדוֹר יְשַׁבַּח מַעֲשֶׂיךָ, וּגְבוּרֹתֶיךָ יַגִּידוּ.

≪ they will ⟨
recount. ⟨ and Your
mighty deeds ≪ Your
actions, ⟨ will
praise ⟨ to
generation ⟨ Gen-
eration ≪ is beyond
investigation.

הֲדַר כְּבוֹד הוֹדֶךָ, וְדִבְרֵי נִפְלְאֹתֶיךָ אָשִׂיחָה. וֶעֱזוּז

⟨ And of
the might ≪ I shall
discuss. ⟨ that are
wondrous ⟨ and Your
deeds ⟨ of Your
majesty ⟨ glory ⟨ The
splendrous

נוֹרְאֹתֶיךָ יֹאמֵרוּ, וּגְדוּלָּתְךָ אֲסַפְּרֶנָּה. זֵכֶר רַב טוּבְךָ

⟨ of Your abun-
dant goodness ⟨ A recol-
lection ⟨ I shall
relate. ⟨ and Your
greatness ≪ they will
speak, ⟨ of Your
awesome deeds

יַבִּיעוּ, וְצִדְקָתְךָ יְרַנֵּנוּ. חַנּוּן וְרַחוּם יהוה, אֶרֶךְ אַפַּיִם

⟨ to
anger, ⟨ slow ≪ is
HASHEM, ⟨ and
merciful ⟨ Gracious ≪ they will
sing joyfully. ⟨ and of Your
righteousness ≪ they
will utter,

וּגְדָל חָסֶד. טוֹב יהוה לַכֹּל, וְרַחֲמָיו עַל כָּל מַעֲשָׂיו.

≪ His
creations. ⟨ all ⟨ are
on ⟨ His
mercies ≪ to all; ⟨
HASHEM
is good ≪ in [bestowing]
kindness. ⟨ and
great

יוֹדוּךָ יהוה כָּל מַעֲשֶׂיךָ, וַחֲסִידֶיךָ יְבָרְכוּכָה. כְּבוֹד

⟨ Of the
glory ≪ will
bless You. ⟨ and Your
devout ones ≪ Your
creations — ⟨ — all ≪ HASHEM ⟨ They will
thank You,

---

(1) Psalms 84:5. (2) 144:15.

מַלְכוּתְךָ יֹאמֵרוּ, וּגְבוּרָתְךָ יְדַבֵּרוּ. **לְהוֹדִיעַ לִבְנֵי הָאָדָם**

‹ mankind ‹ To inform ❮❮ they will ‹ and of Your ❮❮ they will ‹ of Your
                declare.   power   speak,   kingdom

גְּבוּרֹתָיו, וּכְבוֹד הֲדַר מַלְכוּתוֹ. **מַלְכוּתְךָ** מַלְכוּת כָּל

‹ [span- ‹ is a ‹ Your kingdom ❮❮ of His ‹ splendor ‹ and of the ❮❮ of His mighty
ning] all kingdom   kingdom.   glorious   deeds,

עֹלָמִים, וּמֶמְשַׁלְתְּךָ בְּכָל דּוֹר וָדֹר. **סוֹמֵךְ** יהוה

‹ HASHEM ❮❮ after ‹ gen- ‹ is ‹ and Your ❮❮ eternities,
supports   generation. eration throughout   dominion

לְכָל הַנֹּפְלִים, וְזוֹקֵף לְכָל הַכְּפוּפִים. **עֵינֵי** כֹל

‹ of all ‹ The ❮❮ those who ‹ all ‹ and ❮❮ those who ‹ all
    eyes   are bent.   straightens are fallen,

אֵלֶיךָ יְשַׂבֵּרוּ, וְאַתָּה נוֹתֵן לָהֶם אֶת אָכְלָם בְּעִתּוֹ.

❮❮ in its ‹ their food ‹ them ‹ give ‹ and You ❮❮ do look ‹ to You
proper time.   with hope,

CONCENTRATE INTENTLY WHILE RECITING THE VERSE פּוֹתֵחַ, YOU OPEN.

פּוֹתֵחַ אֶת יָדֶךָ, וּמַשְׂבִּיעַ לְכָל חַי רָצוֹן. ❖ **צַדִּיק**

‹ Righteous ❮❮ [with its] ‹ living ‹ every ‹ and satisfy ❮❮ Your hand, ‹ You open
desire.   thing

יהוה בְּכָל דְּרָכָיו, וְחָסִיד בְּכָל מַעֲשָׂיו. **קָרוֹב** יהוה

‹ is ‹ Close ❮❮ His deeds. ‹ in all ‹ and ❮❮ His ways, ‹ in all ‹ is
HASHEM   magnanimous   HASHEM

לְכָל קֹרְאָיו, לְכֹל אֲשֶׁר יִקְרָאֻהוּ בֶאֱמֶת. **רְצוֹן** יְרֵאָיו

‹ of those ‹ The ❮❮ sincerely. ‹ call upon ‹ who ‹ to all ❮❮ who call ‹ to all
who fear Him will   Him   upon Him,

יַעֲשֶׂה, וְאֶת שַׁוְעָתָם יִשְׁמַע וְיוֹשִׁיעֵם. **שׁוֹמֵר** יהוה

‹ HASHEM protects ❮❮ and He will ‹ He will ‹ and their cry ❮❮ He
save them.   hear,   will do;

אֶת כָּל אֹהֲבָיו, וְאֵת כָּל הָרְשָׁעִים יַשְׁמִיד. **תְּהִלַּת**

‹ The praise ❮❮ He will destroy. ‹ the wicked ‹ but all ❮❮ who love Him; ‹ all

יהוה יְדַבֶּר פִּי, וִיבָרֵךְ כָּל בָּשָׂר שֵׁם קָדְשׁוֹ לְעוֹלָם

‹ for ever ‹ of His ‹ the ‹ flesh ‹ may ‹ and bless ❮❮ may my ‹ of
Holiness Name   all   mouth declare, HASHEM

וָעֶד. וַאֲנַחְנוּ נְבָרֵךְ יָהּ מֵעַתָּה וְעַד עוֹלָם; הַלְלוּיָהּ.[1]

❮❮ Halleluyah! ❮❮ eternity. ‹ until ‹ from ‹ God ‹ will ‹ But we ❮❮ and
this time   bless   ever.

(1) *Psalms* 115:18.

THE *CHAZZAN* **RECITES** חֲצִי קַדִּישׁ, *HALF-KADDISH*:

יִתְגַּדַּל וְיִתְקַדַּשׁ שְׁמֵהּ רַבָּא. (.Cong — אָמֵן) בְּעָלְמָא
⟨ Grow exalted ⟨ and be sanctified ⟨ may His Name ⟨ that is great! — 《 (Amen.) ⟨ — in the world

דִּי בְרָא כִרְעוּתֵהּ. וְיַמְלִיךְ מַלְכוּתֵהּ, וְיַצְמַח פֻּרְקָנֵהּ
⟨ that ⟨ He created ⟨ according to His will, 《 and may He give reign ⟨ to His kingship, 《 and cause to sprout ⟨ His salvation,

וִיקָרֵב מְשִׁיחֵהּ. (.Cong — אָמֵן) בְּחַיֵּיכוֹן וּבְיוֹמֵיכוֹן וּבְחַיֵּי
⟨ and bring near ⟨ His Messiah, 《 (Amen.) ⟨ in your lifetimes ⟨ and in your days, ⟨ and in the lifetimes

דְכָל בֵּית יִשְׂרָאֵל, בַּעֲגָלָא וּבִזְמַן קָרִיב. וְאִמְרוּ: אָמֵן.
⟨ of the entire ⟨ Family ⟨ of Israel, 《 swiftly ⟨ and at a time 《 that comes soon. ⟨ Now respond: 《Amen.

CONGREGATION RESPONDS:

אָמֵן. יְהֵא שְׁמֵהּ רַבָּא מְבָרַךְ לְעָלַם וּלְעָלְמֵי עָלְמַיָּא.
《 Amen. 《 May ⟨ His Name ⟨ that is great ⟨ be blessed ⟨ forever 《 and for all eternity.

CHAZZAN CONTINUES:

יְהֵא שְׁמֵהּ רַבָּא מְבָרַךְ לְעָלַם וּלְעָלְמֵי עָלְמַיָּא. יִתְבָּרַךְ
⟨ May ⟨ His Name ⟨ that is great ⟨ be blessed ⟨ forever 《 and for all eternity. ⟨ Blessed,

וְיִשְׁתַּבַּח וְיִתְפָּאַר וְיִתְרוֹמַם וְיִתְנַשֵּׂא וְיִתְהַדָּר וְיִתְעַלֶּה
⟨ praised, ⟨ glorified, ⟨ exalted, ⟨ upraised, ⟨ honored, ⟨ elevated,

וְיִתְהַלָּל שְׁמֵהּ דְּקֻדְשָׁא בְּרִיךְ הוּא (.Cong — בְּרִיךְ הוּא)
⟨ and lauded ⟨ be the Name ⟨ of the Holy One, ⟨ Blessed ⟨ is He 《 (Blessed ⟨ is He 》

— לְעֵלָּא מִן כָּל בִּרְכָתָא וְשִׁירָתָא תֻּשְׁבְּחָתָא וְנֶחֱמָתָא
⟨ beyond ⟨ any ⟨ blessing ⟨ and song, 《 praise ⟨ and consolation 》

דַּאֲמִירָן בְּעָלְמָא. וְאִמְרוּ: אָמֵן. (.Cong — אָמֵן)
⟨ that are uttered 《 in the world. ⟨ Now respond: 《 Amen. 《 (Amen.)

ALL:

לְךָ יהוה הַצְּדָקָה, וְלָנוּ בֹּשֶׁת הַפָּנִים.[1] מַה
⟨ Yours, ⟨ O Lord, 《 is the righteousness, 《 and ours ⟨ is shamefacedness. 《 What 》

נִּתְאוֹנֵן,[3] מַה נֹּאמַר, מַה נְּדַבֵּר, וּמַה נִּצְטַדָּק.[2]
《 complaint can we make? ⟨ What 《 can we say? ⟨ What 《 can we declare? ⟨ What 《 justification can we offer?

---

(1) *Daniel* 9:7. (2) Cf. *Lamentations* 3:39. (3) Cf. *Genesis* 44:16.

נַחְפְּשָׂה דְרָכֵינוּ וְנַחְקֹרָה, וְנָשׁוּבָה אֵלֶיךָ,[1] כִּי יְמִינְךָ

‹ Let us examine ‹ our ways « and investigate them, ‹ and return ‹ to You, « for ‹ Your right hand

פְּשׁוּטָה לְקַבֵּל שָׁבִים. לֹא בְחֶסֶד וְלֹא בְמַעֲשִׂים

‹ is extended ‹ to accept « those who return. « Nei-ther ‹ with [merit] for kindness ‹ nor ‹ with [merit for good] deeds

בָּאנוּ לְפָנֶיךָ, כְּדַלִּים וּכְרָשִׁים דָּפַקְנוּ דְלָתֶיךָ.

‹ do we come « before You; ‹ but as paupers ‹ and as destitute people ‹ we have knocked « on Your doors.

דְלָתֶיךָ דָּפַקְנוּ רַחוּם וְחַנּוּן, נָא אַל תְּשִׁיבֵנוּ

‹ On Your doors ‹ we have knocked ‹ O Compassionate One ‹ and Gracious One. « Please ‹ do not ‹ turn us away

רֵיקָם מִלְּפָנֶיךָ. מִלְּפָנֶיךָ מַלְכֵּנוּ רֵיקָם אַל תְּשִׁיבֵנוּ,

‹ empty-handed « from before You. ‹ From before You, ‹ Our King, ‹ empty-handed ‹ do not « turn us away,

כִּי אַתָּה שׁוֹמֵעַ תְּפִלָּה.

‹ for the One ‹ You are ‹ Who hears « prayer.

שְׁמַע תְּפִלָּה, עָדֶיךָ כָּל בָּשָׂר יָבֹאוּ. יָבוֹא

‹ You Who hears « prayer,[2] ‹ unto You ‹ all ‹ flesh « will come. ‹ Come

כָּל בָּשָׂר לְהִשְׁתַּחֲוֹת לְפָנֶיךָ יהוה.[3] יָבֹאוּ וְיִשְׁתַּחֲווּ

‹ will all flesh ‹ to bow down ‹ before You, « O HASHEM. ‹ They will come ‹ and bow down

לְפָנֶיךָ אֲדֹנָי, וִיכַבְּדוּ לִשְׁמֶךָ.[4] בֹּאוּ נִשְׁתַּחֲוֶה וְנִכְרָעָה,

‹ before You, « O Lord, ‹ and they will show honor ‹ to Your Name. « Come! ‹ Let us prostrate ourselves « and bow,

נִבְרְכָה לִפְנֵי יהוה עֹשֵׂנוּ.[5] נָבוֹאָה לְמִשְׁכְּנוֹתָיו,

‹ let us kneel ‹ before « HASHEM, ‹ our Maker. « Let us come « to His Tabernacles,

נִשְׁתַּחֲוֶה לַהֲדֹם רַגְלָיו.[6] בֹּאוּ שְׁעָרָיו בְּתוֹדָה,

« let us prostrate ourselves ‹ at the stool « for His feet. ‹ Enter ‹ His gates « with thanksgiving,

חֲצֵרֹתָיו בִּתְהִלָּה, הוֹדוּ לוֹ בָּרְכוּ שְׁמוֹ.[7] וַאֲנַחְנוּ

‹ His courtyards « with praise; ‹ give thanks « to Him, « bless « His Name. ‹ But we,

---

(1) Cf. *Lamentations* 3:40. (2) *Psalms* 65:3. (3) Cf. *Isaiah* 66:23.
(4) *Psalms* 86:9. (5) 95:6. (6) 132:7. (7) 100:4.

בְּרֹב חַסְדְּךָ נָבוֹא בֵיתֶךָ, נִשְׁתַּחֲוֶה אֶל הֵיכַל קָדְשְׁךָ

Your Holy Sanctuary ‹ toward ‹ we will prostrate ourselves ‹‹ Your House; ‹ will we enter ‹ of Your kindness ‹ through the abundance

בְּיִרְאָתֶךָ. [1] הִנֵּה בָּרְכוּ אֶת יהוה כָּל עַבְדֵי יהוה,

of HASHEM, ‹ you ‹ all ‹ HASHEM, ‹ bless ‹‹ Indeed, ‹‹ in awe of You. ‹ servants

הָעֹמְדִים בְּבֵית יהוה בַּלֵּילוֹת. [2] שְׂאוּ יְדֵיכֶם קֹדֶשׁ

in the Sanctuary ‹ your hands ‹ Lift ‹‹ in the nights. ‹ of HASHEM ‹ in the House ‹ who stand

וּבָרְכוּ אֶת יהוה. [3] רוֹמְמוּ יהוה אֱלֹהֵינוּ, וְהִשְׁתַּחֲווּ

and bow down ‹ our God, ‹ HASHEM, ‹ Exalt ‹‹ HASHEM. ‹ and bless

לַהֲדֹם רַגְלָיו, קָדוֹשׁ הוּא. [4] רוֹמְמוּ יהוה אֱלֹהֵינוּ,

our God, ‹ HASHEM, ‹ Exalt ‹‹ is He! ‹ holy ‹‹ at His footstool;

[5] וְהִשְׁתַּחֲווּ לְהַר קָדְשׁוֹ, כִּי קָדוֹשׁ יהוה אֱלֹהֵינוּ.

our God. ‹ HASHEM, ‹ is ‹ holy ‹ for ‹‹ of His Holiness; ‹ at the Mount ‹ and bow

הִשְׁתַּחֲווּ לַיהוה בְּהַדְרַת קֹדֶשׁ, חִילוּ מִפָּנָיו כָּל

every-one ‹ before Him, ‹ tremble ‹‹ of holiness; ‹ in the splendor ‹ before HASHEM ‹ Bow down

הָאָרֶץ. [6] נִשְׁתַּחֲוֶה אֶל הֵיכַל קָדְשְׁךָ וְנוֹדֶה אֶת שְׁמֶךָ,

Your Name ‹ and we will thank ‹‹ Your Holy Sanctuary, ‹ toward ‹ We will prostrate ourselves ‹‹ on earth.

עַל חַסְדְּךָ וְעַל אֲמִתֶּךָ, כִּי הִגְדַּלְתָּ עַל כָּל שִׁמְךָ

Your Name — ‹ — even beyond ‹‹ You have exalted ‹ for ‹‹ Your faithfulness; ‹ and for ‹ Your kindness ‹ for

אִמְרָתֶךָ. [7] יהוה אֱלֹהֵי צְבָאוֹת, מִי כָמוֹךָ חֲסִין

O Strong One, ‹ is like ‹ — who ‹‹ of Legions ‹ God ‹ HASHEM, ‹‹ Your promise.

יָהּ, וֶאֱמוּנָתְךָ סְבִיבוֹתֶיךָ. [8] כִּי מִי בַשַּׁחַק יַעֲרֹךְ

can be compared ‹ in the sky ‹ who ‹ For ‹‹ surrounds You. ‹ and Your faithfulness ‹‹ God? —

לַיהוה, יִדְמֶה לַיהוה בִּבְנֵי אֵלִים. [9] כִּי גָדוֹל אַתָּה

are You ‹ great ‹ For ‹‹ among the angels? ‹ to HASHEM ‹ be likened ‹‹ to HASHEM;

וְעֹשֵׂה נִפְלָאוֹת, אַתָּה אֱלֹהִים לְבַדֶּךָ. [10] כִּי גָדוֹל

great ‹ For ‹‹ alone. ‹ O God, ‹ You, ‹‹ of wonders; ‹ and a worker

---

(1) Cf. *Psalms* 5:8. (2) 134:1. (3) 134:2. (4) 99:5. (5) 99:9. (6) 96:9. (7) Cf. 138:2. (8) 89:9. (9) 89:7. (10) 86:10.

גָּדוֹל ¹.מֵעַל שָׁמַיִם חַסְדֶּךָ, וְעַד שְׁחָקִים אֲמִתֶּךָ.

⟨ Great ⟫ is Your ⟨ the upper ⟨ and ⟫ is Your ⟨ the very ⟨ above
truth. heights until kindness, heavens

גָּדוֹל (כִּי) ².יהוה וּמְהֻלָּל מְאֹד, וְלִגְדֻלָּתוֹ אֵין חֵקֶר.

⟨ great ⟨ (For) ⟫ investiga- ⟨ is ⟨ and His ⟫ exceed- ⟨ and ⟨ is
tion. beyond greatness ingly, lauded HASHEM

כִּי ³.יהוה וּמְהֻלָּל מְאֹד, נוֹרָא הוּא עַל כָּל אֱלֹהִים.

⟨For ⟫ heavenly ⟨ all ⟨ above ⟨ is He ⟨ awesome ⟫ exceed- ⟨ and ⟨ is
powers. ingly; lauded HASHEM

אֲשֶׁר ⁴.אֵל גָּדוֹל יהוה, וּמֶלֶךְ גָּדוֹל עַל כָּל אֱלֹהִים.

⟨ For ⟫ heavenly ⟨ all ⟨ above ⟨ and a great King ⟫ is ⟨ a great God
powers. HASHEM,

כְמַעֲשֶׂיךָ אֲשֶׁר יַעֲשֶׂה וּבָאָרֶץ, בַּשָּׁמַיִם אֵל מִי

⟨ like unto ⟨ can do ⟨ that ⟨ or in the ⟨ is there in ⟨ power ⟨ what
Your deeds earth the heaven

לְךָ כִּי הַגּוֹיִם, מֶלֶךְ יִרָאֲךָ לֹא מִי ⁵.וְכִגְבוּרֹתֶיךָ.

⟨ to ⟨ For ⟫ of nations? ⟨ O King ⟫ fear You, ⟨ would ⟨ Who ⟫ and like unto Your
You not mighty acts?

מֵאֵין מַלְכוּתָם וּבְכָל הַגּוֹיִם חַכְמֵי בְּכָל כִּי יָאָתָה,

⟨ there is ⟨ their ⟨ and in all ⟨ of the ⟨ the wise ⟨ among ⟨ for ⟫ [kingship]
none kingdoms nations men all befits;

שְׁמֶךָ וְגָדוֹל אַתָּה גָּדוֹל יהוה, כָמוֹךָ מֵאֵין ⁶.כָּמוֹךָ.

⟨ is Your ⟨ and great ⟨ are You ⟨ Great ⟫ O ⟨ like You, ⟨ There is ⟫ like You.
Name HASHEM! none

תָּרוּם יָדְךָ תָּעֹז גְּבוּרָה, עִם זְרוֹעַ לְךָ ⁷.בִּגְבוּרָה.

⟨ uplifted ⟫ is Your ⟨ strength- ⟫ power; ⟨ with ⟨ is the ⟨ Yours ⟫ in might.
hand, ened arm

מָאוֹר הֲכִינוֹתָ אַתָּה לָיְלָה, לְךָ אַף יוֹם, לְךָ ⁸.יְמִינֶךָ.

⟨ the ⟨ prepared ⟨ You ⟫ is the ⟨ Yours ⟨ also ⟫ is the ⟨ Yours ⟫ is Your
luminary night; day, right hand.

הָרִים וְתוֹעֲפוֹת אָרֶץ, מֶחְקְרֵי בְיָדוֹ אֲשֶׁר ⁹.וָשָׁמֶשׁ.

⟨ of the ⟨ and the ⟫ of the ⟨ are the hidden ⟨ in His ⟨ For ⟫ and the
mountains summits earth, mysteries power sun.

¹¹.לוֹ ¹⁰.מִי יְמַלֵּל גְּבוּרוֹת יהוה, יַשְׁמִיעַ כָּל תְּהִלָּתוֹ.

⟫ of His ⟨ all ⟨ [who] can ⟫ of ⟨ the mighty ⟨ can ⟨ Who ⟫ are
praise? make heard HASHEM; acts express His.

---

(1) *Psalms* 108:5. (2) 145:3. (3) 96:4. (4) 95:3. (5) *Deuteronomy* 3:24.
(6) *Jeremiah* 10:7. (7) 10:6. (8) *Psalms* 89:14. (9) 74:16. (10) 95:4. (11) 106:2.

לְךָ יהוה הַגְּדֻלָּה וְהַגְּבוּרָה, וְהַתִּפְאֶרֶת וְהַנֵּצַח

⟨ the triumph, ⟨ the glory, ⟨ the strength, ⟨ is the greatness, ⟨ HASHEM, ⟨ Yours,

וְהַהוֹד, כִּי כֹל בַּשָּׁמַיִם וּבָאָרֶץ; לְךָ יהוה הַמַּמְלָכָה,

⟨ is the kingdom ⟨ HASHEM, ⟨ Yours, ⟨⟨ and on earth [is Yours]; ⟨ in heaven ⟨ every-thing ⟨ for ⟨⟨ and the majesty;

וְהַמִּתְנַשֵּׂא לְכֹל לְרֹאשׁ.¹ לְךָ שָׁמַיִם, אַף לְךָ אָרֶץ,

⟨⟨ is the earth; ⟨ Yours ⟨ also ⟨⟨ are the heavens, ⟨ Yours ⟨⟨ leader. ⟨ over every ⟨ and the sovereignty

תֵּבֵל וּמְלֹאָהּ אַתָּה יְסַדְתָּם.² אַתָּה הִצַּבְתָּ כָּל גְּבוּלוֹת

⟨ the boundaries ⟨ all ⟨ established ⟨ You ⟨⟨ founded them. ⟨ You ⟨ and its fullness, ⟨ the world

אָרֶץ, קַיִץ וָחֹרֶף אַתָּה יְצַרְתָּם.³ אַתָּה רִצַּצְתָּ רָאשֵׁי

⟨ the heads ⟨ crushed ⟨ You ⟨⟨ fashioned them. ⟨ You ⟨ and winter, ⟨ summer ⟨⟨ of earth;

לִוְיָתָן, תִּתְּנֶנּוּ מַאֲכָל לְעָם לְצִיִּים. אַתָּה בָקַעְתָּ מַעְיָן

⟨ fountain ⟨ split open ⟨ You ⟨⟨ [destined] for the desolate people ⟨ to the wilderness. ⟨ as food ⟨ You will ⟨⟨ serve it ⟨ of Leviathan;

וָנָחַל, אַתָּה הוֹבַשְׁתָּ נַהֲרוֹת אֵיתָן.⁴ אַתָּה פוֹרַרְתָּ

⟨ shattered ⟨ You ⟨⟨ that are mighty. ⟨ rivers ⟨ dried ⟨ You ⟨⟨ and stream;

בְעָזְּךָ יָם, שִׁבַּרְתָּ רָאשֵׁי תַנִּינִים עַל הַמָּיִם.⁵ אַתָּה

⟨ You ⟨⟨ the water. ⟨ upon ⟨ of sea serpents ⟨ the heads ⟨ You ⟨⟨ the sea; ⟨ with Your might

מוֹשֵׁל בְּגֵאוּת הַיָּם, בְּשׂוֹא גַלָּיו אַתָּה תְשַׁבְּחֵם.⁶

⟨⟨ calm them. ⟨ You ⟨ its waves, ⟨ when it raises ⟨⟨ of the sea; ⟨ the grandeur ⟨ rule

גָּדוֹל יהוה וּמְהֻלָּל מְאֹד, בְּעִיר אֱלֹהֵינוּ הַר קָדְשׁוֹ.⁷

⟨⟨ of His Holiness. ⟨ Mount ⟨ of our God, ⟨ in the City ⟨ and much praised, ⟨ is HASHEM ⟨ Great

יהוה צְבָאוֹת, אֱלֹהֵי יִשְׂרָאֵל, יוֹשֵׁב הַכְּרֻבִים, אַתָּה

⟨ it is You ⟨⟨ upon the Cherubim, ⟨ en-throned ⟨ of Israel, ⟨ God ⟨ Master of Legions, ⟨ HASHEM,

הוּא הָאֱלֹהִים לְבַדֶּךָ.⁸ אֵל נַעֲרָץ בְּסוֹד קְדֹשִׁים רַבָּה,

⟨⟨ in the great assemblage of the holy [angels], ⟨ is revered ⟨ God ⟨⟨ alone. ⟨ God ⟨ Who are

---

(1) *I Chronicles* 29:11. (2) *Psalms* 89:12. (3) 74:17. (4) 74:14-15. (5) 74:13. (6) 89:10. (7) 48:2. (8) *Isaiah* 37:16.

וְנוֹרָא עַל כָּל סְבִיבָיו.[1] וְיוֹדוּ שָׁמַיִם פִּלְאֲךָ יהוה, אַף

⟨ also ⟨ HASHEM, ⟨ Your ⟨ will the ⟨ Acknowl- ⟨ who sur- ⟨ all ⟨ over ⟨ and is
    wonders,   heavens   edge   round Him.   awesome

אֱמוּנָתְךָ בִּקְהַל קְדֹשִׁים.[2] לְכוּ נְרַנְּנָה לַיהוה, נָרִיעָה

⟨ let us ⟨ to ⟨ Let us sing ⟨ Come! ⟨ of holy ⟨ in the ⟨ Your
call out   HASHEM,   joyfully   ones.   assembly   faithfulness,

לְצוּר יִשְׁעֵנוּ. נְקַדְּמָה פָנָיו בְּתוֹדָה, בִּזְמִירוֹת נָרִיעַ

⟨ let us ⟨ with praiseful ⟨ with ⟨ Him ⟨ Let us greet ⟨ of our ⟨ to the
call out   songs   thanksgiving,   salvation.   Rock

לוֹ.[3] צֶדֶק וּמִשְׁפָּט מְכוֹן כִּסְאֶךָ, חֶסֶד וֶאֱמֶת יְקַדְּמוּ

⟨ precede ⟨ and ⟨ kindness ⟨ of Your ⟨ are the ⟨ and ⟨ Righteous- ⟨ to
   truth   throne;   foundation   justice   ness   Him.

פָנֶיךָ.[4] אֲשֶׁר יַחְדָּו נַמְתִּיק סוֹד, בְּבֵית אֱלֹהִים נְהַלֵּךְ

⟨ let us ⟨ of God ⟨ in the ⟨ counsel; ⟨ let us ⟨ together ⟨ For ⟨ Your coun-
walk   House   take sweet   tenance.

בְּרָגֶשׁ.[5] אֲשֶׁר לוֹ הַיָּם וְהוּא עָשָׂהוּ, וְיַבֶּשֶׁת יָדָיו

⟨ His ⟨ and the ⟨ perfected ⟨ and He ⟨ is the ⟨ His ⟨ For ⟨ in company.
hands   dry land,   it,   sea

יָצָרוּ.[6] אֲשֶׁר בְּיָדוֹ נֶפֶשׁ כָּל חָי, וְרוּחַ כָּל בְּשַׂר אִישׁ.[7]

⟨ mankind. ⟨ of all ⟨ and the ⟨ the ⟨ of ⟨ is the ⟨ in His ⟨ For ⟨ fashioned.
     spirit   living   all   soul   hand

❖ הַנְּשָׁמָה לָךְ וְהַגּוּף פָּעֳלָךְ, חוּסָה עַל עֲמָלָךְ.

⟨ Your ⟨ on ⟨ take pity ⟨ is Your ⟨ and the ⟨ is ⟨ The soul
labor.   handiwork;   body   Yours

הַנְּשָׁמָה לָךְ וְהַגּוּף שֶׁלָּךְ, יהוה עֲשֵׂה לְמַעַן שְׁמֶךָ.

⟨ of Your ⟨ for the ⟨ act ⟨ O ⟨ is Yours; ⟨ and the ⟨ is ⟨ The soul
Name.   sake   HASHEM,   body   Yours

אָתָאנוּ עַל שְׁמֶךָ, יהוה, עֲשֵׂה לְמַעַן שְׁמֶךָ. בַּעֲבוּר

⟨ [act] ⟨ of Your ⟨ for the ⟨ act ⟨ O ⟨ Your ⟨ [relying] ⟨ We have
because of   Name;   sake   HASHEM;   Name,   on   come

כְּבוֹד שְׁמֶךָ, כִּי אֵל חַנּוּן וְרַחוּם שְׁמֶךָ. לְמַעַן

⟨ For the ⟨ is Your ⟨ and ⟨ Who is ⟨ God ⟨ for ⟨ of Your ⟨ the glory
sake   Name.   Merciful   Gracious   Name,

שְׁמֶךָ יהוה, וְסָלַחְתָּ לַעֲוֹנֵנוּ כִּי רַב הוּא.[8]

⟨ it is great. ⟨ though ⟨ our ⟨ forgive ⟨ HASHEM, ⟨ of Your
    iniquity,   Name,

---

(1) *Psalms* 89:8. (2) 89:6. (3) 95:1-2. (4) 89:15. (5) 55:15. (6) 95:5. (7) *Job* 12:10. (8) Cf. *Psalms* 25:11.

CONGREGATION, THEN *CHAZZAN:*

סְלַח לָנוּ אָבִינוּ, כִּי בְרוֹב אִוַּלְתֵּנוּ שָׁגִינוּ,

《 we have 〈 of our folly 〈 in the 〈 for 〈 our Father, 〈 us, 〈 Forgive
erred; abundance

מְחַל לָנוּ מַלְכֵּנוּ, כִּי רַבּוּ עֲוֹנֵינוּ.

《 our 〈 many 〈 for 〈 our King, 〈 us, 〈 pardon
iniquities. are

ALL, WHILE STANDING

אֵל אֶרֶךְ אַפַּיִם אַתָּה,

《 You are, 〈 to anger, 〈 Who is slow 〈 God

וּבַעַל הָרַחֲמִים נִקְרֵאתָ, וְדֶרֶךְ תְּשׁוּבָה הוֹרֵיתָ.

《 You have 〈 of 〈 and the 《 You are 〈 of Mercy 〈 and
taught. repentance way called; Master

גְּדֻלַּת רַחֲמֶיךָ וַחֲסָדֶיךָ,

〈 and Your 〈 of Your 〈 The
kindness mercy greatness

תִּזְכּוֹר הַיּוֹם וּבְכָל יוֹם לְזֶרַע יְדִידֶיךָ.

《 of Your 〈 for the 《 day, 〈 and 〈 this day 〈 may You
beloved ones. offspring every remember,

תֵּפֶן אֵלֵינוּ בְּרַחֲמִים,

《 in mercy, 〈 to us 〈 Turn

כִּי אַתָּה הוּא בַּעַל הָרַחֲמִים.

《 of Mercy. 〈 the Master 〈 are 〈 You 〈 for

בְּתַחֲנוּן וּבִתְפִלָּה פָּנֶיךָ נְקַדֵּם, כְּהוֹדַעְתָּ לֶעָנָיו מִקֶּדֶם.

《in ancient 〈 to the 〈 in the manner 《 we 〈 Your 〈 and prayer 《 With
times. humble one that You made approach, Presence supplication
[Moses] known

מֵחֲרוֹן אַפְּךָ שׁוּב,¹ כְּמוֹ בְּתוֹרָתְךָ כָּתוּב.²

《 it is 〈 in Your Torah 〈 as 《 turn 〈 of Your 〈 From the
written. back, anger fierceness

וּבְצֵל כְּנָפֶיךָ נֶחֱסֶה³ וְנִתְלוֹנָן, כְּיוֹם וַיֵּרֶד יהוה בֶּעָנָן.

《 in a 〈 when HASHEM 〈 as on 《 and may 〈 may we find 〈 of Your 〈 In the
cloud. descended the day we dwell shelter wings shadow

❖ תַּעֲבוֹר עַל פֶּשַׁע וְתִמְחֶה אָשָׁם,

《 guilt, 〈 and erase 〈 sin 〈 Overlook

---

(1) Cf. *Exodus* 32:12. (2) See 32:14. (3) Cf. *Psalms* 36:8.

כְּיוֹם וַיִּתְיַצֵּב עִמּוֹ שָׁם.

《 there. 〈 with him 〈 when He 〈 as on the
[Moses] [God] stood day

תַּאֲזִין שַׁוְעָתֵנוּ וְתַקְשִׁיב מֶנּוּ מַאֲמַר,

《 [our] 〈 from 〈 and hear 〈 to our cry 〈 Give heed
declaration, us

כְּיוֹם וַיִּקְרָא בְשֵׁם יהוה,[1] וְשָׁם נֶאֱמַר:

《 it was said: 〈 and 《 of HASHEM, 〈 with the 〈 when He 〈 as on
there Name called out the day

CONGREGATION, THEN *CHAZZAN*:

וַיַּעֲבֹר יהוה עַל פָּנָיו וַיִּקְרָא:

《 and 《 [Moses'] 〈 before 〈 And HASHEM passed
proclaimed: face,

CONGREGATION AND *CHAZZAN* RECITE LOUDLY AND IN UNISON:

יהוה, יהוה, אֵל, רַחוּם, וְחַנּוּן, אֶרֶךְ אַפַּיִם,

〈 to anger, 〈 Slow 《 and Gracious, 〈 Compassionate 〈 God, 〈 HASHEM, 〈 HASHEM,

וְרַב חֶסֶד, וֶאֱמֶת, נֹצֵר חֶסֶד לָאֲלָפִים, נֹשֵׂא עָוֹן,

〈 of 〈 Forgiver 《 for thousands 〈 of 〈 Preserver 《 and 〈 in 〈 and
iniquity, [of generations], kindness Truth, Kindness Abundant

וָפֶשַׁע, וְחַטָּאָה, וְנַקֵּה.[2] וְסָלַחְתָּ לַעֲוֹנֵנוּ וּלְחַטָּאתֵנוּ

《 and our sins, 〈 our 〈 May You 《 and Who 〈 and inadvertent 〈 willful sin,
iniquities forgive absolves. sin,

וּנְחַלְתָּנוּ.[3] סְלַח לָנוּ אָבִינוּ כִּי חָטָאנוּ, מְחַל לָנוּ

〈 us, 〈 pardon 《 we have 〈 for 《 our Father, 〈 us, 〈 Forgive 《 and make us
sinned; Your heritage.

מַלְכֵּנוּ כִּי פָשָׁעְנוּ. כִּי אַתָּה אֲדֹנָי טוֹב וְסַלָּח, וְרַב

〈 and 《 and 〈 are 〈 O Lord, 〈 You, 〈 For 《 we have 〈 for 《 our King,
abundantly forgiving, good willfully sinned.

חֶסֶד לְכָל קֹרְאֶיךָ.[4]

《 who call 〈 to all 〈 kind
upon You.

פְּסוּקֵי הַקְדָּמָה לִסְלִיחָה כ / PREFATORY VERSES TO SELICHAH 20

אַתָּה יהוה לֹא תִכְלָא רַחֲמֶיךָ מִמֶּנּוּ, חַסְדְּךָ

〈 may Your 《 from me; 〈 Your mercy 〈 withhold 〈 do 〈 HASHEM, 〈 You,
kindness not

---

(1) *Exodus* 34:5. (2) 34:6-7. (3) 34:9. (4) *Psalms* 86:5.

וַאֲמִתְּךָ תָּמִיד יִצְּרוּנִי.¹ שׁוּבָה יִשְׂרָאֵל עַד יהוה

‹ HASHEM, ‹ unto ‹ O Israel, ‹ Return, « protect me. ‹ always ‹ and Your truth

אֱלֹהֶיךָ, כִּי כָשַׁלְתָּ בַּעֲוֹנֶךָ.² כִּי שֹׁמֵעַ אֶל אֶבְיוֹנִים

‹ the ‹ to ‹ listen ‹ For « in your ‹ you have ‹ for « your God,
destitute   iniquity.   stumbled

יהוה; וְאֶת אֲסִירָיו לֹא בָזָה.³

« He has not ‹ and His prisoners « does
despised.   HASHEM,

כְּרַחֵם אָב עַל בָּנִים, כֵּן תְּרַחֵם יהוה עָלֵינוּ.⁴

« on us. ‹ HASHEM, ‹ have ‹ so « his ‹ toward ‹ a ‹ As merciful as
mercy,   children,   father is

לַיהוה הַיְשׁוּעָה, עַל עַמְּךָ בִרְכָתֶךָ סֶּלָה.⁵ יהוה

‹ HASHEM, « Selah. ‹ is Your ‹ Your ‹ upon ‹ is salvation, ‹ To HASHEM
blessing,   people

צְבָאוֹת עִמָּנוּ, מִשְׂגָּב לָנוּ אֱלֹהֵי יַעֲקֹב סֶלָה.⁶

« Selah. ‹ of Jacob, ‹ is the God ‹ for us ‹ a « is with us, ‹ Master of
stronghold   Legions,

יהוה צְבָאוֹת, אַשְׁרֵי אָדָם בֹּטֵחַ בָּךְ.⁷ יהוה הוֹשִׁיעָה,

« save! ‹ HASHEM, « in ‹ who ‹ is the ‹ — praise- « Master of ‹ HASHEM,
You.   trusts   man   worthy   Legions

הַמֶּלֶךְ יַעֲנֵנוּ בְיוֹם קָרְאֵנוּ.⁸

« we call. ‹ on the ‹ answer us ‹ May the
day   King

**IN MOST CONGREGATIONS THE FOLLOWING VERSES ARE RECITED ALOUD RESPONSIVELY,
AS INDICATED; IN OTHERS THEY ARE RECITED SILENTLY.**

CONGREGATION, ALOUD, FOLLOWED BY *CHAZZAN*, ALOUD:

סְלַח נָא לַעֲוֹן הָעָם הַזֶּה כְּגֹדֶל חַסְדֶּךָ, וְכַאֲשֶׁר

‹ just as « of Your ‹ according to ‹ of this people ‹ the ‹ please, ‹ Forgive,
kindness, the greatness   iniquity

נָשָׂאתָה לָעָם הַזֶּה מִמִּצְרַיִם וְעַד הֵנָּה,⁹ וְשָׁם נֶאֱמַר:

« it was ‹ And « now. ‹ until ‹ from Egypt ‹ this people ‹ You have
said: there   forgiven

ALL, ALOUD AND IN UNISON:

וַיֹּאמֶר יהוה סָלַחְתִּי כִּדְבָרֶךָ.¹⁰

« according ‹ I have forgiven « And HASHEM said:
to your word!

---

(1) Cf. *Psalms* 40:12. (2) *Hosea* 14:2. (3) *Psalms* 69:34. (4) *Jeremiah* 31:6.
(5) Cf. *Psalms* 103:13. (6) 3:9. (7) 46:8. (8) 84:13. (9) *Numbers* 14:19. (10) 14:20.

ALL CONTINUE:

הַטֵּה אֱלֹהַי אָזְנְךָ וּשֲׁמָע, פְּקַח עֵינֶיךָ וּרְאֵה
⟨ and see ⟨ Your eyes ⟨ open ⟪ and listen; ⟨ Your ear, ⟨ my God, ⟨ Incline,

שֹׁמְמֹתֵינוּ, וְהָעִיר אֲשֶׁר נִקְרָא שִׁמְךָ עָלֶיהָ, כִּי לֹא
⟨ not ⟨ for ⟪ upon; ⟨ Your Name is ⟨ which ⟨ and that ⟨ our desolation
proclaimed [of] the city

עַל צִדְקֹתֵינוּ אֲנַחְנוּ מַפִּילִים תַּחֲנוּנֵינוּ לְפָנֶיךָ,
⟪ before ⟨ our ⟨ cast ⟨ do we ⟨ of our ⟨ because
You; supplications righteousness

כִּי עַל רַחֲמֶיךָ הָרַבִּים. אֲדֹנָי שְׁמָעָה, אֲדֹנָי סְלָחָה,
⟪ forgive; ⟨ O Lord, ⟪ heed; ⟨ O Lord, ⟪ which is ⟨ of Your ⟨ be- ⟨ but
abundant. compassion, cause

אֲדֹנָי הַקְשִׁיבָה, וַעֲשֵׂה אַל תְּאַחַר, לְמַעַנְךָ אֱלֹהַי,
⟪ my God, ⟨ for Your sake, ⟪ delay; ⟨ do not ⟪ and act, ⟨ be attentive, ⟨ O Lord,

כִּי שִׁמְךָ נִקְרָא עַל עִירְךָ וְעַל עַמֶּךָ.¹
⟪ Your ⟨ and ⟨ Your ⟨ upon ⟨ is ⟨ Your ⟨ for
people. upon City proclaimed Name

סליחה כ / SELICHAH 20

ALL:

אֱלֹהֵינוּ וֵאלֹהֵי אֲבוֹתֵינוּ:
⟪ of our forefathers: ⟨ and the God ⟨ Our God

אֲנַחְנוּ הַחֹמֶר* וְאַתָּה יוֹצְרֵנוּ,²
⟪ our molder; ⟨ and You are ⟨ the clay* ⟨ We are

אֲמִתְּךָ וְחַסְדְּךָ תָּמִיד יִצְּרוּנוּ,³
⟪ protect us. ⟨ always ⟨ and Your ⟨ may Your
kindness truth

בְּאַפְּךָ אַל תּוֹכִיחֵנוּ צוּרֵנוּ,
⟪ O our ⟨ rebuke us ⟨ do ⟪ In Your
Rock; not anger,

בְּשֶׁצֶף חֲמָתְךָ אַל תְּיַסְּרֵנוּ.⁴
⟪ chastise us. ⟨ do not ⟨ of Your rage ⟨ in the stream

---

(1) *Daniel* 9:18-19. (2) *Isaiah* 64:7. (3) Cf. *Psalms* 40:12. (4) Cf. 6:2.

---

§ אֲנַחְנוּ הַחֹמֶר — *We are the clay.* This unsigned *selichah* contains a double alphabetical acrostic. Recognizing that Israel's sins
led to its long exile, the nation beseeches
Hashem for the fulfillment of His promised
Redemption.

גְּשְׁתֵּנוּ אֵלֶיךָ בְּקִיחַת דְּבָרִים,[1]

《words [of remorse- 〈 is by taking 〈 to You 〈 Our
ful confession]; 　　　　　　　　　　　　 approach

גַּלְגֵּל רַחֲמֶיךָ מְשׁוּב חֲפוּרִים,

《 in shame. 〈 that we not 〈 Your mercy 〈 arouse
be turned back

דָּרַשְׁנוּ שְׁכִנְךָ בְּלִבּוֹת נִשְׁבָּרִים,

《 that are 〈 with 〈 Your dwelling- 〈 We have
broken; 　 hearts 　 place 　 sought out

דְּלֵנוּ מֵרֶפֶשׁ וְרַפֵּא שְׁבָרִים.

《 the broken 〈 and heal 《 out of 〈 draw us
[hearts]! 　　　　 [exile's] mud, 　 up

הַעֲבֵר חֶרְפָּתֵנוּ אֲשֶׁר נָגוּר,[2]

《 we fear. 〈 that 〈 our disgrace 〈 Remove
[of sin]

הַאֲלֵם מְלָשְׁנִי וְהַגְבֵּר סַנֵּיגוֹר,

《 the 〈 and 〈 the Accuser 〈 Strike
Advocate. 　 strengthen 　　　　 dumb

וְשַׁעֲרֵי תְפִלָּתֵנוּ בַּל תִּסְגֹּר,

《 close; 〈 do 〈 of our prayer 〈 But the
not 　　　　　　　 gateways

וְעַל שׂוֹטְנֵנוּ חֵמוֹת תַּחְגֹּר.

《You should don. 〈 rather 〈 our Adversary 〈 against

זַכֵּנוּ מֵחֵטְא וְהַחֲסֵנוּ בְּצִלָּךְ,

《 in Your 〈 and shelter 〈 from sin 〈 Exonerate
shade; 　　 us 　　　　　　　 us

זְדוֹנֵנוּ תִּמְחֶה וְתַשְׁלִיךְ בִּמְצוּלָךְ,

《 into the depths 〈 and throw it 〈 wipe away 〈 our willful
of Your sea. 　　　　　　　　　　　　 sin

חַבְּאֵנוּ וְהַסְתִּירֵנוּ בְּסֵתֶר אָהֳלָךְ,[3]

《 of Your tent. 〈 in the con- 〈 and conceal us 〈 Hide us,
cealment

חוּסָה עַל עֲמָלָךְ[4] וּקְהָלָךְ.

《 and Your 〈 Your handi- 〈 on 〈 Take pity
congregation. 　 work

---

(1) Cf. *Hosea* 14:3. (2) Cf. *Psalms* 119:39. (3) Cf. 27:5.
(4) Some editions read עַל עַמָּךְ, *on Your people;* see *Joel* 2:17.

טִמֵּאתָנוּ טַהֵר וְעָרְלַת לְבָבֵנוּ מוֹל,[1]

《 cut away. 〈 of our heart 〈 the blockage 《 purify [us]; 〈 [Of] our contamination

טוּב מִדָּתְךָ לָנוּ תִגְמֹל,

《 grant recompense; 〈 to us 《 —Your Attribute — 《According to Goodness

יַעַן וּבְיַעַן* אוֹתָנוּ מִלִּגְמֹל,

《 do not repay, 〈 to us, 〈 indeed because ...,* 〈 [with] Because

יֶהֱמוּ מֵעֶיךָ, סְגֻלָּתְךָ תַּחְמֹל.

《 You have compassion. 〈 that on Your treasured people 〈 within You 《May there be aroused

כְּמוֹ הָרָה תָּחִיל וְתִזְעַק,* כֵּן מִפָּנֶיךָ נָחִיל וְנִזְעַק,[2]

《 and scream. 〈 we are in pain 〈 in the face [of Your anger], too, 《 so 《 and screams,* 〈 suffers pain 〈 a pregnant woman [in labor] 〈 As

לֹא תִבְזֶה עֱנוּת זַעַק, לֹא תְשַׁקֵּץ עֵרֶךְ צֶעַק.[3]

《 outcry. 〈 our ordered 〈 loathe 〈 nor 〈 that is screamed, 〈 the supplication 〈 disdain 〈 Do not

מְשׁוּבָה יִשְׂרָאֵל הַבַּת הַשּׁוֹבֵבָה,[4]

《 who is wayward — 〈 the daughter 《 [is] Israel, 〈 [Even though] rebellious

מַלֵּא דְבָרֶךָ וּלְנָוֶהָ תְּשׁוֹבֵבָה,

《 bring her back! 〈 and to her home 〈 Your word 〈 [nevertheless] fulfill

---

(1) Cf. *Deuteronomy* 10:16. (2) Cf. *Isaiah* 26:17. (3) Cf. *Psalms* 22:25. (4) Cf. *Jeremiah* 31:21.

יַעַן וּבְיַעַן — *Because indeed because....* In the תּוֹכָחָה, *Admonition* (*Leviticus* 26:14-43), the Torah describes the punishments that will befall the Jewish people if they fail to live up to their obligation as God's Chosen Nation. These verses end: *Because indeed because My ordinances they detested and My decrees were found abhorrent by their soul.* According to the Vilna Gaon, the expression, יַעַן וּבְיַעַן, *because indeed because,* teaches a cause and effect relationship between sin and retribution. In the same measure that they took disgust in God's laws and their spirit rejected God's decrees, did God take disgust in them and reject them (*Aderes Eliyahu*).

The *paytan* pleads that God not punish us as we are deserving according to the principle of "because indeed because ...." Rather, He should grant our recompense commensurate with His Attribute of Goodness (*Pardes*).

כְּמוֹ הָרָה תָּחִיל וְתִזְעַק — *As a pregnant woman suffers pain and screams.* Just as a woman in travail suffers greater and greater pain as her term nears, yet she never loses her love for her husband who brought her into this state, so even as our time draws near and retribution for our sins causes us to shudder and wail, we do not lose our love for God Whose castigation brought us into this state (*Radak* to *Isaiah* 26:17, citing his father, R' Yosef Kimchi).

נָאוֹר, הֲשִׁיבֵנוּ אֵלֶיךָ וְנָשׁוּבָה,¹

《 O Luminous One, 〈 bring us back 《 to You 〈 and we will return,

נְאֻם הַגֶּבֶר תְּסוֹבֵב נְקֵבָה.*²

《 as it is said, 〈 The man [God] 〈 shall be 〈 sought 《 by the woman [Israel].*

שְׂרוּפָה בָאֵשׁ כְּסוּחָה מִגַּעֲרָתֶךָ,³

《 Burnt 〈 by the fire, 《 razed 〈 by Your angry shout,

סָלוּהָ וְאָרוּהָ מוֹאֲסֵי בְרִיתֶךָ,

《 trample her 〈 and pluck her fruit 〈 did those who despise 〈 Your covenant.

עוֹלָלֶיהָ תְּעוֹלֵל וְתָחוֹן שְׁאֵרִיתֶךָ,⁴

《 Her few remaining grapes 〈 gather up 〈 and be gracious 〈 to Your remnant;

עוֹד כְּקֶדֶם תִּכּוֹן עֲדָתֶךָ.⁵

《 once again, 〈 as of old, 《 established 〈 let Your congregation be.

פְּקֹד גֶּפֶן זֹאת הַבְּקוּקָה,⁶

《 that is ravaged! 〈 of this vine 〈 Be mindful

פְּרַע בּוֹקְקֶיהָ כְּחֻקָּה הַחֲקוּקָה,

《 that is inscribed. 〈 according to the law 〈 her ravagers 《 Pay back

צָרְרוּהָ צָרִים בְּבוּקָה וּמְבֻלָּקָה,

《 and plundering. 〈 ravaging 《 have her enemies, 〈 Oppressed her

צוֹרְרֶיהָ תָּצוּר לְהַבְהֵב עֲלוּקָה.⁷

《 leech [Gehinnom]. 〈 to the flaming 〈 You should attach firmly 〈 Her oppressors

---

(1) Cf. *Lamentations* 5:21. (2) Cf. *Jeremiah* 31:21. (3) Cf. *Psalms* 80:17. (4) Cf. *Jeremiah* 6:9. (5) Cf. 30:20. (6) Cf. *Psalms* 80:15; *Hosea* 10:1. (7) Cf. *Proverbs* 30:15.

הַגֶּבֶר תְּסוֹבֵב נְקֵבָה — *The man [God] shall be sought by the woman [Israel]*. According to the prophet there will be a new world order in which the woman will seek the man (*Jeremiah* 31:21). In this world, it is the man who seeks a mate. As the Talmud states: When a person loses a piece of property, who searches for whom? It is the owner who searches for his lost article [and not the article that seeks its owner]. Thus, it is Man who lost his rib [that was fashioned into Woman] who seeks that which he has lost [his rib/mate] (*Kiddushin* 2b). Similarly, in this world, it is God Who is constantly seeking a closeness with His wayward people. But there will come a time of a new world order in which all of Israel will ardently seek to return to its origin, to God its Creator (see *Hosea* Ch. 2). In the *selichah*, we declare that we seek this closeness to Him now.

קוֹמֵם נְפוּלָה כַּמָּה שָׁנִים,

《 years, 〈 for so many 〈 the [nation] 〈 Raise fallen

קְדוֹרַנִּית יוֹשֶׁבֶת בְּמַחֲשַׁכֵּי אִישׁוֹנִים,

《 of nights. 〈 in the darkness 〈 sits 〈 who drearily

רָם תִּזְכֹּר בְּרִית רִאשׁוֹנִים,[1]

《 of the original ancestors; 〈 the covenant 〈 re-member 《O Exalted One,

רוֹמֵם דְּבִירְךָ מֵחָרְבָנִים רִאשׁוֹנִים.

《 that are ancient! 〈 out of [its] ruins 〈 Your Holy Temple 〈 raise up

❖ שְׁעֵה שַׁוְעָה וְקַבֵּל פְּגִיעָה,

《 supplication; 〈 and accept 〈 to [our] outcry, 〈 Turn

שְׁבֹר רִשְׁעָה, חֲבֹשׁ צוֹלֵעָה,

《 the lame. 〈 bandage 《 the wicked [nation]; 〈 break

תָּקִים שְׁבוּעָה תָּחִישׁ יְשׁוּעָה,

《[our] redemption; 〈 hasten 《 [Your] oath; 〈 Uphold

תַּמָּה הוֹשִׁיעָה כִּי גָעָה קֵץ וְשָׁעָה.

《 and time! 〈 has [redemp-tion's] date 〈 come 〈 for 《 save, 〈 the whole-some [nation]

ALL, WHILE STANDING:

אֵל מֶלֶךְ יוֹשֵׁב עַל כִּסֵּא רַחֲמִים, מִתְנַהֵג

〈 Who acts 《 of mercy, 〈 the throne 〈 on 〈 Who sits 〈 King 〈 O God,

בַּחֲסִידוּת, מוֹחֵל עֲוֹנוֹת עַמּוֹ, מַעֲבִיר רִאשׁוֹן

〈 [sins,] one 〈 Who removes 《 of His people, 〈 the sins 〈 Who pardons 《 with kindness,

רִאשׁוֹן,[2] מַרְבֶּה מְחִילָה לְחַטָּאִים וּסְלִיחָה לַפּוֹשְׁעִים,

《 to willful sinners, 〈 and forgiveness 〈 to unintentional sinners 〈 pardon 〈 Who abun-dantly grants 《 by one,

עֹשֶׂה צְדָקוֹת עִם כָּל בָּשָׂר וָרוּחַ, לֹא כְרָעָתָם

〈 in accord with their wickedness 〈 — not 《 and spirit 〈 [beings of] flesh 〈 all 〈 with 〈 acts of generosity 〈 Who performs

---

(1) Cf. *Leviticus* 26:45. (2) *Rosh Hashanah* 17a.

תִּגְמוֹל. ❖ אֵל הוֹרֵיתָ לָּנוּ לוֹמַר שְׁלֹשׁ עֶשְׂרֵה, וּזְכוֹר

⟨ remem- ⟨⟨ the Thirteen ⟨ to ⟨ us ⟨ You ⟨ O God, ⟨⟨ do You
ber [Attributes of Mercy]; recite taught repay them!

לָּנוּ הַיּוֹם בְּרִית שְׁלֹשׁ עֶשְׂרֵה, כְּמוֹ שֶׁהוֹדַעְתָּ לֶעָנָיו

⟨ to the ⟨ You made ⟨ as ⟨⟨ of [these] Thirteen, ⟨ the ⟨ today ⟨ for us
humble one known covenant
[Moses]

מִקֶּדֶם, כְּמוֹ שֶׁכָּתוּב, וַיֵּרֶד יהוה בֶּעָנָן וַיִּתְיַצֵּב עִמּוֹ

⟨ with ⟨ and stood ⟨ in a ⟨ And HASHEM ⟨⟨ it is written: ⟨ as ⟨⟨ in ancient
him cloud descended times,

שָׁם, וַיִּקְרָא בְשֵׁם יהוה.[1]

⟨⟨ of ⟨ with the ⟨ and He ⟨⟨ there,
HASHEM. Name called out

CONGREGATION, THEN *CHAZZAN:*

וַיַּעֲבֹר יהוה עַל פָּנָיו וַיִּקְרָא:

⟨⟨ and ⟨⟨ [Moses'] ⟨ before ⟨ And HASHEM passed
proclaimed: face,

CONGREGATION AND *CHAZZAN* **RECITE LOUDLY AND IN UNISON:**

יהוה, יהוה, אֵל, רַחוּם, וְחַנּוּן, אֶרֶךְ אַפַּיִם,

⟨ to anger, ⟨ Slow ⟨⟨ and ⟨ Compassionate ⟨ God, ⟨ HASHEM, ⟨ HASHEM,
Gracious,

וְרַב חֶסֶד, וֶאֱמֶת, נֹצֵר חֶסֶד לָאֲלָפִים, נֹשֵׂא עָוֹן,

⟨ of ⟨ Forgiver ⟨⟨ for thousands ⟨ of ⟨ Preserver ⟨⟨ and ⟨ in ⟨ and
iniquity, [of generations], kindness Truth, Kindness Abundant

וָפֶשַׁע, וְחַטָּאָה, וְנַקֵּה.[2] וְסָלַחְתָּ לַעֲוֹנֵנוּ וּלְחַטָּאתֵנוּ

⟨⟨ and our sins, ⟨ our ⟨ May You ⟨⟨ and Who ⟨ and inadvertent ⟨ willful sin,
iniquities forgive absolves. sin,

וּנְחַלְתָּנוּ.[3] סְלַח לָנוּ אָבִינוּ כִּי חָטָאנוּ, מְחַל לָנוּ

⟨ us, ⟨ pardon ⟨⟨ we have ⟨ for ⟨⟨ our ⟨ us, ⟨ Forgive ⟨⟨ and make us
sinned; Father, Your heritage.

מַלְכֵּנוּ כִּי פָשָׁעְנוּ. כִּי אַתָּה אֲדֹנָי טוֹב וְסַלָּח,

⟨⟨ and ⟨ are ⟨ O Lord, ⟨ You, ⟨ For ⟨⟨ we have ⟨ for ⟨⟨ our King,
forgiving, good willfully sinned.

וְרַב חֶסֶד לְכָל קֹרְאֶיךָ.[4]

⟨⟨ who call ⟨ to all ⟨ kind ⟨ and
upon You. abundantly

---

(1) *Exodus* 34:5. (2) 34:6-7. (3) 34:9. (4) *Psalms* 86:5.

פסוקי הקדמה לסליחה כא / PREFATORY VERSES TO SELICHAH 21

וְנַפְשִׁי נִבְהֲלָה מְאֹד, וְאַתָּה יהוה עַד מָתָי.[1]

My soul « is terrified ‹ utterly, » and You, ‹ Hashem, ‹ until ‹ when? »

עַד מָתַי רְשָׁעִים, יהוה, עַד מָתַי רְשָׁעִים יַעֲלֹזוּ.[2]

Until ‹ when ‹ the wicked, » O Hashem, » until ‹ when ‹ will the wicked » exult?

עַד מָתַי אֱלֹהִים יְחָרֶף צָר, יְנַאֵץ אוֹיֵב שְׁמֶךָ

Until ‹ when, ‹ O God, » will the tormentor, « revile ‹ the foe ‹ will blaspheme ‹ Your Name

לָנֶצַח. אֲדֹנָי שָׁמְעָה בְקוֹלֵנוּ, תִּהְיֶינָה אָזְנֶיךָ קַשֻּׁבוֹת[3]

for eternity? » O Lord, « hear ‹ our voice; » may they be « — Your ears — » attentive

לְקוֹל תַּחֲנוּנֵינוּ.[4]

to the sound ‹ of our pleas. »

כְּרַחֵם אָב עַל בָּנִים, כֵּן תְּרַחֵם יהוה עָלֵינוּ.[5]

As merciful as ‹ a father is ‹ toward ‹ his » children, « so ‹ have mercy, » Hashem, ‹ on us. »

לַיהוה הַיְשׁוּעָה, עַל עַמְּךָ בִרְכָתֶךָ סֶּלָה.[6] יהוה

To Hashem ‹ is salvation, » upon ‹ Your people ‹ Your blessing, ‹ is Your » Selah. « Hashem, ‹

צְבָאוֹת עִמָּנוּ, מִשְׂגָּב לָנוּ אֱלֹהֵי יַעֲקֹב סֶלָה.[7]

Master of Legions, ‹ is with us, » a stronghold ‹ for us ‹ is the God ‹ of Jacob, « Selah. »

יהוה צְבָאוֹת, אַשְׁרֵי אָדָם בֹּטֵחַ בָּךְ.[8] יהוה הוֹשִׁיעָה,

Hashem, ‹ Master of ‹ Legions, « — praise- ‹ worthy ‹ is the ‹ man ‹ who trusts « in You. ‹ Hashem, ‹ save! »

הַמֶּלֶךְ יַעֲנֵנוּ בְיוֹם קָרְאֵנוּ.[9]

May the King ‹ answer ‹ us ‹ on the day ‹ we call. »

---

(1) *Psalms* 6:4. (2) 94:3. (3) 74:10. (4) Cf. 130:2. (5) Cf. 103:13. (6) 3:9 (7) 46:8. (8) 84:13. (9) 20:10.

סליחה כא / SELICHAH 21

ALL:

אֱלֹהֵינוּ וֵאלֹהֵי אֲבוֹתֵינוּ:

《 of our forefathers: 〈 and God 〈 Our God

אַרְיֵה בַיַּעַר*¹ דָּמִיתִי* וְנִמְשַׁלְתִּי בְּחוֹבַי,

《 because of 〈 and am 〈 I resemble,* 〈 in the 〈 A lion
my sins; likened to forest*

בִּטוּיִי נוֹאַל, מִלָּתִי לְשׁוֹן הֲבַי,

《 is nonsense; 〈 my word 《 is foolish, 〈 my speech

גָּדַעְתִּי מַקִּישׁ כְּבֶן קִישׁ וּמִסְפָּר בִּגְוָי,*²

《 and Mispar Bigvai.* 〈 like [Mordechai] 〈 from [intercessors] 〈 I am
the son of Kish who could knock [on cut off
the Gates of Mercy]

כָּל רֹאשׁ לָחֳלִי וְכָל לֵבָב דַּוָּי.³

《 is 〈 heart 〈 every 《 is [smitten] 〈 head 〈 Every
suffering. with sickness;

(1) Cf. *Jeremiah* 12:8. (2) See *Ezra* 2:2. (3) *Isaiah* 1:5.

אַרְיֵה בַיַּעַר — *A lion in the forest.* The first three verses of the respective stanzas form an *aleph-beis* acrostic, followed by the composer's signature — אֵלִיָּה בַּר שְׁמַעְיָה חֲזַק, *Eliyah bar Shemayah, may he be strong* [see prefatory comment to *Selichah* 14]. The last word of each stanza is also the first word of the following one.

אַרְיֵה בַיַּעַר דָּמִיתִי — *A lion in the forest I resemble.* The prophet Jeremiah, speaking in God's voice, admonished: *To me, My heritage-people was like a lion in the forest; she raised her voice against Me; therefore have I hated her* (*Jeremiah* 12:8). The Talmud interprets the phrase *she raised her voice against Me* as an allusion to a person who, because of character flaws and sinful ways, is unfit to serve as *chazzan*, yet fills the role solely because of his fine voice (*Taanis* 16b, see *Maharsha*). Sending a wicked person, one despised by God, to represent the congregation in its prayers, is a travesty. About such a congregation does God add, *therefore have I hated her.* The *paytan*, in the voice of the *chazzan*, humbly stands before the Ark,

and pleads that his prayers be answered. Although he knows that he is really unworthy, his speech is foolish, and he cannot set the words of the prayer properly, nevertheless, since truly righteous intercessors are no longer available to us, he has no choice but to lead the service, despite his shortcomings.

כְּבֶן קִישׁ וּמִסְפָּר בִּגְוָי — *Like [Mordechai] the son of Kish and Mispar Bigvai.* In the Book of *Esther*, Kish is listed as one of Mordechai's forebears. Although the genealogy there (2:5) is incomplete, three of Mordechai's progenitors are mentioned: *Mordechai son of Yair son of Shimi son of Kish.* The Talmud explains that these names were chosen to be listed because they describe Mordechai's prowess in prayer: יָאִיר, *Yair*, from the root אוֹר, *light*, indicates that he lit up Israel's eyes with his prayers; שִׁמְעִי, *Shimi*, from שָׁמַע, *hear*, because his prayers were heard by God; and קִישׁ, *Kish*, a word related to מַקִּישׁ, *to pound*, for he pounded on the Gates of Mercy until they were opened for him. Furthermore, Scripture calls Mordechai בִּלְשָׁן, *Bilshan*

דַּוָּי גּוֹלֶה וְנִקְלֶה הִכְאַבְתִּי וְנֶעֱכַּרְתִּי,

《 and depressed, 〈 I have become 《 and 〈 exiled, 〈 **Suffering,**
pained   demeaned,

הוּנֵעְתִּי חַגְתִּי וְרָוִיתִי רוֹשׁ וְנִשְׁכַּרְתִּי,

《 I have become 《 with 〈 I was 《 I was 〈 I have been
drunk.   gall,   satiated   reeling,   tossed about,

וּמִדְּחַק אֲדוֹנִים חִנָּם לָהֶם נִמְכַּרְתִּי,[1]

《 was I sold, 〈 to 〈 [that] for 〈 of masters 〈 Yet from the
them   naught   oppression

בְּהִתְעַטֵּף עָלַי נַפְשִׁי, אֶת יהוה זָכַרְתִּי.[2]

《 I remembered. 〈   HASHEM 〈 was my soul, 〈 within me 〈 while faint

זָכַרְתִּי חַסְדֶּךָ וְאַהֲבָתֶךָ[3] עָלַי כְּהַדְגִּילוֹ,[4]

《 when [travelling] with ban- 〈 for me 〈 and Your love 〈 Your 〈 I
ners [in the Wilderness];   kindness   **remembered**

חוֹבוֹת הֶעֱבִירוּ וְאוֹתִי לְךָ הִסְגִּילוּ,

《 Your beloved 〈 made 〈 and 〈 they [Your kindness 〈 [my]
treasure.   me,   and love] removed,   sins

טְלָאֶיךָ עַתָּה בְתַחַן וָפֶלֶל יַרְגִּילוּ,

《 is 〈 and 〈 in 〈 now 〈 Your flock
accustomed: prayer   supplication

אֶבְיוֹנֵי אָדָם בִּקְדוֹשׁ יִשְׂרָאֵל יָגִילוּ.[5]

《 may they 〈 of Israel 〈 in the Holy 〈 of men 〈 The
rejoice!   One   poorest

יָגִילוּ יָרֹנּוּ עֲבָדֶיךָ בְּפֶקֶד חוֹמוֹתַי,

《 my [Holy 〈 when You 〈 shall Your 〈 and 〈 **Rejoice**
City's] walls!   remember   servants   sing
   to restore

כַּדְכֹּד וְאַבְנֵי חֵפֶץ תַּגְבִּילֵם[6] אֵימָתַי,

《 — O when? 《 You will 〈 that are 〈 and 〈 With
surround them   precious   stones   rubies

---

(1) Cf. *Isaiah* 52:3; see commentary to *Selichah* 11, s.v. לְמֹכְרֵי חִנָּם. (2) *Jonah* 2:8.
(3) Cf. *Jeremiah* 2:2. (4) Cf. *Song of Songs* 2:4. (5) Cf. *Isaiah* 29:19. (6) Cf. 54:12.

(*Ezra* 2:2; *Nehemiah* 7:7), a word derived from בִּיל לָשׁוֹן, *he mixed language,* because of his mastery with words (*Menachos* 65a).

Mispar Bigvai is listed in *Ezra* (2:2) among the colleagues of Mordechai who returned with Zerubavel to Jerusalem at the end of the seventy-year exile follow-ing the Destruction of the First Temple. Some commentaries read the two words as the name of one person (since there is no conjunctive prefix ו); others read them as the names of two people (since these names appear in the middle of the list, there is no need for the conjunctive prefix).

לְתֵל עוֹלָם עִירִי[1] וְלַשֵּׁפֶל רָמוֹתַי,

《 my heights, 〈 and into 〈 has my 〈 forever 〈 Into a
lowliness City [been mound
reduced] of ruin

וְאַתָּה יהוה עַד מָתַי.[2]

《 when? 〈 — until 《 O HASHEM 〈 and You,

מָתַי תְּחַיֵּנוּ וּמִתְּהוֹמוֹת תַּעֲלֵנוּ,[3]

《 raise us up? 〈 and from the 〈 will You 《 When
depths revivify us

נָאוֹר,[4] הָסֵר וְהָקֵל סִמְלוֹן עָלֵנוּ,

《 of our 〈 the 〈 and 〈 remove 《 O
yoke. harness loosen [our Illuminated
burden] One,

שָׂבַע מַלֵּא אֲסָמֵינוּ,[5] וְהַצְלִיחָה מִפְעָלֵנוּ,

《 to our 〈 and bring 〈 our granaries, 〈 fill 〈 With
endeavors; success satiation

יְהִי חַסְדְּךָ יהוה עָלֵינוּ.[6]

《 be upon us. 〈 HASHEM, 〈 Your 〈 may
kindness,

עָלֵינוּ הַמָּלֵא רַחֲמִים בְּצָרָה דְרַשְׁתִּיךָ,

《 do I seek You. 〈 for in 《 of mercy, 〈 may [You] 〈 Upon us
distress be full

פֵּרַשְׂתִּי יָדַי אֵלֶיךָ[7] בְּקִרְבִּי שְׁחַרְתִּיךָ,[8]

《 I seek You. 〈 [as long as 《 to You, 〈 my 〈 I spread
my soul is] hands forth
within me

צָמְאָה לְךָ נַפְשִׁי[9] בַּלַּיְלָה כִּי אִוִּיתִיךָ,[10]

《 I desire You; 〈 for 《 in the 〈 does my 〈 for 〈 Thirst
[exile-]night, soul You

יהוה אַל אֵבוֹשָׁה כִּי קְרָאתִיךָ.[11]

《 I have called 〈 for 〈 let me not be shamed, 〈 HASHEM,
upon You.

קְרָאתִיךָ מֵעֹמֶק[12] דָּלוּ עֵינַי,

《 are my 〈 turned 《 from the 〈 I have called
eyes, upward depths, upon You

---

(1) Cf. *Deuteronomy* 13:17. (2) *Psalms* 6:4. (3) Cf. *Psalms* 71:20. (4) See commentary to *Selichah 18*.
(5) Cf. *Proverbs* 3:10. (6) *Psalms* 33:22. (7) *143:6*. (8) Cf. *Isaiah* 26:9. (9) *Psalms* 63:2.
(10) *Isaiah* 26:9. (11) *Psalms* 31:18. (12) Cf. *130:1*.

רוֹם יָדַי נָשָׂאתִי הֲפִיצוֹתִי מַעְיָנָי,

《 my wellsprings 〈   I cause   《   I lift,   〈 my 〈 Heaven-
[of tears].   to flow forth   hands   ward

שׁוּר כְּשִׁרוֹן מְחֵה וְהַעֲבֵר זְדוֹנָי,

《 [even] my 〈   and   〈 wipe 《 [my] proper 〈 Look at
willful sins.   dismiss   away   deeds;

יהוה שָׁמְעָה תְפִלָּתִי הַאֲזִינָה אֶל **תַּחֲנוּנָי**.

《   my   〈 to 〈 be attentive 《 my prayer; 〈   hear   〈 HASHEM,
supplications.

תַּחֲנוּנַי אֲזֵן אוֹמְנִי מְחוֹלְלִי וּפַדְגוּגִי,

《 my Teacher! 〈 my Maker, 〈   my   《 be at- 〈 To my
Nurturer,   tentive, **supplications,**

לְךָ גָּלוּי וְצָפוּי תַּאַב רְגוּגִי,

《   of my   《   the   〈 and 〈 is open 〈 To
yearning.   desire   revealed   You

יִצְלַל זָדוֹן וִיכֻפַּר חֵטְא שְׁגָגִי,

《   that was 〈 my sin 〈   and let   〈 my inten- 〈 Let be
inadvertent;   be atoned   tional sin, sunk deep

אֲמָרַי הַאֲזִינָה יהוה, בִּינָה **הֲגִיגִי**.

《   my   〈 compre- 《 HASHEM; 〈 be attentive, 〈   to my
thought.   hend   words

הֲגִיגִי בַּר יֵחָשֵׁב וְיִכּוֹן פְּלוּלִי,

《   may my   〈 and stand 〈 may it be 〈 to be 〈   My
prayer.   firm   adjudged,   pure   **thought,**

שְׁמַע יָהּ סְלָחָה דְּפִי עֲקוּלִי,

《   of my   〈   the   〈 and forgive 〈 O 〈   Hear,
perversity.   iniquities   God,

חַזֵּק מַאֲמִירֶךָ וּלְרָצוֹן יְהִי מִלּוּלִי,

〈 my words 《 may 〈   and find   《 those who 〈 Strength-
favor   exalt You;   en

הֶגְיוֹן לִבִּי לְפָנֶיךָ יהוה צוּרִי וְגוֹאֲלִי.

《   and my   〈   my   〈 HASHEM, 《   before   〈 of my 〈 and the
Redeemer.   Rock   You,   heart   thoughts

ALL, WHILE STANDING:

אֵל **מֶלֶךְ** יוֹשֵׁב עַל כִּסֵּא רַחֲמִים, מִתְנַהֵג

〈 Who acts   《   of mercy,   〈 the throne 〈 on 〈 Who sits 〈   King   〈 O God,

---

(1) Cf. *Habakkuk* 3:10. (2) Cf. *Psalms* 143:1. (3) 5:2. (4) 19:15.

בַּחֲסִידוּת, מוֹחֵל עֲוֹנוֹת עַמּוֹ, מַעֲבִיר רִאשׁוֹן רִאשׁוֹן,[1]

by one, ⟨ [sins,] one ⟨ Who ⟨ of His ⟨ the sins ⟨ Who ⟨ with kindness,
removes   people,   pardons

מַרְבֶּה מְחִילָה לַחַטָּאִים וּסְלִיחָה לַפּוֹשְׁעִים, עֹשֶׂה

⟨ Who ⟨ to willful ⟨ and ⟨ to unintentional ⟨ pardon ⟨ Who abun-
performs   sinners,   forgiveness   sinners   dantly grants

צְדָקוֹת עִם כָּל בָּשָׂר וָרוּחַ, לֹא כְרָעָתָם תִּגְמוֹל.

do You ⟨ in accord with ⟨ — not ⟨ and ⟨ [beings ⟨ all ⟨ with ⟨ acts of
repay them! their wickedness   spirit   of] flesh   generosity

❖ אֵל הוֹרֵיתָ לָּנוּ לוֹמַר שְׁלֹשׁ עֶשְׂרֵה, וּזְכוֹר

⟨ remem- ⟨ the Thirteen ⟨ to ⟨ us ⟨ You ⟨ O God,
ber   [Attributes of Mercy];   recite   taught

לָּנוּ הַיּוֹם בְּרִית שְׁלֹשׁ עֶשְׂרֵה, כְּמוֹ שֶׁהוֹדַעְתָּ לֶעָנָיו

⟨ to the humble ⟨ You made ⟨ as ⟨ of [these] Thirteen, ⟨ the ⟨ today ⟨ for us
one [Moses]   known   covenant

מִקֶּדֶם, כְּמוֹ שֶׁכָּתוּב, וַיֵּרֶד יהוה בֶּעָנָן וַיִּתְיַצֵּב עִמּוֹ

⟨ with ⟨ and stood ⟨ in a ⟨ And HASHEM ⟨ it is written: ⟨ as ⟨ in ancient
him   cloud   descended   times,

שָׁם, וַיִּקְרָא בְשֵׁם יהוה.[2]

⟨ of ⟨ with the ⟨ and He ⟨ there,
HASHEM. Name   called out

CONGREGATION, THEN *CHAZZAN*:

וַיַּעֲבֹר יהוה עַל פָּנָיו וַיִּקְרָא:

⟨ and ⟨ [Moses'] ⟨ before ⟨ And HASHEM passed
proclaimed: face,

CONGREGATION AND *CHAZZAN* RECITE LOUDLY AND IN UNISON:

יהוה, יהוה, אֵל, רַחוּם, וְחַנּוּן, אֶרֶךְ אַפַּיִם,

⟨ to anger, ⟨ Slow ⟨ and ⟨ Compassionate ⟨ God, ⟨ HASHEM, ⟨ HASHEM,
Gracious,

וְרַב חֶסֶד, וֶאֱמֶת, נֹצֵר חֶסֶד לָאֲלָפִים, נֹשֵׂא עָוֹן,

⟨ of ⟨ Forgiver ⟨ for thousands ⟨ of ⟨ Preserver ⟨ and ⟨ in ⟨ and
iniquity,   [of generations],   kindness   Truth,   Kindness Abundant

וָפֶשַׁע, וְחַטָּאָה, וְנַקֵּה.[3] וְסָלַחְתָּ לַעֲוֹנֵנוּ וּלְחַטָּאתֵנוּ

⟨ and our sins, ⟨ our ⟨ May You ⟨ and Who ⟨ and inadvertent ⟨ willful sin,
iniquities   forgive   absolves.   sin,

(1) *Rosh Hashanah* 17a. (2) *Exodus* 34:5. (3) 34:6-7.

וּנְחַלְתָּנוּ.[1] סְלַח לָנוּ אָבִינוּ כִּי חָטָאנוּ, מְחַל לָנוּ

⟨ us, ⟨ pardon ⟪ we have ⟨ for ⟨ our ⟨ us, ⟨ Forgive ⟪ and make us
sinned; Father, Your heritage.

מַלְכֵּנוּ כִּי פָשָׁעְנוּ. כִּי אַתָּה אֲדֹנָי טוֹב וְסַלָּח,

⟪ and ⟨ are ⟨ O Lord, ⟨ You, ⟨ For ⟪ we have ⟨ for ⟪ our King,
forgiving, good willfully sinned.

וְרַב חֶסֶד לְכָל קֹרְאֶיךָ.[2]

⟪ who call ⟨ to all ⟨ kind ⟨ and
upon You. abundantly

סְלִיחָה כב / SELICHAH 22

(פזמון)

CHAZZAN, THEN CONGREGATION:

יֹשֵׁב* בְּסֵתֶר עֶלְיוֹן,*[3] מָגִנִּי וְצִנָּתִי,*[4]

⟨ and my ⟨ my ⟪ in the celestial ⟨ in ⟨ O You
Armor,* Shield heights,* concealment Who sits*

צַעֲקָתִי הַקְשִׁיבָה, וְהַאֲזִינָה רִנָּתִי,[5]

⟪ to my prayerful song. ⟨ and listen ⟪ attend, ⟨ to my outcry

חַטָּא אֶת חַטָּאתִי, קָדוֹשׁ תֵּן תִּקְוָתִי,[6]

⟪ my hope: ⟨ grant ⟪ O Holy ⟪ my sin; ⟨ Cleanse
One,

נַפְשִׁי בִּשְׁאֵלָתִי, וְעַמִּי בְּבַקָּשָׁתִי.[7]

⟪ as my ⟨ and my ⟨ as my request ⟨ [Spare]
petition. people my life

CONGREGATION, THEN CHAZZAN:

צְדָקָה עֲשֵׂה לְעַמֶּךָ, קָדוֹשׁ לְמַעַן שְׁמֶךָ,

⟪ of Your ⟨ for the ⟨ O Holy ⟪ with Your ⟨ deal ⟨ With right-
Name; sake One, people, eousness

---

(1) Exodus 34:9. (2) Psalms 86:5. (3) 91:1. (4) Cf. 35:2. (5) Cf. 17:1. (6) Cf. Job 6:8. (7) Esther 7:3.

יֹשֵׁב ﱠ — O You Who sits. The acrostic
reads יִצְחָק חֲזַק, Yitzchak, may he be strong,
but the identity of the composer is otherwise
unknown.

יֹשֵׁב בְּסֵתֶר עֶלְיוֹן — O You Who sits in concealment in the celestial heights. Although
in its context in Psalms (91:1) this phrase refers to the righteous person who sits in the
refuge of the Exalted One, the paytan has
borrowed the phrase and applied it to God.

מָגִנִּי וְצִנָּתִי — My Shield and my Armor.
Rashi (to Jeremiah 46:3) states that מָגֵן refers to a leather shield coated with oil before
a battle; and צִנָּה to a wooden shield. Midrash Shocher Tov (1:4) describes מָגֵן as a
shield that affords protection on three sides
of the bearer's body, and צִנָּה as a shield that
completely surrounds the carrier (see also
Rashi to Psalms 91:4). Therefore we have
translated מָגֵן as a shield and צִנָּה as armor.

כִּי פָסוּ תְמִימֶיךָ, מַעֲבִירֵי זַעֲמֶךָ, וּמַגִּישֵׁי לַחְמֶךָ,*

《 Your flour-offering* [to the Altar], 〈 and [the Kohanim] who brought 《 Your anger, 〈 those [whose merit] caused to pass 《 are Your wholesome ones, 〈 vanished 〈 for

לָכֵן עַתָּה בָאתִי,¹

《 I have come [to plead], 〈 indeed 〈 now, therefore,

נַפְשִׁי בִּשְׁאֵלָתִי, וְעַמִּי בְּבַקָּשָׁתִי.

《 as my petition. 〈 and my people 〈 as my request 〈 [Spare] my life

CONGREGATION, THEN *CHAZZAN:*

חַטֹּאת נְעוּרַי תַּצְלִיל, וְיָם יֶהָפְכוּ כִּצְלִיל,*

《 like [a barley] roll.* 〈 let them turn over 〈 and [in the] sea 〈 cause to sink, 〈 of my youth 〈 The sins

וְצֶדֶק זְקֵנִים² תַּסְלִיל, וְשַׁוְעַת נְכָאִים תַּכְלִיל,*

《 make a crown [for Yourself].* 〈 of the downtrodden 〈 and from the desperate prayers 《 celebrate, 〈 of [our] ancestors 〈 The righteousness

וְעֵת תְּנַקֵּנִי כְּבַעֲלִיל, מַסְטִינִי אָז יְיֵלִיל,

《 will wail [in despair], 〈 then 〈 my Adversary 《 as if in a crucible, 〈 when You cleanse me [of sin] 〈 Then, at the time

---

(1) Cf. *Joshua* 5:14. (2) Some editions read וְצֶדֶק זְקוּנִים, *the righteousness of [our] old age.*

לַחְמֶךָ — *Your flour-offering* [lit., *Your bread*]. The translation follows that of the parallel phrase in *Malachi* 3:3. In reality, however, all Altar offerings, whether flour or animal, are called לֶחֶם, *bread* (see, for example, *Leviticus* 3:11, *Numbers* 28:2).

כִּצְלִיל — *Like a [barley] roll.* The *paytan* prays, "May the sins of my youth be overturned and purified as if they were a barley roll that rolled into the sea." The strange metaphor of a barley roll turning over alludes to an episode that occurred when Gideon went to attack Midian. God had instructed Gideon to reduce his forces from 32,000 to a mere three hundred men, lest a victorious Israel deny the miraculous nature of its win. As a sign that his skeleton army would prevail over the huge Midianite army, God told Gideon, "If you are apprehensive about descending [to attack Midian in the valley], then just you and your servant Purah

should go down to their camp. Listen to what they say and you will be encouraged." That night Gideon and Purah went down to spy on the Midianites and their Amalekite allies. There they overheard one soldier tell another, "I have dreamt that a roll of barley bread was spinning through the Midianite camp. It came upon a tent, struck it, turned it upside down, and the tent collapsed." His friend replied, "It is naught but the sword of Gideon ben Joash, the Israelite; God has given Midian into his hand!" (see *Judges* Ch. 7).

Alternatively, the word צְלִיל means *clear* or *pure*, and the stich reads: *Let the sea turn [the sins of my youth] around [so that they will be] like a pure object.*

וְשַׁוְעַת נְכָאִים תַּכְלִיל — *And from the desperate prayers of the downtrodden make a crown [for Yourself].* When all the synagogues have concluded their service, the

כִּי לִבִּי לְךָ כָּלִיל, עַתָּה הִנֵּה בָאתִי,¹

《 I have come 〈 indeed 〈 so now 《 utterly; 〈 is 〈 my 〈 for
[to plead],   Yours   heart

נַפְשִׁי בִּשְׁאֵלָתִי, וְעַמִּי בְּבַקָּשָׁתִי.

《   as my   〈 and my 〈 as my request 〈 [Spare]
petition.   people   my life

CONGREGATION, THEN *CHAZZAN:*

חַנּוּן חַי חָנֵּנִי, לְקוֹל זַעֲקִי בִּגְרוֹנִי,*

《   that is in   〈 of my 〈 to the 《 be 〈 Living 〈 O
my throat.*   shout   sound   gracious,   One, Gracious,
                     to me,

בְּשָׁמְעֲךָ תַּעֲנֵנִי, סְלִיחָתְךָ תַּרְבֵּנִי,²

《 be abundant 〈 and let Your 《 answer me; 〈 As soon as
for me.   forgiveness   You hear me,

חַיִּים תִּכְתְּבֵנִי, וְעָנְתָה בִּי צִדְקָתִי,³

《   shall my   〈 for 〈 and testify 〈 write me 〈 For life
righteousness.   me   down,

נַפְשִׁי בִּשְׁאֵלָתִי, וְעַמִּי בְּבַקָּשָׁתִי.

《   as my   〈 and my 〈 as my request 〈 [Spare]
petition.   people   my life

CONGREGATION, THEN *CHAZZAN:*

זֶה אֵלִי⁴ הוֹשִׁיעָה, וּזְכִיּוֹת הַכְרִיעָה,

《 tilt the scales. 〈 and to 《 save [us], 《 is my 〈 O [You of
           [the side of]   God,   Whom we
            merit   said,] *This*

וּמִזְּבוּלְךָ הוֹפִיעָה, חֹן סֹעֲרָה וְסֹעָה,

《   and   〈 to [the 〈 [and] be 〈 appear 〈 From Your
tempest.   nation] beset gracious   dwelling-place
         by storm   [in Heaven]

וּמַלְשִׁנִי הַבְלִיעָה, צֹאנְךָ מִלְּהַפְשִׁיעָה,

《   no more to accuse, 〈 Your 《 be obliterated, 〈 And let my
               flock   Denouncer

---

(1) Cf. *Numbers* 22:38. (2) Cf. *Isaiah* 55:7. (3) *Genesis* 30:33. (4) *Exodus* 15:2.

angel Sandalfon stations himself behind the Divine Chariot, where he weaves all the congregational prayers into wreaths with which he crowns God, so to speak (see *Chagigah* 13b with *Tosafos*; *Shemos Rabbah* 21:4).

לְקוֹל זַעֲקִי בִּגְרוֹנִי — *To the sound of my shout*

that is in my throat. The prophet proclaimed in the name of God, *"And it will be that before they have called, I shall answer; while they yet speak, I shall hear"* (*Isaiah* 65:24). Thus, we pray that God respond to us while our shout is still in our throat.

פֶּן אֶרְאֶה בָרָעָה,[1] בְּאָבְדַן מוֹלַדְתִּי,[2]

《 of my family. 〈 the extermination 《 the tragedy, 〈   I see   〈 lest

נַפְשִׁי בִּשְׁאֵלָתִי, וְעַמִּי בְּבַקָּשָׁתִי.

《   as my   〈 and my 〈 as my request   〈 [Spare]
petition.   people   my life

CONGREGATION, THEN *CHAZZAN:*

קַדֵּשׁ שֵׁם קָדְשֶׁךָ, חִלְּלוּ בְּמִקְדָּשֶׁךָ,[3]

《 in [destroying] 〈 that [the conquer- 〈 Your Holy 〈 Sanctify
Your Temple,   ors] desecrated   Name

וְאַהֲרוֹנִים קְדוֹשֶׁיךָ,* מַגִּישֵׁי אִשֶּׁיךָ,[4]

《 Your fire- 〈 who [would] 〈 Your holy 〈 and the children
offerings.   bring   ones,*   of Aaron,

וּמַה יַּעֲשׂוּ קְדוֹשֶׁיךָ, כְּפֶסוּ קָדָשֶׁיךָ,

《 have Your sancti- 〈 now that 《 — Your holy 〈 can they 〈 What
fied offerings?   vanished   ones —   do

שְׁעֵה נָא מַקְדִּישֶׁיךָ, כְּפָרִים אִם שְׁלַמְתִּי,[5]

《 I brought 〈 let [my pray- 〈 [in place 《 those who sancti- 〈 please, 〈 Turn
an offering. er] be as if of] bulls fy You [in prayer];   toward,

נַפְשִׁי בִּשְׁאֵלָתִי, וְעַמִּי בְּבַקָּשָׁתִי.

《   as my   〈 and my 〈 as my request   〈 [Spare]
petition.   people   my life

CONGREGATION, THEN *CHAZZAN:*

יֵרָצוּ עֲבָדֶיךָ, לְמַעַן שֵׁם כְּבוֹדֶךָ,

《   of Your glorious 〈 for the 〈 may Your 〈 Find favor
Name,   sake   servants   [with You]

מְיַחֲדֶיךָ מְעִידֶיךָ, כִּי אֵין בִּלְעָדֶיךָ,[6]

《 besides You. 〈 there is 〈 that 〈 and bear 〈 those who
none   witness of You proclaim
Your Oneness

בַּקֵּשׁ נָא אוֹבְדֶיךָ, הֵן בָּאוּ עָדֶיךָ,

《 to You, 〈 have 〈 they 《 Your lost 〈 please, 〈 Seek,
come   ones;

---

(1) Cf. *Genesis* 44:34. (2) *Esther* 8:6. (3) Cf. *Ezekiel* 36:23.
(4) Cf. *Leviticus* 21:6. (5) Cf. *Hosea* 14:3. (6) Cf. *Isaiah* 44:8.

וְאַהֲרוֹנִים קְדוֹשֶׁיךָ — *And the children of
Aaron, Your holy ones.* It is unclear to
which verb this phrase belongs: Either it is
the second subject of קַדֵּשׁ, *sanctify,* and the
stich means, *Sanctify Your Name ... and
the children of Aaron* [so that they might

once again] bring Your fire-offerings;
or its antecedent verb is חִלְּלוּ, *that they
desecrated,* and the line means, *Sanctify
Your Name and the children of Aaron,
Your holy ones, that [the gentiles] desecrated ....*

כִּי טוֹבִים דּדֶיךָ,[1] פָּנֶיךָ בִּקַּשְׁתִּי,[2]

《 have I sought. 〈 Your 《 is Your 〈 dear 〈 for
Presence closeness;

נַפְשִׁי בִּשְׁאֵלָתִי, וְעַמִּי בְּבַקָּשָׁתִי.

《 as my 〈 and my 〈 as my request 〈 [Spare]
petition. people my life

CONGREGATION, THEN *CHAZZAN:*

קוֹלִי יֶעֱרַב נָא, כְּמֵחִים תּוֹךְ צִיּוֹנָה,

《 of Zion; 〈 in the 〈 as [the aroma 〈 please, 〈 let it be as 〈 My voice
midst of] fattened ani- pleasant [in prayer],
mal [offerings] [before You],

לְטוֹבָה הִפָּנֶה נָא, לְהַמְצִיאֵנִי חֲנִינָה,

《 with [Your] 〈 that You may 〈 please, 〈 turn 〈 for good
graciousness. provide me [to me],

כִּי אֶל מִי אֶפְנֶה נָא, בְּאֵין מִשְׁעָן וּמַשְׁעֵנָה,[3]

《 or women? 〈 support from 〈 when 〈 now, 〈 could I 〈 whom 〈 to 〈 For
[righteous] men there is no turn [else]

לְמִיחֲלֶיךָ סְלַח נָא, הַשְׁמִיעֵם סָלַחְתִּי,[4]

《 I have 《 and let them 〈 please, 〈 forgive, 〈 Those who put
forgiven. hear [You say], their hope in You

נַפְשִׁי בִּשְׁאֵלָתִי, וְעַמִּי בְּבַקָּשָׁתִי.

《 as my 〈 and my 〈 as my request 〈 [Spare]
petition. people my life

ALL, WHILE STANDING:

אֵל מֶלֶךְ יוֹשֵׁב עַל כִּסֵּא רַחֲמִים, מִתְנַהֵג

〈 Who acts 《 of mercy, 〈 the throne 〈 on 〈 Who sits 〈 King 〈 O God,

בַּחֲסִידוּת, מוֹחֵל עֲוֹנוֹת עַמּוֹ, מַעֲבִיר רִאשׁוֹן רִאשׁוֹן,[5]

《 by one, 〈 [sins] one 〈 Who 《 of His 〈 the sins 〈 Who 《 with kindness,
removes people, pardons

מַרְבֶּה מְחִילָה לַחַטָּאִים וּסְלִיחָה לַפּוֹשְׁעִים, עֹשֶׂה

〈 Who 《 to willful 〈 and 〈 to unintentional 〈 pardon 〈 Who abun-
performs sinners, forgiveness sinners dantly grants

צְדָקוֹת עִם כָּל בָּשָׂר וָרוּחַ, לֹא כְרָעָתָם תִּגְמוֹל.

《 do You 〈 in accord with 《 — not 《 and spirit 〈 [beings 〈 all 〈 with 〈 acts of
repay them! their wickedness of] flesh generosity

---

(1) *Song of Songs* 1:2. (2) Cf. *Psalms* 27:8. (3) Cf. *Isaiah* 3:1. (4) *Numbers* 14:20. (5) *Rosh Hashanah* 17a.

‎❖ אֵל הוֹרֵיתָ לָּנוּ לוֹמַר שְׁלֹשׁ עֶשְׂרֵה, וּזְכוֹר לָנוּ הַיּוֹם

⟨ today ⟨ for us ⟨ remem- ⟪   the Thirteen   ⟨ to ⟨ us ⟨ You ⟨ O God,
                ber   [Attributes of Mercy]; recite   taught

‎בְּרִית שְׁלֹשׁ עֶשְׂרֵה, כְּמוֹ שֶׁהוֹדַעְתָּ לֶעָנָיו מִקֶּדֶם,

⟪ in ancient ⟨ to the humble ⟨ You made ⟨ as ⟪ of [these] Thirteen, ⟨ the
   times,   one [Moses]   known   covenant

‎כְּמוֹ שֶׁכָּתוּב, וַיֵּרֶד יהוה בֶּעָנָן וַיִּתְיַצֵּב עִמּוֹ שָׁם,

⟪ there, ⟨ with ⟨ and stood ⟨ in a ⟨ And HASHEM ⟪ it is written: ⟨ as
          him   cloud   descended

‎וַיִּקְרָא בְשֵׁם יהוה.[1]

⟪   of   ⟨ with the ⟨ and He
    HASHEM.   Name   called out

CONGREGATION, THEN *CHAZZAN*:

‎וַיַּעֲבֹר יהוה עַל פָּנָיו וַיִּקְרָא:

⟪ and proclaimed: ⟪[Moses'] face, ⟨ before ⟨ And HASHEM passed

CONGREGATION AND *CHAZZAN* **RECITE LOUDLY AND IN UNISON:**

‎יהוה, יהוה, אֵל, רַחוּם, וְחַנּוּן, אֶרֶךְ אַפַּיִם,

⟨ to anger, ⟨ Slow ⟪ and Gracious, ⟨ Compassionate ⟨ God, ⟨ HASHEM, ⟨ HASHEM,

‎וְרַב חֶסֶד, וֶאֱמֶת, נֹצֵר חֶסֶד לָאֲלָפִים, נֹשֵׂא עָוֹן,

⟨ of ⟨ Forgiver ⟪ for thousands ⟨ of ⟨ Preserver ⟪ and ⟨ in ⟨ and
iniquity,   [of generations], kindness   Truth, Kindness Abundant

‎וָפֶשַׁע, וְחַטָּאָה, וְנַקֵּה.[2] וְסָלַחְתָּ לַעֲוֹנֵנוּ וּלְחַטָּאתֵנוּ

⟪ and our sins, ⟨ our ⟨ May You ⟪ and Who ⟨ and inadvertent ⟨ willful sin,
                iniquities forgive absolves.   sin,

‎וּנְחַלְתָּנוּ.[3] סְלַח לָנוּ אָבִינוּ כִּי חָטָאנוּ, מְחַל לָנוּ

⟨ us, ⟨ pardon ⟪ we have ⟨ for ⟪ our ⟨ us, ⟨ Forgive ⟪ and make us
              sinned;   Father,   Your heritage.

‎מַלְכֵּנוּ כִּי פָשָׁעְנוּ. כִּי אַתָּה אֲדֹנָי טוֹב וְסַלָּח, וְרַב

⟨ and ⟪ and ⟨ are ⟨ O Lord, ⟨ You, ⟨ For ⟪ we have ⟨ for ⟪ our King,
abundantly forgiving, good   willfully sinned.

‎חֶסֶד לְכָל קֹרְאֶיךָ.[4]

⟪ who call upon You. ⟨ to all ⟨ kind

ALL:

‎זְכֹר רַחֲמֶיךָ יהוה וַחֲסָדֶיךָ, כִּי מֵעוֹלָם הֵמָּה.[5]

⟪ are they. ⟨ eternal ⟨ for ⟪ and Your ⟨ HASHEM, ⟨ Your mercies, ⟨ Remember
                              kindnesses,

---

(1) *Exodus* 35:4. (2) 34:6-7. (3) 34:9. (4) *Psalms* 86:5. (5) 25:6.

זָכְרֵנוּ יהוה בִּרְצוֹן עַמֶּךָ, פָּקְדֵנוּ בִּישׁוּעָתֶךָ.¹ זְכֹר

‹ Re- ‹‹ with Your ‹ recall us ‹‹ to Your ‹ when You ‹ HASHEM, ‹ Remem-
member　salvation.　　　people;　show favor　　　　ber us,

עֲדָתְךָ קָנִיתָ קֶּדֶם, גָּאַלְתָּ שֵׁבֶט נַחֲלָתֶךָ, הַר צִיּוֹן זֶה

‹the one‹ of ‹ the ‹‹ of Your ‹ the ‹ You ‹‹ long ‹which You‹ Your con-
[where] Zion, mountain　heritage;　tribe　redeemed　ago,　acquired　gregation,

שָׁכַנְתָּ בּוֹ.² זְכֹר יהוה חִבַּת יְרוּשָׁלַיִם, אַהֲבַת

‹ the love ‹‹ of Jerusalem; ‹ the ‹ HASHEM, ‹ Remem- ‹‹there. ‹ You rested
　　　　　affection　　　　ber,　　　Your Presence

צִיּוֹן אַל תִּשְׁכַּח לָנֶצַח.³ אַתָּה תָקוּם תְּרַחֵם צִיּוֹן כִּי

‹ for ‹‹ to ‹ and show ‹ will arise ‹ You ‹‹ forever. ‹ forget ‹ do not ‹ of
　　Zion,　mercy　　　　　　　　　　　　　Zion

עֵת לְחֶנְנָהּ, כִּי בָא מוֹעֵד.⁴ זְכֹר יהוה לִבְנֵי אֱדוֹם

‹ of ‹ [to repay] ‹ HASHEM, ‹ Re- ‹‹ the appointed time ‹ for ‹‹ [there will come]
Edom　the offspring,　　member,　will have come.　　　the time to favor her,

אֵת יוֹם יְרוּשָׁלָיִם, הָאֹמְרִים עָרוּ עָרוּ עַד הַיְסוֹד בָּהּ.⁵

‹‹of it! ‹ the very ‹ to‹Destroy‹‹Destroy! ‹‹ [to repay] ‹‹ of Jerusalem; ‹ for the day
　　foundation　　　　　　　　　those who say,

זְכֹר לְאַבְרָהָם לְיִצְחָק וּלְיִשְׂרָאֵל עֲבָדֶיךָ, אֲשֶׁר נִשְׁבַּעְתָּ

‹ You ‹ that ‹‹ Your ‹ and for Israel, ‹ for Isaac, ‹ for ‹Remem-
swore　　　　servants,　　　　　　　Abraham,　ber

לָהֶם בָּךְ, וַתְּדַבֵּר אֲלֵהֶם, אַרְבֶּה אֶת זַרְעֲכֶם כְּכוֹכְבֵי

‹ like the ‹ Your offspring ‹ I shall ‹‹ to them, ‹ and ‹‹ by Your‹ to
stars　　　　　increase　　　　　You said　Being,　them

הַשָּׁמָיִם, וְכָל הָאָרֶץ הַזֹּאת אֲשֶׁר אָמַרְתִּי, אֶתֵּן

‹ I will give ‹ I spoke ‹ of which ‹ of this land ‹ and all ‹‹of the heavens;

לְזַרְעֲכֶם, וְנָחֲלוּ לְעֹלָם.⁶ זְכֹר לַעֲבָדֶיךָ לְאַבְרָהָם

‹ of Abraham, ‹ of Your ‹ Remember ‹‹ forever. ‹ and they ‹ to your
　　　　servants,　[the merits]　　　will inherit it　offspring,

לְיִצְחָק וּלְיַעֲקֹב, אַל תֵּפֶן אֶל קְשִׁי הָעָם הַזֶּה וְאֶל

‹ to ‹‹ of this people, ‹ the stub- ‹ to ‹ pay ‹ do ‹‹ and of Jacob; ‹ of Isaac,
　　　　　　bornness　attention　not

רִשְׁעוֹ וְאֶל חַטָּאתוֹ.⁷ זְכוֹר לָנוּ בְּרִית אָבוֹת, כַּאֲשֶׁר

‹ as ‹‹ of the ‹ the ‹ for‹ Remember ‹‹ its ‹ and ‹‹ its
　　Patriarchs,　covenant　us　　sinfulness.　　to　wickedness,

---

(1) Cf. *Psalms* 106:4. (2) 74:2. (3) This is not a Scriptural verse.
(4) *Psalms* 102:14. (5) 137:7. (6) *Exodus* 32:13. (7) *Deuteronomy* 9:27.

אָמַרְתָּ: וְזָכַרְתִּי אֶת בְּרִיתִי יַעֲקוֹב, וְאַף אֶת בְּרִיתִי

⟨ My covenant　⟨ and also　《 [with] Jacob,　⟨ My covenant　⟨ And I will remember　《 You said:

יִצְחָק, וְאַף אֶת בְּרִיתִי אַבְרָהָם אֶזְכֹּר, וְהָאָרֶץ אֶזְכֹּר.[1]

《 I will remember.　⟨ and the Land　《 I will remember;　⟨ [with] Abraham　⟨ My covenant　⟨ and also　《 [with] Isaac,

זְכוֹר לָנוּ בְּרִית רִאשׁוֹנִים, כַּאֲשֶׁר אָמַרְתָּ: וְזָכַרְתִּי

⟨ And I will remember　《 You said:　⟨ as　《 of the ancient ones,　⟨ the covenant　⟨ for us　⟨ Remember

לָהֶם בְּרִית רִאשׁוֹנִים, אֲשֶׁר הוֹצֵאתִי אֹתָם מֵאֶרֶץ

⟨ from the land　⟨ I took them out　⟨ that　《 of the ancient ones,　⟨ the covenant　⟨ for them

מִצְרַיִם לְעֵינֵי הַגּוֹיִם, לִהְיוֹת לָהֶם לֵאלֹהִים, אֲנִי

⟨ I am　《 a God;　⟨ to them　⟨ to be　《 of the nations,　⟨ in the very sight　⟨ of Egypt

יהוה.[2] עֲשֵׂה עִמָּנוּ כְּמָה שֶׁהִבְטַחְתָּנוּ: וְאַף גַּם

⟨ all ⟨ And despite　《 You promised us:　⟨ as　⟨ with us　⟨ Do　《 HASHEM.

זֹאת בִּהְיוֹתָם בְּאֶרֶץ אֹיְבֵיהֶם, לֹא מְאַסְתִּים וְלֹא

⟨ nor　⟨ despise them　⟨ I will not　《 of their enemies,　⟨ in the land　⟨ when they will be　《 this,

גְעַלְתִּים לְכַלֹּתָם לְהָפֵר בְּרִיתִי אִתָּם, כִּי אֲנִי יהוה

⟨ HASHEM, ⟨ I am　⟨ for　《 with them,　⟨ My covenant　⟨ to annul　《 to destroy them,　⟨ abhor them

אֱלֹהֵיהֶם.[3] הָשֵׁב שְׁבוּתֵנוּ וְרַחֲמֵנוּ, כְּמָה שֶׁכָּתוּב:

《 it is written:　⟨ as　《 and have mercy on us,　⟨ our captivity　⟨ Bring back　《 their God.

וְשָׁב יהוה אֱלֹהֶיךָ אֶת שְׁבוּתְךָ וְרִחֲמֶךָ, וְשָׁב וְקִבֶּצְךָ

⟨ gather you in　⟨ and He will once again　《 and He will have mercy upon you,　⟨ your captivity,　⟨ your God,　⟨ will HASHEM,　⟨ Then bring back

מִכֹּל הָעַמִּים אֲשֶׁר הֱפִיצְךָ יהוה אֱלֹהֶיךָ שָׁמָּה.[4]

《 thereto.　⟨ your God　⟨ has scattered you　⟨ that　⟨ the peoples　⟨ from all　⟨ HASHEM

קַבֵּץ נִדְחֵינוּ, כְּמָה שֶׁכָּתוּב: אִם יִהְיֶה נִדַּחֲךָ בִּקְצֵה

⟨ at the ends　⟨ your dispersed will be　⟨ If　⟨ it is written:　⟨ as　⟨ our dispersed ones,　⟨ Gather

(1) *Leviticus* 26:42. (2) 26:45. (3) 26:44. (4) 30:3.

הַשָּׁמָיִם, מִשָּׁם יְקַבֶּצְךָ יהוה אֱלֹהֶיךָ, וּמִשָּׁם יִקָּחֶךָ.[1]

‹ He will take you. › ‹ and from there › ‹ your God, › ‹ will HASHEM, › ‹ gather you in › ‹ from there › ‹ of heaven,

מְחֵה פְשָׁעֵינוּ כָּעָב וְכֶעָנָן, כְּמָה שֶׁכָּתוּב: מָחִיתִי

‹ I have wiped away › ‹ it is written: › ‹ as › ‹ and like a cloud, › ‹ like a mist › ‹ our sins › ‹ Wipe away

כָעָב פְּשָׁעֶיךָ וְכֶעָנָן חַטֹּאתֶיךָ, שׁוּבָה אֵלַי כִּי

‹ for › ‹ to Me, › ‹ return › ‹ your transgressions; › ‹ and like a cloud › ‹ your willful sins, › ‹ like a mist

גְאַלְתִּיךָ.[2] מְחֵה פְשָׁעֵינוּ לְמַעֲנָךְ, כַּאֲשֶׁר אָמָרְתָּ:

‹ You have said: › ‹ as › ‹ for Your sake, › ‹ our sins › ‹ Wipe away › ‹ I have redeemed you.

אָנֹכִי אָנֹכִי הוּא מֹחֶה פְשָׁעֶיךָ לְמַעֲנִי, וְחַטֹּאתֶיךָ לֹא

‹ I shall not › ‹ and your transgressions › ‹ for My sake, › ‹ your willful sins › ‹ Who wipes away › ‹ am the One › ‹ [only] I, › ‹ I,

אֶזְכֹּר.[3] הַלְבֵּן חֲטָאֵינוּ כַּשֶּׁלֶג וְכַצֶּמֶר, כְּמָה שֶׁכָּתוּב:

‹ it is written: › ‹ as › ‹ and like wool, › ‹ like snow › ‹ our sins › ‹ Whiten › ‹ recall.

לְכוּ נָא וְנִוָּכְחָה, יֹאמַר יהוה, אִם יִהְיוּ חֲטָאֵיכֶם

‹ your sins may be › ‹ Though › ‹ HASHEM. › ‹ says › ‹ let us reason together, › ‹ now, › ‹ Come,

כַּשָּׁנִים כַּשֶּׁלֶג יַלְבִּינוּ, אִם יַאְדִּימוּ כַתּוֹלָע, כַּצֶּמֶר

‹ like [white] wool › ‹ as crimson, › ‹ they may be red › ‹ though › ‹ they will be whitened; › ‹ like snow › ‹ like scarlet,

יִהְיוּ.[4] זְרוֹק עָלֵינוּ מַיִם טְהוֹרִים וְטַהֲרֵנוּ, כְּמָה שֶׁכָּתוּב:

‹ it is written: › ‹ as › ‹ and purify us, › ‹ pure water › ‹ upon us › ‹ Pour › ‹ they will become.

וְזָרַקְתִּי עֲלֵיכֶם מַיִם טְהוֹרִים וּטְהַרְתֶּם, מִכֹּל

‹ from all › ‹ and you will become pure; › ‹ pure water › ‹ upon you › ‹ I shall pour

טֻמְאוֹתֵיכֶם וּמִכָּל גִּלּוּלֵיכֶם אֲטַהֵר אֶתְכֶם.[5] רַחֵם

‹ Have mercy › ‹ you. › ‹ I will purify › ‹ your abominations › ‹ and from all › ‹ your contaminations

עָלֵינוּ וְאַל תַּשְׁחִיתֵנוּ, כְּמָה שֶׁכָּתוּב: כִּי אֵל רַחוּם

‹ a merciful God › ‹ For › ‹ it is written: › ‹ as › ‹ destroy us, › ‹ and do not › ‹ on us

יהוה אֱלֹהֶיךָ, לֹא יַרְפְּךָ וְלֹא יַשְׁחִיתֶךָ, וְלֹא יִשְׁכַּח

‹ will He forget › ‹ nor › ‹ will He destroy you, › ‹ nor › ‹ relinquish you › ‹ He will not › ‹ your God; › ‹ is HASHEM,

---

(1) *Leviticus* 30:4. (2) *Isaiah* 44:22. (3) 43:25. (4) 1:18. (5) *Ezekiel* 36:25.

מוֹל   לָהֶם.¹   נִשְׁבַּע   אֲשֶׁר   אֲבֹתֶיךָ   בְּרִית   אֶת

‹ Circumcise ‹‹ to them. ‹ He swore ‹ which ‹ with your forefathers, ‹ the covenant

אֶת לְבָבֵנוּ לְאַהֲבָה וּלְיִרְאָה אֶת שְׁמֶךָ, כְּמָה שֶׁכָּתוּב:

‹‹ it is written: ‹ as ‹‹ Your Name, ‹ and to fear ‹ to love ‹   our hearts

וּמָל יהוה אֱלֹהֶיךָ אֶת לְבָבְךָ וְאֶת לְבַב זַרְעֶךָ, לְאַהֲבָה

‹ to love ‹‹ of your ‹ and the ‹ your heart ‹   HASHEM, your God,
offspring,   heart   will circumcise

אֶת יהוה אֱלֹהֶיךָ, בְּכָל לְבָבְךָ וּבְכָל נַפְשְׁךָ, לְמַעַן

‹ so that ‹‹ your soul, ‹ and with all ‹ your heart ‹ with all ‹ your God, ‹   HASHEM,

חַיֶּיךָ.² הַמָּצֵא לָנוּ בְּבַקָּשָׁתֵנוּ, כְּמָה שֶׁכָּתוּב: וּבִקַּשְׁתֶּם

‹ And you ‹‹ it is written: ‹ as ‹‹ in our quest, ‹ to us ‹ Be ‹‹ you may
will seek   accessible   live.

מִשָּׁם אֶת יהוה אֱלֹהֶיךָ וּמָצָאתָ, כִּי תִדְרְשֶׁנּוּ בְּכָל

‹ with ‹ you search ‹ when ‹‹ and you will ‹ your God, ‹   HASHEM, ‹ from
all   Him out   find [Him],   there

לְבָבְךָ וּבְכָל נַפְשֶׁךָ.³ ❖ תְּבִיאֵנוּ אֶל הַר קָדְשֶׁךָ,

‹ Your holy mountain ‹ to ‹ Bring us ‹‹ your soul. ‹ and with all ‹ your heart

וְשַׂמְּחֵנוּ בְּבֵית תְּפִלָּתֶךָ, כְּמָה שֶׁכָּתוּב: וַהֲבִיאוֹתִים

‹ And I will bring them ‹‹ it is written: ‹ as ‹‹ of Prayer, ‹ in Your House ‹ and gladden us

אֶל הַר קָדְשִׁי, וְשִׂמַּחְתִּים בְּבֵית תְּפִלָּתִי, עוֹלֹתֵיהֶם

‹ their burnt- ‹‹ of Prayer; ‹ in My ‹ and I will ‹‹ My holy ‹ to
offerings   House   gladden them   mountain,

וְזִבְחֵיהֶם לְרָצוֹן עַל מִזְבְּחִי, כִּי בֵיתִי בֵּית תְּפִלָּה

‹ of ‹ "a ‹ My ‹ for ‹‹ My Altar, ‹ on ‹ will find ‹ and their feast-
Prayer" House House   favor   offerings

יִקָּרֵא לְכָל הָעַמִּים.⁴

‹‹   nations. ‹ for all ‹ will be called

THE ARK IS OPENED.

CHAZZAN, THEN CONGREGATION:

שְׁמַע קוֹלֵנוּ יהוה אֱלֹהֵינוּ, חוּס וְרַחֵם עָלֵינוּ,

‹‹ on us, ‹ and have ‹ have ‹‹ our God; ‹ HASHEM, ‹ our voice, ‹ Hear
compassion pity

וְקַבֵּל בְּרַחֲמִים וּבְרָצוֹן אֶת תְּפִלָּתֵנוּ.⁵

‹‹   our prayer. ‹ and favor ‹ with compassion ‹ and accept

(1) *Deuteronomy* 4:31. (2) 30:6. (3) 4:29. (4) *Isaiah* 56:7. (5) From the weekday *Shemoneh Esrei.*

CHAZZAN, THEN CONGREGATION:

הֲשִׁיבֵנוּ יהוה אֵלֶיךָ וְנָשׁוּבָה, חַדֵּשׁ יָמֵינוּ כְּקֶדֶם.[1]

《 as of old. 〈 our days 〈 renew 《 and we shall return, 〈 to You, 〈 HASHEM, 〈 Bring us back,

CHAZZAN, THEN CONGREGATION:

אֲמָרֵינוּ הַאֲזִינָה יהוה, בִּינָה הֲגִיגֵנוּ.[2]

《 our thoughts. 〈 perceive 《 HASHEM; 〈 hear, 〈 Our words

THE FOLLOWING VERSE IS RECITED QUIETLY:

יִהְיוּ לְרָצוֹן אִמְרֵי פִינוּ וְהֶגְיוֹן לִבֵּנוּ לְפָנֶיךָ,

《 before You, 《 of our heart — 〈 and the thoughts 〈 of our mouth 〈 — the expressions 《 find favor 〈 May they

יהוה צוּרֵנוּ וְגוֹאֲלֵנוּ.[3]

《 and our Redeemer. 〈 our Rock 〈 HASHEM,

CHAZZAN, THEN CONGREGATION:

אַל תַּשְׁלִיכֵנוּ מִלְּפָנֶיךָ, וְרוּחַ קָדְשְׁךָ אַל תִּקַּח מִמֶּנּוּ.[4]

《 from us. 〈 take 〈 do not 〈 of Your Holiness 〈 and the Spirit 《 from Your Presence, 〈 cast us away 〈 Do not

CHAZZAN, THEN CONGREGATION:

אַל תַּשְׁלִיכֵנוּ לְעֵת זִקְנָה, כִּכְלוֹת כֹּחֵנוּ אַל תַּעַזְבֵנוּ.[5]

《 forsake us not. 〈 does our strength, 〈 when fail 〈 of old age; 〈 in time 〈 cast us away 〈 Do not

ALL CONTINUE (SOME CONGREGATIONS RECITE THE NEXT VERSE RESPONSIVELY):

אַל תַּעַזְבֵנוּ יהוה, אֱלֹהֵינוּ אַל תִּרְחַק מִמֶּנּוּ.[6]

《 from us. 〈 be not distant 〈 our God, 《 O HASHEM; 〈 Forsake us not,

עֲשֵׂה עִמָּנוּ אוֹת לְטוֹבָה, וְיִרְאוּ שׂוֹנְאֵינוּ וְיֵבֹשׁוּ,

《 and be ashamed, 〈 may our enemies 〈 so that see it 《 for good; 〈 a sign 〈 for us 〈 Display

כִּי אַתָּה יהוה עֲזַרְתָּנוּ וְנִחַמְתָּנוּ.[7] כִּי לְךָ יהוה

〈 HASHEM, 〈 for 〈 Because 《 and consoled us. 〈 will have helped us 〈 HASHEM, 〈 You, 〈 for

הוֹחָלְנוּ, אַתָּה תַעֲנֶה אֲדֹנָי אֱלֹהֵינוּ.[8]

《 our God. 〈 O Lord, 〈 will answer, 〈 You 《 do we wait;

THE ARK IS CLOSED.

(1) *Lamentations* 5:21. (2) Cf. *Psalms* 5:2. (3) Cf. 19:15.
(4) 51:13. (5) Cf. 71:9. (6) Cf. 38:22. (7) Cf. 86:17. (8) Cf. 38:16.

EACH INDIVIDUAL CONTINUES UNTIL THE END OF *SELICHOS*.

CONFESSION / וִדּוּי

DURING THE RECITATION OF THE וִדּוּי, *CONFESSION*, STAND WITH HEAD AND BODY SLIGHTLY BOWED, IN SUBMISSIVE CONTRITION.

אֱלֹהֵינוּ וֵאלֹהֵי אֲבוֹתֵינוּ, תָּבֹא לְפָנֶיךָ תְּפִלָּתֵנוּ,[1]

《 may our 〈 before 〈 come 《 of our 〈 and the 〈 Our God
prayer, You forefathers, God

וְאַל תִּתְעַלַּם מִתְּחִנָּתֵנוּ,[2] שֶׁאֵין אָנוּ עַזֵּי פָנִים

〈 faced 〈 so brazen- 〈 For we are not 《 our supplication. 〈 ignore 〈 and do not

וּקְשֵׁי עֹרֶף, לוֹמַר לְפָנֶיךָ יהוה אֱלֹהֵינוּ וֵאלֹהֵי

〈 and the God 〈 our God, 〈 HASHEM, 《 before You, 〈 as to say 〈 necked 〈 and stiff-

אֲבוֹתֵינוּ, צַדִּיקִים אֲנַחְנוּ וְלֹא חָטָאנוּ, אֲבָל

《—for indeed, 《 sinned 〈 and have not 〈 we are, 〈 that righteous 《 of our forefathers,

אֲנַחְנוּ וַאֲבוֹתֵינוּ חָטָאנוּ.[3]

《 have sinned. 〈 and our forefathers 〈 we

STRIKE THE LEFT SIDE OF THE CHEST WITH THE RIGHT FIST WHILE RECITING EACH OF THE SINS OF THE FOLLOWING CONFESSIONAL LITANY:

אָשַׁמְנוּ, בָּגַדְנוּ, גָּזַלְנוּ, דִּבַּרְנוּ דֹפִי. הֶעֱוִינוּ,

《 We have com- 《 slander. 〈 we have 《 we have 《 we have 《 We have been
mitted iniquity; spoken robbed; betrayed; guilty;

וְהִרְשַׁעְנוּ, זַדְנוּ, חָמַסְנוּ, טָפַלְנוּ שֶׁקֶר. יָעַצְנוּ

〈 We have 《 false 〈 we have 《 we have 《 we have sinned 《 we have commit-
given advice accusations. made extorted; willfully; ted wickedness;

רָע, כִּזַּבְנוּ, לַצְנוּ, מָרַדְנוּ, נִאַצְנוּ, סָרַרְנוּ,

《 we have 《 we have provoked 《 we have 《 we have 《 we have been 《 that is
strayed; [God's anger]; rebelled; scorned; deceitful; bad;

עָוִינוּ, פָּשַׁעְנוּ, צָרַרְנוּ, קִשִּׁינוּ עֹרֶף. רָשַׁעְנוּ,

《 We have 《 our 〈 we have 《 we have caused 《 we have sinned 《 we have been
been wicked; necks. stiffened distress; rebelliously; iniquitous;

שִׁחַתְנוּ, תִּעַבְנוּ, תָּעִינוּ, תִּעְתָּעְנוּ.

《 we have 《 we have 《 we have 《 we have
scoffed. gone astray; committed been corrupt;
abominations;

סַרְנוּ מִמִּצְוֹתֶיךָ וּמִמִּשְׁפָּטֶיךָ הַטּוֹבִים, וְלֹא שָׁוָה

〈 worth- 〈 and it 《 that are 〈 and from 〈 from Your 〈 We have
while was not good, Your laws commandments turned away

---

(1) Cf. *Psalms* 88:3. (2) Cf. 55:2. (3) Cf. 106:6, *Jeremiah* 3:25.

לָנוּ.¹ וְאַתָּה צַדִּיק עַל כָּל הַבָּא עָלֵינוּ, כִּי

‹ for   « upon us, ‹ that has come ‹ all   « in ‹ are righteous ‹ And You   « for us.

אֱמֶת עָשִׂיתָ וַאֲנַחְנוּ הִרְשָׁעְנוּ.²

« have acted wickedly. ‹ while we « have You acted, ‹ truthfully

אָשַׁמְנוּ מִכָּל עָם, בּשְׁנוּ מִכָּל דּוֹר, גָּלָה מִמֶּנוּ

‹ from ‹ Departed «genera- ‹ more ‹ We have «people. ‹ more than ‹ We have
us   tion.   than any   been   any other   been guilty
     other   ashamed

מְשׂוֹשׂ, דָּוָה לִבֵּנוּ בַּחֲטָאֵינוּ, הֻחֲבַּל אִוּוּיֵנוּ, וְנִפְרַע

‹ uncov- « was our de- ‹ Seized « because of ‹ is our ‹ Sickened « has joy.
ered   sired [Temple],   our sins.   heart

פְּאָרֵנוּ, זְבוּל בֵּית מִקְדָּשֵׁנוּ חָרַב בַּעֲוֹנֵינוּ, טִירָתֵנוּ

‹ Our Palace « because of ‹ has been ‹ our Holy Temple ‹ for [His] « was our
     our iniquities. destroyed   abode,   splendor;

הָיְתָה לְשַׁמָּה, יְפִי אַדְמָתֵנוּ לְזָרִים, כֹּחֵנוּ לְנָכְרִים.

« [was given] ‹ our « is controlled ‹ of our ‹ [Jerusalem,] «desolate. ‹ has
to foreigners. wealth by strangers,   Land   the beauty   become

וַעֲדַיִן לֹא שַׁבְנוּ מִטָּעוּתֵנוּ וְהֵיךְ נָעִיז פָּנֵינוּ וְנַקְשֶׁה

‹ and ‹ faced ‹ can we be ‹ So « from our ‹ we have not ‹ But still
stiffen   so brazen- how   willful errors.   repented

עָרְפֵּנוּ, לוֹמַר לְפָנֶיךָ יהוה אֱלֹהֵינוּ וֵאלֹהֵי אֲבוֹתֵינוּ,

« of our ‹ and the ‹ our God ‹ HASHEM, ‹ before ‹ so as to ‹ our neck
forefathers,   God   You,   say

צַדִּיקִים אֲנַחְנוּ וְלֹא חָטָאנוּ, אֲבָל אֲנַחְנוּ וַאֲבוֹתֵינוּ

‹ and our ‹ both we ‹ for in « and we have « we are ‹ that
fathers   truth,   not sinned,   righteous

חָטָאנוּ.³

« have sinned.

**STRIKE THE LEFT SIDE OF THE CHEST WITH THE RIGHT FIST WHILE RECITING
EACH OF THE SINS OF THE FOLLOWING CONFESSIONAL LITANY:**

אָשַׁמְנוּ, בָּגַדְנוּ, גָּזַלְנוּ, דִּבַּרְנוּ דֹּפִי. הֶעֱוִינוּ,

« We have com- « slander. ‹ we have « we have « we have « We have been
mitted iniquity;   spoken   robbed;   betrayed;   guilty;

וְהִרְשַׁעְנוּ, זַדְנוּ, חָמַסְנוּ, טָפַלְנוּ שֶׁקֶר. יָעַצְנוּ

‹ We have « false ‹ we have « we have «we have sinned «we have commit-
given advice accusations.   made   extorted;   willfully;   ted wickedness;

רָע, בָּזַבְנוּ, לַצְנוּ, מָרַדְנוּ, נִאַצְנוּ, סָרַרְנוּ,

« we have strayed; « we have provoked [God's anger]; « we have rebelled; « we have scorned; « we have been deceitful; « that is bad;

עָוִינוּ, פָּשַׁעְנוּ, צָרַרְנוּ, קִשִּׁינוּ עֹרֶף. רָשַׁעְנוּ,

« We have been wicked; « our necks. ‹ we have stiffened « we have caused distress; « we have sinned rebelliously; « we have been iniquitous;

שִׁחַתְנוּ, תִּעַבְנוּ, תָּעִינוּ, תִּעְתָּעְנוּ.

« we have scoffed. « we have gone astray; « we have committed abominations; « we have been corrupt;

סַרְנוּ מִמִּצְוֹתֶיךָ וּמִמִּשְׁפָּטֶיךָ הַטּוֹבִים, וְלֹא שָׁוָה

‹ worth- while ‹ and it was not « that are good, ‹ and from Your laws ‹ from Your commandments ‹ We have turned away

לָנוּ.[1] וְאַתָּה צַדִּיק עַל כָּל הַבָּא עָלֵינוּ, כִּי אֱמֶת

‹ truth- fully ‹ for « upon us, ‹ that has come ‹ all ‹ in ‹ are ‹ And You « for us. righteous

עָשִׂיתָ וַאֲנַחְנוּ הִרְשָׁעְנוּ.[2]

« have acted ‹ while we « have You acted, wickedly.

לְעֵינֵינוּ עָשְׁקוּ עֲמָלֵנוּ, מִמֶּשֶׁךְ וּמְמוֹרָט מִמֶּנּוּ,

« from us. ‹ and cut off ‹ [it was] pulled away « the product of our labor; ‹ have they stolen ‹ Before our eyes

נָתְנוּ עֹלָם עָלֵינוּ, סָבַלְנוּ עַל שִׁכְמֶנוּ, עֲבָדִים

‹ Slaves « our shoulders. ‹ upon ‹ we bore it « upon us, ‹ their yoke ‹ They have placed

מָשְׁלוּ בָנוּ, פֹּרֵק אֵין מִיָּדָם, צָרוֹת רַבּוֹת

‹ that are manifold ‹ Troubles « from their hand. there was not ‹ a redeemer « over us; ‹ have ruled

סְבָבוּנוּ, קְרָאנוּךָ יהוה אֱלֹהֵינוּ, רָחַקְתָּ מִמֶּנּוּ

‹ from us ‹ but You have dis- tanced Yourself « our God, ‹ HASHEM, ‹ we called upon You, « have surrounded us,

בַּעֲוֹנֵינוּ, שַׁבְנוּ מֵאַחֲרֶיךָ, תָּעִינוּ וְאָבָדְנוּ.

« we have become lost. « we have gone astray; « from following after You; ‹ We have turned away « because of our iniquities.

(1) Cf. *Job* 33:27. (2) *Nehemiah* 9:33.

וַעֲדַיִן לֹא שַׁבְנוּ מִטָּעוּתֵנוּ וְהֵיךְ נָעִיז פָּנֵינוּ וְנַקְשֶׁה
and ⟨ faced ⟨ can we be ⟨ So ⟪ from our ⟨ we have not ⟨ But still
stiffen   so brazen-   how   willful errors.   repented

עָרְפֵּנוּ, לוֹמַר לְפָנֶיךָ יהוה אֱלֹהֵינוּ וֵאלֹהֵי אֲבוֹתֵינוּ,
⟪ of our ⟨ and the ⟨ our God ⟨ HASHEM, ⟨ before ⟨ so as to ⟨ our neck
forefathers,   God   You,   say

צַדִּיקִים אֲנַחְנוּ וְלֹא חָטָאנוּ, אֲבָל אֲנַחְנוּ וַאֲבוֹתֵינוּ
⟨ and our ⟨ both we ⟨ for in ⟪ and we have ⟪ we are ⟨ that
fathers   truth,   not sinned,   righteous

חָטָאנוּ.[1]
⟪ have sinned.

**STRIKE THE LEFT SIDE OF THE CHEST WITH THE RIGHT FIST WHILE RECITING
EACH OF THE SINS OF THE FOLLOWING CONFESSIONAL LITANY:**

אָשַׁמְנוּ, בָּגַדְנוּ, גָּזַלְנוּ, דִּבַּרְנוּ דְפִי. הֶעֱוִינוּ,
⟪ We have com- ⟪ slander. ⟨ we have ⟪ we have ⟪ we have ⟪ We have been
mitted iniquity;   spoken   robbed;   betrayed;   guilty;

וְהִרְשַׁעְנוּ, זַדְנוּ, חָמַסְנוּ, טָפַלְנוּ שֶׁקֶר. יָעַצְנוּ
⟨ We have ⟪ false ⟨ we have ⟪ we have ⟪we have sinned ⟪we have commit-
given advice accusations.   made   extorted;   willfully;   ted wickedness;

רָע, כִּזַּבְנוּ, לַצְנוּ, מָרַדְנוּ, נִאַצְנוּ, סָרַרְנוּ,
⟪ we have ⟪ we have provoked ⟪ we have ⟪ we have ⟪ we have been ⟨ that is
strayed;   [God's anger];   rebelled;   scorned;   deceitful;   bad;

עָוִינוּ, פָּשַׁעְנוּ, צָרַרְנוּ, קִשִּׁינוּ עֹרֶף. רָשַׁעְנוּ,
⟪ We have ⟪ our ⟨ we have ⟪we have caused ⟪we have sinned ⟪we have been
been wicked;   necks.   stiffened   distress;   rebelliously;   iniquitous;

שִׁחַתְנוּ, תִּעַבְנוּ, תָּעִינוּ, תִּעְתָּעְנוּ.
⟪   we have ⟪ we have ⟪we have commit- ⟪ we have
scoffed.   gone astray;   ted abominations;   been corrupt;

סַרְנוּ מִמִּצְוֹתֶיךָ וּמִמִּשְׁפָּטֶיךָ הַטּוֹבִים, וְלֹא שָׁוָה
⟨ worth- ⟨ and it ⟪ that are ⟨ and from ⟨ from Your ⟨ We have
while   was not   good,   Your laws   commandments turned away

לָנוּ.[2] וְאַתָּה צַדִּיק עַל כָּל הַבָּא עָלֵינוּ, כִּי אֱמֶת
⟨ truth- ⟨ for ⟪ upon us, ⟨ that has ⟨ all ⟨ in ⟨ are ⟨ And You ⟪ for us.
fully   come   righteous

עָשִׂיתָ וַאֲנַחְנוּ הִרְשָׁעְנוּ.[3]
⟪ have acted wickedly. ⟨ while we ⟪ have You acted,

---

(1) Cf. *Psalms* 106:6; *Jeremiah* 3:25. (2) Cf. *Job* 33:27. (3) *Nehemiah* 9:33.

הִרְשַׁעְנוּ וּפָשַׁעְנוּ, לָכֵן לֹא נוֹשָׁעְנוּ. וְתֵן בְּלִבֵּנוּ

⟨ in our ⟨ Place ≪ been ⟨ we have ⟨ there- ≪ and we ⟨ We have acted
hearts saved. not fore have sinned wickedly
rebelliously;

לַעֲזוֹב דֶּרֶךְ רֶשַׁע, וְחִישׁ לָנוּ יֶשַׁע, כַּכָּתוּב עַל יַד

⟨ the ⟨ by ⟨ as it is ≪ salvation; ⟨ to us ⟨ and ≪ of ⟨ the ⟨ [the will]
hand written hasten wickedness, path to abandon

נְבִיאֶךָ: יַעֲזֹב רָשָׁע דַּרְכּוֹ, וְאִישׁ אָוֶן מַחְשְׁבֹתָיו,

≪ [abandon] ⟨ of ⟨ and ≪ his way, ⟨ the wicked ⟨ Let ≪ of Your
his thoughts; iniquity the man one abandon prophet:

וְיָשֹׁב אֶל יהוה וִירַחֲמֵהוּ, וְאֶל אֱלֹהֵינוּ כִּי

⟨ for ⟨ our God, ⟨ and to ≪ and He will have ⟨ HASHEM, ⟨ to ⟨ and let
compassion on him, him return

יַרְבֶּה לִסְלוֹחַ.[1]

≪ forgiving. ⟨ He is
abundantly

מְשִׁיחַ צִדְקֶךָ אָמַר לְפָנֶיךָ, שְׁגִיאוֹת מִי יָבִין,

≪ can ⟨ who ⟨ Mistakes ≪ before You: ⟨ said ⟨ who is righteous ⟨ Your
discern? [David] anointed one

מִנִּסְתָּרוֹת נַקֵּנִי.[2] נַקֵּנוּ יהוה אֱלֹהֵינוּ מִכָּל פְּשָׁעֵינוּ,

⟨ our sins ⟨ of all ⟨ our God, ⟨ HASHEM, ⟨ Cleanse ≪ cleanse ⟨ From
us, me. unperceived faults

וְטַהֲרֵנוּ מִכָּל טֻמְאוֹתֵינוּ, וּזְרוֹק עָלֵינוּ מַיִם טְהוֹרִים

⟨ pure water ⟨ upon us ⟨ Pour ≪ our contaminations. ⟨ of all ⟨ and purify us

וְטַהֲרֵנוּ, כַּכָּתוּב עַל יַד נְבִיאֶךָ: וְזָרַקְתִּי עֲלֵיכֶם

⟨ upon you ⟨ I shall pour ≪ of Your ⟨ the ⟨ by ⟨ as it is ≪ and purify us,
prophet: hand written

מַיִם טְהוֹרִים וּטְהַרְתֶּם, מִכֹּל טֻמְאוֹתֵיכֶם וּמִכָּל

⟨ and ⟨ your ⟨ from ≪ and you will ⟨ pure water
from all contaminations all become pure;

גִּלּוּלֵיכֶם אֲטַהֵר אֶתְכֶם.[3] עַמְּךָ וְנַחֲלָתֶךָ, רְעֵבֵי

⟨ who ≪ and Your ⟨ Your ≪ you. ⟨ I will purify ⟨ your
hunger heritage, people abominations

טוּבְךָ, צְמֵאֵי חַסְדֶּךָ, תְּאֵבֵי יִשְׁעֶךָ, יַכִּירוּ וְיֵדְעוּ

⟨ and ⟨ — may they ≪ for Your ⟨ and ≪ for Your ⟨ who ≪ for Your
know recognize salvation who long kindness, thirst goodness,

---

(1) *Isaiah* 55:7. (2) *Psalms* 19:13. (3) *Ezekiel* 36:25.

כִּי לַיהוה אֱלֹהֵינוּ הָרַחֲמִים וְהַסְּלִיחוֹת.

⟨ and forgiveness. ⟨ belong mercy ⟨ our God, ⟨ to HASHEM, ⟨ that

אֵל רַחוּם שְׁמֶךָ, אֵל חַנּוּן שְׁמֶךָ,[1] בָּנוּ נִקְרָא שְׁמֶךָ.[2]

⟨ is Your Name ⟨ upon ⟨ is Your ⟨ *Gracious God* ⟨ is Your ⟨ *Merciful God*
proclaimed, us Name, Name

יהוה עֲשֵׂה לְמַעַן שְׁמֶךָ,[3] עֲשֵׂה לְמַעַן אֲמִתָּךְ, עֲשֵׂה

⟨ act ⟨ Your truth; ⟨ for the ⟨ Act ⟨ Your ⟨ for the ⟨ act ⟨ HASHEM,
sake of Name. sake of

לְמַעַן בְּרִיתָךְ, עֲשֵׂה לְמַעַן גָּדְלָךְ וְתִפְאַרְתָּךְ, עֲשֵׂה

⟨ act ⟨ and Your ⟨ Your ⟨ for the ⟨ act ⟨ Your ⟨ for the
splendor; greatness sake of covenant; sake of

לְמַעַן דָּתָךְ, עֲשֵׂה לְמַעַן הוֹדָךְ, עֲשֵׂה לְמַעַן וְעוּדָךְ,

⟨ Your Meet- ⟨ for the ⟨ act ⟨ Your ⟨ for the ⟨ act ⟨ Your ⟨ for the
ing House; sake of glory; sake of Law; sake of

עֲשֵׂה לְמַעַן זִכְרָךְ,[4] עֲשֵׂה לְמַעַן חַסְדָּךְ, עֲשֵׂה לְמַעַן

⟨ for the ⟨ act ⟨ Your ⟨ for the ⟨ act ⟨ Your ⟨ for the ⟨ act
sake of kindness; sake of remembrance; sake of

טוּבָךְ, עֲשֵׂה לְמַעַן יִחוּדָךְ, עֲשֵׂה לְמַעַן כְּבוֹדָךְ, עֲשֵׂה

⟨ act ⟨ Your ⟨ for the ⟨ act ⟨ Your ⟨ for the ⟨ act ⟨ Your
honor; sake of Oneness; sake of goodness;

לְמַעַן לִמּוּדָךְ,[6] עֲשֵׂה לְמַעַן מַלְכוּתָךְ, עֲשֵׂה לְמַעַן

⟨ for the ⟨ act ⟨ Your kingship; ⟨ for the ⟨ act ⟨ Your ⟨ for the
sake of sake of students; sake of

נִצְחָךְ, עֲשֵׂה לְמַעַן סוֹדָךְ,[7] עֲשֵׂה לְמַעַן עֻזָּךְ, עֲשֵׂה

⟨ act ⟨ Your ⟨ for the ⟨ act ⟨ Your secret [re- ⟨ for the ⟨ act ⟨ Your eternal
power; sake of vealed to those sake of [Name];
who fear You];

לְמַעַן פְּאֵרָךְ, עֲשֵׂה לְמַעַן צִדְקָתָךְ, עֲשֵׂה לְמַעַן

⟨ for the ⟨ act ⟨ Your ⟨ for the ⟨ act ⟨ Your ⟨ for the
sake of righteousness; sake of glory; sake of

קְדֻשָּׁתָךְ, עֲשֵׂה לְמַעַן רַחֲמֶיךָ הָרַבִּים, עֲשֵׂה לְמַעַן

⟨ for the ⟨ act ⟨ that is ⟨ Your mercy ⟨ for the ⟨ act ⟨ Your sanctity;
sake of abundant; sake of

שְׁכִינָתָךְ, עֲשֵׂה לְמַעַן תְּהִלָּתָךְ, עֲשֵׂה לְמַעַן אוֹהֲבֶיךָ

⟨ those who ⟨ for the ⟨ act ⟨ Your praise; ⟨ for the ⟨ act ⟨ Your Divine
loved You sake of sake of Presence;

---

(1) Cf. *Exodus* 34:6. (2) Cf. *Deuteronomy* 28:10. (3) *Jeremiah* 14:7.
(4) Cf. *Exodus* 3:15. (5) *Psalms* 6:5. (6) Cf. *Isaiah* 54:13. (7) Cf. *Psalms* 25:14.

שׁוֹכְנֵי עָפָר,¹ עֲשֵׂה לְמַעַן אַבְרָהָם יִצְחָק וְיַעֲקֹב,

《 and Jacob; 〈 Isaac, 〈 Abraham, 〈 for the sake of 〈 act 《 in the dust; 〈 who rest

עֲשֵׂה לְמַעַן מֹשֶׁה וְאַהֲרֹן, עֲשֵׂה לְמַעַן דָּוִד וּשְׁלֹמֹה,

《 and 〈 David 〈 for the 〈 act 《 and Aaron; 〈 Moses 〈 for the 〈 act
Solomon;   sake of   sake of

עֲשֵׂה לְמַעַן יְרוּשָׁלַיִם עִיר קָדְשֶׁךָ,² עֲשֵׂה לְמַעַן צִיּוֹן

〈 Zion, 〈 for the 〈 act 《 of Your 〈 the 〈 Jerusalem, 〈 for the 〈 act
    sake of   Holiness; City   sake of

מִשְׁכַּן כְּבוֹדֶךָ,³ עֲשֵׂה לְמַעַן שִׁמְמוֹת⁴ הֵיכָלֶךָ, עֲשֵׂה

〈 act 《 of Your 〈 the 〈 for the 〈 act 《 of Your 〈 the
      Temple; desolation sake of   glory; abode

לְמַעַן הֲרִיסוּת⁵ מִזְבְּחֶךָ, עֲשֵׂה לְמַעַן הֲרוּגִים עַל

〈 for 〈 those killed 〈 for the 〈 act 《 of Your 〈 the 〈 for the
          sake of   Altar; devastation sake of

שֵׁם קָדְשֶׁךָ, עֲשֵׂה לְמַעַן טְבוּחִים עַל יִחוּדֶךָ, עֲשֵׂה

〈 act 《 Your 〈 for 〈 those 〈 for the 〈 act 《 Your holy Name;
     Oneness;   slaughtered sake of

לְמַעַן בָּאֵי בָאֵשׁ וּבַמַּיִם עַל קִדּוּשׁ שְׁמֶךָ, עֲשֵׂה לְמַעַן

〈 for the 〈 act 《 of Your 〈 the 〈 for 〈 and water 〈 fire 〈 those who 〈 for the
  sake of   Name; sanctification   entered sake of

יוֹנְקֵי שָׁדַיִם⁶ שֶׁלֹּא חָטָאוּ, עֲשֵׂה לְמַעַן גְּמוּלֵי חָלָב

〈 from 〈 the [babies] 〈 for the 〈 act 《 sin; 〈 who did 〈 at the 〈 the [infants]
milk   weaned sake of   not   breast sucking

שֶׁלֹּא פָשְׁעוּ, עֲשֵׂה לְמַעַן תִּינוֹקוֹת שֶׁל בֵּית רַבָּן,⁸

《 their teachers' 〈 of 〈 the children 〈 for the 〈 act 《 transgress; 〈 who
      school;   sake of   did not

עֲשֵׂה לְמַעַנְךָ אִם לֹא לְמַעֲנֵנוּ, עֲשֵׂה לְמַעַנְךָ וְהוֹשִׁיעֵנוּ.

《 and save us. 〈 for Your 〈 act 《 for our 〈 not 〈 if 〈 for Your 〈 act
        sake   sake;   sake

עֲנֵנוּ יהוה עֲנֵנוּ, עֲנֵנוּ אֱלֹהֵינוּ עֲנֵנוּ, עֲנֵנוּ אָבִינוּ⁹

〈 our 〈 answer 《 answer 〈 our God, 〈 answer 《 answer 〈 HASHEM, 〈 Answer
Father, us; us;   us, us;   us;

עֲנֵנוּ, עֲנֵנוּ בוֹרְאֵנוּ¹⁰ עֲנֵנוּ, עֲנֵנוּ גוֹאֲלֵנוּ¹¹ עֲנֵנוּ, עֲנֵנוּ

〈 answer 《 answer 〈 our 〈 answer 《 answer 〈 our Creator, 〈 answer 《 answer
us; us; Redeemer, us; us;   us, us;

(1) *Isaiah* 26:19. (2) Cf. *Daniel* 9:16,24. (3) *Psalms* 26:8. (4) Cf. *Jeremiah* 51:26. (5) Cf. *Isaiah* 49:19.
(6) *Joel* 2:16. (7) *Isaiah* 28:9. (8) *Shabbos* 119b. (9) *Isaiah* 64:7. (10) Cf. 43:1. (11) 47:4.

דּוֹרְשֵׁנוּ¹ עֲנֵנוּ, עֲנֵנוּ הָאֵל הַנֶּאֱמָן² עֲנֵנוּ, עֲנֵנוּ וָתִיק

‹ stead- ‹ answer « answer ‹ Who is ‹ God ‹ answer « answer ‹ You Who
fast us, us, faithful, us, us; searches us out,

וְחָסִיד עֲנֵנוּ, עֲנֵנוּ זַךְ וְיָשָׁר³ עֲנֵנוּ, עֲנֵנוּ חַי וְקַיָּם⁴

‹ and endur- ‹ living ‹ answer « answer ‹ and ‹ pure ‹ answer « answer ‹ and kind
ing One, One, us, us; upright One us, us; One,

עֲנֵנוּ, עֲנֵנוּ טוֹב וּמֵטִיב⁵ עֲנֵנוּ, עֲנֵנוּ יוֹדֵעַ יֵצֶר⁶ עֲנֵנוּ,

« answer ‹ of incli- ‹ Knower ‹ answer « answer ‹ and bene- ‹ good ‹ answer « answer
us; nations, us, us; ficent One, us; us;

עֲנֵנוּ כּוֹבֵשׁ כְּעָסִים עֲנֵנוּ, עֲנֵנוּ לוֹבֵשׁ צְדָקוֹת⁷ עֲנֵנוּ,

« answer ‹ of ‹ Donner ‹ answer « answer ‹ of wrath, ‹ Suppressor ‹ answer
us; righteousness, us, us; us,

עֲנֵנוּ מֶלֶךְ מַלְכֵי הַמְּלָכִים⁸ עֲנֵנוּ, עֲנֵנוּ נוֹרָא וְנִשְׂגָּב⁹

‹ and power- ‹ awesome ‹ answer « answer ‹ of kings, ‹ over ‹ King ‹ answer
ful One, One, us, us; kings us,

עֲנֵנוּ, עֲנֵנוּ סוֹלֵחַ וּמוֹחֵל עֲנֵנוּ, עֲנֵנוּ עוֹנֶה בְּעֵת

‹ in time ‹ You Who ‹ answer « answer ‹ and ‹ You Who ‹ answer « answer
answers us, us; pardons forgives us, us;

צָרָה¹⁰ עֲנֵנוּ, עֲנֵנוּ פּוֹדֶה וּמַצִּיל¹¹ עֲנֵנוּ, עֲנֵנוּ צַדִּיק

‹ righteous ‹ answer « answer ‹ and ‹ Redeemer ‹ answer « answer ‹ of
us, us; Rescuer, us, us; distress,

וְיָשָׁר¹² עֲנֵנוּ, עֲנֵנוּ קָרוֹב לְקוֹרְאָיו¹³ עֲנֵנוּ, עֲנֵנוּ קָשֶׁה

‹ You Who ‹ answer « answer ‹ to those who ‹ He Who ‹ answer « answer ‹ and up-
with difficulty us, us; call upon Him, is close us, us; right One,

לִכְעוֹס¹⁴ עֲנֵנוּ, עֲנֵנוּ רַךְ לִרְצוֹת¹⁵ עֲנֵנוּ, עֲנֵנוּ רַחוּם

‹ merciful ‹ answer « answer ‹ appeased, ‹ You Who ‹ answer « answer ‹ becomes
us, us; are easily us, us; angry,

וְחַנּוּן¹⁶ עֲנֵנוּ, עֲנֵנוּ שׁוֹמֵעַ אֶל אֶבְיוֹנִים¹⁷ עֲנֵנוּ, עֲנֵנוּ

‹ answer « answer ‹ the destitute, ‹ to ‹ You Who ‹ answer « answer ‹ and gra-
us, us; listens us, us; cious One,

תּוֹמֵךְ תְּמִימִים עֲנֵנוּ, עֲנֵנוּ אֱלֹהֵי אֲבוֹתֵינוּ עֲנֵנוּ,

« answer ‹ of our ‹ God ‹ answer « answer ‹ the ‹ You Who
us; forefathers, us, us; wholesome, supports

עֲנֵנוּ אֱלֹהֵי אַבְרָהָם¹⁸ עֲנֵנוּ, עֲנֵנוּ פַּחַד יִצְחָק עֲנֵנוּ,

« answer ‹ of Isaac, ‹ Awesome ‹ answer « answer ‹ of Abraham, ‹ God ‹ answer
us; One, us, us; us,

(1) Cf. Ezekiel 34:11. (2) Deuteronomy 7:9. (3) Job 8:6; cf. Proverbs 20:11. (4) Cf. Daniel 6:27. (5) Cf. Psalms 119:68. (6) Cf. 103:14. (7) Cf. Isaiah 59:17. (8) Ethics of the Fathers 3:1. (9) Psalms 47:3; 148:13. (10) Cf. Isaiah 49:8; Psalms 37:39. Alternate text: בְּעֵת רָצוֹן, in time of favor. (11) Cf. 34:23,18. (12) Deuteronomy 32:4. (13) Cf. Psalms 145:18. (14) Ethics of the Fathers 5:14. (15) Cf. 5:14. (16) Exodus 34:6. (17) Psalms 69:34. (18) Genesis 31:42.

עֲנֵנוּ אֲבִיר יַעֲקֹב¹ עֲנֵנוּ, עֲנֵנוּ עֶזְרַת הַשְּׁבָטִים עֲנֵנוּ,

《answer 〈 of the tribes, 〈 Helper 〈 answer 《answer 〈 of Jacob, 〈 Mighty 〈 answer
us;   us,   us;   One   us,

עֲנֵנוּ מִשְׂגַּב אִמָּהוֹת עֲנֵנוּ, עֲנֵנוּ עוֹנֶה בְּעֵת רָצוֹן² עֲנֵנוּ,

《answer 〈 of favor, 〈 in a 〈 You Who 〈 answer 《answer 〈 of the 〈 Stronghold 〈 answer
us;   time   answers   us,   us;   Matriarchs,   us,

עֲנֵנוּ אֲבִי יְתוֹמִים³ עֲנֵנוּ, עֲנֵנוּ דַּיַּן אַלְמָנוֹת³ עֲנֵנוּ.

《 answer 〈 of widows, 〈 Judge 〈 answer 《answer 〈 of orphans, 〈 Father 〈 answer
us.   us,   us;   us,

מִי שֶׁעָנָה לְאַבְרָהָם אָבִינוּ בְּהַר הַמּוֹרִיָּה⁴

《 Moriah 〈 on Mount 〈 our father 〈 Abraham 〈 Who answered 〈 He

הוּא יַעֲנֵנוּ.

《 answer 〈 — may
us.   He

מִי שֶׁעָנָה לְיִצְחָק בְּנוֹ כְּשֶׁנֶּעֱקַד עַל גַּבֵּי הַמִּזְבֵּחַ⁴

《 of the altar 〈 top 〈 on 〈 when he 〈 his son 〈 Isaac 〈 Who 〈 He
was bound   answered

הוּא יַעֲנֵנוּ.

《 answer 〈 — may
us.   He

מִי שֶׁעָנָה לְיַעֲקֹב בְּבֵית אֵל⁵

《 in Beth-el 〈 Jacob 〈 Who 〈 He
answered

הוּא יַעֲנֵנוּ.

《 answer 〈 — may
us.   He

מִי שֶׁעָנָה לְיוֹסֵף בְּבֵית הָאֲסוּרִים⁶

《 in the prison 〈 Joseph 〈 Who 〈 He
answered

הוּא יַעֲנֵנוּ.

《 answer 〈 — may
us.   He

מִי שֶׁעָנָה לַאֲבוֹתֵינוּ עַל יַם סוּף⁷

《 of 〈 the 〈 at 〈 our forefathers 〈 Who 〈 He
Reeds Sea   answered

הוּא יַעֲנֵנוּ.

《 answer 〈 — may
us.   He

מִי שֶׁעָנָה לְמֹשֶׁה בְּחוֹרֵב⁸

《 in Horeb 〈 Moses 〈 Who 〈 He
answered

הוּא יַעֲנֵנוּ.

《 answer 〈 — may
us.   He

מִי שֶׁעָנָה לְאַהֲרֹן בַּמַּחְתָּה⁹

《 with the fire-pan 〈 Aaron 〈 Who 〈 He
answered

הוּא יַעֲנֵנוּ.

《 answer 〈 — may
us.   He

---

(1) *Isaiah* 49:26. (2) Cf. 49:8; *Psalms* 69:14. Alternate text: בְּעֵת צָרָה, *in time of distress.*
(3) 68:6. (4) *Genesis* 22:12. (5) 35:3. (6) 39:21. (7) *Exodus* Ch. 14.
(8) 17:6,11; *Deuteronomy* 9:19. (9) *Numbers* 17:11-13.

מִי שֶׁעָנָה לְפִינְחָס בְּקוּמוֹ מִתּוֹךְ הָעֵדָה[1]

‹ He ‹ Who ‹ Phinehas ‹ when he ‹ from ‹ the
answered arose amid congregation «

הוּא יַעֲנֵנוּ.

‹ may ‹ answer
He — us. «

מִי שֶׁעָנָה לִיהוֹשֻׁעַ בַּגִּלְגָּל[2]

‹ He ‹ Who ‹ Joshua ‹ in Gilgal «
answered

הוּא יַעֲנֵנוּ.

‹ may ‹ answer
He — us. «

מִי שֶׁעָנָה לִשְׁמוּאֵל בַּמִּצְפָּה[3]

‹ He ‹ Who ‹ Samuel ‹ in Mizpah «
answered

הוּא יַעֲנֵנוּ.

‹ may ‹ answer
He — us. «

מִי שֶׁעָנָה לְדָוִד וּשְׁלֹמֹה בְנוֹ בִּירוּשָׁלַיִם[4]

‹ He ‹ Who ‹ David ‹ and ‹ his ‹ in Jerusalem ‹ may ‹ answer
answered Solomon son He — us. «

הוּא יַעֲנֵנוּ.

מִי שֶׁעָנָה לְאֵלִיָּהוּ בְּהַר הַכַּרְמֶל[5]

‹ He ‹ Who ‹ Elijah ‹ on ‹ Carmel «
answered Mount

הוּא יַעֲנֵנוּ.

‹ may ‹ answer
He — us. «

מִי שֶׁעָנָה לֶאֱלִישָׁע בִּירִיחוֹ[6]

‹ He ‹ Who ‹ Elisha ‹ in Jericho «
answered

הוּא יַעֲנֵנוּ.

‹ may ‹ answer
He — us. «

מִי שֶׁעָנָה לְיוֹנָה בִּמְעֵי הַדָּגָה[7]

‹ He ‹ Who ‹ Jonah ‹ in the ‹ of the «
answered innards fish

הוּא יַעֲנֵנוּ.

‹ may ‹ answer
He — us. «

מִי שֶׁעָנָה לְחִזְקִיָּהוּ מֶלֶךְ יְהוּדָה בְּחָלְיוֹ[8]

‹ He ‹ Who ‹ Hezekiah, ‹ king ‹ of Judah, ‹ in his «
answered illness

הוּא יַעֲנֵנוּ.

‹ may ‹ answer
He — us. «

מִי שֶׁעָנָה לַחֲנַנְיָה מִישָׁאֵל וַעֲזַרְיָה

‹ He ‹ Who ‹ Hananiah, ‹ Mishael, ‹ and Azariah ‹
answered

בְּתוֹךְ כִּבְשַׁן הָאֵשׁ[9]

‹ inside ‹ the furnace ‹ of fire «

הוּא יַעֲנֵנוּ.

‹ may ‹ answer
He — us. «

מִי שֶׁעָנָה לְדָנִיֵּאל בְּגוֹב הָאֲרָיוֹת[10]

‹ He ‹ Who ‹ Daniel ‹ in the ‹ of lions «
answered den

הוּא יַעֲנֵנוּ.

‹ may ‹ answer
He — us. «

(1) *Numbers* 25:7-13. (2) *Joshua* 6:1-20; 7:6-15; 10:12-14. (3) *I Samuel* 7:9.
(4) *II Samuel* 7:5-16; 21:1,14; 24:25; *I Kings* 9:3. (5) 18:36-38. (6) *II Kings* 2:21.
(7) *Jonah* 2:2-11. (8) *II Kings* 20:2-6; *Isaiah* 38:2-8. (9) *Daniel* 3:21-27. (10) 6:17-23.

מִי שֶׁעָנָה לְמָרְדְּכַי וְאֶסְתֵּר בְּשׁוּשַׁן הַבִּירָה¹

⟪ the capital ⟨ in Shushan ⟨ and Esther ⟨ Mordechai ⟨ Who ⟨ He
answered

הוּא יַעֲנֵנוּ.

⟪ answer ⟨ — may
us. He

מִי שֶׁעָנָה לְעֶזְרָא בַּגּוֹלָה²

הוּא יַעֲנֵנוּ.

⟪ in the exile ⟨ Ezra ⟨ Who ⟨ He
answered

⟪ answer ⟨ — may
us. He

מִי שֶׁעָנָה לְכָל הַצַּדִּיקִים וְהַחֲסִידִים וְהַתְּמִימִים

⟨ the wholesome, ⟨ the devout, ⟨ the righteous, ⟨ all ⟨ Who ⟨ He
answered

וְהַיְשָׁרִים

הוּא יַעֲנֵנוּ.

⟪ answer ⟨ — may
us. He

⟪ and the
upright

רַחֲמָנָא דְּעָנֵי לַעֲנִיֵּי, עֲנֵינָן. רַחֲמָנָא דְּעָנֵי לִתְבִירֵי

⟨ those of ⟨ Who ⟨ Merciful ⟪ answer ⟪ the poor, ⟨ Who ⟨ Merciful One
broken answers One us! answers

לִבָּא, עֲנֵינָן. רַחֲמָנָא דְּעָנֵי לְמַכִּיכֵי רוּחָא, עֲנֵינָן.

⟪ answer ⟪ spirit, ⟨ those of ⟨ Who ⟨ Merciful ⟪ answer ⟪ hearts,
us! crushed answers One us!

רַחֲמָנָא עֲנֵינָן. רַחֲמָנָא חוּס. רַחֲמָנָא פְּרוֹק. רַחֲמָנָא

⟨ Merciful ⟪ redeem! ⟨ Merciful ⟪ have ⟨ Merciful ⟪ answer ⟨ Merciful
One, One, pity! One, us! One,

שֵׁזִיב. רַחֲמָנָא רְחַם עֲלָן, הַשְׁתָּא בַּעֲגָלָא וּבִזְמַן קָרִיב.

⟪ that comes ⟨ and at ⟨ swiftly, ⟨ — now, ⟪ on us ⟨ have ⟨ Merciful ⟪ save!
soon. a time mercy One,

PUTTING DOWN THE HEAD / נפילת אפים

RECITE UNTIL יֵבֹשׁוּ רָגַע WITH THE HEAD RESTING ON THE LEFT ARM,
PREFERABLY WHILE SEATED.

(וַיֹּאמֶר דָּוִד אֶל גָּד, צַר לִי מְאֹד, נִפְּלָה נָּא בְיַד יהוה,

⟪ of ⟨ into the ⟨ now ⟨ Let us ⟪ exceed- ⟨ am ⟨ Dis- ⟪ Gad, ⟨ to ⟨ (And David said
HASHEM, hand fall ingly. I tressed

כִּי רַבִּים רַחֲמָיו, וּבְיַד אָדָם אַל אֶפְּלָה.)³

⟪ let me not fall.) ⟨ but into human ⟪ are His ⟨ abundant ⟨ for
hands mercies,

(1) Esther Ch. 8. (2) Ezra 8:21-23. (3) II Samuel 24:14.

רַחוּם וְחַנּוּן חָטָאתִי לְפָנֶיךָ. יהוה מָלֵא רַחֲמִים,

‹ of mercy, ‹ Who is full ‹ HASHEM, ‹ before You. ‹ I have sinned ‹ and gracious One, ‹ O merciful

רַחֵם עָלַי וְקַבֵּל תַּחֲנוּנָי.

‹ my supplications. ‹ and accept ‹ on me ‹ have mercy

—— *Psalms 6:2-11* / תהלים ו:ב-יא ——

יהוה, אַל בְּאַפְּךָ תוֹכִיחֵנִי, וְאַל בַּחֲמָתְךָ תְיַסְּרֵנִי.

‹ chastise me. ‹ in Your wrath ‹ nor ‹ rebuke me, ‹ in Your anger ‹ do not ‹ HASHEM,

חָנֵּנִי יהוה כִּי אֻמְלַל אָנִי, רְפָאֵנִי יהוה כִּי נִבְהֲלוּ

‹ shudder with terror ‹ for ‹ HASHEM, ‹ heal me, ‹ am I; ‹ feeble ‹ for ‹ HASHEM, ‹ Favor me,

עֲצָמָי. וְנַפְשִׁי נִבְהֲלָה מְאֹד, וְאַתָּה יהוה עַד מָתָי.

‹ when? ‹ until ‹ HASHEM, ‹ and You, ‹ utterly, ‹ is terrified ‹ My soul ‹ do my bones.

שׁוּבָה יהוה חַלְּצָה נַפְשִׁי, הוֹשִׁיעֵנִי לְמַעַן חַסְדֶּךָ.

‹ Your kindness. ‹ as befits ‹ save me ‹ my soul; ‹ release ‹ HASHEM, ‹ Desist,

כִּי אֵין בַּמָּוֶת זִכְרֶךָ, בִּשְׁאוֹל מִי יוֹדֶה לָךְ. יָגַעְתִּי

‹ I am wearied ‹ You? ‹ will praise ‹ who ‹ in the grave ‹ is there mention of You; ‹ in death ‹ not ‹ For

בְּאַנְחָתִי, אַשְׂחֶה בְכָל לַיְלָה מִטָּתִי, בְּדִמְעָתִי

‹ with my tears ‹ my bed; ‹ night ‹ every ‹ I drench ‹ with my sigh;

עַרְשִׂי אַמְסֶה. עָשְׁשָׁה מִכַּעַס עֵינִי, עָתְקָה בְּכָל

‹ by all ‹ aged ‹ is my eye, ‹ because of anger ‹ Dimmed ‹ I soak. ‹ my couch

צוֹרְרָי. סוּרוּ מִמֶּנִּי כָּל פֹּעֲלֵי אָוֶן, כִּי שָׁמַע יהוה

‹ HASHEM has heard ‹ for ‹ of evil, ‹ doers ‹ all ‹ from me, ‹ Depart ‹ my tormentors.

קוֹל בִּכְיִי. שָׁמַע יהוה תְּחִנָּתִי, יהוה תְּפִלָּתִי יִקָּח.

‹ will accept. ‹ my prayer ‹ HASHEM ‹ my plea, ‹ HASHEM has heard ‹ of my weeping. ‹ the sound

יֵבֹשׁוּ וְיִבָּהֲלוּ מְאֹד כָּל אֹיְבָי, יָשֻׁבוּ יֵבֹשׁוּ רָגַע.

‹ in an instant. ‹ and be shamed ‹ may they regret ‹ my enemies; ‹ all ‹ utterly, ‹ and confounded ‹ Let them be shamed

מָחֵי וּמַסֵּי מֵמִית וּמְחַיֶּה, מַסִּיק מִן שְׁאוֹל

‹ the grave ‹ from ‹ Who raises [the dead] ‹ and Who restores life, ‹ Who causes death ‹ and Who ‹ heals, ‹ [O God,] Who wounds

לְחַיֵּי עָלְמָא, בְּרָא כַּד חָטֵי אֲבוּהִי לַקְיֵהּ, אֲבוּהִי

‹ to life ‹ eternal: ‹ A son ‹ should he ‹ sin, ‹ his father ‹ would ‹ but a father strike him,

דְחָיֵס אַסֵי לִכְאֵבֵהּ. עַבְדָּא דְמָרִיד נָפִיק בְּקוֹלָר,

‹ who is com-passionate ‹ will heal ‹ his [son's] pain. ‹ A slave ‹ who rebels, ‹ he is led out ‹ in chains,

מָרֵהּ תָּאִיב וְתַבִּיר קוֹלָרֵהּ.

‹ but [if] his master ‹ desires, ‹ he breaks ‹ his chains.

בְּרָךְ בְּכְרָךְ אֲנָן וְחָטִינָן קַמָּךְ, הָא רָוֵי נַפְשִׁין

‹ Your son, ‹ Your firstborn, ‹ we are, ‹ and we have sinned ‹ before You; ‹ indeed ‹ has our soul been satiated

בִּגְּדִין מְרָרִין, עַבְדָּךְ אֲנָן וּמְרוֹדִינָן קַמָּךְ,

‹ with wormwood ‹ that is bitter. ‹ Your ‹ servants ‹ we are ‹ and we have rebelled ‹ before You;

הָא בִּבְזְתָא, הָא בִּשְׁבְיָא, הָא בְּמַלְקִיוּתָא.

‹ [indeed we have looting, suffered,] some ‹ from ‹ some ‹ in captivity, ‹ and some ‹ by the lash.

בְּמָטוּ מִנָּךְ בְּרַחֲמָךְ דִּנְפִישִׁין, אַסֵי לִכְאֵבִין

‹ We beg ‹ of You, ‹ in Your compassion ‹ that is abundant, ‹ heal ‹ the pains

דִּתְקוֹף עֲלָן, עַד דְּלָא נֶהֱוֵי גְמִירָא בְּשִׁבְיָא.

‹ that have overwhelmed ‹ us, ‹ while yet ‹ we are not ‹ completely annihilated ‹ in captivity.

מַכְנִיסֵי רַחֲמִים, הַכְנִיסוּ רַחֲמֵינוּ, לִפְנֵי בַעַל

‹ O you who usher in ‹ [pleas for] mercy, ‹ may you usher in ‹ our [plea for] mercy ‹ before ‹ the Master

הָרַחֲמִים. מַשְׁמִיעֵי תְפִלָּה, הַשְׁמִיעוּ תְפִלָּתֵנוּ, לִפְנֵי

‹ of mercy. ‹ O you who aid the hearing ‹ of prayer, ‹ may you aid the hearing ‹ of our prayer ‹ before

שׁוֹמֵעַ תְּפִלָּה. מַשְׁמִיעֵי צְעָקָה, הַשְׁמִיעוּ צַעֲקָתֵנוּ,

‹ the Hearer ‹ of prayer. ‹ O you who aid the hearing ‹ of outcries, ‹ may you aid the hearing ‹ of our outcries

לִפְנֵי שׁוֹמֵעַ צְעָקָה. מַכְנִיסֵי דִמְעָה, הַכְנִיסוּ

‹ before ‹ the Hearer ‹ of outcries. ‹ O you who usher in ‹ tears, ‹ may you usher in

דִמְעוֹתֵינוּ, לִפְנֵי מֶלֶךְ מִתְרַצֶּה בִּדְמָעוֹת.

‹ our tears ‹ before ‹ the King ‹ Who is appeased ‹ through tears.

הִשְׁתַּדְּלוּ וְהַרְבּוּ תְּחִנָּה וּבַקָּשָׁה, לִפְנֵי מֶלֶךְ אֵל
‹ God, ‹ the King, ‹ before ‹ and pleas ‹ supplications ‹ and intensify ‹ Exert yourselves

רָם וְנִשָּׂא. הַזְכִּירוּ לְפָנָיו, הַשְׁמִיעוּ לְפָנָיו תּוֹרָה
‹ the Torah ‹ before Him, ‹ aid to be heard « before Him, ‹ Mention « and uplifted. ‹ exalted

וּמַעֲשִׂים טוֹבִים שֶׁל שׁוֹכְנֵי עָפָר.
« in the dust. ‹ [the Patriarchs and Matriarchs] who dwell ‹ of ‹ that are good ‹ and the deeds

יִזְכֹּר אַהֲבָתָם וִיחַיֶּה זַרְעָם, שֶׁלֹּא תֹאבַד שְׁאֵרִית
‹ shall the remnant ‹ lost ‹ so that not ‹ to their offspring, ‹ and grant ‹ their love ‹ May He remember life

יַעֲקֹב. כִּי צֹאן רוֹעֶה נֶאֱמָן הָיָה לְחֶרְפָּה,
« a disgrace; ‹ has become ‹ who is faith-ful [Moses] ‹ of the shepherd ‹ the flock ‹ For « of Jacob be.

יִשְׂרָאֵל גּוֹי אֶחָד לְמָשָׁל וְלִשְׁנִינָה.
« and a simile. ‹ a parable « that is unique, ‹ the nation « Israel,

מַהֵר עֲנֵנוּ אֱלֹהֵי יִשְׁעֵנוּ, וּפְדֵנוּ מִכָּל גְּזֵרוֹת קָשׁוֹת
« that are harsh; ‹ decrees ‹ from all ‹ and re-deem us ‹ of our salvation, ‹ O God ‹ answer us, ‹ Swiftly

וְהוֹשִׁיעָה בְּרַחֲמֶיךָ הָרַבִּים, מְשִׁיחַ צִדְקֶךָ וְעַמֶּךָ.
« and Your people. ‹ Your righteous anointed one ‹ that is abundant, ‹ in Your mercy ‹ and may You save,

מָרַן דְּבִשְׁמַיָּא לָךְ מִתְחַנְּנַן, כְּבָר שְׁבִיָא דְמִתְחַנֵּן
‹ who supplicates ‹ in captivity ‹ as one « do we supplicate, ‹ to You « Who is in heaven, ‹ Our Master

לִשְׁבוּיֵהּ. כֻּלְּהוֹן בְּנֵי שְׁבִיָא בְּכַסְפָּא מִתְפָּרְקִין,
« are redeemed, ‹ through money ‹ in captivity, ‹ those ‹ [for] all « before his captors;

וְעַמָּךְ יִשְׂרָאֵל בְּרַחֲמֵי וּבְתַחֲנוּנֵי, הַב לָן שְׁאִילְתִּין
‹ our requests ‹ us ‹ O grant « and supplication. ‹ through compassion ‹ Israel ‹ but Your people

וּבָעוּתִין, דְּלָא נְהָדַר רֵיקָם מִן קֳדָמָךְ.
« before You. ‹ from ‹ empty-handed ‹ that we not be turned away ‹ and our prayers

מָרָן דִּבְשְׁמַיָּא לָךְ מִתְחַנְּנַן, כְּעַבְדָּא דְּמִתְחַנֵּן

Our Master ⟩ Who is in heaven, ⟨ to You ⟩ do we supplicate, ⟨ as a slave ⟩ who supplicates

לְמָרֵיהּ, עֲשִׁיקֵי אֲנָן וּבַחֲשׁוֹכָא שָׁרֵינַן, מְרִירָן נַפְשִׁין

to his master: ⟩ Oppressed ⟨ are we ⟩ and in darkness ⟨ do we abide, ⟩ embittered ⟨ are [our] souls

מֵעָקָתִין דִּנְפִישִׁין, חֵילָא לֵית בָּן לְרַצוּיָךְ. מָרָן,

from distress ⟩ that is excessive. ⟨ Strength ⟩ is ⟨ lacking ⟩ within us ⟩ to appease You. ⟨ Our Master,

עֲבִיד בְּדִיל קְיָמָא דִּגְזַרְתָּ עִם אֲבָהָתָנָא.

act ⟩ for the sake ⟨ of the covenant ⟩ that You established ⟨ with ⟩ our Patriarchs.

שׁוֹמֵר יִשְׂרָאֵל, שְׁמוֹר שְׁאֵרִית יִשְׂרָאֵל, וְאַל

O Guardian ⟩ of Israel, ⟨ safeguard ⟩ the remnant ⟨ of Israel; ⟩ let not

יֹאבַד יִשְׂרָאֵל, הָאֹמְרִים שְׁמַע יִשְׂרָאֵל.¹

Israel be destroyed — ⟩ those who proclaim: ⟨ Hear, ⟩ O Israel.

שׁוֹמֵר גּוֹי אֶחָד, שְׁמוֹר שְׁאֵרִית עַם אֶחָד, וְאַל

O Guardian ⟩ of the nation ⟨ that is unique, ⟩ safeguard ⟨ the remnant ⟩ of the people ⟨ unique; ⟩ let not

יֹאבַד גּוֹי אֶחָד, הַמְּיַחֲדִים שְׁמֶךָ, יהוה אֱלֹהֵינוּ

be nation destroyed ⟩ the unique, ⟨ that is ⟩ those who proclaim ⟨ of Your Name: ⟩ the Oneness ⟨ HASHEM ⟩ is our God,

יהוה אֶחָד.

the One [and Only]! ⟩ HASHEM ⟨ is

שׁוֹמֵר גּוֹי קָדוֹשׁ, שְׁמוֹר שְׁאֵרִית עַם קָדוֹשׁ, וְאַל

O Guardian ⟩ of the ⟨ nation ⟩ that is holy, ⟨ safeguard ⟩ the remnant ⟨ of the people ⟩ holy; ⟨ let not

יֹאבַד גּוֹי קָדוֹשׁ, הַמְּשַׁלְּשִׁים בְּשָׁלֹשׁ קְדֻשּׁוֹת לְקָדוֹשׁ.

be ⟩ nation destroyed ⟨ the ⟩ holy, ⟨ that is ⟩ those who proclaim ⟨ three times ⟩ the threefold ⟨ sanctifications ⟩ to the Holy One.

מִתְרַצֶּה בְּרַחֲמִים וּמִתְפַּיֵּס בְּתַחֲנוּנִים, הִתְרַצֶּה

You Who becomes favorable ⟩ through compassion ⟨ and Who becomes conciliatory ⟩ through supplications, ⟨ be favorable

---

(1) *Deuteronomy* 6:4.

וְהִתְפַּיֵּס לְדוֹר עָנִי, כִּי אֵין עוֹזֵר. אָבִינוּ מַלְכֵּנוּ,

‹‹ our King, ‹ Our Father, ‹‹ helper. ‹ there is no ‹ for ‹‹ that is ‹ to the ‹ and be conciliatory
poor, generation

חָנֵּנוּ וַעֲנֵנוּ, כִּי אֵין בָּנוּ מַעֲשִׂים, עֲשֵׂה עִמָּנוּ

‹ us ‹ treat ‹‹ worthy deeds; ‹ we have no ‹ though ‹ and ‹ be gracious
answer us, with us

צְדָקָה וָחֶסֶד וְהוֹשִׁיעֵנוּ.

‹‹ and save us. ‹ and kindness, ‹ with charity

STAND AFTER THE WORDS וַאֲנַחְנוּ לֹא נֵדַע UNTIL CONCLUSION OF THE PARAGRAPH.

וַאֲנַחְנוּ לֹא נֵדַע מַה נַּעֲשֶׂה, כִּי עָלֶיךָ עֵינֵינוּ.[1]

‹‹ are our eyes. ‹ upon You ‹ rather, ‹‹ we should do, ‹ what ‹ know not ‹ We

זְכֹר רַחֲמֶיךָ יהוה וַחֲסָדֶיךָ, כִּי מֵעוֹלָם הֵמָּה.[2] יְהִי

‹ May ‹‹ are they. ‹ eternal ‹ for ‹ and Your kindnesses, ‹‹ Hashem, ‹ Your mercies, ‹ Remember

חַסְדְּךָ יהוה עָלֵינוּ, כַּאֲשֶׁר יִחַלְנוּ לָךְ.[3] אַל תִּזְכָּר

‹ recall ‹ Do not ‹‹ You. ‹ we awaited ‹ just as ‹‹ be upon us, ‹ Hashem, ‹ Your kindness,

לָנוּ עֲוֺנוֹת רִאשׁוֹנִים, מַהֵר יְקַדְּמוּנוּ רַחֲמֶיךָ, כִּי

‹ for ‹‹ may Your mercies, ‹ advance to meet us ‹ swiftly ‹‹ of the ancients; ‹ the sins ‹ against us

דַלּוֹנוּ מְאֹד.[4] עֶזְרֵנוּ בְּשֵׁם יהוה, עֹשֵׂה שָׁמַיִם

‹ of heaven ‹ Maker ‹ of Hashem, ‹ is through the Name ‹ Our help ‹‹ exceedingly. ‹ we have become impoverished

וָאָרֶץ.[5] חָנֵּנוּ יהוה חָנֵּנוּ, כִּי רַב שָׂבַעְנוּ בוּז.[6] בְּרֹגֶז

‹‹ Amid wrath, ‹‹ with contempt. ‹ sated ‹ we are fully ‹ for ‹‹ favor us, ‹ Hashem, ‹ Favor us, ‹‹ and earth.

רַחֵם תִּזְכּוֹר.[7] בְּרֹגֶז עֲקֵדָה תִּזְכּוֹר. בְּרֹגֶז תְּמִימוֹת

‹ the perfect ones ‹‹ Amid wrath, ‹‹ You should remember! ‹ the binding [of Isaac] ‹‹ Amid wrath, ‹‹ You should remember! ‹ to be merciful

תִּזְכּוֹר. יהוה הוֹשִׁיעָה, הַמֶּלֶךְ יַעֲנֵנוּ בְיוֹם קָרְאֵנוּ.[8]

‹‹ we call. ‹ on the day ‹ answer us ‹ May the King ‹‹ save! ‹ Hashem, ‹‹ You should remember!

כִּי הוּא יָדַע יִצְרֵנוּ, זָכוּר כִּי עָפָר אֲנָחְנוּ.[9]

‹‹ are we. ‹ dust ‹ that ‹ He is mindful ‹‹ our nature, ‹ knew ‹ He ‹ For

---

(1) *II Chronicles* 20:12. (2) *Psalms* 25:6. (3) 33:22. (4) 79:8. (5) 121:1.
(6) 123:3. (7) *Habakkuk* 3:2. (8) *Psalms* 20:10. (9) 103:14.

✢ עָזְרֵנוּ אֱלֹהֵי יִשְׁעֵנוּ עַל דְּבַר כְּבוֹד שְׁמֶךָ, וְהַצִּילֵנוּ

⟨ rescue us ⟪ of Your ⟨ of the ⟨ the ⟨ for ⟨ of our ⟨ O God ⟨ Assist us,
Name; glory sake salvation

וְכַפֵּר עַל חַטֹּאתֵינוּ לְמַעַן שְׁמֶךָ.[1]

⟪ of Your ⟨ for the ⟨ our sins ⟨ for ⟨ and grant
Name. sake atonement

FULL KADDISH / קדיש שלם

THE *CHAZZAN* RECITES קַדִּישׁ שָׁלֵם, FULL *KADDISH.*

יִתְגַּדַּל וְיִתְקַדַּשׁ שְׁמֵהּ רַבָּא. (.אָמֵן — Cong.) בְּעָלְמָא

⟨ — in the ⟪ (Amen.) ⟪ that is ⟨ may His ⟨ and be ⟨ Grow
world great!— Name sanctified exalted

דִּי בְרָא כִרְעוּתֵהּ. וְיַמְלִיךְ מַלְכוּתֵהּ, וְיַצְמַח פֻּרְקָנֵהּ

⟨ His ⟨ and cause ⟪ to His ⟨ and may He ⟪ according ⟨ He ⟨ that
salvation, to sprout kingship, give reign to His will, created

וִיקָרֵב מְשִׁיחֵהּ. (.אָמֵן — Cong.) בְּחַיֵּיכוֹן וּבְיוֹמֵיכוֹן וּבְחַיֵּי

⟨ and in the ⟨ and in ⟨ in your ⟪ (Amen.) ⟪ His Messiah, ⟨ and bring
lifetimes your days, lifetimes near

דְכָל בֵּית יִשְׂרָאֵל, בַּעֲגָלָא וּבִזְמַן קָרִיב. וְאִמְרוּ: אָמֵן.

⟪Amen. ⟨ Now ⟪ that comes ⟨ and at a ⟨ swiftly ⟪ of Israel, ⟨ Family ⟨ of the
respond: soon. time entire

CONGREGATION RESPONDS:

אָמֵן. יְהֵא שְׁמֵהּ רַבָּא מְבָרַךְ לְעָלַם וּלְעָלְמֵי עָלְמַיָּא.

⟪ and for all eternity. ⟨ forever ⟨ be ⟨ that is ⟨ His ⟨ May ⟪ Amen.
blessed great Name

CHAZZAN CONTINUES:

יְהֵא שְׁמֵהּ רַבָּא מְבָרַךְ לְעָלַם וּלְעָלְמֵי עָלְמַיָּא. יִתְבָּרַךְ

⟨ Blessed, ⟪ and for all eternity. ⟨ forever ⟨ be ⟨ that is ⟨ His ⟨ May
blessed great Name

וְיִשְׁתַּבַּח וְיִתְפָּאַר וְיִתְרוֹמַם וְיִתְנַשֵּׂא וְיִתְהַדָּר וְיִתְעַלֶּה

⟨ elevated, ⟨ honored, ⟨ upraised, ⟨ exalted, ⟨ glorified, ⟨ praised,

וְיִתְהַלָּל שְׁמֵהּ דְּקֻדְשָׁא בְּרִיךְ הוּא (.הוּא בְּרִיךְ — Cong.)

⟪ is He) ⟨ (Blessed ⟪ is He ⟨ Blessed ⟨ of the Holy ⟨ be the ⟨ and lauded
One, Name

— לְעֵלָּא מִן כָּל בִּרְכָתָא וְשִׁירָתָא תֻּשְׁבְּחָתָא וְנֶחֱמָתָא

⟨ and ⟨ praise ⟪ and song, ⟨ blessing ⟨ any ⟨ beyond
consolation

---

(1) *Psalms* 79:9.

דַּאֲמִירָן בְּעָלְמָא. וְאִמְרוּ: אָמֵן. (.Cong — אָמֵן.)

《 (Amen.) 　 《 Amen. 〈 Now respond: 　 《 in the world. 〈 that are uttered

CONGREGATION:

(קַבֵּל בְּרַחֲמִים וּבְרָצוֹן אֶת תְּפִלָּתֵנוּ.)

《 our prayers.) 〈 and with favor 〈 with mercy 〈 (Accept

CHAZZAN CONTINUES:

תִּתְקַבֵּל צְלוֹתְהוֹן וּבָעוּתְהוֹן דְּכָל בֵּית יִשְׂרָאֵל קֳדָם

〈 before 〈 Israel 〈 Family of 〈 of the entire 〈 and supplications 〈 the prayers 〈 May accepted be

אֲבוּהוֹן דִּי בִשְׁמַיָּא. וְאִמְרוּ: אָמֵן. (.Cong — אָמֵן.)

《 (Amen.) 　 《 Amen. 〈 Now respond: 　 《 is in Heaven. 〈 Who 〈 their Father

CONGREGATION:

(יְהִי שֵׁם יהוה מְבֹרָךְ, מֵעַתָּה וְעַד עוֹלָם.[1])

《 eternity.) 〈 until 〈 from this time 《 be blessed, 〈 of 〈 the HASHEM Name 〈 (Let

CHAZZAN CONTINUES:

יְהֵא שְׁלָמָא רַבָּא מִן שְׁמַיָּא וְחַיִּים טוֹבִים עָלֵינוּ וְעַל כָּל

〈 all 〈 and upon 〈 upon us 〈 that is good, 〈 and life 〈 Heaven 〈 from 〈 that is abundant 〈 peace 〈 May there be

יִשְׂרָאֵל. וְאִמְרוּ: אָמֵן. (.Cong — אָמֵן.)

《 (Amen.) 　 《 Amen. 〈 Now respond: 　 《 Israel.

CONGREGATION:

(עֶזְרִי מֵעִם יהוה, עֹשֵׂה שָׁמַיִם וָאָרֶץ.[2])

《 and earth.) 〈 of heaven 〈 Maker 《 HASHEM, 〈 is from 〈 (My help

CHAZZAN BOWS; TAKES THREE STEPS BACK. BOWS LEFT AND SAYS "... עֹשֶׂה שָׁלוֹם, HE WHO MAKES PEACE ..."; BOWS RIGHT AND SAYS "... הוּא, MAY HE ..."; BOWS FORWARD AND SAYS "... וְעַל כָּל יִשְׂרָאֵל, AND UPON ALL ISRAEL ..."; REMAINS IN PLACE FOR A FEW MOMENTS, THEN TAKES THREE STEPS FORWARD.

עֹשֶׂה שָׁלוֹם בִּמְרוֹמָיו, הוּא יַעֲשֶׂה שָׁלוֹם עָלֵינוּ, וְעַל כָּל

〈 all 〈 and upon 〈 upon us, 〈 peace 〈 make 〈 may He 《 in His heights, 〈 peace 〈 He Who makes

יִשְׂרָאֵל. וְאִמְרוּ: אָמֵן. (.Cong — אָמֵן.)

《 (Amen.) 　 《 Amen. 〈 Now respond: 　 《 Israel.

---

(1) *Psalms* 113:2. (2) 121:2.

≈{ **EREV ROSH HASHANAH** / ערב ראש השנה }≈

אַשְׁרֵי יוֹשְׁבֵי בֵיתֶךָ, עוֹד יְהַלְלוּךָ סֶּלָה.[1] אַשְׁרֵי

⟨ Praise- « Selah. « they will ⟨ con- « in Your ⟨ are those ⟨ Praiseworthy
worthy   praise You, tinually house,   who dwell

הָעָם שֶׁכָּכָה לוֹ, אַשְׁרֵי הָעָם שֶׁיהוה אֱלֹהָיו.[2]

« is their   ⟨ that   ⟨ is the   ⟨ praise- « is   ⟨ that such   ⟨ is the
God.   people   worthy their lot;   people

———— תהלים קמה / Psalm 145 ————

תְּהִלָּה לְדָוִד, אֲרוֹמִמְךָ אֱלוֹהַי הַמֶּלֶךְ, וַאֲבָרְכָה

⟨ and I   « the King, ⟨ my God ⟨ I will exalt You, « by David: ⟨ A psalm of
will bless   praise

שִׁמְךָ לְעוֹלָם וָעֶד. בְּכָל יוֹם אֲבָרְכֶךָ, וַאֲהַלְלָה שִׁמְךָ

⟨ Your ⟨ and I   « I will   ⟨ day ⟨ Every « and ⟨ for ever ⟨ Your
Name will laud bless You,   ever.   Name

לְעוֹלָם וָעֶד. גָּדוֹל יהוה וּמְהֻלָּל מְאֹד, וְלִגְדֻלָּתוֹ

⟨ and His   «exceedingly, ⟨ and   ⟨ is   ⟨ Great « and ⟨ for ever
greatness   lauded HASHEM   ever.

אֵין חֵקֶר. דּוֹר לְדוֹר יְשַׁבַּח מַעֲשֶׂיךָ, וּגְבוּרֹתֶיךָ יַגִּידוּ.

«they will ⟨ and Your   « Your   ⟨ will   ⟨ to   ⟨ Gen- « is beyond
recount.   mighty deeds actions. praise generation eration investigation.

הֲדַר כְּבוֹד הוֹדֶךָ, וְדִבְרֵי נִפְלְאֹתֶיךָ אָשִׂיחָה. וֶעֱזוּז

⟨ And of « I shall   ⟨ that are   ⟨ and Your ⟨ of Your ⟨ glory ⟨ The
the might discuss.   wondrous   deeds   majesty   splendrous

נוֹרְאֹתֶיךָ יֹאמֵרוּ, וּגְדוּלָּתְךָ אֲסַפְּרֶנָּה. זֵכֶר רַב טוּבְךָ

⟨ of Your abun- ⟨ A recol- « I shall   ⟨ and Your « they will ⟨ of Your
dant goodness   lection relate.   greatness   speak,   awesome deeds

יַבִּיעוּ, וְצִדְקָתְךָ יְרַנֵּנוּ. חַנּוּן וְרַחוּם יהוה, אֶרֶךְ אַפַּיִם

⟨ to   ⟨ slow « is   ⟨ and ⟨ Gracious «they will ⟨ and of Your « they
anger,   HASHEM, merciful   sing joyfully. righteousness will utter,

וּגְדָל חָסֶד. טוֹב יהוה לַכֹּל, וְרַחֲמָיו עַל כָּל מַעֲשָׂיו.

«   His   ⟨ all ⟨ are ⟨ His   « to all; ⟨ HASHEM «in [bestowing] ⟨ and
creations.   on mercies   is good kindness.   great

יוֹדוּךָ יהוה כָּל מַעֲשֶׂיךָ, וַחֲסִידֶיךָ יְבָרְכוּכָה. כְּבוֹד

⟨ Of the «   will   ⟨ and Your « Your   ⟨ — all «HASHEM ⟨ They will
glory   bless You. devout ones creations —   thank You,

———————————

(1) *Psalms* 84:5. (2) 144:15.

מַלְכוּתְךָ יֹאמֵרוּ, וּגְבוּרָתְךָ יְדַבֵּרוּ. **לְהוֹדִיעַ** לִבְנֵי הָאָדָם

⟨ mankind ⟨ To inform ⟪ they will ⟨ and of Your ⟪ they will ⟨ of Your
declare. power speak, kingdom

גְּבוּרֹתָיו, וּכְבוֹד הֲדַר מַלְכוּתוֹ. **מַלְכוּתְךָ** מַלְכוּת כָּל

⟨[span- ⟨ is a ⟨ Your kingdom ⟪ of His ⟨ splendor ⟨ and of the ⟨ of His mighty
ning] all kingdom kingdom. glorious deeds,

עֹלָמִים, וּמֶמְשַׁלְתְּךָ בְּכָל דּוֹר וָדֹר. **סוֹמֵךְ** יהוה

⟨ HASHEM ⟪ after ⟨ gen- ⟨ is ⟨ and Your ⟪ eternities,
supports generation. eration throughout dominion

לְכָל הַנֹּפְלִים, וְזוֹקֵף לְכָל הַכְּפוּפִים. **עֵינֵי** כֹל

⟨ of all ⟨ The ⟪ those who ⟨ all ⟨ and ⟪ those who ⟨ all
eyes are bent. straightens are fallen,

אֵלֶיךָ יְשַׂבֵּרוּ, וְאַתָּה נוֹתֵן לָהֶם אֶת אָכְלָם בְּעִתּוֹ.

⟪ in its ⟨ their food ⟨ them ⟨ give ⟨ and You ⟪ do look ⟨ to You
proper time. with hope,

CONCENTRATE INTENTLY WHILE RECITING THE VERSE פּוֹתֵחַ, YOU OPEN.

פּוֹתֵחַ אֶת יָדֶךָ, וּמַשְׂבִּיעַ לְכָל חַי רָצוֹן. ⟐**צַדִּיק**

⟨ Righteous ⟪ [with its] ⟨ living ⟨ every ⟨ and satisfy ⟪ Your hand, ⟨ You open
desire. thing

יהוה בְּכָל דְּרָכָיו, וְחָסִיד בְּכָל מַעֲשָׂיו. **קָרוֹב** יהוה

⟨ is ⟨ Close ⟪ His deeds. ⟨ in all ⟨ and ⟪ His ways, ⟨ in all ⟨ is
HASHEM magnanimous HASHEM

לְכָל קֹרְאָיו, לְכֹל אֲשֶׁר יִקְרָאֻהוּ בֶאֱמֶת. **רְצוֹן** יְרֵאָיו

⟨ of those ⟨ The ⟪ sincerely. ⟨ call upon ⟨ who ⟨ to all ⟪ who call ⟨ to all
who fear Him will Him upon Him,

יַעֲשֶׂה, וְאֶת שַׁוְעָתָם יִשְׁמַע וְיוֹשִׁיעֵם. **שׁוֹמֵר** יהוה

⟨ HASHEM protects ⟪ and He will ⟨ He will ⟨ and their cry ⟪ He
save them. hear, will do;

אֶת כָּל אֹהֲבָיו, וְאֵת כָּל הָרְשָׁעִים יַשְׁמִיד. **תְּהִלַּת**

⟨ The praise ⟪ He will destroy. ⟨ the wicked ⟨ but all ⟪ who love Him; ⟨ all

יהוה יְדַבֶּר פִּי, וִיבָרֵךְ כָּל בָּשָׂר שֵׁם קָדְשׁוֹ לְעוֹלָם

⟨ for ever ⟨ of His ⟨ the ⟨ flesh ⟨ may ⟨ and bless ⟪ may my ⟨ of
Holiness Name all mouth declare, HASHEM

וָעֶד. וַאֲנַחְנוּ נְבָרֵךְ יָהּ מֵעַתָּה וְעַד עוֹלָם; הַלְלוּיָהּ.¹

⟪ Halleluyah! ⟪ eternity. ⟨ until ⟨ from ⟨ God ⟨ will ⟨ But we ⟪ and
this time bless ever.

---

(1) *Psalms* 115:18.

THE *CHAZZAN* RECITES חֲצִי קַדִּישׁ, HALF-*KADDISH*:

יִתְגַּדַּל וְיִתְקַדַּשׁ שְׁמֵהּ רַבָּא. (Cong. — אָמֵן.) בְּעָלְמָא
⟨ Grow ⟩ and be ⟨ may His ⟩ that is ⟨ (Cong.) ⟨⟨ (Amen.) ⟩ ⟨ — in the
exalted sanctified Name great! —   world

דִּי בְרָא כִרְעוּתֵהּ. וְיַמְלִיךְ מַלְכוּתֵהּ, וְיַצְמַח פֻּרְקָנֵהּ
⟨ that ⟨ He ⟨⟨ according ⟨ and may He ⟨ to His ⟨⟨ and cause ⟨ His
created to His will, give reign kingship, to sprout salvation,

וִיקָרֵב מְשִׁיחֵהּ. (Cong. — אָמֵן.) בְּחַיֵּיכוֹן וּבְיוֹמֵיכוֹן וּבְחַיֵּי
⟨ and bring ⟨ His Messiah, ⟨⟨ (Amen.) ⟨ in your ⟨ and in ⟨ and in the
near   lifetimes your days, lifetimes

דְכָל בֵּית יִשְׂרָאֵל, בַּעֲגָלָא וּבִזְמַן קָרִיב. וְאִמְרוּ: אָמֵן.
⟨ of the ⟨ Family ⟨ of Israel, ⟨⟨ swiftly ⟨ and at a ⟨ that comes ⟨⟨ Now ⟨⟨Amen.
entire   time soon. respond:

CONGREGATION RESPONDS:

אָמֵן. יְהֵא שְׁמֵהּ רַבָּא מְבָרַךְ לְעָלַם וּלְעָלְמֵי עָלְמַיָּא.
⟨⟨ Amen. ⟨⟨ May ⟨ His ⟨ that is ⟨ be ⟨ forever ⟨ and for all eternity. ⟨⟨
Name great blessed

CHAZZAN CONTINUES:

יְהֵא שְׁמֵהּ רַבָּא מְבָרַךְ לְעָלַם וּלְעָלְמֵי עָלְמַיָּא. יִתְבָּרַךְ
⟨ May ⟨ His ⟨ that is ⟨ be ⟨ forever ⟨ and for all eternity. ⟨⟨ Blessed, ⟩
Name great blessed

וְיִשְׁתַּבַּח וְיִתְפָּאַר וְיִתְרוֹמַם וְיִתְנַשֵּׂא וְיִתְהַדָּר וְיִתְעַלֶּה
⟨ praised, ⟨ glorified, ⟨ exalted, ⟨ upraised, ⟨ honored, ⟨ elevated,

וְיִתְהַלָּל שְׁמֵהּ דְּקֻדְשָׁא בְּרִיךְ הוּא (Cong. — בְּרִיךְ הוּא)
⟨ and lauded ⟨ be the ⟨ of the Holy ⟨ Blessed ⟨ is He ⟨⟨ ⟨(Blessed ⟨⟨ is He)
Name One,

— לְעֵלָּא מִן כָּל בִּרְכָתָא וְשִׁירָתָא תֻּשְׁבְּחָתָא וְנֶחֱמָתָא
⟨ beyond ⟨ any ⟨ blessing ⟨ and song, ⟨⟨ praise ⟨ and consolation ⟩

דַּאֲמִירָן בְּעָלְמָא. וְאִמְרוּ: אָמֵן. (Cong. — אָמֵן.)
⟨ that are ⟨⟨ in the ⟨⟨ Now ⟨ Amen. ⟨⟨ (Amen.) ⟩
uttered world. respond:

ALL:

לְךָ יהוה הַצְּדָקָה, וְלָנוּ בֹּשֶׁת הַפָּנִים.[1] מַה
⟨ Yours, ⟨ O Lord, ⟨ is the ⟨⟨ and ⟨ is shamefacedness. ⟨⟨ ⟨⟨What
righteousness, ours

נִּתְאוֹנֵן,[2] מַה נֹּאמַר, מַה נְּדַבֵּר, וּמַה נִּצְטַדָּק.[3]
⟨⟨ complaint ⟨ What ⟨⟨can we say? ⟨ What ⟨can we ⟨ What ⟨⟨ justification
can we make? declare? can we offer?

(1) *Daniel* 9:7. (2) Cf. *Lamentations* 3:39. (3) Cf. *Genesis* 44:16.

נַחְפְּשָׂה דְרָכֵינוּ וְנַחְקְרָה, וְנָשׁוּבָה אֵלֶיךָ,¹ כִּי יְמִינְךָ

‹ Your right hand ‹ for ‹‹ to You, ‹ and return ‹ and investigate ‹ our ways ‹ Let us examine them,

פְּשׁוּטָה לְקַבֵּל שָׁבִים. לֹא בְחֶסֶד וְלֹא בְמַעֲשִׂים

‹ with [merit for good] deeds ‹ nor ‹ with [merit] for kindness ‹ Nei- ther ‹‹ those who return. ‹ to accept ‹ is extended

בָּאנוּ לְפָנֶיךָ, כְּדַלִּים וּכְרָשִׁים דָּפַקְנוּ דְלָתֶיךָ.

‹‹ on Your doors. ‹ we have knocked ‹ and as destitute people ‹ but as paupers ‹‹ before You; ‹ do we come

דְלָתֶיךָ דָּפַקְנוּ רַחוּם וְחַנּוּן, נָא אַל תְּשִׁיבֵנוּ

‹ turn us away ‹ do not ‹ Please ‹‹ and Gra- cious One. ‹ O Compas- sionate One ‹ we have knocked, ‹ On Your doors

רֵיקָם מִלְּפָנֶיךָ. מִלְּפָנֶיךָ מַלְכֵּנוּ רֵיקָם אַל תְּשִׁיבֵנוּ,

‹‹ turn us away, ‹ do not ‹ empty- handed ‹ Our King, ‹ From before You, ‹‹ from before You. ‹ empty- handed

כִּי אַתָּה שׁוֹמֵעַ תְּפִלָּה.

‹‹ prayer. ‹ Who hears ‹ You are ‹ for the One

שֹׁמֵעַ תְּפִלָּה, עָדֶיךָ כָּל בָּשָׂר יָבֹאוּ.² יָבוֹא

‹ Come ‹‹ will come. ‹ flesh ‹ all ‹ unto You ‹‹ prayer, ‹ You Who hears

כָל בָּשָׂר לְהִשְׁתַּחֲוֹת לְפָנֶיךָ יהוה.³ יָבֹאוּ וְיִשְׁתַּחֲווּ

‹ and bow down ‹ They will come ‹‹ O HASHEM. ‹ before You, ‹ to bow down ‹ will all flesh

לְפָנֶיךָ אֲדֹנָי, וִיכַבְּדוּ לִשְׁמֶךָ.⁴ בֹּאוּ נִשְׁתַּחֲוֶה וְנִכְרָעָה,

‹‹ and bow, ‹ Let us prostrate ourselves ‹ Come! ‹‹ to Your Name. ‹ and they will show honor ‹‹ O Lord, ‹ before You,

נִבְרְכָה לִפְנֵי יהוה עֹשֵׂנוּ.⁵ נָבוֹאָה לְמִשְׁכְּנוֹתָיו,

‹‹ to His Tabernacles, ‹ Let us come ‹ our Maker. ‹ HASHEM, ‹ before ‹ let us kneel

נִשְׁתַּחֲוֶה לַהֲדֹם רַגְלָיו.⁶ בֹּאוּ שְׁעָרָיו בְּתוֹדָה,

‹‹ with thanksgiving, ‹ His gates ‹ Enter ‹ for His feet. ‹ at the stool ‹ let us prostrate ourselves

חֲצֵרֹתָיו בִּתְהִלָּה, הוֹדוּ לוֹ בָּרְכוּ שְׁמוֹ.⁷ וַאֲנַחְנוּ

‹ But we, ‹‹ His Name. ‹ bless ‹‹ to Him ‹ give thanks ‹‹ with praise; ‹ His courtyards

(1) Cf. *Lamentations* 3:40. (2) *Psalms* 65:3. (3) Cf. *Isaiah* 66:23.
(4) *Psalms* 86:9. (5) 95:6. (6) 132:7. (7) 100:4.

בְּרֹב חַסְדְּךָ נָבוֹא בֵיתֶךָ, נִשְׁתַּחֲוֶה אֶל הֵיכַל קָדְשְׁךָ

‹ Your Holy ‹ toward ‹ we will pros- ≪ Your ‹ will we ‹ of Your ‹ through the
Sanctuary 　　 trate ourselves 　 House; 　 enter 　 kindness 　 abundance

בְּיִרְאָתֶךָ.[1] הִנֵּה בָּרְכוּ אֶת יהוה כָּל עַבְדֵי יהוה,

‹ of 　 ‹ you 　 ‹ all 　 ‹ HASHEM, 　 ‹ bless 　 ≪ Indeed, ≪ 　 in awe
HASHEM, 　 servants 　　　　　　　　　　　　　　　　 of You.

הָעֹמְדִים בְּבֵית יהוה בַּלֵּילוֹת.[2] שְׂאוּ יְדֵיכֶם קֹדֶשׁ

‹ in the 　 ‹ your 　 ‹ Lift ≪ in the nights. ‹ of 　 ‹ in the ‹ who stand
Sanctuary 　 hands 　　　　　　　　　　 HASHEM 　 House

וּבָרְכוּ אֶת יהוה.[3] רוֹמְמוּ יהוה אֱלֹהֵינוּ, וְהִשְׁתַּחֲווּ

‹ and bow down ‹ our God, ‹ HASHEM, ‹ Exalt ≪ HASHEM. ‹ and bless

לַהֲדֹם רַגְלָיו, קָדוֹשׁ הוּא.[4] רוֹמְמוּ יהוה אֱלֹהֵינוּ,

‹ our God, ‹ HASHEM, ‹ Exalt ≪ is He! ‹ holy ≪ at His footstool;

וְהִשְׁתַּחֲווּ לְהַר קָדְשׁוֹ, כִּי קָדוֹשׁ יהוה אֱלֹהֵינוּ.[5]

≪ our God. ‹ is 　 ‹ holy 　 ‹ for ≪ of His ‹ at the 　 ‹ and bow
　　　　　 HASHEM, 　　　　　　　 Holiness; 　 Mount

הִשְׁתַּחֲווּ לַיהוה בְּהַדְרַת קֹדֶשׁ, חִילוּ מִפָּנָיו כָּל

‹ every- ‹ before ‹ tremble ≪ of 　 ‹ in the 　 ‹ before 　 ‹ Bow down
one 　 Him, 　　　　　　 holiness; 　 splendor 　 HASHEM

הָאָרֶץ.[6] נִשְׁתַּחֲוֶה אֶל הֵיכַל קָדְשְׁךָ וְנוֹדֶה אֶת שְׁמֶךָ,

‹ Your Name ‹ and we ≪ Your Holy ‹ toward ‹ We will pros- ≪ on earth.
　　　　 will thank 　 Sanctuary, 　　　 trate ourselves

עַל חַסְדְּךָ וְעַל אֲמִתֶּךָ, כִּי הִגְדַּלְתָּ עַל כָּל שִׁמְךָ

≪ Your ‹ — even ≪ You have ‹ for ≪ Your ‹ and ‹ Your ‹ for
Name — 　 beyond 　 exalted 　　 faithfulness; 　 for 　 kindness

אִמְרָתֶךָ.[7] יהוה אֱלֹהֵי צְבָאוֹת, מִי כָמוֹךָ חֲסִין

‹ O Strong ‹ is like ‹ — who ≪ of 　 ‹ God ‹ HASHEM, ≪ Your promise.
One, 　 You, 　　　　 Legions

יָה, וֶאֱמוּנָתְךָ סְבִיבוֹתֶיךָ.[8] כִּי מִי בַשַּׁחַק יַעֲרֹךְ

‹ can be ‹ in the sky ‹ who ‹ For ≪ surrounds You. ‹ and Your ≪ God? —
compared 　　　　　　　　　　　　　　　　 faithfulness

לַיהוה, יִדְמֶה לַיהוה בִּבְנֵי אֵלִים.[9] כִּי גָדוֹל אַתָּה

‹ are You ‹ great ‹ For ≪ among the angels? ‹ to HASHEM ‹ be likened ≪ to HASHEM;

וְעֹשֵׂה נִפְלָאוֹת, אַתָּה אֱלֹהִים לְבַדֶּךָ.[10] כִּי גָדוֹל

‹ great ‹ For ≪ alone. ‹ O God, ‹ You, ≪ of wonders; ‹ and a worker

---

(1) Cf. *Psalms* 5:8. (2) 134:1. (3) 134:2. (4) 99:5. (5) 99:9. (6) 96:9. (7) Cf. 138:2. (8) 89:9. (9) 89:7. (10) 86:10.

גָּדוֹל 1.אֲמִתֶּךָ. שְׁחָקִים וְעַד חַסְדֶּךָ, שָׁמַיִם מֵעַל

⟨ Great ⟩ ⟨ is Your truth. ⟩ ⟨ the upper heights ⟩ ⟨ and until ⟩ ⟨ is Your kindness, ⟩ ⟨ the very heavens ⟩ ⟨ above ⟩

גָּדוֹל (כִּי) 2.חֵקֶר. אֵין וְלִגְדֻלָּתוֹ מְאֹד, וּמְהֻלָּל יהוה

⟨ great ⟩ ⟨ (For) ⟩ ⟨ investigation. ⟩ ⟨ is beyond ⟩ ⟨ and His greatness ⟩ ⟨ exceedingly, ⟩ ⟨ and lauded ⟩ ⟨ is HASHEM ⟩

כִּי 3.אֱלֹהִים. כָּל עַל הוּא נוֹרָא מְאֹד, וּמְהֻלָּל יהוה

⟨ For ⟩ ⟨ heavenly powers. ⟩ ⟨ all ⟩ ⟨ above ⟩ ⟨ is He ⟩ ⟨ awesome ⟩ ⟨ exceedingly; ⟩ ⟨ and lauded ⟩ ⟨ is HASHEM ⟩

אֲשֶׁר 4.אֱלֹהִים. כָּל עַל גָּדוֹל וּמֶלֶךְ יהוה, גָּדוֹל אֵל

⟨ For ⟩ ⟨ heavenly powers. ⟩ ⟨ all ⟩ ⟨ above ⟩ ⟨ and a great King ⟩ ⟨ is ⟩ ⟨ HASHEM, ⟩ ⟨ a great God ⟩

כְמַעֲשֶׂיךָ יַעֲשֶׂה אֲשֶׁר וּבָאָרֶץ, בַּשָּׁמַיִם אֵל מִי

⟨ like unto Your deeds ⟩ ⟨ can do ⟩ ⟨ that ⟩ ⟨ or in the earth ⟩ ⟨ is there in the heaven ⟩ ⟨ in power ⟩ ⟨ what ⟩

לְךָ כִּי הַגּוֹיִם, מֶלֶךְ יִרָאֲךָ לֹא מִי 5.וְכִגְבוּרֹתֶיךָ.

⟨ to You ⟩ ⟨ For ⟩ ⟨ of nations? ⟩ ⟨ O King ⟩ ⟨ fear You, ⟩ ⟨ would not ⟩ ⟨ Who ⟩ ⟨ and like unto Your mighty acts? ⟩

מֵאֵין מַלְכוּתָם וּבְכָל הַגּוֹיִם חַכְמֵי בְּכָל כִּי יָאָתָה,

⟨ there is none ⟩ ⟨ their kingdoms ⟩ ⟨ and in all ⟩ ⟨ of the nations ⟩ ⟨ the wise men ⟩ ⟨ among all ⟩ ⟨ for ⟩ ⟨ [kingship] befits; ⟩

שְׁמֶךָ וְגָדוֹל אַתָּה גָּדוֹל יהוה, כָמוֹךָ מֵאֵין 6.כָּמוֹךָ.

⟨ is Your Name ⟩ ⟨ and great ⟩ ⟨ are You ⟩ ⟨ Great ⟩ ⟨ O HASHEM! ⟩ ⟨ like You, ⟩ ⟨ There is none ⟩ ⟨ like You. ⟩

תָּרוּם יָדְךָ תָּעֹז גְּבוּרָה, עִם זְרוֹעַ לְךָ 7.בִּגְבוּרָה.

⟨ uplifted ⟩ ⟨ is Your hand, ⟩ ⟨ strengthened ⟩ ⟨ power; ⟩ ⟨ with ⟩ ⟨ is the arm ⟩ ⟨ Yours ⟩ ⟨ in might. ⟩

מָאוֹר הֲכִינוֹתָ אַתָּה לָיְלָה, לְךָ אַף יוֹם, לְךָ 8.יְמִינֶךָ.

⟨ the luminary ⟩ ⟨ prepared ⟩ ⟨ You ⟩ ⟨ is the night; ⟩ ⟨ Yours ⟩ ⟨ also ⟩ ⟨ is the day, ⟩ ⟨ Yours ⟩ ⟨ is Your right hand. ⟩

הָרִים וְתוֹעֲפוֹת אָרֶץ, מֶחְקְרֵי בְיָדוֹ אֲשֶׁר 9.וָשָׁמֶשׁ.

⟨ of the mountains ⟩ ⟨ and the summits ⟩ ⟨ of the earth, ⟩ ⟨ are the hidden mysteries ⟩ ⟨ in His power ⟩ ⟨ For ⟩ ⟨ and the sun. ⟩

לוֹ. 10.מִי יְמַלֵּל גְּבוּרוֹת יהוה, יַשְׁמִיעַ כָּל תְּהִלָּתוֹ. 11.

⟨ of His praise? ⟩ ⟨ all ⟩ ⟨ [who] can make heard ⟩ ⟨ of ⟩ ⟨ the mighty acts ⟩ ⟨ can express ⟩ ⟨ Who ⟩ ⟨ are His. ⟩

---

(1) *Psalms* 108:5. (2) 145:3. (3) 96:4. (4) 95:3. (5) *Deuteronomy* 3:24.
(6) *Jeremiah* 10:7. (7) 10:6. (8) *Psalms* 89:14. (9) 74:16. (10) 95:4. (11) 106:2.

לְךָ יהוה הַגְּדֻלָּה וְהַגְּבוּרָה, וְהַתִּפְאֶרֶת וְהַנֵּצַח
⟨ the ⟨ the glory, ⟨ the strength, ⟨ is the ⟨ HASHEM, ⟨ Yours,
triumph,　　　　　　　　　　greatness,

וְהַהוֹד, כִּי כֹל בַּשָּׁמַיִם וּבָאָרֶץ; לְךָ יהוה הַמַּמְלָכָה,
⟨ is the ⟨ HASHEM, ⟨ Yours, « and on ⟨ in heaven ⟨ every- ⟨ for « and the
kingdom　　　　　　　earth　　　　thing　　majesty;
　　　　　　　　　　　[is Yours];

וְהַמִּתְנַשֵּׂא לְכֹל לְרֹאשׁ.[1] לְךָ שָׁמַיִם, אַף לְךָ אָרֶץ,
« is the ⟨ Yours ⟨ also « are the ⟨ Yours « leader. ⟨ over ⟨ and the
earth;　　　　　heavens,　　　　　　every　　sovereignty

תֵּבֵל וּמְלֹאָהּ אַתָּה יְסַדְתָּם.[2] אַתָּה הִצַּבְתָּ כָּל גְּבוּלוֹת
⟨ the ⟨ all ⟨ established ⟨ You « founded ⟨ You ⟨ and its ⟨ the
boundaries　　　　　them.　　　　　　fullness,　world

אָרֶץ, קַיִץ וָחֹרֶף אַתָּה יְצַרְתָּם.[3] אַתָּה רִצַּצְתָּ רָאשֵׁי
⟨ the ⟨ crushed ⟨ You « fashioned ⟨ You ⟨ and ⟨ summer « of
heads　　　　　them.　　　　　winter,　　earth;

לִוְיָתָן, תִּתְּנֶנּוּ מַאֲכָל לְעָם לְצִיִּים. אַתָּה בָקַעְתָּ מַעְיָן
⟨ fountain ⟨ split ⟨ You « [destined] for ⟨ to the ⟨ as food ⟨ You will « of
open　　　　the desolate people　　　　serve it　Leviathan;
　　　　　wilderness.

וָנָחַל, אַתָּה הוֹבַשְׁתָּ נַהֲרוֹת אֵיתָן.[4] אַתָּה פוֹרַרְתָּ
⟨ shattered ⟨ You « that are mighty. ⟨ rivers ⟨ dried ⟨ You « and stream;

בְעָזְּךָ יָם, שִׁבַּרְתָּ רָאשֵׁי תַנִּינִים עַל הַמָּיִם.[5] אַתָּה
⟨ You « the water. ⟨ upon ⟨ of sea ⟨ the heads ⟨ You « the « with Your
serpents　　　　　smashed　sea;　might

מוֹשֵׁל בְּגֵאוּת הַיָּם, בְּשׂוֹא גַלָּיו אַתָּה תְשַׁבְּחֵם.[6]
« calm them. ⟨ You ⟨ its ⟨ when it « of the ⟨ the ⟨ rule
waves,　raises　sea;　grandeur

גָּדוֹל יהוה וּמְהֻלָּל מְאֹד, בְּעִיר אֱלֹהֵינוּ הַר קָדְשׁוֹ.[7]
« of His ⟨ Mount ⟨ of our God, ⟨ in the ⟨ and much praised, ⟨ is ⟨ Great
Holiness.　　　　　City　　　　　　　HASHEM

יהוה צְבָאוֹת, אֱלֹהֵי יִשְׂרָאֵל, יוֹשֵׁב הַכְּרֻבִים, אַתָּה
⟨ it is « upon the ⟨ en- ⟨ of Israel, ⟨ God ⟨ Master of ⟨ HASHEM,
You　Cherubim,　throned　　　　　　　Legions,

הוּא הָאֱלֹהִים לְבַדֶּךָ.[8] אֵל נַעֲרָץ בְּסוֹד קְדֹשִׁים רַבָּה,
« in the great assemblage ⟨ is ⟨ God « alone. ⟨ God ⟨ Who
of the holy [angels],　revered　　　　　　　are

(1) *I Chronicles* 29:11. (2) *Psalms* 89:12. (3) 74:17. (4) 74:14-15. (5) 74:13. (6) 89:10. (7) 48:2. (8) *Isaiah* 37:16.

וְנוֹרָא עַל כָּל סְבִיבָיו.¹ וְיוֹדוּ שָׁמַיִם פִּלְאֲךָ יהוה, אַף

‹ also ‹‹ HASHEM, ‹ Your ‹ will the ‹ Acknowl- ‹‹ who sur- ‹ all ‹ over ‹ and is
wonders, heavens edge round Him. awesome

אֱמוּנָתְךָ בִּקְהַל קְדֹשִׁים.² לְכוּ נְרַנְּנָה לַיהוה, נָרִיעָה

‹ let us ‹‹ to ‹ Let us sing ‹ Come! ‹‹ of holy ‹ in the ‹ Your
call out HASHEM, joyfully ones. assembly faithfulness,

לְצוּר יִשְׁעֵנוּ. נְקַדְּמָה פָנָיו בְּתוֹדָה, בִּזְמִירוֹת נָרִיעַ לוֹ.³

‹‹ to ‹ let us ‹ with praiseful ‹‹ with ‹ Him ‹ Let us greet ‹‹ of our ‹ to the
Him. call out songs thanksgiving, salvation. Rock

CHAZZAN, THEN CONGREGATION:

אַשְׁרֵי הָעָם יוֹדְעֵי תְרוּעָה

‹‹ the shofar's ‹ that ‹ is the ‹ Praise-
cry; knows people worthy

יהוה בְּאוֹר פָּנֶיךָ יְהַלֵּכוּן.⁴

‹‹ they walk. ‹ of Your ‹ by the ‹ HASHEM,
countenance illumination

CHAZZAN, THEN CONGREGATION:

בַּחֲצֹצְרוֹת וְקוֹל שׁוֹפָר הָרִיעוּ לִפְנֵי הַמֶּלֶךְ יהוה.⁵

‹‹ HASHEM. ‹ the King, ‹ before ‹ call out ‹‹ of shofar, ‹ and sound ‹ With trumpets

CHAZZAN, THEN CONGREGATION:

צֶדֶק וּמִשְׁפָּט מְכוֹן כִּסְאֶךָ, חֶסֶד וֶאֱמֶת יְקַדְּמוּ פָנֶיךָ.⁶

‹‹ Your coun- ‹ precede ‹ and ‹ kindness ‹ of Your ‹ are the ‹ and ‹ Righteous-
tenance. truth throne; foundation justice ness

ALL CONTINUE:

אֲשֶׁר יַחְדָּו נַמְתִּיק סוֹד, בְּבֵית אֱלֹהִים נְהַלֵּךְ

‹ let us ‹ of God ‹ in the ‹‹ counsel; ‹ let us ‹ together ‹ For
walk House take sweet

בְּרָגֶשׁ.⁷ אֲשֶׁר לוֹ הַיָּם וְהוּא עָשָׂהוּ, וְיַבֶּשֶׁת יָדָיו

‹ His ‹‹ and the ‹‹ perfected ‹ and He ‹ is the ‹ His ‹ For ‹‹ in company.
hands dry land, it, sea

יָצָרוּ.⁸ אֲשֶׁר בְּיָדוֹ נֶפֶשׁ כָּל חָי, וְרוּחַ כָּל בְּשַׂר אִישׁ.⁹

‹‹ mankind. ‹ of all ‹ and the ‹‹ the ‹ of ‹ is the ‹ in His ‹ For ‹‹ fashioned.
spirit living all soul hand

❖ הַנְּשָׁמָה לָךְ וְהַגּוּף פָּעֳלָךְ, חוּסָה עַל עֲמָלָךְ.

‹‹ Your ‹ on ‹ take pity ‹‹ is Your ‹ and the ‹ is ‹ The soul
labor. handiwork; body Yours

(1) *Psalms* 89:8. (2) 89:6. (3) 95:1-2. (4) 89:16. (5) 98:6. (6) 89:15. (7) 55:15. (8) 95:5. (9) *Job* 12:10.

הַנְּשָׁמָה לָךְ וְהַגּוּף שֶׁלָּךְ, יהוה עֲשֵׂה לְמַעַן שְׁמֶךָ.

‎《 of Your 〈 for the 〈 act 〈 O 《 is Yours; 〈 and the 〈 is 〈 The soul
Name.   sake   HASHEM,   body   Yours

אָתָאנוּ עַל שְׁמֶךָ, יהוה, עֲשֵׂה לְמַעַן שְׁמֶךָ. בַּעֲבוּר

‎〈 [act] 《 of Your 〈 for the 〈 act 《 O 《 Your 〈 [relying] 〈 We have
because of Name;   sake   HASHEM; Name,   on   come

כְּבוֹד שְׁמֶךָ, כִּי אֵל חַנּוּן וְרַחוּם שְׁמֶךָ. לְמַעַן

‎〈 For the 《 is Your 〈 and 〈 Who is 〈 God 〈 for 《 of Your 〈 the glory
sake   Name.   Merciful Gracious   Name,

שְׁמֶךָ יהוה, וְסָלַחְתָּ לַעֲוֺנֵנוּ כִּי רַב הוּא.[1]

‎〈 it is great. 〈 though 〈 our 〈 forgive 《 HASHEM, 〈 of Your
                        iniquity,   Name,

CONGREGATION, THEN CHAZZAN:

סְלַח לָנוּ אָבִינוּ, כִּי בְרֹב אִוַּלְתֵּנוּ שָׁגִינוּ,

‎《 we have 〈 of our folly 〈 in the 〈 for 〈 our Father, 〈 us, 〈 Forgive
erred;   abundance

מְחַל לָנוּ מַלְכֵּנוּ, כִּי רַבּוּ עֲוֺנֵינוּ.

‎《 our 〈 many 〈 for 〈 our King, 〈 us, 〈 pardon
iniquities. are

סְלִיחָה כג / SELICHAH 23
(פְּתִיחָה)

ALL:

אֲדֹנָי אֱלֹהֵי הַצְּבָאוֹת,*[2] נוֹרָא בָּעֶלְיוֹנִים,

‎《 on high, 〈 revered 〈 of Legions,* 〈 God 〈 O Lord,

אָמַרְתָּ שׁוּבוּ בָּנִים סָרְבָנִים.[3]

‎《 who are stubborn! 〈 children 〈 Return, 《 You said,

---

(1) Cf. *Psalms* 25:11. (2) Cf. *Amos* 3:13; 9:5. (3) Cf. *Jeremiah* 3:22.

אֲדֹנָי אֱלֹהֵי הַצְּבָאוֹת — *O Lord, God of Legions.* After a double alphabet, the acrostic of this *pesichah* (introductory *selichah*) reads שְׁלֹמֹה בַּר יִצְחָק, *Shlomo bar Yitzchak.* The composer, better known as *Rashi* (the acronym for רַבִּי שְׁלֹמֹה יִצְחָקִי), is considered the greatest of all teacher-commentators on Scripture and the Talmud. *Rashi* was born in Troyes, France in 1040, and passed away there in 1105 (29 Tammuz 4865). He received his earlier education in his native city, but eventually traveled to Mainz, Germany, and

Worms, France, to study under the students of Rabbeinu Gershom [see prefatory comment to *Selichah* 12]. *Rashi*'s commentary to the Talmud opened what would have otherwise remained a closed book, inaccessible to the masses. His Torah commentary is the fundamental tool of Biblical interpretation for schoolchild and scholar alike. Literally hundreds of commentaries have been written on *Rashi*'s work.

Rashi's later years were marred by the excruciating suffering of the Jews during the

בֹּֽאוּ עָדַי בְּתוֹדָה וּבִרְנָנִים,[1]
《 and joyous 〈 with thanksgiving- 〈 up 〈 Come
  songs;   offerings   to Me

בַּקְּשׁוּ פָנַי[2] בְּבִכְיִי וּבְתַחֲנוּנִים.[3]
《 and supplications. 〈 with 〈 My 〈 seek
              weeping Presence

גַּם כִּי נִסְתְּמָה תְפִלַּת[4] הַגִּיוֹנִים,
《 that is 〈 is [our] 〈 shut out 〈 though 〈 Even
thoughtful, prayer

גַּלֵּי שָׁבִים פְּתוּחִים כֵּיוֹנִים.[5]
《 straight 〈 are open 〈 for the 〈 the
  ahead.   pentitents gates

דְּבָרְךָ נִצָּב לְעוֹלְמֵי עֲדָנִים,[6]
《 of eternity, 〈 for the 〈 stands 〈 Your
              worlds   firm   word

דַּרְכֵי טוּבְךָ נֶֽצַח לֹא שׁוֹנִים.
《 change. 〈 will 〈 forever 〈 of Your 〈 [and] the
         not   goodness ways

הִנְנוּ אָתָֽנוּ לְךָ[7] כְּדַלִּים וְאֶבְיוֹנִים,
《 and destitute 〈 as needy 〈 to 〈 we have 《 Here
  people,   You   come   we are;

הַצְּדָקוֹת לְךָ, וְלָֽנוּ הָעֲוֹנִים.
《 are the 〈 and 《 is 〈 [for]
  iniquities. ours Yours, righteousness

וְעָדֶֽיךָ שַֽׁבְנוּ בְּבֹֽשֶׁת הַפָּנִים,[8]
facedly, 〈 shame- 〈 we have 〈 To You
          returned

וְעַל דַּלְתוֹתֶֽיךָ הוֹגִים כַּיּוֹנִים.[9]
《 like doves. 〈 cooing 〈 Your doors 〈 at

זָכְרֵֽנוּ לְחַיִּים מְתֻקָּנִים,[10]
《 that is properly 〈 for a life 〈 Remem-
  prepared;   ber us

(1) Cf. *Psalms* 100:2,4. (2) 27:8. (3) Cf. *Jeremiah* 3:21. (4) Cf. *Lamentations* 3:8.
(5) Some editions read כַּחַלּוֹנִים, windows (cf. *Daniel* 6:11); *the gates are like open windows.*
(6) Cf. *Psalms* 119:89. (7) *Jeremiah* 3:22. (8) Cf. *Daniel* 9:7. (9) Cf. *Isaiah* 59:11, 38:14.
(10) Some editions read מְתוּקָנִים, *sweet.*

First Crusade in 1096, when many impor-   memorial, *Rashi* composed *selichos* to plead
tant Jewish communities were destroyed. In   the case of his suffering people before God.

זַכֵּה כְּתָמֵינוּ צַחִים מַלְבָּנִים.

《 and whitened. 〈 and make 〈 our stains 〈 purify
them] clear [of sin

חַטֹּאת נְעוּרֵינוּ[1] מְחֵה כֶּעָנָנִים,[2]

《 like clouds, 〈 wipe out 〈 of our youth 〈 The sins

חַדֵּשׁ יָמֵינוּ כְּיָמִים קַדְמוֹנִים.[3]

《　　 of old. 〈 like the days 〈 our days 〈 [and] renew

טֻמְאָה הַעֲבֵר וְהָתֵם הַזְּדוֹנִים,

《　willful sin; 〈 and bring 〈 remove 〈 [Our]
to an end impurity

טָהֳרָה תִּזְרֹק מֵיִם[4] הַנֶּאֱמָנִים.[5]

《 that is unfailing. 〈 the 〈 throw 〈 for purity
water [upon us]

יָדַעְנוּ רִשְׁעֵנוּ[6] סָרְבִים וְסַלּוֹנִים,[7]

《　　 and 〈 [how] 《 our 〈 We know
thorn-like, rebellious wickedness,

יַקְשׁוּת עָרְפֵּנוּ חָסֹן כָּאַלּוֹנִים.[8]

《　 as oaks. 〈 as 〈 of our 〈 the stiffness
mighty neck,

כֶּרֶם נְטַעֲנוּ סָגְסַג נְצָנִים,[9]

《 by weeds, 〈 has been 〈 we 〈 The
overgrown planted vineyard

כָּסּוּ פָנָיו חֲרֻלִּים קִמְשׂוֹנִים.[10]

《 and brambles. 〈 with thorns 〈 is its 〈 covered
face over

לִמְדֵי הָרֵעַ[11] צְמוּדֵי חַמָּנִים,

《　 to sun 〈 attached 《 to do 〈 Men
worship, evil, accustomed

לוֹקְחֵי שֹׁחַד רוֹדְפֵי שַׁלְמוֹנִים.*[12]

《 of graft payments.* 〈 pursuers 《 of bribes, 〈 takers

---

(1) Cf. *Psalms* 25:7. (2) Cf. *Isaiah* 44:22. (3) Cf. *Lamentations* 5:21. (4) Cf. *Ezekiel* 36:25. (5) Cf. *Isaiah* 33:16.
(6) Cf. *Jeremiah* 14:20. (7) *Ezekiel* 2:6. (8) Cf. *Amos* 2:9. (9) Cf. *Isaiah* 17:11. (10) Cf. *Proverbs* 24:31;
the word קִמְשׂוֹנִים appears only once in Scripture; some editions read קִמְשׁוֹנִים, both here and
in *Proverbs*, but the meaning is the same. (11) Cf. *Jeremiah* 13:23. (12) Cf. *Isaiah* 1:23.

רוֹדְפֵי שַׁלְמוֹנִים — *Pursuers of graft payments.*
This phrase describes dishonest judges who
pervert justice by conspiring to protect one
another's interest. While being prosecuted

before his colleague, a judge would say,
"You champion my cause today. Tomor-
row, when you are hauled before my court,
I will vindicate you!" (*Rashi* to *Isaiah* 1:23).

מַהֵר קִלְקַלְנוּ חֻפַּת חֲתוּנִים,*
《 of our wedding,* 〈 the canopy 〈 we ruined 〈 Speedily

מֵאָז הֻסַּגְנוּ לְאָחוֹר וְלֹא לְפָנִים.
《 forward. 〈 and 〈 backward 〈 we have 〈 and
not moved since then

נָעוּ זִבְחֵי הַכָּרִים הַמְשֻׁנִּים,*
《 and fattened 〈 of fat sheep 〈 are the 〈 Gone
bulls;* offerings

נִיחֹחֵי רֵיחַ קְטֹרֶת סַמָּנִים.*
《 spices;* 〈 and 〈 aroma of [the flour- 〈 the
of the offerings and the satisfying
incense wine libations]

שַׂר חֲמִשִּׁים יוֹעֵץ וּנְשׂוּא פָנִים,*¹
《 countenance;* 〈 and the man 《 the 〈 over fifty; 〈 the
of respected counselor; captain

סֶגֶן מָשׁוּחַ לְוִיִּים וְאַהֲרֹנִים.
《 and the children 《 the 〈 the 《 the
of Aaron. Levites; anointed deputy;
[Kohen Gadol];

עֲמִידָתֵנוּ רְאֵה דַּלִּים וְרֵיקָנִים,
《 and empty, 〈 destitute 《 see — 〈 Our [spiritual]
position

עַצְבֵי רוּחַ² מְרוֹרִים כְּלַעֲנִים.³
《 as wormwood. 〈 bitter 《 in spirit, 〈 saddened

---

(1) Cf. *Isaiah* 3:3. (2) Cf. 63:10. (3) Cf. *Proverbs* 5:4.

חֻפַּת חֲתוּנִים — *The canopy of our wedding.* The phrase בְּיוֹם חֲתֻנָּתוֹ, *the day of his wedding (Song of Songs* 3:11), alludes to the Giving of the Torah (*Taanis* 26b). While yet at the *chuppah* (Mount Sinai), the bride (Israel) was unfaithful to her betrothed (God) by worshiping the Golden Calf.

הַמְשֻׁנִּים — *And fattened bulls.* The translation follows *Rashi* (to *I Samuel* 15:9), who derives the word from שְׁנַיִם, *two,* and interprets it as a reference to fat, healthy animals that have twice as much meat as others.

נִיחֹחֵי רֵיחַ קְטֹרֶת סַמָּנִים — *The satisfying aroma of [the flour-offerings and the wine libations] and of the incense spices.* The translation follows *Pardes.* Most other

commentaries interpret the entire stich as one topic: *The satisfying aroma of the spice-compounded incense.* However, the term רֵיחַ נִיחֹחַ, *satisfying aroma,* as used in Scripture, refers to either animal and meal-offerings or to wine libations. Since the animal offerings are already mentioned in the preceding stich, this one must mean the flour-offerings and the wine libations.

שַׂר חֲמִשִּׁים יוֹעֵץ וּנְשׂוּא פָנִים — *The captain over fifty; the counselor; and the man of respected countenance.* The Talmud interprets these three terms homiletically. שַׂר חֲמִשִּׁים refers to one who is a master of the Five Books of Moses, for the word חֲמִשִּׁים may be vowelized חֲמָשִׁים (חֲמִשִּׁים),

פְּקַדְנוּךָ בַּצַּר לַחַשׁ צְקוּנִים,[1]

‹‹ outpouring, ‹ with ‹ in [our] ‹ We
whispered distress remembered
[prayer] You

פַּחַד דִּינֶךָ דּוֹאֲגִים וּמִתְאוֹנְנִים.

‹‹ and lamenting. ‹ worrying ‹ of Your ‹ in fear
judgment,

צֶמַח צְדָקָה הַצְמַח לְנֶאֱמָנִים,

‹‹ for [Your] ‹ bring ‹ of ‹ A sprout
faithful; forth righteousness

צַוֵּה לְהַעֲבִיר עֲוֹנוֹת רִאשֹׁנִים.

‹‹ from of old. ‹ [our] sins ‹ to remove ‹ command

קוֹל הַקּוֹרֵא יַשְׁבִּית מְדָיָנִים,[2]

‹‹ with the ‹ do away ‹ of the ‹ Let the
contentious; chazzan voice

קַטְגוֹר יַהַס וְיַשְׁתִּיק נִרְגָּנִים.

‹‹ the defamer. ‹ and silence ‹ hush, ‹ the Accuser

רוּחַ נִכְאָה, דְּכָאוּת לֵב שְׁבְרוֹנִים,[3]

‹ that is broken ‹ of a ‹ [and] the ‹ that is ‹ [May our]
heart humility crippled spirit

רָצוֹן יַעֲלוּ כְּחֶלְבֵי קָרְבָּנִים.

‹‹ of the ‹ like the fats ‹ ascend ‹ with
offerings. favor

שְׁבוּעַת אָבוֹת הָקֵם לַבָּנִים,

‹‹ for their ‹ establish ‹ to the ‹ [Your] vow
children. Patriarchs

שַׁוְעַת קוֹרְאֶיךָ תִּשְׁמַע מִמְּעוֹנִים.

‹‹ from Your [Heavenly] ‹ may You ‹ of those who ‹ The
dwelling-place. hear call to You, outcry

תָּכִין לִבָּם[4] לְיִרְאָתְךָ מוּכָנִים,

‹‹ they are ‹ so that for rev- ‹ their ‹ Focus
prepared; erence of You heart

---

(1) Cf. *Isaiah* 26:16. (2) Cf. *Proverbs* 18:18; some editions of *Selichos* read
מְדָינִים, but the meaning is unchanged. (3) Cf. *Psalms* 51:19. (4) Cf. 10:17.

Chumashim. A יוֹעֵץ is one who is familiar with the laws of establishing the New
Moon and intercalation of years. And נְשׂוּא
פָנִים is the person in whose merit Heaven

sustains an entire generation (*Chagigah*
14a). Due to the length and intensity of the
present exile, this caliber of people no longer
can be found.

תַּקְשִׁיב¹ אָזְנְךָ שִׂיחַ חֲנוּנִים.

‹ attentive › ‹ let Your ear be › ‹ to [their] prayers › « of pleading.

❖ שׁוּב לְהַעֲלוֹת עַמְּךָ מִשְּׁאוֹנִים,²

‹ Once again › ‹ lift up › ‹ Your people › « from the raging sea;

מַהֵר יְקַדְּמוּנוּ רַחֲמֶיךָ³ קַדְמוֹנִים.

‹ swiftly › ‹ advance to meet us › ‹ may Your mercy › « as of old.

בְּרִיבָם יֵצְאוּ חֲנוּנֶיךָ כֵּנִים,

‹ From their judgment › « may they come forth › « — those whom You favor — › « vindicated,

קֽוּם חֲסָדֶיךָ וְעַל רַחֲמֶיךָ שְׁעוּנִים.

‹ for they hope › ‹ for Your kindness › ‹ and upon › ‹ Your mercy › « depend.

ALL:

כִּי עַל רַחֲמֶיךָ הָרַבִּים⁴ אָנוּ בְטוּחִים, וְעַל צִדְקוֹתֶיךָ

‹ For › ‹ upon › ‹ Your mercy › ‹ that is abundant › ‹ we › ‹ trust, › « and upon › ‹ Your righteousness

אָנוּ נִשְׁעָנִים, וְלִסְלִיחוֹתֶיךָ אָנוּ מְקַוִּים, וְלִישׁוּעָתְךָ

‹ we › ‹ rely, › « and for Your forgiveness › ‹ we › ‹ hope, › « and for Your salvation

אָנוּ מְצַפִּים. אַתָּה הוּא מֶלֶךְ, אוֹהֵב צִדְקוֹת מִקֶּדֶם,

‹ we › ‹ await eagerly. › « You › ‹ are › ‹ the King › ‹ Who loves › ‹ righteous-ness › « since the beginning of time,

מַעֲבִיר עֲוֹנוֹת עַמּוֹ, וּמֵסִיר חַטֹּאת יְרֵאָיו. כּוֹרֵת

‹ Who overlooks › ‹ the iniquities › ‹ of His people › ‹ and removes › ‹ the sins › « of those who revere Him. › ‹ He established

בְּרִית לָרִאשׁוֹנִים, וּמְקַיֵּם שְׁבוּעָה לָאַחֲרוֹנִים. אַתָּה

‹ a covenant › ‹ with the ancestors › ‹ and fulfills › ‹ [His] oath › « to the descendants. › ‹ You

הוּא, שֶׁיָּרַדְתָּ בֶּעָנָן כִּבוֹדְךָ עַל הַר סִינַי,⁵ וְהִרְאֵיתָ

‹ are the One › ‹ Who descended › ‹ in the cloud › ‹ of Your glory › ‹ upon › ‹ Mount › ‹ Sinai, › « and You showed

---

(1) Cf. *Psalms* 10:17. (2) Cf. 40:3. (3) 79:8. (4) *Daniel* 9:18. (5) Cf. *Exodus* 34:5.

דַּרְכֵי טוּבְךָ לְמֹשֶׁה עַבְדֶּךָ. וְאָרְחוֹת חֲסָדֶיךָ גִּלִּיתָ[1]

‹ You revealed ‹ of Your kindness ‹ The paths « Your servant. ‹ to Moses ‹ of Your goodness ‹ the ways

לוֹ, וְהוֹדַעְתּוֹ כִּי אַתָּה אֵל רַחוּם וְחַנּוּן, אֶרֶךְ אַפַּיִם

‹ to anger ‹ Slow « and ‹ Compassionate ‹ God, ‹ You are ‹ that ‹ and You « to him, let him know

וְרַב חֶסֶד[2] וּמַרְבֶּה לְהֵטִיב, וּמַנְהִיג אֶת כָּל הָעוֹלָם

‹ world ‹ the whole ‹ and Who guides « beneficent, ‹ Who is ‹ in ‹ and abundantly Kindness, Abundant

כֻּלּוֹ בְּמִדַּת הָרַחֲמִים. ❖וְכֵן כָּתוּב, וַיֹּאמֶר אֲנִי אַעֲבִיר

‹ shall cause to pass ‹ I « And He said, « it is written: ‹ And so « of Mercy. ‹ with the ‹ in its entirety Attribute

כָּל טוּבִי עַל פָּנֶיךָ, וְקָרָאתִי בְשֵׁם יהוה לְפָנֶיךָ,

« before you; ‹ HASHEM « with the Name ‹ and I shall call out « your face, ‹ before ‹ My goodness ‹ all

וְחַנֹּתִי אֶת אֲשֶׁר אָחֹן, וְרִחַמְתִּי אֶת אֲשֶׁר אֲרַחֵם.[3]

« I choose to show mercy. ‹ whomever ‹ to ‹ and I shall show favor, « I choose to show favor ‹ whomever ‹ to ‹ I shall show favor

ALL, WHILE STANDING

אֵל אֶרֶךְ אַפַּיִם אַתָּה,

« You are, ‹ to anger, ‹ Who is slow ‹ God

וּבַעַל הָרַחֲמִים נִקְרֵאתָ, וְדֶרֶךְ תְּשׁוּבָה הוֹרֵיתָ.

« You have taught. ‹ of repentance ‹ and the way « You are called; ‹ of Mercy ‹ and Master

גְּדֻלַּת רַחֲמֶיךָ וַחֲסָדֶיךָ,

‹ and Your kindness ‹ of Your mercy ‹ The greatness

תִּזְכּוֹר הַיּוֹם וּבְכָל יוֹם לְזֶרַע יְדִידֶיךָ.

« of Your beloved ones. ‹ for the offspring « day, ‹ and every ‹ this day ‹ may You remember,

תֵּפֶן אֵלֵינוּ בְּרַחֲמִים,

« in mercy, ‹ to us ‹ Turn

כִּי אַתָּה הוּא בַּעַל הָרַחֲמִים.

« of Mercy. ‹ the Master ‹ are ‹ You ‹ for

---

(1) Cf. *Exodus* 33:13. (2) 34:6. (3) 33:19.

בְּתַחֲנוּן וּבִתְפִלָּה פָּנֶיךָ נְקַדֵּם, כְּהוֹדַעְתָּ לֶעָנָיו מִקֶּדֶם.

With supplication ⟨ and prayer ⟩ Your ⟨ Presence ⟩ we ⟨ approach, ⟩ in the manner ⟨ that You made known ⟩ to the humble one [Moses] ⟨ in ancient times. ⟩⟩

מֵחֲרוֹן אַפְּךָ שׁוּב,¹ כְּמוֹ בְתוֹרָתְךָ כָּתוּב.²

From the fierceness ⟨ of Your anger ⟩⟩ turn back, ⟨ as ⟩ in Your Torah ⟨ it is written. ⟩⟩

וּבְצֵל כְּנָפֶיךָ נֶחֱסֶה³ וְנִתְלוֹנָן, כְּיוֹם וַיֵּרֶד יהוה בֶּעָנָן.

In the shadow ⟨ of Your wings ⟩ may we find shelter ⟨ and may we dwell, ⟩⟩ as on the day ⟨ when HASHEM descended ⟩ in a cloud. ⟩⟩

❖ תַּעֲבוֹר עַל פֶּשַׁע וְתִמְחֶה אָשָׁם,

Overlook ⟨ sin ⟩ and erase ⟨ guilt, ⟩⟩

כְּיוֹם וַיִּתְיַצֵּב עִמּוֹ שָׁם.

as on the day ⟨ when He [God] stood ⟩ with him [Moses] ⟨ there. ⟩⟩

תַּאֲזִין שַׁוְעָתֵנוּ וְתַקְשִׁיב מֶנּוּ מַאֲמָר,

Give heed ⟨ to our cry ⟨ and hear ⟨ from us ⟩ [our] declaration, ⟩⟩

כְּיוֹם וַיִּקְרָא בְשֵׁם יהוה,⁴ וְשָׁם נֶאֱמָר:

as on the day ⟨ when He ⟨ called out ⟩ with the Name ⟨⟨ of HASHEM, ⟩ and there ⟨ it was said: ⟩⟩

CONGREGATION, THEN *CHAZZAN*:

וַיַּעֲבֹר יהוה עַל פָּנָיו וַיִּקְרָא:

And HASHEM passed ⟨ before ⟩ [Moses'] face, ⟨⟨ [Moses'] face, ⟩ and proclaimed: ⟩⟩

CONGREGATION AND *CHAZZAN* RECITE LOUDLY AND IN UNISON:

יהוה, יהוה, אֵל, רַחוּם, וְחַנּוּן, אֶרֶךְ אַפַּיִם,

HASHEM, ⟨ HASHEM, ⟨ God, ⟨ Compassionate ⟨ and Gracious, ⟩⟩ Slow ⟨ to anger, ⟩

וְרַב חֶסֶד, וֶאֱמֶת, נֹצֵר חֶסֶד לָאֲלָפִים, נֹשֵׂא עָוֹן,

and Abundant ⟨ in Kindness ⟨ and Truth, ⟩⟩ Preserver ⟨ of kindness ⟨ for thousands [of generations], ⟩⟩ Forgiver ⟨ of iniquity, ⟩

וָפֶשַׁע, וְחַטָּאָה, וְנַקֵּה.⁵ וְסָלַחְתָּ לַעֲוֹנֵנוּ וּלְחַטָּאתֵנוּ

willful sin, ⟨ and inadvertent sin, ⟨ and our sins, ⟩⟩ absolves. ⟨ and Who ⟨⟨ May You forgive ⟨ our iniquities ⟨ and our sins, ⟩⟩

---

(1) Cf. *Exodus* 32:12. (2) See 32:14. (3) Cf. *Psalms* 36:8. (4) *Exodus* 34:5. (5) 34:6-7

וּנְחַלְתָּנוּ.¹ סְלַח לָנוּ אָבִינוּ כִּי חָטָאנוּ, מְחַל לָנוּ

⟨ us, ⟨ pardon ≪ we have ⟨ for ≪ our Father, ⟨ us, ⟨ Forgive ≪ and make us
sinned; Your heritage.

מַלְכֵּנוּ כִּי פָשָׁעְנוּ. כִּי אַתָּה אֲדֹנָי טוֹב וְסַלָּח, וְרַב

⟨ and ≪ and ⟨ are ⟨ O Lord, ⟨ You, ⟨ For ≪ we have ⟨ for ≪ our King,
abundantly forgiving, good willfully sinned.

חֶסֶד לְכָל קֹרְאֶיךָ.²

≪ who call ⟨ to all ⟨ kind
upon You.

פסוקי הקדמה לסליחה כד / PREFATORY VERSES TO SELICHAH 24

אֱלֹהֵינוּ, בֹּשְׁנוּ בְמַעֲשֵׂינוּ וְנִכְלַמְנוּ בַּעֲוֹנֵינוּ.

≪ by our ⟨ and humiliated ⟨ by our deeds ⟨ we are ≪ Our God,
iniquities, shamed

אֱלֹהֵינוּ, בֹּשְׁנוּ וְנִכְלַמְנוּ לְהָרִים אֱלֹהֵינוּ פָּנֵינוּ

⟨ our ⟨ O God, ⟨ to lift, ⟨ and ⟨ we are too ⟨ Our God,
faces humiliated ashamed

אֵלֶיךָ,³ אֵין לָנוּ פֶּה לְהָשִׁיב, וְלֹא מֵצַח לְהָרִים

⟨ to lift up ⟨ the ⟨ nor ≪ to respond, ⟨ [words in ⟨ We have ≪ toward
audacity our] mouth no You,

רֹאשׁ. יָדַעְנוּ כִּי חָטָאנוּ, וְאֵין מִי יַעֲמוֹד בַּעֲדֵנוּ,

≪ for us; ⟨ can stand ⟨ who ⟨ and there ≪ we have ⟨ that ⟨ We ≪ our
up is no one sinned know heads.

שִׁמְךָ הַגָּדוֹל יַעֲמָד לָנוּ בְּעֵת צָרָה.⁴

≪ of ⟨ in time ⟨ for ⟨ will stand ⟨ that is ⟨ Your
trouble. us up great Name

כְּרַחֵם אָב עַל בָּנִים, כֵּן תְּרַחֵם יהוה עָלֵינוּ.⁵

≪ on us. ⟨ HASHEM, ⟨ have ⟨ so ≪ his ⟨ toward ⟨ a ⟨ As merciful as
mercy, children, father is

לַיהוה הַיְשׁוּעָה, עַל עַמְּךָ בִרְכָתֶךָ סֶּלָה.⁶ יהוה

⟨ HASHEM, ≪ Selah. ≪ is Your ⟨ Your ⟨ upon ≪ is salvation, ⟨ To HASHEM
blessing, people

צְבָאוֹת עִמָּנוּ, מִשְׂגָּב לָנוּ אֱלֹהֵי יַעֲקֹב סֶלָה.⁷ יהוה

⟨ HASHEM, ≪ Selah. ≪ of Jacob, ⟨ is the ⟨ for us ⟨ a ≪ is with us, ⟨ Master of
God stronghold Legions,

---

(1) *Exodus* 34:9. (2) *Psalms* 86:5. (3) Cf. *Ezra* 9:6. (4) From the Monday
and Thursday *Tachanun* prayer. (5) Cf. *Psalms* 103:13. (6) 3:9. (7) 46:8.

צְבָאוֹת, אַשְׁרֵי אָדָם בֹּטֵחַ בָּךְ.¹ יהוה הוֹשִׁיעָה,

‹‹ save! ‹ HASHEM, ‹‹ in You. ‹ who trusts ‹ is the man ‹ — praise-worthy ‹‹ Master of Legions

הַמֶּלֶךְ יַעֲנֵנוּ בְיוֹם קָרְאֵנוּ.²

‹‹ we call. ‹ on the day ‹ answer us ‹ May the King

IN MOST CONGREGATIONS THE FOLLOWING VERSES ARE RECITED ALOUD RESPONSIVELY, AS INDICATED; IN OTHERS THEY ARE RECITED SILENTLY.

CONGREGATION, ALOUD, FOLLOWED BY *CHAZZAN,* **ALOUD:**

סְלַח נָא לַעֲוֹן הָעָם הַזֶּה כְּגֹדֶל חַסְדֶּךָ, וְכַאֲשֶׁר

‹ just as ‹‹ of Your kindness, ‹ according to the greatness ‹ of this people ‹ the ‹ please, ‹ Forgive, iniquity

נָשָׂאתָה לָעָם הַזֶּה מִמִּצְרַיִם וְעַד הֵנָּה,³ וְשָׁם נֶאֱמַר:

‹‹ it was said: ‹ And there ‹‹ now. ‹ until ‹ from Egypt ‹ this people ‹ You have forgiven

ALL, ALOUD AND IN UNISON:

וַיֹּאמֶר יהוה סָלַחְתִּי כִּדְבָרֶךָ.⁴

‹‹ according to your word! ‹ I have forgiven ‹‹ And HASHEM said:

ALL CONTINUE:

הַטֵּה אֱלֹהַי אָזְנְךָ וּשְׁמָע, פְּקַח עֵינֶיךָ וּרְאֵה

‹ and see ‹ Your eyes ‹ open ‹‹ and listen; ‹ Your ear, ‹ my God, ‹ Incline,

שֹׁמְמֹתֵינוּ, וְהָעִיר אֲשֶׁר נִקְרָא שִׁמְךָ עָלֶיהָ, כִּי לֹא

‹ not ‹ for ‹‹ upon; ‹ Your Name is proclaimed ‹ which ‹ and that ‹ our desolation [of] the city

עַל צִדְקֹתֵינוּ אֲנַחְנוּ מַפִּילִים תַּחֲנוּנֵינוּ לְפָנֶיךָ, כִּי

‹ but ‹‹ before You; ‹ our supplications ‹ cast ‹ do we ‹ of our righteousness ‹ because

עַל רַחֲמֶיךָ הָרַבִּים. אֲדֹנָי שְׁמָעָה, אֲדֹנָי סְלָחָה,

‹‹ forgive; ‹ O Lord, ‹‹ heed; ‹ O Lord, ‹‹ which is abundant. ‹ of Your compassion, ‹ because

אֲדֹנָי הַקְשִׁיבָה, וַעֲשֵׂה אַל תְּאַחַר, לְמַעַנְךָ אֱלֹהַי,

‹‹ my God, ‹ for Your sake, ‹‹ delay; ‹ do not ‹‹ and act, ‹ be attentive, ‹ O Lord,

כִּי שִׁמְךָ נִקְרָא עַל עִירְךָ וְעַל עַמֶּךָ.⁵

‹‹ Your people. ‹ and ‹ Your City ‹ upon ‹ is proclaimed ‹ Your Name ‹ for

---

(1) *Psalms* 84:13. (2) 20:10. (3) *Numbers* 14:19. (4) 14:20. (5) *Daniel* 9:18-19.

סְלִיחָה כד / SELICHAH 24

ALL:

אֱלֹהֵינוּ וֵאלֹהֵי אֲבוֹתֵינוּ:
《 of our forefathers:《 and God 《 Our God

אֵיכָכָה אֶפְצֶה פֶה,* וְאֵיךְ אֶשָּׂא עַיִן,
《 an eye [entreating Heaven]? 《 raise 《 can I 《 and how 《 [my] mouth [in prayer],* 《 can I open 《 How

בִּי אֵין מַעַשׂ, וּבְיָדִי זְכוּת אַיִן,
《 is not there. 《 merit 《 in my hand, 《 deeds [to my credit]; 《 there are no 《 With me

גָּעִיתִי הָיֵיתִי כְּשִׁכּוֹר,* וּכְגֶבֶר עֲבָרוֹ יַיִן,¹
《 by wine; 《 overcome 《 like a person 《 like a drunk,* 《 [for] I am 《 I moan,

דָּמִיתִי לְגִבּוֹר שֶׁאֵין בְּיָדוֹ כְּלֵי זַיִן.*
《 of war.* 《 imple- ments 《 in his hand 《 without 《 a warrior 《 I am like

הֶחֱרַד לֵב דַּל, וְחָדַל הַהוּקָם סַרְסוֹר,
《 as intermediary [to God], 《 is the one appointed 《 paralyzed 《 that is impoverished [of good deeds]; 《 does the 《 Tremble 《 heart

וּמַה יִּפְעַר נִבְעַר מִדֵּעַת² וּבִין חָסוֹר,
《 lacking? 《 of understanding 《 without wisdom, 《 — a boor 《 can he open [his mouth] 《 and how

זְדוֹנוֹ בְּחֻבּוֹ טָמוּן³ וְאָוֶן⁴ בְּקִרְבּוֹ אָסוּר,
《 is locked; 《 within him 《 wrong- doing 《 is hidden, 《 inside him 《 His willful sin

---

(1) Cf. *Jeremiah* 23:9; some editions of *Selichos* read כְּאִישׁ שִׁכּוֹר for כְּשִׁכּוֹר, thus quoting the Scriptural verse verbatim; the meaning is the same. (2) Cf. *Jeremiah* 10:14. (3) Cf. *Job* 31:33. (4) Some editions read וַחֹובוֹ, *and his guilt.*

◆§ אֵיכָכָה אֶפְצֶה פֶה — *How can I open [my] mouth [in prayer]?* This *selichah* contains an alphabetic scheme followed by the *paytan's* name — אֵלִיָּה בַּר שְׁמַעְיָה, *Eliyah bar Shemayah* [see prefatory comment to *Selichah* 14].

The theme that echoes and re-echoes through this *selichah* is the anguished words of the humble and contrite *chazzan,* who pours out his heart because he feels unqualified and unsuitable to fulfill the role of intermediary between the congregation and God.

כְּשִׁכּוֹר ... לְגִבּוֹר שֶׁאֵין בְּיָדוֹ כְּלֵי זַיִן — *Like a drunk ... I am like a warrior without in his hand implements of war.* Israel's power is in its mouth (see *Bereishis Rabbah* 65:20; *Bamidbar Rabbah* 20:4). But a drunk cannot arrange his words properly. Hence, since I am like a drunk, I have no weaponry with which to fight (YL).

חוֹטֵא וְרַב מֶרִי, בְּיַד מְנֻוָּל* מָסוּר.

《 is he 〈 of the foul 〈 into the 《 rebel- 〈 and 〈 he is a
turned over. [Evil Inclination]* power lious, greatly sinner,

טָרַד לֵב נִבְזֶה הַלָּזֶה הַבָּא לְבַקֵּשׁ,

《 to ask 〈 who 《 of this 〈 is the 〈 Confused
[mercy]; comes despicable one, heart

יָשָׁר הֶעֱוָה,¹ תּוֹכָחוֹת קָץ,² פְּתַלְתּוֹל וְעִקֵּשׁ,³

《 and warped 〈 — a twisted 《 he has 〈 rebuke 《 he has 〈 that
[soul]. despised made which was
crooked, straight

כָּשֵׁל בִּרְכָּיו⁴ אַשְׁמָתוֹ,* וְצַחֲנָתוֹ לוֹ לְמוֹקֵשׁ,

《 a stumbling 〈 is for 〈 the stench 《 from his guilt,* 〈 do his 〈 Totter
block, him [of his sin] knees

לִבּוֹ אָוֶן חוֹרֵשׁ,⁵ בְּפֹעַל כַּפָּיו נוֹקֵשׁ.⁶

《 he is 〈 of his 〈 by the 《 plots, 〈 wrong- 〈 [for] his
entrapped. hands action doing heart

מַעַן טַעַן בִּפְיצָה לְהָשִׁיב מַה אֶמְצָא,

《 can I find? 〈 — what 《 to refute 〈 when I open 〈 or a 〈 As an
[the charges] my mouth counter- answer
claim

נִתְעַבְתִּי וְנֶאֱלַחְתִּי⁷ כִּי מָלֵאתִי דֹפִי וְשִׂמְצָה,

《 and disgrace. 〈 of 〈 I am full 〈 for 《 and depraved, 〈 I have become
infamy loathsome

סְפָק מֵימַי* לֹא נֶאֶמְנוּ כְּאַכְזָב⁸ מוֹצָא,

《 is its 〈 disillusion- 《 been 〈 has 〈 of my 〈 The
source; ing constant, not water* supply

---

(1) Cf. *Job* 33:27. (2) Cf. *Proverbs* 3:11. (3) Cf. *Deuteronomy* 32:5. (4) Cf. *Isaiah* 35:3; *Psalms* 109:24.
(5) Cf. *Proverbs* 6:18. (6) *Psalms* 9:17. (7) Cf. *Job* 15:16. (8) Cf. *Jeremiah* 15:18.

מְנֻוָּל — *The foul [Evil Inclination].* The
Talmud refers to the יֵצֶר הָרַע [*Yetzer Hara*],
Evil Inclination, as מְנֻוָּל זֶה, *this foul crea-
ture* (*Succah* 52b).

כָּשֵׁל בִּרְכָּיו אַשְׁמָתוֹ — *Totter do his knees
from his guilt* [lit., *stumble*]. The prophet
often used the root כשל, *to stumble,* in
conjunction with sin: *Israel and Ephraim,*
יִכָּשְׁלוּ בַּעֲוֹנָם, *shall stumble in their iniquity*
(*Hosea* 5:5); *Return, O Israel, unto HASHEM,
your God,* כִּי כָשַׁלְתָּ, *for you have stumbled
in your iniquity* (ibid. 14:2). Thus, the *chazzan* blames his weak, tottery knees on his
own misdeeds (*Masbir*).

Alternatively: This stich is based on the
verse, בִּרְכַּי כָּשְׁלוּ מִצּוֹם, *My knees totter from
fasting* (*Psalms* 109:24), and alludes to the
custom of fasting on Erev Rosh Hashanah,
the day on which this *selichah* is recited.
This stich then means: *Although his knees
[the chazzan speaks of himself in the third
person] totter from penitential fasting,
nevertheless, his guilt and the stench of his
sins is for him a stumbling block.*

סְפָק מֵימַי — *The supply of my water.* Even
my tears are unreliable. They should be falling without end, yet have ceased to flow.
They are not constant, and thus are false.

עֲצָרוֹתַי* אָוֶן¹ וּמִרְמָה וְצוֹמוֹתַי* לְרִיב וּמַצָּה.²

《 and strife. ‹ grievance 《 and my fasts,* 《 and ‹ [occasion] ‹ my
deceit, wrongdoing assemblies

פֶּשַׁע* מְחֵה וְעָוֹן שָׂא וְאָשָׁם כַּפֵּר,

《 atone ‹ guilt ‹ for- ‹ iniq- ‹ wipe 《 Rebellious
for! give, uity away, sin*

צָעַקְתִּי מִכְּאֵב לֵב,³ נִכְלָם בּוּשׁ וְחָפֵר,

《 and ‹ ashamed, ‹ mortified, 《 heart, ‹ from ‹ I cry
embarrassed. pained

קֶצֶף שַׁכֵּךְ וְרֹגֶז הַנַּח וְכַעַס* הָפֵר,

《 cancel! ‹ anger* 《 lay down, ‹ rage 《 silence, ‹ Fury

רְצֵה מְרַצֶּה וּמְחַבֵּב, וְעַרְבֵּב גּוֹמֵץ חוֹפֵר.*⁴

《 digger.* ‹ [the Accuser,] ‹ and 《 the arouser ‹ the appeaser ‹ Accept [the
the pit confound of love, [the chazzan], prayers of]

שִׁבְטֵי פְלִיטֵי יִשְׂרָאֵל הָכִינוּ בְּלֵב נָבָר,

《 purified! ‹ with ‹ prepare 《 of Israel, ‹ of the ‹ Tribes
hearts yourselves survivors

תֹּם הַחֲזִיקוּ,* וְתַחַן הָפִיקוּ, נַשְּׁקוּ בַר.*⁵

《 purity [of ‹ embrace 《 bring ‹ supplication 《 hold on ‹ With
heart].* forth, to [God's whole-
mitzvos],* someness

---

(1) Cf. *Isaiah* 1:13. (2) Cf. 58:4; see also *Joel* 2:15. (3) Cf. *Isaiah* 65:14; some editions of *Selichos*
read צָעַקְתִּי מִצָּרָה לִי, *I cry from my distress*; cf. *Jonah* 2:3. (4) Cf. *Ecclesiastes* 10:8. (5) *Psalms* 2:12.

עֲצָרוֹתַי ... וְצוֹמוֹתַי — *My assemblies ...
and my fasts*. True, we have fulfilled the
prophet's words regarding repentance: קַדְּשׁוּ
צוֹם, *sanctify a fast*, קִרְאוּ עֲצָרָה, *summon an
assembly* (*Joel* 2:15), but our good intentions have deteriorated into wrongdoing
and deceit, grievance and strife.

פֶּשַׁע ... וְכַעַס — *Rebellious sin ... anger*.
Our sinfulness has been three-pronged:
rebellious sin, iniquity, and guilt. So our
remorse is threefold: mortification, shame,
and abasement. And we beseech God to
respond to our repentance in three ways:
silencing the fury, laying down the rage,
and canceling the anger brought about by
our sins (*Masbir*).

גּוֹמֵץ חוֹפֵר — *[The Accuser,] the pit digger*.
The Talmud teaches that the Evil Inclination entices man in this world, then testifies

against him in the World to Come (*Succah*
52b). Thus, the *Yetzer Hara* digs pits in this
world to ensnare man into sinfulness, then
points an accusing finger at him before the
Heavenly Tribunal. May You, O God, accept favorably the prayers of the *chazzan*
[or, the words of the Defender angel] as he
attempts to vindicate us and arouse Your
love for us, and at the same time confuse the
claims of the Accuser angel who caused the
iniquities he blames on us.

תֹּם הַחֲזִיקוּ ... בַר — *With wholesomeness
hold on to [God's mitzvos] ... purity [of
heart]*. The translation follows *Matteh Levi*.
According to *Masbir*, the stich is punctu-
ated, תֹּם הַחֲזִיקוּ תַחַן, הָפִיקוּ נַשְּׁקוּ בַר and is
rendered: *Cling wholeheartedly to supplication, bring forth a striving for the purity
of Torah.*

אֶת יהוה בְּהִמָּצְאוֹ* לְדָרְשׁוֹ¹ חַיִל יִגְבַּר,²

» be ‹ may ‹ — to seek ‹ when He can be ‹ HASHEM,
increased, strength Him found*

לֹא בָזָה וְלֹא שִׁקַּץ עֱנוּת עָנִי³ וְנִשְׁבָּר.

» and broken. ‹ of the ‹ the sup- ‹ loathed ‹ nor ‹ [for He] has nei-
poor plication ther despised

יוֹם יְשׁוּעָה* וְעֵת רָצוֹן* אֶמְצָא לְפָנֶיךָ,⁴

» before You; ‹ let me find ‹ of favor* ‹ a time ‹ of salvation* ‹ A day

הָגוּן וְרָאוּי וְשָׁלֵם אֵחָשֵׁב⁵ בְּעֵינֶיךָ,

» in Your eyes. ‹ let me be ‹ and whole ‹ worthy, ‹ proper,
considered

בְּעָמְדִי לְהִתְפַּלֵּל וּלְבַקֵּשׁ רַחֲמִים עַל בָּנֶיךָ,

» Your children, ‹ for ‹ for mercy ‹ and to ask ‹ to pray ‹ As I stand

רָצִיתִי אֶתְכֶם הַשְׁמִיעֵנוּ,⁶ סָלַחְתִּי⁷ נִתְבַּשֵּׂר מִמְּעוֹנֶךָ.

» from Your ‹ may we be ‹ I have ‹ let us hear; ‹ you, ‹ With favor I
abode. informed forgiven, will accept

שִׁקְדוּ נָא פְּנֵי עֶלְיוֹן⁸ וְהִמּוֹלוּ קָשׁוֹת,⁹

» [your hearts'] ‹ and ‹ » of the ‹ the ‹ now ‹ Hurry
stubbornness; circumcise Most High, Presence [to entreat]

מִכְשׁוֹל* הָרִימוּ, פַּנּוּ דֶרֶךְ¹⁰ וְיַשְּׁרוּ מַעֲקַשּׁוֹת,¹¹

» the crooked ‹ and ‹ » the ‹ clear » remove, ‹ the stumbling
places. straighten road, block*

---

(1) Cf. Isaiah 55:6. (2) Cf. Ecclesiastes 10:10. (3) Psalms 22:25. (4) Cf. Isaiah 49:8.
(5) Some editions of Selichos add וְזָקֵן, and scholarly or וְרָצוּי, and favorable, to this list;
see Taanis 16a. (6) Cf. Ezekiel 43:27. (7) Numbers 14:20. (8) Lamentations 3:35; some editions of
Selichos read שִׁקְדוּ נָא בְּנֵי עֶלְיוֹן, Be diligent, O children of the Most High; cf. Psalms 82:6.
(9) Jeremiah 4:4; cf. Deuteronomy 10:16. (10) Cf. Isaiah 57:14. (11) Cf. 42:16.

בְּהִמָּצְאוֹ — When He can be found. When does God allow Himself to be found? During the ten days from Rosh Hashanah [1 Tishrei] until Yom Kippur [10 Tishrei] (Yevamos 49b).

יוֹם יְשׁוּעָה — A day of salvation. According to all the major commentaries (Targum, Rashi, Radak to Isaiah 49:8), the phrase יוֹם יְשׁוּעָה, a day of salvation, means a day that requires salvation, a day of troubles. Here, however, the paytan obviously does not plead for such a day. Rather, the phrase must be understood as a day in which God sends us salvation from our present troubles.

וְעֵת רָצוֹן — A time of favor. When is a time of favor? When the congregation prays (Berachos 8a).

מִכְשׁוֹל — The stumbling block. The Talmud (Succah 52a) records seven names for the Evil Inclination: God called it רָע, Evil (Genesis 8:21); Moses called it עָרֵל, Uncircumcised (Deuteronomy 10:16); King David called it טָמֵא, Unclean (Psalms 51:12); King Solomon called it שׂוֹנֵא, Foe (Proverbs 25:21); Isaiah called it מִכְשׁוֹל, Stumbling block (57:14); Ezekiel called it אֶבֶן, Stone (36:26); and Joel called it צְפוֹנִי, Hidden (2:20).

עָוֹן עִזְבוּ וְהִתְוַדּוּ[1] וְאַל תּוֹסִיפוּ לְהַקְשׁוֹת,[2]

‹ be stubborn, ‹ any longer ‹ and do not ‹ and confess ‹ forsake ‹ Sin

יוֹדֵעַ יָשׁוּב וְנִחָם[3] וְיִקַּח דִּבְרֵי כְבוּשִׁים[4] וּבַקָּשׁוֹת.

and supplication. ‹ of self-reproof ‹ words ‹ and bring [with him] ‹ and regret, ‹ let him repent ‹ and whoever knows [he has sinned]

הַקְשִׁיבָה אֲדוֹן חַנּוּן הַאֲזִינָה עֵרֶךְ שַׁוְעָתִי,[5]

‹ of my prayer. ‹ to the service ‹ listen ‹ Who is gracious, ‹ O Lord ‹ Be attentive,

זַעֲקָתִי רְצֵה וְהִתְרַצֵּה וְהִתְפַּיֵּס וְקַבֵּל שַׁוְעָתִי,

‹ my prayer. ‹ and accept ‹ and become conciliatory ‹ become favorable ‹ accept ‹ My cry

קְרָאתֶיךָ מִמֵּצַר,[6] קָרַב אֵלַי וּלְכָה לִישׁוּעָתִי,

‹ to my rescue; ‹ and come ‹ to me ‹ draw near ‹ out of distress; ‹ I call to You

חוּשָׁה לְעֶזְרָתִי אֲדֹנָי תְּשׁוּעָתִי.[7]

‹ my Salvation. ‹ O Lord, ‹ to my assistance, ‹ hasten

ALL, WHILE STANDING:

אֵל מֶלֶךְ יוֹשֵׁב עַל כִּסֵּא רַחֲמִים, מִתְנַהֵג

‹ Who acts ‹ of mercy, ‹ the throne ‹ on ‹ Who sits ‹ King ‹ O God,

בַּחֲסִידוּת, מוֹחֵל עֲוֹנוֹת עַמּוֹ, מַעֲבִיר רִאשׁוֹן רִאשׁוֹן,[8]

‹ by one, ‹ [sins,] one ‹ Who removes ‹ of His people, ‹ the sins ‹ Who pardons ‹ with kindness,

מַרְבֶּה מְחִילָה לְחַטָּאִים וּסְלִיחָה לַפּוֹשְׁעִים, עֹשֶׂה

‹ Who performs ‹ to willful sinners, ‹ and forgiveness ‹ to unintentional sinners ‹ pardon ‹ Who abundantly grants

צְדָקוֹת עִם כָּל בָּשָׂר וָרוּחַ, לֹא כְרָעָתָם תִּגְמוֹל.

‹ do You repay them! ‹ in accord with their wickedness ‹ — not ‹ and spirit ‹ [beings of] flesh ‹ all ‹ with ‹ acts of generosity

אֵל הוֹרֵיתָ לָּנוּ לוֹמַר שְׁלֹשׁ עֶשְׂרֵה, וּזְכוֹר לָנוּ

‹ for us ‹ remember ‹ the Thirteen [Attributes of Mercy]; ‹ to recite ‹ us ‹ You taught ‹ O God,

הַיּוֹם בְּרִית שְׁלֹשׁ עֶשְׂרֵה, כְּמוֹ שֶׁהוֹדַעְתָּ לֶעָנָיו

‹ to the humble one [Moses] ‹ You made known ‹ as ‹ of [these] Thirteen; ‹ the covenant ‹ today

---

(1) Cf. *Proverbs* 28:13. (2) Cf. *Deuteronomy* 10:16. (3) *Joel* 2:14. (4) Cf. *Hosea* 14:3.
(5) Cf. *Job* 36:19. (6) Cf. *Psalms* 118:5. (7) 38:23. (8) *Rosh Hashanah* 17a.

מִקֶּדֶם, כְּמוֹ שֶׁכָּתוּב, וַיֵּרֶד יהוה בֶּעָנָן וַיִּתְיַצֵּב עִמּוֹ

‹ with ‹ and stood ‹ in a ‹ And HASHEM ≪ it is written: ‹ as ≪ in ancient
him　　　　　　cloud　　descended　　　　　　　　　　　times,

שָׁם, וַיִּקְרָא בְשֵׁם יהוה.[1]

≪ of ‹ with the ‹ and He ≪ there,
HASHEM. Name called out

CONGREGATION, THEN *CHAZZAN*:

וַיַּעֲבֹר יהוה עַל פָּנָיו וַיִּקְרָא:

≪ and ≪ [Moses'] ‹ before ‹ And HASHEM passed
proclaimed: face,

CONGREGATION AND *CHAZZAN* RECITE LOUDLY AND IN UNISON:

יהוה, יהוה, אֵל, רַחוּם, וְחַנּוּן, אֶרֶךְ אַפַּיִם,

‹ to anger, ‹ Slow ≪ and Gracious, ‹ Compassionate ‹ God, ‹ HASHEM, ‹ HASHEM,

וְרַב חֶסֶד, וֶאֱמֶת, נֹצֵר חֶסֶד לָאֲלָפִים, נֹשֵׂא עָוֹן,

‹ of ‹ Forgiver ≪ for thousands ‹ of ‹ Preserver ≪ and ‹ in ‹ and
iniquity, [of generations], kindness Truth, Kindness Abundant

וָפֶשַׁע, וְחַטָּאָה, וְנַקֵּה.[2] וְסָלַחְתָּ לַעֲוֹנֵנוּ וּלְחַטָּאתֵנוּ

≪ and our sins, ‹ our ‹ May You ≪ and Who ‹ and inadvertent ‹ willful sin,
iniquities forgive absolves. sin,

וּנְחַלְתָּנוּ.[3] סְלַח לָנוּ אָבִינוּ כִּי חָטָאנוּ, מְחַל לָנוּ

‹ us, ‹ pardon ≪ we have ‹ for ≪ our ‹ us, ‹ Forgive ≪ and make us
sinned; Father, Your heritage.

מַלְכֵּנוּ כִּי פָשָׁעְנוּ. כִּי אַתָּה אֲדֹנָי טוֹב וְסַלָּח,

≪ and ‹ are ‹ O Lord, ‹ You, ‹ For ≪ we have ‹ for ≪ our King,
forgiving, good willfully sinned.

וְרַב חֶסֶד לְכָל קֹרְאֶיךָ.[4]

≪ who call ‹ to all ‹ kind ‹ and
upon You. abundantly

פסוקי הקדמה לסליחה כה / PREFATORY VERSES TO SELICHAH 25

שׁוּבָה יהוה אֶת שְׁבִיתֵנוּ, כַּאֲפִיקִים בַּנֶּגֶב.[5] שׁוּבָה

‹ Return, ≪ in the ‹ like springs ≪ our captivity, ‹ O ‹ Return,
desert. HASHEM,

יהוה חַלְּצָה נַפְשֵׁנוּ, וְהוֹשִׁיעֵנוּ לְמַעַן חַסְדֶּךָ.[6]

≪ of Your ‹ as ‹ save us ≪ our soul, ‹ Release ≪ HASHEM!
kindness. benefits

---

(1) *Exodus* 34:5. (2) 34:6-7. (3) 34:9. (4) *Psalms* 86:5. (5) 126:4. (6) Cf. 6:5.

דִּרְשׁוּ יהוה בְּהִמָּצְאוֹ, קְרָאֻהוּ בִּהְיוֹתוֹ קָרוֹב.

» near. ‹ when ‹ call upon » when He ‹ HASHEM ‹ Seek
He is Him can be found;

יַעֲזֹב רָשָׁע דַּרְכּוֹ וְאִישׁ אָוֶן מַחְשְׁבֹתָיו, וְיָשֹׁב אֶל

‹ to ‹ and let » his thoughts; ‹ of ‹ and the » his way, ‹ Let the wicked
him return iniquity man one abandon

יהוה וִירַחֲמֵהוּ, וְאֶל אֱלֹהֵינוּ כִּי יַרְבֶּה לִסְלוֹחַ.¹

» in forgiving. ‹ He will be ‹ for ‹ our God ‹ and ‹ and He will ‹ HASHEM
abundant [return] to show him mercy,

כְּרַחֵם אָב עַל בָּנִים, כֵּן תְּרַחֵם יהוה עָלֵינוּ.²

» on us. ‹ HASHEM, ‹ have ‹ so » his ‹ toward ‹ a ‹ As merciful as
mercy, children, father is

לַיהוה הַיְשׁוּעָה, עַל עַמְּךָ בִרְכָתֶךָ סֶּלָה.³ יהוה

‹ HASHEM, » Selah. » is Your ‹ Your ‹ upon » is salvation, ‹ To HASHEM
blessing, people

צְבָאוֹת עִמָּנוּ, מִשְׂגָּב לָנוּ אֱלֹהֵי יַעֲקֹב סֶלָה.⁴

» Selah. » of Jacob, ‹ is the God ‹ for us ‹ a » is with us, ‹ Master of
stronghold Legions,

יהוה צְבָאוֹת, אַשְׁרֵי אָדָם בֹּטֵחַ בָּךְ.⁵ יהוה

‹ HASHEM, » in You. ‹ who ‹ is the ‹ — praiseworthy » Master ‹ HASHEM,
trusts man of Legions

הוֹשִׁיעָה, הַמֶּלֶךְ יַעֲנֵנוּ בְיוֹם קָרְאֵנוּ.⁶

» we call. ‹ on the ‹ answer ‹ May the » save!
day us King

סְלִיחָה כה / SELICHAH 25

ALL:

אֱלֹהֵינוּ וֵאלֹהֵי אֲבוֹתֵינוּ:

» of our forefathers: ‹ and God ‹ Our God

אָנָּא עוֹרְרָה אַהֲבָתְךָ הַיְשָׁנָה,*⁷

» from ancient times,* ‹ Your love ‹ awaken ‹ Please,

---

(1) *Isaiah* 55:6-7. (2) Cf. *Psalms* 103:13. (3) 3:9. (4) 46:8. (5) 84:13. (6) 20:10. (7) Cf. *Song of Songs* 2:7.

◆§ **אָנָּא עוֹרְרָה אַהֲבָתְךָ הַיְשָׁנָה** — *Please,*
awaken Your love from ancient times. This
selichah follows an *aleph-beis* acrostic with
each odd-numbered letter (א,ג,ה ...) appear-

ing twice and each even-numbered letter
(ב,ד,ו ...) only once. The remainder of the
acrostic spells שְׁלֹמֹה חֲזַק, *Shlomo, may he be*
strong [see prefatory comment to *Selichah*

אֲשֶׁר אָהַבְתָּ לַעֲדַת מִי מָנָה,[1]

‹‹ has counted ‹ [it was ‹ the congrega- ‹ You loved ‹ with
[them]; said] who tion of whom which

בְּכָל כִּנּוּי חִבָּה וְאַחֲוָה* וְרֵעוּת* מְכֻנָּה,

‹‹ are ‹ and ‹ brotherhood, ‹ of love, ‹ term ‹ [who]
called — friendship* by every

לְמַעַן אַחַי וְרֵעַי אֲדַבְּרָה נָּא.[2]

‹‹ if You ‹ I [the chazzan] ‹ and my ‹ of my ‹ for the
please. shall speak friends brothers sake

גַּם בְּצֵעַדְךָ עַל הַר גַּבְנוּנִי,*

‹‹ of majestic ‹ the ‹ upon ‹ when You ‹ Also,
peaks [Sinai],* mount stepped forth

גִּיל לְשַׁעֲשֵׁעַ חֶמְדָּ קַדְמוֹנִי,

‹‹ primordial, ‹ with [the Torah ‹ to delight ‹ rejoicing
Your] treasure, [Israel]

דִּמִּיתָ מַמְלֶכֶת כֹּהֲנִים וְגוֹי קָדוֹשׁ,[3] וּבְנִי,[4]

‹‹ and [as] ‹ that is ‹ and a ‹ of priests ‹ a ‹ You envisaged
My son; holy, nation kingdom [Israel as]

וְהִיא גַם הִיא אָמְרָה, אָחִי הוּא,[5] מַלְכִּי וַאדוֹנִי.

‹‹ my Lord! ‹ — my ‹ is He ‹ My ‹‹ said, ‹ she, ‹ also ‹ and she
King, brother [Israel],

הוֹרַשְׁתָּ נַחֲלַת צְבִי,[6] חֶבֶל הַנָּעִים,[7]

‹‹ that is ‹ a ‹‹ that is ‹ an ‹ You bequeathed
pleasant, portion cherished, inheritance [to Israel]

(1) Cf. *Numbers* 23:10. (2) *Psalms* 122:8. (3) *Exodus* 19:6.
(4) 4:22. (5) *Genesis* 20:5. (6) *Jeremiah* 3:19. (7) Cf. *Psalms* 16:6.

2]. The last line of each stanza includes some form of the word אָח, *brother* (see next comment).

חִבָּה וְאַחֲוָה וְרֵעוּת — *Love, brotherhood, and friendship.* Each of these terms is used in Scripture to describe the relationship between God and Israel: חִבָּה, *love,* in the passages חֹבֵב עַמִּים, *He loves the tribes [of Israel]* (*Deuteronomy* 33:3), and *You shall be unto Me,* סְגֻלָּה מִכָּל הָעַמִּים (which *Targum Onkelos* renders חַבִּיבִין מִכָּל עַמְמַיָּא), *the most beloved of all peoples* (*Exodus* 19:5); אַחֲוָה, *brotherhood,* and רֵעוּת, *friendship,* in the verse *[He said,] ''Open [your heart] to Me,* אֲחֹתִי, *My sister,* רַעְיָתִי, *My friend!''* (*Song of Songs* 5:2). And it is the theme of brotherly

friendship and love between God and Israel that permeates this *piyut.* Thus, the last line of each stanza is a Scriptural fragment that includes some form of the word אָח, *brother.*

הַר גַּבְנוּנִי — *The mount of majestic peaks, [Sinai].* According to the Midrash (*Tanchuma, Bamidbar* 7). Scripture records six names for Mount Sinai: (a) הַר [הָ]אֱלֹהִים, *[the] Mountain of Elokim (Exodus* 3:1; 18:5; *Psalms* 68:16); (b) הַר בָּשָׁן, *Mount Bashan* (*Psalms* 68:16); (c) הַר גַּבְנֻנִּים, *Mount Gavnunim* (ibid.); (d) הָהָר חָמַד, *the Desired Mountain* (ibid. v. 17); (e) הַר חוֹרֵב, *Mount Horeb* (*Exodus* 3:1, 33:6; *I Kings* 19:8); and (f) הַר סִינַי, *Mount Sinai* (*Exodus* 19:18).

הִסְתּוֹפֵף לִכְבוֹדְךָ,* בְּלִוְיוֹת צַעֲצֻעִים,¹

were the child- ⟨ where ⟨ in Your honor* ⟨ [where] they stood
like Cherubim. ⟨ entwined ⟨ [in the Temple], ⟨ at the threshold

וְהֵן עַתָּה טִלְטְלוּהָ זָרִים, זֵדִים מְרֵעִים,²

evildoers. ⟨ and ⟨ have ⟨ tossed her ⟨ now, ⟨ But
willful ⟨ strangers ⟨ about ⟨ indeed,

בְּאֶרֶץ לֹא לָהֶם, הֲלוֹא אַחֶיךָ רוֹעִים.³

pasturing? ⟨ Your **brothers** ⟨ are not ⟨ theirs, ⟨ not ⟨ In a land

זְכֹר אַל תִּשְׁכָּח,⁴ וְאַל תֶּחֱרַשׁ וְאַל תִּשְׁקֹט אֵל,⁵

O ⟨ still, ⟨ and ⟨ deaf ⟨ be not ⟨ forget, ⟨ Do Remem-
God! ⟨ be not ⟨ not ⟨ ber!

זָמְמוּ לְהַכְחִידִי⁶ אֱדוֹם וְיִשְׁמָעֵאל,

and Ishmael. ⟨ have been ⟨ to obliterate me ⟨ Plotting
Edom

חַנּוּן, אַתָּה יָדַעְתָּ אֶת כָּל הַתְּלָאוֹת הָאֵל,

that are ⟨ [our] ⟨ all ⟨ know ⟨ You ⟨ O Gracious
these ⟨ tribulations ⟨ One,

כֹּה אָמַר אָחִיךָ יִשְׂרָאֵל.⁷

Israel. ⟨ Your **brother**, ⟨ said ⟨ — so

טָפְלוּ עָלַי⁸ וּבְקָקוּנִי בּוֹקְקִים,⁹

have ⟨ and ⟨ upon ⟨ Piled
plunderers, ⟨ plundered me ⟨ me ⟨ [lies]

טָהֳרָה בְּטֻמְאָה לְהָמִיר,¹⁰ לְחָצוּנִי דּוֹחֲקִים,

— the ⟨ have they ⟨ to exchange ⟨ for defiled ⟨ [the] pure
oppressors. ⟨ pressured me ⟨ [idolatry] ⟨ [Torah]

יוֹם יוֹם, הִנֵּה עֲבָדֶיךָ מֻכִּים¹¹ וְלוֹקִים,

and whipped ⟨ beaten ⟨ are Your ⟨ indeed, ⟨ [after] ⟨ Day
servants ⟨ day,

קוֹל דְּמֵי אָחִיךָ צוֹעֲקִים.¹²

are crying ⟨ of Your ⟨ of the ⟨ — the
out! ⟨ **brother** ⟨ bloods ⟨ voice

---

(1) Cf. *I Kings* 7:29, *II Chronicles* 3:10. (2) In many editions this line omits one or two
of the words זָרִים, strangers, זֵדִים, willful, מְרֵעִים, evildoers. (3) *Genesis* 15:13; 37:13.
(4) *Deuteronomy* 9:7. (5) *Psalms* 83:2. (6) 83:5. (7) *Numbers* 20:14. (8) *Psalms* 119:69.
(9) Cf. *Nahum* 2:3. (10) Some editions omit this phrase. (11) Cf. *Exodus* 5:16. (12) *Genesis* 4:10.

הִסְתּוֹפֵף לִכְבוֹדְךָ — *[Where] they stood at*   You caused Your honor [the Shechinah] to
the threshold in Your honor. Alternatively,   *stand.*

כָּרוּ לִי שִׂיחוֹת¹ לְמוֹקֵשׁ,

They have dug ‹ for me ‹ pits ‹ as a trap; 《

כָּלְתָה וְנִכְסְפָה נַפְשִׁי² עֶזְרָתָה³ לְבַקֵּשׁ,

pine ‹ and yearn ‹ does my soul ‹ help ‹ to seek, 《

לִישׁוּעָתָה לִי עַל פְּתָחַי לִנְקֹשׁ,

[that] ‹ with salvation ‹ for me ‹ on ‹ my doors ‹ You should knock 《

אֶת אַחַי אָנֹכִי מְבַקֵּשׁ.⁴

My brothers — ‹ do I ‹ seek. 《

מִיּוֹם כֶּסֶה, בְּשִׁבְתְּךָ עַל כִּסֵּא כְבוֹדֶךָ,⁶

From the day ‹ of the covered [moon, Rosh Hashanah], ‹ as You sit ‹ upon ‹ Your Throne ‹ of Glory, 《

מַבִּיט לִסְקֹר יַחַד, לֵב מוֹרְדֶיךָ וְעוֹבְדֶיךָ,

gazing out ‹ to survey ‹ together ‹ the hearts ‹ of those who rebel against You ‹ and of those who serve You, 《

נִגָּשׂ כָּל בַּעַל מַשָּׁאת בּוֹגְדֶיךָ,

demand debt payment ‹ from all ‹ who owe ‹ a debt ‹ of those who are disloyal to You, 《

וַאֲשֶׁר יִהְיֶה לְךָ אֶת אָחִיךָ, תַּשְׁמֵט יָדֶךָ.⁷

but over what ‹ is ‹ Yours ‹ that is with ‹ Your brother, ‹ You shall remit ‹ Your authority. 《

סְפָרִים עֵת יִקָּרְאוּ, לִבְרוּאֵי עוֹלָמָךְ,

The Books [of Life and of Death] ‹ at the time ‹ they are read ‹ for those created ‹ in Your world, 《

שֵׂאת חַיִּים וְחִלּוּף, לְשׁוֹעַ וָמָךְ,

bearing the gift ‹ of life ‹ or its opposite ‹ to rich ‹ and to poor, 《

עֶלְיוֹן, חֵן וָחֶסֶד בְּאֻלָמָךְ,

Most High! ‹ favor ‹ and kindness ‹ Let be in Your hall [of justice]; 《

---

(1) Cf. *Psalms* 119:85. (2) Cf. 84:3. (3) Some editions read עֶזְרָתְךָ, *Your help.*
(4) *Genesis* 37:16. (5) Cf. *Psalms* 81:4. (6) *Jeremiah* 14:21. (7) *Deuteronomy* 15:3.

עֶרֹב עַבְדְּךָ לְטוֹב,[1] וְחִי אָחִיךָ עִמָּךְ.[2]

《 with You. 〈 that Your **brother** may live 〈 for good, 〈 for Your servant 〈 be the guarantor

פְּנֵה אֵלַי וְחָנֵּנִי,[3] וּתְנֵנִי עֶלְיוֹן

《 supreme; 〈 and place me 《 and show me favor, 〈 to me 〈 Turn

פַּגֵּר מְנַאֲצֶיךָ בְּעֹנִי וְרִשָּׁיוֹן,

《 and impov- erishment. 〈 [afflicting them] with poverty 〈 those who anger You, 〈 devastate

צָרְכֵי חֹק טֶרֶף, בְּחַלְּקְךָ אַפְסַנְיוֹן,

《 annual stipends, 〈 when You apportion 〈 of nour- ishment, 〈 mea- sure 〈 [As for our] needed

לֹא תִקְפֹּץ אֶת יָדְךָ, מֵאָחִיךָ הָאֶבְיוֹן.[4]

《 who is destitute. 〈 from [giving] to Your **brother** 〈 Your hand 〈 You shall not close

קִדַּמְתִּי בַנֶּשֶׁף, וָאֲשַׁוֵּעַ[5] לְךָ מְחוֹלְלִי,

《 my Creator; 〈 to You, 〈 and I cried out 〈 while still night 〈 I arose

קַדְּמָה חַסְדֶּךָ, וְשָׂא פִּשְׁעִי וּמַעֲלִי,

《 and my treachery! 〈 my willful sin 〈 and forgive 〈 Your kindness 〈 Put forward

רַחֲמֶיךָ יִתְגּוֹלְלוּ עָלַי, כִּמְנַחֵם אֶבְלִי,

《 my mourning; 〈 as if comforting 〈 me 〈 roll over 〈 Let Your mercy

מִי יִתֶּנְךָ כְּאָח לִי.[6]

《 to me! 〈 like a comfort- ing **brother** 〈 You could be 〈 if only

שָׁעָה שַׁוְעַת עֲנִיֶּךָ וְצַעֲקָתָם,

《 and to their shout, 〈 of Your poor ones 〈 to the outcry 〈 Turn

שְׂבְעָה בְרָעוֹת נַפְשָׁם[7] וְחַיָּתָם,

《 and their life force. 〈 are their souls 〈 with troubles 〈 [for] satiated

תַּשְׁלִיךְ בִּמְצֻלוֹת יָם כָּל חַטֹּאתָם,[8]

《 their sins; 〈 all 〈 of the sea 〈 into the depths 〈 You will cast

---

(1) *Psalms* 119:122. (2) *Leviticus* 25:36. (3) *Psalms* 25:16. (4) Cf. *Deuteronomy* 15:7.
(5) *Psalms* 119:147. (6) *Song of Songs* 8:1. (7) Cf. *Psalms* 88:4. (8) Cf. *Micah* 7:19.

אָנָּא, שָׂא נָא פֶּשַׁע אַחֶיךָ, וְחַטָּאתָם.[1]

O please, forgive, please, the flagrant offense of Your brothers, and their sin. »

שָׂשׂ אָנֹכִי עַל אִמְרַת מִבְטָחֶיךָ,[2]

Rejoice do I over the statement of Your assurance; »

לִבַּבְתִּנִי, עַל יְדֵי צִירִים שְׁלוּחֶיךָ,

You have captured my heart through the hands of the emissaries, of Your messengers [the prophets]. »

מָתַי תַּחְשֹׂף זְרוֹעֲךָ בְּכֹחֶךָ,[3]

When will You bare Your arm, « [revealing] Your strength? »

לֶךְ נָא רְאֵה אֶת שְׁלוֹם אַחֶיךָ.[4]

Go, please, and see about the welfare of Your brothers. »

❖ הָיִיתָ מִקֶּדֶם מִקְוֵה יִשְׂרָאֵל, וְחֶרֶב גַּאֲוָתָם,[5]

You have been since antiquity the Hope of Israel, « and the Sword of their grandeur; »

חַי, זְקֹף גַּם עַתָּה קוֹמָתָם,

O Living One, straighten even now their [bent] stature, »

וְאַמֵּץ זְרֹעָם וְתִשְׁכֹּן בֵּינוֹתָם,

strengthen their arm, « and let [Your Presence] dwell among them — »

וְאֶת אַחֶיךָ תִּפְקֹד לְשָׁלוֹם, וְאֶת עֲרֻבָּתָם.[6]

and « Your brothers, inquire about their welfare « and about their families. »

ALL, WHILE STANDING:

אֵל מֶלֶךְ יוֹשֵׁב עַל כִּסֵּא רַחֲמִים, מִתְנַהֵג

O God, King Who sits on the throne of mercy, « Who acts

בַּחֲסִידוּת, מוֹחֵל עֲוֹנוֹת עַמּוֹ, מַעֲבִיר רִאשׁוֹן

with kindness, Who pardons the sins of His people, « Who removes [sins,] one

רִאשׁוֹן, מַרְבֶּה מְחִילָה לַחַטָּאִים וּסְלִיחָה לַפּוֹשְׁעִים,[7]

by one, Who abundantly grants pardon to unintentional sinners « and forgiveness to willful sinners, »

(1) Cf. *Genesis* 50:17. (2) Cf. *Psalms* 119:162. (3) Cf. *Isaiah* 52:10. (4) *Genesis* 37:14. (5) Cf. *Deuteronomy* 33:29. (6) *I Samuel* 17:18. (7) *Rosh Hashanah* 17a.

עֹשֶׂה צְדָקוֹת עִם כָּל בָּשָׂר וָרוּחַ, לֹא כְרָעָתָם

⟨ in accord with ⟨ — not ⟪ and ⟨ [beings ⟨ all ⟨ with ⟨ acts of ⟨ Who
their wickedness spirit of] flesh generosity performs

תִּגְמוֹל. ❖ אֵל הוֹרֵיתָ לָּנוּ לוֹמַר שְׁלֹשׁ עֶשְׂרֵה, וּזְכוֹר

⟨ remem- ⟪ the Thirteen ⟨ to ⟨ You ⟨ O God, ⟪ do You
ber [Attributes of Mercy]; recite us taught repay them!

לָּנוּ הַיּוֹם בְּרִית שְׁלֹשׁ עֶשְׂרֵה, כְּמוֹ שֶׁהוֹדַעְתָּ לֶעָנָיו

⟨ to the humble ⟨ You made ⟨ as ⟪ of [these] Thirteen, ⟨ the ⟨ today ⟨ for us
one [Moses] known covenant

מִקֶּדֶם, כְּמוֹ שֶׁכָּתוּב, וַיֵּרֶד יהוה בֶּעָנָן וַיִּתְיַצֵּב עִמּוֹ

⟨ with ⟨ and stood ⟨ in a ⟨ And HASHEM ⟪ it is written: ⟨ as ⟪ in ancient
him cloud descended times,

שָׁם, וַיִּקְרָא בְשֵׁם יהוה.[1]

⟪ of ⟨ with the ⟨ and He ⟪ there,
HASHEM. Name called out

CONGREGATION, THEN CHAZZAN:

וַיַּעֲבֹר יהוה עַל פָּנָיו וַיִּקְרָא:

⟪ and ⟪ [Moses'] ⟨ before ⟨ And HASHEM passed
proclaimed: face,

CONGREGATION AND CHAZZAN RECITE LOUDLY AND IN UNISON:

יהוה, יהוה, אֵל, רַחוּם, וְחַנּוּן, אֶרֶךְ אַפַּיִם,

⟨ to anger, ⟨ Slow ⟪ and Gracious, ⟨ Compassionate ⟨ God, ⟨ HASHEM, ⟨ HASHEM,

וְרַב חֶסֶד, וֶאֱמֶת, נֹצֵר חֶסֶד לָאֲלָפִים, נֹשֵׂא עָוֹן,

⟨ of ⟨ Forgiver ⟪ for thousands ⟨ of ⟨ Preserver ⟪ and ⟨ in ⟨ and
iniquity, [of generations], kindness Truth, Kindness Abundant

וָפֶשַׁע, וְחַטָּאָה, וְנַקֵּה.[2] וְסָלַחְתָּ לַעֲוֹנֵנוּ וּלְחַטָּאתֵנוּ

⟪ and our sins, ⟨ our ⟨ May You ⟪ and Who ⟨ and inadvertent ⟨ willful sin,
iniquities forgive absolves. sin,

וּנְחַלְתָּנוּ.[3] סְלַח לָנוּ אָבִינוּ כִּי חָטָאנוּ, מְחַל לָנוּ

⟨ us, ⟨ pardon ⟪ we have ⟨ for ⟪ our ⟨ us, ⟨ Forgive ⟪ and make us
sinned; Father, Your heritage.

מַלְכֵּנוּ כִּי פָשָׁעְנוּ. כִּי אַתָּה אֲדֹנָי טוֹב וְסַלָּח,

⟪ and ⟨ are ⟨ O Lord, ⟨ You, ⟨ For ⟪ we have ⟨ for ⟪ our King,
forgiving, good willfully sinned.

וְרַב חֶסֶד לְכָל קֹרְאֶיךָ.[4]

⟪ who call ⟨ to all ⟨ kind ⟨ and
upon You. abundantly

(1) Exodus 34:5. (2) 34:6-7. (3) 34:9. (4) Psalms 86:5.

PREFATORY VERSES TO SELICHAH 26 / פסוקי הקדמה לסליחה כו

לֹא כַחֲטָאֵינוּ תַּעֲשֶׂה לָנוּ, וְלֹא כַעֲוֹנֹתֵינוּ תִּגְמֹל

‹ shall You repay ‹ according to our iniquities ‹ nor ‹‹ us, ‹ shall You treat ‹ according to our sins ‹ Not

עָלֵינוּ.¹ כִּי רַבּוּ מְשׁוּבֹתֵינוּ לְךָ חָטָאנוּ.² תְּחַטְּאֵנוּ

‹ Purge me of sin ‹‹ have we sinned ‹ unto You ‹‹ are our rebellious deeds; ‹ so many ‹ for ‹‹ us.

בְאֵזוֹב וְנִטְהָר, תְּכַבְּסֵנוּ וּמִשֶּׁלֶג נַלְבִּין.³ אַל תִּקְצֹף,

‹ be enraged, ‹ Do not ‹‹ shall I be white. ‹ and more than snow ‹ cleanse me ‹‹ and I shall be pure ‹ with hyssop

יהוה, עַד מְאֹד, וְאַל לָעַד תִּזְכֹּר עָוֹן, הֵן הַבֶּט

‹ see ‹ indeed, ‹‹ iniquity; ‹ shall You remember ‹ forever ‹ and not ‹‹ an extreme, ‹ to ‹ HASHEM,

נָא עַמְּךָ כֻלָּנוּ.⁴

‹‹ are we all. ‹ that Your people ‹ now

כְּרַחֵם אָב עַל בָּנִים, כֵּן תְּרַחֵם יהוה עָלֵינוּ.⁵

‹‹ on us. ‹ HASHEM, ‹ have mercy, ‹ so ‹‹ his children, ‹ toward ‹ a father is ‹ As merciful as

לַיהוה הַיְשׁוּעָה, עַל עַמְּךָ בִרְכָתֶךָ סֶּלָה.⁶ יהוה

‹ HASHEM, ‹‹ Selah. ‹‹ is Your blessing, ‹ Your people ‹ upon ‹‹ is salvation, ‹ To HASHEM

צְבָאוֹת עִמָּנוּ, מִשְׂגָּב לָנוּ אֱלֹהֵי יַעֲקֹב סֶּלָה.⁷

‹‹ Selah. ‹‹ of Jacob, ‹ is the God ‹ for us ‹ a stronghold ‹‹ is with us, ‹ Master of Legions,

יהוה צְבָאוֹת, אַשְׁרֵי אָדָם בֹּטֵחַ בָּךְ.⁸ יהוה

‹ HASHEM, ‹‹ in You. ‹ who trusts ‹ is the man ‹ — praiseworthy ‹‹ Master of Legions ‹ HASHEM,

הוֹשִׁיעָה, הַמֶּלֶךְ יַעֲנֵנוּ בְיוֹם קָרְאֵנוּ.⁹

‹‹ we call. ‹ on the day ‹ answer us ‹ May the King ‹‹ save!

---

(1) Cf. *Psalms* 103:10. (2) *Jeremiah* 14:7. (3) Cf. *Psalms* 51:9.
(4) *Isaiah* 64:8. (5) Cf. *Psalms* 103:13. (6) 3:9. (7) 46:8. (8) 84:13. (9) 20:10.

סליחה כו / SELICHAH 26

ALL:

אֱלֹהֵינוּ וֵאלֹהֵי אֲבוֹתֵינוּ:
《 of our forefathers:《 and God 《 Our God

אֵל אֱלוֹהַ דָּלְפָה עֵינִי,*¹ אֲשַׁוֵּעַ וְיֹאמַר הִנֵּנִי,²
《 Here I 《 and He 《 I shall cry 《 does my 《 drip [tears] 《 God, 《 To
am! shall say, out, eye,*

אֲמָרַי הַאֲזִינָה בְּהִתְחַנְנִי,³
《 as I supplicate, 《 listen 《 To my words

עֲנֵנִי יהוה עֲנֵנִי.⁴
《 answer 《 HASHEM, 《 Answer
me! me,

בְּמֹאזְנַיִם כִּי תְפַלֵּס דַּרְכִּי,⁵
《 my path, 《 You weigh 《 when 《 On the scales

בְּמִצְוֹתֶיךָ דַּלּוֹתִי חֶלְקִי וְחִשְׁקִי,*
《 and in my 《 [both] in 《 I am poor 《 regarding Your
desire;* my portion mitzvos

וְאִם כְּפָעֳלִי תַּשְׁלִים חֻקִּי, וָאִירָא כִּי עֵירֹם אָנֹכִי.⁶
《 am I. 《 naked 《 for 《 I am afraid, 《 my 《 You should 《 according to 《 if
sustenance, mete out my actions

גָּרֵשׁ כַּלֵּה חֵטְא וּמֶרִי, גַּלֵּה נַרְתֵּק מַרְפֵּא* וְצָרִי,
《 and 《 [to provide] 《 the 《 reveal 《 and 《 sin 《 annihilate 《 Chase
balm, healing* sheath rebellion; out,

---

(1) *Job* 16:20. (2) Cf. *Isaiah* 58:9. (3) Cf. *Psalms* 5:2; 86:6.
(4) *I Kings* 18:37. (5) Cf. *Proverbs* 16:11. (6) *Genesis* 3:10.

אֵל אֱלוֹהַ דָּלְפָה עֵינִי ❦ — *To God, drip [tears] does my eye.* This *selichah* follows a double *aleph-beis* as indicated by the bold type. The fourth line of each quatrain is a Scriptural fragment. The last two stanzas bear the author's signature — יוֹאֵל בַּר יִצְחָק הַלֵּוִי, *Yoel son of Yitzchak the Levite.* R' Yoel studied under R' Ephraim of Regensburg [see prefatory comment to *Selichah* 34] and was the son-in-law of the well-known Tosafist and *paytan*, R' Eliezer ben Nassan (*Ravan*). He lived in Bonn, Germany, but in his later years became rabbi of Cologne. His famous son, R' Eliezer (*Ravyah*), took over that position when R' Yoel passed away in the year 1200.

בְּמִצְוֹתֶיךָ דַּלּוֹתִי חֶלְקִי וְחִשְׁקִי — *Regarding Your mitzvos I am poor [both] in my portion and in my desire.* The translation follows virtually all the commentaries. Alternatively,

חֶלְקִי, *my Portion* (see *Psalms* 119:57) and חִשְׁקִי, *my Desire* (see 91:14) refer to God, and the stich reads: *Regarding Your mitzvos I am poor, O my Portion, my Desire* [YL].

גַּלֵּה נַרְתֵּק מַרְפֵּא — *Reveal the sheath [to provide] healing.* The primeval light created at the beginning of the world enabled man to see from one end of the world to other. But when God looked into the future and saw the perverse deeds of the generations of the Flood (see *Genesis* 6:5-12) and of the Dispersion (see ibid. 11:1-9), He concealed that light. In Time to Come, He will unveil that light for the righteous (*Chagigah* 12a).

In Time to Come, God will remove the sun מִנַּרְתִּיקָהּ, *from its sheath.* The wicked will be punished by it, and the righteous will be healed by it (*Avodah Zarah* 3b). Thus, we pray that God remove the sheath from the

וְעָנְתָה בִּי צִדְקָתִי לְיוֹצְרִי,

《 to my   〈 shall my   〈 for 〈 and testify
Creator,   integrity   me

בְּיוֹם מָחָר* כִּי תָבוֹא עַל שְׂכָרִי.[1]

《 my   〈 to   〈 You   〈when 〈 of the mor- 〈 on the
reward.   consider   come   row [Rosh   day
Hashanah],*

דְּפִי כַּבֵּס וְלַבֵּן אֲדַמְדָּם, דְּרֹשׁ אֶת עֲפַר יְסוֹדָם,[3][2]

《 that is their 〈 the dust 〈 consider 《 [sin's bloody] 〈 and 〈 wash 〈 Imper-
foundation,   redness;   whiten   away,   fection

וְאַל תְּשַׁלֵּם כִּגְמוּל יָדָם, כִּי רַבָּה רָעַת הָאָדָם.[5][4]

《 of man. 〈 is the 〈 great 〈 for 《 for the work 〈 as they 〈 repay 〈 and
wickedness   of their hands, deserve   them   do not

הַנֶּפֶשׁ הַחֹטֵאת בַּמֶּה תִּתְכַּפֵּר,

《 will it atone 〈 — with 《 that sins 〈 The soul
for itself?   what

הוֹן לֹא יוֹעִיל וְרֹב כֹּפֶר,[6]

《 ransom. 〈 [nor] 〈 avail, 〈 will 〈Wealth
abundant   not

הֶעֱמַדְתָּ עֵד* מְמַהֵר לִסְפֵּר, מִבַּיִת וּמִחוּץ בַּכֹּפֶר.[7]

《exhibiting 〈 and [deeds] 〈 [thoughts] 〈 to recount 〈 swift 〈 a 〈 You have
lack of belief.   from without   from within   witness*   appointed

---

(1) Cf. *Genesis* 30:33. (2) Cf. *Isaiah* 1:18. (3) Cf. *Job* 4:19. (4) Cf. *Isaiah* 3:11.
(5) *Genesis* 6:5. (6) Cf. *Proverbs* 11:4; *Job* 36:18. (7) *Genesis* 6:14.

sun, that it may become a vessel of healing for us.

בְּיוֹם מָחָר — *On the morrow [Rosh Hasha-nah].* The translation reflects most of the commentaries. Alternatively, this stanza is based on three well-known Aggadic passages: (a) The word מָחָר refers to the Day of Reckoning in Time to Come (see preceding comment), for יֵשׁ מָחָר שֶׁהוּא עַכְשָׁיו, *there is an immediate "tomorrow,"* וְיֵשׁ מָחָר שֶׁהוּא לְאַחַר זְמָן, *and there is a future "tomorrow"* (*Tanchuma, Rashi* to *Exodus* 13:14); (b) שָׂכָר מִצְוָה בְּהַאי עָלְמָא לֵיכָּא, *a mitzvah's [prime] reward is not given in this world [but in the World to Come]* (*Kiddushin* 39b); and (c) all the *mitzvos* that Israel does in this world will come forward to testify on their behalf in the World to Come (*Avodah Zarah* 2a).

הֶעֱמַדְתָּ עֵד — *You have appointed a witness.* According to most commentaries this refers to the Evil Inclination, which becomes Satan, the Accuser. For, as the Talmud teaches: The Evil Inclination leads a man astray in this world, then testifies against him in the World to Come (*Succah* 52b).

According to *Matteh Levi,* however, the stich is translated, *You have appointed [Yourself] a witness,* and is based on the Mishnah (*Avos* 4:29): He is God; He is the Fashioner; He is the Creator; He is the Discerner; He is the Judge; He is the Witness ....

A third interpretation is that a different witness is appointed for each deed. This is based on the Talmud's response to the question: And what if a person will ask, "Who will testify against me?" Four opinions are cited regarding this point: (a) The stones and

וּמַה יְכַפֵּר וּבְיָדוֹ סְדוּרוֹת,*

‹ are ‹ when by his ‹ can man ‹ How
delineated* own hand deny,

(וְתֵק) עֲוַת מַעֲשָׂיו וְכָל הַקּוֹרוֹת,

« [his life's] ‹ and ‹ deeds ‹ his ‹ (from of
events? all corrupted old)

וְאֵיךְ יֹאמַר מִי יוֹדֵעַ סְפוֹרוֹת,[1] וְהִנֵּה הַנֶּגַע בַּקִּירוֹת.[2]

« is [visible] ‹ the ‹ when « their ‹ knows ‹ Who ‹ can he ‹ How
on the walls? affliction indeed number? say,

זַכִּים הַמְלַוּים עִמָּךְ בְּכָל פֶּלֶךְ,

« place, ‹ in every ‹ you ‹ who escort ‹ The pure
[angels]

זְרִיזִים לְשָׁמְרָךְ בְּכָל אֲשֶׁר תֵּלֵךְ,[3]

« you go, ‹ that ‹ in all [places] ‹ guarding You ‹ zealously

וְשׁוֹכֶבֶת בְּחֵיק, תָּעִיד בְּעָשִׁיר וָהֵלֶךְ,*

« as well ‹ against rich ‹ testify ‹ in man's ‹ and the [soul]
as poor,* breast that rests

וְעָמְדָה לִפְנֵי הַמֶּלֶךְ.[4]

« the King. ‹ [every night] ‹ and it [the
before soul] will stand

חָלְתִּי לֹא יִכָּחֵד כֹּל מֶנְהוּ,[5]

« from ‹ will any- ‹ hidden ‹ — not « I tremble
Him; thing be

---

(1) Cf. *Psalms* 71:15. (2) *Leviticus* 14:37. (3) Cf. *Genesis* 28:15.
(4) *I Kings* 1:2. (5) Cf. *II Samuel* 18:13.

beams of a person's house will testify against him; (b) two ministering angels escort a man wherever he goes and will bear witness; (c) a man's own soul will speak against him; and (d) a person's own limbs will testify (*Taanis* 11a). Following this interpretation, the next stich, מִבַּיִת וּמִחוּץ בַּכֹּפֶר, would be translated, *whether the disbeliever's acts took place inside* — so that the stones and beams of his house will testify against him — *or outside* — where his angelic escort becomes his witness. Alternatively, his own soul testifies to his inner thoughts, while his limbs testify against his outward deeds. The *selichah* continues by elaborating on the role of each of these witnesses.

וּבְיָדוֹ סְדוּרוֹת — *When by his own hand are*

delineated. At the time of a person's departure to his eternal home, all his wordly deeds take leave of him. And they say to him, "Did you do thus and thus at such-and-such place on such-and-such day?" He responds, "Yes!" They say, "Sign!" And he signs [to attest to the record's accuracy]. This is all in accord with the verse (*Job* 37:7), בְּיַד כָּל אָדָם יַחְתּוֹם, *He has it signed by the hand of every man* (*Taanis* 11a). Thus, *his own hand has delineated* the litany of his sins.

וָהֵלֶךְ — *As well as poor* [lit., *traveler* or *vagrant*]. The Midrash (*Vayikra Rabbah* 34:6; cf. *Midrash Mishlei* 23) lists eight names by which Scripture calls a pauper: עָנִי, *afflicted* (*Exodus* 22:24); אֶבְיוֹן, *unfulfilled* (ibid. 23:6); מִסְכֵּן, *endangered* (*Ecclesiastes*

חַוּוֹת לְאָדָם מַה שִּׂיחֵהוּ,[1]

《 will be [even] what 〈 to a man 〈 conveyed
he spoke casually —

וְאִם עַל הַמִּשְׁכָּב הוּא,*

《 he is —* 〈 [his] bed 〈 upon 〈 and
even if

וְחִשַּׁב עִם קוֹנֵהוּ.[2]

《 his 〈 with 〈 he must make
Maker.   a reckoning

טֶרֶם יִתְנַגְּפוּ רַגְלֶיךָ[3] בְּעֶרָבוֹן,*

《 in [their] 〈 do your 〈 stub 〈 Before
pledge,*   feet   themselves

טַהֵר עַצְמְךָ מִכָּל עָוֹן,

《 iniquity! 〈 from every 〈 yourself 〈 purify

לֹא יוּכַל לְהִמָּלֵט בְּכָל עִזָּבוֹן,*

《 the wealth he 〈 [not even] 《 to escape, 〈 able 〈 One
leaves behind,*   for all   is not

---

(1) Cf. *Amos* 4:13. (2) *Leviticus* 25:50. (3) Cf. *Jeremiah* 13:16.

4:13); רָשׁ, *impoverished* (*I Samuel* 18:23);
דַּל, *detached* [from his ancestral property]
(*Exodus* 23:3); דָּךְ, *oppressed* (*Psalms* 9:10);
מָךְ, *trampled upon* (*Leviticus* 27:8); and
הֵלֶךְ, *vagrant* (*II Samuel* 12:4).

וְאִם עַל הַמִּשְׁכָּב הוּא — *And even if upon [his]
bed he is.* There is a triple meaning here:
(a) Each night while the body lies asleep in
bed, the soul leaves the body and ascends to
heaven, where it must make an accounting
for its day; (b) upon his death, all a man's
life activities are recounted to him, even his
casual words with his wife during their in-
timacy (*Chagigah* 5b); and (c) "bed" alludes
to man's final resting place, his grave, for
each person must give an accounting for his
entire life "before the King Who reigns over
kings, the Holy One, Blessed is He" (*Avos*
3:1). According to (a) and (c), this stich is connected to the next one: *And even when he is
on his bed, he must make a reckoning with
his Master.* According to (b), the stich is a
continuation of the previous one: *Man will
be told even his casual talk, and even [that
which he speaks] when he is on his bed.*

טֶרֶם יִתְנַגְּפוּ רַגְלֶיךָ בְּעֶרָבוֹן — *Before stub themselves do your feet in [their] pledge.* This is
an allusion to death, as the Talmud (*Succah*
53a) states: A man's feet are his guarantors;
[on the day he is to die] they lead him to the

place decreed for him [to die].

The Talmud tells a story to illustrate this
point. King Solomon had two handsome
scribes, Elicharaf and Achiyah the sons of
Shisha. One day, the king saw the Angel
of Death looking very sad. He asked, "Why
are you so sad?"

"I am to take the souls of the two handsome men that reside here," replied the
Angel of Death.

Solomon hastily dispatched them to the
town of Luz [where the Angel of Death was
not permitted entry (see *Nedarim* 46b)]. As
they were about to enter the town, they died.

The next day, the king spied the Angel of
Death laughing. "Why are you laughing?"
he asked.

"You sent them to the exact spot [the
gateway to Luz] where I was to take their
souls." [Yesterday's sadness was not because
I had to take their souls; it was because they
were not in the right place and I did not
know how to get them there.]

Immediately, Solomon said, "A man's feet
are his guarantors; they lead him to the place
decreed for him."

עִזָּבוֹן — *The wealth he leaves behind.* In
Scripture, this word is found only in Chapter
27 of *Ezekiel* (vs. 12-33), where it is used to
describe exported merchandise. Its derivation

יֹאמְרוּ הַמּוֹשְׁלִים בֹּאוּ חֶשְׁבּוֹן.¹

[then] ⟨ those who rule, ⟨ *Come* ⟨ **to an**
will say   accounting! ⟩⟩

יִעַד אַרְבָּעָה פְרָקִים* וְהֶחֱרִית,

⟨ and engraved ⟨ junctures ⟨ four ⟨ He des-
[their nature in them]: [in the year]*   ignated ⟩⟩⟩

יָדוּן בָּמוֹ נַחֲלַת שְׁאֵרִית,

⟨ who are the ⟨ [the people] ⟨ on ⟨ He would
remnant.   of His heritage   them   judge ⟩⟩⟩

וְאִם מָעֲלוּ בְךָ, הַבֵּט לַבְּרִית,

⟨ to the ⟨ look ⟨ You, ⟨ they have ⟨ And if
covenant,   betrayed ⟩⟩⟩

וְאַל תַּעֲמֹד עַל הַפֶּרֶק לְהַכְרִית.²

⟨ to cut down. ⟨ the juncture ⟨ at ⟨ stand ⟨ and do
[of the year]   not ⟩⟩⟩

כִּי בְיוֹם כֶּסֶה* יָבֹא³ כָּל מִקְרֶה אִישׁ לִפְנֵי חוֹצְבוֹ,

⟨ his ⟨ before ⟨ of a man ⟨ event ⟨ every ⟨ there ⟨ [when the ⟨ on the day ⟨ For
Shaper;   comes   moon is]   [Rosh
                                              concealed,* Hashanah] ⟩⟩⟩⟩⟩⟩

אִם דַּל אִם עָשִׁיר בְּרִיבוֹ, עוֹלִים וְיוֹרְדִים בּוֹ.⁴

⟨ based ⟨ and ⟨ ascending ⟨ [it will come] to ⟨ rich, ⟨ or ⟨ poor ⟨ whether
on it.   descending   his judgment, ⟩⟩⟩⟩⟩⟩

---

(1) *Numbers* 21:27. (2) *Obadiah* 1:14. (3) Cf. *Proverbs* 7:20; *Psalms* 81:4. (4) *Genesis* 28:12.

from the root עזב, *to forsake* or *leave behind*, is discussed by the commentaries. Some of the explanations given are: A dealer *forsakes* his merchandise in the country to which it is exported (*Ibn Janach, Shorashim*); a merchant may sell his wares cheaply, *forsaking* part of its value, in order to attract customers (*R' Eliezer of Beaugency*); any article that is sold is *forsaken* by the seller (*HaKesav VeHaKabbalah* to *Deuteronomy* 32:36); and goods are often *forsaken* in warehouses for long periods of time (*Malbim*). Interestingly, *Targum* (to *Ezekiel*) alternates between *wares* and *storage houses* for the word עֶזָּבוֹן.

In post-Biblical times, the word took on a more specific meaning: the legacy or heritage that one forsakes and passes on to his heirs when he leaves this world.

יִעַד אַרְבָּעָה פְרָקִים — *He designated four junctures [in the year].* The Mishnah teaches: At four junctures [of the year] the world is judged: on Pesach for the grain; on Shavuos for the fruit of the tree; on Rosh Hashanah all who walk the earth pass before Him like young sheep; and on Succos for the water (*Rosh Hashanah* 16a).

בְּיוֹם כֶּסֶה — *On the day [Rosh Hashanah when the moon is] concealed.* The full Scriptural verse reads: תִּקְעוּ בַחֹדֶשׁ שׁוֹפָר, *Blow the shofar at the moon's renewal*, בַּכֶּסֶה לְיוֹם חַגֵּנוּ, *when it [the moon] is covered for our festive day* (*Psalms* 81:4). All Jewish holidays other than Rosh Hashanah occur in the middle of the month, when the major part of the moon is visible. Only Rosh Hashanah occurs at the very beginning of the month, when the moon is still covered (*Rosh Hashanah* 8a).

Alternatively, the word כֶּסֶה means *appointed time* (*Rashi, Radak, Ibn Ezra*).

לְעַמְּךָ מֵלִיץ יֹשֶׁר תְּמַנֶּה, לְעֵת יָבֹאוּ כָּל בְּנֵי

‹ the ‹ all ‹ when ‹ for the ‹ You should ‹ who is ‹ an ‹ For Your
sons shall time [Rosh appoint, righteous advocate people
come Hashanah],

אָדָם בְּשִׁבְטוֹ לְהִמָּנֶה,

《 to be counted, ‹ under His rod ‹ of Man

תַּעֲבֹרְנָה הַצֹּאן עַל יְדֵי מוֹנֶה.[1]

《 of the one ‹ the ‹ before ‹ do the ‹ [just as] pass
who counts hands flock
[them].

מִשְׁפָּט עַמּוֹ תְּחִלָּה* בְּקֶרֶב,

《 should be brought ‹ first of all* ‹ of His ‹ The
[before Him], people judgment

מִשַּׁחַת תַּעַל חַיָּתָם לְטוֹב תַּעֲרֹב,

《 ensure their ‹ and for ‹ their ‹ You may ‹ so that
welfare. good souls raise from ruin

וְיָדִין לְאֻמִּים לְבַדָּם מִלַּעֲרֹב,

《 not to 《 by ‹ the peoples ‹ Then
mix them, themselves, judge

לְבִלְתִּי הֱיוֹת שָׁם עָרֹב.[2]

《 intermingling ‹ there ‹ be ‹ so that
[of judgments]. there not

נָאוֹר[3] אֵלֶיךָ מִי יֵחָבֵר,

《 can be ‹ who ‹ to You 《 O Source
compared? of Light,

נוֹהֵג שֶׁבָּעוֹלָם, אֵין מִשְׁתַּמֵּשׁ בִּכְלִי מְשֻׁבָּר,

《 that is broken, ‹ a vessel ‹ to use ‹ is not ‹ of the world ‹ The way

וְלֹא תִבְזֶה לֵב נִדְכֶּה וְנִשְׁבָּר,[4]

《 and broken. ‹ that is ‹ a ‹ yet You do not
crushed heart despise

הֲיִפָּלֵא מֵיהוה דָּבָר.[5]

《 any- ‹ of ‹ Is there beyond
thing?! HASHEM the capability

(1) Jeremiah 33:13. (2) Exodus 8:18. (3) See commentary to Selichah 18.
(4) Cf. Psalms 51:19. (5) Genesis 18:14.

תְּחִלָּה — First of all. When a king and his nation are brought before the Heavenly Tribunal for judgment, the king is judged first, lest his fate be sealed by the Divine wrath unleashed by the sins of his people. Similarly, when all the world stands in judgment before the Heavenly Tribunal, Israel is judged first, lest its fate be sealed by the Divine wrath unleashed by the sins of the nations (Rosh Hashanah 8b).

סַתְּתוּ אֶבֶן נֶגֶף* לְעֵמֶק שָׁוֶה,

《 that is 〈 until it is 〈 that strikes 〈 the 〈 Chip away
level;   a plain   people*   stone   at

סוּרוּ טָמֵא, קְרְאוּ¹ כְּסִיל הַמַּחְבָא,

《who is hidden; 〈 to the 〈 call 《 the 〈 Remove,
fool   defilement,

כִּי אֵין הַצָּר בְּנֶזֶק שׁוֶה,²

《 care. 〈 about the 〈 the Adversary 〈 for
damage   does not
[he causes us]

הָבָה נִתְחַכְּמָה לוֹ פֶּן יִרְבֶּה.³

《 he 〈 lest 〈 with 〈 let us deal 〈 Come,
increase.   him,   wisely

עוֹבֵד שְׁנֵי אֲדוֹנִים כְּפִי שָׁנָיו,

《 his 〈 through- 〈 masters 〈 two 〈 [A man,]
years,   out   who serves

עֲשׂוֹת לְיוֹצְרוֹ וּלְיִצְרוֹ כִּרְצוֹנָיו,

《 according to 〈 or for his [Evil] 〈 for his 〈 doing
his own will —   Inclination,   Maker

וְטוֹב הִדָּבֵק לְבוֹרְאוֹ כָּל זְמַנָּיו,

《 his days, 〈 all 〈 to his 《 to cling 〈 better
Creator   for him

וְעֶבֶד חָפְשִׁי מֵאֲדוֹנָיו.⁴

《 from his 〈 free 《 [until he dies]
[evil] masters.   and is like a slave,

פְּנוֹת הַיּוֹם* סְעוּדָתוֹ יָכֵן,

《 one 〈 his meal 〈 of the day 〈 If toward
prepares,   [Friday]*   the end

פָּעֳלוֹ לָזֶה וְלַבָּא יְהִי נָכוֹן,

《 ready. 〈 will 〈 and in the 〈 both in this 〈 his
be [World] to Come   [world]   deeds

---

(1) Cf. *Lamentations* 4:15. (2) Cf. *Esther* 7:4. (3) *Exodus* 1:10. (4) *Job* 3:18.

אֶבֶן נֶגֶף — *The stone that strikes people.* This alludes to the Evil Inclination. See commentary to *Selichah* 24 (s.v. מִכְשׁוֹל) regarding the various names by which the Evil Inclination is known.

פְּנוֹת הַיּוֹם — *If toward the end of the day [Friday].* The Talmud compares the World to Come to the Sabbath: If one exerts himself on the eve of the Sabbath [he performs *mitzvos* in this world], he will eat on the Sabbath [he will reap his reward in the World to Come]; but one who does not exert himself on the eve of the Sabbath, what will he eat on the Sabbath? (*Avodah Zarah* 3a).

1. וְעוֹשֵׂהוּ בַּשַׁבָּת מַה יִּסְכָּן, מְעֻוָּת לֹא יוּכַל לְתַקֵּן.

« to be made ‹ able ‹ that is ‹ It is a « does it « what « on the ‹ But if he
straight. not twisted thing avail? Sabbath, makes it

צְעָקָה לָכֵן קִדַּמְנוּ לְיוֹם הַדִּין, וְתַקְשִׁיב,

« and You « of ‹ the Day ‹ we began ‹ there- ‹ Crying out
will listen. Judgment, before

צוֹם* וּתְשׁוּבָה שְׁלֵמָה חֲמָתְךָ יָשִׁיב,

« will ‹ Your « that is ‹ and ‹ [Our]
conciliate. anger complete, repentance fasting,*

3. וְלֹא כְּשָׁב עַל קֵאוֹ בְּאֶחֱטָא וְאָשִׁיב,

« and I will ‹ [saying,] ‹ his ‹ to ‹ like one ‹ [We will]
repent. I will sin vomit, who returns not [be]

4. לֹא מָצְאָה יָדוֹ דֵּי הָשִׁיב.

« repent. ‹ to ‹ at hand ‹ find ‹ but
fully [the time] does not

קוּמוּ יְשֵׁנֵי מַכְפֵּל* לְסַעֲדִי, קַלּוֹתִי וּמַעַשׂ אֵין בְּיָדִי,

« in my ‹ are ‹ and [good] « I am « to my aid! ‹ in the ‹ O [you] ‹ Arise
hand. not deeds embarrassed, Machpelah* sleepers

וְזַעֲקוּ וְהִתְפַּלְלוּ לְאֵל עִמָּדִי,

« along with me, ‹ to God ‹ and pray ‹ Shout

5. וּמִכֹּחֲכֶם שַׁחֲדוּ בַעֲדִי.

« for me. ‹ offer a ‹ and from your
bribe wealth [of mitzvos]

6. רַחֲמִים תְּעוֹרֵר, לָתֵת עָצְמָה לְאֵין אוֹנִים,

« might, ‹ to those ‹ strength ‹ to give ‹ awaken, ‹ Mercy
who have no

רָם, כִּי נִשְׁכְּחוּ זֶה כַּמֶּה שָׁנִים,

« a year. ‹ many ‹ this ‹ they have ‹ for « O Lofty
been forgotten One,

7. שַׁעֲרֵי דְמָעוֹת תִּפְתַּח לְנִטְעֵי נַעֲמָנִים,

« that are ‹ to [Israel, ‹ open ‹ of Tears ‹ The Gates
pleasant; Your] plantings

(1) *Ecclesiastes* 1:15. (2) Cf. *Proverbs* 26:11. (3) See *Yoma* 85b.
(4) *Leviticus* 25:28. (5) *Job* 6:22. (6) Cf. *Isaiah* 40:29. (7) Cf. 17:10.

צוֹם — *[Our]fasting.* Some editions of *Selichos*
read צְדָקָה, *charity.* It has been suggested that
those people who follow the ancient custom
of fasting on Erev Rosh Hashanah should
recite the word צוֹם. However, those who are

unable to fast should substitute the word
צְדָקָה, so their words do not sound false.

יְשֵׁנֵי מַכְפֵּל — *O [you] sleepers in the Mach-*
pelah. Four patriarchal couples were buried
in the Cave of Machpelah: Adam and Eve;

בִּבְכִי יָבֹאוּ וּבְתַחֲנוּנִים.[1]

《 and with supplications. 〈 they will come 〈 with weeping

שַׁדַּי, בְּמֶרְיֵנוּ הֲלוֹא כִּנָכְרִים נֶחְשַׁבְנוּ,[2]

《 regarded [by You]? 〈 as strangers 〈 were we 〈 when we not 〈 rebelled 〈 O Almighty,

שַׁבְנוּ אֵלֶיךָ, וּכְאָב עַל בֵּן תְּרַחֲמֵנוּ,[3]

《 have mercy on us. 〈 [his] child 〈 to-ward 〈 [so now] as a father 《 to You; 〈 [But] we have returned

זְכֹר כִּי בָנִים[4] קְרָאתָנוּ, וְאָב אֶחָד לְכֻלָּנוּ,[5]

《 for us all; 〈 and that there is one Father 〈 You called us 〈 children 〈 that 〈 Re-member

לָמָה יִגָּרַע שֵׁם אָבִינוּ.[6]

《 of our Father? 〈 the name 〈 should be diminished 〈 why

תְּשׁוּרָה אֵין בְּיָדִי לְפָנַי,

《 [to send] in my hand 〈 there is not 〈 Tribute before me;

תְּמוּרָתָה תִּכּוֹן תְּפִלָּתִי וְתַחֲנוּנִי,[7]

《 and my supplication. 〈 should be my prayer 〈 consid-ered 《 in its place,

קַח נָא אֶת הַמִּנְחָה הַהוֹלֶכֶת לְפָנַי,[8]

《before me, 〈 that goes 〈 this offering 〈 please, 〈 Take,

וְיֵדְעוּ (כָל) הָעָם הַזֶּה כִּי אַתָּה יהוה.[9]

《 HASHEM. 〈 You are 〈 that 《 — this (entire) people — 《 and let them know

יָדַע וְהֵכִין[10] מֵרֵאשִׁית תְּשׁוּבָה,*

《 repentance —* 〈 from before Creation 〈 so He prepared 《He knew [man would sin],

---

(1) *Jeremiah* 31:8. (2) Cf. *Genesis* 31:15. (3) Cf. *Psalms* 103:13. (4) See *Deuteronomy* 14:1.
(5) Cf. *Malachi* 2:10. (6) *Numbers* 27:4. (7) Cf. *Psalms* 141:2. (8) Cf. *Genesis* 32:21.
(9) *I Kings* 18:37. (10) Some editions read: יִדַע וְהֵכִין, *He made known that He had prepared.*

Abraham and Sarah; Isaac and Rebecca; Jacob and Leah (*Eruvin* 53a; *Genesis* 49:31).

וְהֵכִין מֵרֵאשִׁית תְּשׁוּבָה — *So He prepared from before Creation repentance.* Seven things were created before the creation of the world [God laid out their creation in His

thoughts (*Rabbeinu Nissim*)]: Torah, *teshuvah* (repentance), *Gan Eden, Gehinnom,* the Throne of Glory, the *Beis HaMikdash,* and the name of the Messiah …. That *teshuvah* preceded Creation is derived from *Psalms* 90:2-3: *Before the mountains were born and*

אֱלֹהִים חֲשָׁבָהּ לְטוֹבָה,¹ בְּכֵן רַצֵנוּ עָדֶיךָ לָשׁוּבָה,

《 to repent; 〈 to You 〈 we run 〈Therefore 《 for [man's] 〈 intended it 〈 God
benefit.

הֲשִׁיבֵנוּ יהוה אֵלֶיךָ וְנָשׁוּבָה.²

《 and we shall 〈 to You, 〈 HASHEM, 〈bring us back,
return.

❖ יְדִידִים צָעֲקוּ חֵלוּ,³ קָרוֹת בִּמְהוּמִים,

《 in tumultuous 〈 calling 《 they 〈 cry out, 〈 [His] beloved
assembly; [to Him] tremble, ones

הַקּוֹל לִמְכוֹן וְעוֹדוֹ יִשָּׁמַע מִמְּרוֹמִים,

《 [there] on high. 〈 be heard 〈 of His 〈 [come] 〈 may the
assembly to the hall sound

יִכָּמְרוּ רַחֲמָיו, בִּזְכוּת שְׁלֹשֶׁת תְּמִימִים,

《wholesome ones 〈 of the three 〈 in the 〈 may His 〈 Aroused
[the Patriarchs] — merit mercy be

אֵל שַׁדַּי, יִתֵּן לָכֶם רַחֲמִים.⁴

《 mercy. 〈 you 〈 grant 〈Almighty 〈 may
God

ALL, WHILE STANDING:

אֵל מֶלֶךְ יוֹשֵׁב עַל כִּסֵּא רַחֲמִים, מִתְנַהֵג

〈 Who acts 《 of mercy, 〈 the throne 〈 on 〈Who sits 〈 King 〈 O God,

בַּחֲסִידוּת, מוֹחֵל עֲוֹנוֹת עַמּוֹ, מַעֲבִיר רִאשׁוֹן

〈[sins,] one 〈 Who 《 of His 〈 the sins 〈 Who 《 with kindness,
removes people, pardons

רִאשׁוֹן,⁵ מַרְבֶּה מְחִילָה לַחֲטָאִים וּסְלִיחָה לַפּוֹשְׁעִים,

《 to willful 〈 and 〈 to unintentional 〈 pardon 〈 Who abun- 《 by one,
sinners, forgiveness sinners dantly grants

עוֹשֶׂה צְדָקוֹת עִם כָּל בָּשָׂר וָרוּחַ, לֹא כְרָעָתָם

〈 in accord with 〈 — not 《 and 〈 [beings 〈 all 〈 with 〈 acts of 〈 Who
their wickedness spirit of] flesh generosity performs

תִּגְמוֹל. ❖ אֵל הוֹרֵיתָ לָנוּ לוֹמַר שְׁלֹשׁ עֶשְׂרֵה, וּזְכוֹר

〈 remem- 《 the Thirteen 〈 to 〈 us 〈 You 〈 O God, 《 do You
ber [Attributes of Mercy]; recite taught repay them!

---

(1) *Genesis* 50:20. (2) *Lamentations* 5:21. (3) Some editions read: חָלוּ, *they pray.*
(4) Cf. *Genesis* 43:14. (5) *Rosh Hashanah* 17a.

You had not yet fashioned the earth ... You   39b; see also commentary to *Selichah* 42, s.v.
say, "Repent, O sons of man!" (Nedarim   אָז טֶרֶם).

לָנוּ הַיּוֹם בְּרִית שְׁלֹשׁ עֶשְׂרֵה, כְּמוֹ שֶׁהוֹדַעְתָּ לֶעָנָיו

⟨ to the humble ⟨ You made ⟨ as ⟪ of [these] Thirteen, ⟨ the ⟨ today ⟨ for us
one [Moses] known　　　　　　　　　　　　　covenant

מִקֶּדֶם, כְּמוֹ שֶׁכָּתוּב, וַיֵּרֶד יהוה בֶּעָנָן וַיִּתְיַצֵּב עִמּוֹ

⟨ with ⟨ and stood ⟨ in a ⟨ And HASHEM ⟪ it is written: ⟨ as ⟪ in ancient
him　　　　　　cloud　descended　　　　　　　　times,

שָׁם, וַיִּקְרָא בְשֵׁם יהוה.[1]

⟪ of ⟨ with the ⟨ and He ⟪ there,
HASHEM.　Name　called out

CONGREGATION, THEN *CHAZZAN*:

וַיַּעֲבֹר יהוה עַל פָּנָיו וַיִּקְרָא:

⟪ and ⟪ [Moses'] ⟨ before ⟨ And HASHEM passed
proclaimed:　face,

CONGREGATION AND *CHAZZAN* RECITE LOUDLY AND IN UNISON:

יהוה, יהוה, אֵל, רַחוּם, וְחַנּוּן, אֶרֶךְ אַפַּיִם,

⟨ to anger, ⟨ Slow ⟪ and ⟨ Compassionate ⟨ God, ⟨ HASHEM, ⟨ HASHEM,
Gracious,

וְרַב חֶסֶד, וֶאֱמֶת, נֹצֵר חֶסֶד לָאֲלָפִים, נֹשֵׂא עָוֹן,

⟨ of ⟨ Forgiver ⟪ for ⟨ of ⟨ Preserver ⟪ and ⟨ in ⟨ and
iniquity,　　　thousands　kindness　　　Truth,　Kindness Abundant
[of generations],

וָפֶשַׁע, וְחַטָּאָה, וְנַקֵּה.[2] וְסָלַחְתָּ לַעֲוֹנֵנוּ וּלְחַטָּאתֵנוּ

⟪ and our sins, ⟨ our ⟨ May You ⟪ and Who ⟨ and inadvertent ⟨ willful sin,
iniquities　forgive　absolves.　sin,

וּנְחַלְתָּנוּ.[3] סְלַח לָנוּ אָבִינוּ כִּי חָטָאנוּ, מְחַל לָנוּ

⟨ us, ⟨ pardon ⟪ we have ⟨ for ⟪ our ⟨ us, ⟨ Forgive ⟪ and make us
sinned;　　Father,　　　　Your heritage.

מַלְכֵּנוּ כִּי פָשָׁעְנוּ. כִּי אַתָּה אֲדֹנָי טוֹב וְסַלָּח,

⟪ and ⟨ are ⟨ O Lord, ⟨ You, ⟨ For ⟪ we have ⟨ for ⟪ our King,
forgiving,　good　　　　　　　willfully sinned.

וְרַב חֶסֶד לְכָל קֹרְאֶיךָ.[4]

⟪ who call ⟨ to all ⟨ kind ⟨ and
upon You.　　　　　abundantly

---

(1) *Exodus* 34:5. (2) 34:6-7. (3) 34:9. (4) *Psalms* 86:5.

פסוקי הקדמה לסליחה כז / PREFATORY VERSES TO SELICHAH 27

1. יְהוֹה, בְּקֶר תִּשְׁמַע קוֹלֵנוּ, בְּקֶר נַעֲרָךְ לְךָ וַנְצַפֶּה.

» and we wait ‹ to ‹as we arrange‹ at » our ‹ hear ‹ at ‹ HASHEM, expectantly. You [our prayer] dawn voice; dawn

2. וְאַתָּה יְהוֹה מָגֵן בַּעֲדֵנוּ, כְּבוֹדֵנוּ וּמֵרִים רֹאשֵׁנוּ.

» our ‹ and the One » for our » for us, ‹ are a ‹ HASHEM, ‹ For You, heads. Who raises soul; shield

3. אַתָּה יְהוֹה לְעוֹלָם תֵּשֵׁב, כִּסְאֲךָ לְדוֹר וָדוֹר. אֹהֵב

‹ He » to gen- ‹ is from ‹ Your » are ‹ forever ‹ HASHEM, ‹ Yet You, loves eration generation throne enthroned;

4. צְדָקָה וּמִשְׁפָּט, חֶסֶד יְהוֹה מָלְאָה הָאָרֶץ. רַחֲמֶיךָ

‹ Your » the earth. ‹ fills ‹ of ‹ the » and justice; ‹ righteous- mercies HASHEM kindness ness

5. רַבִּים יְהוֹה, כְּמִשְׁפָּטֶיךָ חַיֵּנוּ. וְאַל תָּבוֹא בְמִשְׁפָּט

‹ into strict ‹ Do not enter » preserve ‹ as is » HASHEM; ‹ are judgment me. Your practice, abundant,

6. עִמָּנוּ, כִּי לֹא יִצְדַּק לְפָנֶיךָ כָּל חָי.

» living ‹ any » before ‹ vindicated ‹ for » with us, creature. You, would not be,

7. **כְּרַחֵם** אָב עַל בָּנִים, כֵּן תְּרַחֵם יְהוֹה עָלֵינוּ.

» on us. ‹ HASHEM, ‹ have ‹ so » his ‹ toward ‹ a ‹ As merciful as mercy, children, father is

8. לַיהוֹה הַיְשׁוּעָה, עַל עַמְּךָ בִרְכָתֶךָ סֶּלָה. יְהוֹה

‹ HASHEM, » Selah. » is Your » Your ‹ upon » is salvation, ‹ To HASHEM blessing, people

9. צְבָאוֹת עִמָּנוּ, מִשְׂגָּב לָנוּ אֱלֹהֵי יַעֲקֹב סֶּלָה.

» Selah. » of Jacob, ‹ is the God ‹ for us ‹ a » is with us, ‹ Master of stronghold Legions,

10. יְהוֹה צְבָאוֹת, אַשְׁרֵי אָדָם בֹּטֵחַ בָּךְ. יְהוֹה

‹ HASHEM, » in You. ‹ who ‹ is the ‹ — praiseworthy » Master ‹ HASHEM, trusts man of Legions

11. הוֹשִׁיעָה, הַמֶּלֶךְ יַעֲנֵנוּ בְיוֹם קָרְאֵנוּ.

» we call. ‹ on the ‹ answer ‹ May the » save! day us King

---

(1) Cf. *Psalms* 5:4. (2) Cf. 3:4. (3) *Lamentations* 5:19. (4) Cf. *Psalms* 33:5. (5) Cf. 119:156. (6) Cf. 143:2. (7) Cf. 103:13. (8) 3:9. (9) 46:8. (10) 84:13. (11) 20:10.

סליחה כז / SELICHAH 27

ALL:

(אֱלֹהֵינוּ וֵאלֹהֵי אֲבוֹתֵינוּ:)

《 of our forefathers:)〈 and God 〈 (Our God

אָדוֹן מוֹעֵד כְּתִקַּח,* מֵישָׁרִים לִשְׁפּוֹט¹ בְּתַעֲצוּמֶיךָ,

《 in Your 〈 to judge 〈 in fairness 《 when You 〈 — the ap- 《 O Lord
omnipotence, [the world] designate*— pointed time

אֶתְיַצְּבָה בְּפֶלֶץ לְחַלּוֹת פָּנֶיךָ לְרוֹמְמֶךָ,

《 [and] to exalt 〈 before 〈 to entreat 〈 in 〈 I stand forth
You. You [mercy] trepidation

בְּמַעֲשַׂי לֹא נִשְׁעַנְתִּי, כִּי אִם בְּרַחֲמֶיךָ,²

《 on Your mercy 〈 rather 〈 but 《 I rely not, 〈 On my deeds

יהוה עֲשֵׂה לְמַעַן שְׁמֶךָ.³

《 of Your 〈 for the 〈 act 〈 — O
Name! sake HASHEM,

גֵּזּוּ אֱמוּנִים,⁴ גִּבּוֹרֵי כֹחַ בְּמֶרֶץ,

《 in the rapid fluency 〈 in 〈 those 《 are the 〈 Cut
[of their prayer]; strength mighty faithful, off

גַּם גּוֹדְרֵי גֶדֶר וְעוֹמְדֵי בַפֶּרֶץ,⁴

《 in the 〈 and stand 〈 the fence 〈 are those 〈 also
breach, [of Torah] who build [gone]

דּוֹרְשֵׁי חֶפְצָם בְּכֹחַ, מִשׁוֹכֵן שְׁמֵי עֶרֶץ,

《 that are 〈 in the 〈 from the 〈 forcefully 〈 their 〈 [and] those
revered Heavens Dweller needs who [merited
to] demand

---

(1) Cf. *Psalms* 75:3; some editions of *Selichos* reverse the wording, כְּתִקַּח מוֹעֵד לִשְׁפֹּט מֵישָׁרִים, but the meaning is unchanged. (2) Cf. *Isaiah* 10:20. (3) *Jeremiah* 14:7. (4) Cf. *Psalms* 90:10, 12:2.

אָדוֹן מוֹעֵד כְּתִקַּח §— *O Lord — the appointed time when You designate.* This *selichah* and the one that begins מְרֻבִּים צָרְכֵי עַמְּךָ, *Your people's needs are many* (recited during *Neilah* on Yom Kippur), are actually one. They are divided because the theme changes halfway through the composition. In the first half, the *chazzan* speaks of his own lack of worth and his inability to achieve the level of perfection attained by the congregational emissaries of earlier generations. The second half continues with the

same theme, but in the plural, because this time the *chazzan* speaks of the shortcomings of the people who sent him, and of their desire to repent.

In *Nusach Ungarin*, the *selichah* is not divided, but is recited without interruption. In *Nusach Lita*, both halves are recited on Erev Rosh Hashanah, but as separate *selichos*.

The complete work contains an *aleph-beis* acrostic [odd-numbered letters — א,ג... — appear twice; even-numbered letters — ב,ד... — appear only once], followed by

אָבַד חָסִיד מִן הָאָֽרֶץ.[1]

《 the land. 〈 from 〈 is the 〈 — gone
pious one

הֵן קַלּוֹתִי וּמַה אָשִׁיב בְּמוֹ פִי,[2]

《 with my 〈 can I 〈 what 《 I am insig- 〈 Indeed,
mouth itself? answer nificant;

הִנְנִי צָעִיר, בְּאֵין מִפְעָלוֹת בְּכַפִּי,[3]

《 in my 〈 [good] deeds 〈 without 〈 but 〈 Indeed
hand. young, I am

וְאֵיךְ אֲקַוֶּה וַאֲנִי רַב דֹּפִי,

《 of 〈 full 〈 when I 〈 can I 〈 How,
imperfection, am hope, then,

הֱיוֹת לְרָצוֹן אִמְרֵי פִי.[4]

《 of my 〈 — the ex- 《 find 〈 that they
mouth? pressions favor will

זָחַלְתִּי וָאִירָא מֵחַוּוֹת דֵּעִי,[5]

《 my 〈 to express 〈 and I 〈 I trembled
thought; feared

זְדוֹנִי יָגֹרְתִּי וּמֶֽרֶד רִשְׁעִי,[6]

《 of my 〈 and 〈 I am 〈 [From the con-
wickedness. [from] the fright- sequences of]
rebellion ened my willful sin

חַנּוּן, רַחֲמֵֽנִי בְּהִתְוַדּוֹתִי וְעָזְבִי פְּשָׁעִי,[7]

《 my 〈 and 〈 as I confess 〈 have mercy 〈 O Gracious
sinfulness abandon on me, One,

שְׁמַע קוֹל תַּחֲנוּנַי, אֵלֶֽיךָ בְּשַׁוְּעִי.[8]

《 when I cry 〈 to You 〈 of my 〈 the 〈 — hear
out. supplications sound

טָעִֽיתִי וְהִנְנִי שָׁב וּמִתְוַדֶּה, עֲשׂוֹת רְצוֹנֶֽךָ,

《 Your will. 〈 [thus] 《 and confess, 〈 repent 〈 and 〈 I have
doing now I erred,

---

(1) Cf. *Ezekiel* 22:30. (2) *Micah* 7:2. (3) Cf. *Job* 40:4. Some editions read וּכְאַיִן מִפְעָלוֹת כַּפָּי,
and the deeds of my hand are as nothing. (4) Cf. *Psalms* 19:15. (5) *Job* 32:6.
(6) Some editions read וּמֶֽרֶד פִּשְׁעִי, *the rebellion of my sinfulness.* (7) Cf. *Proverbs* 28:13;
some editions of *Selichos* read וְעָזְבִי רִשְׁעִי, *and I abandon my wickedness.* (8) Cf. *Psalms* 28:2.

---

the composer's name — יוֹסֵף בַּר יִצְחָק, *Yosef*
bar Yitzchak. R' Yosef was a 12th-century

Tosafist who lived in Orleans, France, and is
better known as R' Yosef Bechor Shor.

טְהוֹר עֵינַיִם,¹ חָשְׁבֵנִי כְּשָׁלֵם לְפָנֶיךָ,

‹ O Pure › of Eye, ‹ consider me › as if perfect › before You. »

יָהּ, הִכָּנֵס לִי לִפְנִים מִשּׁוּרַת דִּינֶךָ,*

‹ O God, › go › for my sake › more leniently › than the strict line › of Your law* »

וְאֵדָעֲךָ לְמַעַן אֶמְצָא חֵן בְּעֵינֶיךָ.²

‹ — that I may comprehend You, » so that › I may find › favor › in Your eyes. »

❖ כֹּחֲךָ יִגְדַּל נָא³ וּבִתְפִלָּתִי הִתְנָאֵה,*

‹ Your strength, › let it be magnified, » please, › and with my prayer › adorn Yourself,* »

כִּתְפִלַּת זָקֵן וְרָגִיל וּפִרְקוֹ נָאֶה,

‹ as if [it were] the prayer › of a sage, › experienced [in prayer], › whose youth › was well spent. »

לְבָבִי הַנִּשְׁבָּר הַנִּדְכֶּה וְהַנִּכְאֶה,⁴

‹ My heart › that is broken, › humbled, › and shattered »

הַבֵּט מִשָּׁמַיִם וּרְאֵה.⁵

‹ — O look down › from Heaven › and see [it]! »

ALL, WHILE STANDING:

אֵל מֶלֶךְ יוֹשֵׁב עַל כִּסֵּא רַחֲמִים, מִתְנַהֵג

‹ O God, › King › Who sits › on › the throne › of mercy, » Who acts ›

בַּחֲסִידוּת, מוֹחֵל עֲוֹנוֹת עַמּוֹ, מַעֲבִיר רִאשׁוֹן

» with kindness, › Who pardons › the sins › of His people, » Who removes › one [sins,] ›

רִאשׁוֹן,⁶ מַרְבֶּה מְחִילָה לַחַטָּאִים וּסְלִיחָה לַפּוֹשְׁעִים,

» by one, › Who abundantly grants › pardon › to unintentional sinners › and forgiveness › to willful sinners, »

---

(1) *Habakkuk* 1:13. (2) *Exodus* 33:13. (3) Cf. *Numbers* 14:17. (4) Cf. *Psalms* 51:19; 109:16. (5) 80:15. (6) *Rosh Hashanah* 17a.

לִפְנִים מִשּׁוּרַת דִּינֶךָ — *More leniently than the strict line of Your law.* The word לִפְנִים means *within*; however, the English expression *within the line of the law* has the opposite meaning of the Hebrew expression. The phrase לִפְנִים מִשּׁוּרַת הַדִּין implies a merciful lenience that goes far beyond the letter of the law.

וּבִתְפִלָּתִי הִתְנָאֵה — *And with my prayer adorn Yourself.* There is an angel ... named Sandalfon ... who stands behind the Divine Chariot weaving crowns for his Creator (*Chagigah* 13b). These crowns are woven from the prayers of the righteous (*Tosafos*). This is the meaning of the *Kedushah* recited at *Mussaf* [*Nusach Sefard*] which begins: כֶּתֶר יִתְּנוּ

עֹשֶׂה צְדָקוֹת עִם כָּל בָּשָׂר וָרוּחַ, לֹא כְרָעָתָם

⟨ in accord with ⟨ — not ⟪ and ⟨ [beings ⟨ all ⟪ with ⟨ acts of ⟨ Who
their wickedness   spirit   of] flesh   generosity   performs

תִגְמוֹל. ❖ אֵל הוֹרֵיתָ לָּנוּ לוֹמַר שְׁלֹשׁ עֶשְׂרֵה, וּזְכוֹר

⟨ remem- ⟪ the Thirteen ⟨ to ⟨ us ⟨ You ⟨ O God, ⟪ do You
ber   [Attributes of Mercy];   recite   taught   repay them!

לָנוּ הַיּוֹם בְּרִית שְׁלֹשׁ עֶשְׂרֵה, כְּמוֹ שֶׁהוֹדַעְתָּ לֶעָנָיו

⟨ to the humble ⟨ You made ⟨ as ⟪ of [these] Thirteen, ⟨ the ⟨ today ⟨ for us
one [Moses]   known   covenant

מִקֶּדֶם, כְּמוֹ שֶׁכָּתוּב, וַיֵּרֶד יהוה בֶּעָנָן וַיִּתְיַצֵּב עִמּוֹ

⟨ with ⟨ and stood ⟨ in a ⟨ And HASHEM ⟪ it is written: ⟨ as ⟪ in ancient
him   cloud   descended   times,

שָׁם, וַיִּקְרָא בְשֵׁם יהוה.[1]

⟪ of ⟨ with the ⟨ and He ⟪ there,
HASHEM.   Name   called out

CONGREGATION, THEN CHAZZAN:

וַיַּעֲבֹר יהוה עַל פָּנָיו וַיִּקְרָא:

⟪ and ⟪ [Moses'] ⟨ before ⟨ And HASHEM passed
proclaimed: face,

CONGREGATION AND CHAZZAN RECITE LOUDLY AND IN UNISON:

יהוה, יהוה, אֵל, רַחוּם, וְחַנּוּן, אֶרֶךְ אַפַּיִם,

⟨ to anger, ⟨ Slow ⟪ and ⟨ Compassionate ⟨ God, ⟨ HASHEM, ⟨ HASHEM,
Gracious,

וְרַב חֶסֶד, וֶאֱמֶת, נֹצֵר חֶסֶד לָאֲלָפִים, נֹשֵׂא עָוֹן,

⟨ of ⟨ Forgiver ⟪ for thousands ⟨ of ⟨ Preserver ⟪ and ⟨ in ⟨ and
iniquity,   [of generations],   kindness   Truth,   Kindness Abundant

וָפֶשַׁע, וְחַטָּאָה, וְנַקֵּה.[2] וְסָלַחְתָּ לַעֲוֹנֵנוּ וּלְחַטָּאתֵנוּ

⟪ and our sins, ⟨ our ⟨ May You ⟪ and Who ⟨ and inadvertent ⟨ willful sin,
iniquities   forgive   **absolves.**   sin,

וּנְחַלְתָּנוּ.[3] סְלַח לָנוּ אָבִינוּ כִּי חָטָאנוּ, מְחַל לָנוּ

⟨ us, ⟨ pardon ⟪ we have ⟨ for ⟪ our ⟨ us, ⟨ Forgive ⟪ and make us
sinned;   Father,   Your heritage.

מַלְכֵּנוּ כִּי פָשָׁעְנוּ. כִּי אַתָּה אֲדֹנָי טוֹב וְסַלָּח,

⟪ and ⟨ are ⟨ O Lord, ⟨ You, ⟨ For ⟪ we have ⟨ for ⟪ our King,
forgiving,   good   willfully sinned.

(1) *Exodus* 34:5. (2) 34:6-7. (3) 34:9.

לְךָ, *A crown will they give You, O* HASHEM,   *above, together with Your people, Israel, as-*
our God — the angels of the multitudes of   *sembled below (Rabbeinu Chananel).*

וְרַב חֶסֶד לְכָל קֹרְאֶיךָ.¹

《 who call 〈 to all 〈 kind 〈 and
upon You.　　　　　　　　　abundantly

PREFATORY VERSES TO SELICHAH 28 / פסוקי הקדמה לסליחה כח

הָאֱנוֹשׁ מֵאֱלוֹהַּ יִצְדָּק, אִם מֵעֹשֵׂהוּ יִטְהַר גָּבֶר.²

《 be a 〈 purified 〈 — more than 《 can 《 be 〈 — more 〈 Can a man
man.　　　　his Maker —　　　righteous;　　than God —

טוֹב יהוה לַכֹּל, וְרַחֲמָיו עַל כָּל מַעֲשָׂיו.³ חַנּוּן יהוה

〈 is 〈 Gracious 〈 His 〈 all 〈 are 〈 His mercies 《 to all; 〈 HASHEM is good
HASHEM　　　　creations.　on

וְצַדִּיק, וֵאלֹהֵינוּ מְרַחֵם.⁴ הֵן בַּעֲבָדָיו לֹא יַאֲמִין,

《 He does not 〈 in His 〈 Indeed, 《 is 〈 our God 《 and
have faith;　servants　　　　　merciful.　　　　righteous,

וּבְמַלְאָכָיו יָשִׂים תָּהֳלָה.⁵ יָדַעְנוּ כִּי חָטָאנוּ, וְאֵין

〈 and there 〈 we have 〈 that 〈 We know 《 fault. 〈 He finds 〈 and with His
is no one　sinned　　　　　　　　　　　　　　angels

מִי יַעֲמֹד בַּעֲדֵנוּ, שִׁמְךָ הַגָּדוֹל יַעֲמָד לָנוּ בְּעֵת צָרָה.⁶

《 of 〈 in time 〈 for us 〈 will 〈 that is 〈 Your 《 for us; 〈 can 〈 who
trouble.　　　　　　　stand up　great　Name　　　　　stand up

כְּרַחֵם אָב עַל בָּנִים, כֵּן תְּרַחֵם יהוה עָלֵינוּ.⁷

《 on us. 〈 HASHEM, 〈 have 〈 so 《 his 〈 toward 〈 a 〈 As merciful as
　　　　　　　mercy,　　　children,　father is

לַיהוה הַיְשׁוּעָה, עַל עַמְּךָ בִרְכָתֶךָ סֶּלָה.⁸ יהוה

〈 HASHEM, 《 Selah. 《 is Your 〈 Your 〈 upon 《 is salvation, 〈 To HASHEM
　　　　　blessing,　people

צְבָאוֹת עִמָּנוּ, מִשְׂגָּב לָנוּ אֱלֹהֵי יַעֲקֹב סֶלָה.⁹

《 Selah. 《 of Jacob, 〈 is the God 〈 for us 〈 a 《 is with us, 〈 Master of
　　　　　　　　stronghold　　　　　　　Legions,

יהוה צְבָאוֹת, אַשְׁרֵי אָדָם בֹּטֵחַ בָּךְ.¹⁰ יהוה

〈 HASHEM, 《 in You. 〈 who 〈 is the 〈 — praiseworthy 《 Master 〈 HASHEM,
　　　　　trusts　man　　　　　　of Legions

הוֹשִׁיעָה, הַמֶּלֶךְ יַעֲנֵנוּ בְיוֹם קָרְאֵנוּ.¹¹

《 we call. 〈 on the 〈 answer 〈 May the 《 save!
　　　　　day　us　King

---

(1) *Psalms* 86:5. (2) *Job* 4:17. (3) *Psalms* 145:9. (4) 116:5. (5) *Job* 4:18. (6) From the Monday
and Thursday *Tachanun* service. (7) Cf. *Psalms* 103:13. (8) 3:9. (9) 46:8. (10) 84:13. (11) 20:10.

סליחה כח / SELICHAH 28
(שלישיה)

(אֱלֹהֵינוּ וֵאלֹהֵי אֲבוֹתֵינוּ:)

《 of our forefathers:) 〈 and the God 〈 (Our God

אָדוֹן דִּין אִם יְדַקְדֵּק,* בְּחֵקֶר פֹּעַל אִם יְבַדֵּק,

《 were 〈 if it 〈 each 〈 [if] through 《 to be 〈 if it 〈 judg- 《 O Lord,
to be action, an rigorously were ment,
examined, investigation, precise,*

גֶּבֶר לְפָנֶיךָ לֹא יִצְדָּק.[1]

《 be 〈 will 〈 before You 〈 man
vindicated. never

דֹּפִי תִּתֵּן[2] בִּצְבָא מַעְלָה, הֵן בְּמַלְאָכֶיךָ תָּשִׂים תָּהֳלָה,[3]

《 with 〈 You 〈 among Your 〈 indeed 《 celestial, 〈 even in 〈 You 〈 Fault
folly — charge angels the hosts find

וְאַף שׁוֹתֶה כַמַּיִם עַוְלָה.[4]

《 sin. 《 like 〈 who 《 certainly
water, drinks so [man],

זְכוּת וּצְדָקָה אֵין בָּנוּ, חֵטְא וָרֶשַׁע כֻּלָּנוּ,

《 is our entire 〈 and 〈 sin 《 within 〈 are 〈 and right- 〈 Merit
being, wickedness us, not eousness

טוֹב, אַל תָּבֹא בְמִשְׁפָּט עִמָּנוּ.[5]

《 with us. 〈 into strict 〈 enter 〈 do 《 O Benefi-
judgment not cent One,

יֶהֱמוּ מֵעֶיךָ עָלֵינוּ,[6] כְּרוֹב רַחֲמֶיךָ פְּנֵה אֵלֵינוּ,[7]

《 to us. 〈 turn 〈 mercies 〈 in accord with 《 for us; 〈 Your 〈 Let
Your abundant inner being yearn

לְבִלְתִּי כִרְעַ מַעֲלָלֵינוּ.

《 of our deeds. 〈 with the 〈 but not to be
evil [in accord]

מְשׁוּבוֹתֵינוּ רַבּוּ מִלִּמְנוֹת,[8] נִיחוֹחִים אֵין וְקָרְבָּנוֹת,

〈 nor offerings 〈 there are 《 Satisfying 《 to count. 〈 are too 〈 Our wayward
none, aromas — numerous deeds

---

(1) Cf. *Psalms* 143:2. (2) See 50:20 with *Rashi*. (3) Cf. *Job* 4:18. (4) Cf. 15:16.
(5) Cf. *Psalms* 143:2. (6) Cf. *Jeremiah* 31:19. (7) Cf. *Psalms* 69:17. (8) Cf. *Jeremiah* 14:7.

אָדוֹן דִּין אִם יְדַקְדֵּק — *O Lord, judgment,
if it were to be rigorously precise.* The
acrostic of this *selichah* forms the *aleph-*

beis followed by the *paytan's* name —
זְבַדְיָה חֲזַק, *Zevadiah, may he be strong* [see
prefatory comment to *Selichah* 63].

סְלִיחָה מְצָא לַעֲוֹנוֹת.

《 for [our] 〈 would 〈 that
iniquities. evoke forgiveness

עַל צִדְקוֹתֵינוּ אֵין אָנוּ סְמוּכִים,[1]

《 rely, 〈 we do not 〈 our righteousness 〈 Upon

פֶּשַׁע וְעָוֹן מִלְכְלָכִים, צְדָקָה מְצָא תְּחַן עוֹרְכִים.

《 do we 〈 [that our] 《we would 〈 [rather,] so 《 we are filthy; 〈 and 〈 for from
arrange. supplication find, that charity iniquity willful sin

קַו אַל תִּמְתַּח בִּאוֹרְחוֹתֵינוּ,

《 over our ways; 〈 extend 〈 do 〈[Therefore,]
not a measur-
ing line

רִמָּה וְתוֹלֵעָה אַחֲרִיתֵנוּ,[2] שָׁוְא וְהֶבֶל שְׁנוֹתֵינוּ.

《 are our years. 〈 and 〈 worth- 《 are our end, 〈 and maggot 〈 worm
emptiness lessness

תָּשׁוּב עַל הָרָעָה תִּנָּחֵם,[3] זֶה דַרְכְּךָ חִנָּם מְרַחֵם,

《 compas- 〈 being 〈 is Your 〈 [for] 《 reconsider, 《 the evil 〈 regard- 《 Relent
sionate; graciously way, this [judgment], ing [from Your
anger],

בְּרַחֲמֶיךָ הָרַבִּים עָלֵינוּ רַחֵם.

《 may You 〈 on us 《 that are 〈 O, with Your
have mercy. great, mercies

דְּרָכֶיךָ הוֹדַעְתָּ[4] לֶעָנָו לְהוֹרוֹת,

《 so that 〈 to the hum- 〈 You made 〈 Your ways
he may teach; ble [Moses] known

יְדַעְתּוֹ שְׁלֹשׁ עֶשְׂרֵה סְדוּרוֹת,

《 are arranged; 〈 [how] the Thirteen 〈 You let
[Attributes] him know

הִבְטַחְתּוֹ שֶׁאֵין רֵיקָם חוֹזְרוֹת.[5]

《 come back. 〈 ineffective 〈 they would 〈 You promised
never him

❖ חַנּוּן,[6] בָּם סְדַרְנוּ לְפָנֶיךָ, זַעַק קְשֹׁב מִמִּתְחַנְּנֶיךָ,

《of those who sup- 〈 attend 〈 To the 《 before 〈we have arranged 〈 with 《 O Gracious
plicate before You, cries You. [our prayer] them One,

וְאַל תְּשִׁיבֵנוּ רֵיקָם מִלְפָנֶיךָ.

《 from before 〈 empty- 〈 turn us away 〈 and
You. handed do not

---

(1) Cf. *Daniel* 9:18. (2) Cf. *Job* 25:6; *Mishnah, Avos* 3:1. (3) Cf. *Exodus* 32:12. (4) Cf. 33:13.
(5) See *Rosh Hashanah* 17b. (6) Some editions read חִנּוּן, [*our*] *supplication*.

ALL, WHILE STANDING:

אֵל מֶלֶךְ יוֹשֵׁב עַל כִּסֵּא רַחֲמִים, מִתְנַהֵג

⟨ Who acts ⟨ of mercy, ⟨ the throne ⟨ on ⟨ Who sits ⟨ King ⟨ O God,

בַּחֲסִידוּת, מוֹחֵל עֲוֹנוֹת עַמּוֹ, מַעֲבִיר רִאשׁוֹן

⟨ [sins,] one ⟨ Who removes ⟨ of His people, ⟨ the sins ⟨ Who pardons ⟨ with kindness,

רִאשׁוֹן, מַרְבֶּה מְחִילָה לְחַטָּאִים וּסְלִיחָה לַפּוֹשְׁעִים,

⟨ to willful sinners, ⟨ and forgiveness ⟨ to unintentional sinners ⟨ pardon ⟨ Who abundantly grants ⟨ by one,

עֹשֶׂה צְדָקוֹת עִם כָּל בָּשָׂר וָרוּחַ, לֹא כְרָעָתָם

⟨ in accord with their wickedness ⟨ — not ⟨ and spirit ⟨ [beings of] flesh ⟨ all ⟨ with ⟨ acts of generosity ⟨ Who performs

תִּגְמוֹל. ❖ אֵל הוֹרֵיתָ לָנוּ לוֹמַר שְׁלֹשׁ עֶשְׂרֵה, וּזְכוֹר

⟨ remember ⟨ the Thirteen [Attributes of Mercy]; ⟨ to recite ⟨ us ⟨ You taught ⟨ O God, ⟨ do You repay them!

לָנוּ הַיּוֹם בְּרִית שְׁלֹשׁ עֶשְׂרֵה, כְּמוֹ שֶׁהוֹדַעְתָּ לֶעָנָיו

⟨ to the humble one [Moses] ⟨ You made known ⟨ as ⟨ of [these] Thirteen, ⟨ the covenant ⟨ today ⟨ for us

מִקֶּדֶם, כְּמוֹ שֶׁכָּתוּב, וַיֵּרֶד יהוה בֶּעָנָן וַיִּתְיַצֵּב עִמּוֹ

⟨ with him ⟨ and stood ⟨ in a cloud ⟨ And HASHEM descended ⟨ it is written: ⟨ as ⟨ in ancient times,

שָׁם, וַיִּקְרָא בְשֵׁם יהוה.2

⟨ of HASHEM. ⟨ with the Name ⟨ and He called out ⟨ there,

CONGREGATION, THEN CHAZZAN:

וַיַּעֲבֹר יהוה עַל פָּנָיו וַיִּקְרָא:

⟨ and proclaimed: ⟨ [Moses'] face, ⟨ before ⟨ And HASHEM passed

CONGREGATION AND CHAZZAN RECITE LOUDLY AND IN UNISON:

יהוה, יהוה, אֵל, רַחוּם, וְחַנּוּן, אֶרֶךְ אַפַּיִם,

⟨ to anger, ⟨ Slow ⟨ and Gracious, ⟨ Compassionate ⟨ God, ⟨ HASHEM, ⟨ HASHEM,

וְרַב חֶסֶד, וֶאֱמֶת, נֹצֵר חֶסֶד לָאֲלָפִים, נֹשֵׂא עָוֹן,

⟨ of iniquity, ⟨ Forgiver ⟨ for thousands [of generations], ⟨ of kindness ⟨ Preserver ⟨ and Truth, ⟨ in Kindness ⟨ and Abundant

---

(1) Rosh Hashanah 17a. (2) Exodus 34:5.

וָפֶשַׁע, וְחַטָאָה, וְנַקֵּה.¹ וְסָלַחְתָּ לַעֲוֹנֵנוּ וּלְחַטָּאתֵנוּ

《 and our sins, 〈 our 〈 May You 《 *and Who* 〈 *and inadvertent* 〈 *willful sin,*
iniquities forgive *absolves.* sin,

וּנְחַלְתָּנוּ.² סְלַח לָנוּ אָבִינוּ כִּי חָטָאנוּ, מְחַל לָנוּ

〈 us, 〈 pardon 《 we have 〈 for 《 our 〈 us, 〈 Forgive 《 and make us
sinned; Father, Your heritage.

מַלְכֵּנוּ כִּי פָשָׁעְנוּ. כִּי אַתָּה אֲדֹנָי טוֹב וְסַלָּח,

《 and 〈 are 〈 O Lord, 〈 You, 〈 For 《 we have 〈 for 《 our King,
forgiving, good willfully sinned.

וְרַב חֶסֶד לְכָל קֹרְאֶיךָ.³

《 who call 〈 to all 〈 kind 〈 and
upon You. abundantly

PREFATORY VERSES TO SELICHAH 29 / פסוקי הקדמה לסליחה כט

מָה אֱנוֹשׁ כִּי יִזְכֶּה, וְכִי יִצְדַּק יְלוּד אִשָּׁה.⁴ מָה

〈What 《 of 〈 — one 〈 he be found 〈 or 《 he might 〈 that 〈 [frail] 〈 What is
is woman? born righteous can be vindicated man

אֱנוֹשׁ כִּי תִפְקְדֶנּוּ לִבְקָרִים, לִרְגָעִים תִּבְחָנֶנּוּ.⁵ יהוה

〈 HASHEM, 《 test him? 〈 or at times 《 in the 〈 You should be 〈 that 〈 [frail]
mornings, mindful of him man

אַל בְּאַפְּךָ תוֹכִיחֵנוּ, וְאַל בַּחֲמָתְךָ תְיַסְּרֵנוּ.⁶ אַף

〈 Even 《 chastise us. 〈 in Your wrath 〈 nor 《 rebuke us, 〈 in Your 〈 do
anger not

עַל זֶה פָּקַחְתָּ עֵינֶךָ, וְאֹתָנוּ תָבִיא בְמִשְׁפָּט עִמָּךְ.⁷

《 with 〈 to judgment 〈 You will 〈 and us 《 Your 〈 have You 〈 this 〈 on
You. bring eyes, fixed

כְּרַחֵם אָב עַל בָּנִים, כֵּן תְּרַחֵם יהוה עָלֵינוּ.⁸

《 on us. 〈 HASHEM, 〈 have 〈 so 《 his 〈 toward 〈 a 〈 As merciful as
mercy, children, father is

לַיהוה הַיְשׁוּעָה, עַל עַמְּךָ בִרְכָתֶךָ סֶּלָה.⁹ יהוה

〈 HASHEM, 《 Selah. 《 is Your 〈 Your 〈 upon 《 is salvation, 〈 To HASHEM
blessing, people

צְבָאוֹת עִמָּנוּ, מִשְׂגָּב לָנוּ אֱלֹהֵי יַעֲקֹב סֶלָה.¹⁰

《 Selah. 《 of Jacob, 〈 is the God 〈 for us 〈 a 《 is with us, 〈 Master of
stronghold Legions,

---

(1) *Exodus* 34:6-7. (2) 34:9. (3) *Psalms* 86:5. (4) *Job* 15:14. (5) Cf. *Psalms* 8:5; *Job* 7:18.
(6) Cf. *Psalms* 6:2. (7) Cf. *Job* 14:3. (8) Cf. *Psalms* 103:13. (9) 3:9. (10) 46:8.

יהוה צְבָאוֹת, אַשְׁרֵי אָדָם בֹּטֵחַ בָּךְ.[1] יהוה

《 HASHEM, 《 in You. 〈 who 〈 is the 〈 — praiseworthy 《 Master 〈 HASHEM,
trusts man of Legions

הוֹשִׁיעָה, הַמֶּלֶךְ יַעֲנֵנוּ בְיוֹם קָרְאֵנוּ.[2]

《 we call. 〈 on the 〈 answer 〈 May the 《 save!
day us King

סליחה כט / SELICHAH 29

(שנייה)

ALL:

(אֱלֹהֵינוּ וֵאלֹהֵי אֲבוֹתֵינוּ:)

《of our forefathers:)〈 and God 〈 (Our God

אָדוֹן, בְּפָקְדְּךָ אֱנוֹשׁ* לַבְּקָרִים,

《 every 〈 mankind* 〈 when You 〈 Lord,
morning, consider

בְּמִצּוּי הַדִּין אַל תְּמַתַּח.

《 stretch 〈 do 〈 of the 〈 to the last
[judgment]. not law rigorous point

גּוּף וּנְשָׁמָה אִם תְּרִיבֵם,* דְּחוּ וְלֹא יוּכְלוּ קוּם.[3]

《 to rise. 〈 be able 〈 and 〈 they would 《 You should 〈 if 《 and soul, 〈 Body
not be thrust judge
down, [together],*

---

(1) *Psalms* 84:13. (2) 20:10. (3) Cf. 36:13.

‎◄§ אָדוֹן בְּפָקְדְּךָ אֱנוֹשׁ — *Lord, when You consider mankind.* This *selichah* contains an *aleph-beis* acrostic, which is followed by the author's signature — יִצְחָק הַכֹּהֵן הֶחָבֵר, חֲזַק וֶאֱמַץ, *Yitzchak the Kohen, the chaver* [an ancient title bestowed on certain exceptional people], *may he be strong and persevere.* Nothing is known about R' Yitzchak, except that he lived sometime before 1234, the year in which the commentary *Arugas HaBosem* was written. This *selichah,* as well as the next, is composed entirely of couplets and is therefore classified as a *sheniyah.* Interestingly, both are from among the few *selichos* that are unrhymed.

גּוּף וּנְשָׁמָה אִם תְּרִיבֵם — *Body and soul, if You should judge [together].* The Talmud relates an insightful discussion between Rabbi [Yehudah HaNassi] and the Roman emperor Antoninus.

The emperor claimed that man's body and soul could exonerate themselves on Judgment Day. The body could argue, *The soul was the guilty one; for since it left me, I have been lying like a mute rock in the grave;* and the soul could counter, *The body was the guilty one; for since I left it, I have been flying free as a bird.*

Rabbi responded with a parable: A king ordered two men to guard an orchard of fruit-laden trees. One was lame, the other blind. The lame sighted one said to his blind companion, *I see beautiful fruit in the orchard. Let me ride on your shoulders and I will guide you to the trees. We will then be able to eat from them.* And so they did for some time, eating the fruit they were set to protect. When the king returned, he asked what had happened to the ripened figs. The cripple said, *Do I have feet to walk over to the*

הֲיוּכַל גֶּבֶר לִזְכּוֹת בַּמִּשְׁפָּט,

⟨ in judgment, ⟨ to be ⟨ for a ⟨ Is it
vindicated man possible

וְאִם אֵין בְּיָדוֹ מַעֲשׂ לְהִצְטַדָּק.

《 with which to ⟨ good ⟨ in his ⟨ there ⟨ if
justify himself? deeds hand are not

זֵרוּי יְחוּמוֹ מִלֵּחָה סְרוּחָה,[1]

《 that is ⟨ is from ⟨ of his ⟨ The
putrid; [a drop of] conception injected
moisture [seed]

חָבוּי אָרְבוֹ בְּקִרְבּוֹ מֵעֵת הִוָּלְדוֹ.*

《 of his ⟨ from the ⟨ within him ⟨ is the ⟨ con-
birth.* time Ambusher cealed

טָמוּן בְּחֶבּוֹ[2] כְּרֶשֶׁת לְרַגְלָיו,

《 for his feet, ⟨ like a net ⟨ within him, ⟨ Hidden

יְסִיתֵהוּ בְּכָל יוֹם לְשַׁחַת לְהַפִּילוֹ.

《 to cast ⟨ so as into ⟨ day ⟨ every ⟨ it incites him
him down. Gehinnom [to sin],

כֹּחַ וּגְבוּרָה בַּגּוּף אֵין לְפָנָיו לַעֲמֹד וּלְהִתְיַצֵּב.

《 and to remain ⟨ to stand ⟨ against it ⟨ there ⟨ in the ⟨ and ⟨ Strength
firm. is not body might

מִיּוֹם עָמְדוֹ עַל דַּעְתּוֹ,

《 of his ⟨ in ⟨ a man ⟨ From
reason, control stands the day

נַפְשׁוֹ יָשִׂים בְּכַפּוֹ לְהָבִיא לַחְמוֹ.[3]

《 his bread. ⟨ to provide ⟨ in his ⟨ he places ⟨ his life
hands

---

(1) See *Avos* 3:1. (2) Cf. *Job* 31:33. (3) Cf. *Lamentations* 5:9.

trees? The blind one said, *Do I have eyes to see the fruit?* But the wise king had the lame man hoisted onto the blind man's shoulders and judged them as one. So, too, on Judgment Day, God hurls the soul back into its body and judges them as one (*Sanhedrin* 91a).

מֵעֵת הִוָּלְדוֹ — *From the time of his birth.* Another question posed by Antoninus (ibid.) is: *Does the Evil Inclination enter a person when the embryo is formed or at birth?* Rabbi replied, *From the formation of the embryo.*

Antoninus retorted, *If so, it would rebel and kick its way out of its mother. It cannot enter a person until he is born.*

Rabbi acceded, saying, *This matter have I been taught by Antoninus, and I have found a Scriptural verse to support his view; for it is written,* לַפֶּתַח חַטָּאת רֹבֵץ, *"Sin crouches at the door" (Genesis 4:7).* [Although the verse speaks in the context of an unrepentant sinner, Rabbi gave it a novel interpretation: The cause of sin, namely, the Evil Inclination, crouches at the door of the womb, ready to enter the baby as it emerges.]

שָׂבֵעַ כָּל יָמָיו כַּעַס וּמַכְאוֹבוֹת,¹

《 and heartache; 〈 with 〈 his 〈 all 〈 [He is]
      frustration   days   sated

עַד שׁוּבוֹ לַעֲפָרוֹ² לֹא יִשְׁקֹט.

《 he has no rest. 〈 to his dust 〈 he returns 〈 until

פְּנֵה אָדוֹן בְּעֶצְבּוֹן רוּחַ, צְפֵה בְּשִׁבְרוֹן לֵב.

《 hearts. 〈 [our] broken 〈 look at 《 spirit; 〈 [our] aching 〈 Lord, 〈 Consider,

קָרוֹב אַתָּה לָרְחוֹקִים, רוֹצֶה תְּשׁוּבַת רְשָׁעִים.³

《 of the wicked. 〈 the repentance 〈 You desire 《 to those far away, 〈 You are 〈 Near

שַׁדַּי, הִמָּצֵא לְדוֹרְשֶׁיךָ, תֹּאמַר הִנְנִי לִמְבַקְשֶׁיךָ.

《 to those who 〈 Here I 《 say, 《 to those who 〈 manifest 〈 Almighty,
seek You.   am,   search for You.   Yourself

יְבֻשְּׂרוּ סָלַחְתִּי⁴ קוֹרְאֵי בִשְׁמֶךָ,

《 in Your 〈 — those 《 I have 《 Let them
name;   who call out   forgiven   be told,

צַדֵּק בַּמִּשְׁפָּט עַם מְיַחֲדֶךָ.

《 who proclaim 〈 the 〈 in 〈 vindicate
Your unity.   people   judgment

חֲסֹם מְנֻוָּל⁵ מִלְּהַרְשִׁיעַ, קְצֹף בְּמַסְטִין מִלְּהַסְטִין.

《 so that he 〈 [Satan] 〈 rebuke 《 so that he cannot 〈 the foul 〈 Muzzle
cannot accuse.   the Accuser   prosecute;   [Satan]

הָקֵם לָנוּ מֵלִיץ יֹשֶׁר.

《 to speak 〈 an advocate 〈 on our 〈 Establish
well [of us];   [angel]   behalf

כַּפֵּר מְצָאתִי תַּשְׁמִיעַ לַשּׁוֹבָבִים.

《 — Your wayward 《 let them 《 have I found 〈 Atone-
children.   hear   [for you],   ment

הִשְׁלַכְנוּ עָלֶיךָ יְהָבֵנוּ,⁶ נָא אַתָּה תְכַלְכְּלֵנוּ.

《 Who sustains us. 〈 let it 〈 please, 《 our 〈 upon 〈 We have cast
be You   burden;   You

הֵעָתֵר לָנוּ בִּתְפִלָּתֵנוּ.

《 as we pray; 〈 us 〈 Answer

חֶפְצֵנוּ וּבַקָּשָׁתֵנוּ מַלֵּא בְרַחֲמִים.

《 with mercy. 〈 fulfill 〈 and our request 〈 our desire

---

(1) Cf. *Ecclesiastes* 2:23. (2) Cf. 3:20. (3) Cf. *Ezekiel* 18:23. (4) *Numbers* 14:20.
(5) See commentary to *Selichah* 24. (6) Cf. *Psalms* 55:23.

◈ בְּךָ תָלֵינוּ בִטְחוֹנֵנוּ, **רַ**חֲמֶיךָ מְהֵרָה יְקַדְּמוּנוּ.

《 come forth 〈 speedily 〈 let Your 《 our trust; 〈 we have put 〈 In You
to greet us.   mercy

חָזָק וְאַמִּיץ שִׁמְךָ לֹא שְׁכַחְנוּ,

《 we have not 〈 Your 〈 Mighty 〈 Strong,
forgotten;   Name   One,

אָנָּא, לָנֶצַח אַל תִּשְׁכָּחֵנוּ.[1]

《 forget us. 〈 do not 〈 eternally 〈 please,

ALL, WHILE STANDING:

אֵל מֶלֶךְ יוֹשֵׁב עַל כִּסֵּא רַחֲמִים, מִתְנַהֵג

〈 Who acts 《 of mercy, 〈 the throne 〈 on 〈 Who sits 〈 King 〈 O God,

בַּחֲסִידוּת, מוֹחֵל עֲוֹנוֹת עַמּוֹ, מַעֲבִיר רִאשׁוֹן

〈 [sins,] one 〈 Who 《 of His 〈 the sins 〈 Who 《 with kindness,
removes   people,   pardons

רִאשׁוֹן,[2] מַרְבֶּה מְחִילָה לְחַטָּאִים וּסְלִיחָה לַפּוֹשְׁעִים,

《 to willful 〈 and 〈 to unintentional 〈 pardon 〈 Who abun- 《 by one,
sinners, forgiveness   sinners   dantly grants

עֹשֶׂה צְדָקוֹת עִם כָּל בָּשָׂר וָרוּחַ, לֹא כְרָעָתָם

〈 in accord with 〈 — not 《 and 〈 [beings 〈 all 〈 with 〈 acts of 〈 Who
their wickedness   spirit   of] flesh   generosity   performs

תִּגְמוֹל. ◈ אֵל הוֹרֵיתָ לָנוּ לוֹמַר שְׁלֹשׁ עֶשְׂרֵה, וּזְכוֹר

〈 remem- 《 the Thirteen 〈 to 〈 us 〈 You 〈 O God, 《 do You
ber   [Attributes of Mercy];   recite   taught   repay them!

לָנוּ הַיּוֹם בְּרִית שְׁלֹשׁ עֶשְׂרֵה, כְּמוֹ שֶׁהוֹדַעְתָּ לֶעָנָיו

〈 to the humble 〈 You made 〈 as 《 of [these] Thirteen, 〈 the 〈 today 〈 for us
one [Moses]   known   covenant

מִקֶּדֶם, כְּמוֹ שֶׁכָּתוּב, וַיֵּרֶד יהוה בֶּעָנָן וַיִּתְיַצֵּב עִמּוֹ

〈 with 〈 and stood 〈 in a 〈 And HASHEM 《 it is written: 〈 as 《 in ancient
him   cloud   descended   times,

שָׁם, וַיִּקְרָא בְשֵׁם יהוה.[3]

《 of 〈 with the 〈 and He 《 there,
HASHEM.   Name   called out

CONGREGATION, THEN *CHAZZAN:*

וַיַּעֲבֹר יהוה עַל פָּנָיו וַיִּקְרָא:

《 and 《 [Moses'] 〈 before 〈 And HASHEM passed
proclaimed: face,

(1) Cf. *Lamentations* 5:20. (2) *Rosh Hashanah* 17a. (3) *Exodus* 34:5.

CONGREGATION AND *CHAZZAN* RECITE LOUDLY AND IN UNISON:

יְהוָה, יהוה, אֵל, רַחוּם, וְחַנּוּן, אֶרֶךְ אַפַּיִם,
⟨ to anger, ⟨ Slow ⟪ and Gracious, ⟨ Compassionate ⟨ God, ⟨ HASHEM, ⟨ HASHEM,

וְרַב חֶסֶד, וֶאֱמֶת, נֹצֵר חֶסֶד לָאֲלָפִים, נֹשֵׂא עָוֹן,
⟨ of ⟨ Forgiver ⟪ for thousands ⟨ of ⟨ Preserver ⟪ and ⟨ in ⟨ and
iniquity,   [of generations],   kindness   Truth,   Kindness Abundant

וָפֶשַׁע, וְחַטָּאָה, וְנַקֵּה.¹ וְסָלַחְתָּ לַעֲוֹנֵנוּ וּלְחַטָּאתֵנוּ
⟪ and our sins, ⟨ our ⟨ May You ⟪ and Who ⟨ and inadvertent ⟨ willful sin,
iniquities   forgive   absolves.   sin,

וּנְחַלְתָּנוּ.² סְלַח לָנוּ אָבִינוּ כִּי חָטָאנוּ, מְחַל לָנוּ
⟨ us, ⟨ pardon ⟪ we have ⟨ for ⟪ our ⟨ us, ⟨ Forgive ⟪ and make us
sinned;   Father,   Your heritage.

מַלְכֵּנוּ כִּי פָשָׁעְנוּ. כִּי אַתָּה אֲדֹנָי טוֹב וְסַלָּח,
⟪ and ⟨ are ⟨ O Lord, ⟨ You, ⟨ For ⟪ we have ⟨ for ⟪ our King,
forgiving,   good   willfully sinned.

וְרַב חֶסֶד לְכָל קֹרְאֶיךָ.³
⟪ who call ⟨ to all ⟨ kind ⟨ and
upon You.   abundantly

פסוקי הקדמה לסליחה ל / PREFATORY VERSES TO SELICHAH 30

אֲדֹנָי יֱהֹוִה, אַל תַּשְׁחֵת עַמְּךָ וְנַחֲלָתְךָ אֲשֶׁר
⟨ that ⟨ and Your ⟨ Your ⟪ destroy ⟨ do ⟪ HASHEM/ ⟨ O Lord
heritage   people   not   ELOHIM,

פָּדִיתָ בְּגָדְלֶךָ, אֲשֶׁר הוֹצֵאתָ מִמִּצְרַיִם בְּיָד חֲזָקָה.⁴
⟪ that is ⟨ with a ⟨ of Egypt ⟨ You took out ⟨ that ⟨ in Your ⟨ You
strong.   hand   greatness,   redeemed

וּמַה יִּצְדַּק אֱנוֹשׁ עִם אֵל, וּמַה יִּזְכֶּה יְלוּד אִשָּׁה.⁵
⟪ of ⟨ — one ⟨ he be ⟨ how ⟪ God; ⟨ before ⟨ — [frail] ⟨ he be found ⟨ How
woman?   born   vindicated   can   man —   righteous   can

הַאֱנוֹשׁ מֵאֱלוֹהַּ יִצְדָּק, אִם מֵעֹשֵׂהוּ יִטְהַר גָּבֶר.⁶
⟪ be a ⟨ purified ⟨ — more than ⟨ can ⟪ be ⟨ — more ⟪ Can a man
man?   his Maker —   righteous   than God —

כְּרַחֵם אָב עַל בָּנִים, כֵּן תְּרַחֵם יהוה עָלֵינוּ.⁷
⟪ on us. ⟨ HASHEM, ⟨ have ⟨ so ⟪ his ⟨ toward ⟨ a ⟨ As merciful as
mercy,   children,   father is

---

(1) *Exodus* 34:6-7. (2) 34:9. (3) *Psalms* 86:5. (4) *Deuteronomy* 9:26.
(5) *Job* 25:4. (6) 4:17. (7) Cf. *Psalms* 103:13.

לַיהוה הַיְשׁוּעָה, עַל עַמְּךָ בִרְכָתֶךָ סֶּלָה.¹ יהוה
⟨ HASHEM, ⟩ Selah. ⟩ is Your ⟨ Your ⟨ upon ⟩ is salvation, ⟨ To HASHEM
                        blessing, people

צְבָאוֹת עִמָּנוּ, מִשְׂגָּב לָנוּ אֱלֹהֵי יַעֲקֹב סֶּלָה.²
⟩ Selah. ⟩ of Jacob, ⟨ is the God ⟨ for us ⟨ a ⟩ is with us, ⟨ Master of
                                          stronghold   Legions,

יהוה צְבָאוֹת, אַשְׁרֵי אָדָם בֹּטֵחַ בָּךְ.³ יהוה
⟨ HASHEM, ⟩ in You. ⟨ who ⟨ is the ⟨ — praiseworthy ⟩ Master ⟨ HASHEM,
                    trusts   man   of Legions

הוֹשִׁיעָה, הַמֶּלֶךְ יַעֲנֵנוּ בְיוֹם קָרְאֵנוּ.⁴
⟩ we call. ⟨ on the ⟨ answer ⟨ May the ⟩ save!
            day   us   King

סליחה ל / SELICHAH 30

(שניה)

ALL:

(אֱלֹהֵינוּ וֵאלֹהֵי אֲבוֹתֵינוּ:)

⟩ of our forefathers:)⟨ and God ⟨ (Our God

אָדוֹן, בְּשָׁפְטְךָ* אֱנוֹשׁ רִמָּה, תִּזְכֹּר בְּרֹגֶז חַנּוֹת רַחֵם.⁵
⟩ and ⟨ [Your] ⟨ in Your ⟨ remember ⟩ [whose ⟨ man, ⟨ when You ⟨ Lord,
  [Your] grace   wrath   end is] the   judge*
  mercy.   maggot,

בְּעֶרְכְּךָ דִין אֲשֵׁמִים לְוַכֵּחַ, שׁוֹגֶה וּפֶתִי⁶ זַכֵּה וְהַצְדֵּק.
⟩ and ⟨ find ⟨ or ⟨ those ⟩ to ⟨ those ⟩ a trial, ⟨ As You hold
  vindicate. innocent through [who sinned] censure, guilty
                    ignorance unwittingly

גְּמֹל חֶסֶד וְטוֹבָה לְחַיָּבִים, רִיב אַל תִּמְתַּח לְמָצוּי.
⟩ to the last ⟨ stretch ⟨ do ⟨ judgment ⟩ to the ⟨ and ⟨ with ⟨ Act
  rigorous point.   not   guilty; goodness kindness

דַּלֵּי מַעַשׂ וְרֵיקֵי כִשְׁרוֹן, קוֹרְאִים אֵלֶיךָ לֵמוֹ הִמָּצֵא.
⟩ You be ⟨ [that] ⟨ to You ⟨ are calling ⟨ of proper ⟨ and ⟨ in ⟨ [A people]
  accessible. to them   actions   empty deeds poor

---

(1) *Psalms* 3:9. (2) 46:8. (3) 84:13. (4) 20:10. (5) Cf. *Habakkuk* 3:2. (6) Cf. *Ezekiel* 45:20.

אָדוֹן בְּשָׁפְטְךָ §⁀ — *Lord, when You judge.* This unrhymed *selichah*, by R' Eliyah ben Shemayah [see prefatory comment to *Selichah* 14], follows an אֵי׳ת בַּ׳ש format. That is, the respective letters from the beginning of the *aleph-beis* are paired with their counterparts from the opposite end. Thus, א, the first letter, is coupled with ת, the last letter; ב, the second, with ש, the second to last; etc. This is followed with a word-by-word acrostic of the *paytan's* name, as indicated by the bold type.

הִנְנוּ לְפָנֶיךָ בְּאַשְׁמָה רַבָּה, צִפְצוּף מֵעַן בְּשְׁנוּ לִפוֹצֵץ.

Here we are before You, [confessing our] guilt that is vast; to chirp a prayer — we are too ashamed to open [our mouths].

וְאִם מֵאֱלוֹהַּ אֱנוֹשׁ הַיִּצְדָּק, פְּנֵי עֹשֵׂהוּ גֶּבֶר הַיִּטְהָר.[1]

Can it be that from [before] God a man be vindicated? Can, before his Maker, a person be reckoned pure?

זָדוֹן בְּחֻבּוֹ[2] אָוֶן בְּקִרְבּוֹ, עָוֹן מָלֵא וָפֶשַׁע רָב.

Willful sin is hidden in his heart, evil is within him, of iniquity he is full, and rebellious sins, many.

חֶשְׁבּוֹן וְדִין לְמֶלֶךְ מַלְכֵי הַמְּלָכִים,

A reckoning and an accounting to the King over kings of kings

סוֹפוֹ לִתֵּן[3] בְּבֹא חֲלִיפָתוֹ.

in the end he must give, when there comes his time to pass on.

טֶבַע חוֹתָם בְּכַפּוֹ נֶחֱרַת,[4] נֶגֶד פָּנָיו רִשְׁעוֹ יַעֲנֶה.

The imprint of the seal, with his own hand was impressed; before his face, his wickedness will testify.

יוֹרֶה[5] כָּפִיס מֵעֵץ וְיַגִּיד, מְקִיר אֶבֶן תִּזְעַק וְתִקְרָא.[6]

Point a splinter [to him] will a beam [of his house] from the wall, and bear witness; from the stones will cry out the and proclaim.

כּוֹבֵשׁ פָּנָיו נָדוֹן וְנִכְלָם, לְאַיִן חָשׁוּב בְּעָמְדוֹ לְפָנֶיךָ.

He covers his face, convicted and shamed, as naught is he considered, as he stands before You.

אָנָּא לְמַעֲשֵׂה יָדֶיךָ הַרְצֵה,

Please to the work of Your hands show favor;

בְּשִׁבְרוֹן רְאֵה שְׁמֹר מִדֶּחִי.

his brokenness observe and protect him from being pushed down.

❖ עֲבָדֶיךָ יִמְצְאוּ הַיּוֹם חֲנִינָה,

May Your servants find today mercy;

---

(1) Cf. *Job* 4:17. (2) Cf. 31:33. (3) See *Avos* 3:1. (4) See commentary to *Selichah* 26, s.v. וּבְיָדוֹ סְדוּרוֹת. (5) Some editions read יוֹדֶה, *will admit.* (6) Cf. *Habakkuk* 2:11; see commentary to *Selichah* 26, s.v. הַעֲמָדְתָּ עַד.

זַכֵּם קָרְבָתְךְ חֲפוֹץ כְּבָרִאשׁוֹנָה.

⟪ as of old. ⟨ they desire, ⟨ for nearness to You ⟨ vindicate them,

וְכַשֶּׁלֶג וְכַצֶּמֶר הַלְבֵּן חֲטָאֵי שׁוֹשַׁנָה,[1]

⟪ [of the people compared to] a rose. ⟨ the sins ⟨ whiten ⟨ and like [white] wool ⟨ And like snow

מַלְּטֵם מִכָּל רָעוֹת בְּזֹאת הַשָּׁנָה.

⟨ year! ⟨ in this [coming] ⟨ evil ⟨ from all ⟨ Save them

ALL, WHILE STANDING:

אֵל מֶלֶךְ יוֹשֵׁב עַל כִּסֵּא רַחֲמִים, מִתְנַהֵג

⟨ Who acts ⟪ of mercy, ⟨ the throne ⟨ on ⟨ Who sits ⟨ King ⟨ O God,

בַּחֲסִידוּת, מוֹחֵל עֲוֹנוֹת עַמּוֹ, מַעֲבִיר רִאשׁוֹן

⟨ [sins,] one ⟨ Who removes ⟨ of His people, ⟨ the sins ⟨ Who pardons ⟪ with kindness,

רִאשׁוֹן,[2] מַרְבֶּה מְחִילָה לְחַטָּאִים וּסְלִיחָה לַפּוֹשְׁעִים,

⟪ to willful sinners, ⟨ and forgiveness ⟨ to unintentional sinners ⟨ pardon ⟨ Who abundantly grants ⟪ by one,

עֹשֶׂה צְדָקוֹת עִם כָּל בָּשָׂר וָרוּחַ, לֹא כְרָעָתָם

⟨ in accord with their wickedness ⟨ — not ⟪ and spirit ⟨ [beings of] flesh ⟨ all ⟨ with ⟨ acts of generosity ⟨ Who performs

תִּגְמוֹל. ❖ אֵל הוֹרֵיתָ לָּנוּ לוֹמַר שְׁלֹשׁ עֶשְׂרֵה, וּזְכוֹר

⟨ remember ⟪ the Thirteen [Attributes of Mercy]; ⟨ to recite ⟨ us ⟨ You taught ⟨ O God, ⟪ do You repay them!

לָנוּ הַיּוֹם בְּרִית שְׁלֹשׁ עֶשְׂרֵה, כְּמוֹ שֶׁהוֹדַעְתָּ לֶעָנָיו

⟨ to the humble one [Moses] ⟨ You made ⟨ as ⟪ of [these] Thirteen, ⟨ the covenant ⟨ today ⟨ for us

מִקֶּדֶם, כְּמוֹ שֶׁכָּתוּב, וַיֵּרֶד יהוה בֶּעָנָן וַיִּתְיַצֵּב עִמּוֹ

⟨ with him ⟨ and stood ⟨ in a cloud ⟨ And HASHEM descended ⟪ it is written: ⟨ as ⟪ in ancient times,

שָׁם, וַיִּקְרָא בְשֵׁם יהוה.[3]

⟪ of ⟨ with the Name ⟨ and He called out ⟪ there, HASHEM.

CONGREGATION, THEN CHAZZAN:

וַיַּעֲבֹר יהוה עַל פָּנָיו וַיִּקְרָא:

⟪ and proclaimed: ⟪ [Moses'] face, ⟨ before ⟨ And HASHEM passed

(1) Cf. *Isaiah* 1:18. (2) *Rosh Hashanah* 17a. (3) *Exodus* 34:5.

CONGREGATION AND *CHAZZAN* RECITE LOUDLY AND IN UNISON:

יהוה, יהוה, אֵל, רַחוּם, וְחַנּוּן, אֶרֶךְ אַפַּיִם,
⟨ to anger, ⟨ Slow ⟪ and Gracious, ⟨ Compassionate ⟨ God, ⟨ HASHEM, ⟨ HASHEM,

וְרַב חֶסֶד, וֶאֱמֶת, נֹצֵר חֶסֶד לָאֲלָפִים, נֹשֵׂא עָוֹן,
⟨ of ⟨ Forgiver ⟪ for thousands ⟨ of ⟨ Preserver ⟪ and ⟨ in ⟨ and
iniquity,   [of generations],   kindness   Truth,   Kindness Abundant

וָפֶשַׁע, וְחַטָּאָה, וְנַקֵּה. ¹ וְסָלַחְתָּ לַעֲוֹנֵנוּ וּלְחַטָּאתֵנוּ
⟪ and our sins, ⟨ our ⟨ May You ⟪ and Who ⟨ and inadvertent ⟨ willful sin,
  iniquities   forgive   absolves.   sin,

וּנְחַלְתָּנוּ. ² סְלַח לָנוּ אָבִינוּ כִּי חָטָאנוּ, מְחַל לָנוּ
⟨ us, ⟨ pardon ⟪ we have ⟨ for ⟪ our ⟨ us, ⟨ Forgive ⟪ and make us
  sinned;   Father,   Your heritage.

מַלְכֵּנוּ כִּי פָשָׁעְנוּ. כִּי אַתָּה אֲדֹנָי טוֹב וְסַלָּח,
⟪ and ⟨ are ⟨ O Lord, ⟨ You, ⟨ For ⟪ we have ⟨ for ⟪ our King,
forgiving, good   willfully sinned.

וְרַב חֶסֶד לְכָל קֹרְאֶיךָ. ³
⟪ who call ⟨ to all ⟨ kind ⟨ and
upon You.   abundantly

פסוקי הקדמה לסליחה לא / PREFATORY VERSES TO SELICHAH 31

זְכָר נָא כִּי כַחֹמֶר עֲשִׂיתָנוּ, וְאֶל עָפָר תְּשִׁיבֵנוּ. ⁴
⟪ You will ⟨ dust ⟨ and to ⟪ You have ⟨ like clay ⟨ that ⟨ please, ⟨ Remember
return us.   made us   ber

יָדַעְנוּ כִּי אֵין בָּנוּ מַעֲשִׂים, צְדָקָה עֲשֵׂה עִמָּנוּ לְמַעַן
⟨ for the ⟨ with us ⟨ deal ⟨ with ⟪ any worthy ⟨ in us ⟨ there ⟨ that ⟨ We
sake   charity   deeds;   are not   know

שְׁמֶךָ. ⁵ קוּמָה עֶזְרָתָה לָּנוּ, וּפְדֵנוּ לְמַעַן חַסְדֶּךָ. ⁶
⟪ of Your ⟨ for the ⟨ And ⟪ us! ⟨ Assist ⟪ Arise! ⟪ of Your
kindness!   sake   redeem us   Name.

כְּרַחֵם אָב עַל בָּנִים, כֵּן תְּרַחֵם יהוה עָלֵינוּ. ⁷
⟪ on us. ⟨ HASHEM, ⟨ have ⟪ his ⟨ so ⟪ toward ⟨ a ⟨ As merciful as
  mercy,   children,   father is

לַיהוה הַיְשׁוּעָה, עַל עַמְּךָ בִרְכָתֶךָ סֶּלָה. ⁸ יהוה
⟨ HASHEM, ⟪ Selah. ⟪ is Your ⟨ Your ⟨ upon ⟪ is salvation, ⟨ To HASHEM
  blessing,   people

---

(1) *Exodus* 34:6-7. (2) 34:9. (3) *Psalms* 86:5. (4) Cf. *Job* 10:9.
(5) From the Monday and Thursday *Tachanun* service. (6) *Psalms* 44:27. (7) Cf. 103:13. (8) 3:9.

צְבָאוֹת עִמָּנוּ, מִשְׂגָּב לָנוּ אֱלֹהֵי יַעֲקֹב סֶלָה.¹

‹ Master of　‹ is the God ‹ for us ‹　a　《 is with us, ‹ Master of
Legions,　　　　　　　　　　stronghold

יהוה צְבָאוֹת, אַשְׁרֵי אָדָם בֹּטֵחַ בָּךְ.² יהוה

‹ HASHEM, 《 Master 《 — praiseworthy ‹ is the ‹ who 《 in You. ‹ HASHEM,
　　　of Legions　　　　　　　　man　　trusts

הוֹשִׁיעָה, הַמֶּלֶךְ יַעֲנֵנוּ בְיוֹם קָרְאֵנוּ.³

《　save!　《 May the ‹ answer ‹ on the 《 we call.
　　　　　　King　　us　　day

SELICHAH 31 / סליחה לא

ALL:

אֱלֹהֵינוּ וֵאלֹהֵי אֲבוֹתֵינוּ:

《 of our forefathers: ‹ and the God ‹　Our God

אַךְ בְּךָ* לַדַּל* מָעוֹז,⁴ בַּצַּר לוֹ מָצָא סֵתֶר,⁵

《 shelter; ‹ he can ‹ for ‹ when there 《 is there ‹ for the 《 in ‹ Only
　　　　find　　him, is trouble　refuge;　poor man* You,*

גּוֹנֵז⁶ חֵטְא גּוֹעֵל⁶ רֶשַׁע, דָּן⁶ לִזְכוּת מְחַפֵּשׂ צֶדֶק.

《 right- ‹ searching 《 favorably, ‹ Who 《 wickedness, ‹ Who 《 sins, ‹ [You]
eousness.　for　　　　　judges　　　despises　　　　Who hides

הַכֹּל לְךָ מְפֹרָשׁ שֵׂכֶל,⁷ וּבַל תַּחְפֹּץ הִתְבּוֹנֵן אָוֶן,⁸

《 wrong- ‹ to ‹ desire ‹ but 《 and wise, ‹ is clear ‹ to ‹ Every-
doing.　investigate　　　do not　　　　　　　You　thing

זֹאת דַּעְתֵּנוּ כִּי כֵן דַּרְכֶּךָ, חֲסוֹת בְּצִלְּךָ הִנֵּה בָאנוּ.

《 we ‹ indeed, 《 in Your ‹ [therefore,] 《 Your ‹ it is ‹ for 《 we know, ‹ This
have　　shadow,　to take　　way,
come.　　　　　shelter

טוֹב חִנָּם תּוֹשִׁיט לָנוּ. יְמִין סַעַד פְּרוּסַת פֶּתַח,

‹ at the ‹ [extend] 《 to ‹ a right ‹ to us ‹ extend ‹ [though 《 O
door　a piece　help —　hand　　　　　we are] un- Good
of bread　　　　　　　　　　　deserving, One,

---

(1) *Psalms* 46:8. (2) 84:13. (3) 20:10. (4) See commentary to *Selichah 26*, s.v. וְהֵלֵךְ, *And poor*.
(5) Cf. *Isaiah* 25:4. (6) Some editions phrase these words in the imperative, גְּנוֹז, *bury*,
גְּעוֹל, *despise*, דּוּן, *judge*. (7) Cf. *Nehemiah* 8:7. (8) Cf. *Job* 11:11.

אַךְ בְּךָ‏ — *Only in You.* The acrostic
of this *sheniyah* forms the *aleph-beis.*
Although it bears no signature, the composition is ascribed to R' Shlomo HaBavli
[see prefatory comment to *Selichah 2*].

לַדַּל — *For the poor man.* According to the
Midrash, the three synonymous expressions for *poor man* — דַּל עָנִי אֶבְיוֹן — are
used throughout Scripture as a metaphor
for Israel (*Bereishis Rabbah* 71:1).

בְּהַקִּישׁ רָשׁ שׁוֹאֵל חֶסֶד, לוֹ קַח טוֹב* תַּעַן.¹

When there knocks a poor man, asking for kindness — "Take [of My] goodness," You answer.*

מִדָּתְךָ כִּי כֵן הַשֶּׁבַח, נָעוּר וָרֵק² מַחֲזִיר מָלֵא,

This accords with Your Attribute [of kindness], for so is [Your] praise: [Someone] who comes to You shaken out and empty — You send him back full.

סְמוֹךְ נוֹפֵל לֹא תִבְזֶה, עֱנוּת עָנִי³ קִרְבוֹת תֵּרֶץ.

Support the falling; do not disdain the prayer of a poor man; find his nearness desirable.

פִּנְקַס חוֹב יִמָּרְקוּ חֶסֶד, צַו סוֹפֵר כְּתוֹב שׁוֹבֵר,

The ledger of sins — let it be expunged by kindness; command the [Heavenly] scribe to write a Paid release.

קוֹל הַקַּל יַחֲלִיף קָשֶׁה, רְצוֹן יוֹצֵר תָּכוֹף יֵצֶר.

Let the soft voice [of remorse] take the place of harsh [punishment]; to the will of the Creator bend [our Evil] Inclination.

שָׁוֶה לְכַף שִׂית הַקֶּרֶב, שְׁלוֹךְ שֶׁרֶץ טְבִילָה תָּעַל,*

*Level [raised in prayer] with hands, let be lifted [the inner thoughts of] the heart! Cast away the [dead] crawling creature, so that immersion may be effective.**

תְּבַעֵר רַע תַּעֲבִיר טָמֵא, תֵּת טָהוֹר לְכֶת חֻקֶּיךָ.

Extirpate the evil [from within us] and thereby remove contamination; place purity [in our hearts] so that we may follow Your decrees.

---

(1) Cf. *Hosea* 14:3. (2) *Nehemiah* 5:13. (3) Cf. *Psalms* 22:25.

קַח טוֹב — *Take [of My] goodness.* The translation follows the major commentaries and is based on the Midrash (*Pesikta Rabbasi*) which expounds on the verse אִמְרוּ אֵלָיו כָּל תִּשָּׂא עָוֹן וְקַח טוֹב, *Say [in prayer] before Him: Forgive all iniquity, and take goodness* (*Hosea* 14:3). When a man comes before a human king, he comes [with his arms] full [of gifts], but leaves [with] empty [arms]. Not so the Holy One, Blessed is He. Those who come to Him empty, leave full — as it is written: [They say to Him,] "*Forgive all iniquity!*" [and He replies,] "*Take [of My] goodness!*"

שְׁלוֹךְ שֶׁרֶץ טְבִילָה תָּעַל — *Cast away the [dead] crawling creature, so that immersion may be effective.* The Talmud compares the feigned confession of an unremorseful sinner to one who immerses in a *mikveh* while still holding a dead crawling creature (the original source of his contamination). Even if he were to immerse in all the world's waters, he would not be cleansed of his contamination until he casts the dead crawling creature from his hand (*Taanis* 16a).

ALL, WHILE STANDING:

אֵל מֶלֶךְ יוֹשֵׁב עַל כִּסֵּא רַחֲמִים, מִתְנַהֵג

⟨ Who acts ⟪ of mercy, ⟨ the throne ⟨ on ⟨ Who sits ⟨ King ⟨ O God,

בַּחֲסִידוּת, מוֹחֵל עֲוֹנוֹת עַמּוֹ, מַעֲבִיר רִאשׁוֹן

⟨ [sins,] one ⟨ Who ⟪ of His ⟨ the sins ⟨ Who ⟪ with kindness,
　　　　　　removes　　people,　　　　　pardons

רִאשׁוֹן,[1] מַרְבֶּה מְחִילָה לַחַטָּאִים וּסְלִיחָה לַפּוֹשְׁעִים,

⟪ to willful ⟨ and ⟨ to unintentional ⟨ pardon ⟨ Who abun- ⟪ by one,
　sinners,　forgiveness　sinners　　　　　dantly grants

עֹשֶׂה צְדָקוֹת עִם כָּל בָּשָׂר וָרוּחַ, לֹא כְרָעָתָם

⟨ in accord with ⟨— not ⟪ and ⟨ [beings ⟨ all ⟨ with ⟨ acts of ⟨ Who
　their wickedness　　　spirit　of] flesh　　　generosity　performs

תִגְמוֹל. ⋰ אֵל הוֹרֵיתָ לָנוּ לוֹמַר שְׁלֹשׁ עֶשְׂרֵה, וּזְכוֹר

⟨ remem- ⟪ the Thirteen ⟨ to ⟨ us ⟨ You ⟨ O God, ⟪ do You
　ber　[Attributes of Mercy];　recite　　taught　　　repay them!

לָנוּ הַיּוֹם בְּרִית שְׁלֹשׁ עֶשְׂרֵה, כְּמוֹ שֶׁהוֹדַעְתָּ לֶעָנָיו

⟨ to the ⟨ You made ⟨ as ⟪ of [these] Thirteen, ⟨ the ⟨ today ⟨ for us
　humble one　known　　　　　　　　　covenant
　[Moses]

מִקֶּדֶם, כְּמוֹ שֶׁכָּתוּב, וַיֵּרֶד יהוה בֶּעָנָן וַיִּתְיַצֵּב עִמּוֹ

⟨ with ⟨ and stood ⟨ in a ⟨ And HASHEM ⟪ it is written: ⟨ as ⟪ in ancient
　him　　　　cloud　descended　　　　　　　times,

שָׁם, וַיִּקְרָא בְשֵׁם יהוה.[2]

⟪ of ⟨ with the ⟨ and He ⟪ there,
　HASHEM.　Name　called out

CONGREGATION, THEN CHAZZAN:

וַיַּעֲבֹר יהוה עַל פָּנָיו וַיִּקְרָא:

⟪ and ⟪ [Moses'] ⟨ before ⟨ And HASHEM passed
　proclaimed:　face,

CONGREGATION AND CHAZZAN RECITE LOUDLY AND IN UNISON:

יהוה, יהוה, אֵל, רַחוּם, וְחַנּוּן, אֶרֶךְ אַפַּיִם,

⟨ to anger, ⟨ Slow ⟪ and ⟨ Compassionate ⟨ God, ⟨ HASHEM, ⟨ HASHEM,
　　　　　　　Gracious,

וְרַב חֶסֶד, וֶאֱמֶת, נֹצֵר חֶסֶד לָאֲלָפִים, נֹשֵׂא עָוֹן,

⟨ of ⟨ Forgiver ⟪ for thousands ⟨ of ⟨ Preserver ⟪ and ⟨ in ⟨ and
　iniquity,　[of generations],　kindness　　Truth,　Kindness Abundant

---

(1) *Rosh Hashanah* 17a. (2) *Exodus* 34:5.

וָפֶשַׁע, וְחַטָּאָה, וְנַקֵּה.¹ וְסָלַחְתָּ לַעֲוֹנֵנוּ וּלְחַטָּאתֵנוּ

‹‹ and our sins, ‹ our iniquities ‹ May You forgive ‹‹ and Who absolves. ‹ and inadvertent sin, ‹ willful sin,

וּנְחַלְתָּנוּ.² סְלַח לָנוּ אָבִינוּ כִּי חָטָאנוּ, מְחַל לָנוּ

‹ us, ‹ pardon ‹‹ we have sinned; ‹ for ‹‹ our Father, ‹ us, ‹ Forgive ‹‹ and make us Your heritage.

מַלְכֵּנוּ כִּי פָשָׁעְנוּ. כִּי אַתָּה אֲדֹנָי טוֹב וְסַלָּח,

‹‹ and forgiving, ‹ are good ‹ O Lord, ‹ You, ‹ For ‹‹ we have willfully sinned. ‹ for ‹‹ our King,

וְרַב חֶסֶד לְכָל קֹרְאֶיךָ.³

‹‹ who call upon You. ‹ to all ‹ kind ‹ and abundantly

PREFATORY VERSES TO SELICHAH 32 / פסוקי הקדמה לסליחה לב

כִּי אָדָם אֵין צַדִּיק בָּאָרֶץ אֲשֶׁר יַעֲשֶׂה טוֹב וְלֹא

‹ and never ‹ [only] good ‹ he does ‹ that ‹ on the earth ‹ who is [so] righteous ‹ does not exist ‹ the man ‹ For

יֶחֱטָא.⁴ אָדָם יְלוּד אִשָּׁה, קְצַר יָמִים וּשְׂבַע רֹגֶז.⁵ אַף

‹ Even ‹‹ of troubles. ‹ but full ‹ of years, ‹ he is short ‹‹ of woman, ‹ is born ‹ Man ‹‹ sins.

עַל זֶה פָּקַחְתָּ עֵינֶךָ, וְאֹתָנוּ תָבִיא בְמִשְׁפָּט עִמָּךְ.⁶

‹‹ with You. ‹ to judgment ‹ You will bring ‹ and us ‹‹ Your eyes, ‹ have You ‹ this ‹ on

כְּרַחֵם אָב עַל בָּנִים, כֵּן תְּרַחֵם יהוה עָלֵינוּ.⁷

‹‹ on us. ‹ HASHEM, ‹ have mercy, ‹ so ‹‹ his children, ‹ toward ‹ a father is ‹ As merciful as

לַיהוה הַיְשׁוּעָה, עַל עַמְּךָ בִרְכָתֶךָ סֶּלָה.⁸ יהוה

‹ HASHEM, ‹‹ Selah. ‹‹ is Your blessing, ‹ Your people ‹ upon ‹‹ is salvation, ‹ To HASHEM

צְבָאוֹת עִמָּנוּ, מִשְׂגָּב לָנוּ אֱלֹהֵי יַעֲקֹב סֶלָה.⁹

‹‹ Selah. ‹‹ of Jacob, ‹ is the God ‹ for us ‹ a stronghold ‹‹ is with us, ‹ Master of Legions,

יהוה צְבָאוֹת, אַשְׁרֵי אָדָם בֹּטֵחַ בָּךְ.¹⁰ יהוה

‹ HASHEM, ‹‹ in You. ‹ who trusts ‹ is the man ‹ — praiseworthy ‹‹ Master of Legions ‹ HASHEM,

---

(1) *Exodus* 34:6-7. (2) 34:9. (3) *Psalms* 86:5. (4) *Ecclesiastes* 7:20.
(5) *Job* 14:1. (6) Cf. 14:3. (7) Cf. *Psalms* 103:13. (8) 3:9. (9) 46:8. (10) 84:13.

הוֹשִׁיעָה, הַמֶּלֶךְ יַעֲנֵנוּ בְיוֹם קָרְאֵנוּ.¹

《 we call. 〈 on the 〈 answer 〈 May the 《 save!
　　　　　　day　　us　　King

סליחה לב / SELICHAH 32

ALL:

אֱלֹהֵינוּ וֵאלֹהֵי אֲבוֹתֵינוּ:

《of our forefathers: 〈 and the God 〈 Our God

אָדָם אֵיךְ יִזְכֶּה,* בְּכָל יוֹם לַמָּוֶת מְחַכֶּה.

《 he awaits? 〈 for death 〈 day 〈 when 《 can he 〈 how 《 Man,
　　　　　　　　each　　find merit,*

בָּשָׂר מַה יְּדַבֵּר, וְהוּא מוּבָל לַקֶּבֶר.

《 to the 〈 is being 〈 when it 〈 can it say, 〈 what 《 Flesh,
　grave?　led

גְּוִיוֹ לַבּוֹר נוֹפֵל, לִמְקוֹם חֹשֶׁךְ וְאֹפֶל.

《 and 〈 of 〈 to a place 《 falls, 〈 into the 〈 His
　gloom.　darkness　　　　　pit　body

דְּמְיוֹנוֹ* לַהֶבֶל דָּמָה,² וְגַם נִמְשַׁל כַּבְּהֵמוֹת נִדְמָה.*³

《 that 〈 to the animals 〈 is he 〈 and 《 is 〈 to a 〈 His
　perish.*　　　likened　also　compared,　breath　appearance*

הֲלֹא כָל יָמָיו מְעַט וְרָעִים,⁴

《 and bad? 〈 but few, 〈 his days 〈 all 〈 Are not

וְכָל מַעֲשָׂיו עֲוֹנוֹת וּפְשָׁעִים.

《 and willful 〈 iniquities 〈 his deeds 〈 And
　sins?　　　　　　　　　　　all

וּבִלְבָבוֹ יָבִין וָשָׁב, וְרָפָא לוֹ⁵ לְקוֹלוֹ כִּיקְשַׁב.

《 will be 〈 when his 〈 for 〈 there will 《 and 〈 he will 〈 But if in his
　listened to.　voice　him　be healing　repent,　under-　heart
　　　　　[in prayer]　　　　　　　　　stand

---

(1) *Psalms* 20:10. (2) Cf. 144:4. (3) Cf. 49:13. (4) Cf. *Genesis* 47:9. (5) Cf. *Isaiah* 6:10.

◆§ אָדָם אֵיךְ יִזְכֶּה — *Man, how can he find
merit?* This anonymous *sheniyah* contains
an alphabetic acrostic. Although one commentator on *Selichos* claims to have found
the author's signature in the last stanza, his
discovery seems to be more imaginative
than substantive.

דְּמְיוֹנוֹ — *His appearance.* The translation
follows the commentaries to *Psalms* 17:12,

the only place where this word appears
in Scripture. Alternatively, it means *his
thought.*

כַּבְּהֵמוֹת נִדְמָה — *To the animals that perish.* Unlike man, animals do not possess an
immortal soul. When they die, they perish
completely. So it is also with the wicked
(*Radak* to *Psalms* 49:13). Alternatively,
the phrase means *to the animals that are*

זְכוּת וּמִישׁוֹר אִם יַעֲשֶׂה, בָּהֶם יִמְצָא מָנוֹס וּמַחְסֶה.

[Deeds] that are meritorious › and › if » he does › through « them, › he will find › refuge › and shelter. »

חַיָּיו כְּאַיִן חָשׁוּב, וְסוֹפוֹ לְעָפָר יָשׁוּב.

His life [in this world] › as naught › is considered, « and his end will be › that to dust › he will return. »

טוֹב לוֹ שֶׁלֹּא נִבְרָא,* מִשֶּׁנִּבְרָא לְיוֹם צָרָה וְעֶבְרָה.

Better › for him › had he not › been created,* « than to have been created › for a › day › of trouble › and wrath. »

יָמָיו כָּלִים בְּעֹנִי וְעֶלְבּוֹן, וְאַחֲרִיתוֹ לָתֵן דִּין וְחֶשְׁבּוֹן.¹

His days › pass › in › poverty › and embarrassment, « and at his end › he must › render › an › accounting › and a reckoning. »

בְּעֶבֶד יִשְׁאַף צֵל,² וּמִיַּד שְׁאוֹל לֹא יִנָּצֵל.

Like a slave › he longs › for [the evening's] › shadows › — but « the hand › of the grave › he cannot › escape. »

לָמָּה מֵרֶחֶם יָצָא,³ וְהוּא שָׁמוּר לְרִיב וּמַצָּה.

Why › from the womb › did he › leave, « since he › is › destined › to strife › and discord? »

מַה יּוֹעִילֶנּוּ רֹב הוֹנוֹ,⁴ וּלְיוֹם עֶבְרָה מִכְבֶּה עֵינוֹ.⁵

What › will benefit him › his › abundant › wealth, « when on the day › of wrath › dimmed › will his eye be. »

נִשְׁמָתוֹ מֶנּוּ תִפָּרֵד, בִּשְׁעַת מִיתָתוֹ לִמְאֹד יֶחֱרַד.

His soul › from him › will be separated; « at the time › of his death, › greatly › will he tremble. »

סוּפָה וּסְעָרָה⁵ יְבַעֲתוּהוּ, חֶבְלֵי מָוֶת יְסוֹבְבוּהוּ.

Tempest › and storm › will terrorize him, « the › agonies › of death › will surround him. »

---

(1) Avos 3:1. (2) Job 7:2. (3) Cf. Jeremiah 20:18. (4) Cf. Proverbs 11:4. (5) Isaiah 29:6.

without speech (Rashi, ibid.).

In Psalms the phrase reads: כַּבְּהֵמוֹת נִדְמוּ, with both words in their plural forms. The paytan, however, uses the singular modifier נִדְמָה with the plural noun בְּהֵמוֹת. It is possible that the paytan originally wrote both words in the singular — כַּבְּהֵמָה נִדְמָה — as the phrase appears in some editions. A copyist may have subsequently changed the noun to the plural so that it would

coincide with the Scriptural verse. The modifier, however, was not tampered with so that the rhyme would be preserved. [See Minchas Shai to Psalms 49:13 for another approach to the singular-plural anomaly.]

טוֹב לוֹ שֶׁלֹּא נִבְרָא — Better for him had he not been created. For two and a half years, the academies of Shammai and Hillel debated. These said: It would have been better for a person had he not been

עָרֹם יָצָא מִבֶּטֶן אִמּוֹ, וְעָרֹם יָשׁוּב לָבֵית עוֹלָמוֹ.¹

《 for eternity. 〈 to his 〈 he shall 〈 and 《 of his 〈 from the 〈 he came 〈 Naked
　　　　　　home　　return　　　　naked　mother,　womb　forth

פִּתְאֹם יִלָּכֵד בִּמְצוּדָה רָעָה, וְאֵין מִי אוֹתוֹ לְפָדְעָה.

《 to 〈 him 《 any- 〈 and there 《 that is 〈 in a trap 〈 he will 〈 Suddenly
redeem.　　　　one, will not be　evil,　　　　　be caught

צָרָה וְצַלְמָוֶת יִירָשׁ, מִבֵּיתוֹ וּמֵהוֹנוֹ יִפְרָשׁ.

《 he will be 〈 and his 〈 — from his 《 he will 〈 and the 〈 Trouble
separated.　possessions　home　inherit　shadow of death

קָרַב קִצּוֹ וְנֶהְפַּךְ שִׂבְרוֹ, כָּבָה נֵרוֹ* וְאָבַד זִכְרוֹ.

《 is the remem- 〈 gone 《 is his 〈 extin- 《 is his 〈 overturned 《 is his 〈 Near
brance of him.　　lamp,*　guished　hope,　　　　　end,

רִמָּה תוֹרִישֶׁנּוּ, תוֹלֵעָה תִּשְׁלְטֶנּוּ.

《 rules over him. 〈 the worm 〈 will inherit 〈 The
　　　　　　　his [body],　　maggot

❖ שׁוֹמֵעַ זֹאת יִבְכֶּה וְיִדְאַג,

《 and worry, 〈 must 〈 this 〈 Whoever
　　　　　weep　　　　hears

בִּבְכִי וּבְתַחֲנוּנִים כִּלָבִיא יִשְׁאָג.²

《 he must roar. 〈 like a lion 〈 and supplications, 〈 with tears

תְּפִלָּה וּצְדָקָה יַרְבֶּה, אוּלַי מִיִּסּוּרִין יֵחָבֵא.

《 he may be 〈 from 〈 perhaps 《 he will 〈 and charity 〈 Prayers
spared.　suffering　　　increase,

ALL, WHILE STANDING:

אֵל מֶלֶךְ יוֹשֵׁב עַל כִּסֵּא רַחֲמִים, מִתְנַהֵג

〈 Who acts 《 of mercy, 〈 the throne 〈 on 〈 Who sits 〈 King 〈 O God,

בַּחֲסִידוּת, מוֹחֵל עֲוֹנוֹת עַמּוֹ, מַעֲבִיר רִאשׁוֹן

〈 [sins,] one 〈 Who 《 of His 〈 the sins 〈 Who 《 with kindness,
　　　　　removes　people,　　　pardons

---

(1) Cf. *Job* 1:21. (2) See commentary to *Selichah* 7, s.v. אֲרָיוֹת, *Lions*.

created than to have been created [for the
allure of sin is difficult to withstand]. And
those said: It is better for a man that he
has been created than had he not been created [for he can now perform God's will].
They finally took the matter to a vote and
concluded: It would have been better for
a person had he not been created than to
have been created; however, since he has

been created, let him search his deeds [of
the past that he may repent his sins]. Others read the conclusion: ... let him examine
his [future] deeds [before doing them to be
certain they are free of sin] (*Eruvin* 13b).

כָּבָה נֵרוֹ — *Extinguished is his lamp.* This
refers to man's soul, as the wise king
wrote: *The lamp of* H*ASHEM is man's soul*
(*Proverbs* 20:27).

רִאשׁוֹן,¹ מַרְבֶּה מְחִילָה לַחֲטָאִים וּסְלִיחָה לַפּוֹשְׁעִים,

by one, ≪ Who abun- ⟨ pardon ⟨ to unintentional ⟨ and ⟨ to willful
dantly grants   sinners   forgiveness   sinners,

עֹשֶׂה צְדָקוֹת עִם כָּל בָּשָׂר וָרוּחַ, לֹא כְרָעָתָם

Who ⟨ acts of ⟨ with ⟨ all ⟨ [beings ⟨ and ⟨— not ⟨ in accord with
performs   generosity   of] flesh   spirit   their wickedness

תִּגְמוֹל. ❖ אֵל הוֹרֵיתָ לָּנוּ לוֹמַר שְׁלֹשׁ עֶשְׂרֵה, וּזְכוֹר

do You ≪ O God, ⟨ You ⟨ to ⟨ recite ⟨ the Thirteen ≪ remem-
repay them!   taught   us   [Attributes of Mercy];   ber

לָנוּ הַיּוֹם בְּרִית שְׁלֹשׁ עֶשְׂרֵה, כְּמוֹ שֶׁהוֹדַעְתָּ לֶעָנָיו

to the ⟨ You made ⟨ as ⟨ of [these] Thirteen, ⟨ the ⟨ today ⟨ for us
humble one   known   covenant
[Moses]

מִקֶּדֶם, כְּמוֹ שֶׁכָּתוּב, וַיֵּרֶד יהוה בֶּעָנָן וַיִּתְיַצֵּב עִמּוֹ

with ⟨ and stood ⟨ in a ⟨ And HASHEM ≪ it is written: ⟨ as ≪ in ancient
him   cloud   descended   times,

שָׁם, וַיִּקְרָא בְשֵׁם יהוה.²

≪ of ⟨ with the ⟨ and He ≪ there,
HASHEM.   Name   called out

CONGREGATION, THEN CHAZZAN:

וַיַּעֲבֹר יהוה עַל פָּנָיו וַיִּקְרָא:

≪ and ≪ [Moses'] ⟨ before ⟨ And HASHEM passed
proclaimed: face,

CONGREGATION AND CHAZZAN RECITE LOUDLY AND IN UNISON:

יהוה, יהוה, אֵל, רַחוּם, וְחַנּוּן, אֶרֶךְ אַפַּיִם,

⟨ to anger, ⟨ Slow ≪ and ⟨ Compassionate ⟨ God, ⟨ HASHEM, ⟨ HASHEM,
Gracious,

וְרַב חֶסֶד, וֶאֱמֶת, נֹצֵר חֶסֶד לָאֲלָפִים, נֹשֵׂא עָוֹן,

⟨ of ⟨ Forgiver ≪ for thousands ⟨ of ⟨ Preserver ≪ and ⟨ in ⟨ and
iniquity,   [of generations],   kindness   Truth,   Kindness Abundant

וָפֶשַׁע, וְחַטָּאָה, וְנַקֵּה.³ וְסָלַחְתָּ לַעֲוֹנֵנוּ וּלְחַטָּאתֵנוּ

≪ and our sins, ⟨ our ⟨ May You ≪ and Who ⟨ and inadvertent ⟨ willful sin,
iniquities forgive absolves. sin,

וּנְחַלְתָּנוּ.⁴ סְלַח לָנוּ אָבִינוּ כִּי חָטָאנוּ, מְחַל לָנוּ

⟨ us, ⟨ pardon ≪ we have ⟨ for ≪ our ⟨ us, ⟨ Forgive ≪ and make us
sinned; Father, Your heritage.

(1) Rosh Hashanah 17a. (2) Exodus 34:5. (3) 34:6-7. (4) 34:9.

מַלְכֵּנוּ כִּי פָשָׁעְנוּ. כִּי אַתָּה אֲדֹנָי טוֹב וְסַלָּח,

《 and forgiving, 〈 are good 〈 O Lord, 〈 You, 〈 For 《 we have willfully sinned. 〈 for 《 our King,

וְרַב חֶסֶד לְכָל קֹרְאֶיךָ.[1]

《 who call upon You. 〈 to all 〈 kind 〈 and abundantly

PREFATORY VERSES TO SELICHAH 33 / פסוקי הקדמה לסליחה לג

מַה נֹּאמַר לְפָנֶיךָ יוֹשֵׁב מָרוֹם, וּמַה נְּסַפֵּר לְפָנֶיךָ

〈 before You, 〈 can we relate 〈 and what 《 on high, 〈 Who dwells 〈 before You, 〈 can we say 〈 What

שׁוֹכֵן שְׁחָקִים.[2] מַה נְּדַבֵּר וּמַה נִּצְטַדָּק.[3] הֵן בַּעֲבָדָיו

〈 in His servants 〈 Indeed, 《 can we justify 〈 And 《 can we declare? 〈 What 《 in the highest Heavens. 〈 who abides

לֹא יַאֲמִין, וּבְמַלְאָכָיו יָשִׂים תָּהֳלָה.[4]

《 fault. 〈 He finds 〈 and with His angels 《 He does not have faith;

כְּרַחֵם אָב עַל בָּנִים, כֵּן תְּרַחֵם יהוה עָלֵינוּ.[5]

《 on us. 〈 HASHEM, 〈 have mercy, 〈 so 《 his children, 〈 toward 〈 a father is 〈 As merciful as

לַיהוה הַיְשׁוּעָה, עַל עַמְּךָ בִרְכָתֶךָ סֶּלָה.[6] יהוה

〈 HASHEM, 《 Selah. 《 is Your blessing, 〈 Your people 〈 upon 《 is salvation, 〈 To HASHEM

צְבָאוֹת עִמָּנוּ, מִשְׂגָּב לָנוּ אֱלֹהֵי יַעֲקֹב סֶלָה.[7]

《 Selah. 〈 of Jacob, 〈 is the God 〈 for us 〈 a stronghold 《 is with us, 〈 Master of Legions,

יהוה צְבָאוֹת, אַשְׁרֵי אָדָם בֹּטֵחַ בָּךְ.[8] יהוה

〈 HASHEM, 《 in You. 〈 who trusts 〈 is the man 〈 — praiseworthy 《 Master of Legions 〈 HASHEM,

הוֹשִׁיעָה, הַמֶּלֶךְ יַעֲנֵנוּ בְיוֹם קָרְאֵנוּ.[9]

《 we call. 〈 on the day 〈 answer us 〈 May the King 《 save!

---

(1) *Psalms* 86:5. (2) From the *Viduy* of Yom Kippur. (3) Cf. *Genesis* 44:16.
(4) *Job* 4:18. (5) Cf. *Psalms* 103:13. (6) 3:9. (7) 46:8. (8) 84:13. (9) 20:10.

סליחה לג / SELICHAH 33

(שניה)

ALL:

אֱלֹהֵינוּ וֵאלֹהֵי אֲבוֹתֵינוּ:

《 of our forefathers: 〈 and the God 〈 Our God

אַךְ בְּמֶתַח דִּין* וּמֵרוּץ חֶבֶל,

《 destructive 〈 and 〈 judg- 〈 Through 《 Just this
[punishment],   powerful,   ment*   strict   [request]:

בְּנֵי אֱמוּנֶיךָ אַל נָא תְחַבֵּל.[1]

《 destroy. 〈 please, 〈 do 〈 of Your 〈 the
not,   faithful ones   children

גְּלוּי הָרִיב לָהֶם נְטֹשׁ,[2]

《 forgo 〈 with them 〈 of the 〈 [Before]
[punishing   [over   dispute   the rev-
them];   their sins]   elation

דְּרֹשׁ עֶלְבּוֹנָם וְאַל תִּטֹּשׁ.

《 forsake 〈 do not 《 their 〈 avenge
them.   disgrace;

הוֹאַלְתָּ לַעֲשׂוֹתָם לְךָ לְעָם,[3]

《 a people; 〈 for You 〈 to make them 〈 You decided

וְאַל תְּשַׁלְּחֵם בְּיַד פִּשְׁעָם.*[4]

《 of their sin.* 〈 into the 〈 send them 〈 [now]
hand   do not

זְדוֹנוֹת חֲשֹׁב כִּשְׁגָגוֹת,*

《 as unintended,* 〈 consider 〈 Deliberate sins

חֲשֹׁךְ מְזִדִים[5] נְפָשׁוֹת לְךָ עוֹרְגוֹת.

《 long. 〈 that 〈 the souls 〈 from inten- 〈 and
for You   tional sins   restrain

---

(1) Cf. *Micah* 2:10. (2) Cf. *Proverbs* 17:14. (3) Cf. *I Samuel* 12:22. (4) Cf. *Job* 8:4. (5) Cf. *Psalms* 19:14.

אַךְ בְּמֶתַח דִּין§ — *Just this [request]: Through strict judgment.* This *sheniyah* of unknown authorship contains an alphabetical acrostic.

בְּיַד פִּשְׁעָם — *Into the hand of their sin.* The commission of a sin creates a destructive angel which becomes the agent to carry out punishment for that sin (*Rashi* to *Job* 8:4). Alternatively, בְּיַד means *in the place of.* The place where a person sins is the place where he is tried (*Metzudos David* based on *Targum Yonasan*).

זְדוֹנוֹת חֲשֹׁב כִּשְׁגָגוֹת — *Deliberate sins consider as unintended.* Moses prayed that when Israel sins and subsequently repents, their deliberate sins should be ameliorated and considered as unintentional (*Yoma* 36b; see also *Yoma* 86b).

טֶנֶף טַהֵר וְתַדִּיחַ כְּתָמִים,

《 the stains, 〈 wash away 《 cleanse, 〈 The filth
[of our sins]

יִצְלַל בְּצוּל כְּבֶד אֲשָׁמִים.[1]

《 of [our] guilt. 〈 the 〈 into the 〈 and
heaviness depths plunge

כָּלָה אַל תַּעַשׂ וְנֶחֱרָצָה,[2]

《 even though 〈 cause 〈 do 〈 Destruc-
it is decreed; not tion

לְקוּחֶיךָ לְקַח מִכַּף הַנְּטוּיָה וְעֵצָה הַיְעוּצָה.[3]

《 that was 〈 and from 《 that is out- 〈 from the 〈 extract 〈 those You
schemed. plot stretched, [foe's] have taken
hand [as Yours]

מוֹעֵד כִּתְקַח לִשְׁפּוֹט מֵישָׁרִים,[4]

《 with fairness, 〈 to judge 〈 when You 《 At the
[the world] choose appointed
time,

נְזֹף בְּמַשְׂטִין מִלְּלַמֵּד קַטֵגוֹרִים.

《 accusations. 〈 that he may 〈 the 〈 censure
not present Adversary,

סֵפֶר זִכְרוֹנוֹת לְפָנֶיךָ בְּהִתְגּוֹלֵל,

《 when it is 〈 before 《 of Remem- 〈 The
unrolled, You brance, Scroll

עֲוֹן עֲקֵבִים לֹא יְסוֹבֵב[5] לְבָעַמִּים מִתְבּוֹלֵל.

《 is mingled. 〈 [Israel] who 〈 surround 〈 let 《 that are 〈 the
among the [with them trodden iniqui-
peoples retribution] not upon, ties

פֶּשֶׁר הַדִּין וּתְבַצַּע הַשּׁוּרָה,*

《 the [strict] line 〈 break 《 on the 〈 Reach a
of the law;* sentence, compromise

צְרוֹף כַּבּוֹר סִיגִים,[6] וּמַהֵר בְּדִיל לְהָסִירָה.

《 remove. 〈 the tin 〈 and 《 [the] dross, 〈 as with 〈 Refine
alloy quickly lye

---

(1) Cf. *Micah* 7:19. (2) Cf. *Isaiah* 10:23. (3) Cf. 14:26. (4) Cf. *Psalms* 75:3. (5) Cf. 49:6. (6) Cf. *Isaiah* 1:25.

פֶּשֶׁר הַדִּין וּתְבַצַּע הַשּׁוּרָה — *Reach a compromise on the sentence, break the [strict] line of the law.* The execution of justice according to the strict letter of the law is called שׁוּרַת הַדִּין, *the line of the law,* or *the wall of the law.* When a dispute is brought before a *beis din,* the judges try to effect a compromise (בִּצּוּעַ or פְּשָׁרָה) between the disputants. As long as the two parties are willing to "bargain" with each other, the judges do not decide the case. Only when the litigants fail to reach an agreement do

קָפוּי וּמִתָּךְ[1] וְכַדּוֹנַג נִמְסָה,

《 that is   〈 and like 《   yet   《Congealed
melted,   wax   [originally]   [like
soft [as milk], cheese],

רֶגַע יִגְעַשׁ אִם בְּמִשְׁפָּט עָלָיו תִּנָּשֵׂא.

《 You would 〈 against 〈 in judgment 〈 if 《 [Man] 〈 in an
rise up.   him   would be   instant
convulsing,

❖ שַׁלֵּם לוֹ כְּמַעֲשֵׂה הַחֶסֶד וְלֹא כִגְמוּלוֹ,

《 as he   〈 and 〈 of [Your] 〈 as an act 〈 him 〈 Reward
deserves;   not   kindness

תַּכְרִיעַ הַכַּף לְזַכּוֹתוֹ[2] וְלֹא לְחַבְּלוֹ.

《 to destroy 〈 and 〈 to vindicate 〈 the 〈 tip
him.   not   him,   scales

תִּפְשֹׁט יָד וּתְקַבְּלוֹ, תְּחָנֵּנוּ בְּבוֹר שַׁחַת מִלְּהַטְבִּילוֹ.

《 do not immerse 〈 of de- 〈 and into 〈 be gracious 《 and accept 〈 Your 〈 Extend
him.   struction   the pit   unto him   him;   hand

ALL, WHILE STANDING:

אֵל מֶלֶךְ יוֹשֵׁב עַל כִּסֵּא רַחֲמִים, מִתְנַהֵג

〈 Who acts 《 of mercy, 〈 the throne 〈 on 〈 Who sits 〈 King 〈 O God,

בַּחֲסִידוּת, מוֹחֵל עֲוֹנוֹת עַמּוֹ, מַעֲבִיר רִאשׁוֹן

〈 [sins,] one 〈 Who 《 of His 〈 the sins 〈 Who 《 with kindness,
removes   people,   pardons

רִאשׁוֹן,[3] מַרְבֶּה מְחִילָה לַחַטָּאִים וּסְלִיחָה לַפּוֹשְׁעִים,

《 to willful 〈 and 〈 to unintentional 〈 pardon 〈 Who abun- 《 by one,
sinners,   forgiveness   sinners   dantly grants

עֹשֶׂה צְדָקוֹת עִם כָּל בָּשָׂר וָרוּחַ, לֹא כְרָעָתָם

〈 in accord 〈 — not 《 and 〈 [beings] 〈 all 〈 with 〈 acts of 〈 Who
with their   spirit   of] flesh   generosity   performs
wickedness

---

(1) Cf. *Job* 10:10. (2) See commentary, p. 27, s.v. מַעֲבִיר רִאשׁוֹן רִאשׁוֹן,
He removes [sins] one by one. (3) *Rosh Hashanah* 17a.

the judges deliberate the merits of each claim
and render a decision. But their decision
must be strictly within the line of the law.

Similarly, when judging a criminal case,
the *beis din* may only judge by the evi-
dence presented and according to the strict
line of the law. The Heavenly Tribunal,
on the other hand, takes a lot more into

consideration. Remorse, repentance, and a
changed outlook all play a role. Thus, the
sentence can be mitigated or even eliminated by the guilty one's attitude.

And so we stand penitentially before
God, pleading with Him to compromise, to
break the strict line of the law and judge
us favorably.

תִּגְמוֹל. ❖ אֵל הוֹרֵיתָ לָנוּ לוֹמַר שְׁלֹשׁ עֶשְׂרֵה, וּזְכוֹר

⟨ remember ⟨⟨ the Thirteen ⟨ to ⟨ us ⟨ You ⟨ O God, ⟨⟨ do You repay them!
[Attributes of Mercy]; recite taught

לָנוּ הַיּוֹם בְּרִית שְׁלֹשׁ עֶשְׂרֵה, כְּמוֹ שֶׁהוֹדַעְתָּ לֶעָנָיו

⟨ to the humble one [Moses] ⟨ You made known ⟨ as ⟨⟨ of [these] Thirteen, ⟨ the covenant ⟨ today ⟨ for us

מִקֶּדֶם, כְּמוֹ שֶׁכָּתוּב, וַיֵּרֶד יהוה בֶּעָנָן וַיִּתְיַצֵּב עִמּוֹ

⟨ with him ⟨ and stood ⟨ in a cloud ⟨ And HASHEM descended ⟨⟨ it is written: ⟨ as ⟨⟨ in ancient times,

שָׁם, וַיִּקְרָא בְשֵׁם יהוה.¹

⟨⟨ of ⟨ with the Name ⟨ and He called out ⟨⟨ there, HASHEM.

CONGREGATION, THEN *CHAZZAN*:

וַיַּעֲבֹר יהוה עַל פָּנָיו וַיִּקְרָא:

⟨⟨ and proclaimed: ⟨⟨ [Moses'] face, ⟨ before ⟨ And HASHEM passed

CONGREGATION AND *CHAZZAN* RECITE LOUDLY AND IN UNISON:

יהוה, יהוה, אֵל, רַחוּם, וְחַנּוּן, אֶרֶךְ אַפַּיִם,

⟨ to anger, ⟨ Slow ⟨⟨ and Gracious, ⟨ Compassionate ⟨ God, ⟨ HASHEM, ⟨ HASHEM,

וְרַב חֶסֶד, וֶאֱמֶת, נֹצֵר חֶסֶד לָאֲלָפִים, נֹשֵׂא עָוֹן,

⟨ of iniquity, ⟨ Forgiver ⟨⟨ for thousands [of generations], ⟨ of kindness ⟨ Preserver ⟨⟨ and Truth, ⟨ in Kindness Abundant ⟨ and

וָפֶשַׁע, וְחַטָּאָה, וְנַקֵּה.² וְסָלַחְתָּ לַעֲוֹנֵנוּ וּלְחַטָּאתֵנוּ

⟨⟨ and our sins, ⟨ our iniquities ⟨ May You forgive ⟨⟨ and Who absolves. ⟨ and inadvertent sin, ⟨ willful sin,

וּנְחַלְתָּנוּ.³ סְלַח לָנוּ אָבִינוּ כִּי חָטָאנוּ, מְחַל לָנוּ

⟨ us, ⟨ pardon ⟨⟨ we have sinned; ⟨ for ⟨⟨ our Father, ⟨ us, ⟨ Forgive ⟨⟨ and make us Your heritage.

מַלְכֵּנוּ כִּי פָשָׁעְנוּ. כִּי אַתָּה אֲדֹנָי טוֹב וְסַלָּח,

⟨⟨ and forgiving, ⟨ are good ⟨ O Lord, ⟨ You, ⟨ For ⟨⟨ we have willfully sinned. ⟨ for ⟨⟨ our King,

וְרַב חֶסֶד לְכָל קֹרְאֶיךָ.⁴

⟨⟨ who call upon You. ⟨ to all ⟨ kind ⟨ and abundantly

---

(1) *Exodus* 34:5. (2) 34:6-7. (3) 34:9. (4) *Psalms* 86:5.

PREFATORY VERSES TO SELICHAH 34 / פסוקי הקדמה לסליחה לד

לְמִשְׁפָּטֶיךָ עָמְדוּ הַיּוֹם, כִּי הַכֹּל עֲבָדֶיךָ.¹ וְהוּא

‹ And He › ‹« are Your servants. › ‹ all › ‹ for «› until › they [Heaven and earth] stand › ‹ this day, › ‹To fulfill Your decree

יִשְׁפֹּט תֵּבֵל בְּצֶדֶק, לְאֻמִּים בְּמֵישָׁרִים.² מִלְּפָנֶיךָ

‹ From before You › ‹« with fairness. › ‹ and nations «› with right-eousness, › ‹ the world › ‹ will judge

מִשְׁפָּטֵנוּ יֵצֵא, עֵינֶיךָ תֶּחֱזֶינָה מֵישָׁרִים.³

‹« uprightness. › ‹ behold › ‹ and Your eyes «› go forth, › ‹ may our judgment

בְּרַחֵם אָב עַל בָּנִים, כֵּן תְּרַחֵם יהוה עָלֵינוּ.⁴

‹« on us. › ‹ HASHEM, › ‹ have mercy, › ‹ so «› his children, › ‹ toward › ‹ a father is › ‹ As merciful as

לַיהוה הַיְשׁוּעָה, עַל עַמְּךָ בִרְכָתֶךָ סֶּלָה.⁵ יהוה

‹ HASHEM, «› Selah. › ‹« is Your blessing, › ‹ Your people › ‹ upon «› is salvation, › ‹ To HASHEM

צְבָאוֹת עִמָּנוּ, מִשְׂגָּב לָנוּ אֱלֹהֵי יַעֲקֹב סֶלָה.⁶

‹« Selah. › ‹ of Jacob, › ‹ is the God › ‹ for us › ‹ a stronghold › ‹« is with us, › ‹ Master of Legions,

יהוה צְבָאוֹת, אַשְׁרֵי אָדָם בֹּטֵחַ בָּךְ.⁷ יהוה

‹ HASHEM, «› in You. › ‹ who trusts › ‹ is the man › ‹ — praiseworthy «› Master of Legions › ‹ HASHEM,

הוֹשִׁיעָה, הַמֶּלֶךְ יַעֲנֵנוּ בְיוֹם קָרְאֵנוּ.⁸

‹« we call. › ‹ on the day › ‹ answer us › ‹ May the King «› save!

SELICHAH 34 / סליחה לד
(שְׁלִישִׁיָּה)

ALL:

אֵל אֱמוּנָה* עֶזְרָה הָבָה, לְעַמְּךָ כֻּלָּם הֵיטִיבָה,

‹« do good; › ‹ all of them, «› For Your people, «› bring [to us]! › ‹ assistance «› Who is faithful,* › ‹ O God

---

(1) *Psalms* 119:91. (2) 9:9. (3) Cf. 17:2. (4) Cf. 103:13. (5) 3:9. (6) 46:8. (7) 84:13. (8) 20:10.

---

§ אֵל אֱמוּנָה — *O God Who is faithful.* This *selichah* comprises twenty-four triplets, and is thus called a שְׁלִישִׁיָּה, *threesome.* The first twenty-two follow an alphabeti-cal acrostic, and the twenty-third bears the author's signature — אֶפְרַיִם, *Ephraim.* This *paytan* is usually identified as R' Ephraim of Regensburg [see prefatory comment to

יַחַד **לַמִּשְׁפָּט** נִקְרָבָה.¹

《 let us approach. 〈 for **judgment** 〈 together

בּוֹחֵן לִבּוֹת כֻּלָּם, מוֹשֵׁל בִּגְבוּרָתוֹ עוֹלָם,*²

《 forever,* 〈 with His might 〈 Who rules 《 all of 《 [men's] 〈 He Who
them, hearts, searches

יָבִיא **בְמִשְׁפָּט** עַל כָּל נֶעְלָם.³

《 hidden [intention]. 〈 every 〈 for 〈 to **judgment** 〈 brings [us]

גָּבוֹהַּ **בַּמִּשְׁפָּט** הָאֵל, נִקְדָּשׁ בִּצְדָקוֹתָיו⁴ כְּהַרְרֵי אֵל,⁵

《 that is like the 〈 by His 〈 hallowed 《 is God, 〈 in judgment 〈 Lofty
mighty mountains, righteousness

וּמִשְׁפָּטָיו עִם יִשְׂרָאֵל.⁶

《 Israel. 〈 of 〈 and [by] His
judgments

דְּלֵה מֵעֹנֶשׁ נְשׂוּאֶיךָ, בְּחֶסֶד וֶאֱמֶת מְנַשְׂאֶיךָ,*

《 exalt You,* 〈 and 〈 who with 《 those You 〈 from 〈 Draw
truth kindness have borne, punishment up

צֶדֶק **וּמִשְׁפָּט** מְכוֹן כִּסְאֶךָ.⁷

《 of Your 〈 are the 〈 and **justice** 〈 [for]
Throne. foundation righteousness

הַיְשֵׁר לְפָנֶיךָ לֵב עָקֹב, דִּינֶךָ הָהָר יִקֹּב,*

《 pierce,* 〈 the 《 let Your 《 that is 〈 the heart 〈 before 〈 Straighten
mountain law, crooked; [of man] You

---

(1) Cf. *Isaiah* 41:1. (2) *Psalms* 66:7. (3) *Ecclesiastes* 12:14. (4) Cf. *Isaiah* 5:16.
(5) Cf. *Psalms* 36:7. (6) *Deuteronomy* 33:21. (7) Cf. *Psalms* 89:15.

Selichah 74]. The third line of each triplet is a fragment of a Scriptural verse and contains some form of the word מִשְׁפָּט, which can mean *judgment, justice,* or *law.*

עוֹלָם — *Forever.* The translation follows *Radak* and *Ibn Ezra* (*Psalms* 66:7), who understand the word as if it read לְעוֹלָם. *Targum,* however, renders עוֹלָם, *the world;* thus the stich means: *He rules the world with His might.*

... בְּחֶסֶד וֶאֱמֶת מְנַשְׂאֶיךָ — *Who with kindness and truth exalt You ....* This stich may allude either to God's kindness and truth for which Israel praises Him, or to Israel's kindness and truth by which they sanctify and exalt God. Alternatively, this and the next stich form a quotation: *They exalt You by [reciting the verse (Psalms*

89:15)], *"Righteousness and justice are Your Throne's foundation; kindness and truth [precede Your countenance]."*

דִּינֶךָ הָהָר יִקֹּב — *Let Your law the mountain pierce.* This Talmudic expression describes the job of the *beis din* once the litigants stand before the court and the proceedings have started. Until that point, it is proper to attempt mediation that will lead to a settlement agreed upon by both parties. But once the court hearing has begun, "let the law pierce the mountain," for nothing in the world, not even the loftiest mountain, can stand in the way of God's justice; the judges must render their decision based on the principles of *halachah* and not continue to attempt a mediated settlement (see *Sanhedrin* 6b).

מִשְׁפָּט לֵאלֹהֵי יַעֲקֹב.[1]

« of Jacob. ‹ of the God ‹ [for] it is the **judgment**

וְיֹשֶׁר מִדּוֹתֶיךָ נֶחְמְדוּ, יוֹשְׁבֵי תֵבֵל צֶדֶק לָמָדוּ,[2]

« have ‹ — who ‹ of ‹ [to] the ‹ are ‹ of Your ‹ And the
learned, righteousness earth inhabitants desirous Attributes uprightness

לְמִשְׁפָּטֶיךָ עָמֵדוּ.[3]

« they stand to ‹ [when] Your
[receive]. **judgments**

זְקוּקָה צְרוּפָה חוֹתֶמֶת, בְּפֹעַל אָדָם נֶחְתֶּמֶת,*

« is it sealed,* ‹ of man ‹ by the « is the seal ‹ and refined ‹ Clear
himself deed [of Your verdict]:

מִשְׁפְּטֵי יהוה אֱמֶת.[4]

« are true. ‹ of ‹ [for] the
HASHEM **judgments**

חָרַד כָּל מִדִּין בּוֹדֵק, טוֹחֵן וְשׁוֹחֵק הָדֵק,[5]

« [to examine ‹ and pulverizes ‹ Who « of the ‹ before ‹ do all ‹ Tremble
them] [men's deeds Examiner, the [men]
minutely, and hearts] grinds judgment

מִשְׁפְּטֵי יהוה אֱמֶת וָצֶדֶק.[6]

« and ‹ are true ‹ of ‹ the **judgments**
righteous. HASHEM

טוֹב לְמָעוֹז כִּנְאָמוֹ, יוֹם זֶה יִשְׁכַּח זַעְמוֹ,[7]

‹ His fury ‹ He will ‹ On this day « as He ‹ a fortress [in «Beneficent
forget has said. time of trouble], He is,

לַעֲשׂוֹת מִשְׁפָּט עַמּוֹ.[8]

« on His ‹ judgment ‹ when
people. passing

יֵחַלּוּ בְצִקּוֹן דְּבֵקֶיךָ, יְסַלְסְלוּ בְשָׁלוֹם חֻקֶּיךָ,

‹ of Your ‹ for the ‹ they exalt «will those who ‹with outpouring ‹ Pray
decrees perfection [You] cling to You; [of their heart]

---

(1) *Psalms* 81:5. (2) Cf. *Isaiah* 26:9. (3) Cf. *Psalms* 119:91. (4) 19:10. (5) Cf. *Exodus* 30:36.
(6) Unlike the closing stich of the other stanzas, this one is not a Scriptural verse;
some editions read מִשְׁפָּט אֱמֶת וָצֶדֶק, *a true and righteous judgment,*
cf. *Zechariah* 7:9; *Psalms* 119:121. (7) *Nahum* 1:7. (8) Cf. *I Kings* 8:59.

בְּפֹעַל אָדָם נֶחְתֶּמֶת — *By the deed of man himself is it sealed.* See commentary to *Selichah* 26 (s.v. וּבְיָדוֹ סְדוּרוֹת). Alternatively, the stich means that it is man's deed that seals his fate, for Divine judgment is based upon man's actions; he is always judged in accordance with his deeds.

עַל מִשְׁפְּטֵי צִדְקֶךָ.[1]

《 that are 〈 Your 〈 and
righteous. **judgments** for

כַּלֵּה פֶּשַׁע נִכְתָּם, וְאַל יֵבוֹשׁוּ מְיַחֲלֶיךָ בְּמַבָּטָם,

《 in their 〈 those who place 〈 be 〈 and 《 that stain, 〈 of [their] 〈 Make
aspiration, their hope in You shamed let not sins an end

וְעָשִׂיתָ מִשְׁפָּטָם.[2]

《 judgment on them. 〈 when You pass

לְשִׁמְךָ וּלְזִכְרְךָ הוּקַמְנוּ, לִבְרִית עוֹלָם הוּשָׂמְנוּ,[3]

《 were we set; 〈 everlasting 〈 as a 《 were we 〈 and of Your 〈 For the sake
covenant established; remembrance of Your Name

וְאַל תָּבוֹא בְמִשְׁפָּט עִמָּנוּ.[4]

《 with us. 〈 into strict 〈 enter 〈 so
judgment do not

מֶלֶךְ בִּקְדוֹשֵׁי אֶרֶץ,[5] בְּרַחֲמָיו יִגְדֹּר פֶּרֶץ,[6]

《 the breach 〈 He will 〈 in His mercy 〈 awesome 〈 over holy 〈 He Who
[in Israel's wall], mend [angels], is King

בְּמִשְׁפָּט יַעֲמִיד אֶרֶץ.[7]

《 the 〈 He will 〈 and with
world. establish **judgment**

נְגִינוֹתַי כָּל הַיּוֹם[8] יְאַשְּׁרוּהוּ, שַׂגִּיא כֹחַ לֹא מְצָאנוּהוּ,[9]

《 have we 〈 never 〈 in 〈 to be 《 praise Him, 〈 day long 〈 all 〈 My songs
found Him, His over-
strength bearing

כִּי הַמִּשְׁפָּט לֵאלֹהִים הוּא.[10]

《 it is [and He is merciful]. 〈 by God 〈 the **judgment**, 〈 for

שַׂגֵּב חַסְדְּךָ לְעַמֶּךָ, לְשַׁוְעָתָם פְּתַח שָׁמֶיךָ,

《 Your 〈 open 〈 to their outcry 《 to Your 〈 Your 〈 Strength-
heavens, people; kindness en

בְּמִשְׁפָּט לְאֹהֲבֵי שְׁמֶךָ.[11]

《 Your 〈 to those 〈 as is [Your]
Name. who love **practice**

עָלֶיךָ נַשְׁלִיךְ כָּל יְהָבִים,[12] כַּף צֶדֶק תַּכְרִיעַ בָּאֲהָבִים,

《 with love, 〈 may You 〈 of 〈 the 《 [our] 〈 all 〈 we will 〈 Upon
tilt, vindication scales burdens; cast You

---

(1) *Psalms* 119:62. (2) *I Kings* 8:45. (3) Cf. *II Samuel* 23:5. (4) Cf. *Psalms* 143:2. (5) Cf. 89:5.
(6) Cf. *Amos* 9:11. (7) *Proverbs* 29:4. (8) Cf. *Lamentations* 3:14. (9) Cf. *Job* 37:23, see *Rashi* there.
(10) *Deuteronomy* 1:17. (11) *Psalms* 119:132. (12) Cf. 55:23.

כִּי מִשְׁפָּטֶיךָ טוֹבִים.[1]

‹ for › Your **judgments** ‹ are good. «

פָּנֶיךָ הָאֵר לִמְחִילָתִי, בִּבְצָעִי אַל תְּכַבֶּה גַחַלְתִּי,[2]

‹ Let Your ‹ shine › in forgiveness ‹ despite my › do ‹ extinguish › my [soul's]
countenance for me; wrongdoing not ember, «

כִּי לְמִשְׁפָּטֶיךָ יִחָלְתִּי.[3]

‹ for › to Your **judgments** ‹ I look expectantly. «

צַדְּקֵנוּ כְּאַחַת חֲטִיבָה, חָשְׁכֵנוּ מִלַּהַט הַיּוֹם הַבָּא,[4]

‹ Vindicate ‹ as a single › group, « and save us › from the ‹ of the ‹ to
us flame Day Come —

מִשְׁפָּטֶיךָ תְּהוֹם רַבָּה.[5]

‹ Your **judgments** ‹ are like the › that are «
deep waters vast.

קָרֵב יֵשַׁע[6] שְׁבָטֶיךָ, אֲחוּזִים בְּחֶבְלֵי[7] שְׁפָטֶיךָ,

‹ Bring ‹ the › of Your « who are ‹ in the labor ‹ of Your trial
closer salvation tribes, caught pains

וְיוֹשֶׁר מִשְׁפָּטֶיךָ.[8]

‹ and the › of Your «
righteousness **judgments.**

רֶנֶן מִלֵּב וּבָשָׂר וּנְשָׁמָה, יַעֲלֶה לְךָ הַשָּׁמַיְמָה,

« Song › — from « and flesh › and soul — « will rise › to « Heavenward, «
heart up You

מְקוֹם הַמִּשְׁפָּט שָׁמָּה.[9]

‹ the place › where Your ‹ is there. «
judgment

שׁוֹפְטֵנוּ מְחוֹקְקֵנוּ בְּכַפֶּיךָ,*[10] לַמֵּד דְּרָכֶיךָ מְצַפֶּיךָ,

‹ Our Judge, ‹ You Who have « on Your palm,* ‹ teach › Your › to those who
engraved us ways await You

---

(1) *Psalms* 119:39. (2) Cf. *II Samuel* 14:7. (3) *Psalms* 119:43. (4) Cf. *Malachi* 3:19. (5) *Psalms* 36:7. (6) Cf. *85:10*. (7) Cf. *Jeremiah* 13:21. (8) Cf. *Psalms* 119:137. (9) *Ecclesiastes* 3:16. (10) Cf. *Isaiah* 33:22; 49:16.

מְחוֹקְקֵנוּ בְּכַפֶּיךָ — *You Who have engraved us on Your palm.*

The Talmud (*Taanis* 4a) relates an exchange between Israel and God: Israel requested of God, "Master of the Universe, *place me as a seal on Your heart, as a seal on Your arm*" (*Song of Songs* 8:6).

God replied, "My daughter, you request something that at times can be seen and at other times cannot be seen. [A seal placed on the heart or arm cannot be seen when a person is clothed.] However, I shall make of you something that can be seen at all times, הֵן עַל כַּפַּיִם חַקּוֹתִיךְ, *behold, on [My] palms have I engraved you*" (*Isaiah* 49:16).

וְכֹל **מִשְׁפְּטֵי** פִֽיךָ.[1]

《of Your mouth. 〈 the **judgments** 〈 and all

תַּשְׁפִּֽיעַ חַסְדְּךָ דַיֵּֽנוּ, תִּגְבֹּֽרֶת רַחֲמֶֽיךָ לְמַאֲוַיֵּֽינוּ,

《 to [answer] 〈 of Your 〈 a strength- 《 sufficiently 〈 Your 〈 Cause to flow
our desires.　mercy　ening　for our needs; kindness　in abundance

כְּמִשְׁפָּטֶֽיךָ חַיֵּֽנוּ.[2]

《 sustain 《　As is Your
us in life!　**just** way,

אַפִּרְיוֹן לְעִי הַשָּׂדֶה, מַהֵר לְשַׁכְלֵל יְסוֹדָהּ,

《 its 〈 to 〈 quickly 《 in the 〈 has become 〈 [Your]
foundation,　reestablish　come　field —　a heap　Temple
　　　　　　　　　　　　　[of rubble]

צִיּוֹן **בְּמִשְׁפָּט** תִּפָּדֶֽה.[3]

《 be 〈 through 〈 and let
redeemed.　**justice**　Zion

❖ מֵאוֹיְבַי אֶנָּקְמָה פִּזְּרוּנִי, גֻּדַּע קַרְנוֹת[4] זֵרוּנִי,

《 of those who 〈 the pride 〈 cut 《 those who 《 may I have 〈 On my
scattered me,　　　　down　have dispersed　vengeance,　enemies
　　　　　　　　　　　　　me [in Exile];

וּמִשְׁפָּטֶֽיךָ יַעְזְרֽוּנִי.[5]

《 assist me. 〈 and let Your **judgments**

ALL, WHILE STANDING:

אֵל **מֶֽלֶךְ** יוֹשֵׁב עַל כִּסֵּא רַחֲמִים, מִתְנַהֵג

〈 Who acts 《 of mercy, 〈 the throne 〈 on 《 Who sits 〈 King 〈 O God,

בַּחֲסִידוּת, מוֹחֵל עֲוֹנוֹת עַמּוֹ, מַעֲבִיר רִאשׁוֹן

〈 [sins,] one 〈 Who 《 of His 〈 the sins 〈 Who 《 with kindness,
　　　removes　people,　　　pardons

רִאשׁוֹן,[6] מַרְבֶּה מְחִילָה לְחַטָּאִים וּסְלִיחָה לַפּוֹשְׁעִים,

《 to willful 〈 and 〈 to unintentional 〈 pardon 〈 Who abun- 《 by one,
sinners,　forgiveness　sinners　　　dantly grants

עֹשֶׂה צְדָקוֹת עִם כָּל בָּשָׂר וָרֽוּחַ, לֹא כְרָעָתָם

〈 in accord with 〈 — not 《 and 〈 [beings 〈 all 〈 with 〈 acts of 〈 Who
their wickedness　　　spirit　of] flesh　　　generosity　performs

תִּגְמוֹל. ❖ אֵל הוֹרֵֽיתָ לָֽנוּ לוֹמַר שְׁלֹשׁ עֶשְׂרֵה, וּזְכוֹר

〈 remem- 《 the Thirteen 〈 to 〈 us 〈 You 〈 O God, 《 do You
ber　[Attributes of Mercy];　recite　　taught　　repay them!

---

(1) Cf. *Psalms* 119:13. (2) Cf. 119:156. (3) *Isaiah* 1:27. (4) Cf. *Psalms* 75:11. (5) 119:175. (6) *Rosh Hashanah* 17a.

לָנוּ הַיּוֹם בְּרִית שְׁלֹשׁ עֶשְׂרֵה, כְּמוֹ שֶׁהוֹדַעְתָּ לֶעָנָיו

⟨ to the   ⟨ You made   ⟨ as   ⟪ of [these] Thirteen,   ⟨ the   ⟨ today   ⟨ for us
humble one   known   covenant
[Moses]

מִקֶּדֶם, כְּמוֹ שֶׁכָּתוּב, וַיֵּרֶד יהוה בֶּעָנָן וַיִּתְיַצֵּב עִמּוֹ

⟨ with   ⟨ and stood   ⟨ in a   And HASHEM   ⟪ it is written: ⟨ as   ⟪ in ancient
him   cloud   descended   times,

שָׁם, וַיִּקְרָא בְשֵׁם יהוה.[1]

⟪ of   ⟨ with the   ⟨ and He   ⟪ there,
HASHEM.   Name   called out

CONGREGATION, THEN CHAZZAN:

וַיַּעֲבֹר יהוה עַל פָּנָיו וַיִּקְרָא:

⟪   and   ⟪ [Moses'] ⟨ before ⟨   And HASHEM passed
proclaimed: face,

CONGREGATION AND CHAZZAN RECITE LOUDLY AND IN UNISON:

יהוה, יהוה, אֵל, רַחוּם, וְחַנּוּן, אֶרֶךְ אַפַּיִם,

⟨ to anger,   ⟨ Slow   ⟪ and   ⟨ Compassionate ⟨ God,   ⟨ HASHEM,   ⟨ HASHEM,
Gracious,

וְרַב חֶסֶד, וֶאֱמֶת, נֹצֵר חֶסֶד לָאֲלָפִים, נֹשֵׂא עָוֹן,

⟨ of ⟨ Forgiver ⟪   for   ⟨ of   ⟨ Preserver ⟨ and   ⟨ in ⟨ and
iniquity,   thousands   kindness   Truth,   Kindness Abundant
[of generations],

וָפֶשַׁע, וְחַטָּאָה, וְנַקֵּה.[2] וְסָלַחְתָּ לַעֲוֹנֵנוּ וּלְחַטָּאתֵנוּ

⟪ and our sins,   ⟨ our   ⟨ May You   ⟪ and Who ⟨ and inadvertent ⟨ willful sin,
iniquities   forgive   absolves.   sin,

וּנְחַלְתָּנוּ.[3] סְלַח לָנוּ אָבִינוּ כִּי חָטָאנוּ, מְחַל לָנוּ

⟨ us,   ⟨ pardon   ⟪ we have   ⟨ for ⟪   our   ⟨ us,   ⟨ Forgive   ⟪ and make us
sinned;   Father,   Your heritage.

מַלְכֵּנוּ כִּי פָשָׁעְנוּ. כִּי אַתָּה אֲדֹנָי טוֹב וְסַלָּח,

⟪ and   ⟨ are   ⟨ O Lord,   ⟨ You,   ⟨ For ⟪   we have   ⟨ for   ⟪ our King,
forgiving,   good   willfully sinned.

וְרַב חֶסֶד לְכָל קֹרְאֶיךָ.[4]

⟪ who call   ⟨ to all   ⟨ kind ⟨ and
upon You.   abundantly

---

(1) *Exodus* 34:5. (2) 34:6-7. (3) 34:9. (4) *Psalms* 86:5.

פסוקי הקדמה לסליחה לה / PREFATORY VERSES TO SELICHAH 35

רַחֲמֶיךָ רַבִּים יהוה, כְּמִשְׁפָּטֶיךָ חַיֵּנוּ.[1] יְחַיֵּנוּ

‹ He will 《 preserve ‹ as is Your practice, 《 Hashem; ‹ are ‹ Your mercies
revivify us   me.   abundant

מִיָּמִים, בַּיּוֹם הַשְּׁלִישִׁי יְקִמֵנוּ וְנִחְיֶה לְפָנָיו.[2] כִּי

‹For 《 in His ‹ and we ‹ He will ‹ on the third day 《 from our two days
Presence.   will live   raise us up   [of redemption]   [of destruction];

שָׁם צִוָּה יהוה אֶת הַבְּרָכָה, חַיִּים עַד הָעוֹלָם.[3]

《 eternity. ‹ until ‹ May there 《 blessing. ‹ the ‹ Hashem has ‹ there
be life   commanded

כְּרַחֵם אָב עַל בָּנִים, כֵּן תְּרַחֵם יהוה עָלֵינוּ.[4]

《 on us. ‹ Hashem, ‹ have ‹ so 《 his ‹ toward ‹ a ‹ As merciful as
mercy,   children,   father is

לַיהוה הַיְשׁוּעָה, עַל עַמְּךָ בִרְכָתֶךָ סֶּלָה.[5] יהוה

‹ Hashem, 《 Selah. ‹ is Your ‹ Your ‹ upon 《 is salvation, ‹ To Hashem
blessing,   people

צְבָאוֹת עִמָּנוּ, מִשְׂגָּב לָנוּ אֱלֹהֵי יַעֲקֹב סֶלָה.[6]

《 Selah. 《 of Jacob, ‹ is the God ‹ for us ‹ a 《 is with us, ‹ Master of
stronghold   Legions,

יהוה צְבָאוֹת, אַשְׁרֵי אָדָם בֹּטֵחַ בָּךְ.[7] יהוה

‹ Hashem, 《 in You. ‹ who ‹ is the ‹ — praiseworthy 《 Master ‹ Hashem,
trusts   man   of Legions

הוֹשִׁיעָה, הַמֶּלֶךְ יַעֲנֵנוּ בְיוֹם קָרְאֵנוּ.[8]

《 we call. ‹ on the day ‹ answer us ‹ May the King 《 save!

סליחה לה / SELICHAH 35
(שלמונית)

ALL:

(אֱלֹהֵינוּ וֵאלֹהֵי אֲבוֹתֵינוּ:)

《 of our forefathers:) ‹ and God ‹ (Our God

חַיִּים אֲרוּכִים תִּכְתְּבֵנוּ* נָטוּעַ בְּלִי לַעֲקוֹר,

《 to be ‹ but ‹ [Israel] 《 may You ‹ of longevity ‹ **Life**
uprooted.   not   planted   inscribe for us,*

---

(1) Cf. *Psalms* 119:156. (2) *Hosea* 6:2. (3) *Psalms* 133:3. (4) Cf. 103:13. (5) 3:9. (6) 46:8. (74) 84:13. (8) 20:10.

§◄ חַיִּים אֲרוּכִים תִּכְתְּבֵנוּ — *Life of longevity may You inscribe for us.* This is the third
in a series of four *selichos*, each of which revolves around a key word that begins and

בְּשִׁבְתְּךָ עַל כִּסֵּא מַעֲשִׂים לִסְקוֹר,

《 to review, 〈 [men's] 〈 [Your] 〈 upon 〈 As You sit
deeds Throne

הַטּוֹב צָפֹה וְהָרָע אַל תַּחְקוֹר,

《 investigate, 〈 do not 〈 but the bad 《 look 〈 at the good

כִּי עִמְּךָ מְקוֹר חַיִּים.[1]

《 of **life.** 〈 is the source 〈 with you 〈 for

חַיִּים בִּרְצוֹנוֹ וְרֶגַע בְּאַפּוֹ[2] נִרְאֵית,*

《 apparent.* 〈 is His 〈 for but a 《 [is granted] 〈 **Life**
anger moment from His favor;

לֹא לָנֶצַח תָּרִיב[3] נַחֲלַת הַנִּלְאָת,[4]

《 who are 〈 [His] heritage- 〈 will He 〈 forever 〈 not
wearied. people punish

הַשְׁמִיעֵנִי נָא סָלַחְתִּי[5] עָוֹן לָשֵׂאת,

《 will be 〈 the 《 I have 《 please, 〈 Let me hear,
absolved; iniquity forgiven,

רְאֵה נָתַתִּי לְפָנֶיךָ הַיּוֹם אֶת הַחַיִּים.[6]

《 **life.** 〈 today 〈 before 〈 — I have 《 see
you placed

חַיִּים גְּאוֹל מִשַּׁחַת, תְּעַטְּרֵנִי חֶסֶד[7] אֶזְרָח,[8]

《 [in the merit] of [Ab- 〈 with 〈 crown me 《 from ruin; 〈 and redeem 〈 **Life**
raham] the Ezrahite. kindness [me] [grant me]

וֶאֱמֶת יַשְׁרֵשׁ יַעֲקֹב יָצִיץ וּפָרַח,[9]

《 and 〈 bud 〈 by Jacob 〈 implanted 〈 Let the
blossom. [in us] truth

תַּרְחִיק פְּשָׁעֵינוּ כִּרְחוֹק מַעֲרָב מִמִּזְרָח,[10]

《 from east; 〈 as west 〈 as far away 〈 our willful sins 〈 Distance

תּוֹדִיעֵנוּ אֹרַח חַיִּים.[11]

《 of **life.** 〈 the path 〈 make known to us

---

(1) *Psalms* 36:10. (2) Cf. 30:6. (3) Cf. *Isaiah* 57:16. (4) Cf. *Psalms* 68:10. (5) See *Numbers* 14:20.
(6) *Deuteronomy* 30:15. (7) Cf. *Psalms* 103:4. (8) See commentary to *Selichah 58*, s.v. אִיתָן לִמֵּד דַּעַת.
(9) *Isaiah* 27:6. (10) Cf. *Psalms* 103:12. (11) Cf. 16:11.

---

ends each stanza. In the present *selichah*, the theme is חַיִּים, *life* (or *live, living, alive*). [See prefatory comment to *Selichah 26* regarding authorship of this work.]

וְרֶגַע בְּאַפּוֹ נִרְאֵית — *For but a moment is His*

anger apparent. The Talmud states that God's anger lasts for a רֶגַע, *a moment.* And the length of a moment is the amount of time it takes to utter the two syllables of its name, רֶ-גַע (*Berachos* 7a).

חַיִּים דְּבָרְךָ יַדְּעֵנוּ*, אֵל גִּבּוֹר וְיוֹעֵץ,[1]

《 and Who 〈 Who is 〈 O 《 make it 《 is Your 〈 **Live**
Advises, Mighty God known to us,* word;

לְהִדָּבֵק בְּתוֹרָתֶךָ, אוֹתָנוּ בְּטוֹבָה לְהוֹעֵץ,

《 provide 〈 well 〈 to us 《 to Your Torah, 〈 [how we may]
advice. cling

הַגְבֵּר טוֹב עַל צְפוֹנִי[2] לְהָרֵעַ,

《 to break 〈 my hidden 〈 over 〈 the 〈 Strengthen
[its power], [Evil Good
Inclination] [Inclination]

לִשְׁמוֹר אֶת דֶּרֶךְ עֵץ הַחַיִּים.[3]

《 of **Life**. 〈 [to] the Tree〈 the way 〈 to guard

חַיִּים הִיא לַמַּחֲזִיקִים בָּהּ,[4] וְרִפְאוּת וּמֶרְוֹחַ,

《 and salve. 〈 and healing 《 it, 〈 for those who grasp 〈 it is 〈 **Life**

תוֹמְכֶיהָ מְאָשָּׁרִים[4] בְּאוֹר זָרוּעַ זָרוּחַ,

《 that 〈 that is sown 〈 [meriting] 〈 are 〈 Those who
shines [for the the light praiseworthy, support it
[for them]; righteous

וְכָל הַדָּבֵק בָּהּ יִהְיֶה סָרוּחַ,

〈 a surplus 〈 will be 〈 to it 〈 who cling 〈 and
[of blessing] granted all

כָּל בָּשָׂר אֲשֶׁר בּוֹ רוּחַ חַיִּים.[5]

《 of **life**. 〈 the 〈 has 〈 that 〈 flesh 〈 [over]
spirit in it all

חַיִּים וְשָׁלוֹם תִּסְמְכֵנוּ, בְּיִרְאָה אוֹתְךָ לַעֲבוֹד,[6]

《 we will be able 〈 for You 〈 [so that] 〈 may You 〈 and peace 〈 With **life**
to serve [You], with awe support us

וְנָגִילָה וְנִשְׂמְחָה בָךְ,[7] רְשָׁעִים בַּאֲבוֹד,[8]

《 are lost. 〈 while the 《 with 〈 and be glad 〈 let us
wicked You, rejoice

שְׁלשׁ מֵאוֹת וַעֲשָׂרָה* אוֹתָנוּ לִזְבּוֹד,

《 will be 〈 to us 〈 and ten 〈 hundred 〈 Three
apportioned; [worlds]*

---

(1) Cf. *Isaiah* 9:5. (2) See commentary to *Selichah* 24, s.v. מִכְשׁוֹל. (3) *Genesis* 3:24. (4) Cf. *Proverbs* 3:18. (5) Cf. *Genesis* 6:17. (6) Cf. the conclusion of the Blessing on the Temple Service when the Priestly Blessing is said. (7) Cf. *Psalms* 118:24; *Song of Songs* 1:4. (8) Cf. *Proverbs* 11:10.

חַיִּים דְּבָרְךָ יַדְּעֵנוּ — *Live is Your word; make it known to us.* Alternatively: *O Living One, make Your word known to us.*

שְׁלשׁ מֵאוֹת וַעֲשָׂרָה — *Three hundred and ten [worlds].* The very last Mishnah in the Talmud states: In the future, the Holy One,

יִרְאַת יהוה עֹשֶׁר וְכָבוֹד וְחַיִּים.[1]

» and **life**. ‹ honor, ‹ is riches, ‹ of ‹ [the result of]
HASHEM fear

חַיִּים זְבָדַנִי זֶבֶד טוֹב,[2] גְּדוֹל הָעֵצָה,[3]

» of Counsel. ‹ [by] the ‹ that is ‹ an ‹ I was ‹ **Of life,**
One Who good endow- endowed
is Great ment

מַחְסֶה לָנוּ עֶזְרָה בַצָּרוֹת נִמְצָא,[4]

» is ‹ [Who] ‹ a help » for ‹ [He is]
accessible. in distress us, a shelter

שׁוּבָה אֵלַי וְאָשׁוּבָה,[5] אָמַר בִּפְצִיחָה,

» in a clear ‹ He has » and I will return ‹ to Me ‹ Return
utterance, spoken [to you],

כִּי מוֹצְאִי מָצָא חַיִּים.[6]

» **life**. ‹ has ‹ he who ‹ For
found finds Me

חַיִּים חִנָּם חָנֵּנִי, אֵל אֱלֹהֵי הָרוּחוֹת,[*7]

» of the spirits;* ‹ God » O ‹ grant me ‹ as a ‹ **Life**
God, undeserved, free gift

עָוֹן תִּמְחֹל חָרוּת עַל הַלֻּחוֹת,[8]

» stone tablets. ‹ upon ‹ [though it ‹ forgive, ‹ [my]
be] engraved iniquity

וְשׂוֹנְאֶיךָ יִלְבְּשׁוּ בֹשֶׁת בִּיסוֹר תּוֹכָחוֹת,[9]

» of censure. ‹ with the » with ‹ be clad ‹ May Your
suffering shame, enemies

לֹא יְשׁוּבוּן וְלֹא יַשִּׂיגוּ אָרְחוֹת חַיִּים.[10]

» of **life**. ‹ the paths ‹ reach ‹ nor ‹ May they
neither return

חַיִּים טוֹבִים גְּמוֹל לַעֲבָדֶיךָ,[11] נַפְשָׁם לִגְאוֹל

‹ to redeem ‹ their souls » to Your ‹ may you ‹ that is ‹ **Life**
servants, grant good

---

(1) *Proverbs* 22:4. (2) Cf. *Genesis* 30:20. (3) *Jeremiah* 32:19.
(4) Cf. *Psalms* 46:2. (5) *Malachi* 3:7. (6) *Proverbs* 8:35. (7) *Numbers* 16:22.
(8) *Exodus* 32:16. (9) Cf. *Job* 8:22. (10) *Proverbs* 2:19. (11) Cf. *Psalms* 119:17.

Blessed is He, will grant a heritage of three hundred and ten worlds to each and every righteous person (*Uktzin* 3:12). Thus, we pray that we be found righteous when our judgment is issued, and are among those who receive that portion.

אֱלֹהֵי הָרוּחוֹת — *God of the spirits*. According to *Rashi* (*Numbers* 16:22), this phrase describes God as the One Who knows the spirits, the innermost thoughts, of man. It is synonymous with יוֹדֵעַ מַחְשָׁבוֹת, *Knower of thoughts*. According to *Ibn Ezra* (ibid.),

מַרְאוֹת שַׁחַת,[1] כְּנָם נִשְׁאַל נִשְׁאָל,[2]*

《 a request. 〈 the one who requested 〈 as stated* 《 Gehinnom, 〈 not to witness

לֹא כֵן הָרְשָׁעִים[3] שֶׁפָּרְקוּ עוֹל,

《Your yoke; 〈 who threw off 〈 for the wicked 〈 so 〈 Not

יַשִּׂיא מָוֶת עָלֵימוֹ, יֵרְדוּ שְׁאוֹל חַיִּים.[4]

《 alive. 〈 to the grave 〈 may they descend 《 against them, 〈 death 〈 incite

חַיִּים יוֹדוּךָ כָּמוֹנוּ, וְלֹא קְרוּצֵי קֶרֶץ,*

《 those completely cut off [from life].* 〈 but not 《 as we do; 〈 will thank 〈 **Those Alive**

אָב לַבָּנִים יוֹדִיעַ[5] שִׁבְחֲךָ בְּמֶרֶץ,

《 through forceful [teaching], 〈 Your praise 〈 will make known 〈 to his children 〈 Each father

וַאֲנַחְנוּ נְבָרֵךְ יָהּ,[6] שִׁבְחֲךָ לְהַעֲרֵץ,

《 exalting, 〈 Your praise 《 God, 〈 will bless 〈 and we

לִרְאוֹת בְּטוּב יהוה בְּאֶרֶץ הַחַיִּים.[7]

《 of **life**. 〈 in the land 〈 of HASHEM 〈 the goodness 〈 thus, we will see

חַיִּים כֻּלְּכֶם הַיּוֹם,[8] תַּשְׁמִיעַ טֶרֶף חֻקָּם,[9]

《 of their daily allotment. 〈 [together with] the food 〈 may You announce 《 today, 〈 are all of you 〈 **Alive**

מֵחַטָּאתָם טַהֲרֵם[10] וְאַל תְּשִׁיבֵם רֵיקָם,

《 empty-handed. 〈 turn them away 〈 and do not 〈 purify them 〈 From their sin

---

(1) Cf. *Psalms* 16:10. (2) Cf. *I Samuel* 20:28. (3) *Psalms* 1:4. (4) 55:16. (5) Cf. *Isaiah* 38:19. (6) *Psalms* 115:18. (7) Cf. 27:13. (8) *Deuteronomy* 4:4. (9) Cf. *Proverbs* 30:8. (10) Cf. *Psalms* 51:4.

---

it means that God is Master of all living creatures.

כְּנָם נִשְׁאַל נִשְׁאָל — *As stated ....* King David, the Psalmist, said: *You will not abandon my soul to the grave; You will not allow Your devout one to witness Gehinnom* (*Psalms* 16:10). King David is called נִשְׁאָל נִשְׁאַל [lit., *ask did he ask* — he asked earnestly] by the *paytan* based on the words of Jonathan when he explained David's absence to King Saul (see *I Samuel* 20:28).

חַיִּים יוֹדוּךָ ... וְלֹא קְרוּצֵי קֶרֶץ — *Those alive will thank You ... but not those completely cut off [from life].* The verse states: לֹא הַמֵּתִים יְהַלְלוּ יָהּ, *Neither [can] the dead praise God* (*Psalms* 115:17). The people who fail to recognize God's Omnipresence and influence over the world resemble *the dead*, who are insensitive to all external stimuli and who are oblivious to reality (*R' Azariah Figo*). However, the righteous, who are stirred by God's Presence,

מְמְתִים יָדְךָ* יהוה, מַלֵּא סִפְקָם,

《 their need, 〈 fulfill 《 O 《 by Your 〈 Those des-
HASHEM, hand,* tined to die

מְמְתִים מֵחֶלֶד חֶלְקָם בַּחַיִּים.[1]*

《 be among 〈 let their 〈 of old age 〈 even those
the **living.*** portion who die

חַיִּים לְמַעְלָה לְמַשְׂכִּיל, לְמַעַן סוּר מֵחֶרֶךְ,[2]

《 being burned 〈 he 〈 in order 〈 for the 〈 is an 〈 **Life**
[in *Gehinnom*]. avoid that wise man, advantage

אַךְ אֱלֹהִים יִפְדֶּה נַפְשִׁי מִפֶּרֶךְ,[3]

《from backbreak-〈 my soul 〈 redeem 〈 that God 〈 But,
ing oppression. [I ask,]

וִיחִי עוֹד לָנֶצַח[4] לְיָמִים אֹרֶךְ,

《 of longevity, 〈 for days 《 eternity, 〈 until 〈 Let it live

כִּי נֵר מִצְוָה וְתוֹרָה אוֹר וְדֶרֶךְ חַיִּים.[5]

《 of **life**. 〈 and the 〈 is a 〈 and Torah 〈 is a 〈 like a 〈 for
road light *mitzvah*, lamp

חַיִּים מִסֵּפֶר יִמָּחוּ[6] גְּבָל וּמוֹאָב הַגְּבֹהִים,

《who are haughty, 〈 and Moab 〈 Geval 〈 should be 〈 — from 《 **Life**
erased its book

לְבוּל עֵץ סוֹגְדִים[7] וְקוֹדִים וּמַאֲלִיהִים,

《 and deify. 〈 kneel, 〈 bow down, 〈 of 〈 who to
wood a block

בַּל יֻחַן רָשָׁע[8] הַמַּדְכֶּה יְדוֹן בִּשְׁלוּהִים,

《 to termination, 〈 should be 〈 the 《 to the 〈 be 〈 Let
judged oppressor wicked granted there
one, favor not

כִּי חֵרֵף מַעַרְכוֹת אֱלֹהִים חַיִּים.[9]

《 of **life**. 〈 of the God 〈 the 〈 he has 〈 for
battalions blasphemed

---

(1) Cf. *Psalms* 17:14. (2) Cf. *Proverbs* 15:24. (3) Cf. *Psalms* 49:16. (4) Cf. 49:10. (5) *Proverbs* 6:23.
(6) Cf. *Psalms* 69:29. (7) Cf. *Isaiah* 44:19; this line (מַאֲלִיהִים ... לְבוּל).
has been censored out of some editions of *Selichos*. (8) Cf. *Isaiah* 26:10. (9) *I Samuel* 17:36.

---

continue to praise God even after their
souls depart from their bodies (*Ibn Ezra*).

מְמְתִים יָדְךָ — *Those destined to die by
Your hand.* This alludes to the righteous
who will die in their sleep by the hand of

God and not suffer violent death (*Rashi* to
Psalms 17:14).

בַּחַיִּים — *Be among the living.* The translation follows *Radak* (to *Psalms* 17:14).
Targum renders *eternal life.*

חַיִּים נִשְׁבַּעְתָּ בּוֹ לִבְנְךָ יְחִידֶךָ,[1]

《 *your only* 〈 that *to* 〈 by it [to 〈 You swore 《 *[Your]*
　　son!　　　*your son,* Abraham]　　　　　**Life,**

שַׁעַר אוֹיְבָיו לְהַנְחִילוֹ[2] תִּתָּה בְּיָדֶךָ,

《 with Your 〈 You gave 〈　　　as　　　〈 of his 〈 the
　might.　　[him]　　　his heritage　　enemies　　gates

אָנַפְתָּ וְתָשׁוּב עַל כֵּן אוֹדֶךָ,[3]

《 I thank 〈　and　　《 You will 〈 Though You
　You,　　therefore　　　return　　were angry
　　　　　　　　　　　　[to us],　　[with us],

כִּי טוֹב חַסְדְּךָ מֵחַיִּים.[4]

《 than **life.**　〈 is Your 〈 better 〈 for
　　　　　　　kindness

חַיִּים שְׂבַע שְׂמָחוֹת אֶת פָּנֶיךָ[5] נוֹרָאוֹת,

《　　　that is　　〈 Your 〈 in 〈 of joys 〈 is the 〈 **Life**
　　awesome;　　Presence　　　　　　　fullness

חַדֵּשׁ יָמֵינוּ[6] חֵן חֵן תְּשׁוּאוֹת,[7]

《 all acclaim us. 〈 *Beauty!* 〈 [until with] 〈　our　〈 renew
　　　　　　　　　　　　Beauty!　　days

תָּשׁוּב תְּרַחֲמֵנוּ[8] יהוה אֱלֹהִים צְבָאוֹת,[9]

《 Master of 〈　　God,　　〈　O　《　and have 〈 Return
　Legions,　　　　　　　　HASHEM,　 mercy on us,　[to us]

כִּי מִמֶּנּוּ תּוֹצְאוֹת חַיִּים.[10]

《　life.　〈 flows forth 〈 from Him 〈 for
　　　　　　　　　　　　[HASHEM]

חַיִּים עַל הָאֲדָמָה[11] יְבֻשַּׂר עַמְּךָ מִמְּעוֹנוֹת,

《 from Heaven. 〈 to Your 〈 — may it be 《　earth　〈 on 〈 **Life**
　　　　　　people　announced

וְתַשְׁלִיךְ בִּמְצוּלוֹת יָם חֵטְא וַעֲוֹנוֹת,[12]

《　　and　　〈　sin　〈 of the 〈 into the depths 〈 May You
　iniquities.　　　sea　　　　　　　　　　throw

לֵב טָהוֹר בְּרָא לָנוּ[13] וְהַמְצִיאֵנוּ חֲנִינוֹת,[14]

〈　favor,　〈 and provide for us 《 for us, 〈 create 〈 that is pure 〈A heart

אֹרֶךְ יָמִים וּשְׁנוֹת חַיִּים.[15]

《 of **life.**　〈 and years 〈 of days, 〈 length

---

(1) Cf. *Genesis* 22:16. (2) Cf. 22:17. (3) Cf. *Isaiah* 12:1. (4) *Psalms* 63:4. (5) 16:11. (6) *Lamentations* 5:21.
(7) Cf. *Zechariah* 4:7. (8) Cf. *Micah* 7:19. (9) *Psalms* 80:5. (10) *Proverbs* 4:23. (11) *Deuteronomy* 4:10.
(12) Cf. *Micah* 7:19. (13) Cf. *Psalms* 51:12. (14) Cf. *Proverbs* 3:4. (15) 3:2.

חַיִּים פִּי צַדִּיק וּפִי רְשָׁעִים מְחִתָּה,[1]

Life   [flows]   of the   [but from]   of the   [flows   [flows]
  destruction.   wicked   the   righteous;   from]
  mouth   the mouth

בְּקָצְבְּךָ מִלְחָמוֹת וְשָׁלוֹם וּפַלְצוּת וּבְעָתָה,

and panic,   fear   and peace,   wars   As You apportion

שֹׂבַע וְרָזוֹן וְחַיִל[2] הַחַיִּים וְהַמָּוֶתָה,

and death,   life   and   and   plenty
  trembling,   famine

הַבְּרָכָה וְהַקְּלָלָה וּבָחַרְתָּ **בַּחַיִּים**.[3]

life.   — may You   and curse   blessing
  chose

חַיִּים צְדָקָה וְכָבוֹד[4] תַּגְדִּיל לְיָפָה כִתְרְצָה,[5]

Life,   righteous-   and   honor   may You   for [Israel]   when she
  ness,   increase   who is   fulfills Your
  beautiful   desire,

הַזּוֹרַעַת חֶסֶד וְקוֹצֶרֶת בְּלִי שִׂמְצָה,[6]

embarrassing   without   and harvests   kindness   who sows
[the recipient].   [its reward]   [in private]

תְּכוֹנֵן צַדִּיק יהוה וּגְדוֹר פִּרְצָה,

to seal the   and build   O   the   Establish
breach —   a wall   HASHEM,   righteous,

רֹדֵף צְדָקָה וָחֶסֶד יִמְצָא **חַיִּים**.[7]

life.   will find   and   righteous-   so that he
  kindness   ness   who pursues

חַיִּים קַיָּמִים תַּנְחִילֵנוּ, וְחָכְמָה וָדַעַת בְּמוֹעֵצוֹת,[8]

through the   and under-   and   grant us as an   everlasting   Life
[Torah's] counsel;   standing   wisdom   inheritance,

שָׂשׂוֹן וְשִׂמְחָה תַּשְׁמִיעַ מֵעִיר חֻצוֹת,[9]

streets.   from the   let us hear   and gladness   joy
[Holy] City's   [once again]

וְהַעֲבֵר מֵעָלַי עָוֹן, וְהַלְבֵּשׁ מַחֲלָצוֹת,[10]

in fresh   and dress   iniquity   from   Remove
garments;   [me]   upon me

---

(1) Cf. *Proverbs* 10:11. (2) Some editions read וְחַיִל; the translation is then either *plenty and famine and* [*invading*] *armies,* or, *plenty and famine and wealth.* (3) *Deuteronomy* 30:19. (4) *Proverbs* 21:21. (5) Cf. *Song of Songs* 6:4. (6) Cf. *Hosea* 10:12. (7) *Proverbs* 21:21. (8) Cf. 22:20. (9) Cf. *Jeremiah* 33:10-11. (10) Cf. *Zechariah* 3:4.

אֶתְהַלֵּךְ לִפְנֵי יהוה בְּאַרְצוֹת הַחַיִּים.[1]

» of the living.* ‹ in the lands ‹ HASHEM ‹ before ‹ that I may walk

חַיִּים רְאֵה עַם סְגֻלָּתֶךְ כְּקֶדֶם לְמָתוֹב,[2]

» they return ‹ when as ‹ of Your ‹ the ‹ look to ‹ Living
[to You]. of old treasure people One,

לֹא תַחְפּוֹץ בְּמוֹת הַמֵּת, עַד דִּיתוֹב,[3]

» that they ‹ but ‹ of the ‹ the death ‹ You do not wish
repent; rather wicked

נִשְׁבָּר וְנִדְכֶּה לְפָנֶיךָ חָשׁוּב, הַטּוֹב,

» the ‹ are ‹ before ‹ and crushed ‹ the
good; considered You [hearts] broken

קָדוֹשׁ יֵאָמֵר לוֹ, כָּל הַכָּתוּב לַחַיִּים.[4]

» for life. ‹ inscribed ‹ of each ‹ of ‹ shall be ‹ Holy
one him, said

חַיִּים שָׁאַל מִמְּךָ נָתַתָּה לוֹ,[5] חַיֵּיהוּ מִיּוֹמָיִם,[6]

» despite the two ‹ — revivify » to ‹ and You ‹ of You ‹ he ‹ Life
periods [of Temple him, him* gave it requested
Destruction].

---

(1) *Psalms* 116:9. (2) Cf. *Lamentations* 5:21 with *Targum*. (3) Cf. *Ezekiel* 18:32.
(4) *Isaiah* 4:3. (5) *Psalms* 21:5. (6) Cf. *Hosea* 6:2; see *Rashi*.

בְּאַרְצוֹת הַחַיִּים — *In the lands of the living.* Numerous Midrashim identify *Eretz Yisrael* as the *land of the living,* for it is there that the dead are destined to be revivified. For this reason, the Patriarchs and righteous Sages in all generations yearned to be buried in the holy soil. Those who are interred in foreign soil will roll to Israel through subterranean passages prior to their revivification (*Pesikta Rabbasi* 1; *Yerushalmi, Kesubos* 12:3).

According to *Rashi* (*Psalms* 116:9), *Eretz Yisrael* is called by this name because it is the home of the Living God; in foreign lands, however, idolaters worship lifeless gods. Moreover, the very air of the Holy Land makes men healthy and robust and the holy atmosphere grants the mind renewed vitality and alertness. Indeed, the Land of Israel deserves to be called the *land of the living,* for the exiled Jew lives in constant fear of death, but in *Eretz Yisrael* he dwells in safety (*Radak*).

The *Talmud* (*Yoma* 71a) cites the opinion of Rav Yehudah, who identifies the *land of* the living as מָקוֹם שְׁוָוקִים, *the marketplace.* When Israel wanders in exile, they lack the income to provide the necessities of life. Therefore a marketplace becomes of vital importance for them (*Rashi* and *Tosafos Yeshanim, Yoma* 71a).

Rambam (Hil. *Teshuvah* 3:5, 8:7) identifies *the land of the living* as the World to Come.

חַיִּים שָׁאַל מִמְּךָ נָתַתָּה לוֹ — *Life he requested of You and You gave it to him.* The "he" of this verse alludes to King David's descendant, the Messiah. The Talmud (*Succah* 52a) relates: God will [in the future] say to *Mashiach ben David,* may he be revealed speedily in our days, *Ask anything of Me and I shall grant it to you* (*Psalms* 2:8). Having seen that his precursor *Mashiach ben Yosef* had been killed, *Mashiach ben David* will reply, *I ask nothing of You but life!* To this God will respond, *Long before you asked this of Me, your ancestor David already prophesied, "Life he requested of You and You gave it to him!"* (ibid. 21:5).

גָּדוֹל כְּבוֹדוֹ¹ בִּישׁוּעָתֶךָ כִּפַת פַּעֲמָיִם,²

Great ‹ is his honor ‹ in Your salvations, ‹ as at the beautiful « footsteps of the Pilgrimage [Festivals].

הַשְׁקִיפָה מִמְּעוֹן קָדְשְׁךָ מִן הַשָּׁמַיִם,³

Gaze down ‹ from Your abode « that is holy, ‹ from « the Heavens;

בַּיּוֹם הַהוּא יֵצְאוּ מַיִם חַיִּים.⁴

on that day ‹ there will flow out ‹ waters ‹ of life. «

חַיִּים תַּאֲוָה בָאָה⁵ סְלוֹחַ אֶל חַטֹּאתֵיכֶם,

"Life" [for us] « — as Your desire — « has been attained « [with] ‹ for ‹ forgiveness [tell us], your sins! «

תַּשְׁמִיעַ וְאֶת רוּחִי אֶתֵּן בְּקִרְבְּכֶם,⁶

Let us hear, « My spirit ‹ I will place ‹ in your midst. «

לֵאמֹר מָצָאתִי כֹפֶר,⁷ רָצִיתִי אֶתְכֶם,⁸

Say [to us], « I have found « atonement ‹ I will show favor [for you], ‹ to you. «

וְאַתֶּם הַדְּבֵקִים בַּיהוה אֱלֹהֵיכֶם חַיִּים.⁹

And you ‹ who cling ‹ to HASHEM, ‹ your God, ‹ have life. «

חַיִּים מִמְּךָ הָאֵל סָמְכָה יוֹנָתְךָ הַמְשׁוּכָה

Life ‹ is from You, ‹ O God, « support ‹ Your dove [Israel], ‹ who is drawn

אַחֲרֶיךָ,¹⁰ לְהִדָּבֵק בָּךְ כַּדָּת וְכַהֲלָכָה,

after You, « clinging ‹ to ‹ You according to the Torah ‹ and [its] law. «

תְּבִיאֵנוּ לְהַר צִיּוֹן וְתָשִׁיב הַמְּלוּכָה,

Bring us ‹ to Mount ‹ Zion ‹ and restore ‹ the monarchy, «

כִּי שָׁם צִוָּה יהוה אֶת הַבְּרָכָה חַיִּים.¹¹

for ‹ there ‹ HASHEM commanded ‹ the ‹ blessing ‹ of life. «

❖ חַיִּים מִמֶּנּוּ נוֹחִיל וְלִישׁוּעָתוֹ קַוִּינוּ,¹²

Life ‹ from Him « we await, « as for His salvation ‹ we long. «

---

(1) Psalms 21:6. (2) Cf. Song of Songs 7:2. (3) Deuteronomy 26:15. (4) Zechariah 14:8. (5) Proverbs 13:12. (6) Ezekiel 36:27. (7) Job 33:24. (8) Cf. Ezekiel 43:27. (9) Deuteronomy 4:4. (10) Psalms 21:6. (11) Cf. Song of Songs 7:2. (12) Deuteronomy 26:15.

עַתָּה יַרְחִיב יהוה לָנוּ וּפָרִינוּ,[1]

⟨ Now ⟨ may HASHEM grant ⟨ to us ⟨ so that we may be fruitful. ample space

יְחַיֵּינוּ מִיּוֹמַיִם בַּיּוֹם הַשְּׁלִישִׁי יְקִימֵנוּ,[2]

⟨ May He ⟨ despite the ⟨ on the ⟨ [of] the Third ⟨ may He revivify us, two periods [of Temple Destruction] — day [Temple] raise us up,

אֲנַחְנוּ אֵלֶּה פֹה הַיּוֹם כֻּלָּנוּ חַיִּים.[3]

⟨ we, ⟨ those who ⟨ are here ⟨ today, ⟨ all of us ⟨ alive.

ALL, WHILE STANDING:

אֵל מֶלֶךְ יוֹשֵׁב עַל כִּסֵּא רַחֲמִים, מִתְנַהֵג

⟨ O God, ⟨ King ⟨ Who sits ⟨ on ⟨ the throne ⟨ of mercy, ⟨ Who acts

בַּחֲסִידוּת, מוֹחֵל עֲוֹנוֹת עַמּוֹ, מַעֲבִיר רִאשׁוֹן

⟨ with kindness, ⟨ Who pardons ⟨ the sins ⟨ of His people, ⟨ Who removes ⟨ [sins,] one

רִאשׁוֹן,[4] מַרְבֶּה מְחִילָה לַחֲטָאִים וּסְלִיחָה לַפּוֹשְׁעִים,

⟨ by one, ⟨ Who abundantly grants ⟨ pardon ⟨ to unintentional sinners ⟨ and forgiveness ⟨ to willful sinners,

עֹשֶׂה צְדָקוֹת עִם כָּל בָּשָׂר וָרוּחַ, לֹא כְרָעָתָם

⟨ Who performs ⟨ acts of generosity ⟨ with ⟨ all ⟨ [beings of] flesh ⟨ and ⟨ spirit ⟨ — not ⟨ in accord with their wickedness

תִּגְמוֹל. ❖ אֵל הוֹרֵיתָ לָּנוּ לוֹמַר שְׁלֹשׁ עֶשְׂרֵה, וּזְכוֹר

⟨ do You repay them! ⟨ O God, ⟨ You taught ⟨ us ⟨ to recite ⟨ the Thirteen [Attributes of Mercy]; ⟨ remember

לָּנוּ הַיּוֹם בְּרִית שְׁלֹשׁ עֶשְׂרֵה, כְּמוֹ שֶׁהוֹדַעְתָּ לֶעָנָיו

⟨ for us ⟨ today ⟨ the covenant ⟨ of [these] Thirteen, ⟨ as ⟨ You made known ⟨ to the humble one [Moses]

מִקֶּדֶם, כְּמוֹ שֶׁכָּתוּב, וַיֵּרֶד יהוה בֶּעָנָן וַיִּתְיַצֵּב עִמּוֹ

⟨ in ancient times, ⟨ as ⟨ it is written: ⟨ And HASHEM descended ⟨ in a cloud ⟨ and stood ⟨ with him

שָׁם, וַיִּקְרָא בְשֵׁם יהוה.[5]

⟨ there, ⟨ and He called out ⟨ with the Name ⟨ of HASHEM.

---

(1) Cf. *Genesis* 26:22. (2) Cf. *Hosea* 6:2. (3) *Deuteronomy* 5:3.
(4) *Rosh Hashanah* 17a. (5) *Exodus* 34:5.

CONGREGATION, THEN *CHAZZAN*:

וַיַּעֲבֹר יהוה עַל פָּנָיו וַיִּקְרָא:

《 and 《 [Moses'] 〈 before 〈 And HASHEM passed
proclaimed: face,

CONGREGATION AND *CHAZZAN* RECITE LOUDLY AND IN UNISON:

יהוה, יהוה, אֵל, רַחוּם, וְחַנּוּן, אֶרֶךְ אַפַּיִם,

〈 to anger, 〈 Slow 《 and 〈 Compassionate 〈 God, 〈 HASHEM, 〈 HASHEM,
Gracious,

וְרַב חֶסֶד, וֶאֱמֶת, נֹצֵר חֶסֶד לָאֲלָפִים, נֹשֵׂא עָוֹן,

〈 of 〈 Forgiver 《 for thousands 〈 of 〈 Preserver 《 and 〈 in 〈 and
iniquity, [of generations], kindness Truth, Kindness Abundant

וָפֶשַׁע, וְחַטָּאָה, וְנַקֵּה.[1] וְסָלַחְתָּ לַעֲוֹנֵנוּ וּלְחַטָּאתֵנוּ

《 and our sins, 〈 our 〈 May You 《 and Who 〈 and inadvertent 〈 willful sin,
iniquities forgive absolves. sin,

וּנְחַלְתָּנוּ.[2] סְלַח לָנוּ אָבִינוּ כִּי חָטָאנוּ, מְחַל לָנוּ

〈 us, 〈 pardon 《 we have 〈 for 《 our 〈 us, 〈 Forgive 《 and make us
sinned; Father, Your heritage.

מַלְכֵּנוּ כִּי פָשָׁעְנוּ. כִּי אַתָּה אֲדֹנָי טוֹב וְסַלָּח,

《 and 〈 are 〈 O Lord, 〈 You, 〈 For 《 we have 〈 for 《 our King,
forgiving, good willfully sinned.

וְרַב חֶסֶד לְכָל קֹרְאֶיךָ.[3]

《 who call 〈 to all 〈 kind 〈 and
upon You. abundantly

פְּסוּקֵי הַקְדָּמָה לִסְלִיחָה לו / PREFATORY VERSES TO SELICHAH 36

לָמָה רָגְשׁוּ גוֹיִם, וּלְאֻמִּים יֶהְגּוּ רִיק.[4] לָמָה

〈 Why, 《 in vain? 〈 talk 〈 and regimes 〈 do nations throng, 〈 Why

יהוה תַּעֲמֹד בְּרָחוֹק, תַּעְלִים לְעִתּוֹת בַּצָּרָה.[5]

《 of 〈 in times 〈 do You conceal 《 at a 〈 do You 〈 HASHEM,
trouble? Yourself distance, stand

לָמָה לָנֶצַח תִּשְׁכָּחֵנוּ, תַּעַזְבֵנוּ לְאֹרֶךְ יָמִים.[6] לָמָה

〈 Why, 《 of days? 〈 for the length 〈 forsake us 《do You forget us, 〈 eternally 〈 Why

יהוה תִּזְנַח מִשְּׁלוֹם נַפְשִׁי.[7]

《 my soul. 〈 from achiev- 〈 should 〈 HASHEM,
ing peace You reject

---

(1) *Exodus* 34:6-7. (2) 34:9. (3) *Psalms* 86:5. (4) 2:1.
(5) 10:1. (6) *Lamentations* 5:20. (7) Cf. 3:17, *Psalms* 88:15.

כְּרַחֵם אָב עַל בָּנִים, כֵּן תְּרַחֵם יהוה עָלֵינוּ.¹

‹ As merciful as › a ‹ toward › his ‹ so ‹‹ have ‹ HASHEM, ‹ on us.¹
father is children, mercy,

לַיהוה הַיְשׁוּעָה, עַל עַמְּךָ בִרְכָתֶךָ סֶּלָה.² יהוה

‹ To HASHEM ‹ is salvation, ‹ upon ‹‹ Your ‹ is Your ‹‹ Selah. ‹ HASHEM,² יהוה
people blessing,

צְבָאוֹת עִמָּנוּ, מִשְׂגָּב לָנוּ אֱלֹהֵי יַעֲקֹב סֶלָה.³

Master of ‹‹ is with us, ‹‹ a ‹ for us ‹ is the God ‹ of Jacob, ‹‹ Selah.³
Legions, stronghold

יהוה צְבָאוֹת, אַשְׁרֵי אָדָם בֹּטֵחַ בָּךְ.⁴ יהוה

‹ HASHEM, ‹‹ Master ‹‹ — praiseworthy ‹ is the ‹ who ‹ in You.⁴ ‹ HASHEM,
of Legions man trusts

הוֹשִׁיעָה, הַמֶּלֶךְ יַעֲנֵנוּ בְיוֹם קָרְאֵנוּ.⁵

‹‹ save! ‹‹ May the ‹ answer ‹ on the ‹‹ we call.⁵
King us day

(שלמונית)

ALL:

אֱלֹהֵינוּ וֵאלֹהֵי אֲבוֹתֵינוּ:

‹‹ of our forefathers: ‹ and God ‹ Our God

CHAZZAN, THEN CONGREGATION:

שְׁלֹשׁ עֶשְׂרֵה מִדּוֹת* הָאֲמוּרוֹת בַּחֲנִינָה,

‹‹ with grace, ‹ pronounced ‹ Attributes* ‹ [In the merit of Your]
Thirteen

נָא כָל מִדָּה נְכוֹנָה, אֲחַלֶּה פְּנֵי מַלְכִּי בִּתְחִנָּה,

‹‹ in ‹ my King ‹ before ‹ I shall ‹‹ that is readied ‹ [through] ‹ O please,
supplication, [You] pray [for mercy]: every Attribute [HASHEM,]

לְחַפֵּשׂ זְכוּת כְּנוּיִם, קְרוּאִים שׁוֹשַׁנָּה,⁶

‹‹ a rose.⁶ ‹ and called ‹ for [the people] ‹ merit ‹ to seek out
labeled

מַלְּטֵם מִכָּל רָעוֹת בְּזֹאת הַשָּׁנָה.

‹‹ year. ‹ during this ‹ evil ‹ from all ‹ Save them

---

(1) Cf. *Psalms* 103:13. (2) 3:9. (3) 46:8. (4) 84:13. (5) 20:10. (6) See *Song of Songs* 2:1-2.

שְׁלֹשׁ עֶשְׂרֵה מִדּוֹת §— *Thirteen Attributes.*
This is another of those *selichos* that apparently address some "higher beings" pleading that they intervene with the Heavenly

Tribunal on our behalf. In this case the higher beings are not angels, but God's own Thirteen Attributes of Mercy. The propriety and permissibility of such prayer is

CONGREGATION, THEN *CHAZZAN:*

אִם אַשְׁמָתָם גָּדְלָה עַד שְׁמֵי רוֹם וְכוֹכְבֵיהֶם,

If ‹ their guilt ‹ has grown ‹ to ‹ the heavens high ‹ up ‹ and their stars, »

נָא כָּל מִדָּה נְכוֹנָה, אֲבַקֵּשׁ רַחֲמִים עֲלֵיהֶם,

O please, ‹ [through] ‹ every Attribute [HASHEM,] ‹ that is readied [for mercy]: ‹ I shall request ‹ mercy ‹ for them, »

לְבַטֵּל מֵהֶם כָּתוּב, אָמַרְתִּי אַפְאֵיהֶם,[1]

to annul ‹ regarding them ‹ that which is written: » I said ‹ "I will scatter them to the corners."

לָמָה יֹאמְרוּ הַגּוֹיִם, אַיֵּה נָא אֱלֹהֵיהֶם.[2]

Why ‹ should they say ‹ the nations, — ‹ » Where ‹ now ‹ is their God? »

CONGREGATION, THEN *CHAZZAN:*

אִם גָּבְרוּ עֲוֹנוֹת וְעָצְמוּ מִלְּסַפְּרָה,[3]

If ‹ over-whelming ‹ have [Israel's] iniquities become, ‹ and too powerful ‹ to recount, »

נָא כָּל מִדָּה נְכוֹנָה, דְּחֵה אוֹתָם יהוה לְהַסְתִּירָה,

O please, ‹ [through] ‹ every Attribute [HASHEM,] ‹ that is readied [for mercy]: ‹ push them aside ‹ HASHEM, ‹ into concealment. »

דִּבּוּבֵי עֹז בְּתַחַן, לְבַטֵּל מֵהֶם כָּתוּב, אַסְתִּירָה,[4]

Words ‹ strong ‹ [I utter] in supplication, ‹ to ‹ annul ‹ regarding them ‹ what is written: » I shall hide [my face from them]. »

לָמָה יהוה תַּעֲמֹד בְּרָחוֹק, תַּעְלִים לְעִתּוֹת בַּצָּרָה.[5]

Why, ‹ HASHEM, ‹ do You stand ‹ at a distance, ‹ do You conceal Yourself ‹ in times ‹ of trouble? »

CONGREGATION, THEN *CHAZZAN:*

אִם הֶעֱווּ פְּנֵי מַלְכָּם בְּעַזּוּת פָּנִים וּמֵצַח,

If ‹ they have wronged ‹ the coun-tenance ‹ of their King ‹ with ‹ brazen ‹ face ‹ and shamelessly, »

---

(1) *Deuteronomy* 32:26. (2) *Psalms* 115:2. (3) Cf. 40:6. (4) *Deuteronomy* 32:20. (5) *Psalms* 10:1.

discussed in the introduction to this volume. Presumably to avoid this issue, the original text of this *selichah* (as it appears in various manuscripts and in the medieval commentary *Arugas HaBosem*) was altered centuries ago. In its present form the supplication addresses God directly, and passages that asked for in-tercession are now in the first-person active voice. For example, in place of the original words, בַּקְּשִׁי רַחֲמִים, *[you Attributes] seek mercy*, the second stanza now reads, אֲבַקֵּשׁ רַחֲמִים, *I shall request mercy*. Other passages were changed by adding God's Name as the object of the supplication. Thus, in the third

נָא כָּל מִדָּה נְכוֹנָה, אֶתְחַנֵּן לוֹ בְּפֶצַח,

《 with open 〈 to 〈 I will 《 that is readied 〈 [through] 〈 O please,
mouth. Him supplicate [for mercy]: every Attribute [HASHEM,]

וְנַפְשִׁי שְׁפְכִי כַמַּיִם לִבֵּךְ,[1] נְכַח אָדֹם וָצַח,[2]

《 and white 〈 Him Who 《 before 〈 your 〈 like water 〈 pour out 《 And O
[with for- is red [with heart my soul
giveness]. vengeance]

לָמָה אֱלֹהִים זָנַחְתָּ לָנֶצַח.[3]

《 for an 〈 have You 〈 O God, 〈 Why,
eternity? abandoned [us]

CONGREGATION, THEN *CHAZZAN:*

אִם זְדוֹנוֹת הִשִּׂיאוּ לֵב טִפֵּשׁ[4] וְנִשְׁחָץ,

《 and 〈 covered 〈 their 〈 have led 〈 willful sins 〈 If
arrogant, in thick fat heart astray

נָא כָּל מִדָּה נְכוֹנָה, חַלֵּץ אוֹתָם יהוה מִמַּחַץ,

《 from the 〈 O 〈 them, 〈 extricate 《 that is readied 〈 [through] 〈 O please,
crushing blow. HASHEM, [for mercy]: every Attribute [HASHEM,]

חוּשׁ וּבֹא, וְשָׂא קוֹל נַחַץ,

《 that is 〈 [their] 〈 and 〈 come, 〈 Hurry,
urgent: outcry accept

לָמָה קֹדֵר אֶתְהַלֵּךְ בְּלַחַץ.[5]

《 under 〈 must I walk 〈 in 〈 Why
oppression? about gloom

CONGREGATION, THEN *CHAZZAN:*

אִם טָפְלוּ שֶׁקֶר[6] בְּהֶגֶה וְהַוּוֹת לְעָמֶךְ,

《 against 〈 or in 〈 in speech 〈 false 〈 they have 〈 If
you, thought accusations piled

נָא כָּל מִדָּה נְכוֹנָה, יְדִידוּת תִּזְכֹּר מִמַּנְעִימֶיךָ,

《 of those who sing 〈 remember 〈 the love 《 that is readied 〈 [through] 〈 O please,
sweetly to You. [for mercy]: every Attribute [HASHEM,]

---

(1) *Lamentations* 2:19. (2) Cf. *Song of Songs* 5:10.
(3) *Psalms* 74:1. (4) Cf. 119:70. (5) Cf. 42:10. (6) Cf. 119:69.

stanza, דְּחֵה אוֹתָם, *[you Attributes] push
them aside*, has been changed to, דְּחֵה אוֹתָם
ה', *push them aside*, HASHEM. The present
translation conforms to the spirit of these
emendations, even in the stiches that have
remained unaltered from the original. Thus,
כָּל מִדָּה נְכוֹנָה is not translated *every proper
Attribute*, but *[through] every Attribute*

that is readied [for mercy].

　The *selichah* was composed by שְׁלֹמֹה בֶּן
מְנַחֵם, *Shlomo ben Menachem*, whose name
appears in the acrostic of the first two stanzas.
In the original version, the *paytan's* signature was more obvious, for there the first two
lines read שְׁלֹשׁ עֶשְׂרֵה מִדּוֹת הָאֲמוּרוֹת בַּחֲנִינָה
R' Shlomo. נָא מִדָּה נְכוֹנָה חַלִּי מַלְכֵּךְ בְּתִחְנָה

יִתְגּוֹלְלוּ רַחֲמֶיךָ[1] עַל שְׁאֵרִית עַמֶּךָ,

《 of Your people. 〈 the remnant 〈 over 〈 Your mercy 〈 Let roll out

לָמָה יהוה יֶחֱרֶה אַפְּךָ בְּעַמֶּךָ[2].

《 against 〈 Your 〈 should 〈 HASHEM, 〈 Why,
Your people?   anger   flare up

CONGREGATION, THEN *CHAZZAN:*

אִם כָּבְדוּ אְֹזֶן,[3] לְסַלֵּף מִנִּי הַדֶּרֶךְ,

《 the 〈 from 〈 causing 《 [their] 〈 they have 〈 If
[Torah's]   before   them to   ear [to   hardened
way,   Me   corrupt   rebuke],

נָא כָּל מִדָּה נְכוֹנָה, אֶלְחַשׁ עַל עַמִּי בְּעֶרְךְ,

《 in my ordered 〈 my 〈 for 〈 I will 《 that is readied 〈 [through] 〈 O please,
prayer.   people   whisper   [for mercy]: every Attribute [HASHEM,]

וְנַפְשִׁי שִׁפְכִי לִבֵּךְ, פְּנֵי[4] קוֹנֵךְ וְצוּרֵךְ,

《 and your 〈 your 〈 before 〈 your 〈 pour out 《 And O
Rock [saying]: Creator   heart   my soul,

לָמָה פָּרַצְתָּ גְדֵרֶיהָ, וְאָרוּהָ כָּל עֹבְרֵי דָרֶךְ.[5]

《 the 〈 who 〈 do 〈 so that 〈 [Israel's] 〈 have You 〈 Why
way?   pass by   all   pluck its fruit   fences,   breached

CONGREGATION, THEN *CHAZZAN:*

אִם מָרְדוּ בְרֹב פִּשְׁעָם,[6] לְצוּר מַלְכִּי וּקְדוֹשִׁי,

《 and my 〈 my King, 〈 against 〈 sins 〈 with their 〈 they have 〈 If
Holy One,   the Rock,   many   rebelled

נָא כָּל מִדָּה נְכוֹנָה, נַפְשִׁי נְעַם עֲלֵיהֶם תְּבַקְשִׁי,

《 request. 〈 for them 〈 serenity 〈 O my 《 that is readied 〈 [through] 〈 O please,
soul,   [for mercy]: every Attribute [HASHEM,]

לְנוֹרָא מָרוֹם וְקָדוֹשׁ, בְּעֶתֶר אֵלָיו תִּדְרְשִׁי,

《 seek out: 〈 to Him 〈 in powerful 〈 and Holy 〈 Lofty, 〈 The
prayer   One   Awesome,

לָמָה יהוה תִּזְנַח מִשָּׁלוֹם נַפְשִׁי.[7]

《 my 〈 without 〈 should You 〈 HASHEM, 〈 Why,
soul?   peace   abandon

---

(1) Cf. *Berachos* 7b. (2) *Exodus* 32:11. (3) Cf. *Zechariah* 7:11, *Isaiah* 59:1.
(4) Cf. *Lamentations* 2:19. (5) *Psalms* 80:13. (6) Cf. *Ezekiel* 2:3. (7) Cf. *Psalms* 88:15.

---

lived sometime before 1234, ,when the commentary *Arugas HaBosem* [which includes this *piyut*] was written.

In each quatrain (after the first), the first line begins with the word אִם, *if,* followed by a word beginning with the respective letter of the *aleph-beis;* the second line begins with the phrase נָא כָּל מִדָּה נְכוֹנָה, followed by a word beginning with the next letter of the alphabet; the third line repeats the

CONGREGATION, THEN *CHAZZAN:*

אִם סָרְרוּ כְּפָרָה, מֶרֹב עֵתִים וְיָמִים,

« and years ‹ periods ‹ because of ‹ like a cow ‹ they have ‹ If
[in Exile], overlong strayed

נָא כָּל מִדָּה נְכוֹנָה, אֶשָּׂא עַיִן לַמְּרוֹמִים,[1]

« to the heavens; ‹ my ‹ I will «that is readied‹ [through] ‹ O please,
eye raise [for mercy]: every Attribute [HASHEM,]

עַל עַמִּי אֶפְצֶה פֶּה, מְעַטֵּי עַמִּים,

« of nations ‹ – the « my ‹ I will ‹ of my ‹ on
[saying]: smallest mouth, open wide people behalf

לָמָה לָנֶצַח תִּשְׁכָּחֵנוּ, תַּעַזְבֵנוּ לְאֹרֶךְ יָמִים.[2]

« of days? ‹ for the length ‹ forsake us «do You forget us, ‹ eternally ‹ Why

CONGREGATION, THEN *CHAZZAN:*

אִם פְּשָׁעִים עָצְמוּ, וְגָבְרוּ מְאֹד כִּתְלָא,

« like a tall ‹ to the ‹ become over-‹ have ‹ [their] ‹ If
mound, extreme whelming strengthened, willful sins

נָא כָּל מִדָּה נְכוֹנָה, אֲצַפְצֵף קוֹל לְהַפְלִא,

« that You do ‹ in a ‹ I will chirp «that is readied‹ [through] ‹ O please,
wonders. voice [my prayer] [for mercy]: every Attribute [HASHEM,]

צְרוּפָה אִמְרָתֶךָ, לְחַלּוֹת עַל עַם אֵלֶּה,

« of this people: ‹ on ‹ to beseech ‹ are Your ‹ Pure
behalf [You] [Torah's] words enough

לָמָה תָשִׁיב יָדְךָ וִימִינֶךָ, מִקֶּרֶב חֵיקְךָ כַלֵּה.[3]

«remove ‹ Your ‹ From « even Your « Your ‹ do You ‹ Why
[it]! bosom within right hand? hand, withdraw

CONGREGATION, THEN *CHAZZAN:*

אִם קִלְקְלוּ מַעֲשִׂים, לְהָזִיד וּלְהַרְשִׁיעַ,

« and wickedly, ‹ to act ‹ [their] deeds, ‹ they have ‹ If
willfully corrupted

נָא כָּל מִדָּה נְכוֹנָה, רָחַשׁ לִבִּי[4] לְהוֹשִׁיעַ,

« to save [them]. ‹ is my ‹ excited «that is readied‹ [through] ‹ O please,
heart [for mercy]: every Attribute [HASHEM,]

קוּמִי רֹנִּי בַלַּיְלָה[5] לָאֵל הַמּוֹשִׁיעַ,

« Who saves! ‹ to God ‹ in the night ‹ cry out ‹ Arise,

---

(1) Cf. *Isaiah* 40:26. (2) *Lamentations* 5:20. (3) *Psalms* 74:11. (4) 45:2. (5) *Lamentations* 2:19.

second line's letter; and the fourth line is
a Scriptural fragment that begins with the
word לָמָה, *why*. Some lines deviate from

this formula, but that is because the changes
incorporated over the years did not take the
acrostic into account.

לָמָּה תִהְיֶה כְּאִישׁ נִדְהָם, כְּגִבּוֹר לֹא יוּכַל לְהוֹשִׁיעַ.[1]

《 to save? 〈 able 〈 who 〈 like a 《 in shock, 〈 like 〈 should 〈 Why
is not   warrior   a man   You be

CONGREGATION, THEN *CHAZZAN:*

אִם אָמְנָם שָׁבוּ כֻלָּם, בְּלֵב וָנֶפֶשׁ לַחֲלוֹתֶךָ,

《 beseeching 〈 and soul 〈 with 《 — all of 《 they have 〈 indeed 〈 If
You,   heart   them —   repented

נָא כָּל מִדָּה נְכוֹנָה, תַּסְכִּים עִמָּם בְּמִחִילָתֶךָ,

《 with Your pardon. 〈 to them 〈 assent 《 that is readied 〈 [through] 〈 O please,
[for mercy]: every Attribute [HASHEM,]

וַעֲשֵׂה אָדוֹן לְמַעַנְךָ, סְלַח וּמְחַל לַעֲדָתֶךָ,

《 Your flock; 〈 and pardon 〈 forgive 《 for Your sake, 〈 O Lord, 〈 Act,

שׁוּב לְמַעַן עֲבָדֶיךָ, שִׁבְטֵי נַחֲלָתֶךָ.[2]

《 that are 〈 the tribes 〈 of Your 〈 for the 〈 return
Your heritage.   servants,   sake   [to us]

ALL, WHILE STANDING:

אֵל מֶלֶךְ יוֹשֵׁב עַל כִּסֵּא רַחֲמִים, מִתְנַהֵג

〈 Who acts 《 of mercy, 〈 the throne 〈 on 〈 Who sits 〈 King 〈 O God,

בַּחֲסִידוּת, מוֹחֵל עֲוֹנוֹת עַמּוֹ, מַעֲבִיר רִאשׁוֹן

〈 [sins,] one 〈 Who 《 of His 〈 the sins 〈 Who 《 with kindness,
removes   people,   pardons

רִאשׁוֹן,[3] מַרְבֶּה מְחִילָה לַחַטָּאִים וּסְלִיחָה לַפּוֹשְׁעִים,

《 to willful 〈 and 〈 to unintentional 〈 pardon 〈 Who abun- 《 by one,
sinners,   forgiveness   sinners   dantly grants

עֹשֶׂה צְדָקוֹת עִם כָּל בָּשָׂר וָרוּחַ, לֹא כְרָעָתָם

〈 in accord with 〈 — not 《 and 〈 [beings 〈 all 〈 with 〈 acts of 〈 Who
their wickedness   spirit   of] flesh   generosity   performs

תִגְמוֹל. ❖ אֵל הוֹרֵיתָ לָּנוּ לוֹמַר שְׁלֹשׁ עֶשְׂרֵה, וּזְכוֹר

〈 remem- 《 the Thirteen 〈 to 〈 You 〈 O God, 《 do You
ber   [Attributes of Mercy];   recite   taught   repay them!

לָנוּ הַיּוֹם בְּרִית שְׁלֹשׁ עֶשְׂרֵה, כְּמוֹ שֶׁהוֹדַעְתָּ לֶעָנָיו

〈 to the humble 〈 You made 〈 as 《 of [these] Thirteen, 〈 the 〈 today 〈 for us
one [Moses]   known   covenant

מִקֶּדֶם, כְּמוֹ שֶׁכָּתוּב, וַיֵּרֶד יהוה בֶּעָנָן וַיִּתְיַצֵּב עִמּוֹ

〈 with 〈 and stood 〈 in a 〈 And HASHEM 《 it is written: 〈 as 《 in ancient
him   cloud   descended   times,

---

(1) *Jeremiah* 14:9. (2) *Isaiah* 63:17. (3) *Rosh Hashanah* 17a.

שָׁם, וַיִּקְרָא בְשֵׁם יהוה.¹

《 of 〈 with the 〈 and He 《 there,
HASHEM.   Name   called out

CONGREGATION, THEN *CHAZZAN:*

וַיַּעֲבֹר יהוה עַל פָּנָיו וַיִּקְרָא:

《 and 《 [Moses'] 〈 before 〈 And HASHEM passed
proclaimed: face,

CONGREGATION AND *CHAZZAN* **RECITE LOUDLY AND IN UNISON:**

יהוה, יהוה, אֵל, רַחוּם, וְחַנּוּן, אֶרֶךְ אַפַּיִם,

〈 to anger, 〈 Slow 《and Gracious,〈 Compassionate 〈 God, 〈 HASHEM, 〈 HASHEM,

וְרַב חֶסֶד, וֶאֱמֶת, נֹצֵר חֶסֶד לָאֲלָפִים, נֹשֵׂא עָוֹן,

〈 of 〈 Forgiver 《 for thousands 〈 of 〈 Preserver 《 and 〈 in 〈 and
iniquity,   [of generations],   kindness   Truth,   Kindness Abundant

וָפֶשַׁע, וְחַטָּאָה, וְנַקֵּה.² וְסָלַחְתָּ לַעֲוֹנֵנוּ וּלְחַטָּאתֵנוּ

《 and our sins, 〈 our 〈 May You 《 and Who 〈 and inadvertent 〈 willful sin,
  iniquities   forgive   absolves.   sin,

וּנְחַלְתָּנוּ.³ סְלַח לָנוּ אָבִינוּ כִּי חָטָאנוּ, מְחַל לָנוּ

〈 us, 〈 pardon 《 we have 〈 for 《 our 〈 us, 〈 Forgive 《 and make us
  sinned;   Father,   Your heritage.

מַלְכֵּנוּ כִּי פָשָׁעְנוּ. כִּי אַתָּה אֲדֹנָי טוֹב וְסַלָּח,

《 and 〈 are 〈 O Lord, 〈 You, 〈 For 《 we have 〈 for 《 our King,
forgiving,   good   willfully sinned.

וְרַב חֶסֶד לְכָל קֹרְאֶיךָ.⁴

《 who call 〈 to all 〈 kind 〈 and
upon You.   abundantly

סליחה לז / SELICHAH 37

THE ARK IS OPENED.

CHAZZAN, **THEN CONGREGATION:**

אַל תָּבוֹא בְמִשְׁפָּט עִמָּנוּ,* כִּי לֹא יִצְדַּק לְפָנֶיךָ כָל חָי.⁵

《 living 〈 any 〈 before 〈 vindicated 〈 for 《 with 〈 into strict 〈 enter 〈 Do
creature.   You   would not be   us,*   **judgment**   not

---

(1) *Exodus* 34:5. (2) 34:6-7. (3) 34:9. (4) *Psalms* 86:5. (5) Cf. 143:2.

אַל תָּבוֹא בְמִשְׁפָּט עִמָּנוּ §⊷ — *Do not enter into strict judgment with us.* Although *pizmon-im* are not usually preceded by Scriptural verses as are other *selichos,* an exception is made here and not only are verses recited,

they are recited responsively, and before the open Ark. Since the theme of the *pizmon* is the judgment that will take place on Rosh Hashanah, each of the nine verses contains some form of the root שפט, *to judge.*

CHAZZAN, THEN CONGREGATION:

צֶדֶק וּמִשְׁפָּט מְכוֹן כִּסְאֶךָ, חֶסֶד וֶאֱמֶת יְקַדְּמוּ פָנֶיךָ.1

» Your 〈 precede 〈 and truth 〈 kindness » of Your 〈 are the 〈 and 〈 Right-
countenance. throne; foundation justice eousness

CHAZZAN, THEN CONGREGATION:

מִלְּפָנֶיךָ מִשְׁפָּטֵנוּ יֵצֵא, עֵינֶיךָ תֶּחֱזֶינָה מֵישָׁרִים.2

» uprightness. 〈 behold 〈 may Your » go 〈 may our 〈 From before
eyes forth; judgment You

CHAZZAN, THEN CONGREGATION:

וְהוּא יִשְׁפֹּט תֵּבֵל בְּצֶדֶק, יָדִין לְאֻמִּים בְּמֵישָׁרִים.3

» in uprightness. 〈 nations 〈 He will » with right- 〈 the 〈 will judge 〈 And He
judge eousness; world

CHAZZAN, THEN CONGREGATION:

רַחֲמֶיךָ רַבִּים, יהוה, כְּמִשְׁפָּטֶיךָ חַיֵּינוּ.4

〈 preserve 〈 as is Your 〈 HASHEM; 〈 are 〈 Your
me. practice; abundant, mercies

CHAZZAN, THEN CONGREGATION:

הִנָּשֵׂא שֹׁפֵט הָאָרֶץ, הָשֵׁב גְּמוּל עַל גֵּאִים.5

» the haughty. 〈 to 〈 retribution 〈 render » of the earth; 〈 O Judge 〈 Arise

CHAZZAN, THEN CONGREGATION:

כִּי יהוה שֹׁפְטֵנוּ, יהוה מְחֹקְקֵנוּ,

» is our Lawgiver, 〈 HASHEM » is our Judge, 〈 HASHEM 〈 For

יהוה מַלְכֵּנוּ הוּא יוֹשִׁיעֵנוּ.6

» will save us. 〈 He » is our King, 〈 HASHEM

CHAZZAN, THEN CONGREGATION:

חָלִלָה לְּךָ מֵעֲשֹׂת כַּדָּבָר הַזֶּה, לְהָמִית צַדִּיק

〈 the 〈 to kill » as this, 〈 such a 〈 to have 〈 to 〈 It would be
righteous thing done You sacrilegious

עִם רָשָׁע, וְהָיָה כַצַּדִּיק כָּרָשָׁע, חָלִלָה לָּךְ, הֲשֹׁפֵט

〈 Shall it be » to 〈 It would be » so to the 〈 just as to the 〈 that it » the 〈 along
that the Judge You! sacrilegious wicked; righteous will be wicked; with

כָּל הָאָרֶץ לֹא יַעֲשֶׂה מִשְׁפָּט.7

» justice? 〈 will not do 〈 the earth 〈 of all

IN SOME CONGREGATIONS THE ARK IS CLOSED AT THIS POINT.

(1) *Psalms* 89:15. (2) Cf. 17:2. (3) Cf. 9:9. (4) 119:156. (5) 94:2. (6) *Isaiah* 33:22. (7) *Genesis* 18:25.

סליחה לח / SELICHAH 38

(פזמון)

CHAZZAN, THEN CONGREGATION:

שֹׁפֵט כָּל הָאָרֶץ,*¹ וְאַתָּה בַּמִּשְׁפָּט יַעֲמִיד,²

》sets in order, 〈 through justice 〈 [Who] it 》 the earth,* 〈 of all 〈 Judge

נָא חַיִּים וָחֶסֶד, עַל עַם עָנִי תַּצְמִיד,

》 link. 〈 that is 〈 the 〈 for 〈 and 〈 life 》please,
afflicted nation　　　　kindness

אֶת תְּפִלַּת הַשַּׁחַר, בִּמְקוֹם עוֹלָה* תַּעֲמִיד,

》 establish; 〈 of a burnt- 〈 in place 〈 of the 〈 The prayer
offering* 　　　　morning

כְּעוֹלַת הַבְּקֶר, אֲשֶׁר לְעוֹלַת הַתָּמִיד.³

》 burnt- 〈 of the 〈 which is 〈 of the 〈 [let it be] like the
offering. continual part morning burnt-offering

CONGREGATION, THEN CHAZZAN:

לוֹבֵשׁ צְדָקָה וּמַעֲטֵה⁴ לְךָ לְבַד הַיִּתְרוֹן,

》 have the 〈 alone 〈 You 》 and wraps 〈 [a garment of] 〈 You
ultimate power. 　　　Yourself in it, righteousness Who dons

אִם אֵין בָּנוּ מַעֲשִׂים, זָכְרָה יְשֵׁנֵי חֶבְרוֹן,⁵

》 in Hebron, 〈 those 〈 then 》 any [good] 〈 to our 〈 there 〈 If
who sleep remember deeds, merit are not

וְהֵם יַעֲלוּ לְזִכָּרוֹן לִפְנֵי יהוה תָּמִיד,⁶

》constantly, 〈 HASHEM 〈 before 〈 as a 〈 will 〈 and
remembrance ascend they

כְּעוֹלַת הַבְּקֶר, אֲשֶׁר לְעוֹלַת הַתָּמִיד.

》 burnt- 〈 of the 〈 which is 〈 of the 〈 like the
offering. continual part morning burnt-offering

---

(1) Cf. *Genesis* 18:25. (2) Cf. *Proverbs* 29:4. (3) Cf. *Numbers* 28:23. (4) Cf. *Isaiah* 59:17.
(5) See commentary to *Selichah* 26, s.v. יִשֵׁנֵי מַכְפֵּל. (6) *Exodus* 28:29.

---

§⊷ שֹׁפֵט כָּל הָאָרֶץ — *Judge of all the earth.*
Opinions vary widely regarding the identity of the author of this *selichah*, whose
name — שְׁלמה, *Shlomo* — appears in the
acrostic. The opening and closing stanzas
each contains four lines; the three middle
stanzas have three lines each. Apparently
some lines were lost over the centuries; indeed, the Yemenite rite has additional lines
in this *selichah*.

תְּפִלַּת הַשַּׁחַר בִּמְקוֹם עוֹלָה — *The prayer of
the morning in place of a burnt-offering.*
The Talmud records a dispute regarding
the origin of the three daily prayers. According to R' Yose bar R' Chanina, the
Patriarchs Abraham, Isaac, and Jacob,
respectively, instituted the morning, afternoon, and nighttime prayers. According to
R' Yehoshua ben Levi, the morning prayer
was enacted in place of the morning

CONGREGATION, THEN *CHAZZAN:*

מַטֶּה כְּלַפֵּי חֶסֶד, לְהַטּוֹת אִישׁ לִתְחִיָּה,

« toward ‹ man ‹ turning « kindness, ‹ toward ‹ You
[renewed]   Who tip
life,   [the scales]

עַמְּךָ לְחֶסֶד הַטֶּה, גְּמֹל נָא עָלָיו וְחָיָה,

« that they ‹ upon ‹ please, « bestow « tip their ‹ toward « Your
may live.   them   [kindness], scales;   kindness   people,

כְּתֹב תָּו חַיִּים,* וְהָיָה עַל מִצְחוֹ תָּמִיד,[1]

« constantly, ‹ [the people's] ‹ on ‹ let it be « of life,* ‹ the ‹ Inscribe
         forehead   sign

כְּעוֹלַת הַבְּקֶר, אֲשֶׁר לְעוֹלַת הַתָּמִיד.

« burnt- ‹ of the ‹ which is ‹ of the ‹ like the
offering.   continual   part   morning   burnt-offering

CONGREGATION, THEN *CHAZZAN:*

הֵטִיבָה בִרְצוֹנְךָ אֶת צִיּוֹן,[2] עִיר קְדוֹשַׁי,

« of my ‹ the « Zion, ‹ unto ‹ in Your favor ‹ Do good
holy ones,   City

וְנָתַתָּ יָד וָשֵׁם בְּבֵיתְךָ[3] לְמִקְדָּשַׁי,

« for my ‹ in Your ‹ and a ‹ a me- ‹ and
sanctified ones;   House   monument   morial   make

וַעֲרִיכַת נֵר לְבֶן יִשַׁי,[4] לְהַעֲלוֹת נֵר תָּמִיד.[5]

« continually, ‹ a ‹ to kindle « of Jesse, ‹ for the ‹ lamp ‹ and a
       lamp   [the Messiah,]   son   prepared

---

(1) *Exodus* 28:38. (2) *Psalms* 51:20. (3) Cf. *Isaiah* 56:5. (4) Cf. *Psalms* 132:17. (5) *Exodus* 27:20.

burnt-offering (see below); the afternoon prayer, in place of the afternoon burnt-offering; and the nighttime prayer, in place of the organs and fats of the previous day's offerings, which were usually placed on the Altar fire at night (*Berachos* 26b).

The burnt-offering was an animal offering that was burnt in its entirety on the Altar. No parts of it were eaten either by the bringer or by the *Kohanim*. The Torah ordained that two lambs be offered daily, one each morning, one each afternoon, as the first and last Altar offerings of the day. These are called the תָּמִיד [*tamid*], continual or perpetual offerings (see *Numbers* 28:1-8). The constantly repeated theme of

this *selichah* is that some aspect of Israel's existence be constantly before God. In the respective verses these aspects are: their prayers; the Patriarchs and Matriarchs; the sign of life; the Messiah; and those who seek God's Presence.

כְּתֹב תָּו חַיִּים — *Inscribe the sign of life.* The prophet Ezekiel states that God told an angel [Gabriel] to *pass in the midst of Jerusalem, and mark a sign on the foreheads of the* [righteous] *men who sigh* [in agony over the abominations of the wicked] *and* [of the wicked men] *who groan* [in the death throes about to befall them because of their sinfulness] *for all the abominations that are done within it.*

כְּעוֹלַת הַבֹּקֶר, אֲשֶׁר לְעוֹלַת הַתָּמִיד.

《 burnt-offering. 〈 of the continual 〈 which is part 〈 of the morning 〈 like the burnt-offering

CONGREGATION, THEN CHAZZAN:

חִזְקוּ וְאִמְצוּ לְבַבְכֶם, עַמִּי בְּאֵל מָעֻזּוֹ,[1]

《 Who is their fortress. 〈 through God 〈 my people, 〈 your hearts, 〈 and encourage 〈 Strengthen

עֵדוֹתָיו כִּי תִנְצָרוּ, גַּם אֶת זוֹ לְעֻמַּת זוֹ,[2]

《 that [measure]; 〈 parallel to 〈 with this [measure] 〈 [He will act] also 〈 you will safeguard, 〈 when 〈 His commandments

יְכַפֵּר בְּעַד חַטֹּאתֵיכֶם, וְיִזְכֹּר רַחֵם בְּרָגְזוֹ,[3]

《 [even] amidst His rage, 〈 to be merciful 〈 and He will remember 〈 your sins 〈 for 〈 He will provide atonement

דִּרְשׁוּ יהוה וְעֻזּוֹ, בַּקְּשׁוּ פָנָיו תָּמִיד,[4]

《 always, 〈 His Presence 〈 seek 《 and His might, 〈 HASHEM 〈 search out

כְּעוֹלַת הַבֹּקֶר, אֲשֶׁר לְעוֹלַת הַתָּמִיד.

《 burnt-offering. 〈 of the continual 〈 which is part 〈 of the morning 〈 like the burnt-offering

THE ARK IS CLOSED.

ALL, WHILE STANDING:

אֵל מֶלֶךְ יוֹשֵׁב עַל כִּסֵּא רַחֲמִים, מִתְנַהֵג

〈 Who acts 《 of mercy, 〈 the throne 〈 on 〈 Who sits 〈 King 〈 O God,

בַּחֲסִידוּת, מוֹחֵל עֲוֹנוֹת עַמּוֹ, מַעֲבִיר רִאשׁוֹן

〈 [sins,] one 〈 Who removes 《 of His people, 〈 the sins 〈 Who pardons 《 with kindness,

רִאשׁוֹן,[5] מַרְבֶּה מְחִילָה לַחַטָּאִים וּסְלִיחָה לַפּוֹשְׁעִים,

《 to willful sinners, 〈 and forgiveness 〈 to unintentional sinners 〈 pardon 〈 Who abundantly grants 《 by one,

---

(1) Cf. *Psalms* 31:25. (2) Cf. *Ecclesiastes* 7:14. (3) Cf. *Habakkuk* 3:2.
(4) *Psalms* 105:4. (5) *Rosh Hashanah* 17a.

According to the Talmud (*Shabbos* 55a), the mark was to be the letter ת, and it was to be written in ink on the foreheads of the righteous, but in blood on the foreheads of the wicked. Various opinions are offered by the Sages regarding the implication of this letter. Among them: Rav says that the ink ת stands for תִּחְיֶה, *you shall live*, while the blood ת indicates תָּמוּת, *you shall die*. R' Shmuel bar Nachmani says that the ink ת testifies that these people observed the Torah from א to ת (from A to Z), and that the blood ת alludes to those who desecrated the Torah from א to ת.

עֹשֶׂה צְדָקוֹת עִם כָּל בָּשָׂר וָרוּחַ, לֹא כְרָעָתָם

‹ in accord with ‹ — not « and ‹ [beings ‹ all « with ‹ acts of ‹ Who
their wickedness   spirit   of] flesh   generosity   performs

תִּגְמוֹל. ❖ אֵל הוֹרֵיתָ לָּנוּ לוֹמַר שְׁלֹשׁ עֶשְׂרֵה, וּזְכוֹר

‹ remem- « the Thirteen ‹ to ‹ us ‹ You ‹ O God, « do You
ber   [Attributes of Mercy];   recite   taught   repay them!

לָּנוּ הַיּוֹם בְּרִית שְׁלֹשׁ עֶשְׂרֵה, כְּמוֹ שֶׁהוֹדַעְתָּ לֶעָנָיו

‹ to the ‹ You made ‹ as « of [these] Thirteen, ‹ the ‹ today ‹ for us
humble one   known   covenant
[Moses]

מִקֶּדֶם, כְּמוֹ שֶׁכָּתוּב, וַיֵּרֶד יהוה בֶּעָנָן וַיִּתְיַצֵּב עִמּוֹ

‹ with ‹ and stood ‹ in a ‹ And HASHEM « it is written: ‹ as «in ancient
him   cloud   descended   times,

שָׁם, וַיִּקְרָא בְשֵׁם יהוה.[1]

« of ‹ with the ‹ and He « there,
HASHEM.   Name   called out

CONGREGATION, THEN *CHAZZAN*:

וַיַּעֲבֹר יהוה עַל פָּנָיו וַיִּקְרָא:

« and « [Moses'] ‹ before ‹ And HASHEM passed
proclaimed: face,

CONGREGATION AND *CHAZZAN* RECITE LOUDLY AND IN UNISON:

יהוה, יהוה, אֵל, רַחוּם, וְחַנּוּן, אֶרֶךְ אַפַּיִם,

‹ to anger, ‹ Slow « and ‹ Compassionate ‹ God, ‹ HASHEM, ‹ HASHEM,
                Gracious,

וְרַב חֶסֶד, וֶאֱמֶת, נֹצֵר חֶסֶד לָאֲלָפִים, נֹשֵׂא עָוֹן,

‹ of ‹ Forgiver « for thousands ‹ of ‹ Preserver « and ‹ in ‹ and
iniquity,   [of generations],   kindness   Truth,   Kindness Abundant

וָפֶשַׁע, וְחַטָּאָה, וְנַקֵּה.[2] וְסָלַחְתָּ לַעֲוֹנֵנוּ וּלְחַטָּאתֵנוּ

« and our sins, ‹ our ‹ May You « and Who ‹ and inadvertent ‹ willful sin,
          iniquities   forgive   absolves.   sin,

וּנְחַלְתָּנוּ.[3] סְלַח לָנוּ אָבִינוּ כִּי חָטָאנוּ, מְחַל לָנוּ

‹ us, ‹ pardon « we have ‹ for « our ‹ us, ‹ Forgive « and make us
         sinned;   Father,   Your heritage.

מַלְכֵּנוּ כִּי פָשָׁעְנוּ. כִּי אַתָּה אֲדֹנָי טוֹב וְסַלָּח,

« and ‹ are ‹ O Lord, ‹ You, ‹ For « we have ‹ for « our King,
forgiving,   good   willfully sinned.

---

(1) *Exodus* 34:5. (2) 34:6-7. (3) 34:9.

וְרַב חֶסֶד לְכָל קֹרְאֶיךָ.1

《 who call ⟨ to all ⟨ kind ⟨ and
upon You.   abundantly

פסוקי הקדמה לסליחה לט / PREFATORY VERSES TO SELICHAH 39

יִזְכֹּר אֱלֹהִים אֶת בְּרִיתוֹ, אֶת אַבְרָהָם אֶת יִצְחָק

⟨ Isaac, ⟨ with ⟨ Abraham, ⟨ with ⟨ His covenant ⟨ May God remember

וְאֶת יַעֲקֹב.2 טֶרֶף נָתַן לִירֵאָיו, יִזְכֹּר לְעוֹלָם

⟨ eternally ⟨ He ⟨ for those who ⟨ He ⟨ Food ⟨ Jacob. ⟨ and
remembers   fear Him,   provided   with

בְּרִיתוֹ.3 כִּי בָרֵךְ אֲבָרֶכְךָ, וְהַרְבָּה אַרְבֶּה אֶת זַרְעֲךָ

⟨ your ⟨ shall I ⟨ and greatly ⟨ I shall surely ⟨ [I swear] 《 His
offspring   increase   bless you   that   covenant.

כְּכוֹכְבֵי הַשָּׁמַיִם, וְכַחוֹל אֲשֶׁר עַל שְׂפַת הַיָּם, וְיִרַשׁ

⟨ and 《 of the ⟨ the ⟨ on ⟨ that is ⟨ and like ⟨ of the ⟨ like
inherit   sea;   shore   the sand   heavens   the stars

זַרְעֲךָ אֵת שַׁעַר אֹיְבָיו.4

《 of his ⟨ the gates ⟨ will your
enemies.   offspring

כְּרַחֵם אָב עַל בָּנִים, כֵּן תְּרַחֵם יהוה עָלֵינוּ.5

《 on us. ⟨ HASHEM, ⟨ have ⟨ so 《 his ⟨ toward ⟨ a ⟨ As merciful as
      mercy,   children,   father is

לַיהוה הַיְשׁוּעָה, עַל עַמְּךָ בִרְכָתֶךָ סֶּלָה.6 יהוה

⟨ HASHEM, 《 Selah. 《 is Your ⟨ Your ⟨ upon 《 is salvation, ⟨ To HASHEM
        blessing,   people

צְבָאוֹת עִמָּנוּ, מִשְׂגָּב לָנוּ אֱלֹהֵי יַעֲקֹב סֶלָה.7

《 Selah. 《 of Jacob, ⟨ is the God ⟨ for us ⟨ a 《 is with us, ⟨ Master of
            stronghold   Legions,

יהוה צְבָאוֹת, אַשְׁרֵי אָדָם בֹּטֵחַ בָּךְ.8 יהוה

⟨ HASHEM, 《 in You. ⟨ who ⟨ is the ⟨ — praiseworthy 《 Master ⟨ HASHEM,
      trusts   man   of Legions,

הוֹשִׁיעָה, הַמֶּלֶךְ יַעֲנֵנוּ בְיוֹם קָרְאֵנוּ.9

《 we call. ⟨ on the ⟨ answer ⟨ May the 《 save!
      day   us   King

---

(1) *Psalms* 86:5. (2) Cf. *Exodus* 2:24. (3) *Psalms* 111:5. (4) *Genesis* 22:17.
(5) Cf. *Psalms* 103:13. (6) 3:9. (7) 46:8. (8) 84:13. (9) 20:10.

סליחה לט / SELICHAH 39

(עקדה)

**THIS PIYUT SHOULD BE RECITED FOLLOWING THE PUNCTUATION —
NOT THE POETIC LINE ENDINGS (SEE COMMENTARY).**

ALL:

אֱלֹהֵינוּ וֵאלֹהֵי אֲבוֹתֵינוּ:

❰ of our forefathers: ❰ and God ❰ Our God

מְפַלְטִי* אֵלִי צוּרִי סִתְרִי וּמָגִנִּי,

❰ and my ❰ my Con- ❰ my ❰ my ❰ My Rescuer,*
Shield, cealment, Rock, God,

וְקֶרֶן יִשְׁעִי מִשְׂגַּבִּי¹ בְּיוֹם צַר לִי וְאוֹנִי,

❰ and ❰ I am ❰ on the ❰ my ❰ of my ❰ the
grieving — troubled day Stronghold Salvation, Horn

הִשְׁכַּמְתִּי לְחַלּוֹתְךָ מֶלֶךְ רָב. וַאֲנִי

❰ and ❰ Who is ❰ O King ❰ to pray ❰ I have risen
I — great, to You, early

אֵלֶיךָ יהוה שִׁוַּעְתִּי בַּבֹּקֶר.²

❰ in the morning. ❰ I cry out ❰ HASHEM, ❰ to You,

בֹּקֶר רַחֵם תִּזְכֹּר חֶסֶד אַבְרָהָם אָב אֵיתָנַי,

❰ [of those called] ❰ the ❰ of Abraham, ❰ the ❰ remember ❰ to have mer- ❰ In the
My mighty ones, father kindness cy [on me] morning

אֲשֶׁר בְּחַרְתּוֹ וְהֶאֱמִין בְּךָ רֹאשׁ לְמַאֲמִינַי,

❰ of my [people's] ❰ — the ❰ in ❰ and who ❰ You chose ❰ whom
believers. first You believed him,

זְכֹר בְּרִיתוֹ וְהוֹשִׁיעֵנִי מִטֻּמְאָתִי, יהוה

❰ HASHEM, ❰ from my ❰ and save me ❰ his ❰ Remem-
defilement — covenant ber

בֹּקֶר תִּשְׁמַע קוֹלִי בֹּקֶר.³

❰ — in the ❰ my ❰ hear ❰ in the
morning! voice morning

---

(1) Cf. *Psalms* 18:3, 119:114. (2) Cf. 88:14. (3) 5:4.

◆§ מְפַלְטִי — *My Rescuer.* During the period from Erev Rosh Hashanah until Yom Kippur, an *akeidah* is added to the *Selichos* service. As the name implies, an *akeidah* is a *piyut* that describes עֲקֵדַת יִצְחָק, *the Binding of Isaac* (*Genesis* Ch. 22), and pleads that, in its merit, the descendants of Abraham and Isaac be endowed with Divine mercy and forgiveness.

In this *piyut*, the word בֹּקֶר, *[in the] morning*, begins and ends each stanza. The initial letters of the respective second words of each stanza spell the composer's name — מָרְדְּכַי הָאָרֹךְ, *Mordechai HaAruch*

בְּקֶר דִּבַּרְתָּ עִמּוֹ, וְנִסִּיתוֹ לְשַׁלֵּם לוֹ מַשְׂכֹּרֶת,

《 a reward, ⟨ him ⟨ so as ⟨ and You ⟨ with ⟨ You spoke ⟨ **In the**
to pay   tested him   him   **morning**

וְכָרוֹת עִמּוֹ הַבְּרִית[1] לִהְיוֹת לוֹ לְמִשְׁמֶרֶת,

《 a guardian. ⟨ for ⟨ to become ⟨ the ⟨ with ⟨ and You
him   covenant   him   established

אֲהַבְתּוֹ וּרְצִיתוֹ וְקִבַּלְתּוֹ כִּקְטֹרֶת

⟨ like the ⟨ accepted ⟨ and favored ⟨ You loved
incense   him   him,   him,

סַמִּים בַּבֹּקֶר **בַּבֹּקֶר**.[2]

《 each and every **morning.** ⟨ spices,

בְּקֶר כּוֹכְבוֹ הֵאִיר, כְּחָפַצְתָּ לְהַרְאוֹת צִדְקָתוֹ הַגְּדוֹלָה,

《 that was ⟨ his right- ⟨ to show ⟨ when You 《 shone ⟨ when his ⟨ **In the**
great,   eousness   desired   brightly,   star   **morning**

נִסִּיתוֹ בָּעֲשִׂירִי,* וַתֹּאמֶר לוֹ קַח נָא אֶת בִּנְךָ וְאַל תִּכְלָא,

《 withhold ⟨ – do 《 your ⟨ please, ⟨Take, 《 to ⟨ and You ⟨ the tenth ⟨ You
him –   not   son   him,   said   time,*   tested him

עַל אַחַד הֶהָרִים וְהַעֲלֵהוּ שָׁם לְעוֹלָה,[3]

《 as an ⟨ there ⟨ and bring 《 of the ⟨ one ⟨upon
offering.   him up   mountains,

אֶת הַכֶּבֶשׂ אֶחָד תַּעֲשֶׂה בַּבֹּקֶר.[4]

《 in the ⟨ You shall ⟨ The one lamb
morning.   do

---

(1) *Nehemiah* 9:8. (2) Cf. *Exodus* 30:7. (3) *Genesis* 22:2. (4) *Numbers* 28:4.

[the tall one]. Only two things are known about R' Mordechai: He flourished before 1234, when the commentary *Arugas HaBosem* [which includes this *akeidah*] was written; and he wrote another *selichah* for *Minchah* of Yom Kippur which has become part of the Yom Kippur Kattan *Selichos* service. That latter composition is signed *Mordechai ben Shabsi Aruch*.

The stanzas each comprises four lines, three of which rhyme; the fourth is a Scriptural fragment ending with the word בֹּקֶר, *morning*. In an unusual departure, in many stanzas the words of the third and fourth lines flow together, with the third line ending in the middle of a thought. Therefore, it is important that this *piyut* be recited according to the punctuation, not the rhyme

scheme; otherwise it will not make sense.

נִסִּיתוֹ בָּעֲשִׂירִי — *You tested him the tenth time.* Abraham's faith was tested ten times by God. The ten trials are enumerated in *Avos deR'Nosson* (33:2): (a) King Nimrod threw him into the fiery furnace for destroying his father's idols (see *Genesis* 11:28); (b) God commanded him to leave his home to travel to an unknown land (12:1); (c) when he got to that land, there was a hunger and he had to move again (12:10); (d) in Egypt, his wife Sarah was kidnaped by the king (12:15); (e) in order to save his nephew Lot, he had to fight the armies of four mighty kings (14:13-16); (f) he was told that his children would be slaves in a foreign land (15:13); (g) he was commanded to have a *bris milah* (17:9-14); (h) his wife

בְּקֶר יִחַד שִׁמְךָ וְשָׁמַע לְקוֹלֶךָ וְהֶרְאָה אַהֲבָתוֹ,

In the morning ≪ the Oneness ⟨ he declared ⟨ of Your Name; ≪ and he listened ⟨ to Your voice ⟨ and demonstrated ≪ his love.

וְשָׂשׂ בְּכָל לֵב עַל אִמְרָתְךָ לַעֲשׂוֹתוֹ,

He rejoiced ⟨ whole- ⟨heartedly⟨ re-garding ≪ Your word, ≪ to fulfill it.

הָאַהֲבָה קִלְקְלָה הַשּׁוּרָה,* וַיָּקָם בְּשִׂמְחָתוֹ,

Love ⟨ obliterated ⟨ the line,* ⟨ and he rose ⟨ in his joy; ≪

¹**וַיַּשְׁכֵּם אַבְרָהָם בַּבֹּקֶר.**

and Abraham rose early ⟨ ≪**in the morning.**

בְּקֶר הֵכִינוּ לִבָּם שְׁנֵיהֶם לַעֲשׂוֹת רְצוֹנְךָ, אָיוֹם,

In the morning ⟨ they focused ≪ their hearts ⟨ — both of them — ≪ to do ⟨ Your will, ≪**O Awesome One.**

הַבֵּן לָקַח עֵצִים וְהָאָב לָקַח מַאֲכֶלֶת,

The son ⟨ took ⟨ wood, ≪ and the father ⟨ took ⟨ a knife, ⟨

לִשְׁחֹט בְּלִי פְּדִיוֹם,

[determined] to slaughter him. ⟨ without ⟨ [thought of] redeeming ≪

²קְרוּאִים וְהוֹלְכִים לְתָמָם, וְרָאוּ כְבוֹדֶךָ בַּיּוֹם

Summoned, ⟨ they went ⟨ with pure heart, ⟨ and they saw ⟨ Your glory ⟨ on day

³**הַשְּׁלִישִׁי בִּהְיוֹת הַבֹּקֶר.**

three ⟨ when it was ⟨ ≪**the morning.**

---

(1) Genesis 22:3. (2) II Samuel 15:11. (3) Cf. Exodus 19:16.

Sarah was kidnaped by Abimelech, King of Gerar (20:2); (i) he was commanded to send away Hagar and Ishmael (21:10-12); (j) he was commanded to offer his son Isaac as a sacrifice (22:1-2).

הָאַהֲבָה קִלְקְלָה הַשּׁוּרָה — *Love obliterated the line.* The Torah relates that *Abraham rose early in the morning and saddled his donkey* (Genesis 22:3) on the morning after he was commanded to sacrifice his son. This teaches that love obliterates the line [that distinguishes between servant and master]. Abraham had many servants to saddle his donkey for him, yet his love of God and his desire to fulfill His command immediately caused Abraham to act the servant and saddle his donkey on his own. The same lesson is taught by the verse, *Joseph [himself] harnessed his chariot* (ibid. 46:29), when he went to meet his father. Conversely, hatred also obliterates the line, for we find that *[Pharaoh] harnessed his own chariot* (Exodus 14:6) when he pursued Israel; and *Balaam arose early in the morning and saddled his own donkey* (Numbers 22:21) when he set out to curse Israel (Bereishis Rabbah 55:8).

בְּקֶר אָזַר כְּגִבּוֹר חֲלָצָיו¹ וְלַעֲקֹד בְּנוֹ קֶדֶם,

《 went ⟨ his ⟨ and to bind ⟨ around his ⟨ like a ⟨ [Abraham] ⟨ **In the**
forward.   son   waist   warrior   tightened **morning,**
                                                                  the belt

וַיִּקַּח מַאֲכֶלֶת לִשְׁחָטוֹ וְלֹא חָשַׁב אָדָם,*

《 a man.* ⟨ think ⟨ and did ⟨ to slaughter ⟨ the knife ⟨ He took
                     not   him,   up

וַיֹּאמֶר הַיּוֹם אַקְרִיב עוֹלָתִי וְאֶזְרֹק דַּם

⟨ the ⟨ and I will throw ⟨ my burnt- ⟨ I will offer ⟨ Today ⟨ 《 He said,
blood [on the altar]   offering

זִבְחִי לֹא יָלִין עַד בְּקֶר.²

《 the ⟨ [until ⟨ remain ⟨ [it shall] 《 of my
morning.   overnight   not   sacrifice;

בְּקֶר רַחֲמֶיךָ נִכְמְרוּ עַל בֵּן יָחִיד וְעָלָיו זָרֶחוּ,

《 it ⟨ and ⟨ the only ⟨ the ⟨ for ⟨ was ⟨ Your mercy ⟨ **In the**
shone. upon him one,   son,   enkindled   **morning**

וַיִּקְרָא אֵלָיו מַלְאַךְ יהוה, אֶל הַנַּעַר יָדֶיִם אַל יִשְׁלָחוּ,³

《 send forth, ⟨ do ⟨ [your] ⟨ the lad ⟨ Against 《 of ⟨ did the ⟨ to him ⟨ Call
              not   hands   HASHEM, angel [Abraham]

כִּי בְיִצְחָק יִקָּרֵא לְךָ זָרַע,⁴ וְזִכְרוֹ לְדוֹרוֹת הַנִּיחוּ

⟨ shall you ⟨ for [all] ⟨ And remem- 《 off- ⟨ your ⟨ will they ⟨ [only] ⟨ for
retain   generations brance of   spring.   be con-   through   Isaac
                           [his binding]   sidered

לָכֶם לְמִשְׁמֶרֶת עַד הַבֹּקֶר.⁵

《 [Redemption's] ⟨ until ⟨ a security ⟨ that it be
morning.   guarantee   unto you

בְּקֶר כָּשְׁרוֹ וְיָשְׁרוֹ וְצִדְקוֹ יָלִיץ בְּעַד עַם אֵלֶיךָ קָרֵב,

《 draws ⟨ that to ⟨ of the ⟨ on ⟨ advocate ⟨ and his ⟨ his up- ⟨ let his ⟨ **In the**
close,   You   people   behalf   righteous- rightness, [Isaac's] **morning**
                                            ness   proper deeds,

---

(1) Cf. *Job* 38:3. (2) Cf. *Exodus* 23:18; 34:25. (3) Cf. *Genesis* 22:11-12. (4) 21:12. (5) *Exodus* 16:23.

וְלֹא חָשַׁב אָדָם — *And did not think a man.*
The translation of this line has purposely
been left ambiguous and arcane. The *paytan* may have meant any of three things
with these words. According to many commentaries, Abraham overcame his paternal
instinct to spare his son by thinking of Isaac
not as a person, but as an animal to be used
in God's service. This view is difficult to
accept. For one, God commanded Abraham

to sacrifice *your son, your only son, whom
you love, Isaac* (*Genesis* 22:2). By imagining
Isaac to be an animal, or anything less than
your son, your only son …, Abraham would,
in effect, fail the test placed before him. Another problem is that if this view is correct,
the phrase should have read לֹא חָשְׁבוֹ אָדָם,
he did not think him a man, which would
retain the meter while being more explicit.

Two other possible interpretations are: *No*

וְאַפְרוֹ תָּמִיד יֵרָאֶה לְפָנֶיךָ לְכַבְּסֵם הֶרֶב,

‹ and let › always › appear › before › for You to ‹ thoroughly
his ashes   You,   cleanse them   [of their sins].

תִּנָּתֶן לָהֶם נַפְשָׁם בִּשְׁאֵלָתָם,¹ כִּי לְךָ נִכְסְפָה. וּבָעֶרֶב

‹ Grant › them › their life ‹ since ‹ as their request, › for ‹ [the Nation] › and in
    You   yearns,   the evening

הִיא בָאָה וּבַבֹּקֶר.²

› it ‹ comes [to You ‹ as well as ‹
in prayer],   in the morning.

בֹּקֶר קוֹלָם שְׁמַע,³ וּתְכַפֵּר עֲוֹנוֹתֵיהֶם,

‹ In the › their ‹ hear › and provide ‹ for their
morning › voices   atonement   iniquities;

וְעֶרֶךְ תְּפִלָּתָם תֵּחָשֵׁב כְּעֵרֶךְ קָרְבְּנוֹתֵיהֶם,

‹ let the › order › of their ‹ be ‹ as the ‹ of their sacrifices.
order   prayers   considered › order

לָקְחוּ⁴ וּבָאוּ בְּזִכְרוֹן צִדְקַת אֲבוֹתֵיהֶם,

‹ They have taken › and ‹ in the ‹ of the ‹ of their fathers,
[words of prayer] › come, › remembrance › righteousness

וְהֵם הֵבִיאוּ אֵלָיו עוֹד נְדָבָה בַּבֹּקֶר בַּבֹּקֶר.⁵

‹ And › bring ‹ to Him ‹ another ‹ voluntary ‹ each and every
they   [prayer]   morning.
                      offering

❖ בֹּקֶר תֵּפֶן אֵלֵינוּ לְרַחֲמֵנוּ, וְרַחֲמֶיךָ עָלֵינוּ יִכְמֹרוּ,

‹ In the › turn › toward ‹ to have mercy ‹ and let ‹ on our ‹ be
morning,   us   on us,   Your mercy › behalf › enkindled;

וְתַשְׁלִיךְ בִּמְצֻלוֹת יָם כָּל חַטֹּאתֵינוּ⁶ וְלֹא יִזָּכְרוּ,

‹ and may › into the ‹ of ‹ all ‹ our sins, ‹ that they not be
You cast › depths › the sea   remembered.

צוּר הַעֲבֵר עֲוֹנֵנוּ מִלְּפָנֶיךָ, וְלֹא יַשְׁאִירוּ

‹ O ‹ expel ‹ our ‹ from Your ‹ and let ‹ be left over
Rock,   iniquities › presence, › nothing

מִמֶּנּוּ עַד בֹּקֶר.⁷

‹ from ‹ until ‹ the
them   morning.

---

(1) Cf. *Esther* 7:3. (2) 2:14. (3) Cf. *Psalms* 5:4. (4) Cf. *Hosea* 14:3.
(5) *Exodus* 36:3. (6) Cf. *Micah* 7:19. (7) *Numbers* 9:12.

man thought that Abraham would do such a thing; and, *He* [Abraham] *did not think of*   what *any other man* would say regarding his actions.

ALL, WHILE STANDING:

אֵל מֶלֶךְ יוֹשֵׁב עַל כִּסֵּא רַחֲמִים, מִתְנַהֵג

⟨ Who acts 《 of mercy, ⟨ the throne ⟨ on ⟨ Who sits ⟨ King ⟨ O God,

בַּחֲסִידוּת, מוֹחֵל עֲוֹנוֹת עַמּוֹ, מַעֲבִיר רִאשׁוֹן

⟨ [sins,] one ⟨ Who ⟨ of His ⟨ the sins ⟨ Who 《 with kindness,
　　　　　removes　　people,　　　　　pardons

רִאשׁוֹן, מַרְבֶּה מְחִילָה לַחַטָּאִים וּסְלִיחָה לַפּוֹשְׁעִים,

《 to willful ⟨ and ⟨ to unintentional ⟨ pardon ⟨ Who abun- 《 by one,
　sinners,　forgiveness　sinners　　　　　　dantly grants

עֹשֶׂה צְדָקוֹת עִם כָּל בָּשָׂר וָרוּחַ, לֹא כְרָעָתָם

⟨ in accord ⟨ — not 《 and ⟨ [beings ⟨ all ⟨ with ⟨ acts of ⟨ Who
with their　　　spirit　of] flesh　　　　　generosity　performs
wickedness

תִּגְמוֹל. ❖ אֵל הוֹרֵיתָ לָּנוּ לוֹמַר שְׁלֹשׁ עֶשְׂרֵה, וּזְכוֹר

⟨ remem- 《 the Thirteen ⟨ to ⟨ us ⟨ You ⟨ O God, 《 do You
ber　[Attributes of Mercy];　recite　　taught　　　　repay them!

לָנוּ הַיּוֹם בְּרִית שְׁלֹשׁ עֶשְׂרֵה, כְּמוֹ שֶׁהוֹדַעְתָּ לֶעָנָיו

⟨ to the humble ⟨ You made ⟨ as 《 of [these] Thirteen, ⟨ the ⟨ today ⟨ for us
one [Moses]　known　　　　　　　　　　　covenant

מִקֶּדֶם, כְּמוֹ שֶׁכָּתוּב, וַיֵּרֶד יהוה בֶּעָנָן וַיִּתְיַצֵּב עִמּוֹ

⟨ with ⟨ and stood ⟨ in a ⟨ And HASHEM 《 it is written: ⟨ as 《 in ancient
him　　　　cloud　descended　　　　　　　times,

שָׁם, וַיִּקְרָא בְשֵׁם יהוה.

《 of ⟨ with the ⟨ and He 《 there,
HASHEM.　Name　called out

CONGREGATION, THEN *CHAZZAN*:

וַיַּעֲבֹר יהוה עַל פָּנָיו וַיִּקְרָא:

《 and 《 [Moses'] ⟨ before ⟨ And HASHEM passed
proclaimed:　face,

CONGREGATION AND *CHAZZAN* RECITE LOUDLY AND IN UNISON:

יהוה, יהוה, אֵל, רַחוּם, וְחַנּוּן, אֶרֶךְ אַפַּיִם,

⟨ to anger, ⟨ Slow 《 and ⟨ Compassionate ⟨ God, ⟨ HASHEM, ⟨ HASHEM,
　　　　　　　　Gracious,

וְרַב חֶסֶד, וֶאֱמֶת, נֹצֵר חֶסֶד לָאֲלָפִים, נֹשֵׂא עָוֹן,

⟨ of ⟨ Forgiver 《 for thousands ⟨ of ⟨ Preserver 《 and ⟨ in ⟨ and
iniquity,　[of generations],　kindness　　　Truth,　Kindness Abundant

(1) *Rosh Hashanah* 17a. (2) *Exodus* 34:5.

וָפֶשַׁע, וְחַטָאָה, וְנַקֵּה.[1] וְסָלַחְתָּ לַעֲוֹנֵנוּ וּלְחַטֹּאתֵנוּ
and our sins, ‹ our iniquities ‹ May You forgive ≪ and Who absolves. ‹ and inadvertent sin, ‹ willful sin,

וּנְחַלְתָּנוּ.[2] סְלַח לָנוּ אָבִינוּ כִּי חָטָאנוּ, מְחַל לָנוּ
us, ‹ pardon ≪ we have sinned; ‹ for ‹ our Father, ‹ us, ‹ Forgive ≪ and make us Your heritage.

מָלְכֵּנוּ כִּי פָשָׁעְנוּ. כִּי אַתָּה אֲדֹנָי טוֹב וְסַלָּח,
≪ and forgiving, ‹ are good ‹ O Lord, ‹ You, ‹ For ≪ we have willfully sinned. ‹ for ≪ our King,

וְרַב חֶסֶד לְכָל קֹרְאֶיךָ.[3]
≪ who call upon You. ‹ to all ‹ kind ‹ and abundantly

ALL:

זְכֹר רַחֲמֶיךָ יהוה וַחֲסָדֶיךָ, כִּי מֵעוֹלָם הֵמָּה.[4]
≪ are they. ‹ eternal ‹ for ≪ and Your kindnesses, ‹ HASHEM, ‹ Your mercies, ‹ Remember

זָכְרֵנוּ יהוה בִּרְצוֹן עַמֶּךָ, פָּקְדֵנוּ בִּישׁוּעָתֶךָ.[5] זְכֹר
‹ Re-member ≪ with Your salvation. ‹ recall us ≪ to Your people; ‹ when You show favor ‹ HASHEM, ‹ Remem-ber us,

עֲדָתְךָ קָנִיתָ קֶּדֶם, גָּאַלְתָּ שֵׁבֶט נַחֲלָתֶךָ, הַר צִיּוֹן זֶה
‹ the one ‹ of ‹ the ≪ of Your ‹ the ≪ You ≪ long ‹ which You ‹ Your con-[where] Zion, mountain heritage; tribe redeemed ago, acquired gregation,

שָׁכַנְתָּ בּוֹ.[6] זְכֹר יהוה חִבַּת יְרוּשָׁלָיִם, אַהֲבַת
‹ the love ≪ of Jerusalem; ‹ the affection ‹ HASHEM, ‹ Remem-ber, ≪ there. ‹ You rested Your Presence

צִיּוֹן אַל תִּשְׁכַּח לָנֶצַח.[7] אַתָּה תָקוּם תְּרַחֵם צִיּוֹן כִּי
‹ for ≪ to ‹ and show ‹ will arise ‹ You ≪ forever. ‹ forget ‹ do not ‹ of Zion, mercy Zion

עֵת לְחֶנְנָה, כִּי בָא מוֹעֵד.[8] זְכֹר יהוה לִבְנֵי אֱדוֹם
‹ of ‹ [to repay] ‹ HASHEM, ‹ Re-≪ the appointed time ‹ for ≪ [there will come] Edom the offspring, member, will have come. the time to favor her,

אֵת יוֹם יְרוּשָׁלָיִם, הָאֹמְרִים עָרוּ עָרוּ עַד הַיְסוֹד
‹ the very ‹ to ‹ Destroy ≪ Destroy! ≪ [to repay] ≪ of Jerusalem; ‹ for the day foundation those who say,

בָּהּ.[9] זְכֹר לְאַבְרָהָם לְיִצְחָק וּלְיִשְׂרָאֵל עֲבָדֶיךָ,
≪ Your servants, ‹ and for Israel, ‹ for Isaac, ‹ for Abraham, ‹ Remember ≪ of it!

---

(1) *Exodus* 34:6-7. (2) 34:9. (3) *Psalms* 86:5. (4) 25:6. (5) Cf. 106:4. (6) 74:2.
(7) This is not a Scriptural verse. (8) *Psalms* 102:14. (9) 137:7.

אֲשֶׁר נִשְׁבַּעְתָּ לָהֶם בָּךְ וַתְּדַבֵּר אֲלֵהֶם, אַרְבֶּה
‹ I shall   « to them,   ‹ and   « by Your ‹ to   ‹ You   ‹ that
increase   You said   Being,   them   swore

אֶת זַרְעֲכֶם כְּכוֹכְבֵי הַשָּׁמָיִם, וְכָל הָאָרֶץ הַזֹּאת
‹   of this land   ‹ and all « of the heavens; ‹ like the stars ‹ Your offspring

אֲשֶׁר אָמַרְתִּי, אֶתֵּן לְזַרְעֲכֶם, וְנָחֲלוּ לְעֹלָם.¹ זְכֹר
‹ Remember «forever. ‹ and they ‹ to your ‹ I will give ‹ I spoke ‹ of which
[the merits]   will inherit it   offspring,

לַעֲבָדֶיךָ לְאַבְרָהָם לְיִצְחָק וּלְיַעֲקֹב, אַל תֵּפֶן אֶל
‹ to ‹ pay   ‹ do « and of Jacob; ‹ of Isaac, ‹ of Abraham, ‹ of Your
attention   not   servants,

קְשִׁי הָעָם הַזֶּה וְאֶל רִשְׁעוֹ וְאֶל חַטָּאתוֹ.² זְכוֹר לָנוּ
‹ for ‹ Remember « its   ‹ and « its   ‹ to « of this people, ‹ the stub-
us   sinfulness. to wickedness,   bornness

בְּרִית אָבוֹת, כַּאֲשֶׁר אָמַרְתָּ: וְזָכַרְתִּי אֶת בְּרִיתִי
‹ My covenant ‹ And I will « You said: ‹   as   « of the ‹ the
remember   Patriarchs, covenant

יַעֲקוֹב, וְאַף אֶת בְּרִיתִי יִצְחָק, וְאַף אֶת בְּרִיתִי
‹ My covenant ‹ and also « [with] Isaac, ‹ My covenant ‹ and also «[with] Jacob,

אַבְרָהָם אֶזְכֹּר, וְהָאָרֶץ אֶזְכֹּר.³
« I will ‹ and the « I will ‹ [with]
remember.   Land   remember;   Abraham

SELICHAH 40 / סליחה מ
(פזמון)

THE ARK IS OPENED.

CHAZZAN, THEN CONGREGATION:

זְכוֹר בְּרִית אַבְרָהָם* וַעֲקֵדַת יִצְחָק,
« of Isaac; ‹ and the ‹ of Abraham* ‹ the   ‹ Remem-
binding   covenant   ber

וְהָשֵׁב שְׁבוּת אָהֳלֵי יַעֲקֹב,⁴ וְהוֹשִׁיעֵנוּ לְמַעַן שְׁמֶךָ.⁵
« of Your ‹ for the ‹ and save us « of Jacob, ‹ of the ‹ the ‹ Restore
Name.   sake   tents   captivity

---

(1) *Exodus* 32:13. (2) *Deuteronomy* 9:27. (3) *Leviticus* 26:42. (4) Cf. *Jeremiah* 30:18.(5) Cf. *Psalms* 106:8.

◆§ זְכוֹר בְּרִית אַבְרָהָם — *Remember the cove-*
nant of Abraham. This *pizmon* differs from
others by virtue of its two refrains, which
alternate after each stanza. Only seven of

the original fourteen stanzas appear in this
selichah; another three appear in *Selichah*
50. The acrostic of the full composition
forms a double *aleph-beis* followed by the

CONGREGATION, THEN *CHAZZAN:*

אָבַדְנוּ מֵאֶרֶץ טוֹבָה¹ בְּחִפָּזוֹן,

» in   » that is ‹ from our ‹ We have
great haste;   good,   Land   been banished

אָרְכוּ הַיָּמִים וּדְבַר כָּל חָזוֹן,²

» prophetic ‹ of ‹ and the ‹ have been ‹ prolonged
vision [has   every   message   the days
come about].   [of exile],

בְּיִשְׂרָאֵל חָדְלוּ פְרָזוֹן,³ בְּמִשְׁמַנֵּינוּ שֻׁלַּח רָזוֹן,⁴

» a wasting plague ‹ was ‹ for against our fat » in unforti- ‹ can no lon- ‹ Israel
of leanness.   sent   and strong ones   fied cities,   ger [dwell]

וְשׁוּב בְּרַחֲמִים עַל שְׁאֵרִית יִשְׂרָאֵל,

» of Israel, ‹ the remnant ‹ to ‹ with mercy ‹ And return

וְהוֹשִׁיעֵנוּ לְמַעַן שְׁמֶךָ.

» of Your ‹ for the ‹ and save us
Name.   sake

CONGREGATION, THEN *CHAZZAN:*

גּוֹלָה אַחַר גּוֹלָה, גָּלְתָה יְהוּדָה כֻּלָּה,⁵

» entirely; ‹ Judah ‹ was exiled ‹ exile ‹ after ‹ Exile

דָּוָה כָל הַיּוֹם⁶ וְכָלָה, דּוֹרֵשׁ וּמְבַקֵּשׁ אֵין לָהּ.⁷

» for ‹ there ‹ or seek » as they are ‹ day ‹ all «suffering
her.   is not   them   ask about   being decimated   long
    yet one to   [by the nations],

וְהָשֵׁב שְׁבוּת אָהֳלֵי יַעֲקֹב, וְהוֹשִׁיעֵנוּ לְמַעַן שְׁמֶךָ.

» of Your ‹ for the ‹ and save us ‹ of Jacob, ‹ of the ‹ the ‹ Restore
Name.   sake   tents   captivity

CONGREGATION, THEN *CHAZZAN:*

הָעִיר הַקֹּדֶשׁ וְהַמְּחוֹזוֹת,* הָיוּ לְחֶרְפָּה וּלְבִזּוֹת,

» and to spoils; ‹ to shame ‹ have ‹ and the ‹ The Holy City
turned   surrounding regions*

---

(1) Cf. *Deuteronomy* 11:17. (2) Cf. *Ezekiel* 12:22-23. (3) Cf. *Judges* 5:7; see commentary to *Selichah* 18, s.v. וּפְרָזוֹן. (4) Cf. *Isaiah* 10:16. (5) *Lamentations* 1:3. (6) Cf. 1:13. (7) Cf. *Ezekiel* 34:6; *Jeremiah* 30:17.

---

paytan's signature — גֵּרְשֹׁם בַּר יְהוּדָה חֲזַק, *Gershom bar Yehudah, may he be strong* [see prefatory comment to *Selichah* 12].

הָעִיר הַקֹּדֶשׁ וְהַמְּחוֹזוֹת — *The Holy City and the surrounding regions.* Some would translate: *The city [of Jerusalem], the Holy [Temple], and the [outlying] regions.* This

is based on *Daniel* 9:26, where עִיר and קֹדֶשׁ refer to Jerusalem and the *Beis HaMikdash*. We have not used this translation for two reasons. In *Daniel* the phrase contains only two words, הָעִיר וְהַקֹּדֶשׁ, *the city and the holy*, which are joined by the conjunctive prefix ו, *and*; in our stich the conjunction is

וְכָל מַחֲמַדֶּיהָ טְבוּעוֹת וּגְנוּזוֹת,*

《 and hidden,* 〈 lie sunken 〈 her treasures 〈 all

וְאֵין שִׁיּוּר רַק הַתּוֹרָה הַזֹּאת.

《 for this Torah. 〈 except 〈 remnant 〈 and there is no

וְשׁוּב בְּרַחֲמִים עַל שְׁאֵרִית יִשְׂרָאֵל,

《 of Israel, 〈 the remnant 〈 to 〈 with mercy 〈 And return

וְהוֹשִׁיעֵנוּ לְמַעַן שְׁמֶךָ.

《 of Your 〈 for the 〈 and save us
Name. sake

CONGREGATION, THEN *CHAZZAN:*

גּוֹאֵל חָזָק לְמַעַנְךָ פְּדֵנוּ, רְאֵה כִּי אָזְלַת יָדֵנוּ,[1]

《 our strength 〈 that 〈 See 《 deliver 〈 for Your 〈 Who is 〈 O
is gone. us! Own sake mighty, Redeemer

שׁוּר כִּי אָבְדוּ חֲסִידֵינוּ,[2] מַפְגִּיעַ אֵין בַּעֲדֵנוּ.[3]

《 for us. 〈 there is 〈 and to 《 our devout ones, 〈 lost are 〈 that 〈 Observe
no one intercede,

וְהָשֵׁב שְׁבוּת אָהֳלֵי יַעֲקֹב, וְהוֹשִׁיעֵנוּ לְמַעַן שְׁמֶךָ.

《 of Your 〈 for the 〈 and save us 《 of Jacob, 〈 of the 〈 the 〈 Restore
Name. sake tents captivity

CONGREGATION, THEN *CHAZZAN:*

בְּרִית אָבוֹת וְאִמָּהוֹת וְהַשְּׁבָטִים,

《 and Tribes, 〈 the Matriarchs, 〈 of the 〈 The
Patriarchs, covenant

רַחֲמֶיךָ וַחֲסָדֶיךָ בְּרַבּוֹת עִתִּים,[4]

《 times — 〈 through 〈 and Your 〈 Your mercy
so many kindness

יָהּ זְכֹר לְמֻכִּים וְנִמְרָטִים,[5]

〈 and having [their hair 〈 on behalf of 〈 remember 〈 O
and beards] torn out those beaten [all this,] God,

---

(1) Cf. *Deuteronomy* 32:36. (2) Cf. *Micah* 7:2. (3) Cf. *Isaiah* 59:16. (4) Cf. *Nehemiah* 9:28. (5) Cf. 13:25.

absent and so הַקֹּדֶשׁ is more likely an adjective modifying הָעִיר than an independent noun. Additionally, the order of the stich — city, Temple, outlying regions — would be illogical. The list should be in order of either ascending holiness (outlying, city, Temple) or descending (Temple, city, outlying), and not haphazard.

וְכָל מַחֲמַדֶּיהָ טְבוּעוֹת וּגְנוּזוֹת — *All her treasures lie sunken and hidden.* This follows the opinion that before Nebuchadnezzar captured the First Temple, the Holy Ark was hidden beneath the Temple so that it would not be taken by the enemy (see *Yoma* 53b and *Shekalim* 6:1). *Its treasures* refers to the Ark and its contents.

וְעָלֶיךָ כָּל הַיּוֹם נֶשְׁחָטִים.¹

《 are slaughtered. 〈 day long 〈 all 〈 and who for Your sake

וְשׁוּב בְּרַחֲמִים עַל שְׁאֵרִית יִשְׂרָאֵל,

《 of Israel, 〈 the remnant 〈 to 〈 with mercy 〈 And return

וְהוֹשִׁיעֵנוּ לְמַעַן שְׁמֶךָ.

《 of Your Name. 〈 for the sake 〈 and save us

CONGREGATION, THEN *CHAZZAN*:

דּוֹרֵשׁ דָּמִים² דּוֹן דִּינֵנוּ,

《 our vengeance! 〈 avenge 〈 of blood, 〈 Avenger

הָשֵׁב שִׁבְעָתַיִם אֶל חֵיק מְעַנֵּינוּ,³

《 of our tormentors. 〈 the bosom 〈 into 〈 sevenfold 〈 Restore

חִנָּם נִמְכַּרְנוּ, וְלֹא בְכֶסֶף פְּדֻנוּ,⁴

《 redeem us. 〈 with money 〈 so not 〈 were we sold [into Exile], 〈 Without payment

זְקֹף בֵּית מִקְדָּשְׁךָ הַשָּׁמֵם לְעֵינֵינוּ.⁵

《 before our eyes. 〈 that is desolate, 〈 Your Holy Temple 〈 Erect

וְהָשֵׁב שְׁבוּת אָהֳלֵי יַעֲקֹב, וְהוֹשִׁיעֵנוּ לְמַעַן שְׁמֶךָ.

《 of Your Name. 〈 for the sake 〈 and save us 《 of Jacob, 〈 of the tents 〈 the captivity 〈 Restore

THE ARK IS CLOSED.

ALL CONTINUE:

זְכוֹר לָנוּ בְּרִית רִאשׁוֹנִים, כַּאֲשֶׁר אָמַרְתָּ: וְזָכַרְתִּי

〈 And I will remember 《 You said: 〈 as 《 of the ancient ones, 〈 the covenant 〈 for us 〈 Remember

לָהֶם בְּרִית רִאשׁוֹנִים, אֲשֶׁר הוֹצֵאתִי אֹתָם מֵאֶרֶץ

〈 from the land 〈 I took them out 〈 that 《 of the ancient ones, 〈 the covenant 〈 for them

מִצְרַיִם לְעֵינֵי הַגּוֹיִם, לִהְיוֹת לָהֶם לֵאלֹהִים, אֲנִי

〈 I am 《 a God; 〈 to them 〈 to be 《 of the nations, 〈 in the very sight 〈 of Egypt

---

(1) Cf. *Psalms* 44:23. (2) 9:13. (3) Cf. 79:12; some editions of *Selichos* omit this stich.
(4) Cf. *Isaiah* 52:3; see commentary to *Selichah* 11, s.v. לִמְכּוּרֵי חִנָּם. (5) Cf. *Daniel* 9:17.

יהוה.[1] עֲשֵׂה עִמָּנוּ כְּמָה שֶׁהִבְטַחְתָּנוּ: וְאַף גַּם

‹ all ‹ And despite ‹‹ You promised us: ‹ as ‹ with us ‹ Do ‹‹ HASHEM.

זֹאת בִּהְיוֹתָם בְּאֶרֶץ אֹיְבֵיהֶם, לֹא מְאַסְתִּים וְלֹא

‹ nor ‹ despise them ‹ I will not ‹‹ of their enemies, ‹ in the land ‹ when they will be ‹‹ this,

גְעַלְתִּים לְכַלֹּתָם לְהָפֵר בְּרִיתִי אִתָּם, כִּי אֲנִי יהוה

‹ HASHEM, ‹ I am ‹ for ‹‹ with them, ‹ My covenant ‹ to annul ‹‹ to destroy them, ‹ abhor them

אֱלֹהֵיהֶם.[2] הָשֵׁב שְׁבוּתֵנוּ וְרַחֲמֵנוּ, כְּמָה שֶׁכָּתוּב:

‹‹ it is written: ‹ as ‹‹ and have mercy on us, ‹ our captivity ‹ Bring back ‹‹ their God.

וְשָׁב יהוה אֱלֹהֶיךָ אֶת שְׁבוּתְךָ וְרִחֲמֶךָ, וְשָׁב וְקִבֶּצְךָ

‹ gather you in ‹ and He will once again ‹‹ and He will have mercy upon you, ‹ your captivity, ‹ your God, ‹ will ‹ HASHEM, ‹ Then bring back

מִכָּל הָעַמִּים אֲשֶׁר הֱפִיצְךָ יהוה אֱלֹהֶיךָ שָׁמָּה.[3]

‹‹ thereto. ‹ your God ‹ has HASHEM ‹ scattered you ‹ that ‹ the peoples ‹ from all

קַבֵּץ נִדָּחֵינוּ, כְּמָה שֶׁכָּתוּב: אִם יִהְיֶה נִדַּחֲךָ בִּקְצֵה

‹ at the ends ‹ your dispersed will be ‹ If ‹ it is written: ‹ as ‹ our dispersed ones, ‹ Gather

הַשָּׁמָיִם, מִשָּׁם יְקַבֶּצְךָ יהוה אֱלֹהֶיךָ, וּמִשָּׁם יִקָּחֶךָ.[4]

‹‹ He will take you. ‹ and from there ‹‹ your God, ‹ will ‹ gather you in ‹ from ‹‹ of heaven, ‹ HASHEM,

מְחֵה פְשָׁעֵינוּ כָּעָב וְכֶעָנָן, כְּמָה שֶׁכָּתוּב: מָחִיתִי

‹ I have wiped away ‹‹ it is written: ‹ as ‹‹ and like a cloud, ‹ like a mist ‹ our sins ‹ Wipe away

כָעָב פְּשָׁעֶיךָ וְכֶעָנָן חַטֹּאתֶיךָ, שׁוּבָה אֵלַי כִּי

‹ for ‹ to Me, ‹ return ‹‹ your transgressions; ‹ and like a cloud ‹ your willful sins, ‹ like a mist

גְאַלְתִּיךָ.[5] מְחֵה פְשָׁעֵינוּ לְמַעַנְךָ, כַּאֲשֶׁר אָמָרְתָּ:

‹‹ You have said: ‹ as ‹‹ for Your sake, ‹ our sins ‹ Wipe away ‹‹ I have redeemed you.

אָנֹכִי אָנֹכִי הוּא מֹחֶה פְשָׁעֶיךָ לְמַעֲנִי, וְחַטֹּאתֶיךָ לֹא

‹ I shall not ‹ and your transgressions ‹‹ for My sake, ‹ your willful sins ‹ Who wipes away ‹ am the One ‹ [only] I, ‹ I,

---

(1) *Leviticus* 26:45. (2) 26:44. (3) 30:3. (4) 30:4. (5) *Isaiah* 44:22.

אֶזְכֹּר.¹ הַלְבֵּן חֲטָאֵינוּ כַּשֶּׁלֶג וְכַצֶּמֶר, כְּמָה שֶׁכָּתוּב:

recall. « Whiten ‹ our sins ‹ like snow ‹ and « as ‹ it is written:
like wool,

לְכוּ נָא וְנִוָּכְחָה, יֹאמַר יהוה, אִם יִהְיוּ חֲטָאֵיכֶם

Come, ‹ now, ‹ let us reason « says ‹ HASHEM. « Though ‹ your sins may be
together,

כַּשָּׁנִים כַּשֶּׁלֶג יַלְבִּינוּ, אִם יַאְדִּימוּ כַתּוֹלָע, כַּצֶּמֶר

like « like ‹ they will be « though ‹ they may ‹ as crimson, « like [white]
scarlet, snow whitened; be red wool

יִהְיוּ.² זְרוֹק עָלֵינוּ מַיִם טְהוֹרִים וְטַהֲרֵנוּ, כְּמָה שֶׁכָּתוּב:

they will « Pour ‹ upon us ‹ pure water ‹ and « as « it is
become. purify us, written:

וְזָרַקְתִּי עֲלֵיכֶם מַיִם טְהוֹרִים וּטְהַרְתֶּם, מִכֹּל

I shall pour ‹ upon you ‹ pure water ‹ and you will « from
become pure; all

טֻמְאוֹתֵיכֶם וּמִכָּל גִּלּוּלֵיכֶם אֲטַהֵר אֶתְכֶם.³ רַחֵם

your ‹ and ‹ your ‹ I will ‹ you. « Have
contaminations from all abominations purify mercy

עָלֵינוּ וְאַל תַּשְׁחִיתֵנוּ, כְּמָה שֶׁכָּתוּב: כִּי אֵל רַחוּם

on us ‹ and ‹ destroy us, « as ‹ it is written: For ‹ a merciful
do not God

יהוה אֱלֹהֶיךָ, לֹא יַרְפְּךָ וְלֹא יַשְׁחִיתֶךָ, וְלֹא יִשְׁכַּח

is ‹ your God; « He will ‹ relinquish ‹ nor ‹ will He « nor ‹ will He
HASHEM, not you destroy you, forget

אֶת בְּרִית אֲבֹתֶיךָ אֲשֶׁר נִשְׁבַּע לָהֶם.⁴ מוֹל

the covenant ‹ with your ‹ which ‹ He swore ‹ to them. « Circum-
forefathers, cise

אֶת לְבָבֵנוּ לְאַהֲבָה וּלְיִרְאָה אֶת שְׁמֶךָ, כְּמָה שֶׁכָּתוּב:

our hearts ‹ to love ‹ and to fear ‹ Your Name, « as ‹ it is
written:

וּמָל יהוה אֱלֹהֶיךָ אֶת לְבָבְךָ וְאֶת לְבַב זַרְעֶךָ, לְאַהֲבָה

to love ‹ of your « and the ‹ your heart ‹ HASHEM, your God,
offspring, heart will circumcise

אֶת יהוה אֱלֹהֶיךָ, בְּכָל לְבָבְךָ וּבְכָל נַפְשְׁךָ, לְמַעַן

so that « your ‹ and ‹ your heart ‹ with all ‹ your God, ‹ HASHEM,
soul, with all

<hr>

(1) *Isaiah* 43:25. (2) 1:18. (3) *Ezekiel* 36:25. (4) *Deuteronomy* 4:31.

חַיֶּיךָ.¹ הַמָּצֵא לָנוּ בְּבַקָּשָׁתֵנוּ, כְּמָה שֶׁכָּתוּב: וּבִקַּשְׁתֶּם

And you will seek ⟨ it is written: ⟨ as ⟨ in our quest, ⟨ to us ⟨ Be accessible ⟨ you may live.

מִשָּׁם אֶת יהוה אֱלֹהֶיךָ, כִּי תִדְרְשֶׁנּוּ בְּכָל

with all ⟨ you search Him out ⟨ when ⟨ and you will find [Him], ⟨ your God, ⟨ HASHEM, ⟨ from there

לְבָבְךָ וּבְכָל נַפְשֶׁךָ.² ❖ תְּבִיאֵנוּ אֶל הַר קָדְשֶׁךָ,

Your holy mountain ⟨ to ⟨ Bring us ⟨ your soul. ⟨ and with all ⟨ your heart

וְשִׂמַּחְתִּים בְּבֵית תְּפִלָּתֶךָ, כְּמָה שֶׁכָּתוּב: וַהֲבִיאוֹתִים

And I will bring them ⟨ it is written: ⟨ as ⟨ of Prayer, ⟨ in Your House ⟨ and gladden us

אֶל הַר קָדְשִׁי, וְשִׂמַּחְתִּים בְּבֵית תְּפִלָּתִי, עוֹלֹתֵיהֶם

their burnt-offerings ⟨ of Prayer; ⟨ in My House ⟨ and I will gladden them ⟨ My holy mountain, ⟨ to

וְזִבְחֵיהֶם לְרָצוֹן עַל מִזְבְּחִי, כִּי בֵיתִי בֵּית תְּפִלָּה

of Prayer" ⟨ "a House ⟨ My House ⟨ for ⟨ My Altar, ⟨ on ⟨ will find favor ⟨ and their feast-offerings

יִקָּרֵא לְכָל הָעַמִּים.³

nations. ⟨ for all ⟨ will be called

THE ARK IS OPENED.

CHAZZAN, THEN CONGREGATION:

שְׁמַע קוֹלֵנוּ יהוה אֱלֹהֵינוּ, חוּס וְרַחֵם עָלֵינוּ,

on us, ⟨ and have compassion ⟨ have pity ⟨ our God; ⟨ HASHEM, ⟨ our voice, ⟨ Hear

וְקַבֵּל בְּרַחֲמִים וּבְרָצוֹן אֶת תְּפִלָּתֵנוּ.⁴

our prayer. ⟨ and favor ⟨ with compassion ⟨ and accept

CHAZZAN, THEN CONGREGATION:

הֲשִׁיבֵנוּ יהוה אֵלֶיךָ וְנָשׁוּבָה, חַדֵּשׁ יָמֵינוּ כְּקֶדֶם.⁵

as of old. ⟨ our days ⟨ renew ⟨ and we shall return, ⟨ to You, ⟨ HASHEM, ⟨ Bring us back,

(1) *Deuteronomy* 30:6. (2) 4:29. (3) *Isaiah* 56:7.
(4) From the weekday *Shemoneh Esrei*. (5) *Lamentations* 5:21.

CHAZZAN, THEN CONGREGATION:

אֲמָרֵינוּ הַאֲזִינָה יהוה, בִּינָה הֲגִיגֵנוּ.[1]

《 our 《 perceive 《 HASHEM; 〈 hear, 〈 Our words
thoughts.

THE FOLLOWING VERSE IS RECITED QUIETLY:

יִהְיוּ לְרָצוֹן אִמְרֵי פִינוּ וְהֶגְיוֹן לִבֵּנוּ לְפָנֶיךָ,

《 before 《 of our 〈 and the 〈 of our 〈 — the ex- 《 find 〈 May
You, heart — thoughts mouth pressions favor they

יהוה צוּרֵנוּ וְגוֹאֲלֵנוּ.[2]

《 and our 〈 our Rock 〈 HASHEM,
Redeemer.

CHAZZAN, THEN CONGREGATION:

אַל תַּשְׁלִיכֵנוּ מִלְּפָנֶיךָ, וְרוּחַ קָדְשְׁךָ אַל תִּקַּח מִמֶּנּוּ.[3]

《 from us. 〈 take 〈 do 〈 of Your 〈 and the 《 from Your 〈 cast us away 〈 Do
not Holiness Spirit Presence, not

CHAZZAN, THEN CONGREGATION:

אַל תַּשְׁלִיכֵנוּ לְעֵת זִקְנָה, כִּכְלוֹת כֹּחֵנוּ אַל תַּעַזְבֵנוּ.[4]

《 forsake us not. 〈 does our 〈 when fail 《 of old 〈 in time 〈 cast us away 〈 Do
strength, age; not

ALL CONTINUE (SOME CONGREGATIONS RECITE THE NEXT VERSE RESPONSIVELY):

אַל תַּעַזְבֵנוּ יהוה, אֱלֹהֵינוּ אַל תִּרְחַק מִמֶּנּוּ.[5]

《 from us. 〈 be not distant 〈 our God, 《 O HASHEM; 〈 Forsake us not,

עֲשֵׂה עִמָּנוּ אוֹת לְטוֹבָה, וְיִרְאוּ שׂוֹנְאֵינוּ וְיֵבֹשׁוּ,

《 and be 〈 may our 〈 so that 《 for good; 〈 a sign 〈 for us 〈 Display
ashamed, enemies see it

כִּי אַתָּה יהוה עֲזַרְתָּנוּ וְנִחַמְתָּנוּ.[6] כִּי לְךָ יהוה

〈 HASHEM, 〈 for 〈 Because 《 and 〈 will have 〈 HASHEM, 〈 You, 〈 for
You, consoled us. helped us

הוֹחָלְנוּ, אַתָּה תַעֲנֶה אֲדֹנָי אֱלֹהֵינוּ.[7]

《 our God. 〈 O Lord, 〈 will 〈 You 《 do we wait;
answer,

THE ARK IS CLOSED.

(1) Cf. *Psalms* 5:2. (2) Cf. 19:15. (3) 51:13. (4) Cf. 71:9.
(5) Cf. 38:22. (6) Cf. 86:17. (7) Cf. 38:16.

ENTREATIES / בקשות

ALL CONTINUE:

יְהִי רָצוֹן* מִלְּפָנֶיךָ, יהוה אֱלֹהֵינוּ וֵאלֹהֵי אֲבוֹתֵינוּ,

May it be ‹ *the will** ‹ before You, ‹ HASHEM, ‹ our God ‹ and God ‹ of our forefathers,

שֶׁתְּהֵא הַשָּׁנָה הַזֹּאת הַבָּאָה עָלֵינוּ וְעַל כָּל

that it should be — this year ‹ coming ‹ for us, ‹ and for ‹ all

עַמְּךָ בֵּית יִשְׂרָאֵל, קֵץ וְתַכְלִית לִשְׁבִי עַמְּךָ בֵּית

Your people ‹ the House ‹ of Israel — ‹ the conclusion ‹ and the finish ‹ the captivity ‹ of Your people ‹ the House

יִשְׂרָאֵל, וְעֵת סוֹף לְגָלוּתֵנוּ וּלְאָבְלֵנוּ, וְאַחֲרִית טוֹב

of Israel; ‹ the time ‹ of the end ‹ of our Exile ‹ and our mourning; ‹ and an ending ‹ that is favorable

לִימֵי עָנְיֵנוּ וּמְרוּדֵנוּ.¹ כִּי מָשַׁךְ עָלֵינוּ הַשִּׁעְבּוּד, וְאָרַךְ

for the days ‹ of our oppression ‹ and our sorrows. ‹ For ‹ long drawn out ‹ upon us ‹ has the servitude been, ‹ and

עָלֵינוּ עֹל גָּלִיּוֹת. וְהִנְנוּ בְּכָל יוֹם הוֹלְכִים וְדַלִּים,

upon us ‹ has the yoke been. ‹ of exile ‹ And here we are, ‹ each ‹ day ‹ growing ‹ weaker;

בְּרֻבּוֹת הַשָּׁנִים אָנוּ נִמְעָטִים, וּבִסְגוֹת הַזְּמַנִּים אָנוּ

with the increase ‹ of the years, ‹ we ‹ decrease; ‹ and with the piling up ‹ of time, ‹ we

נִצְעָרִים. וְאֵין לָנוּ לֹא מְנַהֵל וְלֹא מַחֲזִיק בְּיָדֵנוּ,

diminish. ‹ There is not ‹ for us ‹ neither ‹ a leader, ‹ nor ‹ someone to hold ‹ our hand,

כַּאֲשֶׁר אָמַרְתָּ.² כִּי מִי יַחְמֹל עָלָיִךְ יְרוּשָׁלָיִם, וּמִי

as ‹ You said: ‹ For ‹ who ‹ will have pity ‹ on you, ‹ Jerusalem? ‹ Who

---

(1) Cf. *Lamentations* 1:7. (2) Some editions have the following additional passage here: אֵין מְנַהֵל לָהּ מִכָּל בָּנִים יָלָדָה, *There is no leader for her from all the children she bore*, וְאֵין מַחֲזִיק בְּיָדָהּ מִכָּל בָּנִים גִּדֵּלָה, *there is no one to hold her hand from all the children she raised* (Isaiah 51:18). וְאֵין מִי יַחֲמוֹל עָלֵינוּ וּמִי יְנַחֲמֶנוּ כַּאֲשֶׁר אָמַרְתָּ, *And there is no one to have pity on us, and who will comfort us, as You said.*

יְהִי רָצוֹן — May it be the will. This lengthy prayer, whose parts are interspersed between the three recitals of the *Viduy/Confession*, is taken mostly from two supplications written by R' Saadiah Gaon more than a thousand years ago. Over the centuries, the prayer has been enhanced with additions, but remains basically R' Saadiah's work.

According to his sons' testimony, R' Saadiah was born in 882 in the Al-Fayyum area west of the Nile Delta. He was appointed *Gaon* of Sura at the unprecedented young age of only forty-five, in 927. Although he was banished from Sura for a seven-year period beginning two years after he assumed his office, R' Saadiah was

יָנוּד לָךְ, וּמִי יָסוּר לִשְׁאָל לִשְׁלוֹם לָךְ.[1] אוֹ מִי

‹who ‹Or « about your welfare? ‹ to inquire ‹ will turn ‹ Who « over ‹will shake
aside you? [his head]

יִגְדֹּר גֶּדֶר, אוֹ מִי יַעֲמֹד בַּפֶּרֶץ (בַּעֲדֵנוּ).[2] וְאֵין עוֹד

‹longer ‹There « (for us)? ‹ in the ‹ will ‹who ‹ or « a fence, ‹ will
is no breach stand build

נָבִיא וְחוֹזֶה,[3] וְאֵין קוֹרֵא בְשִׁמְךָ בֶּאֱמֶת, מִתְעוֹרֵר

‹ who arouses « truthfully, ‹ in Your ‹ anyone ‹ nor is « or seer, ‹ a
himself Name who calls there prophet

לְהַחֲזִיק בָּךְ.[4] כִּי כֻלָּנוּ כַּצֹּאן תָּעִינוּ, אִישׁ אִישׁ

‹ each one [of us] « have ‹ like a flock ‹all of us ‹ For « to ‹ to cling
strayed, of sheep You.

לְדַרְכּוֹ הָרָעָה פָּנִינוּ,[5] כָּל גֶּבֶר אַחֲרֵי בִצְעוֹ, וְכָל

‹ every « his ‹ after ‹ man ‹Every « did we ‹ that is ‹ toward
plunder, turn aside. evil his path

אִישׁ אַחֲרֵי שְׁרִירוּת לִבּוֹ הָרָע.[6] וְלֹא דַי לָנוּ

‹for us ‹enough ‹ Not « the evil vision of his heart. ‹ after ‹ person

בַּעֲוֹנוֹת הָרִאשׁוֹנִים, כִּי אִם הוֹסַפְנוּ עֲלֵיהֶם חֲדָשִׁים.

« new ones. ‹ on top of ‹ we have ‹ rather ‹ — but « from before ‹ were [our]
them added iniquities

וְלֹא הִזְהַרְנוּ בְּכָל הָאַזְהָרוֹת אֲשֶׁר הִזְהַרְתָּנוּ,

«You warned us; ‹ with which ‹ the warnings ‹ by all ‹ We were not warned

וְלֹא הוֹכַחְנוּ מִכָּל הַתּוֹכָחוֹת אֲשֶׁר הוֹכַחְתָּנוּ.

«You chastised us. ‹with which ‹ the chastisements ‹ by all ‹ we were not chastened

וּמַה יֵּשׁ לָנוּ עוֹד צְדָקָה, וְלִזְעֹק עוֹד אֶל

‹ to ‹ anymore ‹ to cry out ‹ justification ‹ further ‹ for us ‹ is there ‹ So how

הַמֶּלֶךְ.[7]

« the King?

(1) Jeremiah 15:5. (2) Cf. Ezekiel 22:30. (3) Cf. Psalms 74:9.
(4) Isaiah 64:6. (5) Cf. 53:6. (6) Cf. Jeremiah 18:12. (7) II Samuel 19:29.

subsequently reinstated. Among his many works were an Arabic commentary/translation of Scriptures; *HaEmunos VehaDeos* (*Faith and Belief*) — the first major work that set forth Jewish philosophy in an organized fashion; many liturgical compositions; and a listing of the 613 *mitzvos* according to his system of counting, written in verse form.

R' Saadiah passed away on 26 Iyar 942, about one month before his sixtieth birthday.

וְאַתָּה יהוה חָשַׁבְתָּ לְצָרֵף סִיגֵנוּ, וּלְהָסִיר בְּדִילֵנוּ,[1]

You,   HASHEM,   decided   to refine   of our dross,   to remove   our base metal;

וְלִשְׁבֹּר אֶת לִבֵּנוּ הַזּוֹנֶה,[2] וּלְהָתֵם טֻמְאָתֵנוּ מִמֶּנּוּ. עַל

For   from within us.   our   to terminate   that strays;   our heart   to break   defilement

כֵּן הִגְלִיתָנוּ וּבַגּוֹיִם זֵרִיתָנוּ.[3] הִנֵּה בִּשְׁאוֹן הַמַּלְכִיּוֹת

that reason   You exiled us,   and among the nations   scattered us.   Indeed,   among the clamorous [waves]   of the kingdoms

הִצְלַלְנוּ, וּכְהִתּוּךְ כֶּסֶף בְּתוֹךְ כּוּר נִתָּכְנוּ.[4] וְלֹא מִקֹּצֶר

we have been sunk;   like the melting   silver   inside the furnace   we have been melted.   It is not   from the shortness

יָדְךָ לֹא הוֹשַׁעְתָּנוּ, וְלֹא מִכֹּבֶד אָזְנְךָ לֹא שָׁמַעְתָּ

of Your hand   that You have not redeemed us;   it is not   from the dullness   of Your ears   that You have not heard

תְּפִלָּתֵנוּ, כִּי הִבְדִּילוּ עֲוֹנוֹתֵינוּ בֵּינֵינוּ וּבֵין יְשׁוּעָתֶךָ.[5]

our prayer;   because   but   have our sins   made a barrier   between us   and between   Your salvation.

וְאַתָּה צַדִּיק עַל כָּל הַבָּא עָלֵינוּ, כִּי אֱמֶת עָשִׂיתָ

And You   are righteous   in   all   that has come   upon us,   for   truthfully   have You acted,

וַאֲנַחְנוּ הִרְשָׁעְנוּ.[6] לְךָ אֲדֹנָי הַצְּדָקָה, וְלָנוּ בֹּשֶׁת

while we   have acted wickedly.   Yours,   O Lord,   is the righteousness;   and ours   is the shame-

הַפָּנִים.[7] לַאֲדֹנָי אֱלֹהֵינוּ הָרַחֲמִים וְהַסְּלִיחוֹת, כִּי

facedness.   To the Lord,   our God,   are mercy   and forgiveness,   for

מָרַדְנוּ בוֹ.[8] וּלְךָ אֲדֹנָי חֶסֶד, כִּי אַתָּה תְשַׁלֵּם

we have rebelled   against Him.   And   O Lord,   is   kindness,   for   You   reward

לְאִישׁ כְּמַעֲשֵׂהוּ.[9] וְאַתָּה יהוה אֱלֹהֵינוּ, גּוֹאֵל יִשְׂרָאֵל

man   according to his deeds.   And You,   HASHEM,   our God,   are the Redeemer   of Israel

וּקְדוֹשׁוֹ,[10] הַלְעוֹלָם תֶּאֱנַף בָּנוּ, תִּמְשֹׁךְ אַפְּךָ לְדֹר

and their Holy One: Is it for eternity   that You will be angry   with us,   extending   Your wrath   for generation

---

(1) Cf. *Isaiah* 1:25. (2) Cf. *Ezekiel* 6:9. (3) *Psalms* 44:12. (4) Cf. *Ezekiel* 22:22. (5) Cf. *Isaiah* 59:1-2.
(6) *Nehemiah* 9:33. (7) *Daniel* 9:7. (8) 9:9. (9) Cf. *Psalms* 62:13. (10) Cf. *Isaiah* 49:7.

וָדֹר,[1] חָלִילָה. הָעוֹלָם תִּזְנַח, וְלֹא תֹסִיף לִרְצוֹת

‹ to be ap- ‹ will You ‹ never ≪that You will ‹ Is it for ≪ It would be ≪ after gen-
peased [by us] continue   abandon [us],   eternity   a sacrilege!   eration?

עוֹד, חָלִילָה. כִּי לֹא אָפְסוּ לָנֶצַח חֲסָדֶיךָ,[2] וְלֹא

‹ not ≪ is Your ‹ forever ‹ ended ‹ not ‹ For ≪ It would be ≪ again?
   kindness,   a sacrilege!

כָלוּ רַחֲמֶיךָ, כִּי הֵמָּה חֲדָשִׁים לַבְּקָרִים,[3] יָחִילוּ

‹ reborn ≪ every morning, ‹ renewed ‹ they ‹ for ≪ is Your ‹ exhausted
         are   mercy;

בְּכָל עֵת וּבְכָל רֶגַע.

≪ moment. ‹ and at ‹ time ‹ at every
        every

וּלְמַעַן שִׁמְךָ יהוה, עֲשֵׂה עִמָּנוּ, כִּי הִיא תְהִלָּתֶךָ.

≪ Your ‹ this is ‹ for ≪ with us, ‹ do ‹ HASHEM, ‹ of Your ‹ So for
praise —   [kindness]   Name,   the sake

כִּי שִׁמְךָ נִקְרָא עָלֵינוּ,[4] יהוה אֱלֹהֵי יִשְׂרָאֵל. וּלְמַעַן

‹ for the ≪ of Israel; ‹ God ‹ HASHEM, ≪ upon us, ‹ is ‹ Your ‹ for
sake   proclaimed   Name

בְּרִית אֲבוֹתֵינוּ, אַבְרָהָם יִצְחָק וְיַעֲקֹב, אֲשֶׁר כָּרַתָּ

‹ You ‹ that ‹ and Jacob, ‹ Isaac, ‹ Abraham, ‹ with our ‹ of the
established   forefathers,   covenant

לָהֶם, כִּי לֹא תִשָּׁכַח מִפִּי זַרְעָם,[5] וּדְבָרַי אֲשֶׁר

‹ that ‹ And My ≪ of [Jacob's] ‹ from ‹ be ‹ that it ≪with them,
   words   seed: the mouth   forgotten   would never

שַׂמְתִּי בְּפִיהֶם לֹא יָמוּשׁוּ.[6] וּלְמַעַן עַמְּךָ וְנַחֲלָתֶךָ

‹ and Your ‹ of Your ‹ for the ≪ be withdrawn ‹ shall ‹ in their ‹ I have
heritage,   people   sake   [from your mouth];   not   mouths   placed

אֲשֶׁר נִשְׁאֲרוּ מְעַט מֵהַרְבֵּה,[7] כַּתֹּרֶן בְּרֹאשׁ הָהָר,

≪ of a ‹ on the ‹ like an [isolated] ≪ out of ‹ a few ‹ are left ‹ who
mountain,   top   signal-post   many,

וְכַנֵּס עַל הַגִּבְעָה.[8] וּלְמַעַן יְרוּשָׁלַיִם עִיר קָדְשֶׁךָ,

‹ of ‹ Your ‹ of Jerusalem, ‹ for the ≪ a hill; ‹ on ‹ like a [forsak-
Holiness   City   sake   en] banner

אֲשֶׁר הָיְתָה מִדְבָּר שְׁמָמָה, וְיָצָא מִמֶּנָּה כָל הֲדָרָהּ.[9]

≪ its ‹ is all ‹ from it ‹ gone ≪ that is ‹ a ‹ has ‹ that
splendor;   desolate,   wasteland   become

---

(1) Psalms 85:6. (2) Cf. 77:8-9. (3) Cf. Lamentations 3:22-23. (4) Cf. Daniel 9:19. (5) Cf. Deuteronomy 31:21. (6) Cf. Isaiah 59:21. (7) Cf. Jeremiah 42:2. (8) Cf. Isaiah 30:17. (9) Cf. Lamentations 1:6.

וּבֵית קָדְשֵׁנוּ וְתִפְאַרְתֵּנוּ, אֲשֶׁר הָיָה לִשְׂרֵפַת אֵשׁ,

and for / the House / [the Temple,] / of our / holiness / and our glory, / which / was / consumed / by fire,

וּרְאֵה כִּי אָזְלַת יָד, וְאֶפֶס עָצוּר וְעָזוּב.[1]

See / that / gone / is [their] / power, / and there / is none / saved / or / assisted.

וְהִנֵּה כָּל הַגּוֹיִם יוֹשְׁבִים שְׁלֵוִים וּשְׁקֵטִים, וְאֶבְיוֹנֵי

Indeed, / all / the / nations / dwell / serenely / and / tranquilly, / while the / impoverished

עַמְּךָ דְּוֵוִיִּים סְחוּפִים וּמְדֻלְדָּלִים. וּמְבַקְשִׁים פָּנֶיךָ,

of Your / people / are full / of pain, / swept aside / and exhausted. / And they / seek / Your / countenance,

וּמַפִּילִים תְּחִנָּתָם מוּל אֲרוֹן בְּרִיתֶךָ. יְהוה אֱלֹהִים

and cast / their / supplication / before / the Ark / of Your / covenant. / HASHEM, / God,

צְבָאוֹת, עַד מָתַי לֹא תְרַחֵם אֶת עָרֵי יְהוּדָה

Master of / Legions, / until / when / will You not / have mercy / on / the / cities / of / Judah,

וִירוּשָׁלַיִם אֲשֶׁר זָעַמְתָּ זֶה כַּמֶּה שָׁנִים.[2] וּרְאֵה

and on / Jerusalem / which / You have / been enraged / [against them] / for / so / this / many / years? / See

אֶת עַמְּךָ יִשְׂרָאֵל מְרוּדִים מְאֹד. פָּנִינוּ לְיָמִין

Your people, / Israel / oppressed / greatly. / We turn / to our right,

וְאֵין עוֹזֵר, לִשְׂמֹאל וְאֵין סוֹמֵךְ,[3] וַאֲנַחְנוּ אֵין לָנוּ

and / there is no / helper; / to our left, / and there / is no one / to support / [us]; / so as for us, / there / is not / for / us

עַל מִי לְהִשָּׁעֵן, כִּי אִם עָלֶיךָ אָבִינוּ שֶׁבַּשָּׁמָיִם.[4]

on / whom / [anyone] / to lean / except / upon / You, / our Father / Who is in / Heaven.

וְהִנֵּה הָעֵת וְהָעוֹנָה יָאַתָה לְךָ לְהוֹשִׁיעֵנוּ.

And / indeed, / the time / and the / season / are / propitious / for / You / to save [us].

---

(1) *Deuteronomy* 32:36. (2) *Zechariah* 1:12.
(3) Some editions read תּוֹמֵךְ, but the meaning is unchanged. (4) Cf. *Sotah* 49a.

אֱלֹהֵינוּ בֹּשְׁנוּ בְּמַעֲשֵׂינוּ וְנִכְלַמְנוּ בַּעֲוֹנֵינוּ, כִּי

⟨ for ⟩ by our ⟨ humiliated ⟩ of our deeds, ⟨ we are ⟨ Our God,
iniquities,   ashamed

הִשְׁחַרוּ פָנֵינוּ מִפְּנֵי חַטֹּאתֵינוּ, וְנִכְפְּפָה קוֹמָתֵנוּ

⟨ is our ⟨ Bowed ⟨⟨ our sins. ⟨ because ⟨ have our ⟨ turned black
stature   of   faces

מִפְּנֵי אַשְׁמָתֵנוּ, וְאֵין לָנוּ פֶּה לְהָשִׁיב וְלֹא

⟨ nor ⟨ to ⟨ [words in ⟨ and we ⟨⟨ our guilt, ⟨ because
answer, our] mouth do not have   of

מֵצַח לְהָרִים רֹאשׁ.

⟨⟨ our heads. ⟨ to lift ⟨ the [auda-
cious] brow

CONFESSION / וִדּוּי

**DURING THE RECITATION OF THE וִדּוּי, *CONFESSION*, STAND WITH
HEAD AND BODY SLIGHTLY BOWED, IN SUBMISSIVE CONTRITION.**

אָנָּא תָבֹא לְפָנֶיךָ תְּפִלָּתֵנוּ,[1] וְאַל תִּתְעַלַּם מִתְּחִנָּתֵנוּ,[2]

⟨⟨ our ⟨ ignore ⟨ and ⟨⟨ may our ⟨ before ⟨ come ⟨ Please,
supplication.   do not   prayer,   You

שֶׁאֵין אָנוּ עַזֵּי פָנִים וּקְשֵׁי עֹרֶף, לוֹמַר לְפָנֶיךָ

⟨⟨ before You, ⟨ as to say ⟨ necked ⟨ and stiff- ⟨ faced ⟨ so brazen- ⟨ For we are not

יהוה אֱלֹהֵינוּ וֵאלֹהֵי אֲבוֹתֵינוּ, צַדִּיקִים אֲנַחְנוּ וְלֹא

⟨ and ⟨ we are, ⟨ that ⟨⟨ of our ⟨ and the ⟨ our God, ⟨ HASHEM,
have not   righteous forefathers, God

חָטָאנוּ, אֲבָל אֲנַחְנוּ וַאֲבוֹתֵינוּ חָטָאנוּ.[3]

⟨⟨ have sinned. ⟨ and our ⟨ we ⟨⟨ —for ⟨⟨ sinned
forefathers   indeed,

**STRIKE THE LEFT SIDE OF THE CHEST WITH THE RIGHT FIST WHILE RECITING
EACH OF THE SINS OF THE FOLLOWING CONFESSIONAL LITANY:**

אָשַׁמְנוּ, בָּגַדְנוּ, גָּזַלְנוּ, דִּבַּרְנוּ דְפִי. הֶעֱוִינוּ,

⟨⟨ We have com- ⟨⟨ slander. ⟨ we have ⟨⟨ we have ⟨⟨ we have ⟨⟨ We have
mitted iniquity;   spoken   robbed;   betrayed; been
guilty;

וְהִרְשַׁעְנוּ, זַדְנוּ, חָמַסְנוּ, טָפַלְנוּ שֶׁקֶר. יָעַצְנוּ

⟨ We have ⟨⟨ false ⟨ we have ⟨⟨ we have ⟨⟨ we have sinned ⟨⟨ we have commit-
given advice accusations. made   extorted; willfully;   ted wickedness;

רָע, כִּזַּבְנוּ, לַצְנוּ, מָרַדְנוּ, נִאַצְנוּ, סָרַרְנוּ,

⟨⟨ we have ⟨⟨ we have provoked ⟨ we have ⟨⟨ we have ⟨⟨ we have been ⟨⟨ that is
strayed;   [God's anger];   rebelled; scorned; deceitful;   bad;

(1) Cf. *Psalms* 88:3. (2) 55:2. (3) Cf. 106:6, *Jeremiah* 3:25.

עָוִינוּ, פָּשַׁעְנוּ, צָרַרְנוּ, קִשִּׁינוּ עֹרֶף. רָשַׁעְנוּ,

《 We have been wicked; 《 our necks. 〈 we have stiffened 《 we have caused distress; 《 we have sinned rebelliously; 《 we have been iniquitous;

שִׁחַתְנוּ, תִּעַבְנוּ, תָּעִינוּ, תִּעְתָּעְנוּ.

《 we have scoffed. 《 we have gone astray; 《 we have committed abominations; 《 we have been corrupt;

סַרְנוּ מִמִּצְוֹתֶיךָ וּמִמִּשְׁפָּטֶיךָ הַטּוֹבִים, וְלֹא שָׁוָה

〈 worthwhile 〈 and it was not 《 that are good, 〈 and from Your laws 〈 from Your commandments 〈 We have turned away

לָנוּ.[1] וְאַתָּה צַדִּיק עַל כָּל הַבָּא עָלֵינוּ, כִּי אֱמֶת

〈 truthfully 〈 for 《 upon us, 〈 that has come 〈 all 〈 in 〈 are righteous 〈 And You 《 for us.

עָשִׂיתָ וַאֲנַחְנוּ הִרְשָׁעְנוּ.[2]

《 have acted wickedly. 〈 while we 《 have You acted,

שָׁכַחְנוּ אֶת טוֹבוֹתֶיךָ, וְנָשִׁינוּ אֶת רֹב חֲסָדֶיךָ,

《 of Your kindnesses; 〈 overwhelming number 〈 the 〈 we have ignored 《 Your good gifts; 〈 We have forgotten

וּמָרִינוּ אֶת פִּיךָ, וּמִמִּשְׁפָּטֶיךָ סַרְנוּ.[3] וּבְהַבְלֵי

〈 With the empty follies 《 we have strayed. 〈 and from Your laws 《 Your word; 〈 against 〈 we have rebelled

הָעוֹלָם הַזֶּה נִהֲבַלְנוּ,[4] אֶל רְהָבִים וְשָׁטֵי כָזָב

〈 after falsehood 〈 and strayers 〈 the arrogant 〈 to 《 we have become empty [of value]; 〈 of this world

פָּנִינוּ.[5] וְהִסְכַּלְנוּ הַרְבֵּה מְאֹד.[6] וְאָהַבְנוּ רַע מִטּוֹב,

《 more than good, 〈 evil 〈 We have loved 《 exceedingly. 〈 We have been foolish 《 we have turned.

וְשֶׁקֶר מִדַּבֵּר צֶדֶק סֶלָה.[7] וְטֻמְאָה תַּחַת טָהֳרָה,

《 purity, 〈 instead of 〈 [We have chosen] 《 Selah. 《 righteously, 〈 more than speaking 〈 lies

וְשִׁקּוּץ תַּחַת זְכוּת. וְהֶחֱלַפְנוּ עוֹלָם עוֹמֵד בְּעוֹלָם

〈 for a world 〈 that is eternal 〈 a world 〈 We have exchanged 《 merit. 〈 instead of 〈 loathsomeness

(1) Cf. *Job* 33:27. (2) *Nehemiah* 9:33. (3) Cf. *Psalms* 119:102. (4) Cf. *Job* 27:12. (5) Cf. *Psalms* 40:5. (6) Cf. *II Samuel* 24:10. (7) Cf. *Psalms* 52:5.

עוֹבֵר, מִדֵּי יוֹם בְּיוֹמוֹ הַשְׁכֵּם וַחֲטוֹא, עַד אֲשֶׁר

‹ when ‹ until » to sin, ‹ rising early ‹ to day ‹ day ‹ From » that is ephemeral.

עֲוֹנוֹתֵינוּ עָבְרוּ רֹאשֵׁנוּ.[1] וְרַבּוּ מִשַּׂעֲרוֹתֵינוּ, וְעָצְמוּ

‹ stronger » than our hairs, ‹ They are more numerous » our heads. ‹ have risen above » our iniquities

מִדִּבְרֵי פִינוּ, וְגָדְלוּ מִצַּעֲדֵי רַגְלֵינוּ, וְגָבְהוּ מִנִּשְׁמַת

‹ than the soul ‹ taller » of our legs, ‹ than the strides ‹ longer » of our mouths, ‹ than the words

רוּחַ אַפֵּנוּ. טָבַעְנוּ בִּיוֵן מְצוּלָה וְאֵין מָעֳמָד,

» foothold; ‹ and there is no ‹ of the shadowy depths, ‹ in the mire ‹ We have sunk » in our nostrils. ‹ that gives breath

בָּאנוּ בְמַעֲמַקֵּי מַיִם וְשִׁבֹּלֶת שְׁטָפָתְנוּ.[2] וְלֹא לְךָ

‹ to You, ‹ Not » sweeps us away. ‹ and a rushing current ‹ of the water, ‹ the depths ‹ we have entered

יהוה אֱלֹהֵינוּ הֲרֵעֹנוּ כִּי אִם לְנַפְשֵׁנוּ, וְלֹא אוֹתְךָ

‹ You ‹ it is not » to our own souls; ‹ rather ‹ but » have we done harm, ‹ our God, ‹ HASHEM,

הִכְעַסְנוּ כִּי אִם אוֹתָנוּ. כִּי אֱנוֹשׁ אִם חָטָא מַה

‹ has he ‹ what ‹ if he ‹ a man ‹ For » ourselves. ‹ rather ‹ but » that we have made angry, sins,

יִּפְעַל לָךְ, וְאִם רַבּוּ פְשָׁעָיו מַה יַּעֲשֶׂה לָּךְ. אֲבָל

‹ Yet » to You? ‹ has he done ‹ what » are his sins, ‹ many ‹ Even if » to You? ‹ done

אוֹי לִבְנֵי אָדָם אֲשֶׁר חָטְאוּ לָךְ, וְאוֹי לְנַפְשָׁם, כִּי

‹ for ‹ to their souls, ‹ and woe » against You, ‹ have sinned ‹ who ‹ of Man ‹ to the Sons ‹ woe

גָּמְלוּ לָהֶם רָעָה.[3] אֱלֹהֵינוּ בֹּשְׁנוּ וְנִכְלַמְנוּ לְהָרִים

» to lift ‹ and we are ashamed ‹ we are embarrassed » Our God, » evil. ‹ on themselves ‹ they have brought

אֱלֹהֵינוּ פָּנֵינוּ אֵלֶיךָ,[4] כִּי אָנוּ כִּכְלִי נִמְאָס. כֵּן נִבְזֵינוּ

‹ are we ‹ So » that has been befouled. ‹ like a utensil ‹ we ‹ for » to You, ‹ our faces » — our God —
disgraced

בְּעֵינֵי נַפְשֵׁנוּ, כְּגֶבֶר אֲשֶׁר הֻטְבַּל בְּשַׁחַת, וְתַעֲבוּהוּ

‹ and is made odious ‹ in a pit, ‹ who was sunk ‹ like a man » of our [inner] self, ‹ in the eyes

---

(1) Cf. *Psalms* 38:5. (2) Cf. 69:3. (3) Cf. *Isaiah* 3:9. (4) Cf. *Ezra* 9:6.

שַׁלְמוֹתָיו.2 וּכְמוֹ בְעָוֹן חוֹלֶלְנוּ, כֵּן בְּשֶׁת פָּנֵינוּ כִּסָּתְנוּ.

« by his own clothes. ‹ of our faces ‹ has the shame **«** so ‹ we were born, ‹ in iniquity ‹ Just as **«** covered us.

אָשַׁמְנוּ מִכָּל עָם, בְּשְׁנוּ מִכָּל דּוֹר, גָּלָה מִמֶּנּוּ

‹ from us ‹ Departed **«** generation. ‹ more than any other ‹ We have been ashamed **«** people. ‹ more than any other ‹ We have been guilty

מָשׂוֹשׂ, דָּוָה לִבֵּנוּ בַּחֲטָאֵינוּ, הֶחְבַּל אַוּוּיֵנוּ, וְנִפְרַע

‹ uncovered **«** was our desired [Temple], ‹ Seized **«** because of our sins. ‹ is our heart ‹ Sickened **«** has joy.

פְּאֵרֵנוּ, זְבוּל בֵּית מִקְדָּשֵׁנוּ חָרַב בַּעֲוֹנֵינוּ, טִירָתֵנוּ

‹ Our Palace **«** because of our iniquities. ‹ has been destroyed ‹ our Holy Temple ‹ for [His] abode, **«** was our splendor;

הָיְתָה לְשַׁמָּה, יְפִי אַדְמָתֵנוּ לְזָרִים, בֹּחֵנוּ לְנָכְרִים.

« to foreigners. ‹ our wealth **«** is controlled by strangers, ‹ of our Land **«** [Jerusalem,] the beauty **«** desolate. ‹ has become

וַעֲדַיִן לֹא שַׁבְנוּ מִטָּעוּתֵנוּ וְהֵיךְ נָעִיז פָּנֵינוּ וְנַקְשֶׁה

‹ and stiffen ‹ faced ‹ can we be ‹ So how **«** from our willful errors. ‹ we have not repented ‹ But still

עָרְפֵּנוּ, לוֹמַר לְפָנֶיךָ יהוה אֱלֹהֵינוּ וֵאלֹהֵי אֲבוֹתֵינוּ,

« of our forefathers, ‹ and the God ‹ our God ‹ HASHEM, ‹ before You, ‹ so as to say ‹ our neck

צַדִּיקִים אֲנַחְנוּ וְלֹא חָטָאנוּ, אֲבָל אֲנַחְנוּ וַאֲבוֹתֵינוּ

‹ and our fathers ‹ both we ‹ for in truth, **«** and we have not sinned, **«** we are ‹ that righteous

חָטָאנוּ.3

« have sinned.

**STRIKE THE LEFT SIDE OF THE CHEST WITH THE RIGHT FIST WHILE RECITING
EACH OF THE SINS OF THE FOLLOWING CONFESSIONAL LITANY:**

אָשַׁמְנוּ, בָּגַדְנוּ, גָּזַלְנוּ, דִּבַּרְנוּ דְפִי. הֶעֱוִינוּ,

« We have committed iniquity; **«** slander. ‹ we have spoken **«** we have robbed; **«** we have betrayed; **«** We have been guilty;

וְהִרְשַׁעְנוּ, זַדְנוּ, חָמַסְנוּ, טָפַלְנוּ שֶׁקֶר. יָעַצְנוּ

‹ We have given advice **«** false ‹ accusations. ‹ we have made **«** we have extorted; **«** we have sinned willfully; **«** we have committed wickedness;

(1) Cf. *Job* 9:31. (2) Cf. *Psalms* 44:16. (3) Cf. 106:6; *Jeremiah* 3:25.

רָע, כִּזַּבְנוּ, לַצְנוּ, מָרַדְנוּ, נִאַצְנוּ, סָרַרְנוּ,

that is bad; we have been deceitful; we have scorned; we have rebelled; we have provoked [God's anger]; we have strayed;

עָוִינוּ, פָּשַׁעְנוּ, צָרַרְנוּ, קִשִּׁינוּ עֹרֶף. רָשַׁעְנוּ,

We have been iniquitous; we have sinned rebelliously; we have caused distress; we have stiffened our necks. We have been wicked;

שִׁחַתְנוּ, תִּעַבְנוּ, תָּעִינוּ, תִּעְתָּעְנוּ.

we have been corrupt; we have committed abominations; we have gone astray; we have scoffed.

סַרְנוּ מִמִּצְוֹתֶיךָ וּמִמִּשְׁפָּטֶיךָ הַטּוֹבִים, וְלֹא שָׁוָה

We have turned away from Your commandments and from Your laws that are good, and it was not worth-while

לָנוּ.[1] וְאַתָּה צַדִּיק עַל כָּל הַבָּא עָלֵינוּ, כִּי אֱמֶת

for us. And You are righteous in all that has come upon us, for truthfully

עָשִׂיתָ וַאֲנַחְנוּ הִרְשָׁעְנוּ.[2]

have You acted, while we have acted wickedly.

וְעַתָּה יהוה אֱלֹהֵינוּ, אַחֲרֵי שׁוּבֵנוּ נִחַמְנוּ,

And now, HASHEM, our God, after our repenting we regretted [our past misdeeds];

וְאַחֲרֵי הִוָּדְעֵנוּ, סָפַקְנוּ עַל יָרֵךְ, בֹּשְׁנוּ וְגַם נִכְלָמְנוּ,

and after being made aware [of our sins], we slapped our thighs [in anguish]; we were ashamed and also humiliated,

כִּי נָשָׂאנוּ חֶרְפַּת נְעוּרֵינוּ.[3] וְעַל זֹאת נִשָּׂא בְשָׂרֵנוּ

for we take this of our youthful [sins]. And for the disgrace we must bear for our flesh

בְּשִׁנֵּינוּ, וְנַפְשֵׁנוּ נָשִׂים בְּכַפֵּנוּ.[4] וּבַמֶּה נִקַדְּמָה פָנֶיךָ

in our teeth [not complaining about our punishment], and our souls we place in our hands [accepting our punishment]. For with what [merit] can we come before You,

(1) Cf. Job 33:27. (2) Nehemiah 9:33. (3) Cf. Jeremiah 31:18. (4) Cf. Job 13:14.

יהוה אֱלֹהֵינוּ, וּבַמֶּה נְכַף לְךָ אֱלֹהֵי מָרוֹם, וּבַמֶּה[1]

⟨ With ⟨⟨ most high? ⟨ O God ⟨⟨ to ⟨ shall we ⟨ With ⟨⟨ our God? ⟨ HASHEM,
what You, humble what
ourselves

תִּתְרַצֶּה, וּתְכַפֵּר לָנוּ עַל כָּל חַטֹּאתֵנוּ, אֲשֶׁר חָלְפוּ

⟨ that have passed ⟨ our sins ⟨ all ⟨ for ⟨ for us ⟨ and atone ⟨ will You find
us favorable

וְעָבְרוּ, כַּמַּיִם הַמֻּגָּרִים אַרְצָה, אֲשֶׁר לֹא יֵאָסֵפוּ.[2]

⟨⟨ be ⟨ cannot ⟨ that ⟨ along the ⟨ flowing ⟨ like water ⟨⟨ and gone
collected? ground by,

אִם בִּתְשׁוּבָה וִוִדּוּי תִּתְרַצֶּה, הִנְנוּ שָׁבִים וּמִתְוַדִּים

⟨ and ⟨ repenting ⟨ here ⟨⟨ You will find ⟨ and ⟨ through ⟨ If
confessing we are, [us] favorable, confession repentance

לְפָנֶיךָ יהוה אֱלֹהֵינוּ. חָטָאנוּ וּפָשַׁעְנוּ וְיָשַׁר הֶעֱוִינוּ,

⟨⟨ we have ⟨ what was ⟨⟨ and we ⟨ we have ⟨⟨ our God: ⟨ HASHEM, ⟨ before
made straight have sinned sinned You,
crooked, willfully; inadvertently,

וְלֹא שָׁוֶה לָנוּ.[3] וְאִם בִּתְפִלָּה וּבְתַחֲנוּנִים תִּמְחָל,

⟨⟨ You par- ⟨ and supplication ⟨ through ⟨ But if ⟨⟨ to us. ⟨ of ⟨ and it
don [us], prayer benefit is not

הִנְנוּ מַפִּילִים תַּחֲנוּנֵינוּ לְפָנֶיךָ כְּעֵינֵי עֲבָדִים אֶל

⟨ [look] ⟨ of ⟨ just as ⟨⟨ before ⟨ our ⟨ we pour ⟨ then here
to servants the eyes You, supplications out we are,

יַד אֲדוֹנֵיהֶם, וּכְעֵינֵי שִׁפְחָה אֶל יַד גְּבִרְתָּהּ, כֵּן

⟨ so ⟨⟨ of her ⟨ to the ⟨ of a maid- ⟨ and just ⟨⟨ of their ⟨ the
mistress, hand servant [look] as the eyes masters, hand

עֵינֵינוּ נְשׂוּאוֹת אֵלֶיךָ.[4]

⟨⟨ toward You. ⟨ lifted ⟨ are our eyes

וְאִם בִּבְכִי וּזְעָקָה תִּסְלַח, הִנֵּה בַּמִּסְתָּרִים

⟨ in [its] ⟨ indeed, ⟨⟨ You will ⟨ and crying ⟨ through ⟨ Or if
hidden places forgive [us], out weeping

תִּבְכֶּה נַפְשֵׁנוּ מִפְּנֵי חַטֹּאתֵינוּ, וּבַחֲדָרִים תֶּאֱנַח[5]

⟨ sighs ⟨ in [its] chambers ⟨⟨ our inadvertent ⟨ because ⟨ our soul ⟨ weeps
sins; of

רוּחֵנוּ עַל רֹב פְּשָׁעֵינוּ.

⟨⟨ of our ⟨ the ⟨ because ⟨ our
willful sins. multitude of spirit

(1) Cf. *Micah* 6:6. (2) Cf. *II Samuel* 14:14. (3) Cf. *Job* 33:27. (4) Cf. *Psalms* 123:2. 5) Cf. *Jeremiah* 13:17.

וְאִם בְּשֶׁבֶר רוּחַ תְּכַפֵּר, הִנֵּה נִשְׁבַּר לִבֵּנוּ בְּקִרְבֵּנוּ,

Or if / because of a broken / spirit / indeed, / You will atone [for us], / broken / are our hearts / within us,

וְנִדְכְּאָה רוּחֵנוּ¹ מִן הַצָּרוֹת וּמִן הַתְּלָאוֹת אֲשֶׁר

and crushed / is our spirit / by / the troubles / and hardships / that

עָבְרוּ עָלֵינוּ, עַד אֲשֶׁר לֹא נוֹתַר מְתוֹם בִּבְשָׂרֵנוּ.²

have happened / to us, / until / there is not / left / [any part] that is whole / in our flesh.

לוּלֵי רַחֲמֶיךָ וַחֲסָדֶיךָ, אָז אָבַדְנוּ בַּעֲוֹנֵינוּ.³

Were it not / for Your mercy / and Your kindness, / then / we would have been lost / because of our iniquities.

לְעֵינֵינוּ עָשְׁקוּ עֲמָלֵנוּ, מִמְּשָׁךְ וּמְמוֹרָט מִמֶּנּוּ,

Before our eyes / have they stolen / the product of our labor; / [it was] pulled away / and cut off / from us.

נָתְנוּ עֹלָם עָלֵינוּ, סָבַלְנוּ עַל שִׁכְמֵנוּ, עֲבָדִים

They have placed / their yoke / upon us, / we bore it / upon / our shoulders. / Slaves

מָשְׁלוּ בָנוּ, פֹּרֵק אֵין מִיָּדָם, צָרוֹת רַבּוֹת

have ruled / over us; / there was not / a redeemer / from their hand. / Troubles / that are manifold

סְבָבוּנוּ, קְרָאנוּךָ יהוה אֱלֹהֵינוּ, רָחַקְתָּ מִמֶּנּוּ

have surrounded us, / we called upon You, / HASHEM, / our God, / but You have distanced Yourself / from us

בַּעֲוֹנֵינוּ, שַׁבְנוּ מֵאַחֲרֶיךָ, תָּעִינוּ וְאָבַדְנוּ.

because of our iniquities. / We have turned away / from following after You; / we have gone astray; / we have become lost.

וַעֲדַיִן לֹא שַׁבְנוּ מִטָּעוּתֵנוּ וְהֵיךְ נָעִיז פָּנֵינוּ וְנַקְשֶׁה

But still / we have not repented / from our willful errors. / So how / can we be so brazen-faced / and stiffen

עָרְפֵּנוּ, לוֹמַר לְפָנֶיךָ יהוה אֱלֹהֵינוּ וֵאלֹהֵי אֲבוֹתֵינוּ,

our neck / so as to say / before You, / HASHEM, / our God / and the God / of our forefathers,

צַדִּיקִים אֲנַחְנוּ וְלֹא חָטָאנוּ, אֲבָל אֲנַחְנוּ וַאֲבוֹתֵינוּ

that righteous / we are / and we have not sinned, / for in truth, / both we / and our fathers

(1) Cf. *Psalms* 51:19. (2) Cf. 38:4. (3) Cf. 119:92.

חָטָאנוּ.1

《 have sinned.

**STRIKE THE LEFT SIDE OF THE CHEST WITH THE RIGHT FIST WHILE RECITING
EACH OF THE SINS OF THE FOLLOWING CONFESSIONAL LITANY:**

אָשַׁמְנוּ, בָּגַדְנוּ, גָּזַלְנוּ, דִּבַּרְנוּ דְפִי. הֶעֱוִינוּ,

| 《 We have committed iniquity; | 《 slander. | 〈 we have spoken | 《 we have robbed; | 《 we have betrayed; | 《 We have been guilty; |

וְהִרְשַׁעְנוּ, זַדְנוּ, חָמַסְנוּ, טָפַלְנוּ שֶׁקֶר. יָעַצְנוּ

| 〈 We have given advice | 《 false accusations. | 〈 we have made | 《 we have extorted; | 《we have sinned willfully; | 《we have committed wickedness; |

רָע, כִּזַּבְנוּ, לַצְנוּ, מָרַדְנוּ, נִאַצְנוּ, סָרַרְנוּ,

| 《 we have strayed; | 《 we have provoked [God's anger]; | 《 we have rebelled; | 《 we have scorned; | 《 we have been deceitful; | 《 that is bad; |

עָוִינוּ, פָּשַׁעְנוּ, צָרַרְנוּ, קִשִּׁינוּ עֹרֶף. רָשַׁעְנוּ,

| 《 We have been wicked; | 《 our necks. | 〈 we have stiffened | 《we have caused distress; | 《we have sinned rebelliously; | 《we have been iniquitous; |

שִׁחַתְנוּ, תִּעַבְנוּ, תָּעִינוּ, תִּעְתָּעְנוּ.

| 《 we have scoffed. | 《 we have gone astray; | 《we have committed abominations; | 《 we have been corrupt; |

סַרְנוּ מִמִּצְוֹתֶיךָ וּמִמִּשְׁפָּטֶיךָ הַטּוֹבִים, וְלֹא שָׁוָה

| 〈 worth-while | 〈 and it was not | 《 that are good, | 〈 and from Your laws | 〈 from Your commandments | 〈 We have turned away |

לָנוּ.2 וְאַתָּה צַדִּיק עַל כָּל הַבָּא עָלֵינוּ, כִּי אֱמֶת

| 〈 truth-fully | 〈 for | 《 upon us, | 〈 that has come | 〈 all | 〈 in | 〈 are righteous | 〈 And You | 《 for us. |

עָשִׂיתָ וַאֲנַחְנוּ הִרְשָׁעְנוּ.3

| 《 have acted wickedly. | 〈 while we | 《 have You acted, |

אָנָּא יהוה, הָאֵל הַגָּדוֹל הַגִּבּוֹר וְהַנּוֹרָא, שׁוֹמֵר

| 〈 Who keeps | 《 and Who is awesome, | 〈 Who is mighty, | 〈 Who is great, | 〈 God | 《 HASHEM, | 〈 Please, |

הַבְּרִית וְהַחֶסֶד, אַל יִמְעֲטוּ לְפָנֶיךָ כָּל הַצָּרוֹת וְכָל

| 〈 and all | 〈 the troubles | 〈 all | 〈 before You | 〈 be minimized | 〈 let not | 《 and the Kindness, | 〈 the Covenant |

(1) Cf. *Psalms* 106:6; *Jeremiah* 3:25. (2) Cf. *Job* 33:27. (3) *Nehemiah* 9:33.

הַתְּלָאוֹת אֲשֶׁר מָצְאוּ אֶת עֲבָדֶיךָ, מִיּוֹם הֱיוֹתָם עַל
‹ upon ‹ they ‹ from the ‹‹ Your servants, ‹ have ‹ that ‹ the sufferings
came to be day befallen

הָאֲדָמָה עַד הַיּוֹם הַזֶּה. הַבֵּט בַּעֲמָלֵנוּ וְאַל תַּבֵּט
‹ look at ‹ but do ‹ our toil, ‹ Look at ‹‹ this very day. ‹ until ‹ the earth
not

בְּמַעֲלָלֵינוּ, שׁוּר נָא בְעָנְיֵנוּ וְאַל תָּשׁוּר אֶל עֲוֹנֵינוּ,
‹‹ our sins; ‹ at ‹ look ‹ but do ‹ our ‹ please, ‹ see, ‹‹ our misdeeds;
not oppression,

וּפְנֵה אֶל עָשְׁקֵנוּ וְאַל תֵּפֶן אֶל קַשְׁיֵנוּ, שִׂים נָא
‹ please, ‹ Deem, ‹‹ our stub- ‹ toward ‹ turn ‹ but do ‹ our ‹ toward ‹ turn
bornness. not subjugation,

צָרוֹתֵינוּ כֹּפֶר לְחַטֹּאתֵינוּ וְלִפְשָׁעֵינוּ, וּמְצוּקוֹתֵינוּ
‹ our persecution ‹‹ and our ‹ for our ‹ as ‹ our troubles
willful sins; inadvertent sins atonement

תַּחַת אַשְׁמָתֵנוּ, וְעֶלְבּוֹן נֶפֶשׁ תַּחַת עֲוֹן נָפֶשׁ.
‹‹ of [our] ‹ the ‹ in place ‹ of [our] ‹ and the ‹‹ our guilt; ‹ in place
soul. iniquity of soul humiliation of

וְעַתָּה יהוה אֱלֹהֵינוּ אִם עָשִׂינוּ כְּאִוַּלְתֵּנוּ,
‹‹ according to ‹ we have ‹ although ‹ our God, ‹ HASHEM, ‹ And now,
our wicked folly, acted

עֲשֵׂה אַתָּה כְּאֱמָנוּתֶךָ וּסְלַח, כִּי תְמִים דֵּעִים אָתָּה.
‹‹ are ‹ knowledge ‹ of ‹ for ‹‹ and ‹ as is Your ‹ may You act
You. perfect forgive, practice

אִם שִׁלַּמְנוּ רָעָה תַּחַת טוֹבָה, גְּמָלֵנוּ טוֹב וְלֹא
‹ and ‹ good ‹ [nevertheless,] ‹ goodness, ‹ in place ‹ evil ‹ we have ‹ If
not grant us of paid back

רָע. כִּי יֵתֵר מֵרֵעֵהוּ צַדִּיק,¹ וְכָל שֹׁכֵן הַבּוֹרֵא
‹ the ‹ so ‹ all the ‹‹ is a righteous ‹ than his ‹ greater ‹ For ‹‹ bad.
Creator, more person; fellow [in soul]

יִתְבָּרַךְ שְׁמוֹ. וְאִם הִרְבִּינוּ לִפְשֹׁעַ, אַתָּה הוּא
‹ the One ‹ You ‹‹ we have will- ‹ many times ‹ And if ‹‹ is His ‹ Blessed
Who is are fully sinned, Name.

רַב חֶסֶד וּמַרְבֶּה לִסְלֹחַ, אֲשֶׁר צִדְקוֹתֶיךָ וַחֲסָדֶיךָ
‹ and Your ‹ Your ‹ for ‹‹ forgiving, ‹ and ‹ in ‹ Abun-
kindnesses righteousness profusely Kindness dant

(1) Cf. *Proverbs* 12:26.

רַבּוּ מֵהַרְרֵי אֵל וְעָמְקוּ מִתְּהוֹם רַבָּה.¹ כִּסָּה שָׁמַיִם

‹ the heavens ‹ Cover « that are vast. ‹ than the deep waters ‹ and deeper ‹ than the mighty mountains ‹ are greater

הוֹדְךָ וּתְהִלָּתְךָ מָלְאָה הָאָרֶץ.² יהוה שְׁמַעֲנוּ

‹ we have heard ‹ HASHEM, « the earth. ‹ filled ‹ and Your praise « did Your glory,

שְׁמַעֲךָ,³ כִּי בְאַחַת הַמִּדוֹת תִּסְלַח לַאֲשֶׁר חָטְאוּ

‹ have sinned ‹ those who ‹ You forgive ‹ of [Your] Attributes ‹ with just one ‹ that « of Your tidings,

לָךְ, וְאַף כִּי בְכֻלָּם. סְלַח נָא לַעֲוֹנֵינוּ וּלְחַטֹּאתֵינוּ.⁴

« and our sins, ‹ our iniquities ‹ please ‹ Forgive « with all of them. ‹ so ‹ certainly « against You;

וּלְכָל חַטֹּאת וַעֲוֹנוֹת יִשְׂרָאֵל. וְכַבְּסֵנוּ מֵעֲוֹנֵינוּ

« of our iniquities; ‹ Wash us clean « of Israel. ‹ and iniquities ‹ the sins ‹ and all

וּמֵחַטֹּאתֵינוּ טַהֲרֵנוּ. וְאַל תִּקְצֹף עָלֵינוּ עַד מְאֹד.⁵

« an extreme; ‹ to ‹ with us ‹ be angry ‹ Do not « purify us. ‹ of our sins

וְאַל לָעַד תִּזְכֹּר עָוֹן כִּי מַה בֶּצַע בְּדָמֵנוּ אִם

‹ if ‹ from our blood ‹ benefit is there ‹ what ‹ For « iniquity. ‹ remember ‹ forever ‹ do not

תַּשְׁחִיתֵנוּ, וּמַה כִּשְׁרוֹן אִם תּוֹרִידֵנוּ לִבְאֵר שַׁחַת

‹ of destruction ‹ to the pit ‹ You will lower us ‹ if ‹ is it appropriate ‹ and how « You destroy us;

בַּחֲטָאֵינוּ, וּמַה יִּתְרוֹן אִם תִּפְקוֹד עָלֵינוּ כִּדְרָכֵינוּ.

« according to our ways. ‹ us ‹ You will punish ‹ if ‹ advantage is there ‹ and what « because of our sins;

לֹא בְאֵלֶּה שְׁבָחֶיךָ וְלֹא בְאֵלֶּה תְהִלָּתֶךָ. אֲבָל

‹ Rather, « is Your praise. ‹ in these ways ‹ and not ‹ is Your adoration, ‹ in these ways ‹ Not

הַדָּבָר שֶׁהוּא לְךָ לְשֵׁם וְלִתְהִלָּה לְהִתְנַהֵג עִם בָּנֶיךָ

‹ Your children ‹ toward ‹ is to act ‹ and praise ‹ renown ‹ to ‹ that is ‹ the response

בְּמִדַּת רַחֲמִים, וּלְגַלְגֵּל עֲלֵיהֶם מִדַּת חֲסָדֶיךָ,

« of Your kindness ‹ the Attribute ‹ upon them ‹ and to invoke « of Mercy, ‹ with [Your] Attribute

---

(1) Cf. *Psalms* 36:7. (2) Cf. *Habakkuk* 3:3. (3) Cf. 3:2. (4) Cf. *Exodus* 34:9. (5) Cf. *Psalms* 51:4.

כַּאֲשֶׁר אָמַרְתָּ, לְמַעַן שְׁמִי אַאֲרִיךְ אַפִּי וּתְהִלָּתִי

‹ and for [the sake of] My praise ‹ « My anger, ‹ I will delay ‹ of My Name ‹ For the sake ‹ « You have said:

אֶחֱטָם לָךְ לְבִלְתִּי הַכְרִיתֶךָ.[1] וְגַם הַמִּדָּה אֲשֶׁר הִיא

‹ is ‹ which ‹ the Attribute ‹ In addition, ‹ « to annihilate you. ‹ so as not ‹ against you, ‹ I will block My anger

לָךְ לְשֵׁם וּלְתִפְאֶרֶת, הַסְּלִיחָה וַעֲבוֹר עַל פֶּשַׁע,

‹ « sin ‹ and overlooking ‹ is forgiveness ‹ and splendor ‹ renown ‹ for Your

כַּאֲשֶׁר אָמַרְתָּ עַל בְּרִיּוֹתֶיךָ, שֶׂכֶל אָדָם הַאֲרִיךְ

‹ to be slow ‹ in a man ‹ It shows wisdom ‹ « Your creations: ‹ concerning ‹ You have said ‹ — as

אַפּוֹ, וְתִפְאַרְתּוֹ עֲבֹר עַל פֶּשַׁע.[2] וּלְמַעְלָה מִזֹּאת

‹ this ‹ Beyond ‹ « sin. ‹ to overlook ‹ and it is his splendor ‹ « to anger,

עֲשֵׂה עִמָּנוּ.

‹ « with us. ‹ act

אָנָּא הַבֵּט בְּצִדְקַת עֲבָדֶיךָ חֲסִידֶיךָ, אֲשֶׁר הֶעֱרוּ

‹ poured forth ‹ who ‹ « Your pious ones, ‹ of Your servants, ‹ to the righteousness ‹ look ‹ Please

נַפְשָׁם לָמוּת עָלֶיךָ,[3] וְלֹא חָסוּ עַל נַפְשָׁם וְעַל

‹ [nor] for ‹ their souls ‹ for ‹ They did not have pity ‹ « for You. ‹ [prepared] to die ‹ their souls

זַרְעָם, וְקֵצוּ וּמָאֲסוּ בְּחַיֵּי הָעוֹלָם הַזֶּה. וּבִטְּלוּ

‹ They put aside ‹ « of this world. ‹ the life ‹ and disdained ‹ rather, they scorned ‹ « their children;

רְצוֹנָם מִפְּנֵי רְצוֹנֶךָ,[4] וְקִדְּשׁוּ שִׁמְךָ הַגָּדוֹל וְלֹא

‹ and did not ‹ that is great ‹ Your Name ‹ They sanctified ‹ « Your will. ‹ before ‹ their will

חִלְּלוּהוּ. וְרָצוּ לַזֶּבַח, וּפָשְׁטוּ צַוָּארָם וְעָמְדוּ

‹ They stood firm ‹ « their necks. ‹ and stretched forth ‹ to the sacrifice ‹ They ran ‹ « desecrate it.

בְּנִסָּיוֹן וְנֶאֶמְנוּ, וְנִבְחֲנוּ בְּצֵרוּף, וְנִמְצְאוּ תְּמִימִים.

‹ « wholesome. ‹ and were found ‹ in the crucible ‹ They were tested ‹ « and proved faithful. ‹ in the trial

---

(1) *Isaiah* 48:9. (2) *Proverbs* 19:11. (3) Cf. *Isaiah* 53:12. (4) See *Avos* 2:2.

וְנָגְעוּ דְּמֵי אָבוֹת וּבָנִים, וּדְמֵי רַחֲמָנִיּוֹת וְיַלְדֵיהֶן,

‹ and their ‹ of compassionate ‹ the ‹ and sons; ‹ of fathers ‹ did the ‹ Touch
children; women bloods bloods [each other]

וְנִתְעָרְבוּ דְּמֵי אַחִים וַאֲחָיוֹת, וּדְמֵי חֲתָנִים וְכַלּוֹת,

‹ and ‹ of grooms ‹ the ‹ and sisters; ‹ of ‹ were the ‹ mixed
brides; bloods brothers bloods together

וּדְמֵי חֲכָמִים וַחֲכָמוֹת, וּדְמֵי הֲגוּנִים וַהֲגוּנוֹת,

‹ and worthy ‹ of worthy ‹ the ‹ and wise ‹ of wise men ‹ the
women men bloods women bloods

וּדְמֵי חֲסִידִים וַחֲסִידוֹת, וּדְמֵי זְקֵנִים וּזְקֵנוֹת, וּדְמֵי

‹ the ‹ and elderly ‹ of elderly ‹ the ‹ and pious ‹ of pious men ‹ the
bloods women; men bloods women; bloods

בַּחוּרִים וּבְחוּרוֹת, וּדְמֵי פַּרְנָסִים וְחַזָּנֵיהֶם, וּדְמֵי

‹ the ‹ and their ‹ of community ‹ the ‹ and young girls; ‹ of young boys
bloods deputies; leaders bloods

דַּיָּנִים וְסוֹפְרֵיהֶם, וּדְמֵי מְלַמְּדִים וְתַלְמִידֵיהֶם, וּדְמֵי

‹ the ‹ and their students; ‹ of teachers ‹ the ‹ and their ‹ of judges
bloods bloods recorders;

אֲנָשִׁים וּנְשׁוֹתֵיהֶם, וְנֶהֶרְגוּ כֻּלָּם יַחַד, עַל קִדּוּשׁ

‹ the sancti- ‹ in ‹ together ‹ all of ‹ They were ‹ and their wives. ‹ of men
fication of them, slain,

שִׁמְךָ הַמְיֻחָד. אֶרֶץ אַל תְּכַסִּי דָמָם, וְאַל יְהִי

‹ be ‹ and let ‹ their ‹ cover ‹ do ‹ Earth, ‹ that is ‹ Your
there not blood; not Unique. Name

מָקוֹם לְזַעֲקָתָם.[1] עַד יַשְׁקִיף וְיֵרֶא יהוה מִשָּׁמָיִם.[2]

‹ from ‹—HASHEM— ‹ and takes ‹ He gazes ‹ until ‹ that contains ‹ a place
Heaven, notice down their outcry;

וְיִנְקֹם נִקְמָתוֹ, וְנִקְמַת עַמּוֹ, וְנִקְמַת תּוֹרָתוֹ, וְנִקְמַת

‹ and the ‹ of His ‹ the ‹ of His ‹ the ‹ His ‹ and
vengeance Torah, vengeance people, vengeance vengeance, avenges

דַּם עֲבָדָיו, אֲשֶׁר שָׁפְכוּ דָמָם כַּמָּיִם, כְּהִבְטַחְתָּנוּ

‹ For so You ‹ like ‹ their ‹ [the enemy] ‹ who ‹ of His ‹ of the
promised us water. blood spilled servants blood

בְּיַד אָבִי חוֹזֶה, הַרְנִינוּ גוֹיִם עַמּוֹ, כִּי דַם עֲבָדָיו

‹ of His ‹ the ‹ for ‹ for His ‹ O ‹ Sing ‹ of ‹ of [Moses] ‹ at the
servants blood people, nations, praises Prophets: the Father hand

(1) Cf. *Job* 16:18. (2) *Lamentations* 3:50.

יָקוּם, וְנָקָם יָשִׁיב לְצָרָיו, וְכִפֶּר אַדְמָתוֹ עַמּוֹ.[1]

He will ‹ and ‹ His ‹ upon His ‹ will He ‹ and ‹ He will
people. » Land » and He foes; » bring retribution avenge;
            will placate

אֶת אֵלֶּה מִזְבְּחוֹת זְכוֹר, וְאֵלֶּה עֲקֵדוֹת תִּרְאֶה,

see. ‹ bindings for ‹ and ‹ remember, ‹ altars ‹ These
»   the sacrifice   these

וְהִנָּחֵם, וְשַׁכֵּךְ אַף, וְכַלֵּה חֵמָה, וְתַשְׁבִּית שׁוֹד וָשֶׁבֶר

and ‹ pillage ‹ and ‹ [Your] ‹ and bring ‹ [Your] ‹ [then] » Reconsider,
destruction   terminate   wrath,   to an end anger   calm

מֵעַמֶּךָ. חוּס וְרַחֵם אֶת יֶתֶר הַפְּלֵיטָה, וְתוֹצִיאֵנָה

and take » of our ‹ on the ‹ and have ‹ Have » from Your
them out   remnant, remainder compassion pity   people.

מֵאֲפֵלָה לְאוֹרָה. וְחַדֵּשׁ עָלֵינוּ שָׁנָה טוֹבָה, שְׁנַת רָצוֹן

of ‹ a year ‹ that is ‹ a year ‹ for us ‹ Renew » into light. ‹ from
favor   good,   darkness

וְעֵת גְּאֻלָּה. שַׁדַּי תִּזְכֹּר לָנוּ בְּרִית אֶזְרָח, וְתִפְקֹד

recall ‹ of [Abraham] ‹ the ‹ in our ‹ remember » O » of ‹ and a
         the Ezrachite; covenant favor   Almighty, redemption. time

לָנוּ זְכוּת הַנֶּעֱקָד, וּתְרַחֲמֵנוּ בְּצִדְקַת אִישׁ תָּם.

» who was ‹ of the ‹ [in the merit] ‹ and have » of [Isaac,] the ‹ the ‹ for our
whole-   man   of the   mercy on us one bound;   merit   sake
some.   [Jacob,] righteousness

וּכְשֶׁחָטְאוּ יִשְׂרָאֵל בַּמִּדְבָּר, עָמַד מֹשֶׁה רַבֵּנוּ

our ‹ did ‹ stand » in the ‹ When Israel sinned
Teacher Moses   Wilderness,

בִּתְפִלָּה לְפָנֶיךָ, וּבִקֵּשׁ רַחֲמִים עַל עַמְּךָ בֵּית יִשְׂרָאֵל.

» of Israel. ‹ the ‹ Your ‹ for ‹ for mercy ‹ and he » before ‹ in prayer
House people   asked   You,

וְכָךְ אָמַר בִּתְפִלָּתוֹ, מַלְכִּי וֵאלֹהַי, סְלַח נָא לַעֲוֹן

the ‹ now, ‹ Forgive, » and my ‹ My King » in his prayer: ‹ did ‹ And
iniquity   God!   he say so

הָעָם הַזֶּה כְּגֹדֶל חַסְדֶּךָ, וְכַאֲשֶׁר נָשָׂאתָה לָעָם הַזֶּה

this people ‹ You have ‹ and as ‹ of Your ‹ according to ‹ of this
            forgiven   kindness the greatness people

מִמִּצְרַיִם וְעַד הֵנָּה.[2]

» now. ‹ until ‹ from Egypt

---

(1) *Deuteronomy* 32:43. (2) *Numbers* 14:19.

סליחה מ' * / SELICHAH 40*

אִישׁ עָנָו* חִלָּה פָנֶיךָ בְּעַד עֲדָתֶךָ,
《 of Your 〈 on 〈 Your 〈 be- 〈 who was 〈 The
people: behalf Presence seeched humble man
[Moses]*

בְּרַחֲמִים אָנָּא נְהוֹג בְּחֶמְלָתֶךָ.
《 according to Your 〈 act 〈 please, 〈 With mercy,
compassion.

גְּאַלְתָּם מִנֹּף* בְּחֹזֶק יָד,
《 of Your 〈 by the 〈 from 〈 You redeemed
hand, strength Nof* them

דָּתְךָ הִנְחַלְתָּם תַּתָּה לָמוֹ[1] שֵׁם וָיָד.[2]
《 and 〈 fame 〈 them 〈 You 《 You made their 〈 Your law
renown. gave inheritance,

הֵם עַמְּךָ וְנַחֲלָתֶךָ,[3] וַעֲלֵימוֹ חֲפוֹף בְּחֶמְלָתֶךָ.
《 in Your 〈 hover 〈 over them 《 and Your 〈 Your 〈 They
compassion. heritage; people are

זְכוֹר לָנוּ בְּרִית[4] אָבוֹת,
《 of the 〈 the 〈 for us 〈 Remem-
Patriarchs, covenant ber

חֵשֶׁק אַהֲבָתָם אֵין מַיִם לְכַבּוֹת.[5]
《 that can 〈 water 〈 that there 〈 of their love 〈 the
extinguish [it]. is no passion

טְעַנְתָּם נְשָׂאתָם עַל כַּנְפֵי נֶשֶׁר,[6]
《 of an 〈 the 〈 on 〈 You carried 《 You bore
eagle, wings them them,

---

(1) Some editions of *Selichos* read לָנוּ, *to us*. (2) Cf. *Isaiah* 56:5. (3) Cf. *Deuteronomy* 9:29.
(4) Some editions of *Selichos* read צִדְקַת, *the righteousness*. (5) Cf. *Song of Songs* 8:7.
(6) Cf. *Exodus* 19:4; some editions of *Selichos* read נְשָׁרִים, *eagles*, in the plural, presumably
to conform to the Scriptural verse; however, that reading overlooks the rhyme scheme.

אִישׁ עָנָו 🙠 — *The man who was humble
[Moses]*. Although the alphabetical acrostic
and rhymed couplets of this section prove
that it is a *piyut*, it is unnumbered and appears in almost all editions of Selichos as
a prose paragraph. Moreover, in most editions some words have been omitted and
the *piyut* has been punctuated in a way

that obliterates the poetics. The author is
unknown.

מִנֹּף — *From Nof*. This Egyptian city is usually identified as Memphis. *Isaiah* (19:13),
Jeremiah (2:16, etc.) and *Ezekiel* (30:13,16)
call it נֹף, *Nof*. *Hosea* (9:6), however,
refers to it as מֹף, *Mof* (see *Targum* and
Radak).

יַשֵּׁר צַעֲדֵיהֶם לֶכֶת יוֹשֶׁר.[1]

《 uprightly. 〈 to walk 〈 their steps 〈 straight-
ening

כִּי תָשׁוּב לָשׂוּשׂ עֲלֵיהֶם לְטוֹב,[2]

《 for good, 〈 over them 〈 to rejoice 〈 You will 〈 When
return

(לָמוֹ חֲקֹתָ* כְּדָת לֶקַח טוֹב.[3])

《 that is 〈 the 《 according 《 You 〈 (them
good). teaching to should [on Your
[Scripture], engrave,* palm]

מִצְרַיִם אִם יִשְׁמְעוּ כִּי הֶאֱבַדְתָּם,

《 You have destroyed 〈 that 〈 they should 〈 — if 《 Egypt
them [Israel], hear

נוֹאֲמִים בְּרָעָה הוֹצֵאתָם לְכַלֹּתָם.[4]

《 to annihilate 〈 You brought them 〈 With evil 《 they will say,
them. out [of Egypt] intent

סְלַח נָא לַעֲוֹן הָעָם הַזֶּה,[5]

《 of this people; 〈 the 〈 now, 〈 Forgive,
iniquity

עֲוֹת פִּשְׁעָם מְחַל נָא הַיּוֹם הַזֶּה.

《 this very day. 〈 please, 〈 absolve, 〈 of their 〈 the cor-
willful sin ruption

פְּנֵה נָא לְצִדְקַת אָבוֹת, (צַדְּקֵם) וְאַל תִּשְׁכַּח חֲנוֹת.[6]

《 gracious- 〈 forget 〈 and do 〈 (vindicate 《 of the 〈 toward the 〈 please, 〈 Turn,
ness. not them) Patriarchs; righteousness

קְרָאתָם בָּנִים[7] וְאַתָּה לָמוֹ אָב, רַחֲמֵם כְּרַחֵם אָב.[8]

《 a father 〈 like the 〈 Have mercy 《 a 〈 to 〈 and You 《 [Your] 〈 You called
has; mercy on them father them are children, them

(1) Cf. *Proverbs* 15:21; some editions of *Selichos* read לֶכֶת בְּכֹשֶׁר, *to walk in proper ways.*
(2) Cf. *Deuteronomy* 30:9. (3) This line does not appear in all editions.
(4) Cf. *Exodus* 32:12; see *Rashi* to *Exodus* 10:10. (5) *Numbers* 14:19. (6) Cf. *Psalms* 77:10; many
edition of *Selichos* read, פְּנֵה נָא לְצִדְקַת אָבוֹת וְאַל תִּשְׁכַּח, *Turn, please, toward the righteousness of
the Patriarchs, and do not forget,* חַנּוּן קְרָאתָם בָּנִים, *O Gracious One, You have called them [Your]
children . . .*, a reading that follows neither the alphabetic acrostic nor the rhyme scheme.
(7) See *Deuteronomy* 14:1; *Exodus* 4:22. (8) Cf. *Psalms* 103:13.

לָמוֹ חֲקֹתָ — *Them [on Your palm] You
should engrave.* The prophet Isaiah proclaimed: *And Zion said, "HASHEM has
forsaken me, and God has forgotten me!"*
[But God replied,] *"Can a woman forget*

*her baby, not to feel compassion for the
child of her womb? Even were these to
forget, I will not forget you. Indeed, upon
[My] palms have I engraved you ..."*
(Isaiah 49:14-16).

שַׁדַּי עֲשֵׂה לְמַעַן שְׁמֶךָ,
‹‹ of Your ‹ for the ‹ act ‹‹ Almighty,
Name, sake

תִּמְחוֹל וְתִסְלַח לִפְשָׁעֵי עַמֶּךָ.
‹‹ of Your ‹ the willful ‹ and forgive ‹ pardon
people: sins

אָנָּא סְלַח נָא לַעֲוֹן הָעָם הַזֶּה.[1] וְאִם לֹא תִסְלַח
‹‹ You will ‹ but if ‹‹ of this people, ‹ the ‹ now ‹ forgive ‹ Please,
not forgive, iniquity

מְחֵנִי.[2] וְאַף אַתָּה הֲשֵׁבוֹתָ לוֹ כְּדַרְכֵי טוּבְךָ. בְּשָׁרְתּוֹ
‹ You ‹‹ of Your ‹ according ‹ him ‹ answered ‹ You ‹ Indeed, ‹‹ then erase
informed goodness: to the ways me [from
him Your book].

וְאָמַרְתָּ לוֹ סָלַחְתִּי כִּדְבָרֶךָ.[3] וּסְלַח נָא לַעֲנִיֵּי עַמֶּךָ
‹‹ of ‹ the ‹ please, ‹ So ‹‹ in accordance ‹ I have ‹‹ to ‹ and said
Your [spiritually] forgive, with your word. forgiven him,
people, poor

וְדַלֵּי הַצֹּאן. כִּי תְמִים דֵּעִים[4] אָתָּה. אִם הִרְבִּינוּ
‹ we have ‹ If ‹‹ are You. ‹ Knowledge ‹ the One ‹ for ‹‹ flock, ‹ [Your] im-
been excessive of Perfect poverished

לִפְשׁוֹעַ אַתָּה מַרְבֶּה לִסְלוֹחַ. אֲדֹנָי שְׁמָעָה, אֲדֹנָי
‹ O Lord, ‹‹ heed; ‹ O Lord, ‹‹ in forgiving. ‹ abundant ‹ You are ‹‹ in sinning,

סְלָחָה, אֲדֹנָי הַקְשִׁיבָה, וַעֲשֵׂה אַל תְּאַחַר.[5]
‹‹ delay! ‹ do not ‹‹ and act; ‹ be attentive ‹ O Lord, ‹‹ forgive;

מְשִׁיחַ צִדְקֶךָ אָמַר לְפָנֶיךָ, שְׁגִיאוֹת מִי יָבִין,
‹‹ can ‹ who ‹ Mistakes ‹‹ before You: ‹ said ‹ who is righteous ‹ Your
discern? [David] anointed one

מִנִּסְתָּרוֹת נַקֵּנִי.[6] נַקֵּנוּ יהוה אֱלֹהֵינוּ מִכָּל פְּשָׁעֵינוּ,
‹ our sins ‹ of all ‹ our God, ‹ HASHEM, ‹ Cleanse ‹‹ cleanse ‹ From
us, me. unperceived faults

וְטַהֲרֵנוּ מִכָּל טֻמְאוֹתֵינוּ, וּזְרוֹק עָלֵינוּ מַיִם טְהוֹרִים
‹ pure water ‹ upon us ‹ Pour ‹‹ our contaminations. ‹ of all ‹ and purify us

וְטַהֲרֵנוּ, כַּכָּתוּב עַל יַד נְבִיאֶךָ: וְזָרַקְתִּי עֲלֵיכֶם
‹ upon you ‹ I shall pour ‹‹ of Your ‹ the ‹ by ‹ as it is ‹‹ and purify us,
prophet: hand written

---

(1) Cf. *Numbers* 14:19. (2) Cf. *Exodus* 32:32. (3) Cf. *Numbers* 14:20. (4) *Job* 37:16.
(5) From the Monday and Thursday *Tachanun* service. (6) *Psalms* 19:13.

מַיִם טְהוֹרִים וּטְהַרְתֶּם, מִכֹּל טֻמְאוֹתֵיכֶם וּמִכָּל
⟨ and   ⟨ your   ⟨ from   ⟪ and you will   ⟨ pure water
from all   contaminations   all   become pure;

גִּלּוּלֵיכֶם אֲטַהֵר אֶתְכֶם.¹
⟪ you.   ⟨ I will purify   ⟨ your
abominations

מִיכָה עַבְדְּךָ אָמַר לְפָנֶיךָ: מִי אֵל כָּמוֹךָ נֹשֵׂא
⟨ Who   ⟪ like You,   ⟨ is a   ⟨ Who   ⟪ before   ⟨ said   ⟨ Your   ⟨ Micah
pardons   God   You: servant

עָוֹן וְעֹבֵר עַל פֶּשַׁע לִשְׁאֵרִית נַחֲלָתוֹ, לֹא הֶחֱזִיק
⟨ He has not   ⟪ of His   ⟨ for the remnant   ⟨ transgression   ⟨ and   ⟨ iniquity
retained   heritage?   overlooks

לָעַד אַפּוֹ, כִּי חָפֵץ חֶסֶד הוּא, יָשׁוּב יְרַחֲמֵנוּ, יִכְבֹּשׁ
⟨ He will   ⟪ be merciful   ⟨ He will   ⟪ is He.   ⟨ of   ⟨ desirous   ⟨ for   ⟪ His   ⟨ eternally
suppress   to us;   again   kindness   wrath,

עֲוֹנֹתֵינוּ, וְתַשְׁלִיךְ בִּמְצֻלוֹת יָם כָּל חַטֹּאתָם. (וְכָל
⟨ (And   ⟪ their sins.   ⟨ all   ⟨ of the   ⟨ into the   ⟨ And You   ⟪ our iniquities.
all   sea   depths   will cast

חַטֹּאת עַמְּךָ בֵּית יִשְׂרָאֵל תַּשְׁלִיךְ בִּמְקוֹם אֲשֶׁר
⟨ where   ⟨ to a place   ⟨ cast away   ⟨ of Israel,   ⟨ the   ⟨ of Your   ⟨ the sins
House   people,

לֹא יִזָּכְרוּ, וְלֹא יִפָּקְדוּ, וְלֹא יַעֲלוּ עַל לֵב לְעוֹלָם.)
⟪ ever.)   ⟨ mind   ⟨ to   ⟨ be   ⟨ nor   ⟨ be   ⟨ nor   ⟨ be remem-   ⟨ they
brought   considered   bered   will not

תִּתֵּן אֱמֶת לְיַעֲקֹב חֶסֶד לְאַבְרָהָם אֲשֶׁר נִשְׁבַּעְתָּ
⟨ You swore   ⟨ as   ⟪ to Abraham,   ⟨ kindness   ⟪ to Jacob,   ⟨ truth   ⟨ Grant

לַאֲבֹתֵינוּ מִימֵי קֶדֶם.³
⟪ of old.   ⟨ from days   ⟨ to our
forefathers

דָּנִיֵּאל אִישׁ חֲמוּדוֹת שִׁוַּע לְפָנֶיךָ: הַטֵּה אֱלֹהַי
⟨ my   ⟨ Incline,   ⟪ before   ⟨ cried   ⟨ greatly   ⟨ the   ⟨ Daniel,
God,   You: out   beloved,   man

אָזְנְךָ וּשְׁמָע, פְּקַח עֵינֶיךָ וּרְאֵה שֹׁמְמֹתֵינוּ וְהָעִיר
⟨ and [that]   ⟨ our   ⟨ and see   ⟨ Your eyes   ⟨ open   ⟪ and listen;   ⟨ Your ear,
of] the City   desolation

---

(1) *Ezekiel* 36:25. (2) *Micah* 7:18-19. (3) 7:20.

אֲשֶׁר נִקְרָא שִׁמְךָ עָלֶיהָ, כִּי לֹא עַל צִדְקֹתֵינוּ אֲנַחְנוּ

⟨ do we ⟨ of our ⟨ because ⟨ not ⟨ for ⟪ upon; ⟨ Your Name is ⟨ which
righteousness   proclaimed

מַפִּילִים תַּחֲנוּנֵינוּ לְפָנֶיךָ, כִּי עַל רַחֲמֶיךָ הָרַבִּים.

⟪ which is ⟨ of Your ⟨ because ⟨ but ⟪ before ⟨ our ⟨ cast
abundant.   compassion,   You;   supplications

אֲדֹנָי שְׁמָעָה, אֲדֹנָי סְלָחָה, אֲדֹנָי הַקְשִׁיבָה, וַעֲשֵׂה

⟪ and act, ⟨ be attentive ⟨ O Lord, ⟪ forgive; ⟨ O Lord, ⟪ heed; ⟨ O Lord,

אַל תְּאַחַר, לְמַעַנְךָ אֱלֹהַי, כִּי שִׁמְךָ נִקְרָא עַל

⟨ upon ⟨ is ⟨ Your ⟨ for ⟪ my God, ⟨ for Your sake, ⟪ delay; ⟨ do not
proclaimed Name

עִירְךָ וְעַל עַמֶּךָ.¹

⟪ Your people. ⟨ and upon ⟨ Your City

עֶזְרָא הַסּוֹפֵר אָמַר לְפָנֶיךָ: אֱלֹהַי, בֹּשְׁתִּי

⟨ I am ⟨ My God, ⟪ before ⟨ said ⟨ the Scribe ⟨ Ezra
embarrassed   You:

וְנִכְלַמְתִּי לְהָרִים, אֱלֹהַי, פָּנַי אֵלֶיךָ, כִּי עֲוֹנֹתֵינוּ

⟨ our iniquities ⟨ for ⟪ to You, ⟨ my face ⟪ —my God— ⟪ to lift ⟨ and I am ashamed

רָבוּ לְמַעְלָה רֹּאשׁ, וְאַשְׁמָתֵנוּ גָדְלָה עַד לַשָּׁמָיִם.²

⟪ to the ⟨ up ⟨ have ⟨ and our sins ⟪ [our] ⟨ over ⟨ have
heavens.   expanded   heads,   multiplied

וְאַתָּה³ אֱלוֹהַּ סְלִיחוֹת, חַנּוּן וְרַחוּם, אֶרֶךְ

⟨ Slow ⟪ and Compassionate, ⟨ Gracious ⟪ of forgiveness, ⟨ are the God ⟨ But You

אַפַּיִם וְרַב חֶסֶד, וְלֹא עֲזַבְתָּנוּ.⁴

⟪ forsaken us. ⟨ and You ⟪ in ⟨ and ⟨ to anger
have not Kindness; Abundant

אַל תַּעַזְבֵנוּ אָבִינוּ וְאַל תִּטְּשֵׁנוּ בּוֹרְאֵנוּ, וְאַל

⟨ do not ⟪ our Creator; ⟨ cast us away, ⟨ do not ⟪ our Father; ⟨ forsake us, ⟨ Do not

תַּזְנִיחֵנוּ יוֹצְרֵנוּ, וְאַל תַּעַשׂ עִמָּנוּ כָּלָה כְּחַטֹּאתֵינוּ.

⟪ as our ⟨ annihila- ⟨ our ⟨ cause ⟨ and ⟪ our Molder; ⟨ abandon us,
sins merit. tion,   do not

וְקַיֵּם לָנוּ יהוה אֱלֹהֵינוּ, אֶת הַדָּבָר שֶׁהִבְטַחְתָּנוּ

⟨ that You pledged ⟨ the declaration ⟨ our God, ⟪ HASHEM, ⟨ for us, ⟨ Fulfill
to us

---

(1) *Daniel* 9:18-19. (2) *Ezra* 9:6. (3) Some editions of *Selichos*
insert the word אֱלֹהֵינוּ, *our God*, at this point. (4) Cf. *Nehemiah* 9:17.

בְּקַבָּלָה עַל יְדֵי יִרְמְיָהוּ חוֹזָךְ, כָּאָמוּר: בַּיָּמִים הָהֵם
‹ In those days ‹‹ as it is said: ‹‹ Your ‹ of Jeremiah, ‹ the ‹ by ‹ in the
seer, hand tradition,

וּבָעֵת הַהִיא, נְאֻם יהוה, יְבֻקַּשׁ אֶת עֲוֺן יִשְׂרָאֵל
‹ of Israel, ‹ the iniquity ‹ sought ‹‹ of ‹ —the ‹‹ and at that time
shall be HASHEM— word

וְאֵינֶנּוּ וְאֶת חַטֹּאת יְהוּדָה וְלֹא תִמָּצֶאנָה, כִּי
‹ for ‹ but [they] will not ‹ of Judah [shall ‹ and the sins ‹‹ but it will be
be found, be sought], [found] nonexistent,

אֶסְלַח לַאֲשֶׁר אַשְׁאִיר.[1] עַמְּךָ וְנַחֲלָתְךָ, רְעֵבֵי טוּבְךָ,
‹‹ for Your ‹ who ‹‹ and Your ‹ Your ‹‹ I will ‹ those ‹ I shall
goodness, hunger heritage, people leave over. whom forgive

צְמֵאֵי חַסְדֶּךָ, תְּאֵבֵי יִשְׁעֶךָ, יַכִּירוּ וְיֵדְעוּ כִּי לַיהוה
‹ to ‹ that ‹ and ‹ — may they ‹‹ for Your ‹ and ‹‹ for Your ‹ who
HASHEM, know recognize salvation who long kindness, thirst

אֱלֹהֵינוּ הָרַחֲמִים וְהַסְּלִיחוֹת.
‹‹ and forgiveness. ‹ belong mercy ‹ our God,

אֵל רַחוּם שְׁמֶךָ, אֵל חַנּוּן שְׁמֶךָ, בָּנוּ נִקְרָא שְׁמֶךָ.[3]
‹‹ is Your Name ‹ upon ‹‹ is Your ‹ Gracious God ‹‹ is Your ‹ Merciful God
proclaimed, us Name, Name,

יהוה עֲשֵׂה לְמַעַן שְׁמֶךָ,[4] עֲשֵׂה לְמַעַן אֲמִתָּךְ, עֲשֵׂה
‹ act ‹‹ Your truth; ‹ for the ‹ Act ‹‹ Your ‹ for the ‹ act ‹ HASHEM,
sake of Name. sake of

לְמַעַן בְּרִיתָךְ, עֲשֵׂה לְמַעַן גָּדְלָךְ וְתִפְאַרְתָּךְ, עֲשֵׂה
‹ act ‹‹ and Your ‹ Your ‹ for the ‹ act ‹‹ Your ‹ for the
splendor; greatness sake of covenant; sake of

לְמַעַן דָּתָךְ, עֲשֵׂה לְמַעַן הוֹדָךְ, עֲשֵׂה לְמַעַן וְעוּדָךְ,
‹‹ Your Meet- ‹ for the ‹ act ‹‹ Your ‹ for the ‹ act ‹‹ Your ‹ for the
ing House; sake of glory; sake of Law; sake of

עֲשֵׂה לְמַעַן זִכְרָךְ,[5] עֲשֵׂה לְמַעַן חַסְדָּךְ, עֲשֵׂה לְמַעַן
‹ for the ‹ act ‹‹ Your ‹ for the ‹ act ‹‹ Your ‹ for the ‹ act
sake of kindness; sake of remembrance; sake of

טוּבָךְ, עֲשֵׂה לְמַעַן יְחוּדָךְ, עֲשֵׂה לְמַעַן כְּבוֹדָךְ, עֲשֵׂה
‹ act ‹‹ Your ‹ for the ‹ act ‹‹ Your ‹ for the ‹ act ‹‹ Your
honor; sake of Oneness; sake of goodness;

---

(1) Jeremiah 50:20. (2) Cf. Exodus 34:6. (3) Cf. Deuteronomy 28:10.
(4) Jeremiah 14:7. (5) Cf. Exodus 3:15. (6) Psalms 6:5.

לְמַעַן **לְמוּדָךְ**,¹ עֲשֵׂה לְמַעַן **מַ**לְכוּתָךְ, עֲשֵׂה לְמַעַן

⟨ for the sake of ⟨ act ⟪ Your kingship; ⟨ for the sake of ⟨ act ⟪ Your students; ⟨ for the sake of

נִצְחָךְ, עֲשֵׂה לְמַעַן **סוֹ**דָךְ,² עֲשֵׂה לְמַעַן **עֻ**זָּךְ, עֲשֵׂה

⟨ act ⟪ Your power; ⟨ for the sake of ⟨ act ⟪ Your secret [revealed to those who fear You]; ⟨ for the sake of ⟨ act ⟪ Your eternal [Name];

לְמַעַן **פְּ**אֵרָךְ, עֲשֵׂה לְמַעַן **צִ**דְקָתָךְ, עֲשֵׂה לְמַעַן

⟨ for the sake of ⟨ act ⟪ Your righteousness; ⟨ for the sake of ⟨ act ⟪ Your glory; ⟨ for the sake of

קְדֻשָּׁתָךְ, עֲשֵׂה לְמַעַן **רַ**חֲמֶיךָ הָרַבִּים, עֲשֵׂה לְמַעַן

⟨ for the sake of ⟨ act ⟪ that is abundant; ⟨ Your mercy ⟨ for the sake of ⟨ act ⟪ Your sanctity;

שְׁכִינָתָךְ, עֲשֵׂה לְמַעַן **תְּ**הִלָּתָךְ, עֲשֵׂה לְמַעַן אוֹהֲבֶיךָ

⟨ those who loved You ⟨ for the sake of ⟨ act ⟪ Your praise; ⟨ for the sake of ⟨ act ⟪ Your Divine Presence;

שׁוֹכְבֵי עָפָר,³ עֲשֵׂה לְמַעַן **אַ**בְרָהָם יִצְחָק וְיַעֲקֹב,

⟪ and Jacob; ⟨ Isaac, ⟨ Abraham, ⟨ for the sake of ⟨ act ⟪ in the dust; ⟨ who rest

עֲשֵׂה לְמַעַן **מֹ**שֶׁה וְאַהֲרֹן, עֲשֵׂה לְמַעַן **דָּ**וִד וּשְׁלֹמֹה,

⟪ and Solomon ⟨ David ⟨ for the sake of ⟨ act ⟪ and Aaron; ⟨ Moses ⟨ for the sake of ⟨ act

עֲשֵׂה לְמַעַן **יְ**רוּשָׁלַיִם עִיר קָדְשֶׁךָ,⁴ עֲשֵׂה לְמַעַן **צִ**יּוֹן

⟨ Zion, ⟨ for the sake of ⟨ act ⟪ of Your Holiness ⟨ the City ⟨ Jerusalem, ⟨ for the sake of ⟨ act

מִשְׁכַּן כְּבוֹדֶךָ,⁵ עֲשֵׂה לְמַעַן שִׁמְמוֹת⁶ הֵיכָלֶךָ, עֲשֵׂה

⟨ act ⟪ of Your Temple; ⟨ the desolation ⟨ for the sake of ⟨ act ⟪ of Your glory; ⟨ the abode

לְמַעַן **הֲ**רִיסוּת⁷ מִזְבְּחֶךָ, עֲשֵׂה לְמַעַן **הֲ**רוּגִים עַל

⟨ for ⟨ those killed ⟨ for the sake of ⟨ act ⟪ of Your Altar; ⟨ the devastation ⟨ for the sake of

שֵׁם קָדְשֶׁךָ, עֲשֵׂה לְמַעַן טְבוּחִים עַל יִחוּדֶךָ, עֲשֵׂה

⟨ act ⟪ Your Oneness; ⟨ for ⟨ those slaughtered ⟨ for the sake of ⟨ act ⟪ Your holy Name;

לְמַעַן בָּאֵי בָאֵשׁ וּבַמַּיִם עַל קִדּוּשׁ שְׁמֶךָ, עֲשֵׂה לְמַעַן

⟨ for the sake of ⟨ act ⟪ of Your Name; ⟨ the sanctification ⟨ for ⟨ and water ⟨ fire ⟨ those who entered ⟨ for the sake of

---

(1) Cf. *Isaiah* 54:13. (7) Cf. *Psalms* 25:14. (3) *Isaiah* 26:19. (4) Cf. *Daniel* 9:16,24.
(5) *Psalms* 26:8. (6) Cf. *Jeremiah* 51:26. (7) Cf. *Isaiah* 49:19.

יוֹנְקֵי שָׁדַיִם¹ שֶׁלֹּא חָטָאוּ, עֲשֵׂה לְמַעַן גְּמוּלֵי חָלָב²

⟨ from the [babies] ⟨ the [infants] ⟨ for the ⟨ act ⟪ sin; ⟨ who did ⟨ at the ⟨ the [infants]
milk weaned sake of not breast sucking

שֶׁלֹּא פָשָׁעוּ, עֲשֵׂה לְמַעַן תִּינוֹקוֹת שֶׁל בֵּית רַבָּן,³

⟪ their teachers' ⟨ of ⟨ the children ⟨ for the ⟨ act ⟪ transgress; ⟪ who
school; sake of did not

עֲשֵׂה לְמַעַנְךָ אִם לֹא לְמַעֲנֵנוּ, עֲשֵׂה לְמַעַנְךָ וְהוֹשִׁיעֵנוּ.

⟪ and save us. ⟨ for Your sake ⟨ act ⟪ for our sake; ⟨ not ⟨ if ⟨ for Your sake ⟨ act

עֲנֵנוּ יהוה עֲנֵנוּ, עֲנֵנוּ אֱלֹהֵינוּ עֲנֵנוּ, עֲנֵנוּ אָבִינוּ⁴

⟨ our ⟨ answer ⟪ answer ⟨ our God, ⟨ answer ⟪ answer ⟨ HASHEM, ⟨ Answer
Father, us, us; us; us;

עֲנֵנוּ, עֲנֵנוּ **בּוֹרְאֵנוּ**⁵ עֲנֵנוּ, עֲנֵנוּ **גּוֹאֲלֵנוּ**⁶ עֲנֵנוּ, עֲנֵנוּ

⟨ answer ⟪ answer ⟨ our ⟨ answer ⟪ answer ⟨ our Creator, ⟨ answer ⟪ answer
us, us; Redeemer, us, us; us, us;

דּוֹרְשֵׁנוּ⁷ עֲנֵנוּ, עֲנֵנוּ **הָאֵל** הַנֶּאֱמָן⁸ עֲנֵנוּ, עֲנֵנוּ וָתִיק

⟨ stead- ⟨ answer ⟪ answer ⟨ Who is ⟨ God ⟨ answer ⟪ answer ⟨ You Who
fast us, us; faithful, us, us; searches us out,

וְחָסִיד עֲנֵנוּ, עֲנֵנוּ זַךְ וְיָשָׁר⁹ עֲנֵנוּ, עֲנֵנוּ חַי וְקַיָּם¹⁰

⟨and endur- ⟨living ⟨answer ⟪answer⟨ and ⟨ pure ⟨ answer ⟪ answer ⟨ and kind
ing One, us, us; upright One us, us; One,

עֲנֵנוּ, עֲנֵנוּ **טוֹב** וּמֵטִיב¹¹ עֲנֵנוּ, עֲנֵנוּ **יוֹדֵעַ** יֵצֶר¹² עֲנֵנוּ,

⟪answer ⟨ of incli- ⟨ Knower ⟨answer ⟪ answer ⟨ and bene- ⟨ good ⟨answer ⟪ answer
us; nations, us, us; ficent One, us, us;

עֲנֵנוּ **כּוֹבֵשׁ** כְּעָסִים עֲנֵנוּ, עֲנֵנוּ **לוֹבֵשׁ** צְדָקוֹת¹³ עֲנֵנוּ,

⟪ answer ⟨ of ⟨ Donner ⟨ answer ⟪ answer ⟨ of wrath, ⟨ Suppressor ⟨ answer
us; righteousness, us, us; us,

עֲנֵנוּ **מֶלֶךְ** מַלְכֵי הַמְּלָכִים¹⁴ עֲנֵנוּ, עֲנֵנוּ **נוֹרָא** וְנִשְׂגָּב¹⁵

⟨and power- ⟨awesome ⟨answer⟪ answer ⟨ of kings, ⟨ over ⟨ King ⟨ answer
ful One, us, us; kings us,

עֲנֵנוּ, עֲנֵנוּ **סוֹלֵחַ** וּמוֹחֵל עֲנֵנוּ, עֲנֵנוּ **עוֹנֶה** בְּעֵת

⟨ in time ⟨ You Who ⟨ answer ⟪ answer ⟨ and ⟨ You Who ⟨ answer ⟪ answer
answers us, us; pardons, forgives us, us;

צָרָה¹⁶ עֲנֵנוּ, עֲנֵנוּ **פּוֹדֶה** וּמַצִּיל¹⁷ עֲנֵנוּ, עֲנֵנוּ צַדִּיק

⟨righteous ⟨answer ⟪ answer ⟨ and ⟨ Redeemer ⟨ answer ⟪ answer ⟨ of
us, us; Rescuer, us, us; distress,

וְיָשָׁר¹ עֲנֵנוּ, עֲנֵנוּ קָרוֹב לְקוֹרְאָיו² עֲנֵנוּ, עֲנֵנוּ קָשֶׁה

⟨ You Who ⟨ answer ⟪answer⟨ to those who ⟨ He Who ⟨ answer ⟪ answer ⟨ and up-
with difficulty us, us; call upon Him, is close us, us; right One,

לִכְעוֹס³ עֲנֵנוּ, עֲנֵנוּ רַךְ לִרְצוֹת⁴ עֲנֵנוּ, עֲנֵנוּ רַחוּם

⟨ merciful ⟨ answer ⟪ answer ⟨ appeased, ⟨ You Who ⟨ answer ⟪ answer ⟨ becomes
us, us; are easily us, us; angry,

וְחַנּוּן⁵ עֲנֵנוּ, עֲנֵנוּ שׁוֹמֵעַ אֶל אֶבְיוֹנִים⁶ עֲנֵנוּ, עֲנֵנוּ

⟨answer ⟪answer ⟨ the destitute, ⟨ to ⟨ You Who ⟨ answer ⟪answer ⟨ and gra-
us, us; listens us, us; cious One,

תּוֹמֵךְ תְּמִימִים עֲנֵנוּ, עֲנֵנוּ אֱלֹהֵי אֲבוֹתֵינוּ עֲנֵנוּ,

⟪answer ⟨ of our ⟨ God ⟨ answer ⟪ answer ⟨ the ⟨ You Who
us; forefathers, us, us; wholesome, supports

עֲנֵנוּ אֱלֹהֵי אַבְרָהָם⁷ עֲנֵנוּ, עֲנֵנוּ פַּחַד יִצְחָק⁷ עֲנֵנוּ,

⟪answer ⟨ of Isaac, ⟨ Awesome ⟨answer ⟪ answer ⟨ of Abraham, ⟨ God ⟨ answer
us; One us, us; us,

עֲנֵנוּ אֲבִיר יַעֲקֹב⁸ עֲנֵנוּ, עֲנֵנוּ עֶזְרַת הַשְּׁבָטִים עֲנֵנוּ,

⟪answer ⟨ of the tribes, ⟨ Helper ⟨ answer ⟪ answer ⟨ of Jacob, ⟨ Mighty ⟨ answer
us; us, us; One us,

עֲנֵנוּ מִשְׂגַּב אִמָּהוֹת עֲנֵנוּ, עֲנֵנוּ עוֹנֶה בְּעֵת רָצוֹן⁹ עֲנֵנוּ,

⟪answer ⟨ of favor, ⟨ in a ⟨ You Who ⟨answer ⟪answer ⟨ of the ⟨ Stronghold ⟨answer
us; time answers us, us; Matriarchs, us,

עֲנֵנוּ אֲבִי יְתוֹמִים¹⁰ עֲנֵנוּ, עֲנֵנוּ דַּיַּן אַלְמָנוֹת¹⁰ עֲנֵנוּ.

⟪ answer ⟨ of widows, ⟨ Judge ⟨ answer ⟪answer ⟨ of orphans, ⟨ Father ⟨ answer
us. us; us,

מִי שֶׁעָנָה לְאַבְרָהָם אָבִינוּ בְּהַר הַמּוֹרִיָּה¹¹

⟪ Moriah ⟨ on Mount ⟨ our father ⟨ Abraham ⟨ Who answered ⟨ He

הוּא יַעֲנֵנוּ.

⟪ answer ⟨ — may
us. He

מִי שֶׁעָנָה לְיִצְחָק בְּנוֹ כְּשֶׁנֶּעֱקַד עַל גַּבֵּי הַמִּזְבֵּחַ¹¹

⟪ of the altar ⟨ top ⟨ on ⟨ when he ⟨ his son ⟨ Isaac ⟨ Who ⟨ He
was bound answered

הוּא יַעֲנֵנוּ.

⟪ answer ⟨ — may
us. He

---

(1) *Deuteronomy* 32:4. (2) Cf. *Psalms* 145:18. (3) *Ethics of the Fathers* 5:14. (4) Cf. 5:14.
(5) *Exodus* 34:6. (6) *Psalms* 69:34. (7) *Genesis* 31:42. (8) *Isaiah* 49:26.
(9) Cf. 49:8; *Psalms* 69:14. Alternate text: בְּעֵת צָרָה, *in time of distress.* (10) 68:6. (11) *Genesis* 22:12.

הוּא יַעֲנֵנוּ. מִי שֶׁעָנָה לְיַעֲקֹב בְּבֵית אֵל[1]

He › may — › answer us. « in Beth-el « Jacob ‹ Who answered ‹ He

הוּא יַעֲנֵנוּ. מִי שֶׁעָנָה לְיוֹסֵף בְּבֵית הָאֲסוּרִים[2]

He › may — › answer us. « in the prison ‹ Joseph ‹ Who answered ‹ He

הוּא יַעֲנֵנוּ. מִי שֶׁעָנָה לַאֲבוֹתֵינוּ עַל יַם סוּף[3]

He › may — › answer us. « of the at ‹ our forefathers ‹ Who answered ‹ He
Reeds Sea

הוּא יַעֲנֵנוּ. מִי שֶׁעָנָה לְמֹשֶׁה בְּחוֹרֵב[4]

He › may — › answer us. « in Horeb ‹ Moses ‹ Who answered ‹ He

הוּא יַעֲנֵנוּ. מִי שֶׁעָנָה לְאַהֲרֹן בַּמַּחְתָּה[5]

He › may — › answer us. « with the fire-pan ‹ Aaron ‹ Who answered ‹ He

מִי שֶׁעָנָה לְפִינְחָס בְּקוּמוֹ מִתּוֹךְ הָעֵדָה[6]

He › Who ‹ Phinehas ‹ when he ‹ from « the
answered arose amid congregation

הוּא יַעֲנֵנוּ.

He › may — › answer us. «

הוּא יַעֲנֵנוּ. מִי שֶׁעָנָה לִיהוֹשֻׁעַ בַּגִּלְגָּל[7]

He › may — › answer us. « in Gilgal ‹ Joshua ‹ Who answered ‹ He

הוּא יַעֲנֵנוּ. מִי שֶׁעָנָה לִשְׁמוּאֵל בַּמִּצְפָּה[8]

He › may — › answer us. « in Mizpah ‹ Samuel ‹ Who answered ‹ He

מִי שֶׁעָנָה לְדָוִד וּשְׁלֹמֹה בְנוֹ בִּירוּשָׁלָיִם[9] הוּא יַעֲנֵנוּ.

He › may — › answer us. « in Jerusalem ‹ his ‹ and ‹ David ‹ Who ‹ He
son Solomon answered

הוּא יַעֲנֵנוּ. מִי שֶׁעָנָה לְאֵלִיָּהוּ בְּהַר הַכַּרְמֶל[10]

He › may — › answer us. « Carmel ‹ on ‹ Elijah ‹ Who answered ‹ He
Mount

הוּא יַעֲנֵנוּ. מִי שֶׁעָנָה לֶאֱלִישָׁע בִּירִיחוֹ[11]

He › may — › answer us. « in Jericho ‹ Elisha ‹ Who answered ‹ He

(1) Genesis 35:3. (2) 39:21. (3) Exodus Ch. 14. (4) Exodus 17:6,11; Deuteronomy 9:19.
(5) Numbers 17:11-13. (6) 25:7-13. (7) Joshua 6:1-20; 7:6-15; 10:12-14. (8) I Samuel 7:9.
(9) II Samuel 7:5-16; 21:1,14; 24:25; I Kings 3:9. (10) 18:36-38. (11) II Kings 2:21.

מִי שֶׁעָנָה לְיוֹנָה בִּמְעֵי הַדָּגָה[1] הוּא יַעֲנֵנוּ.

He › Who › Jonah › in the › of the ‹ — may ‹ answer ‹‹
answered innards fish He us.

מִי שֶׁעָנָה לְחִזְקִיָּהוּ מֶלֶךְ יְהוּדָה בְּחָלְיוֹ[2] הוּא יַעֲנֵנוּ.

He › Who › Hezekiah, › king › of Judah, › in his ‹ — may ‹ answer ‹‹
answered illness He us.

מִי שֶׁעָנָה לַחֲנַנְיָה מִישָׁאֵל וַעֲזַרְיָה

He › Who › Hananiah, ‹ Mishael, ‹ and Azariah ‹
answered

בְּתוֹךְ כִּבְשַׁן הָאֵשׁ[3] הוּא יַעֲנֵנוּ.

inside ‹ the furnace ‹ of fire ‹‹ — may ‹ answer ‹‹
He us.

מִי שֶׁעָנָה לְדָנִיֵּאל בְּגוֹב הָאֲרָיוֹת[4] הוּא יַעֲנֵנוּ.

He › Who › Daniel › in the ‹ of lions ‹‹ — may ‹ answer ‹‹
answered den He us.

מִי שֶׁעָנָה לְמָרְדְּכַי וְאֶסְתֵּר בְּשׁוּשַׁן הַבִּירָה[5]

He › Who › Mordechai ‹ and Esther ‹ in Shushan ‹ the capital ‹‹
answered

הוּא יַעֲנֵנוּ.

— may ‹ answer ‹‹
He us.

מִי שֶׁעָנָה לְעֶזְרָא בַּגּוֹלָה[6] הוּא יַעֲנֵנוּ.

He › Who › Ezra › in the exile ‹‹ — may ‹ answer ‹‹
answered He us.

מִי שֶׁעָנָה לְכָל הַצַּדִּיקִים וְהַחֲסִידִים וְהַתְּמִימִים

He › Who › all › the righteous, ‹ the devout, ‹ the wholesome, ‹
answered

וְהַיְשָׁרִים הוּא יַעֲנֵנוּ.

and the ‹‹ — may ‹ answer ‹‹
upright He us.

רַחֲמָנָא דְּעָנֵי לַעֲנִיֵּי, עֲנֵינָן. רַחֲמָנָא דְּעָנֵי לִתְבִירֵי

Merciful One › Who ‹ the poor, ‹ answer ‹‹ answer ‹‹ Merciful One ‹ Who ‹ those of ‹
answers us! answers broken

לִבָּא, עֲנֵינָן. רַחֲמָנָא דְּעָנֵי לִמְכִיכֵי רוּחָא, עֲנֵינָן.

hearts, ‹‹ answer ‹‹ Merciful One ‹ Who ‹ those of ‹ spirit, ‹‹ answer ‹‹
us! answers crushed us!

---

(1) *Jonah* 2:2-11. (2) *II Kings* 20:2-6; *Isaiah* 38:2-8.
(3) *Daniel* 3:21-27. (4) 6:17-23. (5) *Esther* Ch. 8. (6) *Ezra* 8:21-23.

רַחֲמָנָא עֲנֵינָן. רַחֲמָנָא חוּס. רַחֲמָנָא פְּרוֹק. רַחֲמָנָא

‹ Merciful 《redeem! ‹ Merciful 《 have ‹ Merciful 《 answer ‹ Merciful
One,   One,   pity!   One,   us!   One,

שֵׁזִיב. רַחֲמָנָא רְחַם עֲלָן, הַשְׁתָּא בַּעֲגָלָא וּבִזְמַן קָרִיב.

《that comes‹ and at ‹ swiftly, ‹ — now, 《 on us ‹ have ‹ Merciful 《 save!
soon.   a time   mercy   One,

PUTTING DOWN THE HEAD / נפילת אפים

RECITE UNTIL יָבֵשׁ רָגַע WITH THE HEAD RESTING ON THE LEFT ARM,
PREFERABLY WHILE SEATED.

(וַיֹּאמֶר דָּוִד אֶל גָּד, צַר לִי מְאֹד, נִפְּלָה נָּא בְיַד יהוה,

《 of ‹ into the‹ now ‹ Let us ‹ exceed-‹ am ‹ Dis-《 Gad, ‹ to ‹ (And David said
HASHEM, hand   fall   ingly.   I   tressed

כִּי רַבִּים רַחֲמָיו, וּבְיַד אָדָם אַל אֶפֹּלָה.[1]

《 let me not fall.) ‹ but into human 《 are His ‹ abundant ‹ for
            hands   mercies,

רַחוּם וְחַנּוּן חָטָאתִי לְפָנֶיךָ. יהוה מָלֵא רַחֲמִים,

《 of mercy, ‹ Who ‹ HASHEM, 《 before ‹ I have ‹ and gracious ‹ O merciful
      is full   You.   sinned   One,

רַחֵם עָלַי וְקַבֵּל תַּחֲנוּנָי.

《 my ‹ and ‹ on me ‹ have
supplications. accept   mercy

— *Psalms 6:2-11 / תהלים ו:ב-יא* —

יהוה, אַל בְּאַפְּךָ תוֹכִיחֵנִי, וְאַל בַּחֲמָתְךָ תְיַסְּרֵנִי.

《chastise me. ‹ in Your wrath ‹ nor ‹ rebuke me, ‹in Your anger ‹ do not ‹ HASHEM,

חָנֵּנִי יהוה כִּי אֻמְלַל אָנִי, רְפָאֵנִי יהוה כִּי נִבְהֲלוּ

‹ shudder ‹ for ‹ HASHEM, ‹ heal me, 《 am I; ‹ feeble ‹ for ‹ HASHEM, ‹ Favor
with terror   me,

עֲצָמָי. וְנַפְשִׁי נִבְהֲלָה מְאֹד, וְאַתָּה יהוה עַד מָתָי.

《when?‹ until ‹ HASHEM, ‹ and You, 《 utterly, ‹ is terrified ‹ My soul 《 do my
                                           bones.

שׁוּבָה יהוה חַלְּצָה נַפְשִׁי, הוֹשִׁיעֵנִי לְמַעַן חַסְדֶּךָ.

《 Your ‹ as befits ‹ save me 《 my soul; ‹ release ‹ HASHEM, ‹ Desist,
kindness.

כִּי אֵין בַּמָּוֶת זִכְרֶךָ, בִּשְׁאוֹל מִי יוֹדֶה לָּךְ. יָגַעְתִּי

‹ I am 《 You? ‹ will ‹ who ‹ in the 《 is there men-‹ in ‹ not ‹ For
wearied   praise   grave   tion of You;   death

---

(1) *II Samuel* 24:14.

בְּאַנְחָתִי, אַשְׂחֶה בְכָל לַיְלָה מִטָּתִי, בְּדִמְעָתִי
⟨ with my tears ⟨ my bed; ⟨ night ⟨ every ⟨ I drench ⟨ with my sigh;

עַרְשִׂי אַמְסֶה. עָשְׁשָׁה מִכַּעַס עֵינִי, עָתְקָה בְּכָל
⟨ by all ⟨ aged ⟨ is my eye, ⟨ because of anger ⟨ Dimmed ⟨ I soak. ⟨ my couch

צוֹרְרָי. סְוּרוּ מִמֶּנִּי כָּל פֹּעֲלֵי אָוֶן, כִּי שָׁמַע יהוה
⟨ HASHEM has heard ⟨ for ⟨ of evil, ⟨ doers ⟨ all ⟨ from me, ⟨ Depart ⟨ my tormentors.

קוֹל בִּכְיִי. שָׁמַע יהוה תְּחִנָּתִי, יהוה תְּפִלָּתִי יִקָּח.
⟨ will accept. ⟨ my prayer ⟨ HASHEM ⟨ my plea, ⟨ HASHEM has heard ⟨ of my weeping. ⟨ the sound

יֵבֹשׁוּ וְיִבָּהֲלוּ מְאֹד כָּל אֹיְבָי, יָשֻׁבוּ יֵבֹשׁוּ רָגַע.
⟨ in an instant. ⟨ and be shamed ⟨ may they regret ⟨ my enemies; ⟨ all ⟨ utterly, ⟨ and confounded ⟨ Let them be shamed

מַחֵי וּמַסֵּי מֵמִית וּמְחַיֶּה, מַסִּיק מִן שְׁאוֹל
⟨ the grave ⟨ from ⟨ Who raises [the dead] ⟨ and Who restores life, ⟨ Who causes death ⟨ and Who heals, ⟨ [O God,] Who wounds

לְחַיֵּי עָלְמָא, בְּרָא כַּד חָטֵי אֲבוּהִי לַקְיֵהּ, אֲבוּהִי
⟨ but a father ⟨ would strike him, ⟨ his father ⟨ sin, ⟨ should he ⟨ A son ⟨ eternal: ⟨ to life

דְּחַיֵּס אַסֵּי לִכְאָבֵהּ. עַבְדָּא דְמָרִיד נָפִיק בְּקוֹלָר,
⟨ in chains, ⟨ he is led out ⟨ who rebels, ⟨ A slave ⟨ his [son's] pain. ⟨ will heal ⟨ who is compassionate

מָרֵהּ תָּאִיב וְתַבִּיר קוֹלָרֵהּ.
⟨ his chains. ⟨ he breaks ⟨ desires, ⟨ but [if] his master

בְּרָךְ בְּכְרָךְ אֲנָן וְחָטִינָן קַמָּךְ, הָא רָוֵי נַפְשִׁין בְּגִידִין
⟨ with wormwood ⟨ has our soul been ⟨ satiated ⟨ indeed ⟨ before You; ⟨ and we have sinned ⟨ we ⟨ Your firstborn, ⟨ Your son,

מְרָרִין, עַבְדָּךְ אֲנָן וּמְרוֹדִינָן קַמָּךְ, הָא בְּבִזְּתָא, הָא
⟨ some looting, ⟨ from [indeed we have suffered,] some ⟨ before You; ⟨ and we have rebelled ⟨ we are ⟨ Your servants ⟨ that is bitter.

בְּשִׁבְיָא, הָא בְּמַלְקִיּוּתָא. בְּמָטוּ מִנָּךְ בְּרַחֲמָךְ דִּנְפִישִׁין,
⟨ that is abundant, ⟨ in Your compassion ⟨ of You, ⟨ We beg ⟨ by the lash. ⟨ and some ⟨ in captivity,

אַסֵּי לִכְאָבִין דִּתְקוֹף עֲלָן, עַד דְּלָא נֶהֱוֵי גְמִירָא בְּשִׁבְיָא.
⟨ in captivity. ⟨ completely annihilated ⟨ we are not ⟨ while yet ⟨ us, ⟨ that have overwhelmed ⟨ the pains ⟨ heal

סליחה מא / SELICHAH 41
(תחנה)

ALL:

תְּפִלָּה תִּקַּח* תְּחִנָּה תִבְחַר,

⟨ select ⟨ and [our] ⟨ accept,* ⟨ [Our]
supplication prayer

תְּמוּר נִיחֹחַ תָּמִיד הַשַּׁחַר.

« of the ⟨ of the ⟨ the ⟨ in place
morning. continual- satisfying of
offering aroma

שְׁקֹל לָעוֹמְדִים שִׁמְךָ לְשַׁבֵּחַ, כְּאִלּוּ זָכוּ תְּרֹם מִזְבֵּחַ.[1]

« [from] ⟨ of ⟨ they had ⟨ as if « to praise, ⟨ Your ⟨ those who ⟨ Consider
the Altar. lifting up won the Name stand forth
[the ashes] privilege

רְצֵה עֲבוֹדָתָם בְּמִקְדַּשׁ שְׁבִיתָם,

« in Captivity, ⟨ in their ⟨ their service ⟨ Be favor-
Temple [of prayer] able to

---

(1) See *Tamid* 1:2,4.

∞§ **תְּפִלָּה תִּקַּח** — *[Our] prayer accept.*
Beginning on Erev Rosh Hashanah and
continuing until the day before Erev Yom
Kippur, a *piyut* is added just after the recital of *Tachanun*. Because of its juxtaposition with *Tachanun*, this type of *selichah*
is called a תְּחִנָּה, *techinah*.

R' Meir bar R' Yitzchak (often called
R' Meir *Sheliach Tzibbur*) of mid-11th-
century Germany was a great Torah
scholar often quoted by Rashi and his students. He composed forty-nine *piyutim*,
forty in Hebrew and nine in Aramaic, of
which about fifteen are extant. His most
celebrated work is *Akdamus*, an awesome
exultation of the Torah, God, and Israel,
recited on Shavuos. Tradition records that
R' Meir's compositions were so beautiful and inspiring that angels would sing
them before the Throne of Glory, as if they
themselves had written them.

The daily Temple service began with
the preparations for and offering of the
morning *tamid* or continual-offering.
Likewise, the Altar offering that completed each day's Temple service was the after-

noon *tamid*. One Talmudic tractate, aptly
named *Tamid*, delineates the various ceremonies, rites, and procedures involved in
the bringing of these two daily offerings.

R' Meir *Sheliach Tzibbur*, in fifty-four
pithy lines, captures the essence of the
service. And he pleads with God to accept
our prayers as if we were performing the
Temple and Altar services being described.

Because of the nature of this *selichah*, a knowledge of Tractate *Tamid*
is required, and a full commentary on
this *selichah* would require an exhaus-
tive commentary on the *mishnayos* of
Tractate *Tamid*, an endeavor not within
the purview of this work. Therefore, the
commentary will be limited to points
about which even the student of *Tamid*
will need clarification. (Unless otherwise indicated, the footnotes refer to the
mishnayos, not *gemara*, of Tractate
Tamid.)

The acrostic forms a reverse *aleph-beis*
מֵאִיר בְּרַבִּי יִצְחָק חֲזַק (תשר״ק) followed by
וֶאֱמָץ, *Meir bar R' Yitzchak, may he be
strong and persevere.*

כִּבְבֵית עוֹלָמִים לְעוֹשֵׂי חֲבִיתָם.*¹

» of their ‹ to the ‹ Eternal ‹ as [You are]
chavittin.*   makers   in the Temple

קְשֹׁב מִקְרָאוֹת וְחִנּוּן סְדָרִים,*

» that was ‹ and their ‹ to [their] ‹ Be
structured,* supplication reading of verses attentive

כְּעֵין אֲבָרִים וְעִכּוּל פְּדָרִים.²

» fats [on the ‹ and the [not ‹ to the ‹ similar to [Your
Altar pyre]. yet] consumed limbs   attention]

צָרֵף שָׁטוּחַ* פְּנֵי טָפוּחַ, כְּמַעֲלֶה אֵפֶר עַל גַּב תַּפּוּחַ.²

» of a mound ‹ top ‹ on ‹ of ‹ as if to the ‹ Heaven, ‹ before ‹ spread ‹ Combine
[on the Altar].   ashes   heaping   out*   [our hands],

פְּאַת קָדִימָה פְּנֵיהֶם יִזְרָח,

» shine, ‹ let their ‹ of east ‹ In the
faces   [as they pray] direction

כְּסוֹדְרֵי חָזִית כְּלַפֵּי מִזְרָח.³

» east. ‹ facing ‹ the pyre with ‹ as for those
an opening who arranged
[to kindle it]

עֲרֹב מַחְבֶּרֶת לִמְדוֹת עֲרוּכוֹת,*

» in their order ‹ with the ‹ may [our] ‹ Pleasant
[be],*   [Thirteen] combining [unto You]
Attributes [prayer]

---

(1) See Tamid 1:3. (2) 1:5. (3) See Tamid 2:4.

חֲבִיתָם — *Their chavittin.* The *chavittin*-offering consisted of one-tenth *ephah* of fine wheat flour that was kneaded with boiling water, shaped into twelve loaves, and baked in an oven. Then the loaves were fried in olive oil in a pan called a מַחֲבַת, hence their name חֲבִיתִין, *chavittin.*

The Torah ordains that the *Kohen Gadol* bring this offering each day — half of it with the morning *tamid*, half with the afternoon *tamid* (*Leviticus* 6:12-16). The Talmud derives from these verses that the ordinary *Kohen* must also bring a *chavittin*-offering. But, unlike the *Kohen Gadol*, the ordinary *Kohen* brings it only once in his lifetime — the very first day he participates in the Temple service (*Menachos* 51b).

The *chavittin* makers are mentioned because they were the first Temple functionaries to begin their morning preparations (see *Tamid* 1:3).

מִקְרָאוֹת וְחִנּוּן סְדָרִים — *[Their] reading of verses and their supplication that was structured.* This refers to the Scriptural verses and *selichah* prayers recited in the *Selichos* service (*Pardes*). Or, "verses" alludes to the recital of *Shema* and "supplication" means *Tachanun* (*Masbir*). Alternatively: they refer to *Shema* and *Shemoneh Esrei* (*Matteh Levi*).

צָרֵף שָׁטוּחַ — *Combine [our hands], spread out,* our hands that are spread to the heavens in prayer (*Pardes*). Or, we who are prostrated in prayer (*Masbir*). According to *Arugas HaBosem*, the last word of this stich is תָּפוּחַ, *bloated.* The line then refers to the *chazzan* whose face is contorted in anguish, *spread out and bloated* from torment.

מַחְבֶּרֶת לִמְדוֹת עֲרוּכוֹת — *[Our] combining [prayer] with the [Thirteen] Attributes*

כִּשֵׁרֶת כָּשֵׁר שְׁתֵּי מַעֲרָכוֹת.1

《 Altar pyres. 〈 [arranging] 〈 of the 〈 as
the two worthy [Kohen] service

סְפֹר לִצְעָדִים לְעָבְדְּךָ גָשִׁים,*

《 approach 〈 of those who 〈 the steps 〈 Count
[in prayer],* to serve You

כְּמוֹ בָּעֲזָרָה לְפַיֵּס רוֹגְשִׁים.2

《 thronged. 〈 for those who for 〈 in the 〈 as
the lot-casting Temple Court [You did]

נָכוֹן הַשַּׁחַר וְכוֹכָבִים בְּרָן,

《 [and Israel already] 〈 and the stars 〈 is the dawn, 〈 When
sings [to You], [are yet visible] ready

בָּרַק הַשַּׁחַר זְכוּת שֶׁבְּחֶבְרוֹן.3

《 [of the Patriarchs 〈 [recalling] 〈 did the dawn 〈 flash
buried] in Hebron. the merit [until Hebron]

מְמֻנֶּה מִזֵרֵז* לְהָבִיא טָלֶה,

〈 a lamb 〈 to have 〈 hurried* 〈 The supervis-
brought ing [Kohen]

מִלִּשְׁכַּת טְלָאִים בְּבִקּוּר מוּפְלָא.4

《 with great 〈 [where it had 〈 of Lambs, 〈 from the
care. been] inspected Chamber

לְכוֹס שֶׁל זָהָב יִשְׁלַח לְהַשְׁקוֹת,

《 to be given to drink, 〈 it was sent 〈 gold 〈 of 〈 To a cup

בְּבַקְּרוֹ שֵׁנִית לְאוֹר הָאֲבוּקוֹת.5

《 of the torches. 〈 by the light 〈 again 〈 then it was
inspected

---

(1) See *Tamid* 2:5. (2) 3:1. (3) 3:2. (4) 3:3. (5) 3:4.

---

in their order [be]. The translation follows *Arugas HaBosem* and *Pardes;* the stich refers to the joining of our blessings, prayers, and supplications with our recital of the Thirteen Attributes. According to *Masbir,* it is Israel that is joining to the Thirteen Attributes. Alternatively: the word מִדּוֹת, lit., *measures,* alludes to footsteps, and by extension, to feet in general. The stich then refers to our feet, joined together while we recite the *Shemoneh Esrei* (*Matteh Levi*).

סְפֹר לִצְעָדִים לְעָבְדְּךָ גָשִׁים — *Count the steps of those who to serve You approach [in*

prayer]. According to *Matteh Levi* (see above), this would refer to the three steps back and three steps forward taken at the beginning of *Shemoneh Esrei.* According to the others, it alludes to שְׂכַר הֲלִיכָה, *the reward for going* to do a *mitzvah* (see *Avos* 5:17), which is given over and above the *mitzvah's* own reward.

מְמֻנֶּה מִזֵרֵז — *The supervising [Kohen] hurried.* From this point until near the end of the *selichah,* the *paytan* no longer compares our synagogue service with the Altar service. Rather, he continues to recount the *tamid* service in all its detail.

בִּזְכָה בְּתָמִיד וְזָכָה אֶחָיו,

《 to [twelve] 〈 and extends 〈 to offer 〈 He who won
colleagues the privilege the *tamid* the privilege

מְשָׁכוּ וְהוֹלֵךְ לְבֵית מִטְבָּחָיו.[1]

《 of slaughtering. 〈 to the place 〈 and go 〈 would lead it

יְדֵי שְׁחִיטָתוֹ זְבֹחַ יַחְדֹּל, עֲדֵי יִפְתַּח הַשַּׁעַר הַגָּדוֹל.[2]

《 that was 〈 the Gate 〈 would be 〈 until 《 he would 〈 to 〈 of slaugh- 《 As to the re-
Great. opened refrain, slaughter tering it — quirement

טָרַד עַד שֶׁחִי פָתוֹחַ כֵּיוָן,

《 [the second 〈 to open 〈 his 〈 up 〈 He had
opened] easily, [the first gate] armpit to to strain

שְׁתֵּי מַפְתְּחוֹת לְפָתְחוֹ כִּוֵּן.[3]

《 he had 〈 [needed] 〈 keys 〈 the
in mind. to open it two

חֲרָצָיו* בְּגַלְגְּלוֹ וְצִירֵי* צְרִיחוֹ,

《 shrieked; 〈 the hinge 〈 as he rotated 〈 In its hinge
pegs* [the door] sockets*

וְנִשְׁמַע קוֹלוֹ בְּבִקְעַת יְרִיחוֹ.[4]

《 of Jericho. 〈 in the valley 〈 was the 〈 heard
sound of it

זְרִיזִים זְהִירִים עֲקֵדָה לִגְמֹר,

《 to 〈 the binding 〈 are 〈 The [Kohanim]
complete, [of the animal] careful who act
with alacrity

בְּיָד וְרֶגֶל[5] כְּיִצְחָק בְּהַר מוֹר.[6]

《 Moriah. 〈 on Mount 〈 like Isaac 〈 to hind leg, 〈 foreleg

וְזָכוּ שְׁנִיוֹת* שְׁחִיטָה לְשַׁמֵּשׁ,

《 to serve, 〈 for the 《 — the second 《 They
slaughtering [slaughtering- merited
rings]* —

שַׁחַר וָאֶמֶשׁ לְמוּל הַשֶּׁמֶשׁ.[5]*

《 the sun.* 〈 facing 〈 and evening, 〈 morning

---

(1) See *Tamid* 3:5. (2) 3:7. (3) 3:6. (4) 3:8. (5) 4:1. (6) Talmud *Tamid* 31b.

צִירֵי ... חֲרָצָיו — *In its hinge sockets ... the hinge pegs.* The hinges on the Temple doors did not connect them to the doorposts as do the hinges we usually see today. The צִירִים were two *pegs* or *spikes* set into the bottom

and top surfaces of the door. They fit into חֲרָצִים, *sockets*, in the doorway, one under the door in the threshold, and the other above the door in the lintel.

הַשֶּׁמֶשׁ לְמוּל ... שְׁנִיוֹת — *The second*

הֲרָמַת שְׁתַּיִם לְאַרְבַּע יִתְרֹם,*

《 placement,* 〈 as a 〈 twice, 〈 Then placing
       four-sided   [the blood]

לְמִזְרָח צָפוֹן לְמַעֲרָב דָּרוֹם.[1]

《 south 〈 and the 〈 north 〈 on the east-
  [corner].   west-   [corner]
            [corner]

דְּמֵי שִׁירַיִם יְסוֹד הַדָּרוֹם,[1]

《 on the 〈 onto the 〈 remaining 〈 The
  south,   [Altar's] base [was poured] blood

וְטָעוּן הֶפְשֵׁט וְכָלִיל לַמָּרוֹם.[2]

《 for the sake 〈 and burnt 〈 being 〈 then [the
of Heaven.   entirely   skinned   sacrifice]
                 required

גְּלַל הַנְּתִיחָה מְרֻבָּה בְדִבּוּר,[3]

《 to tell, 〈 is so long 〈 cutting up 〈 But
      the limbs   since

שְׁתִיקָה יָפָה וְאֵימַת צִבּוּר.

《 for the 〈 out of 〈 is 〈 silence
congregation. respect   better

בְּתִשְׁעָה קָרֵב בְּצֵרוּף זוֹכִים,

〈 those privileged 〈 together 〈 it was brought 〈 By nine
   [to bear]   with   [to the Altar], [Kohanim]

חֲבִתִּים וְסֹלֶת וְיֵין הַנְּסָכִים.[4]

《 of the 〈 and 〈 the fine- 〈 the chavittin,
  libation. the wine   flour-
           offering

אֲזַי יַם הַכֶּבֶשׁ מְלָחוּם וּבָאוּ,

〈 and 〈 they salted 〈 of the 〈 at the 〈 Then
came   [the limbs]   Altar ramp   west
                [upper half]

---

(1) Talmud Tamid 31b. (2) See Tamid 4:2-3. (3) See Zevachim 5:4. (4) See Tamid 4:2-3.

[slaughtering-rings] ... facing the sun. The Talmud (*Tamid* 31b) derives from Scriptural verses that the slaughter of the *tamid* had to be done by the light of the sun. Thus, although the usual slaughter of every burnt-offering could take place anywhere in the northern half of the Temple Courtyard, the *tamid* (which was a burnt-offering) could only be slaughtered in an area that received direct sunlight. But since the Altar was ten *amos* tall (15-20 feet), it cast a shadow on its northern side that sometimes reached until the second of six rows of slaughtering-rings (about ten *amos* from the Altar). Consequently, that was the nearest spot to the Altar that the *tamid* could be slaughtered.

הֲרָמַת שְׁתַּיִם לְאַרְבַּע יִתְרֹם — *Then placing [the blood] twice, as a four-sided placement.* Immediately after slaughter, the blood

בְּלִשְׁכַּת גָּזִית שְׁמַע יִקְרָאוּ.¹

《 to recite. 〈 the 〈 of Hewn 〈 to the
Shema Stone Chamber

מְבָרְכִים בְּמִנּוּי בְּרָכָה אַחַת,

《 one blessing 〈 at the command 〈 They
[before Shema], of the recited
supervising Kohen

עֲשֶׂרֶת הַדִּבְּרוֹת וּמוֹסִיף בְּנַחַת.²

〈 on the Day 〈 and would 〈 Commandments, 〈 then
of Rest, add an extra the Ten
blessing

אֱמֶת וַעֲבוֹדָה וּבִרְכַּת כֹּהֲנִים,

〈 of the Priests 〈 and the 〈 Service 〈 [the bless-
[and Sim Shalom]; Blessing [Retzei], ings] Emes
[veyatziv],

יְבָרְכוּ הָעָם² בְּרָכָה נֶהֱנִים.

《 be 〈 that the 〈 the 〈 they
beneficial. blessing people, blessed

יִבְרְרוּ חֲדָשִׁים לְפַיֵּס קְטֹרֶת,³

《 for the 〈 to draw 〈 new 〈 They chose
incense, a lot [Kohanim]

וְלֹא שָׁנוּ בָהּ וְהִיא מְעַשֶּׁרֶת.⁴

brings wealth [to the 〈 for it 〈 it, 〈 repeat 〈 a [Kohen]
Kohen offering it]. could not

רְבִיעִי פַּיִס בְּיַחַד נִקְבָּע,

《 was 〈 for all 〈 lot 〈 The
established, [Kohanim] cast fourth

נִתָּחִים לְהַעֲלוֹת לְגַב הַמְּרֻבָּע.³

《 the square 〈 on top 〈 [to determine] 〈 the limbs
[Altar]. of who would
bring up

בְּקוֹל מַגְרֵפָה מַרְבִּים זְמָרִים,⁵

《 songs, 〈 were 〈 of the 〈 With the
produced many magreifah, sound

---

(1) See *Tamid* 4:3. (2) 5:1. (3) 5:2. (4) See *Yoma* 26a. (5) See *Tamid* 5:6.

of the *tamid* was caught by a *Kohen* in a sacred utensil and dashed on the northeast and southwest corners of the Altar. Blood thrown at one corner would spread out to the two adjacent sides, so there would be some blood on each of the Altar's four sides. Thus, the twice-thrown blood counted as four applications.

וְקוֹלָהּ נִשְׁמַע בָּעִיר הַתְּמָרִים.[1]

« of Date-Palms. ‹ in [Jericho,] ‹ was heard ‹ its sound the City

רְגִילִים לְקוֹלָהּ לְוִים וְכֹהֲנִים,

« and the ‹ the ‹ that at its ‹ Trained Kohanim, Leviim sound

לָשִׁיר וּלְהִשְׁתַּחֲוָיָה הֱיוֹת מְזֻמָּנִים.[2]

« would be ready. ‹ and prostrating ‹ for song themselves

בְּמַעֲלוֹת אוּלָם עָלוֹת בִּמְרוּצָה,

« running ‹ he ‹ of the ‹ Then up the ascended, Sanctuary stairs

מְדַשֵּׁן פְּנִימִי טֶנִי נָטַל וְיָצָא.[3]

« and left. ‹ he ‹ the « from ‹ — the [Kohen] took basket the Inner who was to re- [of ashes] [Altar] move the ashes

יְדַשֵּׁן מְנוֹרָה וְכָבָה יַעַרְכוֹ, וְהַכּוּז נָטַל וְנָחַץ לְדַרְכּוֹ.[3]

« on his ‹ and ‹ the ‹ the urn « it was ‹ and if [its ‹ was the ‹ Cleaned way. hurried [Kohen] [holding rekindled; western Menorah, took ash and lamp] had wicks] gone out

יְרַדֵּד זוֹכֶה בְּשׁוּלֵי מַחְתָּה,

‹ of the ‹ with the « — the [Kohen] « He fire-pan bottom privileged would [to bring the smooth coals] — out

לְגַחֲלֵי הָאֵשׁ וְשָׁחָה וְאָתָה.[4]

« and came ‹ then he pros- « that were ‹ the coals out. trated himself, glowing,

צָבוּר הַקְּטֹרֶת פְּנִימָה חוּץ לוֹ,

« from ‹ away « on the inner ‹ the ‹ To pile him, side [of the Altar], incense

מְלַמְּדִין מַקְטִיר בְּלִי כַּוֵּות אֲצִילוֹ.[5]

« his arm. ‹ burning ‹ [on placing ‹ the one ‹ they would the incense] offering instruct without the incense

חֲרֵדִים לִפְרשׁ בְּעֵת הַקְטָרָה,[5]

« [the incense] ‹ at the ‹ to exit ‹ They was burned; time [the Sanctuary] hastened

_____

(1) See *Tamid* 3:8. (2) 5:6. (3) 6:1. (4) See 6:2. (5) 6:3.

חֲשָׁאִי כַּפָּרָה לְחֵץ מַטָרָה.¹

《 shot at 〈 for the 〈 is the 〈 in
the target. [tongue's] atonement seclusion
arrows

קְבוּעוֹת הָיוּ לְמוּל הַפְּרָצוֹת,

《 the breaches 〈— opposite 《 were 〈 Established
[in the *soreig* wall] —

בְּהִשְׁתַּחֲוָיוֹת* *² לְאֵל חַי לִרְצוֹת.

《 with which 《 Who is 〈 to God 〈 prostrations*
to find favor. Living,

חֲגוּרֵי חֶרֶב* כְּתָב* וְלֹא בִכְנוּי,

《 in its 〈 and 〈 [they 《 with 〈 Girded
alternative not pronounced [blessing
pronunciation, the Name] as with]
as it is written* a sword,

מְבָרְכִין אַחַת וְעַל רֹאשׁ* מָנוּי.³

《 as they were 〈 [their] 〈 [their hands] 《 as 〈 they pronounced
commanded. head* raised over one, the [triple] blessing

---

(1) See *Yoma* 44a; *Jeremiah* 9:7. (2) See *Middos* 2:3; *Yerushalmi, Shekalim* 6:2. (3) See *Tamid* 7:2.

קְבוּעוֹת הָיוּ לְמוּל הַפְּרָצוֹת בְּהִשְׁתַּחֲוָיוֹת — *Established were — opposite the breaches [in the soreig wall] — prostrations.* At a distance of ten cubits outside the walls of the Temple Courtyard stood a low (ten handbreadths, about 30-40 inches) latticework fence called the סוֹרֵג, *soreig*. It served to demarcate the point past which neither non-Jews nor Jews contaminated by contact with a corpse were permitted entry. When the Greeks conquered the Temple compound, they showed their defiance by punching thirteen holes in the *soreig*, symbolically removing the ban. When the Hasmoneans regained control of the Temple, they mended the breaches and enacted that at each breach one must stop and prostrate himself (*Tamid* 2:3; *Yerushalmi Shekalim* 6:2).

[The insertion of these stiches here is strange. Although the Mishnah does mention that the *Kohanim* prostrated themselves before leaving the *Beis HaMikdash* when they concluded their respective duties inside, no mention is made of the prostrations at the *soreig*, which was not even within the courtyard! Perhaps the *paytan* understood the enactment in the following manner: Every time one was required to prostrate himself in the Temple, he had to make thirteen prostrations, corresponding to the breaches.]

Alternatively: The stich is translated, *[the aforementioned services were] necessary to oppose* [rectify] *the* [sinful] *breaches* [of the people] (see *Rashi* to Ezekiel 13:5), [and were accompanied] *by prostrations with which to find favor* [atonement] *before the Living God.* Both interpretations of this stich are cited in *Pardes.*

חֲגוּרֵי חֶרֶב — *Girded with [blessing as with] a sword.* Behold the couch [the Holy Temple] *of the King of peace, sixty warriors round about it . . . all gripping the sword . . .* (*Song of Songs* 3:7-8). According to the Midrash, this verse alludes to the Priestly Blessing: the *sixty warriors* are the sixty letters contained in the Blessing; *the sword* alludes to God's Name within the Blessing, for the Sages proclaimed that any blessing containing God's Name is like a sword that cuts through all obstacles.

The *paytan* therefore refers to the *Kohanim* who pronounced the Priestly Blessing as *girded as with a sword.*

כְּתָב ... וְעַל רֹאשׁ — *As it is written . . . raised over [their] head.* The bestowal of the

זְמַן הַגָּדוֹל לְחֶלְקוֹ כוֹבֵשׁ,

At the time when ⟨ the [Kohen] ⟨ as his ⟨ took over « [the daily tasks], prerogative Gadol

סֶגֶן מִימִינוֹ עֲלוֹת בַּכֶּבֶשׁ.[1]

the Deputy ⟩ at his ⟨ up ⟨ the [Altar] « [would go] right ramp.

קְרֵבִים אֶצְלוֹ וְלוֹ מַגִּישִׁים,

The ⟨ near to ⟨ and to ⟨ they would « [nine priests] him him hand would come

נְתָחִים לִסְמֹךְ זְרַק לָאִשִּׁים.[1]

the pieces ⟨ upon which ⟨ then ⟨ into the fire. « to lay his hand, throw

וְאָז בַּשִּׁיתִין נְסָכִים סִדֵּר, וְסֶגֶן עוֹמֵד וּמֵנִיף בַּסּוּדָר.[1]

Then ⟨ into the ⟨ the [wine] ⟨ he ⟨ while ⟨ stood ⟨ and sig- ⟨ with «
channels libation poured, the naled [to a cloth.
[in the Altar] Deputy the Levites]

מַחְצְרִים בָּאִים עָמַד לוֹ אֵצֶל

Trumpeters ⟨ came ⟨ and ⟨ them- ⟨ next «
stood selves to

(בֶּן אַרְזָא) צְרָדָה מַקִּישׁ לְשֶׁמַע צִלְצֵל.[1]

(Ben Arza), ⟨ who with his ⟨ would « to sound ⟨ the cymbal. «
snapping strike,
[middle] finger

לְוִים דִּבְּרוּ בְּשִׁיר הַחֲוָיָה, לְפֶרֶק תְּקִיעָה וְהִשְׁתַּחֲוָיָה.[1]

The ⟨ sang ⟨ with ⟨ conveying « after each ⟨ trumpeting ⟨ and prostration. «
Levites out song [praise], section,

וְזֶה סֵדֶר עֲבוֹדַת תָּמִיד,

This ⟨ was the ⟨ of the ⟨ of the continual- ⟨
order service offering

בְּבֵית אֱלֹהֵינוּ מְהֵרָה לְהַעֲמִיד.[1]

in the House ⟨ of our God, « may it soon ⟨ be reestablished. «

---

(1) See *Tamid* 7:3.

Priestly Blessings in three ways differed in the Temple from its bestowal in the synagogue: (a) In the synagogue the Tetragrammaton (Four-Letter Divine Name) is pronounced as if it were spelled אֲדֹנָי, but in the *Beis HaMikdash* it was pronounced as it is written; (b) in the synagogue it is recited as three verses, with the congregation responding אָמֵן, *Amen*, after each verse, but in the Temple it was recited as one long sentence; and (c) in the synagogue the *Kohanim* raise their hands to shoulder level, but in the *Beis HaMikdash* above their heads (*Tamid* 7:2). The *paytan* records all three differences.

תָּמִיד הַבְּקֶר יְשֻׁלַּם בְּסִפּוּר,[1]

《 by being retold, 〈 be fulfilled 〈 of the morning 〈 May the continual-offering

וּלְעוֹלָם זֹאת עַל יְשֻׁרוּן כִּפּוּר.

《 an atonement. 〈 Jeshurun 〈 for 〈 may this be 〈 and forever

כְּסִדְרוֹ בַּמִּנְחָה וְנֶסֶךְ קָרֵב, עֵסַק בַּשֵּׁנִי לְעִתּוֹת עָרֶב.

《 of evening; 〈 toward the time 〈 for a second time 〈 they were involved 《 it was brought, 〈 and libation 〈 with the flour-offering 〈 According to the same order,

בְּאֶחָד עָשָׂר זְכוּת בּוֹ מְחֻזָּרִים,

《 [was] repeated, 〈 to do it 〈 the privilege 〈 [except that] on eleven [priests]

שְׁנַיִם בְּיָדָם שְׁנֵי גְזִירִים.[2]

《 logs [of wood]. 〈 two 〈 held in their hands 〈 two [additional]

כְּבָשִׂים כֹּבְשִׁים עֲוֹנוֹת מְכַבְּסִים,

《 washed away, 〈 and iniquity [our sins] 〈 overpowered 〈 [The *tamid*] lambs

כְּתִינוֹק בֶּן שְׁנָתוֹ* סְגֻלָּה עוֹשִׂים.

《 are transformed. 〈 the treasured [people] 〈 first year* 〈 within its 〈 into a [blemish-free] child

---

(1) Cf. *Hosea* 14:3. (2) See *Yoma* 2:5.

כְּבָשִׂים ... כְּתִינוֹק בֶּן שְׁנָתוֹ — *[The tamid] lambs ... into a [blemish-free] child within its first year.* God assigned Adam the task of naming the animals He had created, *and whatever Adam called each living being, that is its [proper] name* (*Genesis* 2:19). The Midrash states that this task was so complicated that even the ministering angels were unable to do it, and thus had to concede Adam's superior intelligence (*Bereishis Rabbah* 17:4). It follows from the Midrash that choosing a name is not merely coining a new set of syllables. The name must imply the nature of its object. Thus, every noun in the Holy Tongue, including those assigned by Adam to the various animals, contains within it the essence of the object named.

The *tamid*-offering comprised כְּבָשִׂים שְׁנַיִם ... בְּנֵי שָׁנָה — *two lambs in their first year* (*Numbers* 28:3), and the Sages seek an interpretation of the name כְּבָשִׂים, *lambs*, and its relationship to sacrificial atonement. The Midrash cites three opinions: Beis Shammai, reading the word as if it were spelled כֹּבְשִׁים, cognate with כּוֹבֵשׁ, *conquerer*, interprets *they overpower Israel's iniquities* (see *Micah* 7:19); Beis Hillel, reading the word as if it were spelled כְּבָסִים, as in כּוֹבֵס, *launderer*, understands that the lambs *wash away Israel's iniquities* (see *Isaiah* 1:18); Ben Azzai agrees with Beis Hillel, but adds that כְּבָשִׂים בְּנֵי שָׁנָה means *they wash away Israel's iniquities so that the nation remains as sin-free as a year-old baby* (*Pesikta Rabbasi* 16). The *paytan* includes all three opinions in this stich.

פְּרַקְלִיט סַנֵּגוֹר בְּצֶדֶק לְלוֹנָנָה,*¹

《 they could lie 〈 so that in 〈and defender〈 [They were]
down [at night],* righteousness [for Israel] advocate

בְּעִיר אֱלֹהֵינוּ אֱלֹהִים יְכוֹנְנָהּ.

《reestablish it. 〈 may God 〈 of our God, 〈 in the City

דֳּמִי אַל תִּתְּנוּ² מַמְנִּים שֹׁמְרִים,³

《 as watchmen [over 〈 you [angels]《 give 〈 do 〈 Quiet
Jerusalem's walls], appointed yourselves, not

וְאַתָּה תָקוּם תְּרַחֵם⁴ אוֹמְרִים.

《 [you shall] 《 and show 〈 will arise 〈 and You
proclaim. mercy [to Zion]! [God]

יְרוּשָׁלַיִם בְּנוּיַת עֶרֶץ, יְכוֹנֵן וְיָשִׂים לְשֵׁם בָּאָרֶץ.³

《 in the 〈 a source 〈 and 〈 may He 〈with fortress-〈[formerly] 〈 Jerusalem,
Land. of praise make it reestablish like strength, built

וְיַעֲמֹד הַמִּמְשָׁל* הַשַּׂר הַגָּדוֹל,

《 who is 〈 the [angelic] 〈 dominion,* 〈 May there
great, prince [Michael] stand

בְּעַד בְּנֵי עַמּוֹ לַחַנֵּן רַע מֵחֲדַל.

《 may cease [from 〈 that 〈 to plead 〈 of his 〈 of the 〈 on
among them]. evil people children behalf

תְּחִנַּת שַׁוְעָם לְהַכְתִּיר תֶּעֱרַב,

《 be found 〈 to be made into a 〈 outcry 〈 May their
pleasant, crown [for God] pleading

לְמִזְבֵּחַ מַעֲלָה כְּכָלִיל יִקְרַב.

《 may it 〈 as a completely 〈 of 〈 on the Altar
be offered. consumed offering Heaven

וְשַׂר הַפַּחַד* אֲחוֹרֵי הַפַּרְגּוֹד,*

《 the [heavenly] 〈 standing 《 of dread 〈 The [angel-
partition,* behind [Gabriel],* ic] prince

---

(1) Cf. Isaiah 1:21. (2) Cf. 62:7; the propriety and permissibility of addressing prayer to
an angel is discussed in the introduction to this volume. (3) Cf. 62:6. (4) Cf. Psalms 102:14.

בְּצֶדֶק לְלוֹנָנָה — So that in righteousness they
could lie down [at night]. No one in ancient
Jerusalem would ever retain his sins, for the
morning tamid would atone for the sins of
the night and the afternoon tamid would
atone for the sins of the day (Bamidbar Rabbah 21:21).

הַמִּמְשָׁל ... הַפַּחַד — Dominion [Michael] ...
dread [Gabriel]. Job's friend Bildad said to
him: הַמְשֵׁל וָפַחַד, Dominion and dread are
with Him; He brings about peace in His
heights (Job 25:2). Targum paraphrases:
Michael at His right is composed of fire;
Gabriel at His left is composed of water; in

בְּיֹשֶׁר תַּמְלִיץ וּבִזְכוּת תֶּאֱגֹד.

《 bundle ⟨ and [our] ⟨ may you ⟨ with words
together, merits advocate [for us] of justice

כְּאָז לַחֲמוּדוֹת בְּלַמְּדָךְ זְכוּת,

《 [his] ⟨ you ⟨ when for the beloved ⟨ as
merit, showed one [Daniel's] behalf then,

וְזָכִיתָ לַחֲזוֹר לְמֶמְשָׁל וּנְסִיכוּת.*

《 and ⟨ to rule ⟨ to return ⟨ and merited
princehood.* thereby

❖ בְּעַד יִשְׂרָאֵל צֶדֶק לִמְדוּ, פְּנֵי הָאָדוֹן יהוה עָמְדוּ.

《 stand, ⟨ HASHEM ⟨ the ⟨ before 《 show, ⟨ their right- ⟨ of Israel ⟨ On
Master, eousness behalf

צְדָקוֹת לְגַלְגֵּל כְּמוֹ נְחוּמִים,

《 consolation, ⟨ arousing ⟨ unroll, ⟨ and all our
good deeds

לְפָנָיו תָּבֹאוּ בְּמִדַּת הָרַחֲמִים.

《 of Mercy. ⟨ with the ⟨ come ⟨ and
Attribute before Him

ALL:

מַכְנִיסֵי רַחֲמִים, הַכְנִיסוּ רַחֲמֵינוּ, לִפְנֵי בַּעַל

⟨ the ⟨ before ⟨ our [plea for] ⟨ may you 《 [pleas for] mercy, ⟨ O you who
Master mercy usher in usher in

הָרַחֲמִים. מַשְׁמִיעֵי תְפִלָּה, הַשְׁמִיעוּ תְפִלָּתֵנוּ, לִפְנֵי

⟨ before ⟨ of our prayer ⟨ may you aid 《 of prayer, ⟨ O you who aid 《 of mercy.
the hearing the hearing

שׁוֹמֵעַ תְּפִלָּה. מַשְׁמִיעֵי צְעָקָה, הַשְׁמִיעוּ צַעֲקָתֵנוּ,

⟨ of our ⟨ may you aid 《 of outcries, ⟨ O you who aid 《 of ⟨ the Hearer
outcries the hearing the hearing prayer.

לִפְנֵי שׁוֹמֵעַ צְעָקָה. מַכְנִיסֵי דִמְעָה, הַכְנִיסוּ

⟨ may you 《 tears, ⟨ O you who 《 of outcries. ⟨ the Hearer ⟨ before
usher in usher in

His holy creation, He kneaded fire with water, and with His dominion and dread made
peace in His highest heavens.

Thus, the *paytan* refers to Michael and
Gabriel as הַמְּשָׁל and הַפַּחַד, respectively.

אֲחוֹרֵי הַפַּרְגּוֹד ... לְמֶמְשָׁל וּנְסִיכוּת — *Behind the*
[heavenly] partition ... to rule and prince-
hood. The Talmud relates that Gabriel had
been banished from his exalted position and

had been exiled behind the *heavenly par-*
tition. He was not restored to his original
status until he had interceded on behalf of
Daniel. We ask him now to do the same
for us. [The propriety and permissibility
of praying for angelic intercession or of
directing prayer through intermediaries
is discussed in the introduction to this
volume.]

דִּמְעוֹתֵינוּ, לִפְנֵי מֶלֶךְ מִתְרַצֶּה בִּדְמָעוֹת.
≪ through tears. ⟨ Who is appeased ⟨ the King ⟨ before ⟨ our tears

הִשְׁתַּדְּלוּ וְהַרְבּוּ תְּחִנָּה וּבַקָּשָׁה, לִפְנֵי מֶלֶךְ אֵל
⟨ God, ⟨ the King, ⟨ before ⟨ and pleas ⟨ supplications ⟨ and ⟨ Exert
intensify yourselves

רָם וְנִשָּׂא. הַזְכִּירוּ לְפָנָיו, הַשְׁמִיעוּ לְפָנָיו תּוֹרָה
⟨ the ⟨ before ⟨ aid to ≪ before ⟨ Mention ≪ and ⟨ exalted
Torah Him, be heard Him, uplifted.

וּמַעֲשִׂים טוֹבִים שֶׁל שׁוֹכְנֵי עָפָר.
≪ in the ⟨ [the Patriarchs ⟨ of ⟨ that are ⟨ and the deeds
dust. and Matriarchs] good
who dwell

יִזְכֹּר אַהֲבָתָם וִיחַיֶּה זַרְעָם, שֶׁלֹּא תֹאבַד שְׁאֵרִית
⟨ shall the ⟨ lost ⟨ so that ⟨ to their ⟨ and grant ⟨ their love ⟨ May He
remnant not offspring, life remember

יַעֲקֹב. כִּי צֹאן רוֹעֶה נֶאֱמָן הָיָה לְחֶרְפָּה,
≪ a disgrace; ⟨ has ⟨ who is faith- ⟨ of the ⟨ the ⟨ For ≪ of Jacob
become ful [Moses] shepherd flock be.

יִשְׂרָאֵל גּוֹי אֶחָד לְמָשָׁל וְלִשְׁנִינָה.
≪ and a simile. ⟨ a parable ≪ that is ⟨ the ≪ Israel,
unique, nation

מַהֵר עֲנֵנוּ אֱלֹהֵי יִשְׁעֵנוּ, וּפְדֵנוּ מִכָּל גְּזֵרוֹת קָשׁוֹת
≪ that are ⟨ decrees ⟨ from all ⟨ and re- ⟨ of our ⟨ O God ⟨ answer ⟨ Swiftly
harsh; deem us salvation, us,

וְהוֹשִׁיעָה בְּרַחֲמֶיךָ הָרַבִּים, מְשִׁיחַ צִדְקֶךָ וְעַמֶּךָ.
≪ and Your ⟨ Your righteous ⟨ that is ⟨ in Your mercy ≪ and may You
people. anointed one abundant, save,

מָרָן דְּבִשְׁמַיָּא לָךְ מִתְחַנְּנַן, כְּבָר שְׁבִיָּא דְּמִתְחַנַּן
⟨ who ⟨ in ⟨ as one ≪ do we ⟨ to You ≪ Who is in ⟨ Our
supplicates captivity supplicate, heaven, Master

לְשִׁבוּיֵהּ. כֻּלְּהוֹן בְּנֵי שְׁבִיָּא בְּכַסְפָּא מִתְפָּרְקִין,
≪ are redeemed, ⟨ through ⟨ in ⟨ those ⟨ [for] all ≪ before his
money captivity, captors;

וְעַמָּךְ יִשְׂרָאֵל בְּרַחֲמֵי וּבְתַחֲנוּנֵי, הַב לָן שְׁאֵילָתִין
⟨ our requests ⟨ us ⟨ O ≪ and ⟨ through ⟨ Israel ⟨ but Your
grant supplication. compassion people

וּבָעוּתִין, דְּלָא נֶהְדַּר רֵיקָם מִן קֳדָמָךְ.

《 before / 《 from 〈 empty- 〈 that we not be 〈 and our prayers
You. 　　　　　 handed 　　turned away

מָרָן דִּבִשְׁמַיָּא לָךְ מִתְחַנְּנָן, כְּעַבְדָּא דְמִתְחַנַּן

〈 who 〈 as a slave 《 do we 〈 to You 《 Who is in 〈 Our
supplicates 　　　　supplicate, 　　heaven, 　　Master

לְמָרֵיהּ, עֲשִׁיקֵי אֲנָן וּבַחֲשׁוֹכָא שָׁרֵינָן, מְרִירָן נַפְשִׁין

〈 are [our] 〈 embittered 《 do we 〈 and in darkness 〈 are 〈 Oppressed 《 to his
souls 　　　　　　　abide, 　　　　　　 we 　　　　　　　　master:

מֵעַקָּתִין דִּנְפִישִׁין, חֵילָא לֵית בָּן לְרַצּוּיָךְ. מָרָן,

〈 Our 　《 to appease 〈 within 〈 is 〈 Strength 《 that is 〈 from distress
Master, 　　　　You. 　　us 　lacking 　　　　excessive.

עֲבִיד בְּדִיל קָיָמָא דִּגְזַרְתָּ עִם אֲבָהָתָנָא.

《 our Patriarchs. 〈 with 〈 that You 〈 of the 〈 for the 〈 act
established 　covenant 　 sake

שׁוֹמֵר יִשְׂרָאֵל, שְׁמוֹר שְׁאֵרִית יִשְׂרָאֵל, וְאַל

〈 let not 《 of Israel; 〈 the remnant 〈 safeguard 《 of Israel, 〈 O Guardian

יֹאבַד יִשְׂרָאֵל, הָאֹמְרִים שְׁמַע יִשְׂרָאֵל.[1]

《 O Israel. 〈 Hear, 〈 those who 《 Israel be destroyed —
proclaim:

שׁוֹמֵר גּוֹי אֶחָד, שְׁמוֹר שְׁאֵרִית עַם אֶחָד, וְאַל

〈 let not 《 that is 〈 of the 〈 the remnant 〈 safeguard 《 that is 〈 of the 〈 O Guardian
unique; 　people 　　　　　　　　　　　 unique, 　nation

יֹאבַד גּוֹי אֶחָד, הַמְיַחֲדִים שִׁמְךָ, יהוה אֱלֹהֵינוּ

〈 is our God, 〈 HASHEM 《 of Your 〈 those who proclaim 《 that is 〈 the 〈 be
Name: 　　　the Oneness 　　　　 unique, 　nation destroyed

יהוה אֶחָד.

《 the One 〈 HASHEM
[and Only]! 　is

שׁוֹמֵר גּוֹי קָדוֹשׁ, שְׁמוֹר שְׁאֵרִית עַם קָדוֹשׁ, וְאַל

〈 let not 《 that is 〈 of the 〈 the remnant 〈 safeguard 《 that is 〈 of the 〈 O Guardian
holy; 　people 　　　　　　　　　　　 holy, 　nation

יֹאבַד גּוֹי קָדוֹשׁ, הַמְשַׁלְּשִׁים בְּשָׁלֹשׁ קְדֻשּׁוֹת לְקָדוֹשׁ.

《 to the 〈 sancti- 〈 the 〈 those who proclaim 《 that is 〈 the 〈 be
Holy One. 　fications 　threefold 　three times 　　　holy, 　nation destroyed

---

(1) *Deuteronomy* 6:4.

מִתְרַצֶּה בְּרַחֲמִים וּמִתְפַּיֵּס בְּתַחֲנוּנִים, הִתְרַצֵּה
be favorable < « through < and Who becomes < through < You Who becomes
through   supplications,   conciliatory   compassion   favorable

וְהִתְפַּיֵּס לְדוֹר עָנִי, כִּי אֵין עוֹזֵר. אָבִינוּ מַלְכֵּנוּ,
« our King, < Our « helper. < there < for « that is < to the « and be
Father,   is no   poor,   generation   conciliatory

חָנֵּנוּ וַעֲנֵנוּ, כִּי אֵין בָּנוּ מַעֲשִׂים, עֲשֵׂה עִמָּנוּ
< us < treat « worthy deeds; < we have no < though < and < be gracious
answer us,   with us

צְדָקָה וָחֶסֶד וְהוֹשִׁיעֵנוּ.
« and save us. < and kindness, < with charity

STAND AFTER THE WORDS וַאֲנַחְנוּ לֹא נֵדַע UNTIL CONCLUSION OF THE PARAGRAPH.

וַאֲנַחְנוּ לֹא נֵדַע מַה נַּעֲשֶׂה, כִּי עָלֶיךָ עֵינֵינוּ.[1]
« are our < upon < rather, « we should < what < know not <
eyes.   You   do,

זְכֹר רַחֲמֶיךָ יהוה וַחֲסָדֶיךָ, כִּי מֵעוֹלָם הֵמָּה.[2] יְהִי
< May « are they. < eternal < for < and Your < HASHEM, < Your < Remem-
kindnesses,   mercies,   ber

חַסְדְּךָ יהוה עָלֵינוּ, כַּאֲשֶׁר יִחַלְנוּ לָךְ.[3] אַל תִּזְכָּר
< recall < Do not « You. < we awaited < just as « be upon us, < HASHEM, < Your kindness,

לָנוּ עֲוֹנוֹת רִאשׁוֹנִים, מַהֵר יְקַדְּמוּנוּ רַחֲמֶיךָ, כִּי
< for « may Your < advance to < swiftly « of the ancients; < the sins < against
mercies,   meet us   us

דַלּוֹנוּ מְאֹד.[4] עֶזְרֵנוּ בְּשֵׁם יהוה, עֹשֵׂה שָׁמַיִם
< of < Maker « of HASHEM, < is through < Our help « exceed- < we have
heaven   the Name   ingly.   become
impoverished

וָאָרֶץ.[5] חָנֵּנוּ יהוה חָנֵּנוּ, כִּי רַב שָׂבַעְנוּ בוּז.[6] בְּרָגֶז
« Amid « with < sated « we are < for « favor us, < HASHEM, < Favor us, « and earth.
wrath, contempt.   fully

רַחֵם תִּזְכּוֹר.[7] בְּרָגֶז עֲקֵדָה תִּזְכּוֹר. בְּרָגֶז תְּמִימוֹת
< the perfect « Amid « You should < the binding « Amid « You should < to be
ones wrath, remember! [of Isaac] wrath, remember! merciful

תִּזְכּוֹר. יהוה הוֹשִׁיעָה, הַמֶּלֶךְ יַעֲנֵנוּ בְיוֹם קָרְאֵנוּ.[8]
« we call. < on the < answer < May the « save! < HASHEM, « You should
day   us   King   remember!

(1) II Chronicles 20:12. (2) Psalms 25:6. (3) 33:22. (4) 79:8.
(5) 121:2. (6) 123:3. (7) Habakkuk 3:2. (8) Psalms 20:10.

כִּי הוּא יָדַע יִצְרֵנוּ, זָכוּר כִּי עָפָר אֲנָחְנוּ.¹

‹ For › He ‹ knew ›› our nature, ‹ that › that ‹ He is mindful › dust ‹ are we.

❖ עָזְרֵנוּ אֱלֹהֵי יִשְׁעֵנוּ עַל דְּבַר כְּבוֹד שְׁמֶךָ, וְהַצִּילֵנוּ

‹ Assist us, ›› O God ‹ of our salvation ‹ for › the sake ‹ of the glory ›› of Your Name; ‹ and rescue us

וְכַפֵּר עַל חַטֹּאתֵינוּ לְמַעַן שְׁמֶךָ.²

‹ and grant atonement › for ‹ our sins › for the sake ›› of Your Name.

קַדִּיש שָׁלֵם / FULL KADDISH

THE *CHAZZAN* RECITES קַדִּיש שָׁלֵם, FULL *KADDISH*.

יִתְגַּדַּל וְיִתְקַדַּשׁ שְׁמֵהּ רַבָּא. (אָמֵן. — Cong.) בְּעָלְמָא

‹ Grow exalted ‹ and be sanctified ‹ may His Name ‹ that is great! — ›› (Amen.) ‹ — in the world

דִּי בְרָא כִרְעוּתֵהּ. וְיַמְלִיךְ מַלְכוּתֵהּ, וְיַצְמַח פֻּרְקָנֵהּ

‹ that ‹ He created ‹ according to His will, ›› and may He give reign ‹ to His kingship, ›› and cause to sprout ‹ His salvation,

וִיקָרֵב מְשִׁיחֵהּ. (אָמֵן. — Cong.) בְּחַיֵּיכוֹן וּבְיוֹמֵיכוֹן וּבְחַיֵּי

‹ and bring near ‹ His Messiah, ›› (Amen.) ›› in your lifetimes ‹ and in your days, ‹ and in the lifetimes

דְכָל בֵּית יִשְׂרָאֵל, בַּעֲגָלָא וּבִזְמַן קָרִיב. וְאִמְרוּ: אָמֵן.

‹ of the entire ‹ Family ›› of Israel, ‹ swiftly ‹ and at a time ›› that comes soon. ‹ Now respond: ›› Amen.

CONGREGATION RESPONDS:

אָמֵן. יְהֵא שְׁמֵהּ רַבָּא מְבָרַךְ לְעָלַם וּלְעָלְמֵי עָלְמַיָּא.

›› Amen. ‹ May ‹ His Name ‹ that is great ‹ be blessed ‹ forever ‹ and for all eternity.

CHAZZAN CONTINUES:

יְהֵא שְׁמֵהּ רַבָּא מְבָרַךְ לְעָלַם וּלְעָלְמֵי עָלְמַיָּא. יִתְבָּרַךְ

‹ May ‹ His Name ‹ that is great ‹ be blessed ‹ forever ›› and for all eternity. ›› Blessed,

וְיִשְׁתַּבַּח וְיִתְפָּאַר וְיִתְרוֹמַם וְיִתְנַשֵּׂא וְיִתְהַדָּר וְיִתְעַלֶּה

‹ praised, ‹ glorified, ‹ exalted, ‹ upraised, ‹ honored, ‹ elevated,

וְיִתְהַלָּל שְׁמֵהּ דְּקֻדְשָׁא בְּרִיךְ הוּא (— Cong. בְּרִיךְ הוּא)

‹ and lauded ‹ be the Name ‹ of the Holy One, ‹ Blessed ‹ is He ›› (Blessed ‹ is He)

(1) *Psalms* 103:14. (2) 79:9.

לְעֵלָּא מִן כָּל בִּרְכָתָא וְשִׁירָתָא תֻּשְׁבְּחָתָא וְנֶחֱמָתָא —
‹ and consolation ‹ praise « and song, ‹ blessing ‹ any ‹ beyond

דַּאֲמִירָן בְּעָלְמָא. וְאִמְרוּ: אָמֵן. (.Cong — אָמֵן.)
« (Amen.) « Amen. ‹ Now respond: « in the world. ‹ that are uttered

CONGREGATION:

(קַבֵּל בְּרַחֲמִים וּבְרָצוֹן אֶת תְּפִלָּתֵנוּ.)
« our prayers.) ‹ and with favor ‹ with mercy ‹ (Accept

CHAZZAN CONTINUES:

תִּתְקַבֵּל צְלוֹתְהוֹן וּבָעוּתְהוֹן דְּכָל בֵּית יִשְׂרָאֵל קֳדָם
‹ before ‹ Israel ‹ Family of ‹ of the entire ‹ and supplications ‹ the prayers ‹ May accepted be

אֲבוּהוֹן דִּי בִשְׁמַיָּא. וְאִמְרוּ: אָמֵן. (.Cong — אָמֵן.)
« (Amen.) « Amen. ‹ Now respond: « is in Heaven. ‹ Who ‹ their Father

CONGREGATION:

(יְהִי שֵׁם יהוה מְבֹרָךְ, מֵעַתָּה וְעַד עוֹלָם.[1])
« eternity.) ‹ until ‹ from this time « be blessed, ‹ of HASHEM ‹ the Name ‹ (Let

CHAZZAN CONTINUES:

יְהֵא שְׁלָמָא רַבָּא מִן שְׁמַיָּא וְחַיִּים טוֹבִים עָלֵינוּ וְעַל כָּל
‹ all ‹ and upon ‹ upon us ‹ that is good, ‹ and life ‹ Heaven ‹ from ‹ that is abundant ‹ peace ‹ May there be

יִשְׂרָאֵל. וְאִמְרוּ: אָמֵן. (.Cong — אָמֵן.)
« (Amen.) « Amen. ‹ Now respond: « Israel.

CONGREGATION:

(עֶזְרִי מֵעִם יהוה, עֹשֵׂה שָׁמַיִם וָאָרֶץ.[2])
« and earth.) ‹ of heaven ‹ Maker « HASHEM, ‹ is from ‹ (My help

CHAZZAN BOWS; TAKES THREE STEPS BACK. BOWS LEFT AND SAYS "... עֹשֶׂה שָׁלוֹם, *HE WHO MAKES PEACE ...*"; BOWS RIGHT AND SAYS "... הוּא, *MAY HE ...*"; BOWS FORWARD AND SAYS "... וְעַל כָּל יִשְׂרָאֵל, *AND UPON ALL ISRAEL ...*"; REMAINS IN PLACE FOR A FEW MOMENTS, THEN TAKES THREE STEPS FORWARD.

עֹשֶׂה שָׁלוֹם בִּמְרוֹמָיו, הוּא יַעֲשֶׂה שָׁלוֹם עָלֵינוּ, וְעַל כָּל
‹ all ‹ and upon ‹ upon us, ‹ peace ‹ make ‹ may He « in His heights, ‹ peace ‹ He Who makes

יִשְׂרָאֵל. וְאִמְרוּ: אָמֵן. (.Cong — אָמֵן.)
« (Amen.) « Amen. ‹ Now respond: « Israel.

(1) *Psalms* 113:2. (2) 121:2.

❧ ANNULMENT OF VOWS / סדר התרת נדרים ❧

IT IS MERITORIOUS TO ANNUL VOWS ON THE MORNING BEFORE ROSH HASHANAH (SEE COMMENTARY). THE THREE "JUDGES" SIT WHILE THE PETITIONER SEEKING ANNULMENT STANDS BEFORE THEM AND STATES:

שִׁמְעוּ נָא רַבּוֹתַי, דַּיָּנִים מוּמְחִים. כָּל נֶדֶר אוֹ

⟨ or ⟨ vow ⟨ Any ⟫   expert judges: ⟨ my masters ⟨ if you please, ⟨   Hear,

שְׁבוּעָה אוֹ אִסּוּר אוֹ קוֹנָם אוֹ חֵרֶם שֶׁנָּדַרְתִּי

⟨ that I vowed ⟫   ban;   ⟨ or ⟨ [vow using the ⟨ or ⟨ prohibition ⟨ or ⟨   oath
                         term] *konam*

אוֹ נִשְׁבַּעְתִּי בְּהָקִיץ אוֹ בַחֲלוֹם, אוֹ נִשְׁבַּעְתִּי

⟨ that I swore ⟨ or ⟫ in a dream; ⟨ or ⟨ while awake ⟨ I swore ⟨ or

בִּשְׁמוֹת הַקְּדוֹשִׁים שֶׁאֵינָם נִמְחָקִים, וּבְשֵׁם הוי"ה

⟨ *HASHEM*, ⟨ or using ⟫ be erased, ⟨ that may not ⟨ that are Holy ⟨ using [one of
       the Name   God's] Names

בָּרוּךְ הוּא, וְכָל מִינֵי נְזִירוּת שֶׁקִּבַּלְתִּי עָלַי, חוּץ

⟨ except ⟫ upon myself, ⟨ that I accepted ⟨ of *nezirus* ⟨ forms ⟨ or any ⟫ is He; ⟨ Blessed

מִנְּזִירוּת שִׁמְשׁוֹן, וְכָל שׁוּם אִסּוּר, וַאֲפִלּוּ אִסּוּר

⟨ a prohibition ⟨ even ⟫ prohibition at all, ⟨ or any ⟨ of Samson; ⟨ the *nezirus*

הֲנָאָה שֶׁאָסַרְתִּי עָלַי אוֹ עַל אֲחֵרִים, בְּכָל לָשׁוֹן

⟨ expres- ⟨ with ⟨ others ⟨ upon ⟨ or ⟨ upon ⟨ that I imposed ⟨ to derive
  sion   any   myself   benefit

שֶׁל אִסּוּר, בֵּין בִּלְשׁוֹן אִסּוּר אוֹ חֵרֶם אוֹ קוֹנָם,

⟫ *konam*; ⟨ or ⟨   ban ⟨ or ⟨ *prohibition* ⟨ with the term ⟨ whether ⟫ prohibition, ⟨ of

וְכָל שׁוּם קַבָּלָה אֲפִילוּ שֶׁל מִצְוָה שֶׁקִּבַּלְתִּי עָלַי

⟫ upon ⟨   that I   ⟫ relating to [perform- ⟨ — even ⟫ commitment at all ⟨ or any
  myself,   accepted   ing] a *mitzvah* —

בֵּין בִּלְשׁוֹן נֶדֶר, בֵּין בִּלְשׁוֹן נְדָבָה, בֵּין בִּלְשׁוֹן

⟨ with an ⟨ whether ⟫ [denoting] ⟨   with an ⟨ whether ⟫ [denoting] ⟨ with an ⟨ whether
  expression   a specific gift,   expression   a vow,   expression

---

❧ **הַתָּרַת נְדָרִים / ANNULMENT OF VOWS** ❧

The Torah permits people to accept upon themselves personal obligations and prohibitions, and it gives an owner the right to forbid others to benefit from his property. Such undertakings, known as שְׁבוּעוֹת וּנְדָרִים, *oaths and vows*, must be carried out and have the force of a positive commandment, כְּכָל הַיֹּצֵא מִפִּיו יַעֲשֶׂה, *he shall do whatever he has uttered*, and their violation carries the penalty

of a negative commandment, לֹא יַחֵל דְּבָרוֹ, *he shall not desecrate his word* (*Numbers* 30:3). So serious are these matters that they are the primary subject of three tractates of the Talmud: *Nedarim, Nazir,* and *Shevuos.*

That a person's freely chosen wishes can have the force of Torah law is a striking indication of the sanctity that God attaches to a person's word. Consequently, it is considered a fearsome sin for one to violate his vows and

שְׁבוּעָה, בֵּין בִּלְשׁוֹן נְזִירוּת, בֵּין בְּכָל לָשׁוֹן, וְגַם

⟨ as well as ⟩ ⟨ expression, ⟩ ⟨ with any [other] ⟩ ⟨ whether ⟩ ⟨ [denoting] nezirus, ⟩ ⟨ with an expression ⟩ ⟨ whether ⟩ ⟨ [denoting] an oath,

הַנַּעֲשֶׂה בִּתְקִיעַת כָּף, בֵּין כָּל נֶדֶר, וּבֵין כָּל נְדָבָה,

⟨ specific gift, ⟩ ⟨ any ⟩ ⟨ whether ⟩ ⟨ vow, ⟩ ⟨ any ⟩ ⟨ whether ⟩ ⟨ a hand; ⟩ ⟨ through shaking ⟩ ⟨ [a commitment] made

וּבֵין שׁוּם מִנְהָג שֶׁל מִצְוָה שֶׁנָּהַגְתִּי אֶת עַצְמִי, וְכָל

⟨ and any ⟩ ⟨ myself; ⟩ ⟨ by which I conducted ⟩ ⟨ a good deed ⟩ ⟨ of ⟩ ⟨ of practice ⟩ ⟨ any kind ⟩ ⟨ whether

מוֹצָא שְׂפָתַי שֶׁיָּצָא מִפִּי, אוֹ שֶׁנָּדַרְתִּי וְגָמַרְתִּי בְּלִבִּי

⟨ in my heart ⟩ ⟨ or I decided ⟩ ⟨ that I vowed ⟩ ⟨ or ⟩ ⟨ of my mouth, ⟩ ⟨ that came out ⟩ ⟨ of my lips ⟩ ⟨ utterance

לַעֲשׂוֹת שׁוּם מִצְוָה מֵהַמִּצְוֹת, אוֹ אֵיזֶה הַנְהָגָה טוֹבָה

⟨ good practice, ⟩ ⟨ some ⟩ ⟨ or ⟩ ⟨ among the mitzvos, ⟩ ⟨ mitzvah ⟩ ⟨ any ⟩ ⟨ to perform

אוֹ אֵיזֶה דָּבָר טוֹב שֶׁנָּהַגְתִּי שָׁלֹשׁ פְּעָמִים, וְלֹא

⟨ and did not ⟩ ⟨ times ⟩ ⟨ three ⟩ ⟨ that I practiced ⟩ ⟨ good act ⟩ ⟨ some ⟩ ⟨ or

הִתְנֵיתִי שֶׁיְּהֵא בְּלִי נֶדֶר, הֵן דָּבָר שֶׁעָשִׂיתִי, הֵן

⟨ both ⟩ ⟨ that I did: ⟩ ⟨ any-thing ⟩ ⟨ includ-ing ⟩ ⟨ [the force of] a vow; ⟩ ⟨ without ⟩ ⟨ that it should be ⟩ ⟨ stipulate

עַל עַצְמִי, הֵן עַל אֲחֵרִים, הֵן אוֹתָן הַיְדוּעִים לִי,

⟨ to me ⟩ ⟨ that are known ⟩ ⟨ those ⟩ ⟨ both ⟩ ⟨ others; ⟩ ⟨ relating to ⟩ ⟨ as well as ⟩ ⟨ myself ⟩ ⟨ relating to

oaths, and the Sages regard it as an extremely serious matter for one to approach the Days of Judgment with such a transgression in hand.

However, the Torah provides a means for one to be released from such obligations. A "court" composed of three knowledgeable people has the authority to decide that the oath or vow was undertaken under a mistaken impression and they may annul the obligation retroactively. [This is an oversimplified explanation of the process of annulment, but the key is that the court has retroactive powers.] One of the pleas that one can make to the court is that he regrets ever having accepted the obligation as a vow or oath.

In order to free oneself of the sin of such violations before being judged on Rosh Hashanah and Yom Kippur, the halachic authorities urge that one convene a court of at least three people — preferably ten — and seek release from his vows and oaths.

However, as the declaration makes clear, this annulment applies only to vows for which the halachah permits annulment and for which there is a halachically acceptable reason for doing so. Likewise, annulment is valid only if the vows involve just oneself. If, however, the vows were adopted for the sake of, or involve someone else, they cannot be annulled without the consent of the other party. Also, for an annulment to be effective, the regret must be complete and, preferably, be accompanied by a valid reason for regret (Yoreh Deah 228:7). And, as the declaration makes clear, the halachah requires that the vow be specified [to at least one member of the court (228:14)]. Consequently, the present declaration should be seen primarily as a means of repentance from the sin of having abused vows.

A second aspect of the Annulment of Vows is the concluding declaration, in which one makes the legal declaration that his future

הֵן אוֹתָן שֶׁכְּבָר שָׁכַחְתִּי, בְּכֻלְּהוֹן אִתְחֲרַטְנָא בְהוֹן

‹ [having made] them ‹ I regret [now] ‹ — regarding all of them, « I have forgotten ‹ that ‹ already ‹ those ‹ as well as

מֵעִקָּרָא, וְשׁוֹאֵל וּמְבַקֵּשׁ אֲנִי מִמַּעֲלַתְכֶם הַתָּרָה

‹ annulment ‹ of your eminences ‹ and I request ‹ and I ask « from the onset,

עֲלֵיהֶם. כִּי יָרֵאתִי פֶּן אֶכָּשֵׁל וְנִלְכַּדְתִּי, חַס וְשָׁלוֹם,

‹ Heaven forbid, ‹ and I become entangled ‹ I stumble ‹ lest ‹ I am fearful ‹ For « for them.

בַּעֲוֹן נְדָרִים וּשְׁבוּעוֹת וּנְזִירוּת וַחֲרָמוֹת וְאִסּוּרִין

‹ prohibitions, ‹ bans, ‹ nezirus ‹ oaths, ‹ of [violation of] vows, ‹ in the sin

וְקוֹנָמוֹת וְהַסְכָּמוֹת. וְאֵין אֲנִי תוֹהֵא, חַס וְשָׁלוֹם,

‹ Heaven forbid, ‹ have regret, ‹ But I do not « and agreements. ‹ konams,

עַל קִיּוּם הַמַּעֲשִׂים הַטּוֹבִים הָהֵם שֶׁעָשִׂיתִי. רַק אֲנִי

‹ I ‹ rather, « that I have done; ‹ of those good deeds ‹ the performance ‹ for

מִתְחָרֵט עַל קַבָּלַת הָעִנְיָנִים בִּלְשׁוֹן נֶדֶר אוֹ שְׁבוּעָה

‹ of an oath ‹ or ‹ of a vow ‹ with an expression ‹ those ‹ matters ‹ having accepted ‹ regret

אוֹ נְזִירוּת אוֹ אִסּוּר אוֹ חֵרֶם אוֹ קוֹנָם אוֹ הַסְכָּמָה

‹ of an agreement ‹ or ‹ of a konam ‹ or ‹ of a ban ‹ or ‹ of a prohibition ‹ or ‹ of nezirus ‹ or

אוֹ קַבָּלָה בְּלֵב, וּמִתְחָרֵט אֲנִי עַל זֶה שֶׁלֹּא אָמַרְתִּי,

« that I did not say, ‹ the fact ‹ for ‹ and I have regret « in [my] heart, ‹ of acceptance ‹ or

---

undertakings should not have the force of a vow or oath. As he declares, this prior nullification is effective only if the person making the vow had forgotten it while making the vow. If he did have the nullification in mind and made the vow anyway, the vow is binding (211:2). This declaration does not free him from the obligation to keep his word; it merely removes the severity of sin that attaches to formally proclaimed vows and oaths.

Briefly defined, the variety of terms listed are:

□ נֶדֶר [neder], vow. This is a vow through which one accepts a prohibition upon himself. The standard means to do so is to say, "This item should be forbidden as if it were a Temple offering." Thus the prohibition rests on the item.

□ שְׁבוּעָה [shevuah], oath. By means of a shevuah one obligates himself either to do or to refrain from doing or benefiting from something. Thus, in contrast to a neder, a shevuah rests on the person.

□ אִסּוּר [issur], prohibition. Technically, this falls under one of the above categories. It is mentioned to indicate that the speaker used the word prohibit, rather than the usual formulation of neder or shevuah as explained by the Talmud.

□ קוֹנָם [konam]. In a common form of neder, one says, "This item should be forbidden as if it were a korban [Temple offering]." Konam is a slang word that came to be used instead of the word korban. Such slang terms are valid.

□ חֵרֶם [cherem]. This is a declaration used to dedicate something as the property of the Kohanim or as the property of the Temple.

הִנְנִי עוֹשֶׂה דָבָר זֶה בְּלִי נֶדֶר וּשְׁבוּעָה וּנְזִירוּת

⟨ nezirus, ⟨ an oath, ⟨ [the force ⟨ without ⟨ this act ⟨ doing ⟨ I am
of] a vow,   hereby

וְחֵרֶם וְאִסּוּר וְקוֹנָם וְקַבָּלָה בְּלֵב. לָכֵן אֲנִי שׁוֹאֵל

⟨ request ⟨ I ⟨ There- ⟪ in [my] ⟨ or ⟨ konam, ⟨ prohibition, ⟨ ban,
fore, heart. acceptance

הַתָּרָה בְּכֻלְּהוֹן. אֲנִי מִתְחָרֵט עַל כָּל הַנִּזְכָּר, בֵּין אִם

⟨ if ⟨ whether ⟪ the afore- ⟨ all ⟨ regret ⟨ I ⟪ for them all. ⟨ annulment
mentioned,

הָיוּ הַמַּעֲשִׂים מֵהַדְּבָרִים הַנּוֹגְעִים בְּמָמוֹן, בֵּין

⟨ whether ⟪ to money, ⟨ relating ⟨ of matters ⟨ these acts were

מֵהַדְּבָרִים הַנּוֹגְעִים בְּגוּף, בֵּין מֵהַדְּבָרִים הַנּוֹגְעִים

⟨ relating ⟨ of matters ⟨ or ⟪ to the body ⟨ relating ⟨ of matters

אֶל הַנְּשָׁמָה. בְּכֻלְּהוֹן אֲנִי מִתְחָרֵט עַל לְשׁוֹן נֶדֶר

⟨ of ⟨ [using] the ⟨ regret ⟨ I ⟪ Regarding ⟪ the soul. ⟨ to
vow, terminology them all,

וּשְׁבוּעָה וּנְזִירוּת וְאִסּוּר וְחֵרֶם וְקוֹנָם וְקַבָּלָה

⟨ and acceptance ⟨ konam ⟨ ban, ⟨ prohibition, ⟨ nezirus, ⟨ oath,

בְּלֵב. וְהִנֵּה מִצַּד הַדִּין, הַמִּתְחָרֵט וְהַמְבַקֵּשׁ הַתָּרָה

⟨ annulment ⟨ and who seeks ⟨ one who regrets ⟨ to the law, ⟨ according ⟨ Now ⟪ in the heart.

צָרִיךְ לִפְרוֹט הַנֶּדֶר, אַךְ דְּעוּ נָא רַבּוֹתַי, כִּי אִי

⟨ it is ⟨ that ⟪ my ⟨ please, ⟨ be ⟨ However, ⟪ the ⟨ specify ⟨ must
not masters, informed, vow.

אֶפְשָׁר לְפוֹרְטָם כִּי רַבִּים הֵם. וְאֵין אֲנִי מְבַקֵּשׁ

⟨ seek ⟨ And I do not ⟪ are they. ⟨ many ⟨ for ⟨ to specify them, ⟨ possible

הַתָּרָה עַל אוֹתָם הַנְּדָרִים שֶׁאֵין לְהַתִּיר אוֹתָם.

⟪ them. ⟨ annul ⟨ that one may not ⟨ vows ⟨ those ⟨ for ⟨ annulment

עַל כֵּן יִהְיוּ נָא בְעֵינֵיכֶם כְּאִלּוּ הָיְיתִי פוֹרְטָם.

⟪ specified them. ⟨ I had ⟨ as if ⟨ in your view ⟨ please, ⟨ may they be ⟨ Therefore,

THE JUDGES DECLARE THREE TIMES IN UNISON:

הַכֹּל יִהְיוּ מֻתָּרִים לָךְ, הַכֹּל מְחוּלִים לָךְ, הַכֹּל

⟨ all of ⟪ for ⟨ shall be ⟨ all of ⟪ for ⟨ annulled ⟨ shall ⟨ All of
them you, forgiven them you, be them

שְׁרוּיִם לָךְ, אֵין כָּאן לֹא נֶדֶר וְלֹא שְׁבוּעָה

⟨ oath, ⟨ nor ⟨ vow, ⟨ neither ⟨ now ⟨ There is ⟪ for you. ⟨ shall be canceled

וְלֹא נְזִירוּת וְלֹא חֵרֶם וְלֹא אִסּוּר וְלֹא קוֹנָם וְלֹא

‹ nor ‹ *konam,* ‹ nor ‹ prohibition, ‹ nor ‹ ban, ‹ nor ‹ *nezirus,* ‹ nor

נִדּוּי וְלֹא שַׁמְתָּא וְלֹא אָרוּר. אֲבָל יֵשׁ כַּאן מְחִילָה

‹ pardon, ‹ now ‹ there ‹ Rather, « curse. ‹ nor ‹ excommu- ‹ nor ‹ ostracism,
        is   nication,

וּסְלִיחָה וְכַפָּרָה. וּכְשֵׁם שֶׁמַּתִּירִים בְּבֵית דִּין שֶׁל

‹ of ‹ of ‹ in the ‹ as we annul ‹ And just « and ‹ forgiveness,
     justice   court   [them]   atonement.

מַטָּה, כַּךְ יִהְיוּ מֻתָּרִים בְּבֵית דִּין שֶׁל מַעְלָה.

« [Heaven] ‹ of ‹ of ‹ in the ‹ annulled ‹ may ‹ so « [Earth]
   above   justice   court   they be   below,

THE PETITIONER MAKES THE FOLLOWING DECLARATION:

הֲרֵי אֲנִי מוֹסֵר מוֹדָעָה לִפְנֵיכֶם, וַאֲנִי מְבַטֵּל

‹ cancel ‹ [by ‹ before you, ‹ a declaration ‹ conveying ‹ I am ‹ Here
      which] I   [of cancellation]   now

מִכַּאן וּלְהַבָּא כָּל הַנְּדָרִים וְכָל שְׁבוּעוֹת וּנְזִירוּת

‹ *nezirus,* ‹ oaths, ‹ and all ‹ the vows ‹ all ‹ onward ‹ from this time

וְאִסּוּרִין וְקוֹנָמוֹת וַחֲרָמוֹת וְהַסְכָּמוֹת וְקַבָּלָה

‹ and acceptance ‹ agreements, ‹ bans, ‹ konams, ‹ prohibitions,

בְּלֵב שֶׁאֲקַבֵּל עָלַי בְּעַצְמִי, הֵן בְּהָקִיץ, הֵן בַּחֲלוֹם,

« in a dream, ‹ as ‹ while awake ‹ both « on my own, ‹ upon ‹ that I will ‹ of the
      well as   myself   accept   heart

חוּץ מִנִּדְרֵי תַעֲנִית בִּשְׁעַת מִנְחָה. וּבְאִם שֶׁאֶשְׁכַּח

‹ I forget ‹ In case « of ‹ [undertaken] ‹ to fast ‹ for vows ‹ except
           Minchah.   at the time

לִתְנַאי מוֹדָעָה הַזֹּאת, וְאֶדּוֹר מֵהַיּוֹם עוֹד, מֵעַתָּה אֲנִי

‹ I ‹ from this « onward, ‹ from this ‹ and I make ‹ [set forth] in this decla- ‹ the
    moment   day   a vow   ration [cancellation],   condition

מִתְחָרֵט עֲלֵיהֶם, וּמַתְנֶה עֲלֵיהֶם, שֶׁיִּהְיוּ כֻּלָּן בְּטֵלִין

‹ null ‹ all of ‹ that they « regarding ‹ and ‹ them ‹ regret
      them, shall be,   them,   stipulate

וּמְבֻטָּלִין, לָא שְׁרִירִין וְלָא קַיָּמִין, וְלָא יְהוֹן חָלִין

‹ take ‹ and they « validity ‹ and ‹ effect ‹ without « and void,
  effect   shall not   without

כְּלָל וּכְלָל. בְּכֻלָּן אִתְחֲרַטְנָא בְּהוֹן מֵעַתָּה וְעַד עוֹלָם.

« eternity. ‹ until ‹ from this ‹ them ‹ I regret ‹ Regarding « at all.
           time   them all,

﷽ צום גדליה / FAST OF GEDALIAH ﷽

אַשְׁרֵי יוֹשְׁבֵי בֵיתֶךָ, עוֹד יְהַלְלוּךָ סֶּלָה. אַשְׁרֵי[1]

⟨ Praise-worthy ⟨⟨ Selah. ⟨⟨ they will praise You, ⟨ con-tinually ⟨⟨ in Your house, ⟨ are those who dwell ⟨ Praiseworthy

הָעָם שֶׁכָּכָה לּוֹ, אַשְׁרֵי הָעָם שֶׁיהוה אֱלֹהָיו.[2]

⟨⟨ is their God. ⟨ that HASHEM ⟨ is the people ⟨ praise-worthy ⟨⟨ is their lot; ⟨ that such ⟨ is the people

———— תהלים קמה / Psalm 145 ————

תְּהִלָּה לְדָוִד, **אֲרוֹמִמְךָ** אֱלוֹהַי הַמֶּלֶךְ, וַאֲבָרְכָה

⟨ and I will bless ⟨⟨ the King, ⟨ my God ⟨ I will exalt You, ⟨⟨ by David: ⟨ A psalm of praise

שִׁמְךָ לְעוֹלָם וָעֶד. **בְּכָל** יוֹם אֲבָרְכֶךָּ, וַאֲהַלְלָה שִׁמְךָ

⟨ Your Name ⟨ and I will laud ⟨⟨ I will bless You, ⟨ day ⟨ Every ⟨⟨ and ever. ⟨ for ever ⟨ Your Name

לְעוֹלָם וָעֶד. **גָּדוֹל** יהוה וּמְהֻלָּל מְאֹד, וְלִגְדֻלָּתוֹ

⟨ and His greatness ⟨⟨ exceedingly, ⟨ and lauded ⟨ is ⟨ Great ⟨⟨ and ever. ⟨ for ever

אֵין חֵקֶר. **דּוֹר** לְדוֹר יְשַׁבַּח מַעֲשֶׂיךָ, וּגְבוּרֹתֶיךָ יַגִּידוּ.

⟨⟨ they will recount. ⟨ and Your mighty deeds ⟨⟨ Your actions, ⟨ will ⟨ to praise ⟨ Gen-eration ⟨ generation ⟨⟨ is beyond investigation.

הֲדַר כְּבוֹד הוֹדֶךָ, וְדִבְרֵי נִפְלְאֹתֶיךָ אָשִׂיחָה. וֶעֱזוּז

⟨ And of the might ⟨⟨ I shall discuss. ⟨ that are wondrous ⟨ and Your deeds ⟨ of Your majesty ⟨ glory ⟨ The splendrous

נוֹרְאֹתֶיךָ יֹאמֵרוּ, וּגְדוּלָּתְךָ אֲסַפְּרֶנָּה. **זֵכֶר** רַב טוּבְךָ

⟨ of Your abun-dant goodness ⟨ A recol-lection ⟨⟨ I shall relate. ⟨ and Your greatness ⟨⟨ they will speak, ⟨ of Your awesome deeds

יַבִּיעוּ, וְצִדְקָתְךָ יְרַנֵּנוּ. **חַנּוּן** וְרַחוּם יהוה, אֶרֶךְ אַפַּיִם

⟨ to anger, ⟨ slow ⟨⟨ is ⟨ and ⟨ Gracious ⟨⟨ they will sing joyfully. ⟨ and of Your righteousness ⟨⟨ they will utter, ⟨ merciful ⟨ HASHEM,

וּגְדָל חָסֶד. **טוֹב** יהוה לַכֹּל, וְרַחֲמָיו עַל כָּל מַעֲשָׂיו.

⟨⟨ His creations. ⟨ all ⟨ are on ⟨ His mercies ⟨⟨ to all; ⟨ HASHEM is good ⟨⟨ in [bestowing] ⟨ kindness. ⟨ and great

יוֹדוּךָ יהוה כָּל מַעֲשֶׂיךָ, וַחֲסִידֶיךָ יְבָרְכוּכָה. **כְּבוֹד**

⟨ Of the glory ⟨⟨ will ⟨ and Your devout ones ⟨ Your creations — ⟨ — all ⟨⟨ HASHEM ⟨ They will thank You, ⟨ bless You.

———

(1) *Psalms* 84:5. (2) 144:15.

מַלְכוּתְךָ יֹאמֵרוּ, וּגְבוּרָתְךָ יְדַבֵּרוּ. **לְהוֹדְיעַ לִבְנֵי הָאָדָם**

‹ mankind ‹ To inform ❯❯ they will ‹ and of Your ❯❯ they will ‹ of Your
         declare.   power   speak,   kingdom

גְּבוּרֹתָיו, וּכְבוֹד הֲדַר מַלְכוּתוֹ. **מַלְכוּתְךָ** מַלְכוּת כָּל

‹ [span- ‹ is a ‹ Your kingdom ❯❯ of His ‹ splendor ‹ and of the ❯❯ of His mighty
ning] all kingdom   kingdom.   glorious   deeds,

עֹלָמִים, וּמֶמְשַׁלְתְּךָ בְּכָל דּוֹר וָדֹר. **סוֹמֵךְ** יהוה

‹ HASHEM ❯❯ after ‹ gen- ‹ is ‹ and Your ❯❯ eternities,
supports generation. eration throughout dominion

לְכָל הַנֹּפְלִים, וְזוֹקֵף לְכָל הַכְּפוּפִים. **עֵינֵי** כֹל

‹ of all ‹ The ❯❯ those who ‹ all ‹ and ❯❯ those who ‹ all
  eyes   are bent.   straightens are fallen,

אֵלֶיךָ יְשַׂבֵּרוּ, וְאַתָּה נוֹתֵן לָהֶם אֶת אָכְלָם בְּעִתּוֹ.

❯❯ in its ‹ their food ‹ them ‹ give ‹ and You ❯❯ do look ‹ to You
proper time.   with hope,

CONCENTRATE INTENTLY WHILE RECITING THE VERSE פּוֹתֵחַ, *YOU OPEN.*

פּוֹתֵחַ אֶת יָדֶךָ, וּמַשְׂבִּיעַ לְכָל חַי רָצוֹן. ✧ **צַדִּיק**

‹ Righteous ❯❯ [with its] ‹ living ‹ every ‹ and satisfy ❯❯ Your hand, ‹ You open
    desire.   thing

יהוה בְּכָל דְּרָכָיו, וְחָסִיד בְּכָל מַעֲשָׂיו. **קָרוֹב** יהוה

‹ is ‹ Close ❯❯ His deeds. ‹ in all ‹ and ❯❯ His ways, ‹ in all ‹ is
HASHEM   magnanimous   HASHEM

לְכָל קֹרְאָיו, לְכֹל אֲשֶׁר יִקְרָאֻהוּ בֶאֱמֶת. **רְצוֹן** יְרֵאָיו

‹ of those ‹ The ❯❯ sincerely. ‹ call upon ‹ who ‹ to all ❯❯ who call ‹ to all
who fear Him will   Him   upon Him,

יַעֲשֶׂה, וְאֶת שַׁוְעָתָם יִשְׁמַע וְיוֹשִׁיעֵם. **שׁוֹמֵר** יהוה

‹ HASHEM protects ❯❯ and He will ‹ He will ‹ and their cry ❯❯ He
      save them. hear,   will do;

אֶת כָּל אֹהֲבָיו, וְאֵת כָּל הָרְשָׁעִים יַשְׁמִיד. **תְּהִלַּת**

‹ The praise ❯❯ He will destroy. ‹ the wicked ‹ but all ❯❯ who love Him; ‹ all

יהוה יְדַבֶּר פִּי, וִיבָרֵךְ כָּל בָּשָׂר שֵׁם קָדְשׁוֹ לְעוֹלָם

‹ for ever ‹ of His ‹ the ‹ flesh ‹ may ‹ and bless ❯❯ may my ‹ of
  Holiness Name   all   mouth declare, HASHEM

וָעֶד. וַאֲנַחְנוּ נְבָרֵךְ יָהּ מֵעַתָּה וְעַד עוֹלָם; הַלְלוּיָהּ.[1]

❯❯ Halleluyah! ❯❯ eternity. ‹ until ‹ from ‹ God ‹ will ‹ But we ❯❯ and
        this time   bless   ever.

---

(1) *Psalms* 115:18.

THE *CHAZZAN* RECITES חֲצִי קַדִּישׁ, HALF-*KADDISH*:

יִתְגַּדַּל וְיִתְקַדַּשׁ שְׁמֵהּ רַבָּא. (Cong. — אָמֵן.) בְּעָלְמָא
⟨ — in the ⟨ (Amen.) ⟨ that is ⟨ may His ⟨ and be ⟨ Grow
world great! — Name sanctified exalted

דִּי בְרָא כִרְעוּתֵהּ. וְיַמְלִיךְ מַלְכוּתֵהּ, וְיַצְמַח פֻּרְקָנֵהּ
⟨ His ⟨ and cause ⟨ to His ⟨ and may He ⟨ according ⟨ He ⟨ that
salvation, to sprout kingship, give reign to His will, created

וִיקָרֵב מְשִׁיחֵהּ. (Cong. — אָמֵן.) בְּחַיֵּיכוֹן וּבְיוֹמֵיכוֹן וּבְחַיֵּי
⟨ and in the ⟨ and in ⟨ in your ⟨ (Amen.) ⟨ His Messiah, ⟨ and bring
lifetimes your days, lifetimes near

דְכָל בֵּית יִשְׂרָאֵל, בַּעֲגָלָא וּבִזְמַן קָרִיב. וְאִמְרוּ: אָמֵן.
⟨Amen. ⟨ Now ⟨ that comes ⟨ and at a ⟨ swiftly ⟨ of Israel, ⟨ Family ⟨ of the
respond: soon. time entire

CONGREGATION RESPONDS:

אָמֵן. יְהֵא שְׁמֵהּ רַבָּא מְבָרַךְ לְעָלַם וּלְעָלְמֵי עָלְמַיָּא.
⟨ and for all eternity. ⟨ forever ⟨ be ⟨ that is ⟨ His ⟨ May ⟨ Amen.
blessed great Name

CHAZZAN CONTINUES:

יְהֵא שְׁמֵהּ רַבָּא מְבָרַךְ לְעָלַם וּלְעָלְמֵי עָלְמַיָּא. יִתְבָּרַךְ
⟨ Blessed, ⟨ and for all eternity. ⟨ forever ⟨ be ⟨ that is ⟨ His ⟨ May
blessed great Name

וְיִשְׁתַּבַּח וְיִתְפָּאַר וְיִתְרוֹמַם וְיִתְנַשֵּׂא וְיִתְהַדָּר וְיִתְעַלֶּה
⟨ elevated, ⟨ honored, ⟨ upraised, ⟨ exalted, ⟨ glorified, ⟨ praised,

וְיִתְהַלָּל שְׁמֵהּ דְּקֻדְשָׁא בְּרִיךְ הוּא (Cong. — בְּרִיךְ הוּא)
⟨is He) ⟨(Blessed ⟨ is He ⟨ Blessed ⟨ of the Holy ⟨ be the ⟨ and lauded
One, Name

— לְעֵלָּא [וּ]לְעֵלָּא מִכָּל בִּרְכָתָא וְשִׁירָתָא תֻּשְׁבְּחָתָא
⟨ praise ⟨ and song, ⟨ blessing ⟨ any ⟨ exceedingly beyond

וְנֶחֱמָתָא דַּאֲמִירָן בְּעָלְמָא. וְאִמְרוּ: אָמֵן. (Cong. — אָמֵן.)
⟨ (Amen.) ⟨ Amen. ⟨ Now ⟨ in the ⟨ that are ⟨ and
respond: world. uttered consolation

ALL:

לְךָ יהוה הַצְּדָקָה, וְלָנוּ בּשֶׁת הַפָּנִים.[1] מַה
⟨What ⟨ is shamefacedness. ⟨ and ⟨ is the ⟨ O Lord, ⟨ Yours,
ours righteousness,

נִּתְאוֹנֵן,[2] מַה נֹּאמַר, מַה נְּדַבֵּר, וּמַה נִּצְטַדָּק.[3]
⟨ justification ⟨ What ⟨ can we ⟨ What ⟨can we say? ⟨ What ⟨ complaint
can we offer? declare? can we make?

(1) *Daniel* 9:7. (2) Cf. *Lamentations* 3:39. (3) Cf. *Genesis* 44:16.

נַחְפְּשָׂה דְרָכֵינוּ וְנַחְקְרָה, וְנָשׁוּבָה אֵלֶיךָ,¹ כִּי יְמִינְךָ

‹ Let us examine ‹ our ways ‹ and investigate ‹ and return « to You, ‹ for « Your right hand

פְּשׁוּטָה לְקַבֵּל שָׁבִים. לֹא בְחֶסֶד וְלֹא בְמַעֲשִׂים

‹ is extended ‹ to accept « those who return. « Nei- ther ‹ with [merit] for kindness ‹ nor ‹ with [merit for good] deeds

בָּאנוּ לְפָנֶיךָ, כְּדַלִּים וּכְרָשִׁים דָּפַקְנוּ דְלָתֶיךָ.

‹ do we come « before You; ‹ but as paupers ‹ and as destitute people ‹ we have knocked « on Your doors.

דְלָתֶיךָ דָּפַקְנוּ רַחוּם וְחַנּוּן, נָא אַל תְּשִׁיבֵנוּ

‹ On Your doors ‹ we have knocked, ‹ O Compas- sionate One « and Gra- cious One. ‹ Please ‹ do not ‹ turn us away

רֵיקָם מִלְּפָנֶיךָ. מִלְּפָנֶיךָ מַלְכֵּנוּ רֵיקָם אַל תְּשִׁיבֵנוּ,

‹ empty- handed « from before You. ‹ From before You, ‹ Our King, ‹ empty- handed « do not ‹ turn us away,

כִּי אַתָּה שׁוֹמֵעַ תְּפִלָּה.

‹ for ‹ You are the One ‹ Who hears « prayer.

שֹׁמֵעַ תְּפִלָּה, עָדֶיךָ כָּל בָּשָׂר יָבֹאוּ.² יָבֹא

‹ You Who hears « prayer, ‹ unto You ‹ all ‹ flesh ‹ will come. « Come

כָּל בָּשָׂר לְהִשְׁתַּחֲוֹת לְפָנֶיךָ יהוה.³ יָבֹאוּ וְיִשְׁתַּחֲווּ

‹ will all flesh ‹ to bow down ‹ before You, « O HASHEM. ‹ They will come ‹ and bow down

לְפָנֶיךָ אֲדֹנָי, וִיכַבְּדוּ לִשְׁמֶךָ. בֹּאוּ נִשְׁתַּחֲוֶה וְנִכְרָעָה,⁴

‹ before You, « O Lord, ‹ and they will show honor ‹ to Your Name. « Come! ‹ Let us prostrate ourselves ‹ and bow,

נִבְרְכָה לִפְנֵי יהוה עֹשֵׂנוּ. נָבוֹאָה לְמִשְׁכְּנוֹתָיו,⁵

« let us kneel ‹ before ‹ HASHEM, « our Maker. ‹ Let us come « to His Tabernacles,

נִשְׁתַּחֲוֶה לַהֲדֹם רַגְלָיו.⁶ בֹּאוּ שְׁעָרָיו בְּתוֹדָה,

« let us prostrate ourselves ‹ at the stool « for His feet. ‹ Enter « His gates ‹ with thanksgiving,

חֲצֵרֹתָיו בִּתְהִלָּה, הוֹדוּ לוֹ בָּרְכוּ שְׁמוֹ.⁷ וַאֲנַחְנוּ

‹ His courtyards « with praise; ‹ give thanks « to Him ‹ bless « His Name. ‹ But we,

---

(1) Cf. *Lamentations* 3:40. (2) *Psalms* 65:3. (3) Cf. *Isaiah* 66:23.
(4) *Psalms* 86:9. (5) 95:6. (6) 132:7. (7) 100:4.

בְּרֹב חַסְדְּךָ נָבוֹא בֵיתֶךָ, נִשְׁתַּחֲוֶה אֶל הֵיכַל קׇדְשְׁךָ

through the / abundance ⟩ of Your ⟨ will we ⟨ Your ⟩ we will pros- ⟩ toward ⟩ Your Holy
kindness ⟩ enter ⟩ House; ⟩ trate ourselves ⟩ Sanctuary

בְּיִרְאָתֶךָ.¹ הִנֵּה בָּרְכוּ אֶת יהוה כׇּל עַבְדֵי יהוה,

in awe ⟩ Indeed, ⟨ bless ⟩ HASHEM, ⟩ all ⟩ you ⟩ of
of You. ⟩ servants ⟩ HASHEM,

הָעֹמְדִים בְּבֵית יהוה בַּלֵּילוֹת.² שְׂאוּ יְדֵיכֶם קֹֽדֶשׁ

who stand ⟩ in the ⟩ of ⟩ in the nights. ⟨ Lift ⟩ your ⟩ in the
Sanctuary ⟩ House ⟩ HASHEM ⟩ hands

וּבָרְכוּ אֶת יהוה.³ רוֹמְמוּ יהוה אֱלֹהֵינוּ, וְהִשְׁתַּחֲווּ

and bless ⟨ HASHEM. ⟩ Exalt ⟨ HASHEM, ⟩ our God, ⟨ and bow down

לַהֲדֹם רַגְלָיו, קָדוֹשׁ הוּא.⁴ רוֹמְמוּ יהוה אֱלֹהֵינוּ.

at His footstool; ⟩ holy ⟨ is He! ⟩ Exalt ⟨ HASHEM, ⟩ our God,

וְהִשְׁתַּחֲווּ לְהַר קׇדְשׁוֹ, כִּי קָדוֹשׁ יהוה אֱלֹהֵינוּ.⁵

and bow ⟩ at the ⟩ of His ⟩ for ⟨ holy ⟩ is ⟩ HASHEM, ⟨ our God. ⟩ ⟨
Mount ⟩ Holiness;

הִשְׁתַּחֲווּ לַיהוה בְּהַדְרַת קֹֽדֶשׁ, חִֽילוּ מִפָּנָיו כׇּל

Bow down ⟨ before ⟩ in the ⟩ of ⟩ tremble ⟩ before ⟩ every-
HASHEM ⟩ splendor ⟩ holiness; ⟩ Him, ⟩ one

הָאָֽרֶץ.⁶ נִשְׁתַּחֲוֶה אֶל הֵיכַל קׇדְשְׁךָ וְנוֹדֶה אֶת שְׁמֶֽךָ,

on earth. ⟨ We will pros- ⟩ toward ⟨ Your Holy ⟩ and we ⟨ Your Name ⟨
trate ourselves ⟩ Sanctuary, ⟩ will thank

עַל חַסְדְּךָ וְעַל אֲמִתֶּֽךָ, כִּי הִגְדַּֽלְתָּ עַל כׇּל שִׁמְךָ

for ⟩ Your ⟩ and ⟩ Your ⟩ for ⟨ You have ⟨ — even ⟨ Your
kindness ⟩ for ⟩ faithfulness; ⟩ exalted ⟩ beyond ⟩ Name —

אִמְרָתֶֽךָ.⁷ יהוה אֱלֹהֵי צְבָאוֹת, מִי כָמֽוֹךָ חֲסִין

Your promise. ⟨ HASHEM, ⟩ God ⟩ of ⟨ — who ⟨ is like ⟩ O Strong
Legions ⟩ You, ⟩ One,

יָהּ, וֶאֱמוּנָתְךָ סְבִיבוֹתֶֽיךָ.⁸ כִּי מִי בַשַּֽׁחַק יַעֲרֹךְ

can be ⟩ in the sky ⟩ who ⟩ For ⟨ surrounds You. ⟨ and Your ⟨ God? —
compared ⟩ faithfulness

לַיהוה, יִדְמֶה לַיהוה בִּבְנֵי אֵלִים.⁹ כִּי גָדוֹל אַתָּה

are You ⟨ great ⟨ For ⟨ among the angels? ⟨ to HASHEM ⟨ be likened ⟨ to HASHEM;

וְעֹשֵׂה נִפְלָאוֹת, אַתָּה אֱלֹהִים לְבַדֶּֽךָ.¹⁰ כִּי גָדוֹל

great ⟨ For ⟨ alone. ⟨ O God, ⟩ You, ⟩ of wonders; ⟨ and a worker

(1) Cf. *Psalms* 5:8. (2) 134:1. (3) 134:2. (4) 99:5. (5) 99:9. (6) 96:9. (7) Cf. 138:2. (8) 89:9. (9) 89:7. (10) 86:10.

מֵעַל שָׁמַיִם חַסְדֶּךָ, וְעַד שְׁחָקִים אֲמִתֶּךָ.¹ גָּדוֹל
⟨ Great ⟨ is Your ⟨ the upper ⟨ and ⟨ is Your ⟨ the very ⟨ above
　　　　truth.　　　heights　until　kindness,　　heavens

יהוה וּמְהֻלָּל מְאֹד, וְלִגְדֻלָּתוֹ אֵין חֵקֶר. (כִּי) ² גָּדוֹל
⟨ great ⟨ (For) ⟨ investiga- ⟨ is ⟨ and His ⟨ exceed- ⟨ and ⟨ is
　　　　　　tion.　beyond　greatness　ingly,　lauded　HASHEM

יהוה וּמְהֻלָּל מְאֹד, נוֹרָא הוּא עַל כָּל אֱלֹהִים.³ כִּי
⟨ For ⟨ heavenly ⟨ all ⟨ above ⟨ is He ⟨ awesome ⟨ exceed- ⟨ and ⟨ is
　　　powers.　　　　　　　　　　　ingly;　lauded　HASHEM

אֵל גָּדוֹל יהוה, וּמֶלֶךְ גָּדוֹל עַל כָּל אֱלֹהִים.⁴ אֲשֶׁר
⟨ For ⟨ heavenly ⟨ all ⟨ above ⟨ and a great King ⟨ is ⟨ a great God
　　　powers.　　　　　　　　　　　　　HASHEM,

מִי אֵל בַּשָּׁמַיִם וּבָאָרֶץ, אֲשֶׁר יַעֲשֶׂה כְמַעֲשֶׂיךָ
⟨ like unto ⟨ can do ⟨ that ⟨ or in the ⟨ is there in ⟨ power ⟨ what
　Your deeds　　　　　earth　　the heaven

וְכִגְבוּרֹתֶיךָ.⁵ מִי לֹא יִרָאֲךָ מֶלֶךְ הַגּוֹיִם, כִּי לְךָ
⟨ to ⟨ For ⟨ of nations? ⟨ O King ⟨ fear You, ⟨ would ⟨ Who ⟨ and like unto Your
You　　　　　　　　　　　　　not　　　　mighty acts?

יָאָתָה, כִּי בְכָל חַכְמֵי הַגּוֹיִם וּבְכָל מַלְכוּתָם מֵאֵין
⟨ there is ⟨ their ⟨ and in all ⟨ of the ⟨ the wise ⟨ among ⟨ for ⟨ [kingship]
　none　kingdoms　　　nations　men　all　　befits;

כָּמוֹךָ.⁶ מֵאֵין כָּמוֹךָ יהוה, גָּדוֹל אַתָּה וְגָדוֹל שְׁמֶךָ
⟨ is Your ⟨ and great ⟨ are You ⟨ Great ⟨ O ⟨ like You, ⟨ There is ⟨ like You.
Name　　　　　　　　　HASHEM!　　　none

בִּגְבוּרָה.⁷ לְךָ זְרוֹעַ עִם גְּבוּרָה, תָּעֹז יָדְךָ תָּרוּם
⟨ uplifted ⟨ is Your ⟨ strength- ⟨ power; ⟨ with ⟨ is the ⟨ Yours ⟨ in might.
　　　hand,　ened　　　　　arm

יְמִינֶךָ.⁸ לְךָ יוֹם, אַף לְךָ לָיְלָה, אַתָּה הֲכִינוֹתָ מָאוֹר
⟨ the ⟨ prepared ⟨ You ⟨ is the ⟨ Yours ⟨ also ⟨ is the ⟨ Yours ⟨ is Your
luminary　　　　night;　　　　　day,　　　right hand.

וָשָׁמֶשׁ.⁹ אֲשֶׁר בְּיָדוֹ מֶחְקְרֵי אָרֶץ, וְתוֹעֲפוֹת הָרִים
⟨ of the ⟨ and the ⟨ of the ⟨ are the hidden ⟨ in His ⟨ For ⟨ and the
mountains　summits　earth,　mysteries　power　　sun.

לוֹ.¹⁰ מִי יְמַלֵּל גְּבוּרוֹת יהוה, יַשְׁמִיעַ כָּל תְּהִלָּתוֹ.¹¹
⟨ of His ⟨ all ⟨ [who] can ⟨ of ⟨ the mighty ⟨ can ⟨ Who ⟨ are
praise?　　make heard　HASHEM;　acts　express　　His.

(1) Psalms 108:5. (2) 145:3. (3) 96:4. (4) 95:3. (5) Deuteronomy 3:24.
(6) Jeremiah 10:7. (7) 10:6. (8) Psalms 89:14. (9) 74:16. (10) 95:4. (11) 106:2.

לְךָ יהוה הַגְּדֻלָּה וְהַגְּבוּרָה, וְהַתִּפְאֶרֶת וְהַנֵּצַח
⟨ the triumph, ⟨ the glory, ⟨ the strength, ⟨ is the greatness, ⟨ HASHEM, ⟨ Yours,

וְהַהוֹד, כִּי כֹל בַּשָּׁמַיִם וּבָאָרֶץ; לְךָ יהוה הַמַּמְלָכָה,
⟨ is the kingdom ⟨ HASHEM, ⟨ Yours, « and on earth [is Yours]; ⟨ in heaven ⟨ every-thing ⟨ for « and the majesty;

וְהַמִּתְנַשֵּׂא לְכֹל לְרֹאשׁ.¹ לְךָ שָׁמַיִם, אַף לְךָ אָרֶץ,
« is the earth; ⟨ Yours also « are the heavens, ⟨ Yours « leader. ⟨ over every ⟨ and the sovereignty

תֵּבֵל וּמְלֹאָהּ אַתָּה יְסַדְתָּם.² אַתָּה הִצַּבְתָּ כָּל גְּבוּלוֹת
⟨ the boundaries ⟨ all ⟨ established ⟨ You « founded them. ⟨ You ⟨ and its fullness, ⟨ the world

אָרֶץ, קַיִץ וָחֹרֶף אַתָּה יְצַרְתָּם.³ אַתָּה רִצַּצְתָּ רָאשֵׁי
⟨ the heads ⟨ crushed ⟨ You « fashioned them. ⟨ You ⟨ and winter, ⟨ summer « of earth;

לִוְיָתָן, תִּתְּנֶנּוּ מַאֲכָל לְעָם לְצִיִּים. אַתָּה בָקַעְתָּ מַעְיָן
⟨ fountain ⟨ split open ⟨ You « [destined] for the desolate wilderness. ⟨ to the people ⟨ as food ⟨ You will serve it « of Leviathan;

וָנָחַל, אַתָּה הוֹבַשְׁתָּ נַהֲרוֹת אֵיתָן.⁴ אַתָּה פוֹרַרְתָּ
⟨ shattered ⟨ You « that are mighty. ⟨ rivers ⟨ dried ⟨ You « and stream;

בְעָזְּךָ יָם, שִׁבַּרְתָּ רָאשֵׁי תַנִּינִים עַל הַמָּיִם.⁵ אַתָּה
⟨ You « the water. ⟨ upon ⟨ of sea serpents ⟨ the heads ⟨ You « the sea; ⟨ with Your might

מוֹשֵׁל בְּגֵאוּת הַיָּם, בְּשׂוֹא גַלָּיו אַתָּה תְשַׁבְּחֵם.⁶
« calm them. ⟨ You ⟨ its waves, ⟨ when it raises « of the sea; ⟨ the grandeur ⟨ rule

גָּדוֹל יהוה וּמְהֻלָּל מְאֹד, בְּעִיר אֱלֹהֵינוּ הַר קָדְשׁוֹ.⁷
« of His Holiness. ⟨ Mount ⟨ of our God, ⟨ in the City ⟨ and much praised, ⟨ is ⟨ Great HASHEM

יהוה צְבָאוֹת, אֱלֹהֵי יִשְׂרָאֵל, יוֹשֵׁב הַכְּרֻבִים, אַתָּה
⟨ it is You « upon the Cherubim, ⟨ en-throned ⟨ of Israel, ⟨ God ⟨ Master of Legions, ⟨ HASHEM,

הוּא הָאֱלֹהִים לְבַדֶּךָ.⁸ אֵל נַעֲרָץ בְּסוֹד קְדוֹשִׁים רַבָּה,
« in the great assemblage of the holy [angels], ⟨ is revered ⟨ God « alone. ⟨ God ⟨ Who are

(1) I Chronicles 29:11. (2) Psalms 89:12. (3) 74:17. (4) 74:14-15. (5) 74:13. (6) 89:10. (7) 48:2. (8) Isaiah 37:16.

וְנוֹרָא עַל כָּל סְבִיבָיו.[1] וְיוֹדוּ שָׁמַיִם פִּלְאֲךָ יהוה, אַף

also ≫ HASHEM, ⟨ Your ⟨ will the ⟨ Acknowl- ≫ who sur- ⟨ all ⟨ over ⟨ and is
wonders, heavens edge round Him. awesome

אֱמוּנָתְךָ בִּקְהַל קְדֹשִׁים.[2] לְכוּ נְרַנְּנָה לַיהוה, נָרְיעָה

let us ≫ to ⟨ Let us sing ⟨ Come! ≫ of holy ⟨ in the ⟨ Your
call out HASHEM, joyfully ones. assembly faithfulness,

לְצוּר יִשְׁעֵנוּ. נְקַדְּמָה פָנָיו בְּתוֹדָה, בִּזְמִרוֹת נָרִיעַ

let us ⟨ with praiseful ≫ with ⟨ Him ⟨ Let us greet ≫ of our ⟨ to the
call out songs thanksgiving, salvation. Rock

לוֹ.[3] צֶדֶק וּמִשְׁפָּט מְכוֹן כִּסְאֶךָ, חֶסֶד וֶאֱמֶת יְקַדְּמוּ

precede ⟨ and ⟨ kindness ≫ of Your ⟨ are the ⟨ and ⟨ Righteous- ≫ to
truth throne; foundation justice ness Him.

פָנֶיךָ.[4] אֲשֶׁר יַחְדָּו נַמְתִּיק סוֹד, בְּבֵית אֱלֹהִים נְהַלֵּךְ

let us ⟨ of God ⟨ in the ≫ counsel; ⟨ let us ⟨ together ⟨ For ≫ Your coun-
walk House take sweet tenance.

בְּרָגֶשׁ.[5] אֲשֶׁר לוֹ הַיָּם וְהוּא עָשָׂהוּ, וְיַבֶּשֶׁת יָדָיו

His ≫ and the ≫ perfected ⟨ and He ⟨ is the ⟨ His ⟨ For ≫ in company.
hands dry land, it, sea

יָצָרוּ.[6] אֲשֶׁר בְּיָדוֹ נֶפֶשׁ כָּל חָי, וְרוּחַ כָּל בְּשַׂר אִישׁ.[7]

≫ mankind. ⟨ of all ⟨ and the ≫ the ⟨ of ⟨ is the ⟨ in His ⟨ For ≫ fashioned.
spirit living all soul hand

❖ הַנְּשָׁמָה לָךְ וְהַגּוּף פָּעֳלָךְ, חוּסָה עַל עֲמָלָךְ.

≫ Your ⟨ on ⟨ take pity ≫ is Your ⟨ and the ⟨ is ⟨ The soul
labor. handiwork; body Yours

הַנְּשָׁמָה לָךְ וְהַגּוּף שֶׁלָּךְ, יהוה עֲשֵׂה לְמַעַן שְׁמֶךָ.

≫ of Your ⟨ for the ⟨ act ⟨ O ≫ is Yours; ⟨ and the ⟨ is ⟨ The soul
Name. sake HASHEM, body Yours

אָתָאנוּ עַל שִׁמְךָ, יהוה, עֲשֵׂה לְמַעַן שְׁמֶךָ. בַּעֲבוּר

[act] ≫ of Your ⟨ for the ⟨ act ≫ O ≫ Your ⟨ [relying] ⟨ We have
because of Name; sake HASHEM; Name, on come

כְּבוֹד שִׁמְךָ, כִּי אֵל חַנּוּן וְרַחוּם שְׁמֶךָ. לְמַעַן

For the ≫ is Your ⟨ and ⟨ Who is ⟨ God ⟨ for ≫ of Your ⟨ the glory
sake Name. Merciful Gracious Name,

שִׁמְךָ יהוה, וְסָלַחְתָּ לַעֲוֹנֵנוּ כִּי רַב הוּא.[8]

⟨ it is great. ⟨ though ⟨ our ⟨ forgive ≫ HASHEM, ⟨ of Your
iniquity, Name,

---

(1) *Psalms* 89:8. (2) 89:6. (3) 95:1-2. (4) 89:15. (5) 55:15. (6) 95:5. (7) *Job* 12:10. (8) Cf. *Psalms* 25:11.

CONGREGATION, THEN *CHAZZAN*:

סְלַח לָנוּ אָבִינוּ, כִּי בְרוֹב אִוַּלְתֵּנוּ שָׁגִינוּ,

« we have ‹ of our folly ‹ in the ‹ for ‹ our Father, ‹ us, ‹ Forgive
erred;　　　　　　　　abundance

מְחַל לָנוּ מַלְכֵּנוּ, כִּי רַבּוּ עֲוֹנֵינוּ.

« our ‹ many ‹ for ‹ our King, ‹ us, ‹ pardon
iniquities.　are

סליחה מב / SELICHAH 42

(פתיחה)

ALL:

אָז טֶרֶם* נִמְתְּחוּ נִבְלֵי שְׁחָקִים.[1]

« to be brought ‹ the water- ‹ were spread ‹ before* ‹ Then,
down [as rainfall], skin clouds　out

בָּאָרֶץ עַד לֹא דֻּבְּקוּ רְגָבִים.[2]

« were the clods [that ‹ stuck ‹ not ‹ while ‹ on earth
would form the earth], together　yet

גַּבְּךָ שִׁבְעָה דְבָרִים הָיוּ מְגֻבָּבִים.

« gathered: ‹ were ‹ things ‹ seven ‹ with You

דָּת[3] וָכֵס[4] וּרְטִיַּת בָּנִים שׁוֹבָבִים.[5]

‹ who are ‹ for ‹ and the ‹ the ‹ The
wayward, children healing [of Throne Torah,
repentance] [of Glory],

הוֹד גַּן עֵדֶן וְעָלֵק הַבְהָבִים.[6]

‹ that is always ‹ and the leech ‹ of ‹ of the ‹ the
asking for more, [Gehinnom] Eden, Garden glory

---

(1) Cf. *Job* 38:37. (2) Cf. 38:38. (3) See *Deuteronomy* 33:2.
(4) See *Exodus* 17:16. (5) See *Jeremiah* 3:14. (6) See *Proverbs* 30:15.

---

§⊸אָז טֶרֶם — *Then, before.* This *pesichah* (introductory *selichah*) was composed by *Rashi*, the best known and greatest of all commentators on Scripture and the Talmud [see prefatory comment to *Selichah* 23]. The acrostic of the stiches comprises the *aleph-beis* followed by *Rashi's* signature — שְׁלֹמֹה בְּרַבִּי יִצְחָק, *Shlomo son of R' Yitzchak.*

The *selichah* is based on the Talmud's teaching that seven things were created before the world itself: Torah, the concept of *teshuvah* (repentance), *Gan Eden, Gehinnom*, the Throne of Glory, the [heavenly] *Beis HaMikdash*, and the name of the Messiah (*Nedarim* 39b; *Pesachim* 54a).

The Midrash describes the scene: Seven things preceded the world by two thousand years .... The Torah, written with black fire [as the ink] on white fire [as the parchment], is lying on God's knees [so to speak]. God is sitting on the Throne of Glory ... with *Gan Eden* at His right [south], *Gehinnom* at His left [north]. The *Beis HaMikdash* is before Him, with the Messiah's name engraved on a precious stone upon the Altar. A heavenly voice calls out, "Repent! O sons

וּמְקוֹם כַּפָּרָה עַל יְדֵי מַקְרִיבִים.

⟨ [Altar] offerings, ⟨ through ⟨ of atonement ⟨ the place

זְהַר שֵׁם יִנּוֹן*[1] מְחוֹלָל מֵחוֹבִים.[2]

《 by [our] sins — ⟨ that was ⟨ of the [Messiah's] ⟨ the
        profaned   name Yinon*   radiance

חֻבְּרוּ אַלְפַּיִם קֹדֶם בְּרִיאַת יְשׁוּבִים.

《 of settlements, ⟨ the creation ⟨ before ⟨ two ⟨ these were
      thousand   joined
      [years]   [before Him]

טְכוּסִים עַל רָקִיעַ בּוֹטִים כִּשְׁבִיבִים.

《 like sparks of fire, ⟨ looking 《 the firmament, ⟨ over ⟨ arrayed

יְעוּרִים וּמְשֹׁרָשִׁים פְּנֵי יוֹשֵׁב הַכְּרוּבִים.

《   on the   ⟨ Him ⟨ before ⟨ well-rooted ⟨ burgeoning,
    Cherubim.   Who sits

כִּסֵּא הָיָה מֻנָּח בָּרָקִיעַ בִּיצוּבִים.

《   firmly,   ⟨ upon the ⟨ posi- ⟨ was ⟨ The
      Heavens   tioned   Throne

לְמוֹשַׁב מֶלֶךְ וְנוֹרָא עַל סְבִיבִים.[3]

《   [all] who   ⟨ over ⟨ who is ⟨ for the ⟨ as a seat
    surround Him;   awesome   King

מִימִינוֹ אֵשׁ דָּת[4] חֲקוּקָה בִּכְתָבִים.

《   in writing,   ⟨ which was ⟨ Torah, ⟨ [He present- ⟨ from His
      engraved   ed] the fiery   right Hand

נְתוּנָה עַל בִּרְכּוֹ בְּשַׁעֲשׁוּעַ[5] אֲהָבִים.

《   love;   ⟨ in playful ⟨ His knee ⟨ on ⟨ placed

סָדוּר עַל הַדָּרוֹם* גַּן רְטוּבִים.

《   well   ⟨ was the Gar- ⟨ the ⟨ to ⟨ set
   watered;   den [of Eden]   south*

עָרוּךְ עַל הַצָּפוֹן* תֹּפֶת[6] שַׁלְהֵבִים.

《   flaming.   ⟨ was the Tofeth ⟨ the north* ⟨ to ⟨ arranged
      [Gehinnom]

---

(1) Cf. *Psalms* 72:17. (2) Cf. *Isaiah* 53:5. (3) Cf. *Psalms* 89:8. (4) *Deuteronomy* 33:2.
(5) Cf. *Proverbs* 8:30-31; *Isaiah* 66:12. (6) See *Jeremiah* 7:32.

---

of man ..." (*Shocheir Tov* 90:12).

שֵׁם יִנּוֹן — *The [Messiah's] ... name*, "Yinon." According to one opinion in the Talmud, the Messiah's name is יִנּוֹן, *Yinon*, as it is
stated (*Psalms* 72:17): May his name endure

forever; before the sun [was created], יִנּוֹן
שְׁמוֹ, *his name was Yinon* (*Sanhedrin* 98b).

סָדוּר עַל הַדָּרוֹם ... עָרוּךְ עַל הַצָּפוֹן — *Set to the
south ... arranged to the north*. The *paytan*
has changed right and left (of the Midrash's

פְּנֵי הַמִּזְרָח יְרוּשָׁלַיִם הַבְּנוּיָה בְּמַחֲצָבִים.
《 of hewn stones, 〈 built 〈 was Jerusalem, 〈 to the east 〈Facing,

צָפוֹן בְּתוֹכָהּ מִקְדָשׁ אֵל בִּישׁוּבִים.
《[paralleling the Temple] 〈 of 〈 the Temple 〈 within it 〈 and
on inhabited earth, God, secreted

קָבוּעַ בְּאֶמְצַע מִזְבַּח כִּפּוּר חַיָּבִים.¹
《 for sinners, 〈of atonement 〈the Altar 〈 in its center, 〈 fixed

רְבוּצָה עָלָיו אֶבֶן שְׁתִיַּת חֲטוּבִים.*
《 was hewn.* 〈 from which 〈 is the 〈 upon [the 〈 and resting
the foundation stone Altar above]

שָׁם יִנּוֹן עָלֶיהָ חָקוּק בְּמִכְתָּבִים.
《 in letters, 〈 is 〈 upon it 〈 The [Messiah's]
engraved name Yinon

תֹּאַר שֵׁם הַמְפֹרָשׁ* בְּתָוֵי גְלוּבִים.
《 that are 〈 in letters 〈 that is 〈 of [God's] 〈 and the
engraved. Ineffable,* Name description

---

(1) Some editions read מִזְבַּח כִּפּוּר חַיָּבִים, *the Altar, to atone for sinners.*

---

description) to south and north respectively. From the viewpoint of the *Shechinah* (Divine Presence) resting upon the top of the Ark in the Holy of Holies, facing the entranceway to the Sanctuary, east is before Him, west behind Him, south to His right and north to His left. Thus, east is called קֶדֶם, *before,* and west is called אָחוֹר, *behind* (see *Psalms* 139:5; *Chagigah* 12a with *Rashi*); south is called יָמִין, *right,* and north is called שְׂמֹאל, *left* (see *Targum Onkelos* to *Genesis* 13:9).

אֶבֶן שְׁתִיַּת חֲטוּבִים — *The stone from which the foundation was hewn.* The Talmud states that there was a rock that protruded three handbreadths above the floor of the Holiest of the Holies. That stone was called אֶבֶן שְׁתִיָּה, *Foundation Stone,* for it was the basis, or central point, from which the world was created (*Yoma* 54b). The *paytan* borrows the term אֶבֶן שְׁתִיָּה and uses it to describe another stone in the *Beis HaMikdash,* namely, the אֶבֶן יְקָרָה, *precious stone,* that the Midrash cited above states was on the Altar and had the Messiah's name engraved upon it. Moreover, he identifies that stone with another upon which King David had engraved the Ineffable Name of God. The Talmud

relates that when King David prepared the foundations for the future Temple that his son Solomon would build, he excavated deep pits beneath the site of the Altar, into which the wine and water libations would flow. David dug so deep that he penetrated the subterranean reservoirs of water that had been stored beneath the earth's crust since Creation. The waters erupted from the reservoir and threatened to inundate the world. David then inscribed a Divine Name on a shard and cast it into the waters, which receded ... (*Succah* 53).

תֹּאַר שֵׁם הַמְפֹרָשׁ — *And the description of [God's] Name that is Ineffable.* See the preceding comment for the interpretation of this phrase. Alternatively, the stich should be understood in its literal sense, and connected to the one before it. Thus, the Messiah's name that is carved into the stone takes the same form as God's Name. Just as in God's Name the first and third letters are י and ו, so in the Messiah's name, Yinon, the first and third letters are י and ו. And just as in God's Name the second and fourth letters are the same (ה), so in the name Yinon are the second and fourth letters the same (נ). Moreover, in

שָׁמָּה בַּתָּוֶךְ לִפְנֵי מַאֲזִין מֵאֲשְׁנַבִּים,*¹

‹ There, › in the mid- › before › Him Who › from the windows »
dle [of the listens [of Heaven],*
firmament], [to prayer]

לִוּוּי תְּשׁוּבָה אֶרֶךְ לִנְדוּים וְכָאֵבִים.

‹ was › to › healing — › for those › and pained »
the link repentance » suffering [from their sins],

מֵעֻתֶּדֶת לְכַבּוּס צוֹאִים, וּלְהַלְבִּישׁ מוּטָבִים.*²

‹ prepared › to launder › [their] befouled › and to dress › with proper »
[garments]* [them] ones,*

הָרֵק שֶׁמֶן הַטּוֹב עַל רֹאשׁ שָׁבִים.

‹ to pour › oil › that is › on › the › of the »
beneficial heads repentant.

בְּכֵן אָתָנוּ לְךָ עֲלָמִים וְשָׁבִים.

‹ There- › we have › to You, » young, › and old, »
fore come

רַחֵץ מִצַּחַן וְהַשְׁלֵךְ טְמוּס סְאָבִים.

‹ to wash › off the stench › and to › the › of our »
[of sin] cast away ledgers defiling deeds.

בִּתְפִלָּה יְקַדְּמוּךָ בָּנִים שׁוֹבֵבִים.

‹ With prayer › shall they › — Your › who are »
approach You children wayward,

יוֹם יוֹם לְדָרְשֶׁךָ בְּפִיץ נִיבִים.

‹ day › by › seeking You › by › words »
day speaking [of prayer].

❖ יֵחָשֵׁב אֲמָרֵינוּ כְּהַקְטֵר דָּמִים וַחֲלָבִים.*

‹ Let be › our words › as the burning › of bloods › and fats;* »
considered [on the Altar]

---

(1) Some editions read מְזִיב מַשְׁאַבִּים; see commentary. (2) Cf. Zechariah 3:4.

one of the Kabbalistic permutations of the aleph-beis (known as אַ״ט בַּ״ח), the letters ה and נ form a pair in which one may be substituted for the other. Accordingly, the two stiches read: *The [Messiah's] name Yinon is engraved upon it in letters that form the Ineffable* ....

מֵאֲזִין מֵאֲשְׁנַבִּים — *Him Who listens [to prayer] from the windows [of Heaven].* Some editions of *Selichos* read מְזִיב מַשְׁאַבִּים, *from which the waters flow.* The phrase then refers to the אֶבֶן שְׁתִיָה, *Foundation Stone,* mentioned earlier, from which flow all the waters of the world.

צוֹאִים . . . מוּטָבִים — *[Their] befouled [garments] . . . with proper ones.* The prophet (*Zechariah* 3:2) describes the effects of sin as befouled garments and repentance as the donning of fresh clothing.

כְּהַקְטֵר דָּמִים וַחֲלָבִים — *As the burning [on the Altar] of bloods and fats.* The expression הַקְטֵר דָּמִים, *burning bloods,* is difficult. We do not find in Scripture or Talmud blood placed upon the Altar fire. Blood from sacrificial

צִפְצוּפֵנוּ יְקַבֵּל כְּפִסוּגֵי פָּרִים וּכְשָׂבִים.

‹ and sheep ‹ of bulls ‹ as [You would] ‹ accept ‹ our chirping
[on the Altar].   the severed parts   [prayer]

חֲטָאֵינוּ הַצְלֵל בְּקַרְקַע נִטְפֵי מַרְזֵבִים.

‹ [flows] from ‹ where the ‹ into the ‹ sink ‹ Our sins
the drainpipes;   dripping   [earth's]
water   depths

קָרְבֵנוּ אֵלֶיךָ בִּרְחִיפַת רַחֲמֶיךָ הָרַבִּים.

‹ that is great. ‹ of Your ‹ with the ‹ to You ‹ bring
mercy   hovering over us   us near

ALL:

כִּי עַל רַחֲמֶיךָ הָרַבִּים[1] אָנוּ בְּטוּחִים, וְעַל צִדְקוֹתֶיךָ

‹ Your ‹ and ‹ trust, ‹ we ‹ that is ‹ Your ‹ upon ‹ For
righteousness   upon   abundant   mercy

אָנוּ נִשְׁעָנִים, וְלִסְלִיחוֹתֶיךָ אָנוּ מְקַוִּים, וְלִישׁוּעָתְךָ

‹ and for Your ‹ hope, ‹ we ‹ and for Your ‹ rely, ‹ we
salvation   forgiveness

אָנוּ מְצַפִּים. אַתָּה הוּא מֶלֶךְ, אוֹהֵב צְדָקוֹת מִקֶּדֶם,

‹ since the ‹ righteous- ‹ Who ‹ the King ‹ are ‹ You ‹ await ‹ we
beginning   ness   loves   eagerly.
of time,

מַעֲבִיר עֲוֹנוֹת עַמּוֹ, וּמֵסִיר חַטֹּאת יְרֵאָיו. כּוֹרֵת

‹ He ‹ of those who ‹ the sins ‹ and ‹ of His ‹ the ‹ Who
established   revere Him.   removes   people   iniquities   overlooks

בְּרִית לָרִאשׁוֹנִים, וּמְקַיֵּם שְׁבוּעָה לָאַחֲרוֹנִים. אַתָּה

‹ You ‹ to the ‹ [His] oath ‹ and fulfills ‹ with the ‹ a covenant
descendants.   ancestors

הוּא, שֶׁיָּרַדְתָּ בַּעֲנַן כְּבוֹדֶךָ עַל הַר סִינַי[2], וְהֶרְאֵיתָ

‹ and You ‹ Sinai, ‹ Mount ‹ upon ‹ of Your ‹ in the ‹ Who ‹ are the
showed   glory   cloud   descended   One

דַּרְכֵי טוּבְךָ לְמֹשֶׁה עַבְדֶּךָ. וְאָרְחוֹת חֲסָדֶיךָ גִּלִּיתָ[3].

‹ You ‹ of Your ‹ The paths ‹ Your ‹ to Moses ‹ of Your ‹ the
revealed   kindness   servant.   goodness   ways

---

(1) *Daniel* 9:18. (2) Cf. *Exodus* 34:5. (3) Cf. 33:13.

animals was placed on the sides or corners of the Altar, not on the fire. Interestingly, none of the commentaries raise this question. There is, however, at least one ancient manuscript that reads סַמִּים, *spices*, instead of דָּמִים, *blood*. If so, the word refers to the Incense offered twice daily on the Golden (Inner) Altar.

לוֹ, וְהוֹדַעְתּוֹ כִּי אַתָּה אֵל רַחוּם וְחַנּוּן, אֶרֶךְ אַפַּיִם

‹ to ‹ Slow « and ‹ Compas- ‹ God, ‹ You are ‹ that ‹ and You « to
anger sionate Gracious, let him know him,

וְרַב חֶסֶד[1] וּמַרְבֶּה לְהֵטִיב, וּמַנְהִיג אֶת כָּל הָעוֹלָם

‹ world ‹ the whole ‹ and Who « beneficent, ‹ Who is ‹ in Kind- ‹ and
guides abundantly ness, Abundant

כֻּלּוֹ בְּמִדַּת הָרַחֲמִים. ❖ וְכֵן כָּתוּב, וַיֹּאמֶר אֲנִי אַעֲבִיר

‹ shall cause ‹ "I « And He « it is ‹ And so « of Mercy. ‹ with the ‹ in its
to pass said, written: Attribute entirely

כָּל טוּבִי עַל פָּנֶיךָ, וְקָרָאתִי בְשֵׁם יהוה לְפָנֶיךָ,

« before ‹ HASHEM ‹ with the ‹ and I shall « your ‹ before ‹ My ‹ all
you; Name call out face, goodness

וְחַנֹּתִי אֶת אֲשֶׁר אָחֹן, וְרִחַמְתִּי אֶת אֲשֶׁר אֲרַחֵם.[2]

« I choose to ‹ whom- ‹ to ‹ and I shall « I choose to ‹ whom- ‹ to ‹ I shall
show mercy." ever show mercy show favor, ever show favor

ALL, WHILE STANDING

אֵל אֶרֶךְ אַפַּיִם אַתָּה,

« You are, ‹ to anger, ‹ Who is slow ‹ God

וּבַעַל הָרַחֲמִים נִקְרֵאתָ, וְדֶרֶךְ תְּשׁוּבָה הוֹרֵיתָ.

« You have ‹ of ‹ and the « You are ‹ of Mercy ‹ and
taught. repentance way called; Master

גְּדֻלַּת רַחֲמֶיךָ וַחֲסָדֶיךָ,

‹ and Your ‹ of Your ‹ The
kindness mercy greatness

תִּזְכּוֹר הַיּוֹם וּבְכָל יוֹם לְזֶרַע יְדִידֶיךָ.

« of Your ‹ for the « day, ‹ and ‹ this day ‹ may You
beloved ones. offspring every remember,

תֵּפֶן אֵלֵינוּ בְּרַחֲמִים,

« in mercy, ‹ to us ‹ Turn

כִּי אַתָּה הוּא בַּעַל הָרַחֲמִים.

« of Mercy. ‹ the Master ‹ are ‹ You ‹ for

בְּתַחֲנוּן וּבִתְפִלָּה פָּנֶיךָ נְקַדֵּם, כְּהוֹדַעְתָּ לֶעָנָיו מִקֶּדֶם.

« in ancient ‹ to the ‹ in the manner « we ‹ Your ‹ and prayer « With
times. humble one that You made approach, Presence supplication
[Moses] known

---

(1) *Exodus* 34:6. (2) 33:19.

מֵחֲרוֹן אַפְּךָ שׁוּב,[1] כְּמוֹ בְּתוֹרָתְךָ כָּתוּב.[2]

‹ it is ⟨ in Your Torah ⟨ as ⟪ turn ⟨ of Your ⟨ From the
written. back, anger fierceness

וּבְצֵל כְּנָפֶיךָ נֶחֱסֶה[3] וְנִתְלוֹנָן, כְּיוֹם וַיֵּרֶד יהוה בֶּעָנָן.

⟪ in a ⟨ when HASHEM ⟨ as on ⟪ and may ⟨ may we find ⟨ of Your ⟨ In the
cloud. descended the day we dwell, shelter wings shadow

❖ תַּעֲבוֹר עַל פֶּשַׁע וְתִמְחֶה אָשָׁם,

⟪ guilt, ⟨ and erase ⟨ sin ⟨ Overlook

כְּיוֹם וַיִּתְיַצֵּב עִמּוֹ שָׁם.

⟪ there. ⟨ with him ⟨ when He ⟨ as on the
[Moses] [God] stood day

תַּאֲזִין שַׁוְעָתֵנוּ וְתַקְשִׁיב מֶנּוּ מַאֲמָר,

⟪ [our] ⟨ from ⟨ and hear ⟨ to our cry ⟨ Give heed
declaration, us

כְּיוֹם וַיִּקְרָא בְּשֵׁם יהוה,[4] וְשָׁם נֶאֱמַר:

⟪ it was said: ⟨ and ⟪ of HASHEM, ⟨ with the ⟨ when He ⟨ as on
there Name called out the day

CONGREGATION, THEN *CHAZZAN:*

וַיַּעֲבֹר יהוה עַל פָּנָיו וַיִּקְרָא:

⟪ and ⟪ [Moses'] ⟨ before ⟨ And HASHEM passed
proclaimed: face,

CONGREGATION AND *CHAZZAN* **RECITE LOUDLY AND IN UNISON:**

יהוה, יהוה, אֵל, רַחוּם, וְחַנּוּן, אֶרֶךְ אַפַּיִם,

⟨ to anger, ⟨ Slow ⟪ and ⟨ Compassionate ⟨ God, ⟨ HASHEM, ⟨ HASHEM,
Gracious,

וְרַב חֶסֶד, וֶאֱמֶת, נֹצֵר חֶסֶד לָאֲלָפִים, נֹשֵׂא עָוֹן,

⟨ of ⟨ Forgiver ⟪ for ⟨ of ⟨ Preserver ⟪ and ⟨ in ⟨ and
iniquity, thousands kindness Truth, Kindness Abundant
[of generations],

וָפֶשַׁע, וְחַטָּאָה, וְנַקֵּה.[5] וְסָלַחְתָּ לַעֲוֹנֵנוּ וּלְחַטָּאתֵנוּ

⟪ and our sins, ⟨ our ⟨ May You ⟪ and Who ⟨ and inadvertent ⟨ willful sin,
iniquities forgive absolves. sin,

וּנְחַלְתָּנוּ.[6] סְלַח לָנוּ אָבִינוּ כִּי חָטָאנוּ, מְחַל לָנוּ

⟨ us, ⟨ pardon ⟪ we have ⟨ for ⟪ our Father, ⟨ us, ⟨ Forgive ⟪ and make us
sinned; Your heritage.

---

(1) Cf. *Exodus* 32:12. (2) See 32:14. (3) Cf. *Psalms* 36:8. (4) *Exodus* 34:5. (5) 34:6-7 (6) 34:9.

מַלְכֵּנוּ כִּי פָשָׁעְנוּ. כִּי אַתָּה אֲדֹנָי טוֹב וְסַלָּח, וְרַב

‹ and « and ‹ are ‹ O Lord, ‹ You, ‹ For « we have ‹ for « our King,
abundantly forgiving, good   willfully sinned.

חֶסֶד לְכָל קֹרְאֶיךָ.[1]

« who call ‹ to all ‹ kind
upon You.

דִּרְשׁוּ יהוה בְּהִמָּצְאוֹ, קְרָאֻהוּ בִּהְיוֹתוֹ קָרוֹב.

« when He is near. ‹ call upon « when He ‹ HASHEM ‹ Seek
Him   can be found;

יַעֲזֹב רָשָׁע דַּרְכּוֹ וְאִישׁ אָוֶן מַחְשְׁבֹתָיו, וְיָשֹׁב אֶל

‹ to ‹ and let « his thoughts; ‹ of ‹ and the « his way, ‹ Let the wicked
him return   iniquity man   one abandon

יהוה וִירַחֲמֵהוּ, וְאֶל אֱלֹהֵינוּ כִּי יַרְבֶּה לִסְלוֹחַ.[2]

« in ‹ He will be ‹ for ‹ our God ‹ and « and He will ‹ HASHEM
forgiving. abundant   [return] to show him mercy,

אֲדֹנָי שִׁמְעָה בְקוֹלֵנוּ, תִּהְיֶינָה אָזְנֶיךָ קַשֻּׁבוֹת לְקוֹל

‹ to the ‹ attentive « — Your « may they be « our voice; ‹ hear ‹ O Lord,
sound   ears —

תַּחֲנוּנֵינוּ.[3] תִּכּוֹן תְּפִלָּתֵנוּ קְטֹרֶת לְפָנֶיךָ.[4]

« before You. ‹ as incense ‹ should be ‹ Consid- « of our pleas.
our prayer   ered

כְּרַחֵם אָב עַל בָּנִים, כֵּן תְּרַחֵם יהוה עָלֵינוּ.[5]

« on us. ‹ HASHEM, ‹ have ‹ so « his ‹ toward ‹ a ‹ As merciful as
mercy,   children, father is

לַיהוה הַיְשׁוּעָה, עַל עַמְּךָ בִרְכָתֶךָ סֶּלָה.[6] יהוה

‹ HASHEM, « Selah. « is Your ‹ Your ‹ upon « is salvation, ‹ To HASHEM
blessing, people

צְבָאוֹת עִמָּנוּ, מִשְׂגָּב לָנוּ אֱלֹהֵי יַעֲקֹב סֶלָה.[7]

« Selah. « of Jacob, ‹ is the God ‹ for us ‹ a « is with us, ‹ Master of
stronghold   Legions,

יהוה צְבָאוֹת, אַשְׁרֵי אָדָם בֹּטֵחַ בָּךְ.[8] יהוה הוֹשִׁיעָה,

« save! ‹ HASHEM, « in ‹ who ‹ is the ‹ — praise- « Master of ‹ HASHEM,
You. trusts man worthy Legions

הַמֶּלֶךְ יַעֲנֵנוּ בְיוֹם קָרְאֵנוּ.¹

《 we call. 〈 on the 〈 answer us 〈 May the
day   King

IN MOST CONGREGATIONS THE FOLLOWING VERSES ARE RECITED ALOUD RESPONSIVELY, AS INDICATED; IN OTHERS THEY ARE RECITED SILENTLY.

CONGREGATION, ALOUD, FOLLOWED BY *CHAZZAN,* **ALOUD:**

סְלַח נָא לַעֲוֹן הָעָם הַזֶּה כְּגֹדֶל חַסְדֶּךָ, וְכַאֲשֶׁר

〈 just as 《 of Your 〈 according to 〈 of this people 〈 the 〈 please, 〈 Forgive,
kindness, the greatness   iniquity

נָשָׂאתָה לָעָם הַזֶּה מִמִּצְרַיִם וְעַד הֵנָּה,² וְשָׁם נֶאֱמַר:

《 it was 〈 And 《 now. 〈 until 〈 from Egypt 〈 this people 〈 You have
said: there   forgiven

ALL, ALOUD AND IN UNISON:

וַיֹּאמֶר יהוה סָלַחְתִּי כִּדְבָרֶךָ.³

《 *according to* 〈 *I have forgiven* 《 *And* HASHEM *said:*
your word!

ALL CONTINUE:

הַטֵּה אֱלֹהַי אָזְנְךָ וּשְׁמָע, פְּקַח עֵינֶיךָ וּרְאֵה

〈 and see 〈 Your eyes 〈 open 《 and listen; 〈 Your ear, 〈 my God, 〈 Incline,

שֹׁמְמֹתֵינוּ, וְהָעִיר אֲשֶׁר נִקְרָא שִׁמְךָ עָלֶיהָ, כִּי לֹא

〈 not 〈 for 《 upon; 〈 Your Name is 〈 which 〈 and that 〈 our desolation
proclaimed [of] the city

עַל צִדְקֹתֵינוּ אֲנַחְנוּ מַפִּילִים תַּחֲנוּנֵינוּ לְפָנֶיךָ,

《 before 〈 our 〈 cast 〈 do we 〈 of our 〈 because
You; supplications righteousness

כִּי עַל רַחֲמֶיךָ הָרַבִּים. אֲדֹנָי שְׁמָעָה, אֲדֹנָי סְלָחָה,

《 forgive; 〈 O Lord, 《 heed; 〈 O Lord, 《 which is 〈 of Your 〈 be- 〈 but
abundant. compassion, cause

אֲדֹנָי הַקְשִׁיבָה, וַעֲשֵׂה אַל תְּאַחַר, לְמַעַנְךָ אֱלֹהַי,

《 my God, 〈 for Your sake, 《 delay; 〈 do not 《 and act, 〈 be attentive, 〈 O Lord,

כִּי שִׁמְךָ נִקְרָא עַל עִירְךָ וְעַל עַמֶּךָ.⁴

《 Your 〈 and 〈 Your 〈 upon 〈 is 〈 Your 〈 for
people. upon City proclaimed Name

---

(1) *Psalms* 20:10. (2) *Numbers* 14:19. (3) 14:20. (4) *Daniel* 9:18-19.

סְלִיחָה מג / SELICHAH 43

ALL:

אֶת יהוה בְּהִמָּצְאוֹ* לְדָרְשׁוֹ¹ קִדַּמְתִּי,*

《 have I come early 〈 to seek Him 《 when He is 〈 HASHEM
[in the morning],*   to be found,*

בְּעַד עֲוֹנוֹת לְכַפֵּר, כִּי כַתּוֹלָע נֶאֱדַמְתִּי,²

《 I am reddened 〈 like a 〈 for 《 [asking Him] 〈 my 〈 for
[with sin].   crimson thread   to atone,   iniquities

גִּלְגַּל הַלֵּב וְטִמְטַם, וּכְיָשֵׁן נִרְדַּמְתִּי,

《 in a deep sleep. 〈 and like 《 and blocked 〈 is My 〈 Confused
     one sleeping   up;   heart

כִּמְעַט כִּסְדוֹם הָיִיתִי וְלַעֲמוֹרָה דָּמִיתִי.³

《 I am likened. 《 and to Amorah, 《 have I become; 〈 like Sodom 〈 Almost

דָּמִיתִי לְסוֹטָה פְּרוּעָה⁴ מְנָאֶפֶת וַחֲלָלָה,⁵

《 to a desecrated 〈 to an 《 her hair 〈 to a wife 〈 I am likened
   woman.   adulteress,   uncovered;   suspected
                        of adultery,

הָיִיתִי כְּבֶגֶד עֵדִים,⁶

《 worn out, 〈 like a 〈 I have
     garment   been

וְהוּשַׁמְתִּי כְּשִׂמְלָה בְּדָמִים מְגוֹלָלָה,⁷

《 wallows. 〈 that in blood 〈 like a cloak 〈 I am considered

וְחָסַרְתִּי מַפְגִּיעַ, וְיוֹדֵעַ אֵין לְפַלְלָה,

《 how to pray. 〈 for there is none 〈 one to pray 〈 Now I lack
           who knows   for me,

רְאֵה יהוה וְהַבִּיטָה, כִּי הָיִיתִי זוֹלֵלָה.⁸

《 degraded. 〈 I have become 〈 that 〈 and observe 〈 HASHEM, 〈 Look,

---

(1) Cf. *Isaiah* 55:6. (2) Cf. 1:18. (3) Cf. 1:9. (4) See *Numbers* Ch. 5.
(5) See *Leviticus* 21:9. (6) Cf. *Isaiah* 64:5. (7) Cf. 9:4. (8) *Lamentations* 1:11.

◆§ אֶת ה' בְּהִמָּצְאוֹ — *HASHEM when He is to be found.* In the intricate tapestry of this *selichah*, the first three lines of the respective quatrains form an *aleph-beis* acrostic followed by the composer's name — אֵלִיָּה בַּר שְׁמַעְיָה חֲזַק, *Eliyah bar Shemayah, may he be strong* [see prefatory comment to *Selichah* 14]. The last line of each stanza is a Scriptural fragment, the last word of which is repeated as the first word of the next stanza.

אֶת ה' בְּהִמָּצְאוֹ לְדָרְשׁוֹ קִדַּמְתִּי — *HASHEM when He is to be found, to seek Him have I come early [in the morning].* This opening stich has a double significance for the Fast of Gedaliah: (a) It is based on *Isaiah* 55:6, the first verse of the *haftarah* read at *Minchah* on fast days; and (b) the Talmud (*Rosh Hashanah* 18a) states that "when He is to be found" refers to the ten-day period from Rosh Hashanah to Yom Kippur, and today

זוֹלֵלָה כְּבוּדָה נֶהְפְּכָה בְּיַד מְגָאֵל,

‹ of the defiler. ‹ at the hand ‹ become ‹ has the respected woman ‹ **Degraded**

חִנָּם נִמְכְּרָה לִצְמִיתוּת, וְאֵין גּוֹאֵל,[1]

‹ a redeemer. ‹ without ‹ eternally, ‹ has she been sold, ‹ For naught

טֻבַּע נָכוֹן וְנִשָּׂא[2] וְחָרַב אֲרִיאֵל,*

‹ is Ariel*; ‹ destroyed ‹ exalted ‹ is the firmly [Temple], established, ‹ Sunken

הִשְׁלִיךְ מִשָּׁמַיִם אֶרֶץ תִּפְאֶרֶת יִשְׂרָאֵל.[3]

‹ of **Israel**. ‹ the glory ‹ to earth ‹ from Heaven ‹ He cast down

יִשְׂרָאֵל לְבוֹזְזִים וְלִמְשִׁסָּה,[4] עַד מָתַי,

‹ when? ‹ — until ‹ and to oppressors ‹ [given over] to looters ‹ **Israel**

כְּאַרְבֶּה רַבּוּ עוֹרְקַי, וְעָצְמוּ מַצְמִיתַי,[5]

‹ who would cut me off. ‹ mighty are those ‹ my pursuers; ‹ were numerous ‹ Like locusts

לַלֵּב בְּשׂוּמִי, הֲרִיסוֹתַי חָרְבוֹתַי וְשׁוֹמְמוֹתַי,[6]

‹ and my desolation, ‹ my ruins, ‹ my wreckage, ‹ to heart ‹ When I take

וַתִּבְחַר מַחֲנָק נַפְשִׁי, מָוֶת מֵעַצְמוֹתַי.[7]

‹ rather than [life in] **my bones**. ‹ death ‹ does my soul, ‹ suffocation ‹ choose

מֵעַצְמוֹתַי הַמְּפֻצָּחוֹת וְהַמְּפֻלָּחוֹת,

‹ and split ‹ that are broken ‹ **Because of my bones**

מִמַּכְעִיסֶיךָ וּמִמַּזְעִימֶיךָ,

‹ and who enrage You, ‹ by those who anger You

נָאֲמְתִּי, נִלְאֵיתִי נְשֹׂא חֲרוֹנְךָ וְזַעְמֶךָ,

‹ and Your rage. ‹ Your fury ‹ of bearing ‹ I am wearied ‹ I declare,

---

(1) Cf. *Isaiah* 52:3; *Leviticus* 25:30. (2) *Isaiah* 2:2. (3) *Lamentations* 2:1.
(4) Cf. *Isaiah* 42:24. (5) *Psalms* 69:5. (6) Cf. *Isaiah* 49:19. (7) *Job* 7:15.

---

is the first day during that period on which *Selichos* is recited.

אֲרִיאֵל — *Ariel.* This compound word literally means *lion of God.* In the Book of *Ezekiel* (43:15-16), it refers to the Altar fire, for the fire that originally descended from heaven when King Solomon inaugurated the Temple (*II Chronicles* 7:1) was in the

shape of a crouching lion (*Yoma* 21b). In *Isaiah* (29:1-2) it refers either to the Altar (*Targum* to v. 1; *Rashi*); the Temple itself, which, like a crouching lion, was wider in front and narrower in back (*Rashi* based on *Berachos* 18a); or the City of Jerusalem in which the Temple and the Altar stood (*Targum* to *Isaiah* loc. cit. v. 2; *Ibn Ezra*).

שִׂים לֵב לִגְאֹל חַיַּת נְעִימֶיךָ,

《 of those who ⟨ the ⟨ to ⟨ to ⟨ Take
sing of Your   lifeblood   redeem   heart
pleasantness,

כִּי שִׁמְךָ נִקְרָא, עַל עִירְךָ וְעַל עַמֶּךָ.[1]

《 **Your** ⟨ and ⟨ Your city ⟨ upon ⟨ is ⟨ Your ⟨ for
people.   upon   proclaimed   Name

עַמְּךָ זְרוּיִים פְּזוּרִים בְּכָל מוֹשָׁבוֹת,

《 settled places, ⟨ in all ⟨ and ⟨ are strewn ⟨ **Your**
scattered   **people**

פְּקָדוּךָ בַּצַּר, פְּחָדוּךָ בְּמַעַשׂ וּבְמַחֲשָׁבוֹת,

《 and in thought. ⟨ in deed ⟨ expressing ⟨ in their ⟨ remember-
fear of You   distress,   ing You

צְלַל זָדוֹן, וְהַעֲבֵר וְרַפֵּא מְשׁוּבוֹת,[2]

《 waywardness. ⟨ and heal ⟨ remove 《 willful ⟨ Sink in
sins;   deep water

אֲדֹנָי, שִׁמְעָה בְקוֹלֵנוּ, תִּהְיֶינָה אָזְנֶיךָ קַשֻּׁבוֹת.[3]

《 **attentive.** 《 — Your 《 may they be 《 our voice; ⟨ hear ⟨ O Lord,
ears —

קַשֻּׁבוֹת תִּהְיֶינָה אָזְנֶיךָ, לְשֶׁפֶךְ שִׂיחֵנוּ,

《 of our ⟨ to the 《 — Your 《 may they be ⟨ **Attentive**
prayer;   outpouring   ears —

רֹן שְׂפָתֵינוּ קַבֵּל כְּרֵיחַ נִיחֹחֵינוּ,[4]

《 that is ⟨ like the aroma ⟨ accept ⟨ of our lips ⟨ the
pleasing.   [of our Temple   song
offerings]

שַׁחֲרְנוּךָ מָגִנֵּנוּ וּבְךָ יַהַב מִבְטָחֵנוּ,

《 our trust. ⟨ is ⟨ and 《 our ⟨ We seek You in
placed   in You   Shield;   the morning,

וְשִׁמְךָ עָלֵינוּ נִקְרָא אַל תַּנִּיחֵנוּ.[5]

《 **abandon us.** ⟨ do 《 is pro- ⟨ upon us ⟨ Your
not   claimed;   Name

תַּנִּיחֵנוּ אָדוֹן זֶה כַּמֶּה שָׁנִים לָמָּה,

《 — why? 《 years ⟨ many ⟨ these ⟨ O Lord, ⟨ **Abandoned**
us have You,

---

(1) *Daniel* 9:19. (2) Cf. *Hosea* 14:5. (3) Cf. *Psalms* 130:2. (4) See *Hosea* 14:3. (5) *Jeremiah* 14:9.

לְשַׁמָּה לְמָשָׁל וְלִשְׁנִינָה¹ לְלַעַג לְבֹשֶׁת וְלִכְלִמָּה,

To be a [paradigm of] desolation, ⟨ an example ⟩ and a lesson, ⟨ a mockery, ⟩ an embarrassment ⟨ and a disgrace?

יֵאָמֵן וְיוּחַשׁ הַמִּבְטָח, שֶׁהִבְטַחְתָּ לַשּׁוֹמֵמָה,

Let be made true ⟨ speedily ⟩ the promise ⟨ that You promised ⟩ about the desolate [Land]:

אֲנִי יהוה בָּנִיתִי הַנֶּהֱרָסוֹת, נָטַעְתִּי **הַנְּשַׁמָּה**.²

I, ⟨ HASHEM, ⟩ have rebuilt ⟨ the ruins, ⟩ I have replanted ⟨ the wasteland.

❖ **הַנְּשַׁמָּה בְּרַחֲמִים** גְדוֹלִים תִּבְנֶה וּתְכוֹנְנָה,

The wasteland ⟨ — with mercy ⟩ that is great ⟨ may You rebuild ⟩ and re-establish it.

שְׁמַע יָהּ חִנּוּנָה, כִּי בָא עֵת לְחֶנְנָה,³

Hear, ⟨ O ⟩ God, ⟨ her ⟩ supplication, ⟨ for ⟩ come ⟨ has ⟩ the time ⟨ to show her favor.

חַזֵּק מַאֲמִירֶיךָ, בְּצֵל יָדְךָ לְגוֹנְנָה,

Strengthen ⟨ those who set You apart, ⟩ in the shadow ⟨ of Your hand ⟩ shielding them,

וּפְדוּיֵי יהוה יְשֻׁבוּן וּבָאוּ צִיּוֹן בְּרִנָּה.⁴

and may those redeemed ⟨ by HASHEM ⟩ return, ⟨ and ⟩ may they come ⟨ to Zion ⟩ with glad song.

ALL, WHILE STANDING:

אֵל מֶלֶךְ יוֹשֵׁב עַל כִּסֵּא רַחֲמִים, מִתְנַהֵג

O God, ⟨ King ⟩ Who sits ⟨ on ⟩ the throne ⟨ of mercy, ⟩ Who acts

בַּחֲסִידוּת, מוֹחֵל עֲוֹנוֹת עַמּוֹ, מַעֲבִיר רִאשׁוֹן

with kindness, ⟨ Who pardons ⟩ the sins ⟨ of His people, ⟩ Who removes ⟨ [sins,] one

רִאשׁוֹן,⁵ מַרְבֶּה מְחִילָה לַחַטָּאִים וּסְלִיחָה לַפּוֹשְׁעִים,

by one, ⟨ Who abundantly grants ⟩ pardon ⟨ to unintentional sinners ⟩ and forgiveness ⟨ to willful sinners,

עֹשֶׂה צְדָקוֹת עִם כָּל בָּשָׂר וָרוּחַ, לֹא כְרָעָתָם

Who performs ⟨ acts of generosity ⟩ with ⟨ all ⟩ [beings] of flesh ⟨ and ⟩ spirit ⟨ — not ⟩ in accord with their wickedness

---

תִּגְמוֹל. ❖ אֵל הוֹרֵיתָ לָנוּ לוֹמַר שְׁלֹשׁ עֶשְׂרֵה, וּזְכוֹר
⟨ remem- ⟪ the Thirteen ⟨ to ⟨ us ⟨ You ⟨ O God, ⟪ do You
ber [Attributes of Mercy]; recite taught repay them!

לָנוּ הַיּוֹם בְּרִית שְׁלֹשׁ עֶשְׂרֵה, כְּמוֹ שֶׁהוֹדַעְתָּ לֶעָנָיו
⟨ to the humble ⟨ You made ⟨ as ⟪ of [these] Thirteen, ⟨ the ⟨ today ⟨ for us
one [Moses] known covenant

מִקֶּדֶם, כְּמוֹ שֶׁכָּתוּב, וַיֵּרֶד יהוה בֶּעָנָן וַיִּתְיַצֵּב עִמּוֹ
⟨ with ⟨ and stood ⟨ in a ⟨ And HASHEM ⟪ it is written: ⟨ as ⟪ in ancient
him cloud descended times,

שָׁם, וַיִּקְרָא בְשֵׁם יהוה.[1]
⟪ of ⟨ with the ⟨ and He ⟪ there,
HASHEM. Name called out

CONGREGATION, THEN *CHAZZAN*:

וַיַּעֲבֹר יהוה עַל פָּנָיו וַיִּקְרָא:
⟪ and ⟪ [Moses'] ⟨ before ⟨ And HASHEM passed
proclaimed: face,

CONGREGATION AND *CHAZZAN* **RECITE LOUDLY AND IN UNISON**:

יהוה, יהוה, אֵל, רַחוּם, וְחַנּוּן, אֶרֶךְ אַפַּיִם,
⟨ to anger, ⟨ Slow ⟪ and ⟨ Compassionate ⟨ God, ⟨ HASHEM, ⟨ HASHEM,
Gracious,

וְרַב חֶסֶד, וֶאֱמֶת, נֹצֵר חֶסֶד לָאֲלָפִים, נֹשֵׂא עָוֹן,
⟨ of ⟨ Forgiver ⟪ for thousands ⟨ of ⟨ Preserver ⟪ and ⟨ in ⟨ and
iniquity, [of generations], kindness Truth, Kindness Abundant

וָפֶשַׁע, וְחַטָּאָה, וְנַקֵּה.[2] וְסָלַחְתָּ לַעֲוֹנֵנוּ וּלְחַטָּאתֵנוּ
⟪ and our sins, ⟨ our ⟪ May You ⟪ and Who ⟨ and inadvertent ⟨ willful sin,
iniquities forgive absolves. sin,

וּנְחַלְתָּנוּ.[3] סְלַח לָנוּ אָבִינוּ כִּי חָטָאנוּ, מְחַל לָנוּ
⟨ us, ⟨ pardon ⟪ we have ⟨ for ⟪ our ⟨ us, ⟨ Forgive ⟪ and make us
sinned; Father, Your heritage.

מַלְכֵּנוּ כִּי פָשָׁעְנוּ. כִּי אַתָּה אֲדֹנָי טוֹב וְסַלָּח,
⟪ and ⟨ are ⟨ O Lord, ⟨ You, ⟨ For ⟪ we have ⟨ for ⟪ our King,
forgiving, good willfully sinned.

וְרַב חֶסֶד לְכָל קֹרְאֶיךָ.[4]
⟪ who call ⟨ to all ⟨ kind ⟨ and
upon You. abundantly

---

(1) *Exodus* 34:5. (2) 34:6-7. (3) 34:9. (4) *Psalms* 86:5.

PREFATORY VERSES TO SELICHAH 44 / פסוקי הקדמה לסליחה מד

בֵּית קָדְשֵׁנוּ וְתִפְאַרְתֵּנוּ אֲשֶׁר הִלְלוּךָ אֲבֹתֵינוּ

« did our   ‹ praise You   ‹ where   « and our splendor,   ‹ of our   ‹ The
fathers,   holiness   Temple

הָיָה לִשְׂרֵפַת אֵשׁ, וְכָל מַחֲמַדֵּינוּ הָיָה לְחָרְבָּה.[1]

« a ruin.   ‹ became   ‹ that we desired   ‹ and all « by fire,   ‹ burned   ‹ was

שִׁלְחוּ בָאֵשׁ מִקְדָּשֶׁךָ, לָאָרֶץ חִלְּלוּ מִשְׁכַּן שְׁמֶךָ.[2]

« of Your   ‹ the   ‹ they have   « to the   « Your   ‹ in flames ‹ The have
Name.   Abode   desecrated   ground   Sanctuary;   sent up

הוֹשִׁיעָה יהוה כִּי גָמַר חָסִיד, כִּי פַסּוּ אֱמוּנִים

‹ have truth- ‹ vanished ‹ for « is the   ‹ gone   ‹ for ‹ Hashem, ‹ Save [us],
ful people   devout one,

מִבְּנֵי אָדָם.[3]

« from mankind.

בְּרַחֵם אָב עַל בָּנִים, כֵּן תְּרַחֵם יהוה עָלֵינוּ.[4]

« on us.   ‹ Hashem,   ‹ have   ‹ so « his   ‹ toward ‹ a   ‹ As merciful as
mercy,   children,   father is

לַיהוה הַיְשׁוּעָה, עַל עַמְּךָ בִרְכָתֶךָ סֶּלָה.[5] יהוה

‹ Hashem, « Selah.   « is Your   ‹ Your ‹ upon « is salvation, ‹ To Hashem
blessing,   people

צְבָאוֹת עִמָּנוּ, מִשְׂגָּב לָנוּ אֱלֹהֵי יַעֲקֹב סֶלָה.[6]

« Selah.   « of Jacob, ‹ is the God ‹ for us ‹ a   « is with us, ‹ Master of
stronghold   Legions,

יהוה צְבָאוֹת, אַשְׁרֵי אָדָם בֹּטֵחַ בָּךְ.[7] יהוה

‹ Hashem, « in You.   ‹ who   ‹ is the ‹ — praiseworthy « Master ‹ Hashem,
trusts   man   of Legions

הוֹשִׁיעָה, הַמֶּלֶךְ יַעֲנֵנוּ בְיוֹם קָרְאֵנוּ.[8]

« we call.   ‹ on the ‹ answer ‹ May the « save!
day   us   King

---

(1) *Isaiah* 64:10. (2) *Psalms* 74:7. (3) 12:2. (4) Cf. 103:13.
(5) 3:9. (6) 46:8. (7) 84:13. (8) 20:10.

סליחה מד / SELICHAH 44

אֱלֹהֵינוּ וֵאלֹהֵי אֲבוֹתֵינוּ:

⟨ of our forefathers: ⟩ and the God ⟨ Our God

אָבְלָה נַפְשִׁי* וְחָשַׁךְ תָּאֳרִי,

⟨ was my ⟨ and ⟨ did my ⟨ Mourn
visage — darkened soul,*

בֵּית תִּפְאַרְתִּי כִּנְשַׁף* בּוֹ הָאֲרִי,[1]

⟨ did the lion ⟨ against ⟨ when ⟨ of ⟨ the
[Nebuchadnezzar]. it Splendor — House
breathe out
[destruction]*

גַּם פְּלֵיטָתִי אֲשֶׁר עָזְבוּ וּשְׁאֵרִי,

⟨ and my ⟨ they left ⟨ whom ⟨ my refugees ⟨ Even
remnant, [in the Land]

דֹּעֲכוּ כְּהַיּוֹם בִּשְׁלֹשָׁה בְּתִשְׁרֵי.

⟨ of Tishrei. ⟨ on the Third ⟨ on ⟨ [had their life]
this day, extinguished

הָאֵשׁ וְהַמַּיִם הַזֵּידוֹנִים שְׁטָפוּנוּ[2] בְּדָלְקָם,

⟨ in their ⟨ have ⟨ that are ⟨ and the ⟨ The fire
pursuit; inundated us treacherous waters

וּבָסְסוּ מִקְדָּשׁ[3] וּבָזְזוּ חֶלְקָם,[4]

⟨ their ⟨ and ⟨ the Temple ⟨ they
portion. looted trampled

זִקְנֵי שְׁאֵרִית אֲשֶׁר פָּלְטוּ מִיּוֹם נָקָם,

⟨ of ⟨ the day ⟨ escaped ⟨ who ⟨ of our ⟨ The
vengeance, remnant, elders

חֻבְּלוּ עַתָּה בְּיוֹם צוֹם גְּדַלְיָה בֶּן אֲחִיקָם.

⟨ Achikam. ⟨ son ⟨ of ⟨ of the ⟨ on the ⟨ now, ⟨ were
of Gedaliah Fast day stricken

---

(1) See *Jeremiah* 50:17. (2) Cf. *Psalms* 124:4-5. (3) Cf. *Isaiah* 63:18. (4) *Jeremiah* 12:10.

אָבְלָה נַפְשִׁי — *Mourn did my soul.* This *selichah* contains an *aleph-beis* acrostic. It is written by R' Saadiah Gaon [see commentary, page 497].

כִּנְשַׁף — *When breathe out [destruction].* The translation follows the commentaries to *Isaiah* 40:24. With a mere puff of breath, that is, in a comparatively easy manner, was Nebuchadnezzar able to capture the *Beis HaMikdash (Masbir).*

According to others, the word is cognate to נֶשֶׁף, *evening,* and means *when he lodged there.* Thus did Nebuchadnezzar fulfill the verse (*Isaiah* 1:21), *Righteousness had once lodged there [in Jerusalem], but now murderers (Beis Levi).*

Others relate the word to יְשׁוּפְךָ and תְּשׁוּפֶנּוּ (*Genesis* 3:15), which *Ibn Ezra* renders *he will smite you* and *you will smite him,* respectively.

טׇרְפוּ דַלַּת עַם הָאָֽרֶץ,

《 of the 〈 of the 〈 were the 〈 Torn
land;   people   poor   asunder

יֶֽתֶר הַגָּזָם אָכַל הָאַרְבֶּה*[1] בְּמֶֽרֶץ,

《 with 〈 by the *arbeh** 〈 was 〈 by the 〈 what was
alacrity.   devoured   *gazam*   left over

כּוֹרְמִים וְיוֹגְבִים[2] פְּקֻדַּת מַרְגִּיז הָאָֽרֶץ[3]

〈 of the 〈 of the one 〈 at the 《 and in fields, 〈 Workers in
earth   who caused   command   vineyards
    the trembling

לְהָטוּ, וְלֹא הָיָה בָם גֹּדֵר גָּדֵר וְעוֹמֵד בַּפֶּֽרֶץ.[4]

《 in the 〈 or to stand 〈 a fence 〈 to 〈 among 〈 there was 《 were
breach.   build   them   no one   burnt up,

מָה אֲסַפֵּר וְאַנְחוֹתַי עֲצוּמוֹת,

《 are so intense; 〈 when my sighs 〈 can I recount 〈 What

נָקְטָה נַפְשִׁי,*[5] וּמַקְהֵלוֹתַי עֲגוּמוֹת.

《 are sorrowful. 〈 my communities 《 is my soul 〈 disgusted
[with my life],*

שָׂרִיגֵֽינוּ אֲשֶׁר נִשְׁאֲרוּ מִיקוֹד אֵשׁ לְתַעֲצוּמוֹת.

《 that was intense, 〈 of fire 〈 from the 〈 were left 〈 that 〈 The branches
conflagration   of our vine

עוֹד הֵם לֹא נִתְקַֽיְּמוּ וְנִתְּשׁוּ בְּחֵמוֹת.

《 with fury. 〈 but they were 《 remained 〈 had 〈 they 〈 also
driven out   [in place],   not

פָּנֶֽיךָ עַד מָתַי מִמֶּֽנּוּ תַּסְתִּיר,[6]

《 will You hide? 〈 from us 〈 when 〈 until 《 Your countenance,

---

(1) *Joel* 1:4. (2) See *Jeremiah* 52:16. (3) See *Isaiah* 14:16.
(4) *Ezekiel* 22:30. (5) *Job* 10:1. (6) Cf. *Psalms* 13:2.

יֶֽתֶר הַגָּזָם אָכַל הָאַרְבֶּה — *What was left over
by the gazam was devoured by the ar-
beh.* During the days of the prophet Joel,
four species of locust — *gazam, arbeh,
yelek,* and *chasil* — plagued the land in
rapid succession: *What the gazam left
over, the arbeh devoured; what the arbeh
left over, the yelek devoured; and what
the yelek left over, the chasil devoured*
(*Joel* 1:4). Similarly, after the Destruction,
Nebuchadnezzar had allowed a remnant
of Israel to remain in the Land. But when

Ishmael ben Nesaniah slew Gedaliah ben
Achikam, even that remnant was banished. Thus, what Nebuchadnezzar left
over, Ishmael ben Nesaniah devoured.

נָקְטָה נַפְשִׁי — *Disgusted is my soul [with
my life].* The translation follows *Rashi*
to *Job* 10:1, which also contains the interpolated phrase. According to *Targum,*
the word נָקְטָה means *cut off.* Thus, *my
soul is cut off even while I am yet alive*
(*Metzudas David*). Others translate *my
soul is melancholy* (*Masbir*).

צַעֲקָתֵנוּ שְׁמַע וַאֲסִירֵינוּ תַּתִּיר,

《 release! 〈 and our prisoners 〈 hear 〈 Our cry

קָדוֹשׁ בְּיטָה כִּי אֵין בַּעֲדֵנוּ מַעְתִּיר,

《 will pray; 〈 [who] for us 〈 there is that 〈 observe 《 O Holy One, no one

רְאֵה בְּדַלּוּתֵנוּ וְשִׁבְחֲךָ בְּפֶה נַכְתִּיר.

《 we will crown You. 〈 in [our] mouth 〈 then with Your praise 《 our poverty [and redeem us], 〈 see

❖ שֻׁדַּדְנוּ מִדּוֹר לְדוֹר וּמִקֵּץ לְקֵץ,

《 to [another] time; 〈 and from one time 《 to gen- eration, 〈 from generation 〈 We have been pillaged

שֹׁרֶשׁ צֶפַע מְעוֹפֵף אוֹתָנוּ עוֹקֵץ,

《 to bite. 〈 after us 〈 darts 〈 of the viper 〈 [the enemy,] from the root

תַּקִּיף, לְמִשְׁפָּטֵנוּ הָעֵר וְהָקֵץ,[1]

《 and awaken! 〈 arouse yourself 〈 to our judgment 〈 O Forceful One,

תְּכַפֵּר לַעֲוֹנוֹתֵינוּ וְנֹאמַר קֵץ.

《 the approach of the end [to our exile]. 〈 and declare 〈 for our sins 〈 May You atone

ALL, WHILE STANDING:

אֵל מֶלֶךְ יוֹשֵׁב עַל כִּסֵּא רַחֲמִים, מִתְנַהֵג

〈 Who acts 《 of mercy, 〈 the throne 〈 on 〈 Who sits 〈 King 〈 O God,

בַּחֲסִידוּת, מוֹחֵל עֲוֹנוֹת עַמּוֹ, מַעֲבִיר רִאשׁוֹן

〈 [sins,] one 〈 Who removes 《 of His people, 〈 the sins 〈 Who pardons 《 with kindness,

רִאשׁוֹן,[2] מַרְבֶּה מְחִילָה לַחַטָּאִים וּסְלִיחָה לַפּוֹשְׁעִים,

《 to willful sinners, 〈 and forgiveness 〈 to unintentional sinners 〈 pardon 〈 Who abun- dantly grants 《 by one,

עֹשֶׂה צְדָקוֹת עִם כָּל בָּשָׂר וָרוּחַ, לֹא כְרָעָתָם

〈 in accord with their wickedness 〈 — not 《 and spirit 〈 [beings of] flesh 〈 all 〈 with 〈 acts of generosity 〈 Who performs

תִּגְמוֹל. ❖ אֵל הוֹרֵיתָ לָנוּ לוֹמַר שְׁלשׁ עֶשְׂרֵה, וּזְכוֹר

〈 remem- ber 《 the Thirteen [Attributes of Mercy]; 〈 to recite 〈 us 〈 You taught 〈 O God, 《 do You repay them!

---

(1) Cf. *Psalms* 35:23. (2) *Rosh Hashanah* 17a.

לָנוּ הַיּוֹם בְּרִית שְׁלֹשׁ עֶשְׂרֵה, כְּמוֹ שֶׁהוֹדַעְתָּ לֶעָנָיו

‹ to the humble one [Moses] ‹ You made known ‹ as ≪ of [these] Thirteen, ‹ the covenant ‹ today ‹ for us

מִקֶּדֶם, כְּמוֹ שֶׁכָּתוּב, וַיֵּרֶד יהוה בֶּעָנָן וַיִּתְיַצֵּב עִמּוֹ

‹ with him ‹ and stood ‹ in a cloud ‹ And HASHEM descended ≪ it is written: ‹ as ≪ in ancient times,

שָׁם, וַיִּקְרָא בְשֵׁם יהוה.¹

≪ of HASHEM. ‹ with the Name ‹ and He called out ≪ there,

CONGREGATION, THEN *CHAZZAN:*

וַיַּעֲבֹר יהוה עַל פָּנָיו וַיִּקְרָא:

≪ and proclaimed: ≪ [Moses'] ‹ before ‹ And HASHEM passed face,

CONGREGATION AND *CHAZZAN* **RECITE LOUDLY AND IN UNISON:**

יהוה, יהוה, אֵל, רַחוּם, וְחַנּוּן, אֶרֶךְ אַפַּיִם,

‹ to anger, ‹ Slow ≪ and Gracious, ‹ Compassionate ‹ God, ‹ HASHEM, ‹ HASHEM,

וְרַב חֶסֶד, וֶאֱמֶת, נֹצֵר חֶסֶד לָאֲלָפִים, נֹשֵׂא עָוֹן,

‹ of ‹ Forgiver ≪ for thousands ‹ of ‹ Preserver ≪ and ‹ in ‹ and iniquity, [of generations], kindness Truth, Kindness Abundant

וָפֶשַׁע, וְחַטָאָה, וְנַקֵּה.² וְסָלַחְתָּ לַעֲוֹנֵנוּ וּלְחַטָּאתֵנוּ

≪ and our sins, ‹ our iniquities ‹ May You forgive ≪ and Who absolves. ‹ and inadvertent sin, ‹ willful sin,

וּנְחַלְתָּנוּ.³ סְלַח לָנוּ אָבִינוּ כִּי חָטָאנוּ, מְחַל לָנוּ

‹ us, ‹ pardon ≪ we have sinned; ‹ for ≪ our Father, ‹ us, ‹ Forgive ≪ and make us Your heritage.

מַלְכֵּנוּ כִּי פָשָׁעְנוּ. כִּי אַתָּה אֲדֹנָי טוֹב וְסַלָּח,

≪ and forgiving, ‹ are good ‹ O Lord, ‹ You, ‹ For ≪ we have willfully sinned. ‹ for ≪ our King,

וְרַב חֶסֶד לְכָל קֹרְאֶיךָ.⁴

≪ who call upon You. ‹ to all ‹ kind ‹ and abundantly

שׁוּבָה יִשְׂרָאֵל עַד יהוה אֱלֹהֶיךָ, כִּי כָשַׁלְתָּ בַּעֲוֹנֶךָ.⁵

≪ in your iniquity. ‹ you have stumbled ‹ for ≪ your God, ‹ HASHEM, ‹ unto ‹ O Israel, ‹ Return,

---

(1) *Exodus* 34:5. (2) 34:6-7. (3) 34:9. (4) *Psalms* 86:5. (5) *Hosea* 14:2.

תָּשֵׁב אֱנוֹשׁ עַד דַּכָּא, וַתֹּאמֶר, שׁוּבוּ בְנֵי אָדָם.[1]

《 of man! 〈 O 〈 Repent 《 and You say, 〈 pulp 〈 to 〈 man 〈 You
sons   reduce

קָרוֹב יהוה לְכָל קֹרְאָיו, לְכֹל אֲשֶׁר יִקְרָאֻהוּ בֶאֱמֶת.[2]

《 sincerely. 〈 call 〈 who 〈 to all 《 who call 〈 to all 〈 is 〈 Close
       upon Him   upon Him,   HASHEM

כְּרַחֵם אָב עַל בָּנִים, כֵּן תְּרַחֵם יהוה עָלֵינוּ.[3]

《 on us. 〈 HASHEM, 〈 have 〈 so 《 his 〈 toward 〈 a 〈 As merciful as
             mercy,   children,   father is

לַיהוה הַיְשׁוּעָה, עַל עַמְּךָ בִרְכָתֶךָ סֶּלָה.[4] יהוה

〈 HASHEM, 《 Selah. 《 is Your 〈 Your 〈 upon 《 is salvation, 〈 To HASHEM
          blessing,   people

צְבָאוֹת עִמָּנוּ, מִשְׂגָּב לָנוּ אֱלֹהֵי יַעֲקֹב סֶלָה.[5]

《 Selah. 《 of Jacob, 〈 is the God 〈 for us 〈 a 《 is with us, 〈 Master of
                    stronghold   Legions,

יהוה צְבָאוֹת, אַשְׁרֵי אָדָם בֹּטֵחַ בָּךְ.[6] יהוה הוֹשִׁיעָה,

《 save! 〈 HASHEM, 《 in You. 〈 who 〈 is the 〈 — praise- 《 Master of 〈 HASHEM,
            trusts   man   worthy   Legions

הַמֶּלֶךְ יַעֲנֵנוּ בְיוֹם קָרְאֵנוּ.[7]

《 we call. 〈 on the 〈 answer 〈 May the
          day   us   King

סליחה מה / SELICHAH 45

אֱלֹהֵינוּ וֵאלֹהֵי אֲבוֹתֵינוּ:

《 of our forefathers: 〈 and the God 〈 Our God

אֲמַנְתָּ מֵאָז* אֲרֶשֶׁת נִיב שְׂפָתָיִם,

〈 of [our] lips 〈 of the 〈 how the 〈 from of 〈 You guaran-
          speech   utterance   old*   teed [to us]

בִּתְפִלָּה וּבְתַחֲנוּן דְּפַק שַׁעֲרֵי דְלָתָיִם,

《 of [Your] 〈 on the 〈 knocking 〈 and 〈 in prayer
  doors —   gates   supplication

גָּשְׁתֵּנוּ עָדֶיךָ בִּזְרִיזוּת וְלֹא בַעֲצַלְתָּיִם,

《 with laziness — 〈 and not 〈 with alacrity 〈 toward You 〈 approaching

---

(1) *Psalms* 90:3. (2) 145:18. (3) Cf. 103:13. (4) 3:9. (5) 46:8. (6) 84:13. (7) 20:10.

§<< אֲמַנְתָּ מֵאָז — *You guaranteed [to us]
from of old.* The *selichah* contains an
alphabetical acrostic, followed by the au-

thor's name — בִּנְיָמִן, *Binyamin* [see introductory comment to *Selichah* 1].

דְּחוֹת רָע פֻּרְעָנִיּוֹת הַמִּתְרַגְּשׁוֹת לְעִתּוֹתֵיִם.

« from time to time. ‹ that gather themselves ‹ the catastrophes ‹ will ward off

הִנְנוּ אָתָנוּ לָךְ¹ בְּשִׁבְרוֹן רוּחַ וְדִכְאוּת לֵב,²

« heart, ‹ and crushed ‹ spirit ‹ with broken ‹ to You ‹ we have come ‹ Here we are,

וַדּוֹת לְפָנֶיךָ כָּל פְּתוּל וְעִקְשׁוּת לֵב,

« of heart. ‹ and stubbornness ‹ [our] devi- ousness ‹ all ‹ before You ‹ confessing

זֶה³ חוֹקֵר לְבָבוֹת, הָרוֹפֵא לִשְׁבוּרֵי לֵב,⁴

« hearted. ‹ of the broken- ‹ the Healer ‹ of Hearts, ‹ the Searcher [my God,] ‹ This is

חַדֵּשׁ רוּחַ נָכוֹן בְּקִרְבֵּנוּ, וּבְרָא לָנוּ טְהוֹר לֵב.⁵

« a heart that is pure. ‹ for us ‹ and create « within us, ‹ that is steadfast ‹ a spirit ‹ Renew

טִכַּסְתָּ מִקֶּדֶם אֵלּוּ יָמִים עֲשָׂרָה,

« — ten, « Days [of Repentance] ‹ these ‹ from of old ‹ You planned

יָחִיד בָּם לָשׁוּב וְלִמְצֹא כַפָּרָה,

« atonement — ‹ and find ‹ can repent ‹ during them ‹ when [even] an individual

כָּל הַשָּׁנָה כֻּלָהּ לָרַבִּים מְסוּרָה,

« it is given over, ‹ to the community ‹ entirely, ‹ of the year, ‹ all the rest

לְשַׁוֵּעַ וְלַעֲנוֹת בְּכָל עֵת צוּקָה וְצָרָה.

« and of trouble. ‹ distress ‹ time ‹ in every ‹ and respond aloud [in prayer] ‹ to cry out

מִהֵר הַיָּחִיד וְשָׁב בֵּינָתַיִם, מוֹחֲלִין לוֹ,

« him; ‹ they [the Heavenly Tribunal] pardon ‹ during these [days], ‹ and repents ‹ does the individual ‹ If hurry

נוֹאָשׁ וְלֹא שָׁב, אֵין תַּקָּנָה לְעַוְולוֹ,

« for his sinfulness; ‹ remedy ‹ there is no ‹ repent, ‹ and does not ‹ if he despairs

סַדֵּר וְעָרַךְ כָּל אֵילֵי נְבָיוֹת לְהוֹעִילוֹ,

« on his behalf; ‹ from Nevayos [that are the best] ‹ the rams ‹ all ‹ and arrange as [offerings] ‹ though he were to prepare

---

(1) *Jeremiah* 3:22. (2) Cf. *Psalms* 51:19. (3) *Exodus* 15:2; *Isaiah* 25:9. (4) *Psalms* 147:3. (5) Cf. 51:12.

עוֹתֵר וְצוֹעֵק וְאֵין שׁוֹמֵעַ לוֹ.

《 to ⟨ who will ⟨ there is 《and shout, ⟨ [though]
him.   listen   no one   he plead

פְּגִיעַת הָרַבִּים וְהַיָּחִיד לְךָ לְבַד עוֹלָה,

⟨ ascends, ⟨ alone ⟨ to ⟨ and of the ⟨ of the many ⟨ The
                      You   individual   entreaty

צוּר, כִּי אַתָּה שׁוֹמֵעַ תְּפִלָּה,

《 of Prayer. ⟨ the Hearer ⟨ You are ⟨ for ⟨ O Rock,

קַבְּלֵנוּ בְרָצוֹן וְהַמְצִיאֵנוּ מְחִילָה,

《 a pardon; ⟨ and make ⟨ favorably ⟨ Accept us
                available to us

רְצֵנוּ כְּקָרְבַּן כָּלִיל וְעוֹלָה.[1]

《 and [with] ⟨ in its ⟨ as You are ⟨ be
burnt-offerings. entirety with a [meal-] pleased
               consumed   offering, with us

❖ שָׁפוֹט תִּשְׁפֹּט אוֹתָנוּ בְּרַחֲמִים וְחֶמְלָה,

《and compassion, ⟨ with mercy ⟨ us [these days] ⟨ May You judge

בָּנֶיךָ יְחוּסֶיךָ לְקוּחִים לְךָ לִסְגֻלָּה,

《 as [Your] ⟨ to ⟨ who are ⟨ who are ⟨ [for we
beloved   You   taken   associated are] Your
treasure.   with You,   children

יֻקַשׁ מֶרְיָם יְצְלַל בִּמְצוּלָה,

《 in the deep sea, ⟨ be sunk ⟨ of their ⟨ May the
                            rebelliousness snare

נֵצַח לְהַלֵּלְךָ בְּכָל מִינֵי תְהִלָּה.

《 of praise. ⟨ kind ⟨ with ⟨ praise ⟨ that they
                      every   You   may eternally

ALL, WHILE STANDING:

אֵל מֶלֶךְ יוֹשֵׁב עַל כִּסֵּא רַחֲמִים, מִתְנַהֵג

⟨ Who acts 《 of mercy, ⟨ the throne ⟨ on ⟨ Who sits ⟨ King ⟨ O God,

בַּחֲסִידוּת, מוֹחֵל עֲוֹנוֹת עַמּוֹ, מַעֲבִיר רִאשׁוֹן

⟨ [sins,] one ⟨ Who 《 of His ⟨ the sins ⟨ Who 《 with kindness,
            removes people,   pardons

רִאשׁוֹן,[2] מַרְבֶּה מְחִילָה לַחַטָּאִים וּסְלִיחָה לַפּוֹשְׁעִים,

《 to willful ⟨ and ⟨ to unintentional ⟨ pardon ⟨ Who abun- 《 by one,
sinners,   forgiveness sinners   dantly grants

---

(1) See last comment to *Selichah 4*. (2) *Rosh Hashanah* 17a.

עוֹשֶׂה צְדָקוֹת עִם כָּל בָּשָׂר וָרוּחַ, לֹא כְרָעָתָם

⟨ in accord with ⟨ — not ⟪ and ⟨ [beings ⟨ all ⟨ with ⟨ acts of ⟨ Who
their wickedness   spirit   of] flesh   generosity   performs

תִּגְמוֹל. ּ∻ אֵל הוֹרֵיתָ לָּנוּ לוֹמַר שְׁלֹשׁ עֶשְׂרֵה, וּזְכוֹר

⟨ remem- ⟪ the Thirteen ⟨ to ⟨ us ⟨ You ⟨ O God, ⟪ do You
ber   [Attributes of Mercy];   recite   taught   repay them!

לָנוּ הַיּוֹם בְּרִית שְׁלֹשׁ עֶשְׂרֵה, כְּמוֹ שֶׁהוֹדַעְתָּ לֶעָנָיו

⟨ to the humble ⟨ You made ⟨ as ⟪ of [these] Thirteen, ⟨ the ⟨ today ⟨ for us
one [Moses]   known   covenant

מִקֶּדֶם, כְּמוֹ שֶׁכָּתוּב, וַיֵּרֶד יהוה בֶּעָנָן וַיִּתְיַצֵּב עִמּוֹ

⟨ with ⟨ and stood ⟨ in a ⟨ And HASHEM ⟪ it is written: ⟨ as ⟪ in ancient
him   cloud   descended   times,

שָׁם, וַיִּקְרָא בְשֵׁם יהוה.[1]

⟪ of ⟨ with the ⟨ and He ⟪ there,
HASHEM.   Name   called out

CONGREGATION, THEN *CHAZZAN:*

וַיַּעֲבֹר יהוה עַל פָּנָיו וַיִּקְרָא:

⟪ and ⟪ [Moses'] ⟨ before ⟨ And HASHEM passed
proclaimed: face,

CONGREGATION AND *CHAZZAN* RECITE LOUDLY AND IN UNISON:

יהוה, יהוה, אֵל, רַחוּם, וְחַנּוּן, אֶרֶךְ אַפַּיִם,

⟨ to anger, ⟨ Slow ⟪ and Gracious, ⟨ Compassionate ⟨ God, ⟨ HASHEM, ⟨ HASHEM,

וְרַב חֶסֶד, וֶאֱמֶת, נֹצֵר חֶסֶד לָאֲלָפִים, נֹשֵׂא עָוֹן,

⟨ of ⟨ Forgiver ⟨ for thousands ⟨ of ⟨ Preserver ⟪ and ⟨ in ⟨ and
iniquity,   [of generations],   kindness   Truth,   Kindness Abundant

וָפֶשַׁע, וְחַטָּאָה, וְנַקֵּה.[2] וְסָלַחְתָּ לַעֲוֹנֵנוּ וּלְחַטָּאתֵנוּ

⟪ and our sins, ⟨ our ⟨ May You ⟪ and Who ⟨ and inadvertent ⟨ willful sin,
iniquities   forgive   absolves.   sin,

וּנְחַלְתָּנוּ.[3] סְלַח לָנוּ אָבִינוּ כִּי חָטָאנוּ, מְחַל לָנוּ

⟨ us, ⟨ pardon ⟪ we have ⟨ for ⟪ our ⟨ us, ⟨ Forgive ⟪ and make us
sinned;   Father,   Your heritage.

מַלְכֵּנוּ כִּי פָשָׁעְנוּ. כִּי אַתָּה אֲדֹנָי טוֹב וְסַלָּח,

⟪ and ⟨ are ⟨ O Lord, ⟨ You, ⟨ For ⟪ we have ⟨ for ⟪ our King,
forgiving,   good   willfully sinned.

וְרַב חֶסֶד לְכָל קֹרְאֶיךָ.[4]

⟪ who call ⟨ to all ⟨ kind ⟨ and
upon You.   abundantly

---

(1) *Exodus* 34:5. (2) 34:6-7. (3) 34:9. (4) *Psalms* 86:5.

PREFATORY VERSES TO SELICHAH 46 / פסוקי הקדמה לסליחה מו

הֵיטִיבָה בִרְצוֹנְךָ אֶת צִיּוֹן, תִּבְנֶה חוֹמוֹת

⟨ the walls ⟨ build ⟪ Zion; ⟨ unto ⟨ in Your favor ⟨ Do good

יְרוּשָׁלָיִם.[1] הוֹשִׁיעֵנוּ אֱלֹהִים, כִּי בָאוּ מַיִם עַד נָפֶשׁ.[2]

⟪ the ⟨ until ⟨ the waters ⟨ for ⟨ O God, ⟨ Save us ⟪ of Jerusalem.
soul!   have reached

הַרְאֵנוּ יהוה חַסְדֶּךָ, וְיֶשְׁעֲךָ תִּתֶּן לָנוּ.[3]

⟪ us. ⟨ grant ⟨ and Your ⟪ Your ⟨ HASHEM, ⟨ Show us,
salvation   kindness,

כְּרַחֵם אָב עַל בָּנִים, כֵּן תְּרַחֵם יהוה עָלֵינוּ.[4]

⟪ on us. ⟨ HASHEM, ⟨ have ⟨ so ⟪ his ⟨ toward ⟨ a ⟨ As merciful as
mercy,   children,   father is

לַיהוה הַיְשׁוּעָה, עַל עַמְּךָ בִרְכָתֶךָ סֶּלָה.[5] יהוה

⟨ HASHEM, ⟪ Selah. ⟪ is Your ⟨ Your ⟨ upon ⟪ is salvation, ⟨ To HASHEM
blessing,   people

צְבָאוֹת עִמָּנוּ, מִשְׂגָּב לָנוּ אֱלֹהֵי יַעֲקֹב סֶלָה.[6]

⟪ Selah. ⟪ of Jacob, ⟨ is the God ⟨ for us ⟨ a ⟪ is with us, ⟨ Master of
stronghold   Legions,

יהוה צְבָאוֹת, אַשְׁרֵי אָדָם בֹּטֵחַ בָּךְ.[7] יהוה הוֹשִׁיעָה,

⟪ save! ⟨ HASHEM, ⟪ in You. ⟨ who ⟨ is the ⟨ — praise- ⟪ Master of ⟨ HASHEM,
trusts   man   worthy   Legions

הַמֶּלֶךְ יַעֲנֵנוּ בְיוֹם קָרְאֵנוּ.[8]

⟪ we call. ⟨ on the ⟨ answer ⟨ May the
day   us   King

SELICHAH 46 / סליחה מו

אֱלֹהֵינוּ וֵאלֹהֵי אֲבוֹתֵינוּ:

⟪ of our forefathers: ⟨ and the God ⟨ Our God

אוֹרְךָ וַאֲמִתְּךָ שְׁלַח,*[9] אֱמוּנֶיךָ בְּטוֹב הַצְלַח,

⟪ give ⟪ for good ⟨ to Your ⟪ send [us];* ⟨ and Your ⟨ Your light
success,   faithful ones   truth

---

(1) *Psalms* 51:20. (2) Cf. 69:2. (3) 85:8. (4) Cf. 103:13. (5) 3:9. (6) 46:8. (7) 84:13. (8) 20:10. (9) Cf. 43:3.

אוֹרְךָ וַאֲמִתְּךָ שְׁלַח — *Your light and Your truth send [us].* The acrostic of this selichah spells the *aleph-beis*. The last line bears the signature שִׁמְעוֹן, *Shimon* [see prefatory comment to *Selichah 18*].

1.כִּי אַתָּה אֲדֹנָי טוֹב וְסַלָּח.

《 and 〈 are 〈 O Lord, 〈 You, 〈 for
forgiving. good

בִּיטָה בְעָנוּי נֶפֶשׁ, בְּטוּבְךָ הוֹצִיאֵנוּ לַחְפֶשׁ,

《 to freedom, 〈 bring us out 〈 [and] in 《 of soul, 〈 at the 〈 Look
Your goodness affliction

2.כִּי בָאוּ מַיִם עַד נָפֶשׁ.

《 the 〈 until 〈 the waters 〈 for
soul. have reached

גַעֲיוֹתֵינוּ יְהוּ נִקְשָׁבִים, גָלוּתֵנוּ הָשֵׁב לְיִשׁוּבִים,

《 to [our] 〈 return 〈 Our Exile 《 be heard: 〈 let 〈 Our cries
settlements, them [in prayer]

3.כִּי גֵרִים אֲנַחְנוּ וְתוֹשָׁבִים.

《 and residents. 〈 are we 〈 aliens 〈 for

דָּפַקְנוּ דְלָתֶיךָ לִתְמֹד, דָּבַקְנוּ אֵלֶיךָ לִצְמֹד,

《 to become united, 〈 to You 〈 we cling 《 continually, 〈 on Your doors 〈 We knock

4.כִּי דַלּוֹנוּ מְאֹד.

《 exceed- 〈 we have 〈 for
ingly. become
impoverished

הֱלִיצוּנוּ זֵדִים בִּמְצָרֵינוּ, הַצִּילֵנוּ וְנוֹדְךָ צוּרֵנוּ,5

《 our Rock, 〈 and we will 《 save us 《 in our straits; 〈 did willful 〈 Taunt us
thank You, sinners

6.כִּי הוֹשַׁעְתָּנוּ מִצָּרֵינוּ.

《 from our 〈 You have 〈 for
oppressors. saved us

זְרוּיֶּיךָ מְיַחֲלִים לְעוֹדְדָם, זַכֵּם7 בְּיִרְאָתְךָ לְסַעֲדָם,

《 You will 〈 so that in [their] 〈 purify 〈 for You to 〈 anxiously 〈 Your scat-
support them, fear of You them encourage them; wait tered people

8.*כִּי זֶה כָּל הָאָדָם.

《 [reason for] 〈 the 〈 that 〈 because
man['s creation].* whole is

---

(1) Psalms 86:5. (2) 69:2. (3) Cf. I Chronicles 29:15, Genesis 23:4. (4) Psalms 79:8. (5) Cf. 119:51. (6) 44:8.
(7) See Job 9:30; some editions of Selichos read זַכִּים, the pure ones, the righteous. (8) Ecclesiastes 12:13.

בְּיִרְאָתְךָ . . . כִּי זֶה כָּל הָאָדָם — So that in [their] fear of You, You will support them, because that is the whole [reason for] man['s creation]. After two hundred and twenty verses of mussar, ethical teachings, admonishment, and deep insights into man, his duties, and the purpose of his existence, the wise King Solomon writes in the penultimate verse of Ecclesiastes (12:13): The sum of the matter, when all has been

חֻקּוֹת הָעַמִּים תֹּהוּ,¹ חֲשׁוּקֶיךָ אַחֲרֶיךָ יִנָּהוּ,²

《 are drawn, 〈 after You 〈 those who 《 are 〈 of the 〈 The
      desire You,   vacuous;   nations   customs

כִּי חַנּוּן וְרַחוּם הוּא.³

《 is He. 〈 and merciful 〈 gracious 〈 For

טִירָתְךָ הַשְּׁמָמָה לְעִיִּים,⁴ טַיְּבָה בְחוֹמוֹת בְּנוּיִים,⁵

《 that are 〈 with walls 〈 Repair it 《 to heaps 〈 has been 〈 Your
built up,   [of rubble]!   turned   Temple-tower

כִּי טוֹב חַסְדְּךָ מֵחַיִּים.⁶

《 than life. 〈 is Your 〈 better 〈 for
     kindness

יָגַעְתִּי⁷ וְאָשִׂיחָה בְמַעֲנִי, יֵבוֹשׁ וְיִכָּלֵם מְעַנִּי,

《 let my 〈 and 〈 Shamed 《 in my 〈 yet I speak out 〈 I am
tormentor be! humiliated   prayer: exhausted,

כִּי יַעֲשֶׂה יהוה דִּין עָנִי.⁸

《of the 〈 the 〈 HASHEM will 〈 for
poor. cause   champion

כָּבְדוּ שְׂפָתֵי קָמַי, כָּל הַיּוֹם⁹ מַזְעִימָי,

《 they enrage 〈 day long 〈 all 《 of my an- 〈 do the 〈Weigh heavily
me,   tagonists;   lips   [upon me]

כִּי כָלוּ בְעָשָׁן יָמָי.¹⁰

《 are 〈 in 〈 consumed 〈 for
my days. smoke

לָהֶם יָשִׁיב כְּפָעֳלָם,*¹¹ לְעַמּוֹ יְלַמֵּד לְהוֹעִילָם,¹²

《 for their benefit, 〈 He will 〈 and to 《 according 〈 He shall 〈 To them
      teach   His people   to their deeds,*   pay back

כִּי לֹא יִזְנַח לְעוֹלָם.¹³

《 forever. 〈 reject 〈 [He will] 〈 for
[them] not

---

(1) Cf. *Jeremiah* 10:3; in some editions of *Selichos* this stanza has been censored to read
חֶלְקֵנוּ אַתָּה הוּא, *It is You Who are our portion,* חֲשׁוּקָיו אַחֲרָיו יִנָּהוּ, *those who desire Him follow
after Him . . .*; in some editions the first two stiches of the stanza have been omitted.
(2) Cf. *I Samuel* 7:2. (3) *Joel* 2:13. (4) Cf. *Psalms* 79:1. (5) Cf. 51:20. (6) 63:4.
(7) Some editions read יָדַעְתִּי, *I am aware.* (8) *Psalms* 140:13. (9) Cf. *Lamentations* 3:62.
(10) *Psalms* 102:4. (11) Cf. *Jeremiah* 25:14. (12) Cf. *Isaiah* 48:17. (13) *Lamentations* 3:31.

---

considered: *God you should fear, and His
commandments you should keep, because
that is the whole [reason for] man's [cre-
ation]* (following *Rashi*).

In the same vein, the Talmud teaches:
הַכֹּל בִּידֵי שָׁמַיִם חוּץ מִיִּרְאַת שָׁמַיִם, *Everything*

*is in the hands of Heaven, except fear of
HASHEM (Berachos 33b).*

כְּפָעֳלָם — *According to their deeds.* This
stich is ambiguous and could mean either *He
shall reward the righteous for their deeds,*
or *He shall punish the oppressors for theirs.*

מְרַחֲמוֹ יִתֵּן מַאֲוָיו, מִמֶּנּוּ יָסִיר דָּפְיוֹ,

《 [the blemishes] ‹ He will ‹ and from 《 his desire, ‹ will ‹ He Who has
of his sins,   remove   him   grant   mercy on
          him [Israel]

כִּי מַה טּוּבוֹ וּמַה יָּפְיוֹ.[1]

《 beautiful he ‹ and ‹ good ‹ how ‹ for
will then be. how

נְשַׁמּוֹת הוּשַׁתּוּ עָרַי,[2] וְנָכְרִים בָּאוּ שְׁעָרַי,[3]

《 our gates; ‹ have ‹ gentiles 《 our ‹ have been ‹ Into
entered   cities;   transformed   desolation

כִּי נָשָׂאתִי חֶרְפַּת נְעוּרָי.[4]

《 of my youth- ‹ the ‹ I have borne ‹ for
[ful sins].   shame

שׂוֹשׂ אָשִׂישׂ עָלֶיךָ,[5] שִׂיחַ לַעֲנוֹת גְּאוּלֶיךָ,

《 of Your ‹ the spoken 《 when You 《 over You, ‹ Yet I will rejoice
redeemed ones,   prayer   answer   intensely

כִּי שִׂמַּחְתַּנִי יהוה בְּפָעֳלֶךָ.[6]

《 with Your ‹ HASHEM, ‹ You have ‹ for
deeds.   gladdened me,

עִזּוּז נוֹרָא וְאָיוֹם, עַתָּה הַמְצִיאֵנוּ פִדְיוֹם,

《 redemption, ‹ bring forth ‹ now 《 and Fear- ‹ Awesome, ‹ O
for us   some One,   Mighty,

כִּי עָלֶיךָ הֹרַגְנוּ כָּל הַיּוֹם.[7]

《 day ‹ all ‹ we are ‹ for Your ‹ because
long.   killed   sake

פַּנֵּה דֶּרֶךְ עֲקֹב,[8] פְּאֵר הֲלוּלֶךְ לִנְקֹב,

《 [we may] ‹ of Your ‹ so that 《 that is ‹ the ‹ Clear
pronounce: praise   the glory   circuitous,   road

כִּי גָאַל יהוה אֶת יַעֲקֹב.[9]

《   Jacob. ‹ HASHEM has redeemed ‹ For

צָרִים לְכַלּוֹת בְּחֶרֶץ,[10] צָפֵה מִשְּׁמֵי עֶרֶץ,

《 mighty, ‹ from the ‹ look 《 with intensity,* ‹ [strive] to ‹ As the
heavens,   down   destroy [us]   oppressors

---

(1) *Zechariah* 9:17. (2) Cf. *Isaiah* 54:3. (3) Cf. *Obadiah* 1:11. (4) *Jeremiah* 31:18. (5) Cf. *Isaiah* 61:10.
(6) *Psalms* 92:5. (7) 44:23. (8) Cf. *Isaiah* 40:3-4. (9) *Jeremiah* 31:10. (10) Cf. *Isaiah* 10:22.

צָרִים לְכַלּוֹת בְּחֶרֶץ — *As the oppressors*
[strive] to destroy [us] with intensity.
The stich is ambiguous and may also be

rendered: *The oppressors — [may You]*
[strive] to destroy [them] with inten-
sity.

כִּי צֵל יָמֵינוּ עֲלֵי אָרֶץ.[1]

« the earth. ‹ upon ‹ are our days ‹ like a shadow ‹ [and see] that

קָרֵב קֵץ עֶדְנַי,[2] קוֹל לְהַשְׁמִיעַ לְעוֹנַי,[3]

‹ by my enemies ‹ let be heard ‹ the sound « my time [of Redemption]; the « End, ‹ Bring near

כִּי קָרוֹב יוֹם יהוה.[4]

« of HASHEM. ‹ is the Day ‹ near ‹ that

רָם זְרֹעֲךָ תַּרְאֶה,[5] רַעֲיָתְךָ פָּנִים הִתְרָאֶה,

« appear, ‹ let Your countenance ‹ To Your beloved [Israel] « display! ‹ Your strong arm ‹ Lofty One,

כִּי רָם יהוה וְשָׁפָל יִרְאֶה.[6]

« He notices. ‹ the lowly « is ‹ [though] HASHEM, exalted ‹ for

שְׁמַע קוֹל תַּחֲנוּנַי,[7] שַׁוְעָתִי תַּעֲלֶה לִמְעוֹנַי,[8]

« [to You,] my eternal abode, ‹ rise ‹ let my outcry « of my supplications, ‹ the sound ‹ Hear

כִּי שׁוֹמֵעַ אֶל אֶבְיוֹנִים, יהוה.[9]

« does HASHEM. ‹ the destitute ‹ to ‹ listen ‹ for

תַּחַן כְּתוֹדָה תִּרְצֶה, תֹּאמַר לְעַמְּךָ אֶתְרַצֶּה,

I am appeased, « to Your people, ‹ say « You should ‹ favor; ‹ as a thanksgiving-offering ‹ Our supplication

כִּי תוֹרָה מֵאִתִּי תֵצֵא.[10]

« goes forth. ‹ from Me ‹ the principle [of equivalence] ‹ for

שְׁקֹל מֹאזְנַיִם יְכַבֵּשׁ, עֹז (נֶצַח) יַעֲטֶה וְיִלְבָּשׁ,[11]

« and wearing, ‹ donning ‹ (eternal) ‹ strength « He should tip [toward mercy], ‹ in the scales [of justice] ‹ The weighing

כִּי הוּא יַכְאִיב וְיֶחְבָּשׁ.[12]

« and He bandages. ‹ inflicts pain ‹ He ‹ for

---

(1) *Job* 8:9. (2) Cf. *Lamentations* 4:18. (3) Cf. *Isaiah* 30:30. (4) *Joel* 1:15. (5) Cf. *Isaiah* 30:30. (6) *Psalms* 138:6. (7) 28:2. (8) See 90:1. (9) 69:34. (10) *Isaiah* 51:4. (11) Cf. *Psalms* 93:1. (12) *Job* 5:18.

ALL, WHILE STANDING:

אֵל מֶלֶךְ יוֹשֵׁב עַל כִּסֵּא רַחֲמִים, מִתְנַהֵג

‹ Who acts ‹‹ of mercy, ‹ the throne ‹ on ‹ Who sits ‹ King ‹ O God,

בַּחֲסִידוּת, מוֹחֵל עֲווֹנוֹת עַמּוֹ, מַעֲבִיר רִאשׁוֹן

‹ [sins,] one ‹ Who ‹‹ of His ‹ the sins ‹ Who ‹‹ with kindness,
removes people, pardons

רִאשׁוֹן,[1] מַרְבֶּה מְחִילָה לַחַטָּאִים וּסְלִיחָה לַפּוֹשְׁעִים,

‹‹ to willful ‹ and ‹ to unintentional ‹ pardon ‹ Who abun- ‹‹ by one,
sinners, forgiveness sinners dantly grants

עֹשֶׂה צְדָקוֹת עִם כָּל בָּשָׂר וָרוּחַ, לֹא כְרָעָתָם

‹ in accord with ‹ — not ‹‹ and ‹ [beings ‹ all ‹ with ‹ acts of ‹ Who
their wickedness spirit of] flesh generosity performs

תִּגְמוֹל. ❖ אֵל הוֹרֵיתָ לָנוּ לוֹמַר שְׁלֹשׁ עֶשְׂרֵה, וּזְכוֹר

‹ remem- ‹‹ the Thirteen ‹ to ‹ You ‹ O God, ‹‹ do You
ber [Attributes of Mercy]; recite taught repay them!

לָנוּ הַיּוֹם בְּרִית שְׁלֹשׁ עֶשְׂרֵה, כְּמוֹ שֶׁהוֹדַעְתָּ לֶעָנָיו

‹ to the ‹ You made ‹ as ‹‹ of [these] Thirteen, ‹ the ‹ today ‹ for us
humble one known covenant
[Moses]

מִקֶּדֶם, כְּמוֹ שֶׁכָּתוּב, וַיֵּרֶד יהוה בֶּעָנָן וַיִּתְיַצֵּב עִמּוֹ

‹ with ‹ and stood ‹ in a ‹ And HASHEM ‹‹ it is written: ‹ as ‹‹ in ancient
him cloud descended times,

שָׁם, וַיִּקְרָא בְשֵׁם יהוה.[2]

‹‹ of ‹ with the ‹ and He ‹‹ there,
HASHEM. Name called out

CONGREGATION, THEN *CHAZZAN:*

וַיַּעֲבֹר יהוה עַל פָּנָיו וַיִּקְרָא:

‹‹ and ‹‹ [Moses'] ‹ before ‹ And HASHEM passed
proclaimed: face,

CONGREGATION AND *CHAZZAN* **RECITE LOUDLY AND IN UNISON:**

יהוה, יהוה, אֵל, רַחוּם, וְחַנּוּן, אֶרֶךְ אַפַּיִם,

‹ to anger, ‹ Slow ‹‹ and ‹ Compassionate ‹ God, ‹ HASHEM, ‹ HASHEM,
Gracious,

וְרַב חֶסֶד, וֶאֱמֶת, נֹצֵר חֶסֶד לָאֲלָפִים, נֹשֵׂא עָוֹן,

‹ of ‹ Forgiver ‹‹ for thousands ‹ of ‹ Preserver ‹ and ‹ in ‹ and
iniquity, [of generations], kindness Truth, Kindness Abundant

───────────────
(1) *Rosh Hashanah* 17a. (2) *Exodus* 34:5.

וָפֶ֫שַׁע, וְחַטָאָה, וְנַקֵּה.¹ וְסָלַחְתָּ לַעֲוֹנֵנוּ וּלְחַטָּאתֵנוּ

《 and our sins, 〈 our 〈 May You 《 *and Who* 〈 *and inadvertent* 〈 *willful sin,*
iniquities forgive *absolves.* *sin,*

וּנְחַלְתָּנוּ.² סְלַח לָנוּ אָבִינוּ כִּי חָטָאנוּ, מְחַל לָנוּ

〈 us, 〈 pardon 《 we have 〈 for 《 our 〈 us, 〈 Forgive 《 and make us
sinned; Father, Your heritage.

מַלְכֵּנוּ כִּי פָשָׁעְנוּ. כִּי אַתָּה אֲדֹנָי טוֹב וְסַלָּח,

《 and 〈 are 〈 O Lord, 〈 You, 〈 For 《 we have 〈 for 《 our King,
forgiving, good willfully sinned.

וְרַב חֶסֶד לְכָל קֹרְאֶיךָ.³

《 who call 〈 to all 〈 kind 〈 and
upon You. abundantly

פסוקי הקדמה לסליחה מז / PREFATORY VERSES TO SELICHAH 47

תָּשׁוּב תְּרַחֲמֵנוּ, תִּכְבּוֹשׁ עֲוֹנֹתֵינוּ, וְתַשְׁלִיךְ בִּמְצֻלוֹת

〈 into the 〈 and may 《 our 〈 may You 《 be merciful 〈 May You
depths You cast iniquities, suppress to us; again

יָם כָּל חַטֹּאתֵינוּ. (וְכָל חַטֹּאת עַמְּךָ בֵּית יִשְׂרָאֵל,⁴

〈 of Israel, 〈 the 〈 of Your 〈 the sins 〈 (And all 《 our sins. 〈 all 〈 of the
House people sea

תַּשְׁלִיךְ בִּמְקוֹם אֲשֶׁר לֹא יִזָּכְרוּ, וְלֹא יִפָּקְדוּ, וְלֹא

〈 nor 〈 be con- 〈 nor 〈 they will not be 〈 where 〈 to a place 〈 cast away
sidered, remembered,

יַעֲלוּ עַל לֵב לְעוֹלָם.)⁵ שׁוּב מֵחֲרוֹן אַפֶּךָ וְהִנָּחֵם

〈 and 〈 of Your 〈 from the 〈 Relent 《 ever.) 〈 mind 〈 to 〈 be
reconsider anger flaring brought

עַל הָרָעָה לְעַמֶּךָ. תָּשֵׁב אֱנוֹשׁ עַד דַּכָּא, וַתֹּאמֶר,⁶

《 and You 〈 pulp 〈 to 〈 man 〈 You 《 [meant] for 〈 the evil 〈 re-
say, reduce your people. garding

שׁוּבוּ בְּנֵי אָדָם.⁷

《 of man! 〈 O sons 〈 Repent

כְּרַחֵם אָב עַל בָּנִים, כֵּן תְּרַחֵם יהוה עָלֵינוּ.⁸

《 on us. 〈 HASHEM, 〈 have 〈 so 《 his 〈 toward 〈 a 〈 As merciful as
mercy, children, father is

---

(1) *Exodus* 34:6-7. (2) 34:9. (3) *Psalms* 86:5. (4) Cf. *Micah* 7:19.
(5) This is not a Scriptural verse. (6) *Exodus* 32:12. (7) *Psalms* 90:3. (8) Cf. 103:13.

לַיהוה הַיְשׁוּעָה, עַל עַמְּךָ בִרְכָתֶךָ סֶּלָה.[1] יהוה

⟨ HASHEM, ⟩⟩ Selah. ⟨⟨ is Your ⟨ Your ⟨ upon ⟩⟩ is salvation, ⟨ To HASHEM
blessing, people

צְבָאוֹת עִמָּנוּ, מִשְׂגָּב לָנוּ אֱלֹהֵי יַעֲקֹב סֶלָה.[2]

⟨⟨ Selah. ⟨⟨ of Jacob, ⟨ is the God ⟨ for us ⟨⟨ a ⟨⟨ is with us, ⟨ Master of
stronghold Legions,

יהוה צְבָאוֹת, אַשְׁרֵי אָדָם בֹּטֵחַ בָּךְ.[3] יהוה הוֹשִׁיעָה,

⟨⟨ save! ⟨ HASHEM, ⟨⟨ in You. ⟨ who ⟨ is the ⟨ — praise- ⟨⟨ Master of ⟨ HASHEM,
trusts man worthy Legions

הַמֶּלֶךְ יַעֲנֵנוּ בְיוֹם קָרְאֵנוּ.[4]

⟨⟨ we call. ⟨ on the ⟨ answer ⟨ May the
day us King

סליחה מז / SELICHAH 47
(שלמונית)

אֱלֹהֵינוּ וֵאלֹהֵי אֲבוֹתֵינוּ:

⟨⟨ of our forefathers: ⟨ and the God ⟨ Our God

תָּשׁוּב תְּרַחֲמֵנוּ,*[5] שׁוּב שְׁבִיתֵנוּ[6] כְּנֶאֱמֶךָ,

⟨⟨ as You ⟨ our captivity ⟨ return ⟨⟨ be merciful ⟨ May You
have said. to us;* again

שׁוּב כְּקֶדֶם חַדֵּשׁ חִבַּת לְאֻמֶּךָ,

⟨⟨ for Your ⟨ Your ⟨ renew ⟨ as of old, ⟨ Once
nation. love again,

רַחֵק רְגֶז וְקָרֵב שֹׁךְ זַעֲמֶךָ,

⟨⟨ of Your ⟨ the ⟨ and draw ⟨ rage ⟨ Distance
fury; assuaging near

שׁוּב מֵחֲרוֹן אַפֶּךָ, וְהִנָּחֵם עַל הָרָעָה לְעַמֶּךָ.[7]

⟨⟨ against Your ⟨ the evil ⟨ re- ⟨ and ⟨ of Your ⟨ from the ⟨ relent
people. garding reconsider anger flaring

קַבֵּץ וּבַקֵּשׁ אֹבְדוֹת וְחַזֵּק נַחֲלָתֶךָ,[8]

⟨⟨ Your heritage- ⟨ and ⟨ the lost ⟨ and seek ⟨ Gather
people, strengthen ones, out together

---

(1) Psalms 3:9. (2) 46:8. (3) 84:13. (4) 20:10. (5) Cf. Micah 7:19. (6) Cf. Psalms 126:4. (7) Exodus 32:12. (8) Cf. Ezekiel 34:16.

⸺§ תָּשׁוּב תְּרַחֲמֵנוּ — May You again be merciful to us. The respective first three lines of each quatrain form a reverse alphabetical acrostic (תשר״ק) followed by

the author's signature — שְׁלֹמֹה, Shlomo [see prefatory comment to Selichah 2]. The fourth line of each stanza is a Scriptural fragment that begins with some form of

צֹאן הַהֲרֵגָה וְהַגְּזוּזָה בִּדְחִילָתֶךְ,[1]
for fearing You. ‹ shorn ≪ of the ‹ the
[by the gentiles] slaughter, flock

פֶּשַׁע אִם רַב בִּבְנֵי מְחִילָתֶךְ,*
Your ‹ among those ‹ [it] is ‹ even ≪ Sin,
forgiveness,* who regularly wide- if
receive spread

שׁוּב לְמַעַן עֲבָדֶיךָ שִׁבְטֵי נַחֲלָתֶךְ.[2]
of Your ‹ and the ‹ of Your servants ‹ for the ‹ return
heritage. tribes [the Patriarchs], sake [to us]

עֲוֹן אֲבוֹתֵינוּ הִטְעִינָנוּ, וּבֹסֶר הִטְעִימָנוּ,[3]
they caused ‹ and sour ≪ placed a heavy yoke ‹ of our ‹ The
us to taste. grapes [of exile] upon us, fathers iniquity

סַף רַעַל הִשְׁקָנוּ[4] הֶלְעִינָנוּ וְהִזְעִימָנוּ,
≪ and with rage. ‹ filling us with ≪ they gave us ‹ of ‹ A
wormwood to drink, poison bowl

נָא כְּאָז בְּשֶׁכֶן יַחַד הִנְעִימָנוּ,[5]
≪ and our life ‹ in ‹ when [we] ‹ as of ‹ Please,
was pleasant, unity dwelt old,

שׁוּבֵנוּ* אֱלֹהֵי יִשְׁעֵנוּ, וְהָפֵר כַּעַסְךָ עִמָּנוּ.[6]
≪ with us. ‹ Your anger ‹ and ≪ of our ‹ O God ‹ return us,*
annul salvation,

מָאוֹס לֹא מָאַסְתָּ[7] חוֹסֶיךָ מְעִידֶיךָ,
≪ who bear ‹ those who take ‹ You have not utterly rejected
witness to You; shelter with You,

לוֹקִים כְּסוֹרְחַ, וּלְהִתְמָרֵחַ סִבְרָם עָדֶיךָ,
≪ to You, ‹ they look ‹ for the balm ≪ when ‹ though they
[of atonement] they sin, are punished

---

(1) Many editions of *Selichos* [and almost all manuscript versions] read וְהַגְּזוּזָה בְּרַחֲלוֹתֶיךָ,
and the shorn of Your ewes, or כְּרַחֲלוֹתֶיךָ, *like Your ewes.* (2) *Isaiah* 63:17.
(3) Cf. *Jeremiah* 31:29. (4) Cf. *Zechariah* 12:2; some editions of *Selichos* read סַף רַעַל רִשְׁעֵנוּ,
Our wickedness is a bowl of poison [for us]. (5) Cf. *Psalms* 133:1. (6) 85:5.
(7) Cf. *Jeremiah* 14:19; *Lamentations* 5:22; *Leviticus* 26:44.

---

the word שׁוּב, *return* or *turn back*.

בִּבְנֵי מְחִילָתֶךְ — *Among those who regular-ly receive Your forgiveness.* The transla-tion follows *Arugas HaBosem*. According to *Masbir*, the phrase means *those who seek Your forgiveness*.

כְּאָז בְּשֶׁכֶן יַחַד הִנְעִימָנוּ שׁוּבֵנוּ ... — *As of old*
when [we] dwelt in unity and our life was pleasant, return us ....* The translation follows *Arugas HaBosem*. However, *Matteh Levi* (based on *Targum* and *Rashi* to *Psalms* 85:5) renders, *As of old when Your Presence dwelt among us and made our life pleasant, so return to us ....*

כַּעַס לְרַצּוֹת כְּמִדַּת יְשֶׁר מַעְבָּדֶיךָ,

of Your ⟪ to the ⟨ as is ⟨ to assuage ⟨ [Your]
deeds. uprightness appropriate anger

שׁוּבָה יהוה עַד מָתַי, וְהִנָּחֵם עַל עֲבָדֶיךָ.[1]

Your ⟪ con- ⟨ And ⟪ until when? ⟨ HASHEM, ⟨ **Return,**
servants. cerning relent

יוֹם יוֹם נְצַפֶּה גִּלּוּי סוֹדֶךָ,

of Your ⟨ to the ⟨ we look ⟨ after ⟨ Day
secret, revelation forward day

טָמוּם וְעָמוּם וּבָלָה בִּשַׂר[2] חֲסִידֶיךָ,

of Your ⟪ is the ⟨ and ⟨ and ⟨ yet it is
pious ones. flesh [meanwhile,] covered, sealed
worn away

חֶרְפָּה שָׁבְרָה לִבֵּנוּ[3] מְקַוִּים חֲסָדֶיךָ,

Your ⟨ that [still] ⟨ our ⟨ has broken ⟨ Humiliation
kindness. hope for hearts

שׁוּבָה יהוה חַלְּצָה נַפְשֵׁנוּ, וְהוֹשִׁיעֵנוּ לְמַעַן חַסְדֶּךָ.[4]

of Your ⟨ for the ⟨ and save us ⟪ our soul; ⟨ release ⟨ HASHEM, ⟨ **Return,**
kindness. sake

זָנַחְנוּ וְנֶחְשַׁבְנוּ עִם יוֹרְדֵי רֶגֶב,

⟪ to the ⟨ those who ⟨ with ⟨ we are ⟨ We are
grave, descend reckoned abandoned,

וַיְהִי לְאֵבֶל כִּנּוֹר וְשִׁיר וְעֻגָב,[5]

⟪ and flute. ⟨ and song ⟨ have ⟨ to ⟨ turned
harp mourning

הַקּוֹדְרִים בְּרִנָּה וְתוֹדָה הִתְהַלֵּךְ בְּשֶׂגֶב,[6]

⟪ with vigor, ⟨ will stride ⟨ and ⟨ with glad ⟪Those [who walk]
thanksgiving song in gloom,

שׁוּבָה יהוה אֶת שְׁבִיתֵנוּ כַּאֲפִיקִים בַּנֶּגֶב.[7]

⟪ in the ⟨ like springs ⟨ our captivity ⟨ O ⟨ [when You]
desert. HASHEM, **return,**

דִּמְעָה לֶחֶם[8] חוֹסֶיךָ צוּרִי אֵל,

⟪ God, ⟨ my ⟨ of those who ⟨ are the ⟨ Tears
Rock, seek refuge bread
with You,

---

(1) *Psalms* 90:13. (2) Cf. *Lamentations* 3:4; some editions of *Selichos* read וְכָלָה,
cf. *Proverbs* 5:10, but the meaning is unchanged. (3) Cf. *Psalms* 69:21.
(4) Cf. 6:5. (5) Cf. *Job* 30:31. (6) Cf. 5:11; *Psalms* 43:2. (7) 126:4. (8) Cf. 80:6.

גּוֹאֵל אַיֵּה בְּחֵרֶף צָרֵי אֵל,[1]

« of ⟨ [ask] the ⟨ in **«** — where **«**[while] *The*
God. enemies blasphemy *is he?* *redeemer*

בְּחָזוֹן אָז כְּדִבַּרְתָּ[2] לִישָׁרֵי אֵל,

« of ⟨ to the upright ⟨ You spoke ⟨ once ⟨ As in
God, [prophets] visions

שׁוּבָה יהוה רִבְבוֹת אַלְפֵי יִשְׂרָאֵל.[3]

« of Israel. ⟨ thou- ⟨ to the ⟨ HASHEM, ⟨ **return,**
sands myriad

❖ שִׁמְעָה יהוה הַטֵּה אָזְנְךָ[4] וְהַקְשִׁיבָה,

« and be attentive; ⟨ Your ear ⟨ incline **«** HASHEM; ⟨ Hear,

לִמְחַלֵּי סְלַח נָא סָלַחְתִּי הָשִׁיבָה,[5]

« answer. **«** I have **«** Forgive please! **«** to those
forgiven! who beg,

מְשׁוּבוֹתֵינוּ רַבּוּ וּפָתַחְתָּ יִשְׂרָאֵל שׁוּבָה,[6]

« return! ⟨ Israel, **«** yet You **«** has ⟨ Our waywardness
have opened been
[the door, saying], great,

הֲשִׁיבֵנוּ יהוה אֵלֶיךָ וְנָשׁוּבָה.[7]

« and we ⟨ to You ⟨ HASHEM, ⟨ **Return** us,
will return.

ALL, WHILE STANDING:

אֵל מֶלֶךְ יוֹשֵׁב עַל כִּסֵּא רַחֲמִים, מִתְנַהֵג

⟨ Who acts **«** of mercy, ⟨ the throne ⟨ on ⟨ Who sits ⟨ King ⟨ O God,

בַּחֲסִידוּת, מוֹחֵל עֲווֹנוֹת עַמּוֹ, מַעֲבִיר רִאשׁוֹן

⟨ [sins,] one ⟨ Who **«** of His ⟨ the sins ⟨ Who **«** with kindness,
removes people,   pardons

רִאשׁוֹן,[8] מַרְבֶּה מְחִילָה לַחַטָּאִים וּסְלִיחָה לַפּוֹשְׁעִים,

« to willful ⟨ and ⟨ to unintentional ⟨ pardon ⟨ Who abun- **«** by one,
sinners, forgiveness sinners dantly grants

עֹשֶׂה צְדָקוֹת עִם כָּל בָּשָׂר וָרוּחַ, לֹא כְרָעָתָם

⟨ in accord ⟨ — not **«** and ⟨ [beings ⟨ all ⟨ with ⟨ acts of ⟨ Who
with their spirit of] flesh generosity performs
wickedness

---

(1) Cf. *Psalms* 74:10. (2) Cf. 89:20. (3) *Numbers* 10:36. (4) Cf. *Daniel* 9:18.
(5) See *Numbers* 14:19-20. (6) Cf. *Hosea* 14:2. (7) *Lamentations* 5:21. (8) *Rosh Hashanah* 17a.

תִּגְמוֹל. ❖ אֵל הוֹרֵיתָ לָּנוּ לוֹמַר שְׁלֹשׁ עֶשְׂרֵה, וּזְכוֹר

⟨ remem- ⟨⟨ the Thirteen ⟨ to ⟨ us ⟨ You ⟨ O God, ⟨⟨ do You
ber   [Attributes of Mercy];   recite   taught   repay them!

לָּנוּ הַיּוֹם בְּרִית שְׁלֹשׁ עֶשְׂרֵה, כְּמוֹ שֶׁהוֹדַעְתָּ לֶעָנָיו

⟨ to the humble ⟨ You made ⟨ as ⟨⟨ of [these] Thirteen, ⟨ the ⟨ today ⟨ for us
one [Moses]   known   covenant

מִקֶּדֶם, כְּמוֹ שֶׁכָּתוּב, וַיֵּרֶד יהוה בֶּעָנָן וַיִּתְיַצֵּב עִמּוֹ

⟨ with ⟨ and stood ⟨ in a ⟨ And HASHEM ⟨⟨ it is written: ⟨ as ⟨⟨ in ancient
him   cloud   descended   times,

שָׁם, וַיִּקְרָא בְשֵׁם יהוה.[1]

⟨⟨ of ⟨ with the ⟨ and He ⟨⟨ there,
HASHEM.   Name   called out

CONGREGATION, THEN CHAZZAN:

וַיַּעֲבֹר יהוה עַל פָּנָיו וַיִּקְרָא:

⟨⟨ and ⟨⟨ [Moses'] ⟨ before ⟨ And HASHEM passed
proclaimed: face,

CONGREGATION AND CHAZZAN RECITE LOUDLY AND IN UNISON:

יהוה, יהוה, אֵל, רַחוּם, וְחַנּוּן, אֶרֶךְ אַפַּיִם,

⟨ to anger, ⟨ Slow ⟨⟨ and ⟨ Compassionate ⟨ God, ⟨ HASHEM, ⟨ HASHEM,
    Gracious,

וְרַב חֶסֶד, וֶאֱמֶת, נֹצֵר חֶסֶד לָאֲלָפִים, נֹשֵׂא עָוֹן,

⟨ of ⟨ Forgiver ⟨⟨ for thousands ⟨ of ⟨ Preserver ⟨⟨ and ⟨ in ⟨ and
iniquity,   [of generations],   kindness   Truth,   Kindness Abundant

וָפֶשַׁע, וְחַטָּאָה, וְנַקֵּה.[2] וְסָלַחְתָּ לַעֲוֹנֵנוּ וּלְחַטָּאתֵנוּ

⟨⟨ and our sins, ⟨ our ⟨ May You ⟨⟨ and Who ⟨ and inadvertent ⟨ willful sin,
   iniquities   forgive   absolves.   sin,

וּנְחַלְתָּנוּ.[3] סְלַח לָנוּ אָבִינוּ כִּי חָטָאנוּ, מְחַל לָנוּ

⟨ us, ⟨ pardon ⟨⟨ we have ⟨ for ⟨⟨ our ⟨ us, ⟨ Forgive ⟨⟨ and make us
   sinned;   Father,   Your heritage.

מַלְכֵּנוּ כִּי פָשָׁעְנוּ. כִּי אַתָּה אֲדֹנָי טוֹב וְסַלָּח,

⟨⟨ and ⟨ are ⟨ O Lord, ⟨ You, ⟨ For ⟨⟨ we have ⟨ for ⟨⟨ our King,
forgiving,   good   willfully sinned.

וְרַב חֶסֶד לְכָל קֹרְאֶיךָ.[4]

⟨⟨ who call ⟨ to all ⟨ kind ⟨ and
upon You.   abundantly

---

(1) *Exodus* 34:5. (2) 34:6-7. (3) 34:9. (4) *Psalms* 86:5.

סליחה מח / SELICHAH 48

(פזמון)

CHAZZAN, THEN CONGREGATION:

הוֹרֵיתָ דֶּרֶךְ תְּשׁוּבָה,* לְבַת הַשּׁוֹבֵבָה,[1]

《 who is 〈 to the 〈 of 〈 the way 〈 You have
wayward, daughter repentance* taught

בֵּין כֶּסֶה לֶעָשׂוֹר,* עָדֶיךָ לָשׁוּבָה,

《 to return. 〈 to You 〈 and 〈 Rosh 〈 be-
Yom Kippur* Hashanah tween

הֲשִׁיבֵנוּ יהוה אֵלֶיךָ, וְנָשׁוּבָה.[2]

《 and we shall return! 〈 to You, 〈 HASHEM, 〈 Bring us back,

CONGREGATION, THEN CHAZZAN:

אָז מֵאָז מִקֶּדֶם, הִקְדַּמְתָּ תְּשׁוּבָה,[3]

《 made 〈 You first 〈 from of old 《 back 《Then,
repentance, then,

בְּטֶרֶם הִמְתַּחְתָּ אֶרֶץ וִיסוֹדֵי רְגוּבָה,

《of [earth formed 〈 and the 〈 the 〈 You stretched 〈 before
from] clumps. foundations heavens out

גַּם לְכָל הַשָּׁבִים,* צֳרִי וּמַרְפֵּא חֲשׁוּבָה,

《it is considered,〈 and healing 〈 balm 〈 penitents,* 〈 for all 〈 Also

---

(1) Cf. Jeremiah 31:21. (2) Lamentations 5:21. (3) See commentary to Selichah 4, s.v. כּוֹנַנְתָּ מֵאָז תֶּרֶף.

הוֹרֵיתָ דֶּרֶךְ תְּשׁוּבָה — You have taught the way of repentance. Various Scriptural personalities sinned and were given the opportunity to repent. Some even become paradigms for the penitent to emulate; others were contrite, but in their own way. Their stories are related in Tanach to teach the lesson of teshuvah, repentance, on different levels — individual, communal, royal .... Six of them are mentioned in this selichah: Adam, Cain, Reuben, Judah, Ahab, and the citizens of Nineveh in Jonah's time.

The paytan's signature — בְּנְיָמֵן, Binyamin [see prefatory note to Selichah 1] — appears after the alphabetical acrostic.

Although the refrain of this pizmon comprises the entire introductory stanza, many congregations repeat only the third line.

בֵּין כֶּסֶה לֶעָשׂוֹר — Between Rosh Hashanah and Yom Kippur. The word כֶּסֶה means covered, and the phrase from which it is taken, בַּכֶּסֶה לְיוֹם חַגֵּנוּ (Psalms 81:4), means on the festive day when the moon is covered. But that can refer only to Rosh Hashanah, which coincides with the New Moon, for all other Scripturally ordained festivals fall between the first quarter and third quarter of their respective months (Rosh Hashanah 8a).

Alternatively, the word כֶּסֶה is cognate to כִּסֵּא and means either appointed time (Rashi) or throne (Sforno), and alludes to Rosh Hashanah as the day appointed for judgment, or the day on which God sits on the Throne of Judgment.

The term עָשׂוֹר, tenth, refers to Yom Kippur, the tenth of Tishrei. Taken together, the Ten Days of Penitence — from Rosh Hashanah to Yom Kippur — are thus called בֵּין כֶּסֶה לֶעָשׂוֹר.

גַּם לְכָל הַשָּׁבִים — Also for all penitents. Not only those mentioned in this piyut, but also all others who are contrite and remorseful

דּוֹפְקֵי דְלָתֶיךָ רֵיקָם מִלְּהָשִׁיבָה.

《 not be sent back. 〈 empty- 《 on Your 〈 so that those
handed doors, who knock

(הוֹרֵיתָ . . .) הֲשִׁיבֵנוּ יהוה אֵלֶיךָ, וְנָשׁוּבָה.

《 and we 〈 to You, 〈 HASHEM, 〈 Bring us 〈 (You have taught . . .)
shall return! back,

CONGREGATION, THEN *CHAZZAN*:

הֵן רֹאשׁ עַפְרוֹת תֵּבֵל,¹ אֲשֶׁר רִאשׁוֹן נוֹצָר,

《 to be 〈 the first 〈 who was 〈 of the 〈 of the dust 〈 the 〈 Indeed,
created, earth, first [Adam,]

וְנִסִּיתוֹ בְּמִצְוָה קַלָּה,* וְאוֹתָהּ לֹא נָצָר,

《 he did not 〈 but it 《 that was 〈 with a 〈 You tested
keep. easy,* commandment him

זָעַמְתָּ וְאָנַפְתָּ עָלָיו, שְׁנוֹתָיו לְקַצֵּר,

《 to cut 〈 [You decreed] 《 at him, 〈 and were 〈 You raged
short, his years furious

חָזַר בִּתְשׁוּבָה² וְכְאִישׁוֹן הַנָּצַר.

《 You 〈 like the pupil 《 in 〈 [yet] when
guarded him. of the eye repentance, he returned

(הוֹרֵיתָ . . .) הֲשִׁיבֵנוּ יהוה אֵלֶיךָ, וְנָשׁוּבָה.

《 and we 〈 to You, 〈 HASHEM, 〈 Bring us 〈 (You have taught . . .)
shall return! back,

CONGREGATION, THEN *CHAZZAN*:

טָעָה גִזְעוֹ דְּמֵי אָחִיו בְּשָׁפְכוֹ,³

《 he spilled; 〈 of his 〈 [when] 《 did his 〈 Go
brother child astray
blood [Cain],

יִסַּרְתּוֹ בְּנָע וָנָד,⁴ לֶכֶת כֹּה וָכֹה,

《 and 〈 here 〈 traveling 〈 and an 〈 to be a 〈 You pun-
there. exile, wanderer ished him

כָּעֵת שָׁב אֵלֶיךָ, וְעָזַב רְעַ דַּרְכּוֹ,⁵

《 of his way, 〈 the 〈 and 〈 to You 〈 he 〈 [Yet] at the
evil abandoned returned moment

---

(1) Cf. *Proverbs* 8:26. (2) See *Eruvin* 18b. (3) See *Genesis* 4:8. (4) 4:12. (5) See 4:13.

about their sinful past may find balm and
healing in *teshuvah*.

בְּמִצְוָה קַלָּה — *With a commandment that was easy.* While yet in the Garden of Eden, Adam

had been given but one *mitzvah: Of every tree of the garden you may freely eat, but of the Tree of Knowledge of Good and Bad, you must not eat thereof* (*Genesis* 2:16-17).

לְשִׁבְעָתַיִם הֶאֱרַכְתּוֹ, כָּל מוֹצְאוֹ בְּלִי לְהַכּוֹ.[1]

For seven ⟨ You lengthened ⟨ that ⟨ who would ⟨ should ⟨ smite
generations [his life], anyone meet him not him.

(הוֹרֵיתָ . . .) הֲשִׁיבֵנוּ יהוה אֵלֶיךָ, וְנָשׁוּבָה.

(You have taught . . .) ⟨ Bring us ⟨ HASHEM, ⟨ to You, ⟨ and we
back, shall return!

CONGREGATION, THEN *CHAZZAN:*

מְחַלֵּל[2] יְצוּעֵי יוֹלְדוֹ, אֲשֶׁר פֶּחַז כַּמַּיִם,[3]

[Reuben,] who ⟨ the ⟨ of his ⟨ he was ⟨ like water, ⟨
desecrated couch progenitor, impetuous

נָטָיוּ רַגְלָיו כִּמְעַט,[4] לוּלֵי שָׁפַךְ לֵב כַּמַּיִם,[5]

turn him ⟨ did his ⟨ almost, ⟨ had ⟨ poured ⟨ his ⟨ like
astray feet he not out heart water.

סָרַח גּוּר אַרְיֵה, בִּקְדֵשָׁה הִיא בָעֵינָיִם,[6]

Sin ⟨ did the ⟨ of the lion ⟨ with a harlot, ⟨ the ⟨ at the
[Judah] cub one crossroads;

עֲוֹנוֹ הוֹדָה,[7] וְהִכְרַעְתּוֹ לְצֶדֶק בְּמֹאזְנָיִם.

his trans- ⟨ he ⟨ and You tipped ⟨ to the side of ⟨ on the scales
gression confessed, for him righteousness [of justice].

(הוֹרֵיתָ . . .) הֲשִׁיבֵנוּ יהוה אֵלֶיךָ, וְנָשׁוּבָה.

(You have taught . . .) ⟨ Bring us ⟨ HASHEM, ⟨ to You, ⟨ and we
back, shall return!

CONGREGATION, THEN *CHAZZAN:*

פָּרַץ גְּדֵרוֹת עוֹלָם, בֶּן עָמְרִי בְּרֶשַׁע,

Breach ⟨ all the ⟨ of the ⟨ did [Ahab] ⟨ of ⟨ in [his]
fences world the son Omri wickedness;

צַלְמֵי אֲשֵׁרִים חָשַׁק, וְהוֹסִיף עַל חַטָּאתוֹ פֶּשַׁע,[8]

idols ⟨ of Asheirah ⟨ lusting for, ⟨ adding ⟨ onto ⟨ his sin ⟨ rebellion.

קָרַעְתָּ גְּזַר דִּינוֹ בְּשׁוּבוֹ מִלְפִשַׁע,[9]

Yet You ⟨ his ⟨ of retri- ⟨ when he ⟨ his sins,
tore up decree bution repented

רְחַם כְּמוֹדֶה וְעוֹזֵב,[10] וּבְךָ נוֹשָׁע.

and he re- ⟨ who confesses ⟨ as befits one ⟨ and for- ⟨ and ⟨ he was
ceived mercy, sakes sin, with You saved.

---

(1) Cf. *Genesis* 4:15. (2) See commentaries to 35:22 and 49:4. (3) Cf. 49:4. (4) Cf. *Psalms* 73:2.
(5) Cf. *Lamentations* 2:19; see *Sotah* 7b. (6) See *Genesis* Ch. 38. (7) See 38:26; see *Sotah* 7b.
(8) See *I Kings* 16:29ff; *Sanhedrin* 102b. (9) See *I Kings* 21:27-29. (10) Cf. *Proverbs* 28:13.

(הוֹרֵיתָ . . .) הֲשִׁיבֵנוּ יהוה אֵלֶיךָ, וְנָשׁוּבָה.

《 and we shall return! 〈 to You, 〈 HASHEM, 〈 Bring us back, 〈 (You have taught . . .)

CONGREGATION, THEN *CHAZZAN*:

שָׁנְנוּ לְשׁוֹנָם כְּחֵץ, אַנְשֵׁי עִיר הַגְּדוֹלָה,

《 that was great; 〈 of [Nineveh] the city 〈 did the people 〈 like arrows [against You] 〈 their tongues 〈 Sharpen

שִׁגְיוֹנָם וּזְדוֹנָם רַבּוּ עַד לְמָעְלָה,

《 up high. 〈 until 〈 in-creased 〈 and willful ones 〈 their inadver-tent sins

תִּתְּךָ חֲזוֹן הֲפֵיכָתָם, אֲחָזוּם רֶתֶת וְחַלְחָלָה,

《 and trembling; 〈 did shuddering 〈 seize them 〈 of their overthrow, 〈 the vision 〈 When You revealed

תְּשׁוּבָה עָשׂוּ כְּהֹגֶן, וְלִפְנֵי כִסֵּא כְבוֹדְךָ נִתְקַבְּלָה.

《 it was accepted. 〈 of Your Glory 〈 the Throne 〈 and before 〈 properly 〈 they went through 〈 repentance

(הוֹרֵיתָ . . .) הֲשִׁיבֵנוּ יהוה אֵלֶיךָ, וְנָשׁוּבָה.

《 and we shall return! 〈 to You, 〈 HASHEM, 〈 Bring us back, 〈 (You have taught . . .)

CONGREGATION, THEN *CHAZZAN*:

בּוֹחֵן כְּלָיוֹת וָלֵב, נֶאְזָר בִּגְבוּרָה,

《 with might, 〈 [You Who are] belted 〈 and hearts, 〈 of thoughts 〈 O Searcher

יַדְּעֵנוּ מַדַּע לֶכֶת בְּאֹרַח יְשָׁרָה,

《 that is straight. 〈 in the path 〈 of 〈 the walking 〈 knowledge 〈 teach us

מְשׁוּבוֹתֵינוּ אִם רַבּוּ בְּפֶשַׁע וּסְרָרָה,

《 and straying, 〈 with rebellious sin 〈 it has grown great 〈 if 〈 Our waywardness,

נָא לְמַעַנְךָ הֲשִׁיבֵנוּ, עֲשׂוֹת תְּשׁוּבָה כְּשׁוּרָה.

《 properly. 〈 repentance 〈 that we may go through 〈 bring us back 〈 for Your own sake, 〈 please,

(הוֹרֵיתָ . . .) הֲשִׁיבֵנוּ יהוה אֵלֶיךָ, וְנָשׁוּבָה.

《 and we shall return! 〈 to You, 〈 HASHEM, 〈 Bring us back, 〈 (You have taught . . .)

---

(1) See *Jonah* 1:2. (2) See 3:4. (3) See 3:5-8. (4) See 3:10. (5) Cf. *Jeremiah* 14:7.

ALL, WHILE STANDING:

אֵל מֶלֶךְ יוֹשֵׁב עַל כִּסֵּא רַחֲמִים, מִתְנַהֵג

⟨ O God, ⟩ King ⟨ Who sits ⟩ on ⟨ the throne ⟨ of mercy, ⟩ Who acts

בַּחֲסִידוּת, מוֹחֵל עֲוֹנוֹת עַמּוֹ, מַעֲבִיר רִאשׁוֹן

⟨ with kindness, ⟩ Who pardons ⟨ the sins ⟨ of His people, ⟩ Who removes ⟨ [sins,] one

רִאשׁוֹן,¹ מַרְבֶּה מְחִילָה לַחַטָּאִים וּסְלִיחָה לַפּוֹשְׁעִים,

⟨ by one, ⟩ Who abun-dantly grants ⟨ pardon ⟨ to unintentional sinners ⟩ and forgiveness ⟨ to willful sinners,

עֹשֶׂה צְדָקוֹת עִם כָּל בָּשָׂר וָרוּחַ, לֹא כְרָעָתָם

⟨ Who performs ⟨ acts of generosity ⟨ with ⟨ all ⟨ [beings of] flesh ⟩ and spirit ⟨ — not ⟨ in accord with their wickedness

תִּגְמוֹל. ❖ אֵל הוֹרֵיתָ לָּנוּ לוֹמַר שְׁלֹשׁ עֶשְׂרֵה, וּזְכוֹר

⟨ do You repay them! ⟨ O God, ⟩ You taught ⟨ us ⟨ to recite ⟨ the Thirteen [Attributes of Mercy]; ⟩ and remember

לָנוּ הַיּוֹם בְּרִית שְׁלֹשׁ עֶשְׂרֵה, כְּמוֹ שֶׁהוֹדַעְתָּ לֶעָנָיו

⟨ for us ⟨ today ⟨ the covenant ⟨ of [these] Thirteen, ⟩ as ⟨ You made known ⟨ to the humble one [Moses]

מִקֶּדֶם, כְּמוֹ שֶׁכָּתוּב, וַיֵּרֶד יהוה בֶּעָנָן וַיִּתְיַצֵּב עִמּוֹ

⟨ in ancient times, ⟩ as ⟨ it is written: ⟨ And HASHEM descended ⟨ in a cloud ⟨ and stood ⟨ with him

שָׁם, וַיִּקְרָא בְשֵׁם יהוה.²

⟨ there, ⟩ and He called out ⟨ with the Name ⟨ of HASHEM.

CONGREGATION, THEN *CHAZZAN:*

וַיַּעֲבֹר יהוה עַל פָּנָיו וַיִּקְרָא:

⟨ And HASHEM passed ⟨ before ⟨ [Moses'] face, ⟩ and ⟨ proclaimed:

CONGREGATION AND *CHAZZAN* **RECITE LOUDLY AND IN UNISON:**

יהוה, יהוה, אֵל, רַחוּם, וְחַנּוּן, אֶרֶךְ אַפַּיִם,

⟨ HASHEM, ⟨ HASHEM, ⟨ God, ⟨ Compassionate ⟩ and Gracious, ⟨ Slow ⟨ to anger,

(1) *Rosh Hashanah* 17a. (2) *Exodus* 34:5.

וְרַב חֶסֶד, וֶאֱמֶת, נֹצֵר חֶסֶד לָאֲלָפִים, נֹשֵׂא עָוֹן,
⟨ of ⟨ Forgiver ≪ for thousands ⟨ of ⟨ Preserver ≪ and ⟨ in ⟨ and
iniquity, [of generations], kindness Truth, Kindness Abundant

וָפֶשַׁע, וְחַטָּאָה, וְנַקֵּה.[1] וְסָלַחְתָּ לַעֲוֹנֵנוּ וּלְחַטָּאתֵנוּ
≪ and our sins, ⟨ our ⟨ May You ≪ and Who ⟨ and inadvertent ⟨ willful sin,
iniquities forgive absolves. sin,

וּנְחַלְתָּנוּ.[2] סְלַח לָנוּ אָבִינוּ כִּי חָטָאנוּ, מְחַל לָנוּ
⟨ us, ⟨ pardon ≪ we have ⟨ for ≪ our ⟨ us, ⟨ Forgive ≪ and make us
sinned; Father, Your heritage.

מַלְכֵּנוּ כִּי פָשָׁעְנוּ. כִּי אַתָּה אֲדֹנָי טוֹב וְסַלָּח,
≪ and ⟨ are ⟨ O Lord, ⟨ You, ⟨ For ≪ we have ⟨ for ≪ our King,
forgiving, good willfully sinned.

וְרַב חֶסֶד לְכָל קֹרְאֶיךָ.[3]
≪ who call ⟨ to all ⟨ kind ⟨ and
upon You. abundantly

הֵיטִיבָה בִרְצוֹנְךָ אֶת צִיּוֹן, תִּבְנֶה חוֹמוֹת
⟨ the walls ⟨ build ≪ Zion; ⟨ unto ⟨ in Your favor ⟨ Do good

יְרוּשָׁלָיִם. אָז תַּחְפֹּץ זִבְחֵי צֶדֶק, עוֹלָה וְכָלִיל,
≪and whole- ⟨ burnt- ⟨ of right- ⟨ the ⟨ You will ⟨ Then ≪ of Jerusalem.
offering; offering eousness, offerings desire

אָז יַעֲלוּ עַל מִזְבַּחֲךָ פָרִים.[4] זִבְחֵי אֱלֹהִים רוּחַ
⟨ are a ⟨ God ⟨ The ⟨ [will be] ⟨ Your Altar ⟨ upon ⟨ offered ⟨then
spirit desires sacrifices bulls. up

נִשְׁבָּרָה, לֵב נִשְׁבָּר וְנִדְכֶּה אֱלֹהִים לֹא תִבְזֶה.[5]
≪ You will not ⟨ O God ⟨ and ⟨ broken ⟨ a ≪ that is
despise. humbled, heart broken;

וְהִתְבָּרְכוּ בְזַרְעֲךָ כֹּל גּוֹיֵי הָאָרֶץ, עֵקֶב אֲשֶׁר
⟨ you ⟨ because ⟨ of the ⟨ the ⟨ will ⟨ by your ⟨ And bless
have earth, nations all offspring themselves

שָׁמַעְתָּ בְּקֹלִי.[6]
≪ to My ⟨ listened
voice.

---

(1) *Exodus* 34:6-7. (2) 34:9. (3) *Psalms* 86:5. (4) 51:20-21. (5) 51:19. (6) *Genesis* 22:18.

סליחה מט / SELICHAH 49
(עקדה)

אֱלֹהֵינוּ וֵאלֹהֵי אֲבוֹתֵינוּ:

《of our forefathers:〈 and the God〈 Our God

אָז בְּהַר מֹר* דָּץ יוֹנַת אֵלֶם,[1]

《 of 〈 [Isaac,]〈 rejoiced〈 Moriah,*〈 on 〈 Then,
silence, the dove   Mount

בְּקַחְתוֹ אֵיתָן[2] לְעוֹלָה וְשֶׁלֶם,[3]

《 without 〈 for a burnt-〈 did the 〈 when take
blemish. offering mighty one him
[Abraham]

גֵּאֶה בְּחָנוּ קַח נָא זֶה הָעֶלֶם,

〈 youth 〈 this〈 please,〈 Take, 《 tested 〈The Grand
[Abraham], One

תְּרוּמָה לַיהוה קֹדֶשׁ.[4]

《 as **holy**.〈 unto HASHEM〈 to be raised up

דָּת הַטֶּנֶא לְפָנַי לְהַנִּיחֵהוּ,[5]

《 it is to be placed. 〈 before 《 of the [first 〈 Such is
Me fruits] basket, the law

הֵן קַח נָא אֶת בִּנְךָ[6] לְאֶשְׁכָּר סְפָחֵהוּ,

《 attach him, 〈 as part of 〈 your son 〈 now 〈 take 〈 So,
your offering indeed

וְאֹנִי בְחַרְתִּיו קוּם מְשָׁחֵהוּ,[7] שֶׁמֶן מִשְׁחַת קֹדֶשׁ.[8]

《 that is 〈 of anointing 〈 with 〈 anoint him 〈 rise, 〈 have chosen 〈 for I
holy. the oil him;

זָךְ בְּשָׁמְעוֹ לִבּוֹ לֹא דָאַב, חָפֵץ צוּרוֹ חָשַׁק וְתָאַב,

《and desired〈 he 〈 of his 〈 the will 《 pained;〈 was 〈 his 《 heard 〈 When the
[to do]. wished Molder not heart this, pure[-hearted
Abraham]

טָפְלוּ שְׁנֵיהֶם הַבֵּן וְהָאָב,[9]

《 and the 〈 the 《 did the two,〈 Join
father, son together

(1) *Psalms* 56:1. (2) See commentary to *Selichah* 58, s.v. אֵיתָן לֻמֵּד דַּעַת.
(3) See *Amos* 5:22. (4) *Ezekiel* 45:1. (5) See *Deuteronomy* 26:4.
(6) *Genesis* 22:2. (7) *I Samuel* 16:12. (8) *Exodus* 30:25. (9) Cf. *Genesis* 22:6,8.

אָז בְּהַר מֹר 🅈 — *Then, on Mount Moriah.* This *selichah*, of the *akeidah* genre, contains an *aleph-beis* acrostic, followed by

the *paytan's* signature — שְׁלֹמֹה בַּר יְהוּדָה גַּבִּירוֹל, *Shlomo bar Yehudah [ibn] Gabirol* [see prefatory comment to *Selichah* 71]. The

וְהִשְׁתַּחֲווּ¹ לַיהוה בְּהַדְרַת קֹדֶשׁ.²

《 of   〈 in the   〈 to HASHEM   《 and prostrated
holiness.   splendor   themselves

יִעֵד עֵצִים וְלִשְׁפֹת עָרַךְ, כַּמָּה וְתָמַהּ יָחִיד וָרָךְ,

《 of tender 〈 did the 〈 and 〈 While 《 arranged 〈 and for 〈 wood 〈 He pre-
age,   only [son] wondered longed   it.   the pyre   pared

לַהַג אַיֵּה הַשֶּׂה³ הַנֶּעֱרָךְ, לְהַקְדִּישׁוֹ בְּמִקְדַּשׁ קֹדֶשׁ.⁴

《 of   〈 into the 〈 to be   〈 prepared, 〈 the lamb 〈 Where 〈 he
holiness?   sanctity   consecrated   is   asked,

מָרוֹם יִרְאֶה לּוֹ הַשֶּׂה⁵ וְהוּא יָשִׁיב,

〈 He will revive   《 the 〈 for 〈 will seek 〈 The Most
     lamb. Himself out   High

נֶפֶשׁ אֵם עֲקֶרֶת שְׂמֵחָה לְהָשִׁיב,⁶

〈 to restore 〈 in joy 〈 who is 〈 of the 〈 the
   [her].   barren, mother soul

סוֹקֵר סְפוּנוֹת בְּנִי שַׁוְעָךְ יַקְשִׁיב,

《 will be 〈 to your 〈 my 《 of hidden 〈 The
attentive, prayer son, things,   Examiner

יִשְׁלַח עֶזְרְךָ מִקֹּדֶשׁ.⁷

《 from the 〈 His aid 〈 and He
Sanctuary.   will send

עֲמָד נָא אָבִי וּקְשֹׁר הַטֶּבַח, פֶּן אָגוּר מִפְּנֵי הָאֶבַח,

《 the 〈 because 〈 I shudder 〈 lest 〈 [for] the 〈 and bind 〈 my 〈 now, 〈 Rise,
blade.   of   in fear   slaughter, [me]   father,

צַמְּדֵנִי פֶּן אֲחַלֵּל הַזֶּבַח, וּלְהַבְדִּיל בֵּין הַקֹּדֶשׁ.⁸*

《 that is 〈 from being 〈 and be 《 the 〈 I invalidate 〈 lest 〈 Bind me
holy.*   [an offering] separated   sacrifice,   tight

קָפַץ לִבְכּוֹת כֹּפֶר אֶשְׁכּוֹל,

《 of henna, 〈 did [Isaac,] 〈 to weep 〈 Begin
    the cluster   suddenly

---

(1) Cf. *Genesis* 22:5. (2) Cf. *Psalms* 29:2. (3) Cf. *Genesis* 22:7. (4) Cf. *I Chronicles* 23:13.
(5) *Genesis* 22:8. (6) Cf. *Psalms* 113:9. (7) 20:3. (8) *Leviticus* 10:10.

---

fourth line of each stanza is a Scriptural fragment that ends in the word קֹדֶשׁ, *holy*, *holiness*, or *Sanctuary*.

וּלְהַבְדִּיל בֵּין הַקֹּדֶשׁ — *And be separated from being [an offering] that is holy.* Isaac asked that he be bound tightly for two reasons: (a) lest he shudder and cause the knife to make an invalid incision; and (b) to distinguish between the slaughter of a well-tied altar offering and a hastily bound animal to be slaughtered for food (*Pardes*).

According to *Arugas HaBosem* the conjunctive וּ, *and*, is omitted from the text. Thus, Isaac gave only one reason: that he not invalidate the offering, but that it remain holy.

רְאוֹתוֹ אָבִיו נִשְׁכַּל שָׁכוּל,

《 left childless.〈 bereaved,〈 his father 〈 seeing

שָׁלַח יָדוֹ לַעֲשׂוֹת אֶת כֹּל מְלֶאכֶת עֲבוֹדַת הַקֹּדֶשׁ.[1]

《 that is **holy**. 〈 for 〈 the tasks 〈 all 〈 to perform 〈 But he [Abraham] stretched forth his hand
　　　　　　the work

תַּרְשִׁישִׁים* צָעֲקוּ בִּשְׁמֵי מְרוֹמִי,

《 heights, 〈 in the 〈 cried out 〈 The angels*
　　　　Heavenly

שְׁחֹט יוֹנַת אֵלֶם הֲיוּכַל יֶחֱזֶה מִי,

《 who is 〈 seeing it 〈 able to 《 of 〈 of the 〈 The
　there?　　　　bear　silence —　dove　slaughter

לָז לְלָז יֶהְגּוּ אַל תִּתְּנוּ דָמִי, שְׂאוּ יְדֵיכֶם קֹדֶשׁ.[3]

《 in 〈 your hands 〈 Lift up 《 silence! 〈 give 〈 Do 《 said, 〈 to 〈 One
holiness.　[to pray]　　　　[Him]　not　　　　another

מָרוֹם הִבִּיט עוֹקֵד וְנֶעֱקַד,

《 and the 〈 the 〈 observed 〈 When the
　bound,　binder　　　　Most High

הַשֶּׂה עָקוּד וְהָאֵשׁ תּוּקַד,

《 kindled, 〈 and the fire 〈 bound 〈 the lamb

בּוֹחֵן טְהָר לֵב זָכַר וּפָקַד,

《 and 〈 remem- 〈 of 〈 of 〈 the
recalled,　bered　heart　purity　Tester

וְנִשְׁמַע קוֹלוֹ בְּבֹאוֹ אֶל הַקֹּדֶשׁ.[4]

《 the 〈 into 〈 as He 〈 was His 〈 and heard
Sanctuary.　entered　voice

רָחַשׁ מֵלִיץ בְּקַחְתּוֹ מְשֻׁלַּחַת,

《 the knife, 〈 as he 〈 did the 〈 Call out
　　　　　[Abraham]　advocate
　　　　　took　[angel],

---

(1) Cf. *Exodus* 36:1. (2) Cf. *Isaiah* 62:7. (3) *Psalms* 134:2. (4) *Exodus* 28:35.

Alternatively: Isaac said, "Bind me tight lest I desecrate the sacrifice and thus separate myself from God's Holiness!" (*Masbir*).

תַּרְשִׁישִׁים — *The angels*. Rambam (*Yesodei HaTorah* 2:7) notes that there are ten levels of angels. Their names are *Chayos*, *Ofanim*, *Erelim*, *Chashmalim*, *Seraphim*, *Malachim*, *Elohim*, *Bnei Elohim*, *Cherubim*, and *Ishim*.

[We do not have the vocabulary to translate these names.] The prophet (*Ezekiel* 1:16) describes the appearance of the *Ofanim* as similar to that of תַּרְשִׁישׁ, *tarshish*, a beautiful, clear gem that *Rashi* identifies as crystal. The *paytanim* have borrowed the term *Tarshishim* for the *Ofanim* in particular, and all angels in general.

יְחִידְךָ פְּדָעֵהוּ מֵרֶדֶת שַׁחַת,[1]

《 to the   〈 from   〈 redeem him 《 Your only
grave!   descending   son,

הִנֵּה כְתוּבָה לְפָנַי[2] פֶּתַח מְפֻתָּחַת,

《   deeply engraved,   《 before Me, 〈 it is written 〈 Indeed,

פִּתּוּחֵי חֹתָם קֹדֶשׁ.[3]

《 made in 〈 like a   〈 with
holiness.   signet   engraving

וַאֲנִי יָדַעְתִּי דַרְכְּךָ בְּשֶׁפֶר,

《 is lovely; 〈 your way 〈 I know that 《 And as
for Me,

דּוּץ וְרוּץ וְקַח אַיִל תַּחַת עֹפֶר,

《 [Isaac,] 〈 instead of 〈 a ram 〈 and take 〈 run, 〈 rejoice,
the gazelle.

הֲכִינוֹתִי כֹפֶר לְאֶשְׁכֹּל הַכֹּפֶר,

《 of henna, 〈 for the cluster 〈 a ransom 〈 I have prepared

וְהָיָה הוּא וּתְמוּרָתוֹ יִהְיֶה קֹדֶשׁ.[4]

《 holy. 〈 shall be 〈 and his 〈 [that both] 〈 and then
     substitute   he   it shall be

גָּמוּל נִמְלַט מֵאַבַּח הַנִּשְׁחַז,

《 that was 〈 from the 〈 was 〈 The young
sharpened;   blade   rescued   [Isaac]

בְּפָשְׁטוֹ צַוָּארוֹ דָּמוֹ לֹא נִפְחַז,

《 [shed] to flow 〈 was 〈 his 〈 his neck, 〈 though he had
impetuously.   not   blood   stretched out

יְמִינוֹ אָחַז בְּיוֹבֵל הַנֶּאֱחַז, לְהַקְדִּישׁוֹ לַיהוה קֹדֶשׁ.[5]

《 as **holy.** 〈 to Hashem 〈 to sanctify it, 《 tangled 〈 the ram 〈 grasped 〈 His right
[in the thicket],   hand

❖ רַחוּם תִּתֵּן שָׁלוֹם לְאַחֲרִיתוֹ,

《 to his posterity, 〈 peace 〈 grant 《 O Merciful
One,

וּזְכוֹר הַיּוֹם לִגְזָעוֹ בְּרִיתוֹ,

《 his 〈 for his descen- 〈 today 〈 and
covenant.   dants' [benefit],   remember

---

(1) *Job* 33:24. (2) *Isaiah* 65:6. (3) *Exodus* 28:36. (4) *Leviticus* 27:10. (5) Cf. *I Chronicles* 23:13.

לְיֶתֶר הַפְּלֵיטָה וּשְׁאָר שְׁאֵרִיתוֹ,

《 of his survivors, 〈 and those 〈 remnant 〈 For the
                          left   remaining

תִּהְיֶה פְּלֵיטָה וְהָיָה קֹדֶשׁ.[1]

《 holy. 〈 and may it be 〈 a refuge, 〈 may there be

ALL, WHILE STANDING:

אֵל מֶלֶךְ יוֹשֵׁב עַל כִּסֵּא רַחֲמִים, מִתְנַהֵג

〈 Who acts 《 of mercy, 〈 the throne 〈 on 〈 Who sits 〈 King 〈 O God,

בַּחֲסִידוּת, מוֹחֵל עֲוֹנוֹת עַמּוֹ, מַעֲבִיר רִאשׁוֹן

〈 [sins,] one 〈 Who removes 《of His people, 〈 the sins 〈 Who pardons 《 with kindness,

רִאשׁוֹן,[2] מַרְבֶּה מְחִילָה לַחַטָּאִים וּסְלִיחָה לַפּוֹשְׁעִים,

《 to willful 〈 and 〈 to unintentional 〈 pardon 〈 Who abun- 《 by one,
    sinners,   forgiveness   sinners   dantly grants

עֹשֶׂה צְדָקוֹת עִם כָּל בָּשָׂר וָרוּחַ, לֹא כְרָעָתָם

〈 in accord with 〈 — not 《 and 〈 [beings 〈 all 〈 with 〈 acts of 〈 Who
their wickedness   spirit   of] flesh   generosity   performs

תִּגְמוֹל. ❖ אֵל הוֹרֵיתָ לָנוּ לוֹמַר שְׁלֹשׁ עֶשְׂרֵה, וּזְכוֹר

〈 remem- 《 the Thirteen 〈 to 〈 us 〈 You 〈 O God, 《 do You
    ber   [Attributes of Mercy]; recite   taught   repay them!

לָנוּ הַיּוֹם בְּרִית שְׁלֹשׁ עֶשְׂרֵה, כְּמוֹ שֶׁהוֹדַעְתָּ לֶעָנָיו

〈 to the humble 〈 You made 〈 as 《 of [these] Thirteen, 〈 the 〈 today 〈 for us
one [Moses]   known   covenant

מִקֶּדֶם, כְּמוֹ שֶׁכָּתוּב, וַיֵּרֶד יהוה בֶּעָנָן וַיִּתְיַצֵּב עִמּוֹ

〈 with 〈 and stood 〈 in a 〈 And HASHEM 《 it is written: 〈 as 《in ancient
   him   cloud   descended   times,

שָׁם, וַיִּקְרָא בְשֵׁם יהוה.[3]

《 of 〈 with the 〈 and He 《 there,
   HASHEM.   Name   called out

CONGREGATION, THEN *CHAZZAN:*

וַיַּעֲבֹר יהוה עַל פָּנָיו וַיִּקְרָא:

《 and 《 [Moses'] 〈 before 〈 And HASHEM passed
proclaimed: face,

CONGREGATION AND *CHAZZAN* **RECITE LOUDLY AND IN UNISON:**

יהוה, יהוה, אֵל, רַחוּם, וְחַנּוּן, אֶרֶךְ אַפַּיִם,

〈 to anger, 〈 Slow 《and Gracious, 〈 Compassionate 〈 God, 〈 HASHEM, 〈 HASHEM,

(1) *Obadiah* 1:17. (2) *Rosh Hashanah* 17a. (3) *Exodus* 34:5.

וְרַב חֶסֶד, וֶאֱמֶת, נֹצֵר חֶסֶד לָאֲלָפִים, נֹשֵׂא עָוֹן,

‹ of ‹ Forgiver « for thousands ‹ of ‹ Preserver ‹ and ‹ in ‹ and
iniquity,   [of generations], kindness   Truth,   Kindness Abundant

וָפֶשַׁע, וְחַטָּאָה, וְנַקֵּה.[1] וְסָלַחְתָּ לַעֲוֹנֵנוּ וּלְחַטָּאתֵנוּ

« and our sins, ‹ our ‹ May You « and Who ‹ and inadvertent « willful sin,
iniquities forgive absolves. sin,

וּנְחַלְתָּנוּ.[2] סְלַח לָנוּ אָבִינוּ כִּי חָטָאנוּ, מְחַל לָנוּ

‹ us, ‹ pardon « we have ‹ for « our ‹ us, ‹ Forgive « and make us
sinned; Father, Your heritage.

מַלְכֵּנוּ כִּי פָשָׁעְנוּ. כִּי אַתָּה אֲדֹנָי טוֹב וְסַלָּח,

« and ‹ are ‹ O Lord, ‹ You, ‹ For « we have ‹ for « our King,
forgiving, good willfully sinned.

וְרַב חֶסֶד לְכָל קֹרְאֶיךָ.[3]

« who call ‹ to all ‹ kind ‹ and
upon You. abundantly

ALL:

זְכֹר רַחֲמֶיךָ יהוה וַחֲסָדֶיךָ, כִּי מֵעוֹלָם הֵמָּה.[4]

«are they. ‹ eternal ‹ for « and Your ‹ HASHEM, ‹ Your mercies, ‹ Remember
kindnesses,

זָכְרֵנוּ יהוה בִּרְצוֹן עַמֶּךָ, פָּקְדֵנוּ בִּישׁוּעָתֶךָ.[5] זְכֹר

‹ Re- « with Your ‹ recall us « to Your ‹ when You ‹ HASHEM, ‹ Remem-
member salvation. people; show favor ber us,

עֲדָתְךָ קָנִיתָ קֶּדֶם, גָּאַלְתָּ שֵׁבֶט נַחֲלָתֶךָ, הַר צִיּוֹן זֶה

‹ the one ‹ of ‹ the « of Your ‹ the ‹ You « long ‹ which You ‹ Your con-
[where] Zion, mountain heritage; tribe redeemed ago, acquired gregation,

שָׁכַנְתָּ בּוֹ.[6] זְכֹר יהוה חִבַּת יְרוּשָׁלָיִם, אַהֲבַת

‹ the love « of Jerusalem; ‹ the ‹ HASHEM, ‹ Remem- «there. ‹ You rested
affection ber, Your Presence

צִיּוֹן אַל תִּשְׁכַּח לָנֶצַח.[7] אַתָּה תָקוּם תְּרַחֵם צִיּוֹן כִּי

‹ for « to ‹ and show ‹ will arise ‹ You « forever. ‹ forget ‹ do not ‹ of
Zion, mercy Zion

עֵת לְחֶנְנָהּ, כִּי בָא מוֹעֵד.[8] זְכֹר יהוה לִבְנֵי אֱדוֹם

‹ of ‹ [to repay] ‹ HASHEM, ‹ Re- « the appointed time ‹ for « [there will come]
Edom the offspring, member, will have come. the time to favor her,

אֵת יוֹם יְרוּשָׁלָיִם, הָאֹמְרִים עָרוּ עָרוּ עַד הַיְסוֹד בָּהּ.[9]

«of it! ‹ the very ‹ to ‹ Destroy «Destroy! « [to repay] « of Jerusalem; ‹ for the day
foundation those who say,

(1) Exodus 34:6-7. (2) 34:9. (3) Psalms 86:5. (4) 25:6. (5) Cf. 106:4.
(6) 74:2. (7) This is not a Scriptural verse. (8) Psalms 102:14. (9) 137:7.

זְכֹר לְאַבְרָהָם לְיִצְחָק וּלְיִשְׂרָאֵל עֲבָדֶיךָ, אֲשֶׁר

⟨ that ⟩ ⟪ Your servants, ⟨ and for Israel, ⟨ for Isaac, ⟨ for Abraham, ⟨Remember

נִשְׁבַּעְתָּ לָהֶם בָּךְ וַתְּדַבֵּר אֲלֵהֶם, אַרְבֶּה אֶת זַרְעֲכֶם

⟨ Your offspring ⟨ I shall ⟪ to them, ⟨ and ⟪ by Your ⟨ to ⟨ You
　　　　　increase　　　　　You said Being, them swore

כְּכוֹכְבֵי הַשָּׁמָיִם, וְכָל הָאָרֶץ הַזֹּאת אֲשֶׁר אָמַרְתִּי,

⟨ I spoke ⟨ of which ⟨ of this land ⟨ and all ⟪ of the heavens;⟨ like the stars

אֶתֵּן לְזַרְעֲכֶם, וְנָחֲלוּ לְעֹלָם.¹ זְכֹר לַעֲבָדֶיךָ לְאַבְרָהָם

⟨ of Abraham, ⟨ of Your ⟨Remember ⟪ forever. ⟨ and they ⟨ to your ⟨ I will
　　　　　servants, [the merits] will inherit it offspring, give

לְיִצְחָק וּלְיַעֲקֹב, אַל תֵּפֶן אֶל קְשִׁי הָעָם הַזֶּה וְאֶל

⟨ to ⟪ of this people, ⟨ the stub- ⟨ to ⟨ pay ⟨ do ⟪ and of Jacob; ⟨ of Isaac,
　　　　　　bornness　　attention not

רִשְׁעוֹ וְאֶל חַטָּאתוֹ.² זְכוֹר לָנוּ בְּרִית אָבוֹת, כַּאֲשֶׁר

⟨ as ⟪ of the ⟨ the ⟨ for ⟨Remember ⟪ its ⟨ and ⟪ its
　　　Patriarchs, covenant us　　sinfulness.　　to wickedness,

אָמָרְתָּ: וְזָכַרְתִּי אֶת בְּרִיתִי יַעֲקוֹב, וְאַף אֶת בְּרִיתִי

⟨ My covenant ⟨ and ⟪[with] Jacob, ⟨ My covenant ⟨ And I will ⟪ You said:
　　　also　　　　　　　　　　　　　　remember

יִצְחָק, וְאַף אֶת בְּרִיתִי אַבְרָהָם אֶזְכֹּר, וְהָאָרֶץ אֶזְכֹּר.³

⟪ I will ⟨ and the ⟪ I will ⟨ [with] ⟨ My covenant ⟨ and ⟪ [with]
remember. Land remember; Abraham　　　　also Isaac,

סליחה נ / SELICHAH 50
(פזמון)

THE ARK IS OPENED.

CHAZZAN, THEN CONGREGATION:

זְכוֹר בְּרִית אַבְרָהָם* וַעֲקֵדַת יִצְחָק,

⟪ of Isaac; ⟨ and the ⟨ of Abraham* ⟨ the ⟨ Remem-
　　　binding　　　　covenant ber

וְהָשֵׁב שְׁבוּת אָהֳלֵי יַעֲקֹב,⁴ וְהוֹשִׁיעֵנוּ לְמַעַן שְׁמֶךָ.⁵

⟪ of Your ⟨ for the ⟨ and save us ⟪ of Jacob, ⟨ of the ⟨ the ⟨ Restore
Name. sake　　　　　　　　　　tents captivity

(1) *Exodus* 32:13. (2) *Deuteronomy* 9:27. (3) *Leviticus* 26:42.
(4) Cf. *Jeremiah* 30:18. (5) Cf. *Psalms* 106:8.

◆§ זְכוֹר בְּרִית אַבְרָהָם — *Remember the* 　selichah 40 are both parts of a longer work
covenant of Abraham. This *selichah* and 　(see prefatory comment to *Selichah* 40).

CONGREGATION, THEN *CHAZZAN:*

טָס כַּנֶּשֶׁר¹ מְבַקֵּשׁ נַפְשָׁם,

《 their death, 〈 did he who 〈 like an 〈 Fly
sought   eagle

טָבֹחַ בְּחוּרֵיהֶם בְּבֵית מִקְדָּשָׁם,²

《 in their Holy Temple. 〈 their young men 〈 to slaughter

יָסַפְתָּ לְיַסְּרָם³ וּלְעָנְשָׁם,

《 and punishing 〈 afflicting 〈 You
them,   them   increased

יְלָדִים וְאֵם לַבָּנִים לְרַטְּשָׁם,⁴

《   tearing 〈 of the 〈 and the 〈 through
asunder.   children   mother   children

וְשׁוּב בְּרַחֲמִים עַל שְׁאֵרִית יִשְׂרָאֵל,

《 of Israel, 〈 the remnant 〈 to 〈 with mercy 〈 And return

וְהוֹשִׁיעֵנוּ לְמַעַן שְׁמֶךָ.

《 of Your 〈 for the 〈 and save us
Name.   sake

CONGREGATION, THEN *CHAZZAN:*

כְּבֶּשְׁנוּ לַעֲבָדִים⁵ וְנִתְיַגְּעְנוּ,

《 and worked 〈 as slaves 〈 We have been
to exhaustion;   subjugated

כְּנַסְנוּ מֵהָאֲרִי* וְהַדֹּב* פְּגָעְנוּ,⁶

《 attacked us. 〈 and the 〈 from the 〈 we were
bear*   lion,*   brought back

לַחַץ נָמֵר* עַד כִּי יָגֵעְנוּ, לָחַם בָּנוּ וְלֹא הִרְגַּעְנוּ.

《 and we had no relief. 〈 against 〈 he 《 we were 〈 until 〈 did the 〈 Oppress
us   fought   exhausted;   leopard*   us

וְהָשֵׁב שְׁבוּת אָהֳלֵי יַעֲקֹב, וְהוֹשִׁיעֵנוּ לְמַעַן שְׁמֶךָ.

《 of Your 〈 for the 〈 and save us 《 of Jacob, 〈 of the 〈 the 〈 Restore
Name.   sake   tents   captivity

---

(1) Cf. *Job* 9:26. (2) Cf. *II Chronicles* 36:17. (3) Cf. *Leviticus* 26:18.
(4) Cf. *Hosea* 10:14. (5) Cf. *II Chronicles* 28:10. (6) Cf. *Amos* 5:19.

מֵהָאֲרִי וְהַדֹּב ... נָמֵר — *From the lion, and the bear ... the leopard.* In his vision, Daniel (Ch. 7) saw four beasts, each of which represented one of the exiles to which Israel had been or would be subjected. The first, a lion, alluded to Babylon. The second, a bear, was an allusion to Persia (*Megillah* 11a). The third, a leopard, represented Greece. The fourth beast, not identified by species, referred to the fourth *galus*, that of the Roman Empire (in all its metamorphoses) from which we still seek redemption.

CONGREGATION, THEN *CHAZZAN:*

מִכָּל מְשַׁעְבְּדֵי שְׁלִישִׁיָה, מָשְׁכָה רְבִיעִיָה,*

《 is this fourth 〈 prolonged 《 from the group 〈 the 〈 More
[enslavement].* of three, enslavements than all

נָתְנָה עֹל עַל עֲנִיָה, וְנִהְיָתָה תַּאֲנִיָה וַאֲנִיָה.[1]

《 and grief. 〈 have 〈 and come 《the afflict-〈 upon〈 a 〈 It placed
mourning upon us ed people, yoke

וְשׁוּב בְּרַחֲמִים עַל שְׁאֵרִית יִשְׂרָאֵל,

《 of Israel, 〈 the remnant 〈 to 〈 with mercy 〈And return

וְהוֹשִׁיעֵנוּ לְמַעַן שְׁמֶךָ.

《 of Your 〈 for the 〈 and save us
Name. sake

CONGREGATION, THEN *CHAZZAN:*

גּוֹאֵל חָזָק לְמַעַנְךָ פְּדֵנוּ, רְאֵה כִּי אָזְלַת יָדֵנוּ,[2]

《 our strength 〈 that 〈 See 《 deliver 〈 for Your 〈 Who is 〈 O
is gone. us! Own sake mighty, Redeemer

שׁוּר כִּי אָבְדוּ חֲסִידֵינוּ,[3] מַפְגִּיעַ אֵין בַּעֲדֵנוּ.[4]

《 for us. 〈 there is 《 and to 《 our devout ones, 〈 lost are 〈 that 〈 Observe
no one intercede,

וְהָשֵׁב שְׁבוּת אָהֳלֵי יַעֲקֹב, וְהוֹשִׁיעֵנוּ לְמַעַן שְׁמֶךָ.

《 of Your 〈 for the 〈 and save us 《 of Jacob, 〈 of the 〈 the 〈 Restore
Name. sake tents captivity

CONGREGATION, THEN *CHAZZAN:*

בְּרִית אָבוֹת וְאִמָּהוֹת וְהַשְּׁבָטִים,

《 and Tribes, 〈 the Matriarchs, 〈 of the 〈 The
Patriarchs, covenant

רַחֲמֶיךָ וַחֲסָדֶיךָ בְּרִבּוֹת עִתִּים,[5]

《 times — 〈 through 〈 and Your 〈 Your mercy
so many kindness

יָהּ זְכֹר לְמֻכִּים וְנִמְרָטִים,[6]

〈 and having [their hair 〈 on behalf of 〈 remember 〈 O
and beards] torn out those beaten [all this,] God,

---

(1) *Lamentations* 2:5. (2) Cf. *Deuteronomy* 32:36. (3) Cf. *Micah* 7:2.
(4) Cf. *Isaiah* 59:16. (5) Cf. *Nehemiah* 9:28. (6) Cf. 13:25.

However, the Talmud (*Pesachim* 118b, based on *Psalms* 80:14) identifies this beast as a type of wild boar.

רְבִיעִיָה — *Is this fourth [enslavement],* Edom.

וְעָלֶיךָ כָּל הַיּוֹם נֶהֱרָגְנוּ.[1]

《 are slaughtered. 〈 day long 〈 all 〈 and who for
                                                      Your sake

וְשׁוּב בְּרַחֲמִים עַל שְׁאֵרִית יִשְׂרָאֵל,

《 of Israel, 〈 the remnant 〈 to 〈 with mercy 〈 And return

וְהוֹשִׁיעֵנוּ לְמַעַן שְׁמֶךָ.

《 of Your 〈 for the 〈 and save us
   Name.   sake

CONGREGATION, THEN *CHAZZAN*:

דּוֹרֵשׁ דָּמִים[2] דּוֹן דִּינֵנוּ,

《 our 〈 avenge 〈 of blood, 〈 Avenger
vengeance!

הָשֵׁב שִׁבְעָתַיִם אֶל חֵיק מְעַנֵּינוּ,[3]

《 of our 〈 the 〈 into 〈 sevenfold 〈 Restore
   tormentors.   bosom

חִנָּם נִמְכַּרְנוּ, וְלֹא בְכֶסֶף פִּדְנוּ,[4]

《 redeem 〈 with 〈 so not 〈 were we sold 〈 Without
   us.   money   [into Exile],   payment

זְקוֹף בֵּית מִקְדָּשְׁךָ הַשָּׁמֵם לְעֵינֵינוּ.[5]

《 before 〈 that is 〈 Your Holy Temple 〈 Erect
   our eyes.   desolate,

וְהָשֵׁב שְׁבוּת אָהֳלֵי יַעֲקֹב, וְהוֹשִׁיעֵנוּ לְמַעַן שְׁמֶךָ.

《 of Your 〈 for the 〈 and save us 〈 of Jacob, 〈 of the 〈 the 〈 Restore
   Name.   sake   tents   captivity

THE ARK IS CLOSED.

ALL CONTINUE:

זְכוֹר לָנוּ בְּרִית רִאשׁוֹנִים, כַּאֲשֶׁר אָמַרְתָּ: וְזָכַרְתִּי

〈 And I will 《 You said: 〈 as 《 of the 〈 the 〈 for us 〈 Remember
   remember   ancient ones,   covenant

לָהֶם בְּרִית רִאשׁוֹנִים, אֲשֶׁר הוֹצֵאתִי אֹתָם מֵאֶרֶץ

〈 from 〈 I took them out 〈 that 《 of the 〈 the 〈 for
   the land   ancient ones,   covenant   them

מִצְרַיִם לְעֵינֵי הַגּוֹיִם, לִהְיוֹת לָהֶם לֵאלֹהִים, אֲנִי

〈 I am 《 a God; 〈 to them 〈 to be 《 of the 〈 in the 〈 of Egypt
                                         nations,   very sight

---

(1) Cf. *Psalms* 44:23. (2) 9:13. (3) Cf. 79:12; some editions of *Selichos* omit this stich.
(4) Cf. *Isaiah* 52:3; see commentary to *Selichah* 11, s.v. לְמִכּוּרֵי חִנָּם. (5) Cf. *Daniel* 9:17.

יהוה.[1] עֲשֵׂה עִמָּנוּ כְּמָה שֶׁהִבְטַחְתָּנוּ: וְאַף גַּם
《 all 〈 And despite 《 You promised us: 〈 as 〈 with us 〈 Do 《 HASHEM.

זֹאת בִּהְיוֹתָם בְּאֶרֶץ אֹיְבֵיהֶם, לֹא מְאַסְתִּים וְלֹא
〈 nor 〈 despise them 〈 I will 《 of their 〈 in the land 〈 when they 《 this,
                              not   enemies,   will be

גְעַלְתִּים לְכַלֹּתָם לְהָפֵר בְּרִיתִי אִתָּם, כִּי אֲנִי יהוה
〈 HASHEM, 〈 I am 〈 for 《 with 〈 My 〈 to annul 《 to destroy 〈 abhor them
                          them,   covenant   them,

אֱלֹהֵיהֶם.[2] הָשֵׁב שְׁבוּתֵנוּ וְרַחֲמֵנוּ, כְּמָה שֶׁכָּתוּב:
《 it is 〈 as 《 and have 〈 our captivity 〈 Bring 《 their God.
written: mercy on us,   back

וְשָׁב יהוה אֱלֹהֶיךָ אֶת שְׁבוּתְךָ וְרִחֲמֶךָ, וְשָׁב וְקִבֶּצְךָ
〈 gather 〈 and He 《 and He will 〈 your captivity, 〈 your 〈 will 〈 Then bring
you in   will once have mercy   God,   HASHEM, back
         again   upon you,

מִכָּל הָעַמִּים אֲשֶׁר הֱפִיצְךָ יהוה אֱלֹהֶיךָ שָׁמָּה.[3]
《 thereto. 〈 your God 〈 has 〈 scattered 〈 that 〈 the 〈 from
                        HASHEM   you   peoples   all

קַבֵּץ נִדָּחֵינוּ, כְּמָה שֶׁכָּתוּב: אִם יִהְיֶה נִדַּחֲךָ בִּקְצֵה
〈 at the 〈 your dispersed 〈 If 〈 it is written: 〈 as 〈 our 〈 Gather
ends   will be   dispersed ones,

הַשָּׁמָיִם, מִשָּׁם יְקַבֶּצְךָ יהוה אֱלֹהֶיךָ, וּמִשָּׁם יִקָּחֶךָ.[4]
《 He will 〈 and from 《 your God, 〈 will 〈 gather 〈 from 《 of heaven,
take you.   there   HASHEM   you in   there

מְחֵה פְשָׁעֵינוּ כָּעָב וְכָעָנָן, כְּמָה שֶׁכָּתוּב: מָחִיתִי
〈 I have 《 it is written: 〈 as 《 and like a 〈 like a 〈 our sins 〈 Wipe
wiped away   cloud,   mist   away

כָעָב פְּשָׁעֶיךָ וְכֶעָנָן חַטֹּאתֶיךָ, שׁוּבָה אֵלַי כִּי
〈 for 〈 to 〈 return 《 your 〈 and like 〈 your willful 〈 like a
        Me,   transgressions; a cloud   sins,   mist

גְאַלְתִּיךָ. מְחֵה פְשָׁעֵינוּ לְמַעַנְךָ, כַּאֲשֶׁר אָמַרְתָּ:[5]
《 You have 〈 as 《 for Your 〈 our sins 〈 Wipe 《 I have
said: sake,   away   redeemed you.

אָנֹכִי אָנֹכִי הוּא מֹחֶה פְשָׁעֶיךָ לְמַעֲנִי, וְחַטֹּאתֶיךָ לֹא
〈 I shall 〈 and your 《 for 〈 your 〈 Who wipes 〈 am the 〈 [only] I, 〈 I,
not   transgressions My sake, willful sins away   One

(1) Leviticus 26:45. (2) 26:44. (3) 30:3. (4) 30:4. (5) Isaiah 44:22.

אֶזְכֹּר. הַלְבֵּן חֲטָאֵינוּ כַּשֶּׁלֶג וְכַצֶּמֶר, כְּמָה שֶׁכָּתוּב:

‹ it is written: ‹ as « and like wool, ‹ like snow ‹ our sins ‹ Whiten « recall.

לְכוּ נָא וְנִוָּכְחָה, יֹאמַר יהוה, אִם יִהְיוּ חֲטָאֵיכֶם

‹ your sins may be ‹ Though « HASHEM. ‹ says « let us reason ‹ now, ‹ Come, together,

כַּשָּׁנִים כַּשֶּׁלֶג יַלְבִּינוּ, אִם יַאְדִּימוּ כַתּוֹלָע, כַּצֶּמֶר

‹ like [white] « as crimson, ‹ they may ‹ though « they will be ‹ like « like wool   be red   whitened; snow   scarlet,

יִהְיוּ. זְרוֹק עָלֵינוּ מַיִם טְהוֹרִים וְטַהֲרֵנוּ, כְּמָה שֶׁכָּתוּב:

« it is written: ‹ as « and purify us, ‹ pure water ‹ upon us ‹ Pour « they will become.

וְזָרַקְתִּי עֲלֵיכֶם מַיִם טְהוֹרִים וּטְהַרְתֶּם, מִכֹּל

‹ from « and you will ‹ pure water ‹ upon you ‹ I shall pour all   become pure;

טֻמְאוֹתֵיכֶם וּמִכָּל גִּלּוּלֵיכֶם אֲטַהֵר אֶתְכֶם. רַחֵם

‹ Have « you. ‹ I will ‹ your ‹ and ‹ your mercy   purify   abominations   from all   contaminations

עָלֵינוּ וְאַל תַּשְׁחִיתֵנוּ, כְּמָה שֶׁכָּתוּב: כִּי אֵל רַחוּם

‹ a merciful God ‹ For « it is written: ‹ as « destroy us, ‹ and do not ‹ on us

יהוה אֱלֹהֶיךָ, לֹא יַרְפְּךָ וְלֹא יַשְׁחִיתֶךָ, וְלֹא יִשְׁכַּח

‹ will He ‹ nor « will He ‹ nor ‹ relinquish « He will ‹ your God; ‹ is forget   destroy you,   you   not   HASHEM,

אֶת בְּרִית אֲבֹתֶיךָ אֲשֶׁר נִשְׁבַּע לָהֶם. מוֹל

‹ Circum- « to them. ‹ He swore ‹ which ‹ with your ‹ the covenant cise   forefathers,

אֶת לְבָבֵנוּ לְאַהֲבָה וּלְיִרְאָה אֶת שְׁמֶךָ, כְּמָה שֶׁכָּתוּב:

« it is written: ‹ as « Your Name, ‹ and to fear ‹ to love ‹ our hearts

וּמָל יהוה אֱלֹהֶיךָ אֶת לְבָבְךָ וְאֶת לְבַב זַרְעֶךָ, לְאַהֲבָה

‹ to love « of your ‹ and the ‹ your heart ‹ HASHEM, your God, offspring,   heart   will circumcise

אֶת יהוה אֱלֹהֶיךָ, בְּכָל לְבָבְךָ וּבְכָל נַפְשְׁךָ, לְמַעַן

‹ so that « your soul, ‹ and with all ‹ your heart ‹ with all ‹ your God, ‹ HASHEM,

חַיֶּיךָ. הִמָּצֵא לָנוּ בְּבַקָּשָׁתֵנוּ, כְּמָה שֶׁכָּתוּב: וּבִקַּשְׁתֶּם

‹ And you « it is written: ‹ as « in our quest, ‹ to us ‹ Be « you may will seek   accessible   live.

---

(1) *Isaiah* 43:25. (2) 1:18. (3) *Ezekiel* 36:25. (4) *Deuteronomy* 4:31. (5) 30:6.

מִשָּׁם אֶת יהוה אֱלֹהֶיךָ וּמָצָאתָ, כִּי תִדְרְשֶׁנּוּ בְּכָל
⟨ with all ⟨ you search Him out ⟨ when ⟨ and you will find [Him], ⟨ your God, ⟨ HASHEM, ⟨ from there

לְבָבְךָ וּבְכָל נַפְשֶׁךָ.¹ ❖ תְּבִיאֵנוּ אֶל הַר קָדְשֶׁךָ,
⟨ Your holy mountain ⟨ to ⟨ Bring us 》 your soul. ⟨ and with all ⟨ your heart

וְשַׂמַּחְנוּ בְּבֵית תְּפִלָּתֶךָ, כְּמָה שֶׁכָּתוּב: וַהֲבִיאוֹתִים
⟨ And I will bring them 》 it is written: ⟨ as 》 of Prayer, ⟨ in Your House ⟨ and gladden us

אֶל הַר קָדְשִׁי, וְשִׂמַּחְתִּים בְּבֵית תְּפִלָּתִי,
》 of Prayer; ⟨ in My House ⟨ and I will gladden them 》 My holy mountain, ⟨ to

עוֹלֹתֵיהֶם וְזִבְחֵיהֶם לְרָצוֹן עַל מִזְבְּחִי, כִּי בֵיתִי
⟨ My House ⟨ for 》 My Altar, ⟨ on ⟨ will find favor ⟨ and their feast-offerings ⟨ their burnt-offerings

בֵּית תְּפִלָּה יִקָּרֵא לְכָל הָעַמִּים.²
》 nations. ⟨ for all ⟨ will be called ⟨ of Prayer" ⟨ "a House

THE ARK IS OPENED.

CHAZZAN, THEN CONGREGATION:

שְׁמַע קוֹלֵנוּ יהוה אֱלֹהֵינוּ, חוּס וְרַחֵם עָלֵינוּ,
》 on us, ⟨ and have compassion ⟨ have pity 》 our God; ⟨ HASHEM, ⟨ our voice, ⟨ Hear

וְקַבֵּל בְּרַחֲמִים וּבְרָצוֹן אֶת תְּפִלָּתֵנוּ.³
》 ⟨ our prayer. ⟨ and favor ⟨ with compassion ⟨ and accept

CHAZZAN, THEN CONGREGATION:

הֲשִׁיבֵנוּ יהוה אֵלֶיךָ וְנָשׁוּבָה, חַדֵּשׁ יָמֵינוּ כְּקֶדֶם.⁴
》 as of old. ⟨ our days ⟨ renew 》 and we shall return, ⟨ to You, ⟨ HASHEM, ⟨ Bring us back,

CHAZZAN, THEN CONGREGATION:

אֲמָרֵינוּ הַאֲזִינָה יהוה, בִּינָה הֲגִיגֵנוּ.⁵
》 our thoughts. ⟨ perceive 》 HASHEM; ⟨ hear, ⟨ Our words

THE FOLLOWING VERSE IS RECITED QUIETLY:

יִהְיוּ לְרָצוֹן אִמְרֵי פִינוּ וְהֶגְיוֹן לִבֵּנוּ לְפָנֶיךָ,
》 before You, 》 of our heart — ⟨ and the thoughts ⟨ of our mouth ⟨ — the ex-pressions 》 find favor ⟨ May they

יהוה צוּרֵנוּ וְגוֹאֲלֵנוּ.⁶
》 and our Redeemer. ⟨ our Rock ⟨ HASHEM,

---

(1) *Deuteronomy* 4:29. (2) *Isaiah* 56:7. (3) From the weekday *Shemoneh Esrei*.
(4) *Lamentations* 5:21. (5) Cf. *Psalms* 5:2. (6) Cf. 19:15.

CHAZZAN, THEN CONGREGATION:

אַל תַּשְׁלִיכֵנוּ מִלְּפָנֶיךָ, וְרוּחַ קָדְשְׁךָ אַל תִּקַּח מִמֶּנּוּ.[1]

《 from us. 〈 take 〈 do not 〈 of Your Holiness 〈 and the Spirit 《 from Your Presence, 〈 cast us away 〈 Do not

CHAZZAN, THEN CONGREGATION:

אַל תַּשְׁלִיכֵנוּ לְעֵת זִקְנָה, כִּכְלוֹת כֹּחֵנוּ אַל תַּעַזְבֵנוּ.[2]

《 forsake us not. 〈 does our strength, 〈 when fail 〈 of old age; 〈 in time 〈 cast us away 〈 Do not

ALL CONTINUE (SOME CONGREGATIONS RECITE THE NEXT VERSE RESPONSIVELY):

אַל תַּעַזְבֵנוּ יהוה, אֱלֹהֵינוּ אַל תִּרְחַק מִמֶּנּוּ.[3]

《 from us. 〈 be not distant 〈 our God, 《 O Hashem; 〈 Forsake us not,

עֲשֵׂה עִמָּנוּ אוֹת לְטוֹבָה, וְיִרְאוּ שׂוֹנְאֵינוּ וְיֵבֹשׁוּ,

《 and be ashamed, 〈 may our enemies 〈 so that see it 《 for good; 〈 a sign 〈 for us 〈 Display

כִּי אַתָּה יהוה עֲזַרְתָּנוּ וְנִחַמְתָּנוּ. כִּי לְךָ יהוה

〈 Hashem, 〈 for You, 〈 Because 《 and consoled us. 〈 will have helped us 〈 Hashem, 〈 You, 〈 for

הוֹחָלְנוּ, אַתָּה תַעֲנֶה אֲדֹנָי אֱלֹהֵינוּ.[5]

《 our God. 〈 O Lord, 〈 will answer, 〈 You 《 do we wait;

THE ARK IS CLOSED.

EACH INDIVIDUAL CONTINUES UNTIL THE END OF SELICHOS.

CONFESSION / וִדּוּי

DURING THE RECITATION OF THE וִדּוּי, CONFESSION, STAND WITH HEAD AND BODY SLIGHTLY BOWED, IN SUBMISSIVE CONTRITION.

אֱלֹהֵינוּ וֵאלֹהֵי אֲבוֹתֵינוּ, תָּבֹא לְפָנֶיךָ תְּפִלָּתֵנוּ,[6]

《 may our prayer, 〈 before You 〈 come 《 of our forefathers, 〈 and the God 〈 Our God

וְאַל תִּתְעַלַּם מִתְּחִנָּתֵנוּ, שֶׁאֵין אָנוּ עַזֵּי פָנִים

〈 faced 〈 so brazen- 〈 For we are not 《 our supplication. 〈 ignore 〈 and do not

וּקְשֵׁי עֹרֶף, לוֹמַר לְפָנֶיךָ יהוה אֱלֹהֵינוּ וֵאלֹהֵי

〈 and the God 〈 our God, 〈 Hashem, 《 before You, 〈 as to say 〈 necked 〈 and stiff-

אֲבוֹתֵינוּ, צַדִּיקִים אֲנַחְנוּ וְלֹא חָטָאנוּ, אֲבָל

《 —for indeed, 《 sinned 〈 and have not 〈 we are, 〈 that righteous 《 of our forefathers,

---

(1) *Psalms* 51:13. (2) Cf. 71:9. (3) Cf. 38:22. (4) Cf. 86:17. (5) Cf. 38:16. (6) Cf. 88:3. (7) Cf. 55:2.

אֲנַחְנוּ וַאֲבוֹתֵינוּ חָטָאנוּ.¹

《 have sinned. 〈 and our forefathers 〈 we

**STRIKE THE LEFT SIDE OF THE CHEST WITH THE RIGHT FIST WHILE RECITING
EACH OF THE SINS OF THE FOLLOWING CONFESSIONAL LITANY:**

אָשַׁמְנוּ, בָּגַדְנוּ, גָּזַלְנוּ, דִּבַּרְנוּ דֹפִי. הֶעֱוִינוּ,

《 We have com- 《 slander. 〈 we have   《 we have   《 we have   《 We have been
mitted iniquity;   spoken   robbed;   betrayed;   guilty;

וְהִרְשַׁעְנוּ, זַדְנוּ, חָמַסְנוּ, טָפַלְנוּ שֶׁקֶר. יָעַצְנוּ

〈 We have   《 false   〈 we have   《 we have 《we have sinned 《we have commit-
given advice accusations. made   extorted; willfully;   ted wickedness;

רָע, כִּזַּבְנוּ, לַצְנוּ, מָרַדְנוּ, נִאַצְנוּ, סָרַרְנוּ,

《 we have 《 we have provoked 《 we have   《 we have 《 we have been 《 that is
strayed;   [God's anger];   rebelled;   scorned;   deceitful;   bad;

עָוִינוּ, פָּשַׁעְנוּ, צָרַרְנוּ, קִשִּׁינוּ עֹרֶף. רָשַׁעְנוּ,

《 We have 《 our   〈 we have 《 we have caused 《 we have sinned 《we have been
been wicked;   necks.   stiffened   distress;   rebelliously;   iniquitous;

שִׁחַתְנוּ, תִּעַבְנוּ, תָּעִינוּ, תִּעְתָּעְנוּ.

《 we have   《 we have   《 we have   《 we have
scoffed.   gone astray; committed   been corrupt;
                         abominations;

סַרְנוּ מִמִּצְוֹתֶיךָ וּמִמִּשְׁפָּטֶיךָ הַטּוֹבִים, וְלֹא שָׁוָה

〈 worth- 〈 and it   《 that are 〈   and from   〈 from Your   〈 We have
while   was not   good,   Your laws   commandments turned away

לָנוּ.² וְאַתָּה צַדִּיק עַל כָּל הַבָּא עָלֵינוּ, כִּי אֱמֶת

〈 truthfully 〈 for 《 upon us, 〈 that has 〈 all 〈 in 〈 are 〈 And You 《 for us.
                                 come   righteous

עָשִׂיתָ וַאֲנַחְנוּ הִרְשָׁעְנוּ.³

《 have acted, 〈 while we 《 have You
wickedly.   acted,

אָשַׁמְנוּ מִכָּל עָם, בֹּשְׁנוּ מִכָּל דוֹר, גָּלָה מִמֶּנּוּ

〈 from 〈 Departed 《 genera- 〈 more 〈 We have 《 people. 〈 more than 〈 We have
us   tion.   than any   been   any other   been guilty
                            other   ashamed

מָשׂוֹשׂ, דָּוָה לִבֵּנוּ בַּחֲטָאֵינוּ, הֻחֲבַּל אַוֵּינוּ, וְנִפְרַע

〈 uncov- 《 was our de- 〈 Seized 《 because of 〈 is our 〈 Sickened 《 has joy.
ered   sired [Temple],   our sins.   heart

---

(1) Cf. *Psalms* 106:6, *Jeremiah* 3:25. (2) Cf. *Job* 33:27. (3) *Nehemiah* 9:33.

פְּאֵרֵנוּ, זְבוּל בֵּית מִקְדָּשֵׁנוּ חָרַב בַּעֲוֹנֵינוּ, טֵרַתֵנוּ

⟨ Our Palace ⟩ ⟨ because of ⟨ has been ⟨ our Holy Temple ⟨ for [His] ⟨ was our
our iniquities. destroyed abode, splendor;

הָיְתָה לְשַׁמָּה, יְפִי אַדְמָתֵנוּ לְזָרִים, כֹּחֵנוּ לְנָכְרִים.

⟨ [was given] ⟨ our ⟨ is controlled ⟨ of our ⟨ [Jerusalem,] ⟨ desolate. ⟨ has
to foreigners. wealth by strangers, Land the beauty become

וַעֲדַיִן לֹא שַׁבְנוּ מִטָּעוּתֵנוּ וְהֵיךְ נָעִיז פָּנֵינוּ וְנַקְשֶׁה

⟨ and ⟨ faced ⟨ can we be ⟨ So ⟨ from our ⟨ we have not ⟨ But still
stiffen so brazen- how willful errors. repented

עָרְפֵּנוּ, לוֹמַר לְפָנֶיךָ יהוה אֱלֹהֵינוּ וֵאלֹהֵי אֲבוֹתֵינוּ,

⟨ of our ⟨ and the ⟨ our God ⟨ HASHEM, ⟨ before ⟨ so as to ⟨ our neck
forefathers, God You, say

צַדִּיקִים אֲנַחְנוּ וְלֹא חָטָאנוּ, אֲבָל אֲנַחְנוּ וַאֲבוֹתֵינוּ

⟨ and our ⟨ both we ⟨ for in ⟨ and we have ⟨ we are ⟨ that
fathers truth, not sinned, righteous

חָטָאנוּ.[1]

⟨ have sinned.

STRIKE THE LEFT SIDE OF THE CHEST WITH THE RIGHT FIST WHILE RECITING EACH OF THE SINS OF THE FOLLOWING CONFESSIONAL LITANY:

אָשַׁמְנוּ, בָּגַדְנוּ, גָּזַלְנוּ, דִּבַּרְנוּ דְפִי. הֶעֱוִינוּ,

⟨ We have com- ⟨ slander. ⟨ we have ⟨ we have ⟨ we have ⟨ We have been
mitted iniquity; spoken robbed; betrayed; guilty;

וְהִרְשַׁעְנוּ, זַדְנוּ, חָמַסְנוּ, טָפַלְנוּ שֶׁקֶר. יָעַצְנוּ

⟨ We have ⟨ false ⟨ we have ⟨ we have ⟨ we have sinned ⟨ we have commit-
given advice accusations. made extorted; willfully; ted wickedness;

רָע, כִּזַּבְנוּ, לַצְנוּ, מָרַדְנוּ, נִאַצְנוּ, סָרַרְנוּ,

⟨ we have ⟨ we have provoked ⟨ we have ⟨ we have ⟨ we have been ⟨ that is
strayed; [God's anger]; rebelled; scorned; deceitful; bad;

עָוִינוּ, פָּשַׁעְנוּ, צָרַרְנוּ, קִשִּׁינוּ עֹרֶף. רָשַׁעְנוּ,

⟨ We have ⟨ our ⟨ we have ⟨ we have ⟨ we have ⟨ we have
been wicked; necks. stiffened caused sinned been
distress; rebelliously; iniquitous;

שִׁחַתְנוּ, תִּעַבְנוּ, תָּעִינוּ, תִּעְתָּעְנוּ.

⟨ we have ⟨ we have ⟨ we have ⟨ we have
scoffed. gone astray; committed been corrupt;
abominations;

---

(1) Cf. *Psalms* 106:6; *Jeremiah* 3:25.

סַרְנוּ מִמִּצְוֹתֶיךָ וּמִמִּשְׁפָּטֶיךָ הַטּוֹבִים, וְלֹא שָׁוָה

⟨ worth- while ⟨ and it was not ⟨⟨ that are good, ⟨ and from Your laws ⟨ from Your commandments ⟨ We have turned away

לָנוּ.[1] וְאַתָּה צַדִּיק עַל כָּל הַבָּא עָלֵינוּ, כִּי אֱמֶת

⟨ truth-fully ⟨ for ⟨⟨ upon us, ⟨ that has come ⟨ all ⟨ in ⟨ are righteous ⟨ And You ⟨⟨ for us.

עָשִׂיתָ וַאֲנַחְנוּ הִרְשָׁעְנוּ.[2]

⟨⟨ have acted wickedly. ⟨ while we ⟨⟨ have You acted,

לְעֵינֵנוּ עָשְׁקוּ עֲמָלֵנוּ, מִמְּשַׁךְ וּמְמוֹרָט מִמֶּנּוּ,

⟨⟨ from us. ⟨ and cut off ⟨ [it was] pulled away ⟨⟨ the product of our labor; ⟨ have they stolen ⟨ Before our eyes

נָתְנוּ עֻלָּם עָלֵינוּ, סָבַלְנוּ עַל שִׁכְמֵנוּ, עֲבָדִים

⟨ Slaves ⟨⟨ our shoulders. ⟨ upon ⟨ we bore it ⟨⟨ upon us, ⟨ their yoke ⟨ They have placed

מָשְׁלוּ בָנוּ, פֹּרֵק אֵין מִיָּדָם, צָרוֹת רַבּוֹת

⟨ that are manifold ⟨ Troubles ⟨⟨ from their hand. ⟨ there was not ⟨ a redeemer ⟨⟨ over us; ⟨ have ruled

סְבָבוּנוּ, קְרָאנוּךָ יהוה אֱלֹהֵינוּ, רָחַקְתָּ מִמֶּנּוּ

⟨ from us ⟨ but You have dis- tanced Yourself ⟨⟨ our God, ⟨ HASHEM, ⟨ we called upon You, ⟨⟨ have surrounded us,

בַּעֲוֹנֵינוּ, שַׁבְנוּ מֵאַחֲרֶיךָ, תָּעִינוּ וְאָבַדְנוּ.

⟨⟨ we have become lost. ⟨⟨ we have gone astray; ⟨⟨ from following after You; ⟨ We have turned away ⟨⟨ because of our iniquities.

וַעֲדַיִן לֹא שַׁבְנוּ מִטָּעוּתֵנוּ וְהֵיךְ נָעִיז פָּנֵינוּ וְנַקְשֶׁה

⟨ and stiffen ⟨ faced ⟨ can we be ⟨ So how ⟨⟨ from our willful errors. ⟨ we have not repented ⟨ But still

עָרְפֵּנוּ, לוֹמַר לְפָנֶיךָ יהוה אֱלֹהֵינוּ וֵאלֹהֵי אֲבוֹתֵינוּ,

⟨⟨ of our forefathers, ⟨ and the God ⟨ our God ⟨ HASHEM, ⟨ before You, ⟨ so as to say ⟨ our neck

צַדִּיקִים אֲנַחְנוּ וְלֹא חָטָאנוּ, אֲבָל אֲנַחְנוּ וַאֲבוֹתֵינוּ

⟨ and our fathers ⟨ both we ⟨ for in ⟨⟨ and we have not sinned, ⟨⟨ we are ⟨ that righteous truth,

חָטָאנוּ.[3]

⟨⟨ have sinned.

---

(1) Cf. *Job* 33:27. (2) *Nehemiah* 9:33. (3) Cf. *Psalms* 106:6; *Jeremiah* 3:25.

**STRIKE THE LEFT SIDE OF THE CHEST WITH THE RIGHT FIST WHILE RECITING
EACH OF THE SINS OF THE FOLLOWING CONFESSIONAL LITANY:**

אָשַׁמְנוּ, בָּגַדְנוּ, גָּזַלְנוּ, דִּבַּרְנוּ דֹפִי. הֶעֱוִינוּ,

《 We have com- 《 slander. 〈 we have 《 we have 《 we have 《 We have been
mitted iniquity; spoken robbed betrayed guilty;

וְהִרְשַׁעְנוּ, זַדְנוּ, חָמַסְנוּ, טָפַלְנוּ שֶׁקֶר. יָעַצְנוּ

〈 We have 《 false 〈 we have 《 we have 《we have sinned 《we have commit-
given advice accusations. made extorted; willfully; ted wickedness;

רָע, כִּזַּבְנוּ, לַצְנוּ, מָרַדְנוּ, נִאַצְנוּ, סָרַרְנוּ,

《 we have 《 we have provoked 《 we have 《 we have 《 we have been 〈 that is
strayed; [God's anger]; rebelled; scorned; deceitful; bad;

עָוִינוּ, פָּשַׁעְנוּ, צָרַרְנוּ, קִשִּׁינוּ עֹרֶף. רָשַׁעְנוּ,

《 We have 《 our 〈 we have 《we have caused 《we have sinned 《we have been
been wicked; necks. stiffened distress; rebelliously; iniquitous;

שִׁחַתְנוּ, תִּעַבְנוּ, תָּעִינוּ, תִּעְתָּעְנוּ.

《 we have 《 we have 《we have commit- 《 we have
scoffed. gone astray; ted abominations; been corrupt;

סַרְנוּ מִמִּצְוֹתֶיךָ וּמִמִּשְׁפָּטֶיךָ הַטּוֹבִים, וְלֹא שָׁוָה

〈 worth- 〈 and it 《 that are 〈 and from 〈 from Your 〈 We have
while was not good, Your laws commandments turned away

לָנוּ.[1] וְאַתָּה צַדִּיק עַל כָּל הַבָּא עָלֵינוּ, כִּי אֱמֶת

〈 truth- 〈 for 《 upon us, 〈 that has 〈 all 〈 in 〈 are 〈 And You 《 for us.
fully come righteous

עָשִׂיתָ וַאֲנַחְנוּ הִרְשָׁעְנוּ.[2]

《 have acted 〈 while we 《 have You
wickedly. acted,

הִרְשַׁעְנוּ וּפָשַׁעְנוּ, לָכֵן לֹא נוֹשָׁעְנוּ. וְתֵן בְּלִבֵּנוּ

〈 in our 〈 Place 《 been 〈 we have 〈 there- 《 and we 〈 We have acted
hearts saved. not fore have sinned wickedly
rebelliously;

לַעֲזוֹב דֶּרֶךְ רֶשַׁע, וְחִישׁ לָנוּ יֶשַׁע, כַּכָּתוּב עַל יַד

〈 the 〈 by 〈 as it is 《 salvation; 〈 to us 〈 and 《 of 〈 the 〈 [the will]
hand written hasten wickedness, path to abandon

נְבִיאֶךָ: יַעֲזֹב רָשָׁע דַּרְכּוֹ, וְאִישׁ אָוֶן מַחְשְׁבֹתָיו,

《 [abandon] 〈 of 〈 and 《 his way, 〈 the wicked 〈 Let 《 of Your
his thoughts; iniquity the man one abandon prophet:

_____

(1) Cf. *Job* 33:27. (2) *Nehemiah* 9:33.

וְיָשֹׁב אֶל יהוה וִירַחֲמֵהוּ, וְאֶל אֱלֹהֵינוּ כִּי

and let him return / to / HASHEM, / and He will have compassion on him, / and to / our God, / for

יַרְבֶּה לִסְלוֹחַ.¹

He is abundantly / forgiving.

מְשִׁיחַ צִדְקְךָ אָמַר לְפָנֶיךָ, שְׁגִיאוֹת מִי יָבִין,

Your anointed one [David] / who is righteous / said / before You: / Mistakes / who / can discern?

מִנִּסְתָּרוֹת נַקֵּנִי.² נַקֵּנוּ יהוה אֱלֹהֵינוּ מִכָּל פְּשָׁעֵינוּ,

From unperceived faults / cleanse me. / Cleanse us, / HASHEM, / our God, / of all / our sins

וְטַהֲרֵנוּ מִכָּל טֻמְאוֹתֵינוּ, וּזְרוֹק עָלֵינוּ מַיִם טְהוֹרִים

and purify us / of all / our contaminations. / Pour / upon us / pure water

וְטַהֲרֵנוּ, כַּכָּתוּב עַל יַד נְבִיאֶךָ: וְזָרַקְתִּי עֲלֵיכֶם

and purify us, / as it is written / by / the hand / of Your prophet: / I shall pour / upon you

מַיִם טְהוֹרִים וּטְהַרְתֶּם, מִכֹּל טֻמְאוֹתֵיכֶם וּמִכָּל

pure water / and you will become pure; / from all / your contaminations / and from all

גִּלּוּלֵיכֶם אֲטַהֵר אֶתְכֶם.³ עַמְּךָ וְנַחֲלָתֶךָ, רְעֵבֵי

your abominations / I will purify / you. / Your people / and Your heritage, / who hunger

טוּבְךָ, צְמֵאֵי חַסְדֶּךָ, תְּאֵבֵי יִשְׁעֶךָ, יַכִּירוּ וְיֵדְעוּ

for Your goodness, / who thirst / for Your kindness, / who long / for Your salvation / — may they recognize / and know

כִּי לַיהוה אֱלֹהֵינוּ הָרַחֲמִים וְהַסְּלִיחוֹת.

that / to HASHEM, / our God, / belong mercy / and forgiveness.

אֵל רַחוּם שְׁמֶךָ, אֵל חַנּוּן שְׁמֶךָ,⁴ בָּנוּ נִקְרָא שְׁמֶךָ.⁵

Merciful God / is Your Name, / Gracious God / is Your Name, / upon us / is Your Name proclaimed.

יהוה עֲשֵׂה לְמַעַן שְׁמֶךָ,⁶ עֲשֵׂה לְמַעַן אֲמִתֶּךָ, עֲשֵׂה

HASHEM, / act / for the sake of / Your Name. / Act / for the sake of / Your truth; / act

---

(1) *Isaiah* 55:7. (2) *Psalms* 19:13. (3) *Ezekiel* 36:25.
(4) Cf. *Exodus* 34:6. (5) Cf. *Deuteronomy* 28:10. (6) *Jeremiah* 14:7.

לְמַעַן בְּרִיתָךְ, עֲשֵׂה לְמַעַן גָּדְלָךְ וְתִפְאַרְתָּךְ, עֲשֵׂה

for the sake of Your covenant; act for the sake of Your greatness and Your splendor; act

לְמַעַן דָּתָךְ, עֲשֵׂה לְמַעַן הוֹדָךְ, עֲשֵׂה לְמַעַן וְעוּדָךְ,

for the sake of Your Law; act for the sake of Your glory; act for the sake of Your Meeting House;

עֲשֵׂה לְמַעַן זִכְרָךְ,[1] עֲשֵׂה לְמַעַן חַסְדָּךְ,[2] עֲשֵׂה לְמַעַן

act for the sake of Your remembrance; act for the sake of Your kindness; act for the

טוּבָךְ, עֲשֵׂה לְמַעַן יִחוּדָךְ, עֲשֵׂה לְמַעַן כְּבוֹדָךְ, עֲשֵׂה

Your goodness; act for the sake of Your Oneness; act for the sake of Your honor; act

לְמַעַן לִמּוּדָךְ,[3] עֲשֵׂה לְמַעַן מַלְכוּתָךְ, עֲשֵׂה לְמַעַן

for the sake of Your students; act for the sake of Your kingship; act for the sake of

נִצְחָךְ, עֲשֵׂה לְמַעַן סוֹדָךְ,[4] עֲשֵׂה לְמַעַן עֻזָּךְ, עֲשֵׂה

Your eternal [Name]; act for the sake of Your secret [revealed to those who fear You]; act for the sake of Your power; act

לְמַעַן פְּאֵרָךְ, עֲשֵׂה לְמַעַן צִדְקָתָךְ, עֲשֵׂה לְמַעַן

for the sake of Your glory; act for the sake of Your righteousness; act for the sake of

קְדֻשָּׁתָךְ, עֲשֵׂה לְמַעַן רַחֲמֶיךָ הָרַבִּים, עֲשֵׂה לְמַעַן

Your sanctity; act for the sake of Your mercy that is abundant; act for the sake of

שְׁכִינָתָךְ, עֲשֵׂה לְמַעַן תְּהִלָּתָךְ, עֲשֵׂה לְמַעַן אוֹהֲבֶיךָ

Your Divine Presence; act for the sake of Your praise; act for the sake of those who loved You

שׁוֹכְנֵי עָפָר,[5] עֲשֵׂה לְמַעַן אַבְרָהָם יִצְחָק וְיַעֲקֹב,

who rest in the dust; act for the sake of Abraham, Isaac, and Jacob;

עֲשֵׂה לְמַעַן מֹשֶׁה וְאַהֲרֹן, עֲשֵׂה לְמַעַן דָּוִד וּשְׁלֹמֹה,

act for the sake of Moses and Aaron; act for the sake of David and Solomon;

עֲשֵׂה לְמַעַן יְרוּשָׁלַיִם עִיר קָדְשֶׁךָ,[6] עֲשֵׂה לְמַעַן צִיּוֹן

act for the sake of Jerusalem the City of Your Holiness; act for the sake of Zion,

---

(1) Cf. *Exodus* 3:15. (2) *Psalms* 6:5. (3) Cf. *Isaiah* 54:13. (4) Cf. *Psalms* 25:14. (5) *Isaiah* 26:19. (6) Cf. *Daniel* 9:16,24.

מִשְׁכַּן כְּבוֹדֶךָ,[1] עֲשֵׂה לְמַעַן שְׁמָמוֹת[2] הֵיכָלֶךָ, עֲשֵׂה

לְמַעַן הֲרִיסוֹת[3] מִזְבְּחֶךָ, עֲשֵׂה לְמַעַן הֲרוּגִים עַל

שֵׁם קָדְשֶׁךָ, עֲשֵׂה לְמַעַן טְבוּחִים עַל יִחוּדֶךָ, עֲשֵׂה

לְמַעַן בָּאֵי בָאֵשׁ וּבַמַּיִם עַל קִדּוּשׁ שְׁמֶךָ, עֲשֵׂה לְמַעַן

יוֹנְקֵי שָׁדַיִם[4] שֶׁלֹּא חָטָאוּ, עֲשֵׂה לְמַעַן גְּמוּלֵי חָלָב[5]

שֶׁלֹּא פָשְׁעוּ, עֲשֵׂה לְמַעַן תִּינוֹקוֹת שֶׁל בֵּית רַבָּן,[6]

עֲשֵׂה לְמַעַנְךָ אִם לֹא לְמַעֲנֵנוּ, עֲשֵׂה לְמַעַנְךָ וְהוֹשִׁיעֵנוּ.

עֲנֵנוּ[7] יהוה עֲנֵנוּ, עֲנֵנוּ אֱלֹהֵינוּ עֲנֵנוּ, עֲנֵנוּ אָבִינוּ

עֲנֵנוּ, עֲנֵנוּ בּוֹרְאֵנוּ[8] עֲנֵנוּ, עֲנֵנוּ גוֹאֲלֵנוּ[9] עֲנֵנוּ, עֲנֵנוּ

דּוֹרְשֵׁנוּ[10] עֲנֵנוּ, עֲנֵנוּ הָאֵל הַנֶּאֱמָן[11] עֲנֵנוּ, עֲנֵנוּ וָתִיק

וְחָסִיד עֲנֵנוּ, עֲנֵנוּ זַךְ וְיָשָׁר[12] עֲנֵנוּ, עֲנֵנוּ חַי וְקַיָּם[13]

---

(1) *Psalms* 26:8. (2) Cf. *Jeremiah* 51:26. (3) Cf. *Isaiah* 49:19. (4) *Joel* 2:16. (5) *Isaiah* 28:9.
(6) *Shabbos* 119b. (7) *Isaiah* 64:7. (8) Cf. 43:1. (9) 47:4. (10) Cf. *Ezekiel* 34:11.
(11) *Deuteronomy* 7:9. (12) *Job* 8:6; cf. *Proverbs* 20:11. (13) Cf. *Daniel* 6:27.

עֲנֵנוּ, עֲנֵנוּ טוֹב וּמֵטִיב¹ עֲנֵנוּ, עֲנֵנוּ יוֹדֵעַ יֵצֶר² עֲנֵנוּ,

‹‹answer us; / ‹answer us; / ‹of inclinations, / ‹Knower / ‹answer us; / ‹‹answer us; / ‹and beneficent One, / ‹good / ‹answer us; / ‹‹answer us;

עֲנֵנוּ כּוֹבֵשׁ כְּעָסִים עֲנֵנוּ, עֲנֵנוּ לוֹבֵשׁ צְדָקוֹת³ עֲנֵנוּ,

‹answer us; / ‹of righteousness, / ‹Donner / ‹answer us; / ‹‹answer us; / ‹of wrath, / ‹Suppressor / ‹answer us;

עֲנֵנוּ מֶלֶךְ מַלְכֵי הַמְּלָכִים⁴ עֲנֵנוּ, עֲנֵנוּ נוֹרָא וְנִשְׂגָּב⁵

‹and powerful One, / ‹awesome / ‹answer us; / ‹‹answer us; / ‹of kings, / ‹over kings, / ‹King / ‹answer us;

עֲנֵנוּ, עֲנֵנוּ סוֹלֵחַ וּמוֹחֵל עֲנֵנוּ, עֲנֵנוּ עוֹנֶה בְּעֵת

‹in time / ‹You Who answers / ‹answer us; / ‹‹answer us; / ‹and pardons, / ‹You Who forgives / ‹answer us; / ‹‹answer us;

צָרָה⁶ עֲנֵנוּ, עֲנֵנוּ פּוֹדֶה וּמַצִּיל⁷ עֲנֵנוּ, עֲנֵנוּ צַדִּיק

‹righteous / ‹answer us; / ‹‹answer us; / ‹and Rescuer, / ‹Redeemer / ‹answer us; / ‹‹answer us; / ‹of distress,

וְיָשָׁר⁸ עֲנֵנוּ, עֲנֵנוּ קָרוֹב לְקוֹרְאָיו⁹ עֲנֵנוּ, עֲנֵנוּ קָשֶׁה

‹You Who with difficulty / ‹answer us; / ‹‹answer us; / ‹to those who call upon Him, / ‹He Who is close / ‹answer us; / ‹‹answer us; / ‹and upright One,

לִכְעוֹס¹⁰ עֲנֵנוּ, עֲנֵנוּ רַךְ לִרְצוֹת¹¹ עֲנֵנוּ, עֲנֵנוּ רַחוּם

‹merciful / ‹answer us; / ‹‹answer us; / ‹appeased, / ‹You Who are easily / ‹answer us; / ‹‹answer us; / ‹becomes angry,

וְחַנּוּן¹² עֲנֵנוּ, עֲנֵנוּ שׁוֹמֵעַ אֶל אֶבְיוֹנִים¹³ עֲנֵנוּ, עֲנֵנוּ

‹answer us; / ‹‹answer us; / ‹the destitute, / ‹to / ‹You Who listens / ‹answer us; / ‹‹answer us; / ‹and gracious One,

תּוֹמֵךְ תְּמִימִים עֲנֵנוּ, עֲנֵנוּ אֱלֹהֵי אֲבוֹתֵינוּ עֲנֵנוּ,

‹‹answer us; / ‹of our forefathers, / ‹God / ‹answer us; / ‹‹answer us; / ‹the wholesome, / ‹You Who supports

עֲנֵנוּ אֱלֹהֵי אַבְרָהָם¹⁴ עֲנֵנוּ, עֲנֵנוּ פַּחַד יִצְחָק¹⁴ עֲנֵנוּ,

‹‹answer us; / ‹of Isaac, / ‹Awesome One / ‹answer us; / ‹‹answer us; / ‹of Abraham, / ‹God / ‹answer us;

עֲנֵנוּ אֲבִיר יַעֲקֹב¹⁵ עֲנֵנוּ, עֲנֵנוּ עֶזְרַת הַשְּׁבָטִים עֲנֵנוּ,

‹‹answer us; / ‹of the tribes, / ‹Helper / ‹answer us; / ‹‹answer us; / ‹of Jacob, / ‹Mighty One / ‹answer us;

---

(1) Cf. *Psalms* 119:68. (2) Cf. *103:14*. (3) Cf. *Isaiah* 59:17. (4) *Ethics of the Fathers* 3:1. (5) *Psalms* 47:3; 148:13. (6) Cf. *Isaiah* 49:8; *Psalms* 37:39. Alternate text: בְּעֵת רָצוֹן, *in time of favor*. (7) Cf. *34:23,18*. (8) *Deuteronomy* 32:4. (9) Cf. *Psalms* 145:18. (10) *Ethics of the Fathers* 5:14. (11) Cf. *5:14*. (12) *Exodus* 34:6. (13) *Psalms* 69:34. (14) *Genesis* 31:42. (15) *Isaiah* 49:26.

עֲנֵנוּ מִשְׂגַּב אִמָּהוֹת עֲנֵנוּ, עֲנֵנוּ עוֹנֶה בְּעֵת רָצוֹן עֲנֵנוּ,¹

answer us; of favor, in a You Who answer answer of the Stronghold answer us, time answers us, us; Matriarchs, us,

עֲנֵנוּ אֲבִי יְתוֹמִים² עֲנֵנוּ, עֲנֵנוּ דַּיַּן אַלְמָנוֹת² עֲנֵנוּ.

answer of widows, Judge answer answer of orphans, Father answer us. us; us; us,

מִי שֶׁעָנָה לְאַבְרָהָם אָבִינוּ בְּהַר הַמּוֹרִיָּה³

Moriah on Mount our father Abraham Who answered He

הוּא יַעֲנֵנוּ.

answer — may us. He

מִי שֶׁעָנָה לְיִצְחָק בְּנוֹ כְּשֶׁנֶּעֱקַד עַל גַּבֵּי הַמִּזְבֵּחַ³

of the altar top on when he his son Isaac Who He was bound answered

הוּא יַעֲנֵנוּ.

answer — may us. He

הוּא יַעֲנֵנוּ.　　מִי שֶׁעָנָה לְיַעֲקֹב בְּבֵית אֵל⁴

answer — may in Beth-el Jacob Who He us. answered

הוּא יַעֲנֵנוּ.　　מִי שֶׁעָנָה לְיוֹסֵף בְּבֵית הָאֲסוּרִים⁵

answer — may in the prison Joseph Who He us. answered

הוּא יַעֲנֵנוּ.　　מִי שֶׁעָנָה לַאֲבוֹתֵינוּ עַל יַם סוּף⁶

answer — may of the at our forefathers Who He us. Reeds Sea answered

הוּא יַעֲנֵנוּ.　　מִי שֶׁעָנָה לְמֹשֶׁה בְּחוֹרֵב⁷

answer — may in Horeb Moses Who He us. answered

הוּא יַעֲנֵנוּ.　　מִי שֶׁעָנָה לְאַהֲרֹן בַּמַּחְתָּה⁸

answer — may with the fire-pan Aaron Who He us. answered

מִי שֶׁעָנָה לְפִינְחָס בְּקוּמוֹ מִתּוֹךְ הָעֵדָה⁹ הוּא יַעֲנֵנוּ.

answer — may He the from when he Phinehas Who He us. congregation amid arose answered

---

(1) Cf. *Isaiah* 49:8; *Psalms* 69:14. Alternate text: בְּעֵת צָרָה, *in time of distress.*
(2) 68:6. (3) *Genesis* 22:12. (4) 35:3. (5) 39:21. (6) *Exodus* Ch. 14.
(7) *Exodus* 17:6,11; *Deuteronomy* 9:19. (8) *Numbers* 17:11-13. (9) 25:7-13.

מִי שֶׁעָנָה לִיהוֹשֻׁעַ בַּגִּלְגָּל¹ הוּא יַעֲנֵנוּ.

He ⟨ Who answered ⟨ Joshua ⟨ in Gilgal ⟩⟩ He — may answer us.

מִי שֶׁעָנָה לִשְׁמוּאֵל בַּמִּצְפָּה² הוּא יַעֲנֵנוּ.

He ⟨ Who answered ⟨ Samuel ⟨ in Mizpah ⟩⟩ He — may answer us.

מִי שֶׁעָנָה לְדָוִד וּשְׁלֹמֹה בְנוֹ בִּירוּשָׁלַיִם³ הוּא יַעֲנֵנוּ.

He ⟨ Who answered ⟨ David ⟨ and Solomon ⟨ his son ⟨ in Jerusalem ⟩⟩ He — may answer us.

מִי שֶׁעָנָה לְאֵלִיָּהוּ בְּהַר הַכַּרְמֶל⁴ הוּא יַעֲנֵנוּ.

He ⟨ Who answered ⟨ Elijah ⟨ on Mount ⟨ Carmel ⟩⟩ He — may answer us.

מִי שֶׁעָנָה לֶאֱלִישָׁע בִּירִיחוֹ⁵ הוּא יַעֲנֵנוּ.

He ⟨ Who answered ⟨ Elisha ⟨ in Jericho ⟩⟩ He — may answer us.

מִי שֶׁעָנָה לְיוֹנָה בִּמְעֵי הַדָּגָה⁶ הוּא יַעֲנֵנוּ.

He ⟨ Who answered ⟨ Jonah ⟨ in the innards ⟨ of the fish ⟩⟩ He — may answer us.

מִי שֶׁעָנָה לְחִזְקִיָּהוּ מֶלֶךְ יְהוּדָה בְּחָלְיוֹ⁷ הוּא יַעֲנֵנוּ.

He ⟨ Who answered ⟨ Hezekiah, ⟨ king ⟨ of Judah, ⟨ in his illness ⟩⟩ He — may answer us.

מִי שֶׁעָנָה לַחֲנַנְיָה מִישָׁאֵל וַעֲזַרְיָה

He ⟨ Who answered ⟨ Hananiah, ⟨ Mishael, ⟨ and Azariah

בְּתוֹךְ כִּבְשַׁן הָאֵשׁ⁸ הוּא יַעֲנֵנוּ.

inside ⟨ the furnace ⟨ of fire ⟩⟩ He — may answer us.

מִי שֶׁעָנָה לְדָנִיֵּאל בְּגוֹב הָאֲרָיוֹת⁹ הוּא יַעֲנֵנוּ.

He ⟨ Who answered ⟨ Daniel ⟨ in the den ⟨ of lions ⟩⟩ He — may answer us.

מִי שֶׁעָנָה לְמָרְדֳּכַי וְאֶסְתֵּר בְּשׁוּשַׁן הַבִּירָה¹⁰

He ⟨ Who answered ⟨ Mordechai ⟨ and Esther ⟨ in Shushan ⟨ the capital

הוּא יַעֲנֵנוּ.

He — may answer us.

(1) *Joshua* 6:1-20; 7:6-15; 10:12-14. (2) *I Samuel* 7:9. (3) *II Samuel* 7:5-16; 21:1,14; 24:25; *I Kings* 9:3. (4) 18:36-38. (5) *II Kings* 2:21. (6) *Jonah* 2:2-11. (7) *II Kings* 20:2-6; *Isaiah* 38:2-8. (8) *Daniel* 3:21-27. (9) 6:17-23. (10) *Esther* Ch. 8.

מִי שֶׁעָנָה לְעֶזְרָא בַּגּוֹלָה¹   הוּא יַעֲנֵנוּ.

He ⟩ Who ⟩ Ezra ⟩ in the exile ⟨   He — may ⟩ answer ⟨ us.

מִי שֶׁעָנָה לְכָל הַצַּדִּיקִים וְהַחֲסִידִים וְהַתְּמִימִים

He ⟩ Who ⟩ all ⟩ the righteous, ⟩ the devout, ⟩ the wholesome,

וְהַיְשָׁרִים   הוּא יַעֲנֵנוּ.

and the upright   He — may ⟩ answer ⟨ us.

רַחֲמָנָא דְעָנֵי לַעֲנִיֵּי, עֲנֵינָן. רַחֲמָנָא דְעָנֵי לִתְבִירֵי

Merciful One ⟩ Who answers ⟩ the poor, ⟩ answer us! ⟩ Merciful One ⟩ Who ⟩ those of broken

לִבָּא, עֲנֵינָן. רַחֲמָנָא דְעָנֵי לְמַכִּיכֵי רוּחָא, עֲנֵינָן.

hearts, ⟩ answer us! ⟩ Merciful One ⟩ Who answers ⟩ those of crushed ⟩ spirit, ⟩ answer us!

רַחֲמָנָא עֲנֵינָן. רַחֲמָנָא חוּס. רַחֲמָנָא פְּרוֹק. רַחֲמָנָא

Merciful One, ⟩ answer us! ⟩ Merciful One, ⟩ have pity! ⟩ Merciful One, ⟩ redeem! ⟩ Merciful One,

שְׁזִיב. רַחֲמָנָא רְחַם עֲלָן, הַשְׁתָּא בַּעֲגָלָא וּבִזְמַן קָרִיב.

save! ⟩ Merciful One, ⟩ have mercy ⟩ on us ⟩ — now, ⟩ swiftly, ⟩ and at a time ⟩ that comes soon.

PUTTING DOWN THE HEAD / נפילת אפים

RECITE UNTIL יִבֹּשׁוּ רָגַע WITH THE HEAD RESTING ON THE LEFT ARM,
PREFERABLY WHILE SEATED.

(וַיֹּאמֶר דָּוִד אֶל גָּד, צַר לִי מְאֹד, נִפְּלָה נָא בְיַד יהוה,

(And David said ⟩ to ⟩ Gad, ⟩ Dis- ⟩ am ⟩ I ⟩ tressed ⟩ exceed- ⟩ ingly. ⟩ Let us ⟩ now ⟩ fall ⟩ into the ⟩ hand ⟩ of HASHEM,

כִּי רַבִּים רַחֲמָיו, וּבְיַד אָדָם אַל אֶפְּלָה.²)

for ⟩ abundant ⟩ are His mercies, ⟩ but into human hands ⟩ let me not fall.)

רַחוּם וְחַנּוּן חָטָאתִי לְפָנֶיךָ. יהוה מָלֵא רַחֲמִים,

O merciful ⟩ and gracious One, ⟩ I have sinned ⟩ before You. ⟩ HASHEM, ⟩ Who is full ⟩ of mercy,

רַחֵם עָלַי וְקַבֵּל תַּחֲנוּנָי.

have mercy ⟩ on me ⟩ and accept ⟩ my supplications.

_____

(1) Ezra 8:21-23. (2) II Samuel 24:14.

—— *Psalms* 6:2-11 / תהלים ו:ב-יא ——

יְהוה, אַל בְּאַפְּךָ תוֹכִיחֵנִי, וְאַל בַּחֲמָתְךָ תְיַסְּרֵנִי.
《 chastise me. 〈 in Your wrath 〈 nor 〈 rebuke me, 〈 in Your anger 〈 do not 〈 HASHEM,

חָנֵּנִי יהוה כִּי אֻמְלַל אָנִי, רְפָאֵנִי יהוה כִּי נִבְהֲלוּ
〈 shudder
with terror 〈 for 〈 HASHEM, 〈 heal me, 《 am I; 〈 feeble 〈 for 〈 HASHEM, 〈 Favor
me,

עֲצָמָי. וְנַפְשִׁי נִבְהֲלָה מְאֹד, וְאַתָּה יהוה עַד מָתָי.
《 when? 〈 until 〈 HASHEM, 〈 and You, 《 utterly, 〈 is terrified 〈 My soul 《 do my bones.

שׁוּבָה יהוה חַלְּצָה נַפְשִׁי, הוֹשִׁיעֵנִי לְמַעַן חַסְדֶּךָ.
《 Your kindness. 〈 as befits 〈 save me 《 my soul; 〈 release 〈 HASHEM, 〈 Desist,

כִּי אֵין בַּמָּוֶת זִכְרֶךָ, בִּשְׁאוֹל מִי יוֹדֶה לָּךְ. יָגַעְתִּי
〈 I am
wearied 《 You? 〈 will
praise 〈 who 〈 in the
grave 《 is there men-
tion of You; 〈 in 〈 not 〈 For
death

בְּאַנְחָתִי, אַשְׂחֶה בְכָל לַיְלָה מִטָּתִי, בְּדִמְעָתִי
〈 with my tears 《 my bed; 〈 night 〈 every 〈 I drench 《 with my sigh;

עַרְשִׂי אַמְסֶה. עָשְׁשָׁה מִכַּעַס עֵינִי, עָתְקָה בְּכָל
〈 by all 〈 aged 〈 is my
eye, 〈 because of
anger 〈 Dimmed 《 I soak. 〈 my couch

צוֹרְרָי. סוּרוּ מִמֶּנִּי כָּל פֹּעֲלֵי אָוֶן, כִּי שָׁמַע יהוה
〈 HASHEM has heard 〈 for 《 of evil, 〈 doers 〈 all 〈 from me, 〈 Depart 《 my
tormentors.

קוֹל בִּכְיִי. שָׁמַע יהוה תְּחִנָּתִי, יהוה תְּפִלָּתִי יִקָּח.
《 will
accept. 〈 my prayer 〈 HASHEM 《 my plea, 〈 HASHEM
has heard 《 of my
weeping. 〈 the
sound

יֵבֹשׁוּ וְיִבָּהֲלוּ מְאֹד כָּל אֹיְבָי, יָשֻׁבוּ יֵבֹשׁוּ רָגַע.
《 in an
instant. 〈 and be
shamed 〈 may they
regret 《 my
enemies; 〈 all 〈 utterly, 〈 and confounded 〈 Let them
be shamed

מָחֵי וּמַסֵּי מֵמִית וּמְחַיֶּה, מַסִּיק מִן שְׁאוֹל
〈 the
grave 〈 from 〈 Who raises
[the dead] 《 and Who
restores life, 〈 Who causes
death 《 and Who 〈 [O God,]
heals, Who wounds

לְחַיֵּי עָלְמָא, בְּרָא כַּד חָטֵי אֲבוּהִי לַקְיֵהּ, אֲבוּהִי
〈 but a
father 《 would
strike him, 〈 his father 〈 sin, 〈 should
he 〈 A son 〈 eternal: 〈 to life

דְּחָיֵּס אַסֵּי לִכְאֵבֵהּ. עַבְדָּא דְּמָרִיד נָפִיק בְּקוֹלָר,
《 in chains, 〈 he is
led out 《 who rebels, 〈 A slave 〈 his [son's]
pain. 〈 will 〈 who is com-
heal passionate

מָרֵה תָּאִיב וְתַבִּיר קוֹלָרֵהּ.

《 his chains. 〈 he breaks 〈 desires, 〈 but [if] his master

בְּרָךְ בְּכְרָךְ אֲנַן וְחָטֵינָן קַמָּךְ, הָא רָוֵי נַפְשִׁין

〈 has our 〈 satiated 〈 indeed 《 before 〈 and we have 〈 we 〈 Your 〈 Your
soul been   You;   sinned   are,   firstborn,   son

בְּגִידִין מְרָרִין, עַבְדָּךְ אֲנַן וּמְרוֹדֵינָן קַמָּךְ,

《 before 〈 and we have 〈 we 〈 Your 《 that is bitter. 〈 with
You;   rebelled   are   servants   wormwood

הָא בְּבִזְתָא, הָא בְּשִׁבְיָא, הָא בְּמַלְקִיוּתָא.

《 by the lash. 〈 and 〈 in captivity, 〈 some 〈 from 〈 [indeed we have
       some   looting, suffered,] some

בְּמָטוּ מִנָּךְ בְּרַחֲמָךְ דִּנְפִישִׁין, אַסֵּי לִכְאֵבִין

〈 the pains 〈 heal 〈 that is 〈 in Your 〈 of You, 〈 We beg
               abundant,   compassion

דִּתְקוֹף עֲלָן, עַד דְּלָא נֶהֱוֵי גְּמִירָא בְּשִׁבְיָא.

《 in captivity. 〈 completely 〈 we are not 〈 while 〈 us, 〈 that have
          annihilated   yet   overwhelmed

סליחה נא / SELICHAH 51

(תחנה)

ALL:

תּוֹרָה הַקְּדוֹשָׁה,* הִתְחַנְּנִי בְּבַקָּשָׁה,*[1]

《 through a request,*〈 beseech 《 that is Holy,* 〈 Torah

פְּנֵי הַצּוּר נַעֲרָץ בִּקְדֻשָּׁה.

《 in [His] holiness. 〈 revered 〈 the Rock 〈 before

---

(1) See the introduction to this volume regarding the propriety of requesting intervention from another source in bringing our prayers before God.

§ **תּוֹרָה הַקְּדוֹשָׁה** — *Torah that is Holy.* The *paytan* recalls Israel's acceptance of the Torah in the face of the gentiles' rejection of it; describes Israel's devotion to its study and its mitzvos; and beseeches the Torah to pray for Israel's redemption. [See the introduction to this volume regarding the propriety and permissibility of requesting outside intervention in our prayers.]

This תְּחִנָּה, *supplication*, consists of a series of triplets the acrostic of which forms a reverse *aleph-beis* (תשר״ק), followed by the composer's signature — שִׁמְעוֹן בַּר יִצְחָק חָזָק,

Shimon bar Yitzchak, may he be strong [see prefatory comment to *Selichah* 18]. In an unusual departure, R' Shimon combined the word חֲזַק with his father's name. Instead of writing יִצְחָק חֲזַק, he inserted the ז of חֲזַק between the ח and ק of יִצְחָק, so that the signature ends יצחזק.

הִתְחַנְּנִי בְּבַקָּשָׁה — *Beseech through a request.* The Torah itself prayed for Israel on a previous occasion. As the Midrash relates: Israel asked two things of God, that they might see His glory and hear His voice. At Mount Sinai, this request was granted. But the

שִׁפְכִי שִׂיחַ עֶרֶב, וְזִכְרִי מַעֲשֵׂה חֹרֵב,[1]

》at Mount 〈 the event 〈 and 》 that is 〈 a prayer 〈 Pour out
Horeb, mention mellifluous,

בְּנַעֲשֶׂה וְנִשְׁמַע[2] נֵמוּ לְהִתְקָרֵב.

》 to be able 〈 they 》 and we will 〈 [where] We
to approach. proclaimed, listen! will do

רָגְנוּ שֵׂעִיר וּפָארָן, דָּתוֹתֶיךָ לְשָׁמְרָן,*

》 to be kept;* 〈 about your laws 〈 and Paran 〈 did Seir 〈 Complain

עָמַד וּמִדָּדָן רָאָה וְהִתִּירָן.[3]

》 and excused 〈 and saw, 〈 and mea- 〈 so He
them. sured them, got up

קָדוֹשׁ הִתִּיקָם, לְלֹא שָׁמְרוּ חֻקָּם,

》 [even] their 〈 keeping 〈 — for 》 cut them off 〈 The Holy
own law — not One

בְּאַף וּבְחֵמָה עֲשׂוֹת בָּהֶם נָקָם.[4]

》 ven- 〈 from 〈 exacting 〈 and wrath 〈 with
geance. them anger

---

(1) See commentary to *Selichah* 25, s.v. הַר גַּבְנוּנִּי.
(2) See *Exodus* 24:7. (3) Cf. *Habakkuk* 3:6. (4) Cf. *Micah* 5:14.

---

nation did not have the strength to endure that great revelation, and so their souls flew out of their bodies. Then the Torah pleaded mercy on their behalf, "Does a King [God] marry off his daughter [the Torah], then slay his household [Israel]? Shall the whole world celebrate [the Giving of the Torah], while Your children are dead?" With that their souls returned (*Shemos Rabbah* 29:4).

דָּתוֹתֶיךָ לְשָׁמְרָן — *About your laws to be kept.* The wording is ambiguous. The other nations' complaints about the Torah and its *mitzvos* are twofold: First, they refused to accept the Torah when it was offered to them, before the Jews accepted it at Sinai — "We cannot live up to its laws, our lifestyle is based on killing [or, stealing, or adultery]!" Each nation had a different reason for rejecting it. Second, in the future, when the nations will witness Israel's reward for its loyalty to the Torah, they will complain that they never had the chance to fulfill as many *mitzvos* as Israel had — "Had the Torah been given to us, we would have been just as loyal" (*Avodah Zarah* 2b).

It is not clear to which of these complaints the *paytan* refers: Seir [Edom] and Paran [Ishmael] complained that they could not keep the Torah and so rejected it; or, Seir and Paran complained that they were not given a chance to observe all 613 *mitzvos*.

The Talmud continues that because of their complaints, God reviewed their observance of the seven Noahide *mitzvos* and found them lacking in their fulfillment. Seeing this, He released them from their obligations. But, the Talmud asks, isn't that rewarding the sinner? The Talmud concludes, He didn't release them completely, He lessened their reward; even if they would fulfill their *mitzvos*, their reward would be only that of one who is not commanded but does the *mitzvah* on his own, a level of performance that the Sages find less exalted than a *mitzvah* performed by one who is commanded in its fulfillment (ibid.). Thus, the *paytan* continues: *So He got up and measured [their fulfillment of their own seven mitzvos], and saw [their performance as inadequate], and excused them.*

צָעַד מֵרְבָבוֹת, וְנִקְדַּשׁ בַּעֲרָבוֹת,*

《 in Aravos,* 〈 and was 《 from the myriads 〈 He
sanctified [of angels], strode out

מִימִינוֹ אֵשׁ דָּת,¹ וְלַהַב שַׁלְהֶבֶת.

《 conflagration. 〈 the flaming 《 of Law, 〈 the fire 〈 at His right

פָּנִים מַסְבִּירוֹת, אֵלָיו מִתְחַבְּרוֹת,

《 they [Israel 〈 to Him 〈 beaming 〈 Faces
sought to] cling, with favor,

הֻנְשְׁקוּ מִפִּיו עֲשֶׂרֶת הַדִּבְּרוֹת.*

《 Command- 〈 with the 〈 from His 〈 and they
ments.* Ten mouth were kissed

עוֹלָם נִתְבַּסָּס, אֲשֶׁר מִתְּנָאוֹ נִמְסָס,

《 [their heart] 〈 because of 〈 whereas 《 then became 〈 The
was melting, His condition [until now] firmly world
[at Creation] established,

וּכְמוֹצֵא שָׁלָל רָב עַל אִמְרָתְךָ שָׂשׂ.²

《 it 〈 your word 〈 over 《 that are 〈 spoils 〈 and like one
rejoiced. [O Torah] abundant, who finds

---

(1) Cf. *Deuteronomy* 33:2. (2) Cf. *Psalms* 119:162.

וְנִקְדַּשׁ בַּעֲרָבוֹת — *And was sanctified in Aravos.* This stich alludes to God, Who is sanctified in the seven heavens. The Talmud names and describes the seven heavens. In ascending order, they are:

(1) וִילוֹן, *Vilon* [lit., *curtain*]; although nothing happens within this heaven, in the morning it withdraws [like a curtain, allowing the daylight to shine through (*Rashi*)], and in the evening it goes forth [preventing the light of the sun from reaching Earth (*Rashi*)], thus it renews the work of Creation each day …

(2) רָקִיעַ, *Rakia* [lit., *firmament*]; in which the sun, moon, stars, and constellations are suspended …

(3) שְׁחָקִים, *Shechakim* [lit., *powders* or *pulverizers*]; in which stand millstones that grind manna for the righteous …

(4) זְבוּל, *Zevul* [lit., *Temple*]; in which are built the heavenly Jerusalem, Temple, and the Altar upon which the great angelic prince Michael sacrifices offerings …

(5) מָעוֹן, *Maon* [lit., *dwelling*]; in which groups of ministering angels recite songs [of

praise to God] through the night, but remain silent by day in deference to Israel …

(6) מָכוֹן, *Machon* [lit., *foundation* or *establishment*]; in which are storehouses of snow, storehouses of hail, the attics in which harmful dew and heavy rainfall are stored, and the chamber of the whirlwind and the tempest, the grotto of smoke with its doors of fire [all of them used for retribution against the wicked (*Rashi*)] …

and (7) עֲרָבוֹת, *Aravos* [lit., *willows* or *darkenings* or *mixtures*]; in which are Righteousness, Justice, and Charity; caches of Life, Peace, and Blessing; the souls of the righteous, the spirits and souls that are destined to be born; and the life-giving dew with which God will revivify the dead … (*Chagigah* 12b).

הֻנְשְׁקוּ מִפִּיו עֲשֶׂרֶת הַדִּבְּרוֹת — *And they were kissed from His mouth with the Ten Commandments.* The Midrash relates that the personification of each of the Ten Commandments approached each Jew at Mount Sinai and said, "Accept me upon yourself! I entail so-and-so many *mitzvos*; so-and-so

סוֹדֵי פִּקוּדֶיךָ, נִמְסְרוּ לִדוֹדֶיךָ,

« to your / were / of your / The
beloved ones, transmitted commandments secrets

מֵאָז וְעַד עַתָּה הֵמָּה מְכַבְּדֶיךָ.

« who honor / they are / now / until / and from
you. the ones then

נָדִים וְגַם נָעִים, וּבְרֹגֶז שְׂבֵעִים,

« satiated, / and with « also / and / Exiled
torment wandering,

בְּנֹפֶת צוּפֶיךָ[1] תָּמִיד מִשְׁתַּעְשְׁעִים.

« delight. / they / from the « with [your words,
constantly [honey] sweeter than]
combs the dripping

מַסֹּרֶת לְיַפֵּה, בִּכְתָב וּבְעַל פֶּה,

« and Oral; / both / they / The
Written enhance, tradition

יָקְרוּ אֲמָרֶיךָ מִשֹּׁהַם וְיָשְׁפֵה.*

« and / than / are your / more
yashpeh.* shoham words, valuable

לִבִּי לְחוֹקְקֶיךָ, בַּעֲלִיל מְזוֹקְקֶיךָ,[2]

« refine / who with « is to those who / My
you[r words], clarity decide your Law, heart

קוֹבְעֵי עִתּוֹתָם לְפַלֵּשׁ פְּקָקֶיךָ.

« your sealed / to clarify / their time / who
[teachings]. devote

כְּלָלוֹת וּפְרָטוֹת, לִרְאוֹת וּלְהַטּוֹת,*

« and to incline / to see / and / [Studying]
toward,* specifications, generalizations

שְׁנָתָם נוֹדֶדֶת בַּחֲדַר הַמִּטּוֹת.

« of their beds. / [even] in « eludes / their sleep
the room them,

---

(1) See *Psalms* 19:11. (2) Cf. 12:7.

many laws; so-and-so many punishments; so-and-so many decrees; so-and-so many leniencies and stringencies; so-and-so many rewards." Each Jew replied, "Yes! Yes!" And the Commandment kissed him on his mouth (*Shir HaShirim Rabbah* to 1:2).

מִשֹּׁהַם וְיָשְׁפֵה — *Than shoham and yash-peh.* These are two of the twelve precious stones worn by the *Kohen Gadol* on his חֹשֶׁן, *breastplate* (*Exodus* 28:20).

לִרְאוֹת וּלְהַטּוֹת — *To see and to incline toward.* An opinion may be accepted by the *Hala-chah* in one of three ways: הֲלָכָה, *halachah,* מַטִּין, *inclining toward,* or נִרְאִין, *appear-ing indicated* (*Eruvin* 46b). According to *Rashi,* statements regarded as הֲלָכָה may be

יוֹם יוֹם יִדְרְשׁוּן,[1] בְּלִבָּם יַחֲרְשׁוּן,

⟨ they contemplate ⟨ in their hearts ⟪ they investigate [the Law], ⟨ after day ⟨ Day

לֶאֱסֹר וּלְהַתִּיר בְּפִיהֶם יְפָרְשׁוּן.

⟪ they explain [their decision]. ⟨ and orally ⟨ or to permit, ⟨ [whether] to forbid

טֻמְאוֹת וּטְהוֹרוֹת, לְהַבְדִּיל וּלְהוֹרוֹת,[2]

⟪ and to render decisions; ⟨ to distinguish ⟪ and the pure, ⟨ [Between] the contaminated

מִלַּחַץ וּדְחַק עֵינֵיהֶם מַנְהִירוֹת.[3]

⟪ shine bright. ⟨ their eyes ⟨ and ⟨ despite [Exile's] affliction, oppression

חֻקִּים וּמִשְׁפָּטִים, עַל פִּימוֹ שְׁפוּטִים,

⟪ are judged, ⟨ their word ⟨ accord-ing to ⟨ and statutes ⟨ Laws

וְאוֹיְבֵיהֶם פְּלִילִים[4] וּבָהֶם נִשְׁפָּטִים.

⟪ are they judged. ⟨ and by them ⟪ have become their judges, ⟨ yet their enemies

זִכְרִי זֹאת תְּעוּדָה, הוֹגַיִךְ לְהִתְעוֹדְדָה,

⟪ to encourage, ⟨ those who study you ⟪ O Torah, ⟨ this, ⟨ Remember

וּמְלִיצֵי הֶגְיוֹנַיִךְ לַעֲזֹר וּלְסַעֲדָה.

⟪ and support. ⟨ to aid ⟨ your ideas ⟨ and those who expound

וְחָנְּנִי פְּנֵי קוֹנֵךְ, בְּמַעַן חִנּוּנֵךְ,

⟪ supplication, ⟨ with your well-spoken ⟪ your Maker, ⟨ before ⟨ Plead

כִּי הוּא אֱלֹהַיִךְ יוֹצְרֵךְ וַאֲדוֹנֵךְ.

⟪ and your Lord. ⟨ your Creator, ⟨ your God, ⟨ He is ⟨ for

---

(1) *Isaiah* 58:2. (2) Cf. *Leviticus* 10:10-11. (3) Some editions read נוֹהֲרוֹת; the stich then reads, *even though their eyes are dimmed by [Exile's] oppression and affliction*. (4) Cf. *Deuteronomy* 32:31.

---

publicized at popular lectures and may be relied upon as practical halachic guidelines; those considered מַתִּין may be followed in individual cases, under certain circumstances, but are not to be publicized to the masses at public lectures; and those opinions classified as נִרְאִין are not to be relied upon in rendering decisions, but if one in fact did rely on such a view, the decision is not reversed.

הֲלֹא אִם אֵין תַּמָּה, הוֹגָה בִּתְמִימָה,

« the perfect [Torah], ‹ pondering ‹ [Israel] the ‹ that if there ‹ Is it wholesome [nation] were not not so

הֵן בְּקֶרֶן זָוִית נְתוּנָה וּמְשֻׁתּוֹמָמָה.[1]

« and [all would be] ‹ it would ‹ in the corner ‹ indeed confounded. be left,

דֹּק וָחֶלֶד עֲבוּרָהּ, עוֹמְדִים בִּגְבֶרָה,

« strong, ‹ stand ‹ because of her ‹ and earth ‹ Heaven

בְּיִרְאָה הַטְּהוֹרָה, וּבְמִצְוָה בָרָה.[2]

« that ‹ and com- ‹ that is pure ‹ with are clear. mandments reverence

גַּבְּרִי רְנוּנִים,[3] וְשִׁפְכִי תַחֲנוּנִים,

« supplication, ‹ [your] prayer ‹ pour forth ‹ [O Torah,] [for us], sing loud

עֲבֹר תִּפְלָתֵנוּ בְּאֵין סְכוּךְ עֲנָנִים.[4]

« of clouds. ‹ obstruction ‹ with ‹ may our ‹ that pass no prayers through [to God]

בָּאֵי עָדָיו בְּתַחַן, לְנַקּוֹתָם מִצַּחַן,[5]

« of [sin's] ‹ that they be « with sup- ‹ to Him ‹ Those stench — cleansed plications, who come

מַאֲוַיִם יִתֵּן יִכְמֹר וְגַם יָחוֹן.

« be ‹ and ‹ may He « may ‹ their wish gracious. also be com- He grant, passionate

אֱסֹף עֲדַת מִי מָנָה,[6] לְקִרְיָה נֶאֱמָנָה,[7]

« that is ‹ to the City ‹ can ‹ that ‹ the con- ‹ Gather faithful; [Jerusalem,] count no one gregation

וּכְעֵדֶר בְּתוֹךְ הַדָּבְרוֹ, מֵאָדָם תְּהִימֶנָה.[8]

« let it resound. ‹ with [the « its fold, ‹ in ‹ and as a noise of] men flock

שְׁבוּיִם יְמַלֵּט, מֵאַשְׁמַנֵּי עָלֶט,

« thick ‹ from the grave- ‹ may He ‹ The darkness; like [Exile's] set free captives

---

(1) See *Kiddushin* 66a. (2) Cf. *Psalms* 19:9-10; some editions of *Selichos* read בְּיִרְאָה הַקְּדוֹשָׁה, *with holy reverence.* (3) Some editions read גַּבְּרִי תַחֲנוּנִים, *give forth strong supplication.* (4) Cf. *Lamentations* 3:44. (5) Some editions read עָדֶיךָ, *to You.* (6) See *Numbers* 23:10. (7) *Isaiah* 1:21. (8) Cf. *Micah* 2:12.

עֲדֵי עַד יְסוֹבְבָם עֹז, רָנֵּי פַלֵּט.¹

‹ of ‹ [with] ‹‹ may the ‹ surround ‹ eternally
rescue.   glad   might [of]   them
      songs   the Torah]

וּבְשׁוּבָה* וָנַחַת, נוֹשָׁעִים מִשָּׁחַת,²

‹‹ from ‹ they will ‹ and ‹ With calm
ruin —   be saved   serenity   spirit*

בַּקֵּשׁ צֹאן אוֹבְדוֹת וְגַם הַנִּדָּחַת.³

‹‹ those ‹ and ‹ that are lost ‹ the ‹ O seek
straying!   also   sheep   out

רְפָאוֹת הַנַּחְלָה, יָסִיר כָּל מַחְלָה,

‹‹ sickness, ‹ all ‹ remove ‹‹ the sick, ‹ May he heal

צִיּוֹן לְמַלֹּאות עִיר הַמְּהֻלָּלָה.

‹‹ that is praised. ‹ the ‹‹ repopulate — ‹ and
     City   Zion

❖ חֲבשׁ הַנִּשְׁבֶּרֶת, ³ זַלְזֵל הַגְּבֶרֶת,

‹‹ the [gentile] ‹ and ‹‹ the broken ‹ Bandage
mistress;   ridicule   people,

קַנֵּא קִנְאָה גְדוֹלָה, לְעִיר הַמְּחֻבֶּרֶת.⁴

‹‹ that is reunited. ‹ for the city ‹ that is great ‹ ven- ‹ and
       [Jerusalem,]   geance   take

ALL:

מַכְנִיסֵי רַחֲמִים, הַכְנִיסוּ רַחֲמֵינוּ, לִפְנֵי בַּעַל

‹ the ‹ before ‹ our [plea for] ‹ may you ‹ [pleas for] mercy, ‹ O you who
Master   mercy   usher in   usher in

הָרַחֲמִים. מַשְׁמִיעֵי תְפִלָּה, הַשְׁמִיעוּ תְפִלָּתֵנוּ, לִפְנֵי

‹ before ‹ of our prayer ‹ may you aid ‹‹ of prayer, ‹ O you who aid ‹‹ of mercy.
        the hearing   the hearing

שׁוֹמֵעַ תְּפִלָּה. מַשְׁמִיעֵי צְעָקָה, הַשְׁמִיעוּ צַעֲקָתֵנוּ,

‹ of our ‹ may you aid ‹‹ of outcries, ‹ O you who aid ‹‹ of ‹ the Hearer
outcries   the hearing   the hearing   prayer.

לִפְנֵי שׁוֹמֵעַ צְעָקָה. מַכְנִיסֵי דִמְעָה, הַכְנִיסוּ

‹ may you usher in ‹‹ tears, ‹ O you who usher in ‹‹ of outcries. ‹ the Hearer ‹ before

---

(1) Cf. *Psalms* 32:7. (2) Cf. *Isaiah* 30:15. (3) Cf. *Ezekiel* 34:16. (4) Cf. *Psalms* 122:3.

וּבְשׁוּבָה — *With calm spirit.* The translation is literal and follows the commentaries to *Isaiah* 30:15. The Talmud understands the word homiletically as an allusion to תְּשׁוּבָה, | *repentance.* Thus, it is through repentance that Israel will attain serenity on its own land (*Sanhedrin* 97b).

דִּמְעוֹתֵינוּ, לִפְנֵי מֶלֶךְ מִתְרַצֶּה בִּדְמָעוֹת.

הִשְׁתַּדְּלוּ וְהַרְבּוּ תְּחִנָּה וּבַקָּשָׁה, לִפְנֵי מֶלֶךְ אֵל

רָם וְנִשָּׂא. הַזְכִּירוּ לְפָנָיו, הַשְׁמִיעוּ לְפָנָיו תּוֹרָה

וּמַעֲשִׂים טוֹבִים שֶׁל שׁוֹכְנֵי עָפָר.

יִזְכֹּר אַהֲבָתָם וִיחַיֶּה זַרְעָם, שֶׁלֹּא תֹאבַד שְׁאֵרִית

יַעֲקֹב. כִּי צֹאן רוֹעֶה נֶאֱמָן הָיָה לְחֶרְפָּה,

יִשְׂרָאֵל גּוֹי אֶחָד לְמָשָׁל וְלִשְׁנִינָה.

מַהֵר עֲנֵנוּ אֱלֹהֵי יִשְׁעֵנוּ, וּפְדֵנוּ מִכָּל גְּזֵרוֹת קָשׁוֹת

וְהוֹשִׁיעָה בְּרַחֲמֶיךָ הָרַבִּים, מְשִׁיחַ צִדְקֶךָ וְעַמֶּךָ.

מָרַן דְּבִשְׁמַיָּא לָךְ מִתְחַנְּנַן, כְּבַר שְׁבִיָּא דְמִתְחַנַּן

לִשְׁבוּיֵהּ. כֻּלְּהוֹן בְּנֵי שְׁבִיָּא בְּכַסְפָּא מִתְפָּרְקִין,

וְעַמָּךְ יִשְׂרָאֵל בְּרַחֲמֵי וּבְתַחֲנוּנֵי, הַב לָן שְׁאִילָתִין

וּבָעוּתִין, דְּלָא נֶהֱדַר רֵיקָם מִן קֳדָמָךְ.

‹ before ‹ from ‹ empty- ‹ that we not be ‹ and our prayers
You. handed turned away

מָרַן דִּבְשְׁמַיָּא לָךְ מִתְחַנְּנָן, כְּעַבְדָּא דְּמִתְחַנֵּן

‹ who ‹ as a slave » do we ‹ to You » Who is in ‹ Our
supplicates supplicate, heaven, Master

לְמָרֵיהּ, עֲשִׁיקֵי אֲנָן וּבַחֲשׁוֹכָא שָׁרֵינָן, מְרִירָן נַפְשִׁין

‹ are [our] ‹ embittered » do we ‹ and in darkness ‹ are ‹ Oppressed » to his
souls abide, we master:

מֵעַקְתִין דִּנְפִישִׁין, חֵילָא לֵית בָּן לְרַצּוּיָךְ. מָרַן,

‹ Our » to appease ‹ within ‹ is ‹ Strength » that is ‹ from distress
Master, You. us lacking excessive.

עֲבִיד בְּדִיל קְיָמָא דִּגְזַרְתָּ עִם אֲבָהָתָנָא.

» our Patriarchs. ‹ with ‹ that You ‹ of the ‹ for the ‹ act
established covenant sake

שׁוֹמֵר יִשְׂרָאֵל, שְׁמוֹר שְׁאֵרִית יִשְׂרָאֵל, וְאַל

‹ let not » of Israel; ‹ the remnant ‹ safeguard » of Israel, ‹ O Guardian

יֹאבַד יִשְׂרָאֵל, הָאוֹמְרִים שְׁמַע יִשְׂרָאֵל.[1]

» O Israel. ‹ Hear, ‹ those who » Israel be destroyed —
proclaim:

שׁוֹמֵר גּוֹי אֶחָד, שְׁמוֹר שְׁאֵרִית עַם אֶחָד, וְאַל

‹ let not » that is ‹ of the ‹ the remnant ‹ safeguard » that is ‹ of the ‹ O Guardian
unique; people unique, nation

יֹאבַד גּוֹי אֶחָד, הַמְיַחֲדִים שִׁמְךָ, יְהוה אֱלֹהֵינוּ

‹ is our God, ‹ HASHEM ‹ of Your ‹ those who proclaim » that is ‹ the ‹ be
Name: the Oneness unique, nation destroyed

יְהוה אֶחָד.

» the One ‹ HASHEM
[and Only]! is

שׁוֹמֵר גּוֹי קָדוֹשׁ, שְׁמוֹר שְׁאֵרִית עַם קָדוֹשׁ, וְאַל

‹ let not » that is ‹ of the ‹ the remnant ‹ safeguard » that is ‹ of the ‹ O Guardian
holy; people holy, nation

יֹאבַד גּוֹי קָדוֹשׁ, הַמְשַׁלְּשִׁים בְּשָׁלֹשׁ קְדֻשּׁוֹת לְקָדוֹשׁ.

» to the ‹ sancti- ‹ the ‹ those who proclaim » that is ‹ the ‹ be
Holy One. fications threefold three times holy, nation destroyed

---

(1) *Deuteronomy* 6:4.

מִתְרַצֶּה בְּרַחֲמִים וּמִתְפַּיֵּס בְּתַחֲנוּנִים, הִתְרַצֵּה

‹ be favorable « through supplications, ‹ and Who becomes conciliatory ‹ through compassion ‹ You Who becomes favorable

וְהִתְפַּיֵּס לְדוֹר עָנִי, כִּי אֵין עוֹזֵר. אָבִינוּ מַלְכֵּנוּ,

« our King, ‹ Our Father, « helper. ‹ there is no ‹ for « that is ‹ to the generation poor, and be conciliatory

חָנֵּנוּ וַעֲנֵנוּ, כִּי אֵין בָּנוּ מַעֲשִׂים, עֲשֵׂה עִמָּנוּ

‹ us ‹ treat « worthy deeds; ‹ we have no ‹ though ‹ and ‹ be gracious answer us, with us

צְדָקָה וָחֶסֶד וְהוֹשִׁיעֵנוּ.

« and save us. ‹ and kindness, ‹ with charity

STAND AFTER THE WORDS וַאֲנַחְנוּ לֹא נֵדַע UNTIL CONCLUSION OF THE PARAGRAPH.

וַאֲנַחְנוּ לֹא נֵדַע מַה נַּעֲשֶׂה, כִּי עָלֶיךָ עֵינֵינוּ.[1]

« are our eyes. ‹ upon You ‹ rather, « we should do, ‹ what ‹ know not ‹ We

זְכֹר רַחֲמֶיךָ יהוה וַחֲסָדֶיךָ, כִּי מֵעוֹלָם הֵמָּה.[2] יְהִי

‹ May « are they. ‹ eternal ‹ for ‹ and Your kindnesses, ‹ Hashem, ‹ Your mercies, ‹ Remember

חַסְדְּךָ יהוה עָלֵינוּ, כַּאֲשֶׁר יִחַלְנוּ לָךְ.[3] אַל תִּזְכָּר

‹ recall ‹ Do not « be upon us, ‹ Hashem, ‹ Your kindness, ‹ You. ‹ we awaited ‹ just as

לָנוּ עֲוֹנוֹת רִאשׁוֹנִים, מַהֵר יְקַדְּמוּנוּ רַחֲמֶיךָ, כִּי

‹ for « may Your mercies, ‹ advance to meet us ‹ swiftly « of the ancients; ‹ the sins ‹ against us

דַלּוֹנוּ מְאֹד.[4] עֶזְרֵנוּ בְּשֵׁם יהוה, עֹשֵׂה שָׁמַיִם

‹ of heaven ‹ Maker « of Hashem, ‹ is through the Name ‹ Our help « exceedingly. ‹ we have become impoverished

וָאָרֶץ.[5] חָנֵּנוּ יהוה חָנֵּנוּ, כִּי רַב שָׂבַעְנוּ בוּז.[6] בְּרֹגֶז

« Amid wrath, « with contempt. ‹ sated ‹ we are fully ‹ for « favor us, ‹ Hashem, ‹ Favor us, « and earth.

רַחֵם תִּזְכּוֹר.[7] בְּרֹגֶז עֲקֵדָה תִּזְכּוֹר. בְּרֹגֶז תְּמִימוֹת

‹ the perfect ones « Amid wrath, « You should remember! ‹ the binding [of Isaac] « Amid wrath, « You should remember! ‹ to be merciful

תִּזְכּוֹר. יהוה הוֹשִׁיעָה, הַמֶּלֶךְ יַעֲנֵנוּ בְיוֹם קָרְאֵנוּ.[8]

« we call. ‹ on the day ‹ answer us ‹ May the King « save! ‹ Hashem, « You should remember!

(1) II Chronicles 20:12. (2) Psalms 25:6. (3) 33:22. (4) 79:8.
(5) 121:2. (6) 123:3. (7) Habakkuk 3:2. (8) Psalms 20:10.

כִּי הוּא יָדַע יִצְרֵנוּ, זָכוּר כִּי עָפָר אֲנָחְנוּ.¹

⟨ For ⟨ He ⟨ knew ⟨ our nature, ⟪ He is ⟨ that ⟨ dust ⟨ are we. ⟫
mindful

❖ עֶזְרֵנוּ אֱלֹהֵי יִשְׁעֵנוּ עַל דְּבַר כְּבוֹד שְׁמֶךָ, וְהַצִּילֵנוּ

⟨ Assist us, ⟨ O God ⟨ of our ⟨ the ⟨ for ⟨ the ⟨ of the ⟪ of Your ⟨ rescue us
salvation sake glory Name;

וְכַפֵּר עַל חַטֹּאתֵינוּ לְמַעַן שְׁמֶךָ.²

⟨ and grant ⟨ for ⟨ our sins ⟨ for the ⟨ of Your ⟫
atonement sake Name.

קדיש שלם / FULL KADDISH

THE *CHAZZAN* RECITES קַדִּישׁ שָׁלֵם, FULL *KADDISH.*

יִתְגַּדַּל וְיִתְקַדַּשׁ שְׁמֵהּ רַבָּא. (אָמֵן. — Cong.) בְּעָלְמָא

⟨ Grow ⟨ and be ⟨ may His ⟨ that is ⟪ (Amen.) ⟨ — in the
exalted sanctified Name great! — world

דִּי בְרָא כִרְעוּתֵהּ. וְיַמְלִיךְ מַלְכוּתֵהּ, וְיַצְמַח פֻּרְקָנֵהּ

⟨ that ⟨ He ⟨ according ⟪ to His ⟨ and may He ⟪ to His ⟨ and cause ⟨ His
created to His will, kingship, give reign sprout salvation,

וִיקָרֵב מְשִׁיחֵהּ. (אָמֵן. — Cong.) בְּחַיֵּיכוֹן וּבְיוֹמֵיכוֹן וּבְחַיֵּי

⟨ and bring ⟨ His Messiah, ⟪ (Amen.) ⟪ in your ⟨ and in ⟨ and in the
near lifetimes your days, lifetimes

דְכָל בֵּית יִשְׂרָאֵל, בַּעֲגָלָא וּבִזְמַן קָרִיב. וְאִמְרוּ: אָמֵן.

⟨ of the ⟨ Family ⟨ of Israel, ⟪ swiftly ⟨ and at a ⟨ that comes ⟪ Now ⟨ Amen. ⟫
entire time soon. respond:

CONGREGATION RESPONDS:

אָמֵן. יְהֵא שְׁמֵהּ רַבָּא מְבָרַךְ לְעָלַם וּלְעָלְמֵי עָלְמַיָּא.

⟪ Amen. ⟨ May ⟨ His ⟨ that is ⟨ be ⟨ forever ⟪ and for all eternity.
Name great blessed

CHAZZAN CONTINUES:

יְהֵא שְׁמֵהּ רַבָּא מְבָרַךְ לְעָלַם וּלְעָלְמֵי עָלְמַיָּא. יִתְבָּרַךְ

⟨ May ⟨ His ⟨ that is ⟨ be ⟨ forever ⟪ and for all eternity. ⟪ Blessed,
Name great blessed

וְיִשְׁתַּבַּח וְיִתְפָּאַר וְיִתְרוֹמַם וְיִתְנַשֵּׂא וְיִתְהַדָּר וְיִתְעַלֶּה

⟨ praised, ⟨ glorified, ⟨ exalted, ⟨ upraised, ⟨ honored, ⟨ elevated,

וְיִתְהַלָּל שְׁמֵהּ דְּקֻדְשָׁא בְּרִיךְ הוּא (בְּרִיךְ הוּא — Cong.)

⟨ and lauded ⟨ be the ⟨ of the Holy ⟨ Blessed ⟨ is He ⟪ (Blessed ⟨ is He) ⟫
Name One,

---

(1) *Psalms* 103:14. (2) 79:9.

לְעֵלָּא [וּ]לְעֵלָּא מִכָּל בִּרְכָתָא וְשִׁירָתָא תֻּשְׁבְּחָתָא —
exceedingly beyond ‹ *any* › *blessing* ‹ *and song,* ›› *praise* ‹

וְנֶחֱמָתָא דַּאֲמִירָן בְּעָלְמָא. וְאִמְרוּ: אָמֵן. (Cong. — אָמֵן.)
and ‹ *consolation* › *that are* ‹ *uttered* › *in the* « *world.* ‹ *Now* « *respond:* *Amen.* ‹ « (*Amen.*)

CONGREGATION:

(קַבֵּל בְּרַחֲמִים וּבְרָצוֹן אֶת תְּפִלָּתֵנוּ.)
(*Accept* ‹ *with mercy* ‹ *and with favor* › *our prayers.*) «

CHAZZAN CONTINUES:

תִּתְקַבֵּל צְלוֹתְהוֹן וּבָעוּתְהוֹן דְּכָל בֵּית יִשְׂרָאֵל קֳדָם
May accepted be ‹ *the prayers* › *and supplications* ‹ *of the entire* › *Family of* ‹ *Israel* ‹ *before* ‹

אֲבוּהוֹן דִּי בִשְׁמַיָּא. וְאִמְרוּ: אָמֵן. (Cong. — אָמֵן.)
their Father ‹ *Who* ‹ *is in Heaven.* « *Now respond:* ‹ *Amen.* « (*Amen.*) »

CONGREGATION:

(יְהִי שֵׁם יהוה מְבֹרָךְ, מֵעַתָּה וְעַד עוֹלָם.[1])
(*Let* ‹ *Name* HASHEM *be* « *blessed,* ‹ *of* ‹ *from this time* › *until* ‹ *eternity.*) «

CHAZZAN CONTINUES:

יְהֵא שְׁלָמָא רַבָּא מִן שְׁמַיָּא וְחַיִּים טוֹבִים עָלֵינוּ וְעַל כָּל
May there be ‹ *peace* ‹ *that is abundant* › *from* ‹ *Heaven* ‹ *and life* › *that is good,* ‹ *upon us* › *and upon* ‹ *all* ‹

יִשְׂרָאֵל. וְאִמְרוּ: אָמֵן. (Cong. — אָמֵן.)
Israel. « *Now respond:* ‹ *Amen.* « (*Amen.*) »

CONGREGATION:

(עֶזְרִי מֵעִם יהוה, עֹשֵׂה שָׁמַיִם וָאָרֶץ.[2])
(*My help* ‹ *is from* ‹ HASHEM, ‹ *Maker* « *of heaven* › *and earth.*) «

CHAZZAN BOWS; TAKES THREE STEPS BACK. BOWS LEFT AND SAYS "... עֹשֶׂה שָׁלוֹם, HE WHO MAKES
PEACE ...*"; BOWS RIGHT AND SAYS "*... הוּא, MAY HE ...*"; BOWS FORWARD AND SAYS "*... וְעַל כָּל יִשְׂרָאֵל,
AND UPON ALL ISRAEL ...*"; REMAINS IN PLACE FOR A FEW MOMENTS, THEN TAKES THREE STEPS FORWARD.*

עֹשֶׂה [הַ]שָׁלוֹם בִּמְרוֹמָיו, הוּא יַעֲשֶׂה שָׁלוֹם עָלֵינוּ, וְעַל
He Who makes ‹ [*the*] *peace* ‹ *in His heights,* › *may He* « *make* ‹ *peace* ‹ *upon us,* › *and upon* ‹

כָּל יִשְׂרָאֵל. וְאִמְרוּ: אָמֵן. (Cong. — אָמֵן.)
all ‹ *Israel.* « *Now respond:* ‹ *Amen.* « (*Amen.*) »

---

(1) *Psalms* 113:2. (2) 121:2.

יום שני של עשרת ימי תשובה

SECOND DAY OF REPENTANCE

אַשְׁרֵי יוֹשְׁבֵי בֵיתֶךָ, עוֹד יְהַלְלוּךָ סֶּלָה.¹ אַשְׁרֵי

⟨ Praise- ⟫ Selah. ⟫ they will ⟨ con- ⟫ in Your ⟨ are those ⟨ Praiseworthy
worthy   praise You,   tinually   house,   who dwell

הָעָם שֶׁכָּכָה לּוֹ, אַשְׁרֵי הָעָם שֶׁיהוה אֱלֹהָיו.²

⟫ is their ⟨ that ⟨ is the ⟨ praise- ⟫ is ⟨ that such ⟨ is the
God.   HASHEM   people   worthy   their lot;   people

—— תהלים קמה / Psalm 145 ——

תְּהִלָּה לְדָוִד, אֲרוֹמִמְךָ אֱלוֹהַי הַמֶּלֶךְ, וַאֲבָרְכָה

⟨ and I ⟫ the King, ⟨ my God ⟨ I will exalt You, ⟫ by David: ⟨ A psalm of
will bless   praise

שִׁמְךָ לְעוֹלָם וָעֶד. בְּכָל יוֹם אֲבָרְכֶךָ, וַאֲהַלְלָה שִׁמְךָ

⟨ Your ⟨ and I ⟫ I will ⟨ day ⟨ Every ⟫ and ⟨ for ever ⟨ Your
Name   will laud   bless You,   ever.   Name

לְעוֹלָם וָעֶד. גָּדוֹל יהוה וּמְהֻלָּל מְאֹד, וְלִגְדֻלָּתוֹ

⟨ and His ⟫ exceedingly, ⟨ and ⟨ is ⟨ Great ⟫ and ⟨ for ever
greatness   lauded   HASHEM   ever.

אֵין חֵקֶר. דּוֹר לְדוֹר יְשַׁבַּח מַעֲשֶׂיךָ, וּגְבוּרֹתֶיךָ יַגִּידוּ.

⟫ they will ⟨ and Your ⟫ Your ⟨ will ⟨ Gen- ⟨ to ⟫ is beyond
recount.   mighty deeds   actions,   praise   generation   eration   investigation

הֲדַר כְּבוֹד הוֹדֶךָ, וְדִבְרֵי נִפְלְאֹתֶיךָ אָשִׂיחָה. וֶעֱזוּז

⟨ And of ⟫ I shall ⟨ that are ⟨ and Your ⟨ of Your ⟨ glory ⟨ The
the might   discuss.   wondrous   deeds   majesty   splendrous

נוֹרְאֹתֶיךָ יֹאמֵרוּ, וּגְדוּלָּתְךָ אֲסַפְּרֶנָּה. זֵכֶר רַב טוּבְךָ

⟨ of Your abun- ⟨ A recol- ⟫ I shall ⟨ and Your ⟫ they will ⟨ of Your
dant goodness   lection   relate.   greatness   speak,   awesome deeds

יַבִּיעוּ, וְצִדְקָתְךָ יְרַנֵּנוּ. חַנּוּן וְרַחוּם יהוה, אֶרֶךְ אַפַּיִם

⟨ to ⟨ slow ⟫ is ⟨ and ⟨ Gracious ⟫ they will ⟨ and of Your ⟫ they
anger,   HASHEM,   merciful   sing joyfully.   righteousness   will utter,

וּגְדָל חָסֶד. טוֹב יהוה לַכֹּל, וְרַחֲמָיו עַל כָּל מַעֲשָׂיו.

⟫ His ⟨ all ⟨ are ⟨ His ⟫ to all; ⟨ HASHEM ⟫ in [bestowing] ⟨ and
creations.   on   mercies   is good   kindness.   great

יוֹדוּךָ יהוה כָּל מַעֲשֶׂיךָ, וַחֲסִידֶיךָ יְבָרְכוּכָה. כְּבוֹד

⟨ Of the ⟫ will ⟨ and Your ⟫ Your ⟨ — all ⟫ HASHEM ⟨ They will
glory   bless You.   devout ones   creations —   thank You,

(1) *Psalms* 84:5. (2) 144:15.

מַלְכוּתְךָ יֹאמֵרוּ, וּגְבוּרָתְךָ יְדַבֵּרוּ. **לְהוֹדִיעַ** לִבְנֵי הָאָדָם

⟨ mankind ⟨ To inform ⟫ they will ⟨ and of Your ⟫ they will ⟨ of Your
declare. power speak, kingdom

גְּבוּרֹתָיו, וּכְבוֹד הֲדַר מַלְכוּתוֹ. **מַלְכוּתְךָ** מַלְכוּת כָּל

⟨[span- ⟨ is a ⟨ Your kingdom ⟫ of His ⟨ splendor ⟨ and of the ⟫ of His mighty
ning] all kingdom kingdom. glorious deeds,

עֹלָמִים, וּמֶמְשַׁלְתְּךָ בְּכָל דּוֹר וָדֹר. **סוֹמֵךְ** יהוה

⟨ HASHEM ⟫ after ⟨ gen- ⟨ is ⟨ and Your ⟫ eternities,
supports generation. eration throughout dominion

לְכָל הַנֹּפְלִים, וְזוֹקֵף לְכָל הַכְּפוּפִים. **עֵינֵי** כֹל

⟨ of all ⟨ The ⟫ those who ⟨ all ⟨ and ⟫ those who ⟨ all
eyes are bent. straightens are fallen.

אֵלֶיךָ יְשַׂבֵּרוּ, וְאַתָּה נוֹתֵן לָהֶם אֶת אָכְלָם בְּעִתּוֹ.

⟫ in its ⟨ their food ⟨ them ⟨ give ⟨ and You ⟫ do look ⟨ to You
proper time. with hope,

CONCENTRATE INTENTLY WHILE RECITING THE VERSE **פּוֹתֵחַ**, YOU OPEN.

פּוֹתֵחַ אֶת יָדֶךָ, וּמַשְׂבִּיעַ לְכָל חַי רָצוֹן. ❖ **צַדִּיק**

⟨ Righteous ⟫ [with its] ⟨ living ⟨ every ⟨ and satisfy ⟫ Your hand, ⟨ You open
desire. thing

יהוה בְּכָל דְּרָכָיו, וְחָסִיד בְּכָל מַעֲשָׂיו. **קָרוֹב** יהוה

⟨ is ⟨ Close ⟫ His deeds. ⟨ in all ⟨ and ⟫ His ways, ⟨ in all ⟨ is
HASHEM magnanimous HASHEM

לְכָל קֹרְאָיו, לְכֹל אֲשֶׁר יִקְרָאֻהוּ בֶאֱמֶת. **רְצוֹן** יְרֵאָיו

⟨ of those ⟨ The ⟫ sincerely. ⟨ call upon ⟨ who ⟨ to all ⟫ who call ⟨ to all
who fear Him will Him upon Him,

יַעֲשֶׂה, וְאֶת שַׁוְעָתָם יִשְׁמַע וְיוֹשִׁיעֵם. **שׁוֹמֵר** יהוה

⟨ HASHEM protects ⟫ and He will ⟨ He will ⟨ and their cry ⟫ He
save them. hear, will do;

אֶת כָּל אֹהֲבָיו, וְאֵת כָּל הָרְשָׁעִים יַשְׁמִיד. **תְּהִלַּת**

⟨ The praise ⟫ He will destroy. ⟨ the wicked ⟨ but all ⟫ who love Him; ⟨ all

יהוה יְדַבֶּר פִּי, וִיבָרֵךְ כָּל בָּשָׂר שֵׁם קָדְשׁוֹ לְעוֹלָם

⟨ for ever ⟨ of His ⟨ the ⟨ flesh ⟨ may ⟨ and bless ⟫ may my ⟨ of
Holiness Name all mouth declare, HASHEM

וָעֶד. וַאֲנַחְנוּ נְבָרֵךְ יָהּ מֵעַתָּה וְעַד עוֹלָם; הַלְלוּיָהּ.[1]

⟫ Halleluyah! ⟫ eternity. ⟨ until ⟨ from ⟨ God ⟨ will ⟨ But we ⟫ and
this time bless ever.

_____

(1) *Psalms* 115:18.

THE *CHAZZAN* RECITES חֲצִי קַדִּישׁ, HALF-*KADDISH*:

יִתְגַּדַּל וְיִתְקַדַּשׁ שְׁמֵהּ רַבָּא. (Cong. — אָמֵן.) בְּעָלְמָא

⟨ Grow exalted ⟩ and be sanctified ⟨ may His Name ⟩ that is great! — ⟨ (Amen.) ⟩ — in the world ⟩

דִּי בְרָא כִרְעוּתֵהּ. וְיַמְלִיךְ מַלְכוּתֵהּ, וְיַצְמַח פֻּרְקָנֵהּ

⟨ that ⟨ He created ⟨ according to His will, ⟩ and may He give reign ⟨ to His kingship, ⟩ and cause to sprout ⟨ His salvation, ⟩

וִיקָרֵב מְשִׁיחֵהּ. (Cong. — אָמֵן.) בְּחַיֵּיכוֹן וּבְיוֹמֵיכוֹן וּבְחַיֵּי

⟨ and bring near ⟨ His Messiah, ⟨ (Amen.) ⟩ in your lifetimes ⟨ and in your days, ⟨ and in the lifetimes ⟩

דְכָל בֵּית יִשְׂרָאֵל, בַּעֲגָלָא וּבִזְמַן קָרִיב. וְאִמְרוּ: אָמֵן.

⟨ of the entire ⟨ Family ⟨ of Israel, ⟨ swiftly ⟨ and at a time ⟨ that comes soon. ⟨ Now respond: ⟨ Amen. ⟩

CONGREGATION RESPONDS:

אָמֵן. יְהֵא שְׁמֵהּ רַבָּא מְבָרַךְ לְעָלַם וּלְעָלְמֵי עָלְמַיָּא.

⟨ Amen. ⟨ May ⟨ His Name ⟨ that is great ⟨ be blessed ⟨ forever ⟨ and for all eternity. ⟩

CHAZZAN CONTINUES:

יְהֵא שְׁמֵהּ רַבָּא מְבָרַךְ לְעָלַם וּלְעָלְמֵי עָלְמַיָּא. יִתְבָּרַךְ

⟨ May ⟨ His Name ⟨ that is great ⟨ be blessed ⟨ forever ⟨ and for all eternity. ⟨ Blessed, ⟩

וְיִשְׁתַּבַּח וְיִתְפָּאַר וְיִתְרוֹמַם וְיִתְנַשֵּׂא וְיִתְהַדָּר וְיִתְעַלֶּה

⟨ praised, ⟨ glorified, ⟨ exalted, ⟨ upraised, ⟨ honored, ⟨ elevated, ⟩

וְיִתְהַלָּל שְׁמֵהּ דְּקֻדְשָׁא בְּרִיךְ הוּא (Cong. — בְּרִיךְ הוּא)

⟨ and lauded ⟨ be the Name ⟨ of the Holy One, ⟨ Blessed ⟨ is He ⟨ (Blessed is He) ⟩

— לְעֵלָּא [וּ]לְעֵלָּא מִכָּל בִּרְכָתָא וְשִׁירָתָא תֻּשְׁבְּחָתָא

⟨ exceedingly beyond ⟨ any ⟨ blessing ⟨ and song, ⟨ praise ⟩

וְנֶחֱמָתָא דַּאֲמִירָן בְּעָלְמָא. וְאִמְרוּ: אָמֵן. (Cong. — אָמֵן.)

⟨ and consolation ⟨ that are ⟨ uttered ⟨ in the world. ⟨ Now respond: ⟨ Amen. ⟨ (Amen.) ⟩

ALL:

לְךָ יהוה הַצְּדָקָה, וְלָנוּ בְּשֶׁת הַפָּנִים.[1] מַה

⟨ Yours, ⟨ O Lord, ⟨ is the righteousness, ⟨ and ours ⟨ is shamefacedness. ⟨ What ⟩

נִּתְאוֹנֵן, מַה נֹּאמַר, מַה נְּדַבֵּר, וּמַה נִּצְטַדָּק.[3]

⟨ complaint can we make? ⟨ What can we say? ⟨ What can we declare? ⟨ What justification can we offer? ⟩[2]

(1) *Daniel* 9:7. (2) Cf. *Lamentations* 3:39. (3) Cf. *Genesis* 44:16.

נַחְפְּשָׂה דְרָכֵינוּ וְנַחְקְֹרָה, וְנָשׁוּבָה אֵלֶיךָ,¹ כִּי יְמִינְךָ

⟨ Your   ⟨ for ⟪ to You, ⟨ and return ⟨ and investigate ⟨ our ways ⟨ Let us
right hand   them,   examine

פְּשׁוּטָה לְקַבֵּל שָׁבִים. לֹא בְחֶסֶד וְלֹא בְמַעֲשִׂים

⟨ with [merit for ⟨ nor ⟨ with [merit] ⟨ Nei- ⟪ those who ⟨ to accept ⟨ is extended
good] deeds   for kindness   ther   return.

בָּאנוּ לְפָנֶיךָ, כְּדַלִּים וּכְרָשִׁים דָּפַקְנוּ דְלָתֶיךָ.

⟪ on Your ⟨ we have ⟨ and as destitute ⟨ but as ⟪ before You; ⟨ do we
doors.   knocked   people   paupers   come

דְלָתֶיךָ דָּפַקְנוּ רַחוּם וְחַנּוּן, נָא אַל תְּשִׁיבֵנוּ

⟨ turn us ⟨ do ⟨ Please ⟪ and Gra- ⟨ O Compas- ⟨ we have ⟨ On Your
away   not   cious One.   sionate One   knocked,   doors

רֵיקָם מִלְּפָנֶיךָ. מִלְּפָנֶיךָ מַלְכֵּנוּ רֵיקָם אַל תְּשִׁיבֵנוּ,

⟪ turn us ⟨ do ⟨ empty- ⟨ Our King, ⟨ From before ⟪ from before ⟨ empty-
away   not   handed   You,   You.   handed

כִּי אַתָּה שׁוֹמֵעַ תְּפִלָּה.

⟪ prayer. ⟨ Who hears ⟨ You are ⟨ for
the One

שׁוֹמֵעַ תְּפִלָּה, עָדֶיךָ כָּל בָּשָׂר יָבֹאוּ.² יָבֹא

⟨ Come ⟪ will come. ⟨ flesh ⟨ all ⟨ unto You ⟪ prayer, ⟨ You Who
hears

כָל בָּשָׂר לְהִשְׁתַּחֲוֹת לְפָנֶיךָ יהוה.³ יָבֹאוּ וְיִשְׁתַּחֲווּ

⟨ and bow ⟨ They will ⟪ O ⟨ before ⟨ to bow down ⟨ will all flesh
down   come   HASHEM.   You,

לְפָנֶיךָ אֲדֹנָי, וִיכַבְּדוּ לִשְׁמֶךָ.⁴ בֹּאוּ נִשְׁתַּחֲוֶה וְנִכְרָעָה,

⟪ and bow, ⟨ Let us prostrate ⟨ Come! ⟪ to Your ⟨ and they will ⟪ O Lord, ⟨ before
ourselves   Name.   show honor   You,

נִבְרְכָה לִפְנֵי יהוה עֹשֵׂנוּ.⁵ נָבוֹאָה לְמִשְׁכְּנוֹתָיו,

⟪ to His Tabernacles, ⟨ Let us come ⟪ our Maker. ⟨ HASHEM, ⟨ before ⟨ let us kneel

נִשְׁתַּחֲוֶה לַהֲדֹם רַגְלָיו.⁶ בֹּאוּ שְׁעָרָיו בְּתוֹדָה,

⟪ with ⟨ His ⟨ Enter ⟪ for His feet. ⟨ at the ⟨ let us prostrate
thanksgiving,   gates   stool   ourselves

חֲצֵרֹתָיו בִּתְהִלָּה, הוֹדוּ לוֹ בָּרְכוּ שְׁמוֹ.⁷ וַאֲנַחְנוּ

⟨ But we, ⟪ His ⟨ bless ⟪ to ⟨ give ⟪ with praise; ⟨ His courtyards
Name.   Him,   thanks

---

(1) Cf. *Lamentations* 3:40. (2) *Psalms* 65:3. (3) Cf. *Isaiah* 66:23.
(4) *Psalms* 86:9. (5) 95:6. (6) 132:7. (7) 100:4.

בְּרֹב חַסְדְּךָ נָבוֹא בֵיתֶךָ, נִשְׁתַּחֲוֶה אֶל הֵיכַל קָדְשְׁךָ

Your Holy Sanctuary ⟨ toward ⟨ we will pros- trate ourselves ⟨ Your House; ⟨ will we enter ⟨ of Your kindness ⟨ through the abundance

בְּיִרְאָתֶךָ.[1] הִנֵּה בָּרְכוּ אֶת יהוה כָּל עַבְדֵי יהוה,

of HASHEM, ⟨ you servants ⟨ all ⟨ HASHEM, ⟨ bless ⟨⟨ Indeed, ⟨⟨ in awe of You.

הָעֹמְדִים בְּבֵית יהוה בַּלֵּילוֹת.[2] שְׂאוּ יְדֵיכֶם קֹדֶשׁ

in the Sanctuary ⟨ your hands ⟨ Lift ⟨⟨ in the nights. ⟨ of HASHEM ⟨ in the House ⟨ who stand

וּבָרְכוּ אֶת יהוה.[3] רוֹמְמוּ יהוה אֱלֹהֵינוּ, וְהִשְׁתַּחֲווּ

and bow down ⟨ our God, ⟨ HASHEM, ⟨ Exalt ⟨⟨ HASHEM. ⟨ and bless

לַהֲדֹם רַגְלָיו, קָדוֹשׁ הוּא.[4] רוֹמְמוּ יהוה אֱלֹהֵינוּ,

our God, ⟨ HASHEM, ⟨ Exalt ⟨⟨ is He! ⟨ holy ⟨⟨ at His footstool;

וְהִשְׁתַּחֲווּ לְהַר קָדְשׁוֹ, כִּי קָדוֹשׁ יהוה אֱלֹהֵינוּ.[5]

our God. ⟨⟨ is ⟨ holy ⟨ for ⟨⟨ of His Holiness; ⟨ at the Mount ⟨ and bow

הִשְׁתַּחֲווּ לַיהוה בְּהַדְרַת קֹדֶשׁ, חִילוּ מִפָּנָיו כָּל

every- one ⟨ before Him, ⟨ tremble ⟨⟨ of holiness; ⟨ in the splendor ⟨ before HASHEM ⟨ Bow down

הָאָרֶץ.[6] נִשְׁתַּחֲוֶה אֶל הֵיכַל קָדְשְׁךָ וְנוֹדֶה אֶת שְׁמֶךָ,

Your Name ⟨ and we will thank ⟨⟨ Your Holy Sanctuary, ⟨ toward ⟨ We will pros- trate ourselves ⟨⟨ on earth.

עַל חַסְדְּךָ וְעַל אֲמִתֶּךָ, כִּי הִגְדַּלְתָּ עַל כָּל שִׁמְךָ

Your Name — ⟨⟨ Your ⟨ — even beyond ⟨⟨ You have exalted ⟨ for ⟨⟨ Your faithfulness; ⟨ and for ⟨ Your kindness

אִמְרָתֶךָ.[7] יהוה אֱלֹהֵי צְבָאוֹת, מִי כָמוֹךָ חֲסִין

O Strong One, ⟨⟨ is like ⟨ You, ⟨ — who ⟨⟨ of Legions ⟨ God ⟨ HASHEM, ⟨⟨ Your promise.

יָהּ, וֶאֱמוּנָתְךָ סְבִיבוֹתֶיךָ.[8] כִּי מִי בַשַּׁחַק יַעֲרֹךְ

can be compared ⟨ in the sky ⟨ who ⟨ For ⟨⟨ surrounds You. ⟨ and Your faithfulness ⟨⟨ God? —

לַיהוה, יִדְמֶה לַיהוה בִּבְנֵי אֵלִים.[9] כִּי גָדוֹל אַתָּה

are You ⟨ great ⟨ For ⟨⟨ among the angels? ⟨ to HASHEM ⟨ be likened ⟨⟨ to HASHEM;

וְעוֹשֵׂה נִפְלָאוֹת, אַתָּה אֱלֹהִים לְבַדֶּךָ.[10] כִּי גָדוֹל

great ⟨ For ⟨⟨ alone. ⟨ O God, ⟨ You, ⟨⟨ of wonders; ⟨ and a worker

(1) Cf. *Psalms* 5:8. (2) 134:1. (3) 134:2. (4) 99:5. (5) 99:9. (6) 96:9. (7) Cf. 138:2. (8) 89:9. (9) 89:7. (10) 86:10.

מֵעַל שָׁמַיִם חַסְדֶּךָ, וְעַד שְׁחָקִים אֲמִתֶּךָ.¹ גָּדוֹל
‹ Great « is Your ‹ the upper ‹ and « is Your ‹ the very ‹ above
truth. heights until kindness, heavens

יהוה וּמְהֻלָּל מְאֹד, וְלִגְדֻלָּתוֹ אֵין חֵקֶר.² (כִּי) גָּדוֹל
‹ great ‹ (For) « investiga- ‹ is ‹ and His « exceed- ‹ and ‹ is
tion. beyond greatness ingly, lauded HASHEM

יהוה וּמְהֻלָּל מְאֹד, נוֹרָא הוּא עַל כָּל אֱלֹהִים.³ כִּי
‹ For « heavenly ‹ all ‹ above ‹ is He ‹ awesome « exceed- ‹ and ‹ is
powers. ingly; lauded HASHEM

אֵל גָּדוֹל יהוה, וּמֶלֶךְ גָּדוֹל עַל כָּל אֱלֹהִים.⁴ אֲשֶׁר
‹ For « heavenly ‹ all ‹ above ‹ and a great King « is ‹ a great God
powers. HASHEM,

מִי אֵל בַּשָּׁמַיִם וּבָאָרֶץ, אֲשֶׁר יַעֲשֶׂה כְמַעֲשֶׂיךָ
‹ like unto ‹ can do ‹ that ‹ or in the ‹ is there in ‹ power ‹ what
Your deeds earth the heaven

וְכִגְבוּרֹתֶיךָ.⁵ מִי לֹא יִרָאֲךָ מֶלֶךְ הַגּוֹיִם, כִּי לְךָ
‹ to ‹ For « of nations? ‹ O King ‹ fear You, ‹ would ‹ Who « and like unto Your
You not mighty acts?

יָאָתָה, כִּי בְכָל חַכְמֵי הַגּוֹיִם וּבְכָל מַלְכוּתָם מֵאַיִן
‹ there is ‹ their ‹ and in all ‹ of the ‹ the wise ‹ among ‹ for « [kingship]
none kingdoms nations men all befits;

כָּמוֹךָ.⁶ מֵאֵין כָּמוֹךָ יהוה, גָּדוֹל אַתָּה וְגָדוֹל שְׁמֶךָ
‹ is Your ‹ and great ‹ are You ‹ Great « O ‹ like You, ‹ There is « like You.
Name HASHEM! none

בִּגְבוּרָה.⁷ לְךָ זְרוֹעַ עִם גְּבוּרָה, תָּעֹז יָדְךָ תָּרוּם
‹ uplifted « is Your ‹ strength- « power; ‹ with ‹ is the ‹ Yours « in might.
hand, ened arm

יְמִינֶךָ.⁸ לְךָ יוֹם, אַף לְךָ לָיְלָה, אַתָּה הֲכִינוֹתָ מָאוֹר
‹ the ‹ prepared ‹ You « is the ‹ Yours ‹ also « is the ‹ Yours « is Your
luminary night; day, right hand.

וָשָׁמֶשׁ.⁹ אֲשֶׁר בְּיָדוֹ מֶחְקְרֵי אָרֶץ, וְתוֹעֲפוֹת הָרִים
‹ of the ‹ and the « of the ‹ are the hidden ‹ in His ‹ For « and the
mountains summits earth, mysteries power sun.

לוֹ.¹⁰ מִי יְמַלֵּל גְּבוּרוֹת יהוה, יַשְׁמִיעַ כָּל תְּהִלָּתוֹ.¹¹
« of His ‹ all ‹ [who] can « of ‹ the mighty ‹ can ‹ Who « are
praise? make heard HASHEM; acts express His.

---

(1) *Psalms* 108:5. (2) 145:3. (3) 96:4. (4) 95:3. (5) *Deuteronomy* 3:24.
(6) *Jeremiah* 10:7. (7) 10:6. (8) *Psalms* 89:14. (9) 74:16. (10) 95:4. (11) 106:2.

לְךָ יהוה הַגְּדֻלָּה וְהַגְּבוּרָה, וְהַתִּפְאֶרֶת וְהַנֵּצַח
Yours, ⟩ HASHEM, ⟩ is the greatness, ⟩ the strength, ⟩ the glory, ⟩ the triumph, ⟩

וְהַהוֹד, כִּי כֹל בַּשָּׁמַיִם וּבָאָרֶץ; לְךָ יהוה הַמַּמְלָכָה,
and the majesty; ⟪ for ⟩ every-thing ⟩ in heaven ⟩ and on earth [is Yours]; ⟪ Yours, ⟩ HASHEM, ⟩ is the kingdom ⟩

וְהַמִּתְנַשֵּׂא לְכֹל לְרֹאשׁ.¹ לְךָ שָׁמַיִם, אַף לְךָ אָרֶץ,
and the sovereignty ⟩ over every ⟩ leader. ⟪ Yours ⟩ are the heavens, ⟩ also ⟩ Yours ⟩ is the earth; ⟪

תֵּבֵל וּמְלֹאָהּ אַתָּה יְסַדְתָּם.² אַתָּה הִצַּבְתָּ כָּל גְּבוּלוֹת
the world ⟩ and its fullness, ⟩ You ⟩ founded them. ⟪ You ⟩ established ⟩ all ⟩ the boundaries ⟩

אָרֶץ, קַיִץ וָחֹרֶף אַתָּה יְצַרְתָּם.³ אַתָּה רִצַּצְתָּ רָאשֵׁי
of earth; ⟪ summer ⟩ and winter, ⟩ You ⟩ fashioned them. ⟪ You ⟩ crushed ⟩ the heads ⟩

לִוְיָתָן, תִּתְּנֶנּוּ מַאֲכָל לְעָם לְצִיִּים. אַתָּה בָקַעְתָּ מַעְיָן
of Leviathan; ⟪ You will serve it ⟩ as food ⟩ to the ⟩ the desolate people ⟩ [destined] for ⟪ You ⟩ split open ⟩ fountain ⟩
wilderness.

וָנָחַל, אַתָּה הוֹבַשְׁתָּ נַהֲרוֹת אֵיתָן.⁴ אַתָּה פוֹרַרְתָּ
and stream; ⟪ You ⟩ dried ⟩ rivers ⟩ that are mighty. ⟪ You ⟩ shattered ⟩

בְעָזְּךָ יָם, שִׁבַּרְתָּ רָאשֵׁי תַנִּינִים עַל הַמָּיִם.⁵ אַתָּה
with Your might ⟩ the sea; ⟪ You ⟩ smashed ⟩ the heads ⟩ of sea serpents ⟩ upon ⟩ the water. ⟪ You ⟩

מוֹשֵׁל בְּגֵאוּת הַיָּם, בְּשׂוֹא גַלָּיו אַתָּה תְשַׁבְּחֵם.⁶
rule ⟩ the grandeur ⟩ of the sea; ⟪ when it raises ⟩ its waves, ⟩ You ⟩ calm them. ⟪

גָּדוֹל יהוה וּמְהֻלָּל מְאֹד, בְּעִיר אֱלֹהֵינוּ הַר קָדְשׁוֹ.⁷
Great ⟩ is HASHEM ⟩ and much praised, ⟩ in the City ⟩ of our God, ⟩ Mount ⟩ of His Holiness. ⟪

יהוה צְבָאוֹת, אֱלֹהֵי יִשְׂרָאֵל, יוֹשֵׁב הַכְּרֻבִים, אַתָּה
HASHEM, ⟩ Master of Legions, ⟩ God ⟩ of Israel, ⟩ en-throned ⟩ upon the Cherubim, ⟪ it is You ⟩

הוּא הָאֱלֹהִים לְבַדֶּךָ.⁸ אֵל נַעֲרָץ בְּסוֹד קְדוֹשִׁים רַבָּה,
Who ⟩ are God ⟪ alone. ⟩ God ⟪ is ⟩ revered ⟩ in the great assemblage of the holy [angels], ⟪

---

(1) *I Chronicles* 29:11. (2) *Psalms* 89:12. (3) 74:17. (4) 74:14-15. (5) 74:13. (6) 89:10. (7) 48:2. (8) *Isaiah* 37:16.

וְנוֹרָא עַל כָּל סְבִיבָיו.[1] וְיוֹדוּ שָׁמַיִם פִּלְאֲךָ יהוה, אַף

〈 also 《 Hashem, 〈 Your 〈 will the 〈 Acknowl- 《 who sur- 〈 all 〈 over 〈 and is
wonders, heavens edge round Him. awesome

אֱמוּנָתְךָ בִּקְהַל קְדֹשִׁים.[2] לְכוּ נְרַנְּנָה לַיהוה, נָרִיעָה

〈 let us 《 to 〈 Let us sing 〈 Come! 《 of holy 〈 in the 〈 Your
call out Hashem, joyfully ones. assembly faithfulness,

לְצוּר יִשְׁעֵנוּ. נְקַדְּמָה פָנָיו בְּתוֹדָה, בִּזְמִרוֹת נָרִיעַ

〈 let us 〈 with praiseful 《 with 〈 Him 〈 Let us greet 《 of our 〈 to the
call out songs thanksgiving, salvation. Rock

לוֹ.[3] צֶדֶק וּמִשְׁפָּט מְכוֹן כִּסְאֶךָ, חֶסֶד וֶאֱמֶת יְקַדְּמוּ

〈 precede 〈 and 〈 kindness 《 of Your 〈 are the 〈 and 〈 Righteous- 《 to
truth throne; foundation justice ness Him.

פָנֶיךָ.[4] אֲשֶׁר יַחְדָּו נַמְתִּיק סוֹד, בְּבֵית אֱלֹהִים נְהַלֵּךְ

〈 let us 〈 of God 〈 in the 《 counsel; 〈 let us 〈 together 〈 For 《 Your coun-
walk House take sweet tenance.

בְּרָגֶשׁ.[5] אֲשֶׁר לוֹ הַיָּם וְהוּא עָשָׂהוּ, וְיַבֶּשֶׁת יָדָיו

〈 His 《 and the 《 perfected 〈 and He 〈 is the 〈 His 〈 For 《 in company.
hands dry land, it, sea

יָצָרוּ.[6] אֲשֶׁר בְּיָדוֹ נֶפֶשׁ כָּל חָי, וְרוּחַ כָּל בְּשַׂר אִישׁ.[7]

《 mankind. 〈 of all 〈 and the 《 the 〈 of 〈 is the 〈 in His 〈 For 《 fashioned.
spirit living all soul hand

❖ הַנְּשָׁמָה לָךְ וְהַגּוּף פָּעֳלָךְ, חוּסָה עַל עֲמָלָךְ.

《 Your 〈 on 〈 take pity 《 is Your 〈 and the 〈 is 〈 The soul
labor. handiwork; body Yours

הַנְּשָׁמָה לָךְ וְהַגּוּף שֶׁלָּךְ, יהוה עֲשֵׂה לְמַעַן שְׁמֶךָ.

《 of Your 〈 for the 〈 act 〈 O 《 is Yours; 〈 and the 〈 is 〈 The soul
Name. sake Hashem, body Yours

אָתָאנוּ עַל שִׁמְךָ, יהוה, עֲשֵׂה לְמַעַן שְׁמֶךָ. בַּעֲבוּר

〈 [act] 《 of Your 〈 for the 〈 act 《 O 《 Your 〈 [relying] 〈 We have
because of Name; sake Hashem; Name, on come

כְּבוֹד שִׁמְךָ, כִּי אֵל חַנּוּן וְרַחוּם שְׁמֶךָ. לְמַעַן

〈 For the 《 is Your 〈 and 〈 Who is 〈 God 〈 for 《 of Your 〈 the glory
sake Name. Merciful Gracious Name,

שִׁמְךָ יהוה, וְסָלַחְתָּ לַעֲוֺנֵנוּ כִּי רַב הוּא.[8]

〈 it is great. 〈 though 〈 our 〈 forgive 《 Hashem, 〈 of Your
iniquity, Name,

---

(1) Psalms 89:8. (2) 89:6. (3) 95:1-2. (4) 89:15. (5) 55:15. (6) 95:5. (7) Job 12:10. (8) Cf. Psalms 25:11.

CONGREGATION, THEN *CHAZZAN:*

סְלַח לָֽנוּ אָבִֽינוּ, כִּי בְרוֹב אִוַּֽלְתֵּֽנוּ שָׁגִֽינוּ,

《 we have 〈 of our folly 〈 in the 〈 for 〈 our Father, 〈 us, 〈 Forgive
erred;   abundance

מְחַל לָֽנוּ מַלְכֵּֽנוּ, כִּי רַבּוּ עֲוֹנֵֽינוּ.

《   our   〈 many 〈 for 〈 our King, 〈 us, 〈 pardon
iniquities.   are

סליחה נב / SELICHAH 52
(פתיחה)

ALL:

אֵלֶֽיךָ לֵב וָנֶֽפֶשׁ נִשְׁפָּךְ* כַּמַּֽיִם,[1]

《 like water, 〈 we pour out*〈 and soul 〈 heart 〈 To You

כֻּלָּֽנוּ אֶל אֵל בַּשָּׁמָֽיִם.[2]

《 in Heaven. 〈 God 〈 to 〈 all of us,

אֵתָֽיוּ זְקֵנִים עִם עוֹלְלֵיכֶם,

《 your children; 〈 with 〈 O elders, 〈 Come,

הִזַּכּוּ וְהָסִֽירוּ רֹעַ מַעַלְלֵיכֶם.[3]

《 of your deeds. 〈 the 〈 and 〈 purify
evil   remove   yourselves

לְפָנָיו נַרְבֶּה תְּחִנָּה וּבַקָּשָׁה,

《 and entreaty, 〈 supplication 〈 let us 〈 Before
increase   Him,

עַל זֹאת מֵאֱלֹהֵֽינוּ נְבַקֵּֽשָׁה.[4]

《 let us request: 〈 of our God 〈 this 〈 for

יִרְגַּז הַטּוֹב עַל מְנֻוָּל,[5] דַּרְכּוֹ יַעֲזֹב פּוֹשֵֽׁעַ וְעָוָּל.[6]

《 and 〈 — the 《 let him 〈 his 《 the 〈 against 〈 the 〈 Let
evildoer.   willful   abandon   way   immoral [Evil   Good   angered
sinner   Inclination];   [Inclination]   be

הָכִֽינוּ לֵב וְהֵטִֽיבוּ מַחֲשָׁבָה, כִּי גָדוֹל כֹּחַ הַתְּשׁוּבָה.[7]

《 of repentance. 〈 is the 〈 great 〈 for 《 our thought, 〈 turn to 〈 [our] 〈 Prepare
power   good   heart,

---

(1) Cf. *Lamentations* 2:19. (2) 3:41. (3) Cf. *Isaiah* 1:16. (4) Cf. *Ezra* 8:23.
(5) See *Berachos* 5a; see also commentary to *Selichah* 24. (6) Cf. *Isaiah* 55:7. (7) See *Yoma* 86a.

◈§ **אֵלֶֽיךָ לֵב וָנֶֽפֶשׁ נִשְׁפָּךְ** — *To You heart and
soul we pour out.* This פְּתִיחָה, *introductory selichah,* contains the signature אֵלִיָה

בַּר שְׁמַעְיָה חֲזַק, *Eliyah bar Shemayah, may
he be strong* [see prefatory comment to
Selichah 14].

בִּקְהַל עַם מִלִּין נַכְבִּיר,[1] וְלֹא יִמְאַס אֵל כַּבִּיר.[2]

‹‹ Almighty. ‹ will ‹ show ‹ for not ‹‹ let us ‹ words ‹ people, ‹ Among the
the God contempt increase, [of prayer] congregated

רוֹצֶה תְשׁוּבַת בּוֹגֵד וְנִשְׁחָת,[3] לְהָשִׁיב נַפְשׁוֹ מִנִּי שָׁחַת.[4]

‹‹ ruin. ‹ from ‹ his ‹ to retrieve ‹‹ and ‹ of the ‹ the ‹ He
soul corrupt, rebellious repentance desires

שְׁמַע תַּחֲנוּן הַעֲתֵר לִמְבַקְשֶׁיךָ,

‹‹ of those who ‹ accede ‹‹ [our] sup- ‹ O Hear
appeal to You, [to the prayer] plication;

בְּנָשְׂאֵנוּ יָדֵינוּ אֶל דְּבִיר קָדְשֶׁךָ.[5]

‹‹ Your Holy Sanctuary. ‹ toward ‹ our hands ‹ as we raise

יִהְיוּ נָא אִמְרֵי פִינוּ לְרָצוֹן,[6]

‹‹ find favor, ‹‹ of our ‹‹ —the ex- ‹‹ please, ‹ May
mouths — pressions they,

וְכַפֵּר עַל חַטֹּאתֵינוּ[7] אֹנֶס וְרָצוֹן.

‹‹ and ‹ both ‹‹ our sins, ‹ for ‹ and
deliberate. accidental atone

חֲשֹׁב זְכֹר קְרִיאַת נְעִימֶיךָ,

‹‹ of Your pleasing ‹ the call ‹ re- ‹‹ Consider,
ones [our Patriarchs], member

וְהִנָּחֵם עַל הָרָעָה לְעַמֶּךָ.[8]

‹‹ [meant] for ‹ the evil ‹ from ‹ and relent
Your people.

וַעֲשֵׂה חֵפֶץ עֲבָדֶיךָ וִישַׁעַשְׁעוּן תַּנְחוּמֶיךָ,[9]

‹‹ delight them, ‹ and let ‹‹ of Your ‹ the ‹ Grant
Your solace servants, desire

סְמוּכִים בְּחַסְדֶּךָ וּבְטוּחִים עַל רַחֲמֶיךָ.

‹‹ Your mercy. ‹ in ‹ and trust ‹ on Your kindness, ‹ [for] they rely

ALL:

כִּי עַל רַחֲמֶיךָ הָרַבִּים[10] אָנוּ בְטוּחִים, וְעַל צִדְקוֹתֶיךָ

‹ Your ‹ and ‹‹ trust, ‹ we ‹ that is ‹ Your ‹ upon ‹ For
righteousness upon abundant mercy

אָנוּ נִשְׁעָנִים, וְלִסְלִיחוֹתֶיךָ אָנוּ מְקַוִּים, וְלִישׁוּעָתֶךָ

‹ and for Your ‹‹ hope, ‹ we ‹ and for Your ‹‹ rely, ‹ we
salvation forgiveness

---

(1) *Job* 35:16. (2) Cf. 36:5. (3) See *Ezekiel* 18:23. (4) *Job* 33:30. (5) Cf. *Psalms* 28:2.
(6) Cf. 19:15. (7) 79:9. (8) *Exodus* 32:12. (9) Cf. *Psalms* 94:19. (10) *Daniel* 9:18.

אָנוּ מְצַפִּים. אַתָּה הוּא מֶלֶךְ, אוֹהֵב צְדָקוֹת מִקֶּדֶם,

‹ since the ‹ righteous- ‹ Who ‹ the King ‹ are ‹ You ‹ await ‹ we
beginning ness loves eagerly.
of time,

מַעֲבִיר עֲוֹנוֹת עַמּוֹ, וּמֵסִיר חַטֹּאת יְרֵאָיו. כּוֹרֵת

‹ He ‹ of those who ‹ the sins ‹ and ‹ of His ‹ the ‹ Who
established revere Him. removes people iniquities overlooks

בְּרִית לָרִאשׁוֹנִים, וּמְקַיֵּם שְׁבוּעָה לָאַחֲרוֹנִים. אַתָּה

‹ You ‹ to the descendants. ‹ [His] oath ‹ and fulfills ‹ with the ancestors ‹ a covenant

הוּא, שֶׁיָּרַדְתָּ בַּעֲנַן כְּבוֹדֶךָ עַל הַר סִינַי,[1] וְהֶרְאֵיתָ

‹ and You ‹ Sinai, ‹ Mount ‹ upon ‹ of Your ‹ in the ‹ Who ‹ are the
showed glory cloud descended One

דַּרְכֵי טוּבְךָ לְמֹשֶׁה עַבְדֶּךָ.[2] וְאָרְחוֹת חֲסָדֶיךָ גִּלִּיתָ

‹ You ‹ of Your ‹ The paths ‹ Your ‹ to Moses ‹ of Your ‹ the
revealed kindness servant. goodness ways

לוֹ, וְהוֹדַעְתּוֹ כִּי אַתָּה אֵל רַחוּם וְחַנּוּן, אֶרֶךְ אַפַּיִם

‹ to ‹ Slow ‹ and ‹ Compas- ‹ God, ‹ You are ‹ that ‹ and You ‹ to
anger Gracious, sionate let him know him,

וְרַב חֶסֶד[3] וּמַרְבֶּה לְהֵיטִיב, וּמַנְהִיג אֶת כָּל הָעוֹלָם

‹ world ‹ the whole ‹ and Who ‹ beneficent, ‹ Who is ‹ in Kind- ‹ and
guides ness, Abundant
abundantly

כֻּלּוֹ בְּמִדַּת הָרַחֲמִים. ❖ וְכֵן כָּתוּב, וַיֹּאמֶר אֲנִי אַעֲבִיר

‹ shall cause ‹ "I ‹ And He ‹ it is ‹ And so ‹ of Mercy. ‹ with the ‹ in its
to pass said, written: Attribute entirety

כָּל טוּבִי עַל פָּנֶיךָ, וְקָרָאתִי בְשֵׁם יהוה לְפָנֶיךָ,

‹ before ‹ HASHEM ‹ with the ‹ and I shall ‹ your ‹ before ‹ My ‹ all
you; Name call out face, goodness

וְחַנֹּתִי אֶת אֲשֶׁר אָחֹן, וְרִחַמְתִּי אֶת אֲשֶׁר אֲרַחֵם.[4]

‹ I choose to ‹ whom- ‹ to ‹ and I shall ‹ I choose to ‹ whom- ‹ to ‹ I shall
show mercy." ever show mercy show favor, ever show favor

ALL, WHILE STANDING

אֵל אֶרֶךְ אַפַּיִם אַתָּה,

‹ You are, ‹ to anger, ‹ Who is slow ‹ God

וּבַעַל הָרַחֲמִים נִקְרֵאתָ, וְדֶרֶךְ תְּשׁוּבָה הוֹרֵיתָ.

‹ You have ‹ of ‹ and the ‹ You are ‹ of Mercy ‹ and
taught. repentance way called; Master

(1) Cf. *Exodus* 34:5. (2) Cf. 33:13. (3) 34:6. (4) 33:19.

גְּדֻלַּת רַחֲמֶיךָ וַחֲסָדֶיךָ,
⟨ and Your ⟨ of Your ⟨ The
   kindness   mercy   greatness

תִּזְכּוֹר הַיּוֹם וּבְכָל יוֹם לְזֶרַע יְדִידֶיךָ.
《 of Your ⟨ for the 《 day, ⟨ and ⟨ this day ⟨ may You
  beloved ones. offspring   every   remember,

תֵּפֶן אֵלֵינוּ בְּרַחֲמִים,
《 in mercy, ⟨ to us ⟨ Turn

כִּי אַתָּה הוּא בַּעַל הָרַחֲמִים.
《 of Mercy. ⟨ the Master ⟨ are ⟨ You ⟨ for

בְּתַחֲנוּן וּבִתְפִלָּה פָּנֶיךָ נְקַדֵּם, כְּהוֹדַעְתָּ לֶעָנָיו מִקֶּדֶם.
《 in ancient ⟨ to the   ⟨ in the manner 《 we ⟨ Your ⟨ and prayer ⟨ With
   times.   humble one that You made approach, Presence   supplication
             [Moses]   known

מֵחֲרוֹן אַפְּךָ שׁוּב,[1] כְּמוֹ בְתוֹרָתְךָ כָּתוּב.[2]
《 it is   ⟨ in Your Torah ⟨ as   《 turn ⟨ of Your ⟨ From the
  written.   back,   anger   fierceness

וּבְצֵל כְּנָפֶיךָ נֶחֱסֶה[3] וְנִתְלוֹנָן, כְּיוֹם וַיֵּרֶד יהוה בֶּעָנָן.
《 in a ⟨ when HASHEM ⟨ as on 《 and may ⟨ may we find ⟨ of Your ⟨ In the
 cloud.   descended   the day   we dwell,   shelter   wings   shadow

❖ תַּעֲבוֹר עַל פֶּשַׁע וְתִמְחֶה אָשָׁם,
《 guilt, ⟨ and erase ⟨ sin ⟨ Overlook

כְּיוֹם וַיִּתְיַצֵּב עִמּוֹ שָׁם.
《 there. ⟨ with him ⟨ when He ⟨ as on the
         [Moses]   [God] stood   day

תַּאֲזִין שַׁוְעָתֵנוּ וְתַקְשִׁיב מֶנּוּ מַאֲמַר,
《 [our]   ⟨ from ⟨ and hear ⟨ to our cry ⟨ Give heed
 declaration, us

כְּיוֹם וַיִּקְרָא בְשֵׁם יהוה,[4] וְשָׁם נֶאֱמַר:
《 it was said: ⟨ and 《 of HASHEM, ⟨ with the ⟨ when He ⟨ as on
              there   Name   called out   the day

CONGREGATION, THEN *CHAZZAN:*

וַיַּעֲבֹר יהוה עַל פָּנָיו וַיִּקְרָא:
《   and   《 [Moses'] ⟨ before ⟨ And HASHEM passed
 proclaimed: face,

(1) Cf. *Exodus* 32:12. (2) See 32:14. (3) Cf. *Psalms* 36:8. (4) *Exodus* 34:5.

CONGREGATION AND *CHAZZAN* RECITE LOUDLY AND IN UNISON:

יְהֹוָה, יְהֹוָה, אֵל, רַחוּם, וְחַנּוּן, אֶרֶךְ אַפַּיִם,

⟨ to anger, ⟨ Slow 《 and ⟨ Compassionate ⟨ God, ⟨ HASHEM, ⟨ HASHEM,
Gracious,

וְרַב חֶסֶד, וֶאֱמֶת, נֹצֵר חֶסֶד לָאֲלָפִים, נֹשֵׂא עָוֹן,

⟨ of ⟨ Forgiver 《 for thousands ⟨ of ⟨ Preserver 《 and ⟨ in ⟨ and
iniquity, [of generations], kindness Truth, Kindness Abundant

וָפֶשַׁע, וְחַטָּאָה, וְנַקֵּה.[1] וְסָלַחְתָּ לַעֲוֹנֵנוּ וּלְחַטָּאתֵנוּ

《 and our sins, ⟨ our ⟨ May You 《 and Who ⟨ and inadvertent ⟨ willful sin,
iniquities forgive **absolves.** sin,

וּנְחַלְתָּנוּ.[2] סְלַח לָנוּ אָבִינוּ כִּי חָטָאנוּ, מְחַל לָנוּ

⟨ us, ⟨ pardon 《 we have ⟨ for 《 our Father, ⟨ us, ⟨ Forgive 《 and make us
sinned; Your heritage.

מַלְכֵּנוּ כִּי פָשָׁעְנוּ. כִּי אַתָּה אֲדֹנָי טוֹב וְסַלָּח, וְרַב

⟨ and 《 and ⟨ are ⟨ O Lord, ⟨ You, ⟨ For 《 we have ⟨ for 《 our King,
abundantly forgiving, good willfully sinned.

חֶסֶד לְכָל קֹרְאֶיךָ.[3]

《 who call ⟨ to all ⟨ kind
upon You.

פסוקי הקדמה לסליחה נג / PREFATORY VERSES TO SELICHAH 53

כִּי דֹרֵשׁ דָּמִים אוֹתָם זָכָר, לֹא שָׁכַח צַעֲקַת עֲנָוִים.[4]

《 of the ⟨ the cry ⟨ He has not 《 has remembered ⟨ of ⟨ the ⟨ For
humble. forgotten them; blood Avenger

שׁוּב מֵחֲרוֹן אַפֶּךָ, וְהִנָּחֵם עַל הָרָעָה לְעַמֶּךָ.[5] תָּבֹא

⟨ Come 《 against Your ⟨ the evil ⟨ re- ⟨ and ⟨ of Your ⟨ from the ⟨ Relent
people. garding reconsider anger flaring

אֵלֶיךָ תְּפִלָּתֵנוּ אֶל הֵיכַל קָדְשֶׁךָ.[6]

《 Your holy Temple. ⟨ to ⟨ shall our prayer ⟨ to You

כְּרַחֵם אָב עַל בָּנִים, כֵּן תְּרַחֵם יהוה עָלֵינוּ.[7]

《 on us. ⟨ HASHEM, ⟨ have ⟨ so 《 his ⟨ toward ⟨ a ⟨ As merciful as
mercy, children, father is

לַיהוה הַיְשׁוּעָה, עַל עַמְּךָ בִרְכָתֶךָ סֶּלָה.[8] יהוה

⟨ HASHEM, 《 Selah. 《 is Your ⟨ Your ⟨ upon 《 is salvation, ⟨ To HASHEM
blessing, people

---

(1) *Exodus* 34:6-7 (2) 34:9. (3) *Psalms* 86:5. (4) 9:13. (5) *Exodus* 32:12.
(6) Cf. *Jonah* 2:8.(7) Cf. *Psalms* 103:13. (8) 3:9.

צְבָאוֹת עִמָּנוּ, מִשְׂגָּב לָנוּ אֱלֹהֵי יַעֲקֹב סֶלָה.[1]

‹ Master of ‹ is the God ‹ for us ‹ a ≪ is with us, ‹ of Jacob, ≪ Selah.
Legions,   stronghold

יהוה צְבָאוֹת, אַשְׁרֵי אָדָם בֹּטֵחַ בָּךְ.[2] יהוה הוֹשִׁיעָה,

≪ HASHEM, ‹ Master of ≪ praise- ‹ — ‹ is the ‹ who ‹ in ≪ HASHEM, ‹ save!
Legions, worthy man trusts You.

הַמֶּלֶךְ יַעֲנֵנוּ בְיוֹם קָרְאֵנוּ.[3]

≪ we call. ‹ on the ‹ answer us ‹ May the
day King

IN MOST CONGREGATIONS THE FOLLOWING VERSES ARE RECITED ALOUD RESPONSIVELY,
AS INDICATED; IN OTHERS THEY ARE RECITED SILENTLY.

CONGREGATION, ALOUD, FOLLOWED BY *CHAZZAN,* ALOUD:

סְלַח נָא לַעֲוֹן הָעָם הַזֶּה כְּגֹדֶל חַסְדֶּךָ, וְכַאֲשֶׁר

‹ just as ≪ of Your ‹ according to ‹ of this people ‹ the ‹ please, ‹ Forgive,
kindness, the greatness iniquity

נָשָׂאתָה לָעָם הַזֶּה מִמִּצְרַיִם וְעַד הֵנָּה,[4] וְשָׁם נֶאֱמַר:

≪ it was ‹ And ≪ now. ‹ until ‹ from Egypt ‹ this people ‹ You have
said: there forgiven

ALL, ALOUD AND IN UNISON:

וַיֹּאמֶר יהוה סָלַחְתִּי כִּדְבָרֶךָ.[5]

≪ according to ‹ *I have forgiven* ≪ *And HASHEM said:*
your word!

ALL CONTINUE:

הַטֵּה אֱלֹהַי אָזְנְךָ וּשֲׁמָע, פְּקַח עֵינֶיךָ וּרְאֵה

‹ and see ‹ Your eyes ‹ open ≪ and listen; ‹ Your ear, ‹ my God, ‹ Incline,

שֹׁמְמֹתֵינוּ, וְהָעִיר אֲשֶׁר נִקְרָא שִׁמְךָ עָלֶיהָ, כִּי לֹא

‹ not ‹ for ≪ upon; ‹ Your Name is ‹ which ‹ and that ‹ our desolation
proclaimed [of] the city

עַל צִדְקֹתֵינוּ אֲנַחְנוּ מַפִּילִים תַּחֲנוּנֵינוּ לְפָנֶיךָ,

≪ before ‹ our ‹ cast ‹ do we ‹ of our ‹ because
You; supplications righteousness

כִּי עַל רַחֲמֶיךָ הָרַבִּים. אֲדֹנָי שְׁמָעָה, אֲדֹנָי סְלָחָה,

≪ forgive; ‹ O Lord, ≪ heed; ‹ O Lord, ≪ which is ‹ of Your ‹ be- ‹ but
abundant. compassion, cause

---

(1) *Psalms* 46:8. (2) 84:13. (3) 20:10. (4) *Numbers* 14:19. (5) 14:20.

אֲדֹנָי הַקְשִׁיבָה, וַעֲשֵׂה אַל תְּאַחַר, לְמַעַנְךָ אֱלֹהָי,

《 my God, 〈 for Your sake, 《 delay; 〈 do not 《 and act, 〈 be attentive, 〈 O Lord,

כִּי שִׁמְךָ נִקְרָא עַל עִירְךָ וְעַל עַמֶּךָ.[1]

《 Your 〈 and 〈 Your 〈 upon 〈 is 〈 Your 〈 for
people. upon City proclaimed Name

סְלִיחָה נג / SELICHAH 53

ALL:

אֱלֹהֵינוּ וֵאלֹהֵי אֲבוֹתֵינוּ:

《 of our forefathers: 〈 and God 〈 Our God

אֲנִי קְרָאתִיךָ* כִּי תַעֲנֵנִי אֵל,[2]

《 O 〈 [I am certain]〈 for 〈 have called 〈 I
God; that You will to You,*
answer me,

בִּקַּשְׁתִּי רַחֲמִים כְּרָשׁ בְּפֶתַח שׁוֹאֵל,

《 begs. 〈 [who] at the 〈 like a 〈 for mercy 〈 I ask
door pauper

גְּדֶל נוֹרְאוֹתֶיךָ בְּצֶדֶק עֲנוֹת הוֹאֵל,[3]

《 [show] 〈 to answer 〈 with 〈 of Your 〈 [In] the
Your desire, [my prayers] righteousness awesomeness, greatness

---

(1) *Daniel* 9:18-19. (2) *Psalms* 17:6. (3) Cf. 65:6.

◆§ אֲנִי קְרָאתִיךָ — *I have called to You.* The first twenty-two lines of this *selichah* form an *aleph-beis* acrostic. This is followed by the *paytan*'s signature — שִׁמְעוֹן בַּר יִצְחָק, חֲזַק וֶאֱמָץ, *Shimon bar Yitzchak, may he be strong and persevere.* Known as R' Shimon HaGadol, he lived in Mainz, Germany, about 950-1020, and he served on that city's *beis din* together with R' Gershom Meor HaGolah [see prefatory comment to *Selichah* 12].

Because of his great wisdom and impressive appearance, R' Shimon was often sent by the community to persuade monarchs and clergymen to abolish harsh decrees proposed against the Jews, and in many cases he succeeded. In a responsum, Rabbeinu Tam describes him as, "R' Shimon ben Yitzchak HaGadol, with whom miracles were common."

According to a popular story, R' Shimon had two sons, Yitzchak and Elchanan. Elchanan was kidnaped by the family's

trusted gentile maid, who handed him over to a monastery where he was raised in the Christian faith. His keen mind absorbed so much knowledge that he was continually raised in rank, until he eventually became pope. Some time after his son's election, R' Shimon journeyed to Rome in order to gain an audience with the new pope and plead with him to nullify a cruel edict against the Jews. During this visit the pope invited his guest to play a game of chess. R' Shimon, a master at chess who had never before been defeated, was stunned when the pope checkmated him. R' Shimon, who had taught chess to his sons, suspected that the pope might have acquired his chess training from him. When he questioned the pope concerning his skills, the truth surfaced, and father and son embraced.

After issuing many decrees in favor of the Jews, Elchanan disappeared with his father and became an outstanding scholar.

דֵּעַת הַכֹּל כִּי יֵשׁ אֱלֹהִים בְּיִשְׂרָאֵל.¹

in Israel. ‹ a God ‹ there ‹ that ‹ by all ‹ [so that] it
                is   be known

הֲלוֹא אַתָּה מִקֶּדֶם אֱלֹהַי קְדֹשִׁי,²

my Holy ‹ been my ‹ from days ‹ You ‹ Have not
One?   God,   of old

וְלָמָּה נָמוּת* בְּלַחַץ וּבְקְשִׁי,

and ‹ through ‹ must we ‹ Then why
hardship?   oppression   die,*

זְכֹר וְעוֹרֵר חֶסֶד כְּאָז³ לְחַדְּשִׁי,

[You] ‹ so that ‹ [Your] ‹ and ‹ Re-
renew us; [to the good] kindness   arouse   member
        times of old

חָרְבוֹתַי תָּשִׁיב וְכוֹנֵן מְקוֹם מִקְדָּשִׁי.

of my ‹ the place ‹ and re- ‹ restore, ‹ my ruins
Sanctuary.   establish

טוֹב אַתָּה לְקוֹיֶךָ* לְנֶפֶשׁ תִּדְרְשֶׁךָ,⁴

that seeks You; ‹ to the soul ‹ to those who ‹ You are ‹ Good
                 trust in You,*

יִחַלְנוּ לָךְ בְּעֵת צָרָה לְדָרְשֶׁךָ,

to seek You. ‹ of ‹ in [our] ‹ for ‹ we have
        trouble   time   You,   hoped

---

(1) Cf. *I Samuel* 17:46. (2) Cf. *Habakkuk* 1:12. (3) Cf. *Jeremiah* 2:2. (4) Cf. *Lamentations* 3:25.

וְלָמָּה נָמוּת — *Then why must we die.* The *paytan* often switches from singular to plural. Sometimes, he speaks as an individual Jew; at other times, he is the voice of the nation collectively. Alternatively, he uses the singular to indicate the nation as a whole, and the plural to show the nation as a group of individuals. [This phenomenon is far from rare in *piyutim*.]

In some cases it is possible to trace the shift in number to the Scriptural source verses upon which the *paytan* bases his words. For example, since the first two stanzas of this *selichah* are written in the first person, we would expect the phrase וְלָמָּה אָמוּת, *then why must I die*. But that form does not appear in *Tanach*. However, the plural form וְלָמָּה נָמוּת appears three times (*Genesis* 47:15,19; *Deuteronomy* 5:22). Thus, the *paytan* uses the plural here. Similarly, the later stiches are

based on Scriptural verses that appear in the plural and so they are also in the plural here.

טוֹב אַתָּה לְקוֹיֶךָ — *Good You are to those who trust in You.* The Talmud resolves two contradictory verses. One verse (*Psalms* 145:9) states: טוֹב ה׳ לַכֹּל, *HASHEM is good to all*; while a second verse (*Lamentations* 3:25) states: טוֹב ה׳ לְקוֹו, *HASHEM is good to those who trust in Him!* R' Elazar explains this with a parable. When one waters his garden, he waters the entire garden [i.e., once he turns on the hose for the healthy thriving plants, he simultaneously waters every plant in the garden, because little or no extra effort is needed]. However, when he performs chores such as digging and pruning that require additional effort for each plant, he attends to the thriving plants and ignores the others.

Similarly, with regard to sustenance, with-

כָּל הַיּוֹם הֹרַגְנוּ עֲלֶיךָ¹ עַל שֵׁם קָדְשֶׁךָ,

《 of Your ⟨ of the ⟨ for the ⟨ for Your ⟨ we are ⟨ day ⟨ Every
   holiness,   Name   sake   sake,   killed

לֹא נָסוֹג לִבֵּנוּ² מִלְּבָרֶכְךָ וּלְהַקְדִּישֶׁךָ.

《 and sanctifying ⟨ from blessing ⟨ has our ⟨ turned ⟨ [yet]
   You.   You   heart   [back]   not

מִתִּגְרַת יָדְךָ, כָּלֵינוּ בְּאַף וּבְחֵמָה,³

《 and by ⟨ by ⟨ we are ⟨ of Your ⟨ From the
   wrath;   anger   devastated   hand   attack

נִדְמֵינוּ כִּכְלִי רֵיק וְכִסָּתְנוּ כְלִמָּה,⁴

《 with ⟨ and we are ⟨ that is ⟨ a vessel ⟨ we are like
   humiliation.   covered   empty,

סְכַּרְנוּ בְּיַד אֲדוֹנִים קָשִׁים לְהוֹמְמָה,⁵

《 causing us to ⟨ who are ⟨ of masters ⟨ into the ⟨ We are
   panic,   hard,   hands   delivered

עַד יַשְׁקִיף וְיֵרֶא יהוה מִן הַשָּׁמֶיְמָה.⁶

《 Heaven. ⟨ from 《 — HASHEM — 《 and ⟨ He gazes ⟨ until
   takes notice   down

פְּצֵנוּ וְהַצִּילֵנוּ מִיַּד בְּנֵי נֵכָר,⁷

《 of strangers. ⟨ from ⟨ and ⟨ Release
   the hand   rescue us   us

צוֹמְתִים חַיֵּינוּ בְּשָׁפְךְ דָּמֵנוּ לְהַעֲכֵר,

《 to torment us. ⟨ our blood ⟨ spilling 《 our life, ⟨ They close off

קְרָא שְׁלוּמַת זָרִים גְּמוּל וְשָׂכָר,

《 and ⟨ [their] 《 against the ⟨ retribution ⟨ Decree
   repayment,   punishment   strangers,

רְאוֹת כִּי דֹרֵשׁ דָּמִים אוֹתָם זָכָר.⁸

《 has remembered ⟨ of blood ⟨ the ⟨ that ⟨ [that all
   them.   Avenger   may] see

שׁוּבֵנוּ אֵלֶיךָ וַחֲרוֹן אַפְּךָ הָפֵר,⁹

《 annul; ⟨ of Your ⟨ and the 《 to You, ⟨ Return us
   wrath   flaring

---

(1) Cf. *Psalms* 44:23. (2) Cf. 44:19. (3) Cf. 39:11, 90:7. (4) Cf. *Jeremiah* 3:25, *Psalms* 69:8.
(5) Cf. *Isaiah* 19:4; some editions of *Selichos* read צוֹרְרִים קָשִׁים, *enemies who are hard*.
(6) Cf. *Lamentations* 3:50. (7) Cf. *Psalms* 144:11. (8) 9:13. (9) Cf. 85:5.

---

out which man cannot survive, HASHEM *is good to all.* But regarding special Divine protection, HASHEM *is good to those who trust in Him (Sanhedrin 39b).*

תִּכְבֹּשׁ עֲוֹנוֹתֵינוּ¹ וְחַטֹּאתֵינוּ תְכַפֵּר,

» provide ‹ and for ‹ our iniquities ‹ suppress
atonement. our sins

שֵׁפֶל מְרוּדֵנוּ עֲלֵה וְלֹא נֵחָפֵר,

« that we not « elevate, ‹ of our ‹ The
be ashamed, wretched state lowliness

בְּרֶשֶׁם יְקָרְךָ צוּפָם חָקְקֵנוּ לְחַיִּים בַּסֵּפֶר.

«in the Book. ‹ for life ‹ etch us « look ‹ [who to the ‹ as You
forward, revelation] of inscribe
Your glory [those]

❖ חַזֵּק וְאַמֵּץ יָדַיִם וּבִרְכַּיִם כּוֹשְׁלוֹת,²

« that are failing; ‹ and knees ‹ [our] ‹ and ‹ Strengthen
hands support

פַּנֵּה דֶרֶךְ עַמֶּךָ וְהָרֵם מִכְשׁוֹלוֹת,³

« the obstacles. ‹ remove « for Your ‹ the ‹ clear
people; road

יֶעֱרַב לְפָנֶיךָ תַּחַן כִּשַׁי וְעוֹלוֹת,

« and burnt- ‹ as ‹ may [our] sup- ‹ to You ‹ As
offerings, presents plications be pleasing

וְאַתָּה קָדוֹשׁ יוֹשֵׁב תְּהִלּוֹת.*⁴

« the praises ‹ enthroned ‹ the Holy ‹ for You
[of Israel]. upon One are

ALL, WHILE STANDING:

אֵל מֶלֶךְ יוֹשֵׁב עַל כִּסֵּא רַחֲמִים, מִתְנַהֵג

‹ Who acts « of mercy, ‹ the throne ‹ on ‹ Who sits ‹ King ‹ O God,

בַּחֲסִידוּת, מוֹחֵל עֲוֹנוֹת עַמּוֹ, מַעֲבִיר רִאשׁוֹן

‹ [sins,] one ‹ Who « of His ‹ the sins ‹ Who « with kindness,
removes people, pardons

רִאשׁוֹן,⁵ מַרְבֶּה מְחִילָה לְחַטָּאִים וּסְלִיחָה לַפּוֹשְׁעִים,

« to willful ‹ and ‹ to unintentional « pardon ‹ Who abun- « by one,
sinners, forgiveness sinners dantly grants

---

(1) Cf. *Micah* 7:19. (2) Cf. *Isaiah* 35:3. (3) Cf. 57:14. (4) *Psalms* 22:4. (5) *Rosh Hashanah* 17a.

וְאַתָּה קָדוֹשׁ יוֹשֵׁב תְּהִלּוֹת — *For You are the Holy One enthroned upon the praises [of Israel].* The translation follows *Rabbi Samson Raphael Hirsch* (to *Psalms* 22:4). *Targum* renders: *You are the Holy One, Who established the world upon Israel's praises;* the world was created for the sake of Israel's

performance of the Divine service [which, in the absence of the *Beis HaMikdash*, is limited to verbal praise]. This is in accord with the Mishnah (*Avos* 1:2) that states: "The world depends on three things: on Torah study; on the [Divine] service, and on kind deeds." [See also *Taanis* 27b.]

עֹשֶׂה צְדָקוֹת עִם כָּל בָּשָׂר וָרוּחַ, לֹא כְרָעָתָם

⟨ in accord with ⟨ — not ⟨⟨ and ⟨ [beings ⟨ all ⟨ with ⟨ acts of ⟨ Who
their wickedness   spirit   of] flesh   generosity   performs

תִּגְמוֹל. ❖ אֵל הוֹרֵיתָ לָּנוּ לוֹמַר שְׁלֹשׁ עֶשְׂרֵה, וּזְכוֹר

⟨ remem- ⟨⟨ the Thirteen ⟨ to ⟨ us ⟨ You ⟨ O God, ⟨⟨ do You
ber   [Attributes of Mercy];   recite   taught   repay them!

לָּנוּ הַיּוֹם בְּרִית שְׁלֹשׁ עֶשְׂרֵה, כְּמוֹ שֶׁהוֹדַעְתָּ לֶעָנָיו

⟨ to the humble ⟨ You made ⟨ as ⟨⟨ of [these] Thirteen, ⟨ the ⟨ today ⟨ for us
one [Moses]   known   covenant

מִקֶּדֶם, כְּמוֹ שֶׁכָּתוּב, וַיֵּרֶד יהוה בֶּעָנָן וַיִּתְיַצֵּב עִמּוֹ

⟨ with ⟨ and stood ⟨ in a ⟨ And HASHEM ⟨⟨ it is written: ⟨ as ⟨⟨ in ancient
him   cloud   descended   times,

שָׁם, וַיִּקְרָא בְשֵׁם יהוה.[1]

⟨⟨ of ⟨ with the ⟨ and He ⟨⟨ there,
HASHEM.   Name   called out

CONGREGATION, THEN *CHAZZAN*:

וַיַּעֲבֹר יהוה עַל פָּנָיו וַיִּקְרָא:

⟨⟨ and ⟨⟨ [Moses'] ⟨ before ⟨ And HASHEM passed
proclaimed: face,

CONGREGATION AND *CHAZZAN* RECITE LOUDLY AND IN UNISON:

יהוה, יהוה, אֵל, רַחוּם, וְחַנּוּן, אֶרֶךְ אַפַּיִם,

⟨ to anger, ⟨ Slow ⟨⟨and Gracious,⟨ Compassionate ⟨ God, ⟨ HASHEM, ⟨ HASHEM,

וְרַב חֶסֶד, וֶאֱמֶת, נֹצֵר חֶסֶד לָאֲלָפִים, נֹשֵׂא עָוֹן,

⟨ of ⟨ Forgiver ⟨⟨ for thousands ⟨ of ⟨ Preserver ⟨⟨ and ⟨ in ⟨ and
iniquity,   [of generations],   kindness   Truth,   Kindness Abundant

וָפֶשַׁע, וְחַטָּאָה, וְנַקֵּה.[2] וְסָלַחְתָּ לַעֲוֹנֵנוּ וּלְחַטָּאתֵנוּ

⟨⟨ and our sins, ⟨ our ⟨ May You ⟨ and Who ⟨ and inadvertent ⟨ willful sin,
iniquities   forgive   absolves.   sin,

וּנְחַלְתָּנוּ.[3] סְלַח לָנוּ אָבִינוּ כִּי חָטָאנוּ, מְחַל לָנוּ

⟨ us, ⟨ pardon ⟨⟨ we have ⟨ for ⟨⟨ our ⟨ us, ⟨ Forgive ⟨⟨ and make us
sinned;   Father,   Your heritage.

מַלְכֵּנוּ כִּי פָשָׁעְנוּ. כִּי אַתָּה אֲדֹנָי טוֹב וְסַלָּח,

⟨⟨ and ⟨ are ⟨ O Lord, ⟨ You, ⟨ For ⟨⟨ we have ⟨ for ⟨⟨ our King,
forgiving,   good   willfully sinned.

וְרַב חֶסֶד לְכָל קֹרְאֶיךָ.[4]

⟨⟨ who call ⟨ to all ⟨ kind ⟨ and
upon You.   abundantly

---

(1) *Exodus* 34:5. (2) 34:6-7. (3) 34:9. (4) *Psalms* 86:5.

PREFATORY VERSES TO SELICHAH 54 / פסוקי הקדמה לסליחה נד

קוֹלֵנוּ שָׁמָעְתָּ, אַל תַּעְלֵם אָזְנְךָ לְרַוְחָתֵנוּ
Our voice ≫ You have heard; ⟨ do not ⟨ shut ⟨ Your ear ⟨ to [our prayer for] our relief,

לְשַׁוְעָתֵנוּ.¹ אַל תִּנְאַץ לְמַעַן שְׁמָךְ, אַל תְּנַבֵּל כִּסֵּא
to our cry. ≫ Do not ⟨ reject [us] ≫ for the sake ⟨ of Your Name; ⟨ do not ⟨ abominate ⟨ the Throne

כְבוֹדֶךָ, זְכֹר אַל תָּפֵר בְּרִיתְךָ אִתָּנוּ.² אַל תִּשְׁטְפֵנוּ
of Your Glory. ⟨ Re- member, ⟨ do not ⟨ annul ⟨ Your covenant ≫ with us. ⟨ Let us not be swept away

שִׁבֹּלֶת מַיִם, וְאַל תִּבְלָעֵנוּ מְצוּלָה, וְאַל תֶּאְטַר
by the rushing current ⟨ of water, ≫ nor ⟨ let swallow us ≫ the shadowy depths; ⟨ and do not ⟨ let close

עָלֵינוּ בְּאֵר פִּיהָ.³
over us ⟨ the mouth of the pit. ≫

בְּרַחֵם אָב עַל בָּנִים, כֵּן תְּרַחֵם יהוה עָלֵינוּ.⁴
As merciful as ⟨ a father is ⟨ toward ⟨ his children, ≫ so ⟨ have mercy, ⟨ HASHEM, ⟨ on us. ≫

לַיהוה הַיְשׁוּעָה, עַל עַמְּךָ בִרְכָתֶךָ סֶּלָה.⁵ יהוה
To HASHEM ⟨ is salvation, ≫ upon ⟨ Your people ⟨ is Your blessing, ≫ Selah. ≫ HASHEM, ⟨

צְבָאוֹת עִמָּנוּ, מִשְׂגָּב לָנוּ אֱלֹהֵי יַעֲקֹב סֶלָה.⁶
Master of Legions, ⟨ is with us, ≫ a stronghold ⟨ for us ⟨ is the God ⟨ of Jacob, ≫ Selah. ≫

יהוה צְבָאוֹת, אַשְׁרֵי אָדָם בֹּטֵחַ בָּךְ.⁷ יהוה
HASHEM, ⟨ Master of Legions ≫ — praiseworthy ⟨ is the ⟨ man ⟨ who trusts ⟨ in You. ≫ HASHEM, ⟨

הוֹשִׁיעָה, הַמֶּלֶךְ יַעֲנֵנוּ בְיוֹם קָרְאֵנוּ.⁸
save! ≫ May the King ⟨ answer us ⟨ on the day ⟨ we call. ≫

---

(1) Cf. *Lamentations* 3:56. (2) *Jeremiah* 14:21. (3) Cf. *Psalms* 69:16.
(4) Cf. 103:13. (5) 3:9. (6) 46:8. (7) 84:13. (8) 20:10.

סליחה נד / SELICHAH 54

ALL:

אֱלֹהֵינוּ וֵאלֹהֵי אֲבוֹתֵינוּ:

《 of our forefathers: 〈 and the God 〈   Our God

אֵלְכָה וְאָשׁוּבָה* אֶל אִישִׁי הָרִאשׁוֹן,[1]

《   my first husband,   〈   to 〈 and I shall return* 〈   I shall go

אֲשֶׁר מֵאָז נְצָרַנִי כְּאִישׁוֹן,[2]

《 like the pupil 〈 protected 〈 from the 〈   who
[of an eye.]   me   beginning

בָּחוּר כָּאֲרָזִים[3] תְּהִלָּתוֹ בְּכָל לָשׁוֹן,*

《 tongue* — 〈 is in every 〈 His praise 《   as a cedar, 〈 As strong

בְּזָכְרִי בוֹ אֵינֶנּוּ מַנִּיחַ לִי לִישׁוֹן.[4]

《 to sleep. 〈 me 〈 allow 〈[His memory]《Him, 〈   when I
                               does not   remember

---

(1) *Hosea* 2:9. (2) Cf. *Deuteronomy* 32:10. (3) *Song of Songs* 5:15. (4) Cf. *Ecclesiastes* 5:11.

---

§ אֵלְכָה וְאָשׁוּבָה — *I shall go and I shall return.* The double *aleph-beis* acrostic of this *selichah* is followed by the *paytan's* name — יִצְחָק, *Yitzchak.* Nothing more is known of his identity, except that he flourished sometime before 1234 when *Arugas HaBosem* (which comments on this *selichah*) was written. [See prefatory comment to *Selichah* 13.]

Rashi, in his introduction to שִׁיר הַשִּׁירִים, *Song of Songs,* writes:

… King Solomon foresaw through רוּחַ הַקֹּדֶשׁ, *the Holy Spirit,* that Israel was destined to suffer a series of exiles and would lament, nostalgically recalling her former status as God's chosen beloved. She would say, *I shall go and return to my first husband* [to God] *for it was better with me then than now (Hosea* 2:9). The Children of Israel will recall His beneficence and *the trespasses which they trespassed (Leviticus* 26:40). And they will recall the goodness which He promised for the End of Days.

In *Song of Songs,* Solomon allegorizes the relationship between God and Israel as that of a loving husband angered by a straying wife who betrayed him. He portrays a passionate dialogue between the husband [God]

who still loves his exiled wife [Israel], and the wife who feels deserted *as if widowed from a living husband (II Samuel* 20:3), who longs for her husband and seeks to endear herself to him once more, as she recalls her youthful love for him and admits her guilt.

God, too, is *afflicted by her afflictions (Isaiah* 63:9), and He recalls the kindness of her youth, her beauty, and her skillful deeds for which He loved her [Israel] so. He proclaimed that He has *not afflicted her capriciously (Lamentations* 3:33), nor is she cast away permanently. For she is still His "wife" and He her "husband," and He will yet return to her.

The *paytan* here, too, uses the images of a wife longing for the husband she had wantonly abandoned, but to whom she now seeks to return.

תְּהִלָּתוֹ בְּכָל לָשׁוֹן — *His praise is in every tongue.* Since HASHEM's Name is praised, *from [the place of] the sun's rising to [the place of] its setting (Psalms* 113:3), from the far east to the far west, therefore it must be praised in every language under the sun (*Arugas HaBosem*).

Alternatively, the phrase means, *His praise is on every [man's] tongue.*

גְּאָלַנִי בִּזְרוֹעַ¹ מִבֵּין קְדֵשִׁים,

《 the licentious 〈 from 〈 with His 〈He redeemed
[Egyptians];   among   powerful arm   me

גַּם כִּלְלַנִי יְפִי וְכֵלִים חֲדָשִׁים,*

《 that are new.* 〈 and 〈 with 〈 perfected 〈 and
   garments   beauty   me   also

דִּבֶּר בִּי עַל פִּי קְדוֹשִׁים,

《 the holy men 〈 through 〈 to 〈 He
[Moses and Aaron],   me   spoke

דִּבְּקַנִי אֶצְלוֹ בִּכְתָבָה וְקִדּוּשִׁים.

《 and betrothal. 〈 with marriage 〈 to Him 〈 and [at
   contract   Mount Sinai]
     connected me

הִרְבָּה מְהַר וּמִקְנֶה וְקִנְיָן,*

《 and possession 〈 the acquisition 〈a dowry, 〈 He lavished
[of the Holy Temple].* [of Torah],   upon me

הִגְדִּיל הַשִּׂמְחָה בְּכָל עִנְיָן,

《 way. 〈 in every 〈 the rejoicing 〈He increased

וְסִיֵּד וְכִיֵּר בֵּית חַתְנוּת בִּנְיָן,

《 the 《 for the 〈 the 〈and deco- 〈 He
Tabernacle, wedding, house rated plastered

וּמָסַר לְשָׁרְתֵנִי עֲלָמוֹת אֵין מִנְיָן.²*

《 count.* 〈 with- 〈handmaidens 〈 to serve me 〈 and
    out   presented

זֶבַח הֵכִין וְשִׁלֵּם נְדָרָיו,

《 His vows, 〈 and 〈 He pre- 〈 Slaugh-
   fulfilled   pared [for   tered
     the feast]   animals

---

(1) Cf. *Psalms* 77:16. (2) Cf. *Song of Songs* 6:8.

וְכֵלִים חֲדָשִׁים — *And garments that are new*
[lit., *new vessels*]. This refers to either: the
clothing that the Egyptians gave the de-
parting Jews on the eve of the Exodus (see
Exodus 3:22, 12:35-36); the *Mishkan* and its
vessels; the *mitzvos*; or the Torah.

וּמִקְנֶה וְקִנְיָן — *The acquisition [of Torah]
and possession [of the Holy Temple].* The
Midrash (*Avos* 6:10) enumerates five קִנְיָנִים,
possessions, that God קָנָה, *acquired*, for
Himself in this world and adduces Scriptural verses regarding each of the five.

They are: (a) Torah; (b) heaven and earth;
(c) Abraham; (d) the people of Israel; and
(e) the Holy Temple. Of these, only Torah
and the Holy Temple were presented to Israel.

עֲלָמוֹת אֵין מִנְיָן — *Handmaidens without
count.* According to *Arugas HaBosem*, this
refers to the nations of the world; but he does
not explain their connection to the *Mishkan*
or *Beis HaMikdash,* which are the subject
of the preceding and following verses.

Perhaps *Arugas HaBosem* alludes to the
Midrash (*Shir HaShirim Rabbah*) that in-

זִבְּדַנִי זֶבֶד טוֹב¹ בַּחֲדָרָיו,

《 in His Temple- 《 that is 〈 an 〈 He
chambers.   good,   endow- endowed
                       ment   me

חֲצֵרוֹת קְטוֹרוֹת תִּכֵּן סְדָרָיו,

《 in their   〈 He 《 open [for smoke 《 Courtyards,
order;   laid out   dissipation,]

חֲתָנִי הַמֶּלֶךְ הֱבִיאַנִי חֲדָרָיו.²

《 into His   〈 brought me 〈 the King, 〈 my
chambers.   Groom,

טָבַלְתִּי* וּבָאתִי בַּעֲדִי עֲדָיִים,*³

《 of   〈 with the 〈 and came 〈 I immersed in
ornaments;*   most   to be   the mikveh*
             beautiful adorned

טָהֲרוֹתַי נָתְנוּ רֵיחַ דּוּדָאִים,*⁴

《 of mandrakes,* 〈 the scent 〈 emitted 〈 my pure ones

יְצוּעִי* עָלָה וְלָן בֵּין שָׁדַיִם,*⁵

《 the staves   〈 between 〈 and [His 《 he   〈 to my
[of the Ark],*   Presence] came   Temple
                         dwelled   up,*

---

(1) Cf. *Genesis* 30:20. (2) Cf. *Song of Songs* 1:4.
(3) Cf. *Ezekiel* 16:7. (4) Cf. *Song of Songs* 7:14. (5) Cf. 1:13.

---

terprets the verse, *Sixty are the queens and eighty the concubines, and maidens without number* (*Song of Songs* 6:8), as a reference to the Israelite masses that left Egypt. *Sixty* are the sixty myriad men, *eighty* are the eighty myriad youngsters, and *maidens without number* are the uncountable proselytes who joined the Israelites. Elsewhere (e.g., *Joshua* 9:27), we learn that many of the proselytes became servants in the *Mishkan*.

טָבַלְתִּי — *I immersed in the mikveh.* According to *Ibn Ezra* (based on *Mechilta*), the phrase וְקִדַּשְׁתָּם, *and sanctity them*, used regarding the preparation of the Jews for receiving the Torah (*Exodus* 9:10), refers to immersing in a *mikveh*.

בַּעֲדִי עֲדָיִים — *With the most beautiful of ornaments.* When Israel was asked to accept the Torah, the nation cried out, "נַעֲשֶׂה וְנִשְׁמָע, *We will do and we will hear*" (*Exodus* 24:7), placing נַעֲשֶׂה, *we will do*, before נִשְׁמָע, *we will hear*. Thus they undertook to fulfill all

of God's commandments, even before they knew what was expected of them. This devotion was rewarded when 600,000 ministering angels approached Israel and placed two crowns upon each Jew's head — one for נַעֲשֶׂה and one for נִשְׁמָע (*Shabbos* 88a).

טָהֲרוֹתַי נָתְנוּ רֵיחַ דּוּדָאִים — *My pure ones emitted the scent of mandrakes.* The Talmud (*Eruvin* 21b) interprets דּוּדָאִים, *mandrakes,* as an allusion to "the youth of Israel who have never partaken of the taste of sin."

יְצוּעִי — *My Temple* [lit., *my couch*]. The *Beis HaMikdash* was surrounded on three sides by a three-story edifice, which contained thirty-four chambers called יְצִיעִים (see *I Kings* 6:5-6 with *Rashi*). The *paytan* borrowed the name יְצִיעַ and applied it to the Temple itself (*Arugas HaBosem*).

בֵּין שָׁדַיִם — *Between the staves [of the Ark].* The staves on either side of the Ark were extremely long. When the Ark was placed in the Inner Sanctum of the Temple, the

יְמִינוּ חִבְּקַנִי חָבוּק יָדָיִם.¹ בִּמְעַט רֶגַע אֶרַע דָּבָר,²

« an ⟨ happened ⟨ moment ⟨ But in   « hands. ⟨ with ⟨ enveloped ⟨ while the
event: a brief   enveloping my [deeds] right arm [of His Law]

כָּבוֹד הֵמִיר*³ וְחֹק חָק שָׁבָר,

« [Moses] ⟨ that were ⟨ when ⟨ he ⟨ [My]
broke, engraved [the Tablets] exchanged* glory
of the Law

לְכָתִּי דֶרֶךְ בְּרוּחַ⁴ וְלֹא לְהָבָר,⁵

« [the way] ⟨ and ⟨ of the ⟨ the way ⟨ because
of cleansing. not wind I went

לַצְתִּי וְאָצְתִּי וְדוֹדִי חָמַק עָבָר.⁶

« and dis- ⟨ turned away ⟨ — and my « and rushed ⟨ I mocked
appeared. [from me] Beloved [to evil]

מֵעַי הָמוּ לְדוֹדִי⁷ קָנֵנִי,

« Who had taken ⟨ for my ⟨ longed ⟨ My
me for His own; Beloved innards

מַה לִידִידִי בִּטֵּל אֲשֶׁר הִתְנַנִי,

« He had ⟨ what ⟨ to ⟨ my ⟨ What
promised me? cancel Beloved brought

נָסַע מֵעָלַי וְלֹא חַנָּנִי,

« pardon ⟨ and ⟨ from me ⟨ He went
me. would not away

נְאָם בִּקַשְׁתִּיו וְלֹא מְצָאתִיו* קְרָאתִיו וְלֹא עָנָנִי.⁸

« but He would not ⟨ I called out « but did not find Him; ⟨ I sought Him « As is
answer me. to Him said:

---

(1) Cf. *Song of Songs* 2:6. (2) *Isaiah* 26:20. (3) Cf. *Psalms* 106:20; *Jeremiah* 2:11.
(4) *Arugas HaBosem*, based on *Job* 6:18, reads לַמְּתֵּי דֶרֶךְ בְּרוֹחַ, and renders, *I gathered*
[my people] to flee. (5) Cf. *Jeremiah* 4:11. (6) *Song of Songs* 5:6. (7) Cf. 5:4. (8) Cf. 5:6.

Holiest of the Holies, its staves stretched from the Ark in the center of the chamber to beyond the Dividing Curtain — as Scripture describes: *The staves extended until the tips of the staves could be seen from the Holy, the front of the Temple, yet they could not be seen outside* (*I Kings* 8:8). The contradictory statements "the staves could be seen" and "they could not be seen" are reconciled by the Talmud. Because of their great length, the twin poles pressed against the curtain that separated the Holiest of the Holies from the Holy. Thus, two bosom-like protrusions

were visible from the outside, even though the staves themselves were not visible behind the curtain (*Yoma* 54a; *Menachos* 98a).

כָּבוֹד הֵמִיר — *[My] glory he exchanged.* The Psalmist described the worship of the Golden Calf with the words וַיָּמִירוּ אֶת כְּבוֹדָם בְּתַבְנִית שׁוֹר, *They exchanged their Glory* [i.e., God] *for the likeness of an ox* (*Psalms* 106:20). The *paytan* uses the same phrase to refer to Moses' reaction of breaking the Tablets.

נְאָם בִּקַשְׁתִּיו וְלֹא מְצָאתִיו — *As is said: I sought Him but did not find Him.* The word

סוּרָה אֲדוֹנִי סוּרָה¹ חִנַּנְתִּיו כַּמָּה,

》so often. 〈 I pleaded 》 turn aside 〈 my Lord, 〈 Turn
with Him [to me]! aside,

סָב וְלֹא פָנָה, הוֹחַלְתִּי עַד מֶה,

》when? 〈 [but] 〈 I waited 》 turning 〈 not 〈 [But] He
until [to me]; turned away,

עָלַי לִבִּי כַּכִּנּוֹר יֶהֱמֶה,² עֵינִי נִגְּרָה וְלֹא תִדְמֶה.³

》 still. 〈 and is 〈 flows 〈 my eye 》 moans, 〈 like a harp 〈 my 〈 Within
not [with tears], heart me

פִּקְפֵּק בִּכְבוֹד לְמוֹרַד עֲנִיּוּת, פִּתְחֵי נִדָּה שָׁם נְקִיּוֹת,⁴

》[even my 〈 he 〈 of 〈 into con- 》 of 〈 until I slid 〈 my glory 〈 He
acts that turned niddah tamination poverty; to the debased
were] pure. depths

צָנוֹף צְנָפַנִי כַּדּוּר דְּחִיּוֹת,⁵

》 thrown 〈 like a ball 》 like a 〈 He wound
around, turban, me around
[with enemies]

צְרוּרָה צְעוּרָה אַלְמְנוּת חַיּוּת.⁶

》from a living 〈 as if widowed 〈 distressed, 〈 tied up,
[husband].

קַוֹּה קִוֵּיתִי (יהוה) יוֹם נֶחָמָה,⁷

》 of 〈 for the 〈 (O HASHEM) 〈 I have placed
comforting, day great hope

קִרְבַת נְטוּשָׁה בְּאַף וּבְחֵמָה,

》 and fury! 〈 in anger 〈 the one 〈 when will be
forsaken drawn close
[to You]

רִשְׁפֵּי אֵשׁ הָיָה לָהּ לְחוֹמָה,⁸

》 a wall, 〈 for her 〈 will be 〈 of fire 〈 Sparks

רַחֵם תְּרַחֵם אֶת לֹא רֻחָמָה.⁹

》 the one called 〈 on 〈 and You will surely
Unmercied. have mercy

(1) Cf. *Judges* 4:18. (2) Cf. *Isaiah* 16:11. (3) *Lamentations* 3:49.
(4) See *Ezekiel* 36:17. (5) Cf. *Isaiah* 22:18. (6) Cf. *II Samuel* 20:3.
(7) *Psalms* 40:2. (8) Cf. *Zechariah* 2:9. (9) See *Hosea* 1:2-2:3, 2:25.

נְאֻם, *as is said, saying, or, the word of,* is
very difficult here and seems to be thrown in
just to begin the line with the letter נ. Some

ancient manuscripts and the commentary
Arugas HaBosem read מְצָאתִיו וְלֹא נָס, *He*
fled and I could not find Him.

שׁוּבִי שׁוּבִי הַשּׁוּלַמִּית מִבֵּין שׁוֹסָיִךְ,

《 your despoilers; ⟨ from among ⟨ Shulamis, ⟨ come back, ⟨ Come back,

שׁוּבִי וְנֶחֱזֶה בָּךְ[1] יֹאמַר עוֹשָׂיִךְ,

《 the One Who made you. ⟨ so will say ⟨ you, ⟨ and let us see ⟨ come back

תִּקְעִי כַף מִלְּבָנוֹן רָצִיתִי מַעֲשָׂיִךְ,

《 your deeds. ⟨ for I have accepted favorably 《 you who [had been exiled] from Lebanon, 《 your hands, ⟨ Clap

תְּעוֹרֵר אַהֲבָתֵךְ כִּי בַעֲלָיִךְ עֹשָׂיִךְ.[2]

《 is your Maker. ⟨ your Husband ⟨ for 《 your love, ⟨ Awaken

❖ יָדֹע תֵּדַע פְּנֵי צֹאנֶךָ,[3]

《 Your flock; ⟨ with all ⟨ May You again be well-acquainted

צִיּוֹן מִכְלַל יֹפִי הֵיטִיבָה בִּרְצוֹנֶךָ,[4]

《 in Your favorable will. ⟨ do good 《 of beauty — ⟨ — consummation — 《 for Zion

חֲסִידֶיךָ רַנֵּן יְרַנְּנוּ צִדְקוֹת פִּרְזוֹנֶךָ,*[5]

《 of Your dispersal.* ⟨ the charity ⟨ will sing aloud ⟨ Your pious ones

קוֹלִי שָׁמַעְתָּ אַל תַּעְלֵם אָזְנֶךָ.[6]

《 Your ear [from it]! ⟨ turn away ⟨ do not 《 You have heard; ⟨ My voice

ALL, WHILE STANDING:

אֵל מֶלֶךְ יוֹשֵׁב עַל כִּסֵּא רַחֲמִים, מִתְנַהֵג

⟨ Who acts 《 of mercy, ⟨ the throne ⟨ on ⟨ Who sits ⟨ King ⟨ O God,

בַּחֲסִידוּת, מוֹחֵל עֲוֹנוֹת עַמּוֹ, מַעֲבִיר רִאשׁוֹן

⟨ [sins,] one ⟨ Who removes 《 of His people, ⟨ the sins ⟨ Who pardons 《 with kindness,

רִאשׁוֹן,[7] מַרְבֶּה מְחִילָה לַחַטָּאִים וּסְלִיחָה לַפּוֹשְׁעִים,

《 to willful sinners, ⟨ and forgiveness ⟨ to unintentional sinners ⟨ pardon ⟨ Who abundantly grants 《 by one,

---

(1) Cf. *Song of Songs* 7:1. (2) *Isaiah* 54:5. (3) *Proverbs* 27:23. (4) *Psalms* 50:2; 51:20.
(5) Cf. *Judges* 5:11. (6) Cf. *Lamentations* 3:56. (7) *Rosh Hashanah* 17a.

צִדְקוֹת פִּרְזוֹנֶךָ — *The charity of Your dispersal.* God was charitable to Israel when He dis- persed them among many nations, for none could destroy them as one (*Pesachim* 87b).

עֹשֶׂה צְדָקוֹת עִם כָּל בָּשָׂר וָרוּחַ, לֹא כְרָעָתָם

⟨ in accord ⟨ — not ⟪ and ⟨ [beings ⟨ all ⟨ with ⟨ acts of ⟨ Who
with their 　　　　 spirit of] flesh 　　　　 generosity performs
wickedness

תִּגְמוֹל. ❖ אֵל הוֹרֵיתָ לָּנוּ לוֹמַר שְׁלֹשׁ עֶשְׂרֵה, וּזְכוֹר

⟨ remem- ⟪ the Thirteen ⟨ to ⟨ us ⟨ You ⟨ O God, ⟪ do You
ber 　 [Attributes of Mercy]; recite 　 taught 　 repay them!

לָנוּ הַיּוֹם בְּרִית שְׁלֹשׁ עֶשְׂרֵה, כְּמוֹ שֶׁהוֹדַעְתָּ לֶעָנָיו

⟨ to the ⟨ You made ⟨ as ⟪ of [these] Thirteen, ⟨ the ⟨ today ⟨ for us
humble one known 　　　　　　　 covenant
[Moses]

מִקֶּדֶם, כְּמוֹ שֶׁכָּתוּב, וַיֵּרֶד יהוה בֶּעָנָן וַיִּתְיַצֵּב עִמּוֹ

⟨ with ⟨ and stood ⟨ in a ⟨ And HASHEM ⟪ it is written: ⟨ as ⟪ in ancient
him 　　 cloud descended 　　　　　　 times,

שָׁם, וַיִּקְרָא בְשֵׁם יהוה.[1]

　　⟪ of ⟨ with the ⟨ and He ⟪ there,
　　 HASHEM. Name called out

CONGREGATION, THEN *CHAZZAN:*

וַיַּעֲבֹר יהוה עַל פָּנָיו וַיִּקְרָא:

⟪ 　 and ⟪ [Moses'] ⟨ before ⟨ And HASHEM passed
proclaimed: 　 face,

CONGREGATION AND *CHAZZAN* **RECITE LOUDLY AND IN UNISON:**

יהוה, יהוה, אֵל, רַחוּם, וְחַנּוּן, אֶרֶךְ אַפַּיִם,

⟨ to anger, ⟨ Slow ⟪ and ⟨ Compassionate ⟨ God, ⟨ HASHEM, ⟨ HASHEM,
　　　　　　 Gracious,

וְרַב חֶסֶד, וֶאֱמֶת, נֹצֵר חֶסֶד לָאֲלָפִים, נֹשֵׂא עָוֹן,

⟨ of ⟨ Forgiver ⟪ for ⟨ of ⟨ Preserver ⟪ and ⟨ in ⟨ and
iniquity, 　 thousands [of kindness 　 Truth, Kindness Abundant
　　　　 generations],

וָפֶשַׁע, וְחַטָּאָה, וְנַקֵּה.[2] וְסָלַחְתָּ לַעֲוֹנֵנוּ וּלְחַטָּאתֵנוּ

⟪ and our sins, ⟨ our ⟪ May You ⟪ and Who ⟨ and inadvertent ⟨ willful sin,
　　　　 iniquities forgive absolves. 　 sin,

וּנְחַלְתָּנוּ.[3] סְלַח לָנוּ אָבִינוּ כִּי חָטָאנוּ, מְחַל לָנוּ

⟨ us, ⟨ pardon ⟪ we have ⟨ for ⟪ our ⟨ us, ⟨ Forgive ⟪ and make us
　　　　 sinned; 　 Father, 　　　　 Your heritage.

(1) *Exodus* 34:5. (2) 34:6-7. (3) 34:9.

מַלְכֵּנוּ כִּי פָשָׁעְנוּ. כִּי אַתָּה אֲדֹנָי טוֹב וְסַלָּח,
our King, « for « we have « For « You, « O Lord, « are « and
willfully sinned. good forgiving,

וְרַב חֶסֶד לְכָל קֹרְאֶיךָ.[1]
« and « kind « to all « who call
abundantly upon You.

יהוה, בְּקֶר תִּשְׁמַע קוֹלֵנוּ, בְּקֶר נַעֲרָךְ לְךָ, וּנְצַפֶּה.[2]
« HASHEM, « at « hear « our « at « as we « before « and we
dawn voice, dawn arrange You, wait ex-
[our prayer] pectantly.

אַל תִּנְאַץ לְמַעַן שְׁמֶךָ, אַל תְּנַבֵּל כִּסֵּא כְבוֹדֶךָ,
« Do « reject [us] « for « of Your « do « abominate « the « of Your
Not the sake Name; not Throne Glory.

זְכֹר אַל תָּפֵר בְּרִיתְךָ אִתָּנוּ.[3] וַאֲנִי, תְּפִלָּתִי לְךָ יהוה
« Re- « do « annul « Your « with us. « As for « may my « to « HASHEM,
member, not covenant me, prayer You,

עֵת רָצוֹן, אֱלֹהִים, בְּרָב חַסְדֶּךָ, עֲנֵנִי בֶּאֱמֶת יִשְׁעֶךָ.[4]
« [be] at « a time « O God, « in the « of Your « answer « with the « of Your
favorable; abundance kindness, me truth salvation.

בְּרַחֵם אָב עַל בָּנִים, כֵּן תְּרַחֵם יהוה עָלֵינוּ.[5]
« As merciful as « a « toward « his « so « have « HASHEM, « on us.
father is children, mercy,

לַיהוה הַיְשׁוּעָה, עַל עַמְּךָ בִרְכָתֶךָ סֶּלָה.[6] יהוה
« To HASHEM « is salvation, « upon « Your « is Your « Selah. « HASHEM,
people blessing,

צְבָאוֹת עִמָּנוּ, מִשְׂגָּב לָנוּ אֱלֹהֵי יַעֲקֹב סֶלָה.[7]
« Master of « is with us, « a « for us « is the God « of Jacob, « Selah.
Legions, stronghold

יהוה צְבָאוֹת, אַשְׁרֵי אָדָם בֹּטֵחַ בָּךְ.[8] יהוה הוֹשִׁיעָה,
« HASHEM, « Master of « praise- « is the « who « in You. « HASHEM, « save!
Legions worthy man trusts

הַמֶּלֶךְ יַעֲנֵנוּ בְיוֹם קָרְאֵנוּ.[9]
« May the « answer « on the « we call.
King us day

---

(1) *Psalms* 86:5. (2) Cf. 5:4. (3) *Jeremiah* 14:21. (4) *Psalms* 69:14.
(5) Cf. 103:13. (6) 3:9. (7) 46:8. (8) 84:13. (9) 20:10.

סליחה נה / SELICHAH 55
(שלישיה)

ALL:

אֱלֹהֵינוּ וֵאלֹהֵי אֲבוֹתֵינוּ:
《 of our forefathers: 〈 and God 〈 Our God

אֶזְעַק אֶל אֱלֹהִים* קוֹלִי,[1]
《 with my voice; 〈 God* 〈 to 〈 I cry

בְּקֶר אֶעֱרָךְ לָּךְ[2] בְּעַד קְהָלִי, יהוה צוּרִי וְגֹאֲלִי.[3]
《 and my 〈 my 〈 HASHEM, 《 my 〈 on 〈 to 〈 I arrange 〈 at
Redeemer. Rock congregation, behalf of You [my prayer] dawn

גִּשְׁנוּ בְּתַחֲנוּן וּבִתְפִלָּה, דְּלָתֶיךָ שַׁקֵּדְנוּ רַב עֲלִילָה,
《Deeds — 〈[O Doer] 《 we 〈 to Your 《 and with 〈 with 〈 We come
of Great hasten, doors prayer, supplication forward

הָסֵר מֵעָלֵינוּ נֶגַע וּמַחֲלָה.
《and sickness! 〈plague 〈 from us 〈 remove

הַמְצֵא לָנוּ סְלִיחוֹת,
《 forgiveness, 〈 for us 〈 Provide

וְהַעֲבֵר רָעָה מִנַּפְשׁוֹת הָאֲנוּחוֹת,
《 that are sighing, 〈 from [our] souls 〈 evil 〈 and remove

אֵל אֱלֹהֵי הָרוּחוֹת.[4]
《 of the spirits. 〈 God 〈 O God,

---

(1) *Psalms* 142:2. (2) 5:4. (3) 19:15. (4) *Numbers* 16:22; see commentary to *Selichah* 35.

אֶזְעַק אֶל אֱלֹהִים § — *I cry to God.* This *selichah* comprises thirteen triplets and is therefore called a *shelishiyah*. The first and second stiches of the respective stanzas contain an *aleph-beis* acrostic. The *paytan's* signature appears in the final two stanzas and is the subject of controversy. All agree that he signed שְׁלֹמֹה, *Shlomo*, in the twelfth stanza and הַקָּטָן, *the lesser*, in the thirteenth. In some editions of *Selichos*, the order of the stiches in the last stanza is הַחוֹסִיךְ ... נְדִיבִי ... מַהֵר ...; accordingly, the words שְׁלֹמֹה הַקָּטָן form the complete signature. Many editions therefore list the author as *R' Shlomo HaBavli* [see prefatory comment to *Selichah* 2] who often signed his composi-

tions in this manner. In most editions (as in this one), however, the stiches are arranged נְדִיבִי ... הַחוֹסִיךְ ... מַהֵר ...; accordingly, the name נַעֲמָן, *Naaman*, appears in the acrostic between the words שְׁלֹמֹה and הַקָּטָן. The name Naaman is akin to Naomi and was given to one of Benjamin's sons (see *Genesis* 46:21, and *Rashi* to *Genesis* 43:30) and one of his grandsons (see *Numbers* 26:40). It is unlikely that R' Shlomo HaBavli would use this signature. Moreover, most of R' Shlomo HaBavli's *selichos* are commented upon by *Arugas HaBosem*, while this one is notably absent from that work. Following this view, the *selichah* is by an otherwise unknown *paytan*, R' Shlomo Naaman.

זָעַקְתִּי לְךָ בְּעֹנִוּי וּתְלָאָה,
《 and   〈 out of 〈 to 〈 I have
hardship;   torment   You   cried out

חַיָּתִי פְּדֵה נָא מִשַּׁחַת וּשְׁאוֹלָה,
《 and the grave — 〈 from ruin 〈 please, 〈 deliver, 〈 my life

קָרְבָה אֶל נַפְשִׁי גְאָלָהּ.[1]
《redeem it! 〈 my soul, 〈 to 〈 draw near

טוֹב מִבֶּטֶן גֹּחִי,[2] יוֹצְרִי וְשִׂבְרִי וּמִבְטָחִי,
《 and my Security, 〈 my Hope, 〈 my Maker, 《drew me 〈 who from 〈 O Good
  forth,   the womb   One,

בְּיָדְךָ אַפְקִיד רוּחִי.[3]
《my spirit. 〈 I entrust 〈 into Your hand

כְּבֹשׁ כַּעַסְךָ מִידִידֶיךָ,
《 from Your 〈 Your 〈 Suppress
beloved ones;   anger

לִרְאוֹת שַׁחַת אַל תִּתֵּן חֲסִידֶיךָ,[4]
《Your devout ones. 〈 allow 〈 do not 〈 destruction 〈 to witness

עֲנֵנִי יהוה כִּי טוֹב חַסְדֶּךָ.[5]
《 is Your 〈 good 〈 for 〈 HASHEM, 〈 Answer
kindness.   me,

מַכָּה בְּלִי תְרוּפָה, נֶצַח לְחוֹרְפֶיךָ תִּשְׁלַח בְּהַקְצָפָה,
《 with fury, 〈 send 〈 to those who 〈 eternally, 〈 healing, 〈 without 〈 A
revile You   wound

וּבְעַמְּךָ לֹא לְמַגֵּפָה.[6]
《 a 〈 there should 〈 but against
plague. not be   Your people

סְגַּפְנוּ בְיוֹם זֶה,* עֲנוּתֵנוּ לֹא תְשַׁקֵּץ וְלֹא תִבְזֶה,[7]
《disparage, 〈 nor 〈 loathe 〈 do 〈 our 《 this day;* 〈 We have
not   supplication   been afflicted

סְלַח נָא לַעֲוֹן הָעָם הַזֶּה.[8]
《 of this people. 〈 the iniquity 〈 now 〈 forgive

---

(1) Psalms 69:19. (2) Cf. 22:10. (3) 31:6. (4) Cf. 16:10. (5) 69:17.
(6) I Chronicles 21:17. (7) Cf. Psalms 22:25. (8) Numbers 14:19.

סְגַּפְנוּ בְיוֹם זֶה — *We have been afflicted this day.* Some commentaries understand this as an allusion to the custom of fasting on Erev Rosh Hashanah and render, "We are afflicting ourselves today." However, the verb form סְגַּפְנוּ is not reflexive and so we have translated *we have been afflicted.*

פָּשַׁעְנוּ וּמָעַלְנוּ, צוּר לְךָ חָבוֹל חָבַלְנוּ,[1]

We have / sinned / rebelliously / and we / have betrayed / Your trust. / O / Rock, / to / You / we have been / most destructive;

לָכֵן (כִּמְעַט) כָּלִינוּ בְאַפֶּךָ, וּבַחֲמָתְךָ נִבְהָלְנוּ.[3]

therefore, / we are (almost) / consumed / by Your / anger, / and by Your / wrath / we are / confounded.

קָדוֹשׁ, רִיב אַל תִּמְתַּח, רְאֵה כִּי כַפַּי לְךָ אֶשְׁטָח,[3]

Holy / One, / judgment / do / not / stretch / out! / See / how / my / hands / to / You / I stretch / out:

יוֹם אִירָא אֲנִי אֵלֶיךָ אֶבְטָח.[4]

on the / day / that / I fear, / I / in You / trust.

שְׁפֹךְ שִׂיחַ עַמֶּךָ, תָּחֹן וְתַעַן שְׁלֵמֶיךָ,

The out- / pouring / of the / prayer / of Your / people / accept / graciously, / and / answer / Your whole- / some ones.

אַל תִּנְאַץ לְמַעַן שְׁמֶךָ.[5]

Do / not / scorn [us], / for the / sake / of Your / Name.

שְׁעֵה שַׁוְעַת אֲנוּנִים,

Turn / toward / the / outcry / of those who / are grieving;

לְקוֹרְאֶיךָ מִדֹּחַק הַסְכֵּת מִמְּעוֹנִים,

to those / who call You / out of / oppression / pay / attention / from [Your] / heavenly abode,

שׁוֹמֵעַ אֶל אֶבְיוֹנִים.[6]

O You / Who hearken / to / the destitute.

❖ נְדִיבֵי עַם[7] מַטַּע נַעֲמָנִים,[8]

the noblest / [Israel] / of / peoples / — like a / planting / that is / pleasant,

הַחוֹסִים קֹוֶיךָ טְהוֹרֶיךָ נִמְנִים,

who take shel- / ter with You, / and place their / hope in You, / and as Your / pure ones / are / accounted —

מַהֵר תְּרַחֲמֵם, כְּרַחֵם אָב עַל בָּנִים.[9]

quickly / have mercy / on them, / as / merciful as / is / a father / toward / his / children.

(1) Cf. *Nehemiah* 1:7. (2) *Psalms* 90:7. (3) Cf. 88:10. (4) 56:4. (5) *Jeremiah* 14:21. (6) *Psalms* 69:34. (7) Cf. 47:10. (8) Cf. *Isaiah* 17:10. (9) *Psalms* 103:13.

ALL, WHILE STANDING:

אֵל מֶלֶךְ יוֹשֵׁב עַל כִּסֵּא רַחֲמִים, מִתְנַהֵג

‹ Who acts ‹‹ of mercy, ‹ the throne ‹ on ‹‹ Who sits ‹ King ‹ O God,

בַּחֲסִידוּת, מוֹחֵל עֲוֹנוֹת עַמּוֹ, מַעֲבִיר רִאשׁוֹן

‹ [sins,] one ‹ Who removes ‹‹ of His people, ‹ the sins ‹ Who pardons ‹‹ with kindness,

רִאשׁוֹן,¹ מַרְבֶּה מְחִילָה לַחַטָּאִים וּסְלִיחָה לַפּוֹשְׁעִים,

‹‹ to willful sinners, ‹ and forgiveness ‹ to unintentional sinners ‹ pardon ‹ Who abun-dantly grants ‹‹ by one,

עֹשֶׂה צְדָקוֹת עִם כָּל בָּשָׂר וָרוּחַ, לֹא כְרָעָתָם

‹ in accord with their wickedness ‹ — not ‹‹ and spirit ‹ [beings of] flesh ‹ all ‹ with ‹ acts of generosity ‹ Who performs

תִּגְמוֹל. ❖ אֵל הוֹרֵיתָ לָּנוּ לוֹמַר שְׁלֹשׁ עֶשְׂרֵה, וּזְכוֹר

‹ remem-ber ‹‹ the Thirteen [Attributes of Mercy]; ‹ to recite ‹ us ‹ You taught ‹ O God, ‹‹ do You repay them!

לָנוּ הַיּוֹם בְּרִית שְׁלֹשׁ עֶשְׂרֵה, כְּמוֹ שֶׁהוֹדַעְתָּ לֶעָנָיו

‹ to the humble one [Moses] ‹ You made known ‹ as ‹‹ of [these] Thirteen, ‹ the covenant ‹ today ‹ for us

מִקֶּדֶם, כְּמוֹ שֶׁכָּתוּב, וַיֵּרֶד יהוה בֶּעָנָן וַיִּתְיַצֵּב עִמּוֹ

‹ with him ‹ and stood ‹ in a cloud ‹ And HASHEM descended ‹‹ it is written: ‹ as ‹‹ in ancient times,

שָׁם, וַיִּקְרָא בְשֵׁם יהוה.²

‹‹ of HASHEM. ‹ with the Name ‹ and He called out ‹‹ there,

CONGREGATION, THEN *CHAZZAN*:

וַיַּעֲבֹר יהוה עַל פָּנָיו וַיִּקְרָא:

‹‹ and proclaimed: ‹‹ [Moses'] face, ‹ before ‹ And HASHEM passed

CONGREGATION AND *CHAZZAN* RECITE LOUDLY AND IN UNISON:

יהוה, יהוה, אֵל, רַחוּם, וְחַנּוּן, אֶרֶךְ אַפַּיִם,

‹ to anger, ‹ Slow ‹‹ and Gracious, ‹ Compassionate ‹ God, ‹ HASHEM, ‹ HASHEM,

וְרַב חֶסֶד, וֶאֱמֶת, נֹצֵר חֶסֶד לָאֲלָפִים, נֹשֵׂא עָוֹן

‹ of iniquity, ‹ Forgiver ‹‹ for thousands [of generations], ‹ of kindness ‹ Preserver ‹‹ and Truth, ‹ in ‹ and Kindness Abundant

וָפֶשַׁע, וְחַטָּאָה, וְנַקֵּה.³ וְסָלַחְתָּ לַעֲוֹנֵנוּ וּלְחַטָּאתֵנוּ

‹‹ and our sins, ‹ our iniquities ‹ May You forgive ‹‹ and Who absolves. ‹ and inadvertent sin, ‹ willful sin,

---

(1) *Rosh Hashanah* 17a. (2) *Exodus* 34:5. (3) 34:6-7.

וּנְחַלְתָּנוּ.¹ סְלַח לָנוּ אָבִינוּ כִּי חָטָאנוּ, מְחַל לָנוּ

‹ us, ‹ pardon « we have ‹ for « our ‹ us, ‹ Forgive « and make us
sinned; Father, Your heritage.

מַלְכֵּנוּ כִּי פָשָׁעְנוּ. כִּי אַתָּה אֲדֹנָי טוֹב וְסַלָּח,

« and ‹ are ‹ O Lord, ‹ You, ‹ For « we have ‹ for « our King,
forgiving, good willfully sinned.

וְרַב חֶסֶד לְכָל קֹרְאֶיךָ.²

« who call ‹ to all ‹ kind ‹ and
upon You. abundantly

PREFATORY VERSES TO SELICHAH 56 / פסוקי הקדמה לסליחה נו

עַל גַּבֵּנוּ חָרְשׁוּ חֹרְשִׁים, הֶאֱרִיכוּ לְמַעֲנִיתָם.³

« their furrow. ‹ they lengthened « the plowers, ‹ plowed ‹ our back ‹ On

כִּי שָׁחָה לֶעָפָר נַפְשֵׁנוּ, דָּבְקָה לָאָרֶץ בִּטְנֵנוּ.⁴

« is our belly. ‹ to the earth ‹ stuck « is our soul, ‹ to the dust ‹ prostrated ‹ For

יהוה מָה רַבּוּ צָרֵינוּ, רַבִּים קָמִים עָלֵינוּ.⁵ קוּמָה

« Arise! « against us! ‹ rise up « The great « are our ‹ numer- ‹ how ‹ HASHEM,
ones tormentors! ous

עֶזְרָתָה לָּנוּ, וּפְדֵנוּ לְמַעַן חַסְדֶּךָ.⁶

« of Your ‹ for the ‹ And « us! ‹ Assist
kindness! sake redeem us

כְּרַחֵם אָב עַל בָּנִים, כֵּן תְּרַחֵם יהוה עָלֵינוּ.⁷

« on us. ‹ HASHEM, ‹ have ‹ so « his ‹ toward ‹ a ‹ As merciful as
mercy, children, father is

לַיהוה הַיְשׁוּעָה, עַל עַמְּךָ בִרְכָתֶךָ סֶּלָה.⁸ יהוה

‹ HASHEM, « Selah. « is Your ‹ Your ‹ upon « is salvation, ‹ To HASHEM
blessing, people

צְבָאוֹת עִמָּנוּ, מִשְׂגָּב לָנוּ אֱלֹהֵי יַעֲקֹב סֶלָה.⁹

« Selah. « of Jacob, ‹ is the God ‹ for us ‹ a « is with us, ‹ Master of
stronghold Legions,

יהוה צְבָאוֹת, אַשְׁרֵי אָדָם בֹּטֵחַ בָּךְ.¹⁰ יהוה

‹ HASHEM, « in You. ‹ who ‹ is the ‹ — praise- « Master of ‹ HASHEM,
trusts man worthy Legions

הוֹשִׁיעָה, הַמֶּלֶךְ יַעֲנֵנוּ בְיוֹם קָרְאֵנוּ.¹¹

« we call. ‹ on the day ‹ answer us ‹ May the King « save!

---

(1) *Exodus* 34:9. (2) *Psalms* 86:5. (3) Cf. 129:3. (4) 44:26. (5) Cf. 3:2.
(6) 44:27. (7) Cf. 103:13. (8) 3:9. (9) 46:8. (10) 84:13. (11) 20:10.

סליחה נו / SELICHAH 56
(שלמונית)

ALL:

אֱלֹהֵינוּ וֵאלֹהֵי אֲבוֹתֵינוּ:

《 of our forefathers: 〈 and the God 〈 Our God

אָמַרְנוּ נִגְזַרְנוּ* לָנוּ¹ וְאֵין דּוֹרֵשׁ,²

《 who seeks 〈 and there 〈 on our 〈 We are 《 We said,
us. is no one own, cut off*

אֲבָל אֲשֵׁמִים אֲנַחְנוּ³ וְקָרוֹב⁴ פּוֹרֵשׁ,

《 separates 〈 so He Who 《 are we, 〈 guilty 〈 But
[from us]. was close

בַּעֲוֹן בִּצְעֵנוּ צוּר לַצָּר יַחֲרֵשׁ,

《 remains 〈 to our 〈 the 《 of our 〈 For the
silent, foes Rock, thievery sin

בּוֹלֵעַ וּמַדִּיק וְרָד וְרוֹפֵס הַחוֹרֵשׁ.⁵

《 [He allows] 〈 and to 〈 to rule 〈 to grind 〈 to swallow
the plowman. trample us, over us, us down, us,

גַּל אַחַר גַּל וְאֵין דּוֹבֵר,

《 a ship captain, 〈 without 《 wave, 〈 after 〈 Wave

גּוֹלֵל וְצָף עֲלֵי רֹאשׁ גּוֹבֵר,⁶

《 rising ever 〈 our 〈 over 〈 and 〈 [the wave]
higher. heads, washes crests

דָּבַק שֶׁבֶר עַל שֶׁבֶר חוֹבֵר,

《 merging 《 disaster, 〈 to 〈 does 〈 Adhere
together; disaster

דַּאֲבוֹן הַבָּא קָשֶׁה יְשַׁכַּח הָעוֹבֵר.⁷

《 of past 〈 it obliterates 〈 is so 〈 that is 〈 the grief
[troubles]. the memory intense, impending

---

(1) Cf. *Lamentations* 3:54; cf. *Ezekiel* 37:11. (2) 34:6. (3) *Genesis* 42:21. (4) See *Psalms* 145:18.
(5) Cf. *Daniel* 7:7. (6) Cf. *Lamentations* 3:54. (7) Cf. *Berachos* 13a: צָרוֹת אַחֲרוֹנוֹת
מְשַׁכְּחוֹת אֶת הָרִאשׁוֹנוֹת, *The later troubles cause the earlier ones to be forgotten.*

⧼ אָמַרְנוּ נִגְזַרְנוּ — *We said, ''We are cut off.''* This *selichah* bewails the plight of Israel in exile. Using various metaphors — the storm-tossed, captainless ship; the tortured slaves; the overworked draft animal — for the downtrodden nation, the *paytan* pleads for the forgiveness of our sins which brought about the exile in the first place, and for the final Redemption.

The acrostic of the verses forms a double *aleph-beis* followed by the signature of the author — שְׁלֹמֹה הַקָּטָן, *Shlomo the lesser* — the prolific *paytan* R' Shlomo HaBavli [see prefatory comment to *Selichah* 2].

הֶמֶס יִמַּס הַלֵּב[1] מֵרֹב הַמִּכְשׁוֹל,

《 is the 〈 so 《 — the 《 Certainly
foundering; great heart — will it melt

הוֹלֵךְ וְסוֹעֵר כִּי רַב הַנַּחְשׁוֹל,[2]

《 the tempest. 〈strong is 〈 for 〈storm tossed,〈increasingly

וּמוֹשִׁיעַ וְרַב אֵין עוֹד לִמְשׁל,

《 to rule 〈 any 〈 there 〈 and 〈 And a savior
[the ship]; longer is not captain

וְאָבַד הַמַּנְהִיג וְעָיֵף שׁוֹל נָשׁוֹל.

《 will certainly drop 〈 and the 《 is the leader, 〈 lost
[into the sea]. weary

זָנַחְנוּ טוֹב[3] וְעַל כָּכָה הִגִּיעַ,[4]

《 this [evil] has 〈 that 〈 for 《 what 〈 We
come upon us; reason is good; forsook

זוֹכְרֶיךָ זָעַמְתָּ בְּיַד עֲוֹנֵינוּ לְהַפְגִּיעַ,

《 to punish us. 〈 our sins, 〈because〈 You raged 〈 [even] those
of against who remem-
ber You

חַיִּים לִרְצוֹת וְסִתְּךָ אַף לְהַרְגִּיעַ,[5]

《 to assuage; 〈 and Your 〈 is Your 〈 to desire 〈 Life
anger way

חוּשָׁה לַעֲזֹר כִּי אֵין מַפְגִּיעַ.[6]

《 to intercede 〈 there is 〈 for 《 to help, 〈 hurry
[on our behalf]. no one

טֹרַדְנוּ וַנְּהִי כַטָּמֵא וּכְבֶגֶד עֵדִים,[7]

《 worn out; 〈 like a 〈 like one 〈 and we 《 We have
garment unclean, have been
become expelled,

טֹרַפְנוּ וַנָּבֶל וְרוֹדְפִים קַלִּים חַדִּים,

《 and keen. 〈 are swift 〈 and the 《 and 〈 we are
pursuers withered, ripped apart

יוֹצְאִים חוּצוֹת מְלֵאֵי גַּעַר כִּמְנֻדִּים,[8]

《 like those 〈 with 〈 are filled 〈 Those who go out
excommunicated, censure [to seek food]

יוֹשְׁבֵי חֹשֶׁךְ צָגִים כְּרֵקִים כַּדִּים.

《 that are empty 〈 like 〈 stand 《 [inside] in 〈 while those
[with no food in them]. pitchers about darkness, who dwell

---

(1) Cf. *II Samuel* 17:10. (2) Cf. *Targum* to *Jonah* 1:4. (3) Cf. *Hosea* 8:3.
(4) Cf. *Esther* 9:26. (5) Cf. *Psalms* 30:6. (6) *Isaiah* 59:16. (7) Cf. 64:5. (8) Cf. 51:20.

בִּלְמוֹת וָרֹק פָּנֵינוּ מְצַפִּים צָפֹה,¹

《 are well covered, 〈 our 〈 and 〈 With
faces spit humiliation

כִּי גָדַל הַכְּאֵב² מִפֹּה וּמִפֹּה,

《 and on 〈 on this 〈 has the 〈 grown 〈 for
that. side pain great

לַיּוֹצֵא בְּעֵתָה וְלַבָּא אֵין רָפֹא,

《 healing; 〈 there 〈 and for whom- 《 terror 〈 For whom-
is no ever returns awaits, ever goes out

לָחוֹן וּלְרַחֵם תִּקְוָה אַיֵּה אֵפוֹא.³

《 now? 〈 — where 《 or for 〈 for mercy, 〈 for
is there any hope grace,

מַה כֹּחִי לְיַחֵל וּמַתֶּשֶׁת גְּבִרְתָּנִית,

《 by the tyrant 〈 while I continue 《 to hope 〈 is my 〈 What
mistress? to be weakened on, strength

מוֹסִיף מֶשֶׁךְ קֵץ מַעֲנִית גּוֹתָנִית,

《 across 〈 of the plow 〈 [dug by] 〈 is the 〈 Increased
my back: the sharp length of
edge the furrow

נֵטֶל נַשְׁכָנִית נַגְחָנִית עֶשֶׂר שַׁלְטָנִית,*⁴

《 ruler,* 〈 ten-horned, 〈 goring, 〈 of the biting, 〈 The
and tenfold burden

נֶגַע יִיגַע רֹדִינִית חִנָּם וְחַלְטָנִית.

《 yet utterly. 〈 who op- 《 gratuitously 〈 who op- 《 and ex- 〈 who
presses us hausts us, smites

סִמְלוֹנִי רֶשַׁע לְקַצֵּץ נָקָם תִּלְבֹּשׁ,

《 may You 〈 vengeance 《 — to 《 of wick- 〈 The harness
don. cut them, edness

---

(1) Cf. *Isaiah* 50:6. (2) *Job* 2:13. (3) Cf. 17:15. (4) See *Daniel* 7:7.

נֵטֶל נַשְׁכָנִית נַגְחָנִית עֶשֶׂר שַׁלְטָנִית — *The burden of the biting, goring, ten-horned, and
tenfold ruler.* Daniel (Chapter 7) records
his prophetic vision of four immense beasts
which represented the four kingdoms that
successively would rule the world, and to
whom Israel would be subjugated in four
periods of exile. The first beast, a lion with
eagle's wings, represented Babylon. The second, a bear, symbolized Persia. The third, a
four-headed, four-winged leopard, stood for
Greece, which — after the death of Alexander

the Great — was split up among four of his
generals.

The fourth beast, unnamed in Daniel's
vision, is described (*Daniel* 7:7) as *exces-
sively terrifying, awesome, and strong;
with immense iron teeth, eating and crum-
bling, trampling the rest with its feet; it
was different from all the beasts that preceded it, and it had ten horns.* This beast
represented the present exile, considered to
have begun with Julius Caesar's ascension
to the Roman Empire.

סֵבֶר קַוֶּיךָ¹ וְסִכּוּיִם תַּעֲמִיד מַלְבּוֹשׁ,

《 that they be not 〈 may You 〈 and their 〈 of those who 〈 The
embarrassed.   uphold,   anticipation   place their   aspiration
                                                    hope in You

עֶגְלַת לִמּוּדֶיךָ² מַחַץ וְשֶׁבֶר תַּחְבֹּשׁ,³

《 bandage; 〈 and broken 〈 [their] 《 You have 〈 They are
                bones   wounds   trained;   the calf

עֲבֹד עֲבוֹדָתְךָ שְׁכֶם אֶחָד⁴ תִּכְבֹּשׁ.

《 may You over- 〈 united, 〈 with 〈 Your service 〈 so that
come [their]   shoulders   they may
stubborn heart].   perform

פָּקַרְנוּ בְאֵמוּן כְּבֵן הָפְכָן וְסַרְבָן,

《 and 〈 who is 〈 like 〈 from 〈 We broke
obstinate,   perverse,   a son   faith   loose

פִּדְיוֹן לְחִזּוּק יִסּוּרִים חִלַּפְתָּ קָרְבָּן,⁵

《 of the 〈 in place 〈 [our] 〈 You 〈 but as redemp-
sacrifices [that   suffering   strength-   tion [from
would atone]:   ened   annihilation]

צָרוֹת רָעוֹת וְנָחָשׁ וְעַקְרָב רַבְרְבָן,

《 that is huge, 〈 and the 〈 the snake 《 that are 〈 Troubles
                 scorpion   severe,

צִמָּאוֹן*⁶ וְחִסֵּר כֹּל מִשְׁנֶה הַדְרִבָן.

《 prod 〈 a strange 《 of every- 〈 and lack 〈 thirst*
[to guide us].   thing,

קוֹבְלִים הַסְתֵּר פָּנֶיךָ עַם טָרְחָן,

《 that is 〈 — does 《 of Your 〈 regarding 〈 Complain
troublesome. the   counte-   the hiding
              nation nance

קָנוּי וְהָרוּג אָכוּל וּמָכוּר וּמֻרְחָן,

《 their [oppression] is 《 or sold; 〈 and 〈 to be 〈 [They are]
measured precisely.   devoured slaughtered bought

---

(1) Cf. *Yoma* 72a and *Succah* 45b. (2) Cf. *Hosea* 10:11. (3) Cf. *Isaiah* 30:26.
(4) Cf. *Zephaniah* 3:9. (5) See *Avodah Zarah* 4a. (6) Cf. *Deuteronomy* 8:15.

צָרוֹת רָעוֹת וְנָחָשׁ וְעַקְרַב רַבְרְבָן *— Troubles*
that are severe, the snake and the scor-
pion that is huge, thirst. Moses described
the wilderness through which the Israelites
traveled as a place of נָחָשׁ שָׂרָף וְעַקְרָב וְצִמָּאוֹן,
snake, fiery serpent and scorpion, and
thirst (*Deuteronomy* 8:15). According to
various Midrashim (some of which have

been tampered with by the censors), Moses
prophesied regarding the Four Exiles [see
commentary to *Selichah* 18, s.v. דְּרוּסָה בְּעוּטָה
נְגוּחָה נְשׁוּכָה]: The snake is the Babylonian exile; the fiery serpent is the Persian-Medean;
the scorpion is the Greek or Macedonian;
and the thirst represents the present Edomite
galus (*Midrash Tehillim* 63:2).

רָגַלְנוּ כְּעֶבֶד רַב פֶּשַׁע וְסוֹרְחָן,

We are wont ‹ like ‹ full ‹ of ‹ and
to behave ‹ a slave ‹ rebellion ‹ perfidious —

רַבָּה לְהֵיטִיב רַב חֶסֶד וְסוֹלְחָן.

but You] ‹ in Your good- ‹ You are ‹ Kind ‹ and the
are grand ‹ ness [to us], ‹ Abundantly ‹ Forgiver!

שִׁקַּרְנוּ בָךְ וְסַטְנוּ מִמְּךָ לָסוּר,

We have ‹ toward ‹ we have ‹ from ‹ straying
been false ‹ You; ‹ strayed ‹ You, ‹ [from Your path].

שְׁכַחֲנוּךְ מֵרֹב כֹּל בְּלִי חָסוּר,

We have ‹ because ‹ of ‹ without ‹ lack.
forgotten You, ‹ we had an ‹ every- ‹
‹ abundance ‹ thing,

תָּעִינוּ אַחַר יֵצֶר וְתוֹעַ רְעַ וְסוּר,

We have ‹ after ‹ our [Evil] ‹ who ‹ and ‹ leads
wandered off ‹ Inclination, ‹ misleads, ‹ to evil ‹ astray.

תַּרְנוּ אַחַר הַזּוּג לַעֲבֵרָה סַרְסוּר.*

We have ‹ follow- ‹ the pair ‹ that to sin ‹ are
explored, ‹ ing ‹ [our heart ‹ ‹ panderers.*
‹ and eyes]

שְׁרִירוּת לֵב יַשֵּׁר וּפְשֹׁט עֲקַמּוּמִית,

The willfulness ‹ of our ‹ straighten, ‹ smooth ‹ its crookedness,
‹ heart ‹ out

לֹא יִרְגַּז עוֹד בְּהִרְהוּר שַׁעֲמוּמִית,

so that ‹ agitate ‹ anymore ‹ with fancies ‹ from boredom.
it not

מַהֵר מִלְּעַכֵּב טְמוּי תְּפִישַׁת שְׂמָמִית,*1

Hurry, ‹ that we be ‹ by the ‹ of the ‹ of the spider.*
not held back ‹ uncleanness ‹ grasp

הֶרֶב כַּבֵּס כְּתָמֵינוּ2 וְלַבֵּן אַדְמוּמִית.3

Thoroughly ‹ wash ‹ our stains; ‹ whiten ‹ [their] redness.
away

---

(1) Cf. *Proverbs* 30:28. (2) Cf. *Psalms* 51:4. (3) Cf. *Isaiah* 1:18.

הַזּוּג לַעֲבֵרָה סַרְסוּר — *The pair [our heart
and eyes] that to sin are panderers.* The
Torah states: *Do not explore after your
heart and after your eyes after which
you stray (Numbers* 15:39). The heart and
the eyes are spies for the body, offering it

an array of sins: The eye sees; the heart
desires; and the body sins (*Rashi* based on
Yerushalmi, Berachos 1:8).

שְׂמָמִית — *The spider,* the *Yetzer Hara*
(*Arugas HaBosem*) or *Edom* (*Mishlei*
30:23).

❖ הֲגוּנִים לְךָ לְעָם אוֹתָנוּ נַוֶּה,

⟪ beautify us: ⟪ as a ⟨ to be ⟨ So that we
people, to You be fit

קָטֹן וְגָדוֹל דַּעַת דְּרָכֶיךָ שַׁוֵּה,

⟪ equally. ⟨ Your ways ⟨ know ⟨ and great ⟨ Let small

יְשׁוּעַת יִשְׂרָאֵל חֵלֶק יַעֲקֹב צַוֵּה,[1]

⟪ command. ⟪ of ⟨ the ⟪ of Israel, ⟨ The
Jacob, portion salvation

הֲלֹא אַתָּה אֱלֹהֵינוּ וּלְךָ נְקַוֶּה.[2]

⟪ we will put ⟨ and ⟨ our God ⟨ that ⟨ Is it
our hope? in You You are not so

ALL, WHILE STANDING:

אֵל מֶלֶךְ יוֹשֵׁב עַל כִּסֵּא רַחֲמִים, מִתְנַהֵג

⟨ Who acts ⟪ of mercy, ⟨ the throne ⟨ on ⟨ Who sits ⟨ King ⟨ O God,

בַּחֲסִידוּת, מוֹחֵל עֲווֹנוֹת עַמּוֹ, מַעֲבִיר רִאשׁוֹן

⟨ [sins,] one ⟨ Who ⟪ of His ⟨ the sins ⟨ Who ⟪ with kindness,
removes people, pardons

רִאשׁוֹן,[3] מַרְבֶּה מְחִילָה לַחַטָּאִים וּסְלִיחָה לַפּוֹשְׁעִים,

⟪ to willful ⟨ and ⟨ to unintentional ⟨ pardon ⟨ Who abun- ⟪ by one,
sinners, forgiveness sinners dantly grants

עֹשֶׂה צְדָקוֹת עִם כָּל בָּשָׂר וָרוּחַ, לֹא כְרָעָתָם

⟨ in accord with ⟨ — not ⟪ and ⟨ [beings ⟨ all ⟨ with ⟨ acts of ⟨ Who
their wickedness spirit of] flesh generosity performs

תִּגְמוֹל. ❖ אֵל הוֹרֵיתָ לָּנוּ לוֹמַר שְׁלֹשׁ עֶשְׂרֵה, וּזְכוֹר

⟨ remem- ⟪ the Thirteen ⟨ to ⟨ us ⟨ You ⟨ O God, ⟪ do You
ber [Attributes of Mercy]; recite taught repay them!

לָנוּ הַיּוֹם בְּרִית שְׁלֹשׁ עֶשְׂרֵה, כְּמוֹ שֶׁהוֹדַעְתָּ לֶעָנָיו

⟨ to the humble ⟨ You made ⟨ as ⟪ of [these] Thirteen, ⟨ the ⟨ today ⟨ for us
one [Moses] known covenant

מִקֶּדֶם, כְּמוֹ שֶׁכָּתוּב, וַיֵּרֶד יהוה בֶּעָנָן וַיִּתְיַצֵּב עִמּוֹ

⟨ with ⟨ and stood ⟨ in a ⟨ And HASHEM ⟪ it is written: ⟨ as ⟪ in ancient
him cloud descended times,

שָׁם, וַיִּקְרָא בְשֵׁם יהוה.[4]

⟪ of ⟨ with the ⟨ and He ⟪ there,
HASHEM. Name called out

---

(1) Cf. *Psalms* 14:7; 44:5; *Deuteronomy* 32:9. (2) Cf. *Jeremiah* 14:22.
(3) *Rosh Hashanah* 17a. (4) *Exodus* 34:5.

CONGREGATION, THEN *CHAZZAN*:

וַיַּעֲבֹר יהוה עַל פָּנָיו וַיִּקְרָא:

《 and 《 [Moses'] 〈 before 〈 And HASHEM passed
proclaimed: face,

CONGREGATION AND *CHAZZAN* RECITE LOUDLY AND IN UNISON:

יהוה, יהוה, אֵל, רַחוּם, וְחַנּוּן, אֶרֶךְ אַפַּיִם,

〈 to anger, 〈 Slow 《 and 〈 Compassionate 〈 God, 〈 HASHEM, 〈 HASHEM,
Gracious,

וְרַב חֶסֶד, וֶאֱמֶת, נֹצֵר חֶסֶד לָאֲלָפִים, נֹשֵׂא עָוֹן,

〈 of 〈 Forgiver 《 for thousands 〈 of 〈 Preserver 《 and 〈 in 〈 and
iniquity,   [of generations], kindness   Truth,   Kindness Abundant

וָפֶשַׁע, וְחַטָּאָה, וְנַקֵּה.[1] וְסָלַחְתָּ לַעֲוֹנֵנוּ וּלְחַטָּאתֵנוּ

《 and our sins, 〈 our 〈 May You 《 and Who 〈 and inadvertent 〈 willful sin,
iniquities forgive absolves.   sin,

וּנְחַלְתָּנוּ.[2] סְלַח לָנוּ אָבִינוּ כִּי חָטָאנוּ, מְחַל לָנוּ

〈 us, 〈 pardon 《 we have 《 for 《 our 〈 us, 〈 Forgive 《 and make us
sinned;   Father,   Your heritage.

מַלְכֵּנוּ כִּי פָשָׁעְנוּ. כִּי אַתָּה אֲדֹנָי טוֹב וְסַלָּח,

《 and 〈 are 〈 O Lord, 〈 You, 〈 For 《 we have 〈 for 《 our King,
forgiving, good   willfully sinned.

וְרַב חֶסֶד לְכָל קֹרְאֶיךָ.[3]

《 who call 〈 to all 〈 kind 〈 and
upon You.   abundantly

סליחה נז / SELICHAH 57
(פזמון)

CHAZZAN, THEN CONGREGATION:

בֵּין כֶּסֶה לֶעָשׂוֹר* הִשְׁלַכְנוּ רְעַ שְׂאוֹר,*

《 Inclination;* 〈 the 〈 we cast off 〈 and 〈 Rosh 〈 Between
Evil   Yom Kippur* Hashanah

---

(1) *Exodus* 34:6-7. (2) 34:9. (3) *Psalms* 86:5.

בֵּין כֶּסֶה לֶעָשׂוֹר — *Between Rosh Hashanah and Yom Kippur*. [See *Selichah* 48 for the derivation of this expression.] The acrostic of this *pizmon* reads, אֱלִיעֶזֶר בְּרַבִּי שְׁלֹמֹה הָאֵל יִגְמְלֵהוּ חֶסֶד, *Eliezer son of R' Shlomo, may God grant him kindness.* He is thought to be the former disciple of Rabbeinu Tam [France, 1100-1171] whose correspondence with R' Tam appears in *Sefer HaYashar* (§58-59).

In this *pizmon*, the *paytan* refers repeatedly to a well-known Talmudic teaching: Three books are opened [before the Heavenly Tribunal] on Rosh Hashanah — one for the unquestionably wicked; one for the unquestionably righteous; and one for those between [these extremes]. The unquestionably righteous are immediately inscribed and sealed for life; the unquestionably wicked

צַדְּקֵנוּ בַּמִּשְׁפָּט בְּאוֹר הַחַיִּים לְאוֹר,[1]

《 [we] may 〈 of life 〈 so that in 〈 in the 〈 vindicate
bask. the light judgment, us

הִנְנוּ אָתָנוּ לְךָ[2] אַדִּיר וְנָאוֹר,[3]

《 and Illumi- 〈 O 《 to 〈 We have 《 Here
nated One, Mighty You, come we are!

כִּי עִמְּךָ מְקוֹר חַיִּים, בְּאוֹרְךָ נִרְאֶה אוֹר.[4]

《 light. 〈 may we 〈 by Your 《 of life; 〈 is the 〈 with 〈 for
see light source You

CONGREGATION, THEN *CHAZZAN*:

אָדוֹן עִמְּךָ סְלִיחָה,[5] סְלַח וּמְחַל לְשָׁבֶיךָ,

《 those who 〈 and 〈 forgive 《 is forgiveness, 〈 with 〈 O Lord,
return to You. pardon You

לְעֵת חִתּוּם גְּזַר דִּינֶךָ, לְטוֹבָה זָכְרָה אֲהוּבֶיךָ,

《 Your beloved 〈 remember 〈 for benefi- 《 of Your 〈 of the 〈 of the 〈 At the
[people]. cence judgment, verdict sealing time

יִוָּדַע כִּי אֱלֹהִים[6] בִּישֻׁרוּן קְרוֹבֶיךָ,

《 the people 〈 is among 〈 God 〈 that 〈 Let it be
close to You, Jeshurun, known

וְשִׂימֵנִי כַחוֹתָם עַל לִבֶּךָ.[7]   בֵּין כֶּסֶה לֶעָשׂוֹר...

《 and Yom 〈 Rosh 〈 between 《 Your 〈 upon 〈 as a seal 〈 and place
Kippur... Hashanah heart — me

CONGREGATION, THEN *CHAZZAN*:

עֲבָדֶיךָ לְטוֹב תַּעֲרֹב,[8] צַו כִּתְמָם לְמָחְקָה,

《 be erased. 〈 that their 〈 command 《 be their 〈 for good 〈 Your
[sin's] stain guarantor; servants

זָכְרָה מְצוּקֵי תֵבֵל,[9] פְּעֻלָּתָם אִם פָּסְקָה,

《 they are 〈 even 〈 their 《 of the 〈 the 〈 Re-
used up, if [meritorious] world; [patriarchal] member
deeds pillars

---

(1) Cf. *Job* 33:30. (2) *Jeremiah* 3:22. (3) Cf. *Psalms* 76:5. (4) 36:10. (5) Cf. 130:4.
(6) Cf. *I Kings* 18:36. (7) Cf. *Song of Songs* 8:6. (8) Cf. *Psalms* 119:122. (9) Cf. *I Samuel* 2:8.

are immediately inscribed and sealed for death. [But the judgment of] those between stands in abeyance from Rosh Hashanah until Yom Kippur. If they are found worthy, they are inscribed for life; if they are not found worthy, they are inscribed for death (*Rosh Hashanah* 6b).

הִשְׁלַכְנוּ רַע שְׂאוֹר — *We cast off the Evil Inclination* [lit., *the evil yeast*]. The Talmud refers to the Evil Inclination as שְׂאוֹר שֶׁבָּעִיסָה, *the yeast in the batter* (*Berachos* 17a), because it leavens the heart, causing it to ferment (*Rashi*), and leading man to sin.

רַחֵם בְּרֹגֶז תִּזְכּוֹר,¹ בָּנֶיךָ עֵת חֲקוּקָה,

《 to inscribe it, 〈 when 〈 Your 《 remember. 〈 amidst 〈 mercy
the time children['s   anger
comes judgment],

כָּתְבָה עַל לוּחַ אִתָּם וְעַל סֵפֶר חֻקָּה.²

《 inscribe 〈 the Book 〈 and 《 in their 〈 a 〈 on 〈 write it
it — [of Life] in presence; tablet down

בֵּין כֶּסֶה לֶעָשׂוֹר...

《 and Yom 〈 Rosh 〈 between
Kippur … Hashanah

CONGREGATION, THEN *CHAZZAN:*

בְּתַחֲנוּנִים כְּרָשׁ וְדַל, לְפָנֶיךָ קָרְבוּ,

《 they have 〈 before 〈 and 〈 like one im- 〈 With
drawn near; You needy poverished supplications,

רְאֵה עֲנִיִּם מֹרֶה מְאֹד,³ בְּלַחַץ בַּשֵּׁפֶל יֵשֵׁבוּ,

〈 they 〈 in 〈 in 《 to the 〈 severe 《 their 〈 see
dwell, degradation oppression, extreme; suffering,

בְּיוֹם חִפּוּשׂ תַּעֲלוּמוֹת, עֶלְיוֹן בְּךָ עֵינֵיךָ יֵיטִיבוּ,

《 may they be 《 in Your 《 to 《 O Exalted 《 hidden things, 〈 for searching 〈 On
found good, eyes, You, One, out the day

וְעַל סִפְרְךָ כֻּלָּם יִכָּתֵבוּ.⁴ בֵּין כֶּסֶה לֶעָשׂוֹר...

《 and Yom 〈 Rosh 〈 between 《 be 〈 may 〈 and in Your Book
Kippur … Hashanah written — they all [of Life]

CONGREGATION, THEN *CHAZZAN:*

שׁוֹחֲרֶיךָ הַמָּצֵא לְחַנְּנָךְ עוֹמְדִים הַשְׁכֵּם,

《 early, 〈 they rise 〈 to beseech Your 《 be 〈 To those who
[forgiveness] accessible, seek You,

לְבַל יָעֹז קַטֵּגוֹר בְּעֵינֶיךָ בַּל יִתְחַכֵּם,

《 seem cogent. 〈 not 〈 and in 《 shall the 〈 bold 〈 that not
Your eyes Adversary be

מְלִיצִים וּפְרַקְלִיטִים בְּחַסְדְּךָ עִמָּם הַסְכֵּם,

《 concur; 〈 with 〈 — in Your 《 and defenders 〈 [Our angelic]
them kindness, advocates

כִּתְבוּ עַל הַיְּהוּדִים כַּטּוֹב בְּעֵינֵיכֶם.⁵

《 in Your eyes — 〈 whatever 〈 the Jews 〈 concerning 〈 write
is favorable

---

(1) Cf. *Habakkuk* 3:2. (2) *Isaiah* 30:8; many editions of *Selichos* paraphrase this verse,
כָּתְבָה עַל לוּחַ אוֹתָם . . . , *write them [Your children] on a tablet. . .*; some editions read,
כָּתוֹב עַל לוּחַ חוֹתָם . . . , *write on the tablet seal. . . .* (3) Cf. *II Kings* 14:26. (4) *Psalms* 139:16. (5) *Esther* 8:8.

בֵּין כֶּסֶה לֶעָשׂוֹר...

《 and Yom 〈 Rosh 〈between
Kippur... Hashanah

CONGREGATION, THEN *CHAZZAN:*

הֵן רוּחַ וְלֵב עַמְּךָ שָׁבוּר וְחוֹלֶה,

《 and sick; 〈 are 〈 of Your 〈 and 〈 the 《 In-
broken people heart spirit deed,

הֵן חַטָּאת וְאָשָׁם וְנֶדֶר אֲשֶׁר יַפְלָא,

《 he 〈 that 〈 and [to sat- 〈 and guilt- 〈 [their own] 〈 they
articulated. isfy] a vow offering sin-offering are

אֱמוּנִים וּבֵינוֹנִים חֲתָם חוֹתָם מָלֵא,

《 that is full 〈 with a seal 〈 seal 〈 and the 〈 The faithful
intermediates [righteous]

אֵלֶּה לְחַיֵּי עוֹלָם וְאֵלֶּה.¹ בֵּין כֶּסֶה לֶעָשׂוֹר...

《 and Yom 〈 Rosh 〈between 《 and these 《 eternal, 〈 are for 〈 — these
Kippur... Hashanah [the interme- life [the
diates also] — righteous]

CONGREGATION, THEN *CHAZZAN:*

לֹא לְפִי רְאוּיִים תִּשְׁפֹּט הֲמוֹנַי,

《 my 〈 should 〈 their 〈 accord- 〈 Not
multitudes, You judge worthiness ing to

יְשֻׁרוּן מִיַחֲדֶיךָ אַף בְּלַחַץ מוֹנַי,

《 by my 〈 when 〈 even 〈 declares Your 〈 for
oppressors. coerced Oneness Jeshurun

גְּלִיפַת כְּתָב צַוֵּה לְשֶׁבַח וְלֹא לִגְנַאי,

《 disgrace, 〈 and 〈 for praise 《 You 〈 be 〈 That their
not should written inscription [of
command, their verdict]

מִפְתַּח פִּתּוּחֵי חוֹתָם קֹדֶשׁ לַיהוה.²

《 to HASHEM — 〈 Holy 《 of a signet 〈 like the 〈 an
[ring], engraving engraving

בֵּין כֶּסֶה לֶעָשׂוֹר...

《 and Yom 〈 Rosh 〈between
Kippur... Hashanah

CONGREGATION, THEN *CHAZZAN:*

לְפַתּוֹתְךָ בְּתַחַן, עֲבָדֶיךָ מַסְכִּימִים,

《 have agreed; 〈 Your 〈 with 〈 To persuade
servants supplication You

_____

(1) *Daniel* 12:2. (2) Cf. *Exodus* 39:30.

הַפְּתַח לָמוֹ וּזְכֹר נְחוּמִים,

《 [Your promised] 〈 and re- 〈 to 〈 let
comfort. member them, [Your Gates]
be opened

חַסְדְּךָ הַפְלֵא, וְהַעֲבֵר כְּתָמִים,

《 the stains 〈 and remove 〈 show 〈 [With] Your
[of their sins], wonders kindness

אֵל מֶלֶךְ יוֹשֵׁב עַל כִּסֵּא רַחֲמִים.

《 of Mercy — 〈 the Throne 〈 on 〈 Who sits 〈 King 〈 O God,

בֵּין כֶּסֶה לֶעָשׂוֹר...

《 and Yom 〈 Rosh 〈 between
Kippur ... Hashanah

ALL, WHILE STANDING:

אֵל מֶלֶךְ יוֹשֵׁב עַל כִּסֵּא רַחֲמִים, מִתְנַהֵג

〈 Who acts 《 of mercy, 〈 the throne 〈 on 〈 Who sits 〈 King 〈 O God,

בַּחֲסִידוּת, מוֹחֵל עֲוֹנוֹת עַמּוֹ, מַעֲבִיר רִאשׁוֹן

〈 [sins,] one 〈 Who 《 of His 〈 the sins 〈 Who 《 with kindness,
removes people, pardons

רִאשׁוֹן,[1] מַרְבֶּה מְחִילָה לַחַטָּאִים וּסְלִיחָה לַפּוֹשְׁעִים,

《 to willful 〈 and 〈 to unintentional 〈 pardon 〈 Who abun- 《 by one,
sinners, forgiveness sinners dantly grants

עֹשֶׂה צְדָקוֹת עִם כָּל בָּשָׂר וָרוּחַ, לֹא כְרָעָתָם

〈 in accord with 〈 — not 《 and 〈 [beings 〈 all 〈 with 〈 acts of 《 Who
their wickedness spirit of] flesh generosity performs

תִּגְמוֹל. ❖ אֵל הוֹרֵיתָ לָנוּ לוֹמַר שְׁלֹשׁ עֶשְׂרֵה, וּזְכוֹר

〈 remem- 《 the Thirteen 〈 to 〈 You 〈 O God, 《 do You
ber [Attributes of Mercy]; recite taught repay them!

לָנוּ הַיּוֹם בְּרִית שְׁלֹשׁ עֶשְׂרֵה, כְּמוֹ שֶׁהוֹדַעְתָּ לֶעָנָיו

〈 to the humble 〈 You made 〈 as 《 of [these] Thirteen, 〈 the 〈 today 〈 for us
one [Moses] known covenant

מִקֶּדֶם, כְּמוֹ שֶׁכָּתוּב, וַיֵּרֶד יהוה בֶּעָנָן וַיִּתְיַצֵּב עִמּוֹ

〈 with 〈 and stood 〈 in a 〈 And HASHEM 《 it is written: 〈 as 《 in ancient
him cloud descended times,

שָׁם, וַיִּקְרָא בְשֵׁם יהוה.[2]

《 of 〈 with the 〈 and He 〈 there,
HASHEM. Name called out

---

(1) *Rosh Hashanah* 17a. (2) *Exodus* 34:5.

CONGREGATION, THEN *CHAZZAN*:

וַיַּעֲבֹר יהוה עַל פָּנָיו וַיִּקְרָא:

《 and 《 [Moses'] 〈 before 〈 And HASHEM passed
proclaimed: face,

CONGREGATION AND *CHAZZAN* RECITE LOUDLY AND IN UNISON:

יהוה, יהוה, אֵל, רַחוּם, וְחַנּוּן, אֶרֶךְ אַפַּיִם,

〈 to anger, 〈 Slow 《 and 〈 Compassionate 〈 God, 〈 HASHEM, 〈 HASHEM,
Gracious,

וְרַב חֶסֶד, וֶאֱמֶת, נֹצֵר חֶסֶד לַאֲלָפִים, נֹשֵׂא עָוֹן,

〈 of 〈 Forgiver 《 for thousands 〈 of 〈 Preserver 《 and 〈 in 〈 and
iniquity, [of generations], kindness Truth, Kindness Abundant

וָפֶשַׁע, וְחַטָּאָה, וְנַקֵּה.[1] וְסָלַחְתָּ לַעֲוֹנֵנוּ וּלְחַטָּאתֵנוּ

《 and our sins, 〈 our 〈 May You 《 and and Who 〈 and inadvertent 〈 willful sin,
iniquities forgive absolves. sin,

וּנְחַלְתָּנוּ.[2] סְלַח לָנוּ אָבִינוּ כִּי חָטָאנוּ, מְחַל לָנוּ

〈 us, 〈 pardon 《 we have 〈 for 《 our 〈 us, 〈 Forgive 《 and make us
sinned; Father, Your heritage.

מַלְכֵּנוּ כִּי פָשָׁעְנוּ. כִּי אַתָּה אֲדֹנָי טוֹב וְסַלָּח,

《 and 〈 are 〈 O Lord, 〈 You, 〈 For 《 we have 〈 for 《 our King,
forgiving, good willfully sinned.

וְרַב חֶסֶד לְכָל קֹרְאֶיךָ.[3]

《 who call 〈 to all 〈 kind 〈 and
upon You. abundantly

PREFATORY VERSES TO SELICHAH 58 / פסוקי הקדמה לסליחה נח

כְּאַיָּל תַּעֲרֹג עַל אֲפִיקֵי מָיִם, כֵּן נַפְשֵׁנוּ תַעֲרֹג אֵלֶיךָ

〈 for You, 〈 longs 〈 our soul 〈 so 《 of water, 〈 brooks 〈 for 〈 longs 〈 As the deer

אֱלֹהִים.[4] כִּי שָׁחָה לֶעָפָר נַפְשֵׁנוּ, דָּבְקָה לָאָרֶץ בִּטְנֵנוּ.

《 is our 〈 to the 〈 stuck 《 is our 〈 to the 〈 prostrated 〈 For 《 O God.
belly. earth soul, dust

וַיֹּאמֶר, בִּי נִשְׁבַּעְתִּי נְאֻם יהוה, כִּי יַעַן אֲשֶׁר עָשִׂיתָ

〈 you have done 〈 since 〈 that 《 of 〈 — the 〈 I swear 〈 By 《 And he
HASHEM — word Myself said,

אֶת הַדָּבָר הַזֶּה, וְלֹא חָשַׂכְתָּ אֶת בִּנְךָ אֶת יְחִידֶךָ.[6]

《 your only one. 〈 your son, 〈 withheld 〈 and have 《 this thing
not

---

(1) *Exodus* 34:6-7. (2) 34:9. (3) *Psalms* 86:5. (4) Cf. 42:2. (5) 44:26. (6) *Genesis* 22:16.

כְּרַחֵם אָב עַל בָּנִים, כֵּן תְּרַחֵם יהוה עָלֵינוּ.[1]

⟪ on us. ⟨ HASHEM, ⟨ have mercy, ⟨ so ⟪ his children, ⟨ toward ⟨ a father is ⟨ As merciful as

לַיהוה הַיְשׁוּעָה, עַל עַמְּךָ בִרְכָתֶךָ סֶּלָה.[2] יהוה

⟨ HASHEM, ⟪ Selah. ⟪ is Your blessing, ⟨ Your people ⟨ upon ⟪ is salvation, ⟨ To HASHEM

צְבָאוֹת עִמָּנוּ, מִשְׂגָּב לָנוּ אֱלֹהֵי יַעֲקֹב סֶלָה.[3]

⟪ Selah. ⟪ of Jacob, ⟨ is the God ⟨ for us ⟨ a stronghold ⟪ is with us, ⟨ Master of Legions,

יהוה צְבָאוֹת, אַשְׁרֵי אָדָם בֹּטֵחַ בָּךְ.[4] יהוה

⟨ HASHEM, ⟪ in You. ⟨ who trusts ⟨ is the man ⟨ — praise-worthy ⟪ Master of Legions ⟨ HASHEM,

הוֹשִׁיעָה, הַמֶּלֶךְ יַעֲנֵנוּ בְיוֹם קָרְאֵנוּ.[5]

⟪ we call. ⟨ on the day ⟨ answer us ⟨ May the King ⟪ save!

סליחה נח / SELICHAH 58

(עקדה)

אֱלֹהֵינוּ וֵאלֹהֵי אֲבוֹתֵינוּ:

⟪ of our forefathers: ⟨ and God ⟨ Our God

אֵיתָן לִמֵּד דֵעַת,* טֶרֶם לַכֹּל מוּדַעַת.

⟪ it was known. ⟨ to all ⟨ before ⟪ knowledge [of God],* ⟨ taught ⟨ The mighty one [Abraham]

בֵּאֵר שִׁמְךָ לְכָל בָּאֵי עוֹלָם, גִּלָּה כָּל סָתוּם וְנֶעְלָם.

⟪ and hidden. ⟨ obscure ⟨ every-thing ⟪ he re-vealed ⟨ [into] ⟨ who come ⟨ to all ⟨ Your Name ⟨ He elucidated

גְּלוּלִים מָאַס וְשָׁבֵּר,* תּוֹעִים לְשִׁמְךָ חִבֵּר.

⟨ he connected [by conversion]. ⟨ to Your Name ⟨ the errant ⟪ and ⟨ he ⟨ [His father's] idols ⟪ shattered;* ⟨ disdained ⟨ idols

---

(1) Cf. *Psalms* 103:13. (2) 3:9. (3) 46:8. (4) 84:13. (5) 20:10.

‎◆§ אֵיתָן לִמֵּד דֵעַת — *The mighty one [Abraham] taught knowledge [of God].* The Psalmist records a psalm by אֵיתָן הָאֶזְרָחִי, *Ethan the Ezrachite,* whom the Talmud identifies as the Patriarch Abraham (*Bava Basra* 15a; see also *Rashi* to *I Kings* 5:11). He is called אֵיתָן, literally, *the mighty one,* for the Patriarchs are the pillars of the world (see *Rosh Hashanah* 11a); and הָאֶזְרָחִי, literally, *the Easterner,* because he hailed from Aram, which is to the east of *Eretz Yisrael* (see *Sanhedrin* 108b).

All *akeidah piyutim* extol the virtues and merits of Abraham and Isaac when they went forth to fulfill God's command to sacrifice Isaac. This *akeidah,* however, goes a few steps further than most, for it also invokes the merit of Jacob, the Matriarchs, and the twelve sons of Jacob. The initial letters of the twenty-two couplets form the *aleph-beis.*

גְּלוּלִים מָאַס וְשָׁבֵּר — *[His father's] idols he disdained and shattered.* Terach, an idol manufacturer, asked his young son Abram

דֶּרֶךְ מִישׁוֹר בָּחַר, תּוֹרָה וּמִצְוֹת שָׁמַר וְלֹא אֵחַר.

《 delay. 〈 without 〈 he 〈 and 〈 Torah 《 he 〈 that was 〈 He
observed   mitzvos   chose,   straight   path

הִצַּלְתּוֹ מֵאוּר כַּשְׂדִּים, גְּנַנְתּוֹ בְּעֵמֶק הַשִּׂדִּים.*

《 of Siddim.* 〈 in the 〈 and pro- 《 of the 〈 from Ur 〈 You saved
Valley   tected him   Chaldees,   him

וְעַדְתּוֹ שְׂכָרְךָ הַרְבֵּה מְאֹד,¹ וַתְּתַקְתוֹ רֹב עֹשֶׁר וְכָבוֹד.

《 and 〈 wealth 〈 with 〈 and forti- 《 is very great! 〈 Your 《 You prom-
honor.   abundant   fied him   reward   ised him,

זָעַק וְהֵשִׁיב מַה תִּתֶּן לִי,² שֹׁרֶשׁ וְעָנָף אֵין לִי.

《 have I not? 〈 and 〈 when 〈 me, 〈 can You 〈 What 《 and 〈 He cried
branch   root   give   answered,   out

חִזַּלְתּוֹ בִּרְאִיַּת מַחֲזֶה, בְּשָׂרְתּוֹ לֹא יִירָשְׁךָ זֶה.³

《 would this 〈 Not inherit 《 You informed 《 a vision, 〈 through 〈 You strength-
[Eliezer].   you   him,   his seeing   ened him

טֶנֶא בִּכּוּרִים לִמְאָה חֲנַנְתּוֹ, לְקָרְבַּן נִיחוֹחַ חֲשַׁקְתּוֹ.

《 You desired 〈 that is 〈 then for 《 you 〈 at a hundred 〈 of first 〈 A
[that son].   pleasant-   an offering   granted   [years of age]   fruits   basket
scented   him,

יַחְדָּו בְּכָל לִבָּם דָּצוּ, לַעֲשׂוֹת רְצוֹנְךָ רָצוּ.

《 they 〈 Your will 〈 to carry out 《 they 〈 their 〈 with all 〈 Together,
ran.   rejoiced;   hearts

(1) *Genesis* 15:1. (2) 15:2. (3) 15:4.

to mind the business. When his father had left, Abram took a club and smashed all the idols except the largest one. Then he placed the club into that idol's hands.

Upon returning, Terach demanded, "Who did this to my idols?"

Abram explained, "When I placed food before them, the idols began arguing, each claiming the right to the first portion. Finally, the largest of them settled the argument by smashing the others with his club."

"What are you saying?" cried the incredulous Terach. "Do they know what's happening?"

To which Abram replied, "Would that your ears would hear what your mouth just said [Why do you worship them if they do not know what is happening?]!"

Not knowing how to handle his son's "blasphemy," Terach hauled Abram before King Nimrod. The king ordered the lad to bow to the fire. Abram replied, "But water extinguishes fire; perhaps we should bow to the water?" The king agreed. Then Abram said, "But the clouds are stronger for they carry the water; perhaps we should bow to the clouds?" Nimrod agreed. Once again Abram argued, "But the wind blows the clouds wherever it pleases; perhaps we should bow to the wind?"

Finally, Nimrod got the point. "You are trying to sidetrack me with your words. I bow only to the fire. And I shall throw you into it. Let us see whether the God to Whom you bow can save you from it." Thereupon, he had Abram cast into a fiery furnace; but the fire miraculously had no power over the young Patriarch, and he emerged unscathed. For this reason the place became known as אוּר כַּשְׂדִּים, Ur [lit., *fire*] *of the Chaldees* (*Bereishis Rabbah* 38:13).

בְּעֵמֶק הַשִּׂדִּים — *In the Valley of Siddim*, where he battled and defeated the four kings

כָּבַשׁ רַחֲמָיו לַעֲשׂוֹת רְצוֹנֶךָ,*

« Your will;* ‹ to carry out ‹ his ‹ He [Abraham]
                mercy   overcame

כֵּן יִכְבְּשׁוּ רַחֲמֶיךָ אֶת כַּעַסְךָ מֵעַל צֹאנֶךָ.

« Your ‹ from ‹ Your anger ‹ may Your ‹ conquer ‹ therefore,
  flock.   upon   mercy   so

לִבָּם וְנַפְשָׁם הָיָה נָכוֹן,[1]

« ready; ‹ were ‹ and their ‹ Their
              soul   heart

לָכֵן תְּפִלָּתֵנוּ לְפָנֶיךָ כִּקְטֹרֶת תִּכּוֹן.[2]

« be ‹ as incense ‹ before ‹ may our ‹ therefore
considered.   You   prayer

מִהֵר וְלָקַח מַאֲכֶלֶת,[3]

« a knife; ‹ and ‹ [Abraham]
     took   hurried

לָכֵן זַרְעָם תַּצִּיל מִמִּיתָה מְשַׁכֶּלֶת.

« that causes ‹ from death ‹ may You ‹ their ‹ therefore
bereavement.   rescue   seed

נֶעֱקַד יָחִיד כְּשֶׂה לַטֶּבַח,

« for ‹ like a ‹ was the ‹ Bound
slaughter;   sheep   only son

לָכֵן תְּפִלָּתֵנוּ תִּרְצֶה כְּעוֹלָה וָזֶבַח.

« and ‹ as with ‹ may You ‹ our prayer ‹ therefore,
sacrifice.   burnt-   accept
       offering   with favor

סִדֵּר עֵצִים וְהִצִּית עֲלֵיהֶם אֵשׁ,

« the ‹ upon them ‹ and ‹ the logs ‹ He
fire;   kindled   arranged

לָכֵן בַּעֲמִידָתֵנוּ הַיּוֹם לֹא נִתְבַּיֵּשׁ.

« be ‹ let us ‹ today ‹ when we stand ‹ therefore,
embarrassed.   not   [in prayer]

עֲנִיתוֹ מִשְּׁמֵי שָׁמַיִם, לָכֵן נִשְׁבַּעְתָּ לּוֹ בִּשְׁמְךָ פַּעֲמָיִם.[4]

« [now] a ‹ in Your ‹ to ‹ You swore ‹ there- « heavens; ‹ from the ‹ You had an-
second time. Name   him   fore,   highest   swered him

---

(1) Cf. *Psalms* 78:37. (2) Cf. 141:2. (3) Cf. *Genesis* 22:10.
(4) See 13:16, 15:5 and 22:15. See *Ramban* 22:16.

---

who had taken his nephew Lot captive (see
Genesis Ch. 14).

כָּבַשׁ רַחֲמָיו לַעֲשׂוֹת רְצוֹנֶךָ — *He [Abraham]*
overcame his mercy to carry out Your

פָּדִיתָ אוֹתוֹ בְּאַיִל בַּסְּבַךְ אֲחוּז,¹

《 caught; 〈 in the 〈 with a 〈 him 〈 You
thicket   ram   [Isaac]   redeemed

לָכֵן עֲמִידָתֵנוּ וְעִנּוּיֵנוּ לֹא תָבוּז.

《   You will   〈 and our afflicting 〈 our standing 〈 therefore
not despise. ourselves [in fasting] [in prayer]

צַעֲקָתֵנוּ שְׁמַע וְשַׁוְעָתֵנוּ סְכֹת,

《 listen, 〈 and to our shout 〈 hear 〈 Our cry,

בִּזְכוּת אָב נָסַע סֻכּוֹת,²

《 to Succos. 〈 who   〈 of the 〈 by the
traveled Patriarch   merit
[Jacob],

קוֹל מְבַשֵּׂר יִשָּׁמַע בָּעוֹלָם,

《 in the world, 〈 be heard 〈 of the 〈 Let the
herald   voice

לִגְאֹל עַם גֶּזַע גִּבְעוֹת עוֹלָם.³

《 eternal [as is 〈 of the hills [the 〈 the de- 《 the 〈 to
their merit].   Matriarchs] scendants people, redeem

רַחֵם קְהַל עֲדַת מְקֻשָּׁטִים, טִיעַת שְׁנֵים עָשָׂר שְׁבָטִים.

《 tribes. 〈 of the twelve 〈 the   《 adorned   〈 of the 〈 on the 〈 Have
planting   [with Your assembly, congre- mercy
commandments],   gation

❖ שְׁכִינָתְךָ תִּשְׁכֹּן בְּתוֹכֵנוּ, תְּנַהֲגֵנוּ לִגְבוּל אַדְמָתֵנוּ.

《 of our land. 〈 to the 〈 and may 《 in our midst, 〈 dwell 〈 May Your
borders   You lead us   Presence

תֵּפֶן אֵלֵינוּ בְּרַחֲמִים, כִּי כֵן נִקְרֵאתָ מָלֵא רַחֲמִים.

《 of mercy. 〈 [God] full 《 are You called: 〈 so 〈 for 〈 with mercy, 〈 to us 〈 Turn

ALL, WHILE STANDING:

אֵל מֶלֶךְ יוֹשֵׁב עַל כִּסֵּא רַחֲמִים, מִתְנַהֵג

〈 Who acts 《 of mercy, 〈 the throne 〈 on 〈 Who sits 〈 King 〈 O God,

בַּחֲסִידוּת, מוֹחֵל עֲוֹנוֹת עַמּוֹ, מַעֲבִיר רִאשׁוֹן

〈 [sins,] one 〈 Who 《 of His 〈 the sins 〈 Who 《 with kindness,
removes   people,   pardons

---

(1) Cf. *Genesis* 22:13. (2) See 33:17.
(3) See *Targum Yerushalmi* to *Genesis* 49:26 and *Deuteronomy* 33:15.

---

will. According to the Midrash, after God
told Abraham to sacrifice the ram in place
of Isaac, Abraham prayed, "... just as I

overcame my mercy to do Your will, so
may it be Your will ..." (*Bereishis Rabbah*
56:10).

רִאשׁוֹן,[1] מַרְבֶּה מְחִילָה לַחֲטָאִים וּסְלִיחָה לַפּוֹשְׁעִים,

《 by one, 》 Who abun- 〈 pardon 〈 to unintentional 〈 and 〈 to willful
dantly grants   sinners   forgiveness   sinners,

עֹשֶׂה צְדָקוֹת עִם כָּל בָּשָׂר וָרְוּחַ, לֹא כְרָעָתָם

〈 Who 〈 acts of 〈 with 〈 all 〈 [beings 《 and 《 — not 〈 in accord
performs generosity   of] flesh   spirit   with their
                                                            wickedness

תִּגְמוֹל. ❖ אֵל הוֹרֵיתָ לָּנוּ לוֹמַר שְׁלֹשׁ עֶשְׂרֵה, וּזְכוֹר

《 do You 〈 O God, 〈 You 〈 us 〈 to 〈 the Thirteen 《 remem-
repay them!   taught   recite   [Attributes of Mercy];   ber

לָּנוּ הַיּוֹם בְּרִית שְׁלֹשׁ עֶשְׂרֵה, כְּמוֹ שֶׁהוֹדַעְתָּ לֶעָנָיו

〈 to the humble 〈 You made 〈 as 《 of [these] Thirteen, 〈 the 〈 today 〈 for us
one [Moses]   known   covenant

מִקֶּדֶם, כְּמוֹ שֶׁכָּתוּב, וַיֵּרֶד יהוה בֶּעָנָן וַיִּתְיַצֵּב עִמּוֹ

〈 with 〈 and stood 〈 in a 〈 And HASHEM 《 it is written: 〈 as 《 in ancient
him   cloud   descended   times,

שָׁם, וַיִּקְרָא בְשֵׁם יהוה.[2]

《 of 〈 with the 〈 and He 《 there,
HASHEM.   Name   called out

CONGREGATION, THEN *CHAZZAN:*

וַיַּעֲבֹר יהוה עַל פָּנָיו וַיִּקְרָא:

《 and 《 [Moses'] 〈 before 〈 And HASHEM passed
proclaimed: face,

CONGREGATION AND *CHAZZAN* RECITE LOUDLY AND IN UNISON:

יהוה, יהוה, אֵל, רַחוּם, וְחַנּוּן, אֶרֶךְ אַפַּיִם,

〈 to anger, 〈 Slow 《 and 〈 Compassionate 〈 God, 〈 HASHEM, 〈 HASHEM,
Gracious,

וְרַב חֶסֶד, וֶאֱמֶת, נֹצֵר חֶסֶד לָאֲלָפִים, נֹשֵׂא עָוֹן,

〈 of 〈 Forgiver 《 for thousands 〈 of 〈 Preserver 《 and 〈 in 〈 and
iniquity,   [of generations], kindness   Truth,   Kindness Abundant

וָפֶשַׁע, וְחַטָּאָה, וְנַקֵּה.[3] וְסָלַחְתָּ לַעֲוֹנֵנוּ וּלְחַטָּאתֵנוּ

《 and our sins, 〈 our 〈 May You 《 and Who 〈 and inadvertent 〈 willful sin,
iniquities   forgive   absolves.   sin,

וּנְחַלְתָּנוּ.[4] סְלַח לָנוּ אָבִינוּ כִּי חָטָאנוּ, מְחַל לָנוּ

〈 us, 〈 pardon 《 we have 〈 for 《 our 〈 us, 〈 Forgive 《 and make us
sinned;   Father,   Your heritage.

---

(1) *Rosh Hashanah* 17a. (2) *Exodus* 34:5. (3) 34:6-7. (4) 34:9.

מַלְכֵּנוּ כִּי פָשֶׁעְנוּ. כִּי אַתָּה אֲדֹנָי טוֹב וְסַלָּח,

וְרַב חֶסֶד לְכָל קֹרְאֶיךָ.[1]

ALL:

זְכֹר רַחֲמֶיךָ יהוה וַחֲסָדֶיךָ, כִּי מֵעוֹלָם הֵמָּה.[2]

זָכְרֵנוּ יהוה בִּרְצוֹן עַמֶּךָ, פָּקְדֵנוּ בִּישׁוּעָתֶךָ.[3] זְכֹר

עֲדָתְךָ קָנִיתָ קֶּדֶם, גָּאַלְתָּ שֵׁבֶט נַחֲלָתֶךָ, הַר צִיּוֹן זֶה

שָׁכַנְתָּ בּוֹ.[4] זְכֹר יהוה חִבַּת יְרוּשָׁלַיִם, אַהֲבַת

צִיּוֹן אַל תִּשְׁכַּח לָנֶצַח.[5] אַתָּה תָקוּם תְּרַחֵם צִיּוֹן כִּי

עֵת לְחֶנְנָהּ, כִּי בָא מוֹעֵד.[6] זְכֹר יהוה לִבְנֵי אֱדוֹם

אֵת יוֹם יְרוּשָׁלָיִם, הָאֹמְרִים עָרוּ עָרוּ עַד הַיְסוֹד בָּהּ.[7]

זְכֹר לְאַבְרָהָם לְיִצְחָק וּלְיִשְׂרָאֵל עֲבָדֶיךָ, אֲשֶׁר

נִשְׁבַּעְתָּ לָהֶם בָּךְ וַתְּדַבֵּר אֲלֵהֶם, אַרְבֶּה אֶת זַרְעֲכֶם

כְּכוֹכְבֵי הַשָּׁמָיִם, וְכָל הָאָרֶץ הַזֹּאת אֲשֶׁר אָמַרְתִּי,

---

(1) *Psalms* 86:5. (2) 25:6. (3) Cf. 106:4. (4) 74:2. (5) This is not a Scriptural verse. (6) *Psalms* 102:14. (7) 137:7.

1. אֶתֵּן לְזַרְעֲכֶם, וְנָחֲלוּ לְעֹלָם. זְכֹר לַעֲבָדֶיךָ לְאַבְרָהָם

⟨ of Abraham, ⟨ of Your servants, ⟨ Remember [the merits] ⟨ forever. ⟨ and they will inherit it ⟨ to your offspring, ⟨ I will give

לְיִצְחָק וּלְיַעֲקֹב, אַל תֵּפֶן אֶל קְשִׁי הָעָם הַזֶּה וְאֶל

⟨ to ⟨ of this people, ⟨ the stubbornness ⟨ to ⟨ pay attention ⟨ do not ⟨ and of Jacob; ⟨ of Isaac,

רִשְׁעוֹ וְאֶל חַטָּאתוֹ. 2. זְכֹר לָנוּ בְּרִית אָבוֹת, כַּאֲשֶׁר

⟨ as ⟨ of the Patriarchs, ⟨ the covenant ⟨ for us ⟨ Remember ⟨ its sinfulness. ⟨ and ⟨ its wickedness, to

אָמַרְתָּ: וְזָכַרְתִּי אֶת בְּרִיתִי יַעֲקוֹב, וְאַף אֶת בְּרִיתִי

⟨ My covenant ⟨ and also ⟨ [with] Jacob, ⟨ My covenant ⟨ And I will remember ⟨ You said:

3. יִצְחָק, וְאַף אֶת בְּרִיתִי אַבְרָהָם אֶזְכֹּר, וְהָאָרֶץ אֶזְכֹּר.

⟨ I will remember. ⟨ and the Land ⟨ I will remember; ⟨ [with] Abraham ⟨ My covenant ⟨ and also ⟨ [with] Isaac,

זְכוֹר לָנוּ בְּרִית רִאשׁוֹנִים, כַּאֲשֶׁר אָמַרְתָּ: וְזָכַרְתִּי

⟨ And I will remember ⟨ You said: ⟨ as ⟨ of the ancient ones, ⟨ the covenant ⟨ for us ⟨ Remember

לָהֶם בְּרִית רִאשׁוֹנִים, אֲשֶׁר הוֹצֵאתִי אֹתָם מֵאֶרֶץ

⟨ from the land ⟨ I took them out ⟨ that ⟨ of the ancient ones, ⟨ the covenant ⟨ for them

מִצְרַיִם לְעֵינֵי הַגּוֹיִם, לִהְיוֹת לָהֶם לֵאלֹהִים, אֲנִי

⟨ I am ⟨ a God; ⟨ to them ⟨ to be ⟨ of the nations, ⟨ in the very sight ⟨ of Egypt

4. יהוה. עָשָׂה עִמָּנוּ כְּמָה שֶׁהִבְטַחְתָּנוּ: וְאַף גַּם

⟨ all ⟨ And despite ⟨ You promised us: ⟨ as ⟨ with us ⟨ Do ⟨ HASHEM.

זֹאת בִּהְיוֹתָם בְּאֶרֶץ אֹיְבֵיהֶם, לֹא מְאַסְתִּים וְלֹא

⟨ nor ⟨ despise them ⟨ I will not ⟨ of their enemies, ⟨ in the land ⟨ when they will be ⟨ this,

גְעַלְתִּים לְכַלֹּתָם לְהָפֵר בְּרִיתִי אִתָּם, כִּי אֲנִי יהוה

⟨ HASHEM, ⟨ I am ⟨ for ⟨ with them, ⟨ My covenant ⟨ to annul ⟨ to destroy them, ⟨ abhor them

5. אֱלֹהֵיהֶם. הָשֵׁב שְׁבוּתֵנוּ וְרַחֲמֵנוּ, כְּמָה שֶׁכָּתוּב:

⟨ it is written: ⟨ as ⟨ and have mercy on us, ⟨ our captivity ⟨ Bring back ⟨ their God.

---

(1) *Exodus* 32:13. (2) *Deuteronomy* 9:27. (3) *Leviticus* 26:42. (4) 26:45. (5) 26:44.

וְשָׁב יהוה אֱלֹהֶיךָ אֶת שְׁבוּתְךָ וְרִחֲמֶךָ, וְשָׁב וְקִבֶּצְךָ

⟨ gather you in ⟨ and He will once again ⟪ and He will have mercy upon you, ⟨ your captivity, ⟨ your God, ⟨ will ⟨Then bring back HASHEM,

מִכָּל הָעַמִּים אֲשֶׁר הֱפִיצְךָ יהוה אֱלֹהֶיךָ שָׁמָּה.[1]

⟪ thereto. ⟨ your God ⟨ has HASHEM ⟨ scattered you ⟨ that ⟨ the peoples ⟨ from all

קַבֵּץ נִדָחֵינוּ, כְּמָה שֶׁכָּתוּב: אִם יִהְיֶה נִדַחֲךָ בִּקְצֵה

⟨ at the ends ⟨ your dispersed will be ⟨ If ⟨ it is written: ⟨ as ⟨ our dispersed ones, ⟨ Gather

הַשָּׁמָיִם, מִשָּׁם יְקַבֶּצְךָ יהוה אֱלֹהֶיךָ, וּמִשָּׁם יִקָּחֶךָ.[2]

⟪ He will take you. ⟨ and from there ⟪ your God, ⟨ will HASHEM, ⟨ gather you in ⟨ from there ⟪ of heaven,

מָחֶה פְשָׁעֵינוּ כָּעָב וְכֶעָנָן, כְּמָה שֶׁכָּתוּב: מָחִיתִי

⟨ I have wiped away ⟪ it is written: ⟨ as ⟪ and like a cloud, ⟨ like a mist ⟨ our sins ⟨ Wipe away

כָּעָב פְּשָׁעֶיךָ וְכֶעָנָן חַטֹּאתֶיךָ, שׁוּבָה אֵלַי כִּי

⟨ for ⟨ to Me, ⟨ return ⟪ your transgressions; ⟨ and like a cloud ⟨ your willful sins, ⟨ like a mist

גְאַלְתִּיךָ.[3] מָחֶה פְשָׁעֵינוּ לְמַעַנָךְ, כַּאֲשֶׁר אָמָרְתָּ:

⟪ You have said: ⟨ as ⟪ for Your sake, ⟨ our sins ⟨ Wipe away ⟪ I have redeemed you.

אָנֹכִי אָנֹכִי הוּא מֹחֶה פְשָׁעֶיךָ לְמַעֲנִי, וְחַטֹּאתֶיךָ לֹא

⟨ I shall ⟨ and your ⟪ for ⟨ your ⟨Who wipes ⟨ am the ⟨ [only] I, ⟨ I, not transgressions My sake, willful sins away One

אֶזְכֹּר.[4] הַלְבֵּן חֲטָאֵינוּ כַּשֶּׁלֶג וְכַצֶּמֶר, כְּמָה שֶׁכָּתוּב:

⟪ it is written: ⟨ as ⟪ and like wool, ⟨ like snow ⟨ our sins ⟨ Whiten ⟪ recall.

לְכוּ נָא וְנִוָּכְחָה, יֹאמַר יהוה, אִם יִהְיוּ חֲטָאֵיכֶם

⟨ your sins may be ⟨ Though ⟪ HASHEM. ⟨ says ⟪ let us reason together, ⟨ now, ⟨ Come,

כַּשָּׁנִים כַּשֶּׁלֶג יַלְבִּינוּ, אִם יַאְדִּימוּ כַתּוֹלָע, כַּצֶּמֶר

⟨ like [white] wool ⟪ as crimson, ⟨ they may be red ⟨ though ⟪ they will be whitened; ⟨ like snow ⟪ like scarlet,

יִהְיוּ.[5] זָרֹק עָלֵינוּ מַיִם טְהוֹרִים וְטַהֲרֵנוּ, כְּמָה שֶׁכָּתוּב:

⟪ it is written: ⟨ as ⟪ and purify us, ⟨ pure water ⟨ upon us ⟨ Pour ⟪ they will become.

---

(1) *Leviticus* 30:3. (2) 30:4. (3) *Isaiah* 44:22. (4) 43:25. (5) 1:18.

וְזָרַקְתִּי עֲלֵיכֶם מַיִם טְהוֹרִים וּטְהַרְתֶּם, מִכֹּל
‹ from all   « and you will become pure;   ‹ pure water   ‹ upon you   ‹ I shall pour

טֻמְאוֹתֵיכֶם וּמִכָּל גִּלּוּלֵיכֶם אֲטַהֵר אֶתְכֶם.[1] רַחֵם
‹ Have mercy   « you.   ‹ I will purify   ‹ your abominations   ‹ and from all   ‹ your contaminations

עָלֵינוּ וְאַל תַּשְׁחִיתֵנוּ, כְּמָה שֶׁכָּתוּב: כִּי אֵל רַחוּם
‹ a merciful God   ‹ For « it is written: ‹ as   « destroy us,   ‹ and do not ‹ on us

יהוה אֱלֹהֶיךָ, לֹא יַרְפְּךָ וְלֹא יַשְׁחִיתֶךָ, וְלֹא יִשְׁכַּח
‹ will He forget   ‹ nor   « will He destroy you,   ‹ nor   ‹ relinquish you   ‹ He will not « your God;   ‹ is HASHEM,

אֶת בְּרִית אֲבֹתֶיךָ אֲשֶׁר נִשְׁבַּע לָהֶם.[2] מוֹל
‹ Circumcise   « to them.   ‹ He swore   ‹ which   ‹ with your forefathers,   ‹ the covenant

אֶת לְבָבֵנוּ לְאַהֲבָה וּלְיִרְאָה אֶת שְׁמֶךָ, כְּמָה שֶׁכָּתוּב:
« it is written: ‹ as   « Your Name,   ‹ and to fear   ‹ to love   ‹ our hearts

וּמָל יהוה אֱלֹהֶיךָ אֶת לְבָבְךָ וְאֶת לְבַב זַרְעֶךָ, לְאַהֲבָה
‹ to love   « of your offspring,   ‹ and the heart   ‹ your heart   ‹ HASHEM, your God, will circumcise

אֶת יהוה אֱלֹהֶיךָ, בְּכָל לְבָבְךָ וּבְכָל נַפְשְׁךָ, לְמַעַן
‹ so that   « your soul, ‹ and with all ‹ your heart ‹ with all   ‹ your God,   ‹ HASHEM,

חַיֶּיךָ.[3] הִמָּצֵא לָנוּ בְּבַקָּשָׁתֵנוּ, כְּמָה שֶׁכָּתוּב: וּבִקַּשְׁתֶּם
‹ And you will seek   « it is written: ‹ as   « in our quest,   ‹ to us ‹ Be accessible   « you may live.

מִשָּׁם אֶת יהוה אֱלֹהֶיךָ וּמָצָאתָ, כִּי תִדְרְשֶׁנּוּ בְּכָל
‹ with all   ‹ you search Him out ‹ when   « and you will find [Him],   ‹ your God,   ‹ HASHEM,   ‹ from there

לְבָבְךָ וּבְכָל נַפְשֶׁךָ.[4] ❖ תְּבִיאֵנוּ אֶל הַר קָדְשֶׁךָ,
‹ Your holy mountain   ‹ to   ‹ Bring us   « your soul.   ‹ and with all ‹ your heart

וְשַׂמְּחֵנוּ בְּבֵית תְּפִלָּתֶךָ, כְּמָה שֶׁכָּתוּב: וַהֲבִיאוֹתִים
‹ And I will bring them   « it is written: ‹ as   « of Prayer,   ‹ in Your House   ‹ and gladden us

אֶל הַר קָדְשִׁי, וְשִׂמַּחְתִּים בְּבֵית תְּפִלָּתִי, עוֹלֹתֵיהֶם
‹ their burnt-offerings   « of Prayer;   ‹ in My House   ‹ and I will gladden them   « My holy mountain,   ‹ to

---

(1) *Ezekiel* 36:25. (2) *Deuteronomy* 4:31. (3) 30:6. (4) 4:29.

וְזִבְחֵיהֶם לְרָצוֹן עַל מִזְבְּחִי, כִּי בֵיתִי בֵּית תְּפִלָּה
‹ of ‹ "a House ‹ My ‹ for ≪ My Altar, ‹ on ‹ will find ‹ and their feast-
Prayer" House favor offerings

יִקָּרֵא לְכָל הָעַמִּים.¹
≪ nations. ‹ for all ‹ will be
called

THE ARK IS OPENED.

CHAZZAN, THEN CONGREGATION:

שְׁמַע קוֹלֵנוּ יהוה אֱלֹהֵינוּ, חוּס וְרַחֵם עָלֵינוּ,
≪ on us, ‹ and have ‹ have ≪ our God; ‹ HASHEM, ‹ our voice, ‹ Hear
compassion pity

וְקַבֵּל בְּרַחֲמִים וּבְרָצוֹן אֶת תְּפִלָּתֵנוּ.²
≪ our prayer. ‹ and favor ‹with compassion ‹ and accept

CHAZZAN, THEN CONGREGATION:

הֲשִׁיבֵנוּ יהוה אֵלֶיךָ וְנָשׁוּבָה, חַדֵּשׁ יָמֵינוּ כְּקֶדֶם.³
≪ as of old. ‹ our ‹ renew ≪ and we shall ‹ to You, ‹ HASHEM, ‹Bring us back,
days return,

CHAZZAN, THEN CONGREGATION:

אֲמָרֵינוּ הַאֲזִינָה יהוה, בִּינָה הֲגִיגֵנוּ.⁴
≪ our thoughts. ‹ perceive ≪ HASHEM; ‹ hear, ‹ Our words

THE FOLLOWING VERSE IS RECITED QUIETLY:

יִהְיוּ לְרָצוֹן אִמְרֵי פִינוּ וְהֶגְיוֹן לִבֵּנוּ לְפָנֶיךָ,
≪ before ≪ of our ‹ and the ‹ of our ‹ — the ex- ≪ find ‹ May
You, heart — thoughts mouth pressions favor they

יהוה צוּרֵנוּ וְגוֹאֲלֵנוּ.⁵
≪ and our Redeemer. ‹ our Rock ‹ HASHEM,

CHAZZAN, THEN CONGREGATION:

אַל תַּשְׁלִיכֵנוּ מִלְּפָנֶיךָ, וְרוּחַ קָדְשְׁךָ אַל תִּקַּח מִמֶּנּוּ.⁶
≪ from us. ‹ take ‹ do ‹ of Your ‹ and the ≪ from Your ‹ cast us away ‹ Do
not Holiness Spirit Presence, not

CHAZZAN, THEN CONGREGATION:

אַל תַּשְׁלִיכֵנוּ לְעֵת זִקְנָה, כִּכְלוֹת כֹּחֵנוּ אַל תַּעַזְבֵנוּ.⁷
≪ forsake us not. ‹ does our ‹ when fail ≪ of old ‹ in time ‹ cast us away ‹ Do
strength, age; not

---

(1) *Isaiah* 56:7. (2) From the weekday *Shemoneh Esrei.*
(3) *Lamentations* 5:21. (4) Cf. *Psalms* 5:2. (5) Cf. 19:15. (6) 51:13. (7) Cf. 71:9.

ALL CONTINUE (SOME CONGREGATIONS RECITE THE NEXT VERSE RESPONSIVELY):

אַל תַּעַזְבֵנוּ יהוה, אֱלֹהֵינוּ אַל תִּרְחַק מִמֶּנּוּ.¹

《 from us. 〈 be not distant 〈 our God, 《 O Hashem; 〈 Forsake us not,

עֲשֵׂה עִמָּנוּ אוֹת לְטוֹבָה, וְיִרְאוּ שׂוֹנְאֵינוּ וְיֵבֹשׁוּ,

《 and be 〈 may our 〈 so that 《 for good; 〈 a sign 〈 for us 〈 Display
ashamed, enemies see it

כִּי אַתָּה יהוה עֲזַרְתָּנוּ וְנִחַמְתָּנוּ.² כִּי לְךָ יהוה

〈 Hashem, 〈 for 〈 Because 《 and 〈 will have 〈 Hashem, 〈 You, 〈 for
You, consoled us. helped us

הוֹחָלְנוּ, אַתָּה תַעֲנֶה אֲדֹנָי אֱלֹהֵינוּ.³

《 our God. 〈 O Lord 〈 will answer 〈 You 《 do we wait;

THE ARK IS CLOSED.

EACH INDIVIDUAL CONTINUES.

CONFESSION / ודוי

**DURING THE RECITATION OF THE ודוי, CONFESSION, STAND WITH
HEAD AND BODY SLIGHTLY BOWED, IN SUBMISSIVE CONTRITION.**

אֱלֹהֵינוּ וֵאלֹהֵי אֲבוֹתֵינוּ, תָּבֹא לְפָנֶיךָ תְּפִלָּתֵנוּ,⁴

《 may our 〈 before 〈 come 《 of our 〈 and the 〈 Our God
prayer, You forefathers,

וְאַל תִּתְעַלַּם מִתְּחִנָּתֵנוּ,⁵ שֶׁאֵין אָנוּ עַזֵּי פָנִים

〈 faced 〈 so brazen- 〈 For we are not 《 our supplication. 〈 ignore 〈 and do not

וּקְשֵׁי עֹרֶף, לוֹמַר לְפָנֶיךָ יהוה אֱלֹהֵינוּ וֵאלֹהֵי

〈 and the God 〈 our God, 〈 Hashem, 《 before You, 〈 as to say 〈 necked 〈 and stiff-

אֲבוֹתֵינוּ, צַדִּיקִים אֲנַחְנוּ וְלֹא חָטָאנוּ, אֲבָל

《 —for 《 sinned 〈 and 〈 we are, 〈 that righteous 《 of our
indeed, have not forefathers,

אֲנַחְנוּ וַאֲבוֹתֵינוּ חָטָאנוּ.⁶

《 have sinned. 〈 and our forefathers 〈 we

**STRIKE THE LEFT SIDE OF THE CHEST WITH THE RIGHT FIST WHILE RECITING
EACH OF THE SINS OF THE FOLLOWING CONFESSIONAL LITANY:**

אָשַׁמְנוּ, בָּגַדְנוּ, גָּזַלְנוּ, דִּבַּרְנוּ דֹפִי. הֶעֱוִינוּ,

《 We have com- 《 slander. 〈 we have 《 we have 《 we have 《 We have been
mitted iniquity; spoken robbed; betrayed; guilty;

---

(1) Cf. *Psalms* 38:22. (2) Cf. 86:17. (3) Cf. 38:16. (4) Cf. 88:3. (5) Cf. 55:2. (6) Cf. 106:6, *Jeremiah* 3:25.

וְהִרְשַׁעְנוּ, זַדְנוּ, חָמַסְנוּ, טָפַלְנוּ שֶׁקֶר. יָעַצְנוּ

≪ we have committed wickedness; ≪ we have sinned willfully; ≪ we have extorted; ‹ we have made ≪ false accusations. ‹ We have given advice

רָע, כִּזַּבְנוּ, לַצְנוּ, מָרַדְנוּ, נִאַצְנוּ, סָרַרְנוּ,

≪ we have strayed; ≪ we have provoked [God's anger]; ≪ we have rebelled; ≪ we have scorned; ≪ we have been deceitful; ≪ that is bad;

עָוִינוּ, פָּשַׁעְנוּ, צָרַרְנוּ, קִשִּׁינוּ עֹרֶף. רָשַׁעְנוּ,

≪ We have been wicked; ≪ our necks. ‹ we have stiffened ≪ we have caused distress; ≪ we have sinned rebelliously; ≪ we have been iniquitous;

שִׁחַתְנוּ, תִּעַבְנוּ, תָּעִינוּ, תִּעְתָּעְנוּ.

≪ we have scoffed. ≪ we have gone astray; ≪ we have committed abominations; ≪ we have been corrupt;

סַרְנוּ מִמִּצְוֹתֶיךָ וּמִמִּשְׁפָּטֶיךָ הַטּוֹבִים, וְלֹא שָׁוָה

‹ worthwhile ‹ and it was not ≪ that are good, ‹ and from Your laws ‹ from Your commandments ‹ We have turned away

לָנוּ.[1] וְאַתָּה צַדִּיק עַל כָּל הַבָּא עָלֵינוּ, כִּי אֱמֶת

‹ truthfully ‹ for ≪ upon us, ‹ that has come ‹ all ‹ in ‹ are righteous ‹ And You ≪ for us.

עָשִׂיתָ וַאֲנַחְנוּ הִרְשָׁעְנוּ.[2]

≪ have acted wickedly. ‹ while we ≪ have You acted,

אָשַׁמְנוּ מִכָּל עָם, בֹּשְׁנוּ מִכָּל דּוֹר, גָּלָה מִמֶּנּוּ

‹ from us ‹ Departed ≪ generation. ‹ more than any other ‹ We have been ashamed ≪ people. ‹ more than any other ‹ We have been guilty

מָשׂוֹשׂ, דָּוָה לִבֵּנוּ בַּחֲטָאֵינוּ, הֻחְבַּל אֻוְּיֵנוּ, וְנִפְרַע

‹ uncovered ≪ was our desired [Temple], ‹ Seized ≪ because of our sins. ‹ is our heart ‹ Sickened ≪ has joy.

פְּאָרֵנוּ, זְבוּל בֵּית מִקְדָּשֵׁנוּ חָרַב בַּעֲוֹנֵינוּ, טִירָתֵנוּ

‹ Our Palace ≪ because of our iniquities. ‹ has been destroyed ‹ our Holy Temple ‹ for [His] abode, ≪ was our splendor;

הָיְתָה לְשַׁמָּה, יְפִי אַדְמָתֵנוּ לְזָרִים, בֹּחֵנוּ לְנָכְרִים.

≪ [was given] to foreigners. ‹ our ≪ is controlled by strangers, ‹ of our Land ‹ [Jerusalem,] ≪ desolate. ‹ the beauty ‹ has become
   wealth

---

(1) Cf. *Job* 33:27. (2) *Nehemiah* 9:33.

וַעֲדַיִן לֹא שַׁבְנוּ מִטָּעוּתֵנוּ וְהֵיךְ נָעִיז פָּנֵינוּ וְנַקְשֶׁה

‹ and ‹ faced ‹ can we be ‹ So » from our ‹ we have not ‹ But still
stiffen so brazen- how willful errors. repented

עָרְפֵּנוּ, לוֹמַר לְפָנֵיךָ יהוה אֱלֹהֵינוּ וֵאלֹהֵי אֲבוֹתֵינוּ,

» of our ‹ and the ‹ our God ‹ HASHEM, ‹ before ‹ so as to ‹ our neck
forefathers, God You, say

צַדִּיקִים אֲנַחְנוּ וְלֹא חָטָאנוּ, אֲבָל אֲנַחְנוּ וַאֲבוֹתֵינוּ

‹ and our ‹ both we ‹ for in » and we have » we are ‹ that
fathers truth, not sinned, righteous

חָטָאנוּ.[1]

» have sinned.

**STRIKE THE LEFT SIDE OF THE CHEST WITH THE RIGHT FIST WHILE RECITING
EACH OF THE SINS OF THE FOLLOWING CONFESSIONAL LITANY:**

אָשַׁמְנוּ, בָּגַדְנוּ, גָּזַלְנוּ, דִּבַּרְנוּ דְפִי. הֶעֱוִינוּ,

» We have com- » slander. ‹ we have » we have » we have » We have been
mitted iniquity; spoken robbed; betrayed; guilty;

וְהִרְשַׁעְנוּ, זַדְנוּ, חָמַסְנוּ, טָפַלְנוּ שֶׁקֶר. יָעַצְנוּ

‹ We have » false ‹ we have » we have »we have sinned »we have commit-
given advice accusations. made extorted; willfully; ted wickedness;

רָע, כִּזַּבְנוּ, לַצְנוּ, מָרַדְנוּ, נִאַצְנוּ, סָרַרְנוּ,

» we have » we have provoked » we have » we have » we have been » that is
strayed; [God's anger]; rebelled; scorned; deceitful; bad;

עָוִינוּ, פָּשַׁעְנוּ, צָרַרְנוּ, קִשִּׁינוּ עֹרֶף. רָשַׁעְנוּ,

» We have » our ‹ we have » we have caused » we have sinned » we have been
been wicked; necks. stiffened distress; rebelliously; iniquitous;

שִׁחַתְנוּ, תִּעַבְנוּ, תָּעִינוּ, תִּעְתָּעְנוּ.

» we have » we have » we have commit- » we have
scoffed. gone astray; ted abominations; been corrupt;

סַרְנוּ מִמִּצְוֹתֶיךָ וּמִמִּשְׁפָּטֶיךָ הַטּוֹבִים, וְלֹא שָׁוָה

‹ worth- ‹ and it » that are ‹ and from ‹ from Your ‹ We have
while was not good, Your laws commandments turned away

לָנוּ.[2] וְאַתָּה צַדִּיק עַל כָּל הַבָּא עָלֵינוּ, כִּי אֱמֶת

‹ truth- ‹ for » upon us, ‹ that has ‹ all ‹ in ‹ are ‹ And You » for us.
fully come righteous

עָשִׂיתָ וַאֲנַחְנוּ הִרְשָׁעְנוּ.[3]

» have acted ‹ while we » have You
wickedly. acted,

---

(1) Cf. *Psalms* 106:6; *Jeremiah* 3:25. (2) Cf. *Job* 33:27. (3) *Nehemiah* 9:33.

לְעֵינֵינוּ עָשְׁקוּ עֲמָלֵנוּ, מְמֻשָּׁךְ וּמְמוֹרָט מִמֶּנּוּ,

⟨ Before our eyes ⟩ have they stolen ⟨ the product of our labor; ⟨ [it was] pulled away ⟨ and cut off ⟨ from us.

נָתְנוּ עֻלָּם עָלֵינוּ, סְבַלְנוּ עַל שִׁכְמֵנוּ, עֲבָדִים

⟨ They have placed ⟨ their yoke ⟨ upon us, ⟨ we bore it ⟨ upon ⟨ our shoulders. ⟨ Slaves

מָשְׁלוּ בָנוּ, פֹּרֵק אֵין מִיָּדָם, צָרוֹת רַבּוֹת

⟨ have ruled ⟨ over us; ⟨ a redeemer ⟨ there was not ⟨ from their hand. ⟨ Troubles ⟨ that are manifold

סְבָבוּנוּ, קְרָאנוּךְ יהוה אֱלֹהֵינוּ, רָחַקְתָּ מִמֶּנּוּ

⟨ have surrounded us, ⟨ we called upon You, ⟨ HASHEM, ⟨ our God, ⟨ but You have distanced Yourself ⟨ from us

בַּעֲוֹנֵינוּ, שַׁבְנוּ מֵאַחֲרֶיךָ, תָּעִינוּ וְאָבָדְנוּ.

⟨ because of our iniquities. ⟨ We have turned away ⟨ from following after You; ⟨ we have gone astray; ⟨ we have become lost.

וַעֲדַיִן לֹא שַׁבְנוּ מִטָּעוּתֵנוּ וְהֵיךְ נָעִיז פָּנֵינוּ וְנַקְשֶׁה

⟨ But still ⟨ we have not repented ⟨ from our willful errors. ⟨ So how ⟨ can we be so brazen- ⟨ faced ⟨ and stiffen

עָרְפֵּנוּ, לוֹמַר לְפָנֶיךָ יהוה אֱלֹהֵינוּ וֵאלֹהֵי אֲבוֹתֵינוּ,

⟨ our neck ⟨ so as to say ⟨ before You, ⟨ HASHEM, ⟨ our God ⟨ and the God ⟨ of our forefathers,

צַדִּיקִים אֲנַחְנוּ וְלֹא חָטָאנוּ, אֲבָל אֲנַחְנוּ וַאֲבוֹתֵינוּ

⟨ that righteous ⟨ we are ⟨ and we have not sinned, ⟨ in truth, ⟨ for ⟨ both we ⟨ and our fathers

חָטָאנוּ.[1]

⟨ have sinned.

STRIKE THE LEFT SIDE OF THE CHEST WITH THE RIGHT FIST WHILE RECITING EACH OF THE SINS OF THE FOLLOWING CONFESSIONAL LITANY:

אָשַׁמְנוּ, בָּגַדְנוּ, גָּזַלְנוּ, דִּבַּרְנוּ דֹפִי. הֶעֱוִינוּ,

⟨ We have committed iniquity; ⟨ We have been guilty; ⟨ we have betrayed; ⟨ we have robbed; ⟨ we have spoken ⟨ slander. ⟨ We have com-

וְהִרְשַׁעְנוּ, זַדְנוּ, חָמַסְנוּ, טָפַלְנוּ שֶׁקֶר. יָעַצְנוּ

⟨ mitted wickedness; ⟨ we have sinned willfully; ⟨ we have extorted; ⟨ we have made ⟨ false accusations. ⟨ We have given advice

רָע, כִּזַּבְנוּ, לַצְנוּ, מָרַדְנוּ, נִאַצְנוּ, סָרַרְנוּ,

⟨ that is bad; ⟨ we have been deceitful; ⟨ we have scorned; ⟨ we have rebelled; ⟨ we have provoked [God's anger]; ⟨ we have strayed;

---

(1) Cf. *Psalms* 106:6; *Jeremiah* 3:25.

עָוִינוּ, פָּשַׁעְנוּ, צָרַרְנוּ, קִשִּׁינוּ עֹרֶף. רָשַׁעְנוּ,

《 We have been iniquitous; 《 we have sinned rebelliously; 《 we have caused distress; 《 we have stiffened 《 our necks. 《 We have been wicked;

שִׁחַתְנוּ, תִּעַבְנוּ, תָּעִינוּ, תִּעְתָּעְנוּ.

《 we have been corrupt; 《 we have committed abominations; 《 we have gone astray; 《 we have scoffed.

סַרְנוּ מִמִּצְוֹתֶיךָ וּמִמִּשְׁפָּטֶיךָ הַטּוֹבִים, וְלֹא שָׁוָה

‹ We have turned away ‹ from Your commandments ‹ and from Your laws 《 that are good, 《 and it was not ‹ worthwhile

לָנוּ.[1] וְאַתָּה צַדִּיק עַל כָּל הַבָּא עָלֵינוּ, כִּי אֱמֶת

‹ for us. 《 And You ‹ are righteous ‹ in ‹ all 《 that has come ‹ upon us, 《 for ‹ truthfully

עָשִׂיתָ וַאֲנַחְנוּ הִרְשָׁעְנוּ.[2]

《 have You acted, ‹ while we 《 have acted wickedly.

הִרְשַׁעְנוּ וּפָשַׁעְנוּ, לָכֵן לֹא נוֹשָׁעְנוּ. וְתֵן בְּלִבֵּנוּ

‹ We have acted wickedly 《 and we have sinned rebelliously; ‹ there-fore 《 we have not ‹ been saved. 《 Place ‹ in our hearts

לַעֲזוֹב דֶּרֶךְ רֶשַׁע, וְחִישׁ לָנוּ יֶשַׁע, כַּכָּתוּב עַל יַד

‹ [the will] to abandon ‹ the path 《 of wickedness, 《 and hasten ‹ to us 《 salvation; ‹ as it is written ‹ by ‹ the hand

נְבִיאֶךָ: יַעֲזֹב רָשָׁע דַּרְכּוֹ, וְאִישׁ אָוֶן מַחְשְׁבֹתָיו,

《 of Your prophet: ‹ Let abandon ‹ the wicked one 《 his way, ‹ and the man ‹ of iniquity 《 [abandon] his thoughts;

וְיָשֹׁב אֶל יהוה וִירַחֲמֵהוּ, וְאֶל אֱלֹהֵינוּ כִּי

‹ and let him return ‹ to ‹ HASHEM, 《 and He will have compassion on him, 《 and to ‹ our God, ‹ for

יַרְבֶּה לִסְלוֹחַ.[3]

《 forgiving. ‹ He is abundantly

מְשִׁיחַ צִדְקֶךָ אָמַר לְפָנֶיךָ, שְׁגִיאוֹת מִי יָבִין,

《 can ‹ who ‹ Mistakes 《 before You: ‹ said ‹ who is righteous ‹ Your anointed one discern? [David]

---

(1) Cf. Job 33:27. (2) Nehemiah 9:33. (3) Isaiah 55:7.

מִנִּסְתָּרוֹת נַקֵּנִי.¹ נַקֵּנוּ יהוה אֱלֹהֵינוּ מִכָּל פְּשָׁעֵינוּ,

⟨ our sins ⟨ of all ⟨ our God, ⟨ HASHEM, ⟨ Cleanse 《 cleanse ⟨ From
us, me. unperceived faults

וְטַהֲרֵנוּ מִכָּל טֻמְאוֹתֵינוּ, וּזְרוֹק עָלֵינוּ מַיִם טְהוֹרִים

⟨ pure water ⟨ upon us ⟨ Pour 《 our contaminations. ⟨ of all ⟨ and purify us

וְטַהֲרֵנוּ, כַּכָּתוּב עַל יַד נְבִיאֶךָ: וְזָרַקְתִּי עֲלֵיכֶם

⟨ upon you ⟨ I shall pour 《 of Your ⟨ the ⟨ by ⟨ as it is 《 and purify us,
prophet: hand written

מַיִם טְהוֹרִים וּטְהַרְתֶּם, מִכֹּל טֻמְאוֹתֵיכֶם וּמִכָּל

⟨ and ⟨ your ⟨ from 《 and you will ⟨ pure water
from all contaminations all become pure;

גִּלּוּלֵיכֶם אֲטַהֵר אֶתְכֶם.² עַמְּךָ וְנַחֲלָתְךָ, רְעֵבֵי

⟨ who 《 and Your ⟨ Your 《 you. ⟨ I will purify ⟨ your
hunger heritage, people abominations

טוּבְךָ, צְמֵאֵי חַסְדֶּךָ, תְּאֵבֵי יִשְׁעֶךָ, יַכִּירוּ וְיֵדְעוּ

⟨ and ⟨ — may they 《 for Your ⟨ and 《 for Your ⟨ who 《 for Your
know recognize salvation who long kindness, thirst goodness,

כִּי לַיהוה אֱלֹהֵינוּ הָרַחֲמִים וְהַסְּלִיחוֹת.

《 and forgiveness. ⟨ belong mercy ⟨ our God, ⟨ to HASHEM, ⟨ that

אֵל רַחוּם שְׁמֶךָ, אֵל חַנּוּן שְׁמֶךָ,³ בָּנוּ נִקְרָא שְׁמֶךָ.⁴

《 is Your Name ⟨ upon 《 is Your ⟨ Gracious God 《 is Your ⟨ Merciful God
proclaimed, us Name, Name,

יהוה עֲשֵׂה לְמַעַן שְׁמֶךָ,⁵ עֲשֵׂה לְמַעַן אֲמִתָּךָ, עֲשֵׂה

⟨ act 《 Your truth; ⟨ for the ⟨ Act 《 Your ⟨ for the ⟨ act ⟨ HASHEM,
sake of Name. sake of

לְמַעַן בְּרִיתָךָ, עֲשֵׂה לְמַעַן גָּדְלָךְ וְתִפְאַרְתָּךְ, עֲשֵׂה

⟨ act 《 and Your ⟨ Your ⟨ for the ⟨ act 《 Your ⟨ for the
splendor; greatness sake of covenant; sake of

לְמַעַן דָּתָךְ, עֲשֵׂה לְמַעַן הוֹדָךְ, עֲשֵׂה לְמַעַן וְעוּדָךְ,

《 Your Meet- ⟨ for the ⟨ act 《 Your ⟨ for the ⟨ act 《 Your ⟨ for the
ing House; sake of glory; sake of Law; sake of

עֲשֵׂה לְמַעַן זִכְרָךְ,⁶ עֲשֵׂה לְמַעַן חַסְדֶּךָ, עֲשֵׂה לְמַעַן

⟨ for the ⟨ act 《 Your ⟨ for the ⟨ act 《 Your ⟨ for the ⟨ act
sake of kindness; sake of remembrance; sake of

(1) Psalms 19:13. (2) Ezekiel 36:25. (3) Cf. Exodus 34:6. (4) Cf. Deuteronomy 28:10.
(5) Jeremiah 14:7. (6) Cf. Exodus 3:15. (7) Psalms 6:5.

טוּבָךְ, עֲשֵׂה לְמַעַן יִחוּדָךְ, עֲשֵׂה לְמַעַן כְּבוֹדָךְ, עֲשֵׂה

act « Your / for the « act « Your / for the « act « Your
goodness; sake of Oneness; sake of honor;

לְמַעַן **לִמּוּדָךְ**,[1] עֲשֵׂה לְמַעַן מַלְכוּתָךְ, עֲשֵׂה לְמַעַן

for the act « Your kingship; / for the act « Your / for the
sake of sake of students; sake of

נִצְחָךְ, עֲשֵׂה לְמַעַן **סוֹדָךְ**,[2] עֲשֵׂה לְמַעַן עֻזָּךְ, עֲשֵׂה

act « Your / for the « act « Your secret [re- / for the « act « Your eternal
power; sake of vealed to those sake of [Name];
who fear You];

לְמַעַן **פְּאֵרָךְ**, עֲשֵׂה לְמַעַן צִדְקָתָךְ, עֲשֵׂה לְמַעַן

for the act « Your / for the act « Your / for the
sake of righteousness; sake of glory; sake of

קְדֻשָּׁתָךְ, עֲשֵׂה לְמַעַן רַחֲמֶיךָ הָרַבִּים, עֲשֵׂה לְמַעַן

for the act « that is « Your mercy / for the act « Your sanctity;
sake of abundant; sake of

שְׁכִינָתָךְ, עֲשֵׂה לְמַעַן תְּהִלָּתָךְ, עֲשֵׂה לְמַעַן אוֹהֲבֶיךָ

those who / for the « act « Your praise; / for the act « Your Divine
loved You sake of sake of Presence;

שׁוֹכְנֵי עָפָר,[3] עֲשֵׂה לְמַעַן אַבְרָהָם יִצְחָק וְיַעֲקֹב,

« and Jacob; « Isaac, « Abraham, / for the sake of « act « in the dust; « who rest

עֲשֵׂה לְמַעַן מֹשֶׁה וְאַהֲרֹן, עֲשֵׂה לְמַעַן דָּוִד וּשְׁלֹמֹה,

« and / David / for the « act « and Aaron; « Moses / for the « act
Solomon; sake of sake of

עֲשֵׂה לְמַעַן יְרוּשָׁלַיִם עִיר קָדְשֶׁךָ,[4] עֲשֵׂה לְמַעַן צִיּוֹן

« Zion, / for the « act « of Your « the « Jerusalem, / for the « act
sake of Holiness; City sake of

מִשְׁכַּן כְּבוֹדָךְ,[5] עֲשֵׂה לְמַעַן שִׁמְמוֹת[6] הֵיכָלֶךָ, עֲשֵׂה

act « of Your « the / for the « act « of Your « the
Temple; desolation sake of glory; abode

לְמַעַן הָרִיסוּת[7] מִזְבְּחֶךָ, עֲשֵׂה לְמַעַן הַהֲרוּגִים עַל

for / those killed / for the « act « of Your / the / for the
Altar; devastation sake of

שֵׁם קָדְשֶׁךָ, עֲשֵׂה לְמַעַן טְבוּחִים עַל יִחוּדָךְ, עֲשֵׂה

act « Your / for / those / for the « act « Your holy Name;
Oneness; slaughtered sake of

---

(1) Cf. *Isaiah* 54:13. (2) Cf. *Psalms* 25:14. (3) *Isaiah* 26:19. (4) Cf. *Daniel* 9:16,24.
(5) *Psalms* 26:8. (6) Cf. *Jeremiah* 51:26. (7) Cf. *Isaiah* 49:19.

לְמַעַן בָּאֵי בָאֵשׁ וּבַמַּיִם עַל קִדּוּשׁ שְׁמֶךָ, עֲשֵׂה לְמַעַן

‹ for the sake of › act ‹ of Your Name; › the sanctification ‹ for › and water ‹ fire ‹ those who entered › for the sake of

יוֹנְקֵי שָׁדַיִם¹ שֶׁלֹּא חָטְאוּ, עֲשֵׂה לְמַעַן גְּמוּלֵי חָלָב²

‹ from milk › the [babies] weaned ‹ for the sake of › act « sin; ‹ who did not › at the breast ‹ the [infants] sucking

שֶׁלֹּא פָשְׁעוּ, עֲשֵׂה לְמַעַן תִּינוֹקוֹת שֶׁל בֵּית רַבָּן,³

« their teachers' school; ‹ of ‹ the children ‹ for the sake of ‹ act « transgress; ‹ who did not

עֲשֵׂה לְמַעַנְךָ אִם לֹא לְמַעֲנֵנוּ, עֲשֵׂה לְמַעַנְךָ וְהוֹשִׁיעֵנוּ.

« and save us. ‹ for Your sake ‹ act « for our sake; ‹ not ‹ if ‹ for Your sake ‹ act

עֲנֵנוּ יהוה עֲנֵנוּ, עֲנֵנוּ אֱלֹהֵינוּ עֲנֵנוּ, עֲנֵנוּ אָבִינוּ⁴

‹ our Father, ‹ answer us, « answer us; ‹ our God, ‹ answer us, « answer us; ‹ HASHEM, ‹ Answer us;

עֲנֵנוּ, עֲנֵנוּ בּוֹרְאֵנוּ⁵ עֲנֵנוּ, עֲנֵנוּ גּוֹאֲלֵנוּ⁶ עֲנֵנוּ, עֲנֵנוּ

‹ answer us, « answer us; ‹ our Redeemer, ‹ answer us, « answer us; ‹ our Creator, ‹ answer us, « answer us;

דּוֹרְשֵׁנוּ⁷ עֲנֵנוּ, עֲנֵנוּ הָאֵל הַנֶּאֱמָן⁸ עֲנֵנוּ, עֲנֵנוּ וָתִיק

‹ steadfast ‹ answer us, « answer us; ‹ Who is faithful ‹ God ‹ answer us, « answer us; ‹ You Who searches us out,

וְחָסִיד עֲנֵנוּ, עֲנֵנוּ זַךְ וְיָשָׁר⁹ עֲנֵנוּ, עֲנֵנוּ חַי וְקַיָּם¹⁰

‹ and enduring One, ‹ living ‹ answer us, « answer us; ‹ and upright One ‹ pure ‹ answer us, « answer us; ‹ and kind One,

עֲנֵנוּ, עֲנֵנוּ טוֹב וּמֵטִיב¹¹ עֲנֵנוּ, עֲנֵנוּ יוֹדֵעַ יֵצֶר¹² עֲנֵנוּ,

« answer us; ‹ of inclinations, ‹ Knower ‹ answer us « answer us; ‹ and beneficent One, ‹ good ‹ answer us « answer us;

עֲנֵנוּ כּוֹבֵשׁ כְּעָסִים עֲנֵנוּ, עֲנֵנוּ לוֹבֵשׁ צְדָקוֹת¹³ עֲנֵנוּ,

« answer us; ‹ of righteousness, ‹ Donner ‹ answer us « answer us; ‹ of wrath, ‹ Suppressor ‹ answer us,

עֲנֵנוּ מֶלֶךְ מַלְכֵי הַמְּלָכִים¹⁴ עֲנֵנוּ, עֲנֵנוּ נוֹרָא וְנִשְׂגָּב¹⁵

‹ and powerful One, ‹ awesome ‹ answer us « answer us; ‹ of kings, ‹ over kings ‹ King ‹ answer us,

---

(1) Joel 2:16. (2) Isaiah 28:9. (3) Shabbos 119b. (4) Isaiah 64:7. (5) Cf. 43:1. (6) 47:4.
(7) Cf. Ezekiel 34:11. (8) Deuteronomy 7:9. (9) Job 8:6; cf. Proverbs 20:11.
(10) Cf. Daniel 6:27. (11) Cf. Psalms 119:68. (12) Cf. 103:14.
(13) Cf. Isaiah 59:17. (14) Ethics of the Fathers 3:1. (15) Psalms 47:3; 148:13.

עֲנֵנוּ, עֲנֵנוּ סוֹלֵחַ וּמוֹחֵל עֲנֵנוּ, עֲנֵנוּ עוֹנֶה בְּעֵת

answer us; answer us, You Who answers, and pardons, answer us; You Who forgives, answer us; in time

צָרָה¹ עֲנֵנוּ, עֲנֵנוּ פּוֹדֶה וּמַצִּיל² עֲנֵנוּ, עֲנֵנוּ צַדִּיק

of distress, answer us, answer us; Redeemer and Rescuer, answer us, answer us; righteous

וְיָשָׁר³ עֲנֵנוּ, עֲנֵנוּ קָרוֹב לְקוֹרְאָיו⁴ עֲנֵנוּ, עֲנֵנוּ קָשֶׁה

and upright One, answer us, answer us; He Who is close to those who call upon Him, answer us, answer us; You Who with difficulty

לִכְעוֹס⁵ עֲנֵנוּ, עֲנֵנוּ רַךְ לִרְצוֹת⁶ עֲנֵנוּ, עֲנֵנוּ רַחוּם

becomes angry, answer us, answer us; You Who are easily appeased, answer us, answer us; merciful

וְחַנּוּן⁷ עֲנֵנוּ, עֲנֵנוּ שׁוֹמֵעַ אֶל אֶבְיוֹנִים⁸ עֲנֵנוּ, עֲנֵנוּ

and gracious One, answer us, answer us; You Who listens to the destitute, answer us, answer us;

תּוֹמֵךְ תְּמִימִים עֲנֵנוּ, עֲנֵנוּ אֱלֹהֵי אֲבוֹתֵינוּ עֲנֵנוּ,

You Who supports the wholesome, answer us, answer us; God of our forefathers, answer us;

עֲנֵנוּ אֱלֹהֵי אַבְרָהָם⁹ עֲנֵנוּ, עֲנֵנוּ פַּחַד יִצְחָק עֲנֵנוּ,

answer us, God of Abraham, answer us, answer us; Awesome One of Isaac, answer us;

עֲנֵנוּ אֲבִיר יַעֲקֹב¹⁰ עֲנֵנוּ, עֲנֵנוּ עֶזְרַת הַשְּׁבָטִים עֲנֵנוּ,

answer us, Mighty One of Jacob, answer us, answer us; Helper of the tribes, answer us;

עֲנֵנוּ מִשְׂגַּב אִמָּהוֹת עֲנֵנוּ, עֲנֵנוּ עוֹנֶה בְּעֵת רָצוֹן¹¹ עֲנֵנוּ,

answer us, Stronghold of the Matriarchs, answer us, answer us; You Who answers in a time of favor, answer us;

עֲנֵנוּ אֲבִי יְתוֹמִים¹² עֲנֵנוּ, עֲנֵנוּ דַּיַּן אַלְמָנוֹת עֲנֵנוּ.

answer us, Father of orphans, answer us, answer us; Judge of widows, answer us.

מִי שֶׁעָנָה לְאַבְרָהָם אָבִינוּ בְּהַר הַמּוֹרִיָּה¹³

He Who answered Abraham our father on Mount Moriah

הוּא יַעֲנֵנוּ.

may He answer us.

---

(1) Cf. *Isaiah* 49:8; *Psalms* 37:39. Alternate text: בְּעֵת רָצוֹן, *in time of favor.* (2) Cf. 34:23,18.
(3) *Deuteronomy* 32:4. (4) Cf. *Psalms* 145:18. (5) *Ethics of the Fathers* 5:14. (6) Cf. 5:14.
(7) *Exodus* 34:6. (8) *Psalms* 69:34. (9) *Genesis* 31:42. (10) *Isaiah* 49:26. (11) Cf. 49:8;
Psalms 69:14. Alternate text: בְּעֵת צָרָה, *in time of distress.* (12) 68:6. (13) *Genesis* 22:12.

מִי שֶׁעָנָה לְיִצְחָק בְּנוֹ כְּשֶׁנֶּעֱקַד עַל גַּבֵּי הַמִּזְבֵּחַ[1]

‹ He ‹ Who answered ‹ Isaac ‹ his son ‹ when he was bound ‹ on ‹ top ‹ of the altar

הוּא יַעֲנֵנוּ.

‹ — may He ‹ answer us.

מִי שֶׁעָנָה לְיַעֲקֹב בְּבֵית אֵל[2]   הוּא יַעֲנֵנוּ.

‹ He ‹ Who answered ‹ Jacob ‹ in Beth-el   ‹ — may He ‹ answer us.

מִי שֶׁעָנָה לְיוֹסֵף בְּבֵית הָאֲסוּרִים[3]   הוּא יַעֲנֵנוּ.

‹ He ‹ Who answered ‹ Joseph ‹ in the prison   ‹ — may He ‹ answer us.

מִי שֶׁעָנָה לַאֲבוֹתֵינוּ עַל יַם סוּף[4]   הוּא יַעֲנֵנוּ.

‹ He ‹ Who answered ‹ our forefathers ‹ at ‹ the ‹ Sea of Reeds   ‹ — may He ‹ answer us.

מִי שֶׁעָנָה לְמֹשֶׁה בְּחוֹרֵב[5]   הוּא יַעֲנֵנוּ.

‹ He ‹ Who answered ‹ Moses ‹ in Horeb   ‹ — may He ‹ answer us.

מִי שֶׁעָנָה לְאַהֲרֹן בַּמַּחְתָּה[6]   הוּא יַעֲנֵנוּ.

‹ He ‹ Who answered ‹ Aaron ‹ with the fire-pan   ‹ — may He ‹ answer us.

מִי שֶׁעָנָה לְפִינְחָס בְּקוּמוֹ מִתּוֹךְ הָעֵדָה[7] הוּא יַעֲנֵנוּ.

‹ He ‹ Who answered ‹ Phinehas ‹ when he arose ‹ from amid ‹ the congregation ‹ — may He ‹ answer us.

מִי שֶׁעָנָה לִיהוֹשֻׁעַ בַּגִּלְגָּל[8]   הוּא יַעֲנֵנוּ.

‹ He ‹ Who answered ‹ Joshua ‹ in Gilgal   ‹ — may He ‹ answer us.

מִי שֶׁעָנָה לִשְׁמוּאֵל בַּמִּצְפָּה[9]   הוּא יַעֲנֵנוּ.

‹ He ‹ Who answered ‹ Samuel ‹ in Mizpah   ‹ — may He ‹ answer us.

מִי שֶׁעָנָה לְדָוִד וּשְׁלֹמֹה בְנוֹ בִּירוּשָׁלַיִם[10] הוּא יַעֲנֵנוּ.

‹ He ‹ Who answered ‹ David ‹ and Solomon ‹ his son ‹ in Jerusalem ‹ — may He ‹ answer us.

מִי שֶׁעָנָה לְאֵלִיָּהוּ בְּהַר הַכַּרְמֶל[11]   הוּא יַעֲנֵנוּ.

‹ He ‹ Who answered ‹ Elijah ‹ on Mount ‹ Carmel   ‹ — may He ‹ answer us.

(1) *Genesis* 22:12. (2) 35:3. (3) 39:21. (4) *Exodus* Ch. 14. (5) 17:6,11; *Deuteronomy* 9:19. (6) *Numbers* 17:11-13. (7) 25:7-13. (8) *Joshua* 6:1-20; 7:6-15; 10:12-14. (9) *I Samuel* 7:9. (10) *II Samuel* 7:5-16; 21:1,14; 24:25; *I Kings* 9:3. (11) 18:36-38.

מִי שֶׁעָנָה לֶאֱלִישָׁע בִּירִיחוֹ[1]   הוּא יַעֲנֵנוּ.

⟨ He ⟩ Who answered ⟨ Elisha ⟨ in Jericho ⟩⟩   He — may ⟨ answer us.

מִי שֶׁעָנָה לְיוֹנָה בִּמְעֵי הַדָּגָה[2]   הוּא יַעֲנֵנוּ.

⟨ He ⟩ Who answered ⟨ Jonah ⟨ in the innards ⟨ of the fish ⟩⟩   He — may ⟨ answer us.

מִי שֶׁעָנָה לְחִזְקִיָּהוּ מֶלֶךְ יְהוּדָה בְּחָלְיוֹ[3]   הוּא יַעֲנֵנוּ.

⟨ He ⟩ Who answered ⟨ Hezekiah, ⟨ king ⟨ of Judah, ⟨ in his illness ⟩⟩   He — may ⟨ answer us.

מִי שֶׁעָנָה לַחֲנַנְיָה מִישָׁאֵל וַעֲזַרְיָה

⟨ He ⟩ Who answered ⟨ Hananiah, ⟨ Mishael, ⟨ and Azariah ⟩

בְּתוֹךְ כִּבְשַׁן הָאֵשׁ[4]   הוּא יַעֲנֵנוּ.

⟨ inside ⟨ the furnace ⟨ of fire ⟩⟩   He — may ⟨ answer us.

מִי שֶׁעָנָה לְדָנִיֵּאל בְּגוֹב הָאֲרָיוֹת[5]   הוּא יַעֲנֵנוּ.

⟨ He ⟩ Who answered ⟨ Daniel ⟨ in the den ⟨ of lions ⟩⟩   He — may ⟨ answer us.

מִי שֶׁעָנָה לְמָרְדְּכַי וְאֶסְתֵּר בְּשׁוּשַׁן הַבִּירָה[6]

⟨ He ⟩ Who answered ⟨ Mordechai ⟨ and Esther ⟨ in Shushan ⟨ the capital ⟩⟩   הוּא יַעֲנֵנוּ.

He — may ⟨ answer us.

מִי שֶׁעָנָה לְעֶזְרָא בַּגּוֹלָה[7]   הוּא יַעֲנֵנוּ.

⟨ He ⟩ Who answered ⟨ Ezra ⟨ in the exile ⟩⟩   He — may ⟨ answer us.

מִי שֶׁעָנָה לְכָל הַצַּדִּיקִים וְהַחֲסִידִים וְהַתְּמִימִים

⟨ He ⟩ Who answered ⟨ all ⟨ the righteous, ⟨ the devout, ⟨ the wholesome, ⟩

וְהַיְשָׁרִים   הוּא יַעֲנֵנוּ.

and the upright ⟨⟩   He — may ⟨ answer us.

רַחֲמָנָא דְּעָנֵי לַעֲנִיֵּי, עֲנֵינַן. רַחֲמָנָא דְּעָנֵי לִתְבִירֵי

⟨ Merciful One ⟨ Who answers ⟨ the poor, ⟨ answer us! ⟨ Merciful One ⟨ Who answers ⟨ those of broken

---

(1) *II Kings* 2:21. (2) *Jonah* 2:2-11. (3) *II Kings* 20:2-6; *Isaiah* 38:2-8.
(4) *Daniel* 3:21-27. (5) 6:17-23. (6) *Esther* Ch. 8. (7) *Ezra* 8:21-23.

לִבָּא, עֲנֵינָן. רַחֲמָנָא דְּעָנֵי לִמַכִּיכֵי רוּחָא, עֲנֵינָן.

‹‹ answer us! / ‹‹ spirit, / ‹ those of crushed / ‹ Who answers / ‹ Merciful One / ‹‹ answer us! / ‹‹ hearts,

רַחֲמָנָא עֲנֵינָן. רַחֲמָנָא חוּס. רַחֲמָנָא פְּרוּק. רַחֲמָנָא

‹ Merciful One, / ‹‹ redeem! / ‹ Merciful One, / ‹‹ have pity! / ‹ Merciful One, / ‹‹ answer us! / ‹ Merciful One,

שְׁזִיב. רַחֲמָנָא רְחַם עֲלָן, הַשְׁתָּא בַּעֲגָלָא וּבִזְמַן קָרִיב.

‹‹ that comes soon. / ‹ and at a time / ‹‹ swiftly, / ‹ — now, / ‹‹ on us / ‹ have mercy / ‹ Merciful One, / ‹‹ save!

PUTTING DOWN THE HEAD / נפילת אפים

**RECITE UNTIL יִבֹשׁוּ רֶגַע WITH THE HEAD RESTING ON THE LEFT ARM,
PREFERABLY WHILE SEATED.**

(וַיְּאֹמֶר דָּוִד אֶל גָּד, צַר לִי מְאֹד, נִפְּלָה נָּא בְיַד יהוה,

‹‹ of HASHEM, / ‹ into the hand / ‹ now / ‹ Let us fall / ‹‹ exceedingly. / ‹ am I / ‹ Distressed / ‹‹ Gad, / ‹ to / ‹ (And David said

כִּי רַבִּים רַחֲמָיו, וּבְיַד אָדָם אַל אֶפְּלָה.[1])

‹‹ let me not fall.) / ‹ but into human hands / ‹‹ are His mercies, / ‹ abundant / ‹ for

רָחוּם וְחַנּוּן חָטָאתִי לְפָנֶיךָ. יהוה מָלֵא רַחֲמִים,

‹‹ of mercy, / ‹ Who is full / ‹ HASHEM, / ‹‹ before You. / ‹ I have sinned / ‹ and gracious One, / ‹ O merciful

רַחֵם עָלַי וְקַבֵּל תַּחֲנוּנָי.

‹‹ my supplications. / ‹ and accept / ‹ on me / ‹ have mercy

——— *Psalms 6:2-11* / תהלים ו:ב-יא ———

יהוה, אַל בְּאַפְּךָ תוֹכִיחֵנִי, וְאַל בַּחֲמָתְךָ תְיַסְּרֵנִי.

‹‹ chastise me. / ‹ in Your wrath / ‹ nor / ‹ rebuke me, / ‹ in Your anger / ‹ do not / ‹ HASHEM,

חָנֵּנִי יהוה כִּי אֻמְלַל אָנִי, רְפָאֵנִי יהוה כִּי נִבְהֲלוּ

‹ shudder with terror / ‹ for / ‹ HASHEM, / ‹ heal me, / ‹‹ am I; / ‹ feeble / ‹ for / ‹ HASHEM, / ‹ Favor me,

עֲצָמָי. וְנַפְשִׁי נִבְהֲלָה מְאֹד, וְאַתָּה יהוה עַד מָתָי.

‹‹ when? / ‹ until / ‹ HASHEM, / ‹ and You, / ‹‹ utterly, / ‹ is terrified / ‹ My soul / ‹‹ do my bones.

שׁוּבָה יהוה חַלְּצָה נַפְשִׁי, הוֹשִׁיעֵנִי לְמַעַן חַסְדֶּךָ.

‹‹ Your kindness. / ‹ as befits / ‹ save me / ‹‹ my soul; / ‹ release / ‹ HASHEM, / ‹ Desist,

---

(1) *II Samuel* 24:14.

כִּי אֵין בַּמָּוֶת זִכְרֶךָ, בִּשְׁאוֹל מִי יוֹדֶה לָּךְ. יָגַעְתִּי

‹ I am ‹ You? » will ‹ who ‹ in the » is there men- ‹ in ‹ not ‹ For
wearied   praise   grave   tion of You;   death

בְאַנְחָתִי, אַשְׂחֶה בְכָל לַיְלָה מִטָּתִי, בְּדִמְעָתִי

‹ with my tears » my bed; ‹ night ‹ every ‹ I drench » with my sigh;

עַרְשִׂי אַמְסֶה. עָשְׁשָׁה מִכַּעַס עֵינִי, עָתְקָה בְּכָל

‹ by all ‹ aged ‹ is my ‹ because of ‹ Dimmed » I soak. ‹ my couch
eye,   anger

צוֹרְרָי. סוּרוּ מִמֶּנִּי כָּל פֹּעֲלֵי אָוֶן, כִּי שָׁמַע יהוה

‹ HASHEM has heard ‹ for » of evil, ‹ doers ‹ all ‹ from me, ‹ Depart » my
tormentors.

קוֹל בִּכְיִי. שָׁמַע יהוה תְּחִנָּתִי, יהוה תְּפִלָּתִי יִקָּח.

» will ‹ my prayer ‹ HASHEM » my plea, ‹ HASHEM » of my ‹ the
accept.   has heard   weeping. sound

יֵבֹשׁוּ וְיִבָּהֲלוּ מְאֹד כָּל אֹיְבָי, יָשֻׁבוּ יֵבֹשׁוּ רָגַע.

» in an ‹ and be ‹ may they » my ‹ all ‹ utterly, ‹ and con- ‹ Let them
instant. shamed regret enemies;   founded be shamed

מַחֵי וּמַסֵּי מֵמִית וּמְחַיֶּה, מַסִּיק מִן שְׁאוֹל

‹ the ‹ from ‹ Who raises » and Who ‹ Who causes » and Who ‹ [O God,]
grave   [the dead] restores life,   death   heals, Who wounds

לְחַיֵּי עָלְמָא, בְּרָא כַּד חָטֵי אֲבוּהִי לַקְיֵהּ, אֲבוּהִי

‹ but a » would ‹ his father ‹ sin, ‹ should ‹ A son ‹ eternal: ‹ to life
father strike him,   he

דְחָיֵס אַסֵּי לִכְאֵבֵהּ. עַבְדָּא דְמָרִיד נָפִיק בִּקוֹלָר,

» in chains, ‹ he is » who rebels, ‹ A slave ‹ his [son's] ‹ will ‹ who is com-
led out   pain.   heal passionate

מָרֵהּ תָּאִיב וְתַבִּיר קוֹלָרֵהּ.

» his chains. ‹ he breaks ‹ desires, ‹ but [if]
his master

בְּרָךְ בִּכְרָךְ אֲנָן וְחָטֵינָן קַמָּךְ, הָא רְוֵי נַפְשִׁין

‹ has our ‹ satiated ‹ indeed » before ‹ and we have ‹ we ‹ Your ‹ Your
soul been   You;   sinned   are, firstborn, son,

בִּגִידִין מְרָרִין, עַבְדָּךְ אֲנָן וּמְרוֹדִינָן קַמָּךְ,

» before ‹ and we have ‹ we ‹ Your » that is bitter. ‹ with
You;   rebelled   are servants   wormwood

הָא בְּבִזְתָא, הָא בְּשִׁבְיָא, הָא בְּמַלְקִיּוּתָא.

» by the lash. ‹ and ‹ in captivity, ‹ some ‹ from ‹ [indeed we have
some   looting, suffered,] some

בְּמָטוּ מִנָּךְ בְּרַחֲמָךְ דִּנְפִישִׁין, אַסֵּי לִכְאֵבִין

‹ the pains ‹ heal ‹ that is abundant, ‹ in Your compassion ‹ of You, ‹ We beg

דְּתִתְקוֹף עֲלָן, עַד דְּלָא נֶהֱוֵי גְּמִירָא בְּשִׁבְיָא.

« in captivity. ‹ completely annihilated ‹ we are not ‹ while yet ‹ us, ‹ that have overwhelmed

---

SELICHAH 59 / סליחה נט
(תחנה)

שַׁעֲרֵי שָׁמַיִם,* בְּלוּלֵי אֵשׁ וּמַיִם,*

« with water,* ‹ of fire ‹ which is a mixture « of Heaven,* ‹ O Gates

שַׁעֲרֵי שָׁמַיִם — *O Gates of Heaven.* The Talmud names and describes seven heavens, each a higher level than the preceding one. They are:

(1) וִילוֹן, *Vilon* [lit., *curtain*], although nothing happens within this heaven, in the morning it withdraws [like a curtain, allowing the daylight to shine through (*Rashi*)] and in the evening it goes forth [preventing the light of the sun from reaching Earth (*Rashi*)], thus it renews the work of Creation each day;

(2) רָקִיעַ, *Rakia* [lit., *firmament*], in which the sun, moon, stars, and constellations are suspended;

(3) שְׁחָקִים, *Shechakim* [lit., *powders* or *pulverizers*], in which stand millstones that grind manna for the righteous;

(4) זְבוּל, *Zevul* [lit., *Temple*], in which stands the Jerusalem of heaven, Temple, and Altar upon which the great angelic prince Michael sacrifices offerings;

(5) מָעוֹן, *Maon* [lit., *dwelling*], in which groups of ministering angels recite songs [of praise to God] through the night, but remain silent by day in deference to Israel;

(6) מָכוֹן, *Machon* [lit., *foundation* or *establishment*], in which are storehouses of snow and of hail, the attics in which harmful dew and heavy rainfall are stored, and the chamber of the whirlwind and the tempest, the grotto of smoke with its doors of fire [all of them used for retribution against the wicked (*Rashi*)];

and (7) עֲרָבוֹת, *Aravos* [lit., *willows* or *darkenings* or *mixtures*], in which are Righteousness, Justice, and Charity; caches of Life, Peace, and Blessing; the souls of the righteous, the spirits and souls that are destined to be born; and the life-giving dew with which God will revivify the dead (*Chagigah* 12b).

The *paytan* petitions all the heavens to open so that Israel's prayers may pour through them to the Throne of Glory. The first stanza speaks to all seven heavens at once, while each of the remaining stanzas addresses a particular heaven. The order of the heavens as enumerated in the *selichah* does not follow that of the Talmud (although in some editions the stanzas have been re-arranged to conform to the Talmudic listing). The propriety and permissibility of directing prayer to any entity other than God is discussed in the introduction to this volume.

Although this *selichah* is apparently unsigned, some attribute it to R' Shimon ben Yitzchak [see prefatory comment to *Selichah* 53].

בְּלוּלֵי אֵשׁ וּמַיִם — *Which is a mixture of fire with water.* This phrase describes not the Gates of Heaven, but Heaven itself. According to one view in the Talmud (*Chagigah* 12a; see also *Rashi* to *Genesis* 1:8) the word שָׁמַיִם, *heavens,* is a composite of אֵשׁ וּמַיִם, *fire and water,* because God combined these two elements and formed the heavens.

שְׁלֹשׁ מֵאוֹת וְתִשְׁעִים כְּמִנְיַן שָׁמַיִם,*

《 [of the letters]《 like the 《 and ninety 《 hundred 《 three
of שָׁמַיִם,* sum of values [in all],

הִפָּתְחוּ לְחַנּוּן יְפַת פְּעָמַיִם,

《 [pilgrimage] 《 beautiful 《 for the   **open up**
footsteps, supplication of
[Israel, who have]

וְתַעַל תְּפִלָּתָם לְאֵל הַשָּׁמַיִם.[1]

《of the Heavens. 《 to God 《 **their prayer** 《 **and let ascend**

שַׁעֲרֵי רָקִיעַ, בּוֹ מְאוֹרוֹת הִתְקִיעַ,

《 are fixed, 《 the stars 《— in which 《of Rakia 《 **O Gates**

וּמִמֶּנּוּ זוֹרְחִים בִּמְקוֹמָם לְהַשְׁקִיעַ,

《 to set [at the end 《 and in their 《 they shine 《 from
of their cycle]— places forth whence

הִפָּתְחוּ לְחַנּוּן יָם לָמוֹ הִבְקִיעַ,

《 He split, 《 for 《 the 《for the sup- **open up**
them sea plication of
[Israel whom]

וְתַעַל תְּפִלָּתָם פְּנֵי מַעֲבִיב רָקִיעַ.

《the sky. 《Him Who brings 《before 《 **their** 《 **and let**
clouds to cover **prayer** **ascend**

שַׁעֲרֵי זְבוּל, שֶׁבּוֹ מִזְבֵּחַ סָבוּל,

《 is borne, 《 the Altar 《— in which 《 of Zevul 《 **O Gates**

וְהַשַּׂר מַקְטִיר עָלָיו כְּמִכַהֵן בְּכַרְבּוּל,

《 wearing a 《 like the 《 on it 《 raises 《 and the
turban — Kohen smoke angel

הִפָּתְחוּ לְחַנּוּן נִדְחָקִים בְּחִבּוּל,

《 and wounded 《 oppressed 《 for the sup- **open up**
[in exile], plication of
[Israel, who are]

---

(1) Some editions read אֶל הַשָּׁמַיִם, to the heavens.

שְׁלֹשׁ מֵאוֹת וְתִשְׁעִים כְּמִנְיַן שָׁמַיִם — Three hundred and ninety [in all], like the sum of
values [of the letters] of שָׁמַיִם. The gematria of the word שָׁמַיִם is 390 [ש=300; מ=40;
י=10; ם=40]. The stich refers to the Aggadah
(Derech Eretz Rabbah 2) that states: God is
One, His Name is One, and He sits among
three hundred and ninety firmaments, each
with its name upon it.

The paytan cites this teaching here to
answer a question regarding the previously
cited Talmudic proem (see preceding comment): If the heavens are compounded of אֵשׁ
and מַיִם, they should be called אֶשְׁמַיִם; why
was the א dropped from their name? The
answer is that the name שָׁמַיִם alludes to the
number of firmaments the heavens comprise
(Masbir).

וְתַעַל תְּפִלָּתָם פְּנֵי יָשַׁב לַמַּבּוּל.[1]

《 at the 〈 Who sat 〈 before 〈 **their prayer** 〈 **and let**
Flood.　enthroned　Him　　　　　　　　　**ascend**

שַׁעֲרֵי וִילוֹן, נִכְנָס וְיוֹצֵא בְּגִלְלוֹן,*

《 unfolding,* 〈 and spreads 〈 that retracts 〈 of Vilon, 〈 **O Gates**
　　　　　open　　[in the
　　　　　[at night]　morning]

וּמְחַדֵּשׁ בְּכָל יוֹם מִפִּתְחֵי חַלּוֹן,

《 of the [celes- 〈 the 〈 day 〈 each 〈 thereby
tial] window,　opening　　　　　　renewing

הִפָּתְחוּ לְחִנּוּן מַצַּבְתָּה כָּאַלּוֹן,

《 like an oak, 〈 stood sturdy 〈 for the sup- 〈 **open up**
　　　　　　　　plication of
　　　　　　　　[Israel, who]

וְתַעַל תְּפִלָּתָם פְּנֵי רוּם וִילוֹן.

《 Vilon. 〈 dwells in 〈 before 〈 **their prayer** 〈 **and let**
　　the high [Him Who]　　　　　**ascend**

שַׁעֲרֵי שְׁחָקִים, שֶׁבּוֹ רֵחַיִם שׁוֹחֲקִים,

《 grind, 〈 the 〈 — in 《 of Shechakim 〈 **O Gates**
　　millstones　which

עוֹמְדוֹת וְטוֹחֲנוֹת מָן לַצַּדִּיקִים,

《 for the righteous — 〈 manna 〈 and grind 〈 that stand

הִפָּתְחוּ לְחִנּוּן זְרוּיִים בִּמְרְחַקִּים,

《 in far-off places, 〈 scattered 〈 for the sup- 〈 **open up**
　　　　　　　　　plication of
　　　　　　　　　[Israel, who are]

וְתַעַל תְּפִלָּתָם פְּנֵי שׁוֹכֵן שְׁחָקִים.

《 in 〈 Him Who 〈 before 〈 **their prayer** 〈 **and let**
Shechakim.　dwells　　　　　　　**ascend**

שַׁעֲרֵי מָכוֹן, שֶׁבּוֹ שְׁלָגִים יִתָּכוֹן,

《 are 〈 snows 〈 — in 《 of 〈 **O Gates**
prepared,　　which　Machon

---

(1) Cf. *Psalms* 29:10; see *Rashi* there; some editions
of *Selichos* read יוֹשֵׁב בִּזְבוּל, *Who is enthroned in Zevul.*

נִכְנָס וְיוֹצֵא בְּגִלְלוֹן — *That retracts [in the
morning] and spreads open [at night] unfolding.* This describes the function of *Vilon,*

not its gates (see the Talmudic passage cited
in the prefatory comment).

וּמְעָרַת קִיטוֹר וְסַעַר בּוֹ יִשְׁכּוֹן,

« dwell — ‹ and ‹ mists ‹ wherein ‹ and the cavern
storm winds

הִפָּתְחוּ לְחִנּוּן עַם לִבּוֹ יִכּוֹן,

« is ‹ whose ‹ the ‹ for the sup- ‹ open up
steadfast, heart nation plication of [Israel,]

וְתַעַל תְּפִלָּתָם פְּנֵי דָר רוֹם מָכוֹן.

« Machon. ‹ in the ‹ Him Who ‹ before ‹ their prayer ‹ and let
high dwells ascend

שַׁעֲרֵי מָעוֹן, בּוֹ מְשׁוֹרְרִים יִשְׁעוֹן,

« [angelic] choirs sing [at night] ‹ — in « of Maon ‹ O Gates
which

וּבַיּוֹם הֵם חָשִׁים לִסְגֻל יִשְׁמָעוּן.

« to hear — ‹ the treasured « are silent, ‹ they ‹ and by day
[people's prayers]

הִפָּתְחוּ לְחִנּוּן נִמְרָרִים לַלְעוֹן,

« [that is] like ‹ embittered ‹ for the sup- ‹ open up
wormwood, [by suffering plication of exile] of [Israel,]

וְתַעַל תְּפִלָּתָם פְּנֵי דָר רוֹם מָעוֹן.

« Maon. ‹ in the ‹ Him Who ‹ before ‹ their prayer ‹ and let
high dwells ascend

שַׁעֲרֵי עֲרָבוֹת, שֶׁבּוֹ בִּרְכוֹת רַבּוֹת,

« that are ‹ are ‹ — in « of Aravos ‹ O Gates
plentiful, blessings which

וְגִנְזֵי צְדָקָה וָחֶסֶד וְכָל טוֹבוֹת,

« good — ‹ and all ‹ kindness, ‹ of right- ‹ and the
eousness, treasure houses

הִפָּתְחוּ לְחִנּוּן בְּנֵי שְׁלֹשֶׁת אָבוֹת,

« Patriarchs, ‹ of the three ‹ the « for the sup- ‹ open up
children plication of [Israel,]

וְתַעַל תְּפִלָּתָם פְּנֵי רוֹכֵב עֲרָבוֹת.[1]

« upon ‹ Who ‹ to ‹ their prayer ‹ and let
Aravos. rides Him ascend

---

(1) Cf. *Psalms* 68:5.

ALL:

מַכְנִיסֵי רַחֲמִים, הַכְנִיסוּ רַחֲמֵינוּ, לִפְנֵי בַּעַל
‹ the Master ‹ before ‹ our [plea for] mercy ‹ may you usher in ‹ [pleas for] mercy, ‹ O you who usher in

הָרַחֲמִים. מַשְׁמִיעֵי תְפִלָּה, הַשְׁמִיעוּ תְּפִלָּתֵנוּ, לִפְנֵי
‹ before ‹ of our prayer ‹ may you aid the hearing ≪ of prayer, ‹ O you who aid the hearing ≪ of mercy.

שׁוֹמֵעַ תְּפִלָּה. מַשְׁמִיעֵי צְעָקָה, הַשְׁמִיעוּ צַעֲקָתֵנוּ,
‹ of our outcries ‹ may you aid the hearing ≪ of outcries, ‹ O you who aid the hearing ≪ of prayer. ‹ the Hearer

לִפְנֵי שׁוֹמֵעַ צְעָקָה. מַכְנִיסֵי דִמְעָה, הַכְנִיסוּ
‹ may you usher in ≪ tears, ‹ O you who usher in ≪ of outcries. ‹ the Hearer ‹ before

דִמְעוֹתֵינוּ, לִפְנֵי מֶלֶךְ מִתְרַצֶּה בִדְמָעוֹת.
≪ through tears. ‹ Who is appeased ‹ the King ‹ before ‹ our tears

הִשְׁתַּדְּלוּ וְהַרְבּוּ תְּחִנָּה וּבַקָּשָׁה, לִפְנֵי מֶלֶךְ אֵל
‹ God, ‹ the King, ‹ before ‹ and pleas ‹ supplications ‹ and intensify ‹ Exert yourselves

רָם וְנִשָּׂא. הַזְכִּירוּ לְפָנָיו, הַשְׁמִיעוּ לְפָנָיו תּוֹרָה
‹ the Torah ‹ before Him, ‹ aid to be heard ≪ before Him, ‹ Mention ≪ and uplifted. ‹ exalted.

וּמַעֲשִׂים טוֹבִים שֶׁל שׁוֹכְנֵי עָפָר.
≪ in the dust. ‹ [the Patriarchs and Matriarchs] who dwell ‹ of ‹ that are good ‹ and the deeds

יִזְכֹּר אַהֲבָתָם וִיחַיֶּה זַרְעָם, שֶׁלֹּא תֹאבַד שְׁאֵרִית
‹ shall the remnant ‹ lost ‹ so that not ‹ to their offspring, ‹ and grant life ‹ their love ‹ May He remember

יַעֲקֹב. כִּי צֹאן רוֹעֵה נֶאֱמָן הָיָה לְחֶרְפָּה,
≪ a disgrace; ‹ has become ‹ who is faithful [Moses] ‹ of the shepherd ‹ the flock ‹ For ≪ of Jacob be.

יִשְׂרָאֵל גּוֹי אֶחָד לְמָשָׁל וְלִשְׁנִינָה.
≪ and a simile. ‹ a parable ‹ that is unique, ‹ the nation ≪ Israel,

מַהֵר עֲנֵנוּ אֱלֹהֵי יִשְׁעֵנוּ, וּפְדֵנוּ מִכָּל גְּזֵרוֹת קָשׁוֹת
≪ that are harsh; ‹ decrees ‹ from all ‹ and redeem us ‹ of our salvation, ‹ O God ‹ answer us, ‹ Swiftly

וְהוֹשִׁיעָה בְּרַחֲמֶיךָ הָרַבִּים, מְשִׁיחַ צִדְקֶךָ וְעַמֶּךָ.
and Your ‹ Your righteous ‹ that is ‹ in Your mercy ‹ and may You
people.   anointed one   abundant,   save,

מָרָן דְּבִשְׁמַיָּא לָךְ מִתְחַנְּנַן, כְּבַר שִׁבְיָא דְּמִתְחַנַּן
‹ who   ‹ in   ‹ as one **«** do we ‹ to You **«** Who is in ‹ Our
supplicates   captivity   supplicate,   heaven,   Master

לְשִׁבְיֵהּ. כֻּלְּהוֹן בְּנֵי שִׁבְיָא בְּכַסְפָּא מִתְפָּרְקִין,
« are redeemed, ‹ through ‹ in ‹ those ‹ [for] all **«** before his
money   captivity,   captors;

וְעַמָּךְ יִשְׂרָאֵל בְּרַחֲמֵי וּבְתַחֲנוּנֵי, הַב לָן שְׁאִילְתִּין
‹ our requests ‹ us ‹ O **«** and ‹ through ‹ Israel ‹ but Your
grant   supplication. compassion   people

וּבָעוּתִין, דְּלָא נֶהֱדַר רֵיקָם מִן קֳדָמָךְ.
« before ‹ from ‹ empty- ‹ that we not be ‹ and our prayers
You.   handed   turned away

מָרָן דְּבִשְׁמַיָּא לָךְ מִתְחַנְּנַן, כְּעַבְדָּא דְּמִתְחַנַּן
‹ who   ‹ as a slave **«** do we ‹ to You **«** Who is in ‹ Our
supplicates   supplicate,   heaven,   Master

לְמָרֵיהּ, עֲשִׁיקֵי אֲנַן וּבַחֲשׁוֹכָא שָׁרֵינָן, מְרִירָן נַפְשִׁין
‹ are [our] ‹ embittered **«** do we ‹ and in darkness ‹ are **«** Oppressed **«** to his
souls   abide,   we   master:

מֵעַקְתִין דִּנְפִישִׁין, חֵילָא לֵית בָּן לִרְצוּיָךְ. מָרָן,
‹ Our **«** to appease ‹ within ‹ is ‹ Strength **«** that is ‹ from distress
Master,   You.   us   lacking   excessive.

עֲבִיד בְּדִיל קַיָּמָא דִּגְזַרְתְּ עִם אֲבָהָתָנָא.
« our Patriarchs. ‹ with ‹ that You ‹ of the ‹ for the ‹ act
established   covenant   sake

שׁוֹמֵר יִשְׂרָאֵל, שְׁמוֹר שְׁאֵרִית יִשְׂרָאֵל, וְאַל
‹ let not **«** of Israel; ‹ the remnant ‹ safeguard ‹ of Israel, ‹ O Guardian

יֹאבַד יִשְׂרָאֵל, הָאֹמְרִים שְׁמַע יִשְׂרָאֵל.[1]
« O Israel. ‹ Hear, ‹ those who **«** Israel be destroyed —
proclaim:

שׁוֹמֵר גּוֹי אֶחָד, שְׁמוֹר שְׁאֵרִית עַם אֶחָד, וְאַל
‹ let not **«** that is ‹ of the ‹ the remnant ‹ safeguard **«** that is ‹ of the ‹ O Guardian
unique; people   unique,   nation

___
(1) *Deuteronomy* 6:4.

יֹאבַד גּוֹי אֶחָד, הַמְּיַחֲדִים שְׁמֶךָ, יהוה אֱלֹהֵינוּ
⟨ is our God, ⟨ HASHEM ⟩⟩ of Your ⟨ those who proclaim ⟩⟩ that is ⟨ the ⟨ be
                    Name: the Oneness   unique,   nation destroyed

יהוה אֶחָד.
⟩⟩ the One ⟨ HASHEM
[and Only]!   is

שׁוֹמֵר גּוֹי קָדוֹשׁ, שְׁמוֹר שְׁאֵרִית עַם קָדוֹשׁ,
⟩⟩ that is ⟨ of the ⟨ the remnant ⟨ safeguard ⟩⟩ that is ⟨ of the ⟨ O Guardian
holy;   people   holy,   nation

וְאַל יֹאבַד גּוֹי קָדוֹשׁ, הַמְּשַׁלְּשִׁים בְּשָׁלֹשׁ קְדֻשּׁוֹת
⟨ sancti- ⟨ the ⟨ those who proclaim ⟩⟩ that is ⟨ the ⟨ be ⟨ let
fications threefold three times   holy, nation destroyed not

לְקָדוֹשׁ.
⟩⟩ to the
Holy One.

מִתְרַצֶּה בְּרַחֲמִים וּמִתְפַּיֵּס בְּתַחֲנוּנִים, הִתְרַצֶּה
⟨ be ⟩⟩ through ⟨ and Who becomes ⟨ through ⟨ You Who becomes
favorable supplications, conciliatory compassion favorable

וְהִתְפַּיֵּס לְדוֹר עָנִי, כִּי אֵין עוֹזֵר. אָבִינוּ מַלְכֵּנוּ,
⟩⟩ our King, ⟨ Our ⟩⟩ helper. ⟨ there ⟨ for ⟩⟩ that is ⟨ to the ⟨ and be
             Father,   is no   poor, generation conciliatory

חָנֵּנוּ וַעֲנֵנוּ, כִּי אֵין בָּנוּ מַעֲשִׂים, עֲשֵׂה עִמָּנוּ
⟨ us ⟨ treat ⟩⟩ worthy deeds; ⟨ we have no ⟨ though ⟨ and ⟨ be gracious
                                             answer us, with us

צְדָקָה וָחֶסֶד וְהוֹשִׁיעֵנוּ.
⟩⟩ and save us. ⟨ and ⟨ with
                kindness, charity

STAND AFTER THE WORDS וַאֲנַחְנוּ לֹא נֵדַע UNTIL CONCLUSION OF THE PARAGRAPH.

וַאֲנַחְנוּ לֹא נֵדַע מַה נַּעֲשֶׂה, כִּי עָלֶיךָ עֵינֵינוּ.[1]
⟩⟩ are our ⟨ upon ⟨ rather, ⟩⟩ we should ⟨ what ⟨ know not ⟨ We
eyes.   You   do,

זְכֹר רַחֲמֶיךָ יהוה וַחֲסָדֶיךָ, כִּי מֵעוֹלָם הֵמָּה.[2] יְהִי
⟨ May ⟩⟩ are they. ⟨ eternal ⟨ for ⟨ and Your ⟨ HASHEM, ⟨ Your ⟨ Remem-
                                kindnesses,   mercies,   ber

---

(1) *II Chronicles* 20:12. (2) *Psalms* 25:6.

חַסְדְּךָ יהוה עָלֵינוּ, כַּאֲשֶׁר יִחַלְנוּ לָךְ.[1] אַל תִּזְכָּר

‹ recall ‹ Do not ‹‹ You. ‹ we awaited ‹ just as ‹‹ be upon us, ‹ HASHEM, ‹ Your kindness,

לָנוּ עֲוֹנוֹת רִאשׁוֹנִים, מַהֵר יְקַדְּמִוּנוּ רַחֲמֶיךָ, כִּי

‹for ‹‹ may Your mercies, ‹ advance to meet us ‹ swiftly ‹‹ of the ancients; ‹ the sins ‹against us

דַלּוֹנוּ מְאֹד.[2] עֶזְרֵנוּ בְּשֵׁם יהוה, עֹשֵׂה שָׁמַיִם

‹ of heaven ‹ Maker ‹ of HASHEM, ‹ is through the Name ‹ Our help ‹‹ exceedingly. ‹ we have become impoverished

וָאָרֶץ.[3] חָנֵּנוּ יהוה חָנֵּנוּ, כִּי רַב שָׂבַעְנוּ בוּז.[4] בְּרֹגֶז

‹‹ Amid wrath, ‹‹ with contempt. ‹ sated ‹ we are ‹ for ‹‹ favor us, ‹ HASHEM, ‹ Favor us, ‹‹ and earth. fully

רַחֵם תִּזְכּוֹר.[5] בְּרֹגֶז עֲקֵדָה תִּזְכּוֹר. בְּרֹגֶז תְּמִימוֹת

‹ the perfect ones ‹‹ Amid wrath, ‹‹ You should remember! ‹ the binding [of Isaac] ‹‹ Amid wrath, ‹‹ You should remember! ‹ to be merciful

תִּזְכּוֹר. יהוה הוֹשִׁיעָה, הַמֶּלֶךְ יַעֲנֵנוּ בְיוֹם קָרְאֵנוּ.[6]

‹‹ we call. ‹ on the day ‹ answer us ‹ May the King ‹‹ save! ‹ HASHEM, ‹‹ You should remember!

כִּי הוּא יָדַע יִצְרֵנוּ, זָכוּר כִּי עָפָר אֲנָחְנוּ.[7]

‹‹ are we. ‹ dust ‹ that ‹ He is mindful ‹‹ our nature, ‹ knew ‹ He ‹ For

❖ עָזְרֵנוּ אֱלֹהֵי יִשְׁעֵנוּ עַל דְּבַר כְּבוֹד שְׁמֶךָ, וְהַצִּילֵנוּ

‹ rescue us ‹‹ of Your Name; ‹ of the glory ‹ the sake ‹ for ‹ of our salvation ‹ O God ‹ Assist us,

וְכַפֵּר עַל חַטֹּאתֵינוּ לְמַעַן שְׁמֶךָ.[8]

‹‹ of Your Name. ‹ for the sake ‹ our sins ‹ for ‹ and grant atonement

FULL KADDISH / קדיש שלם

THE CHAZZAN RECITES קַדִּישׁ שָׁלֵם, FULL KADDISH.

יִתְגַּדַּל וְיִתְקַדַּשׁ שְׁמֵהּ רַבָּא. (.Cong — אָמֵן) בְּעָלְמָא

‹ — in the world ‹‹ (Amen.) ‹ Cong. ‹‹ that is great! — ‹ may His Name ‹ and be sanctified ‹ Grow exalted

דִּי בְרָא כִרְעוּתֵהּ. וְיַמְלִיךְ מַלְכוּתֵהּ, וְיַצְמַח פֻּרְקָנֵהּ

‹ His salvation, ‹ and cause to sprout ‹‹ to His kingship, ‹ and may He give reign ‹‹ according to His will, ‹ He created ‹ that

---

(1) Psalms 33:22. (2) 79:8. (3) 121:2. (4) 123:3. (5) Habakkuk 3:2. (6) Psalms 20:10. (7) 103:14. (8) 79:9.

וִיקָרֵב מְשִׁיחֵהּ. (אָמֵן. — Cong.) בְּחַיֵּיכוֹן וּבְיוֹמֵיכוֹן וּבְחַיֵּי
‹ and in the ‹ and in ‹ in your ‹‹ (Amen.) ‹‹ His Messiah, ‹ and bring
lifetimes   your days,   lifetimes   near

דְכָל בֵּית יִשְׂרָאֵל, בַּעֲגָלָא וּבִזְמַן קָרִיב. וְאִמְרוּ: אָמֵן.
‹‹Amen. ‹ Now ‹‹ that comes ‹ and at a ‹ swiftly ‹‹ of Israel, ‹ Family ‹ of the
respond: soon.   time   entire

CONGREGATION RESPONDS:

אָמֵן. יְהֵא שְׁמֵהּ רַבָּא מְבָרַךְ לְעָלַם וּלְעָלְמֵי עָלְמַיָּא.
‹‹ and for all eternity. ‹ forever ‹ be ‹ that is ‹ His ‹ May ‹‹ Amen.
blessed   great   Name

CHAZZAN CONTINUES:

יְהֵא שְׁמֵהּ רַבָּא מְבָרַךְ לְעָלַם וּלְעָלְמֵי עָלְמַיָּא. יִתְבָּרַךְ
‹ Blessed, ‹‹ and for all eternity. ‹ forever ‹ be ‹ that is ‹ His ‹ May
blessed   great   Name

וְיִשְׁתַּבַּח וְיִתְפָּאַר וְיִתְרוֹמַם וְיִתְנַשֵּׂא וְיִתְהַדָּר וְיִתְעַלֶּה
‹ elevated, ‹ honored, ‹ upraised, ‹ exalted, ‹ glorified, ‹ praised,

וְיִתְהַלָּל שְׁמֵהּ דְּקֻדְשָׁא בְּרִיךְ הוּא (בְּרִיךְ הוּא — Cong.)
‹‹ is He) ‹ (Blessed ‹‹ is He ‹ Blessed ‹ of the Holy ‹ be the ‹ and lauded
One,   Name

לְעֵלָּא [וּ]לְעֵלָּא מִכָּל בִּרְכָתָא וְשִׁירָתָא תֻּשְׁבְּחָתָא —
‹ praise ‹‹ and song, ‹ blessing ‹ any ‹ exceedingly beyond

וְנֶחֱמָתָא דַּאֲמִירָן בְּעָלְמָא. וְאִמְרוּ: אָמֵן. (אָמֵן. — Cong.)
‹‹ (Amen.) ‹‹ Amen. ‹ Now ‹‹ in the ‹ that are ‹ and
respond: world.   uttered   consolation

CONGREGATION:

(קַבֵּל בְּרַחֲמִים וּבְרָצוֹן אֶת תְּפִלָּתֵנוּ.)
‹‹ our prayers.) ‹ and with ‹ with mercy ‹ (Accept
favor

CHAZZAN CONTINUES:

תִּתְקַבֵּל צְלוֹתְהוֹן וּבָעוּתְהוֹן דְּכָל בֵּית יִשְׂרָאֵל קֳדָם
‹ before ‹ Israel ‹ Family ‹ of the ‹ and ‹ the prayers ‹ May
of   entire   supplications   accepted be

אֲבוּהוֹן דִּי בִשְׁמַיָּא. וְאִמְרוּ: אָמֵן. (אָמֵן. — Cong.)
‹‹ (Amen.) ‹‹ Amen. ‹ Now ‹‹ is in ‹ Who ‹ their
respond: Heaven.   Father

CONGREGATION:

(יְהִי שֵׁם יהוה מְבֹרָךְ, מֵעַתָּה וְעַד עוֹלָם.[1])
‹‹ eternity.) ‹ until ‹ from ‹‹ be ‹ of ‹ the ‹ (Let
this time   blessed,   HASHEM Name

---

(1) *Psalms* 113:2.

CHAZZAN CONTINUES:

יְהֵא שְׁלָמָא רַבָּא מִן שְׁמַיָּא וְחַיִּים טוֹבִים עָלֵינוּ וְעַל כָּל

⟨ all ⟨ and ⟨ upon us ⟨ that is ⟨ and life ⟨ Heaven ⟨ from ⟨ that is ⟨ peace ⟨ May
upon good, abundant there be

יִשְׂרָאֵל. וְאִמְרוּ: אָמֵן. (Cong. — אָמֵן.)

《 (Amen.) 《 Amen. ⟨ Now 《 Israel.
respond:

CONGREGATION:

(עֶזְרִי מֵעִם יהוה, עֹשֵׂה שָׁמַיִם וָאָרֶץ.[1])

《 and ⟨ of ⟨ Maker 《HASHEM, ⟨ is ⟨ (My
earth.) heaven from help

CHAZZAN BOWS; TAKES THREE STEPS BACK. BOWS LEFT AND SAYS "... עֹשֶׂה שָׁלוֹם, *HE WHO MAKES
PEACE* ..."; BOWS RIGHT AND SAYS "... הוּא, *MAY HE* ..."; BOWS FORWARD AND SAYS "... וְעַל כָּל יִשְׂרָאֵל,
AND UPON ALL ISRAEL ..."; REMAINS IN PLACE FOR A FEW MOMENTS, THEN TAKES THREE STEPS FORWARD.*

עֹשֶׂה [הַ]שָּׁלוֹם בִּמְרוֹמָיו, הוּא יַעֲשֶׂה שָׁלוֹם עָלֵינוּ, וְעַל

⟨ and ⟨ upon us, ⟨ peace ⟨ make ⟨ may 《 in His ⟨ [the] peace ⟨ He Who
upon He heights, makes

כָּל יִשְׂרָאֵל. וְאִמְרוּ: אָמֵן. (Cong. — אָמֵן.)

《 (Amen.) 《 Amen. ⟨ Now 《 Israel. ⟨ all
respond:

(1) *Psalms* 121:2.

ﭏ יום שלישי של עשרת ימי תשובה ﭏ

ﭏ THIRD DAY OF REPENTANCE ﭏ

אַשְׁרֵי יוֹשְׁבֵי בֵיתֶךָ, עוֹד יְהַלְלוּךָ סֶּלָה.[1] אַשְׁרֵי

⟨ Praise- ⟨⟨ Selah. ⟨⟨ they will ⟨ con- ⟨⟨ in Your ⟨ are those ⟨ Praiseworthy
worthy praise You, tinually house, who dwell

הָעָם שֶׁכָּכָה לּוֹ, אַשְׁרֵי הָעָם שֶׁיהוה אֱלֹהָיו.[2]

⟨⟨ is their ⟨ that ⟨ is the ⟨ praise- ⟨⟨ is ⟨ that such ⟨ is the
God. HASHEM people worthy their lot; people

———— Psalm 145 / תהלים קמה ————

תְּהִלָּה לְדָוִד, אֲרוֹמִמְךָ אֱלוֹהַי הַמֶּלֶךְ, וַאֲבָרְכָה

⟨ and I ⟨⟨ the King, ⟨ my God ⟨ I will exalt You, ⟨⟨ by David: ⟨ A psalm of
will bless praise

שִׁמְךָ לְעוֹלָם וָעֶד. בְּכָל יוֹם אֲבָרְכֶךָ, וַאֲהַלְלָה שִׁמְךָ

⟨ Your ⟨ and I ⟨⟨ I will ⟨ day ⟨ Every ⟨⟨ and ⟨ for ever ⟨ Your
Name will laud bless You, ever. Name

לְעוֹלָם וָעֶד. גָּדוֹל יהוה וּמְהֻלָּל מְאֹד, וְלִגְדֻלָּתוֹ

⟨ and His ⟨⟨exceedingly, ⟨ and ⟨ is ⟨ Great ⟨⟨ and ⟨ for ever
greatness lauded HASHEM ever.

אֵין חֵקֶר. דּוֹר לְדוֹר יְשַׁבַּח מַעֲשֶׂיךָ, וּגְבוּרֹתֶיךָ יַגִּידוּ.

⟨⟨they will ⟨ and Your ⟨⟨ Your ⟨ will ⟨ to ⟨ Gen- ⟨⟨ is beyond
recount. mighty deeds actions, praise generation eration investigation.

הֲדַר כְּבוֹד הוֹדֶךָ, וְדִבְרֵי נִפְלְאֹתֶיךָ אָשִׂיחָה. וֶעֱזוּז

⟨ And of ⟨⟨ I shall ⟨ that are ⟨ and Your ⟨ of Your ⟨ glory ⟨ The
the might discuss. wondrous deeds majesty splendrous

נוֹרְאֹתֶיךָ יֹאמֵרוּ, וּגְדוּלָּתְךָ אֲסַפְּרֶנָּה. זֵכֶר רַב טוּבְךָ

⟨ of Your abun- ⟨ A recol- ⟨⟨ I shall ⟨ and Your ⟨⟨ they will ⟨ of Your
dant goodness lection relate. greatness speak, awesome deeds

יַבִּיעוּ, וְצִדְקָתְךָ יְרַנֵּנוּ. חַנּוּן וְרַחוּם יהוה, אֶרֶךְ אַפַּיִם

⟨ to ⟨ slow ⟨ is ⟨ and ⟨ Gracious ⟨⟨they will ⟨ and of Your ⟨⟨ they
anger, HASHEM, merciful sing joyfully. righteousness will utter,

וּגְדָל חָסֶד. טוֹב יהוה לַכֹּל, וְרַחֲמָיו עַל כָּל מַעֲשָׂיו.

⟨⟨ His ⟨ all ⟨ are ⟨ His ⟨⟨ to all; ⟨ HASHEM ⟨⟨ in [bestowing] ⟨ and
creations. on mercies is good kindness. great

יוֹדוּךָ יהוה כָּל מַעֲשֶׂיךָ, וַחֲסִידֶיךָ יְבָרְכוּכָה. כְּבוֹד

⟨ Of the ⟨⟨ will ⟨ and Your ⟨⟨ Your ⟨ — all ⟨⟨ HASHEM ⟨ They will
glory bless You. devout ones creations — thank You,

———————————

(1) *Psalms* 84:5. (2) 144:15.

מַלְכוּתְךָ יֹאמֵרוּ, וּגְבוּרָתְךָ יְדַבֵּרוּ. **לְהוֹדִיעַ** לִבְנֵי הָאָדָם

⟨ mankind ⟨ To inform « they will ⟨ and of Your « they will ⟨ of Your
declare. power speak, kingdom

גְּבוּרֹתָיו, וּכְבוֹד הֲדַר מַלְכוּתוֹ. **מַלְכוּתְךָ** מַלְכוּת כָּל

⟨[span-⟨ is a ⟨ Your kingdom « of His ⟨ splendor ⟨ and of the « of His mighty
ning] all kingdom kingdom. glorious deeds,

עֹלָמִים, וּמֶמְשַׁלְתְּךָ בְּכָל דּוֹר וָדֹר. **סוֹמֵךְ** יהוה

⟨ HASHEM « after ⟨ gen- ⟨ is ⟨ and Your « eternities,
supports generation. eration throughout dominion

לְכָל הַנֹּפְלִים, וְזוֹקֵף לְכָל הַכְּפוּפִים. **עֵינֵי** כֹל

⟨ of all ⟨ The « those who ⟨ all ⟨ and « those who ⟨ all
eyes are bent. straightens are fallen,

אֵלֶיךָ יְשַׂבֵּרוּ, וְאַתָּה נוֹתֵן לָהֶם אֶת אָכְלָם בְּעִתּוֹ.

« in its ⟨ their food ⟨ them ⟨ give ⟨ and You « do look ⟨ to You
proper time. with hope,

CONCENTRATE INTENTLY WHILE RECITING THE VERSE פּוֹתֵחַ, *YOU OPEN.*

פּוֹתֵחַ אֶת יָדֶךָ, וּמַשְׂבִּיעַ לְכָל חַי רָצוֹן. ❖**צַדִּיק**

⟨ Righteous «[with its] ⟨living ⟨ every ⟨ and satisfy « ⟨ Your hand, ⟨ You open
desire. thing

יהוה בְּכָל דְּרָכָיו, וְחָסִיד בְּכָל מַעֲשָׂיו. **קָרוֹב** יהוה

⟨ is ⟨ Close « His deeds. ⟨ in all ⟨ and « His ways, ⟨ in all ⟨ is
HASHEM magnanimous HASHEM

לְכָל קֹרְאָיו, לְכֹל אֲשֶׁר יִקְרָאֻהוּ בֶאֱמֶת. **רְצוֹן** יְרֵאָיו

⟨ of those ⟨ The « sincerely. ⟨ call upon ⟨ who ⟨ to all « who call ⟨ to all
who fear Him will Him upon Him,

יַעֲשֶׂה, וְאֶת שַׁוְעָתָם יִשְׁמַע וְיוֹשִׁיעֵם. **שׁוֹמֵר** יהוה

⟨ HASHEM protects « and He will ⟨ He will ⟨ and their cry « He
save them. hear, will do;

אֶת כָּל אֹהֲבָיו, וְאֵת כָּל הָרְשָׁעִים יַשְׁמִיד. **תְּהִלַּת**

⟨ The praise «He will destroy. ⟨ the wicked ⟨ but all « who love Him; ⟨ all

יהוה יְדַבֶּר פִּי, וִיבָרֵךְ כָּל בָּשָׂר שֵׁם קָדְשׁוֹ לְעוֹלָם

⟨ for ever ⟨ of His ⟨ the ⟨ flesh ⟨ may ⟨ and bless « may my ⟨ of
Holiness Name all mouth declare, HASHEM

וָעֶד. וַאֲנַחְנוּ נְבָרֵךְ יָהּ מֵעַתָּה וְעַד עוֹלָם; הַלְלוּיָהּ.[1]

« Halleluyah! « eternity. ⟨ until ⟨ from ⟨ God ⟨ will ⟨ But we « and
this time bless ever.

---

(1) *Psalms* 115:18.

THE *CHAZZAN* RECITES חֲצִי קַדִּישׁ, HALF-*KADDISH*:

יִתְגַּדַּל וְיִתְקַדַּשׁ שְׁמֵהּ רַבָּא. (.אָמֵן — Cong.) בְּעָלְמָא

⟨ — in the world ⟨⟨ (Amen.) ⟨⟨ that is great! — ⟨ may His Name ⟨ and be sanctified ⟨ Grow exalted

דִּי בְרָא כִרְעוּתֵהּ. וְיַמְלִיךְ מַלְכוּתֵהּ, וְיַצְמַח פֻּרְקָנֵהּ

⟨ His salvation, ⟨ and cause to sprout ⟨⟨ to His kingship, ⟨ and may He give reign ⟨⟨ according to His will, ⟨ He created ⟨ that

וִיקָרֵב מְשִׁיחֵהּ. (.אָמֵן — Cong.) בְּחַיֵּיכוֹן וּבְיוֹמֵיכוֹן וּבְחַיֵּי

⟨ and in the lifetimes ⟨ and in your days, ⟨ in your lifetimes ⟨⟨ (Amen.) ⟨⟨ His Messiah, ⟨ and bring near

דְכָל בֵּית יִשְׂרָאֵל, בַּעֲגָלָא וּבִזְמַן קָרִיב. וְאִמְרוּ: אָמֵן.

⟨⟨Amen. ⟨ Now respond: ⟨⟨ that comes soon. ⟨ and at a time ⟨ swiftly ⟨⟨ of Israel, ⟨ Family ⟨ of the entire

CONGREGATION RESPONDS:

אָמֵן. יְהֵא שְׁמֵהּ רַבָּא מְבָרַךְ לְעָלַם וּלְעָלְמֵי עָלְמַיָּא.

⟨⟨ and for all eternity. ⟨ forever ⟨ be blessed ⟨ that is great ⟨ His Name ⟨ May ⟨⟨ Amen.

CHAZZAN CONTINUES:

יְהֵא שְׁמֵהּ רַבָּא מְבָרַךְ לְעָלַם וּלְעָלְמֵי עָלְמַיָּא. יִתְבָּרַךְ

⟨ Blessed, ⟨⟨ and for all eternity. ⟨ forever ⟨ be blessed ⟨ that is great ⟨ His Name ⟨ May

וְיִשְׁתַּבַּח וְיִתְפָּאַר וְיִתְרוֹמַם וְיִתְנַשֵּׂא וְיִתְהַדָּר וְיִתְעַלֶּה

⟨ elevated, ⟨ honored, ⟨ upraised, ⟨ exalted, ⟨ glorified, ⟨ praised,

וְיִתְהַלָּל שְׁמֵהּ דְּקֻדְשָׁא בְּרִיךְ הוּא (.בְּרִיךְ הוּא — Cong.)

⟨⟨ is He) ⟨ (Blessed ⟨⟨ is He ⟨ Blessed ⟨ of the Holy One, ⟨ be the Name ⟨ and lauded

— לְעֵלָּא [וּ]לְעֵלָּא מִכָּל בִּרְכָתָא וְשִׁירָתָא תֻּשְׁבְּחָתָא

⟨ praise ⟨⟨ and song, ⟨ blessing ⟨ any ⟨ exceedingly beyond

וְנֶחֱמָתָא דַּאֲמִירָן בְּעָלְמָא. וְאִמְרוּ: אָמֵן. (.אָמֵן — Cong.)

⟨⟨ (Amen.) ⟨⟨ Amen. ⟨ Now respond: ⟨⟨ in the world. ⟨ that are uttered ⟨ and consolation

ALL:

לְךָ יהוה הַצְּדָקָה, וְלָנוּ בֹּשֶׁת הַפָּנִים.¹ מַה

⟨⟨What ⟨⟨ is shamefacedness. ⟨ and ours ⟨⟨ is the ⟨ righteousness, ⟨ O Lord, ⟨ Yours,

נִּתְאוֹנֵן,³ מַה נֹּאמַר, מַה נְּדַבֵּר, וּמַה נִּצְטַדָּק.³

⟨⟨ justification can we offer? ⟨ What ⟨⟨ can we declare? ⟨ What ⟨⟨can we say? ⟨ What ⟨⟨ complaint can we make?

---

(1) *Daniel* 9:7. (2) Cf. *Lamentations* 3:39. (3) Cf. *Genesis* 44:16.

נַחְפְּשָׂה דְרָכֵינוּ וְנַחְקֹרָה, וְנָשׁוּבָה אֵלֶיךָ, כִּי יְמִינְךָ[1]

Let us examine / our ways / and investigate them / and return / to You, / for / Your right hand

פְּשׁוּטָה לְקַבֵּל שָׁבִים. לֹא בְחֶסֶד וְלֹא בְמַעֲשִׂים

is extended / to accept / those who return. / Neither / with [merit] for kindness / nor / with [merit for good] deeds

בָּאנוּ לְפָנֶיךָ, כְּדַלִּים וּכְרָשִׁים דָּפַקְנוּ דְלָתֶיךָ.

do we come / before You; / but as paupers / and as destitute people / we have knocked / on Your doors.

דְלָתֶיךָ דָּפַקְנוּ רַחוּם וְחַנּוּן, נָא אַל תְּשִׁיבֵנוּ

On Your doors / we have knocked, / O Compassionate One / and Gracious One. / Please / do not / turn us away

רֵיקָם מִלְּפָנֶיךָ. מִלְּפָנֶיךָ מַלְכֵּנוּ רֵיקָם אַל תְּשִׁיבֵנוּ,

empty-handed / from before You. / From before You, / Our King, / empty-handed / do not / turn us away,

כִּי אַתָּה שׁוֹמֵעַ תְּפִלָּה.

for / You are the One / Who hears / prayer.

שׁוֹמֵעַ תְּפִלָּה, עָדֶיךָ כָּל בָּשָׂר יָבֹאוּ.[2] יָבוֹא

You Who hears / prayer, / unto You / all / flesh / will come. / Come

כָּל בָּשָׂר לְהִשְׁתַּחֲוֹת לְפָנֶיךָ יהוה.[3] יָבֹאוּ וְיִשְׁתַּחֲווּ

will all flesh / to bow down / before You, / O HASHEM. / They will come / and bow down

לְפָנֶיךָ אֲדֹנָי, וִיכַבְּדוּ לִשְׁמֶךָ.[4] בֹּאוּ נִשְׁתַּחֲוֶה וְנִכְרָעָה,

before You, / O Lord, / and they will show honor / to Your Name. / Come! / Let us prostrate ourselves / and bow,

נִבְרְכָה לִפְנֵי יהוה עֹשֵׂנוּ.[5] נָבוֹאָה לְמִשְׁכְּנוֹתָיו,

let us kneel / before / HASHEM, / our Maker. / Let us come / to His Tabernacles,

נִשְׁתַּחֲוֶה לַהֲדֹם רַגְלָיו.[6] בֹּאוּ שְׁעָרָיו בְּתוֹדָה,

let us prostrate ourselves / at the stool / for His feet. / Enter / His gates / with thanksgiving,

חֲצֵרֹתָיו בִּתְהִלָּה, הוֹדוּ לוֹ בָּרְכוּ שְׁמוֹ.[7] וַאֲנַחְנוּ

His courtyards / with praise; / give thanks / to Him, / bless / His Name. / But we,

---

(1) Cf. *Lamentations* 3:40. (2) *Psalms* 65:3. (3) Cf. *Isaiah* 66:23.
(4) *Psalms* 86:9. (5) 95:6. (6) 132:7. (7) 100:4.

בְּרֹב חַסְדְּךָ נָבוֹא בֵיתֶךָ, נִשְׁתַּחֲוֶה אֶל הֵיכַל קָדְשְׁךָ
‹ Your Holy　‹ toward ‹ we will pros-　« Your　‹ will we ‹ of Your ‹ through the
Sanctuary　　　 trate ourselves　 House;　 enter　kindness　abundance

בְּיִרְאָתֶךָ.¹ הִנֵּה בָּרְכוּ אֶת יהוה כָּל עַבְדֵי יהוה,
‹ of　　　　‹ you ‹ all ‹　HASHEM,　‹ bless « Indeed, «　 in awe
HASHEM,　servants　　　　　　　　　　　　　　　　　　of You.

הָעֹמְדִים בְּבֵית יהוה בַּלֵּילוֹת.² שְׂאוּ יְדֵיכֶם קֹדֶשׁ
‹ in the　‹ your　‹ Lift « in the nights. ‹　of　‹ in the ‹ who stand
Sanctuary hands　　　　　　　　　　　 HASHEM　House

וּבָרְכוּ אֶת יהוה.³ רוֹמְמוּ יהוה אֱלֹהֵינוּ, וְהִשְׁתַּחֲווּ
‹ and bow down ‹ our God,　‹ HASHEM, ‹ Exalt　« HASHEM. ‹ and bless

לַהֲדֹם רַגְלָיו, קָדוֹשׁ הוּא.⁴ רוֹמְמוּ יהוה אֱלֹהֵינוּ,
‹ our God, ‹ HASHEM, ‹ Exalt « is He! ‹ holy « at His footstool;

וְהִשְׁתַּחֲווּ לְהַר קָדְשׁוֹ, כִּי קָדוֹשׁ יהוה אֱלֹהֵינוּ.⁵
« our God. ‹　is　‹ holy ‹ for « of His ‹ at the ‹ and bow
　　　　　HASHEM,　　　　　　Holiness;　Mount

הִשְׁתַּחֲווּ לַיהוה בְּהַדְרַת קֹדֶשׁ, חִילוּ מִפָּנָיו כָּל
‹ every- ‹ before ‹ tremble « of　‹ in the ‹ before ‹ Bow down
one　Him,　　　　　holiness;　splendor　HASHEM

הָאָרֶץ.⁶ נִשְׁתַּחֲוֶה אֶל הֵיכַל קָדְשְׁךָ וְנוֹדֶה אֶת שְׁמֶךָ,
‹ Your Name ‹ and we « Your Holy ‹ toward ‹ We will pros- « on earth.
will thank Sanctuary,　trate ourselves

עַל חַסְדְּךָ וְעַל אֲמִתֶּךָ, כִּי הִגְדַּלְתָּ עַל כָּל שְׁמֶךָ
« Your ‹ — even « You have ‹ for « Your ‹ and ‹ Your ‹ for
Name — beyond　exalted　faithfulness; for　kindness

אִמְרָתֶךָ.⁷ יהוה אֱלֹהֵי צְבָאוֹת, מִי כָמוֹךָ חֲסִין
‹ O Strong « is like ‹ — who « of　‹ God ‹ HASHEM, « Your promise.
One,　You,　Legions

יָהּ, וֶאֱמוּנָתְךָ סְבִיבוֹתֶיךָ.⁸ כִּי מִי בַשַּׁחַק יַעֲרֹךְ
‹ can be ‹ in the sky ‹ who ‹ For « surrounds You. ‹ and Your « God? —
compared　　　　　　　　　　　　　 faithfulness

לַיהוה, יִדְמֶה לַיהוה בִּבְנֵי אֵלִים.⁹ כִּי גָדוֹל אַתָּה
‹ are You ‹ great ‹ For « among the angels? ‹ to HASHEM ‹ be likened « to HASHEM;

וְעֹשֵׂה נִפְלָאוֹת, אַתָּה אֱלֹהִים לְבַדֶּךָ.¹⁰ כִּי גָדוֹל
‹ great ‹ For « alone. ‹ O God, ‹ You, « of wonders; ‹ and a worker

(1) Cf. *Psalms* 5:8. (2) 134:1. (3) 134:2. (4) 99:5. (5) 99:9. (6) 96:9. (7) Cf. 138:2. (8) 89:9. (9) 89:7. (10) 86:10.

גָּדוֹל 1.אֲמִתֶּךָ. שְׁחָקִים וְעַד חַסְדֶּךָ, שָׁמַיִם מֵעַל

〈 Great 》 is Your 〈 the upper 〈 and 》 is Your 〈 the very 〈 above
truth. heights until kindness, heavens

גָּדוֹל (כִּי) 2.חֵקֶר. אֵין וְלִגְדֻלָּתוֹ מְאֹד, וּמְהֻלָּל יהוה

〈 great 〈 (For) 》 investiga- 〈 is 〈 and His 》 exceed- 〈 and 〈 is
tion. beyond greatness ingly, lauded HASHEM

כִּי אֱלֹהִים. כָּל עַל הוּא נוֹרָא מְאֹד, וּמְהֻלָּל יהוה 3.

〈 For 》 heavenly 〈 all 〈 above 〈 is He 〈 awesome 》 exceed- 〈 and 〈 is
powers. ingly; lauded HASHEM

אֲשֶׁר 4.אֱלֹהִים. כָּל עַל גָּדוֹל וּמֶלֶךְ יהוה, גָּדוֹל אֵל

〈 For 》 heavenly 〈 all 〈 above 〈 and a great King 》 is 〈 a great God
powers. HASHEM,

כְמַעֲשֶׂיךָ יַעֲשֶׂה אֲשֶׁר וּבָאָרֶץ, בַּשָּׁמַיִם אֵל מִי

〈 like unto 〈 can do 〈 that 〈 or in the 〈 is there in 〈 power 〈 what
Your deeds earth the heaven

לְךָ כִּי הַגּוֹיִם, מֶלֶךְ יִרָאֲךָ לֹא מִי 5.וְכִגְבוּרֹתֶיךָ.

〈 to 〈 For 》 of nations? 〈 O King 》 fear You, 〈 would 〈 Who 》 and like unto Your
You not mighty acts?

מֵאֵין מַלְכוּתָם וּבְכָל הַגּוֹיִם חַכְמֵי בְּכָל כִּי יָאָתָה,

〈 there is 〈 their 〈 and in all 〈 of the 〈 the wise 〈 among 〈 for 》 [kingship]
none kingdoms nations men all befits;

שְׁמֶךָ וְגָדוֹל אַתָּה גָּדוֹל יהוה, כָּמוֹךָ מֵאֵין 6.כָּמוֹךָ.

〈 is Your 〈 and great 〈 are You 〈 Great 》 O 〈 like You, 〈 There is 》 like You.
Name HASHEM! none

תָּרוּם יָדְךָ תָּעֹז גְּבוּרָה, עִם זְרוֹעַ לְךָ 7.בִּגְבוּרָה.

〈 uplifted 》 is Your 〈 strength- 》 power; 〈 with 〈 is the 〈 Yours 》 in might.
hand, ened arm

מָאוֹר הַכִינוֹתָ אַתָּה לַיְלָה, לְךָ אַף יוֹם, לְךָ 8.יְמִינֶךָ.

〈 the 〈 prepared 〈 You 》 is the 〈 Yours 〈 also 》 is the 〈 Yours 》 is Your
luminary night; day, right hand.

הָרִים וְתוֹעֲפוֹת אָרֶץ, מֶחְקְרֵי בְיָדוֹ אֲשֶׁר 9.וָשָׁמֶשׁ.

〈 of the 〈 and the 》 of the 〈 are the hidden 〈 in His 〈 For 》 and the
mountains summits earth, mysteries power sun.

לוֹ. 10. מִי יְמַלֵּל גְּבוּרוֹת יהוה, יַשְׁמִיעַ כָּל תְּהִלָּתוֹ. 11.

》 of His 〈 all 〈 [who] can 》 of 〈 the mighty 〈 can 〈 Who 》 are
praise? make heard HASHEM; acts express His.

---

(1) *Psalms* 108:5. (2) 145:3. (3) 96:4. (4) 95:3. (5) *Deuteronomy* 3:24.
(6) *Jeremiah* 10:7. (7) 10:6. (8) *Psalms* 89:14. (9) 74:16. (10) 95:4. (11) 106:2.

לְךָ יהוה הַגְּדֻלָּה וְהַגְּבוּרָה, וְהַתִּפְאֶרֶת, וְהַנֵּצַח

〈 the triumph, 〈 the glory, 〈 the strength, 〈 is the greatness, 〈 HASHEM, 〈 Yours,

וְהַהוֹד, כִּי כֹל בַּשָּׁמַיִם וּבָאָרֶץ; לְךָ יהוה הַמַּמְלָכָה,

〈 is the kingdom 〈 HASHEM, 〈 Yours, 《 and on earth [is Yours]; 〈 in heaven 〈 everything 〈 for 《 and the majesty;

וְהַמִּתְנַשֵּׂא לְכֹל לְרֹאשׁ.¹ לְךָ שָׁמַיִם, אַף לְךָ אָרֶץ,

《 is the earth; 〈 Yours 〈 also 《 are the heavens, 〈 Yours 《 leader. 〈 over every 〈 and the sovereignty

תֵּבֵל וּמְלֹאָהּ אַתָּה יְסַדְתָּם.² אַתָּה הִצַּבְתָּ כָּל גְּבוּלוֹת

〈 the boundaries 〈 all 〈 established 〈 You 《 founded them. 〈 You 〈 and its fullness, 〈 the world

אָרֶץ, קַיִץ וָחֹרֶף אַתָּה יְצַרְתָּם.³ אַתָּה רִצַּצְתָּ רָאשֵׁי

〈 the heads 〈 crushed 〈 You 《 fashioned them. 〈 You 〈 and winter, 〈 summer 《 of earth;

לִוְיָתָן, תִּתְּנֶנּוּ מַאֲכָל לְעָם לְצִיִּים. אַתָּה בָקַעְתָּ מַעְיָן

〈 fountain 〈 split open 〈 You 《 [destined] for 〈 to the desolate people 〈 as food 〈 You will serve it 《 of Leviathan;

וָנָחַל, אַתָּה הוֹבַשְׁתָּ נַהֲרוֹת אֵיתָן.⁴ אַתָּה פוֹרַרְתָּ

〈 shattered 〈 You 《 that are mighty. 〈 rivers 〈 dried 〈 You 《 and stream;

בְעָזְּךָ יָם, שִׁבַּרְתָּ רָאשֵׁי תַנִּינִים עַל הַמָּיִם.⁵ אַתָּה

〈 You 《 the water. 〈 upon 〈 of sea serpents 〈 the heads 〈 You 《 the sea; 〈 with Your might

מוֹשֵׁל בְּגֵאוּת הַיָּם, בְּשׂוֹא גַלָּיו אַתָּה תְשַׁבְּחֵם.⁶

《 calm them. 〈 You 〈 its waves, 〈 when it raises 《 of the sea; 〈 the grandeur 〈 rule

גָּדוֹל יהוה וּמְהֻלָּל מְאֹד, בְּעִיר אֱלֹהֵינוּ הַר קָדְשׁוֹ.⁷

《 of His Holiness. 〈 Mount 〈 of our God, 〈 in the City 〈 and much praised, 〈 is HASHEM 〈 Great

יהוה צְבָאוֹת, אֱלֹהֵי יִשְׂרָאֵל, יוֹשֵׁב הַכְּרֻבִים, אַתָּה

〈 it is You 《 upon the Cherubim, 〈 enthroned 〈 of Israel, 〈 God 〈 Master of Legions, 〈 HASHEM,

הוּא הָאֱלֹהִים לְבַדֶּךָ.⁸ אֵל נַעֲרָץ בְּסוֹד קְדוֹשִׁים רַבָּה,

《 in the great assemblage of the holy [angels], 〈 is revered 〈 God 《 alone. 〈 God 〈 Who are

---

(1) I Chronicles 29:11. (2) Psalms 89:12. (3) 74:17. (4) 74:14-15. (5) 74:13. (6) 89:10. (7) 48:2. (8) Isaiah 37:16.

וְנוֹרָא עַל כָּל סְבִיבָיו.¹ וְיוֹדוּ שָׁמַיִם פִּלְאֲךָ יהוה, אַף

‹ also » HASHEM, ‹ Your wonders, ‹ will the heavens ‹ Acknowledge ‹ who surround Him. ‹ all ‹ over ‹ and is awesome

אֱמוּנָתְךָ בִּקְהַל קְדֹשִׁים.² לְכוּ נְרַנְּנָה לַיהוה, נָרִיעָה

‹ let us call out » to HASHEM, ‹ Let us sing joyfully ‹ Come! » of holy ones. ‹ in the assembly ‹ Your faithfulness,

לְצוּר יִשְׁעֵנוּ. נְקַדְּמָה פָנָיו בְּתוֹדָה, בִּזְמִרוֹת נָרִיעַ

‹ let us call out ‹ with praiseful songs » with thanksgiving, ‹ Him ‹ Let us greet » of our salvation. ‹ to the Rock

לוֹ.³ צֶדֶק וּמִשְׁפָּט מְכוֹן כִּסְאֶךָ, חֶסֶד וֶאֱמֶת יְקַדְּמוּ

‹ precede ‹ and truth ‹ kindness » of Your throne; ‹ are the foundation ‹ and justice ‹ Righteousness » to Him.

פָנֶיךָ.⁴ אֲשֶׁר יַחְדָּו נַמְתִּיק סוֹד, בְּבֵית אֱלֹהִים נְהַלֵּךְ

‹ let us walk ‹ of God ‹ in the House » counsel; ‹ let us take sweet ‹ together ‹ For » Your countenance.

בְּרָגֶשׁ.⁵ אֲשֶׁר לוֹ הַיָּם וְהוּא עָשָׂהוּ, וְיַבֶּשֶׁת יָדָיו

‹ His hands » and the dry land, » perfected it, ‹ and He ‹ is the sea ‹ His ‹ For » in company.

יָצָרוּ.⁶ אֲשֶׁר בְּיָדוֹ נֶפֶשׁ כָּל חָי, וְרוּחַ כָּל בְּשַׂר אִישׁ.⁷

» mankind. ‹ of all ‹ and the spirit » the living ‹ of ‹ all ‹ is the soul ‹ in His hand ‹ For » fashioned.

❖ הַנְּשָׁמָה לָךְ וְהַגּוּף פָּעֳלָךְ, חוּסָה עַל עֲמָלָךְ.

» Your labor. ‹ on ‹ take pity » is Your handiwork; ‹ and the body ‹ is Yours ‹ The soul

הַנְּשָׁמָה לָךְ וְהַגּוּף שֶׁלָּךְ, יהוה עֲשֵׂה לְמַעַן שְׁמֶךָ.

» of Your Name. ‹ for the sake ‹ act ‹ O » HASHEM, » is Yours; ‹ and the body ‹ is Yours ‹ The soul

אָתָאנוּ עַל שִׁמְךָ, יהוה, עֲשֵׂה לְמַעַן שְׁמֶךָ. בַּעֲבוּר

‹ [act] because of » of Your Name; ‹ for the sake ‹ act » O HASHEM; » Your Name, ‹ [relying] on ‹ We have come

כְּבוֹד שְׁמֶךָ, כִּי אֵל חַנּוּן וְרַחוּם שְׁמֶךָ. לְמַעַן

‹ For the sake » is Your Name. ‹ and Merciful ‹ Who is Gracious ‹ God ‹ for » of Your Name, ‹ the glory

שִׁמְךָ יהוה, וְסָלַחְתָּ לַעֲוֺנֵנוּ כִּי רַב הוּא.⁸

‹ it is great. ‹ though ‹ our iniquity, ‹ forgive » HASHEM, ‹ of Your Name,

---

(1) *Psalms* 89:8. (2) 89:6. (3) 95:1-2. (4) 89:15. (5) 55:15. (6) 95:5. (7) *Job* 12:10. (8) Cf. *Psalms* 25:11.

CONGREGATION, THEN *CHAZZAN:*

סְלַח לָנוּ אָבִינוּ, כִּי בְרוֹב אִוַּלְתֵּנוּ שָׁגִינוּ,

《 we have 〈 of our folly 〈 in the 〈 for 〈 our Father, 〈 us, 〈 Forgive
erred; abundance

מְחַל לָנוּ מַלְכֵּנוּ, כִּי רַבּוּ עֲוֹנֵינוּ.

《 our 〈 many 〈 for 〈 our King, 〈 us, 〈 pardon
iniquities. are

סליחה ס / SELICHAH 60

(פְּתִיחָה)

ALL:

(אֱלֹהֵינוּ וֵאלֹהֵי אֲבוֹתֵינוּ:)

《of our forefathers:) 〈 and the God 〈 (Our God

שְׁחַרְנוּךְ בְּקַשְׁנוּךְ* יוֹצֵר הָרִים,

《 of the 〈 Maker 《 we have 〈 We have
mountains, beseeched You,* sought You,

מַגִּיד לְאָדָם שִׂיחַ*[1] וּדְבָרִים,

《 and words; 〈 what were 〈 to a man 〈 Who
[his] deeds* recounts

וְחִלִּינוּךְ וּדְרַשְׁנוּךְ בּוֹשִׁים וַחֲפוּרִים,

《 and disgraced, 〈 shamed 〈 we seek You, 〈 we beseech You

אֶת חַטֹּאתֵינוּ הַיּוֹם[2] אָנוּ מְסַפְּרִים.

《 relate. 〈 we 〈 that today 〈 our sins 〈 for

לְהָקְנוּ וְעָדְנוּ זְקֵנִים וּנְעָרִים,

〈 and young 〈 old 〈 gathered 〈 We have
together assembled,

בְּבֵית הַתְּפִלָּה מִקְדַּשׁ מִזְעָרִים,[3]

《 in Miniature, 〈 the Temple 〈 of prayer, 〈 in the house

---

(1) Cf. *Amos* 4:13. (2) Cf. *Genesis* 41:9. (3) See *Ezekiel* 11:16 with *Targum*.

שְׁחַרְנוּךְ בְּקַשְׁנוּךְ § — *We have sought You, we have beseeched You.* The composer of this *selichah* signed his name — שְׁמוּאֵל בְּרַבִּי אַבְרָהָם חֲזַק, *Shmuel bar R' Avraham, may he be strong* — in the initial letters of the respective stiches. He is identified as R' Shmuel bar R' Avraham HaLevi Bonfant, a disciple of R' Simchah of Speyer of late-12th–early-13th-century Germany.

מַגִּיד לְאָדָם שִׂיחַ — *Who recounts to a man what were [his] deeds ....* When a person is brought before the Heavenly Tribunal for his final judgment, his entire life is displayed before him, even his casual conversations with his wife. Can one hope to save himself from retribution when his every word has been recorded and the testimony against him is irrefutable? (*Chagigah* 5b, based on *Amos* 4:13).

רְפוּיֵי יָדַיִם מְעוּדֵי אֵבָרִים,

《 limbs, 〈 faltering 〈 hands, 〈 with weakened

בְּהוּלִים וּסְעוּרִים מִכָּל עֲבָרִים.

《 sides. 〈 about [events on] all 〈 and frantic 〈 panicked

יָגוֹרְנוּ וְדָאַגְנוּ מִשְּׁנֵי גוֹלְיָרִים,

《 minor angelic functionaries, 〈 about Your two 〈 and we worry 〈 We fear

אַף וְחֵמָה*¹ שְׁנֵיהֶם קַטֵגוֹרִים,

《 accusers. 〈 who are both 〈 and Cheimah* 〈 Af

בְּפַשְׁפֵּשֵׁנוּ מַעֲשִׂים וְהִנָּם מְכֹעָרִים,

《 reprehensible. 〈 we see 《 [our] they are 〈 deeds, 〈 As we probe

רֶתֶת אֲחָזַתְנוּ חֲבָלִים וְצִירִים.²

《 and pangs. 〈 [with] pains 《 we are seized, 〈 With trembling

הֻשְׁחֲרוּ פָנֵינוּ וְהָלַכְנוּ קוֹדְרִים,

《 in gloom, 〈 we walk 《 are our faces, 〈 Darkened

מוֹט הִתְמוֹטַטְנוּ וְנַעֲשֵׂינוּ פֵרוּרִים,³

《 crumbs. 〈 and broken into 《 are we trembling 〈 Trembling

✧ חַלְחָלוּ מָתְנֵינוּ וְכַיּוֹלֵדָה מְצִירִים,⁴

《 in labor pains, 〈 like a woman 〈 does our waist 〈 Shudder

זָחַלְנוּ וַנִּירָא מֵעֲוֹנוֹתֵינוּ הַיְתֵרִים,

《 that are excessive. 〈 because of our sins 〈 and we fear 〈 we are scared

קַחְנוּ דְבָרִים בְּשִׁלּוּם פָּרִים,⁵

《 for bull-offerings, 〈 in substitution 〈 words 〈 We bring

תְמוּכִים בְּטוּחִים וּלְרַחֲמֶיךָ מְסַבְּרִים.

《 looking with hope. 〈 and for Your mercy 〈 confident, 〈 trusting,

---

(1) Cf. *Deuteronomy* 9:19. (2) Cf. *Isaiah* 13:8. (3) Cf. 24:19. (4) Cf. 21:3. (5) Cf. *Hosea* 14:3.

---

§• גוֹלְיָרִים אַף וְחֵמָה — *Minor angelic functionaries, Af and Cheimah.* Moses' relationship with the celestial beings changed after the sin of the Golden Calf. At first even the archangels Michael and Gabriel were unable to look Moses in the face. But after Israel sinned, Moses was unable to look directly at even the minor angels אַף וְחֵמָה, *Af and Cheimah* [lit., *Anger and Fury*] (*Pesikta Rabbasi* 15:3).

ALL:

כִּי עַל רַחֲמֶיךָ הָרַבִּים¹ אָנוּ בְטוּחִים, וְעַל צִדְקוֹתֶיךָ

‹ For ‹ upon ‹ Your mercy ‹ that is abundant ‹ we ‹ trust, ‹ and upon ‹ Your righteousness

אָנוּ נִשְׁעָנִים, וְלִסְלִיחוֹתֶיךָ אָנוּ מְקַוִּים, וְלִישׁוּעָתְךָ

‹ we ‹ rely, ‹ and for Your forgiveness ‹ we ‹ hope, ‹ and for Your salvation

אָנוּ מְצַפִּים. אַתָּה הוּא מֶלֶךְ, אוֹהֵב צְדָקוֹת מִקֶּדֶם,

‹ we ‹ await eagerly. ‹ You ‹ are ‹ the King ‹ Who loves ‹ righteous-ness ‹ since the beginning of time,

מַעֲבִיר עֲוֹנוֹת עַמּוֹ, וּמֵסִיר חַטְּאת יְרֵאָיו. כּוֹרֵת

‹ Who ‹ overlooks ‹ the iniquities ‹ of His people ‹ and ‹ removes ‹ the sins ‹ of those who revere Him. ‹ He established

בְּרִית לָרִאשׁוֹנִים, וּמְקַיֵּם שְׁבוּעָה לָאַחֲרוֹנִים. אַתָּה

‹ a covenant ‹ with the ancestors ‹ and fulfills ‹ [His] oath ‹ to the descendants. ‹ You

הוּא, שֶׁיָּרַדְתָּ בַּעֲנַן כְּבוֹדֶךָ עַל הַר סִינַי,² וְהֶרְאֵיתָ

‹ are the One ‹ Who ‹ descended ‹ in the cloud ‹ of Your glory ‹ upon ‹ Mount ‹ Sinai, ‹ and You showed

דַּרְכֵי טוּבְךָ לְמֹשֶׁה עַבְדֶּךָ.³ וְאָרְחוֹת חֲסָדֶיךָ גִּלִּיתָ

‹ the ways ‹ of Your goodness ‹ to Moses ‹ Your servant. ‹ The paths ‹ of Your kindness ‹ You revealed

לוֹ, וְהוֹדַעְתּוֹ כִּי אַתָּה אֵל רַחוּם וְחַנּוּן, אֶרֶךְ אַפַּיִם

‹ to him, ‹ and You let him know ‹ that ‹ You are ‹ God, ‹ Compas-sionate ‹ and Gracious, ‹ Slow ‹ to anger

וְרַב חֶסֶד⁴ וּמַרְבֶּה לְהֵטִיב, וּמַנְהִיג אֶת כָּל הָעוֹלָם

‹ and ‹ Abundant ‹ in Kind-ness, ‹ Who is ‹ beneficent, ‹ and Who guides ‹ the whole ‹ world

כֻּלּוֹ בְּמִדַּת הָרַחֲמִים. וְכֵן כָּתוּב, וַיֹּאמֶר אֲנִי אַעֲבִיר

‹ in its entirety ‹ with the Attribute ‹ of Mercy. ‹ And so ‹ it is written: ‹ And He said, ‹ "I ‹ shall cause to pass

כָּל טוּבִי עַל פָּנֶיךָ, וְקָרָאתִי בְשֵׁם יהוה לְפָנֶיךָ,

‹ all ‹ My goodness ‹ before ‹ your face, ‹ and I shall call out ‹ with the Name ‹ HASHEM ‹ before you;

וְחַנֹּתִי אֶת אֲשֶׁר אָחֹן, וְרִחַמְתִּי אֶת אֲשֶׁר אֲרַחֵם.⁵

‹ I shall show favor ‹ to ‹ whom-ever ‹ I choose to show favor, ‹ and I shall show mercy ‹ to ‹ whom-ever ‹ I choose to show mercy."

(1) *Daniel* 9:18. (2) Cf. *Exodus* 34:5. (3) Cf. 33:13. (4) 34:6. (5) 33:19.

ALL, WHILE STANDING

אֵל אֶרֶךְ אַפַּיִם אַתָּה,
《 You are, ⟨ to anger, ⟨ Who ⟨ God
is slow

וּבַעַל הָרַחֲמִים נִקְרֵאתָ, וְדֶרֶךְ תְּשׁוּבָה הוֹרֵיתָ.
《 You have ⟨ of ⟨ and the 《 You are ⟨ of Mercy ⟨ and
taught. repentance way called; Master

גְּדֻלַּת רַחֲמֶיךָ וַחֲסָדֶיךָ,
⟨ and Your ⟨ of Your ⟨ The
kindness mercy greatness

תִּזְכּוֹר הַיּוֹם וּבְכָל יוֹם לְזֶרַע יְדִידֶיךָ.
《 of Your ⟨ for the 《 day, ⟨ and ⟨ this day ⟨ may You
beloved ones. offspring every remember,

תֵּפֶן אֵלֵינוּ בְּרַחֲמִים,
《 in mercy, ⟨ to us ⟨ Turn

כִּי אַתָּה הוּא בַּעַל הָרַחֲמִים.
《 of Mercy. ⟨ the Master ⟨ are ⟨ You ⟨ for

בְּתַחֲנוּן וּבִתְפִלָּה פָּנֶיךָ נְקַדֵּם, כְּהוֹדַעְתָּ לֶעָנָיו מִקֶּדֶם.
《in ancient ⟨ to the ⟨ in the manner 《 we ⟨ Your ⟨ and prayer ⟨ With
times. humble one that You made approach, Presence supplication
[Moses] known

מֵחֲרוֹן אַפְּךָ שׁוּב,[1] כְּמוֹ בְתוֹרָתְךָ כָּתוּב.[2]
《 it is ⟨ in Your Torah ⟨ as 《 turn ⟨ of Your ⟨ From the
written. back, anger fierceness

וּבְצֵל כְּנָפֶיךָ נֶחֱסֶה[3] וְנִתְלוֹנָן, כְּיוֹם וַיֵּרֶד יהוה בֶּעָנָן.
《 in a ⟨ when HASHEM ⟨ as on 《 and may ⟨ may we find ⟨ of Your ⟨ In the
cloud. descended the day we dwell, shelter wings shadow

❖ תַּעֲבוֹר עַל פֶּשַׁע וְתִמְחֶה אָשָׁם,
《 guilt, ⟨ and erase ⟨ sin ⟨ Overlook

כְּיוֹם וַיִּתְיַצֵּב עִמּוֹ שָׁם.
《 there. ⟨ with him ⟨ when He ⟨ as on the
[Moses] [God] stood day

תַּאֲזִין שַׁוְעָתֵנוּ וְתַקְשִׁיב מֶנּוּ מַאֲמָר,
《 [our] ⟨ from ⟨ and hear ⟨ to our cry ⟨ Give heed
declaration, us

---

(1) Cf. *Exodus* 32:12. (2) See 32:14. (3) Cf. *Psalms* 36:8.

כְּיוֹם וַיִּקְרָא בְשֵׁם יהוה,¹ וְשָׁם נֶאֱמַר:

《 it was said: 〈 and 《 of HASHEM, 〈 with the 〈 when He 〈 as on
                    there   Name   called out   the day

CONGREGATION, THEN *CHAZZAN:*

וַיַּעֲבֹר יהוה עַל פָּנָיו וַיִּקְרָא:

《   and   《 [Moses'] 〈 before 〈 And HASHEM passed
proclaimed: face,

CONGREGATION AND *CHAZZAN* **RECITE LOUDLY AND IN UNISON:**

יהוה, יהוה, אֵל, רַחוּם, וְחַנּוּן, אֶרֶךְ אַפַּיִם,

〈 to anger, 〈 Slow 《 and 〈 Compassionate 〈 God, 〈 HASHEM, 〈 HASHEM,
                          Gracious,

וְרַב חֶסֶד, וֶאֱמֶת, נֹצֵר חֶסֶד לָאֲלָפִים, נֹשֵׂא עָוֹן,

〈 of 〈 Forgiver 《 for thousands 〈 of 〈 Preserver 《 and 〈 in 〈 and
iniquity,   [of generations], kindness   Truth, Kindness Abundant

וָפֶשַׁע, וְחַטָּאָה, וְנַקֵּה.• ²וְסָלַחְתָּ לַעֲוֹנֵנוּ וּלְחַטָּאתֵנוּ

《   and our sins, 〈 our 〈 May You 《 and Who 〈 and inadvertent 〈 willful sin,
                 iniquities forgive absolves.   sin,

וּנְחַלְתָּנוּ.³ סְלַח לָנוּ אָבִינוּ כִּי חָטָאנוּ, מְחַל לָנוּ

〈 us, 〈 pardon 《 we have 〈 for 《 our Father, 〈 us, 〈 Forgive 《 and make us
                 sinned;   Your heritage.

מַלְכֵּנוּ כִּי פָשָׁעְנוּ. כִּי אַתָּה אֲדֹנָי טוֹב וְסַלָּח, וְרַב

〈 and 《 and 〈 are 〈 O Lord, 〈 You, 〈 For 《 we have 〈 for 《 our King,
abundantly forgiving, good   willfully sinned.

חֶסֶד לְכָל קֹרְאֶיךָ.⁴

《   who call 〈 to all 〈 kind
upon You.

כְּרַחֵם אָב עַל בָּנִים, כֵּן תְּרַחֵם יהוה עָלֵינוּ.⁵

《 on us. 〈 HASHEM, 〈 have 〈 so 《 his 〈 toward 〈 a 〈 As merciful as
                 mercy,   children, father is

לַיהוה הַיְשׁוּעָה, עַל עַמְּךָ בִרְכָתֶךָ סֶּלָה.⁶ יהוה

〈 HASHEM, 《 Selah. 《 is Your 〈 Your 〈 upon 《 is salvation, 〈 To HASHEM
                    blessing, people

צְבָאוֹת עִמָּנוּ, מִשְׂגָּב לָנוּ אֱלֹהֵי יַעֲקֹב סֶלָה.⁷

《 Selah. 《 of Jacob, 〈 is the God 〈 for us 〈 a 《 is with us, 〈 Master of
                                   stronghold   Legions,

---

(1) *Exodus* 34:5. (2) 34:6-7 (3) 34:9. (4) *Psalms* 86:5. (5) Cf. 103:13. (6) 3:9. (7) 46:8.

יהוה צְבָאוֹת, אַשְׁרֵי אָדָם בֹּטֵחַ בָּךְ.¹ יהוה הוֹשִׁיעָה,
save! ⟪   HASHEM, ⟪ in   who   is the   — praise- ⟪ Master of   HASHEM,
       You.   trusts   man   worthy   Legions

הַמֶּלֶךְ יַעֲנֵנוּ בְיוֹם קָרְאֵנוּ.²
⟪ we call.   on the   answer us   May the
       day   King

IN MOST CONGREGATIONS THE FOLLOWING VERSES ARE RECITED ALOUD RESPONSIVELY, AS INDICATED; IN OTHERS THEY ARE RECITED SILENTLY.

CONGREGATION, ALOUD, FOLLOWED BY *CHAZZAN,* **ALOUD:**

סְלַח נָא לַעֲוֹן הָעָם הַזֶּה כְּגֹדֶל חַסְדֶּךָ, וְכַאֲשֶׁר
just as   ⟪ of Your   according to   of this people   the   please,   Forgive,
      kindness,   the greatness   iniquity

נָשָׂאתָה לָעָם הַזֶּה מִמִּצְרַיִם וְעַד הֵנָּה,³ וְשָׁם נֶאֱמַר:
⟪ it was   And   ⟪ now.   until   from Egypt   this people   You have
said: there   forgiven

ALL, ALOUD AND IN UNISON:

וַיֹּאמֶר יהוה סָלַחְתִּי כִּדְבָרֶךָ.⁴
⟪ *according to*   *⟨ I have forgiven* ⟪   *And* HASHEM *said:*
your word!

ALL CONTINUE:

הַטֵּה אֱלֹהַי אָזְנְךָ וּשְׁמָע, פְּקַח עֵינֶיךָ וּרְאֵה
and see   Your eyes   open   ⟪ and listen;   Your ear,   my God,   Incline,

שֹׁמְמֹתֵינוּ, וְהָעִיר אֲשֶׁר נִקְרָא שִׁמְךָ עָלֶיהָ, כִּי לֹא
not   for ⟪ upon;   Your Name is   which   and that   our desolation
      proclaimed   [of] the city

עַל צִדְקֹתֵינוּ אֲנַחְנוּ מַפִּילִים תַּחֲנוּנֵינוּ לְפָנֶיךָ,
⟪ before   our   cast   do we   of our   because
You;   supplications   righteousness

כִּי עַל רַחֲמֶיךָ הָרַבִּים. אֲדֹנָי שְׁמָעָה, אֲדֹנָי סְלָחָה,
⟪ forgive;   O Lord, ⟪ heed;   O Lord, ⟪ which is   of Your   be-   but
      abundant.   compassion,   cause

אֲדֹנָי הַקְשִׁיבָה, וַעֲשֵׂה אַל תְּאַחַר, לְמַעַנְךָ אֱלֹהַי,
⟪ my God,   for Your sake, ⟪ delay;   do not ⟪ and act,   be attentive,   O Lord,

כִּי שִׁמְךָ נִקְרָא עַל עִירְךָ וְעַל עַמֶּךָ.⁵
⟪ Your   and   Your   upon   is   Your   for
people.   upon   City   proclaimed   Name

(1) *Psalms* 84:13. (2) 20:10. (3) *Numbers* 14:19. (4) 14:20. (5) *Daniel* 9:18-19.

סליחה סא / SELICHAH 61

ALL:

(אֱלֹהֵינוּ וֵאלֹהֵי אֲבוֹתֵינוּ:)

《 of our forefathers:) 〈 and the God 〈   (Our God

אַךְ בְּךָ מִקְוֵה יִשְׂרָאֵל יהוה,*¹

《 HASHEM,* 《   of Israel, 〈 is the hope 〈 in You 〈 Only

אָחוֹר וָקֶדֶם עַם נוֹשַׁע בַּיהוה,²

《 by HASHEM. 〈 is saved 〈 the 《 until the 〈 from the
                         people future beginning,
                         [Israel]   end,

וּמַדּוּעַ בּוֹשֵׁשׁ יוֹם זֶה כַּמָּה עִדָּנַי,

《 periods 〈 for so 《 — this day 《   does it 〈 Why, then,
of time?   many [of Redemption] —   delay

לִישׁוּעָתְךָ קִוִּיתִי יהוה.³

《O HASHEM. 《do I **long**, 〈 For Your salvation

גַּרְתִּי וָאֵחַר⁴ מֶשֶׁךְ יְמֵי עֲגוּנַי,

《 of aban- 〈 of my 〈 for the 〈   and 〈 I so-
donment, period length   lingered journed

גֵּיא גוֹי נָבָל וְעַם גְּנַאי,

《 that is 〈 the 《 that is 〈 of the 〈 in the
vile.   people sordid, nation valley

וּמַדּוּעַ דַּל כָּבָה⁵ כָּבוֹד וְלִי דִינַי,

《 judged 〈 [Why] 《 is [my] 〈 to such 〈 impov- 〈 Why,
[so harshly]? am I esteem? an extent erished then,

קַוֵּה אֶל יהוה, חֲזַק וְיַאֲמֵץ לִבֶּךָ, וְקַוֵּה אֶל יהוה.⁶

《 HASHEM. 〈 and place your 《 in your 〈 and He 〈 strengthen 《HASHEM; 〈 Place your
hope in heart, will instill yourself **hope** in
courage

---

(1) *Jeremiah* 17:13. (2) *Deuteronomy* 33:29; cf. *Isaiah* 45:17.
(3) *Genesis* 49:18. (4) 32:5. (5) Cf. *II Samuel* 13:4. (6) *Psalms* 27:14.

◈§ אַךְ בְּךָ מִקְוֵה יִשְׂרָאֵל ה' — *Only in You is
the hope of Israel,* HASHEM. The acrostic
forms the *aleph-beis* with odd-numbered
letters (א,ג,ה ...) appearing twice, and even-
numbered letters (ב,ד,ו ...) appearing
once and that after the word וּמַדּוּעַ, *Why,
then?* The fourth line of each alphabetical

stanza is a Scriptural fragment that contains some form of the root קוה, *hope.*
The *paytan* signed his name — שְׁלֹמֹה
הַקָּטָן יִגְדַּל בִּתְשׁוּבָה, *Shlomo the lesser, may
he grow in repentance* [see prefatory
comment to *Selichah 2*], in the last three
stanzas.

הֲלֹא אַתָּה מִקֶּדֶם חֶרֶב גַּאֲוָתֵנוּ,

《 of our Grandeur? 〈 were the Sword 〈 from long ago 〈 that You 〈 Is it not so

הִקְוִינְוּךָ[1] אַף אֹרַח מִשְׁפָּטֶיךָ תַּאֲוָתֵנוּ,

《 is our desire. 〈 of judgment 〈 Your way 〈 indeed 《We have placed our hope in You;

וּמַדּוּעַ וְאֵין אִישׁ מְכַפֵּר[2] עַל חוֹבוֹתֵינוּ,

《 our sins? 〈 for 〈 to atone 〈 man 〈 is there no 〈 Why, then,

וּמִדַּאֲבוֹנֵינוּ אוֹמְרִים

《 we say, 〈 And due to our anguish

יָבְשׁוּ עַצְמוֹתֵינוּ אָבְדָה תִקְוָתֵנוּ.[3]

《 is our hope! 〈 Lost 《 are our bones! 〈 Dried out

זָכַרְנוּ חֶשְׁבּוֹנוֹת מִקֶּדֶם וּמִדָּתָם קָצְרָה,

《 was short; 〈 and their duration 〈 from long ago 〈 reckonings [of exiles] 〈 We re-member

זֶה פַעֲמַיִם קָצִיר* וְעוֹד עָצְרָה,[4]

《 reigns strong. 〈 yet still 〈 harvest,* 〈 has been a double 〈 this [exile]

וּמַדּוּעַ חֶשַּׁבְנוּ כִּבְהֵמָה וְנִטְמִינוּ[5] מִשְׁפַּט הַשּׁוּרָה,

《 from the principle of the line [of fair justice], 《 and we are blocked off 〈 like animals [for slaughter], 〈 are we considered 〈 Why, then,

מִקְוֵה יִשְׂרָאֵל יהוה מוֹשִׁיעוֹ בְּעֵת צָרָה.[6]

《 of trouble. 〈 in time 〈 their Redeemer 《 is 〈 HASHEM, 〈 of Israel 〈 Yet the **Hope**

---

(1) Cf. *Isaiah* 26:8. (2) Cf. 50:2, *Proverbs* 16:14. (3) Cf. *Ezekiel* 37:11. (4) Many editions read זֶה פַעֲמַיִם קָצְרָה וְעוֹד פָּצְרָה, *But this one has been twice the short term, yet still presses hard.* (5) Cf. *Job* 18:3; many editions read וְחֻשַּׁבְנוּ instead of חֻשַּׁבְנוּ, a reading that does not change the meaning and is a more direct quote from the Scriptural source; however, the expected initial letter after the word וּמַדּוּעַ is ח, not נ. (6) Cf. *Jeremiah* 14:8.

זֶה פַעֲמַיִם קָצִיר — *This [exile] has been a double harvest.* The present exile is more difficult than the previous ones because of both its severity and its duration. The *paytan* speaks of its intensity as *a double harvest*: so many more have been slaughtered during our present exile than during earlier exiles.

Additionally, according to *Arugas HaBosem*, the *paytan* had another meaning in mind with the expression פַעֲמַיִם קָצִיר. The word קָצִיר has a *gematria* (numerical value) of 400 [ק=100, צ=90, י=10, ר=200]; double

קָצִיר is then 800. Thus, the stich means, *this exile is already eight hundred years long, yet still reigns strong.* Based on this interpretation, some commentaries claim that this *selichah* must have been written soon after the year 870, eight hundred years after the Destruction of the Second Temple. Nevertheless, most feel that the composer, R' Shlomo HaBavli, lived about a century later. [Perhaps the mathematical calculation should include the word וְעוֹד, *and still,* which can also mean *and more.* How much more? The

טוֹעֲנִים וּפוֹרְקִים בָּנִים הַכָּתוּב סִבְלָם,*

« accepts ‹ the Torah ‹ as [God's] « or cast off [their ‹ [Whether]
them;* children load of mitzvos], they bear

טְרוּדֵי חֶבְלָם וְחָרֵב בֵּית זְבוּלָם,

« is their Temple. ‹ and ‹ from their ‹ [yet] they
destroyed heritage, are evicted

וּמַדּוּעַ יַסְתִּיר הָאָב¹ שְׁבִילָם הָאָמוּר בִּגְלָלָם,

« for their sake, ‹ of which ‹ their path, « — the « should He ‹ Why, then,
it is said Father — conceal

וְיֵשׁ תִּקְוָה לְאַחֲרִיתֵךְ נְאֻם יהוה, וְשָׁבוּ בָנִים לִגְבוּלָם.²

« to their ‹ shall your ‹ and « of ‹ — the « for your future ‹ **hope** ‹ There
border? children return HASHEM — word is

בִּמְעַט נָטָיוּ רַגְלָי וְשֻׁפְּכוּ אֲשׁוּרִים,

« were my ‹ washed « were ‹ turned ‹ Almost
steps, aside my feet, astray

כִּי קִנֵּאתִי בַּהוֹלְלִים³ מְעַרְבְּבֵי מֵישָׁרִים,

« of the straight. ‹ the perverters «the unruly revelers, ‹ we envied ‹ for

וּמַדּוּעַ לֹא תִקְצַר וְתִשָּׁבֵר רָמַת הַקּוֹשְׁרִים,

« of the plotters; ‹ the ‹ and be ‹ be cut ‹should ‹ Why,
arrogance broken short not then,

וְקֹוֵי* יהוה יַחֲלִיפוּ כֹחַ, יַעֲלוּ אֵבֶר כַּנְּשָׁרִים.⁴

« like the ‹ wings ‹ grow- «strength,‹ will have ‹ in ‹ while those who
eagles? ing renewed HASHEM place their **hope***

מָלֵא רֻדַּפְתִּי וְחָסְרָה שְׁנַת גְּאוּלִי,*

« of my ‹ is the ‹ but ‹ have I been ‹ Fully
redemption,* year incomplete chased,

---

(1) Cf. *I Samuel* 20:2. (2) *Jeremiah* 31:16. (3) Cf. *Psalms* 73:2-3. (4) *Isaiah* 40:31.

gematria of וְעוֹד, which is 86. This would then date the work from about 956, and the stich would mean: *Even though this exile is already 886 years long, it still reigns strong.*]

טוֹעֲנִים וּפוֹרְקִים בָּנִים הַכָּתוּב סִבְלָם — *[Whether] they bear or cast off [their load of mitzvos], as [God's] children the Torah accepts them.* The Jewish people are God's children even when they do not uphold His commands. Various Scriptural verses describe them as foolish (*Jeremiah* 4:22), untrustworthy (*Deuteronomy* 32:20), or destructive (*Isaiah* 1:4), yet call them His children (*Arugas Ha-Bosem*, based on *Kiddushin* 36a).

Others understand the stich as a description of Israel's fate to constantly load (טוֹעֲנִים) and unload (פוֹרְקִים) the burdens of the evil taskmasters in whose lands they have been exiled (*Masbir*).

וְקֹוֵי — *While those who place their hope.* The vowelization follows virtually all editions. However, according to *Radak* (*Isaiah* 40:31), the word is pronounced as if it were spelled וְקוֹיֵי.

מָלֵא רֻדַּפְתִּי וְחָסְרָה שְׁנַת גְּאוּלִי — *Fully have I been chased, but incomplete is the year of my redemption.* The Midrash states that whenever the word רוֹדֵף, *pursuer,* appears in

מְסוּרִים לְמַכִּים וּמוֹרְטִים וּלְתִקְוָה אוּלַי,[2][1]

given over ⟨ to those that ⟩ to those who ⟨ beat [me] ⟩ and to those who pull out [my] hairs, ⟩ and hope [of salvation] ⟩ is uncertain.

וּמַדּוּעַ נִסְחֲפוּ אַבִּירַי[3] וּמְתֵי שִׁיר אֵילַי,*

*Why, then, ⟨ have been swept away ⟩ my warriors, ⟨ along with ⟩ of the people ⟩ the song ⟨ accompanying my ram-offerings?**

קַוֹּה קִוִּיתִי (אֶל) יהוה וַיֵּט אֵלָי.[4]

*I have placed great **hope** ⟨ (in) ⟩ HASHEM, ⟨ and ⟩ He has inclined ⟨ toward me.*

סוּגֶיךָ שָׂרִיגֶיךָ בְּקָקוּם בּוֹקְקִים וְהֵבֵאִישׁוּ,[5]

Your fenced-off ⟨ branching vines [Israel] ⟩ — stripped ⟨ have plunderers, ⟩ her bare ⟨ [its fruit] lies rotting;

סִירִים סוּרֶיךָ גָּבְשׁוּ וְלֹא עָבְשׁוּ,

but the thorns ⟨ who turn away from You ⟩ climb high, ⟨ without ⟩ blight.

וּמַדּוּעַ עָתְקוּ גָּבְרוּ כִּמְדֻבָּר לֹא יֵבוֹשׁוּ,

Why, then, ⟨ do they grow old, ⟩ gain ⟨ strength, ⟩ yet [unlike] ⟨ what was said, ⟩ do not ⟨ come to shame?

מִקְוֵה יִשְׂרָאֵל יהוה כָּל עוֹזְבֶיךָ יֵבוֹשׁוּ.[6]

***Hope** ⟨ of Israel ⟩ is ⟨ HASHEM! ⟩ All ⟨ who forsake You ⟩ will be shamed.*

---

(1) Cf. *Isaiah* 50:6. (2) Cf. *Lamentations* 3:29. (3) Cf. *Jeremiah* 46:15. (4) *Psalms* 40:2. (5) Cf. *Nahum* 2:3; *Hosea* 10:1. (6) *Jeremiah* 17:13.

Scripture, it is spelled deficiently (רֹדֵף, without the letter ו), except once: וַיֵּלְכוּ בְלֹא כֹחַ לִפְנֵי רוֹדֵף, *they walked on without strength before the pursuer* (*Lamentations* 1:6). This indicates that the enemy after the Destruction of Jerusalem set out after the remaining Jews in full pursuit. Similarly, the word גֹּאֵל, *Redeemer*, is always spelled deficiently (גֹּאֵל), except once: וּבָא לְצִיּוֹן גּוֹאֵל, *Come to Zion shall a Redeemer* (*Isaiah* 59:20). This indicates that just as their pursuit was a full pursuit, so will their Redemption be a full Redemption (*Eichah Rabbasi* 1:33).

Rashi (to *Lamentations* 1:6), however, seems to have had a different reading in the Midrash (or based his commentary on another Midrash that is no longer extant). He explains that the word גְּאוּלִי, *my redemption*, is spelled deficiently [without the ו] in the verse: שְׁנַת גְּאוּלַי בָּאָה, *The year of my redemption has come* (*Isaiah* 63:4). This, says *Rashi*, is what the *paytan* means by the stich מָלֵא רְדַפְתִּי, *I have been chased to the full* [as indicated by the full spelling of רוֹדֵף], וְחָסְרָה, *but the year of my redemption is lacking* [as indicated by the missing ו of גְּאוּלִי].

וּמְתֵי שִׁיר אֵילַי — *Along with the people of the song accompanying my ram-offerings.* Each day in the Temple, the Levite choir would sing the Song of the Day during the service of the *tamid* [continual] offering. That offering was a male sheep in its first year. Although such a sheep is usually called a כֶּבֶשׁ, the *paytan* here calls it an אַיִל, a name that specifies a male sheep from thirteen to twenty-four months old, possibly to fit the rhyme scheme. [See prefatory commentary to *Selichah* 41.]

פּוֹעֲלֵי שֶׁקֶר יִתְאַמְּרוּ¹ אוֹיְנוּ רָאִינוּ,

《 we have 〈 What we 《 glorify 〈 of 〈 The
seen! longed for, themselves, falsehood perpetrators

פָּשְׁטוּ אֱמֶת אוֹתוֹתֵינוּ שַׂמְנוּ² הִתְוֵינוּ,

《 and 〈 that we set 〈 are our signs 〈 True 《 They
inscribed! expound,

וּמַדּוּעַ צָלְחָה דַרְכָּם,³ וְחַסְדְּךָ דְמִינוּ⁴ נִדְוֵינוּ,

《 yet we 〈 we hope 〈 while 《 this way 《 is it 〈 Why,
grieve? for Your of theirs successful — then,
kindness [against us],

יהוה חָנֵּנוּ לְךָ קִוִּינוּ.⁵

《 we place 〈 in 《 be gracious 〈 HASHEM,
our **hope**! You toward us;

קִימַת סֻכַּת שָׁלֹשׁ עֶשְׂרֵה פֶּרֶץ,⁶

《 breaches, 〈 [in which were made] 〈 of Your 〈 The recon-
thirteen Temple- struction
succah

קִצָּה רָחַק, וּלְמִקְרָא עָלָה הַפּוֹרֵץ,⁷

《 has the King 〈 Ascended 《 as is [the prom- 〈 is far off, 〈 its time
[Messiah]! ise of] the verse,

וּמַדּוּעַ רְשָׁעִים יִחְיוּ⁸ וְלֹא יִדְּמוּ קָרֶץ, *

《 with 〈 be 〈 and 《 go on 〈 should the 〈 Why,
slaughter?* stilled, not living, wicked then,

וְקֹוֵי יהוה הֵמָּה יִירְשׁוּ אָרֶץ.⁹

《 the 〈 shall 〈 they 〈 in 〈 But those
earth. inherit HASHEM, who place
their **hope**

שׁוֹסֵי נַחֲלַת¹⁰ חֶבֶל מֵחֶלְקְךָ לְגָרְשֵׁנוּ,

《 [seek] 〈 from Your 《 portion, 〈 [Your] 〈 Those who
to evict us, Land heritage trample

שׁוּבִי שׁוּבִי הַשּׁוּלַמִּית¹¹ בְּפִיהֶם לְהַפְרִישֵׁנוּ,

《 to separate us 〈 is in their 《 O Shulamite! 〈 Turn 〈 [the call,]
[from You]. mouths, away, Turn away!

---

(1) Cf. *Psalms* 94:4. (2) Cf. 74:4. (3) Cf. *Jeremiah* 12:1. (4) Cf. *Psalms* 48:10. (5) *Isaiah* 33:2.
(6) Cf. *Amos* 9:11; see commentary to *Selichah* 41, s.v. קְבוּעוֹת הָיוּ לְמוּל הַפְּרָצוֹת בְּהִשְׁתַּחֲוָיוֹת.
(7) Cf. *Micah* 2:13. (8) *Job* 21:7. (9) *Psalms* 37:9. (10) Cf. *Jeremiah* 50:11. (11) *Song of Songs* 7:1.

וְלֹא יִדְּמוּ קָרֶץ — *And not be stilled with slaughter.* The translation follows *Radak* and *Metzudos* (to *Jeremiah* 46:20). *Targum*, however, renders *murderous nations;*

accordingly, the translation would read either *and not be stilled by murderous nations,* or *and the murderous nation not be stilled.*

וּמַדּוּעַ תִּתְנַשְּׂאוּ¹ וְזֶה לָזֶה תִּנָּאֲמוּ נַפְרִישֵׁנוּ,

《 "Let us separate them 《 exhorting: 〈 to 〈 one 〈 should you be 〈 But [we
[from their God]!"?   another   so pompous,   reply:] Why

טוֹב יהוה לְקֹוָיו לְנֶפֶשׁ תִּדְרְשֶׁנוּ.²

《 that seeks 〈 to the 《 to those 〈 [Do you not
Him.   soul   who place their   know that]
     hope in Him,   HASHEM is good

שַׁדַּי תְּשׁוּבַת מַדּוּעֵינוּ פִּינוּ נְמַלֵּא,

《 we will fill: 〈 our 〈 to our 〈 Why, 〈 with the 〈 Almighty,
   mouths   then's   answer

לַיהוה אֱלֹהֵינוּ חָטָאנוּ³ וַתִּקְרֶאנָה אוֹתָנוּ כָּאֵלֶּה,⁴

《 such things. 〈 us 〈 and so befell 〈 we have 〈 our God, 〈 Against
     sinned   HASHEM,

מִשְׁפָּטֶיךָ אֱמֶת וְאַתָּה מָרוֹם מִתְעַלֶּה,

《 and exalted — 〈 lofty 〈 and You 〈 are true 〈 Your judgments
     are

הַצְּדָקָה לְךָ וְלָנוּ הַבֹּשֶׁת⁵ נִגְלָה.

《 is 〈 the embar- 〈 and 〈 is 〈 righteousness
revealed.   rassment   for us   Yours,

הַעֵדֹתָ רַבּוֹת וַנֹּאמֶר לֹא נַקְשִׁיב,⁶

《 We will not 《 yet 〈 many 〈 You cau-
pay attention!   we said,   times,   tioned us

קוֹל טִיף נְבִיאֶיךָ בְּזֵינוּ לְהַקְשִׁיב,

《 [refusing] 《 we 〈 of Your 〈 of the ad- 〈 The
to pay heed.   ridiculed,   prophets   monitions   voice

יִגְדַּל כֹּחַ⁷ סֶלָה יְחִידִים מוֹשִׁיב,⁸

《 [into a family] 〈 [You] Who 《 forever, 〈 may 〈 Magni-
settle;   the solitary   [Your]   fied
     strength be

בִּתְשׁוּבָה שְׁלֵמָה אוֹתָנוּ לְהָשִׁיב.

《 return 〈 us 《 that is whole- 〈 and in
[to You].   hearted,   repentance

❖ מַדּוּעַ אָדָם לִלְבוּשֶׁךָ⁹ תִּקְרַב עוֹנָתוֹ,

《 that time 〈 O bring 〈 are your 〈 stained 〈 [The oppres-
[of vengeance].   near   clothes?   red   sors saying:]
     Why

---

(1) *Numbers* 16:3. (2) *Lamentations* 3:25. (3) *Jeremiah* 3:25. (4) Cf. *Leviticus* 10:19.
(5) Cf. *Daniel* 9:7. (6) Cf. *Jeremiah* 6:17. (7) Cf. *Numbers* 14:17. (8) Cf. *Psalms* 68:7. (9) *Isaiah* 63:2.

וְיֵז נִצְחָם עַל בִּגְדֵי עֲטִיתוֹ,

《 they are 〈 the 〈 over 〈 will their 〈 when
wrapped in! clothes lifeblood splatter

נוֹדֶה סֶלָה יוֹם הַבָּא בְּשַׁעְתוֹ,

《 in its 〈 comes 〈 when 《 forever, 〈 We will
due time: that day praise [You]

זֶה יהוה **קִוְּינוּ** לוֹ, נָגִילָה וְנִשְׂמְחָה בִּישׁוּעָתוֹ.[1]

《 at His 〈 and be glad 〈 we shall 《 for 〈 we have 〈 HASHEM; 〈 This
salvation. rejoice Him; **hoped** is

ALL, WHILE STANDING:

אֵל מֶלֶךְ יוֹשֵׁב עַל כִּסֵּא רַחֲמִים, מִתְנַהֵג

〈 Who acts 《 of mercy, 〈 the throne 〈 on 〈 Who sits 《 King 〈 O God,

בַּחֲסִידוּת, מוֹחֵל עֲוֹנוֹת עַמּוֹ, מַעֲבִיר רִאשׁוֹן

〈 [sins,] one 〈 Who 《 of His 〈 the sins 〈 Who 《 with kindness,
removes people, pardons

רִאשׁוֹן,[2] מַרְבֶּה מְחִילָה לַחֲטָאִים וּסְלִיחָה לַפּוֹשְׁעִים,

《 to willful 〈 and 〈 to unintentional 〈 pardon 〈 Who abun- 《 by one,
sinners, forgiveness sinners dantly grants

עֹשֶׂה צְדָקוֹת עִם כָּל בָּשָׂר וָרוּחַ, לֹא כְרָעָתָם

〈 in accord 〈 — not 《 and 〈 [beings 〈 all 〈 with 〈 acts of 〈 Who
with their spirit of] flesh generosity performs
wickedness

תִּגְמוֹל. ❖ אֵל הוֹרֵיתָ לָנוּ לוֹמַר שְׁלֹשׁ עֶשְׂרֵה, וּזְכוֹר

〈 remem- 《 the Thirteen 〈 to 〈 us 〈 You 〈 O God, 《 do You
ber [Attributes of Mercy]; recite taught repay them!

לָנוּ הַיּוֹם בְּרִית שְׁלֹשׁ עֶשְׂרֵה, כְּמוֹ שֶׁהוֹדַעְתָּ לֶעָנָיו

〈 to the 〈 You made 《 as 《 of [these] Thirteen, 〈 the 〈 today 〈 for us
humble one known covenant
[Moses]

מִקֶּדֶם, כְּמוֹ שֶׁכָּתוּב, וַיֵּרֶד יהוה בֶּעָנָן וַיִּתְיַצֵּב עִמּוֹ

〈 with 〈 and stood 〈 in a 〈 And HASHEM 《 it is written: 〈 as 《 in ancient
him cloud descended times,

שָׁם, וַיִּקְרָא בְשֵׁם יהוה.[3]

《 of 〈 with the 〈 and He 《 there,
HASHEM. Name called out

---

(1) *Isaiah* 25:9. (2) *Rosh Hashanah* 17a. (3) *Exodus* 34:5.

CONGREGATION, THEN *CHAZZAN*:

וַיַּעֲבֹר יהוה עַל פָּנָיו וַיִּקְרָא:

《 and   《 [Moses'] 〈 before 〈 And HASHEM passed
proclaimed: face,

CONGREGATION AND *CHAZZAN* RECITE LOUDLY AND IN UNISON:

יהוה, יהוה, אֵל, רַחוּם, וְחַנּוּן, אֶרֶךְ אַפַּיִם,

〈 to anger, 〈 Slow 《 and 〈 Compassionate 〈 God, 〈 HASHEM, 〈 HASHEM,
    Gracious,

וְרַב חֶסֶד, וֶאֱמֶת, נֹצֵר חֶסֶד לָאֲלָפִים, נֹשֵׂא עָוֹן,

〈 of 〈 Forgiver 《 for thousands 〈 of 〈 Preserver 《 and 〈 in 〈 and
iniquity,   [of generations], kindness   Truth, Kindness Abundant

וָפֶשַׁע, וְחַטָּאָה, וְנַקֵּה.¹ וְסָלַחְתָּ לַעֲוֹנֵנוּ וּלְחַטָּאתֵנוּ

《 and our sins, 〈 our 〈 May You 《 and Who 〈 and inadvertent 〈 willful sin,
    iniquities forgive   absolves. sin,

וּנְחַלְתָּנוּ.² סְלַח לָנוּ אָבִינוּ כִּי חָטָאנוּ, מְחַל לָנוּ

〈 us, 〈 pardon 《 we have 〈 for 《 our 〈 us, 〈 Forgive 《 and make us
   sinned;   Father,   Your heritage.

מַלְכֵּנוּ כִּי פָשָׁעְנוּ. כִּי אַתָּה אֲדֹנָי טוֹב וְסַלָּח,

《 and 〈 are 〈 O Lord, 〈 You, 〈 For 《 we have 〈 for 《 our King,
forgiving, good   willfully sinned.

וְרַב חֶסֶד לְכָל קֹרְאֶיךָ.³

《 who call 〈 to all 〈 kind 〈 and
upon You.   abundantly

PREFATORY VERSES TO SELICHAH 62 / פסוקי הקדמה לסליחה סב

מַה בֶּצַע בְּדָמֵנוּ, בְּרִדְתֵּנוּ אֶל שָׁחַת,

《 the Pit? 〈 to 〈 in our descent 〈 in our death, 〈 gain is there 〈 What

הֲיוֹדְךָ עָפָר, הֲיַגִּיד אֲמִתֶּךָ.⁴ כִּי תְבַקֵּשׁ לַעֲוֹנֵנוּ,

〈 out 〈 You search 〈 For 《 Your truth? 〈 Will it 《 Will the dust
iniquities out   declare   acknowledge You?

וּלְחַטָּאתֵנוּ תִדְרוֹשׁ.⁵ כִּי אָדָם אֵין צַדִּיק בָּאָרֶץ,

〈 on the 〈 who is [so] 〈 does 〈 the man 〈 For 〈 You seek. 〈 and our
earth righteous not exist   transgressions

אֲשֶׁר יַעֲשֶׂה טוֹב וְלֹא יֶחֱטָא.⁶ וְאַתָּה אֲדֹנָי אֵל

〈 are 〈 O Lord, 〈 But You, 《 sins. 〈 and 〈 [only] 〈 he does 〈 that
God   never good

---

(1) *Exodus* 34:6-7. (2) 34:9. (3) *Psalms* 86:5. (4) Cf. 30:10. (5) Cf. *Job* 10:6. (6) *Ecclesiastes* 7:20.

רַחוּם וְחַנּוּן, אֶרֶךְ אַפַּיִם וְרַב חֶסֶד וֶאֱמֶת.¹

《 and Truth. 〈 in 〈Abundant 〈 to 〈 Slow 《 and Com- 〈 the
Kindness Anger, passionate, Merciful

כְּרַחֵם אָב עַל בָּנִים, כֵּן תְּרַחֵם יהוה עָלֵינוּ.²

《 on us. 〈 HASHEM, 〈 have 〈 so 《 his 〈 toward 〈 a 〈 As merciful as
mercy, children, father is

לַיהוה הַיְשׁוּעָה, עַל עַמְּךָ בִרְכָתֶךָ סֶּלָה.³ יהוה

〈 HASHEM, 《 Selah. 《 is Your 〈 Your 〈 upon 《 is salvation, 〈 To HASHEM
blessing, people

צְבָאוֹת עִמָּנוּ, מִשְׂגָּב לָנוּ אֱלֹהֵי יַעֲקֹב סֶלָה.⁴

《 Selah. 《 of Jacob, 〈 is the God 〈 for us 〈 a 《 is with us, 〈 Master of
stronghold Legions,

יהוה צְבָאוֹת, אַשְׁרֵי אָדָם בֹּטֵחַ בָּךְ.⁵ יהוה

〈 HASHEM, 《 in You. 〈 who 〈 is the 〈 — praiseworthy 《 Master 〈 HASHEM,
trusts man of Legions

הוֹשִׁיעָה, הַמֶּלֶךְ יַעֲנֵנוּ בְיוֹם קָרְאֵנוּ.⁶

《 we call. 〈 on the 〈 answer 〈 May the 《 save!
day us King

סְלִיחָה סב / SELICHAH 62

אֱלֹהֵינוּ וֵאלֹהֵי אֲבוֹתֵינוּ:

《 of our forefathers: 〈 and the God 〈 Our God

אֵלֶיךָ יהוה שִׁוַּעְתִּי,⁷* בְּתַחֲן פָּנֶיךָ קִדַּמְתִּי,

《 I hasten. 〈before Your〈 with sup- 《 I cry out;* 〈 HASHEM, 〈 To You,
presence plication

גֹּדֶל רַחֲמֶיךָ נִסְמַכְתִּי, אֱלֹהַי בְּךָ בָטַחְתִּי.⁸

《 I trust. 〈 in 〈 My God, 《 I depend: 〈 of Your 〈On the
You mercy greatness

דְּרָכֶיךָ יהוה הוֹדִיעֵנִי,⁹ הַדְרִיכֵנִי בַאֲמִתֶּךָ וְלַמְּדֵנִי,¹⁰

《 and teach 〈 in Your truth 〈 guide me 《 inform me; 〈 HASHEM, 〈 Of Your
me; ways,

---

(1) *Psalms* 86:15. (2) Cf. 103:13. (3) 3:9. (4) 46:8. (5) 84:13. (6) 20:10. (7) 88:14. (8) 25:2. (9) 25:4. (10) 25:5.

Ⱔ אֵלֶיךָ ה' שִׁוַּעְתִּי — *To You,* HASHEM, *I cry out.* The acrostic of the first three lines of each quatrain in this *selichah* comprises

the *aleph-beis* followed by the author's signature, זְבַדְיָה, *Zevadyah* [see prefatory comment to *Selichah 63*].

וּנְתִיב מִצְוֹתֶיךָ יַדְּעֵנִי,¹ אֱלֹהַי אַל תִּרְחַק מִמֶּנִּי.²

《 from me. 〈 be far 〈 do 《 My 《 let me 〈 of Your 〈 and the
not God, know: commandments path

זְכֹר רַחֲמֶיךָ וַחֲסָדֶיךָ יהוה,³ חַנּוּן לְךָ נָשָׂאתִי עֵינַי,⁴

《 my 〈 I lift 〈 to 《Gracious 《 HASHEM! 〈 and Your 〈 Your mercy 〈 Re-
eyes. You One, kindness, member

טוּבְךָ קִוִּיתִי יהוה, הַאֲזִינָה יהוה קוֹל תַּחֲנוּנִי,⁵

《 of my 〈 to the 〈 HASHEM, 〈 Listen, 《 HASHEM: 〈 I place 〈 In Your
supplication. sound my hope, goodness

יָהּ שִׂיחִי לְפָנֶיךָ יֶעֱרַב,⁶

〈 be found 〈 before 〈 may my 〈 God,
sweet You prayer

כְּכָלִיל אֲשֶׁר בְּמִזְבַּחֲךָ נִקְרָב,⁷

《 is 〈 on Your Altar 〈 that 〈 as a burnt-
brought. offering

לְפָנֶיךָ תְּחִנָּתִי תִקְרַב,⁸ וְסָלַחְתָּ לַעֲוֹנִי כִּי רָב.⁹

《 it is 〈 though 〈 my sin, 〈 and may 《 approach, 〈 let my 〈 Before You
great. You forgive supplication

מַה נֹּאמַר לְפָנֶיךָ אֲדוֹן נִשְׁמָתֵנוּ,

《 of our souls? 〈 O Lord 《 before You, 〈 can we say 〈 What

נִכְלַמְנוּ מְאֹד בַּעֲוֹנֵינוּ,

《 of our iniquities. 〈 greatly 〈 We are ashamed

סְלַח נָא לְכָל אַשְׁמוֹתֵינוּ,

《 our guilty deeds: 〈 all 〈 please, 〈 Forgive,

תַּשְׁלִיךְ בִּמְצוֹלוֹת יָם כָּל חַטֹּאתֵינוּ.¹⁰

《 our sins. 〈 all 〈 of the sea 〈 into the depths 〈 You shall cast

עֲצֹר חֲמָתְךָ וְאַל נָא תֶחֱרֶה,

《 let it rage. 〈 please, 〈 do not, 《 Your rage; 〈 Hold back

פּוֹעֵל הַכֹּל יוֹצֵר וּבוֹרֵא,

《 and Creator, 〈 Molder 〈 of All, 〈 Maker

צֶדֶק דֶּרֶךְ תְּשׁוּבָה לָנוּ תוֹרֶה,¹¹

《 may You 〈 to us 〈 of 〈 way 〈 the
teach, repentance righteous

---

(1) Cf. *Psalms* 119:35. (2) 38:22. (3) Cf. 25:6. (4) Cf. 123:1. (5) 140:7.
(6) Cf. 104:34. (7) Cf. *Deuteronomy* 33:10. (8) Cf. *Psalms* 119:169-170.
(9) 25:11. (10) Cf. *Micah* 7:19. (11) Cf. *Psalms* 25:8.

כִּי עִמְּךָ הַסְּלִיחָה לְמַעַן תִּוָּרֵא.[1]

《 You may 〈 so that 《 is forgiveness, 〈 with 〈 for
be feared. 　　　　　　　　　　　　　You

קוֹלֵנוּ תִשְׁמַע יוֹשֵׁב כְּרוּבִים,

《 upon the 〈 O You 《 may You 〈 Our voice
Cherubim; enthroned hear,

רַחֲמָן גְּמֹל טוֹבָה לְחַיָּבִים,

《 upon the 〈 good 〈 bestow 《 Merciful
guilty — 　　　　　　　　　　　One,

שֶׁלֹּא עַל צִדְקוֹתֵינוּ תְּחַן מַרְבִּים,

《 we 〈 that sup- 〈 our 〈 depend- 〈 for it
increase, plications righteousness ing on is not

כִּי עַל רַחֲמֶיךָ הָרַבִּים.[2]

《 that is abundant. 〈 Your mercy 〈 on 〈 but

תַּעֲבִיר חֵטְא וְתִמְחֶה פְּשָׁעִים,

《 rebellious 〈 and wipe 〈 sin 〈 May You
deeds, away overlook

זְדוֹנוֹת וּשְׁגָגוֹת סְתָרִים וִידוּעִים,

《 or known. 〈 [whether] 《 or 〈 [whether]
hidden inadvertent, deliberate

בַּטֵּל מִמֶּנּוּ מַחְשְׁבוֹת שׂוֹנְאֵינוּ וַחֲלָיִם רָעִים,

《 that are 〈 and [nullify] 《 of those 〈 the plots 〈 from us 〈 Nullify
harsh, diseases who hate us,

מַרְבֶּה מְחִילָה לַחֲטָאִים וּסְלִיחָה לְפוֹשְׁעִים.

《 to willful sinners. 〈 and 〈 to inadvertent 〈 pardon 〈 You abun-
forgiveness sinners dantly grant

❖ דַּלֵּנוּ מֵחֵטְא נַקֵּנוּ מֵאֲשָׁמִים,

《 of guilty deeds, 〈 cleanse 《 out of sin, 〈 Draw
us us up

יוֹדֵעַ כָּל סִתְרֵי נֶעְלָמִים,

《 that are 〈 secrets 〈 all 〈 You Who
hidden away. know

הַגִּיגֵנוּ שְׁעֵה כְּעוֹלוֹת וּשְׁלָמִים,

《 and peace- 〈 as if they were 〈 turn [Your 〈 To our
offerings, burnt-offerings attention] thoughts

---

(1) *Psalms* 130:4. (2) Cf. *Daniel* 9:18.

אֵל מֶלֶךְ יוֹשֵׁב עַל כִּסֵּא רַחֲמִים.

‹ of Mercy! ‹ the Throne ‹ on ‹ who sits ‹ King ‹ O God,

ALL, WHILE STANDING:

אֵל מֶלֶךְ יוֹשֵׁב עַל כִּסֵּא רַחֲמִים, מִתְנַהֵג

‹ Who acts ‹ of mercy, ‹ the throne ‹ on ‹ Who sits ‹ King ‹ O God,

בַּחֲסִידוּת, מוֹחֵל עֲוֹנוֹת עַמּוֹ, מַעֲבִיר רִאשׁוֹן

‹ [sins,] one ‹ Who removes ‹ of His people, ‹ the sins ‹ Who pardons ‹ with kindness,

רִאשׁוֹן,[1] מַרְבֶּה מְחִילָה לַחֲטָאִים וּסְלִיחָה לַפּוֹשְׁעִים,

‹ to willful sinners, ‹ and forgiveness ‹ to unintentional sinners ‹ pardon ‹ Who abundantly grants ‹ by one,

עֹשֶׂה צְדָקוֹת עִם כָּל בָּשָׂר וָרוּחַ, לֹא כְרָעָתָם

‹ in accord with their wickedness ‹ — not ‹ and spirit ‹ [beings of] flesh ‹ all ‹ with ‹ acts of generosity ‹ Who performs

תִּגְמוֹל. ❖ אֵל הוֹרֵיתָ לָנוּ לוֹמַר שְׁלֹשׁ עֶשְׂרֵה, וּזְכוֹר

‹ remember ‹ the Thirteen [Attributes of Mercy]; ‹ to recite ‹ us ‹ You taught ‹ O God, ‹ do You repay them!

לָנוּ הַיּוֹם בְּרִית שְׁלֹשׁ עֶשְׂרֵה, כְּמוֹ שֶׁהוֹדַעְתָּ לֶעָנָיו

‹ to the humble one [Moses] ‹ You made known ‹ as ‹ of [these] Thirteen, ‹ the covenant ‹ today ‹ for us

מִקֶּדֶם, כְּמוֹ שֶׁכָּתוּב, וַיֵּרֶד יהוה בֶּעָנָן וַיִּתְיַצֵּב עִמּוֹ

‹ with him ‹ and stood ‹ in a cloud ‹ And HASHEM descended ‹ it is written: ‹ as ‹ in ancient times,

שָׁם, וַיִּקְרָא בְשֵׁם יהוה.[2]

‹ of HASHEM. ‹ with the Name ‹ and He called out ‹ there,

CONGREGATION, THEN *CHAZZAN:*

וַיַּעֲבֹר יהוה עַל פָּנָיו וַיִּקְרָא:

‹ and proclaimed: ‹ [Moses'] face, ‹ before ‹ And HASHEM passed

CONGREGATION AND *CHAZZAN* **RECITE LOUDLY AND IN UNISON:**

יהוה, יהוה, אֵל, רַחוּם, וְחַנּוּן, אֶרֶךְ אַפַּיִם,

‹ to anger, ‹ Slow ‹ and Gracious, ‹ Compassionate ‹ God, ‹ HASHEM, ‹ HASHEM,

---

(1) *Rosh Hashanah* 17a. (2) *Exodus* 34:5.

וְרַב חֶסֶד, וֶאֱמֶת, נֹצֵר חֶסֶד לָאֲלָפִים, נֹשֵׂא עָוֹן,

‹ of ‹ Forgiver « for thousands ‹ of ‹ Preserver « and ‹ in ‹ and
iniquity, [of generations], kindness Truth, Kindness Abundant

וָפֶשַׁע, וְחַטָּאָה, וְנַקֵּה.¹ וְסָלַחְתָּ לַעֲוֹנֵנוּ וּלְחַטָּאתֵנוּ

« and our sins, ‹ our ‹ May You « and Who ‹ and inadvertent ‹ willful sin,
iniquities forgive absolves. sin,

וּנְחַלְתָּנוּ.² סְלַח לָנוּ אָבִינוּ כִּי חָטָאנוּ, מְחַל לָנוּ

‹ us, ‹ pardon « we have ‹ for « our ‹ us, ‹ Forgive « and make us
sinned; Father, Your heritage.

מַלְכֵּנוּ כִּי פָשָׁעְנוּ. כִּי אַתָּה אֲדֹנָי טוֹב וְסַלָּח,

« and ‹ are ‹ O Lord, ‹ You, ‹ For « we have ‹ for « our King,
forgiving, good willfully sinned.

וְרַב חֶסֶד לְכָל קֹרְאֶיךָ.³

« who call ‹ to all ‹ kind ‹ and
upon You. abundantly

פסוקי הקדמה לסליחה סג / PREFATORY VERSES TO SELICHAH 63

אֱלֹהִים לָנוּ מַחֲסֶה וָעֹז, עֶזְרָה בְצָרוֹת נִמְצָא מְאֹד.⁴

« very accessible. ‹ in distress, ‹ a help « and ‹ a ‹ is for ‹ God
strength, refuge us

אֱלֹהִים, אַל דֳּמִי לָךְ, אַל תֶּחֱרַשׁ וְאַל תִּשְׁקֹט אֵל.⁵

« O ‹ still, ‹ and ‹ deaf ‹ be « hold Yourself ‹ do ‹ O God,
God. be not not silent; not

אַל תִּרְחַק מִמֶּנּוּ כִּי צָרָה קְרוֹבָה, כִּי אֵין עוֹזֵר.⁶

« to help. ‹ there is ‹ for « is near; ‹ trouble ‹ for ‹ from us, ‹ distanced ‹ Be not
no one

וַיֹּאמְרוּ, לֹא יִרְאֶה יָּהּ, וְלֹא יָבִין אֱלֹהֵי יַעֲקֹב. לָמָה⁷

‹ Why, « of Jacob. ‹ will ‹ understand « will ‹ See not ‹ And they say,
the God not God,

אֱלֹהִים זָנַחְתָּ לָנֶצַח, יֶעְשַׁן אַפְּךָ בְּצֹאן מַרְעִיתֶךָ.⁸

« of Your ‹ against ‹ does ‹ [Why] ‹ for an ‹ have You ‹ O God,
pasture? the sheep Your smolder eternity? abandoned
wrath [us]

כְּרַחֵם אָב עַל בָּנִים, כֵּן תְּרַחֵם יהוה עָלֵינוּ.⁹

« on us. ‹ HASHEM, ‹ have ‹ so « his ‹ toward ‹ a ‹ As merciful as
mercy, children, father is

---

(1) *Exodus* 34:6-7. (2) 34:9. (3) *Psalms* 86:5. (4) 46:2. (5) 83:2. (6) Cf. 22:12. (7) 94:7. (8) 74:1. (9) Cf. 103:13.

לַיהוה הַיְשׁוּעָה, עַל עַמְּךָ בִרְכָתֶךָ סֶּלָה.[1] יהוה
To Hashem ⟩ is salvation, ⟨ upon ⟩ Your ⟨ Your ⟩ Selah. ⟨ Hashem,
                           people   blessing,

צְבָאוֹת עִמָּנוּ, מִשְׂגָּב לָנוּ אֱלֹהֵי יַעֲקֹב סֶלָה.[2]
Master of ⟩ is with us, ⟨ a ⟩ for us ⟨ is the God ⟩ of Jacob, ⟨ Selah.
Legions,   stronghold

יהוה צְבָאוֹת, אַשְׁרֵי אָדָם בֹּטֵחַ בָּךְ.[3] יהוה הוֹשִׁיעָה,
Hashem, ⟩ Master of ⟨ praise- ⟩ is the ⟨ who ⟩ in You. ⟨ Hashem, ⟩ save!
    Legions ⟨ worthy   man   trusts

הַמֶּלֶךְ יַעֲנֵנוּ בְיוֹם קָרְאֵנוּ.[4]
May the ⟩ answer ⟨ on the ⟩ we call.
King   us   day

SELICHAH 63 / סליחה סג

(שלישיה)

אֱלֹהִים אֵין בִּלְתֶּךָ,[*5] לְדוֹר דּוֹרִים מֶמְשַׁלְתֶּךָ,[6]
God, ⟩ there is none ⟨ besides ⟩ unto ⟨ after ⟩ Your rule
    You;* ⟨ generation ⟩ generation ⟨ extends,

וְלָעַד קִיּוּם בְּרִיתֶךָ.
and forever ⟩ stands ⟨ Your covenant.

בִּימִינְךָ אֵין מַעֲצָר,[7] יָדְךָ לֹא תִקְצָר,[8]
In Your ⟩ there ⟨ restraint; ⟩ Your ⟨ is not ⟩ limited,
right hand   is no   hand

אֵל עוֹנֶה בַּצָּר.[9]
O ⟩ Who ⟨ in
God answers [us] distress.

גָּבְרוּ מְאֹד נִפְלְאוֹתֶיךָ, וְלָעַד שִׁלְטוֹן מַלְכוּתֶךָ,
Powerful ⟩ extremely ⟨ are Your ⟩ forever ⟨ is the ⟩ of Your
wonders; ⟨ dominion ⟨ kingship,

---

(1) *Psalms* 3:9. (2) 46:8. (3) 84:13. (4) 20:10. (5) *I Samuel* 2:2. (6) Cf. *Psalms* 145:13.
(7) Cf. *I Samuel* 14:6. (8) Cf. *Numbers* 11:23; *Isaiah* 59:1. (9) Cf. *Genesis* 35:3.

אֱלֹהִים אֵין בִּלְתֶּךָ — *God, there is none besides You.* The acrostic follows the *aleph-beis*, then spells the *paytan's* name זְבַדְיָה, *Zevadiah.* Not much is known about him, except that he wrote many *piyutim* that appear in various liturgies. He is thought to have lived in 9th- or 10th-century Southern Italy.

The translation regards the opening word, אֱלֹהִים, *God,* as sacred. Thus, as in every *selichah* that begins with a Divine Name, the introductory phrase אֱלֹהֵינוּ וַאלֹהֵי אֲבוֹתֵינוּ, *Our God and the God of our forefathers,* is omitted. Alternatively: the word is not sacred but refers to idols: and the stich is rendered: *There is no other god besides You.* If so, the introductory phrase should be recited.

וְלֹא יִתַּמּוּ שְׁנוֹתֶיךָ.[1]

《 are Your years. 〈 ending 〈 and never

דּוֹרֵשׁ דָּמִים,[2] הִצַּלְתָּנוּ כַּמָּה פְעָמִים,

《 times, 〈 so many 〈 You have saved us 《 of blood, 〈 Avenger

וְהִשְׁפַּלְתָּ מְלָכִים רָמִים.[3]

《 who are haughty! 〈 kings 〈 You have humbled

הֵן אַתָּה לֹא שָׁנִיתָ,[4] וְאַתָּה הוּא שֶׁהָיִיתָ,

《 always were, 〈 Who 〈 for it is You 《 changed, 〈 have not 〈 You 《 Indeed,

בְּנֵי יַעֲקֹב לֹא כִלִּיתָ.[4]

《 You have not annihilated. 〈 of Jacob 〈 the Children

וּמִבְּנֵי בְנֵיהֶם אֲנַחְנוּ, לָמָה לָנֶצַח זְנַחְנוּ,[5]

《 are we abandoned, 〈 eternally 〈 Why 《 are we! 〈 of their children 〈 But from the children

וְכַמֵּת מִלֵּב נִשְׁכָּחְנוּ.[6]

《 we are forgotten? 〈 from the heart 《 and like the dead,

זְרוּיִים בְּכָל פִּנָּה, עֲבוּדִים בְּכָל מְדִינָה,

《 province, 〈 in every 〈 enslaved 《 corner 〈 to every 〈 Scattered [of the world],

וְאֵין לָנוּ חֲנִינָה.[7]

《 leniency. 〈 granted 〈 there to us is not

חֲשׁוּכִים[8] בֵּין כָּל אֻמָּה, נְתוּנִים לְבֹשֶׁת וְלִכְלִמָּה,[9]

〈 and humiliation 〈 to shame 〈 given over 《 nation, 〈 every 〈 among 〈 Darkened [by exile]

לְגוֹיֵי אֲדָמָה.

《 of the earth. 〈 among the peoples

טָבַעְנוּ בְּצוּל מַעֲמַקִּים,[10] יָרַדְנוּ וְאֵין מֵקִים,[11]

《 to lift [us] up; 〈 and there is no one 〈 we have 《 depths; 〈 in the shadowy 〈 We have descended, 　　　sunk

---

(1) Cf. *Psalms* 102:28. (2) 9:13. (3) Cf. *II Samuel* 22:28; some editions of *Selichos* read
וְהִשְׁפַּלְתָּ גֵּאִים וְרָמִים, *You have humbled the proud and the haughty.* (4) Cf. *Malachi* 3:6.
(5) Cf. *Psalms* 74:1. (6) Cf. 31:13. (7) Cf. *Jeremiah* 16:13. (8) Some editions read חֲשׂוּכִים, *deprived.*
(9) Cf. *Psalms* 35:26. (10) Cf. 69:3. (11) Cf. *Jeremiah* 50:32.

לְךָ לְבַד נוֹאֲקִים.

« do we cry. ‹ alone ‹ to You

יוֹשְׁבִים כְּעֵדֵי שְׁקָרִים, בְּלִי רֹאשׁ לְהָרִים,

« to lift, ‹ our heads ‹ unable « exposed ‹ like ‹ We sit
as false, witnesses [in shame]

לַעֲנָה וָרֹאשׁ שְׁכוּרִים.

« intoxicated. ‹ and gall ‹ with
wormwood

בָּשַׁלְנוּ בַצָּהֳרַיִם כְּבַלַּיְלָה, כְּעִוְרִים נְגַשֵׁשׁ בָּאֲפֵלָה,[1]

« through ‹ we grope ‹ like blind « as if at night; ‹ at noon ‹ We stumble
the gloom, men

וְאֵין לֵידַע קֵץ הַגְּאֻלָּה.

« of the ‹ the ‹ to know ‹ unable
Redemption. time

לְקוּחֵי כֶסֶף* לְחֵרוּת יוֹצְאִים, וַאֲנַחְנוּ יוֹם וָלֵיל נִלְאִים,

« are ‹ and ‹ day « yet we, « go out, ‹ to freedom ‹ for ‹ Those
wearied, night money* bought

וּמָנוֹחַ לֹא מוֹצְאִים.[2]

« we cannot find. ‹ a respite

מַה כֹּחִי לִסְבֹּל טִיט רְפָשִׁי,[3]

« and mire? ‹ this ‹ to bear ‹ is my ‹ What
mud strength

וּמַה קִּצִּי כִּי אַאֲרִיךְ נַפְשִׁי,[4]

« [in] my ‹ I should ‹ that ‹ is my ‹ And
soul, extend [hope] [exile's] end, what

עַד זְמַן תּוֹצִיאֵנִי לַחָפְשִׁי.

« into freedom? ‹ You bring ‹ the ‹ until
me out time

נֹאמַר בְּקֹר מִי יִתֵּן עֶרֶב, וּבָעֶרֶב מִי יִתֵּן בְּקֶר יִקְרָב,

« draw ‹ that ‹ can ‹ Who « and in « that evening ‹ can ‹ Who ‹ in the ‹ We say
nigh! morning grant the evening, [arrive], grant morning,

---

(1) Cf. *Isaiah* 59:9-10. (2) Cf. *Lamentations* 1:3. (3) Cf. *Isaiah* 57:20. (4) Cf. *Job* 6:11.

לְקוּחֵי כֶסֶף — *Those bought for money.* Even slaves for whom the master has paid a tidy sum are often able to have themselves set free (see *Kiddushin* 22b). Yet we, who were given over to our oppressors without any cost to them (see *Isaiah* 52:3,5), cannot acquire our freedom (*Masbir*).

Alternatively: לְקוּחֵי כֶסֶף is to be understood as לוֹקְחֵי כֶסֶף, *those who took the silver*, those who looted the Temple treasury (see *Joel* 4:5), לְחֵרוּת יוֹצְאִים, *go about freely* (*Pardes*).

מִפַּחַד לֵב וָקֶרֶב.¹

《　and　〈　of　〈　from the
innards.　heart　fright

שֶׂה פְזוּרָה² אָנוּ מְשׁוּלִים, כָּל מוֹצְאֵינוּ אוֹתָנוּ אוֹכְלִים,

《　they　〈 ourselves 《 who find us, 〈　all 《 compared: 〈 we 〈 that are 〈 To
devour,　　　　　　　　　　　　　　　　　　are　scattered　sheep

וְעַל נַפְשׁוֹתֵינוּ לֹא חוֹמְלִים.

《 compassion. 〈 they have no 〈 our souls 〈 and upon

עֵינַי סָבִיב הֲרִימוֹתִי, שְׂמֹאל וְיָמִין צָפִיתִי,

《 I looked, 〈 and 〈 left 《 I raised; 〈 all around 〈 My
right　　　　　　　　　[me]　eyes

וּמַכִּיר לִי לֹא רָאִיתִי.³

《　I did not see.　〈　but anyone who
recognized me

פָּנִיתִי לְכָל צַד וְאֵין עֶזְרָה, צָעַקְתִּי לְךָ וָאֶקְרָא,

《 and called 〈 to 〈 I have 《 aid; 〈 and there 〈 side, 〈 to 〈 I have
out,　You　shouted　　　　was no　every　turned

אֵל עוֹנֶה בְּעֵת צָרָה.⁴

《　of　〈 in time 〈 Who 〈 O
trouble!　answers　God,

צוּר יָדְךָ לֹא קָצְרָה,⁵ לְךָ הַכֹּחַ וְהַגְּבוּרָה,

《 and the might. 〈 is the 〈 Yours 《 limited; 〈 is not 〈 Your 《 O
power　　　　　　　　　　hand　Rock,

לָמָּה תִישַׁן עוּרָה.⁶

《 Awaken! 《do You [seem 〈 Why
to] sleep?

קְשֹׁב תַּחַן שִׂיחֵנוּ, רְאֵה בְּתַשׁוּת כֹּחֵנוּ,

《 of our 〈 the failing 〈 see 《 of our 〈 to the sup- 〈 Be
strength,　　　　　　　　prayer;　plication　attentive

וְאַל בְּאַפְּךָ תוֹכִיחֵנוּ.⁷

《　rebuke us.　〈 in Your 〈 and
anger　do not

שׁוּר בְּשִׁפְלוּת דּוֹרֵנוּ, תַּבִּיט בְּכֹבֶד צַעֲרֵנוּ,

《 of our pain, 〈 the 〈 look at 《 of our 〈 the 〈 See
intensity　generation;　degradation

---

(1) Cf. *Deuteronomy* 28:67. (2) Cf. *Jeremiah* 50:17. (3) Cf. *Psalms* 142:5.
(4) Cf. 20:2; *Genesis* 35:3. (5) Cf. *Isaiah* 59:1. (6) Cf. *Psalms* 44:24. (7) Cf. 6:20.

וְאַל בַּחֲמָתְךָ תְיַסְּרֵנוּ.[1]

» chastise us. ‹ in Your wrath ‹ and do not

זַעֲקָתֵנוּ שָׁעֵה מִמְּעוֹנֶךָ, בִּיטָה בְּאַנְקַת בָּנֶיךָ,

» of Your ‹ the groans ‹ look at » from Your heav- ‹ turn ‹ Our outcry
children, enly abode; toward

וְאַל תְּשִׁיבֵנוּ רֵיקָם מִלְּפָנֶיךָ.

» from before ‹ empty- ‹ turn us away ‹ and do
You. handed not

❖ דְּרַשְׁנוּךָ בְּחִין וְשַׁוְעָה, יָהּ הַרְצֵה לָנוּ בְּזוּ הַשָּׁעָה,

» time, ‹ at ‹ to us ‹ be ‹ O » and cry; ‹ with sup- ‹ We have
this favorable God, plication sought You

וְתַחֲנוּנֵינוּ[2] יהוה שְׁמָעָה.

» hear! ‹ HASHEM, ‹ and our
supplications,

ALL, WHILE STANDING:

אֵל מֶלֶךְ יוֹשֵׁב עַל כִּסֵּא רַחֲמִים, מִתְנַהֵג

‹ Who acts » of mercy, ‹ the throne ‹ on ‹ Who sits ‹ King ‹ O God,

בַּחֲסִידוּת, מוֹחֵל עֲוֹנוֹת עַמּוֹ, מַעֲבִיר רִאשׁוֹן

‹ [sins,] one ‹ Who » of His ‹ the sins ‹ Who » with kindness,
removes people, pardons

רִאשׁוֹן,[3] מַרְבֶּה מְחִילָה לַחַטָּאִים וּסְלִיחָה לַפּוֹשְׁעִים,

» to willful ‹ and ‹ to unintentional ‹ pardon ‹ Who abun- » by one,
sinners, forgiveness sinners dantly grants

עֹשֶׂה צְדָקוֹת עִם כָּל בָּשָׂר וָרוּחַ, לֹא כְרָעָתָם

‹ in accord with ‹ — not » and ‹ [beings ‹ all ‹ with ‹ acts of ‹ Who
their wickedness spirit of] flesh generosity performs

תִּגְמוֹל. ❖ אֵל הוֹרֵיתָ לָּנוּ לוֹמַר שְׁלֹשׁ עֶשְׂרֵה, וּזְכוֹר

‹ remem- » the Thirteen ‹ to ‹ us ‹ You ‹ O God, » do You
ber [Attributes of Mercy]; recite taught repay them!

לָנוּ הַיּוֹם בְּרִית שְׁלֹשׁ עֶשְׂרֵה, כְּמוֹ שֶׁהוֹדַעְתָּ לֶעָנָיו

‹ to the humble ‹ You made ‹ as » of [these] Thirteen, ‹ the ‹ today ‹ for us
one [Moses] known covenant

מִקֶּדֶם, כְּמוֹ שֶׁכָּתוּב, וַיֵּרֶד יהוה בֶּעָנָן וַיִּתְיַצֵּב עִמּוֹ

‹ with ‹ and stood ‹ in a ‹ And HASHEM » it is written: ‹ as » in ancient
him cloud descended times,

---

(1) Cf. *Psalms* 6:2. (2) Some editions read אֲמָרֵינוּ, our words. (3) *Rosh Hashanah* 17a.

שָׁם, וַיִּקְרָא בְשֵׁם יהוה.[1]

《 of 〈 with the 〈 and He 《 there,
HASHEM. Name called out

CONGREGATION, THEN *CHAZZAN*:

וַיַּעֲבֹר יהוה עַל פָּנָיו וַיִּקְרָא:

《 and 《 [Moses'] 〈 before 〈 And HASHEM passed
proclaimed: face,

CONGREGATION AND *CHAZZAN* RECITE LOUDLY AND IN UNISON:

יהוה, יהוה, אֵל, רַחוּם, וְחַנּוּן, אֶרֶךְ אַפַּיִם,

〈 to anger, 〈 Slow 《 and 〈 Compassionate 〈 God, 〈 HASHEM, 〈 HASHEM,
Gracious,

וְרַב חֶסֶד, וֶאֱמֶת, נֹצֵר חֶסֶד לָאֲלָפִים, נֹשֵׂא עָוֹן,

〈 of 〈 Forgiver 《 for 〈 of 〈 Preserver 《 and 〈 in 〈 and
iniquity, thousands kindness Truth, Kindness Abundant
[of generations],

וָפֶשַׁע, וְחַטָּאָה, וְנַקֵּה.[2] וְסָלַחְתָּ לַעֲוֹנֵנוּ וּלְחַטָּאתֵנוּ

《 and our sins, 〈 our 〈 May You 《 and Who 〈 and inadvertent 〈 willful sin,
iniquities forgive absolves. sin,

וּנְחַלְתָּנוּ.[3] סְלַח לָנוּ אָבִינוּ כִּי חָטָאנוּ, מְחַל לָנוּ

〈 us, 〈 pardon 《 we have 〈 for 《 our 〈 us, 〈 Forgive 《 and make us
sinned; Father, Your heritage.

מַלְכֵּנוּ כִּי פָשָׁעְנוּ. כִּי אַתָּה אֲדֹנָי טוֹב וְסַלָּח,

《 and 〈 are 〈 O Lord, 〈 You, 〈 For 《 we have 〈 for 《 our King,
forgiving, good willfully sinned.

וְרַב חֶסֶד לְכָל קֹרְאֶיךָ.[4]

《 who call 〈 to all 〈 kind 〈 and
upon You. abundantly

PREFATORY VERSES TO SELICHAH 64 / פסוקי הקדמה לסליחה סד

תָּבוֹא אֵלֶיךָ תְּפִלָּתֵנוּ אֶל הֵיכַל קָדְשֶׁךָ.[5] תָּבוֹא

〈 Let 《 of Your 〈 the 〈 toward 〈 our prayers 〈 to You 〈 Let come
come holiness Sanctuary

לְפָנֶיךָ אֶנְקַת אָסִיר, כְּגֹדֶל זְרוֹעֲךָ, הוֹתֵר בְּנֵי תְמוּתָה.[6]

《 to die. 〈 those 《 spare 《 of Your 〈 as [befits] 《 of the 〈 the 〈 before
condemned might, the prisoner; groan You
greatness

---

(1) *Exodus* 34:5. (2) 34:6-7. (3) 34:9. (4) *Psalms* 86:5. (5) Cf. *Jonah* 2:8. (6) *Psalms* 79:11.

לִפְקֹחַ עֵינַיִם עִוְרוֹת, לְהוֹצִיא מִמַּסְגֵּר אַסִּיר, מִבֵּית
To open ⟩ eyes ⟩ that are ⟩ to take out ⟪ from jail ⟩ a prisoner; ⟪ from a house

כֶּלֶא יֹשְׁבֵי חֹשֶׁךְ.[1]
of detention ⟩ those dwelling ⟩ in ⟪ darkness.

כְּרַחֵם אָב עַל בָּנִים, כֵּן תְּרַחֵם יהוה עָלֵינוּ.[2]
As merciful as ⟩ a father is ⟩ toward ⟩ his children, ⟪ so ⟩ have mercy, ⟩ HASHEM, ⟩ on us. ⟪

לַיהוה הַיְשׁוּעָה, עַל עַמְּךָ בִרְכָתֶךָ סֶּלָה. יהוה[3]
To HASHEM ⟩ is salvation, ⟪ upon ⟩ Your people ⟩ is Your blessing, ⟪ Selah. ⟪ HASHEM,

צְבָאוֹת עִמָּנוּ, מִשְׂגָּב לָנוּ אֱלֹהֵי יַעֲקֹב סֶלָה.[4]
Master of Legions, ⟩ is with us, ⟪ a stronghold ⟩ for us ⟩ is the God ⟩ of Jacob, ⟪ Selah. ⟪

יהוה צְבָאוֹת, אַשְׁרֵי אָדָם בֹּטֵחַ בָּךְ.[5] יהוה הוֹשִׁיעָה,
HASHEM, ⟩ Master of Legions, ⟪ praise- worthy ⟩ is the man ⟩ who trusts ⟩ in You. ⟪ HASHEM, ⟩ save! ⟪

הַמֶּלֶךְ יַעֲנֵנוּ בְיוֹם קָרְאֵנוּ.[6]
May the King ⟩ answer us ⟩ on the day ⟪ we call. ⟪

סליחה סד / SELICHAH 64
(שלמונית)

ALL:

אֱלֹהֵינוּ וֵאלֹהֵי אֲבוֹתֵינוּ:
Our God ⟩ and the God ⟩ of our forefathers: ⟪

אֵיךְ אוּכַל לָבֹא* עָדֶיךָ,[7]
How ⟩ can I ⟩ come* ⟩ unto You, ⟪

---

(1) *Isaiah* 42:7. (2) Cf. *Psalms* 103:13. (3) 3:9. (4) 46:8. (5) 84:13. (6) 20:10. (7) Cf. 65:3.

∞§ **אֵיךְ אוּכַל לָבֹא** — *How can I come?* In the intricate pattern of this *selichah*, the first line of each stanza begins with the word אֵיךְ, *How*; the third line begins וְהֵמָּה, *And as for them*; and the fourth line is a Scriptural fragment that begins וַאֲנִי, *But as for me.* An *aleph-beis* acrostic is formed by the initial letters of the words following אֵיךְ and וְהֵמָּה respectively. After the

alphabet, the acrostic continues with the *paytan's* signature — יִצְחָק בַּר סַעַדְיָה חֲזַק, *Yitzchak bar Saadiah, may he be strong.* Nothing is known about this *paytan* except that he was highly praised by R' Shimon Duran in his responsa (*Tashbeitz*), and that he lived sometime before 1234 when the commentary *Arugas HaBosem* [which contains this *selichah*] was written.

וְעוֹבְדֵי זוּלָתֶךָ לֹא עֲזָבוּנִי לְעָבְדֶךָ,[1]

《 to serve 〈 allowed 〈 have 〈 other- 〈 when those
You?   me   not   than-You   who serve

וְהֵמָּה בִּקְשׁוּ לְהַפְרִידִי מִמֶּךָּ,

《 from 〈 to separate me 〈 — they 《 And as
You;   attempt   for them

וַאֲנִי לֹא עָזַבְתִּי פִּקֻּדֶיךָ.[2]

《 Your 〈 — I have 《 but as
precepts.   not forsaken   for me

אֵיךְ גָּלִיתִי וָאֵלֵךְ בְּכָל הֵלֶךְ וָפֶלֶךְ,

《 through 〈 along every road, 〈 I go 《 have I 〈 How
every area,   been exiled?

וּמָלְכוּ עָלַי מַמְלִיכִים לְמֹלֶךְ,[1]

《 [the idol,] 〈 have those who 〈 over 〈 while rule
Molech.   accept as king   me

וְהֵמָּה דִּינָם עוֹמֵד וּמַלְכְּכֶם מוֹלֵךְ,[1]

《 rules; 〈 and their 〈 endure, 〈 — their 《 And as
king   laws   for them

וַאֲנִי לֹא נִקְרֵאתִי לָבוֹא אֶל הַמֶּלֶךְ.[3]

《 the King. 〈 to 〈 to come 〈 — I have not been 《 but as
summoned   for me

אֵיךְ הָלְכוּ נְחָלִים מִדֶּלֶף דִּמְעִי הַדָּלוּף,

《 that are 〈 of my 〈 from the 〈 rivers 〈 have there 〈 How
dripping!   tears   drops   flowed

וְנִמְסַרְתִּי לְפוֹעֲלֵי אָוֶן וְסָלוּף,

《 and 〈 of evil 〈 to workers 〈 For I have been
distortion.   turned over

וְהֵמָּה וּבְנֵיהֶם יוֹרוּנִי חֵץ שָׁלוּף,

《 that are drawn 〈 arrows 〈 — they 《 and their 〈 And as
[from their quiver];   shoot at me   children   for them

וַאֲנִי כְּכֶבֶשׂ אַלּוּף.[4]

《 of first quality 〈 — I am like 《 but as
[led to slaughter]. a lamb   for me

אֵיךְ זְמַן קִצִּי נֶחְתָּם וְלֹא נוֹדַע,

《 known, 〈 and 〈 is sealed, 〈 of my 〈 that the 〈 How
not   [exile's] end time   is it

---

(1) This line has been censored out of some editions.
(2) *Psalms* 119:87. (3) *Esther* 4:11; cf. *Hosea* 8:4. (4) *Jeremiah* 11:19.

וְקַרְנִי גָדַע אוֹיְבִי¹ מְשַׁחַת פָּדָע,²

《 is saved? 〈 who from 《 by my 〈 has been 〈 while my
the grave enemy, cut down pride

וְהֵמָּה חוֹשְׁבִים חָכְמָתָם כְּהֵימָן וְדַרְדַּע,*³

《 and his 〈 [equals] that 〈 their wisdom 〈 — they think 《 And as
generation;* of Moses for them

וַאֲנִי בַעַר וְלֹא אֵדָע.⁴

《 know 〈 and 〈 — [they] 《 but as
anything. do not think] I am for me
senseless

אֵיךְ טֹרְפָה מַלְכוּת, מַמְלֶכֶת עַם סְגֻלָּה,

《 that is [Your] 〈 of the 〈 the kingdom 《 is the 〈 torn apart 〈 How
treasured nation, people kingdom,

וְאָרְכָה מְלוּכָה לְמַלְכֵי בְנֵי עַוְלָה,⁵

《 of iniqui- 〈 of the 〈 of the kings 〈 is the reign 〈 while
tous ones! children extended

וְהֵמָּה יוֹשְׁבִים לָבֶטַח בְּשִׂמְחָה וְגִילָה,

《 and 〈 in gladness 〈 securely, 〈 — they 《 And as for
exultation; dwell them

וַאֲנִי בְּתוֹךְ הַגּוֹלָה.⁶

《 of the Exile. 〈 — I am in 《 but as
the midst for me

אֵיךְ כּוֹס הַתַּרְעֵלָה שָׁתִיתִי⁷ וָאֶגְמָע,

《 and 〈 could I 〈 that was 〈 the 〈 How
swallowed? have drunk poisoned cup

---

(1) Cf. *Lamentations* 2:3. (2) Cf. *Job* 33:24. (3) See *I Kings* 5:11. (4) *Psalms* 73:22.
(5) This line has been censored out of some editions. (6) *Ezekiel* 1:1. (7) Cf. *Isaiah* 51:17.

כְּהֵימָן וְדַרְדַּע — *[Equals] that of Moses
and his generation.* The prophet describes
Solomon as wiser מִכָּל אָדָם, *than any man;*
מֵאֵיתָן הָאֶזְרָחִי, *than Eisan the Ezrachite,*
וְהֵימָן וְכַלְכֹּל וְדַרְדַּע, *and Heiman, Chalcal
and Darda,* בְּנֵי מָחוֹל, *the sons of Machol*
(*I Kings* 5:11). *Rashi* and *Radak* cite a
Midrash (*Pesikta*) that interprets these
names homiletically: מִכָּל אָדָם alludes to
Adam, who, in his wisdom, named all
the animals in the world; אֵיתָן is Abraham (see prefatory comment to *Selichah*
58); הֵימָן is Moses, of whom it is stated:
Of all My household, נֶאֱמָן, *he is the*
faithful one (*Numbers* 12:7); וְכַלְכֹּל refers
to Joseph who supplied food (בִּלְכֵּל) during the famine; וְדַרְדַּע alludes to the generation of the Wilderness that received the
Torah at Mount Sinai and therefore was
called דּוֹר דֵעָה, *the generation of knowl-*
edge; and בְּנֵי מָחוֹל also means that same
generation, for they were granted forgiveness (מְחִילָה) for the sin of the Golden
Calf.

Thus, the *paytan* speaks of the idolaters
who place their writings on the same level
as the Torah given through Moses to the
Generation of Knowledge.

בָּכִיתִי וָאֶדְמַע מֵעַל מַשָּׂא וּמִשְׁמָע.*1

《 of two of the children ⟨ from ⟨ and shed ⟨ I have
of Ishmael.*   the yoke   tears   wept

וְהֵמָּה לוֹעֲגִים עָלַי הַקְשִׁיבָה וּשְׁמָע,

《 and listen ⟨ [demanding that I] 《 me, ⟨ — they 《 And as for
[to them];   be attentive   deride   them

וַאֲנִי כְּחֵרֵשׁ לֹא אֶשְׁמָע.2

《 hear. ⟨ and ⟨ — I am like 《 but as
do not   a deaf man   for me

אֵיךְ מְחָצַנִי אֱלֹהַי, וּמַכְאוֹבִי לֹא חֻבָּשׁ,

《 been ⟨ have ⟨ and my 《 — my 《 has He ⟨ How
bandaged!   not   wounds   God —   crushed me

וּמְעִיל תִּפְאַרְתִּי לִבְנֵי אֱדוֹם הֻלְבָּשׁ,

《 is placed. ⟨ of Edom ⟨ upon the ⟨ of splendor ⟨ My cloak
children

וְהֵמָּה נֹפֶת אוֹכְלִים חָלָב וּדְבַשׁ,

《 and ⟨ milk 《 they feast, ⟨ — on 《 And as
honey;   nectar   for them

וַאֲנִי כָּעֵשֶׂב אִיבָשׁ.3

《 I wither ⟨ — like 《 but as
away.   grass   for me

אֵיךְ סְבָבוּנִי קֵדָר* כִּתְּרוּנִי דְדָן וּשְׁבָא,*

《 did the descendants ⟨ and 《— the people 《 have they sur- ⟨ How
of Ham!*   encircle us   of Araby*   rounded us

הַקּוֹרְאִים נָבִיא לְאִישׁ מֵעוֹלָם לֹא נִבָא,

《 prophesied. ⟨ who never ever ⟨ to a man ⟨ the Prophet ⟨ They call

וְהֵמָּה עוֹשִׂים חַיִל גְּדוּד וּצְבָא,

《 and ⟨ troop, ⟨ an ⟨ — they 《 And as
legion;   army,   build   for them

וַאֲנִי אָנָה אֲנִי בָא.4

《 go? ⟨ can I ⟨ — where 《 but as
for me

---

(1) Cf. *Genesis* 25:14. (2) *Psalms* 38:14. (3) 102:12. (4) *Genesis* 37:30.

מַשָּׂא וּמִשְׁמָע — *Of two of the children of Ishmael.* These are two of the children of Ishmael listed in *Genesis* 25:13-15. The *paytan* plays on the name מַשָּׂא which means *a burden*; thus, מֵעַל מַשָּׂא, *from the yoke of the burden.*

קֵדָר — *The people of Araby* [lit., *Kedar*]. This son of Ishmael (*Genesis* 25:13) is identified by *Targum Yonasan* as עֲרַב, *Araby.*

דְדָן וּשְׁבָא — *The descendants of Ham.* Dedan and Sheba were great-grandsons of Ham (see *Genesis* 10:7).

אֵיךְ פָּקַדְתָּ עָלַי כַּאֲשֶׁר הֲרֵעוֹתִי וְהִסְכַּלְתִּי,

≪ and [how] foolish ⟨ how evil I was ⟨ according ⟨ upon ⟨ have You ⟨ How
I have been?   to   me,   brought
              punishment

בְּשִׁנֵּי אֲרָיוֹת וּלְבָאִים נֶאֱכָלְתִּי,

≪ I have been devoured. ⟨ and lionesses ⟨ of lions ⟨ By the teeth

וְהֵמָּה צָעִיר וָרַב אוֹמְרִים מָצָאתִי וְגַם יָכֹלְתִּי,

≪ have I ⟨ and ⟨ I have found ⟨ they declare, ⟨ and ⟨ — both ⟨ And as
prevailed!   also   old,   young   for them

וַאֲנִי כַּאֲשֶׁר שָׁכֹלְתִּי שָׁכָלְתִּי.[1]

≪ so am I [again] ⟨ I have been ⟨ — as ⟨ But as
bereaved.   bereaved,   for me

אֵיךְ קָדְרוּ כּוֹכָבַי וְחָזְרוּ גַלְגַּלַי,

≪ did the spheres ⟨ and turned back ≪ my ⟨ have ⟨ How
[of Heaven]?   [themselves]   stars,   gone dark

וְעוֹבְדֵי גִלּוּלִים גִּלְלוּ גְלִילַי,*

≪ my ⟨ have turned into ⟨ of Idols ⟨ Worshipers
territories.* heaps of rubble

וְהֵמָּה רָחֲקוּ רַגְלַי מֵעֲלוֹת רְגָלַי,

≪ for my ⟨ from ⟨ my feet ⟨ — they ⟨ And as for
pilgrimage ⟨ ascending   have   them
festivals;   distanced

וַאֲנִי כִּמְעַט נָטָיוּ רַגְלָי.[2]

≪ have my ⟨ turned ⟨ — almost ⟨ but as
feet.   astray   for me

אֵיךְ שָׁמַרְתָּ מַעֲוָיַי וּנְטַרְתַּנִי חוֹבִי,

≪ my guilt; ⟨ and ≪ my sins, ⟨ have You ⟨ How
remembered   kept in mind

וּמְרִיבֵי נַפְשִׁי לֹא רַבְתָּ רִיבִי,[3]

≪ my ⟨ champi- ⟨ You ⟨ of my ⟨ but against
cause? ⟨ oned ⟨ have ⟨ soul ⟨ those who are
        not   the adversaries

וְהֵמָּה תָּקְפָּם וְכֹחָם לְהַכְאִיבִי וּלְהַדְאִיבִי,

≪ and to cause ⟨ [they use] ⟨ and their ⟨ — their ⟨ And as for
me grief; ⟨ to cause me pain ⟨ strength ⟨ power   them

---

(1) *Genesis* 43:14. (2) *Psalms* 73:2. (3) Cf. 35:1.

גִּלְלוּ גְלִילַי — *Have turned into heaps of rubble my territories.* The word גִּלְלוּ is cognate with גַּל, *heap* (*Arugas HaBosem*).

Others derive גִּלְלוּ from גָּלָל, *filth*, and translate, *have befouled my territories* (*Masbir*).

וַאֲנִי בְּחַסְדְּךָ בָטַחְתִּי יָגֵל לִבִּי.¹

‹ but as › ‹ — in Your › ‹ I trust, › « and › « will my ‹
for me kindness rejoice heart.

אֵיךְ יָשַׁבְתִּי בָדָד² וָאֱהִי לְנִידָה,³

‹ How › ‹ have I sat › ‹ alone › « and › « a wanderer, ‹
become

מִכָּבוֹד יְרוּדָה בַּגּוֹיִם נְדוּדָה,⁴

‹ from honor › « lowered, › « among › « wandering? ›
the nations

וְהֵמָּה צָלְחוּ וּמָלְכוּ וּמֶמְשַׁלְתָּם עָמְדָה,

« And as for › ‹ — they have › ‹ and › ‹ and their dominion › « has
them succeeded reigned endured;

וַאֲנִי שְׁכוּלָה וְגַלְמוּדָה.⁵

‹ but as › ‹ — I am bereft › « and forsaken. ›
for me [of my children]

אֵיךְ חֵרְפוּנִי מְעוֹלְלַי וּמְהוֹלְלַי⁶ כֻּלָּהֶם,

‹ How › ‹ is it that › ‹ do my › « and my › « all of
vilify me tormentors mockers, them?

צֶלֶם אֶצְלָם לֹא סָר מֵעֲלֵיהֶם,⁷

‹ Their protec- › « is with › « it has › ‹ gone › « from covering
tive shadow them, not away them.

וְהֵמָּה קָרְאוּ הֶאָח הֶאָח⁸ בְּמִלֵּיהֶם,

« And as › « — they › « Aha! › « Aha! › « as their
for them call out, [taunting] word.

וַאֲנִי הָיִיתִי חֶרְפָּה לָהֶם.⁹

« But as › ‹ — I › ‹ an object › ‹ to them. »
for me became of disgrace

אֵיךְ בֵּינֵיהֶם נִשְׁאַרְתִּי דּוֹאֵג וְדוֹאֵב,

‹ How › ‹ among them › ‹ am I left › ‹ worried › « and in pain, »

מִפַּלְגֵי יְגוֹנָם* וּמִמְּקוֹרָם שׁוֹאֵב,

‹ from the › ‹ of their › ‹ and from their › ‹ I [am forced to] »
streams sorrow wellsprings draw?
[of troubles] [directed at me]*

---

(1) *Psalms* 13:6. (2) Cf. *Lamentations* 1:1. (3) Cf. 1:8; many editions of *Selichos* read וָאֱהִי לְנִדָּה, *and I became [like] a menstruant*, cf. *Lamentations* 1:17. (4) Cf. *Hosea* 9:17. (5) *Isaiah* 49:21. (6) Cf. *Psalms* 102:9. (7) Cf. *Numbers* 14:9. (8) Cf. *Psalms* 40:16. (9) 109:25.

מִפַּלְגֵי יְגוֹנָם — *From the streams of their sorrow [directed at me]*, the flood of troubles the oppressors bring upon Israel (*Arugas*

HaBosem). Alternatively: *from [my] flowing [tears] brought on by the sorrows they placed upon me* (*Masbir*).

וְהֵמָּה רוֹבְצִים וְשׁוֹכְבִים כְּעוֹרֵב וְכִזְאָב,¹*

《 and wolf;* 〈 like raven 〈 and lie back 〈 — they 《 And as
sprawl for them

וַאֲנִי עָנִי וְכוֹאֵב.²

《 and 〈— I am 〈 but as
in pain. afflicted for me

אֵיךְ שׂוֹנְאַי כָּל טָהֳרָה שָׁכְנוּ בְצִיּוֹן,

《 in Zion? 〈 now 〈 that is 〈 of all 〈 that 〈 How is it
dwell pure haters

מִי הֶאֱמִין כָּזֶה מִי עָלָה לוֹ בְּרֶצְיוֹן,³*

《 as [his] 〈 would have 〈 Who 《 anything 〈 would have 〈 Who
desire?* thought [this] up like this? believed

וְהֵמָּה עֲשִׁירִים נְשִׂיאִים נְתוּנִים עֶלְיוֹן,

《 supreme; 〈 placed 〈 princes, 〈 — they are 《 And as
rich men, for them

וַאֲנִי עָנִי וְאֶבְיוֹן.⁴

《 and 〈— I am 《 but as
destitute. poor for me

אֵיךְ דָּרוּ בְהֵיכָלוֹתַי וְשָׁכְנוּ בָם שָׁכוֹן,

《 as an ongoing 〈 in 〈 and 〈 in my Temples 〈 have they 〈 How
dwelling, them dwelled come to live

מֵעֶלְיוֹן לְתַחְתּוֹן וּמִתַּחְתּוֹן לְתִיכוֹן,⁵*

《 to the middle?* 〈 and from the 〈 to the lower, 〈 from the
lower upper section

---

(1) Cf. *Judges* 7:25; *Psalms* 83:12. (2) 69:30. (3) Some editions read בְּרַעְיוֹן,
in [his] thought. (4) *Psalms* 40:18. (5) Cf. *Ezekiel* 41:7.

כְּעוֹרֵב וְכִזְאָב — *Like raven and wolf.* Having
robbed us of our all, the oppressor nations
lie comfortably and satiated, just as the
predatory raven and wolf do after devouring
their prey. Alternatively: The phrase alludes
to עוֹרֵב, *Oreb*, and זְאֵב, *Zeeb*, two Midianite
generals who tormented Israel freely, yet
rested securely, until they were defeated by
Gideon's men (see *Judges* 7:25). Both interpretations appear in *Arugas HaBosem*.

בְּרֶצְיוֹן — *As [his] desire*; i.e., "Who could
possibly desire such a thing?" Alternatively:
בְּרַעְיוֹן, *in [His] thought*; i.e., "Who could
imagine that God would do such a thing?"

מֵעֶלְיוֹן לְתַחְתּוֹן וּמִתַּחְתּוֹן לְתִיכוֹן — *From the*

*upper section to the lower, and from
the lower to the middle.* The enemy took
over the entire Temple complex, from the
Temple Mount [עֶלְיוֹן, *heights*] to the Courtyard [which was six cubits *lower* than the
Sanctuary itself] to the Temple [which
stood in the *center* of the complex] (*Arugas
HaBosem*).

Alternatively: The entire stich alludes to
the Temple edifice, which was surrounded
on three sides by a U-shaped structure of
three stories, *the lowest ascending to the
highest by way of the middle* (*Ezekiel* 41:7).
Thus, the *paytan* means that the enemy
made itself at home in every section of the
Temple.

וְהֵמָּה יָרְשׁוּ הוֹן זָהָב וַאֲדַרְכּוֹן,

《 and of coins; 〈 of gold 〈 a 〈 — they 《 And as for
treasure have them
inherited

וַאֲנִי לְצֶלַע נָכוֹן.¹

《 am I 〈 — to crip- 〈 but as
prone. pling pain for me

אֵיךְ חֶשְׁבְּנוֹתַי נָפוֹצוּ וְהֵמָּה עָלוּ בְּמַחְשְׁבוֹתֶיךָ,

《 [only] 〈 were 〈 while 《 been 〈 have my calcula- 〈 How
in Your thoughts? taken up they confounded, tions [of the time
of redemption]

זָכְרֵנוּ נָא וּפָקְדֵנוּ בִּישׁוּעָתֶךָ² מֵעוֹבְדֵי בִלְתֶּךָ,

《 other- 〈 from those 〈 with Your 〈 and 〈 please, 〈 Remem-
than-You. who worship salvation recall us, ber us,

וְהֵמָּה קַלְּעֵם וּבַלְּעֵם מִמְּכוֹן שִׁבְתֶּךָ,

《 of Your 〈 from the 〈 and swallow 〈 — hurl 《 And as
dwelling, place them up them away for them

וַאֲנִי בְּרֹב חַסְדְּךָ אָבוֹא בֵיתֶךָ.³

《 Your 〈 will I 〈 of Your 〈— through 《 but as
house. enter kindness the abun- for me
dance

ALL, WHILE STANDING:

אֵל מֶלֶךְ יוֹשֵׁב עַל כִּסֵּא רַחֲמִים, מִתְנַהֵג

〈 Who acts 《 of mercy, 〈 the throne 〈 on 〈 Who sits 〈 King 〈 O God,

בַּחֲסִידוּת, מוֹחֵל עֲוֹנוֹת עַמּוֹ, מַעֲבִיר רִאשׁוֹן

〈 [sins,] one 〈 Who 《 of His 〈 the sins 〈 Who 《 with kindness,
removes people, pardons

רִאשׁוֹן,⁴ מַרְבֶּה מְחִילָה לַחַטָּאִים וּסְלִיחָה לַפּוֹשְׁעִים,

《 to willful 〈 and 〈 to unintentional 〈 pardon 〈 Who abun- 《 by one,
sinners, forgiveness sinners dantly grants

עֹשֶׂה צְדָקוֹת עִם כָּל בָּשָׂר וָרוּחַ, לֹא כְרָעָתָם

〈 in accord 〈 — not 《 and 〈 [beings 〈 all 〈 with 〈 acts of 〈 Who
with their spirit of] flesh generosity performs
wickedness

תִּגְמוֹל. ❖ אֵל הוֹרֵיתָ לָּנוּ לוֹמַר שְׁלֹשׁ עֶשְׂרֵה, וּזְכוֹר

〈 remem- 《 the Thirteen 〈 to 〈 us 〈 You 〈 O God, 《 do You
ber [Attributes of Mercy]; recite taught repay them!

---

(1) Cf. *Psalms* 38:18. (2) Cf. 106:4. (3) 5:8. (4) *Rosh Hashanah* 17a.

לָנוּ הַיּוֹם בְּרִית שְׁלֹשׁ עֶשְׂרֵה, כְּמוֹ שֶׁהוֹדַעְתָּ לֶעָנָיו

⟨ to the ⟨ You made ⟨ as ⟪ of [these] Thirteen, ⟨ the ⟨ today ⟨ for us
humble one known covenant
[Moses]

מִקֶּדֶם, כְּמוֹ שֶׁכָּתוּב, וַיֵּרֶד יהוה בֶּעָנָן וַיִּתְיַצֵּב עִמּוֹ

⟨ with ⟨ and stood ⟨ in a ⟨ And HASHEM ⟪ it is written: ⟨ as ⟪ in ancient
him cloud descended times,

שָׁם, וַיִּקְרָא בְשֵׁם יהוה.[1]

⟪ of ⟨ with the ⟨ and He ⟪ there,
HASHEM. Name called out

CONGREGATION, THEN *CHAZZAN*:

וַיַּעֲבֹר יהוה עַל פָּנָיו וַיִּקְרָא:

⟪ and ⟪ [Moses'] ⟨ before ⟨ And HASHEM passed
proclaimed: face,

CONGREGATION AND *CHAZZAN* RECITE LOUDLY AND IN UNISON:

יהוה, יהוה, אֵל, רַחוּם, וְחַנּוּן, אֶרֶךְ אַפַּיִם,

⟨ to anger, ⟨ Slow ⟪ and ⟨ Compassionate ⟨ God, ⟨ HASHEM, ⟨ HASHEM,
Gracious,

וְרַב חֶסֶד, וֶאֱמֶת, נֹצֵר חֶסֶד לָאֲלָפִים, נֹשֵׂא עָוֹן,

⟨ of ⟨ Forgiver ⟪ for ⟨ of ⟨ Preserver ⟪ and ⟨ in ⟨ and
iniquity, thousands kindness Truth, Kindness Abundant
[of generations],

וָפֶשַׁע, וְחַטָּאָה, וְנַקֵּה.[2] וְסָלַחְתָּ לַעֲוֺנֵנוּ וּלְחַטָּאתֵנוּ

⟪ and our sins, ⟨ our ⟨ May You ⟪ and Who ⟨ and inadvertent ⟨ willful sin,
iniquities forgive absolves. sin,

וּנְחַלְתָּנוּ.[3] סְלַח לָנוּ אָבִינוּ כִּי חָטָאנוּ, מְחַל לָנוּ

⟨ us, ⟨ pardon ⟪ we have ⟨ for ⟪ our ⟨ us, ⟨ Forgive ⟪ and make us
sinned; Father, Your heritage.

מַלְכֵּנוּ כִּי פָשָׁעְנוּ. כִּי אַתָּה אֲדֹנָי טוֹב וְסַלָּח,

⟪ and ⟨ are ⟨ O Lord, ⟨ You, ⟨ For ⟪ we have ⟨ for ⟪ our King,
forgiving, good willfully sinned.

וְרַב חֶסֶד לְכָל קֹרְאֶיךָ.[4]

⟪ who call ⟨ to all ⟨ kind ⟨ and
upon You. abundantly

---

(1) *Exodus* 34:5. (2) 34:6-7. (3) 34:9. (4) *Psalms* 86:5.

סליחה סה / SELICHAH 65
(פזמון)

THE ARK IS OPENED.

CHAZZAN, THEN CONGREGATION:

יַחְבִּיאֵנוּ* צֵל יָדוֹ¹ תַּחַת כַּנְפֵי הַשְּׁכִינָה,

《 of the Divine 〈 the 〈 beneath 《 of His 〈 in the 〈 May He
Presence;   wings   hand, shelter conceal us*

חֹן יָחֹן* כִּי יִבְחֹן לֵב עָקוֹב לְהָכִינָה,*

《 to re- 〈 that is 〈 the 〈 He 〈when〈 may He act
establish it.* deceitful, heart probes graciously*

קוּמָה נָא אֱלֹהֵינוּ עֻזָּה² עֻזִּי נָא,

《 please! 〈 O my 〈display Your《 our God, 〈please,〈 Rise up,
          Strength, strength,

יהוה לְשַׁוְעָתֵנוּ הַאֲזִינָה.³

《 listen! 〈 to our outcry 〈 HASHEM,

CONGREGATION, THEN CHAZZAN:

אָנָא אֵלֵךְ מֵרוּחֶךָ וְאָנָה מִפָּנֶיךָ אֶבְרָח,⁴

《 can I flee? 〈 from Your 〈 And to 《 from Your 〈 can I go 〈 Where
            Presence where   spirit?   [to hide]

בִּינוֹתִי אֵין מָנוֹס פְּאַת מַעֲרָב וּמִזְרָח,

《 or east; 〈 of west 〈even to the《escape, 〈 that 〈I understand
                    far corners   there is no

---

(1) Cf. *Isaiah* 41:2. (2) Cf. *Psalms* 68:29. (3) Cf. 39:13. (4) 139:7.

§ **יַחְבִּיאֵנוּ** — *May He conceal us.* The first stanza of this *pizmon* contains an acrostic of the *paytan's* name — יִצְחָק, *Yitzchak*. The first three lines of each of the remaining stanzas follow an *aleph-beis* acrostic, while the initial letters of the respective fourth lines complete the composer's signature — בֶּן שְׁמוּאֵל, *son of Shmuel*. R' Yitzchak ben Shmuel (12th-century France), better known as "the Ri," was a great-grandson of *Rashi* and a nephew and disciple of both *Rashbam* and *Rabbeinu Tam*.

Among all the Tosafists, only the name of *Rabbeinu Tam* appears more often than does *Ri's* in our edition of *Tosafos*. After *Rabbeinu Tam* moved from Ramerupt to

Troyes, *Ri* succeeded him as head of the Talmudic academy at Ramerupt and later settled at Dampierre, where he founded a flourishing yeshivah. Under *Ri's* tenure, the Tosafist method of Talmudical analysis reached its fullest expression. His name is mentioned on most pages of the *Tosafos*, and even many of the insights given anonymously are attributed to him in other sources.

חֹן יָחֹן ... לְהָכִינָה — *May He act graciously to reestablish it.* Though God will surely find our hearts filled with deceit, we pray that He will mercifully forgive us and let us begin as if we had not sinned before.

גֻּלְגַּלְתִּי אַחֲרֶיךָ לְשַׁחֲרֶךָ, יַחַד כַּגֵּר כָּאֶזְרָח,*

《 and citizen ⟨proselyte⟨together 《 seeking You, 《 after You, ⟨ I have been
[alike].*　　　　　　[with]　　　　　　　　　　　　drawn

בְּהִשָּׁפְטִי, לְצִדְקָתִי הַשְׂמְאִילָה וְהַיְמִינָה.*

《 and to the ⟨ [search] to the left ⟨ to vindicate 《 When I am
right.*　　　　　　　　　　　　　me　　　　　judged,

יהוה לְשַׁוְעָתֵנוּ הַאֲזִינָה.

《 listen! ⟨ to our outcry ⟨ HASHEM,

CONGREGATION, THEN CHAZZAN:

דּוֹק שָׁמֶיךָ בְּיַרְכְּתֵיהֶם, גַּם שָׁם אִם אֶסַּק,¹

《 I ascend, ⟨ if ⟨ there ⟨— even 《 to its utmost ends ⟨ sky ⟨The out-
spread

הוֹדְךָ שָׁם לְשָׁפְטֵנִי, עַל כָּל הַנֶּעֱסָק,

《 my dealings. ⟨ all ⟨ for ⟨ to judge me ⟨ is ⟨ Your
there　glory

וַהֲגִיגִי בְּרֹב שְׁגָגֵי כְּכִיּוֹר אֵשׁ הֻנְסַק,²

《 was lit: ⟨ that ⟨ that they ⟨ of my ⟨ contain ⟨ My
with　are like　inadver-　so many　thoughts
fire　an oven　tent sins

נִצְרָה דַל שְׂפָתֵינוּ³ וְתֵן לָנוּ חֲנִינָה.

《 grace! ⟨ us ⟨ and ⟨ of our lips ⟨ the ⟨ Guard
grant　door

יהוה לְשַׁוְעָתֵנוּ הַאֲזִינָה.

《 listen! ⟨ to our outcry ⟨ HASHEM,

CONGREGATION, THEN CHAZZAN:

זָוֵי שְׁאוֹל בְּמַחְתַּרְתּוֹ אַף כִּי אַצִּיעַ,⁴

《 [there] I ⟨ if ⟨— even 《 in its tunnel ⟨ of the low- ⟨ In the
make my bed,　　　　　　　　　　　　est depths,　corners

---

(1) Cf. *Psalms* 139:8. (2) Cf. 39:4. (3) Cf. 141:3. (4) Cf. 139:8.

בְּהִשָּׁפְטִי יַחַד כַּגֵּר כָּאֶזְרָח — *Together [with]*
proselyte and citizen [alike]. The introduction of the phrase *together [with]*
proselyte and citizen alike presumably is
based on the juxtaposition of the Scriptural
verses: ... *both the citizen and proselyte*
who dwell in your midst. For on this day
He will grant atonement to you to purify
you; from all your sins, before HASHEM
you will be purified (Leviticus 16:29-30).

הַשְׂמְאִילָה וְהַיְמִינָה — *[Search] to the left and*
to the right]. The prophet Michayhu described his vision of the Heavenly Court: *I*
saw HASHEM sitting on His Throne and all
the legions of heaven standing before Him,
to His right and to His left (I Kings 22:19).
Rashi (based on *Midrash Tanchuma,*
Mishpatim 15) asks: Is there really a left side
in heaven? Is it not stated, *The right hand*
of HASHEM is raised triumphantly; the

חָזִיתִי וְהִנָּךְ שָׁם¹ לְחַבְּרָה וּלְהַפְצִיעַ,

《 and wounds. 〈 to [punish with] 〈 there 〈 and 〈 I look,
bruises   You are

טָפַשׁ לִבִּי וְהֶחֱרַד בִּי כִּי בֵינִי לְבֵין מָוֶת כְּפָסִיעַ,²

《 was but 〈 death 〈 and 〈between〈 for 《within〈 trembling 〈 was my 〈 Stupefied
a step.   between   me,   heart,
                     me

שְׁמֹר שְׁאֵרִית נִדָּחַי בְּכָל פִּנָּה וּפִנָּה.

《 in each and every corner — 〈 of my dis- 〈 the remnant 〈 Guard
persed people

יהוה לְשַׁוְעָתֵנוּ הַאֲזִינָה.

《 listen! 〈 to our outcry 〈 HASHEM,

CONGREGATION, THEN *CHAZZAN:*

יָם גָּדוֹל בְּאַחֲרִיתוֹ אַף כִּי אֶשְׁכּוֹנָה,³

《 I should dwell, 〈 if 〈 even 〈 — at the far end 《 that is 〈 The
great ocean

כַּף יְמִינְךָ תֹּאחֲזֵנִי⁴ וּמַה לְנַפְשִׁי אֶשְׁכּוֹנָה,⁵

《 from my 〈 does my 〈 So what 《 would grasp 〈 Your right hand
living there? soul obtain profit   me.

לוּלֵא רֹב רַחֲמֶיךָ דְּרָכַי לֹא אֶסְכּוֹנָה,⁶

《 I could not maintain; 〈 my ways 〈 mercy, 〈 for Your 〈 Were
abundant   it not

מְשֹׁךְ חֶסֶד לִנְגָּשִׂים תַּחַת יַד עֲדִינָה.

《 of the pleasure- 〈 the 〈 under 〈 to those 〈 kindness 〈 extend
seeking [tyrant]. hand   oppressed

יהוה לְשַׁוְעָתֵנוּ הַאֲזִינָה.

《 listen! 〈 to our outcry 〈 HASHEM,

CONGREGATION, THEN *CHAZZAN:*

מִדַּת לַיְלָה תְּסוֹבְבֵנִי אָז יְשׁוּפֵנִי חֹשֶׁךְ,⁷

《 by 〈 I will be 〈 surely 《 surrounds me, 〈 of night 〈 When the
darkness! obscured then   essence

---

(1) Cf. *Psalms* 139:8. (2) Cf. *I Samuel* 20:3. (3) Cf. *Psalms* 139:9. (4) 139:10.
(5) Some editions read מַה לָּךְ אֱמוּנָה, *So what need my soul [to worry]?*
I shall stand firm. (6) Cf. *Psalms* 139:3. (7) Cf. 139:11.

---

right hand of HASHEM does deeds of valor
(*Psalms* 118:16)? And, *Your right hand,*
HASHEM, is adorned with strength; Your
right hand, HASHEM, smashes the enemy
(*Exodus* 15:6)? Since both verses mention

God's right hand twice, and omit any reference to His left hand, we can infer that God
has no left side. Rather the prophet meant
מִימִינוּ, *those angelic advocates who spoke*
favorably [of the king to whom the prophet

נְגוֹהוֹת לָךְ הָאֲפֵלוֹת¹ כְּאוֹר יָהֶל וּמוֹשָׁךְ,

But bright ⟨ for ⟩ You ⟩⟩ is even ⟨ the gloom, ⟩⟩ like ⟨ daylight's ⟩ dawning ⟨ and ⟩⟩ growing.

סָמַר בְּשָׂרִי מִפַּחְדְּךָ² כְּשֹׁךְ נָחָשׁ נוֹשָׁךְ,

Become ⟨ prickly ⟩ did my ⟨ flesh ⟩⟩ from fear ⟨ of You, ⟩⟩ as if from ⟨ the bite ⟩ of a ⟨ snake ⟩⟩ that is ⟨ venomous,

וְעַל הַדָּם כְּמוֹ נִרְדָּם בְּיַרְכְּתֵי הַסְּפִינָה.³

and ⟨ [in fear] ⟩ for ⟨ my ⟩ blood, ⟩⟩ like ⟨ [Jonah] in a deep sleep ⟨ [Jonah] ⟨ in the bilges ⟩⟩ of the ship.

יהוה לְשַׁוְעָתֵנוּ הַאֲזִינָה.

⟨ HASHEM, ⟩ to our outcry ⟨ listen! ⟩⟩

CONGREGATION, THEN CHAZZAN:

עָלַי שַׁתָּ כַּפֶּכָה אָחוֹר וָקֶדֶם צַרְתָּנִי,⁴

Upon ⟨ me ⟩ You ⟨ placed ⟨ Your ⟩⟩ hand; ⟨ You have ⟨ constrained me ⟨ behind ⟩ both ⟨ and before. ⟩⟩

פְּנֵה אֶפְנֶה אָנָה וְאָנָה אָרְחִי וְרִבְעִי זֵרִיתָנִי,⁵

Turn ⟨ do I turn, ⟩⟩ here ⟨ there: ⟨ [both] ⟩⟩ and ⟨ when I walk on the way ⟨ and when I lie down ⟩ You have circumscribed me. ⟩⟩

צֵרַפְתָּנִי בַּל תִּמְצָא⁶ יהוה חֲקַרְתָּנִי,⁷

You have ⟨ tested me ⟨ and did ⟨ not ⟨ find any [fault]; ⟩⟩ HASHEM, ⟩⟩ You have ⟨ scrutinized me,

אָח וְאָחוֹת וְצַחְצָחוֹת* בְּלַעַג לָשׁוֹן וְאֵין בִּינָה.⁸

[when] ⟨ and sister ⟨ [of Nebaioth, brother his wife] [Esau] ⟨ and sister ⟩⟩ in [their] smooth coaxings [to convert me]* ⟩⟩ [— I heard] ⟩ speech ⟨ garbled ⟨ with no ⟩ understanding. ⟩⟩

יהוה לְשַׁוְעָתֵנוּ הַאֲזִינָה.

⟨ HASHEM, ⟩ to our outcry ⟨ listen! ⟩⟩

---

(1) Cf. *Isaiah* 59:9. (2) Cf. *Psalms* 119:120. (3) Cf. *Jonah* 1:5.
(4) Cf. *Psalms* 139:5. (5) Cf. 139:3. (6) 17:3. (7) 139:1. (8) Cf. *Isaiah* 33:19.

was speaking], וּמִשְׂמֹאלוֹ, *and those angelic accusers who spoke unfavorably.* Thus, the *paytan* pleads that God should turn the left, the accusing angel, into the right, an advocate for Israel (*Arugas HaBosem*).

אָח וְאָחוֹת וְצַחְצָחוֹת — *[When] brother [Esau] and sister [of Nebaioth, his wife] in [their] smooth coaxings [to convert me].* There are an astonishing number of interpretations of this phrase. Our translation is based on the simple meaning of אָח וְאָחוֹת, *brother and sister.* אָח refers to Esau, whom the prophet called אָח לְיַעֲקֹב, *a brother to Jacob* (*Malachi* 1:2); אָחוֹת to Esau's wife, whom the Torah twice calls אֲחוֹת נְבָיוֹת, *the sister of Nebaioth* (*Genesis* 28:9 and 36:3). The word צַחְצָחוֹת is a poetic form of צָחוּת, *smooth language.* Thus אָח וְאָחוֹת are the

CONGREGATION, THEN *CHAZZAN:*

קַדְּמָה נָא רַחֲמֶיךָ¹ כִּי לְךָ טוֹב לְהוֹדוֹת,²

《 to give thanks. 〈 it is 〈 to 〈 for《 may Your 〈please,〈 Advance
good You mercies, to meet us,

רְצֵה שַׁוְעַת גְּדָיֶיךָ וַעֲמַל צֹאן אוֹבְדוֹת,

《 that is lost: 〈 of the 〈 the 《 of Your 〈 toward 〈 Be
flock suffering lambs, the outcry favorable

תְּפַלְּטֵנוּ, הֱיֵה לָנוּ לְצוּר מָעוֹז לְבֵית מְצוּדוֹת,³

《 a fortress! 〈 of 〈 a rock 〈 for us 〈 Be 《 Rescue us!
strength,

לְכָה לָּנוּ לִישׁוּעָה⁴ כְּלְשִׁמְעוֹן וְלֵוִי אֲחֵי דִינָה,⁵

《 of 〈 the 〈 and 〈 as [You did] 《 for our 〈 to us 〈 Come
Dinah. brothers Levi, for Shimon salvation

יהוה לְשַׁוְעָתֵנוּ הַאֲזִינָה.

《 listen! 〈 to our outcry 〈 HASHEM,

ALL, WHILE STANDING:

אֵל מֶלֶךְ יוֹשֵׁב עַל כִּסֵּא רַחֲמִים, מִתְנַהֵג

〈 Who acts 《 of mercy, 〈 the throne 〈 on 〈 Who sits 〈 King 〈 O God,

בַּחֲסִידוּת, מוֹחֵל עֲוֹנוֹת עַמּוֹ, מַעֲבִיר רִאשׁוֹן

〈 [sins,] one 〈 Who 《 of His 〈 the sins 〈 Who 《 with kindness,
removes people, pardons

רִאשׁוֹן,⁶ מַרְבֶּה מְחִילָה לְחַטָּאִים וּסְלִיחָה לַפּוֹשְׁעִים,

《 to willful 〈 and 〈 to unintentional 〈 pardon 〈 Who abun- 《 by one,
sinners, forgiveness sinners dantly grants

עֹשֶׂה צְדָקוֹת עִם כָּל בָּשָׂר וָרוּחַ, לֹא כְרָעָתָם

〈 in accord with 〈— not 《 and 〈 [beings 〈 all 〈 with 〈 acts of 〈 Who
their wickedness spirit of] flesh generosity performs

תִּגְמוֹל. ❖ אֵל הוֹרֵיתָ לָּנוּ לוֹמַר שְׁלֹשׁ עֶשְׂרֵה, וּזְכוֹר

〈 remem- 《 the Thirteen 〈 to 〈 You 〈 O God, 《 do You
ber [Attributes of Mercy]; recite taught repay them!

---

(1) Cf. *Psalms* 79:8. (2) From the blessing after the recitation of *Hallel*; based on *Psalms* 92:2.
(3) Cf. 31:3. (4) Cf. 80:3. (5) Cf. *Genesis* 34:25. (6) *Rosh Hashanah* 17a.

descendants of Esau, the Christians, who with their smooth coaxing speech attempt to convert the Jews. Following the same concept, some interpret *brother and sister* as a reference to Christian clergy: *friar and nun.*

Other interpretations are: אָח and אָחוֹת are types of ovens (see *Jeremiah* 36:22), and צַחְצָחוֹת is thirst or dehydration (see *Isaiah* 58:11); אָח is an expression of anguish akin to "alas" (see *Ezekiel* 6:11), אָחוֹת means *speech* (see *Job* 13:17).

לָנוּ הַיּוֹם בְּרִית שְׁלֹשׁ עֶשְׂרֵה, כְּמוֹ שֶׁהוֹדַעְתָּ לֶעָנָיו

‹ to the   ‹ You made   ‹ as   « of [these] Thirteen,   ‹ the   ‹ today   ‹ for us
humble one   known   covenant
[Moses]

מִקֶּדֶם, כְּמוֹ שֶׁכָּתוּב, וַיֵּרֶד יהוה בֶּעָנָן וַיִּתְיַצֵּב עִמּוֹ

‹ with   ‹ and stood   ‹ in a   ‹ And HASHEM   « it is written: ‹ as   « in ancient
him   cloud   descended   times,

שָׁם, וַיִּקְרָא בְשֵׁם יהוה.[1]

« of   ‹ with the   ‹ and He   « there,
HASHEM.   Name   called out

CONGREGATION, THEN CHAZZAN:

וַיַּעֲבֹר יהוה עַל פָּנָיו וַיִּקְרָא:

« and   « [Moses']   ‹ before   ‹ And HASHEM passed
proclaimed: face,

CONGREGATION AND CHAZZAN RECITE LOUDLY AND IN UNISON:

יהוה, יהוה, אֵל, רַחוּם, וְחַנּוּן, אֶרֶךְ אַפַּיִם,

‹ to anger,   ‹ Slow   « and   ‹ Compassionate ‹ God,   ‹ HASHEM,   ‹ HASHEM,
                 Gracious,

וְרַב חֶסֶד, וֶאֱמֶת, נֹצֵר חֶסֶד לָאֲלָפִים, נֹשֵׂא עָוֹן,

‹ of   ‹ Forgiver   « for   ‹ of   ‹ Preserver   « and   ‹ in   ‹ and
iniquity,   thousands   kindness   Truth,   Kindness Abundant
            [of generations],

וָפֶשַׁע, וְחַטָּאָה, וְנַקֵּה.[2] וְסָלַחְתָּ לַעֲוֹנֵנוּ וּלְחַטָּאתֵנוּ

« and our sins,   ‹ our   ‹ May You   « and Who   ‹ and inadvertent ‹ willful sin,
         iniquities   forgive   absolves.   sin,

וּנְחַלְתָּנוּ.[3] סְלַח לָנוּ אָבִינוּ כִּי חָטָאנוּ, מְחַל לָנוּ

‹ us,   ‹ pardon   « we have   ‹ for   « our   ‹ us,   ‹ Forgive   « and make us
            sinned;   Father,   Your heritage.

מַלְכֵּנוּ כִּי פָשָׁעְנוּ. כִּי אַתָּה אֲדֹנָי טוֹב וְסַלָּח,

« and   ‹ are   ‹ O Lord,   ‹ You,   ‹ For   « we have   ‹ for   « our King,
forgiving,   good   willfully sinned.

וְרַב חֶסֶד לְכָל קֹרְאֶיךָ.[4]

« who call   ‹ to all   ‹ kind   ‹ and
upon You.   abundantly

---

(1) Exodus 34:5. (2) 34:6-7. (3) 34:9. (4) Psalms 86:5.

PREFATORY VERSES TO SELICHAH 66 / פסוקי הקדמה לסליחה סו

תָּבוֹא אֵלֶיךָ תְּפִלָּתֵנוּ אֶל הֵיכַל קָדְשֶׁךָ.¹ תָּבוֹא

❬ Let come ❫ of Your ❬ the ❬ toward ❬ our prayers ❬ to You ❬ Let come
Holiness. Sanctuary

לְפָנֶיךָ אֶנְקַת אָסִיר, כְּגֹדֶל זְרוֹעֶךָ, הוֹתֵר בְּנֵי תְמוּתָה.²

❫ to die. ❬ those ❬ spare ❬ of Your ❬ as befits ❫ of the ❬ the groan ❬ before
condemned might, the prisoner; You
greatness

לִפְקֹחַ עֵינַיִם עִוְרוֹת, לְהוֹצִיא מִמַּסְגֵּר אַסִּיר, מִבֵּית

❬ from a ❫ a ❬ from jail ❬ to take out ❫ that are ❬ eyes ❬ To open
house prisoner; blind;

כֶּלֶא יֹשְׁבֵי חֹשֶׁךְ.³ כִּי לֹא בָזָה וְלֹא שִׁקַּץ עֱנוּת

❬ the sup- ❬ loathed ❬ nor ❬ despised ❬ He has ❬ For ❫ in ❬ those ❬ of
plication neither darkness. dwelling detention

עָנִי, וְלֹא הִסְתִּיר פָּנָיו מִמֶּנּוּ; וּבְשַׁוְּעוֹ אֵלָיו

❬ to ❬ but when ❫ from ❬ His ❬ has He ❬ nor ❫ of the
Him, he cried him; face concealed poor,

שָׁמֵעַ.⁴

❫ He heard.

כְּרַחֵם אָב עַל בָּנִים, כֵּן תְּרַחֵם יהוה עָלֵינוּ.⁵

❫ on us. ❬ HASHEM, ❬ have ❬ so ❫ his ❬ toward ❬ a ❬ As merciful as
mercy, children, father is

לַיהוה הַיְשׁוּעָה, עַל עַמְּךָ בִרְכָתֶךָ סֶּלָה.⁶ יהוה

❬ HASHEM, ❫ Selah. ❫ is Your ❬ Your ❬ upon ❫ is salvation, ❬ To HASHEM
blessing, people

צְבָאוֹת עִמָּנוּ, מִשְׂגָּב לָנוּ אֱלֹהֵי יַעֲקֹב סֶלָה.⁷

❫ Selah. ❫ of Jacob, ❬ is the God ❬ for us ❬ a ❫ is with us, ❬ Master of
stronghold Legions,

יהוה צְבָאוֹת, אַשְׁרֵי אָדָם בֹּטֵחַ בָּךְ.⁸ יהוה הוֹשִׁיעָה,

❫ save! ❬ HASHEM, ❫ in You. ❬ who ❬ is the ❬ — praise- ❫ Master of ❬ HASHEM,
trusts man worthy Legions

הַמֶּלֶךְ יַעֲנֵנוּ בְיוֹם קָרְאֵנוּ.⁹

❫ we call. ❬ on the ❬ answer ❬ May the
day us King

(1) Cf. *Jonah* 2:8. (2) *Psalms* 79:11. (3) *Isaiah* 42:7 (4) *Psalms* 22:25.
(5) Cf. 103:13. (6) 3:9. (7) 46:8. (8) 84:13. (9) 20:10.

סליחה סו / SELICHAH 66

(עקדה)

אֱלֹהֵינוּ וֵאלֹהֵי אֲבוֹתֵינוּ:

《 of our forefathers: 〈 and the God 〈 Our God

אֶזְרָחִי¹ מֵעֵבֶר הַנָּהָר,*² אֵלֶיךָ רָץ וְלֹא אֵחַר.

《 delay. 〈 and did 〈 he 〈 to You 《 the River 〈 from 〈 [Abraham,]
not   ran   [Euphrates],*   across   the Ezrachite,

בְּחַנְתּוֹ בְּנִסְיוֹנוֹת עֶשֶׂר,³ וְנִמְצָא שָׁלֵם בְּלִי חֶסֶר.

《 a 〈 without 〈 whole, 〈 and he 《 ten, 〈 with tests, 〈 You tested
deficiency.   was found   him

גֹּרַשׁ מֵאֶרֶץ מוֹלַדְתּוֹ, גּוֹי בָּעוֹלָם שַׂמְתּוֹ.

You estab- 〈 of the 〈 as the [major] 《 of his 〈 from 〈 [Though] he
lished him.   world   nation   birth,   the land   was driven

דְּבָרְךָ הֵקִים וְלֹא הֵפֵר, וְנָם אָנֹכִי עָפָר וָאֵפֶר.⁴

《 and ashes. 〈 dust 〈 I am 《 and 《 violate 〈 and 〈 he 〈 Your word
he said,   [it],   did not   upheld

הִקְרִיב חָלָב וְחֶמְאָה,⁵ וְנָחֱנַט פְּרִי לִמְאָה.⁶

《 at age one 〈 and bore fruit 《 and butter, 〈 [the angels] 〈 He offered
hundred.   [Isaac]   milk

וְנֶאֱמַת לוֹ הַעֲלֵהוּ לְעוֹלָה, בָּקַע עֵצִים וְעָרַךְ וְהֶעֱלָה.

《 and brought 〈 and ar- 〈 the 〈 so 《 as a burnt- 〈 Bring him up 《 to 〈 Then You
him up.   ranged [it]   wood   he cut   offering,   [on the altar]   him,   said

זְכָר לָנוּ הַיּוֹם עֲקֵדָתוֹ, וְהַשְׁלָמַת יְחִידָתוֹ.*

《 his soul.* 〈 how he willingly 《 his binding 〈 today 〈 in our 〈 Re-
surrendered   [of Isaac],   favor   member

---

(1) See comm. to *Selichah* 58, s.v. אִיתָן לְמֻד דָּעַת. (2) Cf. *Joshua* 24:2.
(3) See *Mishnah, Avos* 5:4. (4) Cf. *Genesis* 18:27. (5) See 18:8. (6) See 21:5.

אֶזְרָחִי מֵעֵבֶר הַנָּהָר — *[Abraham,] the Ezrachite, from across the River [Euphrates].* The Talmud teaches that Ethan the Ezrachite (*Psalms* 89:1) was Abraham. He was called Ezrachite because he came from a country that was to the east [מִזְרָח, *mizrach*] of *Eretz Yisrael* (*Bava Basra* 15a).

This unsigned *selichah* follows an *aleph-beis* acrostic. It is one of the genre called *akeidah*, for it first describes Abraham's binding of Isaac (see *Genesis* Ch. 22), and then pleads for mercy in the merit of that deed.

וְהַשְׁלָמַת יְחִידָתוֹ — *How he willingly surrendered his soul.* The soul is called by five names in Hebrew, but not all of them are translatable into English. The Midrash lists the five names and their implications, as follows: (a) נֶפֶשׁ, the *lifeblood*, so to speak, since Scripture describes the power of life as residing in the blood (*Deuteronomy* 12:23); (b) רוּחַ, the *spirit*, is man's spiritual capability to rise up, but also to fall back down (see *Ecclesiastes* 3:21); (c) חַיָּה, *life* — man's body dies eventually, but the soul lives on forever; (d) נְשָׁמָה, man's higher *soul*; his intelligence

חֵן הַיּוֹם שִׁבְטֵי תָם,¹ וְתִשְׁכֹּן בְּמַקְהֲלוֹתָם.

《 among their ⟨ and let 《 of [Jacob] ⟨ for the ⟨ today ⟨ Show
assemblies.   our spirit the whole- tribes   gracious-
              dwell   hearted,   ness

טִיעַת מַטּוֹת שְׁנֵים עָשָׂר, מֶזֶג מֵהֶם אַל יֶחְסָר.²

《 be ⟨ let it ⟨ from 《 — the appro- 《 twelve ⟨ from ⟨The plantings
lacking. not   them   priate mixture   tribes,   [that sprout]
                       [of things good],

יְדִידוּת מִשְׁבְּנוֹתֶיךָ³ תְּבִיאֵם, בְּהַר נַחֲלָתְךָ תִּטָּעֵם.⁴

《 implant ⟨ of Your ⟨ and on 《 bring them, ⟨ Sanctuary ⟨ To Your
them.   heritage the Mount   beloved

כַּנֵּס כָּל פְּזוּרֵי נִדְּחֵיהֶם, נַהֲגֵם לְבֵית מַאֲוַיֵּיהֶם.

《 of their longing. ⟨ to the ⟨ and bring 《 of their exiles ⟨ the scat- ⟨ all ⟨ Gather
                      Temple   them   tered ones   in

לְקוּחִים⁵ מִמָּוֶת תַּחְשֹׂךְ, פֶּה מַשְׂטִין סְתֹם וַחֲשֹׂךְ.

《 and prevent ⟨ seal ⟨ of the ⟨ the 《 hold them ⟨ from ⟨The people taken
[from accusing].   Adversary mouth back;   death   [to be Yours],

נָשְׂאֵנוּ וְנַטְּלֵנוּ כִּימֵי עוֹלָם,⁶ וְכַפֵּר לָנוּ כָּל זָדוֹן וְנֶעְלָם.

《 or ⟨ delib- ⟨ for ⟨ for ⟨ and 《 of old, ⟨ as in ⟨ and lift ⟨ Carry us
inadvertent erate every us   provide   days   us up
[sin].   atonement

סְלַח וַעֲבֹר עַל פֶּשַׁע,⁷ וּמְחַל אַשְׁמָה וָרֶשַׁע.

《 and ⟨ [our] guilt ⟨ and 《 [our] rebel- ⟨ over ⟨ and pass ⟨ Forgive,
wickedness.   pardon liousness,

עֲנֵה הַיּוֹם כָּל מְיַחֲלֶיךָ, כִּי עֵינֵינוּ נְשׂוּאוֹת אֵלֶיךָ.⁸

《 to You. ⟨ are lifted up ⟨ our eyes ⟨ for 《who place their ⟨ all ⟨ today ⟨ May You
                                            hope in You,   those   answer

(1) See *Genesis* 25:27. (2) Cf. *Song of Songs* 7:3. (3) *Psalms* 84:2. (4) Cf. *Exodus* 15:17.
(5) See 6:7. (6) Cf. *Isaiah* 63:9. (7) Cf. *Micah* 7:18. (8) Cf. *Psalms* 123:1.

and personality; and (c) יְחִידָה, the soul's *uniqueness* among the many components of man, because virtually all of man's limbs and organs come in pairs — even the heart and brain have pairs of chambers or hemispheres — but there is only one soul (*Bereishis Rabbah* 14:9).

Various Midrashim refer to מְסִירַת נֶפֶשׁ, *self-sacrifice*, as הַשְׁלָמַת הַנֶּפֶשׁ. Thus, our stich alludes to Isaac's act of self-sacrifice in allowing himself to be slaughtered.

According to *Masbir* (based on *Psalms* 78:50), the terms חַיָּה and יְחִידָה may also refer to the body of man. Thus, the translation

would be: *how he willingly surrendered his body*. Nevertheless, the stich still alludes to Isaac's self-sacrifice.

Alternatively: הַשְׁלָמָה refers to *wholeheartedness*, and יְחִידָתוֹ to his *one and only [son]*. Thus, the stich alludes to Abraham's act of wholeheartedly offering his one and only son (*Matteh Levi*). [The expected grammatical form in this case would be in the masculine יְחִידוֹ (= יָחִיד שֶׁלוֹ), rather than the feminine יְחִידָתוֹ (= יְחִידָה שֶׁלוֹ). Presumably, according to *Matteh Levi*, the *paytan* used the feminine form יְחִידָתוֹ to fit the rhyme scheme.]

פְּדֵנוּ מִצָּרָה וְצוּקָה, וְתַעֲלֵנוּ מִשּׁוּחָה עֲמֻקָה.

《 that is deep. 〈 from the pit 〈 and raise us 《 and hardship, 〈 from trouble 〈 Redeem us

צַעֲקָתֵנוּ הַיּוֹם תְּקַבֵּל, וְתַצִּילֵנוּ מִידֵי מְחַבֵּל.

《 of [the Adversary] 〈 from the hands 〈 and save us 《 may You accept, 〈 today 〈 Our cry
who seeks to destroy.

קוֹמֵם בֵּית שְׁכִינַת הוֹדֶךְ, וְאַל תְּנַבֵּל כִּסֵּא כְבוֹדֶךְ.[1]

《 of Your Glory. 〈 the Throne 〈 demean 〈 and do not 《 that is glorious, 〈 of Your Presence 〈 the House 〈 Rebuild

רְפָא עַמְּךָ מִכָּל שֶׁבֶר, כִּי בָאוּ בָנִים עַד מַשְׁבֵּר.[2]

《 the birth canal. 〈 at 〈 have [Your] infants 〈 arrived 〈 for 《 fracture, 〈 of every 〈 Your people 〈 Heal

שָׁבֵץ אֲחָזַתְנוּ[3] כַּיּוֹלֵדָה, וְכֹחַ אַיִן לְלֵדָה.[2]

《 to give birth. 〈 there is not 〈 but 《 like a woman in labor, 《 have seized us, 〈 Spasms

❖ תִּגְאַל עַמְּךָ מֵהַבְהָב, כִּי עָלֶיךָ מַשְׁלִיכִים יָהַב.[4]

《 their burden. 〈 they cast 〈 upon You 〈 for 《 from Gehinnom, 〈 Your people 〈 Redeem

תַּנְחֵם לְעִיר הַבְּנוּיָה, תְּמַהֵר תִּשְׁבִּי מְנַחֵם* וּנְחֶמְיָה.*

《 and Nehemiah.* 〈 the Messiah,* 〈 [Elijah] the Tishbite, 〈 hasten 《 that is rebuilt, 〈 to the City 〈 Lead them

ALL, WHILE STANDING:

אֵל מֶלֶךְ יוֹשֵׁב עַל כִּסֵּא רַחֲמִים, מִתְנַהֵג

〈 Who acts 《 of mercy, 〈 the throne 〈 on 〈 Who sits 〈 King 〈 O God,

בַּחֲסִידוּת, מוֹחֵל עֲוֹנוֹת עַמּוֹ, מַעֲבִיר רִאשׁוֹן

〈 [sins,] one 〈 Who removes 《 of His people, 〈 the sins 〈 Who pardons 《 with kindness,

רִאשׁוֹן, מַרְבֶּה מְחִילָה לַחַטָּאִים וּסְלִיחָה לַפּוֹשְׁעִים,[5]

《 to willful sinners, 〈 and forgiveness 〈 to unintentional sinners 〈 pardon 〈 Who abundantly grants 《 by one,

---

(1) Cf. *Jeremiah* 14:21. (2) *II Kings* 19:3. (3) Cf. *II Samuel* 1:9. (4) Cf. *Psalms* 55:23. (5) *Rosh Hashanah* 17a.

מְנַחֵם — *The Messiah.* The Talmud states four opinions regarding the Messiah's given name: מְנַחֵם, *Menachem*; שִׁילֹה, *Shiloh*; יִנּוֹן, *Yinon* (see commentary to *Selichah* 42); and חֲנִינָה, *Chaninah* (*Sanhedrin* 98b). It is noteworthy that the initial letters of these four names spell מָשִׁיחַ, *Messiah*.

וּנְחֶמְיָה — *And Nehemiah.* Some interpret Nehemiah as another form of מְנַחֵם [*Mena-*

chem, lit., *Comforter*], since both are derived from נֶחָמָה, *comfort*. Thus, it is another name for the Messiah (*Masbir*; *Matteh Levi*).

Alternately, it refers to Nehemiah ben Hachaliah, a leader of those who returned from the Babylonian Exile, and the architect and builder of the Second Temple. Thus, we pray for the advent of Elijah, the Messiah, and the builder of the Third Temple (*Pardes*).

עֹשֶׂה צְדָקוֹת עִם כָּל בָּשָׂר וָרוּחַ, לֹא כְרָעָתָם

⟨ in accord with ⟨ — not ⟪ and ⟨ [beings ⟨ all ⟨ with ⟨ acts of ⟨ Who
their wickedness spirit of] flesh generosity performs

תִּגְמוֹל. ❖ אֵל הוֹרֵיתָ לָּנוּ לוֹמַר שְׁלֹשׁ עֶשְׂרֵה, וּזְכוֹר

⟨ remem- ⟪ the Thirteen ⟨ to ⟨ us ⟨ You ⟨ O God, ⟪ do You
ber [Attributes of Mercy]; recite taught repay them!

לָּנוּ הַיּוֹם בְּרִית שְׁלֹשׁ עֶשְׂרֵה, כְּמוֹ שֶׁהוֹדַעְתָּ לֶעָנָיו

⟨ to the humble ⟨ You made ⟨ as ⟪ of [these] Thirteen, ⟨ the ⟨ today ⟨ for us
one [Moses] known covenant

מִקֶּדֶם, כְּמוֹ שֶׁכָּתוּב, וַיֵּרֶד יהוה בֶּעָנָן וַיִּתְיַצֵּב עִמּוֹ

⟨ with ⟨ and stood ⟨ in a ⟨ And HASHEM ⟪ it is written: ⟨ as ⟪ in ancient
him cloud descended times,

שָׁם, וַיִּקְרָא בְשֵׁם יהוה.¹

⟪ of ⟨ with the ⟨ and He ⟪ there,
HASHEM. Name called out

CONGREGATION, THEN *CHAZZAN*:

וַיַּעֲבֹר יהוה עַל פָּנָיו וַיִּקְרָא:

⟪ and ⟪ [Moses'] ⟨ before ⟨ And HASHEM passed
proclaimed: face,

CONGREGATION AND *CHAZZAN* RECITE LOUDLY AND IN UNISON:

יהוה, יהוה, אֵל, רַחוּם, וְחַנּוּן, אֶרֶךְ אַפַּיִם,

⟨ to anger, ⟨ Slow ⟪ and Gracious, ⟨ Compassionate ⟨ God, ⟨ HASHEM, ⟨ HASHEM,

וְרַב חֶסֶד, וֶאֱמֶת, נֹצֵר חֶסֶד לָאֲלָפִים, נֹשֵׂא עָוֹן,

⟨ of ⟨ Forgiver ⟪ for thousands ⟨ of ⟨ Preserver ⟪ and ⟨ in ⟨ and
iniquity, [of generations], kindness Truth, Kindness Abundant

וָפֶשַׁע, וְחַטָּאָה, וְנַקֵּה.² וְסָלַחְתָּ לַעֲוֹנֵנוּ וּלְחַטָּאתֵנוּ

⟪ and our sins, ⟨ our ⟨ May You ⟪ and Who ⟨ and inadvertent ⟨ willful sin,
iniquities forgive absolves. sin,

וּנְחַלְתָּנוּ.³ סְלַח לָנוּ אָבִינוּ כִּי חָטָאנוּ, מְחַל לָנוּ

⟨ us, ⟨ pardon ⟪ we have ⟨ for ⟪ our ⟨ us, ⟨ Forgive ⟪ and make us
sinned; Father, Your heritage.

מַלְכֵּנוּ כִּי פָשָׁעְנוּ. כִּי אַתָּה אֲדֹנָי טוֹב וְסַלָּח,

⟪ and ⟨ are ⟨ O Lord, ⟨ You, ⟨ For ⟪ we have ⟨ for ⟪ our King,
forgiving, good willfully sinned.

וְרַב חֶסֶד לְכָל קֹרְאֶיךָ.⁴

⟪ who call ⟨ to all ⟨ kind ⟨ and
upon You. abundantly

(1) *Exodus* 34:5. (2) 34:6-7. (3) 34:9. (4) *Psalms* 86:5.

ALL:

זְכֹר רַחֲמֶיךָ יהוה וַחֲסָדֶיךָ, כִּי מֵעוֹלָם הֵמָּה.[1]

Remember ‹ Your mercies, ‹ HASHEM, ‹ and Your kindnesses, ‹ for ‹ eternal ‹ are they.

זָכְרֵנוּ יהוה בִּרְצוֹן עַמֶּךָ, פָּקְדֵנוּ בִּישׁוּעָתֶךָ.[2] זְכֹר

Remember us, ‹ HASHEM, ‹ when You show favor ‹ to Your people; ‹ recall us ‹ with Your salvation. ‹ Remember

עֲדָתְךָ קָנִיתָ קֶּדֶם, גָּאַלְתָּ שֵׁבֶט נַחֲלָתֶךָ, הַר צִיּוֹן זֶה

Your congregation, ‹ which You acquired ‹ long ago, ‹ You redeemed ‹ the tribe ‹ of Your heritage; ‹ the ‹ mountain of ‹ Zion, this one [where]

שָׁכַנְתָּ בּוֹ.[3] זְכֹר יהוה חִבַּת יְרוּשָׁלַיִם, אַהֲבַת

You rested Your Presence ‹ there. ‹ Remember, ‹ HASHEM, ‹ the affection ‹ of Jerusalem; ‹ the love

צִיּוֹן אַל תִּשְׁכַּח לָנֶצַח.[4] אַתָּה תָקוּם תְּרַחֵם צִיּוֹן כִּי

of Zion ‹ do not ‹ forget ‹ forever. ‹ You ‹ will arise ‹ and show mercy ‹ to Zion, ‹ for

עֵת לְחֶנְנָהּ, כִּי בָא מוֹעֵד.[5] זְכֹר יהוה לִבְנֵי אֱדוֹם

the time to favor her, ‹ for ‹ the appointed time will have come. ‹ Remember, ‹ HASHEM, ‹ [to repay] ‹ the offspring ‹ of Edom

אֵת יוֹם יְרוּשָׁלָיִם, הָאֹמְרִים עָרוּ עָרוּ עַד הַיְסוֹד בָּהּ.[6]

for the day ‹ of Jerusalem; ‹ those who say, ‹ [to repay] ‹ Destroy! ‹ Destroy ‹ to ‹ the very foundation ‹ of it!

זְכֹר לְאַבְרָהָם לְיִצְחָק וּלְיִשְׂרָאֵל עֲבָדֶיךָ, אֲשֶׁר

Remember ‹ for Abraham ‹ for Isaac, ‹ and for Israel, ‹ Your servants, ‹ that

נִשְׁבַּעְתָּ לָהֶם בָּךְ וַתְּדַבֵּר אֲלֵהֶם, אַרְבֶּה אֶת זַרְעֲכֶם

You swore ‹ to them ‹ by Your Being, ‹ and You said ‹ to them, ‹ I shall increase ‹ Your offspring

כְּכוֹכְבֵי הַשָּׁמָיִם, וְכָל הָאָרֶץ הַזֹּאת אֲשֶׁר אָמַרְתִּי,

like the stars ‹ of the heavens; ‹ and all ‹ of this land ‹ of which ‹ I spoke

אֶתֵּן לְזַרְעֲכֶם, וְנָחֲלוּ לְעֹלָם.[7] זְכֹר לַעֲבָדֶיךָ לְאַבְרָהָם

I will give ‹ to your offspring, ‹ and they will inherit it ‹ forever. ‹ Remember ‹ [the merits] ‹ of Your servants, ‹ of Abraham,

---

(1) *Psalms* 25:6. (2) Cf. 106:4. (3) 74:2. (4) This is not a Scriptural verse.
(5) *Psalms* 102:14. (6) 137:7. (7) *Exodus* 32:13.

לְיִצְחָק וּלְיַעֲקֹב, אַל תֵּפֶן אֶל קְשִׁי הָעָם הַזֶּה וְאֶל
⟨ to ⟫ of this people, ⟨ the stub- ⟨ to ⟨ pay ⟨ do ⟫ and of Jacob; ⟨ of Isaac,
bornness attention not

רִשְׁעוֹ וְאֶל חַטָּאתוֹ.¹ זְכוֹר לָנוּ בְּרִית אָבוֹת, כַּאֲשֶׁר
⟨ as ⟫ of the ⟨ the ⟨ for ⟨ Remember ⟫ its ⟨ and ⟫ its
Patriarchs, covenant us sinfulness. to wickedness,

אָמַרְתָּ: וְזָכַרְתִּי אֶת בְּרִיתִי יַעֲקוֹב, וְאַף אֶת בְּרִיתִי
⟨ My covenant ⟨ and ⟫[with] Jacob, ⟨ My covenant ⟨ And I will ⟫ You said:
also remember

יִצְחָק, וְאַף אֶת בְּרִיתִי אַבְרָהָם אֶזְכֹּר, וְהָאָרֶץ אֶזְכֹּר.²
⟫ I will ⟨ and the ⟫ I will ⟨ [with] ⟨ My covenant ⟨ and ⟫ [with]
remember. Land remember; Abraham also Isaac,

זְכוֹר לָנוּ בְּרִית רִאשׁוֹנִים, כַּאֲשֶׁר אָמַרְתָּ: וְזָכַרְתִּי
⟨ And I will ⟫ You said: ⟨ as ⟫ of the ⟨ the ⟨ for us ⟨ Remember
remember ancient ones, covenant

לָהֶם בְּרִית רִאשׁוֹנִים, אֲשֶׁר הוֹצֵאתִי אֹתָם מֵאֶרֶץ
⟨ from ⟨ I took them out ⟨ that ⟫ of the ⟨ the ⟨ for
the land ancient ones, covenant them

מִצְרַיִם לְעֵינֵי הַגּוֹיִם, לִהְיוֹת לָהֶם לֵאלֹהִים, אֲנִי
⟨ I am ⟫ a God; ⟨ to them ⟨ to be ⟫ of the ⟨ in the ⟨ of Egypt
nations, very sight

יהוה.³ עֲשֵׂה עִמָּנוּ כְּמָה שֶׁהִבְטַחְתָּנוּ: וְאַף גַּם
⟨ all ⟨ And despite ⟫ You promised us: ⟨ as ⟨ with us ⟨ Do ⟫ HASHEM.

זֹאת בִּהְיוֹתָם בְּאֶרֶץ אֹיְבֵיהֶם, לֹא מְאַסְתִּים וְלֹא
⟨ nor ⟨ despise them ⟨ I will ⟫ of their ⟨ in the land ⟨ when they ⟫ this,
not enemies, will be

גְעַלְתִּים לְכַלֹּתָם לְהָפֵר בְּרִיתִי אִתָּם, כִּי אֲנִי יהוה
⟨ HASHEM, ⟨ I am ⟨ for ⟫ with ⟨ My ⟨ to annul ⟫ to destroy ⟨ abhor them
them, covenant them,

אֱלֹהֵיהֶם.⁴ הָשֵׁב שְׁבוּתֵנוּ וְרַחֲמֵנוּ, כְּמָה שֶׁכָּתוּב:
⟫ it is ⟨ as ⟫ and have ⟨ our captivity ⟨ Bring ⟫ their God.
written: mercy on us, back

וְשָׁב יהוה אֱלֹהֶיךָ אֶת שְׁבוּתְךָ וְרִחֲמֶךָ, וְשָׁב וְקִבֶּצְךָ
⟨ gather ⟨ and He ⟫ and He will ⟨ your captivity, ⟨ your ⟨ will ⟨ Then bring
you in will once have mercy God, HASHEM, back
again upon you,

---

(1) *Deuteronomy* 9:27. (2) *Leviticus* 26:42. (3) 26:45. (4) 26:44.

מִכָּל הָעַמִּים אֲשֶׁר הֱפִיצְךָ יהוה אֱלֹהֶיךָ שָׁמָּה.[1]

from all / the peoples / that / scattered you / has HASHEM / your God / thereto.

קַבֵּץ נִדָּחֵינוּ, כְּמָה שֶׁכָּתוּב: אִם יִהְיֶה נִדַּחֲךָ בִּקְצֵה

Gather / our dispersed ones, / as / it is written: / If / your dispersed will be / at the ends

הַשָּׁמָיִם, מִשָּׁם יְקַבֶּצְךָ יהוה אֱלֹהֶיךָ, וּמִשָּׁם יִקָּחֶךָ.[2]

of heaven, / from there / gather you in / HASHEM, / your God, / and from there / He will take you.

מְחֵה פְשָׁעֵינוּ כָּעָב וְכֶעָנָן, כְּמָה שֶׁכָּתוּב: מָחִיתִי

Wipe away / our sins / like a mist / and like a cloud, / as / it is written: / I have wiped away

כָעָב פְּשָׁעֶיךָ וְכֶעָנָן חַטֹּאתֶיךָ, שׁוּבָה אֵלַי כִּי

like a mist / your willful sins, / and like a cloud / your transgressions; / return / to Me, / for

גְאַלְתִּיךָ.[3] מְחֵה פְשָׁעֵינוּ לְמַעַנְךָ, כַּאֲשֶׁר אָמָרְתָּ:

I have redeemed you. / Wipe away / our sins / for Your sake, / as / You have said:

אָנֹכִי אָנֹכִי הוּא מֹחֶה פְשָׁעֶיךָ לְמַעֲנִי, וְחַטֹּאתֶיךָ לֹא

I, / [only] I, / am the One / Who wipes away / your willful sins / for My sake, / and your transgressions / I shall not

אֶזְכֹּר.[4] הַלְבֵּן חֲטָאֵינוּ כַּשֶּׁלֶג וְכַצֶּמֶר, כְּמָה שֶׁכָּתוּב:

recall. / Whiten / our sins / like snow / and like wool, / as / it is written:

לְכוּ נָא וְנִוָּכְחָה, יֹאמַר יהוה, אִם יִהְיוּ חֲטָאֵיכֶם

Come, / now, / let us reason together, / says / HASHEM. / Though / your sins may be

כַּשָּׁנִים כַּשֶּׁלֶג יַלְבִּינוּ, אִם יַאְדִּימוּ כַתּוֹלָע, כַּצֶּמֶר

like scarlet, / like snow / they will be whitened; / though / they may be red / as crimson, / like [white] wool

יִהְיוּ.[5] זְרוֹק עָלֵינוּ מַיִם טְהוֹרִים וְטַהֲרֵנוּ, כְּמָה שֶׁכָּתוּב:

they will become. / Pour / upon us / pure water / and purify us, / as / it is written:

וְזָרַקְתִּי עֲלֵיכֶם מַיִם טְהוֹרִים וּטְהַרְתֶּם, מִכֹּל

I shall pour / upon you / pure water / and you will become pure; / from all

---

(1) *Leviticus* 30:3. (2) 30:4. (3) *Isaiah* 44:22. (4) 43:25. (5) 1:18.

רַחֵם .1 אֲטַהֵר אֶתְכֶם גִּלּוּלֵיכֶם וּמִכָּל טֻמְאוֹתֵיכֶם

⟨ Have / mercy ⟫ ⟨ you. ⟨ I will / purify ⟨ your / abominations ⟨ and / from all ⟨ your / contaminations

עָלֵינוּ וְאַל תַּשְׁחִיתֵנוּ, כְּמָה שֶׁכָּתוּב: כִּי אֵל רַחוּם

⟨ a merciful / God ⟨ For ⟫ it is written: ⟨ as ⟫ destroy us, ⟨ and / do not ⟨ on us

יהוה אֱלֹהֶיךָ, לֹא יַרְפְּךָ וְלֹא יַשְׁחִיתֶךָ, וְלֹא יִשְׁכַּח

⟨ will He / forget ⟨ nor ⟫ will He / destroy you, ⟨ nor ⟨ relinquish / you ⟨ He will / not ⟨ your God; ⟨ is / HASHEM,

אֶת בְּרִית אֲבֹתֶיךָ אֲשֶׁר נִשְׁבַּע לָהֶם. .2 מוֹל

⟨ Circum- / cise ⟫ to them. ⟨ He swore ⟨ which ⟨ with your / forefathers, ⟨ the covenant

אֶת לְבָבְנוּ לְאַהֲבָה וּלְיִרְאָה אֶת שְׁמֶךָ, כְּמָה שֶׁכָּתוּב:

⟫ it is written: ⟨ as ⟫ Your Name, ⟨ and to fear ⟨ to love ⟨ our hearts

וּמָל יהוה אֱלֹהֶיךָ אֶת לְבָבְךָ וְאֶת לְבַב זַרְעֶךָ, לְאַהֲבָה

⟨ to love ⟫ of your / offspring, ⟨ and the / heart ⟨ your heart ⟨ HASHEM, your God, / will circumcise

אֶת יהוה אֱלֹהֶיךָ, בְּכָל לְבָבְךָ וּבְכָל נַפְשְׁךָ, לְמַעַן

⟨ so that ⟫ your / soul, ⟨ and / with all ⟨ your / heart ⟨ with all ⟨ your God, ⟨ HASHEM,

חַיֶּיךָ. .3 הִמָּצֵא לָנוּ בְּבַקָּשָׁתֵנוּ, כְּמָה שֶׁכָּתוּב: וּבִקַּשְׁתֶּם

⟨ And you / will seek ⟫ it is written: ⟨ as ⟫ in our quest, ⟨ to us ⟨ Be / accessible ⟫ you may / live.

מִשָּׁם אֶת יהוה אֱלֹהֶיךָ וּמָצָאתָ, כִּי תִדְרְשֶׁנּוּ בְּכָל

⟨ with / all ⟨ you search / Him out ⟨ when ⟫ and you will / find [Him], ⟨ your God, ⟨ HASHEM, ⟨ from / there

לְבָבְךָ וּבְכָל נַפְשֶׁךָ. .4 ❖ תְּבִיאֵנוּ אֶל הַר קָדְשֶׁךָ,

⟨ Your holy / mountain ⟨ to ⟨ Bring us ⟫ your soul. ⟨ and / with all ⟨ your / heart

וְשִׂמַּחְנוּ בְּבֵית תְּפִלָּתֶךָ, כְּמָה שֶׁכָּתוּב: וַהֲבִיאוֹתִים

⟨ And I will / bring them ⟫ it is written: ⟨ as ⟫ of Prayer, ⟨ in Your / House ⟨ and gladden / us

אֶל הַר קָדְשִׁי, וְשִׂמַּחְתִּים בְּבֵית תְּפִלָּתִי, עוֹלֹתֵיהֶם

⟨ their burnt- / offerings ⟫ of Prayer; ⟨ in My / House ⟨ and I will / gladden them ⟫ My holy / mountain, ⟨ to

(1) *Ezekiel* 36:25. (2) *Deuteronomy* 4:31. (3) 30:6. (4) 4:29.

וְזִבְחֵיהֶם לְרָצוֹן עַל מִזְבְּחִי, כִּי בֵיתִי בֵּית תְּפִלָּה

⟨ of ⟨ "a House ⟨ My ⟨ for ⟪ My Altar, ⟨ on ⟨ will find ⟨ and their feast-
Prayer" House favor offerings

יִקָּרֵא לְכָל הָעַמִּים.¹

⟪ nations. ⟨ for all ⟨ will be
called

THE ARK IS OPENED.

CHAZZAN, THEN CONGREGATION:

שְׁמַע קוֹלֵנוּ יהוה אֱלֹהֵינוּ, חוּס וְרַחֵם עָלֵינוּ,

⟪ on us, ⟨ and have ⟨ have ⟪ our God; ⟨ HASHEM, ⟨ our voice, ⟨ Hear
compassion pity

וְקַבֵּל בְּרַחֲמִים וּבְרָצוֹן אֶת תְּפִלָּתֵנוּ.²

⟪ our prayer. ⟨ and favor ⟨ with compassion ⟨ and accept

CHAZZAN, THEN CONGREGATION:

הֲשִׁיבֵנוּ יהוה אֵלֶיךָ וְנָשׁוּבָה, חַדֵּשׁ יָמֵינוּ כְּקֶדֶם.³

⟪ as of old. ⟨ our ⟨ renew ⟪ and we shall ⟨ to You, ⟨ HASHEM, ⟨Bring us back,
days return,

CHAZZAN, THEN CONGREGATION:

אֲמָרֵינוּ הַאֲזִינָה יהוה, בִּינָה הֲגִיגֵנוּ.⁴

⟪ our thoughts. ⟨ perceive ⟪ HASHEM; ⟨ hear, ⟨ Our words

THE FOLLOWING VERSE IS RECITED QUIETLY:

יִהְיוּ לְרָצוֹן אִמְרֵי פִינוּ וְהֶגְיוֹן לִבֵּנוּ לְפָנֶיךָ,

⟪ before ⟪ of our ⟨ and the ⟨ of our ⟨ — the ex- ⟪ find ⟨ May
You, heart — thoughts mouth pressions favor they

יהוה צוּרֵנוּ וְגוֹאֲלֵנוּ.⁵

⟪ and our Redeemer. ⟨ our Rock ⟨ HASHEM,

CHAZZAN, THEN CONGREGATION:

אַל תַּשְׁלִיכֵנוּ מִלְּפָנֶיךָ, וְרוּחַ קָדְשְׁךָ אַל תִּקַּח מִמֶּנּוּ.⁶

⟪ from us. ⟨ take ⟨ do ⟨ of Your ⟨ and the ⟪ from Your ⟨ cast us away ⟨ Do
not Holiness Spirit Presence, not

CHAZZAN, THEN CONGREGATION:

אַל תַּשְׁלִיכֵנוּ לְעֵת זִקְנָה, כִּכְלוֹת כֹּחֵנוּ אַל תַּעַזְבֵנוּ.⁷

⟪ forsake us not. ⟨ does our ⟨ when fail ⟪ of old ⟨ in time ⟨ cast us away ⟨ Do
strength, age; not

---

(1) *Isaiah* 56:7. (2) From the weekday *Shemoneh Esrei*.
(3) *Lamentations* 5:21. (4) Cf. *Psalms* 5:2. (5) Cf. 19:15. (6) 51:13. (7) Cf. 71:9.

ALL CONTINUE (SOME CONGREGATIONS RECITE THE NEXT VERSE RESPONSIVELY):

אַל תַּעַזְבֵנוּ יהוה, אֱלֹהֵינוּ אַל תִּרְחַק מִמֶּנּוּ.¹

《 from us. 〈 be not distant 〈 our God, 《 O HASHEM; 〈 Forsake us not,

עֲשֵׂה עִמָּנוּ אוֹת לְטוֹבָה, וְיִרְאוּ שׂוֹנְאֵינוּ וְיֵבֹשׁוּ,

《 and be 〈 may our 〈 so that 《 for good; 〈 a sign 〈 for us 〈 Display
ashamed, enemies see it

כִּי אַתָּה יהוה עֲזַרְתָּנוּ וְנִחַמְתָּנוּ.² כִּי לְךָ יהוה

〈 HASHEM, 〈 for 〈 Because 《 and 〈 will have 〈 HASHEM, 〈 You, 〈 for
You, consoled us. helped us

הוֹחָלְנוּ, אַתָּה תַעֲנֶה אֲדֹנָי אֱלֹהֵינוּ.³

《 our God. 〈 O Lord, 〈 will answer, 〈 You 《 do we wait;

THE ARK IS CLOSED.

EACH INDIVIDUAL CONTINUES.

CONFESSION / וִדּוּי

**DURING THE RECITATION OF THE וִדּוּי, *CONFESSION*, STAND WITH
HEAD AND BODY SLIGHTLY BOWED, IN SUBMISSIVE CONTRITION.**

אֱלֹהֵינוּ וֵאלֹהֵי אֲבוֹתֵינוּ, תָּבֹא לְפָנֶיךָ תְּפִלָּתֵנוּ,⁴

《 may our 〈 before 〈 come 《 of our 〈 and the 〈 Our God
prayer, You forefathers, God

וְאַל תִּתְעַלַּם מִתְּחִנָּתֵנוּ,⁵ שֶׁאֵין אָנוּ עַזֵּי פָנִים

〈 faced 〈 so brazen- 〈 For we are not 《 our supplication. 〈 ignore 〈 and do not

וּקְשֵׁי עֹרֶף, לוֹמַר לְפָנֶיךָ יהוה אֱלֹהֵינוּ וֵאלֹהֵי

〈 and the God 〈 our God, 〈 HASHEM, 《 before You, 〈 as to say 〈 necked 〈 and stiff-

אֲבוֹתֵינוּ, צַדִּיקִים אֲנַחְנוּ וְלֹא חָטָאנוּ, אֲבָל

《 —for 《 sinned 〈 and 〈 we are, 〈 that righteous 《 of our
indeed, have not forefathers,

אֲנַחְנוּ וַאֲבוֹתֵינוּ חָטָאנוּ.⁶

《 have sinned. 〈 and our forefathers 〈 we

**STRIKE THE LEFT SIDE OF THE CHEST WITH THE RIGHT FIST WHILE RECITING
EACH OF THE SINS OF THE FOLLOWING CONFESSIONAL LITANY:**

אָשַׁמְנוּ, בָּגַדְנוּ, גָּזַלְנוּ, דִּבַּרְנוּ דֹפִי. הֶעֱוִינוּ,

《 We have com- 《 slander. 〈 we have 《 we have 《 we have 《 We have been
mitted iniquity; spoken robbed; betrayed; guilty;

---

(1) Cf. *Psalms* 38:22. (2) Cf. 86:17. (3) Cf. 38:16. (4) Cf. 88:3. (5) Cf. 55:2. (6) Cf. 106:6, *Jeremiah* 3:25.

וְהִרְשַׁעְנוּ, זַדְנוּ, חָמַסְנוּ, טָפַלְנוּ שֶׁקֶר. יָעַצְנוּ

‹ We have given advice « false accusations. ‹ we have made « we have extorted; « we have sinned willfully; « we have committed wickedness;

רָע, כִּזַּבְנוּ, לַצְנוּ, מָרַדְנוּ, נִאַצְנוּ, סָרַרְנוּ,

« we have strayed; « we have provoked [God's anger]; « we have rebelled; « we have scorned; « we have been deceitful; « that is bad;

עָוִינוּ, פָּשַׁעְנוּ, צָרַרְנוּ, קִשִּׁינוּ עֹרֶף. רָשַׁעְנוּ,

« We have been wicked; « our necks. ‹ we have stiffened « we have caused distress; « we have sinned rebelliously; «we have been iniquitous;

שִׁחַתְנוּ, תִּעַבְנוּ, תָּעִינוּ, תִּעְתָּעְנוּ.

« we have scoffed. « we have gone astray; « we have committed abominations; « we have been corrupt;

סַרְנוּ מִמִּצְוֹתֶיךָ וּמִמִּשְׁפָּטֶיךָ הַטּוֹבִים, וְלֹא שָׁוָה

‹ worth- while ‹ and it was not « that are good, ‹ and from Your laws ‹ from Your commandments ‹ We have turned away

לָנוּ.[1] וְאַתָּה צַדִּיק עַל כָּל הַבָּא עָלֵינוּ, כִּי אֱמֶת

‹ truthfully ‹ for « upon us, ‹ that has come ‹ all ‹ in ‹ are righteous ‹ And You « for us.

עָשִׂיתָ וַאֲנַחְנוּ הִרְשָׁעְנוּ.[2]

« have acted ‹ while we « have You acted,
wickedly.

אָשַׁמְנוּ מִכָּל עָם, בֹּשְׁנוּ מִכָּל דּוֹר, גָּלָה מִמֶּנּוּ

‹ from us ‹ Departed « genera- tion. ‹ more than any other ‹ We have been ashamed «people. ‹ more than any other ‹ We have been guilty

מָשׂוֹשׂ, דָּוָה לִבֵּנוּ בַּחֲטָאֵינוּ, הֻחַבַּל אֲוֵינוּ, וְנִפְרַע

‹ uncov- ered « was our desired [Temple], ‹ Seized « because of our sins. ‹ is our heart ‹ Sickened « has joy.

פֹּאֲרֵנוּ, זְבוּל בֵּית מִקְדָּשֵׁנוּ חָרַב בַּעֲוֹנֵינוּ, טִירָתֵנוּ

‹ Our Palace « because of our iniquities. ‹ has been destroyed ‹ our Holy Temple ‹ for [His] abode, « was our splendor;

הָיְתָה לְשַׁמָּה, יְפִי אַדְמָתֵנוּ לְזָרִים, כֹּחֵנוּ לְנָכְרִים.

« [was given] to foreigners. ‹ our wealth « is controlled by strangers, ‹ of our Land ‹ [Jerusalem,] « desolate. ‹ the beauty « has become

(1) Cf. *Job* 33:27. (2) *Nehemiah* 9:33.

וַעֲדַיִן לֹא שַׁבְנוּ מִטָּעוּתֵנוּ וְהֵיךְ נָעִיז פָּנֵינוּ וְנַקְשֶׁה

⟨ and
stiffen ⟨ faced ⟨ can we be ⟨ So
so brazen- how ⟪ from our
willful errors. ⟨ we have not
repented ⟨ But still

עָרְפֵּנוּ, לוֹמַר לְפָנֶיךָ יהוה אֱלֹהֵינוּ וֵאלֹהֵי אֲבוֹתֵינוּ,

⟪ of our
forefathers, ⟨ and the
God ⟨ our God ⟪ HASHEM, ⟨ before
You, ⟨ so as to
say ⟨ our neck

צַדִּיקִים אֲנַחְנוּ וְלֹא חָטָאנוּ, אֲבָל אֲנַחְנוּ וַאֲבוֹתֵינוּ

⟨ and our
fathers ⟨ both we ⟨ for in
truth, ⟪ and we have
not sinned, ⟪ we are ⟨ that
righteous

חָטָאנוּ.[1]

⟪ have sinned.

**STRIKE THE LEFT SIDE OF THE CHEST WITH THE RIGHT FIST WHILE RECITING
EACH OF THE SINS OF THE FOLLOWING CONFESSIONAL LITANY:**

אָשַׁמְנוּ, בָּגַדְנוּ, גָּזַלְנוּ, דִּבַּרְנוּ דְפִי. הֶעֱוִינוּ,

⟪ We have com-
mitted iniquity; ⟪ slander. ⟨ we have
spoken ⟪ we have
robbed; ⟪ we have
betrayed; ⟪ We have been
guilty;

וְהִרְשַׁעְנוּ, זַדְנוּ, חָמַסְנוּ, טָפַלְנוּ שֶׁקֶר. יָעַצְנוּ

⟨ We have
given advice ⟪ false
accusations. ⟨ we have
made ⟪ we have
extorted; ⟪ we have sinned
willfully; ⟪ we have committed wickedness;

רָע, כִּזַּבְנוּ, לַצְנוּ, מָרַדְנוּ, נִאַצְנוּ, סָרַרְנוּ,

⟪ we have
strayed; ⟪ we have provoked
[God's anger]; ⟪ we have
rebelled; ⟪ we have
scorned; ⟪ we have been
deceitful; ⟪ that is
bad;

עָוִינוּ, פָּשַׁעְנוּ, צָרַרְנוּ, קִשִּׁינוּ עֹרֶף. רָשַׁעְנוּ,

⟪ We have
been wicked; ⟪ our
necks. ⟨ we have
stiffened ⟪ we have caused
distress; ⟪ we have sinned
rebelliously; ⟪ we have been
iniquitous;

שִׁחַתְנוּ, תִּעַבְנוּ, תָּעִינוּ, תִּעְתָּעְנוּ.

⟪ we have
scoffed. ⟪ we have
gone astray; ⟪ we have committed abominations; ⟪ we have
been corrupt;

סַרְנוּ מִמִּצְוֺתֶיךָ וּמִמִּשְׁפָּטֶיךָ הַטּוֹבִים, וְלֹא שָׁוָה

⟨ worth-
while ⟨ and it
was not ⟪ that are
good, ⟨ and from
Your laws ⟨ from Your
commandments ⟨ We have
turned away

לָנוּ.[2] וְאַתָּה צַדִּיק עַל כָּל הַבָּא עָלֵינוּ, כִּי אֱמֶת

⟨ truth-
fully ⟨ for ⟪ upon us, ⟨ that has
come ⟨ all ⟨ in ⟨ are
righteous ⟨ And You ⟪ for us.

עָשִׂיתָ וַאֲנַחְנוּ הִרְשַׁעְנוּ.[3]

⟪ have acted
wickedly. ⟨ while we ⟪ have You
acted,

(1) Cf. *Psalms* 106:6; *Jeremiah* 3:25. (2) Cf. *Job* 33:27. (3) *Nehemiah* 9:33.

לְעֵינֵנוּ עָשְׁקוּ עֲמָלֵנוּ, מִמְשָׁךְ וּמְמוֹרָט מִמֶּנּוּ,
‹ Before our eyes ‹ have they stolen « the product of our labor; ‹ [it was] pulled away ‹ and cut off « from us.

נָתְנוּ עֶלֶם עָלֵינוּ, סָבֵלְנוּ עַל שִׁכְמֵנוּ, עֲבָדִים
‹ They have placed ‹ their yoke « upon us, ‹ we bore it ‹ upon « our shoulders. ‹ Slaves

מָשְׁלוּ בָנוּ, פֹּרֵק אֵין מִיָּדָם, צָרוֹת רַבּוֹת
‹ have ruled « over us; ‹ a redeemer there was not « from their hand. « Troubles ‹ that are manifold

סְבָבוּנוּ, קְרָאנוּךָ יהוה אֱלֹהֵינוּ, רָחַקְתָּ מִמֶּנּוּ
« have surrounded us, « we called upon You, ‹ HASHEM, « our God, ‹ but You have distanced Yourself ‹ from us

בַּעֲוֹנֵינוּ, שַׁבְנוּ מֵאַחֲרֶיךָ, תָּעִינוּ וְאָבָדְנוּ.
« because of our iniquities. ‹ We have turned away « from following after You; « we have gone astray; « we have become lost.

וַעֲדַיִן לֹא שַׁבְנוּ מִטָּעוּתֵנוּ וְהֵיךְ נָעִיז פָּנֵינוּ וְנַקְשֶׁה
‹ But still ‹ we have not repented « from our willful errors. ‹ So how ‹ can we be so brazen- ‹ faced ‹ and stiffen

עָרְפֵּנוּ, לוֹמַר לְפָנֶיךָ יהוה אֱלֹהֵינוּ וֵאלֹהֵי אֲבוֹתֵינוּ,
‹ our neck ‹ so as to say ‹ before You, ‹ HASHEM, ‹ our God ‹ and the God « of our forefathers,

צַדִּיקִים אֲנַחְנוּ וְלֹא חָטָאנוּ, אֲבָל אֲנַחְנוּ וַאֲבוֹתֵינוּ
‹ that righteous ‹ we are « and we have not sinned, « for in truth, ‹ both we ‹ and our fathers

חָטָאנוּ.[1]
« have sinned.

STRIKE THE LEFT SIDE OF THE CHEST WITH THE RIGHT FIST WHILE RECITING EACH OF THE SINS OF THE FOLLOWING CONFESSIONAL LITANY:

אָשַׁמְנוּ, בָּגַדְנוּ, גָּזַלְנוּ, דִּבַּרְנוּ דֹפִי. הֶעֱוִינוּ,
« We have been guilty; « we have betrayed; « we have robbed; ‹ we have spoken « slander. « We have committed iniquity;

וְהִרְשַׁעְנוּ, זַדְנוּ, חָמַסְנוּ, טָפַלְנוּ שֶׁקֶר. יָעַצְנוּ
«we have committed wickedness; «we have sinned willfully; « we have extorted; ‹ we have made « false accusations. ‹ We have given advice

רָע, כִּזַּבְנוּ, לַצְנוּ, מָרַדְנוּ, נִאַצְנוּ, סָרַרְנוּ,
‹ that is bad; « we have been deceitful; « we have scorned; ‹ we have rebelled; « we have provoked [God's anger]; « we have strayed;

(1) Cf. *Psalms* 106:6; *Jeremiah* 3:25.

עָוִינוּ, פָּשַׁעְנוּ, צָרַרְנוּ, קִשִּׁינוּ עֹרֶף. רָשַׁעְנוּ,

《 We have been wicked; 《 our necks. ‹ we have stiffened 《 we have caused distress; 《 we have sinned rebelliously; 《 we have been iniquitous;

שִׁחַתְנוּ, תִּעַבְנוּ, תָּעִינוּ, תִּעְתָּעְנוּ.

《 we have scoffed. 《 we have gone astray; 《 we have committed abominations; 《 we have been corrupt;

סַרְנוּ מִמִּצְוֹתֶיךָ וּמִמִּשְׁפָּטֶיךָ הַטּוֹבִים, וְלֹא שָׁוָה

‹ worthwhile ‹ and it was not 《 that are good, ‹ and from Your laws ‹ from Your commandments ‹ We have turned away

לָנוּ.[1] וְאַתָּה צַדִּיק עַל כָּל הַבָּא עָלֵינוּ, כִּי אֱמֶת

‹ truthfully ‹ for 《 upon us, ‹ that has come ‹ all ‹ in ‹ are righteous ‹ And You 《 for us.

עָשִׂיתָ וַאֲנַחְנוּ הִרְשָׁעְנוּ.[2]

《 have acted wickedly. ‹ while we 《 have You acted,

הִרְשַׁעְנוּ וּפָשַׁעְנוּ, לָכֵן לֹא נוֹשָׁעְנוּ. וְתֵן בְּלִבֵּנוּ

‹ in our hearts ‹ Place 《 been saved. ‹ we have not ‹ therefore 《 and we have sinned rebelliously; ‹ We have acted wickedly

לַעֲזוֹב דֶּרֶךְ רֶשַׁע, וְחִישׁ לָנוּ יֶשַׁע, כַּכָּתוּב עַל יַד

‹ the hand ‹ by ‹ as it is written 《 salvation; ‹ to us ‹ and 《 of wickedness, ‹ the path ‹ to abandon

נְבִיאֶךָ: יַעֲזֹב רָשָׁע דַּרְכּוֹ, וְאִישׁ אָוֶן מַחְשְׁבֹתָיו,

《 [abandon] his thoughts; ‹ of iniquity ‹ and the man 《 his way, ‹ the wicked one ‹ Let abandon 《 of Your prophet:

וְיָשֹׁב אֶל יהוה וִירַחֲמֵהוּ, וְאֶל אֱלֹהֵינוּ כִּי

‹ for ‹ our God, ‹ and to 《 and He will have compassion on him, ‹ HASHEM, ‹ to ‹ and let him return

יַרְבֶּה לִסְלוֹחַ.[3]

《 forgiving. ‹ He is abundantly

מְשִׁיחַ צִדְקֶךָ אָמַר לְפָנֶיךָ, שְׁגִיאוֹת מִי יָבִין,

《 can ‹ who ‹ Mistakes 《 before You: ‹ said ‹ who is righteous [David] ‹ Your anointed one discern?

---

(1) Cf. *Job* 33:27. (2) *Nehemiah* 9:33. (3) *Isaiah* 55:7.

מִנִּסְתָּרוֹת נַקֵּנִי.[1] נַקֵּנוּ יהוה אֱלֹהֵינוּ מִכָּל פְּשָׁעֵינוּ,

‹ our sins ‹ of all ‹ our God, ‹ HASHEM, ‹ Cleanse ‹‹ cleanse ‹ From unperceived faults
us, me.

וְטַהֲרֵנוּ מִכָּל טֻמְאוֹתֵינוּ, וּזְרוֹק עָלֵינוּ מַיִם טְהוֹרִים

‹ pure water ‹ upon us ‹ Pour ‹‹ our contaminations. ‹ of all ‹ and purify us

וְטַהֲרֵנוּ, כַּכָּתוּב עַל יַד נְבִיאֶךָ: וְזָרַקְתִּי עֲלֵיכֶם

‹ upon you ‹ I shall pour ‹‹ of Your ‹ the ‹ by ‹ as it is ‹‹ and purify us,
prophet: hand written

מַיִם טְהוֹרִים וּטְהַרְתֶּם, מִכֹּל טֻמְאוֹתֵיכֶם וּמִכָּל

‹ and ‹ your ‹ from ‹‹ and you will ‹ pure water
from all contaminations all become pure;

גִּלּוּלֵיכֶם אֲטַהֵר אֶתְכֶם.[2] עַמֶּךָ וְנַחֲלָתֶךָ, רְעֵבֵי

‹ who ‹‹ and Your ‹ Your ‹‹ you. ‹ I will purify ‹ your
hunger heritage, people abominations

טוּבֶךָ, צְמֵאֵי חַסְדֶּךָ, תְּאֵבֵי יִשְׁעֶךָ, יַכִּירוּ וְיֵדְעוּ

‹ and ‹ — may they ‹‹ for Your ‹ and ‹‹ for Your ‹ who ‹‹ for Your
know recognize salvation who long kindness, thirst goodness,

כִּי לַיהוה אֱלֹהֵינוּ הָרַחֲמִים וְהַסְּלִיחוֹת.

‹‹ and forgiveness. ‹ belong mercy ‹ our God, ‹ to HASHEM, ‹ that

אֵל רַחוּם שְׁמֶךָ, אֵל חַנּוּן שְׁמֶךָ,[3] בָּנוּ נִקְרָא שְׁמֶךָ.[4]

‹‹ is Your Name ‹ upon ‹‹ is Your ‹ Gracious God ‹‹ is Your ‹ Merciful God
proclaimed, us Name, Name,

יהוה עֲשֵׂה לְמַעַן שְׁמֶךָ,[5] עֲשֵׂה לְמַעַן אֲמִתֶּךָ, עֲשֵׂה

‹ act ‹‹ Your truth; ‹ for the ‹ Act ‹‹ Your ‹ for the ‹ act ‹ HASHEM,
sake of Name. sake of

לְמַעַן בְּרִיתֶךָ, עֲשֵׂה לְמַעַן גָּדְלְךָ וְתִפְאַרְתֶּךָ, עֲשֵׂה

‹ act ‹‹ and Your ‹ Your ‹ for the ‹ act ‹‹ Your ‹ for the
splendor; greatness sake of covenant; sake of

לְמַעַן דָּתֶךָ, עֲשֵׂה לְמַעַן הוֹדֶךָ, עֲשֵׂה לְמַעַן וְעוּדֶךָ,

‹‹ Your Meet- ‹ for the ‹ act ‹‹ Your ‹ for the ‹ act ‹‹ Your ‹ for the
ing House; sake of glory; sake of Law; sake of

עֲשֵׂה לְמַעַן זִכְרֶךָ,[6] עֲשֵׂה לְמַעַן חַסְדֶּךָ, עֲשֵׂה לְמַעַן

‹ for the ‹ act ‹‹ Your ‹ for the ‹ act ‹‹ Your ‹ for the ‹ act
sake of kindness; sake of remembrance; sake of

---

(1) Psalms 19:13. (2) Ezekiel 36:25. (3) Cf. Exodus 34:6. (4) Cf. Deuteronomy 28:10.
(5) Jeremiah 14:7. (6) Cf. Exodus 3:15. (7) Psalms 6:5.

טוּבְךָ, עֲשֵׂה לְמַעַן יִחוּדְךָ, עֲשֵׂה לְמַעַן כְּבוֹדְךָ, עֲשֵׂה

⟨ act ⟨⟨ Your honor; ⟨ for the sake of ⟨ act ⟨⟨ Your Oneness; ⟨ for the sake of ⟨ act ⟨⟨ Your goodness;

לְמַעַן **לִמּוּדָךָ**,[1] עֲשֵׂה לְמַעַן מַלְכוּתָךְ, עֲשֵׂה לְמַעַן

⟨ for the sake of ⟨ act ⟨⟨ Your kingship; ⟨ for the sake of ⟨ act ⟨⟨ Your students; ⟨ for the sake of

נִצְחָךְ, עֲשֵׂה לְמַעַן סוֹדָךְ,[2] עֲשֵׂה לְמַעַן עֻזָּךְ, עֲשֵׂה

⟨ act ⟨⟨ Your power; ⟨ for the sake of ⟨ act ⟨⟨ Your secret [revealed to those who fear You]; ⟨ for the sake of ⟨ act ⟨⟨ Your eternal [Name];

לְמַעַן **פְּאֵרָךְ**, עֲשֵׂה לְמַעַן צִדְקָתָךְ, עֲשֵׂה לְמַעַן

⟨ for the sake of ⟨ act ⟨⟨ Your righteousness; ⟨ for the sake of ⟨ act ⟨⟨ Your glory; ⟨ for the sake of

קְדֻשָּׁתָךְ, עֲשֵׂה לְמַעַן רַחֲמֶיךָ הָרַבִּים, עֲשֵׂה לְמַעַן

⟨ for the sake of ⟨ act ⟨⟨ that is abundant; ⟨ Your mercy ⟨ for the sake of ⟨ act ⟨⟨ Your sanctity;

שְׁכִינָתָךְ, עֲשֵׂה לְמַעַן תְּהִלָּתָךְ, עֲשֵׂה לְמַעַן אוֹהֲבֶיךָ

⟨ those who loved You ⟨ for the sake of ⟨ act ⟨⟨ Your praise; ⟨ for the sake of ⟨ act ⟨⟨ Your Divine Presence;

שׁוֹכְנֵי עָפָר,[3] עֲשֵׂה לְמַעַן אַבְרָהָם יִצְחָק וְיַעֲקֹב,

⟨⟨ and Jacob; ⟨ Isaac, ⟨ Abraham, ⟨ for the sake of ⟨ act ⟨⟨ in the dust; ⟨ who rest

עֲשֵׂה לְמַעַן מֹשֶׁה וְאַהֲרֹן, עֲשֵׂה לְמַעַן דָּוִד וּשְׁלֹמֹה,

⟨⟨ and Solomon; ⟨ David ⟨ for the sake of ⟨ act ⟨⟨ and Aaron; ⟨ Moses ⟨ for the sake of ⟨ act

עֲשֵׂה לְמַעַן יְרוּשָׁלַיִם עִיר קָדְשֶׁךָ,[4] עֲשֵׂה לְמַעַן צִיּוֹן

⟨ Zion, ⟨ for the sake of ⟨ act ⟨⟨ of Your Holiness; ⟨ the City ⟨ Jerusalem, ⟨ for the sake of ⟨ act

מִשְׁכַּן כְּבוֹדֶךָ,[5] עֲשֵׂה לְמַעַן שְׁמְמוֹת[6] הֵיכָלֶךָ, עֲשֵׂה

⟨ act ⟨⟨ of Your Temple; ⟨ the desolation ⟨ for the sake of ⟨ act ⟨⟨ of Your glory; ⟨ the abode

לְמַעַן הֲרִיסוּת[7] מִזְבְּחֶךָ, עֲשֵׂה לְמַעַן הֲרוּגִים עַל

⟨ for ⟨ those killed ⟨ for the sake of ⟨ act ⟨⟨ of Your Altar; ⟨ the devastation ⟨ for the sake of

שֵׁם קָדְשֶׁךָ, עֲשֵׂה לְמַעַן טְבוּחִים עַל יִחוּדְךָ, עֲשֵׂה

⟨ act ⟨⟨ Your Oneness; ⟨ for ⟨ those slaughtered ⟨ for the sake of ⟨ act ⟨⟨ Your holy Name;

---

(1) Cf. *Isaiah* 54:13. (2) Cf. *Psalms* 25:14. (3) *Isaiah* 26:19. (4) Cf. *Daniel* 9:16,24.
(5) *Psalms* 26:8. (6) Cf. *Jeremiah* 51:26. (7) Cf. *Isaiah* 49:19.

לְמַעַן בָּאֵי בָאֵשׁ וּבַמַּיִם עַל קִדּוּשׁ שְׁמֶךָ, עֲשֵׂה לְמַעַן

יוֹנְקֵי שָׁדַיִם¹ שֶׁלֹּא חָטְאוּ, עֲשֵׂה לְמַעַן גְּמוּלֵי חָלָב²

שֶׁלֹּא פָשְׁעוּ, עֲשֵׂה לְמַעַן תִּינוֹקוֹת שֶׁל בֵּית רַבָּן³,

עֲשֵׂה לְמַעַנְךָ אִם לֹא לְמַעֲנֵנוּ, עֲשֵׂה לְמַעַנְךָ וְהוֹשִׁיעֵנוּ.

עֲנֵנוּ יהוה עֲנֵנוּ, עֲנֵנוּ אֱלֹהֵינוּ עֲנֵנוּ, עֲנֵנוּ אָבִינוּ⁴

עֲנֵנוּ, עֲנֵנוּ **בּוֹרְאֵנוּ**⁵ עֲנֵנוּ, עֲנֵנוּ גּוֹאֲלֵנוּ⁶ עֲנֵנוּ, עֲנֵנוּ

דוֹרְשֵׁנוּ⁷ עֲנֵנוּ, עֲנֵנוּ **הָאֵל** הַנֶּאֱמָן⁸ עֲנֵנוּ, עֲנֵנוּ וָתִיק

וְחָסִיד עֲנֵנוּ, עֲנֵנוּ **זַךְ** וְיָשָׁר⁹ עֲנֵנוּ, עֲנֵנוּ **חַי** וְקַיָּם¹⁰

עֲנֵנוּ, עֲנֵנוּ **טוֹב** וּמֵטִיב¹¹ עֲנֵנוּ, עֲנֵנוּ **יוֹדֵעַ** יֵצֶר¹² עֲנֵנוּ,

עֲנֵנוּ **כּוֹבֵשׁ** כְּעָסִים עֲנֵנוּ, עֲנֵנוּ **לוֹבֵשׁ** צְדָקוֹת¹³ עֲנֵנוּ,

עֲנֵנוּ **מֶלֶךְ** מַלְכֵי הַמְּלָכִים¹⁴ עֲנֵנוּ, עֲנֵנוּ **נוֹרָא** וְנִשְׂגָּב¹⁵

(1) Joel 2:16. (2) Isaiah 28:9. (3) Shabbos 119b. (4) Isaiah 64:7. (5) Cf. 43:1. (6) 47:4.
(7) Cf. Ezekiel 34:11. (8) Deuteronomy 7:9. (9) Job 8:6; cf. Proverbs 20:11.
(10) Cf. Daniel 6:27. (11) Cf. Psalms 119:68. (12) Cf. 103:14.
(13) Cf. Isaiah 59:17. (14) Ethics of the Fathers 3:1. (15) Psalms 47:3; 148:13.

עֲנֵנוּ, עֲנֵנוּ סוֹלֵחַ וּמוֹחֵל עֲנֵנוּ, עֲנֵנוּ עוֹנֶה בְּעֵת

‹ in time ‹ You Who « answer « answer ‹ and ‹ You Who ‹ answer « answer
answers us, us; pardons, forgives us, us;

צָרָה¹ עֲנֵנוּ, עֲנֵנוּ פּוֹדֶה וּמַצִּיל² עֲנֵנוּ, עֲנֵנוּ צַדִּיק

‹ righteous ‹ answer « answer ‹ and ‹ Redeemer ‹ answer « answer ‹ of
us, us; Rescuer, us, us; distress,

וְיָשָׁר³ עֲנֵנוּ, עֲנֵנוּ קָרוֹב לְקוֹרְאָיו⁴ עֲנֵנוּ, עֲנֵנוּ קָשֶׁה

‹ You Who ‹ answer « answer ‹ to those who ‹ He Who ‹ answer « answer ‹ and up-
with difficulty us, us; call upon Him, is close us, us; right One,

לִכְעוֹס⁵ עֲנֵנוּ, עֲנֵנוּ רַךְ לִרְצוֹת⁶ עֲנֵנוּ, עֲנֵנוּ רַחוּם

‹ merciful ‹ answer « answer ‹ appeased, ‹ You Who ‹ answer « answer ‹ becomes
us, us; are easily us, us; angry,

וְחַנּוּן⁷ עֲנֵנוּ, עֲנֵנוּ שׁוֹמֵעַ אֶל אֶבְיוֹנִים⁸ עֲנֵנוּ, עֲנֵנוּ

‹ answer « answer ‹ the destitute, ‹ to ‹ You Who ‹ answer « answer ‹ and gra-
us, us; listens us, us; cious One,

תּוֹמֵךְ תְּמִימִים עֲנֵנוּ, עֲנֵנוּ אֱלֹהֵי אֲבוֹתֵינוּ עֲנֵנוּ,

« answer ‹ of our ‹ God ‹ answer « answer ‹ the ‹ You Who
us; forefathers, us, us; wholesome, supports

עֲנֵנוּ אֱלֹהֵי אַבְרָהָם עֲנֵנוּ, עֲנֵנוּ פַּחַד יִצְחָק⁹ עֲנֵנוּ,

« answer ‹ of Isaac, ‹ Awesome ‹ answer « answer ‹ of Abraham, ‹ God ‹ answer
us; One us, us; us,

עֲנֵנוּ אֲבִיר יַעֲקֹב¹⁰ עֲנֵנוּ, עֲנֵנוּ עֶזְרַת הַשְּׁבָטִים עֲנֵנוּ,

« answer ‹ of the tribes, ‹ Helper ‹ answer « answer ‹ of Jacob, ‹ Mighty ‹ answer
us; us, us; One us,

עֲנֵנוּ מִשְׂגַּב אִמָּהוֹת עֲנֵנוּ, עֲנֵנוּ עוֹנֶה בְּעֵת רָצוֹן¹¹ עֲנֵנוּ,

« answer ‹ of favor, ‹ in a ‹ You Who ‹ answer « answer ‹ of the ‹ Stronghold ‹ answer
us; time answers us, us; Matriarchs, us,

עֲנֵנוּ אֲבִי יְתוֹמִים¹² עֲנֵנוּ, עֲנֵנוּ דַיַּן אַלְמָנוֹת¹² עֲנֵנוּ.

« answer ‹ of widows, ‹ Judge ‹ answer « answer ‹ of orphans, ‹ Father ‹ answer
us. us, us; us,

מִי שֶׁעָנָה לְאַבְרָהָם אָבִינוּ בְּהַר הַמּוֹרִיָּה¹³

« Moriah ‹ on Mount ‹ our father ‹ Abraham ‹ Who answered ‹ He

הוּא יַעֲנֵנוּ.

« answer ‹ — may
us. He

---

(1) Cf. *Isaiah* 49:8; *Psalms* 37:39. Alternate text: בְּעֵת רָצוֹן, *in time of favor.* (2) Cf. 34:23,18.
(3) *Deuteronomy* 32:4. (4) Cf. *Psalms* 145:18. (5) *Ethics of the Fathers* 5:14. (6) Cf. 5:14.
(7) *Exodus* 34:6. (8) *Psalms* 69:34. (9) *Genesis* 31:42. (10) *Isaiah* 49:26. (11) Cf. 49:8;
Psalms 69:14. Alternate text: בְּעֵת צָרָה, *in time of distress.* (12) 68:6. (13) *Genesis* 22:12.

מִי שֶׁעָנָה לְיִצְחָק בְּנוֹ כְּשֶׁנֶּעֱקַד עַל גַּבֵּי הַמִּזְבֵּחַ[1]

He › Who answered › Isaac › his son › when he was bound › on › top › of the altar ⟪

הוּא יַעֲנֵנוּ.

may He › — answer us. ⟪

מִי שֶׁעָנָה לְיַעֲקֹב בְּבֵית אֵל[2]

He › Who answered › Jacob › in Beth-el ⟪

הוּא יַעֲנֵנוּ.

may He › — answer us. ⟪

מִי שֶׁעָנָה לְיוֹסֵף בְּבֵית הָאֲסוּרִים[3]

He › Who answered › Joseph › in the prison ⟪

הוּא יַעֲנֵנוּ.

may He › — answer us. ⟪

מִי שֶׁעָנָה לַאֲבוֹתֵינוּ עַל יַם סוּף[4]

He › Who answered › our forefathers › at › the Sea › of Reeds ⟪

הוּא יַעֲנֵנוּ.

may He › — answer us. ⟪

מִי שֶׁעָנָה לְמֹשֶׁה בְּחוֹרֵב[5]

He › Who answered › Moses › in Horeb ⟪

הוּא יַעֲנֵנוּ.

may He › — answer us. ⟪

מִי שֶׁעָנָה לְאַהֲרֹן בַּמַּחְתָּה[6]

He › Who answered › Aaron › with the fire-pan ⟪

הוּא יַעֲנֵנוּ.

may He › — answer us. ⟪

מִי שֶׁעָנָה לְפִינְחָס בְּקוּמוֹ מִתּוֹךְ הָעֵדָה[7] הוּא יַעֲנֵנוּ.

He › Who answered › Phinehas › when he arose › from › amid › the congregation ⟪ may He › — answer us. ⟪

מִי שֶׁעָנָה לִיהוֹשֻׁעַ בַּגִּלְגָּל[8]

He › Who answered › Joshua › in Gilgal ⟪

הוּא יַעֲנֵנוּ.

may He › — answer us. ⟪

מִי שֶׁעָנָה לִשְׁמוּאֵל בַּמִּצְפָּה[9]

He › Who answered › Samuel › in Mizpah ⟪

הוּא יַעֲנֵנוּ.

may He › — answer us. ⟪

מִי שֶׁעָנָה לְדָוִד וּשְׁלֹמֹה בְנוֹ בִּירוּשָׁלַיִם[10] הוּא יַעֲנֵנוּ.

He › Who answered › David › and Solomon › his son › in Jerusalem ⟪ may He › — answer us. ⟪

מִי שֶׁעָנָה לְאֵלִיָּהוּ בְּהַר הַכַּרְמֶל[11]

He › Who answered › Elijah › on Mount › Carmel ⟪

הוּא יַעֲנֵנוּ.

may He › — answer us. ⟪

(1) *Genesis* 22:12. (2) 35:3. (3) 39:21. (4) *Exodus* Ch. 14. (5) *Exodus* 17:6,11; *Deuteronomy* 9:19.
(6) *Numbers* 17:11-13. (7) 25:7-13. (8) *Joshua* 6:1-20; 7:6-15; 10:12-14. (9) *I Samuel* 7:9.
(10) *II Samuel* 7:5-16; 21:1,14; 24:25; *I Kings* 9:3. (11) 18:36-38.

מִי שֶׁעָנָה לֶאֱלִישָׁע בִּירִיחוֹ¹ הוּא יַעֲנֵנוּ.

‹ He › Who ‹ Elisha ‹ in Jericho ≪ — may ‹ answer
answered He us.

מִי שֶׁעָנָה לְיוֹנָה בִּמְעֵי הַדָּגָה² הוּא יַעֲנֵנוּ.

‹ He › Who ‹ Jonah › in the ‹ of the ≪ — may ‹ answer
answered innards fish He us.

מִי שֶׁעָנָה לְחִזְקִיָּהוּ מֶלֶךְ יְהוּדָה בְּחָלְיוֹ³ הוּא יַעֲנֵנוּ.

‹ He › Who ‹ Hezekiah, ‹ king ‹ of Judah, ‹ in his ≪ — may ‹ answer
answered illness He us.

מִי שֶׁעָנָה לַחֲנַנְיָה מִישָׁאֵל וַעֲזַרְיָה

‹ He › Who ‹ Hananiah, ‹ Mishael, ‹ and Azariah ›
answered

בְּתוֹךְ כִּבְשַׁן הָאֵשׁ⁴ הוּא יַעֲנֵנוּ.

‹ inside ‹ the furnace ‹ of fire ≪ — may ‹ answer
He us.

מִי שֶׁעָנָה לְדָנִיֵּאל בְּגוֹב הָאֲרָיוֹת⁵ הוּא יַעֲנֵנוּ.

‹ He › Who ‹ Daniel ‹ in the ‹ of lions ≪ — may ‹ answer
answered den He us.

מִי שֶׁעָנָה לְמָרְדְּכַי וְאֶסְתֵּר בְּשׁוּשַׁן הַבִּירָה⁶

‹ He › Who ‹ Mordechai ‹ and Esther ‹ in Shushan ‹ the capital ≪
answered

הוּא יַעֲנֵנוּ.

‹ — may ‹ answer
He us.

מִי שֶׁעָנָה לְעֶזְרָא בַּגּוֹלָה⁷ הוּא יַעֲנֵנוּ.

‹ He › Who ‹ Ezra ‹ in the exile ≪ — may ‹ answer
answered He us.

מִי שֶׁעָנָה לְכָל הַצַּדִּיקִים וְהַחֲסִידִים וְהַתְּמִימִים

‹ He › Who ‹ all ‹ the righteous, ‹ the devout, ‹ the wholesome,
answered

וְהַיְשָׁרִים הוּא יַעֲנֵנוּ.

≪ and the ≪ — may ‹ answer
upright He us.

רַחֲמָנָא דְּעָנֵי לַעֲנִיֵּי, עֲנֵינָן. רַחֲמָנָא דְּעָנֵי לִתְבִירֵי

‹ Merciful One ‹ Who ‹ the poor, ≪ answer ‹ Merciful ‹ Who ‹ those of
answers us! One answers broken

(1) *II Kings* 2:21. (2) *Jonah* 2:2-11. (3) *II Kings* 20:2-6; *Isaiah* 38:2-8.
(4) *Daniel* 3:21-27. (5) 6:17-23. (6) *Esther* Ch. 8. (7) *Ezra* 8:21-23.

לִבָּא, עֲנֵינָן. רַחֲמָנָא דְּעָנֵי לִמְכִיכֵי רוּחָא, עֲנֵינָן.

‹ hearts, › answer us! › Merciful One › Who answers › those of crushed › spirit, › answer us!

רַחֲמָנָא עֲנֵינָן. רַחֲמָנָא חוּס. רַחֲמָנָא פְּרוֹק. רַחֲמָנָא

‹ Merciful One, › answer us! › Merciful One, › have pity! › Merciful One, › redeem! › Merciful One,

שְׁזִיב. רַחֲמָנָא רְחֵם עֲלָן, הַשְׁתָּא בַּעֲגָלָא וּבִזְמַן קָרִיב.

‹ save! › Merciful One, › have mercy › on us › — now, › swiftly, › and at a time › that comes soon.

PUTTING DOWN THE HEAD / נפילת אפים

RECITE UNTIL יִבֹּשׁוּ רָגַע WITH THE HEAD RESTING ON THE LEFT ARM, PREFERABLY WHILE SEATED.

(וַיֹּאמֶר דָּוִד אֶל גָּד, צַר לִי מְאֹד, נִפְּלָה נָא בְיַד יהוה,

‹ (And David said › to › Gad, › Dis- tressed › am I › exceed- ingly. › Let us now fall › into the hand › of HASHEM,

כִּי רַבִּים רַחֲמָיו, וּבְיַד אָדָם אַל אֶפְּלָה.[1]

‹ for › abundant › are His mercies, › but into human hands › let me not fall.)

רַחוּם וְחַנּוּן חָטָאתִי לְפָנֶיךָ. יהוה מָלֵא רַחֲמִים,

‹ O merciful One, › and gracious › I have sinned › before You. › HASHEM, › Who is full › of mercy,

רַחֵם עָלַי וְקַבֵּל תַּחֲנוּנָי.

‹ have mercy › on me › and accept › my supplications.

———— תהלים ו:ב-יא / Psalms 6:2-11 ————

יהוה, אַל בְּאַפְּךָ תוֹכִיחֵנִי, וְאַל בַּחֲמָתְךָ תְיַסְּרֵנִי.

‹ HASHEM, › do not › in Your anger › rebuke me, › nor › in Your wrath › chastise me.

חָנֵּנִי יהוה כִּי אֻמְלַל אָנִי, רְפָאֵנִי יהוה כִּי נִבְהֲלוּ

‹ Favor me, › for HASHEM, › feeble › am I; › heal me, › for HASHEM, › shudder with terror

עֲצָמָי. וְנַפְשִׁי נִבְהֲלָה מְאֹד, וְאַתָּה יהוה עַד מָתָי.

‹ do my bones. › My soul › is terrified › utterly, › and You, › HASHEM, › until › when?

שׁוּבָה יהוה חַלְּצָה נַפְשִׁי, הוֹשִׁיעֵנִי לְמַעַן חַסְדֶּךָ.

‹ Desist, › HASHEM, › release › my soul; › save me › as befits › Your kindness.

---

(1) *II Samuel* 24:14.

כִּי אֵין בַּמָּוֶת זִכְרֶךָ, בִּשְׁאוֹל מִי יוֹדֶה לָּךְ. יָגַעְתִּי

For / not / in / is there men- / in the / who / will / You? / I am
death / tion of You; / grave / praise / wearied

בְּאַנְחָתִי, אַשְׂחֶה בְכָל לַיְלָה מִטָּתִי, בְּדִמְעָתִי

with my sigh; / I drench / every / night / my bed; / with my tears

עַרְשִׂי אַמְסֶה. עָשְׁשָׁה מִכַּעַס עֵינִי, עָתְקָה בְּכָל

my couch / I soak. / Dimmed / because of / is my / aged / by all
anger / eye,

צוֹרְרָי. סוּרוּ מִמֶּנִּי כָּל פֹּעֲלֵי אָוֶן, כִּי שָׁמַע יהוה

my / Depart / from me, / all / doers / of evil, / for / HASHEM has heard
tormentors.

קוֹל בִּכְיִי. שָׁמַע יהוה תְּחִנָּתִי, יהוה תְּפִלָּתִי יִקָּח.

the / of my / HASHEM / my plea, / HASHEM / my prayer / will
sound / weeping. / has heard / accept.

יֵבֹשׁוּ וְיִבָּהֲלוּ מְאֹד כָּל אֹיְבָי, יָשֻׁבוּ יֵבֹשׁוּ רָגַע.

Let them / and con- / utterly, / all / my / may they / and be / in an
be shamed / founded / enemies; / regret / shamed / instant.

מָחֵי וּמַסֵּי מֵמִית וּמְחַיֶּה, מַסִּיק מִן שְׁאוֹל

[O God,] / and Who / Who causes / and Who / Who raises / from / the
Who wounds / heals, / death / restores life, / [the dead] / grave

לְחַיֵּי עָלְמָא, בְּרָא כַּד חָטֵי אֲבוּהִי לַקְיֵהּ, אֲבוּהִי

to life / eternal: / A son / should / sin, / his father / would / but a
he / strike him, / father

דְחַיֵּס אַסֵּי לִכְאֵבֵהּ. עַבְדָּא דְמָרִיד נָפִיק בְּקוֹלָר,

who is com- / will / his [son's] / A slave / who rebels, / he is / in chains,
passionate / heal / pain. / led out

מָרֵהּ תָּאִיב וְתַבִּיר קוֹלָרֵהּ.

his master / but [if] / desires, / he breaks / his chains.

בְּרָךְ בִּכְרָךְ אֲנָן וְחָטִינָן קַמָּךְ, הָא רְוֵי נַפְשִׁין

Your / Your / we / Your / and we have / indeed / satiated / has our
son, / firstborn, / are, / sinned / before / soul been
You;

בְּגִידִין מְרָרִין אֲנָן עַבְדָּךְ, וּמְרוֹדִינָן קַמָּךְ,

with / that is bitter. / we / Your / and we have / before
wormwood / are / servants / rebelled / You;

הָא בְּבִזְתָא, הָא בְּשִׁבְיָא, הָא בְּמַלְקִיּוּתָא.

some / from / some / in captivity, / and / by the lash.
[indeed we have / looting, / some
suffered,] some

בְּמָטוּ ‹ מִנָּךְ ‹ בְּרַחֲמָךְ ‹ דִּנְפִישִׁין, ‹ אַסִּי ‹ לִכְאָבִין
《 the pains ‹ heal ‹ that is abundant, ‹ in Your compassion ‹ of You, ‹ We beg

דִּתְקוֹף עֲלָן, ‹ עַד ‹ דְּלָא ‹ נֶהֱוֵי ‹ גְּמִירָא ‹ בְּשִׁבְיָא.
《 in captivity. ‹ completely annihilated ‹ we are not ‹ while yet ‹ us, ‹ that have overwhelmed

---

סְלִיחָה סז / SELICHAH 67
(תחנה)

אֱלֹהֵינוּ ‹ וֵאלֹהֵי ‹ אֲבוֹתֵינוּ:
《 of our forefathers: ‹ and the God ‹ Our God

שֶׁבֶת הַכִּסֵּא,* ‹ אֲשֶׁר ‹ לְמַעְלָה ‹ מְנֻשָּׂא,
《 is exalted, ‹ Above ‹ that ‹ of the Throne [of Glory]* ‹ May the seat

יְחַלֶּה בַּעֲדֵנוּ לְצוּר הַמִּתְנַשֵּׂא.
《 Who is Exalted. ‹ before the Rock ‹ for our sake, ‹ pray

מֶלֶךְ ‹ עַל ‹ כִּסֵּא ‹ לְעַמּוֹ ‹ יְהִי ‹ מַחְסֶה,
《 a shelter, ‹ be ‹ for His people ‹ His Throne ‹ on ‹ May the King

וְיַבִּיט ‹ בְּצוּרַת ‹ תָּם ‹ חֲקוּקָה ‹ בַּכִּסֵּא.*
《 in the Throne.* ‹ carved ‹ of [Jacob] the perfect one ‹ at the likeness ‹ and look

עַל הַיָּמִין אַרְיֵה, יְחַלֶּה פְּנֵי אֶהְיֶה,¹
《 [God Who is called] I-shall-be, ‹ before ‹ pray ‹ may the ‹ the right ‹ On
the lion

---

(1) See *Exodus* 3:14.

§§ שֶׁבֶת הַכִּסֵּא — *May the seat of the Throne [of Glory].* R' Shimon HaGadol signed this supplication in the acrostic of the stanzas — שִׁמְעוֹן בַּר יִצְחָק, *Shimon bar Yitzchak* [see prefatory comment to *Selichah* 18].

The first chapter of *Ezekiel* is a deep, mystical record of the angelic forms that the prophet saw in his Vision of the Chariot, that is, the Throne of Glory and the angels that bear it. Four *Chayos*, each with four faces — *As for the likeness of their faces: there was a human face; with the face of a lion to the right of the four of them; the face of an ox*

to the left of the four of them; and the face of an eagle for the four of them (*Ezekiel* 1:10) — were the bearers of the Chariot.

The *paytan* beseeches the Throne and its angelic bearers to pray before God for Israel's welfare. [The propriety and halachic significance of prayer through intercessors are discussed in the introduction to this volume.]

חֲקוּקָה בַּכִּסֵּא — *Carved in the Throne.* The face of a man that was one face of each of the *Chayos* mentioned above was the face of the Patriarch Jacob (*Rashi* to *Ezekiel* 1:5, based on *Bereishis Rabbah* 68:12).

יָחֹן וְיָחוֹס לְזֶרַע כֹּה יִהְיֶה.¹

《 they were 〈 that so 〈 on 〈 and have 〈 that
[promised] [numerous [Abraham's] pity He grant
to be. as the stars] offspring grace

וְיִשְׁעֵנוּ יִהְיֶה וְאוֹתָנוּ יְחַיֶּה,

《 grant life, 〈 and to us 〈 may He be 〈 Our salvation

וְיָשִׁיב הַמְּלוּכָה לְזֶרַע גּוּר אַרְיֵה.²

《 of the lion 〈 of the 〈 to the 〈 the kingdom 〈 and
[Judah]. cub offspring restore

נָא מֵהַשְּׂמֹאל שׁוֹר, פְּגִיעָתֵנוּ יִתְשַׁר,

《 offer as tribute; 〈 our prayer 〈 may the ox 〈 from the left 〈 Please,

לְלַמְּדֵנוּ הֵיטִיב חֲמוּצֵנוּ לְאַשֵּׁר.

《 to vindicate. 〈 our victim 〈 to do 〈 that He may
good, teach us

בִּרְכוֹת יַחֲשַׁר, וּמְרוּדֵינוּ יַעֲשַׁר,

《 make 〈 and our 〈 may He 〈 Blessings
wealthy, destitute rain down

וְיָשִׁיב לְבִצָּרוֹן הַדְרַת הוֹד בְּכוֹר שׁוֹר.*³

《 [with the power 〈 of [Joseph] 〈 the glory 〈 to the walled 〈 and bring
of] the ox.* the firstborn city [Jerusalem] back

רְאִיַּת פְּנֵי אָדָם, תְּחִנָּתֵנוּ יְקַדֵּם,

《 advance 〈 our 〈 of a man 〈 of the 〈 May the
supplication face visage

לִפְנֵי צוּר מָעוֹז יוֹצֵר הָאָדָם.

《 of Man. 〈 the 〈 the Strong- 〈 the 〈 before
Maker hold, Rock,

יַלְבִּין הַמְאָדָם,⁴ וִיעוֹרֵר הַנִּרְדָּם,

《 the slumbering 〈 and awaken 《 that which 〈 May He
[sinners], was reddened whiten
[by sin],

---

(1) Cf. *Genesis* 15:5. (2) 49:9. (3) Cf. *Deuteronomy* 33:17. (4) Cf. *Isaiah* 1:18.

בְּכוֹר שׁוֹר — *[Joseph] the firstborn [with the power of] the ox.* This description of Joseph is found in Moses' blessings to the tribes before his death (see *Deuteronomy* 33:17). But the reference here is not limited to the offspring of Joseph, for why would the *paytan* single out one tribe over the others? All Israel is called by Joseph's name (*Amos* 5:15) for a variety of reasons: Joseph supported and sustained the fledgling tribes when they first came down to Egypt (*Rashi*); most of the kings of the Northern Kingdom were descended from Joseph's sons Ephraim and Menasseh (*Ibn Ezra*); and the Northern Kingdom was called Ephraim [and also Joseph] for the tribe of its first king (*Radak*).

וְיַרְבֶּה הַמִּשְׂרָה לִקְרוּאֵי צֹאן אָדָם.[1]

》 of Man. 〈 the 〈 of [Israel] 〈 the dominion 〈 and
Flocks who are called increase

צִפְצוּף הַנֶּשֶׁר, בִּכְנָפָיו יְחַשֵּׁר,

》 gather and direct the 〈 with its 〈 of the 〈 May the
flow [of prayer to God], wings eagle chirping

וְיָלִיץ צִדְקֵנוּ פְּנֵי אוֹהֵב יֹשֶׁר.

》 upright- 〈 Him 〈before〈 our right- 〈 and rec-
ness. Who loves eousness ommend

חֶלְקֵנוּ יְבַשֵּׂר, וְעַפְעַפֵּינוּ יְיַשֵּׁר,

》 set 〈 and our 〈 may He 〈 Our
straight, [wandering] eyes herald, portion

וִידַבֵּר בִּצְדָקָה לְעַם נְשׂוּאֵי נֶשֶׁר.[2]

》 by the 〈 borne 〈about the〈 charitably 〈 and speak
eagle. people

❖ קְדִישֵׁי עֶלְיוֹנִים, שְׂרָפִים וְאוֹפַנִּים,

》 and Ofanim [of the 〈 Seraphim 》 on high, 〈 Holy ones
Heavenly Chariot],

הַפִּילוּ תְחִנָּתֵנוּ[3] פְּנֵי אֲדוֹנֵי הָאֲדוֹנִים.

》 of the lords! 〈 the Lord 〈before〈 our supplications 〈 lay

וְיִזְכֹּר רִאשׁוֹנִים, וְאַהֲבַת אֵיתָנִים,

》 of the 〈 and the love 〈 our ancestors' 〈 May He
Patriarchs, [merit] remember

וִיקַיֵּם שְׁבוּעָה לְדוֹרוֹת אַחֲרוֹנִים.

》 that come after. 〈 to the generations 〈 the oath 〈 and fulfill

ALL:

מַכְנִיסֵי רַחֲמִים, הַכְנִיסוּ רַחֲמֵינוּ, לִפְנֵי בַּעַל

〈 the 〈 before 〈 our [plea for] 〈 may you 〈 [pleas for] mercy, 〈 O you who
Master mercy usher in usher in

הָרַחֲמִים. מַשְׁמִיעֵי תְפִלָּה, הַשְׁמִיעוּ תְפִלָּתֵנוּ, לִפְנֵי

〈 before 〈 of our prayer 〈 may you aid 》 of prayer, 〈 O you who aid 》 of mercy.
the hearing the hearing

שׁוֹמֵעַ תְּפִלָּה. מַשְׁמִיעֵי צְעָקָה, הַשְׁמִיעוּ צַעֲקָתֵנוּ,

〈 of our 〈 may you aid 》 of outcries, 〈 O you who aid 》 of 〈 the Hearer
outcries the hearing the hearing prayer.

---

(1) Cf. *Ezekiel* 36:37-38. (2) Cf. *Exodus* 19:4.
(3) Some editions read הַשְׁמִיעוּ תְּפִלּוֹתֵנוּ, *cause our prayers to be heard.*

לִפְנֵי שׁוֹמֵעַ צְעָקָה. מַכְנִיסֵי דִמְעָה, הַכְנִיסוּ
‹ may you usher in ›› tears, ‹ O you who usher in ›› of outcries. ‹ the Hearer ‹ before

דִמְעוֹתֵינוּ, לִפְנֵי מֶלֶךְ מִתְרַצֶּה בִּדְמָעוֹת.
›› through tears. ‹Who is appeased ‹ the King ‹ before ‹ our tears

הִשְׁתַּדְּלוּ וְהַרְבּוּ תְּחִנָּה וּבַקָּשָׁה, לִפְנֵי מֶלֶךְ אֵל
‹ God, ‹ the King, ‹ before ‹ and pleas ‹ supplications ‹ and ‹ Exert
intensify yourselves

רָם וְנִשָּׂא. הַזְכִּירוּ לְפָנָיו, הַשְׁמִיעוּ לְפָנָיו תּוֹרָה
‹ the ‹ before ‹ aid to ›› before ‹ Mention ›› and ‹ exalted
Torah Him, be heard Him, uplifted.

וּמַעֲשִׂים טוֹבִים שֶׁל שׁוֹכְנֵי עָפָר.
›› in the ‹ [the Patriarchs ‹ of ‹ that are ‹ and the deeds
dust. and Matriarchs] good
who dwell

יִזְכֹּר אַהֲבָתָם וִיחַיֶּה זַרְעָם, שֶׁלֹּא תֹאבַד שְׁאֵרִית
‹ shall the ‹ lost ‹ so that ‹ to their ‹ and grant ‹ their love ‹ May He
remnant not offspring, life remember

יַעֲקֹב. כִּי צֹאן רוֹעֵה נֶאֱמָן הָיָה לְחֶרְפָּה,
›› a disgrace; ‹ has ‹ who is faith- ‹ of the ‹ the ‹ For ›› of Jacob
become ful [Moses] shepherd flock be.

יִשְׂרָאֵל גּוֹי אֶחָד לְמָשָׁל וְלִשְׁנִינָה.
›› and a simile. ‹ a parable ›› that is ‹ the ›› Israel,
unique, nation

מַהֵר עֲנֵנוּ אֱלֹהֵי יִשְׁעֵנוּ, וּפְדֵנוּ מִכָּל גְּזֵרוֹת קָשׁוֹת
›› that are ‹ decrees ‹ from all ‹ and re- ‹ of our ‹ O God ‹ answer ‹ Swiftly
harsh; deem us salvation, us,

וְהוֹשִׁיעָה בְּרַחֲמֶיךָ הָרַבִּים, מְשִׁיחַ צִדְקֶךָ וְעַמֶּךָ.
›› and Your ‹ Your righteous ‹ that is ‹ in Your mercy ‹ and may You
people. anointed one abundant, save,

מָרָן דְּבִשְׁמַיָּא לָךְ מִתְחַנְּנָן, כְּבָר שְׁבַיָּא דְמִתְחַנֵּן
‹ who ‹ in ‹ as one ›› do we ‹ to You ›› Who is in ‹ Our
supplicates captivity supplicate, heaven, Master

לְשֵׁבוּיֵהּ. כֻּלְּהוֹן בְּנֵי שְׁבַיָּא בְּכַסְפָּא מִתְפָּרְקִין,
›› are redeemed, ‹ through ‹ in ‹ those ‹ [for] all ›› before his
money captivity, captors;

וְעַמְּךָ יִשְׂרָאֵל בְּרַחֲמֵי וּבְתַחֲנוּנֵי, הַב לָן שְׁאִילְתִּין
‹ our requests ‹ us ‹ O » and ‹ through ‹ Israel ‹ but Your
   grant   supplication.   compassion   people

וּבָעוּתִין, דְּלָא נֶהְדַּר רֵיקָם מִן קֳדָמָךְ.
» before ‹ from ‹ empty- ‹ that we not be ‹ and our prayers
   You.   handed   turned away

מָרָן דִּבְשְׁמַיָּא לָךְ מִתְחַנְּנַן, כְּעַבְדָּא דְּמִתְחַנֵּן
‹ who ‹ as a slave » do we ‹ to You » Who is in ‹ Our
supplicates   supplicate,   heaven,   Master

לְמָרֵיהּ, עֲשִׁיקֵי אֲנָן וּבַחֲשׁוֹכָא שָׁרִינַן, מְרִירָן נַפְשִׁין
‹ are [our] ‹ embittered » do we ‹ and in darkness ‹ are ‹ Oppressed » to his
souls   abide,   we   master:

מֵעַקְתִין דִּנְפִישִׁין, חֵילָא לֵית בָּן לְרַצּוּיָךְ. מָרָן,
‹ Our » to appease ‹ within ‹ is ‹ Strength » that is ‹ from distress
Master,   You.   us lacking   excessive.

עֲבִיד בְּדִיל קַיָמָא דִּגְזַרְתָּ עִם אֲבָהָתָנָא.
» our Patriarchs. ‹ with ‹ that You ‹ of the ‹ for the ‹ act
   established   covenant   sake

שׁוֹמֵר יִשְׂרָאֵל, שְׁמוֹר שְׁאֵרִית יִשְׂרָאֵל, וְאַל
‹ let not » of Israel; ‹ the remnant ‹ safeguard » of Israel, ‹ O Guardian

יֹאבַד יִשְׂרָאֵל, הָאֹמְרִים שְׁמַע יִשְׂרָאֵל.[1]
» O Israel. ‹ Hear, ‹ those who » Israel be destroyed —
    proclaim:

שׁוֹמֵר גּוֹי אֶחָד, שְׁמוֹר שְׁאֵרִית עַם אֶחָד, וְאַל
‹ let not » that is ‹ of the ‹ the remnant ‹ safeguard » that is ‹ of the ‹ O Guardian
   unique; people   unique,   nation

יֹאבַד גּוֹי אֶחָד, הַמְיַחֲדִים שִׁמְךָ, יהוה אֱלֹהֵינוּ
‹ is our God, ‹ HASHEM ‹ of Your ‹ those who proclaim » that is ‹ the ‹ be
    Name: the Oneness   unique, nation destroyed

יהוה אֶחָד.
» the One ‹ HASHEM
[and Only]! is

שׁוֹמֵר גּוֹי קָדוֹשׁ, שְׁמוֹר שְׁאֵרִית עַם קָדוֹשׁ,
» that is ‹ of the ‹ the remnant ‹ safeguard » that is ‹ of the ‹ O Guardian
holy, people   holy,   nation

(1) Deuteronomy 6:4.

וְאַל יֹאבַד גּוֹי קָדוֹשׁ, הַמְשַׁלְּשִׁים בְּשָׁלֹשׁ קְדֻשּׁוֹת

⟨ sancti-　⟨ the　⟨ those who proclaim　《 that is　⟨ the　⟨ be　⟨ let
fications　threefold　three times　holy,　nation　destroyed　not

לְקָדוֹשׁ.

《 to the Holy One.

מִתְרַצֶּה בְּרַחֲמִים וּמִתְפַּיֵּס בְּתַחֲנוּנִים, הִתְרַצֵּה

⟨ be　《 through　⟨ and Who becomes　⟨ through　⟨ You Who becomes
favorable　supplications,　conciliatory　compassion　favorable

וְהִתְפַּיֵּס לְדוֹר עָנִי, כִּי אֵין עוֹזֵר. אָבִינוּ מַלְכֵּנוּ,

《 our King,　⟨ Our　《 helper.　⟨ there　⟨ for　《 that is　⟨ to the　⟨ and be
　　　Father,　　　is no　　poor,　generation　conciliatory

חָנֵּנוּ וַעֲנֵנוּ, כִּי אֵין בָּנוּ מַעֲשִׂים, עֲשֵׂה עִמָּנוּ

⟨ us　⟨ treat　《 worthy deeds;　⟨ we have no　⟨ though　⟨ and　⟨ be gracious
　　　　　　　　　　　　　　answer us,　with us

צְדָקָה וָחֶסֶד וְהוֹשִׁיעֵנוּ.

《 and save us.　⟨ and　⟨ with
　　　kindness,　charity

STAND AFTER THE WORDS וַאֲנַחְנוּ לֹא נֵדַע UNTIL CONCLUSION OF THE PARAGRAPH.

וַאֲנַחְנוּ לֹא נֵדַע מַה נַּעֲשֶׂה, כִּי עָלֶיךָ עֵינֵינוּ.[1]

《 are our　⟨ upon　⟨ rather,　《 we should　⟨ what　⟨ know not　⟨ We
eyes.　You　　　　do,

זְכֹר רַחֲמֶיךָ יהוה וַחֲסָדֶיךָ, כִּי מֵעוֹלָם הֵמָּה.[2] יְהִי

⟨ May　《 are they.　⟨ eternal　⟨ for　⟨ and Your　⟨ HASHEM,　⟨ Your　⟨ Remem-
　　　　　　　　　　　kindnesses,　　　　mercies,　ber

חַסְדְּךָ יהוה עָלֵינוּ, כַּאֲשֶׁר יִחַלְנוּ לָךְ.[3] אַל תִּזְכָּר

⟨ recall　⟨ Do not　《 You.　⟨ we awaited　⟨ just as　《 be upon us,　⟨ HASHEM,　⟨ Your kindness,

לָנוּ עֲוֹנוֹת רִאשׁוֹנִים, מַהֵר יְקַדְּמוּנוּ רַחֲמֶיךָ, כִּי

⟨ for　《 may Your　⟨ advance to　⟨ swiftly　《 of the ancients;　⟨ the sins　⟨ against
　　　mercies,　meet us　　　　　　　　　　us

דַלּוֹנוּ מְאֹד.[4] עֶזְרֵנוּ בְּשֵׁם יהוה, עֹשֵׂה שָׁמַיִם

⟨ of　⟨ Maker　《 of HASHEM,　⟨ is through　⟨ Our help　《 exceed-　⟨ we have
heaven　　　　　the Name　　　　ingly.　become
　　　　　　　　　　　　　　　　　　impoverished

וָאָרֶץ.[5] חָנֵּנוּ יהוה חָנֵּנוּ, כִּי רַב שָׂבַעְנוּ בוּז.[6] בְּרֹגֶז

《 Amid　《 with　⟨ sated　⟨ we are　⟨ for　《 favor us,　⟨ HASHEM,　⟨ Favor us,　《 and earth.
wrath,　contempt.　　fully

(1) *II Chronicles* 20:12. (2) *Psalms* 25:6. (3) 33:22. (4) 79:8. (5) 121:2. (6) 123:3.

רַחֵם תִּזְכּוֹר.¹ בְּרְגֶז עֲקֵדָה תִּזְכּוֹר. בְּרְגֶז תְּמִימוֹת

‹ the perfect ones   « Amid wrath,   » You should remember!   ‹ the binding [of Isaac]   « Amid wrath,   › You should remember!   ‹ to be merciful

תִּזְכּוֹר. יהוה הוֹשִׁיעָה, הַמֶּלֶךְ יַעֲנֵנוּ בְיוֹם קָרְאֵנוּ.²

« we call.   ‹ on the day   ‹ answer us   ‹ May the King   « save!   ‹ HASHEM,   « You should remember!

כִּי הוּא יָדַע יִצְרֵנוּ, זְכוֹר כִּי עָפָר אֲנָחְנוּ.³

« are we.   ‹ dust   ‹ that   ‹ He is mindful   « our nature,   ‹ knew   ‹ He   ‹ For

❖ עָזְרֵנוּ אֱלֹהֵי יִשְׁעֵנוּ עַל דְּבַר כְּבוֹד שְׁמֶךָ, וְהַצִּילֵנוּ

‹ rescue us   « of Your Name;   ‹ of the glory   ‹ the   ‹ for   ‹ of our salvation   ‹ O God   ‹ Assist us,

וְכַפֵּר עַל חַטֹּאתֵינוּ לְמַעַן שְׁמֶךָ.⁴

« of Your Name.   ‹ for the sake   ‹ our sins   ‹ for   ‹ and grant atonement

FULL KADDISH / קדיש שלם

THE *CHAZZAN* RECITES קַדִּישׁ שָׁלֵם, FULL *KADDISH.*

יִתְגַּדַּל וְיִתְקַדַּשׁ שְׁמֵהּ רַבָּא. (.אָמֵן — Cong.) בְּעָלְמָא

‹ — in the world   « (Amen.)   « that is great! —   ‹ may His Name   ‹ and be sanctified   ‹ Grow exalted

דִּי בְרָא כִרְעוּתֵהּ. וְיַמְלִיךְ מַלְכוּתֵהּ, וְיַצְמַח פֻּרְקָנֵהּ

‹ His salvation,   « and cause to sprout   ‹ to His kingship,   ‹ and may He give reign   « according to His will,   ‹ He   ‹ that   ‹ created

וִיקָרֵב מְשִׁיחֵהּ. (.אָמֵן — Cong.) בְּחַיֵּיכוֹן וּבְיוֹמֵיכוֹן וּבְחַיֵּי

‹ and in the lifetimes   ‹ and in your days,   ‹ in your lifetimes   « (Amen.)   « His Messiah,   ‹ and bring near

דְכָל בֵּית יִשְׂרָאֵל, בַּעֲגָלָא וּבִזְמַן קָרִיב. וְאִמְרוּ: אָמֵן.

« Amen.   ‹ Now respond: « that comes soon.   ‹ and at a time   ‹ swiftly   « of Israel,   ‹ Family   ‹ of the entire

CONGREGATION RESPONDS:

אָמֵן. יְהֵא שְׁמֵהּ רַבָּא מְבָרַךְ לְעָלַם וּלְעָלְמֵי עָלְמַיָּא.

« and for all eternity.   ‹ forever   ‹ be blessed   ‹ that is great   ‹ His Name   ‹ May   « Amen.

CHAZZAN CONTINUES:

יְהֵא שְׁמֵהּ רַבָּא מְבָרַךְ לְעָלַם וּלְעָלְמֵי עָלְמַיָּא. יִתְבָּרַךְ

‹ Blessed,   « and for all eternity.   ‹ forever   ‹ be blessed   ‹ that is great   ‹ His Name   ‹ May

וְיִשְׁתַּבַּח וְיִתְפָּאַר וְיִתְרוֹמַם וְיִתְנַשֵּׂא וְיִתְהַדָּר וְיִתְעַלֶּה

‹ elevated,   ‹ honored,   ‹ upraised,   ‹ exalted,   ‹ glorified,   ‹ praised,

---

(1) *Habakkuk* 3:2. (2) *Psalms* 20:10. (3) 103:14. (4) 79:9.

וְיִתְהַלָּל שְׁמֵהּ דְּקֻדְשָׁא בְּרִיךְ הוּא (.Cong — בְּרִיךְ הוּא)

‹ and lauded ‹ be the ‹ of the Holy ‹ Blessed ‹ is He » ((Blessed » is He)
　　　　　　　　Name　　One,

— לְעֵלָּא [וּ]לְעֵלָּא מִכָּל בִּרְכָתָא וְשִׁירָתָא תֻּשְׁבְּחָתָא

‹ exceedingly beyond ‹ any ‹ blessing ‹ and song, » and song, ‹ praise

וְנֶחֱמָתָא דַּאֲמִירָן בְּעָלְמָא. וְאִמְרוּ: אָמֵן. (.Cong — אָמֵן.)

‹ and ‹ that are ‹ in the ‹ Now » Amen. ‹ respond: » (Amen.)
consolation　uttered　world.

CONGREGATION:

(קַבֵּל בְּרַחֲמִים וּבְרָצוֹן אֶת תְּפִלָּתֵנוּ.)

‹ (Accept ‹ with mercy ‹ and with favor ‹ our prayers.) »

CHAZZAN CONTINUES:

תִּתְקַבֵּל צְלוֹתְהוֹן וּבָעוּתְהוֹן דְּכָל בֵּית יִשְׂרָאֵל קֳדָם

‹ May ‹ the prayers ‹ and ‹ of the ‹ Israel ‹ before
accepted be　　　supplications　entire　Family of

אֲבוּהוֹן דִּי בִשְׁמַיָּא. וְאִמְרוּ: אָמֵן. (.Cong — אָמֵן.)

‹ their ‹ Who ‹ is in ‹ Now » Amen. ‹ respond: » (Amen.)
Father　Heaven.

CONGREGATION:

(יְהִי שֵׁם יהוה מְבֹרָךְ, מֵעַתָּה וְעַד עוֹלָם.[1])

‹ (Let ‹ the ‹ of ‹ be » be ‹ from ‹ until ‹ eternity.) »
HASHEM　Name　blessed,　this time

CHAZZAN CONTINUES:

יְהֵא שְׁלָמָא רַבָּא מִן שְׁמַיָּא וְחַיִּים טוֹבִים עָלֵינוּ וְעַל כָּל

‹ May ‹ peace ‹ that is ‹ from ‹ Heaven ‹ and life ‹ that is ‹ upon us ‹ and ‹ all ‹
there be　abundant　good,　upon

יִשְׂרָאֵל. וְאִמְרוּ: אָמֵן. (.Cong — אָמֵן.)

» Israel. ‹ Now respond: » Amen. ‹ respond: » (Amen.)

CONGREGATION:

(עֶזְרִי מֵעִם יהוה, עֹשֵׂה שָׁמַיִם וָאָרֶץ.[2])

‹ (My ‹ is ‹ HASHEM, » Maker ‹ of ‹ and
help　from　heaven　earth.)

CHAZZAN BOWS; TAKES THREE STEPS BACK. BOWS LEFT AND SAYS "... עֹשֶׂה שָׁלוֹם, *HE WHO MAKES PEACE* ..."; BOWS RIGHT AND SAYS "... הוּא, *MAY HE* ..."; BOWS FORWARD AND SAYS "... וְעַל כָּל יִשְׂרָאֵל, *AND UPON ALL ISRAEL* ..."; REMAINS IN PLACE FOR A FEW MOMENTS, THEN TAKES THREE STEPS FORWARD.

עֹשֶׂה [הַ]שָׁלוֹם בִּמְרוֹמָיו, הוּא יַעֲשֶׂה שָׁלוֹם עָלֵינוּ, וְעַל

‹ He Who ‹ [the] peace » in His ‹ may ‹ make ‹ peace ‹ upon us, ‹ and ‹
makes　heights,　He　　upon

כָּל יִשְׂרָאֵל. וְאִמְרוּ: אָמֵן. (.Cong — אָמֵן.)

‹ all » Israel. ‹ Now respond: » Amen. ‹ respond: » (Amen.)

(1) *Psalms* 113:2. (2) 121:2.

**WHEN YOM KIPPUR FALLS ON MONDAY OR THURSDAY, SOME CONGREGATIONS
REVERSE THE ORDER OF THE FOURTH AND FIFTH DAYS OF REPENTANCE.**

יום רביעי של עשרת ימי תשובה
FOURTH DAY OF REPENTANCE

אַשְׁרֵי יוֹשְׁבֵי בֵיתֶךָ, עוֹד יְהַלְלוּךָ סֶּלָה. אַשְׁרֵי

⟨ Praise-
worthy   ⟨ Selah.   ⟨ they will
praise You,   ⟨ con-
tinually   ⟨ in Your
house,   ⟨ are those
who dwell   ⟨ Praiseworthy

הָעָם שֶׁכָּכָה לּוֹ, אַשְׁרֵי הָעָם שֶׁיהוה אֱלֹהָיו.

⟨ is their
God.   ⟨ that   ⟨ is the
people   ⟨ praise-
worthy   ⟨ is
their lot;   ⟨ that such   ⟨ is the
people

——— Psalm 145 / תהלים קמה ———

תְּהִלָּה לְדָוִד, אֲרוֹמִמְךָ אֱלוֹהַי הַמֶּלֶךְ, וַאֲבָרְכָה

⟨ and I
will bless   ⟨ the King,   ⟨ my God   ⟨ I will exalt You,   ⟨ by David: ⟨ A psalm of
praise

שִׁמְךָ לְעוֹלָם וָעֶד. בְּכָל יוֹם אֲבָרְכֶךָ, וַאֲהַלְלָה שִׁמְךָ

⟨ Your
Name   ⟨ and I
will laud   ⟨ I will
bless You,   ⟨ day   ⟨ Every   ⟨ and
ever.   ⟨ for ever   ⟨ Your
Name

לְעוֹלָם וָעֶד. גָּדוֹל יהוה וּמְהֻלָּל מְאֹד, וְלִגְדֻלָּתוֹ

⟨ and His
greatness   ⟨ exceedingly,   ⟨ and
lauded   ⟨ is   ⟨ Great   ⟨ and
ever.   ⟨ forever

אֵין חֵקֶר. דּוֹר לְדוֹר יְשַׁבַּח מַעֲשֶׂיךָ, וּגְבוּרֹתֶיךָ יַגִּידוּ.

⟨ they will
recount.   ⟨ and Your
mighty deeds   ⟨ Your
actions,   ⟨ will
praise   ⟨ to   ⟨ Gen-
generation   ⟨ eration   ⟨ is beyond
investigation.

הֲדַר כְּבוֹד הוֹדֶךָ, וְדִבְרֵי נִפְלְאֹתֶיךָ אָשִׂיחָה. וֶעֱזוּז

⟨ And of
the might   ⟨ I shall
discuss.   ⟨ that are
wondrous   ⟨ and Your
deeds   ⟨ of Your
majesty,   ⟨ glory   ⟨ The
splendrous

נוֹרְאֹתֶיךָ יֹאמֵרוּ, וּגְדוּלָּתְךָ אֲסַפְּרֶנָּה. זֵכֶר רַב טוּבְךָ

⟨ of Your abun-
dant goodness   ⟨ A recol-
lection   ⟨ I shall
relate.   ⟨ and Your
greatness   ⟨ they will
speak,   ⟨ of Your
awesome deeds

יַבִּיעוּ, וְצִדְקָתְךָ יְרַנֵּנוּ. חַנּוּן וְרַחוּם יהוה, אֶרֶךְ אַפַּיִם

⟨ to
anger,   ⟨ slow   ⟨ is
HASHEM,   ⟨ and
merciful   ⟨ Gracious   ⟨ they will
sing joyfully.   ⟨ and of Your
righteousness   ⟨ they
will utter,

וּגְדָל חָסֶד. טוֹב יהוה לַכֹּל, וְרַחֲמָיו עַל כָּל מַעֲשָׂיו.

⟨ His
creations.   ⟨ all
on   ⟨ are   ⟨ His
mercies   ⟨ to all;   ⟨ HASHEM
is good   ⟨ in [bestowing]
kindness.   ⟨ and
great

(1) *Psalms* 84:5. (2) 144:15.

יוֹדֽוּךָ יהוה כָּל מַעֲשֶׂיךָ, וַחֲסִידֶיךָ יְבָרְכֽוּכָה. כְּבוֹד

⟨ Of the ⟨⟨ will ⟨ and Your ⟨⟨ Your ⟨ — all ⟨⟨HASHEM ⟨ They will
glory bless You. devout ones creations — thank You,

מַלְכוּתְךָ יֹאמֵֽרוּ, וּגְבוּרָתְךָ יְדַבֵּֽרוּ. לְהוֹדִֽיעַ לִבְנֵי הָאָדָם

⟨ mankind ⟨ To inform ⟨⟨ they will ⟨ and of Your ⟨⟨ they will ⟨ of Your
declare. power speak, kingdom

גְּבוּרֹתָיו, וּכְבוֹד הֲדַר מַלְכוּתוֹ. מַלְכוּתְךָ מַלְכוּת כָּל

⟨[span- ⟨ is a ⟨ Your kingdom ⟨⟨ of His ⟨ splendor ⟨ and of the ⟨⟨ of His mighty
ning] all kingdom kingdom. glorious deeds,

עֹלָמִים, וּמֶמְשַׁלְתְּךָ בְּכָל דּוֹר וָדֹר. סוֹמֵךְ יהוה

⟨ HASHEM ⟨⟨ after ⟨ gen- ⟨ is ⟨ and Your ⟨⟨ eternities,
supports generation. eration throughout dominion

לְכָל הַנֹּפְלִים, וְזוֹקֵף לְכָל הַכְּפוּפִים. עֵינֵי כֹל

⟨ of all ⟨ The ⟨⟨ those who ⟨ all ⟨ and ⟨⟨ those who ⟨ all
eyes are bent. straightens are fallen.

אֵלֶֽיךָ יְשַׂבֵּֽרוּ, וְאַתָּה נוֹתֵן לָהֶם אֶת אָכְלָם בְּעִתּוֹ.

⟨⟨ in its ⟨ their food ⟨ them ⟨ give ⟨ and You ⟨⟨ do look ⟨ to You
proper time. with hope,

CONCENTRATE INTENTLY WHILE RECITING THE VERSE פּוֹתֵחַ, YOU OPEN.

פּוֹתֵֽחַ אֶת יָדֶֽךָ, וּמַשְׂבִּֽיעַ לְכָל חַי רָצוֹן. ∗צַדִּיק

⟨ Righteous ⟨⟨ [with its] ⟨ living ⟨ every ⟨ and satisfy ⟨⟨ Your hand, ⟨ You open
desire. thing

יהוה בְּכָל דְּרָכָיו, וְחָסִיד בְּכָל מַעֲשָׂיו. קָרוֹב יהוה

⟨ is ⟨ Close ⟨⟨ His deeds. ⟨ in all ⟨ and ⟨⟨ His ways, ⟨ in all ⟨ is
HASHEM magnanimous HASHEM

לְכָל קֹרְאָיו, לְכֹל אֲשֶׁר יִקְרָאֻֽהוּ בֶאֱמֶת. רְצוֹן יְרֵאָיו

⟨ of those ⟨ The ⟨⟨ sincerely. ⟨ call upon ⟨ who ⟨ to all ⟨⟨ who call ⟨ to all
who fear Him will Him upon Him,

יַעֲשֶׂה, וְאֶת שַׁוְעָתָם יִשְׁמַע וְיוֹשִׁיעֵם. שׁוֹמֵר יהוה

⟨ HASHEM protects ⟨⟨ and He will ⟨ He will ⟨ and their cry ⟨⟨ He
save them. hear, will do;

אֶת כָּל אֹהֲבָיו, וְאֵת כָּל הָרְשָׁעִים יַשְׁמִיד. תְּהִלַּת

⟨ The ⟨⟨ He will ⟨ the wicked ⟨ but all ⟨⟨ who ⟨ all
praise destroy. love Him;

יהוה יְדַבֶּר פִּי, וִיבָרֵךְ כָּל בָּשָׂר שֵׁם קָדְשׁוֹ לְעוֹלָם

⟨ for ever ⟨ of His ⟨ the ⟨ flesh ⟨ may ⟨ and ⟨⟨ may my ⟨ of
Holiness Name all bless mouth declare, HASHEM

וָעֶד. וַאֲנַחְנוּ נְבָרֵךְ יָהּ מֵעַתָּה וְעַד עוֹלָם; הַלְלוּיָהּ.[1]

| ❮ Halleluyah! | ❮ eternity. | ❮ until | ❮ from this time | ❮ God | ❮ will bless | ❮ But we | ❮ and ever. |

THE CHAZZAN RECITES חֲצִי קַדִּישׁ, HALF-KADDISH:

יִתְגַּדַּל וְיִתְקַדַּשׁ שְׁמֵהּ רַבָּא. (.אָמֵן — .Cong) בְּעָלְמָא

| ❮ — in the world | ❮ (Amen.) | ❮ that is great! — | ❮ may His Name | ❮ and be sanctified | ❮ Grow exalted |

דִּי בְרָא כִרְעוּתֵהּ. וְיַמְלִיךְ מַלְכוּתֵהּ, וְיַצְמַח פֻּרְקָנֵהּ

| ❮ His salvation, | ❮ and cause to sprout | ❮ to His kingship, | ❮ and may He give reign | ❮ according to His will, | ❮ He created | ❮ that |

וִיקָרֵב מְשִׁיחֵהּ. (.אָמֵן — .Cong) בְּחַיֵּיכוֹן וּבְיוֹמֵיכוֹן וּבְחַיֵּי

| ❮ and in the lifetimes | ❮ and in your days, | ❮ in your lifetimes | ❮ (Amen.) | ❮ His Messiah, | ❮ and bring near |

דְכָל בֵּית יִשְׂרָאֵל, בַּעֲגָלָא וּבִזְמַן קָרִיב. וְאִמְרוּ: אָמֵן.

| ❮ Amen. | ❮ Now respond: | ❮ that comes soon. | ❮ and at a time | ❮ swiftly | ❮ of Israel, | ❮ Family | ❮ of the entire |

CONGREGATION RESPONDS:

אָמֵן. יְהֵא שְׁמֵהּ רַבָּא מְבָרַךְ לְעָלַם וּלְעָלְמֵי עָלְמַיָּא.

| ❮ and for all eternity. | ❮ forever | ❮ be blessed | ❮ that is great | ❮ His Name | ❮ May | ❮ Amen. |

CHAZZAN CONTINUES:

יְהֵא שְׁמֵהּ רַבָּא מְבָרַךְ לְעָלַם וּלְעָלְמֵי עָלְמַיָּא. יִתְבָּרַךְ

| ❮ Blessed, | ❮ and for all eternity. | ❮ forever | ❮ be blessed | ❮ that is great | ❮ His Name | ❮ May |

וְיִשְׁתַּבַּח וְיִתְפָּאַר וְיִתְרוֹמַם וְיִתְנַשֵּׂא וְיִתְהַדָּר וְיִתְעַלֶּה

| ❮ elevated, | ❮ honored, | ❮ upraised, | ❮ exalted, | ❮ glorified, | ❮ praised, |

וְיִתְהַלָּל שְׁמֵהּ דְּקֻדְשָׁא בְּרִיךְ הוּא (.Cong — בְּרִיךְ הוּא)

| ❮ is He) | ❮ (Blessed | ❮ is He | ❮ Blessed | ❮ of the Holy One, | ❮ be the Name | ❮ and lauded |

— לְעֵלָּא [וּ]לְעֵלָּא מִכָּל בִּרְכָתָא וְשִׁירָתָא תֻּשְׁבְּחָתָא

| ❮ praise | ❮ and song, | ❮ blessing | ❮ any | ❮ exceedingly beyond |

וְנֶחֱמָתָא דַּאֲמִירָן בְּעָלְמָא. וְאִמְרוּ: אָמֵן. (.Cong — אָמֵן.)

| ❮ (Amen.) | ❮ Amen. | ❮ Now respond: | ❮ in the world. | ❮ that are uttered | ❮ and consolation |

ALL:

לְךָ יהוה הַצְּדָקָה, וְלָנוּ בֹּשֶׁת הַפָּנִים.[2] מַה

| ❮ What | ❮ is shamefacedness. | ❮ and ours | ❮ is the righteousness, | ❮ O Lord, | ❮ Yours, |

---

(1) *Psalms* 115:18. (2) *Daniel* 9:7.

נִתְאוֹנֵן,¹ מַה נֹּאמַר, מַה נְּדַבֵּר, וּמַה נִּצְטַדָּק.²

《 complaint can we make? 〈 What 《 can we say? 〈 What 《 can we declare? 〈 What 《 justification can we offer?

נַחְפְּשָׂה דְרָכֵינוּ וְנַחְקֹרָה, וְנָשׁוּבָה אֵלֶיךָ,³ כִּי יְמִינְךָ

〈 Your right hand 〈 for 《 to You, 〈 and return 〈 and investigate them, 〈 our ways 〈 Let us examine

פְּשׂוּטָה לְקַבֵּל שָׁבִים. לֹא בְחֶסֶד וְלֹא בְמַעֲשִׂים

〈 with [merit for good] deeds 〈 nor 〈 with [merit] for kindness 〈 Neither 《 those who return. 〈 to accept 〈 is extended

בָּאנוּ לְפָנֶיךָ, כְּדַלִּים וּכְרָשִׁים דָּפַקְנוּ דְלָתֶיךָ.

《 on Your doors. 〈 we have knocked 〈 and as destitute people 〈 but as paupers 《 before You; 〈 do we come

דְלָתֶיךָ דָּפַקְנוּ רַחוּם וְחַנּוּן, נָא אַל תְּשִׁיבֵנוּ

〈 turn us away 〈 do not 〈 Please 《 and Gracious One. 〈 O Compassionate One 〈 we have knocked, 〈 On Your doors

רֵיקָם מִלְּפָנֶיךָ. מִלְּפָנֶיךָ מַלְכֵּנוּ רֵיקָם אַל תְּשִׁיבֵנוּ,

《 turn us away, 〈 do not 〈 empty-handed 〈 Our King, 〈 From before You, 《 from before You. 〈 empty-handed

כִּי אַתָּה שׁוֹמֵעַ תְּפִלָּה.

《 prayer. 〈 Who hears 〈 You are 〈 for the One

שֹׁמֵעַ תְּפִלָּה, עָדֶיךָ כָּל בָּשָׂר יָבֹאוּ.⁴ יָבֹא

〈 Come 《 will come. 〈 flesh 〈 all 〈 unto You 《 prayer, 〈 You Who hears

כָּל בָּשָׂר לְהִשְׁתַּחֲוֹת לְפָנֶיךָ יהוה.⁵ יָבֹאוּ וְיִשְׁתַּחֲווּ

〈 and bow down 〈 They will come 《 O HASHEM. 〈 before You, 〈 to bow down 〈 will all flesh

לְפָנֶיךָ אֲדֹנָי, וִיכַבְּדוּ לִשְׁמֶךָ.⁶ בֹּאוּ נִשְׁתַּחֲוֶה וְנִכְרָעָה,

《 and bow, 〈 Let us prostrate ourselves 〈 Come! 《 to Your Name. 〈 and they will show honor 《 O Lord, 〈 before You,

נִבְרְכָה לִפְנֵי יהוה עֹשֵׂנוּ.⁷ נָבוֹאָה לְמִשְׁכְּנוֹתָיו,

《 to His Tabernacles, 〈 Let us come 《 our Maker. 〈 HASHEM, 〈 before 〈 let us kneel

נִשְׁתַּחֲוֶה לַהֲדֹם רַגְלָיו.⁸ בֹּאוּ שְׁעָרָיו בְּתוֹדָה,

《 with thanksgiving, 〈 His gates 〈 Enter 《 for His feet. 〈 at the stool 〈 let us prostrate ourselves

---

(1) Cf. *Lamentations* 3:39. (2) Cf. *Genesis* 44:16. (3) Cf. *Lamentations* 3:40. (4) *Psalms* 65:3. (5) Cf. *Isaiah* 66:23. (6) *Psalms* 86:9. (7) 95:6. (8) 132:7.

חֲצֵרֹתָיו בִּתְהִלָּה, הוֹדוּ לוֹ בָּרְכוּ שְׁמוֹ.¹ וַאֲנַחְנוּ

⟨ But we, ⟨⟨ His ⟨ bless ⟨⟨ to ⟨ give ⟨⟨ with praise; ⟨ His courtyards
Name. Him, thanks

בְּרֹב חַסְדְּךָ נָבוֹא בֵיתֶךָ, נִשְׁתַּחֲוֶה אֶל הֵיכַל קָדְשְׁךָ

⟨ Your Holy ⟨ toward ⟨ we will pros- ⟨⟨ Your ⟨ will we ⟨ of Your ⟨ through the
Sanctuary trate ourselves House; enter kindness abundance

בְּיִרְאָתֶךָ.² הִנֵּה בָּרְכוּ אֶת יהוה כָּל עַבְדֵי יהוה,

⟨ of ⟨ you ⟨ all ⟨ HASHEM, ⟨ bless ⟨⟨ Indeed, ⟨⟨ in awe
HASHEM, servants of You.

הָעֹמְדִים בְּבֵית יהוה בַּלֵּילוֹת.³ שְׂאוּ יְדֵיכֶם קֹדֶשׁ

⟨ in the ⟨ your ⟨ Lift ⟨⟨ in the nights. ⟨ of ⟨ in the ⟨ who stand
Sanctuary hands HASHEM House

וּבָרְכוּ אֶת יהוה.⁴ רוֹמְמוּ יהוה אֱלֹהֵינוּ, וְהִשְׁתַּחֲווּ

⟨ and bow down ⟨ our God, ⟨ HASHEM, ⟨ Exalt ⟨⟨ HASHEM. ⟨ and bless

לַהֲדֹם רַגְלָיו, קָדוֹשׁ הוּא.⁵ רוֹמְמוּ יהוה אֱלֹהֵינוּ,

⟨ our God, ⟨ HASHEM, ⟨ Exalt ⟨⟨ is He! ⟨ holy ⟨⟨ at His footstool;

וְהִשְׁתַּחֲווּ לְהַר קָדְשׁוֹ, כִּי קָדוֹשׁ יהוה אֱלֹהֵינוּ.⁶

⟨⟨ our God. ⟨ is ⟨ holy ⟨ for ⟨⟨ of His ⟨ at the ⟨ and bow
HASHEM, Holiness; Mount

הִשְׁתַּחֲווּ לַיהוה בְּהַדְרַת קֹדֶשׁ, חִילוּ מִפָּנָיו כָּל

⟨ every- ⟨ before ⟨ tremble ⟨⟨ of ⟨ in the ⟨ before ⟨ Bow down
one Him, holiness; splendor HASHEM

הָאָרֶץ.⁷ נִשְׁתַּחֲוֶה אֶל הֵיכַל קָדְשְׁךָ וְנוֹדֶה אֶת שְׁמֶךָ,

⟨ Your Name ⟨ and we ⟨⟨ Your Holy ⟨ toward ⟨ We will pros- ⟨⟨ on earth.
will thank Sanctuary, trate ourselves

עַל חַסְדְּךָ וְעַל אֲמִתֶּךָ, כִּי הִגְדַּלְתָּ עַל כָּל שִׁמְךָ

⟨⟨ Your ⟨ — even ⟨⟨ You have ⟨ for ⟨⟨ Your ⟨ and ⟨ Your ⟨ for
Name — beyond exalted faithfulness; for kindness

אִמְרָתֶךָ.⁸ יהוה אֱלֹהֵי צְבָאוֹת, מִי כָמוֹךָ חֲסִין

⟨ O Strong ⟨⟨ is like ⟨ — who ⟨⟨ of ⟨ God ⟨ HASHEM, ⟨⟨ Your promise.
One, You, Legions

יָהּ, וֶאֱמוּנָתְךָ סְבִיבוֹתֶיךָ.⁹ כִּי מִי בַשַּׁחַק יַעֲרֹךְ

⟨ can be ⟨ in the sky ⟨ who ⟨ For ⟨⟨ surrounds You. ⟨ and Your ⟨⟨ God? —
compared faithfulness

לַיהוה, יִדְמֶה לַיהוה בִּבְנֵי אֵלִים.¹⁰ כִּי גָדוֹל אַתָּה

⟨ are You ⟨ great ⟨ For ⟨⟨ among the angels? ⟨ to HASHEM ⟨ be likened ⟨⟨ to HASHEM;

(1) *Psalms* 100:4. (2) Cf. 5:8. (3) 134:1. (4) 134:2. (5) 99:5. (6) 99:9. (7) 96:9. (8) Cf. 138:2. (9) 89:9. (10) 89:7.

וְעוֹשֶׂה נִפְלָאוֹת, אַתָּה אֱלֹהִים לְבַדֶּךָ.¹ כִּי גָדוֹל

⟨ great ⟨ For ⟪ alone. ⟨ O God, ⟨ You, ⟪ of wonders; ⟨ and a worker

מֵעַל שָׁמַיִם חַסְדֶּךָ, וְעַד שְׁחָקִים אֲמִתֶּךָ.² גָּדוֹל

⟨ Great ⟪ is Your ⟨ the upper ⟨ and ⟪ is Your ⟨ the very ⟨ above
truth. heights until kindness, heavens

יהוה וּמְהֻלָּל מְאֹד, וְלִגְדֻלָּתוֹ אֵין חֵקֶר. (כִּי)³ גָדוֹל

⟨ great ⟨ (For) ⟪ investiga- ⟨ is ⟨ and His ⟪ exceed- ⟨ and ⟨ is
tion. beyond greatness ingly, lauded HASHEM

יהוה וּמְהֻלָּל מְאֹד, נוֹרָא הוּא עַל כָּל אֱלֹהִים.⁴ כִּי

⟨ For ⟪ heavenly ⟨ all ⟨ above ⟨ is He ⟨ awesome ⟪ exceed- ⟨ and ⟨ is
powers. ingly; lauded HASHEM

אֵל גָּדוֹל יהוה, וּמֶלֶךְ גָּדוֹל עַל כָּל אֱלֹהִים.⁵ אֲשֶׁר

⟨ For ⟪ heavenly ⟨ all ⟨ above ⟨ and a great King ⟪ is ⟨ a great God
powers. HASHEM,

מִי אֵל בַּשָּׁמַיִם וּבָאָרֶץ, אֲשֶׁר יַעֲשֶׂה כְמַעֲשֶׂיךָ

⟨ like unto ⟨ can do ⟨ that ⟨ or in the ⟨ is there in ⟨ power ⟨ what
Your deeds earth the heaven

וְכִגְבוּרֹתֶיךָ.⁶ מִי לֹא יִרָאֲךָ מֶלֶךְ הַגּוֹיִם, כִּי לְךָ

⟨ to ⟨ For ⟪ of nations? ⟨ O King ⟪ fear You, ⟨ would ⟨ Who ⟪ and like unto Your
You not mighty acts?

יָאָתָה, כִּי בְכָל חַכְמֵי הַגּוֹיִם וּבְכָל מַלְכוּתָם מֵאֵין

⟨ there is ⟨ their ⟨ and in all ⟨ of the ⟨ the wise ⟨ among ⟨ for ⟪ [kingship]
none kingdoms nations men all befits;

כָּמוֹךָ.⁷ מֵאֵין כָּמוֹךָ יהוה, גָּדוֹל אַתָּה וְגָדוֹל שִׁמְךָ

⟨ is Your ⟨ and great ⟨ are You ⟨ Great ⟪ O ⟨ like You, ⟨ There is ⟪ like You.
Name HASHEM! none

בִּגְבוּרָה.⁸ לְךָ זְרוֹעַ עִם גְּבוּרָה, תָּעֹז יָדְךָ תָּרוּם

⟨ uplifted ⟪ is Your ⟨ strength- ⟪ power; ⟨ with ⟨ is the ⟨ Yours ⟪ in might.
hand, ened arm

יְמִינֶךָ.⁹ לְךָ יוֹם, אַף לְךָ לָיְלָה, אַתָּה הֲכִינוֹתָ מָאוֹר

⟨ the ⟨ prepared ⟨ You ⟪ is the ⟨ Yours ⟨ also ⟪ is the ⟨ Yours ⟪ is Your
luminary night; day, right hand.

וָשָׁמֶשׁ.¹⁰ אֲשֶׁר בְּיָדוֹ מֶחְקְרֵי אָרֶץ, וְתוֹעֲפוֹת הָרִים

⟨ of the ⟨ and the ⟪ of the ⟨ are the hidden ⟨ in His ⟨ For ⟪ and the
mountains summits earth, mysteries power sun.

---

(1) *Psalms* 86:10. (2) 108:5. (3) 145:3. (4) 96:4. (5) 95:3. (6) *Deuteronomy* 3:24.
(7) *Jeremiah* 10:7. (8) 10:6. (9) *Psalms* 89:14. (10) 74:16.

לו. מִי יְמַלֵּל גְּבוּרוֹת יהוה, יַשְׁמִיעַ כָּל תְּהִלָּתוֹ.

Who are His. can express acts can make Who are [who] can of all of His praise?

לְךָ יהוה הַגְּדֻלָּה וְהַגְּבוּרָה, וְהַתִּפְאֶרֶת וְהַנֵּצַח

Yours, HASHEM, is the the strength, the glory, the triumph,

וְהַהוֹד, כִּי כֹל בַּשָּׁמַיִם וּבָאָרֶץ; לְךָ יהוה הַמַּמְלָכָה,

and the majesty; for every-thing in heaven and on earth [is Yours]; Yours, HASHEM, is the kingdom

וְהַמִּתְנַשֵּׂא לְכֹל לְרֹאשׁ. לְךָ שָׁמַיִם, אַף לְךָ אָרֶץ,

and the sovereignty over every leader. Yours are the heavens, also Yours is the earth;

תֵּבֵל וּמְלֹאָהּ אַתָּה יְסַדְתָּם. אַתָּה הִצַּבְתָּ כָּל גְּבוּלוֹת

the world and its fullness, You founded them. You established all the boundaries

אָרֶץ, קַיִץ וָחֹרֶף אַתָּה יְצַרְתָּם. אַתָּה רִצַּצְתָּ רָאשֵׁי

of earth; summer and winter You fashioned them. You crushed the heads

לִוְיָתָן, תִּתְּנֶנּוּ מַאֲכָל לְעַם לְצִיִּים. אַתָּה בָקַעְתָּ מַעְיָן

of Leviathan; You will serve it [destined] for as food to the people the desolate wilderness. You split open fountain

וָנָחַל, אַתָּה הוֹבַשְׁתָּ נַהֲרוֹת אֵיתָן. אַתָּה פוֹרַרְתָּ

and stream; You dried rivers that are mighty. You shattered

בְעָזְּךָ יָם, שִׁבַּרְתָּ רָאשֵׁי תַנִּינִים עַל הַמָּיִם. אַתָּה

with Your might the sea; You smashed the heads of sea serpents upon the water. You

מוֹשֵׁל בְּגֵאוּת הַיָּם, בְּשׂוֹא גַלָּיו אַתָּה תְשַׁבְּחֵם.

rule the grandeur of the sea; when it raises its waves, You calm them.

גָּדוֹל יהוה וּמְהֻלָּל מְאֹד, בְּעִיר אֱלֹהֵינוּ הַר קָדְשׁוֹ.

Great is HASHEM, and much praised, in the City of our God, Mount of His Holiness.

יהוה צְבָאוֹת, אֱלֹהֵי יִשְׂרָאֵל, יוֹשֵׁב הַכְּרֻבִים, אַתָּה

HASHEM, Master of Legions, God of Israel, en-throned upon the Cherubim, You it is

---

(1) *Psalms* 95:4. (2) *106:2. (3) I Chronicles* 29:11. (4) *Psalms* 89:12.
(5) 74:17. (6) 74:14-15. (7) 74:13. (8) 89:10. (9) 48:2.

הוּא הָאֱלֹהִים לְבַדֶּךָ.[1] אֵל נַעֲרָץ בְּסוֹד קְדוֹשִׁים רַבָּה,

Who are the God alone. God is revered in the great assemblage of the holy [angels],

וְנוֹרָא עַל כָּל סְבִיבָיו.[2] וְיוֹדוּ שָׁמַיִם פִּלְאֲךָ יהוה, אַף

and is awesome over all who surround Him. Acknowledge will the heavens Your wonders, HASHEM, also

אֱמוּנָתְךָ בִּקְהַל קְדֹשִׁים.[3] לְכוּ נְרַנְּנָה לַיהוה, נָרִיעָה

Your faithfulness in the assembly of holy ones. Come! Let us sing joyfully to HASHEM, let us call out

לְצוּר יִשְׁעֵנוּ. נְקַדְּמָה פָנָיו בְּתוֹדָה, בִּזְמִרוֹת נָרִיעַ

to the Rock of our salvation. Let us greet Him with thanksgiving, with praiseful songs let us call out

לוֹ.[4] צֶדֶק וּמִשְׁפָּט מְכוֹן כִּסְאֶךָ, חֶסֶד וֶאֱמֶת יְקַדְּמוּ

to Him. Righteousness and justice are the foundation of Your throne; kindness and truth precede

פָנֶיךָ.[5] אֲשֶׁר יַחְדָּו נַמְתִּיק סוֹד, בְּבֵית אֱלֹהִים נְהַלֵּךְ

Your countenance. For together let us take sweet counsel; in the House of God let us walk

בְּרָגֶשׁ.[6] אֲשֶׁר לוֹ הַיָּם וְהוּא עָשָׂהוּ, וְיַבֶּשֶׁת יָדָיו

in company. For His is the sea and He perfected it, and the dry land His hands

יָצָרוּ.[7] אֲשֶׁר בְּיָדוֹ נֶפֶשׁ כָּל חָי, וְרוּחַ כָּל בְּשַׂר אִישׁ.[8]

fashioned. For in His hand is the soul of all living and the spirit of all mankind.

❖ הַנְּשָׁמָה לָךְ וְהַגּוּף פָּעֳלָךְ, חוּסָה עַל עֲמָלָךְ.

The soul is Yours and the body is Your handiwork; take pity on Your labor.

הַנְּשָׁמָה לָךְ וְהַגּוּף שֶׁלָּךְ, יהוה עֲשֵׂה לְמַעַן שְׁמֶךָ.

The soul is Yours and the body is Yours; O HASHEM, act for the sake of Your Name.

אָתָאנוּ עַל שִׁמְךָ, יהוה, עֲשֵׂה לְמַעַן שְׁמֶךָ. בַּעֲבוּר

We have come [relying] on Your Name; O HASHEM, act for the sake of Your Name; because of

כְּבוֹד שְׁמֶךָ, כִּי אֵל חַנּוּן וְרַחוּם שְׁמֶךָ. לְמַעַן

the glory of Your Name, for God Who is Gracious and Merciful is Your Name. For the sake

(1) *Isaiah* 37:16. (2) *Psalms* 89:8. (3) 89:6. (4) 95:1-2. (5) 89:15. (6) 55:15. (7) 95:5. (8) *Job* 12:10.

שִׁמְךָ יהוה, וְסָלַחְתָּ לַעֲוֹנֵנוּ כִּי רַב הוּא.[1]

of Your ⟨ HASHEM, ⟨ forgive ⟨ though ⟨ our ⟨ it is great.
Name, iniquity,

CONGREGATION, THEN *CHAZZAN:*

סְלַח לָנוּ אָבִינוּ, כִּי בְרוֹב אִוַּלְתֵּנוּ שָׁגִינוּ,

Forgive ⟨ us, ⟨ our Father, ⟨ for ⟨ in the ⟨ of our folly ⟨ we have
abundance erred;

מְחַל לָנוּ מַלְכֵּנוּ, כִּי רַבּוּ עֲוֹנֵינוּ.

pardon ⟨ us, ⟨ our King, ⟨ for ⟨ many ⟨ our
are iniquities.

SELICHAH 68 / סליחה סח
(פתיחה)

ALL:

שׁוֹשַׁנַּת* וֶרֶד בֵּין חוֹחִים גְּדוּלֶיהָ,[2]

The rose ⟨ of roses ⟨ among ⟨ thorn- ⟨ does it grow,
[Israel],* [like nations]

אֲשֶׁר כְּמִגְדָּלוֹת שָׁדֶיהָ[3] פַּעֲמֵי נְעָלֶיהָ,[4]

that ⟨ like protecting ⟨ are her synagogues ⟨ whose ⟨ in sandals
fortresses and study halls that pilgrim- [were so
provide breast-like age steps beautiful] —
nourishment,

וְלָמָּה הֻבְקְעוּ חוֹמוֹתֶיהָ וְהָלְכוּ שְׁבִי עוֹלָלֶיהָ,[5]

why then ⟨ are ⟨ her walls ⟨ and gone ⟨ into ⟨ are her young
breached captivity children,

עַל הֶהָרִים הֻפְנוּ רַגְלֶיהָ.

toward ⟨ the mountains ⟨ are ⟨ her feet?
[to Exile] turned

מוֹשֶׁלֶת אַפְסֵי אֶרֶץ שַׁלְטָנִית וּגְבִירָה,

The people [de- ⟨ to the ⟨ of the ⟨ the sovereign ⟨ mistress,
signed to] rule ends earth,

אֲשֶׁר שְׁכִנְךָ אָז בְּתוֹכָהּ שָׁרָה,

that ⟨ Your Presence ⟨ then ⟨ in her midst ⟨ dwelled —

---

(1) Cf. *Psalms* 25:11. (2) Cf. *Song of Songs* 2:2. (3) Cf. 8:10 with *Rashi*; *Pesachim* 87a.
(4) Cf. 7:2 with *Targum* and *Rashi*. (5) Cf. *Lamentations* 1:5.

---

§ שׁוֹשַׁנַּת וֶרֶד — *The rose of roses.* The acros-
tic of this *pesichah's* stanzas spells שְׁמוּאֵל,
Shmuel, who may have been the *paytan* of
Selichah 7 [see prefatory comment there].

In each stanza, the second verse begins with
the word אֲשֶׁר, literally *which, that,* or *who,*
and describes the glory that once was; the
third verse begins with וְלָמָּה, *why then,* and

וְלָמָה כִּסְכָּה בְכֶרֶם וְכִמְלוּנָה נוֹתָרָה,[1]

《 is she left 〈 and like a 〈 in a vine- 〈 like a 〈 why then
alone; gardener's hut yard [after watchman's
the harvest] booth

מַלְכָּה וְשָׂרֶיהָ בַּגּוֹיִם אֵין תּוֹרָה.[2]

《 Torah? 〈 without 〈 are among 〈 and her 〈 her king
the nations, officers

וְעוֹדָה בַנָּשִׁים מֵעַמִּים מְהֻלָּלָה,

《 the most 〈 of all 《 did the 〈 She who gath-
praised, peoples nations, er around her

אֲשֶׁר עַל כָּל עַם וְלָשׁוֹן מִגְדָּלָה,[3]

《 was exalted — 〈 and tongue 〈 people 〈 every 〈 above 〈 who

וְלָמָה (גְרוּשָׁה) כְּאִשָּׁה זוֹנָה וַחֲלָלָה,

《 or has been 〈 who is a 〈 like a 〈 (is she sent away) 〈 why then
desecrated? prostitute woman

פֵּרְשָׂה צִיּוֹן בְּיָדֶיהָ וְאֵין מְנַחֵם לָה.[4]

《 her? 〈 who could 〈 [why] is 《 her hands 〈 does 〈 Spread out
comfort there no one [in prayer], Zion

אֵצֶל בַּת יוֹשֶׁבֶת בְּלִמּוּד תּוֹרוֹתֶיהָ,

《 of her Torah, 〈 in study 〈 would sit 〈 the 〈 Near
daughter where

אֲשֶׁר בְּמֵימֵי רַבִּים שָׁלְחָה שָׁדוֹתֶיהָ,[5]

《 her fields — 〈 extended 〈 that are 〈 by the waters 〈 who
abundant [of its law]

וְלָמָה נָשִׁים מְאֵרוֹת בָּאוֹת[6] מִשְׁבְּנוֹתֶיהָ,

《 her sanctuaries? 〈 come into 〈 that are accursed 〈 do nations 〈 why then

רָאוּהָ צָרִים שָׂחֲקוּ עַל מִשְׁבַּתֶּיהָ.[7]

《 her cessation 〈 at 〈 they 〈 do her 〈 [Why is it that]
[of celebrations]? rejoiced enemies when see her

לְמוּדָה לְקָחֶיהָ הַיּוֹשֶׁבֶת בַּגּוֹיִם[8] כְּמִדְבָּר,

《 as the Torah 《 among the 〈 even when 《 in her 〈 She is
dictates, nations, she is situated teachings, learned

---

(1) Cf. *Isaiah* 1:8. (2) Cf. *Lamentations* 2:9 with *Rashi*. (3) Cf. *Daniel* 3:29. (4) Cf. *Lamentations* 1:17. (5) Some editions read פֹארְתֶיהָ, *her branches,* i.e., her children. (6) Some editions read נָשִׁים בָּאוֹת מְאֵרוֹת, *nations* [lit., *women*] *come to curse;* see *Isaiah* 27:11. (7) *Lamentations* 1:7. (8) Some editions read בַּגַּנִּים, *in gardens,* based on *Song of Songs* 8:13; the translation follows *Rashi* to that verse.

---

asks why that glory was lost and Israel so degraded; and the fourth line (except in the first stanza) is a Scriptural fragment that determines the stanza's rhyme.

אֲשֶׁר לְצִדְּךָ כְּאֵזוֹר מְדֻבֶּקֶת לְהִתְחַבֵּר,[1]

≪ to be connected — ⟨ fastened ⟨ like a belt ⟨ at Your side ⟨ who

וְלָמָּה פְזוּרָה בְּכָל זָוִיּוֹת וּמַעֲבָר,

≪ and passages? ⟨ corners ⟨ to all ⟨ is she ⟨ why then scattered

בַּת עַמִּי לְאַכְזָר כַּיְעֵנִים בַּמִּדְבָּר.[2]

≪ in the desert? ⟨ as ostriches ⟨ been given over to those as cruel ⟨ of my people ⟨ [Why] has the daughter

❖ חֲסִין יָהּ גְּמוֹל חֶסֶד לְחַיָּבִים,

≪ to the unworthy; ⟨ kindness ⟨ bestow ⟨ God, ⟨ O, Strong One,

זְקוֹף קַרְנָהּ וְהוֹצִיאָהּ מִיַּד מַלְעִיבִים,

≪ of those who humiliate her, ⟨ from the control ⟨ and bring her out ⟨ her honor ⟨ raise up

תְּמוּר כִּי לֹא בְּאַחֵר הִשְׁלִיכָה יְהָבִים,[3]

≪ placing her burden, ⟨ on other's [gods] ⟨ not ⟨ for ⟨ in reward

כִּי עַל רַחֲמֶיךָ הָרַבִּים.

≪ that is great. ⟨ Your mercy ⟨ upon ⟨ but only

ALL:

כִּי עַל רַחֲמֶיךָ הָרַבִּים[4] אָנוּ בְטוּחִים, וְעַל צִדְקוֹתֶיךָ

⟨ Your righteousness ⟨ and upon ≪ trust, ⟨ we ⟨ that is abundant ⟨ Your mercy ⟨ upon ⟨ For

אָנוּ נִשְׁעָנִים, וְלִסְלִיחוֹתֶיךָ אָנוּ מְקַוִּים, וְלִישׁוּעָתְךָ

⟨ and for Your salvation ≪ hope, ⟨ we ⟨ and for Your forgiveness ≪ rely, ⟨ we

אָנוּ מְצַפִּים. אַתָּה הוּא מֶלֶךְ, אוֹהֵב צְדָקוֹת מִקֶּדֶם,

≪ since the beginning of time, ⟨ righteous-ness ⟨ Who loves ⟨ the King ⟨ are ⟨ You ≪ await eagerly. ⟨ we

מַעֲבִיר עֲוֹנוֹת עַמּוֹ, וּמֵסִיר חַטֹּאת יְרֵאָיו. כּוֹרֵת

⟨ He established ≪ of those who revere Him. ⟨ the sins ⟨ and removes ⟨ of His people ⟨ the iniquities ⟨ Who overlooks

בְּרִית לָרִאשׁוֹנִים, וּמְקַיֵּם שְׁבוּעָה לָאַחֲרוֹנִים. אַתָּה

⟨ You ≪ to the descendants. ⟨ [His] oath ⟨ and fulfills ⟨ with the ancestors ⟨ a covenant

---

(1) Cf. *Jeremiah* 13:11. (2) *Lamentations* 4:3. (3) See *Psalms* 55:23 with *Targum*. (4) *Daniel* 9:18.

הוּא, שֶׁיָּרַדְתָּ בַּעֲנַן כְּבוֹדְךָ עַל הַר סִינַי,¹ וְהֶרְאֵיתָ

⟨ and You showed ⟩ ⟪ Sinai, ⟩ ⟨ Mount ⟨ upon ⟩ ⟨ of Your glory ⟩ ⟨ in the cloud ⟩ ⟨ Who descended ⟩ ⟨ are the One

דַּרְכֵי טוּבְךָ לְמֹשֶׁה עַבְדֶּךָ.² וְאָרְחוֹת חֲסָדֶיךָ גִּלֵּיתָ

⟨ You revealed ⟩ ⟨ of Your kindness ⟩ ⟨ The paths ⟪ Your servant. ⟩ ⟨ to Moses ⟩ ⟨ of Your goodness ⟩ ⟨ the ways

לוֹ, וְהוֹדַעְתּוֹ כִּי אַתָּה אֵל רַחוּם וְחַנּוּן, אֶרֶךְ אַפַּיִם

⟨ to anger ⟩ ⟨ Slow ⟪ and ⟩ ⟨ Compas-sionate Gracious, ⟩ ⟨ God, ⟨ You are ⟨ that ⟨ and You let him know ⟪ to him,

וְרַב חֶסֶד³ וּמַרְבֶּה לְהֵטִיב, וּמַנְהִיג אֶת כָּל הָעוֹלָם

⟨ world ⟩ ⟨ the whole ⟩ ⟨ and Who guides ⟪ beneficent, ⟩ ⟨ Who is abundantly ⟩ ⟨ in Kind-ness, ⟨ and Abundant

כֻּלּוֹ בְּמִדַּת הָרַחֲמִים. ❖ וְכֵן כָּתוּב, וַיֹּאמֶר אֲנִי אַעֲבִיר

⟨ shall cause to pass ⟨ "I ⟪ And He said, ⟪ it is written: ⟨ And so ⟪ of Mercy. ⟨ with the Attribute ⟨ in its entirety

כָּל טוּבִי עַל פָּנֶיךָ, וְקָרָאתִי בְשֵׁם יהוה לְפָנֶיךָ,

⟪ before you; ⟩ ⟨ HASHEM ⟨ with the Name ⟩ ⟨ and I shall call out ⟪ your face, ⟩ ⟨ before ⟨ My goodness ⟩ ⟨ all

וְחַנֹּתִי אֶת אֲשֶׁר אָחֹן, וְרִחַמְתִּי אֶת אֲשֶׁר אֲרַחֵם.⁴

⟪ I choose to show mercy." ⟩ ⟨ whom-ever ⟩ ⟨ to ⟩ ⟨ and I shall show favor ⟪ I choose to show favor, ⟩ ⟨ whom-ever ⟩ ⟨ to ⟩ ⟨ I shall show favor

ALL, WHILE STANDING

אֵל אֶרֶךְ אַפַּיִם אַתָּה,

⟪ You are, ⟩ ⟨ to anger, ⟩ ⟨ Who is slow ⟩ ⟨ God

וּבַעַל הָרַחֲמִים נִקְרֵאתָ, וְדֶרֶךְ תְּשׁוּבָה הוֹרֵיתָ.

⟪ You have taught. ⟩ ⟨ of repentance ⟩ ⟨ and the way ⟪ You are called; ⟩ ⟨ of Mercy ⟩ ⟨ and Master

גְּדֻלַּת רַחֲמֶיךָ וַחֲסָדֶיךָ,

⟨ and Your kindness ⟩ ⟨ of Your mercy ⟩ ⟨ The greatness

תִּזְכּוֹר הַיּוֹם וּבְכָל יוֹם לְזֶרַע יְדִידֶיךָ.

⟪ of Your beloved ones. ⟩ ⟨ for the offspring ⟪ day, ⟩ ⟨ and every ⟩ ⟨ this day ⟨ may You remember,

תֵּפֶן אֵלֵינוּ בְּרַחֲמִים,

⟪ in mercy, ⟩ ⟨ to us ⟨ Turn

---

(1) Cf. *Exodus* 34:5. (2) Cf. 33:13. (3) 34:6. (4) 33:19.

כִּי אַתָּה הוּא בַּעַל הָרַחֲמִים.

for ⟨ You ⟨ are ⟨ the Master ⟨ of Mercy. ≪

בְּתַחֲנוּן וּבִתְפִלָּה פָּנֶיךָ נְקַדֵּם, כְּהוֹדַעְתָּ לֶעָנָיו מִקֶּדֶם.

With supplication ⟨ and prayer ⟨ Your Presence ⟨ we approach, ≪ in the manner that You made known ⟨ to the humble one [Moses] ⟨ in ancient times. ≪

מֵחֲרוֹן אַפְּךָ שׁוּב,[1] כְּמוֹ בְתוֹרָתְךָ כָּתוּב.[2]

From the fierceness ⟨ of Your anger ⟨ turn back, ≪ as ⟨ in Your Torah ⟨ it is written. ≪

וּבְצֵל כְּנָפֶיךָ נֶחֱסֶה וְנִתְלוֹנָן,[3] כְּיוֹם וַיֵּרֶד יהוה בֶּעָנָן.

In the shadow ⟨ of Your wings ⟨ may we find ⟨ shelter ≪ and may we dwell, ⟨ as on the day ⟨ when HASHEM ⟨ descended ⟨ in a cloud. ≪

❖ תַּעֲבוֹר עַל פֶּשַׁע וְתִמְחֶה אָשָׁם,

Overlook ⟨ sin ⟨ and erase ⟨ guilt, ≪

כְּיוֹם וַיִּתְיַצֵּב עִמּוֹ שָׁם.

as on the day ⟨ when He [God] stood ⟨ with him [Moses] ⟨ there. ≪

תַּאֲזִין שַׁוְעָתֵנוּ וְתַקְשִׁיב מֶנּוּ מַאֲמָר,

Give heed ⟨ to our cry ⟨ and hear ⟨ from us ⟨ [our] declaration, ≪

כְּיוֹם וַיִּקְרָא בְשֵׁם יהוה,[4] וְשָׁם נֶאֱמַר:

as on ⟨ the day ⟨ when He ⟨ called out ⟨ with the Name ⟨ of HASHEM, ⟨ and ⟨ there ⟨ it was said: ≪

CONGREGATION, THEN *CHAZZAN:*

<u>וַיַּעֲבֹר יהוה עַל פָּנָיו וַיִּקְרָא:</u>

And HASHEM passed ⟨ before ⟨ [Moses'] face, ⟨ and ≪ proclaimed: ≪

CONGREGATION AND *CHAZZAN* **RECITE LOUDLY AND IN UNISON:**

יהוה, יהוה, אֵל, רַחוּם, וְחַנּוּן, אֶרֶךְ אַפַּיִם,

HASHEM, ⟨ HASHEM, ⟨ God, ⟨ Compassionate ⟨ and ≪ Gracious, ⟨ Slow ⟨ to anger, ⟨

וְרַב חֶסֶד, וֶאֱמֶת, נֹצֵר חֶסֶד לָאֲלָפִים, נֹשֵׂא עָוֹן,

and ⟨ Abundant ⟨ in Kindness ⟨ and ≪ Truth, ⟨ Preserver ⟨ of ⟨ kindness ⟨ for ⟨ thousands ⟨ [of generations], ⟨ Forgiver ⟨ of ⟨ iniquity, ⟨

---

(1) Cf. *Exodus* 32:12. (2) See 32:14. (3) Cf. *Psalms* 36:8. (4) *Exodus* 34:5.

וָפֶשַׁע, וְחַטָּאָה, וְנַקֵּה.¹ וְסָלַחְתָּ לַעֲוֺנֵנוּ וּלְחַטָּאתֵנוּ

《 and our sins, 〈 our 〈 May You 《 *and Who* 〈 *and inadvertent* 〈 *willful sin,*
iniquities　　forgive　　*absolves.*　　sin,

וּנְחַלְתָּנוּ.² סְלַח לָנוּ אָבִינוּ כִּי חָטָאנוּ, מְחַל לָנוּ

〈 us, 〈 pardon 《 we have 〈 for 《 our Father, 〈 us, 〈 Forgive 《 and make us
sinned;　　　　　　　　　　　　　　　Your heritage.

מַלְכֵּנוּ כִּי פָשָׁעְנוּ. כִּי אַתָּה אֲדֹנָי טוֹב וְסַלָּח, וְרַב

〈 and 〈 and 〈 are 〈 O Lord, 〈 You, 〈 For 《 we have 〈 for 《 our King,
abundantly forgiving, good　　　　　　　　　　willfully sinned.

חֶסֶד לְכָל קֹרְאֶיךָ.³

《 who call 〈 to all 〈 kind
upon You.

פְּסוּקֵי הַקְדָּמָה לִסְלִיחָה סט / PREFATORY VERSES TO SELICHAH 69

וַאֲנִי אֵלֶיךָ יהוה שִׁוַּעְתִּי, וּבַבֹּקֶר תְּפִלָּתִי תְקַדְּמֶךָ.⁴

《 will greet 〈 my 〈 and in the 《 have I 〈 HASHEM, 〈 to You, 《 As for
You.　　prayer　　morning　　cried,　　　　　　　　　me,

מַה נֹּאמַר לְפָנֶיךָ יֹשֵׁב מָרוֹם, וּמַה נְּסַפֵּר לְפָנֶיךָ

〈 before 〈 can we 〈 and 《 on high, 〈 Who 〈 before 〈 can we 〈 What
You　　relate　　what　　　　dwells　　You,　　say

שֹׁכֵן שְׁחָקִים.⁵

《 in the highest 〈 Who
heavens?　　dwells

בְּרַחֵם אָב עַל בָּנִים, כֵּן תְּרַחֵם יהוה עָלֵינוּ.⁶

《 on us. 〈 HASHEM, 〈 have 〈 so 《 his 〈 toward 〈 a 〈 As merciful as
mercy,　　children,　　father is

לַיהוה הַיְשׁוּעָה, עַל עַמְּךָ בִרְכָתֶךָ סֶּלָה.⁷ יהוה

〈 HASHEM, 《 Selah. 《 is Your 〈 Your 〈 upon 《 is salvation, 〈 To HASHEM
blessing,　　people

צְבָאוֹת עִמָּנוּ, מִשְׂגָּב לָנוּ אֱלֹהֵי יַעֲקֹב סֶלָה.⁸

《 Selah. 《 of Jacob, 《 is the God 〈 for us 〈 a 《 is with us, 〈 Master of
stronghold　　　　　　　　　　　　　　Legions,

יהוה צְבָאוֹת, אַשְׁרֵי אָדָם בֹּטֵחַ בָּךְ.⁹ יהוה הוֹשִׁיעָה,

《 save! 〈 HASHEM, 《 in 〈 who 〈 is the 〈 — praise- 《 Master of 〈 HASHEM,
You.　　trusts　　man　　worthy　　Legions

---

(1) *Exodus* 34:6-7 (2) 34:9. (3) *Psalms* 86:5. (4) 88:14.
(5) From the Yom Kippur *Viduy.* (6) Cf. *Psalms* 103:13. (7) 3:9. (8) 46:8. (9) 84:13.

הַמֶּלֶךְ יַעֲנֵנוּ בְיוֹם קָרְאֵנוּ.[1]

《 we call. 〈 on the day 〈 answer us 〈 May the King

IN MOST CONGREGATIONS THE FOLLOWING VERSES ARE RECITED ALOUD RESPONSIVELY, AS INDICATED; IN OTHERS THEY ARE RECITED SILENTLY.

CONGREGATION, ALOUD, FOLLOWED BY *CHAZZAN*, ALOUD:

סְלַח נָא לַעֲוֹן הָעָם הַזֶּה כְּגֹדֶל חַסְדֶּךָ, וְכַאֲשֶׁר

〈 just as 《 of Your kindness, 〈 according to the greatness 〈 of this people 〈 the iniquity 〈 please, 〈 Forgive,

נָשָׂאתָה לָעָם הַזֶּה מִמִּצְרַיִם וְעַד הֵנָּה,[2] וְשָׁם

〈 And there 《 now. 〈 until 〈 from Egypt 〈 this people 〈 You have forgiven

נֶאֱמַר:

《 it was said:

ALL, ALOUD AND IN UNISON:

וַיֹּאמֶר יהוה סָלַחְתִּי כִּדְבָרֶךָ.[3]

《 according to your word! 〈 *I have forgiven* 《 And *HASHEM* said:

ALL CONTINUE:

הַטֵּה אֱלֹהַי אָזְנְךָ וּשְׁמָע, פְּקַח עֵינֶיךָ וּרְאֵה

〈 and see 〈 Your eyes 〈 open 《 and listen; 〈 Your ear, 〈 my God, 〈 Incline,

שֹׁמְמֹתֵינוּ, וְהָעִיר אֲשֶׁר נִקְרָא שִׁמְךָ עָלֶיהָ, כִּי לֹא

〈 not 〈 for 《 upon; 〈 Your Name is proclaimed 〈 which 〈 and that 〈 [of] the city 〈 our desolation

עַל צִדְקֹתֵינוּ אֲנַחְנוּ מַפִּילִים תַּחֲנוּנֵינוּ לְפָנֶיךָ,

《 before You; 〈 our supplications 〈 cast 〈 do we 〈 of our righteousness 《 because

כִּי עַל רַחֲמֶיךָ הָרַבִּים. אֲדֹנָי שְׁמָעָה, אֲדֹנָי סְלָחָה,

《 forgive; 〈 O Lord, 《 heed; 〈 O Lord, 《 which is abundant. 〈 of Your compassion, 〈 be- 〈 but cause

אֲדֹנָי הַקְשִׁיבָה, וַעֲשֵׂה אַל תְּאַחַר, לְמַעַנְךָ אֱלֹהַי,

《 my God, 〈 for Your sake, 《 delay; 〈 do not 《 and act, 〈 be attentive, 〈 O Lord,

כִּי שִׁמְךָ נִקְרָא עַל עִירְךָ וְעַל עַמֶּךָ.[4]

《 Your people. 〈 and 〈 upon 〈 Your City 〈 upon 〈 is proclaimed 〈 Your Name 〈 for

---

(1) *Psalms* 20:10. (2) *Numbers* 14:19. (3) 14:20. (4) *Daniel* 9:18-19.

SELICHAH 69 / סליחה סט

ALL:

אֱלֹהֵינוּ וֵאלֹהֵי אֲבוֹתֵינוּ:

《 of our forefathers: 〈 and the God 〈 Our God

אֵלֶיךָ יהוה אֶקְרָא*[1] אָיֹם וְנוֹרָא,

《 and Awe- 〈 O 《 I call,* 〈 HASHEM, 〈 To You,
some One: Terrifying

אַל תַּסְתִּיר פָּנֶיךָ בְּיוֹם צָרָה,[2]

〈 of trouble 〈 on the day 〈 Your face 〈 hide 〈 Do not

בְּקוּם עָלֵינוּ בַּעֲלֵי מְאֵרָה,

《 who are 〈 do 〈 against 〈 when
accursed, people us rise up

בְּהִוָּסְדָם יַחַד עֵצָה נִבְעָרָה.

《 that is 〈 a plan 〈 together 〈 when they
boorish. conspire

גּוֹזְרִים עָלַי דּוֹדִי וְאָדוֹן מִלְּקְרֹאת,

《 I may not 〈 and Lord 〈 that my 〈 against 〈 They
call upon, Beloved me decree

גּוֹאֲלֵנוּ יהוה צְבָאוֹת,[3]

《 Master of Legions. 〈 HASHEM, 〈 our Redeemer,

דּוֹדִי צַח וְאָדוֹם דָּגוּל מֵרְבָבוֹת,[4]

《 by myriads 〈 surrounded 〈 and red 〈 is white 〈 My
[of angels] — [when [when Beloved,
punishing forgiving
His enemies], my sins]

דִּבְּרוּ לְהַבְזוֹת וְאוֹתוֹ לְהַלְאוֹת.

《 to be weary. 〈 deeming Him 《 they disgrace, 〈 His word

הָעֶצֶב נִבְזֶה לְקַבֵּל[5] לֶאֱלוֹהַּ,

《 as a god, 〈 [shall we] 《 that is 〈 The idol
accept despicable,

---

(1) *Psalms* 28:1; 30:9. (2) Cf. 102:3. (3) *Isaiah* 47:4. (4) Cf. *Song of Songs* 5:10. (5) Cf. *Jeremiah* 22:28.

אֵלֶיךָ ה' אֶקְרָא — *To You, HASHEM, I call.*
The acrostic of this *selichah* forms a double
aleph-beis, followed by the *paytan's* signature — גֵּרְשֹׁם בַּר יְהוּדָה, *Gershom bar Yehudah*
[see prefatory comment to *Selichah* 12].
Having witnessed many of the atrocities com-

mitted in the name of "the prince of peace,"
Rabbeinu Gershom writes seethingly about
the Church of his time. Understandably, this
selichah has felt the full weight of the censor's heavy hand, with various stiches altered
or omitted in many editions.

הִשְׁתַּחֲווֹת לַסֶּמֶל לְפָנָיו לִפְלוֹחַ,[1]
《 to worship, 〈 before it 《 to the 〈 bowing
symbol,

וּלְבִלְתִּי הַקְדִּישׁ הַמַּרְבֶּה לִסְלוֹחַ,
《 Pardons, 〈 the One Who 〈 sanctifying 〈 not
Abundantly

וְגַם לֹא לִירָא אִם אֵים אֱלוֹהַּ.
《 God? 〈 the 〈 not to fear 〈 and
Terrifying also

זֹאת בְּשָׁמְעִי יֶחֱרַד לִבִּי,
《did my heart,〈 tremble 〈 as I heard, 〈 This

זֹאת אָשִׁיב תְּשׁוּבָה לִמְרִיבִי,
《 to my 〈 I answered 〈 response 〈 and
antagonists: this

חָלִילָה לְשַׁכְּחִי וּלְעָזְבִי, חֲטִיבַת[2] אֱלֹהֵי אָבִי.
《 of my 〈 God 〈 the Unique 〈 or for me 〈 for me 〈 'It is
father! to abandon to forget sacrilegious

טָמֵא וּמֵת חָדָשׁ הַבָּא מִקָּרוֹב,[3]
《 recently — 〈 that 〈 the new 《 dead 〈 That
arrived [god] one, defiled

טִבּוֹ מָה אֶצְלִי עֲרָבְתּוֹ לַעֲרֹב,[4]
《 should be 〈 that his 《 to do 〈 what 《 his
security for me? guarantee with me, has he nature,

יוֹצֵר הַכֹּל אֶחָד לְקוֹרְאָיו בֶּאֱמֶת קָרוֹב,[5]
《 is close, 〈 sincerely 〈 the One Who 《 — I 《 of All 〈 The
to those who declare His Creator
call Him Oneness,

יָתוֹם וְאַלְמָנָה יְעוֹדֵד[6] וְאוֹיְבָיו יְזֹרֵב.
《 He 〈 and His 《 He encour- 〈 and widow 〈 Who the
scorches. enemies ages, orphan

כְּשָׁמְעָם אֲמָרַי כִּי נָעֵמוּ,
《 were 〈 that 〈 my words 〈 When they
pleasant, heard

(1) Some editions have been altered to read הָאוֹמְרִים אֵין לְקַבֵּל אֱלוֹהַּ הִשְׁתַּחֲווֹת לְפָנָיו לִפְלוֹחַ,
They say, "Do not accept God, bowing before Him to worship."
(2) See *Chagigah* 3a with *Rashi*. (3) Cf. *Deuteronomy* 32:17;
some editions of *Selichos* read טָפְלוּ עָלַי וְדִבְּרוּ מִקָּרוֹב, *They joined themselves to me*
and spoke of recent [innovations]. (4) See *Jeremiah* 30:21. (5) Cf. *Psalms* 145:19. (6) 146:9.

כֻּלָּם יַחַד חוֹרְקִים שִׁנֵּימוֹ,
《 their teeth [at me]. 〈 gnashed 〈 as one 〈all of them

לִשְׁלֹל וְלָבוֹז עֲמַל יְדֵימוֹ,
《 of their 〈 became 〈 and pil- 〈 To loot
hands, the labor lage [me]

לְהַשְׁמִיד וּלְאַבֵּד מִפְתַח שְׂפָתֵימוֹ.
《 their lips 〈 is what 〈 and to 〈 to destroy
[to say]. they open *annihilate*

מִבֵּית מַאֲוֵיָה סֻכָּתָה וּמְלוֹנָה,
《 its dwelling- 〈 its *succah*, 〈 that was 〈 From the
place, its desire, Temple

מִגְרֶשֶׁת עֲדָתְךָ בְּכָל רוּחַ וּפְנָה,
《 and corner 〈 direction 〈 in every 〈 is Your 〈 expelled
[of the world]. assembly

נַחֲלָתְךָ נִלְאָה עֲלוּבָה וַעֲגוּנָה,
《 and constrained 〈 humiliated, 〈 is 〈 Your heritage-
[in exile], exhausted, people

נוֹשֵׂאת עֵינֶיהָ לְעֶזְרָתָה הַיְשָׁנָה.
《 as of old. 〈 towards her Help 〈 her eyes 〈 lifting

שָׂמָה פָּנֶיהָ לִתְשׁוּבָה וְלִתְפִלָּה,
《 and prayer — 〈 toward repentance 〈 her face 〈 She turns

סֵדֶר אֲבוֹתֶיהָ כְּמִקֶּדֶם תְּחִלָּה,
《 how to start, 〈 as so 〈 [ordained by] 〈 the order
long ago her forefathers [of prayer]

עָרֹךְ שָׂפָה בַּצַּר לָהּ בַּגּוֹלָה,
《 in the Exile, 〈 when she 〈 her [prayerful] 〈 setting
was distressed speech out

עָלֶיךָ מַשְׁלֶכֶת יָהַב לְכַלְכְּלָהּ.¹
《of sustaining her. 〈 the burden 〈 casting 〈 upon You

פְּנֵה נָא לִתְפִלַּת עֲבָדֶיךָ,²
《 of Your servants; 〈 to the prayer 〈 please, 〈 Turn,

פַּצֵּם וְהַצִּילֵם מִכַּף בּוֹגְדֶיךָ,³
《 of those who are 〈 from the 〈 rescue them 〈 release
unfaithful to You. hand them,

---

(1) Cf. *Psalms* 55:23. (2) Cf. 102:18.
(3) Cf. 144:7. Some editions read בְּרוֹב רַחֲמֶיךָ, *in Your abundant mercy,* in lieu of מִכַּף בּוֹגְדֶיךָ.

צַוֵּה יְשׁוּעוֹת זֶרַע חֲסִידֶיךָ,

‹ Com- ‹ salvation ‹ for the ‹ of Your
mand   seed   devout ones, »

צֵאת לִרְוָיָה מִשְּׁאוֹן מוֹרְדֶיךָ.[1]

‹ let them ‹ to ‹ from the ‹ of those who
go out   abundance   tumult   rebel against You. »

קַנֵּא לְשִׁמְךָ אִם לֹא לְמַעֲנֵנוּ,

‹ Be ‹ for the sake ‹ if ‹ not ‹ for ours:
zealous   of Your Name »

קֶצֶף גָּדוֹל קָצוֹף עַל מְעַנֵּינוּ,[2]

‹ With ‹ that is ‹ be ‹ at ‹ our
a fury   great   furious   oppressors, »

רְשָׁעִים פֶּן יֹאמְרוּ אַיֵּה אֱלֹהֵינוּ,[3]

‹ the wicked ‹ — lest ‹ they ask ‹ where is ‹ our God. »

רִיבָם רִיב וְקוּם לְגוֹנְנֵנוּ.

‹ The battle ‹ fight ‹ and ‹ to shield us! ›
against them   arise »

שָׁפְטָה מִשְׁפָּטִי מֵאִישׁ חָמָס,[4]

‹ Judge ‹ my case ‹ against ‹ of
the man   violence. »

שְׁאֵרָם הָמֵק וּלְשׁוֹנָם תִּמַּס,

‹ Make ‹ waste › let their ‹ melt. »
their flesh   away,   tongue

תַּשְׁפִּיל גְּאוֹנָם וּתְנֵם לְמִרְמָס,

‹ Humble ‹ their › subject ‹ to being
pride,   them   trampled; »

תָּפַח רוּחָם וְיִהְיוּ לָמַס.[5]

‹ let fly ‹ their ‹ and let › dissolve. »
from them   breath   them

---

(1) Some editions read לְנָוֶה בֵּיתֶךָ, *to the Temple, Your House*, in lieu of מִשְּׁאוֹן מוֹרְדֶיךָ.
(2) Some editions read קַבְּצֵנוּ לְמַעַנְךָ וּפְדֵנוּ, *Gather us in for Your sake and redeem us.*
(3) Cf. *Psalms* 79:9. (4) Presumably to appease the censors who would understand
אִישׁ חָמָס, *man of violence*, as an allusion to their god, some editions have inserted
the name יִשְׁמָעֵאל, *Ismael*, before *man of violence*; other editions read מֵאַנְשֵׁי חָמָס,
against men of violence, in the plural; still others omit the entire stanza except for
the first phrase, שָׁפְטָה מִשְׁפָּטִי, *judge my case*; see next footnote. (5) See preceding footnote;
some editions substitute a vastly different text for this stanza: שָׁפְטָה מִשְׁפָּטִי מֵאַנְשֵׁי חָמָס,
Judge my case against men of violence, שֶׁלֹּא יִהְיוּ עוֹד לְמַסְמָס, *that they no longer be
recipients of tribute.* תְּהִי לָהֶם לְעֵזֶר וּמָנוֹס, *Be unto them [Israel] as a Helper and Refuge*;
תִּסְעַד לְבָבָם הַנִּשְׁבָּר וְנָמֵס, *sustain their broken and melted hearts.*

גָּאַלְתָּ בְּזְרֹעַ בְּנֵי (יַעֲקֹב וְ)יוֹסֵף,1

《 Joseph; 〈 of (Jacob and) 〈 the 〈 With Your 〈 You
children mighty arm redeemed

גְּאוֹל שְׁאָר עַמְּךָ שֵׁנִית יָד תּוֹסֵף,2

《 shall once 〈 Your 〈 A second 《 of Your 〈 the 〈 redeem
again [redeem]. hand time [as people! remnant
from Egypt]

רִיבָה רִיבָם וּגְאָלָם מִיַּד מְשַׁסֵּף,3

《 of [the enemy] 〈 from the 〈 and redeem 〈 their 〈 Champion
who tears them apart. hand them cause

רְאֵה כִּי אָזְלַת יָד4 וּמִכִּיס תַּם הַכֶּסֶף.5

《 is the 〈 spent 〈 and from 《 is their 〈 gone 〈 that 〈 See
money. their pockets strength,

שׁוּר כִּי אֵין אִישׁ, הִשְׁתּוֹמֵם כִּי אֵין מַפְגִּיעַ,6

《 to entreat, 〈 there 〈 at 〈 be astonished 《[righteous]〈 there 〈 how 〈 Ob-
is no how man; is no [among serve
one them]

שְׂאֵת בַּעֲדָם רִנָּה וּתְפִלָּה לְהַפְגִּיעַ,7

《 of beseeching, 〈 a prayer 〈 a pleading 〈 on their 〈 to lift up
song, behalf

מִדַּת דִּין לְהַרְחִיק וּמִדַּת הָרַחֲמִים לְהַגִּיעַ,

《 draw near, 〈 of Mercy 〈 and the 〈 to distance 〈 of 〈 the At-
Attribute Justice tribute

מֵעֹצֶב וּמֵרֹגֶז לְהַרְגִּיעַ.8

《 bring relief. 〈 and wrath 〈 and from
anguish

בְּצִדְקָתְךָ הַצֵּל פַּלֵּט וְהוֹשִׁיעַ,9

《 deliver; 〈 rescue, 〈 save, 〈 In Your
righteousness,

בִּצְדָקָה מְדַבֵּר וְרַב לְהוֹשִׁיעַ,10

《 able to save. 〈 You 《 it is You 〈 of just
Who are Who deliverance
abundantly speaks,

רַחֵם תִּזְכֹּר וְאַל נָא תַרְשִׁיעַ,

《 condemn us. 〈 please, 〈 do 《 may You 〈 Mercy
not, remember;

---

(1) Cf. *Psalms* 77:16. (2) Cf. *Isaiah* 11:11 with *Rashi*. (3) Cf. *Psalms* 119:154.
(4) Cf. *Deuteronomy* 32:36. (5) See *Sanhedrin* 97a. (6) Cf. *Isaiah* 59:16.
(7) Cf. *Jeremiah* 7:16. (8) Cf. *Isaiah* 14:3. (9) Cf. *Psalms* 31:2-3. (10) Cf. *Isaiah* 63:1.

רְצֵה וְהַצֵּל חוּסָה וְתוֹשִׁיעַ.
《 and rescue 〈 have 〈 and save 〈 Be
[us]! mercy [us], favorable

יַכִּירוּ וְיֵדְעוּ כָּל בָּאֵי עוֹלָם,
《 the 〈 who 〈 — all 《 and 〈 May they
world — come into know recognize

יַחַד יַעֲנוּ וְיֹאמְרוּ כֻלָּם,¹
《 all of 《 and say, 〈 respond 〈 let them
them, together

הֲלֹא אֵין אֱלֹהִים בְּכָל הָעוֹלָם,
〈 the world 〈 in all 〈 God 〈 there 〈 Indeed
is no

כִּי אִם בְּיִשְׂרָאֵל² חָזָק גֹּאֲלָם.³
《 is mighty. 〈 their 《 in Israel; 〈 except
Redeemer

✧וְעַתָּה נוֹדֶה לְךָ וּנְסַפֵּר תְּהִלָּתֶךָ,⁴
《 Your praise, 〈 and relate 〈 You 〈 — And
thank now

דִּין עָלֵינוּ לְהַלֵּלְךָ עֲלֵי תְשׁוּעָתֶךָ,
《 Your salvation. 〈 for 〈 to praise You 〈 obliges 〈 for the
us law

הַדָּבָר הַזֶּה כָּתוּב בְּסֵפֶר תְּהִלָּתֶךָ,
《 of Your praises: 〈 in the Book 〈 is written 〈 This matter

לַיהוה הַיְשׁוּעָה עַל עַמְּךָ בִרְכָתֶךָ.⁵
《 is Your 〈 Your 〈 upon 《 is salvation; 〈 To HASHEM
blessing. people

ALL, WHILE STANDING:

אֵל מֶלֶךְ יוֹשֵׁב עַל כִּסֵּא רַחֲמִים, מִתְנַהֵג
〈 Who acts 《 of mercy, 〈 the throne 〈 on 〈 Who sits 〈 King 〈 O God,

בַּחֲסִידוּת, מוֹחֵל עֲוֹנוֹת עַמּוֹ, מַעֲבִיר רִאשׁוֹן
〈 [sins,] one 〈 Who 《 of His 〈 the sins 〈 Who 《 with kindness,
removes people, pardons

רִאשׁוֹן,⁶ מַרְבֶּה מְחִילָה לְחַטָּאִים וּסְלִיחָה לַפּוֹשְׁעִים,
《 to willful 〈 and 〈 to unintentional 〈 pardon 〈 Who abun- 《 by one,
sinners, forgiveness sinners dantly grants

---

(1) Cf. *Exodus* 19:8. (2) Cf. *II Kings* 5:15. (3) Cf. *Jeremiah* 50:34.
(4) From the daily *Amidah* prayer, based on *Psalms* 79:13. (5) 3:9. (6) *Rosh Hashanah* 17a.

עֹשֶׂה צְדָקוֹת עִם כָּל בָּשָׂר וָרוּחַ, לֹא כְרָעָתָם

⟨ in accord ⟨ — not ⟪ and ⟪ [beings ⟨ all ⟨ with ⟨ acts of ⟨ Who
with their　　　　　　spirit　　of] flesh　　　　　　generosity　performs
wickedness

תִּגְמוֹל. ❖ אֵל הוֹרֵיתָ לָנוּ לוֹמַר שְׁלֹשׁ עֶשְׂרֵה, וּזְכוֹר

⟨ remem- ⟪ the Thirteen ⟨ to ⟨ us ⟨ You ⟨ O God, ⟪ do You
ber　　　[Attributes of Mercy];　recite　　　taught　　　　repay them!

לָנוּ הַיּוֹם בְּרִית שְׁלֹשׁ עֶשְׂרֵה, כְּמוֹ שֶׁהוֹדַעְתָּ לֶעָנָיו

⟨ to the ⟨ You made ⟨ as ⟪ of [these] Thirteen, ⟨ the ⟨ today ⟨ for us
humble one　known　　　　　　　　　　　　　covenant
[Moses]

מִקֶּדֶם, כְּמוֹ שֶׁכָּתוּב, וַיֵּרֶד יהוה בֶּעָנָן וַיִּתְיַצֵּב עִמּוֹ

⟨ with ⟨ and stood ⟨ in a ⟨ And HASHEM ⟪ it is written: ⟨ as ⟪ in ancient
him　　　　　cloud　descended　　　　　　　　　times,

שָׁם, וַיִּקְרָא בְשֵׁם יהוה.[1]

⟪ of ⟨ with the ⟨ and He ⟪ there,
HASHEM.　Name　called out

CONGREGATION, THEN *CHAZZAN*:

וַיַּעֲבֹר יהוה עַל פָּנָיו וַיִּקְרָא:

⟪ and ⟪ [Moses'] ⟨ before ⟨ And HASHEM passed
proclaimed:　face,

CONGREGATION AND *CHAZZAN* RECITE LOUDLY AND IN UNISON:

יהוה, יהוה, אֵל, רַחוּם, וְחַנּוּן, אֶרֶךְ אַפַּיִם,

⟨ to anger, ⟨ Slow ⟪ and ⟨ Compassionate ⟨ God, ⟨ HASHEM, ⟨ HASHEM,
　　　　　　　　Gracious,

וְרַב חֶסֶד, וֶאֱמֶת, נֹצֵר חֶסֶד לָאֲלָפִים, נֹשֵׂא עָוֹן,

⟨ of ⟨ Forgiver ⟪ for ⟨ of ⟨ Preserver ⟪ and ⟨ in ⟨ and
iniquity,　　　　　thousands　kindness　　Truth,　Kindness Abundant
　　　　　　　[of generations],

וָפֶשַׁע, וְחַטָּאָה, וְנַקֵּה.[2] וְסָלַחְתָּ לַעֲוֹנֵנוּ וּלְחַטָּאתֵנוּ

⟪ and our sins, ⟨ our ⟪ May You ⟪ and Who ⟨ and inadvertent ⟨ willful sin,
　　　　iniquities　forgive　absolves.　sin,

וּנְחַלְתָּנוּ.[3] סְלַח לָנוּ אָבִינוּ כִּי חָטָאנוּ, מְחַל לָנוּ

⟨ us, ⟨ pardon ⟪ we have ⟨ for ⟪ our ⟨ us, ⟨ Forgive ⟪ and make us
　　　　sinned;　　Father,　　　　　　　　Your heritage.

---

(1) *Exodus* 34:5. (2) 34:6-7. (3) 34:9.

מַלְכֵּנוּ כִּי פָשָׁעְנוּ. כִּי אַתָּה אֲדֹנָי טוֹב וְסַלָּח,

‹ and forgiving, ‹ are good ‹ O Lord, ‹ You, ‹ For ‹‹ we have willfully sinned. ‹ for ‹‹ our King,

וְרַב חֶסֶד לְכָל קֹרְאֶיךָ.[1]

‹‹ who call upon You. ‹ to all ‹ kind ‹ and abundantly

פסוקי הקדמה לסליחה ע / PREFATORY VERSES TO SELICHAH 70

אַתָּה הוּא מַלְכִּי מִקֶּדֶם, פֹּעֵל יְשׁוּעוֹת בְּקֶרֶב

‹ in the midst ‹ acts of salvations ‹ performing ‹‹ from days of old, ‹ my King ‹ You are

הָאָרֶץ.[2] אַתָּה הוּא מַלְכֵּנוּ אֱלֹהִים, צַוֵּה יְשׁוּעוֹת

‹ the salvations ‹ command ‹‹ O God; ‹ our King, ‹ Who are ‹ It is You ‹‹ of the earth.

יַעֲקֹב.[3] הַאֲזִינָה יהוה תְּפִלָּתֵנוּ, וְהַקְשִׁיבָה בְּקוֹל

‹ the sound ‹ and heed ‹‹ to our prayer, ‹ HASHEM, ‹ Listen, ‹‹ of Jacob.

תַּחֲנוּנוֹתֵינוּ.[4] שׁוּב לְמַעַן עֲבָדֶיךָ שִׁבְטֵי נַחֲלָתֶךָ.[5]

‹‹ that are Your heritage. ‹ the tribes ‹ of Your servants, ‹ for the sake ‹ Return [to us] ‹‹ of our supplications.

כְּרַחֵם אָב עַל בָּנִים, כֵּן תְּרַחֵם יהוה עָלֵינוּ.[6]

‹‹ on us. ‹ HASHEM, ‹ have mercy, ‹ so ‹‹ his children, ‹ toward ‹ a father is ‹ As merciful as

לַיהוה הַיְשׁוּעָה, עַל עַמְּךָ בִרְכָתֶךָ סֶּלָה.[7] יהוה

‹ HASHEM, ‹‹ Selah. ‹‹ is Your blessing, ‹ Your people ‹ upon ‹‹ is salvation, ‹ To HASHEM

צְבָאוֹת עִמָּנוּ, מִשְׂגָּב לָנוּ אֱלֹהֵי יַעֲקֹב סֶלָה.[8]

‹‹ Selah. ‹ of Jacob, ‹ is the God ‹ for us ‹ a stronghold ‹‹ is with us, ‹ Master of Legions,

יהוה צְבָאוֹת, אַשְׁרֵי אָדָם בֹּטֵחַ בָּךְ.[9] יהוה

‹ HASHEM, ‹‹ in You. ‹ who trusts ‹ is the man ‹ — praiseworthy ‹‹ Master of Legions ‹ HASHEM,

הוֹשִׁיעָה, הַמֶּלֶךְ יַעֲנֵנוּ בְיוֹם קָרְאֵנוּ.[10]

‹‹ we call. ‹ on the day ‹ answer us ‹ May the King ‹‹ save!

---

(1) *Psalms* 86:5. (2) Cf. 74:12. (3) Cf. 44:5. (4) Cf. 86:6. (5) *Isaiah* 63:17.
(6) Cf. *Psalms* 103:13. (7) 3:9. (8) 46:8. (9) 84:13. (10) 20:10.

סליחה ע / SELICHAH 70

אֱלֹהֵינוּ וֵאלֹהֵי אֲבוֹתֵינוּ:

《 of our forefathers: 〈 and the God 〈 Our God

אַתָּה מִקֶּדֶם* אֱלֹהֵינוּ אֲדוֹנֵינוּ,[1]

《 our Lord, 〈 our God, 〈 since of old* 〈 You are

וְאָנוּ עֵדֶיךָ כִּי אֵין בִּלְתְּךָ[2] גְּאוֹנֵנוּ,

《 our Pride. 《 besides 〈 there is 〈 that 〈 Your 〈 and we
You, no one witnesses are

בְּךָ בָּטְחוּ אֲבוֹתֵינוּ וַתְּפַלְּטֵמוֹ[3] פַּלְּטֵנוּ,

《 — rescue 《 and You 〈 our fathers 〈 trusted 〈 In
us, [too]! rescued them You

אֵלֶיךָ זָעֲקוּ וְנִמְלָטוּ[4] בְּזַעֲקֵנוּ מַלְּטֵנוּ.

《 save us! 〈 when 《 and were 〈 they 〈 To You
we cry, saved cried

גֵּר צֶדֶק הָרִאשׁוֹן לְכָל הַנְּדִיבִים,*[5]

《 the nobles,* 〈 first 《 who was 〈 The righteous pros-
among all the first, elyte [Abraham,]

בֶּן שָׁלֹשׁ הִכִּירְךָ* יוֹשֵׁב הַכְּרוּבִים,

《 upon the 〈 You Who are 《 he recognized 〈 of 〈 at the
Cherubim. enthroned You,* three age

---

(1) Cf. *Habakkuk* 1:12. (2) Cf. *Isaiah* 44:8. (3) Cf. *Psalms* 22:5. (4) Cf. 22:6. (5) Cf. 47:10.

⤎ אַתָּה מִקֶּדֶם — *You are since of old.* Like the preceding *selichah*, this one contains an alphabetical acrostic followed by גֵּרְשֹׁם בַּר יְהוּדָה, *Gershom bar Yehudah;* is extremely critical of the Church of his time; and has come under the careful scrutiny of the censor. [See prefatory comments to *Selichos* 12 and 69.]

גֵּר צֶדֶק הָרִאשׁוֹן לְכָל הַנְּדִיבִים — *The right-eous proselyte [Abraham,] who was the first, first among all the nobles.* The text is ambiguous: It can mean, גֵּר צֶדֶק הָרִאשׁוֹן, *the first righteous proselyte,* or הָרִאשׁוֹן לְכָל הַנְּדִיבִים, *the first among the nobles.* Our translation includes both interpretations.

Commenting on the verse, נְדִיבֵי עַמִּים נֶאֱסָפוּ, *the nobles of the peoples gathered,* עַם אֱלֹהֵי אַבְרָהָם, *the people of the God of Abraham* (*Psalms* 47:10), the Talmud

asks: Is He not also the God of Isaac and Jacob? And answers: Only Abraham is mentioned because he was the first of the proselytes (*Chagigah* 3a).

בֶּן שָׁלֹשׁ הִכִּירְךָ — *At the age of three he recognized You.* When a mere three years old, Abraham already recognized that the world must have a Creator and Master. The Talmud explicates this from the verse: עֵקֶב אֲשֶׁר שָׁמַע אַבְרָהָם בְּקֹלִי, literally, *because Abraham obeyed My voice...* (*Genesis* 26:5). The *gematria* of the word עֵקֶב is 172 [ע = 70; ק = 100; ב = 2], allowing the verse to be interpreted as, *For one hundred seventy-two years, Abraham obeyed My voice.* But Abraham lived 175 years (ibid. 25:7). Thus, at the age of three, he already served God (*Nedarim* 32a).

דְּמוּ לְהַפְרִידוֹ מִיִּרְאָתֶךָ אוֹיְבִים חַיָּבִים,

≪ who were ⟨ did enemies ⟨ him from Your ⟨ to separate ⟨ Thought
sinful;   reverence

בְּעַצְמְךָ יָרַדְתָּ וְהוֹצֵאתוֹ מֵאוֹר שְׁבִיבִים.

≪ full of flames. ⟨ of the oven ⟨ and took him out ⟨ descended ⟨ but You Yourself

הַנֶּשֶׁר הַגָּדוֹל אֶרֶךְ הָאֶבְרָה,[1]

≪   wings, ⟨ of long ⟨ that was ⟨ When [Nebu-
great,   chadnezzar,]
the eagle

צֶלֶם בַּהֲקִימוֹ בְּבִקְעַת דּוּרָא,[2]

≪ of Dura, ⟨ in the Valley ⟨ he set up ⟨ an idol

וַחֲנַנְיָה וַחֲבֵרָיו פִּיךָ אָצוּ לְשָׁמְרָה,

≪   to keep; ⟨ hurried ⟨ Your mouth's ⟨ and his ⟨ Chananiah
utterance   companions

וְשַׂר אֵשׁ צִוִּיתָ לְהָקֵר אַתּוּן נוֹרָא.[3]

≪ of fire. ⟨ the ⟨ to cool ⟨ You com- ⟨ of ⟨ and the
furnace   manded   Fire ⟨ Angel

זָמְמוּ רְשָׁעִים מָצֹא עֲלִילָה,

⟨ an ⟨ seeking ⟨ did wicked ⟨ Plot
accusation   to find   men

לְהָמִית אִישׁ חֲמוּדוֹת[4] עַל עֵסֶק הַתְּפִלָּה,

≪ in prayers. ⟨ his ⟨ because ⟨ who was be- ⟨ the ⟨ to put
involvement   of   loved [Daniel]   man   to death

חַיָּיו צָמְתוּ בְּבוֹר אֲרָיוֹת וַיַּדּוּ אֶבֶן מִלְמַעְלָה,

≪ over it; ⟨ a ⟨ placing ⟨ of the lions, ⟨ in the pit ⟨ they sought ⟨ His life
boulder   to end

מַלְאָךְ שָׁלַחְתָּ וְסָגַר פִּיהֶם מִלְחַבְּלָה.[5]

≪ so they ⟨ the [lions'] ⟨ who ⟨ You sent ⟨ but an
could not harm.   mouths   closed   angel

טָפַשׁ יְוָנִי הוּא וּמְשָׁרְתָּיו רְשָׁעִים,

≪ all of them ⟨ and his ⟨ — he ≪ [filled ⟨ Thoughts
wicked —   servants,   Antiochus]   of folly
the Greek

לְהַשְׁכִּיחַ מֵעַמְּךָ שִׁמְךָ הַנָּעִים,

≪ that is ⟨ Your ⟨ by Your ⟨ to cause to
pleasant.   Name   people   be forgotten

---

(1) Cf. *Ezekiel* 17:3. (2) Cf. *Daniel* 3:1. (3) See commentary, p. 58, s.v. חֲנַנְיָה, *Chananiah*.
(4) *Daniel* 10:11. (5) See 6:5-23.

יָעַץ לְהַדִּיחַ מִמְּךָ יְלִידֵי שַׁעֲשׁוּעִים,

He took counsel 〉 to distance 〉 from You 〉 the children 〉 in whom You take pleasure; 》

נָפַל וְנִשְׁבַּר וּמֵת בְּתַחֲלוּאִים רָעִים.*

he fell 〉 and was bro- 〉 and 〉 from diseases 〉 that were malignant.*
ken [in spirit] 〉 died

בַּמָּה וְכַמָּה רָעוֹת רַבּוֹת צְרָרוּנוּ מִנְּעוּרֵינוּ,¹

With so many, 〉 evils 〉 multi- 〉 have they 〉 since our youth! 》
tudinous 〉 troubled us

עֶזְרָתֵנוּ הָיִיתָ וְלֹא יָכְלוּ לָנוּ,²

Our Help 〉 You have 〉 so they were not 《 us. 》
been, 〉 able to overcome

לְשִׁמְךָ תֵּן כָּבוֹד לֹא לָנוּ יהוה לֹא לָנוּ,³

For Your 〉 give 〉 glory, 》 not 〉 for our 〉 HASHEM, 〉 not 〉 for our
Name's sake 〉 sake, 〉 sake! 》

בְּקוּם עָלֵינוּ אָדָם הָיוּ תִהְיֶה עִמָּנוּ.⁴

When 〉 against 〉 do men, 《 You will 〉 with us. 》
rise up 〉 us 〉 surely be

מוֹאֲסֵי דָתֶךָ הִמְשַׁלְתָּ עַל עַם דַּלִּים,⁵

Those who 〉 Your 〉 You have 〉 over 〉 a 〉 that is
despise 〉 Law 〉 given rule 〉 people 〉 poor. 《

טוֹבָתְךָ כָּפוּ וְהֶחֱזִיקוּ טוֹבָה לָאֱלִילִים,

For Your 〉 they are 〉 and give 〉 their 〉 to false gods. 《
goodness 〉 ungrateful 〉 gratitude

נוֹשְׂאִים לִבָּם לְהַרְבּוֹת כָּבוֹד לַפְּסִילִים,

The goal 〉 of their 〉 is to increase 〉 the glory 〉 of [their] idols, 《
heart

חֶבֶל נַחֲלָתְךָ לְהַעֲבִיר לַגִּלּוּלִים.

and [Israel] 〉 and Your 〉 to transfer 〉 to idolatry. 《
Your portion 〉 heritage

---

(1) Cf. *Psalms* 129:1. (2) Cf. 129:2. (3) Cf. 115:1. (4) Cf. 124:2. (5) In most editions this stanza has been altered to read: מוֹשְׁלִים וְשָׂרִים הִמְשַׁלְתָּ עַל עַם דַּלִּים, *Rulers and princes You have given rule over a people that is poor.* טוֹבָתְךָ תָּחִישׁ לָנוּ שׁוֹכֵן מְעוֹנִים, *Your goodness may You speed to us, You Who dwell on high!* נֹשְׂאֵי לִבָּם וְעֵינֵיהֶם לְךָ תוֹלִים, *[We are the ones] who set their hearts and eyes on You, depending;* חֶבֶל נַחֲלָתְךָ לְךָ מְיַחֲלִים, *[Your] portion and Your heritage who in You place their hope.*

נָפַל וְנִשְׁבַּר וּמֵת בְּתַחֲלוּאִים רָעִים — *He fell and was broken [in spirit] and died from diseases that were malignant.* Josephus (*Antiquities* 12:9) describes how Antiochus Epiphanes fell into lingering distemper from which he could find no escape. Before his death; he confided to his friends his belief that his malady was a Divine punishment for his sacrilegious acts of looting and desecrating the Jewish Temple in Jerusalem.

סוֹד עֲצָתָם שָׁמַעְנוּ וַתִּרְגַּז בִּטְנֵנוּ,[1]

Their secret ⟩ counsels ⟨ we heard, ⟩ and ⟨ did our «
shudder ⟩ innards.

בְּיָדֵינוּ תָּפַשְׂנוּ אֻמָּנוּת אֲבוֹתֵינוּ,

In our hands ⟩ we seized ⟨ the craft ⟩ of our fathers: «

עָדֶיךָ לָשׁוּב בַּצַּר לָנוּ בְּגָלוּתֵנוּ,

To You ⟩ to return ⟨ when in ⟩ we ⟨ in our exile. «
trouble ⟩ are

רַחוּם שְׁמַע צַעֲקָתֵנוּ וְאַל תַּשְׁחִיתֵנוּ.[2]

O Compas- « hear ⟩ our cry ⟨ and ⟨ destroy us! «
sionate One, ⟩ do not

פַּלְגֵי מַיִם בְּיָדְךָ לֵב מְלָכִים וְשָׂרִים,[3]

Like ⟩ of ⟨ water ⟩ in Your ⟨ are the ⟩ of kings ⟨ and princes; «
streams ⟩ hand ⟩ hearts

הַטֵּה לִבָּם לְצֶדֶק מֵישָׁרִים,

turn ⟩ their ⟨ toward ⟩ and «
hearts ⟩ justice ⟩ uprightness.

צְפֵה כִּי עַמְּךָ רַכִּים וּנְעָרִים,[4]

Observe ⟩ how ⟨ Your ⟩ are ⟨ and young, «
people ⟩ delicate

וְאֵין יְכֹלִים לִסְבּוֹל פֻּרְעָנוּת וְיִסּוּרִים.

and they are not able ⟩ to bear ⟨ calamity ⟩ and suffering. «

קִיּוּם בְּרִית אָבוֹת זְכוֹר[5] לִבְנֵיהֶם,

The ful- ⟩ of the ⟨ of the ⟩ remember ⟨ for their «
fillment ⟩ covenant ⟩ Patriarchs ⟩ children,

כְּמוֹ כָתוּב בְּסֵפֶר תּוֹכְחוֹתֵיהֶם,

as ⟩ is written ⟨ in the Book ⟩ of their rebukes: «

רְצוּצִים[6] בִּהְיוֹתָם בְּאֶרֶץ אוֹיְבֵיהֶם,

Though they ⟩ when they are ⟨ in the land ⟩ of their enemies; «
are broken

לֹא גְעַלְתִּים לְכַלּוֹתָם לְהָפֵר בְּרִיתִי עִמָּהֶם.[7]

I have not found ⟩ to obliterate ⟨ to annul ⟩ My ⟨ with them. «
them abhorrent ⟩ them, ⟩ covenant

---

(1) Cf. *Habakkuk* 3:16. (2) Cf. *Deuteronomy* 4:30-31. (3) Cf. *Proverbs* 21:1.
(4) Cf. *II Chronicles* 13:7. See also *Ramban* to *Exodus* 33:11. (5) Cf. *Deuteronomy* 4:31.
(6) Some editions read רצויים, *they would find [Your favor]*. (7) Cf. *Leviticus* 26:44.

שַׁדַּי בְּשִׁמְךָ נִשְׁבַּעְתָּ לָרִאשׁוֹנִים,

《 to the first [fathers]; 〈 You swore 〈 By Your 《 O
Name Almighty!

כְּשִׁמְךָ קַיָּם כֵּן שְׁבוּעָתְךָ קַיֶּם לָאַחֲרוֹנִים,[1]

《 to the last 〈 fulfill 〈 Your oath 〈 so 《endures〈 as Your
[generations]. [forever], Name

תִּתֵּן אֱמֶת וְחֶסֶד לַבָּנִים,

〈 to the 〈 and 〈 truth 〈 Grant
children kindness

אֲשֶׁר נִשְׁבַּעְתָּ לַאֲבוֹתָם מִימִים קַדְמוֹנִים.[2]

《 of old. 〈 from days 〈 to their forefathers〈 You swore 〈 as

גַּן נָעוּל מַעְיָן חָתוּם[3] וְאֵין מִזְדַּקֵּר,

《 can jump inside 〈 and 《 that is 〈 the 《 that is 〈[Israel,]
[to sin]— no one sealed, spring locked, the
garden

אַל תִּתֵּן לְמִשְׁלַח מִרְמָס[4] וְהֶפְקֵר,

《 and 〈 trampled 〈 a common 〈 let it be 〈 do
uncontrolled. pasture, not

רֵאשִׁית תְּבוּאָתְךָ[5] וְכַרְמְךָ שֶׁבָּם אַתָּה מִתְיַקֵּר,

《 gain glory — 〈 You 〈 that 《 and Your 〈 of Your crop 〈 [Israel,] the
through them vineyard, first-fruits

אַל תִּמְסְרֵם לְמִרְמָס וּלְעַקֵּר.[6]

《 and 〈 to be 〈 give them 〈 do
uprooted. trampled over not

שְׁאֵרִית כְּנֵסִיָּה וּפְלֵיטָה הַנִּשְׁאָרֶת,

《 who remains — 〈 the refugee 《 of Your 〈 The remnant
assembly,

שְׁמוֹר בְּצִלְּךָ תִּהְיֶה לְמִשְׁמֶרֶת,

《 a safeguarded 〈 let her be 《 in Your 〈 guard
treasure. shadow, [her]

מַעֲמָדָהּ חַזֵּק לְבַל תִּפֹּל בְּמַכְמֹרֶת,

《 into the net; 〈 that she not fall 〈 strengthen 〈 Her stance

תֵּן אוֹתָהּ לִתְהִלָּה וּלְתִפְאָרֶת.

《 and for splendor. 〈 for praise 〈 her 〈 place

---

(1) Some editions read בְּשִׁמְךָ כֵּן תְּקַיֵּים לָאַחֲרוֹנִים, *so with Your Name may You fulfill for the last [generations].* (2) Cf. *Micah* 7:20. (3) Cf. *Song of Songs* 4:12. (4) Cf. *Isaiah* 7:25. (5) Cf. *Jeremiah* 2:3. (6) Some editions read לְכַרְסוֹם נֹחֵר וְמַעֲקֵר, *to the boar that grunts and uproots;* cf. *Psalms* 80:14.

בִּנְךָ בְּכוֹרְךָ אֲשֶׁר בְּךָ נוֹשָׁע,

《 is saved, 〈 by 〈 who 〈 Your 〈 [Israel,] You Your son first-born,

תְּשׁוּעַת עוֹלָמִים בְּקָרוֹב יֻוָּשַׁע,[1]

《 be saved. 〈 may he soon 〈 for eternity 〈 a salvation

רָעֵי גוֹיִם[2] חוֹשְׁבִים מַחְשְׁבוֹת רֶשַׁע,

《 of evil: 〈 thoughts 〈 are thinking 〈 among 〈 The most nations wicked

עֲצָתָם קַלְקֵל וְעֵינֵיהֶם הָשַׁע.[3]

《 seal! 〈 and their eyes 〈 spoil 〈 Their scheme

יִהְיוּ לְרָצוֹן אִמְרֵי פִי לְפָנֶיךָ,[4]

《 before 〈 of my 〈 — the ex- 〈 find favor 〈 May You, mouth — pressions they

הַיּוֹם הַזֶּה בְּהִתְפַּלְלִי עַל בָּנֶיךָ,

《 Your children; 〈 for 〈 as I pray 〈 this day,

וְאַל תְּשַׁקֵּץ עֲנוּת עֲנִיֶּיךָ,

《 of Your 〈 the 〈 loathe 〈 and poor — supplication do not

לִשְׁמֹעַ שַׁוְעָתָם[5] תְּהִי נָא קַשֶּׁבֶת אָזְנֶיךָ.[6]

《 Your ear. 〈 be attentive 〈 please, 〈 let, 《 their cry, 〈 to hear

❖ דִּבְרֵי עֲוֹנוֹתֵינוּ וּפְשָׁעֵינוּ הַנִּכְתָּמִים,[7]

《 that are staining, 〈 and willful sins 〈 our iniquities 〈 Regarding

תִּשָּׂא וְתִכְבּוֹשׁ וְתַשְׁלִיךְ בִּמְצֻלוֹת יַמִּים.[8]

《 of the 〈 into the depths 〈 and cast 〈 suppress, 〈 may You seas. [them] forgive,

הַסְּלִיחָה עִמְּךָ סְלַח נָא לַעֲוֹן אֲשֵׁמִים,

《 of the guilty 〈 the 〈 please 〈 forgive 《 is with 〈 Forgiveness people, iniquity You;

אֵל מֶלֶךְ יוֹשֵׁב עַל כִּסֵּא רַחֲמִים.

《 of Mercy! 〈 the 〈 on 〈 Who sits 〈 King, 〈 O Throne God,

---

(1) Cf. *Isaiah* 45:17. (2) In another example of censorship, this phrase appears variously as: רָעִים, *the wicked*; רָעֵי יִשְׁמְעֵאלִים, *the wicked Ishmaelites*; רִיעֵי רְשָׁעִים, *cohorts of the wicked*; רָעֵי חוֹשְׁבֵי, *shepherds of those who plot . . .*; and, . . . רוֹעֵ חוֹשְׁבֵי, *the evil of those who plot . . . .* (3) Cf. *Isaiah* 6:10. (4) Cf. *Psalms* 19:15. (5) Cf. 22:25. (6) Cf. 130:2. (7) Cf. *Jeremiah* 2:23. (8) Cf. *Micah* 7:19.

ALL, WHILE STANDING:

אֵל מֶלֶךְ יוֹשֵׁב עַל כִּסֵּא רַחֲמִים, מִתְנַהֵג

⟨ Who acts ⟪ of mercy, ⟨ the throne ⟨ on ⟨ Who sits ⟨ King ⟨ O God,

בַּחֲסִידוּת, מוֹחֵל עֲווֹנוֹת עַמּוֹ, מַעֲבִיר רִאשׁוֹן

⟨ [sins,] one ⟨ Who removes ⟪ of His people, ⟨ the sins ⟨ Who pardons ⟪ with kindness,

רִאשׁוֹן,¹ מַרְבֶּה מְחִילָה לַחַטָּאִים וּסְלִיחָה לַפּוֹשְׁעִים,

⟪ to willful sinners, ⟨ and forgiveness ⟨ to unintentional sinners ⟨ pardon ⟨ Who abun- dantly grants ⟪ by one,

עֹשֶׂה צְדָקוֹת עִם כָּל בָּשָׂר וָרוּחַ, לֹא כְרָעָתָם

⟨ in accord with their wickedness ⟨ — not ⟪ and spirit ⟨ [beings of] flesh ⟨ all ⟨ with ⟨ acts of generosity ⟨ Who performs

תִּגְמוֹל. ❖ אֵל הוֹרֵיתָ לָּנוּ לוֹמַר שְׁלֹשׁ עֶשְׂרֵה, וּזְכוֹר

⟨ remem- ber ⟪ the Thirteen [Attributes of Mercy]; ⟨ to recite ⟨ us ⟨ You ⟨ O God, ⟪ do You repay them!

לָנוּ הַיּוֹם בְּרִית שְׁלֹשׁ עֶשְׂרֵה, כְּמוֹ שֶׁהוֹדַעְתָּ לֶעָנָיו

⟨ to the humble one [Moses] ⟨ You made known ⟨ as ⟪ of [these] Thirteen, ⟨ the covenant ⟨ today ⟨ for us

מִקֶּדֶם, כְּמוֹ שֶׁכָּתוּב, וַיֵּרֶד יהוה בֶּעָנָן וַיִּתְיַצֵּב עִמּוֹ

⟨ with him ⟨ and stood ⟨ in a cloud ⟨ And HASHEM descended ⟪ it is written: ⟨ as ⟪ in ancient times,

שָׁם, וַיִּקְרָא בְשֵׁם יהוה.²

⟪ of HASHEM. ⟨ with the Name ⟨ and He called out ⟪ there,

CONGREGATION, THEN CHAZZAN:

וַיַּעֲבֹר יהוה עַל פָּנָיו וַיִּקְרָא:

⟪ and proclaimed: ⟪ [Moses'] face, ⟨ before ⟨ And HASHEM passed

CONGREGATION AND CHAZZAN RECITE LOUDLY AND IN UNISON:

יהוה, יהוה, אֵל, רַחוּם, וְחַנּוּן, אֶרֶךְ אַפַּיִם,

⟨ to anger, ⟨ Slow ⟪ and Gracious, ⟨ Compassionate ⟨ God, ⟨ HASHEM, ⟨ HASHEM,

וְרַב חֶסֶד, וֶאֱמֶת, נֹצֵר חֶסֶד לָאֲלָפִים, נֹשֵׂא עָוֹן,

⟨ of iniquity, ⟨ Forgiver ⟪ for thousands [of generations], ⟨ of kindness ⟨ Preserver ⟪ and Truth, ⟨ in Kindness Abundant ⟨ and

(1) *Rosh Hashanah* 17a. (2) *Exodus* 34:5.

וָפֶשַׁע, וְחַטָּאָה, וְנַקֵּה.¹ וְסָלַחְתָּ לַעֲוֹנֵנוּ וּלְחַטָּאתֵנוּ

《 and our sins, 〈 our iniquities 〈 May You forgive 《 and Who absolves. 〈 and inadvertent sin, 〈 willful sin,

וּנְחַלְתָּנוּ.² סְלַח לָנוּ אָבִינוּ כִּי חָטָאנוּ, מְחַל לָנוּ

〈 us, 〈 pardon 《 we have sinned; 〈 for 《 our Father, 〈 us, 〈 Forgive 《 and make us Your heritage.

מַלְכֵּנוּ כִּי פָשָׁעְנוּ. כִּי אַתָּה אֲדֹנָי טוֹב וְסַלָּח,

《 and forgiving, 〈 are good 〈 O Lord, 〈 You, 〈 For 《 we have willfully sinned. 〈 for 〈 our King,

וְרַב חֶסֶד לְכָל קֹרְאֶיךָ.³

《 who call upon You. 〈 to all 〈 kind 〈 and abundantly

PREFATORY VERSES TO SELICHAH 71 / פסוקי הקדמה לסליחה עא

אִם עֲוֹנֵינוּ עָנוּ בָנוּ, יהוה עֲשֵׂה לְמַעַן שְׁמֶךָ.⁴

《 of Your Name. 〈 for the sake 〈 act 《 O HASHEM, 〈 against us, 〈 testify 《 our iniquities 〈 If

אִם עֲוֹנוֹת תִּשְׁמָר יָהּ, יהוה, מִי יַעֲמֹד. כִּי עִמְּךָ

〈 with You [alone] 〈 For 《 could survive? 〈 who 〈 O Lord, 《 O God, 〈 You preserve, 〈 iniquities 〈 If

הַסְּלִיחָה, לְמַעַן תִּוָּרֵא.⁵ כִּי עִם יהוה הַחֶסֶד,

《 is kindness, 〈 HASHEM 〈 with 〈 For 《 You may be feared. 〈 so that 《 is forgiveness,

וְהַרְבֵּה עִמּוֹ פְדוּת.⁶ רְאֵה עָנְיֵנוּ וַעֲמָלֵנוּ, וְשָׂא לְכָל

〈 all 〈 and forgive 《 and our toil, 〈 our afflictions 〈 See 《 is redemption. 〈 with Him 〈 and abundant

חַטֹּאתֵינוּ.⁷

《 our sins.

בְּרַחֵם אָב עַל בָּנִים, כֵּן תְּרַחֵם יהוה עָלֵינוּ.⁸

《 on us. 〈 HASHEM, 〈 have mercy, 〈 so 《 his children, 〈 toward 〈 a father is 〈 As merciful as

לַיהוה הַיְשׁוּעָה, עַל עַמְּךָ בִרְכָתֶךָ סֶּלָה.⁹ יהוה

〈 HASHEM, 《 Selah. 《 is Your blessing, 〈 Your people 〈 upon 《 is salvation, 〈 To HASHEM

---

(1) Exodus 34:6-7. (2) 34:9. (3) Psalms 86:5. (4) Jeremiah 14:7.
(5) Psalms 130:3-4. (6) 130:7. (7) Cf. 25:18. (8) Cf. 103:13. (9) 3:9.

צְבָאוֹת עִמָּנוּ, מִשְׂגָּב לָנוּ אֱלֹהֵי יַעֲקֹב סֶלָה.¹

‹ Selah. ‹ of Jacob, ‹ is the God ‹ for us ‹ a ‹ is with us, ‹ Master of
　　　　　　　　　　　　　　　　　 stronghold　　　　　　　　　Legions,

יהוה צְבָאוֹת, אַשְׁרֵי אָדָם בֹּטֵחַ בָּךְ.² יהוה הוֹשִׁיעָה,

‹ save! ‹ HASHEM, ‹ in You. ‹ who ‹ is the ‹ — praise- ‹ Master of ‹ HASHEM,
　　　　　　　　　　　 trusts　　 man　　worthy　　　Legions

הַמֶּלֶךְ יַעֲנֵנוּ בְיוֹם קָרְאֵנוּ.³

‹ we call. ‹ on the ‹ answer ‹ May the
　　　　　　 day　　　 us　　　King

סְלִיחָה עא / SELICHAH 71
(שְׁלִישִׁיָּה)

אֱלֹהֵינוּ וֵאלֹהֵי אֲבוֹתֵינוּ:

‹ of our forefathers: ‹ and the God ‹ Our God

שׁוֹמַמְתִּי* בְּרֹב יְגוֹנִי, לַיּוֹם יִפְקֹד זְדוֹנִי,

‹ are my ‹ that ‹ On the ‹ anguish. ‹ in my ‹ I am desolate*
　 sins,　 reviewed　 day　　　　　 abundant

מָה אֹמַר לַאדֹנִי.⁴

‹ to the Lord? ‹ will I say ‹ what

אֻמְלַלְתִּי וְנֶאֱלַמְתִּי, בְּזָכְרִי אֲשֶׁר אָשַׁמְתִּי,

‹ guilty deeds ‹ what ‹ when I ‹ and fall silent ‹ I am miserable
　 I have done;　　　　 remember

בֹּשְׁתִּי וְגַם נִכְלַמְתִּי.⁵

‹ humiliated. ‹ and also ‹ I am ashamed

בְּהֶבֶל כָּלוּ יָמַי,⁶ מִפְּנֵי בֹשֶׁת עֲלוּמַי,⁷

‹ of my ‹ the ‹ because ‹ my ‹ are con- ‹ In
　 youth　 shame　 of　　 days;　 sumed　emptiness

---

(1) *Psalms* 46:8. (2) 84:13. (3) 20:10. (4) Cf. *Genesis* 44:16.
(5) *Jeremiah* 31:18. (6) Cf. *Psalms* 102:4. (7) Cf. *Isaiah* 54:4.

◆§ שׁוֹמַמְתִּי — *I am desolate.* R' Shlomo ben
Yehudah ibn Gabirol (Spain, c. 1021-1058)
was a prolific *paytan* and philosopher
about whom R' Moshe ibn Ezra (Spain, c.
1070-1140) writes, "By subduing his natural
instincts and inclinations in order to purify
his body and soul, he achieved sublime holiness and ascended to heights unparalleled
by his contemporaries." From this purity of
soul welled poems and hymns which have
been incorporated into the festival liturgy.
(However, many, if not most, of the *Selichos*
signed Shlomo ben Yehudah are not by Ibn
Gabirol, but by his namesake, R' Shlomo ben
Yehudah HaBavli; see prefatory comment to
Selichah 2.)

R' Shlomo signed his name in the acrostic
of the first stanza. The remaining stanzas follow an *aleph-beis* acrostic, and the last stich
of each is a fragment of a Scriptural verse.

אֵין שָׁלוֹם בַּעֲצָמַי.[1]

《 for my bones. 〈 peace 〈there is no

גַּחַלְתִּי[2] בִּי קוֹדַחַת, כִּי מְגִלָּה נִמְתָּחַת,

〈 is stretched 〈 the scroll 〈 for 《 burns, 〈within 〈 My ember
open   [of misdeeds]   me

וְהַנּוֹשֶׁה בָּא לָקֶחַת.[3]

《 to collect 〈 comes 〈 and the
[payment].   Creditor

דָּבֶקְתִּי בְמַחְשַׁכִּי, וְנַפְשִׁי לֹא יָדְעָה, כִּי

〈 that 〈 know 〈 did 〈 even my 《 to my [ways of] 〈 I have clung
not   soul   darkness;

גֵּר וְתוֹשָׁב אָנֹכִי.[4]

《 am I. 〈 and a foreign 〈 but an
resident   alien
[in this world]

הוֹי כִּי יָבֹא יוֹמִי,[5] אֲזַי אִיקַץ מֵחֲלוֹמִי,

〈 from my dream 〈 shall I 〈 then 《 does 〈approach 〈when 〈 Woe!
awake   my day,

וְאָשׁוּבָה אֶל מְקוֹמִי.[6]

《 my place. 〈 to 〈 and return

וְעַל חֲטָאַי אֲשֶׁר עָבַר, וְעַל פְּשָׁעַי אֲשֶׁר גָּבַר,

《 over- 〈 that is 〈 and my 《are already〈 which 〈 my sins 〈 As for
whelming,   rebelliousness done,

מָה אָשִׁיב שֹׁלְחִי דָּבָר.[7]

《 as an 〈 to the One 〈 should I 〈 what
answer? Who sent me return

זָדוֹן לִבִּי הִשִּׁיאַנִי,[8] עַל עָוֹן אֲשֶׁר הֶלְאַנִי,

《 wearied me; 〈 that 〈 the 〈 about 〈 of my 〈The wick-
iniquity   heart edness

מִבֶּטֶן קְרָאָנִי.[9]

《 it has 〈 from the
called me. womb

חוֹשֵׁב בְּנַפְשׁוֹ נָבָל, כְּעֵץ שָׁתוּל עַל יוּבָל,[10]

《 a stream, 〈along- 〈 deeply 〈 as a tree 〈 does a 〈 of himself 〈 Think
side   rooted   villain

---

(1) *Psalms* 38:4. (2) See *II Samuel* 14:7. (3) *II Kings* 4:1. (4) *Genesis* 23:4. (5) Cf. *Psalms* 37:13. (6) Cf. *Hosea* 5:15. (7) *II Samuel* 24:13. (8) Cf. *Obadiah* 1:3. (9) *Isaiah* 49:1. (10) Cf. *Jeremiah* 17:8.

וְהוּא לִקְבָרוֹת יוּבָל.[1]

《 is borne. 〈　to his grave 〈even as he

טָפַל שֶׁקֶר* בְּתוֹכוֹ, וְנָמֵס מִמַּהֲלָכוֹ,[2]

〈　as he goes 〈but it [the false-《 within 〈 falsehood 〈 He has
[to his grave]　hood] melts　himself,　piled up

וַיִּפֶן כֹּה וָכֹה.*[3]

《　　and that 〈 this 〈 and he
[trying to find it].* way　turns

יֻשְׁלַךְ כְּאֶבֶן דּוּמָה, וְלֹא יִשָּׂא לְבֵית מְהוּמָה,

〈 of tumultuous 〈　to his 〈 carry 〈and does 《 into [the 〈 like a 〈 He is
[crying]　home　not grave's] silence, stone　thrown

מִכָּל אֲשֶׁר לוֹ מְאוּמָה.[4]

《　anything. 〈was his 〈 that 〈 of all

כֹּחוּ לֹא סְמָכַתְהוּ, עֵת נַפְשׁוֹ נְשָׁאַתְהוּ,

〈　bore him 〈 his soul 〈when 〈 support him 〈 did 〈 His
[in life],　not　strength

אַף כִּי אֵשׁ אֲכָלָתְהוּ.[5]

《　devours him. 〈 the 〈 now 〈certainly
fire　that　[not]

לְכָדַתְנִי אַשְׁמָתִי, הֲלֹא זֶה דְּבַר נִשְׁמָתִי,

〈 of my soul 〈　the 〈 this 《Was not 《 by [the seduc- 〈 I have been
assertion　tions of] my guilt!　entrapped

עַד הֱיוֹתִי עַל אַדְמָתִי.[6]

《my [place on] 〈 in 〈 I was 〈 when
earth?　yet

לְזֹאת נַפְשִׁי נְשַׁמָּה, כְּאִישׁ שׁוֹכֵב בְּכִלְמָה,

《　in shame; 〈 lying 〈 like one 《 is desolate, 〈my soul 〈 And
therefore

עֵרֹם אָשׁוּב שָׁמָּה.[7]

《　there. 〈 shall I return 〈for naked

---

(1) *Job* 21:32. (2) Cf. *Psalms* 58:8-9; Cf. *Ezekiel* 21:12. (3) *Exodus* 2:12.
(4) *I Samuel* 25:21. (5) Cf. *Ezekiel* 15:5. (6) Cf. *Jonah* 4:2. (7) Cf. *Job* 1:21.

טָפַל שֶׁקֶר ... כֹּה וָכֹה — *He has piled up falsehood ... this way and that [trying to find
it].* The translation follows *Pardes* (based on
Ezekiel 21:12), who understands the subject
of the verbs "melts" and "turns" as the sinner's heart בְּתוֹכוֹ, *within himself.*

According to *Masbir*, the subject is the
sinner himself, whose strength melts as he
ages. God causes this to happen as a warning that one should begin re-examining
— this way and that — the falsehood with
which he has been living.

מְשׁוּגָתִי נָשָׂאתִי, וּבִלְבָבִי קְרָאתִי, אָנֹכִי חָטָאתִי.[1]

‹‹ have sinned! ‹ I ‹‹ I call out, ‹ and in my heart ‹‹ I bear, ‹ My misdeeds

נְכוֹחָה לֹא חָשַׁקְתִּי, וּבִשְׁרִירוּת לִבִּי דָבַקְתִּי,

‹‹ I held tight; ‹ of my ‹ but to the ‹‹ I did not desire, ‹ What was
heart   obstinate fantasies   upright

מַה לְּךָ כִּי נִזְעַקְתִּי.[2]

‹‹ I cry out? ‹ if ‹ to ‹ so
You   what is it

שְׂאִי נַפְשִׁי אַשְׁמָתֶךָ, רְאִי חַטָּאתֵךְ לְעֻמָּתֵךְ,

‹‹ is before you; ‹ how your sin ‹ See ‹‹ your guilt. ‹‹ O my soul, ‹‹ Bear,

גַּם אַתְּ שְׂאִי כְלִמָּתֵךְ.[3]

‹‹ your shame. ‹ must bear ‹ you ‹ so also

עֵת אֶדְאַג לַעֲוֹנִי, הֱשִׁיבוּנִי רַעְיוֹנַי,

‹‹ do my ‹ respond ‹‹ about ‹ I worry ‹ When
thoughts,   my sins,

נִפְּלָה נָא בְיַד יהוה.[4]

‹‹ of ‹ into the ‹ please, ‹ Let us fall,
HASHEM.   hand

פְּנֵה מִמְּכוֹן שִׁבְתֶּךָ, וּפְתַח לִי דְלָתֶיךָ,

‹‹ Your doors! ‹ for ‹ and open ‹ of Your ‹ from the ‹ Turn to
me   Dwelling,   [heavenly]   me
abode

כִּי אֵין בִּלְתֶּךָ.[5]

‹‹ besides ‹ there is ‹ For
You.   no one

צוּר הָגֵן בַּעֲדִי, וּמֵעֲוֹנִי פְדֵנִי, וְתוֹרָתְךָ לַמְּדֵנִי.

‹‹ teach me. ‹ and Your ‹‹ redeem ‹ from my ‹‹ for me, ‹ be a ‹ O
Torah   me,   iniquity   shield   Rock,

קוֹלִי שִׁמְעָה כְחַסְדֶּךָ,[6] בְּיוֹם אֶעֱמֹד נֶגְדֶּךָ,

‹‹ before ‹ that I stand ‹ on the ‹‹ in accordance ‹ listen to ‹ My
You,   day   with Your   voice
kindness;

אַל תַּט בְּאַף עַבְדֶּךָ.[7]

‹‹ Your servant. ‹ in anger ‹ repel ‹ do not

---

(1) Joshua 7:20. (2) Cf. Judges 18:23. (3) Ezekiel 16:52. (4) II Samuel 24:14.
(5) I Samuel 2:2. (6) Psalms 119:149. (7) 27:9.

רְאֵה עָנְיִי וַעֲנֵנִי, אֲנִי בְיָדְךָ הִנְנִי, וְאַתָּה יהוה חָנֵּנִי.[1]

⟪may You ⟨HASHEM, ⟪ but as ⟪ here I ⟨ in Your ⟪ As ⟪ and ⟨ my ⟨ See
be gracious　for You,　am;　hand　for me,　answer　destitute
toward me.　　　me.　　　state,

❖ שְׁלַח אֲמִתְּךָ וַחֲסָדֶיךָ, לְעַם צוֹעֲקִים נֶגְדֶּךָ,

⟪ before ⟨ who cry out ⟨ to the ⟨ and Your ⟨ Your truth ⟨ Send
You;　　　　nation　kindnesses

וְלִי אֲנִי עַבְדֶּךָ.[2]

⟪ Your servant. ⟨ for I am ⟨and to me,

תִּסְלַח אַשְׁמָתֵנוּ, וְאַל תִּפְקֹד עֲלוּמֵנוּ, כִּי צֵל יָמֵינוּ.[3]

⟪ are our ⟨ like a ⟨ for ⟪ our ⟨ reckon ⟨ and ⟪ our guilt, ⟨ Forgive
days.　shadow　immaturities,　　　do not

ALL, WHILE STANDING:

אֵל מֶלֶךְ יוֹשֵׁב עַל כִּסֵּא רַחֲמִים, מִתְנַהֵג

⟨ Who acts ⟪ of mercy, ⟨ the throne ⟨ on ⟨ Who sits ⟪ King ⟨ O God,

בַּחֲסִידוּת, מוֹחֵל עֲוֹנוֹת עַמּוֹ, מַעֲבִיר רִאשׁוֹן

⟨ [sins,] one ⟨ Who ⟪ of His ⟨ the sins ⟨ Who ⟪ with kindness,
　　　removes　people,　　　pardons

רִאשׁוֹן,[4] מַרְבֶּה מְחִילָה לַחֲטָאִים וּסְלִיחָה לַפּוֹשְׁעִים,

⟪ to willful ⟨ and ⟨ to unintentional ⟨ pardon ⟨ Who abun- ⟪ by one,
sinners,　forgiveness　sinners　　　dantly grants

עֹשֶׂה צְדָקוֹת עִם כָּל בָּשָׂר וָרוּחַ, לֹא כְרָעָתָם

⟨ in accord with ⟨ — not ⟪ and ⟨ [beings ⟨ all ⟨ with ⟨ acts of ⟨ Who
their wickedness　spirit　of] flesh　　　generosity　performs

תִּגְמוֹל. ❖ אֵל הוֹרֵיתָ לָנוּ לוֹמַר שְׁלֹשׁ עֶשְׂרֵה, וּזְכוֹר

⟨ remem- ⟪ the Thirteen ⟨ to ⟨ You ⟨ O God, ⟪ do You
ber　　[Attributes of Mercy];　recite　us　taught　repay them!

לָנוּ הַיּוֹם בְּרִית שְׁלֹשׁ עֶשְׂרֵה, כְּמוֹ שֶׁהוֹדַעְתָּ לֶעָנָיו

⟨ to the humble ⟨ You made ⟨ as ⟪ of [these] Thirteen, ⟨ the ⟨ today ⟨ for us
one [Moses]　known　　　　covenant

מִקֶּדֶם, כְּמוֹ שֶׁכָּתוּב, וַיֵּרֶד יהוה בֶּעָנָן וַיִּתְיַצֵּב עִמּוֹ

⟨ with ⟨ and stood ⟨ in a ⟨ And HASHEM ⟪ it is written: ⟨ as ⟪in ancient
him　　　cloud　descended　　　　times,

שָׁם, וַיִּקְרָא בְשֵׁם יהוה.[5]

⟪ of ⟨ with the ⟨ and He ⟪ there,
HASHEM.　Name　called out

---

(1) Psalms 41:11. (2) I Kings 1:26. (3) Cf. Job 8:9. (4) Rosh Hashanah 17a. (5) Exodus 34:5.

CONGREGATION, THEN *CHAZZAN:*

וַיַּעֲבֹר יהוה עַל פָּנָיו וַיִּקְרָא:

《 and 　　《 [Moses'] 〈 before 〈 And Hashem passed
proclaimed: 　　face,

CONGREGATION AND *CHAZZAN* **RECITE LOUDLY AND IN UNISON:**

יהוה, יהוה, אֵל, רַחוּם, וְחַנּוּן, אֶֽרֶךְ אַפַּֽיִם,

〈 to anger, 〈 Slow 　《 and 〈 Compassionate 〈 God, 〈 HASHEM, 〈 HASHEM,
　　　　　Gracious,

וְרַב חֶֽסֶד, וֶאֱמֶת, נֹצֵר חֶֽסֶד לָאֲלָפִים, נֹשֵׂא עָוֹן,

〈 of 〈 Forgiver 《 for thousands 〈 of 〈 Preserver 《 and 〈 in 〈 and
iniquity, 　　[of generations], kindness 　Truth, 　Kindness Abundant

וָפֶֽשַׁע, וְחַטָּאָה, וְנַקֵּה.¹ וְסָלַחְתָּ לַעֲוֹנֵֽנוּ וּלְחַטָּאתֵֽנוּ

《 and our sins, 〈 our 〈 May You 《 and Who 〈 and inadvertent 〈 willful sin,
　　iniquities forgive 　absolves. 　sin,

וּנְחַלְתָּֽנוּ.² סְלַח לָֽנוּ אָבִֽינוּ כִּי חָטָֽאנוּ, מְחַל לָֽנוּ

〈 us, 〈 pardon 《 we have 〈 for 《 our 〈 us, 〈 Forgive 《 and make us
　　sinned; 　Father, 　　Your heritage.

מַלְכֵּֽנוּ כִּי פָשָֽׁעְנוּ. כִּי אַתָּה אֲדֹנָי טוֹב וְסַלָּח,

《 and 〈 are 〈 O Lord, 〈 You, 〈 For 《 we have 〈 for 《 our King,
forgiving, good 　　willfully sinned.

וְרַב חֶֽסֶד לְכָל קֹרְאֶֽיךָ.³

《 who call 〈 to all 〈 kind 〈 and
upon You. 　　abundantly

פְּסוּקֵי הַקְדָּמָה לִסְלִיחָה עב / PREFATORY VERSES TO SELICHAH 72

שׁוּבָה יהוה אֶת שְׁבִיתֵֽנוּ, כַּאֲפִיקִים בַּנֶּֽגֶב.⁴

《in the desert. 〈 like springs 　《 our captivity, 〈 HASHEM, 〈 Return,

שׁוּבָה יהוה חַלְּצָה נַפְשֵֽׁנוּ, הוֹשִׁיעֵֽנוּ לְמַֽעַן חַסְדֶּֽךָ.⁵

《 of Your 〈 for the 〈 save us 《 our soul, 〈 Release 《HASHEM! 〈 Return,
kindness. sake

וְהָשֵׁב לִשְׁכֵנֵֽינוּ שִׁבְעָתַֽיִם אֶל חֵיקָם, חֶרְפָּתָם אֲשֶׁר

〈 with 〈 their 《 their 〈 into 〈 sevenfold 〈 to our 《 And
which disgrace bosom, 　　neighbors 　repay

חֵרְפֽוּךָ, אֲדֹנָי.⁶

《 O Lord. 〈 they have
disgraced You,

---

(1) *Exodus* 34:6-7. (2) 34:9. (3) *Psalms* 86:5. (4) 126:4. (5) Cf. 6:5. (6) 79:12.

בְּרַחֵם אָב עַל בָּנִים, כֵּן תְּרַחֵם יהוה עָלֵינוּ.¹

‹ on us. ‹ HASHEM, ‹ have mercy, ‹ so ‹ his children, ‹ toward ‹ a father is ‹ As merciful as

לַיהוה הַיְשׁוּעָה, עַל עַמְּךָ בִרְכָתֶךָ סֶּלָה.² יהוה

‹ HASHEM, ‹ Selah. ‹ is Your blessing, ‹ Your people ‹ upon ‹ is salvation, ‹ To HASHEM

צְבָאוֹת עִמָּנוּ, מִשְׂגָּב לָנוּ אֱלֹהֵי יַעֲקֹב סֶלָה.³

‹ Selah. ‹ of Jacob, ‹ is the God ‹ for us ‹ a stronghold ‹ is with us, ‹ Master of Legions,

יהוה צְבָאוֹת, אַשְׁרֵי אָדָם בֹּטֵחַ בָּךְ.⁴ יהוה

‹ HASHEM, ‹ in You. ‹ who trusts ‹ is the man ‹ praiseworthy — ‹ Master of Legions ‹ HASHEM,

הוֹשִׁיעָה, הַמֶּלֶךְ יַעֲנֵנוּ בְיוֹם קָרְאֵנוּ.⁵

‹ we call. ‹ on the day ‹ answer us ‹ May the King ‹ save!

SELICHAH 72 / סליחה עב
(שלמונית)

ALL:

אֱלֹהֵינוּ וֵאלֹהֵי אֲבוֹתֵינוּ:

‹ of our forefathers: ‹ and the God ‹ Our God

תַּחֲרוּת רֹגֶז הָנִיחַ* וְתִזְכֹּר רַחֵם,⁶

‹ mercy. ‹ and remember ‹ set aside,* ‹ wrath ‹ The flaring

תְּמִימֶיךָ חַנּוֹת וְאַל תִּשְׁכַּח בְּיַד לוֹחֵם,

‹ of the enemy ‹ in the hand ‹ forget [them] ‹ and do not ‹ be gracious ‹ To Your wholesome people ‹ warrior.

שְׁאֵרִיתָם חֲמוֹל פְּלֵיטָתָם תְּרַחֵם,

‹ be merciful. ‹ to their survivors ‹ have pity, ‹ On their remainder

שְׁבִיתָם כַּאֲפִיקִים* שׁוֹבֵב וְכַדֶּשֶׁא תַפְרִיחֵם.⁸

‹ make them bloom. ‹ and like grass ‹ return, ‹ like springs [in the desert]* ‹ Their captivity

---

(1) Cf. *Psalms* 103:13. (2) 3:9. (3) 46:8. (4) 84:13. (5) 20:10.
(6) Cf. *Habakkuk* 3:2. (7) Cf. *Psalms* 126:4. (8) Cf. *Isaiah* 66:14.

---

§ תַּחֲרוּת רֹגֶז הָנִיחַ — *The flaring wrath set aside.* The reversed double *aleph-beis* acrostic is followed by the *paytan's* signature — אֵלִיָּה הַקָּטָן יְחִי, *Eliyah the lesser, may he live*

[see prefatory comment to *Selichah* 14].

כַּאֲפִיקִים — *Like springs [in the desert].* Just as water turns a barren desert into a flourishing garden, so may we be transformed

רָפוּ יְדֵי עַם עֲנִיֵּי הַצֹּאן,

⟪ of the flock. ⟨ the impov-erished people, ⟪ of [Your] people, ⟨ have the hands ⟨ Grown weak

רָדוּ בָהֶם שׂוֹנְאֵיהֶם[1] בְּעֹנִי וְלַחַצוֹן,

⟪ and coercion. ⟨ with poverty ⟨ do their enemies ⟨ them ⟨ Rule over

קוּם כִּי עָלֶיךָ לִגְדֹר פִּרְצוֹן,

⟪ the breach. ⟨ to repair ⟨ it is up to You ⟨ For ⟪ Arise!

קוֹחֵם פְּקַח וּקְרָא שְׁנַת רָצוֹן.[2]

⟪ of favor. ⟨ a year ⟨ and declare ⟨ open ⟨ Their prison

צְבִי יִשְׂרָאֵל קֹדֶשׁ חָלָל עַל בָּמוֹת,[3]

⟪ the heights, ⟨ [slain] on corpses ⟨ are ⟪ that is holy, ⟨ Israel ⟨ The precious

צָרָיו עָלָיו יִשָּׁאוּן יַמִּים כַּהֲמוֹת,[4]

⟪ roaring. ⟨ like the seas ⟨ rise up ⟨ against it ⟪ while its foes

פֶּלֶא אַיֵּה שׁוֹאֵל[5] וּזְכוֹר עוֹלָם יְמוֹת,[6]

⟪ the [kindness of] days of yore; ⟨ Remember ⟪ it asks, ⟪ where are they? ⟨ Your wonders,

פְּקֻדַּת מִשְׁנֶה[7] כְּהוֹפַעְתָּ אֵל נְקָמוֹת.[8]

⟪ of Vengeance! ⟨ as God ⟨ when You appear ⟨ that will be doubled ⟨ [where is] the retribution

עוּרִי לְבֻשִׁי עֹז זְרוֹעַ מְחוֹלֶלֶת קָמִים,

⟪ those in opposition! ⟨ that terrifies ⟨ O Arm ⟪ strength, ⟨ don ⟪ Awaken,

עוּרִי כִּימֵי קֶדֶם דּוֹרוֹת עוֹלָמִים,[9]

⟪ of eternity! ⟨ the generations ⟪ of old, ⟨ as in days ⟨ Awaken

סַפַּח כּוֹס חֲמָתְךָ וְאַף שַׁכֵּר לְאֻמִּים,[10]

⟪ — the nations; ⟪ make them drunk [with it] ⟨ and even ⟨ Your anger ⟨ in the cup ⟨ Gather

---

(1) Cf. *Leviticus* 26:17. (2) Cf. *Isaiah* 61:1-2. (3) Cf. *II Samuel* 1:19. (4) Cf. *Isaiah* 17:12-13.
(5) Cf. *Judges* 6:13. (6) Cf. *Deuteronomy* 32:7. (7) Cf. *Jeremiah* 16:18.
(8) Cf. *Psalms* 94:1. (9) Cf. *Isaiah* 51:9. (10) Cf. *Habakkuk* 2:15.

and gladdened when God delivers us of our exile (*Rashi* to *Psalms* 126:4).

סַף רַעַל פְּקֹד בְּשָׁלוֹם נְחוּמִים.

《 the consolations 〈 when You 〈[command]〉 of 〈 the
[promised to Israel]. complete them poison chalice
[to drink]

נֵצַח יִשְׂרָאֵל קֹוֶיךָ חוּשָׁה לְעֶזְרָתָם,

《 to their aid! 〈 rush 《 those who 《 of 〈 Eternal
place their Israel, One
hope in You,

נִגָּשִׂים וְנַעֲנִים וּבְךָ תִקְוָתָם,

《 do they place 〈 in 《 and 〈 Tyrannized
their hope; You tormented,

מְיַחֲדִים שְׁמְךָ וְזִכְרְךָ תַּאֲוָתָם,[1]

《 they long. 〈 and to 《 of Your 〈 they declare
mention Name, the Oneness
Your Name

מְשֹׁל בָּם אַתָּה וַעֲצֹר בְּמַקְהֵלוֹתָם.

《 their congregations. 〈 and 《 Yourself, 〈 over 〈 Rule
govern them

לְךָ יְיַחֲלוּ הֵן אִם תִּקְטְלֵם,[2]

《 You slay 〈 even 《 them- 〈 they will 〈 To
them; though selves, look, You

לְרַוְחָתָם וּלְשַׁוְעָתָם אֹזֶן בַּל תַּעְלֵם,[3]

《 shut. 〈 do 〈 Your 《 and to their 〈 to their
not ear supplication, [prayer for] relief

כָּשַׁל כֹּחָם מְהֵרָה הַצִּילֵם,

《 rescue them! 〈 quickly 《 has their 〈 Failed
strength;

כָּלוּ עֵינֵיהֶם מִתְּהוֹמוֹת מָתַי תַּעְלֵם.

《 You will 〈 when 〈 [to know] 《 are their 〈 Worn
raise them. from the depths eyes [from out
[of exile], longing]

יֶלֶד שַׁעֲשׁוּעַ בְּיַד צָרָיו לָמָּה לְאָכְלָה,

《 is he to be 〈 why 《 of his 〈 in the 《 of [Your] 〈 [Israel,]
devoured? enemies, hands pleasure, the child

יַחַרְקוּ שֵׁן גְּזָרוּהוּ כַּצֹּאן מִמִּכְלָה,[4]

《 from the fold. 〈 like a 〈 cutting him 《 their 〈 They gnash
sheep into pieces teeth,

---

(1) Cf. *Isaiah* 26:8. (2) Cf. *Job* 13:15. (3) Cf. *Lamentations* 3:56. (4) Cf. *Habakkuk* 3:17.

טָבְעוּ פֹּה מַבָּטָם וּלְעֶזְרָה נָסוּ¹ לְבֵית הַתְּפִלָּה,

They [Israel] have fixed ‹ here › their expectant gaze; « for aid ‹ they have fled › to the House › of Prayer. «

טוּבְךָ וְרַחֲמֶיךָ מֵהֶם לֹא תִכְלָא.²

Your goodness ‹ and Your mercy › from them ‹ do not › withhold! «

חִנָּם פְּעוֹל חֶסֶד גְּמוֹל טוֹבָה לְחַיָּבִים,

Without cause ‹ act » with kindness; ‹ grant » good ‹ [even] to the sinful. «

חִלּוּךְ בְּקִדּוּשׁ צוֹם* וּבַעֲצָרָה נִצָּבִים,³

[For] they ‹ petition You › by ‹ decreeing » a fast day,* ‹ and by in assembly › standing. «

זְרוּם כֻּלּוֹם זֵדִים טוֹרְפִים כִּזְאֵבִים,

Scattered ‹ them › and ‹ have destroyed them › ravening ‹ vicious men, › like wolves — «

זוּ לַעֲגָם וְרַב בּוּזָם בְּאַדְמַת שׁוֹבִים.

this ‹ their » great ‹ mockery, › their ‹ scorn › in the land ‹ of their captors. «

וּבַמֶּה יִוָּדַע אֵפוֹא⁴ כִּי אַתָּה גוֹאֲלָם,

And with ‹ what › will it be ‹ made known, › then, ‹ that › You are ‹ their Redeemer? «

וְצַר הַצּוֹרֵר הִקְשָׁה וְהִכְבִּיד עֻלָּם,

When the ‹ oppressing enemy › who is ‹ has made harder › and heavier ‹ their yoke, «

הִקְדִּישָׁם לְיוֹם הֲרֵגָה וְלִטְבִיחָה הִתִּיקָם כֻּלָּם,⁵

preparing them ‹ for a day ‹ of killing, » and for slaughter ‹ taking them out » — all of them. «

---

(1) Cf. *Isaiah* 20:6. (2) Cf. *Psalms* 40:12. (3) Cf. *Joel* 2:15. (4) *Exodus* 33:16. (5) Cf. *Jeremiah* 12:3.

בְּקִדּוּשׁ צוֹם — *By decreeing a fast day.* According to *Arugas HaBosem*, this *selichah* should be recited only on a fast day [lest the supplicant be guilty of an untruth]. For this reason this *selichah* is recited on 20 Sivan in some communities that observe that day as a fast in commemoration of the atrocities of *Tach Vetat* (1648-49). Nevertheless, the *selichah* is recited (according to *nusach Polin*) on the fourth day of the Ten Days of Repentance, for many Jews customarily fast on each of the days between Rosh Hashanah and Erev Yom Kippur. Perhaps those who do not fast should omit the phrases בְּקִדּוּשׁ צוֹם, *by decreeing a fast day,* and (four lines further) גְּבוּרָתָם בְּצוֹם נָשָׁתָה וְדָמָם לְפָנֶיךָ מְמַעֲטִים, *Their strength from fasting has gone from them and their blood before You they deplete.*

הוֹרֵג שִׁבְעָתַיִם יֻקָּם וְשִׁבְעִים וְשִׁבְעָה יְשֻׁלָּם.[1]

《 let him be 〈 paid back! 〉 and seventy-seven-fold 《 vengeance, 〈 suffer sevenfold 〉 Let the slayer

דְּלֵה וְהַצֵּל לְקֻחֵי מָוֶת וְלַהֲרֻג מָטִים,[2]

《 on the verge, 〈 for slaughter 〉 《 to death, 〈 those taken 〉 and rescue 〈 Draw up

דְּחוּפִים לְלַעַג בְּיַד שׁוֹאֲלֵי בִּתְרָפִים[3] וְדוֹרְשֵׁי אִטִּים,*[4]

《 from false gods. 〈 and inquire 〉 of teraphim 〈 of those who ask 〉 at the hand 〈 with the scorn 〉 buffeted

גְּבוּרָתָם בְּצוֹם נָשָׁתָה וְדָמָם לְפָנֶיךָ מִמַּעֲטִים,[5]

《 they deplete; 〈 before You 〉 and their blood 〈 has gone [from them] 〉 from fasting 〈 Their strength

גָּלוּ רִיבָם אֵלֶיךָ גְּאָלֵם מֵחֶרֶב לְהָטִים.

《 that is sharpened! 〈 from the sword 〉 redeem them 《 to You — 〈 their grievance 〉 They have revealed

בִּלְתְּךָ לָמוֹ אַיִן, זוּלָתְךָ לֹא בָחָרוּ,

《 do they choose. 〈 no one 〉 except for You, 《 there is 〈 for them 〉 no one; 〈 Besides You

בְּעָשָׁן כָּלוּ עֵינֵיהֶם וְעַצְמוֹתָם כְּמוֹקֵד נִחָרוּ,[6]

《 are desiccated; 〈 as from a pyre 〉 and their bones 《 do their eyes, 〈 waste away 〉 In smoke

אוֹר חָשַׁךְ בַּעֲדָם, כֹּחַ נֶעֱזָב וְהַלְּבָבוֹת סְחַרְחָרוּ,[7]

《 fibrillate. 〈 and hearts 〉 has deserted 《 before them, 〈 strength 〉 turns dark 〈 light

אַוּוּךָ פְּקָדוּךָ בַּצָּר[8] וּבְעֵת צַר לְךָ יְשַׁחֲרוּ.[9]

《 that they seek. 〈 it is 〉 of You trouble 〈 and in 《 in time 〉 they re- member You 〈 distress, 《 They de- sire You,

❖ אָנָּא לְעֶזְרַת יְדִידֶיךָ הַוָּעֵדָה חוּשָׁה מְהֵרָה,

《 come quickly, 〈 hurry, 《 rally; 〈 of Your beloved ones 〉 to the aid 〈 Please

הַקָּטֹן לָאֶלֶף וְהַצָּעִיר לְהָעֲצִים וּלְהַגְבִּירָה,[10]

《 and strengthen. 〈 enlarge 〉 and the young one 《 increase a thousandfold 〈 the small [people]

---

(1) Cf. *Genesis* 4:15,24. (2) Cf. *Proverbs* 24:11. (3) Cf. *Ezekiel* 21:26.
(4) Cf. *Isaiah* 19:3. (5) Cf. *Berachos* 17a. (6) Cf. *Psalms* 102:4.
(7) Cf. 38:11. (8) Cf. *Isaiah* 26:9,16. (9) Cf. *Hosea* 5:15. (10) Cf. *Isaiah* 60:22.

אִטִּים — *From false gods.* The translation follows *Arugas HaBosem,* and *Rashi* (to *Isaiah* 19:3). According to *Targum Yonasan* and *Radak* the word refers to practitioners of a certain type of sorcery.

יוֹדוּךָ חֲכֵי יִשְׁעֶךָ וִיהַלְלוּךָ עַם נִבְרָא,[1]

‹ Thank ‹ who await ‹ will those › Your ›› and ‹ will the › newborn,
You › salvation, praise You people

מִקְוֵה יִשְׂרָאֵל מוֹשִׁיעוֹ בְּעֵת צָרָה.[2]

‹ O Hope › of Israel, › its Redeemer ›› in time ‹ of trouble. ››

ALL, WHILE STANDING:

אֵל מֶלֶךְ יוֹשֵׁב עַל כִּסֵּא רַחֲמִים, מִתְנַהֵג

‹ O God, › King ‹ Who sits › on ‹ the throne ›› of mercy, ›› Who acts ›

בַּחֲסִידוּת, מוֹחֵל עֲוֹנוֹת עַמּוֹ, מַעֲבִיר רִאשׁוֹן

›› with kindness, ‹ Who › the sins › of His ›› Who › [sins,] one ›
pardons people, removes

רִאשׁוֹן,[3] מַרְבֶּה מְחִילָה לַחַטָּאִים וּסְלִיחָה לַפּוֹשְׁעִים,

›› by one, › Who abun- › pardon › to unintentional ‹ and › to willful ››
dantly grants sinners, forgiveness sinners,

עֹשֶׂה צְדָקוֹת עִם כָּל בָּשָׂר וָרוּחַ, לֹא כְרָעָתָם

‹ Who › acts of ‹ with ‹ all ‹ [beings › and ›› — not ‹ in accord with
performs generosity of] flesh spirit their wickedness

תִּגְמוֹל. ❖ אֵל הוֹרֵיתָ לָּנוּ לוֹמַר שְׁלֹשׁ עֶשְׂרֵה, וּזְכוֹר

‹ do You ›› O God, › You › us ‹ to › the Thirteen ›› and re-
repay them! taught recite [Attributes of Mercy]; member

לָנוּ הַיּוֹם בְּרִית שְׁלֹשׁ עֶשְׂרֵה, כְּמוֹ שֶׁהוֹדַעְתָּ לֶעָנָיו

‹ for us ‹ today › the › of [these] Thirteen, ›› as ‹ You made › to the humble
covenant known one [Moses]

מִקֶּדֶם, כְּמוֹ שֶׁכָּתוּב, וַיֵּרֶד יהוה בֶּעָנָן וַיִּתְיַצֵּב עִמּוֹ

‹ with › and stood ‹ in a › And HASHEM ›› it is written: ‹ as ›› in ancient
him cloud descended times,

שָׁם, וַיִּקְרָא בְשֵׁם יהוה.[4]

›› of ‹ with the ‹ and He ‹ there,
HASHEM. Name called out

CONGREGATION, THEN CHAZZAN:

וַיַּעֲבֹר יהוה עַל פָּנָיו וַיִּקְרָא:

›› and ›› [Moses'] ‹ before ‹ And HASHEM passed
proclaimed: face,

CONGREGATION AND CHAZZAN RECITE LOUDLY AND IN UNISON:

יהוה, יהוה, אֵל, רַחוּם, וְחַנּוּן, אֶרֶךְ אַפַּיִם,

‹ to anger, ‹ Slow ›› and Gracious, ‹ Compassionate ‹ God, ‹ HASHEM, ‹ HASHEM,

---

(1) Cf. Psalms 102:19. (2) Jeremiah 14:8. (3) Rosh Hashanah 17a. (4) Exodus 34:5.

וְרַב חֶסֶד, וֶאֱמֶת, נֹצֵר חֶסֶד לָאֲלָפִים, נֹשֵׂא עָוֹן,

‹ of ‹ Forgiver ≪ for thousands ‹ of ‹ Preserver ≪ and ‹ in ‹ and
iniquity, [of generations], kindness Truth, Kindness Abundant

וָפֶשַׁע, וְחַטָּאָה, וְנַקֵּה.[1] וְסָלַחְתָּ לַעֲוֹנֵנוּ וּלְחַטָּאתֵנוּ

≪ and our sins, ‹ our ‹ May You ≪ and Who ‹ and inadvertent ‹ willful sin,
iniquities forgive absolves. sin,

וּנְחַלְתָּנוּ.[2] סְלַח לָנוּ אָבִינוּ כִּי חָטָאנוּ, מְחַל לָנוּ

‹ us, ‹ pardon ≪ we have ‹ for ≪ our ‹ us, ‹ Forgive ≪ and make us
sinned. Father, Your heritage.

מַלְכֵּנוּ כִּי פָשָׁעְנוּ. כִּי אַתָּה אֲדֹנָי טוֹב וְסַלָּח,

≪ and ‹ are ‹ O Lord, ‹ You, ‹ For ≪ we have ‹ for ≪ our King,
forgiving, good willfully sinned.

וְרַב חֶסֶד לְכָל קֹרְאֶיךָ.[3]

≪ who call ‹ to all ‹ kind ‹ and
upon You. abundantly

סְלִיחָה עג / SELICHAH 73

(פִּזְמוֹן)

CHAZZAN, THEN CONGREGATION:

יַשְׁמִיעֵנוּ* סָלַחְתִּי, יֹשֵׁב בְּסֵתֶר עֶלְיוֹן,[4]

≪ in the celes- ‹ in ‹ [from] Him ≪ I have ≪ Let us hear,*
tial heights;* concealment Who sits forgiven!

---

(1) *Exodus* 34:6-7. (2) 34:9. (3) *Psalms* 86:5. (4) 91:1.

יַשְׁמִיעֵנוּ ‹§ — *Let us hear. Matteh Levi*, perhaps the most popular commentary on *piyutim* in general and *Selichos* in particular, uncharacteristically writes regarding this *pizmon*: "This *piyut* is difficult in its entirety, for the composer desired to tintinnabulate the ears. Thus, he sported with the phraseology, language, and stiches, at almost every word. Due to the pressure and duress of this [task], the meaning is so arcane, that the commentator has become wearied trying to interpret his riddles ..." (from *Matteh Levi*'s preface to this *selichah*).

Beginning with the second stanza, the *paytan* locked himself into the following intricate rhyme scheme: (a) The first three line endings of each stanza rhyme with one another; (b) the fourth line ending rhymes with the refrain; (c) the first half of each line comprises two rhyming words or phrases. In poetic shorthand the rhyme scheme is: aab/ccb/ddb/eef/f/ggh/iih/jjh/kkf/f.

As indicated by the acrostic, the *selichah* was written by שְׁלֹמֹה בְּרַבִּי שְׁמוּאֵל בְּרַבִּי יוֹאֵל, *Shlomo son of R' Shmuel son of R' Yoel*. However, some read the grandfather's name as אֵלִיָּה, *Eliyah* (see commentary, s.v. וַתֵּק ... תַּצְלִיחִי, below). In either case, nothing more is known of the *paytan*, except that he flourished sometime before 1234, the year in which the commentary *Arugas HaBosem* (which includes this *selichah*) was written.

יֹשֵׁב בְּסֵתֶר עֶלְיוֹן — *[From] Him Who sits in concealment in the celestial heights*. In *Psalms* 91:1, this phrase refers to those who trust in God's protection — *he who sits in the refuge of the Most High*. Here the *paytan* borrows the phrase to refer to God Who is concealed from us in the celestial heights.

בִּימִין יֵשַׁע לְהוֹשֵׁעַ,[1] עַם עָנִי וְאֶבְיוֹן.

》 and 〈 that is 〈 — the 》 may they 〈 that effects 〈 with His
destitute. poor people be saved salvation right hand

בְּשַׁוְּעֵנוּ אֵלֶיךָ, נוֹרָאוֹת בְּצֶדֶק תַּעֲנֵנוּ,[2]

》 You will 〈 in 〈 with awesome 》 to You, 〈 When we
answer us. righteousness deeds cry out

יהוה הֱיֵה עוֹזֵר לָנוּ.[3]

》 for 〈 the 〈 be 〈 O
us! Helper HASHEM,

CONGREGATION, THEN *CHAZZAN:*

שִׁוִּיתִי עֶזְרָתִי, עַל גִּבּוֹר[4] וְנִשָּׂא,

》 Who is 〈 the Mighty 〈 upon 〈 [the burden of]〈 I have
Exalted. One my help placed

לִפְנֵי גֹחִי אֶשְׁפֹּךְ שִׂיחִי,[5] אוּלַי פָּנַי יִשָּׂא,[6]

》 He will 〈 my 〈 perhaps 》 my 〈 I pour 〈 Him Who drew 〈 Before
lift up [in face supplications; forth me [from the
forgiveness]. womb],

מִדַּתִי כִּוַּנְתִּי, כַּסֵּדֶר אֲשֶׁר עָשָׂה.

》 He 〈 that 〈 in the 〈 I have 〈 On my
established order focused my [recitation of
[for Moses]; thoughts the Thirteen]
Attributes

הֲלֹא יַקִּיר מְקַרְקַר קִיר,[7]* עוֹד זָכוֹר תִּזְכְּרֶנּוּ,[8]

》 will You indeed 〈 more 》 the 〈 breaking 〈 Your 〈 Is not
remember them. and more [celestial] down precious
barrier;* [Israel]

יהוה הֱיֵה עוֹזֵר לָנוּ.

》 for 〈 the 〈 be 〈 O
us! Helper HASHEM,

---

(1) Cf. *Psalms* 20:7. (2) Cf. 65:6. (3) Cf. 30:11. (4) Cf. 89:20. (5) Cf. 102:1.
(6) Cf. *Genesis* 32:21; *Numbers* 6:26. (7) Cf. *Isaiah* 22:5; most editions of *Selichos*
read מְקַרְקַר, but the source verse reads מְקַרְקַר. (8) Cf. *Jeremiah* 31:19.

מְקַרְקַר קִיר — *Breaking down the [celestial]*
barrier. The phrase is taken from *Isaiah*
22:5, where it refers to the enemies battering
down the walls of Jerusalem. The translation
here follows *Matteh Levi*, who understands
it as an allusion to Israel's prayers breaking
down the spiritual barrier erected by sins
that prevents Israel's prayers from reaching
the Throne of Glory. As the Talmud states
(*Bava Metzia* 59a): Since the day the *Beis*
HaMikdash was destroyed, the Gates of

Prayer have been sealed.
According to *Arugas HaBosem*, קִיר
refers to the Assyrian province of Kir (see
commentaries to *Isaiah* 22:6) and the stich
means: *Kir* [read, *Assyria*] *shatters Your*
precious [Israel]; *therefore, may You yet*
remember us.
The Talmud [*Taanis* 29a, according to
the reading of *Ein Yaakov*] renders מְקַרְקַר,
crowing, and קִיר, *wailing.* Thus, *God,* so to
speak, *cries like a rooster and wails* about

CONGREGATION, THEN *CHAZZAN:*

בְּבֹא כְגַל הַגַּלְגַּל,* לְהַחֲלִיף הַשְׁטָה,

《 the existing 〈 to overturn 〈 the [evil] 〈 like a 〈 When there
structure,　　　　　　　　wheel*　wave　comes

רַעְיָתְךָ יוֹנָתְךָ,¹ לְךָ פוֹנָה הַבִּיטָה,

《 — look! 《 turns 〈 to You 〈 Your dove, 〈 Your mate,

בְּאַוַּת נַפְשָׁהּ² הִגִּישָׁה, לִפְתֹּחַ בַּחֲרָטָה.³

《 of regret. 〈 to begin 〈 she 〈 of her soul 〈 At the
[her expression] approaches　　　　　longing

יָמִין* פְּשׁוּטָה מִלְּמַטָּה, בְּצִפִּיָּתֵנוּ צִפִּינוּ,⁴

《 we look toward 〈 in our 〈 from below, 〈 is 〈 [The] right
[You] —　expectation　　　　outstretched　hand*

יהוה הֱיֵה עוֹזֵר לָנוּ.

《 for 〈 the 〈 be 〈 O
us!　Helper　　HASHEM,

CONGREGATION, THEN *CHAZZAN:*

שׁוֹאֵל חֶסֶד בְּהֻסַד, הִנְנִי תֹאמַר,⁵

You shall 《 Here I 《 do they 〈 for 〈 When to
say.　am!　gather,　kindness　ask

מָרוּת יֵצֶר הַבָּצֶר, קָבוּעַ כְּבְמַסְמָר,

《 as with a nail; 〈 [though it is] 《 will be 〈 The sovereignty 〈
fixed in us　withheld,　the [Evil] Inclination

וּלְצַוָּאר כְּמוֹ סַוָּאר, הוּטַל לְמִשְׁמָר.

《 to hold them [in 〈 it is 〈 a beam of 〈 like 〈 and on the neck
its sway].　placed　wood　　[of the leaders]

---

(1) Cf. *Songs of Songs* 5:2. (2) *Jeremiah* 2:24, Cf. *Deuteronomy* 18:6.
(3) Cf. *Nedarim* 22b. (4) *Lamentations* 4:17. (5) Cf. *Isaiah* 58:9;
many editions of *Selichos* read הִנֵּנִי, but the meaning is the same.

---

the destruction of Zion and Jerusalem. Following this interpretation, our stich means:
*God, as it were, cries and wails over the
plight of His precious [Israel], and shall yet
remember us and redeem us.*

הַגַּלְגַּל — *The [evil] wheel.* Just as a storm
wave may suddenly roll over a ship and
drown it, so does the *Yetzer Hara* (Evil
Inclination) attempt to overwhelm a person
without warning, in order to turn him from
the lane of righteousness and submerge
him in the depths of sin. And, measure for
measure, this will cause God to turn from

His Attribute of Mercy to His Attribute of
Strict Justice.

Alternatively, this alludes to the wheel
of misfortune that may overtake a person
and cause him to lose faith and to abandon
his righteous ways for a life of sin, Heaven
forbid.

יָמִין — *[The] right hand.* According to most
commentaries, this refers to the right hand
of God, as it were, which is extended earth-
ward from under His Throne of Glory to accept penitents. Others, noting the lack of the
possessive suffix (יְמִינְךָ, *Your right hand*),

וּמִי **אָזַר**[1] זָר לְזָר, וּמִי אַכְזָר כִּי יְעִירֶנּוּ,[2]

《 as to displace him? 〈 is so 〈 and 《 the 〈 to 〈 has been 《 Who
aggressive who [satanic] throw girded [with
stranger, off strength]

יהוה הָיָה עוֹזֵר לָנוּ.

《 for 〈 the 〈 be 〈 O
us! Helper HASHEM,

CONGREGATION, THEN *CHAZZAN:*

לַחֲבַצֶּלֶת פְּתַח דֶּלֶת, אֱלוֹהַּ מִמַּעַל,

《 from on high; 〈 O God 《 the door, 〈 open 〈 For the lily

בִּינָה הֲגִיגִי[3] לְהַצִּיגִי, בְּתוֹךְ שַׁעַר הַנִּנְעַל,[4]

《 that is 〈 the Gate 〈 within 〈 and place me 《 my 〈 perceive
locked. [of Prayer] thoughts

רַחֲמֵנוּ קַדְּמֵנוּ,[5] צָרִי וּמָזוֹר הַתְעַל.

《 bringing. 〈 and cure 〈 the 《 come to 〈 Have mercy
[of atonement] balm meet us, on us,

בָּרֵר חִכִּי, לְהַצְדִּיקִי, יְבֻקַּשׁ עָוֹן וְאֵינֶנּוּ,[6]

《 and it is no 〈 let sin 《 Searched 《 that I may be 《 [the words of]〈 Make
longer there. be, for judged righteous. my palate, clear

יהוה הָיָה עוֹזֵר לָנוּ.

《 for 〈 the 〈 be 〈 O
us! Helper HASHEM,

CONGREGATION, THEN *CHAZZAN:*

יוֹנַת אֵלֶם מְשֻׁלָּם,* חֵלֶק יָפֶה תַּגִּיעַ,[7]

《 may she 〈 that is 〈 — a 《 from 〈 of silence 〈 [Israel]
receive, generous portion Jerusalem* [in exile far] the dove

---

(1) *Arugas HaBosem* reads אָזֹר אָזַר, *May He Who has girded Himself . . .* , a reading that better fits the acrostic, but has not been followed in any of the early printed *Selichos.* (2) Cf. *Job* 41:2. (3) *Psalms* 5:2. (4) See commentary to מְקַרְקַר קִיר, above. (5) Cf. *Psalms* 79:8. (6) Cf. *Jeremiah* 50:20. (7) *Psalms* 56:1.

understand this as the penitent's right hand stretched upward toward heaven from earth below.

יוֹנַת אֵלֶם מְשֻׁלָּם — *[Israel] the dove of silence [in exile far] from Jerusalem.* The translation follows the sense of *Psalms* 56:1, which reads, יוֹנַת אֵלֶם רְחֹקִים, *the distant dove of silence*, a reference to King David when he was forced to flee from King Saul and take refuge in Gath, in Philistia.

שָׁלֵם, *Salem*, was an ancient name of Jerusalem. Abraham called the city יִרְאֶה, *Yireh* [Jeru] (see *Genesis* 22:14). Shem, son of Noah [also called Malchi-zedek], called the city שָׁלֵם, *Shalem* [Salem] (see ibid. 14:18). God said, "If I call it *Yireh* as Abraham did, then the righteous Shem will be distraught. But if I call it *Shalem*, the righteous Abraham will be distraught. Instead I will satisfy both these righteous men by calling

אוֹת צֶדֶק בְּהִצְטַדֵּק, בְּיִרְאָתְךָ לְהוֹשִׁיעָה,

《 shall she 〈 through [her] 《 as she achieves 〈 of right- 〈 a sign
be saved. reverence for You righteousness, eousness,

לְךָ תִּקְרָא עֵת לְשַׁחְרְרָהּ, אָדוֹן בְּזוֹ הַשָּׁעָה.

《 very hour. 〈 in 〈 O Lord, 〈 to liberate her, 〈 the 〈 proclaim 〈 For Your
this time sake,

וַתֵּק* תִּיק מִנַּרְתֵּק, כְּאוֹר תּוֹצִיא דִינֵנוּ,

《 our 〈 bring forth 〈 [as clear] 《 from the case 〈 the con- 〈 Remove*
judgment. as light [of medicine tainer [of
for our souls]; atonement]

יהוה הֱיֵה עוֹזֵר לָנוּ.

《 for 〈 the 〈 be 〈 O
us! Helper HASHEM,

CONGREGATION, THEN *CHAZZAN*:

תַּצְלִיחִי* בְּמִשְׁלָחִי,* אָשִׁיב שׁוֹלְחִי דָבָר,[1]

《 an 〈 to those 〈 that I may 〈 in my mission,* 〈 Bring me
answer. who sent me return success*

חִזַּקְתָּ חֹק חֻקַּת, עֶשֶׂר וְשָׁלֹשׁ כְּמִדְבָּר,

《 as were 〈 and three 〈 [that the] 《 You 〈 the 〈 You have
spoken, [Attributes], ten decreed, law strengthened

מַחֲזִיקֶם וְלֹא רֵיקָם,* שָׁלַחְתִּי לְהִתְגַּבֵּר.

《 to overpower [through 〈 I have been 《 be in vain;* 〈 and 〈 will sustain
my recitation]. sent not them [Israel]

---

(1) *II Samuel* 24:13.

it *Yireh-Shalem* [Jeru-Salem]'' (*Bereishis Rabbah* 56:10). [Incidentally, this Midrash provides the answer to an often-asked question: Why is the name יְרוּשָׁלַיִם almost always spelled without the second י when it appears in Scriptures? Because the original spelling of שָׁלֵם is thus retained in the new name. (The change from יראה to ירו can be explained with *gematria*, for both אה and ו have a *gematria* of six. Thus, one may be substituted for the other.)]

Alternatively, שָׁלֵם means *the Perfect One* and refers to God. If so, the stich reads: *Let [Israel] the dove of silence receive a generous portion from the Perfect One.*

וַתֵּק ... תַּצְלִיחִי — *Remove ... Bring me success.* According to *Arugas HaBosem*, these words should be יוּתַּק and הַצְלִיחִי. Although the translation remains the same, this

reading leads us to a different acrostic for the *paytan's* grandfather's name: The initial letters of בִּינָה, רַחֲמֶנוּ, בָּרֵר, יוֹנַת, אוֹת, לְךָ, יוּתַּק, הַצְלִיחִי spell בְּרַבִּי אֵלִיָה, *the son of R' Eliyah.*

תַּצְלִיחִי בְּמִשְׁלָחִי — *Bring me success in my mission.* This stanza was obviously intended for the *chazzan.* Originally, and in some congregations still, only the *chazzan* would chant the stanzas of a *pizmon* (*piyut* with refrain) and the congregation would respond with the refrain.

מַחֲזִיקֶם וְלֹא רֵיקָם — *Will sustain them [Israel] and not be in vain.* The Talmud states that a covenant was sealed with the Thirteen Attributes that whenever Israel recites them in their fast-day prayers, they will not be returned for naught [but will accomplish their purpose] (*Rosh Hashanah* 17b, see *Rashi* there).

וְכֹל תַּעֲשֶׂה עָוֹן נֹשֵׂא, עַתָּה תָּשׁוּב תְּרַחֲמֵנוּ,[1]

‹ be merciful ‹ once again ‹ now, ‹‹ forgives; ‹ You Who‹ may You ‹ And so
to us.   iniquity   do,

יהוה הֱיֵה עוֹזֵר לָנוּ.

‹‹ for ‹ the ‹ be ‹ O
us!   Helper   HASHEM,

ALL, WHILE STANDING:

אֵל מֶלֶךְ יוֹשֵׁב עַל כִּסֵּא רַחֲמִים, מִתְנַהֵג

‹ Who acts ‹‹ of mercy, ‹ the throne ‹ on ‹ Who sits ‹ King ‹ O God,

בַּחֲסִידוּת, מוֹחֵל עֲוֹנוֹת עַמּוֹ, מַעֲבִיר רִאשׁוֹן

‹[sins,] one ‹ Who ‹‹ of His ‹ the sins ‹ Who ‹‹ with kindness,
removes   people,   pardons

רִאשׁוֹן,[2] מַרְבֶּה מְחִילָה לְחַטָּאִים וּסְלִיחָה לַפּוֹשְׁעִים,

‹‹ to willful ‹ and ‹ to unintentional ‹ pardon ‹ Who abun- ‹‹ by one,
sinners,   forgiveness   sinners   dantly grants

עֹשֶׂה צְדָקוֹת עִם כָּל בָּשָׂר וָרוּחַ, לֹא כְרָעָתָם

‹ in accord ‹ — not ‹‹ and ‹ [beings ‹ all ‹ with ‹ acts of ‹ Who
with their   spirit   of] flesh   generosity   performs
wickedness

תִּגְמוֹל. ❖ אֵל הוֹרֵיתָ לָנוּ לוֹמַר שְׁלֹשׁ עֶשְׂרֵה, וּזְכוֹר

‹ remem- ‹‹ the Thirteen ‹ to ‹ us ‹ You ‹ O God, ‹‹ do You
ber   [Attributes of Mercy];   recite   taught   repay them!

לָנוּ הַיּוֹם בְּרִית שְׁלֹשׁ עֶשְׂרֵה, כְּמוֹ שֶׁהוֹדַעְתָּ לֶעָנָיו

‹ to the ‹ You made ‹ as ‹‹ of [these] Thirteen, ‹ the ‹ today ‹ for us
humble one   known   covenant
[Moses]

מִקֶּדֶם, כְּמוֹ שֶׁכָּתוּב, וַיֵּרֶד יהוה בֶּעָנָן וַיִּתְיַצֵּב עִמּוֹ

‹ with ‹ and stood ‹ in a ‹ And HASHEM ‹‹ it is written: ‹ as ‹‹ in ancient
him   cloud   descended   times,

שָׁם, וַיִּקְרָא בְשֵׁם יהוה.[3]

‹‹ of ‹ with the ‹ and He ‹‹ there,
HASHEM.   Name   called out

CONGREGATION, THEN *CHAZZAN:*

וַיַּעֲבֹר יהוה עַל פָּנָיו וַיִּקְרָא:

‹‹ and ‹‹ [Moses'] ‹ before ‹ And HASHEM passed
proclaimed: face,

---

(1) Cf. *Micah* 7:19. (2) *Rosh Hashanah* 17a. (3) *Exodus* 34:5.

CONGREGATION AND *CHAZZAN* RECITE LOUDLY AND IN UNISON:

יְהוָה, יְהוָה, אֵל, רַחוּם, וְחַנּוּן, אֶרֶךְ אַפַּיִם,

⟨ to anger,　⟨ Slow　《 and　⟨ Compassionate ⟨ God,　⟨ HASHEM,　⟨ HASHEM,
　　　　　　　　　　Gracious,

וְרַב חֶסֶד, וֶאֱמֶת, נֹצֵר חֶסֶד לָאֲלָפִים, נֹשֵׂא עָוֹן,

⟨ of ⟨ Forgiver 《 for thousands ⟨ of ⟨ Preserver 《 and ⟨ in ⟨ and
iniquity,　　　　[of generations],　kindness　　　Truth,　Kindness Abundant

וָפֶשַׁע, וְחַטָּאָה, וְנַקֵּה.¹ וְסָלַחְתָּ לַעֲוֹנֵנוּ וּלְחַטָּאתֵנוּ

《 and our sins,　⟨ our　⟨ May You 《 and Who ⟨ and inadvertent ⟨ willful sin,
　　　　　　　iniquities　forgive　absolves.　sin,

וּנְחַלְתָּנוּ.² סְלַח לָנוּ אָבִינוּ כִּי חָטָאנוּ, מְחַל לָנוּ

⟨ us, ⟨ pardon　《 we have ⟨ for 《 our ⟨ us, ⟨ Forgive 《 and make us
　　　　　　sinned;　　Father,　　　　　　　Your heritage.

מַלְכֵּנוּ כִּי פָשָׁעְנוּ. כִּי אַתָּה אֲדֹנָי טוֹב וְסַלָּח,

《 and ⟨ are ⟨ O Lord, ⟨ You, ⟨ For 《 we have ⟨ for 《 our King,
forgiving,　good　　　　　　　　willfully sinned.

וְרַב חֶסֶד לְכָל קֹרְאֶיךָ.³

《 who call ⟨ to all ⟨ kind ⟨ and
upon You.　　　　abundantly

PREFATORY VERSES TO SELICHAH 74 / פסוקי הקדמה לסליחה עד

הֵיטִיבָה בִרְצוֹנְךָ אֶת צִיּוֹן, תִּבְנֶה חוֹמוֹת

⟨ the walls　⟨ build　《 Zion; ⟨ unto ⟨ in Your favor ⟨ Do good

יְרוּשָׁלָיִם. אָז תַּחְפֹּץ זִבְחֵי צֶדֶק, עוֹלָה וְכָלִיל,

《 and whole- ⟨ burnt- ⟨ of right- ⟨ the ⟨ You will ⟨ Then 《 of Jerusalem.
offering;　offering　eousness,　offerings　desire

אָז יַעֲלוּ עַל מִזְבַּחֲךָ פָרִים.⁴ כִּי בָרֵךְ אֲבָרֶכְךָ,

⟨ I shall surely bless you ⟨ For 《 [will be] ⟨ Your Altar ⟨ upon ⟨ offered ⟨ then
　　　　　　　　　　　bulls.　　　　　　　　　　up

וְהַרְבָּה אַרְבֶּה אֶת זַרְעֲךָ כְּכוֹכְבֵי הַשָּׁמַיִם וְכַחוֹל

⟨ and like ⟨ of the ⟨ like the stars ⟨ your offspring ⟨ shall I ⟨ and greatly
the sand　heavens　　　　　　　　　increase

אֲשֶׁר עַל שְׂפַת הַיָּם, וְיִרַשׁ זַרְעֲךָ אֵת שַׁעַר אֹיְבָיו.⁵

《 of his ⟨ the gates ⟨ will your ⟨ and 《 of the ⟨ the ⟨ is ⟨ that
enemies.　　　　offspring　inherit　sea;　shore　on

---

(1) *Exodus* 34:6-7. (2) 34:9. (3) *Psalms* 86:5. (4) 51:20-21. (5) *Genesis* 22:17.

כְּרַחֵם אָב עַל בָּנִים, כֵּן תְּרַחֵם יהוה עָלֵינוּ.[1]

As merciful as ‹ a father is ‹ toward ‹ his children, ‹ so ≪ have mercy, ‹ HASHEM, ≪ on us.

לַיהוה הַיְשׁוּעָה, עַל עַמְּךָ בִרְכָתֶךָ סֶּלָה.[2] יהוה

To HASHEM ‹ is salvation, ≪ upon ‹ Your people ‹ is Your blessing, ≪ Selah. ≪ HASHEM,

צְבָאוֹת עִמָּנוּ, מִשְׂגָּב לָנוּ אֱלֹהֵי יַעֲקֹב סֶלָה.[3]

Master of Legions, ≪ is with us, ≪ a stronghold ‹ for us ‹ is the God ‹ of Jacob, ≪ Selah.

יהוה צְבָאוֹת, אַשְׁרֵי אָדָם בֹּטֵחַ בָּךְ.[4] יהוה

HASHEM, ‹ Master of Legions ≪ praiseworthy — ‹ is the man ‹ who trusts ‹ in You. ≪ HASHEM,

הוֹשִׁיעָה, הַמֶּלֶךְ יַעֲנֵנוּ בְיוֹם קָרְאֵנוּ.[5]

save! ≪ May the King ‹ answer us ‹ on the day ‹ we call. ≪

SELICHAH 74 / סליחה עד
(עקדה)

אֱלֹהֵינוּ וֵאלֹהֵי אֲבוֹתֵינוּ:

Our God ‹ and the God ‹ of our forefathers: ≪

אִם אָפֵס* רְבַע הַקֵּן,* אֹהֶל שָׁכֵן אִם רֵקֵן,

Even if ‹ ceased* ‹ has the ‹ quarter-dinar ‹ nesting-pair [bird offering],* ‹ the ≪ Tabernacle ‹ in which ≪ He dwelt ‹ even if — ‹ it is empty, ≪

אַל נֹאבְדָה עַל כֵּן, יֵשׁ לָנוּ אָב זָקֵן.[6]

perish ‹ we need not ‹ on ‹ account, ≪ that ‹ for we have ≪ of a father ‹ who is old. [Abraham] [the merits] ≪

פָּנִים לוֹ תַכִּיר,[7] וְצִדְקוֹ לְפָנֶיךָ נַזְכִּיר.

Deference ‹ to ‹ him ‹ You should ≪ show, ‹ as his righteousness ‹ before ‹ You ‹ we ‹ mention. ≪

---

(1) Cf. *Psalms* 103:13. (2) 3:9. (3) 46:8. (4) 84:13. (5) 20:10. (6) *Genesis* 44:20. (7) Cf. *Deuteronomy* 16:19.

אִם אָפֵס — *Even if ceased.* The binding of Isaac on the altar on Mount Moriah (see *Genesis* Ch. 22) is described and its merit is invoked in this *piyut* that is appropriately called an עֲקֵידָה, *akeidah.* The composer signed his name — אֶפְרַיִם בַּר רַבִּי יִצְחָק חֲזַק, *Ephraim bar R' Yitzchak, may he be strong* — in the acrostic of the stanzas. R' Ephraim flourished in 12th-century Regensburg, Germany. He

was a disciple of Rabbeinu Tam and author of *Arbaah Panim,* a Talmud commentary that, unfortunately, is no longer extant.

רְבַע הַקֵּן — *The quarter-dinar nesting-pair, [bird offering].* The word רְבַע means *a quarter* of a *dinar,* the price assigned to a קֵן, *nesting pair of doves,* to be brought as a bird offering (see *Rosh Hashanah* 11b). The intent of the stich

צִוִּיתוֹ, קַח נָא אֶת בִּנְךָ¹ יַקִּיר, וְנִמְצָה דָמוֹ עַל קִיר.²*

《 on the 〈 his 〈 and have be 《 who is 〈 your son 〈 please, 〈 Take, 〈 You com-
[altar's] wall.* blood pressed out dear, manded him,

רָץ אֶל הַנַּעַר וְהִקְדִּישׁוֹ, וְנַפְשׁוֹ קְשׁוּרָה בְנַפְשׁוֹ,³

《 with his 〈 was bound 〈 although 《 and consecrated 〈 the boy 〈 to 〈 He
[son's] soul. up his soul him [as a sacrifice], ran

עִטְּרוֹ בָעֵצִים וְאִשּׁוֹ,* וְנֵזֶר אֱלֹהָיו עַל רֹאשׁוֹ.⁴*

《 his head.* 〈 is 〈 of his God 〈 the 《 and his 〈 with 〈 He gar-
upon crown fire,* wood landed him

יָחִיד רַךְ הוּקַל כַּצְּבִי, עָנָה וְאָמַר אָבִי,

〈 My 《 and 〈 he spoke 《 as he ran 〈 felt the load 〈 tender, 〈 The only
father, said, up like a deer; to be light [son],

הִנֵּה הָאֵשׁ וְהָעֵצִים⁵ נָבִיא, וּתְשׁוּרָה אֵין לְהָבִיא.⁶

《 to bring. 〈 there is 〈 but a 《 that we are 《 and the 〈 the fire 〈 here is
none offering bringing, wood

מִלִּין הֵשִׁיבוּ מִלְהַבְהִילוֹ, עָנָה אָבִיו וְאָמַר לוֹ,

《 to 〈 and said 〈 his 〈 Answered 《 that would not 〈 he 〈 With
him, father alarm him. answered him words

אֱלֹהִים יִרְאֶה לּוֹ,⁷ וְיָדַע יהוה אֶת אֲשֶׁר לוֹ.⁸

《 His 〈 who is 〈 the 〈 for HASHEM will 《 for 〈 will seek 〈 God
own. one make known Himself, out

---

(1) *Genesis* 22:2. (2) *Leviticus* 1:15. (3) *Genesis* 44:30. (4) Cf. *Numbers* 6:7.
(5) *Genesis* 22:7. (6) *I Samuel* 9:7. (7) *Genesis* 22:8. (8) *Numbers* 16:5.

is that even the least of the Altar offerings is no longer available to atone for our sins.

וְנִמְצָה דָמוֹ עַל קִיר — *And have be pressed out his blood on the [altar's] wall.* Since the *piyut* began by mentioning the bird offering, the metaphor of Isaac as a bird offering is continued here.

עִטְּרוֹ בָעֵצִים וְאִשּׁוֹ — *He garlanded him with wood and his fire.* A simple rendering of *Genesis* 22:6 yields the following: *Abraham took the wood of the offering and placed it on Isaac his son; he took in his hand the fire and the knife, and the two of them went together.* The logical antecedent of the pronoun "he" in the phrase "he took ... the fire ..." is Abraham. Yet the *paytan* implies that Isaac carried both the wood and the fire! If so, Isaac, not Abraham, is the subject of the clause "he took ...." Perhaps the *paytan* understands the Scriptural passage in the

following manner. Isaac would never allow his father to carry a burden in his presence, as long as Isaac was able to handle it himself. However, the bundle of wood was too heavy for Isaac to swing onto his shoulders unassisted. Therefore, *Abraham took the wood ... and placed it on Isaac.* But the fire and knife were light, so he *[Isaac] took [them] in his hand* without waiting for his father to hand them to him.

וְנֵזֶר אֱלֹהָיו עַל רֹאשׁוֹ — *The crown of his God is upon his head.* Although the Scriptural passage from which this phrase is taken (*Numbers* 6:7) speaks of a *nazir*, the *paytan* borrows the expression to describe Abraham as a *Kohen Gadol* (see *Bereishis Rabbah* 55:7), for one of the eight vestments of the *Kohen Gadol*, the golden צִיץ, *forehead plate*, is also referred to as נֵזֶר הַקֹּדֶשׁ, *the holy crown* (see *Exodus* 29:6).

בְּמִצְוֹתֶיךָ שְׁנֵיהֶם נִזְהָרִים, וְאַחֲרֶיךָ לֹא מְהַרְהֲרִים,

To do Your commandments ⟨ both of ⟨ were ⟩⟩ careful, ⟨ and about Your intentions ⟨ they did not ⟩⟩ harbor doubts. ⟩

חָשׁוּ מְאֹד נִמְהָרִים, עַל אַחַד הֶהָרִים.[1]

They hurried ⟨ very much ⟨ and went with speed, ⟩⟩ upon ⟩⟩ one ⟨ of the mountains. ⟩⟩

רָאוּ אֵשׁ תְּלוּלָה, מִהֲרוּ עֲצֵי עוֹלָה,

They saw ⟨ fire ⟨ extended [between heaven and earth] ⟨ and hurried ⟨ with the wood ⟨ for the offering. ⟩⟩

יַחַד בְּאַהֲבָה כְלוּלָה, יָשְׁרוּ בָּעֲרָבָה מְסִלָּה.[2]

Together, ⟨ with love ⟨ that was complete, ⟨ they went straight, ⟨ through the wilderness, ⟩⟩ forging a path. ⟩⟩

רָאָה יָחִיד כִּי הוּא הַשֶּׂה, נָאַם לְהוֹרוּ הַמְנֻסֶּה,

Realize ⟨ did the only [son] ⟨ that ⟨ he was ⟩⟩ the [sacrificial] lamb, ⟨ and said ⟨ to his father, ⟩⟩ who was being tested [by God], ⟩⟩

אֹתִי כְּכֶבֶשׂ תַּעֲשֶׂה, לֹא תַחְמֹל וְלֹא תְכַסֶּה.[3]

Me ⟨ like a sheep ⟨ bring; ⟩⟩ do not ⟨ have mercy, ⟩⟩ do not ⟩⟩ shelter me. ⟩⟩

כִּי חָפֵץ וְנִכְסָף, לְבָבִי לוֹ אֶחְשֹׂף,

It is ⟨ that He ⟨ wishes ⟨ and He desires; ⟩⟩ my ⟨ heart ⟨ to Him ⟩⟩ I will bare. ⟩⟩

הַאִם תִּמְנָעֵנִי, סוֹף רוּחִי וְנִשְׁמָתִי אֵלָיו יֵאָסֵף.[4]

Even ⟨ were you to ⟨ withhold me, ⟩⟩ in the end ⟨ my spirit ⟨ and my soul ⟩⟩ to Him ⟩⟩ He will [never-theless] gather. ⟩⟩

יָדָיו וְרַגְלָיו עָקַד, וְחַרְבּוֹ עָלָיו פָּקַד,

His [son's] hands ⟨ and his feet ⟨ he ⟩⟩ bound, ⟨ and his blade ⟨ toward him ⟩⟩ readied, ⟩⟩

לְשׂוּמוֹ עַל עֵצִים שָׁקַד, וְהָאֵשׁ עַל הַמִּזְבֵּחַ תּוּקַד.[5]

to place him ⟨ on ⟨ the wood ⟩⟩ he ⟨ hurried, ⟩⟩ and the fire ⟨ on ⟨ the altar ⟩⟩ was burning. ⟩⟩

צַוָּאר פָּשַׁט מֵאֵלָיו, וְאָבִיו נִגַּשׁ אֵלָיו

[His] throat ⟨ he stretched ⟨ on his own, ⟩⟩ and his father ⟨ approached ⟩⟩ him ⟩

לִשְׁחָטוֹ לְשֵׁם בְּעָלָיו,[6] וְהִנֵּה יהוה נִצָּב עָלָיו.[7]

to slaughter him ⟨ in the ⟨ name ⟨ of his ⟩⟩ Master — ⟩⟩ and then ⟨ HASHEM ⟨ was ⟨ standing ⟩⟩ over him. ⟩⟩

---

(1) *Genesis* 22:2. (2) *Isaiah* 40:3. (3) *Deuteronomy* 13:9.
(4) Cf. *Job* 34:14. (5) *Leviticus* 6:5. (6) See *Zevachim* 2a. (7) *Genesis* 28:13.

חָקַר אֶת אֲשֶׁר נַעֲשָׂה, הָאָב עַל בְּנוֹ לֹא חָסָה,

《 pitied; 〈 had 〈 his 〈 for 〈 the 《 was being 〈 which 〈 that 〈[God] in-
not son father done; vestigated

לִבּוֹ אֶל כַּפָּיו נָשָׂא,[1] וַיַּרְא אֱלֹהִים אֶת כָּל אֲשֶׁר עָשָׂה.[2]

《 he had 〈 that 〈 all 〈 And God saw 《 were 〈 his 〈 to- 〈 his
done. lifted hands gether heart [in
up. [in action] with prayer]

קָרָא לִמְרֶחֵם מִשְׁחָר,[3] תְּמוּר בִּנְךָ תִּבְחָר,

《 choose an 〈 of your 〈 In place 《 sought 〈 who [almost] 〈 He called
alternate; son [HASHEM], from birth [to Abraham],

הִנֵּה אַיִל אַחַר,[4] וַעֲשֵׂה וְאַל תְּאַחַר.[5]

《 delay. 〈 do not 《 so 《 behind 〈 a ram 〈 there is
bring it, [you],

חֲלִיפֵי אַזְכָּרָתוֹ, תִּבֵּן הַקְטָרָתוֹ,

《 as if it went up 〈 be con- 〈 of his memo- 〈 May the
in smoke; sidered rial portion exchange

וְתַעֲלֶה תִמְרָתוֹ, וְהָיָה הוּא וּתְמוּרָתוֹ.[6]

《 and his substitute 〈 he 〈 so that it 《 its smoke, 〈 and may
[shall both be holy]. will be that there ascend

זִכָּרוֹן לְפָנֶיךָ בַּשַּׁחַק, לָעַד בְּסֵפֶר יוּחָק,[7]

《inscribed, 〈 in the 〈 forever 《 in Heaven, 〈 before 〈 [Let it be]
Book You a memorial

בְּרִית עוֹלָם לֹא נִמְחַק, אֶת אַבְרָהָם וְאֶת יִצְחָק.[8]

《 Isaac. 〈 and 〈 Abraham 〈 with 《 to be 〈 never 〈 that is 〈 a
with erased: eternal, covenant

❖ קוֹרְאֶיךָ בָּאִים לִקּוֹד, בְּצֶדֶק עֲקֵדָה תִשְׁקֹד,

《 keep in 〈 of the 〈 the right- 《 to bow 〈 are 〈 Those who
mind. Akeidah eous deed [in prayer]; coming call You

צֹאנְךָ בְּרַחֲמִים תִּפְקֹד, פְּנֵי הַצֹּאן אֶל עָקֹד.[9]

《 [the merits of] 〈 looks 〈 of the 〈 for the 《 remember, 〈 with mercy 〈 Your flock
the bound one. to flock face

ALL, WHILE STANDING:

אֵל מֶלֶךְ יוֹשֵׁב עַל כִּסֵּא רַחֲמִים, מִתְנַהֵג

〈 Who acts 《 of mercy, 〈 the throne 〈 on 〈 Who sits 〈 King 〈 O God,

בַּחֲסִידוּת, מוֹחֵל עֲוֹנוֹת עַמּוֹ, מַעֲבִיר רִאשׁוֹן

〈 [sins,] one 〈 Who removes 《of His people, 〈 the sins 〈 Who pardons 《 with kindness,

---

(1) Cf. *Lamentations* 3:41, see *Rashi* there. (2) *Genesis* 1:31. (3) Cf. *Psalms* 110:3. (4) Cf. *Genesis* 22:13.
(5) *Daniel* 9:19. (6) *Leviticus* 27:33. (7) Cf. *Job* 19:23. (8) Cf. *Exodus* 2:24. (9) *Genesis* 30:40.

רִאשׁוֹן,¹ מַרְבֶּה מְחִילָה לַחַטָּאִים וּסְלִיחָה לַפּוֹשְׁעִים,

《 by one, 《 Who abun- 〉 pardon 〉 to unintentional 〉 and 〉 forgiveness 〉 to willful
dantly grants   sinners   sinners

עֹשֶׂה צְדָקוֹת עִם כָּל בָּשָׂר וָרוּחַ, לֹא כְרָעָתָם

〉 Who 〉 acts of 〉 with 〉 all 〉 [beings 《 and 《 — not 〉 in accord with
performs generosity   of] flesh   spirit   their wickedness

תִּגְמוֹל. ❖ אֵל הוֹרֵיתָ לָּנוּ לוֹמַר שְׁלֹשׁ עֶשְׂרֵה, וּזְכוֹר

《 do You 〉 O God, 〉 You 〉 to 〉 us 〉 the Thirteen 《 remem-
repay them!   taught recite   [Attributes of Mercy]; ber

לָּנוּ הַיּוֹם בְּרִית שְׁלֹשׁ עֶשְׂרֵה, כְּמוֹ שֶׁהוֹדַעְתָּ לֶעָנָיו

〉 for us 〉 today 〉 the 《 of [these] Thirteen, 〉 as 〉 You made 〉 to the humble
covenant   known one [Moses]

מִקֶּדֶם, כְּמוֹ שֶׁכָּתוּב, וַיֵּרֶד יהוה בֶּעָנָן וַיִּתְיַצֵּב עִמּוֹ

《 in ancient 〉 as 〉 it is written: 《 And HASHEM 〉 in a 〉 and stood 〉 with
times,   descended cloud   him

שָׁם, וַיִּקְרָא בְשֵׁם יהוה.²

《 there, 《 and He 〉 with the 〉 of
called out Name HASHEM.

CONGREGATION, THEN *CHAZZAN*:

וַיַּעֲבֹר יהוה עַל פָּנָיו וַיִּקְרָא:

《 and 《 [Moses'] 〉 before 〉 And HASHEM passed
proclaimed: face,

CONGREGATION AND *CHAZZAN* RECITE LOUDLY AND IN UNISON:

יהוה, יהוה, אֵל, רַחוּם, וְחַנּוּן, אֶרֶךְ אַפַּיִם,

〉 to anger, 〉 Slow 《 and Gracious, 〉 Compassionate 〉 God, 〉 HASHEM, 〉 HASHEM,

וְרַב חֶסֶד, וֶאֱמֶת, נֹצֵר חֶסֶד לָאֲלָפִים, נֹשֵׂא עָוֹן

〉 of 〉 Forgiver 《 for thousands 〉 of 〉 Preserver 《 and 〉 in 〉 and
iniquity, [of generations], kindness Truth, Kindness Abundant

וָפֶשַׁע, וְחַטָּאָה, וְנַקֵּה.³ וְסָלַחְתָּ לַעֲוֹנֵנוּ וּלְחַטָּאתֵנוּ

《 and our sins, 〉 our 〉 May You 《 and Who 〉 and inadvertent 〉 willful sin,
iniquities forgive absolves. sin,

וּנְחַלְתָּנוּ.⁴ סְלַח לָנוּ אָבִינוּ כִּי חָטָאנוּ, מְחַל לָנוּ

〉 us, 〉 pardon 《 we have 〉 for 《 our 〉 us, 〉 Forgive 《 and make us
sinned;   Father,   Your heritage.

מַלְכֵּנוּ כִּי פָשָׁעְנוּ. כִּי אַתָּה אֲדֹנָי טוֹב וְסַלָּח,

《 and 〉 are 〉 O Lord, 〉 You, 〉 For 《 we have 〉 for 《 our King,
forgiving, good willfully sinned.

(1) *Rosh Hashanah* 17a. (2) *Exodus* 34:5. (3) 34:6-7. (4) 34:9.

וְרַב חֶסֶד לְכָל קֹרְאֶיךָ.[1]

《 who call 〈 to all 〈 kind 〈 and
upon You.   abundantly

ALL:

זְכֹר רַחֲמֶיךָ יהוה וַחֲסָדֶיךָ, כִּי מֵעוֹלָם הֵמָּה.[2]

《 are they. 〈 eternal 〈 for 《 and Your 〈 HASHEM, 〈 Your mercies, 〈 Remember
kindnesses,

זָכְרֵנוּ יהוה בִּרְצוֹן עַמֶּךָ, פָּקְדֵנוּ בִּישׁוּעָתֶךָ.[3] זְכֹר

〈 Re- 《 with Your 〈 recall us 《 to Your 〈 when You 〈 HASHEM, 〈 Remem-
member   salvation.   people;   show favor   ber us,

עֲדָתְךָ קָנִיתָ קֶּדֶם, גָּאַלְתָּ שֵׁבֶט נַחֲלָתֶךָ, הַר צִיּוֹן זֶה

〈 the one 〈 of 〈 the 《 of Your 〈 the 〈 You 《 long 〈 which You 〈 Your con-
[where] Zion, mountain heritage; tribe redeemed   ago, acquired gregation,

שָׁכַנְתָּ בּוֹ.[4] זְכֹר יהוה חִבַּת יְרוּשָׁלַיִם, אַהֲבַת

〈 the love 《 of Jerusalem; 〈 the 〈 HASHEM, 〈 Remem- 《 there. 〈 You rested
affection   ber,   Your Presence

צִיּוֹן אַל תִּשְׁכַּח לָנֶצַח.[5] אַתָּה תָקוּם תְּרַחֵם צִיּוֹן כִּי

〈 for 《 to 〈 and show 〈 will arise 〈 You 《 forever. 〈 forget 〈 do not 〈 of
Zion, mercy   Zion

עֵת לְחֶנְנָהּ, כִּי בָא מוֹעֵד.[6] זְכֹר יהוה לִבְנֵי אֱדוֹם

〈 of 《 [to repay] 〈 HASHEM, 〈 Re- 《 the appointed time 〈 for 《 [there will come]
Edom the offspring,   member,   will have come.   the time to favor her,

אֵת יוֹם יְרוּשָׁלָיִם, הָאֹמְרִים עָרוּ עָרוּ עַד הַיְסוֹד

〈 the very 〈 to 〈 Destroy 《 Destroy! 〈 [to repay] 《 of Jerusalem; 〈 for the day
foundation   those who say,

בָּהּ.[7] זְכֹר לְאַבְרָהָם לְיִצְחָק וּלְיִשְׂרָאֵל עֲבָדֶיךָ, אֲשֶׁר

〈 that 《 Your servants, 〈 and for Israel, 〈 for Isaac, 〈 for Abraham, 〈 Remember 《 of it!

נִשְׁבַּעְתָּ לָהֶם בָּךְ וַתְּדַבֵּר אֲלֵהֶם, אַרְבֶּה אֶת זַרְעֲכֶם

〈 Your offspring 〈 I shall 《 to them, 〈 and 《 by Your 〈 to 〈 You
increase   You said Being, them swore

כְּכוֹכְבֵי הַשָּׁמַיִם, וְכָל הָאָרֶץ הַזֹּאת אֲשֶׁר אָמַרְתִּי,

〈 I spoke 〈 of which 〈 of this land 〈 and all 《 of the 〈 like the
heavens;   stars

אֶתֵּן לְזַרְעֲכֶם, וְנָחֲלוּ לְעֹלָם.[8] זְכֹר לַעֲבָדֶיךָ לְאַבְרָהָם

〈 of Abraham, 〈 of Your 〈 Remember 《 forever. 〈 and they 〈 to your 〈 I will
servants, [the merits]   will inherit it offspring, give

---

(1) *Psalms* 86:5. (2) 25:6. (3) Cf. 106:4. (4) 74:2. (5) This is not a Scriptural verse.
(6) *Psalms* 102:14. (7) 137:7. (8) *Exodus* 32:13.

לִיצְחָק וּלְיַעֲקֹב, אַל תֵּפֶן אֶל קְשִׁי הָעָם הַזֶּה וְאֶל

⟨ to ⟪ of this people, ⟨ the stub- ⟨ to ⟨ pay ⟨ do ⟪ and of Jacob; ⟨ of Isaac,
bornness   attention   not

רִשְׁעוֹ וְאֶל חַטָּאתוֹ.[1] זְכֹר לָנוּ בְּרִית אָבוֹת, כַּאֲשֶׁר

⟨ as ⟪ of the ⟨ the ⟨ for ⟨ Remember ⟪ its ⟨ and ⟪ its
Patriarchs, covenant us   sinfulness. to wickedness,

אָמַרְתָּ: וְזָכַרְתִּי אֶת בְּרִיתִי יַעֲקוֹב, וְאַף אֶת בְּרִיתִי

⟨ My covenant ⟨ and ⟪ [with] Jacob, ⟨ My covenant ⟨ And I will ⟪ You said:
also   remember

יִצְחָק, וְאַף אֶת בְּרִיתִי אַבְרָהָם אֶזְכֹּר, וְהָאָרֶץ אֶזְכֹּר.[2]

⟪ I will ⟨ and the ⟪ I will ⟨ [with] ⟨ My covenant ⟨ and ⟪ [with]
remember. Land   remember; Abraham   also   Isaac,

זְכוֹר לָנוּ בְּרִית רִאשׁוֹנִים, כַּאֲשֶׁר אָמַרְתָּ: וְזָכַרְתִּי

⟨ And I will ⟪ You said: ⟨ as ⟪ of the ⟨ the ⟨ for us ⟨ Remember
remember   ancient ones, covenant

לָהֶם בְּרִית רִאשׁוֹנִים, אֲשֶׁר הוֹצֵאתִי אֹתָם מֵאֶרֶץ

⟨ from ⟨ I took them out ⟨ that ⟪ of the ⟨ the ⟨ for
the land   ancient ones, covenant them

מִצְרַיִם לְעֵינֵי הַגּוֹיִם, לִהְיוֹת לָהֶם לֵאלֹהִים, אֲנִי

⟨ I am ⟪ a God; ⟨ to them ⟨ to be ⟪ of the ⟨ in the ⟨ of Egypt
nations, very sight

יהוה.[3] עֲשֵׂה עִמָּנוּ כְּמָה שֶׁהִבְטַחְתָּנוּ: וְאַף גַּם

⟨ all ⟨ And despite ⟪ You promised us: ⟨ as ⟨ with us ⟨ Do ⟪ HASHEM.

זֹאת בִּהְיוֹתָם בְּאֶרֶץ אֹיְבֵיהֶם, לֹא מְאַסְתִּים וְלֹא

⟨ nor ⟨ despise them ⟨ I will ⟪ of their ⟨ in the land ⟨ when they ⟪ this,
not enemies, will be

גְעַלְתִּים לְכַלֹּתָם לְהָפֵר בְּרִיתִי אִתָּם, כִּי אֲנִי יהוה

⟨ HASHEM, ⟨ I am ⟨ for ⟪ with ⟨ My ⟨ to annul ⟪ to destroy ⟨ abhor them
them, covenant them,

אֱלֹהֵיהֶם.[4] הָשֵׁב שְׁבוּתֵנוּ וְרַחֲמֵנוּ, כְּמָה שֶׁכָּתוּב:

⟪ it is ⟨ as ⟪ and have ⟨ our captivity ⟨ Bring ⟪ their God.
written: mercy on us,   back

וְשָׁב יהוה אֱלֹהֶיךָ אֶת שְׁבוּתְךָ וְרִחֲמֶךָ, וְשָׁב וְקִבֶּצְךָ

⟨ gather ⟨ and He ⟪ and He will ⟨ your captivity, ⟨ your ⟨ will ⟨ Then bring
you in will once have mercy God, HASHEM, back
again upon you,

(1) *Deuteronomy* 9:27. (2) *Leviticus* 26:42. (3) 26:45. (4) 26:44.

מִכָּל הָעַמִּים אֲשֶׁר הֱפִיצְךָ יהוה אֱלֹהֶיךָ שָׁמָּה.[1]

《 thereto. 〈 your God 〈 has HASHEM 〈 scattered you 〈 that 〈 the peoples 〈 from all

קַבֵּץ נִדָּחֵינוּ, כְּמָה שֶׁכָּתוּב: אִם יִהְיֶה נִדַּחֲךָ בִּקְצֵה

〈 at the ends 〈 your dispersed will be 〈 If 〈 it is written: 〈 as 〈 our dispersed ones, 〈 Gather

הַשָּׁמָיִם, מִשָּׁם יְקַבֶּצְךָ יהוה אֱלֹהֶיךָ, וּמִשָּׁם יִקָּחֶךָ.[2]

《 He will take you. 〈 and from there 《 your God, 〈 will HASHEM, 〈 gather you in 〈 from there 《 of heaven,

מְחֵה פְשָׁעֵינוּ כָעָב וְכֶעָנָן, כְּמָה שֶׁכָּתוּב: מָחִיתִי

〈 I have wiped away 《 it is written: 〈 as 《 and like a cloud, 〈 like a mist 〈 our sins 〈 Wipe away

כָעָב פְּשָׁעֶיךָ וְכֶעָנָן חַטֹּאתֶיךָ, שׁוּבָה אֵלַי כִּי

〈 for 〈 to Me, 〈 return 《 your transgressions; 〈 and like a cloud 〈 your willful sins, 〈 like a mist

גְאַלְתִּיךָ.[3]   מְחֵה פְשָׁעֵינוּ לְמַעֲנָךְ, כַּאֲשֶׁר אָמַרְתָּ:

《 You have said: 〈 as 《 for Your sake, 〈 our sins 〈 Wipe away 《 I have redeemed you.

אָנֹכִי אָנֹכִי הוּא מֹחֶה פְשָׁעֶיךָ לְמַעֲנִי, וְחַטֹּאתֶיךָ לֹא

〈 I shall not 〈 and your transgressions 《 for My sake, 〈 your willful sins 〈 Who wipes away 〈 am the One 〈 [only] I, 〈 I,

אֶזְכֹּר.[4] הַלְבֵּן חֲטָאֵינוּ כַּשֶּׁלֶג וְכַצֶּמֶר, כְּמָה שֶׁכָּתוּב:

《 it is written: 〈 as 《 and like wool, 〈 like snow 〈 our sins 〈 Whiten 《 recall.

לְכוּ נָא וְנִוָּכְחָה, יֹאמַר יהוה, אִם יִהְיוּ חֲטָאֵיכֶם

〈 your sins may be 〈 Though 《 HASHEM. 〈 says 《 let us reason together, 〈 now, 〈 Come,

כַּשָּׁנִים כַּשֶּׁלֶג יַלְבִּינוּ, אִם יַאְדִּימוּ כַתּוֹלָע, כַּצֶּמֶר

〈 like [white] wool 《 as crimson, 〈 they may be red 〈 though 《 they will be whitened; 〈 like snow 《 like scarlet,

יִהְיוּ.[5] זָרוֹק עָלֵינוּ מַיִם טְהוֹרִים וְטַהֲרֵנוּ, כְּמָה שֶׁכָּתוּב:

《 it is written: 〈 as 《 and purify us, 〈 pure water 〈 upon us 〈 Pour 《 they will become.

וְזָרַקְתִּי עֲלֵיכֶם מַיִם טְהוֹרִים וּטְהַרְתֶּם, מִכֹּל

〈 from all 《 and you will become pure; 〈 pure water 〈 upon you 〈 I shall pour

---

(1) *Leviticus* 30:3. (2) 30:4. (3) *Isaiah* 44:22. (4) 43:25. (5) 1:18.

טֻמְאוֹתֵיכֶם וּמִכָּל גִּלּוּלֵיכֶם אֲטַהֵר אֶתְכֶם.¹ רַחֵם

⟨ Have ⟪ you. ⟨ I will ⟨ your ⟨ and ⟨ your
mercy   purify   abominations   from all   contaminations

עָלֵינוּ וְאַל תַּשְׁחִיתֵנוּ, כְּמָה שֶׁכָּתוּב: כִּי אֵל רַחוּם

⟨ a merciful ⟨ For ⟪ it is written: ⟨ as ⟪ destroy us, ⟨ and ⟨ on us
God   do not

יהוה אֱלֹהֶיךָ, לֹא יַרְפְּךָ וְלֹא יַשְׁחִיתֶךָ, וְלֹא יִשְׁכַּח

⟨ will He ⟨ nor ⟪ will He ⟨ nor ⟨ relinquish ⟨ He will ⟪ your God; ⟨ is
forget   destroy you,   you   not   HASHEM,

אֶת בְּרִית אֲבֹתֶיךָ אֲשֶׁר נִשְׁבַּע לָהֶם.² מוֹל

⟨ Circum- ⟪ to them. ⟨ He swore ⟨ which ⟨ with your ⟨ the covenant
cise   forefathers,

אֶת לְבָבֵנוּ לְאַהֲבָה וּלְיִרְאָה אֶת שְׁמֶךָ, כְּמָה שֶׁכָּתוּב:

⟪ it is written: ⟨ as ⟪ Your Name, ⟨ and to fear ⟨ to love ⟪ our hearts

וּמָל יהוה אֱלֹהֶיךָ אֶת לְבָבְךָ וְאֶת לְבַב זַרְעֶךָ, לְאַהֲבָה

⟨ to love ⟪ of your ⟨ and the ⟨ your heart ⟨ HASHEM, your God,
offspring,   heart   will circumcise

אֶת יהוה אֱלֹהֶיךָ, בְּכָל לְבָבְךָ וּבְכָל נַפְשְׁךָ, לְמַעַן

⟨ so that ⟪ your ⟨ and ⟨ your ⟨ with all ⟨ your God, ⟨ HASHEM,
soul,   with all   heart

חַיֶּיךָ.³ הִמָּצֵא לָנוּ בְּבַקָּשָׁתֵנוּ, כְּמָה שֶׁכָּתוּב: וּבִקַּשְׁתֶּם

⟨ And you ⟪ it is written: ⟨ as ⟪ in our quest, ⟨ to us ⟨ Be ⟪ you may
will seek   accessible   live.

מִשָּׁם אֶת יהוה אֱלֹהֶיךָ וּמָצָאתָ, כִּי תִדְרְשֶׁנּוּ בְּכָל

⟨ with ⟨ you search ⟨ when ⟪ and you will ⟨ your God, ⟨ HASHEM, ⟨ from
all   Him out   find [Him],   there

לְבָבְךָ וּבְכָל נַפְשֶׁךָ.⁴ ❖ תְּבִיאֵנוּ אֶל הַר קָדְשֶׁךָ,

⟨ Your holy ⟨ to ⟨ Bring us ⟪ your soul. ⟨ and ⟨ your
mountain   with all   heart

וְשַׂמְּחֵנוּ בְּבֵית תְּפִלָּתֶךָ, כְּמָה שֶׁכָּתוּב: וַהֲבִיאוֹתִים

⟨ And I will ⟪ it is written: ⟨ as ⟪ of Prayer, ⟨ in Your ⟨ and gladden
bring them   House   us

אֶל הַר קָדְשִׁי, וְשִׂמַּחְתִּים בְּבֵית תְּפִלָּתִי, עוֹלֹתֵיהֶם

⟨ their burnt- ⟪ of Prayer; ⟨ in My ⟨ and I will ⟪ My holy ⟨ to
offerings   House   gladden them   mountain,

---

(1) *Ezekiel* 36:25. (2) *Deuteronomy* 4:31. (3) 30:6. (4) 4:29.

וְזִבְחֵיהֶם לְרָצוֹן עַל מִזְבְּחִי, כִּי בֵיתִי בֵּית תְּפִלָּה

⟨ of / Prayer" ⟨ "a House ⟨ My / House ⟨ for ≪ My Altar, ⟨ on ⟨ will find / favor ⟨ and their feast-offerings

יִקָּרֵא לְכָל הָעַמִּים.¹

≪ nations. ⟨ for all ⟨ will be / called

THE ARK IS OPENED.

CHAZZAN, THEN CONGREGATION:

שְׁמַע קוֹלֵנוּ יהוה אֱלֹהֵינוּ, חוּס וְרַחֵם עָלֵינוּ,

≪ on us, ⟨ and have / compassion ⟨ have / pity ≪ our God; ⟨ HASHEM, ⟨ our voice, ⟨ Hear

וְקַבֵּל בְּרַחֲמִים וּבְרָצוֹן אֶת תְּפִלָּתֵנוּ.²

≪ our prayer. ⟨ and favor ⟨ with compassion ⟨ and accept

CHAZZAN, THEN CONGREGATION:

הֲשִׁיבֵנוּ יהוה אֵלֶיךָ וְנָשׁוּבָה, חַדֵּשׁ יָמֵינוּ כְּקֶדֶם.³

≪ as of old. ⟨ our / days ⟨ renew ≪ and we shall / return, ⟨ to You, ⟨ HASHEM, ⟨ Bring us back,

CHAZZAN, THEN CONGREGATION:

אֲמָרֵינוּ הַאֲזִינָה יהוה, בִּינָה הֲגִיגֵנוּ.⁴

≪ our thoughts. ⟨ perceive ≪ HASHEM; ⟨ hear, ⟨ Our words

THE FOLLOWING VERSE IS RECITED QUIETLY:

יִהְיוּ לְרָצוֹן אִמְרֵי פִינוּ וְהֶגְיוֹן לִבֵּנוּ לְפָנֶיךָ,

≪ before / You, ≪ of our / heart — ⟨ and the / thoughts ⟨ of our / mouth ⟨ — the ex-/ pressions ≪ find / favor ⟨ May / they

יהוה צוּרֵנוּ וְגוֹאֲלֵנוּ.⁵

≪ and our Redeemer. ⟨ our Rock ⟨ HASHEM,

CHAZZAN, THEN CONGREGATION:

אַל תַּשְׁלִיכֵנוּ מִלְּפָנֶיךָ, וְרוּחַ קָדְשְׁךָ אַל תִּקַּח מִמֶּנּוּ.⁶

≪ from us. ⟨ take ⟨ do / not ⟨ of Your / Holiness ⟨ and the / Spirit ≪ from Your / Presence, ⟨ cast us away ⟨ Do / not

CHAZZAN, THEN CONGREGATION:

אַל תַּשְׁלִיכֵנוּ לְעֵת זִקְנָה, כִּכְלוֹת כֹּחֵנוּ אַל תַּעַזְבֵנוּ.⁷

≪ forsake us not. ⟨ does our / strength, ⟨ when fail ≪ of old / age; ⟨ in time ⟨ cast us away ⟨ Do / not

(1) *Isaiah* 56:7. (2) From the weekday *Shemoneh Esrei*.
(3) *Lamentations* 5:21. (4) Cf. *Psalms* 5:2. (5) Cf. 19:15. (6) 51:13. (7) Cf. 71:9.

ALL CONTINUE (SOME CONGREGATIONS RECITE THE NEXT VERSE RESPONSIVELY):

אַל תַּעַזְבֵנוּ יהוה, אֱלֹהֵינוּ אַל תִּרְחַק מִמֶּנּוּ.¹

》 from us. 〈 be not distant 〈 our God, 》 O HASHEM; 〈 Forsake us not,

עֲשֵׂה עִמָּנוּ אוֹת לְטוֹבָה, וְיִרְאוּ שׂוֹנְאֵינוּ וְיֵבֹשׁוּ,

》 and be 〈 may our 〈 so that 》 for good; 〈 a sign 〈 for us 〈 Display
ashamed, enemies see it

כִּי אַתָּה יהוה עֲזַרְתָּנוּ וְנִחַמְתָּנוּ.² כִּי לְךָ יהוה

〈 HASHEM, 〈 for 〈 Because 》 and 〈 will have 〈 HASHEM, 〈 You, 〈 for
You, consoled us. helped us

הוֹחָלְנוּ, אַתָּה תַעֲנֶה אֲדֹנָי אֱלֹהֵינוּ.³

》 our God. 〈 O Lord, 〈 will answer, 〈 You 》 do we wait;

THE ARK IS CLOSED.

EACH INDIVIDUAL CONTINUES.

CONFESSION / ודוי

**DURING THE RECITATION OF THE ודוי, *CONFESSION*, STAND WITH
HEAD AND BODY SLIGHTLY BOWED, IN SUBMISSIVE CONTRITION.**

אֱלֹהֵינוּ וֵאלֹהֵי אֲבוֹתֵינוּ, תָּבֹא לְפָנֶיךָ תְּפִלָּתֵנוּ,⁴

》 may our 〈 before 〈 come 》 of our 〈 and the 〈 Our God
prayer, You forefathers, God

וְאַל תִּתְעַלַּם מִתְּחִנָּתֵנוּ,⁵ שֶׁאֵין אָנוּ עַזֵּי פָנִים

〈 faced 〈 so brazen- 〈 For we are not 》 our supplication. 〈 ignore 〈 and do not

וּקְשֵׁי עֹרֶף, לוֹמַר לְפָנֶיךָ יהוה אֱלֹהֵינוּ וֵאלֹהֵי

〈 and the God 〈 our God, 〈 HASHEM, 》 before You, 〈 as to say 〈 necked 〈 and stiff-

אֲבוֹתֵינוּ, צַדִּיקִים אֲנַחְנוּ וְלֹא חָטָאנוּ, אֲבָל

》 —for 》 sinned 〈 and 〈 we are, 〈 that righteous 》 of our
indeed, have not forefathers,

אֲנַחְנוּ וַאֲבוֹתֵינוּ חָטָאנוּ.⁶

》 have sinned. 〈 and our forefathers 〈 we

**STRIKE THE LEFT SIDE OF THE CHEST WITH THE RIGHT FIST WHILE RECITING
EACH OF THE SINS OF THE FOLLOWING CONFESSIONAL LITANY:**

אָשַׁמְנוּ, בָּגַדְנוּ, גָּזַלְנוּ, דִּבַּרְנוּ דֹפִי. הֶעֱוִינוּ,

》 We have com- 》 slander. 〈 we have 》 we have 》 we have 》 We have been
mitted iniquity; spoken robbed; betrayed; guilty;

---

(1) Cf. *Psalms* 38:22. (2) Cf. 86:17. (3) Cf. 38:16. (4) Cf. 88:3. (5) Cf. 55:2. (6) Cf. 106:6, *Jeremiah* 3:25.

וְהִרְשַׁעְנוּ, זַדְנוּ, חָמַסְנוּ, טָפַלְנוּ שֶׁקֶר. יָעַצְנוּ

We have given advice ‖ false accusations. ‖ we have made ‖ we have extorted; ‖ we have sinned willfully; ‖ we have committed wickedness;

רָע, כִּזַּבְנוּ, לַצְנוּ, מָרַדְנוּ, נִאַצְנוּ, סָרַרְנוּ,

we have strayed; ‖ we have provoked [God's anger]; ‖ we have rebelled; ‖ we have scorned; ‖ we have been deceitful; ‖ that is bad;

עָוִינוּ, פָּשַׁעְנוּ, צָרַרְנוּ, קִשִּׁינוּ עֹרֶף. רָשַׁעְנוּ,

We have been wicked; ‖ our necks. ‖ we have stiffened ‖ we have caused distress; ‖ we have sinned rebelliously; ‖ we have been iniquitous;

שִׁחַתְנוּ, תִּעַבְנוּ, תָּעִינוּ, תִּעְתָּעְנוּ.

we have scoffed. ‖ we have gone astray; ‖ we have committed abominations; ‖ we have been corrupt;

סַרְנוּ מִמִּצְוֹתֶיךָ וּמִמִּשְׁפָּטֶיךָ הַטּוֹבִים, וְלֹא שָׁוָה

worthwhile ‖ and it was not ‖ that are good, ‖ and from Your laws ‖ from Your commandments ‖ We have turned away

לָנוּ.[1] וְאַתָּה צַדִּיק עַל כָּל הַבָּא עָלֵינוּ, כִּי אֱמֶת

truthfully ‖ for ‖ upon us, ‖ that has come ‖ all ‖ in ‖ are righteous ‖ And You ‖ for us.

עָשִׂיתָ וַאֲנַחְנוּ הִרְשָׁעְנוּ.[2]

have acted wickedly. ‖ while we ‖ have You acted,

אָשַׁמְנוּ מִכָּל עָם, בֹּשְׁנוּ מִכָּל דּוֹר, גָּלָה מִמֶּנּוּ

from us ‖ Departed ‖ generation. ‖ more than any other ‖ We have been ashamed ‖ people. ‖ more than any other ‖ We have been guilty

מָשׂוֹשׂ, דָּוָה לִבֵּנוּ בַּחֲטָאֵינוּ, הֻחְבַּל אִוּוּיֵנוּ, וְנִפְרַע

uncovered ‖ was our desired [Temple], ‖ Seized ‖ because of our sins. ‖ is our heart ‖ Sickened ‖ has joy.

פְּאֵרֵנוּ, זְבוּל בֵּית מִקְדָּשֵׁנוּ חָרַב בַּעֲוֹנֵינוּ, טִירָתֵנוּ

Our Palace ‖ because of our iniquities. ‖ has been destroyed ‖ our Holy Temple ‖ for [His] abode, ‖ was our splendor;

הָיְתָה לְשַׁמָּה, יְפִי אַדְמָתֵנוּ לְזָרִים, כֹּחֵנוּ לְנָכְרִים.

[was given] to foreigners. ‖ our wealth ‖ is controlled by strangers, ‖ of our Land ‖ [Jerusalem,] the beauty ‖ desolate. ‖ has become

---

(1) Cf. *Job* 33:27. (2) *Nehemiah* 9:33.

וַעֲדַיִן לֹא שַׁבְנוּ מִטָּעוּתֵנוּ וְהֵיךְ נָעִיז פָּנֵינוּ וְנַקְשֶׁה

❬ and ❬ faced ❬ can we be ❬ So ❭❭ from our ❬ we have not ❬ But still
stiffen   so brazen-   how   willful errors.   repented

עָרְפֵּנוּ, לוֹמַר לְפָנֶיךָ יהוה אֱלֹהֵינוּ וֵאלֹהֵי אֲבוֹתֵינוּ,

❭❭ of our ❬ and the ❬ our God ❬ HASHEM, ❬ before ❬ so as to ❬ our neck
forefathers,   God   You,   say

צַדִּיקִים אֲנַחְנוּ וְלֹא חָטָאנוּ, אֲבָל אֲנַחְנוּ וַאֲבוֹתֵינוּ

❬ and our ❬ both we ❬ for in ❭❭ and we have ❭❭ we are ❬ that
fathers   truth,   not sinned,   righteous

חָטָאנוּ.[1]

❭❭ have sinned.

**STRIKE THE LEFT SIDE OF THE CHEST WITH THE RIGHT FIST WHILE RECITING
EACH OF THE SINS OF THE FOLLOWING CONFESSIONAL LITANY:**

אָשַׁמְנוּ, בָּגַדְנוּ, גָּזַלְנוּ, דִּבַּרְנוּ דְפִי. הֶעֱוִינוּ,

❭❭ We have com- ❭❭ slander. ❬ we have ❭❭ we have ❭❭ we have ❭❭ We have been
mitted iniquity;   spoken   robbed;   betrayed;   guilty;

וְהִרְשַׁעְנוּ, זַדְנוּ, חָמַסְנוּ, טָפַלְנוּ שֶׁקֶר. יָעַצְנוּ

❬ We have ❭❭ false ❬ we have ❭❭ we have ❭❭ we have sinned ❭❭ we have commit-
given advice   accusations.   made   extorted;   willfully;   ted wickedness;

רָע, כִּזַּבְנוּ, לַצְנוּ, מָרַדְנוּ, נִאַצְנוּ, סָרַרְנוּ,

❭❭ we have ❭❭ we have provoked ❭❭ we have ❭❭ we have ❭❭ we have been ❭❭ that is
strayed;   [God's anger];   rebelled;   scorned;   deceitful;   bad;

עָוִינוּ, פָּשַׁעְנוּ, צָרַרְנוּ, קִשִּׁינוּ עֹרֶף. רָשַׁעְנוּ,

❭❭ We have ❭❭ our ❬ we have ❭❭ we have caused ❭❭ we have sinned ❭❭ we have been
been wicked;   necks.   stiffened   distress;   rebelliously;   iniquitous;

שִׁחַתְנוּ, תִּעַבְנוּ, תָּעִינוּ, תִּעְתָּעְנוּ.

❭❭ we have ❭❭ we have ❭❭ we have commit- ❭❭ we have
scoffed.   gone astray;   ted abominations;   been corrupt;

סַרְנוּ מִמִּצְוֹתֶיךָ וּמִמִּשְׁפָּטֶיךָ הַטּוֹבִים, וְלֹא שָׁוָה

❬ worth- ❬ and it ❭❭ that are ❬ and from ❬ from Your ❬ We have
while   was not   good,   Your laws   commandments   turned away

לָנוּ.[2] וְאַתָּה צַדִּיק עַל כָּל הַבָּא עָלֵינוּ, כִּי אֱמֶת

❬ truth- ❬ for ❭❭ upon us, ❬ that has ❬ all ❬ in ❬ are ❬ And You ❭❭ for us.
fully   come   righteous

עָשִׂיתָ וַאֲנַחְנוּ הִרְשָׁעְנוּ.[3]

❭❭ have acted ❬ while we ❭❭ have You
wickedly.   acted,

---

(1) Cf. *Psalms* 106:6; *Jeremiah* 3:25. (2) Cf. *Job* 33:27. (3) *Nehemiah* 9:33.

לְעֵינֵינוּ עָשְׁקוּ עֲמָלֵנוּ, **מֶמְּשָׁךְ** וּמְמוֹרָט מִמֶּנּוּ,
» from / and cut off / [it was] » the product / have they / Before our
us. pulled away of our labor; stolen eyes

נָתְנוּ עֹלָם עָלֵינוּ, סָבַלְנוּ עַל שִׁכְמֵנוּ, עֲבָדִים
/ Slaves » our / upon / we bore it » upon us, / their / They have
shoulders. yoke placed

מָשְׁלוּ בָנוּ, פֹּרֵק אֵין מִיָּדָם, צָרוֹת רַבּוֹת
/ that are / Troubles » from their / there / a » over / have
manifold hand. was not redeemer us; ruled

סְבָבוּנוּ, קְרָאנוּךְ יהוה אֱלֹהֵינוּ, רָחַקְתָּ מִמֶּנּוּ
/ from / but You have dis- » our God, / Hashem, / we called » have
us tanced Yourself upon You, surrounded us,

בַּעֲוֹנֵינוּ, שַׁבְנוּ מֵאַחֲרֶיךָ, תָּעֵינוּ וְאָבָדְנוּ.
» we have » we have » from following / We have » because of
become lost. gone astray; after You; turned away our iniquities.

וַעֲדַיִן לֹא שַׁבְנוּ מִטָּעוּתֵנוּ וְהֵיךְ נָעִיז פָּנֵינוּ וְנַקְשֶׁה
/ and / faced / can we be / So » from our / we have not / But still
stiffen so brazen- how willful errors. repented

עָרְפֵּנוּ, לוֹמַר לְפָנֶיךָ יהוה אֱלֹהֵינוּ וֵאלֹהֵי אֲבוֹתֵינוּ,
» of our / and the / our God / Hashem, / before / so as to / our neck
forefathers, God You, say

צַדִּיקִים אֲנַחְנוּ וְלֹא חָטָאנוּ, אֲבָל אֲנַחְנוּ וַאֲבוֹתֵינוּ
/ and our / both we / for in » and we have » we are / that
fathers truth, not sinned, righteous

חָטָאנוּ.[1]
» have sinned.

**STRIKE THE LEFT SIDE OF THE CHEST WITH THE RIGHT FIST WHILE RECITING
EACH OF THE SINS OF THE FOLLOWING CONFESSIONAL LITANY:**

אָשַׁמְנוּ, בָּגַדְנוּ, גָּזַלְנוּ, דִּבַּרְנוּ דֹּפִי. הֶעֱוִינוּ,
» We have com- » slander. / we have » we have » we have » We have been
mitted iniquity; spoken robbed; betrayed; guilty;

וְהִרְשַׁעְנוּ, זַדְנוּ, חָמַסְנוּ, טָפַלְנוּ שֶׁקֶר. יָעַצְנוּ
/ We have » false / we have » we have » we have sinned » we have commit-
given advice accusations. made extorted; willfully; ted wickedness;

רָע, כִּזַּבְנוּ, לַצְנוּ, מָרַדְנוּ, נִאַצְנוּ, סָרַרְנוּ,
» we have » we have provoked » we have » we have » we have been » that is
strayed; [God's anger]; rebelled; scorned; deceitful; bad;

(1) Cf. *Psalms* 106:6; *Jeremiah* 3:25.

עָוִינוּ, פָּשַׁעְנוּ, צָרַרְנוּ, קִשִּׁינוּ עֹרֶף. רָשַׁעְנוּ,

‹ We have been wicked; › our necks. ‹ we have stiffened ‹ we have caused ‹ we have sinned ‹ we have been distress; rebelliously; iniquitous;

שִׁחַתְנוּ, תִּעַבְנוּ, תָּעִינוּ, תִּעְתָּעְנוּ.

‹ we have scoffed. ‹ we have gone astray; ‹ we have committed abominations; ‹ we have been corrupt;

סַרְנוּ מִמִּצְוֹתֶיךָ וּמִמִּשְׁפָּטֶיךָ הַטּוֹבִים, וְלֹא שָׁוָה

‹ worth-while ‹ and it was not ‹ that are good, ‹ and from Your laws ‹ from Your commandments ‹ We have turned away

לָנוּ.[1] וְאַתָּה צַדִּיק עַל כָּל הַבָּא עָלֵינוּ, כִּי אֱמֶת

‹ truth-fully ‹ for ‹ upon us, ‹ that has come ‹ all ‹ in ‹ are righteous ‹ And You ‹ for us.

עָשִׂיתָ וַאֲנַחְנוּ הִרְשָׁעְנוּ.[2]

‹ have acted wickedly. ‹ while we ‹ have You acted,

הִרְשַׁעְנוּ וּפָשַׁעְנוּ, לָכֵן לֹא נוֹשָׁעְנוּ. וְתֵן בְּלִבֵּנוּ

‹ in our hearts ‹ Place ‹ been saved. ‹ we have ‹ there-fore ‹ and we have sinned rebelliously; ‹ We have acted wickedly

לַעֲזוֹב דֶּרֶךְ רֶשַׁע, וְחִישׁ לָנוּ יֶשַׁע, כַּכָּתוּב עַל יַד

‹ the hand ‹ by ‹ as it is written ‹ salvation; ‹ to us ‹ and ‹ of ‹ the ‹ [the will] wickedness, path to abandon

נְבִיאֶךָ: יַעֲזֹב רָשָׁע דַּרְכּוֹ, וְאִישׁ אָוֶן מַחְשְׁבֹתָיו,

‹ [abandon] his thoughts; ‹ of iniquity ‹ and the man ‹ his way, ‹ the wicked one ‹ Let abandon ‹ of Your prophet:

וְיָשֹׁב אֶל יהוה וִירַחֲמֵהוּ, וְאֶל אֱלֹהֵינוּ כִּי

‹ for ‹ our God, ‹ and to ‹ and He will have compassion on him, ‹ HASHEM, ‹ to ‹ and let him return

יַרְבֶּה לִסְלוֹחַ.[3]

‹ forgiving. ‹ He is abundantly

מְשִׁיחַ צִדְקֶךָ אָמַר לְפָנֶיךָ, שְׁגִיאוֹת מִי יָבִין,

‹ can discern? ‹ who ‹ Mistakes ‹ before You: ‹ said ‹ who is righteous [David] ‹ Your anointed one

---

(1) Cf. *Job* 33:27. (2) *Nehemiah* 9:33. (3) *Isaiah* 55:7.

מִנִּסְתָּרוֹת נַקֵּנִי.¹ נַקֵּנוּ יהוה אֱלֹהֵינוּ מִכָּל פְּשָׁעֵינוּ,

⟨ our sins ⟨ of all ⟨ our God, ⟨ HASHEM, ⟨ Cleanse ⟪ cleanse ⟨ From
us, me. unperceived faults

וְטַהֲרֵנוּ מִכָּל טֻמְאוֹתֵינוּ, וּזְרוֹק עָלֵינוּ מַיִם טְהוֹרִים

⟨ pure water ⟨ upon us ⟨ Pour ⟪ our contaminations. ⟨ of all ⟨ and purify us

וְטַהֲרֵנוּ, כַּכָּתוּב עַל יַד נְבִיאֶךָ: וְזָרַקְתִּי עֲלֵיכֶם

⟨ upon you ⟨ I shall pour ⟪ of Your ⟨ the ⟨ by ⟨ as it is ⟪ and purify us,
prophet: hand written

מַיִם טְהוֹרִים וּטְהַרְתֶּם, מִכֹּל טֻמְאוֹתֵיכֶם וּמִכָּל

⟨ and ⟨ your ⟨ from ⟪ and you will ⟨ pure water
from all contaminations all become pure;

גִּלּוּלֵיכֶם אֲטַהֵר אֶתְכֶם.² עַמְּךָ וְנַחֲלָתֶךָ, רְעֵבֵי

⟨ who ⟪ and Your ⟨ Your ⟪ you. ⟨ I will purify ⟨ your
hunger heritage, people abominations

טוּבְךָ, צְמֵאֵי חַסְדֶּךָ, תְּאֵבֵי יִשְׁעֶךָ, יַכִּירוּ וְיֵדְעוּ

⟨ and ⟨ — may they ⟪ for Your ⟨ and ⟪ for Your ⟨ who ⟪ for Your
know recognize salvation who long kindness, thirst goodness,

כִּי לַיהוה אֱלֹהֵינוּ הָרַחֲמִים וְהַסְּלִיחוֹת.

⟪ and forgiveness. ⟨ belong mercy ⟨ our God, ⟨ to HASHEM, ⟨ that

אֵל רַחוּם שְׁמֶךָ, אֵל חַנּוּן שְׁמֶךָ,³ בָּנוּ נִקְרָא שְׁמֶךָ.⁴

⟪ is Your Name ⟨ upon ⟪ is Your ⟨ Gracious God ⟪ is Your ⟨ Merciful God
proclaimed, us Name, Name,

יהוה עֲשֵׂה לְמַעַן שְׁמֶךָ,⁵ עֲשֵׂה לְמַעַן אֲמִתָּךְ, עֲשֵׂה

⟨ act ⟪ Your truth; ⟨ for the ⟨ Act ⟪ Your ⟨ for the ⟨ act ⟨ HASHEM,
sake of Name. sake of

לְמַעַן בְּרִיתָךְ, עֲשֵׂה לְמַעַן גָּדְלָךְ וְתִפְאַרְתָּךְ, עֲשֵׂה

⟨ act ⟪ and Your ⟨ Your ⟨ for the ⟨ act ⟪ Your ⟨ for the
splendor; greatness sake of covenant; sake of

לְמַעַן דָּתָךְ, עֲשֵׂה לְמַעַן הוֹדָךְ, עֲשֵׂה לְמַעַן וְעוּדָךְ,

⟪ Your Meet- ⟨ for the ⟨ act ⟪ Your ⟨ for the ⟨ act ⟪ Your ⟨ for the
ing House; sake of glory; sake of Law; sake of

עֲשֵׂה לְמַעַן זִכְרָךְ,⁷ עֲשֵׂה לְמַעַן חַסְדָּךְ, עֲשֵׂה לְמַעַן

⟨ for the ⟨ act ⟪ Your ⟨ for the ⟨ act ⟪ Your ⟨ for the ⟨ act
sake of kindness; sake of remembrance; sake of

---

(1) *Psalms* 19:13. (2) *Ezekiel* 36:25. (3) Cf. *Exodus* 34:6. (4) Cf. *Deuteronomy* 28:10.
(5) *Jeremiah* 14:7. (6) Cf. *Exodus* 3:15. (7) *Psalms* 6:5.

טוּבָךְ, עֲשֵׂה לְמַעַן יְחוּדָךְ, עֲשֵׂה לְמַעַן **כְּבוֹדָךְ**, עֲשֵׂה
⟨ act ⟪ Your ⟨ for the ⟨ act ⟪ Your ⟨ for the ⟨ act ⟪ Your
honor;   sake of   Oneness;   sake of   goodness;

לְמַעַן **לִמּוּדָךְ**,[1] עֲשֵׂה לְמַעַן **מַלְכוּתָךְ**, עֲשֵׂה לְמַעַן
⟨ for the ⟨ act ⟪ Your kingship; ⟨ for the ⟨ act ⟪ Your ⟨ for the
sake of   sake of   students;   sake of

נִצְחָךְ, עֲשֵׂה לְמַעַן **סוֹדָךְ**,[2] עֲשֵׂה לְמַעַן **עֻזָּךְ**, עֲשֵׂה
⟨ act ⟪ Your ⟨ for the ⟨ act ⟪ Your secret [re- ⟨ for the ⟨ act ⟪ Your eternal
power;   sake of   vealed to those   sake of   [Name];
             who fear You];

לְמַעַן **פְּאֵרָךְ**, עֲשֵׂה לְמַעַן **צִדְקָתָךְ**, עֲשֵׂה לְמַעַן
⟨ for the ⟨ act ⟪ Your ⟨ for the ⟨ act ⟪ Your ⟨ for the
sake of   righteousness;   sake of   glory;   sake of

קְדֻשָּׁתָךְ, עֲשֵׂה לְמַעַן **רַחֲמֶיךָ** הָרַבִּים, עֲשֵׂה לְמַעַן
⟨ for the ⟨ act ⟪ that is ⟨ Your mercy ⟨ for the ⟨ act ⟪ Your sanctity;
sake of   abundant;   sake of

שְׁכִינָתָךְ, עֲשֵׂה לְמַעַן **תְּהִלָּתָךְ**, עֲשֵׂה לְמַעַן אוֹהֲבֶיךָ
⟨ those who ⟨ for the ⟨ act ⟪ Your praise; ⟨ for the ⟨ act ⟪ Your Divine
loved You   sake of   sake of   Presence;

שׁוֹכְנֵי עָפָר,[3] עֲשֵׂה לְמַעַן אַבְרָהָם יִצְחָק וְיַעֲקֹב,
⟪ and Jacob; ⟨ Isaac, ⟨ Abraham, ⟨ for the sake of ⟨ act ⟪ in the dust; ⟨ who rest

עֲשֵׂה לְמַעַן מֹשֶׁה וְאַהֲרֹן, עֲשֵׂה לְמַעַן דָּוִד וּשְׁלֹמֹה,
⟪ and ⟨ David ⟨ for the ⟨ act ⟪ and Aaron; ⟨ Moses ⟨ for the ⟨ act
Solomon;   sake of   sake of

עֲשֵׂה לְמַעַן יְרוּשָׁלַיִם עִיר קָדְשֶׁךָ,[4] עֲשֵׂה לְמַעַן צִיּוֹן
⟨ Zion, ⟨ for the ⟨ act ⟪ of Your ⟨ the ⟨ Jerusalem, ⟨ for the ⟨ act
   sake of   Holiness;   City   sake of

מִשְׁכַּן כְּבוֹדֶךָ,[5] עֲשֵׂה לְמַעַן שִׁמְמוֹת[6] הֵיכָלֶךָ, עֲשֵׂה
⟨ act ⟪ of Your ⟨ the ⟨ for the ⟨ act ⟪ of Your ⟨ the
Temple;   desolation   sake of   glory;   abode

לְמַעַן **הֲרִיסוּת**[7] מִזְבְּחֶךָ, עֲשֵׂה לְמַעַן הֲרוּגִים עַל
⟨ for ⟨ those killed ⟨ for the ⟨ act ⟪ of Your ⟨ the ⟨ for the
     sake of   Altar;   devastation   sake of

שֵׁם קָדְשֶׁךָ, עֲשֵׂה לְמַעַן טְבוּחִים עַל יִחוּדָךְ, עֲשֵׂה
⟨ act ⟪ Your ⟨ for ⟨ those ⟨ for the ⟨ act ⟪ Your holy Name;
   Oneness;   slaughtered   sake of

---

(1) Cf. *Isaiah* 54:13. (2) Cf. *Psalms* 25:14. (3) *Isaiah* 26:19. (4) Cf. *Daniel* 9:16,24.
(5) *Psalms* 26:8. (6) Cf. *Jeremiah* 51:26. (7) Cf. *Isaiah* 49:19.

לְמַעַן בָּאֵי בָאֵשׁ וּבַמַּיִם עַל קִדּוּשׁ שְׁמֶךָ, עֲשֵׂה לְמַעַן
⟨ for the sake of ⟨ act ⟨ of Your Name; sanctification ⟨ the ⟨ for ⟨ and water ⟨ fire ⟨ those who entered ⟨ for the sake of

יוֹנְקֵי שָׁדַיִם[1] שֶׁלֹּא חָטָאוּ, עֲשֵׂה לְמַעַן גְּמוּלֵי חָלָב[2]
⟨ from milk ⟨ the [babies] weaned ⟨ for the sake of ⟨ act ⟨⟨ sin; ⟨ who did not ⟨ at the breast ⟨ the [infants] sucking

שֶׁלֹּא פָשֶׁעוּ, עֲשֵׂה לְמַעַן תִּינוֹקוֹת שֶׁל בֵּית רַבָּן,[3]
⟨⟨ their teachers' school; ⟨ of ⟨ the children ⟨ for the sake of ⟨ act ⟨⟨ transgress; ⟨ who did not

עֲשֵׂה לְמַעַנְךָ אִם לֹא לְמַעֲנֵנוּ, עֲשֵׂה לְמַעַנְךָ וְהוֹשִׁיעֵנוּ.
⟨⟨ and save us. ⟨ for Your sake ⟨ act ⟨ for our sake; ⟨ not ⟨ if ⟨ for Your sake ⟨ act

עֲנֵנוּ יהוה עֲנֵנוּ, עֲנֵנוּ אֱלֹהֵינוּ עֲנֵנוּ, עֲנֵנוּ אָבִינוּ[4]
⟨ our Father, ⟨ answer us; ⟨⟨ answer us; ⟨ our God, ⟨ answer us; ⟨⟨ answer us; ⟨ HASHEM, ⟨ Answer us;

עֲנֵנוּ, עֲנֵנוּ בּוֹרְאֵנוּ[5] עֲנֵנוּ, עֲנֵנוּ גוֹאֲלֵנוּ[6] עֲנֵנוּ, עֲנֵנוּ
⟨ answer us; ⟨⟨ answer us; ⟨ our Redeemer, ⟨ answer us; ⟨⟨ answer us; ⟨ our Creator, ⟨ answer us; ⟨⟨ answer us;

דּוֹרְשֵׁנוּ[7] עֲנֵנוּ, עֲנֵנוּ הָאֵל הַנֶּאֱמָן[8] עֲנֵנוּ, עֲנֵנוּ וָתִיק
⟨ stead-fast ⟨ answer us; ⟨⟨ answer us; ⟨ Who is faithful, ⟨ God ⟨ answer us; ⟨⟨ answer us; ⟨ You Who searches us out,

וְחָסִיד עֲנֵנוּ, עֲנֵנוּ זַךְ וְיָשָׁר[9] עֲנֵנוּ, עֲנֵנוּ חַי וְקַיָּם[10]
⟨ and enduring One, ⟨ living One ⟨ answer us; ⟨⟨ answer us; ⟨ and upright One ⟨ pure ⟨ answer us; ⟨⟨ answer us; ⟨ and kind One,

עֲנֵנוּ, עֲנֵנוּ טוֹב וּמֵטִיב[11] עֲנֵנוּ, עֲנֵנוּ יוֹדֵעַ יֵצֶר[12] עֲנֵנוּ,
⟨⟨ answer us; ⟨ of incli-nations, ⟨ Knower ⟨ answer us; ⟨⟨ answer us; ⟨ and bene-ficent One, ⟨ good ⟨ answer us; ⟨⟨ answer us;

עֲנֵנוּ כּוֹבֵשׁ כְּעָסִים עֲנֵנוּ, עֲנֵנוּ לוֹבֵשׁ צְדָקוֹת[13] עֲנֵנוּ,
⟨⟨ answer us; ⟨ of righteousness, ⟨ Donner ⟨ answer us; ⟨⟨ answer us; ⟨ of wrath, ⟨ Suppressor ⟨ answer us,

עֲנֵנוּ מֶלֶךְ מַלְכֵי הַמְּלָכִים[14] עֲנֵנוּ, עֲנֵנוּ נוֹרָא וְנִשְׂגָּב[15]
⟨ and power-ful One, ⟨ awesome ⟨ answer us; ⟨⟨ answer us; ⟨ of kings, ⟨ over kings ⟨ King ⟨ answer us,

(1) *Joel* 2:16. (2) *Isaiah* 28:9. (3) *Shabbos* 119b. (4) *Isaiah* 64:7. (5) Cf. 43:1. (6) 47:4.
(7) Cf. *Ezekiel* 34:11. (8) *Deuteronomy* 7:9. (9) *Job* 8:6; cf. *Proverbs* 20:11.
(10) Cf. *Daniel* 6:27. (11) Cf. *Psalms* 119:68. (12) Cf. 103:14.
(13) Cf. *Isaiah* 59:17. (14) *Ethics of the Fathers* 3:1. (15) *Psalms* 47:3; 148:13.

עֲנֵנוּ, עֲנֵנוּ סוֹלֵחַ וּמוֹחֵל עֲנֵנוּ, עֲנֵנוּ עוֹנֶה בְּעֵת
‹ in time ‹ You Who answers ‹ answer us, « answer us; ‹ and pardons, ‹ You Who forgives ‹ answer us, « answer us;

צָרָה¹ עֲנֵנוּ, עֲנֵנוּ פּוֹדֶה וּמַצִּיל² עֲנֵנוּ, עֲנֵנוּ צַדִּיק
‹ righteous of ‹ answer us, « answer us; ‹ and Rescuer, ‹ Redeemer ‹ answer us, « answer us; ‹ distress,

וְיָשָׁר³ עֲנֵנוּ, עֲנֵנוּ קָרוֹב לְקוֹרְאָיו⁴ עֲנֵנוּ, עֲנֵנוּ קָשֶׁה
‹ You Who with difficulty ‹ answer us, « answer us; ‹ to those who call upon Him, ‹ He Who is close ‹ answer us, « answer us; ‹ and upright One,

לִכְעוֹס⁵ עֲנֵנוּ, עֲנֵנוּ רַךְ לִרְצוֹת⁶ עֲנֵנוּ, עֲנֵנוּ רַחוּם
‹ merciful ‹ answer us, « answer us; ‹ appeased, ‹ You Who are easily ‹ answer us, « answer us; ‹ becomes angry,

וְחַנּוּן⁷ עֲנֵנוּ, עֲנֵנוּ שׁוֹמֵעַ אֶל אֶבְיוֹנִים⁸ עֲנֵנוּ, עֲנֵנוּ
‹ answer us, « answer us; ‹ the destitute, ‹ to ‹ You Who listens ‹ answer us, « answer us; ‹ and gracious One,

תּוֹמֵךְ תְּמִימִים עֲנֵנוּ, עֲנֵנוּ אֱלֹהֵי אֲבוֹתֵינוּ עֲנֵנוּ,
« answer us; ‹ of our forefathers, ‹ God ‹ answer us, « answer us; ‹ the wholesome, ‹ You Who supports

עֲנֵנוּ אֱלֹהֵי אַבְרָהָם⁹ עֲנֵנוּ, עֲנֵנוּ פַּחַד יִצְחָק⁹ עֲנֵנוּ,
« answer us; ‹ of Isaac, ‹ Awesome One ‹ answer us, « answer us; ‹ of Abraham, ‹ God ‹ answer us,

עֲנֵנוּ אֲבִיר יַעֲקֹב¹⁰ עֲנֵנוּ, עֲנֵנוּ עֶזְרַת הַשְּׁבָטִים עֲנֵנוּ,
« answer us; ‹ of the tribes, ‹ Helper ‹ answer us, « answer us; ‹ of Jacob, ‹ Mighty One ‹ answer us,

עֲנֵנוּ מִשְׂגַּב אִמָּהוֹת עֲנֵנוּ, עֲנֵנוּ עוֹנֶה בְּעֵת רָצוֹן¹¹ עֲנֵנוּ,
« answer us; ‹ of favor, ‹ in a time ‹ You Who answers ‹ answer us, « answer us; ‹ of the Matriarchs, ‹ Stronghold ‹ answer us,

עֲנֵנוּ אֲבִי יְתוֹמִים¹² עֲנֵנוּ, עֲנֵנוּ דַּיַּן אַלְמָנוֹת¹² עֲנֵנוּ.
« answer us. ‹ of widows, ‹ Judge ‹ answer us, « answer us; ‹ of orphans, ‹ Father ‹ answer us,

מִי שֶׁעָנָה¹³ לְאַבְרָהָם אָבִינוּ בְּהַר הַמּוֹרִיָּה
« Moriah ‹ on Mount ‹ our father ‹ Abraham ‹ Who answered ‹ He

הוּא יַעֲנֵנוּ.
« answer us. ‹ — may He

---

(1) Cf. *Isaiah* 49:8; *Psalms* 37:39. Alternate text: בְּעֵת רָצוֹן, *in time of favor.* (2) Cf. 34:23,18.
(3) *Deuteronomy* 32:4. (4) Cf. *Psalms* 145:18. (5) *Ethics of the Fathers* 5:14. (6) Cf. 5:14.
(7) *Exodus* 34:6. (8) *Psalms* 69:34. (9) *Genesis* 31:42. (10) *Isaiah* 49:26. (11) Cf. 49:8;
Psalms 69:14. Alternate text: בְּעֵת צָרָה, *in time of distress.* (12) 68:6. (13) *Genesis* 22:12.

מִי שֶׁעָנָה לְיִצְחָק בְּנוֹ כְּשֶׁנֶּעֱקַד עַל גַּבֵּי הַמִּזְבֵּחַ¹

≪ of the altar ⟨ top ⟨ on ⟨ when he was bound ⟨ his son ⟨ Isaac ⟨ Who answered ⟨ He

הוּא יַעֲנֵנוּ.

≪ answer us. ⟨ — may He

מִי שֶׁעָנָה לְיַעֲקֹב בְּבֵית אֵל²

≪ in Beth-el ⟨ Jacob ⟨ Who answered ⟨ He

הוּא יַעֲנֵנוּ.

≪ answer us. ⟨ — may He

מִי שֶׁעָנָה לְיוֹסֵף בְּבֵית הָאֲסוּרִים³

≪ in the prison ⟨ Joseph ⟨ Who answered ⟨ He

הוּא יַעֲנֵנוּ.

≪ answer us. ⟨ — may He

מִי שֶׁעָנָה לַאֲבוֹתֵינוּ עַל יַם סוּף⁴

≪ of the Reeds ⟨ the Sea ⟨ at ⟨ our forefathers ⟨ Who answered ⟨ He

הוּא יַעֲנֵנוּ.

≪ answer us. ⟨ — may He

מִי שֶׁעָנָה לְמֹשֶׁה בְּחוֹרֵב⁵

≪ in Horeb ⟨ Moses ⟨ Who answered ⟨ He

הוּא יַעֲנֵנוּ.

≪ answer us. ⟨ — may He

מִי שֶׁעָנָה לְאַהֲרֹן בַּמַּחְתָּה⁶

≪ with the fire-pan ⟨ Aaron ⟨ Who answered ⟨ He

הוּא יַעֲנֵנוּ.

≪ answer us. ⟨ — may He

מִי שֶׁעָנָה לְפִינְחָס בְּקוּמוֹ מִתּוֹךְ הָעֵדָה⁷ הוּא יַעֲנֵנוּ.

≪ answer us. ⟨ — may He ≪ the congregation ⟨ from amid ⟨ when he arose ⟨ Phinehas ⟨ Who answered ⟨ He

מִי שֶׁעָנָה לִיהוֹשֻׁעַ בַּגִּלְגָּל⁸

≪ in Gilgal ⟨ Joshua ⟨ Who answered ⟨ He

הוּא יַעֲנֵנוּ.

≪ answer us. ⟨ — may He

מִי שֶׁעָנָה לִשְׁמוּאֵל בַּמִּצְפָּה⁹

≪ in Mizpah ⟨ Samuel ⟨ Who answered ⟨ He

הוּא יַעֲנֵנוּ.

≪ answer us. ⟨ — may He

מִי שֶׁעָנָה לְדָוִד וּשְׁלֹמֹה בְנוֹ בִּירוּשָׁלָיִם¹⁰ הוּא יַעֲנֵנוּ.

≪ answer us. ⟨ — may He ≪ in Jerusalem ⟨ his son ⟨ and Solomon ⟨ David ⟨ Who answered ⟨ He

מִי שֶׁעָנָה לְאֵלִיָּהוּ בְּהַר הַכַּרְמֶל¹¹

≪ Carmel ⟨ on Mount ⟨ Elijah ⟨ Who answered ⟨ He

הוּא יַעֲנֵנוּ.

≪ answer us. ⟨ — may He

---

(1) *Genesis* 22:12. (2) 35:3. (3) 39:21. (4) *Exodus* Ch. 14. (5) 17:6,11; *Deuteronomy* 9:19.
(6) *Numbers* 17:11-13. (7) 25:7-13. (8) *Joshua* 6:1-20; 7:6-15; 10:12-14. (9) *I Samuel* 7:9.
(10) *II Samuel* 7:5-16; 21:1,14; 24:25; *I Kings* 9:3. (11) 18:36-38.

מִי שֶׁעָנָה לְאֱלִישָׁע בִּירִיחוֹ[1]   הוּא יַעֲנֵנוּ.
‹ He › Who › Elisha › in Jericho ›   He — may answer us.

מִי שֶׁעָנָה לְיוֹנָה בִּמְעֵי הַדָּגָה[2]   הוּא יַעֲנֵנוּ.
‹ He › Who › Jonah › in the innards › of the fish ›   He — may answer us.

מִי שֶׁעָנָה לְחִזְקִיָּהוּ מֶלֶךְ יְהוּדָה בְּחָלְיוֹ[3]   הוּא יַעֲנֵנוּ.
‹ He › Who › Hezekiah, › king › of Judah, › in his illness ›   He — may answer us.

מִי שֶׁעָנָה לַחֲנַנְיָה מִישָׁאֵל וַעֲזַרְיָה
‹ He › Who › Hananiah, › Mishael, › and Azariah ›

בְּתוֹךְ כִּבְשַׁן הָאֵשׁ[4]   הוּא יַעֲנֵנוּ.
‹ inside › the furnace › of fire ›   He — may answer us.

מִי שֶׁעָנָה לְדָנִיֵּאל בְּגוֹב הָאֲרָיוֹת[5]   הוּא יַעֲנֵנוּ.
‹ He › Who › Daniel › in the den › of lions ›   He — may answer us.

מִי שֶׁעָנָה לְמָרְדְּכַי וְאֶסְתֵּר בְּשׁוּשַׁן הַבִּירָה[6]
‹ He › Who › Mordechai › and Esther › in Shushan › the capital ›

הוּא יַעֲנֵנוּ.
He — may answer us.

מִי שֶׁעָנָה לְעֶזְרָא בַּגּוֹלָה[7]   הוּא יַעֲנֵנוּ.
‹ He › Who › Ezra › in the exile ›   He — may answer us.

מִי שֶׁעָנָה לְכָל הַצַּדִּיקִים וְהַחֲסִידִים וְהַתְּמִימִים
‹ He › Who › all › the righteous, › the devout, › the wholesome, ›

וְהַיְשָׁרִים   הוּא יַעֲנֵנוּ.
‹ and the upright ›   He — may answer us.

רַחֲמָנָא דְּעָנֵי לַעֲנִיֵּי, עֲנֵינָן. רַחֲמָנָא דְּעָנֵי לִתְבִירֵי
‹ Merciful One › Who answers › the poor, › answer us! › Merciful One › Who answers › those of broken ›

(1) II Kings 2:21. (2) Jonah 2:2-11. (3) II Kings 20:2-6; Isaiah 38:2-8. (4) Daniel 3:21-27. (5) 6:17-23. (6) Esther Ch. 8. (7) Ezra 8:21-23.

לִבָּא, עֲנֵינָן. רַחֲמָנָא דְּעָנֵי לִמְכִיכֵי רוּחָא, עֲנֵינָן.

《 answer us! 《 spirit, 〈 those of crushed 〈 Who answers 〈 Merciful One 《 answer us! 《 hearts,

רַחֲמָנָא עֲנֵינָן. רַחֲמָנָא חוּס. רַחֲמָנָא פְּרוֹק. רַחֲמָנָא

〈 Merciful One, 《 redeem! 〈 Merciful One, 《 have pity! 〈 Merciful One, 《 answer us! 〈 Merciful One,

שְׁזִיב. רַחֲמָנָא רְחַם עֲלָן, הַשְׁתָּא בַּעֲגָלָא וּבִזְמַן קָרִיב.

《 that comes soon. 〈 and at a time 〈 swiftly, 〈 — now, 《 on us 〈 have mercy 〈 Merciful One, 《 save!

PUTTING DOWN THE HEAD / נפילת אפים

RECITE UNTIL יֵבשׁוּ רָגַע **WITH THE HEAD RESTING ON THE LEFT ARM, PREFERABLY WHILE SEATED.**

(וַיֹּאמֶר דָּוִד אֶל גָּד, צַר לִי מְאֹד, נִפְּלָה נָּא בְיַד יהוה,

《 of HASHEM, 〈 into the hand 〈 now 〈 Let us fall 《 exceedingly, 〈 am I 〈 Dis- tressed 《 Gad, 〈 to 〈 (And David said

כִּי רַבִּים רַחֲמָיו, וּבְיַד אָדָם אַל אֶפְּלָה.[1])

《 let me not fall.) 〈 but into human hands 《 are His mercies, 〈 abundant 〈 for

רַחוּם וְחַנּוּן חָטָאתִי לְפָנֶיךָ. יהוה מָלֵא רַחֲמִים,

《 of mercy, 〈 Who is full 〈 HASHEM, 《 before You. 〈 I have sinned 〈 and gracious One, 〈 O merciful One,

רַחֵם עָלַי וְקַבֵּל תַּחֲנוּנָי.

《 my supplications. 〈 and accept 〈 on me 〈 have mercy

——— תהלים ו:ב-יא / **Psalms 6:2-11** ———

יהוה, אַל בְּאַפְּךָ תוֹכִיחֵנִי, וְאַל בַּחֲמָתְךָ תְיַסְּרֵנִי.

《 chastise me. 〈 in Your wrath 〈 nor 〈 rebuke me, 〈 in Your anger 〈 do not 〈 HASHEM,

חָנֵּנִי יהוה כִּי אֻמְלַל אָנִי, רְפָאֵנִי יהוה כִּי נִבְהֲלוּ

〈 shudder with terror 〈 for 〈 HASHEM, 〈 heal me, 《 am I; 〈 feeble 〈 for 〈 HASHEM, 〈 Favor me,

עֲצָמָי. וְנַפְשִׁי נִבְהֲלָה מְאֹד, וְאַתָּה יהוה עַד מָתָי.

《 when? 〈 until 〈 HASHEM, 〈 and You, 《 utterly, 〈 is terrified 〈 My soul 《 do my bones.

שׁוּבָה יהוה חַלְּצָה נַפְשִׁי, הוֹשִׁיעֵנִי לְמַעַן חַסְדֶּךָ.

《 Your kindness. 〈 as befits 〈 save me 《 my soul; 〈 release 〈 HASHEM, 〈 Desist,

---

(1) *II Samuel* 24:14.

כִּי אֵין בַּמָּוֶת זִכְרֶךָ, בִּשְׁאוֹל מִי יוֹדֶה לָּךְ. יָגַעְתִּי

בְּאַנְחָתִי, אַשְׂחֶה בְכָל לַיְלָה מִטָּתִי, בְּדִמְעָתִי

עַרְשִׂי אַמְסֶה. עָשְׁשָׁה מִכַּעַס עֵינִי, עָתְקָה בְּכָל

צוֹרְרָי. סוּרוּ מִמֶּנִּי כָּל פֹּעֲלֵי אָוֶן, כִּי שָׁמַע יהוה

קוֹל בִּכְיִי. שָׁמַע יהוה תְּחִנָּתִי, יהוה תְּפִלָּתִי יִקָּח.

יֵבְשׁוּ וְיִבָּהֲלוּ מְאֹד כָּל אֹיְבָי, יָשֻׁבוּ יֵבְשׁוּ רָגַע.

מַחֵי וּמַסֵי מֵמִית וּמְחַיֶּה, מַסִּיק מִן שְׁאוֹל

לְחַיֵּי עָלְמָא, בְּרָא כַּד חָטֵי אֲבוּהִי לָקְיֵהּ, אֲבוּהִי

דְחַיֵּס אַסֵּי לִכְאֵבֵהּ. עַבְדָּא דְּמָרִיד נָפִיק בְּקוֹלָר,

מָרֵהּ תָּאִיב וְתַבִּיר קוֹלָרֵהּ.

בְּרָךְ בְּכְרָךְ אֲנָן וְחָטִינָן קַמָּךְ, הָא רָוֵי נַפְשִׁין

בְּגִידִין מְרִירִין אֲנָן עַבְדָּךְ, וּמְרוֹדִינָן קַמָּךְ,

הָא בְּבִזְתָא, הָא בְּשִׁבְיָא, הָא בְּמַלְקִיּוּתָא.

בְּמָטוּ מִנָּךְ בְּרַחֲמָךְ דִּנְפִישִׁין, אַסִי לִכְאֵבִין
⟨ the pains ⟨ heal ⟨ that is ⟨ in Your ⟨ of You, ⟨ We beg
abundant, compassion

דְּתִקּוֹף עֲלָן, עַד דְּלָא נֶהֱוֵי גְּמִירָא בְּשִׁבְיָא.
≫ in captivity. ⟨ completely ⟨ we are not ⟨ while ⟨ us, ⟨ that have
annihilated yet overwhelmed

SELICHAH 75 / סליחה עה
(תחנה)

ALL:

מֶלֶךְ מַלְכִים* רָם עַל רָמִים.
≫ the high, ⟨ above ⟨ high ⟨ of kings,* ⟨ King

שׁוֹכֵן שְׁחָקִים וְיוֹשֵׁב בַּמְּרוֹמִים.
≫ in the heights, ⟨ and sits ⟨ in heaven ⟨ Who dwells

הַמְּהֻלָּל וְהַמְּשֻׁבָּח לְעוֹלְמֵי עוֹלָמִים.
≫ and ever, ⟨ for ever ⟨ and praised ⟨ Who is lauded

בָּרוּךְ וּמְבֹרָךְ בְּפִי כָּל יְקוּמִים.
≫ living ⟨ of ⟨ by the ⟨ and blessed ⟨ blessed
creatures: all mouth [is He]

רְאֵה בְּעָנוּי אֲנוּנִים וַעֲגוּמִים.
≫ and ⟨ of the ⟨ the ⟨ See
despondent; mourning affliction

שׁוּר נָא בְּשִׁפְלוּת מְעוּטֵי עַמִּים.[1]
≫ among peoples, ⟨ of the smallest ⟨ at the lowliness ⟨ please ⟨ look

מְפֻזָּרִים וּמְפֹרָדִים בֵּין כָּל הָאֻמִּים.[2]
≫ the nations, ⟨ all ⟨ among ⟨ and dispersed ⟨ scattered

וּבְבֹשֶׁת וּכְלִמָּה נֶחְפָּרִים וְנִכְלָמִים.
≫ and humiliated. ⟨ they are ⟨ and ⟨ with shame
disgraced humiliation

אֲבֵלִים וּבְדוּדִים נְזוּפִים וְנִזְעָמִים.
≫ and angrily ⟨ reprimanded, ⟨ alone, ⟨ Mourning,
spurned,

---

(1) Cf. *Deuteronomy* 7:7. (2) Cf. *Esther* 3:8.

᠁ **מֶלֶךְ מַלְכִים** — *King of kings.* The acrostic
spells the *paytan's* name — מֹשֶׁה בַּר שְׁמוּאֵל
בַּר אַבְשָׁלוֹם חֲזַק וֶאֱמָץ, *Moshe bar Shmuel*

*bar Avshalom, may he be strong and
persevere.* Nothing more is known about
him.

לְמַכִּים נְתוּנִים גֵּוְיָם לְמַהֲלֻמִים.[1]

《 to body blows; ⟨ their ⟨ given over, ⟨ to those
backs who beat them

בַּבְּקֶר מִי יִתֵּן עֶרֶב נוֹאֲמִים.

《 they say, ⟨ that it were ⟨ could ⟨ Who 《 in the
evening! grant morning,

רֶמֶשׁ אוֹמְרִים מִי יְקָרֵב אוֹר יָמִים.[2]

《 of the ⟨ the ⟨ could bring ⟨ Who 《 they say, ⟨ and at
day! light sooner dusk

אֵין לָהֶם מְנוּחָה וְשֶׁקֶט וּשְׁלוּמִים.

⟨ or peace ⟨ or quiet ⟨ rest ⟨ for ⟨ There
them is not

בַּמֶּה לְהִתְנַחֵם וְלִמְצֹא תַנְחוּמִים.

《 consolation. ⟨ and to find ⟨ to take comfort ⟨ in which

שָׁלוֹם מְצַפִּים וְהִנָּם נִלְחָמִים.

《 battling, ⟨ but find ⟨ they look ⟨ To peace
themselves forward,

לְטוֹבָה מְקַוִּים וְהִנֵּה רְעַ תַּשְׁלוּמִים.[3]

《 they are paid. ⟨ with ⟨ and 《 they hope, ⟨ for good
bad indeed [times]

וַתִּבְחַר נַפְשָׁם מִיתַת רְדוּמִים.[4]

《 slumber. ⟨ death's ⟨ do their souls ⟨ Choose

מַה נִּתְאוֹנֵן וּמַה נֹּאמַר וַעֲוֹנוֹתֵינוּ גוֹרְמִים.

《 are the ⟨ When our 《 can we ⟨ What 《 can we ⟨ How
cause! own sins say? complain?

חָטָאנוּ רָשַׁעְנוּ סַרְנוּ מֵחֻקֶּיךָ הַנְּעִימִים.

《 that are ⟨ from Your ⟨ we have 《 we have 《 We have
pleasant. decrees turned been sinned,
away wicked,

זְכֹר רַחֲמֶיךָ יהוה וַחֲסָדֶיךָ הָעֲצוּמִים.[5]

《 that are ⟨ and Your ⟨ HASHEM, ⟨ Your ⟨ Re-
powerful. kindnesses mercies, member

קוּמָה וְהִמָּלֵא עָלֵינוּ רַחֲמִים.

《 with mercy, ⟨ for us ⟨ and fill ⟨ Arise,
Yourself

---

(1) Cf. *Isaiah* 50:6. (2) Cf. *Deuteronomy* 28:67. (3) Cf. *Jeremiah* 8:15. (4) Cf. *Job* 7:15. (5) Cf. *Psalms* 25:6.

וְקַבֵּץ פְּזוּרֵינוּ מֵאֲרָצוֹת וְיַמִּים.
⟨⟨ and the ⟨ from the lands ⟨ our scattered ⟨ and
seas. people gather

אֲשֶׁר מָכַרְתָּ חִנָּם לַאֲדוֹמִים.
⟨⟨ to the Edomites, ⟨ for ⟨ You sold ⟨ Those
naught whom

מַהֵר לְגָאֳלָם בְּלֹא כֶסֶף וְדָמִים.[1]
⟨⟨ or price. ⟨ money ⟨ for no ⟨ to redeem ⟨ hasten
them

צַוֵּה יְשׁוּעוֹת יַעֲקֹב,[2] הַצּוּר תָּמִים.
⟨⟨ that is ⟨ O Rock ⟨⟨ for Jacob, ⟨ the ⟨Command
Perfect, salvations

כִּי לְךָ אֲדֹנָי הַסְּלִיחוֹת וְהָרַחֲמִים.[3]
⟨⟨ and mercy. ⟨ are forgiveness ⟨ O Lord, ⟨ Yours, ⟨ for

ALL:

מַכְנִיסֵי רַחֲמִים, הַכְנִיסוּ רַחֲמֵינוּ, לִפְנֵי בַּעַל
⟨ the ⟨ before ⟨ our [plea for] ⟨ may you ⟨ [pleas for] mercy, ⟨ O you who
Master mercy usher in usher in

הָרַחֲמִים. מַשְׁמִיעֵי תְפִלָּה, הַשְׁמִיעוּ תְפִלָּתֵנוּ, לִפְנֵי
⟨ before ⟨ of our prayer ⟨ may you aid ⟨⟨ of prayer, ⟨ O you who aid ⟨⟨ of mercy.
the hearing the hearing

שׁוֹמֵעַ תְּפִלָּה. מַשְׁמִיעֵי צְעָקָה, הַשְׁמִיעוּ צַעֲקָתֵנוּ,
⟨ of our ⟨ may you aid ⟨⟨ of outcries, ⟨ O you who aid ⟨⟨ of ⟨ the Hearer
outcries the hearing the hearing prayer.

לִפְנֵי שׁוֹמֵעַ צְעָקָה. מַכְנִיסֵי דִמְעָה, הַכְנִיסוּ
⟨ may you ⟨⟨ tears, ⟨ O you who ⟨⟨ of outcries. ⟨ the Hearer ⟨ before
usher in usher in

דִמְעוֹתֵינוּ, לִפְנֵי מֶלֶךְ מִתְרַצֶּה בִּדְמָעוֹת.
⟨⟨ through tears. ⟨ Who is appeased ⟨ the King ⟨ before ⟨ our tears

הִשְׁתַּדְּלוּ וְהַרְבּוּ תְּחִנָּה וּבַקָּשָׁה, לִפְנֵי מֶלֶךְ אֵל
⟨ God, ⟨ the King, ⟨ before ⟨ and pleas ⟨ supplications ⟨ and ⟨ Exert
intensify yourselves

רָם וְנִשָּׂא. הַזְכִּירוּ לְפָנָיו, הַשְׁמִיעוּ לְפָנָיו תּוֹרָה
⟨ the ⟨ before ⟨ aid to ⟨⟨ before ⟨ Mention ⟨⟨ and ⟨ exalted
Torah Him, be heard Him, uplifted.

(1) Cf. *Isaiah* 52:3; see commentary to *Selichah* 11, s.v. לִמְכוּרֵי חִנָּם. (2) *Psalms* 44:5. (3) Cf. *Daniel* 9:9.

וּמַעֲשִׂים טוֹבִים שֶׁל שׁוֹכְנֵי עָפָר.

in the dust. » [the Patriarchs and Matriarchs] who dwell ‹ of ‹ that are good ‹ and the deeds

יִזְכֹּר אַהֲבָתָם וִיחַיֶּה זַרְעָם, שֶׁלֹּא תֹאבַד שְׁאֵרִית

shall the remnant ‹ lost ‹ so that not ‹ to their offspring, ‹ and grant life ‹ their love ‹ May He remember

יַעֲקֹב. כִּי צֹאן רוֹעֵה נֶאֱמָן הָיָה לְחֶרְפָּה,

a disgrace; » has become ‹ who is faithful [Moses] ‹ of the shepherd ‹ the flock ‹ For ‹ of Jacob be. »

יִשְׂרָאֵל גּוֹי אֶחָד לְמָשָׁל וְלִשְׁנִינָה.

and a simile. » a parable ‹ that is unique, » the nation ‹ Israel, »

מַהֵר עֲנֵנוּ אֱלֹהֵי יִשְׁעֵנוּ, וּפְדֵנוּ מִכָּל גְּזֵרוֹת קָשׁוֹת

that are harsh; » decrees ‹ from all ‹ and redeem us ‹ of our salvation, ‹ O God ‹ answer us, ‹ Swiftly ‹

וְהוֹשִׁיעָה בְּרַחֲמֶיךָ הָרַבִּים, מְשִׁיחַ צִדְקֶךָ וְעַמֶּךָ.

and Your people. » Your righteous anointed one ‹ that is abundant, ‹ in Your mercy ‹ and may You save, »

מָרָן דְּבִשְׁמַיָּא לָךְ מִתְחַנְּנַן, כְּבַר שְׁבִיָּא דְּמִתְחַנַּן

who supplicates ‹ in captivity ‹ as one » do we ‹ to You » Who is in heaven, » Our Master ‹

לִשְׁבוּיֵהּ. כֻּלְּהוֹן בְּנֵי שְׁבִיָּא בְּכַסְפָּא מִתְפָּרְקִין,

are redeemed, » through money ‹ in captivity, ‹ those ‹ [for] all » before his captors; »

וְעַמָּךְ יִשְׂרָאֵל בְּרַחֲמֵי וּבְתַחֲנוּנֵי, הַב לָן שְׁאִילְתִּין

our requests ‹ us ‹ O » grant ‹ and supplication. ‹ through compassion ‹ Israel ‹ but Your people ‹

וּבְעוּתִין, דְּלָא נֶהְדַּר רֵיקָם מִן קֳדָמָךְ.

before You. » from ‹ emptyhanded ‹ that we not be turned away ‹ and our prayers ‹

מָרָן דְּבִשְׁמַיָּא לָךְ מִתְחַנְּנַן, כְּעַבְדָּא דְּמִתְחַנַּן

who supplicates ‹ as a slave » do we ‹ to You » Who is in heaven, » Our Master ‹

לְמָרֵיהּ, עֲשִׁיקֵי אֲנָן וּבַחֲשׁוֹכָא שָׁרִינָן, מְרִירָן נַפְשִׁין

are [our] ‹ embittered » do we ‹ and in darkness ‹ are we ‹ Oppressed » to his master: ‹ souls

מֵעַקְתִין דְּנְפִישִׁין, חֵילָא לֵית בֵּן לְרַצּוּיָךְ. מָרָן,

‹ Our Master, › « to appease You. › ‹ within us › ‹ is lacking › ‹ Strength › « that is excessive. › ‹ from distress ›

עֲבִיד בְּדִיל קַיָּמָא דִּגְזַרְתָּ עִם אֲבָהָתָנָא.

« our Patriarchs. › ‹ with › ‹ that You established › ‹ of the covenant › ‹ for the sake › ‹ act ›

שׁוֹמֵר יִשְׂרָאֵל, שְׁמוֹר שְׁאֵרִית יִשְׂרָאֵל, וְאַל

‹ let not › ‹ of Israel; › ‹ the remnant › ‹ safeguard › « of Israel, › ‹ O Guardian ›

יֹאבַד יִשְׂרָאֵל, הָאֹמְרִים שְׁמַע יִשְׂרָאֵל.[1]

« O Israel. › ‹ Hear, › ‹ those who proclaim: › « Israel be destroyed — ›

שׁוֹמֵר גּוֹי אֶחָד, שְׁמוֹר שְׁאֵרִית עַם אֶחָד, וְאַל

‹ let not › « that is unique; › ‹ of the people › ‹ the remnant › ‹ safeguard › « that is unique, › ‹ of the nation › ‹ O Guardian ›

יֹאבַד גּוֹי אֶחָד, הַמְּיַחֲדִים שִׁמְךָ, יהוה אֱלֹהֵינוּ

‹ is our God, › ‹ HASHEM › « of Your Name: › ‹ those who proclaim the Oneness › « that is unique, › ‹ the nation › ‹ be destroyed ›

יהוה אֶחָד.

« the One [and Only]! › ‹ HASHEM is ›

שׁוֹמֵר גּוֹי קָדוֹשׁ, שְׁמוֹר שְׁאֵרִית עַם קָדוֹשׁ,

« that is holy; › ‹ of the people › ‹ the remnant › ‹ safeguard › « that is holy, › ‹ of the nation › ‹ O Guardian ›

וְאַל יֹאבַד גּוֹי קָדוֹשׁ, הַמְּשַׁלְּשִׁים בְּשָׁלֹשׁ קְדֻשּׁוֹת

‹ sanctifications › ‹ the threefold › ‹ those who proclaim three times › « that is holy, › ‹ the nation › ‹ be destroyed › ‹ let not ›

לְקָדוֹשׁ.

« to the Holy One. ›

מִתְרַצֶּה בְּרַחֲמִים וּמִתְפַּיֵּס בְּתַחֲנוּנִים, הִתְרַצֵּה

‹ be favorable › « through supplications, › ‹ and Who becomes conciliatory › ‹ through compassion › ‹ You Who becomes favorable ›

וְהִתְפַּיֵּס לְדוֹר עָנִי, כִּי אֵין עוֹזֵר. אָבִינוּ מַלְכֵּנוּ,

« our King, › ‹ Our Father, › « helper. › ‹ there is no › ‹ for › « that is › ‹ to the poor, › ‹ generation › ‹ and be conciliatory ›

---

(1) *Deuteronomy* 6:4.

חָנֵּנוּ וַעֲנֵנוּ, כִּי אֵין בָּנוּ מַעֲשִׂים, עֲשֵׂה עִמָּנוּ

⟨ us ⟨ treat ≪ worthy deeds; ⟨ we have no ⟨ though ⟨ and ⟨ be gracious
answer us, with us

צְדָקָה וָחֶסֶד וְהוֹשִׁיעֵנוּ.

≪ and save us. ⟨ and ⟨ with
kindness, charity

STAND AFTER THE WORDS וַאֲנַחְנוּ לֹא נֵדַע UNTIL CONCLUSION OF THE PARAGRAPH.

וַאֲנַחְנוּ לֹא נֵדַע מַה נַּעֲשֶׂה, כִּי עָלֶיךָ עֵינֵינוּ.[1]

≪ are our ⟨ upon ⟨ rather, ≪ we should ⟨ what ⟨ know not ⟨ We
eyes. You do,

זְכֹר רַחֲמֶיךָ יהוה וַחֲסָדֶיךָ, כִּי מֵעוֹלָם הֵמָּה. יְהִי[2]

⟨ May ≪ are they. ⟨ eternal ⟨ for ⟨ and Your ⟨ Hashem, ⟨ Your ⟨ Remem-
kindnesses, mercies, ber

חַסְדְּךָ יהוה עָלֵינוּ, כַּאֲשֶׁר יִחַלְנוּ לָךְ.[3] אַל תִּזְכָּר

⟨ recall ⟨ Do not ≪ You. ⟨ we ⟨ just as ≪ be ⟨ Hashem, ⟨ Your
awaited upon us, kindness,

לָנוּ עֲוֹנוֹת רִאשׁוֹנִים, מַהֵר יְקַדְּמוּנוּ רַחֲמֶיךָ, כִּי

⟨ for ≪ may Your ⟨ advance to ⟨ swiftly ≪ of the ancients; ⟨ the sins ⟨ against
mercies, meet us us

דַלּוֹנוּ מְאֹד.[4] עָזְרֵנוּ בְּשֵׁם יהוה, עֹשֵׂה שָׁמָיִם

⟨ of ⟨ Maker ≪ of Hashem, ⟨ is through ≪ Our help ≪ exceed- ⟨ we have
heaven the Name ingly. become
impoverished

וָאָרֶץ.[5] חָנֵּנוּ יהוה חָנֵּנוּ, כִּי רַב שָׂבַעְנוּ בוּז.[6] בְּרֹגֶז

≪ Amid ≪ with ⟨ sated ⟨ we are ⟨ for ≪ favor us, ⟨ Hashem, ⟨ Favor us, ≪ and earth.
wrath, contempt. fully

רַחֵם תִּזְכּוֹר.[7] בְּרֹגֶז עֲקֵדָה תִּזְכּוֹר. בְּרֹגֶז תְּמִימוֹת

⟨ the perfect ≪ Amid ≪ You should ⟨ the binding ≪ Amid ≪ You should ⟨ to be
ones wrath, remember! [of Isaac] wrath, remember! merciful

תִּזְכּוֹר. יהוה הוֹשִׁיעָה, הַמֶּלֶךְ יַעֲנֵנוּ בְיוֹם קָרְאֵנוּ.[8]

≪ we call. ⟨ on the ⟨ answer ⟨ May the ≪ save! ⟨ Hashem, ≪ You should
day us King remember!

כִּי הוּא יָדַע יִצְרֵנוּ, זָכוּר כִּי עָפָר אֲנָחְנוּ.[9]

≪ are we. ⟨ dust ⟨ that ≪ He is ≪ our nature, ⟨ knew ⟨ He ⟨ For
mindful

(1) *II Chronicles* 20:12. (2) *Psalms* 25:6. (3) 33:22. (4) 79:8.
(5) 121:2. (6) 123:3. (7) *Habakkuk* 3:2. (8) *Psalms* 20:10. (9) 103:14.

❖ עָזְרֵנוּ אֱלֹהֵי יִשְׁעֵנוּ עַל דְּבַר כְּבוֹד שְׁמֶךָ, וְהַצִּילֵנוּ

⟨ rescue us ⟨⟨ of Your ⟨ of the ⟨ the ⟨ for ⟨ of our ⟨ O God ⟨ Assist us,
Name; glory sake salvation

וְכַפֵּר עַל חַטֹּאתֵינוּ לְמַעַן שְׁמֶךָ.¹

⟨⟨ of Your ⟨ for the ⟨ our sins ⟨ for ⟨ and grant
Name. sake atonement

FULL KADDISH / קדיש שלם

THE *CHAZZAN* RECITES קַדִּישׁ שָׁלֵם, FULL *KADDISH*.

יִתְגַּדַּל וְיִתְקַדַּשׁ שְׁמֵהּ רַבָּא. (.אָמֵן — .Cong) בְּעָלְמָא

⟨ — in the ⟨⟨ (Amen.) ⟨⟨ that is ⟨ may His ⟨ and be ⟨ Grow
world great! — Name sanctified exalted

דִּי בְרָא כִרְעוּתֵהּ. וְיַמְלִיךְ מַלְכוּתֵהּ, וְיַצְמַח פֻּרְקָנֵהּ

⟨ His ⟨ and cause ⟨⟨ to His ⟨ and may He ⟨⟨ according ⟨ He ⟨ that
salvation, to sprout kingship, give reign to His will, created

וִיקָרֵב מְשִׁיחֵהּ. (.אָמֵן — .Cong) בְּחַיֵּיכוֹן וּבְיוֹמֵיכוֹן וּבְחַיֵּי

⟨ and in the ⟨ and in ⟨ in your ⟨⟨ (Amen.) ⟨⟨ His Messiah, ⟨ and bring
lifetimes your days, lifetimes near

דְכָל בֵּית יִשְׂרָאֵל, בַּעֲגָלָא וּבִזְמַן קָרִיב. וְאִמְרוּ: אָמֵן.

⟨⟨Amen. ⟨ Now ⟨⟨ that comes ⟨ and at a ⟨ swiftly ⟨⟨ of Israel, ⟨ Family ⟨ of the
respond: soon. time entire

CONGREGATION RESPONDS:

אָמֵן. יְהֵא שְׁמֵהּ רַבָּא מְבָרַךְ לְעָלַם וּלְעָלְמֵי עָלְמַיָּא.

⟨⟨ and for all eternity. ⟨ forever ⟨ be ⟨ that is ⟨ His ⟨ May ⟨⟨ Amen.
blessed great Name

CHAZZAN CONTINUES:

יְהֵא שְׁמֵהּ רַבָּא מְבָרַךְ לְעָלַם וּלְעָלְמֵי עָלְמַיָּא. יִתְבָּרַךְ

⟨ Blessed, ⟨⟨ and for all eternity. ⟨ forever ⟨ be ⟨ that is ⟨ His ⟨ May
blessed great Name

וְיִשְׁתַּבַּח וְיִתְפָּאַר וְיִתְרוֹמַם וְיִתְנַשֵּׂא וְיִתְהַדָּר וְיִתְעַלֶּה

⟨ elevated, ⟨ honored, ⟨ upraised, ⟨ exalted, ⟨ glorified, ⟨ praised,

וְיִתְהַלָּל שְׁמֵהּ דְּקֻדְשָׁא בְּרִיךְ הוּא (.Cong — בְּרִיךְ הוּא)

⟨⟨ is He ⟨ (Blessed ⟨⟨ is He ⟨ Blessed ⟨ of the Holy ⟨ be the ⟨ and lauded
One, Name

— לְעֵלָּא [וּ]לְעֵלָּא מִכָּל בִּרְכָתָא וְשִׁירָתָא תֻּשְׁבְּחָתָא

⟨ praise ⟨⟨ and song, ⟨ blessing ⟨ any ⟨ exceedingly beyond

וְנֶחֱמָתָא דַּאֲמִירָן בְּעָלְמָא. וְאִמְרוּ: אָמֵן. (.אָמֵן — .Cong)

⟨⟨ (Amen.) ⟨⟨ Amen. ⟨ Now ⟨⟨ in the ⟨ that are ⟨ and
respond: world. uttered consolation

---

(1) *Psalms* 79:9.

CONGREGATION:

(קַבֵּל בְּרַחֲמִים וּבְרָצוֹן אֶת תְּפִלָּתֵנוּ.)

《 our prayers.) 〈 and with 〈 with mercy 《 (Accept
favor

CHAZZAN CONTINUES:

תִּתְקַבֵּל צְלוֹתְהוֹן וּבָעוּתְהוֹן דְּכָל בֵּית יִשְׂרָאֵל קֳדָם

〈 before 〈 Israel 〈 Family 〈 of the 〈 and 〈 the prayers 〈 May
of entire supplications accepted be

אֲבוּהוֹן דִּי בִשְׁמַיָּא. וְאִמְרוּ: אָמֵן. (Cong. — אָמֵן.)

《 (Amen.) 《 Amen. 〈 Now 《 is in 〈 Who 〈 their
respond: Heaven. Father

CONGREGATION:

(יְהִי שֵׁם יהוה מְבֹרָךְ, מֵעַתָּה וְעַד עוֹלָם.[1])

《 eternity.) 〈 until 〈 from 《 be 〈 of 〈 the 《 (Let
this time blessed, HASHEM Name

CHAZZAN CONTINUES:

יְהֵא שְׁלָמָא רַבָּא מִן שְׁמַיָּא וְחַיִּים טוֹבִים עָלֵינוּ וְעַל כָּל

〈 all 〈 and 〈 upon us 〈 that is 〈 and life 〈 Heaven 〈 from 〈 that is 〈 peace 〈 May
upon good, there be

יִשְׂרָאֵל. וְאִמְרוּ: אָמֵן. (Cong. — אָמֵן.)

《 (Amen.) 《 Amen. 〈 Now respond: 《 Israel.

CONGREGATION:

(עֶזְרִי מֵעִם יהוה, עֹשֵׂה שָׁמַיִם וָאָרֶץ.[2])

《 and 〈 of 〈 Maker 《 HASHEM, 〈 is 〈 (My
earth.) heaven from help

CHAZZAN BOWS; TAKES THREE STEPS BACK. BOWS LEFT AND SAYS "… עֹשֶׂה שָׁלוֹם, *HE WHO MAKES PEACE…"; BOWS RIGHT AND SAYS "…* הוּא, *MAY HE…"; BOWS FORWARD AND SAYS "…* וְעַל כָּל יִשְׂרָאֵל, AND UPON ALL ISRAEL…"; REMAINS IN PLACE FOR A FEW MOMENTS, THEN TAKES THREE STEPS FORWARD.*

עֹשֶׂה [הַ]שָּׁלוֹם בִּמְרוֹמָיו, הוּא יַעֲשֶׂה שָׁלוֹם עָלֵינוּ, וְעַל

〈 and 〈 upon us, 〈 peace 〈 make 〈 may 《 in His 〈 [the] peace 〈 He Who
upon He heights, makes

כָּל יִשְׂרָאֵל. וְאִמְרוּ: אָמֵן. (Cong. — אָמֵן.)

《 (Amen.) 《 Amen. 〈 Now 《 Israel. 〈 all
respond:

---

(1) *Psalms* 113:2. (2) 121:2.

**WHEN YOM KIPPUR FALLS ON MONDAY OR THURSDAY, SOME CONGREGATIONS
REVERSE THE ORDER OF THE FOURTH AND FIFTH DAYS OF REPENTANCE.**

יום חמישי של עשרת ימי תשובה

✣ FIFTH DAY OF REPENTANCE ✣

אַשְׁרֵי יוֹשְׁבֵי בֵיתֶךָ, עוֹד יְהַלְלוּךָ סֶּלָה.¹ אַשְׁרֵי
⟨ Praise-   ⟨ Selah.   ⟨ they will   ⟨ con-   ⟨ in Your   ⟨ are those   ⟨ Praiseworthy
worthy   praise You,   tinually   house,   who dwell

הָעָם שֶׁכָּכָה לּוֹ, אַשְׁרֵי הָעָם שֶׁיהוה אֱלֹהָיו.²
⟨ is their   ⟨ that   ⟨ is the   ⟨ praise-   ⟨ is   ⟨ that such   ⟨ is the
God.   HASHEM   people   worthy   their lot;   people

———— תהלים קמה / Psalm 145 ————

תְּהִלָּה לְדָוִד, אֲרוֹמִמְךָ אֱלוֹהַי הַמֶּלֶךְ, וַאֲבָרְכָה
⟨ and I   ⟨ the King,   ⟨ my God   ⟨ I will exalt You,   ⟨ by David: ⟨ A psalm of
will bless   praise

שִׁמְךָ לְעוֹלָם וָעֶד. בְּכָל יוֹם אֲבָרְכֶךָ, וַאֲהַלְלָה שִׁמְךָ
⟨ Your   ⟨ and I   ⟨ I will   ⟨ day   ⟨ Every   ⟨ and   ⟨ for ever   ⟨ Your
Name   will laud   bless You,   ever.   Name

לְעוֹלָם וָעֶד. גָּדוֹל יהוה וּמְהֻלָּל מְאֹד, וְלִגְדֻלָּתוֹ
⟨ and His   ⟨ exceedingly,   ⟨ and   ⟨ is   ⟨ Great   ⟨ and   ⟨ forever
greatness   lauded   HASHEM   ever.

אֵין חֵקֶר. דּוֹר לְדוֹר יְשַׁבַּח מַעֲשֶׂיךָ, וּגְבוּרֹתֶיךָ יַגִּידוּ.
⟨ they will   ⟨ and Your   ⟨ Your   ⟨ will   ⟨ to   ⟨ Gen-   ⟨ is beyond
recount.   mighty deeds   actions,   praise   generation   eration   investigation.

הֲדַר כְּבוֹד הוֹדֶךָ, וְדִבְרֵי נִפְלְאֹתֶיךָ אָשִׂיחָה. וֶעֱזוּז
⟨ And of   ⟨ I shall   ⟨ that are   ⟨ and Your   ⟨ of Your   ⟨ glory   ⟨ The
the might   discuss.   wondrous   deeds   majesty,   splendrous

נוֹרְאֹתֶיךָ יֹאמֵרוּ, וּגְדוּלָּתְךָ אֲסַפְּרֶנָּה. זֵכֶר רַב טוּבְךָ
⟨ of Your abun-   ⟨ A recol-   ⟨ I shall   ⟨ and Your   ⟨ they will   ⟨ of Your
dant goodness   lection   relate.   greatness   speak,   awesome deeds

יַבִּיעוּ, וְצִדְקָתְךָ יְרַנֵּנוּ. חַנּוּן וְרַחוּם יהוה, אֶרֶךְ אַפַּיִם
⟨ to   ⟨ slow   ⟨ is   ⟨ and   ⟨ Gracious   ⟨ they will   ⟨ and of Your   ⟨ they
anger,   HASHEM,   merciful   sing joyfully.   righteousness   will utter,

וּגְדָל חָסֶד. טוֹב יהוה לַכֹּל, וְרַחֲמָיו עַל כָּל מַעֲשָׂיו.
⟨ His   ⟨ all   ⟨ are   ⟨ His   ⟨ to all;   ⟨ HASHEM   ⟨ in [bestowing]   ⟨ and
creations.   on   mercies   is good   kindness.   great

————
(1) *Psalms* 84:5. (2) 144:15.

יוֹדוּךָ יהוה כָּל מַעֲשֶׂיךָ, וַחֲסִידֶיךָ יְבָרְכוּכָה. כְּבוֹד

‹ Of the glory » will bless You. ‹ and Your devout ones » Your creations — ‹ — all «HASHEM ‹ They will thank You,

מַלְכוּתְךָ יֹאמֵרוּ, וּגְבוּרָתְךָ יְדַבֵּרוּ. לְהוֹדִיעַ לִבְנֵי הָאָדָם

‹ mankind ‹ To inform » they will declare. ‹ and of Your power » they will speak, ‹ of Your kingdom

גְּבוּרֹתָיו, וּכְבוֹד הֲדַר מַלְכוּתוֹ. מַלְכוּתְךָ מַלְכוּת כָּל

‹ [span- ning] all ‹ is a kingdom ‹ Your kingdom » of His kingdom. ‹ splendor ‹ and of the glorious « of His mighty deeds,

עֹלָמִים, וּמֶמְשַׁלְתְּךָ בְּכָל דּוֹר וָדֹר. סוֹמֵךְ יהוה

‹ HASHEM supports » after generation. ‹ gen- eration ‹ is throughout ‹ and Your dominion « eternities,

לְכָל הַנֹּפְלִים, וְזוֹקֵף לְכָל הַכְּפוּפִים. עֵינֵי כֹל

‹ of all ‹ The eyes » those who are bent. ‹ all ‹ and straightens « those who are fallen ‹ all

אֵלֶיךָ יְשַׂבֵּרוּ, וְאַתָּה נוֹתֵן לָהֶם אֶת אָכְלָם בְּעִתּוֹ.

« in its proper time. ‹ their food ‹ them ‹ give ‹ and You « do look with hope, ‹ to You

CONCENTRATE INTENTLY WHILE RECITING THE VERSE פּוֹתֵחַ, *YOU OPEN.*

פּוֹתֵחַ אֶת יָדֶךָ, וּמַשְׂבִּיעַ לְכָל חַי רָצוֹן. ❖ צַדִּיק

‹ Righteous « [with its] desire. ‹ living thing ‹ every ‹ and satisfy « Your hand, ‹ You open

יהוה בְּכָל דְּרָכָיו, וְחָסִיד בְּכָל מַעֲשָׂיו. קָרוֹב יהוה

‹ is HASHEM ‹ Close « His deeds. ‹ in all ‹ and magnanimous « His ways, ‹ in all ‹ is HASHEM

לְכָל קֹרְאָיו, לְכֹל אֲשֶׁר יִקְרָאֻהוּ בֶאֱמֶת. רְצוֹן יְרֵאָיו

‹ of those who fear Him ‹ The will « sincerely. ‹ call upon Him ‹ who ‹ to all « who call upon Him, ‹ to all

יַעֲשֶׂה, וְאֶת שַׁוְעָתָם יִשְׁמַע וְיוֹשִׁיעֵם. שׁוֹמֵר יהוה

‹ HASHEM protects « and He will save them. ‹ He will hear, ‹ and their cry « He will do;

אֶת כָּל אֹהֲבָיו, וְאֵת כָּל הָרְשָׁעִים יַשְׁמִיד. תְּהִלַּת

‹ The praise « He will destroy. ‹ the wicked ‹ but all « who love Him; ‹ all

יהוה יְדַבֶּר פִּי, וִיבָרֵךְ כָּל בָּשָׂר שֵׁם קָדְשׁוֹ לְעוֹלָם

‹ for ever ‹ of His Holiness ‹ the Name ‹ flesh ‹ may all ‹ and bless « may my mouth declare, ‹ of HASHEM

וָעֶד. וַאֲנַחְנוּ נְבָרֵךְ יָהּ מֵעַתָּה וְעַד עוֹלָם; הַלְלוּיָהּ.[1]

《 Halleluyah! 《 eternity. 〈 until 〈 from this time 〈 God 〈 will bless 〈 But we 《 and ever.

THE *CHAZZAN* RECITES חֲצִי קַדִּישׁ, HALF-*KADDISH*:

יִתְגַּדַּל וְיִתְקַדַּשׁ שְׁמֵהּ רַבָּא. (אָמֵן. — Cong.) בְּעָלְמָא

〈 — in the world 《 (Amen.) 《 that is great! — 〈 may His Name 〈 and be sanctified 〈 Grow exalted

דִּי בְרָא כִרְעוּתֵהּ. וְיַמְלִיךְ מַלְכוּתֵהּ, וְיַצְמַח פֻּרְקָנֵהּ

〈 His salvation, 〈 and cause to sprout 《 to His kingship, 〈 and may He give reign 《 according to His will, 〈 He created 〈 that

וִיקָרֵב מְשִׁיחֵהּ. (אָמֵן. — Cong.) בְּחַיֵּיכוֹן וּבְיוֹמֵיכוֹן וּבְחַיֵּי

〈 and in the lifetimes 〈 and in your days, 〈 in your lifetimes 《 (Amen.) 《 His Messiah, 〈 and bring near

דְכָל בֵּית יִשְׂרָאֵל, בַּעֲגָלָא וּבִזְמַן קָרִיב. וְאִמְרוּ: אָמֵן.

《Amen. 〈 Now respond: 《 that comes soon. 〈 and at a time 〈 swiftly 《 of Israel, 〈 Family 〈 of the entire

CONGREGATION RESPONDS:

אָמֵן. יְהֵא שְׁמֵהּ רַבָּא מְבָרַךְ לְעָלַם וּלְעָלְמֵי עָלְמַיָּא.

《 and for all eternity. 〈 forever 〈 be blessed 〈 that is great 〈 His Name 〈 May 《 Amen.

CHAZZAN CONTINUES:

יְהֵא שְׁמֵהּ רַבָּא מְבָרַךְ לְעָלַם וּלְעָלְמֵי עָלְמַיָּא. יִתְבָּרַךְ

〈 Blessed, 《 and for all eternity. 〈 forever 〈 be blessed 〈 that is great 〈 His Name 〈 May

וְיִשְׁתַּבַּח וְיִתְפָּאַר וְיִתְרוֹמַם וְיִתְנַשֵּׂא וְיִתְהַדָּר וְיִתְעַלֶּה

〈 elevated, 〈 honored, 〈 upraised, 〈 exalted, 〈 glorified, 〈 praised,

וְיִתְהַלָּל שְׁמֵהּ דְּקֻדְשָׁא בְּרִיךְ הוּא (בְּרִיךְ הוּא — Cong.)

《is He) 〈 (Blessed 《 is He 〈 Blessed 〈 of the Holy One, 〈 be the Name 〈 and lauded

— לְעֵלָּא [וּ]לְעֵלָּא מִכָּל בִּרְכָתָא וְשִׁירָתָא תֻּשְׁבְּחָתָא

〈 praise 《 and song, 〈 blessing 〈 any 〈 exceedingly beyond

וְנֶחֱמָתָא דַּאֲמִירָן בְּעָלְמָא. וְאִמְרוּ: אָמֵן. (אָמֵן. — Cong.)

《 (Amen.) 《 Amen. 〈 Now respond: 《 in the world. 〈 that are uttered 〈 and consolation

ALL:

לְךָ יהוה הַצְּדָקָה, וְלָנוּ בֹּשֶׁת הַפָּנִים.[2] מַה

《What 《 is shamefacedness. 〈 and ours 《 is the righteousness, 〈 O Lord, 〈 Yours,

(1) *Psalms* 115:18. (2) *Daniel* 9:7.

נִתְאוֹנֵן,¹ מַה נֹּאמַר, מַה נְּדַבֵּר, וּמַה נִּצְטַדָּק.²

‹ justification can we offer? ‹ What ≪ can we declare? ‹ What ≪ can we say? ‹ What ≪ complaint can we make?

נַחְפְּשָׂה דְרָכֵינוּ וְנַחְקְרָה, וְנָשׁוּבָה אֵלֶיךָ, כִּי יְמִינְךָ³

‹ Your right hand ‹ for ≪ to You, ‹ and return ‹ and investigate them, ‹ our ways ‹ Let us examine

פְּשׁוּטָה לְקַבֵּל שָׁבִים. לֹא בְחֶסֶד וְלֹא בְמַעֲשִׂים

‹ with [merit for good] deeds ‹ nor ‹ with [merit] for kindness ‹ Neither ≪ those who return. ‹ to accept ‹ is extended

בָאנוּ לְפָנֶיךָ, כְּדַלִּים וּכְרָשִׁים דָּפַקְנוּ דְלָתֶיךָ.

≪ on Your doors. ‹ we have knocked ‹ and as destitute people ‹ but as paupers ≪ before You; ‹ do we come

דְלָתֶיךָ דָּפַקְנוּ רַחוּם וְחַנּוּן, נָא אַל תְּשִׁיבֵנוּ

‹ turn us away ‹ do not ‹ Please ≪ and Gracious One. ‹ O Compassionate One ‹ we have knocked, ≪ On Your doors

רֵיקָם מִלְּפָנֶיךָ. מִלְּפָנֶיךָ מַלְכֵּנוּ רֵיקָם אַל תְּשִׁיבֵנוּ,

≪ turn us away, ‹ do not ‹ empty-handed ‹ Our King, ‹ From before You, ‹ from before You. ‹ empty-handed

כִּי אַתָּה שׁוֹמֵעַ תְּפִלָּה.

≪ prayer. ‹ Who hears ‹ You are ‹ for the One

שֹׁמֵעַ תְּפִלָּה, עָדֶיךָ כָּל בָּשָׂר יָבֹאוּ.⁴ יָבוֹא

‹ Come ≪ will come. ‹ flesh ‹ all ‹ unto You ≪ prayer, ‹ You Who hears

כָל בָּשָׂר לְהִשְׁתַּחֲוֹת לְפָנֶיךָ יהוה.⁵ יָבֹאוּ וְיִשְׁתַּחֲווּ

‹ and bow down ‹ They will come ≪ O HASHEM. ‹ before You, ‹ to bow down ‹ will all flesh

לְפָנֶיךָ אֲדֹנָי, וִיכַבְּדוּ לִשְׁמֶךָ.⁶ בֹּאוּ נִשְׁתַּחֲוֶה וְנִכְרָעָה,

≪ and bow, ‹ Let us prostrate ourselves ‹ Come! ≪ to Your Name. ‹ and they will show honor ≪ O Lord, ‹ before You,

נִבְרְכָה לִפְנֵי יהוה עֹשֵׂנוּ.⁷ נָבוֹאָה לְמִשְׁכְּנוֹתָיו,

≪ to His Tabernacles, ‹ Let us come ≪ our Maker. ‹ HASHEM, ‹ before ‹ let us kneel

נִשְׁתַּחֲוֶה לַהֲדֹם רַגְלָיו.⁸ בֹּאוּ שְׁעָרָיו בְּתוֹדָה,

≪ with thanksgiving, ‹ His gates ‹ Enter ≪ for His feet. ‹ at the stool ‹ let us prostrate ourselves

---

(1) Cf. *Lamentations* 3:39. (2) Cf. *Genesis* 44:16. (3) Cf. *Lamentations* 3:40.
(4) *Psalms* 65:3. (5) Cf. *Isaiah* 66:23. (6) *Psalms* 86:9. (7) 95:6. (8) 132:7.

חֲצֵרֹתָיו בִּתְהִלָּה, הוֹדוּ לוֹ בָּרְכוּ שְׁמוֹ.¹ וַאֲנַחְנוּ

〈 But we, 《 His 〈 bless 《 to 〈 give 《 with praise; 〈 His courtyards
Name. Him, thanks

בְּרֹב חַסְדְּךָ נָבוֹא בֵיתֶךָ, נִשְׁתַּחֲוֶה אֶל הֵיכַל קָדְשְׁךָ

〈 Your Holy 〈 toward 〈 we will pros- 《 Your 〈 will we 〈 of Your 〈 through the
Sanctuary trate ourselves House; enter kindness abundance

בְּיִרְאָתֶךָ.² הִנֵּה בָּרְכוּ אֶת יהוה כָּל עַבְדֵי יהוה,

〈 of 〈 you 〈 all 〈 HASHEM, 〈 bless 《 Indeed, 《 in awe
HASHEM, servants of You.

הָעֹמְדִים בְּבֵית יהוה בַּלֵּילוֹת.³ שְׂאוּ יְדֵיכֶם קֹדֶשׁ

〈 in the 〈 your 〈 Lift 《 in the nights. 〈 of 〈 in the 〈 who stand
Sanctuary hands HASHEM House

וּבָרְכוּ אֶת יהוה.⁴ רוֹמְמוּ יהוה אֱלֹהֵינוּ, וְהִשְׁתַּחֲווּ

〈 and bow down 〈 our God, 〈 HASHEM, 〈 Exalt 《 HASHEM. 〈 and bless

לַהֲדֹם רַגְלָיו, קָדוֹשׁ הוּא.⁵ רוֹמְמוּ יהוה אֱלֹהֵינוּ,

〈 our God, 〈 HASHEM, 〈 Exalt 《 is He! 〈 holy 《 at His footstool;

וְהִשְׁתַּחֲווּ לְהַר קָדְשׁוֹ, כִּי קָדוֹשׁ יהוה אֱלֹהֵינוּ.⁶

《 our God. 〈 is 〈 holy 〈 for 《 of His 〈 at the 〈 and bow
HASHEM, Holiness; Mount

הִשְׁתַּחֲווּ לַיהוה בְּהַדְרַת קֹדֶשׁ, חִילוּ מִפָּנָיו כָּל

〈 every- 〈 before 〈 tremble 《 of 〈 in the 〈 before 〈 Bow down
one Him, holiness; splendor HASHEM

הָאָרֶץ.⁷ נִשְׁתַּחֲוֶה אֶל הֵיכַל קָדְשְׁךָ וְנוֹדֶה אֶת שְׁמֶךָ,

〈 Your Name 〈 and we 《 Your Holy 〈 toward 〈 We will pros- 《 on earth.
will thank Sanctuary, trate ourselves

עַל חַסְדְּךָ וְעַל אֲמִתֶּךָ, כִּי הִגְדַּלְתָּ עַל כָּל שִׁמְךָ

《 Your 〈 — even 《 You have 〈 for 《 Your 〈 and 〈 Your 〈 for
Name — beyond exalted faithfulness; for kindness

אִמְרָתֶךָ.⁸ יהוה אֱלֹהֵי צְבָאוֹת, מִי כָמוֹךָ חֲסִין

〈 O Strong 《 is like 〈 — who 《 of 〈 God 〈 HASHEM, 《 Your promise.
One, You, Legions

יָהּ, וֶאֱמוּנָתְךָ סְבִיבוֹתֶיךָ.⁹ כִּי מִי בַשַּׁחַק יַעֲרֹךְ

〈 can be 〈 in the sky 〈 who 〈 For 《 surrounds You. 〈 and Your 《 God? —
compared faithfulness

לַיהוה, יִדְמֶה לַיהוה בִּבְנֵי אֵלִים.¹⁰ כִּי גָדוֹל אַתָּה

〈 are You 〈 great 〈 For 《 among the angels? 〈 to HASHEM 〈 be likened 《 to HASHEM;

(1) *Psalms* 100:4. (2) Cf. 5:8. (3) 134:1. (4) 134:2. (5) 99:5. (6) 99:9. (7) 96:9. (8) Cf. 138:2. (9) 89:9. (10) 89:7.

וְעוֹשֶׂה נִפְלָאוֹת, אַתָּה אֱלֹהִים לְבַדֶּךָ.[1] כִּי גָדוֹל

‹ great ‹ For ‹‹ alone. ‹ O God, ‹ You, ‹‹ of wonders; ‹ and a worker

מֵעַל שָׁמַיִם חַסְדֶּךָ, וְעַד שְׁחָקִים אֲמִתֶּךָ.[2] גָּדוֹל

‹ Great ‹‹ is Your ‹ the upper ‹ and ‹‹ is Your ‹ the very ‹ above
     truth.   heights   until   kindness,   heavens

יהוה וּמְהֻלָּל מְאֹד, וְלִגְדֻלָּתוֹ אֵין חֵקֶר. (כִּי) גָדוֹל

‹ great ‹ (For) ‹‹ investiga- ‹ is ‹ and His ‹‹ exceed- ‹ and ‹ is
           tion.   beyond   greatness   ingly,   lauded   HASHEM

יהוה וּמְהֻלָּל מְאֹד, נוֹרָא הוּא עַל כָּל אֱלֹהִים.[4] כִּי

‹ For ‹‹ heavenly ‹ all ‹ above ‹ is He ‹ awesome ‹‹ exceed- ‹ and ‹ is
    powers.   ingly;   lauded   HASHEM

אֵל גָּדוֹל יהוה, וּמֶלֶךְ גָּדוֹל עַל כָּל אֱלֹהִים.[5] אֲשֶׁר

‹ For ‹‹ heavenly ‹ all ‹ above ‹ and a great King ‹‹ is ‹ a great God
    powers.   HASHEM,

מִי אֵל בַּשָּׁמַיִם וּבָאָרֶץ, אֲשֶׁר יַעֲשֶׂה כְמַעֲשֶׂיךָ

‹ like unto ‹ can do ‹ that ‹ or in the ‹ is there in ‹ power ‹ what
Your deeds   earth   the heaven

וְכִגְבוּרֹתֶיךָ.[6] מִי לֹא יִרָאֲךָ מֶלֶךְ הַגּוֹיִם, כִּי לְךָ

‹ to ‹ For ‹‹ of nations? ‹ O King ‹ fear You, ‹ would ‹ Who ‹‹ and like unto Your
You   not   mighty acts?

יָאָתָה, כִּי בְכָל חַכְמֵי הַגּוֹיִם וּבְכָל מַלְכוּתָם מֵאֵין

‹ there is ‹ their ‹ and in all ‹ of the ‹ the wise ‹ among ‹ for ‹‹ [kingship]
none   kingdoms   nations   men   all   befits;

כָּמוֹךָ.[7] מֵאֵין כָּמוֹךָ יהוה, גָּדוֹל אַתָּה וְגָדוֹל שִׁמְךָ

‹ is Your ‹ and great ‹ are You ‹ Great ‹‹ O ‹ like You, ‹ There is ‹‹ like You.
Name   HASHEM!   none

בִּגְבוּרָה.[8] לְךָ זְרוֹעַ עִם גְּבוּרָה, תָּעֹז יָדְךָ תָּרוּם

‹ uplifted ‹‹ is Your ‹ strength- ‹‹ power; ‹ with ‹ is the ‹ Yours ‹‹ in might.
        hand,   ened   arm

יְמִינֶךָ.[9] לְךָ יוֹם, אַף לְךָ לָיְלָה, אַתָּה הֲכִינוֹתָ מָאוֹר

‹ the ‹ prepared ‹ You ‹‹ is the ‹ Yours ‹ also ‹‹ is the ‹ Yours ‹‹ is Your
luminary   night;   day,   right hand.

וָשָׁמֶשׁ.[10] אֲשֶׁר בְּיָדוֹ מֶחְקְרֵי אָרֶץ, וְתוֹעֲפוֹת הָרִים

‹ of the ‹ and the ‹‹ of the ‹ are the hidden ‹ in His ‹ For ‹‹ and the
mountains   summits   earth,   mysteries   power   sun.

---

(1) Psalms 86:10. (2) 108:5. (3) 145:3. (4) 96:4. (5) 95:3. (6) Deuteronomy 3:24.
(7) Jeremiah 10:7. (8) 10:6. (9) Psalms 89:14. (10) 74:16.

לוֹ. ¹ מִי יְמַלֵּל גְּבוּרוֹת יהוה, יַשְׁמִיעַ כָּל תְּהִלָּתוֹ. ²

⟨ of His ⟨ all ⟨ [who] can ⟨ of ⟨ the mighty ⟨ can ⟨ Who ⟨ are
praise?　　　make heard HASHEM;　acts　　express　　　His.

לְךָ יהוה הַגְּדֻלָּה וְהַגְּבוּרָה, וְהַתִּפְאֶרֶת וְהַנֵּצַח

⟨ the ⟨ the glory, ⟨ the strength, ⟨ is the ⟨ HASHEM, ⟨ Yours,
triumph,　　　　　　　　　greatness,

וְהַהוֹד, כִּי כֹל בַּשָּׁמַיִם וּבָאָרֶץ; לְךָ יהוה הַמַּמְלָכָה,

⟨ is the ⟨ HASHEM, ⟨ Yours, ⟨ and on earth ⟨ in ⟨ every- ⟨ for ⟨ and the
kingdom　　　　[is Yours];　heaven　thing　　majesty;

וְהַמִּתְנַשֵּׂא לְכֹל לְרֹאשׁ. ³ לְךָ שָׁמַיִם, אַף לְךָ אָרֶץ,

⟨ is the ⟨ Yours ⟨ also ⟨ are the ⟨ Yours ⟨ leader. ⟨ over ⟨ and the
earth;　　　heavens,　　　　　　every　sovereignty

תֵּבֵל וּמְלֹאָהּ אַתָּה יְסַדְתָּם. ⁴ אַתָּה הִצַּבְתָּ כָּל גְּבוּלוֹת

⟨ the ⟨ all ⟨ established ⟨ You ⟨ founded ⟨ You ⟨ and its ⟨ the
boundaries　　　　them.　　　　　fullness,　world

אָרֶץ, קַיִץ וָחֹרֶף אַתָּה יְצַרְתָּם. ⁵ אַתָּה רִצַּצְתָּ רָאשֵׁי

⟨ the ⟨ crushed ⟨ You ⟨ fashioned ⟨ You ⟨ and ⟨ summer ⟨ of
heads　　　　　them.　　　　winter,　　earth;

לִוְיָתָן, תִּתְּנֶנּוּ מַאֲכָל לְעַם לְצִיִּים. אַתָּה בָקַעְתָּ מַעְיָן

⟨ fountain ⟨ split ⟨ You ⟨ [destined] for ⟨ to the ⟨ as food ⟨ You will ⟨ of
　　open　　　the desolate people　　serve it　Leviathan;
　　　　wilderness.

וָנָחַל, אַתָּה הוֹבַשְׁתָּ נַהֲרוֹת אֵיתָן. ⁶ אַתָּה פוֹרַרְתָּ

⟨ shattered ⟨ You ⟨ that are mighty. ⟨ rivers ⟨ dried ⟨ You ⟨ and stream;

בְעָזְּךָ יָם, שִׁבַּרְתָּ רָאשֵׁי תַנִּינִים עַל הַמָּיִם. ⁷ אַתָּה

⟨ You ⟨ the water. ⟨ upon ⟨ of sea ⟨ the heads ⟨ You ⟨ the ⟨ with Your
　　　　　serpents　smashed　sea;　might

מוֹשֵׁל בְּגֵאוּת הַיָּם, בְּשׂוֹא גַלָּיו אַתָּה תְשַׁבְּחֵם. ⁸

⟨ calm them. ⟨ You ⟨ its ⟨ when it ⟨ of the ⟨ the ⟨ rule
　　　waves,　raises　sea;　grandeur

גָּדוֹל יהוה וּמְהֻלָּל מְאֹד, בְּעִיר אֱלֹהֵינוּ הַר קָדְשׁוֹ. ⁹

⟨ of His ⟨ Mount ⟨ of our God, ⟨ in the ⟨ and much praised, ⟨ is ⟨ Great
Holiness.　　　　City　　　　　　HASHEM

יהוה צְבָאוֹת, אֱלֹהֵי יִשְׂרָאֵל, יוֹשֵׁב הַכְּרֻבִים, אַתָּה

⟨ it is ⟨ upon the ⟨ en- ⟨ of Israel, ⟨ God ⟨ Master of ⟨ HASHEM,
You　Cherubim,　throned　　　　　Legions,

---

(1) *Psalms* 95:4. (2) 106:2. (3) *I Chronicles* 29:11. (4) *Psalms* 89:12.
(5) 74:17. (6) 74:14-15. (7) 74:13. (8) 89:10. (9) 48:2.

הוּא הָאֱלֹהִים לְבַדֶּךָ.¹ אֵל נַעֲרָץ בְּסוֹד קְדוֹשִׁים רַבָּה,

⟨ in the great assemblage ⟨ is ⟨ God ⟨ alone. ⟨ God ⟨ Who
of the holy [angels],   revered   are

וְנוֹרָא עַל כָּל סְבִיבָיו.² וְיוֹדוּ שָׁמַיִם פִּלְאֲךָ יהוה, אַף

⟨ also ⟨ HASHEM, ⟨ Your ⟨ will the ⟨ Acknowl- ⟨ who sur- ⟨ all ⟨ over ⟨ and is
   wonders, heavens edge round Him.   awesome

אֱמוּנָתְךָ בִּקְהַל קְדֹשִׁים.³ לְכוּ נְרַנְּנָה לַיהוה, נָרִיעָה

⟨ let us ⟨ to ⟨ Let us sing ⟨ Come! ⟨ of holy ⟨ in the ⟨ Your
call out   HASHEM, joyfully   ones. assembly faithfulness,

לְצוּר יִשְׁעֵנוּ. נְקַדְּמָה פָנָיו בְּתוֹדָה, בִּזְמִרוֹת נָרִיעַ

⟨ let us ⟨ with praiseful ⟨ with ⟨ Him ⟨ Let us greet ⟨ of our ⟨ to the
call out   songs thanksgiving,   salvation. Rock

לוֹ.⁴ צֶדֶק וּמִשְׁפָּט מְכוֹן כִּסְאֶךָ, חֶסֶד וֶאֱמֶת יְקַדְּמוּ

⟨ precede ⟨ and ⟨ kindness ⟨ of Your ⟨ are the ⟨ and ⟨ Righteous- ⟨ to
   truth   throne; foundation justice ness Him.

פָנֶיךָ.⁵ אֲשֶׁר יַחְדָּו נַמְתִּיק סוֹד, בְּבֵית אֱלֹהִים נְהַלֵּךְ

⟨ let us ⟨ of God ⟨ in the ⟨ counsel; ⟨ let us ⟨ together ⟨ For ⟨ Your coun-
walk   House take sweet   tenance.

בְּרָגֶשׁ.⁶ אֲשֶׁר לוֹ הַיָּם וְהוּא עָשָׂהוּ, וְיַבֶּשֶׁת יָדָיו

⟨ His ⟨ and the ⟨ perfected ⟨ and He ⟨ is the ⟨ His ⟨ For ⟨ in company.
hands dry land, it,   sea

יָצָרוּ.⁷ אֲשֶׁר בְּיָדוֹ נֶפֶשׁ כָּל חָי, וְרוּחַ כָּל בְּשַׂר אִישׁ.⁸

⟨ mankind. ⟨ of all ⟨ and the ⟨ the ⟨ of ⟨ is the ⟨ in His ⟨ For ⟨ fashioned.
   spirit living all soul hand

❖ הַנְּשָׁמָה לָךְ וְהַגּוּף פָּעֳלָךְ, חוּסָה עַל עֲמָלָךְ.

⟨ Your ⟨ on ⟨ take pity ⟨ is Your ⟨ and the ⟨ is ⟨ The soul
labor.   handiwork; body Yours

הַנְּשָׁמָה לָךְ וְהַגּוּף שֶׁלָּךְ, יהוה עֲשֵׂה לְמַעַן שְׁמֶךָ.

⟨ of Your ⟨ for the ⟨ act ⟨ O ⟨ is Yours; ⟨ and the ⟨ is ⟨ The soul
Name. sake   HASHEM,   body Yours

אָתָאנוּ עַל שְׁמֶךָ, יהוה, עֲשֵׂה לְמַעַן שְׁמֶךָ. בַּעֲבוּר

⟨ [act] ⟨ of Your ⟨ for the ⟨ act ⟨ O ⟨ Your ⟨ [relying] ⟨ We have
because of Name; sake   HASHEM; Name, on come

כְּבוֹד שְׁמֶךָ, כִּי אֵל חַנּוּן וְרַחוּם שְׁמֶךָ. לְמַעַן

⟨ For the ⟨ is Your ⟨ and ⟨ Who is ⟨ God ⟨ for ⟨ of Your ⟨ the glory
sake Name. Merciful Gracious   Name,

(1) Isaiah 37:16. (2) Psalms 89:8. (3) 89:6. (4) 95:1-2. (5) 89:15. (6) 55:15. (7) 95:5. (8) Job 12:10.

שִׁמְךָ יהוה, וְסָלַחְתָּ לַעֲוֹנֵנוּ כִּי רַב הוּא.[1]

⟨ it is great. ⟨ though ⟨ our ⟨ forgive ⟪ HASHEM, ⟨ of Your
　　　　　　　　iniquity,　　　　　　　　　　　　　Name,

CONGREGATION, THEN *CHAZZAN:*

סְלַח לָנוּ אָבִינוּ, כִּי בְרוֹב אִוַּלְתֵּנוּ שָׁגִינוּ,

⟪ we have ⟨ of our folly ⟨ in the ⟨ for ⟨ our Father, ⟨ us, ⟨ Forgive
　erred;　　　　　　　abundance

מְחַל לָנוּ מַלְכֵּנוּ, כִּי רַבּוּ עֲוֹנֵינוּ.

⟪ our ⟨ many ⟨ for ⟨ our King, ⟨ us, ⟨ pardon
　iniquities.　are

סליחה עו / SELICHAH 76
(פתיחה)

ALL:

עַם יהוה חִזְקוּ* וְנִתְחַזְּקָה,[2]

⟨ and let us strengthen ⟨ be ⟨ of ⟨ People
　[each other],　　strong*　HASHEM,

וְקִרְאוּ אֶל אֱלֹהִים בְּחָזְקָה.[3]

⟪ mightily! ⟨ God ⟨ to ⟨ and call out

אִישׁ אָוֶן יִתְוַדֶּה אַשְׁמֵהוּ,

⟪ his guilt, ⟨ of ⟨ confess ⟨ Let the
　　　　iniquity　　　　　man

וְיָשׁוֹב אֶל יהוה וִירַחֲמֵהוּ.[4]

⟪ and He will ⟨ HASHEM, ⟨ to ⟨ and let
　show him mercy.　　　　him return

לִקְרֹא לְלֹא יָנוּם וְלֹא יִישָׁן,

⟪ sleeps ⟨ nor ⟨ slumbers ⟨ to the One ⟨ To cry
　　　　　　　　　Who neither

שׁוֹמֵר יִשְׂרָאֵל[5] עוּרָה לָמָה תִישָׁן.[6]

⟪ do You ⟨ Why ⟪ awaken! ⟪ of Israel, ⟨ O
　[seem to] sleep?　　　　　　　　Guardian

---

(1) Cf. *Psalms* 25:11. (2) Cf. *I Chronicles* 19:13. (3) Cf. *Jonah* 3:8. (4) *Isaiah* 55:7.
(5) Cf. *Psalms* 121:4; some editions omit these two words. (6) 44:24.

◆§ חִזְקוּ 'ה עַם — *People of* HASHEM, *be
strong.* This *selichah* calls upon Israel to
arouse itself to repentance. The acrostic

reads, אֵלִיָּה בַּר שְׁמַעְיָה חֲזַק, *Eliyah bar
Shemayah, may he be strong* [see prefatory comment to *Selichah* 14].

יִשֶׁר זֵכֶר וְכִשְׁרוֹן מַעֲשֶׂה,

《 deeds. 〈 and proper 〈 re- 〈 Upright-
member ness

וַיהוה הַטּוֹב בְּעֵינָיו יַעֲשֶׂה.[1]

《 He will do. 〈 in His eyes 〈 what is 《 And
good HASHEM,

הִבְטִיחָנוּ אֱלֹהִים אֱמֶת,*

《 of Truth,* 〈 has the God 〈 Promised us

כִּי לֹא אֶחְפֹּץ בְּמוֹת הַמֵּת.[2]

《 of the one 〈 the death 〈 I do not desire 〈 That
that dies.

בְּהִמָּצְאוֹ דִּרְשׁוּהוּ בְּתַחַן לִקְרֹב,

《 to draw near 〈 in suppli- 《 seek Him, 〈 When He
[to Him]; cation can be found

קְרָאֻהוּ בִּהְיוֹתוֹ קָרוֹב.[3]

《 near. 〈 when He is 〈 call upon Him

רַצּוּהוּ חַלּוּהוּ בְּאֵימָה עִבְדוּהוּ,

《 serve Him; 〈 with 《 plead 《 Appease
reverence from Him, Him,

כָּל זֶרַע יַעֲקֹב כַּבְּדוּהוּ.[4]

《 glorify Him! 〈 of Jacob, 〈 the seed 〈 all

שְׁקֹד דַּלְתוֹת אֶרֶךְ אַפַּיִם, נִשָּׂא לְבָבֵנוּ אֶל כַּפָּיִם.[5]

《 our 〈 together 〈 our hearts 〈 let us 《 to 〈 of Him 〈 to the 〈 Hasten
hands. with [in prayer] lift anger; Who is slow doors

מִי יוֹדֵעַ רַצּוֹת וְיוֹאֵל, הִכּוֹן לִקְרַאת אֱלֹהֶיךָ יִשְׂרָאֵל.[6]

《 O Israel! 〈 your God, 〈 to 〈 prepare 《 that He will 〈 how to 〈 Who-
approach be appeased, find favor, ever knows

עִרְכוּ שֶׁוַע וּתְפִלָּה לְצָרָה,

《 in time of 〈 and a prayer 〈 an 〈 Arrange
trouble; outcry

קַדְּשׁוּ צוֹם קִרְאוּ עֲצָרָה.[7]

《 an assembly! 〈 summon 〈 a fast, 〈 decree

---

(1) I Chronicles 19:13. (2) Ezekiel 18:32. (3) Isaiah 55:6. (4) Psalms 22:24.
(5) Lamentations 3:41. (6) Amos 4:12. (7) Joel 2:15.

הִבְטִיחָנוּ אֱלֹהִים אֱמֶת — *Promised us has the God of Truth.* Translation follows the clas-sic Yiddish version of *Selichos.* Alternative-ly, the stich means, *God promised us truly.*

יְבַקֵּשׁ יְפַלֵּל אֱלֹהִים עוֹבֵד,

《 the one who 〈 to God 〈 and pray 〈 Let
serves [Him], [on our behalf] beseech

וְשָׁב מֵחֲרוֹן אַפּוֹ וְלֹא נֹאבֵד.[1]

《 that we 〈 so that 〈 anger, 〈 from 〈 that He
perish. it not be His flaring may turn
away

הֲיִרְצֶה שַׁי וָתֶשֶׁר מֵהַשְׁמֵן,* בְּרִבְבוֹת נַחֲלֵי שָׁמֶן.[2]

《 of oil? 〈 of 〈 or by tens of 《 from the 〈 and an 〈 with 〈 Will He
streams thousands [person] fattened* offering a gift be pleased

חֲפֵץ שְׁמֹעַ מִתְקָרֶבֶת עוֹלִים, לְהַקְשִׁיב מֵחֵלֶב אֵילִים.[3]

《 of rams. 〈 more than 〈 that we 《 of burnt- 〈 more than 〈 obedience 〈 He
the fat heed, offerings; the bringing desires

❖ זְכוּת לַמֵּד וְיַשֵּׁר עָקֹב, [4] זְכֹר אֵלֶּה לְיַעֲקֹב.[5]

《 for the sake 〈 these 〈 remember 《 the 〈 and 〈 advocate 〈 [O God]
of Jacob. crooked; straighten [for us] [to our] merit

קְחוּ עִמָּכֶם דְּבָרִים וְשָׂפָה בְּשִׁלּוּם פָּרִים.

《 [sacrificial] 〈 instead of 〈 and [the 《 words 〈 with you 〈 Take
bulls. speech of [of prayer],
our] lips

ALL:

כִּי עַל רַחֲמֶיךָ הָרַבִּים[6] אָנוּ בְטוּחִים, וְעַל צִדְקוֹתֶיךָ

〈 Your 〈 and 《 trust, 〈 we 〈 that is 〈 Your 〈 upon 〈 For
righteousness upon abundant mercy

אָנוּ נִשְׁעָנִים, וְלִסְלִיחוֹתֶיךָ אָנוּ מְקַוִּים, וְלִישׁוּעָתְךָ

〈 and for Your 《 hope, 〈 we 〈 and for Your 《 rely, 〈 we
salvation forgiveness

אָנוּ מְצַפִּים. אַתָּה הוּא מֶלֶךְ, אוֹהֵב צְדָקוֹת מִקֶּדֶם,

《 since the 〈 righteous- 〈 Who 〈 the King 〈 are 〈 You 《 await 〈 we
beginning ness loves eagerly.
of time,

---

(1) *Jonah* 3:9. (2) *Micah* 6:7. (3) *I Samuel* 15:22. (4) Some editions read זְכוּת וְיִשֶׁר עָקוֹב, [*turn into*]
merit and uprightness that which has been made crooked [*by our sins*]. (5) Cf. *Isaiah* 44:21;
some editions read זְכֹר אֱלֹהֵי יַעֲקֹב, *remember, O God of Jacob.* (6) Cf. *Hosea* 14:3.

מֵהַשְׁמֵן — *From the [person] fattened.* This
describes either: the wicked man whose
heart is so saturated with spiritual fat that it
prevents him from repenting (*Arugas Ha-
Bosem*); the wealthy man who brings many

fat animals as offerings, yet does not repent
in his heart (*Masbir*); or the penitent whose
heart was once stuffed with spiritual fat, but
who has repented and brought many Altar
offerings (*Matteh Levi*).

מַעֲבִיר עֲוֹנוֹת עַמּוֹ, וּמֵסִיר חַטֹּאת יְרֵאָיו. כּוֹרֵת

⟨ He ⟪ of those who ⟨ the sins ⟨ and ⟨ of His ⟨ the ⟨ Who
established revere Him.   removes   people   iniquities   overlooks

בְּרִית לָרִאשׁוֹנִים, וּמְקַיֵּם שְׁבוּעָה לָאַחֲרוֹנִים. אַתָּה

⟨ You ⟪ to the descendants. ⟨ [His] oath ⟨ and fulfills ⟨ with the ancestors ⟨ a covenant

הוּא, שֶׁיָּרַדְתָּ בַּעֲנָן כְּבוֹדֶךָ עַל הַר סִינַי,[1] וְהִרְאֵיתָ

⟨ and You ⟪ Sinai, ⟨ Mount ⟨ upon ⟨ of Your ⟨ in the ⟨ Who ⟨ are the
showed   glory   cloud   descended   One

דַּרְכֵי טוּבְךָ לְמֹשֶׁה עַבְדֶּךָ.[2] וְאָרְחוֹת חֲסָדֶיךָ גִּלֵּיתָ

⟨ You ⟨ of Your ⟨ The paths ⟪ Your ⟨ to Moses ⟨ of Your ⟨ the
revealed kindness   servant.   goodness   ways

לוֹ, וְהוֹדַעְתּוֹ כִּי אַתָּה אֵל רַחוּם וְחַנּוּן, אֶרֶךְ אַפַּיִם

⟨ to ⟨ Slow ⟪ and ⟨ Compas- ⟨ God, ⟨ You are ⟨ that ⟨ and You ⟪ to
anger   Gracious, sionate   let him know   him,

וְרַב חֶסֶד[3] וּמַרְבֶּה לְהֵטִיב, וּמַנְהִיג אֶת כָּל הָעוֹלָם

⟨ world ⟨ the whole ⟨ and Who ⟪ beneficent, ⟨ Who is ⟨ in Kind- ⟨ and
guides   abundantly ness,   Abundant

כֻּלּוֹ בְּמִדַּת הָרַחֲמִים. ⦂ וְכֵן כָּתוּב, וַיֹּאמֶר אֲנִי אַעֲבִיר

⟨ shall cause ⟨ "I ⟪ And He ⟪ it is ⟨ And so ⟪ of Mercy. ⟨ with the ⟨ in its
to pass   said, written: Attribute entirety

כָּל טוּבִי עַל פָּנֶיךָ, וְקָרָאתִי בְשֵׁם יהוה לְפָנֶיךָ,

⟪ before ⟨ HASHEM ⟨ with the ⟨ and I shall ⟪ your ⟨ before ⟨ My ⟨ all
you;   Name   call out face,   goodness

וְחַנֹּתִי אֶת אֲשֶׁר אָחֹן, וְרִחַמְתִּי אֶת אֲשֶׁר אֲרַחֵם.[4]

⟪ I choose to ⟨ whom- ⟨ to ⟨ and I shall ⟪ I choose to ⟨ whom- ⟨ to ⟨ I shall
show mercy." ever   show mercy show favor, ever   show favor

ALL, WHILE STANDING

אֵל אֶרֶךְ אַפַּיִם אַתָּה,

⟪ You are, ⟨ to anger, ⟨ Who ⟨ God
is slow

וּבַעַל הָרַחֲמִים נִקְרֵאתָ, וְדֶרֶךְ תְּשׁוּבָה הוֹרֵיתָ.

⟪ You have ⟨ of ⟨ and the ⟪ You are ⟨ of Mercy. ⟨ and
taught. repentance way   called;   Master

גְּדֻלַּת רַחֲמֶיךָ וַחֲסָדֶיךָ,

⟨ and Your ⟨ of Your ⟨ The
kindness mercy greatness

---

(1) Cf. *Exodus* 34:5. (2) Cf. 33:13. (3) 34:6. (4) 33:19.

תִּזְכּוֹר הַיּוֹם וּבְכָל יוֹם לְזֶרַע יְדִידֶיךָ.

of Your ⟨ for the ⟪ day, ⟨ and ⟨ this day ⟨ may You
beloved ones. offspring   every   remember,

תֵּפֶן אֵלֵינוּ בְּרַחֲמִים,

⟪ in mercy, ⟨ to us ⟨ Turn

כִּי אַתָּה הוּא בַּעַל הָרַחֲמִים.

⟪ of Mercy. ⟨ the Master ⟨ are ⟨ You ⟨ for

בְּתַחֲנוּן וּבִתְפִלָּה פָּנֶיךָ נְקַדֵּם, כְּהוֹדַעְתָּ לֶעָנָיו מִקֶּדֶם.

⟪ in ancient ⟨ to the ⟨ in the manner ⟪ we ⟨ Your ⟨ and prayer ⟨ With
times. humble one that You made approach, Presence   supplication
[Moses] known

מֵחֲרוֹן אַפְּךָ שׁוּב,[1] כְּמוֹ בְתוֹרָתְךָ כָּתוּב.[2]

⟪ it is ⟨ in Your Torah ⟨ as ⟪ turn ⟨ of Your ⟨ From the
written.   back, anger fierceness

וּבְצֵל כְּנָפֶיךָ נֶחֱסֶה וְנִתְלוֹנָן,[3] כְּיוֹם וַיֵּרֶד יהוה בֶּעָנָן.

⟪ in a ⟨ when HASHEM ⟨ as on ⟪ and may ⟨ may we find ⟨ of Your ⟨ In the
cloud. descended the day we dwell, shelter wings shadow

❖ תַּעֲבוֹר עַל פֶּשַׁע וְתִמְחֶה אָשָׁם,

⟪ guilt, ⟨ and erase ⟨ sin ⟨ Overlook

כְּיוֹם וַיִּתְיַצֵּב עִמּוֹ שָׁם.

⟪ there. ⟨ with him ⟨ when He ⟨ as on the
[Moses] [God] stood day

תַּאֲזִין שַׁוְעָתֵנוּ וְתַקְשִׁיב מֶנּוּ מַאֲמַר,

⟪ [our] ⟨ from ⟨ and hear ⟨ to our cry ⟨ Give heed
declaration, us

כְּיוֹם וַיִּקְרָא בְשֵׁם יהוה,[4] וְשָׁם נֶאֱמַר:

⟪ it was said: ⟨ and ⟪ of HASHEM, ⟨ with the ⟨ when He ⟨ as on
there Name called out the day

CONGREGATION, THEN *CHAZZAN*:

וַיַּעֲבֹר יהוה עַל פָּנָיו וַיִּקְרָא:

⟪ and ⟪ [Moses'] ⟨ before ⟨ And HASHEM passed
proclaimed: face,

CONGREGATION AND *CHAZZAN* RECITE LOUDLY AND IN UNISON:

יהוה, יהוה, אֵל, רַחוּם, וְחַנּוּן, אֶרֶךְ אַפַּיִם,

⟨ to anger, ⟨ Slow ⟪ and Gracious, ⟨ Compassionate ⟨ God, ⟨ HASHEM, ⟨ HASHEM,

(1) Cf. *Exodus* 32:12. (2) See 32:14. (3) Cf. *Psalms* 36:8. (4) *Exodus* 34:5.

וְרַב חֶסֶד, וֶאֱמֶת, נֹצֵר חֶסֶד לָאֲלָפִים, נֹשֵׂא עָוֹן,

⟨ of ⟨ Forgiver ≪ for thousands ⟨ of ⟨ Preserver ≪ and ⟨ in ⟨ and
iniquity, [of generations], kindness Truth, Kindness Abundant

וָפֶשַׁע, וְחַטָּאָה, וְנַקֵּה.[1] וְסָלַחְתָּ לַעֲוֹנֵנוּ וּלְחַטָּאתֵנוּ

≪ and our sins, ⟨ our ⟨ May You ≪ and Who ⟨ and inadvertent ⟨ willful sin,
iniquities forgive absolves. sin,

וּנְחַלְתָּנוּ.[2] סְלַח לָנוּ אָבִינוּ כִּי חָטָאנוּ, מְחַל לָנוּ

⟨ us, ⟨ pardon ≪ we have ⟨ for ≪our Father, ⟨ us, ⟨ Forgive ≪ and make us
sinned; Your heritage.

מַלְכֵּנוּ כִּי פָשָׁעְנוּ. כִּי אַתָּה אֲדֹנָי טוֹב וְסַלָּח, וְרַב

⟨ and ≪ and ⟨ are ⟨ O Lord, ⟨ You, ⟨ For ≪ we have ⟨ for ≪ our King,
abundantly forgiving, good willfully sinned.

חֶסֶד לְכָל קֹרְאֶיךָ.[3]

≪ who call ⟨ to all ⟨ kind
upon You.

PREFATORY VERSES TO SELICHAH 77 / פסוקי הקדמה לסליחה עז

וַאֲנַחְנוּ, בְּרֹב חַסְדְּךָ נָבוֹא בֵיתֶךָ, נִשְׁתַּחֲוֶה אֶל

⟨ toward ⟨ we will ≪ Your ⟨ will we ⟨ of Your ⟨ through ⟨ But we,
prostrate House; enter kindness the
ourselves abundance

הֵיכַל קָדְשְׁךָ בְּיִרְאָתֶךָ.[4] וַאֲנִי, תְפִלָּתִי לְךָ יהוה

⟨ Hashem, ⟨ to ⟨ may my ≪ As for ≪ in awe of You. ⟨ of Your ⟨ the
You, prayer me, Holiness Sanctuary

עֵת רָצוֹן, אֱלֹהִים, בְּרָב חַסְדֶּךָ, עֲנֵנִי בֶּאֱמֶת יִשְׁעֶךָ.[5]

≪ of Your ⟨ with the ⟨ answer ⟨ of Your ⟨ in the ⟨ O God, ≪ that is ⟨ [be] at
salvation. truth me kindness, abundance favorable; a time

הַאֲזִינָה יהוה תְפִלָּתֵנוּ, וְהַקְשִׁיבָה בְּקוֹל תַּחֲנוּנוֹתֵינוּ.[6]

≪ of our ⟨ the ⟨ and heed ≪ to our prayer, ⟨ Hashem, ⟨ Listen,
supplications. sound

כְּרַחֵם אָב עַל בָּנִים, כֵּן תְּרַחֵם יהוה עָלֵינוּ.[7]

≪ on us. ⟨ Hashem, ⟨ have ⟨ so ≪ his ⟨ toward ⟨ a ⟨ As merciful as
mercy, children, father is

לַיהוה הַיְשׁוּעָה, עַל עַמְּךָ בִרְכָתֶךָ סֶּלָה.[8] יהוה

⟨ Hashem, ≪ Selah. ≪ is Your ⟨ Your ⟨ upon ≪ is salvation, ⟨ To Hashem
blessing, people

---

(1) *Exodus* 34:6-7 (2) 34:9. (3) *Psalms* 86:5. (4) Cf. 5:8. (5) 69:14. (6) Cf. 86:6. (7) Cf. 103:13. (8) 3:9.

צְבָאוֹת עִמָּנוּ, מִשְׂגָּב לָנוּ אֱלֹהֵי יַעֲקֹב סֶלָה.¹

⟪ Selah. ⟪ of Jacob, ⟨ is the God ⟨ for us ⟨ a stronghold ⟪ is with us, ⟨ Master of Legions,

יהוה צְבָאוֹת, אַשְׁרֵי אָדָם בֹּטֵחַ בָּךְ.²

⟪ in You. ⟨ who trusts ⟨ is the man ⟨ — praise-worthy ⟪ Master of Legions ⟨ HASHEM,

יהוה הוֹשִׁיעָה, הַמֶּלֶךְ יַעֲנֵנוּ בְיוֹם קָרְאֵנוּ.³

⟪ we call. ⟨ on the day ⟨ answer us ⟨ May the King ⟪ save! ⟨ HASHEM,

---

IN MOST CONGREGATIONS THE FOLLOWING VERSES ARE RECITED ALOUD RESPONSIVELY, AS INDICATED; IN OTHERS THEY ARE RECITED SILENTLY.

CONGREGATION, ALOUD, FOLLOWED BY CHAZZAN, ALOUD:

סְלַח נָא לַעֲוֹן הָעָם הַזֶּה כְּגֹדֶל חַסְדֶּךָ, וְכַאֲשֶׁר

⟨ just as ⟪ of Your kindness, ⟨ according to the greatness ⟨ of this people ⟨ the iniquity ⟨ please, ⟨ Forgive,

נָשָׂאתָה לָעָם הַזֶּה מִמִּצְרַיִם וְעַד הֵנָּה,⁴ וְשָׁם נֶאֱמַר:

⟪ it was said: ⟨ And there ⟪ now. ⟨ until ⟨ from Egypt ⟨ this people ⟨ You have forgiven

ALL, ALOUD AND IN UNISON:

וַיֹּאמֶר יהוה סָלַחְתִּי כִּדְבָרֶךָ.⁵

⟪ according to your word! ⟨ I have forgiven ⟪ And HASHEM said:

ALL CONTINUE:

הַטֵּה אֱלֹהַי אָזְנְךָ וּשְׁמָע, פְּקַח עֵינֶיךָ וּרְאֵה

⟨ and see ⟨ Your eyes ⟨ open ⟪ and listen; ⟨ Your ear, ⟨ my God, ⟨ Incline,

שׁמְמֹתֵינוּ, וְהָעִיר אֲשֶׁר נִקְרָא שִׁמְךָ עָלֶיהָ, כִּי לֹא

⟨ not ⟨ for ⟪ upon; ⟨ Your Name is proclaimed ⟨ which ⟨ and that [of] the city ⟨ our desolation

עַל צִדְקֹתֵינוּ אֲנַחְנוּ מַפִּילִים תַּחֲנוּנֵינוּ לְפָנֶיךָ,

⟪ before You; ⟨ our supplications ⟨ cast ⟨ do we ⟨ of our righteousness ⟨ because

כִּי עַל רַחֲמֶיךָ הָרַבִּים. אֲדֹנָי שְׁמָעָה, אֲדֹנָי סְלָחָה,

⟪ forgive; ⟨ O Lord, ⟪ heed; ⟨ O Lord, ⟪ which is abundant. ⟨ of Your compassion, ⟨ be-cause ⟨ but

אֲדֹנָי הַקְשִׁיבָה, וַעֲשֵׂה אַל תְּאַחַר, לְמַעַנְךָ אֱלֹהַי,

⟪ my God, ⟨ for Your sake, ⟪ delay; ⟨ do not ⟪ and act, ⟨ be attentive, ⟨ O Lord,

(1) Psalms 46:8. (2) 84:13. (3) 20:10. (4) Numbers 14:19. (5) 14:20.

כִּי שִׁמְךָ נִקְרָא עַל עִירְךָ וְעַל עַמֶּךָ.[1]

》 Your 〈 and 〈 Your 〈 upon 〈 is 〈 Your 〈 for
people.   upon   City   proclaimed   Name

סליחה עז / SELICHAH 77

ALL:

אֱלֹהֵינוּ וֵאלֹהֵי אֲבוֹתֵינוּ:

》 of our forefathers: 〈 and the God 〈 Our God

אֲנִי בְּרֹב חַסְדְּךָ* אָבוֹא בֵיתֶךָ,

》 Your 〈 will I 〈 of Your 〈through the 》But
house;   enter   kindness*   abundance   I,

אֶשְׁתַּחֲוֶה אֶל הֵיכַל קָדְשְׁךָ בְּיִרְאָתֶךָ,[2]

》 in awe of You. 〈 of Your 〈 the 〈 toward 〈 I will prostrate
     Holiness   Sanctuary   myself

בְּהַשְׁכִּימִי בְּתַחַן לִפְנֵי מְכוֹן שִׁבְתֶּךָ,[3]

》 of Your 〈 the 〈 before 〈 with 〈 When I rise early
dwelling-place, foundation   supplication

בְּעֵת רָצוֹן* עֲנֵנִי בֶּאֱמֶת יִשְׁעֶךָ.[4]

》 of Your 〈 with the 〈 answer 〈 of favor* 〈 at a time
  salvation.   truth   me

גָּדוֹל וְגִבּוֹר עַל כָּל שִׁמְךָ אִמְרָתֶךָ,[5]

》 is Your promise 〈 Your 〈 [exalted] 》and Mighty 〈 O Great
[to forgive]:   Name   even beyond   One,

גְּבוּרַת רַחֲמֶיךָ מֵאָז* וְאֵלֵינוּ מַחְשְׁבוֹתֶיךָ,[6]

》 are Your thoughts. 〈 and toward 》 is of 〈 of Your 〈 The might
     us   old,*   mercy

---

(1) *Daniel* 9:18-19. (2) Cf. *Psalms* 5:8. (3) Cf. *Exodus* 15:17.
(4) Cf. 69:14. (5) Cf. 138:2. (6) Some editions read מְאֹד, *is copious.*

§⊷ **אֲנִי בְּרֹב חַסְדְּךָ** — *But I, through the abun-dance of Your kindness.* This unsigned *seli-chah* contains a double *aleph-beis* acrostic. Unlike most *piyutim* which change rhymes every two or four lines, this *selichah* main-tains the same rhyme throughout.

בְּעֵת רָצוֹן — *At a time of favor.* In the context of *Psalms* 69:14, from where this phrase is borrowed, the supplicant asks that his prayer time should be a time of favor. According to *Masbir*, however, in the con-text of the *selichah*, the phrase refers to the

days between Rosh Hashanah and Yom Kippur. During that period, God makes Himself available to every Jew who seeks him. [See commentary to *Selichah* 43, s.v. אֵת ה' בְּהִמָּצְאוֹ לְדָרְשׁוּ קְדַמְתִּי.]

גְּבוּרַת רַחֲמֶיךָ מֵאָז — *The might of Your mercy is of old.* Even before Creation, God merged His Attribute of Strict Justice (גְּבוּרָה) with His Attribute of Mercy (רַחֲמִים). Thus, *the might of His mercy,* the combination of His might and mercy, is older than Creation itself (*Masbir;* see *Rashi* to *Genesis* 1:1).

דְּבָרְךָ רֹאשׁ אֱמֶת*1 לָנוּ בְּאוּמֶן עֲצוֹתֶיךָ,

《 counsels, 〈 through 〈 given 《 is Truth,* 〈 beginning〈 Your
Your faithful to us Word's

דְּרָכֶיךָ וּמִדּוֹתֶיךָ בְּעָמְדָם לְפָנֶיךָ

〈 before 〈 when Israel 《 and Your 〈 which are
You, stand attributes, Your ways

לְהַקְדִּים לָמוֹ חֲנִינוֹתֶיךָ.

《 Your 〈 for 〈 [entreating You] to
graciousness. them place to the fore

הַמְּחִילָה וְהַסְּלִיחָה שֶׁלְּךָ, וְעֹבֵר עַל פֶּשַׁע תִּפְאַרְתֶּךָ,2

《 is Your glory; 〈 trans- 〈 and Your 《 are 〈 and forgiveness 〈 Pardon
gression overlooking Yours,

הֲדַר כְּבוֹד הוֹדֶךָ וְדִבְרֵי נִפְלְאוֹתֶיךָ,3

《 of Your wonders. 〈 the deeds 《 of Your 〈 glory 〈 [this is] the
majesty, splendrous

וְהִנְנוּ אֲתָאנוּ לְךָ4 בְּעֹצֶם חֶמְלָתֶךָ,

《 of Your mercy, 〈 [knowing] 《 to 〈 we have 《Now here
the might You, come we are,

וּלְךָ לְבַד הוֹחַלְנוּ וְאַתָּה תַעֲנֶה5 מְחִילָתֶךָ.

《 with Your forgiveness. 〈 will answer 〈 and You 《 do we hope, 〈 alone 〈 for You

זְכוֹר עֲדָתְךָ קָנִיתָ קֶּדֶם גָּאַלְתָּ שֵׁבֶט נַחֲלָתֶךָ,6

《 of Your 〈 the 〈[remember]《 long 〈 which 〈 Your con- 〈Remem-
heritage. tribe how You ago; You gregation, ber
redeemed acquired

זְכוֹר אָבוֹת לַבָּנִים יוֹדַע אֶת אֲמִתֶּךָ,7

《 Your truth. 〈 and let 《 for [their] 〈 the Fathers 〈Remem-
be made children, [the ber
known Patriarchs]

---

(1) Cf. *Psalms* 119:160. (2) Cf. *Micah* 7:18. (3) *Psalms* 145:5.
(4) Cf. *Jeremiah* 3:22. (5) Cf. *Psalms* 38:16. (6) 74:2. (7) Cf. *Isaiah* 38:19.

דְּבָרְךָ רֹאשׁ אֱמֶת — *Your Word's beginning is "Truth."* The first word in the Torah — בְּרֵאשִׁית — is followed by the words בָּרָא אֱלֹהִים, *God created*. These three words end in the letters א מ ת. Thus, the very beginning of the Torah is sealed with the word אמת. This is the meaning of the verse, רֹאשׁ דְּבָרְךָ אֱמֶת, *the beginning of Your Word is truth* (Psalms 119:160).

In addition to the allusion mentioned in the preceding paragraph, the word אֱמֶת is hinted at six other times in the story of Creation. All six allusions are found in the respective final letters of three consecutive words. The six are: בָּרָא אֱלֹהִים אֵת, *God created [the heavens...]* (1:1); וַיַּרְא אֱלֹהִים אֶת, *And God saw [the light]* (1:4); וַיִּבְרָא אֱלֹהִים אֶת, *And God created [the fish and fowl]* (1:21); וַיִּבְרָא אֱלֹהִים אֶת, *And God created [man]* (1:27); וַיַּרְא אֱלֹהִים אֶת, *and God saw [all that He had made]* (1:31); בָּרָא אֱלֹהִים לַעֲשׂוֹת, *God created to make* (2:3).

חֶסֶד נְעוּרִים וְאַהֲבַת כְּלוּלוֹתֶיךָ,[1]

《 of Your bridal days, 〈 and the love 《 done in 〈 [Remember] their youth, the kindness

חֲדָשִׁים לַבְּקָרִים רַבָּה אֱמוּנָתֶךָ.[2]

《 is Your 〈 great 《 every 〈 [for Your kindness] is renewed faithfulness. morning;

טוּבְךָ אֲשֶׁר נוֹדַע לְנֶאֱמַן בֵּית, מְשָׁרְתֶךָ,[3]

《 Your servant — 《 of Your 〈 to [Moses,] the 〈 was made 〈 which 《 Your goodness, house, trusted one known

טֶכֶס שֵׁם אַדִּיר בְּאַרְבַּע אוֹתִיּוֹתֶיךָ,*

《 letters* — 〈 [composed] 〈 that is 〈 of the 〈 the of Your four powerful, Name ordering

יָתֵד תְּקוּעָה בִּשְׁלֹשׁ עֶשְׂרֵה תְבוּתֶיךָ,

〈 expressions 〈 that Your thirteen 〈 driven in 〈 as [firmly [of mercy] [is Your rooted] promise] as a stake

יִגְלוּ רַחֲמֶיךָ עַל מִדּוֹתֶיךָ.

《 Your [other] 《 — [as mani- 《 over- attributes. festations of] whelm Your mercy —

כִּי אֲנַחְנוּ עַמְּךָ וְצֹאן מַרְעִיתֶךָ,[4]

《 of Your 〈 the flock 《 Your 〈 we are 〈 For pasturing, people,

כְּדַלִּים וּכְרָשִׁים דָּפַקְנוּ דְלָתֶיךָ,

《 on Your 〈 we have 〈 and as 〈 [and yet] doors. knocked destitute people as paupers

לֹא לְמַעֲנֵנוּ כִּי אִם בְּרֹב צִדְקָתֶךָ,

《righteousness, 〈 in Your 〈 rather 〈 but 〈 for our 〈[Act on abundant sake, our behalf,] not

לָרָעִים וְלַטּוֹבִים וְהִיא תְהִלָּתֶךָ.[5]

《 Your praise. 〈 for that is 《and toward good, 〈 toward bad

---

(1) Cf. *Jeremiah* 2:2. (2) *Lamentations* 3:23, see *Rashi* there. (3) Cf. *Numbers* 12:7. (4) Cf. *Psalms* 79:13. (5) From the Yom Kippur *selichos* prayers.

Alternatively, the phrase may be rendered, *Your word from the very beginning has stood true* (*Radak* to *Psalms* 119:160).

שֵׁם אַדִּיר בְּאַרְבַּע אוֹתִיּוֹתֶיךָ — *Of the Name that is powerful, [composed] of Your four letters.* This refers to the ineffable Tetragrammaton, which is the Name that connotes God's infinite mercy and kindness. This Name is also the first of the Thirteen Attributes of Mercy that God taught Moses [see commentary, p. 19, s.v. ה' ה'].

מַטֶּה כְּלַפֵּי חֶסֶד זוֹ הִיא אֲמָנוּתֶךָ,

《 Your craft. 〈 is 〈 that 《 kindness: 〈 [judgment] 〈 To tilt
toward

מִדָּה וּמִדָּה הִיא לְשַׁבֵּחַ צְפִירָתֶךָ,

《 [thus creating] 〈 to praise 〈 is in 〈 after Attribute 〈 Attribute
Your crown, [You], essence [of kindness]

נוֹהֵג חִנָּם חֶסֶד עִם כָּל בְּרִיּוֹתֶיךָ,

《 Your creations, 〈 all 〈 toward 〈 kindness 〈 with 〈 You act
undeserved

נְתִיבוֹת חֵן וְרַחֲמִים לְנוֹצְרֵי עֵדוֹתֶיךָ.[1]

《 Your 〈 for those 〈 and mercy 〈 of 〈 with
testimonies. who guard love pathways

סְלִיחָה מְבַקְשִׁים תָּכִין לִבָּם[2] לְקָרְאָתֶךָ,

《 to approach You; 〈 their 〈 — [therefore] 《 they ask 〈 Forgiveness
hearts prepare

שִׂימָה דִמְעָתָם בְּנֹאדֶךָ הֲלֹא בְּסִפְרָתֶךָ.[3]

《 in Your record? 〈 are they not 《 in Your flask; 〈 their tears 〈 place

עֳנִי וְעִנּוּי וְעֶלְבּוֹן בְּנֵי בְרִיתֶךָ,

《 of Your cov- 〈 of the 〈 and insult 〈 suffering, 〈 The
enant nation, members poverty,

עֵינֶיךָ תֶחֱזֶינָה[4] יהוה כְּכָל צִדְקוֹתֶיךָ.[5]

《 Your 〈 as 〈 O 〈 see, 〈 let Your
righteousness. befits all HASHEM, eyes

פּוֹקְדֶיךָ בַּצַּר צָקוּן לַחַשׁ תּוֹכְחוֹתֶיךָ,

《 in response to 〈 their silent 〈 who 《 when in 〈 Those who re-
Your rebukes — prayers pour out trouble, member You

פַּלְּטֵם מִשַּׁחַת מֵחֲמֵשֶׁת מִינֵי עֶבְרָתֶךָ,*

《 of Your fury.* 〈 types 〈 from the five 《 from the grave, 〈 rescue them

---

(1) Cf. *Psalms* 119:2. (2) Cf. 10:17. (3) Cf. 56:9. (4) Cf. 17:2. (5) *Daniel* 9:12.

מֵחֲמֵשֶׁת מִינֵי עֶבְרָתֶךָ — *From the five types of
Your fury.* The *Mechilta*, in the well-known
passage cited in the *Haggadah of Pesach*, records a dispute regarding the interpretation
of the verse, יְשַׁלַּח בָּם חֲרוֹן אַפּוֹ עֶבְרָה וָזַעַם וְצָרָה
מִשְׁלַחַת מַלְאֲכֵי רָעִים (*Psalms* 78:49).

According to Rabbi Eliezer, the words
חֲרוֹן אַפּוֹ, *His fierce anger,* is a catchall for
the following four terms. The verse is then
punctuated, *He sent upon them His fierce*

anger: (1) *wrath;* (2) *rage;* (3) *distress; and*
(4) *a band of emissaries of evil.* Accordingly,
God's anger is fourfold. Rabbi Akiva, on the
other hand, understands *His fierce anger*
as another of the many manifestations of
God's fury. The verse thus reads, *He sent
upon them:* (1) *His fierce anger;* (2) *wrath;*
(3) *rage;* (4) *distress,* and (5) *a band of emissaries of evil.* Thus God's fury is fivefold.
The *paytan* accepts Rabbi Akiva's view.

צוֹפֶה לְקַטְרֵג וּלְחַבֵּל אִם רַעְיָתֶךָ,

that is Your ‹ the ‹ and to ‹ to accuse ‹ The one
beloved,   people   harm   who looks

צַוֵּה לִנְעֹל דֶּלֶת וְאַל יִכָּנֵס בִּמְחִצָּתֶךָ.

Your proximate ‹ that he ‹ the ‹ to lock ‹ com-
space.   not enter   door,   mand

קוֹל יַעֲקֹב בְּעֵת יַעַל מִתְּהוֹמוֹתֶיךָ,

from Your deeps ‹ it ‹ when ‹ of Jacob ‹ The
[in exile],   ascends   voice

קַבֵּל בְּרַחֲמִים מִתַּחַת כֵּס יְשִׁיבָתֶךָ,

where ‹ the ‹ from ‹ in mercy ‹ accept
You sit. Throne beneath   it

רַחַשׁ מְשַׁלְּמִים מְקוֹם זְבָחֶיךָ, וְעוֹלוֹתֶיךָ,

and Your ‹ of Your ‹ in place ‹ they ‹ The stirrings
burnt-offerings; peace-   provide [of the heart
              offerings   in prayer]

רְצֵה נִדְבָתָם וַחֲתֹר לָמוֹ חֲתִירָתֶךָ.*

a tunnel ‹ for ‹ and dig ‹ to their offer ‹ be
[under Your them   [of prayer]   favorable
Throne].*

❖ **שׁוּב** לְמַעַן עֲבָדֶיךָ שִׁבְטֵי נַחֲלָתֶךָ,[1]

of Your ‹ the tribes ‹ of Your ‹ for the ‹ Return
heritage!   servants,   sake

שִׁמְךָ יַעֲמֹד לָנוּ וְיָשׁוּב אַפְּךָ וַחֲמָתֶךָ,

and Your ‹ will ‹ and turn ‹ to our ‹ stand ‹ May Your
anger.   Your   back   aid,   Name
        fury   [from us]

תִּתְאַזָּר בַּחֲסִידוּתֶךָ וְתִתְעַטֵּף בַּחֲנִינוּתֶךָ,

in Your ‹ and wrap ‹ with Your ‹ May You gird
graciousness, Yourself kindness   Yourself

וְתָבֹא לְפָנֶיךָ מִדַּת טוּבְךָ וְעַנְוְתָנוּתֶךָ.[2]

and Your humility. ‹ of ‹ — Your ‹ before ‹ and may
              goodness Attribute You   they come

---

(1) *Isaiah* 63:17. (2) Cf. *Berachos* 16b.

וַחֲתֹר לָמוֹ חֲתִירָתֶךָ — *And dig for them a tunnel [under Your Throne].* The Talmud describes how God dug a tunnel, so to speak, through the heavens to allow the wicked Menashe's penitential supplications to reach His Throne, without His Attribute of Strict Justice able to obstruct its passage (*Sanhedrin* 103a).

ALL, WHILE STANDING:

אֵל מֶלֶךְ יוֹשֵׁב עַל כִּסֵּא רַחֲמִים, מִתְנַהֵג

⟨ Who acts ⟪ of mercy, ⟨ the throne ⟨ on ⟨ Who sits ⟨ King ⟨ O God,

בַּחֲסִידוּת, מוֹחֵל עֲוֹנוֹת עַמּוֹ, מַעֲבִיר רִאשׁוֹן

⟨ [sins,] one ⟨ Who ⟪ of His ⟨ the sins ⟨ Who ⟪ with kindness,
                    removes   people,   pardons

רִאשׁוֹן, ¹ מַרְבֶּה מְחִילָה לַחַטָּאִים וּסְלִיחָה לַפּוֹשְׁעִים,

⟪ to willful ⟨ and ⟨ to unintentional ⟨ pardon ⟨ Who abun- ⟪ by one,
   sinners,   forgiveness   sinners   dantly grants

עֹשֶׂה צְדָקוֹת עִם כָּל בָּשָׂר וָרוּחַ, לֹא כְרָעָתָם

⟨ in accord with ⟨ — not ⟪ and ⟨ [beings ⟨ all ⟨ with ⟨ acts of ⟨ Who
  their wickedness   spirit   of] flesh   generosity   performs

תִּגְמוֹל. ❖ אֵל הוֹרֵיתָ לָנוּ לוֹמַר שְׁלֹשׁ עֶשְׂרֵה, וּזְכוֹר

⟨ remem- ⟪ the Thirteen ⟨ to ⟨ us ⟨ You ⟨ O God, ⟪ do You
  ber   [Attributes of Mercy]; recite   taught   repay them!

לָנוּ הַיּוֹם בְּרִית שְׁלֹשׁ עֶשְׂרֵה, כְּמוֹ שֶׁהוֹדַעְתָּ לֶעָנָיו

⟨ to the humble ⟨ You made ⟨ as ⟪ of [these] Thirteen, ⟨ the ⟨ today ⟨ for us
  one [Moses]   known   covenant

מִקֶּדֶם, כְּמוֹ שֶׁכָּתוּב, וַיֵּרֶד יהוה בֶּעָנָן וַיִּתְיַצֵּב עִמּוֹ

⟨ with ⟨ and stood ⟨ in a ⟨ And HASHEM ⟪ it is written: ⟨ as ⟪ in ancient
  him   cloud   descended   times,

שָׁם, וַיִּקְרָא בְשֵׁם יהוה.²

⟪ of ⟨ with the ⟨ and He ⟪ there,
  HASHEM. Name   called out

CONGREGATION, THEN CHAZZAN:

וַיַּעֲבֹר יהוה עַל פָּנָיו וַיִּקְרָא:

⟪ and ⟪ [Moses'] ⟨ before ⟨ And HASHEM passed
  proclaimed: face,

CONGREGATION AND CHAZZAN RECITE LOUDLY AND IN UNISON:

יהוה, יהוה, אֵל, רַחוּם, וְחַנּוּן, אֶרֶךְ אַפַּיִם,

⟨ to anger, ⟨ Slow ⟪ and ⟨ Compassionate ⟨ God, ⟨ HASHEM, ⟨ HASHEM,
                      Gracious,

וְרַב חֶסֶד, וֶאֱמֶת, נֹצֵר חֶסֶד לָאֲלָפִים, נֹשֵׂא עָוֹן,

⟨ of ⟨ Forgiver ⟪ for thousands ⟨ of ⟨ Preserver ⟪ and ⟨ in ⟨ and
  iniquity,   [of generations], kindness   Truth, Kindness Abundant

(1) *Rosh Hashanah* 17a. (2) *Exodus* 34:5.

וָפֶשַׁע, וְחַטָּאָה, וְנַקֵּה.¹ וְסָלַחְתָּ לַעֲוֹנֵנוּ וּלְחַטָּאתֵנוּ

《 and our sins, 〈 our 〈 May You 〈 *and Who* 〈*and inadvertent* 〈 *willful sin,*
iniquities   forgive   *absolves.*   sin,

וּנְחַלְתָּנוּ.² סְלַח לָנוּ אָבִינוּ כִּי חָטָאנוּ, מְחַל לָנוּ

〈 us, 〈 pardon 《 we have 〈 for 《 our 〈 us, 〈 Forgive 《 and make us
sinned;   Father,   Your heritage.

מַלְכֵּנוּ כִּי פָשָׁעְנוּ. כִּי אַתָּה אֲדֹנָי טוֹב וְסַלָּח,

《 and 〈 are 〈 O Lord, 〈 You, 〈 For 《 we have 〈 for 《 our King,
forgiving,   good   willfully sinned.

וְרַב חֶסֶד לְכָל קֹרְאֶיךָ.³

《 who call 〈 to all 〈 kind 〈 and
upon You.   abundantly

PREFATORY VERSES TO SELICHAH 78 / פסוקי הקדמה לסליחה עח

נְשָׂא לְבָבֵנוּ אֶל כַּפָּיִם, אֶל אֵל בַּשָּׁמָיִם.⁴ תָּבוֹא

〈 Let 《 in Heaven. 〈 God 〈 to 〈 our 〈together〈 our hearts 〈 Let us lift
come   hands   with   [in prayer]

לְפָנֶיךָ אֶנְקַת אָסִיר, כְּגֹדֶל זְרוֹעֲךָ, הוֹתֵר בְּנֵי תְמוּתָה.⁵

《 to die. 〈 those 〈 spare 《 of Your 〈 as befits 《 of the 〈 the 〈 before
condemned   might, the greatness prisoner;   groan   You

לַאדֹנָי אֱלֹהֵינוּ הָרַחֲמִים וְהַסְּלִיחוֹת, כִּי מָרַדְנוּ בּוֹ.⁶

《 against 〈 we have 〈 for 《 and forgiveness, 〈 belong mercy 〈 our God 〈 To the Lord,
Him.   rebelled

כְּרַחֵם אָב עַל בָּנִים, כֵּן תְּרַחֵם יהוה עָלֵינוּ.⁷

《 on us. 〈 HASHEM, 〈 have 《 so 《 his 〈 toward 〈 a 〈 As merciful as
mercy,   children,   father is

לַיהוה הַיְשׁוּעָה, עַל עַמְּךָ בִרְכָתֶךָ סֶּלָה.⁸ יהוה

〈 HASHEM, 《 Selah. 《 is Your 〈 Your 〈 upon 《 is salvation, 〈 To HASHEM
blessing,   people

צְבָאוֹת עִמָּנוּ, מִשְׂגָּב לָנוּ אֱלֹהֵי יַעֲקֹב סֶלָה.⁹

《 Selah. 《 of Jacob, 〈 is the God 〈 for us 〈 a 《 is with us, 〈 Master of
stronghold   Legions,

יהוה צְבָאוֹת, אַשְׁרֵי אָדָם בֹּטֵחַ בָּךְ.¹⁰ יהוה

〈 HASHEM, 《 in You. 〈 who 〈 is the 〈 — praiseworthy 《 Master 〈 HASHEM,
trusts   man   of Legions

---

(1) *Exodus* 34:6-7. (2) 34:9. (3) *Psalms* 86:5. (4) *Lamentations* 3:41.
(5) *Psalms* 79:11. (6) *Daniel* 9:9. (7) Cf. *Psalms* 103:13. (8) 3:9. (9) 46:8. (10) 84:13.

הוֹשִׁיעָה, הַמֶּלֶךְ יַעֲנֵנוּ בְיוֹם קָרְאֵנוּ.[1]

《 we call. 〈 on the 〈 answer 〈 May the 《 save!
day us King

סליחה עח / SELICHAH 78
(שניה)

ALL:

אֱלֹהִים בְּיִשְׂרָאֵל* גָּדוֹל נוֹדָעְתָּ,[2]

《 You are known. 〈 to be great 〈 in Israel* 《 God,

אַתָּה יהוה אָבִינוּ אָתָּה.[3]

《 are You. 〈 our Father 《 HASHEM; 〈 You are

בְּכָל קָרְאֵנוּ אֵלֶיךָ[4] קָרְבֵנוּ,

《 draw us close; 《 to You, 〈 we call 〈 Whenever

רָם וְנִשָּׂא אַתָּה בְּקִרְבֵּנוּ.*[5]

《 in our midst.* 〈 are You 〈 and uplifted 〈 exalted

גְּמַלְתָּנוּ הַטוֹבוֹת בְּחוֹבֵנוּ,

《 despite our 〈 good 〈 You have
guilt, things bestowed upon us

לֹא בְצִדְקוֹתֵינוּ וּבְיֹשֶׁר לְבָבֵנוּ.[6]

《of our heart.〈 and the 〈 because of our 〈 not
uprightness righteousness

דּוֹדֵנוּ גַּם כִּי זְנַחְנוּ,[7]

〈 we have been 〈 if 〈 even 《 Our
forsaken Beloved,

גְּאָלֵנוּ כִּי עֲבָדִים אֲנָחְנוּ.*[8]

《 are we.* 〈 [Your] 〈 for 《 redeem
servants us,

---

(1) Psalms 20:10. (2) Cf. 76:2. (3) Cf. Isaiah 64:7. (4) Cf. Deuteronomy 4:7. (5) Cf. Isaiah 57:15. (6) Cf. Deuteronomy 9:5. (7) Some editions read זְנַחְנוּ, we have forsaken [You]. (8) Ezra 9:9.

§◄• **אֱלֹהִים בְּיִשְׂרָאֵל** — God, in Israel. This selichah, of unknown authorship, follows an aleph-beis acrostic.

רָם וְנִשָּׂא אַתָּה בְּקִרְבֵּנוּ — Exalted and uplifted are You in our midst. R' Yochanan taught: Wherever you find God's greatness [mentioned in Scripture], there you find His humility. This phenomenon is written in the Torah, repeated in the Prophets, and stated a third time in the Writings ....

It is repeated in the Prophets, as it is written (Isaiah 57:15): For so says רָם וְנִשָּׂא, the exalted and uplifted One, Who abides forever and Whose Name is holy, "I abide in exaltedness and holiness, but am with the crushed and lowly of spirit, to revive the spirit of the lowly and to revive the heart of the crushed" (Megillah 31a).

כִּי עֲבָדִים אֲנָחְנוּ — For [Your] servants are we. Our translation follows some comment-

הִנְנוּ בַעֲוֹנֵנוּ עַד דַּכָּא,[1] וַתִּקְצַר נֶפֶשׁ לְךָ מְחַכָּה.

《 awaits. 〈 that 〉 is the 〈 filled with 〈 of 〈 at the 〈 because of 〈 Indeed
for You soul anxiety despair; point our sins, we are,

וְאַיֵּה חֲסָדֶיךָ הָרִאשׁוֹנִים[2] עִמָּנוּ,

《 with us, 〈 of old 〈 are Your 〈 Where
kindnesses

מֵעוֹלָם וְעַד עוֹלָם נֶאֱמָנוּ.

《 have been 〈 and ever 〈 [those that]
faithful? for ever

זַעַף נָשָׂא[3] וַתָּשׁ כֹּחֵנוּ, יהוה אַל בְּאַפְּךָ תוֹכִיחֵנוּ.[4]

《 rebuke us. 〈 in Your 〈 do 〈 O 《 is our 〈 and 《 have we 〈 Anger
anger not HASHEM, strength; sapped borne,

חַלְחָלוֹת רַבּוֹת בָּלוּ בִשְׂרֵנוּ, נָא אַל בַּחֲמָתְךָ תְיַסְּרֵנוּ.[4]

《 chastise us. 〈 in Your 〈 do 〈please 《 our 〈 have 〈 Many afflictions
wrath not flesh; withered

טֹרַח הַצָּרוֹת אֵין לְהַסְפֵּר, אַיֵּה שׁוֹקֵל וְאַיֵּה סוֹפֵר.[5]

《 who can 〈 and where 《who can 〈 Where is 《 be 〈 cannot 〈 of our 〈 The
count [it]? is the one weigh [it], the one calculated. troubles burden

יָדַעְנוּ רִשְׁעֵנוּ כִּי פָשָׁעְנוּ,[6]

《 we have 〈 for 〈 our 〈 We
sinned; wickedness, know

כִּי אֱמֶת עָשִׂיתָ וַאֲנַחְנוּ הִרְשָׁעְנוּ.[7]

《 have acted 〈 while we 《 have You 〈 with 〈 for
wickedly. acted, truth

כַּעַס וְחָרוֹן מֶנּוּ יֶחְדָּל,[8] כִּי קָטֹן יַעֲקֹב[9] וָדָל.

《 and 〈 is Jacob['s 〈 small 〈 for 《 cease, 〈 from us 〈 and fury 〈 Let anger
destitute; nation]

לַחַץ יוּסַר וְעֹל (מֶנּוּ) יֶחְבָּל,[10] כִּי כָשַׁל כֹּחַ הַסַּבָּל.[11]

《 of the one 〈 is the 〈 failed 〈 for 《 be broken, 〈 (from 〈 and let 〈 be 〈 let op-
who bears strength us) the yoke removed pression
[them].

---

(1) Cf. *Psalms* 90:3. (2) Cf. 89:50. (3) Cf. *Micah* 7:9. (4) Cf. *Psalms* 6:2.
(5) Cf. *Isaiah* 33:18. (6) Cf. *Jeremiah* 14:20. (7) *Nehemiah* 9:33.
(8) Some editions read כַּעַס יוּפַר וְחָרוֹן יֶחְדָּל, *Let anger be annulled and fury cease*; cf. *Psalms* 85:5.
(9) Cf. *Amos* 7:2,5. (10) Cf. *Isaiah* 10:27. (11) *Nehemiah* 4:4.

---

aries, including the classic Yiddish translation. However, the phrase is taken from
Ezra 9:9. There it states: *Although we are
slaves to Darius, nevertheless, even in our*
slavery, our God has not abandoned us.
Accordingly, the phrase here should be understood: *Redeem us, for we are servants*
to foreign masters.

מְנָת מִדָּתֵנוּ לֹא תִגְבֶּה, כִּי נִשְׁאַרְנוּ מְעַט מֵהַרְבֵּה.[1]

《 out of many. 〈 few 〈 we remain 〈 for 《 exact, 〈 do not 〈 of measurement [of punishment] 〈 The full portion

נִחָם עַל הָרָעָה לְאָמָתֶךָ,[2] מַטֵּה כְּלַפֵּי חֶסֶד אֲמָנוּתֶךָ.[3]

《 as is Your practice. 〈 kindness 〈 toward 〈 tip [the scale] 《 [decreed] for 〈 the evil 〈 from 〈 Relent Your nation,

סְלָחָה אִם עֲוֹנֵינוּ עָנוּ בָנוּ,[4] עָזְרֵנוּ כִּי עָלֶיךָ נִשְׁעָנוּ.[5]

《 we depend. 〈 upon You 〈 for 〈 help us, 《 against us; 〈 testify 〈 our sins 〈 if 〈 Forgive [us]

עָרְפֵּנוּ כֹף לְךָ לְהִשְׁתַּעְבֶּד,

《 to be subservient, 〈 to You 〈 bend 〈 Our [stiff] neck

בְּאַהֲבָה וּבְיִרְאָה אוֹתְךָ לַעֲבֹד וּלְכַבֵּד.[6]

《 and honor [You]. 〈 we will serve You 〈 and with reverence 〈 so that with love

פּוֹקְדֶיךָ[7] קִדְּשׁוּ צוֹמוֹת[8] לִקְבֹּעַ,

《 establishing [them]; 〈 fasts, 〈 have designated 〈 Those who seek You

דַּעְתָּם קְצָרָה[9] צָרְכָּם לִתְבֹּעַ.

《 to request. 〈 their needs 〈 is inadequate 〈 their understanding

צְקוֹן לַחֲשָׁם[7] אֵלֶיךָ תָבֹא,

《 come; 〈 before You 〈 of their whispered [prayer], 〈 May the outpouring

חַתֵּל לְאִישׁ אִישׁ נִגְעוֹ וּמַכְאוֹבוֹ.[10]

《 and his pain. 〈 his wound 〈 for each person 〈 heal

קוֹל יַעֲקֹב נוֹהֶם מִתְּהוֹמוֹתֶיךָ,

《 from Your depths, 〈 groans 〈 of Jacob 〈 The voice

תִּשְׁמַע הַשָּׁמַיִם מְכוֹן שִׁבְתֶּךָ.[11]

《 of Your dwelling. 〈 the abode 〈 in Heaven, 〈 may You hear [it]

רוֹדֶה רוֹדֵף[12] בְּאַף תְּכַלֶּה,

《 destroy, 〈 — in Your anger 《 who pursues 〈 The oppressor

---

(1) *Jeremiah* 42:2. (2) Cf. *Exodus* 32:12; *Joel* 2:13; *Jonah* 4:2.
(3) See commentary p. 27, s.v. מַעֲבִיר רִאשׁוֹן רִאשׁוֹן. (4) *Jeremiah* 14:7.
(5) Cf. *II Chronicles* 14:10. (6) Cf. *Isaiah* 43:23. (7) Cf. 26:16. (8) Cf. *Joel* 1:14,2:15.
(9) Cf. *Berachos* 29b. (10) Cf. *II Chronicles* 6:29. (11) *I Kings* 8:39,43. (12) Cf. *Isaiah* 14:6.

שְׁנַת שִׁלּוּמִים לְרִיב צִיּוֹן¹ תִּגָּלֶה.

《 reveal. 〈 of Zion 〈 for the grievance 〈 of retribution 〈 and a year

שָׂרַתָּ וְרָדְתָּ מִנְּעַר קְנוֹתָנוּ,

《 to acquire us; 〈 in our youth 〈 and descended [to Egypt] 〈 You saw [our op-pression]

וְאַל תַּשְׁלִיכֵנוּ לְעֵת זִקְנָתֵנוּ.²

《 of our old age! 〈 at the time 〈 cast us off 〈 do not

תָּעִינוּ לִשְׂמֹאל וִימִינְךָ תְּקָרְבֵנוּ,

《 draw us near; 〈 but let Your right hand 《 to the left [to sin], 〈 We have strayed

כִּכְלוֹת כֹּחֵנוּ אַל תַּעַזְבֵנוּ.²

《 abandon us. 〈 do not 〈 is our strength, 〈 when finished

❖ תַּבִּיט וְתָצִיץ וְתַשְׁגִּיחַ לִרְחוּמֶיךָ,

《 the recipients of Your mercy; 〈 and oversee 〈 observe, 〈 Look at,

תִּתְאַזַּר בַּחֲנִינוּתֶךָ, תִּתְלַבֵּשׁ בְּצִדְקוֹתֶיךָ,

《 in Your righteousness. 〈 garb Yourself 《 in Your graciousness; 〈 gird Yourself

תִּתְכַּסֶּה בְּרַחֲמֶיךָ, וְתִתְעַטֵּף בַּחֲסִידוּתֶךָ,

《 in Your [Attribute of] kindness, 〈 wrap Yourself 《 in Your [Attribute of] mercy, 〈 Clothe Yourself

וְתָבֹא לְפָנֶיךָ מִדַּת טוּבְךָ וְעַנְוְתָנוּתֶךָ.³

《 and Your humility. 〈 of Your goodness 〈 the Attribute 〈 before You 〈 and may there come

ALL, WHILE STANDING:

אֵל מֶלֶךְ יוֹשֵׁב עַל כִּסֵּא רַחֲמִים, מִתְנַהֵג

〈 Who acts 《 of mercy, 〈 the throne 〈 on 〈 Who sits 〈 King 〈 O God,

בַּחֲסִידוּת, מוֹחֵל עֲוֹנוֹת עַמּוֹ, מַעֲבִיר רִאשׁוֹן

〈 [sins,] one 〈 Who removes 《 of His people, 〈 the sins 〈 Who pardons 《 with kindness,

---

(1) *Isaiah* 34:8; some editions of *Selichos* omit this line. (2) Cf. *Psalms* 71:9.
(3) See *Berachos* 16b; these last few lines (beginning תַּבִּיט וְתָצִיץ, *Look at, observe*)
do not appear in some early manuscripts and may actually belong to another *selichah*.

רִאשׁוֹן,¹ מַרְבֶּה מְחִילָה לְחַטָּאִים וּסְלִיחָה לַפּוֹשְׁעִים,

‹ by one, « Who abun- ‹ pardon ‹ to unintentional ‹ and ‹ to willful
           dantly grants   sinners   forgiveness   sinners,

עֹשֶׂה צְדָקוֹת עִם כָּל בָּשָׂר וָרוּחַ, לֹא כְרָעָתָם

‹ Who ‹ acts of ‹ with ‹ all ‹ [beings « and «— not ‹ in accord with
performs generosity   of] flesh   spirit   their wickedness

תִּגְמוֹל. ❖ אֵל הוֹרֵיתָ לָנוּ לוֹמַר שְׁלֹשׁ עֶשְׂרֵה, וּזְכוֹר

« do You ‹ O God, « You ‹ us ‹ to ‹ the Thirteen « remem-
repay them!   taught   recite [Attributes of Mercy]; ber

לָנוּ הַיּוֹם בְּרִית שְׁלֹשׁ עֶשְׂרֵה, כְּמוֹ שֶׁהוֹדַעְתָּ לֶעָנָיו

‹ for us ‹ today ‹ the « of [these] Thirteen, ‹ as ‹ You made ‹ to the humble
          covenant   known   one [Moses]

מִקֶּדֶם, כְּמוֹ שֶׁכָּתוּב, וַיֵּרֶד יהוה בֶּעָנָן וַיִּתְיַצֵּב עִמּוֹ

« in ancient ‹ as « it is written: ‹ And HASHEM ‹ in a ‹ and stood ‹ with
times,   descended   cloud   him

שָׁם, וַיִּקְרָא בְשֵׁם יהוה.²

« there, « and He ‹ with the ‹ of
          called out   Name   HASHEM.

CONGREGATION, THEN *CHAZZAN*:

וַיַּעֲבֹר יהוה עַל פָּנָיו וַיִּקְרָא:

«   « [Moses'] ‹ before ‹ And HASHEM passed
and
proclaimed: face,

CONGREGATION AND *CHAZZAN* RECITE LOUDLY AND IN UNISON:

יהוה, יהוה, אֵל, רַחוּם, וְחַנּוּן, אֶרֶךְ אַפַּיִם,

‹ to anger, ‹ Slow « and ‹ Compassionate ‹ God, ‹ HASHEM, ‹ HASHEM,
                     Gracious,

וְרַב חֶסֶד, וֶאֱמֶת, נֹצֵר חֶסֶד לָאֲלָפִים, נֹשֵׂא עָוֹן,

‹ of ‹ Forgiver « for thousands ‹ of ‹ Preserver « and ‹ in ‹ and
iniquity,   [of generations], kindness   Truth,   Kindness Abundant

וָפֶשַׁע, וְחַטָּאָה, וְנַקֵּה.³ וְסָלַחְתָּ לַעֲוֹנֵנוּ וּלְחַטָּאתֵנוּ

« and our sins, ‹ our ‹ May You « and Who ‹ and inadvertent ‹ willful sin,
                iniquities forgive   absolves.   sin,

וּנְחַלְתָּנוּ.⁴ סְלַח לָנוּ אָבִינוּ כִּי חָטָאנוּ, מְחַל לָנוּ

‹ us, ‹ pardon « we have ‹ for « our ‹ us, ‹ Forgive « and make us
               sinned;   Father,   Your heritage.

---

(1) *Rosh Hashanah* 17a. (2) *Exodus* 34:5. (3) 34:6-7. (4) 34:9.

מַלְכֵּנוּ כִּי פָשָׁעְנוּ. כִּי אַתָּה אֲדֹנָי טוֹב וְסַלָּח,

and forgiving, / are good / O Lord, / You, / For / we have willfully sinned. / for / our King,

וְרַב חֶסֶד לְכָל קֹרְאֶיךָ.¹

who call upon You. / to all / kind / and abundantly

PREFATORY VERSES TO SELICHAH 79 / פסוקי הקדמה לסליחה עט

תָּבוֹא לְפָנֶיךָ תְּפִלָּתֵנוּ,² וְאַל תִּתְעַלַּם מִתְּחִנָּתֵנוּ.³

our pleas. / disregard / and do not / our prayer; / before You / Let come

תָּבוֹא לְפָנֶיךָ אֶנְקַת אָסִיר, כְּגֹדֶל זְרוֹעֲךָ, הוֹתֵר

spare / of Your might, / as befits the greatness / of the prisoner; / the groan / before You / Let come

בְּנֵי תְמוּתָה. אַתָּה תָקוּם תְּרַחֵם צִיּוֹן, כִּי

for / to Zion, / and show mercy / will arise / You / to die. / those condemned

עֵת לְחֶנְנָהּ כִּי בָא מוֹעֵד.⁵

the appointed time will have come. / for / to favor her, / [there will come] the time

כְּרַחֵם אָב עַל בָּנִים, כֵּן תְּרַחֵם יהוה עָלֵינוּ.⁶

on us. / HASHEM, / have mercy, / so / his children, / toward / a father is / As merciful as

לַיהוה הַיְשׁוּעָה, עַל עַמְּךָ בִרְכָתֶךָ סֶּלָה.⁷ יהוה

HASHEM, / Selah. / is Your blessing, / Your people / upon / is salvation, / To HASHEM

צְבָאוֹת עִמָּנוּ, מִשְׂגָּב לָנוּ אֱלֹהֵי יַעֲקֹב סֶלָה.⁸

Selah. / of Jacob, / is the God / for us / a stronghold / is with us, / Master of Legions,

יהוה צְבָאוֹת, אַשְׁרֵי אָדָם בֹּטֵחַ בָּךְ.⁹ יהוה הוֹשִׁיעָה,

save! / HASHEM, / in You. / who trusts / is the man / — praiseworthy / Master of Legions / HASHEM,

הַמֶּלֶךְ יַעֲנֵנוּ בְיוֹם קָרְאֵנוּ.¹⁰

we call. / on the day / answer us / May the King

---

(1) Psalms 86:5. (2) Cf. 88:3. (3) Cf. 55:2. (4) 79:11. (5) 102:14.
(6) Cf. 103:13. (7) 3:9. (8) 46:8. (9) 84:13. (10) 20:10.

סליחה עט / SELICHAH 79
(שלישיה)

אֱלֹהֵינוּ וֵאלֹהֵי אֲבוֹתֵינוּ:

《 of our forefathers: 〈 and the God 〈 Our God

אַתָּה חֶלְקִי* וְצוּר לְבָבִי,¹

《 of my 〈 the 《 my 〈 You are
heart;   Rock   portion,*

אִוִּיתִיךָ בַּלַּיְלָה² עַל מִשְׁכָּבִי,³

《 my bed. 〈 on 〈 in the night 〈 I long for You

אֵלֶיךָ יהוה אֶקְרָא בַּעֲטֹף לִבִּי.⁴

《 does my 〈 when 〈 I call 〈 HASHEM, 〈 To You,
heart.   grow faint

בָּגַדְנוּ וְהִרְבִּינוּ חֵמוֹת וּכְעָסִים,

《 and angers; 〈 furies 〈 we have 〈 We have be-
increased   trayed [You],

לְמִרְמָס אָנוּ מְעֻשִּׁים, כִּי אֵין בָּנוּ מַעֲשִׂים.

《 worthy deeds. 〈 we have no 〈 for 《 crushed, 〈 and 〈 [we are subjected]
we are   to trampling

גָּבְרוּ מְאֹד מְצוּקוֹתֵינוּ,

《 are our hardships, 〈 to the 〈 Over-
extreme   whelming

בְּרוֹאֶה שָׁגִינוּ פְּלִילוֹת פּוּקוֹתֵינוּ,⁵

《 we perverted, 〈 and justice 〈 we were 〈 in [not] seeing
in error   [the truth]

וּכְבֶגֶד עִדִּים כָּל צִדְקוֹתֵינוּ.⁶

《   our merits. 〈 are 〈 that is 〈 and like
all   dirty   a rag

דַּעַת חָסַרְנוּ פְּתָאִים מֵעָרְמָה,⁷

《 without cunning, 〈 fools 《 we lacked, 〈 Knowledge

---

(1) Cf. *Psalms* 73:26. (2) *Isaiah* 26:9. (3) Cf. *Song of Songs* 3:1. (4) Cf. *Psalms* 61:3; to conform to the Scriptural verse, some editions of *Selichos* omit the Divine Name from this stich. (5) Cf. *Isaiah* 28:7, see *Rashi* there. (6) 64:5. (7) Cf. *Proverbs* 1:4.

◆§ **אַתָּה חֶלְקִי** — *You are my portion.* Comprising twenty-four triplets, this *selichah* follows an alphabetical acrostic. The last two stanzas bear the author's

signature — אֵלִיָּה בַּר שְׁמַעְיָה חֲזַק וֶאֱמָץ, *Eliyah bar Shemayah, may he be strong and persevere* [see prefatory comment to *Selichah* 14].

²תְּהִלָּה תָשִׂים בְּמַלְאָכֵי רוּמָה, ¹אַף כִּי אֱנוֹשׁ רִמָּה.

Fault ⟨ You find ⟨ even in ⟨ on high, ⟨ so ⟨ that [You ⟨ man, ⟨ who is
the angels   it is   will find   but a
certain deficient]   worm.

³הֵן אִיִּם תִּטֹּל כַּדָּק, וְאִם עַוְלָתָה תְּחַפֵּשׂ וְתִבְדֹּק,

Indeed, ⟨ islands ⟨ You will ⟨ like fine ⟨ and if ⟨ for iniquity ⟨ You should ⟨ You should
the   blow away dust;   search,   examine,

⁴מַה נְּדַבֵּר וּמַה נִּצְטַדָּק.

what ⟨ can we ⟨ How ⟨ can we justify
speak?   ourselves?

⁵וָאֲבַקֵּשׁ גּוֹדֵר גָּדֵר וְעוֹמֵד בַּפֶּרֶץ,

I have ⟨ someone ⟨ fences ⟨ and stand ⟨ in the
sought to mend   [in prayer]   breach,

⁶וְיָשָׁר אֵין פָּנִים לְהָרַע, אָבַד חָסִיד מִן הָאָרֶץ.

but an ⟨ there ⟨ who ⟨ could ⟨ gone ⟨ is the ⟨ from ⟨ the earth.
upright is not before appease;   pious man
man   You

זְמַן קִצִּי סָתוּם מִלֵּדַע,

The ⟨ of my [salva- ⟨ is ⟨ beyond
time   tion's] end sealed knowing;

עֲוֹנוֹתַי הִטּוּ⁷ קַרְנִי לְהִגָּדַע, ⁸כִּי פְשָׁעַי אֲנִי אֵדָע.⁹

my sins ⟨ have ⟨ my ⟨ to be cut ⟨ for ⟨ my ⟨ I ⟨ recognize.
overturned pride, down,   transgressions

¹⁰חָמָס אֶזְעַק וְאֵין מוֹשִׁיעַ,

Injustice! ⟨ I shout, ⟨ but there ⟨ savior.
is no

¹¹לָמָה צַדִּיק מַכְתִּיר מַרְשִׁיעַ,

Why ⟨ is the right- ⟨ surrounded ⟨ by the wicked,
eous man

¹²וְלֹא קָצְרָה יָדְךָ מֵהוֹשִׁיעַ.

when ⟨ too short ⟨ is Your ⟨ to save [him]?
not   hand

¹³טְלָאֶיךָ דוֹפְקִים כַּיָּם הוֹמִים,

Your sheep ⟨ are knocking, ⟨ like ⟨ they roar
the sea   [in prayer],

---

(1) Cf. *Job* 4:18. (2) 25:6. (3) Cf. *Isaiah* 40:15. (4) *Genesis* 44:16. (5) Cf. *Ezekiel* 22:30.
(6) *Micah* 7:2. (7) Cf. *Jeremiah* 5:25. (8) Cf. *Lamentations* 2:3. (9) *Psalms* 51:5.
(10) Cf. *Habakkuk* 1:2. (11) Cf. 1:4. (12) Cf. *Isaiah* 59:1. (13) Cf. 17:12, *Jeremiah* 51:55.

אֲנוּסִים חֲמוּסִים בְּיַד אֲמִים,

《 of the 〈 at the 〈 and robbed 〈 coerced
nations. hand

לָמָּה לָנֶצַח תִּשְׁכָּחֵנוּ, תַּעַזְבֵנוּ לְאֹרֶךְ יָמִים.[1]

《 of days? 〈 for the 〈 forsaken us 《 have You 〈 eternally 〈 Why
length forgotten us,

יַעֲקֹב לִמְשִׁסָּה וְיִשְׂרָאֵל לְבוֹזְזִים,[2]

《 to the looters. 〈 Israel 《 [was given over] 〈 Jacob;
to oppression,

כְּבוּדָּה שִׁבְעַת חֻפּוֹת חֲזִיזִים,*

《 of clouds;* 〈 canopies 〈 by seven 〈 Once dignified

כְּרָחֵל נֶאֱלָמָה לִפְנֵי גוֹזְזִים.[3]

《 the 〈 before 〈 she has 〈 Like a
shearers. become mute sheep

בִּילַי וְנָבָל[4] כְּמֶלֶךְ בִּמְסִבּוֹ,

《 on his 〈 are like 〈 and the 〈 The
couch, a king vile man miser

נָדִיב וְשׁוֹעַ[4] נִטְרָד בְּחוֹבוֹ, כִּכְלִי אֵין חֵפֶץ בּוֹ.[5]

《 in it. 〈 interest 〈 that there 〈 like a 《 for his guilt, 〈 is exiled 〈 and 〈 while the
is no vessel noble generous

לֹא לְעוֹלָם תִּטֹּר[6] לְהַחֲרִיבֵנִי,

《 to destroy me; 〈 will You hold 〈 forever 〈 Not
resentment

שְׂמֹאלְךָ דְּחִיתַנִי יְמִינְךָ תְּקָרְבֵנִי.*

《 bring me 〈 may Your 《 pushed me 〈 Your left hand
close.* right hand away,

---

(1) *Lamentations* 5:20; some editions of *Selichos* read אַל תִּשְׁכָּחֵנוּ לָנֶצַח, *do not forget us eternally.*
(2) Cf. *Isaiah* 42:24. (3) Cf. 53:7. (4) Cf. 32:5. (5) *Hosea* 8:8. (6) Cf. *Jeremiah* 3:12.

שִׁבְעַת חֻפּוֹת חֲזִיזִים — *Seven canopies of clouds.* During its forty-year sojourn in the Wilderness, the nation was accompanied by the protective עֲנַנֵי הַכָּבוֹד, *Clouds of Glory.* According to one view in the Midrash (*Bamidbar Rabbah* 1:2), there were seven clouds. Not just ordinary clouds, the four situated to the east, west, north, and south protected Israel from any arrows or missiles that may have been aimed at them; a fifth cloud was overhead to protect them from the heat of the desert sun; a sixth cloud formed a mat beneath their feet, protecting them

from serpents and scorpions and leveling the ground to ease their travel; and a seventh, the עַמּוּד הֶעָנָן, *column of cloud*, stayed some distance ahead of the encampment, leading them through the Wilderness.

שְׂמֹאלְךָ דְּחִיתַנִי יְמִינְךָ תְּקָרְבֵנִי — *Your left hand pushed me away, may Your right hand bring me close.* The Talmud teaches a lesson in pedagogy: Always push away [a wayward student] with the left hand, yet draw him close with the right (*Sanhedrin* 107b). *Maharsha* explains that מִדַּת הַדִּין, *the Attribute of Strict Justice*, is represented

אֲדֹנָי עָשְׁקָה לִי עָרְבֵנִי.[1]

《 and guarantee 〈 steal me away 〈 O Lord,
[my salvation]. [from the oppressors]

מֵאָז תָּמִיד לָנוּ הַדִּבָּה, הִקְוֵיתָ* שָׁבִים בְּרוּחַ נְדִיבָה,

《 that is 〈 with a 〈 to 〈 yet You have 《 has been 〈 on us 〈 always, 〈 From
generous: spirit penitents given hope* the slander, the start,

אֶרְפָּא מְשׁוּבָתָם אֹהֲבֵם נְדָבָה.[2]

《 freely. 〈 I will love 《 their 〈 [by saying:]
them waywardness; I will heal

נוֹבְעוֹת (עֵינַי) כְּנַחַל אֲגָלַי,

《 of [tear] 〈 like a 〈 (do my 〈 Flow
drops, stream eyes)

הוֹלֵל שׁוֹקֵט וְשָׁבְתוּ גִילַי, וַאֲנִי כִּמְעַט נָטְיוּ רַגְלָי.[3]

《 were 〈 turned 〈 — almost 《 but as 《 are my 〈 while 《 is serene, 〈 for the
my feet. astray for me joys; ended scoffer

שֶׂה אֹבֵד בַּקֵּשׁ עַם נוֹשַׁע,

《 saved 〈 the 《 seek, 〈 that 〈 [Your]
[by You], people is lost, sheep

אָוֶן מָצָא מִבֶּטֶן פֶּשַׁע.* צַדִּיק מָט לִפְנֵי רָשָׁע.[4]

《 the 〈 before 〈 bows 〈 [Even if] 《 sinfulness.* 〈 from 《 it has 〈 [even if]
wicked, the right- birth, found, wrong-
eous man doing

עֵדוּת בְּיַעֲקֹב בִּתְעוּדָה נֶחְתָּם,

《 is signed. 〈 in the testimonial 〈 of Jacob's 〈 witness
document future
[the Torah]

---

(1) *Isaiah* 38:14; some editions of *Selichos* read this entire stanza in the plural, using the suffix נו, *us*, in place of יִ, *me*. (2) *Hosea* 14:5. (3) *Psalms* 73:2. (4) *Proverbs* 25:6.

by the left hand; מִדַּת הָרַחֲמִים, *the Attribute of Mercy*, by the right. Thus, even when Justice requires a master to push away his disciple, Mercy demands that he draw him close. According to *Iyun Yaakov* (to *Sotah* 47a), it is only with the weaker left hand that one may punish, but with the stronger right hand one should reward.

In either case, the *paytan* pleads that we have already been pushed away; it is now time for God to draw us close to Him.

הִקְוֵיתָ — *Yet You have given hope.* The translation follows *Pardes* and *Matteh Levi*, who derive the word from תִּקְוָה, *hope — You*

have given hope, You have encouraged. According to *Masbir*, the word is cognate to מִקְוֶה, *a gathering of water*, and means *You have gathered in*.

מִבֶּטֶן פֶּשַׁע — *From birth sinfulness* [lit., *from the womb, waywardness*]. The period of Egyptian enslavement is considered as the womb from which the nation of Israel emerged. From their very birth as a nation, the people were rebellious, as Moses said (*Deuteronomy* 9:7), *From the day when you left the land of Egypt until your arrival at this place, rebels have you been against HASHEM* (based on *Rashi* and *Radak* to *Isaiah* 48:8).

בְּאֶרֶץ אוֹיֵב הִבְטַחְתָּ לְהַחֲיוֹתָם,

《 to nurture them, 〈 You have 〈 of the 〈 In
promised enemy the land

וְאַף גַּם זֹאת בִּהְיוֹתָם.¹

《 while they are [in 〈 this, 〈 despite 〈 But
their enemies' land . . .]. all yet

פְּשָׁעִים תַּעֲבִיר וְחוֹבוֹת תִּמְחֹק,

《 erase; 〈 and guilt 《 remove, 〈 Willful sins

הִרְחִיבָה שְׁאוֹל נַפְשָׁה לִדְחֹק, וּפָעֲרָה פִּיהָ לִבְלִי חֹק.²

《 limit. 〈 without 〈 its 〈 and has 《 to push 〈 [more] 〈 does 〈 for broaden
mouth opened wide in, souls Gehinnom itself

צֹפֶה נַחְשׁוֹל קָרֵב לְחַפְּשֵׁנוּ,³

《 to set us free, 〈 come 《 the storm 〈 See
near [upon us];

דְּלֵנוּ וְהַעֲלֵנוּ מִטִּיט רִפְשֵׁנוּ, שׁוּבָה יהוה חַלְּצָה נַפְשֵׁנוּ.⁴

《 our 〈 release 〈 O 〈 return, 《 and our 〈 out of 〈 lift us up 〈 pull us
soul! HASHEM, mire; the mud out,

קִדַּשְׁנוּ צוֹם בִּתְפִלָּה לְקַדֵּם,

《 to come 〈 with prayer 〈 a fast 〈 We have
to You; sanctified

חֲבֹשׁ וּצְרִי לְמַכָּתֵנוּ הַקְדֵּם, זְכֹר עֲדָתְךָ קָנִיתָ קֶדֶם.⁵

《 long 〈 that You 〈 Your con- 〈 remem- 《 bring 〈 for our 〈 and 〈 bandage
ago. acquired gregation, ber forward; wound balm

רֹגֶז הַנַּח כַּעַס יֵחָשֵׂךְ,

《 be withheld; 〈 let anger 〈 put aside, 〈 Wrath

אֲסוּרִים בַּעֲבוֹתוֹת אֱהַב, וְהַמְשֵׁךְ⁶

〈 and draw forth 《 show love, 〈 in chains 〈 those bound

מִבֵּית כֶּלֶא יוֹשְׁבֵי חֹשֶׁךְ.⁷

《 in 〈 those 〈 of 〈 from a
darkness. dwelling detention house

שִׁלּוּחַ קְרָא לִשְׁבוּרָה וְלִשְׁמוּטָה,

《 and pushed out 〈 for those 〈 declare 〈 Liberation
[in exile]; broken

---

(1) *Leviticus* 26:44. (2) *Isaiah* 5:14. (3) Some editions read לְחַפְּשֵׂנוּ, *to search for us.*
(4) Cf. *Psalms* 6:5. (5) 74:2. (6) Some editions read אֲסוּרִים בַּעֲבוֹתוֹת אֲהַב הַמְשֵׁךְ,
draw forth with chains of love those who are bound, see *Hosea* 11:4; others read,
אֲסוּרֵי אַהַב בַּעֲבוֹתוֹת הַמְשֵׁךְ, *draw forth with chains the prisoners of love.* (7) *Isaiah* 42:7.

בְּרִיחַ גֻּדַּע שֶׁבֶר מוֹטָה, רְפָה שְׁבָרֶיהָ כִּי מָטָה.[1]

‹ the bar ‹ cut ≪ break ‹ Heal ≪ the yoke! ‹ her fragments, ‹ for ‹ she totters.

תְּשׁוּבָה הֲשֵׁבֹתִי לַתַּנִּין וְזוֹחֵל,[2]

‹ An answer ‹ I have answered ‹ to the serpent, ≪ and the slither-ing [creature],

תִּקְוָתִי הוּא סוֹלֵחַ וּמוֹחֵל,≪

‹ My hope I place ‹ in Him ‹ Who forgives ≪ and pardons;

הֵן (אִם) יִקְטְלֵנִי לוֹ אֲיַחֵל.[3]

‹ in-deed ‹ (though) ‹ He may slay me, ≪ for Him ≪ I will yearn.

אֵלֵינוּ הַטֵּה בּוֹרֵא אָזְנֶךָ,

‹ To us ‹ incline, ‹ O Creator, ≪ Your ear!

שְׁמַע יָהּ דּוֹרְשֶׁיךָ הַקְשִׁיבָה מְחַנְּנֶיךָ,[4]

‹ Hear, ‹ O God, ≪ those who seek You, ≪ be attentive ‹ to those who sup-plicate before You.

תִּכּוֹן תְּפִלָּתִי קְטֹרֶת לְפָנֶיךָ.[5]

‹ Considered ‹ should be ‹ as incense ‹ before You. ≪ my prayer

❖ חַזֵּק כּוֹשֵׁל וְאַמֵּץ רִפְיוֹן,[6]

‹ Strengthen ‹ the one who is failing, ‹ fortify ≪ the weak.

מִקְדָּשׁ יַסֵּד, יַשֵּׁב אַפִּרְיוֹן, הֵיטִיבָה בִרְצוֹנְךָ אֶת צִיּוֹן.[7]

‹ The Sanctuary ‹ establish; ≪ restore ‹ the Temple; ≪ do good ‹ in Your favor ‹ unto ‹ Zion.

ALL, WHILE STANDING:

אֵל מֶלֶךְ יוֹשֵׁב עַל כִּסֵּא רַחֲמִים, מִתְנַהֵג

‹ O God, ‹ King ‹ Who sits ‹ on ‹ the throne ‹ of mercy, ≪ Who acts

בַּחֲסִידוּת, מוֹחֵל עֲוֹנוֹת עַמּוֹ, מַעֲבִיר רִאשׁוֹן

≪ with kindness, ‹ Who pardons ‹ the sins ‹ of His people, ≪ Who removes ‹ [sins,] one

רִאשׁוֹן,[8] מַרְבֶּה מְחִילָה לַחַטָּאִים וּסְלִיחָה לַפּוֹשְׁעִים,

≪ by one, ‹ Who abun-dantly grants ‹ pardon ‹ to unintentional sinners ‹ and forgiveness ≪ to willful sinners,

---

(1) *Psalms* 60:4. (2) Cf. *Deuteronomy* 32:24, 33. (3) *Job* 13:15; the word אִם, included in some editions of *Selichos*, does not appear in the Scriptural verse, and does not change the meaning of the stich. (4) Cf. *Daniel* 9:17-18. (5) *Psalms* 141:2. (6) Cf. *Isaiah* 35:3. (7) *Psalms* 51:20. (8) *Rosh Hashanah* 17a.

עֹשֶׂה צְדָקוֹת עִם כָּל בָּשָׂר וָרוּחַ, לֹא כְרָעָתָם

⟨ Who performs ⟨ acts of generosity ⟨ with ⟨ all ⟨ [beings of] flesh ⟨ and spirit ⟨ — not ⟨ in accord with their wickedness

תִּגְמוֹל. ❖ אֵל הוֹרֵיתָ לָּנוּ לוֹמַר שְׁלֹשׁ עֶשְׂרֵה, וּזְכוֹר

⟨ do You repay them! ⟨ O God, ⟨ You taught ⟨ us ⟨ to recite ⟨ the Thirteen [Attributes of Mercy]; ⟨ remember

לָּנוּ הַיּוֹם בְּרִית שְׁלֹשׁ עֶשְׂרֵה, כְּמוֹ שֶׁהוֹדַעְתָּ לֶעָנָיו

⟨ for us ⟨ today ⟨ the covenant ⟨ of [these] Thirteen, ⟨ as ⟨ You made known ⟨ to the humble one [Moses]

מִקֶּדֶם, כְּמוֹ שֶׁכָּתוּב, וַיֵּרֶד יהוה בֶּעָנָן וַיִּתְיַצֵּב עִמּוֹ

⟨ in ancient times, ⟨ as ⟨ it is written: ⟨ And HASHEM ⟨ descended ⟨ in a cloud ⟨ and stood ⟨ with him

שָׁם, וַיִּקְרָא בְשֵׁם יהוה.[1]

⟨ there, ⟨ and He called out ⟨ with the Name ⟨ of HASHEM.

CONGREGATION, THEN *CHAZZAN*:

וַיַּעֲבֹר יהוה עַל פָּנָיו וַיִּקְרָא:

⟨ And HASHEM passed ⟨ before ⟨ [Moses'] face, ⟨ and proclaimed:

CONGREGATION AND *CHAZZAN* RECITE LOUDLY AND IN UNISON:

יהוה, יהוה, אֵל, רַחוּם, וְחַנּוּן, אֶרֶךְ אַפַּיִם,

⟨ HASHEM, ⟨ HASHEM, ⟨ God, ⟨ Compassionate ⟨ and Gracious, ⟨ Slow ⟨ to anger,

וְרַב חֶסֶד, וֶאֱמֶת, נֹצֵר חֶסֶד לָאֲלָפִים, נֹשֵׂא עָוֹן,

⟨ and Abundant Kindness ⟨ in Kindness ⟨ and Truth, ⟨ Preserver ⟨ of kindness ⟨ for thousands [of generations], ⟨ Forgiver ⟨ of iniquity,

וָפֶשַׁע, וְחַטָּאָה, וְנַקֵּה.[2] וְסָלַחְתָּ לַעֲוֹנֵנוּ וּלְחַטָּאתֵנוּ

⟨ willful sin, ⟨ and inadvertent sin, ⟨ and our sins, ⟨ and Who absolves. ⟨ May You forgive ⟨ our iniquities ⟨ and our sins,

וּנְחַלְתָּנוּ.[3] סְלַח לָנוּ אָבִינוּ כִּי חָטָאנוּ, מְחַל לָנוּ

⟨ and make us Your heritage. ⟨ Forgive ⟨ us, ⟨ our Father, ⟨ for ⟨ we have sinned; ⟨ pardon ⟨ us,

(1) *Exodus* 34:5. (2) 34:6-7. (3) 34:9.

מַלְכֵּנוּ כִּי פָשָׁעְנוּ. כִּי אַתָּה אֲדֹנָי טוֹב וְסַלָּח,

《 and   〈 are   〈 O Lord,   〈 You,   〈 For 《 we have   〈 for 《 our King,
forgiving,   good   willfully sinned.

וְרַב חֶסֶד לְכָל קֹרְאֶיךָ.[1]

《 who call   〈 to all   〈 kind 〈 and
upon You.   abundantly

פסוקי הקדמה לסליחה פ / PREFATORY VERSES TO SELICHAH 80

כִּי עִמְּךָ הַסְּלִיחָה, לְמַעַן תִּוָּרֵא.[2] זֹאת נָשִׁיב

〈 we take   〈 This   《 You may   〈 so that   〈 is forgiveness,   〈 with You 〈 For
         be feared.   [alone]

אֶל לִבֵּנוּ, עַל כֵּן נוֹחִיל.[3] כִּי עִם יהוה הַחֶסֶד,

《 is   〈 HASHEM 〈 with   〈 For 《 we have   〈 [and]   《 our   〈 to
kindness,   hope.   therefore   hearts,

וְהַרְבֵּה עִמּוֹ פְדוּת.[4] טוֹב יהוה לְקֹוָו, לְנֶפֶשׁ

〈 to the   《 to those who   〈 is   〈 Good 《 is   〈 with   〈 and
soul   trust in Him,   redemption.   HASHEM   Him   abundant

תִּדְרְשֶׁנּוּ.[5]

《 that seeks Him.

כְּרַחֵם אָב עַל בָּנִים, כֵּן תְּרַחֵם יהוה עָלֵינוּ.[6]

《 on us.   〈 HASHEM, 〈 have   〈 so 《 his   〈 toward 〈 a   〈 As merciful as
          mercy,   children,   father is

לַיהוה הַיְשׁוּעָה, עַל עַמְּךָ בִרְכָתֶךָ סֶּלָה.[7] יהוה

〈 HASHEM, 《 Selah.   《 is Your   〈 Your   〈 upon 《 is salvation,   〈 To HASHEM
        blessing,   people

צְבָאוֹת עִמָּנוּ, מִשְׂגָּב לָנוּ אֱלֹהֵי יַעֲקֹב סֶלָה.[8]

《 Selah.   《 of Jacob,   〈 is the God   〈 for us 〈 a   〈 is with us,   〈 Master of
              stronghold   Legions,

יהוה צְבָאוֹת, אַשְׁרֵי אָדָם בֹּטֵחַ בָּךְ.[9] יהוה

〈 HASHEM, 《 in You.   〈 who   〈 is the 〈 — praiseworthy 《 Master   〈 HASHEM,
             trusts   man   of Legions

הוֹשִׁיעָה, הַמֶּלֶךְ יַעֲנֵנוּ בְיוֹם קָרְאֵנוּ.[10]

《 we call.   〈 on the   〈 answer   〈 May the   《 save!
          day   us   King

---

(1) *Psalms* 86:5. (2) 130:4. (3) Cf. *Lamentations* 3:21. (4) *Psalms* 130:7.
(5) *Lamentations* 3:25. (6) Cf. *Psalms* 103:13. (7) 3:9. (8) 46:8. (9) 84:13. (10) 20:10.

סליחה פ / SELICHAH 80
(שלמונית)

ALL:

אֱלֹהֵינוּ וֵאלֹהֵי אֲבוֹתֵינוּ:

《 of our forefathers: 〈 and the God 〈 Our God

תּוֹחֶלֶת יִשְׂרָאֵל* חֶסֶד לֹא נֶעֱזָב,

《 aban- 〈 that is 〈 is in [God's] 〈 of Israel* 〈 The hope
doned; never kindness

תִּקְוָתָם נֶצַח אֵמוּן לֹא אַכְזָב,

《 fail. 〈 that will 〈 faith- 《 eternal, 〈 it is their
never fulness hope

שׁוֹמְרֵי חֲזוֹן הַמּוֹעֵד[1] רוֹאוֹת כְּמַרְזָב,*

《 through a flow 〈 see 〈 time [of 〈 the 〈 Those who
[of tears];* redemption] envisaged await

שָׁחוּ כֻלּוּ וְעֵמֶק הַבָּכָא[2] זָב.*

《 flows.* 〈 of 〈 and 〈 wasting 〈 they are
Weeping the Vale away, bent over,

רוּם רַעֲנָן,[3] מַטָּה מַטֶּה שָׁפֵל,

《 is it 〈 lower 〈 [now] 〈 verdant 〈 [Israel,]
debased; down, lower, tree the lofty,

רֹאשׁ לְזָנָב וְעִקָּר לַעֲרַאי וְטָפֵל,

《 and 〈 to 〈 the 《 [is turned 〈 the
triviality. transience essence to] the tail, head

קֵץ תַּכְלִית לְיוֹשְׁבֵי חֹשֶׁךְ וּמַאֲפֵל,[4]

《 and the 〈 in the 〈 [is turned 〈 the 〈 The Ulti-
gloom; dark to] sitting goal mate End,

---

(1) Cf. *Habakkuk* 2:3. (2) Cf. *Psalms* 84:7; see *Eruvin* 19a. (3) Cf. *Jeremiah* 11:16.
(4) Many early editions read קֵץ חֹשֶׁךְ תַּכְלִית לְיוֹשְׁבֵי מַאֲפֵל, *The conclusion of the darkness,
the end for those who sit in gloom;* cf. *Job* 28:3.

◆§ תּוֹחֶלֶת יִשְׂרָאֵל — *The hope of Israel.* The
acrostic of this *shalmonis* forms a double
reverse *aleph-beis* (תשר״ק) followed by the
author's signature — שְׁלֹמֹה הַקָּטָן, *Shlomo the
lesser* [see prefatory comment to *Selichah*
2].

רוֹאוֹת כְּמַרְזָב — *See through a flow [of tears].*
The text and translation follow the reading
found in many editions, including *Masbir*
and *Pardes.* However, many editions follow

the reading of *Arugas HaBosem,* רְאוֹת כְּמַרְזָב,
to see a flow. The sense of the verse is then,
*they wait to see a flow of redemption de-
scending from heaven.*

וְעֵמֶק הַבָּכָא זָב — *And the Vale of Weeping
flows.* The literal meaning of עֵמֶק הַבָּכָא
(*Psalms* 84:7) is either *the Vale of Bacha (Ibn
Ezra); the Vale of the Foundation (Rashi);
the Vale of Confusion (Rambam); or the
Vale of Bacha Trees,* a berry tree that grows

קַוֵּה לָאוֹר וְשִׁית עָנָן וַעֲרָפֶל.¹

≪ and fog. ⟨ was ⟨ but set ⟨ for the ⟨ they
cloud upon them light, hoped

צְבִי קֹדֶשׁ הִלַּלְתָּ² רֵאשִׁית לְהַרְשִׁים,³

≪ designating ⟨ as First ⟨ [Israel] whom ⟨ holy, ⟨ Desired,
them — You once praised,

צֵץ הַמַּטֶּה פָּרַח הַזָּדוֹן⁴ לְיוֹרְשִׁים,*

≪ for [the conquerors'] ⟨ has the ⟨ blos- ≪ has the ⟨ budded
heirs.* willful sin somed staff,

פִּנִּיתָ סְלָעִים וּטְרָשִׁים לְהַשְׁבִּיחַ שָׁרָשִׁים,⁵

≪ the roots, ⟨ to enhance ⟨ and rocks ⟨ the ⟨ [Though
boulders once] You
cleared away

פָּרַצְתָּ מְשׂוֹשׂ פְּרָאִים וַעֲמָלֵק חוֹרְשִׁים.⁷

≪ and the Amal- ⟨ of the ⟨ to the ⟨ [Israel's] ⟨ [now] You
akites plowing [Ishmaelite] delight barrier, have burst
[over them]. wild donkeys

עָרִיץ וְכָל הַבָּא בּוֹזֵז וְשׁוֹלֵל,

≪ and pillage; ⟨ plunder ⟨ who ⟨ and all ⟨ The
come, powerful,

עוֹבֵר וָשָׁב וְזִיז שָׂדַי⁸ יְעוֹלֵל,

≪ scavange. ≪ of the ⟨ even the ≪ and ⟨ all who
field, vermin fro, pass, to

סָבָאִים⁹ שְׂבֵעִים שְׁאָר דָּשִׁים לְמוֹלֵל,

≪ and crush, ⟨ they ⟨ what is ≪ are sated, ⟨ The Sabeans
trample left

סוֹכַת יֶתֶר הַבַּז לְזַלְזֵל הִתְעוֹלֵל.

≪ and scorn. ⟨ they ⟨ from the ⟨ that ⟨ and the
ridicule plundering, remain branches

---

(1) Cf. *Jeremiah* 13:16. (2) Some editions read חִלַּלְתָּ, and the stich means, *Beautiful, holy [Israel] have You profaned, those You had designated 'First.'* (3) See *Jeremiah* 2:3. (4) *Ezekiel* 7:10. (5) Cf. *Psalms* 80:10. (6) Many editions read וַחֲזִירֵי חְרְשִׁים, *the boars of the forest,* a reference to the Romans. (7) Cf. 80:13-14; see also *Isaiah* 32:14. (8) Cf. *Psalms* 80:14. (9) *Isaiah* 45:14.

in arid areas (*Radak* to *Psalms* 84:7 and *II Samuel* 5:23).

However, the Talmud (*Eruvin* 19a) interprets the word בָּכָא as if it were spelled בְּכָה, *weeping.* Thus, עֵמֶק הַבָּכָא is *the Vale of Weeping.*

לְיוֹרְשִׁים — *For [the conquerors'] heirs.* This

refers to the generations that succeeded the original conquerors of the Land of Israel (*Arugas HaBosem; Masbir*). Alternatively, it refers to those who were to have inherited the Land — Israel — and the translation is, *[to be used against the Patriarchs'] heirs* (*Pardes*).

נֶטַע כַּנָּתְךָ¹ לְמִגְזַר בַּרְזֶל וַחֲרִיצִים,

« and threshing ⟨ with iron ⟨ is slashed ⟨ vine ⟨ Your
boards —   weapons   planted

נָטַשְׁתָּ וְעָזַבְתָּ וּבָאוּ בָהּ פְּרִיצִים,

«   ruffians.   ⟨ upon ⟨ and there « Your   ⟨ You aban-
                   it   came   deserted it,   doned it,

מִצִּיֶּנֶת חָפוּי כֶּסֶף וִירַקְרַק חֲרוּצִים,³

«   gold,   ⟨ and brilliant ⟨ with   ⟨ covered « [Israel,] the
                               silver   outstanding
                                                 [dove],

מִדְרַס גֵּז וָנֵץ* אֶפְרוֹחֶיהָ קְרוּצִים.

« slaughtered. ⟨   its chicks   « by predatory ⟨ is preyed
                                    birds,*   upon

לְכָל הַבָּא עָלֵינוּ מְעַט קָצַפְתָּ,

« were You angry⟨ only a « upon us, ⟨ that ⟨ In all
   [with us];   little   came

לְרָעָה עָזְרוּ גּוֹי עַז חִצַּפְתָּ,⁴

« whom You « that was ⟨ did the ⟨ help ⟨ but to do
made insolent. brazen, nation   out   [extreme] evil

כַּף עַיִן בְּעַיִן מִפְּרֹעַ אָסַפְתָּ,

« You held « to punish ⟨ for ⟨ — mea- « Your
  back,   [us] —   measure sure   hand

כִּלַּפֵּי חֶסֶד זְרוֹעַ לְרַע גָּבוּי חָשַׂפְתָּ.

«   You   ⟨ to ⟨ for evil ⟨ when « kindness ⟨ as toward
revealed. punish   Your   [You tipped
                           arm   the scales],

יָד לְקַבֵּל פָּשַׁטְתָּ וְנָתַנּוּ סוֹרֶרֶת,

«   with   ⟨ but we « You ⟨ to receive ⟨ A
rebellion; responded extended, [penitents] hand

יָד אָזְלַת⁵ מִקּוֹל כְּקוֹל הַנִּסְרֶת,

«   sawing   ⟨ which is like « because of ⟨ is ⟨ [therefore]
[through   the sound the din [of   gone our power
space].   of [the sun] the nations],

---

(1) Cf. *Psalms* 80:16. (2) Cf. *II Samuel* 12:31. (3) Cf. *Psalms* 68:14.
(4) Cf. *Zechariah* 1:15. (5) Cf. *Deuteronomy* 32:36.

גֵּז וָנֵץ — *By predatory birds.* We do not attempt to identify these birds. According to
Ibn Ezra (*Leviticus* 11:16), the נֵץ is so named
because of its abundance of נוֹצָה, *feathers.*
The name גָּז or גַּז is probably related to וַיָּגָז,

and He caused to fly (see *Rashi* to *Numbers*
11:31). However, according to *Tosafos* (*Chul-
lin* 42a) and *Arugas HaBosem* the word is
spelled גַּס, and means *a large [bird]*; it is a
descriptive term, not a noun (*Masbir*).

טֹר חֶסֶד וּבְרִית לְאָבוֹת¹ מַסְרֶת,

《 handed ⟨ to the ⟨ and the ⟨ the ⟨ Safe-
down to us;   Patriarchs   covenant   kindness   guard

טוֹב טַעַם פְּתַח לְהַתִּיר אֲסֻרֶת.

《 the impris- ⟨ to release ⟨ declare ⟨ reason ⟨ [with]
oned people.   good

חֶשְׁבּוֹן אַחַר חֶשְׁבּוֹן עַמְּךָ יִפְתֹּר,

《 tries to ⟨ Your ⟨ calculation ⟨ after ⟨ Calculation
solve,   people [for the time of
         redemption]

חוֹכֶה וְסוֹכֶה וְדָוֶה וְחוֹזֵר לִפְתֹּר,

《 to ⟨ and ⟨ become ⟨ watching ⟨ hoping [for
calculation.   return   despondent,   for it,   redemption],

זָח אוֹר מַשְׂכִּיל יְכֹלֶת לַחְתֹּר,

《 [them] to ⟨ that would ⟨ is the ⟨ of intellect ⟨ But re-
investigate,   enable   light   moved

זְמַן קוֹל הַתּוֹר מָתַי לִפְתֹּר.²

《 to solve. ⟨ when [it ⟨ of the ⟨ for the ⟨ and the
will be   dove   sound   time
heard]

וּבְכָל זֹאת חָלִילָה בַּאֱמָנָה לְשַׁקֵּר,³

《 to falsify, ⟨ their faith ⟨ it would be ⟨ this, ⟨ Yet with
sacrilegious   all

וְזָר לֹא יוֹעִיל קְלוֹנוּ לְיַקֵּר,⁴

《 to give ⟨ in its ⟨ avail, ⟨ that ⟨ or to a
honor.   degradation   cannot   strange
[god]

הֶעָקֹב רַב וְהַסַּתָּת תָּשׁ לַעֲקֹר,

《 to uproot it; ⟨ is too ⟨ yet the ⟨ is ⟨ [Their]
weak   stonecutter   great,   crooked [Evil
[in us]   Inclination]

הַדָּבָר עָלֶיךָ כְּלָיוֹת חוֹקֵר וּמְבַקֵּר.⁵

《 and inspects. ⟨ probes ⟨ Who of ⟨ is up to ⟨ so the
thoughts   You,   matter

דְּרֹשׁ וּפְקֹד דַּלַּת שְׁפָלוּת שְׁחוֹחַ,

《 and bowed ⟨ of those ⟨ the ⟨ call to ⟨ Seek
low,   lowered   poverty   mind   out,

---

(1) Cf. *Deuteronomy* 7:9. (2) Cf. *Song of Songs* 2:12.
(3) Cf. *Nehemiah* 10:1. (4) Cf. *Jeremiah* 2:11. (5) Cf. 17:10.

דַּל כֶּרֶם וּמְעֹרָבָב צָחֵי צְחוֹחַ,

《 and totally parched. 〈 in disarray 〈 vine-yard 〈 the poor

גָּדֵר עָזוּק עָדַר מִקְמוֹשׂ וָחוֹחַ,

《 and thorns! 〈 of brambles 〈 weed it 《 bound it round, 〈 Fence it,

גֶּפֶן מַטַּע לְהַכְשִׁיר עִנְּבֵי נִיחוֹחַ.

《 for the sweet-smelling [libations]. 〈 to bear grapes 〈 be made fit 〈 You planted 〈 Let the vine

בָּנוּ שִׁמְךָ עֶלְיוֹן נִקְרָא לְכָל תִּכְלָה,

《 has an end; 〈 [and in this world] everything 《 is called, 〈 O Most High, 〈 Your Name, 〈 Upon us

בֹּא בְּמִדַּת חֶסֶד וְלֹא בְכָלָה,

《 with destruction. 〈 and not 〈 of Mercy, 〈 with the Attribute 〈 come to us

אַשְׁמָתֵנוּ גָדְלָה עַד תְּמֶן וְעָבְלָא,

《 even the smallest measures are needed to be filled, 〈 until 〈 is grown great, 〈 Our guilt

אַתָּה יהוה רַחֲמֶיךָ לֹא תִכְלָא.[1]

《 hold back. 〈 never 〈 Your mercy 〈 HASHEM, 〈 but You,

שֶׁבַח הִלּוּל מִדּוֹתֶיךָ אֵין לְשַׁנּוֹת,[2]

《 be changed, 〈 cannot 〈 that Your ways 〈 and lauding 〈 [It is Your] praise

לְבֵית יִשְׂרָאֵל רַב טוּב חֲנוּת,[3]

《 grace. 〈 good-ness 〈 with abundant 〈 of Israel 〈 the House

מְקוֹם מָנוֹחַ* שִׂים בְּרֹאשׁ פִּנּוֹת,

《 as the [world's] cornerstone, 〈 set 〈 of rest* 〈 The place

הָכֵן בְּלִי רֹגֶז וְתוֹסֶפֶת עֲנוּת.[4]

《 suffering. 〈 or any more 〈 anger 〈 with-out 〈 firmly es-tablished,

---

(1) Cf. Psalms 40:12. (2) Cf. Malachi 3:6. (3) Cf. Isaiah 63:7. (4) Cf. II Samuel 7:10.

מְקוֹם מָנוֹחַ — The place of rest. This refers to Eretz Yisrael in general (Arugas HaBosem), and to the Beis HaMikdash in particular (Pardes).

❖ הִמָּצֵא חִישׁ לָנוּ כִּי נוֹחַלְנוּ,¹

《 we are sick; 〈 for 《 to us, 〈 quickly 〈 Manifest Yourself

קָרְבֵנוּ הַט שָׂשׂוֹן יִשְׁעֲךָ לְנַהֲלֵנוּ,

《 to lead us. 〈 of Your salvation 〈 the joy 〈 direct 〈 draw us near,

טוֹב וְסַלָּח² לְךָ לְבַד הוֹחַלְנוּ,³

《 do we wait — 〈 alone 〈 for 《 You and Forgiving One, 〈 Good

נַחֲמֵנוּ נָא יְהִי חַסְדְּךָ עָלֵינוּ.⁴

《 be upon us! 〈 Your kindness 〈 and may 〈 please, 〈 Comfort us,

ALL, WHILE STANDING:

אֵל מֶלֶךְ יוֹשֵׁב עַל כִּסֵּא רַחֲמִים, מִתְנַהֵג

〈 Who acts 《 of mercy, 〈 the throne 〈 on 〈 Who sits 〈 King 〈 O God,

בַּחֲסִידוּת, מוֹחֵל עֲווֹנוֹת עַמּוֹ, מַעֲבִיר רִאשׁוֹן

〈 [sins,] one 〈 Who removes 《 of His people, 〈 the sins 〈 Who pardons 《 with kindness,

רִאשׁוֹן,⁵ מַרְבֶּה מְחִילָה לַחַטָּאִים וּסְלִיחָה לַפּוֹשְׁעִים,

《 to willful sinners, 〈 and forgiveness 〈 to unintentional sinners 〈 pardon 〈 Who abundantly grants 《 by one,

עֹשֶׂה צְדָקוֹת עִם כָּל בָּשָׂר וָרוּחַ, לֹא כְרָעָתָם

〈 in accord with their wickedness 〈 — not 《 and spirit 〈 [beings of] flesh 〈 all 〈 with 〈 acts of generosity 〈 Who performs

תִּגְמוֹל. ❖ אֵל הוֹרֵיתָ לָנוּ לוֹמַר שְׁלֹשׁ עֶשְׂרֵה, וּזְכוֹר

〈 remember 《 the Thirteen [Attributes of Mercy]; 〈 to recite 〈 us 〈 You taught 〈 O God, 《 do You repay them!

לָנוּ הַיּוֹם בְּרִית שְׁלֹשׁ עֶשְׂרֵה, כְּמוֹ שֶׁהוֹדַעְתָּ לֶעָנָיו

〈 to the humble one [Moses] 〈 You made known 〈 as 《 of [these] Thirteen, 〈 the covenant 〈 today 〈 for us

מִקֶּדֶם, כְּמוֹ שֶׁכָּתוּב, וַיֵּרֶד יהוה בֶּעָנָן וַיִּתְיַצֵּב עִמּוֹ

〈 with him 〈 and stood 〈 in a cloud 〈 And Hashem descended 《 it is written: 〈 as 《 in ancient times,

שָׁם, וַיִּקְרָא בְשֵׁם יהוה.⁶

《 of Hashem. 〈 with the Name 〈 and He called out 《 there,

---

(1) See *Rashi* to *Ezekiel* 19:5. (2) *Psalms* 86:5. (3) Cf. 38:16.
(4) 33:22. (5) *Rosh Hashanah* 17a. (6) *Exodus* 34:5.

CONGREGATION, THEN *CHAZZAN:*

וַיַּעֲבֹר יהוה עַל פָּנָיו וַיִּקְרָא:

《 and 《 [Moses'] 〈 before 〈 And HASHEM passed
proclaimed: face,

CONGREGATION AND *CHAZZAN* **RECITE LOUDLY AND IN UNISON:**

יהוה, יהוה, אֵל, רַחוּם, וְחַנּוּן, אֶרֶךְ אַפַּיִם,

〈 to anger, 〈 Slow 《 and 〈 Compassionate 〈 God, 〈 HASHEM, 〈 HASHEM,
Gracious,

וְרַב חֶסֶד, וֶאֱמֶת, נֹצֵר חֶסֶד לָאֲלָפִים, נֹשֵׂא עָוֹן,

〈 of 〈 Forgiver 《 for thousands 〈 of 〈 Preserver 《 and 〈 in 〈 and
iniquity,   [of generations], kindness   Truth,   Kindness Abundant

וָפֶשַׁע, וְחַטָּאָה, וְנַקֵּה.¹ וְסָלַחְתָּ לַעֲוֹנֵנוּ וּלְחַטָּאתֵנוּ

《 and our sins, 〈 our 〈 May You 《 and Who 〈 and inadvertent 〈 willful sin,
iniquities forgive absolves. sin,

וּנְחַלְתָּנוּ.² סְלַח לָנוּ אָבִינוּ כִּי חָטָאנוּ, מְחַל לָנוּ

〈 us, 〈 pardon 《 we have 〈 for 《 our 〈 us, 〈 Forgive 《 and make us
sinned; Father, Your heritage.

מַלְכֵּנוּ כִּי פָשָׁעְנוּ. כִּי אַתָּה אֲדֹנָי טוֹב וְסַלָּח,

《 and 〈 are 〈 O Lord, 〈 You, 〈 For 《 we have 〈 for 《 our King,
forgiving, good willfully sinned.

וְרַב חֶסֶד לְכָל קֹרְאֶיךָ.³

《 who call 〈 to all 〈 kind 〈 and
upon You.   abundantly

פסוקי הקדמה לסליחה פא / PREFATORY VERSES TO SELICHAH 81

הַאֲזִינָה יהוה תְּפִלָּתֵנוּ, וְהַקְשִׁיבָה בְּקוֹל

〈 the sound 〈 and heed 《 to our prayer, 〈 HASHEM, 〈 Listen,

תַּחֲנוּנוֹתֵינוּ.⁴ שְׁמַע יהוה קוֹלֵנוּ נִקְרָא, וְחָנֵּנוּ וַעֲנֵנוּ.⁵

《 and 〈 show us 《 when we 〈 our 〈 HASHEM, 〈 Hear, 《
answer us. favor call, voices of our
supplications.

שִׁמְעָה יהוה צֶדֶק, הַקְשִׁיבָה רִנָּתֵנוּ.⁶ שְׁמַע יהוה

〈 HASHEM, 〈 Hear, 《 to my 〈 and heed 《 what is 〈 HASHEM, 〈 Hear
entreaty. righteous;

וְחָנֵּנוּ, יהוה הֱיֵה עֹזֵר לָנוּ.⁷

《 our helper. 〈 be 〈 HASHEM, 《 and favor
us;

---

(1) *Exodus* 34:6-7. (2) 34:9. (3) *Psalms* 86:5. (4) Cf. 86:6. (5) Cf. 27:7. (6) Cf. 17:1. (7) Cf. 30:11.

כְּרַחֵם אָב עַל בָּנִים, כֵּן תְּרַחֵם יהוה עָלֵינוּ.[1]

‹ As merciful as › ‹ a father is › ‹ toward › ‹ his children, › ‹ so ›« ‹ have mercy, › ‹ HASHEM, ›« ‹ on us. ›«

לַיהוה הַיְשׁוּעָה, עַל עַמְּךָ בִרְכָתֶךָ סֶּלָה.[2] יהוה

‹ To HASHEM › ‹ is salvation, ›« ‹ upon › ‹ Your people › ‹ is Your blessing, ›« ‹ Selah. ›« ‹ HASHEM, ›

צְבָאוֹת עִמָּנוּ, מִשְׂגָּב לָנוּ אֱלֹהֵי יַעֲקֹב סֶלָה.[3]

‹ Master of Legions, › ‹ is with us, ›« ‹ a stronghold › ‹ for us › ‹ is the God › ‹ of Jacob, ›« ‹ Selah. ›«

יהוה צְבָאוֹת, אַשְׁרֵי אָדָם בֹּטֵחַ בָּךְ.[4] יהוה

‹ HASHEM, › ‹ Master of Legions ›« ‹ praiseworthy — › ‹ is the man › ‹ who trusts › ‹ in You. ›« ‹ HASHEM, ›

הוֹשִׁיעָה, הַמֶּלֶךְ יַעֲנֵנוּ בְיוֹם קָרְאֵנוּ.[5]

‹ save! ›« ‹ May the King › ‹ answer us › ‹ on the day › ‹ we call. ›«

סליחה פא / SELICHAH 81

ALL:

אֱלֹהֵינוּ וֵאלֹהֵי אֲבוֹתֵינוּ:

‹ Our God › ‹ and the God › ‹ of our forefathers: ›«

אֲזֹן תַּחַן* וְהַסְכֵּת עֲתִירָה,

‹ Listen › ‹ to supplication;* ›« ‹ heed › ‹ entreaty; ›«

אַף הָפֵר וְשַׁכֵּךְ עֶבְרָה,

‹ [Your] anger › ‹ annul, › ‹ and calm › ‹ fury. ›«

בָּאֵי לְחַלּוֹתֶךָ בְּנֶפֶשׁ מָרָה,

‹ Those who come › ‹ to plead with You › ‹ with a soul › ‹ that is embittered — ›«

בְּשִׁמְךָ הַגָּדוֹל יִמְצְאוּ עֶזְרָה.*[6]

‹ through [invoking] Your Name › ‹ that is Great › ‹ may they find › ‹ help.* ›«

---

(1) Cf. *Psalms* 103:13. (2) 3:9. (3) 46:8. (4) 84:13. (5) 20:10. (6) Cf. 124:8.

אֲזֹן תַּחַן — *Listen to supplication.* This anonymous *selichah* contains a double *aleph-beis* acrostic, although in some editions a few lines are omitted, presumably to appease the censor.

בְּשִׁמְךָ הַגָּדוֹל יִמְצְאוּ עֶזְרָה — *Through [invoking] Your Name that is Great may they find help.* The translation is based on *Metzudos David* to *Psalms* 124:8. According to *Pardes*, the stich means: *For the sake*

גָּעִית נֶאֱנָחִים עֲנוּתָם חֲזֶה,

《 observe; 〈　and their 〈　of those 〈 The wail
　　　　　affliction　who groan

גְּחִינַת קוֹמָתָם נָא אַל תִּבְזֶה,

《 despise.　〈　do 〈 please 〈 of their up- 〈 the bending
　　　　　　not　　　　right bodies over [in prayer]

דְּרֹשׁ עֶלְבּוֹנָם (מִצַּר בּוֹזֶה,

《 and 〈 (from [their] 〈　their 〈 Avenge
　scorner;　oppressor　humiliation

דְּרֹךְ פּוּרָה וְנִצְחָם יַזֶּה).[1]

《 spurt 〈 and let their 〈 [as in] a 〈 trample
　out)!　lifeblood　winepress　[them]

הֲלֹא אַתָּה הָיִיתָ וְהִנֶּךָ,

《 and You 〈 have always 〈　that 〈 Is it not
　still exist?　existed　You　so

הָיוֹ תִהְיֶה בַּהֲדַר גְּאוֹנֶךָ,

《 of Your 〈　in the 〈 You shall always
　majesty.　splendor　exist

וְנֶאֱמָתָ יִכּוֹן זֶרַע אֱמוּנֶיךָ,[2]

《　of Your 〈 the off- 〈　that 〈 And You
　faithful ones;　spring　steadfast declared
　　　　　　　　　　would be

וְהִנָּם כָּלִים מִתִּגְרַת חֲרוֹנֶךָ.[3]

《　of Your 〈　from the 〈　devas- 〈 but in fact
　fury.　provocation　tated　they are

זֹעֲמוּ בְּעֶוּוֹיִם וּמִמַּאֲוַיִם נִסָּחוּ,

《 they were 〈 and from their 《　because 〈 They have
　torn away;　place of delight 　of their　become
　　　　　[the Temple]　　straying,　scorned

זֹרוּ בָּאֲפָסִים וְלֹא נָחוּ,

《 rested. 〈　and 〈　to the ends 〈 They
　　　have　[of the world]　were
　　　not　　　　　scattered

חֻבְּלָה רוּחָם[4] וְלֶעָפָר שָׁחוּ,[5]

《　they are 〈 and to the 《　is their 〈 Devastated
　prostrated;　dust　spirit,

---

(1) Cf. *Isaiah* 63:3; some editions of *Selichos* omit the passage in parentheses.
(2) Cf. *Psalms* 102:29. (3) Cf. 39:11. (4) Cf. *Job* 17:1. (5) Cf. *Psalms* 44:26.

---

of Your Name [that it not be profaned when their prayer is ignored], *let them find help.*

חָרְשׁוּ חוֹרְשִׁים וּמַעֲנִית הִמְתִּיחוּ.[1]

» they stretched ‹ and their ‹ did the ‹ plowed
out.   furrow   plowers,   [over them]

טָבְעוּ בַבִּץ וְאֵין פּוֹצֶה,

» to extricate ‹ and ‹ into the ‹ They
[them].   there is   mire   sank
  no one   [of Exile]

טוֹרְפֵיהֶם שָׁלוּ מִקָּצֶה אֶל קָצֶה,

» the other ‹ to ‹ from one ‹ are ‹ Those who
end.   end [of the   serene   devour them
  world]

יוֹם יוֹם לוֹחֲמָם מְנַצֶּה,

» provoke ‹ their ‹ [after] ‹ Day
fights,   attackers   day

יַד פּוֹרְשִׂים מִלַּחַץ לֵיצֵא.

» to ‹ from ‹ [Israel] ‹ while a
escape.   oppression   extends,   hand [to
  heaven]

כָּלוּ חַיֵּיהֶם בְּיָגוֹן וַאֲנָחָה,

» and ‹ in grief ‹ are their ‹ Con-
sighing;   lives   sumed

כִּשֵּׁל[2] רַבָּה וְעֻרְבָה שִׂמְחָה,

» is ‹ and and ‹ is ‹ faltering
gladness.   dimmed   abundant

לִישַׁע חוֹכִים וְהִנֵּה צְוָחָה,

» there is ‹ but ‹ they yearn, ‹ For
wailing;   instead   salvation

לִבְּטוּם קָמִים וְכָרוּ שׁוּחָה.[3]

» a pit. ‹ and dug ‹ did their ‹ made them
[them]   adversaries,   distraught

מַעֲרִימִים סוֹד מִמְּךָ לְהַדִּיחָם,

» to push them ‹ from ‹ in ‹ They plot
away;   You   secret,   deviously

מַכְבִּידִים עֹל לְהַכְשִׁיל כֹּחָם,

» their ‹ to cause to ‹ the ‹ they weigh
strength.   falter   yoke   down

---

(1) Cf. *Psalms* 129:3. (2) Cf. 31:11. (3) Cf. *Jeremiah* 18:20.

נֹאֲקִים אֵלֶיךָ בְּהִתְעַטֵּף רוּחָם,
《 does their 〈 when grow 〈 to You 〈 They [Israel]
spirit;   faint   cry out

נַחַת לִמְצֹא מִכְּבֶד טׇרְחָם.
《 of their 〈 from the 〈 to find 〈 relief
burden.   weight

שִׂיחַ צְקִים בְּמַעֲמָד צָפוּף,
《 that is 〈 in an 〈 they pour 〈 Prayers
crowded;   assembly   forth

סְלִיחָה מְבַקְּשִׁים בְּקָדְקֹד כָּפוּף,
《 bowed down. 〈 with heads 〈 they seek 〈 forgiveness

עוֹשְׁקֵיהֶם יַקְנִיאוּם, וּנְתָנוּם לִשְׁסוּף,¹
《 to slaughter; 〈 and deliver 〈 provoke 〈 Their
them   them   tormentors

עֲוֹעִים יְמָסְכוּ² וְיִהְיוּ לִסְפוּף.
《 annihilated! 〈 and may 〈 be poured 〈 [may]
they be   upon them   insanity

פְּדֵה דְבֵקֶיךָ מֵחֵרֶץ וְכִלּוּי,
《 and 〈 from [evil] 〈 those who 〈 Redeem
destruction;   decrees   cling to You

פַּלֵּט מְצוֹרָר וּתְנֵם לְעֵלּוּי,
《 supreme. 〈 and make 〈 from 〈 rescue
them   oppressors   them

צַוֵּה יְשׁוּעוֹת מְשַׁחֲרֶיךָ בְּחִלּוּי,
《 with 〈 for those who 〈 salvations 〈 Com-
entreaty;   seek You   mand

צַדְּקֵם בְּדִינֶךָ מִסֵּתֶר וְגָלוּי.³
《 and revealed 〈 from both 〈 in Your 〈 vindicate
[sins].   concealed   judgment,   them

קַנֹּא וְנוֹקֵם קַנֵּא לִשְׁמֶךָ,
《 for Your 〈 be 《 and aveng- 〈 O
Name;   zealous   ing One,   zealous

---

(1) This stich is another instance of censorship; some editions omit all or part of the stich; the original text reads *Their tormentors provoke them*, בְּנֵצֶר נֶאֱפוּף, *with the branch grown from adultery*. (2) Cf. *Isaiah* 19:4. (3) Another censored line; this one originally read צַמֵּת בְּקִצְפְּךָ שׁוֹחֲחֵי לְתָלוּי, *utterly destroy in Your anger those who bow to one hanging*; some editions read, צוּר עוֹלָמִים הוֹשִׁיעֵנוּ בַּגָּלוּי, *O Rock of the Universe, save us openly*.

קַצֵּץ סִמְלוֹנִים מִצַּוַּאר עַמֶּךְ,

‹ of Your ‹ from the ‹ the [the enemies'] ‹ cut off
people.   neck   yoke

רְאֵה עֲמָלֵנוּ וְשׁוּב מִזַּעְמֶךְ,

‹ from Your ‹ and turn ‹ our toil, ‹ See
wrath;   back

רִיבָה רִיבֵנוּ מֵעַם חֶרְמֶךְ.[1]

‹ [destined] to ‹ against ‹ our ‹ champion
be destroyed the people cause
by You.   [Edom],

❖ (שִׁבְעָתַיִם הָשֵׁב לְחֵיק[2] מַאֲנִינַי,

‹ of those ‹ to the ‹ repay ‹ (Sevenfold
who hurt me; bosom

שַׁכֵּר חִצֶּיךָ מִדַּם מְעַנָּי,)[3]

‹ of my ‹ with the ‹ Your ‹ intoxicate
oppressors.) blood   arrows

תַּטֶּה אָזְנְךָ לְקוֹל תַּחֲנוּנַי,[4]

‹ of my ‹ to the ‹ Your ear ‹ Turn
supplications, sound

תִּרְצֵנִי בְּקָרְאִי יהוה יהוה.

‹ HASHEM .... ‹ HASHEM, ‹ as I cry, ‹ accept me
favorably

ALL, WHILE STANDING:

אֵל מֶלֶךְ יוֹשֵׁב עַל כִּסֵּא רַחֲמִים, מִתְנַהֵג

‹ Who acts ‹ of mercy, ‹ the throne ‹ on ‹ Who sits ‹ King ‹ O God,

בַּחֲסִידוּת, מוֹחֵל עֲוֹנוֹת עַמּוֹ, מַעֲבִיר רִאשׁוֹן

‹ [sins,] one ‹ Who ‹ of His ‹ the sins ‹ Who ‹ with kindness,
removes people, pardons

רִאשׁוֹן,[5] מַרְבֶּה מְחִילָה לְחַטָּאִים וּסְלִיחָה לַפּוֹשְׁעִים,

‹ to willful ‹ and ‹ to unintentional ‹ pardon ‹ Who abun- ‹ by one,
sinners, forgiveness sinners   dantly grants

עֹשֶׂה צְדָקוֹת עִם כָּל בָּשָׂר וָרוּחַ, לֹא כְרָעָתָם

‹ in accord with ‹ — not ‹ and ‹ [beings ‹ all ‹ with ‹ acts of ‹ Who
their wickedness spirit of] flesh generosity performs

---

(1) Cf. *Isaiah* 34:5. (2) Cf. *Psalms* 79:12. (3) Cf. *Deuteronomy* 32:42; some editions of *Selichos* omit the passage in parentheses (some also omit the stanza before it); still others have altered versions: שְׁכִינָתְךָ הָשֵׁב לִמְקוֹם מַאֲוַיַי, *Return Your Presence to the place of my longing* [or, לְחֵיק אַרְמוֹנִי, *to the bosom of my Palace*], שָׁבַת בְּצִיּוֹן לְוִיַי וְכֹהֲנַי, *returned to Zion, my Leviim and Kohanim* [or, שַׁאֲנָן הוּשַׁב לְוִיַי וְכֹהֲנַי, *with serenity let be returned my Leviim and Kohanim*]. (4) Cf. *Psalms* 86:1,6. (5) *Rosh Hashanah* 17a.

תִּגְמוֹל. ❖ אֵל הוֹרֵיתָ לָּנוּ לוֹמַר שְׁלֹשׁ עֶשְׂרֵה, וּזְכוֹר

⟨ remem- ⟪ the Thirteen ⟨ to ⟨ us ⟨ You ⟨ O God, ⟪ do You
ber [Attributes of Mercy]; recite taught repay them!

לָּנוּ הַיּוֹם בְּרִית שְׁלֹשׁ עֶשְׂרֵה, כְּמוֹ שֶׁהוֹדַעְתָּ לֶעָנָיו

⟨ to the humble ⟨ You made ⟨ as ⟪ of [these] Thirteen, ⟨ the ⟨ today ⟨ for us
one [Moses] known covenant

מִקֶּדֶם, כְּמוֹ שֶׁכָּתוּב, וַיֵּרֶד יהוה בֶּעָנָן וַיִּתְיַצֵּב עִמּוֹ

⟨ with ⟨ and stood ⟨ in a ⟪ And HASHEM ⟪ it is written: ⟨ as ⟪ in ancient
him cloud descended times,

שָׁם, וַיִּקְרָא בְשֵׁם יהוה.[1]

⟪ of ⟨ with the ⟨ and He ⟪ there,
HASHEM. Name called out

CONGREGATION, THEN *CHAZZAN*:

וַיַּעֲבֹר יהוה עַל פָּנָיו וַיִּקְרָא:

⟪ and ⟪ [Moses'] ⟨ before ⟨ And HASHEM passed
proclaimed: face,

CONGREGATION AND *CHAZZAN* RECITE LOUDLY AND IN UNISON:

יהוה, יהוה, אֵל, רַחוּם, וְחַנּוּן, אֶרֶךְ אַפַּיִם,

⟨ to anger, ⟨ Slow ⟪ and ⟨ Compassionate ⟨ God, ⟨ HASHEM, ⟨ HASHEM,
Gracious,

וְרַב חֶסֶד, וֶאֱמֶת, נֹצֵר חֶסֶד לָאֲלָפִים, נֹשֵׂא עָוֹן,

⟨ of ⟨ Forgiver ⟪ for thousands ⟨ of ⟨ Preserver ⟪ and ⟨ in ⟨ and
iniquity, [of generations], kindness Truth, Kindness Abundant

וָפֶשַׁע, וְחַטָּאָה, וְנַקֵּה.[2] וְסָלַחְתָּ לַעֲוֹנֵנוּ וּלְחַטָּאתֵנוּ

⟪ and our sins, ⟨ our ⟨ May You ⟪ and Who ⟨ and inadvertent ⟨ willful sin,
iniquities forgive absolves. sin,

וּנְחַלְתָּנוּ.[3] סְלַח לָנוּ אָבִינוּ כִּי חָטָאנוּ, מְחַל לָנוּ

⟨ us, ⟨ pardon ⟪ we have ⟨ for ⟪ our ⟨ us, ⟨ Forgive ⟪ and make us
sinned; Father, Your heritage.

מַלְכֵּנוּ כִּי פָשָׁעְנוּ. כִּי אַתָּה אֲדֹנָי טוֹב וְסַלָּח,

⟪ and ⟨ are ⟨ O Lord, ⟨ You, ⟨ For ⟪ we have ⟨ for ⟪ our King,
forgiving, good willfully sinned.

וְרַב חֶסֶד לְכָל קֹרְאֶיךָ.[4]

⟪ who call ⟨ to all ⟨ kind ⟨ and
upon You. abundantly

---

(1) *Exodus* 34:5. (2) 34:6-7. (3) 34:9. (4) *Psalms* 86:5.

סליחה פב / SELICHAH 82
(פזמון)

[IN SOME CONGREGATIONS, THE PARAGRAPH BEGINNING 'ה 'ה, *HASHEM, HASHEM,*
IS REPEATED BY THE CONGREGATION AFTER EACH STANZA.]

CHAZZAN, THEN CONGREGATION:

יהוה, יהוה,* אֵל רַחוּם, וְחַנּוּן, אֶרֶךְ אַפַּיִם, וְרַב

⟨ and ⟩ ⟨ to ⟩ ⟨ Slow ⟩ ⟨ and ⟩ ⟨ Compas- ⟩ ⟨ God, ⟩ ⟨ HASHEM,* ⟩ ⟨ HASHEM, ⟩
Abundant   anger,   Gracious,   sionate

חֶסֶד, וֶאֱמֶת, נֹצֵר חֶסֶד לַאֲלָפִים, נֹשֵׂא עָוֹן,

⟨ of ⟩ ⟨ Forgiver ⟩ ⟨ for thousands ⟩ ⟨ of ⟩ ⟨ Preserver ⟩ ⟨ and ⟩ ⟨ in ⟩
iniquity,   [of generations],   kindness   Truth,   Kindness

וָפֶשַׁע, וְחַטָּאָה, וְנַקֵּה.¹ וְסָלַחְתָּ לַעֲוֹנֵנוּ וּלְחַטּאתֵנוּ

⟨ and our sins ⟩ ⟨ our ⟩ ⟨ May You ⟩ ⟨ and Who ⟩ ⟨ and inad- ⟩ ⟨ willful ⟩
iniquities forgive absolves. vertent sin, sin,

וּנְחַלְתָּנוּ.²

⟨ and make us
Your heritage.

CONGREGATION, THEN CHAZZAN:

אֶזְכְּרָה אֱלֹהִים וְאֶהֱמָיָה,³

⟨ and I shall ⟩ ⟨ O God, ⟩ ⟨ I shall
moan,   remember,

בִּרְאוֹתִי כָּל עִיר עַל תִּלָּהּ בְּנוּיָה,*⁴

⟨ built,* ⟩ ⟨ its hilltop ⟩ ⟨ on ⟩ ⟨ city ⟩ ⟨ every ⟩ ⟨ when I see

וְעִיר הָאֱלֹהִים מֻשְׁפֶּלֶת עַד שְׁאוֹל תַּחְתִּיָה,

⟨ that is ⟩ ⟨ the depth ⟩ ⟨ to ⟩ ⟨ is lowered ⟩ ⟨ of God ⟩ ⟨ while
nethermost.   the City

וּבְכָל זֹאת אָנוּ לְיָהּ וְעֵינֵינוּ לְיָהּ.⁵

⟨ [look] ⟩ ⟨ and our ⟩ ⟨ are ⟩ ⟨ we ⟩ ⟨ this, ⟩ ⟨ But
to God.   eyes   God's   despite all

---

(1) *Exodus* 34:6-7. (2) 34:9. (3) *Psalms* 77:4. (4) Cf. *Jeremiah* 30:18. (5) See *Succah* 51b.

ה' ה' — *HASHEM, HASHEM.* The theme of this *selichah* is, appropriately, the Thirteen Attributes of Mercy, because God promised Moses that those who beseech Him with these sacred words will not be turned away empty-handed (*Rosh Hashanah* 17b).

The acrostic spells the author's name אֲמִתַּי, *Amittai,* son and successor to R' Shephatiah in 9th-century Oria, Italy [see prefatory comment to *Selichah* 10].

עַל תִּלָּהּ בְּנוּיָה — *On its hilltop built.* The prophet (*Jeremiah* 30:18) promises that Israel will be redeemed and Jerusalem rebuilt. Now, in exile, we contrast Jerusalem, which still has mosques on its holiest place, with the proud, arrogant cities of our oppressors and those who have historically been indifferent to our suffering.

CONGREGATION, THEN *CHAZZAN:*

מִדַּת הָרַחֲמִים עָלֵינוּ הִתְגַּלְגְּלִי,*

《 extend,* 〈 upon us 〈 of Mercy, 〈 O Attribute

וְלִפְנֵי קוֹנֵךְ תְּחִנָּתֵנוּ הַפִּילִי,

《 cast; 〈 our 〈 Your 〈 and
supplication Creator before

וּבְעַד עַמֵּךְ רַחֲמִים שַׁאֲלִי,

《 request, 〈 mercy 〈 of Your 〈 and on
people behalf

כִּי כָל לֵבָב דַּוָּי וְכָל רֹאשׁ לָחֳלִי.¹

《 is ill. 〈 head 〈 and every 〈 is pained 〈 heart 〈 every 〈 for

CONGREGATION, THEN *CHAZZAN:*

תָּמַכְתִּי יְתֵדוֹתַי* בִּשְׁלֹשׁ עֶשְׂרֵה תֵבוֹת,

《 words 〈 on the Thirteen 〈 my props* 〈 I have
[Attributes], supported

וּבְשַׁעֲרֵי דְמָעוֹת כִּי לֹא נִשְׁלָבוֹת,*

《 closed.* 〈 they are 〈 for 〈 of Tears 〈 and on
never [in Heaven], the Gates

לָכֵן שָׁפַכְתִּי שִׂיחַ פְּנֵי בּוֹחֵן לִבּוֹת,

《 hearts. 〈 Him 〈 before 〈 my 〈 I have 〈 There-
Who tests prayer poured out fore,

בָּטוּחַ אֲנִי בְּאֵלֶּה* וּבִזְכוּת שְׁלֹשֶׁת אָבוֹת.

《 Patriarchs. 〈 of the three 〈 and in the merit 〈 in these* 〈 do I 〈 Trust

CONGREGATION, THEN *CHAZZAN:*

יְהִי רָצוֹן מִלְּפָנֶיךָ שׁוֹמֵעַ קוֹל בְּכִיוֹת²

《 of weeping, 〈 the 〈 Who hears 《 before You, 〈 the will 〈 May
sound it be

---

(1) Cf. *Isaiah* 1:5. (2) Cf. *Psalms* 6:9.

עָלֵינוּ הִתְגַּלְגְּלִי — *Upon us extend.* In this stanza, we plead "to" God's Attribute of Mercy as
if it were a tangible being that has the power
to determine the fate of people's prayers. The
propriety and permissibility of such prayer is
discussed in the introduction to this volume.

תָּמַכְתִּי יְתֵדוֹתַי — *I have supported my props.*
Since God has promised to take note of
prayers containing the Thirteen Attributes
of Mercy, we express our confidence that
our *Selichos* prayers will help save us from

a harsh decree.

כִּי לֹא נִשְׁלָבוֹת — *For they are never closed.*
Even when the Gates of Prayer are sealed,
the Gates of Tears are always open (*Berachos* 32b).

בָּטוּחַ אֲנִי בְּאֵלֶּה — *Trust do I in these,* in the
efficacy of the Thirteen Attributes and in
the power of tearful prayer. Some editions
have the singular pronoun בְּזֹאת, *in this,* in
the efficacy of the tearful recitation of the
Thirteen Attributes.

שֶׁתָּשִׂים דִּמְעוֹתֵינוּ בְּנֹאדְךָ לִהְיוֹת,[1]

《 to remain there 〈 in Your flask 〈 our tears 〈 that You place

וְתַצִּילֵנוּ מִכָּל גְּזֵרוֹת אַכְזָרִיּוֹת,

《 that are cruel, 〈 decrees 〈 from all 〈 And [that You] rescue us

כִּי לְךָ לְבַד עֵינֵינוּ תְלוּיוֹת.

《 fixed. 〈 are our eyes 〈 alone 〈 on You 〈 for

ALL, WHILE STANDING:

אֵל מֶלֶךְ יוֹשֵׁב עַל כִּסֵּא רַחֲמִים, מִתְנַהֵג

〈 Who acts 《 of mercy, 〈 the throne 〈 on 〈 Who sits 〈 King 〈 O God,

בַּחֲסִידוּת, מוֹחֵל עֲוֹנוֹת עַמּוֹ, מַעֲבִיר רִאשׁוֹן

〈 [sins,] one 〈 Who removes 《 of His people, 〈 the sins 〈 Who pardons 《 with kindness,

רִאשׁוֹן,[2] מַרְבֶּה מְחִילָה לַחֲטָאִים וּסְלִיחָה לַפּוֹשְׁעִים,

《 to willful sinners, 〈 and forgiveness 〈 to unintentional sinners 〈 pardon 〈 Who abundantly grants 《 by one,

עֹשֶׂה צְדָקוֹת עִם כָּל בָּשָׂר וָרוּחַ, לֹא כְרָעָתָם

〈 in accord with their wickedness 〈 — not 《 and spirit 〈 [beings of] flesh 〈 all 〈 with 〈 acts of generosity 〈 Who performs

תִּגְמוֹל. ❖ אֵל הוֹרֵיתָ לָנוּ לוֹמַר שְׁלֹשׁ עֶשְׂרֵה, וּזְכוֹר

〈 remember 《 the Thirteen [Attributes of Mercy]; 〈 to recite 〈 us 〈 You taught 〈 O God, 《 do You repay them!

לָנוּ הַיּוֹם בְּרִית שְׁלֹשׁ עֶשְׂרֵה, כְּמוֹ שֶׁהוֹדַעְתָּ לֶעָנָיו

〈 to the humble one [Moses] 〈 You made known 〈 as 《 of [these] Thirteen, 〈 the covenant 〈 today 〈 for us

מִקֶּדֶם, כְּמוֹ שֶׁכָּתוּב, וַיֵּרֶד יהוה בֶּעָנָן וַיִּתְיַצֵּב עִמּוֹ

〈 with him 〈 and stood 〈 in a cloud 〈 And HASHEM descended 《 it is written: 〈 as 《 in ancient times,

שָׁם, וַיִּקְרָא בְשֵׁם יהוה.[3]

《 of HASHEM. 〈 with the Name 〈 and He called out 〈 there,

CONGREGATION, THEN CHAZZAN:

וַיַּעֲבֹר יהוה עַל פָּנָיו וַיִּקְרָא:

《 and proclaimed: 《 [Moses'] 〈 before 〈 And HASHEM passed face,

---

(1) Cf. *Psalms* 56:9. (2) *Rosh Hashanah* 17a. (3) *Exodus* 34:5.

CONGREGATION AND *CHAZZAN* RECITE LOUDLY AND IN UNISON:

יְהוָה, יְהוָה, אֵל, רַחוּם, וְחַנּוּן, אֶרֶךְ אַפַּיִם,

⟨ to anger, ⟨ Slow ⟪ and ⟨ Compassionate ⟨ God, ⟨ Hashem, ⟨ Hashem,
Gracious,

וְרַב חֶסֶד, וֶאֱמֶת, נֹצֵר חֶסֶד לָאֲלָפִים, נֹשֵׂא עָוֹן,

⟨ of ⟨ Forgiver ⟪ for thousands ⟨ of ⟨ Preserver ⟪ and ⟨ in ⟨ and
iniquity, [of generations], kindness Truth, Kindness Abundant

וָפֶשַׁע, וְחַטָּאָה, וְנַקֵּה.[1] וְסָלַחְתָּ לַעֲוֹנֵנוּ וּלְחַטָּאתֵנוּ

⟪ and our sins, ⟨ our ⟨ May You ⟪ and Who ⟨ and inadvertent ⟨ willful sin,
iniquities forgive absolves. sin,

וּנְחַלְתָּנוּ.[2] סְלַח לָנוּ אָבִינוּ כִּי חָטָאנוּ, מְחַל לָנוּ

⟨ us, ⟨ pardon ⟪ we have ⟨ for ⟪ our ⟨ us, ⟨ Forgive ⟪ and make us
sinned; Father, Your heritage

מַלְכֵּנוּ כִּי פָשָׁעְנוּ. כִּי אַתָּה אֲדֹנָי טוֹב וְסַלָּח,

⟪ and ⟨ are ⟨ O Lord, ⟨ You, ⟨ For ⟪ we have ⟨ for ⟪ our King,
forgiving, good willfully sinned.

וְרַב חֶסֶד לְכָל קֹרְאֶיךָ.[3]

⟪ who call ⟨ to all ⟨ kind ⟨ and
upon You. abundantly

PREFATORY VERSES TO SELICHAH 83 / פסוקי הקדמה לסליחה פג

חָנֵּנוּ אֱלֹהִים כְּחַסְדֶּךָ, כְּרֹב רַחֲמֶיךָ מְחֵה פְשָׁעֵינוּ.

⟪ our trans- ⟨ erase ⟨ of Your ⟨ according ⟪ according ⟨ O God, ⟨ Show us
gressions compassion, to the to Your favor,
vastness kindness,

הֶרֶב כַּבְּסֵנִי מֵעֲוֹנִי וּמֵחַטָּאתִי טַהֲרֵנוּ.[4] זִבְחֵי

⟨ The ⟪ purify us. ⟨ and from our sins ⟨ from our ⟨ cleanse us ⟨ Abun-
sacrifices iniquities dantly

אֱלֹהִים רוּחַ נִשְׁבָּרָה, לֵב נִשְׁבָּר וְנִדְכֶּה, אֱלֹהִים

⟨ O God, ⟨ and ⟨ broken ⟨ a ⟪ that is ⟨ are a ⟨ God
humbled, heart broken; spirit desires

לֹא תִבְזֶה.[5] אָז תַּחְפֹּץ זִבְחֵי צֶדֶק, עוֹלָה וְכָלִיל, אָז

⟨ then ⟪ and whole ⟨ burnt- ⟨ of right- ⟨ the ⟨ You will ⟨ Then ⟪ You will
offering; offering eousness, offerings desire not despise.

יַעֲלוּ עַל מִזְבַּחֲךָ פָרִים.[6] תִּתֵּן אֱמֶת לְיַעֲקֹב, חֶסֶד

⟨ kindness ⟪ to Jacob, ⟨ truth ⟨ Grant ⟪ [will be] ⟨ Your Altar ⟨ upon ⟨ offered
bulls. up

---

(1) *Exodus* 34:6-7. (2) 34:9. (3) *Psalms* 86:5. (4) 51:3-4. (5) 51:19. (6) 51:21.

לְאַבְרָהָם, אֲשֶׁר נִשְׁבַּעְתָּ לַאֲבוֹתֵינוּ מִימֵי קֶדֶם.¹

《 of old. 〈 from days 〈 to our forefathers 〈 You swore 〈 as 《 to Abraham,

בְּרַחֵם אָב עַל בָּנִים, כֵּן תְּרַחֵם יהוה עָלֵינוּ.²

《 on us. 〈 HASHEM, 〈 have mercy, 〈 so 《 his children, 〈 toward 〈 a father is 〈 As merciful as

לַיהוה הַיְשׁוּעָה, עַל עַמְּךָ בִרְכָתֶךָ סֶּלָה.³ יהוה

〈 HASHEM, 《 Selah. 《 is Your blessing, 〈 Your people 〈 upon 《 is salvation, 〈 To HASHEM

צְבָאוֹת עִמָּנוּ, מִשְׂגָּב לָנוּ אֱלֹהֵי יַעֲקֹב סֶלָה.⁴

《 Selah. 《 of Jacob, 〈 is the God 〈 for us 〈 a stronghold 《 is with us, 〈 Master of Legions,

יהוה צְבָאוֹת, אַשְׁרֵי אָדָם בֹּטֵחַ בָּךְ.⁵ יהוה

〈 HASHEM, 《 in You. 〈 who trusts 〈 is the man 〈 — praiseworthy 《 Master of Legions 〈 HASHEM,

הוֹשִׁיעָה, הַמֶּלֶךְ יַעֲנֵנוּ בְיוֹם קָרְאֵנוּ.⁶

《 we call. 〈 on the day 〈 answer us 〈 May the King 《 save!

סליחה פג / SELICHAH 83

(עקדה)

ALL:

אֱלֹהֵינוּ וֵאלֹהֵי אֲבוֹתֵינוּ:

《 of our forefathers: 〈 and the God 〈 Our God

אֶל הַר הַמּוֹר* גִּבְעַת⁷ הֵלְוֹרְיָה,*

《 of teaching,* 〈 the hill 《 of 〈 the 〈 To myrrh,* mountain

---

(1) *Micah* 7:20. (2) Cf. *Psalms* 103:13. (3) 3:9. (4) 46:8. (5) 84:13. (6) 20:10. (7) Cf. *Song of Songs* 4:6.

§**אֶל הַר הַמּוֹר** — *To the mountain of myrrh.* The eleven stanzas of this *akeidah* comprise two *piyutim* written by different *paytanim.* The first eight stanzas contain an alphabetical acrostic followed by the author's signature — מֵאִיר בְּרַבִּי יִצְחָק, *Meir son of R' Yitzchak* [see prefatory comment to *Selichah* 41].

The final three stanzas bear the signature אֶלְעָזָר, *Elazar,* and were written by R' Elazar Rokeach of Worms (12th–13th-century Germany). R' Elazar was a prolific writer whose works include: *Sefer Rokeach* a guide to ethics and halachah; *Maaseh Rokeach,* a

compendium of *halachah*; commentaries on part of the *Tanach*, the prayers, the ancient Kabbalistic work *Sefer Yetzirah,* and at least two volumes of the Talmud. He also wrote some fifty *piyutim.* On 22 Kislev 4958 (December 1197), crusaders burst into R' Elazar's home and savagely attacked his family. Although he and his son survived the stab wounds inflicted upon them, his wife and two daughters were killed. R' Elazar memorialized them in a touching *kinnah* that is recorded in the Worms chronicles.

הַר הַמּוֹר גִּבְעַת הַלְוֹרְיָה — *The mountain of*

בֵּית עֵקֶד הָרוֹעִים* וְתֵשֶׁר הָעֲלֵיהָ,

《 were brought 〈 where 《 of the 〈 of the 〈 the
up — 　　　　offerings　Shepherds,　binding　place

גָּדוֹל בָּעֲנָקִים כְּהִשְׁכִּים לְזֶבַח וְהִשְׁתַּחֲוָיָה,

《 and prostrating 〈 for bringing 〈 when he 〈 among 〈 [Abraham,]
there,　　　a sacrifice　rose early　giants,　the greatest

דְּבַקְתּוֹ חִבַּקְתּוֹ וַתּוֹצִיאוֹ לִרְוָיָה.

《 to ful- 〈 and brought him 〈 embraced 〈 You clasped
fillment.　out [of his plight]　him,　him,

הֵן בָּעֲשִׂירִית כְּנִסִּיתוֹ בְּפִיּוּסִים,

《 with coaxing 〈 You tested 〈 when for the 《 Indeed
words,　him　tenth time

וְזֵרַזְתּוֹ כְּגִבּוֹר מְלֻמָּד בְּמִלְחֶמֶת אֳנָסִים,

《 that are forced 〈 in the wars 〈 seasoned 〈 as a 〈 and Your
upon him —　　　　soldier　urged him on

זָרַח מִמִּזְרָח וְהוֹדִיעַ בְּכָל אֲפָסִים,

《 the ends [of 〈 in all 〈 and made 〈 from 〈 for he had
the earth] —　　　[Your Name]　the east　shone
　　　　　　　known

חַיַּת בְּנוֹ לִיקוֹד כְּקֹדַח אֵשׁ הֲמָסִים.

《 things that 〈 by fire 〈 as would be 〈 he should 〈 of his 〈 the life
melt.　　consumed　burn　son

טוֹב* כְּהִקְרִין וְהֵאִיר הַשַּׁחַר,

《 the dawn — 〈 and lit up 〈 — when [the 《 The good
sun] shone　[Abraham]*

יַחַד בִּשְׁנֵי נְעָרָיו בַּעֲצַלְתַּיִם לֹא אֵחַר,

《 delay. 〈 did 〈 with idleness 〈 of his 〈 with 〈 together
not　　　servants　the two

---

(1) Cf. *II Kings* 10:12. (2) See *Rashi* to *Joshua* 14:15. (3) See *Genesis* 22:5. (4) See commentary to *Selichah* 39 s.v. נְסִיתוֹ בַּעֲשִׂירִי. (5) See prefatory comment to *Selichah* 66. (6) Cf. *Isaiah* 64:1.

---

myrrh, the hill of teaching. Mount Moriah, the mountain upon which Abraham bound his son as an offering and which later became the Temple Mount, was called *the mountain of myrrh, the hill of frankincense* (Song of Songs 4:6), after two of the eleven ingredients of the Incense offered daily in the *Beis HaMikdash* (*Targum* and *Bereishis Rabbah* 52). The name מוֹרִיָּה, *Moriah,* also connotes *teaching* or *legal decisions* (*Bereishis*

Rabbah 52). Here, the *paytan* combines these two implications of the mountain's name.

בֵּית עֵקֶד הָרוֹעִים — *The place of the binding of the Shepherds.* This was the very spot where Adam, Cain, Abel, as well as Noah and his sons, had brought offerings to God (*Pirkei deRebbi Eliezer* 31).

טוֹב — *The good [Abraham].* Abraham was a good man and righteous (*Arugas HaBosem*). According to the Midrash, the Scriptural

כְּהוֹלֵךְ בֶּחָלִיל וְסוֹפוֹ לַחֲזֹר מָחָר,

As one who ‹ goes out › to the music ‹ of pipes › and in ‹ the end › will ‹ return › tomorrow, »

לָקַח בְּנוֹ בִּדְבָרִים וַעֲצֵי הַמַּעֲרָכָה בָּחָר.

He ‹ drew › his ‹ son › with words ‹ and the ‹ wood › for the pyre › he chose. »

מַאֲכֶלֶת שְׁנוּנָה מְרוּטָה לָטֶבַח,[1]

The knife, ‹ sharpened › and polished ‹ for the slaughter ›

נְדָנָהּ נָתַן מִלְּהַבְעִיתוֹ בְּאֶבַח,

into its ‹ sheath › he ‹ inserted › not to frighten him ‹ with [the sight › of] the blade. »

סָב וּבָחוּר לִשְׁנֵיהֶם הַשֶּׁבַח,

Old ‹ man › and youth, ‹ to both ‹ goes the ‹ praise: »

עָרְכוּ עֵצִים לְשֵׁם הַזֶּבַח.

They ‹ arranged › the wood ‹ for the ‹ sake › of the ‹ slaughter. »

פְּרִי צַדִּיק כְּהַאֲזִין בְּמִלָּה,

The off- ‹ spring › of the ‹ righteous [Abraham] › when he ‹ heard › the word: »

צוּר יִרְאֶה לּוֹ הַשֶּׂה וְאִם לֹא בְּנִי לְעוֹלָה,[2]

The ‹ Rock › will see ‹ for ‹ Himself › the ‹ lamb, › and if ‹ not, » my ‹ son › will be the ‹ burnt-offering — »

קָרֵץ עַצְמוֹ הִזְמִין וְתָלָה עַיִן לְמַעְלָה,

For ‹ slaughter › himself ‹ he ‹ prepared › and fixed ‹ an ‹ eye › on high, »

רָחַשׁ לַעֲקֹדוֹ הֵיטֵב מִלְּהִפָּסֵל בִּמְעִילָה.[3]

asking ‹ that he ‹ be bound › tightly, ‹ lest the offering ‹ be made unfit › through a rebellious move. »

שָׁאַג זָקֵן וּבִשְׁנוּנָה אָחַז,

Cry out ‹ did the ‹ old man [in prayer] › and the ‹ sharp knife › grasped — »

(1) Cf. *Ezekiel* 21:33. (2) See *Rashi* to *Genesis* 22:8. (3) See *Numbers* 5:12.

phrase אִישׁ טוֹב, *a good man* (*Proverbs* 14:14) refers to Abraham (*Bereishis Rabbah* 95:3). Another interpretation of this stich understands טוֹב as an allusion to light, which the

Torah describes with the words כִּי טוֹב, *that it is good* (*Genesis* 1:4). The stich then reads *the goodly light*, and "Abraham" must be interpolated into the next line (*Masbir*).

תָּקְפוּ אֶרְאֶלִים¹ וְצָעֲקוּ מִמַּחַז,

‹ Pray powerfully › did the angels, ‹ crying out ‹ at the scene.

מָרוֹם כְּהִסְכִּית צִמְצֵם שְׁכִינָתוֹ כְּחָז,

‹ The Most High ‹ when He heard, ‹ He manifested on earth ‹ His Presence ‹ when He saw,

אַיִל הֶרְאָהוּ אַחַר בַּסְּבַךְ נֶאֱחַז.²

‹ and a ram ‹ He showed [Abraham], ‹ another one ‹ that in the thicket ‹ was caught.

יָחִיד הַנֶּאֱהָב* כְּשָׁלַף הַתַּעַר,

‹ The unique ‹ beloved one,* ‹ as was drawn ‹ the sharp blade,

רָחַף מָגִנּוֹ וְעָמַד בַּשָּׁעַר,

‹ hover over him ‹ did his Shield ‹ and stood ‹ in the gate:

בִּנְךָ יְחִידְךָ אָהוּב³ מִנֹּעַר,

‹ Your son, ‹ your only one, ‹ beloved ‹ since youth —

רַב לָךְ אַל תִּשְׁלַח יָדְךָ אֶל הַנַּעַר.⁴

‹ enough ‹ have You accomplished! ‹ Do not ‹ send forth ‹ your hand ‹ against ‹ the boy!

כִּי נִשְׁבַּעְתִּי⁵ בְּקִיּוּם רָזֶה,

‹ By Myself ‹ I have sworn ‹ with confirmation ‹ that is strong,

יַעַן אֲשֶׁר עָשִׂיתָ אֶת הַדָּבָר הַזֶּה,⁵

‹ that since ‹ you have done ‹ this thing,

צִקּוּן חֲנִיטֶיךָ בַּצַּר לָמוֹ אֶחֱזֶה,

‹ the outpouring of prayer ‹ of your children ‹ when in trouble ‹ they are ‹ I shall attend to

חַקּוֹתָם לַחַיִּים כִּי אֶסְלַח לַעֲוֹן הָעָם הַזֶּה.⁶

‹ and I shall engrave them ‹ for life, ‹ for ‹ I shall forgive ‹ the sin ‹ of this people.

---

(1) Cf. *Isaiah* 33:7. (2) Cf. *Genesis* 22:13. (3) Cf. 22:1. (4) 22:12. (5) 22:16. (6) Cf. *Jeremiah* 31:33; *Numbers* 14:19.

יָחִיד הַנֶּאֱהָב — *The unique beloved one.* This may refer to either Abraham, who was the unique beloved of God (*Masbir*; see *Ezekiel* 33:24 and *Isaiah* 41:8), or Isaac, who was the unique beloved son of Abraham (*Arugas HaBosem*; see *Genesis* 22:1).

אָנָּא* הַשֵּׁם הַנִּכְבָּד וְהַנּוֹרָא,

《 and awesome, 〈 is honored 〈 You Whose 〈 Please,*
Name

לְעֵת צָרָה פְּקַדְנוּךְ וְשִׁחַרְנוּךְ בְּמוֹרָא,

《 with reverence. 〈 and seek You 〈 we remember You 〈 of 〈 in our time trouble

זְנַחְתָּנוּ רִחַקְתָּנוּ, קָרְבֵנוּ וְהָכֵן עֲתִירָה,

《 [our] prayer 〈 and set 〈 [now] draw 《 pushed us away; 〈 You have [before You]. properly us near neglected us,

לֹא נָסוֹג מִמֶּךָ תְּחַיֵּנוּ וּבְשִׁמְךָ נִקְרָא.

《 we will 〈 and on Your 〈 give us 〈 from 〈 We will not call. Name life, You; retreat

חַזְּקֵנוּ וְאַמְּצֵנוּ לְמַעַן כִּסֵּא כְבוֹדֶךָ,

《 of Glory; 〈 of Your 〈 for the 〈 encourage 〈 Strengthen Throne sake us, us,

קוֹמְמֵנוּ וְהַחֲיֵינוּ בְּטַל אוֹרוֹת הוֹדֶךָ,[1]

《 of Your 〈 of the light 〈 with 〈 and 〈 stand us splendor. the dew revivify us erect

וְכַלֵּה דֶּבֶר וְחֶרֶב וְרָעָב[2] מִנַּחֲלַת שְׂרִידֶךָ,

《 that are 〈 from Your 〈 and 〈 sword, 〈 pesti- 〈 Extermi- surviving; heritage- famine lence, nate people

וְתֹאמַר לַמַּלְאָךְ הֶרֶף יָדֶךָ.[3]

《 your 〈 Stay 《 to the [destroy- 〈 and say hand! ing] angel,

❖ קִדַּמְנוּ פָנֶיךָ אַדִּיר וְנָאוֹר,

〈 and Illumi- 〈 O 〈 before 〈 We have nating One, Powerful You, come

בִּתְפִלָּה וּבַקָּשָׁה וּבְהַכְנָעַת שְׂאוֹר,

《 Evil Inclination. 〈 and a humbled 〈 and entreaty, 〈 with prayer

---

(1) Cf. *Isaiah* 26:19. (2) From the *Avinu Malkeinu* prayer. (3) *II Samuel* 24:16.

אָנָּא — *Please*. This is the beginning of the second *piyut* included in this *selichah*. According to the author of *Arugas Ha-Bosem*, who incidentally was a student of the composer R' Elazar Rokeach, this piece was written for the morning service of Yom Kippur. Like many Yom Kippur prayers, it begins with the word אָנָּא, which has the

same *gematria* as ה' ה', HASHEM, HASHEM, the twofold appearance of the Tetragrammaton as the first two of the Thirteen Attributes of Mercy (see page 19). Thus, concludes *Arugas HaBosem*, אָנָּא is a fitting opening for our prayers on the day when the Thirteen Attributes form the core of the service.

הֲקִימֵנוּ בְּאוֹר פָּנֶיךָ אִמְרָתְךָ לְבָאֵר,

《 we may 〈 so that Your 〈 of Your 〈 in the 〈 Stand us
interpret,   Torah   countenance,   light   erect

כִּי עִמְּךָ מְקוֹר חַיִּים בְּאוֹרְךָ נִרְאֶה אוֹר.[1]

《 light. 〈 may we 〈 by Your 《 of life; 〈 is the 〈 with 〈 for
see   light   source   You

ALL, WHILE STANDING:

אֵל מֶלֶךְ יוֹשֵׁב עַל כִּסֵּא רַחֲמִים, מִתְנַהֵג

〈 Who acts 《 of mercy, 〈 the throne 〈 on 〈 Who sits 〈 King 〈 O God,

בַּחֲסִידוּת, מוֹחֵל עֲוֹנוֹת עַמּוֹ, מַעֲבִיר רִאשׁוֹן

〈 [sins,] one 〈 Who 《 of His 〈 the sins 〈 Who 《 with kindness,
removes   people,   pardons

רִאשׁוֹן,[2] מַרְבֶּה מְחִילָה לַחַטָּאִים וּסְלִיחָה לַפּוֹשְׁעִים,

《 to willful 〈 and 〈 to unintentional 〈 pardon 〈 Who abun- 《 by one,
sinners,   forgiveness   sinners   dantly grants

עֹשֶׂה צְדָקוֹת עִם כָּל בָּשָׂר וָרוּחַ, לֹא כְרָעָתָם

〈 in accord with 〈 — not 《 and 〈 [beings 〈 all 〈 with 〈 acts of 〈 Who
their wickedness   spirit   of] flesh   generosity   performs

תִּגְמוֹל. ❖ אֵל הוֹרֵיתָ לָּנוּ לוֹמַר שְׁלֹשׁ עֶשְׂרֵה, וּזְכוֹר

〈 remem- 《 the Thirteen 〈 to 〈 us 〈 You 〈 O God, 《 do You
ber   [Attributes of Mercy]; recite   taught   repay them!

לָּנוּ הַיּוֹם בְּרִית שְׁלֹשׁ עֶשְׂרֵה, כְּמוֹ שֶׁהוֹדַעְתָּ לֶעָנָיו

〈 to the humble 〈 You made 〈 as 《 of [these] Thirteen, 〈 the 〈 today 〈 for us
one [Moses]   known   covenant

מִקֶּדֶם, כְּמוֹ שֶׁכָּתוּב, וַיֵּרֶד יהוה בֶּעָנָן וַיִּתְיַצֵּב עִמּוֹ

〈 with 〈 and stood 〈 in a 〈 And Hashem 《 it is written: 〈 as 《 in ancient
him   cloud   descended   times,

שָׁם, וַיִּקְרָא בְשֵׁם יהוה.[3]

《 of 〈 with the 〈 and He 《 there,
Hashem.   Name   called out

CONGREGATION, THEN CHAZZAN:

וַיַּעֲבֹר יהוה עַל פָּנָיו וַיִּקְרָא:

《 and 《 [Moses'] 〈 before 〈 And Hashem passed
proclaimed: face,

---

(1) *Psalms* 36:10. (2) *Rosh Hashanah* 17a. (3) *Exodus* 34:5.

CONGREGATION AND *CHAZZAN* RECITE LOUDLY AND IN UNISON:

יְהוה, יְהוה, אֵל, רַחוּם, וְחַנּוּן, אֶרֶךְ אַפַּיִם,

⟨ to anger, ⟨ Slow ⟪ and ⟨ Compassionate ⟨ God, ⟨ HASHEM, ⟨ HASHEM,
Gracious,

וְרַב חֶסֶד, וֶאֱמֶת, נֹצֵר חֶסֶד לָאֲלָפִים, נֹשֵׂא עָוֹן,

⟨ of ⟨ Forgiver ⟪ for thousands ⟨ of ⟨ Preserver ⟪ and ⟨ in ⟨ and
iniquity, [of generations], kindness Truth, Kindness Abundant

וָפֶשַׁע, וְחַטָּאָה, וְנַקֵּה.¹ וְסָלַחְתָּ לַעֲוֹנֵנוּ וּלְחַטָּאתֵנוּ

⟪ and our sins, ⟨ our ⟨ May You ⟪ and Who ⟨ and inadvertent ⟨ willful sin,
iniquities forgive absolves. sin,

וּנְחַלְתָּנוּ.² סְלַח לָנוּ אָבִינוּ כִּי חָטָאנוּ, מְחַל לָנוּ

⟨ us, ⟨ pardon ⟪ we have ⟨ for ⟨ our ⟨ us, ⟨ Forgive ⟪ and make us
sinned; Father, Your heritage.

מַלְכֵּנוּ כִּי פָשָׁעְנוּ. כִּי אַתָּה אֲדֹנָי טוֹב וְסַלָּח,

⟪ and ⟨ are ⟨ O Lord, ⟨ You, ⟨ For ⟪ we have ⟨ for ⟪ our King,
forgiving, good willfully sinned.

וְרַב חֶסֶד לְכָל קֹרְאֶיךָ.³

⟪ who call ⟨ to all ⟨ kind ⟨ and
upon You. abundantly

ALL:

זְכֹר רַחֲמֶיךָ יְהוה וַחֲסָדֶיךָ, כִּי מֵעוֹלָם הֵמָּה.⁴

⟪ are they. ⟨ eternal ⟨ for ⟪ and Your ⟨ HASHEM, ⟨ Your mercies, ⟨ Remember
kindnesses,

זָכְרֵנוּ יְהוה בִּרְצוֹן עַמֶּךָ, פָּקְדֵנוּ בִּישׁוּעָתֶךָ.⁵ זְכֹר

⟨ Re- ⟪ with Your ⟨ recall us ⟪ to Your ⟨ when You ⟨ HASHEM, ⟨ Remem-
member salvation. people; show favor ber us,

עֲדָתְךָ קָנִיתָ קֶּדֶם, גָּאַלְתָּ שֵׁבֶט נַחֲלָתֶךָ, הַר צִיּוֹן זֶה

⟨ the one ⟨ of ⟨ the ⟪ of Your ⟨ the ⟨ You ⟪ long ⟨ which You ⟨ Your con-
[where] Zion, mountain heritage; tribe redeemed ago, acquired gregation,

שָׁכַנְתָּ בּוֹ.⁶ זְכֹר יְהוה חִבַּת יְרוּשָׁלַיִם, אַהֲבַת

⟨ the love ⟪ of Jerusalem; ⟨ the ⟨ HASHEM, ⟨ Remem- ⟪ there. ⟨ You rested
affection ber, Your Presence

צִיּוֹן אַל תִּשְׁכַּח לָנֶצַח.⁷ אַתָּה תָקוּם תְּרַחֵם צִיּוֹן כִּי

⟨ for ⟪ to ⟨ and show ⟨ will arise ⟨ You ⟪ forever. ⟨ forget ⟨ do not ⟨ of
Zion, mercy Zion

---

(1) *Exodus* 34:6-7. (2) 34:9. (3) *Psalms* 86:5. (4) 25:6.
(5) Cf. 106:4. (6) 74:2. (7) This is not a Scriptural verse.

עֵת לְחֶנְנָהּ, כִּי בָא מוֹעֵד. זְכֹר יהוה לִבְנֵי אֱדוֹם

אֵת יוֹם יְרוּשָׁלָיִם, הָאֹמְרִים עָרוּ עָרוּ עַד הַיְסוֹד

בָּהּ. זְכֹר לְאַבְרָהָם לְיִצְחָק וּלְיִשְׂרָאֵל עֲבָדֶיךָ, אֲשֶׁר

נִשְׁבַּעְתָּ לָהֶם בָּךְ וַתְּדַבֵּר אֲלֵהֶם, אַרְבֶּה אֶת זַרְעֲכֶם

כְּכוֹכְבֵי הַשָּׁמָיִם, וְכָל הָאָרֶץ הַזֹּאת אֲשֶׁר אָמַרְתִּי,

אֶתֵּן לְזַרְעֲכֶם, וְנָחֲלוּ לְעֹלָם. זְכֹר לַעֲבָדֶיךָ לְאַבְרָהָם

לְיִצְחָק וּלְיַעֲקֹב, אַל תֵּפֶן אֶל קְשִׁי הָעָם הַזֶּה וְאֶל

רִשְׁעוֹ וְאֶל חַטָּאתוֹ. זְכוֹר לָנוּ בְּרִית אָבוֹת, כַּאֲשֶׁר

אָמַרְתָּ: וְזָכַרְתִּי אֶת בְּרִיתִי יַעֲקוֹב, וְאַף אֶת בְּרִיתִי

יִצְחָק, וְאַף אֶת בְּרִיתִי אַבְרָהָם אֶזְכֹּר, וְהָאָרֶץ אֶזְכֹּר.

זְכוֹר לָנוּ בְּרִית רִאשׁוֹנִים, כַּאֲשֶׁר אָמַרְתָּ: וְזָכַרְתִּי

לָהֶם בְּרִית רִאשׁוֹנִים, אֲשֶׁר הוֹצֵאתִי אֹתָם מֵאֶרֶץ

---

(1) *Psalms* 102:14. (2) 137:7. (3) *Exodus* 32:13. (4) *Deuteronomy* 9:27. (5) *Leviticus* 26:42.

מִצְרַיִם לְעֵינֵי הַגּוֹיִם, לִהְיוֹת לָהֶם לֵאלֹהִים, אֲנִי

of Egypt — in the very sight — of the nations, — to be — to them — a God; — I am

יהוה.[1] עָשָׂה עִמָּנוּ כְּמָה שֶׁהִבְטַחְתָּנוּ: וְאַף גַּם

HASHEM. — Do — with us — as — You promised us: — And despite — all

זֹאת בִּהְיוֹתָם בְּאֶרֶץ אֹיְבֵיהֶם, לֹא מְאַסְתִּים וְלֹא

this, — when they will be — in the land — of their enemies, — I will not — despise them — nor

גְעַלְתִּים לְכַלֹּתָם לְהָפֵר בְּרִיתִי אִתָּם, כִּי אֲנִי יהוה

abhor them — to destroy them, — to annul — My covenant — with them, — for — I am — HASHEM,

אֱלֹהֵיהֶם.[2] הָשֵׁב שְׁבוּתֵנוּ וְרַחֲמֵנוּ, כְּמָה שֶׁכָּתוּב:

their God. — Bring back — our captivity — and have mercy on us, — as — it is written:

וְשָׁב יהוה אֱלֹהֶיךָ אֶת שְׁבוּתְךָ וְרִחֲמֶךָ, וְשָׁב וְקִבֶּצְךָ

Then bring back — HASHEM, — your God, — your captivity, — and He will have mercy upon you, — and He will once again — gather you in

מִכָּל הָעַמִּים אֲשֶׁר הֱפִיצְךָ יהוה אֱלֹהֶיךָ שָׁמָּה.[3]

from all — the peoples — that — has scattered you — HASHEM — your God — thereto.

קַבֵּץ נִדָּחֵינוּ, כְּמָה שֶׁכָּתוּב: אִם יִהְיֶה נִדַּחֲךָ בִּקְצֵה

Gather — our dispersed ones, — as — it is written: — If — your dispersed will be — at the ends

הַשָּׁמָיִם, מִשָּׁם יְקַבֶּצְךָ יהוה אֱלֹהֶיךָ, וּמִשָּׁם יִקָּחֶךָ.[4]

of heaven, — from there — gather you in — HASHEM, — your God, — and from there — He will take you.

מְחֵה פְשָׁעֵינוּ כָּעָב וְכֶעָנָן, כְּמָה שֶׁכָּתוּב: מָחִיתִי

Wipe away — our sins — like a mist — and like a cloud, — as — it is written: — I have wiped away

כָעָב פְּשָׁעֶיךָ וְכֶעָנָן חַטֹּאתֶיךָ, שׁוּבָה אֵלַי כִּי

like a mist — your willful sins, — and like a cloud — your transgressions; — return — to Me, — for

גְאַלְתִּיךָ.[5] מְחֵה פְשָׁעֵינוּ לְמַעַנְךָ, כַּאֲשֶׁר אָמָרְתָּ:

I have redeemed you. — Wipe away — our sins — for Your sake, — as — You have said:

---

(1) *Leviticus* 26:45. (2) 26:44. (3) 30:3. (4) 30:4. (5) *Isaiah* 44:22.

אָנֹכִי אָנֹכִי הוּא מֹחֶה פְשָׁעֶיךָ לְמַעֲנִי, וְחַטֹּאתֶיךָ לֹא

‹ I shall ‹ and your ‹‹ for ‹ your ‹ Who wipes ‹ am the ‹ [only] I, ‹ I,
not   transgressions   My sake,   willful sins   away   One

אֶזְכֹּר.¹ הַלְבֵּן חֲטָאֵינוּ כַּשֶּׁלֶג וְכַצֶּמֶר, כְּמָה שֶׁכָּתוּב:

‹‹ it is written: ‹ as ‹‹ and ‹ like snow ‹ our sins ‹ Whiten ‹‹ recall.
like wool,

לְכוּ נָא וְנִוָּכְחָה, יֹאמַר יהוה, אִם יִהְיוּ חֲטָאֵיכֶם

‹ your sins may be ‹ Though ‹‹ HASHEM. ‹ says ‹‹ let us reason ‹ now, ‹ Come,
together,

כַשָּׁנִים כַּשֶּׁלֶג יַלְבִּינוּ, אִם יַאְדִּימוּ כַתּוֹלָע, כַּצֶּמֶר

‹ like [white] ‹‹ as crimson, ‹ they may ‹ though ‹‹ they will be ‹ like ‹‹ like
wool   be red   whitened;   snow   scarlet,

יִהְיוּ.² זְרוֹק עָלֵינוּ מַיִם טְהוֹרִים וְטַהֲרֵנוּ, כְּמָה שֶׁכָּתוּב:

‹‹ it is written: ‹ as ‹‹ and ‹ pure water ‹ upon us ‹ Pour ‹‹ they will
purify us,   become.

וְזָרַקְתִּי עֲלֵיכֶם מַיִם טְהוֹרִים וּטְהַרְתֶּם, מִכֹּל

‹ from ‹‹ and you will ‹ pure water ‹ upon you ‹ I shall pour
all   become pure;

טֻמְאוֹתֵיכֶם וּמִכָּל גִּלּוּלֵיכֶם אֲטַהֵר אֶתְכֶם.³ רַחֵם

‹ Have ‹‹ you. ‹ I will ‹ your ‹ and ‹ your
mercy   purify   abominations   from all   contaminations

עָלֵינוּ וְאַל תַּשְׁחִיתֵנוּ, כְּמָה שֶׁכָּתוּב: כִּי אֵל רַחוּם

‹ a merciful ‹ For ‹‹ it is written: ‹ as ‹‹ destroy us, ‹ and ‹ on us
God   do not

יהוה אֱלֹהֶיךָ, לֹא יַרְפְּךָ וְלֹא יַשְׁחִיתֶךָ, וְלֹא יִשְׁכַּח

‹ will He ‹ nor ‹‹ will He ‹ nor ‹ relinquish ‹ He will ‹‹ your God; ‹ is
forget   destroy you,   you   not   HASHEM,

אֶת בְּרִית אֲבֹתֶיךָ אֲשֶׁר נִשְׁבַּע לָהֶם.⁴ מוֹל

‹ Circum- ‹‹ to them. ‹ He swore ‹ which ‹ with your ‹ the covenant
cise   forefathers,

אֶת לְבָבֵנוּ לְאַהֲבָה וּלְיִרְאָה אֶת שְׁמֶךָ, כְּמָה שֶׁכָּתוּב:

‹‹ it is written: ‹ as ‹‹ Your Name, ‹ and to fear ‹ to love ‹ our hearts

וּמָל יהוה אֱלֹהֶיךָ אֶת לְבָבְךָ וְאֶת לְבַב זַרְעֶךָ, לְאַהֲבָה

‹ to love ‹‹ of your ‹ and the ‹ your heart ‹ HASHEM, your God,
offspring,   heart   will circumcise

---

(1) *Isaiah* 43:25. (2) 1:18. (3) *Ezekiel* 36:25. (4) *Deuteronomy* 4:31.

אֶת יהוה אֱלֹהֶיךָ, בְּכָל לְבָבְךָ וּבְכָל נַפְשְׁךָ, לְמַעַן

⟨ so that ⟨ your soul, ⟨ and with all ⟨ your heart ⟨ with all ⟨ your God, ⟨ HASHEM,

חַיֶּיךָ.[1] הִמָּצֵא לָנוּ בְּבַקָּשָׁתֵנוּ, כְּמָה שֶׁכָּתוּב: וּבִקַּשְׁתֶּם

⟨ And you will seek ⟨ it is written: ⟨ as ⟨ in our quest, ⟨ to us ⟨ Be accessible ⟨ you may live.

מִשָּׁם אֶת יהוה אֱלֹהֶיךָ וּמָצָאתָ, כִּי תִדְרְשֶׁנּוּ בְּכָל

⟨ with all ⟨ you search Him out ⟨ when ⟨ and you will find [Him], ⟨ your God, ⟨ HASHEM, ⟨ from there

לְבָבְךָ וּבְכָל נַפְשֶׁךָ.[2] ❖ תְּבִיאֵנוּ אֶל הַר קָדְשֶׁךָ,

⟨ Your holy mountain ⟨ to ⟨ Bring us ⟨ your soul. ⟨ and with all ⟨ your heart

וְשַׂמְּחֵנוּ בְּבֵית תְּפִלָּתֶךָ, כְּמָה שֶׁכָּתוּב: וַהֲבִיאוֹתִים

⟨ And I will bring them ⟨ it is written: ⟨ as ⟨ of Prayer, ⟨ in Your House ⟨ and gladden us

אֶל הַר קָדְשִׁי, וְשִׂמַּחְתִּים בְּבֵית תְּפִלָּתִי, עוֹלֹתֵיהֶם

⟨ their burnt-offerings ⟨ of Prayer; ⟨ in My House ⟨ and I will gladden them ⟨ My holy mountain, ⟨ to

וְזִבְחֵיהֶם לְרָצוֹן עַל מִזְבְּחִי, כִּי בֵיתִי בֵּית תְּפִלָּה

⟨ of Prayer" ⟨ "a House ⟨ My House ⟨ for ⟨ My Altar, ⟨ on ⟨ will find favor ⟨ and their feast-offerings

יִקָּרֵא לְכָל הָעַמִּים.[3]

⟨ nations. ⟨ for all ⟨ will be called

THE ARK IS OPENED.

CHAZZAN, THEN CONGREGATION:

שְׁמַע קוֹלֵנוּ יהוה אֱלֹהֵינוּ, חוּס וְרַחֵם עָלֵינוּ,

⟨ on us, ⟨ and have compassion ⟨ have pity ⟨ our God; ⟨ HASHEM, ⟨ our voice, ⟨ Hear

וְקַבֵּל בְּרַחֲמִים וּבְרָצוֹן אֶת תְּפִלָּתֵנוּ.[4]

⟨ our prayer. ⟨ and favor ⟨ with compassion ⟨ and accept

CHAZZAN, THEN CONGREGATION:

הֲשִׁיבֵנוּ יהוה אֵלֶיךָ וְנָשׁוּבָה, חַדֵּשׁ יָמֵינוּ כְּקֶדֶם.[5]

⟨ as of old. ⟨ our days ⟨ renew ⟨ and we shall return, ⟨ to You, ⟨ HASHEM, ⟨ Bring us back,

(1) *Deuteronomy* 30:6. (2) 4:29. (3) *Isaiah* 56:7.
(4) From the weekday *Shemoneh Esrei*. (5) *Lamentations* 5:21.

CHAZZAN, THEN CONGREGATION:

אֲמָרֵינוּ הַאֲזִינָה יהוה, בִּינָה הֲגִיגֵנוּ.‎[1]

» ‹ perceive » HASHEM; ‹ hear, ‹ Our words
thoughts. our

THE FOLLOWING VERSE IS RECITED QUIETLY:

יִהְיוּ לְרָצוֹן אִמְרֵי פִינוּ וְהֶגְיוֹן לִבֵּנוּ לְפָנֶיךָ,‎

» before » of our ‹ and the ‹ of our ‹ — the ex- » find ‹ May
You, heart — thoughts mouth pressions favor they

יהוה צוּרֵנוּ וְגוֹאֲלֵנוּ.‎[2]

» ‹ our ‹ HASHEM,
and our Rock
Redeemer.

CHAZZAN, THEN CONGREGATION:

אַל תַּשְׁלִיכֵנוּ מִלְּפָנֶיךָ, וְרוּחַ קָדְשְׁךָ אַל תִּקַּח מִמֶּנּוּ.‎[3]

» from us. ‹ take ‹ do ‹ of Your ‹ and the » from Your ‹ cast us away ‹ Do
not Holiness Spirit Presence, not

CHAZZAN, THEN CONGREGATION:

אַל תַּשְׁלִיכֵנוּ לְעֵת זִקְנָה, כִּכְלוֹת כֹּחֵנוּ אַל תַּעַזְבֵנוּ.‎[4]

» forsake us not. ‹ does our ‹ when fail » of old ‹ in time ‹ cast us away ‹ Do
strength, age; not

ALL CONTINUE (SOME CONGREGATIONS RECITE THE NEXT VERSE RESPONSIVELY):

אַל תַּעַזְבֵנוּ יהוה, אֱלֹהֵינוּ אַל תִּרְחַק מִמֶּנּוּ.‎[5]

» from us. ‹ be not distant ‹ our God, » O HASHEM; ‹ Forsake us not,

עֲשֵׂה עִמָּנוּ אוֹת לְטוֹבָה, וְיִרְאוּ שׂוֹנְאֵינוּ וְיֵבְשׁוּ,‎

» and be ‹ may our ‹ so that » for good; ‹ a sign ‹ for us ‹ Display
ashamed, enemies see it

כִּי אַתָּה יהוה עֲזַרְתָּנוּ וְנִחַמְתָּנוּ. כִּי לְךָ יהוה‎[6]

‹ HASHEM, ‹ for ‹ Because » and ‹ will have ‹ HASHEM, ‹ You, ‹ for
You, consoled us. helped us

הוֹחָלְנוּ, אַתָּה תַעֲנֶה אֲדֹנָי אֱלֹהֵינוּ.‎[7]

» our God. ‹ O Lord, ‹ will answer, ‹ You » do we wait;

THE ARK IS CLOSED.

---

(1) Cf. *Psalms* 5:2. (2) Cf. 19:15. (3) 51:13. (4) Cf. 71:9. (5) Cf. 38:22. (6) Cf. 86:17. (7) Cf. 38:16.

EACH INDIVIDUAL CONTINUES.

CONFESSION / וִדּוּי

**DURING THE RECITATION OF THE וִדּוּי, *CONFESSION*, STAND WITH
HEAD AND BODY SLIGHTLY BOWED, IN SUBMISSIVE CONTRITION.**

אֱלֹהֵינוּ[1] וֵאלֹהֵי אֲבוֹתֵינוּ, תָּבֹא לְפָנֶיךָ תְּפִלָּתֵנוּ,

《 may our 〈 before 〈 come 《 of our 〈 and the 〈 Our God
prayer, You forefathers, God

וְאַל תִּתְעַלַּם מִתְּחִנָּתֵנוּ,[2] שֶׁאֵין אָנוּ עַזֵּי פָנִים

〈 faced 〈 so brazen- 〈 For we are not 《 our supplication. 〈 ignore 〈 and do not

וּקְשֵׁי עֹרֶף, לוֹמַר לְפָנֶיךָ יהוה אֱלֹהֵינוּ וֵאלֹהֵי

〈 and the God 〈 our God, 《 HASHEM, 〈 before You, 〈 as to say 〈 necked 〈 and stiff-

אֲבוֹתֵינוּ, צַדִּיקִים אֲנַחְנוּ וְלֹא חָטָאנוּ, אֲבָל

〈 —for 《 sinned 〈 and 〈 we are, 〈 that righteous 《 of our
indeed, have not forefathers,

אֲנַחְנוּ וַאֲבוֹתֵינוּ חָטָאנוּ.[3]

《 have sinned. 〈 and our forefathers 〈 we

**STRIKE THE LEFT SIDE OF THE CHEST WITH THE RIGHT FIST WHILE RECITING
EACH OF THE SINS OF THE FOLLOWING CONFESSIONAL LITANY:**

אָשַׁמְנוּ, בָּגַדְנוּ, גָּזַלְנוּ, דִּבַּרְנוּ דֹפִי. הֶעֱוִינוּ,

《 We have com- 《 slander. 〈 we have 《 we have 《 we have 《 We have been
mitted iniquity; spoken robbed; betrayed; guilty;

וְהִרְשַׁעְנוּ, זַדְנוּ, חָמַסְנוּ, טָפַלְנוּ שֶׁקֶר. יָעַצְנוּ

〈 We have 《 false 〈 we have 《 we have 《 we have 《 we have
given advice accusations. made extorted; sinned committed
willfully; wickedness;

רָע, כִּזַּבְנוּ, לַצְנוּ, מָרַדְנוּ, נִאַצְנוּ, סָרַרְנוּ,

《 we have 《 we have provoked 《 we have 《 we have 《 we have been 《 that is
strayed; [God's anger]; rebelled; scorned; deceitful; bad;

עָוִינוּ, פָּשַׁעְנוּ, צָרַרְנוּ, קִשִּׁינוּ עֹרֶף. רָשַׁעְנוּ,

《 We have 《 our 〈 we have 《 we have caused 《 we have sinned 《 we have been
been wicked; necks. stiffened distress; rebelliously; iniquitous;

שִׁחַתְנוּ, תִּעַבְנוּ, תָּעִינוּ, תִּעְתָּעְנוּ.

《 we have 《 we have 《 we have 《 we have
scoffed. gone astray; committed been corrupt;
abominations;

---

(1) Cf. *Psalms* 88:3. (2) Cf. 55:2. (3) Cf. 106:6, *Jeremiah* 3:25.

סַרְנוּ מִמִּצְוֹתֶיךָ וּמִמִּשְׁפָּטֶיךָ הַטּוֹבִים, וְלֹא שָׁוָה
‹ worth-   ‹ and it   « that are   ‹   and from   ‹   from Your   ‹ We have
while   was not   good,   Your laws   commandments   turned away

לָנוּ.[1] וְאַתָּה צַדִּיק עַל כָּל הַבָּא עָלֵינוּ, כִּי אֱמֶת
‹ truthfully ‹ for   « upon us, ‹ that has ‹ all ‹ in ‹ are ‹ And You « for us.
                                  come   righteous

עָשִׂיתָ וַאֲנַחְנוּ הִרְשָׁעְנוּ.[2]
          « have acted   ‹ while we « have You
          wickedly.   acted,

אָשַׁמְנוּ מִכָּל עָם, בֹּשְׁנוּ מִכָּל דּוֹר, גָּלָה מִמֶּנּוּ
‹ from ‹ Departed « genera- ‹ more ‹ We have « people. ‹ more than ‹ We have
us   tion.   than any   been   any other   been guilty
                              other   ashamed

מָשׂוֹשׂ, דָּוָה לִבֵּנוּ בַּחֲטָאֵינוּ, הֻחְבַּל אַוּוּיֵנוּ, וְנִפְרַע
‹ uncov- « was our   ‹ Seized « because of ‹ is our ‹ Sickened « has joy.
ered   desired   our sins.   heart
          [Temple],

פְּאֵרֵנוּ, זְבוּל בֵּית מִקְדָּשֵׁנוּ חָרַב בַּעֲוֹנֵינוּ, טִירָתֵנוּ
‹ Our Palace ‹ because of ‹ has been ‹ our Holy Temple ‹ for [His] « was our
              our iniquities. destroyed   abode,   splendor;

הָיְתָה לְשַׁמָּה, יְפִי אַדְמָתֵנוּ לְזָרִים, כֹּחֵנוּ לְנָכְרִים.
« [was given] ‹ our   « is controlled ‹ of our ‹ [Jerusalem,] « desolate. ‹ has
to foreigners. wealth by strangers,   Land   the beauty   become

וַעֲדַיִן לֹא שַׁבְנוּ מִטָּעוּתֵנוּ וְהֵיךְ נָעִיז פָּנֵינוּ וְנַקְשֶׁה
‹ and   ‹ faced ‹ can we be ‹ So   « from our   ‹ we have not ‹ But still
stiffen   so brazen- how   willful errors.   repented

עָרְפֵּנוּ, לוֹמַר לְפָנֶיךָ יהוה אֱלֹהֵינוּ וֵאלֹהֵי אֲבוֹתֵינוּ,
« of our   ‹ and the ‹ our God ‹ HASHEM, ‹ before ‹ so as to ‹ our neck
forefathers, God   You,   say

צַדִּיקִים אֲנַחְנוּ וְלֹא חָטָאנוּ, אֲבָל אֲנַחְנוּ וַאֲבוֹתֵינוּ
‹ and our ‹ both we ‹ for in « and we have   « we are ‹   that
fathers   truth,   not sinned,   righteous

חָטָאנוּ.[3]
« have sinned.

---

(1) Cf. *Job* 33:27. (2) *Nehemiah* 9:33. (3) Cf. *Psalms* 106:6; *Jeremiah* 3:25.

STRIKE THE LEFT SIDE OF THE CHEST WITH THE RIGHT FIST WHILE RECITING EACH OF THE SINS OF THE FOLLOWING CONFESSIONAL LITANY:

אָשַׁמְנוּ, בָּגַדְנוּ, גָּזַלְנוּ, דִּבַּרְנוּ דְפִי. הֶעֱוִינוּ,

We have been guilty; « we have betrayed; « we have robbed; « we have spoken slander. « We have committed iniquity; «

וְהִרְשַׁעְנוּ, זַדְנוּ, חָמַסְנוּ, טָפַלְנוּ שֶׁקֶר. יָעַצְנוּ

we have committed wickedness « we have sinned willfully; «we have extorted; « we have made « false accusations. « We have given advice «

רָע, כִּזַּבְנוּ, לַצְנוּ, מָרַדְנוּ, נִאַצְנוּ, סָרַרְנוּ,

that is bad; « we have been deceitful; « we have scorned; « we have rebelled; « we have provoked [God's anger]; « we have strayed; «

עָוִינוּ, פָּשַׁעְנוּ, צָרַרְנוּ, קִשִּׁינוּ עֹרֶף. רָשַׁעְנוּ,

We have been iniquitous; «we have sinned rebelliously; « we have caused distress; « we have stiffened our necks. « We have been wicked; «

שִׁחַתְנוּ, תִּעַבְנוּ, תָּעִינוּ, תִּעְתָּעְנוּ.

we have been corrupt; « we have committed abominations; « we have gone astray; « we have scoffed. «

סַרְנוּ מִמִּצְוֹתֶיךָ וּמִמִּשְׁפָּטֶיךָ הַטּוֹבִים, וְלֹא שָׁוָה

We have turned away ‹ from Your commandments ‹ and from Your laws ‹ that are good, « and it was not ‹ worthwhile

לָנוּ.[1] וְאַתָּה צַדִּיק עַל כָּל הַבָּא עָלֵינוּ, כִּי אֱמֶת

for us. « And You ‹ are righteous ‹ in ‹ all ‹ that has come ‹ upon us, ‹ for ‹ truthfully

עָשִׂיתָ וַאֲנַחְנוּ הִרְשָׁעְנוּ.[2]

have You acted, « while we ‹ have acted wickedly. «

לְעֵינֵינוּ עָשְׁקוּ עֲמָלֵנוּ, מְמֻשָּׁךְ [it was] וּמְמוֹרָט מִמֶּנּוּ,

Before our eyes ‹ have they stolen ‹ the product of our labor; « [it was] pulled away ‹ and cut off ‹ from us. «

נָתְנוּ עֹלָם עָלֵינוּ, סָבַלְנוּ עַל שִׁכְמֵנוּ, עֲבָדִים

They have placed ‹ their yoke ‹ upon us, « we bore it ‹ upon ‹ our shoulders. « Slaves ‹

מָשְׁלוּ בָנוּ, פֹּרֵק אֵין מִיָּדָם, צָרוֹת רַבּוֹת

have ruled ‹ over us; « a redeemer ‹ there was not ‹ from their hand. « Troubles « that are manifold ‹

---

(1) Cf. *Job* 33:27. (2) *Nehemiah* 9:33.

סְבָבוּנוּ, קְרָאנוּךְ יהוה אֱלֹהֵינוּ, רָחַקְתָּ מִמֶּנּוּ

⟨ from us　⟨ but You have distanced Yourself　« our God,　⟨ HASHEM,　⟨ we called upon You,　« have surrounded us,

בַּעֲוֹנֵינוּ, שַׁבְנוּ מֵאַחֲרֶיךָ, תָּעִינוּ וְאָבְדְנוּ.

« we have become lost.　« we have gone astray;　« from following after You;　⟨ We have turned away　« because of our iniquities.

וַעֲדַיִן לֹא שַׁבְנוּ מִטָּעוּתֵנוּ וְהֵיךְ נָעִיז פָּנֵינוּ וְנַקְשֶׁה

⟨ and stiffen　⟨ faced　⟨ can we be so brazen-　⟨ So how　« from our willful errors.　⟨ we have not repented　⟨ But still

עָרְפֵּנוּ, לוֹמַר לְפָנֶיךָ יהוה אֱלֹהֵינוּ וֵאלֹהֵי אֲבוֹתֵינוּ,

« of our forefathers,　⟨ and the God　⟨ our God　⟨ HASHEM,　⟨ before You,　⟨ so as to say　⟨ our neck

צַדִּיקִים אֲנַחְנוּ וְלֹא חָטָאנוּ, אֲבָל אֲנַחְנוּ וַאֲבוֹתֵינוּ

⟨ and our fathers　⟨ both we　⟨ for in truth,　« and we have not sinned,　« we are　⟨ that righteous

חָטָאנוּ.[1]

« have sinned.

**STRIKE THE LEFT SIDE OF THE CHEST WITH THE RIGHT FIST WHILE RECITING
EACH OF THE SINS OF THE FOLLOWING CONFESSIONAL LITANY:**

אָשַׁמְנוּ, בָּגַדְנוּ, גָּזַלְנוּ, דִּבַּרְנוּ דֹפִי. הֶעֱוִינוּ,

« We have committed iniquity;　« slander.　⟨ we have spoken　« we have robbed;　« we have betrayed;　« We have been guilty;

וְהִרְשַׁעְנוּ, זַדְנוּ, חָמַסְנוּ, טָפַלְנוּ שֶׁקֶר. יָעַצְנוּ

⟨ We have given advice　« false accusations.　⟨ we have made　« we have extorted;　« we have sinned willfully;　« we have committed wickedness;

רָע, כִּזַּבְנוּ, לַצְנוּ, מָרַדְנוּ, נִאַצְנוּ, סָרַרְנוּ,

« we have strayed;　« we have provoked [God's anger];　« we have rebelled;　« we have scorned;　« we have been deceitful;　⟨ that is bad;

עָוִינוּ, פָּשַׁעְנוּ, צָרַרְנוּ, קִשִּׁינוּ עֹרֶף. רָשַׁעְנוּ,

« We have been wicked;　« our necks.　⟨ we have stiffened　« we have caused distress;　« we have sinned rebelliously;　« we have been iniquitous;

שִׁחַתְנוּ, תִּעַבְנוּ, תָּעִינוּ, תִּעְתָּעְנוּ.

« we have scoffed.　« we have gone astray;　« we have committed abominations;　« we have been corrupt;

---

(1) Cf. *Psalms* 106:6; *Jeremiah* 3:25.

סָרְנוּ מִמִּצְוֹתֶיךָ וּמִמִּשְׁפָּטֶיךָ הַטּוֹבִים, וְלֹא שָׁוָה

‹ worth-while ‹ and it was not ‹‹ that are good, ‹ and from Your laws ‹ from Your commandments ‹‹ We have turned away

לָנוּ.[1] וְאַתָּה צַדִּיק עַל כָּל הַבָּא עָלֵינוּ, כִּי אֱמֶת

‹ truth-fully ‹ for ‹‹ upon us, ‹ that has come ‹ all ‹ in ‹ are righteous ‹ And You ‹‹ for us.

עָשִׂיתָ וַאֲנַחְנוּ הִרְשָׁעְנוּ.[2]

‹‹ have acted wickedly. ‹ while we ‹‹ have You acted,

הִרְשַׁעְנוּ וּפָשַׁעְנוּ, לָכֵן לֹא נוֹשָׁעְנוּ. וְתֵן בְּלִבֵּנוּ

‹ in our hearts ‹ Place ‹‹ been saved. ‹ we have not ‹ there-fore ‹‹ and we have sinned rebelliously; ‹ We have acted wickedly

לַעֲזוֹב דֶּרֶךְ רֶשַׁע, וְחִישׁ לָנוּ יֶשַׁע, כַּכָּתוּב עַל יַד

‹ the hand ‹ by ‹ as it is written ‹‹ salvation; ‹ to us ‹ and ‹‹ of wickedness, ‹ the path ‹ [the will] to abandon

נְבִיאֶךָ: יַעֲזֹב רָשָׁע דַּרְכּוֹ, וְאִישׁ אָוֶן מַחְשְׁבֹתָיו,

‹‹ [abandon] his thoughts; ‹ of iniquity ‹ and the man ‹‹ his way, ‹ the wicked one ‹ Let abandon ‹‹ of Your prophet:

וְיָשֹׁב אֶל יהוה וִירַחֲמֵהוּ, וְאֶל אֱלֹהֵינוּ כִּי

‹ for ‹ our God, ‹ and to ‹‹ and He will have compassion on him, ‹ Hashem, ‹ to ‹ and let him return

יַרְבֶּה לִסְלוֹחַ.[3]

‹‹ forgiving. ‹ He is abundantly

מְשִׁיחַ צִדְקֶךָ אָמַר לְפָנֶיךָ, שְׁגִיאוֹת מִי יָבִין,

‹‹ can discern? ‹ who ‹ Mistakes ‹‹ before You: ‹ said ‹ who is righteous [David] ‹ Your anointed one

מִנִּסְתָּרוֹת נַקֵּנִי.[4] נַקֵּנוּ יהוה אֱלֹהֵינוּ מִכָּל פְּשָׁעֵינוּ,

‹ our sins ‹ of all ‹ our God, ‹ Hashem, ‹ Cleanse us, ‹‹ cleanse me. ‹ From unperceived faults

וְטַהֲרֵנוּ מִכָּל טֻמְאוֹתֵינוּ, וּזְרוֹק עָלֵינוּ מַיִם טְהוֹרִים

‹ pure water ‹ upon us ‹ Pour ‹‹ our contaminations. ‹ of all ‹ and purify us

וְטַהֲרֵנוּ, כַּכָּתוּב עַל יַד נְבִיאֶךָ: וְזָרַקְתִּי עֲלֵיכֶם

‹ upon you ‹ I shall pour ‹‹ of Your prophet: ‹ the hand ‹ by ‹ as it is written ‹‹ and purify us

(1) Cf. Job 33:27. (2) Nehemiah 9:33. (3) Isaiah 55:7. (4) Psalms 19:13.

מַיִם טְהוֹרִים וּטְהַרְתֶּם, מִכֹּל טֻמְאוֹתֵיכֶם וּמִכָּל

pure water / and you will become pure; / from all / your contaminations / and / from all

גִּלּוּלֵיכֶם אֲטַהֵר אֶתְכֶם.¹ עַמֶּךָ וְנַחֲלָתֶךָ, רְעֵבֵי

your abominations / I will purify / you. / Your people / and Your heritage, / who hunger

טוּבְךָ, צְמֵאֵי חַסְדֶּךָ, תְּאֵבֵי יִשְׁעֶךָ, יַכִּירוּ וְיֵדְעוּ

for Your goodness, / who thirst / for Your kindness, / and who long / for Your salvation — may they recognize / and know

כִּי לַיהוה אֱלֹהֵינוּ הָרַחֲמִים וְהַסְּלִיחוֹת.

that / to HASHEM, / our God, / belong mercy / and forgiveness.

אֵל רַחוּם שְׁמֶךָ, אֵל חַנּוּן שְׁמֶךָ,² בָּנוּ נִקְרָא שְׁמֶךָ.³

Merciful God / is Your Name, / Gracious God / is Your Name, / upon us / is Your Name proclaimed,

יהוה עֲשֵׂה לְמַעַן שְׁמֶךָ,⁴ עֲשֵׂה לְמַעַן אֲמִתָּךְ, עֲשֵׂה

HASHEM, / act / for the sake of / Your Name. / Act / for the sake of / Your truth; / act

לְמַעַן בְּרִיתָךְ, עֲשֵׂה לְמַעַן גָּדְלָךְ וְתִפְאַרְתָּךְ, עֲשֵׂה

for the sake of / Your covenant; / act / for the sake of / Your greatness / and Your splendor; / act

לְמַעַן דָּתָךְ, עֲשֵׂה לְמַעַן הוֹדָךְ, עֲשֵׂה לְמַעַן וְעוּדָךְ,

for the sake of / Your Law; / act / for the sake of / Your glory; / act / for the sake of / Your Meeting House;

עֲשֵׂה לְמַעַן זִכְרָךְ,⁵ עֲשֵׂה לְמַעַן חַסְדָּךְ,⁶ עֲשֵׂה לְמַעַן

act / for the sake of / Your remembrance; / act / for the sake of / Your kindness; / act / for the sake of

טוּבָךְ, עֲשֵׂה לְמַעַן יִחוּדָךְ, עֲשֵׂה לְמַעַן כְּבוֹדָךְ, עֲשֵׂה

Your goodness; / act / for the sake of / Your Oneness; / act / for the sake of / Your honor; / act

לְמַעַן לִמּוּדָךְ,⁷ עֲשֵׂה לְמַעַן מַלְכוּתָךְ, עֲשֵׂה לְמַעַן

for the sake of / Your students; / act / for the sake of / Your kingship; / act / for the sake of

נִצְחָךְ, עֲשֵׂה לְמַעַן סוֹדָךְ,⁸ עֲשֵׂה לְמַעַן עֶזָּךְ, עֲשֵׂה

Your power; / act / for the sake of / Your secret [revealed to those who fear You]; / act / for the sake of / Your eternal [Name]; / act

---

(1) *Ezekiel* 36:25. (2) Cf. *Exodus* 34:6. (3) Cf. *Deuteronomy* 28:10. (4) *Jeremiah* 14:7.
(5) Cf. *Exodus* 3:15. (6) *Psalms* 6:5. (7) Cf. *Isaiah* 54:13. (8) Cf. *Psalms* 25:14.

לְמַעַן **פְּאֵרֶךְ**, עֲשֵׂה לְמַעַן **צִדְקָתֶךְ**, עֲשֵׂה לְמַעַן

for the sake of — act — Your righteousness; — for the sake of — act — Your glory; — for the sake of

קְדֻשָּׁתֶךָ, עֲשֵׂה לְמַעַן **רַחֲמֶיךָ** הָרַבִּים, עֲשֵׂה לְמַעַן

for the sake of — act — that is abundant; — Your mercy — for the sake of — act — Your sanctity;

שְׁכִינָתֶךָ, עֲשֵׂה לְמַעַן **תְּהִלָּתֶךָ**, עֲשֵׂה לְמַעַן אוֹהֲבֶיךָ

those who loved You — for the sake of — act — Your praise; — for the sake of — act — Your Divine Presence;

שׁוֹכְנֵי עָפָר,¹ עֲשֵׂה לְמַעַן אַבְרָהָם יִצְחָק וְיַעֲקֹב,

and Jacob; — Isaac, — Abraham, — for the sake of — act — in the dust; — who rest

עֲשֵׂה לְמַעַן מֹשֶׁה וְאַהֲרֹן, עֲשֵׂה לְמַעַן דָּוִד וּשְׁלֹמֹה,

and Solomon; — David — for the sake of — act — and Aaron; — Moses — for the sake of — act

עֲשֵׂה לְמַעַן יְרוּשָׁלַיִם עִיר קָדְשֶׁךָ,² עֲשֵׂה לְמַעַן צִיּוֹן

Zion, — for the sake of — act — of Your Holiness; — the City — Jerusalem, — for the sake of — act

מִשְׁכַּן כְּבוֹדֶךָ,³ עֲשֵׂה לְמַעַן שִׁמְמוֹת⁴ הֵיכָלֶךָ, עֲשֵׂה

act — of Your Temple; — the desolation — for the sake of — act — of Your glory; — the abode

לְמַעַן הֲרִיסוּת⁵ מִזְבְּחֶךָ, עֲשֵׂה לְמַעַן הֲרוּגִים עַל

for — those killed — for the sake of — act — of Your Altar; — the devastation — for the sake of

שֵׁם קָדְשֶׁךָ, עֲשֵׂה לְמַעַן טְבוּחִים עַל יִחוּדֶךָ, עֲשֵׂה

act — Your Oneness; — for — those slaughtered — for the sake of — act — Your holy Name;

לְמַעַן בָּאֵי בָאֵשׁ וּבַמַּיִם עַל קִדּוּשׁ שְׁמֶךָ, עֲשֵׂה לְמַעַן

for the sake of — act — of Your Name; — the sanctification — for — and water — fire — those who entered — for the sake of

יוֹנְקֵי שָׁדַיִם⁶ שֶׁלֹּא חָטְאוּ, עֲשֵׂה לְמַעַן גְּמוּלֵי חָלָב⁷

from milk — the [babies] weaned — for the sake of — act — sin; — who did not — at the breast — the [infants] sucking

שֶׁלֹּא פָשְׁעוּ, עֲשֵׂה לְמַעַן תִּינוֹקוֹת שֶׁל בֵּית רַבָּן,⁸

their teachers' school; — of — the children — for the sake of — act — transgress; — who did not

---

(1) *Isaiah* 26:19. (2) Cf. *Daniel* 9:16,24. (3) *Psalms* 26:8. (4) Cf. *Jeremiah* 51:26.
(5) Cf. *Isaiah* 49:19. (6) *Joel* 2:16. (7) *Isaiah* 28:9. (8) *Shabbos* 119b.

עֲשֵׂה לְמַעַנְךָ אִם לֹא לְמַעֲנֵנוּ, עֲשֵׂה לְמַעַנְךָ וְהוֹשִׁיעֵנוּ.

》 and save us. 〈 for Your 〈 act 》 for our 〈 not 〈 if 〈 for Your 〈 act
sake sake; sake

עֲנֵנוּ יהוה עֲנֵנוּ, עֲנֵנוּ אֱלֹהֵינוּ עֲנֵנוּ, עֲנֵנוּ אָבִינוּ[1]

〈 our 〈 answer 》 answer 〈 our God, 〈 answer 》 answer 〈 HASHEM, 〈 Answer
Father, us; us; us; us;

עֲנֵנוּ, עֲנֵנוּ **בּוֹרְאֵנוּ**[2] עֲנֵנוּ, עֲנֵנוּ **גּוֹאֲלֵנוּ**[3] עֲנֵנוּ, עֲנֵנוּ

〈 answer 》 answer 〈 our 〈 answer 》 answer 〈 our Creator, 〈 answer 》 answer
us; us; Redeemer, us; us; us;

דּוֹרְשֵׁנוּ[4] עֲנֵנוּ, עֲנֵנוּ **הָאֵל** הַנֶּאֱמָן[5] עֲנֵנוּ, עֲנֵנוּ וָתִיק

〈 stead- 〈 answer 》 answer 〈 Who is 〈 God 〈 answer 》 answer 〈 You Who
fast us; us; faithful, us; us; searches us out,

וְחָסִיד עֲנֵנוּ, עֲנֵנוּ **זַךְ** וְיָשָׁר[6] עֲנֵנוּ, עֲנֵנוּ חַי וְקַיָּם[7]

〈 and 〈 living 〈 answer 》 answer 〈 and 〈 pure 〈 answer 》 answer 〈 and kind
enduring One, us; us; upright us; us; One,
One, One

עֲנֵנוּ, עֲנֵנוּ **טוֹב** וּמֵטִיב[8] עֲנֵנוּ, עֲנֵנוּ יוֹדֵעַ יֵצֶר[9] עֲנֵנוּ,

》 answer 〈 of incli- 〈 Knower 〈 answer 》 answer 〈 and bene- 〈 good 〈 answer 》 answer
us; nations, us; us; ficent One, us; us;

עֲנֵנוּ **כּוֹבֵשׁ** כְּעָסִים עֲנֵנוּ, עֲנֵנוּ **לוֹבֵשׁ** צְדָקוֹת[10] עֲנֵנוּ,

》 answer 〈 of 〈 Donner 〈 answer 》 answer 〈 of wrath, 〈 Suppressor 〈 answer
us; righteousness, us; us;

עֲנֵנוּ **מֶלֶךְ** מַלְכֵי הַמְּלָכִים[11] עֲנֵנוּ, עֲנֵנוּ **נוֹרָא** וְנִשְׂגָּב[12]

〈 and power- 〈 awesome 〈 answer 》 answer 〈 of kings, 〈 over 〈 King 〈 answer
ful One, us; us; kings us,

עֲנֵנוּ, עֲנֵנוּ **סוֹלֵחַ** וּמוֹחֵל עֲנֵנוּ, עֲנֵנוּ עוֹנֶה בְּעֵת

〈 in time 〈 You Who 〈 answer 》 answer 〈 and 〈 You Who 〈 answer 》 answer
answers us; us; pardons, forgives us, us;

צָרָה[13] עֲנֵנוּ, עֲנֵנוּ **פּוֹדֶה** וּמַצִּיל[14] עֲנֵנוּ, עֲנֵנוּ צַדִּיק

〈 righteous 〈 answer 》 answer 〈 and 〈 Redeemer 〈 answer 》 answer 〈 of
us; us; Rescuer, us; us; distress,

וְיָשָׁר[15] עֲנֵנוּ, עֲנֵנוּ **קָרוֹב** לְקוֹרְאָיו[16] עֲנֵנוּ, עֲנֵנוּ קָשֶׁה

〈 You Who 〈 answer 》 answer 〈 to those who 〈 He Who 〈 answer 》 answer 〈 and up-
with difficulty us, us; call upon Him, is close us, us; right One,

(1) *Isaiah* 64:7. (2) Cf. 43:1. (3) 47:4. (4) Cf. *Ezekiel* 34:11. (5) *Deuteronomy* 7:9.
(6) *Job* 8:6; cf. *Proverbs* 20:11. (7) Cf. *Daniel* 6:27. (8) Cf. *Psalms* 119:68.
(9) Cf. 103:14. (10) Cf. *Isaiah* 59:17. (11) *Ethics of the Fathers* 3:1. (12) *Psalms* 47:3; 148:13.
(13) Cf. *Isaiah* 49:8; *Psalms* 37:39. Alternate text: בְּעֵת רָצוֹן, *in time of favor.* (14) Cf. 34:23,18.
(15) *Deuteronomy* 32:4. (16) Cf. *Psalms* 145:18.

לְכוֹעֵס¹ עֲנֵנוּ, עֲנֵנוּ רַךְ לִרְצוֹת² עֲנֵנוּ, עֲנֵנוּ רַחוּם

‹ becomes angry » answer us; ‹ answer us; ‹ You Who are easily appeased, » answer us; » answer us; ‹ merciful

וְחַנּוּן³ עֲנֵנוּ, עֲנֵנוּ שׁוֹמֵעַ אֶל אֶבְיוֹנִים⁴ עֲנֵנוּ, עֲנֵנוּ

‹ and gracious One, » answer us; ‹ answer us; ‹ You Who listens ‹ to ‹ the destitute, » answer us; ‹ answer us;

תּוֹמֵךְ תְּמִימִים עֲנֵנוּ, עֲנֵנוּ אֱלֹהֵי אֲבוֹתֵינוּ עֲנֵנוּ,

‹ You Who supports ‹ the wholesome, » answer us; » answer us; ‹ God ‹ of our forefathers, » answer us;

עֲנֵנוּ אֱלֹהֵי אַבְרָהָם עֲנֵנוּ, עֲנֵנוּ פַּחַד יִצְחָק⁵ עֲנֵנוּ,

‹ answer us, ‹ God ‹ of Abraham, » answer us; » answer us; ‹ Awesome One ‹ of Isaac, » answer us;

עֲנֵנוּ אֲבִיר יַעֲקֹב⁶ עֲנֵנוּ, עֲנֵנוּ עֶזְרַת הַשְּׁבָטִים עֲנֵנוּ,

‹ answer us, ‹ Mighty One ‹ of Jacob, » answer us; ‹ answer us; ‹ Helper ‹ of the tribes, » answer us;

עֲנֵנוּ מִשְׂגַּב אִמָּהוֹת עֲנֵנוּ, עֲנֵנוּ עוֹנֶה בְּעֵת רָצוֹן⁷ עֲנֵנוּ,

‹ answer us, ‹ Stronghold ‹ of the Matriarchs, » answer us; ‹ answer us; ‹ You Who answers ‹ in a time ‹ of favor, » answer us;

עֲנֵנוּ אֲבִי יְתוֹמִים⁸ עֲנֵנוּ, עֲנֵנוּ דַּיָּן אַלְמָנוֹת⁸ עֲנֵנוּ.

‹ answer us, ‹ Father ‹ of orphans, » answer us; ‹ answer us; ‹ Judge ‹ of widows, » answer us.

מִי שֶׁעָנָה לְאַבְרָהָם אָבִינוּ בְּהַר הַמּוֹרִיָּה⁹

‹ He ‹ Who answered ‹ Abraham ‹ our father ‹ on Mount » Moriah

הוּא יַעֲנֵנוּ.

‹ He ‹ — may » answer us.

מִי שֶׁעָנָה לְיִצְחָק בְּנוֹ כְּשֶׁנֶּעֱקַד עַל גַּבֵּי הַמִּזְבֵּחַ⁹

‹ He ‹ Who answered ‹ Isaac ‹ his son ‹ when he was bound ‹ on ‹ top » of the altar

הוּא יַעֲנֵנוּ.

‹ He ‹ — may » answer us.

מִי שֶׁעָנָה לְיַעֲקֹב בְּבֵית אֵל¹⁰   הוּא יַעֲנֵנוּ.

‹ He ‹ Who answered ‹ Jacob » in Beth-el   ‹ He ‹ — may » answer us.

---

(1) *Ethics of the Fathers* 5:14. (2) Cf. 5:14. (3) *Exodus* 34:6. (4) *Psalms* 69:34. (5) *Genesis* 31:42.
(6) *Isaiah* 49:26. (7) Cf. 49:8; *Psalms* 69:14. Alternate text: בְּעֵת צָרָה, *in time of distress.*]
(8) 68:6. (9) *Genesis* 22:12. (10) 35:3.

מִי שֶׁעָנָה לְיוֹסֵף בְּבֵית הָאֲסוּרִים¹ הוּא יַעֲנֵנוּ.

He › Who answered › Joseph › in the prison ≪ — may He ≪ answer us.

מִי שֶׁעָנָה לַאֲבוֹתֵינוּ עַל יַם סוּף² הוּא יַעֲנֵנוּ.

He › Who answered › our forefathers › at › the › Sea of Reeds ≪ — may He ≪ answer us.

מִי שֶׁעָנָה לְמֹשֶׁה בְּחוֹרֵב³ הוּא יַעֲנֵנוּ.

He › Who answered › Moses › in Horeb ≪ — may He ≪ answer us.

מִי שֶׁעָנָה לְאַהֲרֹן בַּמַּחְתָּה⁴ הוּא יַעֲנֵנוּ.

He › Who answered › Aaron › with the fire-pan ≪ — may He ≪ answer us.

מִי שֶׁעָנָה לְפִינְחָס בְּקוּמוֹ מִתּוֹךְ הָעֵדָה⁵ הוּא יַעֲנֵנוּ.

He › Who answered › Phinehas › when he arose › from › amid ≪ the congregation — may He ≪ answer us.

מִי שֶׁעָנָה לִיהוֹשֻׁעַ בַּגִּלְגָּל⁶ הוּא יַעֲנֵנוּ.

He › Who answered › Joshua › in Gilgal ≪ — may He ≪ answer us.

מִי שֶׁעָנָה לִשְׁמוּאֵל בַּמִּצְפָּה⁷ הוּא יַעֲנֵנוּ.

He › Who answered › Samuel › in Mizpah ≪ — may He ≪ answer us.

מִי שֶׁעָנָה לְדָוִד וּשְׁלֹמֹה בְנוֹ בִּירוּשָׁלָיִם⁸ הוּא יַעֲנֵנוּ.

He › Who answered › David › and Solomon › his son › in Jerusalem ≪ — may He ≪ answer us.

מִי שֶׁעָנָה לְאֵלִיָּהוּ בְּהַר הַכַּרְמֶל⁹ הוּא יַעֲנֵנוּ.

He › Who answered › Elijah › on › Mount › Carmel ≪ — may He ≪ answer us.

מִי שֶׁעָנָה לֶאֱלִישָׁע בִּירִיחוֹ¹⁰ הוּא יַעֲנֵנוּ.

He › Who answered › Elisha › in Jericho ≪ — may He ≪ answer us.

מִי שֶׁעָנָה לְיוֹנָה בִּמְעֵי הַדָּגָה¹¹ הוּא יַעֲנֵנוּ.

He › Who answered › Jonah › in the › innards › of the fish ≪ — may He ≪ answer us.

מִי שֶׁעָנָה לְחִזְקִיָּהוּ מֶלֶךְ יְהוּדָה בְּחָלְיוֹ¹² הוּא יַעֲנֵנוּ.

He › Who answered › Hezekiah, › king › of Judah, › in his illness ≪ — may He ≪ answer us.

(1) Genesis 39:21. (2) Exodus Ch. 14. (3) 17:6,11; Deuteronomy 9:19. (4) Numbers 17:11-13. (5) 25:7-13. (6) Joshua 6:1-20; 7:6-15; 10:12-14. (7) I Samuel 7:9. (8) II Samuel 7:5-16; 21:1,14; 24:25; I Kings 9:3. (9) 18:36-38. (10) II Kings 2:21. (11) Jonah 2:2-11. (12) II Kings 20:2-6; Isaiah 38:2-8.

מִי שֶׁעָנָה לַחֲנַנְיָה מִישָׁאֵל וַעֲזַרְיָה

⟨ He ⟨ Who answered ⟨ Hananiah, ⟨ Mishael, ⟨ and Azariah

הוּא יַעֲנֵנוּ.   בְּתוֹךְ כִּבְשַׁן הָאֵשׁ¹

《 answer us. ⟨ He — may   《 of fire ⟨ the furnace ⟨ inside

הוּא יַעֲנֵנוּ.   מִי שֶׁעָנָה לְדָנִיֵּאל בְּגוֹב הָאֲרָיוֹת²

《 answer us. ⟨ He — may   《 of lions ⟨ in the den ⟨ Daniel ⟨ Who answered ⟨ He

מִי שֶׁעָנָה לְמָרְדְּכַי וְאֶסְתֵּר בְּשׁוּשַׁן הַבִּירָה³

《 the capital ⟨ in Shushan ⟨ and Esther ⟨ Mordechai ⟨ Who answered ⟨ He

הוּא יַעֲנֵנוּ.

《 answer us. ⟨ He — may

הוּא יַעֲנֵנוּ.   מִי שֶׁעָנָה לְעֶזְרָא בַגּוֹלָה⁴

《 answer us. ⟨ He — may   《 in the exile ⟨ Ezra ⟨ Who answered ⟨ He

מִי שֶׁעָנָה לְכָל הַצַּדִּיקִים וְהַחֲסִידִים וְהַתְּמִימִים

⟨ the wholesome, ⟨ the devout, ⟨ the righteous, ⟨ all ⟨ Who answered ⟨ He

הוּא יַעֲנֵנוּ.   וְהַיְשָׁרִים

《 answer us. ⟨ He — may   《 and the upright

רַחֲמָנָא דְּעָנֵי לַעֲנִיֵּי, עֲנֵינָן. רַחֲמָנָא דְּעָנֵי לִתְבִירֵי

⟨ those of broken ⟨ Who answers ⟨ Merciful One 《 answer us! 《 the poor, ⟨ Who answers ⟨ Merciful One

לִבָּא, עֲנֵינָן. רַחֲמָנָא דְּעָנֵי לְמַכִּיכֵי רוּחָא, עֲנֵינָן.

《 answer us! 《 spirit, ⟨ those of crushed ⟨ Who answers ⟨ Merciful One 《 answer us! 《 hearts,

רַחֲמָנָא עֲנֵינָן. רַחֲמָנָא חוּס. רַחֲמָנָא פְּרוֹק. רַחֲמָנָא

⟨ Merciful One, 《 redeem! ⟨ Merciful One, 《 have pity! ⟨ Merciful One, 《 answer us! ⟨ Merciful One,

שֵׁזִיב. רַחֲמָנָא רְחַם עֲלָן, הַשְׁתָּא בַּעֲגָלָא וּבִזְמַן קָרִיב.

《 that comes soon. ⟨ and at a time ⟨ swiftly, ⟨ — now, 《 on us ⟨ have mercy ⟨ Merciful One, 《 save!

---

(1) *Daniel* 3:21-27. (2) 6:17-23. (3) *Esther* Ch. 8. (4) *Ezra* 8:21-23.

PUTTING DOWN THE HEAD / נְפִילַת אַפַּיִם

RECITE UNTIL יָבֵשׁוּ רָגַע WITH THE HEAD RESTING ON THE LEFT ARM,
PREFERABLY WHILE SEATED.

(וַיֹּאמֶר דָּוִד אֶל גָּד, צַר לִי מְאֹד, נִפְּלָה נָּא בְיַד יהוה,

《 of 〈 into the 〉 now 〈 Let us 《 exceed- 〈 am 〉 Dis- 《Gad, 〈 to 〈 (And David said
HASHEM, hand fall ingly. I tressed

כִּי רַבִּים רַחֲמָיו, וּבְיַד אָדָם אַל אֶפֹּלָה.[1]

《 let me not fall.) 〈 but into human 《 are His 〈 abundant 〈 for
hands mercies,

רַחוּם וְחַנּוּן חָטָאתִי לְפָנֶיךָ. יהוה מָלֵא רַחֲמִים,

《 of mercy, 〈 Who 〈 HASHEM, 《 before 〈 I have 〈 and gracious 〈 O merciful
is full You. sinned One,

רַחֵם עָלַי וְקַבֵּל תַּחֲנוּנָי.

《 my 〈 and 〈 on me 〈 have
supplications. accept mercy

——— תהלים ו:ב-יא / Psalms 6:2-11 ———

יהוה, אַל בְּאַפְּךָ תוֹכִיחֵנִי, וְאַל בַּחֲמָתְךָ תְיַסְּרֵנִי.

《chastise me. 〈 in Your wrath 〈 nor 〈 rebuke me, 〈in Your anger 〈 do not 〈 HASHEM,

חָנֵּנִי יהוה כִּי אֻמְלַל אָנִי, רְפָאֵנִי יהוה כִּי נִבְהֲלוּ

〈 shudder 〈 for 〈 HASHEM, 〈 heal me, 《 am I; 〈 feeble 〈 for 〈 HASHEM, 〈 Favor
with terror me,

עֲצָמָי. וְנַפְשִׁי נִבְהֲלָה מְאֹד, וְאַתָּה יהוה עַד מָתָי.

《when? 〈 until 〈 HASHEM, 〈 and You, 《 utterly, 〈 is terrified 〈 My soul 《 do my
bones.

שׁוּבָה יהוה חַלְּצָה נַפְשִׁי, הוֹשִׁיעֵנִי לְמַעַן חַסְדֶּךָ.

《 Your 〈 as befits 〈 save me 《 my soul; 〈 release 〈 HASHEM, 〈 Desist,
kindness.

כִּי אֵין בַּמָּוֶת זִכְרֶךָ, בִּשְׁאוֹל מִי יוֹדֶה לָּךְ. יָגַעְתִּי

〈 I am 《 You? 〈 will 〈 who 〈 in the 《 is there men- 〈 in 〈 not 〈 For
wearied praise grave tion of You; death

בְּאַנְחָתִי, אַשְׂחֶה בְכָל לַיְלָה מִטָּתִי, בְּדִמְעָתִי

〈 with my tears 《 my bed; 〈 night 〈 every 〈 I drench 《 with my sigh;

עַרְשִׂי אַמְסֶה. עָשְׁשָׁה מִכַּעַס עֵינִי, עָתְקָה בְּכָל

〈 by all 〈 aged 〈 is my 〈 because of 〈 Dimmed 《 I soak. 〈 my couch
eye, anger

---

(1) II Samuel 24:14.

צוֹרְרָי. סוּרוּ מִמֶּנִּי כָּל פִּעֲלֵי אָוֶן, כִּי שָׁמַע יהוה

  my   》 HASHEM has heard 》 for 《 of evil, 《 doers 〈 all 〈 from me, 〈 Depart 》 my tormentors.

קוֹל בִּכְיִי. שָׁמַע יהוה תְּחִנָּתִי, יהוה תְּפִלָּתִי יִקָּח.

》 will accept. 〈 my prayer 〈 HASHEM 》 my plea, 〈 HASHEM has heard 》 of my 〈 the weeping. sound

יֵבֹשׁוּ וְיִבָּהֲלוּ מְאֹד כָּל אֹיְבָי, יָשֻׁבוּ יֵבֹשׁוּ רָגַע.

》 in an instant. 〈 and be shamed 《 may they regret 》 my enemies; 〈 all 〈 utterly, 〈 and confounded 〈 Let them be shamed

מַחֵי וּמַסֵּי מֵמִית וּמַחֵיֶה, מַסִּיק מִן שְׁאוֹל

〈 the grave 〈 from 〈 Who raises [the dead] 《 and Who restores life, 〈 Who causes death 《 and Who heals, 〈 [O God,] Who wounds

לְחַיֵּי עָלְמָא, בְּרָא כַּד חָטֵי אֲבוּהִי לַקְיֵהּ, אֲבוּהִי

〈 but a father 》 would strike him, 〈 his father 〈 sin, 〈 should he 〈 A son 〈 eternal: 〈 to life

דְּחַיֵּס אַסֵּי לִכְאֵבֵהּ. עַבְדָּא דְּמָרִיד נָפִיק בְּקוֹלָר,

》 in chains, 〈 he is led out 《 who rebels, 〈 A slave 》 his [son's] pain. 〈 will heal 〈 who is compassionate

מָרֵהּ תָּאִיב וְתַבִּיר קוֹלָרֵהּ.

》 his chains. 〈 he breaks 〈 desires, 〈 but [if] his master

בְּרָךְ בִּכְרָךְ אֲנָן וְחָטֵינָן קַמָּךְ, הָא רְוֵי נַפְשִׁין

〈 has our soul been 〈 satiated 〈 indeed 《 before You; 〈 and we have sinned 〈 we are, 〈 Your firstborn, 〈 Your son,

בְּגִידִין מְרָרִין, עַבְדָּךְ אֲנָן וּמְרוֹדִינָן קַמָּךְ,

》 before You; 〈 and we have rebelled 〈 we are 〈 Your servants 》 that is bitter. 〈 with wormwood

הָא בְּבִזְּתָא, הָא בְּשִׁבְיָא, הָא בְּמַלְקִיּוּתָא.

》 by the lash. 〈 and some 〈 in captivity, 〈 some 〈 from looting, 〈 [indeed we have suffered,] some

בְּמָטוּ מִנָּךְ בְּרַחֲמָךְ דִּנְפִישִׁין, אַסֵּי לִכְאֵבִין

〈 the pains 〈 heal 〈 that is abundant, 〈 in Your compassion 〈 of You, 〈 We beg

דִּתְקוֹף עֲלָן, עַד דְּלָא נֶהֱוֵי גְּמִירָא בְּשִׁבְיָא.

》 in captivity. 〈 completely annihilated 〈 we are not 〈 while yet 〈 us, 〈 that have overwhelmed

סליחה פד / SELICHAH 84
(תחנה)

ALL:

מִקְוֵה יִשְׂרָאֵל* מוֹשִׁיעוֹ בְּעֵת צָרָה.¹
《 of trouble, 〈 in time 〈 its Savior 〈 of Israel,* 〈 Hope

שׁוֹמְרוֹ וְצִלּוֹ² וּמַצִּילוֹ בְּיוֹם עֶבְרָה.
《 of wrath, 〈 on the 〈 and its 〈 its protec- its Guardian,
　　　　　　　day　　Rescuer　tive Shade,

הַמָּלֵא רַחֲמִים עַל עֲנִיָּה סֹעֲרָה.³
《 storm-tossed [nation], 〈 the poor 〈 for 〈 with mercy 〈 be filled

בְּדוּדָה וּשְׁדוּדָה כְּאוּבָה וּצְעוּרָה.
《 and troubled. 〈 aching, 〈 plundered, 〈 lonely,

רְמוּסָה בְּיַד צַר וּבֶעָפָר מְעֻפָּרָה.
《 wallowing, 〈 in the dust 〈 of the 〈 at the She is
　　　　　　　　enemy, hand trampled

שְׁכוּלָה וְגַלְמוּדָה גוֹלָה וְסוּרָה.
《 and wandering, 〈 exiled, 〈 left alone, 〈 bereaved,

מֵאֲרָיוֹת וְדֻבִּים דְּרוּסָה וּשְׁבוּרָה.
《 and broken, 〈 torn 〈 and bears 〈 by lions

וּכְצֹאן בְּלִי רוֹעֶה תּוֹעָה וּפְזוּרָה.
《 and 〈 straying 〈 a 〈 without 〈 and like
scattered.　　　　　shepherd　　　　sheep

אָדוֹן עַד מָתַי לֹא תַבִּיט בַּצָּרָה.
《 at [her] trouble? 〈 will You not look 〈 when 〈 until 《 O Lord,

לָמָּה לָנֶצַח תַּעַזְבֶנָּה בְּיַד עוֹכְרָה.
《 of her 〈 in the 〈 will You 〈 forever 〈 Why
tormentors?　grip　leave her

בְּרַחֲמֶיךָ הוֹצִיאָהּ מֵאֲפֵלָה לְאוֹרָה.
《 into light; 〈 of gloom 〈 bring her out 〈 In Your mercy

אַל תִּנְאַץ לְמַעַן שִׁמְךָ⁴ כַּחַמָּה בָּרָה.⁵
《 is 〈 she who 《 of Your 〈 for the 〈 reject 〈 do
brilliant.　like the sun　Name,　sake　[her]　not

---

(1) Jeremiah 14:8. (2) Cf. Psalms 121:5. (3) Isaiah 54:11. (4) Jeremiah 14:21. (5) Cf. Song of Songs 6:10.

---

§8 **מִקְוֵה יִשְׂרָאֵל** — *Hope of Israel.* The acrostic of this *selichah* reads מֹשֶׁה בַּר שְׁמוּאֵל בַּר אַבְשָׁלוֹם חֲזַק וְאֱמָץ, *Moshe bar Shmuel bar Avshalom, may he be strong and persevere*

בָּחַרְתָּ מִכָּל עַם בְּשָׂפָה בְרוּרָה.1*

‹ You chose her › ‹ from all › ‹peoples,› ‹ with a language › ‹that is clear;*›

שׁוּר נָא בְּעָנְיָהּ וְנַעֲרָה מֵעֲפָרָהּ.2

‹ look, › ‹please,› ‹ at he poverty › ‹ and shake her free › ‹ of her dust. ›

לְחַם לוֹחֲמֶהָ3 וּצְרֹר צוֹרְרֶהָ,4

‹ Battle › ‹ those who do battle with her, › ‹ become an enemy › ‹ to her enemies, ›

וּנְקֹם נִקְמָתָהּ5 וְנִקְמַת בֵּית הַבְּחִירָה.

‹ and avenge › ‹ her vengeance › ‹ and the vengeance › ‹ for the Temple › ‹ that was Chosen. ›

מִגְּרוּ וּפִגְּרוּ וְהִסִּיקוּ בוֹ הַבְעָרָה.

‹They threw it down,› ‹ razed it, › ‹ set › ‹ it › ‹ ablaze, ›

חִלְּלוּ וְנִאֲצוּ שֵׁם הַנִּכְבָּד וְהַנּוֹרָא.6

‹ profaning › ‹ and blaspheming › ‹ [Your] Name › ‹ that is honored › ‹ and that is awesome. ›

זְכֹר חֶרְפַּת נָבָל7 חֵרֵף בַּאֲמִירָה.

‹Remember› ‹ the insolence › ‹ of the degenerate › ‹ when he blasphemed › ‹ in his speaking. ›

קוּמָה יהוה בְּאַפֶּךָ וְהִנָּשֵׂא לְהִתְגַּבְּרָה.8

‹ Arise, › ‹HASHEM,› ‹ in Your wrath › ‹ rise up › ‹ to overpower [him]. ›

וְאַל תִּשְׁכַּח קוֹל צוֹרְרֶיךָ עוֹלֶה בִּתְדִירָה.9

‹Do not› ‹ forget › ‹ the sound › ‹ of Your enemies › ‹ that arises › ‹ continually; ›

❖ אַבֵּד וְגַדַּע מַלְכוּת אֲרוּרָה.

‹destroy› ‹and chop down› ‹ the kingdom › ‹ that is accursed. ›

---

(1) Cf. *Zephaniah* 3:9. (2) Cf. *Isaiah* 52:2. (3) Cf. *Psalms* 35:1. (4) Cf. *Exodus* 23:22.
(5) Cf. *Numbers* 31:2. (6) Cf. *Deuteronomy* 28:58. (7) *Psalms* 39:9. (8) Cf. 7:7. (9) Cf. 74:23.

[see prefatory comment to *Selichah* 75].

בָּחַרְתָּ מִכָּל עַם בְּשָׂפָה בְרוּרָה — *You chose her from all peoples, with a language that is clear.* Human language is capable of capturing sublime and complex ideas, but God chose Israel and granted it the language of the Torah, the language that encompasses God's own wisdom and that is uniquely suited to expressing concepts of holiness.

According to Ibn Ezra (*Zephaniah* 3:9), the Holy Tongue is called שָׂפָה בְרוּרָה, *a language that is clear*, because it is the only language in which God is called by His Holy Name, the Tetragrammaton.

מְבַשֵּׂר שָׁלוֹם לְעַמְּךָ תִּשְׁלַח מְהֵרָה.

《 swiftly, 〈 send 〈 to Your people 〈 of peace 〈 The herald

צִיּוֹן לְנַחֵם וּפִרְצוֹתֶיהָ לְגָדְרָה.[1]

《 to mend, 〈 and her breaches 〈 to comfort 〈 Zion

כִּי לְךָ יהוה הַגְּדֻלָּה וְהַגְּבוּרָה.[2]

《 and the strength. 〈 is the greatness 〈 HASHEM, 〈 Yours, 〈 for

ALL:

מַכְנִיסֵי רַחֲמִים, הַכְנִיסוּ רַחֲמֵינוּ, לִפְנֵי בַּעַל

〈 the Master 〈 before 〈 our [plea for] mercy 〈 may you usher in 〈 [pleas for] mercy, 〈 O you who usher in

הָרַחֲמִים. מַשְׁמִיעֵי תְפִלָּה, הַשְׁמִיעוּ תְפִלָּתֵנוּ, לִפְנֵי

〈 before 〈 of our prayer 〈 may you aid the hearing 《 of prayer, 〈 O you who aid the hearing 《 of mercy.

שׁוֹמֵעַ תְּפִלָּה. מַשְׁמִיעֵי צְעָקָה, הַשְׁמִיעוּ צַעֲקָתֵנוּ,

〈 of our outcries 〈 may you aid the hearing 《 of outcries, 〈 O you who aid the hearing 《 of prayer. 〈 the Hearer

לִפְנֵי שׁוֹמֵעַ צְעָקָה. מַכְנִיסֵי דִמְעָה, הַכְנִיסוּ

〈 may you usher in 《 tears, 〈 O you who usher in 《 of outcries. 〈 the Hearer 〈 before

דִמְעוֹתֵינוּ, לִפְנֵי מֶלֶךְ מִתְרַצֶּה בִּדְמָעוֹת.

《 through tears. 〈 Who is appeased 〈 the King 〈 before 〈 our tears

הִשְׁתַּדְּלוּ וְהַרְבּוּ תְּחִנָּה וּבַקָּשָׁה, לִפְנֵי מֶלֶךְ אֵל

〈 God, 〈 the King, 〈 before 〈 and pleas 〈 supplications 〈 and intensify 〈 Exert yourselves

רָם וְנִשָּׂא. הַזְכִּירוּ לְפָנָיו, הַשְׁמִיעוּ לְפָנָיו תּוֹרָה

〈 the Torah 〈 before Him, 〈 aid to be heard 《 before Him, 〈 Mention 《 and uplifted. 〈 exalted

וּמַעֲשִׂים טוֹבִים שֶׁל שׁוֹכְנֵי עָפָר.

《 in the dust. 〈 [the Patriarchs and Matriarchs] who dwell 〈 of 〈 that are good 〈 and the deeds

---

(1) This stich has been censored out of some editions. (2) *I Chronicles* 29:11.

יִזְכֹּר אַהֲבָתָם וִיחַיֶּה זַרְעָם, שֶׁלֹּא תֹאבַד שְׁאֵרִית
⟨ shall the remnant ⟨ lost ⟨ so that not ⟨ to their offspring, ⟨ and grant life ⟨ their love ⟨ May He remember

יַעֲקֹב. כִּי צֹאן רוֹעֵה נֶאֱמָן הָיָה לְחֶרְפָּה,
《 a disgrace; ⟨ has become ⟨ who is faithful [Moses] ⟨ of the shepherd ⟨ the flock ⟨ For 《 of Jacob be.

יִשְׂרָאֵל גּוֹי אֶחָד לְמָשָׁל וְלִשְׁנִינָה.
《 and a simile. ⟨ a parable ⟨ that is unique, ⟨ the nation ⟨ Israel,

מַהֵר עֲנֵנוּ אֱלֹהֵי יִשְׁעֵנוּ, וּפְדֵנוּ מִכָּל גְּזֵרוֹת
⟨ decrees ⟨ from all ⟨ and redeem us ⟨ of our salvation, ⟨ O God ⟨ answer us, ⟨ Swiftly

קָשׁוֹת וְהוֹשִׁיעָה בְּרַחֲמֶיךָ הָרַבִּים, מְשִׁיחַ צִדְקֶךָ
⟨ Your righteous anointed one ⟨ that is abundant, ⟨ in Your mercy ⟨ and may You save, 《 that are harsh;

וְעַמֶּךָ.
《 and Your people.

מָרָן דְּבִשְׁמַיָּא לָךְ מִתְחַנְּנַן, כְּבַר שִׁבְיָא דְּמִתְחַנַּן
⟨ who supplicates ⟨ in captivity ⟨ as one 《 do we supplicate, ⟨ to You 《 Who is in heaven, ⟨ Our Master

לְשַׁבּוּיֵהּ. כֻּלְּהוֹן בְּנֵי שִׁבְיָא בְּכַסְפָּא מִתְפָּרְקִין,
《 are redeemed, ⟨ through money ⟨ in captivity, ⟨ those ⟨ [for] all 《 before his captors;

וְעַמָּךְ יִשְׂרָאֵל בְּרַחֲמֵי וּבְתַחֲנוּנֵי, הַב לָן שְׁאֵילְתִּין
⟨ our requests ⟨ us ⟨ O grant 《 and supplication. ⟨ through compassion ⟨ Israel ⟨ but Your people

וּבָעוּתִין, דְּלָא נֶהְדַּר רֵיקָם מִן קֳדָמָךְ.
《 before You. ⟨ from ⟨ empty-handed ⟨ that we not be turned away ⟨ and our prayers

מָרָן דְּבִשְׁמַיָּא לָךְ מִתְחַנְּנַן, כְּעַבְדָּא דְּמִתְחַנַּן
⟨ who supplicates ⟨ as a slave 《 do we supplicate, ⟨ to You 《 Who is in heaven, ⟨ Our Master

לְמָרֵיהּ, עֲשִׁיקֵי אֲנַן וּבַחֲשׁוֹכָא שָׁרֵינַן, מְרִירָן נַפְשִׁין
⟨ [our] souls ⟨ embittered 《 do we abide, ⟨ and in darkness ⟨ are we ⟨ Oppressed ⟨ to his master:

מֵעֲקָתִין דִּנְפִישִׁין, חֵילָא לֵית בֵּן לִרְצוּיָךְ. מָרָן,
⟨ Our Master, ⟩ ⟨ to appease You. ⟩ ⟨ within ⟩ ⟨ is lacking ⟩ ⟨ Strength ⟩ ⟨ that is excessive. ⟩ ⟨ from distress ⟩

עֲבִיד בְּדִיל קְיָמָא דִּגְזַרְתְּ עִם אֲבָהָתָנָא.
⟨ our Patriarchs. ⟩ ⟨ with ⟩ ⟨ that You established ⟩ ⟨ of the covenant ⟩ ⟨ for the sake ⟩ ⟨ act ⟩

שׁוֹמֵר יִשְׂרָאֵל, שְׁמוֹר שְׁאֵרִית יִשְׂרָאֵל, וְאַל
⟨ let not ⟩ ⟨ of Israel; ⟩ ⟨ the remnant ⟩ ⟨ safeguard ⟩ ⟨ of Israel, ⟩ ⟨ O Guardian ⟩

יֹאבַד יִשְׂרָאֵל, הָאֹמְרִים שְׁמַע יִשְׂרָאֵל.[1]
⟨ O Israel. ⟩ ⟨ Hear, ⟩ ⟨ those who proclaim: ⟩ ⟨ Israel be destroyed — ⟩

שׁוֹמֵר גּוֹי אֶחָד, שְׁמוֹר שְׁאֵרִית עַם אֶחָד, וְאַל
⟨ let not ⟩ ⟨ that is unique; ⟩ ⟨ of the people ⟩ ⟨ the remnant ⟩ ⟨ safeguard ⟩ ⟨ that is unique, ⟩ ⟨ of the nation ⟩ ⟨ O Guardian ⟩

יֹאבַד גּוֹי אֶחָד, הַמְיַחֲדִים שִׁמְךָ, יהוה אֱלֹהֵינוּ
⟨ is our God, ⟩ ⟨ HASHEM ⟩ ⟨ of Your Name: ⟩ ⟨ those who proclaim the Oneness ⟩ ⟨ that is unique, ⟩ ⟨ the nation ⟩ ⟨ be destroyed ⟩

יהוה אֶחָד.
⟨ the One [and Only]! ⟩ ⟨ HASHEM is ⟩

שׁוֹמֵר גּוֹי קָדוֹשׁ, שְׁמוֹר שְׁאֵרִית עַם קָדוֹשׁ,
⟨ that is holy; ⟩ ⟨ of the people ⟩ ⟨ the remnant ⟩ ⟨ safeguard ⟩ ⟨ that is holy, ⟩ ⟨ of the nation ⟩ ⟨ O Guardian ⟩

וְאַל יֹאבַד גּוֹי קָדוֹשׁ, הַמְשַׁלְּשִׁים בְּשָׁלֹשׁ קְדֻשּׁוֹת
⟨ sanctifications ⟩ ⟨ the threefold ⟩ ⟨ those who proclaim three times ⟩ ⟨ that is holy, ⟩ ⟨ the nation ⟩ ⟨ be destroyed ⟩ ⟨ let not ⟩

לְקָדוֹשׁ.
⟨ to the Holy One. ⟩

מִתְרַצֶּה בְּרַחֲמִים וּמִתְפַּיֵּס בְּתַחֲנוּנִים, הִתְרַצֵּה
⟨ be favorable ⟩ ⟨ through supplications, ⟩ ⟨ and Who becomes conciliatory ⟩ ⟨ through compassion ⟩ ⟨ You Who becomes favorable ⟩

וְהִתְפַּיֵּס לְדוֹר עָנִי, כִּי אֵין עוֹזֵר. אָבִינוּ מַלְכֵּנוּ,
⟨ our King, ⟩ ⟨ Our Father, ⟩ ⟨ helper. ⟩ ⟨ there is no ⟩ ⟨ for ⟩ ⟨ that is poor, ⟩ ⟨ to the generation ⟩ ⟨ and be conciliatory ⟩

---
(1) *Deuteronomy* 6:4.

חָנֵּנוּ וַעֲנֵנוּ, כִּי אֵין בָּנוּ מַעֲשִׂים, עֲשֵׂה עִמָּנוּ

⟨ us ⟨ treat ⟪ worthy deeds; ⟨ we have no ⟨ though ⟨ and ⟨ be gracious
    answer us,   with us

צְדָקָה וָחֶסֶד וְהוֹשִׁיעֵנוּ.

⟪ and save us. ⟨ and ⟨ with
    kindness,   charity

STAND AFTER THE WORDS וַאֲנַחְנוּ לֹא נֵדַע UNTIL CONCLUSION OF THE PARAGRAPH.

וַאֲנַחְנוּ לֹא נֵדַע מַה נַּעֲשֶׂה, כִּי עָלֶיךָ עֵינֵינוּ.[1]

⟪ are our ⟨ upon ⟨ rather, ⟪ we should ⟨ what ⟨ know not ⟨   We
eyes.   You   do,

זְכֹר רַחֲמֶיךָ יהוה וַחֲסָדֶיךָ, כִּי מֵעוֹלָם הֵמָּה.[2] יְהִי

⟨ May ⟪ are they. ⟨ eternal ⟨ for ⟨ and Your ⟨ Hashem, ⟨ Your ⟨ Remem-
   kindnesses,   mercies,   ber

חַסְדְּךָ יהוה עָלֵינוּ, כַּאֲשֶׁר יִחַלְנוּ לָךְ.[3] אַל תִּזְכָּר

⟨ recall ⟨ Do not ⟪ You. ⟨ we ⟨ just as ⟪ be upon ⟨ Hashem, ⟨ Your
    awaited   us,   kindness,

לָנוּ עֲוֹנוֹת רִאשׁוֹנִים, מַהֵר יְקַדְּמוּנוּ רַחֲמֶיךָ, כִּי

⟨for ⟪ may Your ⟨ advance to ⟨ swiftly ⟪ of the ancients; ⟨ the sins ⟨against
mercies,   meet us   us

דַלּוֹנוּ מְאֹד.[4] עֶזְרֵנוּ בְּשֵׁם יהוה, עֹשֵׂה שָׁמַיִם

⟨ of ⟨ Maker ⟪ of Hashem, ⟨ is through ⟨ Our help ⟪ exceed- ⟨ we have
heaven   the Name   ingly.   become
    impoverished

וָאָרֶץ.[5] חָנֵּנוּ יהוה חָנֵּנוּ, כִּי רַב שָׂבַעְנוּ בוּז.[6] בְּרֹגֶז

⟪ Amid ⟪ with ⟨ sated ⟨ we are ⟨ for ⟪ favor us, ⟨ Hashem, ⟨ Favor us, ⟪ and earth.
wrath, contempt.   fully

רַחֵם תִּזְכּוֹר.[7] בְּרֹגֶז עֲקֵדָה תִּזְכּוֹר. בְּרֹגֶז תְּמִימוֹת

⟨ the perfect ⟪ Amid ⟪ You should ⟪ the binding ⟪ Amid ⟪ You should ⟨ to be
ones   wrath, remember! [of Isaac] wrath, remember! merciful

תִּזְכּוֹר. יהוה הוֹשִׁיעָה, הַמֶּלֶךְ יַעֲנֵנוּ בְיוֹם קָרְאֵנוּ.[8]

⟪ we call. ⟨ on the ⟨ answer ⟨ May the ⟪ save! ⟨ Hashem, ⟪ You should
day   us   King   remember!

כִּי הוּא יָדַע יִצְרֵנוּ, זָכוּר כִּי עָפָר אֲנָחְנוּ.[9]

⟪ are we. ⟨ dust ⟨ that ⟨ He is ⟪ our nature, ⟨ knew ⟨ He ⟨ For
    mindful

(1) *II Chronicles* 20:12. (2) *Psalms* 25:6. (3) 33:22. (4) 79:8. (5) 121:2.
(6) 123:3. (7) *Habakkuk* 3:2. (8) *Psalms* 20:10. (9) 103:14.

❖ עָזְרֵנוּ אֱלֹהֵי יִשְׁעֵנוּ עַל דְּבַר כְּבוֹד שְׁמֶךָ, וְהַצִּילֵנוּ

⟨ rescue us　《 of Your Name;　⟨ of the glory　⟨ the　⟨ for　⟨ of our salvation　⟨ O God　⟨ Assist us,

וְכַפֵּר עַל חַטֹּאתֵינוּ לְמַעַן שְׁמֶךָ.¹

《 of Your Name.　⟨ for the sake　⟨ our sins　⟨ for　⟨ and grant atonement

FULL KADDISH / קדיש שלם

THE *CHAZZAN* RECITES **קַדִּישׁ שָׁלֵם**, FULL *KADDISH.*

יִתְגַּדַּל וְיִתְקַדַּשׁ שְׁמֵהּ רַבָּא. (אָמֵן. — Cong.) בְּעָלְמָא

⟨ – in the world　《 (Amen.)　《 that is great! —　⟨ may His Name　⟨ and be sanctified　⟨ Grow exalted

דִּי בְרָא כִרְעוּתֵהּ. וְיַמְלִיךְ מַלְכוּתֵהּ, וְיַצְמַח פֻּרְקָנֵהּ

⟨ His salvation,　⟨ and cause to sprout　《 to His kingship,　⟨ and may He give reign　《 according to His will,　⟨ He created　⟨ that

וִיקָרֵב מְשִׁיחֵהּ. (אָמֵן. — Cong.) בְּחַיֵּיכוֹן וּבְיוֹמֵיכוֹן וּבְחַיֵּי

⟨ and in the lifetimes　⟨ and in your days,　⟨ in your lifetimes　《 (Amen.)　《 His Messiah,　⟨ and bring near

דְכָל בֵּית יִשְׂרָאֵל, בַּעֲגָלָא וּבִזְמַן קָרִיב. וְאִמְרוּ: אָמֵן.

《 Amen.　⟨ Now respond:　《 that comes soon.　⟨ and at a time　⟨ swiftly　《 of Israel,　⟨ Family　⟨ of the entire

CONGREGATION RESPONDS:

אָמֵן. יְהֵא שְׁמֵהּ רַבָּא מְבָרַךְ לְעָלַם וּלְעָלְמֵי עָלְמַיָּא.

《 and for all eternity.　⟨ forever　⟨ be blessed　⟨ that is great　⟨ His Name　⟨ May　《 Amen.

CHAZZAN CONTINUES:

יְהֵא שְׁמֵהּ רַבָּא מְבָרַךְ לְעָלַם וּלְעָלְמֵי עָלְמַיָּא. יִתְבָּרַךְ

⟨ Blessed,　《 and for all eternity.　⟨ forever　⟨ be blessed　⟨ that is great　⟨ His Name　⟨ May

וְיִשְׁתַּבַּח וְיִתְפָּאַר וְיִתְרוֹמַם וְיִתְנַשֵּׂא וְיִתְהַדָּר וְיִתְעַלֶּה

⟨ elevated,　⟨ honored,　⟨ upraised,　⟨ exalted,　⟨ glorified,　⟨ praised,

וְיִתְהַלָּל שְׁמֵהּ דְּקֻדְשָׁא בְּרִיךְ הוּא (בְּרִיךְ הוּא — Cong.)

《 is He) ⟨ (Blessed　《 is He　⟨ Blessed　⟨ of the Holy One,　⟨ be the Name　⟨ and lauded

לְעֵלָּא [וּ]לְעֵלָּא מִכָּל בִּרְכָתָא וְשִׁירָתָא תֻּשְׁבְּחָתָא

⟨ praise　《 and song,　⟨ blessing　⟨ any　⟨ exceedingly beyond

וְנֶחֱמָתָא דַּאֲמִירָן בְּעָלְמָא. וְאִמְרוּ: אָמֵן. (אָמֵן. — Cong.)

《 (Amen.)　《 Amen.　⟨ Now respond:　《 in the world.　⟨ that are uttered　⟨ and consolation

(1) *Psalms* 79:9.

CONGREGATION:

(קַבֵּל בְּרַחֲמִים וּבְרָצוֹן אֶת תְּפִלָּתֵנוּ.)

《   our prayers.) 〈 and with favor 〈 with mercy 〈 (Accept

CHAZZAN CONTINUES:

תִּתְקַבֵּל צְלוֹתְהוֹן וּבָעוּתְהוֹן דְּכָל בֵּית יִשְׂרָאֵל קֳדָם

〈 before 〈   Israel 〈 Family   〈 of the 〈 and   〈 the prayers 〈 May
              of   entire   supplications   accepted be

אֲבוּהוֹן דִּי בִשְׁמַיָּא. וְאִמְרוּ: אָמֵן. (Cong. — אָמֵן.)

《 (Amen.)   《 Amen. 〈 Now   《   is in 〈 Who 〈 their
               respond: Heaven.   Father

CONGREGATION:

(יְהִי שֵׁם יהוה מְבֹרָךְ, מֵעַתָּה וְעַד עוֹלָם.[1])

《 eternity.) 〈 until 《   be 〈 of 〈 the 〈 (Let
       this time   blessed,   HASHEM Name

CHAZZAN CONTINUES:

יְהֵא שְׁלָמָא רַבָּא מִן שְׁמַיָּא וְחַיִּים טוֹבִים עָלֵינוּ וְעַל כָּל

〈 all 〈 and 〈 upon us 〈 that is 〈 and life 〈 Heaven 〈 that is 〈 abundant 〈 peace 〈 May
   upon   good,   there be

יִשְׂרָאֵל. וְאִמְרוּ: אָמֵן. (Cong. — אָמֵן.)

《 (Amen.)   《 Amen. 〈 Now respond: 《 Israel.

CONGREGATION:

(עֶזְרִי מֵעִם יהוה, עֹשֵׂה שָׁמַיִם וָאָרֶץ.[2])

《 and 〈 of 〈 Maker 《 HASHEM, 〈 is 〈 (My
  earth.)   heaven   from   help

CHAZZAN BOWS; TAKES THREE STEPS BACK. BOWS LEFT AND SAYS "... עֹשֶׂה שָׁלוֹם, HE WHO MAKES PEACE ..."; BOWS RIGHT AND SAYS "... הוּא, MAY HE ..."; BOWS FORWARD AND SAYS "... וְעַל כָּל יִשְׂרָאֵל, AND UPON ALL ISRAEL ..."; REMAINS IN PLACE FOR A FEW MOMENTS, THEN TAKES THREE STEPS FORWARD.

עֹשֶׂה [הַ]שָּׁלוֹם בִּמְרוֹמָיו, הוּא יַעֲשֶׂה שָׁלוֹם עָלֵינוּ, וְעַל

〈 and 〈 upon us, 〈 peace 〈 make 〈 may 《 in His 〈 [the] peace 〈 He Who
  upon   He   heights,   makes

כָּל יִשְׂרָאֵל. וְאִמְרוּ: אָמֵן. (Cong. — אָמֵן.)

《 (Amen.)   《 Amen. 〈 Now 《 Israel. 〈 all
                 respond:

---

(1) *Psalms* 113:2. (2) 121:2.

❧ EREV YOM KIPPUR / ערב יום כפור ❧

אַשְׁרֵי יוֹשְׁבֵי בֵיתֶךָ, עוֹד יְהַלְלוּךָ סֶּלָה.¹ אַשְׁרֵי

⟨ Praise-worthy   ⟪ Selah.   ⟨ they will praise You,   ⟨ con-tinually   ⟪ in Your house,   ⟨ are those who dwell   ⟨ Praiseworthy

הָעָם שֶׁכָּכָה לּוֹ, אַשְׁרֵי הָעָם שֶׁיהוה אֱלֹהָיו.²

⟪ is their God.   ⟨ that HASHEM   ⟨ is the people   ⟨ praise-worthy   ⟪ is their lot;   ⟨ that such   ⟨ is the people

——— תהלים קמה / Psalm 145 ———

תְּהִלָּה לְדָוִד, אֲרוֹמִמְךָ אֱלוֹהַי הַמֶּלֶךְ, וַאֲבָרְכָה

⟨ and I will bless   ⟪ the King,   ⟨ my God   ⟨ I will exalt You,   ⟪ by David: ⟨ A psalm of praise

שִׁמְךָ לְעוֹלָם וָעֶד. בְּכָל יוֹם אֲבָרְכֶךָּ, וַאֲהַלְלָה שִׁמְךָ

⟨ Your Name   ⟨ and I will laud   ⟪ I will bless You,   ⟨ day   ⟨ Every   ⟪ and ever.   ⟨ for ever   ⟨ Your Name

לְעוֹלָם וָעֶד. גָּדוֹל יהוה וּמְהֻלָּל מְאֹד, וְלִגְדֻלָּתוֹ

⟨ and His greatness   ⟪ exceedingly,   ⟨ and lauded   ⟨ is HASHEM   ⟨ Great   ⟪ and ever.   ⟨ forever

אֵין חֵקֶר. דּוֹר לְדוֹר יְשַׁבַּח מַעֲשֶׂיךָ, וּגְבוּרֹתֶיךָ יַגִּידוּ.

⟪ they will recount.   ⟨ and Your mighty deeds   ⟪ Your actions,   ⟨ will praise   ⟨ to generation   ⟨ Gen-eration   ⟪ is beyond investigation.

הֲדַר כְּבוֹד הוֹדֶךָ, וְדִבְרֵי נִפְלְאֹתֶיךָ אָשִׂיחָה. וֶעֱזוּז

⟨ And of the might   ⟪ I shall discuss.   ⟨ that are wondrous   ⟨ and Your deeds   ⟪ of Your majesty,   ⟨ glory   ⟨ The splendrous

נוֹרְאֹתֶיךָ יֹאמֵרוּ, וּגְדוּלָּתְךָ אֲסַפְּרֶנָּה. זֵכֶר רַב טוּבְךָ

⟨ of Your abun-dant goodness   ⟨ A recol-lection   ⟨ I shall relate.   ⟨ and Your greatness   ⟪ they will speak,   ⟨ of Your awesome deeds

יַבִּיעוּ, וְצִדְקָתְךָ יְרַנֵּנוּ. חַנּוּן וְרַחוּם יהוה, אֶרֶךְ אַפַּיִם

⟨ to anger,   ⟨ slow   ⟪ is   ⟨ and   ⟨ Gracious   ⟪ they will sing joyfully.   ⟨ and of Your righteousness   ⟪ they will utter,

וּגְדָל חָסֶד. טוֹב יהוה לַכֹּל, וְרַחֲמָיו עַל כָּל מַעֲשָׂיו.

⟪ His creations.   ⟨ all   ⟨ are on   ⟪ His mercies   ⟪ to all;   ⟨ HASHEM   ⟪ in [bestowing]   ⟨ kindness.   ⟨ and great

יוֹדוּךָ יהוה כָּל מַעֲשֶׂיךָ, וַחֲסִידֶיךָ יְבָרְכוּכָה. כְּבוֹד

⟨ Of the glory   ⟪ will bless You.   ⟨ and Your devout ones   ⟪ creations —   ⟨ Your   ⟨ — all   ⟪ HASHEM   ⟨ They will thank You,

———

(1) *Psalms* 84:5. (2) 144:15.

מַלְכוּתְךָ יֹאמֵרוּ, וּגְבוּרָתְךָ יְדַבֵּרוּ. **לְהוֹדִיעַ לִבְנֵי הָאָדָם**

⟨ mankind ⟨ To inform » they will ⟨ and of Your » they will ⟨ of Your
declare. power speak, kingdom

גְּבוּרֹתָיו, וּכְבוֹד הֲדַר מַלְכוּתוֹ. **מַלְכוּתְךָ** מַלְכוּת כָּל

⟨ [span- is a ⟨ Your kingdom » of His ⟨ splendor ⟨ and of the » of His mighty
ning] all kingdom kingdom. glorious deeds,

עֹלָמִים, וּמֶמְשַׁלְתְּךָ בְּכָל דּוֹר וָדֹר. **סוֹמֵךְ** יהוה

⟨ HASHEM » after ⟨ gen- ⟨ is ⟨ and Your » eternities,
supports generation. eration throughout dominion

לְכָל הַנֹּפְלִים, וְזוֹקֵף לְכָל הַכְּפוּפִים. **עֵינֵי** כֹל

⟨ of all ⟨ The » those who ⟨ all ⟨ and » those who ⟨ all
eyes are bent. straightens are fallen,

אֵלֶיךָ יְשַׂבֵּרוּ, וְאַתָּה נוֹתֵן לָהֶם אֶת אָכְלָם בְּעִתּוֹ.

» in its ⟨ their food ⟨ them ⟨ give ⟨ and You » do look ⟨ to You
proper time. with hope,

CONCENTRATE INTENTLY WHILE RECITING THE VERSE פּוֹתֵחַ, *YOU OPEN.*

פּוֹתֵחַ אֶת יָדֶךָ, וּמַשְׂבִּיעַ לְכָל חַי רָצוֹן. ❖**צַדִּיק**

⟨ Righteous » [with its] ⟨ living ⟨ every ⟨ and satisfy » Your hand, ⟨ You open
desire. thing

יהוה בְּכָל דְּרָכָיו, וְחָסִיד בְּכָל מַעֲשָׂיו. **קָרוֹב** יהוה

⟨ is ⟨ Close » His deeds. ⟨ in all ⟨ and » His ways, ⟨ in all ⟨ is
HASHEM magnanimous HASHEM

לְכָל קֹרְאָיו, לְכֹל אֲשֶׁר יִקְרָאֻהוּ בֶאֱמֶת. **רְצוֹן** יְרֵאָיו

⟨ of those ⟨ The » sincerely. ⟨ call upon ⟨ who ⟨ to all » who call ⟨ to all
who fear Him will Him upon Him,

יַעֲשֶׂה, וְאֶת שַׁוְעָתָם יִשְׁמַע וְיוֹשִׁיעֵם. **שׁוֹמֵר** יהוה

⟨ HASHEM protects » and He will ⟨ He will ⟨ and their cry » He
save them. hear, will do;

אֶת כָּל אֹהֲבָיו, וְאֵת כָּל הָרְשָׁעִים יַשְׁמִיד. **תְּהִלַּת**

⟨ The praise » He will destroy. ⟨ the wicked ⟨ but all » who love Him; ⟨ all

יהוה יְדַבֶּר פִּי, וִיבָרֵךְ כָּל בָּשָׂר שֵׁם קָדְשׁוֹ לְעוֹלָם

⟨ for ever ⟨ of His ⟨ the ⟨ flesh ⟨ may ⟨ and bless » may my ⟨ of
Holiness Name all mouth declare, HASHEM

וָעֶד. וַאֲנַחְנוּ נְבָרֵךְ יָהּ מֵעַתָּה וְעַד עוֹלָם; הַלְלוּיָהּ.[1]

» Halleluyah! » eternity. ⟨ until ⟨ from ⟨ God ⟨ will ⟨ But we » and
this time bless ever.

(1) *Psalms* 115:18.

THE *CHAZZAN* RECITES חֲצִי קַדִּישׁ, HALF-*KADDISH*:

יִתְגַּדַּל וְיִתְקַדַּשׁ שְׁמֵהּ רַבָּא. (.אָמֵן — Cong.) בְּעָלְמָא
‹ Grow › and be ‹ may His › that is ‹‹ (Amen.) ‹ – in the
exalted sanctified Name great! — world

דִּי בְרָא כִרְעוּתֵהּ. וְיַמְלִיךְ מַלְכוּתֵהּ, וְיַצְמַח פֻּרְקָנֵהּ
‹ that ‹ He › according ‹‹ and may He › to His ‹‹ and cause › His
created to His will, give reign kingship, to sprout salvation,

וִיקָרֵב מְשִׁיחֵהּ. (.אָמֵן — Cong.) בְּחַיֵּיכוֹן וּבְיוֹמֵיכוֹן וּבְחַיֵּי
‹ and bring › His Messiah, ‹‹ (Amen.) ‹ in your › and in › and in the
near lifetimes your days, lifetimes

דְכָל בֵּית יִשְׂרָאֵל, בַּעֲגָלָא וּבִזְמַן קָרִיב. וְאִמְרוּ: אָמֵן.
‹ of the › Family ‹ of Israel, ‹‹ swiftly › and at a › that comes ‹‹ Now ‹ Amen.‹‹
entire time soon. respond:

CONGREGATION RESPONDS:

אָמֵן. יְהֵא שְׁמֵהּ רַבָּא מְבָרַךְ לְעָלַם וּלְעָלְמֵי עָלְמַיָּא.
‹‹ and for all eternity. ‹ forever › be ‹ that is ‹ His ‹ May ‹‹ Amen.
blessed great Name

CHAZZAN CONTINUES:

יְהֵא שְׁמֵהּ רַבָּא מְבָרַךְ לְעָלַם וּלְעָלְמֵי עָלְמַיָּא. יִתְבָּרַךְ
‹ Blessed, ‹‹ and for all eternity. ‹ forever › be ‹ that is ‹ His ‹ May
blessed great Name

וְיִשְׁתַּבַּח וְיִתְפָּאַר וְיִתְרוֹמַם וְיִתְנַשֵּׂא וְיִתְהַדָּר וְיִתְעַלֶּה
‹ elevated, ‹ honored, ‹ upraised, ‹ exalted, ‹ glorified, ‹ praised,

וְיִתְהַלָּל שְׁמֵהּ דְּקֻדְשָׁא בְּרִיךְ הוּא. (.בְּרִיךְ הוּא — Cong.)
‹‹ is He › Blessed ‹ be the ‹ of the Holy ‹ Blessed ‹ is He ‹‹ (Blessed › (Cong.)
Name One,

— לְעֵלָּא [וּ]לְעֵלָּא מִכָּל בִּרְכָתָא וְשִׁירָתָא תֻּשְׁבְּחָתָא
‹ praise ‹‹ and song, ‹ blessing ‹ any ‹ exceedingly beyond

וְנֶחֱמָתָא דַּאֲמִירָן בְּעָלְמָא. וְאִמְרוּ: אָמֵן. (.אָמֵן — Cong.)
‹‹ (Amen.) ‹‹ Amen. ‹ Now ‹‹ in the ‹ that are ‹ and
respond: world. uttered consolation

ALL:

לְךָ יהוה הַצְּדָקָה, וְלָנוּ בֹּשֶׁת הַפָּנִים.¹ מַה נִּתְאוֹנֵן,²
‹‹ complaint ‹ What ‹‹ is shamefacedness. ‹ and ‹‹ is the ‹ O Lord, ‹ Yours,
can we make? ours righteousness,

מַה נֹּאמַר, מַה נְּדַבֵּר, וּמַה נִּצְטַדָּק. נַחְפְּשָׂה דְרָכֵינוּ³
‹ our ways ‹ Let us ‹‹ justification ‹ What ‹‹ can we ‹ What ‹‹ can ‹ What
examine can we offer? declare? we say?

(1) *Daniel* 9:7. (2) Cf. *Lamentations* 3:39. (3) Cf. *Genesis* 44:16.

וְנַחְקְרָה, וְנָשׁוּבָה אֵלֶיךָ, כִּי יְמִינְךָ פְּשׁוּטָה לְקַבֵּל[1]

and investigate them, ⟨ and return ⟩ to You, ⟪ for ⟩ Your right hand ⟩ is extended ⟩ to accept

שָׁבִים. לֹא בְחֶסֶד וְלֹא בְמַעֲשִׂים בָּאנוּ לְפָנֶיךָ,

those who return. ⟪ Neither ⟩ with [merit] for kindness ⟩ nor ⟩ with [merit for good] deeds ⟩ do we come ⟪ before You;

כְּדַלִּים וּכְרָשִׁים דָּפַקְנוּ דְלָתֶיךָ. דְּלָתֶיךָ דָפֶקְנוּ

but as paupers ⟩ and as destitute people ⟩ we have knocked ⟩ on Your doors. ⟪ On Your doors ⟩ we have knocked

רַחוּם וְחַנּוּן, נָא אַל תְּשִׁיבֵנוּ רֵיקָם מִלְּפָנֶיךָ. מִלְּפָנֶיךָ

O Compassionate One ⟩ and Gracious One. ⟪ Please ⟩ do not ⟩ turn us away ⟩ empty-handed ⟪ from before You. ⟩ From before You

מַלְכֵּנוּ רֵיקָם אַל תְּשִׁיבֵנוּ, כִּי אַתָּה שׁוֹמֵעַ תְּפִלָּה.

Our King, ⟩ empty-handed ⟩ do not ⟩ turn us away, ⟪ for ⟩ You are the One ⟩ Who hears ⟪ prayer.

CONGREGATION, THEN *CHAZZAN* (SOME CONGREGATIONS OMIT THIS VERSE):

סְלַח לָנוּ אָבִינוּ, כִּי בְרוֹב אִוַּלְתֵּנוּ שָׁגִינוּ,

Forgive ⟩ us, ⟩ our Father, ⟩ for ⟩ in the abundance ⟩ of our folly ⟪ we have erred;

מְחַל לָנוּ מַלְכֵּנוּ, כִּי רַבּוּ עֲוֹנֵינוּ.

pardon ⟩ us, ⟩ our King, ⟩ for ⟩ many are ⟩ our iniquities. ⟪

ALL, WHILE STANDING

אֵל אֶרֶךְ אַפַּיִם אַתָּה,

God ⟩ Who is slow ⟩ to anger, ⟩ You are, ⟪

וּבַעַל הָרַחֲמִים נִקְרֵאתָ, וְדֶרֶךְ תְּשׁוּבָה הוֹרֵיתָ.

and Master ⟩ of Mercy ⟩ You are called; ⟪ and the way ⟩ of repentance ⟩ You have taught.

גְּדֻלַּת רַחֲמֶיךָ וַחֲסָדֶיךָ,

The greatness ⟩ of Your mercy ⟩ and Your kindness, ⟨

תִּזְכּוֹר הַיּוֹם וּבְכָל יוֹם לְזֶרַע יְדִידֶיךָ.

may You remember, ⟩ this day ⟩ and ⟪ every ⟩ day, ⟨ for the offspring ⟩ of Your beloved ones. ⟪

תֵּפֶן אֵלֵינוּ בְּרַחֲמִים, כִּי אַתָּה הוּא בַּעַל הָרַחֲמִים.

Turn ⟩ to us ⟪ in mercy, ⟩ for ⟪ You ⟩ are ⟩ the Master ⟩ of Mercy. ⟪

---

(1) Cf. *Lamentations* 3:40.

בְּתַחֲנוּן וּבִתְפִלָּה פָּנֶיךָ נְקַדֵּם, כְּהוֹדַעְתָּ לֶעָנָיו מִקֶּדֶם.

‹ in ancient ‹ to the ‹ in the manner ‹ we ‹ Your ‹ and prayer ‹ With
times. humble one that You made approach, Presence supplication
[Moses] known

מֵחֲרוֹן אַפְּךָ שׁוּב,[1] כְּמוֹ בְּתוֹרָתְךָ כָּתוּב.[2]

‹ it is ‹ in Your Torah ‹ as ‹ turn ‹ of Your ‹ From the
written. back, anger fierceness

וּבְצֵל כְּנָפֶיךָ נֶחֱסֶה[3] וְנִתְלוֹנָן, כְּיוֹם וַיֵּרֶד יהוה בֶּעָנָן.

‹ in a ‹ when HASHEM ‹ as on ‹ and may ‹ may we find ‹ of Your ‹ In the
cloud. descended the day we dwell, shelter wings shadow

✧ תַּעֲבוֹר עַל פֶּשַׁע וְתִמְחֶה אָשָׁם,

‹ guilt, ‹ and erase ‹ sin ‹ Overlook

כְּיוֹם וַיִּתְיַצֵּב עִמּוֹ שָׁם.

‹ there. ‹ with him ‹ when He ‹ as on the
[Moses] [God] stood day

תַּאֲזִין שַׁוְעָתֵנוּ וְתַקְשִׁיב מֶנּוּ מַאֲמָר,

‹ [our] declaration, ‹ from us ‹ and hear ‹ to our cry ‹ Give heed

כְּיוֹם וַיִּקְרָא בְשֵׁם יהוה,[4] וְשָׁם נֶאֱמַר:

‹ it was said: ‹ and ‹ of HASHEM, ‹ with the ‹ when He ‹ as on
there Name called out the day

CONGREGATION, THEN CHAZZAN:

וַיַּעֲבֹר יהוה עַל פָּנָיו וַיִּקְרָא:

‹ and ‹ [Moses'] ‹ before ‹ And HASHEM passed
proclaimed: face,

CONGREGATION AND CHAZZAN RECITE LOUDLY AND IN UNISON:

יהוה, יהוה, אֵל, רַחוּם, וְחַנּוּן, אֶרֶךְ אַפַּיִם,

‹ to anger, ‹ Slow ‹ and Gracious, ‹ Compassionate ‹ God, ‹ HASHEM, ‹ HASHEM,

וְרַב חֶסֶד, וֶאֱמֶת, נֹצֵר חֶסֶד לָאֲלָפִים, נֹשֵׂא עָוֹן,

‹ of ‹ Forgiver ‹ for thousands ‹ of ‹ Preserver ‹ and ‹ in ‹ and
iniquity, [of generations], kindness Truth, Kindness Abundant

וָפֶשַׁע, וְחַטָּאָה, וְנַקֵּה.[5] וְסָלַחְתָּ לַעֲוֹנֵנוּ וּלְחַטָּאתֵנוּ

‹ and our sins, ‹ our ‹ May You ‹ and Who ‹ and inadvertent ‹ willful sin,
iniquities forgive absolves. sin,

וּנְחַלְתָּנוּ.[6] סְלַח לָנוּ אָבִינוּ כִּי חָטָאנוּ, מְחַל לָנוּ

‹ us, ‹ pardon ‹ we have ‹ for ‹ our Father, ‹ us, ‹ Forgive ‹ and make us
sinned; Your heritage.

_____

(1) Cf. *Exodus* 32:12. (2) See 32:14. (3) Cf. *Psalms* 36:8. (4) *Exodus* 34:5. (5) 34:6-7 (6) 34:9.

מַלְכֵּנוּ כִּי פָשָׁעְנוּ. כִּי אַתָּה אֲדֹנָי טוֹב וְסַלָּח, וְרַב

⟨ and ⟪ and ⟨ are ⟨ O Lord, ⟨ You, ⟨ For ⟪ we have ⟨ for ⟪ our King,
abundantly forgiving, good   willfully sinned.

חֶסֶד לְכָל קֹרְאֶיךָ.[1]

⟪ who call ⟨ to all ⟨ kind
upon You.

פסוקי הקדמה לסליחה פה / PREFATORY VERSES TO SELICHAH 85

מָה אֱנוֹשׁ כִּי יִזְכֶּה, וְכִי יִצְדַּק יְלוּד אִשָּׁה.[2] כִּי

⟨ that ⟪ of ⟨ — one ⟨ he be ⟨ or ⟨ he might ⟨ that ⟨ [frail] ⟨ What is
   woman;   born   found   that   be   man
           righteous   vindicated,

תִּפְקְדֶנּוּ לִבְקָרִים לִרְגָעִים תִּבְחָנֶנּוּ.[3] הֵן בַּעֲבָדָיו

⟨ in His ⟨ Indeed, ⟪ test him? ⟨ or at every ⟪ in the ⟨ You should be
servants   moment   mornings,   mindful of him

לֹא יַאֲמִין, וּבְמַלְאָכָיו יָשִׂים תָּהֳלָה.[4] כִּי אָדָם אֵין

⟨ does ⟨ the ⟨ For ⟪ fault. ⟨ He finds ⟨ and with His ⟪ He does not
not exist man   angels   have faith;

צַדִּיק בָּאָרֶץ, אֲשֶׁר יַעֲשֶׂה טּוֹב וְלֹא יֶחֱטָא.[5]

⟪ sins. ⟨ and ⟨ [only] ⟨ he does ⟨ that ⟨ on ⟨ who is [so]
never good   the earth   righteous

כְּרַחֵם אָב עַל בָּנִים, כֵּן תְּרַחֵם יהוה עָלֵינוּ.[6]

⟪ on us. ⟨ HASHEM, ⟨ have ⟨ so ⟪ his ⟨ toward ⟨ a ⟨ As merciful as
         mercy,   children,   father is

לַיהוה הַיְשׁוּעָה, עַל עַמְּךָ בִרְכָתֶךָ סֶּלָה.[7] יהוה

⟨ HASHEM, ⟪ Selah. ⟪ is Your ⟨ Your ⟨ upon ⟪ is salvation, ⟨ To HASHEM,
        blessing, people

צְבָאוֹת עִמָּנוּ, מִשְׂגָּב לָנוּ אֱלֹהֵי יַעֲקֹב סֶלָה.[8]

⟪ Selah. ⟪ of Jacob, ⟨ is the God ⟨ for us ⟨ a ⟪ is with us, ⟨ Master
               stronghold   of Legions,

יהוה צְבָאוֹת, אַשְׁרֵי אָדָם בֹּטֵחַ בָּךְ.[9] יהוה הוֹשִׁיעָה,

⟪ save! ⟨ HASHEM, ⟪ in ⟨ who ⟨ is the ⟨ — praise- ⟪ Master of ⟨ HASHEM,
       You. trusts man worthy   Legions

הַמֶּלֶךְ יַעֲנֵנוּ בְיוֹם קָרְאֵנוּ.[10]

⟪ we call. ⟨ on the ⟨ answer ⟨ May the
day   us   King

---

(1) Psalms 86:5. (2) Job 15:14. (3) Cf. 7:18. (4) 4:18. (5) Ecclesiastes 7:20.
(6) Cf. Psalms 103:13. (7) 3:9. (8) 46:8. (9) 84:13. (10) 20:10.

IN MOST CONGREGATIONS THE FOLLOWING VERSES ARE RECITED ALOUD RESPONSIVELY,
AS INDICATED; IN OTHERS THEY ARE RECITED SILENTLY.

CONGREGATION, ALOUD, FOLLOWED BY *CHAZZAN,* ALOUD:

סְלַח נָא לַעֲוֹן הָעָם הַזֶּה כְּגֹדֶל חַסְדֶּךָ, וְכַאֲשֶׁר

⟨ just as ⟨⟨ of Your ⟨ according to ⟨ of this people ⟨ the ⟨ please, ⟨ Forgive,
kindness, the greatness iniquity

נָשָׂאתָה לָעָם הַזֶּה מִמִּצְרַיִם וְעַד הֵנָּה,¹ וְשָׁם נֶאֱמַר:

⟨⟨ it was ⟨ And ⟨⟨ now. ⟨ until ⟨ from Egypt ⟨ this people ⟨ You have
said: there forgiven

ALL, ALOUD AND IN UNISON:

וַיֹּאמֶר יהוה סָלַחְתִּי כִּדְבָרֶךָ.²

⟨⟨ according to ⟨ I have forgiven ⟨⟨ And HASHEM said:
your word!

ALL CONTINUE:

הַטֵּה אֱלֹהַי אָזְנְךָ וּשְׁמָע, פְּקַח עֵינֶיךָ וּרְאֵה

⟨ and see ⟨ Your eyes ⟨ open ⟨⟨ and listen; ⟨ Your ear, ⟨ my God, ⟨ Incline,

שֹׁמְמֹתֵינוּ, וְהָעִיר אֲשֶׁר נִקְרָא שִׁמְךָ עָלֶיהָ, כִּי לֹא

⟨ not ⟨ for ⟨⟨ upon; ⟨ Your Name is ⟨ which ⟨ and that ⟨ our desolation
proclaimed [of] the city

עַל צִדְקֹתֵינוּ אֲנַחְנוּ מַפִּילִים תַּחֲנוּנֵינוּ לְפָנֶיךָ,

⟨⟨ before ⟨ our ⟨ cast ⟨ do we ⟨ of our ⟨ because
You; supplications righteousness

כִּי עַל רַחֲמֶיךָ הָרַבִּים. אֲדֹנָי שְׁמָעָה, אֲדֹנָי סְלָחָה,

⟨⟨ forgive; ⟨ O Lord, ⟨⟨ heed; ⟨ O Lord, ⟨⟨ which is ⟨ of Your ⟨ be- ⟨ but
abundant. compassion, cause

אֲדֹנָי הַקְשִׁיבָה, וַעֲשֵׂה אַל תְּאַחַר, לְמַעַנְךָ אֱלֹהַי,

⟨⟨ my God, ⟨ for Your ⟨⟨ delay; ⟨ do not ⟨⟨ and act, ⟨ be attentive, ⟨ O Lord,
sake,

כִּי שִׁמְךָ נִקְרָא עַל עִירְךָ וְעַל עַמֶּךָ.³

⟨⟨ Your ⟨ and ⟨ Your ⟨ upon ⟨ is ⟨ Your ⟨ for
people. upon City proclaimed Name

---

(1) *Numbers* 14:19. (2) 14:20. (3) *Daniel* 9:18-19.

סליחה פה / SELICHAH 85
(שלישיה)

(אֱלֹהֵינוּ וֵאלֹהֵי אֲבוֹתֵינוּ:)

⟪ of our forefathers:) ⟨ and the God ⟨ (Our God

אָדוֹן דִּין אִם יְדַקְדֵּק,* בְּחֵקֶר פֹּעַל אִם יְבָדֵּק,

⟪ were to be examined, ⟨ if it ⟨ each action, ⟪ [if] through an investigation, ⟪ to be rigorously precise,* ⟨ if it were ⟪ judg-ment, ⟪ O Lord,

גֶּבֶר לְפָנֶיךָ לֹא יִצְדַּק.[1]

⟪ be vindicated. ⟨ will never ⟨ before You ⟨ man

דֹּפִי תִּתֵּן[2] בִּצְבָא מַעְלָה, הֵן בְּמַלְאָכֶיךָ תָּשִׂים תָּהֳלָה,[3]

⟪ with folly — ⟨ You charge ⟨ among Your angels ⟨ indeed ⟪ celestial, ⟨ even in the hosts ⟨ You find ⟨ Fault

וְאַף שׁוֹתֶה כַמַּיִם עַוְלָה.[4]

⟪ sin. ⟪ like water, ⟨ who drinks ⟪ certainly so [man],

זְכוּת וּצְדָקָה אֵין בָּנוּ, חֵטְא וָרֶשַׁע כֻּלָּנוּ,

⟪ is our entire being, ⟨ and wickedness ⟨ sin ⟪ within us, ⟨ are not ⟨ and right-eousness ⟨ Merit

טוֹב, אַל תָּבֹא בְמִשְׁפָּט עִמָּנוּ.[5]

⟪ with us. ⟨ into strict judgment ⟨ enter ⟪ do not ⟪ O Benefi-cent One,

יֶהֱמוּ מֵעֶיךָ עָלֵינוּ,[6] כְּרוֹב רַחֲמֶיךָ פְּנֵה אֵלֵינוּ,[7]

⟪ to us, ⟨ turn ⟨ mercies ⟨ in accord with Your abundant ⟪ for us; ⟨ Your inner being ⟨ Let yearn

לְבִלְתִּי כְּרֹעַ מַעֲלָלֵינוּ.

⟪ of our deeds. ⟨ with the evil ⟨ but not to be [in accord]

מְשׁוּבֹתֵינוּ רַבּוּ מִלִּמְנוֹת, נִיחוֹחִים אֵין וְקָרְבָּנוֹת,[8]

⟨ nor offerings ⟨ there are none, ⟪ Satisfying aromas — ⟪ to count. ⟨ are too numerous ⟨ Our wayward deeds

---

(1) Cf. *Psalms* 143:2. (2) See 50:20 with *Rashi*. (3) Cf. *Job* 4:18. (4) Cf. 15:16.
(5) Cf. *Psalms* 143:2. (6) Cf. *Jeremiah* 31:19. (7) Cf. *Psalms* 69:17. (8) Cf. *Jeremiah* 14:7.

---

§◆ אָדוֹן דִּין אִם יְדַקְדֵּק — *O Lord, judgment,*
if it were to be rigorously precise. The
acrostic of this *selichah* forms the *aleph-*

beis followed by the *paytan's* name —
זְבַדְיָה חֲזַק, *Zevadiah, may he be strong* [see
prefatory comment to *Selichah* 63].

סְלִיחָה מְצֹא לַעֲוֹנוֹת.

《 for [our] iniquities. 〈 would evoke 〈 that forgiveness

עַל צִדְקוֹתֵינוּ אֵין אָנוּ סְמוּכִים,[1]

《 rely, 〈 we do not 〈 our righteousness 〈 Upon

פֶּשַׁע וְעָוֹן מְלִכְלְכִים, צְדָקָה מְצֹא תַּחַן עוֹרְכִים.

《 do we arrange. 〈 [our] supplication 《 we would [rather,] so find, that charity 《 we are filthy; 〈 and iniquity 〈 for from willful sin

קַו אַל תִּמְתַּח בְּאוֹרְחוֹתֵינוּ,

《 over our ways; 〈 extend 〈 do not 〈 [Therefore,] a measuring line

רִמָּה וְתוֹלֵעָה אַחֲרִיתֵנוּ,[2] שָׁוְא וְהֶבֶל שְׁנוֹתֵינוּ.

《 are our years. 〈 and emptiness 〈 worthlessness 《 are our end, 〈 and maggot 〈 worm

תָּשׁוּב עַל הָרָעָה תִּנָּחֵם,[3] זֶה דַּרְכְּךָ חִנָּם מְרַחֵם,

《 compassionate; 〈 being graciously 《 is Your way, 〈 [for] this 《 reconsider, 《 the evil 〈 regarding [judgment], 《 Relent [from Your anger],

בְּרַחֲמֶיךָ הָרַבִּים עָלֵינוּ רַחֵם.

《 may You have mercy. 〈 on us 《 that are great, 〈 O, with Your mercies

דְּרָכֶיךָ הוֹדַעְתָּ[4] לֶעָנָו לְהוֹרוֹת,

《 so that he may teach; 〈 to the humble [Moses] 〈 You made known 〈 Your ways

יְדַעְתּוֹ שְׁלֹשׁ עֶשְׂרֵה סְדוּרוֹת,

《 are arranged; 〈 [how] the Thirteen [Attributes] 〈 You let him know

הִבְטַחְתּוֹ שֶׁאֵין רֵיקָם חוֹזְרוֹת.[5]

《 come back. 〈 ineffective 〈 they would never 〈 You promised him

❖ חַנּוּן,[6] בָּם סִדַּרְנוּ לְפָנֶיךָ, זַעַק קְשֹׁב מִמִּתְחַנְּנֶיךָ,

《 of those who supplicate before You, 〈 attend 〈 To the cries 《 before You. 〈 we have arranged [our prayer] 〈 with them 《 O Gracious One,

וְאַל תְּשִׁיבֵנוּ רֵיקָם מִלְּפָנֶיךָ.

《 from You. 〈 empty-handed 〈 turn us away 〈 and do not

---

(1) Cf. *Daniel* 9:18. (2) Cf. *Job* 25:6; *Mishnah, Avos* 3:1. (3) Cf. *Exodus* 32:12. (4) Cf. 33:13.
(5) See *Rosh Hashanah* 17b. (6) Some editions read חִנּוּן, [*our*] supplication.

ALL, WHILE STANDING:

אֵל מֶלֶךְ יוֹשֵׁב עַל כִּסֵּא רַחֲמִים, מִתְנַהֵג

⟨ Who acts ⟩ ⟪ of mercy, ⟨ the throne ⟨ on ⟨ Who sits ⟨ King ⟨ O God,

בַּחֲסִידוּת, מוֹחֵל עֲוֹנוֹת עַמּוֹ, מַעֲבִיר רִאשׁוֹן

⟨ [sins,] one ⟨ Who removes ⟪ of His people, ⟨ the sins ⟨ Who pardons ⟪ with kindness,

רִאשׁוֹן,[1] מַרְבֶּה מְחִילָה לְחַטָּאִים וּסְלִיחָה לַפּוֹשְׁעִים,

⟪ to willful sinners, ⟨ and forgiveness ⟨ to unintentional sinners ⟨ pardon ⟨ Who abundantly grants ⟪ by one,

עֹשֶׂה צְדָקוֹת עִם כָּל בָּשָׂר וָרוּחַ, לֹא כְרָעָתָם

⟨ in accord with their wickedness ⟨ — not ⟪ and spirit ⟨ [beings of] flesh ⟨ all ⟨ with ⟨ acts of generosity ⟨ Who performs

תִּגְמוֹל. ❖ אֵל הוֹרֵיתָ לָּנוּ לוֹמַר שְׁלֹשׁ עֶשְׂרֵה, וּזְכוֹר

⟨ remember ⟪ the Thirteen [Attributes of Mercy]; ⟨ to recite ⟨ us ⟨ You taught ⟨ O God, ⟪ do You repay them!

לָנוּ הַיּוֹם בְּרִית שְׁלֹשׁ עֶשְׂרֵה, כְּמוֹ שֶׁהוֹדַעְתָּ לֶעָנָיו

⟨ to the humble one [Moses] ⟨ You made as known ⟪ of [these] Thirteen, ⟨ the covenant ⟨ today ⟨ for us

מִקֶּדֶם, כְּמוֹ שֶׁכָּתוּב, וַיֵּרֶד יהוה בֶּעָנָן וַיִּתְיַצֵּב עִמּוֹ

⟨ with him ⟨ and stood ⟨ in a cloud ⟨ And Hashem descended ⟪ it is written: ⟨ as ⟪ in ancient times,

שָׁם, וַיִּקְרָא בְשֵׁם יהוה.[2]

⟪ of Hashem. ⟨ with the Name ⟨ and He called out ⟪ there,

CONGREGATION, THEN *CHAZZAN:*

וַיַּעֲבֹר יהוה עַל פָּנָיו וַיִּקְרָא:

⟪ and proclaimed: ⟪ [Moses'] face, ⟨ before ⟨ And Hashem passed

CONGREGATION AND *CHAZZAN* **RECITE LOUDLY AND IN UNISON:**

יהוה, יהוה, אֵל, רַחוּם, וְחַנּוּן, אֶרֶךְ אַפַּיִם,

⟨ to anger, ⟨ Slow ⟪ and Gracious, ⟨ Compassionate ⟨ God, ⟨ Hashem, ⟨ Hashem,

וְרַב חֶסֶד, וֶאֱמֶת, נֹצֵר חֶסֶד לָאֲלָפִים, נֹשֵׂא עָוֹן,

⟨ of iniquity, ⟨ Forgiver ⟨ for thousands [of generations], ⟨ of kindness ⟨ Preserver ⟪ and Truth, ⟨ in Kindness Abundant ⟨ and

---

(1) *Rosh Hashanah* 17a. (2) *Exodus* 34:5.

וָפֶשַׁע, וְחַטָּאָה, וְנַקֵּה. ¹ וְסָלַחְתָּ לַעֲוֹנֵנוּ וּלְחַטָּאתֵנוּ

‹ and our sins, ‹ our iniquities ‹ May You forgive « and Who absolves. ‹ and inadvertent sin, « willful sin,

וּנְחַלְתָּנוּ.² סְלַח לָנוּ אָבִינוּ כִּי חָטָאנוּ, מְחַל לָנוּ

‹ us, ‹ pardon « we have sinned; ‹ for « our Father, ‹ us, ‹ Forgive « and make us Your heritage.

מַלְכֵּנוּ כִּי פָשָׁעְנוּ. כִּי אַתָּה אֲדֹנָי טוֹב וְסַלָּח,

« and forgiving, ‹ are good ‹ O Lord, ‹ You, ‹ For « we have willfully sinned. ‹ for « our King,

וְרַב חֶסֶד לְכָל קֹרְאֶיךָ.³

« who call upon You. ‹ to all ‹ kind ‹ and abundantly

PREFATORY VERSES TO SELICHAH 86 / פסוקי הקדמה לסליחה פו

וּמַה יִּצְדַּק אֱנוֹשׁ עִם אֵל, וּמַה יִּזְכֶּה יְלוּד אִשָּׁה.⁴

« of woman? ‹ — one born ‹ might he be vindicated ‹ how ‹ God; ‹ before ‹ — [frail] « can he be found man — ‹ How righteous

מָה אֱנוֹשׁ כִּי תִפְקְדֶנּוּ לִבְקָרִים, לִרְגָעִים תִּבְחָנֶנּוּ.⁵

« test him? ‹ or at every moment « in the mornings, ‹ You should be that ‹ [frail] ‹ What mindful of him man is

יהוה אַל בְּאַפְּךָ תוֹכִיחֵנוּ, וְאַל בַּחֲמָתְךָ תְיַסְּרֵנוּ.⁶ אַף

‹ Even « chastise us. ‹ in Your wrath ‹ nor « rebuke us, ‹ in Your anger ‹ do not ‹ HASHEM,

עַל זֶה פָּקַחְתָּ עֵינֶךָ, וְאֹתָנוּ תָבִיא בְמִשְׁפָּט עִמָּךְ.⁷

« with You. ‹ to judgment ‹ will You bring ‹ and [such as] us « Your eyes, ‹ have You fixed ‹ [such a be-ing as] this ‹ on

כְּרַחֵם אָב עַל בָּנִים, כֵּן תְּרַחֵם יהוה עָלֵינוּ.⁸

« on us. ‹ HASHEM, ‹ have mercy, ‹ so « his children, ‹ toward ‹ a father is ‹ As merciful as

לַיהוה הַיְשׁוּעָה, עַל עַמְּךָ בִרְכָתֶךָ סֶּלָה.⁹ יהוה

‹ HASHEM, « Selah. « is Your blessing, ‹ Your people ‹ upon « is salvation, ‹ To HASHEM

צְבָאוֹת עִמָּנוּ, מִשְׂגָּב לָנוּ אֱלֹהֵי יַעֲקֹב סֶלָה.¹⁰

« Selah. « of Jacob, ‹ is the God ‹ for us « a stronghold « is with us, ‹ Master of Legions,

---

(1) *Exodus* 34:6-7. (2) 34:9. (3) *Psalms* 86:5. (4) *Job* 25:4. (5) Cf. *Psalms* 8:5; *Job* 7:18. (6) Cf. *Psalms* 6:2. (7) Cf. *Job* 14:3. (8) Cf. *Psalms* 103:13. (9) 3:9. (10) 46:8.

יהוה צְבָאוֹת, אַשְׁרֵי אָדָם בֹּטֵחַ בָּךְ.¹ יהוה הוֹשִׁיעָה,

HASHEM, Master of ‹ — praise- ‹ is the ‹ who ‹ in ‹ HASHEM, ‹ save! ›
Legions worthy man trusts You.

הַמֶּלֶךְ יַעֲנֵנוּ בְיוֹם קָרְאֵנוּ.²

May the ‹ answer ‹ on the ‹ we call. ›
King us day

סליחה פו / SELICHAH 86
(שניה)

ALL:

(אֱלֹהֵינוּ וֵאלֹהֵי אֲבוֹתֵינוּ:)

(Our God ‹ and God ‹ of our forefathers:) ›

אָדוֹן, בִּפְקָדְךָ אֱנוֹש* לַבְּקָרִים,

Lord, ‹ when You ‹ mankind* ‹ every ›
consider morning,

בְּמִצּוּי הַדִּין אַל תִּמְתַּח.

to the last ‹ of the ‹ do ‹ stretch ›
rigorous point law not [judgment].

גּוּף וּנְשָׁמָה אִם תְּרִיבֵם,* דְּחוּ וְלֹא יוּבְלוּ קוּם.³

Body ‹ and soul, ‹ if ‹ You should ‹ they would ‹ and ‹ able ‹ to rise. ›
judge be thrust not
[together],* down,

---

(1) Psalms 84:13. (2) 20:10. (3) Cf. 36:13.

אָדוֹן בִּפְקָדְךָ אֱנוֹש — *Lord, when You consider mankind.* This *selichah* contains an *aleph-beis* acrostic, which is followed by the author's signature, יִצְחָק הַכֹּהֵן הֶחָבֵר חֲזַק וְאֱמָץ, *Yitzchak the Kohen, the chaver* [an ancient title bestowed on certain exceptional people], *may he be strong and persevere.* Nothing is known about R' Yitzchak, except that he lived sometime before 1234, the year in which the commentary *Arugas HaBosem* was written. This *selichah*, as well as the next, is composed entirely of couplets and is therefore classified as a *sheniyah*. Interestingly, both are from among the few *selichos* that are unrhymed.

גּוּף וּנְשָׁמָה אִם תְּרִיבֵם — *Body and soul, if You should judge [together].* The Talmud relates an insightful discussion between Rabbi [Yehudah HaNassi] and the Roman emperor Antoninus.

The emperor claimed that man's body and soul could exonerate themselves on Judgment Day. The body could argue, *The soul was the guilty one; for since it left me, I have been lying like a mute rock in the grave;* and the soul could counter, *The body was the guilty one; for since I left it, I have been flying free as a bird.*

Rabbi responded with a parable: A king ordered two men to guard an orchard of fruit-laden trees. One was lame, the other blind. The lame sighted one said to his blind companion, *I see beautiful fruit in the orchard. Let me ride on your shoulders and I will guide you to the trees. We will then be able to eat from them.* And so they did for some time, eating the fruit they were set to protect. When the king returned, he asked what had happened to the ripened figs. The cripple said, *Do I have feet to walk over to the*

הֲיוּכַל גֶּבֶר לִזְכּוֹת בַּמִּשְׁפָּט,

❬ in judgment, ❬ to be ❬ for a ❬ Is it
     vindicated   man   possible

וְאִם אֵין בְּיָדוֹ מַעַשׂ לְהִצְטַדָּק.

《 with which to ❬ good ❬ in his ❬ there ❬ if
justify himself? deeds   hand   are not

זְרוּי יְחוּמוֹ מִלֵחָה סְרוּחָה,[1]

《 that is ❬ is from ❬ of his ❬ The
putrid; [a drop of] conception injected
     moisture   [seed]

חָבוּי אָרְבּוֹ בְּקִרְבּוֹ מֵעֵת הִוָּלְדוֹ.*

《 of his ❬ from the ❬ within him ❬ is the ❬ con-
birth.*   time   Ambusher cealed

טָמוּן בְּחֶבְּוֹ[2] כְּרֶשֶׁת לְרַגְלָיו,

《 for his feet, ❬ like a net ❬ within him, ❬ Hidden

יְסִיתֵהוּ בְּכָל יוֹם לְשַׁחַת לְהַפִּילוֹ.

《 to cast ❬ so as into ❬ day ❬ every ❬ it incites him
him down. Gehinnom [to sin],

כֹּחַ וּגְבוּרָה בַּגּוּף אֵין לְפָנָיו לַעֲמֹד וּלְהִתְיַצֵּב.

《 and to remain ❬ to stand ❬ against it ❬ there ❬ in the ❬ and ❬ Strength
firm.   is not   body   might

מִיּוֹם עָמְדוֹ עַל דַּעְתּוֹ,

《 of his ❬ in ❬ a man ❬ From
reason, control stands the day

נַפְשׁוֹ יָשִׂים בְּכַפּוֹ לְהָבִיא לַחְמוֹ.[3]

《 his bread. ❬ to provide ❬ in his ❬ he ❬ his life
     hands   places

---

(1) See *Avos* 3:1. (2) Cf. *Job* 31:33. (3) Cf. *Lamentations* 5:9.

---

trees? The blind one said, *Do I have eyes to see the fruit?* But the wise king had the lame man hoisted onto the blind man's shoulders and judged them as one. So, too, on Judgment Day, God hurls the soul back into its body and judges them as one (*Sanhedrin* 91a).

מֵעֵת הִוָּלְדוֹ — *From the time of his birth.* Another question posed by Antoninus (ibid.) is: *Does the Evil Inclination enter a person when the embryo is formed or at birth?* Rabbi replied, *From the formation of the embryo.*

Antoninus retorted, *If so, it would rebel and kick its way out of its mother. It cannot enter a person until he is born.*

Rabbi acceded, saying, *This matter have I been taught by Antoninus, and I have found a Scriptural verse to support his view; for it is written,* לַפֶּתַח חַטָּאת רֹבֵץ, *"Sin crouches at the door" (Genesis 4:7).* [Although the verse speaks in the context of an unrepentant sinner, Rabbi gave it a novel interpretation: The cause of sin, namely, the Evil Inclination, crouches at the door of the womb, ready to enter the baby as it emerges.]

שָׂבֵעַ כָּל יָמָיו כַּעַס וּמַכְאוֹבוֹת,¹

[He is] ⟨ all ⟨ his ⟨ with ⟨ and heartache; ⟪
sated   days   frustration

עַד שׁוּבוֹ לַעֲפָרוֹ² לֹא יִשְׁקֹט.

until ⟨ he returns ⟨ to his dust ⟨ he has no rest. ⟪

פְּנֵה אָדוֹן בְּעִצְבוֹן רוּחַ, צְפֵה בְּשִׁבְרוֹן לֵב,

Consider, ⟨ Lord, ⟨ [our] aching ⟨ spirit; ⟪ look at ⟨ [our] broken ⟨ hearts. ⟪

קָרוֹב אַתָּה לָרְחוֹקִים, רוֹצֶה תְּשׁוּבַת רְשָׁעִים.³

Near ⟨ You are ⟨ to those far away, ⟪ You desire ⟨ the repentance ⟨ of the wicked. ⟪

שַׁדַּי, הִמָּצֵא לְדוֹרְשֶׁיךָ, תֹּאמַר הִנְנִי לִמְבַקְשֶׁיךָ.

Almighty, ⟨ manifest ⟨ to those who ⟪ say, ⟨ Here I ⟨ to those who ⟪
Yourself   search for You;   am,   seek You.

יְבֻשְּׂרוּ סָלַחְתִּי⁴ קוֹרְאֵי בִשְׁמֶךָ,

Let them ⟪ I have ⟨ those — ⟨ in Your ⟪
be told,   forgiven   who call out   name;

צַדֵּק בַּמִּשְׁפָּט עַם מְיַחֲדֶךָ.

vindicate ⟨ in ⟨ the ⟨ who proclaim ⟪
judgment   people   Your unity.

חֲסֹם מְנֻוָּל⁵ מִלְּהַרְשִׁיעַ, קָצֹף בְּמַסְטִין מִלְּהַסְטִין.

Muzzle ⟪ the foul ⟨ so that he cannot ⟪ rebuke ⟨ [Satan] ⟨ so that he ⟪
  [Satan]   prosecute;   the Accuser   cannot accuse.

הָקֵם לָנוּ מֵלִיץ יֹשֶׁר.

Establish ⟨ on our ⟨ an advocate ⟨ to speak ⟪
  behalf   [angel]   well [of us];

כִּפֶּר מָצָאתִי תַּשְׁמִיעַ לַשּׁוֹבְבִים.

Atone- ⟨ have I found ⟪ let them ⟪ — Your wayward ⟪
ment   [for you],   hear   children.

הִשְׁלַכְנוּ עָלֶיךָ יְהָבֵנוּ,⁶ נָא אַתָּה תְכַלְכְּלֵנוּ.

We have cast ⟨ upon ⟨ our ⟪ please, ⟨ let it ⟨ Who sustains us. ⟪
  You   burden;   be You

הַעֲתֵר לָנוּ בִּתְפִלָּתֵנוּ.

Answer ⟨ us ⟨ as we pray; ⟪

חֶפְצֵנוּ וּבַקָּשָׁתֵנוּ מַלֵּא בְרַחֲמִים.

our desire ⟨ and our request ⟨ fulfill ⟨ with mercy. ⟪

---

(1) Cf. *Ecclesiastes* 2:23. (2) Cf. 3:20. (3) Cf. *Ezekiel* 18:23. (4) *Numbers* 14:20.
(5) See commentary to *Selichah* 24. (6) Cf. *Psalms* 55:23.

❖ בְּךָ תָלִינוּ בִּטְחוֹנֵנוּ, רַחֲמֶיךָ מְהֵרָה יְקַדְּמוּנוּ.

❮ come forth ❮ speedily ❮ let Your ❮ our trust; ❮ we have put ❮ In You
to greet us.   mercy

חָזָק וְאַמִּיץ שִׁמְךָ לֹא שְׁכַחְנוּ,

❮ we have not ❮ Your ❮ Mighty ❮ Strong,
forgotten;   Name   One,

אָנָּא, לָנֶצַח אַל תִּשְׁכָּחֵנוּ.[1]

❮ forget us. ❮ do not ❮ eternally ❮ please,

ALL, WHILE STANDING:

אֵל מֶלֶךְ יוֹשֵׁב עַל כִּסֵּא רַחֲמִים, מִתְנַהֵג

❮ Who acts ❮ of mercy, ❮ the throne ❮ on ❮ Who sits ❮ King ❮ O God,

בַּחֲסִידוּת, מוֹחֵל עֲוֹנוֹת עַמּוֹ, מַעֲבִיר רִאשׁוֹן

❮ [sins,] one ❮ Who removes ❮ of His people, ❮ the sins ❮ Who pardons ❮ with kindness,

רִאשׁוֹן,[2] מַרְבֶּה מְחִילָה לַחַטָּאִים וּסְלִיחָה לַפּוֹשְׁעִים,

❮ to willful ❮ and ❮ to unintentional ❮ pardon ❮ Who abun- ❮ by one,
sinners,   forgiveness   sinners   dantly grants

עֹשֶׂה צְדָקוֹת עִם כָּל בָּשָׂר וָרוּחַ, לֹא כְרָעָתָם

❮ in accord with ❮ — not ❮ and ❮ [beings ❮ all ❮ with ❮ acts of ❮ Who
their wickedness   spirit   of] flesh   generosity performs

תִּגְמוֹל. ❖ אֵל הוֹרֵיתָ לָנוּ לוֹמַר שְׁלֹשׁ עֶשְׂרֵה, וּזְכוֹר

❮ remem- ❮ the Thirteen ❮ to ❮ us ❮ You ❮ O God, ❮ do You
ber   [Attributes of Mercy]; recite   taught   repay them!

לָנוּ הַיּוֹם בְּרִית שְׁלֹשׁ עֶשְׂרֵה, כְּמוֹ שֶׁהוֹדַעְתָּ לֶעָנָיו

❮ to the humble ❮ You made ❮ as ❮ of [these] Thirteen, ❮ the ❮ today ❮ for us
one [Moses]   known   covenant

מִקֶּדֶם, כְּמוֹ שֶׁכָּתוּב, וַיֵּרֶד יהוה בֶּעָנָן וַיִּתְיַצֵּב עִמּוֹ

❮ with ❮ and stood ❮ in a ❮ And HASHEM ❮ it is written: ❮ as ❮ in ancient
him   cloud   descended   times,

שָׁם, וַיִּקְרָא בְשֵׁם יהוה.[3]

❮ of ❮ with the ❮ and He ❮ there,
HASHEM. Name   called out

CONGREGATION, THEN *CHAZZAN:*

וַיַּעֲבֹר יהוה עַל פָּנָיו וַיִּקְרָא:

❮ and ❮ [Moses'] ❮ before ❮ And HASHEM passed
proclaimed: face,

---

(1) Cf. *Lamentations* 5:20. (2) *Rosh Hashanah* 17a. (3) *Exodus* 34:5.

CONGREGATION AND *CHAZZAN* RECITE LOUDLY AND IN UNISON:

יהוה, יהוה, אֵל, רַחוּם, וְחַנּוּן, אֶרֶךְ אַפַּיִם,

⟨ to anger, ⟨ Slow ⟨ and Gracious, ⟨ Compassionate ⟨ God, ⟨ HASHEM, ⟨ HASHEM,

וְרַב חֶסֶד, וֶאֱמֶת, נֹצֵר חֶסֶד לָאֲלָפִים, נֹשֵׂא עָוֹן,

⟨ of iniquity, ⟨ Forgiver ⟨⟨ for thousands [of generations], ⟨ of kindness ⟨ Preserver ⟨⟨ and Truth, ⟨ in Kindness ⟨ and Abundant

וָפֶשַׁע, וְחַטָּאָה, וְנַקֵּה.[1] וְסָלַחְתָּ לַעֲוֹנֵנוּ וּלְחַטָּאתֵנוּ

⟨⟨ and our sins, ⟨ our iniquities ⟨ May You forgive ⟨⟨ and Who absolves. ⟨ and inadvertent sin, ⟨ willful sin,

וּנְחַלְתָּנוּ.[2] סְלַח לָנוּ אָבִינוּ כִּי חָטָאנוּ, מְחַל לָנוּ

⟨ us, ⟨ pardon ⟨⟨ we have sinned; ⟨ for ⟨⟨ our Father, ⟨ us, ⟨ Forgive ⟨⟨ and make us Your heritage.

מַלְכֵּנוּ כִּי פָשָׁעְנוּ. כִּי אַתָּה אֲדֹנָי טוֹב וְסַלָּח,

⟨⟨ and forgiving, ⟨ are good ⟨ O Lord, ⟨ You, ⟨ For ⟨⟨ we have willfully sinned. ⟨ for ⟨⟨ our King,

וְרַב חֶסֶד לְכָל קֹרְאֶיךָ.[3]

⟨⟨ who call upon You. ⟨ to all ⟨ kind ⟨ and abundantly

סליחה פז / SELICHAH 87

(פזמון)

CHAZZAN, THEN CONGREGATION:

יֵרָצֶה צוֹם עַמְּךָ* אֲשֶׁר דָּמוֹ לְךָ מַזֶּה,

⟨⟨ sprinkles;* ⟨ to You ⟨ its blood ⟨ that ⟨ of Your nation [be] ⟨ may ⟨ Acceptable [to You]

חֲשֹׁב חֶלְבּוֹ כְּעַל זֶבַח* וְקָרְבָּנוֹ אַל תִּבְזֶה,

⟨⟨ disparage. ⟨ do not ⟨ and its offering ⟨⟨ a sacrifice,* ⟨ as if it were ⟨ its fat ⟨ consider

---

(1) *Exodus* 34:6-7. (2) 34:9. (3) *Psalms* 86:5.

§⦿ **יֵרָצֶה צוֹם עַמְּךָ** — *Acceptable [to You] may the fast of Your nation [be]*. This *pizmon* is signed יִצְחָק, *Yitzchak*, in the acrostic of the first four stanzas. Some read בַּר אֲבִיגְדוֹר, *bar Avigdor*, in the acrostic of stanzas five and six. Nothing more is known about this *paytan* except that he wrote before 1234 when the commentary *Arugas HaBosem* [which includes this work] was written.

חֲשֹׁב חֶלְבּוֹ כְּעַל זֶבַח — *Consider its fat as if it were a sacrifice*. The concept that one's fasting is reckoned as if he had sanctified himself on the Altar is the subject of a prayer, originally recited by the Talmudic Sage R' Sheishes (*Berachos* 17a), generally recited at the end of the *Minchah Amidah* on fast days:

"Master of all worlds, it is revealed and

חֲתֹם עָלָיו אוֹת חַיִּים,¹ וּתְפִלָּתוֹ תֶּחֱזֶה —

》 accept. 〈 and its prayer 》 of life, 〈 with a sign 〈 it[s verdict] 〈 Seal

מָחָר יִהְיֶה הָאוֹת הַזֶּה.²

》 this sign. 〈 will happen 〈 Tomorrow

CONGREGATION, THEN *CHAZZAN:*

צִדְקָתְךָ הִתְאַזָּר, שׁוֹכֵן עַד וּמְרוֹמָם,³

》 and Who are 〈 for- 〈 O You 》 gird Yourself, 〈 In righteousness
exalted; ever Who dwell

סְמֹךְ נָא הַנִּכְשָׁלִים, שְׁלַח יָדְךָ לַהֲקִימָם,

》 to raise them, 〈 Your 〈 send 》 those who 〈 please, 〈 support,
hand forth stumble,

אֲשֶׁר דִּמְעָם שִׁקּוּיִם וְאַנְחָתָם הִיא לַחְמָם,⁴

》 is their bread. 〈 and whose 〈 is their 〈 whose tear 〈 those
sigh drink

וְתִנְקֹם דַּם עֲבָדֶיךָ מֵאוֹיְבֶיךָ עַד תֻּמָּם.

》 their 〈 until 〈 from Your 〈 of Your 〈 the 〈 Avenge
annihilation, enemies servants blood

וְתִדְרֹשׁ לְשֶׁפֶךְ דָּמָם, לָדַעַת מַה זֶּה וְעַל מַה זֶּה⁵ —

》 this 〈 what 〈 and 〈 this 》 what 〈 to know 》 of their 〈 the spilling 〈 and avenge
is.* reason for is blood,

מָחָר יִהְיֶה הָאוֹת הַזֶּה.

》 this sign. 〈 will happen 〈 Tomorrow

CONGREGATION, THEN *CHAZZAN:*

חַנּוּן חֹן עַמְּךָ אֲשֶׁר לְשִׁמְךָ הוּא מַאֲמִין,

》 believe, 〈 they 〈 in Your 〈 who 〈 Your 〈 favor 》O Grac-
Name people ious One,

---

(1) See commentary to *Selichah 38*, s.v. כְּתֹב תְּוֵ חַיִּים. (2) Cf. *Exodus* 8:19.
(3) Cf. *Isaiah* 57:15. (4) Cf. *Psalms* 80:6; also 102:10; *Job* 3:24. (5) *Esther* 4:5.

---

known before You that, when the Holy Temple stood, one who sinned would offer an animal — its fat and its blood — upon the Altar, and it would atone for him. Now I have engaged in a fast and my own fat and blood have been diminished. May it be Your will that the diminution of my fat and blood be considered as if I had offered them upon the Altar, and may You show me favor."

לָדַעַת מַה זֶּה וְעַל מַה זֶּה — *To know what this*

is and for what reason this is. The commentaries vary widely on the meaning of this stich:

Investigate to learn why their tears have become their drinks, and why their sighs have become their bread (*Masbir*).

Investigate to determine whether the spilled blood of Your people falls into the category of קִידּוּשׁ הַשֵּׁם, *martyrdom* (*Matteh Levi*).

סַנְגוֹר עָלַי תְּמַנֶּה אֲשֶׁר חַטָאתִי יַטְמִין,

an advocate ⟨ for me ⟨ appoint ⟨ who, ⟨ my inadvertent sin, ⟨ will conceal; ⟩⟩

וְחוֹבִי בִּשְׂמֹאל יַכְמִין, זְכוּתִי יַעֲלֶה בְיָמִין.

[and who] my guilt ⟨ with his left hand ⟨ will suppress, ⟨ and my merit ⟨ elevate ⟨ with his right; ⟩⟩

וְאֵפֶר יִצְחָק* יַזְמִין, אֲשֶׁר יֹאמַר כִּי הוּא זֶה —[1]

[and who] the ashes ⟨ of Isaac* ⟨ will exhibit, ⟨ about which ⟨ he will say ⟨ that, ⟨ It is ⟨ this! ⟩⟩

מָחָר יִהְיֶה הָאוֹת הַזֶּה.

Tomorrow ⟨ will happen ⟨ this sign. ⟩⟩

CONGREGATION, THEN *CHAZZAN*:

קָרֵב וּשְׁמַע רִנָּתִי, לְזַעֲקָתִי תִּפְתַּח שָׁעַר,

Draw near ⟨ and listen ⟨ to my prayerful song, ⟨ before my cry ⟨ open ⟨ the Gate [of Prayer], ⟩⟩

לְזַכּוֹת אֶת חַטָאתִי כְּמוֹ בֶן שָׁנָה נַעַר,*

to cleanse ⟨ my sin ⟨ as if [I were] ⟨ of the age ⟨ of a one-year-old ⟨ child.* ⟩⟩

---

(1) *Exodus* 22:8.

Seek [and refute] the excuses the gentiles used for spilling Jewish blood, so that they will know why Your vengeance is upon them (*Selichos HaMeforash*).

וְאֵפֶר יִצְחָק — *The ashes of Isaac.* Many sources in the Talmud and Midrash speak of God's mercy being evoked by the merit of Isaac's willingness to be offered as a sacrifice. Those merits are referred to as *the ashes of Isaac* (see for example *Taanis* 16a where, according to one view, the fast-day custom of placing ashes on the Ark in which the Torah Scrolls are kept is based on recalling the merit of Isaac's ashes. But our *paytan* asks for more than just a verbal allusion to the *Akeidah*; he asks for an advocate who will *display* Isaac's ashes, as if Isaac were actually burned and his ashes are real!

The Talmud relates that when King David bought the land upon which his son Solomon would eventually build the *Beis HaMikdash*, he was able to determine the exact spot on which the Altar would stand. But how did David know the exact location?

According to one view, he saw the ashes of Isaac heaped up on that spot (*Zevachim* 62a). Similarly, when God sent a destroying angel to visit a death plague on Israel during the days of King David, when the angel began his destruction of Jerusalem, HASHEM *saw and relented about the evil decrees* (*I Chronicles* 21:15). But, asks the Talmud, what did God see that caused him to relent? One opinion answers that He saw Isaac's ashes (*Berachos* 62b). Thus, according to at least two Sages of the Talmud, Isaac's ashes are not just a concept, but are a visible entity. It is to these views that the *paytan* subscribes when he asks that the ashes be displayed.

כְּמוֹ בֶן שָׁנָה נַעַר — *As if [I were] of the age of a one-year-old child.* The simile of a one-year-old as a symbol of innocence is taken from Scripture's description of King Saul: *Saul was a year old when he became king* (*I Samuel* 13:1). The Talmud interprets: [He was as innocent] as a one-year-old child who has not tasted of sin (*Yoma* 22b).

וְתַחְסֹם לְשׁוֹן מַשְׂטִינִי וְאֶת פִּיהוּ לֹא יִפְעַר,

《 he not open. 〈 his mouth 〈 so that 《 of my satanic Accuser, 〈 the speech 〈 Muzzle

יהוה בַּשָּׂטָן יִגְעַר,[1] קוּם רֵד מַהֵר מִזֶּה[2] —

《 from here! 〈 quickly 〈 Descend 《 Get up! 《 rebuke, 〈 the Satan 〈 O HASHEM,

מָחָר יִהְיֶה הָאוֹת הַזֶּה.

《 this sign. 〈 will happen 〈 Tomorrow

CONGREGATION, THEN *CHAZZAN:*

בַּמֶּה אֲקַדֵּם וְאֶכַּף[3] פְּנֵי לֹא יִקַּח שֹׁחַד,[4]

《 a bribe? 〈 Who does not accept 〈 before Him 〈 and humble myself [the *chazzan*] 〈 shall I 〈 With what approach

וּבְיָדִי אֵין מֵעֲשׂ וְעַל זֹאת לִבִּי יִפְחַד,

《 is fearful. 〈 my heart 〈 this 〈 and because of 《 [worthy] deed, 〈 there is no 〈 In my hand

אֲבָל עַתָּה בְּזָכְרִי מַלְכוּת שֵׁם הַמְּיֻחָד,

《 that is uniquely One, 〈 of [Your] Name 〈 [how Israel accepts] the sovereignty 〈 when I recall 〈 now, 〈 Yet,

וְעַל זֹאת אֲנִי בוֹטֵחַ[5] בְּאוֹמְרִים יהוה אֶחָד,

《 is One, 〈 HASHEM 《 when they recite, 《 trust, 〈 do I 〈 this 〈 on

וּמוֹשְׁכִים כֻּלָּם יַחַד, מִזֶּה אֶחָד וּמִזֶּה[6] —

《 and from that side. 〈 the word [of the One, 〈 from this side [of the congregation] 《 all as one, 〈 all of them 〈 and they prolong

מָחָר יִהְיֶה הָאוֹת הַזֶּה.

《 this sign. 〈 will happen 〈 Tomorrow

CONGREGATION, THEN *CHAZZAN:*

רְאֵה אֵין מְכַפֵּר בַּעֲדִי, וְאֵין סוֹדֵר לִי סֵדֶר,

《 the order of the [Yom Kippur Temple] service; 〈 for me 〈 to perform 〈 and no 《 for me, 〈 to atone 〈 there is no one 〈 See,

וּבִגְדֵי לָבָן אַיִן, וְאֵין לוֹבֵשׁ הָאֵדֶר,

《 the [priestly] mantle, 〈 to wear 〈 and there is no one 《 are not here, 〈 of white 〈 the garments

---

(1) Cf. *Zechariah* 3:2. (2) *Deuteronomy* 9:12. (3) Cf. *Micah* 6:6.
(4) Cf. *Deuteronomy* 10:17. (5) Cf. *Psalms* 27:3. (6) *Exodus* 17:12.

וְגַם אֵין קָרְבַּן חוֹבָה וְלֹא נְדָבָה וָנֶדֶר,

וְאַתָּה תְכַפֵּר עָלַי, בּוֹחֵן כְּלָיוֹת וָחֶדֶר,

גְּדֹר פִּרְצַת צֹאנֶךָ וְשִׂים רֶוַח לָעֵדֶר,

וְתִבְנֶה לָמוֹ גֶּדֶר מִזֶּה וּגְדֵר מִזֶּה¹ —

מָחָר יִהְיֶה הָאוֹת הַזֶּה.

CONGREGATION, THEN CHAZZAN:

צֵל קוֹרָתְךָ בָּאוּ² בָּנִים אֲשֶׁר נִגְרָשׁוּ,

בֵּיתְךָ כְּנִתְוַעֲדוּ רָעֲשׁוּ וְגַם נִתְגָּעֲשׁוּ,³

חֶסֶד אֲבוֹתָם תִּזְכֹּר עֵת לָרִיב יִגָּשׁוּ,

אֱמֶת וְשָׁלוֹם נִפְגָּשׁוּ,⁴ גַּם אֶת זֶה לְעֻמַּת זֶה⁵ —

מָחָר יִהְיֶה הָאוֹת הַזֶּה.

ALL, WHILE STANDING:

אֵל מֶלֶךְ יוֹשֵׁב עַל כִּסֵּא רַחֲמִים, מִתְנַהֵג

בַּחֲסִידוּת, מוֹחֵל עֲוֹנוֹת עַמּוֹ, מַעֲבִיר רִאשׁוֹן

---

(1) Numbers 22:24. (2) Cf. Genesis 19:8. (3) Cf. II Samuel 22:8. (4) Cf. Psalms 85:11. (5) Ecclesiastes 7:14.

רִאשׁוֹן,[1] מַרְבֶּה מְחִילָה לַחֲטָאִים וּסְלִיחָה לַפּוֹשְׁעִים,

‹ by one, › Who abun- ‹ pardon › to unintentional ‹ and › to willful
dantly grants sinners forgiveness sinners,

עֹשֶׂה צְדָקוֹת עִם כָּל בָּשָׂר וָרוּחַ, לֹא כְרָעָתָם

‹ Who › acts of ‹ with › all ‹ [beings › and ‹ — not › in accord with
performs generosity of] flesh spirit their wickedness

תִּגְמוֹל. ∴ אֵל הוֹרֵיתָ לָנוּ לוֹמַר שְׁלֹשׁ עֶשְׂרֵה, וּזְכוֹר

‹ do You › O God, › You ‹ to ‹ to › the Thirteen ‹ remem-
repay them! taught us recite [Attributes of Mercy]; ber

לָנוּ הַיּוֹם בְּרִית שְׁלֹשׁ עֶשְׂרֵה, כְּמוֹ שֶׁהוֹדַעְתָּ לֶעָנָיו

‹ for us › today › the ‹ of [these] Thirteen, › as ‹ You made ‹ to the
covenant known humble one
[Moses]

מִקֶּדֶם, כְּמוֹ שֶׁכָּתוּב, וַיֵּרֶד יהוה בֶּעָנָן וַיִּתְיַצֵּב עִמּוֹ

‹ in ancient › as ‹ it is written: › And HASHEM ‹ in a ‹ and stood ‹ with
times, descended cloud him

שָׁם, וַיִּקְרָא בְשֵׁם יהוה.[2]

‹ there, › and He › with the › of
called out Name HASHEM.

CONGREGATION, THEN *CHAZZAN:*

וַיַּעֲבֹר יהוה עַל פָּנָיו וַיִּקְרָא:

‹ and › [Moses'] ‹ before ‹ And HASHEM passed
proclaimed: face,

CONGREGATION AND *CHAZZAN* **RECITE LOUDLY AND IN UNISON:**

יהוה, יהוה, אֵל, רַחוּם, וְחַנּוּן, אֶרֶךְ אַפַּיִם,

‹ to anger, › Slow ‹ and › Compassionate ‹ God, › HASHEM, ‹ HASHEM,
Gracious,

וְרַב חֶסֶד, וֶאֱמֶת, נֹצֵר חֶסֶד לָאֲלָפִים, נֹשֵׂא עָוֹן,

‹ of › Forgiver › for › of › Preserver ‹ and › in ‹ and
iniquity, thousands [of kindness Truth, Kindness Abundant
generations],

וָפֶשַׁע, וְחַטָּאָה, וְנַקֵּה.[3] וְסָלַחְתָּ לַעֲוֹנֵנוּ וּלְחַטָּאתֵנוּ

‹ and our sins, › our › May You ‹ and Who ‹ and inadvertent ‹ willful sin,
iniquities forgive absolves. sin,

וּנְחַלְתָּנוּ.[4] סְלַח לָנוּ אָבִינוּ כִּי חָטָאנוּ, מְחַל לָנוּ

‹ us, › pardon ‹ we have ‹ for ‹ our ‹ us, › Forgive ‹ and make us
sinned; Father, Your heritage.

---

(1) *Rosh Hashanah* 17a. (2) *Exodus* 34:5. (3) 34:6-7. (4) 34:9.

מַלְכֵּנוּ כִּי פָשָׁעְנוּ. כִּי אַתָּה אֲדֹנָי טוֹב וְסַלָּח,

our King, for we have willfully sinned. For You, O Lord, are good and forgiving,

וְרַב חֶסֶד לְכָל קֹרְאֶיךָ.¹

and abundantly kind to all who call upon You.

ALL:

זְכֹר רַחֲמֶיךָ יהוה וַחֲסָדֶיךָ, כִּי מֵעוֹלָם הֵמָּה.²

Remember Your mercies, HASHEM, and Your kindnesses, for eternal are they.

זָכְרֵנוּ יהוה בִּרְצוֹן עַמֶּךָ, פָּקְדֵנוּ בִּישׁוּעָתֶךָ.³ זְכֹר

Remember us, HASHEM, when You show favor to Your people; recall us with Your salvation. Remember

עֲדָתְךָ קָנִיתָ קֶּדֶם, גָּאַלְתָּ שֵׁבֶט נַחֲלָתֶךָ, הַר צִיּוֹן

Your congregation, which You acquired long ago, the tribe You redeemed of Your heritage, the mountain of Zion

זֶה שָׁכַנְתָּ בּוֹ.⁴ זְכֹר יהוה חִבַּת יְרוּשָׁלַיִם, אַהֲבַת

[where] Your Presence rested there. Remember, HASHEM, the affection of Jerusalem; the love

צִיּוֹן אַל תִּשְׁכַּח לָנֶצַח.⁵ אַתָּה תָקוּם תְּרַחֵם צִיּוֹן כִּי

of Zion do not forget forever. You will arise and show mercy to Zion for

עֵת לְחֶנְנָהּ, כִּי בָא מוֹעֵד.⁶ זְכֹר יהוה לִבְנֵי אֱדוֹם

the time to favor her, for the appointed time will have come. Remember, HASHEM, for the offspring of Edom

אֵת יוֹם יְרוּשָׁלָיִם, הָאֹמְרִים עָרוּ עָרוּ עַד הַיְסוֹד

the day of Jerusalem; those who say, Destroy! Destroy! [to repay] the very foundation

בָּהּ.⁷ זְכֹר לְאַבְרָהָם לְיִצְחָק וּלְיִשְׂרָאֵל עֲבָדֶיךָ,

of it! Remember for Abraham, for Isaac and for Israel, Your servants,

אֲשֶׁר נִשְׁבַּעְתָּ לָהֶם בָּךְ וַתְּדַבֵּר אֲלֵהֶם, אַרְבֶּה

that You swore to them by Your Being, and You said to them, I shall increase

אֶת זַרְעֲכֶם כְּכוֹכְבֵי הַשָּׁמָיִם, וְכָל הָאָרֶץ הַזֹּאת אֲשֶׁר

Your offspring like the stars of the heavens; and all this land of which

---

(1) *Psalms* 86:5. (2) 25:6. (3) Cf. 106:4. (4) 74:2. (5) This is not a Scriptural verse. (6) *Psalms* 102:14. (7) 137:7.

אָמַרְתִּי, אֶתֵּן לְזַרְעֲכֶם, וְנָחֲלוּ לְעֹלָם.¹ זְכֹר לַעֲבָדֶיךָ

‹ of Your   ‹ Remember   « forever.   ‹ and they   to your   ‹ I will   ‹ I spoke
servants,   [the merits]   will inherit it   offspring,   give

לְאַבְרָהָם לְיִצְחָק וּלְיַעֲקֹב, אַל תֵּפֶן אֶל קְשִׁי

‹ the stub- ‹ to   ‹ pay   ‹ do   « and of Jacob;   ‹ of Isaac   ‹ of Abraham,
bornness   attention   not

הָעָם הַזֶּה וְאֶל רִשְׁעוֹ וְאֶל חַטָּאתוֹ.² זְכוֹר לָנוּ

‹ for us ‹ Remember « its sinfulness. ‹ and to « its wickedness, ‹ to « of this people,

בְּרִית אָבוֹת, כַּאֲשֶׁר אָמַרְתָּ: וְזָכַרְתִּי אֶת בְּרִיתִי

‹ My covenant   ‹ And I will   « You said: ‹ as   « of the   ‹ the
          remember   Patriarchs,   covenant

יַעֲקוֹב, וְאַף אֶת בְּרִיתִי יִצְחָק, וְאַף אֶת בְּרִיתִי

‹ My covenant   ‹ and   « [with]   ‹ My covenant   ‹ and also « [with] Jacob,
        also   Isaac,

אַבְרָהָם אֶזְכֹּר, וְהָאָרֶץ אֶזְכֹּר.³

« I will   ‹ and the   « I will   ‹ [with]
remember.   Land   remember;   Abraham

THE ARK IS OPENED.

CHAZZAN, THEN CONGREGATION:

שְׁמַע קוֹלֵנוּ יהוה אֱלֹהֵינוּ, חוּס וְרַחֵם עָלֵינוּ,

« on us, ‹ and have ‹ have « our God; ‹ HASHEM, ‹ our voice, ‹ Hear
     compassion   pity

וְקַבֵּל בְּרַחֲמִים וּבְרָצוֹן אֶת תְּפִלָּתֵנוּ.⁴

«   our prayer.   ‹ and favor ‹ with   ‹ and accept
               compassion

CHAZZAN, THEN CONGREGATION:

הֲשִׁיבֵנוּ יהוה אֵלֶיךָ וְנָשׁוּבָה, חַדֵּשׁ יָמֵינוּ כְּקֶדֶם.⁵

« as of old. ‹ our ‹ renew « and we shall ‹ to You, ‹ HASHEM, ‹ Bring us back,
      days   return,

CHAZZAN, THEN CONGREGATION:

אֲמָרֵינוּ הַאֲזִינָה יהוה, בִּינָה הֲגִיגֵנוּ.⁶

«   our   ‹ perceive « HASHEM; ‹ hear,   ‹ Our words
thoughts.

---

(1) *Exodus* 32:13. (2) *Deuteronomy* 9:27. (3) *Leviticus* 26:42.
(4) From the weekday *Shemoneh Esrei.* (5) *Lamentations* 5:21. (6) Cf. *Psalms* 5:2.

THE FOLLOWING VERSE IS RECITED QUIETLY:

יִהְיוּ לְרָצוֹן אִמְרֵי פִינוּ וְהֶגְיוֹן לִבֵּנוּ לְפָנֶיךָ,
《 before 《 of our 〈 and the 〈 of our 〈 — the ex- 《 find 〈 May
　You, 　heart — 　thoughts 　mouth 　pressions 　favor 　they

יהוה צוּרֵנוּ וְגוֹאֲלֵנוּ.¹
　　　　　　　《 and our 〈 our 〈 HASHEM,
　　　　　　　　Redeemer. 　Rock

CHAZZAN, THEN CONGREGATION:

אַל תַּשְׁלִיכֵנוּ מִלְּפָנֶיךָ, וְרוּחַ קָדְשְׁךָ אַל תִּקַּח מִמֶּנּוּ.²
《 from us. 〈 take 〈 do 〈 of Your 〈 and the 《 from Your 〈 cast us away 〈 Do
　　　　　not 　Holiness 　Spirit 　Presence, 　　　　　not

CHAZZAN, THEN CONGREGATION:

אַל תַּשְׁלִיכֵנוּ לְעֵת זִקְנָה, כִּכְלוֹת כֹּחֵנוּ אַל תַּעַזְבֵנוּ.³
《 forsake us not. 〈 does our 〈 when fail 《 of old 〈 in time 〈 cast us away 〈 Do
　　　　　　　strength, 　age; 　　　　　　　　　　　　not

ALL CONTINUE (SOME CONGREGATIONS RECITE THE NEXT VERSE RESPONSIVELY):

אַל תַּעַזְבֵנוּ יהוה, אֱלֹהֵינוּ אַל תִּרְחַק מִמֶּנּוּ.⁴
《 from us. 〈 be not distant 〈 our God, 《 O HASHEM; 〈 Forsake us not,

עֲשֵׂה עִמָּנוּ אוֹת לְטוֹבָה, וְיִרְאוּ שׂוֹנְאֵינוּ וְיֵבְשׁוּ,
《 and be 〈 may our 〈 so that 《 for good; 〈 a sign 〈 for us 〈 Display
　ashamed, 　enemies 　see it

כִּי אַתָּה יהוה עֲזַרְתָּנוּ וְנִחַמְתָּנוּ.⁵ כִּי לְךָ יהוה
〈 HASHEM, 〈 for 〈 Because 《 and 〈 will have 〈 HASHEM, 〈 You, 〈 for
　　　　　You, 　consoled us. 　helped us

הוֹחָלְנוּ, אַתָּה תַעֲנֶה אֲדֹנָי אֱלֹהֵינוּ.⁶
《 our God. 〈 O Lord, 〈 will answer, 〈 You 《 do we wait;

THE ARK IS CLOSED.

EACH INDIVIDUAL CONTINUES UNTIL THE END OF SELICHOS.

CONFESSION / ודוי

**DURING THE RECITATION OF THE ודוי, CONFESSION, STAND WITH
HEAD AND BODY SLIGHTLY BOWED, IN SUBMISSIVE CONTRITION.**

אֱלֹהֵינוּ וֵאלֹהֵי אֲבוֹתֵינוּ, תָּבֹא לְפָנֶיךָ תְּפִלָּתֵנוּ, וְאַל⁷
〈 and 《 may our 〈 before 〈 come 《 of our 〈 and the 〈 Our God
　do not 　prayer, 　You 　forefathers, 　God

(1) Cf. Psalms 19:15. (2) 51:13. (3) Cf. 71:9. (4) Cf. 38:22. (5) Cf. 86:17. (6) Cf. 38:16. (7) Cf. 88:3.

תִּתְעַלַּם מִתְּחִנָּתֵנוּ,¹ שֶׁאֵין אָנוּ עַזֵּי פָנִים וּקְשֵׁי
‹ and ‹ faced ‹ so ‹ For we are not 《 our supplication. ‹ ignore
stiff-   brazen-

עֹרֶף, לוֹמַר לְפָנֶיךָ יהוה אֱלֹהֵינוּ וֵאלֹהֵי אֲבוֹתֵינוּ,
《 of our ‹ and the ‹ our God, ‹ HASHEM, 《 before ‹ as to say ‹ necked
forefathers,   God   You,

צַדִּיקִים אֲנַחְנוּ וְלֹא חָטָאנוּ, אֲבָל אֲנַחְנוּ וַאֲבוֹתֵינוּ
‹ and our ‹ we 《 —for 《 sinned ‹ and ‹ we are, ‹ that
forefathers   indeed,   have not   righteous

חָטָאנוּ.²
《 have sinned.

**STRIKE THE LEFT SIDE OF THE CHEST WITH THE RIGHT FIST WHILE RECITING
EACH OF THE SINS OF THE FOLLOWING CONFESSIONAL LITANY:**

אָשַׁמְנוּ, בָּגַדְנוּ, גָּזַלְנוּ, דִּבַּרְנוּ דֹפִי. הֶעֱוִינוּ,
《 We have com- 《 slander. ‹ we have 《 we have 《 we have 《 We have been
mitted iniquity;   spoken   robbed; betrayed;   guilty;

וְהִרְשַׁעְנוּ, זַדְנוּ, חָמַסְנוּ, טָפַלְנוּ שֶׁקֶר. יָעַצְנוּ
‹ We have 《 false ‹ we have 《 we have 《we have sinned 《we have commit-
given advice accusations. made   extorted; willfully; ted wickedness;

רָע, כִּזַּבְנוּ, לַצְנוּ, מָרַדְנוּ, נִאַצְנוּ, סָרַרְנוּ,
《 we have 《 we have provoked 《 we have 《 we have 《 we have been 《 that is
strayed; [God's anger];   rebelled; scorned; deceitful;   bad;

עָוִינוּ, פָּשַׁעְנוּ, צָרַרְנוּ, קִשִּׁינוּ עֹרֶף. רָשַׁעְנוּ,
《 We have 《 our ‹ we have 《 we have caused 《 we have sinned 《we have been
been wicked; necks. stiffened distress;   rebelliously; iniquitous;

שִׁחַתְנוּ, תִּעַבְנוּ, תָּעִינוּ, תִּעְתָּעְנוּ.
《 we have 《 we have 《we have commit- 《 we have
scoffed. gone astray; ted abominations; been corrupt;

הִרְשַׁעְנוּ וּפָשַׁעְנוּ, לָכֵן לֹא נוֹשָׁעְנוּ. וְתֵן בְּלִבֵּנוּ
‹ in our ‹ Place 《 been ‹ we have ‹ there- 《 and we ‹ We have acted
hearts   saved.   not   fore have sinned   wickedly
                               rebelliously;

לַעֲזוֹב דֶּרֶךְ רֶשַׁע, וְחִישׁ לָנוּ יֶשַׁע, כַּכָּתוּב עַל יַד
‹ the ‹ by ‹ as it is 《 salvation; ‹ to us ‹ and 《 of ‹ the ‹ [the will]
hand written   hasten wickedness, path to abandon

---

(1) Cf. *Psalms* 55:2. (2) Cf. 106:6, *Jeremiah* 3:25.

נְבִיאֶךָ: יַעֲזֹב רָשָׁע דַּרְכּוֹ, וְאִישׁ אָוֶן מַחְשְׁבֹתָיו, וְיָשֹׁב

《 of Your ‹ Let 《 the wicked‹ and ‹ of ‹ [abandon] 《 and let 《
prophet: one abandon his way, the man iniquity his thoughts; him return

אֶל יהוה וִירַחֲמֵהוּ, וְאֶל אֱלֹהֵינוּ כִּי יַרְבֶּה לִסְלוֹחַ.¹

to ‹ Hashem, ‹ and He will ‹ and 《 our God, ‹ for ‹ He is 《 forgiving.
have compassion to abundantly
on him,

מָשִׁיחַ **צִדְקְךָ** אָמַר לְפָנֶיךָ, שְׁגִיאוֹת מִי יָבִין,

Your ‹ who is righteous ‹ said ‹ before 《 Mistakes ‹ who ‹ can 《
anointed one [David] You: discern?

מִנִּסְתָּרוֹת נַקֵּנִי.² נַקֵּנוּ יהוה אֱלֹהֵינוּ מִכָּל פְּשָׁעֵינוּ,

From ‹ cleanse 《 Cleanse ‹ Hashem, ‹ our God, ‹ of all ‹ our sins ‹
unperceived faults me. us,

וְטַהֲרֵנוּ מִכָּל טֻמְאוֹתֵינוּ, וּזְרוֹק עָלֵינוּ מַיִם טְהוֹרִים

and ‹ of all ‹ our 《 Pour ‹ upon us ‹ pure water ‹
purify us contaminations.

וְטַהֲרֵנוּ, כַּכָּתוּב עַל יַד נְבִיאֶךָ: וְזָרַקְתִּי עֲלֵיכֶם

‹ and purify us, 《 as it is ‹ by ‹ the ‹ of Your 《 I shall pour ‹ upon you ‹
written hand prophet:

מַיִם טְהוֹרִים וּטְהַרְתֶּם, מִכֹּל טֻמְאוֹתֵיכֶם וּמִכָּל

pure water ‹ and you will 《 from ‹ your ‹ for Your 《 and ‹
become pure; all contaminations from all

גִּלּוּלֵיכֶם אֲטַהֵר אֶתְכֶם.³

your ‹ I will purify ‹ you. 《
abominations

עַמְּךָ וְנַחֲלָתְךָ, רְעֵבֵי טוּבְךָ, צְמֵאֵי חַסְדֶּךָ, תְּאֵבֵי

‹ Your 《 for Your ‹ who 《 for Your ‹ who hun-《 and Your 《 for Your ‹ and
people heritage, ger goodness, thirst kindness, who long

יִשְׁעֶךָ, יַכִּירוּ וְיֵדְעוּ כִּי לַיהוה אֱלֹהֵינוּ הָרַחֲמִים

‹ for Your 《 — may they ‹ and ‹ that ‹ to ‹ our God, ‹ belong mercy ‹
salvation recognize know Hashem,

וְהַסְּלִיחוֹת.

《 and forgiveness.

---

(1) *Isaiah* 55:7. (2) *Psalms* 19:13. (3) *Ezekiel* 36:25.

FULL KADDISH / קדיש שלם

THE *CHAZZAN* RECITES קדיש שלם, FULL *KADDISH*.

יִתְגַּדַּל וְיִתְקַדַּשׁ שְׁמֵהּ רַבָּא. (.אָמֵן — Cong.) בְּעָלְמָא

⟨ Grow   ⟨ and be   ⟨ may His   ⟨ that is   ⟩⟩ (Amen.)   ⟨ — in the
exalted   sanctified   Name   great! —   world

דִּי בְרָא כִרְעוּתֵהּ. וְיַמְלִיךְ מַלְכוּתֵהּ, וְיַצְמַח פֻּרְקָנֵהּ

⟨ that   ⟨ He   ⟩⟩ according   ⟨ and may He   ⟩⟩ to His   ⟨ and cause   ⟨ His
created   to His will,   give reign   kingship,   to sprout   salvation,

וִיקָרֵב מְשִׁיחֵהּ. (.אָמֵן — Cong.) בְּחַיֵּיכוֹן וּבְיוֹמֵיכוֹן וּבְחַיֵּי

⟨ and bring   ⟩⟩ His Messiah,   ⟩⟩ (Amen.)   ⟨ in your   ⟨ and in   ⟨ and in the
near   lifetimes   your days,   lifetimes

דְכָל בֵּית יִשְׂרָאֵל, בַּעֲגָלָא וּבִזְמַן קָרִיב. וְאִמְרוּ: אָמֵן.

⟨ of the   ⟨ Family   ⟩⟩ of Israel,   ⟨ swiftly   ⟨ and at a   ⟩⟩ that comes   ⟨ Now   ⟩⟩Amen.
entire   time   soon.   respond:

CONGREGATION RESPONDS:

אָמֵן. יְהֵא שְׁמֵהּ רַבָּא מְבָרַךְ לְעָלַם וּלְעָלְמֵי עָלְמַיָּא.

⟩⟩ and for all eternity.   ⟨ forever   ⟨ be   ⟨ that is   ⟨ His   ⟨ May   ⟩⟩ Amen.
blessed   great   Name

CHAZZAN CONTINUES:

יְהֵא שְׁמֵהּ רַבָּא מְבָרַךְ לְעָלַם וּלְעָלְמֵי עָלְמַיָּא. יִתְבָּרַךְ

⟨ Blessed,   ⟩⟩ and for all eternity.   ⟨ forever   ⟨ be   ⟨ that is   ⟨ His   ⟨ May
blessed   great   Name

וְיִשְׁתַּבַּח וְיִתְפָּאַר וְיִתְרוֹמַם וְיִתְנַשֵּׂא וְיִתְהַדָּר וְיִתְעַלֶּה

⟨ elevated,   ⟨ honored,   ⟨ upraised,   ⟨ exalted,   ⟨ glorified,   ⟨ praised,

וְיִתְהַלָּל שְׁמֵהּ דְּקֻדְשָׁא בְּרִיךְ הוּא (.הוּא בְּרִיךְ — Cong.)

⟩⟩ is He   ⟨ Blessed   ⟨ of the Holy   ⟨ be the   ⟨ and lauded   ⟩⟩ is He ⟨ (Blessed
One,   Name

לְעֵלָּא [וּ]לְעֵלָּא מִכָּל בִּרְכָתָא וְשִׁירָתָא תֻּשְׁבְּחָתָא —

⟨ praise   ⟩⟩ and song,   ⟨ blessing   ⟨ any   ⟨ exceedingly beyond

וְנֶחֱמָתָא דַּאֲמִירָן בְּעָלְמָא. וְאִמְרוּ: אָמֵן. (.אָמֵן — Cong.)

⟩⟩ (Amen.)   ⟩⟩ Amen.   ⟨ Now   ⟩⟩ in the   ⟨ that are   ⟨ and
respond: world.   uttered   consolation

CONGREGATION:

(קַבֵּל בְּרַחֲמִים וּבְרָצוֹן אֶת תְּפִלָּתֵנוּ.)

⟩⟩ our prayers.)   ⟨ and with favor ⟨ with mercy ⟨ (Accept

CHAZZAN CONTINUES:

תִּתְקַבֵּל צְלוֹתְהוֹן וּבָעוּתְהוֹן דְּכָל בֵּית יִשְׂרָאֵל קֳדָם

⟨ before   ⟨ Israel   ⟨ Family   ⟨ of the   ⟨ and   ⟨ the prayers   ⟨ May
of   entire   supplications   accepted be

אֲבוּהוֹן דִּי בִשְׁמַיָּא. וְאִמְרוּ: אָמֵן. (Cong. — אָמֵן.)

《 (Amen.)   《 Amen. 〈 Now respond: 《 is in Heaven. 〈 Who 〈 their Father

CONGREGATION:

(יְהִי שֵׁם יהוה מְבֹרָךְ, מֵעַתָּה וְעַד עוֹלָם.[1])

《 eternity.) 〈 until 〈 from 《 be this time 〈 blessed, 〈 of HASHEM 〈 the Name 〈 (Let

CHAZZAN CONTINUES:

יְהֵא שְׁלָמָא רַבָּא מִן שְׁמַיָּא וְחַיִּים טוֹבִים עָלֵינוּ וְעַל כָּל

〈 all 〈 and upon 〈 upon us 〈 that is good, 〈 and life 〈 Heaven 〈 from 〈 that is abundant 〈 peace 〈 May there be

יִשְׂרָאֵל. וְאִמְרוּ: אָמֵן. (Cong. — אָמֵן.)

《 (Amen.)   《 Amen. 〈 Now respond: 《 Israel.

CONGREGATION:

(עֶזְרִי מֵעִם יהוה, עֹשֵׂה שָׁמַיִם וָאָרֶץ.[2])

《 and earth.) 〈 of heaven 〈 Maker 《 HASHEM, 〈 is from 〈 (My help

CHAZZAN BOWS; TAKES THREE STEPS BACK. BOWS LEFT AND SAYS "... עֹשֶׂה שָׁלוֹם, *HE WHO MAKES PEACE* . . ."; BOWS RIGHT AND SAYS "... הוּא, *MAY HE* . . ."; BOWS FORWARD AND SAYS "... וְעַל כָּל יִשְׂרָאֵל, *AND UPON ALL ISRAEL* . . ."; REMAINS IN PLACE FOR A FEW MOMENTS, THEN TAKES THREE STEPS FORWARD.

עֹשֶׂה [הַ]שָׁלוֹם בִּמְרוֹמָיו, הוּא יַעֲשֶׂה שָׁלוֹם עָלֵינוּ, וְעַל

〈 and upon 〈 upon us, 〈 peace 〈 make 〈 may He 《 in His heights, 〈 [the] peace 〈 He Who makes

כָּל יִשְׂרָאֵל. וְאִמְרוּ: אָמֵן. (Cong. — אָמֵן.)

《 (Amen.)   《 Amen. 〈 Now respond: 《 Israel. 〈 all

---

(1) *Psalms* 113:2. (2) 121:2.

ﭏﹸ KAPAROS / סדר כפרות ﭏﹸ

THE *KAPAROS* RITUAL MAY BE PERFORMED BETWEEN ROSH HASHANAH AND YOM KIPPUR.
HOWEVER, THE PREFERRED TIME IS JUST AFTER DAWN OF EREV YOM KIPPUR.
PICK UP THE CHICKEN OR MONEY IN THE RIGHT HAND (SOME SAY נֶפֶשׁ תַּחַת נֶפֶשׁ, *A LIFE FOR A LIFE,* AS THEY PICK UP THE CHICKEN), AND RECITE THE FOLLOWING PARAGRAPH. THEN —
WHILE RECITING THE APPROPRIATE PARAGRAPH ON THE NEXT PAGE — CIRCLE THE CHICKEN OR MONEY AROUND THE HEAD (SOME DO THIS THREE TIMES). THIS ENTIRE PROCEDURE SHOULD BE FOLLOWED THREE TIMES.
MANY FOLLOW A VARIANT FORM OF THE RITUAL. THEY RECITE THE FOLLOWING PARAGRAPHS THREE TIMES, AND THEN — WHILE CIRCLING THE CHICKEN OR THE MONEY AROUND THE HEAD — RECITE THE APPROPRIATE PARAGRAPH (FROM PAGES 1137-1140) THREE TIMES.

בְּנֵי אָדָם* יֹשְׁבֵי חֹשֶׁךְ* וְצַלְמָוֶת,* אֲסִירֵי עֳנִי

⟨ Children ⟨ of man,* ⟨ those who sat ⟨ in darkness* ⟨ and the shadow of death, 《 those shackled ⟨ in affliction

---

⇠§ כַּפָּרוֹת / Atonement

The ancient ritual of *Kaparos*/Atonement is cited by the early *Geonim* (see *Rosh, Yoma* 8:23; *Tur Orach Chaim* 605). *Rashi* (*Shabbos* 81b) describes a vastly different form of this custom. But that form is no longer practiced.

The ritual is designed to imbue people with the awareness that their lives are at stake as Yom Kippur approaches, and that they must repent and seek atonement. The ceremony symbolizes that our sins cry out for atonement, that our good deeds and repentance can save us from the punishment we deserve. The form of the ritual calls for a chicken to be moved in a circular motion around the penitent's head (see instructions accompanying the text). The chicken is later slaughtered [symbolizing the concept that a sinner deserves to forfeit his soul for not having used it to do God's will] and either the chicken or its cash value is given to the poor, for charity is an indispensable part of repentance — and the combination of the two can achieve atonement. [In giving the *Kaparos* chicken to the poor, one must be extremely careful not to embarrass the recipient or to cause him to feel that the donor is ridding himself of his sins and placing them on this poor man's head (*Matteh Ephraim*).] The entrails are left for birds and animals, because this exemplifies the same kind of compassion that we pray God will show us.

Technically, any animal should be acceptable for the *Kaparos* ritual. However, in order that the ritual not be misconstrued as a sacrificial offering — an act prohibited in the absence of the *Beis HaMikdash* — the animal used for *Kaparos* may not be one that is suitable for such sacrifice, e.g., a dove. A chicken was chosen because the Hebrew word גֶּבֶר means both *man* and *rooster*. Thus, use of this particular bird alludes to the person performing the ritual.

In the original and preferable form, a white rooster was taken for a male and a white hen for a female, because the color white symbolizes atonement (see *Isaiah* 1:18). Nevertheless, it is forbidden to make strenuous efforts to find birds of such color, lest it appear that one is following the idolaters' practice of using only white birds in their ceremonies (see *Avodah Zarah* 13b-14a).

Some use a separate chicken for each person while others perform the ritual for all the males simultaneously using one rooster, and for all the females simultaneously with one hen. A pregnant woman uses two hens — one for herself and one in case she is carrying a female child — and one rooster, in case she is carrying a male.

Many people use money for this ritual instead of a rooster. The money is then given to the poor (see *Orach Chaim* §605).

⇠§ בְּנֵי אָדָם — *Children of Man.* The nine verses of this paragraph are all taken directly from Scripture, but this opening phrase was added only for the purpose of this ritual. The term בֶּן אָדָם, literally, *son of Adam,* is used throughout the Book of *Ezekiel,* where it indicates one who remains loyal to the great mission for the sake of which God created Adam, the first human being (see *Overview* to ArtScroll *Yechezkel*). It is used here to stress that we seek atonement for our sins because we want to become worthy of God's purpose.

יֹשְׁבֵי חֹשֶׁךְ — *Those who sat in darkness.*

וּבַרְזֶל.[1] יוֹצִיאֵם* מֵחֹשֶׁךְ וְצַלְמָוֶת, וּמוֹסְרוֹתֵיהֶם
⟨ and their shackles ⟪ and the shadow ⟨ of darkness ⟨ He takes ⟪ and iron.
of death, them out*

יְנַתֵּק.[2] אֱוִלִים* מִדֶּרֶךְ פִּשְׁעָם, וּמֵעֲוֹנֹתֵיהֶם יִתְעַנּוּ.
⟪ were ⟨ and because ⟨ that is sinful ⟨ because of ⟨ Fools,* ⟪ He breaks
afflicted. of their iniquities, their path open.

כָּל אֹכֶל תְּתַעֵב נַפְשָׁם,* וַיַּגִּיעוּ עַד שַׁעֲרֵי מָוֶת.
⟪ of ⟨ the ⟨ until ⟨ and they ⟪ did their ⟨ abhor ⟨ food ⟨ All
death. portals reached soul,*

וַיִּזְעֲקוּ אֶל יהוה בַּצַּר לָהֶם, מִמְּצֻקוֹתֵיהֶם יוֹשִׁיעֵם.*
⟪ He saves ⟨ from their straits ⟪ in their distress; ⟨ HASHEM ⟨ to ⟨ Then they
them.* cried out

יִשְׁלַח דְּבָרוֹ וְיִרְפָּאֵם,* וִימַלֵּט מִשְּׁחִיתוֹתָם. יוֹדוּ
⟨ Let them ⟪ their ⟨ and lets ⟪ and cures ⟨ His ⟨ He
give thanks destruction. them escape them,* word dispatches

_____

(1) *Psalms* 107:10. (2) 107:14

Psalm 107 tells of people who must express their gratitude to God for saving them from mortal danger. The verses from this psalm that are used here refer to a person who was imprisoned and shackled in a dark dungeon and to someone who lay gravely ill. Both afflictions are the fruit of sin. In the first case, imprisonment, one is suddenly cast into darkness by a major transgression that causes a sudden change in his outlook, performance, or life. The second, illness, is the gradual process of a person whose persistent sinning causes a steady change in his character until he becomes gravely ill in a spiritual sense. In either case we pray that God will help us repent so that we can escape the danger (*Radak*).

יוֹצִיאֵם — *He takes them out.* God has many ways of liberating innocent captives from their dark dungeons and the heavy chains. He may even implant a spark of compassion in the hearts of the captors, who will be moved to free their prisoners (*Radak*).

אֱוִלִים — *Fools. Radak* examines the basic difference between captivity and sickness. The captive is seized and imprisoned in one fell swoop, whereas sickness overcomes a person slowly. Indeed, sickness may be compared to a messenger from God

warning a man to repent. At the very first sign of illness a man should immediately repent if he has the wisdom to recognize the Divine signal, but if he is foolish and ignores the first sign, then the illness is progressively intensified until it cannot be ignored. Therefore, one who ignores the early warning signs of sickness is labeled a *fool*.

כָּל אֹכֶל תְּתַעֵב נַפְשָׁם — *All food abhor did their soul.* There are many symptoms of illness — fever, nausea, pain — yet the Psalmist chose abhorrence of food because it indicates the loss of desire to enjoy or even to sustain life. This proves that one has reached the portals of death and has no hope of survival (*Rabbi A. C. Feuer*).

וַיִּזְעֲקוּ אֶל ה׳ בַּצַּר לָהֶם, מִמְּצֻקוֹתֵיהֶם יוֹשִׁיעֵם — *Then they cried out to* HASHEM *in their distress; from their straits He saves them.* The sick man finally realizes that his distresses are his own sins that plague him, and that he can be saved only by sincere prayer and repentance (*Alshich*).

יִשְׁלַח דְּבָרוֹ וְיִרְפָּאֵם — *He dispatches His word and cures them.* No cure is effective on its own. God Himself must speak and decree, "This herb will cure that disease! This doctor will heal that malady!" (*Ibn Ezra; Alshich*).

לַיהוה חַסְדּוֹ, וְנִפְלְאוֹתָיו לִבְנֵי אָדָם.*¹ אִם יֵשׁ

‹ there ‹ If « of man.* ‹ to the ‹ and for « for His ‹ to Hashem
is   children His wonders kindness,

עָלָיו מַלְאָךְ מֵלִיץ אֶחָד* מִנִּי אָלֶף, לְהַגִּיד לְאָדָם

‹ for a ‹ to declare « a ‹ out ‹ — [even] « to defend ‹ an angel ‹ for
man   thousand — of   one*   him   him

יָשְׁרוֹ. וַיְחֻנֶּנּוּ וַיֹּאמֶר, פְּדָעֵהוּ מֵרֶדֶת שָׁחַת, מָצָאתִי

‹ I have « to the Pit; ‹ from ‹ Redeem « and ‹ [God] will be « his up-
found   descending   him   say, gracious to him rightness,

כֹּפֶר.²

« atonement
[for him].

RECITE THE APPLICABLE PARAGRAPH THREE TIMES.
[WHEN MONEY IS USED, SUBSTITUTE THE BRACKETED PHRASE FOR THE PHRASE PRECEDING IT.]
EACH TIME THE PARAGRAPH IS RECITED, THE CHICKEN OR MONEY IS CIRCLED AROUND THE HEAD.

A MAN PERFORMING THE RITUAL FOR HIMSELF:

זֶה חֲלִיפָתִי, זֶה תְּמוּרָתִי, זֶה כַּפָּרָתִי.* זֶה הַתַּרְנְגוֹל

‹ rooster ‹ This « is my ‹ this ‹ is my ‹ this ‹ is my ‹ This
              atonement.   substitute,*   exchange,

יֵלֵךְ לְמִיתָה [זֶה הַכֶּסֶף יֵלֵךְ לִצְדָקָה], וַאֲנִי אֶכָּנֵס

‹ will enter ‹ while I « to charity], ‹ will go ‹ money ‹ [this « to [its] death, ‹ will go

וְאֵלֵךְ לְחַיִּים טוֹבִים אֲרוּכִים וּלְשָׁלוֹם.

« and to peace. ‹ and long, ‹ that is good ‹ to a life ‹ and go

---

(1) *Psalms* 107:17-21. (2) *Job* 33:23-24.

וְנִפְלְאוֹתָיו לִבְנֵי אָדָם — *And for His won-ders to the children of man.* When a king does favors for his subjects it is not necessarily genuine kindness, because every leader tries to ingratiate himself with his followers to inspire their loyalty. Not so is the kindness of God, Who has no need for the assistance of any person. Thus, His wonderful works are truly for the benefit of mankind — not for Himself (*Alshich*).

מַלְאָךְ מֵלִיץ אֶחָד — *An angel to defend him — [even] one.* Commenting on this verse and the next, the Talmud (*Shabbos* 32a) teaches that when someone is in danger and is surrounded by angry accusers on all sides, he can be saved by the pleas of even one defending angel. What is this defend-ing angel? Repentance and good deeds. Sometimes, even a single sincere good deed can save one from destruction.

חֲלִיפָתִי . . . תְּמוּרָתִי — *My exchange ... my substitute.* In the Hebrew idiom, חִלוּף, *ex-change,* refers to putting a superior thing in place of an inferior one. As long as a person is a sinner, even a rooster is considered superior to him. On the other hand תְּמוּרָה, *substitute,* refers to the use of an inferior thing to take the place of a superior one. In the context of *Kaparos,* once someone has repented, he is infinitely better than the rooster that takes his place.

TWO OR MORE MEN PERFORMING THE RITUAL FOR THEMSELVES:

זֶה חֲלִיפָתֵנוּ, זֶה תְּמוּרָתֵנוּ, זֶה כַּפָּרָתֵנוּ. זֶה הַתַּרְנְגוֹל

‹ rooster ‹ This ≪ is our ‹ this ‹ is our ‹ this ‹ is our ‹ This
                  atonement.   substitute,   exchange,

יֵלֵךְ לְמִיתָה [זֶה הַכֶּסֶף יֵלֵךְ לִצְדָקָה], וַאֲנַחְנוּ נִכָּנֵס

‹ will enter ‹ while we ≪ to charity], ‹ will go ‹ money ‹ [this ≪ to [its] death, ‹ will go

וְנֵלֵךְ לְחַיִּים טוֹבִים אֲרוּכִים וּלְשָׁלוֹם.

≪ and to peace. ‹ and long, ‹ that is good ‹ to a life ‹ and go

ONE PERFORMING THE RITUAL FOR A MAN:

זֶה חֲלִיפָתְךָ, זֶה תְּמוּרָתְךָ, זֶה כַּפָּרָתְךָ. זֶה הַתַּרְנְגוֹל

‹ rooster ‹ This ≪ is your ‹ this ‹ is your ‹ this ‹ is your ‹ This
                  atonement.   substitute,   exchange,

יֵלֵךְ לְמִיתָה [זֶה הַכֶּסֶף יֵלֵךְ לִצְדָקָה], וְאַתָּה

‹ while you ≪ to charity], ‹ will go ‹ money ‹ [this ≪ to [its] death, ‹ will go

תִּכָּנֵס וְתֵלֵךְ לְחַיִּים טוֹבִים אֲרוּכִים וּלְשָׁלוֹם.

≪ and to peace. ‹ and long, ‹ that is good ‹ to a life ‹ and go ‹ will enter

ONE PERFORMING THE RITUAL FOR TWO OR MORE MEN:

זֶה חֲלִיפַתְכֶם, זֶה תְּמוּרַתְכֶם, זֶה כַּפָּרַתְכֶם. זֶה

‹This ≪ is your atonement. ‹ this ‹ is your substitute, ‹ this ‹ is your exchange, ‹ This

הַתַּרְנְגוֹל יֵלֵךְ לְמִיתָה [זֶה הַכֶּסֶף יֵלֵךְ לִצְדָקָה],

≪ to charity], ‹ will go ‹ money ‹ [this ≪ to [its] death, ‹ will go ‹ rooster

וְאַתֶּם תִּכָּנְסוּ וְתֵלְכוּ לְחַיִּים טוֹבִים אֲרוּכִים וּלְשָׁלוֹם.

≪ and to peace. ‹ and long, ‹ that is good ‹ to a life ‹ and go ‹ will enter ‹ while you

A WOMAN PERFORMING THE RITUAL FOR HERSELF:

זֹאת חֲלִיפָתִי, זֹאת תְּמוּרָתִי, זֹאת כַּפָּרָתִי. זֹאת

‹ This ≪ is my atonement. ‹ this ‹ is my substitute, ‹ this ‹ is my exchange, ‹ This

הַתַּרְנְגֹלֶת תֵּלֵךְ לְמִיתָה [זֶה הַכֶּסֶף יֵלֵךְ לִצְדָקָה],

≪ to charity], ‹ will go ‹ money ‹ [this ≪ to [its] death ‹ will go ‹ hen

וַאֲנִי אֶכָּנֵס וְאֵלֵךְ לְחַיִּים טוֹבִים אֲרוּכִים וּלְשָׁלוֹם.

≪ and to peace. ‹ and long, ‹ that is good ‹ to a life ‹ and go ‹ will enter ‹ while I

TWO OR MORE WOMEN PERFORMING THE RITUAL FOR THEMSELVES:

זֹאת חֲלִיפָתֵנוּ, זֹאת תְּמוּרָתֵנוּ, זֹאת כַּפָּרָתֵנוּ. זֹאת

〈 This 《 is our atonement.〈 this 〈 is our substitute, 〈 this 〈 is our exchange, 〈 This

הַתַּרְנְגֹלֶת תֵּלֵךְ לְמִיתָה [זֶה הַכֶּסֶף יֵלֵךְ לִצְדָקָה],

《 to charity], 〈 will go 〈 money 〈 [this 《 to [its] death 〈 will go 〈 hen

וַאֲנַחְנוּ נִכָּנֵס וְנֵלֵךְ לְחַיִּים טוֹבִים אֲרוּכִים וּלְשָׁלוֹם.

《 and to peace. 〈 and long, 〈 that is good 〈 to a life 〈 and go 〈 will enter 〈 while we

---

ONE PERFORMING THE RITUAL FOR A WOMAN:

זֹאת חֲלִיפָתֵךְ, זֹאת תְּמוּרָתֵךְ, זֹאת כַּפָּרָתֵךְ. זֹאת

〈 This 《 is your   〈 this 〈 is your   〈 this 〈 is your 〈 This
atonement.   substitute,   exchange,

הַתַּרְנְגֹלֶת תֵּלֵךְ לְמִיתָה [זֶה הַכֶּסֶף יֵלֵךְ לִצְדָקָה],

《 to charity], 〈 will go 〈 money 〈 [this 《 to [its] death, 〈 will go 〈 hen

וְאַתְּ תִּכָּנְסִי וְתֵלְכִי לְחַיִּים טוֹבִים אֲרוּכִים וּלְשָׁלוֹם.

《 and to peace. 〈 and long, 〈 that is good 〈 to a life 〈 and go 〈 will enter 〈 while you

---

ONE PERFORMING THE RITUAL FOR TWO OR MORE WOMEN:

זֹאת חֲלִיפַתְכֶן, זֹאת תְּמוּרַתְכֶן, זֹאת כַּפָּרַתְכֶן. זֹאת

〈 This 《 is your   〈 this 〈 is your   〈 this 〈 is your 〈 This
atonement.   substitute,   exchange,

הַתַּרְנְגֹלֶת תֵּלֵךְ לְמִיתָה [זֶה הַכֶּסֶף יֵלֵךְ לִצְדָקָה],

《 to charity], 〈 will go 〈 money 〈 [this 《 to [its] death, 〈 will go 〈 hen

וְאַתֶּן תִּכָּנַסְנָה וְתֵלַכְנָה לְחַיִּים טוֹבִים אֲרוּכִים

〈 and long, 〈 that is good 〈 to a life 〈 and go 〈 will enter 〈 while you

וּלְשָׁלוֹם.

《 and to peace.

A PREGNANT WOMAN PERFORMING THE RITUAL FOR HERSELF:

אֵלּוּ חֲלִיפוֹתֵינוּ, אֵלּוּ תְּמוּרוֹתֵינוּ, אֵלּוּ כַּפָּרוֹתֵינוּ.

《 are our   〈 these 〈 are our   〈 these 〈 are our 〈 These
atonements.   substitutes,   exchanges,

אֵלּוּ הַתַּרְנְגוֹלִים יֵלְכוּ לְמִיתָה [זֶה הַכֶּסֶף יֵלֵךְ

〈 will go 〈 money 〈 [this 《 to [their] death, 〈 will go 〈 chickens 〈 These

לִצְדָקָה], וַאֲנַחְנוּ נִכָּנֵס וְנֵלֵךְ לְחַיִּים טוֹבִים אֲרוּכִים

‹ and long, ‹ that is good ‹ to a life ‹ and go ‹ will enter ‹ while we ≪ to charity],

וּלְשָׁלוֹם.

≪ and to peace.

ONE PERFORMING THE RITUAL FOR A PREGNANT WOMAN:

אֵלוּ חֲלִיפוֹתֵיכֶם, אֵלוּ תְּמוּרוֹתֵיכֶם, אֵלוּ כַּפָּרוֹתֵיכֶם.

≪ are your atonements. ‹ these ‹ are your substitutes, ‹ these ‹ are your exchanges, ‹ These

אֵלוּ הַתַּרְנְגוֹלִים יֵלְכוּ לְמִיתָה [זֶה הַכֶּסֶף יֵלֵךְ

‹ will go ‹ money ‹ [this ≪ to [their] death, ‹ will go ‹ chickens ‹ These

לִצְדָקָה], וְאַתֶּם תִּכָּנְסוּ וְתֵלְכוּ לְחַיִּים טוֹבִים

‹ that is good ‹ to a life ‹ and go ‹ will enter ‹ while you ≪ to charity],

אֲרוּכִים וּלְשָׁלוֹם.

≪ and to peace. ‹ and long,

This volume is part of
THE ARTSCROLL SERIES

an ongoing project of
translations, commentaries and expositions on
Scripture, Mishnah, Talmud, Midrash, Halachah,
liturgy, history, the classic Rabbinic writings, biographies, and thought

For a brochure of current publications
or to visit our Hebrew bookstore
or contact the publisher

Mesorah Publications, ltd.

4401 Second Avenue
Brooklyn, New York 11232
(718) 921-9000
www.artscroll.com